The Top 6000 Companies in North East England

Companies with assets exceeding £750,000

John D Blackburn
Editor

dp

First Edition

Winter 2018

ISBN-13: 978-1-912736-08-9

ISBN-10: 1-912736-08-X

Printed in 8pt Nimbus Sans L

Designed by URW++ Design and Development GmbH

Dellam Publishing Limited

2 Heath Drive, Sutton, Surrey, SM2 5RP

Fax: 020 8770 7478 email: enquiries@dellam.com

SAN: 0177881 EAN/GLN: 5030670177882

Table of Contents

Acknowledgements

This is a long and detailed publication containing thousands of facts and figures. It is only to be expected, despite continuous and repeated editing and checking, that errors may occur. In such cases, once we are aware of any, we publish a correction on our website.

Readers are encouraged to check regularly at www.dellam.com/books for any corrections and updates.

Although we take extreme care to ensure accuracy and being up-to-date, we cannot accept responsibility for any errors or omissions.

We appreciate your interest in our publications, and your comments and suggestions are always welcome. Please contact us at enquiries@dellam.com.

Introduction

This study looks at all companies registered in North East England and where their total assets are more than £750,000.

North East England covers Northumberland, Co Durham, Tyne and Wear and Cleveland. There are three large conurbations: Teesside, Wearside and Tyneside. There are three cities: Newcastle upon Tyne, Sunderland and Durham; other large towns include Darlington, Gateshead, Hartlepool, Middlesbrough, South Shields, Stockton-on-Tees and Washington.

The aim of this study is to provide an overview of the key movers and shakers in the corporate sector. Only key data has been isolated, particularly the company's net worth and total assets, but also their full name, date incorporated, registered office, activities, shareholders, directors (with date of birth, occupation and nationality) and number of employees.

Two indicators of size are used: net worth and total assets. These are preferable to turnover which is influenced by profit margins and whether the companies are capital or labour intensive.

A short summary of the corporate sector in North East England:

Up until the late 20th century the region's economy was based on traditional heavy industries such as shipbuilding, coal mining, oil refining and chemicals. The key economic characteristic has been one of relative decline during latter part of the 20th century, as evidenced by the growing gap between the region and the national average in terms of economic prosperity.

The region contribution to the UK's GDP is 3% of the UK total. On average, the region's manufacturing base contributes to 4.5% to the UK manufacturing base. In terms of GVA, the three biggest manufacturing industries are chemicals and chemical products, basic metals and metal products, and transport equipment. The region is the only UK region whose economy shrunk with GVA falling by 1%.

In 2017, it had the second lowest employment rate in the UK, nearing 72% and the region with the highest unemployment rate in the UK (7%), far above the national average (4.8%). The region's investment in R&D is one of the lowest in the UK. In 2016, the share of population with tertiary education was 40%, below the UK (48%).

Standard cataloguing guidelines for company names in the profile section have been used, but there will be occurrences when the name may not be strictly alphabetical. A certain licence was adopted where it was felt that strictly alphabetical could lead to improper cataloguing. Some company names have been shortened in the league tables for aesthetic reasons.

John D Blackburn
Editor

This page is intentionally left blank

Total Assets League Table

Company	Value
Virgin Money Holdings (UK) PLC	£35,055,599,616
Virgin Money PLC	£34,915,201,024
Northern Powergrid Holdings Company	£6,051,277,824
Northumbrian Water Group Limited	£4,696,800,256
Northumbrian Water Limited	£4,627,599,872
Sage Treasury Company Limited	£4,396,947,968
Sage Holding Company Limited	£3,605,821,952
Froneri Limited	£3,390,711,040
Northern Powergrid (Yorkshire) PLC	£3,322,706,944
The Sage Group PLC.	£3,223,000,064
Bellway P L C	£3,147,415,040
Bellway Homes Limited	£3,099,051,008
Northern Electric PLC	£2,503,973,120
Northern Powergrid (Northeast) Limited	£2,462,428,928
Nissan Motor Manufacturing (UK) Limited	£2,426,690,048
Grainger Finance Company Limited	£2,272,334,080
Northumbrian Water Finance PLC	£2,267,936,000
DB (UK) Investments Limited	£1,959,042,048
Froneri International Limited	£1,859,410,432
Grainger PLC	£1,767,000,064
Richmond UK Top Holdco Limited	£1,699,299,968
Richmond UK Holdco Limited	£1,699,299,968
The Go-Ahead Group PLC	£1,615,399,936
Sagesoft	£1,490,019,584
Venator Materials PLC	£1,488,084,992
GMF Europe LLP	£1,258,359,424
Parkdean Resorts Limited	£1,119,100,032
Northgate PLC	£1,118,932,992
Vertu Motors PLC	£969,068,032
Northgate (Europe) Limited	£964,588,992
Arriva PLC	£931,694,016
North of England Protecting & Indemnity Assoc Ltd	£915,450,752
Cleveland Potash Limited	£900,454,976
CKI UK Co 6 Limited	£896,153,152
Yorkshire Power Group Limited	£891,595,008
Parkdean Resorts UK Limited	£872,081,984
CKI UK Co 5 Limited	£859,604,096
Nissan Holdings (UK) Limited	£850,251,776
Sabic UK Petrochemicals Limited	£839,699,968
Northern Powergrid Limited	£827,446,976
Go-Ahead Holding Limited	£813,113,984
Northgate Vehicle Hire Limited	£740,851,968
Lucite International Finco Limited	£740,158,080
Arriva International Limited	£733,470,272
Fenwick,Limited	£724,190,976
Northern Powergrid UK Holdings	£718,510,976
Huntsman (Holdings) UK	£698,651,008
Park Resorts Limited	£698,424,000
PD Parks Limited	£681,401,984
NHP Securities No. 3 Limited	£672,915,008
EDF Energy Renewables Holdings Limited	£672,254,976
Atom Bank PLC	£648,836,992
PD Ports Limited	£647,417,984
Bromley Property Investments Limited	£623,097,024
Sage Holdings Limited	£611,094,016
BPT (Bradford Property Trust) Limited	£609,665,024
Ports Holdings Limited	£602,779,008
Libra Careco Limited	£586,443,200
Yorkshire Electricity Group PLC	£577,644,032
Engie Services Holding UK Limited	£573,209,024
Northumberland & Durham Property Trust Limited	£565,209,024
Northgate (CB) Limited	£554,828,992
Enodis Hanover	£534,736,000
HC-ONE Oval Limited	£532,830,016
Sage (UK) Ltd	£522,297,984
PD Teesport Limited	£515,783,008
Monde Nissin (UK) Limited	£513,265,984
Able UK Limited	£508,078,016
Arriva UK Bus Holdings Limited	£505,856,992
PD Portco Limited	£489,836,992
The Gibson O'Neill Company Limited	£486,804,000
Johnson Electric International (UK) Limited	£485,296,992
Engie UK Holding (Services) Limited	£469,782,016
PD Ports Acquisitions (UK) Limited	£465,761,984
Sabic Tees Holdings Limited	£457,437,696
NIAL Finance Limited	£454,656,000
Greggs PLC	£441,270,016
Sage Overseas Limited.	£435,548,992
Getinge Extended Care UK Limited	£433,428,992
Libra Careco CH2 Propco Limited	£422,870,016
Enodis Holdings Limited	£414,900,000
Wirecard Card Solutions Limited	£414,241,984
Govia Thameslink Railway Limited	£410,295,008
MSSL (GB) Limited	£386,374,624
Newcastle International Airport Limited	£384,827,008
Gestamp Tallent Limited	£383,833,984
NHP Limited	£370,082,240
Success Bidco 2 Limited	£358,792,992
PD Ports Group Limited	£354,299,008
NIAL Group Limited	£349,967,008
Arriva International (Northern Europe) Limited	£349,304,224
Arriva International (Southern Europe) Limited	£349,304,224
Retirement Bridge Group Holdings Limited	£337,985,984
BPT Limited	£337,676,000
Nobia Holdings UK Limited	£335,708,992
Arch (Corporate Holdings) Limited	£331,692,544
London & South Eastern Railway Limited	£327,500,992
Enodis Group Limited	£325,000,000
Arriva UK Bus Investments Limited	£315,041,984
Lynemouth Power Limited	£303,292,992
Libra Careco Investments 1 Limited	£302,528,736
Fletcher Challenge Forest Industries Limited	£297,712,992
Northern Powergrid Metering Limited	£296,857,984
PD Ports Management Limited	£295,124,992
Teesside Windfarm Limited	£289,017,984
Fletcher Challenge Building UK Limited	£287,089,984
R&R Ice Cream UK Limited	£285,327,008
Engie Regeneration Limited	£284,984,992
GAP Group Limited	£282,520,000
Bristol Street First Investments Limited	£282,376,992
Hargreaves Services PLC	£281,744,992
Mitsubishi Chemical Lucite Group Limited	£278,780,192
Newcastle Airport Local Authority Holding Co Ltd	£278,606,016
Riviera Acquisitions Limited	£272,101,152
Venator Materials UK Limited	£269,433,984
Lucite International UK Limited	£268,700,000
Venator P&A Holdings UK Limited	£268,370,000
New R & R Ice Cream Limited	£268,284,784
TT2 (Holdings) Limited	£267,644,000
TT2 Limited	£267,643,984
UK Land Estates Partnership (Holdings) Limited	£258,044,992
Engie Regeneration Holdings Limited	£254,730,000
The Station Hotel (Newcastle) Limited	£254,664,000
Northumberland Estates Limited	£254,094,816
Riviera Topco Limited	£254,074,176
The Banks Group Limited	£253,612,000
Northern Electric Finance PLC	£252,998,000
LSL Property Services PLC	£249,620,000
MCC Group Holdings (UK) Limited	£245,717,888
Engie Services Limited	£243,180,000
Bannatyne Fitness Limited	£242,144,992
Newcastle United Limited	£239,424,000
Sunderland Limited	£234,874,000
Newcastle United Football Company Limited	£234,212,000
Jomast Limited	£228,395,360
Cleveland Cable Company (Holdings) Limited	£226,319,936
R&R PIK Limited	£224,768,656
Arch (Commercial Enterprise) Limited	£221,496,912
Engie Regeneration (Apollo) Limited	£217,083,008
GAP Group Leasing Limited	£215,286,000
Reiver Finance Limited	£214,320,992
Grainger Treasury Property (2006) LLP	£209,275,024
Finders Bidco Limited	£208,590,000
Formica Limited	£207,444,992

Company	Amount
Jomast Accommodation Limited	£205,945,808
Arriva London North Limited	£205,327,008
Arriva UK Trains Limited	£205,054,000
Vertu Motors (Property) Limited	£204,256,992
Bromley Property Holdings Limited	£201,808,992
Parkdean Holiday Parks Limited	£194,916,000
Libra Careco Investments 2 Limited	£194,519,488
Libra Careco Ch3 Propco Limited	£193,359,008
Fujifilm Diosynth Biotechnologies UK Limited	£192,900,000
Sunderland Marine Insurance Company Limited	£191,877,520
Cleveland Cable Company Limited	£191,368,320
Lotte Chemical UK Limited	£189,862,000
Caterpillar Skinningrove Limited	£188,894,000
Ruby Acquisitions Limited	£187,855,008
Finders Midco Limited	£187,492,000
BPT (Residential Investments) Limited	£182,394,000
Formica Holdco (UK) Limited	£180,103,008
Jake Acquisitions Limited	£178,904,000
Reversions Financing (No.1) 2011 Limited	£176,675,328
London General Transport Services Limited	£176,364,992
Huntsman Polyurethanes (UK) Limited	£173,428,000
NHP Securities No. 1 Limited	£172,211,376
Unipres (UK) Limited	£168,375,008
Engie FM Limited	£166,484,992
Sage Pay Europe Limited	£164,810,000
NIAL Holdings Limited	£162,728,992
Jake Holdings Limited	£162,668,992
BPT (Assured Homes) Limited	£162,044,112
HC-ONE Limited	£161,444,000
Grainco Limited	£161,034,416
Atlantic Metropolitan (U.K.) Limited	£159,162,240
Sembcorp Utilities (UK) Limited	£158,344,992
Northern Education Trust	£157,928,992
Mayborn (UK) Limited	£156,440,000
True Potential Group Limited	£155,412,000
Hargreaves (UK) Services Limited	£155,030,000
Arriva Rail North Limited	£154,451,008
British Engines Limited	£152,860,000
Mobile Mini UK Limited	£152,312,000
Bristol Street Fourth Investments Limited	£150,779,008
Marlow Foods Limited	£150,028,000
Reece Group Limited	£148,674,000
Student Loans Company Limited	£144,728,992
Sunderland Association Football Club,Limited (The)	£144,671,008
Premier Dawn Properties Limited	£144,588,000
J.Barbour & Sons,Limited	£141,677,088
INEOS Nitriles (UK) Limited	£141,174,000
Stelrad Radiator Group Limited	£140,640,992
Lucite International Holdco Limited	£140,247,536
Komatsu UK Limited	£140,240,992
UK Land Estates (Partnership) Limited	£139,632,000
London & Birmingham Railway Limited	£139,522,000
Cable Properties and Investments Limited	£137,465,568
Northgate (CB 2) Limited	£137,216,000
Svitzer Marine Limited	£137,007,008
Tricomm Housing Limited	£136,250,000
Hays Travel Limited	£135,632,992
Sembcorp Holdings Limited	£134,500,992
Automotive Chassis Products UK Limited	£134,004,000
Go South Coast Limited	£133,782,000
XC Trains Limited	£132,159,000
Enodis Investments Limited	£127,235,000
Grainger Real Estate Limited	£125,816,000
East London Energy Limited	£125,216,000
Arriva Trains Holdings Limited	£124,247,000
Esh Investments Limited	£124,188,000
The Chiltern Railway Company Limited	£123,261,000
Hargreaves Land Limited	£122,555,000
Finders Holdco Limited	£122,090,000
Grainger Europe (No. 2) Limited	£121,027,232
Mechanised Project Management	£119,615,000
Torque Group International Fortune Limited	£117,116,584
Northumbrian Services Limited	£116,700,000
MTL Services Limited	£116,045,000
Albert Farnell Limited	£114,988,000
H.J. Banks and Company Limited	£114,467,000
Grainger Invest No.2 LLP	£114,383,000
PD Group Management Limited	£111,601,000
Esh Holdings Limited	£110,686,000
FC Beamish Bidco Ltd	£109,660,432
Grainger Land & Regeneration Limited	£109,459,312
Lucite International UK Overseas Holdco1 Limited	£107,888,456
A. Share & Sons Limited	£104,130,000
Utilitywise PLC	£102,674,568
Manitowoc Group (UK) Limited	£99,988,000
Svitzer Holding UK Limited	£98,749,000
North East Access To Finance Limited	£98,642,368
Northumbria Healthcare Facilities Management Ltd	£98,137,000
Equity Release (Increments) Limited	£97,649,136
Arriva Motor Holdings Limited	£97,345,000
Ringtons Holdings Limited	£97,098,616
NIAL Investments Limited	£96,414,000
PII Group Limited	£94,730,000
Engie Regeneration (Fhm) Limited	£94,333,000
Sage Online Holdings Limited	£94,311,000
Red Poppy (UK) Limited	£93,162,000
Grainger Invest No . 1 LLP	£91,587,000
Magnet Limited	£90,864,000
Retirement Bridge Housing Limited	£90,830,944
Quantum Pharma Holdings Limited	£90,823,000
Middlesbrough Football & Athletic Company (1986) Ltd	£90,627,000
Community Foundation Serving Tyne & Wear	£90,018,112
Sage Euro Hedgeco 1	£89,184,320
PII Limited	£89,165,000
Dorenell Windfarm Limited	£88,422,000
Torque Group International Wealth Limited	£87,985,232
PD Port Services Limited	£87,778,000
Hanro Limited	£87,748,000
NHP Securities No. 2 Limited	£87,624,400
Northern 2 VCT PLC	£87,177,000
Orca Bidco Limited	£87,025,776
Shepherd Offshore Group Limited	£86,605,840
Blyth Offshore Demonstrator Limited	£86,226,000
Nike (UK) Limited	£86,123,000
Arch (Housing) Limited	£86,067,304
Nissan Trading Europe Limited	£85,946,744
Sage Brazilian Investment One Limited	£84,939,000
Meridian Healthcare Limited	£84,519,000
CPI Books Ltd	£84,269,000
Gainford Care Homes Limited	£84,202,280
Hertel (UK) Limited	£84,011,000
Centre for Process Innovation Limited	£83,460,000
CPI Group (UK) Ltd	£83,438,512
Upperbay Limited	£82,787,000
Faerch Plast Manufacturing Limited	£82,695,000
Sangenic International Ltd.	£82,497,000
Offshore Renewable Energy Catapult	£82,424,000
Corriemoillie Windfarm Limited	£82,280,000
Mayborn Group Limited	£81,922,000
Opsec Security Group Limited	£81,322,000
Arriva London South Limited	£81,090,000
Specialist Machine Developments (Smd) Limited	£80,676,344
John Nixon Limited	£80,121,296
Piramal Healthcare UK Limited	£79,694,360
Arriva Merseyside Limited	£79,443,000
Home Group Developments Limited	£78,655,000
Your-Move.co.uk Limited	£78,148,000
Grainger Unitholder No 1 Limited	£78,037,432
Carrier Rental Systems Limited	£78,029,000
Project Bond Holdco Limited	£77,811,000
Husqvarna UK Limited	£77,737,000
Londinium A & C LLP	£77,325,776
Getinge Holding Ltd	£77,283,000
Al-Shaheen Energy Services Limited	£77,184,416

Company	Value
Northumberland Estates Investments Limited	£77,123,144
Svitzer Eastlands Limited	£76,875,000
Wainstones Investments Limited	£76,700,360
Jomast Developments Limited	£76,402,104
Northern Venture Trust PLC	£76,341,000
Engie Buildings Limited	£75,819,000
Enodis International Limited	£75,564,000
Sabic UK Limited	£75,519,000
Northern 3 VCT PLC	£75,180,000
Calenergy Gas (Holdings) Limited	£74,556,000
Enodis Oxford	£74,520,000
Jake Investment Limited	£74,485,000
Calenergy Resources Limited	£74,293,000
Deepocean 1 UK Limited	£74,094,000
Southview Leisure Park Limited	£73,441,000
Spartan UK Limited	£73,321,768
Grainger Residential Limited	£72,311,816
Hamsard 2517 Limited	£71,996,000
Crown Care Holdings Limited	£71,700,792
Rockliffe Hall Limited	£71,100,000
Quantum Pharma Group Limited	£70,794,000
North East Finance (Holdco) Limited	£70,526,840
Derwent Developments Limited	£70,482,592
Bridgewater Equity Release Limited	£70,205,000
Ensus UK Limited	£70,126,000
Dupont Teijin Films U.K. Limited	£70,097,000
Go North East Limited	£69,391,000
Ben Burgess Holdings Limited	£68,933,784
Tolent Construction Limited	£68,640,504
Hargreaves Services Europe Limited	£67,753,000
The MN Film Partnership No.2, LLP	£67,644,664
Immunodiagnostic Systems Holdings PLC	£67,541,000
Danesmoor Limited	£67,446,480
Grainger Bradley Limited	£67,346,288
Converse Pharma Limited	£67,120,000
Ponton Road LLP	£67,095,916
Quantum Pharmaceutical Limited	£66,999,000
Dragonfly Venture Group Ltd	£66,746,348
Richmond Foods Limited	£66,526,000
Ubisoft Reflections Limited	£66,415,180
M40 Trains Limited	£66,059,000
Tolent PLC	£65,936,000
Leazes Homes Limited	£65,430,000
QE Facilities Limited	£65,142,000
Tees and Hartlepool Pilotage Company Limited	£64,583,000
Esh Construction Limited	£63,759,000
Danesmoor Holdings Limited	£63,654,160
SKR Holdings Limited	£63,311,000
Reece Treasury Management Limited	£62,946,000
Durham Diocesan Board of Finance	£61,943,724
West Waterlooville Developments Limited	£61,569,144
PWS Distributors Limited	£61,485,940
Burnfoot Windfarm Limited	£61,011,000
Vertu Motors (Vmc) Limited	£61,004,000
Sage Global Services Limited	£61,004,000
Cawingredients Limited	£60,866,140
Testerworld Limited	£60,638,000
British Engines (UK) Limited	£60,432,000
Pearson Engineering Limited	£60,357,000
Mammoet (UK) Limited	£60,120,000
Retirement Bridge Limited	£59,488,732
Bel Valves Limited	£59,254,000
Berkeley Exploration Limited	£58,547,624
Frank Recruitment Group Limited	£57,664,000
Grainger Housing & Developments Limited	£57,142,344
Fine Organics Limited	£57,122,000
Hays Tour Operating Limited	£56,845,656
Camerons Brewery Limited	£56,824,420
Sembcorp Utilities Services Limited	£56,752,000
Arriva Bus & Coach Limited	£56,702,000
Frank Recruitment Group Services Limited	£56,452,000
South Lakeland Parks Limited	£56,336,000
Shepherd Offshore Limited	£55,920,536
Nifco UK Limited	£55,782,000
William Leech (Investments) Limited	£55,269,512
Grainger Finance (Tricomm) Limited	£55,209,440
C.A. Group (Holdings) Limited	£55,144,112
True Potential Investments LLP	£55,138,200
Nigel Frank International Limited	£54,994,000
Engie Regeneration (Bramall) Limited	£54,916,000
Malhotra Care Homes Limited	£54,877,152
A&P Group Limited	£54,543,000
Maquet Limited	£54,474,000
Banks Renewables (Kype Muir Wind Farm) Limited	£53,993,000
GIP Limited	£53,932,636
Minhoco 35 Limited	£53,740,164
William Leech Foundation Limited (The)	£53,612,072
PD Logistics Limited	£53,404,000
C Bidco Limited	£53,144,000
Barker & Stonehouse Limited	£53,027,000
Stelrad Radiator Holdings Limited	£53,023,000
Industrial Energy Services Limited	£52,638,000
Draeger Safety UK Ltd	£52,596,000
Govia Limited	£52,481,000
Shield Therapeutics PLC	£52,384,000
Working Links (Employment) Limited	£52,123,000
Project Bond Bidco Limited	£51,936,000
Wellburn Care Homes Limited	£51,841,600
PX UK Holdco1 Limited	£51,714,892
Kitwave Limited	£51,435,652
Holme Dodsworth Metals Limited	£51,144,056
Hall Construction Services Limited	£50,982,644
City Hospitals Independent Commercial Enterprises Ltd	£50,933,280
The Ascent Academies' Trust	£50,637,000
Hargreaves (UK) Limited	£50,406,000
Ben Burgess & Co Limited	£50,098,592
Quantum Pharma 2014 Limited	£50,064,000
Sterling Pharma Solutions Limited	£49,927,000
Crossco Limited	£49,829,320
New College Durham Academies Trust	£49,754,000
Immunodiagnostic Systems Limited	£48,942,620
INEOS Compounds Aycliffe Limited	£48,891,000
Longpark Windfarm Limited	£48,849,000
Northumberland Church of England Academy Trust	£48,763,964
Arriva International Trains (Leasing) Limited	£48,736,736
Arriva Midlands Limited	£48,618,000
Clouston Group Ltd	£48,559,776
Royal IHC Limited	£48,541,000
Jomast Leisure & Property Limited	£48,535,956
Parkdean Caravan Parks Limited	£48,256,000
Reversions Financing Limited	£48,233,416
South Lakeland Group Limited	£48,113,000
Northumberland Estates Ventures Limited	£47,327,652
Kromek Group PLC	£47,180,000
Ouseburn Learning Trust	£47,166,428
Power Topco Limited	£47,107,000
Arriva Durham County Limited	£46,652,000
Atkinson Northern Limited	£46,448,332
Brighton & Hove Bus and Coach Company Limited	£46,234,000
The Auckland Castle Trust	£45,977,720
Arriva Yorkshire Limited	£45,971,000
Kasai UK Ltd	£45,923,820
Northumberland Estates Developments Limited	£45,845,592
IHC Merwede UK Limited	£45,243,000
United Healthcare Developments Limited	£45,081,880
Union Electric Steel UK Limited	£44,689,000
International Centre for Life Trust	£44,672,400
CMP Products Limited	£44,226,000
Luxury Leisure	£44,219,688
The Newcastle upon Tyne Royal Grammar School	£44,153,792
Eden Farm Limited	£44,150,232
Burnhead Moss Wind Farm Limited	£43,766,000
INEOS Compounds Holdings Limited	£43,656,452
Kiplun Limited	£43,638,000

Company	Value
Union Retail Properties Limited	£43,598,580
Global Navigation Solutions Holdings Limited	£43,234,000
Bridgewater Tenancies Limited	£43,194,220
Anglian Water Business (National) Limited	£43,123,000
Arriva Kent & Surrey Limited	£43,088,000
Nitro 2 Limited	£43,000,000
Offshore Support Vessels V Limited	£42,964,000
Stephenson Hotel Limited	£42,788,024
Stelrad Limited	£42,612,000
Beck Burn Windfarm Limited	£42,499,000
S.G. Petch Limited	£42,452,692
Grainger (Clapham) Limited	£42,334,228
Dome Propco Limited	£42,316,000
Cramlington Learning Village	£42,240,552
Gainford Hotels Limited	£42,028,372
The Hospital of God at Greatham	£41,684,312
C.A. Group Limited	£41,254,328
Arlesville Estates Limited	£41,234,956
Arriva UK Bus Limited	£41,227,000
CPI UK Management Company Ltd	£41,156,000
The Laidlaw Schools Trust	£41,086,136
Lucite International China Holdings Limited	£41,008,052
Northern Electric Properties Limited	£40,957,000
Yarm School	£40,910,000
Edgeman Limited	£40,904,240
Ramsdens Financial Limited	£40,709,000
Welbilt (Halesowen) Limited	£40,612,000
Welbilt UK Limited	£40,570,000
On-Hire Limited	£40,438,044
A.V.Dawson Limited	£40,383,444
Kromek Limited	£40,377,000
Arriva Kent Thameside Limited	£40,256,000
AAF-McQuay UK Limited	£40,142,000
Grainger (Aldershot) Limited	£40,075,872
The Gosforth Federated Academies Limited	£40,060,000
Kans and Kandy (Holdings) Ltd	£39,918,856
Crossco (1255) Limited	£39,697,000
Arriva The Shires Limited	£39,685,000
Sabic Global Limited	£39,448,048
Pickerings Europe Limited	£39,284,000
Teesside Learning Trust	£39,141,000
Ashworth and Parker Limited	£38,863,000
Grainger (Octavia Hill) Limited	£38,813,196
CPI Colour Ltd	£38,645,316
Grainger Employees Limited	£38,644,884
Kavli UK Limited	£38,639,340
Paragon Transaction (U.K.) Limited	£38,614,908
Chemoxy International Limited	£38,587,000
Darnley Bidco Limited	£38,457,800
Boasso UK Limited	£38,432,196
Competition Line (U.K.) Limited	£38,383,688
Turnbull Family Investments Limited	£38,361,704
Vertellus Specialties Holdings UK Limited	£38,265,000
LJJ Holdings Limited	£38,061,920
Beamish Museum	£37,807,000
Positive Solutions (Financial Services) Ltd.	£37,638,000
Arriva North West Limited	£37,580,000
International Centre for Life (Property) Limited	£37,531,768
VCS (Holdings UK) Limited	£37,471,528
Emerchantpay Limited	£37,284,060
PX UK Holdco2 Limited	£37,192,212
Tombola Limited	£37,188,032
GNS Acquisitions Limited	£37,110,320
Ringtons Limited	£36,915,668
Rettig (UK) Limited	£36,897,000
Samsung C&T ECUK Limited	£36,701,696
Tanfield Group PLC	£36,613,000
Groveport Logistics Limited	£36,039,000
Northern Powergrid Gas Limited	£36,000,000
SAI Automotive Washington Limited	£35,942,000
Ramside Estates Limited	£35,920,072
Welbeck C P	£35,893,000

Company	Value
Express Engineering (Group) Limited	£35,679,792
Entek International Limited	£35,656,000
Vantec Europe Limited	£35,641,512
PX UK Holdco3 Limited	£35,556,864
Vertellus Specialties UK Limited	£35,513,000
L.B. Foster Rail Technologies (UK) Limited	£35,335,784
The Ballinger Charitable Trust	£35,205,468
Jomast 1 Limited	£35,191,200
Kans and Kandy (Properties) Ltd	£34,992,168
Pure Fishing (UK) Ltd.	£34,838,000
Soil Machine Dynamics Limited	£34,808,352
Vianet Group PLC	£34,717,000
Venator Pigments UK Limited	£34,611,000
Sovereign Reversions Limited	£34,381,000
Cundall Johnston & Partners LLP	£34,231,020
Texon Non Woven Ltd	£34,174,000
The Manydown Company Limited	£34,046,620
Huntsman Advanced Materials (UK) Limited	£34,038,000
Theakston Estates Limited	£34,028,764
Banks Renewables (Middle Muir Wind Farm) Limited	£33,936,000
Zyro Limited	£33,901,000
Middleton Enterprises Ltd	£33,887,072
C. A. Blackwell (Contracts) Limited	£33,882,000
Creambay Limited	£33,843,000
Inoveight Limited	£33,843,000
Arriva Cymru Limited	£33,826,000
Renolit Cramlington Limited	£33,775,000
3R Land & Property Ltd	£33,746,292
Sarens (UK) Ltd	£33,673,000
Paragon Group UK Limited	£33,587,000
Ramside Holdings Limited	£33,555,128
Read Holdings Limited	£33,553,000
Hargreaves Industrial Services Limited	£33,484,000
Genius Bidco Limited	£33,350,060
Billions Europe Ltd	£33,275,236
Eleven Arches	£33,142,104
UKLEP (2003) Limited	£32,933,600
Vehicle Lease and Service Limited	£32,877,600
Gentoo Homes Limited	£32,845,000
Malhotra Property Investments Limited	£32,844,120
Northern Bear PLC	£32,838,000
Grainger Trust Limited	£32,761,044
Borgwarner Gateshead Limited	£32,675,476
Kenton Schools Academy Trust	£32,281,000
Sundram International Limited	£32,280,974
Edmi Europe Limited	£32,130,000
NCFE	£32,113,000
Yorwaste Limited	£32,063,124
Genius Holdco Limited	£31,987,884
Grainger Invest (No.1 Holdco) Limited	£31,744,882
Fairstone Capital Investment Limited	£31,714,000
Den Hartogh Logistics Limited	£31,672,520
Fergusons Blyth Limited	£31,495,500
Tekmar Limited	£31,411,000
Crown Care IV Limited	£31,386,458
Ramsdens Holdings PLC	£31,303,000
Grantham Motor Company Limited	£31,275,000
Welwyn Components Limited	£31,248,000
Encore Envelopes Limited	£31,232,600
PHA Limited	£31,210,886
Centralus Operations LLP	£31,178,336
North Tees Limited	£30,986,164
GNS Midco 1 Limited	£30,848,116
Hilco Europe	£30,800,008
Project Tulip Topco Limited	£30,666,716
South Tyneside Housing Ventures Trust Limited	£30,637,816
M.G.L. Group Limited	£30,548,296
Prince Bishops Homes Limited	£30,425,916
Pearie Law Windfarm Limited	£30,388,000
Boasso Global Limited	£30,132,888
Engie in Partnership Limited	£30,087,000
Banks Property Limited	£30,086,000

Company	Value
Interbulk Group Limited	£30,047,748
Erwin Hymer Group Holdings UK Limited	£29,787,466
AVG Imperial Ltd	£29,631,442
H I Tricomm Holdings Limited	£29,619,720
Getinge UK Limited	£29,608,000
Bell Truck Sales Limited	£29,552,512
Bell Trucks (Holdings) Limited	£29,552,512
Siglion Investments LLP	£29,514,688
North Tees Group Holdings Limited	£29,445,254
Zytronic PLC	£29,318,000
The Three Rivers Learning Trust	£29,293,344
Eyms Group Limited	£29,168,116
Broadband Satellite Services Limited	£29,090,220
Performance Horizon Group Limited	£29,063,000
Grainger Pearl Limited	£28,999,988
Grainger Southwark Limited	£28,976,932
Retirement Housing No. 1 (2007) Limited	£28,889,856
Automatic Retailing (Northern) Limited	£28,855,018
The City of Oxford Motor Services Limited	£28,830,000
Sembcorp Investments (China) Limited	£28,790,000
North Tees Holdings Limited	£28,760,606
Smithers-Oasis Europe Limited	£28,637,000
Arriva Northumbria Limited	£28,443,000
Scott Bros. Holdings Limited	£28,390,208
EDF Energy Renewables Limited	£28,207,000
Tekmar Holdings Limited	£28,179,000
Jomast 5 Limited	£28,158,404
The Davy Roll Company Limited	£28,142,000
Banks Renewables Limited	£28,111,000
GNS Midco 2 Limited	£27,983,560
Cotterhill Limited	£27,972,160
Lucite International Speciality Polymers and Resins Ltd	£27,900,000
Thompsons of Prudhoe Holding Ltd.	£27,896,028
Renolit (U.K.) Limited	£27,839,000
Newcastle Systems Management Limited	£27,792,156
Sir John Fitzgerald,Limited	£27,781,864
Sir John Fitzgerald (Holdings) Limited	£27,781,864
Be Modern Holdings Limited	£27,765,308
Thomas Swan & Co.Limited	£27,576,710
The North East Regional Investment Fund Partner Ltd	£27,540,930
Thomas Swan Holdings Limited	£27,399,000
High Street GRP Limited	£27,329,660
Gosforth Schools' Trust	£27,292,900
Duranta Energy Limited	£27,131,150
The Education Village Academy Trust	£27,130,000
Gestamp Washington UK Limited	£27,005,710
Manor Park Holiday Park Limited	£26,941,000
Bondshold Limited	£26,814,928
East Yorkshire Motor Services Limited	£26,807,044
Thyssenkrupp Access Limited	£26,765,000
Allflex UK Group Limited	£26,571,952
North East Truck & Van Limited	£26,549,000
Enodis Maple Leaf Ltd	£26,544,000
The Welfare Dwellings Trust Limited	£26,501,000
T. Crossling & Co. Limited	£26,438,000
Con Mech Group Limited	£26,221,920
Greencroft Bottling Company Limited	£26,218,898
The Interflex Group Europe Limited	£26,169,644
North East Truck & Van Holdings Limited	£26,162,000
LSLI Limited	£26,031,000
Lake District Leisure Pursuits Limited	£26,021,000
Tyne Region North Limited	£26,020,742
G.T. Group Ltd	£25,970,354
Wainstones Energy Limited	£25,883,276
MSSL Overseas Wiring System Limited	£25,790,792
National Energy Action	£25,610,316
Fairstone Executive Management Limited	£25,608,786
Lanchester Wine Cellars Limited	£25,512,044
Arkgrove Limited	£25,506,312
Elring Klinger (Great Britain) Limited	£25,430,000
Newcastle Diocesan Board of Finance Limited (The)	£25,394,428
Greenoaks (Maidenhead) Limited	£25,362,000
A & P Falmouth Limited	£25,300,004
The Reece Foundation	£25,277,724
Walker Filtration Limited	£25,183,352
The Kerfoot Group Limited	£25,181,402
Markbourn Limited	£25,144,272
Grainger Kensington & Chelsea Limited	£25,091,578
Home Properties Limited	£25,041,860
North East Learning Trust	£25,021,000
Hodgson Newcastle Limited	£24,917,548
Lycetts Holdings Limited	£24,904,208
Everris Limited	£24,793,000
UK Land Estates Limited	£24,747,104
The Percy Hedley Foundation	£24,727,000
Texon International Group Limited	£24,638,000
North East Autism Society	£24,474,494
Cameron Hall Developments Limited	£24,453,000
Newcastle East Mixed Multi Academy Trust	£24,374,000
Beaver Management Services Limited	£24,328,672
Read Limited	£24,317,000
Froneri South Africa Holdings Limited	£24,233,242
Caledonian Trust PLC.	£24,175,000
Engie Urban Energy Limited	£24,005,000
Academy 360	£23,999,000
PD Ports Humber Limited	£23,902,000
Arriva Midlands North Limited	£23,828,000
GMC-Instruments UK Limited	£23,798,802
B.E.L. Properties Limited	£23,738,928
LJJ Ltd	£23,706,242
Nvent Solutions (UK) Limited	£23,693,000
South Hereford Garages Limited	£23,616,000
Wynyard Park Limited	£23,614,882
Vision Academy Learning Trust	£23,558,908
London and North Western Railway Company Limited	£23,525,000
Vaulkhard Group Limited	£23,506,896
Parlour Product Topco Limited	£23,423,000
Ebac Limited	£23,380,876
Tyne & Wear Holdings Limited	£23,364,860
Liebherr Sunderland Works Limited	£23,346,822
Global Navigation Solutions Limited	£23,342,048
Arch (Development Projects) Limited	£23,316,284
GT Timber Limited	£23,295,736
Express Engineering (Gateshead) Limited	£23,275,544
High Hedley Hope Wind Limited	£23,225,000
Faltec Europe Limited	£23,165,462
MTW County Limited	£23,057,126
Sigma Holdings Limited	£22,984,000
CPI Antony Rowe Ltd	£22,938,000
The Callaly Estates Company Limited	£22,828,780
Horatio Holdings Limited	£22,691,204
Mech-Tool Engineering Limited	£22,687,874
H.B.Clark & Co.(Successors) Limited	£22,664,022
Sage USD Hedgeco 1	£22,646,416
Metnor Property Group Limited	£22,644,000
NWG Commercial Solutions Limited	£22,626,000
LSL Corporate Client Services Limited	£22,596,000
High Street Commercial Finance Limited	£22,569,764
Metnor Construction Limited	£22,564,000
Grand Central Railway Company Limited	£22,497,000
Crossling Limited	£22,472,000
Hadrian Learning Trust	£22,387,000
George Allinson (Transport) Limited	£22,334,648
Ebac Holdings Limited	£22,297,326
J.T.Dove,Limited	£22,252,688
Createcity Limited	£22,212,944
Easteye Limited	£22,171,376
UK Independent Medical Services Limited	£22,083,832
C.J. Leonard & Sons Limited	£22,049,778
HMC Group Ltd	£22,033,168
Grainger Residential Management Limited	£21,969,180
Procomm Site Services Limited	£21,830,076
St.John's College,Durham	£21,687,532
Barkers (Northallerton) Limited	£21,671,012

Company	Amount	Company	Amount
Barmoor Wind Power Limited	£21,651,000	Covion Limited	£18,815,000
Wellbark Property Limited	£21,624,724	Ebac Group Limited	£18,777,134
Riverside Acquisitions Limited	£21,602,210	Enodis Property Developments Limited	£18,732,000
Texon Overseas	£21,592,000	Hawkridge Management Limited	£18,692,320
Banks Renewables (Penny Hill Wind Farm) Limited	£21,580,000	J Maguire Holdings Limited	£18,642,422
First Complete Limited	£21,564,000	J. & J. Ward Limited	£18,530,308
Newcastle Park & Fly Limited	£21,542,496	Thompsons of Prudhoe Limited	£18,491,542
Turkey Mill Investments Limited	£21,518,080	Horizons Specialist Academy Trust	£18,486,000
John Wade (Holdings) Limited	£21,502,488	Hargreaves Maltby Limited	£18,453,000
Vale of Mowbray Limited	£21,458,016	Sandco F.P.S. Limited	£18,368,812
Taylormade Timber Products Ltd	£21,421,552	Replay Associates Limited	£18,367,224
Unity City Academy Trust	£21,389,000	Plymouth Citybus Limited	£18,366,000
Southmoor Multi Academy Trust	£21,241,000	NFPA Holdings Limited	£18,305,028
Snorkel Europe Limited	£21,211,000	Modus Seabed Intervention Limited	£18,303,000
Lordstones Developments Limited	£21,203,388	Doncaster Pharmaceuticals Group Limited	£18,294,000
Lycett, Browne-Swinburne & Douglass Limited	£21,187,114	Integrated Utility Services Limited	£18,252,000
Nunthorpe Multi-Academy Trust Limited	£21,057,352	True Potential LLP	£18,232,000
Jomast 6 Limited	£20,989,034	Sacred Heart Partnership of Schools	£18,213,000
Northumbrian Water Projects Limited	£20,966,282	Adderstone 1993 Limited	£18,211,338
Stampflat Limited	£20,951,254	The Riverside Learning Trust	£18,190,746
Banner Contracts (Halnaby) Limited	£20,927,932	Grainger REIT 1 Limited	£18,187,988
FC Tankship I Ltd	£20,846,662	VB Turnbull Limited	£18,170,320
Keelman Homes Limited	£20,784,000	PX Limited	£18,151,180
Ever 1209 Limited	£20,760,146	EEW Offshore Structures (Britain) Limited	£18,078,252
E-Sil Components Ltd	£20,704,000	Aghoco 1085 Limited	£18,070,000
Winn Solicitors Limited	£20,676,104	Bel Engineering (UK) Limited	£18,023,000
Lambton Share Property Company Limited	£20,616,704	Prefere Resins UK Limited	£17,950,000
Leicester District Energy Company Limited	£20,611,000	Outer West Learning Trust	£17,920,552
Richard Irvin & Sons Limited	£20,599,000	W & M Wholesale Limited	£17,860,528
Durham Cricket C.I.C.	£20,596,436	True Potential Adviser Services LLP	£17,852,904
P.C. Henderson Limited	£20,416,000	Foundation of Light	£17,786,566
Learning Curve Group Limited	£20,384,776	James Burrell Limited	£17,707,400
Weststar Holidays Limited	£20,344,000	Skelton Farming Limited	£17,667,380
WHL 2013 Holdings Limited	£20,291,000	The Zurbaran Trust	£17,618,554
The Cyrenians Ltd	£20,260,828	Leven Estates Ltd	£17,578,618
Reece Property Limited	£20,194,204	Newcastle Special Schools Trust	£17,514,612
Erwin Hymer Group UK Ltd	£20,149,680	Esh Developments Limited	£17,476,794
A&P GH 2006 Limited	£20,109,414	Nicholsons Group Limited	£17,297,848
Dragonfly Venture (Trading) Limited	£20,094,048	Mike Pulman Holdings Limited	£17,279,000
The JGW Patterson Foundation	£20,039,826	W & M Holding Company Limited	£17,273,912
Duranta Holding Company Limited	£19,916,456	Wensleydale Dairy Products Limited	£17,249,696
Endeavour Academies Trust	£19,882,000	Union Property Development Limited	£17,223,722
Tekmar Energy Limited	£19,866,000	Armstrong Richardson & Co.Limited	£17,216,364
Cleveland Bridge UK Limited	£19,858,000	Warrens Group Limited	£17,211,688
Latate Limited	£19,857,808	FC Tankship II Ltd	£17,197,016
The Alnwick Garden Trust	£19,857,322	Larkflame Limited	£17,186,352
South Shore Developments Limited	£19,825,640	Responsive Engineering Limited	£17,154,378
Mech-Tool Holdings Limited	£19,823,432	F.T. Construction Group (Holdings) Ltd.	£17,139,340
Worthington Armstrong U.K. Limited	£19,821,532	Engie Energy Services UK Limited	£17,117,000
Berisford Holdings Limited	£19,810,000	Timec 1484 Limited	£17,098,760
Tompkins UK Limited	£19,790,000	Pragmatic Printing Limited	£17,026,104
RPU Group PLC	£19,782,664	Hummersknott Academy Trust	£16,932,000
Duranta Teesside Limited	£19,770,412	Birmingham District Energy Company Limited	£16,900,000
RMB Automotive Ltd	£19,749,696	Convergys CMG UK Limited	£16,872,000
Wynyard Golf Club Ltd.	£19,748,544	Mobile Mini UK Holdings Limited	£16,867,000
J T Atkinson & Sons Limited	£19,683,426	Falck Nutec Ltd	£16,843,660
Crown Care VI Limited	£19,606,132	Leadgates Investments Limited	£16,828,236
Elddis Transport (Consett) Limited	£19,605,308	Dame Allan's Schools	£16,821,080
Jomast 2 Limited	£19,507,420	On Medical Limited	£16,798,716
Miller UK Limited	£19,410,572	Valmont Stainton Limited	£16,793,000
The Clinkard Group Limited	£19,333,000	Vroon Shipping U.K. Ltd.	£16,754,845
Vale of Mowbray Holdings Limited	£19,328,004	A.& J.Scott Limited	£16,735,571
Your Homes Newcastle Limited	£19,304,000	Northumberland Estates Finance LLP	£16,706,744
Opsec Security Limited	£19,296,000	Bath Press Limited	£16,677,391
County Durham Community Foundation	£19,255,472	Heerema Hartlepool Limited	£16,658,000
Turner & Wrights Limited	£19,230,256	Brand New Co (444) Limited	£16,655,207
Fourstones Paper Mill Company Limited	£19,199,940	Mowden Park Estate Company Limited	£16,631,130
Grainger OCCC Limited	£19,166,462	Home and Leisure International Limited	£16,628,625
Mandale Apartments 3 Limited	£19,159,314	Shepherd Offshore Services Limited	£16,608,872
Wemyss Bay Caravan Park Limited	£18,918,000	Arete Learning Trust	£16,561,000
G T Culpitt & Son (Holdings) Limited	£18,902,424	Parmley Graham Limited	£16,546,000
Biddick Academy Trust	£18,860,000	The Hermitage Academy Trust	£16,526,327

Company	Amount
Bannatyne Hotels Limited	£16,511,102
Heraeus Quartz UK Limited	£16,498,501
Vestbrown Limited	£16,479,364
Redcar Bulk Terminal Limited	£16,415,000
Novares Peterlee Limited	£16,406,831
Wilton Engineering Services Limited	£16,391,216
The Belsay Trust	£16,372,485
M.& M.Value Limited	£16,354,993
AD Astra Academy Trust	£16,308,000
Watkins Hire Limited	£16,303,000
Energy Information Centre Limited	£16,280,646
Metabrasive Limited	£16,249,000
Thermodynamix Thermoforming Specialist Services Ltd	£16,247,866
Newquip Limited	£16,221,087
Sembcorp Investments Limited	£16,218,000
Zest Investment Group Limited	£16,178,444
Wellstream Finance Limited	£16,168,000
North East Regeneration Partnership LLP	£16,155,414
Inn Collection Topco Limited	£16,109,880
M & G Solid Fuels LLP	£16,084,499
Clayton Glass Limited	£16,024,951
Norstead Limited	£16,023,000
Banks Renewables (Moor House Wind Farm) Limited	£15,968,000
Whitburn Church of England Academy	£15,933,000
Sirap UK Limited	£15,903,000
West End Schools Trust	£15,878,788
North East Theatre Trust Limited	£15,851,437
Merit Holdings Limited	£15,770,031
Merit Group Services Limited	£15,770,031
Huntsman Advanced Materials Holdings (UK) Limited	£15,756,000
Be Modern Limited	£15,732,189
Virgin Money Unit Trust Managers Limited	£15,731,000
Essex and Suffolk Water Limited	£15,710,000
Scott Logic Limited	£15,701,010
WHL 2013 Limited	£15,673,000
G A Smith Limited	£15,669,003
Hexham Auction Mart Company,Limited	£15,657,445
Polyfoam XPS Limited	£15,545,257
ADM Pressings Limited	£15,541,719
PCCA (UK) Holdings Limited	£15,541,523
Castle View Enterprise Academy	£15,534,000
Manitowoc FSG UK Limited	£15,471,000
SLW (Holdings) Limited	£15,383,942
North East Business and Innovation Centre Limited	£15,380,065
Rainton Construction Limited	£15,375,269
Northumbrian Leisure Limited	£15,288,009
Tyne Region North Stepney Limited	£15,247,644
FB Tankship IV Limited	£15,230,698
Manitowoc Foodservice UK Holding Limited	£15,205,000
Reger Holding Limited	£15,201,488
Forward Sound Limited	£15,184,000
Kans and Kandy (Wholesale) Ltd	£15,172,541
Norham House 2 Limited	£15,145,301
Grainger REIT 3 Limited	£15,133,935
Grainger REIT 2 Limited	£15,133,935
James Cook Discovery Ltd	£15,112,939
TFLX Limited	£15,110,840
LPT Trading Ltd	£15,070,979
Browns Bedrooms & Kitchens Ltd	£15,009,056
NHP Management Limited	£14,994,578
Bulk Logistics Group Ltd	£14,976,294
Walkway Windfarm Limited	£14,966,000
Sage People Limited	£14,958,091
Northumberland Estates Investments 3000 Limited	£14,912,251
Joseph Swan Academy	£14,902,200
Advanced Electronics Limited	£14,849,223
FB Tankship III Limited	£14,841,587
Closegate Hotel Development (Durham) Limited	£14,824,032
Engie Property Services Limited	£14,819,000
Zytronic Displays Limited	£14,808,000
Education and Services for People with Autism Ltd	£14,805,987
S T R Enterprises Limited	£14,802,300

Company	Amount
Hays Beds Limited	£14,772,290
Bywell Home Farms LLP	£14,769,990
Hamsard 2518 Limited	£14,763,800
Riba Enterprises Ltd	£14,732,381
Precision Hydraulic Cylinders (UK) Limited	£14,731,863
Kitwave One Limited	£14,704,827
Pitman Press Limited	£14,693,670
St. Oswald's Hospice Limited	£14,686,304
King James I Academy, Bishop Auckland Limited	£14,652,000
TDX (Europe) Limited	£14,647,826
Tees Valley Community Foundation	£14,638,532
Elanders Ltd	£14,616,346
Allergate Investments Limited	£14,552,768
St. Mary's Catholic School Trust	£14,535,355
Banks Renewables (Armistead Wind Farm) Limited	£14,501,000
Crown Care II LLP	£14,500,518
Conyers Trust	£14,498,668
Exelby Services Limited	£14,453,305
Zonat Limited	£14,452,635
ATFC Limited	£14,435,000
Apartment 1 Limited	£14,431,321
Tudhoe Learning Trust	£14,423,274
Aspire Healthcare Limited	£14,340,762
Surgo Construction Limited	£14,326,285
Technology Services Group Limited	£14,227,000
Grainger Seven Sisters Limited	£14,177,929
Gro-Group Holdings Limited	£14,156,000
PD Co Holdings (UK) Limited	£14,151,332
H.M. Pigs Limited	£14,143,756
Quays Hotels Limited	£14,142,053
Closegate Projects Limited	£14,126,603
Mersen UK Teesside Limited	£14,108,223
Northern General Properties Limited	£14,068,593
Bussey & Armstrong Projects Limited	£14,045,539
Emerald Biogas Ltd	£14,008,520
Calamander Developments Limited	£14,002,368
Leisure World Group Limited	£13,994,411
Dawson & Sanderson Limited	£13,963,118
New Tyne West Development Company LLP	£13,957,009
Mitford F Limited	£13,944,927
Mitford B Limited	£13,944,927
Ever 1855 Limited	£13,943,573
Sistine Properties (Thetford) Limited	£13,941,376
Millfield Enterprises Group Limited	£13,914,260
Fleet Factors Limited	£13,908,752
Bertschi U.K. Limited	£13,857,117
Flaxby Park Limited	£13,844,084
Northgood Industries Limited	£13,826,329
Solehawk Limited	£13,789,525
Wearmouth Construction and Plant Limited	£13,728,367
The Castle Building Services Organisation Limited	£13,708,522
Banks Renewables (Hook Moor Wind Farm) Limited	£13,706,000
Sherwoods (Darlington) Limited	£13,703,086
North of England Estates Limited	£13,649,389
Edward Thompson (Printers) Limited	£13,625,583
Oil NRG Ltd	£13,550,093
H.V.R. International Limited	£13,532,962
Ramscove Limited	£13,530,085
George Washington Golf and Country Club Limited	£13,484,339
Nicholsons Sealing Technologies Limited	£13,478,359
Lingfield Education Trust	£13,448,000
Roundel Manufacturing Limited	£13,407,986
Mulberry Homes Yorkshire Limited	£13,405,606
Middle Caves Ltd	£13,399,682
Extol Academy Trust	£13,397,673
Prima Cheese Limited	£13,346,014
Derek Parnaby Cyclones International Limited	£13,342,263
Upnorth Engineering Services Limited	£13,303,114
Mental Health Concern	£13,303,000
DNR Limited	£13,269,632
Niramax Group Limited	£13,265,251
Niramax Holdings Limited	£13,257,418

Company	Value
Close House Hospitality Limited	£13,234,731
Hawkpost Limited	£13,143,990
Vaulkhard Leisure Limited	£13,141,100
Wise Academies	£13,133,000
Fairstone Group Limited	£13,119,000
NWG Bioenergy Limited	£13,106,000
Tharsus Group Limited	£13,100,259
Hewitson Group Ltd	£13,091,361
Stokesley Hardware Co. Limited	£13,089,360
Tolent Solutions Limited	£13,085,623
F & I Holdings Ltd	£13,083,178
William Hackett Holdings Limited	£13,040,078
Burton Collingwood Limited	£13,029,655
Kilfrost Group Limited	£13,027,000
The Great North Air Ambulance Service	£13,020,887
Malhotra Property Limited	£13,012,289
Eothen Homes Limited	£12,981,601
Orchard Information Systems Limited	£12,947,307
Michael Sehgal Property Company Limited	£12,913,216
St.Julian's Estate Limited (The)	£12,882,843
Carmel Education Trust	£12,842,000
Fradley Residential LLP	£12,841,333
The Bowes Museum	£12,834,297
NFPAS Limited	£12,829,593
QuantuMDx Group Limited	£12,824,881
Park Spring Wind Farm Limited	£12,810,000
Seneca Investments and Developments Limited	£12,809,947
Sunderland FC Hotels Limited	£12,788,000
Roade Windfarm Limited	£12,776,000
Malhotra Commercial Property Limited	£12,762,012
Brims Construction Limited	£12,757,595
Brims Building Group Limited	£12,757,595
Pacifica Group Limited	£12,750,594
Gateshead Regeneration LLP	£12,713,826
North Music Trust	£12,696,555
Remondis JBT Limited	£12,655,831
Barnard Castle School	£12,651,875
Fergusons Transport Limited	£12,645,703
Fergytrux Limited	£12,645,703
Helena Laboratories (U.K.) Limited	£12,635,029
NGP Utilities Limited	£12,634,856
Henry Colbeck Limited	£12,593,097
Bloom Procurement Services Ltd	£12,576,179
Hope Estates Limited	£12,566,565
Partner Group U.K. Limited	£12,557,286
PIMCO 2852 Limited	£12,554,880
W.I.P (Work in Progress) Limited	£12,520,137
Monckton Coke & Chemical Company Limited (The)	£12,518,000
Lucion Environmental Limited	£12,485,076
Michell Bearings Limited	£12,469,000
C.A. (Evenwood) Limited	£12,463,219
Viewpoint Construction Software Ltd	£12,444,966
Nigel Wright Group Holdings Limited	£12,421,000
Connor Solutions Limited	£12,412,955
Kilfrost Limited	£12,405,000
Vishay Ltd.	£12,387,000
Hathaway Roofing Limited	£12,385,601
Swiss Land Limited	£12,380,942
Hoults Limited	£12,351,709
NIAL Services Limited	£12,349,074
The Hambleton Group Limited	£12,341,281
Connor Group Limited	£12,315,802
Stonegrave Aggregates Limited	£12,302,900
Sage Payments (UK) Ltd.	£12,272,000
Cussins Limited	£12,254,032
Fastflow Energy Services Limited	£12,247,000
Smokies Entertainments Limited	£12,244,264
Culpitt Limited	£12,244,218
Springfield Cars Limited	£12,238,890
Intrahealth Limited	£12,231,133
Propharma Group MIS Limited	£12,203,950
The Blyth Quays Trust	£12,172,000

Company	Value
PDZ (UK) Limited	£12,165,678
Sale PFI Limited	£12,142,000
Metcalfe Farms (Haulage) Limited	£12,141,026
Northern Transport Finance Limited	£12,130,000
Saft Limited	£12,098,000
Richard Hardie Limited	£12,080,614
Warren Court Limited	£12,068,604
Rivergreen Limited	£12,059,361
Magnum Packaging (N.E.) Limited	£12,049,399
NYT (Holdings) Limited	£12,042,025
Crossco (1370) Limited	£12,028,481
Partner Construction Limited	£11,987,113
Dixons of Westerhope Limited	£11,982,371
Collins (Seafoods) Limited	£11,950,874
ISP Holdings (U.K.) Ltd.	£11,944,000
Emerchantpay UK Services Ltd	£11,939,234
Leaguenotion	£11,908,000
Inn Collection Bidco Limited	£11,906,486
Findspace Limited	£11,895,524
Tew Engineering Limited	£11,885,437
Discover Learning Trust	£11,854,000
Biss Underwriting Limited	£11,792,501
Newcastle University Students' Union	£11,749,000
GSH 2018 Limited	£11,744,594
Lending Solutions Holdings Limited	£11,740,000
Techflow Marine Ltd	£11,726,640
Global Decontamination Solutions Limited	£11,723,510
J.G. Paxton and Sons Limited	£11,715,955
Flexible Engineered Solutions Limited	£11,704,716
Storage and Handling Equipment Limited	£11,704,218
Grainger Maidenhead Limited	£11,690,924
UK Land Investments Limited	£11,685,315
Tennants of Yorkshire Antique & Fine Art Auctioneers Ltd	£11,683,181
James A. Jobling and Company Limited	£11,681,448
Newcastle Strategic Solutions Limited	£11,678,531
Select Property Developments Limited	£11,672,337
Darrington Healthcare Ltd	£11,671,695
Fletcher Property Investments UK Limited	£11,663,000
Clayside Property Investments Limited	£11,653,775
Hagen Developments Limited	£11,644,763
Cleveland Land Services (Guisborough) Limited	£11,631,934
Chainbridge Steel Group Limited	£11,578,329
J B Tustain Motors Holdings Limited	£11,550,440
GNS Treasury Limited	£11,548,807
Map Group (UK) Limited	£11,545,506
Hytorc (Unex) Limited	£11,528,971
Zetland Estates Limited	£11,515,562
NZR Limited	£11,515,000
Primula Limited	£11,497,000
G. & M. Westgarth Limited	£11,462,633
AKV Group Ltd	£11,453,572
St Aidan's Church of England Academy Limited	£11,448,000
Southampton Geothermal Heating Company Limited	£11,436,000
Remondis Waste Solutions Limited	£11,428,393
D P M Finance LLP	£11,414,686
Oak Learning Trust	£11,397,351
Tharsus Limited	£11,375,646
Bebe Group Limited	£11,372,452
Interbulk (Tankcontainers) Holdings Limited	£11,352,953
M.J. Hickey Plant Hire & Contracts Limited	£11,347,951
Empire Property Holdings 2 Limited	£11,334,046
Cornerstone Chemical Company Limited	£11,326,000
Lucion Services Limited	£11,324,500
Wearmouth Learning Trust	£11,324,077
Smart Multi Academy Trust	£11,315,265
Dynamic CCTV Limited	£11,301,664
Vic Young (South Shields) Limited	£11,299,438
Brandmile Limited	£11,293,968
M.G.L. Demolition Limited	£11,262,293
Banks Renewables (Heysham South Wind Farm) Ltd	£11,255,000
Mercantile Estates Ltd	£11,243,471
Siglion LLP	£11,242,989

MTREC Limited	£11,223,763
Roman Limited	£11,222,885
Stranton Academy Trust	£11,222,664
Derwent Developments (Curzon) Limited	£11,196,000
Evolution Gateshead Developments LLP	£11,176,517
SMH Products Limited	£11,174,139
Potts Print (UK) Limited	£11,157,977
John N Dunn Holdings Limited	£11,146,709
North Yorkshire Timber Company Limited	£11,146,615
Dane & Co., Limited	£11,138,549
Parlour Product Holding Limited	£11,130,000
Cussins (North East) Limited	£11,125,827
Mandale Investments Limited	£11,110,181
Northumbrian Fine Foods Limited	£11,107,337
Clic Time Holdings Limited	£11,091,468
H.Malone and Sons Limited	£11,079,445
True Solicitors LLP	£11,045,120
IKM Testing UK Limited	£11,034,368
CAV Ice Protection Limited	£11,032,427
Lintz Hall Farm Limited	£11,007,206
Salem Tube International Limited	£10,989,730
Excel District Energy Company Limited	£10,985,000
NHP Operations (York) Limited	£10,984,877
Grainger PRS Limited	£10,956,205
Kookaburra Limited	£10,945,332
Grainger Games (Holdings) Limited	£10,912,220
Andrew James UK Ltd	£10,901,169
It's All Good Limited	£10,893,186
Fentimans Ltd.	£10,888,183
Forthcastle LLP	£10,872,047
Ward Bros. (Steel) Limited	£10,867,774
GLPD Property Limited	£10,855,969
Kratos Communications Limited	£10,847,164
Cousins Properties Limited	£10,830,000
Foster Findlay Associates Limited	£10,826,476
Hays Property Services Limited	£10,824,399
St. Chad's College	£10,821,604
Sage Brazilian Investment Two Limited	£10,820,000
Parsons Group Limited	£10,812,148
Templeman Trading Limited	£10,809,070
Inspire Multi Academy Trust	£10,808,000
United Reformed Church (Northern Province) Trust Ltd	£10,795,570
Gala Unity Limited	£10,793,508
Guisborough Hotels Limited	£10,792,803
Almit Group Limited	£10,760,837
Mike Pulman Limited	£10,735,000
North East Finance (Subco) Limited	£10,733,233
W. & M. Thompson (Quarries) Limited	£10,729,145
Sage Far East Investments Limited	£10,721,000
Janus International (UK) Limited	£10,706,087
Montpelier Professional Limited	£10,701,604
First Sight Estates Limited	£10,657,000
HC-ONE Beamish Limited	£10,645,000
Aim High Academy Trust	£10,644,000
St Thomas More Roman Catholic Academy	£10,641,063
HTL Group Limited	£10,627,090
DW Contractors (Oxford) Ltd	£10,610,000
Natzone Limited	£10,605,212
Haskel Europe Ltd	£10,602,379
Scott Bros. Environmental Services Limited	£10,587,841
Port Clarence Logistics Limited	£10,583,534
Nigel Wright Consultancy Limited	£10,580,000
Sam Turner and Sons Limited	£10,559,353
Bulk Tainer Logistics Limited	£10,554,850
Collingwood Business Solutions Limited	£10,552,902
Hydram Engineering Limited	£10,529,852
HMH Civils Limited	£10,517,632
Applebridge Construction Limited	£10,494,699
Holmedale Valley Limited	£10,464,988
Propharma Group MIS Holdings Limited	£10,462,714
Dynamic CCTV Management Ltd	£10,460,035
Rotary Power Ltd.	£10,455,000
J.A.Jewitt	£10,431,761
John N Dunn Group Limited	£10,416,599
Drogo Developments Ltd	£10,399,839
Richard Preston & Son Limited	£10,394,385
The Expanded Metal Company Limited	£10,389,000
Newcastle Theatre Royal Trust Limited	£10,388,675
Tyne Region North Properties Limited	£10,376,637
Nova Marketing Limited	£10,368,147
Durham High School for Girls	£10,366,713
Dane Finance Limited	£10,340,390
Total Recycling Services Limited	£10,322,000
W.D. Close & Sons Limited	£10,320,555
Palintest Limited	£10,320,231
South Tyneside Homes Limited	£10,281,000
The Goshen Trust	£10,266,589
Premier Care Homes Limited	£10,241,008
Aspire Technology Solutions Ltd	£10,234,963
The Excel Academy Partnership	£10,233,000
Newcastle Portland House Limited	£10,211,836
Ravensworth Property Developments LLP	£10,204,771
Langage Energy Park Limited	£10,199,383
Discovery Learning Limited	£10,160,357
Fisher Outdoor Leisure Holdings Limited	£10,158,000
Empire Property Holdings Limited	£10,144,391
Raytec Limited	£10,115,878
Katmex Limited	£10,096,576
Simon Bailes Limited	£10,062,287
ACS Invest UK Limited	£10,047,318
Frecker Limited	£10,040,389
First Windfarm Holdings Limited	£10,031,000
Advance Mortgage Funding Limited	£10,027,000
The Feel Good Group Limited	£10,025,705
Oil Consultants Holdco Limited	£10,009,722
True Potential Wealth Management LLP	£9,965,249
Invertec Holdings Ltd.	£9,922,193
Megabet UK Ltd.	£9,915,485
Schiedel Chimney Systems Limited	£9,905,000
Mason Frank International Limited	£9,886,000
Snop UK Limited	£9,868,865
Derryland Limited	£9,853,932
HD Homes Limited	£9,843,990
Tricomm Housing (Holdings) Limited	£9,843,361
CSD Sealing Systems Limited	£9,816,969
Vardy Property Group Limited	£9,807,455
Northumbrian Roads Limited	£9,795,594
Newham Hall Holdings Limited	£9,792,999
Banks Renewables (Marr Wind Farm) Limited	£9,787,000
SLW Limited	£9,772,270
Materials Processing Institute	£9,759,769
Fordinghall Ltd	£9,749,281
Isotank Services Limited	£9,731,110
SHG Holdings Limited	£9,719,000
Advanced Industrial Solutions Limited	£9,718,151
Hays Transport Limited	£9,697,619
J & B Recycling Limited	£9,697,219
U L Medicines Limited	£9,696,005
Portland House Holdings Limited	£9,667,795
Chapter Homes Durham Limited	£9,643,074
Vauxhall Holiday Park Limited	£9,637,000
Michigan Investments Limited	£9,634,029
St. Martin's Care Limited	£9,629,964
I.T. Professional Services Limited	£9,619,796
Fairfield Windfarm Limited	£9,583,000
ITPS (Holdings) Limited	£9,574,000
Minhoco 27 Limited	£9,558,463
Enhanced Elderly Care Limited	£9,543,604
Maher Entertainments Limited	£9,531,990
Boundary Lane Windfarm Limited	£9,519,000
Expanded Metal Holdings Limited	£9,517,000
Hartlepool Investments Limited	£9,512,277
Exwold Technology Limited	£9,496,290
Crabtree of Gateshead Limited	£9,486,942

Company	Turnover
Warm Zones C.I.C	£9,470,701
Visualsoft Holdings Limited	£9,469,780
And Group Limited	£9,436,400
Durham Care Line Limited	£9,413,397
Riverdale Paper PLC	£9,387,097
Langage Solar Park Limited	£9,376,475
John Harrison (Stockton) Limited	£9,352,106
Petards Joyce-Loebl Limited	£9,343,000
Wingrove Motor Company Limited	£9,339,945
Riddochhill Developments Limited	£9,336,702
Durham School	£9,318,922
J.A. Jewitt (Meat) Limited	£9,317,083
Cardiff Educational Endowment Trust	£9,302,555
Humankind Charity	£9,300,493
Process Control Equipment Limited	£9,295,544
Unika Group Limited	£9,287,312
Dane Architectural Systems Holdings Limited	£9,283,844
Westone Wholesale Limited	£9,282,724
Geordie Jeans Limited	£9,277,110
Electrix International Limited	£9,271,669
The British Electrical & Manufacturing Co Ltd	£9,270,711
Northland Real Estate Properties (UK) Limited	£9,264,906
BJP Corporation Ltd	£9,258,807
St. Cuthbert Newcastle Estates Limited	£9,251,544
VHV Investments UK Limited	£9,241,125
Ravendale Foods Limited	£9,240,603
Whitestone Weavers Limited	£9,238,898
Albert Hill Commercials Limited	£9,236,276
PD Ports Hull Limited	£9,188,000
Hubbway Limited	£9,180,668
Adderstone (Sunderland) LLP	£9,179,356
Bellway Housing Trust Limited	£9,177,523
Fairstone Financial Management Limited	£9,167,831
Catterick Caravan & Camping Centre Limited	£9,157,478
C F Abraham Limited	£9,154,377
J.E. Laidler (North East) Limited	£9,138,066
Hotel Operations Limited	£9,122,808
Alan Jackson (Westcotes) Limited	£9,111,880
Bridgewater Contractual Tenancies Limited	£9,090,747
T J D Properties Limited	£9,079,386
The Gateshead Housing Company	£9,061,000
Stone Hill Park Limited	£9,051,471
Retirement Bridge Management Limited	£9,031,718
R.Manners & Sons Limited	£9,016,888
NAC Trading Limited	£9,015,271
Newcastle School for Boys	£9,012,779
Smithers-Oasis U.K. Limited	£9,004,000
2 Touch BPO Services Ltd	£8,992,000
Franklin Steel Stockholders Ltd	£8,976,992
Grundfos Manufacturing Limited	£8,969,000
Allay Claims Ltd	£8,944,721
4X4 Accessories & Tyres Limited	£8,936,065
Metano Limited	£8,909,672
Sintons Limited Liability Partnership	£8,889,084
Eppleton Quarry Products Limited	£8,883,238
Gosforth Park Hotels Limited	£8,875,352
High Crane Limited	£8,858,034
Arlington Automotive NE Limited	£8,830,000
Green Parks Holdings (Ilfracombe) Ltd	£8,823,383
Stackpole Investments Limited	£8,823,094
Plessey Checks Farming Limited	£8,774,087
Wynyard Homes Limited	£8,773,969
HMY UK Innovation in Retail Ltd	£8,772,000
Holme Farm Residential Village Limited	£8,768,711
The Holy Family Education Trust	£8,760,000
Controle Mesure Regulation (UK) Limited	£8,755,278
Broadacres Services Limited	£8,747,940
Bob Alexander Limited	£8,740,062
Newcastle Rugby Limited	£8,738,960
Sandman Hotel Group (UK) Limited	£8,733,909
Merrychef Limited	£8,728,000
Maxibrite Limited	£8,718,000
Park Electrical Distributors Limited	£8,702,353
Thomas Morris Limited	£8,689,000
Kemel Europe Limited	£8,687,033
United Carlton Office Systems Limited	£8,668,211
Adderstone Developments Limited	£8,651,672
Adderstone Developments (Stock) Limited	£8,625,746
Vision Learning Trust Limited	£8,616,000
Learning Matters Trust Ltd.	£8,599,729
Innerglass Limited	£8,596,429
The McKenzie Corporation Limited	£8,576,478
Meldrum Construction Services Limited	£8,554,870
Analox Sensor Technology Limited	£8,548,763
Lowfield Street Limited	£8,543,860
Mistell Limited	£8,542,256
Lanchester Properties Limited	£8,538,048
Bannatyne Fitness (2) Limited	£8,513,774
The Lakes Distillery Company Limited	£8,505,447
Federal Signal UK Holdings Limited	£8,504,145
The Vindolanda Trust	£8,496,422
Delessert de Maligny LLP	£8,490,749
Greencroft Milk Supplies Limited	£8,480,496
The Punjab Kitchen Ltd	£8,469,262
Carraway Finance Ltd	£8,460,386
Northumberland Estates 2004 Limited	£8,448,167
Sirius Engineering Group Ltd	£8,440,170
Durham Cathedral Open Treasure Limited	£8,434,981
Tynedale Roadstone Limited	£8,421,204
Seaton Trust Limited	£8,415,040
Automotive Group (Newcastle upon Tyne) Limited	£8,405,294
Chan Commercial Ltd	£8,404,748
Business and Enterprise Commercial Limited	£8,364,031
Sirius Renewable Energy Limited	£8,347,450
Fairstone Holdings Limited	£8,331,330
Pipeline Engineering & Supply Co. Limited	£8,317,000
Sunderland Hotels Limited	£8,310,255
Danieli Holdings Limited	£8,273,879
Careline Lifestyles (UK) Ltd	£8,250,608
DHM Vehicle Rental Limited	£8,248,737
Fewsters Limited	£8,220,957
Simpson Print Limited	£8,211,440
Downs Holdings Limited	£8,199,095
Templeman Retailing and Vending Limited	£8,193,989
Genesis Brands Limited	£8,179,729
Lion Care Home Group Limited	£8,176,540
Oil Consultants Limited	£8,172,950
Technimark Limited	£8,146,804
Crafter's Companion Limited	£8,123,055
Tyre Spot Limited	£8,121,714
Harlow Printing Limited	£8,115,879
PCR Holdings Limited	£8,095,104
Fine Environmental Services Limited	£8,089,000
Vestbrown (Esh) Limited	£8,068,915
Apex Cables Limited	£8,058,001
International Cookware Limited	£8,058,000
Washington Metalworks Limited	£8,050,604
Project Genesis Limited	£8,022,312
Ebac Industrial Products Limited	£8,020,379
Crownfold Limited	£8,006,555
Reger Property Limited	£8,005,180
Hambleton Steel Limited	£7,999,759
Gro-Group International Limited	£7,971,000
Land Resources Ltd	£7,969,960
Banks Renewables (Hazlehead Wind Farm) Limited	£7,969,000
Barrier Limited	£7,964,375
Greencroft Estate Company Ltd (The)	£7,963,288
Martel Instruments Holdings Limited	£7,960,248
North East Care Homes Limited	£7,960,247
Coal Contractors Limited	£7,951,347
Brunel Spire LLP	£7,949,834
Park Lets Limited	£7,943,560
A&P Tyne Limited	£7,894,445
Norham Holdings Group Limited	£7,889,852

Company	Value
Cavotec UK Limited	£7,882,004
Hospitaller Order of Saint John of God	£7,878,000
Tyne Logistics Company Limited	£7,873,000
Callaly Leisure Limited	£7,866,130
Popular Care Ltd	£7,858,765
C.F.Motoring Services Ltd	£7,857,394
M.I. Dickson Limited	£7,854,609
Durham Box Company Limited	£7,850,847
Doby Cleats Limited	£7,841,067
Stanley Learning Partnership	£7,838,000
Dyer Engineering Ltd.	£7,830,904
Collingwood Insurance Services (U.K.) Limited	£7,826,272
Crabco Limited	£7,817,096
Newby Foods Limited	£7,806,155
Katmex Holdings Limited	£7,785,428
Autotech Engineering R&D UK Limited	£7,782,000
Prestige Care Limited	£7,781,386
Tyne Properties Limited	£7,774,993
Park View Academy	£7,771,000
Indigo Software Group Limited	£7,764,386
U.C.O.S. Holdings Limited	£7,748,239
Nucleus (GB) Limited	£7,743,490
Hamsard 2342 Limited	£7,733,341
Grainger Europe (No. 4) Limited	£7,718,686
Partner Contracting Limited	£7,717,707
A.T. & P Rentals Ltd.	£7,707,567
Bridgewater (Home Reversions Number 2) Limited	£7,704,999
M.H.Southern & Company Limited	£7,691,385
El Investments Limited	£7,689,559
Crest House Property Limited	£7,679,246
Astley Signs Limited	£7,665,913
Adlink Technology Limited	£7,665,804
Middlesbrough Borough Cars Limited	£7,662,958
Hadrian Healthcare (Knaresborough) Limited	£7,658,913
PBU (UK) Ltd	£7,655,277
St Cuthbert's Care	£7,653,254
Green Lane Primary Academy Limited	£7,645,000
Sunderland Care and Support Limited	£7,641,272
Heck! Food Limited	£7,641,158
Phoenix Steel Holdings Limited	£7,625,791
Seneca Global Energy Limited	£7,616,546
Chemson Limited	£7,611,834
00741078 Limited	£7,608,000
Hellens Investments (Washington) LLP	£7,604,237
Minhoco 24 Limited	£7,595,737
Hodgson Sayers Limited	£7,589,360
St Thomas More Partnership of Schools	£7,589,018
Security Print Solutions Limited	£7,576,065
GB Holiday Parks Limited	£7,575,000
Arc Trinova Limited	£7,563,676
Corrpro Companies Europe Limited	£7,559,269
Kilton Thorpe Specialist Academy	£7,551,837
Roballo Engineering Company Limited	£7,541,000
Gentoo Genie Limited	£7,540,484
TC Industries of Europe Limited	£7,532,934
Yorkshire Tiger Limited	£7,518,000
Bannatyne's Health Club (Fairfield) Limited	£7,514,878
The Mountain Boot Company Limited	£7,511,451
The Darlington Farmers Auction Mart Co Ltd	£7,475,696
Sugarfayre Ltd.	£7,469,580
New Equipment Holdings Limited	£7,459,879
Advance Learning Partnership	£7,454,573
Mandata (Holdings) Limited	£7,451,016
Pensave Limited	£7,442,869
Grainger Serviced Apartments Limited	£7,433,927
Chas. Long & Son (Aggregates) Limited	£7,431,104
Crossco (1256) Limited	£7,431,000
Lindisfarne Inns (Bamburgh Castle) Limited	£7,426,857
Dennis Harley Developments Ltd	£7,409,166
Budget Workspace Limited	£7,408,874
Matfen Hall Hotel LLP	£7,408,647
Brett Bros. Developments Limited	£7,394,173
Kayne Properties UK Limited	£7,391,013
YMCA North Tyneside	£7,390,774
Tyne Subsea Limited	£7,389,055
Lugano Developments Limited	£7,382,995
New Sovereign Reversions Limited	£7,382,000
Carpet Line Direct Limited	£7,379,870
David Summerfield Limited	£7,378,678
Hartley Main Farms Limited	£7,374,841
The Home & Capital Trust Group Limited	£7,366,000
Middleton Hall Limited	£7,342,222
Tropic Properties Limited	£7,332,910
Phoenix Steel Limited	£7,332,680
William Smith Group 1832 Limited	£7,326,137
Phoenix Security Holdings Limited	£7,324,853
Phoenix Eye Ltd	£7,324,753
Subsea Innovation Limited	£7,312,912
McKenzie Real Estates Limited	£7,296,412
M B Distribution (Cleveland) Limited	£7,269,254
Bedmax Limited	£7,262,539
Hewitson Plant Hire Limited	£7,240,052
Bebe Clothing (UK) Limited	£7,237,802
Integrated Display Systems Limited	£7,235,536
Visualsoft Limited	£7,214,059
Teesside Hospice Care Foundation	£7,210,038
Actes Trust	£7,209,431
Barrier Group Limited	£7,205,765
Con Mech Engineers Limited	£7,202,095
Connection Flooring Limited	£7,191,184
Inn Collection Midco Limited	£7,187,312
Crossling Properties Limited	£7,172,000
Covion Holdings Limited	£7,172,000
Finley Structures Ltd	£7,163,446
Pacifica Appliance Services Limited	£7,143,405
Clark Homes Limited	£7,143,082
TGMgroup Limited	£7,141,000
Abri Trading Limited	£7,121,000
North Eastern Y.W.C.A.Trustees Limited	£7,120,879
John Dickinson Transport Limited	£7,117,959
J. Noble & Sons Limited	£7,104,469
Turbo Power Systems Limited	£7,104,000
BHK (UK) Limited	£7,103,290
Firgate Limited	£7,097,760
Springs Roofing Limited	£7,088,116
Ward Recycling Limited	£7,082,529
D.P. Fasteners Limited	£7,080,285
Scholle IPN UK Ltd.	£7,074,504
Whymar Limited	£7,057,458
Bremsen Technik (UK) Limited	£7,047,950
Nova Payroll Management Services Limited	£7,044,406
Ronbar Factors Limited	£7,040,629
MPI Offshore Limited	£7,038,028
Squirrels UK Limited	£7,036,508
Biker Group Limited	£7,031,175
Ideal Caravan Sales Limited	£7,025,826
ZIV Automation UK Ltd	£7,017,907
N A C Trading Holdings Limited	£7,012,896
Longhirst Development Limited	£6,982,148
On A Roll Sandwich Company Limited	£6,978,527
St Aidan's Education Trust	£6,977,272
Walter Thompson (Contractors) Limited	£6,975,379
Newcastle Diocesan Society	£6,972,705
The TTE Technical Training Group	£6,963,288
Invertec Interiors Limited	£6,962,048
Woodham Academy	£6,962,000
Berryvale Ltd	£6,947,396
Silverlink Software Limited	£6,943,765
Bureau of Analysed Samples Limited	£6,936,535
Sage Pay (GB) Limited	£6,930,706
Road Link (A69) Limited	£6,928,667
C.B.L. Cable Contractors Limited	£6,921,724
Daikin Applied (UK) Limited	£6,920,000
Brighter Academy Trust	£6,920,000

Company	Turnover
Wm.Allison & Sons Limited	£6,911,896
Elring Parts Limited	£6,901,178
Hadrian Healthcare (Wetherby) Limited	£6,897,321
Oaks Properties Limited	£6,890,337
Arriva Transport Solutions Limited	£6,889,000
Dysart Developments Limited	£6,887,555
NECA	£6,873,392
Portland Residential Limited	£6,868,598
Red House School Limited	£6,867,039
Bradford Propco Limited	£6,857,756
MH Southern (Holdings) Limited	£6,848,918
Metal Drum Company Limited (The)	£6,842,350
Sharpsmart Limited	£6,837,379
Home & Capital Trust Limited	£6,837,000
Konectbus Limited	£6,836,000
Farah Chemists Limited	£6,834,463
CAV Advanced Technologies Limited	£6,831,578
Millfield Composites Group Limited	£6,823,914
John Flowers Limited	£6,813,687
Offerfair Limited	£6,810,426
D & D Armstrong Limited	£6,797,195
Wearside Accommodation Services Limited	£6,792,571
Henry Williams Limited	£6,784,996
Crown Care V Limited	£6,780,789
Three Tuns Developments Limited	£6,776,183
Elfab Limited	£6,768,904
Herrenknecht International Limited	£6,764,789
Tyne Tees Entertainments Limited	£6,745,649
Express Holdings (Thompson) Limited	£6,745,243
Tavistock Hospitality Limited	£6,744,159
Kymel Limited	£6,714,036
Kymel Trading Limited	£6,713,937
Labone Castleside Limited	£6,708,903
Cavotec International Limited	£6,699,344
J & J Ward Properties Limited	£6,681,400
Dickinson Brothers Limited	£6,680,945
Federation of Mowden Schools Academy Trust	£6,668,000
Fraser Grant Estates Limited	£6,639,509
C G Robinson Limited	£6,638,184
Martel Instruments Limited	£6,627,729
Global Manufacturing Supplies Limited	£6,624,678
Norham Holdings Limited	£6,620,908
Maxwells (Sunderland) Limited	£6,613,887
GES Recycling Ltd.	£6,610,437
Balkan Properties Limited	£6,606,316
Keeping Inn Limited	£6,599,381
Groundwork Services (Durham) Ltd	£6,595,401
T.J.Thomson & Son Limited	£6,585,073
Tan International Limited	£6,570,720
Bruder Property Limited	£6,564,039
Business and Enterprise UK Limited	£6,556,468
Orwin Limited	£6,543,921
GMS (Holdings) Limited	£6,528,697
Wilton Universal Group Limited	£6,527,104
Barbour (Europe) Limited	£6,525,783
International Plastic Systems Limited	£6,513,164
Tynexe Limited	£6,512,122
St. Cuthbert's Hospice Durham	£6,511,757
Mandata (Management and Data Services) Ltd	£6,510,652
Bonds Foundry Company Limited	£6,505,036
Qubic Tax Ltd	£6,501,488
Statebourne (Cryogenic) Limited	£6,472,029
British American Railway Services Limited	£6,471,127
Analox Military Systems Limited	£6,469,344
Osbit Limited	£6,447,530
Crossco (1217) Limited	£6,447,000
Gold Sheen Property Investments Limited	£6,439,355
J.Bradburn & Company,Limited	£6,435,130
Beamish Transport Limited	£6,433,767
MBC Summit Holdings Limited	£6,425,664
Total Oynx Limited	£6,421,439
Hadrian Healthcare (Oulton) Limited	£6,420,810
Angel Homes (Durham) Limited	£6,414,283
Nova International Limited	£6,411,274
M. C. Construction (Cleveland) Limited	£6,381,828
The Five Lamps Organisation	£6,373,343
McVickers Holdings Limited	£6,356,225
Hellens Group Holdings Limited	£6,355,237
Wolviston Group Limited	£6,351,113
TCUK Homes Limited	£6,338,210
Peratech Holdco Ltd	£6,331,262
Scott Bros. Limited	£6,329,881
Northern Saints Catholic Education Trust	£6,329,000
Derek Slack Motors Limited	£6,325,500
Emirates Ltd	£6,323,410
Diesel Marine International Limited	£6,320,000
Ouston Farms Limited	£6,319,523
Montane Ltd	£6,309,816
Witton Care Limited	£6,302,130
D.K. Jones Limited	£6,296,593
Taylored Property Group Limited	£6,292,661
B.& B. Attachments Limited	£6,292,260
Beagle Holdings Limited	£6,284,842
H B Clark Holdings Limited	£6,273,750
P.F.Burridge & Sons Limited	£6,263,887
Zerolight Limited	£6,263,820
Alpha Developments (Bradford2) Ltd	£6,254,889
F. Peter Robinson Limited	£6,250,694
North East Group Limited	£6,249,996
Balmoral Learning Trust	£6,242,000
Atlas Garages (Morpeth) Limited	£6,226,149
Holmesterne Farm Co. Limited	£6,225,867
Green Lane Capital (N/E) LLP	£6,224,558
Nova Holdings Limited	£6,214,447
Sir Joseph Isherwood Limited	£6,211,350
Flexible Engineered Solutions Holdings Limited	£6,200,000
K Hewitt Holdings Limited	£6,199,472
Deerness Fencing & Landscaping Limited	£6,198,756
Connect Health Holdings Ltd	£6,198,638
Newcastle Rugby KP Limited	£6,197,000
Palringo Limited	£6,190,087
Oregon Estates Limited	£6,186,191
Kadmous Holdings (UK) Limited.	£6,183,145
Our Children 1st	£6,183,000
Oskap Limited	£6,179,532
Greenbank Compactors LLP	£6,167,333
K. Hewitt and Co. Limited	£6,139,007
Teward Bros Ltd	£6,135,980
Southlands Management Limited	£6,128,891
Whickham School and Sports College	£6,123,000
Gordon Lamb Limited	£6,122,000
John Livingston (Estates) Limited	£6,121,856
Achieving Real Change in Communities CIC	£6,120,542
MPI Services Stokesley Limited	£6,117,810
Applied Graphene Materials PLC	£6,112,473
Chartres Investment Company Limited	£6,107,656
Muckle LLP	£6,101,091
Teescraft Engineering Limited	£6,089,568
Durham Tees Valley Community Rehabilitation Co Ltd	£6,088,137
Bramley Court (Care Homes) Limited	£6,080,242
Gateshead Bayis Ltd	£6,078,014
K Home International Limited	£6,077,306
A & K Ecofilm Limited	£6,073,447
Alpha Holdings (GB) Ltd	£6,072,264
Hadrian Healthcare (Whickham) Limited	£6,071,231
Mosaic Global Investments Limited	£6,063,459
Tustain Motors Limited	£6,058,699
Geoffrey Robinson Limited	£6,047,398
Lowes Group PLC	£6,046,041
Northern Stage (Theatrical Productions) Limited	£6,037,276
Shildon Estates LLP	£6,034,539
Gary Bluff Projects Limited	£6,033,845
Crown Care VII Limited	£6,028,504
Virgin Money Personal Financial Service Limited	£6,022,000

Company	Value
Coney (York) Limited	£6,017,571
Sycamore Property Developments Limited	£6,007,301
Space Architecture (Europe) Limited	£6,001,696
The Protector Group Limited	£6,000,549
Barkell Limited	£5,996,877
Grainger Asset Management Limited	£5,993,165
Sayers Road Tanker Rentals Limited	£5,988,156
Vardy Property Aberdeen Ltd	£5,981,606
London & Regional Capital Ltd	£5,978,627
Sovereign Reversions Holdings Limited	£5,978,000
Manchester Alloys and Metals Limited	£5,971,251
Dennis Dixon Limited	£5,965,172
Nova Finance Limited	£5,964,672
Todd Waste Management Group Limited	£5,963,408
North Lodge Farming Limited	£5,955,821
Canford Group Limited	£5,952,339
Tyneside Cinema	£5,941,966
Jeave 2 Limited	£5,936,709
Sabic Innovative Plastics Limited	£5,929,000
Swarco Traffic Limited	£5,921,731
Marine Engineering Pipeworks Limited	£5,913,078
Darlington Homes Limited	£5,910,795
Seven Stories, National Centre for Children's Books	£5,906,941
Quickly Group Holdings Limited	£5,904,059
Trumark Properties Limited	£5,902,612
Seaward Electronic Limited	£5,899,074
Procomm Site Services (Holdings) Limited	£5,896,447
Kearton Farms Limited	£5,889,350
Royston Limited	£5,888,640
Pear Tree Projects Limited	£5,868,649
AA Construction Utilities Ltd	£5,866,816
J. R. Adams (Newcastle) Limited	£5,863,681
Underwater Cutting Solutions Ltd	£5,863,254
Weardale Motor Services Limited	£5,861,025
XL Precision Technologies Limited	£5,858,740
The Cedars Academy Trust	£5,850,000
Quickly Finance Limited	£5,845,371
Equity Release Investment Properties Limited	£5,840,548
Northern Ladies Annuity Society	£5,837,171
Stiller Warehousing & Distribution Limited	£5,835,950
Ascot Care North East Limited	£5,825,031
The Chrome Group Limited	£5,824,945
Cosmar Partners LLP	£5,815,451
New Leaf Investments Limited	£5,805,385
P.C.Richardson & Co.(Middlesbrough),Limited	£5,803,552
Hallikeld Limited	£5,803,540
Cramlington Precision Forge Limited	£5,803,393
Northumbrian Ice Cream Company Limited	£5,799,730
Clearly Drinks Limited	£5,796,800
Esh Homes Limited	£5,795,601
CD Johnson Limited	£5,783,424
Lindy Electronics Limited	£5,774,196
William Hackett Lifting Products Limited	£5,774,012
Tompkins Investments Limited	£5,769,000
Hadrian Healthcare (Durham) Limited	£5,768,942
McCaffery Financial Limited	£5,758,349
Peart Property Limited	£5,754,233
Thimbleby Farms Limited	£5,750,857
Close House Golf Club Limited	£5,747,534
Whitchester Farm Limited	£5,744,604
Gale and Phillipson Investment Services Ltd	£5,741,211
NRG Global Power Limited	£5,734,958
Prestige Care (Redcar Sm) Limited	£5,728,066
Northern Recruitment Group Limited	£5,724,000
Ryder Architecture Limited	£5,717,542
Bernex UK Limited	£5,700,000
Greenbale Ltd	£5,699,246
Masterdata Limited	£5,698,957
Edgar F Shepherd Ltd	£5,681,888
Northern Counties Guarantee Corporation Limited	£5,676,055
Actuant Operations UK Limited	£5,672,926
Brick Services Limited	£5,669,599

Company	Value
N & R Gupta Limited	£5,664,508
Lubbers (UK) Limited	£5,663,103
Marblemand Limited	£5,654,960
Cofathec Energy Services Limited	£5,654,000
Mold Systems Limited	£5,652,210
MPI Consultants Limited	£5,647,628
Isotank Depot Services Limited	£5,646,346
Doncaster Pharmaceuticals Limited	£5,645,959
Trout Hotels (Cumbria) Limited	£5,644,545
Northumbria Calvert Trust	£5,639,586
Labman Automation Limited	£5,638,951
Time Properties Limited	£5,635,126
Renown Engineering Limited	£5,632,902
J.H.Cowper Investments Limited	£5,631,418
Derwentside Environmental Testing Services Limited	£5,630,000
National Numbers Limited	£5,623,024
B.Print & Display Limited	£5,618,580
Tees Components Limited	£5,613,356
Procters Coaches (North Yorkshire) Limited	£5,611,037
Rubicon Pastimes Limited	£5,607,015
Ipca Laboratories UK Limited	£5,606,311
Aysgarth School Trust Limited	£5,604,007
Crossco (1371) Limited	£5,592,748
Patrick Parsons Limited	£5,586,990
Moorlands Holdings (N.E.) Limited	£5,582,322
Rivergreen Developments PLC	£5,577,173
Pout and Foster (N E) Limited	£5,576,726
G W Leader Property Limited	£5,568,420
United British Caravans Limited	£5,560,000
Psi Global Ltd	£5,543,335
Lowcock Properties Limited	£5,537,275
Intelect (UK) Limited	£5,536,824
Northumberland Wildlife Trust Limited	£5,536,617
Aceviral.Com Ltd	£5,531,400
Pass (Portable Appliance Safety Services) Ltd	£5,529,521
J.C. Atkinson and Son Limited	£5,525,652
Contact Centre Professional Limited	£5,524,694
Containerships (UK) Ltd	£5,519,164
Sharpness Point Limited	£5,517,755
Minel Venues LLP	£5,516,390
Billingham Headway Limited	£5,507,641
Hare Homes Limited	£5,506,623
Ron Perry & Son Limited	£5,503,728
Country Valley Foods Ltd	£5,492,357
Fellside Properties Limited	£5,491,463
Cleveland Containers Limited	£5,487,735
Loftus Agrius LLP	£5,485,323
K.W. Reader & Sons Limited	£5,484,639
Paragon Financial Investments Limited	£5,473,824
FM Coatings Limited	£5,472,675
Red & Racz Ltd	£5,463,522
Cliff Court (Redcar) Developments Ltd	£5,459,910
Tyne Insulation Supplies Limited	£5,458,228
Xtralite (Rooflights) Limited	£5,456,681
PX Holdings Limited	£5,451,627
Cornucopia Investments Limited	£5,442,490
Shaun Sadler Holdings Limited	£5,441,663
Utility ROV Services Limited	£5,438,560
Finchale Training College	£5,436,707
Etro Properties Limited	£5,428,580
Hacel Lighting Limited	£5,425,369
Ronsbrook Services Limited	£5,423,197
Expertise Properties Limited	£5,422,212
Tripnovel Limited	£5,418,524
Eco Monitoring Utility Systems Limited	£5,414,976
Sansec Development (Stevenage) Limited	£5,413,315
Casa Golf Homes Limited	£5,413,174
Woodside North East Property Limited	£5,410,712
PBI Aqaba Industrial Estate LLP	£5,409,671
Dunelm Optical Co. Limited	£5,392,817
Blackshaw's Garage (Alnwick) Limited	£5,392,343
Dysart Management Limited	£5,389,556

Company	Value
MacGregor (GBR) Limited	£5,382,000
Dapra York Limited	£5,357,964
AKV Cladding Products Ltd	£5,357,911
Ecova, Inc. Limited	£5,355,000
Motherdale Limited	£5,353,504
Royston Power Generation Limited	£5,347,646
A2 Screen Print Limited	£5,343,987
Groveport 2012 Limited	£5,342,000
Hadrian Healthcare (Gosforth) Limited	£5,341,619
CB Farms LLP	£5,338,835
Learning at Work Limited	£5,334,873
Abca Systems Limited	£5,328,557
Whitewell Properties Limited	£5,325,267
Coventry District Energy Company Limited	£5,324,000
Minhoco 12 Limited	£5,313,655
Thermal Transfer Technology Limited	£5,312,342
LGA Developments Limited	£5,306,880
Flexible Support Options Limited	£5,300,708
Josh & Tom Ltd	£5,295,312
Colton Group Limited	£5,295,131
Primex Plastics Limited	£5,290,423
Live Smart @ Home Limited	£5,286,000
Exponential Derivatives Limited	£5,285,184
Ramage Transport Limited	£5,282,436
Beamish Hall Limited	£5,280,403
Wolviston Management Services Limited	£5,271,879
Sonicedge Limited	£5,266,178
Murray Hogg Limited	£5,264,967
IHC FHP Limited	£5,260,000
Wear Referrals Limited	£5,254,638
Lanchester Dairies Limited	£5,253,729
L D H (2010) Limited	£5,253,672
Chainbridge Steel (North East) Ltd	£5,245,596
Superlec Electrical Distributors Limited	£5,245,432
Nuby UK LLP	£5,237,276
Arrowbuild & Civil Engineering Limited	£5,228,263
Whitehead Alloys Limited	£5,224,893
Sterling Property Portfolio Limited	£5,218,721
Drummond Central Limited	£5,216,467
Meadowdale Academy	£5,206,755
Peacocks Medical Group Limited	£5,199,656
Landteam Property Investments Limited	£5,195,989
Hays Foreign Exchange Limited	£5,192,050
Messer Griesheim Limited	£5,190,925
Elaghmore Limited	£5,188,186
Llangwyryfon Windfarm Limited	£5,181,000
Metnor Trafalgar Street Limited	£5,181,000
Cleveland Technologies Limited	£5,175,727
Shared Vision Learning Trust	£5,171,000
Permoid Industries Limited	£5,170,345
Back on the Map Limited	£5,152,028
Akebar Park Leisure Limited	£5,148,893
Fred Mence (Construction) Limited	£5,148,665
Sunnyside Academy	£5,147,996
M C C Properties Newcastle Limited	£5,147,805
M.W. Herdman Forestry Solutions Limited	£5,143,726
Bob Rudd Leisure Limited	£5,140,581
Tom Willoughby Limited	£5,137,864
Niche Technology UK Limited	£5,137,355
GPRB Holdings Limited	£5,136,466
EOS Facades Limited	£5,135,826
Groundwork South Tyneside and Newcastle upon Tyne	£5,131,741
Metallink Fluid Power Systems Limited	£5,127,709
The Reed Group Ltd	£5,113,227
A.M. Strategy Limited	£5,104,259
Aegion Corrosion Protection Holdings Limited	£5,099,411
Wassenburg Limited	£5,098,045
Hodgson Fish Holdings Limited	£5,095,579
Lister House (Fife) Limited	£5,091,314
Mandale Homes North Yorkshire Limited	£5,087,632
T R M Marketing Limited	£5,077,515
Alexander Technologies Europe Limited	£5,076,000
Alan Ransome Sporting Goods Group Limited	£5,075,240
Louie (Holdings) Limited	£5,069,943
South Shore One Limited	£5,069,292
Lindisfarne Inns Limited	£5,061,035
Hughes Bros Construction Limited	£5,045,437
Centre West (Newcastle)	£5,039,553
North East Concrete Limited	£5,036,302
Salecycle Limited	£5,032,800
The Trinity Catholic Multi Academy Trust	£5,031,131
PD Shipping & Inspection Services Limited	£5,029,000
Idec Technical Services Limited	£5,028,103
D.R. Caswell Limited	£5,023,384
Charminster Estates Limited	£5,020,091
Baker Furniture Limited	£5,018,039
Dhillons Investment Properties Limited	£5,012,458
Cross House Buildings Limited	£5,010,813
Golftee LP 4 Limited	£5,010,645
CPI William Clowes Ltd	£5,008,000
Sapphire Technologies Limited	£5,007,000
John Wade (Haulage) Limited	£5,006,957
Victor Products Ltd	£5,001,309
CPI Innovation Services Limited	£4,993,896
Jolan Piccadilly Limited	£4,987,301
The Intraining Group Limited	£4,987,000
Hanover Dairies Limited	£4,986,981
Howick Trustees Limited	£4,986,847
Avid Technology Group Limited	£4,983,387
GW Aviation LLP	£4,978,708
Alt Berg Holdings Limited	£4,978,485
Avid Technology Limited	£4,975,145
Sendrig Construction Limited	£4,970,630
WV Associates Limited	£4,963,336
Devereux Developments Limited	£4,958,816
Midland Steel Traders Limited,	£4,958,335
Midland Steel Traders (Holdings) Limited	£4,958,240
Engineering Support Partnership Ltd.	£4,957,662
Gloag & Sons Limited	£4,951,404
Strathearn Leisure Parks Limited	£4,944,760
River Tees Multi-Academy Trust	£4,930,187
Canford Audio PLC	£4,930,101
Copernicus Adriatic LLP	£4,928,118
A.E. Burt and Company Limited	£4,926,801
Cross Rigg Developments (North East) Limited	£4,923,090
Malhotra Care Homes (Sunderland) Limited	£4,921,265
The Endowment Fund for Tacri	£4,918,366
Northumbria Blow Mouldings Limited	£4,908,597
T&G Automotive Ltd	£4,905,535
LGA Foundation	£4,903,260
Grainger Europe (No. 3) Limited	£4,900,397
Renown Group Limited	£4,900,273
Connect Health Limited	£4,899,838
Harper & Wilkes Limited	£4,899,800
Workwear Express Limited	£4,884,811
Agne Limited	£4,881,100
Belmont View Limited	£4,879,631
Saddlers Land and Property Limited	£4,876,385
Blaydon Holdings Limited	£4,876,168
Ribbon Academy Trust	£4,876,000
EDF Energy Round 3 Isle of Wight Limited	£4,864,000
The John Strutt Conservation Foundation	£4,859,546
St Helen's Farm Limited	£4,856,329
All Saints' Academies Trust	£4,851,143
Wensley Roofing Limited	£4,848,404
Bates Regeneration Limited	£4,842,000
P&R Construction Limited	£4,841,790
Exclusive Bedrooms North East Limited	£4,841,315
Perfect Image Limited	£4,839,737
The Federation of Abbey Schools Academy Trust	£4,837,000
Geofirma Soils Engineering Limited	£4,832,000
Ravensworth Properties Limited	£4,831,743
Cemmaes Windfarm Limited	£4,828,000
Benton House Limited	£4,825,597

Company	Amount
North East England Chamber of Commerce	£4,818,000
Windsor Nursing Home LLP	£4,813,100
Sabre Rail Services Limited	£4,809,061
Millfield Enterprises Limited	£4,806,273
Onyx Scientific Limited	£4,797,612
J.S. Hubbuck Limited	£4,795,195
Hughes Plant Hire Limited	£4,792,132
The Northumbrian Educational Trust Ltd	£4,789,342
Liveco Limited	£4,789,303
Nailsworth (No.2) Limited	£4,783,693
Holmwood Commercial Properties Limited	£4,783,114
Think Limited	£4,778,969
D & A Systems Limited	£4,778,569
Grey Street Newcastle Ltd.	£4,775,332
Be Modern Properties Limited	£4,772,001
Manxguard Limited	£4,768,242
LTS Refurbishment Limited	£4,764,070
Cintra HR & Payroll Services Ltd	£4,762,464
Whitewell Hotels Limited	£4,752,759
NSA (Ventures) Limited	£4,751,579
Blue Barns Poultry Farms Limited	£4,742,350
Glenrock	£4,739,384
Newman Scott Limited	£4,730,828
WJ Drennan Limited	£4,729,509
Groundwork North East	£4,728,013
Neat Active Limited	£4,727,160
Bell Bros.(Ashington) Limited	£4,720,857
Aanco (UK) Limited	£4,720,753
Gus Robinson Developments Limited	£4,718,497
Stessa 3006 Ltd	£4,711,940
Teesside Transport Commercial Services Limited	£4,700,234
AE Europe Limited	£4,693,098
Tait Walker LLP	£4,692,359
Mineral Insulated Cable Company Limited	£4,684,700
Northumberland Estates 2007 Limited	£4,683,681
The Peacock Group Limited	£4,680,894
Northern Retail Consortium Limited	£4,678,158
Pacifica Home Services Limited	£4,677,203
Bellway Properties Limited	£4,675,155
Slaters Electricals Limited	£4,673,704
RBV Energy Limited	£4,671,656
Clifton Holdings (North East) Limited	£4,671,487
Kenworth Limited	£4,671,262
Mandale Construction Limited	£4,669,443
Burnell Fencing Limited	£4,669,161
Nigel Wright Employment Services Limited	£4,669,000
UTS Engineering Limited	£4,668,712
Sanders Plant & Waste Management Limited	£4,662,552
Allure Developments Limited	£4,654,690
Project North East	£4,653,776
Tyne Tees Vehicle Repair Group Limited	£4,637,840
Air Handling Systems Limited	£4,637,446
Excalibur Realty UK Limited	£4,636,584
Flextime Limited	£4,635,945
Texon (Newco 2) Ltd	£4,635,000
NAC Training Limited	£4,633,717
Manners Farms Limited	£4,613,461
Atlantis Management LLP	£4,612,264
Minhoco 30 Limited	£4,604,599
Universal Wolf Limited	£4,604,593
M. & G. Fuels Limited	£4,600,315
PCCA Limited	£4,594,779
Daft as a Brush Cancer Patient Care Charitable Trust	£4,591,316
NVM Private Equity LLP	£4,590,893
Bremsen Technik Holdings Ltd	£4,588,564
Printbylaser Limited	£4,586,529
John Morfield Limited	£4,582,007
Londonderry Garage (S.E.) Limited	£4,581,971
Casper Shipping Limited	£4,580,629
Redcar Racecourse Limited	£4,579,741
Square Peg Properties Limited	£4,569,603
Sirius Remediation Limited	£4,567,870
Joel Memorial Limited	£4,565,502
Esschem Europe Limited	£4,563,748
Endless Stretch Limited	£4,563,602
Zest Investment (Omagh) Limited	£4,550,000
Caledonian Environmental Levenmouth Treatment	£4,545,000
Tanfield Engineering Systems Limited	£4,543,413
Quarrington Renewable Gas Ltd	£4,543,180
George Rye & Sons Limited	£4,542,290
Dibbin Estates & Equipment Limited	£4,541,328
Specialist Alarm Services Limited	£4,540,394
Odyssey Systems Limited	£4,530,604
H F Colton Plant Hire Ltd	£4,529,571
Gill & Schofield Pharmaceutical Chemists Limited	£4,527,285
K W Purvis Limited	£4,526,374
The Pen Shop Limited	£4,523,310
Dane Architectural Systems Limited	£4,522,247
Traidcraft Public Limited Company	£4,518,000
Willow Park Healthcare Limited	£4,517,188
Joyce Construction & Civils Ltd	£4,511,645
Genesis Global Systems Limited	£4,510,870
Geoff Huntley Plant Limited	£4,503,770
Oaktree Homes (Durham) Limited	£4,501,619
Liveworks (Newcastle upon Tyne) Ltd	£4,500,212
Allay (UK) Ltd.	£4,497,055
Premiertec Consulting Limited	£4,496,572
Utex Industries UK Limited	£4,492,028
Ravensworth Homes LLP	£4,491,820
J R Holland Produce Limited Liability Partnership	£4,489,193
Decor Panel Limited	£4,487,897
Graza Limited	£4,487,489
Teatime Tasties Limited	£4,486,292
Hadrian Healthcare (Harrogate) Limited	£4,477,786
S.W. Durham Training Limited	£4,474,378
Tyneside Autoparc Limited	£4,470,473
Real Time Claims Limited	£4,465,118
Carroll & Meynell Transformers Limited	£4,462,158
Anabas (UK 2) Limited	£4,455,062
Sotech Limited	£4,446,908
A & P Tees Limited	£4,443,794
The YW Investment Company Limited	£4,443,055
The Association of North East Councils Limited	£4,441,485
D. Collard Limited	£4,430,434
Teesside High School Limited	£4,427,001
PX (TGPP) Limited	£4,426,914
Teesnap Limited	£4,426,130
Timec 1289 Limited	£4,424,822
Bridgewater (Home Reversions Number 1) Limited	£4,423,021
Kail and Co. Limited	£4,420,291
Cotswold Manufacturing Limited	£4,418,603
North East Plant Sales Limited	£4,417,782
The Medburn Land Company Limited	£4,414,020
Stephenson Quarter Developments Limited	£4,412,963
Alcyone Healthcare North East Ltd	£4,407,071
S and B EPS Limited	£4,404,447
Vertu Motors (Chingford) Limited	£4,403,000
Bannatyne's Health Club (Stratford upon Avon) Limited	£4,401,650
Reviloo Ltd	£4,397,407
Mowden Controls Limited	£4,392,777
SIG Combibloc Limited	£4,389,000
Northumbrian Trust Limited	£4,388,675
McCarrick Construction Company Limited	£4,382,090
LO (Roscommon) Properties Limited	£4,382,070
JL Mechanical and Electrical Services Limited	£4,373,429
Houghton International Electrical Services Limited	£4,372,023
F Jones (Cleveland) Limited	£4,367,137
Hopkins Properties Limited	£4,359,790
Creativity, Culture and Education	£4,354,102
Blyth Investments LLP	£4,352,811
W. Marley Agricultural Contractors Limited	£4,350,334
Bridgewater Lifetime Mortgages Limited	£4,349,993
Wessington Cryogenics Limited	£4,343,826
Azure Charitable Enterprises	£4,343,620

Alpha Developments (Stoke) Ltd	£4,332,270	Marine Court Dover Limited	£4,088,202
Wyn Construction Limited	£4,328,729	Taylored Estates Limited	£4,087,542
Energy24 Limited	£4,323,996	J. Jackson Properties Limited	£4,085,257
Quantum Controls Ltd	£4,323,356	Gate 7 Limited	£4,084,026
Armour Plastics Limited	£4,320,218	William A.Wardman Limited	£4,076,765
Hill Giftware Limited	£4,317,376	J.T. Clough & Son Limited	£4,076,674
PTM Holdings Limited	£4,316,526	Orange Plant Limited	£4,075,382
H.S. Petch & Sons Limited	£4,316,355	Analox Limited	£4,074,364
E.Pearson and Sons (Teesside) Limited	£4,315,542	Team Fostering	£4,069,691
Tew Holdings (2012) Limited	£4,308,390	Prestons Transport Limited	£4,066,173
NBT Integrated Services Limited	£4,304,782	Hartlepool Aspire Trust	£4,065,311
Dipton Care Home Limited	£4,291,206	Boxpipe Limited	£4,064,977
Randstad Limited	£4,280,862	Sabic Innovative Plastics ABS UK Limited	£4,064,000
Engie DE Holding Company Limited	£4,280,000	M Dungait & Sons Limited	£4,061,264
Tees Valley Trailers Limited	£4,276,476	Triple T Engineering Limited	£4,061,168
Coopers Chemist Marske Limited	£4,265,987	Dallas Carpets Limited	£4,059,656
Teesdale South Limited	£4,263,726	Hardware Supply Company (Middlesbrough) Limited	£4,055,278
Woodview Estates Limited	£4,263,553	St Cuthbert's Catholic High School	£4,054,000
Industrial & Community Wind Generation No. 2 Limited	£4,257,888	Paramount Home Improvements (U.K.) Limited	£4,052,277
Thames Travel (Wallingford) Limited	£4,256,000	Wellsprings Properties Ltd	£4,047,622
Lord Lawson of Beamish Academy	£4,251,799	Ray Craggs Ltd	£4,039,702
Zest Investment (Portadown) Limited	£4,250,000	Par Petroleum Limited	£4,039,622
Greenbow Properties Limited	£4,249,696	Geffen Limited	£4,027,077
Chemplas Limited	£4,235,594	Manners (Newcastle) Limited	£4,017,237
Websters (Farmers) Limited	£4,231,946	R.Bland Limited	£4,017,024
Bloomsbury Heat & Power Limited	£4,231,000	Todds Highway Maintenance Limited	£4,008,790
Linden Foods Burradon Limited	£4,227,067	CE Holdings Limited	£4,000,000
Bon Coeur Fine Wines Limited	£4,226,339	Mechplant (North East) Limited	£3,999,751
BLP (Northern) Limited	£4,226,022	Isocom Components 2004 Limited	£3,996,549
Power Wholesale Limited	£4,222,480	P&A Food Management Services Limited	£3,995,927
WPR Farms Ltd	£4,222,379	A.D. Calvert Architectural Stone Supplies Limited	£3,994,428
Grainger Ramp Limited	£4,219,032	Feller (UK) Limited	£3,990,062
MCM Investments (UK & Ire) Ltd	£4,211,581	Abbeyfield Newcastle upon Tyne Society Limited (The)	£3,983,864
Ward Bros. (Plant Hire) Limited	£4,205,428	Peel Street Developments Limited	£3,976,302
Benore Care Limited	£4,205,090	N.P. Alliance Limited	£3,974,479
Nicholas Postgate Catholic Academy Trust	£4,204,000	Oak Park Healthcare Limited	£3,972,666
Non-Fossil Purchasing Agency Limited	£4,195,478	Paragon Rapid Technologies Ltd	£3,972,606
Readman Steel Limited	£4,194,327	GAC Netherlands Limited	£3,967,268
Keith Pattinson Limited	£4,189,725	Tyne Moulds & Machinery Company Limited	£3,963,672
The A1 Steam Locomotive Trust	£4,189,155	Intrahealth Pharmacy Limited	£3,963,288
Ward Bros (Malton) Limited	£4,184,456	Barnwell Academy Trust	£3,960,987
Tolent Living Limited	£4,182,909	M.D. & A.G. Burdon Ltd	£3,955,921
Tom Tappin,Limited	£4,182,842	C.A. Blackwell Group Limited	£3,955,000
Edynamix Global Ltd	£4,181,164	Wyndham Court Limited	£3,951,863
Allerton Steel Limited	£4,175,511	Horizon Products Ltd	£3,951,394
Fred Walker (Estates) Limited	£4,172,242	Leadgates Developments Limited	£3,944,594
Lynx Precast Limited	£4,167,383	W. Hodgson (Hartlepool) Limited	£3,941,101
Ideal Care (North) Limited	£4,163,660	Darlington & District Hospice Movement	£3,938,873
George Fordy Properties Limited	£4,162,923	F.J. Booth Construction Limited	£3,929,910
Stephen A. Sims (Cars) Limited	£4,159,949	Stanley Vickers Limited	£3,929,818
Sekura Trade Frames Limited	£4,159,511	High Force Research Limited	£3,929,128
Branden Property Limited	£4,154,474	Addbudget Limited	£3,927,000
Arcwhiz 2000 Limited	£4,154,388	Jebb Metals (Newcastle) Ltd	£3,918,971
Limekent Limited	£4,154,262	Goldmart Limited	£3,918,669
Fagron UK Ltd	£4,149,983	The Virgin Money Foundation	£3,912,500
Tiger T Investments LLP	£4,145,114	Van Hessen UK Casings Ltd	£3,908,318
Northumbria London Campus Limited	£4,141,586	RS Industrial Services Limited	£3,907,520
Hadrian Architectural Glazing Systems Limited	£4,136,816	Ore Catapult Development Services Limited	£3,907,000
Rowan Specialist Interiors Limited	£4,134,503	FC Shipping Limited	£3,904,693
Magneco Metrel U.K. Limited	£4,127,699	HNM Investments Limited	£3,903,143
Ekwienox Limited	£4,126,315	Cavendish (Northern) Limited	£3,900,897
Hartlepool Hospice Limited (The)	£4,114,731	Aquind Limited	£3,899,694
TYK Limited	£4,113,456	Speedclad Limited	£3,897,494
Osborne Engineering Limited	£4,106,243	Mandale Homes North Limited	£3,894,274
W. Liddy & Company Limited	£4,106,133	Container Sales (UK) Limited	£3,892,391
Punch Bowl Investments Limited	£4,106,048	Aavid Thermacore Europe Limited	£3,890,611
Absolute Civil Engineering Limited	£4,104,023	Flame and Fragrance Limited	£3,887,229
Wm. Noble (Automatics) Limited	£4,102,000	T.James (Bedlington),Limited	£3,885,998
Agricore Ltd	£4,092,927	W.Swinbank & Sons Limited	£3,881,166
Clarkes of Stillington Plate & Profiles Limited	£4,090,777	Islestone Limited	£3,879,988
Hellens Group Limited	£4,090,554	Northern Gas & Power Ltd	£3,877,456
St. Oswald's Catholic Academy Trust	£4,090,000	J. O. Straughan & Co. Limited	£3,875,907

Company	Value
Redesdale Properties LLP	£3,870,597
Butterwick Limited	£3,869,673
Select Prime Sites UK Ltd	£3,869,001
Pharma Nord (UK) Limited	£3,867,796
Tolent Homes Limited	£3,863,199
The Hawthorns Lodge Limited	£3,861,084
Cleveland & Highland Holdings Ltd	£3,860,898
Haswell Moor Developments Ltd	£3,860,070
Implants International Limited	£3,853,176
Alpha Recovery Limited	£3,852,211
Multi-Lab Limited	£3,851,915
JLM Global Foods Limited	£3,851,580
Waters Waste Services Ltd	£3,848,644
Falcombe	£3,843,000
Doocey North East Limited	£3,842,116
Power Efficiency Holdings Limited	£3,838,000
Ionbond UK Limited	£3,837,130
Glasshus Ltd	£3,836,542
Readypay Limited	£3,827,988
Sunderland Lifestyle Partnership Limited	£3,822,857
Faulknerbrowns LLP	£3,819,983
Campuslifestyle (Houses) Ltd	£3,818,382
Mental Health Matters	£3,813,702
Interactive Projects & Design Limited	£3,813,115
The Gibside Hotel Limited	£3,813,030
South Causey Limited	£3,811,572
Indigo Software Limited	£3,808,152
DKB Crop Protection Limited	£3,806,567
High Hedley Hope Farm Limited	£3,806,399
Imbue Property Ltd	£3,804,838
Rosewood Care LLP	£3,801,188
Green & Son Building Services Limited	£3,799,675
Baydale Control Systems Limited	£3,798,632
STP Construction Limited	£3,791,621
Octagon Green Solutions Limited	£3,781,673
Creditscale Limited	£3,775,897
Willow View Care Limited	£3,772,021
Straight Line Holdings North East Limited	£3,770,509
North Tyneside Properties Limited	£3,766,220
Elliston Fine Wines Limited	£3,763,635
Yorhold Limited	£3,750,007
Global Holdings Limited	£3,750,003
Craig Healthcare LLP	£3,747,412
Simco (Engineers) Limited	£3,747,018
LTH Cash & Carry Limited	£3,745,404
UK Industrial Tapes Limited	£3,742,492
Sun Valley Holdings	£3,739,000
DHD Wealth Management Ltd	£3,735,140
Low Grange Quarry Limited	£3,735,079
Thermon (U.K.) Limited	£3,733,115
Alexage Limited	£3,732,875
Spark Ecommerce Group Limited	£3,730,901
Chiltern Farm Chemicals Limited	£3,730,156
Dementia Matters Ltd	£3,730,033
Todd and Cue Limited	£3,728,841
Willowbank Holiday Park Limited	£3,723,613
Millhouse Developments Limited	£3,717,870
Waterloo Estates Limited	£3,715,149
Pennine Newcastle Limited	£3,714,498
Gralenno Limited	£3,714,031
John Livingston & Sons,Limited	£3,709,193
Avenda Estates Limited	£3,701,737
Movesun Limited	£3,701,049
Vardy Property (Teesside) Limited	£3,698,655
Vertu Motors (Amc) Limited	£3,696,815
Leveys Holdings Limited	£3,691,397
Cowie Forestry Limited	£3,690,950
Central Taxis Gateshead Ltd	£3,688,967
Allen Mason & Sons (Herrington) Limited	£3,688,624
Networked Housing Limited	£3,688,058
Glendale Engineering (Milfield) Limited	£3,686,485
Northern Construction Solutions Limited	£3,683,223
International Pipeline Products Limited	£3,682,287
Premier Traffic Management Limited	£3,682,012
Portland Investments (AM) Limited	£3,680,284
Cool Designs Limited	£3,678,799
D.C. Handrails and Ironwork Parts Limited	£3,678,317
Argyle Square Properties Limited	£3,674,128
Accredited Processed Metals Limited	£3,673,114
George W. Barker Limited	£3,671,892
Cleveland Cascades Limited	£3,671,474
Thornton Brothers Limited	£3,653,752
Tricogen Laboratories Limited	£3,653,428
Esh Space The Park Limited	£3,646,898
Ekwienox Holdings Limited	£3,644,564
Maymask (121) Limited	£3,644,158
Lambton House Ltd	£3,643,155
Double Eleven Limited	£3,639,596
Utility Services (N.E.) Limited	£3,636,493
S.A.L. Leisure Limited	£3,632,868
Impress North East Limited	£3,632,748
Eve UK Properties LLP	£3,632,428
Naturalight Systems Limited	£3,631,799
Skelton Primary School	£3,631,308
PX Engineering Consultants Limited	£3,628,231
T E Watson & Co. Limited	£3,616,527
Farmers & Mercantile Insurance Brokers Limited	£3,615,373
Peterlee Glass Company Limited	£3,610,077
Katem Logistics Limited	£3,609,297
Tennant Street Medical Practice LLP	£3,609,114
Q.A. (Weld Tech) Limited	£3,608,837
Armes-Reardon Properties Limited	£3,603,992
Romero Catholic Education Trust	£3,602,377
Transend Solutions Limited	£3,602,209
Fresh Freight Limited	£3,596,337
MCE Group PLC	£3,593,708
Specma Samwon Ltd	£3,591,127
Riverside Primary Academy	£3,586,922
David Miller Frozen Foods Limited	£3,586,831
Amethyst Homes Limited	£3,586,192
Psyche Limited	£3,585,501
The Multiple Sclerosis Research and Relief Fund	£3,578,417
Molekula Limited	£3,577,469
Brazenlight Limited	£3,574,663
Croxdale Service Station Limited	£3,572,755
WHP Investments UK Ltd	£3,571,885
Bannatyne Properties Limited	£3,570,154
Chameleon Bar & Dining Limited	£3,564,028
Hayton & Lamb Limited	£3,563,797
Dunham Leisure Limited	£3,561,509
Cleveland Circuits Limited	£3,560,739
B.E.L. Lift Trucks Limited	£3,560,410
Newroc Ltd	£3,559,408
Consumer Refund Service Ltd	£3,554,791
Supreme Knitwear Manufacturing Company Limited	£3,554,601
Hemlington Hall Academy	£3,553,967
Chisholm Bookmakers Limited	£3,553,856
CDM Recruitment Limited	£3,552,709
David Brown Automotive Limited	£3,551,000
Coolmore Land Limited	£3,549,254
Virgin Money Management Services Limited	£3,548,000
Rose Wood Academy	£3,544,000
Mastclimber Solutions UK Ltd.	£3,538,356
Adventure Sunderland	£3,533,466
Leah Property Limited	£3,533,245
Engie Urban Energy Group Limited	£3,530,000
Juke Box Sales and Rentals Limited	£3,526,599
N.E. Truck Spares Limited	£3,524,386
Hargreaves Services (Blindwells) Limited	£3,520,000
Resource Management Solutions (North East) Ltd	£3,517,428
Waterloo House Rest Home Limited	£3,515,866
John T. Fall Limited	£3,514,200
Grace House North East	£3,512,410
Durham Group Estates Limited	£3,511,186

Company	Value
UNW LLP	£3,502,334
Spark Response Limited	£3,502,056
Moorview Properties Limited	£3,500,941
The Cleveland Dwellings Limited	£3,499,577
S&A Builders Merchants Limited	£3,499,354
Romag PPM Limited	£3,491,702
Libra Seafoods Limited	£3,490,467
T.T.Walker (Newcastle) Limited	£3,486,557
Cundall Limited	£3,482,189
EJM Engineered Systems Limited	£3,481,645
Haswell Moor Farms Ltd	£3,481,076
Summers-Inman Construction & Property Consultants	£3,470,259
Prime Horizontal Limited	£3,468,981
Northallerton Auctions Limited	£3,463,569
Academic Health Science Network for N E & N Cumbria	£3,458,348
Rosen (UK) Limited	£3,457,131
Coopers Studios LLP	£3,456,000
Tyneside Surgical Services Limited	£3,454,748
Musterfield Poultry Growers Ltd	£3,454,456
Axiom Engineering Associates Limited	£3,453,303
M R Robson Electricity Services Ltd	£3,446,554
Brackenshaw Limited	£3,445,654
Lowrie Foods Limited	£3,444,949
D'Addario UK Limited	£3,440,538
Hart Door Systems Limited	£3,440,178
Diamond Chain (UK) Limited	£3,436,799
Service Engines (Newcastle) Limited	£3,436,754
PCL Investments (NE) LLP	£3,436,463
Engie International FM Limited	£3,436,000
Stella Property Investments Limited	£3,435,163
Ambuline Limited	£3,431,000
Red Ridge Residential Limited	£3,429,367
Waterstons Limited	£3,428,285
Northern Commercial Properties Limited	£3,421,248
Velocity UK Limited	£3,419,695
Lamda Pharma Limited	£3,416,319
International Syalons (Newcastle) Limited	£3,407,436
Springboard Sunderland Trust	£3,402,795
Northridge Healthcare Limited	£3,400,255
Katell Limited	£3,396,543
Sunderland Home Care Associates (20-20) Limited	£3,395,038
Town Centre Garage (Sunderland) Limited	£3,394,799
Watson Burton LLP	£3,392,481
Praesto Consulting UK Ltd	£3,391,542
Dean Taxis Limited	£3,389,362
Aston Workshop Limited	£3,386,057
Nxpower (UK) Limited	£3,382,519
Norfolk Hotel Limited	£3,380,864
Millfield Enterprises (Manufacturing) Limited	£3,377,556
St. Anthony of Padua Community Association	£3,376,724
Bay Plastics Limited	£3,376,628
Driven Car Sales Limited	£3,374,693
Whitehall Executive Developments Limited	£3,372,365
Fablink Tank Systems Limited	£3,372,168
TTE International Limited	£3,371,466
Stephen Tuer Farms Ltd	£3,370,990
South Northumberland Cricket Club Limited	£3,370,810
A & P Ship Repairers Limited	£3,367,430
On Track Retail Limited	£3,365,000
Acorn Developments (Kirkby) Limited	£3,357,635
Lanchester Wine Sales Limited	£3,357,063
Red Marine (Holdings) Limited	£3,353,634
Oasis Aquila Housing Ltd	£3,353,358
Mandale Apartments 2 Limited	£3,348,746
J.R. Holland (Food Services) Limited	£3,346,448
Biss 53 Limited	£3,345,098
Masada Developments Limited	£3,343,624
R J Utility Services Ltd	£3,341,732
Bradbury Property Holdings Limited	£3,339,881
John Moody Investments Limited	£3,338,357
Active Northumberland	£3,336,169
PSP Architectural Ltd	£3,332,932
Norsea Group (UK) Limited	£3,332,839
M Rugs Limited	£3,331,937
Falcombe Holdings Limited	£3,330,000
Higher Trevartha Solar Park Limited	£3,329,057
Barrier Architectural Services Limited	£3,323,771
Theakston Estates (Mickle Hill) Limited	£3,323,000
Howarth Litchfield Partnership Limited	£3,321,881
Cleardata UK Limited	£3,321,586
A. & A. Carpets Limited	£3,320,880
Monomarket (Holdings) Limited	£3,315,266
Carlton Power Limited	£3,314,109
Action 4 Equality (Scotland) Limited	£3,312,698
Darlington Arena Limited	£3,310,839
Trend International Group Limited	£3,309,890
Metnor (Great Yarmouth) Limited	£3,308,000
Card Trix [Greetings] Limited	£3,307,402
HMC Land Limited	£3,305,474
Howard Russell Construction Limited	£3,304,101
Premo Fabrications Limited	£3,302,520
Gilesgate Properties Limited	£3,301,879
Brambledown Contracts Group Limited	£3,301,848
Valens Contracts Limited	£3,301,740
Alt Berg Limited	£3,301,337
Bandoffice 2 Limited	£3,300,963
Saferad Limited	£3,300,521
Global Substation Solutions Limited	£3,296,507
Aclet Property Management & Services Limited	£3,294,353
Bekco UK Ltd	£3,294,340
Kader Academy Trust	£3,294,000
Tyneside Foodservice Limited	£3,293,740
Carousel Buses Limited	£3,293,000
Dacre Street Developments Limited	£3,291,443
International Processplants (Europe) Limited	£3,280,528
Newcastle Tool & Gauge Limited	£3,278,164
Wartsila Puregas Solutions Limited	£3,277,834
Northumberland Estates Investments 2000 Limited	£3,275,787
S V Rutter Ltd	£3,273,899
Pola Minerals Limited	£3,273,054
Ebor Leisure World Limited	£3,272,136
Hargreaves Engineering & Contracts Limited	£3,272,000
Barrier Fire Protection Limited	£3,271,307
Bussey and Armstrong Limited	£3,266,250
Parkdean Holidays Limited	£3,262,000
SSL Healthcare Ltd	£3,261,520
Proton Power Systems PLC	£3,260,000
Warren Butterworth Catering Butchers Limited	£3,259,918
H. Jarvis Ltd	£3,254,069
Rohni's International Limited	£3,253,066
Techwax Limited	£3,251,541
Gaskell MacKay Carpets Limited	£3,251,516
Embleton Hall Dairies Limited	£3,247,183
Universal Coatings & Services Limited	£3,245,909
Decadeon Holdings Limited	£3,245,063
Karbon Developments Limited	£3,245,041
Walton Logging Limited	£3,244,535
CPD Bodies Limited	£3,242,275
Tiger Lifting UK Limited	£3,241,138
Moguntia Food Ingredients UK Limited	£3,240,161
Alrahi & Singh Limited	£3,237,333
Fairfield Industries Limited	£3,236,438
A. & J. Keith Limited	£3,235,824
Tynehead (Property) Limited	£3,233,845
Roseberry Care Centres GB Limited	£3,233,534
Crown Care Developments Limited	£3,231,968
Sohech Ltd	£3,231,000
City Leasing (Sunderland) Limited	£3,229,437
Cockerton Green Developments Ltd	£3,227,656
Seaham Harbour Dock Company	£3,227,000
Modrec International Limited	£3,220,867
Bandoffice Limited	£3,215,357
Integrated Polymer Systems (U.K.) Limited	£3,214,780
M.M. Knitwear (1982) Limited	£3,214,719

Company	Amount
Neal Taylor Management Limited	£3,214,549
Ceefox Holdings Limited	£3,210,703
PD Ports Properties Limited	£3,208,000
Donyal Holdings Limited	£3,207,790
Aptec Products Limited	£3,206,732
Weardale Railways CIC	£3,204,679
Mount Gable Estates Limited	£3,203,221
Durham City Transport Limited	£3,203,014
Quayside Frozen Foods (Newcastle) Limited	£3,199,082
Dinsdale Farming Limited	£3,198,814
GSLF Engineering Limited	£3,197,930
Randall Orchard Construction Limited	£3,192,954
Hall & Partners (Special Projects) Limited	£3,192,302
Northern Structures Ltd	£3,183,599
T.Manners & Sons Limited	£3,178,039
Grid Smarter Cities Ltd	£3,177,522
Blundell Production Equipment Limited	£3,175,732
Nova Marketing Consultancy Limited	£3,175,702
Jigsaw Learning Trust	£3,175,169
Dragonfly Venture (UK) Limited	£3,174,495
Healthways Chemists (North East) Limited	£3,172,979
Stevenson of Oxbridge Limited	£3,172,278
Pax Christi Catholic Partnership	£3,166,419
Internet Insurance (Holdings) Limited	£3,165,718
A.R. Calvert (Leyburn) Limited	£3,164,648
John Boyd Associates Limited	£3,163,134
Sekura (Holdings) Limited	£3,157,678
Central Employment Agency (North East) Limited	£3,155,927
Prospero Growth Limited	£3,153,971
Paignton Limited	£3,151,746
Treatview Limited	£3,151,611
J Denham Metals Ltd	£3,150,055
Ergo Flex Enterprises Limited	£3,148,988
Dick Garner & Sons Limited	£3,145,816
Safechem Limited	£3,142,755
Elliott (Holdings) Limited	£3,139,619
Symetri Limited	£3,138,528
George Bolam (Foods) Ltd	£3,138,496
Vehicle Movements (North East) Limited	£3,136,884
M & S Plastics Limited	£3,133,235
IAM-Sold Ltd	£3,133,022
Prestwick Care Limited	£3,127,275
Titan Trailers Industries Limited	£3,125,585
Station Developments Limited	£3,124,965
Icon Plastics Limited	£3,119,528
Cestrian Estates Ltd.	£3,116,210
TCC Holdings Ltd	£3,111,997
Cleves Cross Learning Trust	£3,110,926
W M T Entertainments (No 2) Limited	£3,107,302
Orchidsoft Limited	£3,106,067
Northumbria Care Limited	£3,104,180
Baltic Flour Mills Visual Arts Trust	£3,098,624
Swan Hunter (NE) Limited	£3,094,107
Victor Products Holdings Ltd	£3,088,113
Alderclad Ltd	£3,087,747
Cobalt PSS LLP	£3,084,858
Port of Tyne Distribution Limited	£3,084,000
Propipe Ltd	£3,082,441
ELG Developments Limited	£3,082,111
S.M.Thompson Limited	£3,079,537
Oakdale (Contracts) Limited	£3,075,824
Engelbert Developments Ltd	£3,074,785
Wynyard Hall Limited	£3,071,509
Kingswood Properties (North East) Limited	£3,058,108
Carr & Co Solicitors (NE) Limited	£3,054,332
AG Watson & Sons Limited	£3,053,303
T M A Property Consultants Limited	£3,052,739
Gastronorth Limited	£3,044,222
Tilly Bailey & Irvine LLP	£3,040,562
Sty.Com Limited	£3,039,501
Gem Partnership Limited	£3,039,216
G.T.Gillie & Blair Limited	£3,038,205
Durham County Football Association Limited	£3,036,995
South Tyne Building Supplies Limited	£3,031,695
Compacbrand Limited	£3,030,383
The Media Network Global Limited	£3,029,738
Caring Technology Limited	£3,028,748
Centralus 003 Ltd	£3,026,591
Firthmoor Primary School	£3,026,000
Cormeton Electronics Limited	£3,025,891
C.R.T. Packaging (U.K.) Limited	£3,024,089
Earlsway Holdings Limited	£3,023,800
J & L (North East) Limited	£3,022,631
Heat Tech Tooling Ltd	£3,022,325
Broadmedia Holdings Limited	£3,021,542
Middleton Lodge Events Limited	£3,017,320
Sovereign Adavo (Wallsend) LLP	£3,015,024
RPMR Limited	£3,012,856
Ballentine Properties Ltd	£3,011,933
Grainger (Commercial Developments) Limited	£3,009,043
Elpha Lodge Residential Care Home Limited	£3,007,404
M. & S. Motorcycles Limited	£3,007,220
Steel River Limited	£3,004,838
Nilus Developments Limited	£3,004,518
Blue Aardvark Joinery Limited	£3,000,919
Coquet Trust	£2,999,399
Dalton Homes (North East) Limited	£2,998,461
Istanbul Meats Limited	£2,997,219
Karol Property Company Limited	£2,996,011
Premier Tech Aqua Limited	£2,995,098
Age UK Northumberland	£2,993,867
Altomed Limited	£2,990,960
Perry Process Equipment Limited	£2,988,816
Chemcare Limited	£2,987,992
Bauer Radio's Cash for Kids Charities	£2,982,675
Clarus Limited	£2,982,582
Links Court (Whitley Bay) Limited	£2,981,570
Argentaurum Limited	£2,980,022
Vertu Motors (Knaresborough) Limited	£2,980,000
Empire Property Concepts Limited	£2,979,119
Crow Hall Farms Limited	£2,974,514
Hedley Park Developments Limited	£2,973,521
Keywest No. Three Ltd	£2,972,255
Charterglobe Limited	£2,970,083
A D Plant Hire Limited	£2,969,167
The Van Centre (Richmond) Limited	£2,968,007
Banks Brothers Transport Limited	£2,967,000
Dysart Residential Limited	£2,963,318
Sitelink Communications Limited	£2,958,172
Carbis Filtration Limited	£2,957,031
Bronte Caravan Park Limited	£2,956,796
Vardy Property LLP	£2,956,173
Montagu Hotels Limited	£2,952,770
Pryme Group Limited	£2,950,566
Crystal Galleries Limited	£2,950,371
Cleveland Homes (No.3) Limited	£2,947,278
Flame Heating Spares Limited	£2,946,889
The British Sociological Association	£2,946,044
Cussins Embleton LLP	£2,944,528
Angelbond Limited	£2,943,796
Gracelands Care Home Limited	£2,938,007
A1 Environmental Services Ltd.	£2,934,331
Hewitson Limited	£2,933,545
Prestige Properties (North East) Limited	£2,931,410
Northumberland Golf Club Limited (The)	£2,930,597
Centralus 004 Ltd	£2,928,623
Transcend Bloodstock Limited Liability Partnership	£2,926,951
Sone Products Holdings Ltd	£2,926,445
Thursby Homes Limited	£2,924,962
Valued Properties Limited	£2,924,335
Isotank Transport Services Limited	£2,923,279
Engineering Property Services Limited	£2,923,133
Medical Reporting Solutions Limited	£2,918,981
Taniya Properties Ltd	£2,916,646

Company	Amount
North East Accident Repair Centres Limited	£2,913,130
Athenaeum Developments (Fulwell) Limited	£2,909,880
Sunderland Care and Support (Holding Company) Ltd	£2,909,471
Hawthorns Logistics Limited	£2,908,565
N A College Trust	£2,905,173
J A Sales and Service Limited	£2,903,722
Cambridge Photonics Limited	£2,902,892
Dockleaf Developments Limited	£2,901,269
Grainger European Ventures LLP	£2,901,041
Legacy Resorts Limited	£2,900,973
Dipsticks Research Limited	£2,899,991
Gretpark Properties Limited	£2,898,847
W.H. Forster (Printers) Limited	£2,898,764
Mandale Apartments Limited	£2,896,300
Mastercopy Limited	£2,895,725
Sunderland Marina Ltd	£2,894,154
Marine Fabricators Limited	£2,893,528
Faraday Printed Circuits Limited	£2,892,300
HMC Finance Limited	£2,892,060
Owen Humble Property Investments Limited	£2,891,359
Centrebus Holdings Limited	£2,890,000
McNally and Thompson (UK Contracts) Limited	£2,888,366
Cottam Investments Limited	£2,888,088
Microvention UK Limited	£2,886,881
Extrahold Limited	£2,884,334
Harvey M and A Ltd	£2,881,537
Nulite Ltd	£2,878,952
Vision Building Services Limited	£2,875,983
BGP Consulting Limited	£2,874,596
North West Merchandising Limited	£2,874,504
Martin Tait Redheads Ltd.	£2,873,447
Trotec Laser Limited	£2,873,393
Louietex Ltd	£2,871,560
Westland Way 3 LLP	£2,871,232
Tynemanagement NE Limited	£2,868,704
C.G. Fixings Limited	£2,867,238
Debmat Surfacing Limited	£2,866,621
Halthean Worldwide Limited	£2,866,159
Starstruck Limited	£2,863,854
Murton Farm Estate Limited	£2,863,567
CTG Limited	£2,854,272
Landtime Limited	£2,853,628
The Glendale Gateway Trust	£2,852,230
Viewley Hill Academy	£2,849,000
S.C.H. Site Services Ltd	£2,846,164
Raisco Limited	£2,844,001
Cabe Property Limited	£2,843,561
Starrs Contract Services Limited	£2,843,521
Grainger (Hadston) Limited	£2,841,407
TI Geosciences Ltd	£2,841,000
Reeds (Bray) Cranes Limited	£2,839,424
NAL Asset Management Limited	£2,836,354
The New Pavilion Limited	£2,836,074
Knauf AMF Ceilings Limited	£2,833,208
Mill Masters International Limited	£2,832,533
Dixons Industrial Holdings Limited	£2,830,723
Metro Inns Limited	£2,829,844
Isocom Limited	£2,829,554
Engie Leeds PFI Limited	£2,826,000
Steve Lister Developments Limited	£2,824,071
RMT Accountants & Business Advisors Ltd	£2,823,902
TLC (Car Care) Limited	£2,823,419
NLJIS Holdings Limited	£2,822,668
United Carlton Digital Solutions Limited	£2,820,451
George Ronald Limited	£2,819,798
Colledge Trundle & Hall Limited	£2,816,000
Age UK Sunderland	£2,813,013
Express Engineering (Aerospace) Limited	£2,811,123
Gibson Motorsport Limited	£2,809,788
Stanners Equipment Limited	£2,808,585
Countylife Bamburgh Limited	£2,806,677
Arrowcruit Limited	£2,805,899
Forest Homes Limited	£2,805,489
Scigrip Adhesives Limited	£2,803,708
L A Taxis Ltd	£2,802,889
Maymask (202) Limited	£2,800,939
Steakhouse Holdings Limited	£2,800,000
Armstrong Direct Limited	£2,798,981
Siglion Developments LLP	£2,793,923
Mayford Equities Limited	£2,792,867
V.H. Bio Limited	£2,790,264
Marina Hotels Limited	£2,789,873
MGM Ltd	£2,788,719
2020 Group UK Developments Limited	£2,786,080
Landteam Developments Limited	£2,786,043
Beaumont Colson Ltd.	£2,782,262
Norseal Limited	£2,781,310
P+HS Architects Limited	£2,780,296
Baketime Limited	£2,777,746
Erimus Holdings Teesside Limited	£2,777,431
Intobeige Limited	£2,777,333
Tyne Coast Academy Trust	£2,777,000
M & C Residential Ltd.	£2,775,464
Grab & Deliver Limited	£2,774,927
Minhoco 23 Limited	£2,773,816
Claypath Property Company Limited (The)	£2,773,096
HLA Services Limited	£2,765,412
Chrome PSG Limited	£2,764,993
Tup Tup Palace Limited	£2,758,692
Student Accommodation Services Limited	£2,756,893
Cavu Corporate Finance Limited	£2,754,595
W.G.R. (Steels) Limited	£2,751,327
Interlet Property Investment Consultants Limited	£2,747,739
Monument (Survey:Design:Build) Ltd	£2,747,567
Renaissance Land Regeneration Limited	£2,744,000
Spinks The Chemists Limited	£2,743,868
Cenergist Limited	£2,743,673
Hutton Chemicals Limited	£2,743,302
G.W.Leader Limited	£2,743,087
Alpha Developments (Leicester) Limited	£2,741,660
Townglow Ltd	£2,738,889
Wine World Producers Limited	£2,738,828
Lee's Coaches Limited	£2,738,141
Contract Catering Services (P&A) Holdings Limited	£2,735,906
SW Mawdesley Limited	£2,734,315
Homefair (Holdings) Limited	£2,734,251
Tees Components Property Company Limited	£2,732,788
Bridgman IBC Limited	£2,732,294
Hunley Hall LLP	£2,731,230
Northumberland Rugby Football Union Limited	£2,729,305
Internet Insurance Services UK Ltd	£2,727,020
Jim Hastings Limited	£2,724,147
FB Shipping Limited	£2,724,069
Easterside Academy	£2,723,831
Absolute Pleasure Limited	£2,720,717
Middlesbrough and Stockton Mind Limited	£2,720,026
Newbiggin-By Sea Heritage Partnership Ltd	£2,719,901
Auckland Environmental Services Limited	£2,719,090
Layfield Renewable Ltd	£2,716,832
Jack Coupe & Sons Limited	£2,714,249
MacLeods Pharma UK Limited	£2,713,960
WW Residential Ltd	£2,713,442
Engica Technology Systems International Limited	£2,709,523
UPA (UK) Limited	£2,707,948
Pink Boutique Limited	£2,706,878
McCallum Currie Limited	£2,706,520
RTC North Limited	£2,705,008
Summerhouse Development Limited	£2,703,586
GCA Domestic Limited	£2,702,009
Leda & Swan LLP	£2,700,442
A.M. Fabrication (Northern) Limited	£2,698,290
Transped Limited	£2,698,037
P & P Caravan Services Limited	£2,697,231
Partners in Hygiene Limited	£2,693,231

Fairman Chemists Limited	£2,692,585
Dunelm Optical Holdings Limited	£2,689,691
Appletree Joinery Products Limited	£2,689,677
Proofgolden Limited	£2,688,920
Croxdale Fast-Fit Limited	£2,688,744
Shepherds Dene	£2,686,208
Dalton 009 Limited	£2,684,599
Stockton Casting Company Limited (The)	£2,683,823
Price Right Properties Limited	£2,683,543
Spirit Regeneration & Development Co LLP	£2,683,261
Cool Milk at School Limited	£2,682,297
Abel Yachts Limited	£2,680,046
Bonds Limited	£2,676,301
Andojem Limited	£2,675,616
The Christian Institute	£2,675,219
Eutechnyx Holdings Limited	£2,672,265
P.J.Engineering Products Limited	£2,672,136
Ian Bell (Motor Cycles) Limited	£2,664,328
St. Mary's Chare Developments Limited	£2,663,542
2020 Property Developments Limited	£2,663,313
Corepeople Recruitment Limited	£2,662,480
Hargreaves Technical Resources Limited	£2,661,000
E. J. Stone Limited	£2,660,806
Matthew H. Wilson & Son, Limited	£2,660,040
Nitelites Limited	£2,659,928
King Brothers Bricklaying Contractors Limited	£2,657,970
R and R Hands Road Transport Limited	£2,657,962
S.E.L.F. (North East) Limited	£2,657,674
Ky247 Limited	£2,652,332
Jordan 90 Ltd	£2,651,270
C.P.S. Haulage (Tyneside) Limited	£2,651,016
Addison Plant Limited	£2,648,349
Modern Rugs Limited	£2,647,513
Kaydian Design Limited	£2,647,265
McCarrick Homes Ltd	£2,646,791
Grange Farm Eggs Ltd	£2,645,817
Dunelm Geotechnical & Environmental Limited	£2,645,053
Wylam Garage Limited	£2,644,161
Firgate Estates Limited	£2,642,417
Mesh Marketing Limited	£2,641,633
R. A. & S. Darling Farms (Hartlepool) Limited	£2,641,432
St James' Central Investments Limited	£2,641,320
Charles Lyndon Homes Ltd	£2,635,589
Shapwells Developments Limited	£2,632,933
Hyperdrive Innovation Holdings Limited	£2,632,447
W. Smith (Durham) Limited	£2,624,257
DLI Engineering Limited	£2,622,924
Dedicated Transport Solutions Limited	£2,620,528
D-Line (Europe) Limited	£2,620,383
Newcastle Property Company Limited	£2,618,925
D&K Hire Services Limited	£2,618,160
Belgravia Decor Limited	£2,617,714
Clifton Engineering (North East) Limited	£2,616,421
Air Design Systems Limited	£2,615,877
Specialist IT Services Group Limited	£2,615,641
Peel Jones Copper Products Limited	£2,614,527
Griffith Textile Machines Limited	£2,614,124
Kompass Holdings Limited	£2,613,527
DM Services (Banchory) Ltd	£2,613,343
NAC Property Management Limited	£2,612,509
Immobi Ltd	£2,610,500
Interlink Scaffolding Ltd	£2,609,672
Parsons Containers Limited	£2,609,431
Leavendale Properties Ltd	£2,609,170
Training and Development Resource Limited	£2,607,530
Mazegood Limited	£2,606,617
Indigo Software (Holdings) Limited	£2,606,496
Northern Bear Building Services Limited	£2,604,360
Southbay Civil Engineering Limited	£2,603,724
St Trinity Limited	£2,600,000
J H Harrison Investments Ltd	£2,599,647
Induction Pipe Bending UK Limited	£2,595,763
Cottam Brush Ltd	£2,594,569
Bentincks Ltd	£2,591,333
Invicta Asset Management Limited	£2,591,102
Peacocks (Surgical and Medical Equipment) Limited	£2,590,737
Statex Press (Northern) Limited	£2,588,156
A1 Industrial Trucks Limited	£2,587,074
Jesmond Property Developments Limited	£2,584,786
Andrew Hughes Utility Services Ltd	£2,583,311
Cavendish (Northern) Property Developments Limited	£2,583,243
Ritchie-Bland Estates Ltd	£2,582,549
The Cylinder Service Centre Limited	£2,581,349
Devine Chemicals Limited	£2,580,779
Sunter Limited	£2,577,708
NIS Group Services Limited	£2,574,991
The Northstar Foundation	£2,573,126
Marson Investments Limited	£2,571,565
Teekay Marine Solutions Ltd	£2,571,379
Closewalk Limited	£2,568,490
Grove Information Systems Limited	£2,568,118
Initial Group of Companies Limited	£2,567,516
Ladhar Leisure LLP	£2,564,948
Learning Concepts Limited	£2,561,223
A M I Exchangers Limited	£2,560,535
Total Resources (UK) Limited	£2,559,930
Permatt Fork Lift Trucks Limited	£2,558,397
HMC Ventures Limited	£2,557,823
Anglitemp Limited	£2,553,691
TS Plant Sales (NE) Ltd.	£2,553,615
Wensleydale Bacon Limited	£2,550,963
Regent Leisure Limited	£2,550,505
Vixen Surface Treatments Limited	£2,550,006
Tirsul Limited	£2,549,500
Jules B Limited	£2,547,759
Monitor Coatings Limited	£2,545,942
Pout and Foster Limited	£2,545,189
Indian Kings Walk 1 Limited	£2,544,794
Saint John of God Hospitaller Services	£2,544,000
Tascomp Holdings Limited	£2,541,968
Bellway (Services) Limited	£2,540,994
James Ingleford Scaffolding Limited	£2,537,969
Idec Power Services Limited	£2,537,833
Enviro Property Partners Limited	£2,537,194
Lift-Rite Engineering Services Limited	£2,534,597
Ford Component Manufacturing Limited	£2,534,431
Kid 'n' Play Limited	£2,532,397
Dyce Limited	£2,529,193
Micromix (Northern) Ltd	£2,528,506
Quartztec Europe Limited	£2,526,120
Richmondshire Building Preservation Trust Ltd	£2,523,840
Darlington Residential Limited	£2,523,452
Michael Sehgal & Sons Limited	£2,519,920
Forth England Limited	£2,519,891
Cromex Limited	£2,519,297
F.M. Steelstock Limited	£2,517,708
W. L. Straughan & Son Limited	£2,516,848
Hase Osborne Asset Management Limited	£2,512,917
Stephenson Gobin Limited	£2,512,654
Borders Recycling Limited	£2,510,382
Harry Marsh (Engineers) Limited	£2,510,245
Spreckley Limited	£2,510,222
Sayers Road Tankers Engineering Limited	£2,509,524
Excello Limited	£2,506,516
Robert and Roberts Limited	£2,504,729
Pornic Limited	£2,504,038
Acklam Car Centre Limited	£2,502,589
Amble Development Trust	£2,500,929
Cool Milk Limited	£2,500,651
NTG Group Limited	£2,500,300
Blendspeak Limited	£2,500,000
Peart Property (Bowburn) Limited	£2,498,865
CMP Marketing Limited	£2,497,914
Romanby Golf Course Limited	£2,496,812

Company	Amount
Coolcheck Refrigeration Limited	£2,494,962
G.B. Bandag Ltd	£2,494,236
Distributor Supplies (UK) Limited	£2,492,309
Air Filters Limited	£2,490,000
Polymer Compounders Limited	£2,489,295
RACZ Group Ltd	£2,488,873
P.D.Q. Engineering Limited	£2,487,286
Reid Street Primary School	£2,486,000
Tunstall Developments Limited	£2,485,630
Harbron Legal Ltd	£2,477,688
Square One Law LLP	£2,477,092
Inveniam Home Loans Limited	£2,476,735
AA Construction (North East) Ltd	£2,476,606
Thomas Baty (Newcastle upon Tyne) Limited	£2,475,801
Alex Scott Cars Limited	£2,475,201
Lescost Transport Limited	£2,474,214
North East Actuarial Services Limited	£2,472,917
ICS Integrated Cable Services Limited	£2,472,395
M A Utilities Ltd	£2,471,097
M.Whitfield Limited	£2,465,678
Holystone Civil Engineering Limited	£2,464,135
View Logistics Limited	£2,463,413
Cleveland Alzheimer's Residential Centre Limited	£2,460,246
Tyneside Estate Office Limited	£2,458,323
Diamond Hall Infant Academy	£2,457,200
Urban Lifestyle Limited	£2,454,740
Staithes Lane Properties Limited	£2,453,375
Tsing Hing Limited	£2,448,848
Hyperdrive Innovation Ltd	£2,448,815
Rathbone Training	£2,448,000
Cleveland Homes (No.5) Limited	£2,447,324
Barclay Roofing Limited	£2,447,219
Northumbria Coast and Country Cottages Limited	£2,446,421
Rubb Buildings Limited	£2,446,018
Mechanical Breakdown & General Insurance Services Ltd	£2,445,037
Logical Link Solutions Limited	£2,445,000
Casper Shipping Holdings Limited	£2,444,547
Durham City Property (Holdings) Limited	£2,443,209
Newbridge Engineering Limited	£2,441,643
Eagle Welding & Engineering Supplies Limited	£2,441,142
UK National Limited	£2,438,288
Ryhope Infant School Academy	£2,437,578
Henry Williams Group Limited	£2,436,577
Newcastle Preparatory School Trust Limited (The)	£2,436,307
Wolds Produce Ltd	£2,435,196
Technowash Limited	£2,433,729
R.A. Dalton Limited	£2,431,401
Tesmonard Europe Limited	£2,430,258
REC Consultancy Services Limited	£2,430,255
Peter Milburn Chemist Limited	£2,430,113
Premier Truck Hire Limited	£2,428,702
S&I Developments Ltd	£2,428,653
Sone Products Ltd	£2,428,257
Pebbletree Ltd	£2,427,365
G.C.S. Johnson (Skeeby) Limited	£2,426,688
Tomlinson,Hall & Company Limited	£2,425,983
Two Trees Woolley Limited	£2,422,438
Precision 2000 Limited	£2,420,488
Thornton Print Limited	£2,418,853
Woodhouse Triangle Limited	£2,418,591
Maymask (140) Limited	£2,418,215
Pringle Building Services Limited	£2,417,951
Popcorn Limited	£2,417,057
Burradon Farm Houses and Cottages Limited	£2,417,013
Blue Flames Sporting Club Limited	£2,416,341
My Firms App Limited	£2,415,929
Newcastle Diocesan Education Board Limited	£2,411,425
Adavo Ltd	£2,411,289
Ailantus Hotels Limited	£2,410,970
Theakston Waller Limited	£2,410,004
Armah Switchgear Limited	£2,407,448
Jentone Freight Limited	£2,405,086
Newcastle upon Tyne Y.M.C.A.	£2,402,072
S.J.B. Recycling Limited	£2,400,919
Kail Holdings Limited	£2,399,792
JSB (Metals) Limited	£2,399,725
Cleveland Motorhomes Limited	£2,398,593
N.T.E. Holdings Limited	£2,395,019
Northern Counties LLP	£2,394,121
Applied Graphene Materials UK Limited	£2,391,000
AEDT Operations Limited	£2,389,449
Biochemica Water Limited	£2,388,912
Newburn Riverside Recreation Association Limited	£2,388,835
Tripak Ltd	£2,388,486
Francis Brown Limited	£2,386,043
Geoffrey Forrester & Co Limited	£2,383,658
WW Medical Facilities Limited	£2,383,515
P. Plunkett (Tiling Contractors) Limited	£2,382,160
Business Data Partners Limited	£2,381,309
NRS Media (Europe) Limited	£2,372,435
Airowsafe Limited	£2,372,028
Holmfirth Finance Limited	£2,371,619
Maxim Facilities Management Ltd	£2,369,310
Signature Fencing and Flooring Systems Europe Ltd	£2,363,774
B.M. Stafford & Sons Ltd	£2,360,249
Headlam Leisure Limited	£2,359,056
I D Construction Services Ltd	£2,358,618
Timber Plant & Haulage Ltd.	£2,358,133
Frank Hudson Transport Limited	£2,357,841
Lowe & Simpson Group Limited	£2,356,917
Imad-Muminah Properties Ltd	£2,356,247
SVP Health Care Limited	£2,354,368
Greensfield Moor Development Limited	£2,349,603
Hartlepool Revival Limited	£2,349,584
Teesside Industrial Controls Limited	£2,348,789
Fracks Transport Limited	£2,348,420
Interocean Personnel Services (UK) Limited	£2,347,663
Anglo Scottish Asset Finance Limited	£2,347,354
Delta - North Consett Limited	£2,346,820
Bignall Group Ltd	£2,346,400
Project Advisors International (U.K.) Ltd.	£2,344,667
Moulded Packaging Solutions Ltd	£2,344,367
Fred Henderson Limited	£2,341,550
L.D.H. Plant Limited	£2,341,455
Capital Properties Solutions Limited	£2,339,958
Herrington Mews Ltd	£2,337,867
Robson Laidler Accountants Limited	£2,336,326
Conduit Construction Network Limited	£2,336,204
TLW LLP	£2,335,641
Willington Healthcare Limited	£2,334,420
Kebrico Limited	£2,334,406
Care-Ability Healthcare Limited	£2,332,608
Cramlington Village Primary Ltd	£2,332,545
Turnkey Air Conditioning Limited	£2,332,365
1excellence Multi Academy Trust	£2,332,000
North of England Civic Trust	£2,331,849
Gala Due Limited	£2,331,000
Insight Healthcare Ltd.	£2,330,000
A & SA Properties Limited	£2,329,450
Newcastle Gateshead Initiative Limited	£2,329,000
Transcare Solutions Limited	£2,329,000
Ecco Finishing Supplies Limited	£2,328,425
Liquiform Limited	£2,326,858
Intelect Mechanical Limited	£2,326,300
Hepburn Farm Limited	£2,323,039
Matthew Wood Developments Limited	£2,322,958
Impulsepay Ltd	£2,320,698
Westgarth Haulage Limited	£2,319,600
Site and Field Services Limited	£2,319,339
Silbury Motors Limited	£2,318,920
Aqueous 1st Kwikflow Limited	£2,318,058
Dayspring Trust	£2,317,826
Immi Ltd	£2,317,122
L & G Utilities Ltd	£2,316,142

Company	Value
Horncastle Executive Travel Limited	£2,315,312
Profound Services Limited	£2,314,846
Singh Family Partnership LLP	£2,314,808
John Watson Joinery Ltd	£2,314,380
Rasmi Electronics Limited	£2,314,197
Taemar Limited	£2,314,072
Fitwide Limited	£2,313,499
Parmley Technologies Limited	£2,312,963
G. Whitfield Limited	£2,312,882
Bede Globe LLP	£2,312,183
Saltwell Park Developments Ltd	£2,310,259
JKL Mouldings Limited	£2,310,108
James Paul Services To Industry Limited	£2,309,667
T. M. Ward (Darlington) Limited	£2,309,633
LD Property Management Limited	£2,309,084
The Head of Steam Limited	£2,307,518
Gecomac Limited	£2,306,725
Red Oak Ltd	£2,306,542
Ryka Developments Limited	£2,302,612
Precision Geomatics Limited	£2,301,759
SLJH Limited	£2,300,200
McVickers Limited	£2,298,507
Avenue Pharmacy (Sunderland) Limited	£2,295,965
Woodside Park Estates Limited	£2,294,988
Reed Thermoformed Packaging Ltd.	£2,291,880
Association of International Accountants (The)	£2,291,316
Abbeyfield (Darlington) Society Limited (The)	£2,287,986
Saltwell Park Agencies Limited	£2,287,349
Pallion Engineering Limited	£2,287,074
Primrose House Ltd	£2,285,680
Hedley Hill Developments Limited	£2,285,607
Jim Hughes Coaches Limited	£2,285,488
Vallum Properties Limited	£2,284,587
Wynyard Life Ltd	£2,284,441
Tiles Porcelain Limited	£2,282,525
21st Century Style Limited	£2,279,629
Armstrong Nationwide Ltd.	£2,279,412
Reproflex 3 Limited	£2,277,978
Lawnsward Limited	£2,276,007
Utility Support Solutions Limited	£2,275,205
Erico Europa (G.B.) Limited	£2,274,875
The Wensleydale Property Company Limited	£2,273,447
Polar (N.E.) Limited	£2,271,390
Francis Transport Limited	£2,270,782
Supreme Property Developments Limited	£2,270,127
Protec The Cap Company Limited	£2,266,038
Millfield Composites Limited	£2,265,662
P A Moody Recycling Limited	£2,262,690
Anvil Homes Limited	£2,262,542
Casmaco Limited	£2,262,192
F K Solutions (UK) Limited	£2,260,670
Hepple Engineering Services Limited	£2,260,432
Launchpad Homes Limited	£2,257,813
Hutchinson Transport Limited	£2,254,429
Metrology Software Products Limited	£2,253,266
Christchurch Claypath Durham	£2,252,615
High Warden Farm Limited	£2,251,914
Crabtree of Gateshead (Holdings) Limited	£2,251,373
The Vehicle Group Limited	£2,247,689
Fullwell Mill Limited	£2,245,681
Knightingales Limited	£2,245,332
Underwood Hall Limited	£2,242,686
Grainger Europe Limited	£2,241,794
Ceefox Sports Consultancy Limited	£2,241,385
Melanor Limited	£2,240,427
Thomas Witter Carpets Limited	£2,240,003
R Campbell & Sons Limited	£2,237,896
N.T.E. Limited	£2,236,112
NEA2F Subco Limited	£2,233,881
Matfen Golf Limited	£2,233,721
Swarland Brick Company Limited (The)	£2,233,480
Durham Precision Engineering Limited	£2,233,059
Abletransfer Limited	£2,232,964
Robertson Simpson Limited	£2,232,824
West Denton Indoor Bowls Club Limited	£2,231,219
TGT Holidays Limited	£2,231,083
Spark of Genius North East LLP	£2,230,988
Clevestones Trans Limited	£2,229,944
A.Buckler Haulage Limited	£2,229,797
Westminster Day Nurseries Limited	£2,229,762
Standard Security Services Limited	£2,228,848
Premier Commercial Properties (UK) LLP	£2,228,058
Thermal Insulation Contractors Association	£2,227,485
Angel Distribution Limited	£2,226,819
Eland Homes Limited	£2,225,562
Roseville Asset Management Limited	£2,225,148
CISV International Limited	£2,223,855
Brush Technology Limited	£2,223,156
Cellular Solutions (North East) Ltd.	£2,222,799
Langley Moor B3 Ltd.	£2,221,065
Key Homes (GB) Limited	£2,219,557
R. Thornton & Co. Ltd.	£2,219,205
Goodfellow & Goodfellow Ltd.	£2,217,853
J.W. Wood Limited	£2,216,929
Bede Investments Limited	£2,216,786
Whitworth Hall Developments Limited	£2,216,095
Hart Biologicals Limited	£2,215,729
Drilcorp Limited	£2,215,676
Tyne Mills Motor Company Limited	£2,214,540
Robert Kirkland (Blyth) Limited	£2,214,060
Ford Aerospace Limited	£2,213,324
Dale Care Limited	£2,212,784
Derwentside Hospice Care Foundation	£2,212,677
3 E Investment Ltd	£2,212,193
Hedingham & District Omnibuses Ltd.	£2,212,000
Pulman Seat Limited	£2,212,000
Sterling GP Limited	£2,210,580
Philadelphia Structures Ltd	£2,209,857
Zapego Limited	£2,203,613
Red House Investments Limited	£2,199,902
Ashfield Estates Limited	£2,199,345
W. Robson (Farm) Limited	£2,195,996
Greco Brothers Limited	£2,195,814
Bastion Glassfibre Rod & Sections Limited	£2,195,767
Secon Solar Limited	£2,194,310
I&K International Company Limited	£2,194,130
Intruder Detection & Surveillance Ltd.	£2,192,705
Solmek Limited	£2,192,558
Wheatley Hill Property Company Limited	£2,190,667
GT Cleaning Machines Limited	£2,187,238
Streonshalh Limited	£2,187,201
Geocore Site Investigations Limited	£2,186,604
William Coulthard and Company Limited	£2,186,365
Elite Embroidery Limited	£2,186,299
New Seaham Academy	£2,184,607
Darwins Holdings Limited	£2,184,131
OSO Hotwater (U.K.) Limited	£2,181,630
Go-Ahead London Rail Replacement Services Limited	£2,180,000
Clive Owen LLP	£2,179,186
Heinzmann UK Limited	£2,179,103
Dissington Investments Limited	£2,178,111
Swiftpage International Limited	£2,175,611
J.K. Construction and Joinery Limited	£2,173,257
Ceres Energy Limited	£2,169,582
Vaulkhard Investment Properties Limited	£2,168,876
Donald Pig & Poultry Ltd	£2,167,427
Restaurant Design Associates Ltd	£2,166,830
Eppleton Quarry Products (Scunthorpe) Limited	£2,166,573
Bestmark Properties Limited	£2,165,792
Pipetawse Limited	£2,164,056
Rosh Engineering Limited	£2,163,596
Jeave 4 Limited	£2,162,926
Earsdon Properties LLP	£2,161,410
Percy A.Hudson Limited	£2,160,928

Company	Amount
Ingleby Healthcare Ltd	£2,160,663
Dawn Estates Limited	£2,160,433
KDL Systems Ltd	£2,159,802
Bulman Support Ltd	£2,159,777
M.G.N. Fire Protection Limited	£2,158,926
Tancred Gravel Limited	£2,157,308
Xander Developments Limited	£2,153,497
Cleveland Land Limited	£2,153,341
Michael Drapers Limited	£2,152,622
Valiant Sheep Limited	£2,151,137
D.P. Builders Limited	£2,148,458
Multichem Limited	£2,148,038
Alab Environmental Services Limited	£2,147,501
Hadrian Limited	£2,146,826
XCEL County Durham	£2,143,820
Ovington Boats Limited	£2,142,776
TBT Catering Limited	£2,142,722
Aircon-Refrigeration Limited	£2,142,606
Calibrate Inc Ltd	£2,142,248
SES Securus Limited	£2,140,334
Clarity Informatics Limited	£2,138,588
Seaton Healthcare Limited	£2,138,347
The Morpeth Practice Ltd	£2,137,884
Kenneth Easby Limited	£2,137,681
MJM Developments (Portrack Grange) Limited	£2,137,111
Tao Sustainable Power Solutions (UK) Ltd	£2,137,000
G. Abbott & Co. Limited	£2,136,394
Castleview Group Training Limited	£2,135,588
Hays Credit LLP	£2,134,779
Glendale Transport UK Limited	£2,133,042
Deerness Rubber Company Limited	£2,132,380
Excelsior Services (Student Accommodation) Limited	£2,131,358
Anglian Bus Limited	£2,131,000
Greta Cottage Limited	£2,129,337
JMW (Aluminium) Limited	£2,127,647
Rivermeade Signs Limited	£2,127,367
Easibathe Limited	£2,126,913
Elaghmore (Holdings) Limited	£2,125,933
Moores Leisure (Teesside) Limited	£2,125,496
Twin Services Limited	£2,125,426
Van Mildert Landlord and Tenant Protection Limited	£2,125,280
Parkside Care Limited	£2,123,837
Wharton Construction Limited	£2,123,053
Silvia Properties Limited	£2,121,618
Shire Aggregates Bulk Limited	£2,121,369
Care and Share Associates One (2014) Limited	£2,120,277
Forrest Park (Newton Aycliffe) Limited	£2,120,220
James of Stokesley LLP	£2,119,369
Commercial & Temperance Developments LLP	£2,119,103
Philip Cussins House	£2,118,120
Age UK North Tyneside	£2,116,322
K.Johnson Limited	£2,115,671
Adderstone Developments (104) Limited	£2,115,359
Quartz Electrical & Mechanical Services Limited	£2,113,522
Cecil M. Yuill Limited	£2,112,617
Tyne and Wear Building Preservation Trust Limited	£2,112,139
Swan Kee Limited	£2,111,776
CLC Enterprise Limited	£2,111,588
Lam-Plas (Durham) Limited	£2,110,145
Direct Sports Limited	£2,109,502
M R B Schumag Ltd	£2,108,110
Jesmond Leisure Limited	£2,105,448
IK-UK Limited	£2,105,179
Cool Milk Administration Limited	£2,103,641
Great Orton Windfarm II Limited	£2,103,000
Petersen Stainless Rigging Limited	£2,102,222
Stuart Bell Asset Management Limited	£2,099,069
Deanmoor Limited	£2,097,930
Eco Drill (England) Limited	£2,097,021
D.W. Marshall and Co. Limited	£2,095,247
Normans of Billingham Limited	£2,094,696
UK Warranty Limited	£2,093,891
Berger Closures Limited	£2,093,786
Holy Trinity Church of England Academy (S Shields) Trust	£2,093,000
Mactech Inspection Holdco Limited	£2,091,745
R C McInnes Limited	£2,091,236
Mactech Inspection Limited	£2,089,467
The Minel Group Ltd.	£2,088,637
Total Business Computers Ltd	£2,087,609
TS Developments Ltd	£2,085,513
A.L.M. Products Limited	£2,085,492
N A College Limited	£2,085,189
FPP Design Limited	£2,085,040
Mineral & Chemical Services Ltd	£2,084,051
Leybourne Urwin Limited	£2,083,315
North East Panels Limited	£2,083,249
Henson Property Company Ltd	£2,080,369
Sebastian Enterprises Ltd	£2,079,969
Queensberry Design Limited	£2,079,846
N A Consultants Ltd	£2,078,570
Ashley Timber Limited	£2,078,357
E.S.P. Plastics Ltd	£2,076,496
Gilbert Birdsall Limited	£2,075,203
Philip Makin Transport Limited	£2,074,854
S&A Builders Merchants (Holdings) Limited	£2,073,002
Genhawk Limited	£2,069,763
Dawson Farms Limited	£2,069,758
RS Industrial Services (Tyne & Wear) Limited	£2,069,270
Travelsure Coaches Limited	£2,068,770
AVG Power Limited	£2,067,938
Agma Limited	£2,067,758
Border Traffic Transport Limited	£2,067,059
Longden Walker and Renney (Solicitors) Limited	£2,066,684
C.Donnelly Construction Limited	£2,066,614
Britton Leisure Limited	£2,065,513
Jonsigns Limited	£2,064,578
JPG Property LLP	£2,062,703
Glenrose Developments (Whitburn) Limited	£2,061,126
Protherm (UK) Limited	£2,060,264
Tom Walker and Sons Limited	£2,057,425
Acer Learning Trust	£2,056,000
Cameron's Builders (Newcastle) Limited	£2,053,379
Blue Diamond Engineering Limited	£2,052,683
G H Farms Limited	£2,051,647
Delcor Ltd.	£2,050,934
Ward Timber Limited	£2,049,294
Rosewood HR Services Ltd	£2,048,991
Dunelm Investments Limited	£2,048,180
Sleekburn Estates Limited	£2,047,554
Amtech Automated Micro Technology Limited	£2,044,924
Stuart Wright Funeral Service Limited	£2,043,014
Northeastern Finance Limited	£2,042,249
Property Rental Services Limited	£2,042,197
Thompson (Wholesale Meat) Limited	£2,041,420
Osborne Professional Services Limited	£2,037,442
Murray and Lamb Accountants Limited	£2,037,250
JCM Holdings Limited	£2,037,195
Shelcorp 2008 Ltd	£2,037,000
Richard J Knaggs & Co LLP	£2,036,559
ABS Precision Limited	£2,036,073
South Durham Health C.I.C.	£2,034,796
Check in USA Limited	£2,033,890
Age Concern Durham County	£2,033,070
The Redemption Food Company Limited	£2,032,958
Blacklock Harvesting Ltd	£2,032,699
Bruker JV UK Ltd	£2,031,627
Topside Group Limited	£2,030,825
Reial Property Investments Limited	£2,029,950
Brenda Road Properties Limited	£2,029,800
Healthworks Newcastle	£2,029,602
Engynious Clean Power (UK) Ltd	£2,029,116
Northeast Sheets & Panels Limited	£2,028,834
Richmond Fire Engineers Ltd	£2,024,853
Taylor Packaging (Bishop Auckland) Limited	£2,024,314

Company	Amount	Company	Amount
Geo.A.Carter Limited	£2,022,680	RH Marine UK Ltd	£1,959,000
Holiday at Home Limited	£2,022,078	Sandgate Park Limited	£1,956,974
M M C (Europe) Limited	£2,021,004	TTR Barnes Limited	£1,955,889
Elite Maintenance & Installation Services Limited	£2,019,075	Talbot House Trust North East	£1,955,457
BTS Fabrications Limited	£2,018,113	The Coach Inn Company Limited	£1,954,658
Felton Property and Investments Limited	£2,017,934	Westerhope Limited	£1,954,603
Arcot Grange Developments Limited	£2,017,346	J.J. Blair & Sons Limited	£1,953,781
Harry Swaddle Limited	£2,016,363	Roxburgh Group Limited	£1,952,611
T.W.R. Trade Frames Limited	£2,014,906	Homefair Blinds (U.K.) Limited	£1,952,514
Halls Pharmacy (North East) Limited	£2,013,739	Whiteside Residential Limited	£1,951,507
Wallsend Memorial Hall & People's Centre	£2,012,468	Logic Manufacturing Limited	£1,950,577
1973 Developments Ltd	£2,011,462	Tyne North Training Limited	£1,950,041
Altec Precision Limited	£2,010,000	J.A.Willis (Northallerton) Limited	£1,949,128
Reay Security Limited	£2,009,995	Total Bolt Solutions Limited	£1,948,540
Gnat UK Limited	£2,009,022	South Durham Structures Limited	£1,948,263
SM Farms Limited	£2,007,757	Eaglescliffe Properties Limited	£1,946,128
Theakston Estates (North East) Limited	£2,007,419	JCM Retail Equipment Limited	£1,944,146
John Lilley & Gillie Limited	£2,007,036	Renaissance (Padiham) Limited	£1,944,000
J. & J. Whittaker (Chemist) Limited	£2,006,192	Chrysalis Grant Making Trust	£1,943,377
Modaim Limited	£2,005,973	Seatechs Limited	£1,942,713
Group Tegula Limited	£2,005,780	The Mea Trust	£1,937,827
Leggott Farming Limited	£2,004,260	TVG Vision Ltd	£1,937,494
NEL Technologies Limited	£2,003,054	Match Day Centres Ltd	£1,933,105
H.J. Banks (Construction) Limited	£2,003,000	Brackenburn Holdings Limited	£1,931,558
KBR I.T. and Networking Solutions Limited	£2,002,992	Stephen Willcox Builder Limited	£1,931,439
Sentinel Homes Limited	£2,002,688	Formula Plastics Limited	£1,930,914
Commercial Maintenance Services UK Limited	£2,002,517	L.H. (Quarry Plant) Limited	£1,929,983
Map Construction Services Ltd	£2,001,995	Nano-Purification Solutions Ltd	£1,929,652
Pakway Limited	£2,001,117	Blackwell Grange Golf Club Limited	£1,926,022
2M Food Suppliers Limited	£2,001,095	UK Docks Marine Services Teesside Limited	£1,925,650
Roxburgh Holdings Limited	£2,000,780	Trumeau Limited	£1,925,332
Gill & Robinson Limited	£2,000,559	Momento Vivere Limited	£1,924,794
PJA Distribution Limited	£1,998,815	Biostore Limited	£1,924,203
Old Exchange Darlington Limited	£1,995,323	Junsterik Ltd	£1,922,985
John Clark Valves Limited	£1,993,958	SMH Equipment Limited	£1,922,592
F. Brunton & Sons Limited	£1,993,388	Moorlands Care Homes (N.E.) Limited	£1,919,800
Cambridge Scholars Publishing Ltd	£1,991,827	Manissa Ltd	£1,918,433
Hadrian Technology Limited	£1,991,763	Newcastle Buttress Limited	£1,918,397
Heaton Enterprises Limited	£1,991,440	City Church Newcastle	£1,916,661
Able Construction (Northern) Limited	£1,991,108	CB Inn Limited	£1,916,560
John Hellens (Contracts) Limited	£1,990,973	Samson Aviation Services Limited	£1,916,159
G D Lee Building Services Limited	£1,988,500	M. Pattison & Co. Limited	£1,913,961
Baltic Training Services Limited	£1,988,293	Sage Multi Academy Trust	£1,913,000
GBB Manufacturing Limited	£1,988,255	George Vardy Limited	£1,911,721
Prudhoe Estates LLP	£1,985,800	Chris Quigley Education Limited	£1,911,112
Barrier (Offshore) Engineering Limited	£1,984,241	Arriva UK Bus Properties Limited	£1,911,000
Driving Success Limited	£1,983,934	Greit Limited	£1,910,401
Derwent Manor Ltd	£1,983,719	Peter Stott Properties Ltd	£1,906,521
Electronic Security Solutions Limited	£1,982,437	Arquer Diagnostics Limited	£1,906,166
Flightblade Limited	£1,982,065	Tyneside Leisure World Limited	£1,905,472
Adept Professional Services Ltd	£1,979,327	Clark Residential Limited	£1,903,370
Port Clarence Land Limited	£1,977,763	Northumbrian Land Limited	£1,902,976
Whiterock Bid Support Limited	£1,977,594	CPS Drivelink Limited	£1,902,939
Beis Chaye Rochel (The Gateshead Jewish Academy)	£1,976,357	The Hill Cross Organisation Limited	£1,902,791
Protomed Limited	£1,974,495	North Eastern Glass Limited	£1,902,421
Ubisoft CRC Ltd	£1,973,000	Isoclad Limited	£1,898,397
A.W. Cowan Groundworks Limited	£1,971,456	Allan Liddle (Holding) Limited	£1,897,894
Harraton Properties Limited	£1,970,782	Lewis & Cooper Limited	£1,897,876
Hornby Healthcare Limited	£1,970,515	K & L Groundworks Limited	£1,895,522
CMC North East Ltd	£1,970,216	Derma UK Limited	£1,893,601
Dualbound Limited	£1,968,977	JA Property Limited	£1,893,056
Storage Equipment Safety Service Limited	£1,968,569	Horsley Properties Limited	£1,892,109
B L Training Limited	£1,968,014	Clavering Management Limited	£1,890,894
Lift-Rite Holdings Limited	£1,966,788	Sunley Farms (Richmond) Limited	£1,890,576
Damian Cronin Limited	£1,965,340	Newcastle Jewellers Ltd.	£1,890,203
Interceil Limited	£1,964,879	Turboactive Limited	£1,888,193
Cleveland Homes (No.4) Limited	£1,963,190	Exclusive Care Group Ltd	£1,887,023
GNS 2015 Limited	£1,962,437	Timec 1306 Limited	£1,886,018
Friends of Biala Limited	£1,961,939	Emmanuel Church Durham	£1,885,442
S Hogarth Holdings Limited	£1,960,462	Falconvale Limited	£1,885,333
Medichem (Sunderland) Limited	£1,960,000	Milburn Motors Garages Limited	£1,885,079
Commerce Chambers Ltd	£1,959,148	WBE Limited	£1,884,858

Company	Amount
Purity Global Limited	£1,884,729
B.M.A. Properties Limited	£1,882,095
Country Valley Wholesale Foods Limited	£1,880,919
20/20 Vision Systems Limited	£1,879,258
Pioneering Care Partnership	£1,878,878
Pressed Steel Products Limited	£1,878,246
Mynicehouse Limited	£1,877,897
Brian Robinson Machinery Limited	£1,877,564
Harnham Buddhist Monastery Trust	£1,876,831
Halton Property Services Limited	£1,876,608
Tustain Motors Northumberland Limited	£1,875,979
Hindhaugh Homes Limited	£1,875,675
Lool Shulan Ltd	£1,875,317
Cleveland Homes (No.1) Limited	£1,874,218
Nicholson's Aircraft Seals Limited	£1,872,215
North East Property and Investments Limited	£1,871,019
Middleton Forge Limited	£1,870,430
Red I55 Ltd	£1,869,359
Emsosaru Limited	£1,867,788
St James' Central 4 & 5 Limited	£1,867,420
Fairstone Financial Management (City) Limited	£1,867,012
Aedis Regulatory Services Limited	£1,866,504
Elmfield Trading Limited	£1,865,730
Ray & Company (Hairdressers Sundries Men) Limited	£1,864,499
Gilmour & Associates Limited	£1,864,329
Ropers Caravan World (Catterick) Limited	£1,860,959
Bel Estates Limited	£1,860,912
Dane Group Holdings Limited	£1,860,597
J.G. Windows Limited	£1,859,022
Kura Financial Services Limited	£1,859,000
H.H.R. Investments Limited	£1,857,844
Robinsons Tees Valley Ltd	£1,857,291
Northern Housing Consortium Limited	£1,857,154
Allerton Steel (Property) Limited	£1,855,447
Intumescent Protective Coatings Limited	£1,854,375
Sky Scaffolding (Whitby) Limited	£1,854,180
Youll Construction Ltd	£1,853,593
Contract Design (Northern) Limited	£1,853,011
Kuyt Limited	£1,852,737
Grainger Newbury Limited	£1,850,833
Bishop's Beds Ltd	£1,850,166
Beckleberrys Limited	£1,850,138
JCP Consulting Engineers Limited	£1,848,786
Melorvale Limited	£1,848,711
Bel Group Investments Limited	£1,848,122
Compass Developments (NE) Ltd	£1,848,053
SMD Offshore Support Limited	£1,847,902
Landwood Properties Limited	£1,847,861
Waterseal (Waterbar & Sealants) Limited	£1,847,679
Sunderland Accommodation Services Limited	£1,847,574
Hatton Traffic Management Limited	£1,847,042
Scott Bros. Recycling Limited	£1,846,648
Colmans Caterers Limited	£1,845,336
Billy Shiel Farne Islands Boats Limited	£1,844,722
The Roof Truss Company (Northern) Ltd	£1,844,657
Belle Vue Community, Sports & Youth Centre Limited	£1,844,328
S.M.P. (Services) Limited	£1,842,532
Gibson & Co. Solicitors Ltd	£1,842,507
Ayton Consulting Limited	£1,842,122
Metnor Quays Limited	£1,841,000
Blagdon Farming Limited	£1,840,937
Fine & Performance Chemicals Limited	£1,840,802
Vixen Properties Limited	£1,839,596
LCH Renewables Limited	£1,837,115
Dormor Machine and Engineering Company Limited	£1,836,552
J Harland Haulage Limited	£1,834,670
Stewart & Harris Limited	£1,833,184
Acorn Laser Limited	£1,830,782
Trevor Atkinson & Co Limited	£1,829,901
Midas Cladding Services Limited	£1,829,759
Leftbank Properties Limited	£1,828,566
Zenith People Limited	£1,827,577
Paper Dove Company Limited	£1,826,913
Holywell Farms Ltd	£1,826,581
NST Welding (UK) Limited	£1,826,186
Barnes Academy Trust	£1,826,024
Brandh Academy Limited	£1,826,000
Northern Guild Limited	£1,824,590
G. Rutherford & Co. Limited	£1,823,284
Novatech (UK) Limited	£1,823,270
Hameed Investments Limited	£1,823,018
C. and R. Limited	£1,822,696
Mulberry Leisure Holdings Limited	£1,819,566
Eppleton Academy Primary School	£1,819,106
Milbank Investments Ltd	£1,818,523
C.C. Property Management Limited	£1,816,390
P North Group Limited	£1,816,287
Owens Nutrition Limited	£1,816,022
RDS Driving Services Limited	£1,814,840
LEC Management	£1,814,031
Vardy 1985 Investments Limited	£1,813,330
Cenelec Standards Inspections Limited	£1,812,306
Suffolk Electrical Services Limited	£1,811,803
Northumberland Castle and Country Lodgings Ltd	£1,811,475
Ikonica Furniture Ltd	£1,811,318
Mediaworks UK Limited	£1,809,669
Tourmaster Travel Limited	£1,809,341
Kingston Property Services Limited	£1,809,001
Coble Developments Limited	£1,808,726
I6media Ltd	£1,807,354
Foundation of European Nurses in Diabetes	£1,807,220
Darlington Tyre & Auto Centre Limited	£1,806,987
Sharperton Developments Limited	£1,806,717
County and Northern Limited	£1,806,640
Falcon Engineering & Development Limited	£1,804,175
Bramwells Retail Limited	£1,803,542
D.J.R. Smith Limited	£1,803,239
Daisy Chain Project Teesside	£1,802,886
Pleasant Residential Ltd	£1,802,323
C & V Developments Ltd.	£1,801,806
Thistle Property Developments Ltd.	£1,801,660
Grovekey Limited	£1,801,566
Charlton Blair Limited	£1,800,908
Soccer Sensations Hull Limited	£1,799,771
Technocopy Ltd.	£1,799,186
Fillpack Limited	£1,796,366
Maersk Training Newcastle Limited	£1,796,210
Henderson Site Services Limited	£1,795,594
Geo - Drill Limited	£1,795,261
The Maymask Healthcare Group Limited	£1,795,005
White Bros. (N'cle-on-Tyne) Limited	£1,794,726
Flatliners Limited	£1,792,188
Edenpace Limited	£1,792,000
Manning Limited	£1,790,385
Create Images Ion Limited	£1,789,263
H. Tones & Sons Limited	£1,788,704
Watsons Haulage Limited	£1,785,822
Adept Ecommerce Ltd	£1,784,743
Newcastle Science Central LLP	£1,783,000
C. W. J. Fall & Sons Limited	£1,782,495
Direkt Engineering Holdings Limited	£1,781,852
Argos Inspection Company Limited	£1,781,447
Thomas Potter Limited	£1,780,779
Denemouth Caravan Park Limited	£1,779,104
L & A Reinforcements Ltd.	£1,778,372
Northern Floorcraft (Gateshead) Limited	£1,777,749
Northstar Ventures Limited	£1,777,425
Marshall Inns Limited	£1,776,363
Tax Incentivised Savings Association	£1,776,192
Darlington Rugby Football Club Limited	£1,775,661
Direkt Engineering Services Limited	£1,775,268
EVT Contractors Limited	£1,774,858
W Metcalfe & Sons Limited	£1,774,010
R.Lord & Co.(Newcastle) Limited	£1,773,723

Company	Amount
Lees Cleaning Contractors LLP	£1,773,151
Maval Electrical and Mechanical Engineering Co Ltd	£1,772,696
W. Todd (Builders) Limited	£1,770,906
Van Hessen UK Holding Ltd	£1,770,455
David Gray Solicitors LLP	£1,770,417
Greenlay (Grass Machinery) Limited	£1,768,281
Cyril John Limited	£1,767,945
Darlington Mowden Park Rugby Football Club Limited	£1,766,725
Landteam Northern Limited	£1,766,600
Newcastle Arts Centre Limited	£1,765,453
Harris (U.K.) Limited	£1,764,893
A P Estates Limited	£1,764,536
CML Property Solutions Limited	£1,764,397
Croxdale Farms Limited	£1,764,136
Chemtech Environmental Limited	£1,762,117
Mills Pharmacies Limited	£1,761,405
H.R. Hill Property Co. Limited	£1,761,337
Kenmor Ceilings & Partitions Limited	£1,761,231
Donyal Engineering Limited	£1,761,202
Visitech International Limited	£1,760,372
CLX Ltd	£1,759,475
North East Plant Hire Limited	£1,759,475
TRI Construction Limited	£1,759,323
Integrated Office Systems Limited	£1,758,979
The Artisan Travel Company Limited	£1,758,483
Sudfeld Limited	£1,758,233
J.M.& W.Darling Limited	£1,757,670
Technical Housing Solutions Limited	£1,756,901
Dhammakaya North United Kingdom	£1,756,402
St Bede's Catholic Academy (Lanchester)	£1,755,505
MNP Services Ltd.	£1,754,424
Brambledown Landscape Services Limited	£1,753,827
A.M. Graham Fabrications Limited	£1,753,263
DFP Services Limited	£1,752,586
Colin Marshall Painting Contractors Ltd	£1,752,212
Monkton Infants School	£1,751,720
Clemitsons Limited	£1,751,676
Strathmore Holdings Limited	£1,751,625
Metcalfe Components (Sunderland) Limited	£1,751,113
Cranbourne Estates Limited	£1,750,764
Colena Ltd.	£1,749,751
NFPA Scotland Limited	£1,749,344
AAA Property (North East) Limited	£1,749,315
Millfield Properties Holdings Limited	£1,748,735
Sigma Plantfinder Limited	£1,748,276
Palmer (U.K.) Limited	£1,747,626
Drey Developments Limited	£1,747,115
AVG Holdings (Cleveland) Limited	£1,746,907
John Eliot (Footwear) Limited	£1,745,986
All Saints Developments (NE) Ltd	£1,745,965
Panda Motor Vehicles Ltd	£1,745,860
The Agents Property Auction Limited	£1,745,692
Tyne Gangway (Structures) Limited	£1,743,046
Viscatain Ltd	£1,742,504
Bolam Group Limited	£1,740,937
R. Dinning Limited	£1,740,177
R.D. Kearton & Sons Limited	£1,739,513
Marmax Products Limited	£1,739,375
Harvest Home Limited	£1,738,537
Oubas LLP	£1,738,154
Newcastle Motorcycles Ltd	£1,737,388
A H Engineering (North East) Limited	£1,737,024
Penshaw Estates Limited	£1,735,498
Oakview Properties Limited	£1,735,456
Wescott Industrial Services Ltd	£1,734,529
Stateplus Limited	£1,733,944
Reversionary Assets 2 Limited	£1,733,215
Edgar Lawson Limited	£1,732,974
Historic Property Restoration Limited	£1,732,469
Pearson Caulfield Limited	£1,732,464
Grasmere Academy	£1,732,000
Turbocharger Solutions Limited	£1,731,511
ITL (North East) Limited	£1,730,420
S.T. Swaddle Ltd	£1,729,954
Wyn Limited	£1,728,254
Hopax Europe Limited	£1,728,232
Wallsend Boys Club	£1,728,218
Morfitt Waste Management Ltd	£1,726,653
Precision Labelling Systems Limited	£1,725,124
Fine Industries Limited	£1,725,000
The Endeavour Partnership LLP	£1,722,025
T.P.M. McDonagh (Civil Engineering) Limited	£1,721,875
Freeman Clinics Limited	£1,721,505
BGRP Limited	£1,721,491
Aristou Family Partnership LLP	£1,721,314
North View Academy	£1,720,000
Corespec Ltd	£1,719,056
NSG Limited	£1,718,910
Dunningham Decorators Limited	£1,716,528
Taprich Limited	£1,715,660
Barking Dog (UK) Limited	£1,714,292
Regal Motors (Ashington) Limited	£1,713,929
MKM Investments Limited	£1,711,306
Premier Leisure Limited	£1,711,168
Rock Farms Limited	£1,709,714
Braddan Structures Limited	£1,708,261
Sehgal Commercial Properties Limited	£1,707,846
Metnor (Portland Road) Limited	£1,707,000
Amitex LED Lighting Company Limited	£1,706,229
Snippersgate '88 Limited	£1,705,946
Metec Cathodic Protection Limited	£1,705,147
CACDP	£1,705,110
Eagle Road Services Limited	£1,703,944
Clover Controls Limited	£1,702,803
Commercial Insulation Services Ltd	£1,701,472
Ro-Bal Steel Fabrications Limited	£1,700,752
Argyle House Holdings Limited	£1,700,601
Premier Properties (UK) Limited	£1,699,914
Broomhouse Care Limited	£1,699,489
JHW Estates Limited	£1,699,341
Glassfibre Flagpoles Limited	£1,699,268
Ambic Limited	£1,699,207
HH Community Care Limited	£1,699,197
Jotron UK Ltd	£1,698,479
BNB Fabrications Limited	£1,698,389
Renaissance Land (D20) Limited	£1,697,000
Sturton Grange Developments Limited	£1,696,828
Coupe Group Limited	£1,696,819
Victoria Chemist Ltd	£1,695,941
Hellens Investments (Teal Farm Park) LLP	£1,695,384
Murdock Property Investments Limited	£1,695,114
Cowan Transport Limited	£1,695,104
Lowes Financial Management Limited	£1,695,026
Zig Zag Cars Limited	£1,694,825
Medichem Limited	£1,694,544
S&A Fabrications Limited	£1,693,699
Standard Aviation Limited	£1,692,000
S. & S. Precision Engineering (Washington) Limited	£1,691,875
Aurele-Belle Limited	£1,691,803
Barry Sanderson (Property) Limited	£1,691,629
Newcastle upon Tyne World Headquarters Limited	£1,690,776
R & H Scott Limited	£1,690,475
Socialrel8 Ltd	£1,690,451
Payapps.Com (UK) Ltd	£1,690,394
Avor Garages (North East) Limited	£1,688,977
Mammoet Wind Ltd	£1,686,238
Glen Valley Tours Ltd.	£1,685,949
John Baxter & Company (Newcastle) Limited	£1,685,386
John Arthur and Son Limited	£1,684,794
Asset Manager Solutions Limited	£1,684,452
PFS (Newcastle) Limited	£1,684,096
St Benedict's Hospice, Sunderland	£1,684,081
HLP (Holdings) Limited	£1,683,914
Beckwith Developments Limited	£1,683,729

Company	Value
Durham Vale Developments Limited	£1,683,583
Impress North East (Holdings) Limited	£1,683,494
RPS Switchgear Ltd	£1,682,983
F&I Management Limited	£1,682,617
Collier Properties Limited	£1,682,260
Pinnacle Re-Tec Limited	£1,681,896
R.M. & K. Fashions Limited	£1,681,795
Kingsway Claims Limited	£1,681,529
Stockton Arts Centre	£1,680,926
Michael O'Connor (Carpets) Limited	£1,677,028
Chan Property Group Limited	£1,676,811
Roadsafe Corporate Group Limited	£1,676,600
TRN (Train) Ltd.	£1,676,402
MJR Controls Limited	£1,674,318
Sure Wind Marine Limited	£1,674,181
Beanies The Flavour Co. Ltd.	£1,674,036
Barrington Distribution Ltd	£1,673,820
Temp-Team Limited	£1,671,958
M. & S. Distributors Limited	£1,671,056
Argrennan Manor House Limited	£1,669,659
Cooper & Kime (Cleveland) Limited	£1,669,210
B.T.I.C. Limited	£1,669,108
Tees Valley Community Church	£1,668,643
St. Camillus Care Group Ltd	£1,666,333
Thoroughbred Homes Limited	£1,665,867
CCG Cable Terminations Limited	£1,664,149
NDT Electronic Services Ltd	£1,663,689
D.J.H. (Group) Limited	£1,663,562
Crossco No.3 Unlimited	£1,662,000
Highbury Jewellers Limited	£1,661,406
Alpha Developments (Bradford) Ltd	£1,660,030
M & D Bell Ltd	£1,657,880
Encore Packaging Solutions Limited	£1,657,847
Lycetts Financial Services Limited	£1,655,183
Arix Europe Limited	£1,654,479
TVG Telematics Ltd	£1,653,940
A2M Developments Limited	£1,653,938
Arc Environmental Limited	£1,653,516
Missionbuild Limited	£1,653,056
Dixon Landscapes Limited	£1,651,292
Hadrian Air Conditioning and Refrigeration Co Ltd	£1,650,994
Looprevil (North East) Limited	£1,650,305
Dance North	£1,649,274
Samuel Grant (North East) Limited	£1,648,843
Vapourlites Limited	£1,648,020
Alnwick Garden Enterprises Limited	£1,646,889
Newhall Caravan Park Limited	£1,644,491
Chavtown Properties Ltd	£1,643,937
Collingdon Developments Ltd	£1,643,656
Amakhala Limited	£1,642,328
North East Eye Care Limited	£1,641,750
Oar Properties Limited	£1,640,736
Phoenix Theatre (Blyth)	£1,639,837
PPG (NE) Limited	£1,639,744
Jesmond Community Leisure	£1,639,575
Think Synergy Limited	£1,639,000
Golden Dragon Properties Limited	£1,636,605
UK Docks Marine Services North Limited	£1,636,475
Jamas Building Services Limited	£1,636,148
Agma Holdings Limited	£1,633,068
Hawthorn Parks Limited	£1,632,904
A.C.T Construction Services Limited	£1,632,271
Allsafety Limited	£1,631,297
North Lakes Foods Limited	£1,630,613
Joel A Moseley Transport Limited	£1,630,178
Premier Meats Limited	£1,630,165
Asari Limited	£1,629,471
Robinsons Durham Limited	£1,629,044
Wise Financial Property Limited	£1,628,478
R.H. Orange & Son Limited	£1,628,375
NETA Training Trust	£1,627,973
Whickham Salerooms Limited	£1,627,456
Robinson Dane Limited	£1,627,046
Forte Freehold Management Limited	£1,625,910
John B.Smith Limited	£1,623,623
University of Northumbria at Newcastle Developments Ltd	£1,623,038
Howard House Care Limited	£1,622,560
Melford Contracts Limited	£1,622,077
Williamson Construction Equipment Limited	£1,621,615
Danieli Property Investments Limited	£1,621,596
Community Based Care Health Limited	£1,619,853
Fluid Technology Generation Limited	£1,619,817
Caru Investments Limited	£1,619,575
Court Holdings Limited	£1,618,184
North Tyneside Learning Trust	£1,617,889
P. Dawson Developments Limited	£1,617,680
Buildroute Limited	£1,617,248
Swinburne Horticultural Services Limited	£1,615,219
East Durham Community Development Trust Limited	£1,615,099
Chemplas Roofing Services Ltd	£1,614,917
Ace Aluminium & Architectural Services Ltd	£1,613,715
Silver Street (Durham) Properties Limited	£1,611,647
PGM Investments Ltd	£1,609,889
Safinah Limited	£1,609,622
Aluminium (Bar & Sheet) Limited	£1,609,616
Utilergy Gas Limited	£1,608,138
Peterleefour Limited	£1,607,688
Wraggs Seafoods Limited	£1,607,530
Oakwell Gate Property Company Limited (The)	£1,607,317
Mrs J & J G Gill & Son Limited	£1,606,466
E. Turnbull & Son Limited	£1,606,134
Unity Tech Group Ltd	£1,605,924
Northern Property Partnership LLP	£1,605,701
Cookswell Garage Limited	£1,604,518
Woodtech (Joinery) Limited	£1,603,297
Queribus Ltd	£1,603,085
Furniture Clinic Limited	£1,603,040
Plimsoll Publishing Limited	£1,602,160
Marske Site Services Ltd.	£1,600,817
Safe-Line Marine After Sales Ltd	£1,600,772
Woodhorn Charitable Trust	£1,598,241
Bantel Investments Limited	£1,598,040
Geneius Laboratories Limited	£1,595,900
Waltons Clark Whitehill Limited	£1,594,900
Deepstar Subsea Limited	£1,594,843
Lydon Pharmacy Group Ltd.	£1,594,502
Baileys Blinds Limited	£1,594,138
Strathmore Bondgate Limited	£1,594,090
Charles Porter Holdings Limited	£1,591,671
Fontmerry Ltd	£1,589,632
T C Developments North East Ltd	£1,589,203
Alan Wadkins Limited	£1,587,585
Aquatran House Ltd	£1,586,974
Durham Footwear Distributors Limited	£1,585,678
P. James Construction Limited	£1,585,545
Wing Hong & Company Limited	£1,584,012
Jiahua Europe Limited	£1,582,872
K.E.P. Services (UK) Ltd.	£1,582,109
G.C.S. Johnson Limited	£1,582,054
Copenhagen 1801 Limited	£1,581,979
JSK Property Development (UK) Ltd	£1,581,317
Pro - Fix Installations (North East) Limited	£1,579,899
Ropers Leisure Limited	£1,579,523
Britton & Robson Limited	£1,577,994
Advantex Network Solutions Limited	£1,575,818
J. Freeman & Sons Limited	£1,573,555
Top Line Promotions Limited	£1,573,125
Geffen Construction Limited	£1,573,095
Homeware Essentials Limited	£1,571,560
Dulai Enterprises Limited	£1,571,361
St. Astier Limited	£1,569,942
Meadowcroft Homes Limited	£1,569,643
Matthew Charlton,Limited	£1,567,390
Hartlepool Marina Limited	£1,566,535

Company	Value
Taopix Group Limited	£1,566,497
Swaledale Homes Limited	£1,566,199
Singer Machines Limited	£1,565,939
GJPS Trust Fund	£1,565,688
Pleasure Leisure Limited	£1,565,504
W.I.P. (Workwear) Limited	£1,565,264
Kickpoint Limited	£1,563,550
Inbond Limited	£1,563,331
John Cullerton & Sons Limited	£1,563,053
Proflex Packaging Co Ltd	£1,562,220
Nice Network Ltd	£1,561,760
Castle Construction (North East) Limited	£1,561,694
Thompson Power Tool Services UK Ltd	£1,561,350
Acklam Park Limited Liability Partnership	£1,560,374
Dartford Student Living Limited	£1,558,604
E.B. & C.A. Welsh Limited	£1,558,510
Cares Group Holdings Limited	£1,558,413
Clay's Garden Centre Ltd.	£1,558,208
DH Dowen Limited	£1,557,855
Leader Online Limited	£1,557,111
Regeneration (North East) LLP	£1,556,698
Etro Investments Limited	£1,555,934
Heber Street Limited	£1,555,486
Opus Building Services Limited	£1,555,370
NK Property Ltd	£1,553,686
7 Star (North East) Ltd	£1,553,583
Little Acorns London Beach Farm Limited	£1,553,426
H.C.Chambers & Son Limited	£1,553,000
H E Woolley Limited	£1,552,225
All Car Parts Limited	£1,552,215
Nunthorpe Nurseries Group Ltd	£1,550,575
Bescol Motors Limited	£1,549,655
Blake Newport Associates Limited	£1,548,667
Cafe Twentyone Newcastle Limited	£1,548,562
Euro Contract Leasing Limited	£1,547,347
Washington Direct Mail Limited	£1,547,208
Visual Concept Ltd	£1,545,710
Durham Markets Company Limited	£1,545,479
Terry Deary Limited	£1,545,330
Thompson Ventures Limited	£1,545,034
CPMC Limited	£1,544,911
St. Joseph's Catholic Education Trust	£1,544,486
Landon Engineering (Castle Works) Limited	£1,544,211
C.W. Russell Ltd	£1,543,050
Hyperdrug Pharmaceuticals Ltd	£1,542,481
Advance Automated Systems Limited	£1,541,921
TVG Systems Limited	£1,539,638
Burnell Properties Limited	£1,539,276
PDL Solutions (Europe) Limited	£1,538,811
The Energy Checking Company Limited	£1,538,715
Washington Components Limited	£1,538,284
Inshore Fisheries Limited	£1,538,014
The Vocational Learning Trust	£1,537,759
Dromonby Bridge Farm Limited	£1,537,712
Coquet Island Shellfish Limited	£1,536,540
TDG Brand Communications Limited	£1,535,778
Pinpin Ltd	£1,535,526
Full Circle Investments Limited	£1,535,051
MW Crane Hire Ltd	£1,534,946
Jesres (Property Lets) Co. Limited	£1,534,568
Scott Bros. Enterprises Limited	£1,533,658
Tavistock House Day Nursery Limited	£1,533,525
Arch Building Supplies Limited	£1,533,477
Plant Services (Gateshead) Limited	£1,532,171
Plastic Mouldings Northern Limited	£1,532,096
PC Investments Limited	£1,531,921
Main-Tel (NE) Limited	£1,531,152
Hedgehog Lab Limited	£1,530,549
Lite-On Electronics (Europe) Limited	£1,529,507
Redgate Lodge Limited	£1,527,297
Cathie Associates Limited	£1,526,817
Alchemy Design & Works Limited	£1,526,540

Company	Value
Heating World of Spares Limited	£1,525,880
Northern Estates and Investment Company Limited	£1,525,335
Northumbrian Trust Day Nurseries Limited	£1,523,921
Tofco CPP Limited	£1,523,615
Jack Brodie (Wholesale) Limited	£1,522,830
Sovereign Care (North East) Ltd	£1,521,351
Chris Stonock Limited	£1,521,108
Teesside Estates Limited	£1,517,636
Town Centre Automobiles Ltd.	£1,517,472
Tim Stonock Limited	£1,516,780
Constantine Building Services Limited	£1,516,708
E.E.M.I.T.S. Communications Limited	£1,516,644
Y&I Properties Limited	£1,515,606
Noda Taxis Limited	£1,515,472
Brewing and Distilling Company Limited	£1,514,978
Quality Food Service Limited	£1,514,828
Middlesbrough Environment City Trust Limited	£1,514,130
ITC Plumbing and Heating Services Limited	£1,513,374
Fillworth (UK) Limited	£1,513,195
High Level Contracts Limited	£1,512,674
Oldham & Openshaw DP Limited	£1,512,623
Alnwick Farmers Livestock Auction Company Limited	£1,510,097
Re:Production Limited	£1,509,696
Wensleydale Railway PLC	£1,508,542
Psyche Holdings Limited	£1,508,520
Dinning Farms Limited	£1,508,483
HDC Travel Limited	£1,507,378
Cell Pack Solutions Limited	£1,506,276
Durham Wildlife Trust	£1,503,835
Ben Hoare Bell LLP	£1,502,287
Ago Group Ltd	£1,501,506
George F. White LLP	£1,501,399
Etro Group Ltd	£1,500,240
Carbon8 Ltd	£1,499,867
Northumbria Youth Action Limited	£1,498,887
Silk Family Law Limited	£1,498,477
Tyne Electro Diesel Limited	£1,495,845
OGI Groundwater Specialists Limited	£1,495,273
Springfield Properties (Ncle) Limited	£1,495,172
Industrial Monitoring Systems Limited	£1,495,117
AIS Securus Ltd	£1,494,640
Inn Collection Acquisitionco Limited	£1,493,494
Saks (Education) Limited	£1,492,844
Leighton Corporation Limited	£1,491,816
Durham Action on Single Housing Limited	£1,491,773
Go Geothermal Ltd	£1,491,205
J. M. D. Developments Limited	£1,489,952
Fewsters Services Limited	£1,489,529
Centrex Computing Services Limited	£1,489,280
Ronan Engineering Limited	£1,487,958
Security Systems and Alarms Inspection Board	£1,487,450
Posi-Thread (U.K.) Ltd.	£1,486,358
Lord Technical Limited	£1,484,871
Longstaffs Travel Ltd	£1,484,809
Co-Wheels Car Club Community Interest Company	£1,484,283
Allied Exploration & Geotechnics Limited	£1,484,220
H Clarke & Sons Limited	£1,483,596
Dunhouse Quarry Co.Limited	£1,482,791
Lingscars.Com Limited	£1,480,641
Savona Imports Limited	£1,480,489
Big Hearted Hospitality Company Limited	£1,480,259
Honeyman Group Limited	£1,478,869
Lanof (UK) Ltd	£1,476,978
Calmband Limited	£1,476,194
Medburn Estates Limited	£1,474,877
NOI4 Limited	£1,472,734
Headway Point Limited	£1,471,917
Cablecom Training Limited	£1,470,240
Hewitson Haulage Ltd	£1,468,781
S.I.E. Industrial Limited	£1,468,511
Uber Limited	£1,468,234
Hays Finance Limited	£1,467,615

Company	Value	Company	Value
Ribchesters Group Limited	£1,467,319	Mc Dougall Dodds Limited	£1,422,645
Gunnergate Limited	£1,465,351	Countylife Corbridge Limited	£1,421,650
Kirkhill Fleming Limited	£1,465,214	Phoenix Civil Engineering Limited	£1,421,125
Zigi Enterprises Limited	£1,464,247	Northern Archaeological Associates Limited	£1,420,904
Pauls Property Investment Limited	£1,464,198	Inlec UK Limited	£1,420,061
Clifton Property Investments Limited	£1,464,073	H.S. Carlsteel Engineering Limited	£1,419,844
Roth Properties LLP	£1,462,877	Easington Greyhound Stadium Limited	£1,418,825
Jacksons Commercial & Private Law LLP	£1,462,173	Advanced Cutting Tools Limited	£1,418,384
A1 Alpha Properties (Leicester) Limited	£1,460,923	Beacon View Pharmacy Limited	£1,417,854
Castleson Ltd	£1,460,876	Middleton Coal Depot Limited	£1,417,622
Routes Healthcare (North East) Limited	£1,460,804	JTM Plumbing Limited	£1,416,985
Kearton Crushing and Screening Limited	£1,459,974	Service Engineering Marine Limited	£1,416,877
Newcastle-upon-Tyne & District Property & Investment	£1,459,360	Clever Clogs Day Nurseries Limited	£1,415,979
Isoler Ltd.	£1,459,144	Q9 Cladding Solutions Ltd	£1,415,970
Unwind Me Limited	£1,458,470	The Middlesbrough Empire Limited	£1,415,737
Chamberlin Agencies Limited	£1,458,229	J Kelly Plant Hire Limited	£1,415,360
Felixarc Marine Limited	£1,458,000	Dougal & Railton Limited	£1,415,332
Choice Property NE Limited	£1,457,304	Rail Management Services Limited	£1,415,294
Monkton Junior School	£1,456,971	Cygnet Family Law Limited	£1,414,506
Architectural Powder Coatings Limited	£1,456,701	Amor Healthcare Limited	£1,413,422
Crispin (Pharmacy) Limited	£1,456,114	Vector Power Solutions Limited	£1,413,391
R & A Kay Inspection Services Limited	£1,454,063	GTD Developments Limited	£1,412,924
Wear Valley Renewables C.I.C.	£1,453,928	Eastbourne House Ltd	£1,412,713
Cartridge Tech Limited	£1,453,167	Datasupplies (Stationery) Limited	£1,412,297
Country Harvest Frozen Foods Limited	£1,452,608	ITC Service Limited	£1,410,023
MS Investments (IB) Limited	£1,451,156	H.T.B. Electrical Contractors Limited	£1,409,733
Miresdale Dairy Limited	£1,449,590	Quayside Pharmacy Limited	£1,409,379
Rainton Meadows Arena Limited	£1,448,391	Nielsen,Andersen & Company Limited	£1,409,222
Gillen's Limited	£1,448,367	Jaspia Limited	£1,409,136
Aeolian Energy Limited	£1,447,797	Formica Finance Limited	£1,409,000
Teesside Insurance Consultants Limited	£1,447,194	Ludgate 373 Limited	£1,408,334
Manchester Surgical Services Limited	£1,447,071	PHCC Developments (West Kensington) Limited	£1,407,034
Mitrepoint Limited	£1,446,626	Pneumatic Power Source Limited	£1,406,808
Eyeworks Industries Limited	£1,446,481	T.P. Enterprises Limited	£1,406,561
Nelson Developments (Durham) Limited	£1,446,459	The Durham Company Limited	£1,405,726
Windcrew Workboats Limited	£1,445,308	House and Properties Ltd.	£1,404,577
Gliderol Garage & Industrial Doors Limited	£1,445,204	Darras Consulting Limited	£1,402,657
Pee Gee Limited	£1,443,286	Centre for Sports Injury Surgery Limited	£1,402,479
GFC Group Limited	£1,443,169	The Gilchrist Company (UK) Limited	£1,402,102
Thor Car Parts and Accessories Limited	£1,442,246	Forman Vehicle Services Limited	£1,401,191
Cleveland Systems Engineering Limited	£1,441,906	Corbitts Limited	£1,400,711
Stevenson Properties Limited	£1,441,798	Screen Services (NE) Limited	£1,400,666
European Horseboxes Limited	£1,440,921	LV Valenbeck Limited	£1,399,388
Thompson Contracts Limited	£1,439,177	Izumi Products UK Limited	£1,398,884
Admec Municipal Services Limited	£1,438,650	T.B. Tarn Limited	£1,397,679
Addison & Co (Teesdale) Limited	£1,437,476	KD Plant Services Limited	£1,397,152
Crossco (281) Limited	£1,437,000	Blyth Star Enterprises Limited	£1,397,146
Ward Property Investments Limited	£1,435,871	The Traidcraft Exchange	£1,397,000
Angela Ward Properties LLP	£1,434,922	S.D.S.K Limited	£1,396,870
W.J.(Bill) Tillston Limited	£1,434,443	Portrack Handling Limited	£1,396,686
J A Dent & Sons Limited	£1,433,880	Chancery Investments (NE) Ltd	£1,396,530
Alfol Limited	£1,433,311	Brickwork Direct Limited	£1,395,415
Penton House Limited	£1,431,367	L.& N.Property Investment Co.Limited (The)	£1,395,225
Newchem Technologies Limited	£1,431,148	Tonks 2000 Limited	£1,394,827
Phillips Chemists Limited	£1,429,141	T-Mac Technologies Limited	£1,394,701
Harkers Transport Limited	£1,429,010	Enfield Properties Limited	£1,394,326
Hawks Road Community Nursery Limited	£1,428,051	Middleheads Limited	£1,394,185
Stairrods (UK) Limited	£1,427,999	Student Accommodation (UK) Limited	£1,394,011
Peikko UK Limited	£1,427,339	ADP Precision Engineering Limited	£1,393,971
Southlands Motor Company Ltd	£1,427,102	Consultus Developments Limited	£1,393,965
Cynergy UK Limited	£1,425,977	Great Park Food Company Ltd.	£1,393,520
B. Weightman Ltd.	£1,425,804	Findley Roofing & Building Limited	£1,393,270
Equine Products U.K. Limited	£1,425,655	Independent Air Treatment Technology Limited	£1,393,268
Castlegate Property Company Limited	£1,425,534	Align Property Partners Limited	£1,392,458
Richard Pickles Limited	£1,425,053	4 Cool Technology Limited	£1,392,347
Commercial Vehicle Exports (Northern) Limited	£1,425,039	Datim Building Contractors Limited	£1,392,347
Gordon Brown Law Firm LLP	£1,424,986	Teesside Properties (2) Limited	£1,391,158
Hamsard 2517 (New Business) Limited	£1,424,282	L & G Plant Hire and Sales Limited	£1,390,897
Newcastle NE1 Limited	£1,423,691	Body Engineering Limited	£1,388,741
Williamson Network Limited	£1,423,648	FM Trading (GB) Limited	£1,388,352
McGovern Holdings Limited	£1,423,018	Additional Lengths Ltd	£1,387,229
Lands (North East) Limited	£1,422,894	T.O. Mounter & Sons Limited	£1,385,728

Company	Value
Identity Consult Limited	£1,385,660
Jack Ford Limited	£1,384,937
Jordan Leasing (2005) LLP	£1,384,395
Wilkinson Landscapes Limited	£1,384,271
Apex Radio Systems Limited	£1,383,584
Hindley Circuits Limited	£1,383,132
Wynyard Motor Company Limited	£1,382,078
J & S Taylor (Site Services) Ltd	£1,381,592
Lacegold Electrical and Mechanical Services Limited	£1,381,018
JHT Fabrications Ltd	£1,379,164
Middlesbrough & District Motor Club Limited	£1,378,731
Mignolet Ltd	£1,378,065
Prudhoe Community Partnership	£1,377,310
Brunton Nursery Limited	£1,374,702
John Low Limited	£1,374,653
Washington Waterjet Limited	£1,374,045
Nevesco Limited	£1,373,867
Safe & Sure Fire Protection Limited	£1,373,801
Osborne Orthodontics Ltd	£1,373,775
Mazhar Ltd	£1,373,500
CKW Trading Limited	£1,373,444
Darren McCormick Jewellery Limited	£1,372,993
Northumbria Optical Coatings Limited	£1,372,587
Celtic Aerospace Ventures Limited	£1,372,221
Mash Staffing Payroll Limited	£1,372,006
Lytestream Electrical Engineers & Contractors Limited	£1,371,646
Carrick Contractors Limited	£1,371,573
Last Night Limited	£1,371,135
Blue House Retail Limited	£1,371,118
St John's Church of England Academy	£1,371,000
Blue Rain Limited	£1,370,119
Bede and Cuthbert Developments Limited	£1,369,825
Activ Technology Limited	£1,369,791
B.C. & T. Consultants Limited	£1,369,037
Herrington Industrial Services Limited	£1,368,788
St. Anthony's Girls' Catholic Academy	£1,367,126
Les Rayner Foxhunters Motor Company Ltd.	£1,366,990
Network Ticketing Limited	£1,366,205
P J M Properties Limited	£1,366,187
The Assembly Rooms (Newcastle) Limited	£1,366,105
Mercer Street Security Systems Limited	£1,365,007
Ashington Mews Limited	£1,364,703
James H Ward Properties Limited	£1,364,569
Cramlington Garages Limited	£1,364,434
Scanman UK Limited	£1,364,395
In-House Inspired Room Design Ltd	£1,363,839
C.A.T. Builders Limited	£1,363,084
King Hope Ltd	£1,361,725
Grand Hotel Ltd	£1,361,111
Hutchinsons Fruit & Veg Limited	£1,360,890
Sameach	£1,358,902
Roflow Limited	£1,358,738
Lawson & Cowell Ltd	£1,358,149
Rokshaw Limited	£1,355,438
Barclay Roofing (Holdings) Limited	£1,354,980
Blenheim Homes North East Ltd	£1,354,420
Clarks Coachbuilders Limited	£1,354,343
Soretrac (U.K.) Limited	£1,353,401
Sheers Limited	£1,353,050
Jerry Fried & Co Limited	£1,353,030
Redrose Manufacturing Limited	£1,352,948
MLM (UK) Limited	£1,351,045
Maysan Foods Limited	£1,350,579
Todd and Cue (RMS) Limited	£1,350,000
MD5 Forensics Ltd	£1,350,000
The Waterside Palace Restaurant Co Ltd	£1,349,794
Citizens Advice County Durham	£1,348,291
Darlington Cricket and Athletic Club C.I.C.	£1,347,982
Westside Properties & Developments Limited	£1,347,678
Ravensworth Golf Club,Limited (The)	£1,347,309
Ewart Parsons,Limited	£1,347,096
Elder Properties Ltd	£1,346,226
Stanfam Properties Limited	£1,345,837
Scarlet Band Bus and Coach Limited	£1,345,624
Ouseburn Trust	£1,344,627
Gowland and Dawson Limited	£1,344,397
DHN Property Services Ltd	£1,344,300
GGE Holdings Limited	£1,344,095
J. R. Freeman & Co. (Estates) Limited	£1,343,434
Durham Cathedral Trading Limited	£1,341,929
Otolift Stairlifts Limited	£1,341,522
S.R. Transport Services Limited	£1,341,411
Zubedo Limited	£1,341,293
Datastor (North East) Limited	£1,340,970
Euro GPS Limited	£1,339,592
Allied Domain Limited	£1,338,665
Unasys Limited	£1,337,698
G Mayes Ltd	£1,337,079
Society for Education Limited	£1,336,148
Askews Solicitors Limited	£1,335,813
Phusion IM Limited	£1,335,784
Ravenside Ltd	£1,335,266
The Wine Fusion Limited	£1,335,002
3KB Recruitment Group Ltd	£1,334,920
Starkold Building Services Limited	£1,333,748
Thermalmate UK Limited	£1,333,643
Dinnington Cottages Limited	£1,333,427
PMK Limited	£1,332,504
New Beginnings (North East) Limited	£1,332,312
Pinkney Building Contractors Limited	£1,332,279
Contemporary Franchising Ltd	£1,332,140
Westline Distributors Limited	£1,330,671
Osborne Motor Transport Limited	£1,330,593
Optimus Global Limited	£1,329,846
Claire Errington Limited	£1,329,719
Bremsen Technik Reman Limited	£1,329,082
Warrior Assault Systems Limited	£1,328,839
DC Assets Limited	£1,328,218
TTE Apprenticeships Limited	£1,328,172
Increase Computers Limited	£1,327,878
Matrix Power Limited	£1,327,697
J S Locum Services Limited	£1,326,699
Emperor Investment Property Limited	£1,326,290
Vizsec Holdings Limited	£1,326,187
JW Installations UK Limited	£1,325,477
J A & M Boyes Limited	£1,324,972
Advanced Handling & Storage Limited	£1,324,686
DC Gaming Limited	£1,324,000
Safety Systems Distribution Limited	£1,323,941
Tyne Valves Limited	£1,323,578
Nelson Yard Limited	£1,321,767
Cad 21 Holdings Limited	£1,321,132
Ner Brek,Limited	£1,320,805
MRM Electrical Solutions Limited	£1,319,975
Dunstanburgh Farm Limited	£1,319,515
Razorblue Ltd	£1,319,151
HSA DIY Limited	£1,318,645
M.H.T. Technology Limited	£1,318,538
Walton Robinson Ltd	£1,317,728
Iris Engineering & Technology Limited	£1,317,468
Duil Limited	£1,316,594
J.E.M Road Construction Ltd	£1,316,379
First2print Ltd	£1,315,868
Ex-Pro Products Limited	£1,315,712
RHJ Maintenance Ltd	£1,314,676
Sterling Trust Professional (North East) Limited	£1,314,440
North East Homes Limited	£1,314,139
Coastline Fish and Chip Restaurant Limited	£1,312,227
Redhead Roofing LLP	£1,310,860
Harry Wilson Associates Limited	£1,308,473
JDE Management Limited	£1,307,738
Nala Engineers Limited	£1,306,121
MSM Media Solutions Ltd	£1,305,988
Lyndon Systems Ltd	£1,305,745

J. Dinning (Investments) Limited	£1,305,510	Different Advertising Design and Marketing Limited	£1,268,440
Faraday Printed Circuits (Holdings) Limited	£1,305,377	Molly York Limited	£1,268,363
EWM Hightec Welding UK Limited	£1,305,344	DSONS Limited	£1,268,250
Eaglescliffe and District Golf Company Limited	£1,304,547	Mercer Street Marketing and Consulting Limited	£1,267,862
Owens Business Developments Limited	£1,304,534	Blaydon UK Limited	£1,267,539
R. Mason Chemicals Limited	£1,304,425	Mike Rogerson Estate Agents Limited	£1,266,758
Enigma Interactive Limited	£1,304,424	Elim Properties Ltd	£1,266,718
NY Construction Ltd	£1,304,088	Tendercrave Limited	£1,266,530
Northumberland Luxury Log Cabins Limited	£1,304,055	Kevin Snowdon Groundworks Limited	£1,266,217
R. Parker (Wall & Floor Tiling Contractors) Limited	£1,303,452	Pipe Equipment Specialists Limited	£1,266,146
KCA Cars Limited	£1,303,368	Sirrah Properties Limited	£1,266,103
Solar Solve Limited	£1,303,181	Bans Healthcare Ltd	£1,265,027
Hawik Limited	£1,302,917	R J Construction & Development Limited	£1,263,255
Teesside Precision Engineering Ltd	£1,302,007	Dial-a-Loo Limited	£1,263,246
Avendus Capital (UK) Private Limited	£1,301,945	Fission Recruitment Services Limited	£1,262,861
Homecare Heating Supplies Teesside Limited	£1,301,591	Fox House Ltd	£1,261,690
Cordrow Limited	£1,300,085	Ken Thomas Site Clearance Limited	£1,261,194
AA Construction (Holdings) Limited	£1,300,001	Ken Warne Limited	£1,259,319
NT Enterprises Limited	£1,300,000	Catalyst Stockton-on-Tees Limited	£1,259,161
Lucite International Trading Limited	£1,300,000	Rapid Response Transport (UK) Limited	£1,258,910
SM Comedy Limited	£1,299,592	ULookUBook Travel Limited	£1,258,684
Nonlinear Technologies Limited	£1,298,419	Norman Cornish Limited	£1,258,491
North East Executive Limited	£1,297,476	21 Degrees Limited	£1,258,139
Epro (Wholesale) Limited	£1,297,068	Lily Kunj Properties LLP	£1,257,751
Strathmore Renewables Ltd	£1,296,693	Marlin Assets Limited	£1,256,391
Coles Solicitors Limited	£1,296,632	Synergy Compliance Limited	£1,256,170
Yorkshire Construction Contractors Limited	£1,296,584	W.O.W! (Welcome To Our World) Limited	£1,255,136
One Real Estate Development Limited	£1,296,164	Beyond360 Limited	£1,255,125
NAC Agency Limited	£1,293,957	Digitax Electronics UK Limited	£1,254,572
Clarke Mairs LLP	£1,293,248	HAB Northern Ltd	£1,254,486
Adams Jenkins Properties Limited	£1,293,038	Thornley Properties Limited	£1,254,382
Cosmopolitan Properties North Ltd	£1,292,686	Bridging Funding Limited	£1,254,177
European Vehicle Contracts Limited	£1,291,802	Arrow Commercial Limited	£1,253,981
Thompson Bros (South Shields) Limited	£1,291,039	Acrol Air Conditioning Co. Limited	£1,253,318
Jetsun Ltd	£1,291,025	Owben Ltd	£1,253,002
Theakston Estate Company Limited	£1,290,502	Industrial Technology Systems Limited	£1,252,627
Drinx Leisure Limited	£1,288,903	Cad 21 Limited	£1,252,611
Star Meats Limited	£1,288,540	Heating Trade Supplies Group Limited	£1,252,531
Dulai Property Limited	£1,287,496	Stargate Developments (2015) Limited	£1,249,806
B & T Kitson Limited	£1,287,077	Taradina Number Two Limited	£1,249,626
Webworks Internet (UK) Limited	£1,286,744	Rockbit UK Limited	£1,249,516
Mapleleaf (Northern) Limited	£1,285,676	Ashford Orthodontics Limited	£1,249,120
Ronco Engineering Limited	£1,285,043	Red Ridge Developments Limited	£1,248,857
Ops Catering Limited	£1,284,997	O Kay Automatics Limited	£1,248,591
Hospitality Guaranteed Limited	£1,284,602	Evolution Valves Limited	£1,248,048
Decke (Newcastle) Limited	£1,283,123	Leisure Centre Holdings	£1,248,000
Lincoln Property Investments Ltd	£1,281,264	Meat Zone UK Limited	£1,247,914
Reality Enterprise Ltd	£1,281,137	Mincoffs Solicitors LLP	£1,247,815
Bradshaw Homes Ltd	£1,281,077	B2B Staff Solutions Ltd	£1,246,951
Meadowfield Motors Limited	£1,280,201	Ability Supplies UK Limited	£1,246,933
Broseley Fires Limited	£1,279,927	ATF Supplies Limited	£1,246,743
Ashbrooke Sports Club Limited	£1,279,344	MSD Construction (UK) Ltd	£1,246,712
Woodham Christian Centre Ltd.	£1,278,857	NDT Global Services Limited	£1,246,003
Johnson Wright (Flooring) Limited	£1,278,254	Teesside Properties Limited	£1,245,885
Italica UK Limited	£1,277,266	J.J.Hardy & Sons Limited	£1,245,811
Nudo Sushi Box Ltd	£1,276,843	EMG Solicitors Limited	£1,245,262
Ask Property Services Limited	£1,276,793	Crown Alderney Limited	£1,245,155
Fast Track Sourcing Limited	£1,276,551	Plenary Project Solutions Limited	£1,245,039
Legacy No.1 Limited	£1,275,462	Gibbons (UK) Property Limited	£1,244,749
N.OOR Jewellery Limited	£1,275,443	Flanges Limited	£1,244,542
Shelford Sales LLP	£1,275,443	Nova Stellar Property Management Limited	£1,243,560
Forest Carbon Limited	£1,274,840	RSD Marine Ltd	£1,243,422
G.I. Fox Limited	£1,274,524	McNicholas Estates Ltd.	£1,242,922
Rothbury Estates UK Limited	£1,273,708	C. C. Jensen Limited	£1,242,138
Macey Property Consultancy Limited	£1,272,929	Park Lane Garages (Teeside) Limited	£1,241,595
Northumbria Property Co. Limited	£1,272,913	Hare Bulk Haulage Limited	£1,241,485
Theakston-Laing Limited	£1,271,556	Voicentric Limited	£1,241,192
S&A Fabrications (Holdings) Limited	£1,271,002	Durhamlane Limited	£1,240,861
Awan Properties Limited	£1,270,947	Newland Jem Limited	£1,240,652
Oskap (Commercial) Limited	£1,270,517	Spectrum Industrial Limited	£1,240,598
JR Dynamics Limited	£1,269,515	DVS Autos Limited	£1,240,467
Team Stokes Limited	£1,269,003	Rust Resources Limited	£1,240,446

Queensway Dental Laboratory Limited	£1,239,839
Thomson West Limited	£1,239,645
L. D. Mountain Centre Limited	£1,239,357
Titan Property (Newcastle) Limited	£1,237,808
Wox Agri Services Ltd	£1,237,618
Stablewood Developments Limited	£1,237,603
Adamms Wholesale Carpets Limited	£1,236,914
OFL4 LLP	£1,236,394
Cosmar Properties Ltd	£1,235,898
Durham Estates Limited	£1,235,131
Icicle Vehicle Solutions Limited	£1,234,807
Literary & Philosophical Society of Newcastle upon Tyne	£1,234,763
Storey & Edmondson (Builders) Limited	£1,234,540
Teesside Industrial Solutions Ltd	£1,234,362
Pantheon Macroeconomics Ltd.	£1,233,704
H T Process Control Ltd	£1,233,695
G.B.U. Hire Ltd	£1,233,619
Ford Parts (UK) Limited	£1,232,678
Willow Group Ltd	£1,231,979
PHCC Developments (Commonfield) Limited	£1,231,930
Station Taxis (Sunderland) Limited	£1,231,338
Cowie Properties LLP	£1,231,243
Dealmaster Ltd	£1,231,015
S A Day Care Ltd	£1,230,746
Durham City Coaches Limited	£1,230,563
P & I Design Limited	£1,229,613
Coopers Chemist Redcar Limited	£1,227,232
Truck Technics Limited	£1,226,208
Assembly & Packaging Services Ltd	£1,225,906
Players Bars Investments Limited	£1,225,796
G & G Leisure Limited	£1,225,291
Zerust (UK) Limited	£1,224,988
Window Fitters Warehouse Limited	£1,224,777
Russell Network Solutions Limited	£1,224,527
Prizepay Limited	£1,224,372
Fawcett & Hetherington Funeral Service Limited	£1,223,966
Bradley Hall Farm (South Wylam) Limited	£1,223,840
The Hamilton Portfolio (Care Homes) Limited	£1,223,742
Twice Brewed LLP	£1,223,721
Acornford (Kensington) Limited	£1,222,169
Sanderson Young Ltd	£1,222,113
Peter Weldon & Co Limited	£1,221,727
Flagg Court Pharmacy Limited	£1,221,477
S F Wind Ltd	£1,221,195
A19 Properties Limited	£1,221,015
Management Development Centre International Ltd	£1,221,002
Bluegauge LLP	£1,220,000
The Thoroughbred Agency Ltd	£1,218,878
Allay Redress Ltd.	£1,218,691
Timberway Limited	£1,217,485
Harton Properties Limited	£1,216,874
Carter Steel Limited	£1,216,412
Clearly Drinks Properties Limited	£1,216,402
Warner of Wingate Limited	£1,216,369
Exis Technologies Limited	£1,215,880
Graform Limited	£1,215,304
Westray Recruitment Consultants Limited	£1,213,742
Oakenclough Buildings Limited	£1,213,611
Sirius Civil Engineering Limited	£1,213,008
E W Properties Ltd	£1,212,503
Libra Seafood Processing Limited	£1,211,080
Coffee Design Limited	£1,209,697
Devereux Architecture Limited	£1,209,602
Women's Health in South Tyneside	£1,209,507
Camden Estates (North Shields) Limited	£1,209,280
Wearside Plumbing Supplies Limited	£1,208,771
SDY Limited	£1,208,481
Zenith Jewellery and Accessories UK Limited	£1,208,330
Nusafe Europe Limited	£1,207,885
F.A. Atkinson Limited	£1,207,652
W. McGovern & Co. Limited	£1,207,556
J. D. S. (City Developments) Limited	£1,207,525
Inspired Agency Ltd	£1,207,057
R & D Patterson Limited	£1,206,790
Hawksby Bainbridge Limited	£1,205,665
Aberwood Developments Limited	£1,205,418
Gibson Engineering Limited	£1,204,740
Mortley Estates Limited	£1,203,308
Alnwick District Playhouse Trust	£1,202,786
Dongard Contract Services Limited	£1,201,608
Court Homemakers Limited	£1,201,471
Holme Dodsworth (Est.1879) Limited	£1,200,652
First Class Supply & Training Limited	£1,200,364
Metalis Energy Limited	£1,199,467
Stuart Halbert Foundation	£1,199,409
Tyneside Express Transport Limited	£1,197,405
Bolel Ltd	£1,196,619
Clevechem Limited	£1,196,137
Campbell Properties Limited	£1,195,948
Commercial Edge Consulting Limited	£1,195,605
Bentley Medical Practice Limited	£1,194,710
Returnable Packaging Services Limited	£1,194,564
D.Moody (Haulage) Limited	£1,193,514
The Ashbank Group Limited	£1,193,361
EDM Zone Limited	£1,192,618
Aconpex (UK) Limited	£1,191,998
Rooster Enterprises Limited	£1,191,496
Howard Snaith Limited	£1,190,482
Justships Ltd	£1,190,361
Cellular Solutions Holdings Limited	£1,190,355
Beacon Electrical (N.E.) Limited	£1,187,568
Castle Insurance Services (North East) Ltd	£1,187,346
Invenio Systems Limited	£1,187,180
J & R A Hawkes & Sons Limited	£1,186,830
Newcastle Financial Advisers Limited	£1,186,444
Northern Switchgear & Controls Limited	£1,186,155
Alpha Process Controls (International) Limited	£1,184,384
Bell View (Belford)	£1,183,995
West Hartlepool Rugby Football Club Limited	£1,183,969
MIW Office Solutions Limited	£1,183,925
Crowther Lodge Motor Company Limited	£1,183,729
Firthmoor and District Community Association	£1,182,402
Stadium Export Services Limited	£1,182,165
PHP Architects Limited	£1,181,934
Neasham Estate Limited	£1,181,636
Kevin Richardson Plantmasteruk Ltd	£1,181,571
Longhoughton Community and Sports Centre Trust	£1,181,376
Northumbria Leisure Limited	£1,181,325
Stone Technical Services Group Limited	£1,181,322
Wainstones Estates Limited	£1,180,704
People First Care Ltd	£1,180,586
Kibblesworth Academy	£1,180,474
Eurojag Limited	£1,180,264
Monomarket Limited	£1,180,077
Delta Precision Engineering North East Limited	£1,179,387
Greens Property Developments Limited	£1,178,595
Anderson Barrowcliff LLP	£1,178,037
Nirvana Europe Limited	£1,176,796
Holme Dodsworth (Non-Ferrous) Limited	£1,176,722
The Charlotte Straker Project	£1,175,949
Hagen Homes Ltd	£1,175,920
Thorngate Place Properties Limited	£1,175,799
Willowcrete Manufacturing Company Limited	£1,175,763
Simon Bailes Property LLP	£1,175,585
Middlesbrough DP Ltd	£1,175,517
Maritsave Limited	£1,175,093
Savisto Limited	£1,175,020
Metalpoint Limited	£1,174,742
The Fountain Group Limited	£1,174,425
Westbrook Cycles Limited	£1,174,054
Cowie Holiday Cottage Developments LLP	£1,173,607
Cleveland Fire Brigade Risk Management Services C.I.C.	£1,172,539
Alexander Sinclair (N.E.) Limited	£1,171,973
A-Tech Fabrications Limited	£1,171,639

Level Flooring North East Limited	£1,169,987	Overs and Rich Limited	£1,133,682
Anglesea Terrace Orthodontic Practice Ltd	£1,168,816	Pern Consumer Products Limited	£1,133,240
UK & Ireland SAP User Group Limited	£1,168,575	N H Property Ltd	£1,133,105
Gateshead College Foundation	£1,168,281	KWR Holdings Limited	£1,132,969
Prodrive Property Maintenance Limited	£1,166,678	Green Lane Capital (Boldon) LLP	£1,132,451
Smallburn Properties Ltd	£1,165,403	Lion Garage (Bedlington) Limited	£1,132,369
Shaheen Medical Services Limited	£1,165,350	M.A. Properties Limited	£1,132,125
Eco-Drill Ltd	£1,164,936	Offshore Support Vessels IV Limited	£1,132,000
IK-ECO Limited	£1,164,799	PMK Hague Investments Limited	£1,131,406
Artemis Support Limited	£1,164,058	Turners Fabrications Limited	£1,131,376
Davison Tyne Metal Limited	£1,162,963	N21 Limited	£1,130,522
Indoor Climate Control Holdings Limited	£1,162,936	Winder House Developments Limited	£1,130,470
Theme Bins (International) Ltd	£1,162,917	Zimb Johnson Bespoke Financial Planning Limited	£1,130,341
Claremont IT Services Limited	£1,162,857	HGC Properties Limited	£1,130,062
Be Property Management LLP	£1,162,046	Archers Law Limited Liability Partnership	£1,130,054
Northumbria Vehicle Co Ltd.	£1,161,957	Utility Alliance Ltd	£1,129,537
Crestfix Limited	£1,161,818	Underpressure Pipeline Solutions Limited	£1,129,409
Northumbria Dental Care Limited	£1,161,469	The Tiling Company (Northern) Limited	£1,128,690
The Hawes Farmers' Auction Mart Company, Limited	£1,161,317	David Robert Limited	£1,128,629
Leedawn Properties Limited	£1,160,853	Cool Retail Services Ltd	£1,128,298
Skyline Retail Limited	£1,160,566	Kennedy Services Limited	£1,127,455
Wright Construction (Durham) Limited	£1,160,253	Lexiauk Limited	£1,127,247
Volume Trading (Europe) Limited	£1,160,088	E-Wire Northern Limited	£1,126,699
Aphrodite Clothing Limited	£1,160,052	Jarrow Coachworks Limited	£1,126,443
Sirius Demolition Ltd	£1,159,980	Roland Burgess Limited	£1,126,418
Galleria Retail Limited	£1,159,613	KC Engineering Bearings Ltd	£1,126,405
1st Choice Skip Hire North East Ltd	£1,159,426	Kwik Corporate Lettings Limited	£1,126,345
Ribchester Smith & Law Limited	£1,158,722	Century Composites Limited	£1,126,294
Newcastle United Foundation	£1,158,176	Willson Developments Limited	£1,125,975
SGS Timber Haulage Limited	£1,158,130	Little Haven Beach Limited	£1,125,834
Our Lady of Light Catholic Academy Trust	£1,157,394	Cook & Barker Inn Limited	£1,125,094
Advanced Utility Solutions Limited	£1,157,267	Sashless Window Co. Limited	£1,124,198
Almet Sheet Metal Fabrication Limited	£1,157,253	Smart Real Estate Limited	£1,123,927
Newcastle Council for Voluntary Service	£1,157,038	Scott-Chem Limited	£1,122,564
Tyneside Group Limited	£1,156,293	Isotank (2006) Limited	£1,122,523
Goode Durrant Administration Limited	£1,156,231	Cast Tec Limited	£1,122,205
Inderjeet Medicals Limited	£1,154,241	Baydale Estates Limited	£1,121,681
East Durham Partnership Limited	£1,152,673	The Redemption Holding Company (UK) Limited	£1,120,140
Security Centres Securus Limited	£1,151,656	NEPACS	£1,120,119
Mallen Print Limited	£1,149,308	Armourpost Limited	£1,119,852
Middlesbrough Voluntary Development Agency	£1,149,290	Clearwater Developments Ltd	£1,119,748
Halls of Durham Limited	£1,148,501	Pullan Barnes Limited	£1,119,065
Showermania Limited	£1,148,318	Beecham Peacock North East Limited	£1,118,944
Team Build Construction Limited	£1,148,218	GKC Interiors (NE) Limited	£1,118,797
VMS Live 2011 Ltd	£1,144,260	Kinder Castle Limited	£1,118,634
The Talent Group UK Limited	£1,144,258	A & K Fashions Limited	£1,118,286
Meadownet Limited	£1,143,728	Total Electrical Solutions UK Limited	£1,118,225
Tait Walker Financial Services Limited	£1,143,125	Just Sport (Pro Club) Ltd	£1,117,507
Steadfast Secure Storage Ltd	£1,142,028	Harbour Support Services	£1,117,374
Union Property Services Limited	£1,141,204	John Moody & Son Limited	£1,116,520
Oakwood House Property and Developments (UK) Ltd	£1,140,819	The Ainderby LLP	£1,116,171
Monument Developments Ltd	£1,140,555	AAP Metal Fabrication Services Ltd	£1,116,032
NEG Holdings Limited	£1,140,000	Newcastle Optical Engineering Limited	£1,115,719
First Fix Plastics Ltd	£1,139,899	L. Sampson & Son Limited	£1,115,530
Cleveland Homes (No.2) Limited	£1,139,124	Interactive Development Support Limited	£1,115,061
Swinburne Maddison LLP	£1,138,927	McIntyres Properties Limited	£1,114,918
J.A. Jewitt (Farms) Limited	£1,138,463	Bartram Walker Limited	£1,114,523
Blue Assistance Limited	£1,138,378	Journey Enterprises Ltd	£1,113,954
Enviroclothes Limited	£1,138,175	J Watson Haulage Limited	£1,113,533
Pear Tree Honey Farm Limited	£1,138,093	Vectis Auctions Limited	£1,113,424
JW Colpitts & Co Limited	£1,138,076	McLuckie Projects Limited	£1,113,182
Deanswood Properties Limited	£1,137,990	David Coates Agronomy Limited	£1,113,174
Northern Lights Energy Limited	£1,137,180	Phoenix Passive Fire Protection Limited	£1,112,670
GMA Healthcare Ltd	£1,136,902	Marrick Priory Trust	£1,112,310
Lincoln Healthcare Group Limited	£1,136,025	Barton Environmental Services Limited	£1,112,042
Communicators Training Associates Limited	£1,135,030	Aimgo Limited	£1,111,565
G. Scott of York Limited	£1,134,875	Kidd & Spoor Solicitors Limited	£1,110,442
Tau Properties Limited	£1,134,570	Stephenson Rocket Limited	£1,110,285
Skills Training Academy Limited	£1,134,186	Compac Services (NE) Limited	£1,110,266
MacDee LLP	£1,134,186	Northallerton Properties Limited	£1,110,159
R & R Edwards and Sons Limited	£1,134,176	Forum Centrespace Limited	£1,109,790
Williams & Spenceley Limited	£1,133,951	Inkland Limited	£1,109,395

Company	Amount
Low Carbon Lighting Limited	£1,109,093
Premier Scaffolding Services Limited	£1,108,986
MCQ Investments Limited	£1,108,890
J & H Property and Developments Ltd	£1,108,186
Tandem Properties Limited	£1,107,744
Providence Fishing Company Limited	£1,107,597
Hambleton Steel (South) Limited	£1,107,503
Guy Sports Limited	£1,107,184
Adaptive Trading Limited	£1,107,012
MH Holdings (North) Limited	£1,106,441
Andlaw Holdings Limited	£1,106,360
Mobi Developments Limited	£1,106,196
Ron Perry (A19 Test & Tune) Limited	£1,105,985
Total Gutter Maintenance Limited	£1,105,383
Foster Hill Properties (Bedford) Limited	£1,105,122
At Home Furnishings Outlet Limited	£1,104,603
Baltic Recruitment Services Limited	£1,103,057
I2media Limited	£1,101,480
University of Sunderland Enterprises Limited	£1,101,000
Barker Bros. Limited	£1,099,898
Eshott South Farm Limited	£1,099,822
Hartlepool Golf Club Limited	£1,099,717
T.A. Plastic Supplies Limited	£1,098,954
Carmel Structures Limited	£1,098,683
Cherry Orchards Care Ltd	£1,098,257
Protex (UK) Systems Limited	£1,097,422
J Gunn Scaffolding Limited	£1,096,382
Reynolds & Law (Stainless) Limited	£1,095,688
Allan Liddle (Steel) Limited	£1,095,070
Act Response Ltd	£1,094,972
Lane7 Aberdeen Ltd	£1,094,967
D Jones Construction & Haulage Limited	£1,094,960
Deepdegree Limited	£1,093,965
Artneat Limited	£1,093,167
Beaumont Landscapes Holdings Limited	£1,092,288
Goldshield Securus Limited	£1,091,404
Whale Hill Limited	£1,090,884
Vigilant Homes (UK) Limited	£1,090,552
Hawk Fasteners Limited	£1,089,826
Hoults Enterprises Limited	£1,089,005
GLT Limited	£1,088,957
Montgomery Blue Limited	£1,088,947
The Bedsit Company Limited	£1,088,773
Ultralight Outdoor Gear Limited	£1,088,023
Arcada Trading Limited	£1,087,373
O Communications Ltd	£1,086,412
Tees Insulation (International) Limited	£1,085,522
O Morgan Developments Limited	£1,085,132
Impact 3D Signs Limited	£1,084,861
M & L Associates Design and Build Limited	£1,084,793
Propertees Ltd	£1,084,784
John Aynsley (Architectural Metalwork) Limited	£1,084,671
Red Marine Engineering Limited	£1,084,170
Landscape Matters Limited	£1,083,539
Burlam House Limited	£1,083,504
Tribo - Synthetics Limited	£1,083,468
W A Old & Son Limited	£1,083,382
Interflon (UK) Limited	£1,083,380
T.S.C. Dobbin Limited	£1,083,214
Chuhan & Singh Partnership Limited	£1,083,105
Richmond Contracts Projects Limited	£1,082,886
Health & Safety Training Limited	£1,082,609
UTS Group Limited	£1,082,523
Azure Business Centres Limited	£1,082,411
Patterson Ryan Limited	£1,082,190
M.J. Scaife Limited	£1,081,871
Absolute Medicals Limited	£1,081,559
Bedi Group Limited	£1,081,183
Lenton Marketing Limited	£1,081,163
Bob Rudd Limited	£1,080,989
Ebony Leisure Limited	£1,080,320
Overdrive (North East) Limited	£1,079,988
W.H.Hillerby & Sons Limited	£1,079,306
Autosense Limited	£1,078,894
Zonic Investments Limited	£1,078,290
Michael Brandon Limited	£1,078,257
Robinson Construction Limited	£1,077,898
Grayson Spa Limited	£1,077,210
Simpson Fuels Limited	£1,077,125
Euro Property Management Ltd	£1,076,418
Nemro Properties Limited	£1,075,920
North Bar Properties Limited	£1,075,604
Certax Accounting (Durham) LLP	£1,075,598
Total Communications and Security Limited	£1,075,534
Hadrian Window Systems Limited	£1,074,979
Buy from Us Autopark Limited	£1,074,949
PAC Holdings Limited	£1,074,887
Ovington Holdings Limited	£1,074,718
Kennek Construction Limited	£1,074,676
B2B Property Solutions Limited	£1,074,415
B2B Contracting Services Ltd.	£1,074,153
Hornsey (Hartlepool) Limited	£1,074,146
Primary Care Recruitment Ltd	£1,073,442
Express Engineering (Industrial Products) Limited	£1,072,860
Sunderland Counselling Service	£1,072,817
Durham Pharmaceuticals Limited	£1,072,750
Microchem Limited	£1,072,231
Hexham and Tynedale Community Trust	£1,071,886
Kindred Living Limited	£1,071,784
C.K.& D.Muir Limited	£1,071,497
Chipchase Farms Limited	£1,070,804
Georgian Theatre (Richmond) Trust Limited (The)	£1,070,435
Henzell Enterprises Limited	£1,070,254
Roseberry Specialist Care Centres Limited	£1,070,253
Universal Systems Solutions (Security) Limited	£1,070,174
Higham Ventures Limited	£1,069,917
Newarc (Newcastle) Limited	£1,069,872
Oldgate Finance Limited	£1,069,805
Tweedmouth House Care Limited	£1,069,360
Identec Limited	£1,069,147
Craig Enterprises Limited	£1,069,137
Total Courier Solutions Limited	£1,068,951
Dalts Ltd	£1,068,627
Houghton-le-Spring Golf Club,Limited (The)	£1,068,410
Beecham Peacock LLP	£1,068,056
Stephenson Coates Limited	£1,067,370
B and R Property Limited	£1,066,438
Bench Marque (GBR) Limited	£1,064,129
Woodydog Limited	£1,064,065
EWP Technical Services Limited	£1,064,000
Billingham Machine Company Limited	£1,063,928
Advanced Radiators Limited	£1,063,873
Aardvarc Electrical Engineers Limited	£1,063,752
Tyne Tees Thermal Limited	£1,063,509
Little Learners Sunderland Limited	£1,063,089
Hydraulic & Offshore Supplies Limited	£1,063,018
Cygnet Total Communications Limited	£1,063,004
Edynamix UK Ltd	£1,062,268
Contract Joinery (North East) Limited	£1,061,873
Contract Laboratory Services Limited	£1,061,769
Fivedean Limited	£1,061,505
Kaas Properties (North) Limited	£1,061,233
G.V. Engineering Limited	£1,061,218
Utilergy Limited	£1,061,144
Keyfort Group Limited	£1,059,742
Riverside Leisure Promotions Limited	£1,059,434
Forest B.P. LLP	£1,059,309
Straightline (NE) Limited	£1,058,620
Yorkshire Dales Meat Company Ltd	£1,058,575
Kotur Limited	£1,058,209
Shilbottle Community Hall Limited	£1,057,348
ASL Powerstream Services Limited	£1,057,146
Brancepeth Estates Ltd	£1,056,790
Cool Refrigeration Limited	£1,056,542

Company	Value
Fragrant Harbour Limited	£1,056,525
VA Property Developments Limited	£1,056,366
Phoenix Coaches (NE) Limited	£1,056,308
Hogarth Coachworks Limited	£1,055,475
ICCS Holdings Limited	£1,055,137
DCS Maintenance Solutions NE Ltd	£1,054,957
Stelling LLP	£1,054,937
Nigel Cabourn Marketing Limited	£1,054,802
Premier Estate Properties Ltd	£1,054,761
Yorkshire Independent Building Supplies Limited	£1,054,649
Lamda (UK) Limited	£1,054,146
A. Williamson Limited	£1,053,467
CJW Country Estates Limited	£1,053,001
MC Ware IT Solutions Limited	£1,052,918
D. C. C. (Cars) Limited	£1,052,458
Provenance Developments Limited	£1,052,023
Shout Digital Limited	£1,051,496
Kelt Properties Limited	£1,051,178
Tong Ltd	£1,050,394
Supreme Health Care Limited	£1,050,090
C & R Utilities Ltd	£1,049,307
Quay North LLP	£1,048,388
Spiro-Gills Thermal Products Ltd	£1,048,226
Aycliffe Decorative Supplies Limited	£1,047,788
Christopher Bailey Tax Consultants Limited	£1,047,466
Ors Contracting Limited	£1,046,915
A.V.Taylor Limited	£1,046,761
Regal Amusements (North East) Limited	£1,046,506
Medicentre (Newcastle) Limited	£1,045,556
Loanchoice Limited	£1,045,442
UK Bathrooms Limited	£1,044,845
Bellaine Limited	£1,044,791
NAS Group Durham Limited	£1,044,374
Stokesley Tractors Ltd	£1,044,282
Lescrow Investments Limited	£1,043,290
The People's Kitchen Limited	£1,042,756
Thomson Bros (Newcastle) Limited	£1,042,366
CRS (North-East) Limited	£1,042,100
Darlington Mind Limited	£1,042,000
Daava Developments (UK) Limited	£1,041,942
FLC Durham Limited	£1,041,695
Complete Weed Control Limited	£1,041,590
Thornton Investments Ltd	£1,041,585
Insulation Contractors Limited	£1,041,259
Market Edge Consulting Limited	£1,041,183
Bors Advisory Limited	£1,040,132
Edmondson Logging Ltd	£1,039,313
Maval Investments Limited	£1,039,213
Ichina Wholesale Ltd	£1,039,167
Planit Project Services Limited	£1,038,627
North East Motor Salvage Limited	£1,038,546
First Choice Labels Limited	£1,038,287
Chilcott Limited	£1,036,952
Devon Conversions Limited	£1,036,492
Taopix Limited	£1,036,429
Dutchwest Distribution Limited	£1,036,156
East Coast Fibreglass Supplies Limited	£1,035,941
O'Neill Richmonds Law Firm Limited	£1,035,488
Arodnap Limited	£1,034,656
Dellwood Enterprises Limited	£1,034,354
Digital Office Solutions Limited	£1,034,182
Oldgreen Limited	£1,033,139
Real Time Money Ltd.	£1,032,945
Timec 1526 Limited	£1,032,816
Corinthia Limited	£1,032,279
PDE (NE) Limited	£1,032,117
Graham S Hall Properties Limited	£1,032,092
Swandene Furniture Limited	£1,031,925
Green Team Partnership Ltd	£1,031,757
Lockwell Limited	£1,031,726
Swift Brake & Clutch Limited	£1,031,578
Stelrad Management Limited	£1,031,000

Company	Value
Tyne Tees Ceramics Limited	£1,030,721
DPH Construction (North East) Limited	£1,028,729
Appleton Grange Equestrian Centre Limited	£1,028,614
Licensed Consultancy Services Limited	£1,028,384
Blue Aardvark Holdings Limited	£1,027,968
Hebburn Properties (NE) Limited	£1,027,640
ITEC North East Limited	£1,027,438
T W Eason Limited	£1,027,387
Linhope Farming Company Limited	£1,026,917
Lyrico Securus Limited	£1,026,454
MCM (Spain) Ltd	£1,026,374
Print Ventures Limited	£1,025,231
TGA Consulting Engineers LLP	£1,025,030
Reethorn Investments Limited	£1,023,405
Hartridge Buddhist Monastery Trust	£1,023,023
Brighstone Developments Limited	£1,022,928
MJ & A Taylor Limited	£1,022,858
Ryan Offshore Limited	£1,022,091
Barnaby Side Farms Limited	£1,021,930
Euro Super Abrasives Limited	£1,021,688
Seateks Engineering Limited	£1,021,345
Naturalight Properties Ltd.	£1,021,304
Sound Training for Reading Ltd	£1,021,170
Beadnell Links Limited	£1,020,464
Haven (Tyneside) Ltd.	£1,020,408
Natural Stockcare Limited	£1,020,395
Denton Estates Limited	£1,020,220
Crandus (Contractors) Limited	£1,020,033
Surtec (North East) Limited	£1,019,929
Martin Corney Limited	£1,018,967
Hartlepool People Limited	£1,018,043
Key Stage Recruitment Limited	£1,017,998
Ebsonlodge Limited	£1,017,973
Eciggy UK Limited	£1,016,364
J.E.B. Contractors (UK) Limited	£1,016,267
Thornex Limited	£1,015,925
Maceachern HCH Ltd	£1,014,565
SLW (Thornbury) Limited	£1,014,273
Sandco 830 Limited	£1,014,016
Hartlepool NDC Trust	£1,013,709
Port Ventures Ltd	£1,013,615
Viswanath & Co Limited	£1,013,493
Nicander Limited	£1,013,384
Catcote Futures	£1,012,814
Autoclock Systems Limited	£1,012,613
G.Nicholson (Engineers) Limited	£1,012,208
Ashbrook Construction Services Limited	£1,012,156
Watson Woodhouse Solicitors LLP	£1,011,332
Peter Fergusson Properties Limited	£1,011,237
New Century Services Limited	£1,010,820
Apollo Facility Management Ltd	£1,010,533
Sharewave Limited	£1,010,000
The Customs House Trust Limited	£1,009,913
Aldar Property Limited	£1,009,772
Swale View Caravan Sales Limited	£1,009,328
The Morpeth Golf Club Limited	£1,009,296
Zenith Growth Limited	£1,008,966
ADC Electrical Limited	£1,008,826
Tantallon Homes Limited	£1,008,523
E3 Ecology Ltd	£1,007,480
Make Believe UK Limited	£1,007,299
Wack Wholesale (Building Supplies) Ltd	£1,006,930
Genesis Flooring Limited	£1,005,915
Templeton LPA Limited	£1,005,591
Thirston Property & Investments Limited	£1,004,985
Northdale Rotary Engineering Limited	£1,004,866
Trims Gym Limited	£1,004,806
Rushyford Transport Services Limited	£1,004,562
Arcot Hall Golf Club Limited	£1,004,511
Thrift Energy Limited	£1,004,108
G & H Property Limited	£1,003,422
Katmex Seaham Limited	£1,003,381

Company	Amount
Central Plant (Northern) Limited	£1,003,272
IN2 Developments Limited	£1,003,243
Avec Sport Limited	£1,002,722
Empharm (North East) Limited	£1,002,587
A S & J K Leggott Limited	£1,002,582
Print Demon Holdings Limited	£1,001,950
Iris Project Solutions Ltd	£1,001,464
Country Homes & Estates (Northern) Limited	£1,000,463
Sunderland Engineering Training Association Limited	£1,000,227
Stott Holdings Limited	£1,000,002
Brunton Holdings Limited	£1,000,000
FT Management Consultants Limited	£999,937
Cimex Service (UK) Limited	£998,324
PFC Marine Ltd	£998,203
Invate Limited	£997,140
Shiellow Wood Limited	£997,093
Catterick Service Station Ltd.	£996,791
B.Z. Limited	£996,415
Q Laser Ltd	£996,259
Saks Hair (Holdings) Limited	£996,086
Metro Repro Limited	£995,862
Smithfield Timber Limited	£995,437
The R.D.A. Centre in Cleveland Limited	£994,965
Alex Clark Art Ltd	£994,636
Newcastle Great Park (Estates) Limited	£993,953
Albany Office Equipment (Wholesale) Limited	£993,901
Deetronic Fire Systems Limited	£993,873
Aldona Seals Ltd	£993,344
County Life Homes Limited	£992,788
Tyne Property Limited	£992,430
Sacriston Community and Sports Trust	£992,344
The Original Produce Company (Middlesbrough) Ltd	£991,122
M Spence Surfacing Limited	£990,944
Hesbro Limited	£990,373
Epsom Dental Centre Ltd	£990,365
Tees Licensed Foyboatmens' Association Limited	£990,218
First Call Healthcare Limited	£990,214
Dick Lawson Yorkshire Limited	£990,099
Spark Etail Limited	£990,026
Cliffvalley Limited	£989,958
Ringrose Properties Limited	£989,888
Bob Little & Co Limited	£989,847
Tynedale Agricultural Society Ltd	£989,313
Qubic Tax Advisory Limited	£988,942
Northern Grid for Learning	£988,897
C.R.D. Devices Ltd.	£988,883
Tier One Capital Investments Limited	£988,662
Poppypride Limited	£988,643
Bede Group Limited	£988,244
Youngs RPS Limited	£987,870
Newcastle Flooring Company Limited	£987,854
Rand Rocket Limited	£987,805
Leisure Works (Yorkshire) Limited	£987,415
North East Estates Limited	£986,733
High Sixes Projects Limited	£986,704
Singisetti Srinivas Limited	£986,308
St Bede's RC Primary School	£986,000
Bell Tindle Williamson LLP	£985,809
Pennine Contracts Ltd	£985,719
Technical Investment Solutions Ltd	£985,032
Perfect Care Limited	£984,830
Neue Schule Limited	£984,246
Brynco Ltd	£984,144
CY Partners Recruitment Ltd	£984,038
Brian Noble Fencing Contractors Limited	£983,180
E C Groundworks Ltd	£982,778
Castle Fabrication & Installation Limited	£981,885
Britannia Office Systems Limited	£981,222
Technical Options (Europe) Ltd	£980,940
Patrick Henry Ventures Unlimited	£980,924
Oak Road and Whitby Motor Factors Limited	£980,886
Hudsons 23 Limited	£980,776
Syntex Engineering Services Limited	£980,236
KPL Engineering Limited	£980,007
Chilcott Holdings Limited	£980,000
Roseville (Hillgate) Limited	£979,488
Faverdale Recycling Centre Limited	£979,145
Clean It UK/Gumbusters Limited	£978,937
Superkrush Films Limited	£978,809
J Cotton Agricultural Contractors Limited	£978,548
Durham County Carers Support	£978,467
Seaton Developments Limited	£978,326
Glenwood Paint Supplies Limited	£978,324
Project Bridal Designer Outlet Limited	£978,314
Adina Reay Limited	£978,064
T.A. and N. White Limited	£977,545
DM North Limited	£977,446
Shaw & Company Solicitors Limited	£977,242
Hyena (Northern) Limited	£977,090
Westway Developments (North East) Limited	£976,438
Eco Tyre Disposals Ltd	£976,067
R&R Packaging Limited	£976,035
Mineral & Chemical Services (North East) Limited	£975,432
Evergreen Park Limited	£974,964
Tara Davison Developments Limited	£974,849
Sage Wealth Management Limited	£974,810
Adapt (North East)	£974,270
CEL Securus Ltd	£972,564
The Faraday Centre Limited	£972,311
Doby Verrolec Limited	£972,223
D & S UK Properties Limited	£972,065
Ready Mix Tees Valley Ltd	£972,053
Specialist Castings Ltd	£971,729
Armstrong Foulkes LLP	£970,438
Car Construction (North East) Ltd	£970,311
Render Alarms Limited	£969,603
Chatswell Properties Ltd	£969,120
Hirst (Farmers) Limited	£968,216
Sea Island Developments (Ponteland) Limited	£968,199
Indepak Limited	£968,089
Avenue (North East) Limited	£968,009
Kings Church Darlington	£967,918
Meldon Estates Limited	£967,762
Print Demon Systems Limited	£967,706
Pegasus Material Handling Ltd	£967,619
Coopers Chemist Gt.Ayton Limited	£967,340
Carlton Hill Properties Limited	£966,809
Mandale Homes 1 Limited	£966,643
Teesside Pain Management Limited	£966,443
East Cleveland M.S. Home	£966,206
Mill Poultry Limited	£966,023
Charnley Marketing Limited	£965,844
David Carr (Durham) Limited	£965,209
Fairfield House Limited	£965,081
Andrew Craig Limited	£964,737
Pro-Flex Packaging Europe Ltd	£964,311
Diespeker Holdings Ltd	£963,652
Preferred Management Solutions (PMS) Ltd	£963,556
Rees Turnbull Limited	£963,486
Aztec Print North East Limited	£962,822
HTL Worldwide Ltd	£962,130
Infinity Dental Services (IDS) Ltd	£961,938
Mlgo Limited	£961,434
Richard Reed Ltd	£960,681
Howarth Limited	£960,625
Newgate Investments Limited	£960,575
RMH Lamps, Lighting & Electrical Limited	£959,946
BMM Heaters Limited	£959,905
Eldrett Finch Limited	£959,592
Harden Redstone Company Limited	£959,512
Mio Angelo Limited	£959,209
Garth Thompson Wealth Management Limited	£958,969
Mercantile Partnership Ltd	£958,729
Humbles Real Estate Limited	£958,294

Company	Value
Nigel Wright Group Limited	£958,000
J.Mccheyne Construction Limited	£957,822
Eppleton Quarry Products (Middlesbrough) Ltd	£957,652
Graham Hair and Beauty Limited	£956,989
Juma Corporation Ltd	£956,951
T.A.P. Limited	£956,657
Millfield GRP Products Limited	£956,364
Blue Line Services Ltd	£956,353
Durham City Golf Club Limited	£955,310
Dr W Hassan Ltd	£954,706
Thirteen Properties Limited	£954,705
Euro Foods (GB) Limited	£953,939
Odin Shipping Limited	£953,655
Chemian Technology Limited	£953,527
November 26 Limited	£953,377
The Delsyl Limited	£953,195
Bowers Developments Ltd	£953,025
Dimeplace Limited	£952,094
Document Solutions (UK) Limited	£952,012
Bellingham Camping Limited	£951,707
Esh-MWH Limited	£951,497
Blyth Valley Disabled Forum Ltd	£951,193
Houston Commercial Ltd	£951,139
Apollo Schools Trust	£951,000
Thermodynamix (Holdings) Limited	£950,605
Northprop Limited	£950,364
Kwikbizz Limited	£950,002
NE Property Management Limited	£950,000
Tees Valley Components Limited	£948,169
Henry F. Dodds Limited	£947,683
J.& H.B.Ibbitson (Sunderland) Limited	£947,547
Atlas Washroom Systems Limited	£947,442
The Bedlingtonshire Golf Club Limited	£947,419
Training Support for Industry Limited	£947,050
Specialist Panels UK Limited	£947,040
NOF Energy Ltd	£946,906
YOLO (Newcastle) Limited	£946,878
Clennell Properties Limited	£946,000
Caterpak Limited	£945,824
Twoplustwo Commercial Services Limited	£945,404
Millhouse Group Holdings Limited	£944,781
Dalesend Farms Limited	£943,587
Frith Street LLP	£943,000
Subsea Energy Solutions Ltd	£942,667
Scotts of Whittington Limited	£942,317
Stadium Consumer Products Limited	£942,194
DOH Construction Limited	£941,858
Rootwise Limited	£941,722
Lofthouse and Partners Limited	£941,621
Eversley Management Limited	£941,443
Cleveland Country Store Limited	£941,054
The Cosmetic Dental Clinic Limited	£940,956
John Davey Limited	£940,555
Romaldrose Limited	£939,763
Vickers Scott Investment Company Limited	£939,485
Mapleleaf Property Developments Limited	£938,914
Ezimix Limited	£938,905
Heddon Stables Limited	£938,607
Windmill (Heaton) Orthodontics Limited	£938,451
Endeavour Northern Limited	£938,112
Sincera Ltd	£938,050
Top Drawer Properties Limited	£937,979
Global Enterprise (EU) Limited	£937,873
Alliance Psychological Services Ltd	£937,424
40/46 The Side Newcastle Limited	£937,176
Kiltech Limited	£937,104
Manor House Commercial Acquisitions Limited	£937,077
Age Concern Tyneside South	£936,647
FG Trailers Limited	£936,377
Autoroll UK Limited	£935,996
One Premium Fitness Limited	£935,802
Cliff House Service Station Ltd	£935,208
North East Wholesale Fruit & Vegetable Market Limited	£934,912
Leo Car Company Limited	£934,749
Changing Health Limited	£934,237
Russell Foster Tyne and Wear Sports Foundation	£934,035
HBH Investments Limited	£933,420
Saddle Skedaddle Limited	£933,064
Kings Court (Team Valley) LLP	£932,920
Colton Excavations Limited	£932,575
J.E.B. Contractors Limited	£932,363
Aceda Limited	£932,322
Scollen & Wright Funeral Service Limited	£932,210
Biss 89 Limited	£931,769
Whitley Bay Golf Club Ltd (The)	£931,637
Vale Ventures Limited	£931,266
Frederick Dennison Limited	£931,054
Collingwood Groundworks Limited	£931,052
Argent Wealth Limited	£930,784
A.E.T. Ltd	£929,805
G Ramage & Sons Windows Limited	£929,274
David Jarvis Limited	£929,218
Ruff 'n' Tumble Adventure World Limited	£929,109
Russell Telecom Limited	£929,016
Green Lane Capital (Gibson House Middlesbrough) LLP	£928,328
Sandco 1184 Limited	£927,741
Cherry Hill Garden & Landscape Centre Ltd	£927,684
Gardiner Richardson Limited	£927,674
Campbell & Hall Engineering Limited	£927,633
Whitehouse Funeral Service Limited	£927,492
GR Properties (North East) Limited	£927,257
A E L Systems Ltd	£927,142
Athenaeum Developments Limited	£926,452
Choice Childcare Limited	£926,434
Challenging Learning Ltd	£926,406
Cleveland Heat Treatment Centre Limited	£926,142
H Wood & Sons (Leyburn) Limited	£925,505
Exis (Group) Limited	£925,004
Banks Renewables (Harting Rig Wind Farm) Limited	£925,000
G.W. Seymour Transport Limited	£923,599
I-Evo Ltd	£922,564
R D Consulting and Education Limited	£921,655
Hop Vietnamese Limited	£921,626
Land Factor Limited	£921,603
Lewis Franklin Trading Ltd	£920,558
Heritage Healthcare Limited	£920,316
Arjuna Technologies Limited	£919,437
Northumbrian Property Services Group Limited	£919,109
Epivalence Ltd	£918,684
Bon-Bloemen Ltd	£918,628
Rend-Tech North East Ltd	£917,902
Alfred Cox Limited	£917,802
J3S Ltd	£917,757
Rosedene Nurseries Limited	£917,461
North East Enterprise Agency Limited	£916,948
L & L Braines Limited	£916,941
Omar Najeeb Ltd	£916,757
View Developments Limited	£916,328
Balmoral Interiors Limited	£916,280
C & C Horse Transport Limited	£916,112
Holme Dodsworth (Rock Salt) Limited	£916,086
Ladybird's Childrens Nursery Limited	£916,013
Fitch Taylor Limited	£915,936
R&M Diagnostics Limited	£915,363
Aqualution Systems Ltd	£914,923
A690 Specialist Cars Limited	£914,382
Wheatley Hill Community Association	£914,287
JH Laidler & Son Limited	£914,182
Shield Engineering Cramlington LLP	£913,912
Sedbury Property Limited	£913,777
Braybell Limited	£913,747
T.J. Hazell (Engineering Consultants) Limited	£913,265
Norton Care Limited	£913,170
Bikesport (North East) Limited	£912,588

Sarah Mains Residential Limited	£912,047
Redcar Scaffolding Specialists Ltd	£911,966
DFI Properties Limited	£911,910
D.A.K. Tipper Hire Limited	£911,633
Jewel First Limited	£911,328
Grosvenor Gate Property Management Limited	£911,228
Hutchinsons Fruit&Veg (Gateshead) Limited	£911,123
AW Fabrication Limited	£911,028
UK Docks Marine Services South Limited	£910,181
Flint Properties Limited	£908,429
St Chad's Community Project	£908,352
Engynious Schools PLC	£908,258
S J I Holdings Limited	£908,179
Helme Park Hall Limited	£906,926
THDA Ltd	£906,609
Colewood Internet Ltd	£906,391
J & D Longlands Ltd	£905,964
Devon Motor Caravans Limited	£905,734
Commercial & Industrial Interiors Ltd	£905,682
Arrandene Ltd	£905,121
PGS Law LLP	£904,566
NEOS Protect Limited	£904,516
Kenley Holdings Limited	£904,435
Nextgen Group Limited	£903,936
Fox Formulated Feeds Limited	£903,805
Bahr Academy	£903,631
Northumberland Stone Limited	£903,387
Kenneth M Barrow & Co Limited	£903,136
Classic Masonry Limited	£902,900
ME Cronin Ltd	£902,819
Handyside Fishing Ltd	£902,388
Bewicke Service Station Limited	£902,044
Badgepalm Limited	£901,690
Calmor Limited	£901,590
Hugh Crawford Property Ltd	£900,398
Beauclerc Investments Limited	£900,315
Sea Island Developments Limited	£899,989
Durham Sheet Metal Works Limited	£899,216
Tyneview Diagnostics Limited	£898,383
Eat Fresh Investments Limited	£898,350
WM Utility Services Limited	£897,174
Your Care First Limited	£896,733
Evergreen Pallet Solutions (UK) Limited	£896,412
01906302 Limited	£896,314
Coastline Properties Limited	£896,262
Protection Installation Services Ltd	£896,009
Beyond Leisure Limited	£895,917
Winkfield Properties Limited	£895,793
Building Design (Northern) Limited	£895,244
Cheeseburn Estate Management Company Limited	£894,724
Hopling Properties Limited	£894,535
RB Blackburn Ltd	£894,381
Killashee House Limited	£893,660
Direct Connections Limited	£893,374
McVickers Free Solar Limited	£892,874
Plaxica Limited	£892,654
Gills Fry Fry Limited	£892,464
Otterburn Investments Limited	£892,287
Gledstone Estates Limited	£892,229
Chester Le Street DP Limited	£892,115
Advanced Productivity Group Limited	£890,484
Trading North East Limited	£890,231
RSL One Limited	£889,702
Welkin Investments Ltd	£889,667
Creative Cutting Services Limited	£889,655
Eldon Estates Limited	£889,542
St (Edrom) Limited	£889,472
Mendip (North East) Limited	£889,151
Crown Doors and Shutters Limited	£888,951
Warm Protection Products Limited	£888,604
Fairmoor Holdings Limited	£887,633
EHLUK Building Maintenance & Facility Services Ltd	£887,493

Vega Environmental Consultants Limited	£887,457
North Sport Fishing Industry LLP	£887,272
J Barbour and Sons (Manufacturing) Limited	£887,167
North East Roof Truss Limited	£887,041
Askaris Information Technology Limited	£886,847
Durham Roofing Centre Limited	£886,604
Shining Thought Limited	£886,250
Blue Lake Property Company Limited	£885,787
Lawkell LLP	£885,067
Tyneview Properties Limited	£885,023
James Ingleford Limited	£884,969
Lintron Electronics Limited	£884,818
Dewhirst Holywell Enterprises Limited	£884,650
Redbead Limited	£884,130
Beadnell Bay Caravan Park Ltd	£883,798
Ken Brown Agencies Limited	£883,593
Consett DP Limited	£883,454
Badesha Property Investments Ltd	£881,948
New Pineapple Limited	£881,813
SLP Developments Limited	£880,826
JDP Contracting (Holdings) Limited	£880,820
Hantman Select Limited	£880,404
N-Sign Limited	£879,826
Watson Investments Limited	£879,489
Cable Jointing Services Limited	£879,452
Monitor Marine (C.P.) Limited	£879,420
Complete Cladding Systems Limited	£879,293
Standing Stone Drawing Office Supplies Limited	£879,083
Winning Homes Limited	£878,808
Addisons Surveyors LLP	£878,318
Benchmark Electronics Limited	£878,281
D.W.S. Property Developments Limited	£877,282
Bon Bon Leisure Limited	£875,858
Plasterpiece Limited	£875,379
Tyneside Investments Limited	£875,031
PT Wood Finishes LLP	£874,371
EPG Property Management Ltd	£873,765
Romano's Limited	£872,902
Polyphotonix Limited	£872,850
Barter Books Limited	£872,599
T & G Allan Holdings Limited	£872,391
Validus Investments Limited	£872,050
Cowell's Garden Centre Limited	£871,985
Newarc (Aberdeen) Limited	£871,727
Gavin Reed Limited	£871,586
Deehan Property Limited	£871,220
Foxy Hair Extensions (NE) Ltd	£870,902
Swale Valley Construction Limited	£870,899
Lyndale Robert Limited	£870,613
Karlin Timber Frame (NE) Limited	£870,507
Blenheim Court Properties Limited	£869,905
Flat Free Tyres Limited	£869,895
Optimise Neurotherapy Centre Limited	£869,765
SNS Management & Solutions Limited	£868,718
Custom Design B.A. Limited	£867,744
Alldec (Northern) Limited	£867,339
Crossfield Homes Limited	£867,198
Darren Kelly Transport Limited	£867,070
Hall Farm Foods Limited	£866,391
Quality Tooling (North East) Limited	£866,171
Engineering Recruitment Services Ltd	£865,997
Millennium Conveyor Services Limited	£865,740
J Barthram & Son Limited	£865,583
Mandale Homes North East Limited	£865,361
New Bridge Street Partnership LLP	£864,888
A.H.U.S. Plant Hire Limited	£864,864
Adderstone Developments (103) Limited	£864,808
Technical Engineering Resource (Aerospace) Limited	£864,756
Shark Club (UK) Limited	£864,162
Trewicks Accident Repair Centre Limited	£863,780
James Cooper & Son (Tyneside) Ltd	£863,130
N&T Civils Ltd	£863,074

Ashdown Park Homes Limited	£862,693	Lane7 Ltd	£838,969
M T Haulage Ltd	£862,391	Dickens Self Storage Limited	£838,775
Morley Group Limited	£862,389	Simply Sugar Ltd	£837,608
Hymas & Hall Limited	£862,293	Harbron Properties Ltd	£836,408
Covervale Limited	£862,216	Steadfast Security Solutions Limited	£835,978
Adderstone Developments (101) Limited	£862,028	Billfreehomes Limited	£835,247
Fawside	£861,583	Shellbraes Property Ltd	£835,124
Rasmi Lighting Limited	£861,560	Dancorr Limited	£833,515
Bold Bloc Design Limited	£860,929	Tripsdale Technology Ltd	£832,553
Purification Solutions UK Limited	£860,887	Airport Retail UK Limited	£832,156
Wescott Medical Limited	£860,424	Haswells Homer Hill Farm Shop Limited	£832,085
Hivehome Ltd	£859,590	Dependable Bodies (Newcastle) Limited	£831,070
Hammer Services Ltd	£859,064	Theatre Leisure Limited	£830,347
Group Horizon Limited	£856,546	Mullen Properties Limited	£830,200
WHP Facilities Ltd	£854,880	Blue Diamond Machine Tools Limited	£829,638
Rockliffe Court Healthcare Limited	£854,689	Gisborough Project Services Ltd	£829,151
Whickham Golf Club Limited (The)	£854,526	Fulbeck Limited	£828,872
Belvedere Property Company Limited	£854,402	Peron Limited	£828,837
Robert Attey & Sons Limited	£853,955	KDL Mezzanine Limited	£828,799
Mountgate Caravans Limited	£853,717	J W Bainbridge Contractors Ltd	£828,450
Unsworth Unsworth & Co. Limited	£852,801	E L Denney & Son Limited	£828,352
JJC Engineering Ltd	£852,259	Pennine Enterprises Ltd	£828,298
North Tees Waste Management Limited	£851,933	Trojan Scaffolding (NE) Ltd	£828,128
Actdesign (UK) Ltd	£851,397	HVR Limited	£827,794
SPS Electrical Wholesalers Limited	£851,369	N I Sattar Holdings Limited	£827,687
Metro Rental Limited	£851,220	Euremica Limited	£827,287
D K & L R Davison Ltd	£851,113	Vandewiele UK Limited	£827,026
R & J Farrow Limited	£850,949	DW & FE Butterworth Holdings Limited	£826,782
E.J.Melling Limited	£850,933	Acumen Investigation Services Ltd.	£826,164
Homes Direct 365 Limited	£850,654	Precision Toolroom Services & Machining Limited	£825,446
Bridge End Motors Limited	£850,531	A. McCall & Sons (Houghton-le-Spring) Limited	£825,394
Geneva Brasswind Limited	£850,360	Ultramap Limited	£825,254
Inshore Holdings Limited	£850,003	Advent Development Holdings Ltd	£824,520
Integrated Polymer Systems Limited	£849,882	Oaktree Leasing Ltd	£824,126
Eagle Dreams Ltd	£849,863	Maryport Homes LLP	£824,020
4B Precision Engineering Ltd	£849,042	Ashington Central Limited	£823,656
Advanced Vehicle Leasing (Stockton) Limited	£848,900	Expertcare Limited	£823,232
Malcolm Tempest Limited	£848,437	J and K Training Ltd	£822,769
Orchard Homecare Services Limited	£848,346	Acomb Construction Limited	£822,766
PRD Property Management Limited	£848,281	Howell Cummings Joinery Ltd	£822,480
Copeland Veterinary Practice Limited	£848,088	Fursewood Limited	£822,478
Lord Technical (Holdco) Limited	£847,979	Tenmanor Limited	£821,638
Furniture Solutions (Northumberland) Limited	£847,780	Next2buy Limited	£821,100
Winning Lines Limited	£847,620	Brickwork Services Limited	£821,010
Tynegrain Agriculture Limited	£847,540	SRJ Energy Ltd	£820,993
William Peat (Barnard Castle) Limited	£847,168	Lee Construction (Ldg) Limited	£820,536
P. S. Pendergood Limited	£847,154	Triple Air-Technology Ltd	£820,425
Wave Aluminium Profiles Limited	£846,293	Church Lane Builders Limited	£820,076
J.T.P. (Non-Ferrous Stockholders) Limited	£845,419	M J M Leisure Limited	£819,822
Stargate Precision Engineering Limited	£844,997	Zynk Software Limited	£819,707
Off Shore Fuels Limited	£844,971	Platinum Properties (GB) Limited	£819,120
Autoclock Holdings Limited	£844,952	Ascot Place Properties Limited	£819,009
Select Control Systems Limited	£843,634	Sutton Services International Limited	£818,557
Marityne Marine Projects Limited	£843,620	Monte Cristo Residential Ltd	£818,553
Supportive SRC Ltd	£843,136	Tangent Construction Limited	£818,259
Stockton Machine Company Limited	£843,130	UK Asbestos Specialists Ltd	£818,115
Hancock & Ainsley Limited	£843,094	DJ Camp Ltd	£817,853
SSDOS Limited	£842,861	M & D Travel Limited	£817,639
Total Reclaim Limited	£842,453	Freeman Finance (North East) Limited	£817,459
Simpson Coulson Limited	£841,879	Seatgeek Sport Limited	£817,263
Kirsten Scott Limited	£841,563	Vicari Properties Services Limited	£816,802
Satcom Global Aura Limited	£841,117	North East Building Services Limited	£816,246
Treeview Properties Limited	£840,456	North England Laboratory Supplies Ltd	£816,227
Northumberland CTC (Properties) Limited	£840,187	Lawson Cars Limited	£815,493
G T Project Engineering Limited	£840,143	Southampton Orthodontic Centre Limited	£815,456
Northumbrian Entertainments,Limited	£840,044	Living Lets Ltd	£815,275
Tynedale Family Funeral Directors Limited	£839,854	Presmac Limited	£814,935
Brightlight Management Limited	£839,655	Parnell Products Ltd	£814,649
Ward A Limited	£839,541	Code Property Developments Limited	£814,552
Stannington Estates Limited	£839,297	Sayers Property Limited	£813,882
W & W Peeled Potatoes Limited	£839,214	Outlet Properties Limited	£813,555
Arc Finance Group Limited	£839,075	M S Vernon Limited	£813,520

M62 Developments Limited	£813,348
SRSS Ltd	£813,179
Datatrial Limited	£813,057
Tallantyre Wallcoverings Limited	£812,001
Abbey Plant Ltd	£811,459
IT-IS International Limited	£811,444
Barrington Homes Limited	£810,687
Nursery Properties (N.E.) Limited	£810,668
J. Dinning (Woodlands) Limited	£810,206
Carewell (Health Care) Limited	£810,021
Park Parade Homes LLP	£809,885
Carson Office Environments Limited	£809,759
3.13	£809,027
Ford Castle Adventure Ltd	£808,883
Complete Leasing Solutions Limited	£808,875
Nicholsons Transport Limited	£808,806
The Dove Academy Trust	£808,000
Burncastle Farming Company Ltd	£807,969
TMH Associates Ltd	£807,947
Alpha Developments (Preston) Ltd	£807,702
Northern Bespoke Developments Ltd	£807,254
Proto (GB) Ltd	£807,198
Danco Properties Limited	£806,769
Clearmid Limited	£806,593
The Riverside Events LLP	£805,996
Decorating Direct Limited	£805,986
Dickens Warehousing Limited	£805,940
Joseph Developments Limited	£805,492
Penhill Investments Limited	£805,232
Ashington Leisure Partnership	£804,852
Southhill Farm Services Ltd	£804,735
Parker Prestige Limited	£804,591
B L Training (Holdings) Limited	£804,024
Robin Jessop Holdings Limited	£803,947
Villafirst Investment Properties Limited	£803,905
Pokrok 111 Limited	£803,726
Great North Properties Limited	£803,105
T C & C Ltd	£802,716
G.W. Herdman (Chemists) Limited	£802,667
Foden Spence Construction Limited	£802,660
Tynexe Residential Limited	£802,475
Changing Futures North East	£802,207
Brookleigh Caring Services Limited	£801,833
KMS Property Services Limited	£801,442
Dumark Investment Limited	£800,437
Crafty Apps Limited	£800,098
Windgrove Limited	£798,782
Coatham House	£798,156
Rapid (UK) Engineering Services Limited	£798,026
J H Johnson Shopfitters Limited	£797,521
Tees Valley Chinese Community Centre Ltd	£797,279
Blue Opal Investments Limited	£797,029
Sandwath Contracting Limited	£796,803
Les Woolston Haulage Limited	£796,361
AIS Environmental Ltd	£795,506
Matthew James Services Limited	£795,497
Borthwick Marble & Granite Ltd	£795,042
Encompassed Limited	£793,925
Waggies Limited	£793,497
Commercial Propshaft Services Limited	£793,359
A.& K. Gorham Limited	£793,338
Portalclad Limited	£793,043
Town Farm (Wall) Limited	£792,260
Elliott Westland Insurance Brokers Limited	£792,200
Labourn Property Ltd	£792,066
Axenic Limited	£791,319
Explain Market Research Limited	£789,947
The Leyburn Livestock Auction Mart Company Limited	£789,616
Atlas Cloud Limited	£789,227
RLDOM Ltd	£789,102
Speedbrand Limited	£788,810
Deepfields Property Management Limited	£788,479
A McGann Building Contractors Limited	£787,837
My Sister's Place	£787,548
The Charlton Group Limited	£787,199
The Indie Stone Ltd	£786,557
Total Maintenance & Engineering Limited	£786,384
Just Drama Based Training Ltd	£786,362
Strickland Tucker LLP	£786,187
Applied Ecological Services Limited	£786,146
G.B. Belting Ltd	£785,770
Class Fundraising Limited	£785,515
Wellway Pharmacy Limited	£785,214
Sweetdreams Limited	£785,111
KJT Properties Ltd	£785,064
Prodrive (Joinery & Shop Fitting) Limited	£784,744
Wansbeck (Morpeth) Limited	£784,655
Building Maintenance Services North East Limited	£784,494
Equitvain Limited	£784,402
Hunky Dory Leisure Limited	£784,206
South Shore Developments (Monkton) Limited	£784,000
Rennyco Limited	£783,525
Tivoli Properties Limited	£783,273
Quay Timber Ltd	£783,205
Yayla Enterprises Limited	£783,188
Tysoft Software Ltd	£783,176
Premier Fluid Solutions Limited	£782,626
Filematch Limited	£782,484
MBL Solutions Limited	£781,923
Caledonian Decking & Fencing Limited	£781,823
D J M S Solicitors Ltd	£781,598
BCTQ Maritime Corporate Limited	£781,405
Fishlocks Estates Limited	£781,255
Twizell Poultry (Ponteland) Limited	£780,198
Danick Limited	£779,688
Tees & Hartlepool Yacht Club Limited	£779,599
S.Bainbridge Limited	£779,103
FWS Consultants Limited	£778,668
J Dalby & Son Limited	£778,310
Enviro - Clear Limited	£777,442
Rutherford Association Football Club	£777,175
Grove Reed Joinery Limited	£776,458
Armstrong Hall Social Club Ltd	£775,652
Gray & Son Robe Makers (Durham) Ltd	£775,537
Nigel Lightfoot Electrical Contracting Limited	£774,916
Gateshead Bearings Limited	£774,860
Roseframe Limited	£774,105
Davies Tracey Limited	£773,891
Harbro Electrical Wholesale Limited	£772,973
Voltigeur Estates Ltd.	£772,644
Wentworth Northern Properties Limited	£772,381
RJY Investments (North East) Ltd	£772,115
AAM & Sons Limited	£772,066
Quick Developments Limited	£772,009
21 Hospitality Group Limited	£771,889
Peterlee Fire Company Limited	£771,838
J. Frampton Property Development Limited	£771,807
Allendale Creative Artists CIC	£771,748
Willow Bridge Properties Limited	£771,543
Essential Aluminium Limited	£771,431
Gary Beadle Promotions Limited	£771,273
Complement Genomics Limited	£770,917
Vistech Services Ltd	£770,600
H. & J. Forbes Limited	£770,472
Kilderk Inns Limited	£770,235
GKP Solutions Ltd	£770,015
C & D Leisure Properties Ltd	£769,806
B & S (Rentals) Limited	£769,696
Feld Limited	£769,231
David A Clark Limited	£768,909
Citizens Advice Sunderland	£768,070
The Feed Warehouse Ltd	£767,635
JJ Metcalfe & Son Ltd	£767,193
Amjaf Estates Ltd	£767,125

Company	Value
Kingfield Estates Limited	£766,987
Q.A. International Certification Limited	£766,484
Hedgeco Limited	£766,347
Rock Haulage Limited	£766,308
Tyneside Badminton Centre CIC	£766,020
Bradley Mill Caravan Site Limited	£765,624
Trend International Holdings Limited	£765,599
Mids Auto Services Limited	£765,405
John Donkin Solicitors Ltd	£765,017
Newford Estates Ltd	£764,782
The PNE Foundation	£763,331
Bowes Wealth Management Limited	£763,073
Aquajet Drain Cleaning Limited	£763,005
Wilton Energy Limited	£763,000
Robsons General Wares Limited	£762,632
Deenhall Ltd	£762,483
H Duckworth Limited	£762,467
CMS Holdings UK Limited	£762,041
Maymask (171) Limited	£761,841
Gilligan Engineering Services Limited	£761,305
MacDonald Martin Limited	£761,003
For Skills Limited	£761,000
Decor Cladding Centre Ltd	£760,987
SMC Motors Limited	£760,874
Disability North	£760,664
SGG Property Developments Limited	£760,174
BBL NE Limited	£760,127
Braemore Wood Windfarm Limited	£760,000
Rothco Properties Ltd	£759,906
Finkle Street Properties Limited	£759,757
Dunhill and McGrouther Limited	£759,481
Design and Security Services Limited	£758,846
Sirius Geotechnical Ltd	£758,500
R.F.I. Limited	£757,875
Wise Financial Consulting Limited	£757,727
Joegraphic Ltd	£757,630
Destiny Church Tees Valley	£757,523
Soundbitelearning UK Limited	£757,332
W Dot Homes Limited	£757,263
JD Joinery & Building Services Limited	£756,557
Sycamore Homes Limited	£756,267
Southmoor Golf Club	£756,146
Chevron Taxis Limited	£755,398
Tiplady Tanker Services Ltd	£754,788
RI & Mr Ridley Limited	£754,675
Forge Leisure (UK) Limited	£754,509
Bill Hewison Bespoke Homes Limited	£753,793
The Shiremoor Press Limited	£753,519
CMN Support Services Limited	£753,413
Dasyl Enterprises Limited	£753,326
Bradley Hall Limited	£753,138
ASPP Limited	£751,259
Gilsan Sports Limited	£750,865
N.T. Steel Services Ltd	£750,542
F.E.Maughan Limited	£750,311
Frank Jones (Chemist) Limited	£750,105
Tokyo and York Limited	£750,001

This page is intentionally left blank

Company Profiles

00741078 Limited
Incorporated: 16 November 1962 *Employees:* 1
Net Worth: £534,000 *Total Assets:* £7,608,000
Registered Office: 1 Admiral Way, Doxford International Business Park, Sunderland, Tyne & Wear, SR3 3XP
Activities: Banks
Officers: Lorna Edwards, Secretary; David Graham Johnstone [1963] Director Group Tax

01906302 Limited
Incorporated: 18 April 1985
Net Worth: £379,713 *Total Assets:* £896,314
Registered Office: Bulman House, Regent Centre, Gosforth, Newcastle upon Tyne, NE3 3LS
Activities: Other construction installation
Officers: Valerie Thomas, Secretary; Michael William Craig [1982] Managing Director; David Thomas [1951] Director/Sales Manager; Graham Thomas [1939] Director; Valerie Thomas [1941] Director

1 4 Sale Limited
Incorporated: 6 November 2015
Registered Office: Essell, 29 Howard Street, North Shields, Tyne & Wear, NE30 1AR
Activities: Buying and selling of own real estate
Shareholders: Tracy Michelle Robertson; Russell Robertson
Officers: Russell Stewart Robertson, Secretary; Russell Stewart Robertson [1960] Director/Financial Advisor; Tracy Michelle Robertson [1965] Director/Lecturer

1973 Developments Ltd
Incorporated: 24 February 2003
Net Worth: £575,455 *Total Assets:* £2,011,462
Registered Office: Stoneylea, Stoney Lane, Springwell Village, Gateshead, Tyne & Wear, NE9 7SJ
Activities: Buying and selling of own real estate
Major Shareholder: Stephen John Hudson
Officers: Amelia Caroline Hudson, Secretary; Stephen John Hudson [1973] Director/Manager

1excellence Multi Academy Trust
Incorporated: 14 June 2017 *Employees:* 108
Net Worth: £2,154,000 *Total Assets:* £2,332,000
Registered Office: Pentland Primary School, Pentland Avenue, Billingham, Cleveland, TS23 2RG
Activities: Primary education
Officers: Natasha White, Secretary; David Bowes [1944] Director/Retired; Michael James Fryer [1971] Project Delivery Director; Valerie Ann Hall [1957] Director/Headteacher; Lynda Hobson [1955] Director/Education Adviser; Harry Smith [1943] Director/Retired; Keith Eliot Smith [1972] Director/Financial Controller; Fiona Parker Williams [1964] Director/Independent Reviewing Officer

1st Choice Skip Hire North East Ltd
Incorporated: 11 April 2003
Net Worth: £450,306 *Total Assets:* £1,159,426
Registered Office: 7 Lorton Road, Redcar, Cleveland, TS10 4LY
Activities: Treatment and disposal of non-hazardous waste
Shareholders: Keith Rutherford; Laura Jean Rutherford
Officers: Linda Margaret Wales, Secretary; Keith Rutherford [1976] Director/Business Proprietor; Laura Jean Rutherford [1979] Director

1st Leisure Limited
Incorporated: 19 July 2002
Registered Office: 25a Parkview Road West, Hartlepool, Cleveland, TS25 1PE
Activities: Development of building projects
Officers: Candice Louise Wilkinson [1985] Director

2 Touch BPO Services Ltd
Incorporated: 17 March 2014 *Employees:* 1,147
Net Worth: £473,000 *Total Assets:* £8,992,000
Registered Office: 1 Victory Way, Doxford International Business Park, Sunderland, Tyne & Wear, SR3 3XF
Activities: Activities of call centres
Parent: Kura (CS) Limited
Officers: Brian Bannatyne [1965] Director; Julie McIntosh [1965] Director

20/20 Vision Systems Limited
Incorporated: 2 April 1992
Net Worth: £877,091 *Total Assets:* £1,879,258
Registered Office: 28 Northumberland Square, North Shields, Tyne & Wear, NE30 1PW
Activities: Security systems service activities
Shareholders: Peter James Houlis; Peter Andrew Jones; Peter James Houlis; Peter Andrew Jones
Officers: Peter Andrew Jones, Secretary; Peter James Houlis [1958] Director; Peter Andrew Jones [1968] Director

2020 Group UK Developments Limited
Incorporated: 12 January 2015
Net Worth: £25,765 *Total Assets:* £2,786,080
Registered Office: 1 University Boulevard, Middlesbrough, Cleveland, TS1 3BB
Activities: Development of building projects
Shareholder: Mohammed Arif Mushtaq
Officers: Mohammed Arif Mushtaq [1962] Director

2020 Property Developments Limited
Incorporated: 5 March 2007 *Employees:* 1
Net Worth: £559,094 *Total Assets:* £2,663,313
Registered Office: 1 University Boulevard, Middlesbrough, Cleveland, TS1 3BB
Activities: Development of building projects
Major Shareholder: Mohammed Arif Mushtaq
Officers: Sofia Tabasum Mushtaq, Secretary; Mohammed Arif Mushtaq [1962] Director/Manager

21 Degrees Limited
Incorporated: 13 January 2003 *Employees:* 31
Net Worth: £582,927 *Total Assets:* £1,258,139
Registered Office: Unit 10 Apollo Court, Koppers Way, Monkton Business Park, Hebburn, Tyne & Wear, NE31 2ES
Activities: Plumbing, heat and air-conditioning installation
Shareholders: Steven Redhead; Christine Redhead; Vincent Noble; Deborah Noble
Officers: Steven Redhead, Secretary; Deborah Noble [1969] Director; Vincent Noble [1965] Director; Christine Redhead [1961] Director; Steven Redhead [1961] Director

21 Hospitality Group Limited
Incorporated: 30 October 1996
Net Worth: £66,192 *Total Assets:* £771,889
Registered Office: 25 Broad Chare, Quayside, Newcastle upon Tyne, NE1 3DQ
Activities: Activities of head offices
Shareholders: Laurance Laybourne; Terence Laybourne
Officers: Laurance Laybourne, Secretary; Laurance Laybourne [1944] Director; Terence Laybourne [1955] Director/Chef

21st Century Style Limited
Incorporated: 20 December 1999
Net Worth: £487,881 *Total Assets:* £2,279,629
Registered Office: White Court, Church Lane, Riding Mill, Northumberland, NE44 6AP
Activities: Development of building projects
Shareholders: Paul Sehgal; Lucy Sehgal
Officers: Lucy Sehgal, Secretary; Lucy Sehgal [1974] Director/Manager; Paul Sehgal [1975] Executive Director; Rakesh Kumar Sehgal [1951] Director

2M Food Suppliers Limited
Incorporated: 16 December 2008
Net Worth: £462,438 *Total Assets:* £2,001,095
Registered Office: Exchange Building, 66 Church Street, Hartlepool, Cleveland, TS24 7DN
Activities: Non-specialised wholesale of food, beverages and tobacco
Major Shareholder: Mousa Abid Mousa
Officers: Mousa Abid Mousa [1975] Director

3 E Investment Ltd
Incorporated: 7 May 1993
Net Worth: £1,674,594 *Total Assets:* £2,212,193
Registered Office: 9 Heritage Gardens, The Walled Garden, High Gosforth Park, Newcastle upon Tyne, NE3 5AF
Activities: Buying and selling of own real estate
Officers: Karen Sau Kin Lau, Secretary; James Win Lau [1996] Director; Karen Sau Kin Lau [1969] Director/Restaurateur

3.13
Incorporated: 4 January 1994 *Employees:* 12
Net Worth: £689,305 *Total Assets:* £809,027
Registered Office: 2 Maria Drive, Stockton on Tees, Cleveland, TS19 7JL
Activities: Other residential care activities n.e.c.
Officers: Heather Bunce, Secretary; Christopher Charles Taylor [1951] Director/Marketing Manager; Paul John Winstone [1958] Director/Professional Engineer; Harry Wrigglesworth [1942] Director/General Manager

3KB Recruitment Group Ltd
Incorporated: 4 September 2014 *Employees:* 5
Net Worth: £75,737 *Total Assets:* £1,334,920
Registered Office: Floor 5, Cathedral Buildings, Dean Street, Newcastle upon Tyne, NE1 1PG
Activities: Temporary employment agency activities
Shareholders: Kieran Paul Beaney; Katherine Louise Beaney
Officers: Katherine Louise Beaney, Secretary; Katherine Louise Beaney [1989] Director/Clerical Assistant; Kieran Paul Beaney [1977] Sales Director

3R Land & Property Ltd
Incorporated: 2 January 1973 *Employees:* 7
Net Worth: £15,216,817 *Total Assets:* £33,746,292
Registered Office: RSM UK Tax and Accounting Limited, 1 St James' Gate, Newcastle upon Tyne, NE1 4AD
Activities: Other letting and operating of own or leased real estate
Major Shareholder: Robert Alexander Fulton
Officers: Robert Alexander Fulton, Secretary; Robert Fulton [1988] Director; Robert Alexander Fulton [1960] Director; Shirley Fulton [1963] Director; Chloe Thompson [1985] Director

4 Cool Technology Limited
Incorporated: 5 March 2004
Net Worth: £542,816 *Total Assets:* £1,392,347
Registered Office: Discovery 1, William Armstong Way, NETPark, Sedgefield, Co Durham, TS21 3FH
Activities: Retail sale via mail order houses or via Internet
Major Shareholder: Michael Armstrong
Officers: Elizabeth Armstrong, Secretary; Micheal John Armstrong [1969] Director

40/46 The Side Newcastle Limited
Incorporated: 12 December 1996 *Employees:* 38
Net Worth: £379,438 *Total Assets:* £937,176
Registered Office: 40-46 The Side, Quayside, Newcastle upon Tyne, NE1 3JA
Activities: Licenced restaurants
Major Shareholder: Paul Luigi Bernardelli
Officers: Paul Luigi Bernardelli [1975] Director/Manager

4B Precision Engineering Ltd
Incorporated: 4 March 2010 *Employees:* 16
Net Worth: £628,257 *Total Assets:* £849,042
Registered Office: 10 Ettrick Grove, High Barnes, Sunderland, Tyne & Wear, SR4 8PZ
Activities: Other engineering activities
Shareholders: Stephen Forbister; Lucy Forbister
Officers: Stephen Forbister [1974] Director

4X4 Accessories & Tyres Limited
Incorporated: 14 August 2002 *Employees:* 33
Net Worth: £5,050,510 *Total Assets:* £8,936,065
Registered Office: Meridian Park, Leeming Bar Industrial Estate, Leeming Bar, N Yorks, DL7 9UN
Activities: Wholesale trade of motor vehicle parts and accessories
Shareholder: Timothy Snowden
Officers: Ian Christopher Robinson [1963] Finance Director; Timothy Snowden [1973] Director

7 Star (North East) Ltd
Incorporated: 20 August 2013
Net Worth: £18,428 *Total Assets:* £1,553,583
Registered Office: 283-285 Marton Road, Middlesbrough, Cleveland, TS4 2HF
Activities: Buying and selling of own real estate
Officers: Mourzzam Ali, Secretary; Azram Ali [1971] Director; Mourzzam Ali [1980] Director; Basharit Hussain [1974] Director; Matloob Hussain Majid [1964] Director

A & K Ecofilm Limited
Incorporated: 15 June 1998 *Employees:* 26
Net Worth: £4,360,311 *Total Assets:* £6,073,447
Registered Office: 31 High Street, Stokesley, Cleveland, TS9 5AD
Activities: Manufacture of plastic packing goods
Major Shareholder: Stewart Andrew
Officers: Janet Andrew, Secretary; Stewart Andrew [1962] Director

A & K Fashions Limited
Incorporated: 12 February 2002 *Employees:* 2
Net Worth: £422,249 *Total Assets:* £1,118,286
Registered Office: 9 Stonehouse Street, Middlesbrough, Cleveland, TS5 6HR
Activities: Retail sale of clothing in specialised stores
Officers: Kulwinder Kaur, Secretary; Kulwinder Kaur [1962] Director/Fashion Manufacturer; Kuldip Singh [1962] Director/Fashion Manufacturer

A & P Falmouth Limited
Incorporated: 29 May 1909 *Employees:* 289
Net Worth: £297,752 *Total Assets:* £25,300,004
Registered Office: c/o A & P Tyne Limited, Wagonway Road, Hebburn, Tyne & Wear, NE31 1SP
Activities: Repair and maintenance of ships and boats
Officers: David Thomas McGinley [1955] Director

A & P Ship Repairers Limited
Incorporated: 30 January 1995
Net Worth: £329,006 *Total Assets:* £3,367,430
Registered Office: c/o A & P Tyne Limited, Wagonway Road, Hebburn, Tyne & Wear, NE31 1SP
Activities: Non-trading company
Officers: David Thomas McGinley [1955] Director

A & P Tees Limited
Incorporated: 3 March 2003 *Employees:* 28
Net Worth: £919,698 *Total Assets:* £4,443,794
Registered Office: c/o A & P Tyne Limited, Wagonway Road, Hebburn, Tyne & Wear, NE31 1SP
Activities: Repair and maintenance of ships and boats
Officers: David Thomas McGinley [1955] Director

A & SA Properties Limited
Incorporated: 23 November 2015
Net Worth: £118,136 *Total Assets:* £2,329,450
Registered Office: 48 Runnymede Road, Ponteland, Northumberland, NE20 9HG
Activities: Other letting and operating of own or leased real estate
Shareholders: Ashok Kumar Aggarwal; Shobha Aggarwal
Officers: Ashok Kumar Aggarwal [1956] Director; Shoba Aggarwal [1959] Director

A D Plant Hire Limited
Incorporated: 25 July 2007 *Employees:* 7
Net Worth: £784,309 *Total Assets:* £2,969,167
Registered Office: Hughes House, Cargo Fleet Road, Middlesbrough, Cleveland, TS3 6AG
Activities: Other business support service activities n.e.c.
Shareholders: Donal James Hughes; Lisa Carmen Hughes
Officers: Lisa Hughes, Secretary; Donal James Hughes [1975] Director; Lisa Carmen Hughes [1977] Director

A E L Systems Ltd
Incorporated: 6 January 2003
Net Worth: £280,123 *Total Assets:* £927,142
Registered Office: Innovation House, Leaside, Aycliffe Business Park, Newton Aycliffe, Co Durham, DL5 6DE
Activities: Security systems service activities
Shareholders: Lee Trevor Willis; Victoria Louise Willis
Officers: Lee Trevor Willis, Secretary; Iain Michael Vipond [1981] Technical Director; Lee Trevor Willis [1973] Director/Manager

A H Engineering (North East) Limited
Incorporated: 22 March 1999 *Employees:* 29
Net Worth: £1,549,237 *Total Assets:* £1,737,024
Registered Office: Unit 5 Wagonway Industrial Estate, Wagonway Road, Hebburn, Tyne & Wear, NE31 1SP
Activities: Manufacture of tools
Major Shareholder: Alan Haynes
Officers: Carolyn Clarke, Secretary; Carolyn Clarke [1965] Director/Teacher; Christopher Clarke [1963] Director/Engineer; Alan Haynes [1937] Director/Engineer

A M I Exchangers Limited
Incorporated: 16 December 1988 *Employees:* 32
Net Worth: £584,060 *Total Assets:* £2,560,535
Registered Office: West Chirton Industrial Estate, Gloucester Road, North Shields, Tyne & Wear, NE29 8RQ
Activities: Repair and maintenance of ships and boats
Parent: Valiant Sheep Limited
Officers: Alan Leslie Gray, Secretary/Accountant; Peter Lindsey Jackson [1941] Director; Nicholas Welford [1970] Sales Director

A P Estates Limited
Incorporated: 22 February 2016
Net Worth: £38,266 *Total Assets:* £1,764,536
Registered Office: 4a Front Street, Sedgefield, Stockton on Tees, Cleveland, TS21 3AT
Activities: Buying and selling of own real estate
Major Shareholder: Alpesh Patel
Officers: Alpesh Patel [1975] Director/Property Management

A&P GH 2006 Limited
Incorporated: 25 June 2001 *Employees:* 6
Net Worth: £5,453,320 *Total Assets:* £20,109,414
Registered Office: c/o A & P Tyne Limited, Wagonway Road, Hebburn, Tyne & Wear, NE31 1SP
Activities: Repair and maintenance of ships and boats
Officers: David Thomas McGinley [1955] Director

A&P Group Limited
Incorporated: 31 May 2006 *Employees:* 513
Net Worth: £13,387,000 *Total Assets:* £54,543,000
Registered Office: c/o A & P Tyne Limited, Wagonway Road, Hebburn, Tyne & Wear, NE31 1SP
Activities: Repair and maintenance of ships and boats
Officers: David Thomas McGinley [1955] Director

A&P Tyne Limited
Incorporated: 13 May 2004 *Employees:* 152
Net Worth: £1,603,134 *Total Assets:* £7,894,445
Registered Office: c/o A & P Tyne Limited, Wagonway Road, Hebburn, Tyne & Wear, NE31 1SP
Activities: Repair and maintenance of ships and boats
Officers: David Thomas McGinley [1955] Director

A-Tech Fabrications Limited
Incorporated: 19 July 1994 *Employees:* 30
Net Worth: £454,875 *Total Assets:* £1,171,639
Registered Office: A-Tech Fabrications Limited, Fulbeck Road, Aycliffe Business Park, Newton Aycliffe, Co Durham, DL5 6TX
Activities: Manufacture of lifting and handling equipment
Major Shareholder: John Manners
Officers: Jennifer Manners, Secretary; John Manners [1957] Director/Businessman; William John Manners [1992] Director/Business Development

A. & A. Carpets Limited
Incorporated: 4 February 1988 *Employees:* 37
Net Worth: £1,041,480 *Total Assets:* £3,320,880
Registered Office: View Logistics, Parkview Road East, Hartlepool, Cleveland, TS25 1HT
Activities: Wholesale of household goods (other than musical instruments) n.e.c
Parent: Whitestone Carpets Holdings Ltd
Officers: Tanya Kelly, Secretary; Stephen Maurice Martin Byrne [1960] Director; Geoffrey Brendon Wilding [1963] Director [New Zealander]

A.C.T Construction Services Limited
Incorporated: 5 June 2003 *Employees:* 35
Net Worth: £1,206,871 *Total Assets:* £1,632,271
Registered Office: 34 Frederick Street, Sunderland, Tyne & Wear, SR1 1LP
Activities: Other building completion and finishing
Shareholders: Alan Charles Thompson; Kim Thompson
Officers: Cavan John McNicholas [1972] Director/Estimator; Alan Charles Thompson [1965] Director/Builder; Debbie Thompson [1996] Director; Martin Charles Thompson [1989] Director/Site Manager

A.E.T. Ltd
Incorporated: 6 November 1997
Net Worth: £274,051 *Total Assets:* £929,805
Registered Office: Todhills Farm, Todhills, Bishop Auckland, Co Durham, DL14 8BB
Activities: Other business support service activities n.e.c.
Major Shareholder: Alan John Etherington
Officers: Alan John Etherington [1961] Director/Farmer

A.H.U.S. Plant Hire Limited
Incorporated: 22 July 2010
Net Worth: £39,489 *Total Assets:* £864,864
Registered Office: 32 Saltwell View, Gateshead, Tyne & Wear, NE8 4NT
Activities: Construction of domestic buildings
Officers: Andrew Matthew Hughes [1970] Director; Tracy Ann Hughes [1971] Director

A.L.M. Products Limited
Incorporated: 30 March 1994 *Employees:* 36
Net Worth: £423,270 *Total Assets:* £2,085,492
Registered Office: Grindon Way, Heighington Lane Business Park, Newton Aycliffe, Co Durham, DL5 6SH
Activities: Manufacture of locks and hinges
Shareholders: Anthony William Thompson; Lesley Thompson
Officers: Lesley Thompson, Secretary; Anthony William Thompson [1962] Managing Director; Lesley Thompson [1968] Director

A.M. Fabrication (Northern) Limited
Incorporated: 4 February 1999 *Employees:* 76
Net Worth: £989,031 *Total Assets:* £2,698,290
Registered Office: Unit 1 Franklin Industrial Estate, Patterson Street, Blaydon Haugh, Tyne & Wear, NE21 5TL
Activities: Manufacture of other fabricated metal products n.e.c.
Parent: Consolidated Structures Ltd
Officers: Anthony Peter Nichol, Secretary; Anthony Peter Nichol [1956] Director; James Benjamin Race [1980] Commercial Director; Matthew Reed [1990] Director; Peter Hugh Bellairs Sykes [1956] Director; Michael John Trueman [1959] Director

A.M. Strategy Limited
Incorporated: 6 November 2006 *Employees:* 1
Net Worth: £2,710,824 *Total Assets:* £5,104,259
Registered Office: 3 Batt House Road, Stocksfield, Northumberland, NE43 7QZ
Activities: Other business support service activities n.e.c.
Major Shareholder: Alan Milburn
Officers: Alan Milburn, Secretary; Dr Ruth Cordelia Garnet Briel [1963] Director; Alan Milburn [1958] Director

A.T. & P Rentals Ltd.
Incorporated: 28 November 1988
Net Worth: £6,368,787 *Total Assets:* £7,707,567
Registered Office: Clevestone Works, Whitby Road, Guisborough, Cleveland, TS14 6PZ
Activities: Renting and leasing of construction and civil engineering machinery and equipment
Officers: Charles Joseph Leonard, Secretary; Charles Joseph Leonard [1964] Director/Engineer; Michael Patrick Leonard [1968] Director/Engineer

A1 Alpha Properties (Leicester) Limited
Incorporated: 16 February 2001 *Employees:* 4
Net Worth: £482,958 *Total Assets:* £1,460,923
Registered Office: Valley House, Seventh Avenue, Team Valley Trading Estate, Gateshead, Tyne & Wear, NE11 0JW
Activities: Buying and selling of own real estate
Officers: Derek Arthur Kewley [1973] Director; Nicholas John Spence [1972] Director/Mechanical Engineer; Peter Sullivan [1963] Director

A1 Environmental Services Ltd.
Incorporated: 5 November 1996 *Employees:* 21
Net Worth: £2,486,456 *Total Assets:* £2,934,331
Registered Office: The Paddock, 4 Low Green, Catterick Village, Richmond, N Yorks, DL10 7RZ
Activities: Demolition
Shareholders: Robert Knowles; Danuta Anna Knowles; Michael Knowles
Officers: Danuta Anna Knowles, Company Secretary; Danuta Anna Knowles [1953] Director/Company Secretary; Robert Knowles [1956] Director

A1 Industrial Trucks Limited
Incorporated: 30 March 1990 *Employees:* 24
Net Worth: £2,023,033 *Total Assets:* £2,587,074
Registered Office: Riverside Works, Shelley Road, Newburn Industrial Estate, Newburn, Newcastle upon Tyne, NE15 9RT
Activities: Agents involved in the sale of machinery, industrial equipment, ships and aircraft
Parent: Northern Bear PLC
Officers: Wendy Ann Edgell, Secretary; Graham Roy Jennings [1956] Director; Steven Mark Roberts [1966] Director; Keith Soulsby [1956] Director

The A1 Steam Locomotive Trust
Incorporated: 12 August 1991
Net Worth: £4,094,087 *Total Assets:* £4,189,155
Registered Office: Darlington Locomotive Works, Hopetown Lane, Darlington, Co Durham, DL3 6RQ
Activities: Manufacture of railway locomotives and rolling stock
Officers: David Erwyn Burgess, Secretary; Mark Colin Allatt [1965] Director/Public Relations Manager; Paul Andrew Bruce [1961] Director/Railway Consultant; Graeme Bunker [1974] Director; David Erwyn Burgess [1948] Director/Trust Manager; David Andrew Elliott [1951] Director/Consulting Engineer; Graham Philip Langer [1961] Director/Farmer; Robert John Morland [1955] Director/Consulting Engineer; James Christopher Walker [1943] Director/Retired

A19 Properties Limited
Incorporated: 7 December 2012
Net Worth: £123,160 *Total Assets:* £1,221,015
Registered Office: Beaumont Accountancy Services, First Floor, Enterprise House, 202-206 Linthorpe Road, Middlesbrough, Cleveland, TS1 3QW
Activities: Other letting and operating of own or leased real estate
Major Shareholder: Peter John McGee
Officers: Peter John McGee [1970] Director

A2 Screen Print Limited
Incorporated: 22 February 1999
Net Worth: £2,136,193 *Total Assets:* £5,343,987
Registered Office: Bridge End Works, Ryhope Road, Ryhope, Sunderland, Tyne & Wear, SR2 0NJ
Activities: Management consultancy activities other than financial management
Officers: Linda Gray, Secretary; Linda Gray [1953] Director; Malcolm Robin Gray [1950] Director/Printer; Joseph Edward Laidler [1939] Director

A2M Developments Limited
Incorporated: 26 March 2010
Net Worth: £461,051 *Total Assets:* £1,653,938
Registered Office: UGC House, 136-170 Shields Road, Newcastle upon Tyne, NE6 1DT
Activities: Development of building projects
Major Shareholder: Jagmohan Malhotra
Officers: Rajiv Vadhera [1975] Director

A690 Specialist Cars Limited
Incorporated: 10 December 2008 *Employees:* 12
Net Worth: £347,356 *Total Assets:* £914,382
Registered Office: Belmont Bridge, Carville, Co Durham, DH1 1LU
Activities: Sale of used cars and light motor vehicles
Shareholders: Philip Oldroyd; Joy Oldroyd
Officers: Riad Ketani [1982] Director; Jamie Oldroyd [1984] Director; Joy Oldroyd [1960] Director; Philip Oldroyd [1961] Director

AA Construction (Holdings) Limited
Incorporated: 6 July 2016
Net Worth: £4,408 *Total Assets:* £1,300,001
Registered Office: Highway House, Saltmeadows Road, Gateshead, Tyne & Wear, NE8 3AH
Activities: Activities of other holding companies n.e.c.
Major Shareholder: Ali Attarchian
Officers: Ali Attarchian [1957] Director

AA Construction (North East) Ltd
Incorporated: 13 March 2008 *Employees:* 4
Net Worth: £375,347 *Total Assets:* £2,476,606
Registered Office: Highway House, Saltmeadows Road, Gateshead, Tyne & Wear, NE8 3AH
Activities: Construction of commercial buildings
Major Shareholder: Ali Attarchian
Officers: Carol Attarchian, Secretary; Ali Attarchian [1957] Director/Chartered Civil Engineer

AA Construction Utilities Ltd
Incorporated: 22 June 2010 *Employees:* 21
Net Worth: £1,882,420 *Total Assets:* £5,866,816
Registered Office: Wesley Way, Benton Square Industrial Estate, Newcastle upon Tyne, NE12 9TA
Activities: Construction of roads and motorways
Shareholders: Michael Thorburn; Julie Wilson
Officers: Julie Wilson [1971] Director

AAA Property (North East) Limited
Incorporated: 3 October 2007
Net Worth: £598,382 *Total Assets:* £1,749,315
Registered Office: 4a Front Street, Sedgefield, Stockton on Tees, Cleveland, TS21 3AT
Activities: Buying and selling of own real estate
Officers: Alison Margaret Stephenson, Secretary; Alison Margaret Stephenson [1983] Director/Administrator; Richard Hamlyn Tucker [1958] Director

AAF-McQuay UK Limited
Incorporated: 14 September 1988 *Employees:* 6
Net Worth: £7,871,000 *Total Assets:* £40,142,000
Registered Office: Bassington Lane, Cramlington, Northumberland, NE23 8AF
Activities: Activities of head offices
Parent: Daikin Holdings America Inc
Officers: Ian Phillip Creasey, Secretary; Darren Allsopp [1969] Director; Voon Ping Chen [1965] Director/Corporate Controller [Malaysian]; Ian Phillip Creasey [1961] Director/Accountant; Benny Woon Khin Liow [1957] Director [Malaysian]; Alan Dale Proffitt [1972] Director/Corporate Controller [American]; Katsuhiko Takagi [1943] Director [Japanese]

AAM & Sons Limited
Incorporated: 11 May 2004 *Employees:* 60
Net Worth: £575,764 *Total Assets:* £772,066
Registered Office: Cheeky Monkees Day Nursery, 161 Durham Road, Stockton on Tees, Cleveland, TS19 0DS
Activities: Pre-primary education
Shareholders: Andrew Alan Mehegan; Angela Mehegan
Officers: Angela Mehegan, Secretary; Andrew Alan Mehegan [1966] Director/Child Care; Angela Mehegan [1968] Director/Childcare

Aanco (UK) Limited
Incorporated: 13 December 1983 *Employees:* 93
Net Worth: £1,865,763 *Total Assets:* £4,720,753
Registered Office: Unit 5a Limeoak Way, St Annes Industrial Estate, Stockton on Tees, Cleveland, TS18 2LS
Activities: Manufacture of other plastic products
Shareholder: Bradley John Gaunt
Officers: Carol Lynn Gaunt, Secretary; Austin Richard Gaunt [1946] Director/Company Chairman; Bradley John Gaunt [1982] Managing Director; Carol Lynn Gaunt [1948] Director/Company Secretary

AAP Metal Fabrication Services Ltd
Incorporated: 16 April 2009 *Employees:* 33
Net Worth: £460,864 *Total Assets:* £1,116,032
Registered Office: Bedesway, Bede Trading Estate, Jarrow, Tyne & Wear, NE32 3EG
Activities: Manufacture of metal structures and parts of structures
Shareholder: Paul Vincent Bradley
Officers: Paul Vincent Bradley, Secretary; Paul Vincent Bradley [1959] Director/Engineer; Dean William Close [1965] Director; William Dixon Close [1943] Director

Aardvarc Electrical Engineers Limited
Incorporated: 5 April 2006 *Employees:* 14
Net Worth: £253,489 *Total Assets:* £1,063,752
Registered Office: Unit 4 West Quay Court, West Quay Road, Sunderland, Tyne & Wear, SR5 2TE
Activities: Electrical installation
Officers: Andrea Claire Miller, Secretary; Stuart Danial Stephen [1971] Director

Aavid Thermacore Europe Limited
Incorporated: 29 January 1998 *Employees:* 66
Net Worth: £2,327,763 *Total Assets:* £3,890,611
Registered Office: 12 Wansbeck Business Park, Rotary Parkway, Ashington, Northumberland, NE63 8QW
Activities: Machining
Officers: Eric Karel Struik, Secretary; Mitchell Franklin Aiello [1961] Director [American]; Eric Karel Struik [1968] Director [American]

Abbey Plant Ltd
Incorporated: 25 January 2013
Net Worth: £560,628 *Total Assets:* £811,459
Registered Office: Abbey Plant Ltd, Tyne Mills, Hexham, Northumberland, NE46 1XL
Activities: Renting and leasing of construction and civil engineering machinery and equipment
Shareholders: Joseph William Brown; Daniel Joseph Brown
Officers: Daniel Joseph Brown [1977] Director/Plant; Joseph William Brown [1956] Director/Plant

Abbeyfield (Darlington) Society Limited (The)
Incorporated: 8 December 1970 *Employees:* 12
Net Worth: £2,274,787 *Total Assets:* £2,287,986
Registered Office: 7-8 Priestgate, Darlington, Co Durham, DL1 1NL
Activities: Residential care activities for the elderly and disabled
Officers: Dr Trevor Birnie [1948] Director/Physician - Retired; David Aneurin Bodycombe [1945] Director/Chartered Secretary; Thomas William Harrison [1946] Director/Solicitor; Reverend David James Railton [1966] Director/Clerk in Holy Orders; Heather Irene Scott [1940] Director/Retired; Carole Anne Sobkowiak [1942] Director/Retired; David Lindesay Steel [1952] Director/Chartered Accountant; Judith Watson [1945] Director/Housewife

Abbeyfield Newcastle upon Tyne Society Limited (The)
Incorporated: 12 September 1961 *Employees:* 57
Net Worth: £3,508,723 *Total Assets:* £3,983,864
Registered Office: 40a The Grove, Gosforth, Newcastle upon Tyne, NE3 1NH
Activities: Residential care activities for the elderly and disabled
Officers: William Kevin Parrish, Secretary; Marion Jean Anderson [1938] Director/Retired Administrator; Brian Duell [1936] Director/Retired Foreman Joiner; Carole Lesley Eke [1943] Director/Retired; Anthony William Kay [1965] Director/Chartered Surveyor; Raymond Mackintosh [1934] Director/Retired; Vera Rose Wilkinson [1954] Director/Retired Headteacher

G. Abbott & Co. Limited
Incorporated: 18 October 1982 *Employees:* 14
Net Worth: £2,035,409 *Total Assets:* £2,136,394
Registered Office: The Mansion House, Sheraton, Castle Eden, Co Durham, TS27 4RB
Activities: Other construction installation
Parent: G Abbott & Company (Holdings) Limited
Officers: Norma Abbott, Secretary; Norma Abbott [1951] Director/Company Secretary

Abca Systems Limited
Incorporated: 27 June 2007 *Employees:* 156
Net Worth: £2,563,187 *Total Assets:* £5,328,557
Registered Office: Unit 24 Mylord Crescent, Camperdown Industrial Estate, Killingworth, Tyne & Wear, NE12 5UJ
Activities: Electrical installation
Shareholders: Philip James Miller; Peter Miller
Officers: Philip James Miller, Secretary; Peter Miller [1951] Director; Philip James Miller [1980] Director/Businessman; Christopher Scott [1979] Director

Abel Yachts Limited
Incorporated: 1 October 2014 *Employees:* 3
Net Worth Deficit: £1,109,490 *Total Assets:* £2,680,046
Registered Office: Citygate, St James' Boulevard, Newcastle upon Tyne, NE1 4JE
Activities: Building of pleasure and sporting boats
Shareholders: Arthur McQuade Hughes; Geoffrey Ronald Mayhill; Don Marshall
Officers: Arthur McQuade Hughes [1952] Director; Geoffrey Ronald Mayhill [1958] Director/Lawyer; Grant Richard Willis [1962] Director

Aberwood Developments Limited
Incorporated: 2 February 1994 *Employees:* 2
Net Worth: £1,178,949 *Total Assets:* £1,205,418
Registered Office: 379 Norton Road, Stockton on Tees, Cleveland, TS20 2PJ
Activities: Other letting and operating of own or leased real estate
Major Shareholder: Norman Woodall
Officers: Karen Ann Hallam, Company Secretary; Karen Ann Hallam [1957] Director/Property Manager; Norman Woodall [1950] Director/Property Developer

Ability Supplies UK Limited
Incorporated: 16 August 2005 *Employees:* 26
Net Worth: £1,021,464 *Total Assets:* £1,246,933
Registered Office: 5 Frontier Court, Claymere Road, Leechmere Industrial Estate, Sunderland, Tyne & Wear, SR2 9TX
Activities: Wholesale of hardware, plumbing and heating equipment and supplies
Parent: Bowcroft Commerce Ltd
Officers: Nicola Sanderson, Secretary; Nicola Sanderson [1973] Director; Owen Sanderson [1972] Managing Director

Able Construction (Northern) Limited
Incorporated: 27 June 1997 *Employees:* 18
Net Worth: £1,574,244 *Total Assets:* £1,991,108
Registered Office: Park Works, Sunderland Road, Felling, Gateshead, Tyne & Wear, NE10 9LR
Activities: Other building completion and finishing
Parent: Able Holdings (Northern) Limited
Officers: Peter Fowle, Secretary/Building Contractor; Pauline Fowle [1957] Director/Building Contractor; Peter Fowle [1956] Director/Building Contractor

Able UK Limited
Incorporated: 18 May 1989 *Employees:* 75
Net Worth: £482,915,008 *Total Assets:* £508,078,016
Registered Office: Able House, Billingham Reach Industrial Estate, Haverton Hill Road, Billingham, Cleveland, TS23 1PX
Activities: Remediation activities and other waste management services
Major Shareholder: Peter Melvin Stephenson
Officers: Karen Jewers, Secretary; Richard Michael Cram [1960] Engineering Director; Neil Francis Etherington [1957] Business Development Director; Andrew Jacques [1978] Operations Director; Christopher Patrick McManus [1965] Director/Chief Operating Officer; Peter Melvin Stephenson [1947] Director; Rachel Stephenson [1969] Director/Company Secretary

Abletransfer Limited
Incorporated: 26 January 1994 *Employees:* 62
Net Worth: £751,977 *Total Assets:* £2,232,964
Registered Office: Kitching Road, North West Industrial Estate, Peterlee, Co Durham, SR8 2HP
Activities: Freight transport by road
Shareholder: Ian Lawson
Officers: Lee John Lawson, Secretary; William Graham Giles [1957] Sales Director; Ian Lawson [1973] Director/Transport Logistics; Lee John Lawson [1977] Director/Company Secretary; Heidi Rochester [1966] Director/Financial Controller

C F Abraham Limited
Incorporated: 7 January 1960 *Employees:* 4
Net Worth: £5,199,800 *Total Assets:* £9,154,377
Registered Office: Hall Garth, Carperby, Leyburn, N Yorks, DL8 4DQ
Activities: Maintenance and repair of motor vehicles
Officers: Roger Fenwick Abraham, Secretary; Andrew James Abraham [1970] Director/Engineer; Anthony Fell Poad Abraham [1943] Director; Charles Thomas Fenwick Abraham [1974] Director/Solicitor; Roger Fenwick Abraham [1945] Director/Electrical Engineer

Abri Trading Limited
Incorporated: 10 September 2015
Net Worth: £1,518,000 *Total Assets:* £7,121,000
Registered Office: YHN House, Benton Park Road, Newcastle upon Tyne, NE7 7LX
Activities: Retail of furniture, lighting, and similar (not musical instruments or scores) in specialised store
Parent: Your Homes Newcastle Limited
Officers: Jill Louise Davison, Secretary; Joyce McCarty [1953] Director/Education Advisor; Malcolm Douglas Page [1967] Director/Chief Operating Officer; Paul William Scope [1975] Director/Solicitor

ABS Precision Limited
Incorporated: 17 May 2004 *Employees:* 41
Net Worth: £952,860 *Total Assets:* £2,036,073
Registered Office: 1 Bellway Industrial Estate, Benton, Newcastle upon Tyne, NE12 9SW
Activities: Manufacture of other general-purpose machinery n.e.c.
Shareholders: Brian Brooks; Maurice Atherton; David Stott
Officers: Maurice Atherton, Secretary; Maurice Atherton [1960] Director/Manufacturing Engineer; Brian Brooks [1960] Director/Works Manager; David Stott [1958] Works Director

Absolute Civil Engineering Limited
Incorporated: 1 February 2008 *Employees:* 25
Net Worth: £2,843,149 *Total Assets:* £4,104,023
Registered Office: Mill House, Hownsgill Industrial Park, Consett, Co Durham, DH8 7NU
Activities: Development of building projects
Shareholders: Ann Short; Roland Mark Short
Officers: Richard John Emmerson, Secretary; Patrick Lynch [1964] Director/Civil Engineer; Roland Mark Short [1966] Director/Civil Engineer

Absolute Medicals Limited
Incorporated: 3 November 2004
Net Worth: £162,631 *Total Assets:* £1,081,559
Registered Office: The Cube, Barrack Road, Newcastle upon Tyne, NE4 6DB
Activities: Financial intermediation not elsewhere classified
Parent: Maymask (158) Limited
Officers: Philip Ian Ridley [1962] Director/Practice Manager

Absolute Pleasure Limited
Incorporated: 19 September 2007
Net Worth: £777,386 *Total Assets:* £2,720,717
Registered Office: Flat 40, Low Friar House, Low Friar Street, Newcastle upon Tyne, NE1 5UF
Activities: Sea and coastal passenger water transport
Shareholders: Sheila Winnifred Quadrini; Valerie Ann Stanley
Officers: Sheila Winnifred Quadrini, Secretary/Director; Valerie Ann Stanley, Secretary; Michael Angelo Mario Quadrini [1943] Director; Sheila Winnifred Quadrini [1943] Director

The Academic Health Science Network for The North East and North Cumbria Limited
Incorporated: 10 October 2013 *Employees:* 17
Total Assets: £3,458,348
Registered Office: Loftus House, Colima Avenue, Sunderland Enterprise Park, Sunderland, Tyne & Wear, SR5 3XD
Activities: Other human health activities
Officers: Stephanie Frances Walton, Secretary; Arnab Basu [1973] Director; Ken Bremner [1961] Director/Chief Executive; Professor David John Burn [1961] Director/Pro-Vice-Chancellor, Faculty of Medical Sciences; Dr Mark Richard Dornan [1975] Director/GP/Chair of Newcastle Gateshead CCG; Alan Foster [1957] Director/Chief Executive; Marion Wilson McGeachie Grieves [1954] Director/Dean, School of Health & Social Care; John James Lawlor [1961] Director/Chief Executive; Professor Rosemary Jane MacNaughton [1960] Director/University Professor and Physician; Siobhan Marie McArdle [1968] Director/Chief Executive; Dr Seamus O'Neill [1966] Director; Janet Linda Probert [1963] Director/Accountable Officer for NHS Hambleton, Richmondshire; Dr Jonathan Smith [1979] Director/Doctor

Academy 360
Incorporated: 5 June 2007 *Employees:* 122
Net Worth: £22,147,000 *Total Assets:* £23,999,000
Registered Office: Suite 2, Level 3, St Nicholas Building, St Nicholas Street, Newcastle upon Tyne, NE1 1RF
Activities: Primary education
Officers: Peter Snowdon, Secretary; Christopher Roy Pennison [1999] Director; Simon Walker [1967] Director/General Counsel

Accredited Processed Metals Limited
Incorporated: 4 February 1977 *Employees:* 8
Net Worth: £2,851,073 *Total Assets:* £3,673,114
Registered Office: Stockton House, Grangefield Road, Stockton on Tees, Cleveland, TS18 4AB
Activities: Recovery of sorted materials
Shareholders: James David Turner; David Brian Turner
Officers: James David Turner, Secretary; David Brian Turner [1959] Director; James David Turner [1990] Director

Ace Aluminium & Architectural Services Ltd
Incorporated: 17 October 2011
Net Worth: £732,275 *Total Assets:* £1,613,715
Registered Office: Acklam Hall, Hall Drive, Acklam, Middlesbrough, Cleveland, TS5 7DY
Activities: Glazing
Major Shareholder: Andrew Clifford Platts
Officers: Andrew Clifford Platts [1975] Director/Window & Glass Installation & Project Management

Aceda Limited
Incorporated: 21 October 2002
Net Worth: £286,793 *Total Assets:* £932,322
Registered Office: Ellerbeck House, Ellerbeck Way, Stokesley Industrial Estate, Stokesley, Cleveland, TS9 5JZ
Activities: Other information technology service activities
Major Shareholder: Colin Nicholas Harker
Officers: Susan Pearce, Secretary; Colin Nicholas Harker [1966] Director/Electrical Engineer; Susan Pearce [1956] Director; Paul Warnes [1968] Director/Manager

Acer Learning Trust
Incorporated: 26 July 2012 *Employees:* 35
Net Worth: £1,676,000 *Total Assets:* £2,056,000
Registered Office: Ayton Road, Oxclose, Washington, Tyne & Wear, NE38 0LR
Activities: Primary education
Officers: Glenda Wood, Secretary; Victoria Brown [1968] Director; Richard Chamberlain [1972] Director; Glenn Stephen Cue [1983] Director; David Christopher Dent [1978] Director/Teacher; Douglass Green [1949] Director/Self Employed; David Haw [1954] Director; Sharon Richards [1959] Director/Headteacher; Tricia Steele [1967] Director/Customer Solutions Leader; Glenda Wood [1969] Director/Business Manager

Aceviral.Com Ltd
Incorporated: 20 August 2010 *Employees:* 19
Net Worth: £5,223,546 *Total Assets:* £5,531,400
Registered Office: 16 Birchwood, Sunderland, Tyne & Wear, SR4 0AP
Activities: Other software publishing
Shareholders: Mohammed Shazad; Nosheen Ghafoor
Officers: Nosheen Ghafoor [1983] Director/Software Engineer; Mohammed Shazad [1977] Director/Software Engineer

Achieving Real Change in Communities CIC
Incorporated: 6 February 2014 *Employees:* 177
Net Worth: £2,098,219 *Total Assets:* £6,120,542
Registered Office: Wetherby House, Wetherby Close, Portrack Interchange Business Park, Stockton on Tees, Cleveland, TS18 2SL
Activities: Justice and judicial activities
Officers: John David Bentley [1951] Director/Chief Executive; Julie Danks [1964] Director/Local Government Officer; Sean Duffy [1969] Director/Chief Executive; David Edward Levy [1961] Director/NHS Manager; Michael Maiden [1953] Director/Consultant; Jeanette Redgwell [1971] Director/Probation Manager; John Sampson [1965] Director of Corporate Services; Christine Smith [1962] Managing Director; Sir Peter Vardy [1947] Director/Company Chairman; Christopher Paul Wildsmith [1959] Director

Acklam Car Centre Limited
Incorporated: 5 March 2001 *Employees:* 31
Net Worth: £2,179,699 *Total Assets:* £2,502,589
Registered Office: 237 Acklam Road, Middlesbrough, Cleveland, TS5 7AB
Activities: Sale of used cars and light motor vehicles
Major Shareholder: Kirk Andrews
Officers: Pauline Elizabeth Andrews, Secretary; Kirk Andrews [1970] Director

Acklam Park Limited Liability Partnership
Incorporated: 26 March 2008
Net Worth: £1,530,767 *Total Assets:* £1,560,374
Registered Office: Acklam Park, Green Lane, Middlesbrough, Cleveland, TS5 7SL
Officers: Peter Bates [1944] Member; Keith Bircham [1946] Member; Donald Brydon [1942] Member; Laurence Davison [1942] Member; Phillip Tilson [1970] Member

Aclet Property Management & Services Limited
Incorporated: 24 November 1999 *Employees:* 3
Net Worth Deficit: £988,003 *Total Assets:* £3,294,353
Registered Office: Sherwood, 4 Watling Road, Bishop Auckland, Co Durham, DL14 6RP
Activities: Buying and selling of own real estate
Major Shareholder: Leslie Wood
Officers: Diane Wood, Secretary; Diane Wood [1955] Director/Administrator; Harry Wood [1984] Director/Property Consultant; Leslie Wood [1952] Director/Housing Consultant

Acomb Construction Limited
Incorporated: 9 October 1991 *Employees:* 15
Net Worth: £160,325 *Total Assets:* £822,766
Registered Office: 63 Mercury Road, Gallowfields Trading Estate, Richmond, N Yorks, DL10 4TQ
Activities: Development of building projects
Shareholders: David Patrick Phillips; Lynette Phillips
Officers: Lynette Mary Phillips, Secretary; David Patrick Phillips [1954] Director (Builder)

Aconpex (UK) Limited
Incorporated: 29 May 1990 *Employees:* 12
Net Worth: £956,887 *Total Assets:* £1,191,998
Registered Office: Glenshele House, Westwood Road, Scroggwood, Bardon Mill, Northumberland, NE47 7JQ
Activities: Repair of machinery
Shareholders: Joan Catherine West; James Burns West
Officers: Joan Catherine West, Secretary; James Burns West [1953] Director; Joan Catherine West [1954] Secretary/Director

Acorn Developments (Kirkby) Limited
Incorporated: 13 April 2007 *Employees:* 2
Net Worth: £1,772,984 *Total Assets:* £3,357,635
Registered Office: c/o International Processplants (Europe), Postal Pages, The Grange Business Centre, Belasis Avenue, Billingham, Cleveland, TS23 1LG
Activities: Development of building projects
Shareholder: Vincent Ryan
Officers: Anthony Stephen Field, Secretary; Anthony Stephen Field [1957] Director; Stanley W Sackowitz [1956] Director/Real Estate Management [American]

Acorn Laser Limited
Incorporated: 2 October 1998 *Employees:* 35
Net Worth: £1,217,252 *Total Assets:* £1,830,782
Registered Office: 3 Armstrong Road, Washington, Tyne & Wear, NE37 1PR
Activities: Manufacture of other fabricated metal products n.e.c.
Major Shareholder: Graeme Robert Deanus
Officers: Graeme Robert Deanus [1962] Director/Engineer

Acornford (Kensington) Limited
Incorporated: 12 July 2001 *Employees:* 3
Net Worth: £1,024,878 *Total Assets:* £1,222,169
Registered Office: Tower Buildings, 9 Oldgate, Morpeth, Northumberland, NE61 1PY
Activities: Other letting and operating of own or leased real estate
Shareholders: Ian Charles Cawkwell; Neil Lyndon Yeomans; Sidney Latham
Officers: Paul Andrew Brown, Secretary; Ian Charles Cawkwell [1957] Director; Earle Sidney Latham [1953] Director/Surveyor; Neil Lyndon Yeomans [1958] Director/Surveyor

Acrol Air Conditioning Co. Limited
Incorporated: 25 November 1976 *Employees:* 35
Net Worth: £334,992 *Total Assets:* £1,253,318
Registered Office: Unit 12 Saltmeadows Road, East Gateshead Industrial Estate, Gateshead, Tyne & Wear, NE8 3AH
Activities: Other business support service activities n.e.c.
Shareholders: Michael John Kears; Tom Wood
Officers: Michael John Kears, Secretary/Director; Michael John Kears [1959] Director; Thomas Wood [1954] Director

ACS Invest UK Limited
Incorporated: 8 June 2012
Net Worth: £13,232 *Total Assets:* £10,047,318
Registered Office: 2 Bedford Terrace, North Shields, Tyne & Wear, NE29 0AW
Activities: Activities of financial services holding companies
Officers: Konstantina Athanasopoulou [1956] Director/Entrepreneur [Greek]; Apostolos Georgantzis [1968] Director/Businessman [Greek]; Konstantinos Menegakis [1961] Director/Businessman [Greek]; Evangelos Roussos [1959] Director/Businessman [Greek]

Act Response Ltd
Incorporated: 6 October 1998 *Employees:* 35
Net Worth: £707,732 *Total Assets:* £1,094,972
Registered Office: 384 Linthorpe Road, Middlesbrough, Cleveland, TS5 6HA
Activities: Security systems service activities
Parent: Advanced Consumer Technology Limited
Officers: Brian Boston [1981] Director; Mark Sullivan [1981] Director

Actdesign (UK) Ltd
Incorporated: 19 August 2014
Net Worth: £735,572 *Total Assets:* £851,397
Registered Office: c/o Womble Bond Dickinson (UK) LLP, St Ann's Wharf, 112 Quayside, Newcastle upon Tyne, NE1 3DX
Activities: Business and domestic software development
Major Shareholder: Alex Charles Thompson
Officers: Alex Charles Thompson [1993] Director

Actes Trust
Incorporated: 24 December 2001 *Employees:* 38
Net Worth: £7,021,019 *Total Assets:* £7,209,431
Registered Office: 99 Acklam Road, Acklam, Middlesbrough, Cleveland, TS5 5HR
Activities: Other business support service activities n.e.c.
Officers: Geoffrey Donald Payne, Secretary/Accountant; James William Cooper [1955] Director/Welder; Geoffrey Donald Payne [1954] Director/Accountant; Charles Michael Rooney [1954] Director/Councillor; Sharon Stuttard [1961] Director/School Administrator

Action 4 Equality (Scotland) Limited
Incorporated: 8 June 2005 *Employees:* 1
Net Worth: £3,177,714 *Total Assets:* £3,312,698
Registered Office: Joseph Miller & Co, Floor A, Milburn House, Dean Street, Newcastle upon Tyne, NE1 1LE
Activities: Other service activities n.e.c.
Shareholders: Stefan Tylney Cross; Dr Alison Mary Steele
Officers: Dr Alison Mary Steele, Secretary; Anna Louise Cross [1991] Director/Solicitor; Michael Tylney Cross [1996] Director; Rachel Elizabeth Cross [1993] Director/Medical Student; Stefan Tylney Cross [1960] Director/Solicitor

Activ Technology Limited
Incorporated: 29 April 2006
Net Worth Deficit: £638,873 *Total Assets:* £1,369,791
Registered Office: Hadrian House, Balliol Business Park, Benton Lane, Newcastle upon Tyne, NE12 8EW
Activities: Wireless telecommunications activities
Shareholders: Ian William Gillespie; Lynne Gillespie
Officers: Michael James Hearns, Secretary; Ian William Gillespie [1959] Director; Lynne Gillespie [1965] Director

Active Northumberland
Incorporated: 11 April 2013 *Employees:* 986
Net Worth Deficit: £3,093,714 *Total Assets:* £3,336,169
Registered Office: Blyth Sports Centre, Bolam Park, Blyth, Northumberland, NE24 5BT
Activities: Library activities
Officers: Peter Stonell, Secretary; William Kenneth Dunbar [1960] Director/Consultant; Noel Anthony Gates [1965] Director/Chief Executive [Irish]; David Hall [1966] Director/Head of Leisure, Strategy and Transformation; Councillor Catherine Robson Homer [1967] Director/Northumberland County Council Councillor; James Anthony Murray [1986] Director/Consultant; Judith Stonebridge [1965] Director/Acting Consultant Public Health; Judith Stonebridge [1965] Director/Acting Consultant Public Health

Actuant Operations UK Limited
Incorporated: 8 January 1965 *Employees:* 28
Net Worth: £2,539,589 *Total Assets:* £5,672,926
Registered Office: 5 Coopies Lane, Morpeth, Northumberland, NE61 6JR
Activities: Non-specialised wholesale trade
Parent: Actuant Corporation
Officers: Nicholas James Gemmell, Secretary; Willem Robert Daniel Bakkum [1967] Director [Dutch]; Antony Lloyd Mather [1965] Director/Manager; Richard Martin Roman [1971] Finance Director [American]; Geert Jan Van Der Heijden [1966] Director/EMEA Finance Leader [Dutch]

Acumen Investigation Services Ltd.
Incorporated: 16 January 1997 *Employees:* 8
Net Worth: £700,073 *Total Assets:* £826,164
Registered Office: 16 Kirby's Drive, Chestnut Walk Estate, Bowburn, Co Durham, DH6 5GA
Activities: Investigation activities
Shareholders: Ian Grey; William Harbottle
Officers: Marian Grey, Secretary; Ian Grey [1963] Managing Director; Marian Grey [1938] Director/Retired RGN/Secretary; William Harbottle [1947] Director/Accountant

AD Astra Academy Trust
Incorporated: 12 November 2014 *Employees:* 270
Net Worth: £13,960,000 *Total Assets:* £16,308,000
Registered Office: West View Primary School, Davison Drive, Hartlepool, Cleveland, TS24 9BP
Activities: Primary education
Officers: Andrew Appleton Brown [1957] Director/Headteacher; Garry Brown [1975] Managing Director; Revd Canon Graeme Buttery [1962] Director/Clerk in Holy Orders; Stephen Hall [1960] Non-Executive Director NHS; Adrian Charles Anthony Morris [1964] Director/Solicitor; Albert Pattison [1958] Director; Raymond Priestman [1959] Director/Chartered Accountant; Christopher James Simmons [1944] Director/Retired; Andrew Steel [1962] Director/Assistant Principal

Adamms Wholesale Carpets Limited
Incorporated: 6 March 2000 *Employees:* 11
Net Worth: £902,172 *Total Assets:* £1,236,914
Registered Office: Unit 3 Bugatti Industrial Park, Norham Road, North Shields, Tyne & Wear, NE29 7AH
Activities: Non-specialised wholesale trade
Major Shareholder: Adam Hewett
Officers: Adam Hewett [1963] Director

J. R. Adams (Newcastle) Limited
Incorporated: 19 September 1955 *Employees:* 63
Net Worth: £4,018,699 *Total Assets:* £5,863,681
Registered Office: Hannington Works, Longrigg, Swalwell, Gateshead, Tyne & Wear, NE16 3AS
Activities: Freight transport by road
Shareholders: James Robertson Adams; James Robertson Adams
Officers: James Robertson Adams Jnr, Secretary; Brenda Ann Margaret Adams [1936] Director; Caron Michelle Adams [1963] Director/Accounts; John Robert Adams [1959] Director/Haulage Contractor; Lesley Susan Adams [1956] Director/Credit Controller; James Robertson Adams Jnr [1933] Director/Transport Contractor; James Robertson Adams Minor [1957] Director/Transport Contractor; Kim Henderson [1967] Director/Secretary; Dawn Holmes [1954] Director/Secretary

Adams Jenkins Properties Limited
Incorporated: 23 September 2011
Net Worth: £200,213 *Total Assets:* £1,293,038
Registered Office: 1 Starbeck Avenue, Newcastle upon Tyne, NE2 1RJ
Activities: Development of building projects
Shareholders: David George Jenkins; Alastair David Adams
Officers: Alastair David Adams [1984] Director/Landlord; David George Jenkins [1987] Director/Landlord

Adapt (North East)
Incorporated: 28 July 1998 *Employees:* 32
Net Worth: £579,301 *Total Assets:* £974,270
Registered Office: Old Highways Depot, Burn Lane, Hexham, Northumberland, NE46 3HN
Activities: Other business support service activities n.e.c.
Officers: Elizabeth Anne Prudhoe, Secretary; Anne Marie Bishop [1954] Director/Social Work Consultant; Michael Briggs [1967] Director/Lecturer; Lorraine Hershon [1966] Director; Patricia Maginn [1947] Director; Margaret Louise Makin [1953] Director/Social Worker; Mavis Anne Ostler [1943] Director/Retired; Gillian Renwick [1961] Director/Retired; Anita Louise Stevenson [1948] Director/Educational Support Worker; Rosemary Eileen Theobalds [1940] Director

Adaptive Trading Limited
Incorporated: 21 April 2015
Net Worth: £965,219 *Total Assets:* £1,107,012
Registered Office: Unit 2 Team Valley Business Centre, Earlsway, Team Valley Trading Estate, Gateshead, Tyne & Wear, NE11 0QH
Activities: Wholesale of other intermediate products
Major Shareholder: Andrew Wallace
Officers: Andrew Wallace [1984] Managing Director

Adavo Ltd
Incorporated: 15 May 2014 *Employees:* 6
Net Worth: £997,952 *Total Assets:* £2,411,289
Registered Office: The Town Hall, High Street East, Wallsend, Tyne & Wear, NE28 7AT
Activities: Management of real estate on a fee or contract basis
Shareholders: Kerry Anne Alexander; Mark Henry Black
Officers: Kerry Anne Alexander, Secretary; Kerry Anne Alexander [1981] Director; Mark Henry Black [1981] Director

ADC Electrical Limited
Incorporated: 23 August 2010 *Employees:* 19
Net Worth: £422,783 *Total Assets:* £1,008,826
Registered Office: Burtree Works, Brindley Road, Hertburn Industrial Estate, Washington, Tyne & Wear, NE37 2SF
Activities: Repair of electrical equipment
Major Shareholder: Christopher Carrick
Officers: Christopher Carrick [1962] Director

Addbudget Limited
Incorporated: 23 September 1994
Net Worth: £1,598,000 *Total Assets:* £3,927,000
Registered Office: 1a Dukesway Court, Team Valley Trading Estate, Gateshead, Tyne & Wear, NE11 0PJ
Activities: Activities of other holding companies n.e.c.
Parent: Falcombe Holdings Limited
Officers: Phillip Nigel Blain, Secretary; David James Horrocks [1959] Director/Chartered Accountant; Ian Imrie [1955] Director

Adderstone (Sunderland) LLP
Incorporated: 28 July 2010
Net Worth Deficit: £1,505,199 *Total Assets:* £9,179,356
Registered Office: 3 Austin Boulevard, Quay West Business Park, Sunderland, Tyne & Wear, SR5 2AL
Officers: Ian Robert Baggett [1972] Member; Nicola Baggett [1976] Member

Adderstone 1993 Limited
Incorporated: 7 July 2000 *Employees:* 14
Net Worth: £5,378,927 *Total Assets:* £18,211,338
Registered Office: Unit 5 Maling Court, Union Street, Newcastle upon Tyne, NE2 1BP
Activities: Financial management
Major Shareholder: Ian Robert Baggett
Officers: Ian Robert Baggett [1972] Director/Landlord; Nicola Baggett [1976] Director; Michael Raymond Shipley [1984] Director

Adderstone Developments (101) Limited
Incorporated: 15 April 2016
Net Worth: £2,272 *Total Assets:* £862,028
Registered Office: 5 Maling Court, Union Street, Newcastle upon Tyne, NE2 1BP
Activities: Development of building projects
Parent: Adderstone Developments Limited
Officers: Ian Robert Baggett [1972] Director; Allison Jane Harrison [1964] Director; Michael Raymond Shipley [1984] Director/Chartered Accountant

Adderstone Developments (103) Limited
Incorporated: 14 April 2010
Net Worth: £598,185 *Total Assets:* £864,808
Registered Office: 5 Maling Court, Union Street, Newcastle upon Tyne, NE2 1BP
Activities: Development of building projects
Parent: Adderstone Developments Limited
Officers: Timothy Joseph Clark, Secretary; Ian Robert Baggett [1972] Director; Allison Jane Harrison [1964] Director; Michael Raymond Shipley [1984] Finance Director

Adderstone Developments (104) Limited
Incorporated: 25 June 2015
Net Worth Deficit: £183,161 *Total Assets:* £2,115,359
Registered Office: Unit 5 Maling Court, Union Street, Newcastle upon Tyne, NE2 1BP
Activities: Development of building projects
Major Shareholder: Ian Robert Baggett
Officers: Timothy Joseph Clark, Secretary; Ian Robert Baggett [1972] Director; Allison Jane Harrison [1964] Director; Michael Raymond Shipley [1984] Finance Director

Adderstone Developments (Stock) Limited
Incorporated: 7 July 2015
Net Worth: £287,312 *Total Assets:* £8,625,746
Registered Office: Unit 5 Maling Court, Union Street, Newcastle upon Tyne, NE2 1BP
Activities: Development of building projects
Parent: Adderstone Developments Limited
Officers: Ian Robert Baggett [1972] Director; Allison Jane Harrison [1964] Director; Michael Raymond Shipley [1984] Finance Director

Adderstone Developments Limited
Incorporated: 18 April 2000
Net Worth: £1,481,977 *Total Assets:* £8,651,672
Registered Office: 5 Maling Court, Union Street, Newcastle upon Tyne, NE2 1BP
Activities: Development of building projects
Parent: Adderstone Group Limited
Officers: Timothy Joseph Clark, Secretary; Ian Robert Baggett [1972] Director; Allison Jane Harrison [1964] Director; Michael Raymond Shipley [1984] Finance Director

Addison & Co (Teesdale) Limited
Incorporated: 25 April 2002 *Employees:* 14
Net Worth: £1,038,638 *Total Assets:* £1,437,476
Registered Office: 91 Galgate, Barnard Castle, Co Durham, DL12 8ES
Activities: Accounting and auditing activities
Shareholders: Robert Tarn; David John Addison
Officers: Robert Tarn, Secretary; David John Addison [1961] Director/Chartered Accountant; Robert Tarn [1948] Director/Chartered Accountant

Addison Plant Limited
Incorporated: 1 June 1988 *Employees:* 36
Net Worth: £1,822,789 *Total Assets:* £2,648,349
Registered Office: Belle Vue, Aislaby Road, Eaglescliffe, Stockton-on-Tees, Cleveland, TS16 0QJ
Activities: Other specialised construction activities n.e.c.
Shareholder: William Allan Addison
Officers: Lynne Addison, Secretary; Lynne Addison [1957] Director; William Allan Addison [1954] Director/Drainage Contractor

Addisons Surveyors LLP
Incorporated: 14 June 2010 *Employees:* 20
Net Worth: £275,946 *Total Assets:* £878,318
Registered Office: 13 Galgate, Barnard Castle, Co Durham, DL12 8EQ
Officers: Jane Elizabeth Nixon [1972] Member; Simon William Nixon [1961] Member

Additional Lengths Ltd
Incorporated: 26 January 2007
Net Worth: £1,003,592 *Total Assets:* £1,387,229
Registered Office: Maxwell's Corner, 1-3 Norton Road, Stockton on Tees, Cleveland, TS18 2BW
Activities: Wholesale of perfume and cosmetics
Major Shareholder: Victoria Lynch
Officers: Victoria Lynch [1977] Director

Adelson Limited
Incorporated: 16 April 2004
Registered Office: Nelson Farm, Hart Station, Hartlepool, Cleveland, TS27 3AE
Activities: Construction of domestic buildings
Shareholders: Michael Ford; Colin Ford
Officers: Michael Ronald Ford, Secretary/Farmer; Colin Stephen Ford [1954] Director/Farmer; Michael Ronald Ford [1949] Director/Farmer

Adept Ecommerce Ltd
Incorporated: 15 August 2007 *Employees:* 31
Net Worth: £1,402,621 *Total Assets:* £1,784,743
Registered Office: 37-38 Market Street, Ferryhill, Co Durham, DL17 8JH
Activities: Retail sale of electrical household appliances in specialised stores
Shareholder: Andrew John Tomlinson
Officers: Alan Richard Neal [1951] Financial Director; Andrew John Tomlinson [1973] Director/Transport Manager

Adept Professional Services Ltd
Incorporated: 5 September 2013 *Employees:* 21
Net Worth: £817,409 *Total Assets:* £1,979,327
Registered Office: 37-38 Market Street, Ferryhill, Co Durham, DL17 8JH
Activities: Retail sale via mail order houses or via Internet
Shareholders: Andrew John Tomlinson; James Benjamin Buckle
Officers: Alan Richard Neal [1951] Finance Director; Andrew John Tomlinson [1973] Director

Adlink Technology Limited
Incorporated: 20 November 1991 *Employees:* 38
Net Worth: £2,179,894 *Total Assets:* £7,665,804
Registered Office: The Edge, Fifth Avenue, Team Valley Trading Estate, Gateshead, Tyne & Wear, NE11 0XA
Activities: Business and domestic software development
Parent: Adlink Technology, Inc.
Officers: Elizabeth Waters, Secretary; Jeff Chou [1965] Director [Taiwanese]; Mimi Han [1966] Director/Accountant [American]; Jim Liu [1962] Director [Taiwanese]; Lawrence Ross [1963] Director

ADM Pressings Limited
Incorporated: 17 December 2008 *Employees:* 278
Net Worth: £4,292,386 *Total Assets:* £15,541,719
Registered Office: ADM Pressings Limited, Scotswood Road, Newcastle upon Tyne, NE15 6BZ
Activities: Manufacture of metal structures and parts of structures
Major Shareholder: Gregory Frederick Hutchings
Officers: Cassie Olivia Hutchings, Secretary; Cassie Olivia Hutchings [1983] Director; Gregory Frederick Hutchings [1947] Director; Andrew Wingfield [1964] Director

Admec Municipal Services Limited
Incorporated: 27 April 1998 *Employees:* 36
Net Worth: £432,965 *Total Assets:* £1,438,650
Registered Office: Rowletch Burn Industrial Estate, Station Lane, Birtley, Co Durham, DH2 1AJ
Activities: Other specialised construction activities n.e.c.
Parent: Admec Group (North East) Limited
Officers: Barbara Louise Tweddle, Secretary; Barbara Louise Tweddle [1964] Director/Company Secretary; George Thornton Tweddle [1954] Director

ADP Precision Engineering Limited
Incorporated: 25 November 2002 *Employees:* 20
Net Worth: £827,434 *Total Assets:* £1,393,971
Registered Office: Unit 3 Westway Industrial Park, Throckley, Newcastle upon Tyne, NE15 9HW
Activities: Other business support service activities n.e.c.
Parent: ADP Precision Holdings Limited
Officers: Lorraine Dolan, Secretary; Peter Anthony Cornish [1965] Director; Anthony Ingledew [1974] Director

Advance Automated Systems Limited
Incorporated: 19 September 2003 *Employees:* 44
Net Worth: £610,340 *Total Assets:* £1,541,921
Registered Office: 1 Angels Close, Aycliffe Business Park, Newton Aycliffe, Co Durham, DL5 6BG
Activities: Manufacture of other general-purpose machinery n.e.c.
Shareholders: Zak Jeavons; Bryn Roberts
Officers: Zak Jeavons [1972] Director/Manufacturing Manager; Bryn William Roberts [1969] Director/Project Manager

Advance Learning Partnership
Incorporated: 30 January 2012 *Employees:* 104
Net Worth: £4,227,727 *Total Assets:* £7,454,573
Registered Office: Advance Learning Partnership, Whitworth Road, Whitworth Lane, Spennymoor, Co Durham, DL16 7LN
Activities: General secondary education
Officers: Claire Oates, Secretary; Hilary Armstrong [1945] Director/Cabinet Minister; Ellen Beveridge [1973] Director/Headteacher; Linda Ann Davies [1958] Director/Headteacher; John Deller [1952] Director; David Paul Kingston [1963] Director/Supply Teacher; Steve Leech [1974] Director/Lecturer; David Glenn Liddle [1967] Managing Director; Kevin Reynolds [1965] Director/Headteacher; Marie Roe [1978] Director; Linda Christine Thompson [1954] Director/Retired; Andrea Tomlinson [1972] Director/Head of Finance & Compliance

Advance Mortgage Funding Limited
Incorporated: 4 February 1988 *Employees:* 78
Net Worth: £5,593,000 *Total Assets:* £10,027,000
Registered Office: Newcastle House, Albany Court, Newcastle Business Park, Newcastle upon Tyne, NE4 7YB
Activities: Activities of other holding companies n.e.c.
Parent: LSL Property Services PLC
Officers: Sapna Bedi FitzGenerald, Secretary; Adam Robert Castleton [1964] Director; David Joseph Copland [1960] Director/Sales & Marketing; Richard Stephen Coulson [1960] Director; Kay Leslie [1964] Director; Rajeev Raichura [1979] Director; Jonathan Pearson Round [1964] Director; Toni Smith [1969] Director

Advanced Cutting Tools Limited
Incorporated: 10 August 2006 *Employees:* 20
Net Worth: £376,092 *Total Assets:* £1,418,384
Registered Office: 8 Apollo Court, Koppers Way, Monkton Business Park South, Hebburn, Tyne & Wear, NE31 2ES
Activities: Manufacture of metal forming machinery
Parent: Advanced Productivity Group Limited
Officers: Michael Richardson, Secretary; Michael McCann [1977] Director; Michael Richardson [1949] Director; Michael Mark Dennis Richardson [1971] Managing Director

Advanced Electronics Limited
Incorporated: 9 April 1999 *Employees:* 161
Net Worth: £11,137,704 *Total Assets:* £14,849,223
Registered Office: 34 Moorland Way, Nelson Park, Cramlington, Northumberland, NE23 1WE
Activities: Manufacture of other electrical equipment
Officers: Christopher John Widdas, Secretary; Peter Bell [1972] R&D Director; Aston Bowles [1970] Marketing Director; Raymond James Hope [1954] Director/Manager; Christopher Marston [1957] Operations Director; Christopher John Widdas [1962] Finance Director

Advanced Handling & Storage Limited
Incorporated: 2 October 1991
Net Worth: £720,840 *Total Assets:* £1,324,686
Registered Office: Unit 9A All Saints Industrial Estate, Darlington Road, Shildon, Co Durham, DL4 2RD
Activities: Agents involved in the sale of machinery, industrial equipment, ships and aircraft
Shareholders: Caron Moody; Christopher Andrew Moody
Officers: Caron Moody, Secretary; Caron Moody [1974] Director; Christopher Andrew Moody [1975] Director/Engineer

Advanced Industrial Solutions Limited
Incorporated: 30 October 2006 *Employees:* 121
Net Worth: £1,039,398 *Total Assets:* £9,718,151
Registered Office: 3 & 4 Jupiter Court, Orion Business Park, North Shields, Tyne & Wear, NE29 7SE
Activities: Other building completion and finishing
Parent: Transforming Training with Technology Limited
Officers: Sarah Lesley Richens, Secretary; Kevin Nigel Franklin [1962] Director; Martin Somerville [1977] Director; Paul Malcolm Stonebanks [1976] Director; Graeme David Sword [1968] Director/Partner

Advanced Productivity Group Limited
Incorporated: 14 March 2013
Net Worth: £690,902 *Total Assets:* £890,484
Registered Office: 8 Apollo Court, Koppers Way, Monkton Business Park South, Hebburn, Tyne & Wear, NE31 2ES
Activities: Other retail sale not in stores, stalls or markets
Major Shareholder: Michael Mark Dennis Richardson
Officers: Michael Mark Dennis Richardson [1971] Director

Advanced Radiators Limited
Incorporated: 10 June 1982 *Employees:* 28
Net Worth: £797,697 *Total Assets:* £1,063,873
Registered Office: Unit 8 Bells Close Industrial Estate, Lemington, Newcastle upon Tyne, NE15 6UF
Activities: Other manufacturing n.e.c.
Shareholders: Philip Riches; Mark Riches
Officers: Louise Riches, Secretary; Keith Riches [1949] Director; Mark Riches [1975] Director; Mary Patricia Riches [1949] Director; Philip Riches [1979] Service Director

Advanced Utility Solutions Limited
Incorporated: 17 May 2006 *Employees:* 6
Net Worth: £833,295 *Total Assets:* £1,157,267
Registered Office: 9 Carcut Road, Lawson Industrial Estate, Middlesbrough, Cleveland, TS3 6QL
Activities: Other business support service activities n.e.c.
Shareholders: Gary Richards; Nicola Jane Richards
Officers: Nicola Richards, Secretary; Gary Richards [1966] Director/Civil Engineer

Advanced Vehicle Leasing (Stockton) Limited
Incorporated: 19 January 2004
Net Worth: £300,332 *Total Assets:* £848,900
Registered Office: 10 Barton Road, Riverside Park, Middlesbrough, Cleveland, TS2 1RY
Activities: Financial leasing
Major Shareholder: Stuart Wallace Beagrie
Officers: Clarke Stuart Beagrie, Secretary

Advantex Network Solutions Limited
Incorporated: 3 October 2002 *Employees:* 51
Net Worth: £559,660 *Total Assets:* £1,575,818
Registered Office: 16b Follingsby Close, Gateshead, Tyne & Wear, NE10 8YG
Activities: Wired telecommunications activities
Shareholders: David James O'Connell; Stephen George O'Connell
Officers: David O'Connell, Secretary; David O Connell [1969] Director/Engineer; Stephen George O'Connell [1971] Director/Engineer

Advent Development Holdings Ltd
Incorporated: 29 May 2012 *Employees:* 2
Net Worth: £390,326 *Total Assets:* £824,520
Registered Office: Cold Moor Cote Farm, Chop Gate, Middlesbrough, Cleveland, TS9 7JJ
Activities: Activities of construction holding companies
Shareholder: Timothy James Reeve
Officers: Malcolm John Reeve [1951] Director; Mary Bernadette Reeve [1961] Director; Timothy James Reeve [1968] Director

Adventure Sunderland
Incorporated: 1 February 1996 *Employees:* 13
Net Worth: £2,820,452 *Total Assets:* £3,533,466
Registered Office: Marine Activities Centre, North Dock, Roker, Sunderland, Tyne & Wear, SR6 0PW
Activities: Other education n.e.c.
Officers: Tom Wills, Secretary; Robert Atchison [1947] Director; Fiona Carole Brown [1966] Director/Local Government Officer; Paul Francis Gowans [1956] Director; Michael Hendy [1966] Director/Accountant; Malcolm George Holmes [1954] Director/Chartered Surveyor; Matthew Hunt [1966] Port Director; Martin Ole Olsen Meling [1945] Director/Retired; Ian Michael Simon [1961] Director; Ivan Whitfield [1963] Sports Director; Tom Wills [1981] Director/Solicitor

AE Europe Limited
Incorporated: 14 November 2003 *Employees:* 3
Net Worth: £2,620,272 *Total Assets:* £4,693,098
Registered Office: 17th Floor, Cale Cross House, Pilgrim Street, Newcastle upon Tyne, NE1 6SU
Activities: Other business support service activities n.e.c.
Parent: AE Europe Holdings Inc.
Officers: Heather Mae Gamage [1978] Director/Assistant Treasurer [American]; Nathalie Buki Houder [1968] Director/VP-Finance [American]

Aedis Regulatory Services Limited
Incorporated: 25 February 2009 *Employees:* 85
Net Worth: £236,933 *Total Assets:* £1,866,504
Registered Office: Aedis House, Unit 3 Pioneer Court, Darlington, Co Durham, DL1 4WD
Activities: Other professional, scientific and technical activities n.e.c.
Major Shareholder: Joseph Ayre
Officers: Joseph Ayre [1955] Director; David Barley [1970] Director; Martin Barrett [1970] Director; Kevin Mark Blunden [1964] Director/Building Engineer & Surveyor; Paul Thorpe [1970] Director

AEDT Operations Limited
Incorporated: 20 September 2013
Net Worth: £158,101 *Total Assets:* £2,389,449
Registered Office: 2 St Peters Road, Wallsend, Tyne & Wear, NE28 7LG
Activities: Management of real estate on a fee or contract basis
Major Shareholder: Andrew Edward David Taylor
Officers: Andrew Edward David Taylor [1985] Director

Aegion Corrosion Protection Holdings Limited
Incorporated: 14 July 1988
Net Worth: £2,300,976 *Total Assets:* £5,099,411
Registered Office: Adam Street, Bowesfield Lane, Stockton on Tees, Cleveland, TS18 3HQ
Activities: Activities of head offices
Parent: Corrpro Companies Inc
Officers: Andrew Gillespie, Secretary; Mark Thomas Russell Davies [1965] Director/Chartered Accountant; David Francis Morris [1961] Business Director [American]

Aeolian Energy Limited
Incorporated: 18 January 2001 *Employees:* 1
Net Worth: £1,163,493 *Total Assets:* £1,447,797
Registered Office: Harlequin House, Clayton Road, Jesmond, Newcastle upon Tyne, NE2 4RP
Activities: Management consultancy activities other than financial management
Major Shareholder: Helen Mary Edwards
Officers: Helen Mary Edwards, Secretary/Corporate Body [Canadian]; Helen Mary Edwards [1956] Director [Canadian]; Professor Michael John Whitaker [1953] Director/Professor of Physiology

Age Concern Durham County
Incorporated: 19 November 2007 *Employees:* 23
Net Worth: £1,728,583 *Total Assets:* £2,033,070
Registered Office: Age UK House, Belmont Business Park, Durham, DH1 1TW
Activities: Physical well-being activities
Officers: Harriet Elizabeth Gibbon, Secretary; Anthony Armstrong [1946] Director/Retired; Natalie Davison-Terranova [1969] Director/College Principal; David Robert Haw [1946] Director/Retired; Ann Elizabeth Hitchman [1947] Director/Member Nursing & Midwifery Council [American]; David Martin [1957] Director/Group Treasurer Northumbria Water; Heather Joan Scott [1945] Director/Retired; Ivan Halliday Wood [1961] Director/Retired; Pauline Una York [1954] Director/Head of Housing

Age Concern Tyneside South
Incorporated: 25 July 2016 *Employees:* 36
Net Worth: £493,455 *Total Assets:* £936,647
Registered Office: 29 Beach Road, South Shields, Tyne & Wear, NE33 2QU
Activities: Social work activities without accommodation for the elderly and disabled
Officers: Steven Peter Duckworth [1969] Director/NHS Manager; Ian Johnson [1975] Director/Chief Executive; Raymond Staward [1950] Director/Retired; Joseph Edward Tiernan [1950] Retired Director; Helen Louise Tranter [1979] Director/Supported Housing Manager; Ian Cameron Ward [1962] Director/Management Consultant

Age UK North Tyneside
Incorporated: 21 October 1983 *Employees:* 276
Net Worth: £1,504,665 *Total Assets:* £2,116,322
Registered Office: Bradbury Centre, 13 Saville Street West, North Shields, Tyne & Wear, NE29 6QP
Activities: Social work activities without accommodation for the elderly and disabled
Officers: Richard John Adams [1946] Director/Member/Delegate European Economic Social Committee; William John Booth [1982] Director/Solicitor; William McKenzie Carr [1956] Director/Senior Investment Manager; Julie Gillson [1962] Director/Retired; Tracy Harrison [1969] Commercial Director; Robert Dryden Morton [1949] Director/Chartered Accountant; Carole Jayne Pitkeathley [1961] Director/Consultant; David Charles Sharp [1949] Director/Retired; Christopher Peter Alan Swan [1975] Director/IT Manager

Age UK Northumberland
Incorporated: 25 September 1998 *Employees:* 287
Net Worth: £1,822,692 *Total Assets:* £2,993,867
Registered Office: The Round House, Lintonville Parkway, Ashington, Northumberland, NE63 9JZ
Activities: Social work activities without accommodation for the elderly and disabled
Officers: Antonia Sintra Brindle [1971] Director; Ralph Firth [1946] Director/Retired; Patricia Jane Grahamslaw [1963] Director/Chartered Accountant; George Brown Hall [1960] Director; Graeme Martin James [1959] Director/Retired; Parry Jenkins [1964] Director/Management Consultant; Anu Kaura [1978] Director/Solicitor; Andrew Alexander Marsh [1973] Director; Sophie Clare Milliken [1979] Recruitment Director

Age UK Sunderland
Incorporated: 12 April 2001 *Employees:* 89
Net Worth: £2,495,082 *Total Assets:* £2,813,013
Registered Office: Bradbury Centre, Grange House, Stockton Road, Sunderland, Tyne & Wear, SR2 7AQ
Activities: Social work activities without accommodation for the elderly and disabled
Officers: Tracy Teresa Buck, Secretary; Graham Burt [1958] Director/Trustee; Carol Harries [1952] Health Service Director; Dianne Patricia Hutchinson [1972] Director/Revenues Officer; Matthew Jackson [1982] Director; Ann Lorna Lawson-Mclean [1937] Director/Trustee; Gerard McCormack [1952] Director/Architect; Roy Peter McLachlan [1956] Director/NHS Manager; Graeme Miller [1962] Director/Councillor; Susan Amanda Ritchie [1967] Director/Accountant; Patricia Robinson [1951] Director/Retired; David Teasdale [1955] Financial Adviser/Director

The Agents Property Auction Limited
Incorporated: 8 December 2009 *Employees:* 5
Net Worth: £636,110 *Total Assets:* £1,745,692
Registered Office: 14a Front Street, Prudhoe, Northumberland, NE42 5HN
Activities: Real estate agencies
Shareholders: Alison Louise Francis; Richard Mark Francis
Officers: Sukhvinder Singh Dhillon [1968] Director/Property Development; Alison Louise Francis [1970] Director/Administrator; Richard Mark Francis [1970] Director/Auctioneer

Aghoco 1085 Limited
Incorporated: 28 February 2012 *Employees:* 6
Net Worth Deficit: £5,957,000 *Total Assets:* £18,070,000
Registered Office: 12b Beechburn Industrial Estate, Prospect Road, Crook, Co Durham, DL15 8RA
Activities: Management consultancy activities other than financial management
Parent: Pedes Investments Limited
Officers: Ian Ralph Bailey [1963] Managing Director; Clinton Wayne George Edy [1962] Director; Jonathan Hammond [1975] Finance Director; Hiroaki Kobayashi [1963] Director [Japanese]; Eijiro Nireki [1971] Director [Japanese]; Hitoshi Suyama [1961] Director [Japanese]

Agma Holdings Limited
Incorporated: 27 February 2013 *Employees:* 2
Net Worth: £970,795 *Total Assets:* £1,633,068
Registered Office: Gemini Works, Haltwhistle Industrial Estate, Haltwhistle, Northumberland, NE49 9HA
Activities: Activities of head offices
Shareholders: Maxine Gillian Franklin; Malcolm Philip Franklin
Officers: Malcolm Philip Franklin [1958] Director; Maxine Gillian Franklin [1960] Director

Agma Limited
Incorporated: 26 September 1968 *Employees:* 29
Net Worth: £1,387,076 *Total Assets:* £2,067,758
Registered Office: Gemini Works, Haltwhistle, Northumberland, NE49 9HA
Activities: Manufacture of other chemical products n.e.c.
Parent: Agma Holdings Ltd
Officers: Philippa Jane Franklin, Secretary; Malcolm Philip Franklin [1958] Director; Philippa Jane Franklin [1991] Company Secretary/Director; John David Taylor [1959] Director/Chartered Accountant

Agne Limited
Incorporated: 10 August 2007 *Employees:* 101
Net Worth: £1,274,997 *Total Assets:* £4,881,100
Registered Office: 9 Vanguard Court, Preston Farm, Stockton on Tees, Cleveland, TS18 3TR
Activities: Printing n.e.c.
Shareholders: Andrew Leslie Dalton; Sean Michael Costigan
Officers: Isabelle Jane Dalton, Secretary; Sean Michael Costigan [1969] Director; Andrew Leslie Dalton [1956] Director/Printer

Ago Group Ltd
Incorporated: 3 June 2008
Net Worth: £920,047 *Total Assets:* £1,501,506
Registered Office: Brunel House, Brunel Road, Middlesbrough, Cleveland, TS6 6JA
Activities: Activities of head offices
Major Shareholder: Simon Colin Scotchbrook
Officers: Simon Colin Scotchbrook [1973] Director

Agricore Ltd
Incorporated: 14 June 2011 *Employees:* 11
Net Worth: £1,046,728 *Total Assets:* £4,092,927
Registered Office: Hill Top Farm, Winston, Darlington, Co Durham, DL2 3RR
Activities: Other specialised construction activities n.e.c.
Major Shareholder: Ian Bainbridge
Officers: Ian Bainbridge [1985] Director/Farmer; John Bainbridge [1960] Director/Farmer

Ailantus Hotels Limited
Incorporated: 13 October 2003
Net Worth: £1 *Total Assets:* £2,410,970
Registered Office: Stone Cellar Road, High Usworth, Washington, Tyne & Wear, NE13 8BJ
Activities: Hotels and similar accommodation
Officers: Saroj Rani Chawla, Secretary; Mukesh Raj Chawla [1954] Director; Neel Chawla [1986] Director; Saroj Rani Chawla [1955] Director

Aim High Academy Trust
Incorporated: 13 January 2014 *Employees:* 172
Net Worth: £9,116,000 *Total Assets:* £10,644,000
Registered Office: Newbottle Primary Academy, Houghton Road, Newbottle, Houghton-le-Spring, Co Durham, DH4 4EE
Activities: Primary education
Officers: Patricia Dutton [1957] Director/Retired; Janet Foster [1958] Director/Retired Headteacher; Julie Milner [1966] Director; Graham Roger Stephenson [1971] Director/Headteacher; John Walvin [1964] Director/Retired; James Crawford Westwater [1963] Director/Accountant

Aimgo Limited
Incorporated: 26 October 1989
Net Worth: £1,106,818 *Total Assets:* £1,111,565
Registered Office: Grove Cottage, 2 Villa Real Road, Consett, Co Durham, DH8 6BL
Activities: Other service activities n.e.c.
Major Shareholder: Margaret Ann Mukherjee
Officers: Margaret Ann Mukherjee [1939] Director/Retired; Dr Indira Patra [1946] Director/Doctor

The Ainderby LLP
Incorporated: 8 October 2012
Net Worth: £786,475 *Total Assets:* £1,116,171
Registered Office: Ainderby Manor, Ainderby Steeple, Northallerton, N Yorks, DL7 9PY
Officers: David Arnold Kerfoot [1953] Member; Elizabeth Mary Kerfoot [1954] Member; Thomas David James Kerfoot [1985] LLP Member; Eleanor Jane Wade [1983] LLP Member; Jennifer Elizabeth Wood [1981] LLP Member

Air Design Systems Limited
Incorporated: 28 June 1993
Net Worth: £1,199,788 *Total Assets:* £2,615,877
Registered Office: G22 The Avenues, Eleventh Avenue North, Team Valley Trading Estate, Gateshead, Tyne & Wear, NE11 0NJ
Activities: Other specialised construction activities n.e.c.
Parent: Air Design Systems (Holdings) Limited
Officers: Adam Clare [1983] Director/Design Consultant

Air Filters Limited
Incorporated: 14 January 1998 *Employees:* 28
Net Worth: £885,000 *Total Assets:* £2,490,000
Registered Office: Bassington Lane, Bassington Industrial Estate, Cramlington, Northumberland, NE23 8AF
Activities: Manufacture of other fabricated metal products n.e.c.
Parent: AAF McQuay UK Ltd
Officers: Ian Phillip Creasey, Secretary; Voon Ping Chen [1965] Director/Corporate Controller [Malaysian]; Ian Phillip Creasey [1961] Director/Accountant; Benny Woon Khin Liow [1957] Director [Malaysian]; Alan Dale Proffitt [1972] Director/Corporate Controller [American]; Carmella Marie Serapiglia Wantland [1952] Director/Controller [American]

Air Handling Systems Limited
Incorporated: 25 February 2000 *Employees:* 131
Net Worth: £1,227,765 *Total Assets:* £4,637,446
Registered Office: 3-5 Furnace Industrial Estate, Shildon, Co Durham, DL4 1QB
Activities: Other manufacturing n.e.c.
Major Shareholder: Leonard George Johnson
Officers: Leonard George Johnson, Secretary; Robert Wesley Campbell [1969] Technical Director; Matthew Cherrington [1971] Technical Director; Wayne Hodgson [1969] Operations Director; Lee Hartley Johnson [1974] Finance Director; Leonard George Johnson [1951] Managing Director; Richard Matthew Taylor [1981] Sales Director

Aircon-Refrigeration Limited
Incorporated: 17 September 1963 *Employees:* 42
Net Worth: £1,207,014 *Total Assets:* £2,142,606
Registered Office: 8 Whorlton Road, Riverside Business Park, Middlesbrough, Cleveland, TS2 1QJ
Activities: Plumbing, heat and air-conditioning installation
Shareholders: Stephen Mark Farrell; Bernadette Farrell
Officers: Stephen Mark Farrell, Secretary/Businessman; Robert Paul Dann [1961] Director/Businessman; Stephen Mark Farrell [1959] Director/Businessman

Airowsafe Limited
Incorporated: 3 November 2010
Net Worth: £2,126,866 *Total Assets:* £2,372,028
Registered Office: 14e The Avenues, Eleventh Avenue North, Team Valley Trading Estate, Gateshead, Tyne & Wear, NE11 0NJ
Activities: Other information service activities n.e.c.
Major Shareholder: Robert Wilkinson
Officers: Kim Wilkinson [1959] Director; Robert Wilkinson [1955] Director

Airport Retail UK Limited
Incorporated: 7 February 2012 *Employees:* 60
Net Worth Deficit: £712,770 *Total Assets:* £832,156
Registered Office: 32 Portland Terrace, Newcastle upon Tyne, NE2 1QP
Activities: Retail sale of clothing in specialised stores
Parent: Airport Retail Group AS
Officers: Kristoffer Olsen [1962] Director/Investor [Norwegian]

AIS Environmental Ltd
Incorporated: 24 January 2008 *Employees:* 2
Net Worth: £34,100 *Total Assets:* £795,506
Registered Office: 14 Rectory Drive, Newcastle upon Tyne, NE3 1XT
Activities: Other service activities n.e.c.
Major Shareholder: Marion Hoyle
Officers: Marion Hoyle [1961] Director

AIS Securus Ltd
Incorporated: 7 April 1989
Net Worth Deficit: £593,163 *Total Assets:* £1,494,640
Registered Office: 9-18 Ruby Court, Wesley Drive, Benton Square Industrial Estate, Newcastle upon Tyne, NE12 9UP
Activities: Other business support service activities n.e.c.
Parent: Securus Group Limited
Officers: Anthony Denis Kane [1959] Director; John Stewart [1968] Director

Akebar Park Leisure Limited
Incorporated: 25 March 2014
Net Worth: £1,449,703 *Total Assets:* £5,148,893
Registered Office: Akebar Park, Wensleydale, Leyburn, N Yorks, DL8 5LY
Activities: Recreational vehicle parks, trailer parks and camping grounds
Shareholders: Giles Dominic Procter Ellwood; Judith Mary Ellwood
Officers: Giles Dominic Procter Ellwood [1966] Director; Judith Mary Hodgson [1958] Director

AKV Cladding Products Ltd
Incorporated: 27 June 2011 *Employees:* 66
Net Worth: £1,459,082 *Total Assets:* £5,357,911
Registered Office: Unit 3 Hackworth Industrial Park, Shildon, Co Durham, DL4 1HF
Activities: Other manufacturing n.e.c.
Parent: AKV Group Limited
Officers: Karl James Everitt [1984] Director; Kevin Everitt [1958] Director; Lee Hammond [1978] Director; Mark Jones [1979] Production Director; Andrew Sneddon [1988] Operations Director

AKV Group Ltd
Incorporated: 14 April 2015 *Employees:* 68
Net Worth: £5,831,964 *Total Assets:* £11,453,572
Registered Office: The Old Forge Site, Hackworth Industrial Park, Byerley Road, Shildon, Co Durham, DL4 1HF
Activities: Activities of production holding companies
Officers: Karl James Everitt [1984] Director; Kevin Michael Everitt [1958] Director; Lee Hammond [1978] Director

Al-Shaheen Energy Services Limited
Incorporated: 14 December 2009
Net Worth: £77,184,416 *Total Assets:* £77,184,416
Registered Office: Atley Way, North Nelson Industrial Estate, Cramlington, Northumberland, NE23 1WW
Activities: Activities of head offices
Officers: Michael Bellamy [1962] Director/General Manager; Sanjeet Chadda [1978] Director/Chartered Accountant

Alab Environmental Services Limited
Incorporated: 6 May 1992 *Employees:* 8
Net Worth Deficit: £830,477 *Total Assets:* £2,147,501
Registered Office: Able House, Billingham Reach Industrial Estate, Billingham, Cleveland, TS23 1PX
Activities: Treatment and disposal of non-hazardous waste
Major Shareholder: Peter Melvin Stephenson
Officers: Rachel Stephenson, Secretary; Karen Jewers [1971] Director/PA; Rachel Stephenson [1969] Director/Company Secretary

Albany Office Equipment (Wholesale) Limited
Incorporated: 13 March 1964
Net Worth: £290,480 *Total Assets:* £993,901
Registered Office: Brandling Street, Gateshead, Tyne & Wear, NE8 2BA
Activities: Wholesale of office furniture
Major Shareholder: David Wilkinson
Officers: Daniel David Wilkinson, Secretary/Director; George Anthony Preston [1960] Director; Daniel David Wilkinson [1977] Director; David Wilkinson [1947] Director/Office Furniture Retailer

Alchemy Design & Works Limited
Incorporated: 13 April 1992 *Employees:* 11
Net Worth: £342,143 *Total Assets:* £1,526,540
Registered Office: Hanover House, 13 Victoria Road, Darlington, Co Durham, DL1 5SF
Activities: Manufacture of jewellery and related articles
Shareholders: Jane Frances Wetter-Sanchez; Erik Wetter
Officers: Malcolm George Paget, Secretary/Accountant; Malcolm George Paget [1954] Director/Accountant; Erik Wetter [1959] Director [Swedish]; Jane Frances Wetter-Sanchez [1963] Director/Designer

Alcyone Healthcare North East Ltd
Incorporated: 9 February 2010 *Employees:* 14
Net Worth Deficit: £456,714 *Total Assets:* £4,407,071
Registered Office: 8a Bridge Street, Blyth, Northumberland, NE24 1BL
Activities: Construction of commercial buildings
Major Shareholder: Barry William Elliott
Officers: Barry William Elliott [1966] Director/Developer

Aldar Property Limited
Incorporated: 2 September 2014
Net Worth: £25,875 *Total Assets:* £1,009,772
Registered Office: Exchange Building, 66 Church Street, Hartlepool, Cleveland, TS24 7DN
Activities: Other letting and operating of own or leased real estate
Major Shareholder: Mousa Abid Mousa
Officers: Mousa Abid Mousa [1975] Director

Alderclad Ltd
Incorporated: 28 November 2005
Net Worth: £1,752,620 *Total Assets:* £3,087,747
Registered Office: 69-71 Station Road, Seaham, Co Durham, SR7 0AQ
Activities: Roofing activities
Shareholders: Trevor Alderson; Anthony John Nevison
Officers: Lisa Marie Ibbetson, Secretary; Trevor Alderson [1949] Director; Craig Anthony Dowson [1971] Director/Estimator; Anthony Nevison [1960] Director; Paul Pattison [1967] Director/Cladding Supervisor

Alderson Law LLP
Incorporated: 23 March 2004
Registered Office: Pethgate House, Castle Square, Morpeth, Northumberland, NE61 1YL
Officers: Paul William Dunn [1961] Member; Richard Guy Goodings [1958] Member; Mark Damian Hipkin [1958] Member; Susan Johnson [1957] Member; Tracey Jane Murray [1970] Member; Graham Shannon [1965] Member

Aldona Seals Ltd
Incorporated: 29 July 1988 *Employees:* 22
Net Worth: £663,584 *Total Assets:* £993,344
Registered Office: 3 Traynor Way, Whitehouse Business Park, Peterlee, Co Durham, SR8 2RU
Activities: Manufacture of other rubber products
Parent: Knorr-Bremse AG
Officers: Keith Bendelow [1958] Director; Neil Stuart Conley [1962] Director

Alexage Limited
Incorporated: 24 May 1978 *Employees:* 2
Net Worth: £3,445,129 *Total Assets:* £3,732,875
Registered Office: 7 Brenkley Way, Blezard Business Park, Seaton Burn, Newcastle upon Tyne, NE13 6DS
Activities: Other accommodation
Major Shareholder: Simon Andrew Ellis
Officers: Linda Ann Scott [1963] Director/Sales

Bob Alexander Limited
Incorporated: 23 January 1964 *Employees:* 58
Net Worth: £3,267,767 *Total Assets:* £8,740,062
Registered Office: Chapel Street Garage, Chapel Street, Thornaby, Cleveland, TS17 6BB
Activities: Sale of new cars and light motor vehicles
Major Shareholder: David Robert Alexander
Officers: David Robert Alexander, Secretary; David Robert Alexander [1965] Managing Director

Alexander Technologies Europe Limited
Incorporated: 16 May 1984 *Employees:* 56
Net Worth: £2,167,000 *Total Assets:* £5,076,000
Registered Office: 4 Doxford Drive, South West Industrial Estate, Peterlee, Co Durham, SR8 2RL
Activities: Manufacture of batteries and accumulators
Officers: Scott Mahlon Schooley [1956] Director/Private Investor/Attorney [American]; Michael Shirley [1973] Director/Investment Management [American]

Alfol Limited
Incorporated: 13 June 2000 *Employees:* 13
Net Worth: £697,354 *Total Assets:* £1,433,311
Registered Office: Low Broadwood Hall, Allendale, Hexham, Northumberland, NE47 9AD
Activities: Publishing of consumer and business journals and periodicals
Shareholders: Catherine Elizabeth Handcock; Russell John Handcock
Officers: Catherine Elizabeth Handcock, Secretary/Publisher; Catherine Elizabeth Handcock [1964] Director/Journalist; Russell John Handcock [1930] Director; Laura MacLeod [1983] Director

Algernon Precision Engineering Limited
Incorporated: 12 July 2001
Registered Office: Suite 4, Earlshouse, Earlsway, Team Valley Trading Estate, Gateshead, Tyne & Wear, NE11 0RY
Activities: Manufacture of bearings, gears, gearing and driving elements
Shareholders: Graham Watson; Beverley Watson
Officers: Beverley Jane Watson, Secretary; Graeme Jeffrey Watson [1959] Director/Engineer

Align Property Partners Limited
Incorporated: 20 September 2016 *Employees:* 40
Net Worth: £1,153,175 *Total Assets:* £1,392,458
Registered Office: County Hall, Racecourse Lane, Northallerton, N Yorks, DL7 8AD
Activities: Development of building projects
Parent: North Yorkshire County Council
Officers: David Raymond Bowe [1962] Director/Local Government Officer; Gary Fielding [1969] Corporate Director Strategic Resources; Anthony Hodge [1969] Director/Local Government Officer; Ronnie Walton [1960] Director

Aliweld Limited
Incorporated: 8 October 1991
Registered Office: Unit 9 Star Gate Industrial Estate, Ryton, Newcastle upon Tyne, NE40 3DG
Activities: Manufacture of other fabricated metal products n.e.c.
Officers: Leslie Welch, Secretary/Director-Welder; Trevor Matthew Marshall [1968] Director-Welder; Leslie Welch [1960] Director Welder

All Car Parts Limited
Incorporated: 1 February 2012 *Employees:* 26
Net Worth: £26,187 *Total Assets:* £1,552,215
Registered Office: Vertu House, Fifth Avenue Business Park, Team Valley Trading Estate, Gateshead, Tyne & Wear, NE11 0XA
Activities: Retail sale via mail order houses or via Internet
Parent: Aceparts Limited
Officers: Karen Anderson, Secretary; Karen Anderson [1971] Finance Director; David Paul Crane [1967] Commercial Director; Robert Thomas Forrester [1969] Director; Michael Sherwin [1959] Finance Director

All Floors (Services) Limited
Incorporated: 20 June 2000
Registered Office: Unit 3 Burford Way, Boldon Colliery, Co Durham, NE35 9PY
Activities: Manufacture of other carpets and rugs
Shareholders: Joseph Dorian; Kevin Thompson; Laura Thompson; Joanne Dorian
Officers: Kevin Thompson, Secretary/Accountancy Assistant; Joseph Dorian [1969] Director/Financial Manager; Kevin Thompson [1968] Director/Accountancy Assistant

All Saints Developments (NE) Ltd
Incorporated: 24 October 2013 *Employees:* 10
Net Worth: £170,546 *Total Assets:* £1,745,965
Registered Office: 2nd Floor, Cuthbert House, All Saints Business Centre, Newcastle upon Tyne, NE1 2ET
Activities: Development of building projects
Officers: Gary Ronald Forrest [1968] Director

All Saints' Academies Trust
Incorporated: 15 April 2014 *Employees:* 48
Net Worth: £4,083,923 *Total Assets:* £4,851,143
Registered Office: Cleadon Church of England Academy, Boldon Lane, Cleadon Village, Sunderland, Tyne & Wear, SR6 7RP
Activities: Primary education
Officers: Christine Flynn, Secretary; Paul Eric Bowens [1959] Director/Business Development Manager; Michael James Cuthbertson [1956] Director/Chartered Surveyor (Retired); Beverley George [1963] Director/IT Service Manager; Jayn Gray [1959] Director/Principal; Dean Hall [1959] Director/Business Development Manager (Retired); John Keith Higgin [1937] Director/Retired Bank Manager; Michael James Morris [1974] Director/Accountant

T & G Allan Holdings Limited
Incorporated: 11 June 2010 *Employees:* 13
Net Worth: £180,614 *Total Assets:* £872,391
Registered Office: 24 Newgate Street, Morpeth, Northumberland, NE61 1BA
Activities: Other retail sale of new goods in specialised stores (not commercial art galleries and opticians)
Parent: The Fountain Group Limited
Officers: Colin Peter McClymont [1956] Director

Dame Allan's Schools
Incorporated: 26 May 2000 *Employees:* 150
Net Worth: £8,815,152 *Total Assets:* £16,821,080
Registered Office: Dame Allans Schools, Fowberry Crescent, Newcastle upon Tyne, NE4 9YJ
Activities: Pre-primary education
Officers: Victoria Alyson McDonald, Secretary; Brian William Adcock [1951] Director; David Robson Arthur [1954] Director/Chartered Accountant; Charlotte Anna McLauchlan Bell [1970] Director/Property Manager; Ian John Belsham [1949] Director/Architect; Christopher Bolland [1955] Director/Retired; Eric Grahame Nicol Cross [1953] Director/University Professor; Deborah Ann Cunningham [1959] Director/Housewife; Michael Davison [1946] Director/Retired Accountant; Timothy Rohan Gray [1952] Director/Solicitor; Professor Ruth Gregory [1963] Director/University Professor; Melanie Jane Hinson [1962] Director/Headteacher; Dr Vanessa Jane Morrell [1974] Director/Self Employed Management Consultant; Dr Paul Vincent Paes [1974] Director/Doctor; Professor Ruth Elizabeth Plummer [1965] Director/Doctor

Allay (UK) Ltd.
Incorporated: 12 November 2014 *Employees:* 27
Net Worth: £306,896 *Total Assets:* £4,497,055
Registered Office: 3rd Floor, Generator Studios, Trafalgar Street, Newcastle upon Tyne, NE1 2LA
Activities: Other activities auxiliary to insurance and pension funding
Shareholder: Stuart Phillipson Bell
Officers: Steven Phillipson Bell [1976] Director; Stuart Phillipson Bell [1947] Director; Andrew Mark Stokoe [1988] Director

Allay Claims Ltd
Incorporated: 4 March 2009 *Employees:* 87
Net Worth: £6,093,177 *Total Assets:* £8,944,721
Registered Office: Generator Studios, Trafalgar Street, Newcastle upon Tyne, NE1 2LA
Activities: Activities of call centres
Parent: Allay (UK) Ltd
Officers: Paul Anthony Calland, Secretary; Stuart Phillipson Bell [1947] Director; Andrew Mark Stokoe [1988] Director

Allay Redress Ltd.
Incorporated: 12 November 2014
Net Worth Deficit: £946,519 *Total Assets:* £1,218,691
Registered Office: 3rd Floor, Generator Studios, Trafalgar Street, Newcastle upon Tyne, NE1 2LA
Activities: Financial intermediation not elsewhere classified
Shareholders: Stuart Phillipson Bell; Steven Phillipson Bell
Officers: Steven Phillipson Bell [1976] Director; Stuart Phillipson Bell [1947] Director; Andrew Mark Stokoe [1988] Director

Alldec (Northern) Limited
Incorporated: 9 November 2001 *Employees:* 33
Net Worth: £314,500 *Total Assets:* £867,339
Registered Office: 176 Hylton Road, Sunderland, Tyne & Wear, SR4 7YA
Activities: Painting
Shareholders: David Allen; Gillian Allen
Officers: David Allan, Secretary; David Allan [1963] Director/Decorator; Gillian Allan [1968] Director; Reece Michael Allan [1992] Director

Allendale Creative Artists Community Interest Company
Incorporated: 19 January 2007
Net Worth Deficit: £68,290 *Total Assets:* £771,748
Registered Office: Allendale Forge Studios, Market Place, Allendale, Hexham, Northumberland, NE47 9BD
Activities: Artistic creation
Officers: Denise Sheila Williams, Secretary; Zoe Elizabeth Bell [1985] Director/Cafe Manager; Lindsey Olive Cooper [1957] Director/Retired; Lesley Anne Gosling [1944] Director/PR Consultant; Alexander McEwan Rutherford [1951] Director/Retired

Allergate Investments Limited
Incorporated: 1 August 2003 *Employees:* 3
Net Worth: £4,482,498 *Total Assets:* £14,552,768
Registered Office: Kingfisher House, St Johns Road, Meadowfield, Co Durham, DH7 8TZ
Activities: Other letting and operating of own or leased real estate
Shareholders: Karen Jayne Clark; Steven Eric Clark
Officers: Eric Clark [1947] Director; Joan Clark [1949] Director; Karen Jayne Clark [1981] Director/Marketing Manager; Steven Eric Clark [1978] Director/Technical Officer

Allerton Steel (Property) Limited
Incorporated: 24 March 2009
Net Worth: £668,127 *Total Assets:* £1,855,447
Registered Office: 20 Leases Road, Leeming Bar, Northallerton, N Yorks, DL7 9AW
Activities: Other letting and operating of own or leased real estate
Officers: John Gatenby [1946] Director

Allerton Steel Limited
Incorporated: 24 March 2009 *Employees:* 132
Net Worth: £2,443,591 *Total Assets:* £4,175,511
Registered Office: 20 Leases Road, Leeming Bar, Northallerton, N Yorks, DL7 9AW
Activities: Manufacture of metal structures and parts of structures
Officers: Giles Francis John Penn, Company Secretary; Andrew Robert Gatenby [1974] Director; John Gatenby [1946] Director; Giles Francis John Penn [1967] Managing Director

Allflex UK Group Limited
Incorporated: 29 July 2010 *Employees:* 99
Net Worth: £2,088,107 *Total Assets:* £26,571,952
Registered Office: 1 Greencroft Industrial Park, Stanley, Co Durham, DH9 7YA
Activities: Manufacture of other plastic products
Parent: Merko Acquisition (Belgique)
Officers: Louis-Marie Allain, Secretary; John Ashley Musgrave [1961] Commercial Director; Kevin David Parker [1984] Finance Director; Gregoire Claude Jacques Wambergue [1964] Director/General Manager [French]

Alliance Psychological Services Ltd
Incorporated: 15 March 2006 *Employees:* 127
Net Worth: £252,986 *Total Assets:* £937,424
Registered Office: 24 Yarm Road, Stockton on Tees, Cleveland, TS18 3NA
Activities: Other human health activities
Parent: Alliance Teesside Ltd
Officers: Leanda Kane Fidgeon, Secretary; Elizabeth Anne Drummond [1956] Director/Service Manager; Leanda Mary Kane-Fidgeon [1968] Director/Service Manager

Allied Domain Limited
Incorporated: 11 February 2003
Net Worth: £755,835 *Total Assets:* £1,338,665
Registered Office: 16-17 Marshall Terrace, Gilesgate Moor, Durham, DH1 2HX
Activities: Buying and selling of own real estate
Major Shareholder: George David Crozier
Officers: Tarnya Hickson, Secretary; George David Crozier [1960] Director/Property Investor

Allied Exploration & Geotechnics Limited
Incorporated: 9 December 1987 *Employees:* 59
Net Worth: £494,108 *Total Assets:* £1,484,220
Registered Office: Unit 25 Stella Gill Industrial Estate, Pelton Fell, Chester-le-Street, Co Durham, DH2 2RG
Activities: Test drilling and boring
Major Shareholder: Keith Peacock
Officers: Kevin Warriner, Secretary; Keith Peacock [1947] Managing Director; Nickolas William Vater [1967] Director/Geotechnical; Kevin Warriner [1954] Director/Health Safety Environment & Q

George Allinson (Transport) Limited
Incorporated: 21 August 1969 *Employees:* 117
Net Worth: £18,915,820 *Total Assets:* £22,334,648
Registered Office: Faverdale North, Faverdale Industrial Estate, Darlington, Co Durham, DL3 0PH
Activities: Freight transport by road
Major Shareholder: David Allinson
Officers: David Joseph Jackson, Secretary; David Allinson [1948] Managing Director; Denise Allinson [1959] Director; George William Allinson [1955] Director; Irene Allinson [1949] Director

Wm.Allison & Sons Limited
Incorporated: 19 May 1954 *Employees:* 52
Net Worth: £3,876,170 *Total Assets:* £6,911,896
Registered Office: 7 South Church Road, Bishop Auckland, Co Durham, DL14 7LB
Activities: Mixed farming
Major Shareholder: Michael Nixon Allison
Officers: Paul Richard Allison, Secretary/Director; Michael Nixon Allison [1939] Director; Paul Richard Allison [1965] Director

Allsafety Limited
Incorporated: 5 December 2009 *Employees:* 248
Net Worth: £577,799 *Total Assets:* £1,631,297
Registered Office: Unit 6 Riverside Industrial Estate, Langley Park, Co Durham, DH7 9TT
Activities: Activities of amusement parks and theme parks
Major Shareholder: Hugh Robert Edeleanu
Officers: Hugh Robert Edeleanu [1955] Managing Director

Allure Developments Limited
Incorporated: 23 August 1990 *Employees:* 7
Net Worth: £3,031,498 *Total Assets:* £4,654,690
Registered Office: Hackworth Industrial Park, Byerley Road, Shildon, Co Durham, DL4 1HF
Activities: Other manufacturing n.e.c.
Parent: AKV Holdings Limited
Officers: Kevin Michael Everitt, Secretary; Karl James Everitt [1984] Director; Kevin Michael Everitt [1958] Director/Company Secretary

Almet Sheet Metal Fabrication Limited
Incorporated: 11 May 2007 *Employees:* 17
Net Worth: £824,609 *Total Assets:* £1,157,253
Registered Office: 5 Armstrong Road, Armstrong Industrial Estate, Washington, Tyne & Wear, NE37 1PR
Activities: Manufacture of basic iron and steel and of ferro-alloys
Shareholders: Paul James Almond; Rosalind Almond
Officers: Rosalind Almond, Secretary; Paul James Almond [1957] Director; Rosalind Almond [1961] Director

Almit Group Limited
Incorporated: 28 July 2008 *Employees:* 126
Net Worth: £5,161,843 *Total Assets:* £10,760,837
Registered Office: Faverdale Industrial Estate, Darlington, Co Durham, DL3 0PP
Activities: Activities of head offices
Shareholders: Dr Allan Mitchell; Irene Mitchell
Officers: Irene Mitchell, Secretary/Director; Allan David Mitchell [1970] Director; Dr Allan Mitchell [1941] Director; Irene Mitchell [1941] Director; Mark Mitchell [1980] Director; Stephen Mitchell [1974] Director

Alnwick District Playhouse Trust
Incorporated: 12 December 1990
Net Worth: £1,020,139 *Total Assets:* £1,202,786
Registered Office: The Playhouse, Bondgate Without, Alnwick, Northumberland, NE66 1PQ
Activities: Motion picture projection activities
Officers: Lisa McGeary, Secretary; Martin Allenby [1976] Director/Headmaster; Elizabeth Margaret Anderson [1943] Director/Retired Fundraising Consultant; Dr Alan Fortune [1948] Director/Retired; Philip John Gregory [1962] Director; Norman Luke [1957] Director/Solicitor; Christopher Mark Sayers [1960] Director/Chairman; Roger Styring [1945] Director/Retired; Roy Todd [1937] Director/Retired

Alnwick Farmers Livestock Auction Company Limited
Incorporated: 12 December 1956 *Employees:* 20
Net Worth: £1,028,036 *Total Assets:* £1,510,097
Registered Office: Acklington Auction Market, Acklington, Morpeth, Northumberland, NE65 9BU
Activities: Support activities for animal production (other than farm animal boarding)
Officers: Karen Elizabeth Hill, Secretary; Hugh Henry Annett [1961] Director/Farmer; William John Curry [1969] Director/Farmer; William Arthur Curry [1941] Director/Farmer; Edward John Davy [1977] Director/Farmer; George Andrew Davy [1950] Director/Farmer; Christopher George Manners [1955] Director/Farmer; Joseph Andrew Walton [1962] Director/Farmer

Alnwick Garden Enterprises Limited
Incorporated: 1 November 2002 *Employees:* 130
Net Worth: £79,286 *Total Assets:* £1,646,889
Registered Office: Gardeners Cottage, Alnwick, Northumberland, NE66 1YU
Activities: Other business support service activities n.e.c.
Officers: Mark James Brassell [1971] Managing Director; Jane Northumberland [1958] Director/Mother

The Alnwick Garden Trust
Incorporated: 7 November 2002 *Employees:* 133
Net Worth: £15,930,228 *Total Assets:* £19,857,322
Registered Office: Gardeners Cottage, Greenwell Lane, Alnwick, Northumberland, NE66 1YU
Activities: Other business support service activities n.e.c.
Officers: Jonathan Adam Blackie [1953] Regional Director; Louise Halbert [1956] Director; Richard John Hutton [1968] Finance Director; Ken McMeikan [1965] Director/Group Chief Executive; Jane Northumberland [1958] Director

Aloe Flats Limited
Incorporated: 8 June 1998
Registered Office: Flat 3 Saville Gardens, The Grove, Gosforth, Newcastle upon Tyne, NE3 1NG
Activities: Other letting and operating of own or leased real estate
Shareholders: Michael Brennan; Angela Brennan; Sara Brennan
Officers: Michael Edward Brennan, Secretary; Angela Mary Brennan [1951] Director/Retired; Michael Edward Brennan [1948] Director/Chartered Accountant; Sara Helen Brennan [1989] Marketing Director

Alpha Developments (Bradford) Ltd
Incorporated: 19 November 2015 *Employees:* 2
Net Worth: £1,657,497 *Total Assets:* £1,660,030
Registered Office: Valley House, Kingsway South, Gateshead, Tyne & Wear, NE11 0JW
Activities: Construction of domestic buildings
Officers: Derek Arthur Kewley [1973] Director; Nicholas Spence [1972] Director

Alpha Developments (Bradford2) Ltd
Incorporated: 19 May 2016 *Employees:* 2
Net Worth: £2,234,967 *Total Assets:* £6,254,889
Registered Office: Valley House, Kingsway South, Gateshead, Tyne & Wear, NE11 0JW
Activities: Management of real estate on a fee or contract basis
Officers: Derek Kewley [1973] Director; Nicholas Spence [1972] Director

Alpha Developments (Leicester) Limited
Incorporated: 4 November 2014 *Employees:* 2
Net Worth: £2,677,071 *Total Assets:* £2,741,660
Registered Office: Valley House, Seventh Avenue, Team Valley Trading Estate, Gateshead, Tyne & Wear, NE11 0JW
Activities: Activities of head offices
Officers: Derek Kewley [1973] Director; Nicholas John Spence [1972] Director

Alpha Developments (Preston) Ltd
Incorporated: 25 February 2015 *Employees:* 2
Net Worth: £363,425 *Total Assets:* £807,702
Registered Office: Valley House, Kingsways South, Gateshead, Tyne & Wear, NE11 0JW
Activities: Buying and selling of own real estate
Officers: Derek Kewley [1973] Director; Nicholas John Spence [1972] Director

Alpha Developments (Stoke) Ltd
Incorporated: 1 December 2016 *Employees:* 2
Net Worth: £1,096,692 *Total Assets:* £4,332,270
Registered Office: Valley House, Kingsway South, Gateshead, Tyne & Wear, NE11 0JW
Activities: Other business support service activities n.e.c.
Shareholders: Derek Kewley; Nicholas Spence
Officers: Derek Kewley [1973] Director; Nicholas Spence [1972] Director

Alpha Developments (Stoke1) Ltd
Incorporated: 13 July 2015
Registered Office: Valley House, Kingsway South, Gateshead, Tyne & Wear, NE11 0JW
Activities: Buying and selling of own real estate
Shareholders: Derek Kewley; Steven Turner
Officers: Derek Arthur Kewley [1973] Director; Nicholas Spence [1972] Director

Alpha Holdings (GB) Ltd
Incorporated: 17 October 2013 *Employees:* 2
Net Worth: £6,060,719 *Total Assets:* £6,072,264
Registered Office: Valley House, Kingsway South, Gateshead, Tyne & Wear, NE11 0JW
Activities: Buying and selling of own real estate
Shareholders: Derek Arthur Kewley; Nicholas John Spence
Officers: Derek Kewley [1973] Director; Nicholas John Spence [1972] Director/Property Developer

Alpha Process Controls (International) Limited
Incorporated: 10 August 1978 *Employees:* 6
Net Worth: £624,208 *Total Assets:* £1,184,384
Registered Office: 3 Traynor Way, Whitehouse Business Park, Peterlee, Co Durham, SR8 2RU
Activities: Manufacture of taps and valves
Parent: Knorr-Bremse AG
Officers: Keith Bendelow [1958] Director; Neil Stuart Conley [1962] Director; John Lamb [1954] Managing Director

Alpha Recovery Limited
Incorporated: 22 August 1995 *Employees:* 16
Net Worth: £3,029,733 *Total Assets:* £3,852,211
Registered Office: Weetslade Industrial Estate, Dudley, Cramlington, Northumberland, NE23 7PS
Activities: Other transportation support activities
Major Shareholder: Michael Robert Burke
Officers: Kerry Louise Burke, Secretary; Kerry Louise Burke [1968] Managing Director

Alrahi & Singh Limited
Incorporated: 7 June 2010 *Employees:* 18
Net Worth: £719,200 *Total Assets:* £3,237,333
Registered Office: 113 Lanehouse Road, Thornaby, Stockton on Tees, Cleveland, TS17 8AB
Activities: Dispensing chemist in specialised stores
Shareholders: Asif Alrahi; Sidra Alrahi; Iqbal Singh; Sandeep Kaur
Officers: Iqbal Singh, Secretary; Asif Alrahi [1983] Director/Pharmacist; Iqbal Singh [1979] Director/Pharmacist

Alt Berg Holdings Limited
Incorporated: 23 October 2012 *Employees:* 1
Net Worth: £4,784,334 *Total Assets:* £4,978,485
Registered Office: 14-15 Harelands Courtyard Offices, Moor Road, Melsonby, Richmond, N Yorks, DL10 5NY
Activities: Activities of other holding companies n.e.c.
Major Shareholder: Michael Joseph Sheehan
Officers: Angela Sheehan [1945] Director; Michael Joseph Sheehan [1947] Director

Alt Berg Limited
Incorporated: 28 November 1990 *Employees:* 20
Net Worth: £2,173,539 *Total Assets:* £3,301,337
Registered Office: Unit 2b Racecourse Road, Gallowfields Industrial Estate, Richmond, N Yorks, DL10 4XB
Activities: Manufacture of footwear
Parent: Alt Berg Holdings Limited
Officers: Angela Sheehan, Secretary/Director; Joseph Sheehan [1989] Director; Tara May Sheehan [1971] Director

Alta Vista Global Limited
Incorporated: 6 June 2006
Registered Office: Exchange Building, 66 Church Street, Hartlepool, Cleveland, TS24 7DN
Activities: Development of building projects
Major Shareholder: Riaz Hameed
Officers: Riaz Mohammad Hameed, Secretary; Riaz Mohammad Hameed [1973] Director [Turkish]

Altec Precision Limited
Incorporated: 27 October 2014
Net Worth: £1 *Total Assets:* £2,010,000
Registered Office: Unit 1 Bowburn North Industrial Estate, Bowburn, Co Durham, DH6 5PF
Activities: Manufacture of other fabricated metal products n.e.c.
Parent: Altec Engineering Group Limited
Officers: Martin Reid, Secretary; Simon Alexander McIntosh [1965] Director/Chartered Accountant; Alastair Waite [1960] Director

Altomed Limited
Incorporated: 9 February 1976 *Employees:* 21
Net Worth: £2,267,373 *Total Assets:* £2,990,960
Registered Office: 2 Witney Way, Boldon Business Park, Boldon Colliery, Co Durham, NE35 9PE
Activities: Manufacture of medical and dental instruments and supplies
Major Shareholder: Dr Nicholas James Master
Officers: Dr Nicholas James Master, Secretary; Dr Nicholas James Master [1973] Managing Director; Alan Wilson [1968] Director/Sales Manager

Aluminium (Bar & Sheet) Limited
Incorporated: 9 September 1969
Net Worth: £1,601,034 *Total Assets:* £1,609,616
Registered Office: 59-69 Heaton Park Road, Newcastle upon Tyne, NE6 1SQ
Activities: Wholesale of metals and metal ores
Officers: David George Mutch, Secretary; David George Mutch [1960] Director; Fiona Joan Mutch [1965] Director

Amakhala Limited
Incorporated: 4 July 2005 *Employees:* 1
Net Worth: £1,062,932 *Total Assets:* £1,642,328
Registered Office: 9 Hedley Court, Orion Business Park, North Shields, Tyne & Wear, NE29 7ST
Activities: Solicitors
Major Shareholder: John Gareth Burn
Officers: Peter McKenna, Secretary/Solicitor; John Gareth Burn [1973] Director/Solicitor; Peter McKenna [1980] Director/Solicitor

Ambic Limited
Incorporated: 31 August 2001 *Employees:* 27
Net Worth: £637,772 *Total Assets:* £1,699,207
Registered Office: House of Ambic, Stella Gill Industrial Estate, Pelton Fell, Chester-le-Street, Co Durham, DH2 2RN
Activities: Manufacture of other furniture
Major Shareholder: David Potter
Officers: David Richings, Secretary; David Potter [1944] Director/Engineer

Amble Boat Company Limited
Incorporated: 23 June 1995
Registered Office: 14 The Boatyard, Coquet Street, Amble, Northumberland, NE65 0DJ
Activities: Building of ships and floating structures
Shareholders: Nicholas Spurr; Kate Spurr
Officers: Kate Victoria Spurr, Secretary/Director; Kate Victoria Spurr [1961] Director; Nicholas Roger Spurr [1960] Managing Director

Amble Development Trust
Incorporated: 15 November 1994 *Employees:* 4
Net Worth: £2,429,147 *Total Assets:* £2,500,929
Registered Office: Fourways 2, 6 Dilston Terrace, Amble, Morpeth, Northumberland, NE65 0DT
Activities: Other service activities n.e.c.
Officers: Julia Aston, Secretary; George Robert Arckless [1958] Director/Teaching; Catherine Millar Armstrong [1949] Director; William Redford Armstrong [1943] Director/Fisherman; Terence John Broughton [1943] Director; Maurice Burnett [1951] Director; John Charles Carruthers [1956] Director/Carpet and Bed Retailer; Rodney Alwyn Henderson [1956] Director/Civil Servant; Mary Helena MacLean [1943] Director; Derek Gibson Sproat Nickalls [1950] Director/Accountant; Moyra Evelyn Nyberg [1938] Director/Retired; Paul Harvey Rigby [1969] Director/Kitchen Designer; Andrew Sim [1936] Director/Retired; Jeffrey George Watson [1947] Director/Councillor; Craig Weir [1946] Director/Councillor

Ambuline Limited
Incorporated: 26 March 1993 *Employees:* 67
Net Worth: £1,030,000 *Total Assets:* £3,431,000
Registered Office: 1 Admiral Way, Doxford International Business Park, Sunderland, Tyne & Wear, SR3 3XP
Activities: Other passenger land transport
Officers: Lorna Edwards, Secretary; Carol Bainbridge [1965] Director; Andrew Charles Cullen [1979] Director; Stephen Brien Law [1969] Director; Edward Charles Thomas Potter [1982] Director

Amethyst Homes Limited
Incorporated: 23 May 2013 *Employees:* 17
Net Worth: £1,006,770 *Total Assets:* £3,586,192
Registered Office: Steel House, Ponds Court Business Park, Genesis Way, Consett, Co Durham, DH8 5XP
Activities: Construction of domestic buildings
Shareholder: Roland Mark Short
Officers: Gary Coils [1963] Construction Director; Richard John Emmerson [1968] Director/Accountant; David Robinson [1968] Commercial Director; Roland Mark Short [1966] Director/Civil Engineer

Amitex LED Lighting Company Limited
Incorporated: 26 February 2003
Net Worth: £236,939 *Total Assets:* £1,706,229
Registered Office: Unit 6 Building 2, Airport Freightway, Freight Village, Newcastle International Airport, Newcastle upon Tyne, NE13 8BH
Activities: Wholesale of other intermediate products
Major Shareholder: Alan Morton
Officers: Alan Morton [1958] Director; Alexander William Noble Morton [1989] Operation Director; David William Nesbitt [1971] Finance Director; Johnathan Robert Waugh [1985] Sales Director

Amjaf Estates Ltd
Incorporated: 11 May 2006
Net Worth: £165,275 *Total Assets:* £767,125
Registered Office: 24 Windermere Street, Gateshead, Tyne & Wear, NE8 1TU
Activities: Other letting and operating of own or leased real estate
Officers: Varda Amzalag, Secretary; Aharon Amazalag [1952] Director/Landlord

Amor Healthcare Limited
Incorporated: 19 July 2012 *Employees:* 10
Net Worth: £35,785 *Total Assets:* £1,413,422
Registered Office: 62 Fareham Grove, Harden Park, Boldon Colliery, Co Durham, NE35 9NF
Activities: Other human health activities
Shareholders: Aman Hussain; Omara Nawab
Officers: Aman Hussain, Secretary; Aman Hussain [1987] Director; Omara Nawab [1991] Director

Amtech Automated Micro Technology Limited
Incorporated: 21 January 1998 *Employees:* 4
Net Worth: £1,413,410 *Total Assets:* £2,044,924
Registered Office: Samson Close, Killingworth, Newcastle upon Tyne, NE12 6DX
Activities: Manufacture of computers and peripheral equipment
Shareholders: Stewart Ronald Scott; Elaine Scott
Officers: Elaine Scott, Secretary; Stewart Ronald Scott [1960] Director

Anabas (UK 2) Limited
Incorporated: 18 February 2003 *Employees:* 344
Net Worth: £1,018,582 *Total Assets:* £4,455,062
Registered Office: 2 Pioneer Court, Darlington, Co Durham, DL1 4WD
Activities: Other business support service activities n.e.c.
Major Shareholder: Mark Patrick Cooper
Officers: Mark Patrick Cooper [1967] Director; Alistair Craig [1971] Managing Director

Analox Limited
Incorporated: 23 December 1994 *Employees:* 75
Net Worth: £3,170,871 *Total Assets:* £4,074,364
Registered Office: 15 Ellerbeck Court, Stokesley Business Park, Stokesley, Middlesbrough, Cleveland, TS9 5PT
Activities: Other manufacturing n.e.c.
Major Shareholder: Alan Harbottle
Officers: Julia Harbottle, Secretary; Ian Bachelor [1962] Director/Accountant; Alan Harbottle [1953] Director/Chairman; Emma Clare Harbottle [1988] Operations Director; William Mark Lewis [1963] Managing Director; Simon Andrew Minto [1966] Director; Kathryn Victoria Pigg [1976] Sales Marketing Director

Analox Military Systems Limited
Incorporated: 4 April 2006 *Employees:* 5
Net Worth: £558,950 *Total Assets:* £6,469,344
Registered Office: 15 Ellerbeck Court, Stokesley Business Park, Stokesley, Cleveland, TS9 5PT
Activities: Manufacture of electronic measuring, testing etc. equipment, not for industrial process control
Parent: Analox Ltd
Officers: Ian Bachelor, Secretary; Alan Harbottle [1953] Director/Chairman; William Mark Lewis [1963] Managing Director; Simon Andrew Minto [1966] Director; Kathryn Victoria Pigg [1976] Sales and Marketing Director

Analox Sensor Technology Limited
Incorporated: 18 June 1996 *Employees:* 51
Net Worth: £1,210,152 *Total Assets:* £8,548,763
Registered Office: 15 Ellerbeck Court, Stokesley Business Park, Stokesley, Middlesbrough, Cleveland, TS9 5PT
Activities: Manufacture of electronic measuring, testing etc. equipment, not for industrial process control
Parent: Analox Ltd
Officers: Ian Bachelor, Secretary; Alan Harbottle [1953] Director; William Mark Lewis [1963] Director/Engineer

And Group Limited
Incorporated: 20 September 1988 *Employees:* 59
Net Worth: £1,714,684 *Total Assets:* £9,436,400
Registered Office: Tanners Bank, North Shields, Tyne & Wear, NE30 1JH
Activities: Satellite telecommunications activities
Officers: Robert Alan Howes, Secretary; Robert Alan Howes [1955] Director/Accountant; Ian Andrew Robinson [1961] Director/Chief Operating Officer

Anderson Barrowcliff LLP
Incorporated: 16 January 2008 *Employees:* 44
Net Worth: £711,224 *Total Assets:* £1,178,037
Registered Office: 3 Kingfisher Court, Bowesfield Park, Stockton on Tees, Cleveland, TS18 3EX
Officers: Beverley Susan Blakey [1961] Member; Jerome Quentin James Patrick Bury [1962] Member; James Andrew Dale [1982] Member; Andrew Dewing [1976] Member; David James Robertson [1967] Member; David Robert Shawcross [1966] Member; Helen Frances Wilson [1982] Member

William Anderson Farmers Limited
Incorporated: 18 December 1957
Registered Office: Ainderby Myers, Hackforth, Bedale, N Yorks, DL8 1PF
Activities: Mixed farming
Shareholders: David Anderson; Stuart Anderson; Nicholas Anderson
Officers: David Ian Anderson [1958] Director/Farmer; Nicholas John Anderson [1966] Director; Stuart Timothy Anderson [1961] Director

Andlaw Holdings Limited
Incorporated: 2 March 2010 *Employees:* 2
Net Worth: £1,083,004 *Total Assets:* £1,106,360
Registered Office: Unit J30 The Avenues, Eleventh Avenue North, Team Valley Trading Estate, Gateshead, Tyne & Wear, NE11 0NJ
Activities: Activities of head offices
Shareholders: Mark Joseph Anderson Anderson; Anthony Robert Lawton
Officers: Mark Joseph Anderson [1979] Director; Anthony Robert Lawton [1976] Director

Andojem Limited
Incorporated: 1 December 2011 *Employees:* 1
Net Worth: £484,570 *Total Assets:* £2,675,616
Registered Office: 511 Durham Road, Low Fell, Gateshead, Tyne & Wear, NE9 5EY
Activities: Other service activities n.e.c.
Major Shareholder: Andrew Patterson
Officers: Andrew Patterson [1963] Director; Emma Patterson [1993] Director

Angel Distribution Limited
Incorporated: 4 March 1998 *Employees:* 2
Net Worth: £1,070,145 *Total Assets:* £2,226,819
Registered Office: Regional Distribution Centre, Riverside Road, Southwick, Sunderland, Tyne & Wear, SR5 3JG
Activities: Freight transport by road
Shareholders: Joan Harker; Kevin Harker
Officers: Joan Harker, Company Secretary; Joan Harker [1954] Director/Secretary; Kevin Harker [1957] Director/Haulage Contractor

Angel Homes (Durham) Limited
Incorporated: 23 May 2013
Net Worth: £3,367,221 *Total Assets:* £6,414,283
Registered Office: c/o Workwear Express Ltd, Cathedral Park, Belmont Industrial Estate, Durham, DH1 1TN
Activities: Other letting and operating of own or leased real estate
Major Shareholder: Andrew John Ward
Officers: Andrew Ward, Secretary; Andrew John Ward [1972] Director

Angel of Corbridge Limited
Incorporated: 5 September 2005
Registered Office: Angel Inn, Main Street, Corbridge, Northumberland, NE45 5LA
Activities: Hotels and similar accommodation
Major Shareholder: Ismail Kurdi
Officers: Ismail Kurdi [1968] Director; Kevin James Laing [1966] Director

Angelbond Limited
Incorporated: 28 December 1983 *Employees:* 22
Net Worth: £2,351,355 *Total Assets:* £2,943,796
Registered Office: c/o Begbies Traynor, 2 Collingwood Street, Newcastle upon Tyne, NE1 1JF
Activities: Processing and preserving of fish, crustaceans and molluscs
Officers: Antoine Jean Michel Curunet [1982] Director [French]; Guenole Merveilleux [1973] Director [French]; Ronald Scordia [1971] Director [French]

Anglesea Terrace Orthodontic Practice Ltd
Incorporated: 27 November 2012 *Employees:* 4
Net Worth: £444,219 *Total Assets:* £1,168,816
Registered Office: Third Floor, Citygate, St James Boulevard, Newcastle upon Tyne, NE1 4JE
Activities: Dental practice activities
Parent: Braces for You Limited
Officers: Dr Rupinder Kaur Sidhu [1974] Director

Anglian Bus Limited
Incorporated: 27 May 1976 *Employees:* 62
Net Worth Deficit: £3,840,000 *Total Assets:* £2,131,000
Registered Office: 3rd Floor, 41-51 Grey Street, Newcastle upon Tyne, NE1 6EE
Activities: Other urban, suburban or metropolitan passenger land transport (not underground, metro or similar)
Parent: Go-Ahead Holding Limited
Officers: Carolyn Ferguson, Secretary; David Allen Brown [1960] Director; Simon Patrick Butcher [1967] Finance Director; Jeremy Hugh Cooper [1967] Director; Martin Richard Dean [1963] Director; David Hector Golding [1965] Director

Anglian Water Business (National) Limited
Incorporated: 14 February 1995 *Employees:* 29
Net Worth: £3,812,000 *Total Assets:* £43,123,000
Registered Office: Northumbria House, Abbey Road, Pity Me, Durham, DH1 5FJ
Activities: Water collection, treatment and supply
Parent: Wave Ltd
Officers: Martin Parker, Secretary; Richard Alistair Boucher [1969] Director; Lucy Jean Darch [1970] Director/MD Utilities Retailer; Anthony Donnelly [1964] Director; Stewart Hazon [1971] Director/Group Financial Controller; Martin Parker [1959] Director/Solicitor; Nigel Jonathan Watson [1964] IT Director; Wayne Paul Young [1976] Director/Chartered Accountant

Anglitemp Limited
Incorporated: 28 December 1979 *Employees:* 29
Net Worth: £118,821 *Total Assets:* £2,553,691
Registered Office: Unit A3, Third Avenue, Tyne Tunnel Trading Estate, North Shields, Tyne & Wear, NE29 7SW
Activities: Other manufacturing n.e.c.
Parent: Megastone Limited
Officers: Fiona Lough, Secretary; Gordon James Lough [1961] Director

Anglo Scottish Asset Finance Limited
Incorporated: 13 February 2007 *Employees:* 50
Net Worth: £1,264,272 *Total Assets:* £2,347,354
Registered Office: 12-14 Lumley Court, Drum Industrial Estate, Chester-le-Street, Co Durham, DH2 1AN
Activities: Financial intermediation not elsewhere classified
Parent: Maxxia (UK) Ltd
Officers: Lisa Joanne Edwards, Secretary; Mark Sutherland Blackburn [1957] Director/Chief Financial Officer & Company Secretary [Australian]; David Foster [1970] Director; Geoffrey Robert Kruyt [1968] Director/Business Executive [Australian]; Michael Neil Salisbury [1965] Managing Director and Chief Executive Officer [Australian]; Gareth Shaw [1971] Director/Chief Financial Officer; Murray Anderson Wark [1970] Director

Anvil Homes Limited
Incorporated: 6 October 1994 *Employees:* 4
Net Worth: £645,140 *Total Assets:* £2,262,542
Registered Office: Anvil House, Whittonstall, Consett, Co Durham, DH8 9JN
Activities: Construction of domestic buildings
Shareholders: Walter Carr; Iris Carr
Officers: Jill Tearse, Secretary; Alistair Edward Carr [1969] Managing Director; Andrew William Carr [1970] Director

Apartment 1 Limited
Incorporated: 3 January 2003 *Employees:* 119
Net Worth: £7,168,112 *Total Assets:* £14,431,321
Registered Office: 1st Floor, The Apartment Group Two, Jesmond Three Sixty, Newcastle upon Tyne, NE2 1DB
Activities: Public houses and bars
Major Shareholder: Duncan Fisher
Officers: Amanda Jayne Fisher, Secretary; Duncan Fisher [1968] Managing Director

Apex Cables Limited
Incorporated: 27 December 1979 *Employees:* 63
Net Worth: £6,497,151 *Total Assets:* £8,058,001
Registered Office: St Johns Road, Meadowfield Industrial Estate, Meadowfield, Co Durham, DH7 8RJ
Activities: Manufacture of other electrical equipment
Shareholders: David Francis Lewis; James Michael Lewis
Officers: David Francis Lewis, Secretary/Director; Anthony James Lewis [1978] Operation Director; David Francis Lewis [1956] Director; James Michael Lewis [1960] Director; Richard Lewis [1979] Commercial Director

Apex Radio Systems Limited
Incorporated: 27 March 1990
Net Worth: £564,624 *Total Assets:* £1,383,584
Registered Office: 102 Tantobie Road, Denton Burn, Newcastle upon Tyne, NE15 7DQ
Activities: Wireless telecommunications activities
Shareholder: James Southern Curry
Officers: Ian James Curry [1974] Director; James Southern Curry [1947] Director

Aphrodite Clothing Limited
Incorporated: 13 June 2001 *Employees:* 33
Net Worth: £805,373 *Total Assets:* £1,160,052
Registered Office: 8 Vine Place, Sunderland, Tyne & Wear, SR1 3NE
Activities: Retail sale of clothing in specialised stores
Shareholders: Duncan McKenzie; Andrew McKenzie
Officers: Andrew McKenzie, Secretary; Andrew McKenzie [1972] Director and Secretary; Duncan McKenzie [1975] Director

Apollo Facility Management Ltd
Incorporated: 2 July 2004 *Employees:* 21
Net Worth: £271,481 *Total Assets:* £1,010,533
Registered Office: Unit 5 Parsons Road, Parsons Industrial Estate, Washington, Tyne & Wear, NE37 1HB
Activities: Manufacture of metal structures and parts of structures
Shareholders: Ian Topliff; Lynn Topliff; Helen Simpson
Officers: Colin Simpson [1962] Director/Manager; Ian Topliff [1968] Director

Apollo Schools Trust
Incorporated: 7 August 2013 *Employees:* 17
Net Worth Deficit: £85,000 *Total Assets:* £951,000
Registered Office: Passfield Way, Peterlee, Co Durham, SR8 1AU
Activities: General secondary education
Officers: Lee John Alexander, Secretary; Suzanne Duncan [1971] Director/Principal and Chief Executive; Lesley Anne Powell [1966] Director/Principal; Margaret Patricia Saxton [1951] Director/Semi Retired; Carina Tomlinson [1976] Director/Assistant Principal

Applebridge Construction Limited
Incorporated: 15 October 2013 *Employees:* 100
Net Worth: £4,086,951 *Total Assets:* £10,494,699
Registered Office: Hughes House, Cargo Fleet Road, Middlesbrough, Cleveland, TS3 6AG
Activities: Construction of other civil engineering projects n.e.c.
Major Shareholder: Donal James Hughes
Officers: Christopher Roystone Brown [1981] Commercial Director; Donal James Hughes [1975] Director; Philip Gerard Hughes [1982] Director; Andrew Michael Ray [1978] Construction Director; Martyn Johnathan Strong [1977] Director

Appleton Grange Equestrian Centre Limited
Incorporated: 14 July 2009
Net Worth: £944,358 *Total Assets:* £1,028,614
Registered Office: c/o Isotank Services Limited, Limerick Road, Dormanstown, Cleveland, Redcar, Cleveland, TS10 5JU
Activities: Farm animal boarding and care
Shareholders: Enid Garnett; Brian Garnett Appleton Grange Will Trust
Officers: Enid Garnett, Secretary; Enid Garnett [1937] Director

Appletree Joinery Products Limited
Incorporated: 18 July 1985
Net Worth: £933,907 *Total Assets:* £2,689,677
Registered Office: Howden Road, Aycliffe Industrial Estate, Newton Aycliffe, Co Durham, DL5 6EU
Activities: Manufacture of other products of wood; manufacture of articles of cork, straw and plaiting materials
Parent: Tempest Research Limited
Officers: Fiona Morrison [1963] Director; Nicola Louise Young [1965] Director

Applied Ecological Services Limited
Incorporated: 21 March 1996
Net Worth: £739,475 *Total Assets:* £786,146
Registered Office: Ramshaw House, Ramshaw, Co Durham, DL14 0NG
Activities: Environmental consulting activities
Shareholders: Gary Tudor; Charlotte Tudor
Officers: Charlotte Tudor, Secretary; Charlotte Tudor [1974] Director/Ecologist; Gary Tudor [1960] Director/Ecologist

Applied Graphene Materials PLC
Incorporated: 27 September 2013 *Employees:* 42
Net Worth: £5,315,347 *Total Assets:* £6,112,473
Registered Office: The Wilton Centre, Wilton, Redcar, Cleveland, TS10 4RF
Activities: Manufacture of other inorganic basic chemicals
Officers: Gareth Hywel Jones, Secretary; Michael Sean Christie [1957] Director; Dr Karl Stuart Coleman [1971] Technical Director; Dr Bryan Crawford Dobson [1952] Director; Gareth Hywel Jones [1968] Director/Certified Chartered Accountant; Dr Hugh Adrian Potts [1961] Director/Chief Executive Officer; Michael Charles Nettleton Townend [1962] Director

Applied Graphene Materials UK Limited
Incorporated: 29 July 2010 *Employees:* 38
Net Worth Deficit: £13,833,000 *Total Assets:* £2,391,000
Registered Office: Office 2 Innovation Centre, Wilton Site, Redcar, Cleveland, TS10 4RF
Activities: Manufacture of other inorganic basic chemicals
Parent: Applied Graphene Materials PLC
Officers: Gareth Hywel Jones, Secretary; Dr Karl Stuart Coleman [1971] Director/Research Scientist; Dr Bryan Crawford Dobson [1952] Director; Gareth Hywel Jones [1968] Director/Certified Chartered Accountant; Dr Hugh Adrian Potts [1961] Director/Chief Executive Officer

Aptec Products Limited
Incorporated: 8 June 2006 *Employees:* 35
Net Worth: £2,267,861 *Total Assets:* £3,206,732
Registered Office: Aptec Enterprise Park, Darlington Road, West Auckland, Co Durham, DL14 9PD
Activities: Manufacture of man-made fibres
Shareholders: David Anthony Walker; Roy Stewart Perkins
Officers: David Anthony Walker, Secretary; Ian Hodgson [1950] Director; Roy Stewart Perkins [1951] Director/Financial Planing Consultant; David Anthony Walker [1945] Director/Chartered Accountant

Aquajet Drain Cleaning Limited
Incorporated: 5 October 2001
Net Worth: £277,502 *Total Assets:* £763,005
Registered Office: Unit 24 Drum Industrial Estate, Chester-le-Street, Co Durham, DH2 1AG
Activities: Sewerage
Parent: LP Construction Limited
Officers: Michelle Porter [1984] Director/Housewife

Aqualution Systems Ltd
Incorporated: 2 November 2000 *Employees:* 8
Net Worth Deficit: £856,042 *Total Assets:* £914,923
Registered Office: 19 Fenkle Street, Alnwick, Northumberland, NE66 1HW
Activities: Manufacture of other special-purpose machinery n.e.c.
Shareholders: Richard William Joyce; Arnold Joseph Hill; Nicholas St John Meakin
Officers: Richard William Joyce [1956] Director/Company Chairman; Nicholas St John Meakin [1959] Director/General Manager

Aquatran House Ltd
Incorporated: 17 February 2016
Net Worth: £1,565,848 *Total Assets:* £1,586,974
Registered Office: c/o Mincoffs Solicitors LLP, 5 Osborne Terrace, Jesmond, Newcastle upon Tyne, NE2 1SQ
Activities: Other letting and operating of own or leased real estate
Officers: Odd Egil Andersen [1955] Managing Director [Norwegian]; Per Kristian Hagen [1952] Director [Norwegian]

Aqueous 1st Kwikflow Limited
Incorporated: 28 September 1998
Net Worth: £1,057,017 *Total Assets:* £2,318,058
Registered Office: 71 Kingsway North, Team Valley Trading Estate, Gateshead, Tyne & Wear, NE11 0JH
Activities: Specialised cleaning services
Shareholders: Roy Flemming Bradley; Kevin Mark Waugh
Officers: Diane Eleanor Bradley, Secretary; Roy Fleming Bradley [1966] Director/Drainage Surveyors; Steven Hollis [1968] Director; Kevin Mark Waugh [1962] Director/IT Consultant

Aquind Limited
Incorporated: 26 August 2008 *Employees:* 7
Net Worth Deficit: £463,456 *Total Assets:* £3,899,694
Registered Office: OGN House, Hadrian Way, Wallsend, Tyne & Wear, NE28 6HL
Activities: Other construction installation
Officers: Richard Damien Glasspool [1956] Director/Chartered Accountant; Kirill Glukhovskoy [1974] Director/Manager; Alexander Temerko [1966] Director

Arc Adoption North East Limited
Incorporated: 18 November 2013
Registered Office: Unit 29 Business and Innovation Centre, Sunderland Enterprise Park East, Wearfield, Sunderland, Tyne & Wear, SR5 2TA
Activities: Other social work activities without accommodation n.e.c.
Officers: Terence Fitzpatrick [1958] Director/Social Worker; Lorraine Linda Jefferson [1957] Director/Social Work Manager

Arc Environmental Limited
Incorporated: 18 August 2005 *Employees:* 16
Net Worth: £1,236,188 *Total Assets:* £1,653,516
Registered Office: Solum House, Unit 1 Elliott Court, St Johns Road, Meadowfield, Co Durham, DH7 8PN
Activities: Technical testing and analysis
Officers: Kevin Moir, Secretary; Mark Richard Berriman [1966] Director/Engineer; Terence McMenam [1975] Director/Engineering Geologist; Kevin Charles Moir [1965] Director/Geologist

Arc Finance Group Limited
Incorporated: 18 January 2008 *Employees:* 50
Net Worth: £101,298 *Total Assets:* £839,075
Registered Office: Power House, 20 Haughton Road, Darlington, Co Durham, DL1 1ST
Activities: Activities auxiliary to financial intermediation n.e.c.
Parent: Arc Group Holdings Ltd
Officers: Rachel Chambers, Secretary; Nathen Phillip Lowe [1982] Director; Mark Sleaford [1985] Director; James Matthew Sloan [1987] Director/Financial Advisor

Arc Trinova Limited
Incorporated: 8 September 2015 *Employees:* 73
Net Worth: £3,992,790 *Total Assets:* £7,563,676
Registered Office: Taylor Drive, Alnwick, Northumberland, NE66 2DH
Activities: Research and experimental development on biotechnology
Shareholders: Paul Christopher Ryan; Ian Dermot Shott
Officers: Mark Gunnar Bryant [1962] Director; Dr Mark Philip Chadwick [1971] Director; Robert Paul Dungworth [1961] Director; Dr Michael John Hudson [1958] Director; Gareth Nicholas Jenkins [1969] Director; Paul Christopher Ryan [1965] Director; Ian Dermot Shott [1957] Director

Arcada Trading Limited
Incorporated: 14 October 2005
Net Worth: £1,025,980 *Total Assets:* £1,087,373
Registered Office: 237 Acklam Road, Acklam, Middlesbrough, Cleveland, TS5 7AB
Activities: Real estate agencies
Shareholders: Kirk Andrews; Chrsitopher James Andrews
Officers: Christopher James Andrews, Secretary; Christopher James Andrews [1978] Director; Kirk Andrews [1970] Director

Arch (Commercial Enterprise) Limited
Incorporated: 27 April 1998
Net Worth: £19,660,056 *Total Assets:* £221,496,912
Registered Office: Wansbeck Workspace, Rotary Parkway, Ashington, Northumberland, NE63 8QZ
Activities: Management consultancy activities other than financial management
Parent: Arch (Corporate Holdings) Limited
Officers: Peter Alan Jackson [1958] Director/Farmer; Jeffrey Stewart Reid [1956] Director/Leader of Northumberland Liberal Democrats Party; Christopher Mark Sayers [1960] Director/Chairman; Richard Watson Wearmouth [1981] Director/Engineer; John Crawford Woodman [1955] Director and Trustee

Arch (Corporate Holdings) Limited
Incorporated: 18 January 2011 *Employees:* 113
Net Worth: £59,710,848 *Total Assets:* £331,692,544
Registered Office: Wansbeck Workspace, Rotary Parkway, Ashington, Northumberland, NE63 8QZ
Activities: Activities of head offices
Parent: Northumberland County Council
Officers: Peter Alan Jackson [1958] Director/Farmer; Jeffrey Stewart Reid [1956] Director/Leader of Northumberland Liberal Democrats Party; Christopher Mark Sayers [1960] Director/Chairman; Richard Watson Wearmouth [1981] Director/Engineer; John Crawford Woodman [1955] Director and Trustee

Arch (Development Projects) Limited
Incorporated: 19 January 2011
Net Worth: £178,778 *Total Assets:* £23,316,284
Registered Office: Wansbeck Workspace, Rotary Parkway, Ashington, Northumberland, NE63 8QZ
Activities: Development of building projects
Parent: Arch (Corporate Holdings) Limited
Officers: Peter Alan Jackson [1958] Director/Farmer; Jeffrey Stewart Reid [1956] Director/Leader of Northumberland Liberal Democrats Party; Christopher Mark Sayers [1960] Director/Chairman; Richard Watson Wearmouth [1981] Director/Engineer; John Crawford Woodman [1955] Director and Trustee

Arch (Housing) Limited
Incorporated: 30 July 1986 *Employees:* 113
Net Worth: £39,013,648 *Total Assets:* £86,067,304
Registered Office: Wansbeck Workspace, Rotary Parkway, Ashington, Northumberland, NE63 8QZ
Activities: Other letting and operating of own or leased real estate
Parent: Arch (Corporate Holdings) Limited
Officers: Peter Alan Jackson [1958] Director/Farmer; Jeffrey Stewart Reid [1956] Director/Leader of Northumberland Liberal Democrats Party; Christopher Mark Sayers [1960] Director/Chairman; Richard Watson Wearmouth [1981] Director/Engineer; John Crawford Woodman [1955] Director and Trustee

Arch Building Supplies Limited
Incorporated: 2 February 1983 *Employees:* 11
Net Worth: £1,038,340 *Total Assets:* £1,533,477
Registered Office: Thornton House, Cargo Fleet Lane, Middlesbrough, Cleveland, TS3 8DE
Activities: Dormant company
Parent: Atkinson Northern Limited
Officers: James Edwin Atkinson [1957] Director; Jeremy John Boyd [1955] Director; Robin Jeremy Shuttleworth [1961] Director/Builders Merchant

Archers Law Limited Liability Partnership
Incorporated: 28 January 2004 *Employees:* 66
Net Worth: £627,221 *Total Assets:* £1,130,054
Registered Office: Lakeside House, Kingfisher Way, Stockton on Tees, Cleveland, TS18 3NB
Officers: Christopher David Todd [1968] Member; Angela Kathleen Torrance [1969] Member; David Adams [1983] LLP Member; Kenton David Bazeley [1975] LLP Member; Vicky Browning [1976] LLP Member; Elizabeth Casey [1972] LLP Member; Wendy Lorraine John [1983] LLP Member; Zoe Claire Tansley [1979] LLP Member

Architectural Powder Coatings Limited
Incorporated: 28 February 2002 *Employees:* 28
Net Worth: £628,555 *Total Assets:* £1,456,701
Registered Office: Blaydon Industrial Park, Chainbridge Road, Blaydon on Tyne, Tyne & Wear, NE21 5AB
Activities: Painting
Shareholders: Robin Harvey Orchard; Patricia Daphne Orchard
Officers: Patricia Daphne Orchard, Secretary; Robin Harvey Orchard [1947] Director/Chairman

Arcot Grange Developments Limited
Incorporated: 22 March 2013
Net Worth: £116,197 *Total Assets:* £2,017,346
Registered Office: 24 Apex Business Village, Cramlington, Northumberland, NE23 7BF
Activities: Construction of domestic buildings
Major Shareholder: Stuart Moy
Officers: Stuart Moy [1968] Director

Arcot Hall Golf Club Limited
Incorporated: 15 December 1909 *Employees:* 16
Net Worth: £523,795 *Total Assets:* £1,004,511
Registered Office: Arcot Hall, Dudley, Cramlington, Northumberland, NE23 7QP
Activities: Activities of sport clubs
Officers: Steven Alan Halsall, Secretary; Eleanor Allan [1945] Director/Retired; Peter Clayton [1949] Director/Retired; Steven James Connelly [1973] Director; David Anthony Evans [1938] Director; Steve Alan Halsall [1954] Director/Retired; Simon John Lunn [1967] Director/Civil Servant; Andrew Lynch [1963] Director/Manager; Pat Mattinson [1949] Director/Retired; Neil Melrose [1951] Director/Salesman; Gary Russell [1962] Director/Housing Finance Co-ordinator; David Alan Sanson [1959] Director; Margaret Spence [1943] Director/Retired

Arcwhiz 2000 Limited
Incorporated: 10 January 2000 *Employees:* 40
Net Worth: £3,986,380 *Total Assets:* £4,154,388
Registered Office: Lion House, 400 Durham Road, Birtley, Chester-le-Street, Co Durham, DH3 1LS
Activities: Licenced restaurants
Major Shareholder: Robert Pattinson
Officers: Stevie-Lee Pattinson, Secretary; Robert Pattinson [1934] Director/Theatrical; Stevie-Lee Pattinson [1969] Director/Care Homes

Arete Learning Trust
Incorporated: 4 March 2015 *Employees:* 152
Net Worth: £13,972,000 *Total Assets:* £16,561,000
Registered Office: Stokesley School, Station Road, Stokesley, Cleveland, TS9 5AL
Activities: Primary education
Officers: Paul Donald Bartlett [1960] Director/Chartered Engineer; Stewart William Brennan [1966] Director/Project Manager; Catherine Mary Brooker [1955] Director/Headteacher; Mark Hardwick Foster [1962] Chartered Accountant and Director; Judith Ann Hooton [1948] Director/Education Consultant; Andrew Paul Hutchinson [1965] Director/Minister of Religion; Andrew Peaston Price [1961] Director/University Manager

Argent Wealth Limited
Incorporated: 17 November 2009 *Employees:* 5
Net Worth: £268,691 *Total Assets:* £930,784
Registered Office: Evolve Building, Cygnet Way, Rainton Bridge Business Park, Houghton-le-Spring, Co Durham, DH4 5QY
Activities: Financial intermediation not elsewhere classified
Shareholder: David Hardman
Officers: David Hardman [1965] Director

Argentaurum Limited
Incorporated: 4 September 2014
Net Worth: £2,700,998 *Total Assets:* £2,980,022
Registered Office: 24 Elvet Bridge, Durham, DH1 3AA
Activities: Retail sale of watches and jewellery in specialised stores
Shareholder: William John Bramwell
Officers: Gwendoline Mabel Bramwell, Secretary; Jill Bramwell [1956] Director/Jeweller; Peter Bramwell [1947] Director/Jeweller; William John Bramwell [1954] Director/Jeweller

Argos Inspection Company Limited
Incorporated: 17 March 1980
Net Worth: £1,160,363 *Total Assets:* £1,781,447
Registered Office: Inspection House, Tower Road, Glover Estate, District 11, Washington, Tyne & Wear, NE37 2SH
Activities: Technical testing and analysis
Major Shareholder: Peter William Bauckham
Officers: Evelyn Georgina Margaret Reay, Secretary; Peter William Bauckham [1947] Director; Evelyn Georgina Margaret Reay [1952] Director

Argrennan Manor House Limited
Incorporated: 10 January 2005
Net Worth Deficit: £1,306,189 *Total Assets:* £1,669,659
Registered Office: 3 Kingfisher Court, Bowesfield Park, Stockton on Tees, Cleveland, TS18 3EX
Activities: Other amusement and recreation activities n.e.c.
Major Shareholder: Alistair Flanagan
Officers: Gail Flanagan, Secretary; Alistair Flanagan [1955] Director

Argyle House Holdings Limited
Incorporated: 30 August 2007
Net Worth: £866,070 *Total Assets:* £1,700,601
Registered Office: Argyle House School, 19-20 Thornhill Park, Sunderland, Tyne & Wear, SR2 7LA
Activities: Pre-primary education
Major Shareholder: Christopher Johnson
Officers: Andrea Rose Johnson [1975] Director/Housewife; Christopher Johnson [1975] Director

Argyle Square Properties Limited
Incorporated: 9 September 2003 *Employees:* 3
Net Worth: £142,422 *Total Assets:* £3,674,128
Registered Office: The Barn, Cobshaw Farm, Langthorne, Bedale, N Yorks, DL8 1PJ
Activities: Development of building projects
Officers: Jason Living, Secretary; Bernard Courtney Living [1936] Director/Chartered Surveyor; Jason Living [1966] Director/Chartered Surveyor; Joanna Kirsty Living [1968] Director/Property Investor

Aristou Family Partnership LLP
Incorporated: 11 November 2016
Net Worth: £1,720,314 *Total Assets:* £1,721,314
Registered Office: Yoden House, 30 Yoden Way, Peterlee, Co Durham, SR8 1AL
Officers: Salome Aristou [1954] Member

Arix Europe Limited
Incorporated: 3 November 2009 *Employees:* 6
Net Worth: £755,344 *Total Assets:* £1,654,479
Registered Office: Milfield Enterprise Park, Milfield, Wooler, Northumberland, NE71 6TF
Activities: General cleaning of buildings
Shareholder: Timothy Ernest Myer
Officers: Timothy Ernest Myer [1954] Director

Arjuna Technologies Limited
Incorporated: 27 July 2002 *Employees:* 2
Net Worth: £685,032 *Total Assets:* £919,437
Registered Office: The Urban Sciences Building, Science Square, Science Central, Newcastle upon Tyne, NE4 5TG
Activities: Business and domestic software development
Officers: Dr Stuart Mark Wheater, Secretary; John George Carney [1948] Director/Strategic Consultancy; Stephen Mark I'anson [1955] Director; Stuart Mark Wheater [1963] Director/Software Architect

Arkgrove Limited
Incorporated: 9 February 1982 *Employees:* 19
Net Worth: £17,134,198 *Total Assets:* £25,506,312
Registered Office: Mandale House, 5 Neville Road, North Tees Industrial Estate, Stockton on Tees, Cleveland, TS18 2RD
Activities: Other letting and operating of own or leased real estate
Officers: Joseph Darragh, Secretary; Paula Davidson, Secretary; David Ian Harriman [1956] Director; Richard Thomas Harriman [1990] Director

Arlesville Estates Limited
Incorporated: 7 April 1972 *Employees:* 3
Net Worth: £36,827,716 *Total Assets:* £41,234,956
Registered Office: Fernwood House, Fernwood Road, Jesmond, Newcastle upon Tyne, NE2 1TJ
Activities: Development of building projects
Shareholders: Alexander Ellinson; Uri Ellinson
Officers: Uri Ellinson, Secretary; Alexander Ellinson [1967] Director/Property Dealer; Uri Ellinson [1970] Director

Arlington Automotive NE Limited
Incorporated: 6 March 1984 *Employees:* 103
Net Worth: £4,071,000 *Total Assets:* £8,830,000
Registered Office: Arlington Automotive NE Limited, Gurney Way, Aycliffe Business Park, Newton Aycliffe, Co Durham, DL5 6UJ
Activities: Manufacture of metal structures and parts of structures
Parent: Arlington Automotive Holdings Limited
Officers: Peter William Coates [1971] Director/Engineer; Mark Franckel [1962] Director; Simon George Greenhalgh [1972] Director/Chief Financial Officer; Kevin Morley [1950] Director

Armah Switchgear Limited
Incorporated: 1 February 1991 *Employees:* 63
Net Worth: £326,466 *Total Assets:* £2,407,448
Registered Office: 18 Tower Road, Glover West Industrial Estate, District 11, Washington, Tyne & Wear, NE37 2SH
Activities: Manufacture of electricity distribution and control apparatus
Shareholders: Andrew Robert Mayo; Alan Hawkins
Officers: Alan Hawkins, Secretary; Alan Hawkins [1958] Director/Manager; Andrew Robert Mayo [1961] Director/Manager

Armes-Reardon Properties Limited
Incorporated: 2 November 2012 *Employees:* 2
Net Worth: £172,961 *Total Assets:* £3,603,992
Registered Office: Sandgate House, 102 Quayside, Newcastle upon Tyne, NE1 3DX
Activities: Buying and selling of own real estate
Shareholders: Simon Patrick John Francis Armes-Reardon; Sarah Lesley Armes-Reardon
Officers: Sarah Lesley Armes-Reardon [1969] Director; Simon Patrick John Francis Armes-Reardon [1955] Director

Armour Plastics Limited
Incorporated: 8 June 1971 *Employees:* 63
Net Worth: £3,018,935 *Total Assets:* £4,320,218
Registered Office: Unit 13b, Pennywell Industrial Estate, Sunderland, Tyne & Wear, SR4 9EN
Activities: Manufacture of other plastic products
Shareholders: Sean Michael Mulloy; John Mulloy
Officers: Sean Michael Mulloy, Secretary; Nigel Patrick Clamp [1967] Director; Paul Lindley [1968] Sales Director; John Mulloy [1936] Director; Sean Michael Mulloy [1961] Director; Paul Kenneth Samuel [1977] Director/Engineer

Armourpost Limited
Incorporated: 11 November 1991 *Employees:* 25
Net Worth: £627,831 *Total Assets:* £1,119,852
Registered Office: Saltmeadows Road, East Gateshead Industrial Estate, Gateshead, Tyne & Wear, NE8 3AH
Activities: Other manufacturing n.e.c.
Shareholder: Nicola Scott
Officers: Nicola Scott, Secretary; Nicola Scott [1969] Director/Administration; Mark Spoors [1966] Director; Geoffrey Young [1970] Director/Manager; Victoria Young [1978] Director/Administrator

Armstrong Direct Limited
Incorporated: 24 October 2005 *Employees:* 19
Net Worth: £1,522,679 *Total Assets:* £2,798,981
Registered Office: 194 Thames Road, Billingham, Stockton on Tees, Cleveland, TS22 5EF
Activities: Retail sale via mail order houses or via Internet
Parent: Montgomery Blue Limited
Officers: Kathryn Louise Armstrong, Secretary; Kathryn Louise Armstrong [1969] Director/Administrator; Stephen Neil Armstrong [1971] Director

Armstrong Foulkes LLP
Incorporated: 23 May 2013 *Employees:* 6
Net Worth: £855,376 *Total Assets:* £970,438
Registered Office: Cleveland Business Centre, Watson Street, Middlesbrough, Cleveland, TS1 2RQ
Officers: Robert Hilton Armstrong [1958] Member; Joanne Dennison [1976] LLP Member; Ashleigh Holt [1980] LLP Member

Armstrong Hall Social Club Ltd
Incorporated: 16 February 2012
Net Worth Deficit: £43,892 *Total Assets:* £775,652
Registered Office: 5a Station Terrace, East Boldon, Co Durham, NE36 0LJ
Activities: Licenced clubs
Shareholder: Satnam Singh
Officers: Gurminder Kaur [1961] Director/Manager; Satnam Singh [1963] Director/Manager

D & D Armstrong Limited
Incorporated: 4 April 2003 *Employees:* 21
Net Worth: £3,888,311 *Total Assets:* £6,797,195
Registered Office: The Old Stables, Bebside, Blyth, Northumberland, NE24 4JW
Activities: Sea and coastal freight water transport
Shareholders: David Armstrong; Donna Armstrong
Officers: Donna Armstrong, Secretary; David Armstrong [1963] Director/Sales Executive; Donna Armstrong [1966] Director/Administrator

Armstrong Nationwide Ltd.
Incorporated: 4 February 2000
Net Worth: £2,107,588 *Total Assets:* £2,279,412
Registered Office: 17 Riverside Studios, Amethyst Road, Newcastle upon Tyne, NE4 7YL
Activities: Activities of mortgage finance companies
Major Shareholder: Beverley Armstrong
Officers: Beverly Armstrong, Secretary; Beverly Armstrong [1972] Director/Manager; Stephen Andrew Barber [1970] Finance Director

Armstrong Richardson & Co.Limited
Incorporated: 2 June 1925 *Employees:* 185
Net Worth: £7,275,959 *Total Assets:* £17,216,364
Registered Office: Mount Pleasant Way, Stokesley Business Park, Stokesley, Cleveland, TS9 5NZ
Activities: Wholesale of grain, unmanufactured tobacco, seeds and animal feeds
Shareholders: Nigel Edwin Mitchell Jones; Craig Barclay Mitchell Jones; Mark Duncan Mitchell Jones
Officers: Serena Elizabeth Jones [1991] Director/Manager; Susan Elisabeth Jones [1940] Director; Michael David Sharp [1967] Director/Accountant; Helen Thompson [1980] Director/Wholesale Manager

Arodnap Limited
Incorporated: 20 May 2010 *Employees:* 25
Net Worth: £671,537 *Total Assets:* £1,034,656
Registered Office: 24 Elvet Bridge, Durham, DH1 3AA
Activities: Retail sale of watches and jewellery in specialised stores
Shareholder: William John Bramwell
Officers: William John Bramwell, Secretary; Jill Bramwell [1956] Director; Peter Bramwell [1947] Director; William John Bramwell [1954] Director

Arquer Diagnostics Limited
Incorporated: 18 April 2005 *Employees:* 12
Net Worth: £1,631,539 *Total Assets:* £1,906,166
Registered Office: North East Business & Innovation Centre, Wearfield, Sunderland, Tyne & Wear, SR5 2TA
Activities: Manufacture of electronic measuring, testing etc. equipment, not for industrial process control
Shareholder: Longwall Ventures ECF LP
Officers: Sarah Lucy Couch [1971] Director/Chief Technical Officer; Sarah Lucy Couch [1971] Director/Chief Technical Officer; David James Edmonds Denny [1970] Director; Dr David Nicholas Miller-Jones [1951] Director; Dr Sandy Blackadder Primrose [1944] Director/Technology Consultant; Nadia Whittley [1965] Director [Australian/Italian]

Arrandene Ltd
Incorporated: 19 September 2002
Net Worth Deficit: £252,102 *Total Assets:* £905,121
Registered Office: 28 Morgans Way, Blaydon on Tyne, Tyne & Wear, NE21 4HN
Activities: Other business support service activities n.e.c.
Major Shareholder: Scott Andrew Robson
Officers: Scott Andrew Robson [1975] Director Plumbing Engineer

Arriva Bus & Coach Limited
Incorporated: 4 October 1972 *Employees:* 68
Net Worth: £10,608,000 *Total Assets:* £56,702,000
Registered Office: 1 Admiral Way, Doxford International Business Park, Sunderland, Tyne & Wear, SR3 3XP
Activities: Sale of new cars and light motor vehicles
Officers: Lorna Edwards, Secretary; Carol Bainbridge [1965] Director; Andrew Charles Cullen [1979] Director; Stephen Brien Law [1969] Director; Edward Charles Thomas Potter [1982] Director

Arriva Cymru Limited
Incorporated: 22 May 1919 *Employees:* 546
Net Worth: £23,240,000 *Total Assets:* £33,826,000
Registered Office: 1 Admiral Way, Doxford International Business Park, Sunderland, Tyne & Wear, SR3 3XP
Activities: Other urban, suburban or metropolitan passenger land transport (not underground, metro or similar)
Officers: Lorna Edwards, Secretary; Philip Cummins [1968] Director; Tina Colleen Edwards [1982] Director; Michael John Morton [1958] Director; Philip Martin Stone [1961] Director; John Ian Thompson [1978] Director

Arriva Durham County Limited
Incorporated: 14 July 1989 *Employees:* 812
Net Worth: £30,760,000 *Total Assets:* £46,652,000
Registered Office: 1 Admiral Way, Doxford International Business Park, Sunderland, Tyne & Wear, SR3 3XP
Activities: Other urban, suburban or metropolitan passenger land transport (not underground, metro or similar)
Officers: Lorna Edwards, Secretary; David Cocker [1957] Director; Nigel Paul Featham [1964] Managing Director; Nicholas Robert Knox [1955] Director; Thomas Robert Large [1985] Director

Arriva International (Northern Europe) Limited
Incorporated: 2 December 2004 *Employees:* 3
Net Worth: £173,011,904 *Total Assets:* £349,304,224
Registered Office: 1 Admiral Way, Doxford International Business Park, Sunderland, Tyne & Wear, SR3 3XP
Activities: Activities of head offices
Officers: Lorna Edwards, Secretary; Peter Charles Davison [1965] Director; David Graham Johnstone [1963] Director Group Tax; Piers Darryl St John Marlow [1959] Director

Arriva International (Southern Europe) Limited
Incorporated: 2 December 2004
Net Worth: £173,011,904 *Total Assets:* £349,304,224
Registered Office: 1 Admiral Way, Doxford International Business Park, Sunderland, Tyne & Wear, SR3 3XP
Activities: Activities of head offices
Officers: Lorna Edwards, Secretary; Peter Charles Davison [1965] Director; David Graham Johnstone [1963] Director Group Tax

Arriva International Limited
Incorporated: 8 July 1983
Net Worth: £346,718,784 *Total Assets:* £733,470,272
Registered Office: 1 Admiral Way, Doxford International Business Park, Sunderland, Tyne & Wear, SR3 3XP
Activities: Non-trading company
Officers: Lorna Edwards, Secretary; Richard Piers Sainthill Burgess [1972] Director; Peter Charles Davison [1965] Director; David Graham Johnstone [1963] Director Group Tax; Piers Darryl St John Marlow [1959] Director

Arriva International Trains (Leasing) Limited
Incorporated: 11 December 2001 *Employees:* 4
Net Worth: £14,943,250 *Total Assets:* £48,736,736
Registered Office: 1 Admiral Way, Doxford International Business Park, Sunderland, Tyne & Wear, SR3 3XP
Activities: Other business support service activities n.e.c.
Officers: Lorna Edwards, Secretary; Peter Charles Davison [1965] Director; David Graham Johnstone [1963] Director Group Tax; Piers Darryl St John Marlow [1959] Director

Arriva Kent & Surrey Limited
Incorporated: 22 March 1911 *Employees:* 893
Net Worth: £16,535,000 *Total Assets:* £43,088,000
Registered Office: 1 Admiral Way, Doxford International Business Park, Sunderland, Tyne & Wear, SR3 3XP
Activities: Other urban, suburban or metropolitan passenger land transport (not underground, metro or similar)
Officers: Lorna Edwards, Secretary; Jason Bush [1967] Director; Gavin Craig Hunter [1979] Director; Simon Oliver Loh [1983] Director; Oliver Joseph Monahan [1975] Director; Laura Kiri Wakefield [1982] Director

Arriva Kent Thameside Limited
Incorporated: 1 April 1986 *Employees:* 1,079
Net Worth: £30,007,000 *Total Assets:* £40,256,000
Registered Office: 1 Admiral Way, Doxford International Business Park, Sunderland, Tyne & Wear, SR3 3XP
Activities: Other urban, suburban or metropolitan passenger land transport (not underground, metro or similar)
Officers: Lorna Edwards, Secretary; Jason Bush [1967] Director; Gavin Craig Hunter [1979] Director; Simon Oliver Loh [1983] Director; Oliver Joseph Monahan [1975] Director; Laura Kiri Wakefield [1982] Director

Arriva London North Limited
Incorporated: 14 December 1988 *Employees:* 3,957
Net Worth: £56,462,000 *Total Assets:* £205,327,008
Registered Office: 1 Admiral Way, Doxford International Business Park, Sunderland, Tyne & Wear, SR3 3XP
Activities: Other urban, suburban or metropolitan passenger land transport (not underground, metro or similar)
Officers: Lorna Edwards, Secretary; Pierre Andrew Jonathan Stephen Ayers [1970] Director; Peter John Batty [1961] Commercial Director; Alexander Jones [1963] Director; Harmeet Singh Notay [1987] Director; Robert Scowen [1960] Director

Arriva London South Limited
Incorporated: 14 December 1988 *Employees:* 1,606
Net Worth: £45,047,000 *Total Assets:* £81,090,000
Registered Office: 1 Admiral Way, Doxford International Business Park, Sunderland, Tyne & Wear, SR3 3XP
Activities: Other urban, suburban or metropolitan passenger land transport (not underground, metro or similar)
Officers: Lorna Edwards, Secretary; Pierre Andrew Jonathan Stephen Ayers [1970] Director; Peter John Batty [1961] Commercial Director; Alexander Jones [1963] Director; Harmeet Singh Notay [1987] Director; Robert Scowen [1960] Director

Arriva Merseyside Limited
Incorporated: 18 February 1986 *Employees:* 1,555
Net Worth: £48,381,000 *Total Assets:* £79,443,000
Registered Office: 1 Admiral Way, Doxford International Business Park, Sunderland, Tyne & Wear, SR3 3XP
Activities: Other urban, suburban or metropolitan passenger land transport (not underground, metro or similar)
Officers: Lorna Edwards, Secretary; Philip Cummins [1968] Director; Tina Colleen Edwards [1982] Director; Howard Edge Farrall [1960] Director; Philip Martin Stone [1961] Director; John Ian Thompson [1978] Director

Arriva Midlands Limited
Incorporated: 18 June 1987 *Employees:* 836
Net Worth: £24,454,000 *Total Assets:* £48,618,000
Registered Office: 1 Admiral Way, Doxford International Business Park, Sunderland, Tyne & Wear, SR3 3XP
Activities: Other urban, suburban or metropolitan passenger land transport (not underground, metro or similar)
Officers: Lorna Edwards, Secretary; Mark Antony Bowd [1962] Director; Tina Colleen Edwards [1982] Director; Simon Joseph Finnie [1978] Director; Simon William Mathieson [1979] Director; Kevin Liam O'Leary [1962] Director; Jason Mathew Perkin [1974] Director; Cora Woodhouse [1978] Director

Arriva Midlands North Limited
Incorporated: 15 April 1981 *Employees:* 608
Net Worth: £9,363,000 *Total Assets:* £23,828,000
Registered Office: 1 Admiral Way, Doxford International Business Park, Sunderland, Tyne & Wear, SR3 3XP
Activities: Other urban, suburban or metropolitan passenger land transport (not underground, metro or similar)
Officers: Lorna Edwards, Secretary; Mark Antony Bowd [1962] Director; Tina Colleen Edwards [1982] Director; Simon William Mathieson [1979] Director; Kevin Liam O'Leary [1962] Director; Jason Mathew Perkin [1974] Director; Cora Woodhouse [1978] Director

Arriva Motor Holdings Limited
Incorporated: 4 April 1989 *Employees:* 2
Net Worth: £97,345,000 *Total Assets:* £97,345,000
Registered Office: 1 Admiral Way, Doxford International Business Park, Sunderland, Tyne & Wear, SR3 3XP
Activities: Non-trading company
Officers: Lorna Edwards, Secretary; Lorna Edwards [1984] Director; David Graham Johnstone [1963] Director Group Tax

Arriva North West Limited
Incorporated: 5 September 1953 *Employees:* 919
Net Worth: £4,384,000 *Total Assets:* £37,580,000
Registered Office: 1 Admiral Way, Doxford International Business Park, Sunderland, Tyne & Wear, SR3 3XP
Activities: Other urban, suburban or metropolitan passenger land transport (not underground, metro or similar)
Officers: Lorna Edwards, Secretary; Philip Cummins [1968] Director; Tina Colleen Edwards [1982] Director; Howard Edge Farrall [1960] Director; Philip Martin Stone [1961] Director; John Ian Thompson [1978] Director

Arriva Northumbria Limited
Incorporated: 28 February 1929 *Employees:* 535
Net Worth: £11,978,000 *Total Assets:* £28,443,000
Registered Office: 1 Admiral Way, Doxford International Business Park, Sunderland, Tyne & Wear, SR3 3XP
Activities: Other urban, suburban or metropolitan passenger land transport (not underground, metro or similar)
Officers: Lorna Edwards, Secretary; David Cocker [1957] Director; Nigel Paul Featham [1964] Managing Director; Nicholas Robert Knox [1955] Director; Thomas Robert Large [1985] Director

Arriva PLC
Incorporated: 8 December 1938 *Employees:* 269
Net Worth: £652,729,024 *Total Assets:* £931,694,016
Registered Office: 1 Admiral Way, Doxford International Business Park, Sunderland, Tyne & Wear, SR3 3XP
Activities: Passenger rail transport, interurban
Officers: Peter Charles Davison, Secretary; Alexander Doll [1970] Director [German]; Martin James Hibbert [1967] Director/Chartered Accountant; Berthold Huber [1963] Director [German]; Stefan Klenke [1971] Director/Head of M&A [German]; Dr. Marein Mueller [1967] Director [German]; Dr. Manfred Rudhart [1965] Director/CFO Deutsche Bahn Regional [German]

Arriva Rail North Limited
Incorporated: 11 December 2001 *Employees:* 5,488
Net Worth: £44,193,000 *Total Assets:* £154,451,008
Registered Office: c/o Arriva PLC, 1 Admiral Way, Doxford International Business Park, Sunderland, Tyne & Wear, SR3 3XP
Activities: Passenger rail transport, interurban
Officers: Lorna Edwards, Secretary; Richard Graham Allan [1973] Director; David Brown [1965] Director; Christopher Derek Dyne Burchell [1973] Director; Amanda Furlong [1975] Director; Mary Elisabeth Courtney Hewitt [1979] Director

Arriva The Shires Limited
Incorporated: 30 March 1987 *Employees:* 823
Net Worth: £20,929,000 *Total Assets:* £39,685,000
Registered Office: 1 Admiral Way, Doxford International Business Park, Sunderland, Tyne & Wear, SR3 3XP
Activities: Other urban, suburban or metropolitan passenger land transport (not underground, metro or similar)
Officers: Lorna Edwards, Secretary; Mark Antony Bowd [1962] Director; Tina Colleen Edwards [1982] Director; Simon Joseph Finnie [1978] Director; Kevin Liam O'Leary [1962] Director; Jason Mathew Perkin [1974] Director; Cora Woodhouse [1978] Director

Arriva Trains Holdings Limited
Incorporated: 6 July 1995 *Employees:* 3
Net Worth: £103,964,000 *Total Assets:* £124,247,000
Registered Office: 1 Admiral Way, Doxford International Business Park, Sunderland, Tyne & Wear, SR3 3XP
Activities: Passenger rail transport, interurban
Officers: Lorna Edwards, Secretary; Amanda Furlong [1975] Director; David James Penney [1975] Director; Alexis James Scott [1983] Director

Arriva Transport Solutions Limited
Incorporated: 28 April 1966 *Employees:* 542
Net Worth Deficit: £817,000 *Total Assets:* £6,889,000
Registered Office: 1 Admiral Way, Doxford International Business Park, Sunderland, Tyne & Wear, SR3 3XP
Activities: Other passenger land transport
Officers: Lorna Edwards, Secretary; Carol Bainbridge [1965] Director; Andrew Charles Cullen [1979] Director; Stephen Brien Law [1969] Director; Edward Charles Thomas Potter [1982] Director

Arriva UK Bus Holdings Limited
Incorporated: 23 February 2001
Net Worth: £425,347,008 *Total Assets:* £505,856,992
Registered Office: 1 Admiral Way, Doxford International Business Park, Sunderland, Tyne & Wear, SR3 3XP
Activities: Activities of head offices
Officers: Liam Edward McDermott, Secretary; Ruth Cecilia Abdey [1976] Director; Alistair Jonathon Hands [1971] Director; Iain Mulligan Jago [1970] Director; Mark Richard Noakes [1970] Director

Arriva UK Bus Investments Limited
Incorporated: 28 September 1964 *Employees:* 2
Net Worth: £311,300,992 *Total Assets:* £315,041,984
Registered Office: 1 Admiral Way, Doxford International Business Park, Sunderland, Tyne & Wear, SR3 3XP
Activities: Other business support service activities n.e.c.
Officers: Liam Edward McDermott, Secretary; Ruth Cecilia Abdey [1976] Director; Alistair Jonathon Hands [1971] Director; Iain Mulligan Jago [1970] Director; Mark Richard Noakes [1970] Director

Arriva UK Bus Limited
Incorporated: 19 October 1992 *Employees:* 177
Net Worth: £3,374,000 *Total Assets:* £41,227,000
Registered Office: 1 Admiral Way, Doxford International Business Park, Sunderland, Tyne & Wear, SR3 3XP
Activities: Activities of head offices
Officers: Liam Edward McDermott, Secretary; Ruth Cecilia Abdey [1976] Director; Alistair Jonathon Hands [1971] Director; Iain Mulligan Jago [1970] Director; Mark Richard Noakes [1970] Director

Arriva UK Bus Properties Limited
Incorporated: 8 October 1980 *Employees:* 5
Net Worth: £1,742,000 *Total Assets:* £1,911,000
Registered Office: 1 Admiral Way, Doxford International Business Park, Sunderland, Tyne & Wear, SR3 3XP
Activities: Development of building projects
Parent: Arriva UK Bus Holdings Limited
Officers: Liam Edward McDermott, Secretary; Ruth Cecilia Abdey [1976] Director; Alistair Jonathon Hands [1971] Director; Iain Mulligan Jago [1970] Director; Mark Richard Noakes [1970] Director

Arriva UK Trains Limited
Incorporated: 29 February 1996 *Employees:* 68
Net Worth: £154,460,000 *Total Assets:* £205,054,000
Registered Office: 1 Admiral Way, Doxford International Business Park, Sunderland, Tyne & Wear, SR3 3XP
Activities: Passenger rail transport, interurban
Officers: Lorna Edwards, Secretary; Christopher John Brooks [1975] Director; Christopher Derek Dyne Burchell [1973] Director; Peter Charles Davison [1965] Director; Amanda Furlong [1975] Director; Mary Elisabeth Courtney Hewitt [1979] Director

Arriva Yorkshire Limited
Incorporated: 5 April 1905 *Employees:* 931
Net Worth: £22,156,000 *Total Assets:* £45,971,000
Registered Office: 1 Admiral Way, Doxford International Business Park, Sunderland, Tyne & Wear, SR3 3XP
Activities: Other urban, suburban or metropolitan passenger land transport (not underground, metro or similar)
Officers: Lorna Edwards, Secretary; David Cocker [1957] Finance Director; Jon Lee Croxford [1984] Director; Nigel Paul Featham [1964] Director; Thomas Robert Large [1985] Director

Arrow Commercial Limited
Incorporated: 2 August 1988 *Employees:* 2
Net Worth: £632,903 *Total Assets:* £1,253,981
Registered Office: Victoria House, High Street, Witton-le-Wear, Co Durham, DL14 0AY
Activities: Development of building projects
Shareholders: Philip Gibbs; Valerie Margaret Gibbs
Officers: Valerie Margaret Gibbs, Secretary; Philip Gibbs [1961] Director; Valerie Margaret Gibbs [1960] Director

Arrowbuild & Civil Engineering Limited
Incorporated: 11 November 2009 *Employees:* 146
Net Worth: £2,150,980 *Total Assets:* £5,228,263
Registered Office: c/o Waltons Clark Whitehill, Maritime House, Harbour Walk, The Marina, Hartlepool, Cleveland, TS24 0UX
Activities: Construction of domestic buildings
Parent: Arrowcruit Holdings Ltd
Officers: Carol Ann Hutchinson, Secretary; Carol Ann Hutchinson [1960] Director/Farmer; Robert Owen Hutchinson [1968] Director

Arrowcruit Limited
Incorporated: 22 September 2005 *Employees:* 11
Net Worth: £272,568 *Total Assets:* £2,805,899
Registered Office: c/o Waltons Clark Whtiehill, Maritime House, Harbour Walk, The Marina, Hartlepool, Cleveland, TS24 0UX
Activities: Site preparation
Parent: Arrowcruit Holdings Ltd
Officers: Carol Ann Hutchinson, Secretary/Farmer; Carol Ann Hutchinson [1960] Director/Farmer; Robert Owen Hutchinson [1968] Director

Artemis Support Limited
Incorporated: 9 September 2009 *Employees:* 37
Net Worth: £16,226 *Total Assets:* £1,164,058
Registered Office: 92 Whitton View, Rothbury, Morpeth, Northumberland, NE65 7QN
Activities: Other residential care activities n.e.c.
Shareholders: Clare Lesley Coward; Ciaron Paul Gallagher; Lee James Coward
Officers: Clare Lesley Coward, Secretary; Clare Lesley Coward [1969] Director/Foster Carer

John Arthur and Son Limited
Incorporated: 4 April 1963 *Employees:* 9
Net Worth: £1,546,057 *Total Assets:* £1,684,794
Registered Office: Throckley Industrial Estate, Ponteland Road, Throckley, Newcastle upon Tyne, NE15 9EW
Activities: Freight transport by road
Major Shareholder: Nigel Mark Arthur
Officers: Antony Arthur [1990] Director; Nigel Mark Arthur [1961] Director/Service Engineer

The Artisan Travel Company Limited
Incorporated: 10 July 2002 *Employees:* 28
Net Worth: £403,143 *Total Assets:* £1,758,483
Registered Office: Suite 2, Netherton Park, Stannington, Northumberland, NE61 6EF
Activities: Other business support service activities n.e.c.
Parent: Timec 1650 Limited
Officers: Alistair William McLean, Secretary/Tour Operator; Alistair William McLean [1963] Director/Tour Operator

Artneat Limited
Incorporated: 20 March 1989
Net Worth: £1,047,314 *Total Assets:* £1,093,167
Registered Office: The Walled Garden, Longhirst, Morpeth, Northumberland, NE61 3LJ
Activities: Buying and selling of own real estate
Officers: Anne Marie Carey, Secretary; Laraine Blewitt [1950] Director/Bank Clerk; Thomas William Blewitt [1950] Director; Anne Marie Carey [1952] Director; Doctor Christopher Daniel Carey [1978] Director/Doctor; Daniel Paul Carey [1981] Director/Solicitor; Lawrence Daniel Carey [1951] Director/Chartered Accountant; Gillian Maguire [1974] Director

Asari Limited
Incorporated: 24 September 2012
Net Worth: £1,629,320 *Total Assets:* £1,629,471
Registered Office: 16 Ashtree Close, Rowlands Gill, Tyne & Wear, NE39 1RA
Activities: Activities of head offices
Major Shareholder: Egemen Dogan
Officers: Vivien Sian Dogan, Secretary; Egemen Dogan [1959] Director/Manager

The Ascent Academies' Trust
Incorporated: 8 June 2012 *Employees:* 441
Net Worth: £42,485,000 *Total Assets:* £50,637,000
Registered Office: Portland Academy, Weymouth Road, Chapelgarth, Sunderland, Tyne & Wear, SR3 2NQ
Activities: Pre-primary education
Officers: David Edward Barker [1965] Director/Charity Chief Executive Officer; Carolyn Dunn [1967] Director; Nadine Renae Hudspeth [1973] Director/Trustee; Nicholas Simon Hurn [1961] Director/Headteacher; Valerie Milnes [1949] Director/Retired Head of Service - Registered Social Landlord; Rohit Patel [1977] Director/Self Employed; Michelle Quinn [1966] Director; Patricia Lynn Watson [1957] Director/Trustee; Rachael Whorlton [1980] Director/HR Manager; Paul Richard Wright [1976] Finance Director

Ascot Care North East Limited
Incorporated: 26 March 2009 *Employees:* 109
Net Worth: £1,314,241 *Total Assets:* £5,825,031
Registered Office: Westoe Grange, 4 Horsley Hill Road, South Shields, Tyne & Wear, NE33 3DY
Activities: Residential nursing care facilities
Shareholders: Gareth Nesbit; Gavin Nesbit
Officers: Joan Nesbit, Secretary; Gareth Nesbit [1981] Director/Care Home Operator; Gavin Nesbit [1979] Director/Care Home Operator; Joan Nesbit [1950] Director; Trevor Nesbit [1948] Director/Care Home Operator

Ascot Place Properties Limited
Incorporated: 18 October 1993
Net Worth: £808,041 *Total Assets:* £819,009
Registered Office: 80 Hartington Road, Stockton on Tees, Cleveland, TS18 1HE
Activities: Other accommodation
Officers: Dominic George Collinge Ferard, Secretary/Director; Dominic George Collinge Ferard [1963] Director; Jo Tracy Ferard [1969] Director; Rupert Charles Hawkesworth Ferard [1966] Director; Sally Clare Ferard [1962] Director

The Ashbank Group Limited
Incorporated: 26 March 1970 *Employees:* 7
Net Worth: £636,385 *Total Assets:* £1,193,361
Registered Office: Forty House, Earlsway, Teesside Industrial Estate, Stockton on Tees, Cleveland, TS17 9JU
Activities: Washing and (dry-)cleaning of textile and fur products
Parent: Crossco (1298) Ltd
Officers: Christopher Tyrrell Brockbank [1959] Director; Henry Tyrrell Brockbank [1992] Director

Ashbrook Construction Services Limited
Incorporated: 13 February 2003 *Employees:* 23
Net Worth: £468,424 *Total Assets:* £1,012,156
Registered Office: 11 Leeholme Industrial Estate, Cowpen Lane, Billingham, Stockton on Tees, Cleveland, TS23 3TA
Activities: Construction of other civil engineering projects n.e.c.
Shareholders: Anthony Abel; Michael John Harrison
Officers: Joanne Claire Hopper, Secretary; Anthony Abel [1965] Director/Site Engineer; Michael John Harrison [1952] Director/Quantity Surveyor

Ashbrooke Sports Club Limited
Incorporated: 14 July 2000 *Employees:* 13
Net Worth: £1,011,410 *Total Assets:* £1,279,344
Registered Office: West Lawn, Ashbrooke Road, Sunderland, Tyne & Wear, SR2 7HH
Activities: Activities of sport clubs
Officers: Paul Airey [1962] Director/Estate Agent; Gregory Richard Applegarth [1986] Director/Senior Client Services Executive; Anthony Paul Alexander Clark [1945] Director/Manufacturer; Christopher Johnston [1975] Director/Headmaster

Ashdown Care Homes Ltd
Incorporated: 29 May 2003
Registered Office: 5 Ladyrigg, Darras Hall, Ponteland, Northumberland, NE20 9QS
Activities: Residential care activities for learning difficulties, mental health and substance abuse
Shareholders: Linda Mary Candlish; Gary Craig Candlish
Officers: Linda Mary Candlish, Secretary; Gary Craig Candlish [1966] Director/Care Homes; Linda Mary Candlish [1958] Director/Care Homes

Ashdown Park Homes Limited
Incorporated: 4 August 2015
Net Worth: £220,341 *Total Assets:* £862,693
Registered Office: Barrington House, 41-45 Yarm Lane, Stockton on Tees, Cleveland, TS18 3EA
Activities: Buying and selling of own real estate
Shareholders: John Lee; Joanne Miller
Officers: John Lee [1977] Director; Joanne Miller [1981] Director

Ashfield Estates Limited
Incorporated: 24 August 1979
Net Worth: £810,645 *Total Assets:* £2,199,345
Registered Office: 64 Willow Way, Ponteland, Northumberland, NE20 9RF
Activities: Buying and selling of own real estate
Officers: Raymond Anthony Bates, Secretary; Maureen Ann Bates [1949] Director/Examiner; Raymond Anthony Bates [1945] Director/Solicitor

Ashford Orthodontics Limited
Incorporated: 8 November 2005 *Employees:* 38
Net Worth: £568,927 *Total Assets:* £1,249,120
Registered Office: 115 Chester Road, Sunderland, Tyne & Wear, SR4 7HG
Activities: Dental practice activities
Shareholders: Craig Stevens; Sean Norman Thompson; Graeme Winyard
Officers: Robert Adamson Lye, Secretary; Craig Stevens [1975] Director/Dental Technician; Sean Norman Thompson [1964] Director/Orthodontic Technician; Graeme Winyard [1964] Director/Dental Technician

Ashington & District Estates Company Limited (The)
Incorporated: 8 March 1928
Registered Office: Post Office Chambers, Station Road, Ashington, Northumberland, NE63 8RL
Activities: Other letting and operating of own or leased real estate
Officers: Gillian Elizabeth McLean, Secretary; David Alastair Craigs [1957] Director/Farmer; John James Craigs [1955] Director/Farmer

Ashington Central Limited
Incorporated: 19 November 2007 *Employees:* 18
Net Worth: £444,584 *Total Assets:* £823,656
Registered Office: Lintonville Medical Group, Lintonville Terrace, Ashington, Northumberland, NE63 9UT
Activities: Other human health activities
Officers: Dr Lindsay John Gilfillan, Secretary; Dr Andrew David Bell [1963] Director/Doctor; Rakesh Chopra [1961] Director/Doctor; Susan Margaret Dixon [1960] Director/Pharmacist; Dr Lindsay John Gilfillan [1960] Director/Doctor; Sukhpreet Singh Kullar [1980] Director/Pharmacist

Ashington Leisure Partnership
Incorporated: 14 December 2011
Net Worth: £803,052 *Total Assets:* £804,852
Registered Office: Hirst Welfare Centre, Alexandra Road, Ashington, Northumberland, NE63 9HN
Activities: Other sports activities
Officers: Marcia Bircham [1944] Director/Retired; Lynne Grimshaw [1950] Director/County Councillor; James Aidan Lang [1954] Director/Safety Manager; Jack Pease [1946] Director/Retired; Colin Redpath [1945] Director/Retired; Brian Storey [1946] Director/Retired; Alan Thompson [1936] Director/Chartered Engineer

Ashington Mews Limited
Incorporated: 4 February 2016
Net Worth: £2,438 *Total Assets:* £1,364,703
Registered Office: Alhambra, 15 The Close, Stanhope Road, Edmundbyers, Consett, Co Durham, DH8 9NH
Activities: Other letting and operating of own or leased real estate
Parent: Cross Rigg Developments (North East) Limited
Officers: James Brough [1949] Director

Ashley Timber Limited
Incorporated: 4 May 1988 *Employees:* 18
Net Worth: £1,385,493 *Total Assets:* £2,078,357
Registered Office: Garden Lane, South Shields, Tyne & Wear, NE33 1PS
Activities: Wholesale of wood, construction materials and sanitary equipment
Shareholders: Brian Robert Seales; Elaine Seales
Officers: Brian Robert Seales, Secretary; Anthony Irving [1960] Director; Brian Robert Seales [1959] Director

Ashworth and Parker Limited
Incorporated: 1 April 2009 *Employees:* 238
Net Worth: £32,493,000 *Total Assets:* £38,863,000
Registered Office: Unit C, Merlin Way, New York Industrial Park, Newcastle upon Tyne, NE27 0QG
Activities: Retail sale of clothing in specialised stores
Shareholders: Rupert Christiaan Ashworth; John Douglas Parker
Officers: John Douglas Parker, Secretary; Rupert Christiaan Ashworth [1982] Director/MD Online Retailer; Peter Emerson [1953] Director; Maurice Harold Helfgott [1967] Director; John Douglas Parker [1982] Director/MD Online Retailer; Giuseppe Zocco [1965] Director/Venture Capitalist [Italian]

Ask Property Services Limited
Incorporated: 28 June 2002
Net Worth: £1,217,063 *Total Assets:* £1,276,793
Registered Office: 15 Oakhurst Drive, Newcastle upon Tyne, NE3 4JS
Activities: Other letting and operating of own or leased real estate
Major Shareholder: Anjana Aggarwal
Officers: Anjana Aggarwal, Secretary; Anjana Aggarwal [1946] Director

Askaris Information Technology Limited
Incorporated: 11 November 2009 *Employees:* 4
Net Worth Deficit: £965,973 *Total Assets:* £886,847
Registered Office: Unit 10 Orde Wingate Way, Stockton on Tees, Cleveland, TS19 0GA
Activities: Information technology consultancy activities
Major Shareholder: Richard John Eric Upshall
Officers: Sean Allison, Secretary; Sean Allison [1966] Director

Askews Solicitors Limited
Incorporated: 30 August 2005 *Employees:* 32
Net Worth: £213,564 *Total Assets:* £1,335,813
Registered Office: 92-94 Borough Road, Middlesbrough, Cleveland, TS1 2HJ
Activities: Solicitors
Major Shareholder: Simon Hill Askew
Officers: David Frank Askew [1942] Director/Solicitor; Simon Hill Askew [1974] Director/Solicitor; Kieron Doran [1970] Director/Solicitor

ASL Powerstream Services Limited
Incorporated: 5 June 2009 *Employees:* 18
Net Worth: £256,441 *Total Assets:* £1,057,146
Registered Office: 59 Ullswater Avenue, West Auckland, Bishop Auckland, Co Durham, DL14 9LS
Activities: Other business support service activities n.e.c.
Shareholders: Peter Johnson; Ronald Thomas Heward
Officers: Ronald Thomas Heward [1949] Director/Engineer; Peter Johnson [1968] Director/Engineer; Richard Walton [1966] Director/Engineer

Aspire Healthcare Limited
Incorporated: 11 June 2007 *Employees:* 171
Net Worth: £6,161,640 *Total Assets:* £14,340,762
Registered Office: Unit 6 South Nelson Road, South Nelson Industrial Estate, Cramlington, Northumberland, NE23 1WF
Activities: Other human health activities
Parent: Aspire Wellbeing Ltd
Officers: Cheryl Marie Strutt, Secretary; Anoop Puri [1976] Director/Manager

Aspire Technology Solutions Ltd
Incorporated: 18 December 2006 *Employees:* 125
Net Worth: £5,645,824 *Total Assets:* £10,234,963
Registered Office: Heworth Hall, Shields Road, Gateshead, Tyne & Wear, NE10 0UX
Activities: Information technology consultancy activities
Parent: Aspire Solutions Group Limited
Officers: Nigel Begg [1971] Managing Director; Chris Fraser [1981] Technical Director; Stephen George Laverick [1969] Technical Solutions Director

ASPP Limited
Incorporated: 18 April 2012
Net Worth: £153,871 *Total Assets:* £751,259
Registered Office: 101 Prince Edward Road, South Shields, Tyne & Wear, NE34 8PJ
Activities: Other service activities n.e.c.
Shareholder: Pritam Singh
Officers: Dildar Singh [1982] Director; Pritam Singh [1979] Director/Pharmacist

Assembly & Packaging Services Ltd
Incorporated: 4 May 1989 *Employees:* 215
Net Worth: £658,807 *Total Assets:* £1,225,906
Registered Office: 5 Cowley Road, Blyth Riverside Business Park, Blyth, Northumberland, NE24 5TF
Activities: Other manufacturing n.e.c.
Shareholder: Judith Leighton
Officers: David D'Arcy, Secretary; Judith Leighton [1946] Director

The Assembly Rooms (Newcastle) Limited
Incorporated: 27 April 1998
Net Worth: £601,921 *Total Assets:* £1,366,105
Registered Office: The Assembly Room (Newcastle) Ltd, Fenkle Street, Newcastle upon Tyne, NE1 5XU
Activities: Event catering activities
Officers: Antony George Michaelides, Secretary; Antony George Michaelides [1964] Director; Homer Antoniou Michaelides [1935] Director

Asset Manager Solutions Limited
Incorporated: 14 September 2006 *Employees:* 30
Net Worth: £298,412 *Total Assets:* £1,684,452
Registered Office: Eland House, Eland Lane, Ponteland, Northumberland, NE20 9TP
Activities: Public houses and bars
Shareholders: Kamran Aziz; Guy Thomas Lissimore
Officers: Kamran Aziz, Secretary; Kamran Aziz [1961] Director; Guy Thomas Lissimore [1967] Director

Association of International Accountants (The)
Incorporated: 1 April 1932 *Employees:* 25
Net Worth: £1,467,886 *Total Assets:* £2,291,316
Registered Office: Staithes 3, The Watermark, Metro Riverside, Gateshead, Tyne & Wear, NE11 9SN
Activities: Activities of professional membership organisations
Officers: Philip John Jeffrey Turnbull, Secretary; Joseph Block [1933] Director/Accountant; Leslie David Bradley [1944] Director/Accountant; Venetia Caroline Carpenter [1955] Director/Sole Practitioner; Say Soon Michael Chow [1951] Director [Singaporean]; Philip Martin Ford [1950] Director/Practitioner Accounting; Seth Ebenezer Kwaku Ganu [1944] Director/Financial Consultant [Ghanaian]; Mohd Noh Jidin [1950] Director/Audit Partner [Malaysian]; Koon Sang Jong [1949] Director [Chinese]; George Antoniou Josephakis [1956] Director/Registered Auditor [Cypriot]; Andrew Richard Lamb [1950] Director/International Accountant; Hugh Godfrey McCormack [1949] Director/Accountant [Irish]; Shahram Moallemi [1953] Director/Sole Practitioner Accounting; Gloria Rosemond Murray [1962] Director; Twaraq Oozeerally [1963] Director/Sole Practitioner Accountancy; Linda Mary Frances Richards [1958] Director/Accountant; Maggie Timoney [1966] Director/Consultant [Irish]

The Association of North East Councils Limited
Incorporated: 14 January 2004 *Employees:* 26
Net Worth Deficit: £1,320,941 *Total Assets:* £4,441,485
Registered Office: Civic Centre, Burdon Road, Sunderland, Tyne & Wear, SR2 7DN
Activities: Other business support service activities n.e.c.
Officers: Councillor Christopher Akers - Belcher [1968] Director/Health Watch Manager; Christopher David Budd [1948] Director/Retired; Robert Cook [1952] Director/Councillor/Office Manager; Cllr Nicholas Iain Forbes [1973] Director/Charity Chief Executive; Martin Gannon [1958] Director; Councillor Stephen James Harker [1963] Director/Software Designer; Councillor Simon Antony Henig [1969] Director/Lecturer; Peter Alan Jackson [1958] Director/Farmer; Susan Jennifer Jeffrey [1958] Director/Council Leader; Iain Malcolm [1966] Director; Councillor Graeme Ferguson Miller [1962] Director; Norma Redfearn [1938] Director/Elected Mayor North Tyneside

Astley Signs Limited
Incorporated: 25 April 1990 *Employees:* 157
Net Worth: £4,725,893 *Total Assets:* £7,665,913
Registered Office: Redforrest House, Queens Court North, Earlsway, Team Valley Trading Estate, Gateshead, Tyne & Wear, NE11 0BP
Activities: Other manufacturing n.e.c.
Shareholders: Robert David Redhead; Robert Gavin Redhead; David William Forrester
Officers: David William Forrester [1964] Director; Robert Gavin Redhead [1970] Director/Chartered Surveyor; Robert David Redhead [1942] Director; Gregory David Waugh [1966] Director/Certified Chartered Accountant

Aston Workshop Limited
Incorporated: 9 December 2009 *Employees:* 42
Net Worth: £1,252,433 *Total Assets:* £3,386,057
Registered Office: Gosling Hill, 1 Red Row, Beamish Burn, Beamish, Stanley, Co Durham, DH9 0RW
Activities: Sale of new cars and light motor vehicles
Major Shareholder: Robert Steven Fountain
Officers: Robert Steven Fountain [1954] Director

At Home Furnishings Outlet Limited
Incorporated: 7 December 2000 *Employees:* 32
Net Worth: £155,615 *Total Assets:* £1,104,603
Registered Office: At Home Furnishings, 2a Malleable Way, Stockton on Tees, Cleveland, TS18 2QX
Activities: Retail of furniture, lighting, and similar (not musical instruments or scores) in specialised store
Shareholders: Andrew Marcus Dicken; Ann Dicken
Officers: Ian Huntington, Secretary; Andrew Marcus Dicken [1970] Director/Retail; Ann Dicken [1968] Director/Retail

ATF Supplies Limited
Incorporated: 25 May 2001 *Employees:* 14
Net Worth: £820,220 *Total Assets:* £1,246,743
Registered Office: Units 1 & 2 Tees Court, Wallis Road, Skippers Lane Industrial Estate, Middlesbrough, Cleveland, TS6 6DX
Activities: Wholesale of hardware, plumbing and heating equipment and supplies
Shareholder: David William Usherwood
Officers: Edward John Matthews, Secretary; Kevin Paul Harker [1969] Director/Manager; Edward John Matthews [1967] Director/Accountant; John Egmont Usherwood [1970] Director/Manager

ATFC Limited
Incorporated: 26 March 2003 *Employees:* 533
Net Worth: £5,215,000 *Total Assets:* £14,435,000
Registered Office: 1a Dukesway Court, Team Valley Trading Estate, Gateshead, Tyne & Wear, NE11 0PJ
Activities: Licenced restaurants
Parent: Steakhouse Holdings Limited
Officers: Phillip Nigel Blain, Secretary; David James Horrocks [1959] Director/Chartered Accountant; Ian Imrie [1955] Director

Atha Developments (No. 1) Limited
Incorporated: 24 October 2013
Registered Office: 165 Albert Road, Middlesbrough, Cleveland, TS1 2PX
Activities: Other service activities n.e.c.
Shareholders: Charles Atha;
Officers: Charles Anthony Stewart Atha [1962] Director/Solicitor

Athenaeum Developments (Fulwell) Limited
Incorporated: 26 January 1987
Net Worth: £513,490 *Total Assets:* £2,909,880
Registered Office: The Annexe, The Garden House, Stelling Hall, Newton, Stocksfield, Northumberland, NE43 7UR
Activities: Development of building projects
Major Shareholder: Elizabeth Claire Wright
Officers: Elizabeth Claire Wright [1968] Director; Pamela Wright [1942] Director

Athenaeum Developments Limited
Incorporated: 10 May 1985
Net Worth: £869,094 *Total Assets:* £926,452
Registered Office: The Annexe, The Garden House, Stelling Hall, Newton, Stocksfield, Northumberland, NE43 7UR
Activities: Management of real estate on a fee or contract basis
Major Shareholder: Elizabeth Claire Wright
Officers: Elizabeth Claire Wright [1968] Director; Pamela Wright [1942] Director

Trevor Atkinson & Co Limited
Incorporated: 1 December 2006 *Employees:* 17
Net Worth: £700,120 *Total Assets:* £1,829,901
Registered Office: The Market Place, Mickleton, Barnard Castle, Co Durham, DL12 0JF
Activities: Other specialised construction activities n.e.c.
Shareholders: Richard William Atkinson; Mary Atkinson
Officers: Mary Atkinson, Secretary; Richard William Atkinson [1962] Director/Landscape Contractor

J T Atkinson & Sons Limited
Incorporated: 20 October 1971 *Employees:* 262
Net Worth: £2,535,149 *Total Assets:* £19,683,426
Registered Office: Thornton House, Cargo Fleet Lane, Middlesbrough, Cleveland, TS3 8DE
Activities: Agents involved in the sale of timber and building materials
Parent: Atkinson Northern Ltd
Officers: Jeremy John Boyd, Secretary/Accountant; James David Edwin Atkinson [1985] Director/Builders Merchant; James Edwin Atkinson [1957] Director/Builders Merchant; Mark Robert Atkinson [1967] Director; Jeremy John Boyd [1955] Director/Chartered Accountant; Paul McGill [1965] Director/Builders Merchant; Michael Stalley [1968] Director/Builders Merchant

J.C. Atkinson and Son Limited
Incorporated: 21 April 1966 *Employees:* 113
Net Worth: £2,464,903 *Total Assets:* £5,525,652
Registered Office: Sedling Road, Wear Industrial Estate, Washington, Tyne & Wear, NE38 9BZ
Activities: Funeral and related activities
Major Shareholder: Julian Marcus Atkinson
Officers: Julian Marcus Atkinson [1966] Director

F.A. Atkinson Limited
Incorporated: 1 August 2005 *Employees:* 49
Net Worth: £28,702 *Total Assets:* £1,207,652
Registered Office: Unit 21 Evans Business Centre, Orion Way, Orion Business Park, North Shields, Tyne & Wear, NE29 7SN
Activities: Electrical installation
Shareholder: Christopher John Corkhill
Officers: Paul St John Lloyd Venable, Secretary; Christopher John Corkhill [1953] Director; Colin Peter Reed [1959] Director; Paul St John Lloyd Venable [1963] Director

Atkinson Northern Limited
Incorporated: 24 December 1980 *Employees:* 365
Net Worth: £36,289,960 *Total Assets:* £46,448,332
Registered Office: Thornton House, Cargo Fleet Lane, Middlesbrough, Cleveland, TS3 8DE
Activities: Activities of head offices
Officers: Jeremy John Boyd, Secretary/Chartered Accountant; James David Edwin Atkinson [1985] Director/Builders Merchant; James Edwin Atkinson [1957] Director/Builders Merchant; Jonathan Alan Atkinson [1990] Director/Timber Merchant; Mark Robert Atkinson [1967] Director/Builders Merchant; Jeremy John Boyd [1955] Director/Chartered Accountant

Atlantic Metropolitan (U.K.) Limited
Incorporated: 8 April 1982
Net Worth: £159,035,712 *Total Assets:* £159,162,240
Registered Office: Citygate, St James Boulevard, Newcastle upon Tyne, NE1 4JE
Activities: Other letting and operating of own or leased real estate
Parent: Grainger PLC
Officers: Adam McGhin, Secretary; Helen Christine Gordon [1959] Director; Adam McGhin [1978] Director/Solicitor; Mark Jeremy Robson [1959] Director/Chartered Surveyor; Vanessa Kate Simms [1975] Director

Atlantis Management LLP
Incorporated: 8 December 2005
Net Worth: £4,092,485 *Total Assets:* £4,612,264
Registered Office: West 2, Asama Court, Newcastle Business Park, Newcastle upon Tyne, NE4 7YD
Officers: John Smithson Young [1951] Member

Atlas Care Homes Limited
Incorporated: 21 October 2014
Registered Office: 7 Kyle Road, Gateshead, Tyne & Wear, NE8 2YE
Activities: Residential care activities for the elderly and disabled
Officers: Varghese Thomas, Secretary; Mohammad Amjad Ahmad [1968] Director; Mohammad Afzal Ahmad [1967] Director; Ali Ashgar [1960] Director; Varghese Thomas [1970] Director; Merly Varghese [1972] Director

Atlas Cloud Limited
Incorporated: 28 June 2010 *Employees:* 17
Net Worth: £714,536 *Total Assets:* £789,227
Registered Office: Generator Studios, Trafalgar Street, Newcastle upon Tyne, NE1 2LA
Activities: Computer facilities management activities
Officers: Chris Morris [1980] Technical Director; Peter Thomas Watson [1979] Sales Director

Atlas Garages (Morpeth) Limited
Incorporated: 4 May 1990 *Employees:* 55
Net Worth: £3,473,791 *Total Assets:* £6,226,149
Registered Office: Davidsons of Morpeth, Coopies Way, Morpeth, Northumberland, NE61 6JN
Activities: Sale of new cars and light motor vehicles
Shareholders: Colin Henry Davidson; Peter Edward Davidson
Officers: Mark Edward Hudspith, Secretary; Colin Henry Davidson [1952] Director; Peter Edward Davidson [1956] Director

Atlas Washroom Systems Limited
Incorporated: 20 April 2001 *Employees:* 23
Net Worth: £600,799 *Total Assets:* £947,442
Registered Office: 10 Aptec Enterprise Park, Darlington Road, West Auckland, Co Durham, DL14 9PD
Activities: Manufacture of household and sanitary goods and of toilet requisites
Parent: Atlas Washroom Holdings Ltd
Officers: Lesley Carol Shervington, Secretary; Christopher Hockaday [1979] Director; Generald Thomas Shervington [1962] Managing Director

Atom Bank PLC
Incorporated: 31 July 2013 *Employees:* 216
Net Worth: £103,946,000 *Total Assets:* £648,836,992
Registered Office: The Rivergreen Centre, Aykley Heads, Durham, DH1 5TS
Activities: Banks
Shareholder: Banco Bilbao Vizcaya Argentaria S.A.
Officers: Edward Twiddy, Secretary; Victoria Del Castillo Marchese [1975] Director [Spanish]; Patricia Doreen Jackson [1952] Director; David James McCarthy [1965] Director; Mark Thomas Mullen [1968] Director; Laurel Claire Powers-Freeling [1957] Director; David Andrew Roper [1961] Director; Bridget Clare Rosewell [1951] Director; Sait Ergun Ozen [1960] Director [Turkish]

Robert Attey & Sons Limited
Incorporated: 20 November 1998 *Employees:* 2
Net Worth: £835,615 *Total Assets:* £853,955
Registered Office: 1-3 William Street, Sunderland, Tyne & Wear, SR1 1UL
Activities: Other business support service activities n.e.c.
Major Shareholder: Christopher Michael Attey
Officers: Philippa Jane Attey, Secretary; Christopher Michael Attey [1962] Director/Printer

The Auckland Castle Trust
Incorporated: 1 February 2012 *Employees:* 76
Net Worth: £44,721,104 *Total Assets:* £45,977,720
Registered Office: Vinovium House, Saddler Street, Bishop Auckland, Co Durham, DL14 7BH
Activities: Operation of historical sites and buildings and similar visitor attractions
Officers: Nicholas John Eldred, Secretary; Jane Elizabeth Bonnar Dean [1955] Director of Hospitality and Catering; Lady Sarah Nicholson [1947] Director; Lady Sarah Riddell [1942] Director; Dr Malcolm Austin Rogers [1948] Director/Retired; Nicholas Timothy Turner [1961] Director/Investment Manager; Daniel Richard Wolfe [1972] Director of Communications and Development

Auckland Environmental Services Limited
Incorporated: 28 June 2004 *Employees:* 9
Net Worth: £427,086 *Total Assets:* £2,719,090
Registered Office: 3b Lockheed Court, Preston Farm, Stockton on Tees, Cleveland, TS18 3SH
Activities: Management consultancy activities other than financial management
Major Shareholder: Andrew Mark Bainbridge
Officers: Andrew Mark Bainbridge [1969] Director; Arron Butta [1993] Director

Aurele-Belle Limited
Incorporated: 30 April 2016
Net Worth: £630,767 *Total Assets:* £1,691,803
Registered Office: 11 Whickham Street East, Sunderland, Tyne & Wear, SR6 0EH
Activities: Other business support service activities n.e.c.
Major Shareholder: Alan Callander
Officers: Alan Callander [1951] Director/Administrator

Autoclock Holdings Limited
Incorporated: 12 November 2010
Net Worth: £734,943 *Total Assets:* £844,952
Registered Office: B3 Kingfisher House, Team Valley Trading Estate, Gateshead, Tyne & Wear, NE11 0JQ
Activities: Activities of head offices
Shareholders: Brian Turner; Phyllis Turner
Officers: Stephen Halliday [1969] Director; Brian Turner [1945] Director; Phyllis Turner [1947] Director

Autoclock Systems Limited
Incorporated: 9 December 1982 *Employees:* 15
Net Worth: £564,264 *Total Assets:* £1,012,613
Registered Office: 93-97 Second Avenue, Heaton, Newcastle upon Tyne, NE6 5XT
Activities: Other service activities n.e.c.
Parent: Autoclock Holdings Ltd
Officers: Phyllis Turner, Secretary; Brian Turner [1945] Technical Director; Phyllis Turner [1947] Sales Director

Automatic Retailing (Northern) Limited
Incorporated: 20 December 1988 *Employees:* 72
Net Worth: £10,880,272 *Total Assets:* £28,855,018
Registered Office: Unit S3, Narvik Way, Tyne Tunnel Trading Estate, North Shields, Tyne & Wear, NE29 7XJ
Activities: Wholesale of sugar and chocolate and sugar confectionery
Officers: David Leonard Brind [1972] Director; John Frederick Hope [1969] Group Operations Director; Patricia Ada Rice [1951] Finance Director; Paul Victor Young [1957] Director/Accountant

Automotive Chassis Products UK Limited
Incorporated: 8 June 1988 *Employees:* 1
Net Worth: £133,999,000 *Total Assets:* £134,004,000
Registered Office: 1 Skerne Road, Aycliffe Business Park, Newton Aycliffe, Co Durham, DL5 6EP
Activities: Forging, pressing, stamping and roll-forming of metal; powder metallurgy
Shareholders: Francisco Jose Riberas Mera; Juan Maria Riberas Mera
Officers: David Vázquez Pascual, Secretary; Francisco Jose Riberas Mera [1968] Director [Spanish]

Automotive Group (Newcastle upon Tyne) Limited
Incorporated: 12 December 1991 *Employees:* 55
Net Worth: £6,812,136 *Total Assets:* £8,405,294
Registered Office: Segedunum Domus, Fisher Street, Newcastle upon Tyne, NE6 4NH
Activities: Manufacture of bicycles and invalid carriages
Shareholders: Philip Hind; Jon Hind
Officers: Jon Hind, Secretary/Airline Pilot; Jon Hind [1975] Director/Airline Pilot; Philip Hind [1945] Director/Business Proprietor

Autoroll UK Limited
Incorporated: 3 February 2005
Net Worth: £455,328 *Total Assets:* £935,996
Registered Office: Pinewood Business Park, Wilden Road, Washington, Tyne & Wear, NE38 8QB
Activities: Manufacture of doors and windows of metal
Shareholders: Giles Andrew Bower; Gillian Bower
Officers: Simon Bannister, Secretary; Giles Andrew Bower [1961] Director/Businessman; Gillian Bower [1966] Director/Businesswoman

Autosense Limited
Incorporated: 19 August 1991 *Employees:* 5
Net Worth: £244,751 *Total Assets:* £1,078,894
Registered Office: Clifton Car Sales, Clifton, Morpeth, Northumberland, NE61 6DG
Activities: Sale of new cars and light motor vehicles
Shareholders: William Saville Longridge; George William Coulson
Officers: William Saville Longridge, Secretary; George William Coulson [1955] Director/Car Salesman; William Saville Longridge [1950] Director/Car Salesman

Autotech Engineering R&D UK Limited
Incorporated: 2 October 2012 *Employees:* 61
Net Worth: £5,109,000 *Total Assets:* £7,782,000
Registered Office: 1 Skerne Road, Aycliffe Business Park, Newton Aycliffe, Co Durham, DL5 6EP
Activities: Engineering design activities for industrial process and production
Shareholders: Juan Maria Riberas Mera; Francisco Jose Riberas Mera
Officers: David Vázquez Pascual, Secretary; Maria Jose Armendariz Tellitu [1971] General Director Business Unit Chassis [Spanish]; Francisco Josė Riberas Mera [1964] Director [Spanish]

Avec Sport Limited
Incorporated: 23 January 2001 *Employees:* 4
Net Worth: £458,366 *Total Assets:* £1,002,722
Registered Office: 1 Enterprise City, Meadowfield Avenue, Spennymoor, Co Durham, DL16 6JF
Activities: Other business support service activities n.e.c.
Parent: Just Sport (Group) Ltd
Officers: Judith Smith, Secretary; Peter Crawford [1959] Sales Director

Avenda Estates Limited
Incorporated: 22 June 2004
Net Worth: £1,059,740 *Total Assets:* £3,701,737
Registered Office: 1 Fox Street, Sunderland Road, Gateshead, Tyne & Wear, NE10 0BD
Activities: Other letting and operating of own or leased real estate
Shareholders: Rudi Scott Wright; Gary Owen Lewis
Officers: Joanne Lynn Lewis [1974] Director; Duncan Richard McGregor [1973] Director

Avendus Capital (UK) Private Limited
Incorporated: 23 June 2008 *Employees:* 5
Net Worth: £1,029,852 *Total Assets:* £1,301,945
Registered Office: RMT Accountants & Business Advisors Ltd, Gosforth Park Avenue, Newcastle upon Tyne, NE12 8EG
Activities: Financial intermediation not elsewhere classified
Shareholders: George Roberts; Henry Kravis
Officers: Deepak Rajveerchand Bhandari [1970] Director; Gaurav Deepak [1974] Director [Indian]; Jerome Glynn-Smith [1986] Director

Avenue (North East) Limited
Incorporated: 5 September 2013
Net Worth: £946,391 *Total Assets:* £968,009
Registered Office: 5 Orchard Gardens, Whitburn, Sunderland, Tyne & Wear, SR6 9JW
Activities: Activities of other holding companies n.e.c.
Major Shareholder: Robert Burns
Officers: Doreen Burns [1952] Director; James Robert Burns [1982] Director; Robert Burns [1951] Director

Avenue Pharmacy (Sunderland) Limited
Incorporated: 22 July 2002 *Employees:* 19
Net Worth: £1,601,774 *Total Assets:* £2,295,965
Registered Office: 5 Orchard Gardens, Sunderland, Tyne & Wear, SR6 7JW
Activities: Dispensing chemist in specialised stores
Officers: Doreen Burns, Secretary; James Robert Burns [1982] Director/Trainee Pharmacist; Robert Burns [1951] Director/Pharmacist

AVG Holdings (Cleveland) Limited
Incorporated: 5 December 2014
Net Worth Deficit: £3,274 *Total Assets:* £1,746,907
Registered Office: Hughes House, Cargo Fleet Road, Middlesbrough, Cleveland, TS3 6AG
Activities: Activities of production holding companies
Parent: AVG Power Limited
Officers: Donal James Hughes [1975] Director/C.E.O; Timothy Rodney Spring [1958] Director

AVG Imperial Ltd
Incorporated: 9 December 2014
Net Worth: £217,655 *Total Assets:* £29,631,442
Registered Office: Hughes House, Cargo Fleet Road, Middlesbrough, Cleveland, TS3 6AG
Activities: Remediation activities and other waste management services
Parent: AVG Holdings Limited
Officers: Donal James Hughes [1975] Director/C.E.O; Timothy Rodney Spring [1958] Director; James Arden Bruce Williams [1978] Director

AVG Power Limited
Incorporated: 16 October 2014
Net Worth Deficit: £17,610 *Total Assets:* £2,067,938
Registered Office: Hughes House, Cargo Fleet Road, Middlesbrough, Cleveland, TS3 6AG
Activities: Remediation activities and other waste management services
Officers: Donal James Hughes [1975] Director/C.E.O; James William Routledge [1970] Director; Martyn Johnathan Strong [1977] Managing Director

Avid Technology Group Limited
Incorporated: 13 March 2009 *Employees:* 55
Net Worth: £1,462,927 *Total Assets:* £4,983,387
Registered Office: Unit 3d Nelson Way, Nelson Park West, Cramlington, Northumberland, NE23 1WG
Activities: Activities of other holding companies n.e.c.
Officers: Ryan Ellis Maughan, Secretary; Mauro Andrea Biagioni [1978] Investment Director [British/Italian]; Michael John Hunt [1952] Director; Ryan Ellis Maughan [1979] Director; David Alun Stark [1965] Finance and Operations Director; Keith Ternent [1963] Engineering Director; Iain Young [1965] Director

Avid Technology Limited
Incorporated: 28 November 2003 *Employees:* 55
Net Worth Deficit: £1,382,795 *Total Assets:* £4,975,145
Registered Office: Unit 3d Admiral Business Park, Nelson Way, Cramlington, Northumberland, NE23 1WG
Activities: Manufacture of other transport equipment n.e.c.
Parent: Avid Technology Group Limited
Officers: Ryan Ellis Maughan [1979] Managing Director; David Alun Stark [1965] Finance and Operations Director; Keith Ternent [1963] Engineering Director; Iain Young [1965] Director

Avor Garages (North East) Limited
Incorporated: 11 June 1974 *Employees:* 34
Net Worth: £634,266 *Total Assets:* £1,688,977
Registered Office: 1 Jesmond Business Court, Jesmond Road, Newcastle upon Tyne, NE2 1LA
Activities: Retail sale of automotive fuel in specialised stores
Officers: Anne Lorraine Straker, Secretary; John Straker [1954] Director/Garage Proprietor

AW Fabrication Limited
Incorporated: 2 March 1992
Net Worth: £649,451 *Total Assets:* £911,028
Registered Office: St Nicholas House, St Nicholas Industrial Estate, Dodsworth Street, Albert Hill, Darlington, Co Durham, DL1 2NJ
Activities: Manufacture of metal structures and parts of structures
Major Shareholder: Stephen Whitehead
Officers: Tracey Simpson, Secretary; Damon Stephen Hudson [1993] Director; Stephen Whitehead [1962] Director/Engineer

Awan Properties Limited
Incorporated: 5 July 2001
Net Worth: £583,705 *Total Assets:* £1,270,947
Registered Office: 393-395 Stamfordham Road, Westerhope, Newcastle upon Tyne, NE5 5HA
Activities: Buying and selling of own real estate
Major Shareholder: Mohammed Pervaz
Officers: Nasreen Perwaz, Secretary; Mohammed Perwaz [1942] Director/Landlord

Axenic Limited
Incorporated: 14 May 2009 *Employees:* 6
Net Worth: £411,060 *Total Assets:* £791,319
Registered Office: Netpark Incubator, Thomas Wright Way, Sedgefield, Co Durham, TS21 3FD
Activities: Manufacture of electronic components
Parent: Axenic Holdings Limited
Officers: Stephen John Clements [1958] Director

Axiom Engineering Associates Limited
Incorporated: 6 January 2003 *Employees:* 42
Net Worth: £2,824,006 *Total Assets:* £3,453,303
Registered Office: 14 Woodstock Court, Bowesfield Crescent, Stockton on Tees, Cleveland, TS18 3BL
Activities: Technical testing and analysis
Shareholder: Adam Lee Potter
Officers: Adam Lee Potter, Secretary; Robert Michael Johnson [1971] Director/Mechanical Engineer; Adam Lee Potter [1973] Director

Aycliffe Decorative Supplies Limited
Incorporated: 12 January 1984
Net Worth: £998,817 *Total Assets:* £1,047,788
Registered Office: Horndale Avenue, Aycliffe Industrial Estate, Newton Aycliffe, Co Durham, DL5 6DR
Activities: Retail sale of hardware, paints and glass in specialised stores
Shareholders: Karen Hayton; Paul Gerard Hayton
Officers: Susan Lamb, Secretary; Paul Gerard Hayton [1965] Director

John Aynsley (Architectural Metalwork) Limited
Incorporated: 11 January 1994 *Employees:* 36
Net Worth: £676,709 *Total Assets:* £1,084,671
Registered Office: Unit D3, New Hartley Industrial Estate, Double Row, Seaton Delaval, Whitley Bay, Tyne & Wear, NE25 0PP
Activities: Manufacture of metal structures and parts of structures
Officers: John Fenwick Aynsley, Secretary/Engineer; John Fenwick Aynsley [1949] Director/Engineer; David Joseph Benson [1966] Director/Draughtsman; Paul Richard Brown [1961] Director/Whitesmith; Marian Hedley [1958] Director/Company Secretary; Paul Thomas Hedley [1966] Director/Whitesmith

Aysgarth School Trust Limited
Incorporated: 14 February 1967 *Employees:* 68
Net Worth: £4,829,569 *Total Assets:* £5,604,007
Registered Office: Aysgarth School, Newton-le-Willows, Bedale, N Yorks, DL8 1TF
Activities: Pre-primary education
Officers: Lucinda Mary Hoskyns-Abrahall, Secretary; James Luke Bourne-Arton [1977] Director/Barrister; Melissa Ann Bowring [1960] Director/Housewife; Robert James Brooksbank [1966] Finance Director; David James Christian Faber [1961] Director/Headmaster; Sarah Guthe [1966] Director/Mother; Bennet Mansel Leigh Hoskyns-Abrahall [1971] Director; Hon William James Kay-Shuttleworth [1979] Director/School Teacher; Thomas Edmund Justin Nolan [1969] Director/Deputy Head; William James Roe [1969] Director/Retail Executive; Peter John Stuart Thompson [1946] Director/Lawyer; Mark Clouston Wallace [1971] Director/Investment Manager; Christy York [1968] Director/Farmer

Ayton Consulting Limited
Incorporated: 15 October 2002 *Employees:* 5
Net Worth: £1,742,596 *Total Assets:* £1,842,122
Registered Office: Ayton Banks Farm, Great Ayton, Middlesbrough, Cleveland, TS9 6HW
Activities: Engineering related scientific and technical consulting activities
Shareholders: Robert Jack Bradley; Samuel James Bradley; Susan Kathleen Bradley
Officers: Susan Kathleen Bradley, Secretary; Robert Jack Bradley [1987] Director/Civil Engineer; Stephen Charles Pinch [1961] Director/Engineer

Aztec Print North East Limited
Incorporated: 13 February 1997 *Employees:* 48
Net Worth: £523,356 *Total Assets:* £962,822
Registered Office: 8 Bridgewater Road, Hertburn Industrial Estate, Washington, Tyne & Wear, NE37 2SG
Activities: Printing n.e.c.
Officers: Julie Carman, Secretary; Anthony Joseph Moore [1954] Director/Retired; Margaret Moore [1952] Director/Retired; Lee Redford [1982] Director; Anna Whitter [1969] Director; Michael John Whitter [1968] Director/Printing Manager

Azure Business Centres Limited
Incorporated: 20 January 2003
Net Worth: £990,624 *Total Assets:* £1,082,411
Registered Office: Kielder Avenue, Beacon Lane, Cramlington, Northumberland, NE23 8JT
Activities: Other letting and operating of own or leased real estate
Parent: Azure Charitable Enterprises
Officers: Geoffrey Crosby, Secretary; Geoffrey Crosby [1956] Director/Accountant; Alan Edward Kilburn [1936] Director; Eric Morgan [1945] Director/Chartered Surveyor; Peter James Wilson [1972] Managing Director

Azure Charitable Enterprises
Incorporated: 21 September 1982 *Employees:* 234
Net Worth: £3,182,315 *Total Assets:* £4,343,620
Registered Office: McCallum House, Kielder Avenue, Cramlington, Northumberland, NE23 8JT
Activities: Plant propagation
Officers: Geoffrey Crosby, Secretary; Graham Palmer Barnard [1954] Director/Solicitor; Isobel Hindle [1944] Director/Retired; Ian Alastair Keddie [1951] Director/Retired; Alan Edward Kilburn [1936] Director/Retired; Christine Suzanne Litchfield [1949] Director/Retired; Eric Morgan [1945] Director/Chartered Surveyor; Geoffrey William Robson [1958] Director/Chartered Accountant; Isabelle Trewhitt Turnbull [1943] Director; Annemarie Wood [1946] Director/Housewife

B & S (Rentals) Limited
Incorporated: 19 February 1992 *Employees:* 18
Net Worth: £403,387 *Total Assets:* £769,696
Registered Office: Greencroft Milk Supplies Ltd, Telford Road, Middlesbrough, Cleveland, TS3 8BL
Activities: Renting and leasing of other machinery, equipment and tangible goods n.e.c.
Parent: Greencroft Milk Supplies Limited
Officers: Janice Parker, Secretary; Michael Brian Doyle [1964] Director; Derek Parker [1961] Director; Janice Parker [1965] Director and Company Secretary; Jonathon Parker [1992] Director; Ian Richard Simpson [1956] Director/Management Consultant

B and R Property Limited
Incorporated: 11 July 2002
Net Worth: £220,770 *Total Assets:* £1,066,438
Registered Office: 21 North Bridge Street, Sunderland, Tyne & Wear, SR5 1AB
Activities: Other letting and operating of own or leased real estate
Shareholders: Richard Wooler; Victoria Anne Bianchi
Officers: Victoria Anne Bianchi, Secretary; Richard Wooler [1950] Director

B L Training (Holdings) Limited
Incorporated: 23 October 2008
Net Worth: £24 *Total Assets:* £804,024
Registered Office: 1st Floor, 11 Nelson Street, Newcastle upon Tyne, NE1 5AN
Activities: Technical and vocational secondary education
Major Shareholder: Kelvin Brennan
Officers: Gail Dalton Ayres, Secretary; Kelvin Brennan [1963] Director; Gail Dalton-Ayres [1970] Director/Regional Manager; Julie Elizabeth Ritson [1970] Director/Regional Manager

B L Training Limited
Incorporated: 26 November 1998 *Employees:* 34
Net Worth: £1,707,532 *Total Assets:* £1,968,014
Registered Office: 1st Floor, 11 Nelson Street, Newcastle upon Tyne, NE1 5AN
Activities: Technical and vocational secondary education
Parent: B L Training (Holdings) Limited
Officers: Gail Dalton Ayres, Secretary; Kelvin Brennan [1963] Director; Gail Dalton Ayres [1970] Director/Regional Manager; Julie Elizabeth Ritson [1970] Director/Regional Manager

B.& B. Attachments Limited
Incorporated: 4 December 1980 *Employees:* 69
Net Worth: £1,310,923 *Total Assets:* £6,292,260
Registered Office: Unit 46 Colbourne Avenue, Nelson Park, Cramlington, Northumberland, NE23 1WD
Activities: Manufacture of lifting and handling equipment
Shareholders: Michael Robert Barton; John William Lamberth
Officers: Michael Robert Barton [1949] Managing Director; Neal Watson Fowler [1970] Director; Neil David Jackson [1986] Finance Director; John William Lamberth [1959] Director

B.C. & T. Consultants Limited
Incorporated: 22 September 1986 *Employees:* 7
Net Worth: £1,029,628 *Total Assets:* £1,369,037
Registered Office: Office 314, The Innovation Centre, Vienna Court, Kirkleatham Business Park, Redcar, Cleveland, TS10 5SH
Activities: Engineering design activities for industrial process and production
Major Shareholder: Gareth Lloyd-Jones
Officers: Lisa Bennett, Secretary; Gareth Lloyd Jones [1969] Director/Engineer; Lisa Michelle Lloyd Jones [1971] Director/Solicitor

B.E.L. Lift Trucks Limited
Incorporated: 8 November 1950 *Employees:* 21
Net Worth: £928,924 *Total Assets:* £3,560,410
Registered Office: Bel House, Fisher Street, Newcastle upon Tyne, NE6 4LT
Activities: Maintenance and repair of motor vehicles
Major Shareholder: Leslie Walter Gill
Officers: Lynda Whent, Secretary; Leslie Walter Gill [1951] Managing Director

B.E.L. Properties Limited
Incorporated: 9 April 1990
Net Worth: £7,546,366 *Total Assets:* £23,738,928
Registered Office: 11 Glasshouse Street, St Peters, Newcastle upon Tyne, NE6 1BS
Activities: Other letting and operating of own or leased real estate
Officers: Joanne Alicea Wilkes, Secretary; Laura Joicey [1976] Director/Group Chief Financial Officer; Alexander Harold Lamb [1971] Director; Harold Graham Lamb [1935] Director/Engineer; Jonathan Charles Lamb [1977] Group Manufacturing Director

B.M.A. Properties Limited
Incorporated: 22 August 2007
Net Worth: £1,466,592 *Total Assets:* £1,882,095
Registered Office: Cleveland House, Cleveland Street, Darlington, Co Durham, DL1 2PE
Activities: Other letting and operating of own or leased real estate
Major Shareholder: Billy Ward
Officers: Michelle Ward, Secretary; Billy Ward [1978] Director

B.Print & Display Limited
Incorporated: 3 December 1981 *Employees:* 61
Net Worth: £763,984 *Total Assets:* £5,618,580
Registered Office: 31 Moorland Way, Nelson Park, Cramlington, Northumberland, NE23 1WE
Activities: Printing n.e.c.
Shareholders: William Paul Skelchy; Monique Skelchy
Officers: Monique Skelchy, Secretary; Robert Daglish Rutherford [1973] Director of Customer Services; Daniel Skelchy [1988] Sales & Marketing Director; Monique Skelchy [1963] Director/Administrator; William Paul Skelchy [1959] Sales Director

B.T.I.C. Limited
Incorporated: 23 February 1996 *Employees:* 21
Net Worth: £917,092 *Total Assets:* £1,669,108
Registered Office: 26 Lansdowne Terrace, Gosforth, Newcastle upon Tyne, NE3 1HP
Activities: Non-life insurance
Major Shareholder: Brian William Thompson
Officers: Sherene Thompson, Secretary; Brian William Thompson [1955] Director/Insurance Consultant

B.Z. Limited
Incorporated: 7 November 1990 *Employees:* 1
Net Worth: £902,166 *Total Assets:* £996,415
Registered Office: 9-11 Carliol Square, Newcastle upon Tyne, NE1 6UF
Activities: Other letting and operating of own or leased real estate
Major Shareholder: Sunil Kumar Vadehra
Officers: Anita Vadehra, Secretary; Sunil Kumar Vadehra [1961] Health Club Director

B2B Contracting Services Ltd.
Incorporated: 21 January 2016 *Employees:* 3
Net Worth: £434,546 *Total Assets:* £1,074,153
Registered Office: 11 Ridley Place, Newcastle upon Tyne, NE1 8JQ
Activities: Treatment and disposal of non-hazardous waste
Officers: Pamela Clark, Secretary; James Henry Clark [1943] Director; Nicholas James Clark [1970] Director; Jonathan Dunn [1974] Director

B2B Property Solutions Limited
Incorporated: 11 October 2012
Net Worth: £127,328 *Total Assets:* £1,074,415
Registered Office: 3rd Floor, 11 Ridley Place, Newcastle upon Tyne, NE1 8JQ
Activities: Other letting and operating of own or leased real estate
Officers: James Henry Clark [1943] Director; Nicholas James Clark [1970] Director; Jonathan Dunn [1974] Director/Recruitment Consultant

B2B Staff Solutions Ltd
Incorporated: 9 November 2004 *Employees:* 4
Net Worth: £1,119,242 *Total Assets:* £1,246,951
Registered Office: 2nd Floor, 11 Ridley Place, Newcastle upon Tyne, NE1 8JQ
Activities: Other activities of employment placement agencies
Officers: Pamela Clark, Secretary; James Henry Clark [1943] Director; Nicholas James Clark [1970] Director; Jonathan Dunn [1974] Operations Director

Back on the Map Limited
Incorporated: 23 August 2004 *Employees:* 7
Net Worth: £4,932,023 *Total Assets:* £5,152,028
Registered Office: 67 Toward Road, Hendon, Sunderland, Tyne & Wear, SR2 8JG
Activities: Other letting and operating of own or leased real estate
Officers: Laura Calvert [1984] Director/Solicitor; Marie Hazel Clark [1948] Director; Julie Dawn Gray [1959] Director/Retired; Andrew Collins Jones [1962] Director; Christine Susan McCardle [1955] Director; Glenda Meldrum [1955] Director/Artist; Jean Moore [1943] Director/Retired; Councillor Dale Michael Mordey [1986] Director/Elected Member; Michael Alan Smith [1958] Director/Accountant; Andrew Sneddon [1953] Director/Self Employed

Badesha Property Investments Ltd
Incorporated: 16 June 2010
Net Worth: £179,805 *Total Assets:* £881,948
Registered Office: Badesha, 2 Craghead Road, Pelton Fell, Chester-le-Street, Co Durham, DH2 2NH
Activities: Other letting and operating of own or leased real estate
Officers: Jaswinder Singh [1965] Director/Postmaster

Badgepalm Limited
Incorporated: 9 May 1978
Net Worth: £880,721 *Total Assets:* £901,690
Registered Office: The Penthouse, Bolton Crofts, 42 Quakers Lane, Richmond, N Yorks, DL10 4AX
Activities: Other letting and operating of own or leased real estate
Shareholder: John Lewis Moss
Officers: John Lewis Moss [1943] Director/Property Developer

Bahr Academy
Incorporated: 24 February 2010
Net Worth: £467,309 *Total Assets:* £903,631
Registered Office: 72 Sceptre Street, Elswick, Newcastle upon Tyne, NE4 6PR
Activities: Other education n.e.c.
Officers: Muhammad Abdulmueet [1974] Director/Self Employed; Saddiqur Rahman [1980] Director/Teacher

Simon Bailes Limited
Incorporated: 9 February 1988 *Employees:* 97
Net Worth: £4,976,793 *Total Assets:* £10,062,287
Registered Office: 2-3 Tannery Lane, Northallerton, N Yorks, DL7 8DS
Activities: Sale of new cars and light motor vehicles
Major Shareholder: Simon Dominic Bailes
Officers: Simon Dominic Bailes, Secretary; Simon Dominic Bailes [1952] Director/Dealer Principal; Julie Kirby [1967] Director/Accountant; Tessa Rose Sanderson [1957] Director/Graphic Artist; John Sedgwick [1963] Director

Simon Bailes Property LLP
Incorporated: 21 January 2011
Net Worth: £1,157,854 *Total Assets:* £1,175,585
Registered Office: Tannery Lane, Northallerton, N Yorks, DL7 8DS
Officers: Simon Dominic Bailes [1952] Member

Christopher Bailey Tax Consultants Limited
Incorporated: 4 February 2011 *Employees:* 3
Net Worth: £224,331 *Total Assets:* £1,047,466
Registered Office: 2nd Floor, Yoden House, 30 Yoden Way, Peterlee, Co Durham, SR8 1AL
Activities: Tax consultancy
Shareholder: Christopher Neil Bailey
Officers: Christopher Neil Bailey [1966] Director/Chartered Accountant

Baileys Blinds Limited
Incorporated: 4 May 1993 *Employees:* 15
Net Worth: £120,173 *Total Assets:* £1,594,138
Registered Office: 34 High Street, Spennymoor, Co Durham, DL16 6DB
Activities: Manufacture of soft furnishings
Parent: Crest Properties (Scotland) Ltd
Officers: Morag Blaney, Company Secretary; Alexander Blaney [1963] Director/Retail Manufacturer; Morag Blaney [1962] Director/Company Secretary

J W Bainbridge Contractors Ltd
Incorporated: 14 April 2010 *Employees:* 7
Net Worth: £435,275 *Total Assets:* £828,450
Registered Office: Bogg House, Eggleston, Barnard Castle, Co Durham, DL12 0AX
Activities: Landscape service activities
Major Shareholder: Jonathan William Bainbridge
Officers: Anita Elizabeth Bainbridge, Secretary; Anita Elizabeth Bainbridge [1961] Director/Contractor; Jonathan William Bainbridge [1984] Director/Contractor; Kim Suzanne Bainbridge [1987] Director/Advanced Teaching Assistant; William Miller Bainbridge [1960] Director/Contractor

S.Bainbridge Limited
Incorporated: 18 March 1970
Net Worth: £745,416 *Total Assets:* £779,103
Registered Office: Black Bull Farm, Winston, Darlington, Co Durham, DL2 3PU
Activities: Support activities for crop production
Shareholder: John Bainbridge
Officers: Peter Bainbridge, Secretary; Florence Irene Bainbridge [1931] Director; John Bainbridge [1960] Director/Farmer; Peter Bainbridge [1962] Director/Farmer; Stanley Bainbridge [1932] Director/Farmer

Baker Furniture Limited
Incorporated: 21 September 1994 *Employees:* 30
Net Worth: £4,173,321 *Total Assets:* £5,018,039
Registered Office: Romaldkirk Road, Metz Bridge, Middlesbrough, Cleveland, TS2 1XA
Activities: Wholesale of furniture, carpets and lighting equipment
Shareholders: Richard Joseph Barker; James Thompson Barker
Officers: Peter Soakell, Secretary; Richard Joseph Barker [1939] Director; Mark James Callaghan [1979] Director/Accountant; Peter Soakell [1964] Director/Chartered Accountant

Baketime Limited
Incorporated: 1 July 2010 *Employees:* 51
Net Worth Deficit: £6,907,012 *Total Assets:* £2,777,746
Registered Office: Unit 1 Imperial Food Park, Imperial Avenue, South Bank, Middlesbrough, Cleveland, TS6 6BA
Activities: Manufacture of rusks and biscuits; manufacture of preserved pastry goods and cakes
Officers: Dr Dissanayake Hitihamu [1944] Director; Naushad Mahomed Ismail Abdoola [1960] Director; Shaukat Alli Moosa [1946] Director [South African]

Balkan Properties Limited
Incorporated: 3 September 2015 *Employees:* 3
Net Worth Deficit: £495,364 *Total Assets:* £6,606,316
Registered Office: Carter House, Pelaw Leazes Lane, Durham, DH1 1TB
Activities: Non-trading company
Shareholder: London & Regional Overseas Limited
Officers: Trevor Cartner [1960] Director/Chartered Surveyor; James Patrick Mitchell [1957] Director/Solicitor

Ballentine Properties Ltd
Incorporated: 5 March 2004 *Employees:* 2
Net Worth: £432,059 *Total Assets:* £3,011,933
Registered Office: 7a Studley Terrace, Newcastle upon Tyne, NE4 5PA
Activities: Buying and selling of own real estate
Major Shareholder: Shaban Suleman
Officers: Mohammed Suleman, Secretary; Shaban Suleman [1967] Director

The Ballinger Charitable Trust
Incorporated: 15 November 2007 *Employees:* 1
Net Worth: £35,194,452 *Total Assets:* £35,205,468
Registered Office: 112 Quayside, Newcastle upon Tyne, NE99 1SB
Activities: Other business support service activities n.e.c.
Officers: Jennifer Douthwaite, Secretary; Andrew John Nigel Ballinger [1973] Director/Civil Engineer; Diana Susan Ballinger [1940] Director/Retired; Nicola Jane Crowther [1971] Director/Chartered Accountant; John Flynn [1959] Director/Solicitor

Balmoral Interiors Limited
Incorporated: 25 January 1989
Net Worth: £632,732 *Total Assets:* £916,280
Registered Office: 47-55 Ormonde Street, Jarrow, Tyne & Wear, NE32 3PB
Activities: Retail sale of carpets, rugs, wall and floor coverings in specialised stores
Shareholders: Derek Francis Kerr; Bryan Mills
Officers: Derek Francis Kerr, Secretary; Derek Francis Kerr [1955] Director/Building Surveyor; Bryan Mills [1956] Director/Interior Design Manager

Balmoral Learning Trust
Incorporated: 25 May 2012 *Employees:* 74
Net Worth: £4,929,000 *Total Assets:* £6,242,000
Registered Office: East Herrington Primary Academy, Balmoral Terrace, East Herrington, Sunderland, Tyne & Wear, SR3 3PR
Activities: Primary education
Officers: Wendy Alder, Secretary; Deborah Ann Brown [1958] Director/Retired Teacher; Peter Chapman [1956] Director/Chief Executive; Terry Hambleton [1954] Director/Retired Headteacher; Alison Hodgson [1959] Director/Headteacher; Juli Isabel Poulton [1977] Director; John Mason Robe [1948] Director/Retired; Vicky Talbot [1977] Director/Human Resources; Damien Todd [1989] Director/Solicitor

Baltic Flour Mills Visual Arts Trust
Incorporated: 29 June 1998 *Employees:* 93
Net Worth: £2,401,001 *Total Assets:* £3,098,624
Registered Office: Baltic Centre for Contemporary Art, Gateshead Quays, South Shore Road, Gateshead, Tyne & Wear, NE8 3BA
Activities: Operation of arts facilities
Officers: Sara Dee Bryson [1979] Director/Community Organiser; Professor Stuart Edward Corbridge [1957] Director/Vice Chancellor and Warden, Durham University; Catherine Donovan [1959] Director/Councillor; Joanna Feeley [1975] Managing Director; Tina Gharavi [1972] Director/Filmmaker/Artist/Lecturer [Iranian]; Michael Francis Henry [1947] Director/Councillor; Louise Hunter [1975] Director of Corporate Affairs; Kirsty Patricia Lang [1962] Director/Journalist and Broadcaster; Michaela Dawn Martin [1957] Director/Solicitor (Retired); John Darren Richardson [1965] Director/Designer; Manohari Saravanamuttu [1972] Director/Marketing Consultant; Charlotte Brigid Sexton [1966] Director/Consultant; Graham Simon Thrower [1966] Director; Louise Anne Wilson [1967] Director/Artist

Baltic Recruitment Services Limited
Incorporated: 1 August 2006
Net Worth: £483,117 *Total Assets:* £1,103,057
Registered Office: Baltic House, Hilton Road, Aycliffe Business Park, Newton Aycliffe, Co Durham, DL5 6EN
Activities: Other activities of employment placement agencies
Officers: Charles Frederick Peart, Secretary; Christopher David Kent [1975] Managing Director; Charles Frederick Peart [1966] Managing Director; Roger David Hunter Peart [1972] Director

Baltic Training Services Limited
Incorporated: 6 July 2006 *Employees:* 132
Net Worth: £613,459 *Total Assets:* £1,988,293
Registered Office: Baltic House, Hilton Road, Aycliffe Business Park, Newton Aycliffe, Co Durham, DL5 6EN
Activities: Technical and vocational secondary education
Officers: Roger David Hunter Peart, Secretary/Managing Director; Anthony Russell Hobbs [1970] Managing Director; Laura Jayne Jackson [1981] Director; Charles Frederick Peart [1966] Managing Director; Emily Victoria I'anson Peart [1977] Director; Dr Emma Jane Peart [1966] Director; Roger David Hunter Peart [1972] Managing Director

Bandoffice 2 Limited
Incorporated: 7 September 1993
Net Worth: £3,300,963 *Total Assets:* £3,300,963
Registered Office: Top Floor, Oriel House, Calverts Lane, Bishop Street, Stockton on Tees, Cleveland, TS18 1SW
Activities: Other letting and operating of own or leased real estate
Parent: Jomast Limited
Officers: Stuart John Monk, Secretary/Director; Jennifer Monk [1952] Director; Stuart John Monk [1949] Director

Bandoffice Limited
Incorporated: 9 March 1992
Net Worth: £3,215,357 *Total Assets:* £3,215,357
Registered Office: Top Floor, Oriel House, Calverts Lane, Bishop Street, Stockton on Tees, Cleveland, TS18 1SW
Activities: Other letting and operating of own or leased real estate
Parent: Jomast Limited
Officers: Stuart John Monk, Secretary/Director; Jennifer Monk [1952] Director; Stuart John Monk [1949] Director

H.J. Banks (Construction) Limited
Incorporated: 26 January 1956 *Employees:* 4
Net Worth: £1,983,000 *Total Assets:* £2,003,000
Registered Office: Inkerman House, St Johns Road, Meadowfield, Co Durham, DH7 8XL
Activities: Construction of other civil engineering projects n.e.c.
Parent: The Banks Group Limited
Officers: David Joseph Martin, Secretary; Harry James Banks [1940] Managing Director; Richard John Dunkley [1969] Finance Director; Andrew Simon David Fisher [1971] Director/Accountant; Anthony Martin Kellerman [1961] Contracts Director

H.J. Banks and Company Limited
Incorporated: 8 March 1976 *Employees:* 235
Net Worth: £63,118,000 *Total Assets:* £114,467,000
Registered Office: Inkerman House, St John's Road, Meadowfield, Co Durham, DH7 8XL
Activities: Buying and selling of own real estate
Parent: The Banks Group Limited
Officers: David Joseph Martin, Secretary; Harry James Banks [1940] Managing Director; Richard John Dunkley [1969] Finance Director; Andrew Simon David Fisher [1971] Director/Accountant; Gavin Anthony Styles [1978] Director

Banks Brothers Transport Limited
Incorporated: 14 July 1982 *Employees:* 14
Net Worth: £2,760,000 *Total Assets:* £2,967,000
Registered Office: Inkerman House, St Johns Road, Meadowfield, Co Durham, DH7 8XL
Activities: Freight transport by road
Parent: H J Banks & Company Limited
Officers: David Joseph Martin, Secretary; Harry James Banks [1940] Managing Director; Richard John Dunkley [1969] Finance Director; Andrew Simon David Fisher [1971] Director/Accountant; Freda Styles [1950] Director; Gavin Anthony Styles [1978] Executive Director

The Banks Group Limited
Incorporated: 14 June 1988 *Employees:* 334
Net Worth: £69,185,000 *Total Assets:* £253,612,000
Registered Office: Inkerman House, St John's Road, Meadowfield, Co Durham, DH7 8XL
Activities: Activities of head offices
Shareholders: Janice Ann Banks; Harry James Banks
Officers: David Joseph Martin, Secretary; Harry James Banks [1940] Group Chairman and Managing Director; Andrew Rolland Cunningham [1956] Director; Richard John Dunkley [1969] Executive Director; Andrew Simon David Fisher [1971] Director of Finance; Christopher John Gill [1962] Director/Chartered Accountant; David Joseph Martin [1957] Director/Company Secretary; Gavin Anthony Styles [1978] Director/Head of Legal Services

Banks Property Limited
Incorporated: 18 July 1995 *Employees:* 11
Net Worth: £5,216,000 *Total Assets:* £30,086,000
Registered Office: Inkerman House, St Johns Road, Meadowfield, Co Durham, DH7 8XL
Activities: Buying and selling of own real estate
Parent: Banks Developments Limited
Officers: David Joseph Martin, Secretary; Harry James Banks [1940] Group Chairman and Managing Director; Richard John Dunkley [1969] Finance Director; Andrew Simon David Fisher [1971] Director/Accountant; Paul Bernard Langley [1955] Technical Director; John Michael Shuttleworth [1961] Managing Director

Banks Renewables (Armistead Wind Farm) Limited
Incorporated: 30 May 2007
Net Worth: £153,000 *Total Assets:* £14,501,000
Registered Office: Inkerman House, St Johns Road, Meadowfield, Co Durham, DH7 8XL
Activities: Non-trading company
Parent: Banks Renewables Limited
Officers: David Joseph Martin, Secretary; Richard John Dunkley [1969] Director; Andrew Simon David Fisher [1971] Director/Accountant

Banks Renewables (Harting Rig Wind Farm) Limited
Incorporated: 26 November 2013
Total Assets: £925,000
Registered Office: Inkerman House, St John's Road, Meadowfield, Co Durham, DH7 8XL
Activities: Non-trading company
Parent: Banks Renewables Limited
Officers: David Martin, Secretary; Colin Anderson [1970] Director; Richard John Dunkley [1969] Director; Andrew Simon David Fisher [1971] Director/Accountant

Banks Renewables (Hazlehead Wind Farm) Limited
Incorporated: 11 August 2006
Net Worth Deficit: £451,000 *Total Assets:* £7,969,000
Registered Office: Inkerman House, St Johns Road, Meadowfield, Co Durham, DH7 8XL
Activities: Non-trading company
Parent: Banks Renewables Limited
Officers: David Joseph Martin, Secretary; Richard John Dunkley [1969] Director; Andrew Simon David Fisher [1971] Director/Accountant

Banks Renewables (Heysham South Wind Farm) Limited
Incorporated: 14 October 2009
Net Worth: £505,000 *Total Assets:* £11,255,000
Registered Office: Inkerman House, St Johns Road, Meadowfield, Co Durham, DH7 8XL
Activities: Non-trading company
Parent: Camvo 201 Limited
Officers: David Joseph Martin, Secretary; Richard John Dunkley [1969] Director; Andrew Simon David Fisher [1971] Director/Accountant

Banks Renewables (Hook Moor Wind Farm) Limited
Incorporated: 16 February 2007
Net Worth: £345,000 *Total Assets:* £13,706,000
Registered Office: Inkerman House, St Johns Road, Meadowfield, Co Durham, DH7 8XL
Activities: Non-trading company
Parent: Banks Renewables Limited
Officers: David Joseph Martin, Secretary; Richard John Dunkley [1969] Director; Andrew Simon David Fisher [1971] Director/Accountant

Banks Renewables (Kype Muir Wind Farm) Limited
Incorporated: 28 May 2009
Net Worth: £1,446,000 *Total Assets:* £53,993,000
Registered Office: Inkerman House, St Johns Road, Meadowfield, Co Durham, DH7 8XL
Activities: Non-trading company
Parent: Banks Renewables Limited
Officers: David Joseph Martin, Secretary; Colin Anderson [1970] Managing Director; Richard John Dunkley [1969] Director; Andrew Simon David Fisher [1971] Director/Accountant

Banks Renewables (Marr Wind Farm) Limited
Incorporated: 26 July 2006
Net Worth Deficit: £268,000 *Total Assets:* £9,787,000
Registered Office: Inkerman House, St Johns Road, Meadowfield, Co Durham, DH7 8XL
Activities: Production of electricity
Parent: Banks Renewables Limited
Officers: David Joseph Martin, Secretary; Richard John Dunkley [1969] Director; Andrew Simon David Fisher [1971] Director/Accountant

Banks Renewables (Middle Muir Wind Farm) Limited
Incorporated: 15 September 2010
Net Worth: £704,000 *Total Assets:* £33,936,000
Registered Office: Inkerman House, St Johns Road, Meadowfield, Co Durham, DH7 8XL
Activities: Non-trading company
Parent: Banks Renewables Limited
Officers: David Joseph Martin, Secretary; Colin Anderson [1970] Managing Director; Richard John Dunkley [1969] Director; Andrew Simon David Fisher [1971] Director/Accountant

Banks Renewables (Moor House Wind Farm) Limited
Incorporated: 22 July 2009
Net Worth: £120,000 *Total Assets:* £15,968,000
Registered Office: Inkerman House, St Johns Road, Meadowfield, Co Durham, DH7 8XL
Activities: Non-trading company
Parent: Banks Renewables Limited
Officers: David Joseph Martin, Secretary; Richard John Dunkley [1969] Director; Andrew Simon David Fisher [1971] Director/Accountant

Banks Renewables (Penny Hill Wind Farm) Limited
Incorporated: 3 March 2008
Net Worth Deficit: £1,283,000 *Total Assets:* £21,580,000
Registered Office: Inkerman House, St Johns Road, Meadowfield, Co Durham, DH7 8XL
Activities: Non-trading company
Parent: Banks Renewables Limited
Officers: David Joseph Martin, Secretary; Richard John Dunkley [1969] Director; Andrew Simon David Fisher [1971] Director/Accountant

Banks Renewables Limited
Incorporated: 22 May 1989 *Employees:* 16
Net Worth Deficit: £11,354,000 *Total Assets:* £28,111,000
Registered Office: Inkerman House, St Johns Road, Meadowfield, Co Durham, DH7 8XL
Activities: Buying and selling of own real estate
Parent: The Banks Group Limited
Officers: David Joseph Martin, Secretary; Colin Anderson [1970] Managing Director; Harry James Banks [1940] Group Chairman and Managing Director; Richard John Dunkley [1969] Finance Director; Andrew Simon David Fisher [1971] Director/Accountant

Bannatyne Fitness (2) Limited
Incorporated: 20 June 2011 *Employees:* 60
Net Worth: £4,249,584 *Total Assets:* £8,513,774
Registered Office: Power House, Haughton Road, Darlington, Co Durham, DL1 1ST
Activities: Fitness facilities
Parent: The Bannatyne Group PLC
Officers: Edwin James, Secretary; Kenneth Peter Campling [1963] Director/Chief Financial Officer; Anthony Craig Elliott [1981] Director; Steven Hancock [1965] National Technical Services Director; Edwin Michael Lewis James [1980] Director/Solicitor; Justin Musgrove [1969] Director

Bannatyne Fitness Limited
Incorporated: 4 December 1996 *Employees:* 2,777
Net Worth: £41,972,000 *Total Assets:* £242,144,992
Registered Office: Power House, Haughton Road, Darlington, Co Durham, DL1 1ST
Activities: Fitness facilities
Parent: The Bannatyne Group PLC
Officers: Edwin James, Secretary; Kenneth Peter Campling [1963] Director/Chief Financial Officer; Anthony Craig Elliott [1981] Director; Steven Hancock [1965] National Technical Services Director; Edwin Michael Lewis James [1980] Director/Solicitor; Justin Musgrove [1969] Director

Bannatyne Hotels Limited
Incorporated: 25 October 1996 *Employees:* 226
Net Worth: £6,773,347 *Total Assets:* £16,511,102
Registered Office: Power House, Haughton Road, Darlington, Co Durham, DL1 1ST
Activities: Hotels and similar accommodation
Parent: The Bannatyne Group PLC
Officers: Edwin James, Secretary; Kenneth Peter Campling [1963] Director/Chief Financial Officer; Anthony Craig Elliott [1981] Director; Steven Hancock [1965] National Technical Services Director; Edwin Michael Lewis James [1980] Director/Solicitor; Justin Musgrove [1969] Director

Bannatyne Properties Limited
Incorporated: 20 June 2011 *Employees:* 3
Net Worth: £1,933,901 *Total Assets:* £3,570,154
Registered Office: Power House, Haughton Road, Darlington, Co Durham, DL1 1ST
Activities: Other letting and operating of own or leased real estate
Major Shareholder: Duncan Walker Bannatyne
Officers: Edwin James, Secretary; Duncan Walker Bannatyne [1949] Director; Hollie Nicole Bannatyne [1985] Director; Abigail Victoria Bannatyne-Elliott [1983] Director

Bannatyne's Health Club (Fairfield) Limited
Incorporated: 4 January 2007 *Employees:* 35
Net Worth: £6,942,250 *Total Assets:* £7,514,878
Registered Office: Power House, Haughton Road, Darlington, Co Durham, DL1 1ST
Activities: Fitness facilities
Parent: The Bannatyne Group PLC
Officers: Edwin James, Secretary; Kenneth Peter Campling [1963] Director/Chief Financial Officer; Edwin Michael Lewis James [1980] Director/Solicitor

Bannatyne's Health Club (Stratford upon Avon) Limited
Incorporated: 13 May 1998 *Employees:* 45
Net Worth Deficit: £4,578,934 *Total Assets:* £4,401,650
Registered Office: Power House, Haughton Road, Darlington, Co Durham, DL1 1ST
Activities: Other human health activities
Parent: Bannatyne Fitness Limited
Officers: Edwin Michael Lewis James, Secretary; Kenneth Peter Campling [1963] Director/Accountant; Anthony Craig Elliott [1981] Commercial Director; Steven Hancock [1965] Director; Edwin Michael Lewis James [1980] Director/Solicitor; Justin Musgrove [1969] Director

Banner Contracts (Halnaby) Limited
Incorporated: 24 February 1993 *Employees:* 86
Net Worth: £12,494,721 *Total Assets:* £20,927,932
Registered Office: The Coach House, Halnaby Hall, Croft on Tees, Darlington, Co Durham, DL2 2TJ
Activities: Repair of machinery
Major Shareholder: Michael Stuart Banner
Officers: Andrew Michael Banner [1981] Director; Jonathan Laurence Banner [1978] Director; Michael Stuart Banner [1953] Executive Director

Bans Healthcare Ltd
Incorporated: 28 June 2012 *Employees:* 8
Net Worth: £385,303 *Total Assets:* £1,265,027
Registered Office: Fawdon Park Pharmacy, 9 Fawdon Park Road, Newcastle upon Tyne, NE3 2PE
Activities: General medical practice activities
Shareholders: Bharat Dhir; Neera Dhir
Officers: Bharat Dhir [1964] Director/Pharmacist; Neera Dhir [1970] Director

Bantel Investments Limited
Incorporated: 3 January 1949
Net Worth: £1,552,644 *Total Assets:* £1,598,040
Registered Office: c/o Clements & Company, 2 Eslington Terrace, Jesmond, Newcastle upon Tyne, NE2 4RJ
Activities: Other letting and operating of own or leased real estate
Officers: Peter James Brandon, Secretary; James Thomas Brandon [1944] Director; Jason Adam Barry Brandon [1966] Director; Lisa Dawn Brandon [1963] Director; Michael Francis Brandon [1941] Director; Paul Brandon [1960] Director; Peter James Brandon [1932] Director

J.Barbour & Sons,Limited
Incorporated: 11 September 1912 *Employees:* 962
Net Worth: £110,876,328 *Total Assets:* £141,677,088
Registered Office: Simonside Industrial Estate, South Shields, Tyne & Wear, NE34 9PD
Activities: Manufacture of other wearing apparel and accessories n.e.c.
Shareholders: Dame Margaret Barbour; Helen Mary Barbour
Officers: Dame Margaret Barbour [1940] Director; Ian Melvin Beattie [1953] Director; Helen Mary Humphrey [1966] Director; Ian Richard Sime [1962] Supply Chain Director

Barbour (Europe) Limited
Incorporated: 4 August 1983 *Employees:* 80
Net Worth: £5,832,055 *Total Assets:* £6,525,783
Registered Office: Simonside Industrial Estate, South Shields, Tyne & Wear, NE34 9PD
Activities: Wholesale of clothing and footwear
Parent: J Barbour & Sons Ltd
Officers: Jens Bakker [1965] Director/General Manager [German]; Helen Mary Barbour [1966] Director; Dame Margaret Barbour [1940] Director; Ian Melvin Beattie [1953] Director

J Barbour and Sons (Manufacturing) Limited
Incorporated: 13 January 2009 *Employees:* 153
Net Worth Deficit: £1,984,466 *Total Assets:* £887,167
Registered Office: Simonside Industrial Estate, South Shields, Tyne & Wear, NE34 9PD
Activities: Manufacture of other men's outerwear
Parent: J Barbour & Sons Ltd
Officers: Helen Mary Barbour [1966] Director; Dame Margaret Barbour [1940] Director

Barclay Roofing (Holdings) Limited
Incorporated: 22 November 2001
Net Worth: £1,349,117 *Total Assets:* £1,354,980
Registered Office: Portrack Industrial Estate, Portrack Grange Road, Stockton on Tees, Cleveland, TS18 2PH
Activities: Activities of other holding companies n.e.c.
Shareholders: Paul Trelease; Julie Anne Trelease
Officers: Jeffrey Caine, Secretary; Julie Anne Trelease [1960] Director; Paul Trelease [1958] Director

Barclay Roofing Limited
Incorporated: 10 June 1986
Net Worth: £1,252,733 *Total Assets:* £2,447,219
Registered Office: Portrack Industrial Estate, Portrack Grange Road, Stockton on Tees, Cleveland, TS18 2PH
Activities: Roofing activities
Parent: Barclay Roofing (Holdings) Limited
Officers: Jeffrey Caine, Secretary; Julie Anne Trelease [1960] Director; Paul Trelease [1958] Director

Barkell Limited
Incorporated: 14 October 1981 *Employees:* 120
Net Worth Deficit: £16,473 *Total Assets:* £5,996,877
Registered Office: Unit 22 No 1 Industrial Estate, Consett, Co Durham, DH8 6SZ
Activities: Manufacture of other electrical equipment
Parent: Airedale International Air Conditioning
Officers: Simon Andrew Thorburn, Secretary; Anthony Cole [1963] Director; Steven Joyce [1965] HR Director; Scott Miller [1964] Director/Company Vice President [American]

Barker & Stonehouse Limited
Incorporated: 20 August 1968 *Employees:* 362
Net Worth: £23,273,000 *Total Assets:* £53,027,000
Registered Office: Barker and Stonehouse, Haydock Park Road, Teesside Retail Park, Stockton on Tees, Cleveland, TS17 7BG
Activities: Retail of furniture, lighting, and similar (not musical instruments or scores) in specialised store
Shareholders: Richard Joseph Barker; James Thompson Barker
Officers: Peter Soakell, Secretary; James Thompson Barker [1966] Director/Retailer; Richard Joseph Barker [1939] Director/Retail Furnisher; Shane David Butler [1968] Director/Retailer; Richard Parnell [1959] Commercial Director; Peter Soakell [1964] Director/Chartered Accountant

Barker Bros. Limited
Incorporated: 5 June 2008
Net Worth: £233,024 *Total Assets:* £1,099,898
Registered Office: East Cliff Farm, Cliff Road, Staithes, Saltburn-by-the-Sea, N Yorks, TS13 5AF
Activities: Mixed farming
Shareholders: Samuel Mark Barker; Jane Barker
Officers: Jane Margaret Barker, Secretary; Jane Margaret Barker [1991] Director; Samuel Mark Barker [1990] Director/Farmer

Barker Estate Management Ltd
Incorporated: 8 March 2004
Registered Office: 21 Colegate West, High Heworth, Gateshead, Tyne & Wear, NE10 9AH
Activities: Other letting and operating of own or leased real estate
Officers: George Philip Barker Snr [1944] Board Director

George W. Barker Limited
Incorporated: 24 February 1978 *Employees:* 2
Net Worth: £1,797,205 *Total Assets:* £3,671,892
Registered Office: Manor House Farm, Whitwell Scorton, Richmond, N Yorks, DL10 6AZ
Activities: Mixed farming
Major Shareholder: Benjamin George William Barker
Officers: George William Barker, Secretary; Benjamin George William Barker [1968] Director/Farmer; George William Barker [1940] Director/Farmer

Barkers (Northallerton) Limited
Incorporated: 1 April 1947 *Employees:* 151
Net Worth: £18,205,944 *Total Assets:* £21,671,012
Registered Office: 198-202 High Street, Northallerton, N Yorks, DL7 8LP
Activities: Other retail sale in non-specialised stores
Shareholder: Charles Wilfred Barker
Officers: Robert Baker, Secretary; Charles Wilfred Barker [1951] Department Store Director; Guy Charles Barker [1989] Director; Ian David Barker [1969] Director of Retail Store

Barking Dog (UK) Limited
Incorporated: 14 June 2005 *Employees:* 2
Net Worth: £1,570,438 *Total Assets:* £1,714,292
Registered Office: Hazlett House Farm, Waterhouses, Co Durham, DH7 9HD
Activities: Television programme production activities
Shareholders: Matthew James Baker; Nicola Baker
Officers: Nicola Baker, Secretary; Matthew James Baker [1977] Managing Director; Nicola Baker [1978] Director

Barmoor Wind Power Limited
Incorporated: 10 September 2010
Net Worth: £10,190,000 *Total Assets:* £21,651,000
Registered Office: Alexander House, 1 Mandarin Road, Rainton Bridge Business Park, Houghton-le-Spring, Co Durham, DH4 5RA
Activities: Production of electricity
Parent: EDF Energy Renewables Holdings Limited
Officers: Susan Elizabeth Lind, Secretary; Matthieu Thomas Hue [1975] Director [French]; Hassaan Majid [1968] Director

Barnaby Side Farms Limited
Incorporated: 4 June 1957 *Employees:* 4
Net Worth: £709,057 *Total Assets:* £1,021,930
Registered Office: Barnaby Side Farm, Middlesbrough Road, Guisborough, Cleveland, TS14 6RR
Activities: Mixed farming
Shareholders: John Walter Rider; Maureen Barbara Rider
Officers: Maureen Barbara Rider, Secretary; Suzanne Elizabeth Mack [1967] Director/Designer; John Walter Rider [1938] Director/Farmer; Katherine Barbara Rider [1965] Director/Event Organiser; Maureen Barbara Rider [1939] Director

Barnard Castle School
Incorporated: 19 May 2008 *Employees:* 200
Net Worth: £8,584,007 *Total Assets:* £12,651,875
Registered Office: Newgate, Barnard Castle, Co Durham, DL12 8UN
Activities: Other education n.e.c.
Officers: Suzanne Marie Metcalf, Secretary; Ian Martin Allison [1957] Director/Teacher; Nicholas John Bliss [1959] Director/Lawyer; Ruth Dent [1947] Director; Dr Jonathan Richard Elphick [1970] Director/Consultant Engineer; Alan John Fielder [1948] Director; Norman Peter Hodges [1954] Director/Chartered Builder; John Harvey Hunter [1968] Director/Banker; Robert Iain Moffatt [1961] Director/Chartered Accountant; Peter David Alan Mothersill [1957] Director; Clare Margaret Newman [1967] Director/Sales Account Manager; David Charles Osborne [1970] Director; Erland Robert Rendall [1971] Director/Chartered Surveyor; Cllr George Morland Richardson [1949] Director/Farmer; Donald Frederick Starr [1945] Director/Lecturer; Catherine Jean Sunley [1964] Director; Neil Thorpe [1967] Director/Lecturer; Donna Vinsome [1964] Director/Headmistress

Barnes Academy Trust
Incorporated: 12 June 2014 *Employees:* 51
Net Worth: £1,382,416 *Total Assets:* £1,826,024
Registered Office: Barnes Infant Academy, Mount Road, Sunderland, Tyne & Wear, SR4 7QF
Activities: Primary education
Officers: Patricia Ann Bell [1943] Director/Retired; Julia Anne Belshaw [1961] Director/Headteacher; Ian Laws [1956] Managing Director; Winifred Pennington Lightfoot [1936] Director/Retired; Simon Timothy Mattock [1961] Director/Independent Social Work Consultant

Barnwell Academy Trust
Incorporated: 7 March 2014 *Employees:* 50
Net Worth: £3,295,646 *Total Assets:* £3,960,987
Registered Office: Barnwell Primary School, Whitefield Estate, Penshaw, Houghton-le-Spring, Co Durham, DH4 7RT
Activities: Primary education
Officers: Christopher Nellist, Secretary; Christopher Armstrong [1994] Director/Building Surveyor; Nicola Collinson [1978] Director/Teaching Assistant; Susan Dimmock [1962] Director/Teacher; Ashley Emmerson [1973] Director/Headteacher; Donna Marie Hargrave [1980] Director/Senior Early Years Practitioner; Darren John Morton [1987] Director/Teacher; Nicola Procter [1987] Director/Financial Controller; Debbie Smith [1967] Director/Teaching Assistant; Stephen Joseph Wharton [1970] Director/Programme Co-ordinator; Lindsay Williams [1984] Director/Teacher

Barrasford Park Limited
Incorporated: 8 April 2010
Registered Office: Wynyard Park House, Wynyard Avenue, Wynyard, Billingham, Cleveland, TS22 5TB
Activities: Management of real estate on a fee or contract basis
Shareholders: Anthony Smith; Mary Smith
Officers: Anthony Smith [1952] Director; Mary Smith [1951] Director

Barrier (Offshore) Engineering Limited
Incorporated: 14 September 1982 *Employees:* 18
Net Worth: £603,264 *Total Assets:* £1,984,241
Registered Office: Haverton Hill Industrial Estate, Haverton Hill Road, Billingham, Cleveland, TS23 1PZ
Activities: Manufacture of metal structures and parts of structures
Officers: Alan John Harris, Secretary; David Glenn Anderson [1963] Director; Christopher James Garbutt [1969] Director/Works Manager; Alan John Harris [1966] Director/General Manager; Paul Harris [1971] Director

Barrier Architectural Services Limited
Incorporated: 12 September 2012
Net Worth: £1,160,434 *Total Assets:* £3,323,771
Registered Office: Pearl Buildings, Stephenson Street, Willington Quay, Wallsend, Tyne & Wear, NE28 6UE
Activities: Other professional, scientific and technical activities n.e.c.
Parent: Barrier Group Limited
Officers: Robert Charles Freeman Bowles [1952] Director; Graham Anthony Fuller [1958] Director; Alan Edward Nightingale [1962] Director; Anthony Joseph Scott [1967] Director

Barrier Fire Protection Limited
Incorporated: 24 November 1998
Net Worth: £1,946,238 *Total Assets:* £3,271,307
Registered Office: Pearl Buildings, Stephenson Street, Wallsend, Tyne & Wear, NE28 6UE
Activities: Other specialised construction activities n.e.c.
Parent: Barrier Group Limited
Officers: Robert Charles Freeman Bowles, Secretary/Director; Robert Charles Freeman Bowles [1952] Technical Director; Alan Edward Nightingale [1962] Director; David Shaw [1970] Managing Director; Anthony Patrick Spoors [1960] Director/Contracts Manager

Barrier Group Limited
Incorporated: 25 November 1998 *Employees:* 124
Net Worth: £2,643,081 *Total Assets:* £7,205,765
Registered Office: Pearl Buildings, Stephenson Street, Wallsend, Tyne & Wear, NE28 6UE
Activities: Activities of head offices
Major Shareholder: Robert Charles Freeman Bowles
Officers: Robert Charles Freeman Bowles [1952] Technical Director; Alan Edward Nightingale [1962] Director/Manager

Barrier Limited
Incorporated: 11 September 1975 *Employees:* 121
Net Worth: £4,744,719 *Total Assets:* £7,964,375
Registered Office: Pearl Buildings, Stephenson Street, Willington Quay, Tyne & Wear, NE28 6UE
Activities: Other specialised construction activities n.e.c.
Shareholders: Robert Charles Freeman Bowles; Richard Martin Soloman
Officers: Robert Charles Freeman Bowles, Secretary; Robert Charles Freeman Bowles [1952] Technical Director; Alan Edward Nightingale [1962] Director/Manager

Barrier Surveillance Systems Limited
Incorporated: 29 May 1991
Registered Office: Unit 7 All Saints Industrial Estate, Darlington Road, Shildon, Co Durham, DL4 2RD
Activities: Security systems service activities
Shareholder: Barry Johnson
Officers: Barry Johnson [1961] Director; Vincent Johnson [1952] Director/Quantity Surveyor

Barrington Distribution Ltd
Incorporated: 21 January 2016
Net Worth: £1,592,121 *Total Assets:* £1,673,820
Registered Office: Centra Lofts, 5 Waterloo Square, Newcastle upon Tyne, NE1 4DR
Activities: Operation of warehousing and storage facilities for land transport activities
Officers: Dominick Shelly [1967] Director

Barrington Homes Limited
Incorporated: 31 August 1999
Net Worth Deficit: £146,256 *Total Assets:* £810,687
Registered Office: Barrington Chambers, Victoria Avenue, Bishop Auckland, Co Durham, DL14 7NE
Activities: Development of building projects
Shareholders: Barrington Estates Limited; Meldon Investments Limited
Officers: Anthony Walters, Secretary; Christopher Shields [1947] Director; Anthony Walters [1954] Director/Solicitor

Kenneth M Barrow & Co Limited
Incorporated: 26 July 2012 *Employees:* 18
Net Worth: £640,432 *Total Assets:* £903,136
Registered Office: 15-16 Adelaide Row, Seaham, Co Durham, SR7 7EF
Activities: Solicitors
Officers: Kenneth Malcolm Barrow [1954] Director/Solicitor; Ravi Khosla [1978] Director/Solicitor; Mandeep Sunny Singh Thandi [1985] Director

Barter Books Limited
Incorporated: 15 March 2012 *Employees:* 47
Net Worth: £205,258 *Total Assets:* £872,599
Registered Office: Alnwick Station, Wagonway Road, Alnwick, Northumberland, NE66 2NP
Activities: Retail sale of books in specialised stores
Shareholders: John Stuart Manley; Mary Manley
Officers: David Champion [1948] Director; John Stuart Manley [1942] Director; Mary Manley [1938] Director [American]

J Barthram & Son Limited
Incorporated: 21 March 2011 *Employees:* 12
Net Worth: £443,576 *Total Assets:* £865,583
Registered Office: 47 South Parade, Northallerton, N Yorks, DL7 8SG
Activities: Funeral and related activities
Shareholders: Owen Jame Barthram; Allan Barthram; Kathryn Barthram
Officers: Allan Barthram [1938] Funeral Director; Joy Barthram [1947] Funeral Director; Owen Barthram [1977] Funeral Director

Barton Environmental Services Limited
Incorporated: 10 March 1988 *Employees:* 36
Net Worth: £838,878 *Total Assets:* £1,112,042
Registered Office: 5 Alvis Court, Cowpen Industrial Estate, Billingham, Cleveland, TS23 4JG
Activities: Other specialised construction activities n.e.c.
Parent: Barton Industrial Group Limited
Officers: Derick Beazley [1964] Director; Mark Jason Harrison [1970] Director

Bartram Walker Limited
Incorporated: 18 July 1985 *Employees:* 19
Net Worth: £488,059 *Total Assets:* £1,114,523
Registered Office: Esh House, Bowburn North Industrial Estate, Bowburn, Co Durham, DH6 5PF
Activities: Repair of other equipment
Parent: Esh Holdings Limited
Officers: Mark Sowerby, Secretary; Andrew Edward Radcliffe [1973] Director; Mark Andrew Sowerby [1971] Director; Keith William Walker [1973] Director/Business Development Manager

Bastion Glassfibre Rod & Sections Limited
Incorporated: 14 September 1973
Net Worth: £1,980,280 *Total Assets:* £2,195,767
Registered Office: 13 Patience Avenue, Seaton Burn, Newcastle upon Tyne, NE13 6HF
Activities: Manufacture of glass fibres
Major Shareholder: Jeffrey Leslie Redmayne
Officers: Jeffrey Leslie Redmayne [1944] Director/Glassfibre Manufacturer

Bates Regeneration Limited
Incorporated: 8 May 2009
Net Worth Deficit: £441,000 *Total Assets:* £4,842,000
Registered Office: Inkerman House, St Johns Road, Meadowfield, Co Durham, DH7 8XL
Activities: Buying and selling of own real estate
Shareholders: Banks Property Limited; Harworth Estates Limited
Officers: David Joseph Martin, Secretary; Paul Bernard Langley [1955] Technical Director; Richard Owen Michaelson [1966] Director; Edward Charles Peat [1958] Director/Chartered Surveyor; John Michael Shuttleworth [1961] Director/Surveyor

Bath Press Limited
Incorporated: 24 March 1943 *Employees:* 3
Net Worth Deficit: £3,595,832 *Total Assets:* £16,677,391
Registered Office: 8 Springfield Close, Ovington, Prudhoe, Northumberland, NE42 6EL
Activities: Printing n.e.c.
Parent: Cameron France Holding SAS
Officers: Matthew William Robson, Secretary; Matthew William Robson [1954] Director/Barrister

Thomas Baty (Newcastle upon Tyne) Limited
Incorporated: 16 July 1956
Net Worth: £253,331 *Total Assets:* £2,475,801
Registered Office: Units 7-8 North East, Fruit & Vegetable Market, Team Valley Trading Estate, Gateshead, Tyne & Wear, NE11 0QZ
Activities: Wholesale of fruit and vegetables
Officers: Dudley Colin Alexander Baty, Secretary; Holly Jasmine Barkess [1987] Director; Dudley Colin Alexander Baty [1959] Director/Fruit Merchant

R.Bau Limited
Incorporated: 1 August 2001
Registered Office: 22 Armstrong Road, North East Industrial Estate, Peterlee, Co Durham, SR8 5AJ
Activities: Construction of other civil engineering projects n.e.c.
Shareholders: Paul Webster; Margaret Webster; Praveen Varma
Officers: Margaret Webster, Secretary/Director; Margaret Webster [1952] Director/Sales; Paul Darryl Webster [1959] Director/Manager

Bauer Radio's Cash for Kids Charities
Incorporated: 12 November 2007 *Employees:* 31
Net Worth: £2,381,091 *Total Assets:* £2,982,675
Registered Office: Hampdon House, Falcon Court, Preston Farm Industrial Estate, Stockton on Tees, Cleveland, TS18 3TS
Activities: Other service activities n.e.c.
Officers: Tracey Butler, Secretary; Sally Fiona Aitchison [1964] Managing Director; Martin Ball [1966] Managing Director; Mark James Mahaffy [1963] Managing Director; Sean Patrick Marley [1968] Managing Director; Daniel Simpson [1981] Director; Gary Stein [1968] Director

John Baxter & Company (Newcastle) Limited
Incorporated: 12 August 1918 *Employees:* 3
Net Worth: £1,520,670 *Total Assets:* £1,685,386
Registered Office: Bulman House, Regent Centre, Gosforth, Newcastle upon Tyne, NE3 3LS
Activities: Other letting and operating of own or leased real estate
Officers: Judith Ann Woodford, Secretary; John Donald Woodford [1952] Director/Letting Agent; Judith Ann Woodford [1953] Director

Bay Plastics Limited
Incorporated: 5 December 1988 *Employees:* 55
Net Worth: £1,522,022 *Total Assets:* £3,376,628
Registered Office: Unit H1, High Flatworth, Tyne Tunnel Trading Estate, North Shields, Tyne & Wear, NE29 7UZ
Activities: Manufacture of plastic plates, sheets, tubes and profiles
Major Shareholder: Michael Currell
Officers: Michael Currell, Secretary; Michael Currell [1962] Managing Director

Baydale Control Systems Limited
Incorporated: 29 November 1999 *Employees:* 47
Net Worth: £2,413,722 *Total Assets:* £3,798,632
Registered Office: Unit I6, Morton Park Way, Darlington, Co Durham, DL1 4PH
Activities: Electrical installation
Major Shareholder: Neil James Pentland
Officers: Neil James Pentland, Secretary/Managing Director; Neil James Pentland [1964] Managing Director

Baydale Estates Limited
Incorporated: 26 October 2004 *Employees:* 5
Net Worth: £681,428 *Total Assets:* £1,121,681
Registered Office: c/o GSM, Albert Road, Darlington, Co Durham, DL1 2PD
Activities: Wholesale trade of motor vehicle parts and accessories
Shareholders: Alfred William Moore; George Frank Moore
Officers: George Frank Moore, Secretary; Alfred William Moore [1970] Director; George Frank Moore [1968] Director

BBL NE Limited
Incorporated: 27 January 2004 *Employees:* 4
Net Worth: £381,375 *Total Assets:* £760,127
Registered Office: Stephenson House, Richard Street, Hetton-le-Hole, Co Durham, DH5 9HW
Activities: Licenced restaurants
Officers: Craig Fitzakerly, Secretary; Caroline Fitzakerly [1971] Director/Administrator; Craig Fitzakerly [1970] Director/Architect; Clinton Mysleyko [1979] Director/Architectural Technician; Gemma Mysleyko [1980] Director/Office Worker

BCTQ Maritime Corporate Limited
Incorporated: 6 April 1959 *Employees:* 1
Net Worth: £416,316 *Total Assets:* £781,405
Registered Office: Office 5 Horton Park, Berwick Hill Road, Newcastle upon Tyne, NE13 6BU
Activities: Other professional, scientific and technical activities n.e.c.
Major Shareholder: Barry Edward Kerr Gilmour
Officers: William Allan Plant, Secretary; Brian James Corlett [1953] Director/Naval Architect; Barry Edward Kerr Gilmour [1947] Director; William Allan Plant [1962] Director

Be Modern Holdings Limited
Incorporated: 18 December 2006 *Employees:* 336
Net Worth: £22,557,500 *Total Assets:* £27,765,308
Registered Office: 19-34 Bedesway, Bede Industrial Estate, Jarrow, Tyne & Wear, NE32 3BE
Activities: Activities of head offices
Shareholders: Walter Bloodworth; Gregory Bloodworth
Officers: John Richard Harris, Secretary; Gregory Bloodworth [1965] Production Director; Walter Bloodworth [1940] Joint Managing Director

Be Modern Limited
Incorporated: 26 November 1964 *Employees:* 323
Net Worth: £10,130,495 *Total Assets:* £15,732,189
Registered Office: 19-34 Bedesway, Bede Industrial Estate, Jarrow, Tyne & Wear, NE32 3BE
Activities: Manufacture of other furniture
Shareholders: Walter Bloodworth; Gregory Bloodworth
Officers: John Richard Harris, Secretary; Craig Bloodworth [1985] Director/Business Consultant; Gregory Bloodworth [1965] Executive Director; Walter Bloodworth [1940] Director/Chairman; John Richard Harris [1958] Financial Director; David John MacArthur [1964] Managing Director - Furniture Division

Be Modern Properties Limited
Incorporated: 18 March 2008 *Employees:* 2
Net Worth: £4,314,711 *Total Assets:* £4,772,001
Registered Office: 19-34 Bedesway, Bede Industrial Estate, Jarrow, Tyne & Wear, NE32 3BE
Activities: Other letting and operating of own or leased real estate
Officers: John Richard Harris, Secretary; Gregory Bloodworth [1965] Production Director; Walter Bloodworth [1940] Joint Managing Director

Be Property Management LLP
Incorporated: 18 April 2005
Net Worth: £1,159,562 *Total Assets:* £1,162,046
Registered Office: Louie House, Lancaster Road, Gateshead, Tyne & Wear, NE11 9JR
Officers: Archna Babuta [1968] Member

Beacon Electrical (N.E.) Limited
Incorporated: 27 April 1983 *Employees:* 7
Net Worth: £1,016,111 *Total Assets:* £1,187,568
Registered Office: 1-3 Franklin Street, South Shields, Tyne & Wear, NE33 1PR
Activities: Non-specialised wholesale trade
Major Shareholder: Peter Maughan
Officers: Cherie Michelle Maughan, Secretary; Peter Maughan [1964] Director

Beacon View Pharmacy Limited
Incorporated: 24 March 1999
Net Worth: £319,906 *Total Assets:* £1,417,854
Registered Office: Stanley Vale, Wylam Wood Road, Wylam, Northumberland, NE41 8HZ
Activities: Dispensing chemist in specialised stores
Major Shareholder: Robert George Young
Officers: Jacqueline Ann Young, Secretary; Jacqueline Ann Young [1962] Director; Robert George Young [1960] Director/Pharmacist

Gary Beadle Promotions Limited
Incorporated: 6 December 2013
Net Worth: £682,462 *Total Assets:* £771,273
Registered Office: 2 Gosforth Park Avenue, Newcastle upon Tyne, NE12 8EG
Activities: Television programme production activities
Major Shareholder: Gary Beadle
Officers: Gary Beadle [1988] Director/Entertainer; George McCowie [1942] Director/Chartered Accountant

Beadnell Bay Caravan Park Ltd
Incorporated: 4 June 1971 *Employees:* 5
Net Worth: £809,886 *Total Assets:* £883,798
Registered Office: 27 Portland Terrace, Newcastle upon Tyne, NE2 1QP
Activities: Sale of other motor vehicles
Major Shareholder: Thomas Grenville Holmes
Officers: Dawn Holmes, Secretary; Dawn Holmes [1954] Director/Secretary; Drew Thomas Rennison Holmes [1981] Director/Assistant Campsite Manager; Laura Edwina Holmes [1985] Director/Administration Clerk; Thomas Grenville Holmes [1947] Director/Caravan Dealer

Beadnell Links Limited
Incorporated: 7 January 1958 *Employees:* 9
Net Worth: £974,476 *Total Assets:* £1,020,464
Registered Office: Beadnell Harbour, Beadnell, Northumberland, NE67 5BN
Activities: Recreational vehicle parks, trailer parks and camping grounds
Officers: Richard William Breakey, Secretary; Penelope Ann Breakey [1958] Director; Richard William Breakey [1956] Director/Accountant; Victoria Jane Dungait [1960] Director/Secretary; Jacqueline Ann Hall [1955] Director/Administrator; Jennifer Margaret Hall [1951] Director; William Lambton Hogg [1933] Director/Yacht Chandler

Beagle Holdings Limited
Incorporated: 7 August 1996
Net Worth: £2,954,715 *Total Assets:* £6,284,842
Registered Office: Parsons Business Centre, Brenda Road, Hartlepool, Cleveland, TS25 2BJ
Activities: Activities of head offices
Officers: David Lawn, Secretary; Timothy Dunningham [1953] Director; Richard Christopher Irvine [1952] Director/Fleet Engineer

Beamish Hall Limited
Incorporated: 28 June 2000
Net Worth: £1,555,949 *Total Assets:* £5,280,403
Registered Office: Beamish Hall, Beamish, Stanley, Co Durham, DH9 0YB
Activities: Hotels and similar accommodation
Major Shareholder: David Craggs
Officers: Hilary Craggs, Secretary; Arron Craggs [1989] Director/Gardener; David Craggs [1955] Director; Hilary Craggs [1958] Director; Katie Craggs [1985] Director/Head of Housekeeping; Amy Eveline Tocu [1982] Director/Hotelier

Beamish Museum
Incorporated: 22 March 2006 *Employees:* 423
Net Worth: £33,671,000 *Total Assets:* £37,807,000
Registered Office: Regional Resource Centre, Beamish, Stanley, Co Durham, DH9 0RG
Activities: Other business support service activities n.e.c.
Officers: Helen Mary Lynch, Secretary; Alan Ashburner [1948] Director/Retired Bank Officer; Michael Alexander Barker [1969] Director/Local Government Officer & Solicitor; Councillor Angela Douglas [1960] Director/Local Authority Councillor; Councillor Stephen Paul Foster [1956] Director/Councillor; Oswald Johnson [1946] Director; John Kelly [1962] Director; Councillor Carl Marshall [1980] Director/Councillor; Councillor Nancy Elizabeth Maxwell [1945] Director; Gillian Elizabeth Miller [1967] Regional Director Association of Colleges; Anne Marie Nixon [1978] Director/Chief Executive Officer; John Anthony Pennie [1955] Director/Solicitor; Sarah Elizabeth Salter [1964] Group HR Director; Councillor John-Paul Stephenson [1978] Director/Councillor Higher Education Tutor; Sarah Lesley Stewart [1958] Director/Business Consultant; David Stoker [1952] Director/Management Consultant

Beamish Transport Limited
Incorporated: 16 September 1998 *Employees:* 89
Net Worth: £1,803,235 *Total Assets:* £6,433,767
Registered Office: Junction of Burnt House Bank, Pelton Fell Road, Chester-le-Street, Co Durham, DH2 2AG
Activities: Freight transport by road
Shareholders: Stephen Fenwick; Darrin Lea Pickering
Officers: Darrin LEA Pickering, Secretary; Geoffrey Barlow [1956] Director/Transport Manager; Richard Hedley Foster [1956] Financial Director; Darrin LEA Pickering [1965] Director/Transport Manager

Beanies The Flavour Co. Ltd.
Incorporated: 10 October 2011 *Employees:* 16
Net Worth: £217,124 *Total Assets:* £1,674,036
Registered Office: Beanies The Flavour Co Ltd, Faverdale North, Darlington, Co Durham, DL3 0PH
Activities: Production of coffee and coffee substitutes
Shareholder: John Arthur Evans
Officers: Mark Philip Porteous, Secretary; John Arthur Evans [1950] Managing Director; Mark Philip Porteous [1975] Finance Director; John Duncan Spurr [1958] Director

Beauclerc Investments Limited
Incorporated: 14 September 2004 *Employees:* 1
Net Worth Deficit: £897,149 *Total Assets:* £900,315
Registered Office: Beauclerc, Riding Mill, Northumberland, NE44 6HY
Activities: Buying and selling of own real estate
Shareholders: Feidlim MacLoughlin; Penelope MacLoughlin
Officers: Feidlim Michael MacLoughlin [1941] Director [Irish]; Penelope MacLoughlin [1945] Director

Beaufront Business Park LLP
Incorporated: 22 July 2014
Registered Office: Yours Business Networks, Suite A, 7-8 Delta Bank Road, Gateshead, Tyne & Wear, NE11 9DJ
Officers: Reuben Thomas Coppin Straker [1956] Member; Mark William Tully [1963] Member

Beaumont Colson Ltd.
Incorporated: 12 July 1996 *Employees:* 22
Net Worth: £2,018,671 *Total Assets:* £2,782,262
Registered Office: 129 New Bridge Street, Newcastle upon Tyne, NE1 2SW
Activities: Information technology consultancy activities
Shareholders: Gordon Crosthwaite; Paul Andrew Ryder
Officers: Dr Howard Adamson [1962] Director/Dentist/Software Engineering; Paul Andrew Ryder [1960] Director/IT Consultant

Beaumont Landscapes Holdings Limited
Incorporated: 20 December 2007
Net Worth: £949,778 *Total Assets:* £1,092,288
Registered Office: Beaumont House, Groat Drive, Aycliffe Industrial Estate, Newton Aycliffe, Co Durham, DL5 6HY
Activities: Activities of other holding companies n.e.c.
Shareholders: Mark William Lineton; Sally Anne Lineton
Officers: Sally Anne Lineton, Secretary; Mark William Lineton [1962] Director; Sally Anne Lineton [1961] Director

Beaver Management Services Limited
Incorporated: 20 December 1996 *Employees:* 659
Net Worth: £4,929,622 *Total Assets:* £24,328,672
Registered Office: 20 Manor Way, Belasis Business Park, Billingham, Cleveland, TS23 4HN
Activities: Other business support service activities n.e.c.
Major Shareholder: Bernard Kenneth Goodchild
Officers: Bernard Kenneth Goodchild [1956] Director/Manager; Andrew William Haygarth [1968] Director/Electrical Engineer; Anthony Paul Shipley [1966] Managing Director

Bebe Clothing (UK) Limited
Incorporated: 31 March 2011 *Employees:* 18
Net Worth: £1,584,769 *Total Assets:* £7,237,802
Registered Office: Bebe House, Dukesway, Team Valley Trading Estate, Gateshead, Tyne & Wear, NE11 0PZ
Activities: Wholesale of clothing and footwear
Major Shareholder: Naresh Kumar Jerath
Officers: Naresh Kumar Jerath [1961] Director; Rajnee Jerath [1963] Director

Bebe Group Limited
Incorporated: 27 January 2004 *Employees:* 19
Net Worth: £5,186,855 *Total Assets:* £11,372,452
Registered Office: Bebe House, Dukesway, Team Valley Trading Estate, Gateshead, Tyne & Wear, NE11 0PZ
Activities: Wholesale of clothing and footwear
Major Shareholder: Naresh Kumar Jerath
Officers: Ranjee Jerath, Secretary; Naresh Kumar Jerath [1961] Director

Beck Burn Windfarm Limited
Incorporated: 27 October 2015
Net Worth: £9,642,000 *Total Assets:* £42,499,000
Registered Office: Alexander House, 1 Mandarin Road, Rainton Bridge Business Park, Houghton-le-Spring, Co Durham, DH4 5RA
Activities: Construction of utility projects for electricity and telecommunications
Parent: EDF Energy Renewables Holdings Limited
Officers: Susan Elizabeth Lind, Secretary; Matthieu Thomas Hue [1975] Director [French]; Hassaan Majid [1968] Director

Beckleberrys Limited
Incorporated: 12 October 2005
Net Worth: £1,034,020 *Total Assets:* £1,850,138
Registered Office: Beckleberrys Limited, Cowen Road, Blaydon on Tyne, Tyne & Wear, NE21 5TW
Activities: Manufacture of ice cream
Shareholders: Ian David Craig; Peter James Craig
Officers: Brenda Craig, Secretary; Ian David Craig [1950] Director/Manager; Peter Craig [1977] Director/Manager

Beckside Properties Limited
Incorporated: 7 May 1987
Registered Office: 14 Duke Street, Darlington, Co Durham, DL3 7AA
Activities: Other letting and operating of own or leased real estate
Major Shareholder: Charles Carver
Officers: Charles Nicholas Carver [1956] Director/Estate Agent

Beckwith Developments Limited
Incorporated: 10 April 1978
Net Worth: £1,085,114 *Total Assets:* £1,683,729
Registered Office: The Keepers Cottage, Hebron, Morpeth, Northumberland, NE61 3LA
Activities: Other letting and operating of own or leased real estate
Shareholders: George Leighton Beckwith; Susan Beckwith
Officers: Susan Beckwith, Secretary; Christopher Beckwith [1973] Director/Property Management; George Leighton Beckwith [1946] Director/Quantity Surveyor; Justin George James Beckwith [1987] Director/Property Manager; Susan Beckwith [1951] Director/Property Investment

Bede and Cuthbert Developments Limited
Incorporated: 25 April 2016
Net Worth Deficit: £168,948 *Total Assets:* £1,369,825
Registered Office: Keel House, Garth Heads, Newcastle upon Tyne, NE1 2JE
Activities: Construction of domestic buildings
Shareholders: TOC Property Backed Lending Trust PLC; Bede Homes Limited
Officers: David Barlow [1961] Director; Stephen William Black [1981] Director; Richard Stewart Arran Buckley [1968] Director; Andrew Burnett [1976] Director; Gavin David Cordwell Smith [1976] Director/Chartered Accountant; Ian Michael McElroy [1980] Director

Bede Globe LLP
Incorporated: 22 July 2010
Net Worth: £1,179,610 *Total Assets:* £2,312,183
Registered Office: Unit 5 Maling Court, Union Street, Newcastle upon Tyne, NE2 1BP
Officers: Dr Ian Robert Baggett [1972] Member; Jason Moray Justin MacKay [1973] Member; Matthew James Totham [1972] Member

Bede Group Limited
Incorporated: 10 March 1971
Net Worth: £779,663 *Total Assets:* £988,244
Registered Office: Bede House, Westline Industrial Estate, Birtley, Co Durham, DH2 1AU
Activities: Manufacture of metal structures and parts of structures
Officers: Joy Christine Crawley, Secretary; George Henry Gibbon [1961] Director; Gillian Gibbon [1956] Director/Credit Controller; Julie Gibbon [1962] Director

Bede Investments Limited
Incorporated: 30 July 2015
Net Worth: £74,934 *Total Assets:* £2,216,786
Registered Office: Unit 5 Maling Court, Union Street, Newcastle upon Tyne, NE2 1BP
Activities: Activities of open-ended investment companies
Shareholders: Ian Robert Baggett; Jason Moray Justin MacKay; Matthew James Totham
Officers: Ian Robert Baggett [1972] Director; Jason Moray Justin MacKay [1973] Director; Matthew James Totham [1972] Director

Bedi Group Limited
Incorporated: 19 February 2016
Net Worth: £24,632 *Total Assets:* £1,081,183
Registered Office: Suite 2b, North Sands Business Centre, Liberty Way, Sunderland, Tyne & Wear, SR6 0QA
Activities: Other letting and operating of own or leased real estate
Major Shareholder: Dr Sanjeev Bedi
Officers: Dr Sanjeev Bedi [1975] Director/Dentist

The Bedlingtonshire Golf Club Limited
Incorporated: 27 March 2001 *Employees:* 17
Net Worth: £343,816 *Total Assets:* £947,419
Registered Office: Bedlingtonshire Golf Club, Acorn Bank, Hartford Road, Bedlington, Northumberland, NE22 6AA
Activities: Operation of sports facilities
Officers: Layla Levy, Secretary; Ray Baldwin [1959] Director/Maintenance Manager; Kevin Beaney [1961] Director; Christine Jacklin [1948] Director/Retired; David Jefferson [1966] Director/Fireman; Alan McBride [1958] Director/Retired; Richard Metcalf [1965] Director/Construction

Bedmax Limited
Incorporated: 28 June 1999 *Employees:* 62
Net Worth: £3,326,305 *Total Assets:* £7,262,539
Registered Office: Detchant, Belford, Northumberland, NE70 7PF
Activities: Sawmilling and planing of wood
Parent: Pensave Limited
Officers: Timothy Wyndham Basil Smalley, Secretary; John Haddon Lovett [1951] Director; Jonathan Richard Malton [1964] Director; Timothy Wyndam Basil Smalley [1960] Director/Manufacturer; William Moore Teasdale [1942] Director/Chartered Accountant

The Bedsit Company Limited
Incorporated: 2 March 2003
Net Worth: £361,097 *Total Assets:* £1,088,773
Registered Office: 14 Regent Terrace, Gateshead, Tyne & Wear, NE8 1LU
Activities: Other service activities n.e.c.
Shareholders: Shahid Mohammed; Medina Shahid; Yasmin Shahid
Officers: Shahid Mohammed [1969] Director

Beecham Peacock LLP
Incorporated: 26 May 2009 *Employees:* 39
Total Assets: £1,068,056
Registered Office: 7 Collingwood Street, Newcastle upon Tyne, NE1 1JE
Officers: Sophia Yau-Rosher [1973] Member; Charlotte Talbot [1982] LLP Member

Beecham Peacock North East Limited
Incorporated: 13 June 2016 *Employees:* 37
Net Worth: £301 *Total Assets:* £1,118,944
Registered Office: 7 Collingwood Street, Newcastle upon Tyne, NE1 1JE
Activities: Solicitors
Shareholders: C Talbot Limited; M Laverick Limited; S Yau-Rosher Limited
Officers: David Bruce Dewar [1967] Director/Solicitor; Mark Laverick [1961] Director; Morag Frances Polmear [1955] Director/Solicitor; Charlotte Talbot [1982] Director/Solicitor; Victoria Ann Wanless [1973] Director/Solicitors; Sophia Yau-Rosher [1973] Director/Solicitor

Beis Chaye Rochel (The Gateshead Jewish Academy) Limited
Incorporated: 4 November 2003
Net Worth: £710,956 *Total Assets:* £1,976,357
Registered Office: 138 Coatsworth Road, Gateshead, Tyne & Wear, NE8 4LL
Activities: General secondary education
Officers: Martin Terry Cope [1948] Director/General Practitioner; Avram M Guttentag [1988] Director

Bekco UK Ltd
Incorporated: 29 May 2015
Net Worth: £3,147,217 *Total Assets:* £3,294,340
Registered Office: Unit H, The Waterfront, Kingfisher Boulevard, Newcastle upon Tyne, NE15 8NZ
Activities: Construction of domestic buildings
Officers: Richard Lester, Secretary; Richard Lester [1978] Director; Joyce Newell [1946] Sales Director

Bel Engineering (UK) Limited
Incorporated: 29 February 2012 *Employees:* 233
Net Worth: £711,000 *Total Assets:* £18,023,000
Registered Office: 11 Glasshouse Street, St Peters, Newcastle upon Tyne, NE6 1BS
Activities: Machining
Parent: Bel Valves Limited
Officers: Joanne Alicea Wilkes, Secretary; Laura Joicey [1976] Director/Group Chief Financial Officer; Alexander Harold Lamb [1971] Director/Group Chairman; Jonathan Charles Lamb [1977] Group Manufacturing Director

Bel Estates Limited
Incorporated: 10 May 2013 *Employees:* 3
Net Worth: £1,712,148 *Total Assets:* £1,860,912
Registered Office: 11 Glasshouse Street, St Peters, Newcastle upon Tyne, NE6 1BS
Activities: Other service activities n.e.c.
Parent: British Engines Limited
Officers: Joanne Alicea Wilkes, Secretary; Laura Joicey [1976] Director/Group Chief Financial Officer; Alexander Harold Lamb [1971] Director/Group Chairman; Jonathan Charles Lamb [1977] Group Manufacturing Director

Bel Group Investments Limited
Incorporated: 9 December 1937 *Employees:* 5
Net Worth Deficit: £782,254 *Total Assets:* £1,848,122
Registered Office: 11 Glasshouse Street, St Peters, Newcastle upon Tyne, NE6 1BS
Activities: Other business support service activities n.e.c.
Parent: British Engines Limited
Officers: Joanne Alicea Wilkes, Secretary; Richard Dodd [1974] Director; Laura Joicey [1976] Director/Group Chief Financial Officer; Alexander Harold Lamb [1971] Director/Chairman; Jonathan Charles Lamb [1977] Group Manufacturing Director

Bel Valves Limited
Incorporated: 18 May 1920 *Employees:* 241
Net Worth: £49,343,000 *Total Assets:* £59,254,000
Registered Office: 11 Glasshouse Street, St Peters, Newcastle upon Tyne, NE6 1BS
Activities: Manufacture of taps and valves
Parent: British Engines (UK) Limited
Officers: Joanne Alicea Wilkes, Secretary; Bruce Michael Amos Heppenstall [1970] Director/Bel Valves CEO; Laura Joicey [1976] Director/Group Chief Financial Officer; Neil Kirkbride [1960] Chairman/Director; Alexander Harold Lamb [1971] Director; Jonathan Charles Lamb [1977] Group Manufacturing Director

Belgravia Decor Limited
Incorporated: 2 October 1978
Net Worth: £1,980,570 *Total Assets:* £2,617,714
Registered Office: Belgravia House, Woodbine Street, Sunderland, Tyne & Wear, SR1 2NL
Activities: Manufacture of wallpaper
Major Shareholder: Ferruccio Zambaiti
Officers: Davide Zambaiti [1987] Director [Italian]

Ian Bell (Motor Cycles) Limited
Incorporated: 12 November 1974 *Employees:* 9
Net Worth: £2,418,840 *Total Assets:* £2,664,328
Registered Office: Third Floor, Citygate, St James Boulevard, Newcastle upon Tyne, NE1 4JE
Activities: Sale of other motor vehicles
Major Shareholder: Trudi Anne Bell
Officers: Trudi Anne Bell, Secretary; Trudi Anne Bell [1961] Director

Stuart Bell Asset Management Limited
Incorporated: 15 January 2014
Net Worth: £797,965 *Total Assets:* £2,099,069
Registered Office: Unit 10 Hackworth Industrial Park, Shildon, Co Durham, DL4 1HF
Activities: Management consultancy activities other than financial management
Major Shareholder: Stuart Bell
Officers: Stuart Bell [1967] Director

Bell Bros.(Ashington) Limited
Incorporated: 23 July 1942 *Employees:* 2
Net Worth: £4,540,158 *Total Assets:* £4,720,857
Registered Office: 32 Portland Terrace, Jesmond, Newcastle upon Tyne, NE2 1QP
Activities: Other letting and operating of own or leased real estate
Shareholders: Yvonne Bell; Carolyn Bayne; Bell Bros. (Holdings) Limited
Officers: Yvonne Bell, Secretary/Marketing Director; Carolyn Bayne [1956] Director/Administrator; Yvonne Bell [1960] Director/Administrator

Ben Hoare Bell LLP
Incorporated: 11 August 2005 *Employees:* 80
Net Worth: £936,928 *Total Assets:* £1,502,287
Registered Office: 19 John Street, Sunderland, Tyne & Wear, SR1 1JQ
Officers: Adrian Patrick Dalton [1960] Member; Richard Keith Hardy [1973] Member; Mark Harrison [1959] Member; Andrew Gerard Kelly [1968] Member; Katharine Elizabeth Lawrence [1976] Member; Christine McCurley [1961] Member; Tricia Jane Mytton [1980] Member

M & D Bell Ltd
Incorporated: 7 April 2011
Net Worth: £420,905 *Total Assets:* £1,657,880
Registered Office: Thornbrough Farm, Corbridge, Northumberland, NE45 5LX
Activities: Support activities for crop production
Shareholders: Diane Bell; Martin Bell
Officers: Diane Bell [1968] Director; Martin Bell [1965] Director

Bell Tindle Williamson LLP
Incorporated: 19 August 2005
Net Worth: £108,272 *Total Assets:* £985,809
Registered Office: The Old Post Office, 63 Saville Street, North Shields, Tyne & Wear, NE30 1AY
Officers: John Bell [1953] Member; Judith Cassells [1967] Member; Emma Jane Hartshorne-Ferguson [1980] Member

Bell Truck Sales Limited
Incorporated: 31 July 1973 *Employees:* 198
Net Worth Deficit: £288,920 *Total Assets:* £29,552,512
Registered Office: Bellway Industrial Estate, Whitley Road, Longbenton, Newcastle upon Tyne, NE12 9SW
Activities: Sale of other motor vehicles
Parent: Bell Trucks (Holdings) Limited
Officers: Manjit Singh Powar [1976] Director; Danny Steven Sawrij [1969] Director; Benjamin Sowersby [1977] Managing Director

Bell Trucks (Holdings) Limited
Incorporated: 9 August 2006 *Employees:* 198
Net Worth Deficit: £199,687 *Total Assets:* £29,552,512
Registered Office: Bellway Industrial Estate, Whitley Road, Longbenton, Newcastle upon Tyne, NE12 9SW
Activities: Sale of other motor vehicles
Parent: Leo Group Limited
Officers: Manjit Singh Powar [1976] Director; Danny Steven Sawrij [1969] Director; Benjamin Sowersby [1977] Managing Director

Bell View (Belford)
Incorporated: 16 June 1998 *Employees:* 11
Net Worth: £1,145,155 *Total Assets:* £1,183,995
Registered Office: 33 West Street, Belford, Northumberland, NE70 7QB
Activities: Social work activities without accommodation for the elderly and disabled
Officers: Roger Melville Howell, Secretary; Ethel Bennett [1951] Director/Retired; Malcolm Charles Cresswell [1951] Director/Retired; Eileen Duncan [1948] Director/Retired; Andrew John Harris [1974] Director; Christine Mary Harris [1949] Director/RGN Urology Specialist Nurse; Dr Emma Christina Miller [1967] Director/GP; Guy Renner-Thompson [1991] Director/Farm Salesman; Margaret Todd [1945] Director/Carers Support Worker; Barbara Twiname [1950] Director; Kathleen Mary Williamson [1949] Director/Retired; John Crawford Woodman [1955] Director/Accountant

Bellaine Limited
Incorporated: 28 May 1980 *Employees:* 2
Net Worth: £959,676 *Total Assets:* £1,044,791
Registered Office: 4 Sandwood Park, Guisborough, Cleveland, TS14 8EH
Activities: Other letting and operating of own or leased real estate
Shareholders: Elaine Bell; Leslie Bell
Officers: Elaine Bell, Secretary; Elaine Bell [1953] Director; Leslie Bell [1933] Director

Belle Vue Community, Sports & Youth Centre Limited
Incorporated: 21 January 2002 *Employees:* 48
Net Worth: £1,456,313 *Total Assets:* £1,844,328
Registered Office: Kendal Road, Hartlepool, Cleveland, TS25 1QU
Activities: Activities of sport clubs
Officers: Alan Ronald Clark, Secretary; Alan Ronald Clark [1986] Director; Kevin Henry Cranney [1956] Director/Councillor; Stuart Fraser Drummond [1973] Director/Mayor; Malcolm Walker [1958] Director/Local Government

Belle Vue Developments (Low Fell) Ltd
Incorporated: 17 August 2011
Registered Office: The Warehouse, Well Lane, Gateshead, Tyne & Wear, NE9 6JW
Activities: Development of building projects
Major Shareholder: Stephen Bowler
Officers: Stephen Bowler [1969] Director

Bellingham Camping Limited
Incorporated: 6 March 2013
Net Worth: £8,120 *Total Assets:* £951,707
Registered Office: Tweed House, The Croft, Bellingham, Hexham, Northumberland, NE48 2JY
Activities: Recreational vehicle parks, trailer parks and camping grounds
Shareholders: Dr Johanna Mary Avis; Dr David John Berrisford
Officers: Dr Johanna Mary Avis [1965] Director/University Lecturer; Dr David John Berrisford [1964] Director/University Lecturer

Bellway (Services) Limited
Incorporated: 8 October 1964
Net Worth: £2,048,821 *Total Assets:* £2,540,994
Registered Office: Seaton Burn House, Dudley Lane, Seaton Burn, Newcastle upon Tyne, NE13 6BE
Activities: Other business support service activities n.e.c.
Parent: Bellway P.L.C.
Officers: Simon Scougall, Secretary; Keith Derek Adey [1979] Finance Director; Jason Michael Honeyman [1968] Director; John Knowlton Watson [1954] Director/Chief Executive

Bellway Homes Limited
Incorporated: 16 September 1960 *Employees:* 6,037
Net Worth: £1,570,685,056 *Total Assets:* £3,099,051,008
Registered Office: Seaton Burn House, Dudley Lane, Seaton Burn, Newcastle upon Tyne, NE13 6BE
Activities: Construction of domestic buildings
Parent: Bellway P.L.C.
Officers: Simon Scougall, Secretary; Keith Derek Adey [1979] Finance Director; Jason Michael Honeyman [1968] Director; John Knowlton Watson [1954] Managing Director

Bellway Housing Trust Limited
Incorporated: 14 June 1930
Net Worth: £2,000,835 *Total Assets:* £9,177,523
Registered Office: Seaton Burn House, Dudley Lane, Seaton Burn, Newcastle upon Tyne, NE13 6BE
Activities: Non-trading company
Parent: Bellway P.L.C.
Officers: Simon Scougall, Secretary; Keith Derek Adey [1979] Finance Director; Jason Michael Honeyman [1968] Director; Simon Scougall [1976] Director/Solicitor; John Knowlton Watson [1954] Director/Chief Executive

Bellway P L C
Incorporated: 9 June 1978 *Employees:* 2,544
Net Worth: £2,191,406,080 *Total Assets:* £3,147,415,040
Registered Office: Seaton Burn House, Dudley Lane, Seaton Burn, Newcastle upon Tyne, NE13 6BE
Activities: Development of building projects
Officers: Simon Scougall, Secretary; Keith Derek Adey [1979] Finance Director; Jill Caseberry [1965] Director; John Arthur Cuthbert [1953] Director; Paul Nigel Hampden Smith [1960] Director/Chartered Accountant; Jason Michael Honeyman [1968] Director; Denise Nichola Jagger [1958] Director/Solicitor; Ian Philip McHoul [1960] Director; John Knowlton Watson [1954] Director

Bellway Properties Limited
Incorporated: 30 December 1983 *Employees:* 4
Net Worth Deficit: £2,395,670 *Total Assets:* £4,675,155
Registered Office: Seaton Burn House, Dudley Lane, Seaton Burn, Newcastle upon Tyne, NE13 6BE
Activities: Development of building projects
Parent: Bellway P.L.C.
Officers: Simon Scougall, Secretary; Keith Derek Adey [1979] Finance Director; Jason Michael Honeyman [1968] Director; John Knowlton Watson [1954] Director/Chief Executive

Belmont View Limited
Incorporated: 19 December 2007 *Employees:* 68
Net Worth: £2,605,867 *Total Assets:* £4,879,631
Registered Office: Rosehill, Belmangate, Guisborough, Cleveland, TS14 7BB
Activities: Other residential care activities n.e.c.
Parent: BJP Corporation Limited
Officers: Joan Corinne Parvin, Secretary; Barry Malcolm Parvin [1948] Finance Director

The Belsay Trust
Incorporated: 17 September 2012
Net Worth: £15,648,663 *Total Assets:* £16,372,485
Registered Office: Belsay Estate Office, Belsay, Northumberland, NE20 0DX
Activities: Other letting and operating of own or leased real estate
Officers: Angus Edward Collingwood-Cameron [1963] Director/Consultant; Simon Roger Kirkup [1966] Director/Solicitor; Anne-Marie Belinda Trevelyan [1969] Director/Chartered Accountant; John Antony Scott Walton [1945] Director

Belvedere Property Company Limited
Incorporated: 10 August 1921
Net Worth: £755,892 *Total Assets:* £854,402
Registered Office: 18 Northumberland Square, North Shields, Tyne & Wear, NE30 1PX
Activities: Other letting and operating of own or leased real estate
Major Shareholder: Peter Richard Jackson
Officers: Robert Alan Storey, Secretary/Chartered Surveyor; Caroline Ann Jackson [1953] Director/Housewife; Peter Richard Jackson [1949] Director/Chartered Surveyor; Richard Merlin Jackson [1980] Director/Chartered Surveyor; Robert Alan Storey [1956] Director/Chartered Surveyor

Bench Marque (GBR) Limited
Incorporated: 18 September 2008
Net Worth: £609,798 *Total Assets:* £1,064,129
Registered Office: Swallow House, Parsons Road, Washington, Tyne & Wear, NE37 1EZ
Activities: Retail of furniture, lighting, and similar (not musical instruments or scores) in specialised store
Major Shareholder: Ian McKeag
Officers: Catherine Louise McKeag [1972] Director; Ian McKeag [1968] Director

Benchmark Electronics Limited
Incorporated: 14 November 1997
Net Worth: £747,639 *Total Assets:* £878,281
Registered Office: Brandon Lane, Langley Moor, Co Durham, DH7 8PE
Activities: Manufacture of loaded electronic boards
Shareholders: Gavin Hancock; Karen Louisa Hancock
Officers: Karen Louisa Hancock, Secretary; Clifford Jeffrey Hancock [1934] Director/Chartered Engineer; Gavin Hancock [1964] Director/Engineer; Dr Elliott Makin [1974] Director/Engineer

Benore Care Limited
Incorporated: 19 May 2005 *Employees:* 76
Net Worth: £1,918,348 *Total Assets:* £4,205,090
Registered Office: Cale Cross House, 156 Pilgrim Street, Newcastle upon Tyne, NE1 6SU
Activities: Other human health activities
Officers: Adrian Osborne Hendry [1969] Director; Catherine Joan Hendry [1943] Director; Graeme Allan Hendry [1965] Director

Bentincks Ltd
Incorporated: 1 April 2009
Net Worth: £780,208 *Total Assets:* £2,591,333
Registered Office: Bentinck House, Nest Road, Gateshead, Tyne & Wear, NE10 0ES
Activities: Manufacture of other furniture
Shareholder: Zaffar Iqbal
Officers: Zaffar Iqbal, Secretary; Fozia Ajmee [1982] Director; Zaffar Iqbal [1976] Managing Director; Tajun Nisa [1957] Director

Bentley Medical Practice Limited
Incorporated: 4 July 2014 *Employees:* 44
Net Worth: £981,931 *Total Assets:* £1,194,710
Registered Office: Bentley Medical Practice, Redcar Primary Care Hospital, West Dyke Road, Redcar, Cleveland, TS10 4NW
Activities: General medical practice activities
Shareholders: Noushafarin Farjadnia; Dr Ali Tahmassebi
Officers: Dr Ali Tahmassebi [1969] Director/General Practitioner

Benton House Limited
Incorporated: 15 September 2011 *Employees:* 3
Net Worth: £2,740,412 *Total Assets:* £4,825,597
Registered Office: Benton House, Benton Business Park, Bellway Industrial Estate, Newcastle upon Tyne, NE12 9SW
Activities: Other letting and operating of own or leased real estate
Major Shareholder: Courtney Aldo Clift
Officers: Philip John Rodgers, Secretary; Philip John Rodgers [1970] Director

Berger Closures Limited
Incorporated: 26 July 1988 *Employees:* 19
Net Worth: £1,423,240 *Total Assets:* £2,093,786
Registered Office: 5 Doxford Drive, Southwest Industrial Estate, Peterlee, Co Durham, SR8 2RL
Activities: Manufacture of fasteners and screw machine products
Parent: Ringmetall AG
Officers: Richard John Lofthouse Swart, Secretary; Pierina Fontana [1935] Director [Italian]; Christoph Alexander Petri [1980] Director [German]; Richard John Lofthouse Swart [1962] Managing Director

Berisford Holdings Limited
Incorporated: 15 July 1991 *Employees:* 3
Net Worth: £19,810,000 *Total Assets:* £19,810,000
Registered Office: St Ann's Wharf, 112 Quayside, Newcastle upon Tyne, NE1 3DX
Activities: Activities of other holding companies n.e.c.
Parent: Enodis Group Limited
Officers: Adrian David Gray [1962] Director/Accountant; John Albert James Rourke [1967] Director

Berkeley Exploration Limited
Incorporated: 18 September 2006 *Employees:* 3
Net Worth Deficit: £383,799 *Total Assets:* £58,547,624
Registered Office: Third Floor, Citygate, St James Boulevard, Newcastle upon Tyne, NE1 4JE
Activities: Other business support service activities n.e.c.
Parent: Berkeley Energia Limited
Officers: Dylan Browne, Secretary; Paul Campbell Atherley [1956] Director; Dylan Paul Browne [1985] Director/Executive [Australian]

Bernex UK Limited
Incorporated: 29 May 1997
Net Worth Deficit: £1,305,627 *Total Assets:* £5,700,000
Registered Office: Unit 36 Number One Industrial Estate, Medomsley Road, Consett, Co Durham, DH8 6TS
Activities: Activities of head offices
Parent: Indigo Topco Limited
Officers: Dr Christopher Paul Constable [1975] Managing Director; Jeffrey David Ostman [1968] Regional Managing Director [French/American]; Prof. Gerrit Jan Van Der Kolk [1955] Director [Dutch]

Bernicia Limited
Incorporated: 23 January 2001
Registered Office: 4 Cedar Drive, Jarrow, Tyne & Wear, NE32 4BG
Activities: Buying and selling of own real estate
Officers: Doriza Karin Wetz, Secretary; David Wilkinson [1964] Director/Painter Decorator

Berryvale Ltd
Incorporated: 26 March 1999 *Employees:* 86
Net Worth: £3,495,389 *Total Assets:* £6,947,396
Registered Office: 65 Low Lane, Middlesbrough, Cleveland, TS5 8EG
Activities: Maintenance and repair of motor vehicles
Shareholder: Charles Doocey
Officers: Nuala Theresa Doocey, Secretary [Irish]; Charles Doocey [1954] Director/Civil Engineer [Irish]

Bertschi U.K. Limited
Incorporated: 27 July 1989 *Employees:* 133
Net Worth: £3,291,938 *Total Assets:* £13,857,117
Registered Office: Bertschi UK Ltd, Middlesbrough Road East, Southbank, Middlesbrough, Cleveland, TS6 6TZ
Activities: Freight transport by road
Shareholder: Hans-Jorg Bertschi
Officers: Brigitta Berner, Secretary; Brigitta Berner [1956] Director [Swiss]; Hans-Jorg Bertschi [1957] Director [Swiss]; Nicholas Brown [1958] Managing Director

Bescol Motors Limited
Incorporated: 21 January 2014
Net Worth Deficit: £84,518 *Total Assets:* £1,549,655
Registered Office: 24 Mill Farm Road, Hamsterley Mill, Rowlands Gill, Tyne & Wear, NE39 1NW
Activities: Sale of new cars and light motor vehicles
Parent: Bescol Investments Limited
Officers: Peter Nixon Chapman, Secretary; Caroline Rosemary Jane Chapman [1956] Director; Peter Nixon Chapman [1955] Director

Bespoke Concrete Products Limited
Incorporated: 15 December 1992
Registered Office: Tynedale Works, Princess Court, Low Prudhoe, Northumberland, NE42 6PL
Activities: Other manufacturing n.e.c.
Shareholders: Martin Kay; Elsa Kay
Officers: Elsa Joan Kay, Secretary; Anthony William Kay [1965] Director/Chartered Surveyor; Elsa Joan Kay [1953] Director; Martin Alexander Kay [1957] Managing Director

Bestmark Properties Limited
Incorporated: 29 June 2000
Net Worth: £862,855 *Total Assets:* £2,165,792
Registered Office: 7b Cleveland Drive, Marton, Middlesbrough, Cleveland, TS7 8AE
Activities: Other letting and operating of own or leased real estate
Shareholders: Hamid Shan; Shahaida Parveen Shan
Officers: Hamid Shan, Secretary/Director; Hamid Shan [1963] Director; Shahaida Parveen Shan [1964] Director

Bewicke Service Station Limited
Incorporated: 3 January 2014
Net Worth: £598,160 *Total Assets:* £902,044
Registered Office: 130 Sutherland Avenue, Newcastle upon Tyne, NE4 9NR
Activities: Retail sale of automotive fuel in specialised stores
Major Shareholder: Mohammed Tanvir
Officers: Mohammed Tanvir [1969] Director

Beyond Leisure Limited
Incorporated: 10 October 2002
Net Worth: £624,856 *Total Assets:* £895,917
Registered Office: Ramside Hall Hotel, Carrville, Durham, DH1 1TD
Activities: Public houses and bars
Officers: Karen Wilson, Secretary; John Richard Adamson [1965] Director

Beyond360 Limited
Incorporated: 5 September 2015
Net Worth: £1,253,909 *Total Assets:* £1,255,125
Registered Office: Clavering House, Business Centre, Clavering Place, Newcastle upon Tyne, NE1 3NG
Activities: Other information technology service activities
Shareholders: Rashpal Kaur Shoker; Jason Singh Shoker; Gurpinder Rikky Shoker
Officers: Laurie Jo Bassi [1954] Director/Economist [American]; Maneesh Mehndiratta [1975] Technical Director [Indian]; Dominique Franck Romano [1964] Director/Entrepreneur [French]; Kaldish Singh Shoker [1963] Director; Gayle Patricia Thomas [1974] Director/Teacher

BGP Consulting Limited
Incorporated: 12 March 2014
Net Worth: £1,322,189 *Total Assets:* £2,874,596
Registered Office: Wellington House, Wellington Court, Preston Farm Business Park, Stockton on Tees, Cleveland, TS18 3TA
Activities: Other service activities n.e.c.
Shareholders: James Conway; Ian Richard Walker
Officers: Neville Baines [1959] Director; James Conway [1962] Director; Ian Richard Walker [1966] Director; Paul Arthur Winship [1965] Director

BGRP Limited
Incorporated: 14 April 2005 *Employees:* 40
Net Worth: £842,294 *Total Assets:* £1,721,491
Registered Office: Unit 3 Easter Park, Nelson Park West, Cramlington, Northumberland, NE23 1WQ
Activities: Manufacture of soft furnishings
Shareholders: Jayne Helen Dolder; Mark Dolder
Officers: Jayne Helen Dolder, Secretary/Personal Assistant; Andrew John Atkins [1963] Director/Management Consultant; Jayne Helen Dolder [1971] Director; Mark Dolder [1959] Director; Ian Richard Simpson [1956] Director/Consultant

BHK (UK) Limited
Incorporated: 18 November 1987 *Employees:* 75
Net Worth: £1,953,017 *Total Assets:* £7,103,290
Registered Office: Davy Drive, North West Industrial Estate, Peterlee, Co Durham, SR8 2JF
Activities: Manufacture of other furniture
Major Shareholder: Peter Kottmann
Officers: Christopher Nigel Longley, Secretary; Peter Kottmann [1962] Director [German]; Christopher Nigel Longley [1964] Director/Accountant

Biddick Academy Trust
Incorporated: 9 May 2013 *Employees:* 133
Net Worth: £17,379,000 *Total Assets:* £18,860,000
Registered Office: Biddick Academy Trust, Biddick Lane, Washington, Tyne & Wear, NE38 8AL
Activities: General secondary education
Officers: Graham Patterson, Secretary; Rev Nicholas James Barr-Hamilton [1974] Director/Vicar; Paul Cowen [1982] Director/Headteacher; Paul John Eastwood [1970] Director/Teacher; Christine Elizabeth Ford [1943] Director/Retired; Vivienne May Fox [1968] Director/Local Government Officer; David McDonald [1962] Sales Director; Anne Moran [1938] Director/Retired; Joanne Christine Richardson [1971] Director/Senior Social Worker; Dax Robb [1980] Director/ICT Manager; John Rostron [1955] Director/Retired; Councillor Dianne Elizabeth Snowdon [1964] Director/Councillor; Ian Tindle [1979] Director; Leslie John Todd [1962] Operations Director

Big Hearted Hospitality Company Limited
Incorporated: 24 January 2014
Net Worth Deficit: £852,884 *Total Assets:* £1,480,259
Registered Office: Jesmond Dene House, Jesmond Dene Road, Newcastle upon Tyne, NE2 2EY
Activities: Hotels and similar accommodation
Officers: Terry Bayliff [1949] Director; Peter Haswell Candler [1953] Managing Director; Philip Anthony Ganley [1956] Director; Paul Joseph Morrissey [1952] Director

Bignall Group Ltd
Incorporated: 17 March 1976 *Employees:* 37
Net Worth: £1,705,016 *Total Assets:* £2,346,400
Registered Office: Butler House, Haughton Green, Darlington, Co Durham, DL1 2DD
Activities: Repair of machinery
Shareholders: John Roger Bignall; Oliver Charles Bignall
Officers: John Roger Bignall, Secretary; John Roger Bignall [1944] Director; Oliver Charles Bignall [1970] Director/Engineer; Paul Higginbottom [1958] Director; Frances Anabel Sand [1973] Director/Marketing

Biker Group Limited
Incorporated: 15 June 1993 *Employees:* 126
Net Worth: £2,610,419 *Total Assets:* £7,031,175
Registered Office: Moor Park, Moor Road, Leyburn, N Yorks, DL8 5LA
Activities: Construction of domestic buildings
Major Shareholder: Antony William Biker
Officers: Bruce Shepherd, Secretary; Anthony William Biker [1945] Director/Builder/Plant Operator/Hirer; Benjamin Robert Biker [1978] Director/Quantity Surveyor; Matthew Anthony Biker [1976] Director/Land Agent; Howard Mark Pearson [1968] Financial Director

Bikesport (North East) Limited
Incorporated: 6 July 2009 *Employees:* 7
Net Worth: £483,632 *Total Assets:* £912,588
Registered Office: 208 Westgate Road, Newcastle upon Tyne, NE4 6AN
Activities: Retail trade of motor vehicle parts and accessories
Shareholders: Gavin Roy Linscott; Lydia Margaret Linscott
Officers: Lydia Margaret Linscott, Secretary; Gavin Roy Linscott [1948] Director/Shop Owner

Billfreehomes Limited
Incorporated: 13 January 2004 *Employees:* 12
Net Worth: £196,327 *Total Assets:* £835,247
Registered Office: 85 New Elvet, Durham, DH1 3AQ
Activities: Other letting and operating of own or leased real estate
Shareholders: Deborah Michele Smith; Peter Arthur Smith
Officers: Peter Arthur Smith, Secretary/Salesman; Sean Peter Lawless [1989] Director/Lettings Agent; Deborah Michele Smith [1967] Director; Peter Arthur Smith [1963] Director/Salesman

Billingham Headway Limited
Incorporated: 11 October 2007
Net Worth: £1,022,657 *Total Assets:* £5,507,641
Registered Office: Abbey Health Centre, Finchale Avenue, Billingham, Cleveland, TS23 2DG
Activities: Other letting and operating of own or leased real estate
Officers: Dr Claire Lesley Jackson, Secretary; Dr Judith Ann Donkin [1967] Director/General Practitioner; Dr Hugh Francis Geoghegan [1953] Director/General Medical Practitioner [Irish]; Dr Claire Lesley Jackson [1969] Director/General Practitioner; Mohammad Naseem Khan [1967] Director/General Practitioner; John Patrick O Donoghue [1952] Director/General Practitioner [Irish]; Mark Pritchard [1973] Director/General Practitioner Principal; Dr Shafquth Rasool [1955] Director/General Practitioner; Dr Pawanjit Singh [1975] Director/General Practitioner

Billingham Machine Company Limited
Incorporated: 19 December 1997 *Employees:* 15
Net Worth: £356,488 *Total Assets:* £1,063,928
Registered Office: Bewley House, Alvis Close, Billingham, Cleveland, TS23 4JB
Activities: Manufacture of metal structures and parts of structures
Major Shareholder: Paul Anthony Messham
Officers: Ann Messham, Secretary; Paul Anthony Messham [1965] Director/Engineers

Billions Europe Ltd
Incorporated: 6 November 2014 *Employees:* 13
Net Worth: £3,123,108 *Total Assets:* £33,275,236
Registered Office: Winder House, Kingfisher Way, Stockton on Tees, Cleveland, TS18 3EX
Activities: Manufacture of dyes and pigments
Officers: Fiona Margaret MacLeod [1961] Director/Engineer; Ruiqing Tan [1966] Director/Owner [Chinese]; Ran Xu [1990] Director/Marketing Representative [Chinese]

Biochemica Water Limited
Incorporated: 3 July 2007 *Employees:* 55
Net Worth: £252,516 *Total Assets:* £2,388,912
Registered Office: Unit 4 Daimler Drive, Cowpen Lane Industrial Estate, Billingham, Cleveland, TS23 4JD
Activities: Wholesale of chemical products
Shareholders: Biochemica Group Limited; Dr Timothy Robinson; David Simon Ruddy
Officers: David Simon Ruddy, Secretary; John Fraser [1971] Director; Gary Lumby [1958] Director; Dr Timothy Robinson [1976] Director/Consultant; David Simon Ruddy [1979] Director/Consultant

Biostore Limited
Incorporated: 10 August 2005 *Employees:* 26
Net Worth: £1,150,286 *Total Assets:* £1,924,203
Registered Office: Dobson House, Regent Centre, Gosforth, Newcastle upon Tyne, NE3 3PF
Activities: Other information technology service activities
Shareholders: Nigel Walker; Jonathan David Shuttleworth
Officers: John Bradley [1954] Director/Consultant; Alasdair Duncan Darroch [1956] Director; Paul Greathead [1974] Marketing and Sales Director; Jonathan David Shuttleworth [1965] Director/Technical Manager; Nigel Walker [1964] Managing Director

Gilbert Birdsall Limited
Incorporated: 2 October 2003 *Employees:* 16
Net Worth: £1,534,551 *Total Assets:* £2,075,203
Registered Office: South Farm, South Road, Belford, Northumberland, NE70 7DP
Activities: Manufacture of ready-mixed concrete
Shareholders: Steven Birdsall; George Gilbert Birdsall
Officers: Steven Birdsall, Secretary; George Gilbert Birdsall [1942] Director; Steven Birdsall [1970] Director/Manager

Birmingham District Energy Company Limited
Incorporated: 6 November 2006
Net Worth: £4,954,000 *Total Assets:* £16,900,000
Registered Office: Shared Services Centre, Q3 Office, Quorum Business Park, Benton Lane, Newcastle upon Tyne, NE12 8EX
Activities: Distribution of electricity
Parent: Engie Urban Energy Group Limited
Officers: Sarah Gregory, Secretary; Andrew David Hart [1969] Managing Director; Lee Kitchen [1979] Director/Accountant

Biscuit Vehicle Leasing Limited
Incorporated: 11 September 2008
Registered Office: JFS Torbitt, 58 Durham Road, Birtley, Chester-le-Street, Co Durham, DH3 2QJ
Activities: Sale of used cars and light motor vehicles
Shareholders: Edward Wood; Joan Wood
Officers: Edward Wood [1947] Director; Joan Wood [1942] Director

Bishop's Beds Ltd
Incorporated: 5 September 2005
Net Worth: £980,932 *Total Assets:* £1,850,166
Registered Office: 2 Brindley Road, South West Industrial Estate, Peterlee, Co Durham, SR8 2LT
Activities: Manufacture of mattresses
Major Shareholder: David Alan Gullane
Officers: Keith Michael Robinson, Secretary; David Alan Gullane [1957] Director/Manager; Paul Vinnicombe [1980] Director/Engineer

Biss 53 Limited
Incorporated: 16 June 2014
Net Worth: £1,007 *Total Assets:* £3,345,098
Registered Office: 80 Darras Road, Ponteland, Northumberland, NE20 9PG
Activities: Other letting and operating of own or leased real estate
Major Shareholder: Philip Morris
Officers: Philip Morris [1961] Director

Biss 89 Limited
Incorporated: 20 May 2015
Net Worth Deficit: £33,550 *Total Assets:* £931,769
Registered Office: 80 Darras Road, Ponteland, Northumberland, NE20 9PG
Activities: Buying and selling of own real estate
Major Shareholder: Philip Morris
Officers: Philip Morris [1961] Director

Biss Underwriting Limited
Incorporated: 4 August 2010
Net Worth: £512,459 *Total Assets:* £11,792,501
Registered Office: 80 Darras Road, Ponteland, Northumberland, NE20 9PG
Activities: Non-life insurance
Major Shareholder: Philip Morris
Officers: Jordan Lee Morris [1988] Director/General Manager; Philip Morris [1961] Director

BJP Corporation Ltd
Incorporated: 2 April 2007 *Employees:* 70
Net Worth: £5,198,461 *Total Assets:* £9,258,807
Registered Office: Rosehill, Belmangate, Guisborough, Cleveland, TS14 7BB
Activities: Other business support service activities n.e.c.
Officers: Joan Corinne Parvin, Secretary; Barry Malcolm Parvin [1948] Director/Finance Manager; Joan Corinne Parvin [1956] Director/General Manager

Black Partners Limited
Incorporated: 20 May 2013
Registered Office: 54 Keswick Street, Gateshead, Tyne & Wear, NE8 1TQ
Activities: Buying and selling of own real estate
Officers: Martin Zvi Oppenheimer [1989] Director

RB Blackburn Ltd
Incorporated: 17 February 2015
Net Worth: £416,873 *Total Assets:* £894,381
Registered Office: 103 Station Road, Ashington, Northumberland, NE63 8RS
Activities: Site preparation
Major Shareholder: Ross Barnes Blackburn
Officers: Ross Barnes Blackburn [1986] Director/Groundworks

Blacklock Harvesting Ltd
Incorporated: 22 January 2009 *Employees:* 1
Net Worth: £412,445 *Total Assets:* £2,032,699
Registered Office: Milburn House, Hexham Business Park, Hexham, Northumberland, NE46 3RU
Activities: Other business support service activities n.e.c.
Major Shareholder: John Luke Blacklock
Officers: Sheila Blacklock, Secretary; John Luke Blacklock [1957] Director/Engineer

Blackshaw's Garage (Alnwick) Limited
Incorporated: 27 July 1977 *Employees:* 52
Net Worth: £1,812,503 *Total Assets:* £5,392,343
Registered Office: Blackshaws, Birch Close, Lionheart Enterprise Park, Alnwick, Northumberland, NE66 2EP
Activities: Sale of new cars and light motor vehicles
Shareholders: Jill Blackshaw; William Dixon Blackshaw
Officers: David George Blackshaw, Secretary; David George Blackshaw [1955] Director/Garage Proprietor; Diane Blackshaw [1955] Director; Jill Blackshaw [1981] Director/Accounts Administrator; William Dixon Blackshaw [1984] Director/General Manager

C. A. Blackwell (Contracts) Limited
Incorporated: 22 August 1956 *Employees:* 251
Net Worth: £1,205,000 *Total Assets:* £33,882,000
Registered Office: West Terrace, Esh Winning, Co Durham, DH7 9PT
Activities: Other specialised construction activities n.e.c.
Parent: CA Blackwell Group Limited
Officers: Patrick James Kemp, Secretary; Steven Leslie Anson [1965] Director; Gordon Frank Colenso Banham [1964] Director; Niall Keith Fraser [1970] Director/Operational Contracts Manager; Guy Warwick Pugh [1956] Director/Civil Engineer; David Giles Salmon [1971] Director/Chartered Surveyor; Philip James Smith [1979] Director

Blackwell Grange Golf Club Limited
Incorporated: 2 March 1964 *Employees:* 10
Net Worth: £1,172,690 *Total Assets:* £1,926,022
Registered Office: The Club House, Snipe Lane, Darlington, Co Durham, DL2 2SA
Activities: Operation of sports facilities
Officers: Neil Clarke, Secretary; Nigel Alderson [1970] Director/Butcher; Jonathan Richard Bradley [1966] Director/Senior Plant Manager; Douglas Campbell Christie [1952] Director/Chartered Surveyor; Neil Clarke [1959] Director/Retired; John Alister Edgar [1969] Director/Chartered Accountant; Nicholas Morris Gibson [1962] Director/Warehouseman; Rebecca Louise Gibson [1994] Director/Student; Neil Lawson Sayers [1953] Director/Consultant

C.A. Blackwell Group Limited
Incorporated: 11 July 1960 *Employees:* 7
Net Worth: £3,871,000 *Total Assets:* £3,955,000
Registered Office: West Terrace, Esh Winning, Co Durham, DH7 9PT
Activities: Activities of head offices
Parent: Hargreaves Services PLC
Officers: Patrick James Kemp, Secretary; Steven Leslie Anson [1965] Director; Gordon Frank Colenso Banham [1964] Director; Niall Keith Fraser [1970] Director/Quantity Surveyor; Guy Warwick Pugh [1956] Director/Operational Business Development; Philip James Smith [1979] Director

Blagdon Farming Limited
Incorporated: 14 April 1997
Net Worth: £888,759 *Total Assets:* £1,840,937
Registered Office: Blagdon Estate Office, Seaton Burn, Newcastle upon Tyne, NE13 6DE
Activities: Mixed farming
Major Shareholder: Viscount Matthew White Ridley
Officers: Christopher Brian Stonehouse, Secretary; John McMorrough Carr Ellison [1952] Director/Farmer; Viscount Matthew White Ridley [1958] Director/Land Owner; William Mark Wood [1947] Director/Chartered Surveyor

J.J. Blair & Sons Limited
Incorporated: 20 September 1985 *Employees:* 16
Net Worth: £1,931,856 *Total Assets:* £1,953,781
Registered Office: Skerne Gardens, 82 Barmpton Lane, Darlington, Co Durham, DL1 3HE
Activities: Retail sale via stalls and markets of other goods
Shareholders: Olwen Jean Blair; Robin Victor Blair
Officers: Robin Victor Blair, Secretary; Olwen Jean Blair [1948] Director/Shop Assistant; Robin Victor Blair [1945] Director/Market Gardener

Blake Newport Associates Limited
Incorporated: 17 October 1991
Net Worth: £626,671 *Total Assets:* £1,548,667
Registered Office: Houndgate House, 12 Houndgate, Darlington, Co Durham, DL1 5RF
Activities: Management consultancy activities other than financial management
Shareholders: Richard Howard Tench; David Steven Blake
Officers: Richard Howard Tench, Secretary/Quantity Surveyor; David Steven Blake [1955] Director/Chartered Surveyor; Gregory Richard Stewart Brownlee [1970] Director/Surveyor; John Paul Cinnamond [1971] Director/Quantity Surveyor; George William MacKellar [1960] Director/Management Consultancy; Simon James McGrail [1961] Director/Management Consultancy; Richard Howard Tench [1955] Director/Quantity Surveyor

R.Bland Limited
Incorporated: 9 October 1961 *Employees:* 21
Net Worth: £3,702,906 *Total Assets:* £4,017,024
Registered Office: Morton Road, Yarm Road Business Park, Darlington, Co Durham, DL1 4PT
Activities: Development of building projects
Parent: Chance Investments Ltd
Officers: Graham Jeffrey Bland, Secretary; Graham Jeffrey Bland [1966] Director/Office Manager; Philip Raymond Bland [1964] Director

Blaydon Holdings Limited
Incorporated: 22 May 2014 *Employees:* 120
Net Worth: £1,650,546 *Total Assets:* £4,876,168
Registered Office: Units A & B, Pattison Street, Blaydon on Tyne, Tyne & Wear, NE21 5SD
Activities: Activities of other holding companies n.e.c.
Shareholders: Philiip Theobald Lewis; David Rowland Lewis
Officers: David Rowland Lewis [1970] Director; Philip Theobald Lewis [1940] Director

Blaydon UK Limited
Incorporated: 22 July 2013 *Employees:* 77
Net Worth: £538,661 *Total Assets:* £1,267,539
Registered Office: Units A & B, Pattison Street, Blaydon on Tyne, Tyne & Wear, NE21 5SD
Activities: Other retail sale in non-specialised stores
Officers: Christopher Mark Marchant, Secretary; David Rowland Lewis [1970] Director; Philip Theobald Lewis [1940] Director

Blendspeak Limited
Incorporated: 20 April 2005
Net Worth: £2,229,623 *Total Assets:* £2,500,000
Registered Office: Unit A23 Stonehills, Pelaw, Gateshead, Tyne & Wear, NE10 0HW
Activities: Activities of head offices
Shareholder: Andrew Gerald Donnelly
Officers: Norma Elizabeth Donnelly, Secretary; Andrew Generald Donnelly [1976] Director/Business Manager; Darren Robert Donnelly [1979] Director/Processing Manager

Blenheim Court Properties Limited
Incorporated: 27 January 1993
Net Worth: £850,764 *Total Assets:* £869,905
Registered Office: 80 Hartington Road, Stockton on Tees, Cleveland, TS18 1HE
Activities: Other letting and operating of own or leased real estate
Officers: Dominic George Collinge Ferard, Secretary/Director; Dominic George Collinge Ferard [1963] Director; Jo Tracy Ferard [1969] Director; Rupert Charles Hawkesworth Ferard [1966] Director; Sally Clare Ferard [1962] Director

Blenheim Homes North East Ltd
Incorporated: 27 April 2016
Net Worth Deficit: £35,611 *Total Assets:* £1,354,420
Registered Office: 8a Bridge Street, Blyth, Northumberland, NE24 1BL
Activities: Construction of domestic buildings
Major Shareholder: Barry William Elliott
Officers: Barry William Elliott, Secretary; Barry William Elliott [1966] Director

Bloom Procurement Services Ltd
Incorporated: 25 April 2012 *Employees:* 21
Net Worth: £202,443 *Total Assets:* £12,576,179
Registered Office: Rotterdam House, 116 Quayside, Newcastle upon Tyne, NE1 3DY
Activities: Management consultancy activities other than financial management
Parent: V4 Holdings Limited
Officers: Diane Cheesebrough [1962] Director/Consultant; Adam Jonathan Jacobs [1970] Director/Management Consultant; Robert Isadore Levene [1972] Director/Lead Category Specialist - Professional Services

Bloomsbury Heat & Power Limited
Incorporated: 4 September 1998
Net Worth: £2,575,000 *Total Assets:* £4,231,000
Registered Office: Shared Services Centre, Q3 Office, Quorum Business Park, Benton Lane, Newcastle upon Tyne, NE12 8EX
Activities: Steam and air conditioning supply
Parent: Engie Urban Energy Group Limited
Officers: Sarah Gregory, Secretary; Andrew David Hart [1969] Managing Director; Lee Kitchen [1979] Director/Accountant

BLP (Northern) Limited
Incorporated: 25 April 1991 *Employees:* 130
Net Worth: £834,113 *Total Assets:* £4,226,022
Registered Office: Unit 99/15 North Tyne Industrial Estate, Whitley Road, Benton, Newcastle upon Tyne, NE12 9SZ
Activities: Printing n.e.c.
Shareholders: Leo Kane; Peter Kane
Officers: Valerie Kane, Secretary; Stephen Bertram Dobinson [1960] Director; Bernard Kane [1953] Director; Leo Kane [1950] Director; Patricia Ann Kane [1953] Director/Secretary; Peter Kane [1961] Director; Valerie Kane [1961] Director/Secretary

Blue Aardvark Holdings Limited
Incorporated: 30 September 2015
Net Worth: £919,585 *Total Assets:* £1,027,968
Registered Office: The Purvis Building, Leeholme Road, Billingham, Cleveland, TS23 3TA
Activities: Activities of construction holding companies
Shareholders: Tracy Louise McDonald; Steve McDonald
Officers: Tracy McDonald, Secretary; Steven McDonald [1982] Director

Blue Aardvark Joinery Limited
Incorporated: 6 May 2008 *Employees:* 38
Net Worth: £977,761 *Total Assets:* £3,000,919
Registered Office: The Purvis Building, Leeholme Road, Billingham, Cleveland, TS23 3TA
Activities: Manufacture of other furniture
Parent: Blue Aardvark Holdings Limited
Officers: Craig Drury [1970] Director/Contracts Manager; Peter Marwood [1969] Director/General Manager; Steven McDonald [1982] Director

Blue Assistance Limited
Incorporated: 30 October 2012
Net Worth: £27,547 *Total Assets:* £1,138,378
Registered Office: Wynyard Park House, Wynyard Avenue, Wynyard, Billingham, Cleveland, TS22 5TB
Activities: Non-trading company
Officers: Kevin Colin Howes [1982] Director/Accountant

Blue Barns Poultry Farms Limited
Incorporated: 25 January 2010 *Employees:* 4
Net Worth: £438,595 *Total Assets:* £4,742,350
Registered Office: Southfield Farm, Hamsterley Mill, Rowlands Gill, Tyne & Wear, NE39 1NQ
Activities: Raising of poultry
Shareholders: Keith Stuart Henderson; Christina Henderson
Officers: Christina Henderson, Secretary; Christina Henderson [1969] Director; Keith Stuart Henderson [1969] Director

Blue Diamond Engineering Limited
Incorporated: 19 January 1987
Net Worth: £610,990 *Total Assets:* £2,052,683
Registered Office: Factory BT 6-9, Shildon Industrial Estate, Shildon, Co Durham, DL4 2QN
Activities: Machining
Officers: Carol Jean Brown, Secretary; Carol Jean Brown [1964] Financial Director; John Charles Hedley [1962] Managing Director

Blue Diamond Machine Tools Limited
Incorporated: 12 February 1987
Net Worth: £757,120 *Total Assets:* £829,638
Registered Office: Unit 6b, Hackworth Industrial Park, Shildon, Co Durham, DL4 1HG
Activities: Wholesale of machine tools
Major Shareholder: Brian William Burn
Officers: Brian William Burn [1962] Managing Director

Blue Flames Sporting Club Limited
Incorporated: 21 August 1996
Net Worth: £1,120,944 *Total Assets:* £2,416,341
Registered Office: Whitley Park, Whitley Road, Longbenton, Newcastle upon Tyne, NE12 9SF
Activities: Activities of sport clubs
Officers: Thomas Scarry, Secretary/Retired; Steve Allison [1954] Director/IT Consultant; Darren Atkinson [1973] Director/Head Groundsman; Peter John Carter [1952] Director; Stephen George Charles Crown [1949] Director/Systems Analyst; Roderick John Davey [1951] Director/Human Resource Manager; Terry Dean Fox [1980] Director/Personal Trainer; George William Green [1951] Director/Retired; Amy Estelle Rutherford [1978] Director/Facilities Manager; Thomas Scarry [1948] Director/Retired; Brian Smith [1934] Director/Retired; Laura Jane Stewart [1989] Director/Reception Manager

Blue House Retail Limited
Incorporated: 17 February 2011
Net Worth: £247,893 *Total Assets:* £1,371,118
Registered Office: The Smithy, Rowan Avenue, Washington, Tyne & Wear, NE38 9BP
Activities: Other letting and operating of own or leased real estate
Major Shareholder: Babar Arshad
Officers: Babar Arshad [1987] Director

Blue Lake Property Company Limited
Incorporated: 14 January 1970
Net Worth: £881,440 *Total Assets:* £885,787
Registered Office: 118 High Street, Redcar, Cleveland, TS10 3DH
Activities: Other letting and operating of own or leased real estate
Major Shareholder: Executors of James Morris McKinley Deceased
Officers: David Robert Shawcross [1966] Director

Blue Line Services Ltd
Incorporated: 30 September 2008
Net Worth: £121,338 *Total Assets:* £956,353
Registered Office: 31-33 Sycamore Street, Wallsend, Tyne & Wear, NE28 6TH
Activities: Other letting and operating of own or leased real estate
Shareholders: Ian Gordon Shanks; Paul Thomas Shanks; Jane Bell
Officers: Jane Bell [1958] Director; Paul Thomas Shanks [1961] Director

Blue Opal Investments Limited
Incorporated: 30 September 2011 *Employees:* 3
Net Worth Deficit: £3,466 *Total Assets:* £797,029
Registered Office: Pen Y Dalar, Main Street, Thornton-le-Moor, Northallerton, N Yorks, DL7 9DN
Activities: Other letting and operating of own or leased real estate
Major Shareholder: Simon John Edward Raper
Officers: John Edward Raper [1945] Director; Simon John Edward Raper [1972] Director; Susan Joyce Raper [1946] Director

Blue Rain Limited
Incorporated: 19 November 1996 *Employees:* 2
Net Worth: £1,328,152 *Total Assets:* £1,370,119
Registered Office: 2 The Copse, Prudhoe, Northumberland, NE42 5DA
Activities: Other letting and operating of own or leased real estate
Shareholders: Leslie Savory; Susan Savory
Officers: Leslie Savory, Secretary/Director; Leslie Savory [1955] Director/Railway Safety; Susan Savory [1958] Director

Bluegauge LLP
Incorporated: 14 May 2012
Net Worth: £713,000 *Total Assets:* £1,220,000
Registered Office: 1a Dukesway Court, Team Valley Trading Estate, Gateshead, Tyne & Wear, NE11 0PJ
Officers: David James Horrocks [1959] Member; Ian Imrie [1955] Member; Philip Noble [1955] Member

Gary Bluff Projects Limited
Incorporated: 23 December 2003 *Employees:* 12
Net Worth: £2,009,732 *Total Assets:* £6,033,845
Registered Office: 7 Brenkley Way, Blezard Business Park, Seaton Burn, Tyne & Wear, NE13 6DS
Activities: Other building completion and finishing
Major Shareholder: Gary Roy Bluff
Officers: Annette Walker, Secretary; Gary Roy Bluff [1961] Director; Annette Walker [1964] Director

Blundell Production Equipment Limited
Incorporated: 28 March 1968 *Employees:* 24
Net Worth: £987,256 *Total Assets:* £3,175,732
Registered Office: Unit 7 Brighouse Business Village, Brighouse Road, Middlesbrough, Cleveland, TS2 1RT
Activities: Manufacture of other technical ceramic products
Parent: Blundell Production Holdings Limited
Officers: Inca Ross, Secretary; Neil Martin Blundell [1959] Sales Director; Steven Richard Pell [1983] Director; Hugh Mark Whitcomb [1961] Director

Blyth Investments LLP
Incorporated: 27 May 2010
Net Worth Deficit: £3,443,432 *Total Assets:* £4,352,811
Registered Office: Northumberland Estates, Suite 2a, Quayside House, 110 Quayside, Newcastle upon Tyne, NE1 3DX

Blyth Offshore Demonstrator Limited
Incorporated: 13 June 2014
Net Worth: £30,094,000 *Total Assets:* £86,226,000
Registered Office: Alexander House, 1 Mandarin Road, Rainton Bridge Business Park, Houghton-le-Spring, Co Durham, DH4 5RA
Activities: Production of electricity
Shareholders: EDF EN UK Limited; EDF Energy Renewables Holdings Limited
Officers: Susan Elizabeth Lind, Secretary; Beatrice Buffon [1974] Director [French]; Matthieu Thomas Hue [1975] Director [French]; Denis Rouhier [1966] Director/Engineer [French]

The Blyth Quays Trust
Incorporated: 4 March 2013 *Employees:* 161
Net Worth: £8,144,000 *Total Assets:* £12,172,000
Registered Office: Croftway Primary Academy, William Street, Blyth, Northumberland, NE24 2HP
Activities: Primary education
Officers: Louise Carolyn Doyle [1973] Director/Business Owner; Sandra Garrity [1962] Director/Local Government Officer; Julie-Ann Hewitt [1970] Director/Chief Executive Officer; Jeffrey McCartney [1950] Director/Retired; Claire Ritson [1978] Director HR Bond Dickinson; Lynn Watson [1957] Director/Education Consultant; Christopher Philip Zarraga [1969] Director/Chief Operations Officer

Blyth Star Enterprises Limited
Incorporated: 6 August 1987 *Employees:* 53
Net Worth: £589,705 *Total Assets:* £1,397,146
Registered Office: The Old Chandlery, 30 Ridley Street, Blyth, Northumberland, NE24 3AG
Activities: Growing of vegetables and melons, roots and tubers
Officers: Stephen William Gibson, Secretary; Timothy Paul Chrisp [1965] Director/Chairman; Stephen William Gibson [1955] Director/Solicitor; Sharron Marie Herron [1964] Director/Businesswoman; Bill McHugh [1960] Director/Chief Executive; Teresa Rendall [1951] Director

Blyth Valley Disabled Forum Ltd
Incorporated: 20 March 1997 *Employees:* 84
Net Worth: £904,656 *Total Assets:* £951,193
Registered Office: 20 Stanley Street, Blyth, Northumberland, NE24 2BU
Activities: Other social work activities without accommodation n.e.c.
Officers: John Lawrence Clough, Secretary; John Lawrence Clough [1951] Director; Simpson Crawford [1932] Director/Retired; Alan Hall [1952] Director/Retired; David Thomas Hopper [1942] Director/Retired

Blythman & Partners Limited
Incorporated: 25 February 2002
Registered Office: 16 Elsdon Road, Gosforth, Newcastle upon Tyne, NE3 1JD
Activities: Veterinary activities
Shareholders: Graham Chambers; Heather Grace Barbara Morton
Officers: Susan Innes, Secretary; Graham Chambers [1965] Director/Veterinary Surgeon; Heather Grace Barbara Morton [1965] Director/Veterinary Surgeon

BMM Heaters Limited
Incorporated: 18 November 2004
Net Worth: £10,229 *Total Assets:* £959,905
Registered Office: 16 Limerick Road, Trunk Road Industrial Estate, Redcar, Cleveland, TS10 5JU
Activities: Manufacture of non-domestic cooling and ventilation equipment
Shareholders: Kevin Murray-Myers; Sean Russell Byrne
Officers: Kevin Murray-Myers, Secretary; Sean Byrne [1976] Director; Kevin Murray-Myers [1966] Director

BNB Fabrications Limited
Incorporated: 18 March 1998 *Employees:* 33
Net Worth: £507,923 *Total Assets:* £1,698,389
Registered Office: Unit 1 Stephenson Road, Stephenson Industrial Estate, Washington, Tyne & Wear, NE37 3HR
Activities: Manufacture of other fabricated metal products n.e.c.
Major Shareholder: William Wilson
Officers: Lorna Grieves, Company Secretary; William Wilson [1949] Director/Engineer

Boasso Global Limited
Incorporated: 30 March 2016 *Employees:* 326
Net Worth: £7,403,622 *Total Assets:* £30,132,888
Registered Office: c/o Isotank Services, Limerick Road, Dormanstown, Redcar, Cleveland, TS10 5JU
Activities: Activities of other holding companies n.e.c.
Parent: Gruden Acquisition Inc
Officers: Joseph Troy [1963] Director [American]; John Wilson [1974] Director [American]

Boasso UK Limited
Incorporated: 30 March 2016
Net Worth: £20,715,804 *Total Assets:* £38,432,196
Registered Office: c/o Isotank Services, Limerick Road, Dormanstown, Redcar, Cleveland, TS10 5JU
Activities: Activities of other holding companies n.e.c.
Parent: Boasso Global Limited
Officers: Joseph Troy [1963] Director [American]; John Wilson [1974] Director [American]

Body Engineering Limited
Incorporated: 21 December 1988 *Employees:* 13
Net Worth: £888,715 *Total Assets:* £1,388,741
Registered Office: Randolph Works, Evenwood, Bishop Auckland, Co Durham, DL14 9QL
Activities: Other engineering activities
Shareholders: David Robert Body; Kenneth Paul Body
Officers: Kenneth Paul Body, Secretary; David Robert Body [1970] Director/Engineer; Kenneth Paul Body [1951] Director/Accountant

George Bolam (Foods) Ltd
Incorporated: 8 August 1988 *Employees:* 84
Net Worth: £1,664,224 *Total Assets:* £3,138,496
Registered Office: Sedgefield Industrial Estate, Salters Lane, Sedgefield, Co Durham, TS21 3EE
Activities: Wholesale of meat and meat products
Shareholders: George Bolam; The Estate of Mrs Beatrice Bolam
Officers: George Bolam [1944] Director/Butcher

Bolam Group Limited
Incorporated: 9 June 2016
Net Worth: £375,563 *Total Assets:* £1,740,937
Registered Office: Unit 1 Bolam Business Park, Bassington Drive, Bassington Industrial Estate, Cramlington, Northumberland, NE23 8AL
Activities: Other business support service activities n.e.c.
Shareholder: Alan David Moody
Officers: Gavin Ridley Cape [1971] Director; Caroline Jane Crawford [1971] Director; Alan Richard Moody [1976] Director; Alan David Moody [1945] Director

Bold Bloc Design Limited
Incorporated: 18 November 2009
Net Worth: £382,557 *Total Assets:* £860,929
Registered Office: E7 Morrisons Mall, Morton Park Way, Darlington, Co Durham, DL1 4PJ
Activities: Retail sale via mail order houses or via Internet
Major Shareholder: John Thomas Liddle
Officers: John Thomas Liddle [1982] Director

Bolel Ltd
Incorporated: 4 September 2009
Net Worth: £56,250 *Total Assets:* £1,196,619
Registered Office: 98 Bewick Road, Gateshead, Tyne & Wear, NE8 1RS
Activities: Real estate agencies
Shareholders: Abraham Bolel; Brocha Naomi Bolel
Officers: Brocho Naomi Bolel, Secretary; Abraham Bolel [1976] Director/Residential Landlord; Brocho Naomi Bolel [1977] Director/Residential Landlord

Bon Bon Leisure Limited
Incorporated: 14 August 2013 *Employees:* 90
Net Worth Deficit: £247,084 *Total Assets:* £875,858
Registered Office: The Assembly Rooms, Fenkle Street, Newcastle upon Tyne, NE1 5XU
Activities: Licenced restaurants
Officers: Antony George Michaelides [1964] Director

Bon Coeur Fine Wines Limited
Incorporated: 24 May 2005 *Employees:* 18
Net Worth: £690,964 *Total Assets:* £4,226,339
Registered Office: Moor Park, Moor Road, Melsonby, Richmond, N Yorks, DL10 5PR
Activities: Wholesale of wine, beer, spirits and other alcoholic beverages
Shareholders: James Henry Goodhart; Samantha Jane Goodhart
Officers: Jonathon Timothy Mann, Secretary; James Henry Goodhart [1970] Director/Wine Merchant; Samantha Jane Goodhart [1967] Director; Jonathon Timothy Mann [1976] Finance Director

Bon Marche (Wallsend) Limited
Incorporated: 4 May 1931
Registered Office: 64 Fern Avenue, Jesmond, Newcastle upon Tyne, NE2 2QY
Activities: Other letting and operating of own or leased real estate
Officers: Elke Smith, Secretary; Anina Elizabeth Holmes [1958] Director/Teacher; Elke Smith [1936] Director; Stormont James Eltringham Smith [1961] Director

Bon-Bloemen Ltd
Incorporated: 9 February 2010 *Employees:* 8
Net Worth: £472,074 *Total Assets:* £918,628
Registered Office: Unit 4 Eastern Avenue Trade Park, Team Valley Trading Estate, Gateshead, Tyne & Wear, NE11 0PG
Activities: Retail sale of flowers, plants, seeds, fertilizers, pet animals and pet food in specialised stores
Shareholders: David Bland; Danielle Hannah Horn
Officers: David Bland [1978] Director; Danielle Horn [1985] Director

Bonds Foundry Company Limited
Incorporated: 10 April 2000 *Employees:* 119
Net Worth: £1,561,360 *Total Assets:* £6,505,036
Registered Office: 1 Prospect Road, Crook, Co Durham, DL15 8JL
Activities: Casting of steel
Parent: Bondshold Limited
Officers: Robert Jon Blackett, Secretary/Director; Robert Jon Blackett [1973] Director; Trevor John Machin [1966] Director; Mark Lawrence McCarthy [1963] Group Director; Andrew Shaw [1965] Managing Director

Bonds Limited
Incorporated: 1 May 1997
Net Worth: £2,655,017 *Total Assets:* £2,676,301
Registered Office: Prospect Road, Crook, Co Durham, DL15 8JL
Activities: Activities of head offices
Parent: Bondsteel Ltd
Officers: Melissa Joy Duncan [1968] Director/Head of Communications [American]; Paul Robson Duncan [1948] Managing Director

Bondshold Limited
Incorporated: 10 August 2010 *Employees:* 292
Net Worth: £11,723,407 *Total Assets:* £26,814,928
Registered Office: 1 Prospect Road, Crook, Co Durham, DL15 8JL
Activities: Activities of head offices
Major Shareholder: Paul Robson Duncan
Officers: Robert Jon Blackett, Secretary; Robert Jon Blackett [1973] Director; Melissa Joy Duncan [1968] Director/Head of Communications [American]; Paul Robson Duncan [1948] Director; Andrew Shaw [1965] Director

F.J. Booth Construction Limited
Incorporated: 3 July 2006 *Employees:* 99
Net Worth: £1,425,023 *Total Assets:* £3,929,910
Registered Office: Victoria Court, Rectory Lane, Guisborough, Cleveland, TS14 7GA
Activities: Other specialised construction activities n.e.c.
Major Shareholder: Shaun Muir
Officers: Nicole Denerley Muir, Secretary; Steven Paul Agar [1971] Director; Shaun Nicholas Muir [1966] Director; Geoff Wright [1967] Director

Border Traffic Transport Limited
Incorporated: 7 July 2015 *Employees:* 19
Net Worth: £512,620 *Total Assets:* £2,067,059
Registered Office: 246 Park View, Whitley Bay, Tyne & Wear, NE26 3QX
Activities: Freight transport by road
Shareholders: Drysdale Freight Limited; Olivers Transport Limited
Officers: Kenneth Andrew Oliver [1965] Director/Haulage Contractor; Alexander William Scougall [1960] Director

Borders Recycling Limited
Incorporated: 6 February 2004 *Employees:* 5
Net Worth: £1,670,447 *Total Assets:* £2,510,382
Registered Office: Suite 2, Beaufront Park, Alnwick Road, Hexham, Northumberland, NE46 4TU
Activities: Remediation activities and other waste management services
Parent: Reukema Paper Group B V
Officers: Deborah Scott, Secretary; Lynn Dobson [1961] Director

Borgwarner Gateshead Limited
Incorporated: 6 October 1951 *Employees:* 102
Net Worth: £1,306,510 *Total Assets:* £32,675,476
Registered Office: Eighth Avenue, Princesway, Team Valley Trading Estate, Gateshead, Tyne & Wear, NE11 0QA
Activities: Manufacture of other electrical equipment
Parent: Borgwarner Massachusetts Inc.
Officers: Peter Kaempfer [1970] Director [American]; David John Sidlow [1964] Director

Bors Advisory Limited
Incorporated: 22 October 2003
Net Worth: £470,780 *Total Assets:* £1,040,132
Registered Office: 30 Yoden Way, Peterlee, Co Durham, SR8 1AL
Activities: Activities auxiliary to financial intermediation n.e.c.
Officers: Shaun Christopher Murphy [1959] Director

Borthwick Marble & Granite Ltd
Incorporated: 6 May 2005 *Employees:* 6
Net Worth: £41,368 *Total Assets:* £795,042
Registered Office: Unit 15 Prospect Way, Park View Industrial Estate, Hartlepool, Cleveland, TS25 1UD
Activities: Funeral and related activities
Shareholders: Jamie Borthwick; Sarah Jane Borthwick
Officers: Jamie Borthwick, Secretary; Jamie Borthwick [1980] Director/Engineer; Sarah Jane Borthwick [1980] Director

Boundary Lane Windfarm Limited
Incorporated: 25 November 2002
Net Worth: £4,874,000 *Total Assets:* £9,519,000
Registered Office: Alexander House, 1 Mandarin Road, Rainton Bridge Business Park, Houghton-le-Spring, Co Durham, DH4 5RA
Activities: Production of electricity
Parent: EDF Energy Renewables Holdings Limited
Officers: Susan Elizabeth Lind, Secretary; Matthieu Thomas Hue [1975] Director [French]; Hassaan Majid [1968] Director

Bowers Developments Ltd
Incorporated: 11 January 2013
Net Worth: £8,472 *Total Assets:* £953,025
Registered Office: Unit 1 Gatherley Road Industrial Estate, Brompton on Swale, Richmond, N Yorks, DL10 7JG
Activities: Other letting and operating of own or leased real estate
Shareholders: Peter Bowers; Gavin Richard Bowers
Officers: Gavin Richard Bowers [1978] Director; Peter Bowers [1948] Director

The Bowes Museum
Incorporated: 18 November 1999 *Employees:* 65
Net Worth: £12,249,548 *Total Assets:* £12,834,297
Registered Office: The Bowes Museum, Newgate, Barnard Castle, Co Durham, DL12 8NP
Activities: Museums activities
Officers: Richard Armstrong Welsby, Secretary; Mark Blackett-Ord [1950] Director/Lawyer; Adrian Jenkins [1965] Director/Chief Executive; Peter David Alan Mothersill [1957] Director; Susan Lesley Palmer OBE [1952] Director; Caroline Patricia Peacock [1947] Director; Ann-Marie Marie Robinson [1960] Director; Sir Charles Mark Garmondsway Wrightson [1951] Director

Bowes Wealth Management Limited
Incorporated: 3 October 2008
Net Worth: £545,881 *Total Assets:* £763,073
Registered Office: 27 St Paul's Drive, Mount Pleasant, Houghton-le-Spring, Co Durham, DH4 7SH
Activities: Financial intermediation not elsewhere classified
Shareholders: Shaun Scrimger; Lynn Scrimger
Officers: Lynn Scrimger, Secretary; Lynn Scrimger [1972] Director/Financial Representative; Shaun James Scrimger [1971] Director/Financial Representative

Boxpipe Limited
Incorporated: 4 July 2003 *Employees:* 13
Net Worth Deficit: £779,234 *Total Assets:* £4,064,977
Registered Office: Lugano Building, Melbourne Street, Newcastle upon Tyne, NE1 2JQ
Activities: Hotels and similar accommodation
Officers: Howard Barry Gold, Secretary/Solicitor; Howard Barry Gold [1943] Director/Solicitor; Allan John Henderson [1961] Director/Solicitor; Paul Hughes [1965] Director/Solicitor; Scott Munro [1970] Director/Planner; Ben Zion Rabinowitz [1935] Director/Rabbi [Polish]; Joseph Rabinowitz [1964] Director [Polish]; Allan Rankin [1960] Director; Richard John Robson [1964] Development Director

John Boyd Associates Limited
Incorporated: 3 March 1989 *Employees:* 11
Net Worth: £2,073,299 *Total Assets:* £3,163,134
Registered Office: 17 Evolution Business Park, Wynyard, Billingham, Cleveland, TS22 5TB
Activities: Engineering design activities for industrial process and production
Major Shareholder: Hugh Pilot
Officers: Paul Cockrill, Secretary/Accountant/Director; Paul Cockrill [1974] Accountant/Director; Russell Holmes [1967] Director/Engineer; Simon Jones [1967] Director; Peter Hugh Pilot [1961] Director

J A & M Boyes Limited
Incorporated: 11 February 2010
Net Worth: £289,596 *Total Assets:* £1,324,972
Registered Office: Strathmore House Farm, Cleatlam, Darlington, Co Durham, DL2 3QS
Activities: Raising of other cattle and buffaloes
Shareholders: John Arthur Boyes; Marion Boyes
Officers: Marion Boyes, Secretary; John Arthur Boyes [1956] Director/Farmer; Marion Boyes [1957] Director/Farmer

BPT (Assured Homes) Limited
Incorporated: 29 July 1994
Net Worth: £158,756,128 *Total Assets:* £162,044,112
Registered Office: Citygate, St James Boulevard, Newcastle upon Tyne, NE1 4JE
Activities: Buying and selling of own real estate
Parent: BPT Limited
Officers: Adam McGhin, Secretary; Helen Christine Gordon [1959] Director; Adam McGhin [1978] Director/Solicitor; Mark Jeremy Robson [1959] Director/Chartered Surveyor; Andrew Philip Saunderson [1975] Director; Vanessa Kate Simms [1975] Director

BPT (Bradford Property Trust) Limited
Incorporated: 23 December 1930
Net Worth: £606,617,024 *Total Assets:* £609,665,024
Registered Office: Citygate, St James Boulevard, Newcastle upon Tyne, NE1 4JE
Activities: Buying and selling of own real estate
Parent: BPT Limited
Officers: Adam McGhin, Secretary; Helen Christine Gordon [1959] Director; Adam McGhin [1978] Director/Solicitor; Mark Jeremy Robson [1959] Director/Chartered Surveyor; Andrew Philip Saunderson [1975] Director; Vanessa Kate Simms [1975] Director

BPT (Residential Investments) Limited
Incorporated: 15 February 1940
Net Worth: £179,356,000 *Total Assets:* £182,394,000
Registered Office: Citygate, St James Boulevard, Newcastle upon Tyne, NE1 4JE
Activities: Buying and selling of own real estate
Parent: BPT Limited
Officers: Adam McGhin, Secretary; Helen Christine Gordon [1959] Director; Adam McGhin [1978] Director/Solicitor; Mark Jeremy Robson [1959] Director/Chartered Surveyor; Andrew Philip Saunderson [1975] Director; Vanessa Kate Simms [1975] Director

BPT Limited
Incorporated: 30 March 1928
Net Worth: £206,968,992 *Total Assets:* £337,676,000
Registered Office: Citygate, St James Boulevard, Newcastle upon Tyne, NE1 4JE
Activities: Buying and selling of own real estate
Parent: Bromley Property Investments Limited
Officers: Adam McGhin, Secretary; Helen Christine Gordon [1959] Director; Adam McGhin [1978] Director/Solicitor; Mark Jeremy Robson [1959] Director/Chartered Surveyor; Vanessa Kate Simms [1975] Director

Brackenburn Holdings Limited
Incorporated: 9 March 1970
Net Worth: £1,888,344 *Total Assets:* £1,931,558
Registered Office: 23 West Park, Hartlepool, Cleveland, TS26 0DB
Activities: Buying and selling of own real estate
Shareholder: John Tilly
Officers: John Tilly, Secretary; Kate Fiona Potter [1969] Director/Housewife; John Tilly [1940] Director/Solicitor; Nicholas Charles Tilly [1966] Director/Solicitors Assistant; Veronica Evelyn Tilly [1943] Director/Housewife

Brackenshaw Limited
Incorporated: 3 August 2001
Net Worth: £1,060,650 *Total Assets:* £3,445,654
Registered Office: 22 Osborne Road, Newcastle upon Tyne, NE2 2AD
Activities: Development of building projects
Major Shareholder: Robert Hamish Moody
Officers: Robert Hamish Moody [1966] Director/Property Developer

J.Bradburn & Company,Limited
Incorporated: 27 August 1924 *Employees:* 5
Net Worth: £5,570,194 *Total Assets:* £6,435,130
Registered Office: Helister House, Riding Mill, Northumberland, NE44 6JB
Activities: Development of building projects
Shareholders: Dickon Anthony Russell Wood; Annabel Jane Burchnall; A R Wood Discretionary Settlement
Officers: Susan Margaret Wood, Secretary; Annabel Jane Burchnall [1969] Director; Dickon Anthony Russell Wood [1971] Director/Chartered Surveyor; Susan Margaret Wood [1946] Director

Bradbury Property Holdings Limited
Incorporated: 25 February 2014
Net Worth Deficit: £96,416 *Total Assets:* £3,339,881
Registered Office: Mayfield, Leazes Lane, Wolsingham, Bishop Auckland, Co Durham, DL13 3DR
Activities: Other business support service activities n.e.c.
Parent: Linnaeus Group Bidco Limited
Officers: Paul Daryl Coxon [1965] Director; Lynne Victoria Hill [1954] Director [Irish]

Braddan Structures Limited
Incorporated: 19 February 2008 *Employees:* 33
Net Worth: £342,153 *Total Assets:* £1,708,261
Registered Office: Braddan House, 28 Cleveland Trading Estate, Forge Way, Darlington, Co Durham, DL1 2PB
Activities: Other specialised construction activities n.e.c.
Parent: Braddan Group Ltd
Officers: Marie Caddick, Secretary; Carl Daren Caddick [1968] Director/Steel Erector

Bradford Propco Limited
Incorporated: 13 November 2009
Net Worth: £2,331,355 *Total Assets:* £6,857,756
Registered Office: 2nd Floor, 16 High Street, Yarm, Cleveland, TS15 9AE
Activities: Other letting and operating of own or leased real estate
Officers: Graham Kevin Sizer [1969] Director

Bradley Hall Farm (South Wylam) Limited
Incorporated: 8 July 2011 *Employees:* 1
Net Worth: £358,124 *Total Assets:* £1,223,840
Registered Office: 182 Front Street, Chester-le-Street, Co Durham, DH3 3AZ
Activities: Development of building projects
Major Shareholder: Stewart Ian Pittendrigh
Officers: Stewart Ian Pittendrigh [1970] Director/Farmer

Bradley Hall Limited
Incorporated: 6 March 2007 *Employees:* 29
Net Worth: £209,234 *Total Assets:* £753,138
Registered Office: 1 Hood Street, Newcastle upon Tyne, NE1 6JQ
Activities: Other professional, scientific and technical activities n.e.c.
Shareholders: Neil Thomas Hart; Peter Francis Bartley
Officers: Peter Francis Bartley, Secretary/Chartered Surveyor; Peter Francis Bartley [1968] Director/Chartered Surveyor; Geoffrey Joseph Davis [1957] Director/Chartered Accountant; Neil Thomas Hart [1980] Director/Chartered Surveyor; Richard Omar Rafique [1983] Director/Chartered Surveyor

Bradley Mill Caravan Site Limited
Incorporated: 17 June 1971 *Employees:* 5
Net Worth: £665,618 *Total Assets:* £765,624
Registered Office: Bradley Mill Caravan Site Limited, Wolsingham, Bishop Auckland, Co Durham, DL13 3JH
Activities: Recreational vehicle parks, trailer parks and camping grounds
Officers: John Percival Stephenson, Secretary; Christopher James Stephenson [1973] Director/Farmer; John Percival Stephenson [1941] Director/Farmer

Bradshaw Homes Ltd
Incorporated: 14 February 2014
Net Worth: £19,439 *Total Assets:* £1,281,077
Registered Office: 7 Gowanburn, Fatfield, Washington, Tyne & Wear, NE38 8SG
Activities: Other letting and operating of own or leased real estate
Officers: Eileen Bradshaw [1953] Director/Retired; Robert John Bradshaw [1953] Director/Self Employed

Braemore Wood Windfarm Limited
Incorporated: 25 November 2002
Net Worth Deficit: £2,137,000 *Total Assets:* £760,000
Registered Office: Alexander House, 1 Mandarin Road, Rainton Bridge Business Park, Houghton-le-Spring, Co Durham, DH4 5RA
Activities: Production of electricity
Parent: EDF Energy Renewables Limited
Officers: Susan Elizabeth Lind, Secretary; Matthieu Thomas Hue [1975] Director [French]; Hassaan Majid [1968] Director

L & L Braines Limited
Incorporated: 14 May 2014 *Employees:* 10
Net Worth: £449,341 *Total Assets:* £916,941
Registered Office: Mill House, 10 Mill Street, Millfield, Sunderland, Tyne & Wear, SR4 7BG
Activities: Removal services
Officers: Gary Braines [1962] Director/Office Removals

Brambledown Contracts Group Limited
Incorporated: 18 February 2011 *Employees:* 112
Net Worth: £2,223,477 *Total Assets:* £3,301,848
Registered Office: Quorn Cottage, Brandon Village, Co Durham, DH7 8SU
Activities: Retail sale of flowers, plants, seeds, fertilizers, pet animals and pet food in specialised stores
Major Shareholder: Frank Joseph Curry
Officers: Frank Joseph Curry [1953] Director/Landscape Contractor; Paul Curry [1982] Director; Susan Curry [1953] Director/Manageress; Caroline Walker [1990] Director

Brambledown Landscape Services Limited
Incorporated: 28 September 1972 *Employees:* 70
Net Worth: £936,467 *Total Assets:* £1,753,827
Registered Office: Quorn Cottage, Brandon Village, Co Durham, DH7 8SU
Activities: Construction of other civil engineering projects n.e.c.
Major Shareholder: Frank Joseph Curry
Officers: Frank Joseph Curry, Secretary; Neville Dean Clay [1966] Director; Frank Joseph Curry [1953] Director; Paul Curry [1982] Director; Susan Curry [1953] Director/Company Secretary

Bramley Court (Care Homes) Limited
Incorporated: 20 April 2004 *Employees:* 2
Net Worth: £3,225,413 *Total Assets:* £6,080,242
Registered Office: 2nd Floor, 16 High Street, Yarm, Cleveland, TS15 9AE
Activities: Other human health activities
Parent: Bramley (2007) Limited
Officers: Graham Sizer, Secretary; Philip Henry Scott [1964] Director; Graham Kevin Sizer [1969] Director

Bramwells Retail Limited
Incorporated: 20 May 2010 *Employees:* 26
Net Worth: £292,332 *Total Assets:* £1,803,542
Registered Office: 24 Elvet Bridge, Durham, DH1 3AA
Activities: Retail sale of watches and jewellery in specialised stores
Shareholder: William John Bramwell
Officers: William John Bramwell, Secretary; Jill Bramwell [1956] Director; Peter Bramwell [1947] Director; William John Bramwell [1954] Director

Brancepeth Estates Ltd
Incorporated: 18 February 2015 *Employees:* 2
Net Worth: £230,594 *Total Assets:* £1,056,790
Registered Office: The Paddock, Kirk Merrington, Spennymoor, Co Durham, DL16 7JT
Activities: Buying and selling of own real estate
Major Shareholder: Wayne Andrew Baister
Officers: Wayne Andrew Baister [1971] Director

Brand New Co (444) Limited
Incorporated: 7 December 2010 *Employees:* 115
Net Worth: £9,982,052 *Total Assets:* £16,655,207
Registered Office: Springvale EPS Limited, Coach Lane, Hazlerigg, Newcastle upon Tyne, NE13 7AP
Activities: Other manufacturing n.e.c.
Shareholders: Anthony France; Fiona France
Officers: Neil Tebbutt, Secretary; Jonathan David Ballard [1970] Director/Corporate Finance Advisor; Anthony France [1955] Director; Fiona France [1954] Director

Branden Property Limited
Incorporated: 23 February 2006 *Employees:* 2
Net Worth: £4,146,523 *Total Assets:* £4,154,474
Registered Office: 1st Floor, Finchale House, Belmont Business Park, Durham, DH1 1TW
Activities: Other letting and operating of own or leased real estate
Officers: Helen Austin, Secretary; John Corbitt Barnsley [1948] Director/Accountant; Spencer Glanville [1972] Director; Robert William Jefferson [1950] Director/Chartered Accountant

Brandh Academy Limited
Incorporated: 8 July 2011 *Employees:* 62
Net Worth: £1,264,000 *Total Assets:* £1,826,000
Registered Office: Heighington Cofe Primary School, Hopelands, Heighington Village, Newton Aycliffe, Co Durham, DL5 6PH
Activities: Primary education
Officers: Robert Neville Briscoe [1942] Director/Retired Civil Servant; Lynn Chambers [1966] Director/Headteacher; Richard John Frankland [1953] Director/Solicitor (Retired); David John Halfacre [1946] Company Chairman and Director of Development; Lee Alan Hammond [1978] Director; Michael Neil Parker [1958] Director/Headteacher

Brandmile Limited
Incorporated: 26 May 1999 *Employees:* 154
Net Worth: £8,358,935 *Total Assets:* £11,293,968
Registered Office: 3 Armstrong Road, North East Industrial Estate, Peterlee, Co Durham, SR8 5AE
Activities: Activities of head offices
Shareholder: Geoffrey Herbert
Officers: John Graham Monkhouse, Secretary; Geoffrey Herbert [1945] Director; John Graham Monkhouse [1953] Director

Michael Brandon Limited
Incorporated: 4 May 1970 *Employees:* 5
Net Worth: £95,905 *Total Assets:* £1,078,257
Registered Office: Unit 19 Royal Industrial Estate, Western Road, Jarrow, Tyne & Wear, NE32 3HR
Activities: Sale, maintenance and repair of motorcycles and related parts and accessories
Major Shareholder: Michael Francis Brandon
Officers: Hamish Brandon, Secretary; Hamish Brandon [1979] Director/Company Secretary; Michael Francis Brandon [1941] Director

Braybell Limited
Incorporated: 11 June 1985 *Employees:* 1
Net Worth: £735,297 *Total Assets:* £913,747
Registered Office: 25 Marsden Road, Cleadon Village, Sunderland, Tyne & Wear, SR6 7RA
Activities: Other letting and operating of own or leased real estate
Major Shareholder: Emile Antoine Gabriel
Officers: Emile Auntion Gabriel [1957] Director/Property Management

Brazenlight Limited
Incorporated: 9 December 1999
Net Worth: £315,551 *Total Assets:* £3,574,663
Registered Office: 2nd Floor, Grainger Chambers, Hood Street, Newcastle upon Tyne, NE1 6JQ
Activities: Other letting and operating of own or leased real estate
Major Shareholder: Bryan Percy Beattie
Officers: John Colin Fitzpatrick, Secretary; Bryan Percy Beattie [1932] Director; Kenneth Brian Beattie [1953] Director; Kevin Lee Huntley [1975] Director/Business Manager

Breckonborough Equestrian Limited
Incorporated: 4 November 2003
Registered Office: Breckenbrough Farm, Brough Park, Richmond, N Yorks, DL10 7PL
Activities: Farm animal boarding and care
Major Shareholder: Paul Hodgson
Officers: Judith Mary Hodgson, Secretary; Paul MacGregor Hodgson [1962] Director/Manager

Bremsen Technik (UK) Limited
Incorporated: 14 December 2001 *Employees:* 25
Net Worth: £3,903,018 *Total Assets:* £7,047,950
Registered Office: Unit 6 Easton Way, Colburn, Catterick Garrison, N Yorks, DL9 4GA
Activities: Wholesale trade of motor vehicle parts and accessories
Parent: Bremsen Technik Holdings Ltd
Officers: Robin James Anderson, Secretary; Robin James Anderson [1980] Director; Brian Reginald Hall [1959] Director

Bremsen Technik Holdings Ltd
Incorporated: 25 October 2013 *Employees:* 1
Net Worth: £1,405,699 *Total Assets:* £4,588,564
Registered Office: Unit 6 Easton Way, Colburn, Catterick Garrison, N Yorks, DL9 4GA
Activities: Activities of other holding companies n.e.c.
Major Shareholder: Brian Reginald Hall
Officers: Jane Louise Hall, Secretary; Robin James Anderson [1980] Director; Brian Reginald Hall [1959] Director

Bremsen Technik Reman Limited
Incorporated: 7 October 2016 *Employees:* 19
Net Worth: £46,144 *Total Assets:* £1,329,082
Registered Office: Unit 6 Easton Way, Colburn, Catterick Garrison, N Yorks, DL9 4GA
Activities: Manufacture of other parts and accessories for motor vehicles
Major Shareholder: Brian Reginald Hall
Officers: Robin James Anderson [1980] Director/Accountant; Dean Aaron Gregory [1964] Director; Brian Reginald Hall [1959] Director

Brenda Road Properties Limited
Incorporated: 18 November 1988 *Employees:* 3
Net Worth: £1,079,857 *Total Assets:* £2,029,800
Registered Office: Parsons Business Centre, Brenda Road, Hartlepool, Cleveland, TS25 2BJ
Activities: Other letting and operating of own or leased real estate
Officers: David Lawn, Secretary; Timothy Dunningham [1953] Director; Richard Christopher Irvine [1952] Director/Fleet Engineer

Brett Bros. Developments Limited
Incorporated: 17 April 1986
Net Worth: £4,148,546 *Total Assets:* £7,394,173
Registered Office: 41b High Street South, Langley Moor, Co Durham, DH7 8JW
Activities: Construction of domestic buildings
Shareholder: Michael John Brett
Officers: Michael John Brett, Secretary; Lynda Carol Jane Brett [1958] Director/Secretary; Michael John Brett [1955] Director/Contractor

Brewing and Distilling Company Limited
Incorporated: 23 October 2013
Net Worth Deficit: £875,447 *Total Assets:* £1,514,978
Registered Office: Rowlands House, Portobello Road, Birtley, Chester-le-Street, Co Durham, DH3 2RY
Activities: Manufacture of beer
Major Shareholder: David Patrick Brown
Officers: David Patrick Brown [1955] Director

Brick Services Limited
Incorporated: 25 February 1999 *Employees:* 19
Net Worth: £970,413 *Total Assets:* £5,669,599
Registered Office: Wellington House, Wellington Road, Dunston, Gateshead, Tyne & Wear, NE11 9JL
Activities: Agents involved in the sale of timber and building materials
Parent: Brickability UK Holdings Limited
Officers: Christopher Paul Millican, Secretary/Director; Simon Jess Mellor [1963] Managing Director; Christopher Paul Millican [1969] Director; Alan Jonathan Simpson [1966] Director (Chief Executive Officer); Alan William Virgo [1958] Finance Director

Brickwork Direct Limited
Incorporated: 7 March 2003 *Employees:* 12
Net Worth: £191,431 *Total Assets:* £1,395,415
Registered Office: Unit 210 Henry Robson Way, South Shields, Tyne & Wear, NE33 1RF
Activities: Construction of domestic buildings
Officers: Deborah Collins, Secretary; Kenneth Collins, Secretary/Bricklayer; Julian Bulman [1971] Director/Quantity Surveyor; Deborah Collins [1967] Director/Administrator; Kenneth Collins [1960] Director/Bricklayer

Brickwork Services Limited
Incorporated: 28 September 2005 *Employees:* 90
Net Worth: £375,140 *Total Assets:* £821,010
Registered Office: 3 Kingfisher Court, Bowesfield Park, Stockton on Tees, Cleveland, TS18 3EX
Activities: Other building completion and finishing
Major Shareholder: Stephen Paul Willis
Officers: Joanne Willis, Secretary; Richard David Jowett Ashcroft [1965] Director; Stephen Paul Willis [1961] Director/Builder

Bridge End Motors Limited
Incorporated: 27 November 2007 *Employees:* 12
Net Worth: £458,863 *Total Assets:* £850,531
Registered Office: Hopgarth, Bridge End, Chester-le-Street, Co Durham, DH3 3RF
Activities: Sale of new cars and light motor vehicles
Major Shareholder: Ross Johnson
Officers: James Mullaney, Secretary; Ross Johnson [1974] Director

Bridgewater (Home Reversions Number 1) Limited
Incorporated: 7 January 2002
Net Worth: £4,357,551 *Total Assets:* £4,423,021
Registered Office: Cross House, Westgate Road, Newcastle upon Tyne, NE1 4XX
Activities: Buying and selling of own real estate
Parent: Reversions Financing (No. 1) 2011 Limited
Officers: Paul Trevor Barber [1967] Director; Antony Lewis Pierce [1976] Finance Director

Bridgewater (Home Reversions Number 2) Limited
Incorporated: 8 November 2001
Net Worth: £7,704,975 *Total Assets:* £7,704,999
Registered Office: Cross House, Westgate Road, Newcastle upon Tyne, NE1 4XX
Activities: Buying and selling of own real estate
Parent: Reversions Financing (No. 1) 2011 Limited
Officers: Paul Trevor Barber [1967] Director; Antony Lewis Pierce [1976] Finance Director

Bridgewater Contractual Tenancies Limited
Incorporated: 17 March 2004
Net Worth: £9,090,747 *Total Assets:* £9,090,747
Registered Office: Cross House, Westgate Road, Newcastle upon Tyne, NE1 4XX
Activities: Other letting and operating of own or leased real estate
Parent: Bridgewater Property Holdings Limited
Officers: Paul Trevor Barber [1967] Director; Antony Lewis Pierce [1976] Finance Director

Bridgewater Equity Release Limited
Incorporated: 4 March 2004
Net Worth: £70,204,000 *Total Assets:* £70,205,000
Registered Office: Cross House, Westgate Road, Newcastle upon Tyne, NE1 4XX
Activities: Buying and selling of own real estate
Parent: Reversions Financing (No. 1) 2011 Limited
Officers: Paul Trevor Barber [1967] Director; Ashish Kashyap [1979] Director; Antony Lewis Pierce [1976] Finance Director

Bridgewater Lifetime Mortgages Limited
Incorporated: 5 March 2004
Net Worth: £4,349,058 *Total Assets:* £4,349,993
Registered Office: Cross House, Westgate Road, Newcastle upon Tyne, NE1 4XX
Activities: Other letting and operating of own or leased real estate
Parent: Bridgewater Property Holdings Limited
Officers: Paul Trevor Barber [1967] Director; Antony Lewis Pierce [1976] Finance Director

Bridgewater Tenancies Limited
Incorporated: 4 November 2003
Net Worth: £43,053,960 *Total Assets:* £43,194,220
Registered Office: Cross House, Westgate Road, Newcastle upon Tyne, NE1 4XX
Activities: Buying and selling of own real estate
Parent: Nitro 2 Limited
Officers: Paul Trevor Barber [1967] Director; Antony Lewis Pierce [1976] Finance Director

Bridging Funding Limited
Incorporated: 27 May 2011
Net Worth: £50,231 *Total Assets:* £1,254,177
Registered Office: Yours Business Networks, Suite B, 7-8 Delta Bank Road, Gateshead, Tyne & Wear, NE11 9DJ
Activities: Financial intermediation not elsewhere classified
Shareholders: James Roland Fleming; Reuben Thomas Coppin Straker
Officers: James Roland Fleming [1944] Director/Author; Reuben Thomas Coppin Straker [1956] Director/Property Consultant

Bridgman IBC Limited
Incorporated: 31 March 2004 *Employees:* 73
Net Worth: £693,798 *Total Assets:* £2,732,294
Registered Office: Bridgman IBC Ltd, Greatham Street, Longill Industrial Estate, Hartlepool, Cleveland, TS25 1PU
Activities: Manufacture of other builders' carpentry and joinery
Shareholders: Anthony Phillips; Michael Butler
Officers: Peter Lawrence Henry Bowes, Secretary; Peter Lawrence Henry Bowes [1967] Operations Director; Michael Butler [1957] Managing Director; Anthony Phillips [1954] Sales Director

Brighstone Developments Limited
Incorporated: 11 December 2015 *Employees:* 1
Net Worth Deficit: £7,947 *Total Assets:* £1,022,928
Registered Office: 2nd Floor, Cuthbert House, Newcastle upon Tyne, NE1 2ET
Activities: Development of building projects
Parent: High Street Commercial Finance Limited
Officers: Gary Ronald Forrest [1968] Director

Brighter Academy Trust
Incorporated: 5 June 2013 *Employees:* 133
Net Worth: £5,167,000 *Total Assets:* £6,920,000
Registered Office: Farringdon Community Academy, Allendale Road, Sunderland, Tyne & Wear, SR3 3EL
Activities: General secondary education
Officers: Megan Blacklock [1940] Director/Executive Officer; Alan Eastick [1966] Director/Consultancy; Neal Holder [1972] Director/Headmaster

Brightlight Management Limited
Incorporated: 4 November 2003
Net Worth: £51,878 *Total Assets:* £839,655
Registered Office: 58 Glen Street, Hebburn, Tyne & Wear, NE31 1NG
Activities: Buying and selling of own real estate
Shareholders: John Hambling; David Metcalfe
Officers: John Hambling, Secretary; John Hambling [1959] Director; David Metcalfe [1953] Director/Property Letting

Brighton & Hove Bus and Coach Company Limited
Incorporated: 26 November 1935 *Employees:* 1,463
Net Worth: £4,993,000 *Total Assets:* £46,234,000
Registered Office: 3rd Floor, 41-51 Grey Street, Newcastle upon Tyne, NE1 6EE
Activities: Other passenger land transport
Parent: Go-Ahead Holding Limited
Officers: Carolyn Ferguson, Secretary; Stephen Ambury [1963] Engineering Director; Michael Derek Best [1963] Commercial Director; David Allen Brown [1960] Director; Simon Patrick Butcher [1967] Finance Director; Kevin David Carey [1959] Director; Christopher John Ford [1979] Finance Director; Martin Philip Harris [1957] Commercial Director

Brims Building Group Limited
Incorporated: 27 June 2011 *Employees:* 73
Net Worth: £3,574,915 *Total Assets:* £12,757,595
Registered Office: 3 Austin Boulevard, Quay West, Sunderland, Tyne & Wear, SR5 2AL
Activities: Construction of commercial buildings
Officers: Josie Clements, Secretary; Ian Robert Baggett [1972] Director; Ian Clift [1967] Director; Jason Michael Wood [1969] Director; Richard Jonathon Wood [1972] Director

Brims Construction Limited
Incorporated: 6 December 1996 *Employees:* 73
Net Worth: £3,574,615 *Total Assets:* £12,757,595
Registered Office: 3 Austin Boulevard, Quay West Business Park, Sunderland, Tyne & Wear, SR5 2AL
Activities: Construction of commercial buildings
Parent: Brims Building Group Limited
Officers: Jason Michael Wood, Secretary; Ian Robert Baggett [1972] Director; Ian Clift [1967] Director; Jason Michael Wood [1969] Director; Richard Jonathon Wood [1972] Director

Bristol Street First Investments Limited
Incorporated: 8 October 1930 *Employees:* 1,327
Net Worth: £40,582,000 *Total Assets:* £282,376,992
Registered Office: Vertu House, Fifth Avenue Business Park, Team Valley Trading Estate, Gateshead, Tyne & Wear, NE11 0XA
Activities: Sale of new cars and light motor vehicles
Parent: Vertu Motors PLC
Officers: Karen Anderson, Secretary; Karen Anderson [1971] Finance Director; David Paul Crane [1967] Commercial Director; Robert Thomas Forrester [1969] Director; Ian Harrison [1964] Group Operations Director; Michael Sherwin [1959] Finance Director

Bristol Street Fourth Investments Limited
Incorporated: 20 August 1953 *Employees:* 1,451
Net Worth: £3,131,000 *Total Assets:* £150,779,008
Registered Office: Vertu House, Fifth Avenue Business Park, Team Valley Trading Estate, Gateshead, Tyne & Wear, NE11 0XA
Activities: Sale of new cars and light motor vehicles
Parent: Vertu Motors PLC
Officers: Karen Anderson, Secretary; Karen Anderson [1971] Finance Director; David Paul Crane [1967] Commercial Director; Robert Thomas Forrester [1969] Director; Stephen Paul Gould [1972] Group Operations Director; Ian Harrison [1964] Director; Colin Kent [1957] Director; Mike Rich [1961] Group Operations Director; Michael Sherwin [1959] Finance Director

Britannia Office Systems Limited
Incorporated: 8 October 1997
Net Worth: £894,377 *Total Assets:* £981,222
Registered Office: 17a Front Street, Monkseaton, Whitley Bay, Tyne & Wear, NE25 8AQ
Activities: Repair of other equipment
Shareholder: Caroline Dickie
Officers: Caroline Dickie, Secretary; Caroline Dickie [1974] Company Secretary/Director; Carl Robson [1974] Director/Engineer

British American Railway Services Limited
Incorporated: 8 July 2008 *Employees:* 71
Net Worth Deficit: £10,718,907 *Total Assets:* £6,471,127
Registered Office: Stanhope Station, Station Road, Stanhope, Bishop Auckland, Co Durham, DL13 2YS
Activities: Activities of head offices
Officers: Edwin Ellis [1954] Director/Manager [American]; Hugh Michael McConville [1961] Director [American]

The British Electrical & Manufacturing Company Limited
Incorporated: 17 August 1937 *Employees:* 121
Net Worth: £3,627,218 *Total Assets:* £9,270,711
Registered Office: P O Box 2BD, Clavering Court, Clavering Place, Newcastle upon Tyne, NE1 3NG
Activities: Manufacture of electricity distribution and control apparatus
Officers: Richard John Neville Barkes, Secretary; Bryan Rogerson Barkes [1933] Director/Chairman & Manager; Geoffrey Rogerson Barkes [1927] Director/Manager; Richard John Neville Barkes [1954] Director/Manager; Simon Rogerson Barkes [1957] Director/Manager

British Engines (UK) Limited
Incorporated: 16 February 2010 *Employees:* 75
Net Worth: £18,174,000 *Total Assets:* £60,432,000
Registered Office: 11 Glasshouse Street, St Peters, Newcastle upon Tyne, NE6 1BS
Activities: Activities of head offices
Parent: British Engines Limited
Officers: Joanne Alicea Wilkes, Secretary; Laura Joicey [1976] Director/Group Chief Financial Officer; Alexander Harold Lamb [1971] Director/Group Chairman; Jonathan Charles Lamb [1977] Group Manufacturing Director

British Engines Limited
Incorporated: 17 February 2010 *Employees:* 1,398
Net Worth: £89,687,000 *Total Assets:* £152,860,000
Registered Office: 11 Glasshouse Street, St Peters, Newcastle upon Tyne, NE6 1BS
Activities: Activities of head offices
Officers: Joanne Alicea Wilkes, Secretary; Richard Dodd [1974] Director/Bel Group Chief Operating Officer (COO); Dr Christopher Gordon Floyd [1955] Director/Partner in The Floyd Partnership; Laura Joicey [1976] Director/Group Chief Financial Officer; Alexander Harold Lamb [1971] Director/Bel Group Chairman & CEO; Harold Graham Lamb [1935] Engineer and Director; Jonathan Charles Lamb [1977] Director/Bel Group Chief Manufacturing Officer(CMO); Sheila Claire Longo [1944] Director; Vincent Patterson [1961] Director; Wiiliam Moore Teasdale [1942] Director

The British Sociological Association
Incorporated: 3 December 1999 *Employees:* 15
Net Worth: £1,968,138 *Total Assets:* £2,946,044
Registered Office: Chancery Court, Belmont Business Park, Durham, DH1 1TW
Activities: Activities of professional membership organisations
Officers: Kerry Collins, Secretary; Dr Aminu Musa Audu [1974] Director/Researcher [Nigerian]; Dr John David Bone [1957] Director/Sociologist; Professor Stephanie Forsythe Jackson [1951] Director/Professor; Dr Jieyu Liu [1978] Director/Academic; Professor Linda McKie [1956] Director/University Professor; Professor Janice McLaughlin [1968] Director/Academic; Professor Abdul Nasar Meer [1980] Director/Academic; Professor Henrietta O'Connor [1968] Director/Professor of Sociology; Professor Louise Ryan [1965] Director/Professorial Research Fellow [Irish]; Michael Antony Savage [1959] Director/Professor; Dr Richard David Waller [1964] Director/University Lecturer; Dr Aaron Zave Winter [1971] Director/Academic/Senior Lecturer [Canadian]; Dr Christopher David Yuill [1966] Director/Lecturer

Britton & Robson Limited
Incorporated: 27 April 2007 *Employees:* 15
Net Worth: £510,992 *Total Assets:* £1,577,994
Registered Office: Lakeside House, Kingfisher Way, Stockton on Tees, Cleveland, TS18 3NB
Activities: Dispensing chemist in specialised stores
Major Shareholder: David Graham Jarvis
Officers: David Graham Jarvis [1966] Director/Pharmacist; Hardip Singh Kang [1987] Director/Pharmacist; Kevin Alan Simpson [1958] Director/Pharmacist

Britton Leisure Limited
Incorporated: 3 October 1980
Net Worth: £318,613 *Total Assets:* £2,065,513
Registered Office: Seafield Park, Seahouses, Northumberland, NE68 7SP
Activities: Recreational vehicle parks, trailer parks and camping grounds
Officers: John Kenneth Britton, Secretary/Director; Allison Britton [1976] Director/Caravan Park Manager; Carolyn Britton [1976] Director/Caravan Park Manager; John Kenneth Britton [1947] Director; Marjorie Manners [1946] Director; Simon Ian Manners [1971] Director/Caravan Park Manager

Broadacres Services Limited
Incorporated: 24 September 2002
Net Worth: £970,190 *Total Assets:* £8,747,940
Registered Office: Broadacres House, Mount View, Standard Way Industrial Estate, Northallerton, N Yorks, DL6 2YD
Activities: Buying and selling of own real estate
Parent: Broadacres Housing Association Ltd
Officers: Christopher John Robert Fawcett, Secretary; Jacqui Bateson [1961] Director/Senior Proposition Manager; June Patricia Mulroy [1949] Director/Retired; Peter Anthony Ottowell [1955] Director/Retired; Phil Summers [1960] Director; Martin Warhurst [1974] Director/Chief Executive; Colin Wilkie [1954] Director/Retired

Broadband Satellite Services Limited
Incorporated: 5 September 2012 *Employees:* 117
Net Worth: £2,986,280 *Total Assets:* £29,090,220
Registered Office: Satcom Global, Tanners Bank, North Shields, Tyne & Wear, NE30 1JH
Activities: Satellite telecommunications activities
Shareholders: Robert Alan Howes; Ian Andrew Robinson
Officers: Michael John Butler [1963] Director/Consultant; Robert Alan Howes [1955] Director; Ian Andrew Robinson [1961] Director; Matthew Joseph Widdall [1972] Director/Investment Manager

Broadmedia Holdings Limited
Incorporated: 11 July 2007
Net Worth: £2,679,236 *Total Assets:* £3,021,542
Registered Office: Third Floor, Citygate, St James' Boulevard, Newcastle upon Tyne, NE1 4JE
Activities: Other information technology service activities
Parent: Alex Media Technology Limited
Officers: Harry Francis Drnec [1946] Director [American]; Andrew John Hudson [1947] Director/TV Producer; James Barrett Maclaren Leslie [1957] Director

Jack Brodie (Wholesale) Limited
Incorporated: 27 April 1978 *Employees:* 1
Net Worth: £642,359 *Total Assets:* £1,522,830
Registered Office: 66-76 Scotswood Road, Newcastle upon Tyne, NE4 7JE
Activities: Other accommodation
Major Shareholder: Andrew John Brodie
Officers: Andrew John Brodie [1966] Director

Bromley Property Holdings Limited
Incorporated: 29 December 2000
Net Worth: £157,132,992 *Total Assets:* £201,808,992
Registered Office: Citygate, St James Boulevard, Newcastle upon Tyne, NE1 4JE
Activities: Activities of head offices
Parent: Grainger PLC
Officers: Adam McGhin, Secretary; Helen Christine Gordon [1959] Director; Adam McGhin [1978] Director/Solicitor; Vanessa Kate Simms [1975] Director

Bromley Property Investments Limited
Incorporated: 6 September 2000
Net Worth: £45,641,000 *Total Assets:* £623,097,024
Registered Office: Citygate, St James Boulevard, Newcastle upon Tyne, NE1 4JE
Activities: Activities of head offices
Parent: Bromley Property Holdings Limited
Officers: Adam McGhin, Secretary; Helen Christine Gordon [1959] Director; Adam McGhin [1978] Director/Solicitor; Mark Jeremy Robson [1959] Director/Chartered Surveyor; Vanessa Kate Simms [1975] Director

Bronte Caravan Park Limited
Incorporated: 13 September 2006 *Employees:* 5
Net Worth: £895,730 *Total Assets:* £2,956,796
Registered Office: Ash House, Catterick Bridge, Richmond, N Yorks, DL10 7PH
Activities: Recreational vehicle parks, trailer parks and camping grounds
Major Shareholder: John Christopher Darling
Officers: Richard Henry Darling, Secretary/Director; John Christopher Darling [1978] Director; Judith Anne Darling [1946] Director; Richard Henry Darling [1943] Director

Brookleigh Caring Services Limited
Incorporated: 30 September 2004 *Employees:* 182
Net Worth: £376,104 *Total Assets:* £801,833
Registered Office: 17 St Cuthbert Avenue, Marton, Middlesbrough, Cleveland, TS7 8RG
Activities: Other human health activities
Shareholders: Michelle Caroline Savage; Vernon Tyrone Savage; Michelle Caroline Savage; Vernon Tyrone Savage
Officers: Vernon Tyrone Savage, Secretary; Michelle Caroline Savage [1963] Director; Vernon Tyrone Savage [1959] Director

Broomhouse Care Limited
Incorporated: 19 May 2009 *Employees:* 40
Net Worth: £323,037 *Total Assets:* £1,699,489
Registered Office: 8 Broomhouse Farm Court, Castlefields, Prudhoe, Northumberland, NE42 5FS
Activities: Other business support service activities n.e.c.
Shareholders: Susan Ann Patel; Robert Roney
Officers: Susan Ann Patel [1959] Director; Robert Roney [1960] Director

Broseley Fires Limited
Incorporated: 8 March 1982 *Employees:* 15
Net Worth: £657,149 *Total Assets:* £1,279,927
Registered Office: 19-34 Bedesway, Bede Industrial Estate, Jarrow, Tyne & Wear, NE32 3BE
Activities: Manufacture of other fabricated metal products n.e.c.
Major Shareholder: Walter Bloodworth
Officers: John Richard Harris, Secretary; Gregory Bloodworth [1965] Executive Director; John Richard Harris [1958] Financial Director

Ken Brown Agencies Limited
Incorporated: 31 March 2010
Net Worth: £777,157 *Total Assets:* £883,593
Registered Office: F1 Tanfield Lea Business Centre, Tanfield Lea Industrial Estate North, Tanfield Lea, Stanley, Co Durham, DH9 9DB
Activities: Agents specialised in the sale of other particular products
Major Shareholder: Ken Brown
Officers: Ken Brown [1957] Director/Sales Agent; Heather Wilson-Brown [1959] Director

David Brown Automotive Limited
Incorporated: 1 March 2010
Net Worth Deficit: £3,927,000 *Total Assets:* £3,551,000
Registered Office: 1a Dukesway Court, Team Valley Trading Estate, Gateshead, Tyne & Wear, NE11 0PJ
Activities: Specialised design activities
Parent: Addbudget Limited
Officers: Phillip Nigel Blain, Secretary; David Patrick Brown [1955] Director; David James Horrocks [1959] Financial Director; Ian Imrie [1955] Director

Gordon Brown Law Firm LLP
Incorporated: 23 February 2011 *Employees:* 82
Net Worth: £779,494 *Total Assets:* £1,424,986
Registered Office: Mains House, 143 Front Street, Chester-le-Street, Co Durham, DH3 3AU
Officers: Kathryn Taylor [1975] Member; Simon Dakers [1972] LLP Member; Rebecca Harbron Gray [1980] LLP Member

Francis Brown Limited
Incorporated: 19 December 1947 *Employees:* 75
Net Worth: £384,762 *Total Assets:* £2,386,043
Registered Office: Church Road, Stockton on Tees, Cleveland, TS18 2HL
Activities: Manufacture of other fabricated metal products n.e.c.
Shareholder: David George Brown
Officers: James George Brown, Secretary; David George Brown [1945] Director; James George Brown [1968] Director; Joan Mary Brown [1947] Director; Simon Francis Brown [1971] Director; Mark Roddy [1970] Director

Browns Bedrooms & Kitchens Ltd
Incorporated: 27 August 1999 *Employees:* 53
Net Worth: £2,826,425 *Total Assets:* £15,009,056
Registered Office: Colbourne House, Colbourne Avenue, Nelson Park, Cramlington, Northumberland, NE23 1WD
Activities: Manufacture of kitchen furniture
Shareholders: Peter Alfred Brown; Sylvia Brown
Officers: Gail Farrugia, Secretary; Peter Alfred Brown [1952] Director; Sylvia Brown [1953] Director

Bruder Property Limited
Incorporated: 2 August 2007 *Employees:* 3
Net Worth: £1,812,243 *Total Assets:* £6,564,039
Registered Office: First Floor, Finchale House, Belmont Business Park, Durham, DH1 1TW
Activities: Other letting and operating of own or leased real estate
Officers: Helen Austin, Secretary; John Corbitt Barnsley [1948] Director/Accountant; Spencer Trerise Glanville [1972] Director; Robert William Jefferson [1950] Director/Chartered Accountant

Bruker JV UK Ltd
Incorporated: 8 April 2008 *Employees:* 28
Net Worth Deficit: £2,737,691 *Total Assets:* £2,031,627
Registered Office: Belmont Business Park, Durham, DH1 1TW
Activities: Manufacture of electronic measuring, testing etc. equipment, not for industrial process control
Officers: Avraham Lifshitz, Secretary; Generald Herman [1957] Director/Vice President - Corporate Controller [Canadian]; Avraham Lifshitz [1958] Director/Accountant [Israeli]; Itzhak Mazor [1950] Director/Chief Executive Officer [Israeli]; Brent David Nelson [1959] Director/Vice President of Bruker Nano Inc

Brunel Spire LLP
Incorporated: 16 February 2010 *Employees:* 2
Total Assets: £7,949,834
Registered Office: One Central Parkway, Newcastle upon Tyne, NE1 3BZ
Officers: Rahul Sharma [1975] Member; Dr Swatanter Bahrat Sharma [1946] Member

F. Brunton & Sons Limited
Incorporated: 25 March 1955 *Employees:* 8
Net Worth: £1,502,828 *Total Assets:* £1,993,388
Registered Office: Barnaby Grange, Guisborough, Cleveland, TS14 6RS
Activities: Growing of cereals (except rice), leguminous crops and oil seeds
Shareholder: Andrew James Hall
Officers: Kim Louise Brunton, Secretary [New Zealander]; Andrew James Hall Brunton [1966] Director/Farmer; Ann Christine Brunton [1935] Director/Married Woman; Joanna Elizabeth Oakhill [1964] Director/Married Woman

Brunton Holdings Limited
Incorporated: 28 March 2015
Net Worth: £500,000 *Total Assets:* £1,000,000
Registered Office: Spaceworks, Benton Road, Newcastle upon Tyne, NE7 7LX
Activities: Non-trading company
Shareholders: Robert James Charlton; Diane Charlton
Officers: Neil McGlew, Secretary; Diane Charlton [1964] Director; Mr Robert James Charlton [1969] Director/Architect

Brunton Nursery Limited
Incorporated: 14 October 2010 *Employees:* 36
Net Worth: £333,695 *Total Assets:* £1,374,702
Registered Office: Brunton Nursery, Roseden Way, Newcastle upon Tyne, NE13 9BD
Activities: Pre-primary education
Major Shareholder: Julia Ruth Wilcock
Officers: Graham Wilcock [1962] Production Director; Julia Ruth Wilcock [1964] Director/Chief Executive

Brush Technology Limited
Incorporated: 9 March 1990 *Employees:* 14
Net Worth: £2,005,235 *Total Assets:* £2,223,156
Registered Office: Unit 3 Throckley Industrial Estate, Ponteland Road, Throckley, Newcastle upon Tyne, NE15 9EW
Activities: Manufacture of brooms and brushes
Shareholders: Richard William Renwick; Gillian Renwick
Officers: Gillian Renwick, Secretary; Gillian Renwick [1965] Director/Brush Manufacturer; Jonathan Hugo Renwick [1972] Director/Brush Manufacturer; Richard William Renwick [1963] Director/Brush Manufacturer

Brynco Ltd
Incorporated: 23 February 2010
Net Worth: £869,094 *Total Assets:* £984,144
Registered Office: 25 Coverdale, Hadrian Lodge West, Wallsend, Tyne & Wear, NE28 8TJ
Activities: Other construction installation
Major Shareholder: Bryn Patterson
Officers: Bryn Paterson [1972] Director

BSD (UK) Ltd
Incorporated: 9 May 2002
Registered Office: 113 Bewick Road, Gateshead, Tyne & Wear, NE8 1UA
Activities: Other manufacturing n.e.c.
Major Shareholder: Moishe Fordsham
Officers: Judith Fordsham, Secretary; Joseph Fordsham [1971] Director

BTS Fabrications Limited
Incorporated: 28 February 2006 *Employees:* 37
Net Worth: £831,157 *Total Assets:* £2,018,113
Registered Office: Unit 7 Central Park, Woodham Road, Aycliffe Business Park, Newton Aycliffe, Co Durham, DL5 6HT
Activities: Manufacture of metal structures and parts of structures
Shareholders: David Bryan Atkinson; Philip James Atkinson
Officers: Marcia Atkinson, Secretary; Bryan Atkinson [1941] Director; David Atkinson [1979] Director; Philip James Atkinson [1968] Director; David Robert Precious [1978] Design & Manufacturing Director

A.Buckler Haulage Limited
Incorporated: 21 December 1960 *Employees:* 29
Net Worth: £622,082 *Total Assets:* £2,229,797
Registered Office: Marsh Road Garage, Marsh Road, Middlesbrough, Cleveland, TS1 5LD
Activities: Demolition
Major Shareholder: Mark Stephen Love
Officers: Mark Stephen Love, Secretary; Mark Stephen Love [1958] Director/Demolition Contractor; Richard Mark Love [1986] Director/General Manager

Budget Workspace Limited
Incorporated: 3 November 1997 *Employees:* 2
Net Worth: £4,900,471 *Total Assets:* £7,408,874
Registered Office: Estate Office, Hamsterley Hall, Hamsterley Mill, Rowlands Gill, Tyne & Wear, NE39 1NJ
Activities: Renting and operating of Housing Association real estate
Parent: Budget Workspace Holdings Limited
Officers: William Henry Spry, Secretary; Beryl Spry [1944] Director; Steven George Spry [1978] Director/Manager; William Henry Spry [1943] Director/Developer

Buffalo Power Services Limited
Incorporated: 24 September 2003
Registered Office: Lynwood, Seaton, Seaham, Co Durham, SR7 0NB
Activities: Other specialised construction activities n.e.c.
Shareholders: Thomas Davidson; Hilda Davidson
Officers: Hilda Davidson, Secretary/Executive; Hilda Davidson [1954] Director/Executive; Thomas William Davidson [1955] Director/Executive

Building Design (Northern) Limited
Incorporated: 19 January 1983 *Employees:* 12
Net Worth: £667,541 *Total Assets:* £895,244
Registered Office: Kepier House, Belmont Business Park, Durham, DH1 1TW
Activities: Architectural activities
Shareholders: Gary Ward; Clive Leonard Oliphant; Clive Leonard Oliphant; Gary Ward
Officers: Richard Grahame Marsden [1985] Director/Architect; Clive Leonard Oliphant [1956] Director/Chartered Civil & Structural Engineer; Gary Ward [1965] Director/Project Manager

Building Maintenance Services North East Limited
Incorporated: 22 June 2006
Net Worth: £109,384 *Total Assets:* £784,494
Registered Office: The Clay Pit, 50 Walker Road, Newcastle upon Tyne, NE6 1BG
Activities: Other specialised construction activities n.e.c.
Shareholders: William Robert Daniel Ridley; Charlotte Kate Ridley; William David Ridley
Officers: Charlotte Kate Ridley, Secretary; Charlotte Kate Ridley [1967] Director; William Robert Daniel Ridley [1969] Director

Buildroute Limited
Incorporated: 29 September 1987 *Employees:* 51
Net Worth: £250,547 *Total Assets:* £1,617,248
Registered Office: 27 Scarborough Street, Hartlepool, Cleveland, TS24 7DA
Activities: Other specialised construction activities n.e.c.
Officers: Bridget Ann Towler, Secretary; Guy Dobson [1965] Director; Wayne Dobson [1960] Director

Bulk Logistics Group Ltd
Incorporated: 23 March 2016 *Employees:* 110
Net Worth Deficit: £62,687 *Total Assets:* £14,976,294
Registered Office: The Garage, Patrick Brompton, Bedale, N Yorks, DL8 1JP
Activities: Freight transport by road
Major Shareholder: Michael James Ward
Officers: David Andrew Castle [1952] Director; David Keith Edghill [1979] Director; Paul William Tolmie [1961] Director; Michael James Ward [1968] Director

Bulk Tainer Logistics Limited
Incorporated: 20 January 2009 *Employees:* 31
Net Worth: £732,683 *Total Assets:* £10,554,850
Registered Office: 22 Ellerbeck Court, Stokesley Business Park, Stokesley, Middlesbrough, Cleveland, TS9 5PT
Activities: Freight transport by road
Officers: David Michael Eltherington [1967] Director

Bulman Support Ltd
Incorporated: 13 June 2013
Net Worth: £150,232 *Total Assets:* £2,159,777
Registered Office: 7 Diamond Court, Newcastle upon Tyne, NE3 2EN
Activities: Other professional, scientific and technical activities n.e.c.
Parent: Kielder Investments Limited
Officers: Jamie Patrick Cooke [1985] Director; Benjamin Thomas Ridgway [1985] Director

M.D. & A.G. Burdon Ltd
Incorporated: 17 June 2004
Net Worth: £760,873 *Total Assets:* £3,955,921
Registered Office: 30-32 Front Street, Whickham, Gateshead, Tyne & Wear, NE16 4DT
Activities: Dispensing chemist in specialised stores
Shareholders: Mark David Burdon; Anita Geraldine Burdon
Officers: Anita Generaldine Burdon, Secretary/Pharmacist; Anita Generaldine Burdon [1977] Director/Pharmacist; Mark David Burdon [1977] Director/Pharmacist; Lee Ronald Middleton [1976] Director

Bureau of Analysed Samples Limited
Incorporated: 28 November 1935 *Employees:* 25
Net Worth: £4,190,953 *Total Assets:* £6,936,535
Registered Office: Newham Hall, Newby, Middlesbrough, Cleveland, TS8 9EA
Activities: Manufacture of non-electronic industrial process control equipment
Parent: Newham Hall Holdings Limited
Officers: Geoffrey Colin Flintoft, Secretary; Geoffrey Colin Flintoft [1942] Director/Company Secretary; Jane Caroline Meeres [1954] Director/Secretary; Richard Powys Meeres [1943] Managing Director; Dr Malcolm Stuart Taylor [1934] Director/Chemist

Ben Burgess & Co Limited
Incorporated: 5 March 2001 *Employees:* 205
Net Worth: £10,089,412 *Total Assets:* £50,098,592
Registered Office: Central Square South, Orchard Street, Newcastle upon Tyne, NE1 3XX
Activities: Wholesale of agricultural machinery, equipment and supplies
Officers: Alex Wade, Secretary; David Gerard Fairman [1969] Commercial Director; Martin John Fuller [1970] Commercial Director; Peter James Lockhart [1962] Director; John Ferdinand Rupp [1952] Director; Benjamin Burgess Turner [1956] Managing Director

Ben Burgess Holdings Limited
Incorporated: 24 December 2002 *Employees:* 225
Net Worth: £45,274,184 *Total Assets:* £68,933,784
Registered Office: Central Square South, Orchard Street, Newcastle upon Tyne, NE1 3XX
Activities: Activities of head offices
Officers: Alex Wade, Secretary; David Gerard Fairman [1969] Director; Martin John Fuller [1970] Commercial Director; Peter James Lockhart [1962] Director; John Ferdinand Rupp [1952] Director; Benjamin Burgess Turner [1956] Director

Roland Burgess Limited
Incorporated: 2 January 1922
Net Worth: £1,054,475 *Total Assets:* £1,126,418
Registered Office: The Warehouse, Crowley Road, Swalwell, Gateshead, Tyne & Wear, NE16 3HD
Activities: Wholesale of clothing and footwear
Shareholders: William Roland Edward Burgess; Rosemary Ann Kinghorn
Officers: William Roland Edward Burgess, Secretary; William Roland Edward Burgess [1964] Director; Terrence Knox [1952] Director/General Manager

Burlam House Limited
Incorporated: 28 April 2015
Net Worth Deficit: £51,831 *Total Assets:* £1,083,504
Registered Office: Houghton House, New Road, Team Valley Trading Estate, Gateshead, Tyne & Wear, NE11 0JU
Activities: Residential nursing care facilities
Parent: Exclusive Care Group Ltd
Officers: Jennifer Pamela Houghton [1946] Director; Jill Yvette Houghton [1965] Director

Burncastle Farming Company Ltd
Incorporated: 9 July 1996
Net Worth: £763,109 *Total Assets:* £807,969
Registered Office: Estates Office, Alnwick Castle, Alnwick, Northumberland, NE66 1NQ
Activities: Mixed farming
Major Shareholder: Earl George Dominic Percy
Officers: Lesley Ann Ilderton, Secretary; Colin Leslie Barnes [1960] Director/Town & Country Planner; Lesley Ann Ilderton [1976] Director/Group Financial Controller; Ralph George Algernon Percy [1956] Director/Peer of The Realm; Rory Charles St John Wilson [1961] Director/Land Agent

Burnell Fencing Limited
Incorporated: 1 June 1998 *Employees:* 49
Net Worth: £3,560,302 *Total Assets:* £4,669,161
Registered Office: Light Industrial Estate, West Terrace, Esh Winning, Co Durham, DH7 9PT
Activities: Other construction installation
Shareholders: David Bushby; Donna Maria Bushby
Officers: Donna Maria Bushby, Secretary; David Bushby [1970] Director; Donna Maria Bushby [1969] Director; Shaun Gregory [1979] Director/Operations

Burnell Properties Limited
Incorporated: 9 December 2009
Net Worth: £284,310 *Total Assets:* £1,539,276
Registered Office: The Yard, Light Industrial Estate, Esh Winning, Co Durham, DH7 9PT
Activities: Management of real estate on a fee or contract basis
Shareholders: David Bushby; Donna Maria Bushby
Officers: David Bushby [1970] Director; Donna Maria Bushby [1969] Director

Burnfoot Windfarm Limited
Incorporated: 26 September 2008
Net Worth: £24,447,000 *Total Assets:* £61,011,000
Registered Office: Alexander House, 1 Mandarin Road, Rainton Bridge Business Park, Houghton-le-Spring, Co Durham, DH4 5RA
Activities: Production of electricity
Parent: EDF Energy Renewables Holdings Limited
Officers: Susan Elizabeth Lind, Secretary; Matthieu Thomas Hue [1975] Director [French]; Hassaan Majid [1968] Director

Burnhead Moss Wind Farm Limited
Incorporated: 9 July 2013
Net Worth: £13,006,000 *Total Assets:* £43,766,000
Registered Office: Alexander House, 1 Mandarin Road, Rainton Bridge Business Park, Houghton-le-Spring, Co Durham, DH4 5RA
Activities: Production of electricity
Parent: EDF Energy Renewables Holdings Limited
Officers: Susan Elizabeth Lind, Secretary; Matthieu Thomas Hue [1975] Director [French]; Hassaan Majid [1968] Director

Burradon Farm Houses and Cottages Limited
Incorporated: 6 December 2007
Net Worth: £431,502 *Total Assets:* £2,417,013
Registered Office: Burradon Farm, Cramlington, Northumberland, NE23 7ND
Activities: Other accommodation
Officers: Judith Winifred Younger, Secretary; James Robert Younger [1972] Director/Banker; Judith Winifred Younger [1944] Director & Secretary; William James Edmund Younger [1942] Director/Farmer

James Burrell Limited
Incorporated: 22 December 1926 *Employees:* 190
Net Worth: £3,707,315 *Total Assets:* £17,707,400
Registered Office: Deptford Road, Gateshead, Tyne & Wear, NE8 2BR
Activities: Agents involved in the sale of timber and building materials
Shareholders: Stephen John Richardson; Simon Mark Richardson
Officers: Simon Mark Richardson [1963] Joint Managing Director; Stephen John Richardson [1959] Joint Managing Director

P.F.Burridge & Sons Limited
Incorporated: 23 August 1967 *Employees:* 146
Net Worth: £835,614 *Total Assets:* £6,263,887
Registered Office: Units 8 & 9 Wesley Way, Benton Square Industrial Estate, Newcastle upon Tyne, NE12 9TA
Activities: Construction of commercial buildings
Parent: P.F. Burridge Holdings Limited
Officers: Dawn Burridge [1963] Director/Admin/Accounts; Philip John Burridge [1960] Director; Stephen Christopher McCoy [1967] Commercial Director; Nicholas James Moore [1973] Director/Quantity Surveyor

A.E. Burt and Company Limited
Incorporated: 22 September 1977 *Employees:* 23
Net Worth: £1,027,684 *Total Assets:* £4,926,801
Registered Office: Oakwood House, 80 Eastmount Road, Darlington, Co Durham, DL1 1LA
Activities: Other letting and operating of own or leased real estate
Major Shareholder: Marion Barbara Todd
Officers: Marion Barbara Todd, Secretary; Claire Elizabeth Kerr [1971] Director; Graeme Stuart Kerr [1971] Director; Marion Barbara Todd [1948] Director; Nigel Robert Todd [1975] Director

Burton Collingwood Limited
Incorporated: 6 July 2011 *Employees:* 5
Net Worth: £11,569,005 *Total Assets:* £13,029,655
Registered Office: 34 Howard Street, North Shields, Tyne & Wear, NE30 1AR
Activities: Other letting and operating of own or leased real estate
Shareholders: Christopher Daniel Burton; Peter Timothy Burton; Julie Claire Burton
Officers: Noel Francis Chintillier, Secretary; Christopher Daniel Burton [1981] Director; Garnet Duff Burton [1948] Director; Peter Timothy Burton [1985] Director/Chartered Accountant

Bushnell Limited
Incorporated: 6 November 1991
Registered Office: 14 Cobblestone Court, Hoults Estate, Walker Road, Newcastle upon Tyne, NE6 1AB
Activities: Other service activities n.e.c.
Officers: Barry Fox, Secretary; Antony John Crerar [1966] Director/Project Manager; Pamela Louise Crerar [1970] Director/Manager; Barry Fox [1961] Director/Audio Visual Consultant; Lorraine Fox [1958] Director/Manager

Business and Enterprise Commercial Limited
Incorporated: 19 April 2010 *Employees:* 117
Net Worth: £4,027,085 *Total Assets:* £8,364,031
Registered Office: Spectrum 6, Spectrum Business Park, Seaham, Co Durham, SR7 7TT
Activities: Management consultancy activities other than financial management
Parent: Business and Enterprise UK Limited
Officers: Julia Louise Hatton, Secretary; Nicola Clark [1973] Director; Alastair Angus MacColl [1964] Director

Business and Enterprise UK Limited
Incorporated: 22 July 2009 *Employees:* 114
Net Worth: £2,216,228 *Total Assets:* £6,556,468
Registered Office: Spectrum 6, Spectrum Business Park, Seaham, Co Durham, SR7 7TT
Activities: Management consultancy activities other than financial management
Parent: BE-UK Employee Ownership Trustee Co Limited
Officers: Julia Louise Hatton, Secretary; Nicola Clark [1973] Director; Geoffrey Mark Hodgson [1961] Director; Alastair Angus MacColl [1964] Director; Suzanne McCreedy [1975] National Services Director

Business Data Partners Limited
Incorporated: 23 October 2014 *Employees:* 98
Net Worth: £468,239 *Total Assets:* £2,381,309
Registered Office: Cobalt Business Exchange, Cobalt Park Way, Wallsend, Tyne & Wear, NE28 9NZ
Activities: Other information service activities n.e.c.
Parent: Business Data Partners Holdings Limited
Officers: Jacqueline Hoey [1972] Managing Director; Ian James Huckle [1960] Director

Bussey & Armstrong Projects Limited
Incorporated: 13 September 1999
Net Worth: £11,386,949 *Total Assets:* £14,045,539
Registered Office: Brinkburn, 147 Brinkburn Road, Darlington, Co Durham, DL3 9LA
Activities: Development of building projects
Major Shareholder: Anthony John Cooper
Officers: Angela Edwina Cooper, Company Secretary; Anthony John Cooper [1950] Director

Bussey and Armstrong Limited
Incorporated: 11 February 1949 *Employees:* 31
Net Worth: £3,021,448 *Total Assets:* £3,266,250
Registered Office: Brinkburn, 147 Brinkburn Road, Darlington, Co Durham, DL3 9LA
Activities: Development of building projects
Major Shareholder: Anthony John Cooper
Officers: Angela Edwina Cooper, Secretary; Angela Edwina Cooper [1950] Director; Anthony John Cooper [1950] Director/Builder

Butterfly Riot Limited
Incorporated: 24 May 2010
Registered Office: Hadrian House, Front Street, Chester-le-Street, Co Durham, DH3 3DB
Activities: Buying and selling of own real estate
Shareholders: James Sommerville; Christine Sommerville
Officers: Christine Sommerville [1973] Director/Designer [American]; James Anthony Sommerville [1966] Director/Designer

Butterwick Limited
Incorporated: 17 October 1994 *Employees:* 178
Net Worth: £3,191,523 *Total Assets:* £3,869,673
Registered Office: Butterwick Hospice, Middlefield Road, Stockton on Tees, Cleveland, TS19 8XN
Activities: Other human health activities
Officers: Ian Mortimer, Secretary; Beverley Susan Blakey [1961] Director/Accountant; John Paul Bury [1954] Director/Solicitor; Dr David Carr [1943] Director/Consultant Physician; Judith Cosker Hunter [1956] Director/Registered Nurse; Carol Mary Lancaster [1961] Director/Clinical Quality Officer; Paul Langdon [1964] Director/Banker; Dr Bruce Irving McLain [1959] Director/Consultant Paediatrician; Dr Neil George Reynolds [1953] Director/Retired

Warren Butterworth Catering Butchers Limited
Incorporated: 14 June 1999 *Employees:* 45
Net Worth: £1,561,097 *Total Assets:* £3,259,918
Registered Office: Unit 5 Westway Industrial Park, Ponteland Road, Throckley, Tyne & Wear, NE15 9HW
Activities: Wholesale of meat and meat products
Parent: DW & FE Butterworth Holdings Limited
Officers: Frances Elizabeth Rutherford, Secretary/Director; Duncan Warren Butterworth [1974] Director/Manager; James Warren Butterworth [1948] Director; Susan Elizabeth Butterworth [1949] Director; Frances Elizabeth Rutherford [1977] Director

DW & FE Butterworth Holdings Limited
Incorporated: 3 October 2007
Net Worth: £90,760 *Total Assets:* £826,782
Registered Office: Unit 5 Westway Industrial Park, Ponteland Road, Throckley, Newcastle upon Tyne, NE15 9HW
Activities: Activities of head offices
Shareholders: Duncan Warren Butterworth; Frances Elizabeth Rutherford
Officers: Frances Elizabeth Rutherford, Secretary/Director; Duncan Warren Butterworth [1974] Director/Manager; Frances Elizabeth Rutherford [1977] Director

Buy from Us Autopark Limited
Incorporated: 4 September 2012 *Employees:* 12
Net Worth: £241,145 *Total Assets:* £1,074,949
Registered Office: Unit 1 Meena Drive, Meadowfield Industrial Estate, Meadowfield, Co Durham, DH7 8AA
Activities: Sale of used cars and light motor vehicles
Major Shareholder: Meenakshi Chowdhry
Officers: Meenakshi Chowdhry [1963] Director

Bywell Home Farms LLP
Incorporated: 29 August 2014 *Employees:* 2
Net Worth: £14,076,051 *Total Assets:* £14,769,990
Registered Office: Bywell Castle, Bywell, Stocksfield, Northumberland, NE43 7AB
Officers: Henry Richard Geers Cotterell [1961] Member; William Henry Van Cutsem [1979] Member; The Right Honourable Wentworth Peter Ismay Viscount Allendale [1948] Member; The Right Honourable Theresa Mary Magdalene Viscountess Allendale [1950] Member; Michael Thomas Waterhouse [1949] Member

C & C Horse Transport Limited
Incorporated: 5 January 2007 *Employees:* 19
Net Worth: £293,680 *Total Assets:* £916,112
Registered Office: 1 Mount Pleasant Way, Stokesley Business Park, Stokesley, Cleveland, TS9 5NZ
Activities: Other passenger land transport
Officers: Elizabeth Anne Jones [1961] Operations Director

C & D Leisure Properties Ltd
Incorporated: 24 August 2016
Net Worth Deficit: £43,078 *Total Assets:* £769,806
Registered Office: First Floor, Enterprise House, 202-206 Linthorpe Road, Middlesbrough, Cleveland, TS1 3QW
Activities: Activities of other holding companies n.e.c.
Major Shareholder: Leslie Boswell
Officers: Craig Boswell [1962] Director; Leslie Boswell [1957] Director

C & R Utilities Ltd
Incorporated: 27 July 2010
Net Worth: £759,096 *Total Assets:* £1,049,307
Registered Office: Heavens View, Chilton, Ferryhill, Co Durham, DL17 0EH
Activities: Distribution of gaseous fuels through mains
Shareholders: David James Rothwell; Victoria Ruth Rothwell
Officers: David James Rothwell [1981] Director; Victoria Ruth Rothwell [1969] Director

C & V Developments Ltd.
Incorporated: 21 March 2002 *Employees:* 3
Net Worth: £224,583 *Total Assets:* £1,801,806
Registered Office: 4 Bridge Street, Amble, Morpeth, Northumberland, NE65 0DR
Activities: Other specialised construction activities n.e.c.
Shareholders: Colin Gilholm; Iris Vivienne Gilholm
Officers: Iris Vivienne Gilholm, Secretary/Administrator; Colin Gilholm [1952] Director/Building Contractor; Iris Vivienne Gilholm [1966] Director/Administrator

C Bidco Limited
Incorporated: 2 March 2015 *Employees:* 557
Net Worth Deficit: £28,988,000 *Total Assets:* £53,144,000
Registered Office: Northern Aerospace, Unit 24 Number One Industrial Estate, Consett, Co Durham, DH8 6SR
Activities: Activities of head offices
Major Shareholder: Jonathan Paul Moulton
Officers: Norman Amey [1970] Director; James Anderson Christie [1969] Director; Laurence Shannon McNairn [1955] Director; Jonathan Paul Moulton [1950] Director

C. and R. Limited
Incorporated: 22 August 1984 *Employees:* 22
Net Worth: £1,040,871 *Total Assets:* £1,822,696
Registered Office: The Dunes, Sea Road, South Shields, Tyne & Wear, NE33 2LD
Activities: Other amusement and recreation activities n.e.c.
Officers: Kenneth William Reader [1964] Director/Amusement Caterer

C.A. (Evenwood) Limited
Incorporated: 21 January 2000 *Employees:* 3
Net Worth: £12,353,357 *Total Assets:* £12,463,219
Registered Office: Evenwood Industrial Estate, Evenwood, Bishop Auckland, Co Durham, DL14 9SF
Activities: Other letting and operating of own or leased real estate
Parent: C.A. Group (Holdings) Limited
Officers: Desmond Joseph Webster, Secretary; Steven William Forster [1968] Director; Martin Kenneth Lowther [1967] Director; Desmond Joseph Webster [1963] Director/Accountant

C.A. Group (Holdings) Limited
Incorporated: 9 August 2006 *Employees:* 227
Net Worth: £22,921,366 *Total Assets:* £55,144,112
Registered Office: Evenwood Industrial Estate, Evenwood, Bishop Auckland, Co Durham, DL14 9SF
Activities: Roofing activities
Parent: C.A. Foundation
Officers: Desmond Joseph Webster, Secretary; Neil James Alderson [1976] Director; Steven William Forster [1968] Director; Martin Kenneth Lowther [1967] Director; Peter William Rowe [1961] Director; Desmond Joseph Webster [1963] Managing Director

C.A. Group Limited
Incorporated: 9 August 1983 *Employees:* 220
Net Worth: £10,075,248 *Total Assets:* £41,254,328
Registered Office: Evenwood Industrial Estate, Evenwood, Co Durham, DL14 9SF
Activities: Roofing activities
Parent: C.A. Group (Holdings) Limited
Officers: Desmond Joseph Webster, Secretary; Neil James Alderson [1976] Commercial Director; Stuart Iain Brown [1976] Director; Lee Andrew Davies [1974] Technical Director; Steven William Forster [1968] Commercial Director; Martin Kenneth Lowther [1967] Operations Director; Peter William Rowe [1961] Contracts Director; Desmond Joseph Webster [1963] Managing Director

C.A.T. Builders Limited
Incorporated: 26 April 1989 *Employees:* 4
Net Worth: £1,257,472 *Total Assets:* £1,363,084
Registered Office: Willow Tree House, Mill Lane, Well, Bedale, N Yorks, DL8 2RX
Activities: Construction of other civil engineering projects n.e.c.
Shareholders: Bernard Lewis Thwaites; Bernard Lewis Thwaites
Officers: Bernard Lewis Thwaites [1963] Director/Builder

C.B.L. Cable Contractors Limited
Incorporated: 14 November 1994 *Employees:* 242
Net Worth: £3,759,401 *Total Assets:* £6,921,724
Registered Office: Bensway House, Usworth Road, Hartlepool, Cleveland, TS25 1PD
Activities: Electrical installation
Officers: Andrew William Haygarth, Secretary/Director; Bernard Kenneth Goodchild [1956] Director/Electrical Engineer; Andrew William Haygarth [1968] Director

C.C. Property Management Limited
Incorporated: 10 January 2006
Net Worth: £59,665 *Total Assets:* £1,816,390
Registered Office: Plaster Piece, Shaftesbury Avenue, South Shields, Tyne & Wear, NE34 9PH
Activities: Renting and operating of Housing Association real estate
Officers: Skye Alexander Ferry, Secretary; Christopher Ferry [1959] Director/Self Employed; Skye-Alexander Ferry [1988] Director/Self Employed

C.F.Motoring Services Ltd
Incorporated: 31 January 1995 *Employees:* 193
Net Worth: £2,805,378 *Total Assets:* £7,857,394
Registered Office: Units 1-6 Chainbridge North, Blaydon on Tyne, Tyne & Wear, NE21 5SR
Activities: Maintenance and repair of motor vehicles
Shareholder: Frederick Alexander Calvert
Officers: Mandy Reardon, Secretary/Accounts Manager; Frederick Alexander Calvert [1951] Director/Chief Executive; Patricia Calvert [1954] Director; Philip Colling Calvert [1974] Director; William Michael Calvert [1959] Director/Managing

C.G. Fixings Limited
Incorporated: 14 February 2003 *Employees:* 10
Net Worth: £686,941 *Total Assets:* £2,867,238
Registered Office: Park 2000, Millennium Way, Newton Aycliffe, Co Durham, DL5 6AR
Activities: Non-specialised wholesale trade
Shareholder: Suzanne Guy
Officers: Suzanne Guy, Secretary/Director; Christopher Martin Guy [1971] Director; Suzanne Guy [1971] Director

C.P.S. Haulage (Tyneside) Limited
Incorporated: 23 August 1976 *Employees:* 2
Net Worth: £2,598,242 *Total Assets:* £2,651,016
Registered Office: c/o Tindles LLP, Scotswood House, Teesdale South, Thornaby Place, Stockton on Tees, Cleveland, TS17 6SB
Activities: Development of building projects
Major Shareholder: Robert Ralph Tindle
Officers: Robert Ralph Tindle, Secretary; Robert Ralph Tindle [1957] Director/Chartered Accountant; Michael Whinham [1939] Director

C.R.D. Devices Ltd.
Incorporated: 5 October 1995 *Employees:* 10
Net Worth: £239,864 *Total Assets:* £988,883
Registered Office: Unit 3 All Saints Industrial Estate, Shildon, Co Durham, DL4 2RD
Activities: Manufacture of electronic components
Shareholders: Alison Cockrill; Kathryn Robinson
Officers: Stuart George Charles Cockrill, Secretary/Sales Manager; Stuart George Charles Cockrill [1963] Director; David George Robinson [1963] Director

C.R.T. Packaging (U.K.) Limited
Incorporated: 15 March 1996 *Employees:* 3
Net Worth: £1,457,383 *Total Assets:* £3,024,089
Registered Office: 5 Berrymoor Court, Northumberland Business Park, Cramlington, Northumberland, NE23 7RZ
Activities: Agents specialised in the sale of other particular products
Major Shareholder: Colin Robinson
Officers: Janice Robinson, Secretary; Steven John Halliday [1968] Director/Accountant; Colin Robinson [1961] Director/Sales Manager

Cabe Property Limited
Incorporated: 5 August 2013
Net Worth: £446,438 *Total Assets:* £2,843,561
Registered Office: Ebac Limited, Ketton Way, Aycliffe Industrial Park, Newton Aycliffe, Co Durham, DL5 6SQ
Activities: Other letting and operating of own or leased real estate
Shareholders: Pamela Petty; Amanda Hird; Phillip Elliott
Officers: Pamela Petty, Secretary; John Malcolm Elliott [1943] Director

Cable Jointing Services Limited
Incorporated: 21 July 1981 *Employees:* 14
Net Worth: £530,835 *Total Assets:* £879,452
Registered Office: North Farm House, Warden Law, Houghton-le-Spring, Co Durham, DH5 8LX
Activities: Electrical installation
Officers: Debra Garbutt, Secretary; Christopher Andrew Hunter [1980] Director/HV Jointer

Cable Properties and Investments Limited
Incorporated: 17 August 2005 *Employees:* 14
Net Worth: £128,027,968 *Total Assets:* £137,465,568
Registered Office: Riverside Park Road, Middlesbrough, Cleveland, TS2 1QW
Activities: Buying and selling of own real estate
Officers: Janice Robson, Secretary; Alastair Powell [1952] Director; Michael Powell [1957] Director

Cablecom Training Limited
Incorporated: 28 February 2000 *Employees:* 22
Net Worth: £94,901 *Total Assets:* £1,470,240
Registered Office: 1 Wylam Court, Westland Way, Preston Farm Industrial Estate, Stockton on Tees, Cleveland, TS18 3FB
Activities: Technical and vocational secondary education
Shareholders: Roy Fraser; Sean Ratchford
Officers: Roy Fraser, Secretary; Roy Fraser [1956] Director/Training Manager; Anthony John Horridge [1964] Managing Director

Nigel Cabourn Marketing Limited
Incorporated: 28 July 2008
Net Worth Deficit: £1,573,980 *Total Assets:* £1,054,802
Registered Office: Principal House, 5 Back Grove Avenue, Gosforth, Newcastle upon Tyne, NE3 1NT
Activities: Wholesale of clothing and footwear
Shareholder: Reiko Himeda
Officers: Nigel John Cabourn [1949] Director; Andrew Shane [1954] Director; Isamu Sugure [1943] Director [Japanese]; Naoki Takeda [1965] Director [Japanese]

CACDP
Incorporated: 15 June 1998 *Employees:* 23
Net Worth: £805,101 *Total Assets:* £1,705,110
Registered Office: Mersey House, Mandale Park, Belmont Industrial Estate, Durham, DH1 1TH
Activities: Other education n.e.c.
Officers: Lindsay Jane Foster, Secretary; Helen Jane Beaton [1965] Director/Accountant; Alan Martin Blunt [1962] Director/Consultant; Liz Duncan [1964] Director/Teacher/Youthworker; Mark Hopkinson [1967] Director/Head of Department, Education; Paul Hamilton Keen [1951] Director/Retired; Karen Anne Riley [1958] Director/Retired Headteacher; Ian John Robinson [1958] Director/Trainer and Consultant on Deaf Issues; John David Walker [1972] Director/Lecturer

Cad 21 Holdings Limited
Incorporated: 23 March 2016
Net Worth: £675,117 *Total Assets:* £1,321,132
Registered Office: Unit 12 Berrymoor Court, Northumberland Business Park, Cramlington, Northumberland, NE23 7RZ
Activities: Activities of other holding companies n.e.c.
Shareholders: Garry Melvin Charlton; Peter Graham Ather
Officers: Peter Graham Ather [1971] Director; Garry Melvin Charlton [1972] Director; Tony Eric Grainger [1961] Director/Chartered Engineer

Cad 21 Limited
Incorporated: 24 November 1998 *Employees:* 38
Net Worth: £573,029 *Total Assets:* £1,252,611
Registered Office: 12 Berrymoor Court, Northumberland Business Park, Cramlington, Northumberland, NE23 7RZ
Activities: Other engineering activities
Shareholders: Garry Melvin Charlton; Peter Graham Ather
Officers: Peter Graham Ather [1971] Director/Chartered Engineer; Garry Melvin Charlton [1972] Director/Chartered Engineer

Cafe Twentyone Newcastle Limited
Incorporated: 21 September 1987
Net Worth: £278,256 *Total Assets:* £1,548,562
Registered Office: Pandon House, Trinity Gardens, Newcastle upon Tyne, NE1 2HH
Activities: Licenced restaurants
Parent: 21 Hospitality Group Limited
Officers: Catherine Laybourne, Secretary; Laurance Laybourne [1944] Director

Calamander Developments Limited
Incorporated: 31 July 2001 *Employees:* 8
Net Worth: £12,591,018 *Total Assets:* £14,002,368
Registered Office: 1 Station Lane, Gilesgate Roundabout, Durham, DH1 1LJ
Activities: Other letting and operating of own or leased real estate
Shareholder: Nancy Knight McIntyre
Officers: James Christopher Grimston Luckin, Company Secretary; James Christopher Grimston Luckin [1971] Director/Company Secretary; Philippa Nancy Luckin [1974] Director; Nancy Knight McIntyre [1944] Director

Caledonian Decking & Fencing Limited
Incorporated: 16 May 2014
Net Worth: £488,996 *Total Assets:* £781,823
Registered Office: Bells Close Industrial Estate, Lemington, Newcastle upon Tyne, NE15 6UF
Activities: Other specialised construction activities n.e.c.
Shareholders: John Murray; Susan Lynne Murray
Officers: Susan Lynne Murray, Secretary; John Murray [1960] Director

Caledonian Environmental Levenmouth Treatment Services Limited
Incorporated: 12 May 2000 *Employees:* 16
Net Worth: £3,628,000 *Total Assets:* £4,545,000
Registered Office: Northumbria House, Abbey Road, Pity Me, Durham, DH1 5FJ
Activities: Sewerage
Parent: NWG Commercial Solutions Limited
Officers: Martin Parker, Secretary; James Henry John King [1966] Director; Graham Brinsley Southall [1965] Commercial Director in Water Sector; Richard Warneford [1969] Waste Water Director

Caledonian Trust PLC.
Incorporated: 27 January 1972 *Employees:* 8
Net Worth: £19,055,000 *Total Assets:* £24,175,000
Registered Office: St Anns Wharf, 112 Quayside, Newcastle upon Tyne, NE99 1SB
Activities: Mixed farming
Major Shareholder: Ian Douglas Lowe
Officers: Michael James Baynham, Secretary; Michael James Baynham [1956] Lawyer & Director; Ian Douglas Lowe [1937] Director; Roderick John Pearson [1954] Director/Chartered Surveyor

Calenergy Gas (Holdings) Limited
Incorporated: 9 December 1992
Net Worth: £37,776,000 *Total Assets:* £74,556,000
Registered Office: Lloyds Court, 78 Grey Street, Newcastle upon Tyne, NE1 6AF
Activities: Activities of other holding companies n.e.c.
Parent: Northern Powergrid Gas Limited
Officers: Jennifer Catherine Riley, Secretary; Thomas Edward Fielden [1970] Director/Chartered Accountant; Thomas Hugh France [1985] Director/Lawyer; Dr Philip Antony Jones [1968] Director/President & Chief Executive Officer; Michael Jack Sparkes [1959] Director/Manager

Calenergy Resources Limited
Incorporated: 12 August 2002 *Employees:* 5
Net Worth: £15,588,000 *Total Assets:* £74,293,000
Registered Office: Lloyds Court, 78 Grey Street, Newcastle upon Tyne, NE1 6AF
Activities: Other business support service activities n.e.c.
Parent: Calenergy Gas (Holdings) Limited
Officers: Jennifer Catherine Riley, Secretary; Thomas Edward Fielden [1970] Director/Chartered Accountant; Thomas Hugh France [1985] Director/Lawyer; Dr Philip Antony Jones [1968] Director/President & Chief Executive Officer; Stephen John Lockwood [1965] Director/Accountant; Michael Jack Sparkes [1959] Director/Manager

Calibrate Inc Ltd
Incorporated: 1 November 2012
Net Worth: £512,931 *Total Assets:* £2,142,248
Registered Office: West Cottage, Amerside Law Farm, Chatton, Alnwick, Northumberland, NE66 5RF
Activities: Other engineering activities
Shareholder: Susan Elizabeth McDonald
Officers: Shane Robert McDonald [1979] Director/Engineer [New Zealander]; Susan Elizabeth McDonald [1983] Director/Business Consultant

Calibre Properties Limited
Incorporated: 27 September 2002
Registered Office: c/o Union Property Services Ltd, Cobalt 3.1, Silver Fox Way, Cobalt Business Park, Newcastle upon Tyne, NE27 0QJ
Activities: Renting and operating of Housing Association real estate
Major Shareholder: Manoj Vedhara
Officers: Mukesh Kumar Sehgal [1949] Director; Promila Sehgal [1948] Director

The Callaly Estates Company Limited
Incorporated: 7 March 1940
Net Worth: £21,525,788 *Total Assets:* £22,828,780
Registered Office: Callaly Stables, Whittingham, Alnwick, Northumberland, NE66 4TA
Activities: Mixed farming
Major Shareholder: Alexander Simon Richard Bateson
Officers: Alexander Simon Richard Bateson, Secretary; Alexander Simon Richard Bateson [1954] Director/Farmer; Rupert Peter Conyers Wailes-Fairbairn [1966] Director/Farmer Insurance Broker

Callaly Leisure Limited
Incorporated: 20 December 2005 *Employees:* 39
Net Worth: £1,978,926 *Total Assets:* £7,866,130
Registered Office: Riverside Rothbury Holiday Park, Rothbury, Northumberland, NE65 7QL
Activities: Recreational vehicle parks, trailer parks and camping grounds
Shareholder: Richard Bateson
Officers: Stephanie Warnes, Secretary; Alexander Simon Richard Bateson [1954] Director/Farmer; Andrew Warnes [1966] Director/Developments Manager

Calmband Limited
Incorporated: 17 May 2000
Net Worth: £742,353 *Total Assets:* £1,476,194
Registered Office: 7 Regents Drive, Prudhoe, Northumberland, NE42 6PX
Activities: Activities of head offices
Parent: Converse Pharma
Officers: Mark Gulliford [1969] Director; Derek Andrew Wilson [1964] Director/Chartered Accountant

Calmor Limited
Incorporated: 20 January 2009 *Employees:* 9
Net Worth Deficit: £4,172,205 *Total Assets:* £901,590
Registered Office: 80 Victoria Road, Darlington, Co Durham, DL1 5JG
Activities: Combined office administrative service activities
Shareholders: Eric Dodd; Julian Nicholas Coulthard
Officers: Eric Dodd, Secretary; Julian Nicholas Coulthard [1959] Director; Eric Dodd [1947] Director

A.R. Calvert (Leyburn) Limited
Incorporated: 14 July 1965 *Employees:* 33
Net Worth: £2,739,374 *Total Assets:* £3,164,648
Registered Office: Thornton House, Leyburn Business Park, Harmby Road, Leyburn, N Yorks, DL8 5QA
Activities: Construction of domestic buildings
Shareholders: Andrew Daniel Calvert; Albert Richard Calvert
Officers: Olive Ann Calvert, Secretary; Albert Richard Calvert [1928] Director/Builder; Andrew Daniel Calvert [1971] Director/Builder; Olive Ann Calvert [1944] Director/Secretary; Paul Robert Sadler [1963] Director/Joiner

A.D. Calvert Architectural Stone Supplies Limited
Incorporated: 24 November 2000 *Employees:* 32
Net Worth: £3,515,524 *Total Assets:* £3,994,428
Registered Office: The Stoneyard, Wensley Road, Leyburn, N Yorks, DL8 5ED
Activities: Quarrying of ornamental and building stone, limestone, gypsum, chalk and slate
Parent: Andrew Daniel Calvert
Officers: Peter Eric Reed, Secretary; Allison Jane Calvert [1972] Director; Andrew Daniel Calvert [1971] Director/Stone Supplier

Cambridge Photonics Limited
Incorporated: 26 September 2000 *Employees:* 3
Net Worth: £2,740,785 *Total Assets:* £2,902,892
Registered Office: Administrative Building, Thomas Swan & Co Ltd, Rotary Way, Consett, Co Durham, DH8 7ND
Activities: Other research and experimental development on natural sciences and engineering
Parent: Thomas Swan & Co. Ltd.
Officers: Ian George Bonas [1942] Director; Harry MacKlyn Swan [1976] Managing Director

Cambridge Scholars Publishing Ltd
Incorporated: 4 December 2001
Net Worth: £1,577,507 *Total Assets:* £1,991,827
Registered Office: Lady Stephenson Library, Welbeck Road, Newcastle upon Tyne, NE6 2PA
Activities: Book publishing
Parent: Timec 1306 Limited
Officers: Kourosh Manoucheri [1955] Director; Graeme Robert Campbell Nicol [1968] Director/Chief Executive Officer; Malcolm Andrew Vaughan [1961] Director

Camden Estates (North Shields) Limited
Incorporated: 18 May 1939 *Employees:* 4
Net Worth: £1,006,962 *Total Assets:* £1,209,280
Registered Office: 18 Northumberland Square, North Shields, Tyne & Wear, NE30 1PX
Activities: Other letting and operating of own or leased real estate
Shareholders: Caroline Ann Jackson; Peter Richard Jackson
Officers: Robert Alan Storey, Secretary/Chartered Surveyor; Caroline Ann Jackson [1953] Director/Housewife; Peter Richard Jackson [1949] Director/Chartered Surveyor; Richard Merlin Jackson [1980] Director/Chartered Surveyor; Robert Alan Storey [1956] Director/Chartered Surveyor

Cameron Hall Developments Limited
Incorporated: 19 October 1976 *Employees:* 192
Net Worth: £22,694,000 *Total Assets:* £24,453,000
Registered Office: Wynyard Hall, Billingham, Cleveland, TS22 5NF
Activities: Development of building projects
Officers: Allison Antonopoulos [1960] Director; Paul Anthony MacKings [1961] Director

Cameron's Builders (Newcastle) Limited
Incorporated: 15 March 1973
Net Worth: £1,802,424 *Total Assets:* £2,053,379
Registered Office: 12 Bankside, The Watermark, Gateshead, Tyne & Wear, NE11 9SY
Activities: Construction of other civil engineering projects n.e.c.
Parent: Cameron Builders Newcastle (Holdings) Limited
Officers: John Cameron Wigham, Secretary; Carole Ann Wigham [1945] Director/Married Woman; John Cameron Wigham [1945] Director/Builder

Camerons Brewery Limited
Incorporated: 27 May 1998 *Employees:* 458
Net Worth: £16,029,964 *Total Assets:* £56,824,420
Registered Office: Main Gate House, Waldon Street, Hartlepool, Cleveland, TS24 7QS
Activities: Manufacture of beer
Shareholders: David John Soley; Ramscove Ltd
Officers: John Richard Foots, Secretary; John Richard Foots [1968] Director/Chartered Accountant; Christopher David Soley [1975] Commercial Director; David John Soley [1949] Director/Management Consultant

DJ Camp Ltd
Incorporated: 23 November 2005 *Employees:* 22
Net Worth: £488,121 *Total Assets:* £817,853
Registered Office: 37-38 Market Street, Ferryhill, Co Durham, DL17 8JH
Activities: Manufacture of metal structures and parts of structures
Shareholders: Robert Malcolm Camp; Clare Camp
Officers: Clare Camp, Secretary; Steven John Bassett [1981] Director; Clare Camp [1975] Director/Nursery Nurse; Robert Malcolm Camp [1971] Director/Steel Fabricator

Campbell & Hall Engineering Limited
Incorporated: 8 July 2002
Net Worth: £720,553 *Total Assets:* £927,633
Registered Office: Bewley House, Alvis Close, Cowpen Industrial Estate, Billingham, Cleveland, TS23 4JB
Activities: Activities of other holding companies n.e.c.
Major Shareholder: Paul Anthony Messham
Officers: Edith Ann Messham, Secretary; Paul Anthony Messham [1965] Director/Engineer

R Campbell & Sons Limited
Incorporated: 31 October 2001 *Employees:* 26
Net Worth: £1,771,733 *Total Assets:* £2,237,896
Registered Office: Swan House, Westpoint Road, Thornaby, Stockton on Tees, Cleveland, TS17 6BP
Activities: Other retail sale in non-specialised stores
Shareholder: Kathleen Campbell
Officers: Kathleen Campbell, Secretary; Kathleen Campbell [1973] Director

Campbell Properties Limited
Incorporated: 25 September 1980
Net Worth: £1,114,337 *Total Assets:* £1,195,948
Registered Office: Hollinside Hall, Lanchester, Co Durham, DH7 0RN
Activities: Management of real estate on a fee or contract basis
Shareholders: Walter Brown Morris; Maureen Maria Morris
Officers: Laura Morris, Secretary; Laura Anne Morris [1977] Director; Walter Brown Morris [1946] Director/Builder

Campuslifestyle (Houses) Ltd
Incorporated: 23 February 2004
Net Worth: £739,218 *Total Assets:* £3,818,382
Registered Office: 190 Linthorpe Road, Middlesbrough, Cleveland, TS1 3RF
Activities: Other letting and operating of own or leased real estate
Officers: Stephen Morris, Secretary; Stephen John Michael Morris [1956] Director; Julian Charles Oliver Pilling [1971] Director

Canford Audio PLC
Incorporated: 25 August 1978 *Employees:* 141
Net Worth: £2,311,709 *Total Assets:* £4,930,101
Registered Office: Crowther Road, Washington, Tyne & Wear, NE38 0BW
Activities: Manufacture of electronic components
Parent: Canford Group Limited
Officers: John Stuart Francis, Secretary; Herr Werner Bachmann [1954] Director/Retired CEO; Consultant [Austrian]; Iain Stewart Elliott [1952] Director; John Stuart Francis [1952] Director/Chartered Accountant; John Alexander Slider [1946] Director

Canford Group Limited
Incorporated: 5 February 1996 *Employees:* 145
Net Worth: £3,160,441 *Total Assets:* £5,952,339
Registered Office: Crowther Road, Washington, Tyne & Wear, NE38 0BW
Activities: Other letting and operating of own or leased real estate
Shareholder: Elizabeth Anne Elliott
Officers: John Stuart Francis, Secretary; Herr Werner Bachmann [1954] Director/Retired CEO; Consultant [Austrian]; Iain Stewart Elliott [1952] Director; John Stuart Francis [1952] Director/Chartered Accountant; John Alexander Slider [1946] Director

Capital Properties Solutions Limited
Incorporated: 19 April 2004
Net Worth: £506,351 *Total Assets:* £2,339,958
Registered Office: 53 George Street, Newcastle upon Tyne, NE4 7JN
Activities: Other letting and operating of own or leased real estate
Major Shareholder: Sarwar Hakim
Officers: Sarwar Hakim, Secretary; Saleem Hakim [1967] Director/Manager; Sarwar Hakim [1955] Director/Property Management

Car Construction (North East) Ltd
Incorporated: 3 April 2014 *Employees:* 15
Net Worth: £739,562 *Total Assets:* £970,311
Registered Office: 27 Newhouse Avenue, Esh Winning, Co Durham, DH7 9JH
Activities: Construction of domestic buildings
Major Shareholder: Colin Askew
Officers: Colin Askew [1965] Director/Builder

Carbis Filtration Limited
Incorporated: 24 February 2003 *Employees:* 11
Net Worth: £2,355,508 *Total Assets:* £2,957,031
Registered Office: Barrington House, 41-45 Yarm Lane, Stockton on Tees, Cleveland, TS18 3EA
Activities: Agents involved in the sale of machinery, industrial equipment, ships and aircraft
Shareholders: Michael Riley; Simon Riley
Officers: Michael Riley, Secretary/Managing Director; Michael Riley [1944] Managing Director; Simon Riley [1971] Sales Director

Carbon8 Ltd
Incorporated: 6 May 2010
Net Worth: £501,254 *Total Assets:* £1,499,867
Registered Office: 23 Springhouse Lane, Ebchester, Consett, Co Durham, DH8 0QF
Activities: Manufacture of electric lighting equipment
Shareholders: Alison Murphy; John Ronald Murphy
Officers: Alison Murphy, Secretary; John Ronald Murphy [1966] Director/Computer Engineer

Card Trix [Greetings] Limited
Incorporated: 30 April 2002 *Employees:* 125
Net Worth: £1,345,523 *Total Assets:* £3,307,402
Registered Office: Unit 1 Hall Dene Way, Seaham Grange Industrial Estate, Seaham, Co Durham, SR7 0PU
Activities: Other food services
Officers: Stuart Freeman, Secretary; Andrea Phyllis Freeman [1965] Director; Craig Stevan Freeman [1967] Director; Georgette Edwina Freeman [1963] Director; Stuart Freeman [1960] Director

Cardiff Educational Endowment Trust
Incorporated: 11 February 2008 *Employees:* 110
Net Worth Deficit: £1,949,061 *Total Assets:* £9,302,555
Registered Office: Womble Bond Dickinson (UK) LLP, St Anns Wharf, 112 Quayside, Newcastle upon Tyne, NE1 3DX
Activities: Other business support service activities n.e.c.
Officers: Niaz Ali Khan [1968] Director [Pakistani]; Tubasum Munawar [1989] Director/Pharmacist [Malaysian]

Care and Share Associates One (2014) Limited
Incorporated: 18 July 2014 *Employees:* 1,049
Net Worth Deficit: £396,567 *Total Assets:* £2,120,277
Registered Office: 3 Benton Terrace, Jesmond, Newcastle upon Tyne, NE2 1QU
Activities: Social work activities without accommodation for the elderly and disabled
Shareholders: Bronwyn Burgess; Wendy McIntyre; Mandy Hearn; Ed Robson; Joanne Barr; Stephen McKay; Clare Skipper; Deanne Patricia McBride; Patrick Delisle Burns; Ann Christine Tyler
Officers: Lance Kenneth Gardner [1960] Director/Chairman; Sharon Teresa Lowrie [1978] Managing Director; Hayley Louise Quinn [1972] Director; Craig Slater [1963] Director; Georg Stratenwerth [1960] Director/Partner in Private Equity Firm [German]

Care-Ability Healthcare Limited
Incorporated: 7 June 2011
Net Worth: £971,617 *Total Assets:* £2,332,608
Registered Office: Phoenix House, Walton Road, Pattinson Industrial Estate North, Washington, Tyne & Wear, NE38 8QE
Activities: Other retail sale of new goods in specialised stores (not commercial art galleries and opticians)
Shareholders: David Anthony Tilly; Penny Maureen Tilly
Officers: David Anthony Tilly [1963] Director; Penny Maureen Tilly [1962] Director

Careline Lifestyles (UK) Ltd
Incorporated: 4 December 2006 *Employees:* 263
Net Worth: £1,774,141 *Total Assets:* £8,250,608
Registered Office: Onc Central Parkway, Newcastle upon Tyne, NE1 3BZ
Activities: Residential care activities for learning difficulties, mental health and substance abuse
Shareholders: Rahul Sharma; Dr Swatanter Bahrat Sharma
Officers: Archana Shama, Secretary; Rahul Sharma [1975] Director; Dr Swatanter Bahrat Sharma [1946] Director

Cares Group Holdings Limited
Incorporated: 7 October 1993 *Employees:* 33
Net Worth: £1,061,582 *Total Assets:* £1,558,413
Registered Office: The Old Hall, Byers Green, Spennymoor, Co Durham, DL16 7PS
Activities: Other social work activities without accommodation n.e.c.
Major Shareholder: James David Cassie
Officers: Lilian Isobel Cassie, Secretary; Esther Cassie [1977] Director; James David Cassie [1948] Director; Lilian Isobel Cassie [1949] Director; Laura Wilson [1978] Director/Veterinary Nurse

Carewell (Health Care) Limited
Incorporated: 28 November 1988 *Employees:* 34
Net Worth: £421,602 *Total Assets:* £810,021
Registered Office: Gainford House, Picktree Lane, Chester-le-Street, Co Durham, DH3 3SR
Activities: Medical nursing home activities
Officers: Susan McAlear [1951] Director

Caring Technology Limited
Incorporated: 18 December 2007 *Employees:* 2
Net Worth: £142,972 *Total Assets:* £3,028,748
Registered Office: Hinde House, Elswick East Terrace, George Street Industrial Estate, Newcastle upon Tyne, NE4 7LJ
Activities: Activities of head offices
Shareholders: Daniel Philip Adam Eastwood; Bryan Christopher Smith
Officers: Daniel Philip Adam Eastwood [1970] Technical Director; Bryan Christopher Smith [1965] Sales Director

Carlton Hill Properties Limited
Incorporated: 12 August 1996
Net Worth: £542,643 *Total Assets:* £966,809
Registered Office: 29 Axwell Park Road, Blaydon on Tyne, Tyne & Wear, NE21 5PB
Activities: Other letting and operating of own or leased real estate
Shareholders: Colette Marian Barker; John Keith Barker
Officers: Colette Marian Barker, Secretary; Colette Marian Barker [1954] Director/Teacher; John Keith Barker [1950] Director

Carlton Power Limited
Incorporated: 6 January 2014 *Employees:* 13
Net Worth: £287,554 *Total Assets:* £3,314,109
Registered Office: 4 Ellerbeck Way, Stokesley Business Park, Stokesley, Middlesbrough, Cleveland, TS9 5JZ
Activities: Development of building projects
Major Shareholder: Keith Clarke
Officers: Jayne Margaret Hodgson, Secretary; Michael Fred Shaw Benson [1964] Director; Keith Clarke [1960] Director; Jayne Margaret Hodgson [1963] Director/Company Secretary; David John Philpot [1961] Director/General Counsel; Matthew Ian Shields [1944] Director; Alan White [1961] Finance Director

Carmel Education Trust
Incorporated: 13 October 2011 *Employees:* 557
Net Worth: £5,391,000 *Total Assets:* £12,842,000
Registered Office: Carmel RC College, The Headlands, Darlington, Co Durham, DL3 8RW
Activities: General secondary education
Officers: Rev John Butters [1948] Director/Catholic Priest; James Matthew Cunningham [1961] Director/Police Officer; Peter Malcolm Frank [1946] Director/Retired Headteacher; Councillor Cynthia Beaver Hughes [1961] Director/Political and Legal Researcher; Janice Long [1953] Director/Schools Finance Partner (Retired); Maria Matthews [1952] Director/Headteacher (Retired); Patricia Ann McTimoney [1940] Director/Retired Headteacher; Catherine Alison Powell [1967] Director/Civil Servant; Maura Regan [1957] Director/Principal and Chief Executive Officer; Christopher Ronald Wiper [1956] Director/Solicitor

Carmel Structures Limited
Incorporated: 2 August 2000 *Employees:* 8
Net Worth: £327,333 *Total Assets:* £1,098,683
Registered Office: Birch House, Eastmount Road, Darlington, Co Durham, DL1 1LA
Activities: Other building completion and finishing
Shareholders: Terence Goodchild; Eileen Rita Marie Goodchild; Timothy Dominic Goodchild
Officers: Eileen Rita Marie Goodchild, Secretary; Eileen Rita Marie Goodchild [1954] Director; Terence Goodchild [1948] Managing Director; Timothy Dominic Goodchild [1973] Director/General Manager

Carnaby Steel Structures Limited
Incorporated: 28 January 2005
Registered Office: Brougham Enterprise Centre, Brougham Terrace, Hartlepool, Cleveland, TS24 8EY
Activities: Construction of commercial buildings
Shareholders: Roger Mark Phillips; Paul Johnson
Officers: Paul Johnson, Secretary/Director; Annamarie Johnson [1973] Director/Accounts and Sales; Paul Johnson [1971] Director; Andrea Phillips [1963] Director/Accounts and Sales; Roger Mark Phillips [1957] Director

Carousel Buses Limited
Incorporated: 30 August 2000 *Employees:* 77
Net Worth: £780,000 *Total Assets:* £3,293,000
Registered Office: 3rd Floor, 41-51 Grey Street, Newcastle upon Tyne, NE1 6EE
Activities: Other urban, suburban or metropolitan passenger land transport (not underground, metro or similar)
Parent: Go-Ahead Holding Limited
Officers: Carolyn Ferguson, Secretary; David Allen Brown [1960] Director; Simon Patrick Butcher [1967] Finance Director; Luke Carl Marion [1980] Director/Chartered Accountant; Philip Richard Southall [1976] Director; Raymond Woodhouse [1953] Director

Carpet Line Direct Limited
Incorporated: 31 October 1995 *Employees:* 8
Net Worth: £2,591,189 *Total Assets:* £7,379,870
Registered Office: Park View Road East, Brenda Road, Hartlepool, Cleveland, TS25 1HT
Activities: Wholesale of textiles
Parent: Whitestone Carpets Holdings Limited
Officers: Tanya Kelly, Secretary; Clive Nicholas Beckett [1969] Sales Director; Stephen Maurice Martin Byrne [1960] Director/Carpet Merchant; Nicholas Michael Finlay [1969] Company Sales Director; Geoffrey Brendon Wilding [1963] Director [New Zealander]

Carr & Co Solicitors (NE) Limited
Incorporated: 12 June 2014 *Employees:* 15
Net Worth: £208,103 *Total Assets:* £3,054,332
Registered Office: 229-231 High Street, Gosforth, Newcastle upon Tyne, NE3 1HQ
Activities: Solicitors
Shareholders: Valerie Wormald; Sharon Grace Smith
Officers: Victoria Bell [1977] Director; Sharon Grace Smith [1959] Director; Valerie Wormald [1957] Director

David Carr (Durham) Limited
Incorporated: 11 May 2009 *Employees:* 1
Net Worth: £367,319 *Total Assets:* £965,209
Registered Office: Kepier House, Belmont Business Park, Durham, DH1 1TW
Activities: Construction of other civil engineering projects n.e.c.
Major Shareholder: David Carr
Officers: David Carr [1972] Managing Director

Carraway Finance Ltd
Incorporated: 7 December 2000 *Employees:* 2
Net Worth Deficit: £2,175,148 *Total Assets:* £8,460,386
Registered Office: Nelson House, The Fleming Business Centre, Burdon Terrace, Jesmond, Newcastle upon Tyne, NE2 3AE
Activities: Other credit granting n.e.c.
Parent: Wylie Childrens Settlement
Officers: Kerry Louise McDonnell, Secretary; Andrew William Graham Wylie [1959] Director

Carrick Contractors Limited
Incorporated: 4 December 2002 *Employees:* 6
Net Worth: £1,158,205 *Total Assets:* £1,371,573
Registered Office: Ireshope Plains, Ireshopeburn, Bishop Auckland, Co Durham, DL13 1HG
Activities: Construction of commercial buildings
Shareholders: John Carrick; Kay Carrick
Officers: Kay Louise Carrick, Secretary; John Carrick [1964] Director/Farmer

Carrier Rental Systems Limited
Incorporated: 15 July 1999
Net Worth: £78,029,000 *Total Assets:* £78,029,000
Registered Office: Unit B, Colima Avenue, Sunderland Enterprise Park West, Sunderland, Tyne & Wear, SR5 3XE
Activities: Activities of head offices
Parent: United Technologies Holdings Limited
Officers: Simon Boniface, Secretary; Laura Wilcock, Secretary; Steven Blaby [1979] Director/Accountant; Archibald Ziwanemoyo Hungwe [1973] Director/General Manager; Simon Ross Harden McMullen [1969] Financial Director

Carroll & Meynell Transformers Limited
Incorporated: 10 August 2005 *Employees:* 85
Net Worth: £681,634 *Total Assets:* £4,462,158
Registered Office: Guiseley Way, Durham Lane Industrial Park, Stockton on Tees, Cleveland, TS16 0RF
Activities: Manufacture of electric motors, generators and transformers
Major Shareholder: Michael Meynell
Officers: Michael Meynell [1943] Director/Electrical Engineer

Carson Office Environments Limited
Incorporated: 5 February 1987
Net Worth: £536,077 *Total Assets:* £809,759
Registered Office: 8-10 Saltmeadows Road, Gateshead, Tyne & Wear, NE8 3AH
Activities: Wholesale of office furniture
Major Shareholder: Paul Bernard McIlduff
Officers: Paul Bernard McIlduff [1955] Managing Director

Geo.A.Carter Limited
Incorporated: 18 January 1952
Net Worth: £1,609,659 *Total Assets:* £2,022,680
Registered Office: Romaldkirk Hall, Romaldkirk, Barnard Castle, Co Durham, DL12 9ED
Activities: Buying and selling of own real estate
Major Shareholder: Ivan Carter
Officers: Ivan Seaward Carter Becker [1989] Director; Gillian Carter [1954] Director

Carter Steel Limited
Incorporated: 18 June 1970 *Employees:* 13
Net Worth: £953,414 *Total Assets:* £1,216,412
Registered Office: 43-45 Yarm Lane, Stockton on Tees, Cleveland, TS18 3EA
Activities: Wholesale of metals and metal ores
Shareholders: David Carter; Joan May Carter
Officers: Joan May Carter, Secretary; David Carter [1937] Director/Steel Stockist; James Geoffrey Carter [1966] Sales Director; Joan May Carter [1937] Director/Married Woman

Cartridge Tech Limited
Incorporated: 9 March 2006 *Employees:* 18
Net Worth: £975,849 *Total Assets:* £1,453,167
Registered Office: West 2, Asama Court, Newcastle Business Park, Newcastle upon Tyne, NE4 7YD
Activities: Information technology consultancy activities
Shareholders: Neil Kumar Dutta; Nicholas Chandra Dutta
Officers: Neil Kumar Dutta, Secretary; Neil Kumar Dutta [1981] Director; Nicholas Chandra Dutta [1983] Director

Caru Investments Limited
Incorporated: 3 July 2015
Net Worth: £1,595,948 *Total Assets:* £1,619,575
Registered Office: 6 Osbaldeston Gardens, Newcastle upon Tyne, NE3 4JE
Activities: Activities of head offices
Shareholder: Fiona Campbell Collins Fletcher
Officers: Alan Crawford Fletcher [1969] Director/Solicitor; Fiona Campbell Collins Fletcher [1969] Director

Casa Golf Homes Limited
Incorporated: 19 September 2012 *Employees:* 2
Net Worth: £71,192 *Total Assets:* £5,413,174
Registered Office: 511 Durham Road, Low Fell, Gateshead, Tyne & Wear, NE9 5EY
Activities: Other service activities n.e.c.
Major Shareholder: Andrew Patterson
Officers: Andrew Patterson [1963] Director

Casmaco Limited
Incorporated: 26 January 2012 *Employees:* 22
Net Worth Deficit: £46,792 *Total Assets:* £2,262,192
Registered Office: B3 Kingfisher House, Kingsway, Team Valley Trading Estate, Gateshead, Tyne & Wear, NE11 0JQ
Activities: Business and domestic software development
Parent: Business & Decision UK Limited
Officers: Bruno Pierre Ferdinand Mahieux [1963] Director [French]

Casper Shipping Holdings Limited
Incorporated: 28 August 2014
Net Worth: £135,835 *Total Assets:* £2,444,547
Registered Office: Tees Wharf, Dockside Road, Middlesbrough, Cleveland, TS3 6AH
Activities: Non-trading company
Major Shareholder: Michael Shakesheff
Officers: Helen Mary Shakesheff [1979] Director/Physiotherapist; Michael Shakesheff [1975] Director/Shipbroker

Casper Shipping Limited
Incorporated: 5 July 1990 *Employees:* 37
Net Worth: £587,582 *Total Assets:* £4,580,629
Registered Office: Tees Wharf, Dockside Road, Middlesbrough, Cleveland, TS3 6AH
Activities: Sea and coastal freight water transport
Officers: Alan Appleyard [1981] Director/Chartered Shipbroker; Robert William Bateman [1968] Business Development Director; John Mitchell [1957] Director/Shipping Agent; Michael Shakesheff [1975] Managing Director; Bryan Tismond [1948] Director/Shipping Agent

Cast Tec Limited
Incorporated: 17 September 2002
Net Worth: £163,153 *Total Assets:* £1,122,205
Registered Office: Unit 3b East Side, Tynedock, South Shields, Tyne & Wear, NE33 5SP
Activities: Wholesale of other intermediate products
Major Shareholder: Geoffrey Moore
Officers: Nithiyaraj Ellayathamby, Secretary; Anthony Byrne [1968] Director/Sales Representative; Brian Hart [1966] Director; Geoffrey Moore [1957] Managing Director

The Castle Building Services Organisation Limited
Incorporated: 14 December 2012 *Employees:* 179
Net Worth: £4,552,111 *Total Assets:* £13,708,522
Registered Office: 6 Merchant Court, Monkton Business Park South, Hebburn, Tyne & Wear, NE31 2EX
Activities: Electrical installation
Shareholders: Allan Carr; Anthony Philip Lister
Officers: Allan Carr [1962] Director; Andrew Dawson [1984] Director; Natalie Groom [1969] Director; Simon Groom [1970] Director; David Harland [1966] Director; Jayne Harland [1967] Director; Anthony Philip Lister [1961] Director; Carol Lister [1964] Director

Castle Commercial Services Limited
Incorporated: 11 September 2007
Registered Office: 27 Northumberland Square, North Shields, Tyne & Wear, NE30 1PW
Activities: Other letting and operating of own or leased real estate
Shareholders: Darren Purdy; Andrew Ford
Officers: Andrew David Ford, Secretary/Property Developer; Andrew David Ford [1972] Director/Property Developer; Darren John Joseph Purdy [1968] Director/Property Developer

Castle Construction (North East) Limited
Incorporated: 2 January 1997 *Employees:* 84
Net Worth: £740,631 *Total Assets:* £1,561,694
Registered Office: 12 Emmerson Street, Linthorpe, Middlesbrough, Cleveland, TS5 6JF
Activities: Other building completion and finishing
Shareholders: Colin Dorman; Bernadette Dorman
Officers: Colin Dorman, Secretary; Bernadette Dorman [1958] Director/Administration; Colin Dorman [1958] Director/Building Contractor

Castle Fabrication & Installation Limited
Incorporated: 2 August 1994 *Employees:* 21
Net Worth: £781,647 *Total Assets:* £981,885
Registered Office: Site No 8 Unit 3a, Cold Hesledon Industrial Estate, Cold Hesledon, Seaham, Co Durham, SR7 8ST
Activities: Manufacture of metal structures and parts of structures
Major Shareholder: David Andrew Evans
Officers: Jacqueline Anne Margaret Fenton, Secretary; David Andrew Evans [1967] Managing Director; Paul Whelam [1973] Director/Engineer

Castle Insurance Services (North East) Ltd
Incorporated: 26 February 2009 *Employees:* 20
Net Worth: £892,395 *Total Assets:* £1,187,346
Registered Office: 15 Marshall Terrace, Durham, DH1 2HX
Activities: Activities of insurance agents and brokers
Shareholders: Robert Paul Younger; Colin Phillip Younger
Officers: John Raymond Graham [1960] Director; Colin Philip Younger [1960] Director; Robert Paul Younger [1958] Director

Castle View Enterprise Academy
Incorporated: 4 June 2007 *Employees:* 124
Net Worth: £14,371,000 *Total Assets:* £15,534,000
Registered Office: Castle View Enterprise Academy, Cartwright Road, Sunderland, Tyne & Wear, SR5 3DX
Activities: General secondary education
Officers: Philip James Walker Smith, Secretary; Janet Susan Bridges [1960] Director/Headteacher; Barbara Joan Gubbins [1952] Director/Consultant; Louise Hunter [1975] Director; Richard John Hutton [1968] Finance Director; Rene Koglbauer [1977] University Lecturer/Executive Director [Austrian]; Claire Elizabeth Leighton [1965] Director/Finance Officer; Kieran Joseph McLaughlin [1972] Director/Headteacher; Heidi Mottram [1965] Director/Chief Executive Officer; Lynn Perry [1973] Director/HP Operations Manager; Andrew Edward Radcliffe [1973] Director; Michael Wooler [1955] Director/Headteacher (Retired); Aaron Michael Young [1986] Director/Architect

Castlegate Property Company Limited
Incorporated: 26 April 1947 *Employees:* 2
Net Worth: £1,300,590 *Total Assets:* £1,425,534
Registered Office: Joseph Miller & Co, Floor A, Milburn House, Dean Street, Newcastle upon Tyne, NE1 1LE
Activities: Other letting and operating of own or leased real estate
Officers: Sara Jane Chalmers, Secretary; Robert Anthony Burke [1938] Director/Chartered Architect; Sara Jane Chalmers [1966] Director/Chartered Surveyor

Castleson Ltd
Incorporated: 8 November 2013
Net Worth: £252,047 *Total Assets:* £1,460,876
Registered Office: 4-6 Market Street, Alnwick, Northumberland, NE66 1TL
Activities: Production of electricity
Shareholder: Hardcastle Renewables Limited
Officers: Amy Louise Hardcastle, Secretary; Amy Louise Hardcastle [1986] Director/Accountant; Richard Etherington Hardcastle [1984] Director/Farmer; Andrew Francis Megginson [1963] Director/Farmer; Simon John Megginson [1961] Director/Farmer

Castleview Group Training Limited
Incorporated: 6 November 2001 *Employees:* 42
Net Worth: £294,138 *Total Assets:* £2,135,588
Registered Office: 4 & 5 Lumley Court, Drum Industrial Estate, Chester-le-Street, Co Durham, DH2 1AN
Activities: Pre-primary education
Major Shareholder: Anthony Richard Healer
Officers: Michelle Healer, Secretary; Anthony Richard Healer [1975] Director/Training and Recruitment Consultant; Emma Louise Mawson [1982] Director

D.R. Caswell Limited
Incorporated: 1 September 1972 *Employees:* 40
Net Worth: £1,591,167 *Total Assets:* £5,023,384
Registered Office: Lagonda Road, Cowpen Industrial Estate, Billingham, Cleveland, TS23 4JA
Activities: Non-specialised wholesale trade
Major Shareholder: Peter Caswell
Officers: Geoffrey McCue, Secretary; Derick Robert Caswell [1926] Director; Peter Caswell [1959] Director; Paul Anthony Murphy [1976] Commercial Director

Catalyst Stockton-on-Tees Limited
Incorporated: 16 June 2000 *Employees:* 12
Net Worth: £720,439 *Total Assets:* £1,259,161
Registered Office: Catalyst House, 27 Yarm Road, Stockton on Tees, Cleveland, TS18 3NJ
Activities: Activities of other membership organisations n.e.c.
Officers: Aylia Lucia Atherley, Secretary; Paul Burgum [1979] Managing Director; Lesley Cooke [1954] Director/Teacher; Clara Jane Fawcett [1977] Director/Governance Officer; Oliver Simon Mack [1970] Managing Director; Christopher David Marshall [1986] Director/Area Manager; Guru Dhasaratha Naidoo [1951] Business Support Director; Steven L'anson Nelson [1957] Director/Councillor; William Williams [1949] Director/Principal

Catcote Futures
Incorporated: 21 October 2013 *Employees:* 39
Net Worth: £877,013 *Total Assets:* £1,012,814
Registered Office: c/o Hartlepool Aspire Trust, Catcote Academy, Catcote Road, Hartlepool, Cleveland, TS25 4EZ
Activities: Other education n.e.c.
Officers: Louise Annette Robson, Secretary; Alan Carr Chapman [1952] Director/Headteacher; Clare Ferguson [1952] Director/Retired; Joanne Hodgson [1970] Director/Nurse; Georgina Jones [1957] Director/Retired Teacher; Dr Graham Jones [1969] Director/Engineer; Roger Mark Phillips [1957] Managing Director, Carnaby Steel

Caterpak Limited
Incorporated: 22 April 2005 *Employees:* 11
Net Worth: £257,574 *Total Assets:* £945,824
Registered Office: Caterpak, Double Row, Seaton Delaval, Whitley Bay, Tyne & Wear, NE25 0PP
Activities: Wholesale of other food, including fish, crustaceans and molluscs
Shareholders: Peter Robert Burgon; Gary Robert Burgon; Stephen Philip Burgon
Officers: Gary Robert Burgon, Secretary; Gary Robert Burgon [1971] Director; Peter Robert Burgon [1947] Director; Stephen Philip Burgon [1983] Director

Caterpillar Skinningrove Limited
Incorporated: 2 June 1987 *Employees:* 53
Net Worth: £186,046,000 *Total Assets:* £188,894,000
Registered Office: Skinningrove Works, Carlin How, Saltburn-by-the-Sea, N Yorks, TS13 4EE
Activities: Manufacture of other fabricated metal products n.e.c.
Parent: Caterpillar (U.K.) Limited
Officers: Johanna Elizabeth Deason, Secretary; Neil Frederick Anderson [1960] Managing Director Skinningrove; Nigel John Burroughs [1964] Director/Tax Accountant; Philip Leslie James Handley [1961] Managing Director Peterlee; Kenneth Hoefling [1967] Director/General Manager [American]; Sandeep Virmani [1972] Director/Business Resource Manager; Donald Lee Young [1965] Director/Product Manager [American]

Cathie Associates Limited
Incorporated: 16 January 2006 *Employees:* 18
Net Worth: £515,601 *Total Assets:* £1,526,817
Registered Office: Collingwood Buildings, 38 Collingwood Street, Newcastle upon Tyne, NE1 1JF
Activities: Other engineering activities
Parent: Cathie Associates Holding SCRL
Officers: David Nigel Cathie, Secretary; David Nigel Cathie [1950] Director/Civil Engineer; Robin John Comrie [1968] Director/Engineering Geologist

Catterick Caravan & Camping Centre Limited
Incorporated: 21 November 2006 *Employees:* 61
Net Worth: £1,793,838 *Total Assets:* £9,157,478
Registered Office: Gatherley Road, Catterick Bridge, Richmond, N Yorks, DL10 7JB
Activities: Sale of other motor vehicles
Parent: Leisure World Group Limited
Officers: Christopher Michael Kinsell, Secretary; Christopher Michael Kinsell [1973] Director; Matthew Alexander Kinsell [1979] Sales Director

Catterick Service Station Ltd.
Incorporated: 24 July 1998
Net Worth: £403,033 *Total Assets:* £996,791
Registered Office: Momentum Taxation & Accountancy Ltd, Harelands Courtyard Offices, Moor Road, Melsonby, Richmond, N Yorks, DL10 5NY
Activities: Sale of used cars and light motor vehicles
Major Shareholder: Mary Chisholm
Officers: Mary Chisholm, Secretary/Director; Jonathon Paul Chisholm [1972] Director/Car Salesman; Mark John Chisholm [1970] Director/Car Salesman; Mary Chisholm [1948] Director

CAV Advanced Technologies Limited
Incorporated: 2 October 2008 *Employees:* 16
Net Worth: £6,399,818 *Total Assets:* £6,831,578
Registered Office: Number One Industrial Estate, Consett, Co Durham, DH8 6SR
Activities: Manufacture of air and spacecraft and related machinery
Parent: Caviar Bidco Limited
Officers: Richard John Dent Lowery, Secretary; Richard John Dent Lowery [1966] Director; Michael David Richards [1965] Director

CAV Ice Protection Limited
Incorporated: 3 October 2008 *Employees:* 111
Net Worth: £6,700,469 *Total Assets:* £11,032,427
Registered Office: Number One Industrial Estate, Consett, Co Durham, DH8 6SR
Activities: Manufacture of air and spacecraft and related machinery
Parent: Caviar Bidco Limited
Officers: Richard John Dent Lowery, Secretary; Richard John Dent Lowery [1966] Director; Michael David Richards [1965] Director

Cavendish (Northern) Limited
Incorporated: 21 October 1982
Net Worth: £2,282,284 *Total Assets:* £3,900,897
Registered Office: Beaumont House, Macklin Avenue, Cowpen Lane Industrial Estate, Billingham, Cleveland, TS23 4HF
Activities: Machining
Major Shareholder: Ian Brown
Officers: Vivienne Ann Brown, Secretary; Ian Brown [1956] Director/Engineer; Gillian Carol Hemlin [1957] Financial Director

Cavendish (Northern) Property Developments Limited
Incorporated: 3 December 2002
Net Worth: £951,865 *Total Assets:* £2,583,243
Registered Office: Beaumont House, Macklin Avenue, Cowpen Lane Industrial Estate, Billingham, Cleveland, TS23 4HF
Activities: Management of real estate on a fee or contract basis
Major Shareholder: Ian Brown
Officers: Vivienne Ann Brown, Secretary; Ian Brown [1956] Director/Engineer

Cavotec International Limited
Incorporated: 11 December 1992 *Employees:* 16
Net Worth: £3,927,836 *Total Assets:* £6,699,344
Registered Office: 32 Jay Avenue, Teesside Industrial Estate, Stockton on Tees, Cleveland, TS17 9LZ
Activities: Combined office administrative service activities
Parent: Cavotec Group Holdings NV
Officers: Peter Brandel [1950] Director [Swedish]; Peter Gary Matthews [1966] Director; Mikael Curt Norin [1963] Director [Swedish]; Stefan Lars Widegren [1950] Director/Civil Engineer [Swedish]

Cavotec UK Limited
Incorporated: 10 February 1986 *Employees:* 26
Net Worth: £5,087,463 *Total Assets:* £7,882,004
Registered Office: 32 Jay Avenue, Teesside Industrial Estate, Stockton on Tees, Cleveland, TS17 9LZ
Activities: Manufacture of other special-purpose machinery n.e.c.
Parent: Cavotec International Limited
Officers: Christopher Hammersley [1971] Director/Engineer; Peter Gary Matthews [1966] Director

Cavu Corporate Finance Limited
Incorporated: 22 May 2013 *Employees:* 4
Net Worth: £2,379,998 *Total Assets:* £2,754,595
Registered Office: Suite 6, City Quadrant, 11 Waterloo Square, Newcastle upon Tyne, NE1 4DP
Activities: Accounting and auditing activities
Shareholders: Shawn Bone; Fiona Pauline Douglas
Officers: Shawn Bone [1967] Director/Chartered Accountant; Fiona Pauline Douglas [1969] Director/Chartered Accountant

Cawingredients Limited
Incorporated: 20 June 2008 *Employees:* 173
Net Worth: £22,491,476 *Total Assets:* £60,866,140
Registered Office: Caw House, Conygarth Way, Leeming Bar Business Park, Leeming Bar, Northallerton, N Yorks, DL7 9FD
Activities: Manufacture of soft drinks; production of mineral waters and other bottled waters
Major Shareholder: Andrew James Cawthray
Officers: Mark Kevin Adamson [1984] Director/Chartered Accountant; Elizabeth Burkhardt [1986] Director; Andrew James Cawthray [1957] Director; Susan Cawthray [1958] Director; Hannah Harrison [1983] Director; Peter Richard Harrison [1979] Director; Andrew David Holt [1959] Director/Solicitor

CB Farms LLP
Incorporated: 5 August 2009
Net Worth: £5,295,602 *Total Assets:* £5,338,835
Registered Office: The Hall, Newton-le-Willows, Bedale, N Yorks, DL8 1SW
Officers: John Kenneth Bell [1974] Member; Leonidas Christophilopoulos [1969] Member; Helen Judith Bell [1973] LLP Member; Sorrel Harriet Katherine Scott Christophilopoulos [1970] LLP Member

CB Inn Limited
Incorporated: 6 July 2004
Net Worth: £753,050 *Total Assets:* £1,916,560
Registered Office: The Charles Bathurst Inn, Arkengarthdale, Reeth, Richmond, N Yorks, DL11 6EN
Activities: Hotels and similar accommodation
Shareholder: Charles Cody
Officers: Charles Frederick Cody [1954] Director/Hotelier

CCG Cable Terminations Limited
Incorporated: 15 January 2002 *Employees:* 6
Net Worth: £1,273,360 *Total Assets:* £1,664,149
Registered Office: Unit 31B Metcalfe Road, Skippers Lane Industrial Estate, Middlesbrough, Cleveland, TS6 6PT
Activities: Wholesale of other machinery and equipment
Officers: Nicholas Lackinger, Secretary; Franz Lackinger [1936] Director [German]; Nicholas Lackinger [1967] Director [South African]; Anthony Murray [1964] Director

CDM Recruitment Limited
Incorporated: 30 August 2002 *Employees:* 30
Net Worth: £576,609 *Total Assets:* £3,552,709
Registered Office: 16 Bluesky Way, Monkton Business Park, Hebburn, Tyne & Wear, NE31 2EQ
Activities: Other activities of employment placement agencies
Shareholders: Mark David Bulmer; Christopher Wall
Officers: Mark David Bulmer, Secretary/Recruitment Consultant; Mark David Bulmer [1974] Director/Recruitment Consultant; Christopher Wall [1973] Director/Recruitment Consultant

CE Holdings Limited
Incorporated: 14 June 2007
Net Worth: £673,605 *Total Assets:* £4,000,000
Registered Office: Bede House, St Cuthbert's Way, Aycliffe Industrial Park, Newton Aycliffe, Co Durham, DL5 6DX
Activities: Activities of head offices
Shareholders: Andrew Peter Hinton; Nicholas Andrew Wyatt
Officers: Andrew Peter Hinton [1952] Director; Nicholas Andrew Wyatt [1962] Director

The Cedars Academy Trust
Incorporated: 3 August 2012 *Employees:* 64
Net Worth: £4,569,000 *Total Assets:* £5,850,000
Registered Office: Cedars Academy Trust, Ivy Lane, Low Fell, Gateshead, Tyne & Wear, NE9 6QD
Activities: Other education n.e.c.
Officers: Alan Elders [1950] Director/Casual Athletics Coach; Martin Flowers [1962] Director/Headmaster; Sarah Louise Guy [1984] Director/Housewife; Maria Theresa Hall [1962] Managing Director; Tracey Jayne Higgins [1973] Director/Housewife; Paul William Hills [1967] Director/Civil Servant; Stuart Kay [1970] Director/Principal Engineer; Rachel Lane [1972] Director/HLTA; Lisa Miller [1978] Director/Housewife; Gill Morton [1968] Director/Housewife; Gordon William Neale [1945] Director/Disability Sport; Michelle Patricia O'Reilly [1977] Director/Assistant Headteacher; Julie Vincent [1983] Director/Teacher Business Partnership Development Manager

Ceefox Holdings Limited
Incorporated: 21 August 2015
Net Worth: £3,209,235 *Total Assets:* £3,210,703
Registered Office: 8 Adelaide Row, Seaham, Co Durham, SR7 7EF
Activities: Activities of other holding companies n.e.c.
Shareholders: James Foxcroft; Carol Anne Foxcroft; Lucy Foxcroft-Wardle
Officers: Carol Foxcroft, Secretary; Carol Anne Foxcroft [1962] Director; James Foxcroft [1949] Director; Lucy Foxcroft-Wardle [1988] Director; Robert Gale [1944] Director/Accountant

Ceefox Sports Consultancy Limited
Incorporated: 8 June 2011 *Employees:* 3
Net Worth: £173,255 *Total Assets:* £2,241,385
Registered Office: 8 Adelaide Row, Seaham, Co Durham, SR7 7EF
Activities: Other sports activities
Shareholders: James Foxcroft; Carol Anne Foxcroft; Lucy Foxcroft-Wardle
Officers: Carol Anne Foxcroft [1962] Director; James Foxcroft [1949] Director; Lucy Foxcroft-Wardle [1988] Sales Director; Robert Gale [1944] Director/Chartered Accountant

CEL Securus Ltd
Incorporated: 13 August 2002
Net Worth Deficit: £1,035,824 *Total Assets:* £972,564
Registered Office: 9-18 Ruby Court, Wesley Drive, Benton Square Industrial Estate, Newcastle upon Tyne, NE12 9UP
Activities: Electrical installation
Parent: Securus Group Limited
Officers: Anthony Denis Kane [1959] Director; John Stewart [1968] Director

Cell Pack Solutions Limited
Incorporated: 12 March 2001
Net Worth: £950,071 *Total Assets:* £1,506,276
Registered Office: 6 West Walpole Street, South Shields, Tyne & Wear, NE33 5BY
Activities: Manufacture of batteries and accumulators
Shareholders: Edward Czestochowski; Michelle Czestochowski
Officers: Michelle Czestochowski, Secretary; Edward Czestochowski [1962] Director/Battery Pack Technician; Michelle Czestochowski [1963] Director/Financial Controller

Cellular Solutions (North East) Ltd.
Incorporated: 2 July 1999 *Employees:* 38
Net Worth: £274,552 *Total Assets:* £2,222,799
Registered Office: Ferryboat House, Ferryboat Lane, Sunderland, Tyne & Wear, SR5 3JN
Activities: Wireless telecommunications activities
Shareholders: Michael Angus Bowers; Eileen Marie Bowers
Officers: Eileen Marie Bowers, Secretary; Michael Angus Bowers [1970] Director/Retail Manager

Cellular Solutions Holdings Limited
Incorporated: 5 April 2007
Net Worth: £96,289 *Total Assets:* £1,190,355
Registered Office: Ferryboat House, Ferryboat Lane, Sunderland, Tyne & Wear, SR5 3JN
Activities: Wireless telecommunications activities
Shareholders: Micahel Angus Bowers; Eileen Marie Bowers
Officers: Eileen Marie Bowers, Secretary; Michael Angus Bowers [1970] Director/Retail Manager

Celtic Aerospace Ventures Limited
Incorporated: 23 November 2000
Net Worth Deficit: £70,658,240 *Total Assets:* £1,372,221
Registered Office: c/o Muckle LLP, Time Central, 32 Gallowgate, Newcastle upon Tyne, NE1 4BF
Activities: Other business support service activities n.e.c.
Officers: Andrew David Willis Jones [1959] Director/Chartered Accountant

Cemmaes Windfarm Limited
Incorporated: 20 November 1991
Net Worth: £2,404,000 *Total Assets:* £4,828,000
Registered Office: Alexander House, 1 Mandarin Road, Rainton Bridge Business Park, Houghton-le-Spring, Co Durham, DH4 5RA
Activities: Production of electricity
Parent: EDF Energy Renewables Holdings Limited
Officers: Susan Elizabeth Lind, Secretary; Matthieu Thomas Hue [1975] Director [French]; Hassaan Majid [1968] Director

Cenelec Standards Inspections Limited
Incorporated: 2 September 1986
Net Worth: £855,196 *Total Assets:* £1,812,306
Registered Office: Unit 22 Apex Business Village, Northumberland Business Park, Cramlington, Northumberland, NE23 7BF
Activities: Repair of electrical equipment
Shareholder: Jonathan Lee Gibson
Officers: Pamela Catherine Gibson, Secretary/Director; Alan William Gibson [1948] Director; Jonathan Lee Gibson [1976] Director; Pamela Catherine Gibson [1947] Director; Steven Roy Peter Turner [1982] Director/Project Manager

Cenergist Limited
Incorporated: 24 August 2012 *Employees:* 15
Net Worth: £537,454 *Total Assets:* £2,743,673
Registered Office: 7 Bede House, Glover Industrial Estate, Washington, Tyne & Wear, NE37 2SH
Activities: Combined facilities support activities
Officers: Karolyn Scott, Secretary; Gary James Copeland [1959] Director/Solicitor; Mitesh Dhanak [1966] Director; Joseph Andrew Johnson [1959] Director/Retired; Ian Daniel McLeod [1968] Director; Hayley Louise Peters [1971] Programme Director; David Arthur Routledge [1958] Director; James Waring [1986] Finance Director

Central Employment Agency (North East) Limited
Incorporated: 26 March 1987 *Employees:* 469
Net Worth: £933,916 *Total Assets:* £3,155,927
Registered Office: 34-36 St Mary's Place, Newcastle upon Tyne, NE1 7PQ
Activities: Temporary employment agency activities
Parent: Decadeon Holdings Limited
Officers: Steven Hart, Secretary; Steven Hart [1975] Director; Paul John Ponton [1975] Director; Mark Andrew Trett [1979] Director

Central Plant (Northern) Limited
Incorporated: 6 September 1979
Net Worth: £103,019 *Total Assets:* £1,003,272
Registered Office: Central House, Ninth Avenue, Team Valley Trading Estate, Gateshead, Tyne & Wear, NE11 0EJ
Activities: Wholesale of other intermediate products
Officers: Katherine Clint, Secretary; Anthony Clint [1959] Director; Graham Clint [1965] Managing Director

Central Taxis Gateshead Ltd
Incorporated: 22 April 2009
Net Worth: £1,152,913 *Total Assets:* £3,688,967
Registered Office: Stoneygate House, Stoneygate Lane, Gateshead, Tyne & Wear, NE10 0HJ
Activities: Taxi operation
Major Shareholder: Mark Royal Nellist
Officers: Louise Nellist, Secretary; Mark Royal Nellist [1969] Director

Centralus 003 Ltd
Incorporated: 7 July 2016
Net Worth Deficit: £58,919 *Total Assets:* £3,026,591
Registered Office: Wynyard Park House, Wynyard Avenue, Wynyard, Cleveland, TS22 5TB
Activities: Human resources provision and management of human resources functions
Parent: Centralus Operations LLP
Officers: Jonathan Michael Beckerlegge [1945] Director/Certified Chartered Accountant

Centralus 004 Ltd
Incorporated: 7 October 2016
Net Worth Deficit: £66,987 *Total Assets:* £2,928,623
Registered Office: Wynyard Park House, Wynyard Avenue, Wynyard, Cleveland, TS22 5TB
Activities: Human resources provision and management of human resources functions
Parent: Centralus Operations LLP
Officers: Jonathan Michael Beckerlegge [1945] Director/Certified Chartered Accountant

Centralus Operations LLP
Incorporated: 31 March 2016
Net Worth: £31,166,868 *Total Assets:* £31,178,336
Registered Office: Wynyard Park House, Wynyard Avenue, Wynyard, Cleveland, TS22 5TB
Officers: Jonathan Michael Beckerlegge [1945] Member

Centre for Process Innovation Limited
Incorporated: 23 December 2003 *Employees:* 299
Net Worth: £54,652,000 *Total Assets:* £83,460,000
Registered Office: Wilton Centre, Wilton, Redcar, Cleveland, TS10 4RF
Activities: Research and experimental development on biotechnology
Officers: Nicola Kirtley, Secretary; Alexander Beveridge Anderson [1944] Director/Retired; Professor John Howard Anstee [1943] Director/Retired; Charles David Bragg [1956] Research Director; Mark Gibson [1953] Director; Dr Colin Robert Harrison [1948] Director; Professor Judith Ann Kathleen Howard [1945] Director/University Professor; Professor Trevor Francis Page [1946] Director/Retired; Nigel John Perry [1957] Director/Professional Chartered Engineer; Lady Jennie Veronica Younger [1956] Director

Centre for Sports Injury Surgery Limited
Incorporated: 19 October 2009 *Employees:* 2
Net Worth: £1,338,370 *Total Assets:* £1,402,479
Registered Office: School House, Bolton on Swale, Richmond, N Yorks, DL10 6AQ
Activities: Hospital activities
Shareholders: Anna Michelle Van Niekerk; Lodewicus Johannes Abraham Van Niekerk
Officers: Anna Michelle Van Niekerk [1976] Director; Lodewicus Johannes Abraham Van Niekerk [1963] Director/Orthopaedic Surgeon

Centre West (Newcastle)
Incorporated: 21 January 2002 *Employees:* 14
Net Worth: £4,799,213 *Total Assets:* £5,039,553
Registered Office: 28 Hawthorn Terrace, Elswick, Newcastle upon Tyne, NE4 6RJ
Activities: Other business support service activities n.e.c.
Officers: Revd George Robert Curry [1951] Director/Minister; Sarah Louise Douglas [1982] Director/Recruitment Consultant; Fergus James Laird [1965] Director/Chartered Surveyor; Geoffrey O'Brien [1952] Director/University Lecturer; Councillor Habib Rahman [1985] Director; Christopher Dennis Henry Waugh [1991] Director

Centrebus Holdings Limited
Incorporated: 26 March 2008 *Employees:* 54
Net Worth: £21,000 *Total Assets:* £2,890,000
Registered Office: 1 Admiral Way, Doxford International Business Park, Sunderland, Tyne & Wear, SR3 3XP
Activities: Other urban, suburban or metropolitan passenger land transport (not underground, metro or similar)
Officers: Lorna Edwards, Secretary; Mark Antony Bowd [1962] Director; Tina Colleen Edwards [1982] Director; Simon Joseph Finnie [1978] Director; Simon William Mathieson [1979] Director; Kevin Liam O'Leary [1962] Director; Jason Mathew Perkin [1974] Director; Cora Woodhouse [1978] Director

Centrex Computing Services Limited
Incorporated: 9 October 2006
Net Worth: £155,779 *Total Assets:* £1,489,280
Registered Office: 22 Wansbeck Business Centre, Wansbeck Business Park, Ashington, Northumberland, NE63 8QZ
Activities: Repair of computers and peripheral equipment
Major Shareholder: Michael William Heslop
Officers: Michael William Heslop [1956] Managing Director

Century Composites Limited
Incorporated: 30 June 1978 *Employees:* 23
Net Worth: £996,367 *Total Assets:* £1,126,294
Registered Office: 58-60 Hutton Close, Crowther, Washington, Tyne & Wear, NE38 0AH
Activities: Manufacture of man-made fibres
Shareholders: Anna Victoria Chilcott; Simon Philip Chilcott
Officers: James Chilcott, Secretary; Anna Victoria Chilcott [1953] Director; James Chilcott [1984] Director and Company Secretary; Michael Chilcott [1984] Director; Simon Phillip Chilcott [1950] Director/Fishing Rod Manufacturer

Ceramica Elegance Limited
Incorporated: 25 January 2007
Registered Office: 8 Anderson Green, Saltwell Business Park, Gateshead, Tyne & Wear, NE9 5BQ
Activities: Other service activities n.e.c.
Officers: Levent Gurocak [1970] Managing Director

Ceres Energy Limited
Incorporated: 1 February 2008 *Employees:* 1
Net Worth: £395,567 *Total Assets:* £2,169,582
Registered Office: Harlequin House, Clayton Road, Jesmond, Newcastle upon Tyne, NE2 4RP
Activities: Trade of gas through mains
Shareholders: Richard Harper; Helen Edwards
Officers: Helen Mary Edwards, Secretary/Director [Canadian]; Helen Mary Edwards [1956] Director [Canadian]; Jean Alison Harper [1960] Director/Event Management; Richard Harper [1961] Energy Consultant and Director; Professor Michael John Whitaker [1953] Director/Professor of Physiology

Certax Accounting (Durham) LLP
Incorporated: 9 December 2014
Net Worth: £375,324 *Total Assets:* £1,075,598
Registered Office: Unit 8 & 9 Parsons Court, Welbury Way, Aycliffe Industrial Park, Newton Aycliffe, Co Durham, DL5 6ZE
Officers: Matthew McConnell [1990] Member; Jonathan Gerard Tait [1990] Member

Cestrian Estates Ltd.
Incorporated: 10 March 1989 *Employees:* 3
Net Worth: £2,984,275 *Total Assets:* £3,116,210
Registered Office: 10 Ashfield Terrace, Chester-le-Street, Co Durham, DH3 3PD
Activities: Buying and selling of own real estate
Shareholder: Patrick Keith O'Brien
Officers: Aidan O'Brien, Secretary; Aidan O'Brien [1965] Director; Patrick Keith O'Brien [1960] Director

Chainbridge Steel (North East) Ltd
Incorporated: 14 July 1999 *Employees:* 34
Net Worth: £1,759,011 *Total Assets:* £5,245,596
Registered Office: Stephenson Industrial Estate, Rainhill Road, District 12, Washington, Tyne & Wear, NE37 3HU
Activities: Wholesale of metals and metal ores
Major Shareholder: Shaun Michael Harrison
Officers: Shaun Michael Harrison, Secretary; Shaun Michael Harrison [1963] Director

Chainbridge Steel Group Limited
Incorporated: 23 November 2006 *Employees:* 45
Net Worth: £3,370,911 *Total Assets:* £11,578,329
Registered Office: Rainhill Road, Stephenson Industrial Estate, Washington, Tyne & Wear, NE37 3HU
Activities: Wholesale of metals and metal ores
Major Shareholder: Shaun Michael Harrison
Officers: Shaun Michael Harrison, Secretary; Shaun Michael Harrison [1963] Managing Director

Challenging Learning Ltd
Incorporated: 12 August 2004 *Employees:* 21
Net Worth: £309,566 *Total Assets:* £926,406
Registered Office: 2 Linnet Court, Cawledge Business Park, Alnwick, Northumberland, NE66 2GD
Activities: Other education n.e.c.
Shareholder: James Andrew Nottingham
Officers: Jill Nottingham, Company Secretary; James Andrew Nottingham [1971] Director; Jill Nottingham [1976] Director

Chamberlin Agencies Limited
Incorporated: 13 April 2012 *Employees:* 6
Net Worth: £1,101,029 *Total Assets:* £1,458,229
Registered Office: 22 Basement Office, Foyle Street, Sunderland, Tyne & Wear, SR1 1LE
Activities: Agents involved in the sale of food, beverages and tobacco
Shareholders: Neville Edward Chamberlin; Rebecca Anne Chamberlin
Officers: Neville Edward Chamberlin [1947] Director/Sales; Rebecca Anne Chamberlin [1985] Director/Administration

H.C.Chambers & Son Limited
Incorporated: 3 May 1937 *Employees:* 41
Net Worth: £1,315,000 *Total Assets:* £1,553,000
Registered Office: 3rd Floor, 41-51 Grey Street, Newcastle upon Tyne, NE1 6EE
Activities: Other urban, suburban or metropolitan passenger land transport (not underground, metro or similar)
Parent: Go-Ahead Holding Limited
Officers: Carolyn Ferguson, Secretary; David Allen Brown [1960] Director; Simon Patrick Butcher [1967] Finance Director; Jeremy Hugh Cooper [1967] Director; Martin Richard Dean [1963] Director; David Hector Golding [1965] Director

Chameleon Bar & Dining Limited
Incorporated: 5 March 1999 *Employees:* 128
Net Worth: £973,484 *Total Assets:* £3,564,028
Registered Office: Belasis Business Centre, Coxwold Way, Billingham, Cleveland, TS23 4EA
Activities: Public houses and bars
Shareholders: Alistair Grant Arkley; Barry Whitehead
Officers: Barry Whitehead, Secretary/Director; Alistair Grant Arkley [1947] Managing Director; Barry Whitehead [1948] Director

Chan Commercial Ltd
Incorporated: 27 May 1988
Net Worth: £6,463,424 *Total Assets:* £8,404,748
Registered Office: 1 Norton Court, Norton Road, Stockton on Tees, Cleveland, TS20 2BL
Activities: Wholesale of clothing and footwear
Parent: Chan Property Group Limited
Officers: Apinder Singh Ghura [1963] Director; Khushninder Singh Ghura [1967] Director

Chan Property Group Limited
Incorporated: 22 March 2016
Net Worth: £658,668 *Total Assets:* £1,676,811
Registered Office: 1 Norton Court, Norton Road, Stockton on Tees, Cleveland, TS20 2BL
Activities: Buying and selling of own real estate
Shareholders: Apinder Singh Ghura; Khushninder Singh Ghura
Officers: Apinder Singh Ghura [1963] Director; Khushninder Singh Ghura [1967] Director

Chance Investments Ltd
Incorporated: 22 May 2014
Registered Office: Catterick House, Morton Road, Darlington, Co Durham, DL1 4PT
Activities: Other letting and operating of own or leased real estate
Major Shareholder: Philip Bland
Officers: Graham Jeffrey Bland [1966] Director; Philip Raymond Bland [1964] Director

Chancery Investments (NE) Ltd
Incorporated: 16 December 2015
Net Worth: £9,757 *Total Assets:* £1,396,530
Registered Office: 6 Chancery Rise, Thornaby, Stockton on Tees, Cleveland, TS17 0AZ
Activities: Other letting and operating of own or leased real estate
Officers: Israr Ahmed, Secretary; Israr Ahmed [1980] Director/Manager

Chandlers Ridge Academy
Incorporated: 19 July 2012
Registered Office: Chandlers Ridge Academy, Nunthorpe, Middlesbrough, Cleveland, TS7 0JL
Activities: Primary education

Changing Futures North East
Incorporated: 7 June 2000 *Employees:* 19
Net Worth: £770,752 *Total Assets:* £802,207
Registered Office: 3 Abbey Street, Headland, Hartlepool, Cleveland, TS24 0JR
Activities: Other education n.e.c.
Officers: Anthony Jackson, Secretary; Alison Marie Croymans [1966] Director; Jeanette Henderson [1965] Director; Anthony Nigel Jackson [1947] Director; David Michael Jeffrey [1967] Director; Sheila Statter [1950] Director; Jonathan Martyn Townshend [1975] Director/Commissioning Officer; Gillian Walker [1951] Director/Retired

Changing Health Limited
Incorporated: 18 December 2015 *Employees:* 2
Net Worth Deficit: £225,391 *Total Assets:* £934,237
Registered Office: 3rd Floor, Citygate, St James Boulevard, Newcastle upon Tyne, NE1 4JE
Activities: Educational support services
Officers: Simon Andrew Barnes [1969] Director/Venture Capital Fund Manager; John Paul George Grumitt [1965] Director/Chartered Accountant; Michael Iain Trenell [1975] Director/Medical Researcher

Chapter Homes Durham Limited
Incorporated: 10 August 2015
Net Worth: £1,835,650 *Total Assets:* £9,643,074
Registered Office: County Hall, Durham, DH1 5UL
Activities: Construction of domestic buildings
Parent: Durham County Council
Officers: David Norman Taylor, Secretary; Paul Darby [1970] Director; Alan Napier [1954] Director/Councillor; Sarah English Robson [1971] Director/Local Government Officer; Cllr Kevin Joseph Shaw [1958] Director

Charlton Blair Limited
Incorporated: 9 March 2012
Net Worth: £826,015 *Total Assets:* £1,800,908
Registered Office: 8 Winchester Drive, South West Industrial Estate, Peterlee, Co Durham, SR8 2JD
Activities: Other letting and operating of own or leased real estate
Shareholders: Alastair Blair; Timothy Blair
Officers: Alastair Blair [1987] Director; Timothy Blair [1988] Director

The Charlton Group Limited
Incorporated: 19 February 1999
Net Worth: £717,208 *Total Assets:* £787,199
Registered Office: Highford Cottage, Highford Lane, Hexham, Northumberland, NE46 2NA
Activities: Non-specialised wholesale trade
Major Shareholder: Angus Robert Charlton
Officers: Isabella Catherine Charlton, Secretary; Angus Robert Charlton [1964] Director/Builders Merchant

Matthew Charlton,Limited
Incorporated: 6 January 1939 *Employees:* 27
Net Worth: £653,870 *Total Assets:* £1,567,390
Registered Office: Charlton House, 135 Elswick Road, Newcastle upon Tyne, NE4 6SQ
Activities: Plumbing, heat and air-conditioning installation
Major Shareholder: Michael Joseph Blance
Officers: Lisa de Redder, Secretary; Michael Kristian Blance [1980] Director/Mechanical Services Engineer; Michael Joseph Blance [1946] Director/Heating Engineer

Charminster Estates Limited
Incorporated: 16 January 1995
Net Worth: £1,208,527 *Total Assets:* £5,020,091
Registered Office: 120-122 High Northgate, Darlington, Co Durham, DL1 1UR
Activities: Buying and selling of own real estate
Shareholder: Kenneth Roy Thomason
Officers: Richard Thomas Brooke Thomason, Secretary; Julia Ann Brooke Blower [1978] Director/Regeneration Consultant; Emily Sarah Brooke Close [1981] Director/Administrator; Kenneth Roy Thomason [1944] Director/Solicitor; Richard Thomas Brooke Thomason [1972] Managing Director

Charnley Marketing Limited
Incorporated: 7 June 2001 *Employees:* 2
Net Worth: £306,918 *Total Assets:* £965,844
Registered Office: Mount Pleasant, Scruton, Northallerton, N Yorks, DL7 0QZ
Activities: Agents selling agricultural raw materials, livestock, textile raw materials and semi-finished goods
Parent: Charnley Holdings Limited
Officers: Josephine Charnley, Secretary; James Andrew Charnley [1973] Director

Charterglobe Limited
Incorporated: 30 September 2009
Net Worth: £139,273 *Total Assets:* £2,970,083
Registered Office: Lion House, 400 Durham Road, Birtley, Chester-le-Street, Co Durham, DH3 1LS
Activities: Other letting and operating of own or leased real estate
Major Shareholder: Lucy Del Pattinson
Officers: Lucy Del Pattinson [1965] Director

Chartres Investment Company Limited
Incorporated: 14 June 1950 *Employees:* 4
Net Worth: £3,463,240 *Total Assets:* £6,107,656
Registered Office: Floor A, Milburn House, Dean Street, Newcastle upon Tyne, NE1 1LE
Activities: Buying and selling of own real estate
Officers: Barbara Mary Loffill, Secretary; Peter Cowen [1946] Director/Chartered Surveyor; Colin Dickinson [1940] Director/Solicitor; Simon James Dickinson [1969] Director; Barbara Mary Loffill [1954] Director/Solicitor; James Mark Rainbow [1966] Director/Stockbroker

Chatswell Properties Ltd
Incorporated: 3 June 2003
Net Worth: £410,484 *Total Assets:* £969,120
Registered Office: 15 Walker Terrace, Gateshead, Tyne & Wear, NE8 1EB
Activities: Dormant company
Shareholders: Joseph Schleider; David Schleider; Menachem Schleider
Officers: Joseph Schleider, Secretary; David Schleider [1959] Director/Estate Agent

Chavtown Properties Ltd
Incorporated: 5 August 2010
Net Worth: £616,621 *Total Assets:* £1,643,937
Registered Office: 205 Queen Alexandra Road, Sunderland, Tyne & Wear, SR3 1XS
Activities: Buying and selling of own real estate
Shareholders: Beverley Baxter; James Martin Baxter
Officers: James Martin Baxter, Secretary; Beverley Baxter [1963] Director; James Martin Baxter [1961] Director/Butcher

Check in USA Limited
Incorporated: 27 August 2002
Net Worth: £727,867 *Total Assets:* £2,033,890
Registered Office: Glen C Rodger Ltd, Cragside House, Heaton Road, Newcastle upon Tyne, NE6 1SE
Activities: Travel agency activities
Shareholders: Anthony Blackmore; Carolyn Lesley Blackmore
Officers: Carolyn Lesley Blackmore, Secretary; Anthony Blackmore [1972] Director/Travel Agent; Carolyn Lesley Blackmore [1971] Director

Cheeseburn Estate Management Company Limited
Incorporated: 5 April 2011
Net Worth: £28,987 *Total Assets:* £894,724
Registered Office: Cheeseburn Grange Hall, Stamfordham, Northumberland, NE18 0PT
Activities: Activities of head offices
Shareholders: Edward Simon Riddell; Simon Francis Riddell
Officers: Michael William Orde [1957] Director/Land Agent; Edward Simon Riddell [1989] Director; Joanna Lucy Riddell [1962] Director; Simon Francis Riddell [1961] Director

Chemcare Limited
Incorporated: 28 September 2004 *Employees:* 16
Net Worth: £401,119 *Total Assets:* £2,987,992
Registered Office: 79 Front Street, Stanley, Co Durham, DH9 0TB
Activities: Dispensing chemist in specialised stores
Major Shareholder: Louise Lydon
Officers: Laura Rowley, Secretary/Pharmacist; David Lydon [1978] Director/Pharmacy; Louise Lydon [1979] Director/Pharmacy Owner

Chemian Technology Limited
Incorporated: 22 December 1995
Net Worth: £558,480 *Total Assets:* £953,527
Registered Office: Unit 2 Eastmount Road, Darlington, Co Durham, DL1 1LA
Activities: Manufacture of pesticides and other agrochemical products
Shareholder: Ian Thomas Dell
Officers: Christine Barbara Hodgson, Secretary; Michael Ian Armstrong [1953] Director; Ian Thomas Dell [1958] Director/Salesman

Chemoxy International Limited
Incorporated: 3 March 1939 *Employees:* 147
Net Worth: £31,988,000 *Total Assets:* £38,587,000
Registered Office: All Saints Refinery, Cargo Fleet Road, Middlesbrough, Cleveland, TS3 6AF
Activities: Manufacture of other chemical products n.e.c.
Parent: Crossco (1255) Limited
Officers: Martyn John Bainbridge [1966] Director; Laurent Castor [1967] Director/Vice President Performance Chemical Division [French]; Neil Christopher McLoughlin [1965] Director/Management Accountant; Ian Stark [1957] Director

Chemplas Limited
Incorporated: 16 June 1970 *Employees:* 25
Net Worth: £824,805 *Total Assets:* £4,235,594
Registered Office: Triskell House, Brunswick Industrial Estate, Brunswick Village, Newcastle upon Tyne, NE13 7BA
Activities: Roofing activities
Major Shareholder: Adam John William Stone
Officers: Diana Jane Stone, Secretary; Derek Michael Brown [1963] Director; Adam John William Stone [1960] Managing Director; Diana Stone [1961] Director

Chemplas Roofing Services Ltd
Incorporated: 3 October 2000 *Employees:* 18
Net Worth: £817,335 *Total Assets:* £1,614,917
Registered Office: Triskell House, Brunswick Industrial Estate, Brunswick Village, Newcastle upon Tyne, NE13 7BA
Activities: Roofing activities
Shareholders: Derek Michael Brown; Timothy John Horner; Adam John William Stone
Officers: Diana Jane Stone, Secretary; Glen Vincent Archbold [1970] Director/Quantity Surveyor; Derek Michael Brown [1963] Director/Contract Manager; Timothy John Horner [1964] Director/Commercial Manager; Adam John William Stone [1960] Director

Chemson Limited
Incorporated: 20 January 1986 *Employees:* 74
Net Worth: £3,627,481 *Total Assets:* £7,611,834
Registered Office: Hayhole Works, Northumberland Dock Road, Howdon, Wallsend, Tyne & Wear, NE28 0PB
Activities: Manufacture of other inorganic basic chemicals
Officers: Robin Byron [1959] Operations Director; Gozde Diner [1978] Director/Accounting and Financial Reporting [Turkish]; Suleyman Savas Erdem [1969] Director/General Manager [Turkish]; Toker Ozcan [1969] Director/General Manager [Turkish]

Chemtech Environmental Limited
Incorporated: 10 September 2001 *Employees:* 33
Net Worth: £335,163 *Total Assets:* £1,762,117
Registered Office: Unit 6 Parkhead, Greencroft Industrial Park, Stanley, Co Durham, DH9 7YB
Activities: Environmental consulting activities
Shareholders: John Campbell; Karan Campbell
Officers: John Campbell [1969] Director/Chemist; Karan Campbell [1978] Company Secretary/Director

Cherry Hill Garden & Landscape Centre Ltd
Incorporated: 11 February 2010
Net Worth: £484,456 *Total Assets:* £927,684
Registered Office: Exchange Building, 66 Church Street, Hartlepool, Cleveland, TS24 7DN
Activities: Retail sale of flowers, plants, seeds, fertilizers, pet animals and pet food in specialised stores
Shareholders: Jonathan Peter Wilkinson; Thomas Michael Wilkinson
Officers: Jonathon Peter Wilkinson [1963] Director; Thomas Michael Wilkinson [1961] Director

Cherry Orchards Care Ltd
Incorporated: 28 July 2014
Net Worth: £809,303 *Total Assets:* £1,098,257
Registered Office: Yoden House, 30 Yoden Way, Peterlee, Co Durham, SR8 1AL
Activities: Residential care activities for learning difficulties, mental health and substance abuse
Major Shareholder: Gerald Phillips
Officers: Generald Phillips [1955] Director/Care Co-ordinator

Chester Le Street DP Limited
Incorporated: 4 May 2012 *Employees:* 63
Net Worth: £284,449 *Total Assets:* £892,115
Registered Office: 178 York Road, Hartlepool, Cleveland, TS26 9EA
Activities: Other retail sale of food in specialised stores
Major Shareholder: Mike Racz
Officers: Mike Racz, Secretary; Mike Racz [1982] Director

Chevron Taxis Limited
Incorporated: 28 April 1997 *Employees:* 2
Net Worth: £662,922 *Total Assets:* £755,398
Registered Office: 7 Bankside, The Watermark, Gateshead, Tyne & Wear, NE11 9SY
Activities: Taxi operation
Major Shareholder: James Robson
Officers: James Robson [1948] Director/Taxi Proprietor

Chilcott Holdings Limited
Incorporated: 11 December 2003
Net Worth: £980,000 *Total Assets:* £980,000
Registered Office: Lower Chapel House, Caldwell, Richmond, N Yorks, DL11 7UQ
Activities: Activities of head offices
Shareholder: John Franklin Chilcott Hodges
Officers: Pauline Barrett Hodges, Secretary; John Franklin Chilcott Hodges [1946] Director; Pauline Barrett Hodges [1947] Director/Housewife

Chilcott Limited
Incorporated: 15 February 1985
Net Worth: £971,418 *Total Assets:* £1,036,952
Registered Office: Lower Chapel House, Caldwell, Richmond, N Yorks, DL11 7UQ
Activities: Management consultancy activities other than financial management
Parent: Chilcott Holdings Limited
Officers: Pauline Barrett Hodges, Secretary; John Franklin Chilcott Hodges [1946] Director; Pauline Barrett Hodges [1947] Director

Chiltern Farm Chemicals Limited
Incorporated: 8 October 1980 *Employees:* 2
Net Worth: £3,190,380 *Total Assets:* £3,730,156
Registered Office: East Mellwaters Farm, Stainmore Road, Bowes, Barnard Castle, Co Durham, DL12 9RH
Activities: Manufacture of pesticides and other agrochemical products
Shareholders: Philip Brandon Tavener; Sally Tavener
Officers: Sally Tavener, Secretary; Philip Brandon Tavener [1943] Director/Agrochemical Consultant; Sally Tavener [1943] Director/Agrochemical Consultant

The Chiltern Railway Company Limited
Incorporated: 10 January 1995 *Employees:* 847
Net Worth: £20,866,000 *Total Assets:* £123,261,000
Registered Office: 1 Admiral Way, Doxford International Business Park, Sunderland, Tyne & Wear, SR3 3XP
Activities: Passenger rail transport, interurban
Officers: Lorna Edwards, Secretary; Christopher Derek Dyne Burchell [1973] Director; Amanda Furlong [1975] Director; Mary Elisabeth Courtney Hewitt [1979] Director; Gavin Marc Panter [1972] Director; David James Penney [1975] Director; Matthew James Prosser [1972] Director; Alexis James Scott [1983] Director; Rebecca Ward [1971] HR Director

Chipchase Farms Limited
Incorporated: 18 April 2011 *Employees:* 8
Net Worth: £756,518 *Total Assets:* £1,070,804
Registered Office: Blackhill Farm, Wark, Hexham, Northumberland, NE48 3NU
Activities: Mixed farming
Major Shareholder: Penelope Josephine Torday
Officers: Honourable Charles Richard Beaumont [1954] Director; Jonathan Richard Elkington [1978] Director; David William Hall [1956] Director; Penelope Josephine Torday [1953] Director

Chisholm Bookmakers Limited
Incorporated: 4 February 1986 *Employees:* 147
Net Worth: £1,453,773 *Total Assets:* £3,553,856
Registered Office: Deneside Buildings, Remscheid Way, Jubilee Industrial Estate, Ashington, Northumberland, NE63 8UB
Activities: Gambling and betting activities
Shareholders: Charles Howard Chisholm; Neil Miller Chisholm; David Keith Chisholm
Officers: Charles Howard Chisholm, Secretary; Charles Howard Chisholm [1958] Director; David Keith Chisholm [1962] Director; Neil Miller Chisholm [1959] Director

Choice Childcare Limited
Incorporated: 30 July 2003 *Employees:* 63
Net Worth: £441,205 *Total Assets:* £926,434
Registered Office: 384-388 Stamfordham Road, Westerhope, Newcastle upon Tyne, NE5 5HE
Activities: Pre-primary education
Parent: North East Nurseries Ltd
Officers: Ajeet Chadda, Secretary; Ajeet Chadda [1982] Director; Jagesh Kumar Chadda [1952] Director; Kanchan Chadda [1982] Director

Choice Property NE Limited
Incorporated: 28 May 2014
Net Worth: £154,651 *Total Assets:* £1,457,304
Registered Office: Beaumont Accountancy, First Floor, Enterprise House, 202-206 Linthorpe Road, Middlesbrough, Cleveland, TS1 3QW
Activities: Other letting and operating of own or leased real estate
Major Shareholder: John Richard Robinson
Officers: John Richard Robinson [1959] Director

Christchurch Claypath Durham
Incorporated: 25 June 2004 *Employees:* 7
Net Worth: £2,099,291 *Total Assets:* £2,252,615
Registered Office: Christchurch Durham, Claypath, Durham, DH1 1RH
Activities: Activities of religious organisations
Officers: Dr David Buckley [1982] Director/Doctor; James David Cleave [1987] Finance Director; David Richard Gibb [1968] Director/Christian (Anglican) Minister; Anthony Thomas Jones [1970] Director/Christian (Anglican) Minister; Adam Edward Straker [1985] Director/Businessman

The Christian Institute
Incorporated: 1 August 1991 *Employees:* 48
Net Worth: £2,122,510 *Total Assets:* £2,675,219
Registered Office: Wilberforce House, 4 Park Road, Gosforth Business Park, Newcastle upon Tyne, NE12 8DG
Activities: Activities of religious organisations
Officers: Roderick Leslie Badams [1946] Director/Retired; Revd Rupert Paul Bentley-Taylor [1953] Director/Itinerant Minister; John Burn [1938] Director/Education Consultant; Revd George Robert Curry [1951] Director/Clerk in Holy Orders; Geoffrey Paul Fox [1954] Managing Director; Revd David Ronald James Holloway [1939] Director/Clerk in Holy Orders; Trevor Ernest James [1948] Director/Chartered Accountant; Revd James Henry Aufrere Leggett [1961] Director/Minister of Religion; Kenneth John Nelson [1962] Director/Company Chief Executive; Revd Dr William James Unwin Philip [1967] Director/Minister of Religion; Philip Alexander Robinson [1973] Director/Lecturer; Revd Dr Richard Duncan Turnbull [1960] Director of Research

The Chrome Group Limited
Incorporated: 18 March 2015 *Employees:* 81
Net Worth: £3,192,337 *Total Assets:* £5,824,945
Registered Office: 7-9 Front Street, Chester-le-Street, Co Durham, DH3 3BQ
Activities: Dormant company
Shareholders: Pericles Ataliotis; Aidan David Sunter
Officers: Pericles Ataliotis [1961] Director; Aidan David Sunter [1976] Director

Chrome PSG Limited
Incorporated: 13 December 2013 *Employees:* 81
Net Worth: £92,842 *Total Assets:* £2,764,993
Registered Office: 7-9 Front Street, Chester-le-Street, Co Durham, DH3 3BQ
Activities: Retail sale of mobile telephones
Parent: The Chrome Group Limited
Officers: Stavroulla Ataliotis, Secretary; Katherine Helen Sunter, Secretary; Pericles Ataliotis [1961] Director; Aidan David Sunter [1976] Director

Chrysalis Grant Making Trust
Incorporated: 11 January 2010
Net Worth: £1,940,917 *Total Assets:* £1,943,377
Registered Office: Piper Close, Aydon Road, Corbridge, Northumberland, NE45 5PW
Activities: Non-trading company
Officers: Sarah Catherine Evans, Secretary; Hannah Alba Evans [1995] Director/Student; Mark Price Evans [1963] Director; Sarah Catherine Evans [1965] Director; Thomas Charles Evans [1993] Director; Andrew Michael Playle [1969] Director/Solicitor

Chuhan & Singh Partnership Limited
Incorporated: 23 January 2007
Net Worth: £621,611 *Total Assets:* £1,083,105
Registered Office: 81 Borough Road, Middlesbrough, Cleveland, TS1 3AA
Activities: Accounting and auditing activities
Shareholders: Gursharan Hardeyal Singh; Anthony Blueitt
Officers: Gursharan Hardeyal Singh, Secretary/Accountant; Anthony Blueitt [1965] Director/Chartered Accountant; Gursharan Hardeyal Singh [1962] Director/Accountant

Church Lane Builders Limited
Incorporated: 26 July 2012
Net Worth Deficit: £71,203 *Total Assets:* £820,076
Registered Office: Conifers, Church Lane, Ormesby, Middlesbrough, Cleveland, TS7 9AU
Activities: Construction of domestic buildings
Major Shareholder: Alan Edward Ransome
Officers: Alan Edward Ransome [1946] Director

Cimex Service (UK) Limited
Incorporated: 8 October 1976
Net Worth: £344,199 *Total Assets:* £998,324
Registered Office: Bridge End Works, Ryhope Road, Ryhope, Sunderland, Tyne & Wear, SR2 0NJ
Activities: Construction of domestic buildings
Officers: Joanne Elaine Laidler, Secretary; Joanne Elaine Laidler [1964] Director/Company Secretary; Joseph Edward Laidler [1939] Director

Cintra HR & Payroll Services Ltd
Incorporated: 11 September 1996 *Employees:* 91
Net Worth: £2,754,833 *Total Assets:* £4,762,464
Registered Office: Computer House, 353 High Street, Gateshead, Tyne & Wear, NE8 1ET
Activities: Other business support service activities n.e.c.
Shareholders: Hugh Keegan; John McEvoy
Officers: Gemma Dougal, Secretary/Finance Manager; Hugh Keegan [1943] Director [Irish]; John McEvoy [1946] Director; Carsten Staehr [1963] Managing Director [Danish]

Circle Red Properties (St. James) Limited
Incorporated: 15 May 2006
Registered Office: Henson House, Planet Place, Stephenson Industrial Estate, Newcastle upon Tyne, NE12 6RZ
Activities: Development of building projects
Shareholders: David Wilson; John Morse
Officers: John Bede Morse [1953] Director; David Nathan Wilson [1973] Managing Director

CISV International Limited
Incorporated: 24 November 1998 *Employees:* 12
Net Worth: £1,804,536 *Total Assets:* £2,223,855
Registered Office: MEA House, Ellison Place, Newcastle upon Tyne, NE1 8XS
Activities: Cultural education
Officers: Gabrielle Suzanne Mandell, Secretary; Maarin Cecilia Makalintal Cabato [1974] Director/Lawyer [Filipino]; Gustavo Enrique Cuellar [1986] Director/Economist [Salvadoran]; Einav Dinur [1982] Director/Marketing Manager [Israeli]; Daniel Edelshaim [1979] Director/Project Manager IT [Israeli]; Emmanuel Hugo Richard Keates [1974] Director/Entrepreneur; Dr Calixto Mateos Hanel [1966] Director/Economist [Mexican]; Madhuri Parikh [1964] Financial Planner, Board Director [Canadian]; Vinh Vilhelm Brorson Prag [1980] Director/Coordinator [Danish]; Frank Steffen [1965] Director/Product Manager [German]

Citizens Advice County Durham
Incorporated: 11 January 2013 *Employees:* 68
Net Worth: £1,108,645 *Total Assets:* £1,348,291
Registered Office: Armstrong House, Abbeywoods Business Park, Pity Me, Durham, DH1 5GH
Activities: Activities of business and employers membership organisations
Officers: Neil John Bradbury, Secretary; Angela Cheek [1981] Director/Human Resources; Alison Collins [1980] Director/Volunteer; Kamila Coulson-Patel [1983] Director/Solicitor; Brenda Davidson [1963] Director/Solicitor; David Hall [1975] Director/County Councillor; George Colin McPherson [1959] Director/Retired; Anthony John Pensom [1951] Director/Retired; Alan Keith Roxborough [1942] Director; John Scollen [1962] Director/Retired; Michael Smith [1948] Director/Retired; Councillor Angela Surtees [1970] Director/County Councillor; John William Taylor [1943] Director

Citizens Advice Sunderland
Incorporated: 20 August 2007 *Employees:* 13
Net Worth: £732,072 *Total Assets:* £768,070
Registered Office: 5a Waterloo Place, Sunderland, Tyne & Wear, SR1 3HT
Activities: Other information service activities n.e.c.
Officers: Christopher Graham [1955] Director/Consultant; John Richard Hicks [1971] Ex-Banking Director; Malcolm Hook [1959] Director; Agatha Celeste Kanyangu [1974] Director/Business Researcher [Zimbabwean]; Doctor David William Reed [1964] Director/Head of Governance and Compliance; Tony Taylor [1966] Director/Reach Truck Driver; David Robert Wood [1974] Director/Business Development Manager

City & Commercial Property Company Limited
Incorporated: 18 January 1980
Registered Office: Murky Hill Offices, Cow Lane, Middleton Tyas, Richmond, N Yorks, DL10 6RW
Activities: Other letting and operating of own or leased real estate
Shareholders: Ralph Congreve; Adrian John Speir
Officers: Ralph Congreve, Secretary; Ralph Congreve [1953] Director

City Church Newcastle
Incorporated: 25 July 2009 *Employees:* 4
Net Worth: £1,154,732 *Total Assets:* £1,916,661
Registered Office: The Castlegate, Melbourne Street, Newcastle upon Tyne, NE1 2JQ
Activities: Activities of religious organisations
Officers: James Heath Faraday [1973] Director/Speech and Language Therapist; Ian David Galloway [1958] Director/Church Team Leader; Andrew Robert Kahn [1978] Director/Chartered Surveyor; David Duncan Podbury [1975] Director/Church Leader; Janet Mary Smith [1963] Director/Primary School Teacher; Sarah Catherine Wade [1981] Director/Solicitor

City Hospitals Independent Commercial Enterprises Limited
Incorporated: 10 December 2013
Net Worth: £12,221,774 *Total Assets:* £50,933,280
Registered Office: Sunderland Royal Hospital, Kayll Road, Sunderland, Tyne & Wear, SR4 7TP
Activities: Hospital activities
Officers: Wayne Carr [1975] Director/Chartered Engineer; Dr Ian Kenneth Makinson [1964] Director/General Manager; Paul Robinson [1969] Director/Chartered Accountant; Mark Stouph [1968] Director/Barrister

City Leasing (Sunderland) Limited
Incorporated: 10 October 1961 *Employees:* 3
Net Worth: £2,912,437 *Total Assets:* £3,229,437
Registered Office: Unit 117I Business & Innovation Centre, Wearfield, Sunderland Enterprise Park, Sunderland, Tyne & Wear, SR5 2TJ
Activities: Sale of other motor vehicles
Major Shareholder: Thomas Elves
Officers: Janine Calzini, Secretary; Janine Calzini [1972] Director; Thomas Elves [1945] Director; Suzanne Johnson [1974] Director

The City of Oxford Motor Services Limited
Incorporated: 6 December 1906 *Employees:* 591
Net Worth: £6,243,000 *Total Assets:* £28,830,000
Registered Office: 3rd Floor, 41-51 Grey Street, Newcastle upon Tyne, NE1 6EE
Activities: Other urban, suburban or metropolitan passenger land transport (not underground, metro or similar)
Parent: Go-Ahead Holding Limited
Officers: Carolyn Ferguson, Secretary; David Allen Brown [1960] Director; Simon Patrick Butcher [1967] Finance Director; Luke Carl Marion [1980] Director/Chartered Accountant; Philip Richard Southall [1976] Director; Raymond Woodhouse [1953] Director/Engineering

City Signs and Display Limited
Incorporated: 1 April 1987
Registered Office: The Brinkburn Centre, Brinkburn Street, Byker, Newcastle upon Tyne, NE6 2AR
Activities: Manufacture of other plastic products
Major Shareholder: James Rowe
Officers: Irene Margaret Rowe, Secretary; Irene Margaret Rowe [1947] Director/Clerk; James Rowe [1948] Director

City View (Sunderland) Limited
Incorporated: 17 October 2014
Registered Office: 1 Kingswood Drive, Darras Hall, Ponteland, Newcastle upon Tyne, NE20 9PL
Activities: Buying and selling of own real estate
Parent: SSG Property Limited
Officers: Dr Akash Ghai [1979] Director; Promila Sehgal [1948] Director; Dr Deepinder Singh Somal [1961] Director

CJW Country Estates Limited
Incorporated: 8 November 2012 *Employees:* 1
Net Worth: £251,464 *Total Assets:* £1,053,001
Registered Office: 246 Park View, Whitley Bay, Tyne & Wear, NE26 3QX
Activities: Buying and selling of own real estate
Major Shareholder: Callum James Watson
Officers: Callum James Watson [1990] Director

CKI UK Co 5 Limited
Incorporated: 28 January 2011
Net Worth: £858,058,432 *Total Assets:* £859,604,096
Registered Office: Northumbria House, Abbey Road, Pity Me, Durham, DH1 5FJ
Activities: Activities of other holding companies n.e.c.
Parent: CKI UK Co 6 Limited
Officers: Martin Parker, Secretary; Loi Shun Chan [1962] Director [Chinese]; Andrew John Hunter [1958] Director; Hing Lam Kam [1946] Director [Chinese]; Duncan Nicholas MacRae [1970] Director; Heidi Mottram [1965] Director

CKI UK Co 6 Limited
Incorporated: 28 January 2011
Net Worth: £474,885,312 *Total Assets:* £896,153,152
Registered Office: Northumbria House, Abbey Road, Pity Me, Durham, DH1 5FJ
Activities: Activities of other holding companies n.e.c.
Officers: Martin Parker, Secretary; Loi Shun Chan [1962] Director [Chinese]; Andrew John Hunter [1958] Director; Hing Lam Kam [1946] Director [Chinese]; Duncan Nicholas MacRae [1970] Director; Heidi Mottram [1965] Director

CKW Trading Limited
Incorporated: 20 May 2010 *Employees:* 3
Net Worth: £11,456 *Total Assets:* £1,373,444
Registered Office: Grainger Suite, Dobson House, Regent Centre, Gosforth, Newcastle upon Tyne, NE3 3PF
Activities: Wholesale of wine, beer, spirits and other alcoholic beverages
Shareholders: Peter James Schroeder; Christina Kelway Wotherspoon
Officers: Christina Wotherspoon, Secretary; Peter James Schroeder [1962] Director [Canadian]

Claremont IT Services Limited
Incorporated: 28 June 2012
Net Worth: £12,507 *Total Assets:* £1,162,857
Registered Office: Rotterdam House, 116 Quayside, Newcastle upon Tyne, NE1 3DY
Activities: Activities of other holding companies n.e.c.
Shareholders: Richard Owen MacInnes-Manby; Ian Michael Monaghan; Roland James Miles
Officers: Steven James Anderson [1960] Director; Richard Owen MacInnes Manby [1956] Director/Consultant; Roland James Miles [1970] Director/IT Consultant; Ian Monaghan [1968] Director/IT Consultant; Jonathan Douglas Stuart [1971] Director; Mark Claude James Vivian [1966] Director/IT Consultant

Clarity Informatics Limited
Incorporated: 29 December 2000 *Employees:* 54
Net Worth: £920,525 *Total Assets:* £2,138,588
Registered Office: Deltic House, Kingfisher Way, Silverlink Business Park, Wallsend, Tyne & Wear, NE28 9NX
Activities: Business and domestic software development
Parent: Clarity Informatics Group Limited
Officers: David James Price [1979] Director; Professor Ian Nicholas Purves [1961] Director/Professor of Health Informatic; Timothy James Sewart [1978] Director/Solicitor; Michael Anthony Sowerby [1950] Director

H.B.Clark & Co.(Successors) Limited
Incorporated: 31 July 1913 *Employees:* 311
Net Worth: £5,576,925 *Total Assets:* £22,664,022
Registered Office: Unit S3, Narvik Way, Tyne Tunnel Trading Estate, North Shields, Tyne & Wear, NE29 7XJ
Activities: Manufacture of beer
Officers: Patricia Ada Rice, Secretary; David Leonard Brind [1972] Director; John Frederick Hope [1969] Group Operations Director; Jay MacKay [1966] Managing Director; Patricia Ada Rice [1957] Director; Paul Victor Young [1957] Director

Alex Clark Art Ltd
Incorporated: 12 May 2006 *Employees:* 13
Net Worth: £610,160 *Total Assets:* £994,636
Registered Office: Mallan House, Bridge End, Hexham, Northumberland, NE46 4DQ
Activities: Specialised design activities
Shareholders: Alexandra Clark; Erik Buchanan Nielsen
Officers: Christine Clark, Secretary; Alexandra Clark [1974] Director; Erik Buchanan Nielsen [1968] Director

H B Clark Holdings Limited
Incorporated: 18 October 2016
Net Worth: £6,273,750 *Total Assets:* £6,273,750
Registered Office: Unit S3, Narvik Way, Tyne Tunnel Trading Estate, North Shields, Tyne & Wear, NE29 7XJ
Activities: Activities of other holding companies n.e.c.
Officers: Patricia Ada Rice, Secretary; David Leonard Brind [1972] Director; John Frederick Hope [1969] Group Operations Director; Patricia Ada Rice [1957] Director; Paul Victor Young [1957] Director

Clark Homes Limited
Incorporated: 14 April 1998 *Employees:* 61
Net Worth: £3,622,458 *Total Assets:* £7,143,082
Registered Office: Unit 20b Coopies Haugh, Coopies Lane Industrial Estate, Morpeth, Northumberland, NE61 6JN
Activities: Construction of commercial buildings
Shareholders: Jeffrey Braithwaite Clark; Duncan Edward Clark
Officers: Duncan Edward Clark, Secretary; Duncan Edward Clark [1968] Director/Builder; Jeffrey Braithwaite Clark [1965] Director/Builder

David A Clark Limited
Incorporated: 21 September 2006 *Employees:* 1
Net Worth: £363,280 *Total Assets:* £768,909
Registered Office: 3 Eden Terrace, Kirk Merrington, Co Durham, DL16 7JP
Activities: Construction of other civil engineering projects n.e.c.
Major Shareholder: David Anthony Clark
Officers: Jeanette Tatham, Secretary; David Anthony Clark [1969] Director/Executive

Clark Residential Limited
Incorporated: 8 September 2003
Net Worth Deficit: £738,917 *Total Assets:* £1,903,370
Registered Office: 1 Jesmond Business Court, 217 Jesmond Road, Newcastle upon Tyne, NE2 1LA
Activities: Development of building projects
Major Shareholder: Jonathan Garry Clark
Officers: Helen Nora Clark, Secretary; Helen Nora Clark [1964] Director; Jonathan Garry Clark [1968] Director/Chairman

John Clark Valves Limited
Incorporated: 1 April 1985 *Employees:* 10
Net Worth: £1,259,410 *Total Assets:* £1,993,958
Registered Office: Portrack Industrial Estate, Portrack Grange Road, Stockton on Tees, Cleveland, TS18 2PH
Activities: Agents specialised in the sale of other particular products
Officers: Julie Patricia Roberts, Secretary; Howard Antony Thornill Roberts [1961] Director; Julie Patricia Roberts [1960] Director

H Clarke & Sons Limited
Incorporated: 21 January 2003 *Employees:* 50
Net Worth: £536,486 *Total Assets:* £1,483,596
Registered Office: 2 Moxon Court, Thurston Road, Northallerton, N Yorks, DL6 2NG
Activities: Plumbing, heat and air-conditioning installation
Parent: Harry Clarke Holdings Ltd
Officers: Hazel Laura Houston-Clarke, Secretary; Richard Peter Clarke [1964] Director; Mark Lammey [1962] Operations Director (Scotland); Ashley Smith [1984] Commercial Director; Barry John Taylor [1978] Director/Operations Manager

Clarke Mairs LLP
Incorporated: 3 September 2007 *Employees:* 32
Net Worth: £1,057,589 *Total Assets:* £1,293,248
Registered Office: One Hood Street, Newcastle upon Tyne, NE1 6JQ

Clarkes of Stillington Plate & Profiles Limited
Incorporated: 29 June 1999 *Employees:* 27
Net Worth: £1,572,845 *Total Assets:* £4,090,777
Registered Office: Ironmasters Way, Stillington, Stockton on Tees, Cleveland, TS21 1LF
Activities: Wholesale of metals and metal ores
Shareholders: Darin Robert Knox; Michael Laws; Geoffrey Blair Wilson
Officers: John Alexander Dunn, Secretary; John Alexander Dunn [1949] Director; Darin Robert Knox [1968] Director; Michael Laws [1959] Director; Geoffrey Blair Wilson [1954] Director

Clarks Coachbuilders Limited
Incorporated: 10 September 1942 *Employees:* 43
Net Worth: £771,875 *Total Assets:* £1,354,343
Registered Office: 94/4 Carrmere Road, Leechmere Industrial Estate, Sunderland, Tyne & Wear, SR2 9TE
Activities: Maintenance and repair of motor vehicles
Parent: North East Accident Repair Centres Limited
Officers: Roger Andrew Collings, Secretary; Antoinette Collings [1938] Director; Roger Andrew Collings [1961] Director/Marketing Manager; Peter Sadler [1966] Commercial Director; Robert George Taylor [1957] Managing Director

Clarus Limited
Incorporated: 20 July 1962
Net Worth: £780,330 *Total Assets:* £2,982,582
Registered Office: 17 Linden Road, Gosforth, Newcastle upon Tyne, NE3 4EY
Activities: Other business support service activities n.e.c.
Shareholder: Philip Richard Ternent
Officers: Karen Jane Ternent, Secretary; Joseph Boustead Seery [1936] Director; Vivien Seery [1938] Director/Secretary; Karen Jane Ternent [1962] Director/Secretary; Philip Richard Ternent [1958] Director/Manager

Class Fundraising Limited
Incorporated: 30 July 2010
Net Worth: £548,016 *Total Assets:* £785,515
Registered Office: Suite W9, Vienna Court, The Innovation Centre, Kirkleatham Business Park, Redcar, Cleveland, TS10 5SH
Activities: Printing n.e.c.
Shareholder: Mark Andrew Simpson
Officers: Simon Fulton [1978] Director; Mark Andrew Simpson [1978] Director

Class G5 Locomotive Company Ltd
Incorporated: 18 June 2007
Registered Office: Unit 8s Hackworth Industrial Park, Shildon, Co Durham, DL4 1HF
Activities: Manufacture of railway locomotives and rolling stock
Officers: Timothy Ralph Taylor, Secretary; Ian Alexander Irving [1940] Director/Pharmacist; Richard John Maughan [1960] Director/Retired Civil Engineer; Stephen Raine [1946] Director; Roger Ingham Womersley [1945] Director/Chartered Accountant; Christopher Jeremy Francis Wood [1957] Director/Agronomist; Michael Richard Duncan Wood [1950] Director/General Medical Practitioner

Classic Masonry Limited
Incorporated: 13 February 1991 *Employees:* 32
Net Worth: £439,929 *Total Assets:* £902,900
Registered Office: Sandgate Hall, 36 Albion Road, North Shields, Tyne & Wear, NE30 2RQ
Activities: Other specialised construction activities n.e.c.
Major Shareholder: Michael Moody
Officers: Joanne Elizabeth Regan, Secretary; Anthony William Kay [1965] Commercial Director; Gary Kennedy [1965] Contracts Director; Michael Moody [1965] Managing Director

Clavering Management Limited
Incorporated: 20 February 2004
Net Worth: £1,720,471 *Total Assets:* £1,890,894
Registered Office: 1 St James' Gate, Newcastle upon Tyne, NE1 4AD
Activities: Renting and operating of Housing Association real estate
Officers: Stuart Robson, Secretary; Alan Ernest Brown [1945] Advertising Director; Stuart Robson [1948] Advertising Director

Clay's Garden Centre Ltd.
Incorporated: 28 March 2001 *Employees:* 37
Net Worth: £1,347,309 *Total Assets:* £1,558,208
Registered Office: Peel Retail Park, Washington, Tyne & Wear, NE37 2PA
Activities: Other retail sale of new goods in specialised stores (not commercial art galleries and opticians)
Shareholders: Henry John Clay; Joan Margaret Clay
Officers: Henry John Clay, Secretary/Horticulturalist; Richard Cain [1961] Director/Horticulturalist; David Clay [1968] Director/Horticulturalist; Henry John Clay [1940] Director/Horticulturalist; Joan Margaret Clay [1941] Director/Horticulturist; Wendy Rippon [1959] Director/Horticulturalist

Claypath Property Company Limited (The)
Incorporated: 28 June 1962 *Employees:* 1
Net Worth: £2,404,317 *Total Assets:* £2,773,096
Registered Office: 63 Darlington Road, Hartburn, Stockton on Tees, Cleveland, TS18 5EU
Activities: Buying and selling of own real estate
Major Shareholder: Alexandra Gilllian Coxon
Officers: Robert Coxon, Secretary/Chief Executive Officer; Alexandra Gillian Coxon [1953] Director

Clayside Property Investments Limited
Incorporated: 5 March 1954 *Employees:* 3
Net Worth: £11,121,615 *Total Assets:* £11,653,775
Registered Office: 76 Roman Road, Jarrow, Tyne & Wear, NE32 5EJ
Activities: Other letting and operating of own or leased real estate
Major Shareholder: Malcolm David Jacobson
Officers: Norman Scott, Secretary; Anne Bettina Jacobson [1945] Director/Housewife; Malcolm David Jacobson [1943] Managing Director; Norman Scott [1935] Director

Clayton Glass Limited
Incorporated: 30 December 2004 *Employees:* 315
Net Worth: £2,981,628 *Total Assets:* £16,024,951
Registered Office: Unit 8 Harelaw Industrial Estate, North Road, Stanley, Co Durham, DH9 8UJ
Activities: Shaping and processing of flat glass
Shareholders: Ryan Paul Green; Vanessa Catherine Green
Officers: Ryan Paul Green, Secretary/Accountant; Ryan Paul Green [1976] Director/Accountant; Vanessa Catherine Green [1970] Marketing Director; Jason Matthew McCabe [1971] Sales Director

CLC Enterprise Limited
Incorporated: 30 September 2013 *Employees:* 2
Net Worth: £1,482,762 *Total Assets:* £2,111,588
Registered Office: Coburg House, 1 Coburg Street, Gateshead, Tyne & Wear, NE8 1NS
Activities: Media representation services
Major Shareholder: Charlotte Letitia Crosby
Officers: Charlotte Letitia Crosby [1990] Director/Entertainer; Gary Crosby [1968] Director

Clean It UK/Gumbusters Limited
Incorporated: 5 June 2003 *Employees:* 55
Net Worth: £203,193 *Total Assets:* £978,937
Registered Office: Unit 45 Cuthbert Court, Bede Trading Estate, Jarrow, Tyne & Wear, NE32 3EG
Activities: General cleaning of buildings
Officers: Justine Nipper, Secretary; Elizabeth Jane Moyse [1953] Director/Contract Cleaner; Thomas Clyde Moyse [1950] Director/Contact Cleaner; Kim Moyse Mukhtar [1971] Director; Justine Nipper [1970] Director/Cleaning; Mark Nipper [1967] Director/Cleaning; Lynn Storey [1974] Director/Cleaning

Cleardata UK Limited
Incorporated: 5 May 2000 *Employees:* 92
Net Worth: £1,514,080 *Total Assets:* £3,321,586
Registered Office: Innovation House, Coniston Court, Blyth Riverside Business Park, Blyth, Northumberland, NE24 4RP
Activities: Information technology consultancy activities
Shareholders: David Alexander Bryce; Robert Wood
Officers: Robert Wood, Secretary/Director; David Alexander Bryce [1968] Sales & Marketing Director; Richard Mark LEA Jones [1963] Director; Paul McKeown [1965] Sales Director; Robert Joseph Wood [1960] Director

Clearly Drinks Limited
Incorporated: 26 January 2011 *Employees:* 71
Net Worth: £1,946,960 *Total Assets:* £5,796,800
Registered Office: Riverside Industrial Estate, Riverside Road, Sunderland, Tyne & Wear, SR5 3JG
Activities: Manufacture of soft drinks; production of mineral waters and other bottled waters
Parent: Clearly Drinks Group Limited
Officers: Finian James O'Driscoll [1970] Director [Irish]; Lorraine Ann Quinn [1964] Director; Martin Vincent Thornton [1954] Director

Clearly Drinks Properties Limited
Incorporated: 22 March 2016
Net Worth: £13,012 *Total Assets:* £1,216,402
Registered Office: Riverside Industrial Estate, Riverside Road, Sunderland, Tyne & Wear, SR5 3JG
Activities: Other letting and operating of own or leased real estate
Parent: Clearly Drinks Group Limited
Officers: Finian James O'Driscoll [1970] Director [Irish]; Martin Vincent Thornton [1954] Director

Clearmid Limited
Incorporated: 15 March 1989 *Employees:* 2
Net Worth: £584,183 *Total Assets:* £806,593
Registered Office: Moor Pit Lodge, Harelaw, Stanley, Co Durham, DH9 8DT
Activities: Extraction of crude petroleum
Officers: Tracey Ann Beattie, Secretary; Tracey Ann Beattie [1969] Director/Secretary; Glen Thompson [1957] Director/Instrument Technician

Clearwater Developments Ltd
Incorporated: 7 April 2011
Net Worth: £324,855 *Total Assets:* £1,119,748
Registered Office: Unit 3, 21 North Terrace, Seaham, Co Durham, SR7 7EU
Activities: Buying and selling of own real estate
Major Shareholder: Ranjeet Singh Gill
Officers: Ranjeet Singh Gill [1980] Director; Gursharan Singh Kahlon [1985] Director

Clemitsons Limited
Incorporated: 28 July 1998 *Employees:* 21
Net Worth: £790,862 *Total Assets:* £1,751,676
Registered Office: 25a Hope Street, Crook, Co Durham, DL15 9HS
Activities: Dispensing chemist in specialised stores
Major Shareholder: Rachel Mary Hurst
Officers: Hilary Jane Chapman [1976] Director; Matthew Stuart Hurst [1977] Director; Rachel Mary Hurst [1974] Director/Pharmacist

Clennell Properties Limited
Incorporated: 6 March 1996
Net Worth Deficit: £80,000 *Total Assets:* £946,000
Registered Office: 1a Dukesway Court, Team Valley Trading Estate, Gateshead, Tyne & Wear, NE11 0PJ
Activities: Other letting and operating of own or leased real estate
Parent: Addbudget Limited
Officers: Phillip Nigel Blain, Secretary; David James Horrocks [1959] Director/Chartered Accountant; Ian Imrie [1955] Director

Clevechem Limited
Incorporated: 20 March 1974
Net Worth: £551,564 *Total Assets:* £1,196,137
Registered Office: Redcar Primary Care Hospital, West Dyke Road, Redcar, Cleveland, TS10 4NW
Activities: Dispensing chemist in specialised stores
Shareholders: Coopers Chemist Marske Ltd; Scott Chem Pharmacy
Officers: John Larvin, Secretary; Jonathan Cooper [1962] Director/Pharmacy Proprietor; Nitin Gupta [1970] Director/Pharmacist; John Larvin [1957] Director/Superintendent Pharmacist

Cleveland & Highland Holdings Ltd
Incorporated: 7 April 1922 *Employees:* 10
Net Worth: £3,806,495 *Total Assets:* £3,860,898
Registered Office: Wynyard Park House, Wynyard Avenue, Wynyard, Cleveland, TS22 5TB
Activities: Raising of other cattle and buffaloes
Shareholder: Clifford Keith Wain Schellenberg
Officers: Jillian Barbara Schellenberg, Secretary; Sophie Chaplin [1958] Director/Knitwear Designer Manufacturer; Amy Schellenberg [1971] Director/Interior Designer; Clifford Keith Wain Schellenberg [1929] Director; Jillian Barbara Schellenberg [1946] Director; Nicholas Udny Schellenberg [1966] Director; Rose Joan Schellenberg [1973] Producer/Director; Serena Louise Schellenberg [1961] Director/Freelance Agency Producer; Charles Ward-Jackson [1960] Director/Barrister

Cleveland Alzheimer's Residential Centre Limited
Incorporated: 10 February 1989 *Employees:* 90
Net Worth: £1,413,171 *Total Assets:* £2,460,246
Registered Office: Kirkdale, Radcliffe Crescent, Thornaby, Stockton on Tees, Cleveland, TS17 6BS
Activities: Residential care activities for learning difficulties, mental health and substance abuse
Officers: Geoffrey Skeoch, Secretary; Frances Louise Harding [1956] Director; Henry Alan Kitching [1936] Director/Stockbroker; Helen Louise Lowrie [1966] Director/Chief Executive; Dr Jonathan Mann [1960] Director/Chief Executive Castlebeck

Cleveland Bridge UK Limited
Incorporated: 9 April 1999 *Employees:* 229
Net Worth Deficit: £3,449,000 *Total Assets:* £19,858,000
Registered Office: Cleveland House, Yarm Road, Darlington, Co Durham, DL1 4DE
Activities: Other specialised construction activities n.e.c.
Major Shareholder: Sheikh Abdullah Rushaid Al Rushaid
Officers: Rasheed Abdullah Alrushaid [1973] Director/Chairman [Saudi Arabian]; Christopher John Droogan [1958] Director; John Philip Heathcock [1976] Finance Director

Cleveland Cable Company (Holdings) Limited
Incorporated: 6 August 2012 *Employees:* 506
Net Worth: £195,473,168 *Total Assets:* £226,319,936
Registered Office: c/o Cleveland Cable Company Ltd, Riverside Park Road, Middlesbrough, Cleveland, TS2 1QW
Activities: Activities of other holding companies n.e.c.
Major Shareholder: Alastair Powell
Officers: Janice Robson, Secretary; Alastair Powell [1952] Director; Michael Powell [1957] Director

Cleveland Cable Company Limited
Incorporated: 17 August 2005 *Employees:* 495
Net Worth: £165,267,456 *Total Assets:* £191,368,320
Registered Office: Riverside Park Road, Middlesbrough, Cleveland, TS2 1QW
Activities: Wholesale of other intermediate products
Officers: Janice Robson, Secretary; Alastair Powell [1952] Director; Michael Powell [1957] Director

Cleveland Cascades Limited
Incorporated: 19 November 2003 *Employees:* 38
Net Worth: £2,243,712 *Total Assets:* £3,671,474
Registered Office: Unit 22 Dukesway, Teesside Industrial Estate, Thornaby, Stockton on Tees, Cleveland, TS17 9LT
Activities: Manufacture of other special-purpose machinery n.e.c.
Shareholders: Ian Robert Barnard; Matthew Ian Barnard
Officers: Sally Diane Buckworth, Secretary; Ian Robert Barnard [1953] Director/Chairman; Matthew Ian Barnard [1985] Commercial Director; Sally Diane Buckworth [1969] Managing Director; Peter Luke [1974] Technical Director; Gordon William Patton [1965] Production Director

Cleveland Circuits Limited
Incorporated: 16 July 1971 *Employees:* 46
Net Worth: £3,110,665 *Total Assets:* £3,560,739
Registered Office: Longbeck Road, Marske, Redcar, Cleveland, TS11 6HQ
Activities: Manufacture of electronic components
Parent: Cleveland Technologies Limited
Officers: Karen Gleghorn, Secretary; Andrew Michael Chiles [1965] Director; Andrew Harry Gleghorn [1959] Managing Director

Cleveland Containers Limited
Incorporated: 7 February 2011 *Employees:* 44
Net Worth: £1,698,648 *Total Assets:* £5,487,735
Registered Office: Cleveland House, Eston Road, Grangetown, Middlesbrough, Cleveland, TS6 6UA
Activities: Other transportation support activities
Shareholders: Johnathan Richard Bulmer; Jane Bulmer
Officers: Jane Bulmer [1965] Director; Johnathan Richard Bulmer [1966] Director

Cleveland Country Store Limited
Incorporated: 15 April 2004 *Employees:* 8
Net Worth: £775,480 *Total Assets:* £941,054
Registered Office: Millholme Farm, Brotton, Saltburn-by-the-Sea, N Yorks, TS12 2RY
Activities: Retail sale of flowers, plants, seeds, fertilizers, pet animals and pet food in specialised stores
Shareholder: John Robert Heseltine
Officers: Lynda Heseltine, Secretary/Director; John Robert Heseltine [1954] Director/Farmer; Lynda Heseltine [1961] Director/Farmer

The Cleveland Dwellings Limited
Incorporated: 31 January 1935 *Employees:* 1
Net Worth: £1,517,675 *Total Assets:* £3,499,577
Registered Office: 24 The Grove, Hartlepool, Cleveland, TS26 9NB
Activities: Development of building projects
Major Shareholder: Richard David Ord
Officers: Richard David Ord [1963] Director

Cleveland Fire Brigade Risk Management Services C.I.C.
Incorporated: 30 March 2011
Net Worth: £199,224 *Total Assets:* £1,172,539
Registered Office: Training and Administration Hub, Queens Meadow Business Park, Hartlepool, Cleveland, TS25 5TH
Activities: Risk and damage evaluation
Officers: Karen Winter, Secretary; Peter John Devlin [1959] Director/Legal Advisor/Monitoring Officer; Ian Hayton [1956] Director/Chief Fire Officer; Shaukat Riasat Khaliq [1965] Director Cleveland Fire Brigade; Karen Winter [1963] Director Corporate Services

Cleveland Heat Treatment Centre Limited
Incorporated: 16 December 1987
Net Worth: £881,604 *Total Assets:* £926,142
Registered Office: 17 West Park, Hartlepool, Cleveland, TS26 0DB
Activities: Other specialised construction activities n.e.c.
Shareholder: Sheila Brackstone
Officers: Claire Brackstone, Secretary; William Brackstone [1946] Director/Technician; Kenneth Charlton [1962] Director

Cleveland Homes (No.1) Limited
Incorporated: 22 December 1988
Net Worth: £1,404,526 *Total Assets:* £1,874,218
Registered Office: 80 Hartington Road, Stockton on Tees, Cleveland, TS18 1HE
Activities: Other letting and operating of own or leased real estate
Officers: Dominic George Collinge Ferard, Secretary/Director; Dominic George Collinge Ferard [1963] Director; Jo Tracy Ferard [1969] Director; Rupert Charles Hawkesworth Ferard [1966] Director; Sally Clare Ferard [1962] Director

Cleveland Homes (No.2) Limited
Incorporated: 14 August 1990
Net Worth: £1,125,573 *Total Assets:* £1,139,124
Registered Office: 80 Hartington Road, Stockton on Tees, Cleveland, TS18 1HE
Activities: Other letting and operating of own or leased real estate
Parent: Marblemand Limited
Officers: Dominic George Collinge Ferard, Secretary/Director; Dominic George Collinge Ferard [1963] Director; Jo Tracy Ferard [1969] Director; Rupert Charles Hawkesworth Ferard [1966] Director; Sally Clare Ferard [1962] Director

Cleveland Homes (No.3) Limited
Incorporated: 27 January 1992
Net Worth: £2,901,733 *Total Assets:* £2,947,278
Registered Office: 80 Hartington Road, Stockton on Tees, Cleveland, TS18 1HE
Activities: Other letting and operating of own or leased real estate
Officers: Dominic George Collinge Ferard, Secretary/Director; Dominic George Collinge Ferard [1963] Director; Jo Tracy Ferard [1969] Director; Rupert Charles Hawkesworth Ferard [1966] Director; Sally Clare Ferard [1962] Director

Cleveland Homes (No.4) Limited
Incorporated: 27 January 1993
Net Worth: £1,936,874 *Total Assets:* £1,963,190
Registered Office: 80 Hartington Road, Stockton on Tees, Cleveland, TS18 1HE
Activities: Other letting and operating of own or leased real estate
Officers: Dominic George Collinge Ferard, Secretary/Director; Dominic George Collinge Ferard [1963] Director; Jo Tracy Ferard [1969] Director; Rupert Charles Hawkesworth Ferard [1966] Director; Sally Clare Ferard [1962] Director

Cleveland Homes (No.5) Limited
Incorporated: 21 October 1993
Net Worth: £2,410,429 *Total Assets:* £2,447,324
Registered Office: 80 Hartington Road, Stockton on Tees, Cleveland, TS18 1HE
Activities: Other letting and operating of own or leased real estate
Officers: Dominic George Collinge Ferard, Secretary/Director; Dominic George Collinge Ferard [1963] Director; Jo Tracy Ferard [1969] Director; Rupert Charles Hawkesworth Ferard [1966] Director; Sally Clare Ferard [1962] Director

Cleveland Housing Trust Limited
Incorporated: 16 May 1996
Registered Office: Sopwith House, Sopwith Close, Preston Farm, Stockton on Tees, Cleveland, TS18 3TT
Activities: Renting and operating of Housing Association real estate
Officers: James Barry Parkin [1947] Director/Retired

Cleveland Land Limited
Incorporated: 11 October 1994
Net Worth: £2,149,321 *Total Assets:* £2,153,341
Registered Office: Estate Office, Skelton, Saltburn-by-the-Sea, N Yorks, TS12 2ES
Activities: Buying and selling of own real estate
Major Shareholder: Anthony Charles Philip Wharton
Officers: Neil Colver, Secretary; Elizabeth Anne Millard [1942] Director/Housewife; Anthony Charles Philip Wharton [1946] Director

Cleveland Land Services (Guisborough) Limited
Incorporated: 22 September 1978 *Employees:* 94
Net Worth: £4,690,085 *Total Assets:* £11,631,934
Registered Office: Park Farm, Dunsdale, Guisborough, Cleveland, TS14 6RQ
Activities: Other specialised construction activities n.e.c.
Shareholder: Coleen Miller
Officers: Coleen Miller, Secretary; Brian Stanley Dunn [1961] Director of Operations; Coleen Miller [1939] Director; John Arthur Miller [1961] Managing Director; Lynn Denise Miller [1961] Marketing Director; Stephen John Miller [1985] Contracts Director

Cleveland Motorhomes Limited
Incorporated: 19 May 1971
Net Worth: £1,067,124 *Total Assets:* £2,398,593
Registered Office: 43 Coniscliffe Road, Darlington, Co Durham, DL3 7EH
Activities: Sale of used cars and light motor vehicles
Major Shareholder: Kenneth Jackson
Officers: Craig Kenneth Jackson [1962] Director/Salesman; Neil Andrew Jackson [1966] Director/Salesman

Cleveland Potash Limited
Incorporated: 14 September 1967 *Employees:* 963
Net Worth: £487,575,008 *Total Assets:* £900,454,976
Registered Office: Boulby Mine, Loftus, Saltburn-by-the-Sea, N Yorks, TS13 4UZ
Activities: Mining of chemical and fertilizer minerals
Shareholders: Dead Sea Works Limited; Ashli Chemicals (Holland) B.V.
Officers: Celine Smeets, Secretary; Jacob Ben Hamou [1963] Director [Israeli]; Howard David Clark [1962] Director

Cleveland Sitesafe Limited
Incorporated: 5 November 1987
Registered Office: Riverside Works, Dockside Road, Middlesbrough, Cleveland, TS3 8AT
Activities: Manufacture of metal structures and parts of structures
Parent: Graving Dock Ltd
Officers: John William Hodgson [1970] Director/General Manager; Nadia Whiteley [1983] Director/Company Accountant

Cleveland Systems Engineering Limited
Incorporated: 26 March 1997 *Employees:* 15
Net Worth: £852,698 *Total Assets:* £1,441,906
Registered Office: Unit 12 Code Business Estate, Henson Road, Darlington, Co Durham, DL1 4NZ
Activities: Information technology consultancy activities
Major Shareholder: Thomas Anthony Ashcroft
Officers: Thomas Anthony Ashcroft, Secretary; Thomas Anthony Ashcroft [1959] Director/Engineer

Cleveland Technologies Limited
Incorporated: 16 January 2008 *Employees:* 129
Net Worth: £3,893,427 *Total Assets:* £5,175,727
Registered Office: c/o Weyfringe Limited, Longbeck Road, Marske, Redcar, Cleveland, TS11 6HQ
Activities: Manufacture of electronic components
Major Shareholder: Andrew Harry Gleghorn
Officers: Karen Gleghorn, Secretary; Claire Aydon [1977] Director/Accountant; Andrew Michael Chiles [1965] Director; Andrew Harry Gleghorn [1959] Director; Barbra Walton [1950] Director

Clever Clogs Day Nurseries Limited
Incorporated: 21 April 2006 *Employees:* 57
Net Worth: £646,533 *Total Assets:* £1,415,979
Registered Office: Clever Clogs Nursery, Clever Clogs Childrens Nursery, New Ferens Park, Belmont Business Park, Durham, DH1 1GG
Activities: Pre-primary education
Major Shareholder: Andrea Emma Townsley
Officers: Mark William Townsley, Secretary/Factory Manager; Sharon Susan Lewis [1965] Operational Director; Andrea Emma Townsley [1969] Managing Director; Mark William Townsley [1966] Company Secretary/Director

Cleves Cross Learning Trust
Incorporated: 4 October 2013 *Employees:* 67
Net Worth: £1,504,831 *Total Assets:* £3,110,926
Registered Office: c/o Cleves Cross Primary School, Cleves Cross, Ferryhill, Co Durham, DL17 8QY
Activities: Primary education
Officers: Helen Andrews [1978] Director/Children's Homes Manager; Sara Jane Clasper [1977] Director/Solicitor; Graham Frederick French [1970] Director/IT Consultant; Alison Lazenby [1964] Director/Headteacher; Leigh Lockey [1958] Director/Retired; John Alexander Bell Muir [1955] Director/Retired; Glenys Joan Newby [1966] Director/Self Employed

Clevestones Trans Limited
Incorporated: 21 August 1974 *Employees:* 21
Net Worth: £1,640,591 *Total Assets:* £2,229,944
Registered Office: Moreland Street, Hartlepool, Cleveland, TS24 7NL
Activities: Freight transport by road
Shareholders: David Leslie Swales; Hunter House Developments Limited
Officers: Corinne Diane Darby, Secretary; David Leslie Swales [1949] Director; David Anthony Swales [1982] Director/Plant Operator; Mark John Swales [1971] Director/Transport Manager

Clic Time Holdings Limited
Incorporated: 17 July 2007 *Employees:* 20
Net Worth Deficit: £733,138 *Total Assets:* £11,091,468
Registered Office: 1 Jesmond Business Court, 217 Jesmond Road, Newcastle upon Tyne, NE2 1LA
Activities: Other professional, scientific and technical activities n.e.c.
Shareholder: Jim Richardson
Officers: Claire Richardson, Secretary; Robert Palmer [1987] Finance Director; Claire Richardson [1969] Director; James Joseph Richardson [1965] Director

Cliff Court (Redcar) Developments Ltd
Incorporated: 6 January 2010
Net Worth: £1,601,074 *Total Assets:* £5,459,910
Registered Office: 14 Halegrove Court Cygnet Drive, Bowesfield Park, Stockton on Tees, Cleveland, TS18 3DB
Activities: Buying and selling of own real estate
Shareholders: Dennis Harley Developments Ltd; CJ Leonard & Sons Ltd
Officers: Rosaleen Anne Harley-Rogers, Secretary; James Dennis Harley [1974] Director/Construction; Charles Joseph Leonard [1964] Director

Cliff House Service Station Ltd
Incorporated: 31 March 2009
Net Worth: £257,962 *Total Assets:* £935,208
Registered Office: 130 Sutherland Avenue, Fenham, Newcastle upon Tyne, NE4 9NR
Activities: Retail sale of automotive fuel in specialised stores
Major Shareholder: Mohammed Tanvir
Officers: Rukhsana Tanvir, Secretary; Mohammed Tanvir [1969] Director

Cliffvalley Limited
Incorporated: 22 August 2008
Net Worth Deficit: £82,929 *Total Assets:* £989,958
Registered Office: Murkey Hill Offices, Cow Lane, Middleton Tyas, N Yorks, DL10 6RW
Activities: Buying and selling of own real estate
Major Shareholder: Ralph Congreve
Officers: Ralph Congreve [1953] Director

Clifton Engineering (North East) Limited
Incorporated: 15 April 1993 *Employees:* 32
Net Worth: £1,782,331 *Total Assets:* £2,616,421
Registered Office: Coopies Haugh, Coopies Lane Industrial Estate, Morpeth, Northumberland, NE61 6JN
Activities: Machining
Officers: Dorothy Kerr Pearson, Secretary; Andrew Robert Pearson [1972] Director/Manager; David William Simm [1961] Director/Engineer

Clifton Holdings (North East) Limited
Incorporated: 17 July 2014 *Employees:* 53
Net Worth: £3,448,503 *Total Assets:* £4,671,487
Registered Office: Clifton Engineering, Coopies Haugh, Morpeth, Northumberland, NE61 6JN
Activities: Activities of production holding companies
Officers: Andrew Robert Pearson [1972] Director/Manager

Clifton Property Investments Limited
Incorporated: 10 October 2012
Net Worth: £202,222 *Total Assets:* £1,464,073
Registered Office: Unit 5 Maling Court, Union Street, Newcastle upon Tyne, NE2 1BP
Activities: Management of real estate on a fee or contract basis
Shareholders: Ian Robert Baggett; Jason Moray Justin MacKay; Lauren Emma MacKay; Lorna Louise Crook
Officers: Ian Robert Baggett [1972] Director; Jason Moray Justin MacKay [1973] Director; Michael Raymond Shipley [1984] Director

The Clinkard Group Limited
Incorporated: 4 December 1992 *Employees:* 587
Net Worth: £13,772,000 *Total Assets:* £19,333,000
Registered Office: Eveline House, Cannon Park Way, Cannon Park, Middlesbrough, Cleveland, TS1 5JU
Activities: Wholesale of clothing and footwear
Shareholder: Charles Colin Clinkard
Officers: Jonathan Mankin, Secretary; Graeme Boulton [1985] Director/IT; Charles Jonathan Clinkard [1965] Group Managing Director; Rachel Anne Clinkard [1971] Director/E Commerce; Toby Hewison [1968] Retail Operations Director; Jonathan Mankin [1963] Director/Accountant; Christopher Ian McBride [1943] Director/Management Consultant/CD; Timothy Payne [1977] Director/Merchandiser

W.D. Close & Sons Limited
Incorporated: 27 June 1986 *Employees:* 119
Net Worth: £8,447,186 *Total Assets:* £10,320,555
Registered Office: Units 14-16 Valentia Avenue, Walkergate, Newcastle upon Tyne, NE6 4QR
Activities: Manufacture of other fabricated metal products n.e.c.
Shareholders: William Dixon Close; Ann Helen Close
Officers: Ann Helen Close, Secretary; Ann Helen Close [1954] Director; Christopher Paul Close [1982] Works Director; Dean William Close [1965] Director; William Dixon Close [1943] Director; Kelly Christopher Scott [1972] Works Director

Close House Golf Club Limited
Incorporated: 15 October 2007 *Employees:* 106
Net Worth Deficit: £1,884,810 *Total Assets:* £5,747,534
Registered Office: Golf Club, Close House, Heddon on the Wall, Newcastle upon Tyne, NE15 0HT
Activities: Activities of sport clubs
Parent: Wylie Childrens Settlement Trust
Officers: Kerry Louise McDonnell, Secretary; Alan Graham [1956] Director; Andrew William Graham Wylie [1959] Director

Close House Hospitality Limited
Incorporated: 6 July 2004
Net Worth: £5,246,738 *Total Assets:* £13,234,731
Registered Office: Heddon on the Wall, Newcastle upon Tyne, NE15 0HT
Activities: Hotels and similar accommodation
Major Shareholder: Andrew William Graham Wylie
Officers: Kerry Louise McDonnell, Secretary; Alan Graham [1956] Director; Andrew William Graham Wylie [1959] Director

Closegate Hotel Development (Durham) Limited
Incorporated: 9 April 1925 *Employees:* 69
Net Worth: £7,855,236 *Total Assets:* £14,824,032
Registered Office: Alderman Fenwick's House, 98-100 Pilgrim Street, Newcastle upon Tyne, NE1 6SQ
Activities: Hotels and similar accommodation
Shareholder: Diane Frances Bishop
Officers: Michaela Caroline Hunt, Secretary; Diane Frances Bishop [1949] Director/Administrator; Robert William Bishop [1947] Director; Generaldine Anne Hunt [1950] Director/Manager; Michaela Caroline Hunt [1981] Director/Administrator

Closegate Projects Limited
Incorporated: 8 December 2005 *Employees:* 73
Net Worth: £6,341,563 *Total Assets:* £14,126,603
Registered Office: Alderman Fenwick's House, 98-100 Pilgrim Street, Newcastle upon Tyne, NE1 6SQ
Activities: Development of building projects
Shareholders: Geraldine Ann Hunt; Diane Frances Bishop
Officers: Michaela Caroline Hunt, Secretary; Diane Frances Bishop [1949] Director/Retired; Robert William Bishop [1947] Director; Generaldine Anne Hunt [1950] Director/Manager; Michaela Caroline Hunt [1981] Director/Administrator

Closewalk Limited
Incorporated: 29 March 1965 *Employees:* 7
Net Worth: £1,008,506 *Total Assets:* £2,568,490
Registered Office: 1st Floor Offices, Grandstand Garage, Kenton Road, Gosforth, Newcastle upon Tyne, NE3 4NB
Activities: Buying and selling of own real estate
Shareholders: Nigel John Mills; Susan Mills
Officers: Nigel John Mills, Secretary; Emma Paige Mills [1998] Director/Student; Gregory Bruce Mills [1998] Director/Student; Nigel John Mills [1958] Director/Chartered Accountant; Susan Mills [1961] Director; Martin Geoffrey Stokoe [1964] Director

J.T. Clough & Son Limited
Incorporated: 16 May 1951
Net Worth: £4,016,263 *Total Assets:* £4,076,674
Registered Office: Cranford, 27 Batt House Road, Stocksfield, Northumberland, NE43 7RA
Activities: Renting and operating of Housing Association real estate
Major Shareholder: Thomas Frederick Fagg
Officers: Sheila Rosemary Fagg, Secretary; Sheila Rosemary Fagg [1944] Director/State Registered Nurse; Thomas Frederick Fagg [1944] Director

Clouston Group Ltd
Incorporated: 31 January 1994 *Employees:* 213
Net Worth Deficit: £9,229,708 *Total Assets:* £48,559,776
Registered Office: Stockbridge House, Trinity Gardens, Newcastle upon Tyne, NE1 2HJ
Activities: Activities of head offices
Major Shareholder: William David Clouston
Officers: William David Clouston, Secretary; Martryn Bowes [1964] Director/Financial Consultant; Pamela Fry Clouston [1950] Director; Richard Donald Carr Clouston [1976] Director/Student; William David Clouston [1946] Company Secretary/Director

Clovely Care Limited
Incorporated: 22 June 2009
Registered Office: Oakmere, Belmont Business Park, Durham, DH1 1TW
Activities: Residential nursing care facilities
Shareholder: Kathryn Dunningham
Officers: Kathryn Dunningham [1971] Director

Clover Controls Limited
Incorporated: 20 July 1992 *Employees:* 23
Net Worth: £170,317 *Total Assets:* £1,702,803
Registered Office: Clover House, Princesway North, Team Valley Trading Estate, Gateshead, Tyne & Wear, NE11 0TU
Activities: Manufacture of other electrical equipment
Shareholders: Paul Jackson; Gordon Brown
Officers: Paul Jackson, Secretary; Paul Jackson [1956] Director/Electronics Engineer

CLX Ltd
Incorporated: 13 April 2001
Net Worth: £1,371,391 *Total Assets:* £1,759,475
Registered Office: Unit 30B The Gates Shopping Centre, Lambton Walk, Durham, DH1 4SL
Activities: Licenced restaurants
Major Shareholder: Kit Keung Lau
Officers: Choi Ling Lau, Secretary; Karen Sau Kin Lau, Secretary; Karen Sau Kin Lau [1969] Director/Restaurateur; Kit Keung Lau [1965] Director

CMC North East Ltd
Incorporated: 9 November 2005 *Employees:* 10
Net Worth: £305,173 *Total Assets:* £1,970,216
Registered Office: Unit D6, Princesway, Team Valley Trading Estate, Gateshead, Tyne & Wear, NE11 0TU
Activities: Wholesale of wood, construction materials and sanitary equipment
Major Shareholder: David John Holmes
Officers: David John Holmes [1968] Managing Director; Stephen Wallace [1969] Director/Manager

CML Property Solutions Limited
Incorporated: 19 March 2013
Net Worth: £201,068 *Total Assets:* £1,764,397
Registered Office: Colmas House, West End, Willington, Crook, Co Durham, DL15 0HW
Activities: Renting and operating of Housing Association real estate
Shareholders: Angela Bartlett; Christopher John Bartlett
Officers: Angela Bartlett [1969] Director; Christopher John Bartlett [1971] Director

CMN Support Services Limited
Incorporated: 23 March 1993
Net Worth: £727,715 *Total Assets:* £753,413
Registered Office: Centre for Advanced Industry, Coble Dene, Royal Quays, North Shields, Tyne & Wear, NE29 6DE
Activities: Other business support service activities n.e.c.
Officers: Stephen Charles Thompson, Secretary; Pierre Maurice Jean-Marie Balmer [1955] Director/Chairman [French]; Andrew Paul Hartley [1965] Director/Engineer; Camille Elias Karam [1958] Director/Financial Adviser [American]; Peter Rossiter [1945] Director/Engineer; Dieter Rottsieper [1959] Director [German]; Stephen Charles Thompson [1975] Director/Chartered Accountant

CMP Marketing Limited
Incorporated: 11 May 1921 *Employees:* 8
Net Worth: £2,468,423 *Total Assets:* £2,497,914
Registered Office: 11 Glasshouse Street, St Peters, Newcastle upon Tyne, NE6 1BS
Activities: Other business support service activities n.e.c.
Shareholder: Sheila Claire Longo
Officers: Joanne Alicea Wilkes, Secretary; Richard Dodd [1974] Director; Jonathan Charles Lamb [1977] Group Director; Leona Lamb [1971] Director/Chartered Accountant; Sally Lamb [1939] Director; Vincent Patterson [1961] Director; David Harold Wilson [1966] Director; Shirley Sylvia Wilson [1929] Director

CMP Products Limited
Incorporated: 7 March 2007 *Employees:* 272
Net Worth: £25,091,000 *Total Assets:* £44,226,000
Registered Office: 11 Glasshouse Street, St Peters, Newcastle upon Tyne, NE6 1BS
Activities: Other manufacturing n.e.c.
Parent: British Engines (UK) Limited
Officers: Joanne Alicea Wilkes, Secretary; Laura Joicey [1976] Director/Group Chief Financial Officer; Alexander Harold Lamb [1971] Director; Jonathan Charles Lamb [1977] Group Manufacturing Director; Vincent Patterson [1961] Director/Chief Executive Officer (CEO)

CMS Holdings UK Limited
Incorporated: 22 June 2005 *Employees:* 26
Net Worth: £400,810 *Total Assets:* £762,041
Registered Office: Tyne House, Temple Street, Gateshead, Tyne & Wear, NE10 0HN
Activities: Activities of other holding companies n.e.c.
Shareholders: Nicholas John Smith; Neil William Smith
Officers: Nicholas John Smith, Secretary; Neil William Smith [1964] Director; Nicholas John Smith [1969] Director

Co-Wheels Car Club Community Interest Company
Incorporated: 25 February 2008 *Employees:* 32
Net Worth Deficit: £530,978 *Total Assets:* £1,484,283
Registered Office: 3a Sunderland Road, Gilesgate, Durham, DH1 2LH
Activities: Renting and leasing of cars and light motor vehicles
Shareholders: Paul David Balmont; Richard Morris Falconer
Officers: Paul David Balmont, Secretary; Paul David Balmont [1979] Director/Business Manager; Richard Morris Falconer [1980] Director/Account Manager

The Coach Inn Company Limited
Incorporated: 4 June 1998
Net Worth: £302,056 *Total Assets:* £1,954,658
Registered Office: c/o Censis, Exchange Building, 66 Church Street, Hartlepool, Cleveland, TS24 7DN
Activities: Hotels and similar accommodation
Shareholders: George Thomas Crow; Greta Florence Crow
Officers: George Thomas Crow, Secretary/Leisure Services Manager; George Thomas Crow [1953] Director/Leisure Services Manager; Greta Florence Crow [1961] Director/Leisure Services Manager

Coal Contractors Limited
Incorporated: 29 October 1951 *Employees:* 3
Net Worth: £7,591,918 *Total Assets:* £7,951,347
Registered Office: Stotforth Hill House, Rushyford, Ferryhill, Co Durham, DL17 0NF
Activities: Open cast coal working
Parent: Hall Construction Services Limited
Officers: Neville John Hall [1956] Director; Stephen Hall [1954] Director; Garry Hutchinson [1955] Director

Coast & Country Connections Ltd.
Incorporated: 21 October 1981
Registered Office: Carpenters Court, River Bank Road, Alnmouth, Northumberland, NE66 2RH
Activities: Management of real estate on a fee or contract basis
Major Shareholder: Nicola Brierley
Officers: Nicola Hough Brierley [1955] Director; Alistair Denney Johnson [1948] Director/Farmer

Coastline Fish and Chip Restaurant Limited
Incorporated: 30 August 2001
Net Worth: £1,000,518 *Total Assets:* £1,312,227
Registered Office: B3 Kingsway, Team Valley Trading Estate, Gateshead, Tyne & Wear, NE11 0JQ
Activities: Take-away food shops and mobile food stands
Parent: Gregorio Holdings Limited
Officers: Domenico Gregorio, Company Secretary; Domenico Gregorio [1972] Director; Gino Gregorio [1970] Director

Coastline Properties Limited
Incorporated: 22 November 1989
Net Worth: £549,877 *Total Assets:* £896,262
Registered Office: 6 Highbury, Monkseaton, Whitley Bay, Tyne & Wear, NE25 8EF
Activities: Other letting and operating of own or leased real estate
Major Shareholder: Ian Alexander Dickie
Officers: Caroline Dickie, Secretary; Ian Alexander Dickie [1949] Director

David Coates Agronomy Limited
Incorporated: 31 July 2009 *Employees:* 4
Net Worth: £1,046,375 *Total Assets:* £1,113,174
Registered Office: The Beeches, 28 Merrybent, Darlington, Co Durham, DL2 2LE
Activities: Activities of agricultural holding companies
Officers: Debra Ann Coates, Secretary; David Coates [1960] Director; Debra Ann Coates [1960] Director; Richard Coates [1993] Director

Coatham House
Incorporated: 29 March 1993 *Employees:* 13
Net Worth: £573,433 *Total Assets:* £798,156
Registered Office: 1st Floor, 5a High Street, Redcar, Cleveland, TS10 3BY
Activities: Other accommodation
Officers: Hazel Valerie Yare, Secretary; Andrew Petterson [1978] Director/Social Business Manager; Patricia Mary Rutherford [1932] Director/Retired Headteacher; David Robert Stones [1957] Director/Carer; Hazel Valerie Yare [1945] Director

Cobalt PSS LLP
Incorporated: 28 January 2014
Net Worth: £3,079,588 *Total Assets:* £3,084,858
Registered Office: 2nd Floor, Tirrem House, 16 High Street, Yarm, Cleveland, TS15 9AE
Officers: Andrew Loughran Preston [1966] Member; Graham Michael Senior [1970] Member; Graham Kevin Sizer [1969] Member

Coble Developments Limited
Incorporated: 7 August 2013 *Employees:* 7
Net Worth: £637,297 *Total Assets:* £1,808,726
Registered Office: The Boatyard, 14 Coquet Street, Amble, Morpeth, Northumberland, NE65 0DJ
Activities: Development of building projects
Shareholders: Antony Karl Pull; Nicholas Roger Spurr
Officers: Antony Karl Pull [1963] Director; Nicholas Roger Spurr [1960] Director

Cockerton Green Developments Ltd
Incorporated: 10 August 2009 *Employees:* 2
Net Worth: £1,540,337 *Total Assets:* £3,227,656
Registered Office: Unit 14 Halegrove Court, Cygnet Drive, Stockton on Tees, Cleveland, TS18 3DB
Activities: Buying and selling of own real estate
Shareholders: Dennis Harley Developments Ltd; A T & P Rentals Ltd
Officers: Rosaleen Anne Harley-Rodgers, Secretary/Civil Engineering; James Dennis Harley [1974] Director/Construction; Charles Joseph Leonard [1964] Director

Code Property Developments Limited
Incorporated: 13 September 2005 *Employees:* 1
Net Worth: £58,923 *Total Assets:* £814,552
Registered Office: 65 Duke Street, Darlington, Co Durham, DL3 7AQ
Activities: Development of building projects
Shareholders: Paul Sutton Million; Adam Christian Watson
Officers: Ernest Sutton Million, Secretary; Paul Sutton Million [1971] Director; Adam Christian Watson [1971] Director/Hairdresser Property Developer

Cofathec Energy Services Limited
Incorporated: 25 June 2002 *Employees:* 1
Net Worth Deficit: £1,322,000 *Total Assets:* £5,654,000
Registered Office: Shared Services Centre, Q3 Office, Quorum Business Park, Benton Lane, Newcastle upon Tyne, NE12 8EX
Activities: Dormant company
Parent: Cofathec Energy Limited
Officers: Sarah Gregory, Secretary; Samuel Hockman [1982] Director

Coffee Design Limited
Incorporated: 24 April 2006 *Employees:* 20
Net Worth: £629,719 *Total Assets:* £1,209,697
Registered Office: 16 Great North Road, Jesmond, Newcastle upon Tyne, NE2 4PS
Activities: Advertising agencies
Major Shareholder: Lee Stobbart
Officers: Gary Carr, Secretary; Lee Stobbart [1971] Director/Graphic Designer

Henry Colbeck Limited
Incorporated: 12 October 1964 *Employees:* 138
Net Worth: £7,156,426 *Total Assets:* £12,593,097
Registered Office: Seventh Avenue, Team Valley Trading Estate, Gateshead, Tyne & Wear, NE11 0HG
Activities: Non-specialised wholesale of food, beverages and tobacco
Shareholder: Douglas William Colbeck
Officers: Andrew Mark Naylor, Secretary; Douglas William Colbeck [1967] Sales Director; Georgina Samantha Colbeck [1967] Director; Isobel Colbeck [1936] Personnel Director; William Henry Colbeck [1936] Director/Chairman; Paul David Holliday [1976] Financial Director; David Murdoch [1954] Sales Director; Andrew Mark Naylor [1957] Managing Director; Hugh Terence O'Brien [1967] Operations Director; Michael Shone [1957] Purchasing Director

Colena Ltd.
Incorporated: 17 May 2006 *Employees:* 17
Net Worth: £1,087,698 *Total Assets:* £1,749,751
Registered Office: Unit 9 Jupiter Court, Orion Business Park, North Shields, Tyne & Wear, NE29 7SE
Activities: Other retail sale not in stores, stalls or markets
Shareholders: Joel Charles Peter Ross; Michelle Ann Lucy
Officers: Michelle Ann Lucy, Secretary; Joel Charles Peter Ross [1977] Director/Manager

Coles Solicitors Limited
Incorporated: 4 July 2007
Net Worth: £289,567 *Total Assets:* £1,296,632
Registered Office: Century House, Thornfield Business Park, Standard Way Business Park, Northallerton, N Yorks, DL6 2XQ
Activities: Solicitors
Major Shareholder: Peter Alexander Gibson
Officers: Peter Alexander Gibson, Secretary/Solicitors; Peter Alexander Gibson [1975] Director/Solicitors; Emma Clare Ladd [1979] Director/Solicitor; Alexander Irving Spurr [1980] Director/Solicitor

Colewood Internet Ltd
Incorporated: 17 September 1999 *Employees:* 38
Net Worth: £239,068 *Total Assets:* £906,391
Registered Office: Colewood House, 1 Kingfisher Court, Bowesfield Park, Stockton on Tees, Cleveland, TS18 3EX
Activities: Data processing, hosting and related activities
Shareholder: Travis Michael Coleman
Officers: Travis Michael Coleman [1977] Director; James Wilson [1982] Director

D. Collard Limited
Incorporated: 13 December 1984 *Employees:* 28
Net Worth: £3,462,080 *Total Assets:* £4,430,434
Registered Office: Lily Estate, Ponteland Road, Throckley, Newcastle upon Tyne, NE15 9EP
Activities: Removal services
Officers: Brenda Collard, Secretary; Brenda Collard [1958] Director; David Collard [1956] Director

Colledge Trundle & Hall Limited
Incorporated: 9 July 1996 *Employees:* 25
Net Worth Deficit: £240,000 *Total Assets:* £2,816,000
Registered Office: Shared Services Centre, Q3 Office, Quorum Business Park, Benton Lane, Newcastle upon Tyne, NE12 8EX
Activities: Electrical installation
Parent: Engie Services Holding UK Limited
Officers: Sarah Gregory, Secretary; Mark Gallacher [1979] Director; Graham Oxley [1976] Director

Collier Properties Limited
Incorporated: 23 December 2002 *Employees:* 4
Net Worth: £1,492,728 *Total Assets:* £1,682,260
Registered Office: 466 Linthorpe Road, Middlesbrough, Cleveland, TS5 6JG
Activities: Other letting and operating of own or leased real estate
Shareholder: David Anthony Collier
Officers: David Anthony Collier, Secretary; David Anthony Collier [1958] Director; Judith Ann Collier [1957] Director

Collingdon Developments Ltd
Incorporated: 26 January 1987
Net Worth: £1,006,366 *Total Assets:* £1,643,656
Registered Office: Suite 6, Spencer House, Market Lane, Swalwell, Tyne & Wear, NE16 3DS
Activities: Other letting and operating of own or leased real estate
Shareholders: David Andrew Foggin; Marc David Foggin
Officers: Dorothy Amanda Oloman, Secretary; David Andrew Foggin [1952] Director/Sole Trader Property Developer; Marc David Foggin [1983] Director/Co Manager

Collingwood Business Solutions Limited
Incorporated: 16 August 1996 *Employees:* 89
Net Worth: £3,089,624 *Total Assets:* £10,552,902
Registered Office: Collingwood House, Redburn Court, Earl Grey Way, North Shields, Tyne & Wear, NE29 6AR
Activities: Other activities auxiliary to insurance and pension funding
Parent: Horatio Holdings Limited
Officers: Michelle Beenshill, Secretary; Gary John Fothergill [1971] Director/Certified Accountant; Steven Geoffrey Welton [1968] Director

Collingwood Groundworks Limited
Incorporated: 24 July 2003 *Employees:* 18
Net Worth: £546,868 *Total Assets:* £931,052
Registered Office: Unit 1d, Steetley Terrace, Quarrington Hill Industrial Estate, Quarrington Hill, Co Durham, DH6 4QJ
Activities: Construction of commercial buildings
Shareholder: Renee Collingwood
Officers: Renee Collingwood, Secretary; Ian Anthony Carr [1968] Director; Gareth John Collingwood [1981] Director; John Collingwood [1953] Director/Construction Manager; Renee Collingwood [1953] Director

Collingwood Insurance Services (U.K.) Limited
Incorporated: 7 March 2001 *Employees:* 88
Net Worth: £7,461,878 *Total Assets:* £7,826,272
Registered Office: Collingwood House, Redburn Court, Earl Grey Way, North Shields, Tyne & Wear, NE29 6AR
Activities: Non-life insurance
Parent: Collingwood Business Solutions Limited
Officers: Michelle Beenshill, Secretary; Gary John Fothergill [1971] Director/Certified Accountant; Steven Geoffrey Welton [1968] Director

Collins (Seafoods) Limited
Incorporated: 26 June 1986 *Employees:* 33
Net Worth: £6,000,450 *Total Assets:* £11,950,874
Registered Office: Unit 2 Park 2000, Millennium Way, Aycliffe Industrial Park, Newton Aycliffe, Co Durham, DL5 6AR
Activities: Wholesale of meat and meat products
Parent: Seagold Limited
Officers: Claire Elizabeth Carter, Secretary; Gustaf Baldvinsson [1957] Director [Icelander]; Thorsteinn Mar Baldvinsson [1952] Director [Icelander]; Claire Elizabeth Carter [1979] Director; Richard Collins [1954] Director; Kenneth Gary Lethem [1959] Director

Colmans Caterers Limited
Incorporated: 23 September 2003 *Employees:* 28
Net Worth: £753,635 *Total Assets:* £1,845,336
Registered Office: 182-186 Ocean Road, South Shields, Tyne & Wear, NE33 2JQ
Activities: Licenced restaurants
Shareholders: Frances Ord; Richard Ord
Officers: Frances Ord, Secretary; Richard Ord [1992] Director/Caterer; Richard Ord [1954] Director/Caterer

JW Colpitts & Co Limited
Incorporated: 4 February 1980
Net Worth: £748,847 *Total Assets:* £1,138,076
Registered Office: John Anderson House, Coniston Road, Blyth Riverside Business Park, Blyth, Northumberland, NE24 4RF
Activities: Manufacture of other fabricated metal products n.e.c.
Officers: Prachi Sharma, Secretary; William Emery [1955] Director/Carpenter; Prachi Sharma [1956] Director/Finance

Colthome Limited
Incorporated: 22 September 1982
Registered Office: The Grange, Little Maltby Farm, Low Lane, High Leven, Yarm, Cleveland, TS15 9JT
Activities: Other letting and operating of own or leased real estate
Officers: Brian Malcolm Harriman, Secretary; Brian Malcolm Harriman [1949] Director; Ian Martin Harriman [1975] Director; Susan Elizabeth Harriman [1951] Director

Colton Excavations Limited
Incorporated: 6 December 1999
Net Worth: £20,111 *Total Assets:* £932,575
Registered Office: 6 Drum Industrial Estate, Birtley, Co Durham, DH2 1UR
Activities: Site preparation
Parent: Colton Group Limited
Officers: Marian Teresa Thompson, Secretary; Hugh Finton Colton [1939] Director; Jessie Agnes Colton [1934] Director; Paul Fintan Colton [1964] Director; Marian Teresa Thompson [1963] Director

Colton Group Limited
Incorporated: 29 January 2007 *Employees:* 103
Net Worth: £2,387,149 *Total Assets:* £5,295,131
Registered Office: 6 Drum Industrial Estate, Birtley, Co Durham, DH2 1UR
Activities: Activities of head offices
Shareholders: Hugh Finton Colton; Jessie Agnes Colton
Officers: Marian Teresa Thompson, Secretary; Hugh Finton Colton [1939] Director; Jessie Agnes Colton [1934] Director; Paul Fintan Colton [1964] Director; Marian Teresa Thompson [1963] Director

H F Colton Plant Hire Ltd
Incorporated: 15 May 2002 *Employees:* 76
Net Worth: £2,198,559 *Total Assets:* £4,529,571
Registered Office: 6 Drum Industrial Estate, Birtley, Co Durham, DH2 1UR
Activities: Construction of commercial buildings
Parent: Colton Group Limited
Officers: Marian Teresa Thompson, Secretary; Hugh Finton Colton [1939] Director; Jessie Agnes Colton [1934] Director; Paul Fintan Colton [1964] Director; Marian Teresa Thompson [1963] Director

Commerce Chambers Ltd
Incorporated: 2 October 2015
Net Worth Deficit: £167,048 *Total Assets:* £1,959,148
Registered Office: Keel House, Garth Heads, Newcastle upon Tyne, NE1 2JE
Activities: Other letting and operating of own or leased real estate
Parent: Inperpetuity Limited
Officers: Christopher Bull, Secretary; David Redhead [1980] Director; Alan Selby [1979] Director

Commercial & Industrial Interiors Ltd
Incorporated: 14 November 2005
Net Worth: £422,356 *Total Assets:* £905,682
Registered Office: Commercial House, Princess Way, Low Prudhoe Industrial Estate, Prudhoe, Northumberland, NE42 6HD
Activities: Other building completion and finishing
Shareholders: Philip John Dunnage; John Iain Dunnage; Anita Veronica Dunnage
Officers: John Iain Dunnage, Secretary; Anita Veronica Dunnage [1965] Director/Teacher; John Iain Dunnage [1962] Director

Commercial & Temperance Developments LLP
Incorporated: 16 July 2010
Net Worth: £568,899 *Total Assets:* £2,119,103
Registered Office: 79-84 North East Wholesale Market, Team Valley Trading Estate, Gateshead, Tyne & Wear, NE11 0QY
Officers: John Holland [1960] Member; Michael Anthony Keen [1963] Member

Commercial Edge Consulting Limited
Incorporated: 17 September 2007 *Employees:* 1
Net Worth: £502,077 *Total Assets:* £1,195,605
Registered Office: 8 Moorfield, Newcastle upon Tyne, NE2 3NL
Activities: Management consultancy activities other than financial management
Major Shareholder: Nicholas Stephen Moore
Officers: Nicholas Stephen Moore [1962] Managing Director

Commercial Insulation Services Ltd
Incorporated: 19 October 2011 *Employees:* 6
Net Worth: £536,025 *Total Assets:* £1,701,472
Registered Office: Commercial Insulation Services Limited, Naylor Court, Patterson Street, Blaydon on Tyne, Tyne & Wear, NE21 5SD
Activities: Other construction installation
Shareholder: Ian Neville Marsden
Officers: Richard Brake [1970] Director; Ian Neville Marsden [1971] Director

Commercial Maintenance Services UK Limited
Incorporated: 5 May 2000 *Employees:* 63
Net Worth: £349,713 *Total Assets:* £2,002,517
Registered Office: Tyne House, Temple Street, Felling, Gateshead, Tyne & Wear, NE10 0HN
Activities: Other business support service activities n.e.c.
Parent: CMS Holdings UK Limited
Officers: Nicholas John Smith, Secretary/Director; Neil William Smith [1964] Director; Nicholas John Smith [1969] Director

Commercial Propshaft Services Limited
Incorporated: 19 April 1989
Net Worth: £764,838 *Total Assets:* £793,359
Registered Office: 190 Kingsway South, Team Valley Trading Estate, Gateshead, Tyne & Wear, NE11 0SH
Activities: Wholesale trade of motor vehicle parts and accessories
Major Shareholder: Roy Stanley Carruthers
Officers: Margaret Carruthers, Secretary; Roy Stanley Carruthers [1947] Director

Commercial Vehicle Exports (Northern) Limited
Incorporated: 1 October 1996 *Employees:* 10
Net Worth: £1,069,259 *Total Assets:* £1,425,039
Registered Office: Pottery Road, Low Southwick, Sunderland, Tyne & Wear, SR5 2BP
Activities: Sale of used cars and light motor vehicles
Major Shareholder: Darren Ord
Officers: Mary Jean Baker, Secretary; Malcolm Jack Hewitt [1948] Director/Accountant; Darren Ord [1963] Director

Communicate Technology PLC
Incorporated: 1 December 2011
Registered Office: Wynyard Park House, Wynyard Park, Billingham, Cleveland, TS22 5TB
Activities: Other telecommunications activities
Officers: Simon Pocock, Secretary; Barry Hersh [1934] Director; Christopher Patrick Oliver [1963] Director; Dean Parsons [1963] Director; Konrad Marek Rutkowski [1979] Director/Accountant; Antony Derek Snaith [1965] Director/Communications Executive

Communicators Training Associates Limited
Incorporated: 24 August 2001
Net Worth: £1,042,442 *Total Assets:* £1,135,030
Registered Office: 8 Stoneleigh Court, Newton Aycliffe, Darlington, Co Durham, DL5 4TL
Activities: Management consultancy activities other than financial management
Major Shareholder: Isobel Jane Currie
Officers: Isobel Jane Currie [1964] Director/Training Associate

Community Based Care Health Limited
Incorporated: 11 February 1994 *Employees:* 83
Net Worth: £936,029 *Total Assets:* £1,619,853
Registered Office: Unit 7 Queens Park, Team Valley Trading Estate, Gateshead, Tyne & Wear, NE11 0QD
Activities: General medical practice activities
Officers: Craig Appleby, Secretary; Dr Jeremy Swain Warwick [1964] Director/Doctor; Dr William Don Westwood [1959] Director/GP

Community Estates UK Limited
Incorporated: 12 August 1994
Registered Office: c/o R Toby Raimes Solicitors, Churchill House, 12 Mosley Street, Newcastle upon Tyne, NE1 1DE
Activities: Renting and operating of Housing Association real estate
Major Shareholder: Christopher Watson
Officers: Christopher John Watson [1961] Managing Director

Community Foundation Serving Tyne & Wear and Northumberland
Incorporated: 4 July 1988 *Employees:* 22
Net Worth: £87,023,656 *Total Assets:* £90,018,112
Registered Office: Philanthropy House, Woodbine Road, Gosforth, Newcastle upon Tyne, NE3 1DD
Activities: Other social work activities without accommodation n.e.c.
Officers: Sonia Ellen Waugh, Finance Director; Lady Anna Margaret Blackett [1959] Hotel Director; Alastair Macbeth Conn [1955] Director/Investment Manager; Fiona Crozier [1966] Director; Paul Neil Farquhar [1962] Director; Andrew Scott Haigh [1963] Director/Financial Services; Geoffrey Mark Hodgson [1961] Director; Jon Stuart Mallen-Beadle [1969] Managing Director; Patrick Martin Melia [1967] Director/Chief Executive - Local Government; Jane Elizabeth Robinson [1970] Director/Chief Executive; Sharon Lesley Spurling [1963] Director/Chief Executive; Neil Kenneth Warwick [1968] Director; Kathryn Lucy Hay Winskell OBE DI [1963] Director/Pro Vice-Chancellor; Sally Anne Young [1956] Director/Chief Executive

Compac Services (NE) Limited
Incorporated: 2 February 1988 *Employees:* 16
Net Worth: £501,472 *Total Assets:* £1,110,266
Registered Office: 88 Westoe Road, South Shields, Tyne & Wear, NE33 4NA
Activities: Construction of utility projects for fluids
Parent: The Compac Group
Officers: Valerie Keighery, Secretary; David Malpass [1980] Director; John Paul Malpass [1986] Director

Compacbrand Limited
Incorporated: 15 April 1996
Net Worth: £2,430,317 *Total Assets:* £3,030,383
Registered Office: 18 Orchard Road, Fairfield, Stockton on Tees, Cleveland, TS19 7DA
Activities: Other letting and operating of own or leased real estate
Shareholder: Susan McGee
Officers: Susan McGee, Secretary; Lorena McGee [1946] Director/Housewife; Sara McGee [1975] Director; Susan McGee [1973] Director

Compass Developments (NE) Ltd
Incorporated: 23 January 2009
Net Worth: £231,444 *Total Assets:* £1,848,053
Registered Office: Unit 9 Trafalgar Court, South Nelson Road, South Nelson Industrial Estate, Cramlington, Northumberland, NE23 1WF
Activities: Construction of commercial buildings
Shareholder: Graham John Anderson
Officers: Christopher Morris, Secretary; Graham John Anderson [1976] Managing Director; Christopher Morris [1980] Director/Company Secretary; Stephen James O'Neill [1978] Director; Graham George Williams [1949] Director/Retired; Peter Lawrence Young [1958] Construction Director

Competition Line (U.K.) Limited
Incorporated: 17 May 1982 *Employees:* 129
Net Worth: £8,099,279 *Total Assets:* £38,383,688
Registered Office: Competition Line (UK) Ltd, 91 Eastmount Road, Darlington, Co Durham, DL1 1LA
Activities: Fitness facilities
Parent: Bystad Holdings AB
Officers: Timothy John Morant Curtis [1961] Director; Dr Ulla-Britt Gripenstedt [1962] Director [Swedish]; Kathryn Sarah O'Neil [1984] Finance Director; Claes Gunnar Mathias Palme [1954] Director/Consultant [Swedish]; Tomas Richard Folke Thuresson [1963] Director/Chief Executive [Swedish]

Complement Genomics Limited
Incorporated: 21 February 2000 *Employees:* 12
Net Worth: £394,060 *Total Assets:* £770,917
Registered Office: The Durham Genome Centre, Park House, Station Road, Lanchester, Co Durham, DH7 0EX
Activities: Research and experimental development on biotechnology
Major Shareholder: Dr Neil Fraser Sullivan
Officers: Dr Neil Fraser Sullivan, Secretary; Louise Claire Allcroft [1972] Director

Complete Cladding Systems Limited
Incorporated: 8 December 2000 *Employees:* 9
Net Worth: £155,346 *Total Assets:* £879,293
Registered Office: Newton Cap House, Toronto, Bishop Auckland, Co Durham, DL14 7SD
Activities: Construction of other civil engineering projects n.e.c.
Shareholders: Christopher Tremewan; Cresswell Timothy Robinson
Officers: Christopher Tremewan, Secretary/Director; Cresswell Timothy Robinson [1957] Director/Roofing Contractor; Christopher Tremewan [1971] Director

Complete Leasing Solutions Limited
Incorporated: 3 February 1998
Net Worth: £613,569 *Total Assets:* £808,875
Registered Office: 18 Apex Business Village, Cramlington, Northumberland, NE23 7BF
Activities: Other business support service activities n.e.c.
Shareholders: Joseph Patrick Lloyd; Ian Malcolm Hara
Officers: Joseph Patrick Lloyd, Secretary; David Lee Cummings [1978] Director/Sales Consultant; Ian Malcolm Hara [1976] Director/Leasing Broker; Joseph Patrick Lloyd [1969] Director

Complete Weed Control Limited
Incorporated: 1 July 1993 *Employees:* 9
Net Worth: £287,743 *Total Assets:* £1,041,590
Registered Office: Unit 16 Hurworth Road, Newton Aycliffe, Co Durham, DL5 6UD
Activities: Activities of head offices
Shareholders: Alan Charles Campbell Abel; Ian Graham
Officers: Alan Charles Campbell Abel, Secretary; Alan Charles Campbell Abel [1955] Director; Ian Graham [1970] Director

Con Mech Engineers Limited
Incorporated: 14 December 1960 *Employees:* 66
Net Worth: £6,127,187 *Total Assets:* £7,202,095
Registered Office: Con Mech Engineers Ltd, Hare Law Industrial Estate, Stanley, Co Durham, DH9 8UR
Activities: Manufacture of other fabricated metal products n.e.c.
Parent: Con Mech Group Ltd
Officers: Derek Neil, Secretary; Christine Ames [1962] Managing Director; Joseph Devanney [1962] Director; Robert James Dilley [1972] Director; Robert Howard Stapleton Dilley [1946] Director; Derek Neil [1964] Director

Con Mech Group Limited
Incorporated: 26 October 1949 *Employees:* 295
Net Worth: £16,971,984 *Total Assets:* £26,221,920
Registered Office: c/o Henry Williams Group Ltd, Dodsworth Street, Darlington, Co Durham, DL1 2NJ
Activities: Manufacture of other fabricated metal products n.e.c.
Major Shareholder: Robert Howard Stapleton Dilley
Officers: Robert James Dilley, Secretary; Christine Ames [1962] Director; Hazel Margaret Dilley [1946] Director; Dr Jonathan Charles Dilley [1975] Director; Robert James Dilley [1972] Director; Robert Howard Stapleton Dilley [1946] Director; Teresa Lorraine Heathcote [1980] Director; Derek Neil [1964] Director

Conduit Construction Network Limited
Incorporated: 23 May 2005
Net Worth: £504,901 *Total Assets:* £2,336,204
Registered Office: C E House, 3 Waldridge Way, Simonside East Industrial Estate, South Shields, Tyne & Wear, NE34 9PZ
Activities: Manufacture of other builders' carpentry and joinery
Shareholders: Christopher Jack Maguire; Laurence Edward James Maguire
Officers: Christopher Jack Maguire [1983] Director/Operations Manager; Laurence Edward James Maguire [1952] Director/General Manager

Coney (York) Limited
Incorporated: 21 April 2005
Net Worth: £2,396,045 *Total Assets:* £6,017,571
Registered Office: First Floor, Finchale House, Belmont Business Park, Durham, DH1 1TW
Activities: Other letting and operating of own or leased real estate
Officers: Helen Austin, Secretary; John Corbitt Barnsley [1948] Director; Spencer Trerise Glanville [1972] Director; Robert William Jefferson [1950] Director/Chartered Accountant

Connect Health Holdings Ltd
Incorporated: 15 December 2015 *Employees:* 355
Net Worth: £1,844,514 *Total Assets:* £6,198,638
Registered Office: The Light Box, Quorum Business Park, Benton Lane, Newcastle upon Tyne, NE12 8EU
Activities: Activities of other holding companies n.e.c.
Major Shareholder: Andrew Walton
Officers: Martin Burns, Secretary; Lucy Victoria Winwood Armstrong [1968] Director; Professor Andrew Geoffrey Walton [1962] Director/Physiotherapist

Connect Health Limited
Incorporated: 23 January 1989 *Employees:* 355
Net Worth: £1,373,369 *Total Assets:* £4,899,838
Registered Office: The Light Box, Quorum Business Park, Benton Lane, Newcastle upon Tyne, NE12 8EU
Activities: Other human health activities
Parent: Connect Health Holdings Limited
Officers: Lee Jon Ali, Secretary; Lee Jon Ali [1978] Finance Director; Lucy Victoria Winwood Armstrong [1968] Director; Lisa Marie Davidson [1975] HR Director; Jonathan Christopher Lowe [1964] Director; Michael Dennis Parsons [1950] Director; Michael Edward Turner [1971] Operations Director; Professor Andrew Geoffrey Walton [1962] Director/Physiotherapist; Dr Graeme Wilkes [1961] Medical Director

Connection Flooring Limited
Incorporated: 25 January 2012 *Employees:* 65
Net Worth: £928,601 *Total Assets:* £7,191,184
Registered Office: The Offices & Unit 4-5, The Future Business Park, Shildon, Co Durham, DL4 2RB
Activities: Wholesale of furniture, carpets and lighting equipment
Shareholders: Jason James Maguire; Daniel Richard Foskett
Officers: Kimberley Jane Richardson, Secretary; Daniel Richard Foskett [1988] Managing Director; Jason James Maguire [1973] Director; David Stubbs [1957] Director

Connor Group Limited
Incorporated: 9 April 1999 *Employees:* 173
Net Worth: £2,217,624 *Total Assets:* £12,315,802
Registered Office: Gadwall Road, Houghton-le-Spring, Co Durham, DH4 5NL
Activities: Activities of production holding companies
Major Shareholder: Dermot John Guerin
Officers: Anita Bonser-Hall, Secretary; Dermot John Guerin [1963] Managing Director [Irish]; Philip Cameron Hall [1969] Finance Director

Connor Solutions Limited
Incorporated: 21 May 1999 *Employees:* 171
Net Worth: £2,112,270 *Total Assets:* £12,412,955
Registered Office: Gadwall Road, Houghton-le-Spring, Co Durham, DH4 5NL
Activities: Manufacture of loaded electronic boards
Parent: Connor Group Limited
Officers: Anita Bonser-Hall, Secretary; Dermot John Guerin [1963] Managing Director [Irish]; Philip Cameron Hall [1969] Finance Director

Consett DP Limited
Incorporated: 25 October 2012 *Employees:* 48
Net Worth Deficit: £74,784 *Total Assets:* £883,454
Registered Office: 178 York Road, Hartlepool, Cleveland, TS26 9EA
Activities: Other retail sale of food in specialised stores
Major Shareholder: Mike Racz
Officers: Mike Racz, Secretary; Mike Racz [1982] Director/Franchisee

Constantine Building Services Limited
Incorporated: 16 January 2007
Net Worth: £678,518 *Total Assets:* £1,516,708
Registered Office: c/o Tindle's Chartered Accountants, Scotswood House, Teesdale South, Thornaby Place, Stockton on Tees, Cleveland, TS17 6SB
Activities: Management consultancy activities other than financial management
Parent: CBS Services Group Limited
Officers: Philip John O'Brien, Secretary; Alan Michael Constantine [1947] Director; Mark Alan Constantine [1970] Director

Consultus Developments Limited
Incorporated: 22 October 2007
Net Worth Deficit: £177,302 *Total Assets:* £1,393,965
Registered Office: Somerford Buildings, Norfolk Street, Sunderland, Tyne & Wear, SR1 1EE
Activities: Buying and selling of own real estate
Parent: Consultus Building Consultants Limited
Officers: Jean Gaye Graham, Secretary; Jean Gaye Graham [1959] Director/School Manager; John Alexander Sample [1937] Director

Consumer Refund Service Ltd
Incorporated: 14 December 2011
Net Worth: £2,267,758 *Total Assets:* £3,554,791
Registered Office: Arden House, Regent Centre, Gosforth, Newcastle upon Tyne, NE3 3LU
Activities: Other professional, scientific and technical activities n.e.c.
Parent: Moore House Holdings Ltd
Officers: Phillip Rodger, Secretary; Phillip Rodger [1978] Director/Legal Consultant

Contact Centre Professional Limited
Incorporated: 23 April 2001
Net Worth: £3,615,462 *Total Assets:* £5,524,694
Registered Office: Cuthbert House, City Road, All Saints, Newcastle upon Tyne, NE1 2ET
Activities: Management consultancy activities other than financial management
Major Shareholder: Shona Michelle Harper-Wilkes
Officers: Shona Michelle Harper, Secretary; Shona Michelle Harper [1974] Director; John Wilkes [1968] Consultant & IT Director

Container Sales (UK) Limited
Incorporated: 6 October 1992 *Employees:* 2
Net Worth: £2,719,064 *Total Assets:* £3,892,391
Registered Office: 25 Pallion West Industrial Estate, Sunderland, Tyne & Wear, SR4 6SJ
Activities: Wholesale of other machinery and equipment
Shareholders: Denise Wilson; Keith Wilson
Officers: Denise Wilson, Secretary; Ian Gibson [1966] Director; Carl Allen Hedley [1980] Director/Container Trader; Keith Wilson [1963] Director

Containerships (UK) Ltd
Incorporated: 29 March 1988 *Employees:* 140
Net Worth: £1,450,087 *Total Assets:* £5,519,164
Registered Office: Haverton Hill, Haverton Hill Road, Billingham, Cleveland, TS23 1PS
Activities: Operation of warehousing and storage facilities for land transport activities
Officers: Perttu Matias Noppari [1986] Director/Country Sales Manager [Finnish]; Harri Ragnar Gustaf Nordstrom [1961] Director [Finnish]; Karita Nina Helena Nordstrom [1963] Director [Finnish]; Veli Kimmo Ragnar Nordstrom [1962] Director [Finnish]

Contemporary Franchising Ltd
Incorporated: 7 October 2003 *Employees:* 10
Net Worth: £730,802 *Total Assets:* £1,332,140
Registered Office: 136 Marton Road, Middlesbrough, Cleveland, TS1 2ED
Activities: Activities of head offices
Shareholders: Alan George Simpson; Karen Storr Simpson
Officers: Alan George Simpson, Secretary/Hairdresser; Alan George Simpson [1970] Director/Hairdresser; Karen Storr Simpson [1965] Director/Hairdresser

Contract Catering Services (P&A) Holdings Limited
Incorporated: 19 September 2007
Net Worth: £1,011,117 *Total Assets:* £2,735,906
Registered Office: Suite 1 & 4 Kingsfield House, Carthorpe, Bedale, N Yorks, DL8 2LL
Activities: Activities of head offices
Parent: Contract Catering Services (P&A) Group Limited
Officers: David John Hall, Secretary; Edward Arthur Naylor [1956] Director

Contract Design (Northern) Limited
Incorporated: 10 April 1987 *Employees:* 31
Net Worth: £1,329,292 *Total Assets:* £1,853,011
Registered Office: Suite 7, 3rd Floor, Bulman House, Newcastle upon Tyne, NE3 1DQ
Activities: Engineering design activities for industrial process and production
Major Shareholder: Sidney Douglass
Officers: Peter Bernard Douglass, Secretary/Accountant; Eileen Douglass [1937] Director/Engineer; Peter Bernard Douglass [1961] Director/Accountant; Sidney Douglass [1937] Director/Engineer; Huw Guariento [1963] Director/HR and Business Development

Contract Joinery (North East) Limited
Incorporated: 14 June 2005 *Employees:* 55
Net Worth Deficit: £525,564 *Total Assets:* £1,061,873
Registered Office: Unit 1 Nest Road, Felling, Gateshead, Tyne & Wear, NE10 0ES
Activities: Joinery installation
Major Shareholder: Ian Sanderson
Officers: James Martin Mason, Secretary; Anthony William Graham [1957] Director/Manager; James Martin Mason [1959] Finance Director; Michael Stephen Morritt [1968] Director/Production; Kenneth Smith [1965] Director

Contract Laboratory Services Limited
Incorporated: 27 February 2006 *Employees:* 5
Net Worth: £895,120 *Total Assets:* £1,061,769
Registered Office: Unit 1a Rivergreen Business Centre, Queen's Meadow Business Park, Hartlepool, Cleveland, TS25 2DL
Activities: Other professional, scientific and technical activities n.e.c.
Shareholder: Mark Joseph Scott
Officers: Mark Joseph Scott, Secretary; Mark Joseph Scott [1975] Director/Sales Manager; Helen Elisabeth Tabbener [1974] Director/Finance Manager

Controle Mesure Regulation (UK) Limited
Incorporated: 9 February 1984 *Employees:* 67
Net Worth: £4,040,713 *Total Assets:* £8,755,278
Registered Office: New York Way, New York Industrial Park, Wallsend, Tyne & Wear, NE27 0QF
Activities: Manufacture of other electronic and electric wires and cables
Officers: Maureen Janice Jamieson, Secretary; Yves Barraquand [1960] Director/Group President [French]; Maureen Janice Jamieson [1971] Director/Chartered Accountant; Neil Wilkinson [1966] Managing Director

Convergys CMG UK Limited
Incorporated: 22 October 2003 *Employees:* 1,671
Net Worth: £7,326,000 *Total Assets:* £16,872,000
Registered Office: Q13 Quorum Business Park, Benton Lane, Newcastle upon Tyne, NE12 8BU
Activities: Activities of call centres
Parent: Convergys Corporation
Officers: Andrew Albert Farwig, Secretary; Richard James Evans [1976] Director/Vice President Operations UK Region; Joel Lewis [1963] Director/Vice President, Client Services; Jarrod Blaine Pontius [1971] Director/General Counsel Attorney [American]; Marife Butalid Zamora [1953] Managing Director [Filipino]

Converse Pharma Limited
Incorporated: 26 April 2013 *Employees:* 697
Net Worth: £7,897,000 *Total Assets:* £67,120,000
Registered Office: 7 Regents Drive, Prudhoe, Northumberland, NE42 6PX
Activities: Activities of distribution holding companies
Shareholders: Mark James Gulliford; Derek Andrew Wilson
Officers: Mark James Gulliford [1969] Director; David Horry [1964] Director/Chairman; Haydn Peter Smith [1966] Group IT Director; Derek Andrew Wilson [1964] Director

Conyers Trust
Incorporated: 18 January 2013 *Employees:* 213
Net Worth: £12,507,147 *Total Assets:* £14,498,668
Registered Office: Conyers School, Green Lane, Yarm, Cleveland, TS15 9ET
Activities: General secondary education
Officers: John McCann, Secretary; Christopher Paul Beaumont [1968] Director/Chartered Accountant; Judith Coleman [1939] Director; Frances Anne Johnson [1955] Director; Sandra Marjorie Jones [1952] Director/Retired; Professor Eileen Martin [1949] Director/Retired; Dr Richard John Alan Smith [1959] Director/Business Executive

Cook & Barker Inn Limited
Incorporated: 25 January 1999 *Employees:* 39
Net Worth: £787,373 *Total Assets:* £1,125,094
Registered Office: Newton on the Moor, Felton, Morpeth, Northumberland, NE65 9JY
Activities: Licenced restaurants
Major Shareholder: Philip John Farmer
Officers: Patricia Lynn Farmer, Secretary; Philip John Farmer [1959] Director

James Cook Discovery Ltd
Incorporated: 17 October 2016
Net Worth: £265,730 *Total Assets:* £15,112,939
Registered Office: Cargo Fleet Offices, Middlesbrough Road, Middlesbrough, Cleveland, TS6 6XH
Activities: Buying and selling of own real estate
Shareholders: Martin Russel Johnson; Peter John Broome
Officers: Peter John Broome [1959] Director; Martin Russel Johnson [1959] Director

Cookswell Garage Limited
Incorporated: 9 May 1980 *Employees:* 22
Net Worth: £390,204 *Total Assets:* £1,604,518
Registered Office: Cookswell Garage, Pegswood, Morpeth, Northumberland, NE61 6RF
Activities: Sale of new cars and light motor vehicles
Shareholder: Julie Stephenson
Officers: Julie Stephenson, Secretary; Alan Stephenson [1952] Sales Director/Chairman; Dale Stephenson [1959] Managing Director; Julie Stephenson [1957] Director/Company Secretary

Cool Assets Ltd
Incorporated: 23 June 2009
Registered Office: c/o Tindle's LLP, Scotswood House, Teesdale South, Thornaby Place, Stockton on Tees, Cleveland, TS17 6SB
Activities: Renting and leasing of other machinery, equipment and tangible goods n.e.c.
Major Shareholder: Janet Thornes
Officers: Jonathan Bryan Thornes [1960] Director

Cool Designs Limited
Incorporated: 23 September 2002
Net Worth: £330,254 *Total Assets:* £3,678,799
Registered Office: Unit 8 North Hylton Enterprise Park, Hepworth Road, Sunderland, Tyne & Wear, SR5 3JT
Activities: Other manufacturing n.e.c.
Parent: Cool Designs Holdings Limited
Officers: Jennifer Louise Devine Birkett, Secretary; Darrel Lawrence Birkett [1972] Director/Sales Representative

Cool Milk Administration Limited
Incorporated: 24 August 2010 *Employees:* 24
Net Worth: £409,869 *Total Assets:* £2,103,641
Registered Office: c/o Tindle's LLP, Scotswood House, Teesdale South, Thornaby Place, Stockton on Tees, Cleveland, TS17 6SB
Activities: Other business support service activities n.e.c.
Major Shareholder: Jonathan Bryan Thornes
Officers: John Sedgwick [1960] Director; Jonathan Bryan Thornes [1960] Director

Cool Milk at School Limited
Incorporated: 24 July 1998 *Employees:* 2
Net Worth: £122,902 *Total Assets:* £2,682,297
Registered Office: c/o Tindle's LLP, Scotswood House, Teesdale South, Thornaby Place, Stockton on Tees, Cleveland, TS17 6SB
Activities: Other business support service activities n.e.c.
Major Shareholder: Jonathan Bryan Thornes
Officers: Janet Thornes, Secretary; John Sedgwick [1960] Managing Director; Gordon Peter Smith [1958] Director; Jonathan Bryan Thornes [1960] Director

Cool Milk Limited
Incorporated: 24 July 1998
Net Worth: £123,741 *Total Assets:* £2,500,651
Registered Office: c/o Tindle's LLP, Scotswood House, Teesdale South, Thornaby Place, Stockton on Tees, Cleveland, TS17 6SB
Activities: Other business support service activities n.e.c.
Parent: Cool Milk Group Limited
Officers: Janet Thornes, Secretary; John Sedgwick [1960] Managing Director; Jonathan Bryan Thornes [1960] Director

Cool Refrigeration Limited
Incorporated: 14 September 1999
Net Worth: £72,073 *Total Assets:* £1,056,542
Registered Office: c/o Tindle's LLP, Scotswood House, Teesdale South, Thornaby Place, Stockton on Tees, Cleveland, TS17 6SB
Activities: Other service activities n.e.c.
Parent: Cool Milk Group Limited
Officers: Janet Thornes, Secretary; John Sedgwick [1960] Managing Director; Jonathan Bryan Thornes [1960] Director

Cool Retail Services Ltd
Incorporated: 9 July 2010 *Employees:* 69
Net Worth: £132,121 *Total Assets:* £1,128,298
Registered Office: 3b Wellington House, Wynyard Avenue, Wynyard, Billingham, Cleveland, TS22 5TB
Activities: Operation of warehousing and storage facilities for land transport activities
Shareholder: Malcolm Ibbotson
Officers: Malcolm Ibbotson [1948] Managing Director

Coolcheck Refrigeration Limited
Incorporated: 23 September 1985 *Employees:* 48
Net Worth: £996,812 *Total Assets:* £2,494,962
Registered Office: Unit D4, Bergen Close, Tyne Tunnel Estate, North Shields, Tyne & Wear, NE29 7TA
Activities: Installation of industrial machinery and equipment
Major Shareholder: Steven Gillin
Officers: Steven Gillin, Secretary; Ian Gillin [1964] Director/Sales Engineer; Steven Gillin [1962] Director/Engineer

Coolmore Land Limited
Incorporated: 28 October 2008
Net Worth Deficit: £472,027 *Total Assets:* £3,549,254
Registered Office: Ravensworth House, Fifth Avenue Business Park, Team Valley Trading Estate, Gateshead, Tyne & Wear, NE11 0HF
Activities: Buying and selling of own real estate
Parent: Tolent PLC
Officers: Andrew David Clark, Secretary; Andrew David Clark [1965] Director/Chartered Accountant; Andrew Ian McLeod [1964] Director; Paul William Webster [1962] Director/Engineer; John Gibbon Wood [1944] Director/Engineer

Cooper & Kime (Cleveland) Limited
Incorporated: 16 May 1995 *Employees:* 10
Net Worth: £1,121,480 *Total Assets:* £1,669,210
Registered Office: Lakeside House, Kingfisher Way, Stockton on Tees, Cleveland, TS18 3NB
Activities: Other human health activities
Major Shareholder: David Graham Jarvis
Officers: David Graham Jarvis, Secretary; David Graham Jarvis [1966] Director/Pharmacist; Kevin Alan Simpson [1958] Director/Pharmacist

James Cooper & Son (Tyneside) Ltd
Incorporated: 17 December 2004 *Employees:* 12
Net Worth: £410,218 *Total Assets:* £863,130
Registered Office: Burnside Garage, Annitsford, Cramlington, Northumberland, NE23 7BD
Activities: Maintenance and repair of motor vehicles
Shareholder: Margaret Denise Cooper
Officers: Margaret Denise Cooper, Secretary/Engineer; Margaret Denise Cooper [1960] Director/Engineer

Coopers Chemist Gt.Ayton Limited
Incorporated: 7 March 1978 *Employees:* 16
Net Worth: £481,722 *Total Assets:* £967,340
Registered Office: 112 High Street, Marske-by-the-Sea, Redcar, Cleveland, TS11 7BA
Activities: Dispensing chemist in specialised stores
Shareholder: Coopers Chemist Marske Ltd
Officers: Jonathan Cooper, Secretary; Dr David William Cooper [1960] Director; Jonathan Cooper [1962] Director; Judith Caroline Cooper [1960] Director/Solicitor; Lyn Cooper [1962] Pharmacy Director; Sadie Cooper [1930] Director; John Vincent Evans [1966] Director/Pharmacist

Coopers Chemist Marske Limited
Incorporated: 30 December 1977 *Employees:* 37
Net Worth: £3,009,811 *Total Assets:* £4,265,987
Registered Office: 112 High Street, Marske-by-the-Sea, Redcar, Cleveland, TS11 7BA
Activities: Dispensing chemist in specialised stores
Shareholders: Jonathan Cooper; Dr David William Cooper
Officers: Sadie Cooper, Secretary; Peter Ian Brady [1971] Director/Retail Pharmacy; Dr David William Cooper [1960] Director; George David Cooper [1994] Director/Geologist; Harry Robert Cooper [1994] Director/Neuroscientist; Jonathan Cooper [1962] Director; Judith Caroline Cooper [1960] Director; Lyn Cooper [1962] Director; Sadie Cooper [1930] Director; William John Donald Cooper [1992] Director/Market Researcher

Coopers Chemist Redcar Limited
Incorporated: 5 September 1985 *Employees:* 17
Net Worth: £861,240 *Total Assets:* £1,227,232
Registered Office: 112 High Street, Marske-by-the-Sea, Redcar, Cleveland, TS11 7BA
Activities: Dispensing chemist in specialised stores
Parent: Coopers Chemist Marske Ltd
Officers: Jonathan Cooper, Secretary/Pharmacy Director; Dr David William Cooper [1960] Director/Doctor; Jonathan Cooper [1962] Pharmacy Director; Lyn Cooper [1962] Pharmacy Director; Graham Readman [1959] Director/Pharmacist

Coopers Studios LLP
Incorporated: 29 January 2007
Net Worth: £1,867,000 *Total Assets:* £3,456,000
Registered Office: City Gate House, Bath Lane, Newcastle upon Tyne, NE4 5SQ
Officers: Peter Buchan [1953] Member; Mark Richard Thompson [1965] Member

Copeland Veterinary Practice Limited
Incorporated: 6 February 2013
Net Worth: £568,656 *Total Assets:* £848,088
Registered Office: Myton Park, Myton Road, Ingleby Barwick, Stockton-on-Tees, Cleveland, TS17 0WA
Activities: Veterinary activities
Shareholders: Penny Ann Copeland; Derek John Copeland
Officers: Derek Copeland [1961] Director; Penny Copeland [1961] Director

Copenhagen 1801 Limited
Incorporated: 28 October 2011 *Employees:* 70
Net Worth: £988,946 *Total Assets:* £1,581,979
Registered Office: 14 Scotswood Road, Newcastle upon Tyne, NE4 7JB
Activities: Other business support service activities n.e.c.
Parent: Pleasure Leisure Limited
Officers: David Fisher [1980] Director/Operations Manager; John Michael Little [1965] Director

Copernicus Adriatic LLP
Incorporated: 28 January 2011
Net Worth: £4,335,510 *Total Assets:* £4,928,118
Registered Office: UNW LLP, Citygate, St James Boulevard, Newcastle upon Tyne, NE1 4JE
Officers: Ivana Dotur [1974] Member; Arthur McQuade Hughes [1952] Member; Geoffrey Ronald Mayhill [1958] Member

Coquet Island Shellfish Limited
Incorporated: 21 August 2003 *Employees:* 41
Net Worth: £507,142 *Total Assets:* £1,536,540
Registered Office: 2 Pow Dene Court, North Shields, Tyne & Wear, NE30 1JG
Activities: Processing and preserving of fish, crustaceans and molluscs
Parent: D. R. Collin & Son Ltd
Officers: Thomas Newton, Secretary; James Cowe Cook [1955] Director; Ryan Thomas Mark [1991] Director; Thomas Newton [1973] Director; Shona Alice Wilson [1967] Director/Credit Controller

Coquet Trust
Incorporated: 17 May 2007 *Employees:* 177
Net Worth: £2,736,870 *Total Assets:* £2,999,399
Registered Office: 23 Lansdowne Terrace, Gosforth, Newcastle upon Tyne, NE3 1HP
Activities: Residential care activities for learning difficulties, mental health and substance abuse
Officers: Janet Margaret Bewick [1951] Director/Retired; Susan Welsh [1958] Director/Secretary

Corbitts Limited
Incorporated: 12 May 1986 *Employees:* 6
Net Worth: £1,297,772 *Total Assets:* £1,400,711
Registered Office: 5 Mosley Street, Newcastle upon Tyne, NE1 1YE
Activities: Wholesale of metals and metal ores
Major Shareholder: David Charles McMonagle
Officers: Jaqueline McMonagle, Secretary; David Charles McMonagle [1952] Director/Stamp Dealer; Jaqueline McMonagle [1952] Director/Stamp Dealer

Cordrow Limited
Incorporated: 6 November 2001 *Employees:* 2
Net Worth: £478,311 *Total Assets:* £1,300,085
Registered Office: 7 Brenkley Way, Blezard Business Park, Seaton Burn, Tyne & Wear, NE13 6DS
Activities: Management of real estate on a fee or contract basis
Parent: Redbale Limited
Officers: Stephen Leslie Doberman, Secretary; Christopher Owen Humble [1959] Director/Property Management

Corepeople Recruitment Limited
Incorporated: 11 December 1998 *Employees:* 772
Net Worth: £172,144 *Total Assets:* £2,662,480
Registered Office: Allergate House, Belmont Business Park, Durham, DH1 1TW
Activities: Temporary employment agency activities
Shareholders: Ian John Storer; Victoria Storer
Officers: Susan Marie Jackson, Secretary; Susan Marie Jackson [1976] Director/Company Secretary; Stephen Phillips [1979] Director/Recruitment Consultant; Ian John Storer [1965] Director; Victoria Storer [1977] Director/Recruitment Manager

Corespec Ltd
Incorporated: 3 June 1998 *Employees:* 23
Net Worth: £189,866 *Total Assets:* £1,719,056
Registered Office: Unit 7 Greencroft Industrial Park, Annfield Plain, Stanley, Co Durham, DH9 7YB
Activities: Manufacture of other articles of paper and paperboard n.e.c.
Shareholders: Brian Hodge; Gordon Charles Gregory
Officers: Brian Hodge, Secretary; Gordon Charles Gregory [1947] Director/Sales Manager; Brian Hodge [1955] Director/Operations Manager

Corinthia Limited
Incorporated: 9 June 2014
Net Worth: £504,778 *Total Assets:* £1,032,279
Registered Office: The Old Brewery, Castle Eden, Hartlepool, Cleveland, TS27 4SU
Activities: Other specialised construction activities n.e.c.
Major Shareholder: James Croft
Officers: David James Croft [1979] Director/Surveyor

Cormeton Electronics Limited
Incorporated: 18 May 1989 *Employees:* 57
Net Worth: £1,670,072 *Total Assets:* £3,025,891
Registered Office: 6 Jupiter Court, Orion Business Park, Tyne Tunnel Trading Estate, North Shields, Tyne & Wear, NE29 7SN
Activities: Security systems service activities
Shareholders: John Thomas Aitchison; Barbara Aitchison
Officers: John Thomas Aitchison, Secretary; John Thomas Aitchison [1960] Director; Alan James Anderson [1965] Sales Director; Stephen Christopher Rush [1978] Director/Engineering Manager

Cornerstone Chemical Company Limited
Incorporated: 13 December 2011 *Employees:* 3
Net Worth: £4,337,000 *Total Assets:* £11,326,000
Registered Office: Anson House, Fleming Business Centre, Burdon Terrace, Jesmond, Newcastle upon Tyne, NE2 3AE
Activities: Manufacture of other organic basic chemicals
Parent: Cornerstone Chemical Company Incorporated
Officers: Michael Cyril Driscoll [1970] Director [American]; Ronald James Foster [1967] Director [American]; Eifion Samuel Jones [1967] Director [British/American]

Martin Corney Limited
Incorporated: 24 August 2010
Net Worth: £26,011 *Total Assets:* £1,018,967
Registered Office: Southlands, The Avenue, Eaglescliffe, Stockton on Tees, Cleveland, TS16 9AS
Activities: Buying and selling of own real estate
Officers: Ian Jacob Waller, Secretary; Jarrod Colin Best [1977] Director; Martin Trevor Corney [1965] Director/Property Developer; David James Shann [1973] Director; Ian Jacob Waller [1952] Director/Property Developer

Norman Cornish Limited
Incorporated: 17 October 2014 *Employees:* 1
Net Worth Deficit: £4,994 *Total Assets:* £1,258,491
Registered Office: Portland House, Belmont Business Park, Belmont, Durham, DH1 1TW
Activities: Retail sale in commercial art galleries
Officers: Dorothy Cornish [1957] Director/Teacher; John Cornish [1956] Director/Retired; Ann Thornton [1949] Director/Retired; Michael Thornton [1948] Director/Retired Headteacher

Cornucopia Investments Limited
Incorporated: 21 August 2013
Net Worth: £5,426,907 *Total Assets:* £5,442,490
Registered Office: 140 Coniscliffe Road, Darlington, Co Durham, DL3 7RT
Activities: Security dealing on own account
Officers: Matthew Christopher Bennett [1964] Director/Solicitor; Elizabeth Kate Gardner [1983] Director; Antony William Luckett [1961] Director/Accountant; Janice Rosalind Moyes [1953] Director

Corriemoillie Windfarm Limited
Incorporated: 7 January 2015
Net Worth: £25,283,000 *Total Assets:* £82,280,000
Registered Office: Alexander House, 1 Mandarin Road, Rainton Bridge Business Park, Houghton-le-Spring, Co Durham, DH4 5RA
Activities: Production of electricity
Parent: EDF Energy Renewables Holdings Limited
Officers: Susan Elizabeth Lind, Secretary; Matthieu Thomas Hue [1975] Director [French]; Hassaan Majid [1968] Director

Corrpro Companies Europe Limited
Incorporated: 18 December 1968 *Employees:* 62
Net Worth: £4,549,422 *Total Assets:* £7,559,269
Registered Office: Adam Street, Bowesfield, Stockton on Tees, Cleveland, TS18 3HQ
Activities: Aluminium production
Parent: Aegion Corrosion Protection Holdings Limited
Officers: Andrew Gillespie, Secretary; Mark Thomas Russell Davies [1965] Director/Chartered Accountant; David Francis Morris [1961] Business Director [American]

Cosmar Partners LLP
Incorporated: 22 August 2016
Net Worth: £2,368,267 *Total Assets:* £5,815,451
Registered Office: Yoden House, 30 Yoden Way, Peterlee, Co Durham, SR8 1AL
Officers: Costas Constantinou [1961] Member; Marie Rose Constantinou [1961] Member

Cosmar Properties Ltd
Incorporated: 1 May 2012
Net Worth: £517,678 *Total Assets:* £1,235,898
Registered Office: Yoden House, 30 Yoden Way, Peterlee, Co Durham, SR8 1AL
Activities: Other letting and operating of own or leased real estate
Officers: Marie Rose Judith Constantinou, Secretary; Costas Constantinou [1961] Director

The Cosmetic Dental Clinic Limited
Incorporated: 12 September 2006 *Employees:* 16
Net Worth: £464,268 *Total Assets:* £940,956
Registered Office: 2 Old Eldon Square, Newcastle upon Tyne, NE1 7JG
Activities: Dental practice activities
Shareholder: Andrew John Stafford
Officers: Harold John Stafford, Secretary; Dr Darren Cannell [1976] Director/Dentist; Doctor Andrew John Stafford [1978] Director/Dentist

Cosmopolitan Properties North Ltd
Incorporated: 12 October 1973 *Employees:* 2
Net Worth: £894,796 *Total Assets:* £1,292,686
Registered Office: Joseph Miller & Co, Floor A, Milburn House, Dean Street, Newcastle upon Tyne, NE1 1LE
Activities: Other letting and operating of own or leased real estate
Major Shareholder: Christine Mabel Purdon
Officers: Mabel Patricia Hindmarsh, Secretary/Retired; Mabel Patricia Hindmarsh [1920] Director/Retired; Christine Mabel Purdon [1949] Director

Cotswold Manufacturing Limited
Incorporated: 8 July 2005
Net Worth: £2,176,408 *Total Assets:* £4,418,603
Registered Office: 70a Robson Avenue, Teesside Industrial Estate, Thornaby, Stockton on Tees, Cleveland, TS17 9LS
Activities: Other manufacturing n.e.c.
Shareholders: Kenneth Alexander Napper; Jane Napper; Stuart Burnett; Michelle Burnett
Officers: Kenneth Alexander Napper, Secretary/Director; Stuart James Burnett [1964] Director; Kenneth Alexander Napper [1969] Director

Cottam Brush Ltd
Incorporated: 28 August 1946 *Employees:* 21
Net Worth: £1,867,751 *Total Assets:* £2,594,569
Registered Office: Unit 7 Monkton Business Park North, Hebburn, Tyne & Wear, NE31 2JZ
Activities: Manufacture of brooms and brushes
Parent: Cottam Investments Limited
Officers: David George Cottam, Secretary; Kathy Bevan [1976] Sales Director; Ben Cottam [1977] Director/Engineer; David George Cottam [1951] Director/Chartered Accountant; Alan Crook [1962] Manufacturing Director

Cottam Investments Limited
Incorporated: 5 May 2010
Net Worth: £2,794,177 *Total Assets:* £2,888,088
Registered Office: Unit 7 Monkton Business Park North, Hebburn, Tyne & Wear, NE31 2JZ
Activities: Other letting and operating of own or leased real estate
Officers: Benjamin Jeffrey Cottam [1977] Director; David George Cottam [1951] Director/Chartered Accountant; Alan Crook [1962] Manufacturing Director

Cotterhill Limited
Incorporated: 10 March 2000 *Employees:* 91
Net Worth: £10,268,459 *Total Assets:* £27,972,160
Registered Office: 43 Russell Street, Darlington, Co Durham, DL1 1PT
Activities: Retail sale of textiles in specialised stores
Shareholders: Julie Marie Maguire; William Maguire
Officers: Julie Maguire, Secretary; William Maguire [1965] Director/Carpet Retailer

J Cotton Agricultural Contractors Limited
Incorporated: 20 April 2006 *Employees:* 6
Net Worth: £430,591 *Total Assets:* £978,548
Registered Office: Milburn House, Hexham Business Park, Burn Lane, Hexham, Northumberland, NE46 3RU
Activities: Other business support service activities n.e.c.
Major Shareholder: Jonathan Cotton
Officers: Jonathan Cotton [1965] Director

William Coulthard and Company Limited
Incorporated: 19 April 2010 *Employees:* 21
Net Worth: £1,734,729 *Total Assets:* £2,186,365
Registered Office: 80 Victoria Road, Darlington, Co Durham, DL1 5JG
Activities: Other engineering activities
Parent: Calmor Limited
Officers: Julian Nicholas Coulthard [1959] Director; Eric Dodd [1947] Director

Country Harvest Frozen Foods Limited
Incorporated: 29 May 1991 *Employees:* 26
Net Worth: £427,355 *Total Assets:* £1,452,608
Registered Office: Sutherland House, Cleveland Industrial Estate, Darlington, Co Durham, DL1 2PB
Activities: Other food services
Shareholders: Emma Alexandra Bamlet; Master Samuel Robert Carlyle Bamlet
Officers: Jeffrey Abbott, Secretary; David Bamlet [1955] Director; Emma Alexandra Bamlet [1980] Director

Country Homes & Estates (Northern) Limited
Incorporated: 9 August 2004 *Employees:* 1
Net Worth: £516,015 *Total Assets:* £1,000,463
Registered Office: The Old Post Office, 63 Saville Street, North Shields, Tyne & Wear, NE30 1AY
Activities: Buying and selling of own real estate
Major Shareholder: Christopher John Carlisle
Officers: John Bell, Secretary; Christopher John Carlisle [1960] Director

Country Valley Foods Ltd
Incorporated: 30 December 1971 *Employees:* 110
Net Worth: £2,485,492 *Total Assets:* £5,492,357
Registered Office: Gillander House, Leeholme Road, Billingham, Stockton on Tees, Cleveland, TS23 3TA
Activities: Non-specialised wholesale of food, beverages and tobacco
Officers: James Edward Munro, Secretary; Edward Stewart Munro [1976] Director/Wholesaler; James Edward Munro [1973] Director/Wholesaler; Stewart John Munro [1944] Director/Master Butcher

Country Valley Wholesale Foods Limited
Incorporated: 13 February 2008 *Employees:* 28
Net Worth: £603,782 *Total Assets:* £1,880,919
Registered Office: Gillander House, Leeholme Road, Billingham, Stockton on Tees, Cleveland, TS23 3TA
Activities: Wholesale of meat and meat products
Officers: James Edward Munro, Secretary; Edward Stewart Munro [1976] Director; James Edward Munro [1973] Director; Stewart John Munro [1944] Director

County and Northern Limited
Incorporated: 25 March 1988
Net Worth Deficit: £215,610 *Total Assets:* £1,806,640
Registered Office: Ravensworth House, 1 Ravensworth Street, Bedlington, Northumberland, NE22 7JP
Activities: Development of building projects
Parent: Millhouse Group Holdings Limited
Officers: Viscount Terence Devonport, Secretary; Viscount Terence Devonport [1944] Director/Landowner; Morris Robert Muter [1954] Director

County Durham Community Foundation
Incorporated: 23 June 1995 *Employees:* 11
Net Worth: £17,870,360 *Total Assets:* £19,255,472
Registered Office: Victoria House, Whitfield Court, St Johns Road, Meadowfield Industrial Estate, Meadowfield, Co Durham, DH7 8XL
Activities: Other business support service activities n.e.c.
Officers: Margaret Vaughan, Secretary; Michele Janice Armstrong [1963] Director/Chief Executive Officer; Duncan Colin Barrie [1970] Director/Chartered Accountant; Paul Geoffrey Chandler [1961] Director/Retired; Peter Morrison Cook [1953] Managing Director; Annie Dolphin [1949] Director/Retired; Lesley Anne Fairclough [1967] Director/Partner; James Mark Featherstone Fenwick [1964] Director/Investment Manager; Stephen Hall [1970] Director/Office Senior Partner; Prof Ray Hudson [1948] Director/Deputy Vice-Chancellor

County Life Homes Limited
Incorporated: 3 October 1991 *Employees:* 11
Net Worth: £121,838 *Total Assets:* £992,788
Registered Office: The Hall, Glanton Pyke, Glanton, Northumberland, NE66 4BB
Activities: Construction of domestic buildings
Shareholders: Claire Swanson; John Stewart Richardson Swanson
Officers: Clare Swanson, Secretary; Michael Alexander Pattison [1962] Director/Chartered Surveyor; Clare Swanson [1951] Director & Secretary; John Stewart Richardson Swanson [1945] Director

Countylife Bamburgh Limited
Incorporated: 8 May 2009 *Employees:* 2
Net Worth: £43,989 *Total Assets:* £2,806,677
Registered Office: The Hall, Glanton Pyke, Alnwick, Northumberland, NE66 4BB
Activities: Construction of domestic buildings
Shareholders: John Stewart Richardson Swanson; Michael Alexander Pattison
Officers: Claire Swanson, Secretary; Michael Alexander Pattison [1962] Director; John Stewart Richardson Swanson [1945] Director

Countylife Corbridge Limited
Incorporated: 8 May 2009
Net Worth: £17,044 *Total Assets:* £1,421,650
Registered Office: The Hall, Glanton Pyke, Alnwick, Northumberland, NE66 4BB
Activities: Construction of domestic buildings
Shareholder: John Stewart Richardson Swanson
Officers: Clare Swanson, Secretary; Michael Alexander Pattison [1962] Director; Clare Swanson [1951] Director; John Stewart Richardson Swanson [1945] Director

Jack Coupe & Sons Limited
Incorporated: 22 April 2010 *Employees:* 33
Net Worth: £872,292 *Total Assets:* £2,714,249
Registered Office: Jack Coupe & Sons, Hackworth Industrial Park, Shildon, Co Durham, DL4 1HG
Activities: Other specialised construction activities n.e.c.
Parent: Coupe Group Limited
Officers: Moya McGregor, Secretary; Martin Phillip Coupe [1974] Director; Simon Mark Coupe [1977] Director

Coupe Group Limited
Incorporated: 22 April 2010
Net Worth: £1,438,490 *Total Assets:* £1,696,819
Registered Office: Jack Coupe & Sons, Hackworth Industrial Park, Shildon, Co Durham, DL4 1HG
Activities: Other specialised construction activities n.e.c.
Shareholders: Simon Mark Coupe; Martin Phillip Coupe
Officers: Moya McGregor, Secretary; Martin Phillip Coupe [1974] Director; Simon Mark Coupe [1977] Director

Court Holdings Limited
Incorporated: 13 August 2008 *Employees:* 3
Net Worth: £906,863 *Total Assets:* £1,618,184
Registered Office: Lustrum Avenue, Portrack Lane, Stockton on Tees, Cleveland, TS18 2RB
Activities: Activities of head offices
Officers: Paul Ford Henderson, Secretary; Paul Andrew Davies [1965] Director; Paul Ford Henderson [1966] Director; Christopher James Walker [1974] Director

Court Homemakers Limited
Incorporated: 5 March 1991 *Employees:* 20
Net Worth: £255,557 *Total Assets:* £1,201,471
Registered Office: Lustrum Avenue, off Portrack Lane, Stockton on Tees, Cleveland, TS18 2RB
Activities: Manufacture of other furniture
Officers: Paul Ford Henderson, Secretary/Director; Paul Andrew Davies [1965] Director; Paul Ford Henderson [1966] Director; Christopher James Walker [1974] Director

Courtyard Developments (Newcastle) Limited
Incorporated: 17 August 1990
Registered Office: 43 Lambton Court, High Rickleton, Washington, Tyne & Wear, NE38 9HE
Activities: Other letting and operating of own or leased real estate
Officers: Evelyn Bernice Bright, Secretary; David Bright [1945] Director; Evelyn Bernice Bright [1943] Director

Cousins Properties Limited
Incorporated: 21 March 1956
Net Worth: £10,494,000 *Total Assets:* £10,830,000
Registered Office: Citygate House, Bath Lane, Newcastle upon Tyne, NE4 5SQ
Activities: Other letting and operating of own or leased real estate
Parent: Hanro Limited
Officers: Duncan Colin Barrie, Secretary; Patricia Duncan [1931] Director; William Rankin [1931] Director/Chairman; Adam James Serfontein [1964] Director/Chartered Surveyor

Coventry District Energy Company Limited
Incorporated: 31 May 2012 *Employees:* 2
Net Worth Deficit: £465,000 *Total Assets:* £5,324,000
Registered Office: Shared Services Centre, Q3 Office, Quorum Business Park, Benton Lane, Newcastle upon Tyne, NE12 8EX
Activities: Production of electricity
Parent: Engie Urban Energy Group Limited
Officers: Sarah Gregory, Secretary; Andrew David Hart [1969] Managing Director; Lee Kitchen [1979] Director/Accountant

Covervale Limited
Incorporated: 9 June 1995
Net Worth Deficit: £17,595 *Total Assets:* £862,216
Registered Office: 1 Elmtree Grove, Elmfield Road, Gosforth, Newcastle upon Tyne, NE3 4BG
Activities: Activities of other holding companies n.e.c.
Shareholders: Valerie Moorhouse; Anna Maria Noble; Angela Porter Smith
Officers: Valerie Moorhouse, Secretary; Valerie Moorhouse [1954] Director; Anna Maria Noble [1959] Director; Angela Porter Smith [1962] Director

Covion Holdings Limited
Incorporated: 11 March 2005
Net Worth Deficit: £728,000 *Total Assets:* £7,172,000
Registered Office: Shared Services Centre, Q3 Office, Quorum Business Park, Benton Lane, Newcastle upon Tyne, NE12 8EX
Activities: Non-trading company
Parent: Engie Services Holding UK Limited
Officers: Sarah Gregory, Secretary; Simon David Pinnell [1964] Director

Covion Limited
Incorporated: 21 September 2000 *Employees:* 172
Net Worth: £13,673,000 *Total Assets:* £18,815,000
Registered Office: Shared Services Centre, Q3 Office, Quorum Business Park, Benton Lane, Newcastle upon Tyne, NE12 8EX
Activities: Management of real estate on a fee or contract basis
Parent: Covion Holdings Limited
Officers: Sarah Gregory, Secretary; Mark Gallacher [1979] Director; Nicola Elizabeth Anne Lovett [1969] Director

A.W. Cowan Groundworks Limited
Incorporated: 17 August 1981 *Employees:* 53
Net Worth: £619,716 *Total Assets:* £1,971,456
Registered Office: The Old Offices, Urlay Nook, Eaglescliffe, Yarm, Stockton on Tees, Cleveland, TS16 0LA
Activities: Other specialised construction activities n.e.c.
Shareholders: Alec William Cowan; Wendy Elizabeth Cowan
Officers: Wendy Elizabeth Cowan, Secretary; Alexander William Cowan [1952] Director; Wendy Elizabeth Cowan [1955] Director

Cowan Transport Limited
Incorporated: 12 September 2007 *Employees:* 110
Net Worth: £418,874 *Total Assets:* £1,695,104
Registered Office: Ashfield, Deighton, Northallerton, N Yorks, DL6 2SW
Activities: Freight transport by road
Shareholder: Gillian Fiona Cowan
Officers: Gillian Fiona Cowan, Secretary/Director; David William Cowan [1957] Director; Gillian Fiona Cowan [1964] Director

Cowell's Garden Centre Limited
Incorporated: 18 February 2013 *Employees:* 44
Net Worth: £570,254 *Total Assets:* £871,985
Registered Office: Bulman House, Regent Centre, Gosforth, Newcastle upon Tyne, NE3 3LS
Activities: Retail sale of flowers, plants, seeds, fertilizers, pet animals and pet food in specialised stores
Shareholders: Alan Cowell; Karolyn Mavis Cowell
Officers: Alan Cowell [1944] Director; Karolyn Mavis Cowell [1946] Director; Martin Fenwick Cowell [1973] Director; Jane Suzanne Keating [1971] Director

Cowie Forestry Limited
Incorporated: 18 August 2015
Net Worth: £3,534,440 *Total Assets:* £3,690,950
Registered Office: The Estate Office, Broadwood Hall, Lanchester, Co Durham, DH7 0TD
Activities: Silviculture and other forestry activities
Shareholder: Lady Diana Carole Wentworth Cowie
Officers: Patricia Loraine Maddison, Secretary; Lady Diana Carole Wentworth Cowie [1938] Director; David Andrew Gray [1963] Director/Land Agent

Cowie Holiday Cottage Developments LLP
Incorporated: 21 November 2006
Net Worth: £1,160,638 *Total Assets:* £1,173,607
Registered Office: Estate Office, Broadwood Hall, Lanchester, Co Durham, DH7 0TD
Officers: Peter Rodney Blackett [1947] Member; David Andrew Gray [1963] Member; Lady Diana Carole Wentworth Cowie [1938] LLP Member

Cowie Properties LLP
Incorporated: 14 May 2007
Net Worth: £1,202,496 *Total Assets:* £1,231,243
Registered Office: The Estate Office, Broadwood Hall, Lanchester, Co Durham, DH7 0TD
Officers: Peter Rodney Blackett [1947] Member; David Andrew Gray [1963] Member; Lady Diana Carole Wentworth Cowie [1938] LLP Member

J.H.Cowper Investments Limited
Incorporated: 25 February 1964 *Employees:* 3
Net Worth: £5,242,436 *Total Assets:* £5,631,418
Registered Office: Saville Chambers, 5 North Street, Newcastle upon Tyne, NE1 8DF
Activities: Other service activities n.e.c.
Shareholder: Pauline Jill Nisbet
Officers: Caroline Anna Cowper, Secretary; Pauline Jill Nisbet, Company Secretary; Caroline Anna Cowper [1946] Director; David Scott Cowper [1942] Director/Chartered Surveyor; Pauline Jill Nisbet [1945] Director

Alfred Cox Limited
Incorporated: 30 November 2011
Net Worth: £917,802 *Total Assets:* £917,802
Registered Office: 1 Greencroft Industrial Park, Stanley, Co Durham, DH9 7YA
Activities: Activities of head offices
Parent: Allflex UK Group Limited
Officers: Louis-Marie Allain [1974] Director [French]; Kevin David Parker [1984] Finance Director

CPD Bodies Limited
Incorporated: 2 June 2002 *Employees:* 86
Net Worth: £1,187,004 *Total Assets:* £3,242,275
Registered Office: 97 Bowesfield Lane, Stockton on Tees, Cleveland, TS18 3HF
Activities: Manufacture of other transport equipment n.e.c.
Major Shareholder: Cathal Patrick Doocey
Officers: Nuala Theresa Doocey, Secretary [Irish]; Cathal Patrick Doocey [1983] Director/Surveyor

CPI Antony Rowe Ltd
Incorporated: 2 June 1993 *Employees:* 308
Net Worth: £9,130,000 *Total Assets:* £22,938,000
Registered Office: Portland House, Belmont Business Park, Durham, DH1 1TW
Activities: Printing n.e.c.
Parent: CPI Group (UK) Ltd
Officers: Robson Matthew William, Secretary; Panayiotis Andreou [1968] Director; Joost de Haas [1959] Director [Dutch]; Matthew William Robson [1954] Director/Barrister

CPI Books Ltd
Incorporated: 20 November 1987 *Employees:* 396
Net Worth: £55,061,000 *Total Assets:* £84,269,000
Registered Office: Portland House, Belmont Business Park, Durham, DH1 1TW
Activities: Printing n.e.c.
Parent: CPI UK Mangement Co Ltd
Officers: Matthew William Robson, Secretary; Panayiotis Andreou [1968] Director; Joost de Haas [1959] Director [Dutch]; Matthew William Robson [1954] Director/Barrister

CPI Colour Ltd
Incorporated: 18 November 1971 *Employees:* 136
Net Worth: £31,156,172 *Total Assets:* £38,645,316
Registered Office: Portland House, Belmont Business Park, Durham, DH1 1TW
Activities: Printing n.e.c.
Parent: CPI Group (UK) Ltd
Officers: Matthew William Robson, Secretary; Panayiotis Andreou [1968] Director; Joost de Haas [1959] Director [Dutch]; Matthew William Robson [1954] Director/Barrister

CPI Group (UK) Ltd
Incorporated: 19 September 2005 *Employees:* 3
Net Worth: £25,691,488 *Total Assets:* £83,438,512
Registered Office: Portland House, Belmont Business Park, Durham, DH1 1TW
Activities: Activities of head offices
Major Shareholder: Jacques Veyrat
Officers: Matthew William Robson, Secretary; Panayiotis Andreou [1968] Director; Joost de Haas [1959] Director [Dutch]; Matthew William Robson [1954] Director/Barrister

CPI Innovation Services Limited
Incorporated: 8 March 2006 *Employees:* 47
Net Worth: £2,627,990 *Total Assets:* £4,993,896
Registered Office: The Wilton Centre, Wilton, Redcar, Cleveland, TS10 4RF
Activities: Management consultancy activities other than financial management
Parent: Centre for Process Innovation Limited
Officers: Nicola Kirtley, Secretary; Alexander Beveridge Anderson [1944] Director/Retired; Dr Thomas Mark Cavell-Taylor [1959] Business Unit Director; Graham Stewart Hillier [1958] Technology Director; Francis Joseph Millar [1964] Operations Director; Nigel John Perry [1957] Director/Professional Chartered Engineer

CPI UK Management Company Ltd
Incorporated: 6 October 1993 *Employees:* 61
Net Worth: £26,084,000 *Total Assets:* £41,156,000
Registered Office: Portland House, Belmont Business Park, Durham, DH1 1TW
Activities: Activities of head offices
Parent: CPI Group (UK) Ltd
Officers: Matthew William Robson, Secretary; Panayiotis Andreou [1968] Director; Joost de Haas [1959] Director [Dutch]; Matthew William Robson [1954] Director/Barrister

CPI William Clowes Ltd
Incorporated: 13 May 1997 *Employees:* 84
Net Worth Deficit: £1,566,000 *Total Assets:* £5,008,000
Registered Office: Portland House, Belmont Business Park, Durham, DH1 1TW
Activities: Printing n.e.c.
Parent: CPI Group (UK) Ltd
Officers: Matthew William Robson, Secretary; Matthew William Robson [1954] Director/Barrister

CPMC Limited
Incorporated: 16 May 2002
Net Worth: £1,058,681 *Total Assets:* £1,544,911
Registered Office: 2 The Riding School, Aske, Richmond, N Yorks, DL10 5HQ
Activities: Agents involved in the sale of a variety of goods
Parent: Charles Porter Holdings Limited
Officers: Alison Porter, Secretary; Gerard Holmes [1962] Director; Alison Porter [1965] Director; Charles David Porter [1964] Director/Management Consultant

CPS Drivelink Limited
Incorporated: 24 February 2012 *Employees:* 40
Net Worth: £749,345 *Total Assets:* £1,902,939
Registered Office: 190 Kingsway South, Team Valley Trading Estate, Gateshead, Tyne & Wear, NE11 0SH
Activities: Wholesale trade of motor vehicle parts and accessories
Major Shareholder: Roy Stanley Carruthers
Officers: Roy Stanley Carruthers [1947] Director

Crabco Limited
Incorporated: 21 February 2007 *Employees:* 113
Net Worth: £4,371,578 *Total Assets:* £7,817,096
Registered Office: Kingsway, Team Valley Trading Estate, Gateshead, Tyne & Wear, NE11 0SU
Activities: Manufacture of other special-purpose machinery n.e.c.
Major Shareholder: Stephen McDowell
Officers: Jacqueline Athey, Secretary; William George Athey [1959] Director; Stephen McDowell [1957] Director

Crabtree of Gateshead (Holdings) Limited
Incorporated: 6 September 2005
Net Worth: £1,112,173 *Total Assets:* £2,251,373
Registered Office: Kingsway, Team Valley Trading Estate, Gateshead, Tyne & Wear, NE11 0SU
Activities: Manufacture of other special-purpose machinery n.e.c.
Parent: Crabco Limited
Officers: Jacqueline Athey, Secretary; William George Athey [1959] Director; Stephen McDowell [1957] Director

Crabtree of Gateshead Limited
Incorporated: 15 October 2002 *Employees:* 113
Net Worth: £6,041,424 *Total Assets:* £9,486,942
Registered Office: Kingsway, Team Valley Trading Estate, Gateshead, Tyne & Wear, NE11 0SU
Activities: Manufacture of other special-purpose machinery n.e.c.
Parent: Crabtree of Gateshead (Holdings) Limited
Officers: Jacqueline Athey, Secretary; William George Athey [1959] Spare Parts Director; Stephen McDowell [1957] Director

Crafter's Companion Limited
Incorporated: 8 March 2006 *Employees:* 104
Net Worth: £3,148,919 *Total Assets:* £8,123,055
Registered Office: Unit 1 Horndale Avenue, Aycliffe Business Park, Newton Aycliffe, Co Durham, DL5 6DR
Activities: Retail sale via mail order houses or via Internet
Major Shareholder: Sara Anne Davies
Officers: Sara Anne Davies, Secretary/Craft Designer; Sara Anne Davies [1984] Director/Craft Designer; Simon Christopher Davies [1980] Director/Management Accountant; Gerard Scot Downes [1967] Director; Richard David Harpin [1964] Director; Frank Johnson [1950] Director; Kamala Vijayaraghavan [1961] Director

Crafty Apps Limited
Incorporated: 13 September 2010 *Employees:* 2
Net Worth: £734,890 *Total Assets:* £800,098
Registered Office: 16-17 Marshall Terrace, Gilesgate Moor, Durham, DH1 2HX
Activities: Other retail sale not in stores, stalls or markets
Major Shareholder: Keith Lee Wilmot
Officers: Keith Lee Wilmot [1971] Director/Software Designer

Ray Craggs Ltd
Incorporated: 3 February 2005
Net Worth: £1,808,954 *Total Assets:* £4,039,702
Registered Office: East Close Farm, Sedgefield, Stockton on Tees, Cleveland, TS21 3HW
Activities: Other business support service activities n.e.c.
Shareholders: Angela Susan Craggs; Mark Stephen Craggs; Philip Ian Craggs; Raymond Craggs
Officers: Angela Susan Craggs, Secretary; Angela Susan Craggs [1947] Director/Farmer; Mark Stephen Craggs [1968] Director/Farmer; Philip Ian Craggs [1969] Director/Farmer; Raymond Craggs [1944] Director/Farmer

Craig Enterprises Limited
Incorporated: 29 August 2001
Net Worth: £521,882 *Total Assets:* £1,069,137
Registered Office: Unit 1 Craig Court, Coopies Field Coopies Lane, Morpeth, Northumberland, NE61 6JT
Activities: Sewerage
Major Shareholder: Patricia Mary Craig
Officers: Patricia Mary Craig, Secretary; Patricia Mary Craig [1965] Director/Secretary

Craig Healthcare LLP
Incorporated: 6 August 2009
Net Worth: £733,532 *Total Assets:* £3,747,412
Registered Office: Cramlington House, Bassington Avenue, Cramlington, Northumberland, NE23 8AD
Officers: Lucy Craig [1971] Member; Pamela Craig [1939] Member

Andrew Craig Limited
Incorporated: 16 January 1996 *Employees:* 65
Net Worth: £659,575 *Total Assets:* £964,737
Registered Office: Albert House, Albert Drive, Gateshead, Tyne & Wear, NE9 6EH
Activities: Real estate agencies
Major Shareholder: Andrew Francis Craig
Officers: June McPherson, Secretary; Andrew Francis Craig [1955] Director/Surveyor

Cramlington Garages Limited
Incorporated: 21 January 1991 *Employees:* 24
Net Worth: £795,047 *Total Assets:* £1,364,434
Registered Office: Station Road, Cramlington, Northumberland, NE23 8BH
Activities: Sale of new cars and light motor vehicles
Shareholders: Malcolm Dunn; Suzanne Christine Dunn; Robert Armstrong; Suzanne Claire Armstrong
Officers: Robert Armstrong, Secretary; Malcolm Dunn, Secretary; Robert Armstrong [1970] Director/Garage Manager; Robert William Armstrong [1940] Director; Edward Dunn [1934] Director; Malcolm Dunn [1969] Director/Garage Manager

Cramlington Learning Village
Incorporated: 5 August 2011 *Employees:* 202
Net Worth: £37,888,792 *Total Assets:* £42,240,552
Registered Office: Cramlington Learning Village, Highburn, Cramlington, Northumberland, NE23 6BN
Activities: General secondary education
Officers: Christine Calder, Secretary; Debra Ann Betham [1966] Director/Senior Pastoral Co-ordinator; Tracy Buck [1971] Director/Administration Officer; Peter Clayton [1949] Director/Retired; Dr Carol Jeanette Davenport [1970] Director of Think Physics; Michael Dunn [1964] Director; Phyllis Gordon [1946] Director/Retired; Ian Davison Hall [1954] Director/Retired; Leah Elizabeth Heatley [1977] Director/Solicitor; Wendy Heslop [1959] Director/Headteacher; Lesley Ann Ilderton [1976] Director/Accountant; Jeffrey McCartney [1950] Director/Retired; Dawn Richardson [1974] Commercial Director; Darren Paul Warburton [1971] Finance Director; Patricia Edwina Wright [1959] Director/Assistant Headteacher

Cramlington Precision Forge Limited
Incorporated: 23 July 2003 *Employees:* 61
Net Worth: £2,165,275 *Total Assets:* £5,803,393
Registered Office: Eversheds, Central Square South, Orchard Street, Newcastle upon Tyne, NE1 3XX
Activities: Manufacture of metal structures and parts of structures
Officers: Narayansamy Balakrishnan [1951] Director/President - Fasteners & Hot Forgings [Indian]; David Bartle [1966] Director/General Manager; Stephen John Rose [1957] Director/General Manager

Cramlington Village Primary Ltd
Incorporated: 23 March 2011 *Employees:* 29
Net Worth: £2,157,162 *Total Assets:* £2,332,545
Registered Office: Bowmont Drive, Cramlington, Northumberland, NE23 2SN
Activities: Primary education
Officers: Mark Bernard Atkinson [1968] Director/Civil Servant; Christopher Paul Dale [1986] Director/Management Consultant; Angela Hall [1970] Director; Samantha Jane Harrison [1987] Director/Senior HR Business Partner; Kurt Robert Johnson [1972] Director/Lead Examiner Ofqual Inspector; Paul Kennedy [1978] Director/Solicitor; Alison Malcolm [1973] Director/Accountant; Suzanne McGarva [1979] Director/Project Manager; Irena Dawn Peel [1969] Director/Chartered Accountant; Deborah Jean Westhorpe-Wylie [1968] Director/School Principal

Cranbourne Estates Limited
Incorporated: 19 August 2002 *Employees:* 2
Net Worth: £1,157,383 *Total Assets:* £1,750,764
Registered Office: 27 Reid Park Road, Newcastle upon Tyne, NE2 2ER
Activities: Development of building projects
Shareholders: Philip Peter Ferguson Upton; Nigel Matthew Upton
Officers: Nigel Matthew Upton [1963] Director/Estate Manager; Philip Peter Ferguson Upton [1958] Director/Chartered Accountant

Crandus (Contractors) Limited
Incorporated: 23 August 1956
Net Worth: £195,081 *Total Assets:* £1,020,033
Registered Office: 163 Alexandra Road, Gateshead, Tyne & Wear, NE8 1RB
Activities: Buying and selling of own real estate
Officers: Anita Schleider, Secretary; David Schleider [1959] Director; Joseph Zvi Schleider [1985] Director

Hugh Crawford Property Ltd
Incorporated: 9 April 2005
Net Worth: £228,294 *Total Assets:* £900,398
Registered Office: York House, Market Place, Leyburn, N Yorks, DL8 5AT
Activities: Other letting and operating of own or leased real estate
Major Shareholder: Jonathan Hugh Crawford
Officers: Jonathan Crawford, Secretary; Jonathan Hugh Crawford [1965] Director

Creambay Limited
Incorporated: 10 August 2000
Net Worth: £22,214,000 *Total Assets:* £33,843,000
Registered Office: Titanium House, Hanzard Drive, Wynyard Park, Stockton on Tees, Cleveland, TS22 5FD
Activities: Activities of head offices
Parent: Venator P&A Holdings UK Limited
Officers: Richard Justin James Phillipson, Secretary; Kurt David Ogden [1968] Director/Finance [American]; John Jeffrey Pehrson [1975] Director [American]; Richard Justin James Phillipson [1968] Director/Solicitor; Russell Robert Stolle [1962] Director/Attorney [American]; Simon Turner [1963] Director/President

Create Images Ion Limited
Incorporated: 13 November 1996 *Employees:* 9
Net Worth: £1,474,539 *Total Assets:* £1,789,263
Registered Office: 24 Brenda Road, Hartlepool, Cleveland, TS25 1QE
Activities: Wholesale of perfume and cosmetics
Shareholders: Christine Cesarano; Gerardo Cesarano
Officers: Christine Cesarano, Secretary; Christine Cesarano [1947] Director/Administrator; Gerardo Cesarano [1946] Director [Italian]

Createcity Limited
Incorporated: 3 July 1992 *Employees:* 87
Net Worth: £12,680,994 *Total Assets:* £22,212,944
Registered Office: The Future Business Park, Darlington Road, Shildon, Co Durham, DL4 2RB
Activities: Wholesale of furniture, carpets and lighting equipment
Parent: J Maguire Holdings Limited
Officers: David Stubbs, Secretary; Alice Victoria Maguire [1975] Strategic Development Director; Jason James Maguire [1973] Director/Carpet Retailer; William Maguire [1944] Director; David Stubbs [1957] Director/Accountant

Creative Cutting Services Limited
Incorporated: 7 January 2000 *Employees:* 9
Net Worth: £25,149 *Total Assets:* £889,655
Registered Office: Cochranes Wharf, Dockside Road Industrial Estate, Middlesbrough, Cleveland, TS3 6AU
Activities: Manufacture of metal structures and parts of structures
Shareholders: Julia Wardman; Malcolm Wardman
Officers: Julia Wardman, Secretary; Malcolm Wardman [1966] Sales Director

Creative Management Services Limited
Incorporated: 8 February 2001
Registered Office: 15 Foyle Street, Sunderland, Tyne & Wear, SR1 1LE
Activities: Event catering activities
Major Shareholder: Lynne Brooks
Officers: Lynne June Brooks, Secretary; Lynne June Brooks [1952] Director/Catering Consultant; Carole Henderson [1962] Director/Catering Consultant

Creativity, Culture and Education
Incorporated: 22 May 2008 *Employees:* 7
Net Worth: £4,288,235 *Total Assets:* £4,354,102
Registered Office: 20 Portland Terrace, Jesmond, Newcastle upon Tyne, NE2 1QQ
Activities: Educational support services
Officers: Peter Sean O'Hara, Secretary; Stephanie Elaine Bird [1954] HR Director; Johanne Mica Clifton [1967] Director/Headteacher; Mark Lewis Emmerson [1961] Director/Chief Executive Officer; Rt Hon Fiona Margaret MacTaggart [1953] Director/Consultant; Laurence Richard Simon Newman [1948] Director/Management Consultant; Jane Elizabeth Robinson [1970] Director/Chief Operating Officer; Stephan Vincent-Lancrin [1970] Director of Education [French]

Creditscale Limited
Incorporated: 23 February 1996 *Employees:* 4
Net Worth: £1,585,636 *Total Assets:* £3,775,897
Registered Office: Whinbank Road, Aycliffe Business Park, Newton Aycliffe, Co Durham, DL5 6AY
Activities: Other business support service activities n.e.c.
Shareholders: John Finley; Valerie Finley
Officers: Julie Raistrick, Secretary; John Finley [1952] Director/Manager; Valerie Finley [1952] Director/Manager

Crest House Property Limited
Incorporated: 9 November 1998 *Employees:* 2
Net Worth: £2,864,193 *Total Assets:* £7,679,246
Registered Office: 43 Maxwell Street, South Shields, Tyne & Wear, NE33 4PU
Activities: Buying and selling of own real estate
Major Shareholder: Derek Edward West
Officers: Jane Rosanna Carr, Secretary/Office Manager; Jane Rosanna Carr [1970] Company Secretary/Director; Derek Edward West [1949] Director; Lee West [1967] Director

Crestfix Limited
Incorporated: 30 May 2002 *Employees:* 1
Net Worth: £933,959 *Total Assets:* £1,161,818
Registered Office: 3 De Havilland Drive, Marske-by-the-Sea, Redcar, Cleveland, TS11 6NB
Activities: Construction of bridges and tunnels
Major Shareholder: Gary Leonard Calvert
Officers: Diane Patricia Calvert, Secretary; Gary Leonard Calvert [1958] Director/Joiner

Crispin (Pharmacy) Limited
Incorporated: 4 May 2000 *Employees:* 14
Net Worth: £1,225,636 *Total Assets:* £1,456,114
Registered Office: Oakmere, Belmont Business Park, Durham, DH1 1TW
Activities: General medical practice activities
Shareholder: Elizabeth Ann Crispin
Officers: Elizabeth Ann Crispin [1951] Director/Pharmacy; Iain Phillips Crispin [1978] Director/Pharmacy

Cromex Limited
Incorporated: 25 January 2007 *Employees:* 4
Net Worth: £876,745 *Total Assets:* £2,519,297
Registered Office: 7 Arcot Court, Nelson Park, Cramlington, Northumberland, NE23 1BB
Activities: Plumbing, heat and air-conditioning installation
Shareholders: Claire Henderson; Kevin Henderson
Officers: Claire Henderson, Secretary; Claire Henderson [1976] Director/Engineering; Kevin Henderson [1967] Director/Engineering

Damian Cronin Limited
Incorporated: 2 May 2008 *Employees:* 25
Net Worth: £902,347 *Total Assets:* £1,965,340
Registered Office: 6 Southcroft, Forest Hall, Newcastle upon Tyne, NE12 9LR
Activities: Joinery installation
Major Shareholder: Damian Joseph Cronin
Officers: Wendy Elizabeth Cronin, Secretary; Damian Joseph Cronin [1961] Managing Director [Irish]

ME Cronin Ltd
Incorporated: 9 May 2007 *Employees:* 12
Net Worth: £206,193 *Total Assets:* £902,819
Registered Office: 379 Princesway South, Team Valley Trading Estate, Gateshead, Tyne & Wear, NE11 0TU
Activities: Dispensing chemist in specialised stores
Parent: Northcare Limited
Officers: David James Gulliford [1988] Director; Eric James Gulliford [1947] Director; Dr Peter Gulliford [1949] Director

Cross House Buildings Limited
Incorporated: 4 October 1955
Net Worth: £4,853,581 *Total Assets:* £5,010,813
Registered Office: Styford Hall, Stocksfield, Northumberland, NE43 7TY
Activities: Other letting and operating of own or leased real estate
Major Shareholder: Robert Alexander Dickinson
Officers: Robert Alexander Dickinson, Secretary/Solicitor; Robert Alexander Dickinson [1964] Director/Solicitor; Robert Henry Dickinson [1934] Director/Solicitor

Cross Lanes Organic Farm Limited
Incorporated: 24 January 2007
Registered Office: Levy Pool Farm House, Sled Dale, Bowes, Barnard Castle, Co Durham, DL12 9JE
Activities: Other retail sale of food in specialised stores
Shareholders: Peter William Coverdale; Susan Joyce Coverdale
Officers: Peter William Coverdale, Secretary/Director; Peter William Coverdale [1956] Director; Susan Joyce Coverdale [1959] Director

Cross Rigg Developments (North East) Limited
Incorporated: 21 February 2007
Net Worth: £743,117 *Total Assets:* £4,923,090
Registered Office: Alhambra, 15 The Close, Stanhope Road, Edmundbyers, Consett, Co Durham, DH8 9NH
Activities: Development of building projects
Major Shareholder: James Brough
Officers: Eileen Jordan, Secretary; James Brough [1949] Director

Crossco (1217) Limited
Incorporated: 12 November 2010
Net Worth Deficit: £1,000 *Total Assets:* £6,447,000
Registered Office: 1a Dukesway Court, Team Valley Trading Estate, Gateshead, Tyne & Wear, NE11 0PJ
Activities: Other letting and operating of own or leased real estate
Major Shareholder: Philip Noble
Officers: Phillip Nigel Blain, Secretary; David James Horrocks [1959] Financial Director; Ian Imrie [1955] Director

Crossco (1255) Limited
Incorporated: 23 September 2011 *Employees:* 147
Net Worth: £34,582,000 *Total Assets:* £39,697,000
Registered Office: All Saints Refinery, Cargo Fleet Road, Middlesbrough, Cleveland, TS3 6AF
Activities: Activities of head offices
Parent: Novacap UK Limited
Officers: Martyn John Bainbridge [1966] Director; Laurent Castor [1967] Director/Vice President Performance Chemical Division [French]; Neil Christopher McLoughlin [1965] Director/Management Accountant; Ian Stark [1957] Director

Crossco (1256) Limited
Incorporated: 23 September 2011
Total Assets: £7,431,000
Registered Office: 1a Dukesway Court, Team Valley Trading Estate, Gateshead, Tyne & Wear, NE11 0PJ
Activities: Development of building projects
Major Shareholder: Philip Noble
Officers: Phillip Nigel Blain, Secretary; David James Horrocks [1959] Director/Chartered Accountant; Philip Noble [1955] Director

Crossco (1370) Limited
Incorporated: 3 June 2014 *Employees:* 191
Net Worth Deficit: £930,357 *Total Assets:* £12,028,481
Registered Office: Windermere MRF, Thomlinson Road, Hartlepool, Cleveland, TS25 1NS
Activities: Recovery of sorted materials
Shareholders: BGF GP Limited; Victoria Jackson-Smith
Officers: Christopher Gardner-Boyes [1983] Investment Director; Victoria Jackson-Smith [1971] Director; Ross Stephen Smith [1966] Director/Chairman

Crossco (1371) Limited
Incorporated: 3 June 2014 *Employees:* 3
Net Worth Deficit: £2,035,020 *Total Assets:* £5,592,748
Registered Office: Windermere MRF, Thomlinson Road, Hartlepool, Cleveland, TS25 1NS
Activities: Collection of non-hazardous waste
Officers: Victoria Jackson-Smith [1971] Director; Ross Stephen Smith [1966] Director/Chairman

Crossco (281) Limited
Incorporated: 19 August 1997
Net Worth: £1,392,000 *Total Assets:* £1,437,000
Registered Office: Inkerman House, St Johns Road, Meadowfield, Co Durham, DH7 8XL
Activities: Letting and operating of conference and exhibition centres
Parent: H J Banks & Company Limited
Officers: David Joseph Martin, Secretary; Harry James Banks [1940] Managing Director; Andrew Simon David Fisher [1971] Director/Accountant; Gavin Anthony Styles [1978] Director

Crossco Limited
Incorporated: 15 March 2004
Net Worth: £39,100 *Total Assets:* £49,829,320
Registered Office: First Floor, Finchale House, Belmont Business Park, Durham, DH1 1TW
Activities: Other business support service activities n.e.c.
Officers: Helen Austin, Secretary; John Corbitt Barnsley [1948] Director/Accountant; Spencer Glanville [1972] Director/Chartered Accountant; Robert William Jefferson [1950] Director/Chartered Accountant

Crossco No.3 Unlimited
Incorporated: 10 October 2007
Net Worth Deficit: £17,000 *Total Assets:* £1,662,000
Registered Office: 1a Dukesway Court, Team Valley Trading Estate, Gateshead, Tyne & Wear, NE11 0PJ
Activities: Other letting and operating of own or leased real estate
Parent: Falcombe
Officers: Phillip Nigel Blain, Secretary; David James Horrocks [1959] Director/Chartered Accountant; Ian Imrie [1955] Director

Crossfield Homes Limited
Incorporated: 16 December 2013 *Employees:* 2
Net Worth Deficit: £34,954 *Total Assets:* £867,198
Registered Office: Low Sober Farm, Warlaby, Northallerton, N Yorks, DL7 9JT
Activities: Development of building projects
Shareholders: Timothy John Ratcliffe Wilson; Elizabeth Ann Wilson
Officers: Elizabeth Ann Wilson [1955] Director/Retired; Timothy John Ratcliffe Wilson [1948] Director

T. Crossling & Co. Limited
Incorporated: 21 September 1992 *Employees:* 259
Net Worth: £22,266,000 *Total Assets:* £26,438,000
Registered Office: P O Box 5, Coast Road, Newcastle upon Tyne, NE6 5TP
Activities: Activities of head offices
Shareholders: Charles Peter Hodnett Errington; Richard Roger Errington
Officers: Kevin Cornelius Clifford, Secretary; Kevin Cornelius Clifford [1962] Director; Charles Peter Hodnett Errington [1959] Director; Richard Roger Errington [1957] Director; Susan Margaret Errington [1931] Director

Crossling Limited
Incorporated: 27 January 1910 *Employees:* 259
Net Worth: £18,368,000 *Total Assets:* £22,472,000
Registered Office: P O Box 5, Coast Road, Newcastle upon Tyne, NE6 5TP
Activities: Agents involved in the sale of timber and building materials
Parent: T Crossling & Co Limited
Officers: Kevin Cornelius Clifford, Secretary; David Byerley [1967] Purchasing Director; Paul Cartner [1967] Director; Kevin Cornelius Clifford [1962] Financial Director; Charles Peter Hodnett Errington [1959] Field Sales Director; Richard Roger Errington [1957] Managing Director; Susan Margaret Errington [1931] Director

Crossling Properties Limited
Incorporated: 9 October 1992
Net Worth: £5,390,000 *Total Assets:* £7,172,000
Registered Office: P O Box 5, Coast Road, Newcastle upon Tyne, NE6 5TP
Activities: Other letting and operating of own or leased real estate
Parent: T Crossling & Co Limited
Officers: Kevin Cornelius Clifford, Secretary; Kevin Cornelius Clifford [1962] Director; Charles Peter Hodnett Errington [1959] Director; Richard Roger Errington [1957] Director

Crow Hall Farms Limited
Incorporated: 16 July 1976 *Employees:* 4
Net Worth: £1,591,720 *Total Assets:* £2,974,514
Registered Office: Crow Hall Farm, Bardon Mill, Hexham, Northumberland, NE47 7BJ
Activities: Mixed farming
Shareholders: Michael Edward Dickinson; Mary Elisabeth Dickinson; James Stephen Dickinson; Mills & Reeve Trust Corporation Limited
Officers: Mary Elisabeth Dickinson [1945] Director/Business Consultant; Michael Edward Dickinson [1969] Director/Accountant

Crown Alderney Limited
Incorporated: 8 December 2009
Net Worth: £249,946 *Total Assets:* £1,245,155
Registered Office: 70 Victoria Road, Darlington, Co Durham, DL1 5JG
Activities: Development of building projects
Major Shareholder: Timothy James Wilks
Officers: Gillian Pamela Wilks [1975] Director; Timothy James Wilks [1978] Director

Crown Care Developments Limited
Incorporated: 6 February 2015
Net Worth Deficit: £25,457 *Total Assets:* £3,231,968
Registered Office: Unit 15-16 Stockholm Close, Tyne Tunnel Trading Estate, North Shields, Tyne & Wear, NE29 7SF
Activities: Construction of domestic buildings
Parent: Crown Care Holdings Limited
Officers: Amarjit Singh Ladhar [1956] Director; Baldev Singh Ladhar [1958] Director; Bhagwant Kaur Ladhar [1961] Director

Crown Care Holdings Limited
Incorporated: 9 February 2015 *Employees:* 615
Net Worth: £26,384,776 *Total Assets:* £71,700,792
Registered Office: Unit 15-16 Stockholm Close, Tyne Tunnel Trading Estate, North Shields, Tyne & Wear, NE29 7SF
Activities: Non-trading company
Officers: Amarjit Singh Ladhar [1956] Director; Baldev Singh Ladhar [1958] Director; Bhagwant Kaur Ladhar [1961] Director; Bhupinder Singh Ladhar [1981] Director; Mandeep Singh Ladhar [1985] Director

Crown Care II LLP
Incorporated: 27 May 2009 *Employees:* 114
Net Worth: £6,361,211 *Total Assets:* £14,500,518
Registered Office: Unit 15-16 Stockholm Close, Tyne Tunnel Trading Estate, North Shields, Tyne & Wear, NE29 7SF

Crown Care IV Limited
Incorporated: 15 November 2013 *Employees:* 375
Net Worth: £13,751,571 *Total Assets:* £31,386,458
Registered Office: 15-16 Stockholm Close, Tyne Tunnel Trading Estate, North Shields, Tyne & Wear, NE29 7SF
Activities: Residential nursing care facilities
Shareholder: Baldev Singh Ladhar
Officers: Mandeep Singh Ladhar [1985] Director

Crown Care V Limited
Incorporated: 9 January 2014 *Employees:* 23
Net Worth Deficit: £733,552 *Total Assets:* £6,780,789
Registered Office: 15-16 Stockholm Close, Tyne Tunnel Trading Estate, North Shields, Tyne & Wear, NE29 7SF
Activities: Residential nursing care facilities
Parent: Crown Care Holdings Limited
Officers: Mandeep Singh Ladhar [1985] Director

Crown Care VI Limited
Incorporated: 8 July 2014 *Employees:* 227
Net Worth: £8,106,687 *Total Assets:* £19,606,132
Registered Office: 15-16 Stockholm Close, Tyne Tunnel Trading Estate, North Shields, Tyne & Wear, NE29 7SF
Activities: Residential nursing care facilities
Parent: Crown Care Holdings Ltd
Officers: Mandeep Singh Ladhar [1985] Director

Crown Care VII Limited
Incorporated: 10 February 2017 *Employees:* 40
Net Worth: £23,108 *Total Assets:* £6,028,504
Registered Office: 15-16 Stockholm Close, Tyne Tunnel Trading Estate, North Shields, Tyne & Wear, NE29 7SF
Activities: Residential nursing care facilities
Officers: Baldev Singh Ladhar [1958] Director

Crown Doors and Shutters Limited
Incorporated: 19 January 2007 *Employees:* 21
Net Worth: £272,280 *Total Assets:* £888,951
Registered Office: Unit 32 Bentall Business Park, Washington, Tyne & Wear, NE37 3JD
Activities: Manufacture of doors and windows of metal
Shareholder: Michael Arthur Mersh
Officers: Marilyn Mersh, Secretary; Michael Arthur Mersh [1953] Director

Crownfold Limited
Incorporated: 1 February 1989 *Employees:* 56
Net Worth: £5,334,287 *Total Assets:* £8,006,555
Registered Office: 1c North Tyne Industrial Estate, Whitley Road, Benton, Newcastle upon Tyne, NE12 9SZ
Activities: Construction of other civil engineering projects n.e.c.
Parent: Paramount Home Improvements (U.K.) Limited
Officers: Michael Alexander Giscombe [1967] Director; Sayeda Nusheen Hussain [1974] Marketing Director; Graham Christopher Jenney [1965] Director; Gregory Kane [1975] Director; Mark Tinnion [1977] Brand Director; Sarah Lyn Van Haazel [1975] Director

Crowther Lodge Motor Company Limited
Incorporated: 25 January 2013 *Employees:* 17
Net Worth: £200,622 *Total Assets:* £1,183,729
Registered Office: Crowther Lodge Motor Company, Park Road, Felling By-Pass, Gateshead, Tyne & Wear, NE8 3HL
Activities: Sale of used cars and light motor vehicles
Shareholders: John Robert Houckham; Paul Peacock
Officers: John Robert Houckham [1959] Director/Mortgage Advisor; Paul Peacock [1974] Director

Croxdale Farms Limited
Incorporated: 26 November 1957
Net Worth: £1,531,902 *Total Assets:* £1,764,136
Registered Office: Hett Moor Farm, Hett, Croxdale, Co Durham, DH6 5LJ
Activities: Mixed farming
Major Shareholder: John Hutchinson
Officers: Christine Ann Hutchinson, Secretary; Christine Ann Hutchinson [1944] Director/Farmer; John Hutchinson [1942] Director/Farmer; Mark William Hutchinson [1978] Director/Farming and Contracting

Croxdale Fast-Fit Limited
Incorporated: 19 June 1998 *Employees:* 39
Net Worth: £1,883,992 *Total Assets:* £2,688,744
Registered Office: Scrafton Lodge, Leyburn, N Yorks, DL8 4RR
Activities: Maintenance and repair of motor vehicles
Shareholders: Edward Neil Corner; Nigel Frederick Hartley Corner
Officers: Joanne Richmond, Secretary; Edward Neil Corner [1937] Director; Nigel Frederick Hartley Corner [1965] Director; David Urwin [1968] Director

Croxdale Service Station Limited
Incorporated: 16 August 1967 *Employees:* 33
Net Worth: £371,948 *Total Assets:* £3,572,755
Registered Office: Scrafton Lodge, Leyburn, N Yorks, DL8 4RR
Activities: Sale of new cars and light motor vehicles
Shareholders: Kathleen Freda Corner; Nigel Frederick Hartley Corner
Officers: Joanne Richmond, Secretary; David Atkins [1950] Director; Edward Neil Corner [1937] Director; Kathleen Freda Corner [1941] Director/Secretary; Nigel Frederick Hartley Corner [1965] Director; Anthony Edward Rockingham [1979] Director

CRS (North-East) Limited
Incorporated: 22 September 2011 *Employees:* 6
Net Worth: £351,543 *Total Assets:* £1,042,100
Registered Office: Benton House, Old Arla Foods Site, Benton Business Park, Newcastle upon Tyne, NE12 9SW
Activities: Recovery of sorted materials
Major Shareholder: Philip Rodgers
Officers: Philip Rodgers [1970] Director

Crutes LLP
Incorporated: 13 January 2006
Registered Office: Great North House, Sandyford Road, Newcastle upon Tyne, NE1 8ND
Officers: Helen Louise Ager [1965] Member; David Michael Drewe [1957] Member; Paul John Bell [1961] LLP Member; Paul Maurice Hughes [1962] LLP Member; Rodney Searl [1966] LLP Member

Crystal Galleries Limited
Incorporated: 14 January 1983 *Employees:* 69
Net Worth: £1,361,771 *Total Assets:* £2,950,371
Registered Office: Edwards House, 2 Westerby Road, Middlesbrough, Cleveland, TS3 8TD
Activities: Other manufacturing n.e.c.
Shareholders: Joanne Melanie Ellen Lowes; Jeremy Richard Lowes
Officers: Joanne Melanie Ellen Lowes, Secretary; Jeremy Richard Lowes [1964] Managing Director; Joanne Melanie Ellen Lowes [1962] Finance Director

CSD Sealing Systems Limited
Incorporated: 12 March 1993 *Employees:* 15
Net Worth: £8,623,053 *Total Assets:* £9,816,969
Registered Office: Bulman House, Regent Centre, Gosforth, Newcastle upon Tyne, NE3 3LS
Activities: Non-specialised wholesale trade
Major Shareholder: David Edward Ripley
Officers: David Edward Ripley, Secretary; David Edward Ripley [1973] Sales Director

CTG Limited
Incorporated: 15 January 2008 *Employees:* 83
Net Worth: £737,126 *Total Assets:* £2,854,272
Registered Office: c/o Weyfringe Limited, Longbeck Road, Marske-by-the-Sea, Redcar, Cleveland, TS11 6HQ
Activities: Manufacture of electronic components
Parent: Cleveland Technologies Limited
Officers: Karen Gleghorn, Secretary; Andrew Michael Chiles [1965] Director; Andrew Harry Gleghorn [1959] Director

John Cullerton & Sons Limited
Incorporated: 18 July 2002 *Employees:* 32
Net Worth: £250,200 *Total Assets:* £1,563,053
Registered Office: Unit A, Rennys Lane, Gilesgate Moor, Durham, DH1 2RB
Activities: Electrical installation
Shareholders: Paul Stewart Cook; Darryl John Cullerton; John Cullerton
Officers: Paul Stewart Cook [1976] Director; Darryl John Cullerton [1986] Director/Electrician; John Cullerton [1967] Director; Joshua Phillip Cullerton [1991] Director

G T Culpitt & Son (Holdings) Limited
Incorporated: 15 March 1988 *Employees:* 237
Net Worth: £14,535,149 *Total Assets:* £18,902,424
Registered Office: Jubilee Industrial Estate, Ashington, Northumberland, NE63 8UQ
Activities: Activities of head offices
Parent: Decopac Inc
Officers: Donna George, Secretary; John Anderson [1959] Director [American]; Simon Mark Keogh [1971] Finance Director; Michael McGlynn [1950] Director [American]

Culpitt Limited
Incorporated: 23 December 1931 *Employees:* 111
Net Worth: £10,113,048 *Total Assets:* £12,244,218
Registered Office: Jubilee Industrial Estate, Ashington, Northumberland, NE63 8UQ
Activities: Manufacture of other food products n.e.c.
Parent: G.T. Culpitt & Son (Holdings) Ltd
Officers: Donna George, Secretary; John Anderson [1959] Director [American]; Helen Jane Johnson [1965] Marketing Director; Simon Mark Keogh [1971] Finance Director; Michael McGlynn [1950] Director [American]; Gary Peter Quinn [1982] Supply Chain Director; Thomas Wylie [1967] Managing Director

Cumbria Investments Limited
Incorporated: 5 March 2015
Registered Office: 54-56 Keswick Street, Gateshead, Tyne & Wear, NE8 1TQ
Activities: Buying and selling of own real estate
Officers: Martin Zvi Oppenheimer [1989] Director

Cundall Johnston & Partners LLP
Incorporated: 5 July 2001 *Employees:* 690
Net Worth: £9,717,678 *Total Assets:* £34,231,020
Registered Office: Partnership House, Regent Farm Road, Gosforth, Newcastle upon Tyne, NE3 3AF
Officers: Stephen Cook [1960] Member; David Peter Dryden [1954] Member; Tomas Gerard Neeson [1969] Member; Sarah Louise Prime [1966] Member; James John Allen [1970] LLP Member; Jonathan Rowlatt Allen [1980] LLP Member; Keith Anderson [1958] LLP Member; Rastslav Bartek [1976] LLP Member; Andrew Bishop [1968] LLP Member; Julian Garfield Bott [1977] LLP Member; Geoffrey Alan Carter [1956] LLP Member; Antonio Centola [1965] LLP Member; David Halford Clark [1969] LLP Member; Stephen Clough [1967] LLP Member; Duncan Cox [1972] LLP Member; Neil Angus Dely [1965] LLP Member; Laurence Brendan Dervan [1960] LLP Member; Alan Michael Fogarty [1965] LLP Member; Paul Hards [1968] LLP Member; Kevin William Hayes [1973] LLP Member; Malcolm Robert Howe [1960] LLP Member; John Barnaby Jordan [1964] LLP Member; Paul David Kenyon [1966] LLP Member; Lee Leston-Jones [1972] LLP Member; Peter David Liddle [1975] LLP Member; Stephen John Maddocks [1964] LLP Member; Gary Ian Marshall [1973] LLP Member; Caimin McCabe [1966] LLP Member; Andrew James Moore [1965] LLP Member; Belinda Catherine Morgan [1962] LLP Member; Peter Francis O'Halloran [1957] LLP Member; Carole Penelope O'Neil [1977] LLP Member; Andrew James Parkin [1975] LLP Member; Adrian Roche [1959] LLP Member; Gareth Anthony Victor Rollison [1961] LLP Member; Garrit Schot [1975] LLP Member; Alec Stewart [1965] LLP Member; Timothy James Stidwill [1974] LLP Member; Peter Stocks [1959] LLP Member; Richard Andrew Stratton [1968] LLP Member; Julian Bruce Sutherland [1966] LLP Member; Robert Van Zyl [1966] LLP Member; David Alexander Walker [1959] LLP Member; Craig Sheldon Winter [1962] LLP Member; Simon Wyatt [1982] LLP Member

Cundall Limited
Incorporated: 27 June 2005 *Employees:* 440
Net Worth Deficit: £5,452 *Total Assets:* £3,482,189
Registered Office: Partnership House, Regent Farm Road, Gosforth, Newcastle upon Tyne, NE3 3AF
Activities: Human resources provision and management of human resources functions
Officers: Sarah Louise Prime, Secretary; Stephen Cook [1960] Director; David Peter Dryden [1954] Director; Samantha Jane Hammond Opelt [1967] Legal Director; Tomas Gerard Neeson [1969] Director/Engineer [Irish]; Carole Penelope O'Neil [1977] Human Resources Director; Sarah Louise Prime [1966] Director/Accountant

Cussins (North East) Limited
Incorporated: 9 November 2000 *Employees:* 64
Net Worth: £2,963,935 *Total Assets:* £11,125,827
Registered Office: 12 Bondgate Within, Alnwick, Northumberland, NE66 1TD
Activities: Construction of domestic buildings
Parent: Cussins Limited
Officers: Richard Anthony Johnson Lowry, Secretary; Colin Leslie Barnes [1960] Director/Town & Country Planner; David Mark Derek Brocklehurst [1976] Director; Andrew Rolland Cunningham [1956] Director/Chartered Accountant; Jabin Philip Cussins [1980] Director/Property Developer; Peter Ian Cussins [1949] Director/Property Developer; Lesley Ann Ilderton [1976] Director/Group Financial Controller; Richard Anthony Johnson Lowry [1972] Director; Roderick Charles St John Wilson [1961] Director/Land Agent

Cussins Embleton LLP
Incorporated: 27 August 2015 *Employees:* 2
Net Worth: £2,017,446 *Total Assets:* £2,944,528
Registered Office: 12 Bondgate Within, Alnwick, Northumberland, NE66 1TD

Philip Cussins House
Incorporated: 15 May 1997 *Employees:* 27
Net Worth: £2,079,719 *Total Assets:* £2,118,120
Registered Office: 33 Linden Road, Gosforth, Newcastle upon Tyne, NE3 4EY
Activities: Residential care activities for the elderly and disabled
Officers: Martin Alan Levinson, Secretary; Gabrielle Bernstone [1946] Director/Retired; Alan David Cahill [1948] Director/Retired; Jean Brenda Dinsdale [1947] Director/Retired; Frank Ian Fagleman [1959] Director; David Michael Gold [1945] Director/Solicitor; Anthony Alan Josephs [1951] Director/Chartered Accountants; Martin Alan Levinson [1950] Director/Solicitor; Carole Eve Lurie [1937] Director/Retired; Bernice Susanne Marcus [1947] Director/Retired; Doctor Paul Netts [1965] Director/General Practitioner

Cussins Limited
Incorporated: 8 May 2014 *Employees:* 66
Net Worth: £3,270,717 *Total Assets:* £12,254,032
Registered Office: 12 Bondgate Within, Alnwick, Northumberland, NE66 1TD
Activities: Activities of head offices
Shareholders: Jabin Philip Cussins; Peter Ian Cussins
Officers: Richard Anthony Johnson Lowry, Secretary; Colin Leslie Barnes [1960] Director/Town & Country Planner; David Mark Derek Brocklehurst [1976] Director; Andrew Rolland Cunningham [1956] Director/Chartered Accountant; Jabin Philip Cussins [1980] Director; Peter Ian Cussins [1949] Director; Lesley Ann Ilderton [1976] Director/Group Financial Controller; Richard Anthony Johnson Lowry [1972] Director; Roderick Charles St John Wilson [1961] Director/Land Agent

Custom Design B.A. Limited
Incorporated: 6 June 2000 *Employees:* 20
Net Worth: £443,609 *Total Assets:* £867,744
Registered Office: St Helen Way, St Helens Industrial Estate, St Helens Auckland, Bishop Auckland, Co Durham, DL14 9AZ
Activities: Manufacture of kitchen furniture
Officers: Gary Paul Aldred [1962] Director/Manufacturer; Jillian Aldred [1967] Director; Claire Margaret Alice Steel [1975] Director; Gary Steel [1970] Director/Manufacturer

The Customs House Trust Limited
Incorporated: 26 August 1993 *Employees:* 62
Net Worth: £447,579 *Total Assets:* £1,009,913
Registered Office: The Customs House, Mill Dam, South Shields, Tyne & Wear, NE33 1ES
Activities: Support activities to performing arts
Officers: Claire Louise Burn, Secretary; Yusef Hassen Abdullah [1958] Director/Community Service Coordinator; Shuley Alam [1973] Director [British/Bangladeshi]; Jayden Blacklock [1997] Youth Theatre Junior Group Director; Carol Elizabeth Cooke [1950] Director/Lecturer; David George Cottam [1951] Finance Director; Margaret Fay [1949] Director; Stephanie Finnon [1983] Director/Journalist; Darren Hymers [1973] Director/Consultant; Councillor Alan Kerr [1936] Director/Councillor; Kerry Ann Leng [1978] Director; Simon John Mitchell [1956] Director/Consultant; Claire Simmons [1974] Director/Solicitor; Graeme Thompson [1956] Director/University Dean; Vivienne Claire Wiggins [1972] Director/Actor/Drama Facilitator

CY Partners Recruitment Ltd
Incorporated: 24 May 2011 *Employees:* 30
Net Worth: £866,947 *Total Assets:* £984,038
Registered Office: Suite 2-3 Gateway West Business Centre, Gateway House, Gateway West, Newburn Riverside, Newcastle upon Tyne, NE15 8NX
Activities: Temporary employment agency activities
Shareholders: Probier Chatterjee; Daniel Younger
Officers: Probier Chatterjee [1975] Director; Daniel Younger [1980] Director

Cygnet Family Law Limited
Incorporated: 25 August 2009
Net Worth: £915,477 *Total Assets:* £1,414,506
Registered Office: Portland House, West Dyke Road, Redcar, Cleveland, TS10 1DH
Activities: Solicitors
Officers: Lisa Smith, Secretary; Peter George Medd [1953] Director/Lawyer; John Charles Robinson [1969] Director/Solicitor

Cygnet Total Communications Limited
Incorporated: 25 October 2001 *Employees:* 9
Net Worth: £298,087 *Total Assets:* £1,063,004
Registered Office: 10 Bailey Court, Colburn Business Park, Catterick Garrison, N Yorks, DL9 4QL
Activities: Retail sale of mobile telephones
Shareholders: Christopher James Nichols; Neil Andrew Arkwright
Officers: Margaret Elaine Nichols, Secretary; Neil Andrew Arkwright [1964] Director; Christopher James Nichols [1954] Director

The Cylinder Service Centre Limited
Incorporated: 29 February 1996 *Employees:* 38
Net Worth: £1,249,146 *Total Assets:* £2,581,349
Registered Office: Unit 2 Stephenson Street, Howdon Quays, Wallsend, Tyne & Wear, NE28 6UE
Activities: Repair of machinery
Parent: Benbecula Group Ltd
Officers: Simon Stewart Long [1975] Director/Chartered Accountant; Alasdair MacDonald [1965] Director

Cynergy UK Limited
Incorporated: 18 November 2004 *Employees:* 9
Net Worth Deficit: £123,227 *Total Assets:* £1,425,977
Registered Office: Ranyell House, 10 Ellerbeck Way, Stokesley Business Park, Stokesley, Middlesbrough, Cleveland, TS9 5JZ
Activities: Activities of conference organisers
Major Shareholder: Rebecca Jenna Louise Howard
Officers: Jonathan Heaton Howard, Secretary; Rebecca Jenna Louise Howard [1968] Director/Marketing Consultant

The Cyrenians Ltd
Incorporated: 1 December 1970 *Employees:* 383
Net Worth: £13,286,424 *Total Assets:* £20,260,828
Registered Office: Unit D13 Marquis Court, Team Valley Trading Estate, Gateshead, Tyne & Wear, NE11 0RU
Activities: Other accommodation
Officers: Susan Carr, Secretary/Personal Assistant; Rt Hon Hilary Jane Armstrong [1945] Director/Member of Parliament; Pete Edwin Brown [1955] Director/Retired; Dean Andrew Fielding [1965] Finance/Business Director; Stephen Guyon [1955] Director/Retired; Generaldine Kay [1961] Director/Chief Executive; Maggie Pavlou [1966] HR Director; James David Alexander Ramsbotham [1959] Director/Chief Executive; Lesley Telford [1970] Director/Bank Officer; Fiona Wharton [1971] Director/Solicitor

D & A Systems Limited
Incorporated: 1 March 1993 *Employees:* 43
Net Worth: £2,778,544 *Total Assets:* £4,778,569
Registered Office: Unit 6 Stapylton Court, Bolckow Industrial Estate, Grangetown, Middlesbrough, Cleveland, TS6 7BL
Activities: Electrical installation
Major Shareholder: Neil Andrew Robinson
Officers: Neil Andrew Robinson [1961] Director/Communications Consultant

D & S UK Properties Limited
Incorporated: 8 May 2014
Net Worth: £38,904 *Total Assets:* £972,065
Registered Office: 30 Yoden Way, Peterlee, Co Durham, SR8 1AL
Activities: Buying and selling of own real estate
Shareholders: Sanjay Kumar; Jetinder Singh Sokal
Officers: Sanjay Kumar [1978] Director/Sales Manager; Jetinder Singh Sokal [1981] Director/Builder

D J M S Solicitors Ltd
Incorporated: 22 December 2006
Net Worth: £386,448 *Total Assets:* £781,598
Registered Office: 53 John Street, Sunderland, Tyne & Wear, SR1 1QH
Activities: Solicitors
Officers: Jason Alexander Shaw Smith, Secretary/Solicitor; Joanne Gatens [1975] Director/Solicitor; Paul Kennedy [1978] Director/Solicitor; David Michael Malone [1963] Director/Solicitor; Jason Alexander Shaw Smith [1970] Director/Solicitor

D P M Finance LLP
Incorporated: 4 June 2009
Net Worth: £4,505,746 *Total Assets:* £11,414,686
Registered Office: 12-14 Lumley Court, Drum Industrial Estate, Chester-le-Street, Co Durham, DH2 1AN
Officers: Paul David Rowland [1962] Member; Murray Anderson Wark [1970] Member; Dean Cowley [1974] LLP Member; David Foster [1970] LLP Member; Michael Paul Sargent [1973] LLP Member

D&K Hire Services Limited
Incorporated: 31 December 2010 *Employees:* 30
Net Worth: £106,872 *Total Assets:* £2,618,160
Registered Office: Hadrian House, Beaminster Way East, Newcastle upon Tyne, NE3 2ER
Activities: Renting and leasing of construction and civil engineering machinery and equipment
Shareholders: Kenneth Brown; Richard Norman Mills
Officers: Richard Norman Mills Brown, Secretary; Richard Norman Mills Brown [1972] Director/Chartered Accountant; Paul Moyes [1955] Director

D'Addario UK Limited
Incorporated: 17 September 2009 *Employees:* 22
Net Worth: £1,533,440 *Total Assets:* £3,440,538
Registered Office: 2 Greenfinch Way, Newburn Riverside, Newcastle upon Tyne, NE15 8NX
Activities: Non-specialised wholesale trade
Officers: John D'Addario Iii, Secretary [American]; James D'Addario [1949] Director/Chief Executive [American]; John D'Addario III [1971] Director/President [American]; Simon John Turnbull [1971] Director

D-Line (Europe) Limited
Incorporated: 29 July 2004 *Employees:* 32
Net Worth: £1,933,575 *Total Assets:* £2,620,383
Registered Office: Unit A5, Tromso Close, Tyne Tunnel Trading Estate, North Shields, Tyne & Wear, NE29 7XH
Activities: Manufacture of other electrical equipment
Officers: Duncan Glen Moncrieff, Secretary; Philip Sydney Coates [1955] Director; Michael Francis Hogan [1944] Director; Jeremy Peter Middleton [1960] Director; Duncan Glen Moncrieff [1958] Finance and Operations Director; Nicholas Stephen Moore [1962] Director; Paul David Ruddick [1968] Director

D. C. C. (Cars) Limited
Incorporated: 24 April 2002
Net Worth Deficit: £15,469 *Total Assets:* £1,052,458
Registered Office: Pandon Buildings, Valley Street, Darlington, Co Durham, DL1 1PY
Activities: Sale of used cars and light motor vehicles
Major Shareholder: Neil Plews
Officers: Diane Jones Plews, Secretary; Diane Jones Plews [1971] Director; Neil Plews [1969] Director

D.A.F. Timber Limited
Incorporated: 2 September 1987
Registered Office: Unit 8 Coundon Industrial Estate, Coundon, Bishop Auckland, Co Durham, DL15 8NR
Activities: Manufacture of other products of wood; manufacture of articles of cork, straw and plaiting materials
Shareholders: Dale French; Lesley French
Officers: Lesley French, Secretary; Dale Andrew French [1962] Managing Director; Lesley French [1967] Director

D.A.K. Tipper Hire Limited
Incorporated: 8 July 2003 *Employees:* 15
Net Worth: £282,574 *Total Assets:* £911,633
Registered Office: Unit 4 Adams House, Wesley Drive, Benton Square Industrial Estate, Newcastle upon Tyne, NE12 9UP
Activities: Freight transport by road
Major Shareholder: Kevin Reid
Officers: Karen Reid, Secretary; Kevin Reid [1967] Director/Haulier

D.C. Handrails and Ironwork Parts Limited
Incorporated: 27 February 2001 *Employees:* 18
Net Worth: £3,143,504 *Total Assets:* £3,678,317
Registered Office: Unit 3 Team Valley Brush Factory, Whickham Industrial Estate, Swalwell, Tyne & Wear, NE16 3DA
Activities: Manufacture of metal structures and parts of structures
Shareholders: David Alan Collins; Sandra Ann Collins
Officers: Sandra Ann Collins, Secretary; David Alan Collins [1956] Director/Whitesmith; Sandra Ann Collins [1953] Director/Secretary; Scott Collins [1988] Director/Business Development Manager

D.J.H. (Group) Limited
Incorporated: 15 February 1982
Net Worth: £915,953 *Total Assets:* £1,663,562
Registered Office: Project House, Consett Business Park, Villa Real, Consett, Co Durham, DH8 6BP
Activities: Manufacture of other fabricated metal products n.e.c.
Parent: New Equipment Holdings Limited
Officers: Stephen John Widdows, Secretary; Neil Corner [1937] Director/Chairman; Nigel Frederick Hartley Corner [1965] Finance Director; Stephen John Widdows [1960] Managing Director

D.P. Builders Limited
Incorporated: 4 October 1977 *Employees:* 28
Net Worth: £1,165,420 *Total Assets:* £2,148,458
Registered Office: Coquet Enterprise Park, Amble, Northumberland, NE65 0PE
Activities: Construction of domestic buildings
Shareholders: Douglas Paterson; Eleanor Irene Paterson
Officers: Eleanor Irene Paterson, Secretary; Douglas Paterson [1947] Director/Builder; Eleanor Irene Paterson [1947] Director/Company Secretary; Ewan Douglas Paterson [1975] Director/Construction Foreman; John Charles Patterson [1955] Director/Quantity Surveyor

D.P. Fasteners Limited
Incorporated: 31 October 1986 *Employees:* 12
Net Worth: £5,405,326 *Total Assets:* £7,080,285
Registered Office: 14 Donkin Road, Armstrong Industrial Estate, District 2, Washington, Tyne & Wear, NE37 1PF
Activities: Wholesale of other intermediate products
Major Shareholder: David McMaster
Officers: David McMaster, Secretary; Stephen Crammond [1958] Director/Sales Executive; Carol Mary McMaster [1960] Director; David McMaster [1958] Director; Lindsay McMaster [1989] Director/Sales Administrator; Paul McMaster [1987] Director/Lawyer

D.W.S. Property Developments Limited
Incorporated: 9 February 2004 *Employees:* 2
Net Worth: £2,776 *Total Assets:* £877,282
Registered Office: 37-38 Market Street, Ferryhill, Co Durham, DL17 8JH
Activities: Development of building projects
Shareholders: Derek William Stott; William Stott
Officers: William Stott, Secretary; Derek William Stott [1974] Director; William Stott [1948] Director/Retired

Daava Developments (UK) Limited
Incorporated: 17 December 2012
Net Worth: £482,223 *Total Assets:* £1,041,942
Registered Office: 4 Ivymount Road, Heaton, Newcastle upon Tyne, NE6 5RN
Activities: Development of building projects
Shareholders: Rajesh Kumar Mehan; Ravinder Kumar Mehan
Officers: Rajesh Kumar Mehan [1977] Director/Project Manager; Ravinder Kumar Mehan [1974] Director/Senior Systems Consultant

Dacre Street Developments Limited
Incorporated: 21 July 2015
Net Worth Deficit: £9,785 *Total Assets:* £3,291,443
Registered Office: Pringle Building Services Ltd, Stephenson Way, Barrington Industrial Estate, Bedlington, Northumberland, NE22 7DL
Activities: Construction of domestic buildings
Major Shareholder: David Sean Pringle
Officers: David Sean Pringle [1968] Managing Director

Daft as a Brush Cancer Patient Care Charitable Trust
Incorporated: 9 January 1989 *Employees:* 5
Net Worth: £4,525,503 *Total Assets:* £4,591,316
Registered Office: Daft As A Brush House, Great North Road, Gosforth, Newcastle upon Tyne, NE3 2DR
Activities: Other service activities n.e.c.
Officers: Jean Ross, Secretary; Brian Thomas Burnie [1944] Director; Leslie Austin Caisley [1952] Director/Solicitor; Jean Ross [1941] Director; Derek Paul Warren [1939] Director/Consultant; Ernest Young [1944] Director

Daikin Applied (UK) Limited
Incorporated: 3 February 1998 *Employees:* 94
Net Worth Deficit: £6,998,000 *Total Assets:* £6,920,000
Registered Office: Bassington Lane, Cramlington, Northumberland, NE23 8AF
Activities: Manufacture of other fabricated metal products n.e.c.
Parent: AAF McQuay UK Ltd
Officers: Ian Phillip Creasey, Secretary; Claudio Capozio [1954] Director/VP/GM [Italian]; Voon Ping Chen [1965] Director/Corporate Controller [Malaysian]; Ian Phillip Creasey [1961] Director/Accountant; James Henley [1954] Director/General Manager; Benny Woon Khin Liow [1957] Director [Malaysian]; Alan Dale Proffitt [1972] Director/Corporate Controller [American]; Katsuhiko Takagi [1943] Director [Japanese]

Daisy Chain Project Teesside
Incorporated: 14 May 2003 *Employees:* 75
Net Worth: £1,702,743 *Total Assets:* £1,802,886
Registered Office: Calf Fallow Farm, Calf Fallow Lane, Norton, Stockton-on-Tees, Cleveland, TS20 1PF
Activities: Other social work activities without accommodation n.e.c.
Officers: Leanne Caroline Boyd-Smith [1978] Director/Clinical Lead Speech and Language Therapist; Lesley Clode [1953] Director/Retired; James Andrew Dale [1982] Director/Accountant; Jonathan Richard Dicken [1971] Director; Emma Louise Hansford [1975] Director/Accountant; Ian Dennis Kinnery [1957] Director/Business Coach; Elaine Ann McLaine-Wood [1974] Director/Solicitor; Ian Parker [1956] Director/Retired; Dr Edwin John Pugh [1954] Director/Retired; Alison Jane Tasker [1957] Director

J Dalby & Son Limited
Incorporated: 22 August 2000 *Employees:* 8
Net Worth: £569,318 *Total Assets:* £778,310
Registered Office: Mylord Crescent, Camperdown Industrial Estate, Killingworth, Newcastle upon Tyne, NE12 5UJ
Activities: Other specialised construction activities n.e.c.
Shareholder: Benjamin Dalby
Officers: Benjamin Dalby, Secretary; Benjamin Dalby [1979] Director; John Barrington Dalby [1955] Director/Roofer

Dale Care Limited
Incorporated: 4 March 1993 *Employees:* 654
Net Worth: £776,043 *Total Assets:* £2,212,784
Registered Office: 13 Hope Street, Crook, Co Durham, DL15 9HS
Activities: Social work activities without accommodation for the elderly and disabled
Parent: Clece Care Services Ltd
Officers: Mario Abajo Ménguez [1972] Managing Director [Spanish]; Raul Gutierrez Rodriguez [1967] Director/Chief Financial Officer [Spanish]

Dalesend Farms Limited
Incorporated: 21 February 2012
Net Worth: £940,236 *Total Assets:* £943,587
Registered Office: Hilltop East, Newton-le-Willows, Bedale, N Yorks, DL8 1TP
Activities: Growing of cereals (except rice), leguminous crops and oil seeds
Shareholder: Trustees of Will Jonathan Gray Ropner
Officers: John Bernard Liddle, Secretary; John Joicey Dickinson [1953] Director/Chartered Surveyor; Tobyn Benedict Dickinson [1981] Director/Banker; Charles Guy Corban Ropner [1959] Director; Edith Avril Ropner [1930] Director/Housewife; Paul Benedict Peat Ropner [1963] Director/Financial Consultant

Dallas Carpets Limited
Incorporated: 3 March 1976 *Employees:* 16
Net Worth: £3,352,697 *Total Assets:* £4,059,656
Registered Office: Unit 2 Double Row, Seaton Delaval, Whitley Bay, Tyne & Wear, NE25 0PP
Activities: Wholesale of furniture, carpets and lighting equipment
Shareholders: Vernon Burke; Paul Burke; Patricia Burke
Officers: Paul Burke, Secretary; Patricia Burke [1940] Director; Paul Burke [1968] Director; Vernon Burke [1939] Director; Ian Hughes [1950] Director

Dalton 009 Limited
Incorporated: 16 May 2005
Net Worth: £2,295,460 *Total Assets:* £2,684,599
Registered Office: Sheraton Park, Blackwell, Darlington, Co Durham, DL3 8QY
Activities: Buying and selling of own real estate
Officers: Peter Jeffrey Davison, Secretary; Peter Jeffrey Davison [1955] Director; Peter Arthur Emerson [1953] Director; Brian William Hick [1958] Director; Nigel Pickard [1965] Director; William Lindsay Ross [1949] Director; John Leslie Severs [1954] Director

Dalton Homes (North East) Limited
Incorporated: 17 July 2002
Net Worth: £1,020,142 *Total Assets:* £2,998,461
Registered Office: B3 Kingfisher House, Kingsway, Team Valley Trading Estate, Gateshead, Tyne & Wear, NE11 0JQ
Activities: Construction of commercial buildings
Major Shareholder: Patrick Parkes Duffy
Officers: Patrick Parkes Duffy, Secretary/Heating Engineer; Patrick Parkes Duffy [1969] Director/Heating Engineer; Steven James Reay [1972] Director/Financial Controller; Philip David Warren [1968] Commercial Director

R.A. Dalton Limited
Incorporated: 28 August 2003
Net Worth: £1,463,751 *Total Assets:* £2,431,401
Registered Office: Burtreeford, Cowshill, Bishop Auckland, Co Durham, DL13 1DB
Activities: Sewerage
Shareholder: Alistair Dalton
Officers: Lynn Dalton, Secretary; Richard Alistair Dalton [1969] Director

Dalts Ltd
Incorporated: 17 August 2005
Net Worth: £912,659 *Total Assets:* £1,068,627
Registered Office: Vass House, 7 Fife Cove, Darlington, Co Durham, DL3 7HH
Activities: Accounting and auditing activities
Officers: Denise Vassilounis, Secretary; Denise Vassilounis [1977] Director/Property Manager; Nicholas Antony Vassilounis [1965] Director/Chartered Accountant

Dance North
Incorporated: 9 April 1990 *Employees:* 80
Net Worth: £769,249 *Total Assets:* £1,649,274
Registered Office: Temple Street, Newcastle upon Tyne, NE1 4BR
Activities: Operation of arts facilities
Officers: Ian McKeown, Secretary; Andrew Hammond Bairstow [1964] Marketing Director; Michael Cockburn [1954] Director; Ann Isabel Cooper [1970] Director/Head of Communications; Kiz Crosbie [1979] Director; Jeffrey Martin Dean [1955] Director/Personnel Manager; Philip Douglas [1985] Director/Dance Practitioner; Roshan Israni [1962] Director/Human Resource Consultant; Rosland Jane Kay-Price [1976] Director/Dance Practitioner; Sharon Ann Paterson [1957] Director/Associate Dean; Frank Wilson [1952] Arts Centre Director; Kay Wilson [1961] Director/PR Consultant

Danco Properties Limited
Incorporated: 17 January 2006 *Employees:* 2
Net Worth: £229,716 *Total Assets:* £806,769
Registered Office: 7 North Lodge, Lambton Park, Chester-le-Street, Co Durham, DH3 4BA
Activities: Other letting and operating of own or leased real estate
Shareholders: Lee Anthony Lawrence; James Lawrence; Edna Lawrence
Officers: Lee Anthony Lawrence, Secretary/Director; James Lawrence [1943] Director; Lee Anthony Lawrence [1971] Director

Dancorr Limited
Incorporated: 19 April 1994
Net Worth: £823,101 *Total Assets:* £833,515
Registered Office: 16 Swainby Close, Gosforth, Newcastle upon Tyne, NE3 5JE
Activities: Other transportation support activities
Officers: Peter Kelly [1957] Director/Removals & Storage

Dane & Co., Limited
Incorporated: 21 June 2013 *Employees:* 20
Net Worth: £10,424,943 *Total Assets:* £11,138,549
Registered Office: 17 Floor, Cale Cross House, Pilgrim Street, Newcastle upon Tyne, NE1 6SU
Activities: Activities of other holding companies n.e.c.
Shareholders: Amber Isobel Mary Dane; Michael Robert Leather
Officers: Amber Isobel Mary Dane, Secretary; Zoe Lawson, Secretary; Amber Isobel Mary Dane [1952] Director; Michael Robert Leather [1961] Director/Chartered Accountant

Dane Architectural Systems Holdings Limited
Incorporated: 31 January 2013 *Employees:* 141
Net Worth: £4,461,376 *Total Assets:* £9,283,844
Registered Office: Viking Works, Hamsterley Colliery, Newcastle upon Tyne, NE17 7SY
Activities: Construction of commercial buildings
Shareholder: Gary Stephen Hall
Officers: Gary Alistair Foster, Secretary; William Edourd Field [1956] Director; Gary Alistair Foster [1971] Director/Chartered Accountant; Martin George [1970] Director; Gary Stephen Hall [1962] Managing Director; David Hardie [1969] Contracts Director; Godfrey Edward Monaghan [1950] Director; Robert Patterson [1959] Director

Dane Architectural Systems Limited
Incorporated: 16 September 1971 *Employees:* 141
Net Worth: £2,803,525 *Total Assets:* £4,522,247
Registered Office: Viking Works, Hamsterley, Newcastle upon Tyne, NE17 7SY
Activities: Construction of commercial buildings
Parent: Dane Architecutural Systems Holdings Limited
Officers: Gary Alistair Foster, Secretary; William Edourd Field [1956] Business Development Director; Gary Alistair Foster [1971] Director/Chartered Accountant; Martin George [1970] Director/Quantity Surveyor; Gary Stephen Hall [1962] Director; Godfrey Edward Monaghan [1950] Technical Director; Robert Patterson [1959] Operations Director

Dane Finance Limited
Incorporated: 8 August 2013 *Employees:* 1
Net Worth: £1,205,997 *Total Assets:* £10,340,390
Registered Office: 17th Floor, Cale Cross House, Pilgrim Street, Newcastle upon Tyne, NE1 6SU
Activities: Other credit granting n.e.c.
Parent: Dane & Co., Limited
Officers: Amber Isobel Mary Dane, Secretary; Zoe Lawson, Secretary; Amber Isobel Mary Dane [1952] Director; Michael Robert Leather [1961] Director/Accountant

Dane Group Holdings Limited
Incorporated: 31 January 2013 *Employees:* 13
Net Worth: £1,611,536 *Total Assets:* £1,860,597
Registered Office: Viking Works, Hamsterley Colliery, Newcastle upon Tyne, NE17 7SY
Activities: Activities of head offices
Shareholder: Gary Stephen Hall
Officers: Gary Alistair Foster, Secretary; Gary Alistair Foster [1971] Director/Chartered Accountant; Gary Stephen Hall [1962] Managing Director

Danesmoor Holdings Limited
Incorporated: 13 July 2012 *Employees:* 319
Net Worth: £51,211,672 *Total Assets:* £63,654,160
Registered Office: P O Box 20, Station Road, Aycliffe Business Park, Newton Aycliffe, Co Durham, DL5 6XJ
Activities: Activities of head offices
Major Shareholder: Mark William Winspear Stephenson
Officers: Jonathan Barclay Whisker, Secretary; Mark William Winspear Stephenson [1962] Director; Jonathan Barclay Whisker [1964] Financial Director

Danesmoor Limited
Incorporated: 8 December 1993 *Employees:* 20
Net Worth: £51,978,568 *Total Assets:* £67,446,480
Registered Office: P O Box 20, Station Road, Aycliffe Business Park, Newton Aycliffe, Co Durham, DL5 6XJ
Activities: Agents involved in the sale of furniture, household goods, hardware and ironmongery
Officers: Jonathan Barclay Whisker, Secretary; David Burchnall [1967] Director/Salesman; Marc John Holmes [1965] Director; Mark William Winspear Stephenson [1962] Director; Jonathan Barclay Whisker [1964] Financial Director

Danick Limited
Incorporated: 13 June 1997
Net Worth: £501,322 *Total Assets:* £779,688
Registered Office: 25 Parkshiel, South Shields, Tyne & Wear, NE34 8BU
Activities: Residential care activities for the elderly and disabled
Shareholders: John Craggs Young; Jennifer Young
Officers: Jennifer Young, Secretary/University Lecturer; Jennifer Young [1947] Director/University Lecturer; John Craggs Young [1946] Director/Engineer; Nicola Young [1971] Director/Teacher

Danieli Holdings Limited
Incorporated: 21 May 2008 *Employees:* 591
Net Worth: £2,546,043 *Total Assets:* £8,273,879
Registered Office: Patrick House, Gosforth Park Avenue, Newcastle upon Tyne, NE12 8EG
Activities: Activities of head offices
Shareholders: Neill Aidan Winch; Stephen William Howe
Officers: Neill Aidan Winch, Secretary/Director; Stephen William Howe [1967] Director; Donna Winch [1976] Director; Neill Aidan Winch [1964] Director

Danieli Property Investments Limited
Incorporated: 22 April 2009 *Employees:* 2
Net Worth Deficit: £231,451 *Total Assets:* £1,621,596
Registered Office: Patrick House, Gosforth Park Avenue, Gosforth Business Park, Newcastle upon Tyne, NE12 8EG
Activities: Other business support service activities n.e.c.
Shareholder: Neill Aidan Winch
Officers: Neill Aidan Winch, Secretary; Stephen William Howe [1967] Director; Donna Winch [1976] Director; Neill Aidan Winch [1964] Director

Dapra York Limited
Incorporated: 2 April 2008 *Employees:* 28
Net Worth: £1,735,622 *Total Assets:* £5,357,964
Registered Office: Alexanders, Chapel Street, Teesdale, Thornaby on Tees, Cleveland, TS17 6BB
Activities: Sale of new cars and light motor vehicles
Parent: Bob Alexander Limited
Officers: David Robert Alexander, Secretary; David Robert Alexander [1965] Director

R. A. & S. Darling Farms (Hartlepool) Limited
Incorporated: 26 July 1996
Net Worth: £1,755,775 *Total Assets:* £2,641,432
Registered Office: High Tunstall Farm, Hartlepool, Cleveland, TS26 0BY
Activities: Growing of cereals (except rice), leguminous crops and oil seeds
Shareholders: Sheila Darling; Robert Anthony Darling
Officers: Sheila Darling, Secretary/Farmer; Richard John Darling [1977] Director/Farmer; Robert Anthony Darling [1944] Director/Farmer; Sheila Darling [1945] Director/Farmer

J.M.& W.Darling Limited
Incorporated: 24 March 1930 *Employees:* 25
Net Worth: £1,106,002 *Total Assets:* £1,757,670
Registered Office: Unit 14 Witney Way, Boldon Business Park, Boldon Colliery, Co Durham, NE35 9PE
Activities: Dispensing chemist in specialised stores
Shareholders: Geoffrey William Robson; Ann Edith Darling
Officers: Jacqueline Ann Lockwood, Secretary; Ann Edith Darling [1937] Director; Paul Anthony Darling [1960] Director/Barrister; Jacqueline Ann Lockwood [1958] Director/Bookkeeper

Darlington & District Hospice Movement
Incorporated: 4 December 1986 *Employees:* 131
Net Worth: £3,078,383 *Total Assets:* £3,938,873
Registered Office: The Woodlands, Woodland Road, Darlington, Co Durham, DL3 7UA
Activities: Hospital activities
Officers: Nicola Jane Myers, Secretary; Dr Harry Byrne [1953] Director/General Practitioner [Irish]; Anne Foster [1946] Director/General Nurse; Mary Lovell [1932] Director/Retired Head of Department Technical; Antony William Luckett [1961] Director/Accountant; Dr Helen McLeish [1970] Director/General Practitioner; Nicholas Charles Tristram Millen [1958] Durham School (Director, International); Steve John Rose [1957] Director/Management Consultant; Sasha Warr [1973] Director/HR Consultant

Darlington Arena Limited
Incorporated: 9 June 2011
Net Worth: £2,347,357 *Total Assets:* £3,310,839
Registered Office: Northern Echo Arena, Neasham Road, Darlington, Co Durham, DL2 1DL
Activities: Other sports activities
Parent: Darlington Mowden Park Rugby Football Club Limited
Officers: Michael Birch [1964] Director; Lee Trevor Rust [1980] Director

Darlington Cricket and Athletic Club C.I.C.
Incorporated: 27 February 2016 *Employees:* 3
Net Worth: £1,331,524 *Total Assets:* £1,347,982
Registered Office: Darlington Cricket and Athletic Club, South Terrace, Feethams, Darlington, Co Durham, DL1 5JD
Activities: Activities of sport clubs
Officers: Peter Jonathan Barnes [1968] Director/Business Funding Advisor; David Frank Bentley [1948] Director/Retired; Jeffrey Bessford [1971] Director/Foreman Steel Fixer; Stephen Anthony Charlton [1975] Director/IT Project Manager; Martin Clarke [1974] Director/Head of Learning and Development; David Stanley Coad [1944] Director; Thomas Denys de La Motte [1970] Director; Grant Compton Hopkins [1970] Director/Headteacher; Gloria Margaret Howells [1950] Director; Geoffrey Brian Johnson [1933] Director; John Garry Moody [1967] Director/Joiner; Matthew Charles Crispin Morgan [1976] Director/Bid Manager; Ian James Newell [1969] Director/Sales and Marketing Manager; James Sutton [1991] Director/Optometrist

The Darlington Farmers Auction Mart Company Limited
Incorporated: 20 March 1926 *Employees:* 38
Net Worth: £4,822,652 *Total Assets:* £7,475,696
Registered Office: Bank Top Mart, Clifton Road, Darlington, Co Durham, DL1 5DU
Activities: Support activities for animal production (other than farm animal boarding)
Officers: Andrew Armstrong [1981] Director; James Edward Beadle [1977] Director/Farmer; Eric Blacklock [1964] Director/Farmer; Simon Catterall [1956] Director/Solicitor; Jon Andrew Grieves [1972] Director/Farmer; Richard Heseltine [1972] Director/FCCA; Trevor David Johnson [1953] Director/Farmer; Peter Anthony Guy Monkhouse [1963] Director; John Anthony Ward [1957] Director

Darlington Homes Limited
Incorporated: 17 September 1992
Net Worth: £58,212 *Total Assets:* £5,910,795
Registered Office: Sentinel House, Morton Road, Darlington, Co Durham, DL1 4PT
Activities: Development of building projects
Officers: John Jack Cullen [1954] Director; Christopher Hunter [1977] Director/Chief Risk Officer; Christopher Ben White [1978] Finance Director

Darlington Mind Limited
Incorporated: 9 May 2002 *Employees:* 48
Net Worth: £800,822 *Total Assets:* £1,042,000
Registered Office: St Hildas House, 11 Borough Road, Darlington, Co Durham, DL1 1SQ
Activities: Other social work activities without accommodation n.e.c.
Officers: Gary Henry Emerson, Secretary; Peter Freitag [1929] Director/Estate Agent; Heinz Peter French [1949] Director/Retired; Lesley Gillespie [1947] Director; Reverend Lynda Elizabeth Gough [1954] Director/Vicar; Kenneth Greenfield [1953] Director/Retired; Dr Richard Langrick [1959] Director/Research Chemist; Janice Lincoln [1957] Director/Retired; Melanie Louise Pears [1965] Director/Solicitor; Susan Jane Porteus [1957] Director/Retired; Catherine Ruth Walters [1963] Director/Retired

Darlington Mowden Park Rugby Football Club Limited
Incorporated: 7 December 2005
Net Worth: £1,623,719 *Total Assets:* £1,766,725
Registered Office: Northern Echo, Darlington Arena, Neasham Road, Darlington, Co Durham, DL2 1DL
Activities: Activities of sport clubs
Officers: Michael Birch [1964] Director; Anthony Hugh Copsey [1965] Director/Management Consultant; Andrew Paul Craggs [1965] Director; Daniel Stuart Hunter [1971] Managing Director; Paul Anthony MacKings [1961] Director/Chief Executive; Piers Mitchell [1964] Director; Lee Trevor Rust [1980] Director; Andrew John Westgarth [1965] Director

Darlington Residential Limited
Incorporated: 18 January 2000
Net Worth: £1,096,128 *Total Assets:* £2,523,452
Registered Office: 29a Larchfield Street, Darlington, Co Durham, DL3 7DL
Activities: Buying and selling of own real estate
Officers: Nicholas John Hodgson, Secretary; Nicholas John Hodgson [1957] Director/Retired Solicitor; Richard Anthony Hodgson [1953] Director/Retired Solicitor; Michael Hugh Lindsay [1961] Director/Property Manager

Darlington Rugby Football Club Limited
Incorporated: 31 December 1996 *Employees:* 15
Net Worth: £1,313,544 *Total Assets:* £1,775,661
Registered Office: Blackwell Meadows, Grange Road, Darlington, Co Durham, DL1 5NR
Activities: Activities of sport clubs
Officers: Lynne Murphy, Secretary; Alison Bell [1972] Director/Regional Inventory Manager; Jessica Clare Cheesman [1978] Director/Civil Engineer; Lee Dodsworth [1967] Director/Steel Worker; Andrew Fenner [1956] Sales Director; Lynne Murphy [1960] Director/HR Business Support; Graham Alexander Webster [1969] Director/Project Manager; Michael James Wilkinson [1950] Director; Anita Elisabeth Jane Fall Wilson [1961] Director; Dermot Winters [1967] Director/Solicitor [Irish]

Darlington Tyre & Auto Centre Limited
Incorporated: 31 October 2009 *Employees:* 20
Net Worth: £590,708 *Total Assets:* £1,806,987
Registered Office: 121 Parkgate, Darlington, Co Durham, DL1 1RZ
Activities: Maintenance and repair of motor vehicles
Major Shareholder: Christopher Neil Alexander
Officers: Christopher Neil Alexander, Secretary; Sarah Elizabeth Alexander, Secretary; Christopher Neil Alexander [1969] Director; Sarah Elizabeth Alexander [1974] Director

Darnley Bidco Limited
Incorporated: 20 June 2013 *Employees:* 528
Net Worth: £2,633,683 *Total Assets:* £38,457,800
Registered Office: Anson House, Fleming Business Centre, Burdon Terrace, Newcastle upon Tyne, NE2 3AE
Activities: Residential care activities for the elderly and disabled
Major Shareholder: Kevin Pattison
Officers: Kevin Pattison [1962] Director/Businessman

Darras Consulting Limited
Incorporated: 17 December 2007
Net Worth: £1,272,678 *Total Assets:* £1,402,657
Registered Office: 37 Woodland, Darras Hall, Ponteland, Northumberland, NE20 9EU
Activities: Other activities auxiliary to insurance and pension funding
Major Shareholder: Graeme John Charlton
Officers: Helen Marie Charlton, Secretary; Graeme John Charlton [1967] Director/Actuary

Darrington Healthcare Ltd
Incorporated: 25 October 2012 *Employees:* 166
Net Worth: £2,301,737 *Total Assets:* £11,671,695
Registered Office: RSM Tax and Accounting Limited, 1 St James' Gate, Newcastle upon Tyne, NE1 4AD
Activities: Residential nursing care facilities
Officers: Eric George Dixon [1954] Managing Director; Stephen Dixon [1957] Director; Shaun Ian Lucas [1945] Director; Iain Alston Murphy [1953] Director/Architect

Dartford Student Living Limited
Incorporated: 10 March 2014
Net Worth: £267,593 *Total Assets:* £1,558,604
Registered Office: 22 Ashleigh Gardens, Sunderland, Tyne & Wear, SR6 7PY
Activities: Other accommodation
Major Shareholder: Gurpreet Singh Jagpal
Officers: Gurpreet Singh Jagpal, Secretary; Kuldeep Singh Jagpal [1955] Director/Retailer [Indian]; Balbir Kaur [1958] Director/Retailer [Indian]; Gurpreet Kaur Jagpal [1985] Director/Teacher; Gurpreet Singh Jagpal [1981] Director/Consultant

Darwins Holdings Limited
Incorporated: 4 December 1957 *Employees:* 58
Net Worth: £135,786 *Total Assets:* £2,184,131
Registered Office: Prospect Road, Crook, Co Durham, DL15 8JL
Activities: Casting of steel
Parent: Bonddarwin Limited
Officers: Robert Jon Blackett [1973] Director; Trevor John Machin [1966] Group Technical Director

Dasyl Enterprises Limited
Incorporated: 24 May 1982 *Employees:* 2
Net Worth: £348,442 *Total Assets:* £753,326
Registered Office: 37-38 Market Street, Ferryhill, Co Durham, DL17 8JH
Activities: Activities of head offices
Shareholders: David Cameron Little; Sylvia Little
Officers: Sylvia Little, Secretary; David Cameron Little [1944] Director/Chartered Accountant; Sylvia Little [1943] Director/Secretary

Datastor (North East) Limited
Incorporated: 5 March 2002 *Employees:* 5
Net Worth: £794,308 *Total Assets:* £1,340,970
Registered Office: Wesley Way, Benton Square Industrial Estate, Newcastle upon Tyne, NE12 9TA
Activities: Operation of warehousing and storage facilities for land transport activities
Major Shareholder: Paul Turnbull
Officers: Paul Turnbull [1983] Director

Datasupplies (Stationery) Limited
Incorporated: 19 August 1980
Net Worth: £557,962 *Total Assets:* £1,412,297
Registered Office: Stargate Industrial Estate, Ryton, Tyne & Wear, NE40 3EX
Activities: Printing n.e.c.
Major Shareholder: Christopher Robson
Officers: Steven Miles Sedlacek, Secretary; Christopher Robson [1964] Sales Director; Steven Miles Sedlacek [1960] Commercial Director

Datatrial Limited
Incorporated: 29 February 2000 *Employees:* 20
Net Worth: £277,145 *Total Assets:* £813,057
Registered Office: Unit 2 & 6 The Old Forge, Hoults Yard, Walker Road, Newcastle upon Tyne, NE6 2HL
Activities: Data processing, hosting and related activities
Major Shareholder: Eric Jonathan Lund
Officers: Dr Emma Mary Sonia Banks [1971] Director/Clinical Operations; Eric Jonathan Lund [1967] Director [American]

Datim Building Contractors Limited
Incorporated: 2 April 2007 *Employees:* 24
Net Worth: £385,028 *Total Assets:* £1,392,347
Registered Office: Unit 8 Atley Business Park, Cramlington, Northumberland, NE23 1WP
Activities: Construction of commercial buildings
Shareholders: Timothy John Joseph Barrett; David Hepton
Officers: Timothy John Joseph Barrett, Secretary; Timothy John Joseph Barrett [1970] Director; David Hepton [1974] Director

John Davey Limited
Incorporated: 21 October 1981
Net Worth: £699,898 *Total Assets:* £940,555
Registered Office: Unit 9A Cannon Park Way, Cannon Park Industrial Estate, Middlesbrough, Cleveland, TS1 5JU
Activities: Manufacture of paints, varnishes and similar coatings, mastics and sealants
Major Shareholder: John Edward Sidney Davey
Officers: Alma Davey, Secretary; Malcolm Paul Bell [1971] Sales Director; Alma Davey [1951] Director; John Edward Sidney Davey [1949] Managing Director

Davies Tracey Limited
Incorporated: 31 March 2009 *Employees:* 31
Net Worth: £173,974 *Total Assets:* £773,891
Registered Office: Swan House, Westpoint Road, Teesdale Business Park, Stockton on Tees, Cleveland, TS17 6BP
Activities: Accounting and auditing activities
Major Shareholder: Craig Davies
Officers: Ian George Tracey, Secretary; Craig Davies [1968] Director; Craig Thomas McBride [1961] Director/Chartered Accountant; Ian George Tracey [1957] Director

Tara Davison Developments Limited
Incorporated: 21 October 2015 *Employees:* 2
Net Worth: £13,859 *Total Assets:* £974,849
Registered Office: The Grainger Suite, Regent Centre, Gosforth, Newcastle upon Tyne, NE3 3PF
Activities: Development of building projects
Shareholders: Karen Davison; Gary Davison
Officers: Gary Kenneth Davison [1971] Director; Karen Davison [1973] Director

D K & L R Davison Ltd
Incorporated: 15 January 2015
Net Worth: £60,411 *Total Assets:* £851,113
Registered Office: 3 Balmoral Gardens, Whitley Bay, Tyne & Wear, NE26 3LU
Activities: Other human health activities
Shareholders: David Kevin Davison; Leah Rowanne Davison
Officers: David Kevin Davison [1972] Director/Pharmacist; Leah Rowanne Davison [1970] Director/Personal Trainer

Davison Tyne Metal Limited
Incorporated: 3 February 1983 *Employees:* 2
Net Worth: £1,161,159 *Total Assets:* £1,162,963
Registered Office: 16 Bishops Hill, Acomb, Hexham, Northumberland, NE46 4NH
Activities: Non-trading company
Major Shareholder: Ian Richardson
Officers: Ian Richardson, Secretary/Engineering Director; Ian Richardson [1962] Engineering Director; Olwyn Richardson [1962] Director

The Davy Roll Company Limited
Incorporated: 2 July 1999
Net Worth: £24,030,000 *Total Assets:* £28,142,000
Registered Office: P O Box 21, Union Electric Steel UK Limited, Coulthards Lane, Gateshead, Tyne & Wear, NE8 3DX
Activities: Activities of head offices
Parent: Ampco UES Sub, Inc
Officers: Rose Hoover, Secretary/Corporate Executive [American]; William John Garrett [1972] Managing Director; Rose Hoover [1955] Director/Corporate Executive [American]; Brett McBrayer [1966] Director/CEO Ampco-Pittsburgh Corporation [American]

Dawn Estates Limited
Incorporated: 28 January 2004
Net Worth: £452,811 *Total Assets:* £2,160,433
Registered Office: 20 Lansdowne Terrace, Newcastle upon Tyne, NE3 1HP
Activities: Other letting and operating of own or leased real estate
Officers: Ved Prakash Dhaun, Secretary; Ved Prakash Dhaun [1949] Director/Chartered Accountant

Dawson & Sanderson Limited
Incorporated: 23 November 1962 *Employees:* 259
Net Worth: £4,423,082 *Total Assets:* £13,963,118
Registered Office: 124-130 Northumberland Street, Newcastle upon Tyne, NE1 7DG
Activities: Travel agency activities
Major Shareholder: Thomas Dawson
Officers: Irene Margaret Blackburn, Secretary; Graham Chambers [1968] Director/Golf Course Manager; Ian Clough [1956] Director; Alistair Cormack [1958] Director; Sylvia Dawson [1927] Director; Thomas Dawson [1933] Director; Janice Fawcett [1961] Director; Christopher Robert Harrison [1978] Director; Christopher Clark Pattison [1955] Director/Travel Agency Manager

P. Dawson Developments Limited
Incorporated: 4 March 2010 *Employees:* 1
Net Worth: £1,538,812 *Total Assets:* £1,617,680
Registered Office: Victoria House, Bondgate Within, Alnwick, Northumberland, NE66 1TA
Activities: Development of building projects
Major Shareholder: Paul Dawson
Officers: Paul Dawson [1961] Director

Dawson Farms Limited
Incorporated: 3 February 2004 *Employees:* 5
Net Worth: £1,199,204 *Total Assets:* £2,069,758
Registered Office: Thornhill Farm, Blackhorse Lane, Swainby, Northallerton, N Yorks, DL6 3ET
Activities: Growing of cereals (except rice), leguminous crops and oil seeds
Major Shareholder: Steven Roger Dawson
Officers: Kate Elizabeth Dawson, Secretary; Steven Roger Dawson [1967] Director/Farmer

A.V.Dawson Limited
Incorporated: 24 April 1959 *Employees:* 197
Net Worth: £25,062,464 *Total Assets:* £40,383,444
Registered Office: Riverside Park Road, Middlesbrough, Cleveland, TS2 1UT
Activities: Operation of warehousing and storage facilities for land transport activities
Major Shareholder: Gary Stuart Dawson
Officers: Craig Lloyd, Secretary; Gary Stuart Dawson [1970] Commercial Director; Mr Andrew Kenneth Watkins [1964] Director; John Ellis Young [1970] Financial Director

Dayspring Trust
Incorporated: 28 November 2012 *Employees:* 258
Net Worth Deficit: £654,051 *Total Assets:* £2,317,826
Registered Office: The Venerable Bede C of E Academy, Tunstall Bank, Sunderland, Tyne & Wear, SR2 0SX
Activities: General secondary education
Officers: Lynne O'Leary, Secretary; The Venerable John Venerable John Stuart Bain [1955] Director/Archdeacon of Sunderland; Gillian Ann Booth [1965] Director/Headteacher; Elizabeth Ruth Miller [1970] Director/Independent Social Worker; Christine Rayner [1958] Director/Retired School Improvement Officer; David Malcolm Robinson [1985] Director; Paul James Russell [1973] Director/Watch Manager; Richard Patrick Thorndyke [1944] Director/Retired; Colin Neil Williams [1966] Director

DB (UK) Investments Limited
Incorporated: 11 December 2001
Net Worth: £865,016,000 *Total Assets:* £1,959,042,048
Registered Office: 1 Admiral Way, Doxford International Business Park, Sunderland, Tyne & Wear, SR3 3XP
Activities: Activities of other holding companies n.e.c.
Parent: Deutsche Bahn AG
Officers: Lorna Edwards, Secretary; David Graham Johnstone [1963] Director; Andrea Rossi [1975] Director

DBM Enterprises Limited
Incorporated: 11 February 2008
Registered Office: Unit 8a Bowes Road, Riverside Park Industrial Estate, Middlesbrough, Cleveland, TS2 1LU
Activities: Activities of other holding companies n.e.c.
Major Shareholder: Christopher McGrory
Officers: Christopher McGrory [1971] Director

DC Assets Limited
Incorporated: 25 February 2013 *Employees:* 4
Net Worth: £337,606 *Total Assets:* £1,328,218
Registered Office: Martinet House, Martinet Road, Thornaby, Stockton on Tees, Cleveland, TS17 0AS
Activities: Other passenger land transport
Major Shareholder: Derrick Collin
Officers: Rachael Anne Armstrong, Secretary; Derrick Collin [1948] Director/Entrepreneur; Kristian James Collin [1993] Marketing Director; Stephen Anthony James [1958] Commercial Director

DC Gaming Limited
Incorporated: 22 October 2009
Net Worth: £1,270,000 *Total Assets:* £1,324,000
Registered Office: 1a Dukesway Court, Team Valley Trading Estate, Gateshead, Tyne & Wear, NE11 0PJ
Activities: Activities of other holding companies n.e.c.
Parent: Falcombe Holdings Limited
Officers: Phillip Nigel Blain, Secretary; David James Horrocks [1959] Financial Director; Ian Imrie [1955] Director

DCS Maintenance Solutions NE Ltd
Incorporated: 26 February 2014
Net Worth: £519,626 *Total Assets:* £1,054,957
Registered Office: Jarrow Business Centre, Viking Business Park, Jarrow, Tyne & Wear, NE32 3DT
Activities: Construction of roads and motorways
Major Shareholder: Jonathan Smart
Officers: Jonathan Smart [1967] Director

Dealmaster Ltd
Incorporated: 20 February 2003
Net Worth: £226,547 *Total Assets:* £1,231,015
Registered Office: 43 Picktree Lodge, Chester-le-Street, Co Durham, DH3 4DH
Activities: Other letting and operating of own or leased real estate
Officers: Paul Graham Shepherd [1965] Director

Dean Group Limited
Incorporated: 31 October 2003
Registered Office: Frederick House, Brenda Road, Hartlepool, Cleveland, TS25 2BW
Activities: Buying and selling of own real estate
Major Shareholder: Steve Winspear
Officers: Stuart Winspear, Secretary/Contracts Manager; Steven Winspear [1957] Director/Civil Engineer

Dean Taxis Limited
Incorporated: 1 May 2001 *Employees:* 49
Net Worth: £937,716 *Total Assets:* £3,389,362
Registered Office: 362b Dukesway, Team Valley Trading Estate, Gateshead, Tyne & Wear, NE11 0PZ
Activities: Taxi operation
Parent: Collinsdale Limited
Officers: Daniel Piers Felce [1985] Managing Director; Christopher Martin Hope [1978] Director/Chartered Accountant

Deanmoor Limited
Incorporated: 18 February 2002
Net Worth Deficit: £160,204 *Total Assets:* £2,097,930
Registered Office: 82 Bewick Road, Gateshead, Tyne & Wear, NE8 1RS
Activities: Other letting and operating of own or leased real estate
Shareholder: Shamai Schleider
Officers: Anna Schleider, Secretary [American]; Anna Schleider [1956] Director/Secretary [American]; Sarah Schleider [1981] Director/Company Secretary [Australian]; Shamai Schleider [1953] Director/Property Investor; Ruth Walkin [1983] Director/Graphic Designer [American]

Deanswood Properties Limited
Incorporated: 28 November 1989
Net Worth: £1,107,452 *Total Assets:* £1,137,990
Registered Office: 9 Stephenson Street, Thornaby, Cleveland, TS17 6AL
Activities: Other letting and operating of own or leased real estate
Shareholder: Philip Arthur Thompson
Officers: Susan Evelyn Thompson, Secretary; Philip Arthur Thompson [1945] Director

Terry Deary Limited
Incorporated: 14 April 1998 *Employees:* 3
Net Worth: £1,470,792 *Total Assets:* £1,545,330
Registered Office: Burnhope Flatts, Farm Green Lane, Burnhope, Co Durham, DH7 0DS
Activities: Artistic creation
Shareholder: William Terence Deary
Officers: William Terence Deary, Secretary; Jennifer Rose Sheila Deary [1951] Director/Executive; William Terence Deary [1946] Director/Author

Debmat Surfacing Limited
Incorporated: 23 May 1979 *Employees:* 60
Net Worth: £451,144 *Total Assets:* £2,866,621
Registered Office: 14-15 Harelands Courtyard Offices, Moor Road, Melsonby, Richmond, N Yorks, DL10 5NY
Activities: Construction of roads and motorways
Shareholder: David Buggy
Officers: Kelly Kenny, Secretary; David Buggy [1971] Director/Contract Manager; James Davidson [1976] Director/Office Manager; Kelly Kenny [1973] Director/Secretary; Ernest Albert Turner [1946] Director/Surfacing Contractor; John Turner [1976] Director/Contract Manager

Decadeon Holdings Limited
Incorporated: 25 March 2015
Net Worth: £560,080 *Total Assets:* £3,245,063
Registered Office: 34-36 St Marys Place, Newcastle upon Tyne, NE1 7PQ
Activities: Activities of head offices
Shareholders: William Charles Palmer; Paul John Ponton; Mark Andrew Trett
Officers: Steven Hart, Secretary; Steven Hart [1975] Director; William Charles Palmer [1983] Director; Paul John Ponton [1975] Managing Director; Mark Andrew Trett [1979] Director

Decke (Newcastle) Limited
Incorporated: 26 May 2000
Net Worth: £772,177 *Total Assets:* £1,283,123
Registered Office: 244 Park View, Whitley Bay, Tyne & Wear, NE26 3QX
Activities: Other building completion and finishing
Major Shareholder: George Mather Beeby
Officers: Karen Maria Beeby, Secretary; George Mather Beeby [1953] Director/Estimator; Jason Frank [1970] Director

Decor Cladding Centre Ltd
Incorporated: 5 October 2004
Net Worth: £186,914 *Total Assets:* £760,987
Registered Office: 23 Second Avenue, Drum Industrial Estate, Chester-le-Street, Co Durham, DH2 1AG
Activities: Wholesale of hardware, plumbing and heating equipment and supplies
Major Shareholder: Howard John Cross
Officers: Howard John Cross [1965] Director

Decor Panel Limited
Incorporated: 16 September 1998 *Employees:* 62
Net Worth: £2,054,460 *Total Assets:* £4,487,897
Registered Office: 8 Hetton Lyons Industrial Estate, Hetton-le-Hole, Houghton-le-Spring, Co Durham, DH5 0RH
Activities: Wholesale of wood, construction materials and sanitary equipment
Shareholders: Richard Thomas Ling; Ian David Ling
Officers: Julie Anne Anderson, Secretary; Anthony Joseph Hopps [1969] Director/Salesman; Ian David Ling [1969] Director/Salesman; Richard Thomas Ling [1943] Director/Sales

Decorating Direct Limited
Incorporated: 11 November 1999 *Employees:* 10
Net Worth: £642,889 *Total Assets:* £805,986
Registered Office: Unit G1, Commerce Way, Skippers Lane Industrial Estate, Middlesbrough, Cleveland, TS6 6UR
Activities: Other retail sale not in stores, stalls or markets
Officers: Sharon Bernadette Donnelly, Company Secretary; Max Anthony Bone [1969] Director; Sharon Bernadette Donnelly [1964] Director/Company Secretary; David Norman Troughton [1937] Director; Davina Rose Troughton [1941] Director

Dedicated Transport Solutions Limited
Incorporated: 13 September 2002 *Employees:* 31
Net Worth: £2,187,157 *Total Assets:* £2,620,528
Registered Office: DTS International Freight Terminal, Nelson Park West, Cramlington, Northumberland, NE23 1WG
Activities: Freight transport by road
Major Shareholder: John Joisce
Officers: Sandra Kimberly Thompson, Secretary; John Joisce [1966] Director/Haulage Contractor

Deehan Property Limited
Incorporated: 14 May 2012 *Employees:* 1
Net Worth Deficit: £1,148 *Total Assets:* £871,220
Registered Office: 4 Elgy Road, Gosforth, Newcastle upon Tyne, NE3 4UU
Activities: Other letting and operating of own or leased real estate
Major Shareholder: Dr David John Deehan
Officers: Pamela Mary Deehan [1966] Director/Health Visitor

Deenhall Ltd
Incorporated: 16 October 2006
Net Worth: £354,284 *Total Assets:* £762,483
Registered Office: Evans House, Bewick Road, Gateshead, Tyne & Wear, NE8 4DP
Activities: Buying and selling of own real estate
Shareholder: Jeffrey Steiner
Officers: Jeffrey Steiner, Secretary; David Steiner [1967] Director; Jeffrey Steiner [1961] Director

Deepdegree Limited
Incorporated: 31 May 2002
Net Worth: £718,060 *Total Assets:* £1,093,965
Registered Office: Lambshield, Hexham, Northumberland, NE46 1SF
Activities: Other letting and operating of own or leased real estate
Parent: Rundot Limited
Officers: David Kenneth Young, Secretary; Stephen Campion [1967] Director/Accountant; David Kenneth Young [1957] Director/Accountant

Deepfields Property Management Limited
Incorporated: 13 May 2002
Net Worth: £111,489 *Total Assets:* £788,479
Registered Office: Deepfield, 35 Whitburn Road, Cleadon, Sunderland, Tyne & Wear, SR6 7QP
Activities: Other letting and operating of own or leased real estate
Shareholders: Simon Dodsworth; Elayne Dodsworth
Officers: Elayne Dodsworth, Secretary/Property Manager; Elayne Dodsworth [1962] Director/Property Manager; Simon Dodsworth [1970] Director/Property Manager

Deepocean 1 UK Limited
Incorporated: 12 July 1993 *Employees:* 134
Net Worth: £10,042,000 *Total Assets:* £74,094,000
Registered Office: Coniscliffe House, Coniscliffe Road, Darlington, Co Durham, DL3 7EE
Activities: Other specialised construction activities n.e.c.
Officers: Pierre Harry Caine Boyde [1974] Director/Engineer; Louise Elisabeth Lewin [1981] Director/Solicitor; Ottar Kringen Maeland [1975] Director [Norwegian]; Keith Watson [1958] Director/Accountant

Deepstar Subsea Limited
Incorporated: 10 April 1997
Net Worth: £1,421,152 *Total Assets:* £1,594,843
Registered Office: 301a Sunderland Road, South Shields, Tyne & Wear, NE34 6RB
Activities: Other manufacturing n.e.c.
Shareholder: John Samuel Coulter
Officers: Diane Coulter [1958] Director; John Samuel Coulter [1954] Director/Engineer

Deerness Fencing & Landscaping Limited
Incorporated: 27 September 1985 *Employees:* 106
Net Worth: £4,309,991 *Total Assets:* £6,198,756
Registered Office: Esh House, Bowburn North Industrial Estate, Bowburn, Co Durham, DH6 5PF
Activities: Landscape service activities
Parent: Esh Holdings Limited
Officers: Mark Sowerby, Secretary; James Robert Bates [1969] Director; Andrew Edward Radcliffe [1973] Finance Director; Mark Andrew Sowerby [1971] Director

Deerness Rubber Company Limited
Incorporated: 30 November 1978 *Employees:* 20
Net Worth: £1,879,598 *Total Assets:* £2,132,380
Registered Office: Coulson Street, Spennymoor, Co Durham, DL16 7RS
Activities: Manufacture of other rubber products
Shareholders: Karen McKenna; Stephen McKenna
Officers: Stephen McKenna, Secretary; Mary Marina McKenna [1937] Director/Housewife/Clerk; Paul McKenna [1964] Director-Silicone Moulding Co; Stephen McKenna [1959] Director-Silicone Moulding Company

Deetronic Fire Systems Limited
Incorporated: 13 April 2000
Net Worth: £460,815 *Total Assets:* £993,873
Registered Office: 9-18 Ruby Court, Wesley Drive, Benton Square Industrial Estate, Newcastle upon Tyne, NE12 9UP
Activities: Other business support service activities n.e.c.
Parent: Securus Group Limited
Officers: Anthony Denis Kane [1959] Director; John Stewart [1968] Director

Delcor Ltd.
Incorporated: 14 September 2009
Net Worth: £900,347 *Total Assets:* £2,050,934
Registered Office: Delcor House, Double Row, Seaton Delaval, Northumberland, NE25 0PR
Activities: Manufacture of other furniture
Shareholders: Enrico Ernest Petini; Janet Gail Petini
Officers: Janet Gail Petini, Secretary; Enrico Ernest Petini [1960] Director/Administrator; Janet Gail Petini [1959] Director/Administrator

Delessert de Maligny LLP
Incorporated: 25 February 2009 *Employees:* 2
Net Worth: £7,432,787 *Total Assets:* £8,490,749
Registered Office: Pigdon Hall, Pigdon, Morpeth, Northumberland, NE61 3SE
Officers: Anthony Charles Robson [1943] Member; Dorothea Victoria Robson [1956] Member; Ben Robert William Robson [1984] LLP Member; James Joseph Maligny Robson [1986] LLP Member; Stephanie Delessert de Maligny Alexandra Robson [1989] LLP Member

Dellwood Enterprises Limited
Incorporated: 9 February 1972 *Employees:* 4
Net Worth: £951,585 *Total Assets:* £1,034,354
Registered Office: 18 The Dell, Bishop Auckland, Co Durham, DL14 7HJ
Activities: Other letting and operating of own or leased real estate
Parent: Maymask (213) Limited
Officers: Patricia Anne King, Secretary; Athol Richard Forbes King [1983] Director/Mechanical Engineer; Athol Norman Forbes King [1952] Director/Civil Engineer; Eamonn Thomas Forbes King [1984] Director/Doctor; Patricia Anne King [1955] Director/Superintendent Pharmacist

The Delsyl Limited
Incorporated: 1 March 2002
Net Worth: £72,871 *Total Assets:* £953,195
Registered Office: Old Dairy Farm House, East Barns, Dudley Lane, Seaton Burn, Cramlington, Northumberland, NE23 7JT
Activities: Other letting and operating of own or leased real estate
Officers: John Richard Wordsworth Wordsworth - Goodram, Secretary; John Edward Albert Wordsworth-Goodram [1974] Director/Senior IT Project Manager; John Richard Wordsworth Wordsworth-Goodram [1945] Director/Estate Agent

Delta - North Consett Limited
Incorporated: 5 January 1998
Net Worth: £2,270,643 *Total Assets:* £2,346,820
Registered Office: YMCA, Parliament Street, Consett, Co Durham, DH8 5DH
Activities: Youth hostels
Officers: Julie Margaret Ingham, Secretary; Phillip Curran [1982] Director/Business Development Manager; Alan David Gallagher [1971] Director/Risk Manager; Keith Francis Gill [1951] Director; Jason Mole [1971] Director/Police Officer; Barbara Anne Salkeld [1951] Director/Retired Teacher; Amanda Scott [1968] Director; Reverend Valerie Shedden [1956] Director/Vicar; Peter Sinclair [1944] Director/Retired Clergyman; Roy Reginald Tyerman [1933] Director/Retired; Alexander Watson [1942] Director/County Councillor

Delta Precision Engineering North East Limited
Incorporated: 24 November 2011 *Employees:* 25
Net Worth: £834,874 *Total Assets:* £1,179,387
Registered Office: Site 3 Unit 1, Cold Hesledon Industrial Estate, Seaham, Co Durham, SR7 8ST
Activities: Manufacture of bearings, gears, gearing and driving elements
Shareholders: Derek Sanderson; David Wilkinson
Officers: Derek Sanderson [1958] Director/Engineer; David Wilkinson [1958] Director/Engineer

Dementia Matters Ltd
Incorporated: 19 October 1994 *Employees:* 130
Net Worth: £3,605,297 *Total Assets:* £3,730,033
Registered Office: The Bradbury Centre, Darrell Street, Brunswick Village, Newcastle upon Tyne, NE13 7DS
Activities: Other human health activities
Officers: Fraser Quin, Secretary; Dr Susan Clare Abley [1965] Director/Nurse Consultant; Lee Jon Ali [1978] Director/Accountant; Paul John Bell [1961] Director/Solicitor; Timothy Paul Chrisp [1965] Director; Rosalind Dougal [1963] Director; John Paul Lee [1959] Director/Chief Executive; Professor Moira Margaret Livingston [1961] Director/Independent Consultant; Dr Michael John Nicholds [1960] Managing Director; Paul Harold Taylor [1947] Director/Management Consultant; Russell Ward [1982] Director/Solicitor

Den Hartogh Logistics Limited
Incorporated: 28 May 1974 *Employees:* 68
Net Worth: £22,458,034 *Total Assets:* £31,672,520
Registered Office: Victoria House, Pearson Court, Pearson Way, Teesdale Business Park, Stockton on Tees, Cleveland, TS17 6PT
Activities: Other transportation support activities
Major Shareholder: Klaas Pieter Den Hartogh
Officers: Abraham Cornelius Paape [1959] Financial Director [Dutch]; Klaas Pieter Den Hartogh [1965] Managing Director [Dutch]

Denemouth Caravan Park Limited
Incorporated: 16 December 2005 *Employees:* 3
Net Worth: £952,362 *Total Assets:* £1,779,104
Registered Office: Kensington House, 3 Kensington, Bishop Auckland, Co Durham, DL14 6HX
Activities: Other amusement and recreation activities n.e.c.
Major Shareholder: Edith Lakey
Officers: Darren Thomas Green, Secretary; Darren Thomas Green [1970] Director; Neil William Green [1974] Director; Edith Lakey [1949] Director

J Denham Metals Ltd
Incorporated: 28 July 2009 *Employees:* 22
Net Worth: £2,299,299 *Total Assets:* £3,150,055
Registered Office: Coppycrooks, West Auckland Road, Shildon, Co Durham, DL14 9PN
Activities: Wholesale of waste and scrap
Major Shareholder: Joseph Denham
Officers: Joseph Denham [1949] Director

Denka Limited
Incorporated: 6 December 2005
Registered Office: Begbies Traynor (Central) LLP, 4th Floor, Cathedral Buildings, Dean Street, Newcastle upon Tyne, NE1 1PG
Activities: Wholesale trade of motor vehicle parts and accessories
Officers: Andrew Chin Poh Tan [1977] Director [Malaysian]

E L Denney & Son Limited
Incorporated: 14 March 2008 *Employees:* 11
Net Worth Deficit: £306,424 *Total Assets:* £828,352
Registered Office: 50-55 Esplanade Garage, Redcar, Cleveland, TS10 3AQ
Activities: Maintenance and repair of motor vehicles
Shareholder: Ian Laurence Denney
Officers: Patricia Denney, Secretary; Christopher Laurence Denney [1973] Director/Retailer; Ian Laurence Denney [1934] Director; Patricia Denney [1941] Director/Company Secretary

Frederick Dennison Limited
Incorporated: 24 July 1937 *Employees:* 2
Net Worth: £799,276 *Total Assets:* £931,054
Registered Office: Ground Floor, Finchale House, Belmont Business Park, Durham, DH1 1TW
Activities: Other letting and operating of own or leased real estate
Officers: Peter Beckett Dennison, Secretary; Peter Beckett Dennison [1954] Director/Civil Servant; Philippa Anne Dennison [1958] Director

J A Dent & Sons Limited
Incorporated: 19 May 2011 *Employees:* 15
Net Worth: £450,891 *Total Assets:* £1,433,880
Registered Office: Cote Farm, Walden, West Burton, Leyburn, N Yorks, DL8 4LG
Activities: Mixed farming
Shareholders: John Arnold Dent; Margaret Dent
Officers: Clifford Rowland Dent [1972] Director/Farmer; David Abram Dent [1968] Director/Farmer; John Arnold Dent [1940] Director/Farmer; Margaret Dent [1944] Director/Farmer

Denton Estates Limited
Incorporated: 18 March 1987
Net Worth: £631,789 *Total Assets:* £1,020,220
Registered Office: Eastcroft, Redburn, Hexham, Northumberland, NE47 7EA
Activities: Other letting and operating of own or leased real estate
Shareholder: Alison Allcock
Officers: Nicholas Lindsay Partington, Secretary; Alison Allcock [1965] Director/Housewife

Dependable Bodies (Newcastle) Limited
Incorporated: 24 November 1966
Net Worth: £580,931 *Total Assets:* £831,070
Registered Office: Wellington Road, Gateshead, Tyne & Wear, NE11 9HB
Activities: Manufacture of other transport equipment n.e.c.
Shareholder: Martin Richard John Brown
Officers: Gillian Brown, Secretary; Martin Richard John Brown [1960] Director/Sales Manager

Derek Slack Motors Limited
Incorporated: 11 October 1994 *Employees:* 46
Net Worth: £3,655,439 *Total Assets:* £6,325,500
Registered Office: Prospect Place, A66 Cargo Fleet, Middlesbrough, Cleveland, TS3 8AR
Activities: Sale of used cars and light motor vehicles
Major Shareholder: Derek Norman Slack
Officers: Anthony Derek Slack, Secretary; Anthony Derek Slack [1968] Director/Motor Vehicle Mechanic; Derek Norman Slack [1944] Director/Garage Proprietor

Derma UK Limited
Incorporated: 8 August 1996 *Employees:* 18
Net Worth: £391,210 *Total Assets:* £1,893,601
Registered Office: Toffee Factory, Unit S20 Lower Steenbergs Yard, Quayside, Ouseburn, Walker Road, Newcastle upon Tyne, NE1 2DF
Activities: Wholesale of pharmaceutical goods
Parent: Derma UK (Holdings) Limited
Officers: Nicholas Stephen Pass [1959] Director

Derryland Limited
Incorporated: 8 August 1985
Net Worth: £4,178,372 *Total Assets:* £9,853,932
Registered Office: Albert House, Albert Drive, Gateshead, Tyne & Wear, NE9 6EH
Activities: Other letting and operating of own or leased real estate
Shareholders: Denise Craig; Andrew Francis Craig
Officers: Andrew Francis Craig, Secretary; Alexandra Charlotte Craig [1990] Director; Andrew Francis Craig [1955] Director/Estate Agent; Charlotte Jane Craig [1992] Director; Denise Craig [1956] Director/Secretary; Sarah Frances Craig [1983] Director

Derwent Developments (Curzon) Limited
Incorporated: 26 July 2006
Net Worth Deficit: £10,953,490 *Total Assets:* £11,196,000
Registered Office: Citygate, St James Boulevard, Newcastle upon Tyne, NE1 4JE
Activities: Development of building projects
Parent: Derwent Developments Limited
Officers: Adam McGhin, Secretary; Helen Christine Gordon [1959] Director; Michael Paul Keaveney [1967] Director; Adam McGhin [1978] Director/Solicitor; Vanessa Kate Simms [1975] Director

Derwent Developments Limited
Incorporated: 26 March 1985
Net Worth: £69,962,304 *Total Assets:* £70,482,592
Registered Office: Citygate, St James Boulevard, Newcastle upon Tyne, NE1 4JE
Activities: Development of building projects
Parent: Grainger Housing & Developments Limited
Officers: Adam McGhin, Secretary; Helen Christine Gordon [1959] Director; Adam McGhin [1978] Director/Solicitor; Vanessa Kate Simms [1975] Director

Derwent Manor Ltd
Incorporated: 16 September 2013 *Employees:* 3
Net Worth: £17,100 *Total Assets:* £1,983,719
Registered Office: Suite 2b, North Sands Business Centre, Liberty Way, Sunderland, Tyne & Wear, SR6 0QA
Activities: Hotels and similar accommodation
Officers: Keith David Donkin [1978] Director; Linda Ann Wrout [1956] Director/Care Home Operator; Shelia Wrout [1933] Director/Care Home Operator

Derwentside Environmental Testing Services Limited
Incorporated: 1 February 1999 *Employees:* 116
Net Worth: £1,164,000 *Total Assets:* £5,630,000
Registered Office: Unit 2 Park Road Industrial Estate, South Consett, Consett, Co Durham, DH8 5PY
Activities: Technical testing and analysis
Parent: Suez Advanced Solutions UK Limited
Officers: Joan Knight, Secretary; Julien Joseph Rojo [1981] Director/Vice President [French]; Simon Timothy Dyke Turner [1965] Director

Derwentside Hospice Care Foundation
Incorporated: 2 June 1988 *Employees:* 86
Net Worth: £2,053,551 *Total Assets:* £2,212,677
Registered Office: Willow Burn Hospice, Maiden Law Hospital, Howden Bank, Lanchester, Co Durham, DH7 0QS
Activities: Specialists medical practice activities
Officers: Anne Britton [1952] Director/Retired Local Government Officer; Anita Generaldine Burdon [1977] Director/Pharmacist; Nigel Cook [1968] Director; Mark Davies [1957] Director/Solicitor; Paul Jackson [1945] Chair of The Board of Directors; Mark Henry McArdle [1968] Managing Director

Design and Security Services Limited
Incorporated: 26 January 2004 *Employees:* 32
Net Worth: £178,498 *Total Assets:* £758,846
Registered Office: Unit 1 Hunter Road, South West Industrial Estate, Peterlee, Co Durham, SR8 2LX
Activities: Machining
Shareholders: Andrew Gaskins; Mark David Kelly; Alastair Tennant
Officers: Mark David Kelly, Secretary; Andrew Gaskins [1972] Director; Mark David Kelly [1966] Director; Alastair Tennant [1972] Director

Destiny Church Tees Valley
Incorporated: 29 May 2007 *Employees:* 2
Net Worth: £658,443 *Total Assets:* £757,523
Registered Office: The Destiny Centre, 395 Norton Road, Norton, Stockton on Tees, Cleveland, TS20 2QQ
Activities: Activities of religious organisations
Officers: John Micah, Secretary; Tracy Petrina Chetty [1973] Director/Physiotherapist; Catherine Esther Gladys Harris [1970] Director/Pastor; Jonathan Mark Harris [1962] Director/Pastor; John Micah [1982] Director/Teacher [Ghanaian]; Mabel Micah [1984] Director/Teacher [Ghanaian]; Deveshin Reddy [1973] Director/Accountant

Devereux Architecture Limited
Incorporated: 20 February 2001 *Employees:* 35
Net Worth: £152,724 *Total Assets:* £1,209,602
Registered Office: Cooper's Studios, Westgate Road, Newcastle upon Tyne, NE1 3NN
Activities: Architectural activities
Parent: Ryder Architecture Limited
Officers: Graeme Richard Hurworth, Secretary; Peter Buchan [1953] Director; Mark Thompson [1965] Director

Devereux Developments Limited
Incorporated: 4 March 1977 *Employees:* 172
Net Worth: £2,575,492 *Total Assets:* £4,958,816
Registered Office: Daimler Drive, Cowpen Lane Industrial Estate, Billingham, Cleveland, TS23 4JD
Activities: Freight transport by road
Shareholders: Anthony Deveruex; Kenneth Devereux
Officers: Kenneth Devereux, Secretary; Anthony Devereux [1962] Director/Haulage Contractor; Kenneth Devereux [1952] Director/Haulage Contractor

Devine Chemicals Limited
Incorporated: 13 January 1994 *Employees:* 9
Net Worth: £844,884 *Total Assets:* £2,580,779
Registered Office: Prospect Business Park, Leadgate, Consett, Co Durham, DH8 7PW
Activities: Wholesale of chemical products
Shareholders: James Devine; Eileen Devine
Officers: Eileen Devine, Secretary; Daniel James Devine [1981] Commercial Director; Eileen Devine [1947] Director/Chemical Distributor; James Devine [1946] Director/Chemical Distributor

Devon Conversions Limited
Incorporated: 20 February 1990 *Employees:* 17
Net Worth: £553,382 *Total Assets:* £1,036,492
Registered Office: Mainsforth Road, Ferryhill, Co Durham, DL17 9DE
Activities: Manufacture of motor vehicles
Officers: Heather Ann Gowland, Secretary; Heather Ann Gowland [1959] Director; Peter James Gowland [1952] Director

Devon Motor Caravans Limited
Incorporated: 29 December 2000
Net Worth: £869,426 *Total Assets:* £905,734
Registered Office: c/o Devon Conversions Ltd, Mainsforth Road, Ferryhill, Co Durham, DL17 9DE
Activities: Other letting and operating of own or leased real estate
Major Shareholder: Peter James Gowland
Officers: Heather Ann Gowland, Secretary; Heather Ann Gowland [1959] Director; Peter James Gowland [1952] Director

Dewhirst Holywell Enterprises Limited
Incorporated: 3 February 1998
Net Worth: £808,965 *Total Assets:* £884,650
Registered Office: Holywell House, Brancepeth, Co Durham, DH7 8EH
Activities: Growing of cereals (except rice), leguminous crops and oil seeds
Parent: Holywell Wren Holdings Limited
Officers: Ian Roberts Dewhirst, Secretary/Director; Ian Roberts Dewhirst [1948] Director; Margaret Anne Dewhirst [1947] Director/Housewife

DFI Properties Limited
Incorporated: 27 October 2014
Net Worth: £607,561 *Total Assets:* £911,910
Registered Office: 104 Middle Drive, Darras Hall, Ponteland, Northumberland, NE20 9DW
Activities: Development of building projects
Major Shareholder: Richard John Charles Lawson
Officers: Richard John Charles Lawson [1970] Director

DFP Services Limited
Incorporated: 12 December 2000
Net Worth: £840,493 *Total Assets:* £1,752,586
Registered Office: 1 Artemis Court, St Johns Road, Meadowfield, Co Durham, DH7 8XQ
Activities: Repair of electrical equipment
Parent: DFP Services Holdings Limited
Officers: Jon Paul Seed [1985] Director/Sales and Operations Manager

Dhammakaya North United Kingdom
Incorporated: 19 November 2007
Net Worth: £1,753,402 *Total Assets:* £1,756,402
Registered Office: Dhammakaya Meditation Centre, Church Street, Hebburn, Tyne & Wear, NE31 1DR
Activities: Activities of religious organisations
Officers: Phibul Choompolpaisal, Secretary; Theanchai Chitvicheankul [1962] Director/Sole Trader; Pichit Choompolpaisal [1974] Director [Thai]; Nicholas Thanissaro [1965] Director/Minister of Religion; Wairot Treenet [1963] Director/Minister of Religion [Thai]; Veera Vingvorn [1962] Director/Minister of Religion [Thai]

DHD Wealth Management Ltd
Incorporated: 22 February 2016 *Employees:* 10
Net Worth: £3,526,174 *Total Assets:* £3,735,140
Registered Office: 1 The Bulrushes, Woodstock Way, Boldon Business Park, Boldon Colliery, Co Durham, NE35 9PF
Activities: Financial intermediation not elsewhere classified
Parent: Fairstone Holdings Limited
Officers: Scott Hopkinson, Secretary; Lee Graham Hartley [1976] Director; Scott Hopkinson [1974] Director/Accountant

Dhillons Investment Properties Limited
Incorporated: 6 April 2005 *Employees:* 7
Net Worth: £1,300,355 *Total Assets:* £5,012,458
Registered Office: Old Post House, Hexham Road, Throckley, Newcastle upon Tyne, NE15 9EB
Activities: Development of building projects
Officers: Sirbjit Kaur Dhillon, Secretary; Sukhvinder Singh Dhillon [1968] Director/Retail Manager; Sukhvir Singh Dhillon [1966] Director/Retail Manager [Indian]

DHM Vehicle Rental Limited
Incorporated: 31 January 2014 *Employees:* 8
Net Worth: £816,457 *Total Assets:* £8,248,737
Registered Office: Office 7, Bhive Business Centre, Allum Way, Skelton Industrial Estate, Skelton, N Yorks, TS12 2LQ
Activities: Renting and leasing of cars and light motor vehicles
Major Shareholder: Paul Docherty
Officers: John Adam Docherty [1986] Director; Paul Docherty [1958] Director

DHN Property Services Ltd
Incorporated: 9 August 2002
Net Worth: £451,969 *Total Assets:* £1,344,300
Registered Office: 112 Whitley Road, Whitley Bay, Tyne & Wear, NE26 2NE
Activities: Other letting and operating of own or leased real estate
Shareholders: David Trevor Newton; Dorothy Newton
Officers: Dorothy Newton, Secretary; David Trevor Newton [1970] Director/Self Employed Antiques Business; Dorothy Newton [1943] Director

Dial-a-Loo Limited
Incorporated: 4 March 2003
Net Worth: £923,110 *Total Assets:* £1,263,246
Registered Office: Unit 10 Stonehills, Shields Road, Gateshead, Tyne & Wear, NE10 0HW
Activities: Sewerage
Officers: Christine Bell, Secretary/Administrator; Christine Bell [1954] Director/Administrator; Joseph Bell [1954] Managing Director

Diamond Chain (UK) Limited
Incorporated: 1 February 1999
Net Worth Deficit: £7,402,016 *Total Assets:* £3,436,799
Registered Office: Tundry Way, Chainbridge Industrial Estate, Blaydon on Tyne, Tyne & Wear, NE21 5SJ
Activities: Machining
Officers: Richard Gray [1979] Director [American]; Christopher Marr [1971] Director/President [American]

Diamond Hall Infant Academy
Incorporated: 11 June 2013 *Employees:* 54
Net Worth: £1,699,937 *Total Assets:* £2,457,200
Registered Office: Diamond Hall Infant Academy, Well Street, Millfield, Sunderland, Tyne & Wear, SR4 6JF
Activities: Primary education
Officers: Alison Elizabeth Collingwood [1953] Director/Headteacher; Sandra Duke [1963] Director/School Business Manager; Catherine Yvonne Elston [1950] Director/Retired Supply Teacher; Rebecca Louise Foster-Snook [1978] Director/Teacher/Manager; Reverend Alison Jean Hampton [1961] Director/Reverend; Penny Henry [1951] Director/Retired; Alison Rose Levitt [1965] Director/Project Leader; Kirsty McNicholl [1980] Director/Local Government Officer/Parent; Ann Pickering [1944] Director/Retired; Susan Reed [1969] Director/Headteacher

Dibbin Estates & Equipment Limited
Incorporated: 22 April 2010
Net Worth: £2,362,985 *Total Assets:* £4,541,328
Registered Office: c/o International Processplants (Europe) Ltd, Postal Pages, The Grange Business Centre, Belasis Avenue, Billingham, Cleveland, TS23 1LG
Activities: Other business support service activities n.e.c.
Parent: Newfuturevest Limited
Officers: Anthony Stephen Field [1957] Director; Thomas Elgey Nash [1958] Director/Chartered Surveyor

Dickens Self Storage Limited
Incorporated: 20 April 2005 *Employees:* 6
Net Worth: £177,273 *Total Assets:* £838,775
Registered Office: Unit 2b Guiseley Way, Durham Lane Industrial Park, Eaglescliffe, Stockton on Tees, Cleveland, TS16 0RF
Activities: Other letting and operating of own or leased real estate
Major Shareholder: Jonathan Richard Dicken
Officers: Robert Michael Goodrum, Secretary; Alison Dicken [1970] Director; Jonathan Richard Dicken [1971] Director

Dickens Warehousing Limited
Incorporated: 13 March 2007 *Employees:* 2
Net Worth: £785,188 *Total Assets:* £805,940
Registered Office: Unit 2b Guiseley Way, Durham Lane Industrial Park, Eaglescliffe, Stockton on Tees, Cleveland, TS16 0RF
Activities: Other letting and operating of own or leased real estate
Major Shareholder: Jonathan Richard Dicken
Officers: Robert Michael Goodrum, Secretary; Alison Dicken [1970] Director/Housewife; Jonathan Richard Dicken [1971] Director

Dickinson Brothers Limited
Incorporated: 22 July 1936 *Employees:* 25
Net Worth: £5,553,863 *Total Assets:* £6,680,945
Registered Office: 2 Lambton Road, Jesmond, Newcastle upon Tyne, NE2 4RX
Activities: Retail sale of carpets, rugs, wall and floor coverings in specialised stores
Shareholders: John Conrad Dickinson; John Robert Joel Dickinson; Hilary Anne Dickinson
Officers: Hilary Anne Dickinson, Secretary/Director/Bookkeeper; Dorothy Johnson Dickinson [1928] Director; Hilary Anne Dickinson [1953] Director; John Robert Joel Dickinson [1982] Director; John Conrad Dickinson [1955] Director

John Dickinson Transport Limited
Incorporated: 31 May 2006 *Employees:* 57
Net Worth: £1,649,748 *Total Assets:* £7,117,959
Registered Office: The Old Station, Winston, Darlington, Co Durham, DL2 3QQ
Activities: Freight transport by road
Shareholders: Brenda Dickinson; John Drevor Dickinson
Officers: Mrs Brenda Dickinson, Secretary/Director; Mrs Brenda Dickinson [1937] Director; Mr John Drevor Dickinson [1930] Director

M.I. Dickson Limited
Incorporated: 18 June 1953 *Employees:* 334
Net Worth: £5,853,768 *Total Assets:* £7,854,609
Registered Office: 32 Portland Terrace, Newcastle upon Tyne, NE2 1QP
Activities: Production of meat and poultry meat products
Shareholder: Michael George Dickson
Officers: Haydn Biddle [1946] Director; Elena Dickson [1978] Director; Marisa Michela Dickson [1951] Director; Michael George Dickson [1951] Director/Pork Butcher; Christopher David Hayman [1974] Director; Daniela Parkinson [1976] Director

Diesel Marine International Limited
Incorporated: 6 June 2001 *Employees:* 129
Net Worth: £2,804,000 *Total Assets:* £6,320,000
Registered Office: West Chirton Industrial Estate, Gloucester Road, North Shields, Tyne & Wear, NE29 8RQ
Activities: Activities of head offices
Major Shareholder: Peter Lindsey Jackson
Officers: Alan Leslie Gray, Secretary/Accountant; David Disneur [1978] Director/Marketing Manager; Alan Leslie Gray [1963] Director/Accountant; Clare Jackson [1979] Director/CRM Manager; Peter Lindsey Jackson [1941] Director; Nicholas Welford [1970] Sales Director; Richard Kevin Woodmansey [1954] Director

Diespeker Holdings Ltd
Incorporated: 13 December 1999
Net Worth: £726,743 *Total Assets:* £963,652
Registered Office: Bridge End Works, Ryhope Road, Ryhope, Sunderland, Tyne & Wear, SR2 0NJ
Activities: Other business support service activities n.e.c.
Officers: Joanne Elaine Laidler, Secretary; Joseph Edward Laidler [1939] Director

Different Advertising Design and Marketing Limited
Incorporated: 24 February 1999 *Employees:* 40
Net Worth: £491,602 *Total Assets:* £1,268,440
Registered Office: 6-8 Ravensworth Terrace, Newcastle upon Tyne, NE4 6AU
Activities: Advertising agencies
Parent: Everything Different Limited
Officers: Benjamin John Quigley, Secretary; Yousaf Khalid [1965] Managing Director; Mark Martin [1966] Director/Graphic Designer Account Executive; Ian Millen [1964] Director/Advertising; Benjamin John Quigley [1965] Director/Advertising

Digital Office Solutions Limited
Incorporated: 2 July 1998 *Employees:* 15
Net Worth: £886,003 *Total Assets:* £1,034,182
Registered Office: Middleton House, Durham & Tees Valley Airport, Darlington, Co Durham, DL2 1PD
Activities: Repair of electrical equipment
Shareholders: Jonathan Lester Alexander; Jayne Alexander
Officers: Jayne Alexander, Secretary; Jonathan Lester Alexander [1971] Director

Digitax Electronics UK Limited
Incorporated: 12 May 1989
Net Worth: £810,366 *Total Assets:* £1,254,572
Registered Office: The Old Smoke House, 31 Tanners Bank, North Shields, Tyne & Wear, NE30 1JH
Activities: Other business support service activities n.e.c.
Major Shareholder: Stephen Laidler
Officers: Stephen Laidler, Secretary; Stephen Laidler [1958] Director/General Manager; Thomas James Laidler [1991] Director

Dimeplace Limited
Incorporated: 21 November 1997 *Employees:* 1
Net Worth: £840,195 *Total Assets:* £952,094
Registered Office: The Boathouse, Newburn, Newcastle upon Tyne, NE15 8NL
Activities: Buying and selling of own real estate
Major Shareholder: David Philip Johnson
Officers: David Philip Johnson [1959] Director/Chartered Surveyor

J. Dinning (Investments) Limited
Incorporated: 17 December 2012
Net Worth: £1,067,775 *Total Assets:* £1,305,510
Registered Office: 22 Whitworth Terrace, Spennymoor, Co Durham, DL16 7LD
Activities: Non-trading company
Shareholders: Julie Cowie; William Stewart Cowie
Officers: Julie Cowie [1961] Director/Secretary; William Stewart Cowie [1956] Director/Pharmacist

J. Dinning (Woodlands) Limited
Incorporated: 2 May 2012 *Employees:* 25
Net Worth: £409,560 *Total Assets:* £810,206
Registered Office: 22 Whitworth Terrace, Spennymoor, Co Durham, DL16 7LD
Activities: Dispensing chemist in specialised stores
Shareholders: William Stewart Cowie; Julie Cowie
Officers: Julie Cowie [1961] Director/Secretary; William Stewart Cowie [1956] Director/Pharmacist

Dinning Farms Limited
Incorporated: 5 July 2007
Net Worth: £1,336,627 *Total Assets:* £1,508,483
Registered Office: Milburn House, Hexham Business Park, Burn Lane, Hexham, Northumberland, NE46 3RU
Activities: Other business support service activities n.e.c.
Shareholder: Christopher Paul Dinning
Officers: Joan Margery Dinning, Secretary; Christopher George Dinning [1944] Director/Farmer; Christopher Paul Dinning [1968] Director/Farmer; Joan Margery Dinning [1944] Director/Farmer

R. Dinning Limited
Incorporated: 19 June 1963 *Employees:* 13
Net Worth: £215,674 *Total Assets:* £1,740,177
Registered Office: 5 Stirling Court, Team Valley Trading Estate, Gateshead, Tyne & Wear, NE11 0JF
Activities: Wholesale of radio, television goods & electrical household appliances (other than records, tapes, CDs)
Shareholder: Carol Ann Hebson
Officers: Carol Ann Hebson, Secretary/Civil Servant; Carol Ann Hebson [1951] Director/Civil Servant; Graeme Leslie Hebson [1981] Director; Neil Douglas Hebson [1977] Managing Director

Dinnington Cottages Limited
Incorporated: 27 April 1912
Net Worth: £1,224,332 *Total Assets:* £1,333,427
Registered Office: Spring Cottage, Broomhaugh, Riding Mill, Northumberland, NE44 6EG
Activities: Financial management
Officers: Geoffrey Edward Roland Heslop, Secretary; Benjamin Michael Heslop [1976] Director; Charles William Roland Heslop [1955] Director; Geoffrey Edward Roland Heslop [1927] Director; Jonathan Heslop [1962] Director/Solicitor; Michael Hugh Heslop [1948] Director/Chartered Accountant; Richard James Heslop [1960] Director/Chartered Surveyor

Dinsdale Farming Limited
Incorporated: 18 April 2012 *Employees:* 7
Net Worth: £89,720 *Total Assets:* £3,198,814
Registered Office: Manor House Farm, Low Dinsdale, Neasham, Darlington, Co Durham, DL2 1PN
Activities: Raising of poultry
Shareholders: Harry Trevor Dent; Henry Lloyd Dent; Susan Rachel Dent
Officers: Rachel Dent, Secretary; Harry Trevor Dent [1948] Director/Farmer; Henry Lloyd Dent [1985] Director/Farmer; Susan Rachel Dent [1957] Director/Farmer

Dipsticks Research Limited
Incorporated: 15 April 1999
Net Worth: £1,071,024 *Total Assets:* £2,899,991
Registered Office: The Mill, Hexham Business Park, Burn Lane, Hexham, Northumberland, NE46 3RU
Activities: Market research and public opinion polling
Shareholders: John Raglan; Fiona Dempster Raglan
Officers: John Raglan, Secretary; Dominic Anthony Barnes [1960] Director; Fiona Dempster Raglan [1957] Director/Market Researcher; John Raglan [1961] Director/Marketing Consultant; Angus Christopher Webb [1974] Director/Market Research

Dipton Care Home Limited
Incorporated: 27 October 2009 *Employees:* 103
Net Worth: £274,723 *Total Assets:* £4,291,206
Registered Office: Lion House, 400 Durham Road, Birtley, Chester-le-Street, Co Durham, DH3 1LS
Activities: Residential care activities for the elderly and disabled
Parent: Lion Care Home Group
Officers: Robert Pattinson [1934] Director/Restaurateur; Stevie-Lee Pattinson [1969] Director/Restaurateur

Direct Connections Limited
Incorporated: 5 October 2016 *Employees:* 148
Net Worth: £13,320 *Total Assets:* £893,374
Registered Office: 14 Harelands Courtyard Offices, Melsonby, Richmond, N Yorks, DL10 5NY
Activities: Combined office administrative service activities
Major Shareholder: Duncan Adrian John Crocker
Officers: Colin Robert Hartness [1962] Director

Direct Sports Limited
Incorporated: 27 January 2003 *Employees:* 15
Net Worth: £1,700,529 *Total Assets:* £2,109,502
Registered Office: Evolution, Wynyard Avenue, Wynyard, Stockton on Tees, Cleveland, TS22 5TB
Activities: Retail sale via mail order houses or via Internet
Major Shareholder: Mark Watson
Officers: Helen Smith, Secretary; Mark Watson [1968] Managing Director

Direkt Engineering Holdings Limited
Incorporated: 6 December 2012 *Employees:* 2
Net Worth: £1,255,844 *Total Assets:* £1,781,852
Registered Office: 12 Whickham Bank, Whickham, Gateshead, Tyne & Wear, NE16 4AJ
Activities: Other letting and operating of own or leased real estate
Shareholders: Keith Roy Burn; Patricia Ann Burn
Officers: Keith Roy Burn [1951] Director; Patricia Ann Burn [1954] Director

Direkt Engineering Services Limited
Incorporated: 31 August 1999 *Employees:* 89
Net Worth: £868,390 *Total Assets:* £1,775,268
Registered Office: 12 Whickham Bank, Whickham, Gateshead, Tyne & Wear, NE16 4AJ
Activities: Temporary employment agency activities
Parent: Direkt Engineering Holdings Limited
Officers: Patricia Ann Burn, Secretary; Keith Roy Burn [1951] Director; Patricia Ann Burn [1954] Director/Secretary

Disability North
Incorporated: 30 December 1983 *Employees:* 18
Net Worth: £15,155 *Total Assets:* £760,664
Registered Office: The Dene Centre, Castles Farm Road, Newcastle upon Tyne, NE3 1PH
Activities: Social work activities without accommodation for the elderly and disabled
Officers: Sandra Wheatley, Secretary; Joseph Luke Ayton [1982] Director/Voluntary Work; Alison Elizabeth Blackburn [1956] Director/Disability Consultant; Dr Toby Brandon [1967] Director/Lecturer; Jamie Liam Cairns [1988] Director; Maria Hood [1961] Director; Stuart Knox [1957] Director/Accountant; Malcolm Patrick Albany MacOurt [1947] Director/University Lecturer; David John Pritchard [1976] Director/Digital Marketing Manager; Sandra Wheatley [1956] Director/Volunteer; Doctor Timothy Williams [1964] Director/Hospital Doctor

Discover Learning Trust
Incorporated: 11 October 2012 *Employees:* 188
Net Worth: £9,722,000 *Total Assets:* £11,854,000
Registered Office: Oxclose Community Academy, Dilston Close, Washington, Tyne & Wear, NE38 0LN
Activities: General secondary education
Officers: Karen Atkinson, Secretary; Lynda Elizabeth Brown [1956] Director/Retired; Anthony Paul Cunningham [1957] Director/Executive Headteacher; Julie Cuthbertson [1981] Director/Business Bank Manager; Linda Nixon [1965] Director/Civil Servant; Joanne Quinn [1974] Director; Lynne Simpson [1973] Director/Civil Servant; Linda Williams [1958] Director/Councillor

Discovery Learning Limited
Incorporated: 27 May 2011 *Employees:* 18
Net Worth: £9,653,503 *Total Assets:* £10,160,357
Registered Office: Rye Hill House, Scotswood Road, Newcastle upon Tyne, NE4 7SA
Activities: Technical and vocational secondary education
Officers: Gerard Francis Garvey [1979] Director; Paula Miller [1975] Director/Head of Learner Services and Safeguarding

Dissington Investments Limited
Incorporated: 18 February 2015
Net Worth: £217,974 *Total Assets:* £2,178,111
Registered Office: West 2, Asama Court, Amethyst Road, Newcastle Business Park, Newcastle upon Tyne, NE4 7YD
Activities: Activities of investment trusts
Major Shareholder: Fiona Mary Edwina Nicholson
Officers: Fiona Mary Edwina Nicholson [1966] Director; Stephen Thomas Nicholson [1959] Director

Distributor Supplies (UK) Limited
Incorporated: 11 June 1997
Net Worth: £258,661 *Total Assets:* £2,492,309
Registered Office: IG House, Burdon Drive, Peterlee, Co Durham, SR8 2JH
Activities: Other business support service activities n.e.c.
Major Shareholder: Stephen Hoey
Officers: Stephen Hoey [1958] Managing Director

Dixon Landscapes Limited
Incorporated: 19 August 1998
Net Worth: £1,341,095 *Total Assets:* £1,651,292
Registered Office: Woodbrae, Comb Hill, Haltwhistle, Northumberland, NE49 9EN
Activities: Landscape service activities
Shareholders: Richard Joseph Dixon; Victoria Alice Dixon
Officers: Richard Joseph Dixon [1974] Director/Landscaper; Victoria Alice Dixon [1979] Director/Office Manager

Dennis Dixon Limited
Incorporated: 4 February 1987 *Employees:* 77
Net Worth: £4,549,578 *Total Assets:* £5,965,172
Registered Office: Tilbury Road, South Bank, Middlesbrough, Cleveland, TS6 6AW
Activities: Repair and maintenance of other transport equipment n.e.c.
Shareholders: Dennis Laurence Dixon; Hoyer UK Ltd
Officers: Dennis Laurence Dixon [1938] Director; Steven Paul Dixon [1968] Managing Director; Andreas Theodor Reinhardt [1958] Director [German]

Dixons Industrial Holdings Limited
Incorporated: 11 February 2015
Net Worth: £776,412 *Total Assets:* £2,830,723
Registered Office: Mayfair House, Redburn Road, Newcastle upon Tyne, NE5 1NB
Activities: Activities of other holding companies n.e.c.
Officers: Anthony Dixon [1981] Director; David Marc Dixon [1979] Director; Mary Dixon [1956] Director; David Dixon Jnr [1956] Director

Dixons of Westerhope Limited
Incorporated: 4 September 2002 *Employees:* 90
Net Worth: £4,602,349 *Total Assets:* £11,982,371
Registered Office: Westfield, Newbiggin Lane, Westerhope, Newcastle upon Tyne, NE5 1LX
Activities: Agents involved in the sale of fuels, ores, metals and industrial chemicals
Parent: Air Products PLC
Officers: Mark Jamie Sambrook, Secretary; Sonia de Vasconcelos Borges de Araujo [1975] Accounting Director - Europe [Portuguese]; Mark Jamie Sambrook [1971] Director/Solicitor; Michael Neil Smyth [1971] Director/General Manager

DKB Crop Protection Limited
Incorporated: 12 February 2002 *Employees:* 10
Net Worth: £2,867,255 *Total Assets:* £3,806,567
Registered Office: Hill House, Thrintoft, Northallerton, N Yorks, DL7 0PL
Activities: Landscape service activities
Shareholders: David Barker; Valerie Barker; Vernon John Spinks
Officers: Valerie Barker, Secretary; David Barker [1950] Director/Agronomist; Valerie Barker [1956] Director/Secretary; Vernon John Spinks [1962] Director/Agronomist

DLI Engineering Limited
Incorporated: 8 May 2008 *Employees:* 36
Net Worth: £1,147,591 *Total Assets:* £2,622,924
Registered Office: Trimdon Grange Industrial Estate, Trimdon Grange, Co Durham, TS29 6PA
Activities: Manufacture of taps and valves
Parent: DLI Group Limited
Officers: George Stephen Penchion [1954] Director; Barry Michael Wells [1946] Director

DM North Limited
Incorporated: 27 January 2012
Net Worth: £965,881 *Total Assets:* £977,446
Registered Office: Mandale House, 5 Neville Road, North Tees Industrial Estate, Stockton on Tees, Cleveland, TS18 2RD
Activities: Development of building projects
Major Shareholder: David Ian Harriman
Officers: Joseph Darragh, Secretary; Paula Davidson, Secretary; David Ian Harriman [1956] Director

DM Services (Banchory) Ltd
Incorporated: 27 October 2008 *Employees:* 4
Net Worth: £2,203,267 *Total Assets:* £2,613,343
Registered Office: 43 Coniscliffe Road, Darlington, Co Durham, DL3 7EH
Activities: Support activities for petroleum and natural gas mining
Major Shareholder: David Telford MacKay
Officers: Dr Susan Catherine McHardy, Secretary/Doctor [British/Australian]; David Telford MacKay [1960] Director; Dr Susan Catherine McHardy [1961] Director; Catriona Anne McHardy MacKay [1996] Director

DNR Limited
Incorporated: 1 April 1936 *Employees:* 146
Net Worth: £7,554,206 *Total Assets:* £13,269,632
Registered Office: North Tyne Industrial Estate, Whitley Road, Longbenton, Newcastle upon Tyne, NE12 9SZ
Activities: Other letting and operating of own or leased real estate
Officers: Doreen Mallen [1948] Director; Pamela Helen Louise Mallen [1975] Director/H R Manager; Scott Mallen [1975] Director; Paul David Thompson [1969] Director; Rachel Thompson [1973] Director/Solicitor

T.S.C. Dobbin Limited
Incorporated: 16 October 2000
Net Worth: £951,799 *Total Assets:* £1,083,214
Registered Office: 10 Grange Terrace, Sunderland, Tyne & Wear, SR2 7DF
Activities: Dispensing chemist in specialised stores
Major Shareholder: Timothy Simon Charles Dobbin
Officers: Timothy Simon Charles Dobbin, Secretary/Pharmacist; Janet Dobbin [1967] Director/Bank Official; Timothy Simon Charles Dobbin [1963] Director/Pharmacist

Doby Cleats Limited
Incorporated: 15 April 1969 *Employees:* 60
Net Worth: £2,776,278 *Total Assets:* £7,841,067
Registered Office: Unit 4 Harelaw Industrial Estate, Harelaw, Stanley, Co Durham, DH9 8UJ
Activities: Other non-ferrous metal production
Officers: Thomas Malcolm Moss, Secretary; Terence Dingley [1955] Director/Engineer; Peter Jennissen [1954] Director [German]; Thomas Malcolm Moss [1956] Director

Doby Verrolec Limited
Incorporated: 1 December 1998 *Employees:* 2
Net Worth: £972,223 *Total Assets:* £972,223
Registered Office: Harelaw Industrial Estate, Stanley, Co Durham, DH9 8UJ
Activities: Non-trading company
Officers: Terence Dingley, Secretary; Peter Jennissen [1954] Director [German]; Thomas Malcolm Moss [1956] Director

Dockleaf Corbridge Limited
Incorporated: 21 October 2013
Registered Office: Winders Wood Cottage, Newcastle Road, Corbridge, Northumberland, NE45 5LT
Activities: Development of building projects
Major Shareholder: Timothy John Anderson
Officers: Sally Anderson [1968] Director/Property Developer; Tim John Anderson [1968] Director

Dockleaf Developments Limited
Incorporated: 13 October 2014 *Employees:* 2
Net Worth: £1,007,256 *Total Assets:* £2,901,269
Registered Office: Winders Wood Cottage, Howden Dene, Newcastle Road, Corbridge, Northumberland, NE45 5LT
Activities: Development of building projects
Shareholders: Tim John Anderson; Sally Anderson
Officers: Sally Anderson [1968] Director/Developer; Timothy John Anderson [1968] Director/Developer

Document Solutions (UK) Limited
Incorporated: 23 March 2011 *Employees:* 29
Net Worth: £100,271 *Total Assets:* £952,012
Registered Office: 2 Christon Road, Gosforth Industrial Estate, Newcastle upon Tyne, NE3 1XD
Activities: Renting and leasing of office machinery and equipment (including computers)
Shareholders: Lee John Allinson; David MacArtney; Mark Stewart Friberg
Officers: Caroline Elizabeth Allinson [1978] Director; Lee John Allinson [1974] Sales Director; Linda Friberg [1968] Director; Mark Stewart Friberg [1967] Sales Director; David MacArtney [1968] Sales Directors; Paula MacArtney [1970] Director

Henry F. Dodds Limited
Incorporated: 16 June 1965 *Employees:* 11
Net Worth: £363,310 *Total Assets:* £947,683
Registered Office: 3 St James Street, Newcastle upon Tyne, NE1 4NF
Activities: Activities of insurance agents and brokers
Major Shareholder: Ian Henderson
Officers: Audrey Henderson, Secretary; Ian Henderson [1961] Director/Insurance Broker; Keith Murray Main [1952] Director/Insurance Broker

DOH Construction Limited
Incorporated: 14 June 2005 *Employees:* 42
Net Worth: £354,093 *Total Assets:* £941,858
Registered Office: Lloyd Court, Metrocentre East Industrial Estate, St Omers Road, Dunston, Tyne & Wear, NE11 9EP
Activities: Other building completion and finishing
Shareholder: Scott Hamilton
Officers: Joanne Hamilton, Secretary; Scott Hamilton [1971] Director

Dome Propco Limited
Incorporated: 23 January 2007
Net Worth: £2,261,000 *Total Assets:* £42,316,000
Registered Office: 2nd Floor, One Gosforth Park Way, Gosforth Business Park, Newcastle upon Tyne, NE12 8ET
Activities: Other letting and operating of own or leased real estate
Parent: Parkdean Resorts Limited
Officers: Judith Ann Archibold, Secretary; Ian Kellett [1963] Director; John Anthony Waterworth [1963] Director

Donald Pig & Poultry Ltd
Incorporated: 23 February 2012 *Employees:* 8
Net Worth: £959,270 *Total Assets:* £2,167,427
Registered Office: Mount Pleasant Farm, West Rounton, Northallerton, N Yorks, DL6 2LU
Activities: Raising of swine and pigs
Shareholders: Colin Marshall Donald; Christine Donald; Matthew Marshall Donald
Officers: Christine Donald [1961] Director/Farmer; Colin Marshall Donald [1962] Director/Farmer; Matthew Marshall Donald [1991] Director/Farmer

Doncaster Pharmaceuticals Group Limited
Incorporated: 21 January 1987 *Employees:* 88
Net Worth: £6,882,000 *Total Assets:* £18,294,000
Registered Office: 7 Regents Drive, Prudhoe, Northumberland, NE42 6PX
Activities: Wholesale of pharmaceutical goods
Parent: Doncaster Pharmaceuticals Limited
Officers: Mark James Gulliford [1969] Director; David Horry [1964] Director/Chairman; Haydn Peter Smith [1966] Group IT Director; Derek Andrew Wilson [1964] Director

Doncaster Pharmaceuticals Limited
Incorporated: 10 October 1977
Net Worth: £200 *Total Assets:* £5,645,959
Registered Office: 7 Regents Drive, Prudhoe, Northumberland, NE42 6PX
Activities: Wholesale of pharmaceutical goods
Parent: Converse Pharma Limited
Officers: Mark James Gulliford [1969] Director; Derek Andrew Wilson [1964] Director

Dongard Contract Services Limited
Incorporated: 20 January 2005 *Employees:* 24
Net Worth: £128,667 *Total Assets:* £1,201,608
Registered Office: Baxter Place, Seaton Delaval, Whitley Bay, Tyne & Wear, NE25 0AP
Activities: Construction of commercial buildings
Parent: Dongard Limited
Officers: Josh William Elliott Boyle [1988] Director; Leslie Donaldson [1961] Director/Electrician; Lee Gardner [1970] Director/Managing Executive

John Donkin Solicitors Ltd
Incorporated: 21 November 2008
Net Worth: £409,458 *Total Assets:* £765,017
Registered Office: A3 Kingfisher House, Team Valley Trading Estate, Gateshead, Tyne & Wear, NE11 0JQ
Activities: Solicitors
Shareholders: John Richard Rodger; John Adrian Donkin
Officers: John Adrian Donkin, Secretary; John Adrian Donkin [1978] Director/Solicitors; Graeme Langlands [1974] Director/Solicitor; John Richard Rodger [1962] Director/Solicitor

C.Donnelly Construction Limited
Incorporated: 29 October 2004
Net Worth: £630,607 *Total Assets:* £2,066,614
Registered Office: 14-15 Tame Road, Lawson Industrial Estate, North Ormesby, Middlesbrough, Cleveland, TS3 6LL
Activities: Other specialised construction activities n.e.c.
Shareholders: Conor Joseph Donnelly; Jayne Donnelly
Officers: Jayne Donnelly, Secretary; Conor Joseph Donnelly [1972] Director [Irish]

Donyal Engineering Limited
Incorporated: 9 December 2005 *Employees:* 26
Net Worth: £1,440,706 *Total Assets:* £1,761,202
Registered Office: Hobson Industrial Estate, Burnopfield, Co Durham, NE16 6EA
Activities: Manufacture of metal structures and parts of structures
Parent: Donyal Group Limited
Officers: Kate Amanda Downs, Secretary; Kate Amanda Downs [1970] Director/Company Secretary; Michael Simon Downs [1968] Director

Donyal Holdings Limited
Incorporated: 20 April 1971
Net Worth: £1,956,293 *Total Assets:* £3,207,790
Registered Office: Hobson Industrial Estate, Burnopfield, Co Durham, NE16 6EA
Activities: Activities of head offices
Parent: Donyal Investments Limited
Officers: Kate Amanda Downs, Secretary; Kate Amanda Downs [1970] Director/Company Secretary; Michael Simon Downs [1968] Director/Manager

Doocey North East Limited
Incorporated: 17 June 1997 *Employees:* 60
Net Worth: £1,596,485 *Total Assets:* £3,842,116
Registered Office: 65 Low Lane, Brookfield, Middlesbrough, Cleveland, TS5 8EG
Activities: Construction of utility projects for electricity and telecommunications
Shareholder: Charles Doocey
Officers: Nuala Theresa Doocey, Secretary [Irish]; Charles Doocey [1954] Director/Civil Engineer [Irish]; Mark Riley [1963] Director/General Manager

Dorenell Windfarm Limited
Incorporated: 18 November 2005
Net Worth: £28,935,000 *Total Assets:* £88,422,000
Registered Office: Alexander House, 1 Mandarin Road, Rainton Bridge Business Park, Houghton-le-Spring, Co Durham, DH4 5RA
Activities: Construction of utility projects for electricity and telecommunications
Parent: EDF Energy Renewables Holdings Limited
Officers: Susan Elizabeth Lind, Secretary; Matthieu Thomas Hue [1975] Director [French]; Hassaan Majid [1968] Director

Dormor Machine and Engineering Company Limited
Incorporated: 29 May 1979 *Employees:* 30
Net Worth: £1,546,321 *Total Assets:* £1,836,552
Registered Office: Dormor Way, South Bank, Middlesbrough, Cleveland, TS6 6XH
Activities: Manufacture of metal structures and parts of structures
Major Shareholder: Clive Leslie Wood
Officers: Helen Cameron Clarke, Secretary; Helen Cameron Clarke [1975] Director/Accounts Manager; Clive Leslie Wood [1949] Managing Director; Jean Wood [1949] Director

Double Eleven Limited
Incorporated: 23 December 2009 *Employees:* 42
Net Worth: £3,215,807 *Total Assets:* £3,639,596
Registered Office: Boho One, Bridge Street West, Middlesbrough, Cleveland, TS2 1AE
Activities: Ready-made interactive leisure and entertainment software development
Major Shareholder: Lee Hutchinson
Officers: Shahid Kamal Ahmad [1965] Director; Lee Hutchinson [1980] Director; Samantha Hutchinson [1981] Director; Matthew Shepcar [1980] Director/Software Engineer; Mark Lancey South [1978] Operations Director [Canadian]; Kimberley Anne Turner [1982] Director/Chartered Accountant; Robin Ware [1981] Director/Software Engineer

Dougal & Railton Limited
Incorporated: 24 October 1956 *Employees:* 32
Net Worth: £371,114 *Total Assets:* £1,415,332
Registered Office: Strowger House, Sandy Lane Industrial Estate, Wideopen, Newcastle upon Tyne, NE3 5HE
Activities: Electrical installation
Officers: Christopher Burt, Secretary; Christopher Burt [1965] Director/Estimating Manager; Garrie Paul Forster [1965] Director/Contracts Manager

The Dove Academy Trust
Incorporated: 25 May 2016 *Employees:* 54
Net Worth: £51,000 *Total Assets:* £808,000
Registered Office: High Coniscliffe CE Primary School, Ulnaby Lane, High Coniscliffe, Darlington, Co Durham, DL2 2LL
Activities: Primary education
Officers: Chrissie Broadbent, Secretary; Wendy Aitken [1970] Director/Headteacher; Craig Robert Alderson [1970] Director/Civil Servant; Kath Alley [1962] Director/Head of Change Acceptance; Reverend Damon John Bage [1971] Director/Clerk in Holy Orders; Reverend David James Railton [1966] Director/Clerk in Holy Orders; Martin Stand [1969] Youth Project Director; Dr Jenny Louise Steel [1976] Director/General Practitioner; Professor Timothy James Upton Thompson [1976] Director/University of Teesside - Associate Dean; Rosanne Tweddle [1980] Director/Solicitor

J.T.Dove,Limited
Incorporated: 8 August 1905 *Employees:* 224
Net Worth: £7,786,957 *Total Assets:* £22,252,688
Registered Office: 1 Riversdale Way, Newburn Haugh Industrial Estate, Newcastle upon Tyne, NE15 8SF
Activities: Agents involved in the sale of timber and building materials
Parent: J T Dove Pensions Trust Limited
Officers: Richard James Painter, Secretary; John George Burke [1962] Director/Builders Merchant; Ian James Hindmarsh [1956] Director/Builders Merchant; Richard James Painter [1955] Director/Chartered Accountant; Steven Robinson [1963] Director

DH Dowen Limited
Incorporated: 5 March 2014 *Employees:* 38
Net Worth: £958,104 *Total Assets:* £1,557,855
Registered Office: 6 Jubilee House, York Road, Hartlepool, Cleveland, TS26 9EN
Activities: Real estate agencies
Shareholders: Denis Henry Dowen; Darren Glenn Clayton
Officers: Darren Glenn Clayton [1971] Director; Denis Henry Dowen [1956] Director; Gemma Dowen [1987] Director; Christopher John Elliot [1961] Director

Downs Holdings Limited
Incorporated: 11 August 1977 *Employees:* 150
Net Worth: £1,671,417 *Total Assets:* £8,199,095
Registered Office: Kirklevington Hall Farm, Kirklevington, Yarm, Cleveland, TS15 9LW
Activities: Hotels and similar accommodation
Shareholder: Stephen Michael Downs
Officers: Stephen Michael Downs, Secretary; Anne Downs [1933] Director; Stephen Michael Downs [1957] Director/Accountant

DP Plant Hire Limited
Incorporated: 8 October 1997
Registered Office: 5 Broadoaks, Bishop Middleham, Co Durham, DL17 9BW
Activities: Renting and leasing of other machinery, equipment and tangible goods n.e.c.
Shareholder: Dawn Pickering
Officers: Carole Pickering, Secretary; Dawn Pickering [1967] Director

DPH Construction (North East) Limited
Incorporated: 26 April 2005 *Employees:* 12
Net Worth: £738,346 *Total Assets:* £1,028,729
Registered Office: 9 Frank Place, North Shields, Tyne & Wear, NE29 0LT
Activities: Construction of domestic buildings
Shareholders: Dean Hogarty; Heather Hogarty
Officers: Heather Hogarty, Secretary; Dean Hogarty [1971] Director; Heather Hogarty [1972] Director

Draeger Safety UK Ltd
Incorporated: 16 October 1963 *Employees:* 463
Net Worth: £34,507,000 *Total Assets:* £52,596,000
Registered Office: Draeger Safety UK Limited, Ullswater Close, Blyth Riverside Business Park, Blyth, Northumberland, NE24 4RG
Activities: Manufacture of other special-purpose machinery n.e.c.
Parent: Dragerwerk AG & Co KGaA
Officers: Matthew Bedford, Secretary; Michael Allan Norris [1957] Managing Director [American]

Dragonfly Venture (Trading) Limited
Incorporated: 5 January 2011 *Employees:* 12
Net Worth: £5,937,360 *Total Assets:* £20,094,048
Registered Office: 32 Portland Terrace, Newcastle upon Tyne, NE2 1QP
Activities: Manufacture of footwear
Shareholders: Christopher Patrick Maughan; Dragonfly Venture Group Limited
Officers: Christopher Patrick Maughan [1963] Director

Dragonfly Venture (UK) Limited
Incorporated: 2 August 2004 *Employees:* 1
Net Worth: £720,912 *Total Assets:* £3,174,495
Registered Office: 32 Portland Terrace, Newcastle upon Tyne, NE2 1QP
Activities: Manufacture of footwear
Shareholders: Christopher Patrick Maughan; Dragonfly Venture Group Limited
Officers: Simon Wilkinson, Secretary; Christopher Patrick Maughan [1963] Director

Dragonfly Venture Group Ltd
Incorporated: 19 August 2011 *Employees:* 17
Net Worth: £50,160,904 *Total Assets:* £66,746,348
Registered Office: 32 Portland Terrace, Newcastle upon Tyne, NE2 1QP
Activities: Manufacture of footwear
Major Shareholder: Christopher Patrick Maughan
Officers: Christopher Patrick Maughan [1963] Director

WJ Drennan Limited
Incorporated: 2 July 2007 *Employees:* 5
Net Worth: £87,386 *Total Assets:* £4,729,509
Registered Office: High Hedley Hope Farm, Tow Law, Co Durham, DL13 4PR
Activities: Production of electricity
Major Shareholder: William James Drennan
Officers: Stanley David Thomson, Secretary; William James Drennan [1950] Director; Stanley David Thomson [1966] Director

Drey Developments Limited
Incorporated: 27 April 1998
Net Worth: £1,632,864 *Total Assets:* £1,747,115
Registered Office: 10 The Drey, Darras Hall, Ponteland, Northumberland, NE20 9NS
Activities: Other service activities n.e.c.
Major Shareholder: Beverley Jane Pearson
Officers: Sammyjo Pearson, Secretary; Beverley Jane Pearson [1965] Director/Accounts Manager

Drilcorp Limited
Incorporated: 28 February 1992 *Employees:* 41
Net Worth: £1,194,070 *Total Assets:* £2,215,676
Registered Office: Kinley Hill Farm, Hawthorn, Seaham, Co Durham, SR7 8SW
Activities: Other specialised construction activities n.e.c.
Shareholder: David Gowans
Officers: David Gowans, Secretary; David Gowans [1953] Director/Drilling Operating Manager; Kirsty Gowans [1978] Director; Lyndsey Gowans [1957] Director/Civil Servant; Scott Gowans [1976] Director

Drinx Leisure Limited
Incorporated: 7 May 2013 *Employees:* 18
Net Worth: £1,033,446 *Total Assets:* £1,288,903
Registered Office: 17 Westgate Road, Newcastle upon Tyne, NE1 1SE
Activities: Public houses and bars
Parent: Drinx Holdings Limited
Officers: Jonathan Patrick Dyer [1972] Director; Paul James Pringle [1970] Director; Mark Anthony Wrightson [1971] Director

Driven Car Sales Limited
Incorporated: 21 December 2009 *Employees:* 40
Net Worth: £469,021 *Total Assets:* £3,374,693
Registered Office: Middleway, Mandale Triangle Industrial Estate, Thornaby, Stockton on Tees, Cleveland, TS17 6BZ
Activities: Sale of used cars and light motor vehicles
Shareholders: Jonathan Stephen Hobday; Christopher Dixon Maddren
Officers: Jonathan Stephen Hobday [1984] Director/Car Salesman; Jake Cyril Livermore [1989] Director/Professional Footballer; Christopher Dixon Maddren [1969] Director/Car Salesman

Driving Success Limited
Incorporated: 5 February 2010 *Employees:* 90
Net Worth Deficit: £473,236 *Total Assets:* £1,983,934
Registered Office: Pavilion 6, Coxwold Way, Belasis Hall Technology Park, Billingham, Cleveland, TS23 4EA
Activities: Activities of head offices
Parent: Kelso Place Special Situations Fund LP
Officers: Simon Liddiard Clarke, Secretary; Ian McIntosh [1956] Director; Philip Richard Weston [1966] Director/Private Equity

Drogo Developments Ltd
Incorporated: 4 March 2014
Net Worth: £96,570 *Total Assets:* £10,399,839
Registered Office: 2nd Floor, Cuthbert House, All Saints Business Centre, Newcastle upon Tyne, NE1 2ET
Activities: Development of building projects
Officers: Gary Ronald Forrest [1968] Director

Dromonby Bridge Farm Limited
Incorporated: 14 September 2015 *Employees:* 1
Net Worth: £387,750 *Total Assets:* £1,537,712
Registered Office: Exchange Building, 66 Church Street, Hartlepool, Cleveland, TS24 7DN
Activities: Raising of other animals
Shareholders: Robert Jones; Rachel Smith
Officers: Rachel Jones, Secretary; Rachel Jones [1989] Director

Drummond Central Limited
Incorporated: 23 June 2004 *Employees:* 34
Net Worth: £4,364,281 *Total Assets:* £5,216,467
Registered Office: 70 Jesmond Road West, Newcastle upon Tyne, NE2 4PQ
Activities: Advertising agencies
Shareholders: Julie Drummond; Stephen Michael Drummond
Officers: Matthew John Briggs [1968] Director; Julie Drummond [1971] Marketing Director; Stephen Michael Drummond [1973] Creative Director

DSE (N.E.) Limited
Incorporated: 29 November 2006
Registered Office: 20 Burdon Walk, Castle Eden, Co Durham, TS27 4FD
Activities: Other building completion and finishing
Shareholders: David Slater; Kerry Slater
Officers: David Slater, Secretary; David Slater [1969] Director; Kerry Suzanne Slater [1970] Director

DSONS Limited
Incorporated: 6 August 2009
Net Worth: £293,672 *Total Assets:* £1,268,250
Registered Office: 30 Yoden Way, Peterlee, Co Durham, SR8 1AL
Activities: Management of real estate on a fee or contract basis
Major Shareholder: Jetinder Singh Sokal
Officers: Jetinder Singh Sokal [1981] Director/Builder; Sabina Sokal [1988] Director

Dualbound Limited
Incorporated: 10 August 1987 *Employees:* 44
Net Worth: £1,435,271 *Total Assets:* £1,968,977
Registered Office: Diamond Court, Douglas Close, Preston Farm Industrial Park, Stockton on Tees, Cleveland, TS18 3SB
Activities: Electrical installation
Major Shareholder: Ernest David Newton Corney
Officers: Kendra Lilian Corney, Secretary; Eileen Corney [1935] Director/Clerical Assistant; Ernest David Newton Corney [1938] Director; Kendra Lilian Corney [1967] Director; Martin David Corney [1963] Director/Electrical Engineer

H Duckworth Limited
Incorporated: 11 September 2002 *Employees:* 14
Net Worth: £649,727 *Total Assets:* £762,467
Registered Office: Front Street, Cramlington, Northumberland, NE23 6QH
Activities: Funeral and related activities
Major Shareholder: Elizabeth Burton
Officers: Elizabeth Burton, Secretary; Elizabeth Burton [1945] Funeral Directors; Kim Horrobin [1978] Director

Dufell Roofing Company Limited
Incorporated: 8 November 1972
Registered Office: Alexander House, Unit 28 Faverdale Industrial Estate, Darlington, Co Durham, DL3 0QQ
Activities: Roofing activities
Shareholders: Gillian Wilks; Stephen Riddell
Officers: Gillian Pamela Wilks, Secretary; Barbara Riddell [1948] Director; Neil Anthony Riddell [1947] Director/Roofing Contractor; Stephen Graeme Riddell [1973] Director/Contract Manager; Gillian Pamela Wilks [1975] Director/Office Manager

Duil Limited
Incorporated: 27 October 2009 *Employees:* 2
Net Worth: £128 *Total Assets:* £1,316,594
Registered Office: Cale Cross House, 156 Pilgrim Street, Newcastle upon Tyne, NE1 6SU
Activities: Other business support service activities n.e.c.
Officers: Susan Boyle [1961] Director; Colette Marie Murray [1969] Director

Dulai Enterprises Limited
Incorporated: 9 February 2012 *Employees:* 21
Net Worth: £736,480 *Total Assets:* £1,571,361
Registered Office: 28 West Meadows Road, Cleadon, Sunderland, Tyne & Wear, SR6 7TU
Activities: Take-away food shops and mobile food stands
Shareholders: Gurmail Singh Dulai; Harkamaljit Kaur Dulai
Officers: Gurmail Singh Dulai [1973] Director; Harkamaljit Kaur Dulai [1976] Director

Dulai Property Limited
Incorporated: 23 September 2004
Net Worth: £281,450 *Total Assets:* £1,287,496
Registered Office: 32 Middle Street, Blackhall Colliery, Hartlepool, Cleveland, TS27 4EA
Activities: Other letting and operating of own or leased real estate
Shareholders: Balkar Singh Dulai; Davinder Pal Singh Dulai; Joga Singh Dulai
Officers: Joga Singh Dulai, Secretary; Balkar Singh Dulai [1973] Director; Joga Singh Dulai [1955] Director

Dumark Investment Limited
Incorporated: 29 March 2004
Net Worth: £84,692 *Total Assets:* £800,437
Registered Office: 71 Howard Street, North Shields, Tyne & Wear, NE30 1AF
Activities: Other letting and operating of own or leased real estate
Shareholders: Duncan Charles Turner; Marcus John Turner; Shiela Diane Turner
Officers: Marcus John Turner, Secretary/Property Manager; Duncan Charles Turner [1972] Director; Marcus John Turner [1981] Director; Shiela Diane Turner [1945] Director

Dunelm Geotechnical & Environmental Limited
Incorporated: 19 February 2004 *Employees:* 34
Net Worth: £674,412 *Total Assets:* £2,645,053
Registered Office: Foundation House, St Johns Road, Meadowfield Industrial Estate, Meadowfield, Co Durham, DH7 8TZ
Activities: Test drilling and boring
Major Shareholder: Gary Raymond Dresser
Officers: Gary Raymond Dresser [1965] Director/Engineer; Patricia Ann Ellen Izatt Lowry [1965] Director

Dunelm Investments Limited
Incorporated: 27 September 1985
Net Worth: £1,254,517 *Total Assets:* £2,048,180
Registered Office: The Farmhouse, Hedley Hill Farm, Hedley Hill, Co Durham, DH7 9EX
Activities: Buying and selling of own real estate
Officers: Michael Francis Hogan [1944] Director/Builder

Dunelm Optical Co. Limited
Incorporated: 17 July 1973 *Employees:* 72
Net Worth: £2,949,077 *Total Assets:* £5,392,817
Registered Office: 9 Enterprise Way, Green Lane Industrial Estate, Spennymoor, Co Durham, DL16 6YP
Activities: Other manufacturing n.e.c.
Major Shareholder: Peter Julian Tinker Beaumont
Officers: Anita Deborah Booty, Secretary; David Baker [1965] Managing Director; Angela Gillian Beaumont [1951] Director; Oliver Peter Julian Beaumont [1983] Director; Peter Julian Tinker Beaumont [1949] Director/Manufacturing Optician

Dunelm Optical Holdings Limited
Incorporated: 22 May 2014
Net Worth: £1,344,846 *Total Assets:* £2,689,691
Registered Office: 9 Enterprise Way, Green Lane Industrial Estate, Spennymoor, Co Durham, DL16 6YP
Activities: Activities of other holding companies n.e.c.
Shareholders: Peter Julian Tinker Beaumont; Angela Gillian Beaumont
Officers: Anita Booty, Secretary; Angela Gillian Beaumont [1951] Director; Peter Julian Tinker Beaumont [1949] Director/Chief Executive

M Dungait & Sons Limited
Incorporated: 18 March 1997
Net Worth: £3,895,702 *Total Assets:* £4,061,264
Registered Office: Hebron West Farm, Hebron, Morpeth, Northumberland, NE61 3LA
Activities: Growing of vegetables and melons, roots and tubers
Shareholders: John Dungait; David Maurice Dungait
Officers: Christine Margaret Dungait, Secretary; Ailsa Jane Dungait [1961] Director/Farmer; Christine Margaret Dungait [1968] Director/Farmer; David Maurice Dungait [1958] Director/Farmer; John Dungait [1961] Director/Farmer; Richard Thomas Dungait [1981] Director/Farmer

Dunham Leisure Limited
Incorporated: 10 November 2011 *Employees:* 17
Net Worth: £2,890,487 *Total Assets:* £3,561,509
Registered Office: South Meadows, South Road, Belford, Northumberland, NE70 7DP
Activities: Holiday centres and villages
Shareholders: Simon Paul Dunham; Philip Anthony Whiteway (As Executor)
Officers: Simon Paul Dunham, Secretary; Andrew Philip Dunham [1961] Director; Catherine Dunham [1963] Director; Simon Paul Dunham [1965] Director

Dunhill and McGrouther Limited
Incorporated: 24 March 1950 *Employees:* 9
Net Worth: £50,031 *Total Assets:* £759,481
Registered Office: Palin & Twyford Solicitors, 14-16 Bridge Street, Amble, Morpeth, Northumberland, NE65 0DR
Activities: Other business support service activities n.e.c.
Shareholders: David Alexander McGrouther; Barbara Rose McGrouther
Officers: Barbara Rose McGrouther, Secretary; Barbara Rose McGrouther [1947] Director/Company Secretary; David Alexander McGrouther [1941] Director

Dunhouse Quarry Co.Limited
Incorporated: 12 June 1954 *Employees:* 39
Net Worth: £221,335 *Total Assets:* £1,482,791
Registered Office: Dunhouse Quarry Works, Cleatlam, Darlington, Co Durham, DL2 3QU
Activities: Quarrying of ornamental and building stone, limestone, gypsum, chalk and slate
Officers: Paul Richard Allison, Secretary/Managing Director; Michael Nixon Allison [1939] Director; Paul Richard Allison [1965] Managing Director; Francis William Lillystone [1948] Director

John N Dunn Group Limited
Incorporated: 21 March 2007 *Employees:* 283
Net Worth Deficit: £213,679 *Total Assets:* £10,416,599
Registered Office: Phoenix House, Kingfisher Way, Silverlink Business Park, Wallsend, Tyne & Wear, NE28 9NX
Activities: Electrical installation
Officers: Richard Bertram, Secretary; Richard Bertram [1957] Financial Director; Jane Hilary Bilclough [1979] Director; Stephen Paul Bilclough [1969] Director; Ian Fletcher Steward [1972] Director

John N Dunn Holdings Limited
Incorporated: 8 July 2016 *Employees:* 289
Net Worth: £686,847 *Total Assets:* £11,146,709
Registered Office: Phoenix House, Kingfisher Way, Silverlink Business Park, Wallsend, Tyne & Wear, NE28 9NX
Activities: Activities of construction holding companies
Officers: Richard Bertram, Secretary; Richard Bertram [1957] Financial Director; Jane Hilary Bilclough [1979] Director; Stephen Paul Bilclough [1969] Director; Ian Fletcher Steward [1972] Director

Dunningham Decorators Limited
Incorporated: 12 November 1979 *Employees:* 58
Net Worth: £981,739 *Total Assets:* £1,716,528
Registered Office: 10-13 Bonnersfield, Sunderland, Tyne & Wear, SR6 0AA
Activities: Painting
Shareholders: Rita Dunningham; Neil Stanley Dunningham
Officers: Rita Dunningham, Secretary; Terry Cunningham [1975] Director; Rita Dunningham [1945] Director

Dunstanburgh Farm Limited
Incorporated: 31 January 1997
Net Worth: £1,160,811 *Total Assets:* £1,319,515
Registered Office: Newton House, Newton-by-the-Sea, Embleton, Northumberland, NE66 3ED
Activities: Growing of cereals (except rice), leguminous crops and oil seeds
Shareholders: Victoria Jane Baring; Jonathan Ben Sutherland; Margaret Ann Sutherland
Officers: Margaret Ann Sutherland, Secretary/Farming; Doctor Victoria Jane Baring [1974] Director/Doctor; Jonathan Ben Sutherland [1976] Director/Airline Pilot; Margaret Ann Sutherland [1948] Director/Farming

Dupont Teijin Films U.K. Limited
Incorporated: 25 May 1999 *Employees:* 287
Net Worth: £42,689,000 *Total Assets:* £70,097,000
Registered Office: The Wilton Centre, Wilton Site, Redcar, Cleveland, TS10 4RF
Activities: Manufacture of plastic plates, sheets, tubes and profiles
Shareholders: Du Pont (U.K.) Limited; Teijin Holdings Netherlands B.V
Officers: Mark Richard Jenkins, Secretary; John Cole Miller [1962] Director/Chief Executive Officer; Jan Follings [1954] Director [Dutch]; Osamu Iwai [1975] Director [Japanese]; James Weigand [1955] Director/Chief Executive Officer [American]

Duranta Energy Limited
Incorporated: 29 June 2012 *Employees:* 2
Net Worth Deficit: £7,046,158 *Total Assets:* £27,131,150
Registered Office: Duranta Teesside Limited, Forty Foot Road, Middlesbrough, Cleveland, TS2 1HG
Activities: Activities of head offices
Parent: Duranta Holding Company Limited
Officers: Barry David Collins, Secretary; Divya Seshamani [1978] Director/Managing Partner [Singaporean]

Duranta Holding Company Limited
Incorporated: 25 September 2012 *Employees:* 9
Net Worth Deficit: £17,842,708 *Total Assets:* £19,916,456
Registered Office: Duranta Teesside Ltd, Forty Foot Road, Middlesbrough, Cleveland, TS2 1HG
Activities: Activities of head offices
Shareholders: UK Green Sustainable Waste and Energy Investment L.P.; Shuban Power Limited
Officers: Barry David Collins, Secretary; Divya Seshamani [1978] Director/Managing Partner [Singaporean]

Duranta Teesside Limited
Incorporated: 21 September 2012 *Employees:* 2
Net Worth Deficit: £13,420,957 *Total Assets:* £19,770,412
Registered Office: Duranta Energy Limited, Forty Foot Road, Middlesbrough, Cleveland, TS2 1HG
Activities: Production of electricity
Parent: Duranta Energy Limited
Officers: Barry David Collins, Secretary; Divya Seshamani [1978] Director/Managing Partner [Singaporean]

Durham Action on Single Housing Limited
Incorporated: 10 February 1972 *Employees:* 21
Net Worth: £1,459,957 *Total Assets:* £1,491,773
Registered Office: Hudson House, Gort Place, Durham, DH1 1EY
Activities: Other service activities n.e.c.
Officers: Leslie Andrew Punton, Secretary; Madeleine Mary Ashdown [1953] Director/Practice Manager; Patrick Stephen Conway [1949] Director/Councillor; Catharine Jane Curry [1970] Director/Housing Manager; Alireza Foroozani [1991] Director/Postgrad Student; Marie-Therese Pinder [1948] Director/Retired; Leslie Andrew Punton [1961] Director/Lecturer/Tutor; Mark Conrad Scanlon [1964] Director/Housing Lettings Officer; Joanne Wandless [1971] Director/Administrator

Durham Box Company Limited
Incorporated: 20 April 1989 *Employees:* 67
Net Worth: £4,157,133 *Total Assets:* £7,850,847
Registered Office: Auckland Crescent, St Helen Auckland, Bishop Auckland, Co Durham, DL14 9AD
Activities: Manufacture of other paper and paperboard containers
Officers: Susan Ann Morris, Secretary; Daniel Christian Morris [1976] Director; Michael John Morris [1950] Sales Director; Susan Ann Morris [1952] Director/Company Secretary

Durham Care Line Limited
Incorporated: 3 September 1986 *Employees:* 184
Net Worth: £3,690,484 *Total Assets:* £9,413,397
Registered Office: One Central Parkway, Newcastle upon Tyne, NE1 3BZ
Activities: Other human health activities
Shareholders: Dr Swatanter Bahrat Sharma; Geeta Sharma
Officers: Geeta Sharma, Secretary; Archana Sharma [1977] Director; Geeta Sharma [1949] Director; Rahul Sharma [1975] Director; Dr Swatanter Bahrat Sharma [1946] Medical Director

Durham Cathedral Open Treasure Limited
Incorporated: 28 March 2012 *Employees:* 15
Net Worth: £6,317,829 *Total Assets:* £8,434,981
Registered Office: The Cathedral Office, The College, Durham, DH1 3EH
Activities: Museums activities
Parent: Durham Cathedral
Officers: Elizabeth Jayne Manns, Secretary; Catherine Patricia Barnes [1949] Director/Retired; The Venerable Ian Jagger [1955] Director/Archdeacon; Sophie Jelley [1972] Director/Member of The Clergy; David John Kennedy [1957] Director/Priest; Professor Simon Oliver [1971] Director/University Professor; Ivor Robert Stolliday [1946] Director/Retired

Durham Cathedral Trading Limited
Incorporated: 11 September 2007 *Employees:* 12
Net Worth: £211,447 *Total Assets:* £1,341,929
Registered Office: The Cathedral Office, The College, Durham, DH1 3EH
Activities: Other retail sale of new goods in specialised stores (not commercial art galleries and opticians)
Parent: The Corporate Body of Durham Cathedrral
Officers: Elizabeth Jayne Manns, Secretary; Catherine Patricia Barnes [1949] Director/Retired; The Venerable Ian Jagger [1955] Director/Archdeacon; Sophie Jelley [1972] Director/Member of The Clergy; David John Kennedy [1957] Director/Priest; Professor Simon Oliver [1971] Director/University Professor; Ivor Robert Stolliday [1946] Director/Retired

Durham City Coaches Limited
Incorporated: 7 December 1990
Net Worth Deficit: £28,470 *Total Assets:* £1,230,563
Registered Office: Durham City Coaches Ltd, Brandon Lane, Brandon, Co Durham, DH7 8PG
Activities: Other passenger land transport
Major Shareholder: Derrick Collin
Officers: Derrick Collin [1948] Director; Stephen Anthony James [1958] Director; Michael John Dunn Lightfoot [1962] Managing Director

Durham City Golf Club Limited
Incorporated: 8 December 1927 *Employees:* 25
Net Worth: £389,702 *Total Assets:* £955,310
Registered Office: Littleburn, Langley Moor, Co Durham, DH7 8HL
Activities: Activities of sport clubs
Officers: Jeff Shield, Secretary; Angela Emerson [1946] Director/Retired; Mattew Harper [1988] Director/Engineer; Ian Harries [1960] Director/Retired; Jonathon Hope [1971] Director/Civil Servant; David McColl [1955] Director; Stephen William Park [1967] Director/Export Sales; Christine Pullan [1955] Director/Retired; Christopher Robinson [1960] Director/Retired; Kevin Sample [1974] Director/Local Government Officer - Childrens Services; Colin Sturdy [1959] Director/Engineer

Durham City Property (Holdings) Limited
Incorporated: 12 September 2016
Net Worth: £258,779 *Total Assets:* £2,443,209
Registered Office: Durham City House, St Johns Road, Meadowfield, Co Durham, DH7 8XQ
Activities: Other letting and operating of own or leased real estate
Shareholders: Leslie Stuart Coatman; Christine Coatman
Officers: Leslie Stuart Coatman [1957] Director

Durham City Transport Limited
Incorporated: 9 October 1991 *Employees:* 37
Net Worth: £2,548,909 *Total Assets:* £3,203,014
Registered Office: Durham City House, St Johns Road, Meadowfield Industrial Estate, Meadowfield, Co Durham, DH7 8QX
Activities: Freight transport by road
Parent: Durham City Property (Holdings) Limited
Officers: Darren Coatman [1980] Director/Transport Manager; Leslie Stuart Coatman [1957] Director/Transport Consultant

The Durham Company Limited
Incorporated: 22 April 1999
Net Worth: £346,799 *Total Assets:* £1,405,726
Registered Office: Hawthorne House, Blackthorn Way, Sedgeletch Industrial Estate, Fencehouses, Co Durham, DH4 6JN
Activities: Other building and industrial cleaning activities
Shareholders: Winston Scott Hawthorne; Patrick John Roche
Officers: Donna Marie Ingram, Secretary; Raymond Hawthorne [1949] Director; Winston Scott Hawthorne [1977] Director/Manager; Patrick John Roche [1966] Operations Director

Durham County Carers Support
Incorporated: 25 March 1998 *Employees:* 38
Net Worth: £618,330 *Total Assets:* £978,467
Registered Office: Enterprise House, Enterprise City, Meadowfield Avenue, Spennymoor, Co Durham, DL16 6JF
Activities: Other information service activities n.e.c.
Officers: John Dannell [1950] Director/Manager; Ray Mumford [1950] Director/Driving Instructor; Arthur Ronald Passfield [1939] Director/Supt Registrar Retired; Janet Potts [1970] Director/Legal Executive; Anne Stobbs [1948] Director/Retired; Susan Sumpton [1957] Director/Housewife; Audrey Vasey [1958] Director/Retired; Elizabeth Whiting [1946] Director/Retired

Durham County Football Association Limited
Incorporated: 21 September 2001 *Employees:* 17
Net Worth: £2,803,063 *Total Assets:* £3,036,995
Registered Office: Riverside South, Chester-le-Street, Co Durham, DH3 3SJ
Activities: Other sports activities
Officers: John Charles Topping, Secretary; George Charlton [1950] Director/Chartered Accountant; Ronald Coleman [1947] Director/Retired; John Morton [1954] Director/Retired; Francis Davison Pattison [1936] Director/Solicitor; John Priestley [1939] Director/Retired; David Robinson [1947] Director/Retired; Ian Shuttleworth [1963] Director/Solicitor; Melvyn Spedding [1953] Director/Councillor; John Charles Topping [1954] Director/Company Secretary

Durham Cricket C.I.C.
Incorporated: 22 September 2004 *Employees:* 65
Net Worth: £5,179,326 *Total Assets:* £20,596,436
Registered Office: Emirates Riverside, Riverside, Chester-le-Street, Co Durham, DH3 3QR
Activities: Operation of sports facilities
Officers: David Harker, Secretary/Chief Executive; Timothy Bostock [1962] Director/Chief Executive; Sir Ian Terence Botham [1955] Director; Philip Collins [1961] Director/Management Consultant; Allison Curbishley [1976] Director; Naynesh Gunvant Desai [1960] Director/Solicitor; David Harker [1961] Director/Chief Executive; Councillor Simon Antony Henig [1969] Director/Councillor; Robert Jackson [1936] Director; Paul Ronald Woolston [1955] Director/Accountant

Durham Diocesan Board of Finance
Incorporated: 21 August 1923 *Employees:* 27
Net Worth: £57,373,704 *Total Assets:* £61,943,724
Registered Office: Cuthbert House, Stonebridge, Durham, DH1 3RY
Activities: Activities of religious organisations
Officers: Margaret Louise Vaughan, Secretary; Michael Anthony Banks [1963] Director/Retired; The Revd John William Barron [1966] Director/Clerk in Holy Orders; William Edward Braviner [1966] Director/Priest; Bishop Mark Watts Bryant [1949] Director/Bishop of Jarrow; Paul Roger Butler [1955] Director/Bishop (Minister of Religion); The Venerable Robert Gerard Cooper [1968] Director/Archdeacon of Sunderland; Revd Canon Frances Jane Grieve [1955] Director/Clerk in Holy Orders; James Herbert Harrison [1953] Director/General Medical Practitioner; Hylda Eileen Hopper [1940] Director/Retired; The Venerable Ian Jagger [1955] Director/Archdeacon of Durham; Barrie Kirton [1949] Director/Retired; Stephen Cyndon Pickering [1960] Director/Retired; Dr Alfred Colin Price [1952] Director/Retired; Frank Andrew Rogers [1955] Director; Richard Lee Simpson [1966] Director/Clerk in Holy Orders; Frances Ruth Stenlake [1969] Director/Actuary; David Robert Tomlinson [1963] Director/Minister of Religion; The Very Reverend Andrew Tremlett [1964] Director/Clerk in Holy Orders; Margaret Louise Vaughan [1968] Business Director; Nigel Ralph Wyrley-Birch [1954] Director/Chartered Accountant

Durham Estates Limited
Incorporated: 9 July 1990 *Employees:* 6
Net Worth: £782,200 *Total Assets:* £1,235,131
Registered Office: Temple Chambers, Douro Terrace, Sunderland, Tyne & Wear, SR2 7DX
Activities: Buying and selling of own real estate
Major Shareholder: James Russell Foster
Officers: Fiona Marjory Morton, Secretary; David Neil Armstrong [1960] Director/Chartered Accountant; Nicola Jane Foster-Hird [1972] Director; Mark Hird [1973] Director

Durham Footwear Distributors Limited
Incorporated: 1 August 1975 *Employees:* 15
Net Worth: £1,486,915 *Total Assets:* £1,585,678
Registered Office: The Old Waterloo, High Street, Spennymoor, Co Durham, DL16 6DB
Activities: Wholesale of clothing and footwear
Major Shareholder: Kenneth Tregoning
Officers: Jane Ellen Tregoning, Secretary; Jane Ellen Tregoning [1939] Director; Kenneth Tregoning [1935] Director/Footwear Wholesaler and Retail

Durham Group Estates Limited
Incorporated: 22 October 2003
Net Worth: £2,267,718 *Total Assets:* £3,511,186
Registered Office: Office 10, Unit 5 Fairfield Industrial Park, Bill Quay, Gateshead, Tyne & Wear, NE10 0UR
Activities: Other letting and operating of own or leased real estate
Shareholders: Gurpreet Singh Jagpal; Ian William Wrigglesworth
Officers: Gurpreet Singh Jagpal, Secretary; Gurpreet Singh Jagpal [1981] Finance Director; Sir Ian William Wrigglesworth [1939] Director

Durham High School for Girls
Incorporated: 23 May 2007 *Employees:* 76
Net Worth: £8,902,974 *Total Assets:* £10,366,713
Registered Office: Farewell Hall, South Road, Durham, DH1 3TB
Activities: Pre-primary education
Officers: David Richard Payne, Secretary; Katherine Gertrude Barker [1952] Director/Retired Teacher; Elisa Joanne Berry [1974] Director/Architect; Stephen Jerome George Cheffings [1953] Managing Director; Linda Clark [1953] Director/Retired; Morag McDonald Cummings [1949] Director/Teacher; Kenneth Delanoy [1946] Director/Retired; Dr Christine Joy English [1950] Director/Retired Consultant Occupational Health Physician; Dr Michael John Gilmore [1958] Director/University Manager; Dr Mohammed Azfar Hyder [1969] Director/Dentist; Andrew Michael Lake [1963] Director; Joanne Logan [1964] Director/Church of England Minister; Ian Meston [1967] Director/Minister/Author; Richard James Metcalfe [1949] Director/Retired; Alan Ribchester [1945] Director/Chartered Accountant; Patricia Anne Walker [1954] Director/Retired

Durham Lifting Limited
Incorporated: 5 June 1996
Registered Office: Britannia Test House, Romaldkirk Road, Middlesbrough, Cleveland, TS2 1HB
Activities: Manufacture of lifting and handling equipment
Major Shareholder: Francis Pickersgill
Officers: Amanda Jane Gardiner [1973] Director/Sales Manageress

Durham Markets Company Limited
Incorporated: 1 April 1992
Net Worth: £1,398,804 *Total Assets:* £1,545,479
Registered Office: Ground Floor, Finchale House, Belmont Business Park, Durham, DH1 1TW
Activities: Other retail sale in non-specialised stores
Officers: Alan Ribchester, Secretary; Michael Kenward Crofts [1951] Director; Frank Nicholson [1954] Director; Colin Richard Wilkes [1961] Director; Eileen Rosalind Amy Wood [1950] Director/Shopowner

Durham Pharmaceuticals Limited
Incorporated: 15 February 1950
Net Worth: £214,640 *Total Assets:* £1,072,750
Registered Office: St Aidans Terrace, Trimdon Station, Cleveland, TS29 6BT
Activities: Wholesale of pharmaceutical goods
Major Shareholder: Peter Robert Whitfield Grundy
Officers: Peter Robert Whitfield Grundy, Secretary; Peter Robert Whitfield Grundy [1951] Director

Durham Precision Engineering Limited
Incorporated: 11 December 2007 *Employees:* 44
Net Worth: £1,010,765 *Total Assets:* £2,233,059
Registered Office: DPE, Grindon Way, Heighington Lane Business Park, Newton Aycliffe, Co Durham, DL5 6SH
Activities: Machining
Shareholders: Mark Ashley Saul; Peter William Coates
Officers: Mark Saul, Secretary; Peter William Coates [1971] Director/Engineer; Mark Ashley Saul [1965] Director/Chartered Accountant

Durham Roofing Centre Limited
Incorporated: 9 March 1992 *Employees:* 8
Net Worth: £347,808 *Total Assets:* £886,604
Registered Office: Unit 3 North Point, Belmont Industrial Estate, Durham, DH1 1SE
Activities: Agents involved in the sale of timber and building materials
Officers: Dean Gray [1965] Commercial Director; Trevor O'Neil [1962] Director/Manager; Garry Welsh [1971] Operations Director

Durham School
Incorporated: 4 January 1993 *Employees:* 118
Net Worth: £451,367 *Total Assets:* £9,318,922
Registered Office: The Bursars Office, Durham School, Durham, DH1 4SZ
Activities: General secondary education
Officers: Deborah Joan Leigh, Secretary; Margaret Coates [1960] Director/Headteacher; Joanne Cowie [1966] Director/Solicitor and Notary Public; Simon Patrick Joseph Dobson [1963] Director/Wealth Adviser; Geoffrey Mark Hodgson [1961] Managing Director; David John Kennedy [1957] Director/Canon, Church of England; Jennifer Lynn Kirkley [1989] Director/Procurement Manager; Sharon Eleanor Langridge [1961] Director/Solicitor; Alasdair MacConachie [1946] Managing Director; Maura Regan [1957] Director/Chief Executive Officer; Robert William Ribchester [1981] Director/Accountant; Dr Jacquelyn Marie Robson [1976] Director/Associate Professor (Teaching); John Ritchie Walton Salkeld [1953] Managing Director; Neil Turner [1966] Director/Architect

Durham Sheet Metal Works Limited
Incorporated: 20 January 1955 *Employees:* 40
Net Worth: £339,853 *Total Assets:* £899,216
Registered Office: Templetown, South Shields, Tyne & Wear, NE33 5TE
Activities: Manufacture of metal structures and parts of structures
Shareholder: William Thomas Gracie
Officers: William Thomas Gracie, Secretary; David Gracie [1980] Director; William Thomas Gracie [1949] Director

The Durham Tees Valley Community Rehabilitation Company Limited
Incorporated: 4 December 2013 *Employees:* 177
Net Worth: £2,065,814 *Total Assets:* £6,088,137
Registered Office: Wetherby House, Wetherby Close, Portrack Interchange Business Park, Stockton on Tees, Cleveland, TS18 2SL
Activities: Justice and judicial activities
Officers: Alison Jane Thompson, Secretary; John David Bentley [1951] Director/Chief Executive; Bronwen Joanne Elphick [1969] Director; John Alfred Graham [1967] Director of Operations; Michael Maiden [1953] Director/Consultant; Christine Smith [1962] Director; Alison Jane Thompson [1966] Finance Director; Sir Peter Vardy [1947] Director/Business Executive

Durham Vale Developments Limited
Incorporated: 6 May 2005 *Employees:* 21
Net Worth Deficit: £80,156 *Total Assets:* £1,683,583
Registered Office: Sandgate House, 102 Quayside, Newcastle upon Tyne, NE1 3DX
Activities: Hotels and similar accommodation
Parent: Inn Collection Bidco Limited
Officers: Sean Lee Donkin [1981] Operations Director; Angus Keith Liddell [1955] Director; Iain Stein [1959] Director

Durham Wildlife Trust
Incorporated: 30 July 1971 *Employees:* 30
Net Worth: £1,430,474 *Total Assets:* £1,503,835
Registered Office: Rainton Meadows, Chilton Moor, Houghton-le-Spring, Co Durham, DH4 6PU
Activities: Botanical and zoological gardens and nature reserves activities
Officers: Janice Baker [1956] Director; Peter Thomas Bell [1961] Director/Retired; Faye Butler [1958] Director/Retired; Michael Andrew Coates [1966] Director/Management Consultant; Steven Gater [1952] Director/Part Time Educational Consultant; Christopher Gorman [1943] Director/Retired Chartered Engineer; Georgina Mary Hand [1977] Director/Charity Services Manager; Rachel Helen Hepburn [1984] Director/Ecological Consultant; Alan Keith Holden [1947] Director/Retired; Robert Kirton-Darling [1946] Director/Land Agent; Sarah Elizabeth Lister [1979] Director/Chartered Accountant; Malcolm Dennis Shorney [1942] Director/Retired; Christopher Robin Smith [1940] Director/Chartered Accountant; Amy Sorrell [1987] Director/Lecturer; Ian Thomas [1968] Director/Clerical Officer

Durhamlane Limited
Incorporated: 28 February 2011 *Employees:* 36
Net Worth: £808,057 *Total Assets:* £1,240,861
Registered Office: Deltic House, Kingfisher Way, Wallsend, Tyne & Wear, NE28 9NX
Activities: Other business support service activities n.e.c.
Shareholders: Lee Christopher Durham; Richard Matthew Lane
Officers: Lee Christopher Durham [1972] Director; Richard Matthew Lane [1972] Director

Durorg Limited
Incorporated: 23 May 2015
Registered Office: Grorud Engineering Ltd, Castleside Industrial Estate, Consett, Co Durham, DH8 8JA
Activities: Other service activities n.e.c.
Parent: Arkle Acquisitions Limited
Officers: George Lambert [1967] Director [Irish]

Dutchwest Distribution Limited
Incorporated: 20 January 1978
Net Worth: £542,650 *Total Assets:* £1,036,156
Registered Office: West End Industrial Estate, Haltwhistle, Northumberland, NE49 9HA
Activities: Retail sale of electrical household appliances in specialised stores
Shareholders: Sandra Cogan; Barry Cogan
Officers: Sandra Cogan, Secretary; Barry Cogan [1946] Director/Electrical Wholesalers; Sandra Cogan [1946] Director/Electrical Wholesalers

DVS Autos Limited
Incorporated: 20 August 2007
Net Worth: £63,801 *Total Assets:* £1,240,467
Registered Office: Unit 10 Warrenby Court, Redcar, Cleveland, TS10 5AT
Activities: Renting and leasing of cars and light motor vehicles
Major Shareholder: Darren Darren Lee
Officers: Darren Darren Lee [1966] Director/Motor Trader

DW Contractors (Oxford) Ltd
Incorporated: 18 February 1986 *Employees:* 133
Net Worth: £4,134,000 *Total Assets:* £10,610,000
Registered Office: Units 11 & 12, Parsons Road, Parsons Industrial Estate, Washington, Tyne & Wear, NE37 1HB
Activities: Painting
Parent: Fastflow Group Limited
Officers: Shaun Hastings, Secretary; Neil Patrick Armstrong [1969] Director/Chief Executive [Irish]; Conor Bray [1980] Managing Director [Irish]; Ryan John Brennan [1971] Director/Business Executive; Ian Craggs [1976] Director/Business Executive; Shaun Hastings [1958] Business Director; Colin McMahon [1967] Operations Director; David Michael Rooney [1981] Commercial Director

Dyce Limited
Incorporated: 12 December 2002
Net Worth: £1,820,618 *Total Assets:* £2,529,193
Registered Office: 82 Bewick Road, Gateshead, Tyne & Wear, NE8 1RS
Activities: Buying and selling of own real estate
Officers: Anna Schleider, Secretary [American]; Aidel Schleider [1985] Director/Housewife; Anna Schleider [1956] Director/Secretary [American]; Avi Schleider [1988] Director/Investor; Rivka Schleider [1990] Director/Student; Shamai Schleider [1953] Director/Lecturer; Miriam Silver [1977] Director/Interior Designer; Ruth Walkin [1983] Director/Housewife [American]; Avrohom Wittler [1982] Director/Student

Dyer Engineering Ltd.
Incorporated: 2 November 1987 *Employees:* 130
Net Worth: £4,472,099 *Total Assets:* £7,830,904
Registered Office: Unit 3 & 5, Morrison Road Industrial Estate, Annfield Plain, Stanley, Co Durham, DH9 7RU
Activities: Manufacture of other fabricated metal products n.e.c.
Parent: GPRB Holdings Limited
Officers: Richard Graham Bradley [1967] Finance Director; Graeme James Parkins [1969] Managing Director; James Alexander Robson [1960] Director

Dynamic CCTV Limited
Incorporated: 7 December 1994
Net Worth: £7,071,466 *Total Assets:* £11,301,664
Registered Office: 9b/9c Bowes Road, Middlesbrough, Cleveland, TS2 1LU
Activities: Security systems service activities
Parent: Dynamic CCTV Management Ltd
Officers: Paul Gordon, Secretary; Graham Reece Dunne [1973] Technical Director; Paul Neville Gordon [1974] Sales Director; Diane Tatters [1970] Director

Dynamic CCTV Management Ltd
Incorporated: 13 October 2015 *Employees:* 40
Net Worth: £4,929,837 *Total Assets:* £10,460,035
Registered Office: 9b/9c Bowes Road, Middlesbrough, Cleveland, TS2 1LU
Activities: Security systems service activities
Shareholders: Graham Reece Dunne; Paul Neville Gordon; Diane Tatters
Officers: Graham Reece Dunne [1973] Technical Director; Paul Neville Gordon [1974] Sales Director; Diane Tatters [1970] Finance Director

Dysart Developments Limited
Incorporated: 28 December 1979
Net Worth: £4,245,545 *Total Assets:* £6,887,555
Registered Office: Ravensworth House, 1 Ravensworth Street, Bedlington, Northumberland, NE22 7JP
Activities: Development of building projects
Parent: Dysart Management Limited
Officers: Lyn Joan Binks, Company Secretary; Morris Robert Muter [1954] Director; Roland Mark Short [1966] Director/Civil Engineer

Dysart Management Limited
Incorporated: 31 August 2004
Net Worth: £1,608,417 *Total Assets:* £5,389,556
Registered Office: Mill House, Hownsgill Industrial Park, Knitsley Lane, Consett, Co Durham, DH8 7NU
Activities: Other business support service activities n.e.c.
Shareholders: Morris Robert Muter; Lyn Joan Binks
Officers: Lyn Joan Binks, Secretary; Morris Robert Muter [1954] Director

Dysart Residential Limited
Incorporated: 29 July 2005
Net Worth: £95,385 *Total Assets:* £2,963,318
Registered Office: Mill House, Hownsgill Industrial Park, Knitsley Lane, Consett, Co Durham, DH8 7NU
Activities: Construction of domestic buildings
Parent: Project Genesis Limited
Officers: Lyn Joan Binks, Secretary; Lyn Joan Binks [1960] Director/Manager; Morris Robert Muter [1954] Director/Manager

E C Groundworks Ltd
Incorporated: 9 March 2010 *Employees:* 3
Net Worth: £557,923 *Total Assets:* £982,778
Registered Office: Clifton Lodge, Clifton, Morpeth, Northumberland, NE61 6DG
Activities: Demolition
Shareholders: Steve Anna Redpath; Richard Alexander Johnston
Officers: Anna Redpath, Secretary; Richard Alexander Johnston [1976] Director/Civil Engineer; Steve Anna Redpath [1967] Director

E W Properties Ltd
Incorporated: 22 September 2014
Net Worth: £18,086 *Total Assets:* £1,212,503
Registered Office: Tower Buildings, 9 Oldgate, Morpeth, Northumberland, NE61 1PY
Activities: Other letting and operating of own or leased real estate
Shareholders: Robert Elliot; Michael James Williamson
Officers: Robyn Elliot, Secretary; Jade Williamson, Secretary; Robert Elliot [1986] Director; Michael James Williamson [1983] Director

E-Sil Components Ltd
Incorporated: 13 October 1987 *Employees:* 2
Net Worth: £12,434,000 *Total Assets:* £20,704,000
Registered Office: Suite 7a, Tower House, St Catherines Court, Sunderland Enterprise Park, Sunderland, Tyne & Wear, SR5 3XJ
Activities: Activities of head offices
Parent: Ecomal UK Limited
Officers: Laura Mary Bell, Secretary; Laura Mary Bell [1955] Director; Jeffrey William Wheeler [1949] Director

E-Wire Northern Limited
Incorporated: 12 March 2009 *Employees:* 29
Net Worth: £382,403 *Total Assets:* £1,126,699
Registered Office: WS House, Stapylton Street, Bolckow Industrial Estate, Middlesbrough, Cleveland, TS6 7BH
Activities: Electrical installation
Shareholders: Colin Davies; Jennifer Davies; Colin Davies; Jennifer Davies
Officers: Jennifer Davies, Secretary; Colin Davies [1963] Director; Jennifer Davies [1966] Director

E.E.M.I.T.S. Communications Limited
Incorporated: 25 August 1992 *Employees:* 15
Net Worth: £691,509 *Total Assets:* £1,516,644
Registered Office: Brignell Road, Riverside Park, Middlesbrough, Cleveland, TS2 1PS
Activities: Wireless telecommunications activities
Shareholders: Dr Craig John Matthews; Michelle Matthews
Officers: Michelle Matthews, Secretary; Dr Craig John Matthews [1972] Managing Director; Jessica Leigh Matthews [1998] Director; Michelle Matthews [1971] Director

E.S.P. Plastics Ltd
Incorporated: 16 January 1985
Net Worth: £1,241,475 *Total Assets:* £2,076,496
Registered Office: ESP Commercial Centre, Prospect Road, Crook, Co Durham, DL15 8JL
Activities: Manufacture of other plastic products
Shareholders: Alan Freeman; Paula Ritson
Officers: Violet Freeman, Secretary; Alan Freeman [1954] Director/Operations Manager; Violet Freeman [1954] Director/Company Secretary; Paula Ritson [1978] Director/Financial Controller; Dean Shields [1968] Director/Coach Builder

E3 Ecology Ltd
Incorporated: 22 August 2003 *Employees:* 17
Net Worth: £622,206 *Total Assets:* £1,007,480
Registered Office: Pasture House, Wark, Hexham, Northumberland, NE48 3DG
Activities: Environmental consulting activities
Shareholders: Antony David Martin; Mary Tracy Elizabeth Martin
Officers: Mary Tracy Elizabeth Martin, Secretary; Antony David Martin [1960] Director/Ecology Consultant; Mary Tracy Elizabeth Martin [1963] Director/Consultancy Manager

Eagle Dreams Ltd
Incorporated: 3 March 2017
Net Worth: £27,715 *Total Assets:* £849,863
Registered Office: 99 Bewick Road, Gateshead, Tyne & Wear, NE8 1TY
Activities: Buying and selling of own real estate
Shareholders: Samuel Adler; Hadassah Adler
Officers: Samuel Adler [1978] Director

Eagle Road Services Limited
Incorporated: 20 January 1964 *Employees:* 14
Net Worth: £1,419,542 *Total Assets:* £1,703,944
Registered Office: 16 Union Street, Blyth, Northumberland, NE24 2DX
Activities: Sale, maintenance and repair of motorcycles and related parts and accessories
Officers: Helen Whitaker, Secretary; Alan Ferguson [1954] Director/Haulier; Helen Whitaker [1951] Director/Secretary; Steven Mark Whitaker [1956] Director/Haulier

Eagle Welding & Engineering Supplies Limited
Incorporated: 19 April 1995 *Employees:* 13
Net Worth: £1,158,498 *Total Assets:* £2,441,142
Registered Office: Portrack Industrial Estate, Portrack Grange Road, Stockton on Tees, Cleveland, TS18 2PH
Activities: Wholesale of other machinery and equipment
Parent: GSLF Engineering Limited
Officers: Graham Stuart Lindsay Forrest [1962] Director; Fiona Helen McCafferty [1982] Director

Eaglescliffe and District Golf Company Limited
Incorporated: 13 March 1914 *Employees:* 30
Net Worth: £600,281 *Total Assets:* £1,304,547
Registered Office: Yarm Road, Eaglescliffe, Stockton on Tees, Cleveland, TS16 0DQ
Activities: Operation of sports facilities
Officers: Martin John Ball, Secretary; Richard Michael Chamberlain [1948] Director/Retired; Geoffrey Kevin Spencer [1960] Director/Retired; Roland Todd [1965] Director/Local Government Officer

Eaglescliffe Properties Limited
Incorporated: 28 August 2003
Net Worth: £48,923 *Total Assets:* £1,946,128
Registered Office: Unit 1d Lockheed Close, Preston Farm Industrial Estate, Stockton on Tees, Cleveland, TS18 3BP
Activities: Other letting and operating of own or leased real estate
Major Shareholder: Laura Jane Arnold
Officers: Alexander Neville Hall [1978] Director

Earlsway Holdings Limited
Incorporated: 16 May 2007
Net Worth: £2,663,865 *Total Assets:* £3,023,800
Registered Office: Easter Park, Earlsway, Teesside Industrial Estate, Thornaby, Stockton on Tees, Cleveland, TS17 9NT
Activities: Activities of head offices
Parent: Earlsway Solutions Ltd
Officers: Mary Caffry, Secretary; Michael Lawrence Baum [1967] Sales Director; Mary Caffry [1957] Director/Accountant

Earsdon Properties LLP
Incorporated: 20 March 2003
Net Worth: £2,074,943 *Total Assets:* £2,161,410
Registered Office: Swallow House, Parsons Road, Washington, Tyne & Wear, NE37 1EZ
Officers: Carol Barlow [1950] Member; John Barlow [1947] Member; Graham Carter [1955] Member; Helen Dorothy Carter [1965] Member

Kenneth Easby Limited
Incorporated: 17 December 2009 *Employees:* 37
Net Worth: £1,337,625 *Total Assets:* £2,137,681
Registered Office: Trinity House, Thurston Road, Northallerton, N Yorks, DL6 2NA
Activities: Other business support service activities n.e.c.
Shareholders: Kenneth Graham; Samantha Jane Rainbow
Officers: Sharon Aideen Mei Mei Adams [1968] Director/Chartered Accountant [Malaysian]; Kevin Anthony Bradley [1962] Director/Accountant; Kenneth Graham [1960] Director/Accountant; Samantha Jane Rainbow [1968] Director/Accountant

Easibathe Limited
Incorporated: 24 March 1999 *Employees:* 54
Net Worth: £589,711 *Total Assets:* £2,126,913
Registered Office: Bulman House, Regent Centre, Gosforth, Newcastle upon Tyne, NE3 3LS
Activities: Manufacture of medical and dental instruments and supplies
Shareholders: Martin Cook; Denise Marie Cook
Officers: Denise Marie Cook, Secretary; Martin Cook [1956] Director/Manager

Easington Academy
Incorporated: 14 March 2012
Registered Office: Easington Academy, Stockton Road, Easington Village, Peterlee, Co Durham, SR8 3AY
Activities: General secondary education
Officers: Eileen Adamson [1952] Director/Physiotherapy Technician; Barry Russell Garside [1955] Director/Local Government Officer; Jacqueline Barbara Garside [1973] Director; Malcolm Peter Grinstead [1955] Director/Retired; Joyce Middlemas [1949] Director/Retired; Jacqueline Mary Anne Morris [1964] Director; Helen Louise Rutherford [1972] Director; Toni Spoors [1969] Director; George Andrew Ingram Vest [1943] Director/Retired; Ian Frederick Wright [1962] Managing Director

Easington Greyhound Stadium Limited
Incorporated: 11 May 1995
Net Worth: £716,915 *Total Assets:* £1,418,825
Registered Office: 22 Whitworth Terrace, Spennymoor, Co Durham, DL16 7LD
Activities: Other letting and operating of own or leased real estate
Major Shareholder: William Barry Ford
Officers: Jayne Sophia Mary Auld, Secretary; William Barry Ford [1946] Managing Director

T W Eason Limited
Incorporated: 5 February 2014
Net Worth: £762,204 *Total Assets:* £1,027,387
Registered Office: Willow House, Main Street, Red Row, Morpeth, Northumberland, NE61 5AG
Activities: Construction of roads and motorways
Major Shareholder: Thomas William Eason
Officers: Thomas William Eason [1967] Director/Haulage Contractor

East Cleveland M.S. Home
Incorporated: 29 July 1987 *Employees:* 42
Net Worth: £908,056 *Total Assets:* £966,206
Registered Office: Edenhall Grove, Redcar, Cleveland, TS10 4PR
Activities: Residential care activities for the elderly and disabled
Officers: Clive Victor Greenley, Secretary; Clive Victor Greenley [1945] Director/Retired; Rose Hewitt [1943] Director/Retired; Nicola Idle [1967] Director/Administrator; Susan Jackson-Wilson [1955] Director/Retired; Malcolm Thompson [1941] Director/Retired; Nicola Louise Tizard [1968] Director/Business Analyst; Peter William Wilson [1943] Director/Retired

East Coast Fibreglass Supplies Limited
Incorporated: 5 April 2006 *Employees:* 28
Net Worth: £525,924 *Total Assets:* £1,035,941
Registered Office: 1 Jesmond Business Court, 217 Jesmond Road, Newcastle upon Tyne, NE2 1LA
Activities: Manufacture of glass fibres
Shareholder: Gary Peel Bates
Officers: Donna Marie Bates, Secretary; Donna Bates [1968] Director; Gary Bates [1966] Director; Lee Bates [1969] Director/Manager

East Durham Community Development Trust Limited
Incorporated: 13 September 2006 *Employees:* 13
Net Worth: £1,605,773 *Total Assets:* £1,615,099
Registered Office: Community House, Yoden Road, Peterlee, Co Durham, SR8 5DP
Activities: Activities of other membership organisations n.e.c.
Officers: Peter Coe [1971] Director/Manager; Edna Mary Connor [1947] Director/Retired; Judith Evans [1947] Director/Retired; Rona Hardy [1961] Director/Project Development Worker; Andrea Johnson [1968] Director/HR Advisor; Wendy Kennedy [1941] Director/Retired; Alan David Miller [1942] Director/Retired; Terrence Murray [1944] Director/Retired; Alison Elizabeth Nutter [1956] Director/Project Manager; Sanjee Deshika Ratnatunga [1970] Director/Economic Development Consultant; Tony Walsh [1959] Director/Development Worker

East Durham Partnership Limited
Incorporated: 11 May 1995 *Employees:* 24
Net Worth: £1,121,418 *Total Assets:* £1,152,673
Registered Office: 1 Kilburn Drive, Seaview Industrial Estate, Horden, Peterlee, Co Durham, SR8 4TQ
Activities: Other social work activities without accommodation n.e.c.
Officers: Beverley Hart [1962] Director/Performance Manager; Kay Hawkridge Smith [1941] Director/Retired; John Thomas McLoughlin [1966] Director/Bank Manager; Mark John McNichol [1983] Director/Strategic Manager

East London Energy Limited
Incorporated: 10 July 2007 *Employees:* 3
Net Worth: £33,945,000 *Total Assets:* £125,216,000
Registered Office: Shared Services Centre, Q3 Office, Quorum Business Park, Benton Lane, Newcastle upon Tyne, NE12 8EX
Activities: Production of electricity
Parent: Engie UK Holding (Services) Limited
Officers: Sarah Gregory, Secretary; Andrew David Hart [1969] Managing Director; Wilfrid John Petrie [1965] Director [French]; Simon David Pinnell [1964] Director

East Yorkshire Motor Services Limited
Incorporated: 5 October 1926 *Employees:* 700
Net Worth: £6,565,154 *Total Assets:* £26,807,044
Registered Office: The Go-Ahead Group, 3rd Floor, 41-51 Grey Street, Newcastle upon Tyne, NE1 6EE
Activities: Other urban, suburban or metropolitan passenger land transport (not underground, metro or similar)
Shareholders: Peter John Sidney Shipp; Eyms Group Limited
Officers: Carolyn Ferguson, Secretary; David Allen Brown [1960] Director; Simon Patrick Butcher [1967] Director; Gary Edmundson [1967] Director; Alexander Paul Edwards [1966] Director; Martijn Lee Gilbert [1982] Director; Stephen King [1978] Director

Eastbourne House Ltd
Incorporated: 28 April 2015
Net Worth Deficit: £43,029 *Total Assets:* £1,412,713
Registered Office: Houghton House, New Road, Team Valley Trading Estate, Gateshead, Tyne & Wear, NE11 0JU
Activities: Residential nursing care facilities
Parent: Exclusive Care Group Ltd
Officers: Jennifer Pamela Houghton [1946] Director; Jill Yvette Houghton [1965] Director

Easterside Academy
Incorporated: 21 February 2014 *Employees:* 49
Net Worth: £2,151,279 *Total Assets:* £2,723,831
Registered Office: Easterside Academy, Erith Grove, Easterside, Middlesbrough, Cleveland, TS4 3RG
Activities: Primary education
Officers: Sarah Anderson [1982] Director/Teacher; Dr Daisy Best [1973] Director/Principal Lecturer; Cllr Michael Carr [1947] Director/Retired; Christopher Philip Drew [1971] Director/Headteacher (Principal); David William Elliott [1949] Director/Retired; David Foster [1964] Director/Youth Worker; Linda Rachael Harrison [1962] Director of Teaching and Learning; Delyth Linacre [1974] Director/Headteacher; Ruth Parker [1952] Director/Retired; Dr Jonathon Lee Reay [1978] Director/University Lecturer; Ruth Saber [1981] Director/Housewife; Chris Thomas [1960] Director

Easteye Limited
Incorporated: 13 April 1982 *Employees:* 239
Net Worth: £7,566,481 *Total Assets:* £22,171,376
Registered Office: Units 15-16 Stockholm Close, Tyne Tunnel Trading Estate, North Shields, Tyne & Wear, NE29 7SF
Activities: Public houses and bars
Parent: Ever 1209 Limited
Officers: Bhupinder Singh Ladhar [1981] Director/Self Employed; Mandeep Singh Ladhar [1985] Director

Eat Fresh Investments Limited
Incorporated: 20 March 2009 *Employees:* 60
Net Worth: £363,215 *Total Assets:* £898,350
Registered Office: 7 Canon Grove, Yarm, Cleveland, TS15 9XE
Activities: Take-away food shops and mobile food stands
Major Shareholder: Mark Anthony Millward
Officers: Joanne Louise Millward, Secretary; Mark Anthony Millward [1975] Director

Ebac Group Limited
Incorporated: 13 August 1997
Net Worth: £9,280,265 *Total Assets:* £18,777,134
Registered Office: Ketton Way, Aycliffe Industrial Park, Newton Aycliffe, Co Durham, DL5 6SQ
Activities: Other business support service activities n.e.c.
Parent: Ebac Holdings Ltd
Officers: Amanda Hird, Secretary; Graham Currie [1970] Finance Director; John Malcolm Elliott [1943] Director; Margaret Rose Elliott [1948] Director; Amanda Hird [1969] Operations Director; Robert Anthony Hird [1962] Sales Director; John Clifford Laverick [1942] Director

Ebac Holdings Limited
Incorporated: 7 April 2011 *Employees:* 237
Net Worth: £4,833,875 *Total Assets:* £22,297,326
Registered Office: Ketton Way, Aycliffe Business Park, Newton Aycliffe, Co Durham, DL5 6SR
Activities: Other manufacturing n.e.c.
Parent: Ebac Foundation
Officers: Amanda Hird, Secretary; John Malcolm Elliott [1943] Director; Paul Folkard Elliott [1951] Director/Business Consultant; John Clifford Laverick [1942] Director

Ebac Industrial Products Limited
Incorporated: 12 November 2003 *Employees:* 29
Net Worth: £3,599,854 *Total Assets:* £8,020,379
Registered Office: St Helen Trading Estate, Bishop Auckland, Co Durham, DL14 9AD
Activities: Manufacture of electric domestic appliances
Parent: Ebac Group Ltd
Officers: Amanda Hird, Secretary; John Malcolm Elliott [1943] Director/Engineer; Stephen Robert Lilly [1959] Director

Ebac Limited
Incorporated: 5 January 1973 *Employees:* 208
Net Worth: £9,979,689 *Total Assets:* £23,380,876
Registered Office: Ketton Way, Aycliffe Industrial Park, Newton Aycliffe, Co Durham, DL5 6SR
Activities: Other manufacturing n.e.c.
Parent: Ebac Group Ltd
Officers: Amanda Hird, Secretary; Graham Currie [1970] Finance Director; John Malcolm Elliott [1943] Director/Engineer; Amanda Hird [1969] Operations Director; Robert Anthony Hird [1962] Sales Director

Ebony Leisure Limited
Incorporated: 13 March 2008 *Employees:* 39
Net Worth: £316,134 *Total Assets:* £1,080,320
Registered Office: Ebony Champagne Bar, 8 Walkergate, Durham, DH1 1SQ
Activities: Public houses and bars
Officers: Marcia Ann Watson, Secretary; Jayne Sophia Mary Auld [1975] Director; Ann Ford [1946] Director; William Barry Ford [1946] Director; Javis Manoo Robinson [1968] Director/Civil Engineer; Marcia Ann Watson [1970] Director

Ebor Leisure World Limited
Incorporated: 18 January 2012 *Employees:* 17
Net Worth: £228,778 *Total Assets:* £3,272,136
Registered Office: c/o Catterick Caravan & Camping Centre Limited, Gatherley Road, Brompton on Swale, Richmond, N Yorks, DL10 7JB
Activities: Sale of other motor vehicles
Parent: Leisure World Group Limited
Officers: Christopher Michael Kinsell, Secretary; Christopher Michael Kinsell [1973] Director; Matthew Alexander Kinsell [1979] Director

Ebsonlodge Limited
Incorporated: 17 December 1992 *Employees:* 13
Net Worth: £651,958 *Total Assets:* £1,017,973
Registered Office: Discount Tiles, Portrack Lane, Stockton on Tees, Cleveland, TS18 2HP
Activities: Retail sale of hardware, paints and glass in specialised stores
Major Shareholder: Mark Barrett
Officers: Jane Elizabeth Barrett, Company Secretary; Jane Elizabeth Barrett [1962] Director/Company Secretary; Mark Barrett [1964] Director/Manager

Ecco Finishing Supplies Limited
Incorporated: 12 October 1995 *Employees:* 17
Net Worth: £1,212,238 *Total Assets:* £2,328,425
Registered Office: Unit 6 Letitia Industrial Estate, Middlesbrough, Cleveland, TS5 4BE
Activities: Other retail sale not in stores, stalls or markets
Officers: Carol Ann Miller, Secretary; Keith Miller [1959] Director; Lucy Hannah Miller [1991] Director

Eciggy UK Limited
Incorporated: 9 April 2014
Net Worth: £628,255 *Total Assets:* £1,016,364
Registered Office: Unit 4 & 5 High Street, The Shambles, Stockton on Tees, Cleveland, TS18 1AA
Activities: Retail sale of tobacco products in specialised stores
Shareholders: Derek Pearce; Alan O'Neill
Officers: Alan O'Neill [1970] Director; Derek Pearce [1956] Director

Eco Drill (England) Limited
Incorporated: 21 May 2007 *Employees:* 11
Net Worth: £392,621 *Total Assets:* £2,097,021
Registered Office: Durham Road, Chilton, Co Durham, DL17 0EW
Activities: Electrical installation
Parent: Eco-Drill Ltd
Officers: Michael Andrew Angus [1972] Director/Pipe Layer; John Paul Dunlavey [1978] Director/Civil Engineering

Eco Monitoring Utility Systems Limited
Incorporated: 12 February 2008
Net Worth: £3,073,875 *Total Assets:* £5,414,976
Registered Office: 3 & 4 Cobalt Park Way, Cobalt Business Park, New York, Tyne & Wear, NE28 9EJ
Activities: Manufacture of electronic measuring, testing etc. equipment, not for industrial process control
Parent: Utilitywise PLC
Officers: Richard Stephen Laker [1976] Director; Richard Brinsley Sheridan [1964] Director

Eco Tyre Disposals Ltd
Incorporated: 14 September 2011
Net Worth Deficit: £615,719 *Total Assets:* £976,067
Registered Office: Rosebay Road, Littleburn Industrial Estate, Langley Moor, Co Durham, DH7 8HJ
Activities: Treatment and disposal of non-hazardous waste
Officers: Eliezer Reich [1972] Director; Aron Tzvi Sandler [1969] Director

Eco-Drill Ltd
Incorporated: 24 January 2011
Net Worth: £449,452 *Total Assets:* £1,164,936
Registered Office: 43 Coniscliffe Road, Darlington, Co Durham, DL3 7EH
Activities: Activities of other holding companies n.e.c.
Officers: Charlotte Rachel Angus [1975] Director; Michael Andrew Angus [1972] Director; John Paul Dunlavey [1978] Director; Kay Dunlavey [1982] Director

Ecova, Inc. Limited
Incorporated: 5 August 1999 *Employees:* 74
Net Worth: £3,111,000 *Total Assets:* £5,355,000
Registered Office: Shared Services Centre, Q3 Office, Quorum Business Park, Benton Lane, Newcastle upon Tyne, NE12 8EX
Activities: Management consultancy activities other than financial management
Parent: Power Efficiency Holdings Limited
Officers: Sarah Gregory, Secretary; Mark Gallacher [1979] Director; Nicola Elizabeth Anne Lovett [1969] Director; Graham Oxley [1976] Director

Eden Farm Limited
Incorporated: 25 September 1964 *Employees:* 298
Net Worth: £6,511,727 *Total Assets:* £44,150,232
Registered Office: Unit S3, Narvik Way, Tyne Tunnel Trading Estate, North Shields, Tyne & Wear, NE29 7XJ
Activities: Other food services
Officers: Patricia Ada Rice, Secretary; David Leonard Brind [1972] Director; Stephen Carr [1955] Director/Commercial Manager; Ben Maxted [1983] Frozen Director; Patricia Ada Rice [1957] Director; Paul Victor Young [1957] Director

Eden Transport Limited
Incorporated: 22 June 1978
Registered Office: Eden House, High Hesledon, Hartlepool, Cleveland, TS27 4QF
Activities: Freight transport by road
Major Shareholder: Andrew Cracknell
Officers: Avril Cracknell, Secretary; Andrew Cracknell [1966] Director; Avril Cracknell [1966] Director

Edenpace Limited
Incorporated: 18 July 1983
Net Worth: £1,730,000 *Total Assets:* £1,792,000
Registered Office: 1a Dukesway Court, Team Valley Trading Estate, Gateshead, Tyne & Wear, NE11 0PJ
Activities: Gambling and betting activities
Parent: Wm.Noble (Automatics) Limited
Officers: Phillip Nigel Blain, Secretary; David James Horrocks [1959] Director/Chartered Accountants; Ian Imrie [1955] Director

EDF Energy Renewables Holdings Limited
Incorporated: 28 July 2008
Net Worth: £451,156,992 *Total Assets:* £672,254,976
Registered Office: Alexander House, 1 Mandarin Road, Rainton Bridge Business Park, Houghton-le-Spring, Co Durham, DH4 5RA
Activities: Activities of head offices
Parent: EDF Energy Renewables Limited
Officers: Susan Elizabeth Lind, Secretary; Generaldine Marie Roseline Anceau [1978] Director [French]; Matthieu Thomas Hue [1975] Director [French]; Joseph Eugene Philipsz [1967] Director/Investment Banker [Irish]; Edward Arthur Wilson [1965] Director; Emilio Alessandro Zito [1980] Director [Italian]

EDF Energy Renewables Limited
Incorporated: 18 December 2007 *Employees:* 91
Net Worth: £13,217,000 *Total Assets:* £28,207,000
Registered Office: Alexander House, 1 Mandarin Road, Rainton Bridge Business Park, Houghton-le-Spring, Co Durham, DH4 5RA
Activities: Production of electricity
Shareholders: EDF Energy (Energy Branch) Limited; EDF EN UK Limited
Officers: Susan Elizabeth Lind, Secretary; Generaldine Marie Roseline Anceau [1978] Director [French]; Frederic Marie Albert Belloy [1977] Director [French]; Robert Guyler [1966] Director/Accountant; Denis Rouhier [1966] Director [French]; Matthew Sykes [1962] Director/Chief Nuclear Officer; Emilio Alessandro Zito [1980] Director [Italian]

EDF Energy Round 3 Isle of Wight Limited
Incorporated: 26 November 2002
Net Worth Deficit: £11,904,000 *Total Assets:* £4,864,000
Registered Office: Alexander House, 1 Mandarin Road, Rainton Bridge Business Park, Houghton-le-Spring, Co Durham, DH4 5RA
Activities: Activities of other holding companies n.e.c.
Shareholders: EDF Energy (Energy Branch) Limited; EDF EN UK Limited
Officers: Susan Elizabeth Lind, Secretary; Matthieu Thomas Hue [1975] Director [French]; Hassaan Majid [1968] Director

Edgeman Limited
Incorporated: 21 July 1999 *Employees:* 419
Net Worth: £18,675,440 *Total Assets:* £40,904,240
Registered Office: 24 Woolsington Park South, Woolsington, Newcastle upon Tyne, NE13 8BJ
Activities: Hotels and similar accommodation
Officers: Saroj Rani Chawla, Secretary; Mukesh Raj Chawla [1954] Director; Neel Chawla [1986] Director; Saroj Rani Chawla [1955] Director

Ediscum Properties Limited
Incorporated: 24 March 1960
Registered Office: 3 Saddler Street, Bishop Auckland, Co Durham, DL14 7BH
Activities: Buying and selling of own real estate
Shareholder: Jeremy Alexander Edkins
Officers: Jeremy Alexander Edkins, Secretary/Director; Jeremy Alexander Edkins [1962] Director; Sheila Edkins [1935] Director

EDM Zone Limited
Incorporated: 30 May 2012 *Employees:* 14
Net Worth: £952,463 *Total Assets:* £1,192,618
Registered Office: Unit 10 Hawick Trading Estate, Hawick Crescent, Newcastle upon Tyne, NE6 1AS
Activities: Other engineering activities
Major Shareholder: Paul Wilson
Officers: Paul Wilson [1962] Director/Manager

Edmi Europe Limited
Incorporated: 14 October 2011 *Employees:* 96
Net Worth: £15,793,000 *Total Assets:* £32,130,000
Registered Office: 1 Gosforth Park Avenue, Gosforth Business Park, Newcastle upon Tyne, NE12 8EG
Activities: Wholesale of other machinery and equipment
Officers: Ashley Lawson, Secretary; Willem Hoogers [1969] Finance Director [Dutch]; Alan Masterman [1962] Director/General Manager; How New Seng [1961] Director/Chief Operating Officer [Malaysian]; Kiyoshi Shiina [1959] Director [Japanese]

Edmondson Logging Ltd
Incorporated: 24 August 2005
Net Worth: £360,686 *Total Assets:* £1,039,313
Registered Office: Cheviot Cottage, West Plain, Milfield, Northumberland, NE71 6HP
Activities: Logging
Shareholders: Victoria Estrilde Sutherland Edmondson; Alistair David Edmondson; Charles Timothy Edmondson
Officers: Victoria Estrilde Sutherland Edmondson, Secretary; Alistair David Edmondson [1969] Director/Forester; Charles Timothy Edmondson [1991] Director/Forestry; Victoria Estrilde Sutherland Edmondson [1968] Director/Office Administrator

Education and Services for People with Autism Limited
Incorporated: 18 March 1994 *Employees:* 541
Net Worth: £12,768,762 *Total Assets:* £14,805,987
Registered Office: 2a Hylton Park, Hylton Park Road, Sunderland, Tyne & Wear, SR5 3HD
Activities: Other education n.e.c.
Officers: Karl Thomas Hardy, Secretary; Thomas Peter Berney [1943] Director/Retired Psychiatrist [Irish]; Professor Malcolm Hooper [1934] Director/Professor Medical Chemistry; Professor Rita Jordan [1941] Director/Retired/Freelance Consultant; Philip Michael Moxon [1949] Director/Teacher; Stephanie Robinson [1947] Director/Retired Lecturer Higher Education & Autism Practice; Paul Edward Gilbert Shattock [1942] Director/University Lecturer; Graeme Charles Young [1964] Director/Business Development Manager

The Education Village Academy Trust
Incorporated: 22 August 2011 *Employees:* 316
Net Worth: £21,870,000 *Total Assets:* £27,130,000
Registered Office: The Education Village, Salters Lane South, Darlington, Co Durham, DL1 2AN
Activities: Primary education
Officers: Christopher John Ashford [1964] Director/Multi Agency Safeguarding Trainer; Hanne Tobias Barton [1957] Director/Headteacher [Danish]; Michael Butler [1968] Director; Allan Christopher Dixon [1981] Director/Accountant; Helen Radcliffe [1952] Director/Head of Apprenticeships-Business Development; Ramandeep Singh Sanghera [1987] Director/Chartered Accountant; Heather Irene Scott [1940] Director/Councillor; Shirley Anne Welsh [1966] Director/Headteacher; Deborah Louise Wood [1970] Director/University Administrator

R & R Edwards and Sons Limited
Incorporated: 22 October 2014 *Employees:* 2
Net Worth: £136,427 *Total Assets:* £1,134,176
Registered Office: c/o RMT Accountants & Business Advisors Ltd, Gosforth Park Avenue, Newcastle upon Tyne, NE12 8EG
Activities: Other accommodation
Shareholder: Richard John Edwards
Officers: Dr Richard John Edwards [1970] Director/Doctor; Dr Rona Alicia Lunt [1973] Director/Doctor

Edynamix Global Ltd
Incorporated: 22 August 2014 *Employees:* 2
Net Worth: £471,280 *Total Assets:* £4,181,164
Registered Office: Wansbeck Workspace, Rotary Parkway, Ashington, Northumberland, NE63 8QZ
Activities: Other information technology service activities
Shareholder: Sean Robert Booth
Officers: Sean Robert Booth [1964] Director; Iain Nickalls [1978] Director

Edynamix UK Ltd
Incorporated: 25 September 2014
Net Worth: £926,053 *Total Assets:* £1,062,268
Registered Office: Wansbeck Workspace, Rotary Parkway, Ashington, Northumberland, NE63 8QZ
Activities: Other information technology service activities
Shareholder: Sean Robert Booth
Officers: Sean Robert Booth [1964] Director; Iain Nickalls [1978] Director

EEW Offshore Structures (Britain) Limited
Incorporated: 4 November 2014 *Employees:* 56
Net Worth: £2,329,193 *Total Assets:* £18,078,252
Registered Office: Haverton House, Haverton Hill, Rig Yard, Billingham, Stockton on Tees, Cleveland, TS23 1PZ
Activities: Manufacture of metal structures and parts of structures
Parent: EEW Special Pipe Constructions
Officers: Sascha Hofmeister [1978] Managing Director [German]

EHLUK Building Maintenance & Facility Services Ltd
Incorporated: 4 June 2001 *Employees:* 26
Net Worth: £280,031 *Total Assets:* £887,493
Registered Office: The Oaks Centre, Whinfield Drive, Aycliffe Business Park, Newton Aycliffe, Co Durham, DL5 6AU
Activities: Plumbing, heat and air-conditioning installation
Officers: Barbara Vowles, Secretary; Gary Stainsbury [1969] Director/Business Consultant; Ryan John Stainsby [1996] Financial Director

EJM Engineered Systems Limited
Incorporated: 23 April 1980 *Employees:* 38
Net Worth: £1,207,874 *Total Assets:* £3,481,645
Registered Office: Unit 1a & 1b Thornley Station Industrial Estate, Shotton Colliery, Co Durham, DH6 2QA
Activities: Installation of industrial machinery and equipment
Shareholders: Matthew Morton; Valerie Morton
Officers: Valerie Morton, Secretary; John Bell [1953] Director/Chartered Accountant; Paul James Cable [1970] Director/Refrigeration Engineer; Stephen Jerome George Cheffings [1953] Director/Engineer; Matthew Morton [1945] Director/Engineer

Ekwienox Holdings Limited
Incorporated: 2 November 2015
Net Worth Deficit: £1,770 *Total Assets:* £3,644,564
Registered Office: Third Floor, Citygate, St James Boulevard, Newcastle upon Tyne, NE1 4JE
Activities: Activities of head offices
Major Shareholder: Stephen Lant
Officers: Stephen Lant [1963] Director/Accountant

Ekwienox Limited
Incorporated: 19 November 2003
Net Worth: £948,019 *Total Assets:* £4,126,315
Registered Office: UNW LLP, Citygate, St James Boulevard, Newcastle upon Tyne, NE1 4JE
Activities: Activities of head offices
Parent: Ekwienox Holdings Limited
Officers: Romina Vucic-Pranic, Secretary; Stephen Lant [1963] Director/Accountant

El Investments Limited
Incorporated: 4 August 1959
Net Worth: £7,689,409 *Total Assets:* £7,689,559
Registered Office: Cross House, Westgate Road, Newcastle upon Tyne, NE1 4XX
Activities: Buying and selling of own real estate
Parent: Retirement Bridge Limited
Officers: Paul Trevor Barber [1967] Director; Antony Lewis Pierce [1976] Finance Director

Elaghmore (Holdings) Limited
Incorporated: 11 April 2013
Net Worth: £4,613 *Total Assets:* £2,125,933
Registered Office: c/o Leathers LLP, 17th Floor, Cale Cross House, Pilgrim Street, Newcastle upon Tyne, NE1 6SU
Activities: Activities of other holding companies n.e.c.
Shareholders: Andrew James Ducker; David Brown Manning
Officers: Andrew James Ducker [1963] Director; David Brown Manning [1958] Director

Elaghmore Limited
Incorporated: 16 May 2007
Net Worth: £3,783,368 *Total Assets:* £5,188,186
Registered Office: 17th Floor, Cale Cross House, Pilgrim Street, Newcastle upon Tyne, NE1 6SU
Activities: Management consultancy activities other than financial management
Parent: Elaghmore (Holdings) Limited
Officers: Andrew James Ducker, Secretary; Andrew James Ducker [1963] Director; David Brown Manning [1958] Director

Eland Homes Limited
Incorporated: 7 February 2006
Net Worth Deficit: £251,448 *Total Assets:* £2,225,562
Registered Office: 25 John Street, Sunderland, Tyne & Wear, SR1 1JG
Activities: Development of building projects
Officers: Stephen Treanor, Secretary; Simon Antony Peckham [1962] Director; Stephen Treanor [1960] Director/Solicitor

Elanders Ltd
Incorporated: 14 June 1999 *Employees:* 187
Net Worth: £11,197,140 *Total Assets:* £14,616,346
Registered Office: Merlin Way, New York Business Park, New York, Tyne & Wear, NE27 0QG
Activities: Printing n.e.c.
Parent: Elanders AB
Officers: Paul Richard Jacques, Secretary; Christopher Michael Hewitt [1965] Managing Director; Paul Richard Jacques [1965] Finance Director; Magnus Nilsson [1966] Director [Swedish]

Elddis Transport (Consett) Limited
Incorporated: 6 September 1971 *Employees:* 333
Net Worth: £8,147,927 *Total Assets:* £19,605,308
Registered Office: Delves Lane, Consett, Co Durham, DH8 7LH
Activities: Freight transport by road
Major Shareholder: Geoffrey Robin Cook
Officers: Mark Andrew Rankin, Secretary/Commercial Director; Geoffrey Robin Cook [1936] Director; Nigel Cook [1968] Director; Tony David Hogarth [1968] Operations Director; Austin Lawrie [1938] Director; Lisa Raisbeck [1970] Director; Mark Andrew Rankin [1973] Financial Director; Richard Toner [1983] Commercial Director; Robert Kirtley Whinney [1939] Director

Elder Properties Ltd
Incorporated: 4 June 2007
Net Worth: £411,742 *Total Assets:* £1,346,226
Registered Office: Unit 4 Moreland Street, Hartlepool, Cleveland, TS24 7NL
Activities: Development of building projects
Officers: Brian Elder, Secretary/Property Developer; Brian Elder [1963] Director/Property Developer; Susan Elder [1967] Director

Eldon Estates Limited
Incorporated: 23 July 1982 *Employees:* 1
Net Worth: £854,786 *Total Assets:* £889,542
Registered Office: Brackenwood, 12 Jesmond Park West, Newcastle upon Tyne, NE7 7BU
Activities: Other letting and operating of own or leased real estate
Major Shareholder: Robert William Atwell
Officers: Robert William Atwell [1954] Director/Chartered Surveyor

Eldrett Finch Limited
Incorporated: 4 October 2006 *Employees:* 19
Net Worth: £391,415 *Total Assets:* £959,592
Registered Office: Unit 10 Hatfield Way, South Church Enterprise Park, Bishop Auckland, Co Durham, DL14 6XF
Activities: Manufacture of metal structures and parts of structures
Shareholders: Alexander David Turnbull; Paul Eldrett
Officers: Paul Eldrett, Secretary; Paul Eldrett [1980] Director; Alexander David Turnbull [1976] Sales Director

Electrix International Limited
Incorporated: 25 June 1981 *Employees:* 71
Net Worth: £3,726,817 *Total Assets:* £9,271,669
Registered Office: Dovecot Hill, South Church Enterprise Park, Bishop Auckland, Co Durham, DL14 6XP
Activities: Manufacture of other fabricated metal products n.e.c.
Major Shareholder: Malcolm Thompson
Officers: Dorothy Thompson, Secretary; Christopher Paul Thompson [1982] Operations Director; Malcolm Thompson [1950] Director/Business Manager

Electronic Security Solutions Limited
Incorporated: 7 June 2000 *Employees:* 44
Net Worth: £778,729 *Total Assets:* £1,982,437
Registered Office: ESS Limited, Henson Road, Yarm Road Business Park, Darlington, Co Durham, DL1 4QD
Activities: Other construction installation
Shareholders: Stephen Francis Bellamy; Mark Lee Johnson
Officers: Stephen Francis Bellamy, Secretary/Security; Stephen Francis Bellamy [1969] Director/Security; Mark Lee Johnson [1972] Director/Security

Eleven Arches
Incorporated: 23 May 2014 *Employees:* 13
Net Worth: £26,914,998 *Total Assets:* £33,142,104
Registered Office: Flatts Farm, Toronto, Bishop Auckland, Co Durham, DL14 7SF
Activities: Performing arts
Officers: Louis Stourton Greig [1956] Director/Private Banker; Stefa Janita McManners [1949] Director/Retired Headteacher; Jonathan Garnier Ruffer [1951] Director/Chairman of Auckland Castle Trust; Dennis Tindall [1946] Director/Catholic Priest; Nicholas Timothy Turner [1961] Director/Retired

Elfab Limited
Incorporated: 1 July 1965 *Employees:* 64
Net Worth: £5,330,913 *Total Assets:* £6,768,904
Registered Office: Alder Road, West Chirton Industrial Estate, North Shields, Tyne & Wear, NE29 8SD
Activities: Manufacture of other fabricated metal products n.e.c.
Parent: Halma PLC
Officers: Sharif Moneeb, Secretary; Christopher Andrew Billinge [1972] Commercial Director; Anika Ephraim [1971] Managing Director; Sharif Moneeb [1980] Finance Director [Irish]; Russell Paul Trotter [1965] Business Development Director; Deborah Watson [1981] Marketing Director

ELG Developments Limited
Incorporated: 20 February 2007
Net Worth: £1,021,319 *Total Assets:* £3,082,111
Registered Office: The Willows, Kingswood, Langley Park, Co Durham, DH7 9WA
Activities: Pre-primary education
Shareholder: Trevor Graham
Officers: Richard Hugh Langdon, Secretary; Emma Louise Graham [1983] Director/Nursery Manager; Emma Victoria Pearson [1982] Director

Elim Properties Ltd
Incorporated: 10 April 2012 *Employees:* 2
Net Worth: £121,968 *Total Assets:* £1,266,718
Registered Office: 27a Norton Road, Stockton on Tees, Cleveland, TS18 2BW
Activities: Other letting and operating of own or leased real estate
Shareholders: Manohar Jesuraj; Hepzibah Jesuraj
Officers: Hepzibah Jesuraj [1972] Director; Manohar Jesuraj [1967] Director

John Eliot (Footwear) Limited
Incorporated: 9 March 1978 *Employees:* 117
Net Worth: £775,875 *Total Assets:* £1,745,986
Registered Office: 68 King Street, South Shields, Tyne & Wear, NE33 1HZ
Activities: Retail sale of footwear in specialised stores
Officers: Matthew Jeremy Neville-Eliot [1975] Director; Susan Irene Neville-Eliot [1948] Director

Elite Embroidery Limited
Incorporated: 7 July 2000 *Employees:* 22
Net Worth: £1,829,761 *Total Assets:* £2,186,299
Registered Office: Elite House, Front Street, Bells Close, Lemington, Newcastle upon Tyne, NE15 6YF
Activities: Finishing of textiles
Shareholders: Antony Lee Taylor; Lianne Taylor
Officers: Lianne Taylor, Secretary; Antony Lee Taylor [1973] Director/Embroidery; Lianne Taylor [1977] Director/Accounts and Embroidery

Elite Maintenance & Installation Services Limited
Incorporated: 19 February 2003
Net Worth: £1,023,822 *Total Assets:* £2,019,075
Registered Office: Elite House, 11 Queens Court, Third Avenue, Team Valley Trading Estate, Gateshead, Tyne & Wear, NE11 0BU
Activities: Plumbing, heat and air-conditioning installation
Shareholders: Paul Goodfellow; David Seth Hardingham; Alison Goodfellow; Christine Diane Hardingham
Officers: Paul Goodfellow, Secretary/Commercial Manager; Alison Goodfellow [1972] Director/Catering Supervisor; Paul Goodfellow [1968] Director/Commercial Manager; Christine Diane Hardingham [1958] Director/Office Administrator; David Seth Hardingham [1956] Director/Operations Manager

Elliott (Holdings) Limited
Incorporated: 24 March 1961
Net Worth: £3,032,163 *Total Assets:* £3,139,619
Registered Office: Gallowfield, Thropton, Morpeth, Northumberland, NE65 7NF
Activities: Other letting and operating of own or leased real estate
Shareholders: Caroline Victoria Elliott; Charles William Poore
Officers: Caroline Victoria Elliott, Company Secretary; Caroline Victoria Elliott [1974] Director; Charles William Poore [1971] Director

Elliott Westland Insurance Brokers Limited
Incorporated: 27 November 2000 *Employees:* 16
Net Worth: £71,885 *Total Assets:* £792,200
Registered Office: Unit 1 Lambton House, Newbottle Street, Houghton-le-Spring, Co Durham, DH4 4AR
Activities: Non-life insurance
Officers: Ann Westland, Secretary/Manager; Angela Mary Chell [1959] Commercial Director; John Kevin Elliott [1959] Director/Insurance Broker; Lucy Elliott [1990] Director/Insurance Broker; Ann Westland [1961] Director/Manager; Ian Westland [1958] Director/Insurance Broker

Elliston Fine Wines Limited
Incorporated: 22 September 2003 *Employees:* 3
Net Worth: £39,965 *Total Assets:* £3,763,635
Registered Office: 19 Fenkle Street, Alnwick, Northumberland, NE66 1HW
Activities: Wholesale of wine, beer, spirits and other alcoholic beverages
Shareholders: Piers Harry North Dalrymple Methuen; Rebecca Methuen
Officers: Rebecca Methuen, Secretary; Piers Harry North Dalrymple Methuen [1966] Director/Business Executive; Rebecca Methuen [1969] Director/Secretary

Elmfield Trading Limited
Incorporated: 26 February 2013 *Employees:* 10
Net Worth: £928,374 *Total Assets:* £1,865,730
Registered Office: 60 Horsley Hill Square, South Shields, Tyne & Wear, NE34 6RF
Activities: Other service activities n.e.c.
Major Shareholder: Sunil Maini
Officers: Sunil Maini [1967] Director/Pharmacist

Elpha Lodge Residential Care Home Limited
Incorporated: 21 March 1997
Net Worth: £834,075 *Total Assets:* £3,007,404
Registered Office: South Broomhill, Morpeth, Northumberland, NE65 9RR
Activities: Other human health activities
Major Shareholder: Elsie Dixon
Officers: Elsie Dixon [1943] Director; John James Dixon [1943] Director

Elring Klinger (Great Britain) Limited
Incorporated: 19 October 1987 *Employees:* 298
Net Worth: £17,463,000 *Total Assets:* £25,430,000
Registered Office: Kirkleatham Business Park, Redcar, Cleveland, TS10 5RX
Activities: Forging, pressing, stamping and roll-forming of metal; powder metallurgy
Parent: Elring Klinger AG
Officers: Paul James Alexander, Secretary; Theo Ernst Becker [1959] Director [German]; Kevin John Fletcher [1947] Director/Solicitor; Glen Pearson [1966] Director/General Manager; Jessulat Thomas [1969] Director [German]; Dr Stefan Wolf [1961] Director [German]

Elring Parts Limited
Incorporated: 29 November 1995 *Employees:* 34
Net Worth: £4,553,327 *Total Assets:* £6,901,178
Registered Office: Unit 2 Derwent Court, Earlsway, Team Valley Trading Estate, Gateshead, Tyne & Wear, NE11 0TF
Activities: Wholesale trade of motor vehicle parts and accessories
Parent: Elringklinger AG
Officers: Toni Jensen, Secretary; David Masterman [1953] Managing Director; Jessulat Thomas [1969] Director [German]; Garry Waite [1962] Managing Director; Dirk Willers [1973] Director/General Manager Aftermarket Division [German]; Dr Stefan Wolf [1961] Director [German]

Elvet Developments Ltd
Incorporated: 8 October 2015
Registered Office: P A Brown & Co, 9 Oldgate, Morpeth, Northumberland, NE61 1PY
Activities: Development of building projects
Shareholder: Shaun Joseph Crawley
Officers: Paul Andrew Brown, Secretary; Shaun Joseph Crawley [1981] Director

RS Ember Properties Limited
Incorporated: 4 December 2015
Registered Office: Essell, 29 Howard Street, North Shields, Tyne & Wear, NE30 1AR
Activities: Other letting and operating of own or leased real estate
Shareholders: Ray Shelley; Sandra Shelley
Officers: Raymond Shelley, Secretary; Raymond Shelley [1952] Director/Caretaker; Sandra Shelley [1959] Director/Nurse

Embleton Hall Dairies Limited
Incorporated: 31 May 1984 *Employees:* 48
Net Worth: £2,049,917 *Total Assets:* £3,247,183
Registered Office: Murton Hall Farm, Hurworth Burn, Wingate, Cleveland, TS28 5NU
Activities: Liquid milk and cream production
Shareholder: Michael Thompson
Officers: Christine Emily Nicholson, Secretary; Michael Thompson [1938] Director/Farmer; Paul William Thompson [1967] Director/Farmer; Sally Thompson [1942] Director/Farmer

Emerald Biogas Ltd
Incorporated: 24 April 2009 *Employees:* 11
Net Worth: £3,546,850 *Total Assets:* £14,008,520
Registered Office: Emerald Biogas, Preston Road, Aycliffe Business Park, Newton Aycliffe, Co Durham, DL5 6AB
Activities: Growing of cereals (except rice), leguminous crops and oil seeds
Shareholders: Agricore Ltd; John Warren (Animal By-Products) Limited
Officers: Ian Bainbridge, Secretary; Ian Bainbridge [1985] Director/Farmer; Adam Warren [1972] Director/General Manager; Antony Michael Warren [1978] Director/Technical Manager

Emerchantpay Limited
Incorporated: 14 June 2004 *Employees:* 5
Net Worth: £22,232,438 *Total Assets:* £37,284,060
Registered Office: 29 Howard Street, North Shields, Tyne & Wear, NE30 1AR
Activities: Financial intermediation not elsewhere classified
Officers: Alex Robinson, Secretary; Stephen Ross Dickson [1957] Director/Accountant; Alan Richard Goslar [1947] Director/Finance Executive; Jonas Reynisson [1961] Director/Senior Consultant [Icelander]

Emerchantpay UK Services Ltd
Incorporated: 24 February 2010 *Employees:* 18
Net Worth: £787,539 *Total Assets:* £11,939,234
Registered Office: 29 Howard Street, North Shields, Tyne & Wear, NE30 1AR
Activities: Other professional, scientific and technical activities n.e.c.
Officers: Alex Robinson, Secretary; Laurence Armstrong [1960] Trust Director; Stephen Ross Dickson [1957] Director/Accountant; Susan Mary Hall [1963] Director; Jonas Reynisson [1961] Managing Director [Icelander]

EMG Solicitors Limited
Incorporated: 29 August 2013 *Employees:* 18
Net Worth: £917,630 *Total Assets:* £1,245,262
Registered Office: Abbey House, 1-2 Abbeywoods Business Park, Pity Me, Durham, DH1 5TH
Activities: Solicitors
Major Shareholder: Emma Mary Gaudern
Officers: Emma Mary Gaudern, Secretary; Samantha Margaret Edward [1977] Director; Emma Mary Gaudern [1975] Director/Solicitor; Gwen Angharad Jones [1982] Director; Jemma Claire Morland [1985] Director; Richard Swinbank [1982] Director

Emirates Ltd
Incorporated: 23 August 2012
Net Worth: £1,597,526 *Total Assets:* £6,323,410
Registered Office: 82 Bewick Road, Gateshead, Tyne & Wear, NE8 1RS
Activities: Renting and operating of Housing Association real estate
Parent: Blockdale Limited
Officers: Shamai Schleider, Secretary; Jacob Israel Koenig [1986] Director/Student [American]; Rivka Koenig [1990] Director/Housewife; Anna Schleider [1956] Director/Housewife [American]; Shamai Schleider [1953] Director/Lecturer; Yosef Dov Schleider [1983] Director/Student; Chaya Silver [1998] Director/Student

Emmanuel Church Durham
Incorporated: 13 February 2007 *Employees:* 7
Net Worth: £1,343,244 *Total Assets:* £1,885,442
Registered Office: The Durham Centre, Belmont Industrial Estate, Durham, DH1 1TN
Activities: Activities of religious organisations
Officers: Andrew James Biggs, Secretary/Chartered Accountant; George Alan Bell [1953] Director/Minister of Religion; Jennifer Elizabeth Booth [1973] Director/Paediatric Nurse; Viscount William Robert Enfield [1964] Director/Software Engineer; Ian James Portwine [1971] Director/Church Pastor

Emperor Investment Property Limited
Incorporated: 22 November 2001 *Employees:* 2
Net Worth: £356,531 *Total Assets:* £1,326,290
Registered Office: Sutherland House, 5-7 The Friars, Newcastle upon Tyne, NE1 5XE
Activities: Other letting and operating of own or leased real estate
Shareholders: Ah Pat Leung; Ying Yu Leung
Officers: Ying Yu Leung, Secretary; Ah Pat Leung [1957] Director; Ying Yu Leung [1960] Director

Empharm (North East) Limited
Incorporated: 26 April 2013 *Employees:* 19
Net Worth: £23,207 *Total Assets:* £1,002,587
Registered Office: 22 Cheapside, Spennymoor, Co Durham, DL16 6DJ
Activities: Dispensing chemist in specialised stores
Parent: RPMR Healthcare Limited
Officers: Robert Michael Pitt [1976] Director/Pharmacist; Mark David Roberts [1972] Director/Pharmacist

Empire Property Concepts Limited
Incorporated: 11 June 2009 *Employees:* 9
Net Worth: £523,591 *Total Assets:* £2,979,119
Registered Office: 30 Yoden Way, Peterlee, Co Durham, SR8 1AL
Activities: Other building completion and finishing
Officers: Paul Timothy Rothwell [1982] Director; Jeffrey Kevin Taylor [1972] Director

Empire Property Holdings 2 Limited
Incorporated: 4 October 2016 *Employees:* 2
Net Worth Deficit: £14,062 *Total Assets:* £11,334,046
Registered Office: c/o The Bailey Group, 30 Yoden Way, Peterlee, Co Durham, SR8 1AL
Activities: Buying and selling of own real estate
Shareholders: Paul Timothy Rothwell; Richard Alexander Barrow
Officers: Richard Alexander Barrow, Secretary; Richard Alexander Barrow [1984] Marketing Director; Paul Timothy Rothwell [1982] Director/Property Developer

Empire Property Holdings Limited
Incorporated: 14 August 2015 *Employees:* 2
Net Worth Deficit: £77,292 *Total Assets:* £10,144,391
Registered Office: 30 Yoden Way, Peterlee, Co Durham, SR8 1AL
Activities: Buying and selling of own real estate
Shareholders: Richard Alexander Barrow; Paul Timothy Rothwell
Officers: Richard Alexander Barrow [1984] Director/Property Investment; Paul Timothy Rothwell [1982] Director/Property Investment

Emsosaru Limited
Incorporated: 1 March 2005
Net Worth: £151,239 *Total Assets:* £1,867,788
Registered Office: Unit 2 Kellaw Road, Yarm Road Business Park, Darlington, Co Durham, DL1 4YA
Activities: Other letting and operating of own or leased real estate
Officers: Rupert James Brown, Secretary; Byron William James Robert Brown [1951] Director/Manager

Encompassed Limited
Incorporated: 5 December 2006 *Employees:* 32
Net Worth Deficit: £126,977 *Total Assets:* £793,925
Registered Office: 29-33 Maxwell Street, South Shields, Tyne & Wear, NE33 4PU
Activities: Management consultancy activities other than financial management
Parent: SMH T&SS Limited
Officers: Dean Thomas Rowe, Secretary; Dean Thomas Rowe [1979] Commercial Director

Encore Envelopes Limited
Incorporated: 2 July 1984 *Employees:* 217
Net Worth: £19,450,552 *Total Assets:* £31,232,600
Registered Office: Wessyngton House, Industrial Road, Hertburn, Washington, Tyne & Wear, NE37 2SA
Activities: Manufacture of paper stationery
Parent: Tyne & Wear Holdings Ltd
Officers: Michael John Williamson, Secretary; Craig Lee Allen [1982] Director; David Norris Cooper [1975] Production Director; John Russell Croisdale [1960] Commercial Director; Mark Eyeington [1974] Director; Gary Joyce [1984] Director; Michael John Williamson [1965] Financial Director

Encore Packaging Solutions Limited
Incorporated: 6 February 2013 *Employees:* 25
Net Worth: £346,442 *Total Assets:* £1,657,847
Registered Office: Wessyngton House, Industrial Road, Hertburn Industrial Estate, Washington, Tyne & Wear, NE37 2SA
Activities: Manufacture of corrugated paper and paperboard, sacks and bags
Major Shareholder: John Russell Croisdale
Officers: Michael John Williamson, Secretary; David Norris Cooper [1975] Production Director; John Russell Croisdale [1960] Managing Director; Michael John Williamson [1965] Financial Director

Endeavour Academies Trust
Incorporated: 28 March 1988 *Employees:* 238
Net Worth: £16,831,000 *Total Assets:* £19,882,000
Registered Office: Macmillan Academy, Stockton Road, Middlesbrough, Cleveland, TS5 4AG
Activities: General secondary education
Officers: Louisa Ann Robson, Secretary; Gareth Roger Attwood [1944] Director/Retired; Julian Elliot [1955] Director/University Professor; Sara Louise Ford [1968] Director/Policy Officer; Kenneth Uisdean Fraser [1951] Director/Principal; Glyn Holland [1959] Director/Parish Priest; Phillip Latham [1974] Director/Principal; Sally McGill [1962] Director; Dr Barry Leonard Phillipo [1947] Director; Anthony James Wentworth [1963] Director/Solicitor

Endeavour Northern Limited
Incorporated: 24 March 1994 *Employees:* 16
Net Worth: £350,767 *Total Assets:* £938,112
Registered Office: 7 Bankside, The Watermark, Gateshead, Tyne & Wear, NE11 9SY
Activities: Licenced restaurants
Shareholders: Terence Victor Noble; Joda Developments Limited
Officers: David Macpherson, Secretary/Engineer; David Macpherson [1945] Director/Engineer; Joseph Frederick Wilson [1955] Director

The Endeavour Partnership LLP
Incorporated: 16 July 2002 *Employees:* 44
Net Worth: £1,350,301 *Total Assets:* £1,722,025
Registered Office: Tobias House, St Mark's Court, Teesdale Business Park, Stockton on Tees, Cleveland, TS17 6QW
Officers: Lee Carl Hickton Bramley [1974] Member; James William Brown [1974] Member; John Paul Bury [1954] Member; Stephen Elliott [1972] Member; Gerard Francis Flanagan [1964] Member; Alexander Frey Smith [1978] Member; Niklas Francis Krister Tunley [1979] Member; Simon Wake [1964] Member; Nigel Timothy Williams [1965] Member

Endless Stretch Limited
Incorporated: 5 December 2014 *Employees:* 1
Net Worth Deficit: £742,290 *Total Assets:* £4,563,602
Registered Office: 77 Grey Street, Newcastle upon Tyne, NE1 6EF
Activities: Other letting and operating of own or leased real estate
Parent: MCM Services No 1 Limited
Officers: Louisa Scarlet Uzan [1983] Director

The Endowment Fund for Tacri
Incorporated: 19 April 2006
Net Worth: £4,845,616 *Total Assets:* £4,918,366
Registered Office: St Ann's Wharf, 112 Quayside, Newcastle upon Tyne, NE1 3DX
Activities: Growing of beverage crops
Officers: Hussein Ahmed Mansoor [1959] Director of Research and Development [New Zealander]; Professor Melchior Emeran Mlambiti [1940] Director/Professor [New Zealander]; Henry Moshi [1939] Director/Certified Public Accountant [New Zealander]

The Energy Checking Company Limited
Incorporated: 5 August 2014 *Employees:* 64
Net Worth: £748,933 *Total Assets:* £1,538,715
Registered Office: Unit 4 Waverley Business Park, South Shields, Tyne & Wear, NE33 1LE
Activities: Other business support service activities n.e.c.
Major Shareholder: David Winton
Officers: Paul Comerford [1967] Director/Accountant; David Winton [1985] Managing Director

Energy Information Centre Limited
Incorporated: 7 August 1975 *Employees:* 183
Net Worth: £12,239,518 *Total Assets:* £16,280,646
Registered Office: 3 & 4 Cobalt Park Way, Cobalt Business Park, New York, Tyne & Wear, NE28 9EJ
Activities: Other business support service activities n.e.c.
Parent: Utilitywise PLC
Officers: Richard Stephen Laker [1976] Director; Richard Brinsley Sheridan [1964] Director

Energy24 Limited
Incorporated: 8 May 2006 *Employees:* 3
Net Worth: £1,626,500 *Total Assets:* £4,323,996
Registered Office: PX House, Westpoint Road, Stockton on Tees, Cleveland, TS17 6BF
Activities: Trade of electricity
Parent: PX Holdings Limited
Officers: Mark William Kenrick [1958] Director; Lee Nadine Smail [1971] Director/Accountant; Daniel Philip David Weatherill [1974] Director/Solicitor

Enfield Properties Limited
Incorporated: 25 September 1985
Net Worth: £97,765 *Total Assets:* £1,394,326
Registered Office: Albert House, Albert Drive, Gateshead, Tyne & Wear, NE9 6EH
Activities: Other letting and operating of own or leased real estate
Officers: Andrew Francis Craig, Secretary; Jacqueline Anne Charlton [1949] Director/Legal Secretary; Vincent Charlton [1947] Director/Legal Executive; Andrew Francis Craig [1955] Director/Chartered Surveyor; Denise Craig [1956] Director

Engelbert Developments Ltd
Incorporated: 4 March 2014
Net Worth Deficit: £251,098 *Total Assets:* £3,074,785
Registered Office: 2nd Floor, Cuthbert House, All Saints Business Centre, Newcastle upon Tyne, NE1 2ET
Activities: Development of building projects
Parent: High Street Commercial Finance Limited
Officers: Gary Ronald Forrest [1968] Director

Engica Technology Systems International Limited
Incorporated: 13 October 1988 *Employees:* 43
Net Worth: £1,801,819 *Total Assets:* £2,709,523
Registered Office: 32 Brenkley Way, Blezard Business Park, Seaton Burn, Newcastle upon Tyne, NE13 6DS
Activities: Other software publishing
Major Shareholder: Kenneth William Huskisson
Officers: Kenneth William Huskisson, Secretary/Director; Stephen Edward Adams [1971] Business Commercial Director; Kenneth William Huskisson [1952] Director; Keith Stott [1944] Director/Chartered Engineer; Peter Strassheim [1970] Managing Director

Engie Buildings Limited
Incorporated: 20 July 1999 *Employees:* 607
Net Worth: £10,653,000 *Total Assets:* £75,819,000
Registered Office: Shared Services Centre, Q3 Office, Quorum Business Park, Benton Lane, Newcastle upon Tyne, NE12 8EX
Activities: Development of building projects
Parent: Engie Services Holding UK Limited
Officers: Sarah Gregory, Secretary; Wilfrid John Petrie [1965] Director [French]; Simon David Pinnell [1964] Director

Engie DE Holding Company Limited
Incorporated: 6 April 1988
Net Worth Deficit: £6,157,000 *Total Assets:* £4,280,000
Registered Office: Shared Services Centre, Q3 Office, Quorum Business Park, Benton Lane, Newcastle upon Tyne, NE12 8EX
Activities: Dormant company
Parent: Engie Services Holding UK Limited
Officers: Sarah Gregory, Secretary; Andrew David Hart [1969] Managing Director; Lee Kitchen [1979] Director/Accountant

Engie Energy Services UK Limited
Incorporated: 22 November 1991 *Employees:* 3
Net Worth: £15,524,000 *Total Assets:* £17,117,000
Registered Office: Shared Services Centre, Q3 Office, Quorum Business Park, Benton Lane, Newcastle upon Tyne, NE12 8EX
Activities: Electrical installation
Parent: Cofathec Energy Services Limited
Officers: Sarah Gregory, Secretary; John Michael Jago [1968] Director/Divisional COO; Nicola Elizabeth Anne Lovett [1969] Director; Simon David Pinnell [1964] Director

Engie FM Limited
Incorporated: 21 July 1960 *Employees:* 4,750
Net Worth: £8,521,000 *Total Assets:* £166,484,992
Registered Office: Shared Services Centre, Q3 Office, Quorum Business Park, Benton Lane, Newcastle upon Tyne, NE12 8EX
Activities: Distribution of gaseous fuels through mains
Parent: Engie Services Holding UK Limited
Officers: Sarah Gregory, Secretary; David George Alcock [1965] Director; Nicola Elizabeth Anne Lovett [1969] Director; Wilfrid John Petrie [1965] Director [French]; Simon David Pinnell [1964] Director

Engie in Partnership Limited
Incorporated: 8 January 2001
Net Worth: £18,876,000 *Total Assets:* £30,087,000
Registered Office: Shared Services Centre, Q3 Office, Quorum Business Park, Benton Lane, Newcastle upon Tyne, NE12 8EX
Activities: Construction of domestic buildings
Parent: Engie Regeneration (Apollo) Limited
Officers: Sarah Jane Gregory, Secretary; Wilfrid John Petrie [1965] Director; Simon David Pinnell [1964] Director; Martin Jon Smithurst [1971] Director

Engie International FM Limited
Incorporated: 26 February 2013 *Employees:* 20
Net Worth Deficit: £5,738,000 *Total Assets:* £3,436,000
Registered Office: Shared Services Centre, Q3 Office, Quorum Business Park, Benton Lane, Newcastle upon Tyne, NE12 8EX
Activities: Combined facilities support activities
Parent: Engie Energy Services International S.A.
Officers: Sarah Gregory, Secretary; Nicola Elizabeth Anne Lovett [1969] Director; Wilfrid John Petrie [1965] Director [French]; Simon David Pinnell [1964] Director; Claude Turbet [1958] Director [French]

Engie Leeds PFI Limited
Incorporated: 29 November 2012
Net Worth: £709,000 *Total Assets:* £2,826,000
Registered Office: Shared Services Centre, Q3 Office, Quorum Business Park, Benton Lane, Newcastle upon Tyne, NE12 8EX
Activities: Construction of domestic buildings
Parent: Engie Regeneration Holdings Limited
Officers: Sarah Jane Gregory, Secretary; Wilfrid John Petrie [1965] Director; Simon David Pinnell [1964] Director

Engie Property Services Limited
Incorporated: 23 March 2007
Net Worth: £1,524,000 *Total Assets:* £14,819,000
Registered Office: Shared Services Centre, Q3 Office, Quorum Business Park, Benton Lane, Newcastle upon Tyne, NE12 8EX
Activities: Other specialised construction activities n.e.c.
Parent: Engie Regeneration Limited
Officers: Sarah Jane Gregory, Secretary; Wilfrid John Petrie [1965] Director; Simon David Pinnell [1964] Director; Martin Jon Smithurst [1971] Director

Engie Regeneration (Apollo) Limited
Incorporated: 11 February 1976
Net Worth: £92,565,000 *Total Assets:* £217,083,008
Registered Office: Shared Services Centre, Q3 Office, Quorum Business Park, Benton Lane, Newcastle upon Tyne, NE12 8EX
Activities: Construction of commercial buildings
Parent: Engie Regeneration Limited
Officers: Sarah Jane Gregory, Secretary; Wilfrid John Petrie [1965] Director; Simon David Pinnell [1964] Director; Martin Jon Smithurst [1971] Director

Engie Regeneration (Bramall) Limited
Incorporated: 17 December 1979
Net Worth: £14,270,000 *Total Assets:* £54,916,000
Registered Office: Shared Services Centre, Q3 Office, Quorum Business Park, Benton Lane, Newcastle upon Tyne, NE12 8EX
Activities: Construction of domestic buildings
Parent: Engie Regeneration Limited
Officers: Sarah Jane Gregory, Secretary; Wilfrid John Petrie [1965] Director; Simon David Pinnell [1964] Director

Engie Regeneration (Fhm) Limited
Incorporated: 2 June 1959 *Employees:* 330
Net Worth: £51,303,000 *Total Assets:* £94,333,000
Registered Office: Shared Services Centre, Q3 Office, Quorum Business Park, Benton Lane, Newcastle upon Tyne, NE12 8EX
Activities: Construction of domestic buildings
Parent: Engie Regeneration Limited
Officers: Sarah Jane Gregory, Secretary; Wilfrid John Petrie [1965] Director; Simon David Pinnell [1964] Director; Martin Jon Smithurst [1971] Director

Engie Regeneration Holdings Limited
Incorporated: 2 May 2013
Net Worth: £9,439,000 *Total Assets:* £254,730,000
Registered Office: Shared Services Centre, Q3 Office, Quorum Business Park, Benton Lane, Newcastle upon Tyne, NE12 8EX
Activities: Activities of head offices
Parent: Engie Services Holding UK Limited
Officers: Sarah Jane Gregory, Secretary; Wilfrid John Petrie [1965] Director; Simon David Pinnell [1964] Director

Engie Regeneration Limited
Incorporated: 11 July 1983 *Employees:* 2,239
Net Worth: £75,078,000 *Total Assets:* £284,984,992
Registered Office: Shared Services Centre, Q3 Office, Quorum Business Park, Benton Lane, Newcastle upon Tyne, NE12 8EX
Activities: Construction of domestic buildings
Parent: Engie Regeneration Holdings Limited
Officers: Sarah Jane Gregory, Secretary; Wilfrid John Petrie [1965] Director; Simon David Pinnell [1964] Director

Engie Services Holding UK Limited
Incorporated: 24 July 2012 *Employees:* 3
Net Worth: £408,144,992 *Total Assets:* £573,209,024
Registered Office: Q3 Office, Quorum Business Park, Benton Lane, Newcastle upon Tyne, NE12 8EX
Activities: Non-trading company
Parent: Engie UK Holding (Services) Limited
Officers: Sarah Gregory, Secretary; Wilfrid John Petrie [1965] Director [French]; Simon David Pinnell [1964] Director; Claude Turbet [1958] Director [French]

Engie Services Limited
Incorporated: 4 February 1958 *Employees:* 8,907
Net Worth: £37,943,000 *Total Assets:* £243,180,000
Registered Office: Shared Services Centre, Q3 Office, Quorum Business Park, Benton Lane, Newcastle upon Tyne, NE12 8EX
Activities: Combined facilities support activities
Parent: Engie Services Holding UK Limited
Officers: Sarah Gregory, Secretary; Nicola Elizabeth Anne Lovett [1969] Director; Wilfrid John Petrie [1965] Director [French]; Simon David Pinnell [1964] Director

Engie UK Holding (Services) Limited
Incorporated: 29 January 1996
Net Worth: £438,319,008 *Total Assets:* £469,782,016
Registered Office: Shared Services Centre, Q3 Office, Quorum Business Park, Benton Lane, Newcastle upon Tyne, NE12 8EX
Activities: Activities of head offices
Parent: Engie Energy Services International S.A.
Officers: Sarah Gregory, Secretary; Wilfrid John Petrie [1965] Director [French]; Simon David Pinnell [1964] Director

Engie Urban Energy Group Limited
Incorporated: 16 August 2002
Net Worth: £550,000 *Total Assets:* £3,530,000
Registered Office: Shared Services Centre, Q3 Office, Quorum Business Park, Benton Lane, Newcastle upon Tyne, NE12 8EX
Activities: Activities of head offices
Parent: Engie de Holding Company Limited
Officers: Sarah Gregory, Secretary; Andrew David Hart [1969] Managing Director; Lee Kitchen [1979] Director/Accountant

Engie Urban Energy Limited
Incorporated: 7 July 1980 *Employees:* 116
Net Worth: £5,484,000 *Total Assets:* £24,005,000
Registered Office: Shared Services Centre, Q3 Office, Quorum Business Park, Benton Lane, Newcastle upon Tyne, NE12 8EX
Activities: Installation of industrial machinery and equipment
Parent: Engie Urban Energy Group Limited
Officers: Sarah Gregory, Secretary; Andrew David Hart [1969] Managing Director; Lee Kitchen [1979] Director/Accountant

Engineering Property Services Limited
Incorporated: 7 December 2010 *Employees:* 3
Net Worth: £2,442,343 *Total Assets:* £2,923,133
Registered Office: Engineering Property Services, Ilford Road, Newcastle upon Tyne, NE2 3NX
Activities: Other manufacturing n.e.c.
Shareholders: Paul George Hoyle; Marion Hoyle
Officers: Marion Hoyle, Secretary; Paul George Hoyle [1960] Director/Manager

Engineering Recruitment Services Ltd
Incorporated: 28 July 2006 *Employees:* 49
Net Worth: £513,514 *Total Assets:* £865,997
Registered Office: First Floor, The Southlands Business Centre, Ormesby Road, Middlesbrough, Cleveland, TS3 0HB
Activities: Temporary employment agency activities
Shareholder: Lee Antony McGee
Officers: Susan Casson [1976] Director/Management Accountant; Lee Antony McGee [1973] Director/Contracts Manager

Engineering Support Partnership Ltd.
Incorporated: 13 January 1994 *Employees:* 2
Net Worth: £465,150 *Total Assets:* £4,957,662
Registered Office: Office, Unit 13 Quay Level, St Peters Wharf, St Peters Basin, Newcastle upon Tyne, NE6 1TZ
Activities: Engineering related scientific and technical consulting activities
Major Shareholder: Donald Anthony Lord
Officers: Katie Morton Dodd, Secretary; Jonathan Francis Hall [1972] Director; Donald Anthony Lord [1966] Director/Engineer

Engynious Clean Power (UK) Ltd
Incorporated: 21 March 2013
Net Worth Deficit: £657,716 *Total Assets:* £2,029,116
Registered Office: St Ann's Wharf, 112 Quayside, Newcastle upon Tyne, NE1 3DX
Activities: Combined facilities support activities
Parent: Engynious AG
Officers: Theodor Philip Scheidegger [1958] Director/Merchant [Swiss]

Engynious Schools PLC
Incorporated: 31 March 2014
Net Worth Deficit: £57,549 *Total Assets:* £908,258
Registered Office: St Ann's Wharf, 112 Quayside, Newcastle upon Tyne, NE1 3DX
Activities: Combined facilities support activities
Parent: Engynious AG
Officers: Ann Flaherty [1962] Director/Marketing and Business Development; Theodor Philip Scheidegger [1958] Director [Swiss]

Enhanced Elderly Care Limited
Incorporated: 27 September 2004 *Employees:* 218
Net Worth: £5,994,570 *Total Assets:* £9,543,604
Registered Office: 1 Fox Street, Sunderland Road, Gateshead, Tyne & Wear, NE10 0BD
Activities: Residential nursing care facilities
Major Shareholder: Gary Owen Lewis
Officers: Joanne Lynn Lewis, Secretary; Joanne Lynn Lewis [1974] Director

Enigma Interactive Limited
Incorporated: 25 April 1997
Net Worth: £1,019,538 *Total Assets:* £1,304,424
Registered Office: Quayside Studios, 8-10 Close, Newcastle upon Tyne, NE1 3RE
Activities: Business and domestic software development
Major Shareholder: Steven Granger
Officers: John Grainger, Secretary; Stephen Grainger [1969] Director/Multimedia Designer

Enodis Group Limited
Incorporated: 28 November 2001 *Employees:* 418
Net Worth: £225,500,000 *Total Assets:* £325,000,000
Registered Office: St Ann's Wharf, 112 Quayside, Newcastle upon Tyne, NE1 3DX
Activities: Activities of head offices
Parent: Enodis Holdings Limited
Officers: Adrian David Gray [1962] Director/Accountant; John Albert James Rourke [1967] Director

Enodis Hanover
Incorporated: 19 May 2006 *Employees:* 2
Net Worth: £460,216,000 *Total Assets:* £534,736,000
Registered Office: St Ann's Wharf, 112 Quayside, Newcastle upon Tyne, NE1 3DX
Activities: Activities of other holding companies n.e.c.
Parent: Enodis Regent
Officers: Adrian David Gray [1962] Director/Accountant; John Albert James Rourke [1967] Director

Enodis Holdings Limited
Incorporated: 28 November 2001 *Employees:* 2
Net Worth: £80,300,000 *Total Assets:* £414,900,000
Registered Office: St Anns Wharf, 112 Quayside, Newcastle upon Tyne, NE1 3DX
Activities: Activities of other holding companies n.e.c.
Shareholders: Manitowoc FSG UK Limited; Manitowoc Foodservice UK Holding Limited
Officers: Adrian David Gray [1962] Director/Accountant; John Albert James Rourke [1967] Director

Enodis International Limited
Incorporated: 18 November 1994 *Employees:* 3
Net Worth: £26,527,000 *Total Assets:* £75,564,000
Registered Office: St Ann's Wharf, 112 Quayside, Newcastle upon Tyne, NE1 3DX
Activities: Activities of other holding companies n.e.c.
Parent: Enodis Industrial Holdings Limited
Officers: Adrian David Gray [1962] Director/Accountant; John Albert James Rourke [1967] Director

Enodis Investments Limited
Incorporated: 15 June 1948 *Employees:* 3
Net Worth: £125,995,000 *Total Assets:* £127,235,000
Registered Office: St Ann's Wharf, 112 Quayside, Newcastle upon Tyne, NE1 3DX
Activities: Other letting and operating of own or leased real estate
Shareholders: Enodis Group Limited; Enodis Property Group Limited
Officers: Adrian David Gray [1962] Director/Accountant; John Albert James Rourke [1967] Director

Enodis Maple Leaf Ltd
Incorporated: 21 February 2007 *Employees:* 2
Net Worth: £26,544,000 *Total Assets:* £26,544,000
Registered Office: St Ann's Wharf, 112 Quayside, Newcastle upon Tyne, NE1 3DX
Activities: Activities of other holding companies n.e.c.
Parent: Enodis Hanover
Officers: Adrian David Gray [1962] Director/Accountant; John Albert James Rourke [1967] Director

Enodis Oxford
Incorporated: 19 May 2006 *Employees:* 2
Net Worth Deficit: £33,036,000 *Total Assets:* £74,520,000
Registered Office: St Ann's Wharf, 112 Quayside, Newcastle upon Tyne, NE1 3DX
Activities: Other business support service activities n.e.c.
Parent: Manitowoc Foodservice Inc
Officers: Adrian David Gray [1962] Director/Accountant; John Albert James Rourke [1967] Director

Enodis Property Developments Limited
Incorporated: 30 March 1951 *Employees:* 3
Net Worth: £18,363,000 *Total Assets:* £18,732,000
Registered Office: St Anns Wharf, 112 Quayside, Newcastle upon Tyne, NE1 3DX
Activities: Development of building projects
Parent: Enodis Property Group Limited
Officers: Adrian David Gray [1962] Director/Accountant; John Albert James Rourke [1967] Director

Ensus UK Limited
Incorporated: 15 May 2006 *Employees:* 74
Net Worth: £44,544,000 *Total Assets:* £70,126,000
Registered Office: The Granary, 17a High Street, Yarm, Cleveland, TS15 9BW
Activities: Manufacture of other chemical products n.e.c.
Parent: Cropenergies
Officers: Jacqueline Readman, Secretary; Michael Erich Friedmann [1955] Director [German]; Peter Kay [1975] Operations Director; Joachim Ernst Lutz [1956] Director [German]; Sir Robert John Margetts [1946] Director/Engineer; Dr Stephan Meeder [1970] Director [German]; Grant Pearson [1962] Commercial Director; Jacqueline Readman [1964] Director/Management Accountant

Entek International Limited
Incorporated: 29 June 1988 *Employees:* 143
Net Worth: £27,578,000 *Total Assets:* £35,656,000
Registered Office: Mylord Crescent, Camperdown Industrial Estate, Killingworth, Newcastle upon Tyne, NE12 5XG
Activities: Manufacture of other plastic products
Major Shareholder: Larry Thomas Keith
Officers: Graeme Bell, Secretary; Jeffrey Grimm [1955] Director/Chief Financial Officer [American]; Kirk Hanawalt [1962] Director/Vice-President [American]; Larry Keith [1963] Director/Chief Executive Officer [American]; Rob Keith [1957] Director/President [American]; Richard Pekala [1959] Director/Vice-President of Research and Development [American]

Enviro - Clear Limited
Incorporated: 2 June 1999
Net Worth: £441,499 *Total Assets:* £777,442
Registered Office: 246 Park View, Whitley Bay, Tyne & Wear, NE26 3QX
Activities: Other service activities n.e.c.
Major Shareholder: Michael Anthony Dow
Officers: Elizabeth Dow, Secretary; Michael Anthony Dow [1979] Director

Enviro Property Partners Limited
Incorporated: 3 April 2012 *Employees:* 4
Net Worth Deficit: £200,547 *Total Assets:* £2,537,194
Registered Office: 14 Newgate Street, Morpeth, Northumberland, NE61 1BA
Activities: Construction of domestic buildings
Shareholders: Kenneth Brian Beattie; Bryan Percy Beattie
Officers: Kimberley Aileen Pollard, Secretary; Kenneth Brian Beattie [1953] Sales Director; David Pollard [1962] Director/Gas Engineer

Enviroclothes Limited
Incorporated: 9 December 2009 *Employees:* 12
Net Worth: £506,232 *Total Assets:* £1,138,175
Registered Office: Units 9 and 10 Neptune Court, Orion Business Park, North Shields, Tyne & Wear, NE29 7UW
Activities: Recovery of sorted materials
Shareholders: Drew Gardiner; Steven Gardiner; Laura Gardiner
Officers: Laura Deborah Gardiner, Secretary; Drew Gardiner [1985] Director

EOS Facades Limited
Incorporated: 16 January 2013 *Employees:* 45
Net Worth: £2,779,057 *Total Assets:* £5,135,826
Registered Office: Esh Business Park, Heighington Lane, Aycliffe Business Park, Newton Aycliffe, Co Durham, DL5 6QG
Activities: Manufacture of metal structures and parts of structures
Parent: Engineered Offsite Group Holdings Limited
Officers: Clive Graham Ellwood, Secretary; Neil Alexander Ash [1971] Director; Clive Graham Ellwood [1958] Director; Neil Teesdale [1972] Finance Director; Stephen Anthony Thompson [1965] Managing Director

Eothen Homes Limited
Incorporated: 19 May 1950 *Employees:* 192
Net Worth: £8,940,663 *Total Assets:* £12,981,601
Registered Office: 15 Berrymoor Court, Northumberland Business Park, Cramlington, Northumberland, NE23 7RZ
Activities: Residential care activities for the elderly and disabled
Officers: Barbara Wilson, Secretary; Maureen Janet Erny [1958] Director/Management Consultant; Louise Deborah Marsh [1960] Director/Chief Executive; Alexander Lindsay McIlhinney [1947] Retired Tax Director; Dr Sameh Mishreki [1951] Director/Retired General Practitioner; Dr Andrew David Shepherd [1948] Director/Retired General Medical Practitioner; Ian David Thomson [1953] Retired Director of Town Planning; Dr Alexander Van Den Bos [1974] Director/Trustee

EPG Property Management Ltd
Incorporated: 9 June 2010
Net Worth: £23,649 *Total Assets:* £873,765
Registered Office: 10a Whitburn Road, Cleadon, Sunderland, Tyne & Wear, SR6 7QL
Activities: Other letting and operating of own or leased real estate
Officers: Paul Allwood Green [1954] Director; Eric Parker [1947] Director/Planning Engineer

Epivalence Ltd
Incorporated: 21 May 2014 *Employees:* 9
Net Worth: £707,913 *Total Assets:* £918,684
Registered Office: T404 The Wilton Centre, Redcar, Cleveland, TS10 4RF
Activities: Agents involved in the sale of fuels, ores, metals and industrial chemicals
Shareholders: Nigel Henderson Kennedy; Christopher Paul Richards
Officers: Nigel Henderson Kennedy [1974] Director; Christopher Paul Richards [1974] Director

Eppleton Academy Primary School
Incorporated: 10 May 2012 *Employees:* 29
Net Worth: £1,497,266 *Total Assets:* £1,819,106
Registered Office: Eppleton Academy Primary School, Church Road, Hetton-le-Hole, Houghton-le-Spring, Co Durham, DH5 9AJ
Activities: Primary education
Officers: Kimberley Bushby [1980] Director/Headteacher; Rachel Ann Chapman [1979] Director/Office Manager; Ellen Hagan [1984] Director/Technical Manager; John Francis Hannon [1945] Director/Retired; Margaret Anne Haswell [1946] Director/Retired; Laura Jackson [1980] Director/Deputy Headteacher; Stephanie James [1967] Director/Teacher; Brian Johnson [1949] Director/Retired; Stacey Ann Parkin [1978] Director/School Business Manager; Jayne Rowell [1976] Director/Teacher; David Edward Wallace [1957] Director/Electrician; Claire Marie Webb [1986] Director; Ian Wren [1957] Director/Minister of Religion

Eppleton Quarry Products (Middlesbrough) Ltd
Incorporated: 1 September 2003
Net Worth: £957,652 *Total Assets:* £957,652
Registered Office: Stotforth Hill House, Windlestone, Rushyford, Co Durham, DL17 0NF
Activities: Operation of gravel and sand pits; mining of clays and kaolin
Parent: Eppleton Quarry Products Limited
Officers: Neville John Hall [1956] Director; Stephen Hall [1954] Director; Garry Hutchinson [1955] Director

Eppleton Quarry Products (Scunthorpe) Limited
Incorporated: 26 March 2002
Net Worth: £2,050,473 *Total Assets:* £2,166,573
Registered Office: Stotforth Hill House, Windlestone, Rushyford, Co Durham, DL17 0NF
Activities: Quarrying of ornamental and building stone, limestone, gypsum, chalk and slate
Parent: Eppleton Quarry Products Limited
Officers: Neville John Hall [1956] Director; Stephen Hall [1954] Director; Garry Hutchinson [1955] Director

Eppleton Quarry Products Limited
Incorporated: 26 February 2001 *Employees:* 4
Net Worth: £6,356,870 *Total Assets:* £8,883,238
Registered Office: Stotforth Hill House, Windlestone, Ferryhill, Co Durham, DL17 0NF
Activities: Operation of gravel and sand pits; mining of clays and kaolin
Shareholder: Hall Construction Services Limited
Officers: Neville John Hall [1956] Director; Stephen Hall [1954] Director; Garry Hutchinson [1955] Director

Epro (Wholesale) Limited
Incorporated: 6 July 1962
Net Worth: £1,175,281 *Total Assets:* £1,297,068
Registered Office: 12a Tundry Way, Chainbridge Industrial Estate, Blaydon, Tyne & Wear, NE21 5SJ
Activities: Retail sale of flowers, plants, seeds, fertilizers, pet animals and pet food in specialised stores
Shareholder: Edith Patricia King
Officers: Adam Paul King [1991] Director/Retailer; Edith Patricia King [1953] Director/Teaching Assistant

Epsom Dental Centre Ltd
Incorporated: 11 December 2015 *Employees:* 8
Net Worth: £80,741 *Total Assets:* £990,365
Registered Office: Third Floor, Citygate, St James Boulevard, Newcastle upon Tyne, NE1 4JE
Activities: Dental practice activities
Shareholders: Anika Amin; Chirag Pravinkant Amin
Officers: Chirag Pravinkant Amin [1976] Director/Dentist

Equine Products U.K. Limited
Incorporated: 28 April 1981 *Employees:* 8
Net Worth: £995,634 *Total Assets:* £1,425,655
Registered Office: Unit 8 Gateway West, Newburn Riverside, Newcastle upon Tyne, NE15 8NX
Activities: Manufacture of prepared feeds for farm animals
Parent: Los Alerces Limited
Officers: Ian Williamson, Secretary; Philip Masterson [1966] Director [Irish]; Raoul Patrick Masterson [1963] Director [Irish]

Equitvain Limited
Incorporated: 14 June 1985
Net Worth: £653,641 *Total Assets:* £784,402
Registered Office: Winpenny House, 135-137 High Street, Yarm, Cleveland, TS15 9AY
Activities: Other letting and operating of own or leased real estate
Shareholders: Thomas Malcolm Swanston; Patricia Anne Swanston
Officers: Patricia Anne Swanston, Secretary; Patricia Anne Swanston [1948] Director/Company Secretary; Thomas Malcolm Swanston [1949] Director

Equity Release (Increments) Limited
Incorporated: 4 August 2006
Net Worth: £2,042,754 *Total Assets:* £97,649,136
Registered Office: Cross House, Westgate Road, Newcastle upon Tyne, NE1 4XX
Activities: Buying and selling of own real estate
Parent: Retirement Bridge Limited
Officers: Paul Trevor Barber [1967] Director; Ashish Kashyap [1979] Director; Antony Lewis Pierce [1976] Finance Director

Equity Release Investment Properties Limited
Incorporated: 1 February 2005
Net Worth Deficit: £12,621,789 *Total Assets:* £5,840,548
Registered Office: Cross House, Westgate Road, Newcastle upon Tyne, NE1 4XX
Activities: Buying and selling of own real estate
Parent: Retirement Bridge Limited
Officers: Paul Trevor Barber [1967] Director; Antony Lewis Pierce [1976] Finance Director

Ergo Flex Enterprises Limited
Incorporated: 6 February 2008
Net Worth: £3,132,346 *Total Assets:* £3,148,988
Registered Office: 246 Park View, Whitley Bay, Tyne & Wear, NE26 3QX
Activities: Activities of head offices
Shareholders: Margaret Jack; Gerald Joseph MacEwan
Officers: Margaret Jack, Secretary; Generald Joseph MacEwan [1976] Director

Erico Europa (G.B.) Limited
Incorporated: 9 May 1972
Net Worth: £1,827,915 *Total Assets:* £2,274,875
Registered Office: 3 Rutherford Road, Stephenson Industrial Estate, Washington, Tyne & Wear, NE37 3HX
Activities: Manufacture of other fabricated metal products n.e.c.
Parent: Nvent Electric PLC
Officers: Sylvain Henri Corneel Lemmens [1957] Director/Pentair Project Leader SAP Implementation [Belgian]; Marek Tapsik [1974] Director/Pentair Associate General Counsel EMEA [Czech]

Erimus Holdings Teesside Limited
Incorporated: 20 September 2009
Net Worth: £2,031,925 *Total Assets:* £2,777,431
Registered Office: 2 Kingfisher Court, Kingfisher Way, Bowesfield Park, Stockton on Tees, Cleveland, TS18 3EX
Activities: Activities of insurance agents and brokers
Shareholders: Paul James Davison; Shaun David Edward Hughes
Officers: Paul James Davison [1973] Director; Shaun David Edward Hughes [1962] Director; Ian David Miller [1981] Director; Scott Stephen Pinnell [1976] Director

Claire Errington Limited
Incorporated: 11 July 1958
Net Worth: £1,262,696 *Total Assets:* £1,329,719
Registered Office: 8 Beechfield Road, Gosforth, Newcastle upon Tyne, NE3 4DR
Activities: Activities of open-ended investment companies
Major Shareholder: Hilary Claire Errington
Officers: Hilary Claire Errington, Secretary; Hilary Claire Errington [1959] Director; Richard Roger Errington [1957] Director

Esh Construction Limited
Incorporated: 10 August 1990 *Employees:* 754
Net Worth: £19,754,000 *Total Assets:* £63,759,000
Registered Office: Esh House, Bowburn North Industrial Estate, Bowburn, Co Durham, DH6 5PF
Activities: Construction of commercial buildings
Parent: Esh Holdings Limited
Officers: Mark Sowerby, Secretary; Mr John Peter Davies [1966] Director/Civil Servant; Alistair Law [1971] Director/Accountant; Stephen Leadbitter [1967] Director; Andrew Edward Radcliffe [1973] Finance Director; Mark Andrew Sowerby [1971] Director; Paul Watson [1970] Commercial Director; Stephen Thomas Wilkie [1971] Director

Esh Developments Limited
Incorporated: 24 May 1993 *Employees:* 8
Net Worth: £1,562 *Total Assets:* £17,476,794
Registered Office: Esh House, Bowburn North Industrial Estate, Bowburn, Co Durham, DH6 5PF
Activities: Buying and selling of own real estate
Parent: Esh Holdings Limited
Officers: Mark Sowerby, Secretary; Michael Francis Hogan [1944] Director/Contractor; David Horrocks [1959] Director; Andrew Edward Radcliffe [1973] Finance Director; Mark Andrew Sowerby [1971] Director

Esh Holdings Limited
Incorporated: 3 March 1999 *Employees:* 1,038
Net Worth: £41,382,000 *Total Assets:* £110,686,000
Registered Office: Esh House, Bowburn North Industrial Estate, Bowburn, Co Durham, DH6 5PF
Activities: Development of building projects
Parent: Esh Investments Limited
Officers: Mark Sowerby, Secretary; Anthony John Carroll [1939] Director; John Peter Davies [1966] Director; Michael Francis Hogan [1944] Director; John George Lumsden [1968] Director; Andrew Edward Radcliffe [1973] Director; Mark Andrew Sowerby [1971] Director; Paul Garth Watson [1970] Director; Stephen Thomas Wilkie [1971] Director

Esh Homes Limited
Incorporated: 14 February 2014 *Employees:* 18
Net Worth Deficit: £622,691 *Total Assets:* £5,795,601
Registered Office: Esh House, Bowburn North Industrial Estate, Bowburn, Co Durham, DH6 5PF
Activities: Construction of domestic buildings
Parent: Esh Holdings Limited
Officers: Mark Sowerby, Secretary; Philip James Brown [1970] Director; David Horrocks [1959] Director; Andrew Edward Radcliffe [1973] Director; Mark Andrew Sowerby [1971] Director

Esh Investments Limited
Incorporated: 29 October 2014 *Employees:* 1,038
Net Worth: £54,999,000 *Total Assets:* £124,188,000
Registered Office: Esh House, Bowburn North Industrial Estate, Bowburn, Co Durham, DH6 5PF
Activities: Development of building projects
Shareholder: Vestbrown (Esh) Limited
Officers: Mark Sowerby, Secretary; Anthony John Carroll [1939] Director; Philip Sydney Coates [1955] Director; John Peter Davies [1966] Director; Michael Francis Hogan [1944] Director; John George Lumsden [1968] Director; Andrew Edward Radcliffe [1973] Director; Mark Andrew Sowerby [1971] Director

Esh Space The Park Limited
Incorporated: 13 February 2007
Net Worth Deficit: £3,689,301 *Total Assets:* £3,646,898
Registered Office: The Farm House, Hedley Hill Farm, Cornsay Colliery, Co Durham, DH7 9EX
Activities: Development of building projects
Parent: Vestbrown (ESPL) Ltd
Officers: Philip Sydney Coates, Secretary; Michael Francis Hogan [1944] Director; Andrew Edward Radcliffe [1973] Director; Alexander John Turnbull [1956] Director

Esh-MWH Limited
Incorporated: 21 September 2015 *Employees:* 4
Net Worth: £2 *Total Assets:* £951,497
Registered Office: Esh House, Bowburn North Industrial Estate, Bowburn, Co Durham, DH6 5PF
Activities: Construction of water projects
Shareholders: Esh Construction Limited; MWH UK Limited
Officers: Andrew Radcliffe, Secretary; John Peter Davies [1966] Director; Catherine Margaret Schefer [1968] Director; Stephen Thomas Wilkie [1971] Director; Tracy Ann Worrall [1973] Director

Eshott South Farm Limited
Incorporated: 22 August 1995
Net Worth: £729,549 *Total Assets:* £1,099,822
Registered Office: Eshott South Farm, Felton, Morpeth, Northumberland, NE65 9ES
Activities: Growing of cereals (except rice), leguminous crops and oil seeds
Shareholders: Hugh Glenville Howard Sanderson; Nicola Garbutt Sanderson
Officers: Nicola Garbutt Sanderson, Secretary; Hugh Glenville Howard Sanderson [1951] Director/Farmer

Esschem Europe Limited
Incorporated: 25 October 2000 *Employees:* 24
Net Worth: £2,862,687 *Total Assets:* £4,563,748
Registered Office: Unit 3 Hall Dene Way, Seaham Grange Industrial Estate, Seaham, Co Durham, SR7 0PU
Activities: Manufacture of paints, varnishes and similar coatings, mastics and sealants
Officers: Gary Raymond Shaw, Secretary/Managing Director; Henry Milne Justi [1959] Director/Attorney [American]; Stephen Harvey Morrison III [1960] Director/Financial Officer [American]; Gary Raymond Shaw [1964] Director - Research & Development & Technical Sale

Essential Aluminium Limited
Incorporated: 8 November 2001
Net Worth: £595,647 *Total Assets:* £771,431
Registered Office: Unit 12, Dewley Court, Westway Industrial Estate, Throckley, Tyne & Wear, NE15 9AW
Activities: Manufacture of doors and windows of metal
Shareholder: Victoria Louise Wadds
Officers: Victoria Louise Wadds, Secretary; Stephen Christopher Wadds [1960] Director; Victoria Louise Wadds [1970] Director/Company Administrator

Essex and Suffolk Water Limited
Incorporated: 6 August 1991
Net Worth: £15,684,000 *Total Assets:* £15,710,000
Registered Office: Northumbria House, Abbey Road, Pity Me, Durham, DH1 5FJ
Activities: Non-trading company
Parent: NWG Commercial Solutions Limited
Officers: Martin Parker, Secretary; Christopher Ian Johns [1970] Director/Accountant; Heidi Mottram [1965] Director/Chief Executive Officer; Martin Parker [1959] Director/Solicitor

Etro Group Ltd
Incorporated: 17 September 2013
Net Worth: £1,300,210 *Total Assets:* £1,500,240
Registered Office: Bulman House, Regent Centre, Gosforth, Newcastle upon Tyne, NE3 3LS
Activities: Activities of other holding companies n.e.c.
Shareholders: Suresh Kumar Jerath; Ritu Rajni Jerath
Officers: Suresh Kumar Jerath, Secretary; Ritu Rajni Jerath [1970] Director; Suresh Kumar Jerath [1963] Director

Etro Investments Limited
Incorporated: 16 February 2012
Net Worth: £511,519 *Total Assets:* £1,555,934
Registered Office: Bulman House, Regent Centre, Gosforth, Newcastle upon Tyne, NE3 3LS
Activities: Buying and selling of own real estate
Parent: Etro Group Limited
Officers: Suresh Kumar Jerath, Secretary; Ritu Rajni Jerath [1970] Director; Suresh Kumar Jerath [1963] Director

Etro Properties Limited
Incorporated: 15 March 2011
Net Worth: £2,327,873 *Total Assets:* £5,428,580
Registered Office: Bulman House, Regent Centre, Gosforth, Newcastle upon Tyne, NE3 3LS
Activities: Buying and selling of own real estate
Parent: Etro Group Limted
Officers: Suresh Kumar Jerath, Secretary; Ritu Rajni Jerath [1970] Director/Physiotherapist; Suresh Kumar Jerath [1963] Director

Euremica Limited
Incorporated: 2 June 1967 *Employees:* 3
Net Worth: £805,293 *Total Assets:* £827,287
Registered Office: 21 Belmangate, Guisborough, Cleveland, TS14 7AB
Activities: Other letting and operating of own or leased real estate
Major Shareholder: Mark Berwick Baty
Officers: Natalie Ursula Linford, Secretary; Joy Baty [1949] Director; Mark Berwick Baty [1956] Director/Chairman; Thelma Rose Baty [1934] Director; Natalie Ursula Linford [1969] Finance Director

Euro Contract Leasing Limited
Incorporated: 1 July 1998
Net Worth: £228,458 *Total Assets:* £1,547,347
Registered Office: Cowpen Bewley Road, Haverton Hill, Billingham, Stockton on Tees, Cleveland, TS23 4EX
Activities: Renting and leasing of cars and light motor vehicles
Parent: North East Truck & Van Limited
Officers: Ian Thomas Hopkins [1966] Director; Steven Lane [1963] Aftersales Support Director; Alexander William McDonald [1955] Joint Managing Director; John William McDonald [1989] Director

Euro Foods (GB) Limited
Incorporated: 27 November 2005 *Employees:* 20
Net Worth: £630,736 *Total Assets:* £953,939
Registered Office: 32 Brenkley Way, Blezard Business Park, Seaton Burn, Newcastle upon Tyne, NE13 6DS
Activities: Production of meat and poultry meat products
Shareholders: Haluk Zeki Onenc; Sumer Sardagi
Officers: Haluk Zeki Onenc, Secretary; Ali Ihsan Inan [1971] Director; Haluk Zeki Onenc [1954] Director [Turkish]; Sumer Sardagi [1967] Director [Turkish]

Euro GPS Limited
Incorporated: 30 September 2005 *Employees:* 1
Net Worth: £1,184,964 *Total Assets:* £1,339,592
Registered Office: 30 Rosedale Avenue, South Bents, Sunderland, Tyne & Wear, SR6 8BD
Activities: General medical practice activities
Shareholders: Elahe Khorshidi; Dr Atiqullah Sadeqzada
Officers: Elahe Khorshidi, Secretary/Student [Afghan]; Elahe Khorshidi [1983] Director [Afghan]; Dr Atiqullah Sadeqzada [1963] Director/Doctor [German]

Euro Property Management Ltd
Incorporated: 21 February 2005
Net Worth: £636,122 *Total Assets:* £1,076,418
Registered Office: 7 Bankside, The Watermark, Gateshead, Tyne & Wear, NE11 9SY
Activities: Development of building projects
Major Shareholder: Jonathan Paul Whitfield
Officers: Jonathan Paul Whitfield [1968] Director

Euro Super Abrasives Limited
Incorporated: 23 May 2013 *Employees:* 3
Net Worth: £328,046 *Total Assets:* £1,021,688
Registered Office: 2 Union Square, Central Park, Darlington, Co Durham, DL1 1GL
Activities: Other retail sale not in stores, stalls or markets
Major Shareholder: Richard Arthur Lee
Officers: Philip Robert Davis [1968] Director; Richard Arthur Lee [1955] Director/Business Analyst - Non Financial; Raymond Mason [1958] Director/Salesman

Eurojag Limited
Incorporated: 5 July 1995
Net Worth: £580,615 *Total Assets:* £1,180,264
Registered Office: Sovereign House, Hurworth Moor, Darlington, Co Durham, DL2 1QH
Activities: Retail trade of motor vehicle parts and accessories
Major Shareholder: Peter Francis Robertshaw
Officers: Peter Francis Robertshaw [1957] Director

European Horseboxes Limited
Incorporated: 19 September 2016
Net Worth: £24,076 *Total Assets:* £1,440,921
Registered Office: Hadrian House, Front Street, Chester-le-Street, Co Durham, DH3 3DB
Activities: Sale of used cars and light motor vehicles
Shareholders: David Beckett; Claire Louise Young
Officers: David Beckett [1973] Director; Emily Charlotte Box [1990] Director; Claire Louise Young [1969] Director

European Vehicle Contracts Limited
Incorporated: 12 March 2008 *Employees:* 37
Net Worth: £353,476 *Total Assets:* £1,291,802
Registered Office: 9 Apex Business Village, Annitsford, Cramlington, Northumberland, NE23 7BF
Activities: Other service activities n.e.c.
Parent: Maxxia (UK) Limited
Officers: Lisa Joanne Edwards, Secretary; Mark Sutherland Blackburn [1957] Director [Australian]; Stephen Andrew Dixon [1963] Director; Geoffrey Robert Kruyt [1968] Director/Business Executive [Australian]; Michael Neil Salisbury [1965] Director [Australian]; Gareth Shaw [1971] Director

Eutechnyx Holdings Limited
Incorporated: 29 July 1996 *Employees:* 2
Net Worth: £2,395,968 *Total Assets:* £2,672,265
Registered Office: Live Works, 55-57 Quayside, Newcastle upon Tyne, NE1 3DE
Activities: Activities of head offices
Parent: Prime Ventures
Officers: Brian Henry Jobling [1968] Director; Darren Jobling [1966] Director

G A Evans Roofing Contractors Limited
Incorporated: 25 October 2000
Registered Office: 61 Devonworth Place, Cowpen Estate, Blyth, Northumberland, NE24 5AE
Activities: Roofing activities
Major Shareholder: Glen Anthony Evans
Officers: Gillian Evans, Secretary; Gillian Evans [1969] Director/Roofing; Glen Anthony Evans [1966] Director/Roofing Contractor; Liam Evans [1996] Director; Natalie Marie Evans [1991] Director/Pharmacist

Eve UK Properties LLP
Incorporated: 10 April 2008
Net Worth: £1,725,165 *Total Assets:* £3,632,428
Registered Office: 43 Maxwell Street, South Shields, Tyne & Wear, NE33 4PU
Officers: Derek Edward West [1949] Member; Jean West [1949] Member

Ever 1209 Limited
Incorporated: 15 October 1999 *Employees:* 276
Net Worth: £5,094,338 *Total Assets:* £20,760,146
Registered Office: 15-16 Stockholm Close, Tyne Tunnel Trading Estate, North Shields, Tyne & Wear, NE29 7ST
Activities: Activities of extraterritorial organisations and bodies
Shareholder: Mandeep Singh Ladhar
Officers: Bhupinder Singh Ladhar [1981] Director/Self Employed; Mandeep Singh Ladhar [1985] Director

Ever 1855 Limited
Incorporated: 2 August 2002
Net Worth: £8,986,320 *Total Assets:* £13,943,573
Registered Office: 2nd Floor, Building 7, Queens Park, Queensway, Team Valley Trading Estate, Gateshead, Tyne & Wear, NE11 0QD
Activities: Other business support service activities n.e.c.
Parent: UK Land Estates (Partnership) Limited
Officers: Jerome Christian Kathleen Anselme [1974] Director [French]; Michael O'Shaughnessy [1972] Director [American]; Joseph Martin Pedlow [1962] Director [British/American]; Richard Alexander Pellatt [1976] Director; Stephen Smith [1953] Director; Alan Keith Taylor [1963] Treasury Director; Christopher John Whitfield [1963] Director

Evergreen Pallet Solutions (UK) Limited
Incorporated: 18 April 1996 *Employees:* 17
Net Worth: £617,592 *Total Assets:* £896,412
Registered Office: Unit 7 Albert Hill Industrial Estate, Dodsworth Street, Darlington, Co Durham, DL1 2NG
Activities: Manufacture of wooden containers
Major Shareholder: Paul Graham Tait
Officers: Paul Graham Tait, Secretary; Graham Michael Tait [1984] Director; Paul Graham Tait [1958] Director

Evergreen Park Limited
Incorporated: 23 August 2004 *Employees:* 2
Net Worth: £905,259 *Total Assets:* £974,964
Registered Office: Evergreen Park, Coast Road, Crimdon Dene, Hartlepool, Cleveland, TS27 4BW
Activities: Buying and selling of own real estate
Officers: Robert Douglas Drummond [1957] Director/Park Site Operator

Everris Limited
Incorporated: 1 February 2011 *Employees:* 56
Net Worth: £4,395,000 *Total Assets:* £24,793,000
Registered Office: Boulby Mine, Loftus, Saltburn-by-the-Sea, N Yorks, TS13 4UZ
Activities: Other manufacturing n.e.c.
Parent: Cleveland Potash Limited
Officers: Cornelis Petrus Langeveld [1952] Managing Director [Dutch]; Stephen Squires [1966] Business Director

IC & MJ Evershed Limited
Incorporated: 12 April 2012
Registered Office: Greenbank House, Sotherby Road, Middlesbrough, Cleveland, TS3 8BT
Activities: Remediation activities and other waste management services
Shareholders: Ian Cyril Evershed; Margaret Jane Evershed
Officers: Margaret Jane Evershed, Secretary; Ian Cyril Evershed [1942] Director

Eversley Management Limited
Incorporated: 20 March 2002
Net Worth: £353,203 *Total Assets:* £941,443
Registered Office: Yoden House, 30 Yoden Way, Peterlee, Co Durham, SR8 1AL
Activities: Management consultancy activities other than financial management
Shareholder: Richard Blass
Officers: Joshua Blass, Secretary; Richard Blass [1952] Director/Hairdresser

Evolution Gateshead Developments LLP
Incorporated: 23 March 2012
Net Worth Deficit: £27,481 *Total Assets:* £11,176,517
Registered Office: 2 Esh Plaza, Sir Bobby Robson Way Great Park, Newcastle upon Tyne, NE13 9BA

Evolution Valves Limited
Incorporated: 9 June 2010 *Employees:* 7
Net Worth: £341,408 *Total Assets:* £1,248,048
Registered Office: Evolution House, Limeoak Way, St Anns Industrial Estate, Stockton on Tees, Cleveland, TS18 2LS
Activities: Manufacture of taps and valves
Shareholders: Steven Timothy Heap; Mark Peter Cone
Officers: Mark Peter Cone [1957] Director; Steven Timothy Heap [1962] Managing Director

EVT Contractors Limited
Incorporated: 24 April 2002 *Employees:* 15
Net Worth: £1,520,479 *Total Assets:* £1,774,858
Registered Office: Dunelm Cottage, Park Street, Willington, Crook, Co Durham, DL15 0ER
Activities: Repair of other equipment
Major Shareholder: John Edward (Junior) Wright
Officers: Lisa Bell, Secretary; John Edward Wright Jnr [1967] Director/Construction Industry Contract

Ewart and Dilworth Limited
Incorporated: 21 August 1996
Registered Office: Ferguson Lodge, Fergusons Lane, Old Benwell Village, Newcastle upon Tyne, NE15 7PL
Activities: Other human health activities
Shareholders: Philip Ewart; Robert Ewart
Officers: Philip Laurence Ewart, Secretary/General Services Manager; Philip Laurence Ewart [1972] Director/General Services Manager; Robert Ewart [1942] Director

EWM Hightec Welding UK Limited
Incorporated: 4 November 2008 *Employees:* 9
Net Worth: £516,223 *Total Assets:* £1,305,344
Registered Office: Unit 2 Coopies Way, Coopies Lane Industrial Estate, Morpeth, Northumberland, NE61 6JN
Activities: Wholesale of machine tools
Parent: EWM AG
Officers: Alan Cauchi [1969] Managing Director

EWP Technical Services Limited
Incorporated: 4 March 2002
Net Worth Deficit: £5,752,000 *Total Assets:* £1,064,000
Registered Office: Shared Services Centre, Q3 Office, Quorum Business Park, Benton Lane, Newcastle upon Tyne, NE12 8EX
Activities: Other service activities n.e.c.
Parent: Engie Services Limited
Officers: Sarah Gregory, Secretary; Simon David Pinnell [1964] Director

Ex-Pro Products Limited
Incorporated: 22 December 2011 *Employees:* 18
Net Worth: £529,417 *Total Assets:* £1,315,712
Registered Office: Ex-Pro House, 7 Bradbury Road, Norton, Stockton on Tees, Cleveland, TS20 1LD
Activities: Retail sale via mail order houses or via Internet
Shareholders: Paul Spencer; Virginia Serencio Spencer
Officers: Paul Spencer [1972] Director; Virginia Spencer [1989] Director

Excalibur Realty UK Limited
Incorporated: 13 July 2007
Net Worth: £4,510,243 *Total Assets:* £4,636,584
Registered Office: Titanium House, Hanzard Drive, Wynyard Park, Stockton on Tees, Cleveland, TS22 5FD
Activities: Other letting and operating of own or leased real estate
Parent: Venator Pigments UK Limited
Officers: Richard Justin James Phillipson, Secretary; Kurt David Ogden [1968] Director/Finance [American]; John Jeffrey Pehrson [1975] Director [American]; Richard Justin James Phillipson [1968] Director/Solicitor; Russell Robert Stolle [1962] Director/Attorney [American]; Simon Turner [1963] Director/President

The Excel Academy Partnership
Incorporated: 7 November 2011 *Employees:* 118
Net Worth: £8,262,000 *Total Assets:* £10,233,000
Registered Office: Newton Drive, Framwellgate Moor, Durham, DH1 5BQ
Activities: General secondary education
Officers: Karen Cromarty [1961] Director/Senior Lead Advisor; Angela Freda Darnell [1953] Director/Teacher; Professor Michael Peter Fleming [1951] Director/University Academic - Emeritus Professor; Colin Hillary [1950] Director/Retired Chartered Civil Engineer; Amanda Jayne Hopgood [1970] Director/County Councillor; Rachael McLauchlan [1978] Director/Chief Audit Executive; Karenza Passmore [1966] Director/Resource Centre Manager; Paul Robert Stewart [1970] Director/Solicitor; Richard Warneford [1969] Director

Excel District Energy Company Limited
Incorporated: 27 December 2012 *Employees:* 2
Net Worth: £28,000 *Total Assets:* £10,985,000
Registered Office: Shared Services Centre, Q3 Office, Quorum Business Park, Benton Lane, Newcastle upon Tyne, NE12 8EX
Activities: Production of electricity
Parent: Engie Urban Energy Group Limited
Officers: Sarah Gregory, Secretary; Andrew David Hart [1969] Managing Director; Lee Kitchen [1979] Director/Accountant

Excello Limited
Incorporated: 25 May 2005
Net Worth: £1,987,121 *Total Assets:* £2,506,516
Registered Office: Unit G21, 11th Avenue North, Team Valley Trading Estate, Gateshead, Tyne & Wear, NE11 0NJ
Activities: Unlicensed carriers
Shareholders: Jonathan Wylie Beswick; Antony John Harris
Officers: Jonathan Beswick, Secretary; Jonathan Beswick [1967] Director/Salesman; Anthony Harris [1963] Director/Operations Manager

Excelsior Services (Student Accommodation) Limited
Incorporated: 3 February 2014 *Employees:* 2
Net Worth: £667,639 *Total Assets:* £2,131,358
Registered Office: The Old Hall, Benedict Road, Roker, Sunderland, Tyne & Wear, SR6 0NX
Activities: Electrical installation
Shareholders: Robert Wilson; John Steven Richardson
Officers: John Steven Richardson [1967] Director; Robert Wilson [1966] Director

Exclusive Bedrooms North East Limited
Incorporated: 16 February 1999 *Employees:* 18
Net Worth: £4,205,878 *Total Assets:* £4,841,315
Registered Office: 246 Park View, Whitley Bay, Tyne & Wear, NE26 3QX
Activities: Retail of furniture, lighting, and similar (not musical instruments or scores) in specialised store
Major Shareholder: Gregory Carlisle
Officers: Ayca Carlisle, Secretary; Gregory Carlisle [1971] Director

Exclusive Care Group Ltd
Incorporated: 27 April 2015
Net Worth: £222 *Total Assets:* £1,887,023
Registered Office: Houghton House, New Road, Team Valley Trading Estate, Gateshead, Tyne & Wear, NE11 0JU
Activities: Residential nursing care facilities
Major Shareholder: Jennifer Pamela Houghton
Officers: George Houghton [1940] Director; Jennifer Pamela Houghton [1946] Director/Healthcare Consultant

Exelby Services Limited
Incorporated: 23 December 1976 *Employees:* 82
Net Worth: £12,344,597 *Total Assets:* £14,453,305
Registered Office: Coneygarth House, Leases Road, Leeming Bar, Northallerton, N Yorks, DL7 9FE
Activities: Agents involved in the sale of fuels, ores, metals and industrial chemicals
Major Shareholder: Michael Exelby
Officers: Shaun Bennington, Secretary; Michael Exelby [1957] Director; Robert Exelby [1986] Operations Director

Exis (Group) Limited
Incorporated: 24 March 2014
Net Worth: £475,004 *Total Assets:* £925,004
Registered Office: 3 Trinity Court, Faverdale North, Darlington, Co Durham, DL3 0PH
Activities: Activities of head offices
Officers: Robert Ahlborn [1951] Director [American]; William James Douglas [1960] Director; David George Hallam [1955] Director; Ian Lennard [1964] Director [American]; Shirley Christine Morton [1959] Director/Programmer; Richard Nagle [1958] Director [American]; Kris Wiede [1968] Director [American]

Exis Technologies Limited
Incorporated: 7 March 1986 *Employees:* 17
Net Worth: £584,159 *Total Assets:* £1,215,880
Registered Office: 3 Trinity Court, Faverdale North, Darlington, Co Durham, DL3 0PH
Activities: Information technology consultancy activities
Parent: Exis Holdings Limited
Officers: Robert Ahlborn [1951] Director [American]; William James Douglas [1960] Director; David George Hallam [1955] Director/Programmer; Ian Lennard [1964] Director [American]; Shirley Christine Morton [1959] Director/Programmer; Richard Nagle [1958] Director [American]; Kris Wiede [1968] Director [American]

The Expanded Metal Company Limited
Incorporated: 24 November 2005 *Employees:* 91
Net Worth: £5,557,000 *Total Assets:* £10,389,000
Registered Office: P O Box 14, Longhill Industrial Estate North, Hartlepool, Cleveland, TS25 1PR
Activities: Forging, pressing, stamping and roll-forming of metal; powder metallurgy
Parent: Expanded Metal Holdings Limited
Officers: John Bland Charlton, Secretary; Philip James Astley [1968] Director; John Bland Charlton [1962] Director/Chartered Accountant

Expanded Metal Holdings Limited
Incorporated: 9 October 2006 *Employees:* 93
Net Worth: £6,055,000 *Total Assets:* £9,517,000
Registered Office: P O Box 14, Greatham Street, Longhill Industrial Estate, Hartlepool, Cleveland, TS25 1PR
Activities: Activities of head offices
Parent: Emco Acquisition LLC
Officers: John Bland Charlton, Secretary; Philip James Astley [1968] Director; John Bland Charlton [1962] Director/Chartered Accountant

Expertcare Limited
Incorporated: 28 January 2010 *Employees:* 16
Net Worth: £192,464 *Total Assets:* £823,232
Registered Office: 15 Bentinck Road, Fairfield, Stockton on Tees, Cleveland, TS19 7QB
Activities: Other human health activities
Shareholders: Arif Aziz; Syma Aziz
Officers: Arif Aziz [1980] Director; Syma Aziz [1980] Director

Expertise Properties Limited
Incorporated: 24 December 1990
Net Worth: £385,898 *Total Assets:* £5,422,212
Registered Office: Norman Hurst, Westoe Village, South Shields, Tyne & Wear, NE33 3EB
Activities: Buying and selling of own real estate
Shareholder: Victoria Grace Long
Officers: Michael Albert Long, Secretary; Michael Albert Long [1961] Director; Victoria Grace Long [1964] Director

Explain Market Research Limited
Incorporated: 15 December 1993 *Employees:* 78
Net Worth: £537,667 *Total Assets:* £789,947
Registered Office: 48 Leazes Park Road, Newcastle upon Tyne, NE1 4PG
Activities: Market research and public opinion polling
Shareholders: Gillian Shiel; David James Shiel
Officers: David James Shiel, Secretary/Director; Kim Davis [1975] Research Director; Claire Riley [1971] Director; David James Shiel [1951] Director; Gillian Shiel [1962] Director; Stephen Derek Slater [1968] Director/Chartered Accountant

Exponential Derivatives Limited
Incorporated: 4 January 2011 *Employees:* 2
Net Worth: £5,049,897 *Total Assets:* £5,285,184
Registered Office: 56 Darras Road, Ponteland, Northumberland, NE20 9PG
Activities: Security and commodity contracts dealing activities
Major Shareholder: Ian Alexander Liddle
Officers: Ian Alexander Liddle [1980] Director; Yuqin Zou [1977] Director [Chinese]

Express Engineering (Aerospace) Limited
Incorporated: 5 June 2013 *Employees:* 69
Net Worth Deficit: £2,826,577 *Total Assets:* £2,811,123
Registered Office: c/o Express Engineering, Kingsway North, Team Valley Trading Estate, Gateshead, Tyne & Wear, NE11 0EG
Activities: Manufacture of other general-purpose machinery n.e.c.
Parent: Express Engineering (Holdings) Ltd
Officers: Mark James Morgan Bevan [1969] Finance Director; Eric James Lewis [1947] Director; John Patterson [1963] Director

Express Engineering (Gateshead) Limited
Incorporated: 13 December 1978 *Employees:* 142
Net Worth: £15,478,537 *Total Assets:* £23,275,544
Registered Office: Kingsway North, Team Valley Trading Estate, Gateshead, Tyne & Wear, NE11 0EG
Activities: Machining
Parent: Express Engineering (Holdings) Ltd
Officers: William Barclay [1966] Sales Director; Mark James Morgan Bevan [1969] Finance Director; Eric James Lewis [1947] Director; John Patterson [1963] Director; Kevin Scott [1955] Technical Director

Express Engineering (Group) Limited
Incorporated: 11 July 2013 *Employees:* 202
Net Worth: £17,203,030 *Total Assets:* £35,679,792
Registered Office: Kingsway North, Team Valley Trading Estate, Gateshead, Tyne & Wear, NE11 0EG
Activities: Activities of other holding companies n.e.c.
Shareholder: Christopher Scott Thompson
Officers: Mark James Morgan Bevan [1969] Finance Director; Eric James Lewis [1947] Director; Gareth Marshall [1982] Director; John Patterson [1963] Director; Robin Clive Powell [1965] Director; Christopher Scott Thompson [1956] Director

Express Engineering (Industrial Products) Limited
Incorporated: 24 June 2013 *Employees:* 11
Net Worth: £779,730 *Total Assets:* £1,072,860
Registered Office: c/o Express Engineering, Kingsway North, Team Valley Trading Estate, Gateshead, Tyne & Wear, NE11 0EG
Activities: Machining
Parent: Express Engineering (Holdings) Ltd
Officers: Mark James Morgan Bevan [1969] Finance Director; Eric James Lewis [1947] Director; John Patterson [1963] Director

Express Holdings (Thompson) Limited
Incorporated: 12 December 1996 *Employees:* 10
Net Worth: £5,859,018 *Total Assets:* £6,745,243
Registered Office: Express Group, 398A Princesway North, Team Valley Trading Estate, Gateshead, Tyne & Wear, NE11 0TU
Activities: Buying and selling of own real estate
Parent: Yogo Investments Limited
Officers: Christopher Scott Thompson [1956] Director/Engineer; Lynn Wilson [1969] Director/Accountant

Express Lasers Limited
Incorporated: 8 December 2005
Registered Office: Impress NE Ltd, Ryton Industrial Estate, Newburn Bridge Road, Blaydon on Tyne, Tyne & Wear, NE21 4SQ
Activities: Other engineering activities
Officers: David Haley, Secretary/Accountant; Peter Douglass [1956] Director/Engineer; Lee Heslop [1971] Director/Engineer; George Peel [1957] Director/Engineer; Steven Young [1960] Director/Engineer

Extol Academy Trust
Incorporated: 7 June 2013 *Employees:* 98
Net Worth: £12,123,595 *Total Assets:* £13,397,673
Registered Office: Eldon Grove Academy, Eldon Grove, Hartlepool, Cleveland, TS26 9LY
Activities: Primary education
Officers: Arthur Stephen Blake [1960] Director/Group Treasurer; Margaret Elizabeth Bousfield [1949] Director/Retired; Michael William Bretherick [1957] Director; Jacqueline Butterworth [1963] Director/Medical Professional; Julie Denise Deville [1959] Director/Executive Headteacher; Leo Gillen [1956] Director; Derek Richardson [1960] Programme Director; Philip Michael Tye [1975] Director/Operations Manager

Extrahold Limited
Incorporated: 30 September 2009
Net Worth: £146,418 *Total Assets:* £2,884,334
Registered Office: Lion House, 400 Durham Road, Birtley, Chester-le-Street, Co Durham, DH3 1LS
Activities: Other letting and operating of own or leased real estate
Major Shareholder: Stevie Lee Pattinson
Officers: Stevie-Lee Pattinson [1969] Director

Exwold Technology Limited
Incorporated: 29 July 1992 *Employees:* 105
Net Worth: £4,537,084 *Total Assets:* £9,496,290
Registered Office: P O Box 270, Brenda Road, Hartlepool, Cleveland, TS25 2BW
Activities: Manufacture of pesticides and other agrochemical products
Parent: Hartlepool Investments Ltd
Officers: Andrea Gallant, Secretary; Michael Terence Hird [1946] Director/Investment Manager; Kevin James Martin [1964] Director/Engineer; Samantha Jane Price [1969] Director; James Alexander Robson [1960] Director/Engineer; David Tunney [1958] Director

Eyeworks Industries Limited
Incorporated: 7 March 2007
Net Worth: £54,716 *Total Assets:* £1,446,481
Registered Office: 54 North End, Longhoughton, Alnwick, Northumberland, NE66 3JP
Activities: Agents specialised in the sale of other particular products
Major Shareholder: Douglas James Denholm
Officers: Jamie Denholm [1970] Director

Eyms Group Limited
Incorporated: 17 October 1986 *Employees:* 710
Net Worth: £12,463,972 *Total Assets:* £29,168,116
Registered Office: 41-51 Grey Street, Newcastle upon Tyne, NE1 6EE
Activities: Other urban, suburban or metropolitan passenger land transport (not underground, metro or similar)
Major Shareholder: Peter John Sidney Shipp
Officers: Carolyn Ferguson, Secretary; David Allen Brown [1960] Director; Simon Patrick Butcher [1967] Director; Gary Edmundson [1967] Director; Alexander Paul Edwards [1966] Director; Martijn Lee Gilbert [1982] Director; Stephen King [1978] Director

Ezimix Limited
Incorporated: 3 October 2001
Net Worth: £594,691 *Total Assets:* £938,905
Registered Office: 2 Westmorland Rise, Peterlee, Co Durham, SR8 2EX
Activities: Other manufacturing n.e.c.
Shareholders: Kenneth Fox; Jean Fox; Stephen Fox
Officers: Jean Fox, Secretary/Director; Jean Fox [1946] Director; Kenneth Fox [1942] Director; Stephen Fox [1974] Director

F & I Holdings Ltd
Incorporated: 9 August 2016 *Employees:* 203
Net Worth: £9,426,252 *Total Assets:* £13,083,178
Registered Office: A1 Marquis Court, Team Valley Trading Estate, Gateshead, Tyne & Wear, NE11 0RU
Activities: Activities of construction holding companies
Shareholders: John Flowers; Jenny Flowers
Officers: Jenny Flowers [1956] Director; John Flowers [1957] Director

F K Solutions (UK) Limited
Incorporated: 18 May 2003 *Employees:* 7
Net Worth: £1,830,087 *Total Assets:* £2,260,670
Registered Office: Moguntia Food Ingredients UK Limited, Unit 1 Hetton Lyons Industrial Estate, Hetton-le-Hole, Houghton-le-Spring, Co Durham, DH5 0RH
Activities: Manufacture of other food products n.e.c.
Major Shareholder: Ralph Karl Buchholz
Officers: Frank Campanaro [1958] Director; Colin Hitch [1961] Director

F&I Management Limited
Incorporated: 16 June 2003 *Employees:* 34
Net Worth: £1,336,327 *Total Assets:* £1,682,617
Registered Office: B3 Kingfisher House, Kingsway, Team Valley Trading Estate, Gateshead, Tyne & Wear, NE11 0JU
Activities: Other business support service activities n.e.c.
Parent: F & I Holdings Limited
Officers: Jeanette Flowers, Secretary; Jeanette Flowers [1956] Director; John Flowers [1957] Director; Michael Norman Watson [1971] Director

F.M. Steelstock Limited
Incorporated: 13 January 1987 *Employees:* 22
Net Worth: £1,099,360 *Total Assets:* £2,517,708
Registered Office: Newburn Ford House, Newburn Bridge Road, Newburn, Newcastle upon Tyne, NE15 8NR
Activities: Wholesale of wood, construction materials and sanitary equipment
Shareholders: David Maughan; Brenda Maughan
Officers: Brenda Maughan, Secretary; Brenda Maughan [1953] Director/Secretary; David Maughan [1951] Director; Robert William Walker [1954] Director

F.T. Construction Group (Holdings) Ltd.
Incorporated: 1 February 1996 *Employees:* 193
Net Worth: £9,039,513 *Total Assets:* £17,139,340
Registered Office: Construction House, Northallerton, N Yorks, DL7 8ED
Activities: Development of building projects
Parent: Fordy Thompson (Holdings) Limited
Officers: Derek John Greenwell, Secretary; Paul Blades [1963] Director; Keith Edmund Caygill [1953] Director; Derek John Greenwell [1948] Director Company Secretary; Susan Bridget Greenwell [1958] Director; Keith Brian Noddings [1972] Finance Director; Vincent Phillips [1959] Non-Executive Director Chairman; Sarah Louise Anne Wilkinson [1965] Director

Fablink Tank Systems Limited
Incorporated: 21 May 2009 *Employees:* 134
Net Worth: £296,631 *Total Assets:* £3,372,168
Registered Office: Fablink Tank Systems Ltd, Evenwood, Bishop Auckland, Co Durham, DL14 9NJ
Activities: Manufacture of other fabricated metal products n.e.c.
Officers: Michael Singleton, Secretary; Richard Alan Westley [1974] Director

Faerch Plast Manufacturing Limited
Incorporated: 12 September 2011 *Employees:* 110
Net Worth: £9,457,000 *Total Assets:* £82,695,000
Registered Office: Faerch Plast Manufacturing Ltd, Damson Way, Dragonville Industrial Estate, Durham, DH1 2YN
Activities: Manufacture of plastic packing goods
Officers: Thomas Peter Vikkelso Tranders, Secretary; Tom Sand-Kristensen [1971] Director/Group CFO [Danish]; Thomas Peter Vikkelso Tranders [1972] Director/Attorney-at-Law [Danish]

Fagron UK Ltd
Incorporated: 15 August 2007 *Employees:* 8
Net Worth: £1,232,843 *Total Assets:* £4,149,983
Registered Office: Media Exchange, 4b Coquet Street, Newcastle upon Tyne, NE1 2QB
Activities: Wholesale of pharmaceutical goods
Officers: Karin de Jong, Secretary; Peter Batty [1966] Director/General Manager

Fairfield House Limited
Incorporated: 21 February 2012
Net Worth Deficit: £263,966 *Total Assets:* £965,081
Registered Office: Portland House, Holywood, Wolsingham, Co Durham, DL13 3HE
Activities: Other holiday and other collective accommodation
Shareholders: Simon Heptinstall; Paula Carlington
Officers: Paula Carlington [1966] Director; Simon Heptinstall [1964] Director

Fairfield Industries Limited
Incorporated: 25 September 1987 *Employees:* 9
Net Worth: £2,992,669 *Total Assets:* £3,236,438
Registered Office: The Works, North Ormesby Road, Middlesbrough, Cleveland, TS4 2AG
Activities: Agents involved in the sale of machinery, industrial equipment, ships and aircraft
Parent: John Livingston & Sons Ltd
Officers: John Roger Baker [1930] Director; Robert Cockerill [1965] Director/General Manager; Bernard John Ord [1935] Director

Fairfield Windfarm Limited
Incorporated: 26 September 2008
Net Worth: £3,634,000 *Total Assets:* £9,583,000
Registered Office: Alexander House, 1 Mandarin Road, Rainton Bridge Business Park, Houghton-le-Spring, Co Durham, DH4 5RA
Activities: Production of electricity
Parent: EDF Energy Renewables Holdings Limited
Officers: Susan Elizabeth Lind, Secretary; Matthieu Thomas Hue [1975] Director [French]; Hassaan Majid [1968] Director

Fairman Chemists Limited
Incorporated: 16 June 1986
Net Worth: £1,322,621 *Total Assets:* £2,692,585
Registered Office: 39 High Street, Gosforth, Newcastle upon Tyne, NE3 4AA
Activities: Dispensing chemist in specialised stores
Officers: Julie Forster, Secretary; Christopher Hall Forster [1962] Director; Julie Forster [1963] Director; Lucy Haig [1974] Director/Retail Pharmacy; Christopher Martin Holmes [1978] Director/Retail Pharmacy

Fairmoor Holdings Limited
Incorporated: 4 May 1989
Net Worth: £879,381 *Total Assets:* £887,633
Registered Office: Hadrian Road, Willington Quay, Tyne & Wear, NE28 6NW
Activities: Other letting and operating of own or leased real estate
Major Shareholder: David Bruce Chambers
Officers: Maureen Chambers, Secretary; David Bruce Chambers [1949] Director; Ivan Roddick Chambers [1971] Director/Gas Technician; Maureen Chambers [1950] Director

Fairstone Capital Investment Limited
Incorporated: 23 December 2015 *Employees:* 85
Net Worth: £24,373,000 *Total Assets:* £31,714,000
Registered Office: 1 The Bulrushes, Woodstock Way, Boldon Business Park, Boldon Colliery, Co Durham, NE35 9PF
Activities: Other service activities n.e.c.
Parent: Synova Capital General Partner 5 Limited
Officers: Alexander Charles Spencer Bowden [1974] Investment Director; Matthew Chairman [1987] Director/Investment Manager; Lee Graham Hartley [1976] Director; David Martin James Hickey [1955] Director; Scott Hopkinson [1974] Director; Malcolm James Bowes Kerr [1948] Director; Christian Alexander Rigg [1974] Director; Tom Taylor [1968] Director

Fairstone Executive Management Limited
Incorporated: 6 January 2016
Net Worth: £19,475,724 *Total Assets:* £25,608,786
Registered Office: Boldon Business Park, Boldon Colliery, Co Durham, NE35 9PF
Activities: Other service activities n.e.c.
Parent: Fairstone Capital Investment Limited
Officers: Lee Graham Hartley [1976] Director; Scott Hopkinson [1974] Director/Accountant

Fairstone Financial Management (City) Limited
Incorporated: 7 July 1998 *Employees:* 18
Net Worth: £945,532 *Total Assets:* £1,867,012
Registered Office: Unit 1 The Bulrushes, Woodstock Way, Boldon Business Park, Boldon Colliery, Co Durham, NE35 9PF
Activities: Other business support service activities n.e.c.
Parent: Fairstone Holdings Limited
Officers: Lee Graham Hartley [1976] Director; Scott Hopkinson [1974] Director/Accountant; Sean Larkin [1973] Director/Financial Adviser; Sean McParland [1963] Director/Financial Adviser; Angela Murfitt [1969] Director/Financial Adviser; Robert Reich [1950] Director/Financial Adviser; Peter Savage [1977] Director/Financial Adviser; Ursula Sweis [1978] Compliance Director

Fairstone Financial Management Limited
Incorporated: 26 September 2005
Net Worth: £7,136,279 *Total Assets:* £9,167,831
Registered Office: 1 The Bulrushes, Boldon Business Park, Boldon Colliery, Co Durham, NE35 9PF
Activities: Financial intermediation not elsewhere classified
Parent: Fairstone Holdings Limited
Officers: Lee Graham Hartley [1976] Director; Scott Hopkinson [1974] Director/Accountant; Sean Larkin [1973] Director/Financial Adviser; Sean McParland [1963] Director/Financial Adviser; Angela Murfitt [1969] Director/Financial Adviser; Robert Reich [1950] Director/Financial Adviser; Peter Savage [1977] Director/Financial Adviser; Ursula Sweis [1978] Compliance Director

Fairstone Group Limited
Incorporated: 21 May 2008 *Employees:* 68
Net Worth Deficit: £224,000 *Total Assets:* £13,119,000
Registered Office: 1 The Bulrushes, Boldon Business Park, Boldon Colliery, Co Durham, NE35 9PF
Activities: Financial intermediation not elsewhere classified
Parent: Fairstone Executive Management Limited
Officers: Scott Hopkinson, Secretary; Lee Graham Hartley [1976] Director/Chief Executive Officer; Scott Hopkinson [1974] Director/Accountant

Fairstone Holdings Limited
Incorporated: 21 May 2008
Net Worth: £2,190,384 *Total Assets:* £8,331,330
Registered Office: 1 The Bulrushes, Boldon Business Park, Boldon Colliery, Co Durham, NE35 9PF
Activities: Other business support service activities n.e.c.
Parent: Fairstone Group Limited
Officers: Alexander Hugh Edward Campbell [1961] Director; Stephen Easter [1966] Sales Director; Michael James Hall [1967] Commercial Director; Dennis Lee Reed [1964] Sales Director; Ursula Sweis [1978] Compliance Director

Falck Nutec Ltd
Incorporated: 3 February 1993 *Employees:* 91
Net Worth: £14,427,023 *Total Assets:* £16,843,660
Registered Office: Haverton Hill Industrial Estate, Billingham, Cleveland, TS23 1PZ
Activities: Other service activities n.e.c.
Officers: Duncan Bonner [1960] UK Managing Director; Torben Harring [1972] Director [Danish]; Lizette Kjellerup [1966] Director/Chief Financial Officer [Danish]; Colin Leyden [1968] Managing Director

Falcombe
Incorporated: 11 October 1994
Net Worth Deficit: £1,237,000 *Total Assets:* £3,843,000
Registered Office: 1a Dukesway Court, Team Valley Trading Estate, Gateshead, Tyne & Wear, NE11 0PJ
Activities: Other business support service activities n.e.c.
Parent: Falcombe Holdings Limited
Officers: Phillip Nigel Blain, Secretary; David James Horrocks [1959] Director/Chartered Accountant; Ian Imrie [1955] Director

Falcombe Holdings Limited
Incorporated: 16 November 2007
Net Worth: £3,324,000 *Total Assets:* £3,330,000
Registered Office: 1a Dukesway Court, Team Valley Trading Estate, Gateshead, Tyne & Wear, NE11 0PJ
Activities: Activities of other holding companies n.e.c.
Parent: Red Poppy (UK) Limited
Officers: Phillip Nigel Blain, Secretary; David James Horrocks [1959] Director/Chartered Accountant; Ian Imrie [1955] Director

Falcon Engineering & Development Limited
Incorporated: 24 August 1990 *Employees:* 9
Net Worth Deficit: £85,170 *Total Assets:* £1,804,175
Registered Office: Unit 14 Newcomen Road, Skippers Lane Industrial Estate, Middlesbrough, Cleveland, TS6 6PS
Activities: Other engineering activities
Major Shareholder: Lee Ross Crawford
Officers: Steven Grant Crawford, Secretary; Christopher Richard Crawford [1944] Director/Oilfield Engineer

Falconvale Limited
Incorporated: 21 May 2016
Net Worth: £11,962 *Total Assets:* £1,885,333
Registered Office: 74 Whitehall Road, Gateshead, Tyne & Wear, NE8 4ET
Activities: Other letting and operating of own or leased real estate
Shareholders: Yehuda Green; Ruth Green
Officers: Yehuda Green, Secretary; Ruth Green [1988] Director; Yehuda Green [1985] Director [Swiss]

C. W. J. Fall & Sons Limited
Incorporated: 16 August 1973 *Employees:* 6
Net Worth: £1,677,686 *Total Assets:* £1,782,495
Registered Office: Mile House Farm, Bedale, N Yorks, DL8 2SF
Activities: Growing of cereals (except rice), leguminous crops and oil seeds
Shareholders: Charles David Fall; C. W. J. Fall Discretionary Settlement; A. M. Fall Discretionary Settlement
Officers: Martyn Alton Fall, Secretary; Charles David Fall [1953] Director/Farmer; Martyn Alton Fall [1956] Director/Timber Merchant & Farmer

John T. Fall Limited
Incorporated: 4 April 1977 *Employees:* 12
Net Worth: £2,429,726 *Total Assets:* £3,514,200
Registered Office: Mill Beck, Kirklington, Bedale, N Yorks, DL8 2LX
Activities: Growing of cereals (except rice), leguminous crops and oil seeds
Major Shareholder: Stephen Charles Fall
Officers: Annabel Louise Fall, Secretary; Annabel Louise Fall [1968] Director; Stephen Charles Fall [1963] Director/Farmer

Faltec Europe Limited
Incorporated: 17 May 1989 *Employees:* 396
Net Worth: £6,032,521 *Total Assets:* £23,165,462
Registered Office: Unit 1 Didcot Way, Boldon Business Park, Boldon Colliery, Co Durham, NE35 9PD
Activities: Manufacture of bodies (coachwork) for motor vehicles (except caravans)
Parent: Faltec Co Ltd
Officers: Takayuki Furuuchi [1967] Managing Director [Japanese]; Toshiyuki Tanaka [1963] Director/Chairman [Japanese]; Keith Wakley [1976] Deputy Managing Director

The Faraday Centre Limited
Incorporated: 13 October 1993 *Employees:* 33
Net Worth: £657,159 *Total Assets:* £972,311
Registered Office: The Wilton Centre Annexe, South Building, The Wilton Centre, Redcar, Cleveland, TS10 4RF
Activities: Electrical installation
Major Shareholder: Barry Thomas
Officers: Barry Thomas, Secretary/Electrical Engineer; Barry Thomas [1943] Director/Electrical Engineer; Hannah Grace Thomas [1982] Director; Lynnda Thomas [1949] Director/Company Secretary

Faraday Printed Circuits (Holdings) Limited
Incorporated: 1 July 2004
Net Worth: £649,468 *Total Assets:* £1,305,377
Registered Office: 15-18 Faraday Close, Pattison Industrial Estate North, District 15, Washington, Tyne & Wear, NE38 8QJ
Activities: Other business support service activities n.e.c.
Shareholder: Julia Arkley-Smith
Officers: Jamie Pearson, Secretary; Jamie Pearson [1977] Director

Faraday Printed Circuits Limited
Incorporated: 17 April 1985 *Employees:* 55
Net Worth: £1,068,310 *Total Assets:* £2,892,300
Registered Office: 15 Faraday Close, Pattinson Industrial Estate North, District 15, Washington, Tyne & Wear, NE38 8QJ
Activities: Manufacture of electronic components
Parent: Faraday Printed Circuits (Holdings) Ltd
Officers: Jamie Pearson [1977] Director/Manager; Stephen Robert Spence [1958] Director/Manager; Anthony Thomas Teasdale [1965] Director/Manager

Farah Chemists Limited
Incorporated: 30 October 1996
Net Worth: £2,213,224 *Total Assets:* £6,834,463
Registered Office: 44 Adelaide Terrace, Benwell, Newcastle upon Tyne, NE4 8BL
Activities: Wholesale of pharmaceutical goods
Parent: ISAA Holdings Limited
Officers: Mushtaq Ahmed, Secretary; Mushtaq Ahmed [1953] Director/Pharmacist; Nabeel Ahmed [1988] Director; Shakeel Ahmed [1979] Director/Manager; Shakeela Ahmed [1957] Director/Retailer

Farmers & Mercantile Insurance Brokers Limited
Incorporated: 2 January 1996 *Employees:* 59
Net Worth: £1,215,063 *Total Assets:* £3,615,373
Registered Office: Milburn House, Dean Street, Newcastle upon Tyne, NE1 1PP
Activities: Activities of insurance agents and brokers
Parent: Lycetts Holdings Limited
Officers: Rachael Jane Hall, Secretary; Alastair Charles Herbert Foster [1955] Director; Angus Christopher Keate [1962] Director

Farmtastic Valley Limited
Incorporated: 18 April 2007
Registered Office: Union Hall Farm, Brasside, Co Durham, DH1 5SG
Activities: Other amusement and recreation activities n.e.c.
Shareholders: Marco Calzini; Janine Calzini
Officers: Janine Calzini, Secretary; Janine Calzini [1972] Director; Marco Calzini [1972] Director/Farmer

Albert Farnell Limited
Incorporated: 15 December 1944 *Employees:* 408
Net Worth: £16,830,000 *Total Assets:* £114,988,000
Registered Office: Vertu House, Fifth Avenue Business Park, Team Valley Trading Estate, Gateshead, Tyne & Wear, NE11 0XA
Activities: Sale of new cars and light motor vehicles
Parent: Vertu Motors PLC
Officers: Karen Anderson, Secretary; Karen Anderson [1971] Finance Director; Jatinder Singh Aujla [1973] Group Operations Director; David Paul Crane [1967] Commercial Director; Robert Thomas Forrester [1969] Director; Michael Sherwin [1959] Finance Director

R & J Farrow Limited
Incorporated: 2 August 2006
Net Worth: £338,457 *Total Assets:* £850,949
Registered Office: The Old Vicarage, Redmire, Leyburn, N Yorks, DL8 4EN
Activities: Collection of non-hazardous waste
Shareholders: Shaun Robert Farrow; Wayne Thomas Farrow
Officers: Shaun Robert Farrow, Secretary; Shaun Robert Farrow [1970] Director/Metal Recycler; Wayne Thomas Farrow [1972] Director/Metal Recycler

Fast Track Sourcing Limited
Incorporated: 15 March 2010 *Employees:* 3
Net Worth: £265,272 *Total Assets:* £1,276,551
Registered Office: 5 Osborne Terrace, Jesmond, Newcastle upon Tyne, NE2 1SQ
Activities: Wholesale of pharmaceutical goods
Major Shareholder: William Alasdair Gray
Officers: William Alasdair Gray [1960] Director/General Manager; Andrew William McLeod Lowdon [1963] Director; Nicholas David Sutherland Owen [1963] Director/Businessman

Fastflow Energy Services Limited
Incorporated: 29 May 2012 *Employees:* 110
Net Worth: £5,620,000 *Total Assets:* £12,247,000
Registered Office: Units 11 & 12 Parsons Road Industrial Estate, Washington, Tyne & Wear, NE37 1HB
Activities: Other specialised construction activities n.e.c.
Parent: Fastflow Group Limited
Officers: Shaun Hastings, Secretary; Neil Patrick Armstrong [1969] Director [Irish]; Ryan John Brennan [1971] Director/Business Executive; Anthony Ernest Cottrell [1952] Director; Benn Cottrell [1979] Operations Director; Ian Craggs [1976] Director/Businessman; Paul James Crooks [1972] Commercial Director; Shaun Hastings [1958] Finance Director; Terence Bernard Walsh [1948] Director

Faulknerbrowns LLP
Incorporated: 30 July 2013 *Employees:* 98
Net Worth: £1,759,546 *Total Assets:* £3,819,983
Registered Office: Dobson House, Northumbrian Way, Killingworth, Newcastle upon Tyne, NE12 6QW
Officers: Russell Davenport [1957] Member; Benjamin Mellor Sykes [1967] Member; Nicholas Deeming [1959] LLP Member; Michael John Hall [1964] LLP Member; Andrew Joseph Kane [1964] LLP Member; Stephen Alexander McIntyre [1968] LLP Member; Lee Colin McLaughlin [1982] LLP Member; Paul Richardson [1974] LLP Member; Paul Rigby [1978] LLP Member

Faverdale Recycling Centre Limited
Incorporated: 9 July 1997
Net Worth: £354,332 *Total Assets:* £979,145
Registered Office: Victoria Building, 14 Elwin Lane, Darlington, Co Durham, DL1 5RX
Activities: Other letting and operating of own or leased real estate
Major Shareholder: John Anthony Ward
Officers: John Anthony Ward [1957] Director

Fawcett & Hetherington Funeral Service Limited
Incorporated: 24 February 2014 *Employees:* 16
Net Worth: £236,438 *Total Assets:* £1,223,966
Registered Office: King George House, 92 High Street, Eston, Middlesbrough, Cleveland, TS6 9EG
Activities: Funeral and related activities
Shareholders: Alistair John Fawcett; Pauline Fawcett
Officers: Alistair John Fawcett [1955] Funeral Director; Andrew Robert Fawcett [1978] Funeral Director and Embalmer; Pauline Fawcett [1957] Director/Funeral Service Office Manager; Terry Peter Fawcett [1975] Funeral Director

Fawside
Incorporated: 23 December 2003
Net Worth: £858,466 *Total Assets:* £861,583
Registered Office: Allendale Village Hall, Leadgate, Allendale, Hexham, Northumberland, NE47 9PR
Activities: Other letting and operating of own or leased real estate
Officers: Margaret Stonehouse, Secretary; Carol Maria Dalton [1959] Director/Farmer Licensee; Professor John Edward Dobson [1941] Director/Lecturer; David Herry Humes [1957] Director/Resource Manager; Charlotte Reid [1977] Director/Housewife; Margaret Stonehouse [1951] Director/Farmer; Dr Larry Aldon Winger [1952] Director/Teacher/Driver [Canadian]

FB Shipping Limited
Incorporated: 23 June 2004
Net Worth Deficit: £4,941 *Total Assets:* £2,724,069
Registered Office: Tobias House, St Mark's Court, Teesdale Business Park, Stockton on Tees, Cleveland, TS17 6QW
Activities: Financial leasing
Parent: Santander Asset Finance PLC
Officers: Craig Harvie [1967] Director/Manager; Graeme Paul Sheach [1966] Director/Chartered Accountant

FB Tankship III Limited
Incorporated: 27 August 2004
Net Worth: £3,383,574 *Total Assets:* £14,841,587
Registered Office: Tobias House, St Mark's Court, Teesdale Business Park, Stockton on Tees, Cleveland, TS17 6QW
Activities: Sea and coastal freight water transport
Parent: Vroon Shipping U.K. Limited
Officers: Craig Harvie [1967] Director/Manager; Graeme Paul Sheach [1966] Director/Chartered Accountant

FB Tankship IV Limited
Incorporated: 27 August 2004
Net Worth: £4,324,054 *Total Assets:* £15,230,698
Registered Office: Tobias House, St Mark's Court, Teesdale Business Park, Stockton on Tees, Cleveland, TS17 6QW
Activities: Sea and coastal freight water transport
Parent: Vroon Shipping U.K. Limited
Officers: Craig Harvie [1967] Director/Manager; Graeme Paul Sheach [1966] Director/Chartered Accountant

FC Beamish Bidco Ltd
Incorporated: 6 December 2016
Net Worth: £100,710,656 *Total Assets:* £109,660,432
Registered Office: Southgate House, Archer Street, Darlington, Co Durham, DL3 6AH
Activities: Activities of other holding companies n.e.c.
Parent: FC Skyfall Bidco Limited
Officers: James Justin Hutchens [1974] Director [American]; David Andrew Smith [1974] Director/Accountant

FC Shipping Limited
Incorporated: 26 March 2004
Net Worth Deficit: £3,348 *Total Assets:* £3,904,693
Registered Office: Tobias House, St Mark's Court, Teesdale Business Park, Stockton on Tees, Cleveland, TS17 6QW
Activities: Financial leasing
Parent: Santander Asset Finance PLC
Officers: Craig Harvie [1967] Director/Manager; Graeme Paul Sheach [1966] Director/Chartered Accountant

FC Tankship I Ltd
Incorporated: 6 January 2004
Net Worth: £2,750,692 *Total Assets:* £20,846,662
Registered Office: Tobias House, St Mark's Court, Teesdale Business Park, Stockton on Tees, Cleveland, TS17 6QW
Activities: Sea and coastal freight water transport
Parent: Vroon Shipping U.K. Limited
Officers: Craig Harvie [1967] Director/Manager; Graeme Paul Sheach [1966] Director/Chartered Accountant

FC Tankship II Ltd
Incorporated: 6 January 2004
Net Worth: £456,014 *Total Assets:* £17,197,016
Registered Office: Tobias House, St Mark's Court, Teesdale Business Park, Stockton on Tees, Cleveland, TS17 6QW
Activities: Sea and coastal freight water transport
Parent: Vroon Shipping U.K. Limited
Officers: Craig Harvie [1967] Director/Manager; Graeme Paul Sheach [1966] Director/Chartered Accountant

Federal Signal UK Holdings Limited
Incorporated: 21 September 1993
Net Worth: £8,504,145 *Total Assets:* £8,504,145
Registered Office: c/o Victor Products Ltd, Unit 3a Tyne Dock East Side, Port of Tyne, South Shields, Tyne & Wear, NE33 5SQ
Activities: Activities of head offices
Parent: Federal Signal Corporation
Officers: Daniel Anthony Dupre [1956] Director/Attorney [American]; Ian Hudson [1976] Director/VP Interim CFO; Jennifer Sherman [1964] Director/General Counsel [American]; Svetlana Vinokur [1979] Director/VP Treasurer [American]

The Federation of Abbey Schools Academy Trust
Incorporated: 11 July 2011 *Employees:* 98
Net Worth: £3,878,000 *Total Assets:* £4,837,000
Registered Office: The Federation of Abbey Schools, Infant Building, Cleveland Terrace, Darlington, Co Durham, DL3 8JA
Activities: Primary education
Officers: David Michael Bailey [1975] Director/Educational Consultant/Regional Network Lead; Peter Alan Bibby [1978] Director/Civil Servant; Jonathan Briggs [1970] Director/Headteacher; Laurence Miles Bryant [1971] Director/IT Manager; Emma Louise de La Motte [1972] Director/Secondary School Teacher (MFL); Vicky Folkes [1973] Director/Teacher; Michael James Fryer [1952] Director; Rita Hall [1953] Director/Retired; Rachel Kershaw [1975] Director/Senior Partner; Nigel Peter Little [1951] Director/Retired; Clare Marley [1979] Director [Irish]; Helen Parkinson [1970] Director; Jodie Scott [1978] Director; Catherine Stow Smith [1975] Director; Peter Malcolm Willson [1941] Director/Retired

Federation of Mowden Schools Academy Trust
Incorporated: 12 April 2012 *Employees:* 63
Net Worth: £5,870,000 *Total Assets:* £6,668,000
Registered Office: c/o Mowden Junior School, Conyers Avenue, Darlington, Co Durham, DL3 9DE
Activities: Primary education
Officers: Angela Taylor, Secretary; Alison Cockrill [1967] Director/Office Administrator; David Holmes [1968] Director/Regional Sales Manager; Alan Jones [1982] Director/Teacher; Peter Donald King [1969] Director/Headteacher; Tarryn Dimmock Lloyd-Payne [1976] Director/Local Authority Manager; Jacqueline Saint [1954] Director; Christopher Strong [1976] Director of Education; Diane Turner [1955] Director/Childminder; Anthony John Ward [1984] Director/Civil Servant

The Feed Warehouse Ltd
Incorporated: 3 June 2011
Net Worth: £355,049 *Total Assets:* £767,635
Registered Office: 35 Galgate, Barnard Castle, Co Durham, DL12 8EJ
Activities: Wholesale of grain, unmanufactured tobacco, seeds and animal feeds
Major Shareholder: Sean Martin Kell
Officers: Sean Martin Kell [1978] Director/Pet Food Warehouse

The Feel Good Group Limited
Incorporated: 31 July 2006 *Employees:* 268
Net Worth: £4,591,457 *Total Assets:* £10,025,705
Registered Office: Unit J6, Morton Park Way, Darlington, Co Durham, DL1 4PG
Activities: Other retail sale in non-specialised stores
Parent: The Feel Good Group (Holdings) Limited
Officers: Keith Eliot Smith, Secretary; Adam Leo Mooney [1964] Managing Director [Irish]; Ciaran John Mooney [1968] Franchise Director [Irish]

Feld Limited
Incorporated: 20 March 2012
Net Worth: £72,061 *Total Assets:* £769,231
Registered Office: 26 Cambridge Terrace, Gateshead, Tyne & Wear, NE8 1RP
Activities: Other letting and operating of own or leased real estate
Major Shareholder: Robert Feldman
Officers: Robert Feldman [1993] Director [Belgian]

Felixarc Marine Limited
Incorporated: 23 October 2000 *Employees:* 88
Net Worth Deficit: £444,000 *Total Assets:* £1,458,000
Registered Office: Tees Wharf, Dockside Road, Middlesbrough, Cleveland, TS3 6AB
Activities: Sea and coastal freight water transport
Parent: Svitzer Eastlands Limited
Officers: David Anthony Noakes, Secretary; Anthony Howard Brown [1955] Director/Finance Manager; Kasper Friis Nilaus [1975] Regional Director [Danish]; Matthijs Schot [1975] Finance Director [Dutch]

Feller (UK) Limited
Incorporated: 20 March 1985 *Employees:* 43
Net Worth: £2,384,126 *Total Assets:* £3,990,062
Registered Office: Unit 1 Middlefields Industrial Estate, South Shields, Tyne & Wear, NE34 0NU
Activities: Manufacture of electronic components
Officers: Dr Barbara Ascher, Secretary; Dr Barbara Ascher [1954] Director [Austrian]

Fellside Properties Limited
Incorporated: 15 July 1997 *Employees:* 1
Net Worth: £3,206,819 *Total Assets:* £5,491,463
Registered Office: 2 Benton Terrace, Sandyford, Newcastle upon Tyne, NE2 1QU
Activities: Buying and selling of own real estate
Shareholders: Paul Nicholas Good; Andrew Steven Good
Officers: Paul Nicholas Good [1963] Director

Felmoor Park Limited
Incorporated: 13 May 2008
Registered Office: 5c Linnet Court, Cawledge Business Park, Hawfinch Drive, Alnwick, Northumberland, NE66 2GD
Activities: Recreational vehicle parks, trailer parks and camping grounds
Shareholder: Ian Thornton
Officers: Melvin Thornton, Secretary; Gladys McLean [1962] Director/Clerk; Ian Thornton [1958] Director/Contracts Manager; Melvin Thornton [1956] Director/Finance Manager; Robert Thornton [1964] Director/Contracts Manager

Felton Property and Investments Limited
Incorporated: 12 July 2002 *Employees:* 2
Net Worth: £1,321,135 *Total Assets:* £2,017,934
Registered Office: Bulman House, Regent Centre, Gosforth, Newcastle upon Tyne, NE3 3LS
Activities: Other letting and operating of own or leased real estate
Parent: North East Property and Investments Limited
Officers: John Cooke [1946] Director; Stephen Cowell [1951] Director; Cheryl Patricia Foreman [1958] Managing Director

Fentimans Ltd.
Incorporated: 13 September 1994 *Employees:* 47
Net Worth: £2,779,859 *Total Assets:* £10,888,183
Registered Office: Fearless House, Beaufront Park, Alnwick Road, Hexham, Northumberland, NE46 4TU
Activities: Manufacture of soft drinks; production of mineral waters and other bottled waters
Major Shareholder: Eldon Arthur Robson
Officers: Eldon Arthur Robson, Secretary; Ian David Bray [1963] Director; David Charlton [1952] Director/Chartered Accountant; Eldon Arthur Robson [1950] Director/Manager

Fenwick,Limited
Incorporated: 6 May 1897 *Employees:* 2,256
Net Worth: £588,396,992 *Total Assets:* £724,190,976
Registered Office: Elswick Court, Northumberland Street, Newcastle upon Tyne, NE99 1AR
Activities: Other retail sale in non-specialised stores
Officers: Jill Anders, Secretary; Stephen David Barber [1952] Director/Chartered Accountant; Andrew James Doyle [1967] Director; Robert Feather [1967] Director; Hugo Mark Fenwick [1964] Director; Mia Rose Fenwick [1978] Director; Richard John Pennycook [1964] Director/Chartered Accountant

Fergusons Blyth Limited
Incorporated: 30 October 1959 *Employees:* 38
Net Worth: £10,506,700 *Total Assets:* £31,495,500
Registered Office: Northumberland Business Park West, Cramlington, Northumberland, NE23 7RH
Activities: Other letting and operating of own or leased real estate
Parent: Fergyprops Limited
Officers: Helen Whitaker, Secretary; Alan Ferguson [1954] Director/Haulier; Eileen Isabel Ferguson [1959] Director/Chartered Accountant; Helen Whitaker [1951] Director/Secretary; Steven Mark Whitaker [1956] Director Fuel Co-ordinator

Fergusons Transport Limited
Incorporated: 22 March 1937 *Employees:* 295
Net Worth: £1,542,813 *Total Assets:* £12,645,703
Registered Office: Northumberland Business Park West, Cramlington, Northumberland, NE23 7RH
Activities: Freight transport by road
Parent: Fergytrux Limited
Officers: Helen Whitaker, Secretary; Michael Arkle [1973] Director/Transport Manager; Stuart Arkle [1975] Director/Transport Manager; Alan Ferguson [1954] Director/Haulage Contractor; Eileen Isabel Ferguson [1959] Director/Accountant; John Arthur Redpath [1925] Director; Arthur Wappat [1941] Director/Chartered Accountant; Helen Whitaker [1951] Director; Steven Mark Whitaker [1956] Director

Peter Fergusson Properties Limited
Incorporated: 29 April 2002
Net Worth: £24,032 *Total Assets:* £1,011,237
Registered Office: Rowlands House, Portobello Road, Birtley, Chester-le-Street, Co Durham, DH3 2RY
Activities: Activities of professional membership organisations
Major Shareholder: Peter Ramsay Fergusson
Officers: Peter Ramsay Fergusson, Secretary/Manager; Kathleen Dianne Fergusson [1956] Director/Manager; Peter Ramsay Fergusson [1952] Director/Manager

Fergytrux Limited
Incorporated: 30 August 2006 *Employees:* 295
Net Worth: £1,542,813 *Total Assets:* £12,645,703
Registered Office: Business Park West, Cramlington, Northumberland, NE23 7RH
Activities: Freight transport by road
Major Shareholder: Alan Ferguson
Officers: Helen Whitaker, Secretary; Alan Ferguson [1954] Director; Eileen Isabel Ferguson [1959] Director/Chartered Accountant; Helen Whitaker [1951] Director/Secretary; Steven Mark Whitaker [1956] Director Fuel Co-ordinator

Fewsters Limited
Incorporated: 29 August 1944 *Employees:* 4
Net Worth: £7,410,363 *Total Assets:* £8,220,957
Registered Office: 39 Bridge Street, Seaton Burn, Newcastle upon Tyne, NE13 6EN
Activities: Other letting and operating of own or leased real estate
Shareholder: Christopher James Fewster
Officers: Christopher James Fewster [1968] Director; Michael Fabian Fewster [1967] Director; James Fewster Jnr [1943] Managing Director

Fewsters Services Limited
Incorporated: 30 December 1949 *Employees:* 4
Net Worth Deficit: £24,556 *Total Assets:* £1,489,529
Registered Office: 39 Bridge Street, Seaton Burn, Newcastle upon Tyne, NE13 6EN
Activities: Collection of non-hazardous waste
Parent: Fewsters Limited
Officers: Christopher James Fewster [1968] Director; Michael Fabian Fewster [1967] Director; James Fewster Jnr [1943] Managing Director

FG Trailers Limited
Incorporated: 25 November 2004 *Employees:* 11
Net Worth: £317,677 *Total Assets:* £936,377
Registered Office: Cheryl House, 18 Bedesway, Bede Industrial Estate, Jarrow, Tyne & Wear, NE32 3EG
Activities: Manufacture of other transport equipment n.e.c.
Major Shareholder: Paul Nash
Officers: Lisa Nash, Secretary; Paul Nash [1969] Director/Trailer Constructor

Filematch Limited
Incorporated: 19 March 1990 *Employees:* 2
Net Worth: £513,995 *Total Assets:* £782,484
Registered Office: Aston House, Redburn Road, Newcastle upon Tyne, NE5 1NB
Activities: Publishing of computer games
Officers: Marcia Ann Neffendorf, Secretary; Alice Elizabeth Neffendorf [1988] Director; James Emil Neffendorf [1985] Director [American]; James Edward Neffendorf [1952] Director/Engineer [American]; Marcia Ann Neffendorf [1953] Director

Fillpack Limited
Incorporated: 15 April 1997 *Employees:* 7
Net Worth: £1,646,902 *Total Assets:* £1,796,366
Registered Office: Kenya Lodge, Laneside, Middleton in Teesdale, Barnard Castle, Co Durham, DL12 0RY
Activities: Other business support service activities n.e.c.
Shareholders: Karl Edward Robinson; Loraine Robinson
Officers: Loraine Robinson, Secretary; Karl Edward Robinson [1965] Managing Director; Loraine Robinson [1962] Director

Fillworth (UK) Limited
Incorporated: 27 February 2003 *Employees:* 22
Net Worth: £877,986 *Total Assets:* £1,513,195
Registered Office: Joseph Miller & Co, Floor A, Milburn House, Dean Street, Newcastle upon Tyne, NE1 1LE
Activities: Manufacture of other general-purpose machinery n.e.c.
Shareholders: Mark Mackintosh; Darrin John Cockbain
Officers: Darrin John Cockbain, Secretary/Director; Darrin John Cockbain [1966] Director; Mark Mackintosh [1964] Director

Finchale Training College
Incorporated: 31 July 1990 *Employees:* 28
Net Worth: £4,375,428 *Total Assets:* £5,436,707
Registered Office: Durham, DH1 5RX
Activities: Other education n.e.c.
Officers: Stewart Atkin [1948] Director/Tax Adviser; David George Lawrence Bowles [1941] Director; Doctor Margaret Purnell Collins [1947] Director/Retired; Christopher Cunnington-Shore [1953] Director; Norman Thomas Hart [1943] Director/Solicitor; Edmund William Marchant [1940] Director/Retired; William John McGawley [1949] Director; Simon Robinson [1960] Director/Solicitor; Michael John Hewson Tait [1952] Director/Accountant; Dorothy Winter [1952] HR Director

Finders Bidco Limited
Incorporated: 14 July 2015 *Employees:* 6
Net Worth: £113,272,000 *Total Assets:* £208,590,000
Registered Office: The St Nicholas Building, St Nicholas Street, Newcastle upon Tyne, NE1 1RF
Activities: Activities of other holding companies n.e.c.
Parent: Finders Midco Limited
Officers: James Lloyd Townshend [1973] Director; Lewis Paul Miller [1981] Director/Chief Financial Officer; Nigel Ashley O'Donoghue [1972] Director

Finders Holdco Limited
Incorporated: 21 April 2016
Net Worth: £121,959,000 *Total Assets:* £122,090,000
Registered Office: The St Nicholas Building, St Nicholas Street, Newcastle upon Tyne, NE1 1RF
Activities: Activities of other holding companies n.e.c.
Parent: Finders Topco Limited
Officers: James Lloyd Townshend [1973] Director; Lewis Paul Miller [1981] Director/Chief Financial Officer; Nigel Ashley O'Donoghue [1972] Director

Finders Midco Limited
Incorporated: 14 July 2015 *Employees:* 1,152
Net Worth: £110,508,000 *Total Assets:* £187,492,000
Registered Office: The St Nicholas Building, St Nicholas Street, Newcastle upon Tyne, NE1 1RF
Activities: Dormant company
Parent: Finders Holdco Limited
Officers: James Lloyd-Townshend [1973] Director; Lewis Paul Miller [1981] Director/Chief Financial Officer; Nigel Ashley O'Donoghue [1972] Director

Findley Roofing & Building Limited
Incorporated: 22 April 2009
Net Worth: £451,613 *Total Assets:* £1,393,270
Registered Office: Hackworth Road, Blackhall Colliery, Hartlepool, Cleveland, TS27 4EL
Activities: Roofing activities
Major Shareholder: Grant Matthew Findley
Officers: Hettie Findley, Secretary; Dean Coombe [1985] Director/Manager; Grant Matthew Findley [1981] Director

Findspace Limited
Incorporated: 6 November 1997
Net Worth: £5,473,135 *Total Assets:* £11,895,524
Registered Office: 190 Heaton Road, Newcastle upon Tyne, NE6 5HP
Activities: Other letting and operating of own or leased real estate
Officers: Simon Geoffrey Pickering, Secretary; John Philip Pickering [1954] Director; Kerry May Pickering [1965] Director

Fine & Performance Chemicals Limited
Incorporated: 3 May 1974 *Employees:* 6
Net Worth: £701,694 *Total Assets:* £1,840,802
Registered Office: FPC Skutterskelfe, Hutton Rudby, Yarm, Cleveland, TS15 0JR
Activities: Manufacture of other chemical products n.e.c.
Major Shareholder: Simon Richard Lines
Officers: Tracy Galloway, Secretary; John Ian Lawson [1958] Director/Chartered Accountant; Simon Richard Lines [1962] Director

Fine Environmental Services Limited
Incorporated: 9 March 2010 *Employees:* 9
Net Worth Deficit: £1,783,000 *Total Assets:* £8,089,000
Registered Office: Seal Sands, Middlesbrough, Cleveland, TS2 1UB
Activities: Treatment and disposal of hazardous waste
Parent: Lianhe Chemical Technology Co. Ltd
Officers: Lee Paul Kingsbury [1972] Operations Director; Dr Nigel Christopher Parkinson [1968] Director; Minghui Xu [1971] Finance Director [Chinese]

Fine Industries Limited
Incorporated: 7 August 2008
Net Worth: £614,000 *Total Assets:* £1,725,000
Registered Office: Seal Sands, Middlesbrough, Cleveland, TS2 1UB
Activities: Activities of head offices
Parent: Lianhe Chemical Technology Co. Ltd
Officers: Lee Paul Kingsbury [1972] Director; Dr Nigel Christopher Parkinson [1968] Director; Minghui Xu [1971] Finance Director [Chinese]

Fine Organics Limited
Incorporated: 3 December 1980 *Employees:* 295
Net Worth: £30,472,000 *Total Assets:* £57,122,000
Registered Office: Seal Sands, Middlesbrough, Cleveland, TS2 1UB
Activities: Manufacture of other organic basic chemicals
Parent: Lianhe Chemical Technology Co. Ltd
Officers: Nigel James Bartley, Secretary; Lee Paul Kingsbury [1972] Operations Director; Dr Nigel Christopher Parkinson [1968] Director; Minghui Xu [1971] Finance Director [Chinese]

Finkle Street Properties Limited
Incorporated: 9 May 1988
Net Worth: £111,167 *Total Assets:* £759,757
Registered Office: 11 Finkle Street, Richmond, N Yorks, DL10 4QA
Activities: Other letting and operating of own or leased real estate
Officers: Patricia Mary Fava, Secretary; Anthony Joseph Leopold Fava [1938] Director/Chartered Accountant; Patricia Mary Fava [1943] Director/Retired

Finklegate Properties Limited
Incorporated: 14 May 1984
Registered Office: 5 Henson Close, South Church Enterprise Park, Bishop Auckland, Co Durham, DL14 6WA
Activities: Other letting and operating of own or leased real estate
Officers: Barry Allen, Secretary; Barry Allen [1936] Director/Chartered Accountant; Charles Hope Clarey [1939] Director/Master Builder; Arthur Neville Fairclough [1936] Director/Solicitor

Finley Structures Ltd
Incorporated: 28 July 2000 *Employees:* 63
Net Worth: £2,654,516 *Total Assets:* £7,163,446
Registered Office: Whinbank Road, Aycliffe Industrial Estate, Newton Aycliffe, Co Durham, DL5 6AY
Activities: Manufacture of metal structures and parts of structures
Shareholders: John Finley; Valerie Finley
Officers: Julie Raistrick, Secretary/Office Manager; Gary John Finley [1980] Director; John Finley [1952] Sales Director; Valerie Finley [1952] Director/Fabrication; Julie Raistrick [1975] Director/Office Manager

Firgate Estates Limited
Incorporated: 9 April 2002
Net Worth: £1,307,227 *Total Assets:* £2,642,417
Registered Office: 45 Grasmere Street, Gateshead, Tyne & Wear, NE8 1TR
Activities: Other letting and operating of own or leased real estate
Shareholders: Emily Bodner; Sarah Bodner
Officers: Michael Martin Bodner, Secretary; Michael Martin Bodner [1951] Director; Steven Anthony Bodner [1961] Director

Firgate Limited
Incorporated: 5 April 1977 *Employees:* 24
Net Worth: £5,580,152 *Total Assets:* £7,097,760
Registered Office: 45 Grasmere Street, Gateshead, Tyne & Wear, NE8 1TR
Activities: Wholesale of textiles
Officers: Michael Martin Bodner, Secretary; Fanny Bodner [1952] Director; Marlene Bodner [1963] Director; Michael Martin Bodner [1951] Director; Steven Anthony Bodner [1961] Director

First Call Healthcare Limited
Incorporated: 3 February 2004 *Employees:* 205
Net Worth: £289,309 *Total Assets:* £990,214
Registered Office: Gear House, Saltmeadows Road, Gateshead, Tyne & Wear, NE8 3AH
Activities: Other human health activities
Major Shareholder: Desiree Burdis
Officers: John Robert Burdis, Secretary/Welder; Desiree Burdis [1957] Director; John Robert Burdis [1956] Director

First Choice Labels Limited
Incorporated: 16 September 2004 *Employees:* 17
Net Worth: £400,756 *Total Assets:* £1,038,287
Registered Office: Unit 4 Malmo Court, Kirkleatham Business Park, Redcar, Cleveland, TS10 5SQ
Activities: Printing n.e.c.
Shareholders: Nigel Willis; Lisa Jayne Willis
Officers: Lisa Jayne Willis, Secretary; Lisa Jayne Willis [1972] Director; Nigel Willis [1968] Sales Director

First Class Supply & Training Limited
Incorporated: 20 February 2004 *Employees:* 365
Net Worth: £477,236 *Total Assets:* £1,200,364
Registered Office: 136 Whitley Road, Whitley Bay, Tyne & Wear, NE26 2NA
Activities: Temporary employment agency activities
Shareholder: Stephenie Boulton
Officers: Stephanie Mary Boulton, Secretary/Director; Stephanie Mary Boulton [1963] Director; Dionne Sara Clark [1973] Director/Finance Manager; Frances Alice Mary Hale [1982] Director/Senior Recruitment Consultant; Lesley Robinson [1954] Director

First Complete Limited
Incorporated: 6 April 2005 *Employees:* 90
Net Worth: £10,485,000 *Total Assets:* £21,564,000
Registered Office: Newcastle House, Albany Court, Newcastle Business Park, Newcastle upon Tyne, NE4 7YB
Activities: Financial intermediation not elsewhere classified
Parent: Lending Solutions Holdings Ltd
Officers: Sapna Bedi FitzGenerald, Secretary/Solicitor; Adam Robert Castleton [1964] Director; Richard Stephen Coulson [1960] Director; Kay Leslie [1964] Director; Rajeev Raichura [1979] Director; Jonathan Pearson Round [1964] Director; Toni Smith [1969] Director

First Fix Plastics Ltd
Incorporated: 9 March 2009 *Employees:* 12
Net Worth Deficit: £30,327 *Total Assets:* £1,139,899
Registered Office: Unit D6, Princesway, Team Valley Trading Estate, Gateshead, Tyne & Wear, NE11 0TU
Activities: Non-specialised wholesale trade
Major Shareholder: David John Holmes
Officers: Joanne Dixon [1970] Director; David John Holmes [1968] Director; Neville Potts [1968] Sales Director

First Sight Estates Limited
Incorporated: 3 November 2009 *Employees:* 16
Net Worth: £168,000 *Total Assets:* £10,657,000
Registered Office: Cleveland House, Norton Road, Stockton on Tees, Cleveland, TS20 2AQ
Activities: Hotels and similar accommodation
Major Shareholder: John Donald Read Fothergill
Officers: John Philip Pickering, Secretary; John Donald Read Fothergill [1961] Director; John Philip Pickering [1954] Director/Chartered Accountant

First Windfarm Holdings Limited
Incorporated: 21 November 1991
Net Worth: £7,533,000 *Total Assets:* £10,031,000
Registered Office: Alexander House, 1 Mandarin Road, Rainton Bridge Business Park, Houghton-le-Spring, Co Durham, DH4 5RA
Activities: Activities of head offices
Parent: EDF Energy Renewables Limited
Officers: Susan Elizabeth Lind, Secretary; Matthieu Thomas Hue [1975] Director [French]; Hassaan Majid [1968] Director

First2print Ltd
Incorporated: 27 October 2010 *Employees:* 32
Net Worth: £344,438 *Total Assets:* £1,315,868
Registered Office: Unit 94 Business & Innovation Centre, Wearfield, Sunderland Enterprise Park, Sunderland, Tyne & Wear, SR5 2TQ
Activities: Printing n.e.c.
Parent: Precision Printing Co. Limited
Officers: Clive David Cooper [1947] Director/Chairman; Margaret Anne Howell [1948] Director; Gary Ian Peeling [1971] Director/Group CEO

Firthmoor and District Community Association
Incorporated: 10 November 2011 *Employees:* 24
Net Worth: £1,172,673 *Total Assets:* £1,182,402
Registered Office: Firthmoor Community Centre, Burnside Road, Darlington, Co Durham, DL1 4SU
Activities: Other activities of employment placement agencies
Officers: Kayleigh Tait, Secretary; Rachel Benson [1984] Director/Treasurer; Susan Denise Dulston [1966] Director/Charity Worker; Gillian Garbutt [1962] Director/Shop Assistant; Victoria Hamilton [1972] Director/EE Manager; Lynsey Munro [1984] Director/Trustee; Kevin Nicholson [1988] Director; Steven James Tait [1984] Director/Charity Worker; Darrien Paul Wright [1985] Director/Dance Teacher

Firthmoor Primary School
Incorporated: 12 April 2012 *Employees:* 40
Net Worth: £2,223,000 *Total Assets:* £3,026,000
Registered Office: Firthmoor Primary School, Ingleby Moor Crescent, Darlington, Co Durham, DL1 4RW
Activities: Primary education
Officers: Jannette Brooks, Secretary; Ann Dixon [1960] Director/Headteacher; Patricia Mary Irving [1948] Director/Educational Consultant; Valerie Johnston [1945] Director/Retired; Jayne Newbery [1981] Director/Sales Assistant; David William Owen [1962] Director/Credit Risk Controller; Victoria Helen Pace [1966] Director/Teacher; William Granville Paton [1945] Director; Catherine Shaw [1982] Director/RESH Coordinator

Fisher Outdoor Leisure Holdings Limited
Incorporated: 21 December 2005 *Employees:* 3
Net Worth: £5,530,000 *Total Assets:* £10,158,000
Registered Office: Roundhouse Road, Faverdale Industrial Estate, Darlington, Co Durham, DL3 0UR
Activities: Wholesale of household goods (other than musical instruments) n.e.c
Parent: Power Topco Limited
Officers: Matthew Barker [1979] Director; James Scott Browning [1966] Managing Director; Ian James Calvesbert [1966] Director; Paul Gibson [1980] Director; Richard Damon Smith [1974] Director

Fishlocks Estates Limited
Incorporated: 9 February 2016
Net Worth: £179,936 *Total Assets:* £781,255
Registered Office: 24 St Cuthberts Way, Darlington, Co Durham, DL1 1GB
Activities: Other letting and operating of own or leased real estate
Major Shareholder: Robert James Pickersgill
Officers: Robert James Pickersgill [1947] Director

Fission Recruitment Services Limited
Incorporated: 13 July 2007 *Employees:* 18
Net Worth: £58,977 *Total Assets:* £1,262,861
Registered Office: 5 Royal Road, Stanley, Co Durham, DH9 8AL
Activities: Temporary employment agency activities
Shareholders: Mark David Heatherington; Nicola Heatherington
Officers: Nicola Heatherington, Secretary/Teacher; Mark David Heatherington [1977] Director/Recruitment; Alan Richard William Tarrant [1978] Director

Fitch Taylor Limited
Incorporated: 28 January 2009
Net Worth Deficit: £155,389 *Total Assets:* £915,936
Registered Office: Fernwood House, Fernwood Road, Jesmond, Newcastle upon Tyne, NE2 1TJ
Activities: Other letting and operating of own or leased real estate
Major Shareholder: Robert Laurence Taylor
Officers: Robert Laurence Taylor [1972] Director

Fitwide Limited
Incorporated: 12 November 1986
Net Worth: £1,728,412 *Total Assets:* £2,313,499
Registered Office: The Old Mill, Dalehouse Staithes, Saltburn-by-the-Sea, N Yorks, TS13 5DT
Activities: Other letting and operating of own or leased real estate
Shareholder: Harold Armstrong
Officers: Harold Armstrong, Secretary; Harold Armstrong [1951] Director/Retail Manager

Sir John Fitzgerald (Holdings) Limited
Incorporated: 8 November 2009 *Employees:* 496
Net Worth: £21,689,008 *Total Assets:* £27,781,864
Registered Office: 8 Nelson Street, Newcastle upon Tyne, NE1 5AW
Activities: Activities of head offices
Officers: David Anthony Ridley, Secretary; David Horgan [1947] Managing Director

Sir John Fitzgerald,Limited
Incorporated: 9 June 1926 *Employees:* 496
Net Worth: £21,675,356 *Total Assets:* £27,781,864
Registered Office: Cafe Royal Buildings, 8 Nelson Street, Newcastle upon Tyne, NE1 5AW
Activities: Retail sale in non-specialised stores with food, beverages or tobacco predominating
Parent: Sir John Fitzgerald (Holdings) Limited
Officers: David Anthony Ridley, Secretary; David Horgan [1947] Managing Director; Louise Horgan [1948] Director

The Five Lamps Organisation
Incorporated: 9 November 1989
Net Worth: £4,151,929 *Total Assets:* £6,373,343
Registered Office: Eldon Street, Thornaby, Stockton on Tees, Cleveland, TS17 7DJ
Activities: Other information service activities n.e.c.
Officers: Patricia Chambers [1956] Director/Head of Partners; Vivienne Jane Holmes [1967] Director/Consultant; Michael Poole [1955] Director; Trevor George Watson [1946] Director/Manager; Ian Thomas Wright [1966] Director/Manager

Fivedean Limited
Incorporated: 18 October 2002
Net Worth: £341,693 *Total Assets:* £1,061,505
Registered Office: Harrison Packaging, Teesside Industrial Estate, Earls Way, Thornaby, Stockton on Tees, Cleveland, TS17 9NT
Activities: Activities of head offices
Parent: Earlsway Holdings Limited
Officers: Mary Caffry, Secretary; Michael Lawrence Baum [1967] Director; Mary Caffry [1957] Director/Accountant

Flagg Court Pharmacy Limited
Incorporated: 20 October 2006 *Employees:* 13
Net Worth: £985,929 *Total Assets:* £1,221,477
Registered Office: Saville Chambers, 4 Saville Street, South Shields, Tyne & Wear, NE33 2PR
Activities: Dispensing chemist in specialised stores
Major Shareholder: Joseph Anthony Schofield
Officers: Joseph Anthony Schofield, Secretary; Joseph Anthony Schofield [1954] Director/Pharmacist

Flame and Fragrance Limited
Incorporated: 29 October 2013 *Employees:* 35
Net Worth: £494,003 *Total Assets:* £3,887,229
Registered Office: Units A and B, Patterson Street, Blaydon on Tyne, Tyne & Wear, NE21 5SD
Activities: Non-specialised wholesale trade
Officers: Christopher Mark Marchant, Secretary; David Rowland Lewis [1970] Director; Philip Theobald Lewis [1940] Director

Flame Heating Spares Limited
Incorporated: 15 March 2011 *Employees:* 19
Net Worth: £680,908 *Total Assets:* £2,946,889
Registered Office: Unit 2 Ninth Avenue, Team Valley Trading Estate, Gateshead, Tyne & Wear, NE11 0EH
Activities: Wholesale of hardware, plumbing and heating equipment and supplies
Shareholders: John Savage; Gary Riseborough
Officers: Gary Riseborough [1965] Sales Director; John Savage [1980] Director/Manager

Flanges Limited
Incorporated: 19 September 1962
Net Worth: £1,067,681 *Total Assets:* £1,244,542
Registered Office: Flanges Limited, Blue House, Point Road, Portrack Trading Estate, Stockton on Tees, Cleveland, TS18 2PJ
Activities: Manufacture of other fabricated metal products n.e.c.
Officers: John Roger Northcote Inch, Secretary; Kenneth Gullane Gibb [1946] Director; Keith Harker [1957] Works Director; John Roger Northcote Inch [1929] Director

Flat Free Tyres Limited
Incorporated: 31 January 2006 *Employees:* 21
Net Worth: £275,605 *Total Assets:* £869,895
Registered Office: Simcox Court, Riverside Park Industrial Estate, Middlesbrough, Cleveland, TS2 1UU
Activities: Manufacture of other plastic products
Major Shareholder: Colin Philip Scarsi
Officers: Colin Philip Scarsi, Secretary; Stephen Bell [1968] Director; Robert Ferguson [1979] Director; Colin Philip Scarsi [1951] Director

Flatliners Limited
Incorporated: 7 August 2003
Net Worth: £304,527 *Total Assets:* £1,792,188
Registered Office: 108 Fowler Street, South Shields, Tyne & Wear, NE33 1PZ
Activities: Buying and selling of own real estate
Major Shareholder: Ajay Jagota
Officers: Ajay Jagota [1969] Director

Flaxby Park Limited
Incorporated: 18 April 2016
Net Worth Deficit: £7,571 *Total Assets:* £13,844,084
Registered Office: Wynyard Park House, Wynyard Avenue, Wynyard, Cleveland, TS22 5TB
Activities: Buying and selling of own real estate
Officers: Pauline Anne Bradley [1961] Director; Trevor Cartner [1960] Director; Ann Heron Gloag [1942] Director; Joseph Christopher Musgrave [1965] Director

FLC Durham Limited
Incorporated: 22 February 2010 *Employees:* 18
Net Worth: £745,797 *Total Assets:* £1,041,695
Registered Office: 66 Saddler Street, Durham, DH1 4NP
Activities: Licenced restaurants
Shareholders: Fabio Ciampolillo; Lesley Anne Ciampolillo
Officers: Fabio Ciampolillo [1962] Director/Restaurateur [Italian]; Lesley Anne Ciampolillo [1958] Director/Restaurateur

Fleet Factors Limited
Incorporated: 27 October 1975 *Employees:* 261
Net Worth: £5,636,029 *Total Assets:* £13,908,752
Registered Office: Unit 3-4 Wallis Road, Sotherby Road, Middlesbrough, Cleveland, TS6 6JB
Activities: Retail trade of motor vehicle parts and accessories
Shareholder: Michael John Hunter
Officers: Barnaby James Edward Hunter, Secretary; Barnaby James Edward Hunter [1974] Director/Manager; Joelyon Michael Thomas Hunter [1976] Managing Director; Michael John Hunter [1944] Director/Chairman; David Kevin James [1963] Director/Manager; Thomas William Mather [1966] Director/Manager; Gary Anthony Norris [1961] Director/Manager

Fletcher Challenge Building UK Limited
Incorporated: 28 June 2000 *Employees:* 2
Net Worth Deficit: £625,000 *Total Assets:* £287,089,984
Registered Office: c/o Formica Limited, Coast Road, North Shields, Tyne & Wear, NE29 8RE
Activities: Other business support service activities n.e.c.
Officers: Joanne McGregor, Secretary; Paul Andrew Foreman [1979] Director/Chief Operating Officer; Neil Laurence Mason [1970] Finance Director

Fletcher Challenge Forest Industries Limited
Incorporated: 27 October 1989 *Employees:* 2
Net Worth: £86,027,000 *Total Assets:* £297,712,992
Registered Office: c/o Formica Limited, Coast Road, North Shields, Tyne & Wear, NE29 8RE
Activities: Combined office administrative service activities
Parent: Fletcher Challenge Building UK Ltd
Officers: Joanne McGregor, Secretary; Paul Andrew Foreman [1979] Director/Chief Operating Officer; Neil Laurence Mason [1970] Finance Director

James Fletcher Limited
Incorporated: 11 January 1989
Registered Office: Unit 4 Wolsingham Estate, Durham Road, Wolsingham, Co Durham, DL13 3JW
Activities: Freight transport by road
Shareholders: James Fletcher; Amanda Fletcher
Officers: Amanda Fletcher, Secretary; Adam James Fletcher [1985] Director; Amanda Fletcher [1955] Director/Marquee Hirer; William Morris James Fletcher [1952] Director/Marquee Hirer

Fletcher Property Investments UK Limited
Incorporated: 28 December 1987 *Employees:* 2
Net Worth: £11,506,000 *Total Assets:* £11,663,000
Registered Office: c/o Formica Limited, Coast Road, North Shields, Tyne & Wear, NE29 8RE
Activities: Buying and selling of own real estate
Parent: Fletcher Challenge Forest Industries Ltd
Officers: Joanne McGregor, Secretary; Paul Andrew Foreman [1979] Director/Chief Operating Officer; Neil Laurence Mason [1970] Finance Director

Flexible Engineered Solutions Holdings Limited
Incorporated: 14 November 2008
Net Worth: £2,746,000 *Total Assets:* £6,200,000
Registered Office: Merchant Court, North Seaton Industrial Estate, Ashington, Northumberland, NE63 0YB
Activities: Activities of other holding companies n.e.c.
Officers: Robert Anderson, Secretary; Robert Anderson [1967] Director; Ian Latimer [1965] Director

Flexible Engineered Solutions Limited
Incorporated: 17 March 2004 *Employees:* 44
Net Worth: £10,078,244 *Total Assets:* £11,704,716
Registered Office: Merchant Court, North Seaton Industrial Estate, Ashington, Northumberland, NE63 0YB
Activities: Other business support service activities n.e.c.
Officers: Robert Anderson, Secretary; Robert Anderson [1967] Commercial Director; Ian Latimer [1965] Director; Joseph Oliphant [1949] Director

Flexible Support Options Limited
Incorporated: 23 January 2012 *Employees:* 178
Net Worth: £4,365,133 *Total Assets:* £5,300,708
Registered Office: 15-16 Stockholm Close, Tyne Tunnel Trading Estate, North Shields, Tyne & Wear, NE29 7SF
Activities: Residential care activities for learning difficulties, mental health and substance abuse
Parent: Flexible Support Options Holdings Ltd
Officers: Amarjit Singh Ladhar [1956] Director; Baldev Singh Ladhar [1958] Director

Flextime Limited
Incorporated: 22 September 2010 *Employees:* 6
Net Worth: £3,482,797 *Total Assets:* £4,635,945
Registered Office: Russel House, Mill Road, Langley Moor, Co Durham, DH7 8HJ
Activities: Management consultancy activities other than financial management
Officers: Douglas Mill, Secretary; Patrick Edward Kane [1970] Director; Douglas Mill [1962] Director; Matthew James Powell [1968] Director; Paul John Taylor [1967] Director

Flightblade Limited
Incorporated: 19 September 2006
Net Worth: £239,662 *Total Assets:* £1,982,065
Registered Office: 27 Crossway, Jesmond, Newcastle upon Tyne, NE2 3QH
Activities: Other letting and operating of own or leased real estate
Major Shareholder: Houshang Tahmassebi
Officers: Houshang Tahmassebi [1953] Director

Flint Properties Limited
Incorporated: 13 February 1996
Net Worth Deficit: £118,227 *Total Assets:* £908,429
Registered Office: c/o Magnet Limited, 3 Allington Way, Yarm Road Business Park, Darlington, Co Durham, DL1 4XT
Activities: Other manufacturing n.e.c.
Parent: Magnet Limited
Officers: Nicola Jane Hardcastle, Secretary; Peter Kane [1965] Managing Director

John Flowers Limited
Incorporated: 4 May 1982 *Employees:* 106
Net Worth: £4,419,615 *Total Assets:* £6,813,687
Registered Office: 2 Monument Park, Pattinson Industrial Estate, Washington, Tyne & Wear, NE38 8QU
Activities: Roofing activities
Parent: F & I Holdings Limited
Officers: John Flowers, Secretary; James Harvey Flowers [1986] Director/Contracts Manager; Jeanette Flowers [1956] Director; John Flowers [1957] Director; Jonathan James Flowers [1982] Director/Contracts Manager; Michael Norman Watson [1971] Director/Estimator

Fluid Technology Generation Limited
Incorporated: 30 July 1998 *Employees:* 18
Net Worth: £1,192,508 *Total Assets:* £1,619,817
Registered Office: Drum House, Drum Industrial Estate, Chester-le-Street, Co Durham, DH2 1SR
Activities: Manufacture of other chemical products n.e.c.
Officers: David Bowman [1951] Commercial Director; Christine Bruce [1958] Director/Secretary; Nigel Laurence Bruce [1951] Managing Director; Harold George Cattell [1955] Production Director

FM Coatings Limited
Incorporated: 17 September 2007 *Employees:* 92
Net Worth: £2,028,640 *Total Assets:* £5,472,675
Registered Office: Unit 15 Brooklands Way, Boldon Business Park, Boldon Colliery, Co Durham, NE35 9LZ
Activities: Manufacture of other plastic products
Shareholders: Michael Alan Ford; Sharon Ford
Officers: Michael Alan Ford, Secretary; Michael Alan Ford [1966] Director/Manager; Michael McNicholas [1976] Director

FM Trading (GB) Limited
Incorporated: 10 August 2011
Net Worth: £707,603 *Total Assets:* £1,388,352
Registered Office: The Office, Cromwell Court, Shields Road, Pelaw, Gateshead, Tyne & Wear, NE10 0SG
Activities: Retail sale of carpets, rugs, wall and floor coverings in specialised stores
Shareholders: Montana Marie Maguire; Frank Maguire (Jnr)
Officers: Frank Maguire Jnr [1993] Director

Foden Spence Construction Limited
Incorporated: 27 February 1985 *Employees:* 14
Net Worth: £535,392 *Total Assets:* £802,660
Registered Office: Ellerbeck Court, Stokesley Industrial Park, Stokesley, Cleveland, TS9 5PT
Activities: Construction of commercial buildings
Major Shareholder: Mark Foden
Officers: Janine Brenda Wedgewood, Secretary; Mark Foden [1970] Managing Director

Fontmerry Ltd
Incorporated: 25 June 2003
Net Worth: £1,589,632 *Total Assets:* £1,589,632
Registered Office: Bridge House, 96 High West Street, Gateshead, Tyne & Wear, NE8 1NA
Activities: Buying and selling of own real estate
Officers: Bernard Dunner, Secretary/Manager; Bernard Dunner [1981] Director/Manager; Nechama Dunner [1982] Director/Housewife

For Skills Limited
Incorporated: 29 April 2005
Net Worth: £7,000 *Total Assets:* £761,000
Registered Office: c/o Emma Hoare, Q6 Quorum Business Park, Benton Lane, Newcastle upon Tyne, NE12 8BT
Activities: Other software publishing
Parent: NCFE
Officers: David John Grailey [1967] Director; Myles Frederick Almon Ponsonby [1972] Director; Esme Frances Winch [1958] Director

H. & J. Forbes Limited
Incorporated: 4 February 1986
Net Worth: £470,797 *Total Assets:* £770,472
Registered Office: 8 High Street, Yarm, Stockton on Tees, Cleveland, TS15 9AE
Activities: Manufacture of office and shop furniture
Officers: Susan Jean Wray, Secretary; Ian Forbes [1958] Director/Manager; Stephen Forbes [1953] Director/Manager

Ford Aerospace Limited
Incorporated: 6 January 1944 *Employees:* 70
Net Worth: £1,065,587 *Total Assets:* £2,213,324
Registered Office: East Side, Tyne Dock, South Shields, Tyne & Wear, NE33 5ST
Activities: Manufacture of other fabricated metal products n.e.c.
Shareholder: Robert Geoffrey Ford
Officers: Robert Geoffrey Ford, Secretary; Christopher Geoffrey Ford [1985] Managing Director; Marilyn Ford [1950] Director; Robert Geoffrey Ford [1943] Director/Chartered Accountant; Iain Oates [1963] Director

Ford Castle Adventure Ltd
Incorporated: 20 December 2011 *Employees:* 23
Net Worth: £602,662 *Total Assets:* £808,883
Registered Office: Demesne Hall, Rectory Lane, Wolsingham, Co Durham, DL13 3AJ
Activities: Other holiday and other collective accommodation
Shareholder: Dr Peter Joseph Smith
Officers: Dr Peter Joseph Smith [1950] Director; Ben Wire [1976] Director

Ford Component Manufacturing Limited
Incorporated: 5 August 2008
Net Worth: £996,962 *Total Assets:* £2,534,431
Registered Office: East Side, Tyne Dock, South Shields, Tyne & Wear, NE33 5ST
Activities: Manufacture of metal structures and parts of structures
Shareholder: Robert Geoffrey Ford
Officers: Robert Geoffrey Ford, Secretary; Christopher Geoffrey Ford [1985] Managing Director; Marilyn Ford [1950] Director; Robert Geoffrey Ford [1943] Director/Chartered Accountant; Iain Oates [1963] Director

Jack Ford Limited
Incorporated: 18 July 1977
Net Worth: £1,366,172 *Total Assets:* £1,384,937
Registered Office: 19 Rectory Road, Gosforth, Newcastle upon Tyne, NE3 1XP
Activities: Sale of used cars and light motor vehicles
Shareholders: Ian Watson; Caroline Watson; Emma Watson
Officers: Ian Watson, Secretary; Caroline Watson [1955] Director; Emma Watson [1976] Director/Press Officer; Ian Watson [1950] Managing Director

Ford Parts (UK) Limited
Incorporated: 13 August 1999 *Employees:* 9
Net Worth: £542,756 *Total Assets:* £1,232,678
Registered Office: Unit 14a, Brama Teams Industrial Park, Team Street, Gateshead, Tyne & Wear, NE8 2RG
Activities: Wholesale trade of motor vehicle parts and accessories
Shareholders: Karen Gamble; Trevor Gamble
Officers: Karen Julie Fletcher, Secretary; Trevor Gamble [1969] Director/Car Parts Salesman

Fordinghall Ltd
Incorporated: 25 June 2003 *Employees:* 4
Net Worth: £2,610,586 *Total Assets:* £9,749,281
Registered Office: Bridge House, 96 High West Street, Gateshead, Tyne & Wear, NE8 1NA
Activities: Buying and selling of own real estate
Officers: Bernard Dunner, Secretary/Manager; Bernard Dunner [1981] Director/Manager; Nechama Dunner [1982] Director/Housewife

George Fordy Properties Limited
Incorporated: 24 October 2001 *Employees:* 3
Net Worth: £3,627,227 *Total Assets:* £4,162,923
Registered Office: Construction House, High Street, Northallerton, N Yorks, DL7 8ED
Activities: Other letting and operating of own or leased real estate
Major Shareholder: Susan Bridget Greenwell
Officers: Derek John Greenwell, Secretary; Paul Blades [1963] Director; Derek John Greenwell [1948] Director Company Secretary; Keith Brian Noddings [1972] Finance Director

Forest B.P. LLP
Incorporated: 10 May 2004
Net Worth: £568,333 *Total Assets:* £1,059,309
Registered Office: York House, Thornfield Business Park, Standard Way Business Park, Northallerton, N Yorks, DL6 2XQ
Officers: Charles William Foster [1941] Member; James Richard Foster [1964] Member; Simon Charles Foster [1967] Member

Forest Carbon Limited
Incorporated: 3 January 2007 *Employees:* 1
Net Worth: £547,204 *Total Assets:* £1,274,840
Registered Office: Abbey Road Business Centre, Abbey Road, Durham, DH1 5JZ
Activities: Support services to forestry
Shareholders: Stephen David Prior; James Patrick Hepburne Scott
Officers: Stephen David Prior, Secretary/Director; James Patrick Hepburne Scott [1947] Sales Director; Stephen David Prior [1968] Director

Forest Homes Limited
Incorporated: 7 January 2016 *Employees:* 4
Net Worth Deficit: £800 *Total Assets:* £2,805,489
Registered Office: Holywood House, Wolsingham, Co Durham, DL13 3HE
Activities: Construction of domestic buildings
Shareholders: Anne Hill; Robert Angus Hill
Officers: Anne Hill, Secretary; Andrea Cassidy [1975] Director; Emma Hill [1979] Director; Robert Angus Hill [1950] Director

Forge Leisure (UK) Limited
Incorporated: 25 May 2007
Net Worth: £407,436 *Total Assets:* £754,509
Registered Office: Forge Industrial Centre, Morpeth Road, Ashington, Northumberland, NE63 8QG
Activities: Other manufacturing n.e.c.
Shareholders: Paul Dawson; P. Dawson Developments Limited
Officers: Karen Campbell, Secretary; Christopher Ian Bland [1972] Director; Paul Dawson [1961] Managing Director

Forman Vehicle Services Limited
Incorporated: 19 June 2001 *Employees:* 9
Net Worth: £837,386 *Total Assets:* £1,401,191
Registered Office: 2 Ellerbeck Court, Stokesley Business Park, Stokesley, Middlesbrough, Cleveland, TS9 5PT
Activities: Repair and maintenance of other transport equipment n.e.c.
Shareholders: Terence William Forman; Heather Irene Forman
Officers: Heather Irene Foreman [1958] Director; Scott Foreman [1982] Director; Terence William Foreman [1955] Director/Auto Electrician

Formica Finance Limited
Incorporated: 18 March 2008
Net Worth: £1,409,000 *Total Assets:* £1,409,000
Registered Office: Formica Limited, Coast Road, North Shields, Tyne & Wear, NE29 8RE
Activities: Non-trading company
Parent: Formica Limited
Officers: Joanne McGregor, Secretary; Neil Laurence Mason [1970] Finance Director; Peter John Rush [1962] Director/President

Formica Holdco (UK) Limited
Incorporated: 11 March 1998
Net Worth: £100,094,000 *Total Assets:* £180,103,008
Registered Office: Coast Road, North Shields, Tyne & Wear, NE29 8RE
Activities: Non-trading company
Officers: Joanne McGregor, Secretary; Neil Laurence Mason [1970] Finance Director; Peter John Rush [1962] Director/President

Formica Limited
Incorporated: 23 March 1915 *Employees:* 501
Net Worth: £68,449,000 *Total Assets:* £207,444,992
Registered Office: Coast Road, North Shields, Tyne & Wear, NE29 8RE
Activities: Other manufacturing n.e.c.
Parent: Formica Holdco (UK) Limited
Officers: Joanne McGregor, Secretary; Leigh Jeffrey Box [1955] Director [Australian]; Paul Andrew Foreman [1979] Director; Neil Laurence Mason [1970] Finance Director; Bevan John McKenzie [1977] Finance Director [New Zealander]; Peter John Rush [1962] Director/President

Formula Plastics Limited
Incorporated: 16 February 1996 *Employees:* 52
Net Worth: £563,315 *Total Assets:* £1,930,914
Registered Office: 20 The Broadway, Tynemouth, North Shields, Tyne & Wear, NE30 2LF
Activities: Manufacture of other plastic products
Shareholders: Christopher Smith; Dr John Reginald Suggate
Officers: Dr John Reginald Suggate, Secretary/Managing Director; James Richard Goodliffe [1970] Managing Director; Geoffrey Hodgson [1973] Production Director; Dr John Reginald Suggate [1947] Director/Chairman

Forrest Park (Newton Aycliffe) Limited
Incorporated: 30 March 2016
Net Worth: £2,003,420 *Total Assets:* £2,120,220
Registered Office: c/o Durham County Council, County Hall, Durham, DH1 5UE
Activities: Buying and selling of own real estate
Parent: Durham County Council
Officers: Frederick Jason Forrest [1963] Director/Farmer; Fredrik Kurt Forrest [1971] Director/Surveyor; Joy Forrest [1936] Director/Farming; Antony Forster [1966] Director/Local Government Officer; Andrew Philip Palmer [1965] Director/Local Government Officer; Azhar Ahmed Rafiq [1975] Director/Local Government Officer; David John Wafer [1963] Director/Chartered Civil Engineer

Geoffrey Forrester & Co Limited
Incorporated: 13 June 2012 *Employees:* 23
Net Worth: £729,754 *Total Assets:* £2,383,658
Registered Office: 4 Grange Road West, Jarrow, Tyne & Wear, NE32 3JA
Activities: Solicitors
Shareholders: Geoffrey Michael Forrester; David Forrester
Officers: Joyce Linda Forrester, Secretary; Valerie Ann Bell [1965] Director; David Lewis Forrester [1973] Director/Solicitor; Geoffrey Michael Forrester [1948] Director/Solicitor; Helen Louise Forrester [1975] Director; Julia Margaret Halling [1979] Director/Solicitor; Michelle Stonley [1972] Director/Solicitor

W.H. Forster (Printers) Limited
Incorporated: 25 July 1951
Net Worth: £1,423,506 *Total Assets:* £2,898,764
Registered Office: Doxford Printworks, Pallion Quay, Sunderland, Tyne & Wear, SR4 6TQ
Activities: Printing n.e.c.
Major Shareholder: Malcolm Robin Gray
Officers: Linda Gray, Secretary; Linda Gray [1953] Director/Private Secretary; Malcolm Robin Gray [1950] Director/Printer

Forte Freehold Management Limited
Incorporated: 12 October 2009 *Employees:* 3
Net Worth: £1,397,162 *Total Assets:* £1,625,910
Registered Office: 5 Maling Court, Union Street, Newcastle upon Tyne, NE2 1BP
Activities: Management of real estate on a fee or contract basis
Major Shareholder: Ian Robert Baggett
Officers: Diane Fletcher [1964] Director

Forth England Limited
Incorporated: 26 June 2012
Net Worth: £1,996,902 *Total Assets:* £2,519,891
Registered Office: Denwick House, Denwick Village, Denwick, Alnwick, Northumberland, NE66 3RE
Activities: Other business support service activities n.e.c.
Major Shareholder: Roderick Charles St John Wilson
Officers: Roderick Charles St John Wilson, Secretary; James Hugh St John Wilson [1992] Director; Oliver Harry St John Wilson [1994] Director; Roderick Charles St John Wilson [1961] Director

Forthcastle LLP
Incorporated: 22 September 2004
Net Worth: £10,652,250 *Total Assets:* £10,872,047
Registered Office: 14 Westfield Drive, Gosforth, Newcastle upon Tyne, NE3 4XU
Officers: Peter Armstrong [1948] Member; Malcolm Robertson Croudace [1956] Member; Beverley Ann Scott [1970] Member

Forum Centrespace Limited
Incorporated: 8 October 2001 *Employees:* 7
Net Worth: £403,057 *Total Assets:* £1,109,790
Registered Office: 14 Lansdowne Terrace, Gosforth, Newcastle upon Tyne, NE3 1HN
Activities: Management of real estate on a fee or contract basis
Shareholders: Peter Ling; Kathryn Martha Ling
Officers: Peter Ling, Secretary; Kathryn Martha Ling [1961] Director/Marketing Consultant; Peter Ling [1956] Director/Marketing Consultant

Forward Sound Limited
Incorporated: 14 October 2008 *Employees:* 5
Net Worth: £6,225,000 *Total Assets:* £15,184,000
Registered Office: West Terrace, Esh Winning, Co Durham, DH7 9PT
Activities: Support activities for other mining and quarrying
Parent: Hargreaves Services PLC
Officers: Stephen Nigel Macquarrie, Secretary; Steven Leslie Anson [1965] Director; Gordon Frank Colenso Banham [1964] Director; David Thomas Pearce [1980] Director

Foster Findlay Associates Limited
Incorporated: 22 October 1987 *Employees:* 35
Net Worth: £8,959,456 *Total Assets:* £10,826,476
Registered Office: Generator Studios, Trafalgar Street, Newcastle upon Tyne, NE1 2LA
Activities: Other software publishing
Officers: Nicola Louise Blanshard, Secretary; Nicola Louise Blanshard [1970] Director/Chartered Accountant; John George Carney [1948] Director/Business Strategist; Jan Grimnes [1961] Director [Norwegian]; Helge Tveit [1964] Director [Norwegian]

Foster Hill Properties (Bedford) Limited
Incorporated: 1 April 1960 *Employees:* 2
Net Worth: £810,790 *Total Assets:* £1,105,122
Registered Office: 2 Milbank Road, Darlington, Co Durham, DL3 9NH
Activities: Other letting and operating of own or leased real estate
Major Shareholder: Judith Patricia Potts
Officers: Gemma Fay Charlton, Secretary; Gemma Fay Charlton [1979] Director; Judith Patricia Potts [1953] Director

L.B. Foster Rail Technologies (UK) Limited
Incorporated: 3 March 2000 *Employees:* 86
Net Worth: £30,034,712 *Total Assets:* £35,335,784
Registered Office: 5 Osborne Terrace, Jesmond, Newcastle upon Tyne, NE2 1SQ
Activities: Manufacture of other special-purpose machinery n.e.c.
Officers: Peter David Vaughan Jones [1966] Director; John Francis Kasel [1965] Director [American]; Suzanne Roberts [1974] Director

Russell Foster Tyne and Wear Sports Foundation
Incorporated: 19 March 1997
Net Worth: £929,195 *Total Assets:* £934,035
Registered Office: Temple Chambers, Douro Terrace, Sunderland, Tyne & Wear, SR2 7DX
Activities: Operation of sports facilities
Officers: David Neil Armstrong, Secretary; David Neil Armstrong [1960] Director/Chartered Accountant; Michael Clark [1947] Director; James Russell Foster [1948] Director; George Tilley [1964] Director/Solicitor

Foundation of European Nurses in Diabetes
Incorporated: 31 December 2009 *Employees:* 1
Net Worth: £1,803,774 *Total Assets:* £1,807,220
Registered Office: 37 Earls Drive, Denton Burn, Newcastle upon Tyne, NE15 7AL
Activities: Other human health activities
Officers: Deirdre Cregan [1945] Director/Retired [Irish]; Kristin Debacker [1958] Director/Registered Nurse [Belgian]; Anne-Marie Mary Felton [1943] Director/Retired; Deirdre Anne Kyne Grzebalski [1951] Director/Senior Nurse; Dr Colin Stephen McIntosh [1940] Director; Professor Regina Wredling [1940] Director [Finnish]

Foundation of Light
Incorporated: 28 June 2001 *Employees:* 130
Net Worth: £12,311,903 *Total Assets:* £17,786,566
Registered Office: Beacon of Light, Stadium Park, Sunderland, Tyne & Wear, SR5 1SN
Activities: Other education n.e.c.
Officers: Kathryn Adie [1945] Director/Broadcaster; George Clarke [1974] Director/Architect; Paul David Collingwood [1976] Director/Sports Management; Stephen Cram [1960] Director/Television Presenter; Estelle Morris [1957] Director/Peer; Sir Robert Sydney Murray [1946] Director/Businessman; James David Alexander Ramsbotham [1959] Director; Sir Timothy Miles Bindon Rice [1944] Director/Writer

The Fountain Group Limited
Incorporated: 5 May 2015 *Employees:* 2
Net Worth Deficit: £631,178 *Total Assets:* £1,174,425
Registered Office: 24 Newgate Street, Morpeth, Northumberland, NE61 1BA
Activities: Activities of head offices
Officers: Colin Peter McClymont [1956] Director; Sally McClymont [1961] Director

Fourstones Paper Mill Company Limited
Incorporated: 26 June 1952 *Employees:* 155
Net Worth: £8,448,605 *Total Assets:* £19,199,940
Registered Office: South Tyne Mill, Fourstones, Hexham, Northumberland, NE46 3SD
Activities: Manufacture of paper and paperboard
Parent: Sandco F.P.S Limited
Officers: Pauline Duxbury, Secretary; Peter Gerard Duxbury [1960] Director

Fox Formulated Feeds Limited
Incorporated: 25 July 1995
Net Worth: £394,245 *Total Assets:* £903,805
Registered Office: East Shaws Farm, Westwick, Barnard Castle, Co Durham, DL12 8UT
Activities: Support activities for animal production (other than farm animal boarding)
Shareholders: Allison Fiona Fox; Neale Fox
Officers: Allison Fiona Fox, Secretary; Allison Fiona Fox [1972] Director/Bank Clerk; Neale Fox [1965] Director/Sales Manager

Fox House Ltd
Incorporated: 9 January 2014
Net Worth: £1,185,710 *Total Assets:* £1,261,690
Registered Office: 19 Molineux Court, Heaton Park Road, Newcastle upon Tyne, NE6 1SU
Activities: Renting and operating of Housing Association real estate
Major Shareholder: Luke Gad
Officers: Luke Gad, Secretary; Edward Gad [1977] Director/Manager; Luke Gad [1981] Director/Manager

G.I. Fox Limited
Incorporated: 31 January 2003 *Employees:* 1
Net Worth: £779,242 *Total Assets:* £1,274,524
Registered Office: 80 Borough Road, Middlesbrough, Cleveland, TS1 2JN
Activities: Management of real estate on a fee or contract basis
Major Shareholder: Geoffrey Ian Fox
Officers: Geoffrey Ian Fox [1946] Director/Landlord

Foxy Hair Extensions (NE) Ltd
Incorporated: 13 June 2012 *Employees:* 15
Net Worth: £528,061 *Total Assets:* £870,902
Registered Office: Unit 14d Airport Industrial Estate, Kingston Park, Newcastle upon Tyne, NE3 2EF
Activities: Retail sale via mail order houses or via Internet
Shareholders: Simon Andrew Fox; Hayley Fox
Officers: Hayley Fox [1981] Director; Simon Fox [1979] Director

FPP Design Limited
Incorporated: 8 November 1996 *Employees:* 55
Net Worth: £1,189,632 *Total Assets:* £2,085,040
Registered Office: Felton House, The Courtyard, 1 Dinsdale Place, Sandyford, Newcastle upon Tyne, NE2 1BD
Activities: Advertising agencies
Shareholders: William Edwin Rodger; Christopher Hewison
Officers: David Glendenning [1968] Accounts Director; Christopher Hewison [1946] Director/Design Consultant; William Edwin Rodger [1952] Director/Design Consultant; Neil James Rowley [1979] Director/Chartered Accountant; Nicholas John Taylor [1983] Planning Director

Fracks Transport Limited
Incorporated: 23 February 1982 *Employees:* 36
Net Worth: £1,771,991 *Total Assets:* £2,348,420
Registered Office: Groat Drive, Aycliffe Industrial Estate, Newton Aycliffe, Co Durham, DL5 6HY
Activities: Freight transport by road
Major Shareholder: Stanley Fraquet
Officers: Sandra Elizabeth Watson, Secretary; Sandra Fraquet [1952] Director; Stanley Fraquet [1950] Director

Fradley Residential LLP
Incorporated: 30 October 2015
Net Worth: £919,283 *Total Assets:* £12,841,333
Registered Office: Seaton Burn House, Dudley Lane, Seaton Burn, Newcastle upon Tyne, NE13 6BE

Fragrant Harbour Limited
Incorporated: 9 August 2001
Net Worth: £615,416 *Total Assets:* £1,056,525
Registered Office: 32 Northumberland Avenue, Gosforth, Newcastle upon Tyne, NE3 4XH
Activities: Other letting and operating of own or leased real estate
Shareholder: Nigel Hin for Tsang
Officers: Nigel Hin for Tsang, Secretary; Nigel Hin for Tsang [1966] Finance Director; Sindy Yee Han Tsang [1967] Director

J. Frampton Property Development Limited
Incorporated: 10 January 2002
Net Worth: £340,882 *Total Assets:* £771,807
Registered Office: Kelloe Hall Farm, Town Kelloe, Kelloe, Co Durham, DH6 4PR
Activities: Buying and selling of own real estate
Major Shareholder: John Frampton
Officers: John Frampton, Secretary; Anne Frampton [1955] Director/Executive; John Frampton [1952] Director/Self Employed

Francis Transport Limited
Incorporated: 30 April 1998 *Employees:* 37
Net Worth: £1,262,726 *Total Assets:* £2,270,782
Registered Office: 7 Stephenson Road, Stephenson Industrial Estate, Washington, Tyne & Wear, NE37 3HR
Activities: Freight transport by road
Shareholder: Eric John Francis
Officers: Eric John Francis, Secretary/Haulier; Paul Mark Dollery [1967] Director/Haulier; Eric John Francis [1947] Director/Haulier

Nigel Frank International Limited
Incorporated: 1 November 2006 *Employees:* 596
Net Worth: £22,060,000 *Total Assets:* £54,994,000
Registered Office: The St Nicholas Building, St Nicholas Street, Newcastle upon Tyne, NE1 1RF
Activities: Other activities of employment placement agencies
Parent: Frank Recruitment Group Services Limited
Officers: Nigel Ashley O'Donoghue, Secretary/Director; James Lloyd-Townshend [1973] Director; Lewis Paul Miller [1981] Director; Nigel Ashley O'Donoghue [1972] Director

Frank Recruitment Group Limited
Incorporated: 4 April 2013 *Employees:* 815
Net Worth: £42,283,000 *Total Assets:* £57,664,000
Registered Office: The St Nicholas Building, St Nicholas Street, Newcastle upon Tyne, NE1 1RF
Activities: Activities of other holding companies n.e.c.
Parent: Finders Bidco Limited
Officers: James Lloyd-Townshend [1973] Director; Lewis Paul Miller [1981] Director; Nigel Ashley O'Donoghue [1972] Director

Frank Recruitment Group Services Limited
Incorporated: 13 July 2012 *Employees:* 4
Net Worth: £32,044,000 *Total Assets:* £56,452,000
Registered Office: The St Nicholas Building, St Nicholas Street, Newcastle upon Tyne, NE1 1RF
Activities: Other activities of employment placement agencies
Parent: Frank Recruitment Group Limited
Officers: Nigel Ashley O'Donoghue, Secretary; James Lloyd-Townshend [1973] Director; Lewis Paul Miller [1981] Director; Kashif Shafique Naqshbandi [1969] Director; Nigel Ashley O'Donoghue [1972] Director

Franklin Steel Stockholders Ltd
Incorporated: 28 August 1986
Net Worth: £4,124,252 *Total Assets:* £8,976,992
Registered Office: Franklin Industrial Estate, Patterson Street, Blaydon Haugh, Blaydon, Tyne & Wear, NE21 5TL
Activities: Other retail sale not in stores, stalls or markets
Major Shareholder: Brian Dennis Phillips
Officers: Robert Wealleans, Secretary; Brian Dennis Phillips [1955] Managing Director; Ian Andrew Robinson [1961] Executive Director; Michael St Clair Wallace [1972] Director; Robert Wealleans [1959] Director

Lewis Franklin Trading Ltd
Incorporated: 11 July 2016
Net Worth: £798,339 *Total Assets:* £920,558
Registered Office: Portland House, Belmont Business Park, Durham, DH1 1TW
Activities: Other service activities n.e.c.
Major Shareholder: Albert Francis Gill
Officers: Albert Francis Gill [1954] Director; Pratick Tailor [1996] Director

Frecker Limited
Incorporated: 13 October 1995 *Employees:* 23
Net Worth: £4,479,886 *Total Assets:* £10,040,389
Registered Office: Henson House, Whitley Road, Newcastle upon Tyne, NE12 9SR
Activities: Sale of used cars and light motor vehicles
Major Shareholder: David Nathan Wilson
Officers: Richard Nigel Wilson, Secretary; John Muckian [1971] Director; David Nathan Wilson [1973] Managing Director

J. R. Freeman & Co. (Estates) Limited
Incorporated: 15 March 1988
Net Worth: £786,950 *Total Assets:* £1,343,434
Registered Office: Unit 353 Dukesway Court, Team Valley Trading Estate, Gateshead, Tyne & Wear, NE11 0BH
Activities: Other letting and operating of own or leased real estate
Shareholders: James Robert Freeman; James Robert Freeman; Daniel George Freeman
Officers: Joyce Hepplewhite, Secretary; Daniel George Freeman [1976] Director; James Robert Freeman [1971] Director; James Robert Freeman [1948] Director

J. Freeman & Sons Limited
Incorporated: 11 September 2001 *Employees:* 53
Net Worth: £635,101 *Total Assets:* £1,573,555
Registered Office: Unit 353a Team Valley Trading Estate, Gateshead, Tyne & Wear, NE11 0BH
Activities: Wholesale of meat and meat products
Shareholders: Daniel George Freeman; James Robert Freeman
Officers: Daniel George Freeman, Secretary; Daniel George Freeman [1976] Director; James Robert Freeman [1971] Director; James Robert Freeman [1948] Director

Freeman Clinics Limited
Incorporated: 1 August 2007
Net Worth Deficit: £304,492 *Total Assets:* £1,721,505
Registered Office: RMT, Gosforth Park Avenue, Newcastle upon Tyne, NE12 8EG
Activities: General medical practice activities
Parent: The Newcastle upon Tyne Hospitals NHS Foundation Trust
Officers: Rachel Shakir, Secretary; Teresa Creighton [1963] Director/NHS Manager; David Iain Reynolds [1962] Director/NHS Accountant; Rachel Shakir [1966] Director/Manager; Katharine Adele Simpson [1963] Deputy Director of Business and Development; Dr Ian Stewart Winterton [1948] Director/Retired

Freeman Finance (North East) Limited
Incorporated: 18 November 2014
Net Worth: £812,144 *Total Assets:* £817,459
Registered Office: 353 Dukesway Court, Team Valley Trading Estate, Gateshead, Tyne & Wear, NE11 0BH
Activities: Financial management
Major Shareholder: James Robert Freeman
Officers: Daniel George Freeman [1976] Director; James Robert Freeman [1971] Director; James Robert Freeman [1948] Director/Butcher

Fresh Freight Limited
Incorporated: 5 May 1993 *Employees:* 106
Net Worth: £1,405,231 *Total Assets:* £3,596,337
Registered Office: The Railhead Building, Earlsway, Team Valley Trading Estate, Gateshead, Tyne & Wear, NE11 0QY
Activities: Freight transport by road
Major Shareholder: Dominic Graeme Quigley
Officers: Dominic Graeme Quigley, Secretary; Rhonda Alice Quigley, Secretary; Dominic Graeme Quigley [1970] Director/Transport Manager; Dominic Eamon Quigley [1947] Director/Haulage Contractor; John Toft [1984] Director

Jerry Fried & Co Limited
Incorporated: 24 June 1982 *Employees:* 18
Net Worth: £1,063,641 *Total Assets:* £1,353,030
Registered Office: 2 Richmond Terrace, Gateshead, Tyne & Wear, NE8 1RN
Activities: Wholesale of radio, television goods & electrical household appliances (other than records, tapes, CDs)
Shareholders: Jerry Fried; Judith Fried
Officers: Judith Fried, Secretary [Swiss]; Jerry Fried [1950] Director [American]; Judith Fried [1950] Director [Swiss]

Friends of Biala Limited
Incorporated: 4 May 1964
Net Worth: £1,937,995 *Total Assets:* £1,961,939
Registered Office: 106 High West Street, Gateshead, Tyne & Wear, NE8 1NA
Activities: Other social work activities without accommodation n.e.c.
Officers: Yechezkel Michael Halberstadt, Secretary; Michael Dejong [1981] Director; Moshe Thomas Glausiusz [1950] Director; Yechezkel Michael Halberstadt [1972] Director

Frith Street LLP
Incorporated: 28 September 2012
Net Worth: £876,000 *Total Assets:* £943,000
Registered Office: 1a Dukesway Court, Team Valley Trading Estate, Gateshead, Tyne & Wear, NE11 0PJ

Froneri International Limited
Incorporated: 11 April 2006 *Employees:* 33
Net Worth Deficit: £104,741,536 *Total Assets:* £1,859,410,432
Registered Office: Richmond House, Leeming Bar, Northallerton, N Yorks, DL7 9UL
Activities: Other manufacturing n.e.c.
Parent: New R&R Ice Cream Limited
Officers: Marcello Mattia, Secretary; Phil Karl Griffin [1972] Director; Marcello Mattia [1965] Director [Italian]; Ibrahim Mahmood Ibrahim Najafi [1958] Director

Froneri Limited
Incorporated: 20 April 2016 *Employees:* 12,765
Net Worth: £163,001,840 *Total Assets:* £3,390,711,040
Registered Office: Richmond House, Leeming Bar, Northallerton, N Yorks, DL7 9UL
Activities: Activities of production holding companies
Officers: Philip Graham Mellor, Secretary; Sanjay Bahadur [1959] Director/Senior Vice President [Indian]; Patrice Bula [1956] Director/Executive Vice President [Swiss/French]; Luis Cantarell [1952] Director/Executive Vice President [Spanish]; Martin Richard Glenn [1960] Director; Ibrahim Mahmood Ibrahim Najafi [1958] Director; Colm Paul O'Sullivan [1967] Director/Investment Manager [Irish]; Frederic Jacques Maria Paul Stevenin [1966] Director/Investment Manager [French]

Froneri South Africa Holdings Limited
Incorporated: 16 February 2015
Net Worth: £23,591,466 *Total Assets:* £24,233,242
Registered Office: Richmond House, Leeming Bar, Northallerton, N Yorks, DL7 9UL
Activities: Activities of production holding companies
Parent: Froneri International PLC
Officers: Phil Karl Griffin [1972] Director; Marcello Mattia [1965] Director [Italian]; Ibrahim Mahmood Ibrahim Najafi [1958] Director

FT Management Consultants Limited
Incorporated: 28 May 2008
Net Worth: £247,326 *Total Assets:* £999,937
Registered Office: Unit 8 & 9 Parsons Court, Welbury Way, Aycliffe Industrial Park, Newton Aycliffe, Co Durham, DL5 6ZE
Activities: Activities of other holding companies n.e.c.
Shareholders: Aidan Kevin Tait; David Fisher
Officers: David Fisher [1985] Director/Accountant; Aidan Kevin Tait [1982] Director/Accountant

Fujifilm Diosynth Biotechnologies UK Limited
Incorporated: 3 May 2006 *Employees:* 502
Net Worth: £115,500,000 *Total Assets:* £192,900,000
Registered Office: Fujifilm Diosynth Biotechnologies, Belasis Avenue, Billingham, Cleveland, TS23 1LH
Activities: Manufacture of pharmaceutical preparations
Parent: Fujifilm Holdings Corporation
Officers: Neil Llewellyn Denham, Secretary; Stephen Bagshaw [1964] Director/Engineer; Takatoshi Ishikawa [1954] Director [Japanese]; Akira Kase [1963] Director/Employee [Japanese]; Kenji Orihashi [1962] Director/Employee [Japanese]; Masato Yamamoto [1963] Director [Japanese]

Fulbeck Limited
Incorporated: 27 November 2006 *Employees:* 14
Net Worth: £357,542 *Total Assets:* £828,872
Registered Office: Fulbeck Road, Aycliffe Business Park, Newton Aycliffe, Co Durham, DL5 6TX
Activities: Manufacture of other chemical products n.e.c.
Shareholder: Robin Simon Glover Tallentire
Officers: Robin Simon Glover Tallentire, Secretary/Director; Gillian Constance Tallentire [1957] Director; Robin Simon Glover Tallentire [1957] Director; Douglas Urquhart [1951] Director; Frances Greta Urquhart [1950] Director; Glenn Anderson Urquhart [1977] Director

Full Circle Investments Limited
Incorporated: 5 June 1996
Net Worth: £1,508,755 *Total Assets:* £1,535,051
Registered Office: 190 High Street, Redcar, Cleveland, TS10 3AW
Activities: Other letting and operating of own or leased real estate
Major Shareholder: Neville John Hartwell Holdsworth
Officers: Sally Emma Rose, Secretary; Neville John Hartwell Holdsworth [1955] Director; Sally Emma Rose [1964] Director/Housewife Secretary

Fullwell Mill Limited
Incorporated: 15 September 1988
Net Worth: £599,689 *Total Assets:* £2,245,681
Registered Office: Unit 5d Southwick Industrial Estate, Sunderland, Tyne & Wear, SR5 3TX
Activities: Other food services
Shareholders: Adam Edward Brett; Kate Sebag Montefiore
Officers: Adam Edward Brett [1964] Director; Peter Eric Fawcett [1963] Director; Richard David Friend [1963] Director/Baker; David Nicholson [1953] Director/Accountant

Furniture Clinic Limited
Incorporated: 6 September 2005
Net Worth: £165,248 *Total Assets:* £1,603,040
Registered Office: Unit 10 Hobson Industrial Estate, Burnopfield, Co Durham, NE16 6EA
Activities: Tanning and dressing of leather; dressing and dyeing of fur
Major Shareholder: Ben Harvey Staerck
Officers: Ben Harvey Staerck [1986] Director Sales

Furniture Solutions (Northumberland) Limited
Incorporated: 6 September 2007
Net Worth: £320,042 *Total Assets:* £847,780
Registered Office: 32 Saltwell View, Gateshead, Tyne & Wear, NE8 4NT
Activities: Other specialised construction activities n.e.c.
Major Shareholder: Steven Dall Holmes
Officers: Dorothy Holmes, Secretary; Steven Dall Holmes [1967] Director

Fursewood Limited
Incorporated: 19 October 2004 *Employees:* 9
Net Worth: £93,086 *Total Assets:* £822,478
Registered Office: Hancock & Ainsley Pharmacy, 1 Main Street, Shildon, Co Durham, DL4 1AJ
Activities: Dispensing chemist in specialised stores
Officers: Ruth Louise Percival, Secretary; John David Percival [1971] Director/Pharmacist

FWS Consultants Limited
Incorporated: 9 March 2000 *Employees:* 10
Net Worth: £72,526 *Total Assets:* £778,668
Registered Office: Merrington House, Merrington Lane Industrial Estate, Spennymoor, Co Durham, DL16 7UT
Activities: Environmental consulting activities
Parent: NACL Holdings Limited
Officers: Gary Raymond Dresser [1965] Director; Richard Graeme Izatt-Lowry [1964] Director

G & G Leisure Limited
Incorporated: 21 October 1999
Net Worth: £1,071,170 *Total Assets:* £1,225,291
Registered Office: Exchange Building, 66 Church Street, Hartlepool, Cleveland, TS24 7DN
Activities: Licenced clubs
Shareholders: George Thomas Crow; Greta Florence Crow
Officers: George Thomas Crow, Secretary/Leisure Services Manager; George Thomas Crow [1953] Director/Leisure Services Manager; Greta Florence Crow [1961] Director/Leisure Services Manager

G & H Property Limited
Incorporated: 3 August 2016 *Employees:* 2
Net Worth: £994,679 *Total Assets:* £1,003,422
Registered Office: Joyce Buildings, Haverton Hill Industrial Estate, Billingham, Cleveland, TS23 1PZ
Activities: Other letting and operating of own or leased real estate
Shareholder: Christopher James Garbutt
Officers: Christopher James Garbutt [1969] Director; Alan John Harris [1966] Director

G H Farms Limited
Incorporated: 12 October 2010 *Employees:* 6
Net Worth: £477,095 *Total Assets:* £2,051,647
Registered Office: Grange Hill Farm, Grange Hill, Bishop Auckland, Co Durham, DL14 8EG
Activities: Mixed farming
Shareholders: Jane Louise Westgarth; John Angus Westgarth
Officers: Jane Louise Westgarth [1966] Director; John Angus Westgarth [1967] Director/Farmer

G T Project Engineering Limited
Incorporated: 19 April 1971 *Employees:* 37
Net Worth: £162,283 *Total Assets:* £840,143
Registered Office: Delves Lane, Consett, Co Durham, DH8 7LQ
Activities: Manufacture of other tanks, reservoirs and containers of metal
Parent: Knorr-Bremse AG
Officers: Ann Anderson, Secretary; Keith Bendelow [1958] Director; Neil Stuart Conley [1962] Director

G W Leader Property Limited
Incorporated: 9 October 2003 *Employees:* 3
Net Worth: £1,233,060 *Total Assets:* £5,568,420
Registered Office: 116 Newport Road, Middlesbrough, Cleveland, TS1 5JF
Activities: Other letting and operating of own or leased real estate
Shareholders: Anne Leader; David Leader; Mark John Leader; Helen Leader-Jenkins
Officers: Ann Leader, Secretary; Helen Jenkins [1979] Director; David Leader [1949] Director/Timber Merchant; Mark John Leader [1972] Director

G.B. Bandag Ltd
Incorporated: 28 July 1997
Net Worth: £1,828,072 *Total Assets:* £2,494,236
Registered Office: Unit BT 6-14, Dabbleduck Industrial Estate, Shildon, Co Durham, DL4 2RA
Activities: Manufacture of rubber tyres and tubes; retreading and rebuilding of rubber tyres
Parent: GBB Manufacturing Limited
Officers: Paula Latcham, Secretary; Antony Clark [1966] Director; Paula Latcham [1975] Director/Company Secretary; Stuart William Gilmour Whigham [1968] Director

G.B. Belting Ltd
Incorporated: 28 November 1996 *Employees:* 11
Net Worth: £560,045 *Total Assets:* £785,770
Registered Office: 10 Yarm Road, Stockton on Tees, Cleveland, TS18 3NA
Activities: Manufacture of bearings, gears, gearing and driving elements
Major Shareholder: Jeremy Byrne
Officers: Beverley Kay Byrne, Secretary; Gerard Lawrence Byrne [1937] Director; Jeremy Lawrence Byrne [1961] Director

G.B.U. Hire Ltd
Incorporated: 8 March 2013
Net Worth: £970,400 *Total Assets:* £1,233,619
Registered Office: 4 High Street, Stanley, Co Durham, DH9 0DQ
Activities: Other service activities n.e.c.
Shareholders: Kelly Bainbridge; Heather Bainbridge
Officers: Kelly Bainbridge [1971] Director/Civil Engineer

G.T. Group Ltd
Incorporated: 23 April 1986 *Employees:* 247
Net Worth: £16,169,368 *Total Assets:* £25,970,354
Registered Office: 3 Traynor Way, Whitehouse Business Park, Peterlee, Co Durham, SR8 2RU
Activities: Activities of head offices
Parent: Knorr-Bremse AG
Officers: Keith Bendelow [1958] Director; Neil Stuart Conley [1962] Director/Accountant; John Lamb [1954] Director

G.V. Engineering Limited
Incorporated: 26 April 2000
Net Worth: £798,183 *Total Assets:* £1,061,218
Registered Office: 103 Station Road, Ashington, Northumberland, NE63 8RS
Activities: Machining
Major Shareholder: Alan Scott Richardson
Officers: Alan Scott Richardson [1945] Director/Engineer; Alan Scott Richardson Jnr [1972] Director/Engineer

GAC Netherlands Limited
Incorporated: 24 October 1995 *Employees:* 46
Net Worth Deficit: £6,526,422 *Total Assets:* £3,967,268
Registered Office: Christine House, Sorbonne Close, Thornaby, Stockton on Tees, Cleveland, TS17 6DA
Activities: Service activities incidental to water transportation
Parent: GAC Services (UK) Ltd
Officers: Edward Graham, Secretary; Bengt Ake Ekstrand [1960] Director/Group Vice President [Swedish]; Ivo Rene Monique Verheyen [1962] Director/Manager [Belgian]; Hakan Tommy Bo Wester [1960] Director [Swedish]; Hans Zwerus [1966] Director/Business Controller [Dutch]

Gaelpharm Ltd
Incorporated: 17 March 1994
Registered Office: The Cube, Barrack Road, Newcastle upon Tyne, NE4 6DB
Activities: Dispensing chemist in specialised stores
Parent: Buchanhaven Pharmacy Limited
Officers: Samantha Melrose [1968] Director; John Mitchell [1979] Director/Pharmacist; Elaine Muir [1959] Director/Book-Keeping/Accounting; Dale Winchester [1960] Director/Pharmacist

Gainford Care Homes Limited
Incorporated: 3 June 1994 *Employees:* 1,100
Net Worth: £53,582,432 *Total Assets:* £84,202,280
Registered Office: Gainford House, Picktree Lane, Chester-le-Street, Co Durham, DH3 3SR
Activities: Residential care activities for learning difficulties, mental health and substance abuse
Shareholder: Susan McAlear
Officers: Glenn Martin, Secretary; Susan McAlear [1950] Director/Manager

Gainford Hotels Limited
Incorporated: 13 March 2012 *Employees:* 417
Net Worth: £21,995,396 *Total Assets:* £42,028,372
Registered Office: Gainford House, Picktree Lane, Chester-le-Street, Co Durham, DH3 3SR
Activities: Hotels and similar accommodation
Parent: Gainford Care Homes Limited
Officers: Glenn Martin, Secretary; Imran Khaliq [1987] Director

Gala Due Limited
Incorporated: 13 June 2006
Net Worth: £2,109,397 *Total Assets:* £2,331,000
Registered Office: 142 Manor House Road, Newcastle upon Tyne, NE2 2NA
Activities: Buying and selling of own real estate
Shareholder: Timothy John Richardson
Officers: Timothy John Richardson, Secretary; Brian James McGurk [1959] Director/Chartered Surveyor; Timothy John Richardson [1954] Director/Valuation Surveyor

Gala Unity Limited
Incorporated: 14 March 2001
Net Worth: £9,249,011 *Total Assets:* £10,793,508
Registered Office: 142 Manor House Road, Newcastle upon Tyne, NE2 2NA
Activities: Buying and selling of own real estate
Shareholders: Timothy John Richardson; Brian James McGurk
Officers: Timothy John Richardson, Secretary; Brian James McGurk [1959] Director/Chartered Surveyor; Timothy John Richardson [1954] Director/Valuation Surveyor

Gale and Phillipson Investment Services Ltd
Incorporated: 31 March 2005 *Employees:* 67
Net Worth: £4,896,397 *Total Assets:* £5,741,211
Registered Office: Gallowfields House, Fairfield Way, Richmond, N Yorks, DL10 4TB
Activities: Activities auxiliary to financial intermediation n.e.c.
Parent: Gale and Phillipson Holdings Ltd
Officers: Adam Joseph Galache Brown [1967] Director/Actuary; Alan Robert Sneddon [1962] Director

Henry Gallacher Limited
Incorporated: 24 August 1965
Registered Office: Perry Avenue, Teesside Industrial Estate, Stockton on Tees, Cleveland, TS17 9LN
Activities: Manufacture of other rubber products
Shareholders: Trevor Ford; Malcolm Young (Deceased)
Officers: Nicholas Anthony Whitton, Secretary; Trevor Ford [1952] Director; Nicholas Anthony Whitton [1953] Director/Local Government Officer

Galleria Retail Limited
Incorporated: 13 February 2003 *Employees:* 21
Net Worth: £803,547 *Total Assets:* £1,159,613
Registered Office: 18 Market Place, Hexham, Northumberland, NE46 1XQ
Activities: Retail sale of watches and jewellery in specialised stores
Shareholders: Glenis Goundry; John Goundry
Officers: Glenis Goundry, Secretary; Glenis Goundry [1954] Director; John Goundry [1960] Director

GAP Group Leasing Limited
Incorporated: 8 March 2012
Net Worth: £3,822,000 *Total Assets:* £215,286,000
Registered Office: Gap Group, Blenheim Place, Dunston Industrial Estate, Gateshead, Tyne & Wear, NE11 9HF
Activities: Renting and leasing of construction and civil engineering machinery and equipment
Parent: GAP Group Limited
Officers: Iain Martin Anderson [1958] Director; Chris Alick George Parr [1965] Director/Chartered Accountant

GAP Group Limited
Incorporated: 24 June 1924 *Employees:* 1,713
Net Worth: £93,960,000 *Total Assets:* £282,520,000
Registered Office: Gap Group, Blenheim Place, Dunston Industrial Estate, Gateshead, Tyne & Wear, NE11 9HF
Activities: Renting and leasing of construction and civil engineering machinery and equipment
Parent: GAP Holdings Limited
Officers: Christopher Alick George Parr, Secretary; Iain Martin Anderson [1958] Director/Plant Hire; Mark Douglas Anderson [1984] Director; Kevin McEwan [1965] Operations Director; Daniel O'Neil [1960] Director/Chairman; Chris Alick George Parr [1965] Director/Chartered Accountant

Gardiner Richardson Limited
Incorporated: 29 December 1997
Net Worth: £567,963 *Total Assets:* £927,674
Registered Office: Generator Studios, Trafalgar Street, Newcastle upon Tyne, NE1 2LA
Activities: Other business support service activities n.e.c.
Shareholders: John Darren Richardson; Lucy Victoria Gardiner
Officers: Lucy Victoria Gardiner, Secretary; Dominic James Aldred [1973] Director/Public Relations; Lucy Victoria Gardiner [1970] Company Secretary/Director; Austin Iliffe [1944] Director/Retired; John Darren Richardson [1965] Director

Dick Garner & Sons Limited
Incorporated: 6 October 1943
Net Worth: £2,906,321 *Total Assets:* £3,145,816
Registered Office: Moorhills, Lumley Lane, Kirkby Fleetham, Northallerton, N Yorks, DL7 0SL
Activities: Other letting and operating of own or leased real estate
Officers: Richard Garner, Secretary; Derek Garner [1954] Director; Richard Garner [1957] Director

Garnetts Limited
Incorporated: 26 October 1999
Registered Office: Unit E1, Roman Way Industrial Estate, Tindale Crescent, Bishop Auckland, Co Durham, DL14 9AW
Activities: Other passenger land transport
Major Shareholder: Sylvia Garnett
Officers: Carole Ward, Secretary; Andrew Garnett [1965] Director; Malcolm Garnett [1962] Director/Transport Manager; Paul Garnett [1972] Maintenance Director; Sylvia Garnett [1936] Director; Carole Ward [1959] Administration Director

Gaskell MacKay Carpets Limited
Incorporated: 13 April 2006 *Employees:* 11
Net Worth: £1,830,229 *Total Assets:* £3,251,516
Registered Office: View Logistics, Park View Road East, Hartlepool, Cleveland, TS25 1HT
Activities: Manufacture of woven or tufted carpets and rugs
Parent: Whitestone Carpets Holdings Ltd
Officers: Tanya Kelly, Secretary; Stephen Maurice Martin Byrne [1960] Director; Stephen Donlan [1966] Sales Director; Geoffrey Brendon Wilding [1963] Director [New Zealander]

Gastronorth Limited
Incorporated: 18 November 2002 *Employees:* 26
Net Worth: £1,586,635 *Total Assets:* £3,044,222
Registered Office: Merlin House, Princesway, Team Valley Trading Estate, Gateshead, Tyne & Wear, NE11 0NF
Activities: Other business support service activities n.e.c.
Shareholders: Richard Toye; Timothy Railton Whitfield; Stewart Alan Grierson
Officers: Vickie Grierson, Secretary; Stewart Alan Grierson [1978] Sales Director; Richard Toye [1967] Sales Director; Timothy Railton Whitfield [1973] Director

Gate 7 Limited
Incorporated: 5 July 2000
Net Worth: £3,099,305 *Total Assets:* £4,084,026
Registered Office: Princes Park, Princesway, Team Valley Trading Estate, Gateshead, Tyne & Wear, NE11 0NF
Activities: Printing n.e.c.
Major Shareholder: Keith Wickham
Officers: Audrey Wickham, Secretary/Director; Audrey Wickham [1948] Director; Kate Victoria Wickham [1983] Director; Keith Wickham [1947] Managing Director

Gateshead Bayis Ltd
Incorporated: 11 August 2011
Net Worth: £2,835,004 *Total Assets:* £6,078,014
Registered Office: 82 Bewick Road, Gateshead, Tyne & Wear, NE8 1RS
Activities: Other letting and operating of own or leased real estate
Parent: Latate Limited
Officers: Anna Schleider, Secretary; Anna Schleider [1956] Director [American]; Shamai Schleider [1953] Director; Ruth Elisheva Walkin [1983] Director/Housewife [American]; Aidel Wittler [1985] Director/Counsellor

Gateshead Bearings Limited
Incorporated: 13 July 1983
Net Worth: £313,954 *Total Assets:* £774,860
Registered Office: 1 Station Road, Bill Quay, Gateshead, Tyne & Wear, NE10 0UH
Activities: Other service activities n.e.c.
Major Shareholder: Alan Bell
Officers: Alan Bell, Secretary; Alan Bell [1949] Director; Angela Fallow [1953] Director

Gateshead College Foundation
Incorporated: 18 April 2011
Net Worth: £1,165,702 *Total Assets:* £1,168,281
Registered Office: Baltic Campus, Quarryfield Road, Gateshead, Tyne & Wear, NE8 3BE
Activities: Technical and vocational secondary education
Officers: John Holt, Secretary; Judith Doyle [1961] Director; Darren Lawrence Heathcoate [1978] Director/College Manager; John Holt [1968] Director; Nadine Renae Hudspeth [1973] College Director; Shelley Raine [1981] Director/Administrator

The Gateshead Housing Company
Incorporated: 27 October 2003 *Employees:* 748
Net Worth Deficit: £37,399,000 *Total Assets:* £9,061,000
Registered Office: Civic Centre, Regent Street, Gateshead, Tyne & Wear, NE8 1JN
Activities: Management of real estate on a fee or contract basis
Officers: Jonathan Stuart Mallen Beadle, Secretary; Elizabeth Bird [1946] Tenant Director; Sheila Bouitieh [1958] Director/Tenant; Dr. Robert John Buckley [1960] Director; Joanne Carr [1946] Director of Business Development; George Clark [1956] Director/Inspection Review Specialist; Brenda Clelland [1953] Director/Councillor; Michael Davison [1953] Director/Board Member; Councillor Paul Foy [1964] Director/Councillor; Eileen Gill [1955] Director/Board Member; Helen Mary Hall [1971] Director/Tenant; Tracy Harrison [1969] Commercial Director; Councillor Michael Hood [1954] Director/Councillor; Leigh Kirton [1988] Director/Councillor; Dr Joachim Moussounda Mouanda [1968] Tenant Director [Congolese]; Jim Turnbull [1940] Director/Councillor

Gateshead Regeneration LLP
Incorporated: 29 March 2012
Net Worth: £563,277 *Total Assets:* £12,713,826
Registered Office: Galliford Try, 2 Esh Plaza, Sir Bobby Robson Way, Newcastle upon Tyne, NE13 9BA

GB Holiday Parks Limited
Incorporated: 22 February 2001 *Employees:* 75
Net Worth: £586,000 *Total Assets:* £7,575,000
Registered Office: 2nd Floor, One Gosforth Park Way, Gosforth Business Park, Newcastle upon Tyne, NE12 8ET
Activities: Hotels and similar accommodation
Parent: PD Parks Limited
Officers: Judith Ann Archibold, Secretary; Ian Kellett [1963] Director; John Anthony Waterworth [1963] Director

GBB Manufacturing Limited
Incorporated: 31 July 2012
Net Worth: £49,445 *Total Assets:* £1,988,255
Registered Office: Milburn House, Hexham Business Park, Burn Lane, Hexham, Northumberland, NE46 3RU
Activities: Activities of other holding companies n.e.c.
Shareholders: Paula Latcham; Antony Clark
Officers: Paula Latcham, Secretary; Antony Clark [1966] Director; Paula Latcham [1975] Director; Stuart William Gilmour Whigham [1968] Director

GCA Domestic Limited
Incorporated: 23 December 1976 *Employees:* 41
Net Worth Deficit: £1,068,309 *Total Assets:* £2,702,009
Registered Office: Scott Business Park, Haverton Hill, Billingham, Cleveland, TS23 1PY
Activities: Freight transport by road
Parent: Charles Andre UK
Officers: Delphine Andre [1966] Director [French]; Colomb Antoine [1965] Director [French]; Jean-Louis Cherel [1954] Director/Human Resources Manager [French]; Jacques Yves Marie Duvauchelle [1974] Financial Director [French]

Gecomac Limited
Incorporated: 25 February 2010 *Employees:* 44
Net Worth: £202,623 *Total Assets:* £2,306,725
Registered Office: Kellaw Road, Yarm Road Industrial Estate, Darlington, Co Durham, DL1 4YA
Activities: Manufacture of steam generators, except central heating hot water boilers
Shareholders: Paul Nigel Thompson; Simon James Ruck
Officers: John Anthony Davison [1967] Financial Director; Simon James Ruck [1967] Director; Paul Nigel Thompson [1966] Director

Geffen Construction Limited
Incorporated: 8 December 1995 *Employees:* 10
Net Worth: £248,118 *Total Assets:* £1,573,095
Registered Office: Suite 18, Springboard Business Centre, 24 Ellerbeck Way, Stokesley, Cleveland, TS9 5JZ
Activities: Development of building projects
Major Shareholder: Michael Bernard Anthony Van Geffen
Officers: Jayne Susan Van Geffen, Secretary; Ian David Brown [1962] Director/Site Manager; Jayne Susan Van Geffen [1961] Director; Michael Bernard Anthony Van Geffen [1957] Managing Director

Geffen Limited
Incorporated: 20 April 1999
Net Worth: £765,054 *Total Assets:* £4,027,077
Registered Office: Suite 18, Springboard Business Centre, 24 Ellerbeck Way, Stokesley, Cleveland, TS9 5JZ
Activities: Development of building projects
Major Shareholder: Michael Bernard Anthony Van Geffen
Officers: Jayne Susan Van Geffen, Secretary/Director; Jayne Susan Van Geffen [1961] Director; Michael Bernard Anthony Van Geffen [1957] Director

Gem Partnership Limited
Incorporated: 11 June 2009 *Employees:* 701
Net Worth: £580,421 *Total Assets:* £3,039,216
Registered Office: Fernwood House, Fernwood Road, Jesmond, Newcastle upon Tyne, NE2 1TJ
Activities: Temporary employment agency activities
Shareholders: Lynsey Dunbar; Robert Anthony Dunbar; Kinetic Holdings Limited; Ian Miller; Maria Luisa Miller
Officers: Robert Anthony Dunbar [1968] Director/Recruitment Manager; Ian Miller [1979] Director/Recruitment; Maria Luisa Miller [1981] Director/Recruitment; Lee John Rankin [1970] Director/Recruitment Manager

Geneius Laboratories Limited
Incorporated: 2 January 2007
Net Worth: £428 *Total Assets:* £1,595,900
Registered Office: 44 Colbourne Crescent, Nelson Park, Cramlington, Northumberland, NE23 1WB
Activities: Technical testing and analysis
Parent: Labco UK Group Limited
Officers: Mark Peter Frederick Dollar [1974] Director; Arnaud Guény [1977] Director [French]; Ronald Herman Pluut [1964] Director [Dutch]; Nicholas John Stopford [1972] Director

Genesis Brands Limited
Incorporated: 25 April 2006 *Employees:* 53
Net Worth: £3,626,299 *Total Assets:* £8,179,729
Registered Office: 7 Ellerbeck Way, Stokesley Business Park, Stokesley, Cleveland, TS9 5JZ
Activities: Activities of production holding companies
Major Shareholder: Aidan Simon Bruce
Officers: Adam Edward Pritchard, Secretary; Aidan Simon Bruce [1958] Director; Paul Leonard Gadney [1957] Managing Director; Adam Edward Pritchard [1980] Financial Director

Genesis Flooring Limited
Incorporated: 15 July 2014 *Employees:* 10
Net Worth: £766,387 *Total Assets:* £1,005,915
Registered Office: 7 Ellerbeck Way, Stokesley Business Park, Stokesley, Cleveland, TS9 5JZ
Activities: Other manufacturing n.e.c.
Major Shareholder: Aidan Simon Bruce
Officers: Adam Pritchard, Secretary; Aidan Simon Bruce [1958] Director/Chairman; Michael James Gadney [1983] Sales Director; Paul Leonard Gadney [1957] Managing Director; Adam Edward Pritchard [1980] Financial Director; David Stuart Saunders [1966] Purchasing Director

Genesis Global Systems Limited
Incorporated: 16 July 2014 *Employees:* 40
Net Worth: £2,281,595 *Total Assets:* £4,510,870
Registered Office: 7 Ellerbeck Way, Stokesley Business Park, Stokesley, Cleveland, TS9 5JZ
Activities: Other manufacturing n.e.c.
Major Shareholder: Aidan Simon Bruce
Officers: Adam Pritchard, Secretary; Aidan Simon Bruce [1958] Director/Chairman; Michael James Gadney [1983] Sales Director; Paul Leonard Gadney [1957] Managing Director; Adam Edward Pritchard [1980] Financial Director; David Stuart Saunders [1966] Purchasing Director

Geneva Brasswind Limited
Incorporated: 20 January 2016 *Employees:* 1
Net Worth: £1,398 *Total Assets:* £850,360
Registered Office: 3 Kingfisher Court, Bowesfield Park, Stockton on Tees, Cleveland, TS18 3EX
Activities: Wholesale of musical instruments
Shareholders: Oldshaw Distributions Limited; Timothy Oldroyd
Officers: Timothy Oldroyd [1970] Director

Genhawk Limited
Incorporated: 6 March 1989 *Employees:* 23
Net Worth: £1,768,647 *Total Assets:* £2,069,763
Registered Office: 11 Well Ridge Close, Whitley Bay, Tyne & Wear, NE25 9PN
Activities: Other human health activities
Parent: Broadwake Limited
Officers: Dr Nooh Khan Abdul Salam, Secretary; Dr Annamma Abdul Salam [1944] Director/Medical Practitioner; Dr Nooh Khan Abdul Salam [1937] Director/Medical Practitioner; Reshmi Salam [1981] Director/Student; Seema Salam [1976] Director/MBA Student

Genius Bidco Limited
Incorporated: 13 March 2015 *Employees:* 4
Net Worth Deficit: £2,817,653 *Total Assets:* £33,350,060
Registered Office: Unit 51-53 Innovation House, Longfield Road, South Church Enterprise Park, Bishop Auckland, Co Durham, DL14 6XB
Activities: Post-secondary non-tertiary education
Parent: Genius Holdco Limited
Officers: Jonathan Daniel Cummins [1976] Director; Gavin Stewart Higgins [1977] Director/Chief Financial Officer; Richard Daniel Mayers [1975] Director; Brenda Sophie McLeish [1978] Director; Ian Scott Wallis [1970] Director/Investment Professional

Genius Holdco Limited
Incorporated: 12 March 2015 *Employees:* 233
Net Worth Deficit: £4,013,587 *Total Assets:* £31,987,884
Registered Office: Unit 51-53 Innovation House, Longfield Road, South Church Enterprise Park, Bishop Auckland, Co Durham, DL14 6XB
Activities: Post-secondary non-tertiary education
Parent: MML UK Partners LLP
Officers: Jonathan Daniel Cummins [1976] Director; Gavin Stewart Higgins [1977] Finance Director; Richard Daniel Mayers [1975] Director; Martin McCourt [1956] Director; Brenda Sophie McLeish [1978] Director; Ian Scott Wallis [1970] Director/Investment Professional

Gentoo Genie Limited
Incorporated: 21 November 2009 *Employees:* 4
Net Worth Deficit: £655,860 *Total Assets:* £7,540,484
Registered Office: Emperor House, 2 Emperor Way, Doxford International Business Park, Sunderland, Tyne & Wear, SR3 3XR
Activities: Other credit granting n.e.c.
Officers: Simon Walker, Secretary; Steven Mark Hicks [1963] Director; Simon Walker [1967] Director/Company Secretary & General Counsel

Gentoo Homes Limited
Incorporated: 18 April 2003 *Employees:* 80
Net Worth: £977,000 *Total Assets:* £32,845,000
Registered Office: Emperor House, 2 Emperor Way, Sunderland, Tyne & Wear, SR3 3XR
Activities: Development of building projects
Officers: Simon Walker, Secretary; Colin Blakey [1950] Director; John Harrison [1951] Director/Marketing Manager; Phillip Graham Sean Marsh [1969] Director/Management Consultant; Ian Anthony Charles Parkin [1954] Director/Chartered Surveyor; Jeffrey Arnold Platt [1958] Director/Chartered Surveyor; Claire Louise Warren [1969] Director/Chief Executive

Geo - Drill Limited
Incorporated: 20 July 2006 *Employees:* 21
Net Worth: £1,043,079 *Total Assets:* £1,795,261
Registered Office: 6 Queens Court North, Third Avenue, Team Valley Trading Estate, Gateshead, Tyne & Wear, NE11 0BU
Activities: Test drilling and boring
Shareholders: Paul Turnbull; Susan Turnbull
Officers: Susan Turnbull, Secretary/Driller; Paul Turnbull [1972] Director/Driller

Geocore Site Investigations Limited
Incorporated: 28 July 2000 *Employees:* 28
Net Worth: £1,107,285 *Total Assets:* £2,186,604
Registered Office: Tralee Close, Kirkleatham Business Park, Redcar, Cleveland, TS10 5SG
Activities: Test drilling and boring
Shareholders: Michelle Soo Lin Woodhead; Adam Matthew Miller Woodhead
Officers: Michelle Soo Lin Woodhead, Secretary; Adam Matthew Miller Woodhead [1974] Director/Land Surveyor; Michelle Soo Lin Woodhead [1975] Finance Director

Geofirma Soils Engineering Limited
Incorporated: 20 September 1996 *Employees:* 32
Net Worth: £2,720,000 *Total Assets:* £4,832,000
Registered Office: West Terrace, Esh Winning, Co Durham, DH7 9PT
Activities: Construction of other civil engineering projects n.e.c.
Parent: C A Blackwell (Contracts) Ltd
Officers: Steven Leslie Anson [1965] Director; Stephen John Dunn [1970] Director/Estimator; David Giles Salmon [1971] Director/Quantity Surveyor; Philip James Smith [1979] Director

Geordie Jeans Limited
Incorporated: 15 November 1979 *Employees:* 2
Net Worth: £9,133,041 *Total Assets:* £9,277,110
Registered Office: 18 Marsden Road, Cleadon Village, Sunderland, Tyne & Wear, SR6 7RA
Activities: Other letting and operating of own or leased real estate
Major Shareholder: Derek Keers Robson
Officers: Derek Robson, Secretary; Derek Robson [1947] Director

George Washington Golf and Country Club Limited
Incorporated: 27 January 2003 *Employees:* 96
Net Worth: £7,817,579 *Total Assets:* £13,484,339
Registered Office: 24 Woolsington Park South, Woolsington, Newcastle upon Tyne, NE13 8BJ
Activities: Hotels and similar accommodation
Officers: Saroj Rani Chawla, Secretary; Mukesh Raj Chawla [1954] Director/Manager; Neel Chawla [1986] Director; Saroj Rani Chawla [1955] Director/Manager

Georgian Theatre (Richmond) Trust Limited (The)
Incorporated: 1 January 1960 *Employees:* 8
Net Worth: £988,989 *Total Assets:* £1,070,435
Registered Office: Victoria Road, Richmond, N Yorks, DL10 4DW
Activities: Operation of historical sites and buildings and similar visitor attractions
Officers: Patricia Ann Kassell, Secretary; James Brown [1947] Director/Retired; Malcolm John Bryant [1945] Director/Retired; Amanda Jane Cook [1963] Director/Local Government Manager; Lord Charles James Crathorne [1939] Director/Retired; Murray Edwards [1944] Director/Retired; Katharine Field [1980] Director/Interior Designer; Colin Grant [1947] Director/Retired; Michael John Robinson [1961] Group Legal Director; Hon Caroline Mary Stanley [1948] Director/Marketing Consultant; Nigel Tooze [1967] Director/Retired

GES Recycling Ltd.
Incorporated: 25 September 2012 *Employees:* 22
Net Worth: £1,310,878 *Total Assets:* £6,610,437
Registered Office: Tallent Automotive, Aycliffe Business Park, Newton Aycliffe, Co Durham, DL5 6EP
Activities: Recovery of sorted materials
Parent: Gescrap Desarrollo, S.L.
Officers: Ignacio Velasco [1964] Director/Entrepreneur [Spanish]

Gestamp Tallent Limited
Incorporated: 21 April 1948 *Employees:* 2,474
Net Worth: £131,810,000 *Total Assets:* £383,833,984
Registered Office: 1 Skerne Road, Aycliffe Business Park, Newton Aycliffe, Co Durham, DL5 6EP
Activities: Forging, pressing, stamping and roll-forming of metal; powder metallurgy
Shareholders: Francisco Jose Riberas Mera; Juan Maria Riberas Mera
Officers: David Vázquez Pascual, Secretary; Unai Aguirre Mandaluniz [1968] Director/Economist [Spanish]; Francisco López Peña [1959] Director/Economist [Spanish]; Francisco Jose Riberas Mera [1968] Director [Spanish]

Gestamp Washington UK Limited
Incorporated: 15 April 1998 *Employees:* 230
Net Worth: £16,060,868 *Total Assets:* £27,005,710
Registered Office: Site 10 Rutherford Road, Stephenson Industrial Estate, Washington, Tyne & Wear, NE37 3HX
Activities: Manufacture of other parts and accessories for motor vehicles
Shareholder: Francisco Jose Riberas Mera
Officers: David Vázquez Pascual, Secretary; Francisco Jose Riberas Mera [1964] Director [Spanish]

Getinge Extended Care UK Limited
Incorporated: 28 November 2006 *Employees:* 3
Net Worth: £282,467,008 *Total Assets:* £433,428,992
Registered Office: 14-15 Burford Way, Boldon Business Park, Boldon Colliery, Co Durham, NE35 9PZ
Activities: Activities of head offices
Parent: Getinge Holding Limited
Officers: Martin Forbister, Secretary; Avril Ann Forde [1974] Director/MD [Irish]; Karin Soderlund [1981] Director/FD [Finnish]; Jon Barrie Yard [1967] QA Director

Getinge Holding Ltd
Incorporated: 29 December 1989
Net Worth: £49,321,000 *Total Assets:* £77,283,000
Registered Office: 14-15 Burford Way, Boldon Business Park, Boldon Colliery, Co Durham, NE35 9PZ
Activities: Activities of head offices
Parent: Getinge Arjo Nederland Holdings BV
Officers: Martin Forbister, Secretary; Avril Ann Forde [1974] Director/MD [Irish]; Karin Soderlund [1981] Director/FD [Finnish]; Jon Barrie Yard [1967] QA Director

Getinge UK Limited
Incorporated: 17 February 1983 *Employees:* 194
Net Worth: £11,166,000 *Total Assets:* £29,608,000
Registered Office: 14-15 Burford Way, Boldon Business Park, Boldon Colliery, Co Durham, NE35 9PZ
Activities: Manufacture of basic pharmaceutical products
Parent: Getinge Extended Care UK Limited
Officers: Martin Forbister, Secretary; Avril Ann Forde [1974] Director/Regional President [Irish]; Karin Soderlund [1981] Commercial Excellence Director [Finnish]; Jon Barrie Yard [1967] QA Director

GFC Group Limited
Incorporated: 16 October 2015
Net Worth: £311,536 *Total Assets:* £1,443,169
Registered Office: 7 Bankside, The Watermark, Gateshead, Tyne & Wear, NE11 9SY
Activities: Licensed carriers
Major Shareholder: Nathan Hepurker
Officers: Nathan Hepurker [1984] Director

GGE Holdings Limited
Incorporated: 28 July 2004 *Employees:* 1
Net Worth: £1,165,763 *Total Assets:* £1,344,095
Registered Office: Suite 1, Byron House, Hall Dene Way, Seaham Grange Industrial Estate, Seaham, Co Durham, SR7 0PY
Activities: Activities of head offices
Major Shareholder: Gwilym George Edwards
Officers: Jacqueline Mary Edwards, Secretary; Gwilym George Edwards [1956] Director/Joinery Contractor

GH Group UK (2018) Ltd
Incorporated: 30 May 2003
Registered Office: Houghton House, New Road, Team Valley Trading Estate, Gateshead, Tyne & Wear, NE11 0JU
Activities: Buying and selling of own real estate
Major Shareholder: Gary George Houghton
Officers: George Houghton [1940] Director

Gibbons (UK) Property Limited
Incorporated: 13 June 2008 *Employees:* 1
Net Worth: £534,225 *Total Assets:* £1,244,749
Registered Office: 4a Spectrum Business Park, Blair Way, Seaham, Co Durham, SR7 7PP
Activities: Other letting and operating of own or leased real estate
Major Shareholder: Ian Gibbons
Officers: Ian Gibbons [1968] Director; Lisa Gibbons [1984] Director/Administrator

The Gibside Hotel Limited
Incorporated: 14 June 1973
Net Worth: £3,130,005 *Total Assets:* £3,813,030
Registered Office: The Gibside Arms Hotel, Front Street, Whickham, Gateshead, Tyne & Wear, NE16 4JG
Activities: Hotels and similar accommodation
Shareholder: Malcolm Walker
Officers: Lilian Joy Bell, Secretary; Malcolm Walker, Secretary; Malcolm Walker [1950] Director; William Henry Walker [1948] Director - Hotel Manager

Gibson & Co. Solicitors Ltd
Incorporated: 5 August 2011 *Employees:* 31
Net Worth: £1,160,335 *Total Assets:* £1,842,507
Registered Office: Gibson House, 77-87 West Road, Newcastle upon Tyne, NE15 6PR
Activities: Solicitors
Officers: David Lee Bawn [1978] Director/Solicitor; Andrew Henry Roland Chrisp [1967] Director/Solicitor; Anthony Gair Gibson [1937] Director/Solicitor; Derwent Sebastian Coleridge Gibson [1946] Director/Solicitor; Jane Phoebe Gibson [1967] Director/Solicitor; Toby James Gibson [1969] Director/Solicitor; Michael James MacGregor [1953] Director/Solicitor; Michael Reed [1981] Director/Solicitor

Gibson Engineering Limited
Incorporated: 5 May 2011
Net Worth Deficit: £163,524 *Total Assets:* £1,204,740
Registered Office: Barrington House, 41-45 Yarm Lane, Stockton on Tees, Cleveland, TS18 3EA
Activities: Other manufacturing n.e.c.
Major Shareholder: Paul Francis Gibson
Officers: Paul Francis Gibson [1953] Director

Gibson Motorsport Limited
Incorporated: 5 May 2011 *Employees:* 6
Net Worth Deficit: £258,077 *Total Assets:* £2,809,788
Registered Office: Barrington House, 41-45 Yarm Lane, Stockton on Tees, Cleveland, TS18 3EA
Activities: Other manufacturing n.e.c.
Major Shareholder: Paul Francis Gibson
Officers: Paul Francis Gibson [1953] Director

The Gibson O'Neill Company Limited
Incorporated: 18 November 1994 *Employees:* 98
Net Worth: £224,243,008 *Total Assets:* £486,804,000
Registered Office: Brignell Road, Riverside Park Industrial Estate, Middlesbrough, Cleveland, TS2 1PS
Activities: Activities of head offices
Major Shareholder: Stephen Gibson
Officers: Terry Jackson, Secretary; Stephen Gibson [1958] Director; Michael David O'Neill [1957] Director; Graham John Redman [1953] Director/Chartered Accountant

The Gilchrist Company (UK) Limited
Incorporated: 5 November 2003
Net Worth: £318,579 *Total Assets:* £1,402,102
Registered Office: 11 Hatfield Road, Northallerton, N Yorks, DL7 8QX
Activities: Other letting and operating of own or leased real estate
Shareholders: Caroline Gilchrist; William Gilchrist
Officers: William Gilchrist, Secretary/Director; Caroline Gilchrist [1955] Director; William Gilchrist [1955] Director

Gilesgate Properties Limited
Incorporated: 29 June 1978 *Employees:* 1
Net Worth: £2,076,793 *Total Assets:* £3,301,879
Registered Office: 7 Old Elvet, Durham, DH1 3HL
Activities: Other letting and operating of own or leased real estate
Shareholders: Keith Johnson; Patricia Johnson
Officers: Michael Longstaff, Secretary; Keith Johnson [1947] Director/Chartered Surveyor; Patricia Johnson [1949] Director/Married Woman; Rebecca Sally Powell [1978] Director/Sales Negotiator

Gill & Robinson Limited
Incorporated: 19 August 1975 *Employees:* 10
Net Worth: £70,958 *Total Assets:* £2,000,559
Registered Office: Andrew House, Benton Terrace, Newcastle upon Tyne, NE2 1QU
Activities: Agents involved in the sale of timber and building materials
Major Shareholder: Carsten Kullik
Officers: Carsten Kullik [1966] Director [German]; Lawrence Poole Webster [1965] Managing Director

Gill & Schofield Pharmaceutical Chemists Limited
Incorporated: 22 August 1995 *Employees:* 79
Net Worth: £357,673 *Total Assets:* £4,527,285
Registered Office: Saville Chambers, 4 Saville Street, South Shields, Tyne & Wear, NE33 2PR
Activities: Dispensing chemist in specialised stores
Shareholders: Angela Teresa Gill; Steven Edward Gill; Joseph Anthony Schofield
Officers: Joseph Anthony Schofield, Secretary; Steven Edward Gill [1962] Director/Pharmacist; Joseph Anthony Schofield [1954] Director/Pharmacist

Mrs J & J G Gill & Son Limited
Incorporated: 16 March 2006 *Employees:* 12
Net Worth: £677,014 *Total Assets:* £1,606,466
Registered Office: 91 Galgate, Barnard Castle, Co Durham, DL12 8ES
Activities: Support activities for crop production
Shareholders: Robert William Gill; John David Gill
Officers: Julie Gill, Secretary; John David Gill [1973] Director/Haulier; Robert William Gill [1961] Director/Haulier

John Gill Limited
Incorporated: 16 February 1988
Registered Office: Aiskew Garage, Bedale, N Yorks, DL8 1DD
Activities: Non-trading company
Shareholders: Carol Gill; Bryan Gill
Officers: Carol Anne Gill, Secretary; Gareth Peter Frank [1962] Director; Bryan John Gill [1967] Director; Carol Anne Gill [1965] Director; John George Gill [1942] Director

Gillen's Limited
Incorporated: 26 August 1994 *Employees:* 26
Net Worth: £1,157,778 *Total Assets:* £1,448,367
Registered Office: The Golden Lion, Dunston Road, Hartlepool, Cleveland, TS26 0EN
Activities: Other retail sale in non-specialised stores
Officers: Leigh Walker, Secretary/Director; Leo Gillen [1956] Director; Rhoda Gillen [1927] Director; Tracy Mary Liddle [1966] Director; Leigh Walker [1952] Director

G.T.Gillie & Blair Limited
Incorporated: 1 April 1949 *Employees:* 8
Net Worth: £1,653,793 *Total Assets:* £3,038,205
Registered Office: 178 New Bridge Street, Newcastle upon Tyne, NE1 2TE
Activities: Sea and coastal freight water transport
Shareholders: George Stephen Gillie; Alan Geoffrey Gillie
Officers: Vikki Cunningham, Secretary; Alan Geoffrey Gillie [1963] Director/Shipbroker; George Stephen Gillie [1961] Director/Shipbroker

Gilligan Engineering Services Limited
Incorporated: 14 May 2002 *Employees:* 7
Net Worth: £297,708 *Total Assets:* £761,305
Registered Office: Andrews House, Princess Way, Low Prudhoe Industrial Estate, Prudhoe, Northumberland, NE42 6HB
Activities: Technical testing and analysis
Major Shareholder: Julie Gilligan
Officers: Julie Gilligan, Secretary/Accountant; Brian Gilligan [1939] Director/Engineer; Julie Gilligan [1965] Director/Accountant

Gills Fry Fry Limited
Incorporated: 15 March 2007 *Employees:* 43
Net Worth: £458,500 *Total Assets:* £892,464
Registered Office: 19 North Terrace, Seaham, Co Durham, SR7 7EU
Activities: Other retail sale of food in specialised stores
Officers: Gurmanpreet Kaur Gill [1982] Director; Jagdev Singh Gill [1978] Director/Takeaway Proprietor; Pawandeep Kaur Gill [1981] Director; Sarwan Singh Gill [1955] Director [Indian]; Sukhwinder Kaur Gill [1953] Director [Indian]

Gilmour & Associates Limited
Incorporated: 30 June 2006 *Employees:* 4
Net Worth: £1,716,980 *Total Assets:* £1,864,329
Registered Office: Office 5 Horton Park, Berwick Hill Road, Newcastle upon Tyne, NE13 6BU
Activities: Other professional, scientific and technical activities n.e.c.
Major Shareholder: Barry Edward Kerr Gilmour
Officers: William Allan Plant, Secretary; Barry Edward Kerr Gilmour [1947] Director; William Allan Plant [1962] Director

Gilsan Sports Limited
Incorporated: 17 July 2003
Net Worth: £499,709 *Total Assets:* £750,865
Registered Office: Moor Park, Moor Road, Melsonby, Richmond, N Yorks, DL10 5PR
Activities: Retail sale of sports goods, fishing gear, camping goods, boats and bicycles
Officers: Susan Jean Fenwick, Secretary/Director; Simon Mark Fenwick [1970] Director

GIP Limited
Incorporated: 27 July 1966
Net Worth: £53,695,636 *Total Assets:* £53,932,636
Registered Office: Citygate, St James Boulevard, Newcastle upon Tyne, NE1 4JE
Activities: Other letting and operating of own or leased real estate
Parent: Atlantic Metropolitan (U.K.) Limited
Officers: Adam McGhin, Secretary; Helen Christine Gordon [1959] Director; Michael Paul Keaveney [1967] Director; Adam McGhin [1978] Director/Solicitor; Mark Jeremy Robson [1959] Director/Chartered Surveyor; Vanessa Kate Simms [1975] Director

Gisborough Project Services Ltd
Incorporated: 10 March 2015 *Employees:* 6
Net Worth: £114,850 *Total Assets:* £829,151
Registered Office: 64 Hutton Lane, Guisborough, Cleveland, TS14 8AN
Activities: Development of building projects
Major Shareholder: Alan Barraclough
Officers: Alan Barraclough [1970] Director; Thomas Barraclough [1997] Director

GJPS Trust Fund
Incorporated: 3 July 2006
Net Worth: £1,287,328 *Total Assets:* £1,565,688
Registered Office: Gateshead Jewish Primary School, 18-22 Gladstone Terrace, Gateshead, Tyne & Wear, NE8 4EA
Activities: Other education n.e.c.
Officers: Nathan Hirsch [1977] Director; David Schleider [1959] Director; Mark Steinhaus [1974] Director/Lecturer

GKC Interiors (NE) Limited
Incorporated: 17 October 2009
Net Worth: £548,836 *Total Assets:* £1,118,797
Registered Office: 7 Segedunum Business Centre, Station Road, Wallsend, Tyne & Wear, NE28 6HQ
Activities: Manufacture of other furniture
Major Shareholder: Derrick David Crozier
Officers: Derrick David Crozier [1968] Director

GKP Solutions Ltd
Incorporated: 29 October 2004
Net Worth: £577,767 *Total Assets:* £770,015
Registered Office: Portland House, Belmont Business Park, Durham, DH1 1TW
Activities: Residents property management
Major Shareholder: Majender Bassi
Officers: Majender Bassi [1969] Director/Consultant

Gladglider Limited
Incorporated: 30 May 2012
Registered Office: 12 Carlton Terrace, Newcastle upon Tyne, NE2 4PD
Activities: Other letting and operating of own or leased real estate
Shareholders: Karen Liddle; Simon Christopher Ragg
Officers: Karen Liddle [1967] Director; Simon Christopher Ragg [1965] Director

Glassfibre Flagpoles Limited
Incorporated: 3 November 1987 *Employees:* 40
Net Worth: £555,856 *Total Assets:* £1,699,268
Registered Office: 38 Borough Road, Darlington, Co Durham, DL1 1SW
Activities: Other manufacturing n.e.c.
Officers: Andrew Graham Sellers, Secretary; Adrian Harrison [1973] Managing Director; Jemima Harrison [1972] Director; Simon Craig Lunt [1977] Director; Andrew Graham Sellers [1965] Finance Director

Glasshus Ltd
Incorporated: 4 August 2009 *Employees:* 50
Net Worth: £704,886 *Total Assets:* £3,836,542
Registered Office: Unit 7 Rivergreen Industry Centre, Pallion Industrial Estate, Sunderland, Tyne & Wear, SR4 6AD
Activities: Construction of commercial buildings
Major Shareholder: Simon Tuckwell
Officers: Steven William Henderson [1978] Director; Hayley Ann Scott [1977] Director; Jack Lewis Tuckwell [1997] Director; Joshua James Tuckwell [1995] Director/Manager; Simon Tuckwell [1972] Director

Gledstone Estates Limited
Incorporated: 1 September 2006
Net Worth: £394,187 *Total Assets:* £892,229
Registered Office: 10 Gledstone, Wynyard Woods, Wynyard, Cleveland, TS22 5GF
Activities: Other letting and operating of own or leased real estate
Shareholder: Hassan Al-Faham
Officers: Amal Al-Faham, Secretary; Hassan Ali Al-Faham [1957] Director

Glen Valley Tours Ltd.
Incorporated: 1 February 2006 *Employees:* 21
Net Worth: £280,608 *Total Assets:* £1,685,949
Registered Office: Glen Valley Tours Ltd, Station Road, Wooler, Northumberland, NE71 6SP
Activities: Other passenger land transport
Shareholders: Eric Royston Laidler; Iain David Moffat
Officers: Irene Patricia Laidler, Secretary; Eric Royston Laidler [1940] Director/Travel Manager; Iain David Moffat [1968] Director/Coach Operator

Glendale Engineering (Milfield) Limited
Incorporated: 10 May 1984 *Employees:* 47
Net Worth: £2,248,407 *Total Assets:* £3,686,485
Registered Office: 16 Bondgate Without, Alnwick, Northumberland, NE66 1PP
Activities: Manufacture of metal structures and parts of structures
Shareholders: Gordon Andrew Wilson; Graeme Stewart Wilson
Officers: Gordon Andrew Wilson, Secretary; Paul McKenna [1973] Finance Director; Gordon Andrew Wilson [1956] Director; Graeme Stewart Wilson [1964] Director; Richard John Wilson [1978] Director/Project Manager

The Glendale Gateway Trust
Incorporated: 6 June 1996 *Employees:* 6
Net Worth: £2,661,260 *Total Assets:* £2,852,230
Registered Office: Cheviot Centre, 12 Padgepool Place, Wooler, Northumberland, NE71 6BL
Activities: Other service activities n.e.c.
Officers: Dr Julian Bruce Bales [1947] Director/Retired; Elizabeth Margaret Brown [1960] Director/Farmer; David John Charles Bull [1952] Director/Retired; Patsy Healey [1940] Director/Retired; Frank Ormston Mansfield [1946] Director/Retired; Robert Anthony Marriner [1959] Director/Consultant; Councillor Anthony Harkness Murray [1937] Director/Retailer; Patrick James Sheard [1963] Director/Self Employed

Glendale Transport UK Limited
Incorporated: 13 March 2000 *Employees:* 51
Net Worth: £935,594 *Total Assets:* £2,133,042
Registered Office: Unit 3 Throckley Way, Middlefields Industrial Estate, South Shields, Tyne & Wear, NE34 0NU
Activities: Freight transport by road
Shareholders: Jamie Douglas Moore; Glenn Douglass
Officers: John Carroll, Secretary; Glenn Douglas [1968] Haulage Director; Jamie Douglass Moore [1982] Managing Director; Marjorie Streatfield Moore [1942] Managing Director; Norman Moore [1946] Haulage Director

Glenrock
Incorporated: 4 December 1961
Net Worth: £4,654,283 *Total Assets:* £4,739,384
Registered Office: Rowlands House, Portobello Road, Birtley, Chester-le-Street, Co Durham, DH3 2RY
Activities: Development of building projects
Shareholders: George Henry Jewitt; Dr John Jackson; Ann Lilly
Officers: George Henry Jewitt, Secretary; Dr John Jackson [1941] Director/Retired Medical Practitioner; George Henry Jewitt [1957] Director/Architect; Ann Lilly [1945] Director/Film Producer

Glenrose Developments (Whitburn) Limited
Incorporated: 10 March 2016
Net Worth: £22,528 *Total Assets:* £2,061,126
Registered Office: 246 Park View, Whitley Bay, Tyne & Wear, NE26 3QX
Activities: Buying and selling of own real estate
Major Shareholder: Callum James Watson
Officers: Callum James Watson [1990] Director; Christopher John Watson [1961] Managing Director

Glenwood Paint Supplies Limited
Incorporated: 29 December 1976 *Employees:* 22
Net Worth: £348,759 *Total Assets:* £978,324
Registered Office: Lukes House, 206-210 Yarm Road, Darlington, Co Durham, DL1 1XD
Activities: Painting
Major Shareholder: Robert Charles Greenhalgh
Officers: Janice Hobson, Secretary; Robert Charles Greenhalgh [1949] Director/Master Painter

Gliderol Garage & Industrial Doors Limited
Incorporated: 24 November 1986 *Employees:* 30
Net Worth: £655,218 *Total Assets:* £1,445,204
Registered Office: Kitching Road, North West Industrial Estate, Peterlee, Co Durham, SR8 2HP
Activities: Other manufacturing n.e.c.
Parent: Panacea Standa Holdings Limited
Officers: Andrew David Dick [1965] Director; Steven Mark Roberts [1966] Director; Roy William Sinclair [1974] Managing Director; Daniel Richard Summerfield [1976] Director

Gloag & Sons Limited
Incorporated: 5 April 1960 *Employees:* 6
Net Worth: £8,386 *Total Assets:* £4,951,404
Registered Office: Busby House, Stokesley, Middlesbrough, Cleveland, TS9 5LB
Activities: Growing of cereals (except rice), leguminous crops and oil seeds
Shareholder: Andrew Robert Gloag
Officers: Jane Gloag, Secretary; Andrew Robert Gloag [1963] Director/Farmer

Global Decontamination Solutions Limited
Incorporated: 30 July 2013 *Employees:* 142
Net Worth: £2,065,497 *Total Assets:* £11,723,510
Registered Office: 29-33 Maxwell Street, South Shields, Tyne & Wear, NE33 4PU
Activities: Activities of production holding companies
Major Shareholder: Damian Meehan
Officers: Paul Cameron [1980] Finance Director; James Craig Leese [1968] Operations Director; Damian Meehan [1955] Director/Owner; Dean Thomas Rowe [1979] Commercial Director

Global Enterprise (EU) Limited
Incorporated: 12 November 2014
Net Worth: £42,063 *Total Assets:* £937,873
Registered Office: Ragpath Cottage, Esh Winning, Co Durham, DH7 9QE
Activities: Dormant company
Shareholders: Darren James Grooms; Joanne Grooms
Officers: Darren James Grooms [1969] Director; Joanne Grooms [1970] Director

Global Holdings Limited
Incorporated: 11 December 1991
Net Worth: £3,750,003 *Total Assets:* £3,750,003
Registered Office: The Lodge, Gatherley Moor Farm, Gilling West, Richmond, N Yorks, DL10 5LJ
Activities: Activities of head offices
Officers: Joe Mulhall [1966] Director/Product Research

Global Manufacturing Supplies Limited
Incorporated: 27 November 1998 *Employees:* 22
Net Worth: £2,371,080 *Total Assets:* £6,624,678
Registered Office: 4 Regents Drive, Low Prudhoe Industrial Estate, Prudhoe, Northumberland, NE42 6PX
Activities: Other engineering activities
Parent: GMS (Holdings) Limited
Officers: Ann Marie Ingram, Secretary; Ann Marie Ingram [1963] Director; Owen George Ingram [1961] Director

Global Navigation Solutions Holdings Limited
Incorporated: 4 October 2012 *Employees:* 290
Net Worth Deficit: £35,433,000 *Total Assets:* £43,234,000
Registered Office: 17 Elm Road, North Shields, Tyne & Wear, NE29 8SE
Activities: Activities of distribution holding companies
Officers: Kieron Quinn Abernethy [1965] Director/Chief Revenue Officer; Richard William Daw [1968] Director/Investment Executive; Tim Michael Dunn [1973] Director/Investment Executive; Paul Robert Stanley [1967] Director/Chief Executive; Geoffrey Eric Unwin [1942] Director

Global Navigation Solutions Limited
Incorporated: 23 August 2012 *Employees:* 113
Net Worth: £1,386,348 *Total Assets:* £23,342,048
Registered Office: 17 Elm Road, North Shields, Tyne & Wear, NE29 8SE
Activities: Agents specialised in the sale of other particular products
Parent: GNS Acquisitions Limited
Officers: Kieron Quinn Abernethy [1965] Director/Chief Revenue Officer; Paul Robert Stanley [1967] Director/Chief Executive

Global Substation Solutions Limited
Incorporated: 2 March 2006
Net Worth: £1,987,297 *Total Assets:* £3,296,507
Registered Office: Unit 1 Merchant Court, Monkton Business Park South, Hebburn, Tyne & Wear, NE31 2EX
Activities: Construction of utility projects for electricity and telecommunications
Shareholders: Gary Moore; Alan Bone; Luke de Sousa
Officers: Gary Moore, Secretary; Alan Bone [1960] Director/Engineer; Luke de Sousa [1971] Director/Engineer; Gary Moore [1971] Director/Engineer

GLPD Property Limited
Incorporated: 14 June 2011
Net Worth: £757,955 *Total Assets:* £10,855,969
Registered Office: c/o Leathers LLP, Carter House, Pelaw Leazes Lane, Durham, DH1 1TB
Activities: Other letting and operating of own or leased real estate
Parent: GLPD Holdings Limited
Officers: Amber Isobel Mary Dane, Secretary; Zoe Lawson, Secretary; Amber Isobel Mary Dane [1952] Director; Michael Robert Leather [1961] Director/Chartered Accountant

GLT Limited
Incorporated: 8 November 1935 *Employees:* 2
Net Worth: £1,066,437 *Total Assets:* £1,088,957
Registered Office: Yeavering, Kirknewton, Wooler, Northumberland, NE71 6HG
Activities: Non-trading company
Shareholders: Geoffrey Michael Tate; Linda Gaye Tate
Officers: Linda Gaye Tate, Secretary; Geoffrey Michael Tate [1936] Director/Engineer; Linda Gaye Tate [1938] Director/Secretary

GMA Healthcare Ltd
Incorporated: 26 May 2009 *Employees:* 72
Net Worth: £840,870 *Total Assets:* £1,136,902
Registered Office: Nunthorpe Hall Eastside, Nunthorpe Village, Nunthorpe, Middlesbrough, Cleveland, TS7 0NP
Activities: Residential care activities for the elderly and disabled
Parent: GMA Holdings Limited
Officers: Angela Dixon [1966] Director/Care Home Manager; George Dixon [1961] Director/Care Home Provider

GMC-Instruments UK Limited
Incorporated: 16 June 2015
Net Worth: £9,871,323 *Total Assets:* £23,798,802
Registered Office: 18 Bracken Hill, South West Industrial Estate, Peterlee, Co Durham, SR8 2SW
Activities: Activities of head offices
Parent: Metrawatt International GmbH
Officers: Mark Marsh [1971] Finance Director; Andrew Richard Upton [1969] Managing Director; Matthias Wist [1964] Managing Director [German]

GMF Europe LLP
Incorporated: 7 December 2012
Net Worth: £1,252,235,776 *Total Assets:* £1,258,359,424
Registered Office: c/o Womble Bond Dickinson (UK) LLP, St Ann's Wharf, 112 Quayside, Newcastle upon Tyne, NE1 3DX

GMS (Holdings) Limited
Incorporated: 19 March 2013 *Employees:* 29
Net Worth: £2,323,456 *Total Assets:* £6,528,697
Registered Office: 4 Regents Drive, Low Prudhoe Industrial Estate, Prudhoe, Northumberland, NE42 6PX
Activities: Other engineering activities
Major Shareholder: Owen George Ingram
Officers: Ann Marie Ingram [1963] Director; Owen George Ingram [1961] Director

Gnat UK Limited
Incorporated: 12 October 2005
Net Worth: £1,349,968 *Total Assets:* £2,009,022
Registered Office: Unit 5 Jackson Court, Olympic Way, Gallowfields, Richmond, N Yorks, DL10 4FB
Activities: Demolition
Major Shareholder: Nicholas Anthony Turnbull
Officers: Nicholas Anthony Turnbull [1963] Managing Director

GNS 2015 Limited
Incorporated: 5 November 2012 *Employees:* 3
Net Worth Deficit: £4,711,483 *Total Assets:* £1,962,437
Registered Office: 17 Elm Road, North Shields, Tyne & Wear, NE29 8SE
Activities: Agents specialised in the sale of other particular products
Parent: GNS Acquisitions Limited
Officers: Kieron Quinn Abernethy [1965] Director/Chief Revenue Officer; Paul Robert Stanley [1967] Director/Chief Executive

GNS Acquisitions Limited
Incorporated: 1 May 2012 *Employees:* 6
Net Worth Deficit: £17,412,178 *Total Assets:* £37,110,320
Registered Office: 17 Elm Road, North Shields, Tyne & Wear, NE29 8SE
Activities: Agents specialised in the sale of other particular products
Parent: GNS Midco 2 Limited
Officers: Kieron Quinn Abernerthy [1965] Director/Chief Revenue Officer; Paul Robert Stanley [1967] Director/Chief Executive

GNS Midco 1 Limited
Incorporated: 25 September 2012
Net Worth Deficit: £19,929,120 *Total Assets:* £30,848,116
Registered Office: 17 Elm Road, North Shields, Tyne & Wear, NE29 8SE
Activities: Activities of distribution holding companies
Parent: Global Navigation Solutions Holdings Limited
Officers: Kieron Quinn Abernethy [1965] Director/Chief Revenue Officer; Paul Robert Stanley [1967] Director/Chief Executive

GNS Midco 2 Limited
Incorporated: 25 September 2012
Net Worth Deficit: £11,380,056 *Total Assets:* £27,983,560
Registered Office: 17 Elm Road, North Shields, Tyne & Wear, NE29 8SE
Activities: Activities of distribution holding companies
Parent: GNS Midco 1 Limited
Officers: Kieron Quinn Abernethy [1965] Director/Chief Revenue Officer; Paul Robert Stanley [1967] Director/Chief Executive

GNS Treasury Limited
Incorporated: 22 February 2013
Net Worth: £11,548,807 *Total Assets:* £11,548,807
Registered Office: 17 Elm Road, North Shields, Tyne & Wear, NE29 8SE
Activities: Activities of distribution holding companies
Parent: GNS Acquisitions Limited
Officers: Kieron Quinn Abernethy [1965] Director/Chief Revenue Officer; Paul Robert Stanley [1967] Director/Chief Executive

Go Geothermal Ltd
Incorporated: 16 October 2006 *Employees:* 10
Net Worth: £587,641 *Total Assets:* £1,491,205
Registered Office: Unit 3 Ridgeway, Aycliffe Business Park, Newton Aycliffe, Co Durham, DL5 6SP
Activities: Wholesale of hardware, plumbing and heating equipment and supplies
Shareholders: Sowden David Paul Sowden; Timothy Woodward Williams
Officers: Victoria Louise Sowden, Secretary; Sean David Paul Sowden [1970] Director; Timothy Woodward Williams [1971] Director

Go North East Limited
Incorporated: 23 September 1986 *Employees:* 2,017
Net Worth: £2,135,000 *Total Assets:* £69,391,000
Registered Office: 3rd Floor, 41-51 Grey Street, Newcastle upon Tyne, NE1 6EE
Activities: Other urban, suburban or metropolitan passenger land transport (not underground, metro or similar)
Parent: Go-Ahead Holding Limited
Officers: Carolyn Ferguson, Secretary; David Allen Brown [1960] Director; Simon Patrick Butcher [1967] Finance Director; Gary Edmundson [1967] Director; Alexander Paul Edwards [1966] Director; Martijn Lee Gilbert [1982] Director; Stephen King [1978] Director

Go South Coast Limited
Incorporated: 16 March 2000 *Employees:* 1,835
Net Worth: £6,490,000 *Total Assets:* £133,782,000
Registered Office: 3rd Floor, 41-51 Grey Street, Newcastle upon Tyne, NE1 6EE
Activities: Activities of head offices
Parent: Go-Ahead Holding Limited
Officers: Carolyn Ferguson, Secretary; David Allen Brown [1960] Director; Simon Patrick Butcher [1967] Finance Director; Steven John Hamilton [1962] Engineering Director; David Richard Lee-Kong [1983] Director; Benjamin Matthew Murray [1977] Finance Director [American]; Andrew Rodney Wickham [1966] Managing Director

The Go-Ahead Group PLC
Incorporated: 17 February 1987
Net Worth: £208,300,000 *Total Assets:* £1,615,399,936
Registered Office: 3rd Floor, 41-51 Grey Street, Newcastle upon Tyne, NE1 6EE
Activities: Other passenger land transport
Officers: Carolyn Ferguson, Secretary; Andrew James Allner [1953] Director; David Allen Brown [1960] Director; Simon Patrick Butcher [1967] Finance Director; Adrian James Henry Ewer [1953] Director; Harry Arthur Blair Holt [1968] Director; Katherine Christina Mary Innes Ker [1960] Director; Leanne Wood [1972] Director

Go-Ahead Holding Limited
Incorporated: 24 August 2007
Net Worth: £338,873,984 *Total Assets:* £813,113,984
Registered Office: 3rd Floor, 41-51 Grey Street, Newcastle upon Tyne, NE1 6EE
Activities: Activities of head offices
Officers: Carolyn Ferguson, Secretary; David Allen Brown [1960] Director; Simon Patrick Butcher [1967] Finance Director

Go-Ahead London Rail Replacement Services Limited
Incorporated: 20 June 2013
Net Worth: £1,882,000 *Total Assets:* £2,180,000
Registered Office: 3rd Floor, 41-51 Grey Street, Newcastle upon Tyne, NE1 6EE
Activities: Other urban, suburban or metropolitan passenger land transport (not underground, metro or similar)
Parent: London General Transport Services Limited
Officers: Carolyn Ferguson, Secretary; David Allen Brown [1960] Director; Simon Patrick Butcher [1967] Finance Director; David Arthur Cutts [1969] Operations Director; Richard Harrington [1967] Engineering Director; Michael John Slattery [1967] Finance Director [Irish]; John Trayner [1959] Director

Gold Sheen Property Investments Limited
Incorporated: 17 July 1997 *Employees:* 4
Net Worth: £5,108,409 *Total Assets:* £6,439,355
Registered Office: Joseph Miller & Co, Floor A, Milburn House, Dean Street, Newcastle upon Tyne, NE1 1LE
Activities: Other letting and operating of own or leased real estate
Shareholders: Tracy Elizabeth Shearman; Christopher James Duffy
Officers: Tracy Elizabeth Shearman, Secretary; Jessica Victoria Dixon [1989] Director/Shop Assistant; Stephanie Elizabeth Dixon [1987] Director/Shop Assistant; Christopher James Duffy [1977] Director; Tracy Elizabeth Shearman [1958] Director

Golden Dragon Properties Limited
Incorporated: 12 October 2009 *Employees:* 1
Net Worth: £1,555,970 *Total Assets:* £1,636,605
Registered Office: 32 Portland Terrace, Newcastle upon Tyne, NE2 1QP
Activities: Other letting and operating of own or leased real estate
Shareholders: Dragonfly Venture Properties Limited; Christopher Patrick Maughan
Officers: Christopher Patrick Maughan [1963] Director

Goldmart Limited
Incorporated: 15 November 1984
Net Worth: £3,481,174 *Total Assets:* £3,918,669
Registered Office: 2 Houndgate, Darlington, Co Durham, DL1 5RL
Activities: Retail sale of watches and jewellery in specialised stores
Major Shareholder: Luke Peter Gray Wall-Row
Officers: Mark Stansfield, Secretary; Mark Stansfield [1958] Director/Jeweller; Luke Peter Gray Wallrow [1958] Director/Jeweller

Goldshield Securus Limited
Incorporated: 12 October 1988
Net Worth: £237,410 *Total Assets:* £1,091,404
Registered Office: 9-18 Ruby Court, Wesley Drive, Benton Square Industrial Estate, Newcastle upon Tyne, NE12 9UP
Activities: Electrical installation
Parent: Securus Group Limited
Officers: Anthony Denis Kane [1959] Director; John Stewart [1968] Director

Golftee LP 4 Limited
Incorporated: 1 August 2003 *Employees:* 2
Net Worth Deficit: £12,708,713 *Total Assets:* £5,010,645
Registered Office: First Floor, Finchale House, Belmont Business Park, Durham, DH1 1TW
Activities: Non-trading company
Officers: Helen Austin, Secretary; John Corbitt Barnsley [1948] Director/Accountant; Robert William Jefferson [1950] Director/Chartered Accountant

Goode Durrant Administration Limited
Incorporated: 5 October 1898
Net Worth: £1,156,231 *Total Assets:* £1,156,231
Registered Office: Northgate Centre, Lingfield Way, Darlington, Co Durham, DL1 4PZ
Activities: Renting and leasing of cars and light motor vehicles
Parent: Northgate PLC
Officers: Katie Laura Tasker-Wood, Secretary; Katie Laura Tasker-Wood [1981] Director

Goodfellow & Goodfellow Ltd.
Incorporated: 7 June 2011 *Employees:* 27
Net Worth: £1,432,222 *Total Assets:* £2,217,853
Registered Office: 7-8 Burdon Drive, North West Industrial Estate, Peterlee, Co Durham, SR8 2JH
Activities: Wholesale of china and glassware and cleaning materials
Officers: Valda Goodfellow, Secretary; Paul Goodfellow [1958] Director; Valda Goodfellow [1959] Director

A.& K. Gorham Limited
Incorporated: 19 June 2014
Net Worth: £155,778 *Total Assets:* £793,338
Registered Office: 511 Durham Road, Gateshead, Tyne & Wear, NE9 5EY
Activities: Other letting and operating of own or leased real estate
Shareholders: Austin John Gorham; Kathleen Gorham
Officers: Austin John Gorham [1949] Director; Kathleen Gorham [1950] Director

Gosforth 22 Limited
Incorporated: 16 August 2012
Registered Office: c/o Womble Bond Dickinson (UK) LLP, St Ann's Wharf, 112 Quayside, Newcastle upon Tyne, NE1 3DX
Activities: Buying and selling of own real estate
Major Shareholder: Glenville Hall
Officers: Glenville Lee Hall [1973] Director

The Gosforth Federated Academies Limited
Incorporated: 5 November 2010 *Employees:* 238
Net Worth: £37,066,000 *Total Assets:* £40,060,000
Registered Office: Knightsbridge, Great North Road, Gosforth, Newcastle upon Tyne, NE3 2JH
Activities: General secondary education
Officers: Christine Edwardson, Secretary; Roger Anthony Edwardson [1950] Director/Education Consultant; Jacqueline Slesenger Greene [1938] Director/Member Newcastle City Council; John Hall [1956] Assistant Director; Jeffrey Peter Lough [1956] Director/Retired; Geoffrey Michael Norris [1948] Director/Retired; George Snaith [1954] Director/Retired; Judy Angela Storey [1956] Director/Civil Servant Senior Accountant

Gosforth Park Hotels Limited
Incorporated: 25 October 2013 *Employees:* 98
Net Worth: £4,348,971 *Total Assets:* £8,875,352
Registered Office: 24 Woolsington Park South, Woolsington, Newcastle upon Tyne, NE13 8BJ
Activities: Hotels and similar accommodation
Officers: Mukesh Raj Chawla [1954] Director; Neel Chawla [1986] Director; Rani Chawla [1955] Director; Tina Chawla [1986] Director

Gosforth Schools' Trust
Incorporated: 17 March 2014
Net Worth: £27,291,220 *Total Assets:* £27,292,900
Registered Office: Gosforth Central Middle School, Great North Road, Gosforth, Newcastle upon Tyne, NE3 1UN
Activities: Primary education
Officers: Julia Margaret Bayes [1956] Director/Headteacher; Jeremy Paul Turnbull Bell [1952] Director/Retired Diplomat; Sean Martin Bullick [1967] Director; Sharon Coull [1972] Director/Accountant; Martin William Fletcher [1972] Director/Consultant-Business; Sarah Hawkins [1975] Director/Solicitor; Richard Michael Hukin [1975] Director/Chartered Accountant; Helen McKenna [1970] Director/Headteacher; Sarah Louise Medcalf [1976] Director/Development Manager; Gillian Karen Sanders [1960] Director/Retired; George Snaith [1954] Director; Timothy John Stout [1960] Director; Deborah Mary Tyler [1967] Director/Local Government Officer

The Goshen Trust
Incorporated: 16 February 2007
Net Worth: £10,234,753 *Total Assets:* £10,266,589
Registered Office: Unit 2b Guiseley Way, Durham Lane Industrial Park, Eaglescliffe, Stockton on Tees, Cleveland, TS16 0RF
Activities: Non-trading company
Officers: Robert Michael Goodrum, Secretary; Albert George Dicken [1946] Director; Alison Dicken [1970] Director; Jonathan Richard Dicken [1971] Director; Pauline Bernice Dicken [1946] Director

Govia Limited
Incorporated: 14 November 1996
Net Worth: £9,353,000 *Total Assets:* £52,481,000
Registered Office: 3rd Floor, 41-51 Grey Street, Newcastle upon Tyne, NE1 6EE
Activities: Activities of head offices
Shareholders: Go-Ahead Holding Limited; Keolis (UK) Limited
Officers: Carolyn Ferguson, Secretary; David Allen Brown [1960] Director; Simon Patrick Butcher [1967] Finance Director; Alistair John Francis Gordon [1968] Director; Charles Anthony Hodgson [1979] Managing Director - Rail Development; Bernard Denis Maurice Tabary [1960] Director [French]

Govia Thameslink Railway Limited
Incorporated: 2 February 2012 *Employees:* 6,946
Net Worth: £9,253,000 *Total Assets:* £410,295,008
Registered Office: 3rd Floor, 41-51 Grey Street, Newcastle upon Tyne, NE1 6EE
Activities: Passenger rail transport, interurban
Parent: Govia Limited
Officers: Carolyn Ferguson, Secretary; David Allen Brown [1960] Director; Nicholas James Forster Brown [1959] Director; Simon Patrick Butcher [1967] Finance Director; Alistair John Francis Gordon [1968] Director; Charles Anthony Hodgson [1979] Managing Director - Rail Development; Ian McLaren [1968] Finance and Contracts Director; Bernard Denis Maurice Tabary [1960] Director [French]; Hendrikus Verwer [1960] Managing Director [Dutch]

Gowland and Dawson Limited
Incorporated: 6 April 2001
Net Worth: £974,601 *Total Assets:* £1,344,397
Registered Office: 16 Harvey Close, Crowther Industrial Estate, Washington, Tyne & Wear, NE38 0AB
Activities: Construction of commercial buildings
Shareholders: Michael John Dawson; Steven Dawson; Judith Dawson; Susan Dawson
Officers: Judith Dawson, Secretary; Michael John Dawson [1966] Director; Steven Dawson [1957] Director

GPRB Holdings Limited
Incorporated: 9 May 2013 *Employees:* 130
Net Worth: £634,465 *Total Assets:* £5,136,466
Registered Office: Units 3-5 Morrison Road Industrial Estate, Annfield Plain, Stanley, Co Durham, DH9 7RU
Activities: Other business support service activities n.e.c.
Shareholder: Richard Graham Bradley
Officers: Richard Graham Bradley [1967] Finance Director; Graeme James Parkins [1969] Managing Director

GR Properties (North East) Limited
Incorporated: 15 January 2002 *Employees:* 2
Net Worth: £55,415 *Total Assets:* £927,257
Registered Office: 142 Hatfield Place, Peterlee, Co Durham, SR8 5TG
Activities: Buying and selling of own real estate
Shareholders: Ann Reid; Raymond Reid
Officers: Ann Reid, Secretary; Graeme Reid [1968] Director/Property Developer

Grab & Deliver Limited
Incorporated: 3 March 2006
Net Worth: £1,814,977 *Total Assets:* £2,774,927
Registered Office: 27 Medomsley Road, Consett, Co Durham, DH8 5HE
Activities: Site preparation
Shareholders: Peter Barrass; Thomas Dunn
Officers: Peter Barrass [1969] Director; Thomas Dunn [1968] Director

Grace House North East
Incorporated: 18 April 2002 *Employees:* 6
Net Worth: £3,491,134 *Total Assets:* £3,512,410
Registered Office: Swallow House, Parsons Road, Washington, Tyne & Wear, NE37 1EZ
Activities: Medical nursing home activities
Officers: Claire Miller, Secretary; Simon James William Berry [1974] Director/Optometrist; Simon Briton [1976] Director/Solicitor; David Michael Cook [1969] Director; Neil Henry [1972] Director; Hock Kim Stephen Hinshaw [1959] Director; Claire Elizabeth Miller [1968] Director/Chartered Accountant; Valerie Milnes [1949] Director

Gracelands Care Home Limited
Incorporated: 5 February 1996 *Employees:* 2
Net Worth: £1,655,530 *Total Assets:* £2,938,007
Registered Office: Graceland Nursing Home, Belmangate, Guisborough, Cleveland, TS14 7BB
Activities: Residential care activities for the elderly and disabled
Parent: BJP Corporation Limited
Officers: Joan Corinne Parvin, Secretary; Barry Malcolm Parvin [1948] Director/Finance Manager

Graform Limited
Incorporated: 14 April 2004 *Employees:* 4
Net Worth: £852,657 *Total Assets:* £1,215,304
Registered Office: Witton Hall Farm, Witton Gilbert, Co Durham, DH7 6SU
Activities: Landscape service activities
Shareholders: Christopher David Holmes; John Nigel Holmes
Officers: Christopher David Holmes, Secretary; Christopher David Holmes [1963] Director/Farmer; John Nigel Holmes [1961] Director/Farmer

A.M. Graham Fabrications Limited
Incorporated: 17 July 1997 *Employees:* 34
Net Worth: £1,206,550 *Total Assets:* £1,753,263
Registered Office: Atlas Works, West View Terrace, St Omers Road, Dunston, Tyne & Wear, NE11 9EL
Activities: Casting of steel
Major Shareholder: Anthony Michael Graham
Officers: Anthony Michael Graham [1953] Director

Graham Hair and Beauty Limited
Incorporated: 2 May 1986 *Employees:* 13
Net Worth: £667,790 *Total Assets:* £956,989
Registered Office: MacGregor House, Station Road, Seaton Delaval, Northumberland, NE25 0PT
Activities: Wholesale of perfume and cosmetics
Major Shareholder: Graham Millis Janaway
Officers: Patricia Bennett, Secretary; Graham Millis Janaway [1944] Director/Hairdressing Wholesaler

Grainco Limited
Incorporated: 9 June 1995 *Employees:* 65
Net Worth: £15,261,120 *Total Assets:* £161,034,416
Registered Office: Grainco Limited, Tyne Dock, South Shields, Tyne & Wear, NE34 9PL
Activities: Wholesale of grain, unmanufactured tobacco, seeds and animal feeds
Parent: Tynegrain Limited
Officers: Susan Yvonne Duck, Secretary; Gareth Thomas Gilroy Baird [1957] Director/Farmer; Charles Cummine Birnie [1960] Director; Gary John Bright [1969] Director/Trader; Robert John Davison [1954] Director/Farmer; Susan Yvonne Duck [1965] Director/Accountant; George Stephen Gillie [1961] Director/Shipbroker; John Cameron Hutcheson [1964] Director/Farmer; Peter Alan Jackson [1958] Director/Farmer; Simon Edward Rust [1963] Director; Charles Michael Scholey [1955] Director/Farmer

Grainger (Aldershot) Limited
Incorporated: 23 February 2011
Net Worth: £1,198,141 *Total Assets:* £40,075,872
Registered Office: Citygate, St James Boulevard, Newcastle upon Tyne, NE1 4JE
Activities: Development of building projects
Parent: Grainger PLC
Officers: Adam McGhin, Secretary; Helen Christine Gordon [1959] Director; Michael Paul Keaveney [1967] Director; Adam McGhin [1978] Director/Solicitor; Vanessa Kate Simms [1975] Director

Grainger (Clapham) Limited
Incorporated: 16 May 2001
Net Worth: £41,694,280 *Total Assets:* £42,334,228
Registered Office: Citygate, St James Boulevard, Newcastle upon Tyne, NE1 4JE
Activities: Development of building projects
Parent: GIP Limited
Officers: Adam McGhin, Secretary; Helen Christine Gordon [1959] Director; Michael Paul Keaveney [1967] Director; Adam McGhin [1978] Director/Solicitor; Vanessa Kate Simms [1975] Director

Grainger (Commercial Developments) Limited
Incorporated: 15 March 1990 *Employees:* 4
Net Worth: £2,233,845 *Total Assets:* £3,009,043
Registered Office: The Pele Tower, Corbridge, Northumberland, NE45 5LA
Activities: Development of building projects
Officers: Carol Fletcher, Secretary/Sales Negotiator; Jean Elizabeth Firth [1948] Director; John Philip David Firth [1946] Director; Carol Fletcher [1946] Director/Company Secretary; Peter Scarth Fletcher [1946] Director

Grainger (Hadston) Limited
Incorporated: 11 September 2000
Net Worth: £2,839,010 *Total Assets:* £2,841,407
Registered Office: Citygate, St James Boulevard, Newcastle upon Tyne, NE1 4JE
Activities: Buying and selling of own real estate
Parent: Northumberland & Durham Property Trust Limited
Officers: Adam McGhin, Secretary; Helen Christine Gordon [1959] Director; Michael Paul Keaveney [1967] Director; Adam McGhin [1978] Director/Solicitor; Vanessa Kate Simms [1975] Director

Grainger (Octavia Hill) Limited
Incorporated: 14 December 2005
Net Worth: £36,908,220 *Total Assets:* £38,813,196
Registered Office: Citygate, St James Boulevard, Newcastle upon Tyne, NE1 4JE
Activities: Activities of other membership organisations n.e.c.
Parent: BPT (Residential Investments) Limited
Officers: Adam McGhin, Secretary; Helen Christine Gordon [1959] Director; Adam McGhin [1978] Director/Solicitor; Andrew Philip Saunderson [1975] Director; Vanessa Kate Simms [1975] Director

Grainger Asset Management Limited
Incorporated: 15 April 2002
Net Worth: £5,993,165 *Total Assets:* £5,993,165
Registered Office: Citygate, St James Boulevard, Newcastle upon Tyne, NE1 4JE
Activities: Management of real estate on a fee or contract basis
Parent: Grainger PLC
Officers: Adam McGhin, Secretary; Helen Christine Gordon [1959] Director; Adam McGhin [1978] Director/Solicitor; Mark Jeremy Robson [1959] Director/Chartered Surveyor; Andrew Philip Saunderson [1975] Director; Vanessa Kate Simms [1975] Director

Grainger Bradley Limited
Incorporated: 10 December 2012
Net Worth: £14,180,991 *Total Assets:* £67,346,288
Registered Office: Citygate, St James' Boulevard, Newcastle upon Tyne, NE1 4JE
Activities: Development of building projects
Parent: BPT Limited
Officers: Adam McGhin, Secretary; Helen Christine Gordon [1959] Director; Adam McGhin [1978] Director/Solicitor; Mark Jeremy Robson [1959] Director/Chartered Surveyor; Vanessa Kate Simms [1975] Director

Grainger Employees Limited
Incorporated: 19 January 2004 *Employees:* 215
Net Worth: £33,665,080 *Total Assets:* £38,644,884
Registered Office: Citygate, St James Boulevard, Newcastle upon Tyne, NE1 4JE
Activities: Development of building projects
Parent: Grainger PLC
Officers: Adam McGhin, Secretary; Helen Christine Gordon [1959] Director; Adam McGhin [1978] Director/Solicitor; Mark Jeremy Robson [1959] Director/Chartered Surveyor; Vanessa Kate Simms [1975] Director

Grainger Europe (No. 2) Limited
Incorporated: 27 July 2005
Net Worth: £119,847,776 *Total Assets:* £121,027,232
Registered Office: Citygate, St James Boulevard, Newcastle upon Tyne, NE1 4JE
Activities: Activities of head offices
Parent: Grainger PLC
Officers: Adam McGhin, Secretary; Helen Christine Gordon [1959] Director; Adam McGhin [1978] Director/Solicitor; Vanessa Kate Simms [1975] Director

Grainger Europe (No. 3) Limited
Incorporated: 7 June 2005
Net Worth: £4,900,397 *Total Assets:* £4,900,397
Registered Office: Citygate, St James Boulevard, Newcastle upon Tyne, NE1 4JE
Activities: Other business support service activities n.e.c.
Parent: Grainger PLC
Officers: Adam McGhin, Secretary; Helen Christine Gordon [1959] Director; Adam McGhin [1978] Director/Solicitor; Vanessa Kate Simms [1975] Director

Grainger Europe (No. 4) Limited
Incorporated: 24 August 2007
Net Worth Deficit: £24,207,090 *Total Assets:* £7,718,686
Registered Office: Citygate, St James Boulevard, Newcastle upon Tyne, NE1 4JE
Activities: Other business support service activities n.e.c.
Parent: Grainger PLC
Officers: Adam McGhin, Secretary; Steven Butler [1978] Director/Tax Manager; Helen Christine Gordon [1959] Director; Adam McGhin [1978] Director/Solicitor; Vanessa Kate Simms [1975] Director

Grainger Europe Limited
Incorporated: 29 November 2004
Net Worth: £1,280,895 *Total Assets:* £2,241,794
Registered Office: Citygate, St James' Boulevard, Newcastle upon Tyne, NE1 4JE
Activities: Activities of head offices
Parent: Grainger PLC
Officers: Adam McGhin, Secretary; Richard Flynn [1976] Director/Property Litigator; Helen Christine Gordon [1959] Director; Adam McGhin [1978] Director/Solicitor; Vanessa Kate Simms [1975] Director

Grainger European Ventures LLP
Incorporated: 27 June 2005
Net Worth: £2,901,041 *Total Assets:* £2,901,041
Registered Office: Citygate, St James' Boulevard, Newcastle upon Tyne, NE1 4JE

Grainger Finance (Tricomm) Limited
Incorporated: 19 March 2013
Net Worth: £55,209,440 *Total Assets:* £55,209,440
Registered Office: Citygate, St James' Boulevard, Newcastle upon Tyne, NE1 4JE
Activities: Financial intermediation not elsewhere classified
Parent: Grainger Finance Company Limited
Officers: Adam McGhin, Secretary; Helen Christine Gordon [1959] Director; Adam McGhin [1978] Director/Solicitor; Vanessa Kate Simms [1975] Director

Grainger Finance Company Limited
Incorporated: 30 June 1999
Net Worth: £479,248,992 *Total Assets:* £2,272,334,080
Registered Office: Citygate, St James Boulevard, Newcastle upon Tyne, NE1 4JE
Activities: Financial intermediation not elsewhere classified
Parent: Grainger PLC
Officers: Adam McGhin, Secretary; Helen Christine Gordon [1959] Director; Adam McGhin [1978] Director/Solicitor; Mark Jeremy Robson [1959] Director/Chartered Surveyor; Vanessa Kate Simms [1975] Director

Grainger Games (Holdings) Limited
Incorporated: 16 March 2010 *Employees:* 390
Net Worth: £6,178,005 *Total Assets:* £10,912,220
Registered Office: Unit 4 North Tyne Industrial Estate, Longbenton, Newcastle upon Tyne, NE12 9SZ
Activities: Retail sale of games and toys in specialised stores
Shareholder: Stephen Bowyer
Officers: Stephen Bowyer [1974] Director; Jonathan Fellows [1958] Director

Grainger Housing & Developments Limited
Incorporated: 12 May 1986
Net Worth Deficit: £84,686,696 *Total Assets:* £57,142,344
Registered Office: Citygate, St James Boulevard, Newcastle upon Tyne, NE1 4JE
Activities: Development of building projects
Parent: GIP Limited
Officers: Adam McGhin, Secretary; Helen Christine Gordon [1959] Director; Adam McGhin [1978] Director/Solicitor; Andrew Philip Saunderson [1975] Director; Vanessa Kate Simms [1975] Director

Grainger Invest (No.1 Holdco) Limited
Incorporated: 8 March 2011
Net Worth: £31,671,716 *Total Assets:* £31,744,882
Registered Office: Citygate, St James Boulevard, Newcastle upon Tyne, NE1 4JE
Activities: Activities of head offices
Parent: BPT Limited
Officers: Adam McGhin, Secretary; Helen Christine Gordon [1959] Director; Adam McGhin [1978] Director/Solicitor; Andrew Philip Saunderson [1975] Director; Vanessa Kate Simms [1975] Director

Grainger Invest No . 1 LLP
Incorporated: 23 April 2005
Net Worth: £53,121,000 *Total Assets:* £91,587,000
Registered Office: Citygate, St James Boulevard, Newcastle upon Tyne, NE1 4JE

Grainger Invest No.2 LLP
Incorporated: 22 February 2006
Net Worth: £70,200,000 *Total Assets:* £114,383,000
Registered Office: Citygate, St James Boulevard, Newcastle upon Tyne, NE1 4JE

Grainger Kensington & Chelsea Limited
Incorporated: 20 July 2012
Net Worth: £34,378 *Total Assets:* £25,091,578
Registered Office: Citygate, St James Boulevard, Newcastle upon Tyne, NE1 4JE
Activities: Development of building projects
Parent: Grainger PLC
Officers: Adam McGhin, Secretary; Helen Christine Gordon [1959] Director; Michael Paul Keaveney [1967] Director; Adam McGhin [1978] Director/Solicitor; Vanessa Kate Simms [1975] Director

Grainger Land & Regeneration Limited
Incorporated: 29 September 2004
Net Worth: £5,508,061 *Total Assets:* £109,459,312
Registered Office: Citygate, St James Boulevard, Newcastle upon Tyne, NE1 4JE
Activities: Development of building projects
Parent: Grainger Housing & Developments Limited
Officers: Adam McGhin, Secretary; Helen Christine Gordon [1959] Director; Adam McGhin [1978] Director/Solicitor; Andrew Philip Saunderson [1975] Director; Vanessa Kate Simms [1975] Director

Grainger Maidenhead Limited
Incorporated: 8 February 1999
Net Worth: £11,652,031 *Total Assets:* £11,690,924
Registered Office: Citygate, St James Boulevard, Newcastle upon Tyne, NE1 4JE
Activities: Other letting and operating of own or leased real estate
Parent: Northumberland & Durham Property Trust Limited
Officers: Adam McGhin, Secretary; Helen Christine Gordon [1959] Director; Michael Paul Keaveney [1967] Director; Adam McGhin [1978] Director/Solicitor; Vanessa Kate Simms [1975] Director

Grainger Newbury Limited
Incorporated: 11 January 2000
Net Worth Deficit: £29,503 *Total Assets:* £1,850,833
Registered Office: Citygate, St James Boulevard, Newcastle upon Tyne, NE1 4JE
Activities: Non-trading company
Parent: Grainger Housing & Developments Limited
Officers: Adam McGhin, Secretary; Helen Christine Gordon [1959] Director; Adam McGhin [1978] Director/Solicitor; Vanessa Kate Simms [1975] Director

Grainger OCCC Limited
Incorporated: 9 March 2011
Net Worth: £18,985,948 *Total Assets:* £19,166,462
Registered Office: Citygate, St James Boulevard, Newcastle upon Tyne, NE1 4JE
Activities: Development of building projects
Parent: Atlantic Metropolitan (U.K.) Limited
Officers: Adam McGhin, Secretary; Helen Christine Gordon [1959] Director; Adam McGhin [1978] Director/Solicitor; Mark Jeremy Robson [1959] Director/Chartered Surveyor; Vanessa Kate Simms [1975] Director

Grainger Pearl Limited
Incorporated: 16 April 2012
Net Worth: £11,479,451 *Total Assets:* £28,999,988
Registered Office: Citygate, St James Boulevard, Newcastle upon Tyne, NE1 4JE
Activities: Development of building projects
Parent: Grainger Pearl Holdings Limited
Officers: Adam McGhin, Secretary; Helen Christine Gordon [1959] Director; Adam McGhin [1978] Director/Solicitor; Andrew Philip Saunderson [1975] Director; Vanessa Kate Simms [1975] Director

Grainger PLC
Incorporated: 27 November 1912 *Employees:* 215
Net Worth: £745,299,968 *Total Assets:* £1,767,000,064
Registered Office: Citygate, St James Boulevard, Newcastle upon Tyne, NE1 4JE
Activities: Activities of head offices
Officers: Adam McGhin, Secretary; Andrew Charles Phillip Carr-Locke [1953] Director; Mark Sydney Clare [1957] Director; Helen Christine Gordon [1959] Director; Justin Richard Read [1961] Director; Vanessa Kate Simms [1975] Director; Robert William Ian Wilkinson [1972] Director; Antony Paul Wray [1961] Director

Grainger PRS Limited
Incorporated: 21 April 2006
Net Worth: £1,540,042 *Total Assets:* £10,956,205
Registered Office: Citygate, St James Boulevard, Newcastle upon Tyne, NE1 4JE
Activities: Non-trading company
Parent: Greit Limited
Officers: Adam McGhin, Secretary; Helen Christine Gordon [1959] Director; Adam McGhin [1978] Director/Solicitor; Vanessa Kate Simms [1975] Director

Grainger Ramp Limited
Incorporated: 11 March 2011
Net Worth: £4,185,047 *Total Assets:* £4,219,032
Registered Office: Citygate, St James Boulevard, Newcastle upon Tyne, NE1 4JE
Activities: Management of real estate on a fee or contract basis
Parent: Grainger PLC
Officers: Adam McGhin, Secretary; Helen Christine Gordon [1959] Director; Adam McGhin [1978] Director/Solicitor; Mark Jeremy Robson [1959] Director/Chartered Surveyor; Vanessa Kate Simms [1975] Director; Anish Nathalal Thobhani [1970] Director/Deputy MD

Grainger Real Estate Limited
Incorporated: 28 February 2001
Net Worth: £125,816,000 *Total Assets:* £125,816,000
Registered Office: Citygate, St James Boulevard, Newcastle upon Tyne, NE1 4JE
Activities: Activities of head offices
Parent: Atlantic Metropolitan (U.K.) Limited
Officers: Adam McGhin, Secretary; Helen Christine Gordon [1959] Director; Adam McGhin [1978] Director/Solicitor; Vanessa Kate Simms [1975] Director

Grainger REIT 1 Limited
Incorporated: 30 October 2015
Net Worth: £15,133,935 *Total Assets:* £18,187,988
Registered Office: Citygate, St James Boulevard, Newcastle upon Tyne, NE1 4JE
Activities: Other business support service activities n.e.c.
Parent: Grainger Unitholder No 1 Limited
Officers: Adam McGhin, Secretary; Helen Christine Gordon [1959] Director; Adam McGhin [1978] Director/Solicitor; Vanessa Kate Simms [1975] Director

Grainger REIT 2 Limited
Incorporated: 30 October 2015
Net Worth: £15,133,935 *Total Assets:* £15,133,935
Registered Office: Citygate, St James Boulevard, Newcastle upon Tyne, NE1 4JE
Activities: Other business support service activities n.e.c.
Parent: Grainger Unitholder No 1 Limited
Officers: Adam McGhin, Secretary; Helen Christine Gordon [1959] Director; Adam McGhin [1978] Director/Solicitor; Vanessa Kate Simms [1975] Director

Grainger REIT 3 Limited
Incorporated: 30 October 2015
Net Worth: £15,133,935 *Total Assets:* £15,133,935
Registered Office: Citygate, St James Boulevard, Newcastle upon Tyne, NE1 4JE
Activities: Other business support service activities n.e.c.
Parent: Grainger Unitholder No 1 Limited
Officers: Adam McGhin, Secretary; Helen Christine Gordon [1959] Director; Adam McGhin [1978] Director/Solicitor; Vanessa Kate Simms [1975] Director

Grainger Residential Limited
Incorporated: 15 January 2004
Net Worth Deficit: £1,476,221 *Total Assets:* £72,311,816
Registered Office: Citygate, St James Boulevard, Newcastle upon Tyne, NE1 4JE
Activities: Activities of head offices
Parent: Grainger PLC
Officers: Adam McGhin, Secretary; Helen Christine Gordon [1959] Director; Adam McGhin [1978] Director/Solicitor; Andrew Philip Saunderson [1975] Director; Vanessa Kate Simms [1975] Director

Grainger Residential Management Limited
Incorporated: 24 November 2003
Net Worth: £9,727,882 *Total Assets:* £21,969,180
Registered Office: Citygate, St James Boulevard, Newcastle upon Tyne, NE1 4JE
Activities: Development of building projects
Officers: Adam McGhin, Secretary; Helen Christine Gordon [1959] Director; Adam McGhin [1978] Director/Solicitor; Mark Jeremy Robson [1959] Director/Chartered Surveyor; Vanessa Kate Simms [1975] Director

Grainger Serviced Apartments Limited
Incorporated: 25 June 2004
Net Worth: £7,433,927 *Total Assets:* £7,433,927
Registered Office: Citygate, St James Boulevard, Newcastle upon Tyne, NE1 4JE
Activities: Development of building projects
Parent: Northumberland & Durham Property Trust Limited
Officers: Adam McGhin, Secretary; Helen Christine Gordon [1959] Director; Adam McGhin [1978] Director/Solicitor; Mark Jeremy Robson [1959] Director/Chartered Surveyor; Vanessa Kate Simms [1975] Director

Grainger Seven Sisters Limited
Incorporated: 16 February 2007
Net Worth: £1,084,042 *Total Assets:* £14,177,929
Registered Office: Citygate, St James Boulevard, Newcastle upon Tyne, NE1 4JE
Activities: Development of building projects
Parent: Grainger Housing & Developments Limited
Officers: Adam McGhin, Secretary; Helen Christine Gordon [1959] Director; Adam McGhin [1978] Director/Solicitor; Andrew Philip Saunderson [1975] Director; Vanessa Kate Simms [1975] Director

Grainger Southwark Limited
Incorporated: 10 March 2011
Net Worth: £21,340,212 *Total Assets:* £28,976,932
Registered Office: Citygate, St James Boulevard, Newcastle upon Tyne, NE1 4JE
Activities: Development of building projects
Parent: BPT Limited
Officers: Adam McGhin, Secretary; Helen Christine Gordon [1959] Director; Adam McGhin [1978] Director/Solicitor; Mark Jeremy Robson [1959] Director/Chartered Surveyor; Vanessa Kate Simms [1975] Director

Grainger Treasury Property (2006) LLP
Incorporated: 23 January 2007
Net Worth: £209,275,024 *Total Assets:* £209,275,024
Registered Office: Citygate, St James Boulevard, Newcastle upon Tyne, NE1 4JE

Grainger Trust Limited
Incorporated: 8 January 2003
Net Worth: £29,029,448 *Total Assets:* £32,761,044
Registered Office: Citygate, St James Boulevard, Newcastle upon Tyne, NE1 4JE
Activities: Non-trading company
Parent: Grainger Housing & Developments Limited
Officers: Rodica Damian, Secretary; Gina Amoh [1959] Director/Chief Executive; Toby Edward Austin [1972] Director; Paul McGowan [1969] Director; Calum Mercer [1965] Director/Consultant; Mark Jeremy Robson [1959] Director/Chartered Surveyor; Deborah Frances Shackleton [1952] Director/Retired

Grainger Unitholder No 1 Limited
Incorporated: 19 October 2005
Net Worth: £8,342,969 *Total Assets:* £78,037,432
Registered Office: Citygate, St James Boulevard, Newcastle upon Tyne, NE1 4JE
Activities: Other business support service activities n.e.c.
Parent: Grainger PLC
Officers: Adam McGhin, Secretary; Helen Christine Gordon [1959] Director; Adam McGhin [1978] Director/Solicitor; Vanessa Kate Simms [1975] Director

Gralenno Limited
Incorporated: 15 August 2000 *Employees:* 4
Net Worth Deficit: £442,014 *Total Assets:* £3,714,031
Registered Office: Ringtons Limited, Algernon Road, Newcastle upon Tyne, NE6 2YN
Activities: Non-life insurance
Officers: Peter Nigel Hastings Smith, Secretary; John David Smith [1951] Director; Peter Nigel Hastings Smith [1954] Director; Simon Montgomery Smith [1956] Director; Anthony Ian Godfrey Charles South [1943] Director

Grand Central Railway Company Limited
Incorporated: 25 April 2000 *Employees:* 150
Net Worth: £12,691,000 *Total Assets:* £22,497,000
Registered Office: 1 Admiral Way, Doxford International Business Park, Sunderland, Tyne & Wear, SR3 3XP
Activities: Passenger rail transport, interurban
Officers: Lorna Edwards, Secretary; Christopher Derek Dyne Burchell [1973] Director; Andrew John Cooper [1958] Director; Mark Alan Dale [1976] Director; Sean Gerrard English [1967] Director; Amanda Furlong [1975] Director; David Hatfield [1960] Director; Mary Elisabeth Courtney Hewitt [1979] Director; Richard Henry McClean [1963] Director

Grand Hotel Ltd
Incorporated: 4 November 1997 *Employees:* 2
Net Worth: £1,150,439 *Total Assets:* £1,361,111
Registered Office: 213b Western Way, Darras Hall, Ponteland, Northumberland, NE20 9ND
Activities: Other service activities n.e.c.
Officers: Danesh Kohli, Secretary/Nursing Home Hotelier; Danesh Kohli [1952] Director/Nursing Home Hotelier

Grange Farm Eggs Ltd
Incorporated: 9 April 2010 *Employees:* 11
Net Worth: £1,447,617 *Total Assets:* £2,645,817
Registered Office: Grange Farm, Hornby, Northallerton, N Yorks, DL6 2HF
Activities: Raising of poultry
Shareholders: Martin William Morrison; Gillian Ann Morrison
Officers: Gillian Morrison, Secretary; Gillian Ann Morrison [1958] Director/Secretary; Kenneth Morrison [1986] Director/Farmers; Martin William Morrison [1956] Director/Farmer

Samuel Grant (North East) Limited
Incorporated: 5 September 1984 *Employees:* 17
Net Worth: £350,464 *Total Assets:* £1,648,843
Registered Office: Unit B, Viking Industrial Estate, Rolling Mill Road, Jarrow, Tyne & Wear, NE32 3DP
Activities: Wholesale of other intermediate products
Parent: Samuel Grant (Holdings) Ltd
Officers: Ashley Jon Dean, Secretary; Andrew David Surrey Grant [1970] Director/Packaging Merchant; Matthew Paul Surrey Grant [1974] Director/Packaging Merchant; Ian Laidlaw [1961] Sales Director

Fraser Grant Estates Limited
Incorporated: 25 April 1983
Net Worth: £2,920,154 *Total Assets:* £6,639,509
Registered Office: 27 Acorn Road, Jesmond, Newcastle upon Tyne, NE2 2DJ
Activities: Construction of domestic buildings
Major Shareholder: Charles Gordon Grant
Officers: Wendy Elizabeth Mizen, Secretary; Ellen Alexandra Mizen Grant [1989] Director/Trainee; Wendy Elizabeth Mizen [1952] Director/Personnel

Grantham Motor Company Limited
Incorporated: 4 April 2003 *Employees:* 517
Net Worth: £6,762,000 *Total Assets:* £31,275,000
Registered Office: Vertu House, Fifth Avenue Business Park, Team Valley Trading Estate, Gateshead, Tyne & Wear, NE11 0XA
Activities: Wholesale trade of motor vehicle parts and accessories
Parent: Vertu Motors PLC
Officers: Karen Anderson, Secretary; Karen Anderson [1971] Finance Director; David Paul Crane [1967] Commercial Director; Robert Thomas Forrester [1969] Director; Michael Sherwin [1959] Finance Director; Christopher Leigh Taylor [1973] Managing Director

Graphite Enterprises (DEP) Limited
Incorporated: 30 November 2007
Registered Office: Derwenthaugh Eco Parc, Derwenthaugh Road, Swalwell, Newcastle upon Tyne, NE16 3BJ
Activities: Other letting and operating of own or leased real estate
Parent: Catfoss Renewables Limited
Officers: Nicholas Robert King, Secretary; Andrew Patrick Foreman [1963] Director; Nicholas Robert King [1973] Director

Graphite Resources (DEP) Limited
Incorporated: 30 November 2007
Registered Office: Derwenthaugh Eco Parc, Derwenthaugh Road, Swalwell, Newcastle upon Tyne, NE16 3BJ
Activities: Recovery of sorted materials
Parent: Catfoss Renewables Limited
Officers: Nicholas Robert King, Secretary; Andrew Patrick Foreman [1963] Director

Grasmere Academy
Incorporated: 5 July 2012 *Employees:* 23
Net Worth: £1,509,000 *Total Assets:* £1,732,000
Registered Office: Grasmere Academy, Grasmere Court, Killingworth, Tyne & Wear, NE12 6TS
Activities: Primary education
Officers: Domonique Ellis, Secretary; David Mark Baldwin [1962] Director/Headteacher; Moira Banks [1966] Director/Teacher; Hannah Mary Lind Girvan [1987] Director/Teacher; Lynn Goossens [1959] Director; David Ian Hodgson [1956] Director of Regulatory Compliance; Jacqueline Patricia Lackenby [1985] Director/Student; Kerry Lilico [1978] Director/Headteacher; David James Richardson [1986] Director/Accountant; Louisa Stevenson [1978] Director/Financial Adviser; Richard Stevenson [1977] Director/Education Consultant

Gray & Son Robe Makers (Durham) Ltd
Incorporated: 19 December 1988 *Employees:* 5
Net Worth: £567,919 *Total Assets:* £775,537
Registered Office: Ground Floor, Finchale House, Belmont Business Park, Durham, DH1 1TW
Activities: Other retail sale in non-specialised stores
Major Shareholder: Marion Grace Myers
Officers: Marion Grace Myers, Secretary; Marion Grace Myers [1958] Director/Company Secretary

David Gray Solicitors LLP
Incorporated: 18 March 2011 *Employees:* 65
Net Worth: £1,326,717 *Total Assets:* £1,770,417
Registered Office: Old County Court, 56 Westgate Road, Newcastle upon Tyne, NE1 5XU
Officers: Michael Bishop [1957] Member; Brian Hegarty [1968] Member; Lucy Katrina Mead [1975] Member; Mary Caroline Shaw [1959] Member; Hilary Elspeth Thomson [1967] Member; Lucy Katrina Mead [1975] LLP Member

Grayson Spa Limited
Incorporated: 11 December 2014 *Employees:* 1
Net Worth Deficit: £24,690 *Total Assets:* £1,077,210
Registered Office: 50 The Green, Romanby, Northallerton, N Yorks, DL7 8NR
Activities: Manufacture of other plastic products
Major Shareholder: Anthony Thomas Grayson
Officers: Anthony Thomas Grayson [1963] Director/Engineer

Graza Limited
Incorporated: 20 March 2015
Net Worth: £1,487,489 *Total Assets:* £4,487,489
Registered Office: Time Central, 32 Gallowgate, Newcastle upon Tyne, NE1 4SN
Activities: Non-trading company
Shareholders: Northern Venture Trust PLC; Northern 2 VCT PLC; Northern 3 VCT PLC
Officers: James Kirk Bryce, Secretary; Simon Gregory Barrell [1959] Director; Timothy Roland Levett [1949] Director

The Great North Air Ambulance Service
Incorporated: 13 May 2002 *Employees:* 81
Net Worth: £12,354,860 *Total Assets:* £13,020,887
Registered Office: Northumberland Wing, The Imperial Centre, Grange Road, Darlington, Co Durham, DL1 5NQ
Activities: Non-scheduled passenger air transport
Officers: John Richard Devine [1976] Director/Solicitor; Dawn Catherine Dunn [1962] Director/Marketing Communications Manager; Stephen Groves [1962] Director/National Head of Emergency Preparedness, Resilience; Dr Kyee Han [1951] Clinical Director; James Andrew Harris [1971] Director; Brian Henry Jobling [1968] Director; James Kyle [1976] Director/Wealth Manager; Peter Andrew Neal [1966] Associate Director; Joan Trench [1954] Director/HR Strategic Lead and Executive Coach; Paul Leonard Turner [1953] Director/International Development Consultant

Great North Properties Limited
Incorporated: 11 December 1996
Net Worth: £1,331 *Total Assets:* £803,105
Registered Office: Design Works, William Street, Felling, Gateshead, Tyne & Wear, NE10 0JP
Activities: Other letting and operating of own or leased real estate
Parent: Raj Ashby & Mr Ashby Settlement
Officers: Mary Ruth Ashby, Secretary/Manager; Mary Ruth Ashby [1947] Company Secretary/Director; Councillor Robin Arthur John Ashby [1947] Director; Simon Nicholas Paul Ashby [1975] Director/Builder

Great Orton Windfarm II Limited
Incorporated: 30 July 1998
Net Worth: £1,434,000 *Total Assets:* £2,103,000
Registered Office: Alexander House, 1 Mandarin Road, Rainton Bridge Business Park, Houghton-le-Spring, Co Durham, DH4 5RA
Activities: Production of electricity
Parent: EDF Energy Renewables Holdings Limited
Officers: Susan Elizabeth Lind, Secretary; Matthieu Thomas Hue [1975] Director [French]; Hassaan Majid [1968] Director

Great Park Food Company Ltd.
Incorporated: 27 July 2009 *Employees:* 4
Net Worth: £974,885 *Total Assets:* £1,393,520
Registered Office: The Old Granary, North Brunton, Newcastle upon Tyne, NE3 5HD
Activities: Wholesale of meat and meat products
Shareholders: Ross Frazer Greenhill; Laura Greenhill
Officers: Laura Greenhill, Secretary; Ross Frazer Greenhill [1979] Managing Director

Greco Brothers Limited
Incorporated: 15 May 1947 *Employees:* 20
Net Worth: £1,975,665 *Total Assets:* £2,195,814
Registered Office: 5 Greta Street, Middlesbrough, Cleveland, TS1 5QS
Activities: Manufacture of rusks and biscuits; manufacture of preserved pastry goods and cakes
Major Shareholder: Peter Marino Rovardi
Officers: Lucia Rovardi-Tomlinson, Secretary; Anthony Gerard Rovardi [1977] Director/Cone and Wafer Manufacturers; Peter Marino Rovardi [1953] Director/Biscuit Manufacturer

Green & Son Building Services Limited
Incorporated: 10 May 1965 *Employees:* 21
Net Worth: £3,375,551 *Total Assets:* £3,799,675
Registered Office: Beechwood Depot, Stanghow Road, Lingdale, Saltburn-by-the-Sea, N Yorks, TS12 3JU
Activities: Agents involved in the sale of timber and building materials
Shareholders: Mark Edward Green; Pamela Green
Officers: Pamela Green, Secretary; Mark Edward Green [1975] Director; Pamela Green [1946] Director

Green Lane Capital (Boldon) LLP
Incorporated: 14 February 2014
Net Worth: £760,933 *Total Assets:* £1,132,451
Registered Office: Boho 4, Cleveland Street, Middlesbrough, Cleveland, TS2 1AY
Officers: Andrew Loughran Preston [1966] Member; Christopher Mark Preston [1974] Member

Green Lane Capital (Gibson House Middlesbrough) LLP
Incorporated: 7 May 2010
Net Worth: £418,944 *Total Assets:* £928,328
Registered Office: Boho 4, Cleveland Street, Middlesbrough, Cleveland, TS2 1AY
Officers: Andrew Loughran Preston [1966] Member; Christopher Mark Preston [1974] Member

Green Lane Capital (N/E) LLP
Incorporated: 29 March 2006 *Employees:* 5
Net Worth: £2,826,624 *Total Assets:* £6,224,558
Registered Office: Boho 4, Cleveland Street, Middlesbrough, Cleveland, TS2 1AY
Officers: Andrew Loughran Preston [1966] Member; Christopher Mark Preston [1974] Member

Green Lane Primary Academy Limited
Incorporated: 3 March 2014 *Employees:* 91
Net Worth: £6,637,000 *Total Assets:* £7,645,000
Registered Office: Green Lane Primary Academy, Green Lane, Middlesbrough, Cleveland, TS5 7RU
Activities: Primary education
Officers: Carolyn Armitage [1966] Director/Retail Assistant; Jill Berry [1964] Director/Manager; Kate Bowe [1976] Director/Local Government Officer; Lucy Victoria Donner [1980] Director/Accountant; Helen Ellis [1968] Director/Local Government Officer; Linda Etherington [1957] Director/Teaching Assistant; Saliah Parveen Hameed [1975] Director/Teacher; Helen Elizabeth McLean [1967] Director/Teacher; Mark Victor Pagan [1960] Director/Optometrist; Jessica Lauren Roberts [1977] Director/Teacher; Jacqueline Walsh [1964] Director/Co-Headteacher

Green Mountain Travel Ltd
Incorporated: 23 January 2008
Registered Office: 1 Jesmond Business Court, 217 Jesmond Road, Newcastle upon Tyne, NE2 1LA
Activities: Other passenger land transport
Major Shareholder: Tracey Thorpe
Officers: Patricia Thorpe, Secretary; Tracey Thorpe [1966] Director/Coach Driver

Green Parks Holdings (Ilfracombe) Ltd
Incorporated: 21 July 2015 *Employees:* 2
Net Worth Deficit: £69,293 *Total Assets:* £8,823,383
Registered Office: Valley House, Kingsway South, Gateshead, Tyne & Wear, NE11 0JW
Activities: Buying and selling of own real estate
Shareholders: Derek Arthur Kewley; Nicholas John Spence
Officers: Derek Arthur Kewley [1973] Director; Nicholas John Spence [1972] Director

Green Team Partnership Ltd
Incorporated: 8 November 2011
Net Worth Deficit: £1,295,280 *Total Assets:* £1,031,757
Registered Office: 8 Roe House, Broomley, Stocksfield, Northumberland, NE43 7HP
Activities: Plumbing, heat and air-conditioning installation
Shareholders: Kristopher Anthony Grey; Marie Grey
Officers: Kristopher Anthony Grey [1978] Director; Marie Grey [1973] Director

Greenbale Ltd
Incorporated: 11 June 2009
Net Worth: £969,036 *Total Assets:* £5,699,246
Registered Office: 82 Bewick Road, Gateshead, Tyne & Wear, NE8 1RS
Activities: Renting and operating of Housing Association real estate
Officers: Anna Schleider, Secretary [American]; Anthony Marmorstein [1989] Director/Rabbi; Chana Marmorstein [1993] Director/Housewife; Anna Schleider [1956] Director [American]; Shamai Schleider [1953] Director/Lecturer; Yosef Schleider [1983] Director; Avrohom Wittler [1982] Director/Student

Greenbank Compactors LLP
Incorporated: 23 April 2012 *Employees:* 33
Net Worth: £3,839,368 *Total Assets:* £6,167,333
Registered Office: Greenbank House, Sotherby Road, Middlesbrough, Cleveland, TS3 8BT

Greenbow Properties Limited
Incorporated: 6 November 2003
Net Worth: £1,432,293 *Total Assets:* £4,249,696
Registered Office: 14 Eddleston Avenue, Kenton Park, Newcastle upon Tyne, NE3 4SJ
Activities: Other letting and operating of own or leased real estate
Major Shareholder: Amjed Taj Malik
Officers: Amjed Taj Malik, Secretary/Solicitor; Amjed Taj Malik [1957] Director/Solicitor; Shaheena Malik [1958] Director/Manager

Greencroft Bottling Company Limited
Incorporated: 18 May 2003 *Employees:* 200
Net Worth: £10,954,691 *Total Assets:* £26,218,898
Registered Office: Unit 1 Greencroft Estate, Tower Road, Annfield Plain, Stanley, Co Durham, DH9 7XP
Activities: Wholesale of wine, beer, spirits and other alcoholic beverages
Shareholders: Anthony Austin Cleary; Veronica Anne Cleary
Officers: Alexandra Louise Cleary [1986] Director; Anthony Austin Cleary [1952] Director; Benjamin William Andrew Cleary [1988] Director; Caroline Robyn Cleary [1990] Director; Veronica Anne Cleary [1954] Director; Mark Anthony Satchwell [1964] Managing Director

Greencroft Estate Company Ltd (The)
Incorporated: 15 September 1926 *Employees:* 2
Net Worth: £7,489,871 *Total Assets:* £7,963,288
Registered Office: Ryecroft Glenton & Co, 27 Portland Terrace, Newcastle upon Tyne, NE2 1QP
Activities: Other letting and operating of own or leased real estate
Major Shareholder: Herard Francois Odon Marie de Pins
Officers: Romain Pierre Louis Guiramand [1973] Director [Swiss]

Greencroft Milk Supplies Limited
Incorporated: 17 May 1994 *Employees:* 103
Net Worth: £2,398,693 *Total Assets:* £8,480,496
Registered Office: Greencroft Milk Supplies Limited, Telford Road, Middlesbrough, Cleveland, TS3 8BL
Activities: Other retail sale of food in specialised stores
Shareholders: Derek Parker; Janice Parker
Officers: Janice Parker, Secretary; Michael Brian Doyle [1964] Director; Derek Parker [1961] Director; Janice Parker [1965] Director and Company Secretary; Jonathon Parker [1992] Director; Ian Richard Simpson [1956] Director/Management Consultant

Greenlay (Grass Machinery) Limited
Incorporated: 18 November 1971
Net Worth: £1,250,473 *Total Assets:* £1,768,281
Registered Office: Baker Road, Nelson Park West, Cramlington, Northumberland, NE23 1WL
Activities: Agents involved in the sale of machinery, industrial equipment, ships and aircraft
Major Shareholder: Geoffrey David Clark Lowes
Officers: Geoffrey David Clark Lowes [1967] Managing Director

Greenoaks (Maidenhead) Limited
Incorporated: 21 August 1987 *Employees:* 248
Net Worth: £372,000 *Total Assets:* £25,362,000
Registered Office: Vertu House, Fifth Avenue Business Park, Team Valley Trading Estate, Gateshead, Tyne & Wear, NE11 0XA
Activities: Sale of new cars and light motor vehicles
Parent: Sigma Holdings Limited
Officers: Karen Anderson, Secretary; Karen Anderson [1971] Finance Director; David Paul Crane [1967] Commercial Director; Robert Thomas Forrester [1969] Director; Mike Rich [1961] Group Operations Director; Michael Sherwin [1959] Finance Director

Greens Property Developments Limited
Incorporated: 5 June 2006
Net Worth: £11,057 *Total Assets:* £1,178,595
Registered Office: c/o JFS Torbitt, 58 Durham Road, Birtley, Chester-le-Street, Co Durham, DH3 2QJ
Activities: Other letting and operating of own or leased real estate
Major Shareholder: Mark Green
Officers: Mark Green, Secretary; Mark Green [1964] Director/Nurseryman

Greensfield Moor Development Limited
Incorporated: 15 April 2010 *Employees:* 29
Net Worth: £1,256,263 *Total Assets:* £2,349,603
Registered Office: c/o Ward Hadaway, Sandgate House, 102 Quayside, Newcastle upon Tyne, NE1 3DX
Activities: Hotels and similar accommodation
Parent: Inn Collection Bidco Limited
Officers: Sean Lee Donkin [1981] Operations Director; Angus Keith Liddell [1955] Director; Iain Stein [1959] Director

Greggs PLC
Incorporated: 29 December 1951 *Employees:* 21,549
Net Worth: £304,958,016 *Total Assets:* £441,270,016
Registered Office: Greggs House, Quorum Business Park, Newcastle upon Tyne, NE12 8BU
Activities: Manufacture of bread; manufacture of fresh pastry goods and cakes
Officers: Jonathan Jowett, Secretary; Raymond Robert Reynolds, Secretary; Alicia Marie Ryan, Secretary; Ian Charles Durant [1958] Director; Doctor Helena Louise Ganczakowski [1962] Director; Richard John Hutton [1968] Finance Director; Allison Kirkby [1967] Finance Director; Peter Laurence McPhillips [1951] Director; Sandra Turner [1952] Director; Roger Mark Whiteside [1958] Director/Chief Executive Officer

Greit Limited
Incorporated: 20 April 2006
Net Worth: £1,910,401 *Total Assets:* £1,910,401
Registered Office: Citygate, St James Boulevard, Newcastle upon Tyne, NE1 4JE
Activities: Non-trading company
Parent: Grainger PLC
Officers: Adam McGhin, Secretary; Helen Christine Gordon [1959] Director; Adam McGhin [1978] Director/Solicitor; Vanessa Kate Simms [1975] Director

Greta Cottage Limited
Incorporated: 3 September 1999
Net Worth: £1,203,495 *Total Assets:* £2,129,337
Registered Office: Greta Cottage, Greta Street, Saltburn-by-the-Sea, N Yorks, TS12 1LS
Activities: Residential care activities for the elderly and disabled
Major Shareholder: Heather Yvonne Garcia
Officers: Dr Emilio Jose Garcia, Secretary; Heather Yvonne Garcia [1961] Director/Residential Care Home Owner

Gretpark Properties Limited
Incorporated: 4 April 2001
Net Worth: £2,653,649 *Total Assets:* £2,898,847
Registered Office: The Future Business Park, Darlington Road, Shildon, Co Durham, DL4 2RB
Activities: Buying and selling of own real estate
Shareholders: Frank Maguire; Jason James Maguire; William Maguire
Officers: Frank Maguire [1969] Carpet Director; Jason James Maguire [1973] Director/Carpet Retailer; William Maguire [1965] Director/Carpet Retailer

Grey Street Newcastle Ltd.
Incorporated: 15 March 2013 *Employees:* 19
Net Worth: £1,048,747 *Total Assets:* £4,775,332
Registered Office: Malhotra House, 7-9 Groat Market, Newcastle upon Tyne, NE1 1UQ
Activities: Hotels and similar accommodation
Officers: Devinder Mohan Malhotra [1967] Director

Grid Smarter Cities Ltd
Incorporated: 16 October 2009 *Employees:* 6
Net Worth: £2,760,924 *Total Assets:* £3,177,522
Registered Office: RMT Accountants & Business Advisors Ltd, Gosforth Park Avenue, Newcastle upon Tyne, NE12 8EG
Activities: Business and domestic software development
Shareholders: Neil Andrew Herron; David John Comyn
Officers: Susan Jayne Wingate, Secretary; David John Comyn [1954] Director [Irish]; Neil Andrew Herron [1963] Director; Julian Michael Wrigley [1967] Director/IT Consultant

Griffith Textile Machines Limited
Incorporated: 4 September 1984 *Employees:* 41
Net Worth: £2,173,669 *Total Assets:* £2,614,124
Registered Office: 9 Walton Road, Pattinson Industrial Estate North, District 15, Washington, Tyne & Wear, NE38 8QA
Activities: Manufacture of woven or tufted carpets and rugs
Major Shareholder: David John Watson
Officers: Elaine Ann Evans, Secretary; David Robert Acheson [1967] Director; Christopher Urquhart Clarke [1977] Director; Nicholas David George Coburn [1959] Director; Neil Stanley Grabham [1976] Director; David Taylor [1959] Finance Director; Philip John Turnbull [1975] Director; Carole Lisa Watson [1967] Director; David John Watson [1963] Managing Director

Gro-Group Holdings Limited
Incorporated: 21 November 2012 *Employees:* 43
Net Worth: £154,000 *Total Assets:* £14,156,000
Registered Office: Mayborn House, Balliol Business Park, Newcastle upon Tyne, NE12 8EW
Activities: Wholesale of textiles
Parent: Mayborn Group Limited
Officers: Stephen William Parkin [1969] Director; James William Matthew Taylor [1974] Director

Gro-Group International Limited
Incorporated: 13 April 2004 *Employees:* 34
Net Worth: £918,000 *Total Assets:* £7,971,000
Registered Office: Mayborn House, Balliol Business Park, Newcastle upon Tyne, NE12 8EW
Activities: Wholesale of textiles
Parent: Gro-Group Limited
Officers: Stephen William Parkin [1969] Director; James William Matthew Taylor [1974] Director

Grosvenor Gate Property Management Limited
Incorporated: 21 April 2005
Net Worth: £396,456 *Total Assets:* £911,228
Registered Office: 71 Kingsway North, Team Valley Trading Estate, Gateshead, Tyne & Wear, NE11 0JH
Activities: Management of real estate on a fee or contract basis
Shareholders: Roy Flemming Bradley; Kevin Mark Waugh
Officers: Kevin Mark Waugh, Secretary/Director; Roy Flemming Bradley [1966] Director; Kevin Mark Waugh [1962] Director

Groundwork North East
Incorporated: 31 March 1992 *Employees:* 153
Net Worth: £4,262,768 *Total Assets:* £4,728,013
Registered Office: Grosvenor House, 29 Market Place, Bishop Auckland, Co Durham, DL14 7NP
Activities: Activities of business and employers membership organisations
Officers: Catherine Joanna Culverhouse, Secretary; Peter Brookes [1955] Director/Self Employed; Ian Brown [1952] Director/Consultant; Darush Hossginzadgh Dodds [1984] Director/Head of Corporate Responsibility; Barbara-Anne Johnson [1946] Director/Retired Business Owner; Thomas Justice [1990] Director/Solicitor; David Martin [1957] Director/Treasurer; Diana Catherine Pearce [1952] Director; John Edward Pritchard [1967] Director of Strategic Planning; Professor Graham Street [1942] Director/Retired

Groundwork Services (Durham) Ltd
Incorporated: 29 September 2000 *Employees:* 95
Net Worth: £1,799,797 *Total Assets:* £6,595,401
Registered Office: Thistle Road, Littleburn Industrial Estate, Langley Moor, Co Durham, DH7 8HJ
Activities: Construction of other civil engineering projects n.e.c.
Shareholder: Kim Barron
Officers: Kim Barron, Secretary; Jon Barron [1981] Director; Kim Barron [1959] Director; Michael Barron [1987] Director

Groundwork South Tyneside and Newcastle upon Tyne
Incorporated: 15 March 1991 *Employees:* 62
Net Worth: £4,719,529 *Total Assets:* £5,131,741
Registered Office: The Eco Centre, Windmill Way, Hebburn, Tyne & Wear, NE31 1SR
Activities: Landscape service activities
Officers: Derrick Laland Robson, Secretary; Mark Charlton [1958] Director/Chartered Accountant; Michael James Cuthbertson [1956] Director/Chartered Surveyor; Catherine Anne Donnelly [1968] Director/Head of Human Resources; Dr Geoffrey O'Brien [1952] Director/Senior Lecturer; Jeffrey David Owen [1948] Director/Accountant; Diana Catherine Pearce [1952] Director/Civil Servant; Councillor James Perry [1947] Director/Trust Administrator; Derrick Laland Robson [1945] Director/Solicitor; John Richard Short [1952] Marketing Director; Danielle Turton [1987] Director/Communications Manager; Andrew Whittaker [1965] Director/Local Government Officer

Group Horizon Limited
Incorporated: 13 May 2008 *Employees:* 39
Net Worth: £213,455 *Total Assets:* £856,546
Registered Office: Unit G24 The Avenues, Eleventh Avenue North, Team Valley Trading Estate, Gateshead, Tyne & Wear, NE11 0NJ
Activities: Other business support service activities n.e.c.
Major Shareholder: Peter Behan
Officers: Peter Behan [1978] Director

Group Tegula Limited
Incorporated: 10 January 2011 *Employees:* 41
Net Worth: £759,625 *Total Assets:* £2,005,780
Registered Office: 3 Bracknell Close, Sunderland, Tyne & Wear, SR3 2DE
Activities: Roofing activities
Officers: Elaine Forrest [1958] Financial Director/Company Secretary; Amanda Jane Hennessy [1971] Finance Director; David Murray [1961] Managing Director

Grove Information Systems Limited
Incorporated: 6 May 2004
Net Worth: £703,528 *Total Assets:* £2,568,118
Registered Office: 32 Portland Terrace, Newcastle upon Tyne, NE2 1QP
Activities: Other information technology service activities
Parent: Grove Solutions Limited
Officers: Philip Charles Gilbart Witheridge [1972] Director

Grove Reed Joinery Limited
Incorporated: 4 June 2008 *Employees:* 16
Net Worth: £73,983 *Total Assets:* £776,458
Registered Office: Unit 33/2 Auckland Crescent, St Helen's Industrial Estate, Bishop Auckland, Co Durham, DL14 9AD
Activities: Manufacture of other builders' carpentry and joinery
Major Shareholder: Graeme Leslie Ripley
Officers: Graeme Leslie Ripley [1968] Director

Grovekey Limited
Incorporated: 25 July 1994 *Employees:* 26
Net Worth: £714,563 *Total Assets:* £1,801,566
Registered Office: Rushpool Hall, Saltburn Lane, Saltburn-by-the-Sea, N Yorks, TS12 1HD
Activities: Hotels and similar accommodation
Major Shareholder: James Brennan
Officers: Susan Crane, Secretary; James Brennan [1950] Managing Director; Susan Crane [1961] Director

Groveport 2012 Limited
Incorporated: 28 June 2011
Net Worth: £159,000 *Total Assets:* £5,342,000
Registered Office: 17-27 Queen's Square, Middlesbrough, Cleveland, TS2 1AH
Activities: Activities of head offices
Parent: PD Ports Humber Limited
Officers: Johannes Franciscus Calje [1972] Director [Dutch]; Jeremy Mark Hopkinson [1955] Director; Dermot Michael Russell [1965] Director/Accountant

Groveport Logistics Limited
Incorporated: 1 April 2005 *Employees:* 132
Net Worth: £28,198,000 *Total Assets:* £36,039,000
Registered Office: 17-27 Queens Square, Middlesbrough, Cleveland, TS2 1AH
Activities: Operation of warehousing and storage facilities for land transport activities
Parent: Groveport 2012 Limited
Officers: Johannes Franciscus Calje [1972] Director [Dutch]; Jeremy Mark Hopkinson [1955] Director; Dermot Michael Russell [1965] Director/Accountant

Growth Capital Ventures Limited
Incorporated: 24 July 2012
Registered Office: Carlton House, 15 Parsons Court, Newton Aycliffe, Co Durham, DL5 6ZE
Activities: Fund management activities
Shareholders: Norman Peterson; Craig Alistair Peterson
Officers: Norman Peterson, Secretary; William Alexander Kennedy [1969] Director; Suzanne Jean Lupton [1969] Director; Craig Alistair Peterson [1969] Director; Norman Peterson [1956] Director

Grundfos Manufacturing Limited
Incorporated: 20 December 1973 *Employees:* 157
Net Worth: £2,914,000 *Total Assets:* £8,969,000
Registered Office: Ferry Boat Lane, Castletown, Sunderland, Tyne & Wear, SR5 3JL
Activities: Manufacture of other fabricated metal products n.e.c.
Officers: John Paul Boyer, Secretary; Morten Tordrup Andersen [1975] Supplier Management Director [Danish]; Niels Moller Jensen [1961] Director/Regional VP of Operations [Danish]; Michele Sterlecchini [1975] Director/Group Vice President [Italian]

GSH 2018 Limited
Incorporated: 29 July 1969 *Employees:* 207
Net Worth: £4,515,799 *Total Assets:* £11,744,594
Registered Office: Planet Place, Newcastle upon Tyne, NE12 6DY
Activities: Activities of production holding companies
Officers: Charles Graham Conyers [1948] Director; Hugo Benjamin Day [1964] Director/Property Consultant; Sir Simon James Day [1935] Director; David Alistair Greenwell [1932] Director; Gabrielle Helene Rance [1968] Director/Reflexologist; Joanna Lucy Riddell [1962] Director; Simon Francis Riddell [1961] Director; William Joseph Rusga [1946] Director; Lady Alison Bridget Wakeham [1950] Director

GSLF Engineering Limited
Incorporated: 26 November 2014
Net Worth Deficit: £238,913 *Total Assets:* £3,197,930
Registered Office: Anson House, Fleming Business Centre, Burdon Terrace, Newcastle upon Tyne, NE2 3AE
Activities: Wholesale of other machinery and equipment
Major Shareholder: Graham Stuart Lindsay Forrest
Officers: Graham Stuart Lindsay Forrest [1962] Director; Kay Alberta Forrest [1965] Director; Fiona Helen McCafferty [1982] Director

GT Cleaning Machines Limited
Incorporated: 5 April 2001 *Employees:* 11
Net Worth: £1,315,929 *Total Assets:* £2,187,238
Registered Office: Units 6B-6D Bowburn North Industrial Estate, Bowburn, Co Durham, DH6 5PF
Activities: Agents involved in the sale of machinery, industrial equipment, ships and aircraft
Shareholders: Theresa Brolly; Theresa Brolly
Officers: Aidan Harrison, Secretary; Aidan Harrison [1966] Director/Sales Manager

GT Timber Limited
Incorporated: 16 April 2008 *Employees:* 216
Net Worth: £15,342,968 *Total Assets:* £23,295,736
Registered Office: Sherburn Hill, Co Durham, DH6 1PS
Activities: Other manufacturing n.e.c.
Officers: John Douglas Wentworth, Secretary; Andrea Jane McAuslan [1982] Director; Suzanne Claire Penrose [1987] Finance Director; Douglas John Wentworth [1953] Director; Ericia Wentworth [1950] Director; Jillian Anne Wentworth [1980] Director

GTD Developments Limited
Incorporated: 2 February 2006
Net Worth: £219,991 *Total Assets:* £1,412,924
Registered Office: 41 Greystoke Avenue, Tunstall, Sunderland, Tyne & Wear, SR2 9DS
Activities: Other building completion and finishing
Officers: Dorothy Cummings, Secretary; Graeme Cummings [1976] Director/Architect; Thomas Cummings [1953] Director/Fencing

Guisborough Hotels Limited
Incorporated: 10 March 1972 *Employees:* 105
Net Worth: £4,143,121 *Total Assets:* £10,792,803
Registered Office: Gisborough Hall, Guisborough, Redcar & Cleveland, TS14 6PT
Activities: Hotels and similar accommodation
Shareholders: Andrew Harold Wentworth Sutcliffe; Rupert Roderick Faure Walker; Charles Martin Crawshay
Officers: Roger David Renfree Barons [1962] Director/Accountant; Richard Thomas Chaloner [1927] Director; The Honourable Thomas Peregrine Long Chaloner [1961] Director/Farmer; Nick Holmes [1957] Director

J Gunn Scaffolding Limited
Incorporated: 23 July 2010
Net Worth: £253,824 *Total Assets:* £1,096,382
Registered Office: Beaumont Accountancy Services, First Floor, Enterprise House, 202-206 Linthorpe Road, Middlesbrough, Cleveland, TS1 3QW
Activities: Scaffold erection
Major Shareholder: Jonathan Gunn
Officers: Jonathan Gunn [1975] Director/Scaffolder

Gunnergate Limited
Incorporated: 11 April 2012 *Employees:* 2
Net Worth: £1,440,427 *Total Assets:* £1,465,351
Registered Office: Greenbank House, Sotherby Road, Middlesbrough, Cleveland, TS3 8BT
Activities: Remediation activities and other waste management services
Shareholders: Steven Evershed; Juliet Evershed
Officers: Juliet Evershed, Secretary; Steven Evershed [1976] Director

N & R Gupta Limited
Incorporated: 31 March 1998 *Employees:* 10
Net Worth: £2,845,170 *Total Assets:* £5,664,508
Registered Office: 63 Fatfield Park, Washington, Tyne & Wear, NE38 8BP
Activities: Dispensing chemist in specialised stores
Shareholders: Nitin Gupta; Rachna Gupta
Officers: Nitin Gupta, Secretary/Pharmacist; Nitin Gupta [1970] Director/Pharmacist; Rachna Gupta [1974] Director; Shashi Gupta [1948] Director

Guy Sports Limited
Incorporated: 5 November 2010
Net Worth: £641,534 *Total Assets:* £1,107,184
Registered Office: Quarriston, Houghton Bank, Heighington, Darlington, Co Durham, DL2 2UF
Activities: Operation of sports facilities
Major Shareholder: Guy Wilks
Officers: Guy Philip Wilks [1981] Director; Philip Charles Wilks [1949] Director

GW Aviation LLP
Incorporated: 5 February 2004
Net Worth: £3,047,720 *Total Assets:* £4,978,708
Registered Office: Nelson House, The Fleming Business Centre, Burdon Terrace, Jesmond, Newcastle upon Tyne, NE2 3AE
Officers: Andrea Wylie [1972] Member; Andrew William Graham Wylie [1959] Member

H I Tricomm Holdings Limited
Incorporated: 6 February 2006
Net Worth: £29,619,720 *Total Assets:* £29,619,720
Registered Office: Citygate, St James Boulevard, Newcastle upon Tyne, NE1 4JE
Activities: Development of building projects
Parent: Atlantic Metropolitan (U.K.) Limited
Officers: Adam McGhin, Secretary; Helen Christine Gordon [1959] Director; Adam McGhin [1978] Director/Solicitor; Vanessa Kate Simms [1975] Director

H T Process Control Ltd
Incorporated: 7 April 2011 *Employees:* 7
Net Worth: £507,404 *Total Assets:* £1,233,695
Registered Office: Orchard House, Easterly Grange, Foxton, Sedgefield, Co Durham, TS21 2HX
Activities: Wholesale of other machinery and equipment
Shareholders: Alan Christopher Hayes; Process Control Equipment Limited
Officers: Alan Christopher Hayes [1966] Director/Engineer; Barry James Jackson [1947] Director; Richard Jackson [1974] Director; Ben Williamson [1984] Finance Director

H.H.R. Investments Limited
Incorporated: 25 May 2012 *Employees:* 1
Net Worth: £621,915 *Total Assets:* £1,857,844
Registered Office: Mandale House, 5 Neville Road, North Tees Industrial Estate, Stockton on Tees, Cleveland, TS18 2RD
Activities: Other letting and operating of own or leased real estate
Parent: HHR Investments Holding Company Limited
Officers: Paula Davidson, Secretary; Richard Thomas Harriman [1990] Director; Harriet Frederica Spalding [1987] Director; Helen Catherine Woods [1985] Director

H.M. Pigs Limited
Incorporated: 9 April 1996 *Employees:* 9
Net Worth: £11,269,083 *Total Assets:* £14,143,756
Registered Office: Pond Dale Farm, Gilling West, Richmond, N Yorks, DL10 5LB
Activities: Raising of swine and pigs
Major Shareholder: Timothy Peter Westgarth
Officers: Paul Anthony Hall Westgarth, Secretary; Paul Anthony Hall Westgarth [1967] Director/Manager; Timothy Peter Westgarth [1973] Director/Manager

H.S. Carlsteel Engineering Limited
Incorporated: 13 December 2005 *Employees:* 9
Net Worth: £79,552 *Total Assets:* £1,419,844
Registered Office: Kensington House, 3 Kensington, Bishop Auckland, Co Durham, DL14 6HX
Activities: Construction of other civil engineering projects n.e.c.
Officers: Christopher Charles Springate, Secretary; Carlos Wayne Alleyne [1960] Director; Phillip Healey [1960] Director; Christopher Charles Springate [1962] Director

H.T.B. Electrical Contractors Limited
Incorporated: 9 July 2004
Net Worth: £1,323,389 *Total Assets:* £1,409,733
Registered Office: 41b Carrmere Road, Leechmere Industrial Estate, Sunderland, Tyne & Wear, SR2 9TW
Activities: Electrical installation
Major Shareholder: Angela Hixon
Officers: Angela Hixon, Secretary; Angela Hixon [1960] Director; Sean Paul Hixon [1981] Director; Philip Naylor [1957] Director

H.V.R. International Limited
Incorporated: 7 March 1991 *Employees:* 172
Net Worth: £11,155,564 *Total Assets:* £13,532,962
Registered Office: Bedesway, Bede Industrial Estate, Jarrow, Tyne & Wear, NE32 3EN
Activities: Manufacture of other electrical equipment
Shareholders: Stephen Elliott; Kevin McLaughlin
Officers: Kevin McLaughlin [1953] Technical Director

HAB Northern Ltd
Incorporated: 1 October 2012 *Employees:* 30
Net Worth: £327,782 *Total Assets:* £1,254,486
Registered Office: 43 Coniscliffe Road, Darlington, Co Durham, DL3 7EH
Activities: Construction of other civil engineering projects n.e.c.
Major Shareholder: Michael Edward Hewitson
Officers: Brian Gibson [1971] Director; Henry Michael Hewitson [1993] Director; Michael Edward Hewitson [1960] Director

Hacel Lighting Limited
Incorporated: 10 September 1981 *Employees:* 87
Net Worth: £3,526,905 *Total Assets:* £5,425,369
Registered Office: Hacel House, Kittiwake Close, Wallsend, Tyne & Wear, NE28 9ND
Activities: Manufacture of electric lighting equipment
Major Shareholder: David Cockburn
Officers: Christopher Charles Neal, Secretary; David Cockburn [1955] Managing Director; Stephen Cockburn [1962] Works Director; Paul Wallace [1968] Sales Director

William Hackett Holdings Limited
Incorporated: 23 April 2012 *Employees:* 68
Net Worth: £6,546,504 *Total Assets:* £13,040,078
Registered Office: Oak Drive, Lionheart Enterprise Park, Alnwick, Northumberland, NE66 2EU
Activities: Renting and leasing of other machinery, equipment and tangible goods n.e.c.
Officers: Paul Davies, Secretary; Elizabeth Ann Burgess [1965] Director; Joshua Andrew Burgess [1990] Director; Timothy James Burgess [1965] Director; Adrian Lloyd [1964] Director; Hannah Elizabeth Reynolds [1988] Director

William Hackett Lifting Products Limited
Incorporated: 9 July 2015 *Employees:* 30
Net Worth: £549,758 *Total Assets:* £5,774,012
Registered Office: Oak Drive, Lionheart Enterprise Park, Alnwick, Northumberland, NE66 2EU
Activities: Other manufacturing n.e.c.
Officers: Paul Davies, Secretary; Roderik Thomas Bell [1967] Director; Benjamin Burgess [1964] Director; Joshua Andrew Burgess [1990] Director; Tim Burgess [1964] Director; Adrian Lloyd [1964] Director

Hadrian Air Conditioning and Refrigeration Company Limited
Incorporated: 27 June 1985 *Employees:* 45
Net Worth: £749,317 *Total Assets:* £1,650,994
Registered Office: Hadrian House, Crowther Road, Crowther Industrial Estate, Washington, Tyne & Wear, NE38 0AQ
Activities: Steam and air conditioning supply
Parent: Unsworth Unsworth & Co Ltd
Officers: Elizabeth Rutherford Unsworth, Secretary/Administration; Kevin Armstrong [1983] Sales Director; Michael Robert Hurst [1980] Service Director; Alan John Unsworth [1970] Director/Sales Engineer; Elizabeth Rutherford Unsworth [1979] Director/Administration

Hadrian Architectural Glazing Systems Limited
Incorporated: 3 May 2000 *Employees:* 53
Net Worth: £2,975,346 *Total Assets:* £4,136,816
Registered Office: Unit 5 Haugh Lane, Addison Industrial Estate, Blaydon on Tyne, Tyne & Wear, NE21 4TE
Activities: Aluminium production
Shareholders: Darren Wilfred Nichol; Frances Nichol
Officers: Frances Nichol, Secretary; Darren Wilfred Nichol [1972] Director/Aluminium Glazing; Frances Nichol [1974] Director/Aluminium Glazing

Hadrian Healthcare (Durham) Limited
Incorporated: 15 November 2007 *Employees:* 75
Net Worth: £1,469,836 *Total Assets:* £5,768,942
Registered Office: Hadrian Offices, 3 Keel Row, The Watermark, Gateshead, Tyne & Wear, NE11 9SZ
Activities: Other human health activities
Parent: Hadrian Healthcare Holdings Limited
Officers: Jasvinder Singh Gill, Secretary; Ian Watson [1962] Director

Hadrian Healthcare (Gosforth) Limited
Incorporated: 12 June 2009 *Employees:* 54
Net Worth: £2,000,746 *Total Assets:* £5,341,619
Registered Office: Hadrian Offices, 3 Keel Row, The Watermark, Gateshead, Tyne & Wear, NE11 9SZ
Activities: Other human health activities
Parent: Hadrian Healthcare Holdings Limited
Officers: Jasvinder Singh Gill, Secretary; Ian Watson [1962] Director

Hadrian Healthcare (Harrogate) Limited
Incorporated: 4 July 2014
Net Worth Deficit: £56,395 *Total Assets:* £4,477,786
Registered Office: Hadrian Offices, 3 Keel Row, The Watermark, Gateshead, Tyne & Wear, NE11 9SZ
Activities: Other human health activities
Parent: Hadrian Healthcare Holdings Limited
Officers: Jasvinder Singh Gill, Secretary; Ian Watson [1962] Director

Hadrian Healthcare (Knaresborough) Limited
Incorporated: 15 January 2015 *Employees:* 57
Net Worth Deficit: £141,694 *Total Assets:* £7,658,913
Registered Office: Hadrian Offices, 3 Keel Row, The Watermark, Gateshead, Tyne & Wear, NE11 9SZ
Activities: Residential care activities for the elderly and disabled
Parent: Hadrian Healthcare Holdings Limited
Officers: Jasvinder Singh Gill, Secretary; Ian Watson [1962] Director

Hadrian Healthcare (Oulton) Limited
Incorporated: 3 February 2015 *Employees:* 52
Net Worth Deficit: £505,064 *Total Assets:* £6,420,810
Registered Office: Hadrian Offices, 3 Keel Row, The Watermark, Gateshead, Tyne & Wear, NE11 9SZ
Activities: Residential care activities for the elderly and disabled
Parent: Hadrian Healthcare Holdings Limited
Officers: Jasvinder Singh Gill, Secretary; Ian Watson [1962] Director

Hadrian Healthcare (Wetherby) Limited
Incorporated: 13 May 2009 *Employees:* 79
Net Worth: £1,817,703 *Total Assets:* £6,897,321
Registered Office: Hadrian Offices, 3 Keel Row, The Watermark, Gateshead, Tyne & Wear, NE11 9SZ
Activities: Other human health activities
Parent: Hadrian Healthcare Holdings Limited
Officers: Jasvinder Singh Gill, Secretary; Ian Watson [1962] Director

Hadrian Healthcare (Whickham) Limited
Incorporated: 27 July 2009 *Employees:* 75
Net Worth: £1,152,349 *Total Assets:* £6,071,231
Registered Office: Hadrian Offices, 3 Keel Row, The Watermark, Gateshead, Tyne & Wear, NE11 9SZ
Activities: Other human health activities
Parent: Hadrian Healthcare Holdings Limited
Officers: Jasvinder Singh Gill, Secretary; Ian Watson [1962] Director

Hadrian Learning Trust
Incorporated: 27 July 2016 *Employees:* 24
Net Worth: £16,389,000 *Total Assets:* £22,387,000
Registered Office: Queen Elizabeth High School, Whetstone Bridge Road, Hexham, Northumberland, NE46 3JB
Activities: Primary education
Officers: Graeme David Atkins [1970] Director/Executive Headteacher; Charles Anthony Brown [1964] Director/Management Consultant; Kathryn Chaplin [1967] Director/Chief Executive; David Hartland [1962] Director/Education Technologist; Barbara Margaret Hignett [1960] Director/Learning Support Assistant & Music Teacher; Jonathan Maurice Holmes [1961] Director/Judge; Veryan Steele Johnston [1956] Director; Sarah Caroline Kemp [1954] Theatre Director; Simon Kitchman [1958] Director/Management Consultant

Hadrian Limited
Incorporated: 26 February 1981 *Employees:* 7
Net Worth: £1,673,538 *Total Assets:* £2,146,826
Registered Office: 5 Henson Close, South Church Enterprise Park, Bishop Auckland, Co Durham, DL14 6WA
Activities: Veterinary activities
Shareholders: David McKenzie Leak; Elizabeth Anne Leak
Officers: Elizabeth Anne Leak, Secretary; David McKenzie Leak [1957] Director/Chemist; Elizabeth Anne Leak [1957] Director/Secretary

Hadrian Technology Limited
Incorporated: 21 May 1999 *Employees:* 11
Net Worth: £1,541,227 *Total Assets:* £1,991,763
Registered Office: Unit C, Endeavour Court, Hall Dene Way, Seaham Grange Industrial Estate, Seaham, Co Durham, SR7 0HB
Activities: Other construction installation
Major Shareholder: Stuart Gardner Ferguson
Officers: Stuart Gardner Ferguson [1965] Director/CCTV

Hadrian Window Systems Limited
Incorporated: 14 March 2003
Net Worth: £669,173 *Total Assets:* £1,074,979
Registered Office: Unit 5 Haugh Lane, Addison Industrial Estate, Blaydon-on-Tyne, Tyne & Wear, NE21 4TE
Activities: Other business support service activities n.e.c.
Shareholders: Darren Wilfred Nichol; Christopher Paul Hughes
Officers: Frances Nichol, Secretary; Christopher Paul Hughes [1972] Director; Darren Wilfred Nichol [1972] Director

Hagen Developments Limited
Incorporated: 10 February 1986
Net Worth: £9,784,323 *Total Assets:* £11,644,763
Registered Office: Unit 12 Christon Close, Gosforth Industrial Estate, Newcastle upon Tyne, NE3 1XD
Activities: Buying and selling of own real estate
Officers: Martin Anthony Keegan, Secretary; Martin Anthony Keegan [1958] Director; Jacqueline Reynolds [1957] Director

Hagen Homes Ltd
Incorporated: 4 October 2016
Net Worth: £352,682 *Total Assets:* £1,175,920
Registered Office: Unit 12 Christon Road, Newcastle upon Tyne, NE3 1XD
Activities: Buying and selling of own real estate
Officers: Martin Anthony Keegan [1958] Director; Jacqueline Reynolds [1957] Director

Stuart Halbert Foundation
Incorporated: 8 July 2010
Net Worth: £1,195,089 *Total Assets:* £1,199,409
Registered Office: Albion Works, Haltwhistle, Northumberland, NE49 0HJ
Activities: Other business support service activities n.e.c.
Officers: Gary Lydiate, Secretary; Josephine Clare Halbert [1962] Director/Artist; Louise Halbert [1956] Director; Mark Stuart Halbert [1966] Director; Gary Lydiate [1960] Director

Hall & Partners (Special Projects) Limited
Incorporated: 16 December 1998 *Employees:* 19
Net Worth: £2,967,359 *Total Assets:* £3,192,302
Registered Office: Suites 1 & 2 Cheviot House, Beaminster Way East, Kingston Park, Newcastle upon Tyne, NE3 2ER
Activities: Quantity surveying activities
Shareholder: Timothy Robert Weightman
Officers: Casandra McPherson, Secretary; Alan James Dunn [1954] Director/Quantity Surveyor; Mark Sanderson [1964] Director/Quantity Surveyor; Julia Ann Weightman [1963] Director/Administration; Timothy Robert Weightman [1962] Director/Surveyor

Hall Construction Services Limited
Incorporated: 21 November 1986 *Employees:* 116
Net Worth: £44,547,124 *Total Assets:* £50,982,644
Registered Office: Stotforth Hill House, Windlestone, Rushyford, Co Durham, DL17 0NF
Activities: Open cast coal working
Shareholders: Neville John Hall; Stephen Hall
Officers: Neville John Hall [1956] Director/Civil Engineer; Stephen Hall [1954] Director/Civil Engineer; Garry Hutchinson [1955] Director

Hall Farm Foods Limited
Incorporated: 9 March 2006 *Employees:* 11
Net Worth: £178,130 *Total Assets:* £866,391
Registered Office: Murton Hall Farm, Wingate, Cleveland, TS28 5NU
Activities: Wholesale of dairy products, eggs and edible oils and fats
Major Shareholder: Richard Redfern
Officers: Richard Redfern [1964] Director

Graham S Hall Properties Limited
Incorporated: 14 January 1986 *Employees:* 1
Net Worth: £911,926 *Total Assets:* £1,032,092
Registered Office: Garden Cottage, Southill Hall, Plawsworth, Chester-le-Street, Co Durham, DH3 4EQ
Activities: Buying and selling of own real estate
Major Shareholder: Graham Stephen Hall
Officers: Graham Stephen Hall [1956] Director

Hallikeld Limited
Incorporated: 7 February 2005 *Employees:* 22
Net Worth: £2,813,703 *Total Assets:* £5,803,540
Registered Office: Hallikeld Farm, Long Lane, Brompton, Northallerton, N Yorks, DL6 2UF
Activities: Raising of swine and pigs
Shareholder: Jane Isobel Sanderson
Officers: Jane Isobel Sanderson, Secretary/Farmer; Donald Kirk Sanderson [1956] Director/Farmer; Jane Isobel Sanderson [1958] Director/Farmer

Halls of Durham Limited
Incorporated: 15 January 1975 *Employees:* 2
Net Worth: £1,050,633 *Total Assets:* £1,148,501
Registered Office: Park Farm Studio, Willow Tree Avenue, Shincliffe Village, Durham, DH1 2PA
Activities: Buying and selling of own real estate
Shareholders: John Hall; Margaret Sobo
Officers: Margaret Sobo, Secretary; John Hall [1950] Director; Margaret Sobo [1959] Director

Halls Pharmacy (North East) Limited
Incorporated: 7 December 2012
Net Worth: £227,844 *Total Assets:* £2,013,739
Registered Office: 6 Kensington Avenue, Gosforth, Newcastle upon Tyne, NE3 2HP
Activities: Other human health activities
Officers: Ayaz Akram [1974] Director/Pharmacist; Abdur Razzak [1971] Director/Pharmacist; Monowara Shamsuttabriz [1969] Director

Halthean Worldwide Limited
Incorporated: 20 May 2004
Net Worth: £2,436,726 *Total Assets:* £2,866,159
Registered Office: 6B Planet Business Centre, Planet Place, Killingworth, Newcastle upon Tyne, NE12 6DY
Activities: Management consultancy activities other than financial management
Major Shareholder: Helen Althea Urwin
Officers: Ashley Scott, Secretary; Helen Althea Urwin [1965] Director/Consultant

Halton Property Services Limited
Incorporated: 15 February 1983 *Employees:* 3
Net Worth: £1,772,008 *Total Assets:* £1,876,608
Registered Office: 1 East Shore, Whitburn Bents Road, Sunderland, Tyne & Wear, SR6 8BF
Activities: Other letting and operating of own or leased real estate
Shareholders: Malcolm Halton; Yvonne Halton
Officers: Yvonne Halton, Secretary; Malcolm Halton [1952] Director

The Hambleton Group Limited
Incorporated: 9 October 1979 *Employees:* 78
Net Worth: £6,676,634 *Total Assets:* £12,341,281
Registered Office: Teesside Industrial Estate, Fleck Way, Thornaby, Stockton on Tees, Cleveland, TS17 9JZ
Activities: Other service activities n.e.c.
Shareholders: Bryan Walter Goodall; Georgina Goodall
Officers: Georgina Goodall, Secretary; Bryan Walter Goodall [1948] Director/Company Executive; Georgina Goodall [1947] Director/Company Executive; Jonathan James Goodall [1973] Director/Assistant Manager; Kathryn Holly Goodall [1975] Director; Lisa Margaret Pluves [1976] Director/Accountant; Victoria Weall [1966] Director

Hambleton Steel (South) Limited
Incorporated: 23 June 2006
Net Worth Deficit: £183,448 *Total Assets:* £1,107,503
Registered Office: Gatherley Road, Brompton on Swale, Richmond, N Yorks, DL10 7JH
Activities: Other letting and operating of own or leased real estate
Parent: Hambleton Steel Ltd
Officers: James William Grice, Secretary/Manager; James William Grice [1953] Director/Manager; Colin Richard Watson [1960] Director/Manager

Hambleton Steel Limited
Incorporated: 27 September 1995 *Employees:* 78
Net Worth: £3,378,987 *Total Assets:* £7,999,759
Registered Office: Gatherley Road, Brompton on Swale, Richmond, N Yorks, DL10 7JH
Activities: Construction of commercial buildings
Shareholders: James William Grice; Patricia Grice
Officers: Patricia Grice, Secretary/Housewife; James William Grice [1953] Director/Manager; Patricia Grice [1955] Director/Housewife; Martin Hague Jobbings [1951] Director/Solicitor; Colin Richard Watson [1960] Director/Steel Fabricator

Hameed Investments Limited
Incorporated: 24 May 2002
Net Worth: £1,234,046 *Total Assets:* £1,823,018
Registered Office: Exchange Building, 66 Church Street, Hartlepool, Cleveland, TS24 7DN
Activities: Development of building projects
Major Shareholder: Riaz Mohammad Hameed
Officers: Riaz Mohammad Hameed, Secretary; Riaz Mohammad Hameed [1973] Director [Turkish]

The Hamilton Portfolio (Care Homes) Limited
Incorporated: 26 October 2009 *Employees:* 1
Net Worth Deficit: £118,410 *Total Assets:* £1,223,742
Registered Office: Hindley House, Hindley Estate, Stocksfield, Northumberland, NE43 7SA
Activities: Residential nursing care facilities
Major Shareholder: Andrew Christopher Lapping
Officers: Andrew Christopher Lapping [1963] Director

Hammer Services Ltd
Incorporated: 21 May 1987 *Employees:* 4
Net Worth: £838,391 *Total Assets:* £859,064
Registered Office: The Old Motor House, Townfoot, Rothbury, Northumberland, NE65 7SN
Activities: Maintenance and repair of motor vehicles
Shareholders: Jonathan Philip Radgick; Sandra Olive Nattrass
Officers: Sandra Olive Nattrass, Secretary/Chartered Accountant; Sandra Olive Nattrass [1957] Director/Chartered Accountant; Jonathan Philip Radgick [1957] Director/Chartered Surveyor

Hamsard 2342 Limited
Incorporated: 4 July 2001
Net Worth: £7,702,695 *Total Assets:* £7,733,341
Registered Office: Cross House, Westgate Road, Newcastle upon Tyne, NE1 4XX
Activities: Activities of head offices
Parent: Reversions Financing (No. 1) 2011 Limited
Officers: Paul Trevor Barber [1967] Director; Antony Lewis Pierce [1976] Finance Director

Hamsard 2517 (New Business) Limited
Incorporated: 4 August 2006
Net Worth: £1,419,734 *Total Assets:* £1,424,282
Registered Office: Cross House, Westgate Road, Newcastle upon Tyne, NE1 4XX
Activities: Buying and selling of own real estate
Parent: Hamsard 2517 Limited
Officers: Paul Trevor Barber [1967] Director; Ashish Kashyap [1979] Director; Antony Lewis Pierce [1976] Finance Director

Hamsard 2517 Limited
Incorporated: 10 April 2002
Net Worth: £27,902,000 *Total Assets:* £71,996,000
Registered Office: Cross House, Westgate Road, Newcastle upon Tyne, NE1 4XX
Activities: Buying and selling of own real estate
Parent: Hamsard 2518 Limited
Officers: Paul Trevor Barber [1967] Director; Antony Lewis Pierce [1976] Finance Director

Hamsard 2518 Limited
Incorporated: 10 April 2002
Net Worth Deficit: £24,101,300 *Total Assets:* £14,763,800
Registered Office: Cross House, Westgate Road, Newcastle upon Tyne, NE1 4XX
Activities: Activities of head offices
Parent: Retirement Bridge Group Holdings Limited
Officers: Paul Trevor Barber [1967] Director; Ashish Kashyap [1979] Director; Antony Lewis Pierce [1976] Finance Director

Hancock & Ainsley Limited
Incorporated: 14 February 2003 *Employees:* 10
Net Worth: £677,571 *Total Assets:* £843,094
Registered Office: 1 Main Street, Shildon, Co Durham, DL4 1AJ
Activities: Dispensing chemist in specialised stores
Officers: Ruth Louise Percival, Secretary; John David Percival [1971] Director/Pharmacist

Handyside Fishing Ltd
Incorporated: 6 September 2005
Net Worth: £258,859 *Total Assets:* £902,388
Registered Office: 12 Runciman Way, Amble, Morpeth, Northumberland, NE65 0AW
Activities: Marine fishing
Shareholder: Steven Handyside
Officers: Audrey Handyside, Secretary; Audrey Handyside [1946] Director/Administrator; David Handyside [1966] Director/Share Fisherman; Steven Handyside [1968] Director/Share Fisherman

Hanover Dairies Limited
Incorporated: 1 November 2005 *Employees:* 62
Net Worth: £1,610,209 *Total Assets:* £4,986,981
Registered Office: Unit 2 Blaydon Park, Chainbridge Road, Blaydon, Tyne & Wear, NE21 5ST
Activities: Wholesale of dairy products, eggs and edible oils and fats
Shareholders: Trevor Alan Hanover; Veronica Mary Hanover
Officers: Veronica Mary Hanover, Secretary; Michael Hanover [1980] Director/Milkman; Richard Hanover [1974] Director/Dairyman; Trevor Alan Hanover [1952] Director; Veronica Mary Hanover [1955] Director; Jayne Moore [1977] Director/Manager

Hanro Limited
Incorporated: 18 April 1988 *Employees:* 10
Net Worth: £73,391,000 *Total Assets:* £87,748,000
Registered Office: Citygate House, Bath Lane, Newcastle upon Tyne, NE4 5SQ
Activities: Other letting and operating of own or leased real estate
Shareholder: Katie Reavley
Officers: Duncan Colin Barrie, Secretary; Patricia Duncan [1931] Director; Caroline Emma Mary Rankin Mackness [1965] Director/Florist; Lee Deborah McGill [1950] Director/Support Worker; William Rankin [1931] Director/Chairman; Vanessa Jane Rankin Ramm [1963] Director/Retail Consultant; Katie Reavley [1963] Director/Radiographer; Adam James Serfontein [1964] Director/Chartered Surveyor

Hantman Select Limited
Incorporated: 6 June 2014
Net Worth: £57,877 *Total Assets:* £880,404
Registered Office: The Barns, South High Moor, Bywell, Felton, Northumberland, NE65 9QG
Activities: Other letting and operating of own or leased real estate
Shareholders: Philip Hantman; Louise Raine Hantman
Officers: Louise Raine Hantman, Secretary; Philip Hantman [1960] Director/Property Landlord

Harbour Support Services
Incorporated: 16 January 2001 *Employees:* 123
Net Worth: £967,853 *Total Assets:* £1,117,374
Registered Office: 15 Whitburn Street, Hartlepool, Cleveland, TS24 7QR
Activities: Other residential care activities n.e.c.
Officers: Caroline Skerry, Secretary; Marilyn Davies [1951] Director; Victoria Louise Duncan [1973] Director; Louise Amanda Hurst [1962] Director/Deputy Manager Youth Offending; Wendy Margaret Morris [1965] Director/Senior Lecturer; Christine Mulgrew [1950] Director; Denise Rudkin [1957] Director; Caroline Skerry [1966] Company Secretary/Director

Harbro Electrical Wholesale Limited
Incorporated: 12 November 1998 *Employees:* 9
Net Worth: £137,851 *Total Assets:* £772,973
Registered Office: 6-7 Whitworth Road, South West Industrial Estate, Peterlee, Co Durham, SR8 2LY
Activities: Wholesale of radio, television goods & electrical household appliances (other than records, tapes, CDs)
Shareholders: Philip Andrew Harbord; Jacqueline Harbord; David William Harbord
Officers: David William Harboard, Secretary; David William Harboard [1960] Director; Philip Andrew Harboard [1961] Director; Jacqueline Harbord [1963] Director/Financial Controller

Harbron Legal Ltd
Incorporated: 16 April 2012
Net Worth: £1,988,065 *Total Assets:* £2,477,688
Registered Office: 4 Tyne View, Lemington, Newcastle upon Tyne, NE15 8DE
Activities: Activities of patent and copyright agents; other legal activities n.e.c.
Major Shareholder: David George Harbron
Officers: David George Harbron [1979] Director/Solicitor

Harbron Properties Ltd
Incorporated: 30 April 2014
Net Worth Deficit: £7,233 *Total Assets:* £836,408
Registered Office: 32 Valley Drive, Low Fell, Gateshead, Tyne & Wear, NE9 5DH
Activities: Other letting and operating of own or leased real estate
Major Shareholder: David George Harbron
Officers: David George Harbron [1979] Director/Solicitor

Harden Redstone Company Limited
Incorporated: 31 October 1957 *Employees:* 4
Net Worth: £661,096 *Total Assets:* £959,512
Registered Office: Bulman House, Regent Centre, Gosforth, Newcastle upon Tyne, NE3 3LS
Activities: Other mining and quarrying n.e.c.
Shareholder: Malcolm Douglas Sym
Officers: Alastair Temperley Sym, Secretary/I T Technician; Alastair Temperley Sym [1960] Director/I T Technician; Jane Sym [1960] Director; Malcolm Douglas Sym [1957] Director/Farmer; Thomas William Walker [1960] Director

Richard Hardie Limited
Incorporated: 24 May 1972 *Employees:* 126
Net Worth: £3,858,478 *Total Assets:* £12,080,614
Registered Office: Trafford Road, Southwick, Sunderland, Tyne & Wear, SR5 2DA
Activities: Sale of new cars and light motor vehicles
Shareholders: Richard Philip Hardie; Nicholas Richard Hardie
Officers: Bernadette Hardie [1949] Director/Bookkeeper; Nicholas Richard Hardie [1976] Director/Branch Manager; Richard Philip Hardie [1951] Director; Rachel Luke [1982] Marketing Director

Hardware Supply Company (Middlesbrough) Limited
Incorporated: 21 August 1920 *Employees:* 25
Net Worth: £3,563,623 *Total Assets:* £4,055,278
Registered Office: The Faulkner Building, North Ormesby Road, Middlesbrough, Cleveland, TS4 2AP
Activities: Retail sale of hardware, paints and glass in specialised stores
Major Shareholder: Paul Anthony Faulkner
Officers: Amy Louise Faulkner, Secretary; Paul Anthony Faulkner [1957] Director/Hardware Merchant

J.J.Hardy & Sons Limited
Incorporated: 15 June 1922 *Employees:* 24
Net Worth: £372,914 *Total Assets:* £1,245,811
Registered Office: Brenda Road, Hartlepool, Cleveland, TS25 2BL
Activities: Manufacture of other fabricated metal products n.e.c.
Major Shareholder: Andrew Thomas Pailor
Officers: Andrew Thomas Pailor [1967] Managing Director

Hare Bulk Haulage Limited
Incorporated: 18 March 2011
Net Worth: £309,911 *Total Assets:* £1,241,485
Registered Office: The Garage, Patrick Brompton, Bedale, N Yorks, DL8 1JP
Activities: Freight transport by road
Parent: Bulk Logistics Group Limited
Officers: Andrew David Castle [1952] Director; David Keith Edghill [1979] Finance Director; Michael Anthony Hare [1976] Sales Director; Paul William Tolmie [1961] Director; Michael James Ward [1968] Director

Hare Homes Limited
Incorporated: 10 June 1997 *Employees:* 2
Net Worth: £2,658,254 *Total Assets:* £5,506,623
Registered Office: 25 Edgehill, Darras Hall, Ponteland, Northumberland, NE20 9RW
Activities: Buying and selling of own real estate
Major Shareholder: Balbinder Singh Haire
Officers: Lindsey Haire, Secretary/Director; Balbinder Singh Haire [1969] Director/Builder; Lindsey Haire [1975] Director/Company Secretary

Hargreaves (UK) Limited
Incorporated: 12 January 2001 *Employees:* 60
Net Worth Deficit: £31,405,000 *Total Assets:* £50,406,000
Registered Office: West Terrace, Esh Winning, Co Durham, DH7 9PT
Activities: Freight transport by road
Parent: Hargreaves Services PLC
Officers: Andrew Norman Robertson, Secretary; Gordon Frank Colenso Banham [1964] Director; John William Young Strachan Samuel [1956] Director

Hargreaves (UK) Services Limited
Incorporated: 17 March 1999 *Employees:* 453
Net Worth: £20,448,000 *Total Assets:* £155,030,000
Registered Office: West Terrace, Esh Winning, Co Durham, DH7 9PT
Activities: Wholesale of metals and metal ores
Parent: Hargreaves (UK) Limited
Officers: Andrew Norman Robertson, Secretary; Robert Brotherston [1958] Director/Accountant; John Paul Burks [1964] Director; Neal Sowerby [1962] Operations Director

Hargreaves Engineering & Contracts Limited
Incorporated: 9 March 1998 *Employees:* 36
Net Worth Deficit: £7,156,000 *Total Assets:* £3,272,000
Registered Office: West Terrace, Esh Winning, Co Durham, DH7 9PT
Activities: Machining
Parent: Hargreaves Industrial Services Limited
Officers: Gordon Frank Colenso Banham [1964] Director

Hargreaves Industrial Services Limited
Incorporated: 19 October 1988 *Employees:* 591
Net Worth: £7,401,000 *Total Assets:* £33,484,000
Registered Office: Hargreaves Services PLC, West Terrace, Esh Winning, Co Durham, DH7 9PT
Activities: Management consultancy activities other than financial management
Parent: Hargreaves Services PLC
Officers: Gordon Frank Colenso Banham [1964] Director; Sean Hager [1966] Director; John William Young Strachan Samuel [1956] Director

Hargreaves Land Limited
Incorporated: 18 October 2011 *Employees:* 238
Net Worth Deficit: £4,614,000 *Total Assets:* £122,555,000
Registered Office: West Terrace, Esh Winning, Co Durham, DH7 9PT
Activities: Open cast coal working
Shareholder: Hargreaves Services PLC
Officers: Gordon Frank Colenso Banham [1964] Director; John Paul Burks [1964] Director; Iain Philip Slater [1969] Director

Hargreaves Maltby Limited
Incorporated: 18 October 2012 *Employees:* 5
Net Worth Deficit: £2,917,000 *Total Assets:* £18,453,000
Registered Office: West Terrace, Esh Winning, Co Durham, DH7 9PT
Activities: Dormant company
Parent: Hargreaves Services PLC
Officers: Gordon Frank Colenso Banham [1964] Director

Hargreaves Services (Blindwells) Limited
Incorporated: 27 June 2013 *Employees:* 2
Net Worth Deficit: £102,000 *Total Assets:* £3,520,000
Registered Office: West Terrace, Esh Winning, Co Durham, DH7 9PT
Activities: Support activities for other mining and quarrying
Parent: Hargreaves Services PLC
Officers: Iain Philip Slater [1969] Director

Hargreaves Services Europe Limited
Incorporated: 23 September 2011 *Employees:* 16
Net Worth: £10,059,000 *Total Assets:* £67,753,000
Registered Office: West Terrace, Esh Winning, Co Durham, DH7 9PT
Activities: Other service activities n.e.c.
Shareholders: Hilmar Eller; Hargreaves Services PLC
Officers: Gordon Frank Colenso Banham [1964] Director/Group Chief Executive; Hilmar Eller [1960] Director/Trader [German]; Daniel Kuballa [1968] Director/Trader/Sales Manager [German]

Hargreaves Services PLC
Incorporated: 4 November 2003 *Employees:* 1,960
Net Worth: £137,898,000 *Total Assets:* £281,744,992
Registered Office: West Terrace, Esh Winning, Co Durham, DH7 9PT
Activities: Activities of head offices
Officers: Andrew Norman Robertson, Secretary; Gordon Frank Colenso Banham [1964] Director; Nigel Leslie Halkes [1955] Director; Peter Anthony Jones [1955] Director; Roger Steven McDowell [1955] Director; John William Young Strachan Samuel [1956] Director/Chartered Accountant

Hargreaves Technical Resources Limited
Incorporated: 22 November 2012 *Employees:* 4
Net Worth: £2,106,000 *Total Assets:* £2,661,000
Registered Office: West Terrace, Esh Winning, Co Durham, DH7 9PT
Activities: Support activities for other mining and quarrying
Parent: Hargreaves Services PLC
Officers: Kevin Sabin [1959] Director

Harkers Transport Limited
Incorporated: 13 February 2006 *Employees:* 98
Net Worth: £368,112 *Total Assets:* £1,429,010
Registered Office: Regional Distribution Centre, De Vere Building, Riverside Road, Southwick, Sunderland, Tyne & Wear, SR5 3JG
Activities: Freight transport by road
Parent: Angel Distribution Limited
Officers: Joan Harker, Secretary; Joan Harker [1954] Director; Kevin Harker [1957] Director

J Harland Haulage Limited
Incorporated: 14 August 2003 *Employees:* 8
Net Worth: £1,640,918 *Total Assets:* £1,834,670
Registered Office: Morton Palms Bungalow, Middleton St George, Darlington, Co Durham, DL2 1JZ
Activities: Freight transport by road
Shareholder: John Harland
Officers: Barbara Louise Harland, Secretary; Barbara Louise Harland [1958] Director/Company Secretary; John Harland [1949] Director

Dennis Harley Developments Ltd
Incorporated: 21 December 2004 *Employees:* 4
Net Worth: £2,708,672 *Total Assets:* £7,409,166
Registered Office: 14 Halegrove Court Cygnet Drive, Bowesfield Park, Stockton on Tees, Cleveland, TS18 3DB
Activities: Buying and selling of own real estate
Shareholder: James Dennis Harley
Officers: Rosaleen Anne Harley Rodgers, Secretary; James Dennis Harley [1974] Director/Construction

Harlow Printing Limited
Incorporated: 19 May 1947 *Employees:* 106
Net Worth: £6,044,413 *Total Assets:* £8,115,879
Registered Office: Maxwell Street, South Shields, Tyne & Wear, NE33 4PU
Activities: Printing n.e.c.
Major Shareholder: Brian Walker
Officers: Marjorie Elizabeth Walker, Secretary; Jack Andrew Harrison [1986] Commercial Director; Brian Walker [1931] Director/Chairman; Marjorie Elizabeth Walker [1932] Director/Company Secretary; Richard Brian Walker [1960] Managing Director

Harluk Associates Limited Liability Partnership
Incorporated: 26 April 2007
Registered Office: Gladstone House, 1 Ramside Park, Durham, DH1 1NS
Officers: Marie Hardy [1967] Member; Nigel William Hardy [1964] Member; Stephen James Luke [1957] Member

Harnham Buddhist Monastery Trust
Incorporated: 3 September 2008 *Employees:* 1
Net Worth: £1,867,143 *Total Assets:* £1,876,831
Registered Office: 2 Harnham Hall Cottages, Harnham, Belsay, Northumberland, NE20 0HF
Activities: Activities of religious organisations
Officers: Penelope Barbara Wakefield-Pearce, Secretary; John Bower [1957] Director/Police Officer; Paul Kristian Hansen [1977] Director/Telecoms Data Provisioning Team Manager; Kathleen Ann Jones [1953] Director/Teacher - Retired; Myint-Su Myint-Su [1940] Director/Retired Formerly Lecturer; Philippa Mary Padbury [1960] Director/Social Worker; Dr Michael Pearce [1952] Director/Retired (Formerly Banking)

Harper & Wilkes Limited
Incorporated: 4 October 2011
Net Worth: £4,899,800 *Total Assets:* £4,899,800
Registered Office: Crawley Hall, East Crawleyside, Stanhope, Bishop Auckland, Co Durham, DL13 2DX
Activities: Activities of head offices
Major Shareholder: Shona Wilkes
Officers: John Wilkes [1968] Director; Shona Wilkes [1974] Director

Harraton Properties Limited
Incorporated: 27 July 2006
Net Worth: £345,574 *Total Assets:* £1,970,782
Registered Office: Rowlands House, Portobello Road, Birtley, Co Durham, DH3 2RY
Activities: Buying and selling of own real estate
Major Shareholder: Peter Ramsay Fergusson
Officers: Peter Ramsay Fergusson [1952] Director

Harris (U.K.) Limited
Incorporated: 3 September 1987 *Employees:* 2
Net Worth: £1,748,500 *Total Assets:* £1,764,893
Registered Office: Marrick Moor Barn, Marrick, Richmond, N Yorks, DL11 7LF
Activities: Sale of other motor vehicles
Major Shareholder: Denise Harris
Officers: Denise Harris, Secretary; Ciaran Desmond [1962] Director/Solicitor [Irish]; Denise Harris [1945] Director [Irish]

John Harrison (Stockton) Limited
Incorporated: 11 March 1910 *Employees:* 127
Net Worth: £4,236,143 *Total Assets:* £9,352,106
Registered Office: Easter Park, Earlsway, Teesside Industrial Park, Thornaby, Stockton on Tees, Cleveland, TS17 9NT
Activities: Manufacture of other paper and paperboard containers
Parent: Fivedean Limited
Officers: Mary Caffry, Secretary; Michael Lawrence Baum [1967] Sales Director; Mary Caffry [1957] Finance Director

J H Harrison Investments Ltd
Incorporated: 19 August 2010 *Employees:* 2
Net Worth: £2,544,545 *Total Assets:* £2,599,647
Registered Office: 26 Hawthorn Gardens, Whitley Bay, Tyne & Wear, NE26 3PQ
Activities: Other letting and operating of own or leased real estate
Major Shareholder: Dean Robert Auld
Officers: Wendy Bruce, Secretary; Dean Auld [1968] Director/Solicitor

Harrison Properties Limited
Incorporated: 16 July 1980
Registered Office: 38 Borough Road, Darlington, Co Durham, DL1 1SW
Activities: Other letting and operating of own or leased real estate
Officers: Andrew Graham Sellers, Secretary; Adrian Harrison [1973] Managing Director Designate; Andrew Graham Sellers [1965] Finance Director

Hart Biologicals Limited
Incorporated: 28 August 2002 *Employees:* 42
Net Worth: £1,628,134 *Total Assets:* £2,215,729
Registered Office: 21 Berkeley Avenue, Hartlepool, Cleveland, TS25 3DW
Activities: Manufacture of medical and dental instruments and supplies
Officers: Lynne Pattison, Secretary; Albert Pattison [1958] Director/Manager; Malcolm Pattison [1961] Director

Hart Door Systems Limited
Incorporated: 16 February 1955 *Employees:* 43
Net Worth: £2,622,562 *Total Assets:* £3,440,178
Registered Office: Redburn Road, Newcastle upon Tyne, NE5 1PJ
Activities: Manufacture of other general-purpose machinery n.e.c.
Major Shareholder: Douglas Alexander Hart
Officers: Cynthia Mary Hart, Secretary; Alexander Nicholas Hart [1971] Director/Project Manager; Cynthia Mary Hart [1945] Director; Douglas Alexander Hart [1946] Director/Industrial Door Manufacturer

Hartlepool Aspire Trust
Incorporated: 10 July 2013 *Employees:* 162
Net Worth: £2,374,146 *Total Assets:* £4,065,311
Registered Office: c/o Catcote Academy, Catcote Road, Hartlepool, Cleveland, TS25 4EZ
Activities: General secondary education
Officers: Louise Annette Robson, Secretary; Julie Carter [1971] Director/Housewife; Alan Carr Chapman [1952] Director/Headteacher; Gillian Fletcher [1984] Director/Manager of Care Home; Helen Victoria Gordon [1961] Managing Director; Paul Robert Hewitson [1980] Director; Pauline Holbrook [1955] Director/Retired; Dr Graham Jones [1969] Director/Engineer; Elisa Latimer [1968] Director/Housewife; Anne Malcolm [1972] Director/Former Academy Principal; Roger Mark Phillips [1957] Director

Hartlepool Golf Club Limited
Incorporated: 27 July 1921
Net Worth: £986,214 *Total Assets:* £1,099,717
Registered Office: Golf House, Hart Warren, Hartlepool, Cleveland, TS24 9QF
Activities: Operation of sports facilities
Officers: Carole Wright, Secretary; James Allison [1945] Director/Retired; Graham Chapman [1961] Director; Patrick William Duff [1950] Director/Owner Driver; Linton Gavin Gordon [1941] Director/Retired; Clive Harbron [1964] Director/L & D Consultant; Kevin Jones [1964] Director/UK Trainer; Gerard McIlwrath [1952] Director/Retired; Anthony Waites [1953] Director/Retired; Mark Whitelock [1963] Director/Business Manager; Carole Lesley Wright [1961] Director/Registered Nurse/Infection Prevention Coordinator

Hartlepool Hospice Limited (The)
Incorporated: 31 October 1980 *Employees:* 84
Net Worth: £3,117,513 *Total Assets:* £4,114,731
Registered Office: Alice House, Wells Avenue, Hartlepool, Cleveland, TS24 9DA
Activities: Hospital activities
Officers: James Frederick Ainslie [1947] Director/Retired; Dr Robin William Wylie Armstrong [1963] Director/GP; Mra Annaliese Barber [1975] Director/Solicitor; Malcolm John Cairns [1932] Director/Retired; Sunil Thomas Chacko [1962] Director/Manager; Francis Matthew Gibbon [1939] Director/Solicitor; Lorna Jones [1934] Director/Lecturer; Paul Thomas Jones-King [1976] Director/Registered Nurse; Karen Patricia Martin [1974] Director/Business Owner - Marketing Consultant; Raymond Priestman [1959] Director/Chartered Accountant; Joanne Regan [1971] Director/Chartered Accountant; Clive Shotton [1957] Director/Retail Businessman

Hartlepool Investments Limited
Incorporated: 14 March 2006 *Employees:* 105
Net Worth: £4,553,071 *Total Assets:* £9,512,277
Registered Office: P O Box 270, Units 1-4 Brenda Road, Hartlepool, Cleveland, TS25 2BW
Activities: Activities of other holding companies n.e.c.
Shareholder: Michael Patrick Hamburger
Officers: Andrea Gallant, Secretary; Michael Terence Hird [1946] Director; Kevin James Martin [1964] Director; Samantha Jane Price [1969] Commercial Director; James Alexander Robson [1960] Engineer/Director; David Tunney [1958] Operations Director; Peter William Webb [1954] Technical Director

Hartlepool Marina Limited
Incorporated: 25 February 2002 *Employees:* 18
Net Worth: £574,666 *Total Assets:* £1,566,535
Registered Office: The Lock Office, The Marina, Slake Terrace, Hartlepool, Cleveland, TS24 0RU
Activities: Other amusement and recreation activities n.e.c.
Officers: Adam Edwin Henderson [1987] Director; Allan Rodney Henderson [1955] Managing Director

Hartlepool NDC Trust
Incorporated: 23 June 2008 *Employees:* 5
Net Worth: £952,888 *Total Assets:* £1,013,709
Registered Office: Unit 1-2 Baltic Street, Hartlepool, Cleveland, TS25 1PS
Activities: Activities of head offices
Officers: Stuart Fraser Drummond, Secretary; Michael William Bretherick [1957] Director/Retired; Christopher Mark Dutton [1968] Director/Housing Manager; Julie Rudge [1958] Director; Michael Andrew Sumpter [1961] Branch Director; Malcolm Walker [1958] Director/Local Government; Michael William Ward [1958] Director/Retired

Hartlepool People Limited
Incorporated: 12 June 1986 *Employees:* 3
Net Worth: £996,404 *Total Assets:* £1,018,043
Registered Office: Hartlepool People Centre, Raby Road, Hartlepool, Cleveland, TS24 8AH
Activities: Other social work activities without accommodation n.e.c.
Officers: Linda Jean Craddy, Secretary; Graham Hastings Culley [1940] Director/Self Employed; John Alfred Dinning [1951] Director/Audit Clerk; Jean Lathen [1946] Director/Teacher; Christopher McLoughlin [1954] Director/Retired

Hartlepool Revival Limited
Incorporated: 17 July 2003
Net Worth: £1,746,010 *Total Assets:* £2,349,584
Registered Office: Unit 1-2 Baltic Street, Hartlepool, Cleveland, TS25 1PS
Activities: Other letting and operating of own or leased real estate
Officers: Stuart Fraser Drummond, Secretary; Malcolm Walker, Secretary/Local Government; Christopher Mark Dutton [1968] Director/Housing Manager; Councillor Jean Kennedy [1938] Director

Hartley Main Farms Limited
Incorporated: 8 May 1953 *Employees:* 8
Net Worth: £5,802,469 *Total Assets:* £7,374,841
Registered Office: North Moor Farm, Seaton Delaval, Whitley Bay, Tyne & Wear, NE25 0PX
Activities: Mixed farming
Major Shareholder: Miles Frederick Anthony Capstick
Officers: Margaret Elizabeth Capstick, Secretary; Margaret Elizabeth Capstick [1930] Director/Retired; Miles Frederick Anthony Capstick [1961] Director/Farmer/Landowner

Harton Construction Limited
Incorporated: 15 June 2005
Registered Office: 20 The Square, Fulwell, Sunderland, Tyne & Wear, SR6 8JJ
Activities: Other letting and operating of own or leased real estate
Officers: Anthony William Mordew, Secretary; Mark Edward Harvey [1963] Director; Anthony William Mordew [1969] Director

Harton Properties Limited
Incorporated: 2 November 2006
Net Worth: £14,895 *Total Assets:* £1,216,874
Registered Office: 2-6 Franklin Street, South Shields, Tyne & Wear, NE33 1PR
Activities: Buying and selling of own real estate
Shareholder: Kenneth Ross
Officers: Kenneth Ross, Secretary/Accountant; Mark Edward Harvey [1963] Director; Anthony William Mordew [1969] Director; Kenneth Ross [1965] Director/Accountant

Hartridge Buddhist Monastery Trust
Incorporated: 24 September 2010
Net Worth: £1,022,285 *Total Assets:* £1,023,023
Registered Office: 29 Howard Street, North Shields, Tyne & Wear, NE30 1AR
Activities: Activities of religious organisations
Officers: Janene Lorraine Horton, Secretary; Denise Christa Beal [1950] Director [Irish]; Maxim Alexander MacKay-James [1951] Director/Medical Practitioner; Julian Wall [1956] Director/Software Consultant; Robert Harry Whittle [1941] Director/Retired Civil Engineer/Planner; Anne Patricia Williams [1952] Director

Harvest Home Limited
Incorporated: 9 December 2009 *Employees:* 6
Net Worth: £226,183 *Total Assets:* £1,738,537
Registered Office: Rowlands House, Portobello Road, Birtley, Chester-le-Street, Co Durham, DH3 2RY
Activities: Management consultancy activities other than financial management
Shareholders: Alan Crozier; Colin Crozier; John Crozier
Officers: Alan Crozier [1960] Director/Farmer; Colin Crozier [1965] Director/Farmer; John Crozier [1962] Director/Farmer

Harvey M and A Ltd
Incorporated: 30 June 2005 *Employees:* 2
Net Worth: £1,107,861 *Total Assets:* £2,881,537
Registered Office: 89a Tunstall Road, Sunderland, Tyne & Wear, SR2 7RW
Activities: Other business support service activities n.e.c.
Major Shareholder: Barrie Richard Harvey
Officers: Neil Harvey, Secretary; Barry Harvey [1941] Director; Neil Harvey [1970] Director

Hase Osborne Asset Management Limited
Incorporated: 11 March 2003
Net Worth: £2,229,077 *Total Assets:* £2,512,917
Registered Office: 1 The Bulrushes, Woodstock Way, Boldon Business Park, Boldon Colliery, Co Durham, NE35 9PF
Activities: Financial intermediation not elsewhere classified
Parent: Fairstone Holdings Limited
Officers: Scott Hopkinson, Secretary; Lee Graham Hartley [1976] Director; Scott Hopkinson [1974] Director/Accountant

Haskel Europe Ltd
Incorporated: 27 September 1976 *Employees:* 62
Net Worth: £3,636,173 *Total Assets:* £10,602,379
Registered Office: North Hylton Road, Sunderland, Tyne & Wear, SR5 3JD
Activities: Manufacture of pumps
Officers: Nicholas James Kendall-Jones [1971] Director; Stephen Learney [1958] Director

Dr W Hassan Ltd
Incorporated: 28 May 2009 *Employees:* 2
Net Worth: £829,900 *Total Assets:* £954,706
Registered Office: 7 Bankside, The Watermark, Gateshead, Tyne & Wear, NE11 9SY
Activities: General medical practice activities
Shareholders: Dr Wajahat Hassan; Dr Sharon Anne Scott
Officers: Dr Wajahat Hassan [1958] Director/Doctor; Dr Sharon Anne Scott [1964] Director/Doctor

Jim Hastings Limited
Incorporated: 3 May 1973 *Employees:* 34
Net Worth: £2,098,172 *Total Assets:* £2,724,147
Registered Office: Bainbridge House, 379 Stamfordham Road, Newcastle upon Tyne, NE5 2LH
Activities: Construction of commercial buildings
Shareholders: Fiona Lindsey Hastings; James Stuart Hastings
Officers: Fiona Lindsey Hastings, Secretary; Fiona Lindsey Hastings [1963] Director/Company Secretary; James Stuart Hastings [1959] Director/Civil Engineer

Haswell Moor Developments Ltd
Incorporated: 9 January 2007
Net Worth: £140,807 *Total Assets:* £3,860,070
Registered Office: Haswell Moor Farm, Haswell, Co Durham, DH6 2BD
Activities: Development of building projects
Shareholders: Christine Beatrice Oliver; Leslie Graham Oliver
Officers: Christine Beatrice Oliver, Secretary; Christine Beatrice Oliver [1945] Director; John Alfred Oliver [1972] Director/Farmer; Leslie Graham Oliver [1945] Director/Farmer

Haswell Moor Farms Ltd
Incorporated: 21 January 2003 *Employees:* 1
Net Worth: £1,513,439 *Total Assets:* £3,481,076
Registered Office: Haswell Moor Farm, Haswell, Co Durham, DH6 2BD
Activities: Raising of dairy cattle
Shareholders: Leslie Graham Oliver; Christine Beatrice Oliver
Officers: Christine Beatrice Oliver, Secretary; Christine Beatrice Oliver [1945] Director/Company Secretary; John Alfred Oliver [1972] Director/Farmer; Leslie Graham Oliver [1945] Director/Farmer

Haswells Homer Hill Farm Shop Limited
Incorporated: 18 March 2003 *Employees:* 48
Net Worth: £406,822 *Total Assets:* £832,085
Registered Office: Homer Hill Farm, Pittington Road, Rainton Gate, Houghton-le-Spring, Co Durham, DH5 9RG
Activities: Retail sale of meat and meat products in specialised stores
Shareholders: Joanne Moran; Gillian Hide
Officers: John Glanville Haswell, Secretary; Jean Carroll Haswell [1942] Director/Butcher; John Glanville Haswell [1940] Director/Butcher; Gillian Hide [1963] Director/Butcher; Joanne Moran [1964] Director/Butcher

Hathaway Roofing Limited
Incorporated: 22 April 1997 *Employees:* 82
Net Worth: £4,953,523 *Total Assets:* £12,385,601
Registered Office: Tindale Crescent, Bishop Auckland, Co Durham, DL14 9TL
Activities: Roofing activities
Major Shareholder: Simon David Binks
Officers: Diane Marie Thompson, Secretary; Simon David Binks [1972] Director; Stephen John Godfrey [1956] Contracts Director; Kevin Hall [1959] Managing Director; Andrew Harrison [1965] Technical Director; Steven Price [1969] Director; Diane Marie Thompson [1965] Finance Director; Mark Watson [1964] Director

Hatton Traffic Management Limited
Incorporated: 12 August 1976
Net Worth: £594,571 *Total Assets:* £1,847,042
Registered Office: Unit 10b Brunswick Industrial Estate, Newcastle upon Tyne, NE13 7BA
Activities: Renting and leasing of other machinery, equipment and tangible goods n.e.c.
Major Shareholder: Marshall Graham Bailey
Officers: Lara Juliette Louise Bailey, Secretary; Marshall Graham Bailey [1948] Director; Thomas Robert Bailey [1976] Managing Director

Haven (Tyneside) Ltd.
Incorporated: 23 August 1993 *Employees:* 26
Net Worth: £989,018 *Total Assets:* £1,020,408
Registered Office: 11 Regent Terrace, Gateshead, Tyne & Wear, NE8 1LU
Activities: Other accommodation
Officers: James William Little, Secretary; Clare Michelle Blunt [1975] Director/Training Consultant; Diane Creighton [1957] Director/Housing Officer; Margaret Ferguson [1961] Director/Fundraising Consultant; Russell Hewitson [1963] Director/Enterprise Fellow; Dr Helen Moira Kay [1963] Director/Solicitor; James William Little [1965] Director/Business Improvement Lead; Ian Mackintosh [1957] Director/Financial Administrator; Patrick John Rice [1973] Director/Local Government Officer; Nitin Shukla [1961] Director/Policy & Performance & Scrutiny Officer

The Hawes Farmers' Auction Mart Company, Limited
Incorporated: 16 January 1914 *Employees:* 26
Net Worth: £1,059,563 *Total Assets:* £1,161,317
Registered Office: Burtersett Road, Hawes, N Yorks, DL8 3NP
Activities: Agents selling agricultural raw materials, livestock, textile raw materials and semi-finished goods
Officers: Linda Tennant, Secretary; John Dixon [1963] Director/Farmer; John Christopher Fawcett [1950] Director/Farmer; Wilson Hodgson [1945] Director/Farmer; Henry Allen Kirkbride [1949] Director/Farmer; Phillip Thomas Metcalfe [1972] Director/Farmer; Andrew Thomas Pratt [1961] Director/Farmer; David Leonard Scarr [1971] Director/Farmer; John Edward Thorpe [1974] Director/Farmer; Thomas George Willoughby [1982] Director/Farmer

Hawik Limited
Incorporated: 13 December 1993
Net Worth: £1,012,466 *Total Assets:* £1,302,917
Registered Office: The Walled Garden, Longhirst, Morpeth, Northumberland, NE61 3LJ
Activities: Other letting and operating of own or leased real estate
Officers: Anne Marie Carey, Secretary; Daniel Paul Carey, Secretary; Paula Marie Kennedy, Secretary; Anne Marie Carey [1952] Director; Doctor Christopher Daniel Carey [1978] Director/Medical Doctor; Daniel Paul Carey [1981] Director/Solicitor; Lawrence Daniel Carey [1951] Director/Chartered Accountant

Hawk Fasteners Limited
Incorporated: 11 November 1981 *Employees:* 20
Net Worth: £1,037,242 *Total Assets:* £1,089,826
Registered Office: Brunel Road, Skippers Lane Industrial Estate, South Bank, Middlesbrough, Cleveland, TS6 6JA
Activities: Manufacture of fasteners and screw machine products
Major Shareholder: David Robert Ashworth
Officers: David Robert Ashworth, Secretary; David Robert Ashworth [1946] Director; John Duncan Dodds [1952] Director

J & R A Hawkes & Sons Limited
Incorporated: 3 December 2001 *Employees:* 14
Net Worth: £574,850 *Total Assets:* £1,186,830
Registered Office: Southlands, Yarm Back Lane, Stockton on Tees, Cleveland, TS21 1AR
Activities: Maintenance and repair of motor vehicles
Officers: Andrew Gary Hawkes, Secretary; Andrew Gary Hawkes [1968] Director/Manager; Joseph Hawkes [1944] Director/Engineer; Martin Joseph Hawkes [1971] Director/Engineer; Rita Angela Hawkes [1943] Director/Nurse

Hawkpost Limited
Incorporated: 16 January 2002 *Employees:* 78
Net Worth: £2,036,673 *Total Assets:* £13,143,990
Registered Office: Albany Court, Monarch Road, Newcastle Business Park, Newcastle upon Tyne, NE4 7YB
Activities: Activities of construction holding companies
Major Shareholder: Ian Walker
Officers: Ian Walker [1949] Director; Marilyn Walker [1950] Director

Hawkridge Management Limited
Incorporated: 8 April 2013 *Employees:* 197
Net Worth: £14,903,385 *Total Assets:* £18,692,320
Registered Office: Unit 15-19 Bedesway, Bede Industrial Estate, Jarrow, Tyne & Wear, NE32 3EN
Activities: Manufacture of other electrical equipment
Shareholders: Stephen Mitchell Elliott; Kevin McLaughlin
Officers: Amita Pandit, Secretary; Kevin McLaughlin [1953] Director

Hawks Road Community Nursery Limited
Incorporated: 8 February 1991 *Employees:* 61
Net Worth: £1,397,204 *Total Assets:* £1,428,051
Registered Office: Hawks Road Community Nursery, The Boulevard, Holmes Drive, Gateshead, Tyne & Wear, NE10 0DJ
Activities: Pre-primary education
Officers: Peter James Maughan [1954] Director/Solicitor; Andrew Christopher Miller [1961] Director/Bank Manager; Robert Richardson [1930] Director/Retired

Hawksby Bainbridge Limited
Incorporated: 10 November 2014
Net Worth: £106,441 *Total Assets:* £1,205,665
Registered Office: 5 Anesty Court, Bishopston, Stockton on Tees, Cleveland, TS21 1NP
Activities: Buying and selling of own real estate
Shareholders: Jenifer Bainbridge; Devinia Marson
Officers: Devinia Bainbridge [1983] Director/Primary School Teacher; Jenifer Bainbridge [1945] Director/Retired; Malcolm Christopher Bainbridge [1943] Director/Secretary

Hawthorn Parks Limited
Incorporated: 11 April 2012 *Employees:* 3
Net Worth: £250,848 *Total Assets:* £1,632,904
Registered Office: 36 Haughton Green, Haughton Village, Darlington, Co Durham, DL1 2DF
Activities: Holiday centres and villages
Shareholders: Elizabeth Julie Burnside; Joseph Burnside
Officers: Elizabeth Julie Burnside [1992] Director; Joseph Burnside [1986] Director

The Hawthorns Lodge Limited
Incorporated: 15 February 2006 *Employees:* 146
Net Worth: £979,164 *Total Assets:* £3,861,084
Registered Office: 384 Linthorpe Road, Middlesbrough, Cleveland, TS5 6HA
Activities: Residential care activities for learning difficulties, mental health and substance abuse
Major Shareholder: Justin Ignatius Harrington Russi
Officers: Justin Ignatius Harrington Russi [1961] Director/Residential Care Owner

Hawthorns Logistics Limited
Incorporated: 8 November 2009 *Employees:* 48
Net Worth: £1,286,188 *Total Assets:* £2,908,565
Registered Office: Field Heads Farm, Castleside, Consett, Co Durham, DH8 9AT
Activities: Freight transport by road
Shareholders: Alison Finlay Kilsby; Christian Jordan Kilsby
Officers: Alison Finlay Kilsby, Secretary; Alison Finlay Kilsby [1968] Director/Consultant; Christian Jordan Kilsby [1969] Director/Consultant

Hays Beds Limited
Incorporated: 19 April 2001 *Employees:* 5
Net Worth: £1,774,762 *Total Assets:* £14,772,290
Registered Office: 25 Vine Place, Sunderland, Tyne & Wear, SR1 3NA
Activities: Travel agency activities
Parent: Hays Travel Limited
Officers: Marta Fernandez Varona [1966] Finance Director [Spanish]; John Hays [1949] Director; Jonathan Hays [1978] Director/Legal Adviser

Hays Credit LLP
Incorporated: 1 November 2007 *Employees:* 16
Net Worth: £1,412,887 *Total Assets:* £2,134,779
Registered Office: 5 Vine Place, Sunderland, Tyne & Wear, SR1 3NE
Officers: Donna Hays [1971] Member; Malcolm Thomas Hays [1954] Member

Hays Finance Limited
Incorporated: 3 October 1994
Net Worth: £1,467,615 *Total Assets:* £1,467,615
Registered Office: 5 Vine Place, Sunderland, Tyne & Wear, SR1 3NE
Activities: Other service activities n.e.c.
Major Shareholder: Malcolm Thomas Hays
Officers: Donna Hays [1971] Director; Malcolm Thomas Hays [1954] Managing Director

Hays Foreign Exchange Limited
Incorporated: 8 November 1996 *Employees:* 100
Net Worth: £4,226,309 *Total Assets:* £5,192,050
Registered Office: 25 Vine Place, Sunderland, Tyne & Wear, SR1 3NA
Activities: Travel agency activities
Parent: Hays Travel Limited
Officers: Marta Fernandez Varona [1966] Finance Director [Spanish]; John Hays [1949] Director; Jonathan Hays [1978] Director/Legal Adviser; Jane Elizabeth Schumm [1969] Director

Hays Property Services Limited
Incorporated: 1 June 1934 *Employees:* 4
Net Worth: £10,245,539 *Total Assets:* £10,824,399
Registered Office: 25 Vine Place, Sunderland, Tyne & Wear, SR1 3NA
Activities: Other letting and operating of own or leased real estate
Parent: Hays Travel Limited
Officers: Marta Fernandez Varona [1966] Financial Director [Spanish]; John Hays [1949] Director/Travel Agent; Jonathan Hays [1978] Director/Legal Adviser; Jane Elizabeth Schumm [1969] Director/Travel Agent

Hays Tour Operating Limited
Incorporated: 2 July 1998 *Employees:* 72
Net Worth: £4,178,759 *Total Assets:* £56,845,656
Registered Office: 25 Vine Place, Sunderland, Tyne & Wear, SR1 3NA
Activities: Tour operator activities
Parent: Hays Travel Limited
Officers: Marta Fernandez Varona [1966] Finance Director [Spanish]; John Hays [1949] Director/Travel Agent; Jonathan Hays [1978] Director/Legal Adviser

Hays Transport Limited
Incorporated: 15 November 2007
Net Worth: £15,737 *Total Assets:* £9,697,619
Registered Office: 25 Vine Place, Sunderland, Tyne & Wear, SR1 3NA
Activities: Travel agency activities
Parent: Hays Travel Limited
Officers: Marta Fernandez Varona [1966] Finance Director [Spanish]; John Hays [1949] Director; Jonathan Hays [1978] Director/Legal Adviser; Jane Elizabeth Schumm [1969] Director

Hays Travel Limited
Incorporated: 18 February 1986 *Employees:* 1,201
Net Worth: £32,550,000 *Total Assets:* £135,632,992
Registered Office: 25 Vine Place, Sunderland, Tyne & Wear, SR1 3NA
Activities: Travel agency activities
Shareholders: John Hays; Irene Hays
Officers: Marta Fernandez Varona [1966] Finance Director [Spanish]; Irene Hays [1954] Director/Chief Executive; John Hays [1949] Director/Travel Agent; Jonathan Hays [1978] Director/Legal Adviser; Jane Elizabeth Schumm [1969] Director/Travel Agent

Hayton & Lamb Limited
Incorporated: 20 May 1982 *Employees:* 89
Net Worth: £1,832,687 *Total Assets:* £3,563,797
Registered Office: Eldon Road, Aycliffe Industrial Estate, Newton Aycliffe, Co Durham, DL5 6UL
Activities: Painting
Major Shareholder: Paul Gerard Hayton
Officers: Susan Lamb, Secretary; Paul Gerard Hayton [1965] Director

T.J. Hazell (Engineering Consultants) Limited
Incorporated: 29 June 1979 *Employees:* 18
Net Worth: £424,757 *Total Assets:* £913,265
Registered Office: Wolviston House, 5 Falcon Court, Preston Farm Industrial Estate, Stockton on Tees, Cleveland, TS18 3TS
Activities: Other specialised construction activities n.e.c.
Parent: Wolviston Group Limited
Officers: Samantha Jane Anderson [1974] Director

HBH Investments Limited
Incorporated: 14 September 2012 *Employees:* 2
Net Worth: £5,900 *Total Assets:* £933,420
Registered Office: 7 Meadow Court, Ponteland, Northumberland, NE20 9RB
Activities: Buying and selling of own real estate
Shareholders: Steven Anthony Hughes; Dennis Trevor Hughes
Officers: Dennis Trevor Hughes [1942] Director/Retired; Steven Anthony Hughes [1975] Director

HC-ONE Beamish Limited
Incorporated: 31 August 2004 *Employees:* 1,295
Net Worth: £1,662,000 *Total Assets:* £10,645,000
Registered Office: Southgate House, Archer Street, Darlington, Co Durham, DL3 6AH
Activities: Residential nursing care facilities
Parent: FC Beamish Bidco Limited
Officers: James Justin Hutchens [1974] Director [American]; David Andrew Smith [1974] Director

HC-ONE Limited
Incorporated: 20 July 2011 *Employees:* 10,957
Net Worth: £20,669,000 *Total Assets:* £161,444,000
Registered Office: Southgate House, Archer Street, Darlington, Co Durham, DL3 6AH
Activities: Residential nursing care facilities
Parent: FC Skyfall Bidco Ltd
Officers: David Andrew Smith, Secretary; James Justin Hutchens [1974] Director [American]; Chaitanya Bhupendra Patel [1954] Director; John Anthony Ransford [1948] Director; David Andrew Smith [1974] Director; Sir William Henry Weston Wells [1940] Director

HC-ONE Oval Limited
Incorporated: 30 June 2016 *Employees:* 4,477
Net Worth: £420,136,000 *Total Assets:* £532,830,016
Registered Office: Southgate House, Archer Street, Darlington, Co Durham, DL3 6AH
Activities: Activities of other holding companies n.e.c.
Officers: David Andrew Smith, Secretary; James Justin Hutchens [1974] Director [American]; David Andrew Smith [1974] Director

HD Homes Limited
Incorporated: 19 December 2005
Net Worth: £3,389,973 *Total Assets:* £9,843,990
Registered Office: Unit 2 Blaydon Park, Chainbridge Road, Blaydon, Tyne & Wear, NE21 5ST
Activities: Buying and selling of own real estate
Shareholders: Tevor Hanover; Vera Hanover
Officers: Veronica Mary Hanover, Secretary; Michael Hanover [1980] Director/Milkman; Richard Hanover [1974] Director/Dairyman; Trevor Alan Hanover [1952] Director; Veronica Mary Hanover [1955] Director; Jayne Moore [1977] Director/Manager

HDC Travel Limited
Incorporated: 16 November 2011
Net Worth: £645,893 *Total Assets:* £1,507,378
Registered Office: 3rd Floor, Tyne House, 26 Side, Newcastle upon Tyne, NE1 3JA
Activities: Advertising agencies
Parent: ULookUBook Travel Limited
Officers: Stephen Campion, Secretary; Stephen Campion [1967] Director; Susan Winter [1963] Director; David Kenneth Young [1957] Director

The Head of Steam Limited
Incorporated: 21 November 1979 *Employees:* 87
Net Worth: £1,588,514 *Total Assets:* £2,307,518
Registered Office: Main Gate House, Waldon Street, Hartlepool, Cleveland, TS24 7QS
Activities: Public houses and bars
Parent: Camerons Brewery Limited
Officers: John Richard Foots, Secretary; John Richard Foots [1968] Director/Chartered Accountant; Christopher David Solely [1975] Commercial Director

Headlam Leisure Limited
Incorporated: 4 April 1985 *Employees:* 63
Net Worth: £1,624,636 *Total Assets:* £2,359,056
Registered Office: Headlam Hall Hotel, Headlam, Gainford, Darlington, Co Durham, DL2 3HA
Activities: Hotels and similar accommodation
Officers: Suzanne Clare Metcalfe, Secretary; David James Jackson [1947] Hotel Operations Director; Suzanne Clare Metcalfe [1963] Director; Ann Orton Bond Robinson [1941] Director; John Hugh Robinson [1937] Director; Simon Hugh James Robinson [1965] Director/Farmer; Thomas Giles John Robinson [1971] Managing Director

Headline Pictures (Peter Pan) Limited
Incorporated: 18 June 2014
Registered Office: 5 Charlotte Square, Newcastle upon Tyne, NE1 4XF
Activities: Television programme production activities
Parent: Headline Pictures Limited
Officers: Christian Baute [1971] Director/Film Producer [German/Israeli]; Adrian Clive Gifford [1946] Director/Retired; Stewart MacKinnon [1948] Director/Film & TV Producer; Derek Arthur Stubbs [1943] Director/Consultant

Headway Point Limited
Incorporated: 11 April 2012 *Employees:* 2
Net Worth: £1,445,781 *Total Assets:* £1,471,917
Registered Office: Greenbank House, Sotherby Road, Middlesbrough, Cleveland, TS3 8BT
Activities: Remediation activities and other waste management services
Shareholders: Duncan Evershed; Lucy Colette Evershed
Officers: Lucy Colette Evershed, Secretary; Duncan Evershed [1974] Director

Health & Safety Training Limited
Incorporated: 10 March 2003 *Employees:* 21
Net Worth: £900,852 *Total Assets:* £1,082,609
Registered Office: Unit 6 Wesley Way, Benton Square Industrial Estate, Newcastle upon Tyne, NE12 9TA
Activities: Other business support service activities n.e.c.
Shareholders: Phil Binks; Carla Christie Binks
Officers: Carla Christie Binks, Secretary/Sales Director; Carla Christie Binks [1974] Director; Philip Binks [1962] Director/Sales

Healthways Chemists (North East) Limited
Incorporated: 27 November 1986 *Employees:* 6
Net Worth: £2,963,436 *Total Assets:* £3,172,979
Registered Office: 5 Broom Court, Springwell Village, Gateshead, Tyne & Wear, NE9 7SZ
Activities: Other human health activities
Major Shareholder: Christopher Michael Bishop
Officers: Christopher Michael Bishop, Secretary; Christopher Michael Bishop [1963] Director/Pharmacist

Healthworks Newcastle
Incorporated: 26 July 1994 *Employees:* 76
Net Worth: £1,891,799 *Total Assets:* £2,029,602
Registered Office: Health Resource Centre, Adelaide Terrace, Benwell, Newcastle upon Tyne, NE4 8BE
Activities: Other human health activities
Officers: Diane Creighton [1957] Director/Executive Assistant; Dr Patricia Anne Cresswell [1957] Director/Retired; John Dawson [1943] Director; Professor Christopher Kenneth Drinkwater [1944] Director/Academic University; Kenneth Graham [1944] Director/Retired Teacher; Mark Ions [1976] Managing Director; Joel Hanoch Marks [1967] Director; Rebecca McCready [1979] Director/Learning and Teaching Advisor; Professor Elizabeth Sarah Todd [1958] Director/Professor of Educational Inclusion; Michael Edward Turner [1971] Director/Head of Commercial Strategy

Heat Tech Tooling Ltd
Incorporated: 9 May 2013 *Employees:* 10
Net Worth: £314,904 *Total Assets:* £3,022,325
Registered Office: Heat Tech Tooling Limited, Cygnet Way, Houghton-le-Spring, Co Durham, DH4 5QY
Activities: Installation of industrial machinery and equipment
Shareholders: Roy Williamson; David Rutter
Officers: David Rutter [1958] Operations Director; Sheila Rutter [1959] Director; Roy Williamson [1961] Sales Director; Tracey Williamson [1963] Director

Heating Trade Supplies Group Limited
Incorporated: 30 June 2015 *Employees:* 25
Net Worth: £64,337 *Total Assets:* £1,252,531
Registered Office: Tyne View Terrace, Wallsend, Tyne & Wear, NE28 6SG
Activities: Wholesale of hardware, plumbing and heating equipment and supplies
Shareholders: Mustafa Erdem Baldudak; Mark Matteo
Officers: Mustafa Erdem Baldudak [1988] Director [Turkish]; Mark Matteo [1973] Managing Director

Heating World of Spares Limited
Incorporated: 30 November 2006 *Employees:* 16
Net Worth: £783,580 *Total Assets:* £1,525,880
Registered Office: 1b Henson Close, South Church Enterprise Park, Bishop Auckland, Co Durham, DL14 6WA
Activities: Wholesale of hardware, plumbing and heating equipment and supplies
Shareholders: Kai Raymond Scott; Aaron Luke Scott
Officers: Aaron Luke Scott, Secretary/Director; Aaron Luke Scott [1976] Director; Emmeline Scott [1983] Director/Sales Manager; Kai Raymond Scott [1974] Director; Raymond Scott [1952] Director

Heaton Enterprises Limited
Incorporated: 18 October 1968 *Employees:* 2
Net Worth: £1,874,383 *Total Assets:* £1,991,440
Registered Office: Lauder Grange, Prospect Hill, Corbridge, Northumberland, NE45 5RS
Activities: Other letting and operating of own or leased real estate
Major Shareholder: Christopher James Clavering
Officers: Esther Howe Clavering, Secretary; Christopher James Clavering [1949] Director; Esther Howe Clavering [1960] Director/Secretary

Hebburn Properties (NE) Limited
Incorporated: 30 November 2015
Net Worth: £16,800 *Total Assets:* £1,027,640
Registered Office: 6 Beaumont Street, Hexham, Northumberland, NE46 3LZ
Activities: Residents property management
Officers: Kourosh Manoucheri [1955] Director; Malcolm Andrew Vaughan [1961] Director

Heber Street Limited
Incorporated: 30 May 2007
Net Worth: £1,005,804 *Total Assets:* £1,555,486
Registered Office: 1 Jesmond Business Court, Jesmond Road, Newcastle upon Tyne, NE2 1LA
Activities: Other business support service activities n.e.c.
Shareholder: Elizabeth Averill Leng
Officers: Elizabeth Averill Leng [1980] Director

Heck! Food Limited
Incorporated: 2 July 2004 *Employees:* 80
Net Worth: £762,886 *Total Assets:* £7,641,158
Registered Office: Berry Hills, Kirklington, Bedale, N Yorks, DL8 2NL
Activities: Retail sale of meat and meat products in specialised stores
Shareholders: Deborah Jane Keeble; Andrew Crispin Keeble; Stephen Alexander Campbell
Officers: Deborah Jane Keeble, Secretary/Director; Stephen Alexander Campbell [1965] Director; Andrew Crispin Keeble [1965] Director; Deborah Jane Keeble [1965] Director; William Mark McDavid [1958] Director

Heddon Stables Limited
Incorporated: 16 May 2003
Net Worth: £150,030 *Total Assets:* £938,607
Registered Office: 18 The Holdings, East Heddon, Newcastle upon Tyne, NE15 0HF
Activities: Other letting and operating of own or leased real estate
Officers: Linda Ann Brown, Secretary; Tony Blackburn [1960] Director; Linda Ann Brown [1952] Director

Hedgeco Limited
Incorporated: 24 June 1994
Net Worth: £364,454 *Total Assets:* £766,347
Registered Office: c/o Reah & McBride, Suite 2b, North Sands Business Centre, Sunderland, Tyne & Wear, SR6 0QA
Activities: Management consultancy activities other than financial management
Major Shareholder: Brian Robinson
Officers: Brian Robinson [1956] Director

Hedgehog Lab Limited
Incorporated: 9 November 2006 *Employees:* 68
Net Worth Deficit: £733,399 *Total Assets:* £1,530,549
Registered Office: Generator Studios, Trafalgar Street, Newcastle upon Tyne, NE1 2LA
Activities: Business and domestic software development
Shareholders: Sarat Pediredla; Mark Forster
Officers: Sarat Pediredla, Secretary; Raymond Henry Clarke [1973] Director/Chief Design Officer; Mark Forster [1979] Director/Chief Operating Officer; Sarat Pediredla [1981] Director/Chief Executive Officer; Michael Vassallo [1977] Investment Director

Hedingham & District Omnibuses Ltd.
Incorporated: 10 November 1965 *Employees:* 97
Net Worth: £1,379,000 *Total Assets:* £2,212,000
Registered Office: 3rd Floor, 41-51 Grey Street, Newcastle upon Tyne, NE1 6EE
Activities: Other urban, suburban or metropolitan passenger land transport (not underground, metro or similar)
Parent: Go-Ahead Holding Limited
Officers: Carolyn Ferguson, Secretary; David Allen Brown [1960] Director; Simon Patrick Butcher [1967] Finance Director; Jeremy Hugh Cooper [1967] Director; Martin Richard Dean [1963] Director; David Hector Golding [1965] Director

Hedley Hill Developments Limited
Incorporated: 24 June 2003
Net Worth: £2,283,607 *Total Assets:* £2,285,607
Registered Office: The Farmhouse, Hedley Hill Farm, Cornsay Colliery, Co Durham, DH7 9EX
Activities: Development of building projects
Parent: Vestbrown Limited
Officers: Michael Francis Hogan, Secretary/Director; Michael Francis Hogan [1944] Director

Hedley Park Developments Limited
Incorporated: 19 June 1979
Net Worth: £285,902 *Total Assets:* £2,973,521
Registered Office: Kingfisher House, St Johns Road, Meadowfield, Co Durham, DH7 8TZ
Activities: Development of building projects
Officers: Eric Clark [1947] Director; Joan Clark [1949] Director; Karen Jayne Clark [1981] Director/Marketing Manager; Steven Eric Clark [1978] Director/Technical Officer

Heerema Hartlepool Limited
Incorporated: 24 November 1976 *Employees:* 61
Net Worth: £3,422,000 *Total Assets:* £16,658,000
Registered Office: Greenland Road, Hartlepool, Cleveland, TS24 0RQ
Activities: Other specialised construction activities n.e.c.
Officers: Peter Bernardus Laurentius Huisman [1970] Director [Dutch]; Alan Francis Lloyd [1957] Director; Johannes Jacobus Van Brouwershaven [1961] Director [Dutch]

Heinzmann UK Limited
Incorporated: 14 December 1983 *Employees:* 17
Net Worth: £1,918,628 *Total Assets:* £2,179,103
Registered Office: Stanley House, Wallis Road, Skippers Lane Industrial Estate, Middlesbrough, Cleveland, TS6 6JB
Activities: Manufacture of other special-purpose machinery n.e.c.
Major Shareholder: Markus Gromer
Officers: Christopher Kenneth Jeggo, Secretary; Mike Congdon [1961] Managing Director; Herr Anton Gromer [1931] Director/Engineer [German]; Markus Gromer [1963] Director [German]

Helena Laboratories (U.K.) Limited
Incorporated: 1 March 1984 *Employees:* 139
Net Worth: £7,559,964 *Total Assets:* £12,635,029
Registered Office: Unit B, M361, Queensway South, Team Valley Trading Estate, Gateshead, Tyne & Wear, NE11 0SD
Activities: Other manufacturing n.e.c.
Major Shareholder: Tipton Lee Golias
Officers: Christopher Gibbison, Secretary; Graeme Beales [1967] Director; Dr Jane Lee-Prudhoe [1972] Director; Adam Stephenson [1979] Director

John Hellens (Contracts) Limited
Incorporated: 14 February 1973 *Employees:* 26
Net Worth: £385,953 *Total Assets:* £1,990,973
Registered Office: Teal House, 10 Teal Farm Way, Washington, Tyne & Wear, NE38 8BG
Activities: Construction of other civil engineering projects n.e.c.
Parent: Hellens Group Limited
Officers: Gavin David Cordwell-Smith, Secretary; Gavin David Cordwell-Smith [1976] Director; Kate Cordwell-Smith [1976] Director; Simon David Thorpe [1971] Commercial Director

Hellens Group Holdings Limited
Incorporated: 12 October 2006 *Employees:* 58
Net Worth: £1,424,474 *Total Assets:* £6,355,237
Registered Office: Teal House, 10 Teal Farm Way, Pattinson, Washington, Tyne & Wear, NE38 8BG
Activities: Activities of head offices
Shareholders: Gavin David Cordwell-Smith; Kate Cordwell-Smith
Officers: Gavin David Cordwell-Smith, Secretary; Gavin David Cordwell-Smith [1976] Director; Kate Cordwell-Smith [1976] Director

Hellens Group Limited
Incorporated: 19 February 2003 *Employees:* 2
Net Worth: £1,194,843 *Total Assets:* £4,090,554
Registered Office: Teal House, 10 Teal Farm Way, Washington, Tyne & Wear, NE38 8BG
Activities: Activities of head offices
Parent: Hellens Group Holdings Limited
Officers: Gavin David Cordwell-Smith, Secretary/Director; Gavin David Cordwell Smith [1976] Director; Kate Cordwell Smith [1976] Director; Simon David Thorpe [1971] Director

Hellens Investments (Teal Farm Park) LLP
Incorporated: 1 February 2008
Net Worth: £1,008,749 *Total Assets:* £1,695,384
Registered Office: 10 Teal House, Teal Farm Way, Washington, Tyne & Wear, NE38 8BG
Officers: Gavin David Cordwell Smith [1976] Member; Kate Cordwell Smith [1976] Member

Hellens Investments (Washington) LLP
Incorporated: 27 March 2008
Net Worth: £3,165,557 *Total Assets:* £7,604,237
Registered Office: Teal House, 10 Teal Farm Way, Teal Farm Park, Washington, Tyne & Wear, NE38 8BG
Officers: Gavin David Cordwell-Smith [1976] Member; Kate Cordwell-Smith [1976] Member; Malcolm David Cordwell-Smith [2011] Member; The Cordwell-Smith Trust [2016] Member

Helme Park Hall Limited
Incorporated: 27 October 2003
Net Worth: £603,048 *Total Assets:* £906,926
Registered Office: 49 St Georges Terrace, Jesmond, Newcastle upon Tyne, NE2 2SX
Activities: Hotels and similar accommodation
Major Shareholder: Dr David Peter Ratliff
Officers: Rachael Cunningham, Secretary; David Peter Ratliff [1946] Director/Dental Surgeon

Hemlington Hall Academy
Incorporated: 5 December 2013 *Employees:* 51
Net Worth: £2,987,593 *Total Assets:* £3,553,967
Registered Office: Hemlington Hall Academy, Briscoe Way, Hemlington, Middlesbrough, Cleveland, TS8 9SJ
Activities: Primary education
Officers: Kay Anne Braithwaite [1959] Director/Retired Police Officer; Emma Cook-Smith [1980] Director/Process Engineer; Karen Louise Edmenson [1972] Director/Headteacher; David William Elliott [1949] Director/Retired; Collette Harkin [1981] Director/Carer; Andrea Hurst [1974] Director/Teaching Assistant; Delyth Linacre [1974] Director/Headteacher; Karen Oliver [1969] Director/Classroom Teacher; Alexandra Roberts [1980] Director/Accountant; Peter Robertson [1961] Marketing Director; Catherine Simon [1969] Director/Teaching Assistant; Joanne Tickle [1972] Director/Team Manager; Victoria Walker [1978] Director/Housewife

P.C. Henderson Limited
Incorporated: 25 October 1974 *Employees:* 59
Net Worth: £10,242,000 *Total Assets:* £20,416,000
Registered Office: Bowburn North Industrial Estate, Durham Road, Bowburn, Co Durham, DH6 5NG
Activities: Manufacture of other fabricated metal products n.e.c.
Parent: Assa Abloy Limited
Officers: Simon Bissell, Secretary; Simon Peter Bissell [1975] Finance Director; Trevor Cossins [1965] Director/General Manager; Ronald Gurney [1965] Operations Director; Per Olof Ingemar Hansson [1964] Director/CFO Assa Abloy Entrance Systems [Swedish]; Mogens Ahrens Jensen [1958] Director/President and CEO Assa Abloy Entrance Systems [Danish]; Andrew Terence Royle [1972] Commercial Director

Fred Henderson Limited
Incorporated: 12 January 1999 *Employees:* 29
Net Worth: £1,327,015 *Total Assets:* £2,341,550
Registered Office: Langley Bridge Garage, Langley Moor, Co Durham, DH7 8JZ
Activities: Maintenance and repair of motor vehicles
Major Shareholder: Valerie Henderson
Officers: Valerie Henderson, Secretary/Administrator; David William Henderson [1975] Director; Frederick William Henderson [1945] Director/Garage Proprietor; Valerie Henderson [1946] Director/Administrator

Henderson Site Services Limited
Incorporated: 11 April 1991 *Employees:* 40
Net Worth: £574,746 *Total Assets:* £1,795,594
Registered Office: Unit 5 Banks Court, Dunne Road, Blaydon, Tyne & Wear, NE21 5NH
Activities: Manufacture of other fabricated metal products n.e.c.
Parent: Western Thermal Limited
Officers: Trevor Martin Horsley, Secretary; Shaun George Cassells [1971] Director/Engineering Manager; Trevor Martin Horsley [1955] Director/Businessman; Ankur Sureshmal Lodha [1976] Director/Businessman [Indian]; Suresh Mal Lodha [1951] Director/Businessman [Indian]

Patrick Henry Ventures Unlimited
Incorporated: 7 March 2000
Net Worth: £442,168 *Total Assets:* £980,924
Registered Office: 1a Chaloner Street, Guisborough, Cleveland, TS14 6QD
Activities: Buying and selling of own real estate
Major Shareholder: Patrick Denis Henry
Officers: Trevor Longden, Secretary/Director; Patrick Denis Henry [1957] Managing Director

Henson Property Company Ltd
Incorporated: 11 December 2006
Net Worth: £538,733 *Total Assets:* £2,080,369
Registered Office: Henson Group, Henson House, Planet Place, Stephenson Industrial Estate, Newcastle upon Tyne, NE12 6RZ
Activities: Other letting and operating of own or leased real estate
Major Shareholder: David Nathan Wilson
Officers: John Muckian, Secretary/Director; John Muckian [1971] Director; David Nathan Wilson [1973] Director

Henzell Enterprises Limited
Incorporated: 19 April 2011 *Employees:* 10
Net Worth: £368,488 *Total Assets:* £1,070,254
Registered Office: Elyhaugh Farm, Longframlington, Morpeth, Northumberland, NE65 8BE
Activities: Other business support service activities n.e.c.
Shareholders: Lee Philip Henzell; Philip George Henzell
Officers: Lee Philip Henzell [1984] Director/Contractor; Philip George Henzell [1954] Director

Hepburn Farm Limited
Incorporated: 18 October 1996
Net Worth: £2,095,348 *Total Assets:* £2,323,039
Registered Office: Hepburn Farmhouse, Chatton, Alnwick, Northumberland, NE66 4EG
Activities: Mixed farming
Major Shareholder: Edward Kingston MacAulay
Officers: Roderick Bruce MacAulay, Secretary; Edward Kingston MacAulay [1933] Director; Roderick Bruce MacAulay [1958] Director/Chartered Accountant

Hepple Engineering Services Limited
Incorporated: 28 July 1982
Net Worth: £994,752 *Total Assets:* £2,260,432
Registered Office: 3 Industry Road, Heaton, Newcastle upon Tyne, NE6 5XB
Activities: Electrical installation
Parent: Hepple NE Limited
Officers: Alan Hepple [1948] Director/Engineer; Andrew Hepple [1983] Director/Electrical Engineer; Stephen Kenneth Limerick [1963] Director/Engineer; Eric Benjamin Robson [1960] Director/Accountant

Heraeus Quartz UK Limited
Incorporated: 24 March 1998 *Employees:* 94
Net Worth: £11,949,042 *Total Assets:* £16,498,501
Registered Office: Neptune Road, Wallsend, Tyne & Wear, NE28 6DD
Activities: Manufacture and processing of other glass, including technical glassware
Officers: Simon David Gascoigne, Secretary; Marco Antonio Aloy Groffmann [1967] Director/Vice President Business Services [German]; Thomas Frederick Eyre [1966] Managing Director; Dr Michael Thomas Faatz [1974] Director/Lawyer [German]; Heinz Fabian [1961] Managing Director [German]

G.W. Herdman (Chemists) Limited
Incorporated: 11 May 1995 *Employees:* 23
Net Worth: £326,068 *Total Assets:* £802,667
Registered Office: 10 Grange Terrace, Sunderland, Tyne & Wear, SR2 7DF
Activities: General medical practice activities
Shareholders: Nigel Dale Herdman; Melanie Jane Elizabeth Jones
Officers: Nigel Dale Herdman [1964] Director; Melanie Jane Elizabeth Jones [1966] Director/Teacher

M.W. Herdman Forestry Solutions Limited
Incorporated: 1 April 2008
Net Worth: £2,783,567 *Total Assets:* £5,143,726
Registered Office: Middle Dukesfield, Hexham, Northumberland, NE46 1SQ
Activities: Logging
Shareholders: Claire Alexandria Bisset; Mark William Herdman
Officers: Mark William Herdman, Secretary/Director; Claire Alexandria Bisset [1973] Director; Mark William Herdman [1967] Director

Heritage Healthcare Limited
Incorporated: 9 July 2007
Net Worth Deficit: £62,086 *Total Assets:* £920,316
Registered Office: Heritage House, 10 Houndgate, Darlington, Co Durham, DL1 5RF
Activities: Activities of other holding companies n.e.c.
Shareholders: Glenn Michael Pickersgill; Sally Elizabeth Pickersgill
Officers: Sally Elizabeth Pickersgill, Secretary; Glenn Michael Pickersgill [1960] Director; Sally Elizabeth Pickersgill [1969] Director/Housewife

Heritage South Limited
Incorporated: 24 February 2003
Registered Office: 12 Grangeside, Darlington, Co Durham, DL3 8QJ
Activities: Construction of domestic buildings
Shareholder: Dr James Gordon
Officers: Thomas Guy Gordon, Secretary; Dr Annabelle Jane Ford [1971] Director; Barbara Gordon [1944] Director; Dr James Gordon [1944] Director; Thomas Guy Gordon [1968] Director

The Hermitage Academy Trust
Incorporated: 10 March 2011 *Employees:* 196
Net Worth: £14,191,226 *Total Assets:* £16,526,327
Registered Office: The Hermitage Academy, Waldridge Lane, Chester-le-Street, Co Durham, DH2 3AD
Activities: General secondary education
Officers: Craig Davidge, Secretary; Keith Alderslade [1958] Director; Kathryn Margaret Best [1968] Director/Nurse Practitioner NHS; John Mervyn Bowery [1965] Director; David Ian Clough [1966] Director/Police Officer; Brian David Ebbatson [1945] Director; Adrian Nicholas Elliott Harris [1958] Director/Research Manager; Leanne Marie Kenny [1983] Director/Teacher; Anthony Ronald Lewin [1964] Director/Teacher; Jonathan Jules Ridley [1980] Director/Education; Hilary Elizabeth Jane Rose [1967] Director/Teacher; Felicity Jane Smith [1975] Director/Principal; Andrea Margaret Taylor [1969] Director/Operations Manager; Simon Christopher Lindsay Westrip [1961] Director/University Lecturer

Herrenknecht International Limited
Incorporated: 29 February 1984 *Employees:* 8
Net Worth: £4,306,080 *Total Assets:* £6,764,789
Registered Office: Wearfield, Sunderland Enterprise Park, Sunderland, Tyne & Wear, SR5 2TZ
Activities: Construction of bridges and tunnels
Officers: David John Atkinson, Secretary; David John Atkinson [1968] Director/Certified Chartered Accountant; Richard John Dexter [1964] Director/Tunnel Engineer; Martin Herrenknecht [1942] Director [German]

Herrington Industrial Services Limited
Incorporated: 11 September 1987
Net Worth: £243,058 *Total Assets:* £1,368,788
Registered Office: Somerford Buildings, Norfolk Street, Sunderland, Tyne & Wear, SR1 1EE
Activities: Other business support service activities n.e.c.
Major Shareholder: Valerie Lilian Hodgson
Officers: Valerie Lilian Hidgson, Secretary; Stephen Dabbs [1953] Director/Estimator; Andrew Christopher Hodgson [1986] Director; Valerie Lilian Hodgson [1960] Director

Herrington Mews Ltd
Incorporated: 28 April 2015
Net Worth: £926,901 *Total Assets:* £2,337,867
Registered Office: Houghton House, New Road, Team Valley Trading Estate, Gateshead, Tyne & Wear, NE11 0JU
Activities: Residential nursing care facilities
Parent: Exclusive Care Group Ltd
Officers: Jennifer Pamela Houghton [1946] Director; Jill Yvette Houghton [1965] Director

Hertel (UK) Limited
Incorporated: 6 June 1975 *Employees:* 2,127
Net Worth: £46,414,000 *Total Assets:* £84,011,000
Registered Office: Cargo Fleet Offices, Middlesbrough Road, South Bank, Middlesbrough, Cleveland, TS6 6XJ
Activities: Other construction installation
Major Shareholder: Mohamed Altrad
Officers: Maureen Susan Dawson, Secretary; David Fitzsimons [1963] Managing Director; Seamus Murphy [1978] Finance Director [Irish]

Hesbro Limited
Incorporated: 11 August 2005
Net Worth: £964,280 *Total Assets:* £990,373
Registered Office: 39 Ellesmere Avenue, Walkergate, Newcastle upon Tyne, NE6 4RP
Activities: Joinery installation
Shareholders: Christopher Heseltine; Darren Heseltine
Officers: Diane Smith, Secretary; Christopher Heseltine [1965] Director; Claire Heseltine [1974] Director; Darren Heseltine [1973] Director; Diane Smith [1964] Director

Bill Hewison Bespoke Homes Limited
Incorporated: 15 December 2005 *Employees:* 4
Net Worth: £574,628 *Total Assets:* £753,793
Registered Office: The Old Barn, Robsheugh, Milbourne, Northumberland, NE20 0JQ
Activities: Construction of domestic buildings
Officers: Maxine Louise Hewison, Secretary/Administrator; Maxine Louise Hewison [1967] Director/Administrator; William Douglas Hewison [1955] Director/Engineer

Hewitson Group Ltd
Incorporated: 18 February 2016 *Employees:* 86
Net Worth: £4,804,413 *Total Assets:* £13,091,361
Registered Office: 43 Coniscliffe Road, Darlington, Co Durham, DL3 7EH
Activities: Construction of other civil engineering projects n.e.c.
Major Shareholder: Michael Edward Hewitson
Officers: Henry Michael Hewitson [1993] Director; Jonathan Edward Hewitson [1987] Director; Michael Edward Hewitson [1960] Director; Owen Scott Hewitson [1990] Director

Hewitson Haulage Ltd
Incorporated: 3 June 2013 *Employees:* 14
Net Worth: £339,789 *Total Assets:* £1,468,781
Registered Office: 43 Coniscliffe Road, Darlington, Co Durham, DL3 7EH
Activities: Freight transport by road
Parent: Hewitson Group Ltd
Officers: Phil Cummings [1973] Director; Jonathan Edward Hewitson [1987] Director; Michael Edward Hewitson [1960] Director

Hewitson Limited
Incorporated: 2 November 2004 *Employees:* 41
Net Worth: £1,014,349 *Total Assets:* £2,933,545
Registered Office: 43 Coniscliffe Road, Darlington, Co Durham, DL3 7EH
Activities: Other specialised construction activities n.e.c.
Parent: Hewitson Group Ltd
Officers: Brian Gibson [1971] Director; Henry Michael Hewitson [1993] Director; Michael Edward Hewitson [1960] Director

Hewitson Plant Hire Limited
Incorporated: 26 January 2010 *Employees:* 14
Net Worth: £1,664,502 *Total Assets:* £7,240,052
Registered Office: 43 Coniscliffe Road, Darlington, Co Durham, DL3 7EH
Activities: Renting and leasing of construction and civil engineering machinery and equipment
Parent: Hewitson Group Ltd
Officers: Michael Edward Hewitson [1960] Director/Farmer; Owen Scott Hewitson [1990] Director; David Glynn Jones [1969] Director

K. Hewitt and Co. Limited
Incorporated: 2 March 1983 *Employees:* 33
Net Worth: £5,101,001 *Total Assets:* £6,139,007
Registered Office: Clyde House, Gibbon Street, Bishop Auckland, Co Durham, DL14 7DL
Activities: Plumbing, heat and air-conditioning installation
Parent: K Hewitt Holdings Limited
Officers: Raymond Kevin Dobson [1987] Director; David Wade [1982] Director

J. Hewitt Crane Hire Limited
Incorporated: 19 April 1982
Registered Office: Swan House, Westpoint Road, Teesdale Business Park, Stockton on Tees, Cleveland, TS17 6BP
Activities: Other specialised construction activities n.e.c.
Shareholders: John Hewitt; Norma Hewitt
Officers: Norma Hewitt, Secretary; John Anthony Hewitt [1947] Director/Crane Driver; Norma Hewitt [1944] Director/Office Manageress

K Hewitt Holdings Limited
Incorporated: 8 July 2015
Net Worth: £31 *Total Assets:* £6,199,472
Registered Office: Clyde House, Gibbon Street, Bishop Auckland, Co Durham, DL14 7DL
Activities: Plumbing, heat and air-conditioning installation
Shareholder: David Wade
Officers: Raymond Kevin Dobson [1987] Director; David Wade [1982] Director

Hexham and Tynedale Community Trust
Incorporated: 28 January 2008 *Employees:* 13
Net Worth: £1,070,136 *Total Assets:* £1,071,886
Registered Office: Hexham Community Centre, Gilesgate, Hexham, Northumberland, NE46 3NP
Activities: Activities of other membership organisations n.e.c.
Officers: Jacqueline Judith Hogg, Secretary; Leslie Robert Hare [1959] Director/Business Consultant; Keda Norman [1964] Director/Project Co-ordinator; Ann Reed [1942] Director/Guest House Proprietor; Paul Tait [1958] Director/Retired

Hexham Auction Mart Company,Limited
Incorporated: 23 March 1901 *Employees:* 105
Net Worth: £15,140,375 *Total Assets:* £15,657,445
Registered Office: Hexham Auction Mart, Mart Offices, Tyne Green, Hexham, Northumberland, NE46 3SG
Activities: Support activities for animal production (other than farm animal boarding)
Officers: Brian Rogerson, Secretary; Robert Iveson Addison [1963] Director/Auctioneer; John Atkinson [1945] Director/Farmer; John Longlands Dodd [1941] Director/Farmer; Richard Henry Iveson [1962] Director/Auctioneer; James Brewis Walton [1948] Director/Farmer; Michael Hugh Walton [1952] Director/Farmer; Peter Walton [1952] Director/Farmer; William Walton Woodman [1958] Director/Farmer

HGC Properties Limited
Incorporated: 16 March 2001
Net Worth: £906,090 *Total Assets:* £1,130,062
Registered Office: Rock Villa, Prospect Place, Barnard Castle, Co Durham, DL12 8HQ
Activities: Other accommodation
Shareholders: Stephen John Charnock; Stephen John Green; David William Harper
Officers: David William Harper, Secretary/Manager; Stephen John Charnock [1961] Director; Stephen John Green [1960] Director; David William Harper [1964] Director/Manager

HH Community Care Limited
Incorporated: 3 April 2008 *Employees:* 623
Net Worth: £804,178 *Total Assets:* £1,699,197
Registered Office: St Matthews House, Haugh Lane Industrial Estate, Hexham, Northumberland, NE46 3PU
Activities: Other social work activities without accommodation n.e.c.
Shareholders: Melna Rae Martin; Thomas Joseph Beattie
Officers: Simon Martin, Secretary/Director; Ruth Mary Beattie [1946] Director; Thomas Joseph Beattie [1972] Director; David Michael Harrison [1969] Managing Director; Melna Rae Martin [1944] Director; Simon Martin [1968] Director

M.J. Hickey Plant Hire & Contracts Limited
Incorporated: 8 September 2003 *Employees:* 103
Net Worth: £3,614,194 *Total Assets:* £11,347,951
Registered Office: Linton Industrial Estate, Linton, Morpeth, Northumberland, NE61 5SD
Activities: Site preparation
Shareholders: Thomas Anthony Hickey; Jacqueline Hickey
Officers: Jacqueline Hickey, Secretary; Thomas Anthony Hickey [1964] Director/Contractor

High Crane Limited
Incorporated: 4 December 1996 *Employees:* 3
Net Worth: £8,422,051 *Total Assets:* £8,858,034
Registered Office: High Crane Lodge, Hamsterley, Bishop Auckland, Co Durham, DL13 3QS
Activities: Mixed farming
Major Shareholder: Peter Murray
Officers: Jane Hilton, Secretary; Jane Hilton [1964] Director/Education Officer; Peter Murray [1958] Managing Director

High Force Research Limited
Incorporated: 27 April 1988 *Employees:* 31
Net Worth: £3,385,197 *Total Assets:* £3,929,128
Registered Office: Bowburn North Industrial Estate, Bowburn, Co Durham, DH6 5PF
Activities: Manufacture of other chemical products n.e.c.
Shareholders: Dr Roy Harry Valentine; Stuart John Penny
Officers: Stuart John Penny [1960] Director/Chemist; Dr Roy Harry Valentine [1949] Director/Chemist

High Hedley Hope Farm Limited
Incorporated: 25 January 2013 *Employees:* 5
Net Worth Deficit: £283,056 *Total Assets:* £3,806,399
Registered Office: High Hedley Hope Farm, Tow Law, Co Durham, DL13 4PR
Activities: Raising of dairy cattle
Shareholders: Cyrus Armstrong; William James Drennan
Officers: Stanley Thomson, Secretary; Cyrus Armstrong [1964] Managing Director

High Hedley Hope Wind Limited
Incorporated: 28 September 2000
Net Worth: £19,426,000 *Total Assets:* £23,225,000
Registered Office: Alexander House, 1 Mandarin Road, Rainton Bridge Business Park, Houghton-le-Spring, Co Durham, DH4 5RA
Activities: Production of electricity
Parent: EDF Energy Renewables Holdings Limited
Officers: Susan Elizabeth Lind, Secretary; Matthieu Thomas Hue [1975] Director [French]; Hassaan Majid [1968] Director

High Level Contracts Limited
Incorporated: 17 January 2008 *Employees:* 6
Net Worth: £742,348 *Total Assets:* £1,512,674
Registered Office: Unit 32 Atley Business Park, Atley Way, Cramlington, Northumberland, NE23 1WP
Activities: Construction of commercial buildings
Officers: Lindsay Anne Walker, Secretary; Derren Neil Farrell [1971] Director; Christopher William Jeavans [1973] Director; Helen Susannah Jeavans [1973] Director; Lindsay Anne Walker [1978] Director

High Sixes Projects Limited
Incorporated: 30 April 2012
Net Worth: £2,456 *Total Assets:* £986,704
Registered Office: 7 Holyrood Avenue, Darlington, Co Durham, DL3 8AZ
Activities: Management consultancy activities other than financial management
Officers: George Andrew Fotheringham [1957] Director/Chartered Accountant

High Street Commercial Finance Limited
Incorporated: 9 November 2011 *Employees:* 4
Net Worth: £891,704 *Total Assets:* £22,569,764
Registered Office: Cuthbert House, All Saints Business Centre, Newcastle upon Tyne, NE1 2ET
Activities: Other credit granting n.e.c.
Parent: High Street GRP Limited
Officers: Phillip Lennox Brumwell [1975] Director; Gary Ronald Forrest [1968] Director

The High Street GRP Contact Centre Limited
Incorporated: 24 April 2013
Registered Office: 2nd Floor, Cuthbert House, All Saints Business Centre, Newcastle upon Tyne, NE1 2ET
Activities: Financial intermediation not elsewhere classified
Parent: High Street Commercial Finance Limited
Officers: Colin Roberts Myers [1969] Director

High Street GRP Limited
Incorporated: 2 November 2011 *Employees:* 10
Net Worth: £26,042,738 *Total Assets:* £27,329,660
Registered Office: Cuthbert House, All Saints Business Centre, Newcastle upon Tyne, NE1 2ET
Activities: Development of building projects
Major Shareholder: Gary Ronald Forrest
Officers: Gary Forrest [1968] Director

High Warden Farm Limited
Incorporated: 18 February 1997
Net Worth: £2,097,271 *Total Assets:* £2,251,914
Registered Office: Estate Office, Stable House, High Warden, Hexham, Northumberland, NE46 4SR
Activities: Mixed farming
Major Shareholder: Philip Hugh Straker
Officers: Charlotte Jane Straker, Secretary; Charlotte Jane Straker [1957] Director; Philip Hugh Straker [1949] Director/Chartered Accountant

Higham Ventures Limited
Incorporated: 22 August 2002
Net Worth: £926,894 *Total Assets:* £1,069,917
Registered Office: 8 Gowan Terrace, Newcastle upon Tyne, NE2 2PS
Activities: Buying and selling of own real estate
Shareholder: William Thompson
Officers: William Thompson, Secretary/Director; William Thompson [1970] Director

Highbury Jewellers Limited
Incorporated: 30 October 2001 *Employees:* 1
Net Worth: £1,479,009 *Total Assets:* £1,661,406
Registered Office: Borough Hall, Wellway, Morpeth, Northumberland, NE61 1BN
Activities: Non-specialised wholesale trade
Officers: Gail Alison Preston, Secretary; Gail Preston [1962] Director/Manager; Mitchell Rex Preston [1961] Director/Jeweller

Higher Trevartha Solar Park Limited
Incorporated: 12 July 2012
Net Worth: £473,743 *Total Assets:* £3,329,057
Registered Office: 4 Ellerbeck Way, Stokesley Business Park, Stokesley, Middlesbrough, Cleveland, TS9 5JZ
Activities: Production of electricity
Parent: Carlton Power Limited
Officers: Jayne Margaret Hodgson, Secretary; Michael Fred Shaw Benson [1964] Director/Engineer; Keith Clarke [1960] Director/Engineer; Jayne Margaret Hodgson [1963] Director/Company Secretary; Alan Mark Pankhurst [1965] Director/Engineering Manager; David John Philpot [1961] Director/Solicitor; Matthew Ian Shields [1944] Director/Engineer

Highway Construction Services Limited
Incorporated: 5 October 2000
Registered Office: 2 Wetherby Close, Portrack Interchange Business Park, Stockton on Tees, Cleveland, TS18 2SL
Activities: Construction of other civil engineering projects n.e.c.
Major Shareholder: Brian Robinson
Officers: Kathleen Mary Robinson, Secretary; Stephen James McNeilly [1963] Director/Commercial Manager; Brian Robinson [1954] Director/Chartered Surveyor; Kathleen Mary Robinson [1954] Director/Office Manager

Hilco Europe
Incorporated: 17 March 1981 *Employees:* 109
Net Worth: £1,403,568 *Total Assets:* £30,800,008
Registered Office: Brunt Acres Road, Industrial Estate, Hawes, N Yorks, DL8 3UZ
Activities: Non-specialised wholesale trade
Officers: Melanie Peacock, Secretary; Ross Brownlee [1973] Director/Chief Executive Officer; John Lemay [1965] Director/Investor [American]; Jonathan Pressnell [1982] Director/Principal of Blue Point Capital Partners [American]; Dennis Wu [1969] Director/Investor [Chinese]

Albert Hill Commercials Limited
Incorporated: 28 January 2000 *Employees:* 7
Net Worth: £7,858,439 *Total Assets:* £9,236,276
Registered Office: Riverside Industrial Estate, Dodsworth Street, Darlington, Co Durham, DL1 2NG
Activities: Sale of other motor vehicles
Major Shareholder: Peter William Foster
Officers: Diane Roberts, Secretary; Peter William Foster [1971] Director/Vehicle Trader

The Hill Cross Organisation Limited
Incorporated: 14 February 2000 *Employees:* 65
Net Worth: £483,833 *Total Assets:* £1,902,791
Registered Office: Cramble Cross, North Cowton, Northallerton, N Yorks, DL7 0HL
Activities: Wholesale of household goods (other than musical instruments) n.e.c
Officers: Jennifer Barker, Secretary; Jennifer Kitty Barker [1974] Director; Richard Townson Barker [1970] Director

Hill Giftware Limited
Incorporated: 12 May 1999 *Employees:* 129
Net Worth: £2,085,612 *Total Assets:* £4,317,376
Registered Office: Hill House, Oak Tree, Burneston, Bedale, N Yorks, DL8 2JW
Activities: Wholesale of household goods (other than musical instruments) n.e.c
Parent: Hill House Group Ltd
Officers: Benjamin James Hawkins [1987] Director; Nicholas Graham Hill [1972] Director; Paul Andrew Nel [1984] Director; Julian Earle Potter [1975] Director

H.R. Hill Property Co. Limited
Incorporated: 8 June 1959 *Employees:* 3
Net Worth: £1,357,577 *Total Assets:* £1,761,337
Registered Office: c/o M Palmer, Whorlton Cross, Faceby, Middlesbrough, Cleveland, TS9 7BN
Activities: Other letting and operating of own or leased real estate
Officers: Margaret Palmer, Secretary; David Hill [1948] Director; Margaret Palmer [1945] Director; Elizabeth Stephens [1956] Director/Chartered Accountant

W.H.Hillerby & Sons Limited
Incorporated: 21 February 1956
Net Worth: £944,937 *Total Assets:* £1,079,306
Registered Office: 87 Station Road, Ashington, Northumberland, NE63 8RS
Activities: Roofing activities
Major Shareholder: Paul Hillerby
Officers: Janice Hillerby, Secretary; Paul Hillerby [1955] Director/Slater

Hindhaugh Homes Limited
Incorporated: 2 July 2003 *Employees:* 2
Net Worth: £837,282 *Total Assets:* £1,875,675
Registered Office: Newton Hall, Newton on the Moor, Morpeth, Northumberland, NE65 9JU
Activities: Construction of domestic buildings
Shareholders: Paul Hindhaugh; Susan Anne Hindhaugh
Officers: Susan Anne Hindhaugh, Secretary; Paul Hindhaugh [1976] Director; Susan Anne Hindhaugh [1978] Director

Hindley Circuits Limited
Incorporated: 11 November 2016 *Employees:* 32
Net Worth: £671,881 *Total Assets:* £1,383,132
Registered Office: Unit 2b Admiral Business Park, Nelson Park West, Cramlington, Northumberland, NE23 1WG
Activities: Manufacture of electronic components
Major Shareholder: Richard Whitehead
Officers: Andrew Christopher Lapping [1963] Director; Sarah-Jane Moffat [1977] Director/Chartered Accountant; Christopher Roy Pennison [1967] Operations Director; Richard Whitehead [1965] Director

Hirst (Farmers) Limited
Incorporated: 8 April 1999 *Employees:* 3
Net Worth: £770,492 *Total Assets:* £968,216
Registered Office: Trimdon House Farm, Fishburn, Stockton on Tees, Cleveland, TS21 4BA
Activities: Growing of cereals (except rice), leguminous crops and oil seeds
Shareholder: Gordon Hirst
Officers: Kathleen Hirst, Secretary/Housewife; Andrew John Hirst [1964] Director/Farmer; Kathleen Hirst [1937] Director/Housewife

Historic Property Restoration Limited
Incorporated: 21 September 1995 *Employees:* 57
Net Worth: £983,281 *Total Assets:* £1,732,469
Registered Office: Sandgate Hall, Albion Road, North Shields, Tyne & Wear, NE30 2RQ
Activities: Other specialised construction activities n.e.c.
Shareholders: John Derek Gibson; Michael Moody
Officers: Joanne Elizabeth Regan, Secretary; Paul Barrett [1965] Contracts Director; John Derek Gibson [1961] Managing Director; Peter William Hixon [1969] Director; Michael Moody [1965] Director/Stonemason; Joanne Elizabeth Regan [1967] Director/Electrical Engineer; Stephen Gary Upton [1968] Director/Quantity Surveyor

Hivehome Ltd
Incorporated: 26 February 2003
Net Worth: £233,837 *Total Assets:* £859,590
Registered Office: 15 Walker Terrace, Gateshead, Tyne & Wear, NE8 1EB
Activities: Dormant company
Officers: Joseph Schleider, Secretary; David Schleider [1959] Director/Estate Agent

HLA Services Limited
Incorporated: 12 February 2003 *Employees:* 109
Net Worth: £900,761 *Total Assets:* £2,765,412
Registered Office: 1 Boldon Court, Burford Way, Boldon Colliery, Co Durham, NE35 9PY
Activities: Other specialised construction activities n.e.c.
Shareholders: Neil Henry; Wendy Hodgson; Kay Smith; Paul Smith
Officers: Paul Smith, Secretary; Neil Henry [1972] Director/Engineer; Wendy Hodgson [1971] Director/Sales and Marketing Manager; Kay Smith [1972] Director/Sales and Marketing Manager; Paul Smith [1973] Director/Engineer

HLP (Holdings) Limited
Incorporated: 22 June 2005
Net Worth: £269,684 *Total Assets:* £1,683,914
Registered Office: 4 Old Elvet, Durham, DH1 3HL
Activities: Activities of other holding companies n.e.c.
Shareholders: Jonathan Francis Yates; Neil Turner; David John Pickersgill
Officers: David John Pickersgill [1971] Director/Building Technologist; Neil Turner [1966] Director/Architect; Jonathan Francis Yates [1965] Director/Architect

HMC Finance Limited
Incorporated: 7 June 2005
Net Worth: £1,651,145 *Total Assets:* £2,892,060
Registered Office: Keel Row, 12 The Watermark, Gateshead, Tyne & Wear, NE11 9SZ
Activities: Renting and leasing of other machinery, equipment and tangible goods n.e.c.
Parent: HMC Group Ltd
Officers: John Nigel Dawson [1969] Director; Josephine Helen McArdle [1948] Director; Mark Henry McArdle [1968] Managing Director

HMC Group Ltd
Incorporated: 5 March 2004 *Employees:* 1,306
Net Worth: £13,247,500 *Total Assets:* £22,033,168
Registered Office: Keel Row 12, The Watermark, Gateshead, Tyne & Wear, NE11 9SZ
Activities: Buying and selling of own real estate
Major Shareholder: Michael Matthew Joseph McArdle
Officers: John Nigel Dawson [1969] Director; Josephine Helen McArdle [1948] Director/Chief Executive Officer; Mark Henry McArdle [1968] Managing Director; Michael Matthew Joseph McArdle [1948] Director

HMC Land Limited
Incorporated: 21 December 2005
Net Worth: £2,823,859 *Total Assets:* £3,305,474
Registered Office: Unit 12 Keel Row, The Watermark, Metro Centre, Gateshead, Tyne & Wear, NE11 9SZ
Activities: Development of building projects
Parent: HMC Group Ltd
Officers: John Nigel Dawson [1969] Director; Josephine Helen McArdle [1948] Director; Mark Henry McArdle [1968] Managing Director

HMC Ventures Limited
Incorporated: 20 April 2015
Net Worth Deficit: £58,164 *Total Assets:* £2,557,823
Registered Office: Keel Row 12, The Watermark, Gateshead, Tyne & Wear, NE11 9SZ
Activities: Other letting and operating of own or leased real estate
Parent: HMC Group Ltd
Officers: John Nigel Dawson [1969] Director; Josephine Helen McArdle [1948] Director; Mark Henry McArdle [1968] Director; Matthew Michael Joseph McArdle [1948] Director

HMH Civils Limited
Incorporated: 3 December 2013 *Employees:* 115
Net Worth: £6,113,452 *Total Assets:* £10,517,632
Registered Office: The Rakish, Ayton Road, Stokesley, Middlesbrough, Cleveland, TS9 5JN
Activities: Construction of domestic buildings
Shareholders: John Patrick Hughes; Michael Andrew Hammond
Officers: Michael Andrew Hammond [1969] Director/Civil Engineer; John Patrick Hughes [1972] Director; Gerard May [1974] Director/Property Developer

HMY UK Innovation in Retail Ltd
Incorporated: 19 May 2006 *Employees:* 150
Net Worth Deficit: £5,939,000 *Total Assets:* £8,772,000
Registered Office: Unit 13 Hobson Industrial Estate, Burnopfield, Co Durham, NE16 6EA
Activities: Manufacture of other fabricated metal products n.e.c.
Parent: HMY SAS
Officers: Ian Martin Smith, Secretary; Stuart Archer Geekie [1966] Managing Director; Ignacio Gabriel Marin Villamayor [1962] Director/Chairman [Spanish]; Gerard Renault [1952] Director/General Manager [French]

HNM Investments Limited
Incorporated: 19 October 1929
Net Worth: £3,267,509 *Total Assets:* £3,903,143
Registered Office: Bugatti House, Norham Road, North Shields, Tyne & Wear, NE29 7HA
Activities: Other letting and operating of own or leased real estate
Parent: HNMX Holdings Ltd
Officers: Gwenyth Lillian Snowball, Secretary; Lisa Douglas [1968] Director; Gwenyth Lillian Snowball [1942] Director; Sydney Snowball [1943] Director

W. Hodgson (Hartlepool) Limited
Incorporated: 18 November 1982 *Employees:* 85
Net Worth: £2,482,387 *Total Assets:* £3,941,101
Registered Office: Hodgson Fish, Fish Quay, Southgate, Hartlepool, Cleveland, TS24 0JH
Activities: Wholesale of other food, including fish, crustaceans and molluscs
Parent: Hodgson Fish Holdings Limited
Officers: Jill Hodgson, Secretary; Jill Hodgson [1979] Director/Fish Merchant; Peter William Hodgson [1982] Director/Fish Merchant; Ian Kennedy [1965] Director/Business Manager

Hodgson Fish Holdings Limited
Incorporated: 7 March 2016 *Employees:* 85
Net Worth: £3,550,521 *Total Assets:* £5,095,579
Registered Office: Hodgson Fish, Fish Quay, Southgate, Hartlepool, Cleveland, TS24 0JH
Activities: Wholesale of other food, including fish, crustaceans and molluscs
Shareholders: Peter William Hodgson; Jill Hodgson Wood
Officers: Nicola Hodgson [1980] Director/Fish Merchant; Peter William Hodgson [1982] Director; Jill Hodgson Wood [1979] Director; Andrew Wood [1975] Director

Hodgson Newcastle Limited
Incorporated: 23 January 1992 *Employees:* 173
Net Worth: £17,492,452 *Total Assets:* £24,917,548
Registered Office: Pentagon House, Bittern Close, The Silverlink, Wallsend, Tyne & Wear, NE28 9ND
Activities: Sale of new cars and light motor vehicles
Officers: Elizabeth Spowart Hodgson, Secretary; Holly Rebecca Hodgson [1993] Director; Joel James Hodgson [1992] Director; Lindsay Ann Hodgson [1957] Director/Motor Dealer; Stephen Hodgson [1958] Director/Motor Dealer

Hodgson Sayers Limited
Incorporated: 23 June 1992 *Employees:* 104
Net Worth: £3,283,328 *Total Assets:* £7,589,360
Registered Office: Unit 15 Tanfield Lea (North), Industrial Estate, Tanfield Lea, Stanley, Co Durham, DH9 9NX
Activities: Development of building projects
Major Shareholder: William Hodgson
Officers: Joyce Wardhaugh, Secretary; John Thomas Sayers [1967] Managing Director; Joyce Wardhaugh [1950] Secretary/Director

Hogarth Coachworks Limited
Incorporated: 23 December 1993 *Employees:* 41
Net Worth: £599,941 *Total Assets:* £1,055,475
Registered Office: Unit 10 Durham Road Trading Estate, Birtley, Co Durham, DH3 2BQ
Activities: Repair and maintenance of other transport equipment n.e.c.
Parent: S Hogarth Holdings Limited
Officers: Karen Howard, Secretary; Stephen Hogarth [1960] Director/Engineer

S Hogarth Holdings Limited
Incorporated: 7 July 2009
Net Worth: £1,094,659 *Total Assets:* £1,960,462
Registered Office: Unit 10 Durham Road Trading Estate, Durham Road, Birtley, Co Durham, DH3 2BQ
Activities: Activities of head offices
Officers: Stephen Hogarth [1960] Director

Murray Hogg Limited
Incorporated: 6 February 1974 *Employees:* 127
Net Worth: £2,281,017 *Total Assets:* £5,264,967
Registered Office: Sandy Lane, North Gosforth, Newcastle upon Tyne, NE3 5HE
Activities: Freight transport by road
Officers: Moira Ann Hogg, Secretary; Colin James Hogg [1966] Director; David Hogg [1971] Director; James Murray Hogg [1960] Director; Dr Jennifer Murray Hogg [1963] Director/Doctor; John Murray Hogg [1934] Director/Haulier; Paul Hogg [1973] Director; Deborah Anne Scott [1962] Director; Alyson Mary Summerhill [1959] Director/Secretary; Joanne Topping [1969] Director/Banqueting Coordinator

Holborn Regeneration LLP
Incorporated: 12 February 2008
Registered Office: Esh House, Bowburn North Industrial Estate, Bowburn, Co Durham, DH6 5PF

Holiday at Home Limited
Incorporated: 30 January 2008 *Employees:* 40
Net Worth: £467,423 *Total Assets:* £2,022,078
Registered Office: Brompton Lakes, Easby, Richmond, N Yorks, DL10 7EJ
Activities: Other holiday and other collective accommodation
Shareholders: Roy Alan Stephenson; William Guy Stephenson
Officers: Jane Ascroft, Secretary; Roy Alan Stephenson [1955] Director; William Guy Stephenson [1992] Director

Holiday Travel & Booking Agency Limited
Incorporated: 25 September 1974
Registered Office: 25 Vine Place, Sunderland, Tyne & Wear, SR1 3NA
Activities: Travel agency activities
Parent: Hays Travel Limited
Officers: Marta Fernandez Varona [1966] Financial Director [Spanish]; Jonathan Hays [1978] Director/Legal Adviser

J.R. Holland (Food Services) Limited
Incorporated: 9 March 1995 *Employees:* 80
Net Worth: £2,075,815 *Total Assets:* £3,346,448
Registered Office: 245 Dukesway, Team Valley Trading Estate, Gateshead, Tyne & Wear, NE11 0PZ
Activities: Other food services
Officers: Hazel Marie Fletcher, Secretary/Accountant; Hazel Marie Fletcher [1967] Director/Accountant; John Holland [1960] Director/Fresh Produce Broker; Dennis Christopher Hutchinson [1958] Managing Director

J R Holland Produce Limited Liability Partnership
Incorporated: 20 September 2007 *Employees:* 34
Net Worth: £1,266,379 *Total Assets:* £4,489,193
Registered Office: 78-84 North East Wholesale Fruit & Vegetable Market, Team Valley Trading Estate, Gateshead, Tyne & Wear, NE11 0RF
Officers: John Holland [1960] Member

Holme Dodsworth (Est.1879) Limited
Incorporated: 21 July 1972
Net Worth: £1,095,552 *Total Assets:* £1,200,652
Registered Office: 59-69 Heaton Park Road, Newcastle upon Tyne, NE6 1SQ
Activities: Wholesale of metals and metal ores
Officers: Jill Wendy Mutch, Secretary; Fiona Joan Mutch [1965] Director

Holme Dodsworth (Non-Ferrous) Limited
Incorporated: 19 January 1972
Net Worth: £1,137,053 *Total Assets:* £1,176,722
Registered Office: 59-69 Heaton Park Road, Newcastle upon Tyne, NE6 1SQ
Activities: Wholesale of metals and metal ores
Officers: David George Mutch, Secretary; David George Mutch [1960] Director; Fiona Joan Mutch [1965] Director; Joan Mutch [1935] Director/Company Secretary

Holme Dodsworth (Rock Salt) Limited
Incorporated: 4 November 1977
Net Worth: £863,811 *Total Assets:* £916,086
Registered Office: 59-69 Heaton Park Road, Newcastle upon Tyne, NE6 1SQ
Activities: Non-specialised wholesale trade
Officers: David George Mutch, Secretary; David George Mutch [1960] Director; Joan Mutch [1935] Director/Company Secretary; Kevin Grant Mutch [1963] Director

Holme Dodsworth Metals Limited
Incorporated: 25 March 1965 *Employees:* 107
Net Worth: £29,963,864 *Total Assets:* £51,144,056
Registered Office: 59-69 Heaton Park Road, Newcastle upon Tyne, NE6 1SQ
Activities: Wholesale of metals and metal ores
Officers: David George Mutch, Secretary; David George Mutch [1960] Director; Fiona Joan Mutch [1965] Director

Holme Farm Residential Village Limited
Incorporated: 30 July 2010 *Employees:* 15
Net Worth: £4,363,778 *Total Assets:* £8,768,711
Registered Office: 1 Fox Street, Sunderland Road, Gateshead, Tyne & Wear, NE10 0BD
Activities: Other residential care activities n.e.c.
Major Shareholder: Gary Owen Lewis
Officers: Joanne Lynn Lewis, Secretary; Joanne Lynn Lewis [1974] Director

Holmedale Valley Limited
Incorporated: 14 September 2011 *Employees:* 18
Net Worth: £8,256,595 *Total Assets:* £10,464,988
Registered Office: Pondale Farm, Gilling West, Richmond, N Yorks, DL10 5LB
Activities: Mixed farming
Shareholders: Paul Anthony Hall Westgarth; Timothy Peter Westgarth
Officers: Paul Anthony Hall Westgarth [1967] Director/Farmer; Timothy Peter Westgarth [1973] Director/Farmer

Holmesterne Farm Co. Limited
Incorporated: 25 September 1986 *Employees:* 150
Net Worth: £1,823,922 *Total Assets:* £6,225,867
Registered Office: Gatherley Road Industrial Estate, Brompton on Swale, Richmond, N Yorks, DL10 7JQ
Activities: Processing and preserving of meat
Shareholders: Keith Philip Tindell; Martin Lionel Sterne
Officers: Richard Pridmore, Secretary; Martin Lionel Sterne [1947] Director; Keith Philip Tindell [1956] Director/Butcher

Holmfirth Finance Limited
Incorporated: 20 December 1962
Net Worth: £2,248,032 *Total Assets:* £2,371,619
Registered Office: 27-28 Frederick Street, Sunderland, Tyne & Wear, SR1 1LZ
Activities: Other business support service activities n.e.c.
Shareholders: John Malcolm Rawse; Roger Craig Martin; Adrian Sinclair Martin
Officers: Roger Craig Martin, Secretary; Adrian Sinclair Martin [1964] Director; Roger Craig Martin [1969] Director

Holmwood Commercial Properties Limited
Incorporated: 28 January 1987
Net Worth: £4,552,757 *Total Assets:* £4,783,114
Registered Office: Third Floor, Citygate, St James' Boulevard, Newcastle upon Tyne, NE1 4JE
Activities: Development of building projects
Major Shareholder: Richard Baker
Officers: Ruth Baker, Secretary; Richard Baker [1959] Director

The Holy Family Education Trust
Incorporated: 27 March 2014 *Employees:* 191
Net Worth: £6,734,000 *Total Assets:* £8,760,000
Registered Office: The English Martyrs School and Sixth Form College, Catcote Road, Hartlepool, Cleveland, TS25 4HA
Activities: General secondary education
Officers: Sarah Jane Tait, Secretary; Patricia Anne Connor [1963] Director/Civil Servant; Jane Dolphin [1971] Director/Headmistress; Michael James Griffiths [1953] Director/Priest; Stephen John Hammond [1966] Director/Headmaster; Susan Ann Harrison [1961] Director; David Michael Jeffery [1967] Director/Commercial Manager; Gillian Proudlock [1968] Director; John Relton [1963] Director/Solicitor

Holy Trinity Church of England Academy (South Shields) Trust
Incorporated: 23 June 2014 *Employees:* 32
Net Worth: £1,714,000 *Total Assets:* £2,093,000
Registered Office: Holy Trinity Church of England Academy (South Shields), Brockley Avenue, South Shields, Tyne & Wear, NE34 6QZ
Activities: Primary education
Officers: Christine Henderson, Secretary; Julie Allan [1971] Director/Teaching Assistant; Karen Allan [1975] Director; Elizabeth Clayton [1977] Director; Andrea Gedling [1947] Director; Tina Lorraine Murphy [1960] Director; David John Pickersgill [1971] Director; Richard Swan [1981] Director/Teacher; Rev Mervyn Patrick Thompson [1959] Director

Holystone Civil Engineering Limited
Incorporated: 24 February 1970 *Employees:* 30
Net Worth: £700,536 *Total Assets:* £2,464,135
Registered Office: Unit 6 Franklin Industrial Park, Patterson Street, Blaydon Haugh, Blaydon on Tyne, Tyne & Wear, NE21 5TL
Activities: Construction of roads and motorways
Major Shareholder: Kieron Thomas Geoghegan
Officers: Gerard Geoghegan [1951] Director/Contractor; Kieron Thomas Geoghegan [1968] Director/Contractor; Steven Geoghegan [1986] Director/Contracts Manager; Ryan Peddie [1981] Finance Director; Ian Andrew Robinson [1961] Director/Management Consultant

Holywell Farms Ltd
Incorporated: 28 May 2010 *Employees:* 6
Net Worth: £78,841 *Total Assets:* £1,826,581
Registered Office: Church Farm, East Holywell, Newcastle upon Tyne, NE27 0JW
Activities: Growing of cereals (except rice), leguminous crops and oil seeds
Shareholders: Philip Gawen Watson; Linda Watson
Officers: Linda Watson [1959] Director; Philip Gawen Watson [1959] Director/Farmer

The Home & Capital Trust Group Limited
Incorporated: 9 March 2004
Net Worth: £5,295,000 *Total Assets:* £7,366,000
Registered Office: Cross House, Westgate Road, Newcastle upon Tyne, NE1 4XX
Activities: Activities of head offices
Parent: Sovereign Reversions Holdings Limited
Officers: Paul Trevor Barber [1967] Director/Chief Executive; Antony Lewis Pierce [1976] Finance Director

Home & Capital Trust Limited
Incorporated: 17 February 1987
Net Worth: £6,789,000 *Total Assets:* £6,837,000
Registered Office: Cross House, Westgate Road, Newcastle upon Tyne, NE1 4XX
Activities: Other business support service activities n.e.c.
Parent: The Home & Capital Trust Group Ltd
Officers: Paul Trevor Barber [1967] Director/Chief Executive; Ashish Kashyap [1979] Investment Director; Antony Lewis Pierce [1976] Finance Director

Home and Leisure International Limited
Incorporated: 24 June 1988 *Employees:* 242
Net Worth: £12,394,771 *Total Assets:* £16,628,625
Registered Office: 63 Saville Street, North Shields, Tyne & Wear, NE30 1AY
Activities: Agents specialised in the sale of other particular products
Major Shareholder: Colin Thomas
Officers: Melanie Thomas, Secretary/Director; Colin Thomas [1952] Director; Melanie Thomas [1976] Director; Patricia Thomas [1954] Director

Home Group Developments Limited
Incorporated: 12 February 2003
Net Worth: £47,188,000 *Total Assets:* £78,655,000
Registered Office: 2 Gosforth Park Way, Gosforth Business Park, Newcastle upon Tyne, NE12 8ET
Activities: Buying and selling of own real estate
Parent: Home Group Limited
Officers: Austin Jonathan Woods, Secretary; Brian Anthony Ham [1958] Executive Director; Mark Gideon Henderson [1962] Director/Chief Executive; Dr John Matthew Hudson [1968] Director/Chief Financial Officer

Home Properties Limited
Incorporated: 2 February 1999
Net Worth: £14,896,875 *Total Assets:* £25,041,860
Registered Office: Cross House, Westgate Road, Newcastle upon Tyne, NE1 4XX
Activities: Other letting and operating of own or leased real estate
Parent: Retirement Bridge Group Holdings Limited
Officers: Paul Trevor Barber [1967] Director; Ashish Kashyap [1979] Director; Antony Lewis Pierce [1976] Finance Director

Homecare Heating Supplies Teesside Limited
Incorporated: 11 February 1974 *Employees:* 17
Net Worth: £1,135,594 *Total Assets:* £1,301,591
Registered Office: Valley Street, Darlington, Co Durham, DL1 1PY
Activities: Other retail sale of new goods in specialised stores (not commercial art galleries and opticians)
Shareholders: Jonathan Paul Cheffings; Sarah Elizabeth Cheffings
Officers: Sarah Elizabeth Cheffings, Secretary; Brian Cheffings [1938] Director/Chairman; Jonathan Paul Cheffings [1972] Managing Director; Sarah Elizabeth Cheffings [1969] Company Secretary/Director; Sheila Ann Cheffings [1943] Director/Company Secretary

Homefair (Holdings) Limited
Incorporated: 11 February 2008 *Employees:* 2
Net Worth: £2,497,737 *Total Assets:* £2,734,251
Registered Office: Unit 10 Chevychase Court, Seaham Grange Industrial Estate, Seaham, Co Durham, SR7 0PR
Activities: Non-trading company
Major Shareholder: Jonathan Michael Fitton
Officers: Sarah Fitton, Secretary; Jonathan Michael Fitton [1962] Director; Sarah Fitton [1973] Director

Homefair Blinds (U.K.) Limited
Incorporated: 19 May 1986 *Employees:* 124
Net Worth: £1,420,747 *Total Assets:* £1,952,514
Registered Office: Unit 10 Chevychase Court, Seaham Grange Industrial Estate, Seaham, Co Durham, SR7 0PR
Activities: Other manufacturing n.e.c.
Officers: Claire Anne Ripley, Secretary; Jonathan Michael Fitton [1962] Director

Homes Direct 365 Limited
Incorporated: 17 April 2009 *Employees:* 22
Net Worth: £144,189 *Total Assets:* £850,654
Registered Office: Unit G4, Commerce Way, Skippers Lane Industrial Estate, Middlesbrough, Cleveland, TS6 6UR
Activities: Retail of furniture, lighting, and similar (not musical instruments or scores) in specialised store
Shareholders: Jon Gregory; Karl Andrew Ward
Officers: Karl Andrew Ward, Secretary; Jon Gregory [1972] Director/Manager; Karl Andrew Ward [1979] Director/Manager

Homes Rock Ltd
Incorporated: 19 July 2011
Registered Office: Estate Office, Rock, Alnwick, Northumberland, NE66 3SB
Activities: Other specialised construction activities n.e.c.
Officers: Lalage Ann Bosanquet, Secretary; Charles Jay Bosanquet [1949] Landowner, Farmer & Director; Lalage Ann Bosanquet [1949] Director/Headteacher

Homeware Essentials Limited
Incorporated: 10 December 2002 *Employees:* 24
Net Worth: £516,757 *Total Assets:* £1,571,560
Registered Office: Wandhills Avenue, Skelton Industrial Estate, Skelton in Cleveland, Saltburn-by-the-Sea, N Yorks, TS12 2LQ
Activities: Wholesale of household goods (other than musical instruments) n.e.c
Shareholders: Michelle Brown; Michael Brown
Officers: Michael Brown, Secretary/Wholesale Distributor; Michael Brown [1967] Director/Wholesale Distributor; Michelle Brown [1974] Director/Wholesale Distributor

Honeyman Group Limited
Incorporated: 28 January 1997 *Employees:* 34
Net Worth: £964,865 *Total Assets:* £1,478,869
Registered Office: Harmire Enterprise Park, Harmire Road, Barnard Castle, Co Durham, DL12 8BN
Activities: Other research and experimental development on natural sciences and engineering
Major Shareholder: Trevor Honeyman
Officers: Marcus Booth [1975] Director of Training and Consultancy; Thomas Honeyman [1987] Managing Director; Trevor Honeyman [1956] Director Chairman

Hop Vietnamese Limited
Incorporated: 23 January 2014 *Employees:* 21
Net Worth: £686,119 *Total Assets:* £921,626
Registered Office: 10 Carisbrooke Road, Hartlepool, Cleveland, TS26 0AB
Activities: Licenced restaurants
Shareholder: Paul Andrew Hopper
Officers: Paul Andrew Hopper [1984] Director/Entrepreneur; Justin Wyse [1965] Director

Hopax Europe Limited
Incorporated: 24 March 1999 *Employees:* 5
Net Worth: £44,955 *Total Assets:* £1,728,232
Registered Office: Aston House, Redburn Road, Newcastle upon Tyne, NE5 1NB
Activities: Activities of head offices
Officers: Stuart Seymour, Secretary; Jason Chung Sheng Cheng [1962] Director/Financial Manager [Taiwanese]; Tsung-Tien Kuo [1946] Director/Company President [Taiwanese]

Hope Estates Limited
Incorporated: 25 June 1998 *Employees:* 6
Net Worth: £160,911 *Total Assets:* £12,566,565
Registered Office: 7 Brenkley Way, Blezard Business Park, Seaton Burn, Newcastle upon Tyne, NE13 6DS
Activities: Other letting and operating of own or leased real estate
Major Shareholder: Nicholas Swift
Officers: Nicholas Swift [1971] Director/Landlord

Hopkins Properties Limited
Incorporated: 24 July 2003 *Employees:* 4
Net Worth: £1,080,533 *Total Assets:* £4,359,790
Registered Office: 15 Ropner Gardens, Middleton St George, Darlington, Co Durham, DL2 1FB
Activities: Other letting and operating of own or leased real estate
Shareholders: Richard Anthony Hopkins; Susan Margaret Hopkins
Officers: Susan Margaret Hopkins, Secretary; Richard Anthony Hopkins [1958] Director/Auctioneer; Susan Margaret Hopkins [1956] Director/Retired Dietician

Hopling Properties Limited
Incorporated: 24 November 2003
Net Worth: £156,148 *Total Assets:* £894,535
Registered Office: 8 Hetton Lyons Industrial Estate, Hetton-le-Hole, Houghton-le-Spring, Co Durham, DH5 0RH
Activities: Other letting and operating of own or leased real estate
Officers: Julie Anderson, Secretary; Julie Anderson [1973] Director/Learning & Development Consultant; Anthony Joseph Hopps [1969] Director; Ian David Ling [1969] Director; Richard Thomas Ling [1943] Director/Timber Merchant

Horatio Holdings Limited
Incorporated: 2 June 2015 *Employees:* 181
Net Worth: £1,310,512 *Total Assets:* £22,691,204
Registered Office: Collingwood House, Redburn Court, Earl Grey Way, North Shields, Tyne & Wear, NE29 6AR
Activities: Other activities auxiliary to insurance and pension funding
Shareholder: Michelle Beenshill
Officers: Cheryl Ball [1989] Director/Trainee Solicitor; Andrew James Gibson [1957] Director/Chartered Accountant; Miguel Rueda Hernando [1967] Director/Entrepreneur [Spanish]; Hamish John Garrow Mair [1966] Director/Investment Manager; Steven Geoffrey Welton [1968] Director/Chief Executive Officer; Martin Stephen Northcote Wright [1968] Director

Horizon Products Ltd
Incorporated: 9 April 2009 *Employees:* 33
Net Worth: £2,469,868 *Total Assets:* £3,951,394
Registered Office: Eltringham Works, Eltringham Road, Prudhoe, Northumberland, NE42 6LP
Activities: Other service activities n.e.c.
Shareholders: Joanne Elizabeth Taylor; Paul Taylor
Officers: Joanne Elizabeth Taylor [1966] Director; Paul Taylor [1969] Director

Horizons Specialist Academy Trust
Incorporated: 12 July 2013 *Employees:* 285
Net Worth: £12,991,000 *Total Assets:* £18,486,000
Registered Office: Abbey Hill Academy, Ketton Road, Stockton on Tees, Cleveland, TS19 8BU
Activities: Other education n.e.c.
Officers: Alison Ruth Ascough, Secretary; James Bromiley [1972] Director/Civil Servant; Helen Dyson [1965] Director/Foster Carer; Elizabeth Anne Horne [1959] Director/Chief Executive; Maurice Davison Jones [1947] Director/Retired; Linda Laidler [1946] Director/Retired JP; Susan Richardson [1956] Director/Retired; Baxi Neeraj Prasad Sinha [1972] Director/Consultant; Colin James Whittaker [1946] Director/Retired; Siân Wilson [1980] Director

Hornby Healthcare Limited
Incorporated: 7 March 2011 *Employees:* 101
Net Worth Deficit: £43,153 *Total Assets:* £1,970,515
Registered Office: The Paddock, Hornby, Northallerton, N Yorks, DL6 2JH
Activities: Residential care activities for the elderly and disabled
Shareholders: Sanjai Kumar Ahitan; Madhu Ahitan
Officers: Madhu Ahitan, Secretary; Sanjai Kumar Ahitan [1964] Director

Horncastle Executive Travel Limited
Incorporated: 20 June 1969
Net Worth: £616,118 *Total Assets:* £2,315,312
Registered Office: Hadrian House, Higham Place, Newcastle upon Tyne, NE1 8AF
Activities: Travel agency activities
Officers: Christina Drummond, Secretary; Christina Drummond [1956] Director; Peter John Drummond [1944] Managing Director

Hornsey (Hartlepool) Limited
Incorporated: 16 July 2014
Net Worth: £1,028,702 *Total Assets:* £1,074,146
Registered Office: Tower House, Tower Street, Hartlepool, Cleveland, TS24 7HL
Activities: Activities of other holding companies n.e.c.
Shareholders: Sheila Coleman; John Walters; Sharon Aideen Mei Mei Adams
Officers: Sheila Colman [1947] Director; Darren Hornsey [1967] Electricals Director; Melissa Howlett [1980] Director/Administration Manager

Horsley Properties Limited
Incorporated: 15 March 2001
Net Worth: £120 *Total Assets:* £1,892,109
Registered Office: 60 Horsley Hill Square, South Shields, Tyne & Wear, NE34 6RF
Activities: Other building completion and finishing
Major Shareholder: Bhavna Patel
Officers: Sunil Maini, Secretary; Sunil Maini [1967] Director/Pharmacist; Bhavna Patel [1970] Director/Pharmacist

The Hospital of God at Greatham
Incorporated: 13 March 2008 *Employees:* 174
Net Worth: £41,047,416 *Total Assets:* £41,684,312
Registered Office: The Estate Office, Greatham, Hartlepool, Cleveland, TS25 2HS
Activities: Residential care activities for the elderly and disabled
Officers: David Granath, Secretary/Charity Chief Executive; Margaret Elizabeth Bousfield [1949] Director/Retired Headteacher; John Frank de Martino [1944] Director/Retired Financial Controller; Christopher John Dickinson [1954] Director/Retired; The Venerable Ian Jagger [1955] Director/Archdeacon; Geoffrey Vincent Miller [1956] Director/Archdeacon; Lois Neal [1955] Director/Retired; Annette Elizabeth Nylund [1958] Director/Local Government Officer; John Michael Poole JP Dl [1955] Director/Estate Agent; Peter Shields [1955] Director/Civil Servant; Philippa Lucy Sinclair [1953] Director/Social Worker; Mike Taylerson [1959] Director/Retired

Hospitality Guaranteed Limited
Incorporated: 6 June 2006 *Employees:* 20
Net Worth: £595,274 *Total Assets:* £1,284,602
Registered Office: Hospitality Guaranteed, 10 Chapell Lane, Wynyard Park Business Village, Wynyard, Billingham, Cleveland, TS22 5FG
Activities: Other reservation service activities n.e.c.
Officers: Amanda Joy Cheesey, Secretary; Amanda Joy Cheesey [1973] Director/Manager; Victoria Shanks [1980] Director/Manager

Hospitaller Order of Saint John of God
Incorporated: 31 March 2010 *Employees:* 2
Net Worth: £6,164,000 *Total Assets:* £7,878,000
Registered Office: St Bedes House, Morton Park, Darlington, Co Durham, DL1 4XZ
Activities: Other social work activities without accommodation n.e.c.
Officers: Malachy Brannigan, Secretary; Malachy Brannigan [1947] Director/Brother of a Religious Order [Irish]; William Martin Forkan [1942] Director/Brother of a Religious Order [Irish]; Michael Edward Francis [1941] Director/Retired; John Gallagher [1944] Director/Brother of a Religious Order [Irish]; John Lennon [1945] Director/Brother of a Religious Order [Irish]; Robert Moore [1944] Director/Religious; Michael John Nield [1940] Director/Religious Brother

Hotel Operations Limited
Incorporated: 9 July 2004 *Employees:* 111
Net Worth Deficit: £213,538 *Total Assets:* £9,122,808
Registered Office: Jesmond Dene House, Jesmond Dene Road, Newcastle upon Tyne, NE2 2EY
Activities: Hotels and similar accommodation
Shareholder: Peter Haswell Candler
Officers: Terry Bayliff [1949] Director; Peter Haswell Candler [1953] Director; Philip Anthony Ganley [1956] Director; Paul Joseph Morrissey [1952] Director

Houghton International Electrical Services Limited
Incorporated: 10 September 1984 *Employees:* 111
Net Worth: £2,261,819 *Total Assets:* £4,372,023
Registered Office: Riverside Court, Fisher Street, Newcastle upon Tyne, NE6 4LT
Activities: Manufacture of electric motors, generators and transformers
Major Shareholder: Michael Robert Mitten
Officers: Sally Christine McCarty, Secretary; David Ronald Mitten, Secretary; David Darcy [1942] Director; Jack Dunning [1977] Director/Chartered Accountant; Craig William Hutton [1969] Operations Director; Pamela Lamming [1975] Director; Michael Robert Mitten [1978] Director/Engineer; Christopher Matt Robson [1981] Director

Houghton-le-Spring Golf Club,Limited (The)
Incorporated: 21 March 1934
Net Worth: £661,208 *Total Assets:* £1,068,410
Registered Office: Copt Hill, Houghton-le-Spring, Co Durham, DH5 8LU
Activities: Activities of sport clubs
Officers: David Freeman, Secretary; John Francis Ellison [1946] Director/Retired; Valda Patricia Grant [1952] Director/Retired

Hoults Enterprises Limited
Incorporated: 21 March 2011 *Employees:* 6
Net Worth: £971,604 *Total Assets:* £1,089,005
Registered Office: Ford Depositories, Walker Road, Newcastle upon Tyne, NE6 2HL
Activities: Other letting and operating of own or leased real estate
Officers: Mark Ian Brown, Secretary; Mark Ian Brown [1976] Director/Accountant; Anabel Kate Hoult [1969] Director; Charles Wilson Hoult [1967] Director; Frederick Wilson Hoult [1938] Director; Peta Ann Hoult [1938] Director; Dr Sarah Louise Hoult [1965] Director

Hoults Limited
Incorporated: 11 May 1936 *Employees:* 25
Net Worth: £1,475,453 *Total Assets:* £12,351,709
Registered Office: Ford Depositories, Walker Road, Newcastle upon Tyne, NE6 2HL
Activities: Other letting and operating of own or leased real estate
Parent: Hoults Holdings Limited
Officers: Mark Ian Brown, Secretary; Mark Ian Brown [1976] Director/Accountant; Anabel Kate Hoult [1969] Director; Charles Wilson Hoult [1967] Director; Frederick Wilson Hoult [1938] Director; Peta Ann Hoult [1938] Director/Journalist; Dr Sarah Louise Hoult [1965] Director/General Practitioner

House and Properties Ltd.
Incorporated: 10 March 2004
Net Worth: £236,305 *Total Assets:* £1,404,577
Registered Office: 158 Heaton Park Road, Heaton, Newcastle upon Tyne, NE6 5NR
Activities: Other letting and operating of own or leased real estate
Officers: Dr Helen Barbara Stringer, Secretary/Property; Peter Horne [1957] Director/Property; Wayne McDowell [1970] Director/Property; William Glenn McDowell [1968] Director/Property Developer; Dr Helen Barbara Stringer [1958] Director/Speech Therapist

Houston Commercial Ltd
Incorporated: 9 July 2003
Net Worth: £454,400 *Total Assets:* £951,139
Registered Office: 1 Aerial House, School Aycliffe Lane, Newton Aycliffe, Co Durham, DL5 6QF
Activities: Retail sale of automotive fuel in specialised stores
Officers: Bret Upex, Secretary; Leonard John Upex [1950] Director

Howard House Care Limited
Incorporated: 27 October 2004
Net Worth: £1,462,404 *Total Assets:* £1,622,560
Registered Office: Howard House Care Ltd, Netherton Colliery, Bedlington, Northumberland, NE22 6BB
Activities: Other residential care activities n.e.c.
Shareholders: Allan O'Neil; Angela Louise O'Neil
Officers: Angela Louise O'Neil, Secretary/Care; Allan O'Neil [1961] Director; Angela Louise O'Neil [1967] Director/Care

Howarth Limited
Incorporated: 15 December 1997
Net Worth: £235,114 *Total Assets:* £960,625
Registered Office: Blue Bridge Centre, Horndale Avenue, Aycliffe Business Park, Newton Aycliffe, Co Durham, DL5 6DS
Activities: Printing of newspapers
Shareholder: Raymond Stuart Howarth
Officers: Raymond Stuart Howarth, Secretary; Beverley Louise Howarth [1968] Director; Christopher John Howarth [1969] Director; Joanne Howarth [1969] Director; Michelle Howarth [1972] Director; Paul David Howarth [1962] Director; Raymond Stuart Howarth [1965] Director

Howarth Litchfield Partnership Limited
Incorporated: 11 February 2003 *Employees:* 24
Net Worth: £2,198,376 *Total Assets:* £3,321,881
Registered Office: 4 Old Elvet, Durham, DH1 3HL
Activities: Architectural activities
Parent: HLP (Holdings) Ltd
Officers: Elisa Joanne Berry [1974] Director/Architect; David John Pickersgill [1971] Director/Building Technologist; Neil Turner [1966] Director/Architects; Jonathan Francis Yates [1965] Director/Architect

Howell Cummings Joinery Ltd
Incorporated: 10 June 2014
Net Worth: £77,106 *Total Assets:* £822,480
Registered Office: 9 Enterprise City, Meadowfield Avenue, Spennymoor, Co Durham, DL16 6JF
Activities: Joinery installation
Shareholders: Alan Richardson; Steven Hewitson
Officers: Steven Hewitson [1983] Director/Joiner; Alan Richardson [1956] Director; Paul Surtees [1957] Director

Howick Trustees Limited
Incorporated: 18 April 1975 *Employees:* 11
Net Worth: £4,922,644 *Total Assets:* £4,986,847
Registered Office: Howick Estate Office, Alnwick, Northumberland, NE66 3LB
Activities: Operation of historical sites and buildings and similar visitor attractions
Officers: Diane Spark, Secretary; Judith Ann Woodford, Secretary; Doctor David Charles Evelyn Baring [1975] Director/Doctor of Medicine; Mark George Orlando Bridgeman [1968] Director/Fund Manager; Matthew George Darby [1967] Director/Farmer; Charles MacIntyre Erskine [1940] Director/Retired Horticulturalist; Lord Charles Evelyn Howick of Glendale [1937] Director/Landowner; Lady Clare Howick of Glendale [1942] Director/Married Woman; Richard Michael Landale [1943] Director/Chartered Surveyor; Sir Walter John Buchanan Riddell [1974] Director

HSA DIY Limited
Incorporated: 14 March 2011
Net Worth: £684,416 *Total Assets:* £1,318,645
Registered Office: Beaumont Accountancy, First Floor, Enterprise House, 202-206 Linthorpe Road, Middlesbrough, Cleveland, TS1 3QW
Activities: Retail sale of hardware, paints and glass in specialised stores
Shareholders: Adam Ali; Mourzzam Ali
Officers: Adam Ali [1994] Director; Mourzzam Ali [1980] Director/Takeaway Proprietor

HTL Group Limited
Incorporated: 3 November 1993 *Employees:* 76
Net Worth: £6,378,075 *Total Assets:* £10,627,090
Registered Office: 45 Colbourne Avenue, Nelson Park, Cramlington, Northumberland, NE23 1WD
Activities: Non-specialised wholesale trade
Shareholders: Stephen Jones; Pat Jones; Ray Jones
Officers: Simon Kyle Dixon [1975] Director; Raymond Jones [1945] Director; Stephen Stuart Jones [1973] Director; Paul Antony Storey [1964] Director

HTL Worldwide Ltd
Incorporated: 24 July 2014
Net Worth Deficit: £165,007 *Total Assets:* £962,130
Registered Office: 45 Colbourne Avenue, Nelson Park Industrial Estate, Cramlington, Northumberland, NE23 1WD
Activities: Manufacture of other special-purpose machinery n.e.c.
Shareholders: HTL Group Limited; Stephen Jones
Officers: Simon Kyle Dixon [1975] Director; Stephen Stuart Jones [1973] Director; Paul Antony Storey [1964] Director

J.S. Hubbuck Limited
Incorporated: 17 April 1975 *Employees:* 12
Net Worth: £2,995,776 *Total Assets:* £4,795,195
Registered Office: Unit 1 Hexham Auction Mart, Mart Offices, Tyne Green, Hexham, Northumberland, NE46 3SG
Activities: Agents selling agricultural raw materials, livestock, textile raw materials and semi-finished goods
Shareholders: Geoffrey Raymond Hubbuck; Derek William Hubbuck
Officers: Geoffrey Raymond Hubbuck, Secretary; Derek William Hubbuck [1951] Director; Geoffrey Raymond Hubbuck [1957] Director

Hubbway Limited
Incorporated: 30 December 1977 *Employees:* 39
Net Worth: £5,365,812 *Total Assets:* £9,180,668
Registered Office: Unit 1 Bassington Industrial Estate, Bassington Lane, Cramlington, Northumberland, NE23 8AD
Activities: Renting and leasing of agricultural machinery and equipment
Shareholder: George Edwin Hubb
Officers: Gillian Elsie Hubb, Secretary; Philip Hickey [1981] Director; George Edwin Hubb [1945] Director/Garage Proprietor; Gillian Elsie Hubb [1947] Director/Secretary; Nicholas Hubb [1974] Director/Sales

Percy A.Hudson Limited
Incorporated: 19 June 1936 *Employees:* 28
Net Worth: £1,187,498 *Total Assets:* £2,160,928
Registered Office: Borough Saw Mills, Northumberland Street, North Shields, Tyne & Wear, NE30 1DW
Activities: Sawmilling and planing of wood
Officers: Anne Hudson, Secretary; Douglas Allardyce Hudson [1944] Director/Timber Merchant; Jonathan Allardyce Hudson [1976] Director; Malcolm Allardyce Hudson [1946] Director/Timber Merchant; Mark Allardyce Hudson [1974] Director; Paul Allardyce Hudson [1972] Director/Timber Merchant

Frank Hudson Transport Limited
Incorporated: 27 March 2000 *Employees:* 18
Net Worth: £1,537,620 *Total Assets:* £2,357,841
Registered Office: Hartbriggs Lane, Etherley Bank, High Etherley, Bishop Auckland, Co Durham, DL14 0LG
Activities: Freight transport by road
Shareholders: Frank Hudson; Anne Hudson
Officers: Ann Hudson, Secretary; Ann Hudson [1957] Director/Partner; Frank Hudson [1948] Director/Owner

Hudsons 23 Limited
Incorporated: 21 May 2003 *Employees:* 155
Net Worth: £335,043 *Total Assets:* £980,776
Registered Office: Gordons Place, Mainsforth Terrace, Hartlepool, Cleveland, TS24 7AJ
Activities: Taxi operation
Shareholders: David Hudson; Catherine Hudson
Officers: Kevin Pout [1965] Managing Director

Hughes Bros Construction Limited
Incorporated: 24 November 2005 *Employees:* 32
Net Worth: £1,374,463 *Total Assets:* £5,045,437
Registered Office: Unit 8 Redesdale Court, Forest Grove Business Park, Middlesbrough, Cleveland, TS2 1RL
Activities: Construction of other civil engineering projects n.e.c.
Officers: Gary Dominic Hughes, Secretary; Gary Dominic Hughes [1972] Director; Joseph Hughes [1979] Director; Ian Thomas Pallas [1975] Director

Jim Hughes Coaches Limited
Incorporated: 25 March 2003 *Employees:* 50
Net Worth: £918,364 *Total Assets:* £2,285,488
Registered Office: Fell Bank, Birtley, Chester-le-Street, Co Durham, DH3 2SP
Activities: Other passenger land transport
Officers: John Christopher Shipley, Secretary; Ian Raymond Shipley [1961] Director; John Christopher Shipley [1986] Director

Hughes Plant Hire Limited
Incorporated: 19 May 2003 *Employees:* 4
Net Worth: £3,028,356 *Total Assets:* £4,792,132
Registered Office: 3b Lockheed Court, Preston Farm, Stockton on Tees, Cleveland, TS18 3SH
Activities: Renting and leasing of construction and civil engineering machinery and equipment
Shareholders: John Patrick Hughes; Christine Mary Hughes
Officers: John Patrick Hughes, Secretary; Christine Mary Hughes [1969] Director; John Patrick Hughes [1972] Director

Andrew Hughes Utility Services Ltd
Incorporated: 7 April 2009
Net Worth: £1,039,205 *Total Assets:* £2,583,311
Registered Office: 32 Saltwell View, Gateshead, Tyne & Wear, NE8 4NT
Activities: Construction of domestic buildings
Officers: Tracy Ann Hughes, Secretary; Andrew Matthew Hughes [1970] Director; Tracy Ann Hughes [1971] Director

Humankind Charity
Incorporated: 30 May 1984 *Employees:* 546
Net Worth: £2,620,750 *Total Assets:* £9,300,493
Registered Office: IES Centre, Horndale Avenue, Aycliffe Business Park, Newton Aycliffe, Co Durham, DL5 6DS
Activities: Other residential care activities n.e.c.
Officers: Camila Horner, Secretary; James Black [1944] Director/Retired; Ian Roberts Dewhirst [1948] Director/Retired; Vivienne Jane Holmes [1967] Director/Local Government Officer; Christopher Ranulph George Matthews-Maxwell [1944] Director/Land/Property Owner; Sarah Patricia Shepherd [1957] Director; Professor Roger Smith [1953] Director/Academic; Michael William Treasure [1952] Director

Owen Humble Property Investments Limited
Incorporated: 16 January 2002 *Employees:* 3
Net Worth: £2,050,271 *Total Assets:* £2,891,359
Registered Office: 2 Burdon Place, Jesmond, Newcastle upon Tyne, NE2 2AQ
Activities: Other letting and operating of own or leased real estate
Shareholders: Patricia Humble; Michael Timothy Humble
Officers: Michael Timothy Humble, Secretary; Alison Clare Humble [1965] Director; Michael Timothy Humble [1961] Director/Antique Dealer; Patricia Frances Humble [1931] Director

Humbles Real Estate Limited
Incorporated: 12 November 1997
Net Worth: £612,723 *Total Assets:* £958,294
Registered Office: Century House, Gatherley Road Industrial Estate, Brompton on Swale, Richmond, N Yorks, DL10 7JG
Activities: Renting and leasing of other machinery, equipment and tangible goods n.e.c.
Shareholder: Caroline Howie
Officers: Caroline Howie [1942] Director; Charles John Howie [1974] Director

Hummersknott Academy Trust
Incorporated: 9 June 2011 *Employees:* 211
Net Worth: £12,685,000 *Total Assets:* £16,932,000
Registered Office: Hummersknott Academy, Edinburgh Drive, Darlington, Co Durham, DL3 8AR
Activities: General secondary education
Officers: Ruth Armer [1980] Director/Teacher; Brenda Elizabeth Baines [1953] Director/Catering Manager; Michael Davidson Dodd [1951] Director/Financial Consultant; Alan James Gowling [1970] Director Business Banking; Stephen Dennis Hunnisett [1958] Director/Vice Principal; Penelope Sarah Ann Jones [1957] Director; James Michael Keating [1972] Director/Executive Principal; David Liddle [1962] Director/Property Developer/Manager; Amanda Allison June Pybus-Coates [1965] Director; Michael Richings [1972] Director/Project Services Manager; Susan Sparrow [1971] Director/Bank Manager; Naomi Jane Woods [1978] Director/Business Consultant

Hunky Dory Leisure Limited
Incorporated: 16 March 1994
Net Worth: £742,687 *Total Assets:* £784,206
Registered Office: Hallgarth House Cottage, Hallgarth, High Pittington, Co Durham, DH6 1AB
Activities: Construction of commercial buildings
Parent: Templemead Consultants Limited
Officers: William Walton [1957] Director/Landlord

Hunley Hall LLP
Incorporated: 30 June 2008 *Employees:* 58
Net Worth: £2,276,611 *Total Assets:* £2,731,230
Registered Office: Ings Lane, Brotton, Saltburn-by-the-Sea, N Yorks, TS12 2FT
Officers: Anthony Charles Philip Wharton [1946] Member

Geoff Huntley Plant Limited
Incorporated: 3 May 1989
Net Worth: £1,505,571 *Total Assets:* £4,503,770
Registered Office: Unit 1 Locomotion Way, Camperdown Industrial Estate, Killingworth, Newcastle upon Tyne, NE12 5US
Activities: Renting and leasing of construction and civil engineering machinery and equipment
Major Shareholder: Geoff Huntley
Officers: Sylvia Huntley, Secretary; John Geoffrey Norman Huntley [1949] Managing Director; Stephen John Huntley [1981] Director; Sylvia Huntley [1952] Director/Secretary

Huntsman (Holdings) UK
Incorporated: 6 May 1999
Net Worth: £269,439,008 *Total Assets:* £698,651,008
Registered Office: Concordia House, Glenarm Road, Wynyard Business Park, Billingham, Cleveland, TS22 5FB
Activities: Manufacture of dyes and pigments
Parent: Huntsman Corporation
Officers: Karen Rachel Hall, Secretary; Natasja Edward Denise Degrieck [1965] Director/Associate General Council [Belgian]; Karen Rachel Hall [1960] Director/HR Manager; Gary Robert Hodgson [1964] Director/Compensation & Benefits Manager

Huntsman Advanced Materials (UK) Limited
Incorporated: 17 September 1999 *Employees:* 126
Net Worth Deficit: £14,121,000 *Total Assets:* £34,038,000
Registered Office: Concordia House, Glenarm Road, Wynyard Business Park, Billingham, Cleveland, TS22 5FB
Activities: Manufacture of glues
Parent: Huntsman Advanced Materials Holdings (UK) Limited
Officers: Karen Rachel Hall, Secretary; Karen Rachel Hall [1960] Director/HR Manager; Gary Robert Hodgson [1964] Director/Compensation & Benefits Manager; Jan Lelong [1978] Finance Director [Belgian]; Patrick Albert Peter Verraes [1972] Director/Lawyer [Belgian]; Scott Jason Wright [1971] Director/Vice President Europe, Advanced Materials

Huntsman Advanced Materials Holdings (UK) Limited
Incorporated: 3 November 1999
Net Worth: £1,066,000 *Total Assets:* £15,756,000
Registered Office: Concordia House, Glenarm Road, Wynyard Business Park, Billingham, Cleveland, TS22 5FB
Activities: Activities of other holding companies n.e.c.
Parent: Huntsman Corporation
Officers: Karen Rachel Hall, Secretary; Karen Rachel Hall [1960] Director/HR Manager; Gary Robert Hodgson [1964] Director/Compensation & Benefits Manager; Jan Lelong [1978] Finance Director [Belgian]; Patrick Albert Peter Verraes [1972] Director/Lawyer [Belgian]; Scott Jason Wright [1971] Director/Vice President Europe, Advanced Materials

Huntsman Polyurethanes (UK) Limited
Incorporated: 5 May 1999 *Employees:* 98
Net Worth: £140,272,000 *Total Assets:* £173,428,000
Registered Office: Concordia House, Glenarm Road, Wynyard Business Park, Billingham, Cleveland, TS22 5FB
Activities: Manufacture of other chemical products n.e.c.
Parent: Huntsman (Holdings) UK
Officers: Karen Rachel Hall, Secretary; Karen Rachel Hall [1960] Director/HR Manager; Gary Robert Hodgson [1964] Director/Compensation & Benefits Manager; John Steven Shipman [1968] Director/Operations Manager

Husqvarna UK Limited
Incorporated: 18 March 1970 *Employees:* 331
Net Worth: £19,498,000 *Total Assets:* £77,737,000
Registered Office: Preston Road, Aycliffe Industrial Park, Newton Aycliffe, Co Durham, DL5 6UP
Activities: Manufacture of agricultural and forestry machinery other than tractors
Officers: Yvonne Dockray, Secretary; Gunnar Niklas Broberg [1969] Director/Vice President [Swedish]; Alexander Stuart de Courcy [1970] Director/Vice President; Glen Anthony Instone [1977] Director

Hutchinson Transport Limited
Incorporated: 13 September 2000 *Employees:* 38
Net Worth: £929,526 *Total Assets:* £2,254,429
Registered Office: Fleming Road, Skippers Lane Industrial Estate, Middlesbrough, Cleveland, TS6 6TT
Activities: Cargo handling for land transport activities
Shareholder: Gillian Hutchinson
Officers: Gillian Hutchinson, Secretary/Chemical Logisticator; Gillian Hutchinson [1966] Director/Health & Safety Manager; Peter Bruce Hutchinson [1962] Director/Chemical Logisticator

Hutchinsons Fruit & Veg Limited
Incorporated: 29 March 2010 *Employees:* 53
Net Worth: £854,641 *Total Assets:* £1,360,890
Registered Office: 273 Stanhope Street, Newcastle upon Tyne, NE4 5JU
Activities: Wholesale of fruit and vegetables
Shareholders: David Blair; Kelly Hutchinson; James Hutchinson
Officers: James Anthony Hutchinson [1961] Director

Hutchinsons Fruit&Veg (Gateshead) Limited
Incorporated: 25 March 2010 *Employees:* 11
Net Worth: £539,030 *Total Assets:* £911,123
Registered Office: 273 Stanhope Street, Newcastle upon Tyne, NE4 5JU
Activities: Retail sale of fruit and vegetables in specialised stores
Major Shareholder: James Hutchinson
Officers: David Blair [1980] Director; James Anthony Hutchinson [1961] Director

Hutton Chemicals Limited
Incorporated: 9 December 1991 *Employees:* 4
Net Worth: £2,620,947 *Total Assets:* £2,743,302
Registered Office: HCL House, Rectory Lane, Guisborough, Cleveland, TS14 7DL
Activities: Manufacture of other chemical products n.e.c.
Shareholders: Ian Kemp Alexander; Susan Agnes Alexander
Officers: Susan Agnes Alexander, Secretary/Chemical Trading and Consultant; Ian Kemp Alexander [1947] Director/Chemicals Trading and Consultant; Susan Agnes Alexander [1947] Director/Chemical Trading and Consultancy

HVR Limited
Incorporated: 25 September 2007
Net Worth: £35,365 *Total Assets:* £827,794
Registered Office: Bedesway, Bede Industrial Estate, Jarrow, Tyne & Wear, NE32 3EN
Activities: Manufacture of other electrical equipment
Shareholders: Stephen Mitchell Elliott; Kevin McLaughlin
Officers: Kevin McLaughlin [1953] Technical Director

Hydram Engineering Limited
Incorporated: 30 March 1994 *Employees:* 226
Net Worth: £5,353,537 *Total Assets:* £10,529,852
Registered Office: Avenue 1, Chilton Industrial Estate, Ferryhill, Co Durham, DL17 0SG
Activities: Manufacture of metal structures and parts of structures
Parent: Dynamic Aerospace and Defense Limited
Officers: David James Greatorex, Secretary/Managing Director; David James Greatorex [1969] Managing Director; Donald Daniel Nystrom [1970] Director [American]

Hydraulic & Offshore Supplies Limited
Incorporated: 31 January 1995 *Employees:* 11
Net Worth: £702,669 *Total Assets:* £1,063,018
Registered Office: Offshore House, Unit BT 25-26 D, Southwick Industrial Estate, Sunderland, Tyne & Wear, SR5 3TX
Activities: Manufacture of pumps
Shareholders: Alan Roger Wills; Joanne Elizabeth Wills
Officers: Joanne Elizabeth Wills, Secretary; Don Fenwick [1967] Managing Director; Paul Taylor [1972] Director; Alan Roger Wills [1959] Director/Chairman; Joanne Elizabeth Wills [1969] Director

Hyena (Northern) Limited
Incorporated: 30 December 2004 *Employees:* 31
Net Worth: £527,556 *Total Assets:* £977,090
Registered Office: 17 Leazes Park Road, Newcastle upon Tyne, NE1 4PF
Activities: Public houses and bars
Major Shareholder: Mohammed Ajaib
Officers: Ming Farn Lee, Secretary/Dental Surgeon [Malaysian]; Mohammed Ajaib [1957] Director/Developer

Hymas & Hall Limited
Incorporated: 12 April 1985 *Employees:* 4
Net Worth: £825,028 *Total Assets:* £862,293
Registered Office: The Aitches, 9 School Street, Witton-le-Wear, Co Durham, DL14 0AS
Activities: Construction of domestic buildings
Shareholders: Graham Stuart Hall; Carolynne Hall
Officers: Graham Stuart Hall, Secretary; Carolynne Hall [1958] Director; Graham Stuart Hall [1960] Director/Property Developer

Erwin Hymer Group Holdings UK Limited
Incorporated: 6 May 2016 *Employees:* 2
Net Worth: £19,205,546 *Total Assets:* £29,787,466
Registered Office: Explorer House, Delves Lane, Consett, Co Durham, DH8 7PE
Activities: Manufacture of bodies (coachwork) for motor vehicles (except caravans)
Parent: Erwin Hymer Group AG & Co KG
Officers: Robert George Quine [1962] Managing Director

Erwin Hymer Group UK Ltd
Incorporated: 18 October 1989 *Employees:* 414
Net Worth: £4,930,006 *Total Assets:* £20,149,680
Registered Office: Explorer House, Delves Lane, Consett, Co Durham, DH8 7PE
Activities: Manufacture of bodies (coachwork) for motor vehicles (except caravans)
Parent: Erwin Hymer Group AG & Co KG
Officers: David James Styles, Secretary/Accountant; Martin Anton Brandt [1960] Director [German]; Stefan Junker [1969] Director/Chief Financial Officer [German]; Robert George Quine [1962] Director; Jorg Reithmeier [1969] Director [German]; David James Styles [1969] Director/Accountant

Hyperdrive Innovation Holdings Limited
Incorporated: 27 January 2016 *Employees:* 31
Net Worth Deficit: £435,311 *Total Assets:* £2,632,447
Registered Office: Future Technology Centre, Barmston Court, Nissan Way, Sunderland, Tyne & Wear, SR5 3NY
Activities: Activities of head offices
Shareholder: Neaf LP
Officers: Stephen Irish [1974] Director; Aidan Lannen [1974] Finance Director; Andrew Christopher Lapping [1963] Director/Investor; Christopher Roy Pennison [1967] Director; Tim Rawlinson Sale [1963] Director/Chartered Accountant; Dr David William Sandells [1976] Director/Chartered Engineer; Bimaljit Singh Sandhu [1962] Director

Hyperdrive Innovation Ltd
Incorporated: 14 February 2012 *Employees:* 31
Net Worth Deficit: £927,855 *Total Assets:* £2,448,815
Registered Office: Future Technology Centre, Barmston Court, Nissan Way, Sunderland, Tyne & Wear, SR5 3NY
Activities: Manufacture of batteries and accumulators
Parent: Hyperdrive Innvovation Holding Ltd
Officers: Stephen Irish [1974] Managing Director; Aidan Lannen [1974] Finance Director; Andrew Christopher Lapping [1963] Director/Investor; Christopher Roy Pennison [1967] Director/Engineer; Tim Rawlinson Sale [1963] Director/Chartered Accountant; Dr David William Sandells [1976] Director/Chartered Engineer; Bimaljit Singh Sandhu [1962] Director

Hyperdrug Pharmaceuticals Ltd
Incorporated: 21 March 1985 *Employees:* 22
Net Worth: £123,441 *Total Assets:* £1,542,481
Registered Office: Hyperdrug Pharmaceuticals Ltd, Station Industrial Estate, Barnard Castle, Co Durham, DL12 0NG
Activities: Manufacture of pharmaceutical preparations
Shareholder: Christine Jennifer Watson
Officers: Christine Jennifer Watson, Secretary; Benjamin Nicholas Watson [1974] Director; Christine Jennifer Watson [1946] Director; Geoffrey Walton Watson [1938] Director/Pharmacist; John Geoffrey Frederick Watson [1971] Director/Sales Manager

Hytorc (Unex) Limited
Incorporated: 2 May 1991 *Employees:* 27
Net Worth: £1,351,489 *Total Assets:* £11,528,971
Registered Office: Unit 25 Moorland Way, Nelson Park Industrial Park, Cramlington, Northumberland, NE23 1WE
Activities: Non-specialised wholesale trade
Officers: Sophie Smith, Secretary; Eric Junkers [1982] Director/President [American]; Jason Kurt Junkers [1981] Director/Manager [American]

I D Construction Services Ltd
Incorporated: 3 October 2002 *Employees:* 8
Net Worth: £1,136,109 *Total Assets:* £2,358,618
Registered Office: 16 Back Heaton Road, Heaton, Newcastle upon Tyne, NE6 1SD
Activities: Other construction installation
Officers: Kevin Peter Ingles, Secretary; Martin John Donnelly [1965] Director; Paul Robert Duffy [1962] Director; Kevin Peter Ingles [1966] Director

I&K International Company Limited
Incorporated: 9 June 2005
Net Worth: £784,808 *Total Assets:* £2,194,130
Registered Office: IK House, Queensway North, Team Valley Trading Estate, Gateshead, Tyne & Wear, NE11 0NY
Activities: Retail sale via mail order houses or via Internet
Shareholders: Mengchao Kou; Fen Wang
Officers: Fen Wang, Secretary; Mengchao Kou [1980] Director [Chinese]

I-Evo Ltd
Incorporated: 26 February 2009 *Employees:* 19
Net Worth: £57,110 *Total Assets:* £922,564
Registered Office: Unit 5 Orion Way, Orion Business Park, North Shields, Tyne & Wear, NE29 7SN
Activities: Other service activities n.e.c.
Major Shareholder: Shaun Terry Oakes
Officers: Stuart Ging, Secretary; Stuart Ging [1981] Director/Accountant; Nicholas Stephen Moore [1962] Director; Shaun Terry Oakes [1973] Director

I.T. Professional Services Limited
Incorporated: 21 February 2000 *Employees:* 110
Net Worth: £2,444,530 *Total Assets:* £9,619,796
Registered Office: Unit 2a & 2b Metrocentre East Business Park, Waterside Drive, Gateshead, Tyne & Wear, NE11 9HU
Activities: Other information technology service activities
Parent: ITPS (Holdings) Limited
Officers: Michael John Harold Jopling, Finance Director; Michael John Harold Jopling [1963] Finance Director; Garry Sheriff [1966] Managing Director

I2media Limited
Incorporated: 15 July 2005 *Employees:* 17
Net Worth: £123,940 *Total Assets:* £1,101,480
Registered Office: Unit 2 Bankside, The Watermark, Gateshead, Tyne & Wear, NE11 9SY
Activities: Publishing of consumer and business journals and periodicals
Shareholders: John Irving Josephs; Robert Michael Hewitt
Officers: Robert Michael Hewitt, Secretary; Maurice John Dobson [1942] Director; Robert Michael Hewitt [1974] Director; John Irving Josephs [1944] Director

I6media Ltd
Incorporated: 10 June 2011 *Employees:* 6
Net Worth: £1,603,638 *Total Assets:* £1,807,354
Registered Office: 3 The Poplars, Sunderland, Tyne & Wear, SR4 0PD
Activities: Publishing of computer games
Major Shareholder: Mohammed Ballal Iftikhar
Officers: Isra Ahmed, Secretary; Mohammed Ballal Iftikhar [1986] Director

IAM-Sold Ltd
Incorporated: 21 October 2009 *Employees:* 63
Net Worth: £1,015,281 *Total Assets:* £3,133,022
Registered Office: Unit 7 Diamond Court, Newcastle upon Tyne, NE3 2EN
Activities: Real estate agencies
Parent: Intelligent Services Group Ltd
Officers: Jamie Patrick Cooke [1985] Director; Eoghan Johnston [1987] Director/Chartered Accountant; Benjamin Thomas Ridgway [1985] Director

J.& H.B.Ibbitson (Sunderland) Limited
Incorporated: 23 August 1956 *Employees:* 17
Net Worth: £912,518 *Total Assets:* £947,547
Registered Office: 31 Holly Avenue, Jesmond, Newcastle upon Tyne, NE2 2PU
Activities: Retail sale via stalls and markets of food, beverages and tobacco products
Officers: Joanne Margaret Smith, Secretary; Simon John Ibbitson [1963] Director; Shaun Muldown [1969] Director/Butcher; Joanne Margaret Smith [1952] Director

ICCS Holdings Limited
Incorporated: 19 February 2016
Net Worth: £803,278 *Total Assets:* £1,055,137
Registered Office: 37 Atley Business Park, Cramlington, Northumberland, NE23 1WP
Activities: Activities of other holding companies n.e.c.
Shareholders: Ian Calderwood; William Watson; George Hart
Officers: Ian Calderwood [1971] Director; George Hart [1975] Director; William Watson [1965] Director

Ichina Wholesale Ltd
Incorporated: 24 June 2013
Net Worth: £522,280 *Total Assets:* £1,039,167
Registered Office: 4-9 The Old School Yard, Greta Street, Middlesbrough, Cleveland, TS1 5QF
Activities: Non-specialised wholesale trade
Officers: Fang Li [1987] Director [Chinese]

Icicle Vehicle Solutions Limited
Incorporated: 4 March 2008 *Employees:* 3
Net Worth: £416,011 *Total Assets:* £1,234,807
Registered Office: Blacksmith's House, Bedale Road, Hunton, N Yorks, DL8 1QE
Activities: Sale of used cars and light motor vehicles
Shareholders: Marilyn Francoise Bradford; Sean Fraser Bradford
Officers: Marilyne Francoise Bradford, Secretary; Marilyne Francoise Bradford [1966] Director [French]; Sean Fraser Bradford [1965] Director

Icon Plastics Limited
Incorporated: 17 May 2001 *Employees:* 54
Net Worth: £1,501,579 *Total Assets:* £3,119,528
Registered Office: 4 Sowerby Way, Durham Lane Industrial Park, Eaglescliffe, Stockton on Tees, Cleveland, TS16 0RB
Activities: Other manufacturing n.e.c.
Major Shareholder: Gareth William Thomas
Officers: Louise Thomas, Secretary; Gareth William Thomas [1971] Director

ICS Integrated Cable Services Limited
Incorporated: 15 December 2000 *Employees:* 80
Net Worth: £1,856,242 *Total Assets:* £2,472,395
Registered Office: ICS Integrated Cable Services, Bentley Avenue, Cowpen Lane Industrial Estate, Billingham, Cleveland, TS23 4BU
Activities: Electrical installation
Shareholders: Paul Maiden; Lynn Maiden
Officers: Lynn Maiden, Secretary; Lynn Maiden [1967] Director/Secretary; Paul Maiden [1968] Director/Quality Assurance Manager

Ideal Caravan Sales Limited
Incorporated: 23 August 1972 *Employees:* 29
Net Worth: £2,422,772 *Total Assets:* £7,025,826
Registered Office: Littleburn Lane, Langley Moor, Co Durham, DH7 8HA
Activities: Sale of new cars and light motor vehicles
Shareholders: David Ballantine; Raymond Anthony Ballantine; Linda Spears
Officers: David Ballantine [1958] Managing Director; Raymond Anthony Ballantine [1964] Director/Sales; Linda Spears [1956] Director/Marketing

Ideal Care (North) Limited
Incorporated: 10 March 1998 *Employees:* 69
Net Worth: £3,436,106 *Total Assets:* £4,163,660
Registered Office: Summerfields, St James Fields, Castle Eden, Co Durham, TS27 4TJ
Activities: Residential nursing care facilities
Parent: Motherdale Limited
Officers: Susan Elizabeth Maredia, Secretary; Ben Maredia [1982] Director; Dr Mohamad Noorbhai Maredia [1945] Director/General Medical Practitioner

Idec Power Services Limited
Incorporated: 7 October 2011 *Employees:* 39
Net Worth: £842,385 *Total Assets:* £2,537,833
Registered Office: Concorde House, Concorde Way, Preston Farm Business Park, Stockton on Tees, Cleveland, TS18 3RB
Activities: Engineering design activities for industrial process and production
Shareholder: Andrew Hodgson
Officers: Steven Norman Carter, Secretary; Steven Norman Carter [1954] Director; Andrew Hodgson [1963] Director/General Manager

Idec Technical Services Limited
Incorporated: 24 May 2002 *Employees:* 73
Net Worth: £2,503,589 *Total Assets:* £5,028,103
Registered Office: 43 Yarm Lane, Stockton on Tees, Cleveland, TS18 3EA
Activities: Engineering design activities for industrial process and production
Major Shareholder: Steven Norman Carter
Officers: Steven Norman Carter, Secretary; Steven Norman Carter [1954] Director

Identec Limited
Incorporated: 7 April 1995 *Employees:* 7
Net Worth: £976,339 *Total Assets:* £1,069,147
Registered Office: Mercantile Road, Rainton Bridge Industrial Estate, Houghton-le-Spring, Co Durham, DH4 5PH
Activities: Manufacture of electronic industrial process control equipment
Major Shareholder: Harold Dodd
Officers: Harold Dodd [1944] Director/Engineer; Gary Vasey [1970] Director

Identity Consult Limited
Incorporated: 6 April 2005
Net Worth: £704,070 *Total Assets:* £1,385,660
Registered Office: 6 Pickersgill Court, Quay West Business Village, Sunderland, Tyne & Wear, SR5 2AQ
Activities: Architectural activities
Parent: Identity Consult Group Limited
Officers: Mark Lee Doherty, Secretary; Mark Lee Doherty [1979] Director/Chartered Quantity Surveyor; Peter Johnson [1980] Director

IHC FHP Limited
Incorporated: 7 August 1986 *Employees:* 42
Net Worth: £2,693,000 *Total Assets:* £5,260,000
Registered Office: Neptune Energy Park, Fisher Street, Newcastle upon Tyne, NE6 4LY
Activities: Manufacture of fluid power equipment
Parent: IHC Merwede UK Limited
Officers: Andrew Briggs, Secretary; Paul Craig Hardisty [1961] Director; Dave Alexander Andre Joseph Antoon Georges Vander Heyde [1967] Director [Belgian]

IHC Merwede UK Limited
Incorporated: 17 December 2007 *Employees:* 2
Net Worth: £21,052,000 *Total Assets:* £45,243,000
Registered Office: Unit 11 Stocksfield Hall, Stocksfield, Northumberland, NE43 7TN
Activities: Activities of head offices
Parent: IHC Merwede Guernsey
Officers: Andrew Briggs, Secretary; Paul Craig Hardisty [1961] Director; Dave Alexander Andre Joseph Antoon Georges Vander Heyde [1967] Director/Chief Financial Officer [Belgian]

IK-ECO Limited
Incorporated: 27 June 2000 *Employees:* 24
Net Worth: £681,660 *Total Assets:* £1,164,799
Registered Office: Aim To Recycle, Abbotsford Road, Felling, Gateshead, Tyne & Wear, NE10 0EX
Activities: Recovery of sorted materials
Parent: Aim To Recycle Limited
Officers: Jennifer Gaydon-Lownds, Secretary; Jennifer Gaydon-Lownds [1986] Director; Adam McDonald [1983] Director; Ian McDonald [1955] Director; Joan McDonald [1954] Director

IK-UK Limited
Incorporated: 23 November 2010
Net Worth: £525,382 *Total Assets:* £2,105,179
Registered Office: 1 Grindon Way, Heighington Business Park, Newton Aycliffe, Co Durham, DL5 6SH
Activities: Manufacture of other general-purpose machinery n.e.c.
Parent: IK Group AS
Officers: Christian Bull Eriksson [1956] Director [Norwegian]; John Erik Gotrik [1960] Director [Norwegian]; Christian Knutsen [1958] Technical Director [Norwegian]; Andrew Peter Marwood [1975] Director; Geir Molberg [1975] Director [Norwegian]; Raymond Schofield [1948] Director Non-Executive; John Alphonsius Walsh [1968] Finance Director [Irish]

IKM Testing UK Limited
Incorporated: 18 November 1997 *Employees:* 107
Net Worth: £6,320,086 *Total Assets:* £11,034,368
Registered Office: 42 Colbourne Crescent, Nelson Park Industrial Estate, Cramlington, Northumberland, NE23 1WB
Activities: Other engineering activities
Major Shareholder: Stale Kyllingstad
Officers: Erling Meinich Bache, Secretary; Stale Kyllingstad [1960] Director [Norwegian]; Anthony Stephen Perkin [1957] Director

Ikonica Furniture Ltd
Incorporated: 30 August 2013
Net Worth: £1,715,300 *Total Assets:* £1,811,318
Registered Office: 27a Todds Nook, Westgate Road, Newcastle upon Tyne, NE4 6EX
Activities: Other retail sale in non-specialised stores
Shareholders: Bernard Partridge; James Elster
Officers: Bernard Partridge, Secretary; James Elster [1977] Director/Manager; Bernard Partridge [1978] Director/Manager

Imad-Muminah Properties Ltd
Incorporated: 9 January 2010
Net Worth: £330,616 *Total Assets:* £2,356,247
Registered Office: 29a New Elvet, Durham, DH1 3AL
Activities: Buying and selling of own real estate
Shareholder: Shoukat Ali
Officers: Shoukat Ali, Secretary; Sakhi Sultana Ali [1970] Director; Shoukat Ali [1949] Director

Imbue Property Ltd
Incorporated: 25 March 2014 *Employees:* 2
Net Worth: £322,864 *Total Assets:* £3,804,838
Registered Office: 37-38 Market Street, Ferryhill, Co Durham, DL17 8JH
Activities: Buying and selling of own real estate
Major Shareholder: Andrew John Tomlinson
Officers: Mark Ellison [1965] Director; Alan Richard Neal [1951] Director; Andrew John Tomlinson [1973] Director

Immi Ltd
Incorporated: 21 July 1999 *Employees:* 21
Net Worth: £1,497,556 *Total Assets:* £2,317,122
Registered Office: St Ann's Wharf, 112 Quayside, Newcastle upon Tyne, NE1 3DX
Activities: Manufacture of other transport equipment n.e.c.
Major Shareholder: James Thomas Anthony
Officers: James Thomas Anthony [1960] Director/Chief Executive Officer [American]; James Richard Anthony [1934] Director [American]; Anthony Schelonka [1942] Director [American]

Immobi Ltd
Incorporated: 2 April 2012
Net Worth: £800,332 *Total Assets:* £2,610,500
Registered Office: Mullen Stoker House, Unit 12 Mandale Business Park, Belmont Industrial Estate, Durham, DH1 1TH
Activities: Other letting and operating of own or leased real estate
Shareholders: Claire Roper-Browning; Ervin Meszaros
Officers: Claire Roper-Browning, Secretary; Ervin Meszaros [1978] Director [Hungarian]; Claire Roper-Browning [1977] Marketing Director

Immunodiagnostic Systems Holdings Public Limited Company
Incorporated: 4 June 2004 *Employees:* 283
Net Worth: £56,872,000 *Total Assets:* £67,541,000
Registered Office: 10 Didcot Way, Boldon Business Park, Boldon Colliery, Co Durham, NE35 9PD
Activities: General medical practice activities
Officers: Paul James Martin, Secretary; Klaus Peter Kaspar [1952] Director [German]; Paul James Martin [1977] Director/Accountant; Jaap Stuut [1970] Director [Dutch]; Peter John Williamson [1966] Director; Dr Burkhard Wittek [1953] Director/Investor [German]

Immunodiagnostic Systems Limited
Incorporated: 27 December 1995 *Employees:* 52
Net Worth: £44,351,780 *Total Assets:* £48,942,620
Registered Office: 10 Didcot Way, Boldon Business Park, Boldon Colliery, Co Durham, NE35 9PD
Activities: Other manufacturing n.e.c.
Parent: Immunodiagnostic Systems Holdings PLC
Officers: Paul James Martin [1977] Finance Director; Nicola Mitton [1979] Group HR Director; Jaap Stuut [1970] Director [Dutch]

Impact 3D Signs Limited
Incorporated: 10 February 2000
Net Worth: £995,943 *Total Assets:* £1,084,861
Registered Office: 13 Hutton Street, Boldon Colliery, Co Durham, NE35 9LW
Activities: Other manufacturing n.e.c.
Major Shareholder: Kevin Washbourne
Officers: Dennis Washbourne, Secretary; Cheryl Washbourne [1984] Director; Kevin Washbourne [1960] Director

Implants International Limited
Incorporated: 1 June 2005 *Employees:* 7
Net Worth: £694,105 *Total Assets:* £3,853,176
Registered Office: 71 Jay Avenue, Teesside Industrial Estate, Thornaby on Tees, Cleveland, TS17 9LZ
Activities: Manufacture of medical and dental instruments and supplies
Shareholder: Najma Mohan Emmanuel
Officers: Najma Mohan Emmanuel, Secretary; Najma Mohan Emmanuel [1955] Director

Impress North East (Holdings) Limited
Incorporated: 22 April 2002
Net Worth: £1,486,545 *Total Assets:* £1,683,494
Registered Office: Impress NE Holdings Ltd, Ryton Industrial Estate, Newburn Bridge Road, Blaydon on Tyne, Tyne & Wear, NE21 4SQ
Activities: Activities of production holding companies
Shareholders: Steven Young; George Peel
Officers: David Haley, Secretary/Accountant; David Haley [1953] Director/Accountant; George Peel [1957] Engineer Director; Steven Young [1960] Engineer Director

Impress North East Limited
Incorporated: 27 January 1997 *Employees:* 76
Net Worth: £2,335,842 *Total Assets:* £3,632,748
Registered Office: Ryton Industrial Estate, Newburn Bridge Road, Blaydon on Tyne, Tyne & Wear, NE21 4SQ
Activities: Machining
Officers: David Haley, Secretary/Director; Kevin Dickinson [1954] Sales Director; Jason Forster [1971] Finance Director; David Haley [1953] Director; Stephen Patrick [1985] Technical Sales Director; George Peel [1957] Director; Craig Rogers [1963] Group Quality Assurance Director; Jason Young [1978] Director; Steven Young [1960] Director

Impulsepay Ltd
Incorporated: 15 March 2002 *Employees:* 7
Net Worth: £433,287 *Total Assets:* £2,320,698
Registered Office: The Stables, St Georges Terrace, Jesmond, Newcastle upon Tyne, NE2 2SU
Activities: Wireless telecommunications activities
Major Shareholder: Christopher James Newell
Officers: Henry David Wilson, Secretary/Consultant; Christopher James Newell [1980] Director; Henry David Wilson [1950] Director/Consultant

In Service Limited
Incorporated: 4 October 2001
Registered Office: 6 Queens Court North, Third Avenue, Team Valley Trading Estate, Gateshead, Tyne & Wear, NE11 0BU
Activities: Other letting and operating of own or leased real estate
Officers: Richard Alan Tait, Secretary/Accountant; Ian Atkinson [1950] Director; Nigel Edward Atkinson [1975] Director; Susan Jane Atkinson [1948] Director; Rebecca Jane Wright [1984] Director/Administration Manager

In-House Inspired Room Design Ltd
Incorporated: 1 May 2003
Net Worth: £829,257 *Total Assets:* £1,363,839
Registered Office: Hill Bank, 14 Batt House Road, Stocksfield, Northumberland, NE43 7RA
Activities: Agents specialised in the sale of other particular products
Major Shareholder: Wayne William Dance
Officers: Christopher Dance [1987] Director/Manager; Stuart Dance [1980] Director/Manager; Wayne William Dance [1958] Managing Director; Malo Tasle [1972] Director/Area Manager [French]

IN2 Developments Limited
Incorporated: 21 April 2011
Net Worth: £651,952 *Total Assets:* £1,003,243
Registered Office: B3 Marquis Court, Team Valley Trading Estate, Gateshead, Tyne & Wear, NE11 0RU
Activities: Management consultancy activities other than financial management
Parent: IN2 Management Group Limited
Officers: Thomas Mark Lee-Gough, Secretary; John Aaron Brown [1966] Director; Susan Lynne Brown [1966] Director

Inbond Limited
Incorporated: 12 May 2003 *Employees:* 23
Net Worth: £716,775 *Total Assets:* £1,563,331
Registered Office: Northshore Logistics Centre, Malleable Way, Stockton on Tees, Cleveland, TS18 2QX
Activities: Operation of warehousing and storage facilities for land transport activities
Parent: Inbond Holdings (NE) Limited
Officers: Phillip Lyons [1973] Director; Craig Derek Rye [1984] Director

Increase Computers Limited
Incorporated: 14 December 1982 *Employees:* 11
Net Worth: £899,727 *Total Assets:* £1,327,878
Registered Office: Gear House, Saltmeadows Road, Gateshead, Tyne & Wear, NE8 3AH
Activities: Information technology consultancy activities
Parent: Compactypist Limited
Officers: Aaron Lee Matheson, Secretary/Director; Paul Fairless [1970] Director; Aaron Lee Matheson [1968] Director; Philip Michael Short [1966] Managing Director

Indepak Limited
Incorporated: 22 May 1925
Net Worth: £951,017 *Total Assets:* £968,089
Registered Office: Dashwood, Blewhouse Lane, Finghall, Leyburn, N Yorks, DL8 5NP
Activities: Buying and selling of own real estate
Major Shareholder: Iain Alexander Blair
Officers: Brenda Esme Blair, Secretary; Iain Alexander Blair [1962] Director/Group Manager [Australian]; Jacqueline May Kimber [1959] Director/Interior Designer

Independent Air Treatment Technology Limited
Incorporated: 4 January 2010 *Employees:* 13
Net Worth: £662,863 *Total Assets:* £1,393,268
Registered Office: The Hemmel, West Marlish Farm, Hartburn, Northumberland, NE61 4ER
Activities: Installation of industrial machinery and equipment
Major Shareholder: Trevor Clark
Officers: Trevor Clark [1958] Finance Director

Inderjeet Medicals Limited
Incorporated: 8 April 2011
Net Worth: £1,123,356 *Total Assets:* £1,154,241
Registered Office: 80 Western Way, Ponteland, Northumberland, NE20 9AW
Activities: General medical practice activities
Officers: Kanika Singh, Secretary; Dr Inderjeet Singh [1973] Director/Doctor; Kanika Singh [1981] Director/Administrator

Indian Kings Walk 1 Limited
Incorporated: 5 June 2002
Net Worth: £1,750,426 *Total Assets:* £2,544,794
Registered Office: Time Central, 32 Gallowgate, Newcastle upon Tyne, NE1 4BF
Activities: Other letting and operating of own or leased real estate
Officers: Jane Elizabeth Callan [1956] Director; Simon Goldberg [1977] Director/Barrister; Alan Toby Hedworth [1952] Director/Barrister; Christopher John Knox [1952] Director/Barrister; Antoine Tinnion [1970] Director/Barrister

The Indie Stone Ltd
Incorporated: 14 August 2013 *Employees:* 4
Net Worth: £614,336 *Total Assets:* £786,557
Registered Office: Northern Design Centre, Abbott's Hill, Baltic Business Quarter, Gateshead, Tyne & Wear, NE8 3DF
Activities: Ready-made interactive leisure and entertainment software development
Shareholders: Christopher Simpson; Andrew Hodgetts
Officers: Andrew Hodgetts [1978] Director; William Porter [1980] Director; Christopher Simpson [1979] Director; Marina Siu-Chong [1983] Director [Canadian]

Indigo Software (Holdings) Limited
Incorporated: 2 November 2012
Net Worth: £1,758,366 *Total Assets:* £2,606,496
Registered Office: Indigo House, Belmont Business Park, Durham, DH1 1TW
Activities: Activities of head offices
Parent: Indigo Software Group Limited
Officers: William Ginn, Secretary; William Ginn [1961] Director/Accountant

Indigo Software Group Limited
Incorporated: 21 July 2016 *Employees:* 36
Net Worth: £3,533,860 *Total Assets:* £7,764,386
Registered Office: Indigo House, Belmont Business Park, Belmont, Durham, DH1 1TW
Activities: Business and domestic software development
Shareholders: Darren Robert Baxter; William Ginn
Officers: Darren Robert Baxter [1965] Director; William Ginn [1961] Director; Michael Hill [1959] Director; Peter James McLane [1956] Director; Anthony Sweeney [1955] Director

Indigo Software Limited
Incorporated: 8 December 2005 *Employees:* 34
Net Worth: £1,075,614 *Total Assets:* £3,808,152
Registered Office: Indigo House, Belmont Business Park, Durham, DH1 1TW
Activities: Business and domestic software development
Parent: Clothco 2016 Limited
Officers: Darren Robert Baxter, Secretary; Darren Robert Baxter [1965] Director; William Ginn [1961] Director/Accountant; Michael Hill [1959] Director

Indoor Climate Control Holdings Limited
Incorporated: 16 February 2017
Net Worth: £865,546 *Total Assets:* £1,162,936
Registered Office: Stokoe Rodger, Unit 15 The Watermark, Bankside, Gateshead, Tyne & Wear, NE11 9SY
Activities: Activities of other holding companies n.e.c.
Shareholders: Susan Patricia Tiffin; Brian Tiffin
Officers: Brian Tiffin [1965] Director

Induction Pipe Bending UK Limited
Incorporated: 24 March 2005 *Employees:* 56
Net Worth: £1,323,872 *Total Assets:* £2,595,763
Registered Office: 11 Sedling Road, Wear Industrial Estate, Washington, Tyne & Wear, NE38 9BZ
Activities: Manufacture of other fabricated metal products n.e.c.
Officers: Peter Ian Wharton, Secretary; Phillip George Graham [1954] Director/Production Supervisor; Michael James Last [1966] Director/Machine Operator; Andrew Martin Stewart [1968] Director/Project Manager; Peter Ian Wharton [1965] Director

Industrial & Community Wind Generation No. 2 Limited
Incorporated: 25 April 2012
Net Worth: £2,896,359 *Total Assets:* £4,257,888
Registered Office: 384 Linthorpe Road, Middlesbrough, Cleveland, TS5 6HA
Activities: Production of electricity
Parent: Industrial & Community Wind Generation Limited
Officers: Nicholas Simon Curtis [1966] Director; Theresa Lorraine Curtis [1939] Director; Zoe Mary Curtis [1967] Director

Industrial and Marine Hydraulics Limited
Incorporated: 14 June 1983
Registered Office: 2 Snowdon Road, Middlesbrough, Cleveland, TS2 1LP
Activities: Machining
Shareholders: Paul Griffiths; Teresa Griffiths
Officers: Teresa Griffiths, Secretary; Paul Griffiths [1949] Director/Hydraulic Engineer; Teresa Griffiths [1950] Director/Secretary

Industrial Energy Services Limited
Incorporated: 20 June 1983 *Employees:* 3
Net Worth: £21,491,000 *Total Assets:* £52,638,000
Registered Office: Shared Services Centre, Q3 Office, Quorum Business Park, Benton Lane, Newcastle upon Tyne, NE12 8EX
Activities: Installation of industrial machinery and equipment
Parent: Engie UK Holding (Services) Limited
Officers: Sarah Gregory, Secretary; Simon David Pinnell [1964] Director

Industrial Monitoring Systems Limited
Incorporated: 24 November 1993 *Employees:* 11
Net Worth: £998,174 *Total Assets:* £1,495,117
Registered Office: Temple Chambers, Douro Terrace, Sunderland, Tyne & Wear, SR2 7DX
Activities: Manufacture of other special-purpose machinery n.e.c.
Major Shareholder: James Russell Foster
Officers: Fiona Marjory Morton, Company Secretary; David Neil Armstrong [1960] Director/Chartered Accountant

Industrial Technology Systems Limited
Incorporated: 30 October 1991
Net Worth: £507,922 *Total Assets:* £1,252,627
Registered Office: ITS House, High Force Road, Riverside Park, Middlesbrough, Cleveland, TS2 1RH
Activities: Information technology consultancy activities
Major Shareholder: Malcolm Knott
Officers: Simon Michael Close, Secretary; Simon Michael Close [1965] Director/Accountant; Dr Stanley Derek Higgins [1953] Director; Graham John Ives [1971] Projects Director; Malcolm Knott [1955] Managing Director; Julian Mark Generald Taylor [1968] Business Development Director

INEOS Compounds Aycliffe Limited
Incorporated: 15 August 2013 *Employees:* 205
Net Worth: £5,902,000 *Total Assets:* £48,891,000
Registered Office: School Aycliffe Lane, Newton Aycliffe, Co Durham, DL5 6EA
Activities: Manufacture of other inorganic basic chemicals
Parent: INEOS Compounds Holdings Limited
Officers: Steven Jamieson, Secretary; David John Wright Rey, Secretary; Andrew Brown [1981] Director/Chartered Accountant; Alex Hogan [1976] Director; Anthony White [1961] Director/Accountant

INEOS Compounds Holdings Limited
Incorporated: 14 August 2013 *Employees:* 311
Net Worth Deficit: £4,187,455 *Total Assets:* £43,656,452
Registered Office: School Aycliffe Lane, Newton Aycliffe, Co Durham, DL5 6EA
Activities: Manufacture of other inorganic basic chemicals
Parent: INEOS Enterprises Holdings Limited
Officers: Steven Jamieson, Secretary; David John Wright Rey, Secretary; Andrew Brown [1981] Director/Chartered Accountant; Alex Hogan [1976] Director; Anthony White [1961] Director/Accountant

INEOS Nitriles (UK) Limited
Incorporated: 4 May 2007 *Employees:* 218
Net Worth: £87,470,000 *Total Assets:* £141,174,000
Registered Office: P O Box 62, Seal Sands, Middlesbrough, Cleveland, TS2 1TX
Activities: Manufacture of other chemical products n.e.c.
Parent: INEOS European Holdings Limited
Officers: Caroline Walker, Secretary; Jonathan Paul Howard [1965] Director; Caroline Walker [1983] Director/Accountant

Infinite Sirius (Lounge) Limited
Incorporated: 19 March 2015
Registered Office: Russel House, Mill Road, Langley Moor, Co Durham, DH7 8HJ
Activities: Production of electricity
Parent: Sirius Renewable Energy Ltd
Officers: Douglas Mill [1962] Director

Infinity Dental Services (IDS) Ltd
Incorporated: 3 October 2011
Net Worth: £28,399 *Total Assets:* £961,938
Registered Office: Coxhoe Dental Practice, 2 Blackgate East, Coxhoe, Co Durham, DH6 4AA
Activities: Dental practice activities
Major Shareholder: Asad Razaq
Officers: Asad Razaq [1987] Director/Dentist

Ingleby Healthcare Ltd
Incorporated: 4 April 2011
Net Worth: £33,562 *Total Assets:* £2,160,663
Registered Office: 4 Hadrian Way, Ingleby Barwick, Cleveland, TS17 5LA
Activities: Other business support service activities n.e.c.
Shareholders: N & R Gupta Limited; Seaton Healthcare Limited
Officers: Nitin Gupta [1970] Director/Pharmacist; Rachna Gupta [1974] Director/Kumon Instructor; Harpreet Singh Kullar [1979] Director/Pharmacist; Narinder Dave Singh Sangha [1975] Director/Pharmacist

James Ingleford Limited
Incorporated: 7 February 2000
Net Worth: £443,968 *Total Assets:* £884,969
Registered Office: A1 Marquis Court, Team Valley Trading Estate, Gateshead, Tyne & Wear, NE11 0RU
Activities: Development of building projects
Major Shareholder: John Flowers
Officers: Jeanette Flowers, Secretary; Jeanette Flowers [1956] Director; John Flowers [1957] Director; Michael Norman Watson [1971] Director/Estimator

James Ingleford Scaffolding Limited
Incorporated: 18 October 2010 *Employees:* 97
Net Worth: £616,835 *Total Assets:* £2,537,969
Registered Office: 2 Monument Park, Pattinson Industrial Estate, Washington, Tyne & Wear, NE38 8QU
Activities: Scaffold erection
Parent: F & I Holdings Limited
Officers: Mark Davison [1987] Director/Contracts Manager; Jonathan Flowers [1982] Director

Initial Group of Companies Limited
Incorporated: 8 May 2012 *Employees:* 1
Net Worth: £169,515 *Total Assets:* £2,567,516
Registered Office: The Paddock, Kirk Merrington, Spennymoor, Co Durham, DL16 7JT
Activities: Activities of head offices
Major Shareholder: Wayne Andrew Baister
Officers: Wayne Andrew Baister [1971] Director/Clothing Retailer

Inkland Limited
Incorporated: 25 July 1979
Net Worth: £143,561 *Total Assets:* £1,109,395
Registered Office: Unit 14 Hurworth Road, Aycliffe Business Park, Newton Aycliffe, Co Durham, DL5 6UD
Activities: Agents specialised in the sale of other particular products
Parent: Sandco 802 Ltd
Officers: Jonathan Simpson, Secretary/Financial Director; Darren Robert Eliot [1969] Director; Jonathan Simpson [1965] Financial Director; Michael Alan Taylor [1970] Sales Director

Inlec UK Limited
Incorporated: 19 January 1996 *Employees:* 4
Net Worth: £466,405 *Total Assets:* £1,420,061
Registered Office: Tobias House, St Marks Court, Teesdale Business Park, Stockton on Tees, Cleveland, TS17 6QW
Activities: Renting and leasing of other machinery, equipment and tangible goods n.e.c.
Parent: Ellerbeck Industries Limited
Officers: Clare Ann McCullagh [1969] Director/Chartered Accountant; John Michael McCullagh [1963] Director; Rolf Michael McCullagh [1965] Director; Tim Michael McCullagh [1968] Director

Inn Collection Acquisitionco Limited
Incorporated: 2 August 2013 *Employees:* 19
Net Worth Deficit: £151,250 *Total Assets:* £1,493,494
Registered Office: c/o Ward Hadaway, Sandgate House, 102 Quayside, Newcastle upon Tyne, NE1 3DX
Activities: Hotels and similar accommodation
Parent: Inn Collection Bidco Limited
Officers: Sean Lee Donkin [1981] Operations Director; Angus Keith Liddell [1955] Director; Iain Stein [1959] Director

Inn Collection Bidco Limited
Incorporated: 2 August 2013 *Employees:* 7
Net Worth Deficit: £2,978,007 *Total Assets:* £11,906,486
Registered Office: c/o Ward Hadaway, Sandgate House, 102 Quayside, Newcastle upon Tyne, NE1 3DX
Activities: Activities of other holding companies n.e.c.
Parent: Inn Collection Midco Limited
Officers: Sean Lee Donkin [1981] Operations Director; Angus Keith Liddell [1955] Director; Iain Stein [1959] Director

Inn Collection Midco Limited
Incorporated: 19 July 2013
Net Worth Deficit: £2,492,473 *Total Assets:* £7,187,312
Registered Office: c/o Ward Hadaway, Sandgate House, 102 Quayside, Newcastle upon Tyne, NE1 3DX
Activities: Activities of other holding companies n.e.c.
Parent: Inn Collection Topco Limited
Officers: Sean Lee Donkin [1981] Managing Director; Angus Keith Liddell [1955] Director; Iain Stein [1959] Director

Inn Collection Topco Limited
Incorporated: 15 July 2013 *Employees:* 186
Net Worth Deficit: £2,149,362 *Total Assets:* £16,109,880
Registered Office: c/o Ward Hadaway, Sandgate House, 102 Quayside, Newcastle upon Tyne, NE1 3DX
Activities: Activities of other holding companies n.e.c.
Parent: Vindolanda Bidco Limited
Officers: Sean Lee Donkin [1981] Managing Director; Angus Keith Liddell [1955] Director

Innerglass Limited
Incorporated: 27 May 1981 *Employees:* 140
Net Worth: £2,362,488 *Total Assets:* £8,596,429
Registered Office: Innerglass Ltd (IG Group), Burdon Drive, North West Industrial Estate, Peterlee, Co Durham, SR8 2JH
Activities: Wholesale of china and glassware and cleaning materials
Major Shareholder: Stephen Hoey
Officers: Stephen Hoey, Secretary; Nathan Lewis Hoey [1992] Director; Stephen Daniel Hoey [1988] Director; Stephen Hoey [1958] Managing Director; Lesley Anne Tait [1968] National Sales Director

Inoveight Limited
Incorporated: 6 April 2001 *Employees:* 44
Net Worth: £7,292,000 *Total Assets:* £33,843,000
Registered Office: 12b Beechburn Industrial Estate, Prospect Road, Crook, Co Durham, DL15 8RA
Activities: Wholesale of clothing and footwear
Parent: Inoveight Holdings Limited
Officers: Gary John Mennell, Secretary; Ian Ralph Bailey [1963] Director; Clinton Wayne George Edy [1962] Director; Jonathan Hammond [1975] Finance Director; Hiroaki Kobayashi [1963] Director [Japanese]; Gary John Mennell [1961] Director; Eijiro Nireki [1971] Director [Japanese]; Hitoshi Suyama [1961] Director [Japanese]

Inshore Fisheries Limited
Incorporated: 26 November 2004
Net Worth: £87,582 *Total Assets:* £1,538,014
Registered Office: Inshore Fisheries, Tod Point Road, Warrenby, Redcar, Cleveland, TS10 5AU
Activities: Wholesale of other food, including fish, crustaceans and molluscs
Parent: Inshore Holdings Limited
Officers: Hazel Cook, Secretary/Food Retailer; Hazel Cook [1954] Director/Food Retailer; Paul Lowery [1964] Director/Food Retailer; Micheal Rogerson [1966] Director/Food Retailer

Inshore Holdings Limited
Incorporated: 11 May 2012
Net Worth: £3 *Total Assets:* £850,003
Registered Office: Inshore House, Tod Point Road, Warrenby, Redcar, Cleveland, TS10 5AU
Activities: Activities of other holding companies n.e.c.
Shareholders: Hazel Cook; Paul Lowery; Michael Rogerson
Officers: Hazel Cook [1954] Director; Paul Lowery [1964] Director; Micheal Rogerson [1966] Director

Insight Healthcare Ltd.
Incorporated: 11 March 2002
Net Worth: £330,000 *Total Assets:* £2,330,000
Registered Office: Buttress House, 36 Brenkley Way, Blezard Business Park, Seaton Burn, Newcastle upon Tyne, NE13 6DS
Activities: Other human health activities
Officers: David Keith Belk, Secretary; David Robson Arthur [1954] Director/Accountant; Fiona Sheila Cassells [1953] Director/Retired; Rosemary Caroline Granger [1957] Director/Consultant; Zena Jones [1955] Director/NHS Employee; Richard McEvoy [1962] Director/Banker; Elizabeth Ann Robinson [1950] Director/Retired; David Smith [1973] Director/Management Consultant; Doctor Angela Mary Walsh [1949] Director/GP (Retired)

Inspire Multi Academy Trust
Incorporated: 8 November 2012 *Employees:* 91
Net Worth: £8,346,000 *Total Assets:* £10,808,000
Registered Office: Farringdon Academy, Archer Road, Farringdon, Sunderland, Tyne & Wear, SR3 3DJ
Activities: Primary education
Officers: Simon Kenneth Allan, Secretary; Howard William Brown [1955] Director/Retired; Melanie Byers [1968] Director/Health and Safety Adviser; Dr Kim Gilligan [1963] Director/Senior Lecturer; Allison McCully [1965] Director/School Bursar; Tracey Pizl [1963] Director/Lead Headteacher; Stephen Ruffell [1956] Director/Manager; Elizabeth Scribbins [1955] Director/Retired; Joanne West [1971] Director/Chief Executive Headteacher

Inspired Agency Ltd
Incorporated: 8 March 2007 *Employees:* 24
Net Worth: £586,537 *Total Assets:* £1,207,057
Registered Office: 246 Park View, Whitley Bay, Tyne & Wear, NE26 3QX
Activities: Advertising agencies
Shareholders: Julia Dawn Patterson; Mark Richard Patterson
Officers: Julia Dawn Patterson, Secretary; Julia Dawn Patterson [1969] Operations Director; Mark Richard Patterson [1980] Managing Director

Insulation Contractors Limited
Incorporated: 21 March 2011 *Employees:* 14
Net Worth: £457,771 *Total Assets:* £1,041,259
Registered Office: 5 Naylor Court, Patterson Street, Blaydon Haugh Industrial Estate, Blaydon on Tyne, Tyne & Wear, NE21 5SD
Activities: Other specialised construction activities n.e.c.
Shareholder: Ian Neville Marsden
Officers: Gary Cameron [1966] Director/Thermal Insulation Contractor; Ian Neville Marsden [1971] Director

Integrated Display Systems Limited
Incorporated: 22 February 1980 *Employees:* 12
Net Worth: £7,216,246 *Total Assets:* £7,235,536
Registered Office: Unit 15 Maurice Road, Wallsend, Tyne & Wear, NE28 6BY
Activities: Manufacture of electronic industrial process control equipment
Parent: Clavis IDS Limited
Officers: Mark Errington [1978] Director/Electronics Engineer; Andrew Punton [1983] Director/Software Engineer

Integrated Office Systems Limited
Incorporated: 31 January 1994 *Employees:* 23
Net Worth: £767,378 *Total Assets:* £1,758,979
Registered Office: 89 Willows Court, Teesside Industrial Estate, Stockton on Tees, Cleveland, TS17 9PP
Activities: Non-specialised wholesale trade
Shareholders: Robert Henry Martin; Thomas Richard Henderson
Officers: Robert Henry Martin, Secretary; Thomas Richard Henderson [1966] Director/Salesman; Paul Stuart MacDonald [1976] Director/Salesman; Robert Henry Martin [1965] Director/Salesman; Lindsey Craig Ritchie [1961] Director/Salesman

Integrated Polymer Systems (U.K.) Limited
Incorporated: 23 July 1991
Net Worth: £713,543 *Total Assets:* £3,214,780
Registered Office: Thornton Rust Hall, Thornton Rust, Leyburn, N Yorks, DL8 3AW
Activities: Other retail sale not in stores, stalls or markets
Major Shareholder: Peter Bowers
Officers: Gavin Richard Bowers, Secretary; Gavin Richard Bowers [1978] Director; Peter Bowers [1948] Director/Building Manager

Integrated Polymer Systems Limited
Incorporated: 3 June 1985
Net Worth: £419,159 *Total Assets:* £849,882
Registered Office: Unit 1 Gatherley Road Industrial Estate, Brompton on Swale, Richmond, N Yorks, DL10 7JG
Activities: Roofing activities
Shareholders: Norman Smith; Peter Bowers
Officers: Gavin Richard Bowers, Secretary/Director; Gavin Richard Bowers [1978] Director; Peter Bowers [1948] Director/Manager

Integrated Utility Services Limited
Incorporated: 5 September 1994 *Employees:* 171
Net Worth: £107,000 *Total Assets:* £18,252,000
Registered Office: Lloyds Court, 78 Grey Street, Newcastle upon Tyne, NE1 6AF
Activities: Electrical installation
Parent: Northern Electric PLC
Officers: Jennifer Catherine Riley, Secretary; Thomas Edward Fielden [1970] Director/Chartered Accountant; Thomas Hugh France [1985] Director/Lawyer; Dr Philip Antony Jones [1968] Director/President & Chief Executive Officer; Andrew John MacLennan [1967] Managing Director

Intelect (UK) Limited
Incorporated: 3 October 1997 *Employees:* 100
Net Worth: £3,192,581 *Total Assets:* £5,536,824
Registered Office: Stephenson House, Intelect Court, Riverside Park, Middlesbrough, Cleveland, TS2 1QT
Activities: Electrical installation
Shareholders: Francis Patrick Cormican; John Paul Thompson
Officers: John Paul Thompson, Secretary; Francis Patrick Cormican [1969] Managing Director; Andrew Graham Shaw [1971] Director; John Paul Thompson [1968] Director; Paul Wilcock [1962] Director

Intelect Mechanical Limited
Incorporated: 4 April 2005 *Employees:* 20
Net Worth: £1,327,209 *Total Assets:* £2,326,300
Registered Office: Stephenson House, Intelect Court, Riverside Park, Middlesbrough, Cleveland, TS2 1QT
Activities: Other business support service activities n.e.c.
Officers: John Paul Thompson, Secretary; Francis Patrick Cormican [1969] Director; John Steven Gent [1970] Director; Andrew Graham Shaw [1971] Director; Kevan Thomas [1965] Director; John Paul Thompson [1968] Director

Interactive Development Support Limited
Incorporated: 17 June 2002 *Employees:* 125
Net Worth: £551,564 *Total Assets:* £1,115,061
Registered Office: 3-5 Brenkley Way, Blezard Business Park, Seaton Burn, Newcastle upon Tyne, NE13 6DS
Activities: Other social work activities without accommodation n.e.c.
Major Shareholder: Gordon Stuart Quince
Officers: Gordon Stuart Quince [1969] Director; Vanessa Kate Quince [1970] Director/Personal Assistant

Interactive Projects & Design Limited
Incorporated: 7 May 2003
Net Worth: £2,137,879 *Total Assets:* £3,813,115
Registered Office: Chesnut House, Chesnut Street, Darlington, Co Durham, DL1 1QL
Activities: Development of building projects
Major Shareholder: James Gerald Tully
Officers: Janette Tully, Secretary; Paul George Barber [1967] Director/Manager; James Generald Tully [1958] Director; Janette Tully [1959] Director

Interbulk (Tankcontainers) Holdings Limited
Incorporated: 22 February 2002
Net Worth Deficit: £8,355,072 *Total Assets:* £11,352,953
Registered Office: Victoria House, Pearson Court, Pearson Way, Stockton on Tees, Cleveland, TS17 6PT
Activities: Other transportation support activities
Major Shareholder: Klaas Pieter Den Hartogh
Officers: Klaas Pieter Den Hartogh [1965] Managing Director [Dutch]; Abraham Cornelius Paape [1959] Finance Director [Dutch]

Interbulk Group Limited
Incorporated: 8 December 2004 *Employees:* 5
Net Worth: £21,595,944 *Total Assets:* £30,047,748
Registered Office: Victoria House, Pearson Court, Pearson Way, Thornaby, Stockton on Tees, Cleveland, TS17 6PT
Activities: Activities of head offices
Major Shareholder: Klaas Pieter Den Hartogh
Officers: Klaas Pieter Den Hartogh [1965] Managing Director [Dutch]; Abraham Cornelius Paape [1959] Group Financial Director [Dutch]

Interceil Limited
Incorporated: 2 April 1982 *Employees:* 51
Net Worth: £795,595 *Total Assets:* £1,964,879
Registered Office: Fairholme, Ridley Terrace, Cambois, Blyth, Northumberland, NE24 1QT
Activities: Other building completion and finishing
Shareholder: Josiah Jones Snr
Officers: Philip John Cross, Secretary; Steven Robert Jones [1968] Managing Director

The Interflex Group Europe Limited
Incorporated: 29 December 1999 *Employees:* 229
Net Worth: £6,854,690 *Total Assets:* £26,169,644
Registered Office: West Quay Road, Sunderland Enterprise Park, Sunderland, Tyne & Wear, SR5 2TE
Activities: Activities of head offices
Officers: Adrian Alday, Secretary; Stephen Joseph Doyle [1963] Director/Chief Executive Officer [American]; Steven Jonathan Sherman Glick [1969] Director/Fund Investor [American]; Brett Snyder [1971] Director [American]; Rob Weiss [1969] Director [American]

Interflon (UK) Limited
Incorporated: 17 April 1998 *Employees:* 33
Net Worth: £500,305 *Total Assets:* £1,083,380
Registered Office: Crofton House, Crofton Road, Stockton on Tees, Cleveland, TS18 2QZ
Activities: Other business support service activities n.e.c.
Shareholders: Elizabeth Ann Marwood; Stephen James Marwood
Officers: Elizabeth Ann Marwood, Secretary/Director; Russell Spencer Brown [1970] Sales Director; Elizabeth Ann Marwood [1957] Director; Stephen James Marwood [1953] Director

Interlet Property Investment Consultants Limited
Incorporated: 11 November 2005
Net Worth: £228,417 *Total Assets:* £2,747,739
Registered Office: c/o A1 Accountancy Services, 12 Regent Terrace, Gateshead, Tyne & Wear, NE8 1LU
Activities: Buying and selling of own real estate
Officers: Leslie Roberts, Secretary/Estate Agent Surveyor; Terence Kimmitt [1962] Director/Letting Agent; William Kimmitt [1963] Director/Surveyor; Leslie Roberts [1957] Director/Estate Agent Surveyor

Interlink Scaffolding Ltd
Incorporated: 20 October 2003 *Employees:* 137
Net Worth: £161,346 *Total Assets:* £2,609,672
Registered Office: Unit 11 Station Lane Industrial Estate, Station Lane, Birtley, Co Durham, DH3 1DQ
Activities: Scaffold erection
Shareholders: Mark Eddy; David John Dale; Patrick Darren Maratty
Officers: David John Dale [1966] Director/Estimator; Mark Eddy [1974] Director/Quantity Surveyor; Patrick Darren Maratty [1966] Director/Manager

International Centre for Life (Property) Limited
Incorporated: 9 October 1996 *Employees:* 95
Net Worth: £4,207,938 *Total Assets:* £37,531,768
Registered Office: Management Suite, Times Square, Scotswood Road, Newcastle upon Tyne, NE1 4EP
Activities: Event catering activities
Parent: International Centre for Life Trust
Officers: Claire Helen Adams, Secretary; Delinda Virginia Julia Conlon [1956] Director/Chief Executive; Elizabeth Dean [1957] Director; Andrew David James [1946] Director/Retired; Catherine Jane Little [1966] Director/Chartered Accountant; Frank Nicholson [1954] Director/Self Employed

International Centre for Life Trust
Incorporated: 11 July 1996 *Employees:* 161
Net Worth: £42,005,400 *Total Assets:* £44,672,400
Registered Office: Management Suite, Times Square, Scotswood Road, Newcastle upon Tyne, NE1 4EP
Activities: Other professional, scientific and technical activities n.e.c.
Officers: Claire Helen Adams, Secretary; Councillor Irim Ali [1979] Director/Legal Assistant; Delinda Virginia Julia Conlon [1956] Director/Chief Executive; Clive Michael Cookson [1956] Director/Journalist; Fiona Crozier [1966] Director; Professor Richard John Davies [1967] Director/Pro Vice-Chancellor; Steven Gater [1952] Director/Headteacher; Andrew Hodgson [1964] Director/Chief Executive Officer; Professor Patrick Joseph Hussey [1962] Director/Pro-Vice Chancellor (Science); Professor David Roy Sandbach [1954] Director/Professor of Innovation and Enterprise; Professor Joris Andre Veltman [1971] Director of Institute of Genetic Medicine [Dutch]; Kathryn Lucy Hay Winskell [1963] Director

International Cookware Limited
Incorporated: 21 November 2005 *Employees:* 28
Net Worth: £3,439,000 *Total Assets:* £8,058,000
Registered Office: Unit 1a Hall Dene Way, Seaham Grange Industrial Estate, Seaham, Co Durham, SR7 0PU
Activities: Operation of warehousing and storage facilities for land transport activities
Officers: Didier Yves Andre Le Tirant [1965] Director [French]; Jose-Luis Llacuna [1966] Director [Spanish]

International Pipeline Products Limited
Incorporated: 5 October 1984 *Employees:* 81
Net Worth: £898,022 *Total Assets:* £3,682,287
Registered Office: International Pipeline Products, Gatherley Road, Brompton on Swale, Richmond, N Yorks, DL10 7JH
Activities: Manufacture of other plastic products
Officers: Darren Mark Williams, Secretary; Keith Appleton [1961] Director; Simon Kim Bell [1957] Director; Surendranath Anjhiah Dhanekula [1978] Director [Indian]; Nikhil Goel [1977] Director [Indian]; Sachin Vijayrao Sanghai [1978] Director [Indian]; Darren Mark Williams [1969] Finance Director

International Plastic Systems Limited
Incorporated: 29 May 1990 *Employees:* 45
Net Worth: £4,499,721 *Total Assets:* £6,513,164
Registered Office: Seaham Grange Industrial Estate, Seaham, Co Durham, SR7 0PT
Activities: Wholesale of other intermediate products
Parent: Indutrade AB
Officers: Johan Kallerhult, Secretary; Kevin Curran [1965] Operations Director; Stephen Hunter [1962] Director; Hakan Per-Olow Jansson [1961] Managing Director [Swedish]; Johan Kallerhult [1962] Director [Swedish]; Andrew Lamb [1967] Director/Sales Manager; David Stildolph [1959] Operations Director

International Processplants (Europe) Limited
Incorporated: 22 September 1975 *Employees:* 8
Net Worth: £2,139,319 *Total Assets:* £3,280,528
Registered Office: c/o Postal Pages, The Grange Business Centre, Belasis Avenue, Billingham, Cleveland, TS23 1LG
Activities: Manufacture of other chemical products n.e.c.
Parent: Newfuturevest Limited
Officers: Anthony Stephen Field, Secretary; Harold Bogatz [1938] Director [American]; Anthony Stephen Field [1957] Director/Site Manager; Jan Gale [1954] Director [American]; Ronald Harvey Gale [1951] Director [American]

International Syalons (Newcastle) Limited
Incorporated: 29 June 1994 *Employees:* 37
Net Worth: £2,801,891 *Total Assets:* £3,407,436
Registered Office: Stephenson Street, Willington Quay, Wallsend, Tyne & Wear, NE28 6TT
Activities: Manufacture of other technical ceramic products
Officers: Alain Ennen [1966] Director [Luxembourger]; Johannes Tobias Hölscher [1972] Director [German]; Karl Klaus Wilhelm Tille [1967] Director [German]

Internet Insurance (Holdings) Limited
Incorporated: 23 May 2013
Net Worth Deficit: £590,941 *Total Assets:* £3,165,718
Registered Office: Alton House, 27-31 Grange Road, Darlington, Co Durham, DL1 5NA
Activities: Activities of financial services holding companies
Shareholder: Paul Christopher Meehan
Officers: Stephen David Bradley [1949] Director; Suzanne Eeles [1974] Director/Operations Manager; Paul Christopher Meehan [1949] Director

Internet Insurance Services UK Ltd
Incorporated: 17 February 2000
Net Worth: £2,007,453 *Total Assets:* £2,727,020
Registered Office: Alton House, 27-31 Grange Road, Darlington, Co Durham, DL1 5NA
Activities: Non-life insurance
Major Shareholder: Steven David Bradley
Officers: Stephen David Bradley [1949] Director; Suzanne Eeles [1974] Operations Director; Paul Christopher Meehan [1949] Director

Interocean Personnel Services (UK) Limited
Incorporated: 16 May 1997 *Employees:* 49
Net Worth: £1,771,479 *Total Assets:* £2,347,663
Registered Office: Wellington House, Falcon Court, Preston Farm Business Park, Stockton on Tees, Cleveland, TS18 3TS
Activities: Other activities of employment placement agencies
Parent: IPS Holding BV
Officers: Leonard Theodorus Oostendorp, Secretary [Dutch]; Robert Nicholas Kooijmans [1965] Director/Manager [Dutch]; Leonard Theodorus Oostendorp [1943] Director/Mechanical Engineer [Dutch]; Theodorus Antonius Wilhelmus Gerardus Wanders [1948] Director [Dutch]

Intobeige Limited
Incorporated: 30 March 1983 *Employees:* 53
Net Worth: £2,471,329 *Total Assets:* £2,777,333
Registered Office: 31-40 West Parade, Newcastle upon Tyne, NE4 7LB
Activities: Other human health activities
Shareholders: Aran Handa; Arvan Handa
Officers: Aran Handa [1955] Director; Varghese Thomas [1970] Director

Intrahealth Limited
Incorporated: 7 June 1999 *Employees:* 486
Net Worth: £2,295,585 *Total Assets:* £12,231,133
Registered Office: William Brown Centre, Manor Way, Peterlee, Co Durham, SR8 5TW
Activities: General medical practice activities
Shareholders: Gregory Ernald Moorhouse; Glenn Edward Carroll
Officers: Dr David Guy Anderson [1960] Director/General Practitioner; Glenn Edward Carroll [1960] Director/Chairman; Brian Hunter [1969] Director/Pharmacist; Gregory Ernald Moorhouse [1970] Managing Director; Marie Claire Young [1970] Director/Clinical Pharmacist; Philip Ian Young [1969] Operational Director

Intrahealth Pharmacy Limited
Incorporated: 10 March 2006 *Employees:* 20
Net Worth: £340,522 *Total Assets:* £3,963,288
Registered Office: William Brown Centre, Manor Way, Peterlee, Co Durham, SR8 5TW
Activities: Dispensing chemist in specialised stores
Officers: Dr David Guy Anderson [1960] Organisational Medical Director; Glenn Edward Carroll [1960] Director/Manager; Brian Hunter [1969] Director/Pharmacist; Gregory Ernald Moorhouse [1970] Director/Manager; Marie Claire Young [1970] Director/Pharmacist; Philip Ian Young [1969] Operations Director

The Intraining Group Limited
Incorporated: 20 March 2008 *Employees:* 261
Net Worth: £71,000 *Total Assets:* £4,987,000
Registered Office: Rye Hill House, Scotswood Road, Newcastle upon Tyne, NE4 7SA
Activities: Other education n.e.c.
Parent: NCG Corporation
Officers: Graeme Roland Dodd [1968] Finance Director; Peter Rene Lauener [1954] Director/Retired Civil Servant; Christopher Payne [1964] Group Director; Ian Webber [1971] Managing Director

Intruder Detection & Surveillance Ltd.
Incorporated: 12 May 1999 *Employees:* 35
Net Worth: £527,027 *Total Assets:* £2,192,705
Registered Office: Unit One Waterside Drive, Metro East Business Park, Gateshead, Tyne & Wear, NE11 9HU
Activities: Electrical installation
Shareholders: Colin Dowson; Linda Dowson
Officers: Paul Andrew Brown, Secretary; Colin Dowson [1960] Director/Security; Michael James Tindale [1969] Director

Intumescent Protective Coatings Limited
Incorporated: 30 July 1998 *Employees:* 41
Net Worth: £1,328,223 *Total Assets:* £1,854,375
Registered Office: 2 Jupiter Court, Orion Business Park, North Shields, Tyne & Wear, NE29 7SN
Activities: Other construction installation
Major Shareholder: Christopher Richard Arnott
Officers: Mandy Louise McAllister, Secretary; Dawn Nesbit, Secretary; Christopher Richard Arnott [1973] Operations Director; Stephen Charles McAllister [1966] Sales Director; Graeme Philip Nesbit [1966] Operations Director

Invate Limited
Incorporated: 31 October 2003
Net Worth: £538,919 *Total Assets:* £997,140
Registered Office: 9 Apollo Court, Koppers Way, Monkton Business Park South, Hebburn, Tyne & Wear, NE31 2ES
Activities: Retail sale of computers, peripheral units and software in specialised stores
Major Shareholder: Christopher James Quickfall
Officers: James Robert Chambers [1954] Director; Christopher James Quickfall [1981] Director

Inveniam Home Loans Limited
Incorporated: 10 August 2016
Net Worth Deficit: £18,963 *Total Assets:* £2,476,735
Registered Office: Keel House, Garth Heads, Newcastle upon Tyne, NE1 2JE
Activities: Activities of mortgage finance companies
Shareholders: Gala Tres (Trading) Limited; BIM Enterprises Limited
Officers: Bryan Harvey Irving [1956] Director; Ian Michael Morl [1958] Director

Invenio Systems Limited
Incorporated: 27 April 2015 *Employees:* 13
Net Worth: £718,214 *Total Assets:* £1,187,180
Registered Office: Portland House, Belmont Business Park, Durham, DH1 1TW
Activities: Engineering related scientific and technical consulting activities
Officers: Heather Mary Tooms-Moore [1958] Director; Stephen Tooms-Moore [1962] Director; Kathleen Marie Trow [1956] Director; Stuart William Trow [1955] Director/Engineer

Invertec Holdings Ltd.
Incorporated: 24 September 1999 *Employees:* 196
Net Worth: £3,254,835 *Total Assets:* £9,922,193
Registered Office: Units 1-6 Trimdon Court, Trimdon Grange Industrial Estate, Trimdon Grange, Trimdon Station, Cleveland, TS29 6PE
Activities: Manufacture of veneer sheets and wood-based panels
Parent: Ellison Company Inc.
Officers: Alex Noble, Secretary; John Gray Blount Ellison [1972] Director [American]

Invertec Interiors Limited
Incorporated: 14 November 2006 *Employees:* 68
Net Worth: £837,004 *Total Assets:* £6,962,048
Registered Office: Units 1-6 Trimdon Court, Trimdon Grange Industrial Estate, Trimdon Grange, Trimdon Station, Cleveland, TS29 6PE
Activities: Manufacture of veneer sheets and wood-based panels
Parent: Invertec Holdings Limited
Officers: Alex Noble, Secretary; Kelvin Neil Baird [1972] Operations Director; John Gray Blount Ellison [1972] Managing Director [American]; Ian King [1971] Director

Invicta Asset Management Limited
Incorporated: 12 August 2014
Net Worth Deficit: £124,627 *Total Assets:* £2,591,102
Registered Office: Wynyard Park House, Wynyard Avenue, Wynyard, Billingham, Cleveland, TS22 5TB
Activities: Other service activities n.e.c.
Shareholder: Fuls Limited
Officers: Trevor Cartner [1960] Director; Joseph Christopher Musgrave [1965] Director

Ionbond UK Limited
Incorporated: 20 September 1982 *Employees:* 50
Net Worth: £3,245,887 *Total Assets:* £3,837,130
Registered Office: Unit 36, Number One Industrial Estate, Medomsley Road, Consett, Co Durham, DH8 6TS
Activities: Treatment and coating of metals
Parent: Bernex UK Limited
Officers: Dr Christopher Paul Constable [1975] Managing Director; Jeffrey David Ostman [1968] Regional Managing Director [French/American]; Prof. Gerrit Jan Van Der Kolk [1955] Director [Dutch]

Ipca Laboratories UK Limited
Incorporated: 4 November 2003
Net Worth: £4,637,299 *Total Assets:* £5,606,311
Registered Office: Units 97-98 Silverbriar, Sunderland Enterprise Park East, Sunderland, Tyne & Wear, SR5 2TQ
Activities: Manufacture of pharmaceutical preparations
Parent: Ipca Ltd
Officers: Nathan Vincent Lane, Secretary; Denise Bowser [1971] Commercial Director; Manish Jain [1974] Director/Vice President - Business Development [Indian]; Dr Derek John Londesbrough [1970] R&D Director

IPS Roofing Limited
Incorporated: 13 January 2012
Registered Office: Unit 1 Gatherley Road Industrial Estate, Brompton on Swale, Richmond, N Yorks, DL10 7JG
Activities: Roofing activities
Shareholders: Peter Bowers; Gavin Bowers
Officers: Gavin Richard Bowers [1978] Director; Peter Bowers [1948] Director

Iris Engineering & Technology Limited
Incorporated: 11 July 2005 *Employees:* 30
Net Worth: £462,744 *Total Assets:* £1,317,468
Registered Office: Unit 7 Fern Court, Bracken Hill Business Park, Peterlee, Co Durham, SR8 2RR
Activities: Architectural activities
Officers: Michael Ian Thompson, Secretary; Joanne Ruth Preston [1966] Director; Robert George Preston [1964] Director; Michael Ian Thompson [1962] Director/Chartered Engineer; Vesta Thompson [1961] Director

Iris Project Solutions Ltd
Incorporated: 10 April 2014 *Employees:* 4
Net Worth: £133,307 *Total Assets:* £1,001,464
Registered Office: Unit 7 Fern Court, Bracken Hill Business Park, Peterlee, Co Durham, SR8 2RR
Activities: Engineering related scientific and technical consulting activities
Shareholders: Neil David Hay; Iris Business Services Ltd
Officers: Neil David Hay [1964] Director; Robert George Preston [1964] Director; Michael Ian Thompson [1962] Director

Richard Irvin & Sons Limited
Incorporated: 31 December 1907 *Employees:* 447
Net Worth: £2,310,000 *Total Assets:* £20,599,000
Registered Office: 58 Howard Street, North Shields, Tyne & Wear, NE30 1AL
Activities: Electrical installation
Officers: George Clark Still, Secretary; Robert Brannan [1956] Director/Chairman; Lindsey Allison Cradock [1958] Director; Richard John Emmerson [1968] Director/Chartered Accountant; William Howard Lund [1966] Director; Hugh John Patrick Stewart [1953] Director; George Clark Still [1968] Finance Director

Sir Joseph Isherwood Limited
Incorporated: 12 February 1993 *Employees:* 20
Net Worth: £5,460,148 *Total Assets:* £6,211,350
Registered Office: 5th Floor, Centre for Advanced Industry, Coble Dene, North Shields, Tyne & Wear, NE29 6DE
Activities: Other information technology service activities
Parent: SJI Holdings Limited
Officers: Stephen Charles Thompson, Secretary; Pierre Maurice Jean-Marie Balmer [1955] Director [French]; Andrew Paul Hartley [1965] Director/Engineer; Camille Elias Karam [1958] Director/Financial Adviser [American]; Peter Rossiter [1945] Director/Engineer; Dieter Rottsieper [1959] Director [German]; Stephen Charles Thompson [1975] Director/Chartered Accountant

Islestone Limited
Incorporated: 16 July 2009 *Employees:* 17
Net Worth: £869,491 *Total Assets:* £3,879,988
Registered Office: 379 Princesway South, Team Valley Trading Estate, Gateshead, Tyne & Wear, NE11 0TU
Activities: Wholesale of pharmaceutical goods
Shareholders: David James Gulliford; Dr Peter Gulliford
Officers: David James Gulliford [1988] Director; Dr Peter Gulliford [1949] Director

Isoclad Limited
Incorporated: 13 November 2003 *Employees:* 38
Net Worth: £648,829 *Total Assets:* £1,898,397
Registered Office: 10 Alder Road, West Chirton Industrial Estate North, North Shields, Tyne & Wear, NE29 8SD
Activities: Other manufacturing n.e.c.
Major Shareholder: David Nicholas Owen Williams
Officers: Jane McColl, Secretary; Michael Paul McColl [1963] Director

Isocom Components 2004 Limited
Incorporated: 31 December 2003 *Employees:* 20
Net Worth: £2,563,501 *Total Assets:* £3,996,549
Registered Office: Unit 25b Park View Road West, Park View Industrial Estate, Hartlepool, Cleveland, TS25 1UD
Activities: Manufacture of electronic components
Shareholder: Gerald Chi Keung Chu
Officers: Paul John Gillespie, Secretary/Director; Generald Chi Keung Chu [1953] Director; Justin Robert Elvin [1969] Director/Sales Manager; Paul John Gillespie [1969] Director/Engineer; Anthony George Hemming [1942] Director/Engineer; Colin Frederick Rowe [1939] Director/Engineer

Isocom Limited
Incorporated: 21 October 1994 *Employees:* 10
Net Worth: £1,225,285 *Total Assets:* £2,829,554
Registered Office: 48 Hutton Close, Crowther Industrial Estate, District 3, Washington, Tyne & Wear, NE38 0AH
Activities: Manufacture of electronic components
Major Shareholder: Ghollam Husayn Tahmosynayat
Officers: Ghollam Husayn Tahmosybayat, Secretary; Ghollam Husayn Tahmosybayat [1955] Managing Director

Isoler Ltd.
Incorporated: 23 November 1992 *Employees:* 34
Net Worth: £1,123,551 *Total Assets:* £1,459,144
Registered Office: 333 Dukesway Court, Team Valley Trading Estate, Gateshead, Tyne & Wear, NE11 0BH
Activities: Other specialised construction activities n.e.c.
Parent: Northern Bear PLC
Officers: Wendy Ann Edgell, Secretary; John Gilstin [1950] Director; Graham Roy Jennings [1956] Director; Steven Mark Roberts [1966] Director; Michael Paul Skelton [1976] Director/Commercial Manager; Keith Soulsby [1956] Director

Isotank (2006) Limited
Incorporated: 17 January 2006
Net Worth: £396,094 *Total Assets:* £1,122,523
Registered Office: Limerick Road, Dormanstown, Redcar, Cleveland, TS10 5JU
Activities: Other letting and operating of own or leased real estate
Parent: Isotank Services Limited
Officers: Robert Anthony Bayliss [1955] Director/Engineer; Colin Garnett [1963] Director; Tony Morsovillo [1972] Corporate Operations Director [American]; Joseph Troy [1963] Director [American]; John Wilson [1974] Director [American]

Isotank Depot Services Limited
Incorporated: 4 June 2003 *Employees:* 120
Net Worth: £2,403,456 *Total Assets:* £5,646,346
Registered Office: Limerick Road, Dormanstown, Redcar, Cleveland, TS10 5JU
Activities: Other cleaning services
Parent: Isotank Services Limited
Officers: Robert Anthony Bayliss [1955] Director/Engineer; Colin Garnett [1963] Managing Director; Tony Morsovillo [1972] Corporate Operations Director [American]; Joseph Troy [1963] Director [American]; John Wilson [1974] Director [American]

Isotank Services Limited
Incorporated: 13 September 1979 *Employees:* 27
Net Worth: £3,760,541 *Total Assets:* £9,731,110
Registered Office: Limerick Road, Dormanstown, Redcar, Cleveland, TS10 5JU
Activities: Freight transport by road
Parent: Boasso UK Limited
Officers: Robert Anthony Bayliss [1955] Director/Engineer; Colin Garnett [1963] Managing Director; Tony Morsovillo [1972] Corporate Operations Director [American]; Joseph Troy [1963] Director [American]; John Wilson [1974] Director [American]

Isotank Transport Services Limited
Incorporated: 4 June 2003 *Employees:* 134
Net Worth: £671,483 *Total Assets:* £2,923,279
Registered Office: Limerick Road, Dormanstown, Redcar, Cleveland, TS10 5JU
Activities: Freight transport by road
Parent: Isotank Services Limited
Officers: Robert Anthony Bayliss [1955] Director/Engineer; Colin Garnett [1963] Managing Director; Tony Morsovillo [1972] Corporate Operations Director [American]; Joseph Troy [1963] Director [American]; John Wilson [1974] Director [American]

ISP Holdings (U.K.) Ltd.
Incorporated: 10 August 1999
Net Worth: £11,933,000 *Total Assets:* £11,944,000
Registered Office: Unit 4b Whinbank Park, Whinbank Road, Aycliffe Business Park, Newton Aycliffe, Co Durham, DL5 6AY
Activities: Manufacture of other chemical products n.e.c.
Officers: Julie Charlton, Secretary; Frank Jacob Adriaan Jumelet [1960] Director [Dutch]

Istanbul Meats Limited
Incorporated: 16 July 2001 *Employees:* 23
Net Worth: £2,712,250 *Total Assets:* £2,997,219
Registered Office: Unit 3 First Avenue, Drum Industrial Estate, Chester-le-Street, Co Durham, DH2 1AG
Activities: Processing and preserving of meat
Shareholder: Nuran Adiguzel
Officers: Nuran Adiguzel, Secretary; Ali Adiguzel [1958] Director/Manufacturer Wholesaler; Nuran Adiguzel [1961] Director/Manufacturer Wholesales

It's All Good Limited
Incorporated: 16 August 2011 *Employees:* 137
Net Worth: £1,312,451 *Total Assets:* £10,893,186
Registered Office: 273 Dukesway, Team Valley Trading Estate, Gateshead, Tyne & Wear, NE11 0PZ
Activities: Manufacture of bread; manufacture of fresh pastry goods and cakes
Shareholder: Mauro Andrea Biagioni
Officers: Mauro Andrea Biagioni [1978] Investment Director; Fiona Crozier [1966] Director; Calum Ryder [1964] Director; Lynn Saul [1963] Director; Charlotte Simpson [1982] Sales & Marketing Director; Michael John Weatherhead [1971] Director

IT-IS International Limited
Incorporated: 8 April 2004 *Employees:* 18
Net Worth: £355,349 *Total Assets:* £811,444
Registered Office: 1 Wainstones Court, Stokesley Business Park, Stokesley, Middlesbrough, Cleveland, TS9 5JY
Activities: Other research and experimental development on natural sciences and engineering
Shareholders: James Richard Howell; Benjamin Webster; Dr Roderic Fuerst
Officers: Elizabeth Bruce, Secretary; Dr Roderic Fuerst [1967] Director/Molecular Biologist; James Richard Howell [1980] Director/Consultant; Benjamin Webster [1978] Director/Consultant

Italica UK Limited
Incorporated: 24 November 2008 *Employees:* 19
Net Worth: £893,348 *Total Assets:* £1,277,266
Registered Office: Unit 1 Chainbridge Industrial Estate, Tundry Way, Blaydon on Tyne, Tyne & Wear, NE21 5SJ
Activities: Wholesale of other food, including fish, crustaceans and molluscs
Shareholders: Francesco Marrone; Susan Michelle Marrone
Officers: Susan Michelle Marrone, Secretary; Francesco Marrone [1963] Director [Italian]; Susan Michelle Marrone [1970] Director

ITC Plumbing and Heating Services Limited
Incorporated: 23 June 2003 *Employees:* 23
Net Worth: £879,174 *Total Assets:* £1,513,374
Registered Office: 1-2 Adelaide Row, Seaham, Co Durham, SR7 7EF
Activities: Electrical installation
Shareholders: Ian Thomas Colling; Graeme Cook
Officers: Graeme Cook, Secretary; Ian Thomas Colling [1964] Director/Plumber; Graeme Cook [1978] Director; Matthew John Parry [1987] Director/Estimator

ITC Service Limited
Incorporated: 28 February 2006 *Employees:* 27
Net Worth: £660,494 *Total Assets:* £1,410,023
Registered Office: 9 Merchant Court, Monkton Business Park South, Hebburn, Tyne & Wear, NE31 2EX
Activities: Information technology consultancy activities
Shareholders: Christopher George Potts; Peter Michael Anderson
Officers: Christopher George Potts, Secretary; Peter Michael Anderson [1977] Managing Director; Christopher George Potts [1977] Managing Director

ITEC North East Limited
Incorporated: 12 August 1986 *Employees:* 26
Net Worth: £758,937 *Total Assets:* £1,027,438
Registered Office: The Digital Factory, Durham Way South, Aycliffe Business Park, Newton Aycliffe, Co Durham, DL5 6XP
Activities: Technical and vocational secondary education
Officers: Tracy Ann Wilson, Secretary; Stephen William Bellwood [1955] Managing Director; Geoffrey Brown [1952] Recruitment Director; Tracy Ann Wilson [1973] Director; Graham Wood [1971] Director/Trustee

ITL (North East) Limited
Incorporated: 24 July 2003 *Employees:* 8
Net Worth: £1,293,493 *Total Assets:* £1,730,420
Registered Office: Design Works, William Street, Gateshead, Tyne & Wear, NE10 0JP
Activities: Other service activities n.e.c.
Officers: Guy Charles Hitchman, Secretary; Grace Tia Bon Bon [1958] Director/Interpreting

ITPS (Holdings) Limited
Incorporated: 15 May 2006 *Employees:* 110
Net Worth: £2,373,734 *Total Assets:* £9,574,000
Registered Office: Unit 2a & 2b Metrocentre East Business Park, Waterside Drive, Gateshead, Tyne & Wear, NE11 9HU
Activities: Activities of head offices
Shareholders: Michael John Harold Jopling; Garry Sheriff
Officers: Michael John Harold Jopling, Secretary; Michael John Harold Jopling [1963] Finance Director; Garry Sheriff [1966] Managing Director

Ivic Limited
Incorporated: 21 August 1989
Registered Office: 4 Winchester Drive, South West Industrial Estate, Peterlee, Co Durham, SR8 2RD
Activities: Other specialised construction activities n.e.c.
Shareholders: Thomas Bell; Irene Bell
Officers: Thomas Victor Bell, Secretary; Irene Kipling Bell [1946] Director; Thomas Victor Bell [1945] Director; Sybil Yvonne Blenkinsopp [1941] Director/Secretary/Bookkeeper

Ivybank Limited
Incorporated: 15 April 2004
Registered Office: Fernwood House, Fernwood Road, Jesmond, Newcastle upon Tyne, NE2 1TJ
Activities: Management of real estate on a fee or contract basis
Officers: Rifka Ellinson, Secretary; Uri Ellinson [1970] Director

Izumi Products UK Limited
Incorporated: 13 February 1995
Net Worth: £543,421 *Total Assets:* £1,398,884
Registered Office: Unit 4b Hatfield Way, South Church Enterprise Park, Bishop Auckland, Co Durham, DL14 6XF
Activities: Manufacture of other machine tools
Shareholder: Stephen John Bracher
Officers: Michael Robert Bracher, Secretary; Michael Robert Bracher [1964] Director [South African]; Stephen John Bracher [1970] Director/Engineer [South African]; Jennifer Ann Williams [1965] Director/Administration [South African]; Megan Ann Woolley [1988] Director

J & B Property Services Limited
Incorporated: 3 October 2002
Registered Office: The Rising, 4 Laburnum Grove, Cleadon, Sunderland, Tyne & Wear, SR6 7RJ
Activities: Other letting and operating of own or leased real estate
Shareholder: Barbara Ann Downey
Officers: Barbara Ann Downey, Secretary; Barbara Ann Downey [1956] Director; John Anthony Downey [1957] Director

J & B Recycling Limited
Incorporated: 7 March 1994 *Employees:* 191
Net Worth: £1,879,737 *Total Assets:* £9,697,219
Registered Office: Windemere MRF, Thomlinson Road, Hartlepool, Cleveland, TS25 1NS
Activities: Recovery of sorted materials
Officers: Amanda Jane Farndale [1974] Finance Director; Victoria Jackson-Smith [1971] Director/Company Secretary; Matthew James Tyrie [1980] Operations Director

J & H Property and Developments Ltd
Incorporated: 20 December 2013
Net Worth: £827,633 *Total Assets:* £1,108,186
Registered Office: 18 Blue Bridge Centre, St Cuthberts Way, Aycliffe Business Park, Newton Aycliffe, Co Durham, DL5 6DS
Activities: Development of building projects
Major Shareholder: John Jones
Officers: John Jones [1976] Director

J & L (North East) Limited
Incorporated: 22 July 2003 *Employees:* 3
Net Worth: £436,025 *Total Assets:* £3,022,631
Registered Office: 16a Durham Road, Spennymoor, Co Durham, DL16 6SH
Activities: Buying and selling of own real estate
Shareholders: George Ellis; Jeffrey Ellis; Linda Ellis
Officers: Jeffrey Ellis, Secretary/Executive; George Ellis [1977] Director/Motor Dealer; Jeffrey Ellis [1953] Director/Executive; Linda Ellis [1949] Director/Executive

J A Sales and Service Limited
Incorporated: 6 January 2012 *Employees:* 1
Net Worth: £2,279,225 *Total Assets:* £2,903,722
Registered Office: N Q House, Leeming Bar Business Park, Leeming Bar, Northallerton, N Yorks, DL7 9EE
Activities: Manufacture of other products of wood; manufacture of articles of cork, straw and plaiting materials
Shareholders: Adam Dye; James Dye
Officers: Adam Dye [1980] Director; James Dye [1978] Director

J and K Training Ltd
Incorporated: 19 June 2008 *Employees:* 14
Net Worth: £771,187 *Total Assets:* £822,769
Registered Office: 71 Cockton Hill Road, Bishop Auckland, Co Durham, DL14 6HS
Activities: Other education n.e.c.
Shareholders: Dorothy Ann Johnson; Paul Kelly
Officers: Dorothy Ann Johnson [1965] Operations Director; Paul Kelly [1954] Director/Training Manager

J I J Estates Limited
Incorporated: 3 June 2003
Registered Office: 3 Kingfisher Court, Bowesfield Park, Stockton on Tees, Cleveland, TS18 3EX
Activities: Other letting and operating of own or leased real estate
Shareholders: Ian Alexander Fox; Jane Louise Robson
Officers: Jane Louise Robson, Secretary; Ian Alexander Fox [1973] Director; Jill Marie Fox [1947] Director; Jane Louise Robson [1976] Director

J S Locum Services Limited
Incorporated: 14 October 2010
Net Worth: £263,442 *Total Assets:* £1,326,699
Registered Office: 10 Grange Terrace, Sunderland, Tyne & Wear, SR2 7DF
Activities: Dispensing chemist in specialised stores
Major Shareholder: Jaspal Singh
Officers: Jaspal Singh [1987] Director/Pharmacist

J. D. S. (City Developments) Limited
Incorporated: 11 November 1981 *Employees:* 3
Net Worth: £763,118 *Total Assets:* £1,207,525
Registered Office: Kepier House, Belmont Business Park, Durham, DH1 1TW
Activities: Development of building projects
Shareholders: Fiona Ann Dent; John Martin Dent
Officers: Fiona Ann Dent [1967] Director; John Martin Dent [1969] Director

J. M. D. Developments Limited
Incorporated: 3 July 1978 *Employees:* 4
Net Worth: £854,338 *Total Assets:* £1,489,952
Registered Office: Nursery House, Bradley Hall, Wylam, Northumberland, NE41 8JL
Activities: Buying and selling of own real estate
Shareholders: David Strachan; David Douglass; Linda Helen Isabella Douglass
Officers: David Douglass, Secretary; David Douglass [1948] Director/Solicitor; Linda Helen Isabella Douglass [1951] Director/Married Woman; David Strachan [1944] Director; Jeanette Strachan [1944] Director/Married Woman

J.E.B. Contractors (UK) Limited
Incorporated: 18 April 2013
Net Worth: £1,015,127 *Total Assets:* £1,016,267
Registered Office: Unit 88 Alexandra Avenue, Sunderland Enterprise Park East, Sunderland, Tyne & Wear, SR5 2TB
Activities: Electrical installation
Shareholders: John Donald Burke; Steven Mark Johnson
Officers: Steven Mark Johnson [1970] Director

J.E.B. Contractors Limited
Incorporated: 6 August 1991 *Employees:* 28
Net Worth: £583,434 *Total Assets:* £932,363
Registered Office: Unit 88 Alexandra Avenue, Enterprise Park East, Sunderland, Tyne & Wear, SR5 2TB
Activities: Electrical installation
Parent: JEB Contractors (UK) Limited
Officers: Denise Burke, Secretary; Denise Burke [1961] Director/Secretary; Steven Mark Johnson [1970] Director/Electrical Engineer

J.E.M Road Construction Ltd
Incorporated: 24 November 2005
Net Worth: £469,018 *Total Assets:* £1,316,379
Registered Office: The Greenhouse, Greencroft Industrial Park, Stanley, Co Durham, DH9 7XN
Activities: Other service activities incidental to land transportation, n.e.c.
Shareholders: Wayne Gill Murray; Joanne Louise Murray
Officers: Wayne Gill Murray, Secretary/Plant Transport Manager; Joanne Louise Murray [1971] Director/Clerical Officer; Wayne Gill Murray [1971] Director

J.G. Windows Limited
Incorporated: 24 June 1925 *Employees:* 42
Net Worth: £921,043 *Total Assets:* £1,859,022
Registered Office: 6 Central Arcade, Newcastle upon Tyne, NE1 5BP
Activities: Retail sale of musical instruments and scores
Major Shareholder: Brian Mawson
Officers: Helen Clare Mawson, Secretary; Rupert William Bradbury [1970] Director/Manager; Stewart Hindmarsh [1954] Director; Brian Mawson [1944] Director

J.K. Construction and Joinery Limited
Incorporated: 10 April 2000
Net Worth: £1,756,260 *Total Assets:* £2,173,257
Registered Office: 3 Upsall Grange Gardens, Nunthorpe, Middlesbrough, Cleveland, TS7 0AX
Activities: Construction of other civil engineering projects n.e.c.
Shareholders: Jonathan King; Julie King
Officers: Julie King, Secretary/Director; Jonathon King [1970] Director; Julie King [1971] Director

J.T.P. (Non-Ferrous Stockholders) Limited
Incorporated: 31 December 1998 *Employees:* 11
Net Worth: £247,935 *Total Assets:* £845,419
Registered Office: 59-69 Heaton Park Road, Newcastle upon Tyne, NE6 1SQ
Activities: Wholesale of metals and metal ores
Officers: Carole Wendy Mutch, Secretary; David George Mutch [1960] Managing Director; Kevin Grant Mutch [1963] Director

J3S Ltd
Incorporated: 18 June 2008
Net Worth: £665,596 *Total Assets:* £917,757
Registered Office: 92-98 Newgate Street, Newcastle upon Tyne, NE1 5RQ
Activities: Licenced restaurants
Shareholder: Sun Kit Lau
Officers: Sun Kit Lau [1978] Director

JA Property Limited
Incorporated: 14 February 2001
Net Worth: £1,616,223 *Total Assets:* £1,893,056
Registered Office: The Barn, Rift Farm, Pittington Lane, Low Pittington, Co Durham, DH6 1BN
Activities: Other letting and operating of own or leased real estate
Major Shareholder: John Richard Adamson
Officers: Rachel Elizabeth Morson, Secretary; John Richard Adamson [1965] Director

Alan Jackson (Westcotes) Limited
Incorporated: 20 September 1965 *Employees:* 7
Net Worth: £4,846,884 *Total Assets:* £9,111,880
Registered Office: Westcotes, Ponteland, Northumberland, NE20 0DG
Activities: Mixed farming
Shareholders: Peter Alan Jackson; James Alan Jackson
Officers: Joyce Jackson, Secretary; James Alan Jackson [1927] Director/Farmer; Joyce Jackson [1933] Director/Company Secretary; Peter Alan Jackson [1958] Director/Farmer

J. Jackson Properties Limited
Incorporated: 22 July 2004 *Employees:* 2
Net Worth: £224,949 *Total Assets:* £4,085,257
Registered Office: 78 Lister Street, Hartlepool, Cleveland, TS15 9EP
Activities: Development of building projects
Major Shareholder: Patrick Lawrence Jackson
Officers: Patrick Lawrence Jackson, Secretary; Patrick Lawrence Jackson [1977] Director/Property Manager

Jacksons Commercial & Private Law LLP
Incorporated: 7 July 2003 *Employees:* 61
Net Worth: £773,146 *Total Assets:* £1,462,173
Registered Office: 17 Falcon Court, Preston Farm Industrial Estate, Stockton on Tees, Cleveland, TS18 3TU
Officers: Jane Elizabeth Armitage [1961] Member; Geoffrey Skeoch [1954] Member; Anthony James Wentworth [1963] Member; Stephen Andrew Wiles [1966] Member; Simon Anthony Catterall [1956] LLP Member; Paul Richard Clark [1980] LLP Member; Inderjit Singh Gill [1967] LLP Member; Toby Mattew Joel [1973] LLP Member; Karen Margaret Robinson [1966] LLP Member; Erica Marie Turner [1985] LLP Member

Jade Developments (North East) Limited
Incorporated: 1 August 2006
Registered Office: 537 Durham Road, Low Fell, Gateshead, Tyne & Wear, NE9 5EY
Activities: Development of building projects
Shareholders: Adrian Trevor Barton; Debra Barton; Debra Barton; Adrian Trevor Barton
Officers: Debra Barton, Secretary; Adrian Trevor Barton [1964] Director/Civil Engineer

Jake Acquisitions Limited
Incorporated: 9 May 2006
Net Worth: £160,000 *Total Assets:* £178,904,000
Registered Office: Mayborn House, Balliol Business Park, Newcastle upon Tyne, NE12 8EW
Activities: Activities of other holding companies n.e.c.
Parent: Jake Investment Limited
Officers: Stephen William Parkin [1969] Director; James William Matthew Taylor [1974] Director/Chief Financial Officer

Jake Holdings Limited
Incorporated: 9 May 2006 *Employees:* 1,334
Net Worth: £40,401,000 *Total Assets:* £162,668,992
Registered Office: Mayborn House, Balliol Business Park, Newcastle upon Tyne, NE12 8EW
Activities: Activities of other holding companies n.e.c.
Parent: Success Bidco 2 Limited
Officers: Min Han [1977] Director [Chinese]; Willis Jiao [1973] HR Director [Chinese]; Stephen William Parkin [1969] Director; James William Matthew Taylor [1974] Director/Chief Financial Officer; Wei Yu [1977] Director/Chief Marketing Officer [Chinese]

Jake Investment Limited
Incorporated: 9 May 2006
Net Worth Deficit: £9,796,000 *Total Assets:* £74,485,000
Registered Office: Mayborn House, Balliol Business Park, Newcastle upon Tyne, NE12 8EW
Activities: Activities of other holding companies n.e.c.
Parent: Jake Holdings Limited
Officers: Stephen William Parkin [1969] Director; James William Matthew Taylor [1974] Director/Chief Financial Officer

Jamas Building Services Limited
Incorporated: 20 April 2005
Net Worth: £1,240,527 *Total Assets:* £1,636,148
Registered Office: 9 Bowesfield Crescent, Stockton on Tees, Cleveland, TS18 3BL
Activities: Other business support service activities n.e.c.
Shareholders: Peter Ian Kemp; Ruth Kemp
Officers: Ruth Kemp, Secretary; Peter Ian Kemp [1969] Director/Engineer

T.James (Bedlington),Limited
Incorporated: 24 March 1965 *Employees:* 24
Net Worth: £2,892,270 *Total Assets:* £3,885,998
Registered Office: West Sleekburn Works, Bedlington, Northumberland, NE22 7LQ
Activities: Freight transport by road
Major Shareholder: Alan James
Officers: Suzanne Jones, Secretary; Alan William James [1976] Director/Transport Manager; Alan James [1954] Director/Transport Manager

P. James Construction Limited
Incorporated: 20 February 1997 *Employees:* 39
Net Worth: £1,361,237 *Total Assets:* £1,585,545
Registered Office: 8 Wesley Drive, Benton Square Industrial Estate, Newcastle upon Tyne, NE12 9UP
Activities: Construction of commercial buildings
Major Shareholder: Philip James Richardson
Officers: Philip James Richardson [1964] Director

James of Stokesley LLP
Incorporated: 25 April 2013
Net Worth: £2,016,880 *Total Assets:* £2,119,369
Registered Office: James of Stokesley, John Boyle Road, Middlesbrough, Cleveland, TS6 6TY
Officers: Adrian Dennis James [1948] Member; Antony Adrian James [1970] Member; Barrie Kurt James [1986] Member; Reuben Mark James [1988] Member; Janet Margaret James [1952] LLP Member; Laura James [1975] LLP Member

Matthew James Services Limited
Incorporated: 21 July 1999 *Employees:* 5
Net Worth: £369,710 *Total Assets:* £795,497
Registered Office: Swallow House, Parsons Road, Washington, Tyne & Wear, NE37 1EZ
Activities: Manufacture of other special-purpose machinery n.e.c.
Shareholders: Darren Rainbow; Wilson Geoffrey Brown
Officers: Geoffrey Brown [1967] Director; Darren Rainbow [1966] Director

Andrew James UK Ltd
Incorporated: 27 October 2005 *Employees:* 25
Net Worth: £4,474,607 *Total Assets:* £10,901,169
Registered Office: 37-38 Market Street, Ferryhill, Co Durham, DL17 8JH
Activities: Retail sale of electrical household appliances in specialised stores
Shareholders: Andrew John Tomlinson; James Benjamin Buckle
Officers: Andrew John Tomlinson, Secretary; Mark Ellison [1965] Director; Alan Richard Neal [1951] Director; Andrew John Tomlinson [1973] Director/Transport Manager

Janus International (UK) Limited
Incorporated: 25 July 2005 *Employees:* 64
Net Worth: £2,972,424 *Total Assets:* £10,706,087
Registered Office: Davy Drive, North West Industrial Estate, Peterlee, Co Durham, SR8 2JF
Activities: Manufacture of other fabricated metal products n.e.c.
Officers: Graham Richard Lomax, Secretary/Sales Director; Rachel Catharine Jane Steed, Secretary; David Bryan Curtis [1960] Director [American]; Colin Russell Jeromson [1966] Director

Jarrow Coachworks Limited
Incorporated: 21 January 2005
Net Worth: £1,061,451 *Total Assets:* £1,126,443
Registered Office: No 2 Curlew Road, Jarrow, Tyne & Wear, NE32 3DX
Activities: Repair and maintenance of other transport equipment n.e.c.
Major Shareholder: David John Ellis
Officers: Suzanne Dawn Bolton, Secretary; Suzanne Dawn Bolton [1956] Director/Company Secretary; David John Ellis [1965] Director/Motor Engineer

David Jarvis Limited
Incorporated: 6 August 1999 *Employees:* 8
Net Worth: £723,126 *Total Assets:* £929,218
Registered Office: Lakeside House, Kingfisher Way, Stockton on Tees, Cleveland, TS18 3NB
Activities: Other human health activities
Major Shareholder: David Graham Jarvis
Officers: David Graham Jarvis, Secretary/Pharmacist; David Graham Jarvis [1966] Director/Pharmacist; Salman Khan [1982] Director/Pharmacist; Kevin Alan Simpson [1958] Director/Pharmacist

H. Jarvis Ltd
Incorporated: 23 September 1946 *Employees:* 74
Net Worth: £2,343,615 *Total Assets:* £3,254,069
Registered Office: Longbeck Trading Estate, Marske by Sea, Redcar, Cleveland, TS11 6HH
Activities: Manufacture of other builders' carpentry and joinery
Shareholder: Charles Jarvis
Officers: Paul Martin Christon [1970] Director; David Glendinning [1955] Managing Director; Rachel Clare Hall [1966] Director/Administration Manager; Gina Ing [1971] Director; Charles Jarvis [1939] Director/Woodworker

Jaspia Limited
Incorporated: 25 July 2016
Net Worth Deficit: £202,814 *Total Assets:* £1,409,136
Registered Office: Technology Court, Bradbury Road, Newton Aycliffe, Co Durham, DL5 6DA
Activities: Development of building projects
Shareholders: Seema Jagota; Javaid Nazir
Officers: Seema Jagota [1973] Director/Property Developer; Javaid Nazir [1969] Director/Property Developer

JB Skills Training Ltd
Incorporated: 31 March 2014
Registered Office: Sunderland Software Centre, Tavistock Place, Sunderland, Tyne & Wear, SR1 1PB
Activities: Other activities of employment placement agencies
Major Shareholder: Jeffrey Bentham
Officers: Jeffrey Bentham [1959] Director; Yve Bentham [1954] Director; David Macmillan [1985] Operations Director

JCM Holdings Limited
Incorporated: 26 September 2001 *Employees:* 3
Net Worth Deficit: £566,584 *Total Assets:* £2,037,195
Registered Office: Wynyard Park House, Wynyard Avenue, Wynyard, Billingham, Cleveland, TS22 5TB
Activities: Activities of head offices
Shareholders: Barbara Musgrave; Joseph Christopher Musgrave; Joseph Christopher Musgrave
Officers: Kenneth Hilton Knowlson, Secretary; Joseph Christopher Musgrave [1965] Director/Property Developer

JCM Retail Equipment Limited
Incorporated: 27 August 1997 *Employees:* 6
Net Worth: £1,446,561 *Total Assets:* £1,944,146
Registered Office: Wynyard Park House, Wynyard Avenue, Wynyard, Billingham, Cleveland, TS22 5TB
Activities: Other retail sale not in stores, stalls or markets
Shareholders: John Robert Beamson; JCM Holdings Limited
Officers: Kenneth Hilton Knowlson, Secretary; Joseph Christopher Musgrave [1965] Managing Director

JCP Consulting Engineers Limited
Incorporated: 3 April 2012 *Employees:* 20
Net Worth: £1,100,724 *Total Assets:* £1,848,786
Registered Office: 1-2 Brenkley Way, Blezard Business Park, Seaton Burn, Newcastle upon Tyne, NE13 6DS
Activities: Other engineering activities
Shareholder: Simon David Jackson
Officers: Robert Stanley Jackson [1941] Director; Simon David Jackson [1973] Director; Michael James Kelly [1960] Director

JD Joinery & Building Services Limited
Incorporated: 25 January 2011
Net Worth: £252,267 *Total Assets:* £756,557
Registered Office: 6 Rudby Close, Whitebridge Park, Gosforth, Newcastle upon Tyne, NE3 5JF
Activities: Other construction installation
Shareholder: Joseph John Dixon
Officers: Christine Dixon [1961] Director; Joseph John Dixon [1964] Director

JDE Management Limited
Incorporated: 21 January 2010
Net Worth: £1,245,337 *Total Assets:* £1,307,738
Registered Office: 15 Elmfield Road, Gosforth, Newcastle upon Tyne, NE3 4AY
Activities: Television programming and broadcasting activities
Major Shareholder: Jonathan David Edwards
Officers: Alison Joy Edwards [1965] Director; Jonathan David Edwards [1966] Director; Nathan Mark Edwards [1995] Director; Samuel James Edwards [1993] Director

JDP Contracting (Holdings) Limited
Incorporated: 22 September 2014
Net Worth: £158,392 *Total Assets:* £880,820
Registered Office: Unit 4 Maple Way, Aycliffe Business Park, Newton Aycliffe, Co Durham, DL5 6BF
Activities: Activities of other holding companies n.e.c.
Major Shareholder: Jolyon Leonard Harrison
Officers: Jolyon Leonard Harrison [1948] Director; Christopher Andrew Hyde [1957] Director

Jeave 2 Limited
Incorporated: 16 June 2010 *Employees:* 67
Net Worth: £5,283,147 *Total Assets:* £5,936,709
Registered Office: Bolckow Street, North Skelton, Saltburn-by-the-Sea, N Yorks, TS12 2AP
Activities: Dormant company
Major Shareholder: Clive Leslie Wood
Officers: Clive Leslie Wood [1949] Director

Jeave 4 Limited
Incorporated: 16 June 2010
Net Worth: £2,162,926 *Total Assets:* £2,162,926
Registered Office: Bolckow Street, North Skelton, Saltburn-by-the-Sea, N Yorks, TS12 2AP
Activities: Dormant company
Major Shareholder: Clive Leslie Wood
Officers: Jean Wood, Secretary; Clive Leslie Wood [1949] Director

Jebb Metals (Newcastle) Ltd
Incorporated: 26 September 1980 *Employees:* 20
Net Worth: £2,940,704 *Total Assets:* £3,918,971
Registered Office: Jebb Metals (Newcastle) Limited, Station Road, Walker, Newcastle upon Tyne, NE6 3PN
Activities: Wholesale of waste and scrap
Shareholders: Philip Kenney; Stephen Kenney
Officers: Joan Karen Sheppard, Secretary; Philip Kenney [1965] Director/Metal Trader; Stephen Kenney [1968] Director/Metal Trader

C. C. Jensen Limited
Incorporated: 22 May 1990 *Employees:* 12
Net Worth: £488,908 *Total Assets:* £1,242,138
Registered Office: Unit 26 Enterprise City, Meadowfield Avenue, Spennymoor, Co Durham, DL16 6JF
Activities: Manufacture of other general-purpose machinery n.e.c.
Officers: Stig Due [1957] Director [Danish]; Ulrich Ritsing [1956] Director/International Sales Manager [Danish]

Jentone Freight Limited
Incorporated: 11 August 1998 *Employees:* 24
Net Worth: £1,756,912 *Total Assets:* £2,405,086
Registered Office: 1 John Boyle Road, South Bank, Middlesbrough, Cleveland, TS6 6TY
Activities: Freight transport by road
Shareholder: Anthony William Hill
Officers: Jennifer Ann Hill, Secretary; Anthony William Hill [1968] Director; Jennifer Ann Hill [1970] Director

Jesmond Community Leisure
Incorporated: 13 September 1991 *Employees:* 13
Net Worth: £1,562,897 *Total Assets:* £1,639,575
Registered Office: Jesmond Pool, St Georges Terrace, Jesmond, Newcastle upon Tyne, NE2 2DL
Activities: Operation of sports facilities
Officers: Christopher John Lawrey Clarke [1946] Director/Retired; Duncan Phillip Davies [1974] Director/Accountant; Annette Hames [1957] Director/Retired; Martin Frederick Hunt [1981] Director/Civil Engineer; Michael David Miller [1952] Director/Retired Dental Surgeon; Paul Anthony Rea [1957] Director/Graphic Designer; John Barrie Thompson [1946] Director/Lecturer

Jesmond Court Limited
Incorporated: 7 March 2005
Registered Office: 1st Floor, The Apartment Group Two, Jesmond Three Sixty, Newcastle upon Tyne, NE2 1DB
Activities: Public houses and bars
Officers: Amanda Jayne Fisher, Secretary; Duncan Fisher [1968] Director

Jesmond Holdings Limited
Incorporated: 10 July 2006
Registered Office: 1st Floor, The Apartment Group Two, Jesmond Three Sixty, Newcastle upon Tyne, NE2 1DB
Activities: Licenced restaurants
Shareholder: Duncan Fisher
Officers: Duncan Fisher, Secretary/Director; Duncan Fisher [1968] Director; Stuart John Monk [1949] Director

Jesmond Leisure Limited
Incorporated: 8 November 2004
Net Worth: £1,208,518 *Total Assets:* £2,105,448
Registered Office: 1st Floor, The Apartment Group Two, Jesmond Three Sixty, Newcastle upon Tyne, NE2 1DB
Activities: Licenced restaurants
Officers: Amanda Jayne Fisher, Secretary; Duncan Fisher [1968] Director

Jesmond Property Developments Limited
Incorporated: 28 November 1986
Net Worth: £1,435,923 *Total Assets:* £2,584,786
Registered Office: Kinnair & Company, Aston House, Redburn Road, Newcastle upon Tyne, NE5 1NB
Activities: Other letting and operating of own or leased real estate
Major Shareholder: Mohammed Ajaib
Officers: Ming Farn Lee, Secretary; Mohammed Ajaib [1957] Director/Civil Engineer

Jesres (Property Lets) Co. Limited
Incorporated: 3 May 1996 *Employees:* 2
Net Worth: £256,650 *Total Assets:* £1,534,568
Registered Office: 18 The Crescent, Tynemouth, North Shields, Tyne & Wear, NE30 2LZ
Activities: Real estate agencies
Shareholders: John Noel Astill; Michelle Astill
Officers: John Noel Astill, Secretary; John Noel Astill [1962] Director; Michelle Astill [1961] Director

Jessna 3 Limited
Incorporated: 26 July 1995
Registered Office: 120-122 High Northgate, Darlington, Co Durham, DL1 1UR
Activities: Other letting and operating of own or leased real estate
Officers: Richard Thomas Brooke Thomason, Secretary; Julia Ann Brooke Blower [1978] Director/Regeneration Consultant; Emily Sarah Brooke Close [1981] Director/Property Manager; Kenneth Roy Thomason [1944] Director/Solicitor; Richard Thomas Brooke Thomason [1972] Director

Jessna Properties Limited
Incorporated: 8 January 2009
Registered Office: 120-122 High Northgate, Darlington, Co Durham, DL1 1UR
Activities: Buying and selling of own real estate
Officers: Julia Ann Brooke Blower [1978] Director; Emily Sarah Brooke Close [1981] Director; Kenneth Roy Thomason [1944] Solicitor/Director; Richard Thomas Brooke Thomason [1972] Managing Director

Robin Jessop Holdings Limited
Incorporated: 30 April 2002
Net Worth: £570,805 *Total Assets:* £803,947
Registered Office: Scruton House, Station Road, Scruton, Northallerton, N Yorks, DL7 0QN
Activities: Real estate agencies
Shareholders: William Robinson Jessop; Valerie Jane Jessop
Officers: William Robinson Jessop, Secretary/Chartered Surveyor; Valerie Jane Jessop [1954] Director/Bookkeeper; William Robinson Jessop [1952] Director/Chartered Surveyor; Sarah Emily Sykes [1986] Director/Property Manager

Jetsun Ltd
Incorporated: 8 August 2006
Net Worth: £1,233,131 *Total Assets:* £1,291,025
Registered Office: 22-26 Mediterranean Village, Metrocentre, Gateshead, Tyne & Wear, NE11 9XG
Activities: Licenced restaurants
Shareholders: Chawalit Prapunwong; Sun Ye Lau
Officers: Sun Ye Lau, Secretary; Chawalit Prapunwong [1971] Director/Restaurant Manager

Jewel First Limited
Incorporated: 26 July 2011
Net Worth: £1,163 *Total Assets:* £911,328
Registered Office: 5 Victoria Avenue, Bishop Auckland, Co Durham, DL14 7JH
Activities: Retail sale via mail order houses or via Internet
Major Shareholder: Claire Christine Ketley
Officers: Claire Christine Ketley [1972] Director/Jewellery Retailer

J.A.Jewitt
Incorporated: 14 May 1959 *Employees:* 5
Net Worth: £8,912,795 *Total Assets:* £10,431,761
Registered Office: Low House Farm, Middlestone Moor, Spennymoor, Co Durham, DL16 7QD
Activities: Wholesale of meat and meat products
Shareholders: Verona Jewitt; The Jewitt Trust
Officers: Verona Jewitt, Secretary; Caroline Jane Jewitt [1971] Director/Administrator; Michael David Jewitt [1969] Director/Butcher; Verona Jewitt [1940] Director/Secretary

J.A. Jewitt (Farms) Limited
Incorporated: 20 February 1979
Net Worth: £973,507 *Total Assets:* £1,138,463
Registered Office: Low House Farm, Middlestone Moor, Spennymoor, Co Durham, DL16 7QD
Activities: Wholesale of meat and meat products
Parent: J A Jewitt
Officers: Verona Jewitt, Secretary; Caroline Jane Jewitt [1971] Director/Administrator; Michael David Jewitt [1969] Director/Butcher; Verona Jewitt [1940] Director/Secretary

J.A. Jewitt (Meat) Limited
Incorporated: 20 February 1979 *Employees:* 65
Net Worth: £7,286,642 *Total Assets:* £9,317,083
Registered Office: Low House Farm, Middlestone Moor, Spennymoor, Co Durham, DL16 7QD
Activities: Wholesale of meat and meat products
Shareholders: Michael David Jewitt; Verona Jewitt; J A Jewitt
Officers: Verona Jewitt, Secretary; Caroline Jane Jewitt [1971] Director/Administrator; Michael David Jewitt [1969] Director/Butcher; Verona Jewitt [1940] Director/Secretary

The JGW Patterson Foundation
Incorporated: 7 March 2002
Net Worth: £19,782,140 *Total Assets:* £20,039,826
Registered Office: The Cube, Barrack Road, Newcastle upon Tyne, NE4 6DB
Activities: Buying and selling of own real estate
Officers: Philippa Aitken, Secretary; Professor Timothy Edward Cawston [1949] Director/Dean of Research Medical Sciences Newcastle University; Professor Sir Alan William Craft [1946] Director/Doctor; James Curry Dias [1948] Director; Stephen Thomas Gilroy [1956] Director/Chartered Surveyor; David Robert Gold [1962] Director/Chartered Accountant

JHT Fabrications Ltd
Incorporated: 13 February 2003
Net Worth: £669,895 *Total Assets:* £1,379,164
Registered Office: Site B2 Hobson Industrial Estate, Hobson, Co Durham, NE16 6EA
Activities: Manufacture of other fabricated metal products n.e.c.
Shareholders: Lee John Jackson; Joanne Thompson
Officers: Joanne Thompson, Secretary; Lee John Jackson [1976] Director/Sheet Metal Worker & General Fabrication; Joanne Thompson [1978] Director/Head Stable Girl

JHW Estates Limited
Incorporated: 31 December 2002 *Employees:* 6
Net Worth: £1,558,795 *Total Assets:* £1,699,341
Registered Office: Chipchase Manners, 384 Linthorpe Road, Middlesbrough, Cleveland, TS5 6HA
Activities: Other letting and operating of own or leased real estate
Shareholders: Henrietta Cecilia Williams; John Matthew Williams
Officers: John Matthew Williams, Secretary; Henrietta Cecilia Williams [1961] Director/Teacher; John Matthew Williams [1960] Director; Jonathan Frederick Matthew Williams [1991] Director; Joshua John Ralph Williams [1989] Director; Katherine Mary Elizabeth Williams [1994] Director; Luke Hugo Harald Williams [1999] Director/Student

Jiahua Europe Limited
Incorporated: 20 January 2016 *Employees:* 3
Net Worth: £198,424 *Total Assets:* £1,582,872
Registered Office: Rotterdam House, 116 Quayside, Newcastle upon Tyne, NE1 3DY
Activities: Other professional, scientific and technical activities n.e.c.
Parent: Jiahua Chemicals (Shanghai) Ltd
Officers: Guillaume Lagadec [1978] Director [French]

Jigsaw Learning Trust
Incorporated: 1 November 2012 *Employees:* 56
Net Worth: £2,488,099 *Total Assets:* £3,175,169
Registered Office: Fulwell Infant School Academy, Ebdon Lane, Fulwell, Sunderland, Tyne & Wear, SR6 8ED
Activities: Primary education
Officers: Hilary Akien [1959] Director/Assistant Headteacher; Wendy Ann Angus [1961] Director/Headteacher; Kathryn Mary Barrass [1963] Director; Glen Peter Batten [1988] Director/Accountant; Hilary Hartnack [1961] Director/Retired Teacher; Kenneth Francis Hern [1952] Director/College Lecturer; Dr Anthony Trevor Jackson [1971] Research Director; Anthony Shaw Kingston [1950] Director/Independent Education Consultant; Louise Jane Lavelle [1970] Director/Headteacher

JJC Engineering Ltd
Incorporated: 18 April 2006 *Employees:* 9
Net Worth: £741,559 *Total Assets:* £852,259
Registered Office: Unit 26 Bonlea Trading Estate, Thornaby, Stockton on Tees, Cleveland, TS17 7AQ
Activities: Manufacture of other fabricated metal products n.e.c.
Shareholders: Paul Warren; Julie Ann Warren
Officers: Julie Ann Warren, Secretary/Administrator; Paul Warren [1957] Director/Engineer

JJT Development Limited
Incorporated: 1 September 2006
Registered Office: 1e North Sands Business Centre, Sunderland, Tyne & Wear, SR6 0QA
Activities: Other letting and operating of own or leased real estate
Parent: Pebbletree Ltd
Officers: Robert Thornton, Secretary; Janni Marline Thornton [1980] Director; Robert Thornton [1975] Director

JKL Mouldings Limited
Incorporated: 9 January 2009 *Employees:* 92
Net Worth: £781,418 *Total Assets:* £2,310,108
Registered Office: St Johns Road, Meadowfield Industrial Estate, Brandon, Co Durham, DH7 8XQ
Activities: Manufacture of other plastic products
Major Shareholder: Neil Brooks
Officers: Neil Brooks [1961] Director/Tool Maker

JL Mechanical and Electrical Services Limited
Incorporated: 20 February 2007
Net Worth: £2,899,059 *Total Assets:* £4,373,429
Registered Office: Leona Grove, Houghton Road, Hetton-le-Hole, Houghton-le-Spring, Co Durham, DH5 9PN
Activities: Non-trading company
Major Shareholder: John Steven Richardson
Officers: Lynne Richardson, Secretary; John Steven Richardson [1967] Director

JLM Global Foods Limited
Incorporated: 2 June 2003 *Employees:* 60
Net Worth: £2,101,337 *Total Assets:* £3,851,580
Registered Office: 37 Allington Way, Yarm Road Business Park, Darlington, Co Durham, DL1 4QB
Activities: Manufacture of other food products n.e.c.
Major Shareholder: Joyce May Moore
Officers: James Alan Moore, Secretary; Anthony Michael Dennett [1945] Director/Accountant; Paul Anthony Huggins [1952] Director; Graeme Alan Moore [1964] Director; James Alan Moore [1940] Director

JM Property Investments Limited
Incorporated: 10 January 2013
Registered Office: Franks The Flooring Store, Linden House, Portrack Lane, Stockton on Tees, Cleveland, TS18 2PS
Activities: Buying and selling of own real estate
Major Shareholder: Jason Maguire
Officers: Jason James Maguire [1973] Director

JMW (Aluminium) Limited
Incorporated: 16 July 1971
Net Worth: £1,028,258 *Total Assets:* £2,127,647
Registered Office: Earl Grey House, 75-85 Grey Street, Newcastle upon Tyne, NE1 6EF
Activities: Construction of commercial buildings
Officers: Trisha Joanne Wadds, Secretary; Patricia Wadds [1950] Director; Trevor Wadds [1948] Director/Chairman; Trisha Joanne Wadds [1971] Director; William Henry Wadds [1937] Director

James A. Jobling and Company Limited
Incorporated: 6 April 1976 *Employees:* 47
Net Worth: £5,492,196 *Total Assets:* £11,681,448
Registered Office: Paradise Works, Scotswood Road, Newcastle upon Tyne, NE15 6BZ
Activities: Other manufacturing n.e.c.
Major Shareholder: Timothy Ernest Jobling Purser
Officers: John McCreary, Secretary; Adrienne Isolde Jobling Purser [1941] Director; David Ernest Jobling Purser [1969] Director; Evan William Jobling Purser [1968] Director [Irish]; Timothy Ernest Jobling Purser [1941] Director; John McCreary [1956] Finance Director

Joegraphic Ltd
Incorporated: 11 December 1998
Net Worth: £334,242 *Total Assets:* £757,630
Registered Office: Register House, Zetland Street, Northallerton, N Yorks, DL6 1NA
Activities: Portrait photographic activities
Officers: Jonathan James Cornish [1958] Director/Photographer; Joni Essex [1945] Marketing Director; Joseph Essex [1973] Director/Graphic Designer

Joel Memorial Limited
Incorporated: 10 April 2003
Net Worth: £1,976,851 *Total Assets:* £4,565,502
Registered Office: 2 Richmond Terrace, Gateshead, Tyne & Wear, NE8 1RN
Activities: Activities of religious organisations
Officers: Judith Fried, Secretary/Housewife [Swiss]; Arran Bleier [1974] Director/Research Assistant; Jerry Fried [1950] Director/Sewing Machine Parts [American]; Judith Fried [1950] Director/Housewife [Swiss]

Cyril John Limited
Incorporated: 2 October 1995 *Employees:* 70
Net Worth: £1,249,126 *Total Assets:* £1,767,945
Registered Office: Unit 9 Mercury Orion Way, Orion Business Park, North Shields, Tyne & Wear, NE29 7SN
Activities: Painting
Officers: Paul Howieson, Secretary; Craig George Bell [1980] Director; Paul Howieson [1967] Finance Director; Paul Steedman [1960] Director

G.C.S. Johnson (Skeeby) Limited
Incorporated: 15 February 1974
Net Worth: £1,696,438 *Total Assets:* £2,426,688
Registered Office: Barton Quarry, Barton, Richmond, N Yorks, DL10 6NF
Activities: Freight transport by road
Shareholder: Charlotte Mary Johnson
Officers: Charlotte Mary Johnson, Secretary; Charlotte Mary Johnson [1946] Director/Secretary; Geoffrey Colin Skinner Johnson [1942] Director/Road Haulier

Johnson Electric International (UK) Limited
Incorporated: 21 July 1967 *Employees:* 15
Net Worth: £483,961,984 *Total Assets:* £485,296,992
Registered Office: Office G5, Ground Floor, Metropolitan House, Longrigg Road, Swalwell, Gateshead, Tyne & Wear, NE16 3AS
Activities: Manufacture of other electrical equipment
Officers: Lai Chu Cheng, Secretary; Kevin Stewart Bisset [1970] Director; Christopher John Hasson [1963] Director; Jeffrey Lee Obermayer [1955] Director [American]

K.Johnson Limited
Incorporated: 1 December 1998 *Employees:* 4
Net Worth: £1,470,649 *Total Assets:* £2,115,671
Registered Office: Orchard House, West End, Gayle, Hawes, N Yorks, DL8 3RQ
Activities: Gambling and betting activities
Shareholders: Keith Johnson; Christine Angela Johnson
Officers: Christine Angela Johnson, Secretary; Christine Angela Johnson [1959] Director; Keith Johnson [1955] Director

CD Johnson Limited
Incorporated: 16 February 2012 *Employees:* 67
Net Worth: £1,103,608 *Total Assets:* £5,783,424
Registered Office: Beaufront Park, Alnwick Road, Hexham, Northumberland, NE46 4TU
Activities: Other building completion and finishing
Shareholders: Charles Darren Johnson; Samantha Johnson
Officers: Charlie Johnson, Secretary; Gillian Frances Banks [1956] Finance Director; Charles Darren Johnson [1965] Director

G.C.S. Johnson Limited
Incorporated: 17 October 2002
Net Worth: £36,077 *Total Assets:* £1,582,054
Registered Office: Barton Quarry Industrial Estate, Barton Park, Barton, Richmond, N Yorks, DL10 6NF
Activities: Freight transport by road
Shareholder: Charlotte Mary Johnson
Officers: Charlotte Mary Johnson, Secretary; Alison Mary Johnson [1977] Director/Secretary; Charlotte Mary Johnson [1946] Director/Secretary; Geoffrey Colin Skinner Johnson [1942] Director/Haulier; Joseph Stuart Johnson [1975] Director/Haulier

J H Johnson Shopfitters Limited
Incorporated: 23 December 2010 *Employees:* 10
Net Worth: £130,864 *Total Assets:* £797,521
Registered Office: Unit 1 Baird Close, Stephenson Industrial Estate, Washington, Tyne & Wear, NE37 3HL
Activities: Construction of commercial buildings
Parent: C & D Investments Limited
Officers: Doreen Clayton [1963] Director; Colin Wilkinson [1961] Director

Johnson Wright (Flooring) Limited
Incorporated: 13 November 1991 *Employees:* 11
Net Worth: £591,046 *Total Assets:* £1,278,254
Registered Office: Arcon House, Sunderland Road, Gateshead, Tyne & Wear, NE10 9LQ
Activities: Floor and wall covering
Parent: JWF (Holdings) Ltd
Officers: Greg Wolfe [1972] Contracts Director

Jolan Piccadilly Limited
Incorporated: 23 March 2009 *Employees:* 3
Net Worth: £4,777,495 *Total Assets:* £4,987,301
Registered Office: First Floor, Finchale House, Belmont Business Park, Durham, DH1 1TW
Activities: Other letting and operating of own or leased real estate
Officers: Helen Austin, Secretary; John Corbitt Barnsley [1948] Director/Accountant; Spencer Trerise Glanville [1972] Director; Robert William Jefferson [1950] Director/Chartered Accountant

Jomast 1 Limited
Incorporated: 9 March 2012 *Employees:* 7
Net Worth Deficit: £1,469,642 *Total Assets:* £35,191,200
Registered Office: Oriel House, Calverts Lane, Bishop Street, Stockton on Tees, Cleveland, TS18 1SW
Activities: Other letting and operating of own or leased real estate
Parent: Jomast Limited
Officers: Stuart John Monk, Secretary; Jennifer Monk [1952] Director; Stuart John Monk [1949] Director

Jomast 2 Limited
Incorporated: 9 March 2012 *Employees:* 2
Net Worth Deficit: £513,851 *Total Assets:* £19,507,420
Registered Office: Oriel House, Calverts Lane, Bishop Street, Stockton on Tees, Cleveland, TS18 1SW
Activities: Other letting and operating of own or leased real estate
Parent: Jomast Limited
Officers: Stuart John Monk, Secretary; Jennifer Monk [1952] Director; Stuart John Monk [1949] Director

Jomast 5 Limited
Incorporated: 4 January 2001 *Employees:* 2
Net Worth: £838,460 *Total Assets:* £28,158,404
Registered Office: Top Floor, Oriel House, Calverts Lane, Stockton on Tees, Cleveland, TS18 1SW
Activities: Other letting and operating of own or leased real estate
Parent: Jomast Limited
Officers: Stuart John Monk, Secretary/Director; Jennifer Monk [1952] Director; Stuart John Monk [1949] Director

Jomast 6 Limited
Incorporated: 22 January 2001 *Employees:* 2
Net Worth: £7,995,836 *Total Assets:* £20,989,034
Registered Office: Top Floor, Oriel House, Calverts Lane, Stockton on Tees, Cleveland, TS18 1SW
Activities: Other letting and operating of own or leased real estate
Parent: Jomast Limited
Officers: Stuart John Monk, Secretary/Director; Jennifer Monk [1952] Director; Stuart John Monk [1949] Director

Jomast Accommodation Limited
Incorporated: 5 June 1969 *Employees:* 39
Net Worth: £138,359,696 *Total Assets:* £205,945,808
Registered Office: Top Floor, Oriel House, Calverts Lane, Bishop Street, Stockton on Tees, Cleveland, TS18 1SW
Activities: Other letting and operating of own or leased real estate
Parent: Jomast Limited
Officers: Stuart John Monk, Secretary; Jennifer Monk [1952] Director; Stuart John Monk [1949] Director

Jomast Developments Limited
Incorporated: 12 July 1978 *Employees:* 76
Net Worth: £29,012,430 *Total Assets:* £76,402,104
Registered Office: Top Floor, Oriel House, Calverts Lane, Bishop Street, Stockton on Tees, Cleveland, TS18 1SW
Activities: Construction of commercial buildings
Parent: Jomast Limited
Officers: Stuart John Monk, Secretary; Jennifer Monk [1952] Director; Stuart John Monk [1949] Director; Ian Paul Williams [1960] Director

Jomast Leisure & Property Limited
Incorporated: 29 April 1988 *Employees:* 2
Net Worth: £5,228,078 *Total Assets:* £48,535,956
Registered Office: Top Floor, Oriel House, Calverts Lane, Bishop Street, Stockton on Tees, Cleveland, TS18 1SW
Activities: Other letting and operating of own or leased real estate
Parent: Jomast Limited
Officers: Stuart John Monk, Secretary; Jennifer Monk [1952] Director; Stuart John Monk [1949] Director

Jomast Limited
Incorporated: 8 March 2012 *Employees:* 157
Net Worth: £132,355,840 *Total Assets:* £228,395,360
Registered Office: Oriel House, Calverts Lane, Bishop Street, Stockton on Tees, Cleveland, TS18 1SW
Activities: Non-trading company
Major Shareholder: Stuart John Monk
Officers: Stuart John Monk, Secretary; Jennifer Monk [1952] Director; Stuart John Monk [1949] Director

Frank Jones (Chemist) Limited
Incorporated: 18 January 1941 *Employees:* 18
Net Worth: £356,263 *Total Assets:* £750,105
Registered Office: 18 Ambleside Court, Chester-le-Street, Co Durham, DH3 2EB
Activities: Other human health activities
Shareholders: Helen Kate Clark; Greg Clark
Officers: Greg Clark [1984] Director/Pharmacist; Helen Kate Clark [1984] Director/Pharmacist; Kevin Alan Simpson [1958] Director/Pharmacist

F Jones (Cleveland) Limited
Incorporated: 5 April 1982 *Employees:* 41
Net Worth: £2,916,989 *Total Assets:* £4,367,137
Registered Office: Riverside Park Road, Middlesbrough, Cleveland, TS2 1QW
Activities: Cutting, shaping and finishing of stone
Major Shareholder: Frederick Jones
Officers: Valerie Helen Jones, Secretary; Edward Ian Jones [1950] Director; Frederick Jones [1952] Director; Jeremy Kevin Jones [1962] Director; Simon Paul Jones [1963] Director

D Jones Construction & Haulage Limited
Incorporated: 2 October 2015 *Employees:* 26
Net Worth: £452,794 *Total Assets:* £1,094,960
Registered Office: Chartwell House, Manor Drive, Hilton, Yarm, Cleveland, TS15 9LE
Activities: Construction of other civil engineering projects n.e.c.
Shareholders: Mary Noreen Jones; David Jones
Officers: Mary Noreen Jones, Secretary; David Jones [1961] Director

D.K. Jones Limited
Incorporated: 18 November 1983 *Employees:* 39
Net Worth: £5,123,342 *Total Assets:* £6,296,593
Registered Office: 48-50 West Street, Middlesbrough, Cleveland, TS2 1LZ
Activities: Non-specialised wholesale trade
Major Shareholder: Desmond Keith Jones
Officers: Lynda Jaqueline Mary Cox, Secretary; Lynda Jaqueline Mary Cox [1961] Director/Company Secretary; Christopher Michael Jones [1989] Managing Director; Desmond Keith Jones [1953] Managing Director; Matthew William Jones [1991] Sales Director

Jonsigns Limited
Incorporated: 3 August 2006 *Employees:* 45
Net Worth: £632,382 *Total Assets:* £2,064,578
Registered Office: Cawthorn House, 24 Saltmeadows Road, Gateshead, Tyne & Wear, NE8 3AH
Activities: Other manufacturing n.e.c.
Shareholder: Francis Jonathan Cawthorn
Officers: Joy Cawthorn, Secretary; Francis Jonathan Cawthorn [1974] Director/Signmaker

Jordan 90 Ltd
Incorporated: 19 June 2009
Net Worth: £2,259,624 *Total Assets:* £2,651,270
Registered Office: 17 Loch Lomond, Washington, Tyne & Wear, NE37 1PD
Activities: Other service activities n.e.c.
Major Shareholder: Jordan Henderson
Officers: Brian Henderson [1955] Managing Director; Jordan Henderson [1990] Director/Professional Footballer

Jordan Leasing (2005) LLP
Incorporated: 3 January 2006
Net Worth: £73,131 *Total Assets:* £1,384,395
Registered Office: Andaray House, Shields Road, Gateshead, Tyne & Wear, NE10 0QE
Officers: Peter Karl Jordan [1975] Member; Dionne Taylor [1979] Member

Joseph Developments Limited
Incorporated: 25 October 2001
Net Worth: £721,572 *Total Assets:* £805,492
Registered Office: Wynyard Park House, Wynyard Avenue, Wynyard, Billingham, Cleveland, TS22 5TB
Activities: Activities of head offices
Shareholders: Joseph Christopher Musgrave; Joseph Christopher Musgrave
Officers: Barbara Musgrave [1966] Director; Joseph Christopher Musgrave [1965] Director/Manager; Joseph Musgrave [1933] Managing Director; Mary Musgrave [1935] Director

Josh & Tom Ltd
Incorporated: 3 December 2002 *Employees:* 3
Net Worth: £4,664,375 *Total Assets:* £5,295,312
Registered Office: 43 Maxwell Street, South Shields, Tyne & Wear, NE33 4PU
Activities: Activities of head offices
Major Shareholder: Derek Edward West
Officers: Jane Rosanna Carr, Secretary; Jane Rosanna Carr [1970] Director; Derek Edward West [1949] Director; Lee West [1967] Director

Jotron UK Ltd
Incorporated: 12 November 1980
Net Worth: £790,188 *Total Assets:* £1,698,479
Registered Office: Jotron UK Ltd, Crosland Park, Crowhall Road, Cramlington, Northumberland, NE23 1LA
Activities: Agents specialised in the sale of other particular products
Officers: Vivienne Rose Keillor, Secretary; Arne Berdal [1963] Director/Sales Manager [Norwegian]; Ian Paul Forbes [1963] Operations Director; Morten Gjersoe [1956] Sales Director [Norwegian]; Rune Kristiansen [1970] Director [Norwegian]; Anthony John Parker [1968] Director/Technical Sales Manager; Tor Martin Roed [1967] Maritime & Energy Sales Director [Norwegian]; Paul David Shaw [1961] Managing Director

Journey Enterprises Ltd
Incorporated: 23 December 1983 *Employees:* 35
Net Worth: £913,303 *Total Assets:* £1,113,954
Registered Office: Network House, Acomb, Hexham, Northumberland, NE46 4SA
Activities: Other human health activities
Officers: Ruth Edwards, Secretary; Anthony Gibson [1949] Director; Emma Jennings [1976] Director/Business Executive; Barbara Simpson [1949] Director/Retired; Christian Hugh Stuart Swinburne [1968] Director/Solicitor

Joyce Construction & Civils Ltd
Incorporated: 7 April 1975 *Employees:* 69
Net Worth: £753,025 *Total Assets:* £4,511,645
Registered Office: Corbridge Business Centre, Tinklers Yard, Tinklers Bank, Corbridge, Northumberland, NE45 5SB
Activities: Other specialised construction activities n.e.c.
Shareholders: Alan Christopher Joyce; John Michael Joyce; Miles David Joyce
Officers: Elsie Joyce, Secretary; Sam Fredrick James Farnworth [1980] Director; Alan Christopher Joyce [1952] Director/Drainage Contractor; Miles David Joyce [1948] Director/Quantity Surveyor

JPG Property LLP
Incorporated: 16 July 2008
Net Worth: £1,957,069 *Total Assets:* £2,062,703
Registered Office: The Cube, Barrack Road, Newcastle upon Tyne, NE4 6DB
Officers: Nicky Peng Gillender [1982] Member; Wilfred Gillender [1947] Member

JR Dynamics Limited
Incorporated: 28 November 1996 *Employees:* 20
Net Worth: £1,083,678 *Total Assets:* £1,269,515
Registered Office: Unit 4 Arcot Court, Nelson Road, Nelson Industrial Estate, Cramlington, Northumberland, NE23 1BB
Activities: Other research and experimental development on natural sciences and engineering
Major Shareholder: Professor Jarek Rosinski
Officers: Professor Jarek Rosinski, Secretary/Engineer; Martin Rosinski, Secretary; Steve Lowry [1988] Director; Professor Jarek Rosinski [1958] Engineer Managing Director; Tomas Rosinski [1990] Director

JSB (Metals) Limited
Incorporated: 24 July 1997 *Employees:* 7
Net Worth: £2,071,673 *Total Assets:* £2,399,725
Registered Office: J S B Metals Ltd, Factory Road, Blaydon on Tyne, Tyne & Wear, NE21 5RZ
Activities: Dismantling of wrecks
Major Shareholder: John Stuart Boyd
Officers: John Stuart Boyd [1966] Director

JSK Property Development (UK) Ltd
Incorporated: 6 March 2014 *Employees:* 3
Net Worth: £1,207,385 *Total Assets:* £1,581,317
Registered Office: 48 Bowden Close, Newcastle upon Tyne, NE13 9GB
Activities: Development of building projects
Major Shareholder: Chen Yee Wong
Officers: Chen Yee Wong [1963] Director [Malaysian]; Sean Brandon Hon Loong Wong [1989] Director [Malaysian]; Clint Pui Yin Woo [1959] Director

JTM Plumbing Limited
Incorporated: 9 August 2007 *Employees:* 19
Net Worth: £584,956 *Total Assets:* £1,416,985
Registered Office: 8 Woodburn Drive, Darlington, Co Durham, DL3 8AB
Activities: Retail sale of hardware, paints and glass in specialised stores
Shareholders: Angela Mulroy; Jason Thomas Mulroy
Officers: Angela Mulroy, Secretary; Angela Mulroy [1971] Director

Juke Box Sales and Rentals Limited
Incorporated: 19 April 1960 *Employees:* 5
Net Worth: £2,315,213 *Total Assets:* £3,526,599
Registered Office: Somerford Buildings, Norfolk Street, Sunderland, Tyne & Wear, SR1 1EE
Activities: Other letting and operating of own or leased real estate
Shareholders: Peter George William Smith; Angela Smith
Officers: Angela Smith, Secretary; Lindsey Jane Dunn [1982] Director/Property Developer; Shona Marie Jack [1975] Director/Clerk; Angela Smith [1953] Director/Housewife; Peter George William Smith [1952] Director/Property Developer; Rachel Anne Smith [1974] Director/Accounts Clerk

Jules B Limited
Incorporated: 14 April 1986 *Employees:* 90
Net Worth Deficit: £444,979 *Total Assets:* £2,547,759
Registered Office: Yellow Brick House, Back New Bridge Street, Newcastle upon Tyne, NE1 2TY
Activities: Retail sale of clothing in specialised stores
Shareholders: Julian Edwin Hylton Blades; Rhona Georgette Blades
Officers: Julian Edwin Hylton Blades [1961] Director; Rhona Georgette Blades [1956] Director Buyer

Juma Corporation Ltd
Incorporated: 1 April 2011
Net Worth: £568,878 *Total Assets:* £956,951
Registered Office: 127 Burnmoor Drive, Eaglescliffe, Stockton on Tees, Cleveland, TS16 0HZ
Activities: Taxi operation
Major Shareholder: Alim Hussien Juma
Officers: Alim Hussien Juma [1969] Director/Taxi Driver

Junction Investments Ltd
Incorporated: 18 July 2013
Registered Office: 85b Junction Road, Stockton on Tees, Cleveland, TS20 1PU
Activities: Other letting and operating of own or leased real estate
Shareholders: Dr Craig Matthews; Michelle Matthews
Officers: Michelle Matthews, Secretary; Dr Craig John Matthews [1972] Director; Michelle Matthews [1971] Director

Junsterik Ltd
Incorporated: 7 January 2009
Net Worth: £1,646,135 *Total Assets:* £1,922,985
Registered Office: 104-108 Newgate Street, Newcastle upon Tyne, NE1 5RQ
Activities: Other retail sale in non-specialised stores
Major Shareholder: Jun Lau
Officers: Jun Lau [1982] Director

Just Drama Based Training Ltd
Incorporated: 10 July 2001
Net Worth: £491,086 *Total Assets:* £786,362
Registered Office: 103 Heaton Park Road, Heaton, Newcastle upon Tyne, NE6 5NR
Activities: Other professional, scientific and technical activities n.e.c.
Shareholders: Jacqueline Elizabeth Meyler; Alice Boyd
Officers: Jacqueline Elizabeth Meyler, Secretary; Alice Boyd [1975] Director/Trainer; Jacqueline Elizabeth Meyler [1963] Director/Trainer

Just Sport (Pro Club) Ltd
Incorporated: 3 February 2004 *Employees:* 74
Net Worth: £461,669 *Total Assets:* £1,117,507
Registered Office: 1 Enterprise City, Meadowfield Avenue, Spennymoor, Co Durham, DL16 6JF
Activities: Inland passenger water transport
Parent: Just Sport (Group) Ltd
Officers: Judith Smith, Secretary; Peter Crawford [1959] Director

Justships Ltd
Incorporated: 21 April 2011
Net Worth: £821,243 *Total Assets:* £1,190,361
Registered Office: 5 Shawwell Business Centre, Stagshaw Road, Corbridge, Northumberland, NE45 5PE
Activities: Activities of insurance agents and brokers
Major Shareholder: Stephen Harald Purvis
Officers: Timothy Nichol [1961] Director/Dean, Liverpool Business School; Jeffrey Paul O'Neill [1966] Director/Chartered Accountant; Stephen Harald Purvis [1962] Director

JW Installations UK Limited
Incorporated: 28 January 1999 *Employees:* 15
Net Worth: £793,701 *Total Assets:* £1,325,477
Registered Office: Atley Hill Road, North Cowton, Northallerton, N Yorks, DL7 0JB
Activities: Manufacture of metal structures and parts of structures
Shareholders: James Robert White; Charles John White; John White
Officers: Charles John White [1975] Director/Office Manager; James Robert White [1972] Director/Agricultural Engineer

K & A Properties Limited
Incorporated: 2 July 2001
Registered Office: c/o Union Property Services Ltd, Cobalt 3.1, Silver Fox Way, Cobalt Business Park, Newcastle upon Tyne, NE27 0QJ
Activities: Other letting and operating of own or leased real estate
Shareholders: Naresh Abrol; Rita Abrol
Officers: Promila Sehgal, Secretary/Director; Naresh Abrol [1973] Director; Rita Abrol [1974] Director; Promila Sehgal [1948] Director

K & L Groundworks Limited
Incorporated: 16 March 2009 *Employees:* 50
Net Worth: £258,528 *Total Assets:* £1,895,522
Registered Office: Oakmere, Belmont Business Park, Durham, DH1 1TW
Activities: Construction of other civil engineering projects n.e.c.
Shareholders: Gordon Pickard; Scott Ernest Leather
Officers: Kathleen Laverty, Secretary; Scott Ernest Leather [1974] Director

K Home International Limited
Incorporated: 3 July 1981 *Employees:* 48
Net Worth: £4,339,671 *Total Assets:* £6,077,306
Registered Office: Ingram House, Allensway, Thornaby, Cleveland, TS17 9HA
Activities: Other engineering activities
Major Shareholder: Kenneth Home
Officers: Michael Frederick Home, Secretary; Lee Anderson [1964] Director; Andrew Kenneth Home [1963] Director/Engineer; Dr Kenneth Home [1930] Director/Engineer; Michael Frederick Home [1962] Director/Accountant

K.E.P. Services (UK) Ltd.
Incorporated: 8 January 1998 *Employees:* 8
Net Worth: £1,368,008 *Total Assets:* £1,582,109
Registered Office: Unit 33a Third Avenue, Drum Industrial Estate, Chester-le-Street, Co Durham, DH2 1AY
Activities: Non-specialised wholesale trade
Officers: Catherine Anne Jobson, Secretary; Catherine Anne Jobson [1957] Director/Secretary; Robert Henry Jobson [1954] Director/Engineer

Kaas Properties (North) Limited
Incorporated: 19 September 2003
Net Worth: £435,165 *Total Assets:* £1,061,233
Registered Office: 20 Norham Drive, Morpeth, Northumberland, NE61 2XA
Activities: Other letting and operating of own or leased real estate
Officers: Suroth Miah, Secretary/Director; Afrus Miah [1962] Director; Awlad Miah [1956] Director; Kaptan Miah [1955] Director; Suroth Miah [1965] Director

Kader Academy Trust
Incorporated: 6 March 2014 *Employees:* 41
Net Worth: £2,710,000 *Total Assets:* £3,294,000
Registered Office: Kader Academy, Staindrop Drive, Acklam, Middlesbrough, Cleveland, TS5 8NU
Activities: Primary education
Officers: Lynne Chalk [1958] Director/Principal; Pauline Cunningham [1946] Director/Retired; Sharon Dalton [1970] Director/Housing Manager; Yvonne Ditchburn [1970] Director/Administrator; Mohammed Aslam Hanif M.B.E. [1959] Director/Retired; Paul John Leadbitter [1968] Director; Robert Barry Lomas [1949] Director/Retired; Christine Anne Elizabeth Marchant [1951] Director/Retired; Alison Rebecca Mitchinson [1966] Director/Vice Principal

Kadmous Holdings (UK) Limited.
Incorporated: 30 May 1985 *Employees:* 176
Net Worth: £1,964,017 *Total Assets:* £6,183,145
Registered Office: Horndale Avenue, Aycliffe Industrial Estate, Newton Aycliffe, Co Durham, DL5 6DW
Activities: Other manufacturing n.e.c.
Officers: Walid El Hage, Secretary; Walid El-Hage [1968] Director/Engineer

Kail and Co. Limited
Incorporated: 15 April 1981 *Employees:* 43
Net Worth: £2,406,932 *Total Assets:* £4,420,291
Registered Office: 1 Castletown Road, Sunderland, Tyne & Wear, SR5 3HT
Activities: Manufacture of compressors
Major Shareholder: Steven Pattison
Officers: Judith Anne Pattison, Secretary; Judith Anne Pattison [1958] Director/Clerical Assistant; Steven Pattison [1959] Director/Engineer

Kail Holdings Limited
Incorporated: 28 March 2001 *Employees:* 3
Net Worth: £1,495,557 *Total Assets:* £2,399,792
Registered Office: 1 Castletown Road, Sunderland, Tyne & Wear, SR5 3HT
Activities: Activities of head offices
Shareholders: Judith Anne Pattison; Steven Pattison
Officers: Judith Anne Pattison, Company Secretary; Judith Anne Pattison [1958] Director/Company Secretary; Steven Pattison [1959] Director/Engineer

Kans and Kandy (Holdings) Ltd
Incorporated: 6 January 2006 *Employees:* 23
Net Worth: £16,223,227 *Total Assets:* £39,918,856
Registered Office: 9 Foxcover Distribution Park, Admiralty Way, Seaham, Co Durham, SR7 7DN
Activities: Activities of head offices
Officers: Mohammed Razaq, Secretary/Director; Jawid Iqbal [1963] Director; Ian David Marley [1973] Director; Mohammed Razaq [1964] Director

Kans and Kandy (Properties) Ltd
Incorporated: 6 January 2006
Net Worth: £6,581,844 *Total Assets:* £34,992,168
Registered Office: 9 Foxcover Distribution Park, Admiralty Way, Seaham, Co Durham, SR7 7DN
Activities: Buying and selling of own real estate
Officers: Mohammed Razaq, Secretary/Director; Jawid Iqbal [1963] Director; Ian David Marley [1973] Director; Mohammed Razaq [1964] Director

Kans and Kandy (Wholesale) Ltd
Incorporated: 4 February 2000 *Employees:* 23
Net Worth: £10,850,341 *Total Assets:* £15,172,541
Registered Office: 9 Foxcover Distribution Park, Admiralty Way, Seaham, Co Durham, SR7 7DN
Activities: Non-specialised wholesale trade
Officers: Mohammed Razaq, Secretary/Businessman; Jawid Iqbal [1963] Director/Businessman; Ian David Marley [1973] Director/Businessman; Mohammed Razaq [1964] Director/Businessman

Karbon Developments Limited
Incorporated: 11 September 2003
Net Worth: £355,183 *Total Assets:* £3,245,041
Registered Office: 5 Gosforth Park Avenue, Gosforth Business Park, Newcastle upon Tyne, NE12 8EG
Activities: Buying and selling of own real estate
Parent: Karbon Homes Limited
Officers: Richard Dean Fryer, Secretary; Charlotte Elise Carpenter [1971] Director; Paul Fiddaman [1965] Director/Chief Executive; Mark Reid [1964] Finance Director

Karlin Timber Frame (NE) Limited
Incorporated: 16 November 2009
Net Worth: £132,041 *Total Assets:* £870,507
Registered Office: Unit 9 Maple Way, Aycliffe Business Park, Newton Aycliffe, Co Durham, DL5 6BF
Activities: Construction of commercial buildings
Shareholder: Karen Lunn
Officers: David Edward Clarke, Secretary; Peter Charles Hudson [1960] Director/Financial Services; Colin William Lunn [1963] Director; Karen Lunn [1964] Director

Karol Property Company Limited
Incorporated: 24 October 1986 *Employees:* 2
Net Worth: £1,762,222 *Total Assets:* £2,996,011
Registered Office: 34 Long Meadows, East Herrington, Sunderland, Tyne & Wear, SR3 3SB
Activities: Other letting and operating of own or leased real estate
Major Shareholder: Raymond Stobbart
Officers: Raymond Stobbart, Secretary; Karol Stobbart [1956] Director; Raymond Stobbart [1954] Director/Consultant Engineer

Kasai UK Ltd
Incorporated: 22 March 1991 *Employees:* 824
Net Worth: £34,554,944 *Total Assets:* £45,923,820
Registered Office: Kasai UK Ltd, Stephenson Road, Stephenson Industrial Estate, Washington, Tyne & Wear, NE37 3HR
Activities: Manufacture of other plastic products
Officers: Itaru Nishikawa [1955] Director [Japanese]; Takashi Terada [1952] Managing Director [Japanese]; Peter Russell Watson [1956] Deputy Managing Director

Katell Limited
Incorporated: 2 August 2001 *Employees:* 66
Net Worth: £1,501,688 *Total Assets:* £3,396,543
Registered Office: 478-480 Durham Way North, Aycliffe Industrial Park, Newton Aycliffe, Co Durham, DL5 6HP
Activities: Manufacture of other furniture
Parent: Charlton & Jenrick Ltd
Officers: Andrew John Hurworth, Secretary; Stuart Clark Bailey [1962] Director/Production; Karl Stephen Baines [1973] Sales Director; Barry George Charlton [1946] Director; Andrew John Hurworth [1966] Director/Accountant; William John Jenrick [1940] Director

Katem Logistics Limited
Incorporated: 6 February 2007 *Employees:* 62
Net Worth: £1,758,722 *Total Assets:* £3,609,297
Registered Office: The Stables, Aykley Heads, Durham, DH1 5AN
Activities: Freight transport by road
Major Shareholder: Clare Davison
Officers: David Illingworth, Secretary; Clare Davison [1958] Director; John Davison [1935] Director

Katmex Holdings Limited
Incorporated: 1 March 2010 *Employees:* 174
Net Worth: £4,568,364 *Total Assets:* £7,785,428
Registered Office: Katmex, Bowron Street, Norton, Stockton on Tees, Cleveland, TS20 2BH
Activities: Activities of head offices
Major Shareholder: David Mitchell
Officers: David Mitchell, Secretary; David Mitchell [1956] Director/Engineer

Katmex Limited
Incorporated: 24 March 1999 *Employees:* 141
Net Worth: £7,366,762 *Total Assets:* £10,096,576
Registered Office: Bowron Street, Stockton on Tees, Cleveland, TS20 2BH
Activities: Manufacture of other fabricated metal products n.e.c.
Major Shareholder: David Mitchell
Officers: David Mitchell, Secretary/Engineer; David Mitchell [1956] Director/Engineer

Katmex Seaham Limited
Incorporated: 14 July 1978
Net Worth: £545,394 *Total Assets:* £1,003,381
Registered Office: Londonderry Works, Seaham, Co Durham, SR7 7SL
Activities: Manufacture of basic iron and steel and of ferro-alloys
Major Shareholder: David Mitchell
Officers: David Mitchell [1956] Director/Engineer

Kavli UK Limited
Incorporated: 12 April 2013 *Employees:* 273
Net Worth: £24,216,420 *Total Assets:* £38,639,340
Registered Office: Kingsway, Team Valley Trading Estate, Gateshead, Tyne & Wear, NE11 0ST
Activities: Activities of head offices
Officers: Lynn Hayes, Secretary; Paul Robert Lewney [1967] Director; Erik Volden [1961] Director [Norwegian]

O Kay Automatics Limited
Incorporated: 17 February 1964
Net Worth: £1,079,972 *Total Assets:* £1,248,591
Registered Office: 63 High Street, Marske-by-the-Sea, Cleveland, TS11 6JW
Activities: Public houses and bars
Major Shareholder: Andrea Kay
Officers: Garry Clapton, Secretary; Andrea Kay [1962] Director

Kay Care Services Ltd
Incorporated: 2 December 1996
Registered Office: 1a Burt Terrace, Walbottle, Newcastle upon Tyne, NE15 9RY
Activities: Residential nursing care facilities
Shareholders: Philippa Codd; Christopher Kay
Officers: Andrew Phillip Burns [1962] Director; Philippa Jane Codd [1966] Director; Adrian Mark Williamson [1957] Director/Accountant

R & A Kay Inspection Services Limited
Incorporated: 27 December 1984 *Employees:* 29
Net Worth: £525,321 *Total Assets:* £1,454,063
Registered Office: 140 Coniscliffe Road, Darlington, Co Durham, DL3 7RT
Activities: Other business support service activities n.e.c.
Parent: RAK Global Limited
Officers: Mary Jarrett, Secretary; Philip James Jackson [1979] Director; Duncan Jarrett [1963] Director; Ian Johnston [1950] Director

Kaydian Design Limited
Incorporated: 24 September 2004 *Employees:* 21
Net Worth: £484,649 *Total Assets:* £2,647,265
Registered Office: 4c Redburn House, Redburn Road, Newcastle upon Tyne, NE5 1NB
Activities: Wholesale of furniture, carpets and lighting equipment
Shareholder: Howard James Obbard
Officers: Neville Boyd, Secretary; Neville Boyd [1955] Director; Richard Jeffrey [1970] Director; Howard James Obbard [1974] Director; Ian Leslie Pooler [1950] Director

Kayne Properties UK Limited
Incorporated: 20 April 2015
Net Worth: £240,140 *Total Assets:* £7,391,013
Registered Office: 1st Floor, 5 Cattle Market, Hexham, Northumberland, NE46 1NJ
Activities: Other letting and operating of own or leased real estate
Parent: PF Trust
Officers: Gary Michael Killmister [1958] Director/Accountant

KBR I.T. and Networking Solutions Limited
Incorporated: 27 November 1984 *Employees:* 22
Net Worth: £1,630,393 *Total Assets:* £2,002,992
Registered Office: Station House, Station Lane, Birtley, Chester-le-Street, Co Durham, DH3 1DJ
Activities: Wired telecommunications activities
Shareholder: Robin John Price
Officers: Juliet Grant, Secretary; Michael David Allen [1971] Operations Director; Robin John Price [1955] Managing Director; Richard Gareth Tomlin [1972] Technical Director

KC Engineering Bearings Ltd
Incorporated: 27 January 2016 *Employees:* 29
Net Worth: £125,779 *Total Assets:* £1,126,405
Registered Office: Hownsgill Drive, Delves Lane Industrial Estate, Consett, Co Durham, DH8 9HU
Activities: Manufacture of metal structures and parts of structures
Shareholders: Westebbe Verwaltungs GmbH; Tobias Francois Heintz
Officers: Gary Adam [1969] Director; Tobias Francois Heintz [1968] Director [German]

KCA Cars Limited
Incorporated: 26 January 2010
Net Worth: £665,332 *Total Assets:* £1,303,368
Registered Office: 237 Acklam Road, Acklam, Middlesbrough, Cleveland, TS5 7AB
Activities: Other letting and operating of own or leased real estate
Shareholders: Kirk Andrews; Christopher James Andrews
Officers: Christopher James Andrews, Secretary; Christopher James Andrews [1978] Director; Kirk Andrews [1970] Director

KD Plant Services Limited
Incorporated: 24 March 2009
Net Worth: £652,458 *Total Assets:* £1,397,152
Registered Office: Unit 2 Colliery Workshop, Acorn Close Lane, Sacriston, Co Durham, DH7 6AN
Activities: Other specialised construction activities n.e.c.
Officers: Kevin Devereux [1960] Director/Plant Fitter

KDL Mezzanine Limited
Incorporated: 7 November 2016 *Employees:* 19
Net Worth: £342,527 *Total Assets:* £828,799
Registered Office: Unit 15 Atley Way, Atley Business Park, Cramlington, Northumberland, NE23 1WP
Activities: Other specialised construction activities n.e.c.
Shareholders: Grahame Sinclair; Tracie Sinclair
Officers: Tracie Sinclair, Secretary; Anthony Barrass [1986] Director; Grahame Sinclair [1963] Director; Lewis Sinclair [1992] Director

KDL Systems Ltd
Incorporated: 31 July 1998 *Employees:* 15
Net Worth: £1,058,312 *Total Assets:* £2,159,802
Registered Office: 15 Atley Business Park, Atley Way, Cramlington, Northumberland, NE23 1WP
Activities: Other specialised construction activities n.e.c.
Shareholders: Tracie Sinclair; Grahame Sinclair
Officers: Tracie Sinclair, Secretary; Grahame Sinclair [1963] Director/Installer; Tracie Sinclair [1962] Director/Company Secretary

R.D. Kearton & Sons Limited
Incorporated: 19 November 1987 *Employees:* 12
Net Worth: £1,237,071 *Total Assets:* £1,739,513
Registered Office: Browside, Boldron, Barnard Castle, Co Durham, DL12 9RQ
Activities: Construction of other civil engineering projects n.e.c.
Officers: Margaret Wendy Kearton, Secretary; Christopher Kearton [1960] Director/Manager; John Stephen Kearton [1959] Director/Manager; Patricia Anne Kearton [1962] Director/Secretary

Kearton Crushing and Screening Limited
Incorporated: 9 November 2006 *Employees:* 2
Net Worth: £858,967 *Total Assets:* £1,459,974
Registered Office: East Roods, Boldron, Barnard Castle, Co Durham, DL12 9SW
Activities: Quarrying of ornamental and building stone, limestone, gypsum, chalk and slate
Shareholders: Anne Kearton; Robert William Kearton; John Stephen Kearton
Officers: Anne Kearton, Secretary; Anne Kearton [1963] Director; John Stephen Kearton [1959] Director; Robert William Kearton [1989] Director/Engineer

Kearton Farms Limited
Incorporated: 5 March 2009 *Employees:* 9
Net Worth: £3,524,850 *Total Assets:* £5,889,350
Registered Office: Wyse Hill, High Startforth, Barnard Castle, Co Durham, DL12 9RA
Activities: Other specialised construction activities n.e.c.
Shareholders: Christopher Kearton; Juliet Mary Kearton
Officers: Juliet Mary Kearton, Secretary; Amy Sarah Kearton [1987] Director; Christopher Kearton [1960] Director; Juliet Mary Kearton [1960] Director; Richard David Kearton [1989] Director

Kebrico Limited
Incorporated: 10 July 1978 *Employees:* 8
Net Worth: £2,004,100 *Total Assets:* £2,334,406
Registered Office: Walker House, Skippers Lane Industrial Estate, Middlesbrough, Cleveland, TS6 6HA
Activities: Retail of furniture, lighting, and similar (not musical instruments or scores) in specialised store
Major Shareholder: Kenneth Knott
Officers: Joyce Sullivan, Secretary; Kenneth Knott [1950] Director/Toy Wholesaler

Keelman Homes Limited
Incorporated: 25 July 2009
Net Worth: £9,548,000 *Total Assets:* £20,784,000
Registered Office: Civic Centre, Regent Street, Gateshead, Tyne & Wear, NE8 1JN
Activities: Renting and operating of Housing Association real estate
Officers: Jonathan Stuart Mallen-Beadle, Secretary; Joanne Carr [1946] Director; Anne Elizabeth Connolly [1957] Director/Housing Professional; Councillor Paul Foy [1964] Director/Office Manager Parliamentary Assistant; Linda Hitman [1952] Director; Brian Sidney Kelly [1951] Director/Retired; Leigh Kirton [1988] Director/Councillor; Alistair Jason Wylie [1969] Assistant Director

Keeping Inn Limited
Incorporated: 16 January 1997 *Employees:* 74
Net Worth: £3,692,068 *Total Assets:* £6,599,381
Registered Office: Waverley House, 30 The Oval, Forest Hall, Newcastle upon Tyne, NE12 9PP
Activities: Public houses and bars
Parent: STR Enterprises Limited
Officers: Elizabeth Anne Sanderson, Secretary/Director; Christopher Spencer Sanderson [1974] Director; Elizabeth Anne Sanderson [1945] Director; John Taylor Sanderson [1944] Managing Director; Richard Alexander Sanderson [1979] Director

A. & J. Keith Limited
Incorporated: 23 November 1988 *Employees:* 32
Net Worth: £2,015,769 *Total Assets:* £3,235,824
Registered Office: 189 Vine Street, Wallsend, Tyne & Wear, NE28 6JB
Activities: Electrical installation
Major Shareholder: James McIver
Officers: James McIver [1980] Director/Electrical Contractor

J Kelly Plant Hire Limited
Incorporated: 23 February 2005 *Employees:* 34
Net Worth: £303,617 *Total Assets:* £1,415,360
Registered Office: Plant Depot, Fowberry Road, Scotswood, Newcastle upon Tyne, NE15 6XP
Activities: Renting and leasing of construction and civil engineering machinery and equipment
Officers: Gillian Dixon, Secretary; Gillian Dixon [1975] Director; John Kelly [1946] Director; Judith Kelly [1951] Director; Sharon Kelly [1974] Director

Darren Kelly Transport Limited
Incorporated: 30 September 2008 *Employees:* 8
Net Worth: £561,590 *Total Assets:* £867,070
Registered Office: 2 Sanctuary Close, Middlesbrough, Cleveland, TS5 7BF
Activities: Freight transport by road
Shareholders: Darren Brendan Kelly; Michelle Kelly
Officers: Darren Brendan Kelly [1974] Director/Haulier; Michelle Kelly [1975] Director/Administrator

Kelt Properties Limited
Incorporated: 4 March 2009
Net Worth: £117,012 *Total Assets:* £1,051,178
Registered Office: Beaumont Accountancy, First Floor, Enterprise House, 202-206 Linthorpe Road, Middlesbrough, Cleveland, TS1 3QW
Activities: Other building completion and finishing
Major Shareholder: Elaine Conway
Officers: Elaine Conway [1957] Director; Kevin Conway [1985] Director; Lawrence Conway [1958] Director/Self Employed; Tony Conway [1987] Director

Kemel Europe Limited
Incorporated: 17 November 1999 *Employees:* 8
Net Worth: £6,890,667 *Total Assets:* £8,687,033
Registered Office: Unit 9 Tower Road, Glover Industrial Estate, Washington, Tyne & Wear, NE37 2SH
Activities: Other business support service activities n.e.c.
Parent: Eagle Industry Co Ltd
Officers: Yasuharu Nakanishi, Secretary; Kiyoshi Fujii [1964] Director [Japanese]; Masaru Ikeda [1958] Director [Japanese]; Masaki Nakao [1955] Director [Japanese]; Eiichi Tsuruta [1958] Director/Senior Operating Officer [Japanese]

Kenley Holdings Limited
Incorporated: 12 March 2008 *Employees:* 2
Net Worth: £51,836 *Total Assets:* £904,435
Registered Office: Unit 33/2 Auckland Crescent, St Helen Industrial Estate, Bishop Auckland, Co Durham, DL14 9AD
Activities: Development of building projects
Shareholders: Steven Aitken; Graeme Leslie Ripley
Officers: Steven Aitken, Secretary/Director; Steven Aitken [1973] Director; Graeme Leslie Ripley [1968] Director

Kenmor Ceilings & Partitions Limited
Incorporated: 11 August 1995
Net Worth: £1,295,387 *Total Assets:* £1,761,231
Registered Office: 11-12 Grange Road, Newburn, Newcastle upon Tyne, NE15 8ND
Activities: Plastering
Major Shareholder: John Trevor Kendra
Officers: John Trevor Kendra, Secretary; Paul Anthony Devlin [1960] Director/Construction Manager; John Trevor Kendra [1956] Director/Buildings Manager

Kennedy Services Limited
Incorporated: 14 September 1989 *Employees:* 25
Net Worth: £479,402 *Total Assets:* £1,127,455
Registered Office: Alexander House, Station Road, Columbia, Washington, Tyne & Wear, NE38 7BD
Activities: Electrical installation
Shareholders: Ian Ryan; Deborah Ann Ryan
Officers: Deborah Ann Ryan, Secretary; Deborah Ann Ryan [1964] Director; Ian Ryan [1964] Director/Electrical Contractor

Kennek Construction Limited
Incorporated: 21 August 2001 *Employees:* 16
Net Worth: £720,975 *Total Assets:* £1,074,676
Registered Office: The Bank Line, Woodbine Street, Sunderland, Tyne & Wear, SR1 2NL
Activities: Manufacture of other builders' carpentry and joinery
Officers: Jillian Brown, Secretary; David William Bradley [1974] Director/Builder; Dean Bradley [1979] Director/Builder; Peter Bradley [1976] Director/Builder; Kenneth Bradley Jnr [1969] Director/Builder

Kenton Schools Academy Trust
Incorporated: 24 February 2012 *Employees:* 287
Net Worth: £28,325,000 *Total Assets:* £32,281,000
Registered Office: Kenton School Newcastle, Drayton Road, Newcastle upon Tyne, NE3 3RU
Activities: General secondary education
Officers: Abi Blair Kelly [1969] Executive Director of Corporate Affairs; Kevin Martin McDermid [1953] Director/Child Workforce Education Consultant; Karen Mills [1968] Director/Informatics Trainer; Siobhan Elisabeth O'Neil [1968] Director; Gillian Stafford [1961] Director; Raymond Frederick Steele [1950] Director; Martin Surtees [1964] Director

Kenworth Limited
Incorporated: 9 February 1989 *Employees:* 43
Net Worth: £1,064,678 *Total Assets:* £4,671,262
Registered Office: Beacon Garage, Catterick Road, Catterick Garrison, N Yorks, DL9 4RZ
Activities: Retail sale of automotive fuel in specialised stores
Major Shareholder: Barry Stewart Raw
Officers: Joan Raw, Secretary/Director Kenworth Ltd; Barry Raw [1954] Director; Joan Raw [1957] Director

The Kerfoot Group Limited
Incorporated: 11 June 1980 *Employees:* 123
Net Worth: £11,901,831 *Total Assets:* £25,181,402
Registered Office: The Olive House, Standard Way Industrial Estate, Darlington Road, Northallerton, N Yorks, DL6 2XA
Activities: Manufacture of oils and fats
Parent: Avril Pole Vegetal SAS
Officers: Alison Rachel Atkins [1971] Director; Sarah Bradley [1974] Director/Chief Executive; Simon Matthew Corner [1979] Commercial Director; Olivier Christophe Marcel Delamea [1969] Director/Chairman [French]; Kim Melanie Newell [1971] Finance Director; Sarah Joanne Stokes [1972] Human Resources Director

Key Homes (GB) Limited
Incorporated: 2 February 2004
Net Worth: £1,317,519 *Total Assets:* £2,219,557
Registered Office: Old Maids Farm, Parkgate Lane, Brompton on Swale, Richmond, N Yorks, DL10 7HD
Activities: Other accommodation
Shareholders: Fiona Templeton Limb; Betty Antonio de Silva
Officers: Fiona Templeton Limb, Secretary; Betty Antonio de Silva [1978] Director; Fiona Templeton Limb [1968] Director

Key Stage Recruitment Limited
Incorporated: 20 June 2005
Net Worth: £345,374 *Total Assets:* £1,017,998
Registered Office: 14 High Street, Yarm, Cleveland, TS15 9AE
Activities: Temporary employment agency activities
Major Shareholder: Julie Mary Richardson
Officers: Julie Mary Richardson [1979] Director/Manager

Keyes Limited
Incorporated: 25 April 2002
Registered Office: Coburg House, 1 Coburg Street, Gateshead, Tyne & Wear, NE8 1NS
Activities: Buying and selling of own real estate
Shareholder: Judy Routledge
Officers: Judy Routledge, Secretary/Property Manager; Judy Routledge [1959] Director/Property Manager; James Sweeney [1960] Director/Property Developer

Keyfort Group Limited
Incorporated: 8 November 2005 *Employees:* 341
Net Worth: £678,847 *Total Assets:* £1,059,742
Registered Office: 2 Earls Court, Fifth Avenue, Team Valley Trading Estate, Gateshead, Tyne & Wear, NE11 0HF
Activities: Educational support services
Officers: Emily Victoria Dunn, Secretary; Emily Victoria Dunn [1976] Director; Kelly Marie Dunn [1978] Director

Keywest No. Three Ltd
Incorporated: 4 August 2016 *Employees:* 3
Net Worth Deficit: £27,428 *Total Assets:* £2,972,255
Registered Office: 43 Maxwell Street, South Shields, Tyne & Wear, NE33 4PU
Activities: Development of building projects
Shareholders: Norfad Developments Ltd; Keywest Ltd
Officers: Norman Fada [1966] Director; Stephen Keyworth [1946] Director; Derek Edward West [1949] Director

Kibblesworth Academy
Incorporated: 10 May 2012 *Employees:* 19
Net Worth: £958,686 *Total Assets:* £1,180,474
Registered Office: Kibblesworth Primary School, Kibblesworth, Gateshead, Tyne & Wear, NE11 0XP
Activities: Primary education
Officers: Meredith Sean Ashford [1977] Director/Business Development Manager; Jason John Cochrane [1975] Director/Teacher; Katie Rebecca Collins [1984] Director/Teacher; Clare Davis [1979] Director/Administrator; Rachel Louise Mungnai [1977] Director; Sarah Renton [1983] Director/Teacher; Timothy James Rutter [1981] Director Manufacturing; Craig Steel [1972] Director/Acting Headteacher; Jayne Walsh [1991] Director/Teacher

Kickpoint Limited
Incorporated: 15 February 2002 *Employees:* 4
Net Worth: £122,951 *Total Assets:* £1,563,550
Registered Office: Lugano Building, 57 Melbourne Street, Newcastle upon Tyne, NE1 2JQ
Activities: Buying and selling of own real estate
Major Shareholder: Ben Zion Rabinowitz
Officers: Howard Barry Gold, Secretary; Howard Barry Gold [1943] Director/Solicitor; Paul Hughes [1965] Director/Solicitor; Ben Zion Rabinowitz [1935] Director [Polish]; Joseph Rabinowitz [1964] Director [Polish]

Kid 'n' Play Limited
Incorporated: 7 February 1996 *Employees:* 32
Net Worth: £1,892,358 *Total Assets:* £2,532,397
Registered Office: 20-22 Second Avenue, Heaton, Newcastle upon Tyne, NE6 5XS
Activities: Other business support service activities n.e.c.
Major Shareholder: Randhir Puri
Officers: Randhir Puri, Secretary/Director; Randhir Puri [1973] Director; Surinder Kumar Puri [1947] Director

Kidd & Spoor Solicitors Limited
Incorporated: 19 March 2015 *Employees:* 23
Net Worth: £251,053 *Total Assets:* £1,110,442
Registered Office: 7 Marden Road, Whitley Bay, Tyne & Wear, NE26 2JN
Activities: Solicitors
Shareholders: Noel Dilks; Nigel Peter Miller
Officers: Carol Nattrass, Secretary; Noel Dilks [1959] Director/Solicitor; Nigel Peter Miller [1963] Director/Solicitor; Katherine Jane Monteith [1970] Director; Julia Russell [1971] Director

Kilderk Inns Limited
Incorporated: 11 April 1991
Net Worth: £317,401 *Total Assets:* £770,235
Registered Office: 2 Park View, Middleton Tyas, Richmond, N Yorks, DL10 6SG
Activities: Other letting and operating of own or leased real estate
Officers: Gillian Margaret Wilkinson, Secretary; Robert Anthony Iles [1955] Director; Ralph English Wilkinson [1955] Director

Kilfrost Group Limited
Incorporated: 10 June 2009 *Employees:* 43
Net Worth: £1,631,000 *Total Assets:* £13,027,000
Registered Office: Albion Works, Haltwhistle, Northumberland, NE49 0HJ
Activities: Manufacture of other chemical products n.e.c.
Shareholders: Josephine Clare Halbert; Jane Louise Halbert
Officers: Jane Louise Halbert [1956] Director; Josephine Clare Halbert [1962] Director; Mark Stuart Halbert [1966] Director; Gary Lydiate [1960] Director

Kilfrost Limited
Incorporated: 28 February 1935 *Employees:* 36
Net Worth: £4,355,000 *Total Assets:* £12,405,000
Registered Office: Albion Works, Haltwhistle, Northumberland, NE49 0HJ
Activities: Manufacture of other chemical products n.e.c.
Parent: Kilfrost Group Limited
Officers: Gary Lydiate [1960] Director

Killashee House Limited
Incorporated: 24 January 2013
Net Worth Deficit: £377,211 *Total Assets:* £893,660
Registered Office: Saltergill Park, Low Worsall, Yarm, Cleveland, TS15 9PG
Activities: Raising of horses and other equines
Major Shareholder: Lucy Horner
Officers: Kahlil de Burca [1978] Director [Irish]; Lucy Victoria Horner [1976] Director

Kiltech Limited
Incorporated: 24 January 1994
Net Worth: £926,275 *Total Assets:* £937,104
Registered Office: 66 Hudson Street, North Shields, Tyne & Wear, NE30 1DL
Activities: Other letting and operating of own or leased real estate
Major Shareholder: William Hammerton Smith
Officers: Rachel Elizabeth Elder-Smith [1978] Director/Primary School Teacher; William Hammerton Smith [1967] Director

Kilton Thorpe Specialist Academy
Incorporated: 19 November 2012 *Employees:* 137
Net Worth: £6,280,124 *Total Assets:* £7,551,837
Registered Office: Kilton Thorpe Specialist Academy, Marshall Drive, Brotton, Saltburn-by-the-Sea, N Yorks, TS12 2UW
Activities: Other education n.e.c.
Officers: Robert Paul Anderson, Secretary; Alexandra Betts [1977] Director/Teacher; Mr Ian Bowman [1947] Director; Frances Brown [1958] Director; Mrs Dawn Froom [1964] Director; Sarah Gunn [1976] Director/Assistant Headteacher; Margaret Hadland [1949] Director; Grant Compton Hopkins [1970] Director; David Hamilton Major [1957] Director/School Improvement Advisor; Mark Robinson [1982] Director/Barrister; Ruth Sherris [1974] Director/Nurse; Kevin William Thompson [1959] Director/Headteacher

Kinder Castle Limited
Incorporated: 10 May 2002 *Employees:* 26
Net Worth: £849,190 *Total Assets:* £1,118,634
Registered Office: 4 Tynemouth Road, Tynemouth, North Shields, Tyne & Wear, NE30 4AU
Activities: Primary education
Major Shareholder: Pamela Craig
Officers: Lucy Craig, Secretary; Lucy Craig [1971] Director; Pamela Craig [1939] Director/Rest Home Operator

Kindred Living Limited
Incorporated: 28 June 2016 *Employees:* 9
Net Worth Deficit: £889,698 *Total Assets:* £1,071,784
Registered Office: P O Box 20, Station Road, Aycliffe Business Park, Newton Aycliffe, Co Durham, DL5 6XJ
Activities: Wholesale of household goods (other than musical instruments) n.e.c
Major Shareholder: Mark William Winspear Stepehson
Officers: Jonathan Barclay Whisker, Secretary; David Burchnall [1967] Director; Mark William Winspear Stephenson [1962] Director; Jonathan Barclay Whisker [1964] Director

King Brothers Bricklaying Contractors Limited
Incorporated: 4 April 1997 *Employees:* 7
Net Worth: £2,045,467 *Total Assets:* £2,657,970
Registered Office: Unit 14 Hepworth Road, Sunderland, Tyne & Wear, SR5 3JT
Activities: Construction of commercial buildings
Shareholders: Ian King; Bryan King
Officers: Ian King, Secretary; Bryan King [1978] Director/Builder; Carol King [1965] Director; Ian King [1965] Director/Builder

King Hope Ltd
Incorporated: 13 October 2014 *Employees:* 28
Net Worth: £252,520 *Total Assets:* £1,361,725
Registered Office: 31 Victoria Road, Darlington, Co Durham, DL1 5SB
Activities: Accounting and auditing activities
Shareholders: Stephen Watson Gardner; Sarah Helen Anderson
Officers: Sarah Helen Anderson [1968] Director/Chartered Accountant; Stephen Watson Gardner [1960] Director/Chartered Accountant

King James I Academy, Bishop Auckland Limited
Incorporated: 18 May 2011 *Employees:* 150
Net Worth: £12,617,000 *Total Assets:* £14,652,000
Registered Office: King James I Academy, South Church Road, Bishop Auckland, Co Durham, DL14 7JZ
Activities: General secondary education
Officers: Sharon Boughey [1964] Director/Corporate Complaints Officer; George William Campbell [1953] Director/Local Government Officer Accountant; Mrs Rachael Anna Marie Dobinson [1976] Director/Teacher; Alastair L Gardner [1964] Director/International Trade Advisor; Nicholas Grieveson [1966] Director/Headteacher; Mr Peter Hardy [1962] Director; Shane Jeffery John Northgreaves [1965] Director; Keith Philpott [1963] Director/Local Government Officer; Nicole Suzanne Read [1970] Director/Teacher; Ian Robley [1947] Director/Teacher (Academy); Alan Stephen Rodchester [1955] Director/Consultant Headteacher; Gladys Short [1956] Director/Teacher; Debra Smith [1966] Director; Tanya Tucker [1965] Director/Teacher; Elizabeth Varley [1948] Director/Retired Assistant Headteacher; Keith Anthony Wilkinson [1948] Director

Kingfield Estates Limited
Incorporated: 2 October 1996
Net Worth Deficit: £10,528 *Total Assets:* £766,987
Registered Office: St Oswald House, 32 Victoria Road, Hartlepool, Cleveland, TS26 8DD
Activities: Other letting and operating of own or leased real estate
Shareholder: Julie Dickinson
Officers: Michael George Dickinson, Secretary; Julie Dickinson [1959] Director; Michael George Dickinson [1954] Director/Secretary

Kings Church Darlington
Incorporated: 10 January 2006 *Employees:* 12
Net Worth: £521,395 *Total Assets:* £967,918
Registered Office: The Kings Centre, Prospect Place, Whessoe Road, Darlington, Co Durham, DL3 0QT
Activities: Activities of religious organisations
Officers: Susan Kay Cureton, Secretary; Richard Paul Davison [1959] Director/Consultant; Philip James Hillsdon [1954] Director/Minister of Religion; Nicholas James Millar [1958] Independent Financial Advisor/Director; Carolyn Mary Salt [1961] Director/HR Manager; Mark Andrew Sowerby [1971] Finance Director; Christine Beck Ward [1962] Director/Community Volunteer Manager; Harold John Wilmshurst [1943] Director/Retired

Kings Court (Team Valley) LLP
Incorporated: 20 September 2010
Net Worth: £463,028 *Total Assets:* £932,920
Registered Office: 2 Lintzford Grange, Lintzford, Rowlands Gill, Tyne & Wear, NE39 1HL
Officers: Helen Bernard [1951] Member; Steven Norman Simpson [1959] Member

Kingston Property Services Limited
Incorporated: 12 July 2000
Net Worth: £198,001 *Total Assets:* £1,809,001
Registered Office: Cheviot House, Beaminster Way East, Newcastle upon Tyne, NE3 2ER
Activities: Residents property management
Parent: Cheviot Housing Association Limited
Officers: Ian Archibald Armstrong [1933] Director/Business Consultant; John David Holmes [1955] Director/Operations Manager; John Johnston [1967] Director/Chief Executive; Andrew Michael Pegg [1955] Director and Consultant

Kingsway Claims Limited
Incorporated: 30 July 2013 *Employees:* 49
Net Worth: £369,248 *Total Assets:* £1,681,529
Registered Office: Kingsway House, Riverbank Road, Sunderland, Tyne & Wear, SR5 3JJ
Activities: Management consultancy activities other than financial management
Major Shareholder: Donald Charles Rodger
Officers: David Forster Amis [1969] Finance Director; David Andrew Muirhead [1985] Director; Donald Charles Rodger [1955] Director

Kingswood Properties (North East) Limited
Incorporated: 12 October 2001 *Employees:* 4
Net Worth: £826,313 *Total Assets:* £3,058,108
Registered Office: Finchale House, Belmont Business Park, Durham, DH1 1TW
Activities: Other letting and operating of own or leased real estate
Officers: Paul Copeland, Secretary/Police Officer; James Edward Charlton [1968] Director/Contract Administrator; Paul Copeland [1964] Director/Police Officer

Kiplun Limited
Incorporated: 7 July 2005 *Employees:* 405
Net Worth: £20,877,000 *Total Assets:* £43,638,000
Registered Office: Cleveland House, Norton Road, Stockton on Tees, Cleveland, TS20 2AQ
Activities: Activities of head offices
Major Shareholder: John Donald Read Fothergill
Officers: John Philip Pickering, Secretary; John Donald Read Fothergill [1961] Director; John Philip Pickering [1954] Director/Chartered Accountant

Kirkhill Fleming Limited
Incorporated: 16 September 2002
Net Worth: £312,617 *Total Assets:* £1,465,214
Registered Office: 32 Brenkley Way, Blezard Business Park, Seaton Burn, Newcastle upon Tyne, NE13 6DS
Activities: Other letting and operating of own or leased real estate
Shareholders: Dr Brian Angus; Maureen June Angus
Officers: Maureen June Angus, Secretary; Dr Brian Angus [1951] Director/Consultant Histopathologist; Maureen June Angus [1951] Director/Administrator

Robert Kirkland (Blyth) Limited
Incorporated: 10 October 1973 *Employees:* 29
Net Worth: £1,640,472 *Total Assets:* £2,214,060
Registered Office: 62-66 Bridge Street, Blyth, Northumberland, NE24 2AP
Activities: Plumbing, heat and air-conditioning installation
Major Shareholder: Jim McGlen
Officers: Hilda McGlen, Secretary; Christopher James McGlen [1977] Director/Contracts Engineer; Hilda McGlen [1954] Director/Secretary; James McGlen [1954] Director; Paul Andrew McGlen [1979] Director/Charge Hand Plumber; Michael Simmons [1969] Director/Estimator

Kitchens Plus Ltd.
Incorporated: 4 June 1996
Registered Office: Kitchens Plus Ltd, Airport Industrial Estate, Newcastle upon Tyne, NE3 2EF
Activities: Other specialised construction activities n.e.c.
Officers: David Craigen, Secretary/Electrical Engineer; Derek Bolton [1973] Director; David Craigen [1946] Director/Electrical Engineer; Joseph Heffernan [1951] Director/Electrical Engineer; Adrian Hughes [1966] Director

B & T Kitson Limited
Incorporated: 27 August 2002 *Employees:* 20
Net Worth: £319,113 *Total Assets:* £1,287,077
Registered Office: Momentum Taxation & Accountancy Ltd, Harelands Courtyard Offices, Moor Road, Melsonby, Richmond, N Yorks, DL10 5NY
Activities: Retail sale of meat and meat products in specialised stores
Major Shareholder: Anthony Kitson
Officers: Thelma Kitson, Secretary; Anthony John Kitson [1966] Director/Butcher

Kitwave Limited
Incorporated: 24 March 1987 *Employees:* 1
Net Worth: £14,011 *Total Assets:* £51,435,652
Registered Office: Unit S3, Narvik Way, Tyne Tunnel Trading Estate, North Shields, Tyne & Wear, NE29 7XJ
Activities: Wholesale of wine, beer, spirits and other alcoholic beverages
Officers: Patrica Ada Rice, Secretary; David Leonard Brind [1972] Director; John Frederick Hope [1969] Group Operations Director; Jay MacKay [1966] Director/Retail Manager; Ben Maxted [1983] Frozen Divison Director; Alan McCartney [1980] IT Director; David Terrence Yolland [1965] Director; Michael Young [1988] Commercial Director; Paul Victor Young [1957] Director/Accountant

Kitwave One Limited
Incorporated: 14 March 2011 *Employees:* 8
Net Worth: £1,756,185 *Total Assets:* £14,704,827
Registered Office: Unit S3, Narvik Way, Tyne Tunnel Trading Estate, North Shields, Tyne & Wear, NE29 7XJ
Activities: Wholesale of sugar and chocolate and sugar confectionery
Officers: David Leonard Brind [1972] Director; Patricia Ada Rice [1951] Finance Director; Paul Victor Young [1957] Director

KJT Properties Ltd
Incorporated: 8 June 2016
Net Worth: £15,157 *Total Assets:* £785,064
Registered Office: 2 Twizell Burn, Houghton-le-Spring, Co Durham, DH4 6GD
Activities: Residents property management
Shareholder: Anthony Jaswant Singh
Officers: Kulwant Kaur [1971] Director; Anthony Jaswant Singh [1969] Director

KMS Property Services Limited
Incorporated: 18 August 2014 *Employees:* 2
Net Worth: £671,396 *Total Assets:* £801,442
Registered Office: 2 Apollo Court, Koppers Way, Monkton Business Park South, Hebburn, Tyne & Wear, NE31 2ES
Activities: Other specialised construction activities n.e.c.
Shareholders: Mitchell Ashley Swirles; Kirstie Swirles
Officers: Kirstie Swirles [1971] Director; Mitchell Ashley Swirles [1968] Director

Richard J Knaggs & Co LLP
Incorporated: 30 April 2009 *Employees:* 16
Net Worth: £173,681 *Total Assets:* £2,036,559
Registered Office: 119 High Street, Redcar, Cleveland, TS10 3DG
Officers: Richard John Knaggs [1952] Member; John Christopher Wilson [1965] Member

Knauf AMF Ceilings Limited
Incorporated: 23 February 1998 *Employees:* 29
Net Worth Deficit: £944,787 *Total Assets:* £2,833,208
Registered Office: 1 Swan Road, South West Industrial Estate, Peterlee, Co Durham, SR8 2HS
Activities: Other business support service activities n.e.c.
Officers: Peter John Symons, Secretary; Karl Wenig [1965] Director [German]

Knightingales Limited
Incorporated: 9 May 2006 *Employees:* 2
Net Worth: £448,888 *Total Assets:* £2,245,332
Registered Office: Lakeside House, Kingfisher Way, Stockton on Tees, Cleveland, TS18 3NB
Activities: Other human health activities
Shareholder: David Graham Jarvis
Officers: David Graham Jarvis, Secretary/Pharmacist; David Graham Jarvis [1966] Director/Pharmacist; Alexandra Simpson [1960] Director/Sales Assistant; Kevin Alan Simpson [1958] Director/Pharmacist

Komatsu UK Limited
Incorporated: 20 September 1985 *Employees:* 424
Net Worth: £75,172,000 *Total Assets:* £140,240,992
Registered Office: Durham Road, Birtley, Chester-le-Street, Co Durham, DH3 2QX
Activities: Manufacture of earthmoving equipment
Parent: Komatsu Limited
Officers: Paul Kenneth Blanchard [1966] Manufacturing Director; Tracey Ann Bowman [1963] Director of Human Resources and Corporate Affairs; Peter John Howe [1962] Managing Director; Masatoshi Morishita [1960] Managing Director & CEO [Japanese]; Nozomu Okamoto [1964] Director/Executive Officer, Osaka Plant Manager [Japanese]; Stuart John Reid [1967] Finance Director; Hidehito Tsuji [1975] Director [Japanese]; Robert Malcolm Williams [1959] Director/Senior Manager Design & Development

Kompass Holdings Limited
Incorporated: 11 February 2004 *Employees:* 4
Net Worth: £1,863,067 *Total Assets:* £2,613,527
Registered Office: 34-36 South Parade, Whitley Bay, Tyne & Wear, NE26 2RQ
Activities: Activities of head offices
Officers: Edward James Hastie [1945] Director; Nigel Anton Hastie [1973] Director; Trevor Edward Hastie [1971] Director

Konectbus Limited
Incorporated: 22 January 1996 *Employees:* 169
Net Worth Deficit: £544,000 *Total Assets:* £6,836,000
Registered Office: 3rd Floor, 41-51 Grey Street, Newcastle upon Tyne, NE1 6EE
Activities: Other urban, suburban or metropolitan passenger land transport (not underground, metro or similar)
Parent: Go-Ahead Holding Limited
Officers: Carolyn Ferguson, Secretary; David Allen Brown [1960] Director; Simon Patrick Butcher [1967] Finance Director; Jeremy Hugh Cooper [1967] Director; Martin Richard Dean [1963] Director/Transport Manager; David Hector Golding [1965] Director

Kookaburra Limited
Incorporated: 17 September 1987 *Employees:* 154
Net Worth: £5,033,611 *Total Assets:* £10,945,332
Registered Office: 3 Armstrong Road, North East Industrial Estate, Peterlee, Co Durham, SR8 5AE
Activities: Processing and preserving of poultry meat
Parent: Brandmile Limited
Officers: John Graham Monkhouse, Secretary; Benjamin William Herbert [1973] Director; Geoffrey Herbert [1945] Director; Peter Ardwin Ireland [1964] Sales Director; John Graham Monkhouse [1953] Director/Accountant; Anthony Edward Wilson [1970] Operations Director

Kotur Limited
Incorporated: 16 April 2003
Net Worth: £434,054 *Total Assets:* £1,058,209
Registered Office: 21 Acle Burn, Woodham, Newton Aycliffe, Co Durham, DL5 4XB
Activities: Specialists medical practice activities
Officers: Vijayalaxmi Chintamaran Kotur, Secretary; Dr Chintaharan Fakirayya Kotur [1950] Director/Consultant Anaesthetist; Karuna Chinta Kotur [1981] Director/Consultant Anaesthetist; Vijayalaxmi Chintamaran Kotur [1959] Director/Diversity Officer

KPL Engineering Limited
Incorporated: 26 October 1999
Net Worth: £466,700 *Total Assets:* £980,007
Registered Office: Bowburn North Industrial Estate, Bowburn, Co Durham, DH6 5PF
Activities: Other service activities n.e.c.
Shareholders: Mark Raymond Falshaw; Stephen John Laverick; Anthony Prosser Brown
Officers: Stephen John Laverick, Secretary/Engineer; Mark Raymond Falshaw [1955] Director/Engineer; Stephen John Laverick [1959] Director/Engineer; Anthony Prosser Brown [1965] Director/Engineer

Kramar Limited
Incorporated: 29 July 1996
Registered Office: Station Garage, Bradbury, Stockton on Tees, Cleveland, TS21 2ES
Activities: Renting and leasing of construction and civil engineering machinery and equipment
Shareholders: Deana Meredith; Margaret Anne Markey; Brendan Joseph Markey
Officers: Deana Meredith, Secretary; Margaret Anne Markey [1950] Director/Receptionist; Deana Meredith [1969] Director/Accounts Administration

Kratos Communications Limited
Incorporated: 11 February 2009 *Employees:* 27
Net Worth: £4,118,370 *Total Assets:* £10,847,164
Registered Office: 17 Princes Park, Fourth Avenue, Team Valley Trading Estate, Gateshead, Tyne & Wear, NE11 0LQ
Activities: Technical testing and analysis
Parent: Kratos Holdings UK Limited
Officers: Denise Angela Fay, Secretary; James Kramer [1970] Director [American]; Andrew Geoffrey John Smith [1955] Director/Company President

Kromek Group PLC
Incorporated: 22 August 2013 *Employees:* 108
Net Worth: £40,256,000 *Total Assets:* £47,180,000
Registered Office: Net Park, Thomas Wright Way, Sedgefield, Co Durham, TS21 3FD
Activities: Other manufacturing n.e.c.
Officers: Derek Bulmer, Secretary; Arnab Basu [1973] Director/Chief Executive Officer; Derek Bulmer [1966] Director; Lawrence Henry Neil Kinet [1947] Director [American]; Jerel Heath Whitingham [1962] Director; Jerel Heath Whittingham [1962] Director; Christopher John Wilks [1964] Director; Sir Peter Michael Williams [1945] Director

Kromek Limited
Incorporated: 9 April 2003 *Employees:* 54
Net Worth Deficit: £643,000 *Total Assets:* £40,377,000
Registered Office: Net Park, Thomas Wright Way, Sedgefield, Co Durham, TS21 3FD
Activities: Manufacture of electronic measuring, testing etc. equipment, not for industrial process control
Officers: Arnab Basu [1973] Director; Derek Bulmer [1966] Director; Jerel Heath Whittingham [1962] Director

Lily Kunj Properties LLP
Incorporated: 4 March 2008 *Employees:* 3
Net Worth: £476,652 *Total Assets:* £1,257,751
Registered Office: 7 Bankside, The Watermark, Gateshead, Tyne & Wear, NE11 9SY
Officers: Annu Singh [1952] Member; Dr Bimal Shankar Singh [1951] Member; Dr Guddi Vijaya Rani Singh [1982] Member; Dr Neil Varun Singh [1985] Member

Kura Financial Services Limited
Incorporated: 2 June 2009 *Employees:* 91
Net Worth: £1,372,000 *Total Assets:* £1,859,000
Registered Office: 1 Victory Way, Doxford International Business Park, Sunderland, Tyne & Wear, SR3 3XF
Activities: Activities of call centres
Parent: Kura (CS) Limited
Officers: Brian Bannatyne [1965] Director; Julie McIntosh [1965] Director

Kuyt Limited
Incorporated: 13 March 2007 *Employees:* 1
Net Worth: £1,118,372 *Total Assets:* £1,852,737
Registered Office: Unit 2b Guiseley Way, Durham Lane Industrial Park, Eaglescliffe, Stockton on Tees, Cleveland, TS16 0RF
Activities: Non-trading company
Shareholders: Andrew Marcus Dicken; Ann Dicken
Officers: Robert Michael Goodrum, Secretary; Andrew Marcus Dicken [1970] Director/Retail

Kwik Corporate Lettings Limited
Incorporated: 18 May 2007
Net Worth Deficit: £220,941 *Total Assets:* £1,126,345
Registered Office: 242 Marton Road, Middlesbrough, Cleveland, TS4 2EZ
Activities: Hotels and similar accommodation
Shareholders: Tabassum Hussain; Samina Hussain
Officers: Philip Frederick Gibson [1966] Director

Kwikbizz Limited
Incorporated: 20 October 2004 *Employees:* 2
Net Worth: £2 *Total Assets:* £950,002
Registered Office: 18-26 Bishopton Lane, Stockton on Tees, Cleveland, TS18 2AA
Activities: Activities of head offices
Shareholders: Derek Leslie Moore; Donald Waites
Officers: Donald Waites, Secretary; Derek Leslie Moore [1973] Director/Manager; Donald Waites [1962] Director

KWR Holdings Limited
Incorporated: 26 July 2016
Net Worth: £1,132,969 *Total Assets:* £1,132,969
Registered Office: The Dunes, Sea Road, South Shields, Tyne & Wear, NE33 2LD
Activities: Dormant company
Major Shareholder: Kenneth William Reader
Officers: Kenneth William Reader [1964] Director

Ky247 Limited
Incorporated: 7 April 2004
Net Worth: £1,291,548 *Total Assets:* £2,652,332
Registered Office: 246 Park View, Whitley Bay, Tyne & Wear, NE26 3QX
Activities: Wholesale of other food, including fish, crustaceans and molluscs
Shareholders: Paul Dowse; Tracey Rita Dowse
Officers: Tracey Rita Dowse, Secretary; Paul Dowse [1964] Director/Fisherman; Tracey Rita Dowse [1968] Director

Kymel Limited
Incorporated: 13 June 2013 *Employees:* 140
Net Worth: £1,439,633 *Total Assets:* £6,714,036
Registered Office: 7 Witney Way, Boldon Business Park, Boldon Colliery, Co Durham, NE35 9PE
Activities: Non-trading company
Major Shareholder: Paul Anthony MacKings
Officers: Linda Jane Miller, Secretary; Kyle MacKings [1987] Director; Melissa MacKings [1989] Director; Paul Anthony MacKings [1961] Director; Vivienne Antoinetta MacKings [1961] Director

Kymel Trading Limited
Incorporated: 4 October 2013 *Employees:* 141
Net Worth: £1,439,534 *Total Assets:* £6,713,937
Registered Office: 7 Witney Way, Boldon Business Park, Boldon Colliery, Co Durham, NE35 9PE
Activities: Licenced restaurants
Officers: Linda Jane Miller, Secretary; Kyle MacKings [1987] Director/Chief Executive; Paul Anthony MacKings [1961] Director; Vivienne Antoinetta MacKings [1961] Director; Linda Jane Miller [1957] Director/Administration Manager; Robert Alan Smith [1978] Managing Director

L & A Reinforcements Ltd.
Incorporated: 18 March 2005 *Employees:* 30
Net Worth: £781,792 *Total Assets:* £1,778,372
Registered Office: High Park Farm, Felton, Morpeth, Northumberland, NE65 9EY
Activities: Construction of other civil engineering projects n.e.c.
Major Shareholder: Simon Atkinson
Officers: Nicole Shepherd, Secretary; Simon Atkinson [1964] Director/Business Manager

L & G Plant Hire and Sales Limited
Incorporated: 25 March 2002 *Employees:* 14
Net Worth: £1,275,961 *Total Assets:* £1,390,897
Registered Office: 29 High West Road, Crook, Co Durham, DL15 9NR
Activities: Other specialised construction activities n.e.c.
Major Shareholder: Janice Duke
Officers: Janice Duke, Secretary/Administrator; Garry Leigh Duke [1973] Director/Foreman; Janice Duke [1944] Director/Administrator; Lindsey Steven Duke [1969] Director/Contracts Manager

L & G Utilities Ltd
Incorporated: 27 July 2010 *Employees:* 2
Net Worth: £2,074,819 *Total Assets:* £2,316,142
Registered Office: 7 Oak Crescent, Chilton, Ferryhill, Co Durham, DL17 0EL
Activities: Distribution of gaseous fuels through mains
Shareholders: Lee Thistlethwaite; Gemma Louise Thistlethwaite
Officers: Gemma Louise Thistlethwaite [1982] Director; Lee Thistlethwaite [1981] Director

L A Taxis Ltd
Incorporated: 21 July 2009 *Employees:* 47
Net Worth: £1,249,494 *Total Assets:* £2,802,889
Registered Office: 196 Portland Road, Sandyford, Shieldfield, Newcastle upon Tyne, NE2 1DJ
Activities: Taxi operation
Shareholders: Robin Armstrong; Anthony Minett; George Hickman
Officers: George Hickman [1960] Director; Anthony Minett [1963] Director

L D H (2010) Limited
Incorporated: 16 September 2010 *Employees:* 89
Net Worth Deficit: £1,014,706 *Total Assets:* £5,253,672
Registered Office: Upper Houses Farm, Lanchester, Co Durham, DH7 0RL
Activities: Activities of head offices
Shareholders: Julie Austin; William Austin
Officers: Julie Austin, Secretary; Julie Austin [1966] Director/Dairy Processing; William Austin [1953] Director/Dairy Processing

L. D. Mountain Centre Limited
Incorporated: 6 January 1993 *Employees:* 16
Net Worth: £682,195 *Total Assets:* £1,239,357
Registered Office: 34 Dean Street, Newcastle upon Tyne, NE1 1PG
Activities: Other retail sale of new goods in specialised stores (not commercial art galleries and opticians)
Parent: LD Property Management Limited
Officers: Peter Davison, Secretary; Peter Davison [1974] Director/Retailer; Roderick Vernon MacKay [1967] Director/Manager

L.& N.Property Investment Co.Limited (The)
Incorporated: 10 September 1959 *Employees:* 4
Net Worth: £1,382,628 *Total Assets:* £1,395,225
Registered Office: 77 Kenton Road, Gosforth, Newcastle upon Tyne, NE3 4NL
Activities: Buying and selling of own real estate
Shareholders: Dr Amanda Ruth Lurie; Suzanne Janet Lurie
Officers: Carole Eve Lurie, Secretary; Dr Amanda Ruth Lurie [1963] Director/Clinical Psychologist; Carole Eve Lurie [1937] Director/Retired; Geoffrey Lurie [1934] Director/Solicitor; Suzanne Janet Lurie [1961] Director/Solicitor

L.D.H. Plant Limited
Incorporated: 1 November 1996 *Employees:* 16
Net Worth: £558,128 *Total Assets:* £2,341,455
Registered Office: Londonderry Garage, Londonderry, Northallerton, N Yorks, DL7 9NB
Activities: Wholesale of other machinery and equipment
Parent: Ward Woolston Group Ltd
Officers: Nicholas Edward James Higgins [1979] Director/Surveyor/Business Manager; Robert Karl Edward Vaughan [1969] Director/Administrator; Michael James Ward [1968] Director; Scott Jon Woolston [1977] Director

L.H. (Quarry Plant) Limited
Incorporated: 2 September 1980 *Employees:* 34
Net Worth: £875,813 *Total Assets:* £1,929,983
Registered Office: Unit 2 Longfield Road, South Church Enterprise Park, Bishop Auckland, Co Durham, DL14 6XB
Activities: Manufacture of machinery for mining
Parent: Teescraft Engineering Limited
Officers: John Clifford Laverick [1942] Director; Robert John Yorke [1971] Director

Labman Automation Limited
Incorporated: 13 November 1992
Net Worth: £2,879,754 *Total Assets:* £5,638,951
Registered Office: Seamer Hill, Seamer, Stokesley, Middlesbrough, Cleveland, TS9 5NQ
Activities: Manufacture of other special-purpose machinery n.e.c.
Shareholder: Andrew David Whitwell
Officers: Christine Ann Smith, Secretary; George Alfred Carter [1933] Director/Engineer; Ian James Riley [1981] Technical Director; Christine Ann Smith [1960] Director/Accountant; Andrew David Whitwell [1960] Director; Joanna Caroline Whitwell [1961] Director

Labone Castleside Limited
Incorporated: 4 February 2004 *Employees:* 156
Net Worth: £2,366,680 *Total Assets:* £6,708,903
Registered Office: Castleside Industrial Estate, Consett, Co Durham, DH8 8HF
Activities: Manufacture of other plastic products
Parent: R A Labone and Company Ltd
Officers: Ruth Frances Young, Secretary; Andrew Maiden [1959] Managing Director; Alfred Anthony Stiegler [1938] Director/Chairman; Ann Blanche Stiegler [1940] Director; Dawn Whittle [1971] Director; Christopher Young [1964] Director

Labourn Property Ltd
Incorporated: 2 February 2010
Net Worth: £108,092 *Total Assets:* £792,066
Registered Office: Woodhead Farm, Hedley, Stocksfield, Northumberland, NE43 7SX
Activities: Other letting and operating of own or leased real estate
Major Shareholder: Ann Burnhope
Officers: Ann Burnhope, Secretary; Ann Burnhope [1954] Director; Ross Cavanagh [1984] Director/Quantity Surveyor

Lacegold Electrical and Mechanical Services Limited
Incorporated: 4 June 1984 *Employees:* 17
Net Worth: £1,072,574 *Total Assets:* £1,381,018
Registered Office: 1 Aerial House, School Aycliffe Lane, Newton Aycliffe, Co Durham, DL5 6QF
Activities: Installation of industrial machinery and equipment
Shareholders: Ann Elizabeth Upex; Leonard John Upex
Officers: Ann Elizabeth Upex, Secretary; Leonard John Upex [1950] Director

Ladhar Leisure LLP
Incorporated: 4 June 2009 *Employees:* 42
Net Worth Deficit: £1,562,426 *Total Assets:* £2,564,948
Registered Office: 15-16 Stockholm Close, Tyne Tunnel Trading Estate, North Shields, Tyne & Wear, NE29 7SF
Officers: Singh Ladhar Bhupinder [1981] Member; Singh Ladhar Mandeep [1985] Member

Ladybird's Childrens Nursery Limited
Incorporated: 24 June 2004 *Employees:* 56
Net Worth: £14,630 *Total Assets:* £916,013
Registered Office: 511 Durham Road, Low Fell, Gateshead, Tyne & Wear, NE9 5EY
Activities: Child day-care activities
Shareholders: Keith Briggs; Rebecca Kate Snedden
Officers: Keith Briggs, Secretary; Keith Briggs [1966] Director; Rebecca Kate Snedden [1975] Director

The Laidlaw Schools Trust
Incorporated: 8 March 2006 *Employees:* 415
Net Worth: £36,100,284 *Total Assets:* £41,086,136
Registered Office: St Nicholas Building, St Nicholas Street, Newcastle upon Tyne, NE1 1RF
Activities: Primary education
Officers: Peter Snowdon, Secretary; Peter Charles Fair [1943] Director/Consultant; Lord Irvine Alan Stewart Laidlaw [1942] Director; Graham Alexander Robertson [1960] Director/Management Accountant

JH Laidler & Son Limited
Incorporated: 11 December 2000 *Employees:* 22
Net Worth: £10,021 *Total Assets:* £914,182
Registered Office: Double Row, New Hartley, Whitley Bay, Tyne & Wear, NE25 0PP
Activities: Wholesale of fruit and vegetables
Shareholders: Dawn Laidler; Henry Thomas Laidler
Officers: Dawn Laidler, Secretary; Dawn Laidler [1963] Director; Henry Thomas Laidler [1969] Director/Produce Wholesaler

J.E. Laidler (North East) Limited
Incorporated: 20 March 1973 *Employees:* 5
Net Worth: £6,123,563 *Total Assets:* £9,138,066
Registered Office: Bridge End Works, Ryhope Road, Ryhope, Sunderland, Tyne & Wear, SR2 0NJ
Activities: Other credit granting n.e.c.
Officers: Joanne Elaine Laidler, Secretary; Denise Laidler [1962] Director/Sales Executive; Dorothy Preece Laidler [1940] Director/Housewife; Joanne Elaine Laidler [1964] Director; Joseph Edward Laidler [1939] Director; Angela Laidler Hall [1968] Director/Housewife

Lake District Leisure Pursuits Limited
Incorporated: 15 February 1956 *Employees:* 72
Net Worth: £13,659,000 *Total Assets:* £26,021,000
Registered Office: 2nd Floor, One Gosforth Park Way, Gosforth Business Park, Newcastle upon Tyne, NE12 8ET
Activities: Other accommodation
Parent: South Lakeland Group Limited
Officers: Judith Ann Archibold, Secretary; Ian Kellett [1963] Director; John Anthony Waterworth [1963] Director

The Lakes Distillery Company Limited
Incorporated: 12 September 2011 *Employees:* 58
Net Worth: £5,034,646 *Total Assets:* £8,505,447
Registered Office: 1st Floor Offices, Grandstand Garage, Kenton Road, Gosforth, Newcastle upon Tyne, NE3 4NB
Activities: Distilling, rectifying and blending of spirits
Officers: Andrew John Davison, Secretary; Paul Richard Currie [1964] Director; Timothy Bahram Neville Farazmand [1960] Director; Richard John Hutton [1968] Director; Nigel John Mills [1958] Director; Paul Anthony Neep [1953] Consultant/Director; David Peter Robinson [1984] Director; Dr Alan Gray Rutherford [1942] Director & Consultant

Lam-Plas (Durham) Limited
Incorporated: 16 December 1970 *Employees:* 87
Net Worth: £886,809 *Total Assets:* £2,110,145
Registered Office: Valley Road, Castleside Industrial Estate, Consett, Co Durham, DH8 8JA
Activities: Manufacture of bodies (coachwork) for motor vehicles (except caravans)
Officers: Francis Davison Pattison, Secretary; John Lloyd Hamilton [1936] Director/Business Consultant; Joseph O'Brien [1959] Production Director; Francis Davison Pattison [1936] Director/Retired; Keith John Siddle [1968] Operations Director; Leslie Vipond Siddle [1931] Director/Company Chairman

Gordon Lamb Limited
Incorporated: 23 December 1966 *Employees:* 178
Net Worth: £6,122,000 *Total Assets:* £6,122,000
Registered Office: Vertu House, Fifth Avenue Business Park, Team Valley Trading Estate, Gateshead, Tyne & Wear, NE11 0XA
Activities: Sale of new cars and light motor vehicles
Parent: Gordon Lamb Holdings Limited
Officers: Karen Anderson, Secretary; Karen Anderson [1971] Finance Director; David Paul Crane [1967] Commercial Director; Robert Thomas Forrester [1969] Director; Michael Sherwin [1959] Finance Director

Lambton House Ltd
Incorporated: 19 November 2012 *Employees:* 55
Net Worth: £688,657 *Total Assets:* £3,643,155
Registered Office: Lambton House, New Lambton, Houghton-le-Spring, Co Durham, DH4 6DE
Activities: Residential care activities for the elderly and disabled
Shareholder: Richard Coltman
Officers: Richard Coltman [1942] Director/Care Home Owner; Vivienne Jayne Coltman [1948] Director/Car Home Owner

Lambton Share Property Company Limited
Incorporated: 9 January 2012 *Employees:* 3
Net Worth: £16,652,448 *Total Assets:* £20,616,704
Registered Office: St Ann's Wharf, 112 Quayside, Newcastle upon Tyne, NE1 3DX
Activities: Management of real estate on a fee or contract basis
Shareholders: Womble Bond Dickinson (Trust Corporation) Limited; Ford & Etal (Trustees) Limited
Officers: Robert Alexander Dickinson [1964] Director/Solicitor; Lady Agnes Harriet Frances Mary Joicey [1956] Director; Lord James Michael Joicey [1953] Director

Lamda (UK) Limited
Incorporated: 16 April 2012 *Employees:* 4
Net Worth: £923,924 *Total Assets:* £1,054,146
Registered Office: Quantum House, Hobson Industrial Estate, Burnopfield, Co Durham, NE16 6EA
Activities: Research and experimental development on biotechnology
Officers: Amanda Miller, Secretary; Ipatia Efraimidou [1980] Finance Director [Greek]; Angelos Karatzas [1980] Director [Greek]; Richard John Paling [1970] Director/Group Financial Controller; David Alan Sanson [1959] Quality Director; Xanthippos Xanthakis [1968] Business Development Director [Greek]

Lamda Pharma Limited
Incorporated: 4 February 2015
Net Worth Deficit: £3,784,808 *Total Assets:* £3,416,319
Registered Office: Quantum House, Hobson Industrial Estate, Burnopfield, Hobson, Co Durham, NE16 6EA
Activities: Research and experimental development on biotechnology
Officers: Amanda Miller, Secretary; Ipatia Efraimidou [1980] Finance Director [Greek]; Angelos Karatzas [1980] Director [Greek]; Richard John Paling [1970] Director/Group Financial Controller; David Alan Sanson [1959] Quality Director; Xanthippos Xanthakis [1968] Business Development Director [Greek]

Lanchester Dairies Limited
Incorporated: 10 June 1994 *Employees:* 89
Net Worth Deficit: £1,013,456 *Total Assets:* £5,253,729
Registered Office: Upperhouses Farm, Lanchester, Co Durham, DH7 0RL
Activities: Liquid milk and cream production
Shareholder: Julie Austin
Officers: William Austin, Secretary/Farmer; Julie Austin [1966] Director/Accounts Administration; William Austin [1953] Director/Farmer

Lanchester Garden Centre Limited
Incorporated: 14 November 2009
Registered Office: The Willows, 6 Kingswood, Langley Park, Co Durham, DH7 9WA
Activities: Retail sale of flowers, plants, seeds, fertilizers, pet animals and pet food in specialised stores
Officers: Trevor Graham [1954] Director

Lanchester Properties Limited
Incorporated: 29 March 1999 *Employees:* 5
Net Worth: £2,792,076 *Total Assets:* £8,538,048
Registered Office: Unit 2 Greencroft Estate, Tower Road, Annfield Plain, Stanley, Co Durham, DH9 7XP
Activities: Production of electricity
Shareholders: Anthony Austin Cleary; Veronica Anne Cleary
Officers: Alexandra Louise Cleary [1986] Director; Anthony Austin Cleary [1952] Director/Wine Importer; Benjamin William Andrew Cleary [1988] Director; Caroline Robyn Cleary [1990] Director; Veronica Anne Cleary [1954] Director

Lanchester Wine Cellars Limited
Incorporated: 12 September 1980 *Employees:* 134
Net Worth: £5,605,775 *Total Assets:* £25,512,044
Registered Office: Unit 2 Greencroft Estates, Tower Road, Annfield Plain, Stanley, Co Durham, DH9 7XP
Activities: Wholesale of wine, beer, spirits and other alcoholic beverages
Shareholders: Anothony Austin Cleary; Veronica Anne Cleary
Officers: Adam Richard Black [1968] Director; Anthony Austin Cleary [1952] Director/Wine Importer; Veronica Anne Cleary [1954] Director/Human Resources Manager; Mark Anthony Satchwell [1964] Director

Lanchester Wine Sales Limited
Incorporated: 25 April 2012 *Employees:* 2
Net Worth Deficit: £371,619 *Total Assets:* £3,357,063
Registered Office: Unit 2 Greencroft Estates, Tower Road, Annfield Plain, Stanley, Co Durham, DH9 7XP
Activities: Wholesale of wine, beer, spirits and other alcoholic beverages
Parent: Lanchester Wine Cellars Limited
Officers: Anthony Austin Cleary [1952] Director/Wine Importer; Veronica Anne Cleary [1954] Director; Mark Anthony Satchwell [1964] Director

Land Factor Limited
Incorporated: 29 April 2008 *Employees:* 24
Net Worth: £379,910 *Total Assets:* £921,603
Registered Office: Burnfoot House, Hexham Business Park, Burn Lane, Hexham, Northumberland, NE46 3RU
Activities: Management of real estate on a fee or contract basis
Officers: Jenny Sinclair, Secretary; Peter Anderson Combe [1970] Director; Roderick James Findlay [1973] Director/Chartered Surveyors; Athole Roy McKillop [1964] Director; Thomas St Andrew Warde-Aldam [1959] Director; Matthew Williamson [1983] Director/Surveyor

Land Resources Ltd
Incorporated: 7 May 2008 *Employees:* 2
Net Worth: £4,048,284 *Total Assets:* £7,969,960
Registered Office: The Office, Cromwell Court, Shields Road, Pelaw, Gateshead, Tyne & Wear, NE10 0SG
Activities: Buying and selling of own real estate
Major Shareholder: Elizabeth Maguire
Officers: Elizabeth Maguire [1972] Director; Frank Maguire [1969] Director; Frank Maguire Jnr [1993] Director

Landon Engineering (Castle Works) Limited
Incorporated: 24 October 1984 *Employees:* 47
Net Worth: £877,071 *Total Assets:* £1,544,211
Registered Office: West Chirton Industrial Estate, Gloucester Road, North Shields, Tyne & Wear, NE29 8RQ
Activities: Manufacture of metal structures and parts of structures
Parent: Diesel Marine International Limited
Officers: Alan Leslie Gray, Secretary; Alan Leslie Gray [1963] Director/Accountant; Peter Lindsey Jackson [1941] Director; Richard Kevin Woodmansey [1954] Director

Lands (North East) Limited
Incorporated: 19 March 2001 *Employees:* 4
Net Worth: £107,189 *Total Assets:* £1,422,894
Registered Office: 18 Whitby Drive, Biddick, Washington, Tyne & Wear, NE38 7NW
Activities: Non-specialised wholesale trade
Shareholders: Dougie Singh Pannu; Linda Pannu
Officers: Nikki Singh Pannu, Secretary; Dougie Singh Pannu [1955] Director; Nikki Singh Pannu [1979] Director

Landscape Matters Limited
Incorporated: 30 April 2010 *Employees:* 30
Net Worth: £361,382 *Total Assets:* £1,083,539
Registered Office: 4 Ellerbeck Way, Stokesley Business Park, Stokesley, Middlesbrough, Cleveland, TS9 5JZ
Activities: Landscape service activities
Parent: Carlton Power Limited
Officers: Jayne Margaret Hodgson, Secretary; Keith Clarke [1960] Director

Landteam Developments Limited
Incorporated: 8 November 2000
Net Worth: £164,663 *Total Assets:* £2,786,043
Registered Office: Murky Hill Offices, Cow Lane, Middleton Tyas, Richmond, N Yorks, DL10 6RW
Activities: Buying and selling of own real estate
Major Shareholder: Edward Francis Speir
Officers: Edward Francis Speir, Secretary; Edward Francis Speir [1976] Director

Landteam Northern Limited
Incorporated: 17 August 2000
Net Worth Deficit: £2,691,305 *Total Assets:* £1,766,600
Registered Office: Murky Hill Offices, Cow Lane, Middleton Tyas, Richmond, N Yorks, DL10 6RW
Activities: Buying and selling of own real estate
Shareholders: Adrian John Speir; Ralph Congreve
Officers: Adrian John Speir, Secretary; Ralph Congreve [1953] Director; Adrian John Speir [1949] Director

Landteam Property Investments Limited
Incorporated: 19 July 1999 *Employees:* 1
Net Worth Deficit: £412,984 *Total Assets:* £5,195,989
Registered Office: Murky Hill Offices, Cow Lane, Middleton Tyas, Richmond, N Yorks, DL10 6RW
Activities: Buying and selling of own real estate
Major Shareholder: Edward Francis Speir
Officers: Edward Francis Speir, Secretary; Edward Francis Speir [1976] Director

Landtime Limited
Incorporated: 30 March 1999 *Employees:* 6
Net Worth: £15,468 *Total Assets:* £2,853,628
Registered Office: William Brown Centre, Manor Way, Peterlee, Co Durham, SR8 5TW
Activities: Buying and selling of own real estate
Officers: Dr David Guy Anderson [1960] Director/Doctor; Glenn Edward Carroll [1960] Director/Manager; Brian Hunter [1969] Director/Pharmacist; Gregory Ernald Moorhouse [1970] Director/Pharmacist; Marie Claire Young [1970] Director/Pharmacist; Philip Ian Young [1969] Operational Director

Landwood Properties Limited
Incorporated: 31 January 2005
Net Worth: £464,068 *Total Assets:* £1,847,861
Registered Office: Millennium House, 49a High Street, Yarm, Cleveland, TS15 9BH
Activities: Other letting and operating of own or leased real estate
Shareholders: William Gate; Shirley Anne Gate
Officers: Joseph William Gate, Secretary; Joseph William Gate [1956] Director; Shirley Anne Gate [1962] Director/Secretary

Lane7 Aberdeen Ltd
Incorporated: 13 September 2016
Net Worth Deficit: £46,434 *Total Assets:* £1,094,967
Registered Office: 70 Victoria Road, Darlington, Co Durham, DL1 5JG
Activities: Other amusement and recreation activities n.e.c.
Parent: Lane7 Ltd
Officers: Timothy James Wilks [1978] Director

Lane7 Ltd
Incorporated: 22 July 2013
Net Worth: £71,618 *Total Assets:* £838,969
Registered Office: 70 Victoria Road, Darlington, Co Durham, DL1 5JG
Activities: Activities of other holding companies n.e.c.
Major Shareholder: Timothy Wilks
Officers: Timothy James Wilks [1978] Director

Langage Energy Park Limited
Incorporated: 30 November 1999
Net Worth: £8,768,702 *Total Assets:* £10,199,383
Registered Office: 4 Ellerbeck Way, Stokesley Business Park, Stokesley, Middlesbrough, Cleveland, TS9 5JZ
Activities: Development of building projects
Parent: Langage Developments Limited
Officers: Jayne Margaret Hodgson, Secretary/Office Manager; Michael Fred Shaw Benson [1964] Director/Engineer; Keith Clarke [1960] Director/Engineer; Jayne Margaret Hodgson [1963] Finance Director; David John Philpot [1961] Director/Legal Counsel; Matthew Ian Shields [1944] Director/Engineer; Alan White [1961] Finance Director

Langage Solar Park Limited
Incorporated: 1 December 2010
Net Worth: £7,120,556 *Total Assets:* £9,376,475
Registered Office: 4 Ellerbeck Way, Stokesley Business Park, Stokesley, Middlesbrough, Cleveland, TS9 5JZ
Activities: Production of electricity
Parent: Carlton Power Limited
Officers: Jayne Margaret Hodgson, Secretary; Michael Fred Shaw Benson [1964] Director/Engineer; Keith Clarke [1960] Director; Jayne Margaret Hodgson [1963] Finance Director; David John Philpot [1961] Director/Legal Counsel; Matthew Ian Shields [1944] Director/Engineer; Alan White [1961] Finance Director

Langley Moor B3 Ltd.
Incorporated: 1 December 1999 *Employees:* 1
Net Worth: £997,726 *Total Assets:* £2,221,065
Registered Office: 26a Old Elvet, Durham, DH1 3HN
Activities: Other letting and operating of own or leased real estate
Major Shareholder: Mary Catherine Best
Officers: Paul Andrew Brown, Secretary; Stephen Best [1957] Director/Property Development

Lanof (UK) Ltd
Incorporated: 23 October 2008
Net Worth: £1,141,745 *Total Assets:* £1,476,978
Registered Office: 43 Coniscliffe Road, Darlington, Co Durham, DL3 7EH
Activities: Management consultancy activities other than financial management
Major Shareholder: Richard Edwin Clarke
Officers: Grazyna Barbara Wood, Secretary; Richard Edwin Clarke [1959] Director/Drilling Consultant

Larkflame Limited
Incorporated: 22 November 1993
Net Worth: £7,593,853 *Total Assets:* £17,186,352
Registered Office: c/o Magnet Limited, 3 Allington Way, Yarm Road Business Park, Darlington, Co Durham, DL1 4XT
Activities: Other manufacturing n.e.c.
Parent: Nobia Holdings UK Limited
Officers: Nicola Jane Hardcastle, Secretary; Anjum Ahmed [1970] Director; Daniel Arthur Edward Carr [1975] Director; Nicola Jane Hardcastle [1965] Director/Company Secretary; Peter Kane [1965] Managing Director

Lartington Hall Limited
Incorporated: 4 October 2011
Registered Office: Lartington Hall, Lartington, Barnard Castle, Co Durham, DL12 9BW
Activities: Hotels and similar accommodation
Major Shareholder: Shona Wilkes
Officers: John Wilkes [1968] Director; Shona Wilkes [1974] Director

Last Night Limited
Incorporated: 12 April 2002 *Employees:* 42
Net Worth: £550,974 *Total Assets:* £1,371,135
Registered Office: Statex House, Saltmeadows Road, Gateshead, Tyne & Wear, NE8 3AH
Activities: Other amusement and recreation activities n.e.c.
Shareholders: Dr Suzanne Mavir; Matthew Miles William Mavir
Officers: Dr Suzanne Mavir, Secretary; Andrew John Hindmarch [1976] Director/Web Developer; Garry Hodgson [1976] Director/Tour Operations; Cheryl Hooper [1983] Operations Director; William Edward Johnson [1984] Finance Director; Matthew Miles William Mavir [1977] Director [Australian]; Dr Suzanne Mavir [1978] Director

Latate Limited
Incorporated: 26 November 2001
Net Worth: £12,000,576 *Total Assets:* £19,857,808
Registered Office: 82 Bewick Road, Gateshead, Tyne & Wear, NE8 1RS
Activities: Other business support service activities n.e.c.
Officers: Shamai Schleider, Secretary/Teacher; Harold Emanuel [1962] Director/Lecturer; Anna Schleider [1956] Director/Teacher [American]; Shamai Schleider [1953] Director/Teacher; Yosef Schleider [1983] Director/Student; Miriam Silver [1977] Director/Interior Designer; Louis Wittler [1957] Director/Lecturer

Launchpad Homes Limited
Incorporated: 21 April 2005
Net Worth Deficit: £69,534 *Total Assets:* £2,257,813
Registered Office: Signature House, 3 Azure Court, Doxford International Business Park, Sunderland, Tyne & Wear, SR3 3BE
Activities: Other letting and operating of own or leased real estate
Shareholders: Kevin Wilde; Kevin Wilde
Officers: Evelyn Wilde, Secretary; Kevin Wilde [1959] Director

Lawkell LLP
Incorporated: 7 November 2012
Net Worth: £878,188 *Total Assets:* £885,067
Registered Office: Verdemar House, 230 Park View, Whitley Bay, Tyne & Wear, NE26 3QR
Officers: Kelvyn Gracie [1951] Member; Lawrence Ralph McCaughey [1957] Member; Rachael Beadling [1987] LLP Member; Rebecca Foster [1982] LLP Member; Carl Antoni Gracie [1975] LLP Member; David Gracie [1979] LLP Member; Steven Gracie [1979] LLP Member; Hayley Ann Ikin [1980] LLP Member

Lawnsward Limited
Incorporated: 23 July 1987 *Employees:* 3
Net Worth: £1,431,461 *Total Assets:* £2,276,007
Registered Office: Bulman House, Regent Centre, Gosforth, Newcastle upon Tyne, NE3 3LS
Activities: Other letting and operating of own or leased real estate
Shareholders: Andrew George McCoull; Elizabeth Ann McCoull
Officers: Andrew George McCoull, Secretary; Andrew George McCoull [1956] Director; Elizabeth Ann McCoull [1960] Director; Helen Elizabeth McCoull [1989] Director; William George McCoull [1987] Director

Lawson & Cowell Ltd
Incorporated: 14 March 1988 *Employees:* 49
Net Worth: £739,145 *Total Assets:* £1,358,149
Registered Office: 1 Jesmond Business Court, Jesmond Road, Newcastle upon Tyne, NE2 1LA
Activities: Plastering
Shareholder: Charles Trevor Lawson
Officers: Stephen Lawson, Secretary; Trevor Lawson, Secretary; Dennis Cowell [1946] Director/Plasterer; Trevor Lawson [1947] Director/Plasterer

Lawson Cars Limited
Incorporated: 18 October 2000
Net Worth: £238,762 *Total Assets:* £815,493
Registered Office: South Bank Road, Middlesbrough, Cleveland, TS3 8AB
Activities: Sale of used cars and light motor vehicles
Major Shareholder: Richard William Hudson
Officers: Richard William Hudson, Secretary/Garage Director; Richard William Hudson [1986] Garage Director

Edgar Lawson Limited
Incorporated: 8 October 1945
Net Worth: £1,167,725 *Total Assets:* £1,732,974
Registered Office: Barton Grange, Barton, Richmond, N Yorks, DL10 6HS
Activities: Mixed farming
Major Shareholder: John Paul Lawson
Officers: Edgar John Lawson, Secretary/Farm Manager; Edgar John Lawson [1971] Director; John Paul Lawson [1945] Director; Robert Edward Lawson [1977] Director/Farmer

Dick Lawson Yorkshire Limited
Incorporated: 27 October 2014
Net Worth: £990,099 *Total Assets:* £990,099
Registered Office: Springfield Farm, Darlington Road, North Cowton, Northallerton, N Yorks, DL7 0HD
Activities: Other letting and operating of own or leased real estate
Major Shareholder: Julia Evelyn Atkinson
Officers: Julia Evelyn Atkinson [1955] Director

Layfield Renewable Ltd
Incorporated: 29 March 2012
Net Worth: £691,863 *Total Assets:* £2,716,832
Registered Office: Milkup Bank Farm, Willington, Crook, Co Durham, DL15 0RN
Activities: Production of electricity
Major Shareholder: Richard Alistair Layfield
Officers: Andrea Jayne Layfield [1971] Director; Richard Alistair Layfield [1965] Director/Farmer

LCH Renewables Limited
Incorporated: 9 September 2014
Net Worth: £465,928 *Total Assets:* £1,837,115
Registered Office: Little Coop House Farm, Hawthorn, Seaham, Co Durham, SR7 8SA
Activities: Production of electricity
Shareholders: Mary Moor; Samantha Louise Moor; William Armstrong Moor; Seymour Moor
Officers: Mary Moor [1944] Director; Samantha Louise Moor [1976] Director; Seymour Moor [1944] Director; William Armstrong Moor [1972] Director

LD Property Management Limited
Incorporated: 17 September 2003
Net Worth: £1,631,858 *Total Assets:* £2,309,084
Registered Office: 34 Dean Street, Newcastle upon Tyne, NE1 1PG
Activities: Other letting and operating of own or leased real estate
Major Shareholder: Peter Davison
Officers: Peter Davison, Secretary; Peter Davison [1974] Director/Manager; Roderick Vernon MacKay [1967] Director/Manager

G.W.Leader Limited
Incorporated: 19 December 1958 *Employees:* 8
Net Worth: £2,629,787 *Total Assets:* £2,743,087
Registered Office: 116 Newport Road, Middlesbrough, Cleveland, TS1 5JF
Activities: Other retail sale of new goods in specialised stores (not commercial art galleries and opticians)
Parent: G W Leader (Holdings) Limited
Officers: Mark John Leader, Secretary; David Leader [1949] Director/Timber Merchant

Leader Online Limited
Incorporated: 18 July 2006 *Employees:* 27
Net Worth: £88,272 *Total Assets:* £1,557,111
Registered Office: 103 Whitby Street South, Hartlepool, Cleveland, TS24 7LH
Activities: Retail of furniture, lighting, and similar (not musical instruments or scores) in specialised store
Parent: Leader Online (Holdings) Limited
Officers: Hilary Leader, Secretary; Mark John Leader [1972] Director; Daniel Lee Shine [1966] Director/Manager

Leader Property Limited
Incorporated: 29 September 2005
Registered Office: 103 Whitby Street South, Hartlepool, Cleveland, TS24 7LH
Activities: Renting and operating of Housing Association real estate
Parent: Leader Property (Holdings) Limited
Officers: Hilary Marie Leader, Secretary; Mark John Leader [1972] Director

Leadgates Developments Limited
Incorporated: 15 December 2011 *Employees:* 2
Net Worth: £2,579,152 *Total Assets:* £3,944,594
Registered Office: 19 Millfield Road, Whickham, Gateshead, Tyne & Wear, NE16 4QA
Activities: Other letting and operating of own or leased real estate
Major Shareholder: Robert Thompson
Officers: Robert Frazer Thompson [1973] Director/Flooring Manager; Robert Thompson [1941] Director

Leadgates Investments Limited
Incorporated: 10 June 2014
Net Worth: £2,134,883 *Total Assets:* £16,828,236
Registered Office: Leadgates, Great Whittington, Northumberland, NE19 2HB
Activities: Financial management
Major Shareholder: Robert Thompson
Officers: Robert Thompson [1941] Director

Leaguenotion
Incorporated: 17 September 1990 *Employees:* 224
Net Worth: £8,364,000 *Total Assets:* £11,908,000
Registered Office: 1a Dukesway Court, Team Valley Trading Estate, Gateshead, Tyne & Wear, NE11 0PJ
Activities: Gambling and betting activities
Parent: Linkfield Estates Limited
Officers: Phillip Nigel Blain, Secretary; David James Horrocks [1959] Director/Chartered Accountant; Ian Imrie [1955] Director

Leah Property Limited
Incorporated: 19 February 2007
Net Worth: £1,153,880 *Total Assets:* £3,533,245
Registered Office: The Haven, 2C West Park, Cleadon Village, Sunderland, Tyne & Wear, SR6 7RR
Activities: Development of building projects
Shareholders: Brent McCafferty; Lisa McCafferty
Officers: Lisa McCafferty, Secretary; Brent Peter McCafferty [1963] Director/Property Developer

Learning at Work Limited
Incorporated: 3 October 2007 *Employees:* 7
Net Worth: £4,894,723 *Total Assets:* £5,334,873
Registered Office: 51-53 Innovation House, Longfield Road, South Church Enterprise Park, Bishop Auckland, Co Durham, DL14 6XB
Activities: Other education n.e.c.
Parent: Learning Curve (NE) Group Limited
Officers: Jonathan Daniel Cummins [1976] Director/Training Provider; Gavin Stewart Higgins [1977] Director/Chief Financial Officer; Richard Daniel Mayers [1975] Director/Accountant; Brenda McLeish [1978] Director; Ian Scott Wallis [1970] Director/Investment Professional

Learning Concepts Limited
Incorporated: 30 July 2004 *Employees:* 32
Net Worth: £2,349,937 *Total Assets:* £2,561,223
Registered Office: Learning Concepts Ltd, Jarrow Business Centre, Rolling Mill Road, Viking Industrial Estate, Jarrow, Tyne & Wear, NE32 3DT
Activities: Post-secondary non-tertiary education
Major Shareholder: Gillian Campbell
Officers: Gillian Campbell [1967] Director/Office Manager

Learning Curve Group Limited
Incorporated: 16 September 2004 *Employees:* 184
Net Worth: £16,961,860 *Total Assets:* £20,384,776
Registered Office: Units 51-53 Innovation House, South Church Enterprise Park, Bishop Auckland, Co Durham, DL14 6XB
Activities: Other business support service activities n.e.c.
Parent: Learning Curve (NE) Group Limited
Officers: Jonathan Daniel Cummins [1976] Director; Gavin Stewart Higgins [1977] Director/Chief Financial Officer; Richard Daniel Mayers [1975] Director/Accountant; Brenda McLeish [1978] Director; Ian Scott Wallis [1970] Director/Investment Professional

Learning Matters Trust Ltd.
Incorporated: 5 July 2011 *Employees:* 145
Net Worth: £7,011,918 *Total Assets:* £8,599,729
Registered Office: Kepier, Dairy Lane, Houghton-le-Spring, Co Durham, DH4 5BH
Activities: General secondary education
Officers: Judith Forster, Secretary; Kathryn Ruth Afsahi [1969] Director/Exams Officer; Stephanie Ann Carter-Smith [1968] Director/Operations Manager; Martin Connor [1967] Director/Retired; Nicola Jane Cooper [1968] Director/Principal; Gemma Fenwick [1979] Director/Analyst; Steven Paul Forsyth [1985] Director/Teacher; Deborah Garland [1971] Director/Resource Manager; Lee Harnett [1979] Director/Printing; Keith Hind [1969] Director/Manufacturing Manager; Thomas Mayer [1975] Director/Teacher; Andrew Slassor [1961] Director; Keith James Stout [1952] Director/Manager; Kenneth Ian Tonge [1952] Director/Retired; Gary Wallace [1991] Director/Certified Chartered Accountant

Leavendale Properties Ltd
Incorporated: 23 March 2004
Net Worth: £491,657 *Total Assets:* £2,609,170
Registered Office: Unit 1 Martinet Road, Thornaby, Stockton on Tees, Cleveland, TS17 0AS
Activities: Activities of households as employers of domestic personnel
Officers: Stephen Alan Watson, Secretary; David Jones [1961] Director/Haulage Contractor; Alan McLean [1968] Director/Fireman; Stephen Alan Watson [1968] Director

Leazes Arcade Limited
Incorporated: 28 February 1992
Registered Office: 17 Leazes Park Road, Newcastle upon Tyne, NE1 4PF
Activities: Buying and selling of own real estate
Major Shareholder: Mohammed Ajaib
Officers: Mohammed Ajaib, Secretary; Mohammed Ajaib [1957] Director/Property Developer

Leazes Homes Limited
Incorporated: 27 April 2009
Net Worth: £1,120,000 *Total Assets:* £65,430,000
Registered Office: Jubilee Court, Kenton Road, Newcastle upon Tyne, NE3 3BW
Activities: Other accommodation
Officers: Jon Mitford, Secretary; Michael Thomas Brady [1943] Director/Retired; Anne Veronica Dunn [1949] Director/Councillor; Dawn Marie Keightley [1965] Director/Consultant; Michael Edward Reynolds [1980] Director/Chartered Quantity Surveyor; William Thompson [1970] Director/Bid and Business Development Manager; Cameron William Waddell [1970] Director, Mazars LI.P, Durham; Gerard Joseph Walsh [1963] Director/Chartered Surveyor

Leazes Park Estates Limited
Incorporated: 14 July 1994
Registered Office: 6-10 Leazes Park Road, Newcastle upon Tyne, NE1 1TG
Activities: Buying and selling of own real estate
Officers: Gianfranco Fanelli [1958] Director/Restaurateur

Leazes Park Properties Limited
Incorporated: 17 March 1987
Registered Office: 15 Bankside, The Watermark, Gateshead, Tyne & Wear, NE11 9SY
Activities: Other letting and operating of own or leased real estate
Shareholders: Crawford Cole; Jean Cole
Officers: Crawford William Alexander Cole, Secretary/Chartered Surveyor; Crawford William Alexander Cole [1955] Director/Chartered Surveyor; Jean Margaret Cole [1957] Director/Secretary Administrator

LEC Management
Incorporated: 8 January 1998
Net Worth: £1,606,924 *Total Assets:* £1,814,031
Registered Office: 27 Staindrop Road, Darlington, Co Durham, DL3 9AG
Activities: Management consultancy activities other than financial management
Shareholders: James Gerald Tully; Janette Tully
Officers: Janette Tully, Secretary; James Generald Tully [1958] Director; Janette Tully [1959] Director

Leda & Swan LLP
Incorporated: 14 May 2012
Net Worth: £339,961 *Total Assets:* £2,700,442
Registered Office: The Estate Office, Aske Hall, Richmond, N Yorks, DL10 5HJ
Officers: Lady Eliza Dundas [1998] Member; Lady Flora Dundas [2001] Member; Lady Imogen Dundas [2001] Member; Lady Minna Dundas [2000] Member

G D Lee Building Services Limited
Incorporated: 24 June 2005
Net Worth: £1,757,647 *Total Assets:* £1,988,500
Registered Office: 6 Larch Court, West Chirton Industrial Estate North, North Shields, Tyne & Wear, NE29 8SG
Activities: Other construction installation
Officers: Karen Jane Lee, Secretary; Graeme Dennis Lee [1968] Director/Joiner

Lee Construction (Ldg) Limited
Incorporated: 2 November 2004 *Employees:* 6
Net Worth: £360,167 *Total Assets:* £820,536
Registered Office: Unit 4 Brompton Industrial Park, Station Road, Brompton on Swale, Richmond, N Yorks, DL10 7SN
Activities: Construction of domestic buildings
Major Shareholder: Lee Danial Green
Officers: Anne Isabelle Latham, Secretary; Lee Danial Green [1974] Director/Construction Engineer

Lee's Coaches Limited
Incorporated: 18 May 2003
Net Worth: £1,337,992 *Total Assets:* £2,738,141
Registered Office: Mill Road Garage, Littleburn Industrial Estate, Langley Moor, Co Durham, DH7 8HE
Activities: Other passenger land transport
Major Shareholder: Derrick Collin
Officers: Derrick Collin [1948] Director; Stephen Anthony James [1958] Director; Malcolm Winship Lee [1964] Director

William Leech (Investments) Limited
Incorporated: 11 April 1953 *Employees:* 2
Net Worth: £53,021,448 *Total Assets:* £55,269,512
Registered Office: Saville Chambers, 5 North Street, Newcastle upon Tyne, NE1 8DF
Activities: Financial intermediation not elsewhere classified
Officers: Kenneth Quinn, Secretary; Andrew Charles Brown [1957] Director/Chartered Surveyor; David John Buffham [1959] Director; Paul Geoffrey Chandler [1961] Director; Andrew Goldsworthy Gibbs [1947] Director/Chartered Accountant; John Overend Harrison [1954] Director/Chartered Accountant; Eric Morgan [1945] Director/Retired Surveyor; Philip John Poole [1946] Finance Director; Rev Norman Keith Stephenson [1962] Finance Director; Hugh Benson Welch [1957] Director/Lawyer; Adrian Donald White [1967] Finance Director

William Leech Foundation Limited (The)
Incorporated: 4 July 1960
Net Worth: £53,558,128 *Total Assets:* £53,612,072
Registered Office: Saville Chambers, 5 North Street, Newcastle upon Tyne, NE1 8DF
Activities: Financial intermediation not elsewhere classified
Officers: Kenneth Quinn, Secretary; Andrew Charles Brown [1957] Director/Chartered Surveyor; David John Buffham [1959] Director; Paul Geoffrey Chandler [1961] Director; Andrew Goldsworthy Gibbs [1947] Director/Chartered Accountant; John Overend Harrison [1954] Director/Chartered Accountant; Eric Morgan [1945] Director/Retired Chartered Surveyor; Philip John Poole [1946] Finance Director; Rev Norman Keith Stephenson [1962] Finance Director; Hugh Benson Welch [1957] Director/Lawyer; Adrian Donald White [1967] Finance Director

Leedawn Properties Limited
Incorporated: 13 March 2012 *Employees:* 2
Net Worth: £218,212 *Total Assets:* £1,160,853
Registered Office: 3 South Street, Crook, Co Durham, DL15 8NE
Activities: Other letting and operating of own or leased real estate
Officers: Dawn Murray [1965] Director/Insurance Agent; Lee Robinson [1963] Director/Insurance Agent

Lees Cleaning Contractors LLP
Incorporated: 16 December 2009 *Employees:* 402
Net Worth: £1,150,347 *Total Assets:* £1,773,151
Registered Office: 43 Maxwell Street, South Shields, Tyne & Wear, NE33 4PU
Officers: Jane Rosanna Carr [1970] Member; Derek Edward West [1949] Member; Jean West [1949] Member; Lee West [1967] Member

Leftbank Properties Limited
Incorporated: 13 July 1990
Net Worth: £1,237,574 *Total Assets:* £1,828,566
Registered Office: Holywood House, Wolsingham, Co Durham, DL13 3HE
Activities: Buying and selling of own real estate
Shareholder: Anne Hill
Officers: Robert Angus Hill, Secretary; Anne Hill [1953] Director/Manager

Legacy No.1 Limited
Incorporated: 7 April 2008
Net Worth: £77,053 *Total Assets:* £1,275,462
Registered Office: Exchange Building, 66 Church Street, Hartlepool, Cleveland, TS24 7DN
Activities: Development of building projects
Major Shareholder: Riaz Mohammad Hameed
Officers: Riaz Mohammad Hameed, Secretary; Riaz Mohammad Hameed [1973] Director [Turkish]

Legacy Resorts Limited
Incorporated: 9 July 2013 *Employees:* 14
Net Worth: £447,164 *Total Assets:* £2,900,973
Registered Office: Kings Hall, 4 Imperial Bldgs, Durham Road, Houghton-le-Spring, Co Durham, DH4 4DJ
Activities: Recreational vehicle parks, trailer parks and camping grounds
Shareholder: Mark Seaton
Officers: Christopher James Seaton [1987] Director/Businessman; Mark Seaton [1972] Director/Businessman

Leggott Farming Limited
Incorporated: 2 May 2008
Net Worth: £107,039 *Total Assets:* £2,004,260
Registered Office: Beech Tree Farm, Hutton Bonville, Northallerton, N Yorks, DL7 0NR
Activities: Raising of dairy cattle
Shareholders: Dawn Lorna Leggott; John Henry Leggott; John Herbert Leggott
Officers: Dawn Lorna Leggott [1957] Director/Farmer; John Henry Leggott [1981] Director/Farmer; John Herbert Leggott [1954] Director/Farmer

A S & J K Leggott Limited
Incorporated: 27 February 2015 *Employees:* 3
Net Worth: £4,522 *Total Assets:* £1,002,582
Registered Office: White House Farm, West Lane, Dalton on Tees, Darlington, Co Durham, DL2 2PL
Activities: Mixed farming
Shareholders: Andrew Simon Leggott; Joanne Kathryn Leggott; Joshua Simon Leggott
Officers: Andrew Leggott, Secretary; Andrew Simon Leggott [1961] Director/Farmer; Joanne Kathryn Leggott [1962] Director/Farmer; Joshua Simon Leggott [1993] Director/Farmer

Leicester District Energy Company Limited
Incorporated: 15 June 2006 *Employees:* 2
Net Worth: £5,260,000 *Total Assets:* £20,611,000
Registered Office: Shared Services Centre, Q3 Office, Quorum Business Park, Benton Lane, Newcastle upon Tyne, NE12 8EX
Activities: Production of electricity
Parent: Engie Urban Energy Group Limited
Officers: Sarah Gregory, Secretary; Andrew David Hart [1969] Managing Director; Lee Kitchen [1979] Director/Accountant

Leighton Corporation Limited
Incorporated: 27 January 1997
Net Worth: £672,591 *Total Assets:* £1,491,816
Registered Office: Chase House, Mandarin Road, Rainton Bridge, Houghton-le-Spring, Co Durham, DH4 5RA
Activities: Other information technology service activities
Shareholder: Paul Michael Callaghan
Officers: Gerard Dominic Callaghan [1967] Director/Businessman; John Bernard Callaghan [1959] Director; Paul Michael Callaghan [1952] Director; Steven Nelson [1965] Director/Chartered Accountant; Christopher James Wilds [1975] Director

Leisure Centre Holdings
Incorporated: 23 August 1988
Net Worth: £1,248,000 *Total Assets:* £1,248,000
Registered Office: 1a Dukesway Court, Team Valley Trading Estate, Gateshead, Tyne & Wear, NE11 0PJ
Activities: Non-trading company
Parent: DC Gaming Limited
Officers: Phillip Nigel Blain, Secretary; David James Horrocks [1959] Director/Chartered Accountant; Ian Imrie [1955] Director

Leisure Works (Yorkshire) Limited
Incorporated: 4 February 2004 *Employees:* 2
Net Worth: £980,363 *Total Assets:* £987,415
Registered Office: High Grange, Exelby, Bedale, N Yorks, DL8 2HQ
Activities: Other holiday and other collective accommodation
Major Shareholder: Ian Michael Cottam
Officers: Caroline Rose Cottam, Secretary/Administrator; Caroline Rose Cottam [1961] Director/Administrator; Ian Michael Cottam [1959] Director/Holiday Let Operator

Leisure World Group Limited
Incorporated: 18 January 2012 *Employees:* 95
Net Worth: £2,417,645 *Total Assets:* £13,994,411
Registered Office: c/o Catterick Caravan & Camping Centre Limited, Gatherley Road, Brompton on Swale, Richmond, N Yorks, DL10 7JB
Activities: Activities of other holding companies n.e.c.
Shareholders: Christopher Michael Kinsell; Matthew Alexander Kinsell
Officers: Christopher Michael Kinsell, Secretary; Christopher Michael Kinsell [1973] Director; Matthew Alexander Kinsell [1979] Director

Lending Solutions Holdings Limited
Incorporated: 5 April 2004
Net Worth: £1,888,000 *Total Assets:* £11,740,000
Registered Office: Newcastle House, Albany Court, Newcastle Business Park, Newcastle upon Tyne, NE4 7YB
Activities: Activities of other holding companies n.e.c.
Parent: LSL Property Services PLC
Officers: Sapna Bedi FitzGenerald, Secretary/Solicitor; Helen Elizabeth Buck [1960] Director; Adam Robert Castleton [1964] Director; Jonathan Pearson Round [1964] Director

Lenton Marketing Limited
Incorporated: 22 November 2011
Net Worth: £799,558 *Total Assets:* £1,081,163
Registered Office: 17 Holmlands Crescent, Durham Moor, Durham, DH1 5AR
Activities: Web portals
Major Shareholder: David Lenton
Officers: Avril Joy [1951] Financial Director; David John Lenton [1987] Marketing Director; John Lenton [1949] Managing Director

Leo Car Company Limited
Incorporated: 12 March 2003
Net Worth: £397,797 *Total Assets:* £934,749
Registered Office: Beaumont Accountancy, First Floor, Enterprise House, 202-206 Linthorpe Road, Middlesbrough, Cleveland, TS1 3QW
Activities: Sale of used cars and light motor vehicles
Major Shareholder: John William Woodier
Officers: John William Woodier [1963] Director/Car Salesman

C.J. Leonard & Sons Limited
Incorporated: 5 March 1998 *Employees:* 21
Net Worth: £16,388,800 *Total Assets:* £22,049,778
Registered Office: Clevestone Works, Slapewath, Guisborough, Cleveland, TS14 6PX
Activities: Sale of other motor vehicles
Officers: Michael Patrick Leonard, Secretary/Plant Dealer; Charles Joseph Leonard [1964] Director/Truck Dealer; Michael Patrick Leonard [1968] Director/Plant Dealer; Rose Bridget Leonard [1938] Director

Lescost Transport Limited
Incorporated: 25 March 1980 *Employees:* 58
Net Worth: £1,542,992 *Total Assets:* £2,474,214
Registered Office: 20 Tower Road, Glover Industrial Estate, Washington, Tyne & Wear, NE37 2SH
Activities: Freight transport by road
Shareholders: James Hunter; Maureen Hunter
Officers: Maureen Hunter, Secretary; James Hunter [1948] Transport Director; Maureen Hunter [1948] Technical Director; Michelle Tyler [1979] Director; Leanne Urwin [1974] Director

Lescrow Investments Limited
Incorporated: 10 June 2010
Net Worth: £150,799 *Total Assets:* £1,043,290
Registered Office: Muckle LLP, Time Central, 32 Gallowgate, Newcastle upon Tyne, NE1 4BF
Activities: Activities of other holding companies n.e.c.
Shareholders: Philip Edward Shaw; Lorraine Shaw
Officers: Lorraine Shaw [1972] Director/Housewife; Philip Edward Shaw [1971] Director

Level Flooring North East Limited
Incorporated: 21 December 2011 *Employees:* 4
Net Worth: £1,024,742 *Total Assets:* £1,169,987
Registered Office: 53 Beverley Terrace, Cullercoats, North Shields, Tyne & Wear, NE30 4NX
Activities: Floor and wall covering
Shareholders: Kevin Martin; Patricia Theresa Martin; Rebecca Martin
Officers: Kevin Martin [1960] Director; Patricia Theresa Martin [1967] Director; Rebecca Martin [1991] Director/Administrator

Leven Estates Ltd
Incorporated: 26 October 2010
Net Worth: £10,709,108 *Total Assets:* £17,578,618
Registered Office: Eure Cottage, Easby Hall, Easby, Great Ayton, N Yorks, TS9 6JQ
Activities: Other accommodation
Shareholders: Julie Ellison; Simon James Ellison
Officers: Julie Ellison [1971] Director; Simon James Ellison [1965] Director

Leveys Holdings Limited
Incorporated: 7 December 1990
Net Worth: £3,634,514 *Total Assets:* £3,691,397
Registered Office: Sandgate House, 102 Quayside, Newcastle upon Tyne, NE1 3DX
Activities: Other letting and operating of own or leased real estate
Major Shareholder: Nigel Adrian Levey
Officers: Eva Newman, Secretary; Kevin Cornelius Clifford [1962] Director/Accountant; Anushka Tanya Levey [1974] Director/Barrister; Edward Michael Levey [1974] Director/Barrister; Nigel Adrian Levey [1944] Director; Stephen Julius Levey [1971] Director; Eva Newman [1955] Director/Company Secretary

Lewis & Cooper Limited
Incorporated: 30 January 1903 *Employees:* 52
Net Worth: £1,338,008 *Total Assets:* £1,897,876
Registered Office: 92 High Street, Northallerton, N Yorks, DL7 8PT
Activities: Retail sale in non-specialised stores with food, beverages or tobacco predominating
Shareholders: Jonathan Lewis Hindley; Dr David Gearey
Officers: Gisella Gearey, Secretary; Bettina Mary Bell [1972] Director/General Manager; Dr David Gearey [1939] Director/Lecturer; Lucinda Mary Irene Gearey [1976] Director/Online Development Manager; Jonathan Lewis Hindley [1954] Director/Chartered Surveyor; Victoria Wendy Howard [1972] Director/General Manager; David Pears [1959] Retail Manager/Director

Lexiauk Limited
Incorporated: 3 October 2005 *Employees:* 16
Net Worth: £221,578 *Total Assets:* £1,127,247
Registered Office: York House, Market Place, Leyburn, N Yorks, DL8 5AT
Activities: Other information technology service activities
Shareholder: Robert Jonathan Kay
Officers: Lynn Kay, Secretary; Robert Jonathan Kay [1971] Director/Software Supplier; Judith Pamela Staples [1946] Director/Software Supplier

Leybourne Urwin Limited
Incorporated: 20 November 1935 *Employees:* 31
Net Worth: £1,502,248 *Total Assets:* £2,083,315
Registered Office: Cramar House, Tanfield Industrial Estate, Stanley, Co Durham, DH9 9QT
Activities: Plumbing, heat and air-conditioning installation
Shareholders: Christopher Urwin; Mark Urwin
Officers: Christopher Urwin, Secretary; Kieron Bennett [1971] Director; Christopher Urwin [1968] Director; Mark Urwin [1972] Director

The Leyburn Livestock Auction Mart Company Limited
Incorporated: 18 November 1918 *Employees:* 15
Net Worth: £690,906 *Total Assets:* £789,616
Registered Office: Auction Mart, Richmond Road, Leyburn, N Yorks, DL8 5DP
Activities: Agents selling agricultural raw materials, livestock, textile raw materials and semi-finished goods
Officers: Rachael Margaret Simpson, Secretary; Robert Dixon [1960] Director/Farmer; Peter Dobbing [1957] Director/Farmer; Granville Ernest Fairburn [1949] Director/Farmer; George Kenneth Hird [1941] Director/Farmer; Raymond Hunter [1943] Director/Farmer; Christopher Metcalfe [1963] Director/Farmer; Shaun Alfred Sowray [1960] Director/Farmer; Norman Joseph Sunter [1963] Director; Philip James Terry [1956] Director/Farmer; Richard Leslie Tuer [1945] Director/Farmer

Lezora Limited
Incorporated: 24 April 2014
Registered Office: 12 Eslington Court, Gateshead, Tyne & Wear, NE8 2TU
Activities: Wholesale of other intermediate products
Major Shareholder: Oliver Daniels
Officers: Oliver Daniels [1983] Director

LGA Developments Limited
Incorporated: 24 March 2015
Net Worth: £325,692 *Total Assets:* £5,306,880
Registered Office: Springfield House, Oakfield Road, Gosforth, Newcastle upon Tyne, NE3 4HS
Activities: Buying and selling of own real estate
Officers: John Peter Reece [1961] Director; Susan Elizabeth Reece [1961] Director

LGA Foundation
Incorporated: 9 November 2010
Net Worth: £4,853,312 *Total Assets:* £4,903,260
Registered Office: Westgarth, Brewery Square, Ovington, Prudhoe, Northumberland, NE42 6EB
Activities: Non-trading company
Officers: John Flynn [1959] Director/Retired Solicitor; John Peter Reece [1961] Director; Susan Elizabeth Reece [1961] Director

Libra Careco CH2 Propco Limited
Incorporated: 7 September 2005
Net Worth: £310,822,016 *Total Assets:* £422,870,016
Registered Office: Southgate House, Archer Street, Darlington, Co Durham, DL3 6AH
Activities: Buying and selling of own real estate
Parent: Libra Careco CH2 Propco Holdco Ltd
Officers: James Justin Hutchens [1974] Director [American]; David Andrew Smith [1974] Director

Libra Careco Ch3 Propco Limited
Incorporated: 30 September 2005
Net Worth: £114,603,000 *Total Assets:* £193,359,008
Registered Office: Southgate House, Archer Street, Darlington, Co Durham, DL3 6AH
Activities: Buying and selling of own real estate
Parent: Libra Careco CH3 Propco Holdco Ltd
Officers: James Justin Hutchens [1974] Director [American]; David Andrew Smith [1974] Director

Libra Careco Investments 1 Limited
Incorporated: 25 November 2004
Net Worth: £279,151,520 *Total Assets:* £302,528,736
Registered Office: Southgate House, Archer Street, Darlington, Co Durham, DL3 6AH
Activities: Other business support service activities n.e.c.
Parent: Libra Careco Holdings Ltd
Officers: James Justin Hutchens [1974] Director [American]; David Andrew Smith [1974] Director

Libra Careco Investments 2 Limited
Incorporated: 25 November 2004
Net Worth: £179,123,232 *Total Assets:* £194,519,488
Registered Office: Southgate House, Archer Street, Darlington, Co Durham, DL3 6AH
Activities: Other business support service activities n.e.c.
Parent: Libra Careco Investments 1 Ltd
Officers: James Justin Hutchens [1974] Director [American]; David Andrew Smith [1974] Director

Libra Careco Limited
Incorporated: 25 November 2004
Net Worth Deficit: £137,949,696 *Total Assets:* £586,443,200
Registered Office: Southgate House, Archer Street, Darlington, Co Durham, DL3 6AH
Activities: Other business support service activities n.e.c.
Parent: Libra Careco Investments 2 Ltd
Officers: James Justin Hutchens [1974] Director [American]; David Andrew Smith [1974] Director

Libra Seafood Processing Limited
Incorporated: 26 November 2002
Net Worth: £751,407 *Total Assets:* £1,211,080
Registered Office: Unit D, Viking Business Park, Rolling Mill Road, Jarrow, Tyne & Wear, NE32 3DP
Activities: Processing and preserving of fish, crustaceans and molluscs
Major Shareholder: Andrew Muat
Officers: Anthony Thomas Wynne, Secretary; Andrew Muat [1943] Director; Anthony Thomas Wynne [1964] Director

Libra Seafoods Limited
Incorporated: 26 November 2002 *Employees:* 4
Net Worth: £106,844 *Total Assets:* £3,490,467
Registered Office: Unit D, Viking Business Park, Rolling Mill Road, Jarrow, Tyne & Wear, NE32 3DP
Activities: Wholesale of other food, including fish, crustaceans and molluscs
Major Shareholder: Andrew Muat
Officers: Anthony Thomas Wynne, Secretary; Andrew Muat [1943] Director; Anthony Thomas Wynne [1964] Director

Licensed Consultancy Services Limited
Incorporated: 13 September 2006
Net Worth: £546,912 *Total Assets:* £1,028,384
Registered Office: Glebe House, Village Lane, Washington, Tyne & Wear, NE38 7HY
Activities: Other business support service activities n.e.c.
Shareholders: Christopher Antoni Irwin; Diane Irwin
Officers: Christopher Antoni Irwin, Secretary; Christopher Antoni Irwin [1965] Director/Consultant; Diane Irwin [1968] Director

Allan Liddle (Holding) Limited
Incorporated: 9 January 2014
Net Worth: £1,266,438 *Total Assets:* £1,897,894
Registered Office: A21 Stonehills Complex, Shields Road, Pelaw, Gateshead, Tyne & Wear, NE10 0HW
Activities: Activities of other holding companies n.e.c.
Shareholders: Mark Richard Liddle; Mark Richard Liddle Executor of Allan Thompson Liddle Deceased
Officers: Ashley Jean Liddle [1968] Director; Marie Rosalie Liddle [1935] Director; Mark Richard Liddle [1962] Director

Allan Liddle (Steel) Limited
Incorporated: 6 December 1978 *Employees:* 11
Net Worth: £506,194 *Total Assets:* £1,095,070
Registered Office: A21 Stonehills Complex, Shields Road, Pelaw, Gateshead, Tyne & Wear, NE10 0HW
Activities: Manufacture of basic iron and steel and of ferro-alloys
Parent: Allan Liddle (Holding) Limited
Officers: Ashley Jean Liddle [1968] Director; Marie Rosalie Liddle [1935] Director/Secretary; Mark Richard Liddle [1962] Director/Office Administrator

W. Liddy & Company Limited
Incorporated: 7 October 1993 *Employees:* 469
Net Worth: £2,022,153 *Total Assets:* £4,106,133
Registered Office: Unit 28 Apex Business Village, Cramlington, Northumberland, NE23 7BF
Activities: Unlicenced restaurants and cafes
Major Shareholder: William Liddy
Officers: Emma Louise Vieira, Secretary; William Liddy [1946] Director

Liebherr Sunderland Works Limited
Incorporated: 21 November 2000 *Employees:* 202
Net Worth: £7,727,686 *Total Assets:* £23,346,822
Registered Office: Ayres Quay, Deptford Terrace, Sunderland, Tyne & Wear, SR4 6DD
Activities: Manufacture of metal structures and parts of structures
Officers: Jill Simmons, Secretary; Claudia Maria Binder [1970] Managing Director [German]; Ralph Saelzer [1958] Director/Works Manager

Lift-Rite Engineering Services Limited
Incorporated: 23 March 2004 *Employees:* 22
Net Worth: £1,482,061 *Total Assets:* £2,534,597
Registered Office: Unit 2 Stephenson Street, Howdon Quays, Wallsend, Tyne & Wear, NE28 6UE
Activities: Other service activities n.e.c.
Parent: Lift-Rite Holdings Limited
Officers: Kenneth McDonald, Secretary/Director; Andrew Philip Clark [1969] Director; Glyn Geach [1971] Director; Alasdair MacDonald [1965] Director; Kenneth McDonald [1964] Director; John Peter Reece [1961] Director

Lift-Rite Holdings Limited
Incorporated: 18 July 2008
Net Worth: £1,935,188 *Total Assets:* £1,966,788
Registered Office: Unit 2 Stephenson Street, Howdon Quays, Wallsend, Tyne & Wear, NE28 6UE
Activities: Activities of head offices
Parent: Benbecula Subsea Services Ltd
Officers: Alasdair MacDonald [1965] Director; Kenneth McDonald [1964] Director; John Peter Reece [1961] Director

Nigel Lightfoot Electrical Contracting Limited
Incorporated: 30 January 2003
Net Worth: £573,716 *Total Assets:* £774,916
Registered Office: Unit 3 County Business Park, Darlington Road, Northallerton, N Yorks, DL6 2NQ
Activities: Electrical installation
Major Shareholder: Nigel David Lightfoot
Officers: Helen Ruth Barnard, Secretary; Helen Ruth Barnard [1966] Director/Office Manager; Nigel David Lightfoot [1965] Director/Electrician

John Lilley & Gillie Limited
Incorporated: 25 November 2016 *Employees:* 32
Net Worth: £1,329,380 *Total Assets:* £2,007,036
Registered Office: Unit 8 Neptune Court, Orion Business Park, North Shields, Tyne & Wear, NE29 7UW
Activities: Manufacture of other special-purpose machinery n.e.c.
Parent: Zollner Holding GmbH
Officers: Glenn Heathcote [1957] Director; Dr. Philipp Alexander Murmann [1964] Director [German]

Limekent Limited
Incorporated: 3 May 1985
Net Worth: £4,129,662 *Total Assets:* £4,154,262
Registered Office: Gladstone House, Gladstone Street, Crook, Co Durham, DL15 9ED
Activities: Artistic creation
Major Shareholder: Royston Vasey
Officers: Richard Vasey, Secretary; Royston Vasey [1945] Director/Entertainer

Lincoln Healthcare Group Limited
Incorporated: 4 July 2003 *Employees:* 80
Net Worth: £850,767 *Total Assets:* £1,136,025
Registered Office: Dene Farm House, 34 Hole Lane, Sunniside, Co Durham, NE16 5NH
Activities: Other human health activities
Major Shareholder: David Barrington Lincoln
Officers: Deborah Susan Thompson, Secretary; David Barrington Lincoln [1958] Director

Lincoln Property Investments Ltd
Incorporated: 1 October 2010
Net Worth: £384,629 *Total Assets:* £1,281,264
Registered Office: Whitegates Equestrian Centre, Snippersgate Farm, South Hetton, Co Durham, DH6 2UQ
Activities: Other letting and operating of own or leased real estate
Major Shareholder: Susan Janet Lincoln
Officers: Stephen Leonard Gair [1990] Director; Susan Janet Lincoln [1962] Director

Linden Foods Burradon Limited
Incorporated: 25 March 1963 *Employees:* 54
Net Worth: £1,661,137 *Total Assets:* £4,227,067
Registered Office: Quarry Cottages, Burradon, Tyne & Wear, NE23 7NE
Activities: Processing and preserving of meat
Officers: Oonagh Catherine Chesney, Secretary; Trevor Lockhart [1971] Director/Chief Executive; Frank Thomas Stephenson [1971] Director [Irish]

Lindisfarne Inns (Bamburgh Castle) Limited
Incorporated: 25 October 2007 *Employees:* 29
Net Worth: £3,995,509 *Total Assets:* £7,426,857
Registered Office: c/o Ward Hadaway, Sandgate House, 102 Quayside, Newcastle upon Tyne, NE1 3DX
Activities: Hotels and similar accommodation
Parent: Inn Collection Bidco Limited
Officers: Angus Keith Liddell, Secretary; Sean Lee Donkin [1981] Operations Director; Angus Keith Liddell [1955] Director; Iain Stein [1959] Director

Lindisfarne Inns Limited
Incorporated: 29 June 2006 *Employees:* 17
Net Worth: £664,075 *Total Assets:* £5,061,035
Registered Office: Sandgate House, 102 Quayside, Newcastle upon Tyne, NE1 3DX
Activities: Hotels and similar accommodation
Parent: Inn Collection Bidco Limited
Officers: Angus Keith Liddell, Secretary; Sean Lee Donkin [1981] Operations Director; Sean Lee Donkin [1981] Managing Director; Angus Keith Liddell [1955] Director; Iain Stein [1959] Director

Lindy Electronics Limited
Incorporated: 19 May 1987 *Employees:* 42
Net Worth: £5,370,756 *Total Assets:* £5,774,196
Registered Office: Unit 103 Sadler Forster Way, Teesside Industrial Estate, Thornaby, Stockton on Tees, Cleveland, TS17 9JY
Activities: Other information technology service activities
Shareholders: Coral Elizabeth Casey; Darren Neil Casey; Lesley Jean Gray
Officers: Darren Casey, Secretary; Coral Elizabeth Casey [1942] Director/Manager; Darren Neil Casey [1971] Managing Director; Lesley Jean Gray [1969] Director/Marketing Manager; Jurgen Lindenberg [1958] Director [German]

Lingfield Education Trust
Incorporated: 12 April 2012 *Employees:* 250
Net Worth: £8,705,000 *Total Assets:* £13,448,000
Registered Office: Suite J-K, Lingfield House, Lingfield Point, Darlington, Co Durham, DL1 1RW
Activities: Primary education
Officers: Nicholas John Blackburn [1968] Director/Headteacher; David John Campbell [1951] Director/Semi-Retired Management Consultant; John Stuart Crowther [1945] Director/Retired; Colin William Eglington [1951] Director/Chairman & MD; David William Elliott [1949] Director/Retired Teacher; Graham FitzGenerald [1973] Director/Chartered Accountant; John Martin [1966] Director/Retired; John Richard Steel [1953] Director/Retired; Kathleen Anne Whitmore [1952] Director/Retired

Lingscars.Com Limited
Incorporated: 22 March 2007
Net Worth: £831,653 *Total Assets:* £1,480,641
Registered Office: 7 Vance Business Park, Gateshead, Tyne & Wear, NE11 9NE
Activities: Sale of new cars and light motor vehicles
Shareholders: Jonathon Andrew Valentine; Ling Valentine
Officers: Ling Valentine, Secretary; Jonathan Andrew Valentine [1963] Director; Ling Valentine [1973] Director

Lingy Moor Farming Ltd
Incorporated: 25 October 2013
Registered Office: North Lingy Moor Farm, Moulton, Richmond, N Yorks, DL10 6QN
Activities: Growing of cereals (except rice), leguminous crops and oil seeds
Officers: Hubert Richard Baker [1941] Director/Farmer; June Barker [1947] Director/Farmer; Richard Townson Barker [1970] Director/Farmer & Furniture Maker

Linhope Farming Company Limited
Incorporated: 11 June 1991
Net Worth: £999,067 *Total Assets:* £1,026,917
Registered Office: Estates Office, Alnwick Castle, Alnwick, Northumberland, NE66 1NQ
Activities: Raising of sheep and goats
Shareholder: Lord James Percy
Officers: Lesley Ann Ilderton, Secretary; Lesley Ann Ilderton [1976] Director/Group Financial Controller; Lord James William Eustace Percy [1965] Director/Landowner; Roderick Charles St John Wilson [1961] Director/Land Agent

Links Court (Whitley Bay) Limited
Incorporated: 10 March 1960 *Employees:* 4
Net Worth: £2,685,495 *Total Assets:* £2,981,570
Registered Office: The Old Post Office, 63 Saville Street, North Shields, Tyne & Wear, NE30 1AY
Activities: Other letting and operating of own or leased real estate
Officers: Mark Alder Gofton, Secretary; Irene Barbara Brown [1942] Director; Mark Alder Gofton [1968] Director; Richard Alder Gofton [1935] Director/Builder; William Alder Gofton [1931] Director/Clergyman

Linthorpe Developments Limited
Incorporated: 2 November 2011
Registered Office: Cleveland Business Centre, Watson Street, Middlesbrough, Cleveland, TS1 2RQ
Activities: Other letting and operating of own or leased real estate
Shareholders: Geoffrey Hogg; Victoria Hogg
Officers: Geoffrey Malcolm John Hogg [1971] Director/Property Developer; Victoria Hogg [1977] Director

Lintron Electronics Limited
Incorporated: 26 April 1988
Net Worth: £270,469 *Total Assets:* £884,818
Registered Office: Unit 6b Wansbeck Business Park, Rotary Park Way, Ashington, Northumberland, NE63 8QW
Activities: Manufacture of electronic components
Parent: Lintron Technologies AB
Officers: Gunilla Margit Magnusson, Secretary; Jan Magnusson [1946] Managing Director [Swedish]

Lintz Green Farms Limited
Incorporated: 3 August 1976
Registered Office: Byermoor Farm Cottage, Fellside Road, Burnopfield, Newcastle upon Tyne, NE16 6BE
Activities: Mixed farming
Major Shareholder: Dominic Eamon Quigley
Officers: Dominic Eamon Quigley, Secretary; Christina May Quigley [1977] Director/Teacher; Dominic Graeme Quigley [1970] Director/Haulage Contractor; Dominic Eamon Quigley [1947] Director/Haulage Contractor; Nolan James Alan Quigley [1972] Director

Lintz Hall Farm Limited
Incorporated: 25 March 1975 *Employees:* 53
Net Worth: £1,099,448 *Total Assets:* £11,007,206
Registered Office: Lintz Hall Farm, Burnopfield, Co Durham, NE16 6AS
Activities: Wholesale of dairy products, eggs and edible oils and fats
Officers: Maureen Tulip, Secretary; Margaret Elizabeth Boland [1948] Director/Retired; George Charles Tulip [1946] Director/Farmer; Maureen Tulip [1949] Director; Richard Tulip [1976] Director; Stephen George Tulip [1973] Director

Lion Care Home Group Limited
Incorporated: 11 December 2009 *Employees:* 203
Net Worth: £369,857 *Total Assets:* £8,176,540
Registered Office: Lion House, 400 Durham Road, Birtley, Co Durham, DH3 1LS
Activities: Residential care activities for the elderly and disabled
Major Shareholder: Stevie Lee Pattinson
Officers: Robert Pattinson [1937] Director/Restaurateur; Stevie-Lee Pattinson [1969] Director/Restaurateur

Lion Garage (Bedlington) Limited
Incorporated: 7 April 1955 *Employees:* 8
Net Worth: £849,192 *Total Assets:* £1,132,369
Registered Office: 15 Front Street West, Bedlington, Northumberland, NE22 5TZ
Activities: Retail sale of automotive fuel in specialised stores
Shareholders: Robert Coulson; Dorothy Mary Coulson; Robert Coulson; John Stewart Coulson
Officers: Dorothy Mary Coulson, Secretary; Dorothy Mary Coulson [1945] Director; John Stewart Coulson [1970] Director; Robert Coulson [1967] Director; Robert Coulson [1942] Director

Liquiform Limited
Incorporated: 17 June 2009 *Employees:* 30
Net Worth: £898,458 *Total Assets:* £2,326,858
Registered Office: Unit 21 North Tyne Industrial Estate, Whitley Road, Benton, Newcastle upon Tyne, NE12 9SZ
Activities: Manufacture of other chemical products n.e.c.
Major Shareholder: Doreen Mallen
Officers: Paul David Thompson, Secretary/Director; Doreen Mallen [1947] Director; Scott Mallen [1975] Director; Paul David Thompson [1969] Director; Brian Wiper [1960] Director

Steve Lister Developments Limited
Incorporated: 28 July 1992 *Employees:* 5
Net Worth: £2,519,754 *Total Assets:* £2,824,071
Registered Office: 23 Yarm Road, Stockton on Tees, Cleveland, TS18 3NJ
Activities: Development of building projects
Shareholders: Stephen John Lister; Christine Lister
Officers: Christine Lister, Secretary; Christine Lister [1957] Director/Secretary; David Stephen Lister [1985] Director; Sebastian Martin Lister [1991] Director; Stephen John Lister [1955] Director; Maria Louise Noonan [1979] Director

Lister House (Fife) Limited
Incorporated: 16 November 2006 *Employees:* 100
Net Worth: £864,122 *Total Assets:* £5,091,314
Registered Office: Cale Cross House, 156 Pilgrim Street, Newcastle upon Tyne, NE1 6SU
Activities: Other human health activities
Officers: Adrian Osborne Hendry [1969] Director; Catherine Joan Hendry [1943] Director; Graeme Allan Hendry [1965] Director

Lite-On Electronics (Europe) Limited
Incorporated: 31 December 1998 *Employees:* 21
Net Worth: £1,396,302 *Total Assets:* £1,529,507
Registered Office: 23 Apex Business Village, Annitsford, Cramlington, Northumberland, NE23 7BF
Activities: Other business support service activities n.e.c.
Officers: Afzul Mohammed, Secretary; Kuang-Chung Chen [1949] Director [Taiwanese]; Afzul Mohammed [1955] Director; Kung Yuan Soong [1942] Director/Chairman [Taiwanese]

The Literary & Philosophical Society of Newcastle upon Tyne
Incorporated: 20 April 2007
Net Worth: £1,197,692 *Total Assets:* £1,234,763
Registered Office: 23 Westgate Road, Newcastle upon Tyne, NE1 1SE
Activities: Library activities
Officers: Dr Katherine Isobel Baxter [1976] Director/Academic; Jeremy Paul Turnbull Bell [1952] Director/Retired; Valerie Ann Boyle [1956] Director/Retired; Margaret Bozic [1950] Director/Retired; Dr Alexander Edward Buchan [1964] Director/Investment Manager; Robin Campbell [1967] Director/Train Driver; Hazel Elizabeth Fleming [1946] Director/Retired; Malcolm Geoffrey Gregor [1932] Director/Retired; Christopher Martin Purser [1943] Director/Retired; Richard Sharp [1953] Director/Retired; Anthony Michael Susman [1948] Director/Retired

Bob Little & Co Limited
Incorporated: 3 February 2004 *Employees:* 13
Net Worth: £844,198 *Total Assets:* £989,847
Registered Office: 29 Howard Street, North Shields, Tyne & Wear, NE30 1AR
Activities: Financial intermediation not elsewhere classified
Major Shareholder: Sharon Little
Officers: Robert Aaron Little [1988] Director/Manager

Little Acorns London Beach Farm Limited
Incorporated: 20 February 2002
Net Worth: £1,521,932 *Total Assets:* £1,553,426
Registered Office: B3 Kingfisher House, Team Valley Trading Estate, Gateshead, Tyne & Wear, NE11 0JQ
Activities: Other residential care activities n.e.c.
Officers: Aized Sheikh [1959] Director

Little Haven Beach Limited
Incorporated: 14 March 1997 *Employees:* 65
Net Worth Deficit: £1,686,209 *Total Assets:* £1,125,834
Registered Office: Little Haven Hotel, River Drive, Little Haven, South Shields, Tyne & Wear, NE33 1LH
Activities: Hotels and similar accommodation
Major Shareholder: Heather Hollingsworth
Officers: Paula Taylor, Secretary; Heather Hollingsworth [1954] Director

Little Learners Sunderland Limited
Incorporated: 26 February 2016 *Employees:* 16
Net Worth: £646,393 *Total Assets:* £1,063,089
Registered Office: 47-50 Ettrick Grove, Sunderland, Tyne & Wear, SR3 4AW
Activities: Pre-primary education
Shareholders: Lawrence Smith; Beverly Smith
Officers: Beverly Smith [1964] Director; Lawrence Smith [1952] Director

Live Smart @ Home Limited
Incorporated: 11 July 1997 *Employees:* 1
Net Worth: £4,929,000 *Total Assets:* £5,286,000
Registered Office: 2 Gosforth Park Way, Gosforth Business Park, Newcastle upon Tyne, NE12 8ET
Activities: Other letting and operating of own or leased real estate
Parent: Home Group Limited
Officers: Austin Jonathan Woods, Secretary; Rosemary Du Rose [1965] Executive Director; Mark Gideon Henderson [1962] Director/Chief Executive; Dr John Matthew Hudson [1968] Director/Chief Financial Officer

Liveco Limited
Incorporated: 15 November 2004 *Employees:* 41
Net Worth: £2,236,608 *Total Assets:* £4,789,303
Registered Office: 2 Henson Close, South Church Enterprise Park, Bishop Auckland, Co Durham, DL14 6WA
Activities: Development of building projects
Shareholders: Gavin Vest; Darren Cooke
Officers: Gavin Vest, Secretary/Construction Director; Darren Cooke [1961] Contracts Director; Gavin Vest [1970] Construction Director

Liverpool Portfolio Ltd
Incorporated: 24 October 2014
Registered Office: Portland House, Belmont Business Park, Durham, DH1 1TW
Activities: Other letting and operating of own or leased real estate
Shareholders: Thomas Christopher Hartley; Rhodes Estates Ltd
Officers: Nicholas Cecil John Fortescue [1953] Director/Consultant; Thomas Christopher Hartley [1951] Director/Photographer

Liveworks (Newcastle upon Tyne) Ltd
Incorporated: 7 April 2014
Net Worth Deficit: £136,743 *Total Assets:* £4,500,212
Registered Office: 29 Broad Chare, Newcastle upon Tyne, NE1 3DQ
Activities: Operation of arts facilities
Parent: North East Theatre Trust Ltd
Officers: James Patrick Beirne [1951] Director; Paul Michael Callaghan [1952] Director; Michelle Frances Percy [1968] Director

Living Lets Ltd
Incorporated: 17 March 2015
Net Worth Deficit: £23,732 *Total Assets:* £815,275
Registered Office: 55 Marden Road, Whitley Bay, Tyne & Wear, NE26 2JW
Activities: Other letting and operating of own or leased real estate
Shareholders: John Paul Gardner; Clark Anthony Fielding; Mark Gardner
Officers: Clark Anthony Fielding [1977] Director/Self Employed; John Paul Gardner [1971] Director/Self Employed; Mark Gardner [1974] Director/Self Employed

John Livingston & Sons,Limited
Incorporated: 15 May 1924 *Employees:* 4
Net Worth: £2,767,872 *Total Assets:* £3,709,193
Registered Office: The Works, North Ormesby Road, Middlesbrough, Cleveland, TS4 2AG
Activities: Activities of other holding companies n.e.c.
Shareholder: Bernard John Ord
Officers: Allison Mary McPherson [1962] Director; Andrew John Ord [1964] Director/Stockbroker; Bernard John Ord [1935] Director; Gillian Ann Ord [1958] Director

John Livingston (Estates) Limited
Incorporated: 26 July 1972 *Employees:* 3
Net Worth: £3,247,148 *Total Assets:* £6,121,856
Registered Office: The Works, North Ormesby Road, Middlesbrough, Cleveland, TS4 2AG
Activities: Other letting and operating of own or leased real estate
Parent: John Livingston Estates Holdings Ltd
Officers: Alison Mary McPherson [1962] Director; Andrew John Ord [1964] Director; Bernard John Ord [1935] Director; Gillian Ann Ord [1958] Director

LJJ Holdings Limited
Incorporated: 25 April 2016
Net Worth: £18,252,468 *Total Assets:* £38,061,920
Registered Office: Richmond House, 107 Bowesfield Lane, Stockton on Tees, Cleveland, TS18 3HF
Activities: Activities of head offices
Shareholder: Ian Ronald Rennison
Officers: Johnathan Daly [1968] Operations Director; Ian Ronald Rennison [1960] Managing Director; Ian-Lee Rennison [1978] Finance/Commercial Director; Jai David Rennison [1981] Operations Director

LJJ Ltd
Incorporated: 14 June 2001 *Employees:* 122
Net Worth: £7,075,778 *Total Assets:* £23,706,242
Registered Office: Richmond House, 107 Bowesfield Lane, Stockton on Tees, Cleveland, TS18 3HF
Activities: Other specialised construction activities n.e.c.
Parent: LJJ Holding Ltd
Officers: Stephen John Baines, Secretary; Jonathan Rory Daly [1968] Regional Director; Philip Paul Eykel [1960] Construction Director; Ian Ronald Rennison [1960] Director/Engineering; Jai Rennison [1981] Operations Director; Lee Rennison [1978] Commercial Director

LJWC Limited
Incorporated: 22 May 2015
Registered Office: Malpas House, 11 South Parade, Northallerton, N Yorks, DL7 8SE
Activities: Dental practice activities
Major Shareholder: Dr Luke Joseph Walter Charnley
Officers: Luke Joseph Walter Charnley [1986] Director

Llangwyryfon Windfarm Limited
Incorporated: 20 November 1991
Net Worth: £2,680,000 *Total Assets:* £5,181,000
Registered Office: Alexander House, 1 Mandarin Road, Rainton Bridge Business Park, Houghton-le-Spring, Co Durham, DH4 5RA
Activities: Production of electricity
Parent: EDF Energy Renewables Holdings Limited
Officers: Susan Elizabeth Lind, Secretary; Matthieu Thomas Hue [1975] Director [French]; Hassaan Majid [1968] Director

LO (Roscommon) Properties Limited
Incorporated: 28 November 2014 *Employees:* 2
Net Worth: £864,833 *Total Assets:* £4,382,070
Registered Office: 30 Yoden Way, Peterlee, Co Durham, SR8 1AL
Activities: Management of real estate on a fee or contract basis
Shareholder: Aileen O'Gara
Officers: Jessika O'Gara [1992] Director/Hairdresser [Irish]; Phoebe O'Gara [1997] Director/Student [Irish]

Loanchoice Limited
Incorporated: 10 May 2012
Net Worth: £351,594 *Total Assets:* £1,045,442
Registered Office: 1 Westpark Drive, Darlington, Co Durham, DL3 0TB
Activities: Activities of mortgage finance companies
Shareholder: Neil Rennard
Officers: Neil Rennard [1957] Director; John Richard Robinson [1959] Director

Lockwell Limited
Incorporated: 30 October 1989 *Employees:* 25
Net Worth: £324,018 *Total Assets:* £1,031,726
Registered Office: Unit 269a Queensway South, Team Valley Trading Estate, Gateshead, Tyne & Wear, NE11 0SD
Activities: Repair and maintenance of other transport equipment n.e.c.
Officers: Michelle Storey, Secretary; John David Hutton [1968] Director; Alan Frederick Maidwell [1933] Director; Andrew Philip Maidwell [1962] Managing Director; Fiona Carol Maidwell [1961] Director; Margaret Francis Maidwell [1933] Director and Secretary; Kevin Monaghan [1968] Director

Lofthouse and Partners Limited
Incorporated: 26 November 2001 *Employees:* 6
Net Worth: £301,335 *Total Assets:* £941,621
Registered Office: 51 Frederick Street, Sunderland, Tyne & Wear, SR1 1NF
Activities: Real estate agencies
Shareholders: Mario Jaconelli; Marc John Weaver; Lofthouse & Partners (Holdings) Limited
Officers: Mario Jaconelli, Secretary; Mario Jaconelli [1972] Director/Surveyor; Marc John Weaver [1973] Director/Chartered Surveyor

Loftus Agrius LLP
Incorporated: 10 December 2014
Net Worth: £3,738,505 *Total Assets:* £5,485,323
Registered Office: 7 Calderdale, Skelton in Cleveland, Saltburn-by-the-Sea, N Yorks, TS12 2WD

Logic Manufacturing Limited
Incorporated: 19 May 1986 *Employees:* 28
Net Worth: £1,245,183 *Total Assets:* £1,950,577
Registered Office: Foundry Industrial Estate, Bridge End, Hexham, Northumberland, NE46 4JL
Activities: Manufacture of other general-purpose machinery n.e.c.
Shareholders: Brian Robert Cordiner; Simon James Beniams
Officers: Brian Robert Cordiner, Secretary; Simon James Beniams [1963] Director; Brian Robert Cordiner [1948] Director; John Dennis Purdy [1955] Director

Logical Link Solutions Limited
Incorporated: 16 April 1971 *Employees:* 10
Net Worth: £1,655,000 *Total Assets:* £2,445,000
Registered Office: 17-27 Queen's Square, Middlesbrough, Cleveland, TS2 1AH
Activities: Freight transport by road
Parent: PD Ports Hull Limited
Officers: Dermot Michael Russell, Secretary; Johannes Franciscus Calje [1972] Director [Dutch]; Jeremy Mark Hopkinson [1955] Director; Dermot Michael Russell [1965] Director/Accountant

Londinium A & C LLP
Incorporated: 8 December 2004 *Employees:* 685
Net Worth: £18,590,276 *Total Assets:* £77,325,776
Registered Office: Unit 1 Hetton Lyons Industrial Estate, Hetton-le-Hole, Houghton-le-Spring, Co Durham, DH5 0RH
Officers: Ralph Karl Paul Buchholz [1968] Member; Susanne Sylvia Buchholz-Spillmann [1969] Member

London & Birmingham Railway Limited
Incorporated: 12 May 2006 *Employees:* 2,508
Net Worth: £24,131,000 *Total Assets:* £139,522,000
Registered Office: 3rd Floor, 41-51 Grey Street, Newcastle upon Tyne, NE1 6EE
Activities: Passenger rail transport, interurban
Parent: Govia Limited
Officers: Carolyn Ferguson, Secretary; David Allen Brown [1960] Director; Simon Patrick Butcher [1967] Finance Director; Alistair John Francis Gordon [1968] Director; Ian McLaren [1968] Finance and Contracts Director

London & Regional Capital Ltd
Incorporated: 24 February 1999 *Employees:* 1
Net Worth Deficit: £108,670 *Total Assets:* £5,978,627
Registered Office: Tower Buildings, 9 Oldgate, Morpeth, Northumberland, NE61 1PY
Activities: Dormant company
Parent: Acornford Holdings Ltd
Officers: Paul Andrew Brown, Secretary/Accountant; Ian Charles Cawkwell [1957] Director/Businessman

London & South Eastern Railway Limited
Incorporated: 8 August 2003 *Employees:* 4,186
Net Worth: £50,925,000 *Total Assets:* £327,500,992
Registered Office: 3rd Floor, 41-51 Grey Street, Newcastle upon Tyne, NE1 6EE
Activities: Passenger rail transport, interurban
Parent: Govia Limited
Officers: Carolyn Ferguson, Secretary; Elodie Brian [1979] Finance and Contracts Director [French]; David Allen Brown [1960] Director; Simon Patrick Butcher [1967] Finance Director; Alistair John Francis Gordon [1968] Director; Charles Anthony Hodgson [1979] Managing Director - Rail Development; David Ira Statham [1968] Director; Bernard Denis Maurice Tabary [1960] Director [French]

London and North Western Railway Company Limited
Incorporated: 13 December 1993 *Employees:* 247
Net Worth: £8,406,000 *Total Assets:* £23,525,000
Registered Office: Admiral Way, Doxford International Business Park, Sunderland, Tyne & Wear, SR3 3XP
Activities: Passenger rail transport, interurban
Officers: Lorna Edwards, Secretary; Christopher Derek Dyne Burchell [1973] Director; Sean Peter Forster [1965] Director; Amanda Furlong [1975] Director; Mary Elisabeth Courtney Hewitt [1979] Director; Gillian Ingham [1968] Director

London General Transport Services Limited
Incorporated: 14 December 1988 *Employees:* 7,069
Net Worth: £29,604,000 *Total Assets:* £176,364,992
Registered Office: 3rd Floor, 41-51 Grey Street, Newcastle upon Tyne, NE1 6EE
Activities: Other urban, suburban or metropolitan passenger land transport (not underground, metro or similar)
Parent: Go-Ahead Holding Limited
Officers: Carolyn Ferguson, Secretary; David Allen Brown [1960] Director; Simon Patrick Butcher [1967] Finance Director; David Arthur Cutts [1969] Operations Director; Richard Harrington [1967] Engineering Director; Michael John Slattery [1967] Finance Director [Irish]; John Trayner [1959] Director

Londonderry Garage (S.E.) Limited
Incorporated: 27 February 2015 *Employees:* 46
Net Worth: £281,718 *Total Assets:* £4,581,971
Registered Office: Londonderry Garage, Londonderry, Northallerton, N Yorks, DL7 9NB
Activities: Repair of machinery
Major Shareholder: Michael James Ward
Officers: Scott Woolston [1977] Director

Chas. Long & Son (Aggregates) Limited
Incorporated: 11 March 2003 *Employees:* 67
Net Worth: £3,818,210 *Total Assets:* £7,431,104
Registered Office: Woodside, North Road, Brompton on Swale, Richmond, N Yorks, DL10 7JL
Activities: Wholesale of other intermediate products
Shareholders: Charles Barry Long; Charles David Long; Mark Andrew Long
Officers: Barbara Anne Horn, Secretary; Charles Barry Long [1943] Director/Haulier; Charles David Long [1969] Director/Haulier; Mark Andrew Long [1973] Director/Mechanic

Longden Walker and Renney (Solicitors) Limited
Incorporated: 5 April 2012 *Employees:* 42
Net Worth: £1,549,987 *Total Assets:* £2,066,684
Registered Office: 14 John Street, Sunderland, Tyne & Wear, SR1 1HZ
Activities: Solicitors
Officers: Alison Jane Ainsley [1962] Director/Solicitor; Pamela Ann Ayres [1965] Director/Solicitor; Katie Cummings [1982] Director/Solicitor; Richard Anthony Ebdon [1952] Director/Solicitor; Neil Ian Heavisides [1970] Director/Solicitor; Dermot Hume Kirkwood [1955] Director/Solicitor; John Paul Lowther [1983] Director/Solicitor; David Nesbitt [1958] Director/Solicitor; Zena Warburton [1976] Director

Longfield Academy Trust
Incorporated: 11 July 2011
Registered Office: Longfield Academy, Longfield Road, Darlington, Co Durham, DL3 0HT
Activities: General secondary education
Officers: Glen Hart, Secretary; Robert Bell [1980] Director/Accountant; Hazel Bullock [1951] Director/Retired; Emily Cheesman [1979] Director/Governor Support Manager; Timothy John Fisher [1967] Director/Principal Sixth Form College; Kelly Anne Lyle [1982] Director/Parent; Mark Steven White [1957] Director/Retired

Longhirst Development Limited
Incorporated: 17 April 2015
Net Worth: £108,873 *Total Assets:* £6,982,148
Registered Office: The Farm House, Hedley Hill Farm, Cornsay Colliery, Co Durham, DH7 9EX
Activities: Buying and selling of own real estate
Parent: VB Turnbull Ltd
Officers: Philip Sidney Coates, Secretary; Michael Francis Hogan [1944] Director

Longhoughton Community and Sports Centre Trust
Incorporated: 26 September 2009
Net Worth: £1,180,209 *Total Assets:* £1,181,376
Registered Office: Westfield Park, Park Road, Longhoughton, Alnwick, Northumberland, NE66 3JH
Activities: Activities of other membership organisations n.e.c.
Officers: Adrian William Hinchcliffe, Secretary; Andrew Paul Crosby [1972] Director/Commissioned Officer in The RAF; Adrian William Hinchcliffe [1944] Director/Retired; Victoria Irene Kelly [1974] Director/Civil Servant; Carol Kirkham [1961] Director/Associate Secretary; Fiona Kay Nelson-Van Loon [1972] Director/Self Employed; Eleanor Phillips [1958] Director; Lynsey Punton [1977] Director/Waitress; Scott Rowntree [1971] Director/RAF Officer; James Bowman Wanless [1948] Director/Retired

J & D Longlands Ltd
Incorporated: 16 August 2002 *Employees:* 5
Net Worth: £589,153 *Total Assets:* £905,964
Registered Office: Tone Hall Farm, Birtley, Hexham, Northumberland, NE48 3JL
Activities: Raising of other cattle and buffaloes
Shareholders: John Longlands; David Eddy Longlands
Officers: John Longlands, Secretary/Farmer; David Eddy Longlands [1954] Director/Farmer; John Longlands [1951] Director/Farmer

Longpark Windfarm Limited
Incorporated: 26 September 2008
Net Worth: £17,745,000 *Total Assets:* £48,849,000
Registered Office: Alexander House, 1 Mandarin Road, Rainton Bridge Business Park, Houghton-le-Spring, Co Durham, DH4 5RA
Activities: Production of electricity
Parent: EDF Energy Renewables Holdings Limited
Officers: Susan Elizabeth Lind, Secretary; Matthieu Thomas Hue [1975] Director [French]; Hassaan Majid [1968] Director

Longstaffs Travel Ltd
Incorporated: 30 May 2013
Net Worth: £6,752 *Total Assets:* £1,484,809
Registered Office: Unit 107 Coquet Enterprise Park, Amble, Northumberland, NE65 0PE
Activities: Other passenger land transport
Shareholder: Glyn Griffiths
Officers: Glyn Griffiths [1950] Business Director; Raymond Wilkinson [1950] Director

Lool Shulan Ltd
Incorporated: 27 October 2009
Net Worth: £1,745,301 *Total Assets:* £1,875,317
Registered Office: 43 Coniscliffe Road, Darlington, Co Durham, DL3 7EH
Activities: Specialists medical practice activities
Major Shareholder: Dr Mahfoodh Abdulla Mahyoub Abbas
Officers: Dr Mahfoodh Abdulla Mahyoub Abbas [1965] Director/Doctor

Looprevil (North East) Limited
Incorporated: 11 September 2008
Net Worth: £131,246 *Total Assets:* £1,650,305
Registered Office: Rowlands House, Portobello Road, Birtley, Chester-le-Street, Co Durham, DH3 2RY
Activities: Management of real estate on a fee or contract basis
Shareholders: Peter Ramsay Fergusson; Kathleen Dianne Fergusson
Officers: Peter Ramsay Fergusson [1952] Director

R.Lord & Co.(Newcastle) Limited
Incorporated: 15 June 1971 *Employees:* 62
Net Worth: £1,041,466 *Total Assets:* £1,773,723
Registered Office: 337 Shields Road, Byker Hill, Newcastle upon Tyne, NE6 2UD
Activities: Renting and leasing of construction and civil engineering machinery and equipment
Officers: Christopher John Rowley [1955] Director/General Manager

Lord Lawson of Beamish Academy
Incorporated: 13 January 2012 *Employees:* 148
Net Worth: £1,698,154 *Total Assets:* £4,251,799
Registered Office: Lord Lawson of Beamish Academy, Birtley Lane, Birtley, Co Durham, DH3 2LP
Activities: General secondary education
Officers: Norine Hazel Charlton, Secretary; Councillor Michael Hood [1954] Director/Local Councillor; David Thomas Horn [1966] Director; Albert Hutchinson Leaf [1952] Director/Retired; Alison Jane Logan [1968] Director; Mark Lovatt [1964] Director/Principal; Kim Michelle Marshall [1971] Director/Specialist Community Public Health Nurse; Caroline Matthias [1946] Director/Office Administrator; Elena Maria Ovington [1970] Director/Learning Support Assistant; Angela Robertson [1967] Director/Teaching Assistant; Brian Scurr [1966] Director/Police Service - Detention Officer; Christopher Peter Smith [1986] Director/Solicitor; Tracey Wallace [1969] Director/Development Manager/Lecturer

Lord Technical (Holdco) Limited
Incorporated: 24 May 2012
Net Worth: £348,286 *Total Assets:* £847,979
Registered Office: Lord Technical Limited, Deptford Road, Gateshead, Tyne & Wear, NE8 3AZ
Activities: Other specialised construction activities n.e.c.
Major Shareholder: John Andrew Lightfoot
Officers: John Andrew Lightfoot [1970] Director

Lord Technical Limited
Incorporated: 7 April 1986 *Employees:* 8
Net Worth: £1,274,748 *Total Assets:* £1,484,871
Registered Office: Deptford Road, Gateshead, Tyne & Wear, NE8 3AZ
Activities: Repair of electronic and optical equipment
Major Shareholder: John Andrew Lightfoot
Officers: John Andrew Lightfoot [1970] Director

Lordstones Developments Limited
Incorporated: 22 October 2001
Net Worth: £10,211,559 *Total Assets:* £21,203,388
Registered Office: 4 Ellerbeck Way, Stokesley Business Park, Stokesley, Middlesbrough, Cleveland, TS9 5JZ
Activities: Development of building projects
Parent: Carlton Investment (Holdings) Ltd
Officers: Jayne Margaret Hodgson, Secretary; Michael Fred Shaw Benson [1964] Director/Engineer; Keith Clarke [1960] Director; Jayne Margaret Hodgson [1963] Finance Director; David John Philpot [1961] Director/Legal Counsel; Matthew Ian Shields [1944] Director/Engineer; Alan White [1961] Finance Director

Lotte Chemical UK Limited
Incorporated: 18 December 2009 *Employees:* 121
Net Worth Deficit: £65,334,000 *Total Assets:* £189,862,000
Registered Office: Davies Offices, Wilton International, Redcar, Cleveland, TS10 4XZ
Activities: Manufacture of other chemical products n.e.c.
Officers: Sung Wook Cho [1973] Director/General Manager of Global Management Team [South Korean]; Min Jae Hwang [1971] Director [South Korean]; Myung Chul Jung [1975] Director/General Manager of Corporate Planning Team [Korean]; Jung Neon Kim [1965] Managing Director [South Korean]; Hugh Trenchard [1951] Director/Investment Banker

Louie (Holdings) Limited
Incorporated: 18 May 2007 *Employees:* 4
Net Worth: £5,064,217 *Total Assets:* £5,069,943
Registered Office: Louie House, Lancaster Road, Dunston Industrial Estate, Gateshead, Tyne & Wear, NE11 9JN
Activities: Activities of head offices
Officers: Ashok Kumar Babuta, Secretary; Archna Babuta [1968] Director; Ashok Kumar Babuta [1966] Director/Clothier; Bushan Babuta [1962] Director/Clothier; Rekha Babuta [1961] Director

Louietex Ltd
Incorporated: 6 October 2008 *Employees:* 25
Net Worth: £524,237 *Total Assets:* £2,871,560
Registered Office: Louie House, Lancaster Road, Dunston Industrial Estate, Gateshead, Tyne & Wear, NE11 9JR
Activities: Wholesale of clothing and footwear
Parent: Louie (Holdings Ltd)
Officers: Balraj Babuta, Secretary; Shashi Bushan Babuta [1962] Director

Low Carbon Lighting Limited
Incorporated: 29 March 2010
Net Worth Deficit: £179,441 *Total Assets:* £1,109,093
Registered Office: Unit 12 Easter Park, Cramlington, Northumberland, NE23 1WQ
Activities: Other manufacturing n.e.c.
Officers: Paul David Brown [1979] Director; Michael William McNeill [1965] Director; Dr Clive Taunton Rankin [1946] Director

Low Grange Quarry Limited
Incorporated: 24 April 2003
Net Worth: £2,638,773 *Total Assets:* £3,735,079
Registered Office: Low Grange Quarry, Low Grange, Melsonby, Richmond, N Yorks, DL10 5PN
Activities: Other business support service activities n.e.c.
Officers: David Austin Richardson, Secretary; David Austin Richardson [1976] Director/Farmer; David Richardson [1949] Director/Farmer; Fiona Kathleen Richardson [1971] Director

John Low Limited
Incorporated: 2 February 1954 *Employees:* 21
Net Worth: £1,019,182 *Total Assets:* £1,374,653
Registered Office: 25a Hope Street, Crook, Co Durham, DL15 9HS
Activities: Dispensing chemist in specialised stores
Shareholders: Rachel Mary Hurst; Hilary Chapman
Officers: Hilary Jane Chapman [1976] Director/Dispensing Technician; Matthew Stuart Hurst [1977] Director; Rachel Mary Hurst [1974] Director/Pharmacist

Lowcock Properties Limited
Incorporated: 31 July 1922 *Employees:* 4
Net Worth: £4,951,109 *Total Assets:* £5,537,275
Registered Office: 3 Kingfisher Court, Bowesfield Park, Stockton on Tees, Cleveland, TS18 3EX
Activities: Development of building projects
Shareholders: Richard William Lowcock; Martin James Lowcock
Officers: Beverley Adele Lowcock, Secretary; Martin James Lowcock, Secretary; Beverley Adele Lowcock [1971] Director; John Martin Lowcock [1941] Director/Factory Manager; Richard William Lowcock [1971] Director/Security Systems Engineer

Lowe & Simpson Group Limited
Incorporated: 4 June 1979 *Employees:* 52
Net Worth: £1,095,439 *Total Assets:* £2,356,917
Registered Office: Vickers Close, Preston Farm Industrial Estate, Stockton on Tees, Cleveland, TS18 3HD
Activities: Other manufacturing n.e.c.
Major Shareholder: John Spencer Haddon
Officers: John Spencer Haddon, Secretary; John Spencer Haddon [1955] Director/Estimator/Surveyor; Tony Leach [1963] Director; Paul Frederick Pearson [1967] Director

Lowes Financial Management Limited
Incorporated: 29 May 1973 *Employees:* 42
Net Worth: £1,071,555 *Total Assets:* £1,695,026
Registered Office: Fernwood House, Clayton Road, Newcastle upon Tyne, NE2 1TL
Activities: Financial intermediation not elsewhere classified
Parent: Lowes Group PLC
Officers: Jeremy Hall, Secretary; Ian Hamilton Lowes [1969] Director/Financial Advisor; Neil Anthony McLachlan [1962] Director/Compliance Manager

Lowes Group PLC
Incorporated: 2 November 1989 *Employees:* 51
Net Worth: £3,313,860 *Total Assets:* £6,046,041
Registered Office: Fernwood House, Clayton Road, Newcastle upon Tyne, NE2 1TL
Activities: Activities of head offices
Shareholders: Ian Hamilton Lowes; Peter Hamilton Lowes
Officers: Jeremy Hall, Secretary; Jeremy Hall [1964] Director/Accountant; Ian Hamilton Lowes [1969] Director/Financial Advisor; Neil Anthony McLachlan [1962] Director/Compliance Manager; Caroline Jean Robinson [1956] Director/Administrator

Lowfield Street Limited
Incorporated: 30 July 2015
Net Worth: £3,591,518 *Total Assets:* £8,543,860
Registered Office: Seaton Burn House, Dudley Lane, Seaton Burn, Newcastle upon Tyne, NE13 6BE
Activities: Development of building projects
Parent: Bellway Homes Limited
Officers: Simon Scougall, Secretary; Keith Derek Adey [1979] Director; Jason Michael Honeyman [1968] Director

Lowrie Foods Limited
Incorporated: 3 February 1984 *Employees:* 28
Net Worth: £2,880,981 *Total Assets:* £3,444,949
Registered Office: 153 Brinkburn Street South, Newcastle upon Tyne, NE6 2BU
Activities: Manufacture of other food products n.e.c.
Major Shareholder: Thomas Stewart Lowrie
Officers: Rosalind Tench, Secretary; Martin Alexander Curran [1957] Director; Thomas Stewart Lowrie [1972] Director

LPT Trading Ltd
Incorporated: 22 January 2013
Net Worth: £190 *Total Assets:* £15,070,979
Registered Office: Floor 6, Vinovium House, Saddler Street, Bishop Auckland, Co Durham, DL14 7BH
Activities: Activities of other holding companies n.e.c.
Officers: Peter John Chapman, Secretary; Matthew Charles Arthur Hutton [1953] Director/Farmer; Harriet Cecilia Ruffer [1990] Director/Research Assistant; Dr Jane Mary Ruffer [1956] Director; Jonathan Garnier Ruffer [1951] Director; Nicholas Timothy Turner [1961] Director/Retired; Ashe George Russell Windham [1957] Director (Financial Services)

LSL Corporate Client Services Limited
Incorporated: 29 June 2010 *Employees:* 87
Net Worth: £2,239,000 *Total Assets:* £22,596,000
Registered Office: Newcastle House, Albany Court, Newcastle Business Park, Newcastle upon Tyne, NE4 7YB
Activities: Management of real estate on a fee or contract basis
Parent: LSL Property Services PLC
Officers: Sapna Bedi FitzGenerald, Secretary; Helen Elizabeth Buck [1960] Director; Adam Robert Castleton [1964] Director; Paul Hardy [1976] Director; James Charles McAuley [1954] Director

LSL Property Services PLC
Incorporated: 27 April 2004 *Employees:* 4,630
Net Worth: £128,582,000 *Total Assets:* £249,620,000
Registered Office: Newcastle House, Albany Court, Newcastle Business Park, Newcastle upon Tyne, NE4 7YB
Activities: Activities of other holding companies n.e.c.
Officers: Sapna Bedi FitzGenerald, Secretary/Solicitor; Kumsal Bayazit Besson [1974] Director [Turkish/French]; Helen Elizabeth Buck [1960] Director; Adam Robert Castleton [1964] Director; Ian Denis Crabb [1959] Director; Simon David Embley [1960] Director; William Mervyn Frew Carey Shannon [1949] Director; David Stewart [1965] Director

LSLI Limited
Incorporated: 14 December 2006 *Employees:* 14
Net Worth Deficit: £9,606,000 *Total Assets:* £26,031,000
Registered Office: Newcastle House, Albany Court, Newcastle Business Park, Newcastle upon Tyne, NE4 7YB
Activities: Activities of other holding companies n.e.c.
Parent: LSL Property Services PLC
Officers: Sapna Bedi FitzGenerald, Secretary; Greig Barker [1969] Finance Director; Helen Elizabeth Buck [1960] Director; Adam Robert Castleton [1964] Director; Simon Cox [1967] Director; Andrew Paul Trantum [1967] Financial Services Director; Gregory Winston Young [1966] Director

LTH Cash & Carry Limited
Incorporated: 4 July 2001
Net Worth: £1,879,729 *Total Assets:* £3,745,404
Registered Office: Unit One Storey Court, Dunne Road, Blaydon on Tyne, Tyne & Wear, NE21 5NH
Activities: Non-specialised wholesale trade
Major Shareholder: Kit Keung Lau
Officers: Kit Keung Lau, Secretary; Karen Sau Kin Lau [1969] Director/Restaurateur; Kit Keung Lau [1965] Director; Jian Xiong Zeng [1979] Director

LTS Refurbishment Limited
Incorporated: 13 January 1997 *Employees:* 4
Net Worth: £704,077 *Total Assets:* £4,764,070
Registered Office: Beaufront Park, Alnwick Road, Hexham, Northumberland, NE46 4TU
Activities: Other building completion and finishing
Officers: Charlie Johnson, Secretary; Gillian Frances Banks [1956] Finance Director; Charles Darren Johnson [1965] Director/Building Contractor; Jonathan Tice [1968] Commercial Director; Colin Alister Generald Wint [1969] Contracts Director

Lubbers (UK) Limited
Incorporated: 12 December 1996 *Employees:* 77
Net Worth: £1,761,330 *Total Assets:* £5,663,103
Registered Office: 11 Atley Way, Nelson Industrial Estate, Cramlington, Northumberland, NE23 1WA
Activities: Freight transport by road
Parent: Lubbers Transport Group B.V.
Officers: Johannes Gerardus Engelsman [1965] Director/Chief Executive Officer [Dutch]; Stuart Martin Ferguson [1963] Regional Director UK; Nicholas Falkner Latham [1989] Regional Sales and Marketing Director UK; Dirk Hendrik Mulder [1967] Director/Chief Financial Officer [Dutch]; Anthony Ronald Tailford [1967] Director/Haulier

Lucion Environmental Limited
Incorporated: 6 February 2008 *Employees:* 222
Net Worth: £7,241,131 *Total Assets:* £12,485,076
Registered Office: Unit 7 Halifax Court, Dunston, Gateshead, Tyne & Wear, NE11 9JT
Activities: Environmental consulting activities
Parent: Lucion Services Limited
Officers: Ross Boulton [1982] Director; Ian Jonathan Grant [1949] Director/Chartered Accountant; Dr Patrick Alexander Joseph Morton [1975] Director; Charles Edmund Pickles [1975] Director; Philip Michael Rozier [1979] Director

Lucion Services Limited
Incorporated: 6 March 2015 *Employees:* 240
Net Worth: £6,013,188 *Total Assets:* £11,324,500
Registered Office: Unit 7 Halifax Court, Dunston, Gateshead, Tyne & Wear, NE11 9JT
Activities: Environmental consulting activities
Shareholders: Dr Patrick Alexander Joseph Morton; Charles Edmund Pickles
Officers: Jaclyn Morton, Secretary; Lina Pickles, Secretary; Ross Boulton [1982] Director; Ian Jonathan Grant [1949] Director/Chartered Accountant; Adam Thomas Mead [1982] Director/Chief Operating Officer; Dr Patrick Alexander Joseph Morton [1975] Director; Charles Edmund Pickles [1975] Director; Philip Michael Rozier [1979] Director

Lucite International China Holdings Limited
Incorporated: 15 October 2002
Net Worth: £41,008,052 *Total Assets:* £41,008,052
Registered Office: Cassel Works, New Road, Billingham, Cleveland, TS23 1LE
Activities: Activities of other holding companies n.e.c.
Parent: Lucite International Singapore Holdings Pte. Ltd.
Officers: Heng Fong Dian, Secretary/Finance Controller [Singaporean]; Heng Fong Dian [1965] Director/Finance Controller [Singaporean]; Satoshi Kurokawa [1960] Director [Japanese]; Chee Ming Tok [1970] Director/Commercial & Supply Chain Manager [Singaporean]

Lucite International Finco Limited
Incorporated: 23 August 1999
Net Worth Deficit: £309,797,184 *Total Assets:* £740,158,080
Registered Office: Cassel Works, New Road, Billingham, Cleveland, TS23 1LE
Activities: Other credit granting n.e.c.
Parent: Mitsubishi Chemical Lucite Group Limited
Officers: Colin Neil Cuthill, Secretary; Philip James Bailey [1966] Director/Chemical Site Manager; Colin Neil Cuthill [1967] Director/Accountant; Nigel Scott Jackson [1966] Director/Finance Manager; Dai Oyama [1968] Director [Japanese]

Lucite International Holdco Limited
Incorporated: 23 August 1999
Net Worth: £97,002,688 *Total Assets:* £140,247,536
Registered Office: Cassel Works, New Road, Billingham, Cleveland, TS23 1LE
Activities: Activities of head offices
Parent: Mitsubishi Chemical Lucite Group Limited
Officers: Colin Neil Cuthill, Secretary; Philip James Bailey [1966] Director/Chemical Site Manager; Colin Neil Cuthill [1967] Director/Accountant; Robert Trevor Dunkley [1952] Director/Lawyer; Dai Oyama [1968] Director [Japanese]

Lucite International Speciality Polymers and Resins Limited
Incorporated: 12 January 1933 *Employees:* 61
Net Worth: £9,900,000 *Total Assets:* £27,900,000
Registered Office: Cassel Works, New Road, Billingham, Cleveland, TS23 1LE
Activities: Manufacture of plastics in primary forms
Parent: Lucite International Holdco Limited
Officers: Colin Neil Cuthill, Secretary; Philip James Bailey [1966] Director/Chemical Site Manager; Colin Neil Cuthill [1967] Director/Accountant; Dirk Cornelis Hoogerdijk [1963] Marketing Director [Dutch]; Caroline Prior [1969] Director

Lucite International Trading Limited
Incorporated: 23 August 1999 *Employees:* 11
Net Worth: £1,100,000 *Total Assets:* £1,300,000
Registered Office: Cassel Works, New Road, Billingham, Cleveland, TS23 1LE
Activities: Activities of head offices
Parent: Lucite International Holdco Limited
Officers: Colin Neil Cuthill, Secretary; Philip James Bailey [1966] Director/Chemical Site Manager; Colin Neil Cuthill [1967] Director/Accountant

Lucite International UK Limited
Incorporated: 23 August 1999 *Employees:* 618
Net Worth: £145,900,000 *Total Assets:* £268,700,000
Registered Office: Cassel Works, New Road, Billingham, Cleveland, TS23 1LE
Activities: Manufacture of plastics in primary forms
Parent: Lucite International Holdco Limited
Officers: Colin Neil Cuthill, Secretary; Philip James Bailey [1966] Director/Chemical Site Manager; Colin Neil Cuthill [1967] Director/Accountant; Melanie Jane Jury [1967] Site Director; Clive James Makin [1962] Director/General Manager; Takashi Miyaki [1956] Director/Business Executive [Japanese]; Ansgar Maria Pohl [1958] Director/Executive Officer [German]

Lucite International UK Overseas Holdco1 Limited
Incorporated: 23 August 1999
Net Worth: £107,813,896 *Total Assets:* £107,888,456
Registered Office: Cassel Works, New Road, Billingham, Cleveland, TS23 1LE
Activities: Activities of head offices
Parent: Lucite International Holdco Limited
Officers: Colin Neil Cuthill, Secretary; Philip James Bailey [1966] Director/Chemical Site Manager; Colin Neil Cuthill [1967] Director/Accountant; Dai Oyama [1968] Director [Japanese]

Ludgate 373 Limited
Incorporated: 11 April 2006
Net Worth Deficit: £30,315 *Total Assets:* £1,408,334
Registered Office: Yours Business Networks, Suite B, 7-8 Delta Bank Road, Gateshead, Tyne & Wear, NE11 9DJ
Activities: Other letting and operating of own or leased real estate
Major Shareholder: Reuben Thomas Coppin Straker
Officers: Reuben Thomas Coppin Straker [1956] Director

Lugano Developments Limited
Incorporated: 24 January 2007 *Employees:* 10
Net Worth Deficit: £5,950,274 *Total Assets:* £7,382,995
Registered Office: Lugano Building, 57 Melbourne Street, Newcastle upon Tyne, NE1 2JQ
Activities: Buying and selling of own real estate
Major Shareholder: Ben Zion Rabinowitz
Officers: Joanne Roe, Secretary; Allan John Henderson [1961] Director/Solicitor; Scott Munro [1970] Director/Planner; Allan Rankin [1960] Director; Richard John Robson [1964] Director/Developments Co-ordinator

Luxury Leisure
Incorporated: 30 November 1989 *Employees:* 1,018
Net Worth: £19,669,204 *Total Assets:* £44,219,688
Registered Office: 362c Dukesway, Team Valley Trading Estate, Gateshead, Tyne & Wear, NE11 0PZ
Activities: Gambling and betting activities
Parent: Luxury Leisure Holdings Ltd
Officers: Neil Paramore, Secretary; Tom Allison [1963] Director; Paul David Hyman [1969] Director; Zane Cedomir Mersich [1972] Managing Director; Neil Paramore [1962] Financial Director

Lycett, Browne-Swinburne & Douglass Limited
Incorporated: 19 October 1961 *Employees:* 168
Net Worth: £2,213,881 *Total Assets:* £21,187,114
Registered Office: Milburn House, Newcastle upon Tyne, NE1 1PP
Activities: Activities of insurance agents and brokers
Parent: Lycetts Holdings Limited
Officers: Rachael Jane Hall, Secretary; William Barne [1967] Director/Insurance Broker; Christopher John Godman Cox [1957] Director/Insurance Broker; Alastair Charles Herbert Foster [1955] Director; Simon Robert Harper [1965] Director; Mark Christopher John Hews [1969] Director/Group Chief Executive; Angus Christopher Keate [1962] Director/Financial Advisor; Simon Richard Landale [1976] Director; William Rice Nicholl [1973] Director; Colin David Sadler [1967] Director

Lycetts Financial Services Limited
Incorporated: 24 September 1986 *Employees:* 25
Net Worth: £1,126,332 *Total Assets:* £1,655,183
Registered Office: Milburn House, Dean Street, Newcastle upon Tyne, NE1 1PP
Activities: Life insurance
Parent: Lycett Browne-Swinburn & Douglas Limited
Officers: Rachael Jane Hall, Secretary; William Barne [1967] Director/Insurance Broker; Christopher John Godman Cox [1957] Director/Insurance Broker; Alastair Charles Herbert Foster [1955] Director; Simon Robert Harper [1965] Director; Angus Christopher Keate [1962] Director/Financial Advisor; Simon Richard Landale [1976] Director; William Rice Nicholl [1973] Director; Colin David Sadler [1967] Director; Nicholas David Barclay Straker [1952] Director/Financial Advisor

Lycetts Holdings Limited
Incorporated: 4 July 2006 *Employees:* 257
Net Worth: £5,199,552 *Total Assets:* £24,904,208
Registered Office: Milburn House, Newcastle upon Tyne, NE1 1PP
Activities: Non-trading company
Parent: Ecclesiastical Insurance Group PLC
Officers: Rachael Jane Hall, Secretary; Mark Christopher John Hews [1969] Director/Group Chief Executive; Angus Christopher Keate [1962] Director; David Robert Moore [1966] Director; Alan John Titchener [1965] Compliance Director

Lydon Pharmacy Group Ltd.
Incorporated: 5 May 2000 *Employees:* 39
Net Worth: £922,543 *Total Assets:* £1,594,502
Registered Office: 79 Front Street, Stanley, Co Durham, DH9 0TB
Activities: Dispensing chemist in specialised stores
Parent: Chemcare Limited
Officers: Louise Lydon, Secretary; David Lydon [1978] Director/Pharmacist; Louise Lydon [1979] Director/Pharmacist

Lyndale Robert Limited
Incorporated: 18 June 2001
Net Worth: £325,664 *Total Assets:* £870,613
Registered Office: Spaceworks, Benton Park Road, Newcastle upon Tyne, NE7 7LX
Activities: Other letting and operating of own or leased real estate
Shareholders: Tony Lyndale Crilley; Susan Parker
Officers: Tony Lyndale Crilley, Secretary/Accountant; Tony Lyndale Crilley [1957] Director/Accountant; Susan Parker [1955] Director

Charles Lyndon Homes Ltd
Incorporated: 24 April 1987 *Employees:* 2
Net Worth Deficit: £50,663 *Total Assets:* £2,635,589
Registered Office: Tower Buildings, 9 Oldgate, Morpeth, Northumberland, NE61 1PY
Activities: Development of building projects
Shareholders: Ian Charles Cawkwell; Neil Lyndon Yeomans
Officers: Paul Brown, Secretary; Neil Lyndon Yeomans, Secretary/Surveyor; Ian Charles Cawkwell [1957] Director; Neil Lyndon Yeomans [1958] Director/Surveyor

Lyndon Systems Ltd
Incorporated: 10 October 2002
Net Worth: £597,681 *Total Assets:* £1,305,745
Registered Office: 5a Station Terrace, East Boldon, Co Durham, NE36 0LJ
Activities: Security systems service activities
Shareholders: Stuart George Wilson; Diane Wilson
Officers: Dianne Wilson, Secretary; Dianne Wilson [1967] Director/Secretary; Stuart George Wilson [1964] Director

Lynemouth Power Limited
Incorporated: 30 November 2011 *Employees:* 128
Net Worth: £134,299,008 *Total Assets:* £303,292,992
Registered Office: Lynemouth Power Station, Ashington, Northumberland, NE63 9NW
Activities: Production of electricity
Parent: EP UK Investments Ltd
Officers: John Marcus Nettelton, Secretary; Tarloke Singh Bains [1968] Director/Chartered Accountant; Carl Andrew Hopper [1967] Director/Chartered Mechanical Engineer; Jonathan Paul Scott [1977] Commercial Director; Deborah Walton [1976] Director/Accountant; Jan SPringl [1978] Director [Czech]

Lynx Precast Limited
Incorporated: 7 August 2013 *Employees:* 33
Net Worth: £1,904,040 *Total Assets:* £4,167,383
Registered Office: Lynefield Park, Ashington, Northumberland, NE63 9YH
Activities: Manufacture of concrete products for construction purposes
Parent: Lynx Concrete Holdings Limited
Officers: Kevin Bjelk, Secretary; Paul John Cutler [1971] Director; Andrew Teasdale [1960] Director

Lyrico Securus Limited
Incorporated: 18 April 2006
Net Worth Deficit: £973,954 *Total Assets:* £1,026,454
Registered Office: 9-18 Ruby Court, Wesley Drive, Benton Square Industrial Estate, Newcastle upon Tyne, NE12 9UP
Activities: Other business support service activities n.e.c.
Parent: Securus Group Limited
Officers: Anthony Denis Kane [1959] Director; John Stewart [1968] Director

Lytestream Electrical Engineers & Contractors Limited
Incorporated: 8 February 1993 *Employees:* 19
Net Worth: £866,515 *Total Assets:* £1,371,646
Registered Office: Chesnut House, Chesnut Street, Darlington, Co Durham, DL1 1QL
Activities: Electrical installation
Major Shareholder: James Gerald Tully
Officers: Janette Tully, Secretary; Eugene Thomas Tully [1961] Director/Electrician; James Generald Tully [1958] Director/Electrical Engineer; Janette Tully [1959] Director

M & C Residential Ltd.
Incorporated: 20 October 2015 *Employees:* 9
Net Worth: £466,673 *Total Assets:* £2,775,464
Registered Office: 3 St Georges Square, Morpeth, Northumberland, NE61 1SL
Activities: Buying and selling of own real estate
Shareholders: Alexandra Blair Paton; Chris Paton
Officers: Alexandra Blair Paton [1987] Lettings Director; Christopher Paton [1984] Managing Director

M & D Travel Limited
Incorporated: 15 February 2011
Net Worth: £245,576 *Total Assets:* £817,639
Registered Office: M & D Travel Ltd, Crofton Road, Stockton on Tees, Cleveland, TS18 2QZ
Activities: Other passenger land transport
Officers: Ian Cass [1984] Director/Consultant; Margaret Cass [1962] Director/Administrator; Hayley O'Neill [1985] Director/Administrator

M & G Solid Fuels LLP
Incorporated: 11 January 2008 *Employees:* 13
Net Worth: £11,013,944 *Total Assets:* £16,084,499
Registered Office: Plot 9, Sandgate Industrial Estate, Mainsforth Terrace, Hartlepool, Cleveland, TS25 1TZ
Officers: John Grand [1946] Member; William John Mallabar [1949] Member; David John Grand [1979] LLP Member; Margaret Grand [1949] LLP Member; Robert Linton [1949] LLP Member; Marion Mallabar [1953] LLP Member; Neil Mallabar [1980] LLP Member

M & L Associates Design and Build Limited
Incorporated: 13 March 2007 *Employees:* 5
Net Worth: £389,650 *Total Assets:* £1,084,793
Registered Office: Oakwood, Ebchester, Consett, Co Durham, DH8 0PQ
Activities: Construction of domestic buildings
Shareholders: Kevin Moody; Justine Moody
Officers: Justine Moody, Secretary; Kevin Moody [1960] Director/Builder

M & S Plastics Limited
Incorporated: 19 April 2008 *Employees:* 22
Net Worth: £433,145 *Total Assets:* £3,133,235
Registered Office: 4 Greenhills Business Park, Enterprise Way, Spennymoor, Co Durham, DL16 6JB
Activities: Manufacture of other plastic products
Shareholder: Stephen Peverall
Officers: Simon Christopher Davies [1980] Financial Director; Steven Peverall [1973] Director/Engineer

M A Utilities Ltd
Incorporated: 24 October 2011
Net Worth: £1,393,752 *Total Assets:* £2,471,097
Registered Office: 4 High Street, Stanley, Co Durham, DH9 0DQ
Activities: Construction of other civil engineering projects n.e.c.
Parent: Imperator Group Limited
Officers: Mark Lisgo [1978] Director/Lawyer; Simon James Maughan [1978] Director/Planning Manager

M B Distribution (Cleveland) Limited
Incorporated: 5 November 1987 *Employees:* 65
Net Worth: £5,466,358 *Total Assets:* £7,269,254
Registered Office: 6 Wallis Road, Skippers Lane Industrial Estate, Middlesbrough, Cleveland, TS6 6JB
Activities: Wholesale of hardware, plumbing and heating equipment and supplies
Shareholder: Michael Greenup
Officers: Brenda Greenup, Secretary; Brenda Greenup [1952] Director/Company Secretary; Michael Lee Greenup [1974] National Sales Director; Michael Greenup [1954] Managing Director; Shirley Marie Harding [1971] Accounts Director; Carol Roberts [1963] Director

M C C Properties Newcastle Limited
Incorporated: 14 May 2004 *Employees:* 2
Net Worth: £4,872,210 *Total Assets:* £5,147,805
Registered Office: c/o Nicholson & Morgan Solicitors, 14 Bell Villas, Ponteland, Northumberland, NE20 9BE
Activities: Development of building projects
Parent: Bond Dickinson (Trust Corporation) Ltd
Officers: Andrew William Morgan, Secretary; Philip Roy Barltrop [1955] Director; Michael Charles Clippingdale [1957] Director

M J M Leisure Limited
Incorporated: 7 July 2003 *Employees:* 26
Net Worth: £400,363 *Total Assets:* £819,822
Registered Office: Red Lion Inn, 22 Northumberland Street, Alnmouth, Alnwick, Northumberland, NE66 2RJ
Activities: Licenced restaurants
Shareholder: Jane Heather McHugh
Officers: Jane Heather McHugh, Secretary; Jane Heather McHugh [1960] Director/Pharmaceutical Sales; Kevin McHugh [1957] Director/Aviation Engineer

M M C (Europe) Limited
Incorporated: 28 April 1981 *Employees:* 8
Net Worth: £1,445,924 *Total Assets:* £2,021,004
Registered Office: South Nelson Road, South Nelson Industrial Estate, Cramlington, Northumberland, NE23 1WF
Activities: Manufacture of other special-purpose machinery n.e.c.
Shareholders: Paul Steven Makepeace; Elizabeth Makepeace
Officers: Elizabeth Makepeace, Secretary; William Henry [1939] Director [American]; Elizabeth Makepeace [1941] Director; Paul Steven Makepeace [1963] Managing Director

M R B Schumag Ltd
Incorporated: 31 July 1975
Net Worth Deficit: £557,553 *Total Assets:* £2,108,110
Registered Office: 1 Henson Close, South Church Enterprise Park, Bishop Auckland, Co Durham, DL14 6WA
Activities: Manufacture of metal forming machinery
Officers: Uwe Repschlager [1961] Director [German]; Joern Schulte [1972] Director [German]

M Rugs Limited
Incorporated: 5 March 2014 *Employees:* 2
Net Worth: £424,203 *Total Assets:* £3,331,937
Registered Office: Unit 3 Maple Way, Aycliffe Business Park, Newton Aycliffe, Co Durham, DL5 6BF
Activities: Activities of distribution holding companies
Shareholders: PHD Nominees (MR) Limited; Coalfields Growth Fund
Officers: Benjamin Daniel Dale [1981] Director/Online Retail; Kyle-Gian Mitchell [1987] Director; Gary Pickering [1989] Director

M T Haulage Ltd
Incorporated: 9 April 2013 *Employees:* 9
Net Worth: £29,546 *Total Assets:* £862,391
Registered Office: M T Haulage Ltd, St Cuthbert's Way, Aycliffe Business Park, Newton Aycliffe, Co Durham, DL5 6DX
Activities: Freight transport by road
Shareholders: Michael Tough; Mary Elizabeth Tough
Officers: Mary Elizabeth Tough, Secretary; Michael Tough [1960] Director/Haulier

M. & G. Fuels Limited
Incorporated: 31 December 1984
Net Worth: £4,442,411 *Total Assets:* £4,600,315
Registered Office: Plot 9, Sandgate Industrial Estate, Mainsforth Terrace, Hartlepool, Cleveland, TS25 1TZ
Activities: Agents involved in the sale of fuels, ores, metals and industrial chemicals
Shareholders: John Grand; William John Mallabar
Officers: Edwin Hird, Secretary; John Grand [1946] Director; Margaret Grand [1949] Director/Clerical Assistant; Marion Mallabar [1953] Director/Clerical Assistant; William John Mallabar [1949] Director

M. & S. Distributors Limited
Incorporated: 3 June 1982 *Employees:* 18
Net Worth: £1,359,955 *Total Assets:* £1,671,056
Registered Office: Riverside Works, Shelley Road, Newburn Industrial Estate, Newburn, Newcastle upon Tyne, NE15 9RT
Activities: Other retail sale of new goods in specialised stores (not commercial art galleries and opticians)
Shareholder: Ronald William Slater
Officers: Ronald William Slater, Secretary; Evelyn Mordue [1931] Director; Ian George Mordue [1966] Sales Director; LEA Mordue [1972] Director; Mark Slater [1969] Sales Director; Ronald William Slater [1940] Sales Director; Sandra Slater [1969] Director

M. & S. Motorcycles Limited
Incorporated: 13 December 1957 *Employees:* 29
Net Worth: £1,182,165 *Total Assets:* £3,007,220
Registered Office: 199-203 Westgate Road, Newcastle upon Tyne, NE4 6AB
Activities: Sale, maintenance and repair of motorcycles and related parts and accessories
Shareholders: Ian Paul Myers; Annette Myers
Officers: Annette Myers, Secretary; Annette Myers [1960] Director/Secretary; Ian Paul Myers [1958] Managing Director

M. C. Construction (Cleveland) Limited
Incorporated: 15 October 1974
Net Worth: £2,270,800 *Total Assets:* £6,381,828
Registered Office: Shed 7 Teesport Commerce Park, Dockside Road, South Bank, Middlesbrough, Cleveland, TS6 6UZ
Activities: Other specialised construction activities n.e.c.
Parent: Mormont Group Limited
Officers: Peter David Conlon, Secretary; Peter David Conlon [1964] Director; Mark Serplus [1961] Director

M.& M.Value Limited
Incorporated: 17 March 1960 *Employees:* 49
Net Worth: £1,659,602 *Total Assets:* £16,354,993
Registered Office: Unit S3, Narvik Way, Tyne Tunnel Trading Estate, North Shields, Tyne & Wear, NE29 7XJ
Activities: Wholesale of wine, beer, spirits and other alcoholic beverages
Officers: Patricia Ada Rice, Secretary; David Leonard Brind [1972] Finance Director; John Frederick Hope [1969] Group Operations Director; Patricia Ada Rice [1951] Director/Accountant; Stephen Rycroft [1963] Director/Buyer; Linda Jayne Wilson [1963] Director; Paul Victor Young [1957] Director/Accountant

M.A. Properties Limited
Incorporated: 8 March 1999
Net Worth: £599,836 *Total Assets:* £1,132,125
Registered Office: 17 Woodburn Avenue, Newcastle upon Tyne, NE4 9EN
Activities: Other letting and operating of own or leased real estate
Shareholder: Mohammed Anwar
Officers: Mohammed Anwar, Secretary/Landlord; Kishwar Sultana Anwar [1955] Director/Landlord; Mohammed Anwar [1954] Director/Landlord

M.G.L. Demolition Limited
Incorporated: 24 April 1972 *Employees:* 142
Net Worth: £4,449,818 *Total Assets:* £11,262,293
Registered Office: Davison House, Rennys Lane, Dragonville Industrial Estate, Durham, DH1 2RS
Activities: Demolition
Parent: MGL Group Limited
Officers: Gary Anthony Smith, Secretary/Director; Mark Davison [1964] Director/Businessman; David Anthony Elliott [1969] Director; Kenneth John Forbes [1954] Director; Gary Anthony Smith [1967] Director

M.G.L. Group Limited
Incorporated: 15 February 2008 *Employees:* 410
Net Worth: £8,502,129 *Total Assets:* £30,548,296
Registered Office: Davison House, Rennys Lane, Dragonville Industrial Estate, Durham, DH1 2RS
Activities: Activities of head offices
Officers: Gary Anthony Smith, Secretary; David Anthony Elliott [1969] Director; Gillian Reader [1965] Director/Businesswoman; Gary Anthony Smith [1967] Director

M.G.N. Fire Protection Limited
Incorporated: 8 March 1995
Net Worth: £789,599 *Total Assets:* £2,158,926
Registered Office: The Old Fire Station, Shankhouse, Cramlington, Northumberland, NE23 3JN
Activities: Other construction installation
Officers: Bruce Monaghan, Secretary; Bruce Monaghan [1965] Director/Fire Proofing Specialist; Owen Monaghan [1969] Director/Fire Proofing Specialists; Paul Monaghan [1961] Director/Fire Protection

M.H.Southern & Company Limited
Incorporated: 11 November 1949 *Employees:* 99
Net Worth: £4,258,066 *Total Assets:* £7,691,385
Registered Office: Church Bank Sawmills, Jarrow, Tyne & Wear, NE32 3EB
Activities: Sawmilling and planing of wood
Officers: Dorothy Jane Southern, Secretary; Robert Johnson Bruce [1959] Director/Timber Merchant; Mark Simon Lowis [1973] Director/Timber Importer; James Andrew Southern [1969] Director/Timber Merchant

M.H.T. Technology Limited
Incorporated: 19 April 1994
Net Worth: £1,074,079 *Total Assets:* £1,318,538
Registered Office: Harelands Courtyard Offices, Moor Road, Melsonby, Richmond, N Yorks, DL10 5NY
Activities: Other service activities n.e.c.
Parent: Endress + Hauser GmbH & Co KG
Officers: David Paul Lucas, Secretary; Matthias Altendorf [1967] Managing Director [German]; Dr. Andreas Mayr [1961] Director/Manager [Austrian]; Stephen Christopher Spelman [1956] Managing Director

M.M. Knitwear (1982) Limited
Incorporated: 5 May 1981 *Employees:* 6
Net Worth: £2,120,156 *Total Assets:* £3,214,719
Registered Office: Jamal Building, New Street, Mandale Triangle, Thornaby, Stockton on Tees, Cleveland, TS17 6BU
Activities: Renting and operating of Housing Association real estate
Shareholders: Mehboob Ahmad; Sorreya Ahmad
Officers: Sorreya Ahmad, Secretary/Director; Mehboob Ahmad [1974] Managing Director

M40 Trains Limited
Incorporated: 23 December 1994 *Employees:* 3
Net Worth: £61,292,000 *Total Assets:* £66,059,000
Registered Office: 1 Admiral Way, Doxford International Business Park, Sunderland, Tyne & Wear, SR3 3XP
Activities: Passenger rail transport, interurban
Officers: Lorna Edwards, Secretary; Amanda Furlong [1975] Director; David James Penney [1975] Director; Alexis James Scott [1983] Director

M62 Developments Limited
Incorporated: 26 January 2012
Net Worth: £138,048 *Total Assets:* £813,348
Registered Office: Esh House, Bowburn North Industrial Estate, Bowburn, Co Durham, DH6 5PF
Activities: Buying and selling of own real estate
Shareholders: Esh Developments Limited; VB Turnbull Limited
Officers: Philip Coates, Secretary; Richard Stewart Aran Buckley [1968] Director; Michael Francis Hogan [1944] Director; Andrew Edward Radcliffe [1973] Director; Alexander John Turnbull [1956] Director

MacDee LLP
Incorporated: 9 March 2009
Net Worth: £373,122 *Total Assets:* £1,134,186
Registered Office: Unit 1 Stephenson Road, Stephenson Industrial Estate, Washington, Tyne & Wear, NE37 3HR
Officers: William Wilson [1949] Member; Christine Blair [1976] LLP Member; Lorna Grieves [1974] LLP Member

MacDonald Martin Limited
Incorporated: 24 September 2003
Net Worth: £561,516 *Total Assets:* £761,003
Registered Office: 3a Wellmere Road, Leechmere Industrial Estate, Sunderland, Tyne & Wear, SR2 9TE
Activities: Fire service activities
Shareholders: Andrew Trafford; Jacqueline Trafford
Officers: Kenneth Taylor, Secretary; Andrew Trafford [1963] Director/Fireman; Jacqueline Trafford [1965] Director/Administrator

Maceachern HCH Ltd
Incorporated: 7 September 1993
Net Worth: £621,791 *Total Assets:* £1,014,565
Registered Office: South Lodge, Swarland, Morpeth, Northumberland, NE65 9JA
Activities: Other accommodation
Major Shareholder: Paul Thompson
Officers: Marianne Maceachern, Secretary; Paul Thompson [1959] Director

Macey Property Consultancy Limited
Incorporated: 7 August 2003
Net Worth: £566,913 *Total Assets:* £1,272,929
Registered Office: 14 Queen Street, Redcar, Cleveland, TS10 1AE
Activities: Development of building projects
Shareholder: Andrew Paul Macey
Officers: Karen Macey, Secretary; Andrew Paul Macey [1966] Director; Stephen Macey [1969] Director; Samantha MacEy-Jones [1974] Director

MacGregor (GBR) Limited
Incorporated: 19 March 2013 *Employees:* 41
Net Worth Deficit: £202,000 *Total Assets:* £5,382,000
Registered Office: 11 Hedley Court, Orion Business Park, Wallsend, Tyne & Wear, NE29 7ST
Activities: Other engineering activities
Officers: Steven Arthur James Goodchild [1957] Managing Director; Jani Mikael Oksanen [1975] Director/VP Finance [Finnish]; Soenke Rohweder-Struve [1977] Director [German]

MacLeods Pharma UK Limited
Incorporated: 17 December 2007 *Employees:* 1
Net Worth Deficit: £1,873,830 *Total Assets:* £2,713,960
Registered Office: Wynyard Park House, Wynyard Avenue, Wynyard, Billingham, Cleveland, TS22 5TB
Activities: Manufacture of basic pharmaceutical products
Officers: Suvarna Bhaskar, Secretary; Vijay Girdharilal Agarwal [1977] Director/Service [Indian]

Mactech Inspection Holdco Limited
Incorporated: 19 March 2014 *Employees:* 70
Net Worth: £1,002,808 *Total Assets:* £2,091,745
Registered Office: 23 Claremont Road, Whitley Bay, Tyne & Wear, NE26 3TN
Activities: Activities of other holding companies n.e.c.
Shareholders: Kevin Malcolm Stuart McFarlane; Andrew William McFarlane
Officers: Andrew William McFarlane [1982] Managing Director; Heike McFarlane [1957] Director [German]; Kevin Malcolm Stuart McFarlane [1955] Director

Mactech Inspection Limited
Incorporated: 12 February 1986 *Employees:* 70
Net Worth: £1,002,618 *Total Assets:* £2,089,467
Registered Office: 23 Claremont Road, Whitley Bay, Tyne & Wear, NE26 3TN
Activities: Engineering related scientific and technical consulting activities
Parent: Mactech Inspection Holdco Limited
Officers: Kevin Malcolm Stuart McFarlane, Secretary; Paul William Atkinson [1964] Finance Director; Andrew William McFarlane [1982] Director/MD; Heike McFarlane [1957] Director/Senior Administrator [German]; Kevin Malcolm Stuart McFarlane [1955] Director/Chairman

Maersk Training Newcastle Limited
Incorporated: 26 June 2006
Net Worth: £166,132 *Total Assets:* £1,796,210
Registered Office: 2 Mercury Court, Orion Business Park, Tyne Tunnel Trading Estate, North Shields, Tyne & Wear, NE29 7SN
Activities: Technical and vocational secondary education
Parent: A.P.Moller-Maersk A/S
Officers: John Richard Abate [1964] Managing Director; Johan Uggla [1976] Director [Swedish]; Brian Lundin Weishaupt [1974] Director/Head of European Finance [Danish]

Magneco Metrel U.K. Limited
Incorporated: 14 May 1990 *Employees:* 15
Net Worth: £2,403,342 *Total Assets:* £4,127,699
Registered Office: Hackworth Industrial Park, Shildon, Co Durham, DL4 1HG
Activities: Manufacture of other ceramic products n.e.c.
Parent: Charles W Connors Family Fund Limited Partnership
Officers: Susan Malloy, Company Secretary [American]; Ann Connors [1937] Director [American]; Charles W Connors [1937] Director/Chief Executive Officer [American]; Colleen Connors [1961] Director/Lawyer [American]; Charles Connors Jr [1962] Director/Manufacturing Vice President [American]; Susan Malloy [1964] Director/Company Secretary [American]

Magnet Limited
Incorporated: 6 November 1992
Net Worth: £34,864,000 *Total Assets:* £90,864,000
Registered Office: c/o Magnet Limited, 3 Allington Way, Yarm Road Business Park, Darlington, Co Durham, DL1 4XT
Activities: Other manufacturing n.e.c.
Parent: Nobia Holdings UK Limited
Officers: Nicola Jane Hardcastle, Secretary; Anjum Ahmed [1970] Director; Daniel Arthur Edward Carr [1975] Finance Director; Nicola Jane Hardcastle [1965] Director/Company Secretary; Peter Kane [1965] Director; Kristoffer Ljungfelt [1977] Director [Swedish]

Magnum Packaging (N.E.) Limited
Incorporated: 24 October 1983 *Employees:* 50
Net Worth: £3,553,422 *Total Assets:* £12,049,399
Registered Office: Haverton Hill Road, Haverton Hill Industrial Estate, Billingham, Stockton on Tees, Cleveland, TS23 1PZ
Activities: Non-specialised wholesale trade
Officers: Tariq Bilal Younis [1983] Operational Director; Zubeir Hassan Younis [1985] Director

J Maguire Holdings Limited
Incorporated: 29 April 2009 *Employees:* 87
Net Worth: £9,110,473 *Total Assets:* £18,642,422
Registered Office: The Future Business Park, Darlington Road, Shildon, Co Durham, DL4 2RB
Activities: Activities of other holding companies n.e.c.
Major Shareholder: Jason James Maguire
Officers: David Stubbs, Secretary; Alice Victoria Maguire [1975] Director; Jason James Maguire [1973] Director/Carpet Retailer

Maher Entertainments Limited
Incorporated: 26 February 1982 *Employees:* 4
Net Worth: £2,463,022 *Total Assets:* £9,531,990
Registered Office: Mount Leven, Leven Bank Road, Yarm, Cleveland, TS15 9JJ
Activities: Buying and selling of own real estate
Officers: Nina Majid Khalid [1964] Director/Administrator; Donna Majid [1959] Director; Jacob Abdul Majid [1992] Operations Director; Javed Ahmed Majid [1950] Director/Hotelier

Main-Tel (NE) Limited
Incorporated: 2 October 2000 *Employees:* 9
Net Worth: £722,348 *Total Assets:* £1,531,152
Registered Office: Thorntree Farm, Bassleton Lane, Thornaby, Stockton on Tees, Cleveland, TS17 0AQ
Activities: Other telecommunications activities
Shareholders: Margaret Howson; Thomas Sydney Howson
Officers: Margaret Howson, Secretary; Thomas Sydney Howson [1956] Director/Telephone Engineer

Sarah Mains Residential Limited
Incorporated: 16 November 2001
Net Worth: £313,388 *Total Assets:* £912,047
Registered Office: 8-10 The Square, Whickham, Gateshead, Tyne & Wear, NE16 4JE
Activities: Real estate agencies
Shareholders: Sarah Anne Mains; Paul McKie
Officers: Sarah Anne Mains, Secretary; Sarah Anne Mains [1968] Director/Estate Agent; Paul McKie [1960] Director/Estate Agent

Make Believe UK Limited
Incorporated: 15 June 2005 *Employees:* 3
Net Worth: £769,856 *Total Assets:* £1,007,299
Registered Office: Kirklington Manor, Stapley Lane, Bedale, N Yorks, DL8 2LU
Activities: Management consultancy activities other than financial management
Shareholders: Brent James McCallum; Momento Vivere Limited
Officers: Jayne Wilson, Secretary; David Charles Griffiths [1963] Director/Marketing Consultant; Sean Christopher Francis Key [1982] Director; Brent James McCallum [1968] Managing Director [New Zealander]; Paul Anthony Wilson [1970] Director/Marketing Consultant

Philip Makin Transport Limited
Incorporated: 12 November 2001 *Employees:* 12
Net Worth: £915,641 *Total Assets:* £2,074,854
Registered Office: The Garage, Patrick Brompton, Bedale, N Yorks, DL8 1JP
Activities: Freight transport by road
Major Shareholder: Helen Ward
Officers: Michael James Ward, Secretary/Director; Mark Stephen Ward [1963] Director; Michael James Ward [1968] Director

Malhotra Care Homes (Sunderland) Limited
Incorporated: 22 May 2013 *Employees:* 34
Net Worth: £4,360,660 *Total Assets:* £4,921,265
Registered Office: Malhotra House, 7-9 Groat Market, Newcastle upon Tyne, NE1 1UQ
Activities: Residential care activities for the elderly and disabled
Officers: Chunda Malhotra [1966] Director; Devinder Mohan Malhotra [1967] Director

Malhotra Care Homes Limited
Incorporated: 12 May 2009 *Employees:* 475
Net Worth: £14,327,303 *Total Assets:* £54,877,152
Registered Office: Malhotra House, 7-9 Groat Market, Newcastle upon Tyne, NE1 1UQ
Activities: Residential nursing care facilities
Officers: Devinder Mohan Malhotra [1967] Director

Malhotra Commercial Property Limited
Incorporated: 4 April 1991 *Employees:* 9
Net Worth: £7,380,087 *Total Assets:* £12,762,012
Registered Office: Malhotra House, 7-9 Groat Market, Newcastle upon Tyne, NE1 1UQ
Activities: Other letting and operating of own or leased real estate
Officers: Jagmohan Malhotra, Secretary; Jagmohan Malhotra [1958] Director [Indian]; Manju Malhotra [1961] Director/Retailer [Indian]

Malhotra Property Investments Limited
Incorporated: 25 August 2000 *Employees:* 1
Net Worth: £15,707,641 *Total Assets:* £32,844,120
Registered Office: Malhotra House, 7-9 Groat Market, Newcastle upon Tyne, NE1 1UQ
Activities: Other letting and operating of own or leased real estate
Officers: Devinder Mohan Malhotra, Secretary; Devinder Mohan Malhotra [1967] Director/Care Home Proprietor

Malhotra Property Limited
Incorporated: 13 December 1990 *Employees:* 2
Net Worth: £5,689,271 *Total Assets:* £13,012,289
Registered Office: 1 Runnymede Road, Ponteland, Northumberland, NE20 9HE
Activities: Other accommodation
Officers: Manju Malhotra, Secretary; Jagmohan Malhotra [1958] Director [Indian]; Manju Malhotra [1961] Director/Retailer [Indian]

Mallen Print Limited
Incorporated: 18 September 2008 *Employees:* 4
Net Worth: £417,429 *Total Assets:* £1,149,308
Registered Office: Falstone Close, North Tyne Industrial Estate, Whitley Road, Longbenton, Newcastle upon Tyne, NE12 9SZ
Activities: Printing n.e.c.
Parent: DNR Limited
Officers: Doreen Mallen [1947] Director; Scott Mallen [1975] Director; Paul David Thompson [1969] Director

H.Malone and Sons Limited
Incorporated: 3 April 1964 *Employees:* 141
Net Worth: £2,436,437 *Total Assets:* £11,079,445
Registered Office: Gosforth Industrial Estate, Newcastle upon Tyne, NE3 1XL
Activities: Plumbing, heat and air-conditioning installation
Shareholder: Weston Malone
Officers: Peter Malone, Secretary/Accountant; David Errington [1965] Director/Engineer; David Gourley [1971] Director; Peter Stephen Malone [1976] Finance Director; Weston Malone [1975] Director; Graeme Redford [1972] Director; Graham Reid [1971] Director

Malones Electricals Group Limited
Incorporated: 20 February 2008
Registered Office: Unit K36 Eleveth Avenue, Team Valley Trading Estate, Gateshead, Tyne & Wear, NE11 0NJ
Activities: Other business support service activities n.e.c.
Shareholders: Amanda Malone; John Edward Malone
Officers: Barry Colledge, Secretary; Amanda Malone [1975] Director; John Edward Malone [1978] Director/Electrician

Mammoet (UK) Limited
Incorporated: 30 March 1990 *Employees:* 206
Net Worth: £47,112,000 *Total Assets:* £60,120,000
Registered Office: Beatrix House, Tyne View Terrace, Wallsend, Tyne & Wear, NE28 6SG
Activities: Other specialised construction activities n.e.c.
Parent: Mammoet Holding BV
Officers: Gillian Steward, Secretary; Matthew Conan Gent [1976] Managing Director; Wouter Van Noort [1972] Managing Director [Dutch]

Mammoet Wind Ltd
Incorporated: 19 March 2007 *Employees:* 29
Net Worth Deficit: £2,096,344 *Total Assets:* £1,686,238
Registered Office: Beatrix House, Tyne View Terrace, Wallsend, Tyne & Wear, NE28 6SG
Activities: Other specialised construction activities n.e.c.
Officers: Gillian Steward, Secretary; Peter Johannes Boer [1970] Director Finance and Organization [Dutch]; Markus Nicolaas de Jong [1970] Managing Director [Dutch]; Matthew Conan Gent [1976] Managing Director

Management Development Centre International Limited
Incorporated: 9 November 1993 *Employees:* 9
Net Worth: £140,345 *Total Assets:* £1,221,002
Registered Office: The Old Coach House, Castle Eden, Co Durham, TS27 4SS
Activities: General secondary education
Major Shareholder: Robert Lee Francis Rice
Officers: Glenn Malcolm Aitken, Secretary; Robert Lee Rice [1952] Managing Director

Manchester Alloys and Metals Limited
Incorporated: 7 October 1988 *Employees:* 57
Net Worth: £584,844 *Total Assets:* £5,971,251
Registered Office: 59-69 Heaton Park Road, Newcastle upon Tyne, NE6 1SQ
Activities: Manufacture of tools
Officers: Carole Thompson, Secretary; David George Mutch [1960] Director; Kevin Grant Mutch [1963] Director

Manchester and Regional Limited
Incorporated: 28 May 2015
Registered Office: 54-56 Keswick Street, Gateshead, Tyne & Wear, NE8 1TQ
Activities: Buying and selling of own real estate
Officers: Martin Zvi Oppenheimer [1989] Director

Manchester Surgical Services Limited
Incorporated: 22 October 2009 *Employees:* 10
Net Worth: £755,082 *Total Assets:* £1,447,071
Registered Office: RMT Accountants & Business Advisors, Gosforth Park Avenue, Newcastle upon Tyne, NE12 8EG
Activities: Other business support service activities n.e.c.
Major Shareholder: Amr Ahmed Yacout Saleh
Officers: Hamdy Yousef Hafez Ashour [1957] Director; Mark Andrew Mercer-Jones [1964] Director

Mandale Apartments 2 Limited
Incorporated: 9 February 2016 *Employees:* 3
Net Worth: £1,278,095 *Total Assets:* £3,348,746
Registered Office: Mandale House, 5 Neville Road, North Tees Industrial Estate, Stockton on Tees, Cleveland, TS18 2RD
Activities: Development of building projects
Parent: Mandale Homes Holdings Limited
Officers: Joseph Darragh, Secretary; Paula Davidson, Secretary; David Ian Harriman [1956] Director; Richard Thomas Harriman [1990] Director

Mandale Apartments 3 Limited
Incorporated: 7 July 2016 *Employees:* 2
Net Worth Deficit: £104,985 *Total Assets:* £19,159,314
Registered Office: Mandale House, 5 Neville Road, North Tees Industrial Estate, Stockton on Tees, Cleveland, TS18 2RD
Activities: Development of building projects
Parent: Mandale Homes Holdings Limited
Officers: Joseph Darragh, Secretary; Paula Davidson, Secretary; David Ian Harriman [1956] Director; Richard Thomas Harriman [1990] Director

Mandale Apartments Limited
Incorporated: 3 June 2014 *Employees:* 1
Net Worth: £2,421,703 *Total Assets:* £2,896,300
Registered Office: Mandale House, 5 Neville Road, North Tees Industrial Estate, Stockton on Tees, Cleveland, TS18 2RD
Activities: Development of building projects
Parent: Mandale Homes Holdings Limited
Officers: Joseph Darragh, Secretary; Paula Davidson, Secretary; David Ian Harriman [1956] Director; Richard Thomas Harriman [1990] Director

Mandale Construction Limited
Incorporated: 29 March 2001 *Employees:* 13
Net Worth: £314,897 *Total Assets:* £4,669,443
Registered Office: Mandale House, 5 Neville Road, North Tees Industrial Estate, Stockton on Tees, Cleveland, TS18 2RD
Activities: Construction of commercial buildings
Parent: Arkgrove Limited
Officers: Joseph Darragh, Secretary; Paula Davidson, Secretary; Joseph Darragh [1966] Director; Paula Davidson [1972] Director; David Ian Harriman [1956] Director

Mandale Homes 1 Limited
Incorporated: 29 September 2016
Net Worth Deficit: £4,446 *Total Assets:* £966,643
Registered Office: Mandale House, 5 Neville Road, North Tees Industrial Estate, Stockton on Tees, Cleveland, TS18 2RD
Activities: Development of building projects
Parent: Mandale Homes Holdings Limited
Officers: Joseph Darragh, Secretary; Paula Davidson, Secretary; David Ian Harriman [1956] Director; Richard Thomas Harriman [1990] Director

Mandale Homes North East Limited
Incorporated: 4 October 2012
Net Worth Deficit: £114,395 *Total Assets:* £865,361
Registered Office: Mandale House, 5 Neville Road, North Tees Industrial Estate, Stockton on Tees, Cleveland, TS18 2RD
Activities: Development of building projects
Major Shareholder: David Ian Harriman
Officers: Joseph Darragh, Secretary; Paula Davidson, Secretary; David Ian Harriman [1956] Director; Richard Thomas Harriman [1990] Director

Mandale Homes North Limited
Incorporated: 1 May 2014 *Employees:* 4
Net Worth Deficit: £226,934 *Total Assets:* £3,894,274
Registered Office: Mandale House, 5 Neville Road, North Tees Industrial Estate, Stockton on Tees, Cleveland, TS18 2RD
Activities: Development of building projects
Parent: Mandale Homes Holdings Limited
Officers: Joseph Darragh, Secretary; Paula Davidson, Secretary; David Ian Harriman [1956] Director; Richard Thomas Harriman [1990] Director

Mandale Homes North Yorkshire Limited
Incorporated: 4 October 2012 *Employees:* 5
Net Worth: £265,891 *Total Assets:* £5,087,632
Registered Office: Mandale House, 5 Neville Road, North Tees Industrial Estate, Stockton on Tees, Cleveland, TS18 2RD
Activities: Development of building projects
Parent: Mandale Homes Holdings Limited
Officers: Joseph Darragh, Secretary; Paula Davidson, Secretary; David Ian Harriman [1956] Director; Richard Thomas Harriman [1990] Director

Mandale Investments Limited
Incorporated: 22 May 1995 *Employees:* 3
Net Worth: £10,640,825 *Total Assets:* £11,110,181
Registered Office: Mandale House, 5 Neville Road, North Tees Industrial Estate, Stockton on Tees, Cleveland, TS18 2RD
Activities: Buying and selling of own real estate
Shareholders: Arkgrove Limited; Teesdale South Limited
Officers: Joseph Darragh, Secretary; Paula Davidson, Secretary; David Ian Harriman [1956] Director; Richard Thomas Harriman [1990] Director

Mandata (Holdings) Limited
Incorporated: 12 July 2013 *Employees:* 59
Net Worth: £567,419 *Total Assets:* £7,451,016
Registered Office: 5 Silverton Court, Northumberland Business Park, Cramlington, Northumberland, NE23 7RY
Activities: Business and domestic software development
Parent: Timec 1634 Limited
Officers: Mark Ian Norcliffe [1964] Director/Chartered Accountant; Christopher Wall [1971] Director

Mandata (Management and Data Services) Ltd
Incorporated: 11 June 1997 *Employees:* 58
Net Worth: £4,020,059 *Total Assets:* £6,510,652
Registered Office: 5 Silverton Court, Northumberland Business Park, Cramlington, Northumberland, NE23 7RY
Activities: Other information technology service activities
Parent: Mandata (Holdings) Limited
Officers: Kevin Marshall [1970] Director; Mark Ian Norcliffe [1964] Director/Chartered Accountant; Christopher Wall [1971] Director

Manissa Ltd
Incorporated: 9 May 2005 *Employees:* 9
Net Worth: £605,903 *Total Assets:* £1,918,433
Registered Office: Suite 2B, North Sands Business Centre, Liberty Way, Sunderland, Tyne & Wear, SR6 0QA
Activities: Agents involved in the sale of machinery, industrial equipment, ships and aircraft
Shareholder: Martin Savage
Officers: Amy Hillier Savage, Secretary; Andrew David Saunders [1959] Director/Chartered Accountant; Martin Joseph Savage [1968] Director; David Kerr Warren [1964] Operations Director

Manitowoc Foodservice UK Holding Limited
Incorporated: 23 December 2015 *Employees:* 2
Net Worth: £15,205,000 *Total Assets:* £15,205,000
Registered Office: St Ann's Wharf, 112 Quayside, Newcastle upon Tyne, NE1 3DX
Activities: Activities of other holding companies n.e.c.
Parent: MTW County Limited
Officers: Adrian David Gray [1962] Director/Accountant; John Albert James Rourke [1967] Director

Manitowoc FSG UK Limited
Incorporated: 22 October 2015 *Employees:* 2
Net Worth: £961,000 *Total Assets:* £15,471,000
Registered Office: St Ann's Wharf, 112 Quayside, Newcastle upon Tyne, NE1 3DX
Activities: Activities of other holding companies n.e.c.
Parent: Manitowoc Foodservice Inc
Officers: Adrian David Gray [1962] Director/Accountant; John Albert James Rourke [1967] Director

Manitowoc Group (UK) Limited
Incorporated: 26 May 1910 *Employees:* 3
Net Worth: £99,988,000 *Total Assets:* £99,988,000
Registered Office: St Ann's Wharf, 112 Quayside, Newcastle upon Tyne, NE1 3DX
Activities: Manufacture of machinery for food, beverage and tobacco processing
Parent: Manitowoc Holdings (UK) Limited
Officers: David Antoniuk [1957] Director [American]; Thomas Lee Doerr [1975] Director/Solicitor [American]

Mann Haulage Limited
Incorporated: 6 September 2004
Registered Office: Nest Road, Gateshead, Tyne & Wear, NE10 0ES
Activities: Other transportation support activities
Officers: Kenneth Hepple [1962] Director; Stephen Murray [1963] Director

T.Manners & Sons Limited
Incorporated: 25 February 1916 *Employees:* 68
Net Worth: £1,060,036 *Total Assets:* £3,178,039
Registered Office: Peel House, 2 Dovecot Hill, South Church Enterprise Park, Bishop Auckland, Co Durham, DL14 6XW
Activities: Construction of commercial buildings
Parent: Manners Holdings Limited
Officers: Robert Bion Manners, Secretary/Engineer; Alan William Crawford [1956] Director; Steven Hodges [1963] Director/Construction; Ian Robert Manners [1981] Director; Kathleen Mary Charlton Manners [1955] Director; Robert Bion Manners [1952] Director/Engineer; Simon Oliver Manners [1983] Director; Martin John Wheelhouse [1957] Director/Works Manager

R.Manners & Sons Limited
Incorporated: 30 April 1954 *Employees:* 65
Net Worth: £5,293,371 *Total Assets:* £9,016,888
Registered Office: Meadowfield, Ponteland, Northumberland, NE20 9SF
Activities: Wholesale of meat and meat products
Shareholders: Anthony John Manners; Ian Christopher Manners
Officers: Jayne Marie Manners, Secretary; Anthony John Manners [1973] Director/Butcher; Ian Christopher Manners [1945] Director/Butcher; Jayne Manners [1976] Director

Manners (Newcastle) Limited
Incorporated: 14 November 2007 *Employees:* 114
Net Worth: £770,425 *Total Assets:* £4,017,237
Registered Office: 1st Floor, The Apartment Group Two, Jesmond Three Sixty, Newcastle upon Tyne, NE2 1DB
Activities: Public houses and bars
Major Shareholder: Duncan Fisher
Officers: Amanda Jayne Fisher, Secretary; Duncan Fisher [1968] Director

Manners Farms Limited
Incorporated: 18 December 1957 *Employees:* 6
Net Worth: £2,967,844 *Total Assets:* £4,613,461
Registered Office: Thornton Hall, High Coniscliffe, Darlington, Co Durham, DL2 2NB
Activities: Mixed farming
Shareholders: Michael Preston Manners; Susan Manners
Officers: Ralph Manners, Secretary; Michael Preston Manners [1960] Director/Farmer; Ralph Manners [1926] Director/Farmer; Susan Manners [1962] Director

Manning Limited
Incorporated: 1 November 1983 *Employees:* 17
Net Worth: £973,801 *Total Assets:* £1,790,385
Registered Office: Wolviston House, 5 Falcon Court, Preston Farm Industrial Estate, Stockton on Tees, Cleveland, TS18 3TS
Activities: Temporary employment agency activities
Parent: Wolviston Group Limited
Officers: Samantha Jane Anderson [1974] Director

Manor House Commercial Acquisitions Limited
Incorporated: 23 August 2016
Net Worth Deficit: £27,563 *Total Assets:* £937,077
Registered Office: The Manor House, High Street, Stokesley, Cleveland, TS9 5AD
Activities: Buying and selling of own real estate
Major Shareholder: Margot Mai Heitmann Levy
Officers: Doctor Lynette Levy Bandeira [1970] Director/Doctor; Hak Shiu To [1945] Director/Retired [Hong Kong]

Manor Park Holiday Park Limited
Incorporated: 14 September 2006 *Employees:* 59
Net Worth: £492,000 *Total Assets:* £26,941,000
Registered Office: 2nd Floor, One Gosforth Park Way, Gosforth Business Park, Newcastle upon Tyne, NE12 8ET
Activities: Holiday centres and villages
Parent: PD Parks Limited
Officers: Judith Ann Archibold, Secretary; Ian Kellett [1963] Director; John Anthony Waterworth [1963] Director

Manxguard Limited
Incorporated: 18 April 1980
Net Worth: £2,917,310 *Total Assets:* £4,768,242
Registered Office: 23 Yarm Road, Stockton on Tees, Cleveland, TS18 3NJ
Activities: Other professional, scientific and technical activities n.e.c.
Shareholders: Barry Joseph Smith; David Ian Smith
Officers: David Ian Smith, Secretary/Director; Barry Joseph Smith [1966] Director; David Ian Smith [1965] Director

The Manydown Company Limited
Incorporated: 23 February 1962
Net Worth: £27,363,424 *Total Assets:* £34,046,620
Registered Office: St Ann's Wharf, 112 Quayside, Newcastle upon Tyne, NE1 3DX
Activities: Growing of cereals (except rice), leguminous crops and oil seeds
Parent: Manydown 2007 Limited
Officers: Simon Meyrick Browne [1956] Farmer and Director; Robert Alexander Dickinson [1964] Director/Solicitor; Ian Mighell Monks [1960] Director/Chartered Surveyor; Francis Otho Moore [1979] Director/Corporate Financier; Peter Paul Thomson [1965] Director/Chief Executive Investment Manager

Map Construction Services Ltd
Incorporated: 26 November 2015 *Employees:* 7
Net Worth: £819,723 *Total Assets:* £2,001,995
Registered Office: Cleveland House, 10 Yarm Road, Stockton on Tees, Cleveland, TS18 3NA
Activities: Other construction installation
Shareholders: Michael Gerard Carlin; Gary Richards
Officers: Michael Gerard Carlin [1961] Director; Gary Richards [1966] Director

Map Group (UK) Limited
Incorporated: 15 September 1993 *Employees:* 279
Net Worth: £1,943,197 *Total Assets:* £11,545,506
Registered Office: 3 George Stephenson Court, Westland Way, Preston Farm Industrial Estate, Stockton on Tees, Cleveland, TS18 3FB
Activities: Electrical installation
Shareholders: Michael Gerard Carlin; Peter Mortley Yuill
Officers: Melissa Jayne Carlin, Secretary; Matthew Steven Carlin [1984] Director; Michael Gerard Carlin [1961] Director; Amanda Carter [1968] Director; Sarwjit Singh [1969] Director

Mapleleaf (Northern) Limited
Incorporated: 21 February 2003 *Employees:* 2
Net Worth: £146,424 *Total Assets:* £1,285,676
Registered Office: The Old Post Office, 63 Saville Street, North Shields, Tyne & Wear, NE30 1AY
Activities: Other letting and operating of own or leased real estate
Shareholders: Mt Malcolm Roland McKenzie; Susan McKenzie
Officers: Susan McKenzie, Secretary/Administrator; Malcolm Roland McKenzie [1965] Director/Quantity Surveyor; Susan McKenzie [1963] Director/Administrator

Mapleleaf Property Developments Limited
Incorporated: 22 January 2003 *Employees:* 1
Net Worth: £92,133 *Total Assets:* £938,914
Registered Office: The Old Post Office, 63 Saville Street, North Shields, Tyne & Wear, NE30 1AY
Activities: Other letting and operating of own or leased real estate
Shareholder: Mt Malcolm Roland McKenzie
Officers: Susan McKenzie, Secretary/Administrator; Malcolm Roland McKenzie [1965] Director/Quantity Surveyor

Maquet Limited
Incorporated: 11 November 1987 *Employees:* 105
Net Worth: £28,559,000 *Total Assets:* £54,474,000
Registered Office: 14-15 Burford Way, Boldon Business Park, Boldon Colliery, Co Durham, NE35 9PZ
Activities: Other service activities n.e.c.
Shareholders: Maquet SAS; Getinge AB
Officers: Martin Forbister, Secretary; Avril Ann Forde [1974] Director/Sales and Marketing [Irish]; Karin Söderlund [1981] Commercial Excellence Director [Finnish]; Jon Barrie Yard [1967] QA Director

Marblemand Limited
Incorporated: 24 February 1978
Net Worth: £4,161,675 *Total Assets:* £5,654,960
Registered Office: 80 Hartington Road, Stockton on Tees, Cleveland, TS18 1HE
Activities: Other letting and operating of own or leased real estate
Officers: Dominic George Collinge Ferard, Secretary; Dominic George Collinge Ferard [1963] Director; Jo Tracy Ferard [1969] Director; Rupert Charles Hawkesworth Ferard [1966] Director; Sally Clare Ferard [1962] Director

Marina Hotels Limited
Incorporated: 1 August 2005
Net Worth Deficit: £862,788 *Total Assets:* £2,789,873
Registered Office: 91-95 Blandford Street, Newcastle upon Tyne, NE1 3PZ
Activities: Hotels and similar accommodation
Shareholders: Tripta Malhotra; Darshan Kumar Malhotra
Officers: Tripta Malhotra, Secretary; Darshan Kumar Malhotra [1948] Managing Director; Rajan Malhotra [1986] Director/Hotel Manager; Rajesh Malhotra [1974] Director/Hotel Manager

Marine Court Dover Limited
Incorporated: 27 August 2003
Net Worth: £3,364,154 *Total Assets:* £4,088,202
Registered Office: Yours Business Networks, Suite A, 7-8 Delta Bank Road, Gateshead, Tyne & Wear, NE11 9DJ
Activities: Buying and selling of own real estate
Shareholders: Nicholas John Knight; Reuben Thomas Coppin Straker
Officers: Reuben Thomas Coppin Straker, Secretary/Property Consultant; Nicholas John Knight [1962] Director; Reuben Thomas Coppin Straker [1956] Director/Property Consultant

Marine Engineering Pipeworks Limited
Incorporated: 26 November 1976 *Employees:* 12
Net Worth: £5,350,768 *Total Assets:* £5,913,078
Registered Office: Leechmere Industrial Estate, Grangetown, Sunderland, Tyne & Wear, SR2 9TE
Activities: Manufacture of other fabricated metal products n.e.c.
Shareholder: Philip Harper
Officers: Gary Harper, Secretary; Gary Harper [1965] Technical Director; Philip Harper [1960] Director

Marine Fabricators Limited
Incorporated: 3 November 1998 *Employees:* 54
Net Worth: £2,499,369 *Total Assets:* £2,893,528
Registered Office: Bays 1 and 2, Unit 1 Haverton Hill Industrial Estate, Stockton on Tees, Cleveland, TS23 1PZ
Activities: Manufacture of metal structures and parts of structures
Parent: RSD Marine Ltd
Officers: Christopher Stephen Reed [1984] Director

Maritsave Limited
Incorporated: 18 September 1998
Net Worth: £1,066,196 *Total Assets:* £1,175,093
Registered Office: Moorlands, Edmundbyers, Consett, Co Durham, DH8 9NN
Activities: Other letting and operating of own or leased real estate
Shareholder: Mark Stuart Lee
Officers: Mark Stuart Lee, Secretary; Brian Lee [1945] Director/Consultant; Mark Stuart Lee [1976] Director/Company Secretary

Marityne Marine Projects Limited
Incorporated: 20 September 2005 *Employees:* 4
Net Worth: £784,121 *Total Assets:* £843,620
Registered Office: Normanhurst, Westoe Village, South Shields, Tyne & Wear, NE33 3EB
Activities: Management consultancy activities other than financial management
Shareholders: Christopher Daniel Bond; Patrick Mark Bond
Officers: Patrick Mark Bond, Secretary; Christopher Daniel Bond [1962] Director/Project Manager; William McGuffog [1970] Director/Marine Engineer

Markbourn Limited
Incorporated: 30 September 1997 *Employees:* 8
Net Worth: £14,021,956 *Total Assets:* £25,144,272
Registered Office: 20-22 Second Avenue, Heaton, Newcastle upon Tyne, NE6 5XS
Activities: Activities of business and employers membership organisations
Major Shareholder: Randhir Puri
Officers: Randhir Puri, Secretary/Administrator; Randhir Puri [1973] Director/Administrator; Surinder Kumar Puri [1947] Director

Market Edge Consulting Limited
Incorporated: 12 September 2000 *Employees:* 2
Net Worth: £700,907 *Total Assets:* £1,041,183
Registered Office: 21 Parker Drive, Bedale, N Yorks, DL8 2UD
Activities: Management consultancy activities other than financial management
Major Shareholder: Paul Drees
Officers: Victor John Pogson, Secretary; Paul Drees [1963] Director/Chemist [American]

Market Street Developments Ltd
Incorporated: 2 November 2015
Registered Office: 121 Low Etherley, Bishop Auckland, Co Durham, DL14 0HA
Activities: Development of building projects
Officers: David Aimer, Secretary; David James Aimer [1951] Director/Company Secretary; Michael Anthony Clark [1939] Director

W. Marley Agricultural Contractors Limited
Incorporated: 20 May 1982
Net Worth: £1,854,242 *Total Assets:* £4,350,334
Registered Office: Constantine Farm, North Bitchburn, Crook, Co Durham, DL15 8AQ
Activities: Landscape service activities
Major Shareholder: William Marley
Officers: Claire Louise Glendenning [1979] Director; Ross William Marley [1990] Director; William Marley [1953] Director

Marlin Assets Limited
Incorporated: 9 January 2017
Net Worth Deficit: £22,986 *Total Assets:* £1,256,391
Registered Office: 202-206 Linthorpe Road, Middlesbrough, Cleveland, TS1 3QW
Activities: Buying and selling of own real estate
Major Shareholder: David James Griffiths
Officers: David James Griffiths [1988] Director/Financial Advisor

Marlow Foods Limited
Incorporated: 12 September 1983 *Employees:* 657
Net Worth: £70,385,000 *Total Assets:* £150,028,000
Registered Office: Quorn Foods, Station Road, Stokesley, Cleveland, TS9 7AB
Activities: Manufacture of other food products n.e.c.
Parent: Monde Nissin (UK) Limited
Officers: James Laurence Harvey, Secretary; Kevin Francis Brennan [1962] Director; James Laurence Harvey [1965] Director/Accountant

Marmax Products Limited
Incorporated: 2 September 1982 *Employees:* 30
Net Worth: £1,134,629 *Total Assets:* £1,739,375
Registered Office: Units 9-16 Tanfield Lea Industrial Estate South, Tanfield Lea, Stanley, Co Durham, DH9 9QX
Activities: Manufacture of other plastic products
Parent: Samuel Grant (Group) Ltd
Officers: Ashley Jon Dean, Secretary; Andrew David Surrey Grant [1970] Director/Packaging Merchant; Matthew Paul Surrey Grant [1974] Director/Packaging Merchant; Sheelagh Margaret Grant [1946] Marketing Director; Jacqueline Robshaw [1960] Director/Manager

Marrick Priory Trust
Incorporated: 7 January 2000
Net Worth: £1,090,139 *Total Assets:* £1,112,310
Registered Office: Marrick Priory, Marrick, Richmond, N Yorks, DL11 7LD
Activities: Other education n.e.c.
Officers: Susan Nicholson, Secretary; Judith Mary Clarke [1942] Director/Retired; Rolline Charlotte Frewen [1956] Director; Revd Caroline Joan Hewlett [1968] Director/Vicar; Stephen Jordan [1964] Director/Army Officer; Susan Nicholson [1953] Director/Retired; Emily Lilian Purver [1930] Director/Retired; Rev John Michael Richards [1953] Director/Retired; Catherine Scott Trewby [1949] Director/Retired; Barrie Whitfield [1949] Director/Bank Manager

Harry Marsh (Engineers) Limited
Incorporated: 18 August 1972
Net Worth: £1,912,005 *Total Assets:* £2,510,245
Registered Office: The Parade, Hendon, Sunderland, Tyne & Wear, SR2 8NT
Activities: Construction of commercial buildings
Major Shareholder: Stephen Anthony Coady
Officers: Stephen Anthony Coady, Secretary; Stephen Anthony Coady [1963] Director/Draughtsman; Neil Gibson [1966] Director

D.W. Marshall and Co. Limited
Incorporated: 27 December 1979 *Employees:* 35
Net Worth: £1,094,077 *Total Assets:* £2,095,247
Registered Office: 3b Gresley Road, Southwest Industrial Estate, Peterlee, Co Durham, SR8 2LU
Activities: Non-specialised wholesale trade
Parent: Adams Coach (Supplies) Ltd
Officers: Karen Margaret Adams, Secretary; David Ramage Adams [1989] Director/Manager; Ian Ramage Adams [1936] Director; Paul Ramage Adams [1964] Director; Colin George MoTlon [1969] Director; Graeme Shand Reid [1968] Director; Neil Shackelton [1962] Director

Marshall Inns Limited
Incorporated: 27 March 2001 *Employees:* 21
Net Worth: £984,105 *Total Assets:* £1,776,363
Registered Office: Sandgate House, Quayside, Newcastle upon Tyne, NE1 3DX
Activities: Licenced restaurants
Parent: Inn Collection Bidco Limited
Officers: Sean Lee Donkin [1981] Operations Director; Angus Keith Liddell [1955] Director; Iain Stein [1959] Director

B. Marshall Marine Limited
Incorporated: 12 January 2011
Registered Office: Graving Dock, Dockside Road, Middlesbrough, Cleveland, TS3 8AT
Activities: Building of ships and floating structures
Shareholder: Barry Marshall
Officers: Barry Marshall, Secretary; Anthony James Curtis [1948] Director; Barry Marshall [1948] Director; Benjamin Marshall [1978] Director/Mechanical Engineer

Colin Marshall Painting Contractors Ltd
Incorporated: 24 May 2001 *Employees:* 84
Net Worth: £1,117,188 *Total Assets:* £1,752,212
Registered Office: 2 Bewick Road, Gateshead, Tyne & Wear, NE8 4DP
Activities: Painting
Officers: Deborah Marshall, Secretary; Colin Marshall [1963] Director/Decorator; Deborah Marshall [1964] Director/Admin Manager

Marshall Property Rentals Limited
Incorporated: 22 May 2012
Registered Office: 7 Victoria Road, Darlington, Co Durham, DL1 5SN
Activities: Other letting and operating of own or leased real estate
Major Shareholder: Dr Adrian Marshall
Officers: Dr Adrian John Marshall [1956] Director

Marske Site Services Ltd.
Incorporated: 10 July 1984
Net Worth: £567,561 *Total Assets:* £1,600,817
Registered Office: Tobias House, St Marks Court, Teesdale Business Park, Stockton on Tees, Cleveland, TS17 6QW
Activities: Other engineering activities
Shareholders: John Michael McCullagh; Rolf Michael McCullagh; Tim Michael McCullagh
Officers: John Michael McCullagh [1963] Director/Engineer; Rolf Michael McCullagh [1965] Director/Chartered Engineer; Tim Michael McCullagh [1968] Director/Engineer

Marson Investments Limited
Incorporated: 7 October 2016 *Employees:* 3
Net Worth: £1,846,177 *Total Assets:* £2,571,565
Registered Office: 1i North Sands Business Centre, Liberty Way, Sunderland, Tyne & Wear, SR6 0QA
Activities: Buying and selling of own real estate
Major Shareholder: Walter Veti
Officers: Walter Christopher Veti [1984] Director; Walter Veti [1955] Director

Martel Instruments Holdings Limited
Incorporated: 27 July 2006
Net Worth Deficit: £2,523,132 *Total Assets:* £7,960,248
Registered Office: Stanelaw Way, Tanfield Lea Industrial Estate, Stanley, Co Durham, DH9 9XG
Activities: Activities of head offices
Officers: Colin John Proudfoot, Secretary; Michael Christopher Collis [1965] Director/Chartered Accountant; Colin John Proudfoot [1960] Director/Accountant; Keith John Walker [1955] Director

Martel Instruments Limited
Incorporated: 26 November 1982
Net Worth: £4,190,222 *Total Assets:* £6,627,729
Registered Office: Stanelaw Way, Tanfield Lea Industrial Estate, Stanley, Co Durham, DH9 9XG
Activities: Manufacture of loaded electronic boards
Parent: Martel Instruments Holdings Limited
Officers: Colin John Proudfoot, Secretary; Colin John Proudfoot [1960] Director/Accountant; Keith John Walker [1955] Director

Maryport Homes LLP
Incorporated: 22 March 2008
Net Worth: £824,020 *Total Assets:* £824,020
Registered Office: Houghton House, New Road, Team Valley Trading Estate, Gateshead, Tyne & Wear, NE11 0JU
Officers: George Houghton [1940] Member; Jennifer Pamela Houghton [1946] Member

Masada Developments Limited
Incorporated: 11 February 2000 *Employees:* 3
Net Worth: £1,690,745 *Total Assets:* £3,343,624
Registered Office: Unit 2b Guiseley Way, Durham Lane Industrial Park, Eaglescliffe, Stockton on Tees, Cleveland, TS16 0RF
Activities: Other letting and operating of own or leased real estate
Officers: Robert Michael Goodrum, Secretary; Andrew Marcus Dicken [1970] Director

Mash Staffing Payroll Limited
Incorporated: 5 April 2016
Net Worth Deficit: £26,958 *Total Assets:* £1,372,006
Registered Office: Wynyard Park House, Wynyard Avenue, Wynyard, Cleveland, TS22 5TB
Activities: Human resources provision and management of human resources functions
Officers: Jonathan Beckerlegge [1945] Director/Chartered Accountant

Allen Mason & Sons (Herrington) Limited
Incorporated: 22 May 1973
Net Worth: £3,064,969 *Total Assets:* £3,688,624
Registered Office: 23 Archery Rise, Durham, DH1 4LA
Activities: Construction of domestic buildings
Major Shareholder: Allen John Mason
Officers: Allen John Mason, Secretary; Allen John Mason [1950] Director/Builder

R. Mason Chemicals Limited
Incorporated: 1 November 1960
Net Worth: £1,166,508 *Total Assets:* £1,304,425
Registered Office: Hare Law Industrial Estate, Stanley, Co Durham, DH9 8UL
Activities: Manufacture of other inorganic basic chemicals
Shareholders: Paul Charles Mason; Tonia Emily Mason
Officers: Eileen Mary Mason, Secretary; Eileen Mary Mason [1934] Director/Company Secretary; Paul Charles Mason [1961] Director

Mason Frank International Limited
Incorporated: 7 July 2010 *Employees:* 61
Net Worth: £4,831,000 *Total Assets:* £9,886,000
Registered Office: The St Nicholas Building, St Nicholas Street, Newcastle upon Tyne, NE1 1RF
Activities: Other activities of employment placement agencies
Parent: Frank Recruitment Group Services Limited
Officers: Nigel Ashley O'Donoghue, Secretary; James Lloyd-Townshend [1973] Director; Andrew Stephen Mason [1972] Director; Lewis Paul Miller [1981] Director; Nigel Ashley O'Donoghue [1972] Director/Chief Financial Officer

Mastclimber Solutions UK Ltd.
Incorporated: 15 February 2008
Net Worth Deficit: £224,063 *Total Assets:* £3,538,356
Registered Office: 34 Bedeburn View, Jarrow, Tyne & Wear, NE32 5PQ
Activities: Agents involved in the sale of timber and building materials
Major Shareholder: Thomas John Mulheran
Officers: Thomas John Mulheran [1945] Director/Admin Manager

Mastercopy Limited
Incorporated: 24 February 1989 *Employees:* 20
Net Worth: £1,901,668 *Total Assets:* £2,895,725
Registered Office: Randol House, Martinet Road, Thornaby, Stockton on Tees, Cleveland, TS17 0BA
Activities: Repair of electrical equipment
Major Shareholder: William Michael Preston
Officers: Anne Marie Plews, Secretary; Neil Antony Preston [1974] Director/Service Manager; Stephen Michael Preston [1971] Director/Photocopier Sales Manager; Teresa Mary Preston [1952] Director/Secretary; William Michael Preston [1950] Director/Photocopier Salesman & Maintenance

Masterdata Limited
Incorporated: 18 March 2016
Net Worth: £5,650,929 *Total Assets:* £5,698,957
Registered Office: 38 Collingwood House, Collingwood Street, Newcastle upon Tyne, NE1 1JF
Activities: Other service activities n.e.c.
Officers: Dominick Robert Shelly [1967] Sales Director; Michelle Wood [1980] Director

Match Day Centres Ltd
Incorporated: 30 March 2010 *Employees:* 19
Net Worth: £593,859 *Total Assets:* £1,933,105
Registered Office: 17th Floor, Cale Cross House, Pilgrim Street, Newcastle upon Tyne, NE1 6SU
Activities: Operation of sports facilities
Parent: Dane & Co., Limited
Officers: Trevor Cartner [1960] Director/Chartered Surveyor; Stewart Dawson [1959] Director; Michael Robert Leather [1961] Director/Accountant; Jason Joseph Maguire [1974] Director; Gerard O'Connor [1961] Director

Materials Processing Institute
Incorporated: 3 March 2014 *Employees:* 63
Net Worth: £4,859,572 *Total Assets:* £9,759,769
Registered Office: Materials Processing Institute, Eston Road, Middlesbrough, Cleveland, TS6 6US
Activities: Engineering design activities for industrial process and production
Officers: Carol Patton, Secretary; Alastair Stuart Aitken [1962] Commercial Director; Jonathan Martin Bolton [1962] Director/Chief Executive Officer; Dr Martin Simon Brunnock [1972] Technical Director; Professor Simon Nicholas Hodgson [1963] Director/Pro Vice-Chancellor (Research & Innovation); Paul Kitson [1965] Director/Manager Electronic Systems and Control; Christopher McDonald [1976] Director/Chief Executive Officer; Jonathan Neal [1959] Director/Accountant; Dr Bernard Alan Rickinson [1950] Director/Chief Executive; Robert Ruddlestone [1948] Director/Chairman

Matfen Golf Limited
Incorporated: 7 February 2000
Net Worth: £9,422 *Total Assets:* £2,233,721
Registered Office: Matfen Estate Office, The Old Laundry, Matfen, Northumberland, NE20 0RP
Activities: Activities of sport clubs
Parent: Crossco (940) Limited
Officers: Lady Anna Margaret Blackett, Secretary/Hotelier; Sir Hugh Francis Blackett [1955] Director/Hotelier

Matfen Hall Hotel LLP
Incorporated: 14 March 2003 *Employees:* 133
Net Worth: £1,405,603 *Total Assets:* £7,408,647
Registered Office: Matfen Hall, Matfen, Northumberland, NE20 0RH
Officers: Lady Anna Margaret Blackett [1959] Member; Sir Hugh Francis Blackett [1955] Member

Mathewson Limited
Incorporated: 20 August 1998
Registered Office: Harewood House, Bowburn North Industrial Estate, Bowburn, Co Durham, DH6 5PF
Activities: Plumbing, heat and air-conditioning installation
Shareholders: James Mathewson; Clare Mathewson
Officers: Clare Mathewson, Secretary; Clare Mathewson [1962] Director/Administrator; James Mathewson [1963] Director

Matrix Power Limited
Incorporated: 20 September 2010 *Employees:* 20
Net Worth: £725,632 *Total Assets:* £1,327,697
Registered Office: Unit 4 Mickleton Road, Middlesbrough, Cleveland, TS2 1RQ
Activities: Electrical installation
Shareholders: Neil Stuart Guest; Ian Hugill
Officers: Ian Hugill, Secretary; Andrew Edward Bell [1982] Director/Electrical Commissioning Engineer; Neil Stuart Guest [1959] Director/Electrical Engineer; Ian Hugill [1972] Director/Electrical Engineer; Ian David Spellman [1969] Technical Director

Matwest Ltd
Incorporated: 29 September 2006
Registered Office: Manor House, Southside, Scorton, N Yorks, DL10 6DN
Activities: Residents property management
Officers: Crighton David Mather, Secretary; Amanda Clare Mather [1966] Director; Crighton David Mather [1958] Director

F.E.Maughan Limited
Incorporated: 16 February 1938 *Employees:* 18
Net Worth: £290,690 *Total Assets:* £750,311
Registered Office: Morne House, Holystone, Tyne & Wear, NE27 0DE
Activities: Agents involved in the sale of timber and building materials
Officers: Dorothy Ann Maughan, Secretary; Catherine Ann Maughan [1972] Director; David Allister Maughan [1965] Director; Dorothy Ann Maughan [1941] Director; Michael Edward Maughan [1968] Director

MAV Investments Limited
Incorporated: 17 May 2011
Registered Office: Stow House Farm, Cornsay, Co Durham, DH7 9EN
Activities: Other holiday and other collective accommodation
Officers: Jane Marie Marley [1974] Director/Office Manager; Keith Marley [1970] Director/Manager

Maval Electrical and Mechanical Engineering Company Limited
Incorporated: 25 July 1972 *Employees:* 30
Net Worth: £692,292 *Total Assets:* £1,772,696
Registered Office: Skippers Lane Industrial Estate, South Bank, Middlesbrough, Cleveland, TS6 6HA
Activities: Electrical installation
Parent: Maval Investments Limited
Officers: Derek Routledge [1944] Director/Electrical Engineer; Phillip Andrew Routledge [1961] Director; Darren Trotter [1970] Director

Maval Investments Limited
Incorporated: 4 February 2005 *Employees:* 2
Net Worth: £1,033,803 *Total Assets:* £1,039,213
Registered Office: c/o Maval Electrical Engineering Ltd, Skippers Lane Industrial Estate, South Bank, Middlesbrough, Cleveland, TS6 6HE
Activities: Activities of other holding companies n.e.c.
Shareholder: Phillip Andrew Routledge
Officers: Phillip Andrew Routledge [1961] Director; Darren Trotter [1970] Director

Maxibrite Limited
Incorporated: 2 August 1962 *Employees:* 29
Net Worth: £7,463,000 *Total Assets:* £8,718,000
Registered Office: West Terrace, Esh Winning, Co Durham, DH7 9PT
Activities: Other manufacturing n.e.c.
Parent: Coal 4 Energy Limited
Officers: Gordon Frank Colenso Banham [1964] Director; John Paul Burks [1964] Director

Maxim Facilities Management Ltd
Incorporated: 30 September 2010 *Employees:* 854
Net Worth: £428,134 *Total Assets:* £2,369,310
Registered Office: 60-62 Wearfield, Sunderland Enterprise Park, Sunderland, Tyne & Wear, SR5 2TA
Activities: Combined facilities support activities
Major Shareholder: Graham Hankin Conway
Officers: Graham Hankin Conway [1954] Director; Juliet Conway [1961] Director

Maxwells (Sunderland) Limited
Incorporated: 6 January 1959 *Employees:* 112
Net Worth: £3,527,522 *Total Assets:* £6,613,887
Registered Office: Unit 4 Durham Road Industrial Estate, Birtley, Co Durham, DH3 2BQ
Activities: Retail sale of hardware, paints and glass in specialised stores
Officers: Neil Maxwell, Secretary/Director; Alison Maxwell [1965] Director/Chartered Secretary; Fraser Maxwell [1973] Director/Hardware Merchant; Ian Maxwell [1956] Director/Handicrafts Dealer; Keith Maxwell [1957] Director/Handicrafts Dealer; Neil Maxwell [1959] Director

Mayborn (UK) Limited
Incorporated: 11 March 1985 *Employees:* 141
Net Worth: £2,262,000 *Total Assets:* £156,440,000
Registered Office: Mayborn House, Balliol Business Park, Newcastle upon Tyne, NE12 8EW
Activities: Manufacture of other plastic products
Parent: Mayborn Group Limited
Officers: Neal Austin [1966] Global Operations Director; Edward Chapman [1964] Director; Stephen William Parkin [1969] Director/Marketing; James William Matthew Taylor [1974] Director/Chief Finance Officer

Mayborn Group Limited
Incorporated: 19 September 1946 *Employees:* 1
Net Worth: £76,166,000 *Total Assets:* £81,922,000
Registered Office: Mayborn House, Balliol Business Park, Newcastle upon Tyne, NE12 8EW
Activities: Activities of head offices
Parent: Jake Acquisitions Limited
Officers: Stephen William Parkin [1969] Director; James William Matthew Taylor [1974] Director/Chief Financial Officer

G Mayes Ltd
Incorporated: 7 October 2015
Net Worth: £60,181 *Total Assets:* £1,337,079
Registered Office: 26 Sandringham Avenue, Newcastle upon Tyne, NE12 8JX
Activities: Dispensing chemist in specialised stores
Major Shareholder: Gillian Mayes
Officers: Gillian Mayes [1971] Director

Mayford Equities Limited
Incorporated: 1 December 2005 *Employees:* 1
Net Worth Deficit: £72,058 *Total Assets:* £2,792,867
Registered Office: 26a Old Elvet, Durham, DH1 3HN
Activities: Other business support service activities n.e.c.
Shareholders: Lucy Atkinson; Helen Frankland
Officers: Paul Andrew Brown, Secretary; Lucy Victoria Atkinson [1985] Director; Mary Catherine Best [1960] Director; Stephen Best [1957] Director; Helen Frankland [1988] Director

Maymask (121) Limited
Incorporated: 27 November 2006
Net Worth: £385,829 *Total Assets:* £3,644,158
Registered Office: 17 Windsor Terrace, Jesmond, Newcastle upon Tyne, NE2 4HE
Activities: Other letting and operating of own or leased real estate
Officers: Sayeed Ahmed, Secretary/Director; Sayeed Ahmed [1956] Director; Nasir Rashid [1964] Director; Salim Rashid [1958] Director

Maymask (140) Limited
Incorporated: 19 October 2009
Net Worth: £709,770 *Total Assets:* £2,418,215
Registered Office: The Park Hotel, Grand Parade, Tynemouth, Tyne & Wear, NE30 4JQ
Activities: Other letting and operating of own or leased real estate
Officers: Jaswant Singh Gill [1968] Director; Sewa Singh Gill [1945] Director

Maymask (171) Limited
Incorporated: 6 June 2011
Net Worth: £26,886 *Total Assets:* £761,841
Registered Office: Lady Stephenson Library, Welbeck Road, Newcastle upon Tyne, NE6 2PA
Activities: Other letting and operating of own or leased real estate
Shareholders: Dr Andy Narsesian; Vlatka Narsesian
Officers: Dr Andy Narsesian [1977] Director/Lecturer; Graeme Robert Campbell Nicol [1968] Director

Maymask (202) Limited
Incorporated: 14 October 2013
Net Worth Deficit: £387,032 *Total Assets:* £2,800,939
Registered Office: Units 15-16 Stockholm Close, Tyne Tunnel Trading Estate, North Shields, Tyne & Wear, NE29 7SF
Activities: Licenced clubs
Shareholder: Baldev Singh Ladhar
Officers: Baldev Singh Ladhar [1958] Director; Bhagwant Kaur Ladhar [1961] Director

The Maymask Healthcare Group Limited
Incorporated: 30 March 2005
Net Worth: £1,563,484 *Total Assets:* £1,795,005
Registered Office: Palmer Four, Clervaux Exchange Business Centre, Clervaux Terrace, Jarrow, Tyne & Wear, NE32 5UP
Activities: Other human health activities
Shareholder: Gordon Roy Peters
Officers: Victoria Jane Peters, Secretary; Douglas John Corbitt [1949] Director/Business Consultant; Oliver George Henry Peters [1990] Director; Victoria Jane Peters [1958] Director/Business Consultant

Maysan Foods Limited
Incorporated: 1 October 1963 *Employees:* 19
Net Worth: £1,146,114 *Total Assets:* £1,350,579
Registered Office: Meadowfield, Ponteland, Northumberland, NE20 9SD
Activities: Manufacture of condiments and seasonings
Major Shareholder: Denise Harrison
Officers: Denise Harrison, Secretary; Denise Harrison [1960] Director/Company Secretary

Mazegood Limited
Incorporated: 23 June 2000
Net Worth: £1,105,685 *Total Assets:* £2,606,617
Registered Office: 43-45 Yarm Lane, Stockton on Tees, Cleveland, TS18 3EA
Activities: Other letting and operating of own or leased real estate
Shareholders: Gilbert Roland Wharton; Janet Wharton
Officers: Janet Wharton, Secretary; Christopher Roland Wharton [1968] Director; Gilbert Roland Wharton [1943] Director; Janet Wharton [1939] Director

Mazhar Ltd
Incorporated: 18 May 2006 *Employees:* 30
Net Worth: £1,211,222 *Total Assets:* £1,373,500
Registered Office: 16 South Shore Road, East Gateshead Industrial Estate, Gateshead, Tyne & Wear, NE8 3AE
Activities: Non-specialised wholesale trade
Shareholders: Saleem Shahzada Mazhar; Kaleem Mazhar
Officers: Angela Mazhar, Secretary; Saleem Mazhar, Secretary; Yasmeen Mazhar, Secretary; Kaleem Mazhar [1964] Director; Saleem Mazhar [1960] Director

MBC Summit Holdings Limited
Incorporated: 9 December 2013 *Employees:* 32
Net Worth: £594,695 *Total Assets:* £6,425,664
Registered Office: Unit 5 New York Way, New York Industrial Estate, Wallsend, Tyne & Wear, NE27 0QF
Activities: Wholesale of clothing and footwear
Major Shareholder: Stephen David Roberts
Officers: Spencer James McBride, Secretary; Stephen David Roberts [1973] Director

MBL Solutions Limited
Incorporated: 8 October 2001
Net Worth: £382,425 *Total Assets:* £781,923
Registered Office: 37 Apex Business Village, Cramlington, Northumberland, NE23 7BF
Activities: Activities of call centres
Shareholders: Oliver Edward Hext Stephens; Sally Wallace
Officers: Oliver Edward Hext Stephens, Secretary; Oliver Edward Hext Stephens [1960] Managing Director; Sally Wallace [1963] Financial Director; Stephen Andrew Winfield [1955] Director

Mc Dougall Dodds Limited
Incorporated: 5 May 1960 *Employees:* 3
Net Worth: £918,327 *Total Assets:* £1,422,645
Registered Office: 22 Rectory Road, Gosforth, Newcastle upon Tyne, NE3 1XP
Activities: Other letting and operating of own or leased real estate
Major Shareholder: James Christopher Summers
Officers: James Christopher Summers, Secretary; James Christopher Summers [1958] Director; Katherine Alexandra Summers [1991] Director

MC Ware IT Solutions Limited
Incorporated: 22 April 2013 *Employees:* 11
Net Worth: £776,222 *Total Assets:* £1,052,918
Registered Office: 17 Halegrove Court, Cygnet Drive, Stockton on Tees, Cleveland, TS18 3DB
Activities: Information technology consultancy activities
Major Shareholder: Jamie Lee Scotchbrook
Officers: Jamie Lee Scotchbrook [1977] Director/IT Solutions; Samantha Karen Scotchbrook [1975] Director

MCC Group Holdings (UK) Limited
Incorporated: 19 December 2008
Net Worth: £245,717,888 *Total Assets:* £245,717,888
Registered Office: Cassel Works, New Road, Billingham, Cleveland, TS23 1LE
Activities: Activities of other holding companies n.e.c.
Parent: Mitsubishi Chemical Corporation
Officers: Yasuhiro Kabu [1960] Director/Company Executive [Japanese]; Dai Oyama [1968] Director [Japanese]

McCaffery Financial Limited
Incorporated: 29 May 2014
Net Worth: £5,735,346 *Total Assets:* £5,758,349
Registered Office: 7 Cliffe Court, Sunderland, Tyne & Wear, SR6 9NT
Activities: Factoring
Shareholders: Pamela McCaffery; George McCaffery
Officers: George McCaffery [1949] Director

A. McCall & Sons (Houghton-le-Spring) Limited
Incorporated: 10 August 2004 *Employees:* 3
Net Worth: £593,456 *Total Assets:* £825,394
Registered Office: The Weighbridge, Field House Farm, Houghton-le-Spring, Co Durham, DH5 8AJ
Activities: Collection of non-hazardous waste
Shareholders: Kathryn Bennison; Christine McCall
Officers: Christine McCall, Secretary; Kathryn Bennison [1965] Director/Quarry Restoration Landfill; Christine McCall [1962] Director/Quarry Restoration Landfill

McCallum Currie Limited
Incorporated: 29 March 2016
Net Worth: £115,177 *Total Assets:* £2,706,520
Registered Office: Coburg House, 1 Coburg Street, Gateshead, Tyne & Wear, NE8 1NS
Activities: Activities of open-ended investment companies
Major Shareholder: Angus McCallum Currie
Officers: Angus McCallum Currie [1993] Director/Student; Gail Eve Peters [1957] Director/Retired

McCarrick Construction Company Limited
Incorporated: 18 May 1953 *Employees:* 25
Net Worth: £3,598,728 *Total Assets:* £4,382,090
Registered Office: The Turnpark, Station Road, Chester-le-Street, Co Durham, DH3 3DU
Activities: Construction of commercial buildings
Officers: Melanie Robson, Secretary; Keith Alderslade [1958] Director/Quantity Surveyor; Lynn Norma McCarrick [1953] Director/Maintenance Secretary; Matthew James McCarrick [1981] Director; Michael McCarrick [1950] Director; Anthony Allan Pearce [1963] Director/Construction

McCarrick Homes Ltd
Incorporated: 25 November 2008
Net Worth: £939,538 *Total Assets:* £2,646,791
Registered Office: The Turnpark, Station Road, Chester-le-Street, Co Durham, DH3 3DU
Activities: Construction of domestic buildings
Officers: Keith Alderslade [1958] Director; Lynn Norma McCarrick [1953] Director; Matthew James McCarrick [1981] Director; Michael McCarrick [1950] Director; Anthony Allan Pearce [1953] Director

J.Mccheyne Construction Limited
Incorporated: 5 May 1970
Net Worth: £945,526 *Total Assets:* £957,822
Registered Office: 56 Jesmond Park West, Jesmond, Newcastle upon Tyne, NE7 7BY
Activities: Other letting and operating of own or leased real estate
Major Shareholder: Andrew McCheyne
Officers: Andrew McCheyne, Secretary; Andrew McCheyne [1962] Director

Darren McCormick Jewellery Limited
Incorporated: 23 February 2010
Net Worth Deficit: £914,988 *Total Assets:* £1,372,993
Registered Office: Pandora House, Redworth Road, Shildon, Co Durham, DL4 2JT
Activities: Other retail sale not in stores, stalls or markets
Major Shareholder: Darren Bernard McCormick
Officers: Darren Bernard McCormick [1964] Director

T.P.M. McDonagh (Civil Engineering) Limited
Incorporated: 23 July 1973 *Employees:* 15
Net Worth: £1,359,882 *Total Assets:* £1,721,875
Registered Office: Barrington House, 41-45 Yarm Lane, Stockton on Tees, Cleveland, TS18 3EA
Activities: Construction of commercial buildings
Major Shareholder: Michael Joseph McDonagh
Officers: Norah McDonagh, Secretary; John Gerard McDonagh [1967] Director/Engineer; Michael Kieron McDonagh [1977] Director/Engineer; Thomas Francis McDonagh [1938] Director/Civil Engineering Contractor [Irish]

McDougal & Breen Ltd
Incorporated: 5 January 2007
Registered Office: Unit 4 Wesley Drive, Benton Square Industrial Estate, Newcastle upon Tyne, NE12 9UP
Activities: Sale of used cars and light motor vehicles
Shareholders: Mark Breen; Terry McDougal
Officers: Mark Breen, Secretary; Mark Breen [1975] Director/Secretary; Terrence Ian McDougal [1969] Director

MCE Group PLC
Incorporated: 5 March 1990 *Employees:* 26
Net Worth: £507,971 *Total Assets:* £3,593,708
Registered Office: Haydock House, Wetherby Close, Portrack Interchange Business Park, Stockton on Tees, Cleveland, TS18 2SL
Activities: Repair of fabricated metal products
Major Shareholder: Kevin Francis Hunt
Officers: Deborah Vickers, Secretary; Kevin Francis Hunt [1950] Director [British/American]; Bernard William Thomas McCallum [1967] Director/General Manager

A McGann Building Contractors Limited
Incorporated: 28 February 2003 *Employees:* 5
Net Worth: £301,988 *Total Assets:* £787,837
Registered Office: Unit 2 Northumberland Street, North Shields, Tyne & Wear, NE30 1DS
Activities: Construction of commercial buildings
Shareholders: Andrew McGann; Kevin Andrew McGann
Officers: Kevin Andrew McGann, Secretary; Andrew McGann [1945] Director/Building Contractor; Kevin Andrew McGann [1972] Director/Building Contractor

W. McGovern & Co. Limited
Incorporated: 5 October 1979 *Employees:* 11
Net Worth: £224,823 *Total Assets:* £1,207,556
Registered Office: Albion Street, Felling, Gateshead, Tyne & Wear, NE10 9AJ
Activities: Manufacture of bricks, tiles and construction products, in baked clay
Officers: George Heydon [1961] Director; Andrew James Pickersgill [1978] Managing Director

McGovern Holdings Limited
Incorporated: 6 May 2015 *Employees:* 11
Net Worth: £440,285 *Total Assets:* £1,423,018
Registered Office: Albion Street, Felling, Gateshead, Tyne & Wear, NE10 9AJ
Activities: Agents involved in the sale of timber and building materials
Officers: George Heydon [1961] Director; Robert Hughes [1981] Managing Director

R C McInnes Limited
Incorporated: 21 April 1937
Net Worth: £2,049,134 *Total Assets:* £2,091,236
Registered Office: High Farm, Old Battersby, Great Ayton, Middlesbrough, Cleveland, TS9 6LU
Activities: Raising of sheep and goats
Major Shareholder: Paul Collins McInnes
Officers: Stefanie Jayne McInnes, Secretary; Paul Collins McInnes [1968] Director

McIntyres Properties Limited
Incorporated: 26 June 1961
Net Worth: £1,111,815 *Total Assets:* £1,114,918
Registered Office: Pillar Cottage, Low Skerningham Lane, Barmpton, Darlington, Co Durham, DL1 3JA
Activities: Non-trading company
Officers: Peter James McIntyre, Secretary; Helen Jayne McIntyre [1970] Director/Admin Assistant; Peter James McIntyre [1968] Director/Project Engineering

The McKenzie Corporation Limited
Incorporated: 25 July 1996 *Employees:* 1
Net Worth: £8,149,581 *Total Assets:* £8,576,478
Registered Office: West 2, Asama Court, Newcastle Business Park, Newcastle upon Tyne, NE4 7YD
Activities: Other business support service activities n.e.c.
Major Shareholder: Philip George Walton
Officers: Diane Walton, Secretary; Victoria Jane Ponton [1978] Director; Diane Walton [1952] Director; Edward James Walton [1987] Director; Mark Adam Walton [1974] Director; Philip George Walton [1949] Director

McKenzie Real Estates Limited
Incorporated: 11 September 2002
Net Worth: £1,699,804 *Total Assets:* £7,296,412
Registered Office: West 2, Asama Court, Newcastle Business Park, Newcastle upon Tyne, NE4 7YD
Activities: Other letting and operating of own or leased real estate
Major Shareholder: Philip George Walton
Officers: Diane Walton, Secretary; Victoria Jane Ponton [1978] Director; Edward James Walton [1987] Director; Mark Adam Walton [1974] Director; Philip George Walton [1949] Director

McLuckie Projects Limited
Incorporated: 4 November 1996
Net Worth: £630,597 *Total Assets:* £1,113,182
Registered Office: 1a Cravengate, Richmond, N Yorks, DL10 4RE
Activities: Construction of commercial buildings
Major Shareholder: Dennis McLuckie
Officers: Alan Paul Brown, Secretary; Dennis McLuckie [1953] Director

MCM (Spain) Ltd
Incorporated: 21 June 2016
Net Worth Deficit: £6,903 *Total Assets:* £1,026,374
Registered Office: 3 Keel Row, The Watermark, Gateshead, Tyne & Wear, NE11 9SZ
Activities: Other letting and operating of own or leased real estate
Shareholders: Ian Watson; Claire Watson
Officers: Claire Watson [1968] Director; Ian Watson [1962] Director

MCM Investments (UK & Ire) Ltd
Incorporated: 16 September 2016
Net Worth: £20,024 *Total Assets:* £4,211,581
Registered Office: 3 Keel Row, The Watermark, Gateshead, Tyne & Wear, NE11 9SZ
Activities: Other letting and operating of own or leased real estate
Major Shareholder: Ian Watson
Officers: Claire Watson [1968] Director/Company Secretary; Ian Watson [1962] Director; Mark Watson [1997] Director/Student

McNally and Thompson (UK Contracts) Limited
Incorporated: 18 December 1997 *Employees:* 53
Net Worth: £1,105,653 *Total Assets:* £2,888,366
Registered Office: Unit 1 North Hylton Enterprise Park, North Hylton Road, Sunderland, Tyne & Wear, SR5 3AD
Activities: Electrical installation
Major Shareholder: Fred Gordon Hood
Officers: David Robert Wealleans [1970] Director/Electrical Engineer

James A McNeill Building & Civil Engineering Limited
Incorporated: 14 February 2003
Registered Office: 14 Parkside, Blackhill, Consett, Co Durham, DH8 5XR
Activities: Construction of commercial buildings
Shareholder: James McNeill
Officers: James Anderson McNeill, Secretary; James Anthony McNeill [1968] Director

McNicholas Estates Ltd.
Incorporated: 7 September 1998
Net Worth: £760,511 *Total Assets:* £1,242,922
Registered Office: 3-5 Scarborough Street, Hartlepool, Cleveland, TS24 7DA
Activities: Other letting and operating of own or leased real estate
Major Shareholder: Sean Patrick McNicholas
Officers: Sean Patrick McNicholas [1966] Director

MCQ Investments Limited
Incorporated: 20 December 2011
Net Worth: £485,569 *Total Assets:* £1,108,890
Registered Office: Clifford House, Quebec, Co Durham, DH7 9DN
Activities: Activities of open-ended investment companies
Shareholders: Marie Elizabeth McQuaid; Sean Francis McQuaid
Officers: Marie Elizabeth McQuaid [1976] Director; Sean Francis McQuaid [1977] Director

McVickers Free Solar Limited
Incorporated: 12 July 2016
Net Worth: £27,921 *Total Assets:* £892,874
Registered Office: Unit 2 Woodland Court, Greencroft Industrial Park, Annfield Plain, Stanley, Co Durham, DH9 7BF
Activities: Other business support service activities n.e.c.
Major Shareholder: Aidan Storey
Officers: Andrew Dover [1976] Director/Engineer; Steven Peacock [1969] Director/Estimator; Catherine Anne Ridley [1974] Director/Administrator; Aidan Storey [1965] Director

McVickers Holdings Limited
Incorporated: 9 November 2010 *Employees:* 68
Net Worth: £2,797,138 *Total Assets:* £6,356,225
Registered Office: 2 Woodland Court, Greencroft Industrial Park, Stanley, Co Durham, DH9 7BF
Activities: Other letting and operating of own or leased real estate
Major Shareholder: Aidan Storey
Officers: Catherine Anne Ridley [1974] Financial Director; Aidan Storey [1965] Managing Director

McVickers Limited
Incorporated: 10 December 1975 *Employees:* 68
Net Worth: £258,053 *Total Assets:* £2,298,507
Registered Office: 2 Woodland Court, Greencroft Industrial Park, Stanley, Co Durham, DH9 7BF
Activities: Electrical installation
Major Shareholder: Aidan Storey
Officers: Anne Storey, Secretary; Mark Armstrong [1969] Director/Contracts Engineer; Andrew Dover [1976] Purchasing Manager/Director; Steven Peacock [1969] Estimator/Managing Director (Joint); Catherine Anne Ridley [1974] Managing Director (Joint); Aidan Storey [1965] Director/Chairman

MD5 Forensics Ltd
Incorporated: 29 November 2012
Net Worth: £1,223,770 *Total Assets:* £1,350,000
Registered Office: Beaumont Accountancy Services, First Floor, Enterprise House, 202-206 Linthorpe Road, Middlesbrough, Cleveland, TS1 3QW
Activities: Non-trading company
Shareholder: Adrian John Green
Officers: Catherine Anne Boyd, Secretary; Geoffrey Boyd [1965] Director; Adrian John Green [1971] Director

The Mea Trust
Incorporated: 26 February 1999 *Employees:* 8
Net Worth: £1,760,117 *Total Assets:* £1,937,827
Registered Office: MEA House, Ellison Place, Newcastle upon Tyne, NE1 8XS
Activities: Other letting and operating of own or leased real estate
Officers: Ann Petrice Wynn, Secretary; Ian Alan Burke [1961] Director/Head of Human Resources; Lisa Charlton [1967] Director/Fundraiser; Stephen Thomas Gilroy [1956] Director/Chartered Surveyor; Rosemary Clare Hogg [1979] Director/Councillor; James Lane [1980] Training Director; Gabrielle Suzanne Mandell [1965] Director/Charity CEO [Canadian/British]; William McKay [1977] Director/Solicitor; Antony Lewis Pierce [1976] Financial Director; Michael Ian Spriggs [1956] Director/Retired; Trevor Thurlow [1954] University Director (Retired)

Meadowcroft Homes Limited
Incorporated: 16 December 1998 *Employees:* 2
Net Worth: £1,557,363 *Total Assets:* £1,569,643
Registered Office: 32 Portland Terrace, Newcastle upon Tyne, NE2 1QP
Activities: Construction of domestic buildings
Parent: The R & J Hall 1999 Settlement
Officers: Alasdair Hall, Secretary/Development Director; Alasdair James Hall [1972] Development Director; Raymond Hall [1944] Director/Surveyor

Meadowdale Academy
Incorporated: 12 March 2012 *Employees:* 75
Net Worth: £4,185,414 *Total Assets:* £5,206,755
Registered Office: Meadowdale Academy, Hazelmere Avenue, Bedlington, Northumberland, NE22 6HA
Activities: General secondary education
Officers: Derek Harold Alcraft [1954] Director; Rosemary Brimelow [1969] Director/Banker; Joy Finn [1959] Director/Headteacher; Andrea Gavaghan [1970] Director/Business Accountant; Julie Anne Keogh [1970] Director/Strategic Marketing Manager; Rachel Helen Morgan [1975] Director/Assistant Headteacher; Trevor George Scott [1961] Director/Track Engineer; Helene Frances Turner [1953] Director/Funding/Resource Manager

Meadowfield Motors Limited
Incorporated: 6 January 2003
Net Worth: £1,148,349 *Total Assets:* £1,280,201
Registered Office: Frederick Street North, Meadowfield, Co Durham, DH7 8ND
Activities: Sale of new cars and light motor vehicles
Shareholders: Geoffrey Brown; Robert Gerard Ross
Officers: Robert Gerard Ross, Secretary; Geoffrey Brown [1959] Director; Robert Gerard Ross [1970] Director

Meadownet Limited
Incorporated: 16 January 2002
Net Worth: £744,657 *Total Assets:* £1,143,728
Registered Office: 1 Aston House, Redburn Road, Westerhope, Newcastle upon Tyne, NE5 1NB
Activities: Other letting and operating of own or leased real estate
Officers: Clive Miller Hindle, Secretary; Douglas John Brown [1963] Director; Peter Cuthbert [1956] Director/Property Consultant

Meat Zone UK Limited
Incorporated: 17 April 2002 *Employees:* 12
Net Worth: £843,983 *Total Assets:* £1,247,914
Registered Office: Hadrian House, Front Street, Chester-le-Street, Co Durham, DH3 3DB
Activities: Processing and preserving of poultry meat
Shareholders: Mahmood Reza Arta; Mahmood Reza Akrami; Masoud Chinikar
Officers: Masoud Chinikar, Secretary/Director; Mahmoud Reza Akrami [1954] Director; Mahmood Reza Arta [1959] Director; Masoud Chinikar [1961] Director

Mech-Tool Engineering Limited
Incorporated: 5 October 2000 *Employees:* 216
Net Worth: £6,160,017 *Total Assets:* £22,687,874
Registered Office: Mech Tool House, Whessoe Road, Darlington, Co Durham, DL3 0QT
Activities: Manufacture of metal structures and parts of structures
Shareholders: Veronica Garner; Marshall Kenneth Garner
Officers: Kerry Ann Shotton, Secretary; Marshall Kenneth Garner [1951] Director; Veronica Garner [1950] Director; Anthony George Jones [1972] Director

Mech-Tool Holdings Limited
Incorporated: 6 January 2014 *Employees:* 226
Net Worth: £8,773,704 *Total Assets:* £19,823,432
Registered Office: Mech-Tool House, Whessoe Road, Darlington, Co Durham, DL3 0QT
Activities: Activities of head offices
Shareholders: Marshall Kenneth Garner; Veronica Garner
Officers: Marshall Kenneth Garner [1951] Director; Veronica Garner [1950] Director

Mechanical Breakdown and General Insurance Services Limited
Incorporated: 8 February 1980
Net Worth: £947,561 *Total Assets:* £2,445,037
Registered Office: Cobalt Business Exchange, Cobalt Park Way, Wallsend, Tyne & Wear, NE28 9NZ
Activities: Non-life insurance
Parent: Aros Holdings Limited
Officers: Robert James Clark, Secretary; David Andrew Brock [1962] Managing Director; Robert James Clark [1965] Finance Director; Nicholas Scott Howard [1958] Director

Mechanised Project Management
Incorporated: 1 July 1946 *Employees:* 35
Net Worth: £33,886,000 *Total Assets:* £119,615,000
Registered Office: 1a Dukesway Court, Team Valley Trading Estate, Gateshead, Tyne & Wear, NE11 0PJ
Activities: Other letting and operating of own or leased real estate
Parent: Falcombe Holdings Limited
Officers: Phillip Nigel Blain, Secretary; David James Horrocks [1959] Director/Chartered Accountant; Ian Imrie [1955] Director

Mechplant (North East) Limited
Incorporated: 21 January 2002 *Employees:* 26
Net Worth: £2,215,936 *Total Assets:* £3,999,751
Registered Office: Esh House, Bowburn North Industrial Estate, Bowburn, Co Durham, DH6 5PF
Activities: Renting and leasing of construction and civil engineering machinery and equipment
Parent: Esh Holdings
Officers: Mark Sowerby, Secretary; Stephen Ronald George Makinson [1964] Director/Manager; Andrew Edward Radcliffe [1973] Finance Director; Mark Andrew Sowerby [1971] Director; Brian Wray [1965] Director/Manager

Medburn Estates Limited
Incorporated: 15 January 2003
Net Worth: £724,682 *Total Assets:* £1,474,877
Registered Office: Manor House, Medburn, Northumberland, NE20 0JB
Activities: Buying and selling of own real estate
Shareholders: Robin Armstrong; Anthony Brown
Officers: Angela Brown, Secretary/Property Development; Robin Armstrong [1964] Director; Anthony Brown [1971] Director/Property Development

The Medburn Land Company Limited
Incorporated: 5 August 2015
Net Worth Deficit: £2,442 *Total Assets:* £4,414,020
Registered Office: 118 Queens Road, Whitley Bay, Tyne & Wear, NE26 3AU
Activities: Buying and selling of own real estate
Shareholders: Alastair Henry Woodruff; Alan Ross
Officers: Alan Ross [1955] Director/Solicitor; Alastair Henry Woodruff [1963] Director

The Media Network Global Limited
Incorporated: 12 March 2013 *Employees:* 9
Net Worth: £780,856 *Total Assets:* £3,029,738
Registered Office: 22 Northumberland Square, North Shields, Tyne & Wear, NE30 1PW
Activities: Advertising agencies
Shareholders: Carl David Phillipson; Caroline Sarah Phillipson
Officers: Carl David Phillipson [1974] Director; Caroline Sarah Phillipson [1973] Director

Mediaworks UK Limited
Incorporated: 11 July 2007 *Employees:* 68
Net Worth: £774,142 *Total Assets:* £1,809,669
Registered Office: Express Group, 398A Princesway North, Team Valley Trading Estate, Gateshead, Tyne & Wear, NE11 0TU
Activities: Other information service activities n.e.c.
Shareholders: Brett Coulson Jacobson; Christopher Scott Thompson
Officers: Lynn Wilson, Secretary; Brett Coulson Jacobson [1985] Director/Software Engineer; Mark Andrew Rutherford [1982] Director/Accountant; Gary Smith [1962] Operations Director; Christopher Scott Thompson [1956] Director/Engineer

Medical Reporting Solutions Limited
Incorporated: 11 June 2015 *Employees:* 11
Net Worth: £428,636 *Total Assets:* £2,918,981
Registered Office: Percy House, Percy Street, Newcastle upon Tyne, NE1 4PW
Activities: Other human health activities
Shareholders: Stephen McCourt; Anne Mary Magee
Officers: Peter Andrew Casey [1971] Director; Neil Benjamin Sheldon [1949] Director

Medicentre (Newcastle) Limited
Incorporated: 17 September 2007 *Employees:* 25
Net Worth: £865,829 *Total Assets:* £1,045,556
Registered Office: 40 St Georges Terrace, Jesmond, Newcastle upon Tyne, NE2 2SY
Activities: Dispensing chemist in specialised stores
Officers: Anil Khanna [1958] Director; Anju Khanna [1969] Director; Sunil Paul Khanna [1959] Director; Surbhi Khanna [1960] Director

Medichem (Sunderland) Limited
Incorporated: 26 February 2008
Net Worth: £1,663,933 *Total Assets:* £1,960,000
Registered Office: 10 High Sand Grove, Sunderland, Tyne & Wear, SR6 7RW
Activities: Non-trading company
Major Shareholder: Saileshkumar Ramanlal Patel
Officers: Naomi Patel, Secretary; Naomi Patel [1988] Director; Nina Patel [1991] Director; Sailesh Kumar Patel [1955] Director/Pharmacist; Aysha Strange [1984] Director; Dr Natasha Wallace [1986] Director

Medichem Limited
Incorporated: 2 July 2002 *Employees:* 20
Net Worth: £1,439,354 *Total Assets:* £1,694,544
Registered Office: 10 High Sandgrove, Cleadon Village, Sunderland, Tyne & Wear, SR6 7RW
Activities: Dispensing chemist in specialised stores
Major Shareholder: Saileshkumar Ramanlal Patel
Officers: Naomi Patel, Secretary; Naomi Patel [1988] Director; Nina Patel [1991] Director; Sailesh Kumar Patel [1955] Director/Pharmacist; Aysha Strange [1984] Director; Dr Natasha Wallace [1986] Director

Megabet UK Ltd.
Incorporated: 29 August 1986 *Employees:* 384
Net Worth: £5,904,817 *Total Assets:* £9,915,485
Registered Office: Pinetree Business Centre, Pinetree Centre, Durham Road, Birtley, Chester-le-Street, Co Durham, DH3 2TD
Activities: Gambling and betting activities
Shareholders: Peter Fisher; Dianne Marie Fisher
Officers: Ian Blackburn, Secretary; Ian Blackburn [1966] Director/Accountant; Anne Philomena Fisher [1942] Director; Stephen Daniel Fisher [1944] Director; Euan McCormick [1973] Director

Melanor Limited
Incorporated: 30 May 2012
Net Worth: £316,888 *Total Assets:* £2,240,427
Registered Office: Suite 3, Battalion Court, 5 Battalion Court, Colburn Business Park, Catterick Garrison, N Yorks, DL9 4QN
Activities: Other business support service activities n.e.c.
Shareholder: Montpelier (Trust and Corporate) Services Limited
Officers: Paul William Garrett [1961] Director; Edward Watkin Gittins [1950] Director/Chartered Accountant

Meldon Estates Limited
Incorporated: 30 August 2000
Net Worth: £728,400 *Total Assets:* £967,762
Registered Office: 33 Redesdale Avenue, Winlaton, Tyne & Wear, NE21 6HS
Activities: Other letting and operating of own or leased real estate
Major Shareholder: Peter Michael Tanner
Officers: Peter Michael Tanner [1963] Director/Lettings Agent

Meldrum Construction Services Limited
Incorporated: 11 July 2001 *Employees:* 169
Net Worth: £2,090,146 *Total Assets:* £8,554,870
Registered Office: Pantheon Building, Lancaster Road, Dunston, Gateshead, Tyne & Wear, NE11 9JW
Activities: Construction of commercial buildings
Shareholders: David Martin Meldrum; David Martin Meldrum
Officers: David Finnigan, Secretary; Steven Church [1975] Technical Director; David Thomas Finnigan [1960] Finance Director; Paul Anthony McCabe [1967] Construction Director; David Martin Meldrum [1963] Director/Civil Servant; Johnathan Stuart Mellis [1976] Director of Engineering

Melford Contracts Limited
Incorporated: 23 May 2002
Net Worth: £648,785 *Total Assets:* £1,622,077
Registered Office: 267b Whitley Road, Whitley Bay, Tyne & Wear, NE26 2SS
Activities: Renting and operating of Housing Association real estate
Major Shareholder: Julio Maria Martino
Officers: Julio Martino, Secretary; Aldo Bertorelli [1941] Director/Financier; Julio Martino [1975] Director/Producer

E.J.Melling Limited
Incorporated: 20 September 1961 *Employees:* 5
Net Worth: £740,726 *Total Assets:* £850,933
Registered Office: Studio 114, Maling Exchange, Hoults Yard, Walker Road, Newcastle upon Tyne, NE6 2HL
Activities: Non-specialised wholesale trade
Major Shareholder: Michael Johan Melling
Officers: Ellen Pattison Melling, Secretary/Director; Ellen Pattison Melling [1945] Director; Michael Johan Melling [1948] Director; Richard Michael Melling [1978] Director/Sales Representative

Melorvale Limited
Incorporated: 3 August 1999
Net Worth: £1,015,760 *Total Assets:* £1,848,711
Registered Office: c/o Rosenthal & Co, 106 High West Street, Gateshead, Tyne & Wear, NE8 1NA
Activities: Other letting and operating of own or leased real estate
Officers: Steven Anthony Bodner, Secretary/Director; Michael Martin Bodner [1951] Director; Steven Anthony Bodner [1961] Director

Fred Mence (Construction) Limited
Incorporated: 27 January 1989 *Employees:* 104
Net Worth: £2,417,956 *Total Assets:* £5,148,665
Registered Office: Walton Road, Pattinson Industrial Estate North, Washington, Tyne & Wear, NE38 8QE
Activities: Construction of roads and motorways
Major Shareholder: Paul Mence
Officers: Colin Douglas [1956] Director; Deborah Mence [1968] Director; Frederick Mence [1940] Director; Paul Mence [1964] Director

Mendip (North East) Limited
Incorporated: 15 May 2003
Net Worth: £152,221 *Total Assets:* £889,151
Registered Office: 259 Durham Road, Low Fell, Gateshead, Tyne & Wear, NE9 5AB
Activities: Other letting and operating of own or leased real estate
Shareholders: William Glenn McDowell; Wayne McDowell
Officers: William Glenn McDowell, Secretary/Managing Director; Wayne McDowell [1970] Director; William Glenn McDowell [1968] Managing Director

Mental Health Concern
Incorporated: 12 November 1986 *Employees:* 605
Net Worth: £10,731,000 *Total Assets:* £13,303,000
Registered Office: Buttress House, 36 Brenkley Way, Seaton Burn, Newcastle upon Tyne, NE13 6DS
Activities: Other human health activities
Officers: David Keith Belk, Secretary; David Robson Arthur [1954] Director/Accountant; Fiona Sheila Cassells [1953] Director/Retired; Rosemary Caroline Granger [1957] Director/Management Consultant; Zena Jones [1955] Director; Richard McEvoy [1962] Director/Banker; Elizabeth Ann Robinson [1950] Director/Retired; David Smith [1973] Director/Management Consultant; Doctor Angela Mary Walsh [1949] Director/Retired

Mental Health Matters
Incorporated: 27 January 1984 *Employees:* 271
Net Worth: £1,934,064 *Total Assets:* £3,813,702
Registered Office: Avalon House, St Catherines Court, Sunderland, Tyne & Wear, SR5 3XJ
Activities: Other human health activities
Officers: Sally Jane Baines [1962] NHS Director; Andrew James Britton [1956] Finance Director; David Nicholas Brown [1973] Director/Chief Financial Officer; David Michael Corner [1957] Director; Lynette Claire Eastman [1956] Director/HR Consultant; Naomi Eve Hankinson [1958] Director/Occupational Therapist; Bruce Neville Howorth [1964] Director/Solicitor; Robert Vaughan Jones [1949] Director/Minister; Dr Stirling Moorey [1956] Director/Psychiatrist

Mercantile Estates Ltd
Incorporated: 5 December 2001
Net Worth: £6,128,381 *Total Assets:* £11,243,471
Registered Office: Evans House, Bewick Road, Gateshead, Tyne & Wear, NE8 4DP
Activities: Development of building projects
Shareholder: Jeffrey Steiner
Officers: Jeffrey Steiner, Secretary; Jeffrey Steiner [1961] Director; Marion Steiner [1965] Director

Mercantile Partnership Ltd
Incorporated: 28 November 2012
Net Worth: £343,353 *Total Assets:* £958,729
Registered Office: Evans House, Bewick Road, Gateshead, Tyne & Wear, NE8 4DP
Activities: Development of building projects
Shareholder: Jeffrey Steiner
Officers: Charles Finkelstein [1960] Director [Belgian]; Jeffrey Steiner [1961] Director

Mercer Street Marketing and Consulting Limited
Incorporated: 13 March 2002 *Employees:* 12
Net Worth: £804,836 *Total Assets:* £1,267,862
Registered Office: Anson House, The Fleming Business Centre, Burdon Terrace, Jesmond, Newcastle upon Tyne, NE2 3AE
Activities: Advertising agencies
Shareholder: Fiona Campbell Collins Fletcher
Officers: Margaret Fletcher, Secretary; Alan Crawford Fletcher [1969] Director/Lawyer; Fiona Campbell Collins Fletcher [1969] Director/Lawyer

Mercer Street Security Systems Limited
Incorporated: 14 March 2006
Net Worth Deficit: £609,847 *Total Assets:* £1,365,007
Registered Office: Anson House, The Fleming Business Centre, Burdon Terrace, Jesmond, Newcastle upon Tyne, NE2 3AE
Activities: Activities of other holding companies n.e.c.
Shareholders: Peter Coates; Alan Crawford Fletcher
Officers: Alan Crawford Fletcher, Secretary; Alan Crawford Fletcher [1969] Director/Lawyer; Lord John Stevens [1942] Director/Chairman

Mercury International Solutions Limited
Incorporated: 29 June 2009
Registered Office: 14-15 Harelands Courtyard Offices, Moor Road, Melsonby, Richmond, N Yorks, DL10 5NY
Activities: Management consultancy activities other than financial management
Shareholder: Julian Mark Christopher Croslegh
Officers: Charles Richard Ebsworth Dunley [1975] Director; Trevor William Inch [1965] Director

Meridian Healthcare Limited
Incorporated: 4 October 1985 *Employees:* 1,362
Net Worth: £73,537,000 *Total Assets:* £84,519,000
Registered Office: Southgate House, Archer Street, Darlington, Co Durham, DL3 6AH
Activities: Residential care activities for the elderly and disabled
Parent: Meridian Healthcare (Holdings) Limited
Officers: James Justin Hutchens [1974] Director [American]; David Andrew Smith [1974] Director

Merit Group Services Limited
Incorporated: 14 February 2017 *Employees:* 114
Net Worth: £4,396,791 *Total Assets:* £15,770,031
Registered Office: 3 Silverton Court, Northumberland Business Park, Cramlington, Northumberland, NE23 7RY
Activities: Other specialised construction activities n.e.c.
Officers: Nicky Berriman, Secretary; Christopher Berriman [1958] Director; Kevin Hynes [1965] Contracts Director; Matthew McGrady [1970] Director; Anthony Wells [1964] Managing Director; Dr Kirsty Wells [1971] Director/Chief Executive; David Wilkinson [1954] Director/Accountant

Merit Holdings Limited
Incorporated: 31 July 2002 *Employees:* 114
Net Worth: £4,396,791 *Total Assets:* £15,770,031
Registered Office: 3 Silverton Court, Northumberland Business Park, Cramlington, Northumberland, NE23 7RY
Activities: Other specialised construction activities n.e.c.
Parent: Merit Group Services Ltd
Officers: Nicola Berriman, Secretary; Christopher Berriman [1958] Director; Kevin Hynes [1965] Contracts Director; Matthew McGrady [1970] Financial Director; Nickolas Small [1968] Operations Director; Anthony Wells [1964] Director; Dr Kirsty Wells [1971] Director/Chief Executive; David Wilkinson [1954] Director/Accountant

Merrychef Limited
Incorporated: 14 August 1992 *Employees:* 3
Net Worth: £8,728,000 *Total Assets:* £8,728,000
Registered Office: St Ann's Wharf, 112 Quayside, Newcastle upon Tyne, NE1 3DX
Activities: Dormant company
Parent: Enodis Group Limited
Officers: Adrian David Gray [1962] Director/Accountant; John Albert James Rourke [1967] Director

Mersen UK Teesside Limited
Incorporated: 1 December 1997 *Employees:* 79
Net Worth: £7,981,228 *Total Assets:* £14,108,223
Registered Office: Boltby Way, Durham Lane Industrial Park, Eaglescliffe, Stockton on Tees, Cleveland, TS16 0RH
Activities: Other manufacturing n.e.c.
Parent: Mersen UK Holdings, Ltd
Officers: Ivan Herrero, Secretary; Andrew Freer [1962] Director/General Manager; Luc Themelin [1961] Director/Engineer [French]

Mesh Marketing Limited
Incorporated: 20 February 2004 *Employees:* 44
Net Worth: £1,436,263 *Total Assets:* £2,641,633
Registered Office: 3 Evolution, Wynyard Avenue, Wynyard, Billingham, Cleveland, TS22 5TB
Activities: Advertising agencies
Shareholders: Stewart Andrew Baxter; Christopher James Masterson
Officers: Christopher James Masterson, Secretary/Marketing Consultant; Stewart Andrew Baxter [1970] Director/Marketing Consultant; Christopher James Masterson [1968] Director/Marketing Consultant; Adrian Richard Thomas [1968] Director/Marketing Consultant

Messer Griesheim Limited
Incorporated: 11 April 1960 *Employees:* 15
Net Worth Deficit: £1,111,377 *Total Assets:* £5,190,925
Registered Office: Unit 4c Northumberland Business Park West, Dudley, Cramlington, Northumberland, NE23 7RH
Activities: Manufacture of other special-purpose machinery n.e.c.
Shareholder: Stefan Messer
Officers: Alan Cardwell, Secretary; Joerg Mosser [1968] Director [Austrian]; Peter Schaaf [1953] Director [German]

Metabrasive Limited
Incorporated: 6 February 1980 *Employees:* 25
Net Worth: £11,463,000 *Total Assets:* £16,249,000
Registered Office: Metabrasive Ltd, Ironmasters Way, Stillington, Stockton on Tees, Cleveland, TS21 1LE
Activities: Other business support service activities n.e.c.
Officers: Patrick Rene Joseph Arnaud [1954] Director [French]; Keith Rowbotham [1969] Director/Financial Controller; Marc Vinet [1968] Director [French]

Metal Drum Company Limited (The)
Incorporated: 20 September 1961 *Employees:* 70
Net Worth: £4,859,727 *Total Assets:* £6,842,350
Registered Office: Dene Bridge Road, Chilton, Co Durham, DL17 0NU
Activities: Manufacture of steel drums and similar containers
Major Shareholder: Jonica Britton
Officers: Helen Edwina Britton, Secretary; Jonica Britton [1954] Director; Michael Alan Britton [1951] Director/Engineer; Samuel James Thomas Britton [1984] Director/General Manager

Metalis Energy Limited
Incorporated: 25 November 2008 *Employees:* 7
Net Worth: £703,979 *Total Assets:* £1,199,467
Registered Office: West 2, Asama Court, Newcastle Business Park, Newcastle upon Tyne, NE4 7YD
Activities: Support activities for petroleum and natural gas mining
Major Shareholder: Paul Benedict George McCreton
Officers: Paul Benedict George McCreton [1963] Director

Metallink Fluid Power Systems Limited
Incorporated: 8 November 1996 *Employees:* 54
Net Worth: £3,880,624 *Total Assets:* £5,127,709
Registered Office: Unit BT 35/2 Beechburn Industrial Estate, Crook, Co Durham, DL15 8JL
Activities: Manufacture of other fabricated metal products n.e.c.
Major Shareholder: Alemanna Bianconcini
Officers: Alan Joseph Hook, Secretary; Alemanna Bianconcini [1940] Director/Administration [Italian]; Paolo Borghi [1973] Managing Director [Italian]

Metalpoint Limited
Incorporated: 12 January 1982 *Employees:* 15
Net Worth: £98,435 *Total Assets:* £1,174,742
Registered Office: Factory D Western Approach, Industrial Estate, South Shields, Tyne & Wear, NE33 5NN
Activities: Wholesale of hardware, plumbing and heating equipment and supplies
Shareholders: David Harland; Pamela Harland
Officers: Pamela Harland, Secretary; Colin Cauwood [1960] Sales Director; David Harland [1948] Managing Director; Pamela Harland [1945] Director/Secretary; Ivan Malley [1967] Technical Director

Metano Limited
Incorporated: 31 January 1994 *Employees:* 27
Net Worth: £2,043,781 *Total Assets:* £8,909,672
Registered Office: Unit 14-15 Whinfield Way, Whinfield Industrial Estate, Rowlands Gill, Tyne & Wear, NE39 1EH
Activities: Renting and leasing of other machinery, equipment and tangible goods n.e.c.
Major Shareholder: Ian William Harland
Officers: Colin Gibson, Secretary; Colin Gibson [1979] Director/Chartered Accountant; James Edward Robert Harland [1975] Director

JJ Metcalfe & Son Ltd
Incorporated: 31 March 2009 *Employees:* 7
Net Worth: £656,054 *Total Assets:* £767,193
Registered Office: 43 Coniscliffe Road, Darlington, Co Durham, DL3 7EH
Activities: Manufacture of agricultural and forestry machinery other than tractors
Major Shareholder: Michael John Metcalfe
Officers: Michael John Metcalfe [1961] Director/Agricultural Engineer

W Metcalfe & Sons Limited
Incorporated: 29 October 1998 *Employees:* 21
Net Worth: £342,365 *Total Assets:* £1,774,010
Registered Office: Cornclose, Appersett, Hawes, N Yorks, DL8 3LN
Activities: Freight transport by road
Major Shareholder: Kenneth Peter Metcalfe
Officers: Sheila Jane Banks, Secretary; Kenneth Peter Metcalfe [1969] Director

Metcalfe Components (Sunderland) Limited
Incorporated: 20 May 1976 *Employees:* 16
Net Worth: £779,991 *Total Assets:* £1,751,113
Registered Office: Riverbank Road, North Hylton Road Industrial Estate, Sunderland, Tyne & Wear, SR5 3JJ
Activities: Other engineering activities
Shareholders: Andrew Metcalfe; Ian Metcalfe; John Christopher Metcalfe
Officers: Louise Metcalfe, Secretary; Andrew Metcalfe [1976] Director; Ian Metcalfe [1947] Director/Engineer; John Christopher Metcalfe [1979] Director

Metcalfe Farms (Haulage) Limited
Incorporated: 27 October 2006 *Employees:* 99
Net Worth: £6,995,783 *Total Assets:* £12,141,026
Registered Office: Washfold Farm, Leyburn, N Yorks, DL8 5JZ
Activities: Freight transport by road
Officers: David James Metcalfe, Secretary/Farmer; Andrew Philip Metcalfe [1970] Director/Farmer; Brian John Metcalfe [1966] Director/Farmer; David James Metcalfe [1964] Director/Farmer; John Metcalfe [1942] Director/Farmer; Thora Metcalfe [1944] Director/Farmer

Metec Cathodic Protection Limited
Incorporated: 29 July 2016
Net Worth: £786,933 *Total Assets:* £1,705,147
Registered Office: Visage House, 2 Shaftesbury Avenue, South Shields, Tyne & Wear, NE34 9PH
Activities: Other manufacturing n.e.c.
Parent: Metec Wilson Walton S.R.L
Officers: Robert Lee Forsyth [1987] Commercial Director; Alberto Via [1989] Director/Manager [Italian]

Metnor (Great Yarmouth) Limited
Incorporated: 20 November 1989 *Employees:* 20
Net Worth: £2,988,000 *Total Assets:* £3,308,000
Registered Office: Metnor House, Mylord Crescent, Camperdown Industrial Estate, Killingworth, Newcastle upon Tyne, NE12 5YD
Activities: Manufacture of pumps
Parent: Metnor Group Limited
Officers: Jan McLuckie, Secretary/Accountant; Keith Andrew Atkinson [1961] Director/Accountant; Karl Brooks [1973] Director; Stephen Rankin [1964] Director

Metnor (Portland Road) Limited
Incorporated: 27 March 2006
Net Worth: £47,000 *Total Assets:* £1,707,000
Registered Office: Metnor House, Mylord Crescent, Killingworth, Newcastle upon Tyne, NE12 5YD
Activities: Development of building projects
Parent: Metnor Group Limited
Officers: Dr Adam Boyd Langman, Secretary; Keith Andrew Atkinson [1961] Director/Accountant; Adam Boyd Langman [1962] Director; Stephen Rankin [1964] Director

Metnor Construction Limited
Incorporated: 25 April 2002 *Employees:* 49
Net Worth: £6,634,000 *Total Assets:* £22,564,000
Registered Office: Metnor House, Mylord Crescent, Killingworth, Newcastle upon Tyne, NE12 5YD
Activities: Construction of commercial buildings
Parent: Metnor Group Limited
Officers: Dr Adam Boyd Langman, Secretary; Keith Andrew Atkinson [1961] Director; Christopher Cant [1971] Director; David Gary Laidlaw [1979] Commercial Director; Adam Boyd Langman [1962] Director; Ian Parsons [1955] Pre Construction Director; Stephen Rankin [1964] Director

Metnor Property Group Limited
Incorporated: 26 February 2002 *Employees:* 8
Net Worth: £8,073,000 *Total Assets:* £22,644,000
Registered Office: Metnor House, Mylord Crescent, Newcastle upon Tyne, NE12 5YD
Activities: Development of building projects
Parent: Metnor Group Limited
Officers: Dr Adam Boyd Langman, Secretary; Keith Andrew Atkinson [1961] Director/Accountant; Adam Boyd Langman [1962] Director; Stephen Rankin [1964] Director

Metnor Quays Limited
Incorporated: 27 November 2006
Net Worth Deficit: £1,612,000 *Total Assets:* £1,841,000
Registered Office: Metnor House, Mylord Crescent, Killingworth, Newcastle upon Tyne, NE12 5YD
Activities: Development of building projects
Parent: Metnor Group Limited
Officers: Keith Andrew Atkinson [1961] Director/Accountant; Adam Boyd Langman [1962] Director; Stephen Rankin [1964] Director

Metnor Trafalgar Street Limited
Incorporated: 13 December 2006 *Employees:* 5
Net Worth Deficit: £2,838,000 *Total Assets:* £5,181,000
Registered Office: Metnor House, Mylord Crescent, Killingworth, Newcastle upon Tyne, NE12 5YD
Activities: Other letting and operating of own or leased real estate
Parent: Metnor Property Group Limited
Officers: Dr Adam Boyd Langman, Secretary; Keith Andrew Atkinson [1961] Director/Accountant; Adam Boyd Langman [1962] Director; Stephen Rankin [1964] Director

Metro Inns (Falkirk) Limited
Incorporated: 24 November 2006
Registered Office: Metro Inns, Ponteland Road, Newcastle upon Tyne, NE3 3TY
Activities: Other letting and operating of own or leased real estate
Officers: Kevin Coleman [1952] Director/Consultant

Metro Inns (Newcastle) Limited
Incorporated: 24 November 2006
Registered Office: Metro Inns, Ponteland Road, Kenton Bank, Newcastle upon Tyne, NE3 3TY
Activities: Other letting and operating of own or leased real estate
Officers: Kevin Coleman [1952] Director; Jonathan Doherty [1989] Director/Property Consultant

Metro Inns (Teesside) Limited
Incorporated: 24 November 2006
Registered Office: Metro Inns, Ponteland Road, Kenton Bank, Newcastle upon Tyne, NE3 3TY
Activities: Other letting and operating of own or leased real estate
Officers: Kevin Coleman [1952] Director

Metro Inns Limited
Incorporated: 6 November 2006
Net Worth: £399,989 *Total Assets:* £2,829,844
Registered Office: Ponteland Road, Kenton Bank, Newcastle upon Tyne, NE3 3TY
Activities: Hotels and similar accommodation
Officers: Kevin Coleman [1952] Director; Christopher Joseph Doherty [1986] Marketing Director; Jonathan Doherty [1989] Director/Property Manager

Metro Rental Limited
Incorporated: 13 April 2005 *Employees:* 5
Net Worth: £95,888 *Total Assets:* £851,220
Registered Office: Staithes Road, Dunston, Gateshead, Tyne & Wear, NE11 9DR
Activities: Renting and leasing of cars and light motor vehicles
Officers: Richard Campbell Scott [1963] Director

Metro Repro Limited
Incorporated: 15 June 1992 *Employees:* 9
Net Worth: £901,369 *Total Assets:* £995,862
Registered Office: B I House, Carliol Square, Newcastle upon Tyne, NE1 6UF
Activities: Printing n.e.c.
Shareholders: Heather Harriet Foster; Paul Robert Foster; Robert Henry Foster
Officers: Heather Harriet Foster, Secretary; Heather Harriet Foster [1950] Director/Company Secretary; Paul Robert Foster [1972] Director; Robert Henry Foster [1946] Director

Metrology Software Products Limited
Incorporated: 25 June 2002 *Employees:* 33
Net Worth: £1,866,646 *Total Assets:* £2,253,266
Registered Office: 6f Greensfield Court, Alnwick, Northumberland, NE66 2DE
Activities: Engineering design activities for industrial process and production
Officers: Anthony Brown, Secretary; Anthony Brown [1958] Director; Peter Russell Hammond [1960] Director; Geoffrey McFarland [1968] Director [Irish]; Allen Christopher George Roberts [1949] Director

MGM Ltd
Incorporated: 28 January 1992 *Employees:* 62
Net Worth: £728,249 *Total Assets:* £2,788,719
Registered Office: Unit 333 Dukesway Court, Team Valley Trading Estate, Gateshead, Tyne & Wear, NE11 0BH
Activities: Other specialised construction activities n.e.c.
Parent: Northern Bear PLC
Officers: Wendy Ann Edgell, Secretary; Graham Roy Jennings [1956] Director; Neil Jukes [1972] Managing Director; Steven Mark Roberts [1966] Director; Keith Soulsby [1956] Director

MH Holdings (North) Limited
Incorporated: 12 December 2011
Net Worth: £93,342 *Total Assets:* £1,106,441
Registered Office: Holly House, Ovington, Northumberland, NE42 6DH
Activities: Activities of head offices
Shareholders: Andrew Philip Maidwell; John David Hutton
Officers: John David Hutton, Secretary; John David Hutton [1968] Director/Chartered Accountant; Andrew Philip Maidwell [1962] Director

MH Southern (Holdings) Limited
Incorporated: 26 October 1999 *Employees:* 99
Net Worth: £3,415,599 *Total Assets:* £6,848,918
Registered Office: Church Bank Sawmills, Jarrow, Tyne & Wear, NE32 3EB
Activities: Sawmilling and planing of wood
Shareholder: Mark Simon Lowis
Officers: Dorothy Jane Southern, Secretary; Robert Johnson Bruce [1959] Director/Timber Merchant; Mark Simon Lowis [1973] Director/Timber Importer; James Andrew Southern [1969] Director/Timber Merchant

Michael Drapers Limited
Incorporated: 3 April 1975 *Employees:* 6
Net Worth: £2,105,252 *Total Assets:* £2,152,622
Registered Office: 28-40 Scotswood Road, Newcastle upon Tyne, NE4 7JB
Activities: Management of real estate on a fee or contract basis
Officers: Veena Sehgal, Secretary; Jai Deip Sehgal [1967] Director; Kiran Sehgal [1970] Director/Manager; Purnima Sehgal [1974] Director/Chartered Accountant; Robin Sehgal [1969] Director; Veena Sehgal [1944] Director

Michell Bearings Limited
Incorporated: 15 January 2015 *Employees:* 138
Net Worth: £7,655,000 *Total Assets:* £12,469,000
Registered Office: 11 Glasshouse Street, St Peters, Newcastle upon Tyne, NE6 1BS
Activities: Manufacture of bearings, gears, gearing and driving elements
Shareholders: British Engines (UK) Limited; Malpani Holdings LLP
Officers: Joanne Alicea Wilkes, Secretary; Stephen Dixon [1964] Director; Richard Dodd [1974] Director; Geoffrey Humble [1970] Director; Laura Joicey [1976] Director; Arvind Prakash Malpani [1954] Director [Indian]; Mridula Malpani [1960] Director [Indian]

Michigan Investments Limited
Incorporated: 1 February 2012 *Employees:* 2
Net Worth: £1,313,041 *Total Assets:* £9,634,029
Registered Office: West 2, Asama Court, Newcastle Business Park, Newcastle upon Tyne, NE4 7YD
Activities: Other letting and operating of own or leased real estate
Shareholders: Philip George Walton; Diane Walton
Officers: Mark Adam Walton [1974] Director/Property Agent; Philip George Walton [1949] Director

Microchem Limited
Incorporated: 29 June 1981 *Employees:* 9
Net Worth: £1,035,082 *Total Assets:* £1,072,231
Registered Office: Unit One, Belmont Industrial Estate, Durham, DH1 1TN
Activities: Manufacture of other chemical products n.e.c.
Shareholders: Paulette Monica Wakefield; Michael Wakefield
Officers: Paulette Monica Wakefield, Secretary; Michael Wakefield [1943] Managing Director; Paulette Monica Wakefield [1943] Director/Company Secretary

Micromix (Northern) Ltd
Incorporated: 13 July 2010
Net Worth: £860,080 *Total Assets:* £2,528,506
Registered Office: Greenland Lodge, Hamsteels Lane, Esh, Co Durham, DH7 9RS
Activities: Freight transport by road
Major Shareholder: Charles Allen Ryan
Officers: Jonathan Richard Gordon, Secretary; Dennis William Peveller [1966] Director; Charles Allen Ryan [1949] Director; Aidan Thomas Weir [1962] Director

Microvention UK Limited
Incorporated: 23 July 2002 *Employees:* 11
Net Worth: £1,927,080 *Total Assets:* £2,886,881
Registered Office: Suite 3, The Barracks Building, Cliffords Fort, North Shields, Tyne & Wear, NE30 1JE
Activities: Other human health activities
Officers: William Hughes, Secretary/Vice President COO [American]; Richard Cappetta [1958] Director [American]; William Hughes [1956] Director/Vice President COO [American]

Midas Cladding Services Limited
Incorporated: 2 February 1994 *Employees:* 48
Net Worth: £904,665 *Total Assets:* £1,829,759
Registered Office: Midas House, Units 1-2 Brignell Road, Riverside Park, Middlesbrough, Cleveland, TS2 1PS
Activities: Roofing activities
Shareholder: Gilbey Holdings Ltd
Officers: Martin Allen Gilbey [1982] Director; Kevan Paul Jefferson [1962] Director/Sheeting and Cladding

Middle Caves Ltd
Incorporated: 24 November 2003 *Employees:* 17
Net Worth: £10,831,629 *Total Assets:* £13,399,682
Registered Office: Pond Dale, Gilling West, Richmond, N Yorks, DL10 5LB
Activities: Raising of swine and pigs
Major Shareholder: Paul Anthony Hall Westgarth
Officers: Paul Anthony Hall Westgarth, Secretary; Paul Anthony Hall Westgarth [1967] Director/Farmer; Timothy Peter Westgarth [1973] Director/Farmer

Middleheads Limited
Incorporated: 19 November 2012
Net Worth: £119,614 *Total Assets:* £1,394,185
Registered Office: Middle Heads Farm, Rowley, Consett, Co Durham, DH8 9AF
Activities: Mixed farming
Shareholders: David Dixon; Mark David Dixon; Colin Michael Williams; Fiona Jayne Wiliams
Officers: David Dixon [1943] Director; Mark David Dixon [1972] Director; Colin Michael Williams [1975] Director; Fiona Jayne Williams [1974] Director

Middlesbrough & District Motor Club Limited
Incorporated: 6 January 2015
Net Worth: £1,366,477 *Total Assets:* £1,378,731
Registered Office: Middlesbrough & District Club, Coulby Manor, Coulby Manor Way, Coulby Newham, Middlesbrough, Cleveland, TS8 0RP
Activities: Other amusement and recreation activities n.e.c.
Officers: Colin William Somerset, Secretary; Douglas Hyslop Crosbie [1939] Director; Susan Marshall [1946] Director/Treasurer; Colin William Somerset [1937] Director/Self Employed; William Wood [1948] Director/Retired Chemical Shift Manager

Middlesbrough and Stockton Mind Limited
Incorporated: 24 July 2006 *Employees:* 110
Net Worth: £2,570,127 *Total Assets:* £2,720,026
Registered Office: The Mind Centre, 90-92 Lothian Road, Middlesbrough, Cleveland, TS4 2QX
Activities: Other social work activities without accommodation n.e.c.
Officers: Susan Margaret Cash [1950] Director/Retired; John Harrison [1958] Director/Chartered Accountant; Ruth Ursula Hicks [1943] Director/Retired; Angela Holloway [1963] Director/Doctor; David King [1955] Director/Consultant; Jennifer Morris [1987] Director/Student; Charlie Nettle [1977] Director/Marketing; Angela Papprill [1983] Director/Solicitor; Joanne Ramsay [1971] Director/Midwife; Marian Ann Ramsey [1954] Director/Retired

Middlesbrough Borough Cars Limited
Incorporated: 31 January 1994
Net Worth: £2,194,232 *Total Assets:* £7,662,958
Registered Office: Cambridge Road, Cargo Fleet, Middlesbrough, Cleveland, TS3 8AY
Activities: Taxi operation
Major Shareholder: Mohammed Bashir
Officers: Christine Ann Bell, Secretary/Director; Mohammed Bashir [1964] Director; Christine Ann Bell [1966] Director

Middlesbrough DP Ltd
Incorporated: 25 October 2010 *Employees:* 89
Net Worth Deficit: £36,381 *Total Assets:* £1,175,517
Registered Office: 178 York Road, Hartlepool, Cleveland, TS26 9EA
Activities: Other retail sale of food in specialised stores
Major Shareholder: Mike Racz
Officers: Mike Racz [1982] Director/Franchisee

The Middlesbrough Empire Limited
Incorporated: 4 April 1996
Net Worth: £868,317 *Total Assets:* £1,415,737
Registered Office: The Empire Theatre, Corporation Road, Middlesbrough, Cleveland, TS1 2RT
Activities: Renting and operating of Housing Association real estate
Major Shareholder: Barry Oswald Faulkner
Officers: Barry Oswald Faulkner [1948] Director/Nightclub Proprietor

Middlesbrough Environment City Trust Limited
Incorporated: 13 June 1997 *Employees:* 35
Net Worth: £335,790 *Total Assets:* £1,514,130
Registered Office: Middlesbrough Environment City, Sandy Flatts Lane, Acklam, Middlesbrough, Cleveland, TS5 7YN
Activities: Other education n.e.c.
Officers: Valerie Cunningham [1947] Director/Retired; Jeremy Alexander Garside [1964] Director/Chief Executive; Brian Glover [1954] Director/Retired; Samantha Jane Granger [1977] Director/Manager; Lynne Elizabeth Hammond [1961] Director/Environmental Education Consultant; Martin Havelock Harvey [1964] Director/Manager; Keith Andrew Lewis [1949] Director/Retired; Kelvin Joseph McMonagle [1954] Director/Volunteer; Russell Karl Mills [1972] Director/Project Officer; Cllr Denise Rooney [1956] Director/Local Authority Councillor; Julia Rostron [1947] Director/Councillor; Janet Stevenson [1964] Director/Charity Worker; Councillor Nicola Joy Walker [1955] Director/Councillor

Middlesbrough Football & Athletic Company (1986) Limited
Incorporated: 17 September 1985 *Employees:* 185
Net Worth Deficit: £68,573,000 *Total Assets:* £90,627,000
Registered Office: Riverside Stadium, Middlesbrough, Cleveland, TS3 6RS
Activities: Activities of sport clubs
Parent: Middlesbrough Football & Athletic Club Holdings Limited
Officers: Jeremy Robin Bloom, Secretary; David Simon Joyes, Secretary; Stephen Gibson [1958] Director; Keith Lamb [1946] Director

Middlesbrough Voluntary Development Agency
Incorporated: 12 August 2002 *Employees:* 17
Net Worth: £975,437 *Total Assets:* £1,149,290
Registered Office: St Marys Centre, 82-90 Corporation Road, Middlesbrough, Cleveland, TS1 2RW
Activities: Other information service activities n.e.c.
Officers: Ailsa Mary Adamson [1965] Director/Charity Project Manager; Amanda Buck [1971] Director/Centre Manager; John Martin Daniels [1959] Director/Chief Executive; Matthew Fowler [1976] Director/Manager; Nicola Jane Harkin [1976] Director/Chief Executive Officer; Michelle Rose O'Rourke [1983] Director/Service Development Manager; Nigel Glenn Sayer [1961] Director/Retired

Middleton Coal Depot Limited
Incorporated: 18 June 2013 *Employees:* 13
Net Worth: £300,160 *Total Assets:* £1,417,622
Registered Office: 101 Galgate, Barnard Castle, Co Durham, DL12 8ES
Activities: Freight transport by road
Major Shareholder: Carl Maurice Shield
Officers: Carl Maurice Shield [1979] Director

Middleton Enterprises Ltd
Incorporated: 6 January 1992 *Employees:* 6
Net Worth: £8,578,752 *Total Assets:* £33,887,072
Registered Office: Middleton Enterprises, Quayside Lofts, 62 The Close, Newcastle upon Tyne, NE1 3RJ
Activities: Other service activities n.e.c.
Parent: Middleton Enterprises (Holdings) Limited
Officers: Michael David Elliot, Secretary; David William Alprovich [1987] Commercial Director; Michael David Elliot [1982] Finance Director; Catherine Middleton [1959] Director; Jeremy Peter Middleton [1960] Director/Marketing Consultant; Paul Ronald Woolston [1955] Director/Accountant

Middleton Forge Limited
Incorporated: 12 July 2002 *Employees:* 22
Net Worth: £1,312,369 *Total Assets:* £1,870,430
Registered Office: Station Industrial Estate, Middleton in Teesdale, Barnard Castle, Co Durham, DL12 0NG
Activities: Agents involved in the sale of timber and building materials
Shareholders: Louie Wallace; Scott Michael Wallace; Neil Robert Wallace
Officers: Louie Wallace, Secretary/Clerk; Louie Wallace [1953] Director/Clerk; Neil Robert Wallace [1980] Director/Manager; Scott Michael Wallace [1983] Director/Manager

Middleton Hall Limited
Incorporated: 23 April 1900 *Employees:* 152
Net Worth: £4,235,067 *Total Assets:* £7,342,222
Registered Office: Middleton Hall, Middleton St George, Darlington, Co Durham, DL2 1HA
Activities: Medical nursing home activities
Major Shareholder: Jeremy Michael Hutton Walford
Officers: Lesley Henderson, Secretary; Lesley Henderson [1960] Director; Pamela Lynne Mooney [1961] Operations Director; Jeremy Michael Hutton Walford [1962] Executive Director; Adrian Walker [1950] Director/Chartered Accountant

Middleton Lodge Events Limited
Incorporated: 8 December 2006 *Employees:* 79
Net Worth: £603,128 *Total Assets:* £3,017,320
Registered Office: Middleton Lodge, Middleton Tyas, Richmond, N Yorks, DL10 6NJ
Activities: Hotels and similar accommodation
Major Shareholder: James Jonathon Allison
Officers: James Connolly, Secretary; James Jonathon Allison [1978] Director/Engineer

Midland Steel Traders (Holdings) Limited
Incorporated: 18 January 2012 *Employees:* 91
Net Worth: £562,147 *Total Assets:* £4,958,240
Registered Office: Nortrac Works, Portobello Industrial Estate, Birtley, Co Durham, DH3 2SW
Activities: Other manufacturing n.e.c.
Officers: Leonie Elizabeth Langdale Whitehall, Secretary; Anne Christine Whitehall [1958] Director; John Philip Whitehall [1955] Director; Kenneth Paul Whitehall [1950] Director; Leonie Elizabeth Langdale Whitehall [1951] Director

Midland Steel Traders Limited,
Incorporated: 24 July 1963 *Employees:* 67
Net Worth: £669,698 *Total Assets:* £4,958,335
Registered Office: Nortrac Works, Portobello Industrial Estate, Birtley, Co Durham, DH3 2SW
Activities: Repair and maintenance of other transport equipment n.e.c.
Officers: Leonie Elizabeth Langdale Whitehall, Secretary; Alan Montgomery [1969] Director/Engineering; John Philip Whitehall [1955] Director; Kenneth Paul Whitehall [1950] Director; Rory John Whitehall [1979] Director/Sales

Mids Auto Services Limited
Incorporated: 9 October 2003 *Employees:* 8
Net Worth: £720,153 *Total Assets:* £765,405
Registered Office: Marske Inn Farm, Marske, Redcar, Cleveland, TS11 8AA
Activities: Maintenance and repair of motor vehicles
Shareholders: Andrew Middleton; Gina Middleton
Officers: Gina Middleton, Secretary; Andrew Middleton [1968] Director/Mechanic; Gina Middleton [1964] Director/Secretary

Migdal Developments (UK) Ltd
Incorporated: 8 February 2006
Registered Office: 113 Bewick Road, Gateshead, Tyne & Wear, NE8 1UA
Activities: Buying and selling of own real estate
Major Shareholder: Moishe Fordsham
Officers: Judith Fordsham, Secretary; Moishe Joseph Fordsham [1971] Director

Mignolet Ltd
Incorporated: 13 July 2012 *Employees:* 1
Net Worth: £1,243,498 *Total Assets:* £1,378,065
Registered Office: 3 Pickersgill Court, Quay West Business Village, Sunderland, Tyne & Wear, SR5 2AQ
Activities: Other business support service activities n.e.c.
Major Shareholder: Simon Luc Hildebert Mignolet
Officers: Simon Luc Hildebert Mignolet [1988] Director/Professional Sportsman [Belgian]

Milbank Investments Ltd
Incorporated: 24 November 2014
Net Worth: £3,214 *Total Assets:* £1,818,523
Registered Office: Barningham Park, Richmond, N Yorks, DL11 7DW
Activities: Activities of open-ended investment companies
Shareholders: Sir Edward Mark Somerset Milbank; Lady Natalie Ann Milbank
Officers: Sir Edward Mark Somerset Milbank [1973] Director; Lady Natalie Ann Milbank [1978] Director

Peter Milburn Chemist Limited
Incorporated: 6 September 2002 *Employees:* 19
Net Worth: £560,049 *Total Assets:* £2,430,113
Registered Office: 113 Lanehouse Road, Thornaby, Stockton on Tees, Cleveland, TS17 8AB
Activities: Dispensing chemist in specialised stores
Parent: Alrahi & Singh Limited
Officers: Asif Alrahi [1983] Director/Pharmacist; Sidra Alrahi [1988] Director; Sandeep Kaur [1987] Director; Iqbal Singh [1979] Director/Pharmacist

Milburn Motors Garages Limited
Incorporated: 2 March 1982 *Employees:* 17
Net Worth: £911,359 *Total Assets:* £1,885,079
Registered Office: 11 Freeman Way, Ashington, Northumberland, NE63 0YB
Activities: Sale of new cars and light motor vehicles
Shareholders: Raymond Allington; Christopher Allington
Officers: Christopher Allington, Secretary; Christopher Allington [1959] Director; Raymond Allington [1962] Director

Mill Masters International Limited
Incorporated: 8 May 2014 *Employees:* 28
Net Worth: £726,500 *Total Assets:* £2,832,533
Registered Office: Unit 24d Whinbank Park, Whinbank Road, Aycliffe Business Park, Newton Aycliffe, Co Durham, DL5 6AY
Activities: Manufacture of other machine tools
Major Shareholder: William Ernest Panthofer
Officers: William Thomas Dowdle III [1953] Director [American]; Chris Harford [1951] Director; Anthony Lynn Luna [1956] Director [American]; William Ernest Panthofer [1956] Director [American]

Mill Poultry Limited
Incorporated: 7 March 1995 *Employees:* 2
Net Worth: £63,194 *Total Assets:* £966,023
Registered Office: Uckerby Mill Farm, Scorton, Middleton Tyas, Richmond, N Yorks, DL10 6DA
Activities: Raising of poultry
Shareholders: David William Raw; John Anthony Raw
Officers: David William Raw, Secretary/Farmer; David William Raw [1965] Director/Farmer; John Anthony Raw [1958] Director/Farmer

Millennium Conveyor Services Limited
Incorporated: 21 May 1999 *Employees:* 8
Net Worth: £367,991 *Total Assets:* £865,740
Registered Office: Unit 1 Kings Court, Potter Street, Jarrow, Tyne & Wear, NE32 3QS
Activities: Manufacture of other rubber products
Parent: Brec (Holdings) Limited
Officers: Nicola Jayne Modlin, Secretary; Paul William Haynes [1968] Director/Engineer; Christopher Graham Kennedy [1968] Director; Barry James Longstaff [1960] Director/Sales Executive; Stephen Perruzza [1968] Director; Geoffrey Toft [1948] Director

Millennium Nails Limited
Incorporated: 8 June 1998
Registered Office: 3-5 Scarborough Street, Hartlepool, Cleveland, TS24 7DA
Activities: Wholesale of perfume and cosmetics
Shareholders: Alan Carter; Yvonne Carter
Officers: Alan Charles Carter [1956] Managing Director

David Miller Frozen Foods Limited
Incorporated: 14 August 1997 *Employees:* 60
Net Worth: £1,856,524 *Total Assets:* £3,586,831
Registered Office: Unit S3, Narvik Way, Tyne Tunnel Trading Estate, North Shields, Tyne & Wear, NE29 7XJ
Activities: Non-specialised wholesale of food, beverages and tobacco
Officers: Patricia Ada Rice, Secretary; David Leonard Brind [1972] Director; Ben Maxted [1983] Frozen Director; Patricia Ada Rice [1957] Director; Gareth Wilson [1982] Sales Director; Paul Victor Young [1957] Director

Miller UK Limited
Incorporated: 28 December 1987 *Employees:* 154
Net Worth: £5,150,138 *Total Assets:* £19,410,572
Registered Office: Bassington Industrial Estate, Bassington Lane, Cramlington, Northumberland, NE23 8AD
Activities: Manufacture of other fabricated metal products n.e.c.
Parent: Miller International Holdings Limited
Officers: Christopher Andrew Parkin, Secretary; Christopher Andrew Parkin [1964] Financial Director

Millfield Composites Group Limited
Incorporated: 16 March 2015 *Employees:* 66
Net Worth: £5,182,045 *Total Assets:* £6,823,914
Registered Office: 16 Shelley Road, Newburn Industrial Estate, Newburn, Newcastle upon Tyne, NE15 9RT
Activities: Activities of head offices
Shareholders: John Marshall Dodd; Jonathan Andrew Dodd
Officers: Rachel Cornelius, Secretary; John Marshall Dodd [1941] Director/Chemist; Jonathan Andrew Dodd [1968] Director

Millfield Composites Limited
Incorporated: 30 April 2009 *Employees:* 44
Net Worth: £1,006,370 *Total Assets:* £2,265,662
Registered Office: 16 Newburn Industrial Estate, Shelley Road, Newcastle upon Tyne, NE15 9RT
Activities: Manufacture of other plastic products
Parent: Millfield Composites Group Limited
Officers: Jill Eileen Dodd, Secretary; Jill Eileen Dodd [1941] Director; John Marshall Dodd [1941] Director; Jonathan Andrew Dodd [1968] Director; John Paul Doyle [1971] Business Director

Millfield Enterprises (Manufacturing) Limited
Incorporated: 11 March 1986 *Employees:* 4
Net Worth: £2,581,327 *Total Assets:* £3,377,556
Registered Office: Newburn Industrial Estate, Shelley Road, Newcastle upon Tyne, NE15 9RT
Activities: Manufacture of plastics in primary forms
Parent: Millfield Enterprises Limited
Officers: Jill Eileen Dodd, Secretary; Jill Eileen Dodd [1941] Director/Secretary; John Marshall Dodd [1941] Director/Plastic Component Manufacturer; Jonathan Andrew Dodd [1968] Director/Contracts Manager

Millfield Enterprises Group Limited
Incorporated: 16 March 2015
Net Worth: £12,973,260 *Total Assets:* £13,914,260
Registered Office: 16 Shelley Road, Newburn Industrial Estate, Newburn, Newcastle upon Tyne, NE15 9RT
Activities: Activities of head offices
Shareholders: John Marshall Dodd; Jonathan Andrew Dodd
Officers: Jill Eileen Dodd, Secretary; John Marshall Dodd [1941] Director/Chemist; Jonathan Andrew Dodd [1968] Director

Millfield Enterprises Limited
Incorporated: 24 May 1963 *Employees:* 4
Net Worth: £1,216,513 *Total Assets:* £4,806,273
Registered Office: Millfield Enterprises Ltd, Newburn Industrial Estate, Shelley Road, Newcastle upon Tyne, NE15 9RT
Activities: Manufacture of builders ware of plastic
Parent: Millfield Enterprises Group Limited
Officers: Jill Eileen Dodd, Secretary; Jill Eileen Dodd [1941] Director/Secretary; John Marshall Dodd [1941] Director/Plastic Component Manufacturer; Jonathan Andrew Dodd [1968] Director/Contracts Manager

Millfield GRP Products Limited
Incorporated: 12 November 1996 *Employees:* 15
Net Worth: £729,395 *Total Assets:* £956,364
Registered Office: Shelley Road, Newburn Industrial Estate, Newcastle upon Tyne, NE15 9RT
Activities: Manufacture of builders ware of plastic
Parent: Millfield Composites Group Limited
Officers: Jill Eileen Dodd, Secretary; Jill Eileen Dodd [1941] Director/Company Secretary; John Marshall Dodd [1941] Director; Jonathan Andrew Dodd [1968] Director; John Paul Doyle [1971] Business Director

Millfield Properties Holdings Limited
Incorporated: 29 March 2016
Net Worth: £1,748,735 *Total Assets:* £1,748,735
Registered Office: 16 Shelley Road, Newburn Industrial Estate, Newcastle upon Tyne, NE15 9RT
Activities: Activities of other holding companies n.e.c.
Shareholders: John Marshall Dodd; Jonathan Andrew Dodd
Officers: John Marshall Dodd [1941] Director/Chemist; Jonathan Andrew Dodd [1968] Director

Millhouse Developments Limited
Incorporated: 11 January 1985 *Employees:* 2
Net Worth: £2,606,157 *Total Assets:* £3,717,870
Registered Office: Ravensworth House, 1 Ravensworth Street, Bedlington, Northumberland, NE22 7JP
Activities: Development of building projects
Parent: Millhouse Group Holdings Limited
Officers: Viscount Terence Devonport [1944] Director/Landowner; Morris Robert Muter [1954] Director

Millhouse Group Holdings Limited
Incorporated: 17 May 1990
Net Worth: £927,652 *Total Assets:* £944,781
Registered Office: Ravensworth House, 1 Ravensworth Street, Bedlington, Northumberland, NE22 7JP
Activities: Activities of construction holding companies
Shareholders: Morris Robert Muter; Viscount Terrence Devonport
Officers: Morris Robert Muter, Secretary/Director; Viscount Terence Devonport [1944] Director/Landowner; Morris Robert Muter [1954] Director

Mills Pharmacies Limited
Incorporated: 2 August 2000
Net Worth: £1,712,174 *Total Assets:* £1,761,405
Registered Office: 10 Grange Terrace, Sunderland, Tyne & Wear, SR2 7DF
Activities: Dispensing chemist in specialised stores
Shareholders: Alison Mary Herdman; Nigel Dale Herdman
Officers: Nigel Dale Herdman, Secretary; Alison Mary Herdman [1966] Director/Pharmacist; Blake William Herdman [2001] Director; Felicity Annabel Herdman [1996] Director; Harriet Herdman [1993] Director; Nigel Dale Herdman [1964] Director/Pharmacist; Sebastian Herdman [1998] Director

Mincoffs Solicitors LLP
Incorporated: 6 May 2004 *Employees:* 53
Net Worth: £593,891 *Total Assets:* £1,247,815
Registered Office: 5 Osborne Terrace, Newcastle upon Tyne, NE2 1SQ
Officers: Ryan Peter Bannon [1973] Member; Antony Michael Hall [1981] Member; Paul Hughes [1965] Member; John Phillip Nicholson [1973] Member; Matthew Foster [1976] LLP Member; Stewart William Irvine [1973] LLP Member; Louise Frances Miller [1981] LLP Member; Peter Hume Robinson [1970] LLP Member; Nicholas Smith [1972] LLP Member; Malcolm Graham Wood [1970] LLP Member

The Minel Group Ltd.
Incorporated: 1 June 2000 *Employees:* 3
Net Worth: £890,999 *Total Assets:* £2,088,637
Registered Office: 5th Floor, Cathedral Buildings, Dean Street, Newcastle upon Tyne, NE1 1PG
Activities: Plumbing, heat and air-conditioning installation
Major Shareholder: Timothy John Whiting
Officers: John Wade [1973] Director/Agent

Minel Venues LLP
Incorporated: 4 April 2013
Net Worth: £3,039,219 *Total Assets:* £5,516,390
Registered Office: Cathedral Buildings, Dean Street, Newcastle upon Tyne, NE1 1PG
Officers: John Wade [1973] Member; Deborah Anne Whiting [1972] Member

Mineral & Chemical Services (North East) Limited
Incorporated: 15 June 2012 *Employees:* 2
Net Worth: £26,152 *Total Assets:* £975,432
Registered Office: 1 Brittania Business House, Brittania Business Park, Point Pleasant, Wallsend, Tyne & Wear, NE28 6HA
Activities: Dormant company
Major Shareholder: Patrick Joseph Hegarty
Officers: Helena Piasecka, Secretary; Patrick Joseph Hegarty [1960] Director

Mineral & Chemical Services Ltd
Incorporated: 29 March 2006 *Employees:* 5
Net Worth: £1,350,639 *Total Assets:* £2,084,051
Registered Office: 1 Brittania House, Point Pleasant Industrial Estate, Wallsend, Tyne & Wear, NE28 6HA
Activities: Wholesale of chemical products
Major Shareholder: Patrick Joseph Hegarty
Officers: Carole Arthur, Secretary; Patrick Joseph Hegarty [1960] Managing Director

Mineral Insulated Cable Company Limited
Incorporated: 26 July 2001 *Employees:* 95
Net Worth: £1,039,548 *Total Assets:* £4,684,700
Registered Office: Unit 21 Sedling Road, Wear Industrial Estate, Washington, Tyne & Wear, NE38 9BZ
Activities: Manufacture of other electronic and electric wires and cables
Officers: Michael David Fitzpatrick, Secretary; Kenneth Douglas Dooley [1953] Managing Director; Mark Liddell [1962] Director; Nicholas Michael Morton [1954] Director/Chartered Engineer

Minhoco 12 Limited
Incorporated: 17 September 2010 *Employees:* 49
Net Worth: £2,265,017 *Total Assets:* £5,313,655
Registered Office: Malhotra House, 7-9 Groat Market, Newcastle upon Tyne, NE1 1UQ
Activities: Public houses and bars
Officers: Atul Malhotra [1981] Director; Devinder Mohan Malhotra [1967] Director

Minhoco 23 Limited
Incorporated: 30 August 2013
Net Worth: £1 *Total Assets:* £2,773,816
Registered Office: 2 Hermitage Drive, Walkworth, Morpeth, Northumberland, NE65 0XF
Activities: Other letting and operating of own or leased real estate
Major Shareholder: Richard John Betteridge
Officers: Richard John Betteridge [1963] Director

Minhoco 24 Limited
Incorporated: 3 November 2014 *Employees:* 73
Net Worth: £1,248,607 *Total Assets:* £7,595,737
Registered Office: 31-40 West Parade, Newcastle upon Tyne, NE4 7LB
Activities: Hotels and similar accommodation
Parent: The Station Hotel (Newcastle) Limited
Officers: Aran Handa [1955] Director; Arvan Handa [1952] Director

Minhoco 27 Limited
Incorporated: 2 September 2015
Net Worth Deficit: £175,022 *Total Assets:* £9,558,463
Registered Office: 31-40 West Parade, Newcastle upon Tyne, NE4 7LB
Activities: Hotels and similar accommodation
Parent: The Station Hotel (Newcastle) Limited
Officers: Aran Handa [1955] Director; Arvan Handa [1952] Director; Roshan Lal Handa [1928] Director [Indian]

Minhoco 30 Limited
Incorporated: 3 November 2015 *Employees:* 42
Net Worth Deficit: £64,377 *Total Assets:* £4,604,599
Registered Office: c/o CHG House, 31-40 West Parade, Newcastle upon Tyne, NE4 7LB
Activities: Hotels and similar accommodation
Parent: The Station Hotel (Newcastle) Limited
Officers: Aran Handa [1955] Director; Arvan Handa [1952] Director; Mr Roshan Lal Handa [1928] Director [Indian]

Minhoco 35 Limited
Incorporated: 17 September 2016 *Employees:* 524
Net Worth Deficit: £67,933 *Total Assets:* £53,740,164
Registered Office: c/o CHG House, 31-40 West Parade, Newcastle upon Tyne, NE4 7LB
Activities: Hotels and similar accommodation
Officers: Aran Handa [1955] Director; Arvan Handa [1952] Director

Mio Angelo Limited
Incorporated: 29 November 2016 *Employees:* 15
Net Worth: £430,385 *Total Assets:* £959,209
Registered Office: 6 Queen's Court, Third Avenue, Team Valley Trading Estate, Gateshead, Tyne & Wear, NE11 0BU
Activities: Licenced restaurants
Shareholders: Tony Tams; Giuseppe Iannitello
Officers: Giuseppe Iannitello [1945] Director; Tony Tams [1987] Director/Plasterer

Miresdale Dairy Limited
Incorporated: 13 October 2009 *Employees:* 8
Net Worth Deficit: £135,564 *Total Assets:* £1,449,590
Registered Office: York House, Thornfield Business Park, Standard Way Business Park, Northallerton, N Yorks, DL6 2XQ
Activities: Raising of dairy cattle
Shareholders: Geoffrey Thomas Spence; Linda May Spence
Officers: Geoffrey Thomas Spence, Secretary; Christopher Spence [1984] Director/Farmer; Geoffrey Thomas Spence [1961] Director; Linda May Spence [1962] Director

Missionbuild Limited
Incorporated: 14 January 1994 *Employees:* 1
Net Worth: £983,700 *Total Assets:* £1,653,056
Registered Office: 38 West Sunniside, Sunderland, Tyne & Wear, SR1 1BU
Activities: Other letting and operating of own or leased real estate
Shareholder: Jane Elviss
Officers: Thomas William Elviss, Secretary; Jane Elviss [1981] Director

Mistell Limited
Incorporated: 17 August 2005 *Employees:* 120
Net Worth: £3,108,242 *Total Assets:* £8,542,256
Registered Office: Riverside Park Road, Middlesbrough, Cleveland, TS2 1QW
Activities: Public houses and bars
Major Shareholder: Alastair Powell
Officers: Janice Robson, Secretary; Alastair Powell [1952] Director; Nicholas Michael Powell [1984] Director; Victoria Powell [1981] Director

Mitford B Limited
Incorporated: 11 December 2007
Net Worth: £12,105,632 *Total Assets:* £13,944,927
Registered Office: Offshore Technology Park, 1 Rendle Road, Walker, Newcastle upon Tyne, NE6 3NH
Activities: Other letting and operating of own or leased real estate
Shareholders: Simon Robert Winskell; Philippa Jean Shepherd; Shaun David Ward
Officers: Shaun David Ward, Secretary; Bruce Stewart Shepherd [1946] Director

Mitford F Limited
Incorporated: 11 December 2007
Net Worth: £12,105,632 *Total Assets:* £13,944,927
Registered Office: Offshore Technology Park, 1 Rendle Road, Walker, Newcastle upon Tyne, NE6 3NH
Activities: Other letting and operating of own or leased real estate
Shareholders: Charles Henry Shepherd; Simon Robert Winskell; Shaun David Ward
Officers: Shaun David Ward, Secretary; Bruce Stewart Shepherd [1946] Managing Director; Charles Henry Shepherd [1976] Director

Mitrepoint Limited
Incorporated: 29 November 1978 *Employees:* 70
Net Worth: £392,895 *Total Assets:* £1,446,626
Registered Office: Penshaw Way, Portobello Trading Estate, Birtley, Co Durham, DH3 2SA
Activities: Roofing activities
Major Shareholder: Alexander William Tilley
Officers: Alexander William Tilley [1987] Director/Surveyor/Estimator; David William Tilley [1959] Director

Mitsubishi Chemical Lucite Group Limited
Incorporated: 11 January 2006
Net Worth Deficit: £1,342,082 *Total Assets:* £278,780,192
Registered Office: Cassel Works, New Road, Billingham, Cleveland, TS23 1LE
Activities: Activities of head offices
Parent: MCC Group Holdings (UK) Limited
Officers: Robert Trevor Dunkley, Company Secretary; Yasuhiro Kabu [1960] Director/Company Executive [Japanese]; Takashi Miyaki [1956] Director/Company Executive [Japanese]

MIW Office Solutions Limited
Incorporated: 4 February 2002 *Employees:* 13
Net Worth: £793,992 *Total Assets:* £1,183,925
Registered Office: Bowman House, Oakeys Road, Tanfield Lea South Industrial Estate, Tanfield Lea, Stanley, Co Durham, DH9 9XW
Activities: Wholesale of other office machinery and equipment
Major Shareholder: Michael Ian Winter
Officers: Trevor Humble, Secretary; Michael Ian Winter [1967] Director/General Manager

MJM Developments (Portrack Grange) Limited
Incorporated: 20 December 2006
Net Worth: £554,837 *Total Assets:* £2,137,111
Registered Office: Unit 1 Portrack Grange Close, Stockton on Tees, Cleveland, TS18 2PH
Activities: Management of real estate on a fee or contract basis
Shareholders: Mark James; James Robert McCulloch
Officers: James Robert McCulloch, Secretary; Mark James [1974] Director; James Robert McCulloch [1977] Director

MJR Controls Limited
Incorporated: 20 February 1998 *Employees:* 22
Net Worth: £1,234,456 *Total Assets:* £1,674,318
Registered Office: Unit 85 Willows Court, Thornaby Industrial Estate, Stockton on Tees, Cleveland, TS17 9PP
Activities: Other engineering activities
Shareholder: MEC Marine & Offshore Ltd
Officers: Diane Elizabeth Cairns [1962] Director; Malcolm Vickers Cairns [1938] Director/Engineer; Mark Cairns [1970] Director/Engineer; Paul Robert Cairns [1967] Director; Christopher Milner [1972] Director/Engineer

MKM Investments Limited
Incorporated: 26 November 1997
Net Worth: £1,333,430 *Total Assets:* £1,711,306
Registered Office: Cale Cross House, 156 Pilgrim Street, Newcastle upon Tyne, NE1 6SU
Activities: Other letting and operating of own or leased real estate
Major Shareholder: Marlene Macpherson
Officers: Marlene Macpherson, Secretary; Marlene Macpherson [1950] Director/Property Developer

Mlgo Limited
Incorporated: 16 March 2006
Net Worth: £154,291 *Total Assets:* £961,434
Registered Office: Park Lane, Shiremoor, Tyne & Wear, NE27 0TQ
Activities: Other retail sale of new goods in specialised stores (not commercial art galleries and opticians)
Shareholders: Malcolm David Crone; Paul Crone
Officers: Paul Crone, Secretary; Malcolm David Crone [1946] Director/Retailer; Paul Crone [1974] Director/Retailer

MLM (UK) Limited
Incorporated: 29 July 2008 *Employees:* 11
Net Worth: £520,292 *Total Assets:* £1,351,045
Registered Office: Unit 1 & 2 Bridge Road, Brompton on Swale, Richmond, N Yorks, DL10 7HS
Activities: Construction of commercial buildings
Shareholders: Timothy Michael Benson; Timothy Michael Benson
Officers: Timothy Michael Benson [1967] Director

The MN Film Partnership No.2, LLP
Incorporated: 1 August 2001
Net Worth: £65,600,456 *Total Assets:* £67,644,664
Registered Office: PricewaterhouseCoopers LLP, 89 Sandyford Road, Newcastle upon Tyne, NE1 8HW

MNP Services Ltd.
Incorporated: 24 July 2001 *Employees:* 26
Net Worth: £937,659 *Total Assets:* £1,754,424
Registered Office: Unit 2 Halegrove Court, Cygnet Drive, Stockton on Tees, Cleveland, TS18 3DB
Activities: Plumbing, heat and air-conditioning installation
Shareholders: Michael Priestley; David Nixon
Officers: Michael Priestley, Secretary; David Nixon [1971] Director; Michael Priestley [1965] Director/Plumbing & Heating; Wendy Anne Priestley [1970] Director/Administrator

Mobi Developments Limited
Incorporated: 15 March 2005 *Employees:* 1
Net Worth Deficit: £122,331 *Total Assets:* £1,106,196
Registered Office: Kinnair & Company, Aston House, Redburn Road, Newcastle upon Tyne, NE5 1NB
Activities: Buying and selling of own real estate
Major Shareholder: Mohammed Ajaib
Officers: Mohammed Ajaib, Secretary; Mohammed Ajaib [1957] Director/Developer

Mobile Mini UK Holdings Limited
Incorporated: 21 March 2006
Net Worth: £16,782,000 *Total Assets:* £16,867,000
Registered Office: Ravenstock House, 28 Falcon Court, Preston Farm Business Park, Stockton on Tees, Cleveland, TS18 3TX
Activities: Activities of head offices
Parent: Mobile Mini Inc
Officers: Christopher David Morgan, Secretary; Christopher Miner [1971] Director/Global Legal Counsel [American]; Christopher David Morgan [1969] Managing Director; Erik Olsson [1962] Director/Chief Executive [American]; Graeme Bryan Parkes [1972] Director/Chief Information Officer [American]; Van Welch [1955] Director/Chief Financial Officer [American]

Mobile Mini UK Limited
Incorporated: 14 October 1993 *Employees:* 406
Net Worth: £99,681,000 *Total Assets:* £152,312,000
Registered Office: Ravenstock House, 28 Falcon Court, Preston Farm Business Park, Stockton on Tees, Cleveland, TS18 3TX
Activities: Renting and leasing of other machinery, equipment and tangible goods n.e.c.
Parent: Mobile Mini UK Holdings Limited
Officers: Christopher David Morgan, Secretary; Christopher Miner [1971] Director/General Counsel [American]; Christopher David Morgan [1969] Managing Director; Erik Olsson [1962] Director/Chief Executive [American]; Graeme Bryan Parkes [1972] Director/Chief Information Officer [American]; Van Welch [1955] Director/Chief Financial Officer [American]

Modaim Limited
Incorporated: 15 February 1989 *Employees:* 14
Net Worth: £1,694,100 *Total Assets:* £2,005,973
Registered Office: 71 Howard Street, North Shields, Tyne & Wear, NE30 1AF
Activities: Raising of dairy cattle
Shareholders: Carol Christine Gilbert; George William Gilbert
Officers: Carol Christine Gilbert, Secretary; Carol Christine Gilbert [1949] Director; George William Gilbert [1945] Director

Modern Rugs Limited
Incorporated: 9 July 2009
Net Worth: £1,760,003 *Total Assets:* £2,647,513
Registered Office: Unit 3 Maple Way, Aycliffe Business Park, Newton Aycliffe, Co Durham, DL5 6BF
Activities: Retail sale via mail order houses or via Internet
Shareholders: M Rugs Limited; PHD Nominees (MR) Limited; Coalfields Growth Fund
Officers: Kyle-Gian Mitchell, Secretary; Benjamin Daniel Dale [1981] Director; Kyle-Gian Mitchell [1987] Director; Gary Pickering [1989] Director

Modrec International Limited
Incorporated: 5 February 1987 *Employees:* 14
Net Worth: £1,214,920 *Total Assets:* £3,220,867
Registered Office: Bugatti House, Norham Road, North Shields, Tyne & Wear, NE29 7HA
Activities: Non-specialised wholesale trade
Parent: Modrec Holdings Ltd
Officers: John Anthony Harris Lightfoot [1971] Director; Gwenyth Lillian Snowball [1942] Director; Sydney Snowball [1943] Director

Modus Seabed Intervention Limited
Incorporated: 26 October 1987 *Employees:* 46
Net Worth: £2,451,000 *Total Assets:* £18,303,000
Registered Office: Beaumont House, Beaumont Street, Darlington, Co Durham, DL1 5RW
Activities: Other specialised construction activities n.e.c.
Officers: Jason Edward Tompkins, Secretary; Peter Mark Iain Short [1973] Finance Director; Jason Edward Tompkins [1974] Director/Company Executive; Nigel James Ward [1975] Commercial Director

Moguntia Food Ingredients UK Limited
Incorporated: 21 March 1989 *Employees:* 75
Net Worth: £1,652,075 *Total Assets:* £3,240,161
Registered Office: Hetton Lyons Industrial Estate, Houghton-le-Spring, Co Durham, DH5 0RH
Activities: Manufacture of condiments and seasonings
Major Shareholder: Ralph Karl Paul Buchholz
Officers: Francesco Campanaro [1958] Director; Colin Hitch [1961] Sales and Development Director; Stephen Neale [1965] Director; Paul Yeates [1958] Director

Mold Systems Limited
Incorporated: 6 May 2009 *Employees:* 80
Net Worth: £1,086,488 *Total Assets:* £5,652,210
Registered Office: 1 Millennium Way, Newton Aycliffe Industrial Park, Newton Aycliffe, Co Durham, DL5 6JW
Activities: Manufacture of other plastic products
Major Shareholder: Ivan Harold Bradbury
Officers: David Bradbury [1995] Director; Ivan Harold Bradbury [1946] Director; David McEwan Kinnaird [1959] Director

Molekula Limited
Incorporated: 17 April 2009 *Employees:* 25
Net Worth: £503,423 *Total Assets:* £3,577,469
Registered Office: Lingfield Way, Yarm Road Business Park, Darlington, Co Durham, DL1 4XX
Activities: Wholesale of chemical products
Shareholders: Kalvin Pierre Banks; Kristan Banks; Marina Banks
Officers: Kevin Peter Banks [1956] Director/Chemist; Margaret Elizabeth Banks [1962] Director/Farmer; David Bowen [1952] Director; Kathleen Bowen [1956] Director

Molly York Limited
Incorporated: 3 April 2007
Net Worth: £170,297 *Total Assets:* £1,268,363
Registered Office: 23 Monkton Rise, Guisborough, Cleveland, TS14 6GF
Activities: Other letting and operating of own or leased real estate
Shareholders: Lailany Fallarcuna Conlon; Peter David Conlon
Officers: Lailany Fallarcuna Conlon [1978] Director

Moltin Ltd
Incorporated: 3 April 2013
Registered Office: 15 Carliol Square, Newcastle upon Tyne, NE1 6UF
Activities: Other information technology service activities
Officers: Jamie Holdroyd [1987] Director/Chief Executive Officer; Adam Sturrock [1990] Director/Chief Communications Officer

Momento Vivere Limited
Incorporated: 29 January 2015 *Employees:* 2
Net Worth: £1,889,571 *Total Assets:* £1,924,794
Registered Office: Kirklington Manor, Stapley Lane, Bedale, N Yorks, DL8 2LU
Activities: Activities of other holding companies n.e.c.
Major Shareholder: Paul Anthony Wilson
Officers: Jayne Wilson [1970] Director/Consultant; Paul Anthony Wilson [1970] Director/Consultant

Monckton Coke & Chemical Company Limited (The)
Incorporated: 25 July 1901 *Employees:* 3
Net Worth Deficit: £8,563,000 *Total Assets:* £12,518,000
Registered Office: West Terrace, Esh Winning, Co Durham, DH7 9PT
Activities: Manufacture of coke oven products
Parent: Hargreaves (UK) Limited
Officers: Gordon Frank Colenso Banham [1964] Director

Monde Nissin (UK) Limited
Incorporated: 30 September 2015 *Employees:* 10
Net Worth: £175,292,992 *Total Assets:* £513,265,984
Registered Office: Quorn Foods, Station Road, Stokesley, Middlesbrough, Cleveland, TS9 7AB
Activities: Manufacture of prepared meals and dishes
Parent: Monde Nissin Singapore PTE Ltd
Officers: James Laurence Harvey, Secretary; Kevin Francis Brennan [1962] Director; James Laurence Harvey [1965] Director/Accountant; Henry Kahayu Soesanto [1952] Director [Indonesian]; Jesse Teo [1971] Director [Filipino]; Vijay Champaklal Thakrar [1961] Director

Monitor Coatings Limited
Incorporated: 20 June 2003 *Employees:* 54
Net Worth: £807,077 *Total Assets:* £2,545,942
Registered Office: Monitor House, 2 Elm Road, West Chirton Industrial Estate, North Shields, Tyne & Wear, NE29 8SE
Activities: Treatment and coating of metals
Parent: Fawm Limited
Officers: Colin George Lishman, Secretary; Rebecca Allcock [1970] Director

Monitor Marine (C.P.) Limited
Incorporated: 22 March 1985 *Employees:* 5
Net Worth: £709,640 *Total Assets:* £879,420
Registered Office: 51 Oaklands, Gosforth, Newcastle upon Tyne, NE3 4YP
Activities: Buying and selling of own real estate
Shareholders: Barbara Mary Clare Carr; Michael John Russell Carr
Officers: Barbara Mary Clare Carr, Secretary; Conor Michael Hanratty Carr [1984] Director; Roisin Clara Hanratty Thomas [1988] Director

Monkton Infants School
Incorporated: 9 January 2013 *Employees:* 21
Net Worth: £1,404,010 *Total Assets:* £1,751,720
Registered Office: Monkton Infants School, St Simon Street, South Shields, Tyne & Wear, NE34 9SD
Activities: Pre-primary education
Officers: Janet Lindsay Daglish, Secretary; Walter Featherstone Armstrong [1937] Director/Retired; Clare Elizabeth Askwith [1966] Director/Principal; Richard Cheadle [1952] Director/Retired; Enid Fairbrother [1953] Director/School Improvement Adviser; Rachel Garvin [1980] Director/Stay at Home Parent; Janice Hansen [1954] Director; Michelle Olsen [1976] Director/Local Government Officer; Alison Sharp [1984] Director/Secretary/Office Manager; Jennifer Watkins [1986] Director/Office Manager; Hayley Winter [1984] Director/Teacher

Monkton Junior School
Incorporated: 9 March 2012 *Employees:* 20
Net Worth: £1,268,471 *Total Assets:* £1,456,971
Registered Office: Monkton Junior School, Dame Flora Robson Avenue, South Shields, Tyne & Wear, NE34 9RD
Activities: Primary education
Officers: Christine Flynn, Secretary; Walter Featherstone Armstrong [1937] Director/Solicitor (Retired); Vivian Anne Byass [1955] Director/Home Maker; Louise Joan Heathfield [1984] Director/Acting Principal; Nigel Henderson [1977] Director/Sales Manager; David William Mullen [1962] Director/Chartered Engineer; Michelle Olsen [1976] Director/Local Government Officer; Alison Sharp [1984] Director/Counsellor; Victoria Sheriff [1992] Director/Teacher; Rachel Wood [1975] Director/Learning Support Assistant

Monomarket (Holdings) Limited
Incorporated: 15 November 2007
Net Worth: £2,578,282 *Total Assets:* £3,315,266
Registered Office: 4 High Street, Stanley, Co Durham, DH9 0DQ
Activities: Activities of head offices
Major Shareholder: Gillian Eve Gale
Officers: Gillian Eve Gale, Secretary; Gillian Eve Gale [1962] Director

Monomarket Limited
Incorporated: 16 June 1986 *Employees:* 52
Net Worth: £240,438 *Total Assets:* £1,180,077
Registered Office: 164-170 Newbridge Street, Newcastle upon Tyne, NE1 2TE
Activities: Retail of furniture, lighting, and similar (not musical instruments or scores) in specialised store
Parent: Monomarket (Holdings) Ltd
Officers: Gillian Eve Gale, Secretary; Gillian Eve Gale [1962] Director/Company Secretary

Montagu Hotels Limited
Incorporated: 21 September 2004
Net Worth Deficit: £3,175,700 *Total Assets:* £2,952,770
Registered Office: 14 Grand Parade, Tynemouth, Tyne & Wear, NE30 4JQ
Activities: Development of building projects
Shareholder: Sewa Singh Gill
Officers: Jaspal Kaur Gill [1948] Director; Sewa Singh Gill [1945] Director

Montane Ltd
Incorporated: 12 July 1996 *Employees:* 34
Net Worth: £1,734,918 *Total Assets:* £6,309,816
Registered Office: 3 Freeman Court, North Seaton Industrial Estate, Ashington, Northumberland, NE63 0YF
Activities: Manufacture of other men's outerwear
Shareholder: Jake Doxat
Officers: David Alan Soulsby, Secretary; Jake Doxat [1965] Director; David Alan Soulsby [1980] Finance Director

Monte Cristo Residential Ltd
Incorporated: 6 January 2014
Net Worth: £28,450 *Total Assets:* £818,553
Registered Office: 33 Bellingham Drive, North Tyneside Industrial Estate, Benton, Newcastle upon Tyne, NE12 9SZ
Activities: Buying and selling of own real estate
Officers: Claire Proud [1958] Director/Homemaker

Montgomery Blue Limited
Incorporated: 10 July 2015
Net Worth: £1,087,587 *Total Assets:* £1,088,947
Registered Office: 194 Thames Road, Billingham, Cleveland, TS22 5EF
Activities: Activities of other holding companies n.e.c.
Shareholders: Kathryn Louise Armstrong; Stephen Neil Armstrong
Officers: Kathryn Louise Armstrong [1969] Director; Stephen Neil Armstrong [1971] Director

Montpelier Professional Limited
Incorporated: 14 January 2004
Net Worth Deficit: £1,154,016 *Total Assets:* £10,701,604
Registered Office: Suite 3, 5 Battalion Court, Colburn Business Park, Catterick Garrison, N Yorks, DL9 4QN
Activities: Accounting and auditing activities
Parent: Montpelier Group (Tax Consultants) Limted
Officers: Edward Watkin Gittins [1950] Director/Chartered Accountant

Monument (Survey:Design:Build) Ltd
Incorporated: 30 August 2012 *Employees:* 7
Net Worth: £342,871 *Total Assets:* £2,747,567
Registered Office: 8 Mosley Street, Newcastle upon Tyne, NE1 1DE
Activities: Development of building projects
Shareholders: Michael Carrick; Andrew Richardson; Stephen Rutherford
Officers: Michael Carrick [1981] Director/Professional Footballer; Andrew Richardson [1977] Director; Stephen Rutherford [1981] Director

Monument Developments Ltd
Incorporated: 20 March 2014
Net Worth Deficit: £4,494 *Total Assets:* £1,140,555
Registered Office: 7 Mercury Road, Gallowfields Trading Estate, Richmond, N Yorks, DL10 4TQ
Activities: Development of building projects
Shareholders: Douglas Edward Newton; Newroc Ltd
Officers: Douglas Edward Newton [1964] Director; Graeme Richard Newton [1968] Director

John Moody & Son Limited
Incorporated: 25 August 1981 *Employees:* 1
Net Worth Deficit: £68,571 *Total Assets:* £1,116,520
Registered Office: Unit 1 Renwick Court, Victoria Road, Gateshead, Tyne & Wear, NE8 2SY
Activities: Other specialised construction activities n.e.c.
Parent: John Moody Investments Limited
Officers: Allison Wright, Secretary; John Moody [1932] Director/Private Builder; John Moody [1963] Director/Private Builder; Shirley Moody [1937] Director

D.Moody (Haulage) Limited
Incorporated: 23 May 1960 *Employees:* 38
Net Worth: £688,969 *Total Assets:* £1,193,514
Registered Office: Bolam Business Park, Bassington Drive, Bassington Industrial Estate, Cramlington, Northumberland, NE23 8AL
Activities: Freight transport by road
Parent: Bolam Group Limited
Officers: Gavin Ridley Cape [1971] Director; Caroline Jane Crawford [1971] Director; Alan Richard Moody [1976] Director

John Moody Investments Limited
Incorporated: 27 March 2002 *Employees:* 2
Net Worth: £1,663,522 *Total Assets:* £3,338,357
Registered Office: Unit 1 Renwick Court, Victoria Road, Gateshead, Tyne & Wear, NE8 2SY
Activities: Buying and selling of own real estate
Shareholders: John Moody; Shirley Moody
Officers: Allison Wright, Secretary; John Moody [1963] Director/Builder; John Moody [1932] Director/Builder; Shirley Moody [1937] Director

P A Moody Recycling Limited
Incorporated: 13 April 2005
Net Worth: £191,578 *Total Assets:* £2,262,690
Registered Office: Gap House, Nest Road, Gateshead, Tyne & Wear, NE10 0ES
Activities: Treatment and disposal of non-hazardous waste
Major Shareholder: Peter Anthony Moody
Officers: Sharon Moody, Secretary; Garry Harbottle [1976] Operation Director; Peter Anthony Moody [1965] Director; Andrew Gavin Wiltshire [1971] Technical Director; Peter Young [1967] Logistics Director

Moores Leisure (Teesside) Limited
Incorporated: 12 September 1995 *Employees:* 31
Net Worth: £1,057,331 *Total Assets:* £2,125,496
Registered Office: 18-26 Bishopton Lane, Stockton on Tees, Cleveland, TS18 2AA
Activities: Public houses and bars
Shareholders: Derek Leslie Moore; Donald Waites
Officers: Donald Waites, Secretary; Derek Leslie Moore [1973] Director/Manager; Donald Waites [1962] Director

Moorlands Care Homes (N.E.) Limited
Incorporated: 25 October 2004
Net Worth: £1,579,800 *Total Assets:* £1,919,800
Registered Office: 49 St Georges Terrace, Jesmond, Newcastle upon Tyne, NE2 2SX
Activities: Residential nursing care facilities
Major Shareholder: David Peter Ratliff
Officers: Michael Charles Ratliff, Secretary; David Peter Ratliff [1946] Director

Moorlands Holdings (N.E.) Limited
Incorporated: 10 December 1987
Net Worth: £4,233,070 *Total Assets:* £5,582,322
Registered Office: 49 St Georges Terrace, Jesmond, Newcastle upon Tyne, NE2 2SX
Activities: Hotels and similar accommodation
Shareholder: Dr David Peter Ratliff
Officers: Michael Charles Ratliff, Secretary; David Peter Ratliff [1946] Director/Dental Surgeon

Moorview Properties Limited
Incorporated: 30 October 1958 *Employees:* 1
Net Worth: £3,342,443 *Total Assets:* £3,500,941
Registered Office: 309 Wingrove Road North, Newcastle upon Tyne, NE4 9ED
Activities: Other letting and operating of own or leased real estate
Officers: Jean Carole Moody [1945] Director/Solicitor

John Morfield Limited
Incorporated: 3 December 1962 *Employees:* 49
Net Worth: £1,085,647 *Total Assets:* £4,582,007
Registered Office: 98 Sadler Forster Way, Teesside Industrial Estate, Thornaby on Tees, Cleveland, TS17 9JY
Activities: Agents involved in the sale of machinery, industrial equipment, ships and aircraft
Shareholders: Stephen David Johnston; Thomas Raymond Crabtree
Officers: Ian Geoffrey Myers, Secretary; Thomas Raymond Crabtree [1944] Director; Phillip Davis [1960] Director (Sales); Peter Johnston [1934] Director; Stephen David Johnston [1963] Managing Director; Gary James McMullen [1956] Director (Sales); Ian Geoffrey Myers [1970] Director/Chartered Accountant; Charles Edward Oyston [1951] Director

Morfitt Waste Management Ltd
Incorporated: 18 March 2011
Net Worth: £1,640,160 *Total Assets:* £1,726,653
Registered Office: The Grange, Lower Piercy Farm, Dalton Piercy, Hartlepool, Cleveland, TS27 3HS
Activities: Renting and leasing of other machinery, equipment and tangible goods n.e.c.
Major Shareholder: Richelle Ebony Hunter
Officers: Richelle Ebony Hunter [1980] Director

O Morgan Developments Limited
Incorporated: 1 August 2013
Net Worth: £134,498 *Total Assets:* £1,085,132
Registered Office: 1 Station Road, Low Pittington, Co Durham, DH6 1BJ
Activities: Buying and selling of own real estate
Major Shareholder: Oliver Allan Morgan
Officers: Oliver Allan Morgan [1989] Director

Morley Group Limited
Incorporated: 28 August 1984 *Employees:* 2
Net Worth: £835,376 *Total Assets:* £862,389
Registered Office: Albion Row, Newcastle upon Tyne, NE6 1PQ
Activities: Other letting and operating of own or leased real estate
Major Shareholder: Peter Morley
Officers: Irene Anne Morley, Secretary; Peter Morley [1950] Director

The Morpeth Golf Club Limited
Incorporated: 31 July 1992
Net Worth: £301,516 *Total Assets:* £1,009,296
Registered Office: The Clubhouse, Loansdean, Morpeth, Northumberland, NE61 2BT
Activities: Activities of sport clubs
Officers: Martin Calder [1957] Director; William Edward Cromar [1950] Director/Retired; Tim Duncan Gorman [1960] Director/Solicitor; Steve Jemmett [1964] Director; Ben Maxted [1983] Director; Tommy Turnbull [1948] Director/Retired; Anthony Mark Waller [1971] Director/Accountant

The Morpeth Practice Ltd
Incorporated: 10 March 2005 *Employees:* 12
Net Worth: £1,556,167 *Total Assets:* £2,137,884
Registered Office: Appleby House, Castle Square, Morpeth, Northumberland, NE61 1YD
Activities: Financial management
Shareholders: Peter Tapson Grieves; James Owen Richfield
Officers: Peter Tapson Grieves, Secretary; Peter Tapson Grieves [1968] Director; James Owen Richfield [1971] Director

Thomas Morris Limited
Incorporated: 20 February 2002 *Employees:* 64
Net Worth: £7,905,000 *Total Assets:* £8,689,000
Registered Office: Newcastle House, Albany Court, Newcastle Business Park, Newcastle upon Tyne, NE4 7YB
Activities: Management of real estate on a fee or contract basis
Parent: LSLI Ltd
Officers: Sapna Bedi FitzGenerald, Secretary; Greig Barker [1969] Director; Simon Luther Bradbury [1961] Director/Estate Agent; Gregory Winston Young [1966] Director

Mortley Estates Limited
Incorporated: 25 May 2006
Net Worth: £650,025 *Total Assets:* £1,203,308
Registered Office: c/o Censis, Exchange Building, 66 Church Street, Hartlepool, Cleveland, TS24 7DN
Activities: Other letting and operating of own or leased real estate
Parent: The C M Yuill 1972 Settlement-Peter's Children's Fund
Officers: Peter Mortley Yuill, Secretary; Margaret Helen Yuill [1952] Director; Peter Mortley Yuill [1949] Director

Mosaic Global Investments Limited
Incorporated: 10 June 2014
Net Worth: £1,172,821 *Total Assets:* £6,063,459
Registered Office: B3 Kingfisher House, Team Valley Trading Estate, Gateshead, Tyne & Wear, NE11 0JQ
Activities: Development of building projects
Parent: Knighton Investments Limited (Based in Guernsey)
Officers: Aized Sheikh [1959] Director

Joel A Moseley Transport Limited
Incorporated: 1 April 2008 *Employees:* 17
Net Worth: £902,428 *Total Assets:* £1,630,178
Registered Office: Keepers Cottage, Long Walk, Bedale, N Yorks, DL8 1TY
Activities: Freight transport by road
Shareholders: Joel Anthony Moseley; Adam Joel Moseley
Officers: Adam Joel Moseley, Secretary; Adam Joel Moseley [1979] Director; Joel Anthony Moseley [1945] Director/Haulage Contractor

Motherdale Limited
Incorporated: 11 June 1986 *Employees:* 69
Net Worth: £4,623,437 *Total Assets:* £5,353,504
Registered Office: Summerfields, St James Fields, Castle Eden, Co Durham, TS27 4TJ
Activities: Residential care activities for the elderly and disabled
Shareholders: Kanoda Holdings Ltd; Dr Mohamad Noorbhai Maredia
Officers: Susan Elizabeth Maredia, Secretary; Ben Maredia [1982] Director; Dr Mohamad Noorbhai Maredia [1945] Director/General Medical Practitioner; Susan Elizabeth Maredia [1952] Director/Nurse

Motorcare (Alnwick) Limited
Incorporated: 20 May 1991
Registered Office: Unit 1 South Road Industrial Estate, Alnwick, Northumberland, NE66 2NN
Activities: Sale of new cars and light motor vehicles
Major Shareholder: Bryan Easton
Officers: Helen Brewis, Secretary; Bryan Easton [1954] Director/Garage Proprietor

Moulded Packaging Solutions Ltd
Incorporated: 4 September 2006 *Employees:* 22
Net Worth: £974,319 *Total Assets:* £2,344,367
Registered Office: Ennerdale Business Centre, Ennerdale Road, Blyth, Northumberland, NE24 4RT
Activities: Manufacture of plastic packing goods
Shareholders: Alan Brian Charlton; Iain Douglas McLeod
Officers: Iain Douglas McLeod, Secretary; Alan Brian Charlton [1963] Director; Iain Douglas McLeod [1977] Director

Mount Gable Estates Limited
Incorporated: 1 May 2015
Net Worth: £1,899,184 *Total Assets:* £3,203,221
Registered Office: Lakeside House, Kingfisher Way, Stockton on Tees, Cleveland, TS18 3NB
Activities: Buying and selling of own real estate
Shareholders: Eileen Elizabeth Davidson; Patricia Mary Sumpter; John Patrick Joyce
Officers: Eileen Elizabeth Davidson [1948] Director; John Patrick Joyce [1954] Director/Managing Partner; Patricia Mary Sumpter [1944] Director

The Mountain Boot Company Limited
Incorporated: 14 January 1994 *Employees:* 32
Net Worth: £1,573,343 *Total Assets:* £7,511,451
Registered Office: Unit 5 New York Way, New York Industrial Estate, Wallsend, Tyne & Wear, NE27 0QF
Activities: Agents involved in the sale of textiles, clothing, fur, footwear and leather goods
Major Shareholder: Stephen David Roberts
Officers: Spencer McBride, Secretary; Julie Roberts [1969] PA to Managing Director; Stephen David Roberts [1973] Managing Director

T.O. Mounter & Sons Limited
Incorporated: 18 July 1972 *Employees:* 34
Net Worth: £737,696 *Total Assets:* £1,385,728
Registered Office: The Sawmills, Park Street, Willington, Crook, Co Durham, DL15 0ER
Activities: Sawmilling and planing of wood
Parent: T.O. Mounter & Sons Holdings Limited
Officers: John James Mounter, Secretary; Alan Mounter [1953] Managing Director; Henry Mounter [1944] Director; John James Mounter [1947] Director; Stanleigh Mounter [1942] Director

Mountgate Caravans Limited
Incorporated: 19 November 1996 *Employees:* 4
Net Worth: £437,832 *Total Assets:* £853,717
Registered Office: Silver Carrs Caravan Park, Low Hauxley, Amble, Morpeth, Northumberland, NE65 0JR
Activities: Recreational vehicle parks, trailer parks and camping grounds
Shareholders: Christopher John Phillips; Kevin Richard Phillips; Jonathan Andrew Phillips
Officers: Christopher John Phillips, Secretary; Christopher John Phillips [1964] Director/Administrator; Jonathon Andrew Phillips [1968] Director/Manager; Kevin Richard Phillips [1965] Director/Manager

Movesun Limited
Incorporated: 27 February 2002
Net Worth: £1,781,574 *Total Assets:* £3,701,049
Registered Office: 15-16 Stockholm Close, Tyne Tunnel Trading Estate, North Shields, Tyne & Wear, NE29 7SF
Activities: Hotels and similar accommodation
Parent: Dean Venture Ltd
Officers: Bhupinder Singh Ladhar [1981] Director; Mandeep Singh Ladhar [1985] Director

Mowden Controls Limited
Incorporated: 1 February 1965 *Employees:* 44
Net Worth: £4,028,302 *Total Assets:* £4,392,777
Registered Office: Mowden Controls Ltd, Mount View, Standard Way Industrial Estate, Northallerton, N Yorks, DL6 2YD
Activities: Manufacture of electronic industrial process control equipment
Shareholders: Stephen Lewis Williams; Anne Letitia Kirk; Elizabeth Anne Barber
Officers: Stephen Lewis Williams, Secretary/Managing Director; Elizabeth Anne Barber [1969] Director; Michael John Green [1945] Director/Retired; Anne Letitia Kirk [1935] Director/Retired; Neil MacLean [1958] Technical Director; Stephen Lewis Williams [1966] Managing Director

Mowden Park Estate Company Limited
Incorporated: 6 February 1967 *Employees:* 8
Net Worth: £4,080,923 *Total Assets:* £16,631,130
Registered Office: Unit 2 Jubilee House, York Road, Hartlepool, Cleveland, TS26 9EN
Activities: Other letting and operating of own or leased real estate
Shareholder: Phillip Guy Yuill
Officers: Julie Margaret Rigali, Secretary; Emma Jane Holmes [1982] Director; David Nigel Williams [1943] Director; Edward Richard Thomas Yuill [1978] Director; Phillip Guy Yuill [1954] Director; Victoria Mary Yuill [1951] Director

Mowlem and Company (London) Limited
Incorporated: 18 May 2000
Registered Office: Mowlem House, High Flatworth, Tyne Tunnel Trading Estate, North Shields, Tyne & Wear, NE29 7UT
Activities: Retail of furniture, lighting, and similar (not musical instruments or scores) in specialised store
Shareholders: Gary Mowlem; Rudolf Luder; Neil Lawrence
Officers: Gary Ronald Mowlem, Secretary/Furniture Retailer; Neil Curtis Lawrence [1956] Sales Director; Rudolf Luder [1952] Sales Director [Swiss]; Gary Ronald Mowlem [1960] Director/Furniture Retailer

Mowlem and Company (Newcastle) Limited
Incorporated: 3 December 1998
Registered Office: Mowlem House, High Flatworth, Tyne Tunnel Trading Estate, North Shields, Tyne & Wear, NE29 7UT
Activities: Manufacture of kitchen furniture
Shareholders: Garfield Mowlem; Mowlem & Company (Services) Ltd
Officers: Gary Ronald Mowlem, Secretary/Director; Julia Brown [1980] Director/Bespoke Furniture; Gary Ronald Mowlem [1960] Director

MPI Consultants Limited
Incorporated: 1 June 2006 *Employees:* 63
Net Worth: £2,519,562 *Total Assets:* £5,647,628
Registered Office: Tobias House, St Mark's Court, Teesdale Business Park, Stockton on Tees, Cleveland, TS17 6QW
Activities: Other business support service activities n.e.c.
Parent: MPI Services Stokesley Limited
Officers: Herman Frans Mathilde Marks [1960] Shipping Director [Dutch]; Graeme Paul Sheach [1966] Director/Chartered Accountant

MPI Offshore Limited
Incorporated: 30 March 2006 *Employees:* 36
Net Worth: £595,946 *Total Assets:* £7,038,028
Registered Office: Tobias House, St Mark's Court, Teesdale Business Park, Stockton on Tees, Cleveland, TS17 6QW
Activities: Other business support service activities n.e.c.
Parent: MPI Services Stokesley Limited
Officers: Herman Frans Mathilde Marks [1960] Shipping Director [Dutch]; Graeme Paul Sheach [1966] Director/Chartered Accountant

MPI Services Stokesley Limited
Incorporated: 4 April 2011
Net Worth: £3,039,829 *Total Assets:* £6,117,810
Registered Office: Tobias House, St Mark's Court, Teesdale Business Park, Stockton on Tees, Cleveland, TS17 6QW
Activities: Activities of head offices
Officers: Herman Frans Mathilde Marks [1960] Shipping Director [Dutch]; Graeme Paul Sheach [1966] Director/Chartered Accountant

MRM Electrical Solutions Limited
Incorporated: 8 September 2009
Net Worth: £289,491 *Total Assets:* £1,319,975
Registered Office: Unit 3b Whitehouse Road Industrial Estate, Whitehouse Road, Newcastle upon Tyne, NE15 6LN
Activities: Electrical installation
Shareholders: Michael Robert Muxworthy; Richard Oliver Muxworthy; Nicholas Wright
Officers: Robert Muxworthy, Secretary; Christopher James Darling [1987] Director; Michael Robert Muxworthy [1985] Director/Electrical Engineer; Richard Oliver Muxworthy [1988] Director/Electrical Engineer; Nicholas Wright [1979] Director/Electrical Engineer

MS Investments (IB) Limited
Incorporated: 22 July 2013
Net Worth: £162,366 *Total Assets:* £1,451,156
Registered Office: Roseville Court, Blair Avenue, Ingleby Barwick, Stockton on Tees, Cleveland, TS17 5BL
Activities: Other letting and operating of own or leased real estate
Major Shareholder: Sukhraj Singh
Officers: Sukhraj Singh [1964] Director/Property Developer

MSD Construction (UK) Ltd
Incorporated: 22 May 2003
Net Worth: £1,105,608 *Total Assets:* £1,246,712
Registered Office: First Floor Suite, 6 High Street, Sedgefield, Stockton on Tees, Cleveland, TS21 3AR
Activities: Other construction installation
Major Shareholder: Anthony Moran
Officers: Julie Moran, Secretary; Anthony Moran [1966] Director

MSM Media Solutions Ltd
Incorporated: 26 August 2008
Net Worth: £792,157 *Total Assets:* £1,305,988
Registered Office: BLP Ltd, Unit 99 North Tyne Industrial Estate, Whitley Road, Benton, Tyne & Wear, NE12 9SZ
Activities: Management consultancy activities other than financial management
Shareholders: Mark Clavering; Mark Taylor Harrison; Scott Young
Officers: Mark Clavering [1972] Director; Mark Harrison [1967] Director; Scott Young [1972] Director

MSSL (GB) Limited
Incorporated: 16 March 2004 *Employees:* 52
Net Worth: £324,848,256 *Total Assets:* £386,374,624
Registered Office: Albany Road, Gateshead, Tyne & Wear, NE8 3AT
Activities: Manufacture of other parts and accessories for motor vehicles
Officers: Ashok Tandon, Secretary; Paul Breen [1964] Director/Technical Manager [Irish]; Anurag Gahlot [1974] Director/Engineer [Indian]; Andreas Heuser [1966] Director/Lawyer [German]; Pankaj Kumar Mital [1966] Director [Indian]; Vivek Chaand Sehgal [1956] Director/Industrialist [Australian]; Ashok Tandon [1951] Director/Service [Indian]

MSSL Overseas Wiring System Limited
Incorporated: 27 June 2014
Net Worth: £25,777,496 *Total Assets:* £25,790,792
Registered Office: Albany Road, Gateshead, Tyne & Wear, NE8 3AT
Activities: Activities of other holding companies n.e.c.
Officers: Gaya Nand Gauba [1961] Director/Service [Indian]; Andreas Heuser [1966] Director/Advisor [German]; Laksh Vaaman Sehgal [1982] Director/Entrepreneur [Australian]; Ashok Tandon [1951] Director/Service [Indian]

MTL Services Limited
Incorporated: 14 September 1998 *Employees:* 2
Net Worth: £116,004,000 *Total Assets:* £116,045,000
Registered Office: 1 Admiral Way, Doxford International Business Park, Sunderland, Tyne & Wear, SR3 3XP
Activities: Activities of head offices
Parent: Arriva PLC
Officers: Lorna Edwards, Secretary; Amanda Furlong [1975] Director; Paul Gerard Smith [1969] Director

MTREC Limited
Incorporated: 14 March 2006 *Employees:* 51
Net Worth: £5,451,377 *Total Assets:* £11,223,763
Registered Office: MTREC House, 8 Market Lane, Newcastle upon Tyne, NE1 6QQ
Activities: Temporary employment agency activities
Parent: Trust Tech Inc
Officers: Yuichi Kamata [1970] Corporate Director [Japanese]; David Musgrave [1969] Director; Yutaka Nishida [1963] Director [Japanese]

MTW County Limited
Incorporated: 24 January 2008 *Employees:* 2
Net Worth Deficit: £471,196,064 *Total Assets:* £23,057,126
Registered Office: St Anns Wharf, 112 Quayside, Newcastle upon Tyne, NE1 3DX
Activities: Activities of other holding companies n.e.c.
Parent: Manitowoc Foodservice Inc
Officers: Adrian David Gray [1962] Director/Accountant; John Albert James Rourke [1967] Director

Muckle LLP
Incorporated: 28 September 2005 *Employees:* 129
Net Worth: £3,127,453 *Total Assets:* £6,101,091
Registered Office: c/o Muckle LLP, Time Central, 32 Gallowgate, Newcastle upon Tyne, NE1 4BF
Officers: Philip Clare [1981] Member; Jonathan Woods Combe [1964] Member; Alexandra Jane Craig [1974] Member; Andrew John Davison [1961] Member; Louise Duffy [1969] Member; Anthony Guy Evans [1973] Member; Susan Jane Howe [1964] Member; Christopher James Maddock [1971] Member; William McKay [1977] Member; Charlotte McMurchie [1970] Member; Anthony James Noel McPhillips [1962] Member; Jason Brian Wainwright [1970] Member; Hugh Benson Welch [1957] Member

C.K.& D.Muir Limited
Incorporated: 13 May 1964
Net Worth: £284,959 *Total Assets:* £1,071,497
Registered Office: Grinkle Park Farm, Loftus, Saltburn-by-the-Sea, N Yorks, TS13 4UD
Activities: Mixed farming
Major Shareholder: Richard Muir
Officers: Beverley Muir, Secretary; Dennis Charles Muir [1947] Director/Farmer; Richard Muir [1966] Director/Farmer

Mulberry Homes Yorkshire Limited
Incorporated: 27 October 2009 *Employees:* 6
Net Worth Deficit: £2,744,377 *Total Assets:* £13,405,606
Registered Office: Broadacres House, Mount View, Standard Way Industrial Estate, Northallerton, N Yorks, DL6 2YD
Activities: Development of building projects
Parent: Broadacres Housing Association Ltd
Officers: Chris Fawcett, Secretary; Jacqui Bateson [1961] Director/Senior Manager; Alison Grainger [1969] Housing Association Director; June Patricia Mulroy [1949] Director/Retired; Peter Anthony Ottowell [1955] Director/Retired; Phil Summers [1960] Director/Retired; Martin Warhurst [1974] Director/Chief Executive; Colin Wilkie [1954] Director/Retired

Mulberry Leisure Holdings Limited
Incorporated: 3 February 2005
Net Worth: £80 *Total Assets:* £1,819,566
Registered Office: Angel View Inn, Low Eighton, Eighton Banks, Gateshead, Tyne & Wear, NE9 7UB
Activities: Activities of head offices
Shareholders: Deepak Kumar Chopra; Neela Chopra
Officers: Neela Chopra, Company Secretary; Deepak Kumar Chopra [1951] Director

Mulberry Leisure Limited
Incorporated: 26 May 1993
Registered Office: Angel View Inn, Low Eighton, Eighton Banks, Low Fell, Tyne & Wear, NE9 7UB
Activities: Hotels and similar accommodation
Parent: Mulberry Leisure Holdings Limited
Officers: Neela Chopra, Secretary/Director; Deepak Kumar Chopra [1951] Director; Neela Chopra [1955] Director; Sanjay Chopra [1982] Director

Mullen Properties Limited
Incorporated: 21 May 2003
Net Worth Deficit: £171,905 *Total Assets:* £830,200
Registered Office: 11 Defender Court, Sunderland Enterprise Park, Sunderland, Tyne & Wear, SR5 3PE
Activities: Other letting and operating of own or leased real estate
Shareholders: Claire Dixon; Rodger Mullen
Officers: Claire Dixon, Secretary; Claire Dixon [1977] Director; Rodger Mullen [1978] Director

Multi-Lab Limited
Incorporated: 18 October 1988 *Employees:* 26
Net Worth: £3,112,045 *Total Assets:* £3,851,915
Registered Office: Unit 1 Westway Industrial Park, Throckley, Newcastle upon Tyne, NE15 9HW
Activities: Manufacture and processing of other glass, including technical glassware
Officers: Sarah Louise Edwards, Secretary; Audrey Eva Jackman [1936] Director; Paul Kevin Jackman [1963] Director; Ronald Beuteman Jackman [1935] Director

Multichem Limited
Incorporated: 9 March 1973 *Employees:* 18
Net Worth: £1,281,846 *Total Assets:* £2,148,038
Registered Office: Unit 1 Tyne Mills Industrial Estate, Hexham, Northumberland, NE46 1XL
Activities: Other manufacturing n.e.c.
Major Shareholder: Kaleel George Zibe
Officers: Kaleel George Zibe, Secretary/Director; Michael Nelson [1972] Managing Director; Kaleel George Zibe [1968] Director/Owner and Chairman of The Board; Pauline Marjorie Zibe [1940] Director

The Multiple Sclerosis Research and Relief Fund
Incorporated: 11 March 1964 *Employees:* 12
Net Worth: £3,546,541 *Total Assets:* £3,578,417
Registered Office: Benmar House, Choppington Road, Stobhill, Morpeth, Northumberland, NE61 2HX
Activities: Other social work activities without accommodation n.e.c.
Officers: Debra Woodward, Secretary; Paul Dennis Atkinson [1954] Director/Chairman; Kevin Carr [1958] Director/Trustee; Peter Frederick Dawson [1957] Director/Trustee; Barbara Ellis [1950] Director/Trustee; Margaret Sharp [1946] Director/Trustee; Margery Tate [1945] Director/Trustee

Murdock Property Investments Limited
Incorporated: 19 January 2007
Net Worth: £315,869 *Total Assets:* £1,695,114
Registered Office: Portland House, Belmont Business Park, Durham, DH1 1TW
Activities: Other letting and operating of own or leased real estate
Major Shareholder: Patrick Kevin Murdock
Officers: Patrick Kevin Murdock, Secretary; Arthur Brendan Murdock [1939] Director/Retired Builders Merchant [Irish]; Patrick Kevin Murdock [1971] Director/Chartered Surveyor; Phyllis Bridget Murdock [1941] Director/Retired Nurse [Irish]

Ed.Murray & Sons Limited
Incorporated: 26 May 1971
Registered Office: Southgate Service Station, Brenda Road, Hartlepool, Cleveland, TS25 2BW
Activities: Freight transport by road
Major Shareholder: Peter Mark Murray
Officers: Peter Mark Murray, Secretary/Director; Peter Mark Murray [1967] Director

Murray and Lamb Accountants Limited
Incorporated: 6 October 2005 *Employees:* 44
Net Worth: £1,472,914 *Total Assets:* £2,037,250
Registered Office: 25-27 Medomsley Road, Consett, Co Durham, DH8 5HE
Activities: Accounting and auditing activities
Shareholder: Paul Stuart Smith
Officers: Stephen Lamb, Secretary/Accountant; David Bayles [1967] Director; Stephen Lamb [1958] Director/Accountant; George Stephen Murray [1963] Director/Accountant; Paul Stuart Smith [1977] Director

Murton Farm Estate Limited
Incorporated: 13 November 1944
Net Worth: £2,821,175 *Total Assets:* £2,863,567
Registered Office: 34 Howard Street, North Shields, Tyne & Wear, NE30 1AR
Activities: Mixed farming
Officers: Noel Francis Chintillier, Secretary; Christopher Daniel Burton [1981] Director/Certified Chartered Accountant; Garnet Duff Burton [1948] Director/Builder; Julie Claire Burton [1979] Director/Optometrist; Peter Timothy Burton [1985] Director/Certified Chartered Accountant

Musterfield Poultry Growers Ltd
Incorporated: 23 February 2010 *Employees:* 5
Net Worth: £313,494 *Total Assets:* £3,454,456
Registered Office: Oak House, Market Place, Bedale, N Yorks, DL8 1AU
Activities: Raising of poultry
Shareholders: Diane Royal Mason; Philip Leslie Mason
Officers: Diane Royal Mason [1968] Director/Poultry Farmer; Philip Leslie Mason [1964] Director/Poultry Farmer

MV Print Limited
Incorporated: 11 September 2012
Registered Office: Unit 2c Nelson Street Industrial Estate, South Bank, Middlesbrough, Cleveland, TS6 6BJ
Activities: Printing n.e.c.
Officers: Stevan Roland Allgood [1963] Director; Gary Clapton [1969] Director; Andrew Ian Gornall [1963] Director; Sean Hutchinson Maynard [1963] Director

MW Crane Hire Ltd
Incorporated: 6 April 2000
Net Worth: £701,951 *Total Assets:* £1,534,946
Registered Office: 7 Manor Grove, Great Broughton, Stokesley, Cleveland, TS9 7EJ
Activities: Construction of other civil engineering projects n.e.c.
Major Shareholder: Michael Welch
Officers: Michael Welch [1954] Managing Director

MWJ Developments Limited
Incorporated: 5 August 2015
Registered Office: Quay Corner Training Centre, Church Bank, Jarrow, Tyne & Wear, NE32 3HH
Activities: Other letting and operating of own or leased real estate
Major Shareholder: Malcolm Atkinson
Officers: Joan Atkinson [1952] Director; Malcolm Atkinson [1951] Director; William Ramsey [1945] Director

My Firms App Limited
Incorporated: 29 July 2014 *Employees:* 26
Net Worth Deficit: £151,815 *Total Assets:* £2,415,929
Registered Office: 1st Floor, 37-39 Victoria Road, Darlington, Co Durham, DL1 5SB
Activities: Other information technology service activities
Parent: My Firms App Holdings Limited
Officers: Gavin Disney-May [1962] Director; Joel Oliver [1980] Managing Director

My Sister's Place
Incorporated: 23 April 2010 *Employees:* 20
Net Worth: £772,038 *Total Assets:* £787,548
Registered Office: 123 Borough Road, Middlesbrough, Cleveland, TS1 3AN
Activities: Other information service activities n.e.c.
Officers: Rebecca Rogerson, Secretary; Jennifer Hill [1984] Director/Accountant; Helen Mather [1983] Director/Board Member; Julie McNaughton [1971] Director/Housing Manager; Rebecca Samuels [1980] Director/Solicitor; Susan Smith [1966] Director/Board Member; Emma Louise Thornhill [1991] Director/Graduate Tutor

Mynicehouse Limited
Incorporated: 22 April 2013
Net Worth Deficit: £183,807 *Total Assets:* £1,877,897
Registered Office: 1 Crossway, Jesmond, Newcastle upon Tyne, NE2 3QH
Activities: Construction of domestic buildings
Major Shareholder: Joan Cunningham
Officers: Joan Cunningham [1951] Director/Property Developer

N A C Trading Holdings Limited
Incorporated: 2 June 2014 *Employees:* 1,055
Net Worth: £2,666,521 *Total Assets:* £7,012,896
Registered Office: Unit 1 Spire Road, Washington, Tyne & Wear, NE37 3ES
Activities: Activities of head offices
Major Shareholder: Paul Robson
Officers: Lisa Jane Snaith, Secretary; Paul Robson [1960] Director; Wendy Ann Robson [1964] Director

N A College Limited
Incorporated: 4 May 2005 *Employees:* 292
Net Worth: £413,370 *Total Assets:* £2,085,189
Registered Office: Unit 1 Spire Road, Washington, Tyne & Wear, NE37 3ES
Activities: Other education n.e.c.
Shareholders: N A C Trading Holdings Limited; Paul Robson
Officers: Lisa Jane Snaith, Secretary; Paul Robson [1960] Director

N A College Trust
Incorporated: 26 September 2005 *Employees:* 27
Net Worth: £172,314 *Total Assets:* £2,905,173
Registered Office: Unit 1 Spire Road, Washington, Tyne & Wear, NE37 3ES
Activities: Management consultancy activities other than financial management
Officers: Lisa Jane Snaith, Secretary; Paul Robson [1960] Director

N A Consultants Ltd
Incorporated: 21 November 2002 *Employees:* 15
Net Worth: £226,198 *Total Assets:* £2,078,570
Registered Office: Unit 1 Spire Road, Washington, Tyne & Wear, NE37 3ES
Activities: Management consultancy activities other than financial management
Parent: N A C Trading Holdings Limited
Officers: Lisa Jane Snaith, Secretary; Paul Robson [1960] Managing Director

N H Property Ltd
Incorporated: 18 July 2002
Net Worth: £469,792 *Total Assets:* £1,133,105
Registered Office: Tower Buildings, 9 Oldgate, Morpeth, Northumberland, NE61 1PY
Activities: Other letting and operating of own or leased real estate
Shareholders: Hayley Dunn; Natalie Weston
Officers: Paul Andrew Brown, Secretary; Hayley Dunn [1985] Director; Natalie Weston [1982] Director

N&T Civils Ltd
Incorporated: 28 October 2015 *Employees:* 3
Net Worth: £569,900 *Total Assets:* £863,074
Registered Office: 53 Park Lane, Guisborough, Cleveland, TS14 6NS
Activities: Other construction installation
Major Shareholder: Nicholas Edwin Leat
Officers: Nicholas Edwin Leat [1976] Director

N-Sign Limited
Incorporated: 6 November 2000 *Employees:* 24
Net Worth: £377,514 *Total Assets:* £879,826
Registered Office: Sign House, Baltic Road, Stockton on Tees, Cleveland, TS18 2EZ
Activities: Other manufacturing n.e.c.
Major Shareholder: Aun David Pearson
Officers: Martin Jeffery Harvey, Secretary; Alun David Pearson [1965] Director

N.E. Truck Spares Limited
Incorporated: 25 November 1974 *Employees:* 52
Net Worth: £845,773 *Total Assets:* £3,524,386
Registered Office: Parkgate, Hetton Lyons Industrial Estate, Houghton-le-Spring, Co Durham, DH5 0RH
Activities: Retail trade of motor vehicle parts and accessories
Shareholders: Peter Reed; Ann Reed
Officers: Ann Reed, Secretary; Ann Reed [1947] Director/Secretary; James John Reed [1980] Commercial Director; Mark Reed [1977] Finance Director; Peter Reed [1947] Director

N.OOR Jewellery Limited
Incorporated: 21 April 2010 *Employees:* 5
Net Worth: £488,935 *Total Assets:* £1,275,443
Registered Office: Finchale House, Belmont Business Park, Durham, DH1 1TW
Activities: Agents involved in the sale of a variety of goods
Major Shareholder: Noor Fares
Officers: Noor Fares [1985] Director/Jewellery Designer [French]

N.P. Alliance Limited
Incorporated: 4 December 2001 *Employees:* 151
Net Worth: £2,519,381 *Total Assets:* £3,974,479
Registered Office: The Black Path, Portrack Lane, Stockton on Tees, Cleveland, TS18 2HE
Activities: Wholesale trade of motor vehicle parts and accessories
Officers: Imtiaz Hassan Umarji, Secretary/Director [Seychellois]; John Alistair Martin [1948] Director; Steve Edward Smith [1954] Managing Director; Imtiaz Hassan Umarji [1961] Director [Seychellois]

N.T. Steel Services Ltd
Incorporated: 7 December 2005
Net Worth: £390,396 *Total Assets:* £750,542
Registered Office: Unit 3/3a Metnor Business Park, Hadrian Road, Wallsend, Tyne & Wear, NE28 6HH
Activities: Wholesale of metals and metal ores
Shareholders: Nigel Thomas Swanson; Thomas Swanson
Officers: Nigel Thomas Swanson, Secretary; Nigel Thomas Swanson [1973] Director/Steel Merchant; Thomas Swanson [1947] Director/Steel Merchant

N.T.E. Holdings Limited
Incorporated: 25 January 2017
Net Worth: £448,584 *Total Assets:* £2,395,019
Registered Office: 7 Camberwell Way, Moorside Park, Doxford, Sunderland, Tyne & Wear, SR3 3XN
Activities: Other telecommunications activities
Shareholders: Pauline Herring; Phillip Herring; John Amos Patterson
Officers: Pauline Herring [1971] Director; Phillip Herring [1973] Director; John Amos Patterson [1968] Director

N.T.E. Limited
Incorporated: 17 October 1997 *Employees:* 25
Net Worth: £1,611,784 *Total Assets:* £2,236,112
Registered Office: 7 Camberwell Way, Doxford International Business Park, Sunderland, Tyne & Wear, SR3 3XN
Activities: Other telecommunications activities
Parent: NTE Holdings Limted
Officers: Pauline Herring, Secretary; Pauline Herring [1971] Business Development Director; Phillip Herring [1973] Sales and Service Director; John Amos Patterson [1968] Channel Development Director

N21 Limited
Incorporated: 12 December 2002 *Employees:* 45
Net Worth: £817,104 *Total Assets:* £1,130,522
Registered Office: Studios 2-3, The Kiln, Hoults Estate, Walker Road, Newcastle upon Tyne, NE6 2HL
Activities: Advertising agencies
Shareholders: Neil Anthony Robbins; Julie Ann Robbins
Officers: Neil Anthony Robbins, Secretary/Managing Director; Julie Ann Robbins [1975] Director/Administrator; Neil Anthony Robbins [1977] Managing Director

NAC Agency Limited
Incorporated: 27 October 2009 *Employees:* 379
Net Worth: £300,376 *Total Assets:* £1,293,957
Registered Office: Unit 1 Spire Road, Washington, Tyne & Wear, NE37 3ES
Activities: Other business support service activities n.e.c.
Parent: NAC Trading Limited
Officers: Lisa Jane Snaith, Secretary; Paul Robson [1960] Director

NAC Property Management Limited
Incorporated: 12 June 2014 *Employees:* 2
Net Worth: £264,216 *Total Assets:* £2,612,509
Registered Office: Unit 1 Spire Road, Washington, Tyne & Wear, NE37 3ES
Activities: Other letting and operating of own or leased real estate
Parent: Forty WP Management Services
Officers: Lisa Jane Snaith, Secretary; Paul Robson [1960] Director; Wendy Ann Robson [1964] Director; Lisa Jane Snaith [1972] Director

NAC Trading Limited
Incorporated: 5 March 2004 *Employees:* 1,017
Net Worth: £3,425,524 *Total Assets:* £9,015,271
Registered Office: Unit 1 Spire Road, Washington, Tyne & Wear, NE37 3ES
Activities: Activities of head offices
Parent: NAC Outsourcing Holdings
Officers: Lisa Jane Snaith, Secretary; Wendy Phillips [1964] Director; Paul Robson [1960] Director

NAC Training Limited
Incorporated: 31 March 2010 *Employees:* 36
Net Worth: £2,412,268 *Total Assets:* £4,633,717
Registered Office: Unit 1 Spire Road, Washington, Tyne & Wear, NE37 3ES
Activities: Other education n.e.c.
Shareholders: N A C Trading Holdings Limited; Paul Robson
Officers: Lisa Jane Snaith, Secretary; Paul Robson [1960] Director

Nailsworth (No.2) Limited
Incorporated: 7 July 2000
Net Worth: £1,092,466 *Total Assets:* £4,783,693
Registered Office: 17 Windsor Terrace, Jesmond, Newcastle upon Tyne, NE2 4HE
Activities: Other letting and operating of own or leased real estate
Major Shareholder: Sayeed Ahmed
Officers: Nasir Rashid, Secretary; Sayeed Ahmed [1956] Director/Property Developer; Nasir Rashid [1964] Director/Property Developer

Omar Najeeb Ltd
Incorporated: 15 December 2008 *Employees:* 1
Net Worth Deficit: £3,686 *Total Assets:* £916,757
Registered Office: 7 Grenville Court, Ponteland, Northumberland, NE20 9HT
Activities: Other service activities n.e.c.
Officers: Omar Najeeb [1983] Director

NAL Asset Management Limited
Incorporated: 13 May 2009 *Employees:* 24
Net Worth: £262,421 *Total Assets:* £2,836,354
Registered Office: Naljets Nal Asset Management, Southside, Newcastle International Airport, Woolsington, Newcastle upon Tyne, NE13 8DT
Activities: Non-scheduled passenger air transport
Major Shareholder: Craig Marin McLeod
Officers: Donna Bulman [1969] Director/Manager; Craig Marin McLeod [1971] Director/Pilot; Elizabeth Victoria McLeod [1974] Director/Manager

Nala Engineers Limited
Incorporated: 8 June 1992 *Employees:* 28
Net Worth: £664,065 *Total Assets:* £1,306,121
Registered Office: Nala Engineers Ltd, Tempest Road, Seaham, Co Durham, SR7 7AJ
Activities: Electrical installation
Shareholders: John David Pollard; Patricia Pollard
Officers: Patricia Pollard, Secretary/Personnel Manager; Nicola Duke [1974] Finance Director; David John Pollard [1938] Director/Electrical Contractor; Patricia Pollard [1945] Director/Personnel Manager

Nano-Purification Solutions Ltd
Incorporated: 24 May 2007 *Employees:* 19
Net Worth: £1,351,906 *Total Assets:* £1,929,652
Registered Office: Dukesway, Team Valley Trading Estate, Gateshead, Tyne & Wear, NE11 0PZ
Activities: Manufacture of other special-purpose machinery n.e.c.
Parent: Purification Solutions UK Limited
Officers: Michael Leslie Eccles [1974] Director/Engineer; David Anthony Gilligan [1968] Director/Operations Manager; David Arthur Peters [1962] Managing Director [American]

NAS Group Durham Limited
Incorporated: 24 April 2003 *Employees:* 11
Net Worth: £483,772 *Total Assets:* £1,044,374
Registered Office: Unit A310 Howden Road, Aycliffe Business Park, Newton Aycliffe, Co Durham, DL5 6EU
Activities: Other activities of employment placement agencies
Shareholders: Kevin Pugh; Stuart William Colin Haden
Officers: Stuart William Colin Haden, Secretary; Stuart William Colin Haden [1970] Marketing Director; Kevin Pugh [1969] Director

National Energy Action
Incorporated: 9 October 1984
Net Worth: £4,402,763 *Total Assets:* £25,610,316
Registered Office: 6th Floor, West One, Forth Banks, Newcastle upon Tyne, NE1 3PA
Activities: Other social work activities without accommodation n.e.c.
Officers: Tracey Ann Archer, Secretary; Syed Viqar Ahmed [1967] Director/Policy Adviser; Andrew Mavor Brown [1956] Director/Retired; Alison Jane Cole [1962] Deputy Communications Director; Jacqueline Gardner [1972] HR Director; Philip John Hudson [1960] Director/Lawyer; Norman William Kerr [1955] Director; James Ernest Kirby [1952] Director/Accountant; Derek Arthur Lickorish [1951] Director/Consultant; Helen Christine McLeod [1956] Director/Charitable Fund Executive; Noel Francis Rice [1960] Director/Retired; Tessa Mary Sayers [1961] Director; Professor Christopher Patrick Underwood [1956] Director/Professor

National Numbers Limited
Incorporated: 29 September 1997 *Employees:* 15
Net Worth: £5,211,138 *Total Assets:* £5,623,024
Registered Office: P O Box 20, The Grange, Billingham, Cleveland, TS23 1XY
Activities: Other retail sale not in stores, stalls or markets
Parent: Jepson and Co Limited
Officers: Peter Geoffrey Jepson [1964] Managing Director

Natural Stockcare Limited
Incorporated: 3 October 1984 *Employees:* 5
Net Worth: £739,945 *Total Assets:* £1,020,395
Registered Office: Unit 1b Willows Business Centre, Newburn Bridge Road, Blaydon on Tyne, Tyne & Wear, NE21 4SQ
Activities: Manufacture of prepared feeds for farm animals
Major Shareholder: Jack Ryan
Officers: Patricia Smith, Secretary; Jack Ryan [1953] Director/Sales Executive [Irish]; Patricia Smith [1948] Director/Office Manager

Naturalight Properties Ltd.
Incorporated: 3 March 2011 *Employees:* 1
Net Worth: £313,823 *Total Assets:* £1,021,304
Registered Office: Accessory House, Barrington Industrial Estate, Gooch Avenue, Bedlington, Northumberland, NE22 7DQ
Activities: Management of real estate on a fee or contract basis
Officers: David Derrick [1953] Director

Naturalight Systems Limited
Incorporated: 24 January 2001 *Employees:* 46
Net Worth: £3,172,678 *Total Assets:* £3,631,799
Registered Office: Accessory House, Barrington Industrial Estate, Bedlington, Northumberland, NE22 7DQ
Activities: Manufacture of other plastic products
Parent: Naturalight Holdings Ltd
Officers: Sandra Derrick, Secretary; John Carruthers [1970] Director; David Derrick [1953] Director/Manager; Steven Derrick [1980] Director; Lindsey Patterson [1972] Director

Natzone Limited
Incorporated: 6 June 2012
Net Worth: £8,744,775 *Total Assets:* £10,605,212
Registered Office: Carter House, Pelaw Leazes Lane, Durham, DH1 1TB
Activities: Activities of other holding companies n.e.c.
Major Shareholder: Trevor Cartner
Officers: Trevor Cartner [1960] Director

NBT Integrated Services Limited
Incorporated: 6 April 1951 *Employees:* 29
Net Worth: £348,843 *Total Assets:* £4,304,782
Registered Office: Locomotion Way, Camperdown Industrial Estate, Killingworth, Newcastle upon Tyne, NE12 5US
Activities: Non-specialised wholesale trade
Parent: NBT (Group) Limited
Officers: Toby Mark Bridges, Secretary; Michael Hugh Bridges [1944] Director; Toby Mark Bridges [1971] Managing Director

NCFE
Incorporated: 10 February 1994 *Employees:* 303
Net Worth: £28,258,000 *Total Assets:* £32,113,000
Registered Office: Q6 Quorum Business Park, Benton Lane, Newcastle upon Tyne, NE12 8BT
Activities: Educational support services
Officers: Esme Winch, Secretary; Barbara Heather Ashton [1963] Executive Director of Resources; Michael Gregory Austin [1971] HR Director; Rosalino Anna Cuschieri [1967] Director; Nigel Gary Hudson [1963] Director; Deborah Mary Jenkins [1959] Director; Christopher Mark Victor Peel [1981] Managing Director; David Wilson [1969] Director

NDT Electronic Services Ltd
Incorporated: 10 December 2007 *Employees:* 7
Net Worth: £1,444,985 *Total Assets:* £1,663,689
Registered Office: Unit 30 Royal Industrial Estate, Jarrow, Tyne & Wear, NE32 3HR
Activities: Technical testing and analysis
Major Shareholder: Christopher Ian Armson
Officers: Darren Addison, Secretary; Christopher Ian Armson [1959] Director/Engineer; Paul Anthony Rutherford [1960] Director/Technical

NDT Global Services Limited
Incorporated: 4 December 2006
Net Worth: £851,564 *Total Assets:* £1,246,003
Registered Office: 13 Patience Avenue, Seaton Burn, Newcastle upon Tyne, NE13 6HF
Activities: Other research and experimental development on natural sciences and engineering
Shareholders: Brian James Wilde; Michael Walker; Simon Thomas Walker
Officers: Karen Elizabeth Wilde, Secretary; Michael Walker [1958] Director; Simon Thomas Walker [1967] Director; Brian James Wilde [1960] Director

NE Property Management Limited
Incorporated: 18 November 2014
Net Worth Deficit: £20,689 *Total Assets:* £950,000
Registered Office: New Century House, Crowther Road, Washington, Tyne & Wear, NE38 0AQ
Activities: Combined facilities support activities
Major Shareholder: Martin Coleman
Officers: Martin Coleman, Secretary; Jillian Coleman [1971] Operations Director; Martin Coleman [1968] Director

NEA2F Subco Limited
Incorporated: 27 February 2008
Total Assets: £2,233,881
Registered Office: 3rd Floor, Baltimore House, Abbotts Hill, Gateshead, Tyne & Wear, NE8 3DF
Activities: Other business support service activities n.e.c.
Officers: Andrew James Arkless, Secretary; Hilary Patricia Florek [1960] Director/PR Consultant; Geoffrey Mark Hodgson [1961] Director; Stephen John Lightley [1957] Director/Chief Operating Officer; Kathryn Lucy Hay Winskell [1963] Director/Pro Vice Chancellor

Neasham Estate Limited
Incorporated: 1 April 1936
Net Worth: £868,281 *Total Assets:* £1,181,636
Registered Office: Strutt & Parker, Thornfield Business Park, Standard Way, Northallerton, N Yorks, DL6 2XQ
Activities: Other letting and operating of own or leased real estate
Major Shareholder: Sir Charles Mark Garmondsway Wrightson
Officers: Lady Stella Virginia Wrightson, Secretary; Barnaby Thomas Garmondsway Wrightson [1979] Director/Landscaping; Sir Charles Mark Garmondsway Wrightson [1951] Director/Barrister & Merchant Banker

Neat Active Limited
Incorporated: 13 October 2016 *Employees:* 19
Net Worth: £4,310,384 *Total Assets:* £4,727,160
Registered Office: Benfield School, Benfield Road, Newcastle upon Tyne, NE6 4NU
Activities: Educational support services
Parent: Newcastle East Mixed Multi Academy Trust
Officers: Lisa Bilton, Secretary; Roger Townley Alston [1944] Director/Retired; Charles Turvill [1962] Director of Finance

NECA
Incorporated: 27 June 1984 *Employees:* 113
Net Worth: £6,190,342 *Total Assets:* £6,873,392
Registered Office: Derwent Point, Clasper Way, Swalwell, Gateshead, Tyne & Wear, NE16 3BE
Activities: Other social work activities without accommodation n.e.c.
Officers: Ronald Ian Watson, Secretary; David Gregory [1945] Managing Director; Dr Peter Brian Moore [1950] Director/Psychiatrist; Norman Richardson [1951] Director/Self Employed; Barry Neil Speker [1947] Director/Solicitor; Ronald Ian Watson [1946] Director/Accountant

NEG Holdings Limited
Incorporated: 15 February 2013
Net Worth: £1,140,000 *Total Assets:* £1,140,000
Registered Office: Viking Works, Hamsterley Colliery, Newcastle upon Tyne, NE17 7SY
Activities: Activities of head offices
Shareholder: Gary Stephen Hall
Officers: Gary Alistair Foster, Secretary; Gary Alistair Foster [1971] Director/Chartered Accountant; Gary Stephen Hall [1962] Managing Director; Bryan Thompson [1970] Director; Clifford Graham Francis Thompson [1966] Director; Derrick Thompson [1943] Director

NEL Technologies Limited
Incorporated: 6 April 1984 *Employees:* 19
Net Worth: £1,575,127 *Total Assets:* £2,003,054
Registered Office: Unit 7b Westway Industrial Park, Throckley, Newcastle upon Tyne, NE15 9HW
Activities: Manufacture of other electrical equipment
Major Shareholder: Dr Patrick Ferguson
Officers: Margaret Elizabeth Ferguson, Secretary/Housewife; Dr Patrick Ferguson [1951] Director

Nelson Developments (Durham) Limited
Incorporated: 29 October 2003 *Employees:* 2
Net Worth Deficit: £3,050 *Total Assets:* £1,446,459
Registered Office: The Bracken, Cornsay Colliery, Co Durham, DH7 9DA
Activities: Development of building projects
Shareholders: Michael Nelson; Susan Marie Nelson
Officers: Susan Marie Nelson, Secretary/Executive; Michael Nelson [1954] Director/Executive; Susan Marie Nelson [1958] Director/Executive

Nelson Yard Limited
Incorporated: 3 June 2013
Net Worth: £7,450 *Total Assets:* £1,321,767
Registered Office: 23 Woolsington Park South, Woolsington, Newcastle upon Tyne, NE13 8BJ
Activities: Other letting and operating of own or leased real estate
Shareholders: Dr Rina Miah Thapar; Paul Thapar
Officers: Paul Thapar [1977] Director/Dentist

Nemro Properties Limited
Incorporated: 13 December 2006
Net Worth: £262,743 *Total Assets:* £1,075,920
Registered Office: 20 Lansdowne Terrace, Gosforth, Newcastle upon Tyne, NE3 1HP
Activities: Other letting and operating of own or leased real estate
Officers: Manisha Dhaun, Secretary; Manisha Dhaun [1957] Director/Tax Advisor

NEOS Protect Limited
Incorporated: 15 June 2011
Net Worth: £295,298 *Total Assets:* £904,516
Registered Office: 4 High Street, Stanley, Co Durham, DH9 0DQ
Activities: Manufacture of doors and windows of metal
Officers: Colin Burns [1957] Director/Surveying & Installation Manager; Paul Ralph Sampson [1975] Director/Office & Operations Manager; Steven Thomas [1963] Director/Estimating & Production Manager; Kevin Francis Walker [1953] Sales & Managing Director

NEPACS
Incorporated: 15 May 2001 *Employees:* 81
Net Worth: £950,471 *Total Assets:* £1,120,119
Registered Office: 20 Old Elvet, Durham, DH1 3HW
Activities: Other service activities n.e.c.
Officers: Margaret Smith, Secretary; David Abrahams [1954] Director/Political Consultant; James Black [1944] Director/Retired; Richard John Courtney Booth [1959] Director/Retired; Reverend Katherine Margaret Brooke [1958] Director/Chaplain; James Russell Bruce [1957] Director/Retired; Linda Norfolk Lovell [1947] Director/Housewife; Donald MacKay [1929] Director/Retired; Sareth Ann Nainby Luxmoore [1959] Director/Housewife; Kathleen Ogilvie [1948] Director/Nurse; Sheila Seacroft [1946] Director/Freelance Editor; Margaret Smith [1955] Director/Retired; Margaret Stockdale [1941] Director/Retired; Mark Weeding [1955] Director/Manager

Ner Brek,Limited
Incorporated: 12 October 1948
Net Worth: £1,006,947 *Total Assets:* £1,320,805
Registered Office: 1A Coast Road, Marske-by-the-Sea, Redcar, Cleveland, TS11 7LZ
Activities: Other letting and operating of own or leased real estate
Shareholders: Eric James Boon; Janice Louie Boon
Officers: Janice Louie Boon, Secretary; Eric James Boon [1944] Managing Director; Janice Louie Boon [1945] Director/Company Secretary

NETA Training Trust
Incorporated: 17 August 1976 *Employees:* 64
Net Worth Deficit: £156,532 *Total Assets:* £1,627,973
Registered Office: Pennine Avenue, North Tees Industrial Estate, Portrack Lane, Stockton on Tees, Cleveland, TS18 2RJ
Activities: Other service activities n.e.c.
Officers: Fiona Jane Sharp, Secretary; Philip Michael Cook [1966] Director; Steven Cossins [1952] Director; Jeremy David Faulkner [1957] Director; John Christopher Hornby [1949] Director/Head of Construction; Russell Warren McCallion [1956] Director

Network Ticketing Limited
Incorporated: 24 November 1987 *Employees:* 3
Net Worth: £1,069 *Total Assets:* £1,366,205
Registered Office: Stagecoach Depot, Shields Road, Walkergate, Newcastle upon Tyne, NE6 2BZ
Activities: Other passenger land transport
Officers: Paul de Santis [1957] Director/Head of Commercial Development; John Dowey Fenwick [1969] Director/Accountant; Stephen King [1978] Director; Nicholas Robert Knox [1955] Commercial Director; Huw David Rhodri Lewis [1971] Director/Senior Manager, Local Government; Andrew Peter Tyldsley [1956] Director/Commercial Manager; Steven Walker [1971] Managing Director

Networked Housing Limited
Incorporated: 13 August 2013
Net Worth: £104,916 *Total Assets:* £3,688,058
Registered Office: Yoden House, 30 Yoden Way, Peterlee, Co Durham, SR8 1AL
Activities: Development of building projects
Major Shareholder: David Fallon
Officers: David Fallon [1965] Director

Neue Schule Limited
Incorporated: 12 January 2007 *Employees:* 11
Net Worth: £810,223 *Total Assets:* £984,246
Registered Office: 5 Victoria Avenue, Bishop Auckland, Co Durham, DL14 7JH
Activities: Other manufacturing n.e.c.
Shareholders: Neue Schule Group Limited; Heather Jayne Margaret Hyde-Saddington
Officers: Susan Jane Lesley Cross, Secretary; Dr Graham Hugh Cross [1957] Director/Technical Advisor; Heather Jayne Margaret Hyde Saddington [1952] Director/Sales and Marketing Manager; Sarfraz Alam Mian [1966] Director/Chief Executive Officer

Nevesco Limited
Incorporated: 7 July 1989 *Employees:* 3
Net Worth: £1,109,857 *Total Assets:* £1,373,867
Registered Office: Unit 3 Lee Close, Pattinson Industrial Estate North, District 15, Washington, Tyne & Wear, NE38 8QA
Activities: Non-specialised wholesale trade
Major Shareholder: Timothy Kendil Gordon
Officers: Ann Gordon, Secretary; Timothy Kendil Gordon [1964] Director

New Beginnings (North East) Limited
Incorporated: 1 August 1995 *Employees:* 310
Net Worth: £610,605 *Total Assets:* £1,332,312
Registered Office: 1 The Meadows, Newcastle upon Tyne, NE3 3NA
Activities: Social work activities without accommodation for the elderly and disabled
Officers: Sandra Dorothy Smith, Secretary; David William Gray [1948] Director; Trevor Clive Gray [1953] Director; David Wray [1954] Director

New Bridge Street Partnership LLP
Incorporated: 6 May 2004
Net Worth: £459,258 *Total Assets:* £864,888
Registered Office: Yours Business Networks, Suite B, 7-8 Delta Bank Road, Gateshead, Tyne & Wear, NE11 9DJ
Officers: Robert Skelly [1954] Member; Reuben Thomas Coppin Straker [1956] Member

New Century Services Limited
Incorporated: 6 July 1981 *Employees:* 9
Net Worth: £633,586 *Total Assets:* £1,010,820
Registered Office: Printcentre, Fulwell Road, Sunderland, Tyne & Wear, SR6 0HR
Activities: Printing n.e.c.
Major Shareholder: Peter Watchman
Officers: Peter Watchman, Secretary/Printer; Peter Watchman [1955] Director/Printer

New College Durham Academies Trust
Incorporated: 18 March 2010 *Employees:* 240
Net Worth: £45,135,000 *Total Assets:* £49,754,000
Registered Office: New College Durham, Framwellgate Moor Campus, Durham, DH1 5ES
Activities: General secondary education
Officers: Susan Mary Dring, Secretary; Andrew Broadbent [1971] Director of Finance & Managed Services; Dr John Paul Duggan [1957] Director [Irish]; Karl David Fairley [1965] HR Director; Councillor Ivan Jewell [1948] Director/County Councillor; Alyson Shields [1960] Director/Head of School; Ian Walton [1960] Director/Accountant; Christine Warren [1949] Director/Retired Headteacher; John Furness Widdowson [1954] Director/College Principal

New Equipment Holdings Limited
Incorporated: 23 February 1984 *Employees:* 75
Net Worth: £2,932,196 *Total Assets:* £7,459,879
Registered Office: Scrafton Lodge, Leyburn, N Yorks, DL8 4RR
Activities: Activities of other holding companies n.e.c.
Shareholders: Edward Neil Corner; Nigel Frederick Hartley Corner
Officers: Sandra Davies, Secretary; Edward Neil Corner [1937] Director; Kathleen Freda Corner [1941] Director; Nigel Frederick Hartley Corner [1965] Director

New Forest Developments (Westwood) Ltd
Incorporated: 21 July 2011
Registered Office: The Warehouse, Well Lane, Low Fell, Gateshead, Tyne & Wear, NE9 6JW
Activities: Development of building projects
Shareholders: David George Charlton; Stephen Bowler
Officers: Stephen Bowler [1969] Director; David George Charlton [1966] Director

New Leaf Investments Limited
Incorporated: 31 May 1978 *Employees:* 59
Net Worth: £3,154,853 *Total Assets:* £5,805,385
Registered Office: 55 George Street, Newcastle upon Tyne, NE4 7JN
Activities: Other letting and operating of own or leased real estate
Shareholders: Koon Kiu Cheng; Po Fat Cheng
Officers: Koon Kiu Cheng, Secretary; Koon Kiu Cheng [1947] Director; Po Fat Cheng [1939] Director

The New Pavilion Limited
Incorporated: 13 April 1994
Net Worth: £2,777,019 *Total Assets:* £2,836,074
Registered Office: The Pavilion, Iveston, Consett, Co Durham, DH8 7TE
Activities: Licenced restaurants
Shareholder: Winnie Hing Fun Yip
Officers: Kim Fai Yip, Secretary; Kim Fai Yip [1954] Director/Restaurateur; Koon Wan Yip [1965] Director/Restaurateur

New Pineapple Limited
Incorporated: 5 May 2015
Net Worth: £650,539 *Total Assets:* £881,813
Registered Office: 95 Grainger Street, Newcastle upon Tyne, NE1 5AE
Activities: Other letting and operating of own or leased real estate
Shareholders: Yan Kit Chong; Chun Kit Chong
Officers: Chun Kit Chong, Secretary; Yan Kit Chong [1979] Director/Baker

New R & R Ice Cream Limited
Incorporated: 18 October 2010
Net Worth: £178,119,472 *Total Assets:* £268,284,784
Registered Office: Richmond House, Leeming Bar, Northallerton, N Yorks, DL7 9UL
Activities: Activities of production holding companies
Parent: R&R PIK PLC
Officers: Marcello Mattia, Secretary; Phil Karl Griffin [1972] Director; Marcello Mattia [1965] Director [Italian]; Ibrahim Mahmood Ibrahim Najafi [1958] Director

New Seaham Academy
Incorporated: 19 September 2012 *Employees:* 31
Net Worth: £1,906,225 *Total Assets:* £2,184,607
Registered Office: New Seaham Academy, Byron Terrace, Seaham, Co Durham, SR7 0HX
Activities: Primary education
Officers: Laura Marie Willcock, Secretary; Melissa Baker [1986] Director/Assistant Headteacher; Angela Bell [1958] Director; Steven Bilton [1974] Director/Assistant Headteacher; Gavin Blagden [1971] Director/Coordinator; John Brady [1958] Director/Business Manager; Angela Elizabeth Carling [1968] Director; Katherine Cuthbertson [1973] Director/Businesswoman; Bernadette Dolan [1958] Director/Headteacher; Tina Lorraine Murphy [1960] Director/Headteacher; Eric Southwick [1963] Director/Accountant; Catherine Wheeldon [1979] Director/Administrator

New Sovereign Reversions Limited
Incorporated: 3 May 2011
Net Worth: £5,911,000 *Total Assets:* £7,382,000
Registered Office: Cross House, Westgate Road, Newcastle upon Tyne, NE1 4XX
Activities: Buying and selling of own real estate
Parent: Retirement Bridge Group Holdings Ltd
Officers: Paul Trevor Barber [1967] Director/Chief Executive; Antony Lewis Pierce [1976] Finance Director

New Tyne West Development Company LLP
Incorporated: 11 March 2011 *Employees:* 1
Net Worth: £9,617,843 *Total Assets:* £13,957,009
Registered Office: 3rd Floor, Citygate, St James Boulevard, Newcastle upon Tyne, NE1 4JE

Newarc (Aberdeen) Limited
Incorporated: 9 February 2012 *Employees:* 5
Net Worth: £76,652 *Total Assets:* £871,727
Registered Office: 6 Wincomblee Road, Walker Riverside, Newcastle upon Tyne, NE6 3PF
Activities: Wholesale of other machinery and equipment
Parent: Newarc Limited
Officers: Gilbert Jackson [1945] Director; Richard Thomas Jackson [1949] Director

Newarc (Newcastle) Limited
Incorporated: 25 January 2012
Net Worth: £61,092 *Total Assets:* £1,069,872
Registered Office: 6 Wincomblee Road, Walker Riverside, Newcastle upon Tyne, NE6 3PF
Activities: Manufacture of other general-purpose machinery n.e.c.
Parent: Newarc Limited
Officers: Gilbert Jackson [1945] Director; Richard Thomas Jackson [1949] Director

Newbiggin-By-The Sea Heritage Partnership Ltd
Incorporated: 22 May 2007
Net Worth: £2,718,357 *Total Assets:* £2,719,901
Registered Office: Newbiggin Maritime Centre, Church Point, Newbiggin-by-the-Sea, Northumberland, NE64 6DB
Activities: Activities of other membership organisations n.e.c.
Officers: Eleanor Grace Air [1954] Director/Retired; Sheila Harrison [1944] Director/Teacher (Retired); Barry Mead [1954] Director/Heritage Consultant; Peter Seddon [1943] Director/Retired

Newbridge Engineering Limited
Incorporated: 14 April 1997 *Employees:* 25
Net Worth: £526,741 *Total Assets:* £2,441,643
Registered Office: Tees Bay Business Park, Brenda Road, Hartlepool, Cleveland, TS25 2BU
Activities: Manufacture of metal structures and parts of structures
Major Shareholder: Terence Nugent
Officers: Joyce Welsh, Company Secretary; Pauline Ann Nugent [1944] Director; Terence Nugent [1941] Director; Joyce Welsh [1952] Director/Company Secretary

Newburn Riverside Recreation Association Limited
Incorporated: 14 November 1983 *Employees:* 34
Net Worth: £2,056,532 *Total Assets:* £2,388,835
Registered Office: Newburn Leisure Centre, Grange Road, Newburn, Newcastle upon Tyne, NE15 8ND
Activities: Operation of sports facilities
Officers: James Francis Lambert, Secretary; Malcolm Hogarth [1974] Director/Postal Worker; Christopher Jeffrey [1948] Director/Civil Engineer/Retired; James Francis Lambert [1951] Director/Quantity Surveyor; William Shaw [1947] Director/Quantity Surveyor; Malcolm Herbert Townson [1944] Director/Retired Engineer; Elizabeth Anne Whittaker [1940] Director/Retired; Councillor Linda Isabell Wright [1950] Director/Finance Administrator

Newby Foods Limited
Incorporated: 2 May 2003 *Employees:* 66
Net Worth: £6,301,680 *Total Assets:* £7,806,155
Registered Office: Marylands, Newby Wiske, Northallerton, N Yorks, DL7 9ER
Activities: Production of meat and poultry meat products
Shareholders: Phillip Owen Wallace; Colin Richard Dicker
Officers: Paul Damian Roe, Secretary; Graham John Bishop [1957] Managing Director; Colin Richard Dicker [1953] Director; Douglas Manning [1946] Operations Director; Phillip Owen Wallace [1949] Director

Newcastle Airport Local Authority Holding Company Limited
Incorporated: 1 December 2000 *Employees:* 430
Net Worth Deficit: £170,310,000 *Total Assets:* £278,606,016
Registered Office: Town Hall & Civic Offices, Westoe Road, South Shields, Tyne & Wear, NE33 2RL
Activities: Activities of head offices
Officers: Michael Geoffrey Harding, Secretary; Catherine Donovan [1959] Director/Councillor; Cllr Nicholas Iain Forbes [1973] Director/Local Councillor; Martin Gannon [1958] Director/Councillor; Councillor Simon Antony Henig [1969] Director/Councillor; Peter Alan Jackson [1958] Director/Farmer; Alan Kerr [1936] Director/Councillor; Iain Malcolm [1966] Director/Chief Executive; Councillor Carl Marshall [1980] Director/Rural Development Officer; Joyce McCarty [1953] Director/Retired; Councillor Graeme Ferguson Miller [1962] Director; Dale Michael Mordey [1986] Director/Councillor; Councillor Bruce Charles Pickard [1952] Director/Retired; Norma Redfearn [1938] Director/Mayor of North Tyneside Council

Newcastle Arts Centre Limited
Incorporated: 1 July 1981
Net Worth: £1,006,697 *Total Assets:* £1,765,453
Registered Office: 67 Westgate Road, Newcastle upon Tyne, NE1 1SG
Activities: Other retail sale of new goods in specialised stores (not commercial art galleries and opticians)
Major Shareholder: Michael John Tilley
Officers: Helen Elizabeth Burns, Secretary; Kay Tilley [1982] Director/Venue Manager; Michael John Tilley [1946] Director

Newcastle Buttress Limited
Incorporated: 21 December 2007
Net Worth: £30,263 *Total Assets:* £1,918,397
Registered Office: Lion House, Durham Road, Birtley, Chester-le-Street, Co Durham, DH3 1LS
Activities: Other letting and operating of own or leased real estate
Shareholders: Stevie Lee Pattinson; Lucy Del Pattinson
Officers: Stevie-Lee Pattinson, Secretary; Robert Pattinson [1934] Director; Stevie-Lee Pattinson [1969] Director

Newcastle Christian Life Centre
Incorporated: 24 June 2005
Registered Office: Westgate Hall, Corporation Street, Newcastle upon Tyne, NE4 5QD
Activities: Activities of religious organisations
Officers: Nathan Stephen Bruce [1981] Director/Volunteer Practice Advisor; Jonathan Stephen Cook [1967] Director/Senior Pastor; Alison Dicken [1970] Director/Housewife; Dr Bunmi Eniola [1978] Director/University Researcher [Nigerian]; Bobby Thomas Rawls [1957] Director/Minister of Religion [Australian]; Charles Anthony Sullivan [1986] Director/Engineer

Newcastle Climbing Centre Limited
Incorporated: 27 September 2006
Registered Office: Units 19 & 20 Stane Law Way, Tanfield Lea Industrial Estate, Stanley, Co Durham, DH9 9XB
Activities: Other sports activities
Shareholders: Paul Myers; Steve Jones
Officers: Paul Robert Myers, Secretary; Stephen Jones [1950] Director/Manager; Paul Robert Myers [1959] Director/Designer

Newcastle Council for Voluntary Service
Incorporated: 26 August 2008
Net Worth: £789,626 *Total Assets:* £1,157,038
Registered Office: Higham House, Higham Place, Newcastle upon Tyne, NE1 8AF
Activities: Activities of other membership organisations n.e.c.
Officers: Anne Bonner [1956] Director; Gemma Dyer [1982] Director/Head of Public Sector Partnerships; Simon Peter Elliott [1963] Director/Human Resources Manager; Martin Stuart Horrocks [1963] Director; Katherine Anne Israel [1954] Director; John Litherland [1952] Director/Retired; Joanne Patricia McKenna [1968] Finance Director; Steven Keith Nash [1956] Director/Project Manager; Jamie Michael Oliver Sadler [1979] Managing Director of Social Enterprise; Nitin Shukla [1961] Director/Policy Officer

Newcastle Diocesan Board of Finance Limited (The)
Incorporated: 1 March 1960 *Employees:* 39
Net Worth: £21,924,824 *Total Assets:* £25,394,428
Registered Office: Church House, St Johns Terrace, North Shields, Tyne & Wear, NE29 6HS
Activities: Activities of religious organisations
Officers: Shane Waddle, Secretary; Dr John Christopher Appleby [1956] Director/Head of University Department; Reverend Christine Lilian Brown [1954] Director/Non Stipendiary Priest; Benjamin Huw Carter [1977] Director/Clerk in Holy Orders; Elizabeth Anne Chadwick [1955] Director/Credit Champion; Christine Elizabeth Hardman [1951] Director/Church of England Bishop; Simon Robert Harper [1965] Director/Accountant; Susan May Hart [1949] Director/Retired; Elizabeth Anne Kerry [1950] Director/Vice Chair; Matthew William King [1955] Director/Charity Manager; Isabella McDonald-Booth [1972] Director/Retail Manager; Geoffrey Vincent Miller [1956] Director/Clerk in Holy Orders; Peter John Alan Robinson [1961] Director/Clerk in Holy Orders; Revd Paul Malcolm Scott [1957] Director/Minister of Religion; Reverend John Robert Sinclair [1958] Director/Clerk in Holy Orders; Mark Simon Austin Tanner [1970] Director/Anglican Bishop; Carol Wolstenholme [1943] Director/Consultant; The Reverend Rachel Astrid Wood [1971] Director/Vicar

Newcastle Diocesan Education Board Limited
Incorporated: 30 March 1950 *Employees:* 4
Net Worth: £2,366,163 *Total Assets:* £2,411,425
Registered Office: Church House, St Johns Terrace, North Shields, Tyne & Wear, NE29 6HS
Activities: Activities of religious organisations
Officers: Paul Thompson Rickeard, Secretary; Revd George Robert Curry [1951] Director/Clerk in Holy Orders; John Faulds Hamilton [1946] Director/Retired; Revd Dennis Francis Handley [1957] Director; Christine Elizabeth Hardman [1951] Director/Church of England Bishop; Susan May Hart [1949] Director/Retired Senior Manager; Reverend Ian James Hennebry [1963] Director/Associate Vicar; Reverend Susan Diane Joyner [1958] Director/Headteacher; Revd Mark Christian Victor Nash-Williams [1964] Director/Clerk in Holy Orders; Pauline Hilary Pearson [1954] Director/Professor of Nursing; Richard David Ratcliff [1948] Director/Retired; Richard Restall [1970] Director/Headteacher; Peter John Alan Robinson [1961] Director/Clerk in Holy Orders; Julie Elizabeth Robson [1957] Director/Headteacher; Reverend Elizabeth Jane Scott [1951] Director/Clerk in Holy Orders

Newcastle Diocesan Society
Incorporated: 13 May 1885
Net Worth: £6,968,295 *Total Assets:* £6,972,705
Registered Office: Church House, St Johns Terrace, North Shields, Tyne & Wear, NE29 6HS
Activities: Activities of religious organisations
Officers: Shane Waddle, Secretary; Dr John Christopher Appleby [1956] Director/Head of University Department; Gilfrid John Baker-Cresswell [1939] Director/Solicitor; Christine Elizabeth Hardman [1951] Director/Church of England Bishop; Simon Robert Harper [1965] Director/Chartered Accountant; Geoffrey Vincent Miller [1956] Director/Archdeacon of Northumberland; Peter John Alan Robinson [1961] Director/Archdeacon

Newcastle East Mixed Multi Academy Trust
Incorporated: 12 January 2017 *Employees:* 379
Net Worth: £19,700,000 *Total Assets:* £24,374,000
Registered Office: Heaton Centre, Trewhitt Road, Newcastle upon Tyne, NE6 5DY
Activities: Other education n.e.c.
Officers: Suzanne Lisa Hendey, Secretary; Roger Townley Alston [1944] Director/Retired; Deborah Bailey [1971] Director/Chief Executive; Steven Thomas Beharall [1976] Director/Operations Manager; Shaun Fooy [1971] Director; Nadia Iftkhar [1982] Director; Andrew Lister [1975] Director; Dr Anne McNall [1961] Director/Principal Lecturer University; Susan Margaret Ormerod [1959] Regional Director - Nigel Wright Consultancy; Michael John White [1965] Director

Newcastle Financial Advisers Limited
Incorporated: 13 August 2002 *Employees:* 42
Net Worth: £837,318 *Total Assets:* £1,186,444
Registered Office: Portland House, New Bridge Street West, Newcastle upon Tyne, NE1 8AL
Activities: Financial intermediation not elsewhere classified
Parent: Newcastle Building Society
Officers: Ian Good, Secretary; Stuart John Dodson [1975] Managing Director [Irish]; Stuart Miller [1970] Building Society Customer Director; Ian William Ward [1949] Director

Newcastle Flooring Company Limited
Incorporated: 7 October 1988 *Employees:* 21
Net Worth: £732,035 *Total Assets:* £987,854
Registered Office: 18 Heaton Road, Newcastle upon Tyne, NE6 1SD
Activities: Floor and wall covering
Parent: Newcastle Flooring Company Holdings Limited
Officers: Claire Marie Buzzeo [1974] Director; Joseph Benedict Buzzeo [1972] Director/Flooring Contractor; Gabrielle Annette Michelle Lynch [1979] Director/Teacher; Estelle Maria Naisbitt [1976] Director/Business Manager

Newcastle Gateshead Initiative Limited
Incorporated: 28 July 1988 *Employees:* 52
Net Worth: £276,000 *Total Assets:* £2,329,000
Registered Office: 9th Floor, Baltic Place East, South Shore Road, Gateshead, Tyne & Wear, NE8 3AE
Activities: Activities of business and employers membership organisations
Officers: Robin Michael Earl, Secretary; Nicole Atkin [1976] Director/Head of Business Development; Emily Cox [1978] Director of Public Affairs; Helen Louise Dalby [1979] Director/Editor, Chroniclelive; Judith Frances Doyle [1961] Director/Principal and CEO; Colin Thompson Hewitt [1957] Director/Solicitor; Louise Hunter [1975] Director of Corporate Affairs; Abi Blair Kelly [1969] Executive Director of Corporate Affairs; Tony Lewin [1964] Director/College Principal; Bill MacLeod [1963] Director/Chartered Accountant; John Philip Birkett Marshall [1966] Director/Retired; Graeme Mark Mason [1968] Director/Board Member; Sheena Ramsey [1962] Director/Chief Executive, Gateshead Council; Patricia Ann Ritchie [1959] Director/Chief Executive; Kevin Gerard Robertson [1972] Director/Solicitor; Michael Ian Spriggs [1956] Managing Director; Phillip Robert Steele [1962] Director/General Manager Shopping Centre; Giselle Elizabeth Stewart [1966] Director, UK Corporate Affairs; Mark Richard Thompson [1965] Director; Professor Andrew Brian Wathey [1958] Director/Vice Chancellor and Chief Executive

Newcastle Great Park (Estates) Limited
Incorporated: 26 October 2007 *Employees:* 2
Net Worth Deficit: £20,071 *Total Assets:* £993,953
Registered Office: 3rd Floor, Citygate, St James' Boulevard, Newcastle upon Tyne, NE1 4JE
Activities: Management of real estate on a fee or contract basis
Shareholders: Taylor Wimpey Developments Limited; Persimmon Homes (North East) Limited
Officers: John Driver [1971] Land & Planning Director; John Christopher Eynon [1970] Director

Newcastle International Airport Limited
Incorporated: 26 November 1986 *Employees:* 234
Net Worth: £210,963,008 *Total Assets:* £384,827,008
Registered Office: Woolsington, Newcastle upon Tyne, NE13 8BZ
Activities: Scheduled passenger air transport
Parent: NIAL Finance Limited
Officers: Mark Allan Hunt, Secretary; Nicholas Iain Forbes [1973] Director/Councillor; Councillor Simon Antony Henig [1969] Director/Councillor; Mark Allan Hunt [1977] Director/Chief Financial Officer; Nicholas Vaughan Jones [1973] Director/Chief Executive; Richard Andrew Knight [1967] Operations Director; Iain Malcolm [1966] Director/Chief Executive; David Rocyn Rees [1959] Director/Investment Manager; Hywel Gwyn Rees [1972] Director/Solicitor; John Julian Stent [1955] Director/Consultant

Newcastle Jewellers Ltd.
Incorporated: 3 November 1995 *Employees:* 21
Net Worth: £1,703,432 *Total Assets:* £1,890,203
Registered Office: 36 Pilgrim Street, Newcastle upon Tyne, NE1 6SE
Activities: Other retail sale of new goods in specialised stores (not commercial art galleries and opticians)
Major Shareholder: Robert Hall
Officers: Pamela Jackson, Secretary; Robert Hall [1954] Director/Jeweller

Newcastle Motorcycles Ltd
Incorporated: 14 September 1978 *Employees:* 25
Net Worth: £498,329 *Total Assets:* £1,737,388
Registered Office: 195-199 Scotswood Road, Newcastle upon Tyne, NE4 7DD
Activities: Sale, maintenance and repair of motorcycles and related parts and accessories
Major Shareholder: David Arthur Winfield
Officers: Craig Michael Smith [1974] Director/Sales Manager; David Arthur Winfield [1939] Director

Newcastle NE1 Limited
Incorporated: 11 February 2008 *Employees:* 12
Net Worth: £807,963 *Total Assets:* £1,423,691
Registered Office: Suite A8, Milburn House, Dean Street, Newcastle upon Tyne, NE1 1LE
Activities: Activities of other membership organisations n.e.c.
Officers: Councillor Generald William Bell [1961] Director/Firefighter; Gavin MacFarlane Black [1949] Director/Chartered Surveyor; Thomas Albert Kogba Caulker [1964] Director; Georgina Claire Collingwood Cameron [1968] Managing Director; Arwen Duddington [1973] Director; Joanna Feeley [1975] Managing Director; Steven Hugh Montague Kyffin [1959] Director/Pro Vice-Chancellor (Business & Enterprise); Tania Ruth Stirling Love [1967] Director/Architect; Carl Robert Milton [1976] Retail Director; Stephen Robert Wilford Patterson [1978] Communications Director; Michelle Frances Percy [1968] Director (Property); Julia Fiona Quinn [1988] Director; Darren Richardson [1965] Director; Adam James Serfontein [1964] Director/Chartered Surveyor; Adrian Osborne McCallum Waddell [1959] Operations Director

Newcastle Optical Engineering Limited
Incorporated: 17 July 2000 *Employees:* 10
Net Worth: £931,500 *Total Assets:* £1,115,719
Registered Office: 1b Buddle Industrial Estate, Benton Way, Wallsend, Tyne & Wear, NE28 6DL
Activities: Manufacture and processing of other glass, including technical glassware
Shareholders: Peter Gibson; Clifford Harries
Officers: Peter Gibson, Secretary; John James Bulman Gibson [1935] Director; Peter Gibson [1965] Director/Optical Engineer; Clifford Harries [1961] Director/Optical Engineer

Newcastle Park & Fly Limited
Incorporated: 17 December 1993 *Employees:* 38
Net Worth: £11,374,226 *Total Assets:* £21,542,496
Registered Office: Unit 1 Prestwick Industrial Estate, Ponteland, Northumberland, NE20 9DA
Activities: Other service activities incidental to land transportation, n.e.c.
Parent: NIAL Services Limited
Officers: Mark Allan Hunt, Secretary; Mark Allan Hunt [1977] Director/Chief Financial Officer; Nicholas Vaughan Jones [1973] Director/Chief Executive

Newcastle Portland House Limited
Incorporated: 14 September 1988
Net Worth: £3,108,745 *Total Assets:* £10,211,836
Registered Office: Portland House, New Bridge Street, Newcastle upon Tyne, NE1 8AL
Activities: Management of real estate on a fee or contract basis
Parent: Newcastle Building Society
Officers: Ian Good, Secretary; Sarah Warren [1974] Director/Head of Group Finance; Stephen Watchman [1961] Director

Newcastle Preparatory School Trust Limited (The)
Incorporated: 31 August 1960 *Employees:* 56
Net Worth: £1,836,548 *Total Assets:* £2,436,307
Registered Office: 6 Eslington Road, Jesmond, Newcastle upon Tyne, NE2 4RH
Activities: Primary education
Officers: Susan Gillian Easton, Secretary; Richard Saxton Appleby [1941] Director/Solicitor; Susan Blair [1971] Director; Patricia Kinmond Caine [1948] Director/Retired Teacher; Sharmishta Chatterjee-Banerjee [1972] Director/Head of International Business Relations, Newcastle University; Nigel Dale Herdman [1964] Director/Pharmacist; Rachel Hudson [1963] Director/Barrister; Richard Paul Waterhouse [1966] Director/Chief Executive

Newcastle Property Company Limited
Incorporated: 31 January 2006
Net Worth: £1,391,498 *Total Assets:* £2,618,925
Registered Office: 2 St Peters Road, Wallsend, Tyne & Wear, NE28 7LG
Activities: Other letting and operating of own or leased real estate
Major Shareholder: Timothy Peter Shearing
Officers: Tim Peter Shearing, Secretary; Stephen David Leightley [1963] Director; Tim Peter Shearing [1979] Director

Newcastle Rugby KP Limited
Incorporated: 30 July 2014 *Employees:* 1
Net Worth Deficit: £505,212 *Total Assets:* £6,197,000
Registered Office: Newcastle Falcons RFU, Kingston Park, Brunton Road, Newcastle upon Tyne, NE13 8AF
Activities: Operation of sports facilities
Major Shareholder: Ismail Walid Kurdi
Officers: Ismail Walid Kurdi [1968] Director

Newcastle Rugby Limited
Incorporated: 2 February 1999 *Employees:* 555
Net Worth Deficit: £18,561,824 *Total Assets:* £8,738,960
Registered Office: Newcastle Falcons RFU, Kingston Park, Brunton Road, Kenton Bank Foot, Newcastle upon Tyne, NE13 8AF
Activities: Activities of sport clubs
Major Shareholder: Ismail Kurdi
Officers: Ismail Walid Kurdi [1968] Director; David Ronald Tiplady Thompson [1945] Director

Newcastle School for Boys
Incorporated: 17 January 1975 *Employees:* 85
Net Worth: £5,021,804 *Total Assets:* £9,012,779
Registered Office: 30 West Avenue, Gosforth, Newcastle upon Tyne, NE3 4ES
Activities: Pre-primary education
Officers: Timothy James Care [1961] Director/Solicitor; Claire Jane King [1972] Commercial Director; Dr Neil Daniel Lloyd Jones [1956] Director/General Practitioner; Philip Douglas Parkinson [1948] Director; Jonathan Roger Sykes [1966] Director/Chartered Surveyor

Newcastle Science Central LLP
Incorporated: 7 April 2011
Net Worth: £1,653,000 *Total Assets:* £1,783,000
Registered Office: Barras Bridge, Newcastle upon Tyne, NE99 1RD

Newcastle Special Schools Trust
Incorporated: 10 September 2013
Net Worth: £17,514,012 *Total Assets:* £17,514,612
Registered Office: Thomas Bewick School, Linhope Road, Newcastle upon Tyne, NE5 2LW
Activities: Other education n.e.c.
Officers: June Marjorie Ball [1963] Director/Senior Teacher Head of Extended Service; Ashley Thomas Ferguson [1959] Director/Chartered Civil Engineer; Karen Anne Hamilton [1970] Director/Headteacher; Sheila Kingsland [1959] Director/School Improvement Service Senior Advisor (SEN); Audrey Lindley [1953] Director/Retired Headteacher; Michael Robert Quincey [1949] Director/Education Consultant; Christopher Rollings [1964] Director/Teacher; Diane Elizabeth Scott [1960] Director/Headteacher; Nicholas Timothy Sharing [1955] Director/Retired Headteacher

Newcastle Strategic Solutions Limited
Incorporated: 8 October 2002 *Employees:* 374
Net Worth: £3,750,936 *Total Assets:* £11,678,531
Registered Office: Portland House, New Bridge Street, Newcastle upon Tyne, NE1 8AL
Activities: Other business support service activities n.e.c.
Parent: Newcastle Building Society
Officers: Ian Good, Secretary; David John Buffham [1959] Director; Philip George Grand [1968] Managing Director; Karen Ingham [1965] Customer Service Director; Ronald Joseph McCormick [1949] Director; Philip James Moorhouse [1953] Director; Andrew William Ward [1971] Finance Director

Newcastle Systems Management Limited
Incorporated: 16 April 1997 *Employees:* 18
Net Worth: £3,129,671 *Total Assets:* £27,792,156
Registered Office: Portland House, New Bridge Street, Newcastle upon Tyne, NE1 8AL
Activities: Other information technology service activities
Parent: Newcastle Building Society
Officers: Ian Good, Secretary; David John Buffham [1959] Director; Stuart Leslie Lynn [1960] Director; Philip James Moorhouse [1953] Director; Andrew William Ward [1971] Finance Director; Ian William Ward [1949] Director; Stephen Watchman [1961] Managing Director

Newcastle Theatre Royal Trust Limited
Incorporated: 26 June 1975 *Employees:* 297
Net Worth: £1,655,853 *Total Assets:* £10,388,675
Registered Office: Theatre Royal, Grey Street, Newcastle upon Tyne, NE1 6BR
Activities: Support activities to performing arts
Officers: Marcia Lant, Secretary; Julie Blackie [1954] Finance Director; John Antony Carver [1961] Finance Director; Sheila Mary Chapman [1960] Director/Corporate Strategy Manager; Nicholas Adam Hodnett Fenwick [1960] Retail Director; John Paul Lee [1959] Director/Chief Executive; Joan Eileen Louw [1955] Director/Chartered Accountant; David William Midgley [1942] Director; Raymond Mills [1960] Director/Chartered Accountant; Howard William Tait [1949] Director/MD Advertising

Newcastle Tool & Gauge Limited
Incorporated: 14 December 1978
Net Worth: £2,520,810 *Total Assets:* £3,278,164
Registered Office: 1 Queens Court, Earlsway, Team Valley Trading Estate, Gateshead, Tyne & Wear, NE11 0BP
Activities: Machining
Parent: NTG Group Limited
Officers: Joan Graham, Secretary; Brian Bates [1947] Director; Joan Graham [1947] Director/Company Accountant; Charles Sampy [1965] Director/Works Manager

Newcastle United Football Company Limited
Incorporated: 11 March 1890 *Employees:* 279
Net Worth Deficit: £19,835,000 *Total Assets:* £234,212,000
Registered Office: St James Park, Newcastle upon Tyne, NE1 4ST
Activities: Operation of sports facilities
Parent: Newcastle United Limited
Officers: Lee Charnley [1977] Director and Company Secretary

Newcastle United Foundation
Incorporated: 30 October 2007 *Employees:* 49
Net Worth: £628,882 *Total Assets:* £1,158,176
Registered Office: St James' Park, Newcastle upon Tyne, NE1 4ST
Activities: Other business support service activities n.e.c.
Officers: Claire Alexander [1967] Director; Lee Charnley [1977] Director; Judith Frances Doyle [1961] Director/College Principal; Stephen Alan Harper [1975] Director; John Philip Birkett Marshall [1966] Director/Solicitor; Graeme Mark Mason [1968] Director; Michael Roger Thompson [1961] Director/Chartered Accountant; Brian Jonathan Thorpe [1963] Director

Newcastle United Limited
Incorporated: 10 August 1990 *Employees:* 279
Net Worth Deficit: £10,341,000 *Total Assets:* £239,424,000
Registered Office: St James' Park, Newcastle upon Tyne, NE1 4ST
Activities: Operation of sports facilities
Parent: St James Holdings Limited
Officers: Lee Charnley [1977] Director and Company Secretary

Newcastle University Students' Union
Incorporated: 3 August 2009 *Employees:* 66
Net Worth: £11,103,000 *Total Assets:* £11,749,000
Registered Office: The University of Newcastle upon Tyne, Kings Walk, Newcastle upon Tyne, NE1 8QB
Activities: First-degree level higher education
Officers: Simon Thomas Gerry, Secretary; Jonathan Alan Bennett [1973] Director/Journalist; Bridget Donaldson [1995] Director/Student Trustee; Maggie Grace Elstob [1996] Director/Sabbatical Officer & Trustee; Peter Alexander Gibson [1975] Director/Solicitor; Jack Oliver Green [1997] Director/Sabbatical Officer & Trustee; Jonathan David Hall [1996] Director/Sabbatical Officer & Trustee; Louise Hall [1997] Director/Sabbatical Officer & Trustee; Tom Lowe [1995] Director/Student Trustee; Raffaello Pasquale Marioni [1997] Director/Sabbatical Officer and Trustee; Sophie Lauren McDermott [1997] Director/Sabbatical Officer and Trustee; Benjamin John Sadler [1974] Director/Management Consultant; Christopher Mark Simpson [1988] Director/Accountant

The Newcastle upon Tyne Royal Grammar School
Incorporated: 3 January 2006 *Employees:* 9
Net Worth: £32,728,932 *Total Assets:* £44,153,792
Registered Office: Royal Grammar School, Eskdale Terrace, Newcastle upon Tyne, NE2 4DX
Activities: Other business support service activities n.e.c.
Officers: Dr Michael Jonathan Pitkethly, Secretary; Paul Andrew Campbell [1959] Director/Chief Executive The Amazing Group; Nalini Claris D'Cruz [1971] Director/Barrister; Julie Drummond [1971] Director/Chief Executive; Isaac Osagie Evbuomwan [1962] Director/Consultant Obstetrician & Gynaecologist; Robert Hugh Fell [1961] Director/Chartered Surveyor; Alan Crawford Fletcher [1969] Director/Solicitor; Aarti Gupta [1974] Director/Solicitor; Professor Sophie Hambleton [1967] Director/Academic Paediatrician; Professor Muzlifah Haniffa [1973] Director/Doctor; Tracey Elizabeth Hartley [1969] Director/Chartered Surveyor; Alexander Harold Lamb [1971] Director; Scarlett Milligan [1993] Director/Barrister; Anthony Peter Murphy [1957] Director of Health and Safety; Catherine Sarah Everett Murphy [1964] Director/Charity Adviser; Ian Richard Simpson [1956] Director/Retired Banker; Carole Stonehouse [1958] Director/Retired; Councillor Trevor Norman Thorne [1953] Director/Councillor; Susan Woodroofe [1966] Director/School Principal

Newcastle upon Tyne World Headquarters Limited
Incorporated: 10 August 2000
Net Worth: £1,151,417 *Total Assets:* £1,690,776
Registered Office: 1a Dinsdale Place, Newcastle upon Tyne, NE2 1BD
Activities: Public houses and bars
Major Shareholder: Thomas Albert Kogba Caulker
Officers: Lesley Anne Caulker, Secretary; Thomas Albert Kogba Caulker [1964] Director/DJ Club Promoter

Newcastle upon Tyne Y.M.C.A.
Incorporated: 17 June 1998 *Employees:* 26
Net Worth: £1,875,440 *Total Assets:* £2,402,072
Registered Office: 592-596 Welbeck Road, Walker, Newcastle upon Tyne, NE6 3AB
Activities: Activities of other membership organisations n.e.c.
Officers: Nigel Paul Hurst, Secretary; Jonathan Martin Burns [1981] Director/HR Manager; Sandria Charalambous [1987] Director/Events Manager [Cypriot]; Alan John English [1952] Director; Austin Luke Gibbons [1993] Director/Facilities Manager and Health and Safety Consultant; Neil David Jackson [1986] Director/Chartered Accountant; Stephen Nicholas Joseph Kerry [1952] Director/Solicitor; Thomas David Frederick Lillie [1983] Director/Solicitor; Thomas Alexander Robert Shaw Nisbet [1980] Director/Accountant; Emma Jane Peacock [1973] Director/Business Manager; Tiffany Scott [1986] Director/Marketing Manager; Jennie Whitell [1980] Director/Marketing Consultant

Newcastle-upon-Tyne & District Property & Investment Co Limited (The)
Incorporated: 20 September 1928 *Employees:* 2
Net Worth: £1,366,001 *Total Assets:* £1,459,360
Registered Office: Metropolitan House, Longrigg, Swalwell, Gateshead, Tyne & Wear, NE16 3AS
Activities: Other letting and operating of own or leased real estate
Officers: Melvyn Sidney Frederick Wallhead, Secretary; Christopher Melvyn Wallhead [1975] Finance Director; Melvyn Wallhead [1947] Director/Chartered Surveyor

Newchem Technologies Limited
Incorporated: 8 April 2002 *Employees:* 11
Net Worth: £1,358,003 *Total Assets:* £1,431,148
Registered Office: Holly Lodge, Whitesmocks, Durham, DH1 4LH
Activities: Other research and experimental development on natural sciences and engineering
Shareholders: Dr Robert Graham Tyson; Professor Bernard Thomas Golding
Officers: Dr Robert Tyson, Secretary; Professor Bernard Thomas Golding [1941] Director/Academic; Dr Robert Graham Tyson [1946] Director/Chemist

Newford Estates Ltd
Incorporated: 26 February 2003
Net Worth: £296,826 *Total Assets:* £764,782
Registered Office: Collingwood Buildings, 38 Collingwood Street, Newcastle upon Tyne, NE1 1JF
Activities: Buying and selling of own real estate
Officers: Eliezer Reich [1967] Director; Aharon Tzvi Sandler [1969] Director

Newgate Investments Limited
Incorporated: 5 November 1959 *Employees:* 2
Net Worth: £930,927 *Total Assets:* £960,575
Registered Office: 3 Saddler Street, Bishop Auckland, Co Durham, DL14 7BH
Activities: Other letting and operating of own or leased real estate
Major Shareholder: Jeremy Alexander Edkins
Officers: Jeremy Alexander Edkins, Secretary; Gillian Edkins [1960] Director/Pharmacist; Jeremy Alexander Edkins [1962] Director; Sheila Edkins [1935] Director

Newhall Caravan Park Limited
Incorporated: 17 February 2005
Net Worth: £1,034,896 *Total Assets:* £1,644,491
Registered Office: 91 Galgate, Barnard Castle, Co Durham, DL12 8ES
Activities: Recreational vehicle parks, trailer parks and camping grounds
Major Shareholder: Ian Malcolm Maughan
Officers: Edna Doreen Maughan, Secretary; Ian Malcolm Maughan [1968] Director/Farmer

Newham Hall Holdings Limited
Incorporated: 10 September 2013 *Employees:* 31
Net Worth: £7,000,863 *Total Assets:* £9,792,999
Registered Office: Newham Hall, Newby, Middlesbrough, Cleveland, TS8 9EA
Activities: Other letting and operating of own or leased real estate
Officers: Geoffrey Colin Flintoft [1942] Director; Jane Caroline Meeres [1954] Director; Richard Powys Meeres [1943] Director

Newland Jem Limited
Incorporated: 3 April 1992 *Employees:* 4
Net Worth: £1,171,675 *Total Assets:* £1,240,652
Registered Office: Hall Cottages, 2 The Cedars, Kirkby Fleetham, Northallerton, N Yorks, DL7 0SU
Activities: Other letting and operating of own or leased real estate
Shareholder: Sheila Hazel Ward
Officers: Sheila Hazel Ward, Secretary; Ross Wyndham Badger [1956] Director/Chartered Accountant; Jeffrey Lyn Jones [1944] Director/IT Consultant; Sheila Hazel Ward [1936] Director/Property Manager

Newman Scott Limited
Incorporated: 18 November 1987 *Employees:* 48
Net Worth: £518,870 *Total Assets:* £4,730,828
Registered Office: Unit BT 50-46 Sadler Forster Way, Teesside Industrial Estate, Thornaby, Stockton-on-Tees, Cleveland, TS17 9JY
Activities: Manufacture of office and shop furniture
Major Shareholder: Steven Andrew Bell
Officers: Peter Jeffrey Walker, Secretary; Steven Andrew Bell [1960] Director/Chairman; David Harry Graham [1951] Director; John Graham [1953] Director; Andrew Paxton [1957] Director; Alan James Riley [1970] Director/Contract Manager; Peter Jeffrey Walker [1969] Director/Accountant

Newquip Limited
Incorporated: 27 May 2005 *Employees:* 25
Net Worth: £3,818,648 *Total Assets:* £16,221,087
Registered Office: NQ House, Conygarth Way, Leeming Bar Business Park, Northallerton, N Yorks, DL7 9EE
Activities: Wholesale of agricultural machinery, equipment and supplies
Shareholders: Adam Dye; James Dye
Officers: Adam Dye [1980] Director

Newroc Ltd
Incorporated: 19 November 2003
Net Worth: £1,585,795 *Total Assets:* £3,559,408
Registered Office: 7 Mercury Road, Gallowfields Trading Estate, Richmond, N Yorks, DL10 4TQ
Activities: Activities of construction holding companies
Major Shareholder: Graeme Richard Newton
Officers: Joanne Katherine Newton, Secretary; Graeme Richard Newton [1968] Director

Newton Hall (Northumberland) Limited
Incorporated: 11 October 2006
Registered Office: 1st Floor, The Apartment Group Two, Jesmond Three Sixty, Newcastle upon Tyne, NE2 1DB
Activities: Hotels and similar accommodation
Major Shareholder: Duncan Fisher
Officers: Amanda Jayne Fisher, Secretary; Duncan Fisher [1968] Director

Next2buy Limited
Incorporated: 7 November 2003 *Employees:* 14
Net Worth: £716,087 *Total Assets:* £821,100
Registered Office: Verdemar House, 230 Park View, Whitley Bay, Tyne & Wear, NE26 3QR
Activities: Real estate agencies
Shareholders: Lorna Sayers; Karen Patricia Blight
Officers: Lorna Sayers, Secretary; Karen Patricia Blight [1961] Director/Manager; Lorna Sayers [1970] Director/Manager

Nextgen Group Limited
Incorporated: 27 October 2015
Net Worth: £370,349 *Total Assets:* £903,936
Registered Office: 37 Darras Road, Ponteland, Northumberland, NE20 9PD
Activities: Buying and selling of own real estate
Shareholders: Steve Donald; Susan Donald
Officers: Steve Donald [1970] Director/Accountant

NFPA Holdings Limited
Incorporated: 20 June 2000 *Employees:* 10
Net Worth: £1,840,049 *Total Assets:* £18,305,028
Registered Office: 4th Floor, Higham House, New Bridge Street West, Newcastle upon Tyne, NE1 8AN
Activities: Other business support service activities n.e.c.
Officers: Russell Crowther, Secretary; Adam James Clarke [1978] Director/Senior Manager; John Dallimore [1975] Director/Manager; David Arthur Fernie [1965] Director; Robert Nigel Finch [1964] Director/Deputy Head Regulation; Christopher Patrick Harris [1961] Director/Head of Regulation; Leyre La Casta [1969] Director/Head of Environmental Procurement [Spanish]; James Michael O'Meara [1973] Director/Contract Negotiator; John Christopher Slater [1959] Director/Electrical Engineer; Louise Wright [1969] Director/Head of Asset Commercialisation Europe

NFPA Scotland Limited
Incorporated: 27 July 2005 *Employees:* 10
Net Worth: £2 *Total Assets:* £1,749,344
Registered Office: 4th Floor, Higham House, New Bridge Street West, Newcastle upon Tyne, NE1 8AN
Activities: Other business support service activities n.e.c.
Officers: Russell Crowther, Secretary; Russell Crowther [1960] Director/Accountant; Melanie Reay [1968] Operations Director; Stuart Charles Stephens [1968] Commercial Director; Andrew Richard Wood [1954] Director/Retired

NFPAS Limited
Incorporated: 5 December 2001 *Employees:* 10
Net Worth: £1,839,453 *Total Assets:* £12,829,593
Registered Office: 4th Floor, Higham House, New Bridge Street West, Newcastle upon Tyne, NE1 8AN
Activities: Other business support service activities n.e.c.
Officers: Russell Crowther, Secretary; Russell Crowther [1960] Director/Accountant; Melanie Reay [1968] Operations Director; Stuart Charles Stephens [1968] Commercial Director; Andrew Richard Wood [1954] Director/Retired

NGP Utilities Limited
Incorporated: 9 January 2015 *Employees:* 179
Net Worth: £32,492 *Total Assets:* £12,634,856
Registered Office: Baltic Place, East Tower, South Shore Road, Gateshead, Tyne & Wear, NE8 3AE
Activities: Other business support service activities n.e.c.
Parent: Global Procurement Group Limited
Officers: Fokhrul Islam [1982] Director; Andrew Laird [1987] Director; Sean Francis McCann [1988] Director

NHP Limited
Incorporated: 11 March 1993
Net Worth: £369,454,816 *Total Assets:* £370,082,240
Registered Office: Southgate House, Archer Street, Darlington, Co Durham, DL3 6AH
Activities: Activities of head offices
Parent: Libra Careco Limited
Officers: James Justin Hutchens [1974] Director [American]; David Andrew Smith [1974] Director

NHP Management Limited
Incorporated: 5 December 1996 *Employees:* 2
Net Worth Deficit: £5,213,374 *Total Assets:* £14,994,578
Registered Office: Southgate House, Archer Street, Darlington, Co Durham, DL3 6AH
Activities: Management consultancy activities other than financial management
Parent: NHP Limited
Officers: James Justin Hutchens [1974] Director [American]; David Andrew Smith [1974] Director

NHP Operations (York) Limited
Incorporated: 6 December 2002
Net Worth: £7,323,799 *Total Assets:* £10,984,877
Registered Office: Southgate House, Archer Street, Darlington, Co Durham, DL3 6AH
Activities: Other business support service activities n.e.c.
Parent: NHP Limited
Officers: James Justin Hutchens [1974] Director [American]; David Andrew Smith [1974] Director

NHP Securities No. 1 Limited
Incorporated: 19 September 1995
Net Worth: £146,812,496 *Total Assets:* £172,211,376
Registered Office: Southgate House, Archer Street, Darlington, Co Durham, DL3 6AH
Activities: Other business support service activities n.e.c.
Parent: NHP Limited
Officers: James Justin Hutchens [1974] Director [American]; David Andrew Smith [1974] Director

NHP Securities No. 2 Limited
Incorporated: 5 December 1996
Net Worth: £77,649,456 *Total Assets:* £87,624,400
Registered Office: Southgate House, Archer Street, Darlington, Co Durham, DL3 6AH
Activities: Other business support service activities n.e.c.
Parent: NHP Limited
Officers: James Justin Hutchens [1974] Director [American]; David Andrew Smith [1974] Director

NHP Securities No. 3 Limited
Incorporated: 5 December 1996
Net Worth: £364,319,808 *Total Assets:* £672,915,008
Registered Office: Southgate House, Archer Street, Darlington, Co Durham, DL3 6AH
Activities: Other business support service activities n.e.c.
Parent: NHP Limited
Officers: James Justin Hutchens [1974] Director [American]; David Andrew Smith [1974] Director

NIAL Finance Limited
Incorporated: 6 October 2006
Net Worth: £33,927,000 *Total Assets:* £454,656,000
Registered Office: Nial Finance Limited, Woolsington, Newcastle upon Tyne, NE13 8BZ
Activities: Service activities incidental to air transportation
Parent: NIAL Holdings Limited
Officers: Mark Allan Hunt, Secretary; Nicholas Iain Forbes [1973] Director/Councillor; Councillor Simon Antony Henig [1969] Director/Councillor; Mark Allan Hunt [1977] Director/Chief Financial Officer; Nicholas Vaughan Jones [1973] Director/Chief Executive; Richard Andrew Knight [1967] Operations Director; Iain Malcolm [1966] Director; David Rocyn Rees [1959] Director/Investment Manager; Hywel Gwyn Rees [1972] Director/Solicitor; John Julian Stent [1955] Director/Consultant

NIAL Group Limited
Incorporated: 6 October 2006 *Employees:* 430
Net Worth Deficit: £98,920,000 *Total Assets:* £349,967,008
Registered Office: Nial Group Limited, Woolsington, Newcastle upon Tyne, NE13 8BZ
Activities: Service activities incidental to air transportation
Shareholders: Site UK SPV Limited; Newcastle Airport Local Authority Holding Company Limited
Officers: Mark Allan Hunt, Secretary; Nicholas Iain Forbes [1973] Director/Councillor; Councillor Simon Antony Henig [1969] Director/Councillor; Mark Allan Hunt [1977] Director/Chief Financial Officer; Nicholas Vaughan Jones [1973] Director/Chief Executive; Richard Andrew Knight [1967] Operations Director; Iain Malcolm [1966] Director; David Rocyn Rees [1959] Director/Investment Manager; Hywel Gwyn Rees [1972] Director/Solicitor; John Julian Stent [1955] Director/Consultant

NIAL Holdings Limited
Incorporated: 22 March 2001
Net Worth: £156,238,000 *Total Assets:* £162,728,992
Registered Office: Woolsington, Newcastle upon Tyne, NE13 8BZ
Activities: Activities of head offices
Shareholders: NIAL Investments Limited; NIAL Group Limited
Officers: Mark Allan Hunt, Secretary; Nicholas Iain Forbes [1973] Director/Councillor; Councillor Simon Antony Henig [1969] Director/Councillor; Mark Allan Hunt [1977] Director/Chief Financial Officer; Nicholas Vaughan Jones [1973] Director/Chief Executive; Richard Andrew Knight [1967] Operations Director; Iain Malcolm [1966] Director/Councillor; David Rocyn Rees [1959] Director/Investment Manager; Hywel Gwyn Rees [1972] Director/Solicitor; John Julian Stent [1955] Director/Consultant

NIAL Investments Limited
Incorporated: 22 March 2001
Net Worth: £96,414,000 *Total Assets:* £96,414,000
Registered Office: Woolsington, Newcastle upon Tyne, NE13 8BZ
Activities: Activities of head offices
Parent: NIAL Group Limited
Officers: Mark Allan Hunt, Secretary; Nicholas Iain Forbes [1973] Director/Councillor; Councillor Simon Antony Henig [1969] Director/Councillor; Mark Allan Hunt [1977] Director/Chief Financial Officer; Nicholas Vaughan Jones [1973] Director/Chief Executive; Richard Andrew Knight [1967] Operations Director; Iain Malcolm [1966] Director; David Rocyn Rees [1959] Director/Investment Manager; Hywel Gwyn Rees [1972] Director/Solicitor; John Julian Stent [1955] Director/Consultant

NIAL Services Limited
Incorporated: 30 July 1991 *Employees:* 152
Net Worth: £3,688,229 *Total Assets:* £12,349,074
Registered Office: Unit 1 Prestwick Industrial Estate, Ponteland, Northumberland, NE20 9DA
Activities: Scheduled passenger air transport
Parent: Newcastle International Airport Limited
Officers: Mark Allan Hunt, Secretary; Mark Allan Hunt [1977] Director/Chief Financial Officer; Nicholas Vaughan Jones [1973] Director/Chief Executive; Richard Andrew Knight [1967] Operations Director

Nicander Limited
Incorporated: 17 December 2007 *Employees:* 29
Net Worth: £678,050 *Total Assets:* £1,013,384
Registered Office: 14 Colmans Nook, Belasis Business Park, Billingham, Stockton on Tees, Cleveland, TS23 4EG
Activities: Business and domestic software development
Officers: Derek Stephen Lister, Secretary; Nicholas John Frederick Drew [1960] Director; Derek Stephen Lister [1963] Director/Secretary

Nice Network Ltd
Incorporated: 3 December 1993 *Employees:* 21
Net Worth: £780,643 *Total Assets:* £1,561,760
Registered Office: Comms House, Pennywell Industrial Estate, Hylton Road, Sunderland, Tyne & Wear, SR4 9EN
Activities: Other telecommunications activities
Officers: Wendy Lee, Secretary; Christopher Lee [1959] Managing Director; Peter John Seward [1960] Director/Accountant

Niche Technology UK Limited
Incorporated: 10 May 2004 *Employees:* 9
Net Worth: £1,866,103 *Total Assets:* £5,137,355
Registered Office: Lakeside House, Kingfisher Way, Stockton on Tees, Cleveland, TS18 3NB
Activities: Other information technology service activities
Officers: Roland Dietrich Schneider, Secretary; Christian Reinhard Schneider [1962] Director/Software Developer [Canadian]; Roland Dietrich Schneider [1961] Director/Electrical Engineer [Canadian]

M.E. Nicholls Conversions Limited
Incorporated: 14 September 1960
Registered Office: The Grove, Frenchgate, Richmond, N Yorks, DL10 7AA
Activities: Other letting and operating of own or leased real estate
Officers: Sophia Jane McDonald [1968] Director; Michael John Nicholls [1935] Director; Peter John Nicholls [1967] Director/Barrister

G.Nicholson (Engineers) Limited
Incorporated: 28 June 1956 *Employees:* 23
Net Worth: £606,895 *Total Assets:* £1,012,208
Registered Office: Blue House, Lane, Washington, Tyne & Wear, NE37 2TD
Activities: Manufacture of metal structures and parts of structures
Officers: John Frederick Nicholson [1947] Director; Paul Nicholson [1971] Works Director

Nicholson's Aircraft Seals Limited
Incorporated: 6 August 1973
Net Worth: £1,872,215 *Total Assets:* £1,872,215
Registered Office: Amos Drive, Greencroft Industrial Park, Stanley, Co Durham, DH9 7YE
Activities: Non-trading company
Parent: Nicholsons Sealing Technologies Limited
Officers: Elizabeth Claire Green [1983] Director; Nicholas Peter Green [1975] Director

Nicholsons Group Limited
Incorporated: 12 January 2007 *Employees:* 158
Net Worth: £14,329,516 *Total Assets:* £17,297,848
Registered Office: B3 Kingfisher House, Team Valley Trading Estate, Gateshead, Tyne & Wear, NE11 0JQ
Activities: Activities of other holding companies n.e.c.
Officers: Elizabeth Claire Green [1983] Director; Nicholas Peter Green [1975] Director

Nicholsons Sealing Technologies Limited
Incorporated: 28 February 1923 *Employees:* 142
Net Worth: £5,647,730 *Total Assets:* £13,478,359
Registered Office: Amos Drive, Greencroft Industrial Park, Stanley, Co Durham, DH9 7YE
Activities: Other manufacturing n.e.c.
Parent: Nicholsons Group Limited
Officers: Elizabeth Claire Green [1983] Director; Nicholas Peter Green [1975] Director/Engineer

Nicholsons Transport Limited
Incorporated: 17 January 1989 *Employees:* 41
Net Worth Deficit: £933,583 *Total Assets:* £808,806
Registered Office: Burnside House, ICI West Gate, Chiltons Avenue, Billingham, Cleveland, TS23 1JD
Activities: Freight transport by road
Parent: Nicholson Group Ltd
Officers: David Michael Nicholson, Secretary; David Michael Nicholson [1965] Director/Haulage Contractor

Nielsen,Andersen & Company Limited
Incorporated: 4 February 1920 *Employees:* 2
Net Worth: £1,350,961 *Total Assets:* £1,409,222
Registered Office: 3 Croftlands, Longhoughton Road, Lesbury, Alnwick, Northumberland, NE66 3QW
Activities: Financial intermediation not elsewhere classified
Shareholder: Joseph William Atkinson
Officers: Carolyn Judith Allbrook [1960] Director; Joseph Michael Atkinson [1958] Director; Joseph William Atkinson [1933] Director; Nigel John Brierley Atkinson [1964] Director

Nifco UK Limited
Incorporated: 6 October 1978 *Employees:* 618
Net Worth: £30,435,000 *Total Assets:* £55,782,000
Registered Office: Nifco House, Durham Lane, Eaglescliffe, Stockton on Tees, Cleveland, TS16 0PS
Activities: Manufacture of other plastic products
Officers: Gary Clark, Secretary; Fukuo Iwasaki [1957] Director & Executive Managing Officer Nifco Inc [Japanese]; Michael Matthews [1964] Managing Director; Tsukasa Naganawa [1969] Director Nifco KTS [Japanese]; Toshiyuki Yamamoto [1949] Director/President Nifco Inc [Japanese]

Nike (UK) Limited
Incorporated: 18 February 1985 *Employees:* 271
Net Worth: £37,087,000 *Total Assets:* £86,123,000
Registered Office: Camberwell Way, Doxford International Technology Park, Sunderland, Tyne & Wear, SR3 3XN
Activities: Agents involved in the sale of textiles, clothing, fur, footwear and leather goods
Parent: Nike, Inc
Officers: Tracey Jane Thane, Secretary; William Edward Berner Jr [1967] Director [American]; Nigel David Bond [1972] Finance Director; David Phillip Carmont [1966] Director/General Manager [Australian]

Nilus Developments Limited
Incorporated: 6 July 2016
Net Worth: £298,097 *Total Assets:* £3,004,518
Registered Office: 2nd Floor, Cuthbert House, Newcastle upon Tyne, NE1 2ET
Activities: Development of building projects
Shareholders: High Street Commercial Finance Limited; High Street Commercial Finance Limited
Officers: Gary Ronald Forrest [1968] Director

Niramax Group Limited
Incorporated: 15 May 2001 *Employees:* 51
Net Worth: £8,689,952 *Total Assets:* £13,265,251
Registered Office: John Shadforth House, Thomlinson Road, Longhill Industrial Estate, Hartlepool, Cleveland, TS25 1NS
Activities: Treatment and disposal of non-hazardous waste
Parent: Niramax Holdings Limited
Officers: Neil Elliott [1975] Director

Niramax Holdings Limited
Incorporated: 1 October 2007 *Employees:* 49
Net Worth: £8,411,862 *Total Assets:* £13,257,418
Registered Office: Niramax House, Site 6-8, Tofts Farm Industrial Estate West, Brenda Road, Hartlepool, Cleveland, TS25 2BQ
Activities: Freight transport by road
Major Shareholder: Neil Elliott
Officers: Neil Elliott [1975] Director

Nirvana Europe Limited
Incorporated: 30 April 1999 *Employees:* 13
Net Worth: £401,274 *Total Assets:* £1,176,796
Registered Office: Third Floor, Citygate, St James Boulevard, Newcastle upon Tyne, NE1 4JE
Activities: Other business support service activities n.e.c.
Major Shareholder: Kenneth Morris
Officers: Nigel David Morris, Secretary/Director; Kenneth Morris [1947] Director/Accountant; Nigel David Morris [1979] Director

NIS Group Services Limited
Incorporated: 11 July 1996 *Employees:* 52
Net Worth: £1,184,455 *Total Assets:* £2,574,991
Registered Office: Naylor Court, Blaydon Haugh Industrial Estate, Blaydon, Tyne & Wear, NE21 5SD
Activities: Other construction installation
Officers: Kate Alexandra Marsden, Secretary; Ian Neville Marsden [1971] Managing Director

Nissan Holdings (UK) Limited
Incorporated: 7 February 2000
Net Worth: £850,142,208 *Total Assets:* £850,251,776
Registered Office: Washington Road, Sunderland, Tyne & Wear, SR5 3NS
Activities: Activities of head offices
Parent: Nissan Motor Co., Ltd.
Officers: Paul Robson, Secretary; John Charles Butcher [1964] Finance Director; Laurent Franck Christian David [1971] Director/Senior Vice President Administration and Finance [French]; Alan David Tennant [1954] Director

Nissan Motor Manufacturing (UK) Limited
Incorporated: 6 April 1984 *Employees:* 7,755
Net Worth: £121,313,000 *Total Assets:* £2,426,690,048
Registered Office: Washington Road, Sunderland, Tyne & Wear, SR5 3NS
Activities: Manufacture of motor vehicles
Parent: Nissan Holdings (UK) Limited
Officers: Steven Neil Tiffin, Secretary; Mamoru Aoki [1958] Director [Japanese]; Paul Bevington [1964] Director/General Manager - Finance; John Charles Butcher [1964] Finance Director; Laurent Franck Christian David [1971] Director/Senior Vice President Administration & Finance [French]; Roberto Carlos Delgado [1975] Director/Vice President Finance [Mexican]; Kevin Fitzpatrick [1960] Director/Vice President - Manufacturing UK; Kevin Michael O'Neil [1963] Director; Kenneth Alexander Ramirez [1968] Director [American]; Nobusuke Tokura [1965] Director [Japanese]

Nissan Trading Europe Limited
Incorporated: 22 January 1990 *Employees:* 61
Net Worth: £44,438,768 *Total Assets:* £85,946,744
Registered Office: c/o Nissan Motor Manufacturing UK Ltd, Washington Road, Sunderland, Tyne & Wear, SR5 3NS
Activities: Sale of new cars and light motor vehicles
Parent: Nissan Motor Co., Limited
Officers: Koji Oya, Secretary; Kazunori Arai [1966] Director [Japanese]; Akihiro Ishiwatari [1957] Managing Director [Japanese]; Yoshinori Kanakubo [1958] Director [Japanese]; Kenichi Kitao [1962] Director/Chief Operating Officer [Japanese]

Nitelites Limited
Incorporated: 23 January 2004 *Employees:* 14
Net Worth: £430,529 *Total Assets:* £2,659,928
Registered Office: Unit S4, Second Avenue, Tyne Tunnel Trading Estate, North Shields, Tyne & Wear, NE29 7SY
Activities: Other professional, scientific and technical activities n.e.c.
Shareholders: James Michael Moore; Jamie Moore
Officers: Jamie Moore, Secretary/Director; James Michael Moore [1952] Director/Electrical Engineer; Jamie Moore [1983] Director/Lighting Engineer; Shaun Moore [1986] Director

Nitro 2 Limited
Incorporated: 8 November 2011
Net Worth: £43,000,000 *Total Assets:* £43,000,000
Registered Office: Cross House, Westgate Road, Newcastle upon Tyne, NE1 4XX
Activities: Activities of head offices
Parent: Reversions Financing (No. 1) 2011 Limited
Officers: Paul Trevor Barber [1967] Director; Antony Lewis Pierce [1976] Finance Director

John Nixon Limited
Incorporated: 7 November 1967 *Employees:* 435
Net Worth: £23,670,412 *Total Assets:* £80,121,296
Registered Office: City West Business Park, Scotswood Road, Newcastle upon Tyne, NE4 7DF
Activities: Renting and leasing of construction and civil engineering machinery and equipment
Officers: Neil McDiarmid, Secretary; Alison Lesley Blackwood [1969] Director; Kevin Matthew Blackwood [1964] Director; Beverley Jane Brown [1961] Director; Terry David King [1966] Operations Director; Neil McDiarmid [1961] Director/Chartered Accountant; Christopher Edward Nixon [1972] Director; Graham Richard Nixon [1972] Director; John Nixon [1932] Director; Stephen John Smith [1957] Director

NK Property Ltd
Incorporated: 26 June 2015
Net Worth: £82,514 *Total Assets:* £1,553,686
Registered Office: 71 Eastern Way, Ponteland, Northumberland, NE20 9RE
Activities: Other letting and operating of own or leased real estate
Officers: Dr Neeta Aggarwal [1983] Director/Property Management; Niraj Aggarwal [1980] Director/Property Management

NLJIS Holdings Limited
Incorporated: 10 October 2013
Net Worth: £1,674,683 *Total Assets:* £2,822,668
Registered Office: Victoria House, Toward Road, Sunderland, Tyne & Wear, SR1 2QF
Activities: Activities of head offices
Shareholders: Kenneth Hin Yeow Lee; Robert Newton
Officers: Andrew Jackson [1975] Director/Insurance Broker; Kenneth Hin Yeow Lee [1959] Director/Insurance Broker; Robert Newton [1951] Director/Insurance Broker

Nobia Holdings UK Limited
Incorporated: 21 March 2001 *Employees:* 2,338
Net Worth: £159,656,992 *Total Assets:* £335,708,992
Registered Office: c/o Magnet Limited, 3 Allington Way, Yarm Road Business Park, Darlington, Co Durham, DL1 4XT
Activities: Other manufacturing n.e.c.
Parent: Nobia AB
Officers: Nicola Jane Hardcastle, Secretary; Anjum Ahmed [1970] Director; Daniel Arthur Edward Carr [1975] Finance Director; Nicola Jane Hardcastle [1965] Director/Company Secretary; Peter Kane [1965] Managing Director; Kristoffer Ljungfelt [1977] Director [Swedish]; Paul David Woolston [1963] Director

J. Noble & Sons Limited
Incorporated: 11 February 1977 *Employees:* 151
Net Worth: £5,227,056 *Total Assets:* £7,104,469
Registered Office: 91 Front Street, Chester-le-Street, Co Durham, DH3 3BJ
Activities: Gambling and betting activities
Major Shareholder: John Noble
Officers: Jason Noble [1966] Director/Amusement Caterer; John Noble Jnr [1959] Director/Amusement Caterer

Wm. Noble (Automatics) Limited
Incorporated: 5 April 1978
Net Worth: £3,992,000 *Total Assets:* £4,102,000
Registered Office: 1a Dukesway Court, Team Valley Trading Estate, Gateshead, Tyne & Wear, NE11 0PJ
Activities: Gambling and betting activities
Parent: Falcombe Holdings Limited
Officers: Phillip Nigel Blain, Secretary; David James Horrocks [1959] Director/Chartered Accountant; Ian Imrie [1955] Director

Brian Noble Fencing Contractors Limited
Incorporated: 17 November 1997 *Employees:* 16
Net Worth: £869,642 *Total Assets:* £983,180
Registered Office: Southview Farm, Great Busby, Stokesley, Middlesbrough, Cleveland, TS9 7AX
Activities: Other business support service activities n.e.c.
Major Shareholder: Brian Arthur Noble
Officers: Brian Arthur Noble, Secretary/Contractor; Brian Arthur Noble [1958] Director/Contractor

Noda Taxis Limited
Incorporated: 9 August 2007 *Employees:* 33
Net Worth: £245,841 *Total Assets:* £1,515,472
Registered Office: 37a Hadrian Road, Newcastle upon Tyne, NE4 9HN
Activities: Taxi operation
Officers: Mohammed Rackhman, Secretary; Mohammed Rackhman [1972] Director; Mohammed Shan Ramzan [1973] Director; Mohammed Rangzaib [1976] Director; Mohammed Suleman [1970] Director; Mohammed Tariq [1977] Director

NOF Energy Ltd
Incorporated: 13 September 2006 *Employees:* 12
Net Worth: £598,203 *Total Assets:* £946,906
Registered Office: First Floor, Thames House, Mandale Business Park, Belmont Industrial Estate, Durham, DH1 1TH
Activities: Other business support service activities n.e.c.
Officers: Colin Thompson Hewitt, Secretary; David Armstrong [1955] Director/Quantity Surveyor; James George Brown [1968] Managing Director; Paul William Robert Charlton [1965] Managing Director; Alexandra Jane Hayward [1967] Managing Director; Bruce Michael Amos Heppenstall [1970] Managing Director; Colin Thompson Hewitt [1957] Director/Solicitor; Neil Kirkbride [1960] Group Managing Director; Andrew Nicholas Leigh [1959] Director/Vice President - Operations; Joanne Leng [1969] Director of Business Development; Dr Alan Lowdon [1962] Director/Energy and Water Professional/Chartered Engineer; Andrew Ian Mills [1979] Managing Director; George Rafferty [1955] Director/Chief Executive; Richard Turner [1978] Director/Chief Executive Officer; Margaret Clare Weirs [1968] Director/Accountant

NOI4 Limited
Incorporated: 15 October 2007
Net Worth: £413,645 *Total Assets:* £1,472,734
Registered Office: 6 Osborne Avenue, Jesmond, Newcastle upon Tyne, NE2 1JQ
Activities: Other letting and operating of own or leased real estate
Shareholders: Jonathan Michael Johnson; Maria Johnson
Officers: Maria Johnson, Secretary [Italian]; Jonathan Michael Johnson [1967] Director; Maria Johnson [1971] Director [Italian]

Non-Fossil Purchasing Agency Limited
Incorporated: 28 March 1989 *Employees:* 10
Net Worth: £600 *Total Assets:* £4,195,478
Registered Office: 4th Floor, Higham House, New Bridge Street West, Newcastle upon Tyne, NE1 8AN
Activities: Other business support service activities n.e.c.
Officers: Russell Crowther, Secretary; Russell Crowther [1960] Director/Accountant; Melanie Reay [1968] Operations Director; Stuart Charles Stephens [1968] Commercial Director; Andrew Richard Wood [1954] Director/Retired

Nonlinear Technologies Limited
Incorporated: 21 May 2007
Net Worth: £290,919 *Total Assets:* £1,298,419
Registered Office: 4th Floor, Dean Court, 22 Dean Street, Newcastle upon Tyne, NE1 1PG
Activities: Information technology consultancy activities
Major Shareholder: William Michael Dracup
Officers: David Ian Bramwell [1970] Director; James Crispin Michael Curry [1964] Director; William Michael Dracup [1963] Director; Keith Bertram Milton [1961] Director/Chief Financial Officer; Stephen Graham Purvis [1981] Director

Norfolk Hotel Limited
Incorporated: 25 August 2000 *Employees:* 6
Net Worth: £2,369,265 *Total Assets:* £3,380,864
Registered Office: Oakmere, Belmont Business Park, Durham, DH1 1TW
Activities: Hotels and similar accommodation
Shareholders: Nasser Bahrami; Elfrida Rose Bahrami
Officers: Nasser Bahrami [1957] Director

Norham Holdings Group Limited
Incorporated: 21 March 2007 *Employees:* 3
Net Worth: £1,760,570 *Total Assets:* £7,889,852
Registered Office: Phoenix House, Kingfisher Way, Silverlink Business Park, Wallsend, Tyne & Wear, NE28 9NX
Activities: Other letting and operating of own or leased real estate
Officers: Richard Bertram [1957] Financial Director; James Keith Bilclough [1977] Director; Stephen Paul Bilclough [1969] Director

Norham Holdings Limited
Incorporated: 29 June 1988
Net Worth: £6,573,255 *Total Assets:* £6,620,908
Registered Office: Phoenix House, Kingfisher Way, Silverlink Business Park, Wallsend, Tyne & Wear, NE28 9NX
Activities: Other letting and operating of own or leased real estate
Parent: Norham Holdings Group Limited
Officers: James Keith Bilclough [1977] Director/Commercial Manager; Stephen Paul Bilclough [1969] Director

Norham House 2 Limited
Incorporated: 17 September 2004 *Employees:* 4
Net Worth: £6,351,665 *Total Assets:* £15,145,301
Registered Office: 18 Sheldon Grove, Gosforth, Newcastle upon Tyne, NE3 4JP
Activities: Other letting and operating of own or leased real estate
Shareholders: Rakesh Kumar Sehgal; Carol Sehgal
Officers: Lucy Sehgal, Secretary; Carol Sehgal [1951] Director; Paul Sehgal [1975] Executive Director; Rakesh Kumar Sehgal [1951] Director; Tony Vikram Sehgal [1979] Director

Normans of Billingham Limited
Incorporated: 17 October 1988 *Employees:* 58
Net Worth: £384,673 *Total Assets:* £2,094,696
Registered Office: Unit 5 Royce Avenue, Cowpen Lane Industrial Estate, Billingham, Cleveland, TS23 4BX
Activities: Non-specialised wholesale trade
Shareholder: Matthew Couldry
Officers: Julie Elizabeth Couldry, Secretary; Matthew Couldry [1979] Director; Norman Dudley Couldry [1953] Director/Stationery Supplier

Norsea Group (UK) Limited
Incorporated: 30 November 2007 *Employees:* 17
Net Worth: £409,625 *Total Assets:* £3,332,839
Registered Office: Merchant House, 30 Cloth Market, Newcastle upon Tyne, NE1 1EE
Activities: Operation of warehousing and storage facilities for land transport activities
Parent: Wilh. Wilhelmsen Holding ASA
Officers: Lars Haug [1968] Director [Norwegian]; Steinar Modalslid-Meling [1968] Director [Norwegian]; John Olaf Naesheim [1964] Director/Vice President SMB [Norwegian]; Ola Magne Theun Neergaard [1981] Director/Executive Vice President (CCO) [Norwegian]; Walter Clark Robertson [1958] Director; John Egil Stangland [1964] Director [Norwegian]

Norseal Limited
Incorporated: 6 November 2001 *Employees:* 18
Net Worth: £1,886,092 *Total Assets:* £2,781,310
Registered Office: Norseal House, 5 Regents Drive, Prudhoe, Northumberland, NE42 6PX
Activities: Wholesale of wood, construction materials and sanitary equipment
Officers: Carl Julius Cronenberg [1962] Director/Chairman [German]; Christian Grabitz [1975] Director [German]; Michael Ian Spoors [1969] Managing Director

Norstead Limited
Incorporated: 6 July 1998
Net Worth: £12,247,000 *Total Assets:* £16,023,000
Registered Office: Metnor House, Mylord Crescent, Killingworth, Newcastle upon Tyne, NE12 5YD
Activities: Electrical installation
Parent: Metnor Group Limited
Officers: Dr Adam Boyd Langman, Secretary; Keith Andrew Atkinson [1961] Director/Chartered Accountant; Adam Boyd Langman [1962] Finance Director; Stephen Rankin [1964] Director; William Thoburn [1954] Director/Engineer

North Bar Properties Limited
Incorporated: 5 February 2004
Net Worth: £441,766 *Total Assets:* £1,075,604
Registered Office: Joseph Miller & Co, Floor A, Milburn House, Dean Street, Newcastle upon Tyne, NE1 1LE
Activities: Other letting and operating of own or leased real estate
Shareholders: Abid Islam Nawaz; Sameena Nawaz
Officers: Sameena Nawaz, Secretary; Abid Islam Nawaz [1962] Director

North East Access To Finance Limited
Incorporated: 25 August 2009 *Employees:* 11
Total Assets: £98,642,368
Registered Office: 3rd Floor, Baltimore House, Abbotts Hill, Gateshead, Tyne & Wear, NE8 3DF
Activities: Activities of other holding companies n.e.c.
Officers: Andrew James Arkless, Secretary; Hilary Patricia Florek [1960] Director/PR Consultant; Geoffrey Mark Hodgson [1961] Director; Stephen John Lightley [1957] Director/Chartered Accountant; Kathryn Lucy Hay Winskell [1963] Director/Pro Vice Chancellor

North East Accident Repair Centres Limited
Incorporated: 10 September 2007 *Employees:* 2
Net Worth: £1,138,168 *Total Assets:* £2,913,130
Registered Office: 94/4 Carrmere Road, Leechmere Industrial Estate, Sunderland, Tyne & Wear, SR2 9TE
Activities: Sale, maintenance and repair of motorcycles and related parts and accessories
Shareholders: Roger Andrew Collings; Robert George Taylor
Officers: Roger Andrew Collings, Secretary; Roger Andrew Collings [1961] Director; Robert George Taylor [1957] Managing Director

North East Actuarial Services Limited
Incorporated: 28 January 2000
Net Worth: £2,278,652 *Total Assets:* £2,472,917
Registered Office: 37 Woodlands, Darras Hall, Ponteland, Northumberland, NE20 9EU
Activities: Other activities auxiliary to insurance and pension funding
Officers: Mark Andrew Sander, Secretary; Graeme John Charlton [1967] Director/Actuary; Mark Andrew Sander [1969] Director/Actuary

North East Autism Society
Incorporated: 6 October 1993 *Employees:* 586
Net Worth: £17,533,770 *Total Assets:* £24,474,494
Registered Office: 15 Lumley Court, Drum Industrial Estate, Chester-le-Street, Co Durham, DH2 1AN
Activities: Primary education
Officers: John Jospeh Phillipson, Secretary; Malcolm Bainbridge [1959] Director/Retired Bank Manager; Gavin Bestford [1949] Director/Retired; Dr Rakesh Chopra OBE [1961] Director/Doctor; Jillian Crumbie [1969] Director; John Terence Hodgson [1960] Director/Pre-Construction Manager; Kevin Patrick McAlister [1961] Director/Retired; John O'Sullivan [1958] Director/Barrister; David James Parker [1987] Director/Finance Manager; Captain Donald Cottew Walker [1947] Director/Retired

North East Building Services Limited
Incorporated: 2 February 1999 *Employees:* 19
Net Worth: £401,536 *Total Assets:* £816,246
Registered Office: 19 Bridge House, Bridge Street, Sunderland, Tyne & Wear, SR1 1TE
Activities: Other construction installation
Shareholders: Gemma Richardson; Lawrence Andrew Richardson
Officers: Paul David Evans, Secretary; Paul David Evans [1968] Director/Contracts Manager; Gemma Richardson [1979] Director; Lawrence Andrew Richardson [1971] Director/Surveyor

North East Business and Innovation Centre Limited
Incorporated: 9 November 1989 *Employees:* 69
Net Worth: £12,931,567 *Total Assets:* £15,380,065
Registered Office: Sunderland Enterprise Park, Riverside, Sunderland, Tyne & Wear, SR5 2TA
Activities: Other business support service activities n.e.c.
Officers: Paul John McEldon, Secretary; John Norman Anderson [1945] Managing Director; Kevan Ward Carrick [1947] Director/Property Consultant; Paul John McEldon [1966] Director/Chief Executive

North East Care Homes Limited
Incorporated: 5 April 2004
Net Worth: £386,940 *Total Assets:* £7,960,247
Registered Office: North East Care Homes Limited, Spaceworks, Suites 4b & 4c, Benton Park Road, South Gosforth, Newcastle upon Tyne, NE7 7LX
Activities: Residential care activities for the elderly and disabled
Shareholders: Ravinder Singh Dhugga; Tarsem Lal Chopra
Officers: Tarsem Lal Chopra, Secretary; Tarsem Lal Chopra [1952] Director; Ravinder Singh Dhugga [1959] Director

North East Concrete Limited
Incorporated: 23 May 1997 *Employees:* 75
Net Worth: £3,117,618 *Total Assets:* £5,036,302
Registered Office: High Street, Newburn, Newcastle upon Tyne, NE15 8LN
Activities: Manufacture of ready-mixed concrete
Shareholders: David James Blakelock; Julie Stabler; David Blakelock
Officers: David James Blakelock, Secretary; Julie Stabler, Secretary/Finance Manager; David James Blakelock [1973] Director/Engineer; David Blakelock [1950] Director/Engineer; Julie Stabler [1973] Director/Finance Manager

North East England Chamber of Commerce
Incorporated: 13 June 1994 *Employees:* 126
Net Worth: £3,375,000 *Total Assets:* £4,818,000
Registered Office: Aykley Heads Business Centre, Aykley Heads, Durham, DH1 5TS
Activities: Activities of business and employers membership organisations
Officers: David John Langley, Secretary; Christopher Paul Beaumont [1968] Director/Chartered Accountant; Gillian Courtney [1962] Director; David John Langley [1978] Director/Chartered Accountant; John Philip Birkett Marshall [1966] Director; Michael Matthews [1964] Managing Director; John McCabe [1972] Managing Director; Paul Burnett Moran [1962] Director/Chartered Accountant; Wayham Hutcheson Moran [1947] Director; James David Alexander Ramsbotham [1959] Director; George Joseph Sanger [1958] Regional Director; Richard John Lofthouse Swart [1962] Managing Director; Kathryn Lucy Hay Winskell [1963] Director/Pro Vice Chancellor

North East Enterprise Agency Limited
Incorporated: 11 April 2007
Net Worth: £5,300 *Total Assets:* £916,948
Registered Office: North East Business and Innovation Centre, Sunderland Enterprise Park, Sunderland, Tyne & Wear, SR5 2TA
Activities: Other business support service activities n.e.c.
Officers: Paul John McEldon, Secretary; Denise Joan Fielding [1968] Director/Chief Executive; Alison Jane Machin [1975] Director/General Manager; Paul John McEldon [1966] Director/Chief Executive; Tracey Joanne Moore [1969] Director/Business Development Manager; Graeme K Oram [1959] Director/Chief Executive; Steven James Robson [1980] Director/Chief Executive; Margaret Rosemary Smith [1957] Director/Operations Manager; Philip Keith Teasdale [1973] Director; Carole Ann White [1960] Director/Manager

North East Estates Limited
Incorporated: 27 June 1980
Net Worth: £886,086 *Total Assets:* £986,733
Registered Office: 2a North Sands Business Centre, Sunderland, Tyne & Wear, SR6 0QA
Activities: Other letting and operating of own or leased real estate
Major Shareholder: Sidney Campbell
Officers: Stuart Andrew Campbell, Secretary; Sydney Adam Alfred Campbell [1932] Director/Accountant

North East Executive Limited
Incorporated: 21 December 2009
Net Worth: £267,853 *Total Assets:* £1,297,476
Registered Office: 2a Stephenson Street, Thornaby, Stockton on Tees, Cleveland, TS17 6AL
Activities: Taxi operation
Major Shareholder: Maharban Ali Khan
Officers: Maharban Ali Khan [1971] Managing Director

North East Eye Care Limited
Incorporated: 27 January 2010
Net Worth: £1,527,398 *Total Assets:* £1,641,750
Registered Office: 1 West Beck Grove, Darlington, Co Durham, DL3 8UQ
Activities: General medical practice activities
Shareholders: Saju Thomas; Dimple George
Officers: Saju Thomas [1969] Director/Surgeon

North East Finance (Holdco) Limited
Incorporated: 25 August 2009 *Employees:* 6
Net Worth: £1 *Total Assets:* £70,526,840
Registered Office: First Floor, 33 Grey Street, Newcastle upon Tyne, NE1 6EE
Activities: Fund management activities
Parent: North East Access To Finance Limited
Officers: William Taninhill Blair [1955] Director/Fund Manager; Jason Lee Hobbs [1969] Director; Andrew Darby Mitchell [1958] Director; Helen Rachelle Sinclair [1966] Director; Michael John Stephenson [1943] Director

North East Finance (Subco) Limited
Incorporated: 13 October 2009
Net Worth Deficit: £14,672,811 *Total Assets:* £10,733,233
Registered Office: First Floor, 33 Grey Street, Newcastle upon Tyne, NE1 6EE
Activities: Fund management activities
Parent: North East Finance (Holdco) Limited
Officers: Jason Lee Hobbs [1969] Director; Andrew Darby Mitchell [1958] Director

North East Granite Company Limited
Incorporated: 22 March 2002
Registered Office: Littleburn Industrial Estate, Langley Moor, Co Durham, DH7 8HJ
Activities: Cutting, shaping and finishing of stone
Major Shareholder: George Smith
Officers: George Smith, Secretary; George Smith [1957] Director/Monumental Mason; Gillian Lesley Smith [1957] Director/Administrator; Henry Smith [1984] Director/Monumental Mason; Robert Smith [1986] Director/Monumental Mason

North East Group Limited
Incorporated: 28 August 2015
Net Worth: £6,249,996 *Total Assets:* £6,249,996
Registered Office: High Street, Newburn, Newcastle upon Tyne, NE15 8LN
Activities: Activities of other holding companies n.e.c.
Shareholders: David James Blakelock; Julie Stabler; David Blakelock
Officers: David Blakelock [1950] Director; David James Blakelock [1973] Director; Julie Stabler [1973] Director/Finance Manager

North East Homes Limited
Incorporated: 29 April 2014
Net Worth Deficit: £903 *Total Assets:* £1,314,139
Registered Office: 3 Upsall Grange Gardens, Nunthorpe, Middlesbrough, Cleveland, TS7 0AX
Activities: Construction of other civil engineering projects n.e.c.
Major Shareholder: Jonathan King
Officers: Jonathon King [1970] Director; David McGlynn [1975] Director/Sales Manager

North East Learning Trust
Incorporated: 13 January 2011 *Employees:* 318
Net Worth: £18,125,000 *Total Assets:* £25,021,000
Registered Office: T/A The Academy at Shotton Hall, Passfield Way, Peterlee, Co Durham, SR8 1AU
Activities: General secondary education
Officers: Lee Alexander, Secretary; Brian Burlinson [1956] Director/Head of School; John Cameron [1942] Director; Derek Gibson [1961] Director/Electrical Engineer; Susan McDonnell [1964] Director; Diane Nicholson [1955] Director/Tenancy Management Officer; Lesley Anne Powell [1966] Director/Principal; Margaret Patricia Saxton [1951] Director/Retired; Roy Simpson [1942] Director; Barbara Waugh [1952] Director/Education Consultant

North East Motor Salvage Limited
Incorporated: 12 July 1985 *Employees:* 15
Net Worth: £271,090 *Total Assets:* £1,038,546
Registered Office: 7b Mill Hill, North West Industrial Estate, Peterlee, Co Durham, SR8 2HR
Activities: Retail trade of motor vehicle parts and accessories
Shareholders: Christine Usher; Alan Usher
Officers: Alan Usher, Secretary; Alan Usher [1947] Director; Christine Usher [1950] Director

North East Panels Limited
Incorporated: 18 December 2006
Net Worth: £929,907 *Total Assets:* £2,083,249
Registered Office: Units 3 & 4 Pinewood Business Park, Wilden Road, Pattinson South Industrial Estate, Washington, Tyne & Wear, NE38 8QB
Activities: Manufacture of other plastic products
Shareholders: Michael Knapton; Teresa Maria Oleksik
Officers: Michael Knapton [1953] Director; Teresa Maria Knapton [1952] Director/Secretary

North East Pipelines Limited
Incorporated: 19 September 2008
Registered Office: Rowlands House, Portobello Road, Birtley, Chester-le-Street, Co Durham, DH3 2RY
Activities: Other specialised construction activities n.e.c.
Major Shareholder: Stephen Willey
Officers: Kay Kendall, Secretary; Kay Kendall [1971] Director/Housewife; Stephen Andrew Willey [1969] Director/Utility Contractor

North East Plant Hire Limited
Incorporated: 7 May 2013
Net Worth: £932,318 *Total Assets:* £1,759,475
Registered Office: Unit 2-4 Protection House, Albion Road, North Shields, Tyne & Wear, NE30 2RH
Activities: Renting and leasing of construction and civil engineering machinery and equipment
Major Shareholder: Michael Wilson
Officers: Michael Wilson [1993] Director

North East Plant Sales Limited
Incorporated: 20 March 1998 *Employees:* 75
Net Worth: £2,903,146 *Total Assets:* £4,417,782
Registered Office: High Street, Newburn, Newcastle upon Tyne, NE15 8LN
Activities: Other business support service activities n.e.c.
Officers: David James Blakelock, Secretary; David James Blakelock [1973] Director/Engineer; David Blakelock [1950] Director/Engineer; Julie Stabler [1973] Finance Director

North East Property and Investments Limited
Incorporated: 19 February 2007
Net Worth: £1,755,660 *Total Assets:* £1,871,019
Registered Office: Bulman House, Regent Centre, Gosforth, Newcastle upon Tyne, NE3 3LS
Activities: Other letting and operating of own or leased real estate
Parent: Thirston Property & Investments Limited
Officers: Stephen Cowell, Secretary/Director; Stephen Cowell [1951] Director; Cheryl Patricia Foreman [1958] Director

North East Regeneration Partnership LLP
Incorporated: 11 April 2013 *Employees:* 2
Net Worth Deficit: £994,474 *Total Assets:* £16,155,414
Registered Office: 2nd Floor, Building 7, Queens Park, Queensway, Team Valley Trading Estate, Gateshead, Tyne & Wear, NE11 0QD

The North East Regional Investment Fund Partner Limited
Incorporated: 20 June 2006 *Employees:* 3
Total Assets: £27,540,930
Registered Office: 3rd Floor, Baltimore House, Abbotts Hill, Gateshead, Tyne & Wear, NE8 3DF
Activities: Activities of investment trusts
Officers: Andrew James Arkless, Secretary; Hilary Patricia Florek [1960] Director/PR Consultant; Geoffrey Mark Hodgson [1961] Director; Stephen John Lightley [1957] Director/Chartered Accountant; Kathryn Lucy Hay Winskell [1963] Director/Pro Vice Chancellor

North East Roof Truss Limited
Incorporated: 15 March 2011 *Employees:* 1
Net Worth: £1,716 *Total Assets:* £887,041
Registered Office: 2 Rainhill Close, Stephenson Industrial Estate, Washington, Tyne & Wear, NE37 3HU
Activities: Other manufacturing n.e.c.
Major Shareholder: Kevin Gray
Officers: Kevin Gray [1957] Director; Lisa Marie Short [1975] Director/Finance Manager

North East Theatre Trust Limited
Incorporated: 9 February 1983 *Employees:* 27
Net Worth: £9,112,596 *Total Assets:* £15,851,437
Registered Office: 29 Broad Chare, Newcastle upon Tyne, NE1 3DQ
Activities: Artistic creation
Officers: James Patrick Beirne, Secretary/Manager; Susan Brown [1956] Director of Communications; Paul Michael Callaghan [1952] Director; Susan Emmas [1964] Associate Artistic Director; Professor Peter Michael Fidler [1947] Director/Retired; Michael Francis Henry [1947] Director/Leader of Gateshead Council; James Rhys McKinnell [1976] Director/Restaurateur; Michelle Frances Percy [1968] Marketing Director; Susan Margaret Wilson [1952] Director; Kathryn Lucy Hay Winskell [1963] Director/Solicitor

North East Truck & Van Holdings Limited
Incorporated: 6 August 2014 *Employees:* 228
Net Worth: £1,162,000 *Total Assets:* £26,162,000
Registered Office: Cowpen Bewley Road, Haverton Hill, Billingham, Cleveland, TS23 4EX
Activities: Activities of other holding companies n.e.c.
Shareholders: John William McDonald; Amanda Lauren McDonald; Hugh Benson Welch
Officers: Ian Thomas Hopkins [1966] Director; Alexander William McDonald [1955] Director; John William McDonald [1989] Director

North East Truck & Van Limited
Incorporated: 3 February 1993 *Employees:* 232
Net Worth: £5,336,000 *Total Assets:* £26,549,000
Registered Office: Cowpen Bewley Road, Haverton Hill, Billingham, Cleveland, TS23 4EX
Activities: Sale of new cars and light motor vehicles
Parent: North East Truck & Van Holdings Limited
Officers: Ian Thomas Hopkins [1966] Commercial Director; David Alistair Jackson [1967] Aftersales Quality and Development Director; Paula Marie Knight [1968] Director; Steven Lane [1963] Director; Alexander William McDonald [1955] Managing Director; John William McDonald [1989] Director; Norman Whittaker [1941] Director

North East Wholesale Fruit & Vegetable Market Limited
Incorporated: 31 January 1966
Net Worth: £281,015 *Total Assets:* £934,912
Registered Office: Administration Centre, North East Fruit & Vegetable Market, Gateshead, Tyne & Wear, NE11 0QY
Activities: Wholesale of fruit and vegetables
Officers: Dudley Colin Alexander Baty [1959] Director; John Holland [1960] Director; Michael Robert Orange [1965] Director/Self Employed; Eamon Quigley [1947] Director/Haulage Contractor; David Alan Shield [1972] Director/General Manager

North East Workspace Limited
Incorporated: 22 March 1990
Registered Office: Unit 3, Ground Floor, 7-15 Pink Lane, Newcastle upon Tyne, NE1 5DW
Activities: Other letting and operating of own or leased real estate
Officers: Nathaniel Richard Mathwin Clark [1957] Director/Manager; James Paul Hedland [1965] Director/Chartered Surveyor; Andrew Ceri Jones [1965] Director; Caroline Pilling [1965] Director/Communications Manager; Timothy Ralph Smith [1959] Director/Solicitor

North Eastern Glass Limited
Incorporated: 9 January 1979 *Employees:* 49
Net Worth: £1,116,168 *Total Assets:* £1,902,421
Registered Office: Viking Works, Hamsterley, Newcastle upon Tyne, NE17 7SY
Activities: Glazing
Parent: NEG Holdings Limited
Officers: Gary Alistair Foster, Secretary; Malcolm Carr [1963] Director/Contract Manager; Gary Stephen Hall [1962] Group Managing Director; Bryan Thompson [1970] Works Director; Clifford Graham Francis Thompson [1966] Contracts Director; Derrick Thompson [1943] Managing Director

North Eastern Y.W.C.A.Trustees Limited
Incorporated: 7 September 1961 *Employees:* 25
Net Worth: £6,870,961 *Total Assets:* £7,120,879
Registered Office: Jesmond House, Clayton Road, Newcastle upon Tyne, NE2 1UJ
Activities: Other accommodation
Officers: Peter Lewis Allen, Secretary; Linda Baird Adams [1965] Director/Business Manager; Roger Robert Darsley [1943] Director/Retired Factory Manager; David Mackintosh Gibson [1967] Director/Solicitor; Victoria Gray [1984] Director/HR Coordinator; Linda Hitman [1952] Director/CEO Exclusive North East Ltd; Caroline Mortlock [1976] Director/H E S Manager; Derek James Smith [1950] Director/Retired Electrician; Janet Smith [1957] Director/Retired

North England Laboratory Supplies Ltd
Incorporated: 10 November 2000 *Employees:* 10
Net Worth: £211,151 *Total Assets:* £816,227
Registered Office: 7 Cumbie Way, Aycliffe Industrial Park, Newton Aycliffe, Co Durham, DL5 6YA
Activities: Other business support service activities n.e.c.
Shareholders: Walter Gordon Campbell McQuilkin; Walter Scott Kelso McQuilkin; Lindsay Reid McQuilkin
Officers: Lindsay Reid McQuilkin, Secretary; Scott McQuilkin [1974] Director; Walter Gordon Campbell McQuilkin [1945] Director/Chairman

North Lakes Foods Limited
Incorporated: 30 May 2002 *Employees:* 39
Net Worth: £271,936 *Total Assets:* £1,630,613
Registered Office: c/o Greencroft Milk Supplies Ltd, Telford Road, Middlesbrough, Cleveland, TS3 8BL
Activities: Liquid milk and cream production
Parent: Greencroft Milk Supplies Ltd
Officers: Janice Parker, Secretary; Michael Brian Doyle [1964] Director; Derek Parker [1961] Director; Janice Parker [1965] Director and Company Secretary; Jonathon Parker [1992] Director; Ian Richard Simpson [1956] Director

North Lodge Farming Limited
Incorporated: 6 March 1996
Net Worth: £5,442,880 *Total Assets:* £5,955,821
Registered Office: Elemore Grange Farm, Littletown, Co Durham, DH6 1QE
Activities: Financial intermediation not elsewhere classified
Officers: Eric Brannigan, Secretary; Robert Edward Duncombe-Shafto [1951] Director/Land Owner; Andrew Michael Playle [1969] Director; William Thomas Weston [1937] Director/Land Agent

North Music Trust
Incorporated: 1 August 2000 *Employees:* 449
Net Worth: £7,171,602 *Total Assets:* £12,696,555
Registered Office: Sage Gateshead, St Marys Square, Gateshead, Tyne & Wear, NE8 2JR
Activities: Performing arts
Officers: Colin Johnston, Secretary; Abigail Pogson, Secretary; Alistair Miles Anderson [1948] Director/Musician, Composer & Educator; Councillor David Berry Bradford [1953] Director/Councillor; Emily Cox [1978] Director of Public Affairs; Subashis Das [1984] Theatre Director; Lord Charles Leslie Falconer [1951] Director/Barrister, QC; Hilary Patricia Florek [1960] Managing Director; Martin Gannon [1958] Director/Office Manager for Ian Means MP; Young Herb Kim [1967] Director/Chief Executive [American]; Roy James McEwan-Brown [1951] Director/Retired; Sir Martin James Narey [1955] Director/Semi Retired; Vidya Sarangapani [1980] Director/Doctoral Researcher; Jacinta Mary Scannell [1963] Director [Irish]; Jane Wyman Spiers [1955] Director/Chief Executive; Susan Lois Underwood [1956] Director/Retired; Tony Wadsworth [1956] Director/Chairman

North of England Civic Trust
Incorporated: 29 July 1982 *Employees:* 6
Net Worth: £1,993,111 *Total Assets:* £2,331,849
Registered Office: The Schoolhouse, Trinity Chare, Quayside, Newcastle upon Tyne, NE1 3DF
Activities: Other professional, scientific and technical activities n.e.c.
Officers: Adrian Banford [1961] Director/Heritage Professional; Peter Bromley [1955] Director/Heritage Consultant; Peter Haswell Candler [1953] Managing Director; Barbara Joan Gubbins [1952] Director/Chief Executive; Deborah Mary Jenkins [1959] Director; Celia Katherine MacKenzie [1959] Director/Chief Executive; Michael Moody [1965] Director; Christopher John Mullin [1947] Director/Retired; Prof. Robert David Pickard [1957] Director/Heritage Conservation Consultant; Barry Neil Speker [1947] Director/Solicitor

North of England Estates Limited
Incorporated: 7 May 1934 *Employees:* 258
Net Worth: £9,949,859 *Total Assets:* £13,649,389
Registered Office: 1-3 Lansdowne Terrace, Gosforth, Newcastle upon Tyne, NE3 1HN
Activities: Hotels and similar accommodation
Shareholders: Donald Clive McKeag; Tessa Rosemary McKeag
Officers: John Colin Fitzpatrick, Secretary; John Colin Fitzpatrick [1955] Director/Chartered Accountant; Nigel Galvin [1967] Director/Golf Manager; Donald Clive McKeag [1930] Director/Solicitor; Tessa Rosemary McKeag [1937] Director; Daniel George Smith [1983] Director/Financial Adviser

North of England Protecting and Indemnity Association Limited (The)
Incorporated: 14 March 1952 *Employees:* 363
Net Worth: £182,339,296 *Total Assets:* £915,450,752
Registered Office: North of England P and I Association Limited, The Quayside, Newcastle upon Tyne, NE1 3DU
Activities: Non-life insurance
Officers: Christopher Philip Owen, Secretary; Jacobus Martinus de Groot [1960] Director/Legal & Contracts Manager [Dutch]; Albert Engelsman [1949] Director [Dutch]; Lord Nicholas John Albert Fairfax [1956] Director; Nicholas John Oxleigh Fell [1963] Director; Trevor Frank Hart [1944] Director; Paul Andrew Jennings [1962] Joint Managing Director; Peter Medwell Johnson [1948] Director; Alexander McKay Lynch [1949] Independent Non-Executive Director; Johanna Procopiou [1978] Director; Johann-Philipp Ferdinand Reith [1978] Managing Director [German]; Pratap Baburao Shirke [1948] Director; Nicholas Ronald Taylor [1952] Director/Consultant; James Alexander Tyrrell [1979] Executive Director [Irish]; Alan Andrew Wilson [1955] Joint Managing Director

North Sport Fishing Industry LLP
Incorporated: 20 January 2014
Net Worth Deficit: £3,043 *Total Assets:* £887,272
Registered Office: 9 King Charles Tower, Shield Field, Newcastle upon Tyne, NE2 1XX

North Tees Group Holdings Limited
Incorporated: 10 March 2016
Net Worth: £29,142,268 *Total Assets:* £29,445,254
Registered Office: Sintons LLP, Barrack Road, Newcastle upon Tyne, NE4 6DB
Activities: Activities of other holding companies n.e.c.
Major Shareholder: Ian George Hunter
Officers: Ian George Hunter [1964] Director

North Tees Holdings Limited
Incorporated: 24 June 2010
Net Worth: £26,518,068 *Total Assets:* £28,760,606
Registered Office: The Cube, Barrack Road, Newcastle upon Tyne, NE4 6DB
Activities: Activities of other holding companies n.e.c.
Major Shareholder: Ian George Hunter
Officers: Ian George Hunter [1964] Director

North Tees Limited
Incorporated: 1 March 2005 *Employees:* 2
Net Worth: £26,900,620 *Total Assets:* £30,986,164
Registered Office: The Cube, Barrack Road, Newcastle upon Tyne, NE4 6DB
Activities: Other business support service activities n.e.c.
Parent: North Tees Holdings Limited
Officers: Ian George Hunter [1964] Director

North Tees Waste Management Limited
Incorporated: 15 May 2003 *Employees:* 2
Net Worth: £799,653 *Total Assets:* £851,933
Registered Office: The Cube, Barrack Road, Newcastle upon Tyne, NE4 6DB
Activities: Treatment and disposal of non-hazardous waste
Parent: North Tees Holdings Limited
Officers: Ian George Hunter [1964] Director

North Tyneside Learning Trust
Incorporated: 23 August 2010 *Employees:* 14
Net Worth: £1,399,198 *Total Assets:* £1,617,889
Registered Office: Churchill Community College, Churchill Street, Wallsend, Tyne & Wear, NE28 7TN
Activities: Other education n.e.c.
Officers: Kehri Ellis, Secretary; Laura Jane Baggett [1968] Director/Headteacher; David Mark Baldwin [1962] Director/Headteacher; Richard Peter Carmichael [1979] Partnership Director with Capita; Tracy Ann Crowder-Cloe [1974] Director/Headteacher; Jane Elizabeth Delany [1968] Director/Lecturer; Peter Gerard Earley [1962] Director/HR Consultant; Peter Gannon [1973] Director/Headteacher; Alexander William Giles [1966] Director/Marketing Consultant; David Ian Hodgson [1956] Director, Health Safety & Environment

North Tyneside Properties Limited
Incorporated: 7 July 2016 *Employees:* 2
Net Worth: £3,405,467 *Total Assets:* £3,766,220
Registered Office: Bell Anderson Limited, 264-266 Durham Road, Gateshead, Tyne & Wear, NE8 4JR
Activities: Other business support service activities n.e.c.
Major Shareholder: Sean Simon Heaney
Officers: Debbie Heaney [1970] Director; Sean Simon Heaney [1961] Director

North View Academy
Incorporated: 9 June 2014 *Employees:* 32
Net Worth: £1,120,000 *Total Assets:* £1,720,000
Registered Office: North View Academy, St Luke's Road, Sunderland, Tyne & Wear, SR4 0HB
Activities: Primary education
Officers: Diane Elizabeth Dimmock [1956] Director/Retired; Avril Godfrey [1950] Director/Retired; Kelly Ann Lawton [1977] Director/HR Consultant; Gary Mellefont [1967] Director/Headteacher; Faye Louise Taylor [1988] Director/Housewife; Angela Ward [1971] Director/Specialist Public Health Nurse; Helen Williams [1982] Director/Foster Carer; Lisa Winship [1972] Director/Teacher

North West Merchandising Limited
Incorporated: 20 September 2000
Net Worth: £2,874,504 *Total Assets:* £2,874,504
Registered Office: c/o Nike (UK) Limited, Camberwell Way, Doxford International Technology Park, Sunderland, Tyne & Wear, SR3 3XN
Activities: Other business support service activities n.e.c.
Parent: Nike, Inc.
Officers: Marcus Arnold Keane [1969] Director [American/Dutch]

North Yorkshire Timber Company Limited
Incorporated: 10 May 1979 *Employees:* 199
Net Worth: £4,067,071 *Total Assets:* £11,146,615
Registered Office: Standard House, Thurston Road, Northallerton Business Park, Northallerton, N Yorks, DL6 2NA
Activities: Wholesale of wood, construction materials and sanitary equipment
Parent: NYT (Holdings) Limited
Officers: Victor Paul Bellas [1964] Director/Timber Salesman; John Alexander George Douglas [1964] Finance Director; Nicholas Peter Kershaw [1972] Managing Director; Neil Andrew McGill [1977] Investment Director; Robert Timmens [1966] Director/Timber Salesman; Stuart Whiteford [1990] Director

Northallerton Auctions Limited
Incorporated: 9 April 1912 *Employees:* 25
Net Worth: £3,067,958 *Total Assets:* £3,463,569
Registered Office: Applegarth Mart, Romanby Road, Northallerton, N Yorks, DL7 8LZ
Activities: Other business support service activities n.e.c.
Officers: Brian Weighell, Secretary; Mark Allen Corner [1971] Director/Farmer; Charles Michael Duffus [1959] Director/Farmer; Martin Jeremy Harland [1965] Director/Farmer; Alan Francis Harrison [1951] Director/Investor; Alan Watson [1954] Director/Farmer; Brian Weighell [1958] Director

Northallerton Properties Limited
Incorporated: 24 May 1962
Net Worth: £1,103,887 *Total Assets:* £1,110,159
Registered Office: 5 The Laurels, Northallerton, N Yorks, DL6 1SA
Activities: Other letting and operating of own or leased real estate
Major Shareholder: Mark Gibson Willoughby
Officers: Mark Gibson Willoughby, Secretary; Lynda Jane Willoughby [1961] Director/Shop Assistant; Mark Gibson Willoughby [1959] Director/Newsagent

Northdale Rotary Engineering Limited
Incorporated: 11 March 1981
Net Worth: £894,493 *Total Assets:* £1,004,866
Registered Office: Tofts Farm Industrial Estate West, Brenda Road, Hartlepool, Cleveland, TS25 2BQ
Activities: Machining
Major Shareholder: Susan Gail George
Officers: Susan Gail George, Secretary; Susan Gail George [1960] Director/Accountant

Northeast Sheets & Panels Limited
Incorporated: 16 December 1997
Net Worth: £472,257 *Total Assets:* £2,028,834
Registered Office: Pinnacle House, Harelaw Industrial Estate, Harelaw, Annfield Plain, Stanley, Co Durham, DH9 8UJ
Activities: Manufacture of kitchen furniture
Parent: L & R Holdings Limited
Officers: Lisa Williams [1968] Director; Richard Stephen Williams [1964] Director

Northeastern Finance Limited
Incorporated: 25 June 1985
Net Worth: £1,787,406 *Total Assets:* £2,042,249
Registered Office: 2 Houndgate, Darlington, Co Durham, DL1 5RL
Activities: Financial intermediation not elsewhere classified
Major Shareholder: Luke Peter Gray Wall-Row
Officers: Mark Stansfield, Secretary; Mark Stansfield [1958] Director; Luke Peter Gray Wallrow [1958] Director/Bullion Dealer

Northern 2 VCT PLC
Incorporated: 8 January 1999
Net Worth: £87,043,000 *Total Assets:* £87,177,000
Registered Office: Time Central, 32 Gallowgate, Newcastle upon Tyne, NE1 4SN
Activities: Financial intermediation not elsewhere classified
Officers: James Kirk Bryce, Secretary; Alastair Macbeth Conn [1955] Director/Investment Manager; Simon Devonshire [1967] Director; David Peter Anthony Gravells [1949] Director; Cecilia Ann McAnulty [1963] Director/Fund Management; Frank Leslie George Neale [1950] Director

Northern 3 VCT PLC
Incorporated: 3 September 2001
Net Worth: £69,892,000 *Total Assets:* £75,180,000
Registered Office: Time Central, 32 Gallowgate, Newcastle upon Tyne, NE1 4SN
Activities: Financial intermediation not elsewhere classified
Officers: James Kirk Bryce, Secretary; James Gordon Dickson Ferguson [1947] Director; Christopher John Fleetwood [1951] Director; Timothy Roland Levett [1949] Director; John Maclaren Ogilvie Waddell [1956] Director

Northern Archaeological Associates Limited
Incorporated: 19 March 1999 *Employees:* 70
Net Worth: £1,072,226 *Total Assets:* £1,420,904
Registered Office: 28 Marwood House, Harmire Enterprise Park, Barnard Castle, Co Durham, DL12 8BN
Activities: Environmental consulting activities
Shareholders: Richard Fraser; Helen Mary Fraser
Officers: Helen Mary Fraser, Secretary; Helen Mary Fraser [1958] Director/Archaeologist

Northern Bear Building Services Limited
Incorporated: 19 February 2013
Net Worth: £523,595 *Total Assets:* £2,604,360
Registered Office: Unit 333 Dukesway Court, Team Valley Trading Estate, Gateshead, Tyne & Wear, NE11 0BH
Activities: Other specialised construction activities n.e.c.
Parent: Northern Bear PLC
Officers: Wendy Ann Edgell, Secretary; Graham Roy Jennings [1956] Director; Neil Jukes [1972] Director; Steven Mark Roberts [1966] Director; Keith Soulsby [1956] Director; Brian Wilkinson [1957] Contracts Director

Northern Bear PLC
Incorporated: 13 April 2006 *Employees:* 368
Net Worth: £19,692,000 *Total Assets:* £32,838,000
Registered Office: A1 Grainger, Prestwick Park, Prestwick, Ponteland, Northumberland, NE20 9SJ
Activities: Other specialised construction activities n.e.c.
Officers: Wendy Ann Edgell, Secretary; Howard Barry Gold [1943] Director; Thomas Edward Hayes [1978] Director/Chartered Accountant; Graham Roy Jennings [1956] Managing Director; Ian Thomas McLean [1953] Director; Steven Mark Roberts [1966] Director; Keith Soulsby [1956] Director

Northern Bespoke Developments Ltd
Incorporated: 15 April 2011 *Employees:* 4
Net Worth: £328,403 *Total Assets:* £807,254
Registered Office: 3b Lockheed Court, Preston Farm, Stockton on Tees, Cleveland, TS18 3SH
Activities: Development of building projects
Shareholders: John Patrick Hughes; Gerard May
Officers: John Patrick Hughes [1972] Director; Gerard May [1974] Director

Northern Commercial Properties Limited
Incorporated: 8 October 2001
Net Worth: £2,645,214 *Total Assets:* £3,421,248
Registered Office: Estates Office, Alnwick Castle, Alnwick, Northumberland, NE66 1NQ
Activities: Other letting and operating of own or leased real estate
Major Shareholder: Lord James Percy
Officers: Lesley Ann Ilderton, Secretary; Lesley Ann Ilderton [1976] Director/Group Financial Controller; Lord James Percy [1965] Director; Roderick Charles St John Wilson [1961] Director/Land Agent

Northern Construction Solutions Limited
Incorporated: 3 January 2002 *Employees:* 57
Net Worth: £534,224 *Total Assets:* £3,683,223
Registered Office: 6 Lumley Court, Drum Road, Chester-le-Street, Co Durham, DH2 1AN
Activities: Construction of commercial buildings
Shareholders: NCS Group Holdings Ltd; David Paul Gardner; Sean James Anderson
Officers: Sean James Anderson, Secretary/Director; Sean James Anderson [1965] Director; David Paul Gardner [1965] Director/Commercial

Northern Counties Guarantee Corporation Limited
Incorporated: 24 December 1928
Net Worth: £5,632,545 *Total Assets:* £5,676,055
Registered Office: NCI House, Lowreys Lane, Low Fell, Gateshead, Tyne & Wear, NE9 5JB
Activities: Other letting and operating of own or leased real estate
Shareholders: Carole Belgian; David James Belgian
Officers: Carole Belgian, Secretary; Carole Belgian [1952] Director/Company Secretary; David James Belgian [1951] Director; Fiona Margaret Belgian [1977] Operations Director; Philip Belgian [1975] Director/Insurance Broker

Northern Counties LLP
Incorporated: 22 October 2008 *Employees:* 23
Net Worth: £2,372,446 *Total Assets:* £2,394,121
Registered Office: NCI House, Lowerys Lane, Low Fell, Gateshead, Tyne & Wear, NE9 5JB
Officers: David James Belgian [1951] Member; Carole Belgian [1952] LLP Member; Philip Belgian [1975] LLP Member

Northern Education Trust
Incorporated: 15 March 2010 *Employees:* 1,432
Net Worth: £131,506,000 *Total Assets:* £157,928,992
Registered Office: Cobalt Business Exchange Central, Unit 5 Silver Fox Way, Cobalt Business Park, Wallsend, Tyne & Wear, NE27 0QJ
Activities: Primary education
Officers: Christine Hopkins, Secretary; John Copping [1961] Director/Civil Engineer; Suzanne Duncan [1971] Director/Chief Executive; Gareth Evan Edmunds [1976] Director of Finance; June Foster [1954] Director/Retired; Thomas Grieveson [1953] Director/Retired; Andrew Hodgson [1964] Director; Christopher Anthony Roberts [1950] Director/Consultant; Mark Henry Sanders [1954] Director/Retired; Robert David Tarn [1972] Director/Headteacher; Leslie Howard Walton [1945] Director/Education Advisor

Northern Electric Finance PLC
Incorporated: 20 June 1995
Net Worth Deficit: £1,265,000 *Total Assets:* £252,998,000
Registered Office: Lloyds Court, 78 Grey Street, Newcastle upon Tyne, NE1 6AF
Activities: Financial intermediation not elsewhere classified
Parent: Northern Powergrid (Northeast) Limited
Officers: Jennifer Catherine Riley, Secretary; Thomas Edward Fielden [1970] Director/Chartered Accountant; Thomas Hugh France [1985] Director/Lawyer; Dr Philip Antony Jones [1968] Director/President & Chief Executive Officer; Stephen John Lockwood [1965] Director/Accountant

Northern Electric PLC
Incorporated: 1 April 1989 *Employees:* 1,270
Net Worth: £974,774,016 *Total Assets:* £2,503,973,120
Registered Office: Lloyds Court, 78 Grey Street, Newcastle upon Tyne, NE1 6AF
Activities: Activities of other holding companies n.e.c.
Parent: Northern Powergrid Limited
Officers: Jennifer Catherine Riley, Secretary; Thomas Edward Fielden [1970] Director/Chartered Accountant; Thomas Hugh France [1985] Director/Solicitor; Patrick Jerome Goodman [1966] Director/Senior VP & Chief Financial [American]; Dr Philip Antony Jones [1968] Director/President & Chief Executive Officer; John Nigel Reynolds [1966] Director

Northern Electric Properties Limited
Incorporated: 17 July 1990
Net Worth: £39,953,000 *Total Assets:* £40,957,000
Registered Office: Lloyds Court, 78 Grey Street, Newcastle upon Tyne, NE1 6AF
Activities: Management of real estate on a fee or contract basis
Parent: Northern Electric PLC
Officers: Jennifer Catherine Riley, Secretary; Thomas Edward Fielden [1970] Director/Chartered Accountant; Thomas Hugh France [1985] Director/Lawyer; Dr Philip Antony Jones [1968] Director/President & Chief Executive Officer

Northern Estates and Investment Company Limited (The)
Incorporated: 21 May 1914
Net Worth: £1,221,300 *Total Assets:* £1,525,335
Registered Office: 18 Northumberland Square, North Shields, Tyne & Wear, NE30 1PX
Activities: Other letting and operating of own or leased real estate
Shareholder: Peter Richard Jackson
Officers: Robert Alan Storey, Secretary/Chartered Surveyor; Garnet Duff Burton [1948] Director/Building Contractor; Peter Timothy Burton [1985] Director; Peter Richard Jackson [1949] Director/Chartered Surveyor; Richard Merlin Jackson [1980] Director; Robert Alan Storey [1956] Director

Northern Floorcraft (Gateshead) Limited
Incorporated: 11 April 1973 *Employees:* 31
Net Worth: £930,074 *Total Assets:* £1,777,749
Registered Office: Bensham Trading Estate, Lobley Hill Road, Gateshead, Tyne & Wear, NE8 2XN
Activities: Floor and wall covering
Officers: Anthony Bowles, Secretary; Raymond Arthur Pearson [1941] Director; Warren Mark Pearson [1962] Director/Surveyor

Northern Gas & Power Ltd
Incorporated: 5 March 2013 *Employees:* 8
Net Worth: £1,065,016 *Total Assets:* £3,877,456
Registered Office: Baltic Place, East Tower, South Shore Road, Gateshead, Tyne & Wear, NE8 3AE
Activities: Other business support service activities n.e.c.
Parent: Global Procurement Group Limited
Officers: Fokhrul Islam [1982] Director; Andrew Laird [1987] Director; Sean Francis McCann [1988] Director

Northern General Properties Limited
Incorporated: 2 February 1939 *Employees:* 3
Net Worth: £12,602,672 *Total Assets:* £14,068,593
Registered Office: Thornton House, Cargo Fleet Lane, Middlesbrough, Cleveland, TS3 8DE
Activities: Other letting and operating of own or leased real estate
Parent: Atkinson Northern Ltd
Officers: Jeremy John Boyd, Secretary/Chartered Accountant; James Edwin Atkinson [1957] Director/Builders Merchant; Mark Robert Atkinson [1967] Director/Builders Merchant; Jeremy John Boyd [1955] Director/Accountant

Northern Grid for Learning
Incorporated: 7 July 2003
Net Worth: £297,075 *Total Assets:* £988,897
Registered Office: Langdale Centre, Langdale Gardens, Wallsend, Tyne & Wear, NE28 0HG
Activities: Educational support services
Officers: Jonathan Mark Chicken [1972] Director/School Improvement Officer; Michael John Hamilton [1965] Director/IT Manager; Jane Melanie Wright [1957] Director/Local Authority Officer

Northern Guild Limited
Incorporated: 16 August 2010 *Employees:* 12
Net Worth: £1,140,660 *Total Assets:* £1,824,590
Registered Office: 83 Jesmond Road, Newcastle upon Tyne, NE2 1NH
Activities: Other human health activities
Shareholders: Andrew McNamara; Jennifer McNamara; Christine Anne Lister-Ford
Officers: Jennifer McNamara, Secretary; Christine Anne Lister-Ford [1951] Director/Psychotherapist; Andrew McNamara [1966] Director/Actuary; Jennifer McNamara [1948] Director/Psychotherapist

Northern Housing Consortium Limited
Incorporated: 25 January 2002 *Employees:* 29
Net Worth: £9,198 *Total Assets:* £1,857,154
Registered Office: Loftus House, Colima Avenue, Sunderland Enterprise Park, Sunderland, Tyne & Wear, SR5 3XB
Activities: Activities of business and employers membership organisations
Officers: Catherine Rosemary Wilmot, Secretary; Ian Robert Ankers [1963] Director of Business Development; Nicholas St.John Atkin [1968] Director/Group Chief Executive; Stephen Roy Close [1958] Director/Group Chief Executive; Paul Fiddaman [1965] Director/Group Chief Executive; Michael Laing [1964] Associate Director, Community Services; Karen Jayne Lythe [1966] Director/Service Manager Housing and Regeneration; Thomas Michael Miskell [1955] Director/Chairman; Michael MacKay Palin [1981] Director/Chief Executive; Gregory Maxwell Robinson [1962] Director/Assistant Chief Executive; Sarah English Robson [1971] Director/Head of Economic Development and Housing; Christine Smith [1962] Business Development Director; Barbara Spicer [1964] Director/Chief Executive; Robert Clive Young [1955] Director/Chief Executive

Northern Ladies Annuity Society
Incorporated: 17 March 2003 *Employees:* 2
Net Worth: £5,822,021 *Total Assets:* £5,837,171
Registered Office: MEA House, Ellison Place, Newcastle upon Tyne, NE1 8XS
Activities: Combined office administrative service activities
Officers: Jean Ferry, Secretary; Suzanne Elaine Armstrong [1964] Director/Homemaker; Diana Mary Audrey Barkes [1959] Director; Diana Mary Braithwaite [1955] Director/Housewife; Sarah Westcott Crone [1959] Director/Solicitor; Annabel Jane Dickinson [1965] Director; Fiona Elizabeth Emmerson [1963] Director/Practice Manager; Elizabeth Etridge Inglis [1930] Director; Ursula Elizabeth Martell [1945] Director/Retired Doctor; Claire Morgan [1951] Director/Solicitor; Susan Veronica Ridley [1941] Director; April Freda Claire Stephenson [1930] Director; Catherine Mary Wood [1959] Director/Solicitor and Fee Paid Tribunal Judge; Jane Wood [1947] Director/Housewife

Northern Lights Energy Limited
Incorporated: 9 September 1996 *Employees:* 10
Net Worth: £895,598 *Total Assets:* £1,137,180
Registered Office: Stephenson House, Richard Street, Hetton-le-Hole, Co Durham, DH5 9HW
Activities: Wholesale of wood, construction materials and sanitary equipment
Shareholder: Stanley Nelson
Officers: Jason Nelson, Secretary; Jason Nelson [1971] Director; Stanley Nelson [1945] Director

Northern Powergrid (Northeast) Limited
Incorporated: 9 March 1994 *Employees:* 1,072
Net Worth: £975,708,032 *Total Assets:* £2,462,428,928
Registered Office: Lloyds Court, 78 Grey Street, Newcastle upon Tyne, NE1 6AF
Activities: Distribution of electricity
Parent: Northern Electric PLC
Officers: Jennifer Catherine Riley, Secretary; Thomas Edward Fielden [1970] Director/Chartered Accountant; Thomas Hugh France [1985] Director/Lawyer; Nicholas Michael Gill [1964] Utility Director; Dr Philip Antony Jones [1968] Director/President & Chief Executive Officer; Andrew John MacLennan [1967] Managing Director; Alison Ruth Marshall [1965] Director; Professor Philip Charles Taylor [1970] Director/University Academic

Northern Powergrid (Yorkshire) PLC
Incorporated: 22 November 2000 *Employees:* 1,187
Net Worth: £1,238,896,000 *Total Assets:* £3,322,706,944
Registered Office: Lloyds Court, 78 Grey Street, Newcastle upon Tyne, NE1 6AF
Activities: Distribution of electricity
Parent: Yorkshire Electricity Group PLC
Officers: Jennifer Catherine Riley, Secretary; Thomas Edward Fielden [1970] Director/Chartered Accountant; Thomas Hugh France [1985] Director/Lawyer; Nicholas Michael Gill [1964] Utility Director; Dr Philip Antony Jones [1968] Director/President and Chief Executive Officer; Andrew John MacLennan [1967] Managing Director; Alison Ruth Marshall [1965] Director; Professor Philip Charles Taylor [1970] Director/University Academic

Northern Powergrid Gas Limited
Incorporated: 23 November 2001
Net Worth: £36,000,000 *Total Assets:* £36,000,000
Registered Office: Lloyds Court, 78 Grey Street, Newcastle upon Tyne, NE1 6AF
Activities: Activities of other holding companies n.e.c.
Parent: Northern Powergrid Limited
Officers: Jennifer Catherine Riley, Secretary; Thomas Edward Fielden [1970] Director/Chartered Accountant; Thomas Hugh France [1985] Director/Lawyer; Dr Philip Antony Jones [1968] Director/President & Chief Executive Officer; Michael Jack Sparkes [1959] Director/Manager

Northern Powergrid Holdings Company
Incorporated: 28 November 1997 *Employees:* 2,485
Net Worth: £2,169,636,096 *Total Assets:* £6,051,277,824
Registered Office: Lloyds Court, 78 Grey Street, Newcastle upon Tyne, NE1 6AF
Activities: Activities of other holding companies n.e.c.
Parent: Berkshire Hathaway Inc.
Officers: Jennifer Catherine Riley, Secretary; William Joseph Fehrman [1960] Director/President and Chief Executive Officer [American]; Thomas Edward Fielden [1970] Director/Chartered Accountant; Thomas Hugh France [1985] Director/Solicitor; Patrick Jerome Goodman [1966] Director/Senior VP & Chief Financial [American]; Dr Philip Antony Jones [1968] Director/President & Chief Executive Officer; John Nigel Reynolds [1966] Director

Northern Powergrid Limited
Incorporated: 24 October 1996
Net Worth: £827,086,016 *Total Assets:* £827,446,976
Registered Office: Lloyds Court, 78 Grey Street, Newcastle upon Tyne, NE1 6AF
Activities: Activities of other holding companies n.e.c.
Parent: Northern Powergrid UK Holdings
Officers: Jennifer Catherine Riley, Secretary; Thomas Edward Fielden [1970] Director/Chartered Accountant; Thomas Hugh France [1985] Director/Solicitor; Dr Philip Antony Jones [1968] Director/President & Chief Executive Officer

Northern Powergrid Metering Limited
Incorporated: 25 May 2011 *Employees:* 13
Net Worth: £15,781,000 *Total Assets:* £296,857,984
Registered Office: 2nd Floor, Lloyds Court, 78 Grey Street, Newcastle upon Tyne, NE1 6AF
Activities: Renting and leasing of other machinery, equipment and tangible goods n.e.c.
Parent: Northern Electric PLC
Officers: Jennifer Catherine Riley, Secretary; Thomas Edward Fielden [1970] Director/Chartered Accountant; Thomas Hugh France [1985] Director/Lawyer; Dr Philip Antony Jones [1968] Director/President & Chief Executive Officer; Andrew John MacLennan [1967] Managing Director

Northern Powergrid UK Holdings
Incorporated: 24 October 1996
Net Worth: £451,406,016 *Total Assets:* £718,510,976
Registered Office: Lloyds Court, 78 Grey Street, Newcastle upon Tyne, NE1 6AF
Activities: Activities of other holding companies n.e.c.
Parent: Northern Powergrid Holdings Company
Officers: Jennifer Catherine Riley, Secretary; Thomas Edward Fielden [1970] Director/Chartered Accountant; Thomas Hugh France [1985] Director/Solicitor; Dr Philip Antony Jones [1968] Director/President & Chief Executive Officer

Northern Property Partnership LLP
Incorporated: 4 August 2008
Net Worth: £708,594 *Total Assets:* £1,605,701
Registered Office: Express Group, 398A Princesway North, Team Valley Trading Estate, Gateshead, Tyne & Wear, NE11 0TU
Officers: Christopher Scott Thompson [1956] Member; Lynn Wilson [1969] Member

Northern Recruitment Group Limited
Incorporated: 26 September 1983 *Employees:* 85
Net Worth: £3,173,000 *Total Assets:* £5,724,000
Registered Office: Lloyds Court, 56 Grey Street, Newcastle upon Tyne, NE1 6AH
Activities: Other activities of employment placement agencies
Major Shareholder: Catherine Lorna Moran
Officers: Wayham Hutcheson Moran, Secretary/Director; David James Carss [1973] Executive Search & Selection and Business Director; Leanne Margaret Chambers [1975] Client Solutions Director; Marie-Therese Liddle [1965] Director; Catherine Lorna Moran [1950] Director/Employment Consultant; Wayham Hutcheson Moran [1947] Director; Mark Richard Victor Smales [1985] Finance Director

Northern Retail Consortium Limited
Incorporated: 7 April 1986
Net Worth: £3,888,349 *Total Assets:* £4,678,158
Registered Office: Watson Burton LLP, 1 St James' Gate, Newcastle upon Tyne, NE99 1YQ
Activities: Buying and selling of own real estate
Officers: Helen Pollard, Secretary; Anthony Nigel Leon [1950] Director/Chartered Surveyor; Bryan Keith Reynolds [1950] Director/Chartered Surveyor; Deidre Sheldon [1952] Director

Northern Saints Catholic Education Trust
Incorporated: 7 January 2016 *Employees:* 125
Net Worth: £4,244,000 *Total Assets:* £6,329,000
Registered Office: St Wilfrid's RC College, Temple Park Road, South Shields, Tyne & Wear, NE34 0QA
Activities: General secondary education
Officers: Christine Henderson, Secretary; Alan Cormack [1947] Director/NHS Manager; Claire Defty [1968] Managing Director and Legal Director; Marie Graham [1968] Director/Acting Headteacher; Patrick Martin Melia [1967] Director/Chief Exec, Local Government; Thomas Brendan Tapping [1963] Director/Executive Headteacher; Patricia Judith Train [1963] Director/Activities Coordinator

Northern Stage (Theatrical Productions) Limited
Incorporated: 3 November 1987 *Employees:* 85
Net Worth: £5,175,354 *Total Assets:* £6,037,276
Registered Office: Northern Stage, Barras Bridge, Newcastle upon Tyne, NE1 7RH
Activities: Performing arts
Officers: Helen Graham, Secretary; Natalia Blagburn [1975] Director/Senior Lecturer; Anne Bonner [1956] Director/Charity Chief Executive; Laura Collier [1978] Director/Theatre Producer; Simon Peter Elliott [1963] Director/HR Manager; Vikas Kumar [1973] Director of Arts Organisation; Jemima Levick [1977] Artistic Director; Charles Stephen Penn [1961] Marketing Director; Keith Michael Proudfoot [1952] Director/Chartered Accountant; Professor Julie Christina Sanders [1968] Director/University Pro-Vice Chancellor; Timothy Russell Smith [1969] Director/Teacher

Northern Structures Ltd
Incorporated: 8 April 1976 *Employees:* 38
Net Worth: £1,853,168 *Total Assets:* £3,183,599
Registered Office: Amble Industrial Estate, Amble, Northumberland, NE65 0PE
Activities: Construction of commercial buildings
Shareholder: Anthony Nelson
Officers: Anthony Nelson, Secretary; Andrew David Mawson [1979] Sales Director; Ross William Meins [1982] Director; Anthony Nelson [1975] Managing Director; Ian Young [1968] Director

Northern Switchgear & Controls Limited
Incorporated: 28 April 1994 *Employees:* 17
Net Worth: £672,248 *Total Assets:* £1,186,155
Registered Office: Unit 17 Burford Way, Boldon Business Park, Boldon Colliery, Co Durham, NE35 9PZ
Activities: Manufacture of electricity distribution and control apparatus
Shareholders: Craig Robert Boddy; Andrew Ord; Katrina Louise Ord
Officers: Andrew Ord, Secretary; Craig Robert Boddy [1978] Director/Electrical Engineer; Andrew Ord [1980] Director/Electrical Engineer

Northern Transport Finance Limited
Incorporated: 2 November 1988
Net Worth: £8,971,000 *Total Assets:* £12,130,000
Registered Office: Lloyds Court, 78 Grey Street, Newcastle upon Tyne, NE1 6AF
Activities: Financial intermediation not elsewhere classified
Parent: Northern Electric PLC
Officers: Jennifer Catherine Riley, Secretary; Thomas Edward Fielden [1970] Director/Chartered Accountant; Thomas Hugh France [1985] Director/Lawyer; Dr Philip Antony Jones [1968] Director/President & Chief Executive Officer; Stephen John Lockwood [1965] Director/Accountant

Northern Venture Trust PLC
Incorporated: 11 August 1995
Net Worth: £76,260,000 *Total Assets:* £76,341,000
Registered Office: Time Central, 32 Gallowgate, Newcastle upon Tyne, NE1 4SN
Activities: Financial intermediation not elsewhere classified
Officers: James Kirk Bryce, Secretary; Nigel Jonathan Beer [1954] Director; Simon John Constantine [1959] Director; Richard James Green [1962] Director; Timothy Roland Levett [1949] Director; David Andrew Mayes [1964] Director; Hugh Patrick Younger [1958] Director/Writer to The Signet

Northgate (CB 2) Limited
Incorporated: 9 March 2012
Net Worth: £137,216,000 *Total Assets:* £137,216,000
Registered Office: Northgate Centre, Lingfield Way, Darlington, Co Durham, DL1 4PZ
Activities: Other service activities n.e.c.
Parent: Northgate (Europe) Ltd
Officers: Katie Laura Tasker-Wood, Secretary; Richard David Podmore [1979] Director

Northgate (CB) Limited
Incorporated: 23 April 2010
Net Worth: £554,828,992 *Total Assets:* £554,828,992
Registered Office: Northgate Centre, Lingfield Way, Darlington, Co Durham, DL1 4PZ
Activities: Bookkeeping activities
Parent: Northgate (Europe) Limited
Officers: Katie Laura Tasker-Wood, Secretary; Richard David Podmore [1979] Director

Northgate (Europe) Limited
Incorporated: 12 September 2006
Net Worth: £97,710,000 *Total Assets:* £964,588,992
Registered Office: Northgate Centre, Lingfield Way, Darlington, Co Durham, DL1 4PZ
Activities: Activities of other holding companies n.e.c.
Parent: Northgate PLC
Officers: Katie Laura Tasker-Wood, Secretary; Richard David Podmore [1979] Director

Northgate PLC
Incorporated: 2 July 1897 *Employees:* 2,900
Net Worth: £539,128,000 *Total Assets:* £1,118,932,992
Registered Office: Northgate Centre, Lingfield Way, Darlington, Co Durham, DL1 4PZ
Activities: Activities of other holding companies n.e.c.
Officers: Katie Laura Tasker-Wood, Secretary; Andrew James Allner [1953] Director; Kevin Michael Bradshaw [1969] Director; Gillian Caseberry [1965] Director; Claire Miles [1972] Director; Andrew Page [1958] Director; William Spencer [1959] Director; Philip James Vincent [1969] Director/Chief Finance Officer

Northgate Vehicle Hire Limited
Incorporated: 2 July 1979 *Employees:* 1,779
Net Worth: £103,127,000 *Total Assets:* £740,851,968
Registered Office: Northgate Centre, Lingfield Way, Darlington, Co Durham, DL1 4PZ
Activities: Renting and leasing of cars and light motor vehicles
Parent: Northgate PLC
Officers: Katie Laura Tasker-Wood, Secretary; James Benjamin Feller [1983] Finance Director; Frank Mahon Hayes [1967] Director [Irish]; Katie Laura Tasker-Wood [1981] Director

Northgood Industries Limited
Incorporated: 19 August 1964 *Employees:* 3
Net Worth: £13,337,546 *Total Assets:* £13,826,329
Registered Office: 2 Benton Terrace, Sandyford, Newcastle upon Tyne, NE2 1QU
Activities: Buying and selling of own real estate
Shareholder: Kenneth Good
Officers: Kenneth Good, Secretary; Judith Good [1940] Director/Secretary; Kenneth Good [1930] Director; Paul Nicholas Good [1963] Director/Chartered Surveyor

Northland Real Estate Properties (UK) Limited
Incorporated: 10 February 2009 *Employees:* 72
Net Worth Deficit: £414,298 *Total Assets:* £9,264,906
Registered Office: Sandman Signature Hotel, Gallowgate, Newcastle upon Tyne, NE1 4SD
Activities: Construction of commercial buildings
Officers: Mitchell Rockford Gaglardi [1980] Director/Hotel and Restaurant Consultant [Canadian]

Northprop Limited
Incorporated: 22 December 2011
Net Worth: £686,583 *Total Assets:* £950,364
Registered Office: 54 Keswick Street, Gateshead, Tyne & Wear, NE8 1TQ
Activities: Buying and selling of own real estate
Major Shareholder: Martin Zvi Oppenheimer
Officers: Martin Zvi Oppenheimer [1989] Director

Northridge Healthcare Limited
Incorporated: 5 July 2010 *Employees:* 3
Net Worth: £58,656 *Total Assets:* £3,400,255
Registered Office: Patrick House, Gosforth Park Avenue, Gosforth Business Park, Newcastle upon Tyne, NE12 8EG
Activities: Other residential care activities n.e.c.
Officers: Stephen William Howe [1967] Director; Donna Winch [1976] Director; Neill Aidan Winch [1964] Director

The Northstar Foundation
Incorporated: 12 May 2014
Net Worth: £1,685,337 *Total Assets:* £2,573,126
Registered Office: 5th Floor, Maybrook House, 27-35 Grainger Street, Newcastle upon Tyne, NE1 5JE
Activities: Other social work activities without accommodation n.e.c.
Officers: Emma Ruth O'Rourke, Secretary; Dr Anthony William Henfrey [1944] Director; Stephen Mark I'anson [1956] Director; Antony David Ross [1960] Director

Northstar Ventures Limited
Incorporated: 19 April 2004 *Employees:* 15
Net Worth: £1,581,759 *Total Assets:* £1,777,425
Registered Office: 5th Floor, Maybrook House, 27-35 Grainger Street, Newcastle upon Tyne, NE1 5JE
Activities: Financial intermediation not elsewhere classified
Parent: Northstar Ventures Holdings Limited
Officers: Emma Ruth O'Rourke, Secretary; Alasdair Douglas Michael Greig [1967] Director/Fund Manager; David Martin James Hickey [1955] Director; Emma Ruth O'Rourke [1966] Director/Chartered Accountant; Ian Richards [1965] Director/Fund Manager; Generald White [1946] Director/Venture Capitalist

Northumberland & Durham Property Trust Limited
Incorporated: 28 June 1922
Net Worth: £85,425,000 *Total Assets:* £565,209,024
Registered Office: Citygate, St James Boulevard, Newcastle upon Tyne, NE1 4JE
Activities: Development of building projects
Parent: Grainger Real Estate Limited
Officers: Adam McGhin, Secretary; Helen Christine Gordon [1959] Director; Adam McGhin [1978] Director/Solicitor; Mark Jeremy Robson [1959] Director/Chartered Surveyor; Andrew Philip Saunderson [1975] Director; Vanessa Kate Simms [1975] Director

Northumberland Castle and Country Lodgings Ltd
Incorporated: 20 May 2013 *Employees:* 37
Net Worth: £546,195 *Total Assets:* £1,811,475
Registered Office: Fram Park, Longframlington, Morpeth, Northumberland, NE65 8DA
Activities: Licenced restaurants
Shareholders: Terence Maughan; Heather Maughan
Officers: Heather Maughan, Secretary; Heather Maughan [1970] Director/Secretary; Terence Maughan [1967] Director/Engineer

Northumberland Church of England Academy Trust
Incorporated: 22 July 2008 *Employees:* 545
Net Worth: £44,051,540 *Total Assets:* £48,763,964
Registered Office: Josephine Butler Campus, Academy Road, Ashington, Northumberland, NE63 9FZ
Activities: Pre-primary education
Officers: Richard Bishopp [1950] Director/Consultant; John Richard Brearley [1961] Director/Chartered Accountant; Martin Browell [1977] Director/Assistant Practitioner (Nursing); Alex Cox [1978] Director/Solicitor; Natalie Fountain [1980] Director/Headteacher; Alan Hardie [1966] Director/Headteacher; Jeffrey Hope [1973] Director/Plant Manager; Paul Johnson [1977] Director/Teacher; Marc Kelly [1980] Director/Paramedic; Jim Lang [1954] Director/Retired; John Marshall [1966] Director/Lawyer; Stephen Graham Purvis [1981] Director/Entrepreneur; Rev Elizabeth Jane Scott [1951] Director/Clerk in Holy Orders

Northumberland CTC (Properties) Limited
Incorporated: 23 November 1995
Net Worth: £483,965 *Total Assets:* £840,187
Registered Office: County Lawn Tennis Ground, North Jesmond Avenue, Jesmond, Newcastle upon Tyne, NE2 3JU
Activities: Operation of sports facilities
Parent: Northumberland Lawn Tennis Association
Officers: Christopher John Lott, Secretary; Martin John Clark [1954] Director/Sales Manager; Colin Dickinson [1940] Director/Solicitor; Christopher John Lott [1953] Director/Manager; George Anthony Murphy [1946] Director/Accountant

Northumberland Estates 2004 Limited
Incorporated: 10 December 2004
Net Worth Deficit: £2,764,064 *Total Assets:* £8,448,167
Registered Office: Northumberland Estates, Suite 2a, Quayside House, 110 Quayside, Newcastle upon Tyne, NE1 3DX
Activities: Buying and selling of own real estate
Officers: Lesley Ann Ilderton, Secretary; Colin Leslie Barnes [1960] Director/Town & Country Planner; Colin Davidson [1976] Director/Chartered Surveyor; Lesley Ann Ilderton [1976] Director/Group Financial Controller; Roderick Charles St John Wilson [1961] Director/Land Agent

Northumberland Estates 2007 Limited
Incorporated: 12 February 2007
Net Worth: £2,722,957 *Total Assets:* £4,683,681
Registered Office: Northumberland Estates, Suite 2a, Quayside House, 110 Quayside, Newcastle upon Tyne, NE1 3DX
Activities: Buying and selling of own real estate
Officers: Lesley Ann Ilderton, Secretary; Colin Leslie Barnes [1960] Director/Town & Country Planner; Colin Davidson [1976] Director/Chartered Surveyor; Lesley Ann Ilderton [1976] Director/Group Financial Controller; Roderick Charles St John Wilson [1961] Director/Land Agent

Northumberland Estates Developments Limited
Incorporated: 6 December 2006
Net Worth Deficit: £1,392,486 *Total Assets:* £45,845,592
Registered Office: Northumberland Estates, Suite 2a, Quayside House, 110 Quayside, Newcastle upon Tyne, NE1 3DX
Activities: Buying and selling of own real estate
Officers: Lesley Ann Ilderton, Secretary; Colin Leslie Barnes [1960] Director/Town & Country Planner; Colin Davidson [1976] Director/Chartered Surveyor; Lesley Ann Ilderton [1976] Director/Group Financial Controller; Ralph George Algernon Percy [1956] Director/Peer to The Realm; Roderick Charles St John Wilson [1961] Director/Land Agent

Northumberland Estates Finance LLP
Incorporated: 11 August 2015
Net Worth: £16,697,344 *Total Assets:* £16,706,744
Registered Office: Estate Office, Alnwick Castle, Alnwick, Northumberland, NE66 1NQ
Officers: The Hon George Dominic Earl Percy [1984] Member; Ralph George Algernon Percy [1956] Member; Earl William James Robert Peel [1947] LLP Member; Ralph George Algernon Percy [1956] LLP Member; Lady Victoria Lucy Diana Percy [1949] LLP Member

Northumberland Estates Investments 2000 Limited
Incorporated: 5 March 2002
Net Worth: £713,793 *Total Assets:* £3,275,787
Registered Office: Northumberland Estates, Suite 2a, Quayside House, 110 Quayside, Newcastle upon Tyne, NE1 3DX
Activities: Buying and selling of own real estate
Officers: Colin Leslie Barnes [1960] Director; Colin Davidson [1976] Director/Chartered Surveyor; Lesley Ann Ilderton [1976] Director/Group Financial Controller; Roderick Charles St John Wilson [1961] Director/Land Agent

Northumberland Estates Investments 3000 Limited
Incorporated: 5 March 2002
Net Worth: £1,277,197 *Total Assets:* £14,912,251
Registered Office: Northumberland Estates, Suite 2a, Quayside House, 110 Quayside, Newcastle upon Tyne, NE1 3DX
Activities: Buying and selling of own real estate
Officers: Colin Davidson [1976] Director/Chartered Surveyor; Lesley Ann Ilderton [1976] Director/Group Finance Controller; Rory Charles St John Wilson [1961] Director/Land Agent

Northumberland Estates Investments Limited
Incorporated: 3 October 1997
Net Worth: £17,275,492 *Total Assets:* £77,123,144
Registered Office: Northumberland Estates, Suite 2a, Quayside House, 110 Quayside, Newcastle upon Tyne, NE1 3DX
Activities: Other letting and operating of own or leased real estate
Officers: Lesley Ann Ilderton, Secretary; Colin Leslie Barnes [1960] Director/Town & Country Planner; Colin Davidson [1976] Director/Chartered Surveyor; Lesley Ann Ilderton [1976] Director/Group Financial Controller; Ralph George Algernon Percy [1956] Director/Peer to The Realm; Roderick Charles St John Wilson [1961] Director/Land Agent

Northumberland Estates Limited
Incorporated: 20 September 2006
Net Worth: £29,469,696 *Total Assets:* £254,094,816
Registered Office: Quayside House, 110 Quayside, Newcastle upon Tyne, NE1 3DX
Activities: Buying and selling of own real estate
Shareholders: Duke of Northumberland Ralph George Algernon Percy; Duke of Buccleuch Richard Walter John Buccleuch; Lord Percy James William Eustace Percy; The Most Noble Ralph George Algernon Percy; The Right Honourable Matthew White 5th Viscount Ridley
Officers: Lesley Ann Ilderton, Secretary; Colin Leslie Barnes [1960] Director/Town & Country Planner; Colin Davidson [1976] Director/Chartered Surveyor; Lesley Ann Ilderton [1976] Director/Group Financial Controller; Ralph George Algernon Percy [1956] Director/Peer to The Realm; Roderick Charles St John Wilson [1961] Director/Land Agent

Northumberland Estates Ventures Limited
Incorporated: 5 August 1988
Net Worth: £10,840,268 *Total Assets:* £47,327,652
Registered Office: Northumberland Estates, Suite 2a, Quayside House, 110 Quayside, Newcastle upon Tyne, NE1 3DX
Activities: Buying and selling of own real estate
Officers: Colin Leslie Barnes [1960] Director/Town & Country Planner; Colin Davidson [1976] Director/Chartered Surveyor; Lesley Ann Ilderton [1976] Director/Group Financial Controller; Ralph George Algernon Percy [1956] Director/Peer to The Realm; Roderick Charles St John Wilson [1961] Director/Land Agent

Northumberland Golf Club Limited (The)
Incorporated: 29 March 1898
Net Worth: £1,064,181 *Total Assets:* £2,930,597
Registered Office: High Gosforth Park, Newcastle upon Tyne, NE3 5HT
Activities: Other sports activities
Officers: Richard William Breakey, Secretary; Kevin Gray [1957] Director; Dr Richard Edward Jones [1952] Director/Neurologist; Alan Ross [1952] Director/Retired

Northumberland Luxury Log Cabins Limited
Incorporated: 22 December 2009
Net Worth: £74,506 *Total Assets:* £1,304,055
Registered Office: c/o Templeman Retailing and Vending Limited, Earlsway, Team Valley Trading Estate, Gateshead, Tyne & Wear, NE11 0RQ
Activities: Other holiday and other collective accommodation
Officers: Wendy Margaret Templeman, Secretary; Wendy Margaret Templeman [1965] Director; William Neil Templeman [1962] Director

Northumberland Rugby Football Union Limited
Incorporated: 12 August 2011
Net Worth: £2,619,918 *Total Assets:* £2,729,305
Registered Office: County Office, Druid Park, Woolsington, Newcastle upon Tyne, NE13 8DF
Activities: Other sports activities
Officers: Dr James Coulson, Secretary; Dr. James Coulson [1945] Director; Christopher Davy [1948] Director/Retired; Lawrence Desmond Fletcher [1963] Director/Management Consultant; Terence Carey O'Neill [1951] Director; John Denoon Reid [1946] Director/Solicitor; Mark Graham Vaughan Richard [1957] Director/Management Consultant; Penelope Jane Stewart [1966] Director/Consultant; Andrew William Thomson [1942] Director; LEA Weatherly [1967] Director/Account Manager

Northumberland Stone Limited
Incorporated: 10 September 1998
Net Worth: £670,335 *Total Assets:* £903,387
Registered Office: Onyx House, 7 South Church Road, Bishop Auckland, Co Durham, DL14 7LB
Activities: Quarrying of ornamental and building stone, limestone, gypsum, chalk and slate
Shareholders: Shaun Christopher Braithwaite; Michael Nixon Allison
Officers: Michael Nixon Allison, Secretary; Michael Nixon Allison [1939] Director; Shaun Christopher Braithwaite [1955] Director/Quarry Manager

Northumberland Wildlife Trust Limited
Incorporated: 13 March 1962 *Employees:* 41
Net Worth: £5,086,492 *Total Assets:* £5,536,617
Registered Office: The Garden House, St Nicholas Park, Jubilee Road, Newcastle upon Tyne, NE3 3XT
Activities: Activities of other membership organisations n.e.c.
Officers: Ailsa Hobson, Secretary; Ian Hamilton Armstrong [1931] Director/Retired; Anthony John Douglas Barber [1953] Director/Farmer; Derek Vincent Coates [1957] Director/Retired; James Graham Simpson Gill [1953] Director/Retired; Ailsa Hobson [1983] Director/Solicitor; Ian Jackson [1950] Director/Consultant; Sandra King [1968] Director/Freelance Consultant; Thomas Lloyd [1984] Director; Dr Angus George Lunn [1933] Director/Retired; Rachel Martin [1981] Director/Youth Sector Worker; Karen Statham [1982] Director/Business Executive

Northumbria Blow Mouldings Limited
Incorporated: 8 October 1982 *Employees:* 62
Net Worth: £2,623,320 *Total Assets:* £4,908,597
Registered Office: Unit 7 North Tyne Industrial Estate, Whitley Road, Longbenton, Newcastle upon Tyne, NE12 9SZ
Activities: Manufacture of other plastic products
Parent: DNR Limited
Officers: Doreen Mallen [1947] Director; Scott Mallen [1975] Director; Paul David Thompson [1969] Director/Finance; Brian Wiper [1960] Director/General Manager

Northumbria Calvert Trust
Incorporated: 10 November 1981 *Employees:* 42
Net Worth: £5,281,186 *Total Assets:* £5,639,586
Registered Office: Calvert Trust Kielder, Kielder Water & Forest Park, Hexham, Northumberland, NE48 1BS
Activities: Other sports activities
Officers: Peter John Vincent Cockerill, Secretary; Roger Anderton [1967] Retired Director; John Neville Bridge [1942] Director/Chief Executive; Dr Anna Maria Charlton [1972] Director/Consultant; Charles Ranfurly Drax [1962] Director/Teacher; Christopher Michael Green [1954] Director/Chartered Accountant; Peter Robert Loyd [1942] Director/Farmer; Mark Simon Priestley [1968] Director/Lawyer; Marion Fiona Schooler [1962] Director/Consultant; Peter Henry Straker [1975] Director/Coroner (in spe); Edward Caverley Thornton Trevelyan [1935] Director/Retired

Northumbria Care Limited
Incorporated: 19 May 1995 *Employees:* 55
Net Worth: £1,165,220 *Total Assets:* £3,104,180
Registered Office: 2b North Sands Business Centre, Sunderland, Tyne & Wear, SR6 0QA
Activities: Residential care activities for the elderly and disabled
Shareholder: Philip Damien Carey
Officers: Ashok Kumar, Secretary; Philip Damien Carey [1968] Operations Director; Ashok Kumar [1952] Director; Varinder Kumar [1940] Director

Northumbria Coast and Country Cottages Limited
Incorporated: 31 January 2000 *Employees:* 13
Net Worth: £1,425,905 *Total Assets:* £2,446,421
Registered Office: Carpenters Court, River Bank Road, Alnmouth, Alnwick, Northumberland, NE66 2RH
Activities: Real estate agencies
Major Shareholder: Nicola Hough Brierley
Officers: Nicola Hough Brierley [1955] Director; William Anthony Hough Brierley [1981] Director/Student; Alistair Denney Johnson [1948] Director/Farmer

Northumbria Dental Care Limited
Incorporated: 1 November 2006 *Employees:* 17
Net Worth: £326,584 *Total Assets:* £1,161,469
Registered Office: 45 High Street, Amble, Morpeth, Northumberland, NE65 0LE
Activities: Dental practice activities
Shareholders: Catherine Mary Thomas; Duncan William Thomas
Officers: Catherine Mary Thomas, Secretary; Keldine Jane Hunter [1972] Director/Practice Manager; Catherine Mary Thomas [1966] Director/Bookkeeper/Administrator; Duncan William Thomas [1967] Director/Dental Practitioner

Northumbria Healthcare Facilities Management Limited
Incorporated: 17 January 2012 *Employees:* 140
Net Worth: £10,381,000 *Total Assets:* £98,137,000
Registered Office: Northumbria House, Silver Fox Way, Cobalt Business Park, Wallsend, Tyne & Wear, NE27 0QJ
Activities: Development of building projects
Officers: Sophie Stephenson, Secretary; Arlene Emma Louise Atkinson [1980] Director; Steven Paul Bannister [1962] Managing Director; Leslie William Morgan [1959] Director; Ernest Nixon Rowe [1961] Director; Dr Peter William Sanderson [1946] Director/General Practitioner - Retired

Northumbria Leisure Limited
Incorporated: 10 October 1973 *Employees:* 21
Net Worth: £765,787 *Total Assets:* £1,181,325
Registered Office: High Mickley Farm House, High Mickley, Stocksfield, Northumberland, NE43 7LU
Activities: Other amusement and recreation activities n.e.c.
Major Shareholder: Peter MacKlam
Officers: Peter MacKlam, Secretary; Margaret MacKlam [1942] Director; Peter MacKlam [1944] Managing Director

Northumbria London Campus Limited
Incorporated: 15 January 2014
Net Worth: £1,000 *Total Assets:* £4,141,586
Registered Office: Sutherland Building, College Street, Newcastle upon Tyne, NE1 8ST
Activities: Post-graduate level higher education
Shareholders: Northumbria University at Newcastle; QAHE (NU) Limited
Officers: Adam Peter Dawkins, Secretary; Professor Peter James Francis [1968] Director/University Senior Management; William Robert George Macpherson [1963] Director/Chief Executive Officer; Julie Noone [1966] Managing Director (HE); Kathryn Lucy Hay Winskell [1963] Director/Pro Vice-Chancellor Employability and Partnerships

Northumbria Optical Coatings Limited
Incorporated: 23 December 1994 *Employees:* 21
Net Worth: £1,072,738 *Total Assets:* £1,372,587
Registered Office: Unit 10 Burford Way, Boldon Business Park, Boldon Colliery, Co Durham, NE35 9PZ
Activities: Other manufacturing n.e.c.
Shareholder: Nicholas James Gilland
Officers: Nicholas James Gilland, Secretary/Managing Director; Nicholas James Gilland [1971] Managing Director; Sandra Hawkes [1963] Director; Adam James Huntley [1981] Director

Northumbria Property Co. Limited
Incorporated: 19 April 1977
Net Worth: £1,089,525 *Total Assets:* £1,272,913
Registered Office: The Old Post Office, 63 Saville Street, North Shields, Tyne & Wear, NE30 1AY
Activities: Development of building projects
Officers: John Bell, Secretary; Daniel Harrison [1961] Director; Vickie Harrison [1972] Director/Civil Servant

Northumbria Vehicle Co Ltd.
Incorporated: 8 September 1999 *Employees:* 1
Net Worth: £731,479 *Total Assets:* £1,161,957
Registered Office: Oliver House, Front Street, Seaton Burn, Newcastle upon Tyne, NE13 6ES
Activities: Sale of new cars and light motor vehicles
Major Shareholder: Roderick George Purvis
Officers: Roderick Andrew Purvis, Secretary/Motor Dealer; Roderick Andrew Purvis [1977] Director/Motor Dealer; Roderick George Purvis [1947] Director/Motor Dealer

Northumbria Youth Action Limited
Incorporated: 3 July 1997 *Employees:* 18
Net Worth: £1,334,407 *Total Assets:* £1,498,887
Registered Office: Youth Village, Hudson Street, North Shields, Tyne & Wear, NE30 1DL
Activities: Maintenance and repair of motor vehicles
Officers: Duncan Stuart Campbell [1958] Director/Solicitor; Paul Cook [1952] Director/Retired Social Worker; Councillor Edward Norman Darke [1947] Director; Keith Felton [1949] Director/Retired; Brenda Joan Gildea [1945] Director/Accountant; Susan Ann Hall [1960] Director; Nicholas John Kincaid [1958] Director/Solicitor; John Douglas Lohoar [1943] Director/Retired Local Government; Alan Turner [1956] Director/Solicitor

The Northumbrian Educational Trust Ltd
Incorporated: 13 September 1960 *Employees:* 63
Net Worth: £643,519 *Total Assets:* £4,789,342
Registered Office: Oakfield House, Oakfield Road, Gosforth, Newcastle upon Tyne, NE3 4HS
Activities: Pre-primary education
Officers: Joseph Leese, Secretary; Kris Bainbridge [1982] Director/Head of ICT; Lex Dowie [1951] Director/Solicitor; Iain Francis Greenshields [1967] Director/Solicitor; Ian Henderson [1957] Director/Retired; Jane Margaret Keep [1958] Director/Chartered Physiotherapist; Liz Keightley [1974] Director/Property Management; Dr Kathryn Anne Manzo [1957] Director/University Lecturer [American]; Jacqueline Ann Rowley [1965] Director/Retired Civil Servant; Isabel Smales [1952] Director/Accountant

Northumbrian Entertainments,Limited
Incorporated: 2 March 1936
Net Worth: £20,526 *Total Assets:* £840,044
Registered Office: 84 York Road, Hartlepool, Cleveland, TS26 8AB
Activities: Other letting and operating of own or leased real estate
Major Shareholder: John Mason
Officers: Dorothy Barbara Mason, Secretary; John Edward Mason [1977] Director

Northumbrian Fine Foods Limited
Incorporated: 14 January 2002 *Employees:* 203
Net Worth: £4,077,609 *Total Assets:* £11,107,337
Registered Office: Dukesway, Team Valley Trading Estate, Gateshead, Tyne & Wear, NE11 0QP
Activities: Manufacture of rusks and biscuits; manufacture of preserved pastry goods and cakes
Officers: Bart Franciscus Mattheus Hulsman [1971] Director [Dutch]; Dr Stewart McLelland [1958] Director; Marcel Martinus Johannes Schaap [1968] Director [Dutch]; Giampaolo Guglielmo Umberto Schiratti [1960] Director [French]; Julian Wood [1964] Director/Accountant

Northumbrian Ice Cream Company Limited
Incorporated: 31 January 1994 *Employees:* 38
Net Worth: £2,036,745 *Total Assets:* £5,799,730
Registered Office: Wansbeck Business Park, Rotary Parkway, Ashington, Northumberland, NE63 8QW
Activities: Manufacture of soft drinks; production of mineral waters and other bottled waters
Shareholders: Allison Goldfinch; Paul John Goldfinch
Officers: Allison Goldfinch [1975] Director; Margaret Goldfinch [1936] Director; Paul John Goldfinch [1973] Director; Peter John Goldfinch [1934] Director; Kieran Anthony O'Connor [1961] Director; Michael Reid [1980] Director

Northumbrian Land Limited
Incorporated: 17 February 2005
Net Worth: £1,823,287 *Total Assets:* £1,902,976
Registered Office: Unit 2 Jubilee House, York Road, Hartlepool, Cleveland, TS26 9EN
Activities: Buying and selling of own real estate
Officers: Julie Margaret Rigali, Secretary; Emma Jane Holmes [1982] Director; David Nigel Williams [1943] Director; Edward Richard Thomas Yuill [1978] Managing Director; Phillip Guy Yuill [1954] Director

Northumbrian Leisure Limited
Incorporated: 17 March 1999 *Employees:* 21
Net Worth: £4,942,376 *Total Assets:* £15,288,009
Registered Office: c/o Womble Bond Dickinson (UK) LLP, St Ann's Wharf, 112 Quayside, Newcastle upon Tyne, NE1 3DX
Activities: Recreational vehicle parks, trailer parks and camping grounds
Major Shareholder: Nigel Thompson
Officers: Nigel Thompson [1970] Director; Sandra Margaret Thompson [1969] Director

Northumbrian Property Services Group Limited
Incorporated: 3 March 2015 *Employees:* 2
Net Worth: £37,218 *Total Assets:* £919,109
Registered Office: Lipwood Hall, Haydon Bridge, Hexham, Northumberland, NE47 6DY
Activities: Electrical installation
Major Shareholder: Stephen Mark I'Anson
Officers: Simon Arthur Cross [1968] Director; Stephen Mark I'anson [1955] Director

Northumbrian Roads Limited
Incorporated: 16 June 1988 *Employees:* 74
Net Worth: £4,011,744 *Total Assets:* £9,795,594
Registered Office: Dukesway, Low Prudhoe Industrial Estate, Prudhoe, Northumberland, NE42 6PQ
Activities: Construction of roads and motorways
Shareholders: Sean Anthony Lynch; Christopher John Lynch
Officers: Christopher Dancer, Secretary/Director; Christopher Dancer [1963] Director/Manager; Christopher John Lynch [1971] Director/Manager; Sean Anthony Lynch [1969] Director/Manager

Northumbrian Services Limited
Incorporated: 17 October 1995
Net Worth: £12,200,000 *Total Assets:* £116,700,000
Registered Office: Northumbria House, Abbey Road, Pity Me, Durham, DH1 5FJ
Activities: Activities of head offices
Shareholder: CKI UK Co 5 Limited
Officers: Martin Parker, Secretary; Andrew John Hunter [1958] Director; Christopher Ian Johns [1970] Director; Hing Lam Kam [1946] Director [Chinese]; Duncan Nicholas MacRae [1970] Director; Heidi Mottram [1965] Director/Chief Executive Officer

Northumbrian Trust Day Nurseries Limited
Incorporated: 21 February 1996 *Employees:* 68
Net Worth: £1,076,469 *Total Assets:* £1,523,921
Registered Office: 301 Chillingham Road, Heaton, Newcastle upon Tyne, NE6 5SB
Activities: Pre-primary education
Officers: Joseph Penryth Gould, Secretary/Company Chairman; Elaine Generaldine Gould [1941] Director; James Justin Gould [1966] Director; Joseph Penryth Gould [1939] Director/Company Chairman; Tara Gould [1968] Director

Northumbrian Trust Limited
Incorporated: 1 December 1986 *Employees:* 5
Net Worth: £3,470,960 *Total Assets:* £4,388,675
Registered Office: 301 Chillingham Road, Heaton, Newcastle upon Tyne, NE6 5SB
Activities: Buying and selling of own real estate
Officers: Elaine Generaldine Gould, Secretary; Elaine Generaldine Gould [1941] Director; James Justin Gould [1966] Director; Joseph Penryth Gould [1939] Director; Tara Gould [1968] Director/Personal Assistant

Northumbrian Water Finance PLC
Incorporated: 21 November 2001
Net Worth: £50,000 *Total Assets:* £2,267,936,000
Registered Office: Northumbria House, Abbey Road, Pity Me, Durham, DH1 5FJ
Activities: Other business support service activities n.e.c.
Parent: Northumbrian Water Limited
Officers: Martin Parker, Secretary; Christopher Ian Johns [1970] Director/Accountant; Heidi Mottram [1965] Director/Chief Executive Officer

Northumbrian Water Group Limited
Incorporated: 12 May 2003 *Employees:* 3,283
Net Worth Deficit: £662,200,000 *Total Assets:* £4,696,800,256
Registered Office: Northumbria House, Abbey Road, Pity Me, Durham, DH1 5FJ
Activities: Activities of head offices
Shareholders: CKI UK Co 6 Limited; CKI UK Co 5 Limited
Officers: Martin Parker, Secretary; Loi Shun Chan [1962] Alternate Director [Chinese]; Frank Riddell Frame [1930] Director/Solicitor Retired; Andrew John Hunter [1958] Director; Hing Lam Kam [1946] Director [Chinese]; Duncan Nicholas MacRae [1970] Director; Heidi Mottram [1965] Director/Chief Executive Officer; Wai Che Wendy Tong Barnes [1960] Director/Chief Corporate Affairs Officer

Northumbrian Water Limited
Incorporated: 1 April 1989 *Employees:* 3,128
Net Worth: £598,200,000 *Total Assets:* £4,627,599,872
Registered Office: Northumbria House, Abbey Road, Pity Me, Durham, DH1 5FJ
Activities: Water collection, treatment and supply
Parent: Northumbrian Water Group Limited
Officers: Martin Parker, Secretary; Loi Shun Chan [1962] Alternate Director [Chinese]; Margaret Fay [1949] Managing Director; Frank Riddell Frame [1930] Director/Solicitor Retired; Andrew John Hunter [1958] Director; Christopher Ian Johns [1970] Director/Accountant; Andrew Ceri Jones [1965] Director; Hing Lam Kam [1946] Director [Chinese]; Simon Lyster [1952] Director; Duncan Nicholas MacRae [1970] Director; Heidi Mottram [1965] Director/Chief Executive Officer; Martin Andre Bernard Negre [1946] Director [French]; Paul Francis Rew [1953] Director/Accountant; Wai Che Wendy Tong Barnes [1960] Director/Chief Corporate Affairs Officer

Northumbrian Water Projects Limited
Incorporated: 7 August 1990 *Employees:* 25
Net Worth: £8,080,745 *Total Assets:* £20,966,282
Registered Office: Northumbria House, Abbey Road, Pity Me, Durham, DH1 5FJ
Activities: Sewerage
Parent: NWG Commercial Solutions Limited
Officers: Martin Parker, Secretary; James Henry John King [1966] Director; Graham Brinsley Southall [1965] Commercial Director in Water Sector; Richard Warneford [1969] Waste Water Director

Norton Care Limited
Incorporated: 19 September 2002
Net Worth: £742,823 *Total Assets:* £913,170
Registered Office: 53 Reid Park Road, Jesmond, Newcastle upon Tyne, NE2 2ER
Activities: Other human health activities
Parent: N I Sattar Holdings Limited
Officers: Irrm Nazir Sattar [1969] Director/Pharmacist; Naweed Sattar [1968] Director/Doctor

Nova Finance Limited
Incorporated: 29 August 1980 *Employees:* 55
Net Worth: £3,212,314 *Total Assets:* £5,964,672
Registered Office: c/o Davidsons of Morpeth, Coopies Way, Morpeth, Northumberland, NE61 6JN
Activities: Sale of used cars and light motor vehicles
Shareholders: Colin Henry Davidson; Peter Edward Davidson
Officers: Mark Edward Hudspith, Secretary; Colin Henry Davidson [1952] Director; Peter Edward Davidson [1956] Director

Nova Holdings Limited
Incorporated: 9 November 1987 *Employees:* 20
Net Worth: £1,259,178 *Total Assets:* £6,214,447
Registered Office: Newcastle House, Albany Court, Monarch Road, Newcastle upon Tyne, NE4 7YB
Activities: Activities of head offices
Officers: Gary Wright, Secretary; John Caine [1946] Director; Mike Candlish [1947] Director; Brendan Foster [1948] Director/Chairman; Paul Brendan Foster [1977] Director; John Rowlinson [1948] Director; Eric Malcolm Wilkins [1952] Director

Nova International Limited
Incorporated: 10 January 1997 *Employees:* 27
Net Worth: £910,929 *Total Assets:* £6,411,274
Registered Office: Newcastle House, Albany Court, Monarch Road, Newcastle upon Tyne, NE4 7YB
Activities: Other sports activities
Parent: Nova Holding Limited
Officers: Gary Wright, Secretary; John Flynn [1959] Director/Solicitor; Brendan Foster [1948] Director; Eric Malcolm Wilkins [1952] Director

Nova Marketing Consultancy Limited
Incorporated: 14 April 1997 *Employees:* 28
Net Worth: £886,060 *Total Assets:* £3,175,702
Registered Office: Newcastle House, Albany Court, Newcastle Business Park, Monarch Road, Newcastle upon Tyne, NE4 7YB
Activities: Television programme production activities
Shareholders: Brendan Foster; Susan Foster
Officers: Gary Wright, Secretary; Brendan Foster [1948] Director; Eric Malcolm Wilkins [1952] Director

Nova Marketing Limited
Incorporated: 23 February 2006 *Employees:* 86
Net Worth: £2,362,897 *Total Assets:* £10,368,147
Registered Office: Newcastle House, Albany Court, Monarch Road, Newcastle upon Tyne, NE4 7YB
Activities: Other sports activities
Shareholders: Susan Margaret Foster; Brendan Foster
Officers: Gary Wright, Secretary; Brendan Foster [1948] Director; Eric Malcolm Wilkins [1952] Director

Nova Payroll Management Services Limited
Incorporated: 12 April 2011 *Employees:* 622
Net Worth: £1,517,689 *Total Assets:* £7,044,406
Registered Office: Unit E14 Marquis Court, Team Valley Trading Estate, Gateshead, Tyne & Wear, NE11 0RU
Activities: Temporary employment agency activities
Major Shareholder: Gillian Findlay
Officers: Gillian Findlay [1962] Director

Nova Stellar Property Management Limited
Incorporated: 5 September 2003
Net Worth: £279,874 *Total Assets:* £1,243,560
Registered Office: 1 Harbour View, Littlehaven, South Shields, Tyne & Wear, NE33 1LR
Activities: Other letting and operating of own or leased real estate
Major Shareholder: Stuart Dowie
Officers: Kenneth Edward Dowie, Secretary; Stuart Dowie [1973] Director/Property Development

Novares Peterlee Limited
Incorporated: 21 June 1995 *Employees:* 107
Net Worth: £5,565,024 *Total Assets:* £16,406,831
Registered Office: Fiennes Road, North West Industrial Estate, Peterlee, Co Durham, SR8 2QH
Activities: Manufacture of plastics in primary forms
Parent: Novares Group SAS
Officers: Jonathan Straughan Waters, Secretary; Emmanuel Voituret [1967] Director [French]

Novatech (UK) Limited
Incorporated: 22 May 1989 *Employees:* 4
Net Worth: £1,661,223 *Total Assets:* £1,823,270
Registered Office: Unit 2 Angel Park, Drum Industrial Estate, Chester-le-Street, Co Durham, DH2 1AQ
Activities: Wholesale of other machinery and equipment
Major Shareholder: Robert Edward Stephenson
Officers: Carol Stephenson, Secretary; Carol Stephenson [1952] Director/Secretary; Robert Edward Stephenson [1946] Managing Director

November 26 Limited
Incorporated: 20 October 2014
Net Worth: £8,899 *Total Assets:* £953,377
Registered Office: St Matthews House, Haugh Lane Industrial Estate, Hexham, Northumberland, NE46 3PU
Activities: Other letting and operating of own or leased real estate
Officers: Neil Paterson [1956] Director/Dentist; Susan Jane Paterson [1958] Director

NRG Global Power Limited
Incorporated: 31 January 2006 *Employees:* 8
Net Worth: £4,108,795 *Total Assets:* £5,734,958
Registered Office: Unit 27 Primrose Hill Industrial Estate, Orde Wingate Way, Stockton on Tees, Cleveland, TS19 0GA
Activities: Other engineering activities
Major Shareholder: David Wilson
Officers: David Wilson [1967] Director/Engineer

NRS Media (Europe) Limited
Incorporated: 28 September 2007 *Employees:* 18
Net Worth: £1,497,238 *Total Assets:* £2,372,435
Registered Office: Rotterdam House, 116 Quayside, Newcastle upon Tyne, NE1 3DY
Activities: Management consultancy activities other than financial management
Parent: NRS Media UK Holdings Limited
Officers: Joao Carlos Ribeiro Salazar Antunes [1969] Director [Portuguese]; Neil Tanner [1970] Director [Irish]

NSA (Ventures) Limited
Incorporated: 4 October 2001
Net Worth: £432,041 *Total Assets:* £4,751,579
Registered Office: Unity House, Dudley Road, Darlington, Co Durham, DL1 4GG
Activities: Combined office administrative service activities
Officers: Darren James Combellack [1985] Director/Car Salvage Dealer; Ian Maurice Hill [1970] Director/Salvage Dealer; Hamish Edward Thomson Irvine [1946] Director; Chris James Morgan [1963] Director/Salvage Dealer; Allen William Frederick Prebble [1961] Director/Vehicle Salvage Owner; Marc John Trent [1966] Managing Director

NSG Limited
Incorporated: 22 April 1985 *Employees:* 29
Net Worth: £625,795 *Total Assets:* £1,718,910
Registered Office: Unity House, Dudley Road, Darlington, Co Durham, DL1 4GG
Activities: Combined office administrative service activities
Officers: Darren James Combellack [1985] Director/Car Salvage Dealer; Ian Maurice Hill [1970] Director/Salvage Dealer; Hamish Edward Thomson Irvine [1946] Director/Motor Trade; Chris James Morgan [1963] Director/Salvage Dealer; Allen William Frederick Prebble [1961] Director/Vehicle Salvage Owner; Marc John Trent [1966] Managing Director

NST Welding (UK) Limited
Incorporated: 23 July 1996 *Employees:* 3
Net Worth: £1,266,065 *Total Assets:* £1,826,186
Registered Office: Dedicated Transport Solutions, Nelson Way, Nelson Park West, Cramlington, Northumberland, NE23 1WG
Activities: Wholesale of chemical products
Major Shareholder: Age Ingebretsen
Officers: David William Millar, Secretary; Dag Drolsum [1957] Director/Accountant [Norwegian]; David William Millar [1958] Managing Director

NT Enterprises Limited
Incorporated: 13 May 1997
Net Worth: £2 *Total Assets:* £1,300,000
Registered Office: 5-8 Priestgate, Darlington, Co Durham, DL1 1NL
Activities: Activities of head offices
Officers: Nicholas Dudley Good Winearls, Secretary; Ian Frederick Ledger [1943] Director; Nicholas Dudley Good Winearls [1953] Director

NTG Group Limited
Incorporated: 13 February 2008
Net Worth: £1,698,580 *Total Assets:* £2,500,300
Registered Office: 1 Queens Court, Earlsway, Team Valley Trading Estate, Gateshead, Tyne & Wear, NE11 0BP
Activities: Activities of other holding companies n.e.c.
Shareholders: Brian Bates; Joan Graham; Charles Sampy
Officers: Joan Graham, Secretary; Brian Bates [1947] Managing Director; Joan Graham [1947] Director/Company Accountant; Charles Sampy [1965] Director/Works Manager

Nuby UK LLP
Incorporated: 24 September 2009 *Employees:* 32
Net Worth: £2,564,139 *Total Assets:* £5,237,276
Registered Office: 6 Boldon Court, Burford Way, Boldon Colliery, Co Durham, NE35 9PY
Officers: Jack Allen Hakim [1989] Member; Leah Raquel Hakim [1987] Member; Abraham Joseph Hakim [1983] LLP Member; Abraham Jack Hakim [1977] LLP Member; Abraham Hakim [1986] LLP Member; David Hakim [1986] LLP Member; Eddie Hakim [1979] LLP Member; Hannah Hakim [1990] LLP Member; Joseph Hakim [1992] LLP Member; Kay Hakim [1989] LLP Member; Lisa Hakim [1983] LLP Member; Louise Hakim [1987] LLP Member

Nucleus (GB) Limited
Incorporated: 26 September 2002 *Employees:* 790
Net Worth: £2,128,591 *Total Assets:* £7,743,490
Registered Office: Nucleus House, 3 Brookside Terrace, Sunderland, Tyne & Wear, SR2 7RN
Activities: Unlicenced restaurants and cafes
Major Shareholder: Jasper Alan Stuart Maudsley
Officers: Jacqueline Maudsley, Secretary; Jacqueline Maudsley [1961] Director; Jasper Alan Stuart Maudsley [1958] Director/Fast Food Restaurants

Nudo Sushi Box Ltd
Incorporated: 1 May 2012
Net Worth: £178,975 *Total Assets:* £1,276,843
Registered Office: Unit One Storey Court, Dunne Road, Blaydon on Tyne, Tyne & Wear, NE21 5NH
Activities: Unlicenced restaurants and cafes
Officers: Karen Sau Kin Lau [1969] Director; Kit Keung Lau [1965] Director; Jian Xiong Zeng [1979] Director

Christine Nugent Business Travel Limited
Incorporated: 31 October 1994
Registered Office: 25 Vine Place, Sunderland, Tyne & Wear, SR1 3NA
Activities: Travel agency activities
Shareholders: Hays Travel Limited; Christine Nugent
Officers: Christine Nugent, Secretary/Managing Director; Marta Fernandez Varona [1966] Director [Spanish]; John Hays [1949] Director; Christine Nugent [1962] Managing Director

Nulite Ltd
Incorporated: 8 January 1998
Net Worth: £1,954,729 *Total Assets:* £2,878,952
Registered Office: 28 Biddick Village Centre, Biddick, Washington, Tyne & Wear, NE38 7NP
Activities: Other manufacturing n.e.c.
Major Shareholder: William Harris
Officers: David William Harris, Secretary; William Harris [1959] Director/Glazing

Nunthorpe Multi-Academy Trust Limited
Incorporated: 22 August 2012 *Employees:* 347
Net Worth: £17,875,454 *Total Assets:* £21,057,352
Registered Office: Nunthorpe Academy Limited, Guisborough Road, Nunthorpe, Middlesbrough, Cleveland, TS7 0LA
Activities: General secondary education
Officers: Keith Brentall [1954] Director/Retired; Lee Andrew Brown [1975] Director/Headteacher; Iain Donald Fuller [1964] Director/Chartered Accountant; Stephen Andrew Jones [1974] Commercial Director; Joanne Victoria Liddle [1972] Director/Housewife; Allan Mansfield [1948] Director/Education Consultant; Malcolm Henry Robinson [1943] Director/Architectural Consultant

Nunthorpe Nurseries Group Ltd
Incorporated: 13 July 2000
Net Worth: £1,192,329 *Total Assets:* £1,550,575
Registered Office: 2 The Crescent, Nunthorpe, Middlesbrough, Cleveland, TS7 0JP
Activities: Other service activities n.e.c.
Shareholders: Ian Howlett; Paul Stephen Nelson
Officers: Paul Stephen Nelson, Secretary; Ian Howlett [1957] Director/Nursery Proprietor; Paul Stephen Nelson [1959] Director/Nursery Proprietor

Nursery Properties (N.E.) Limited
Incorporated: 30 May 2007
Net Worth: £380,617 *Total Assets:* £810,668
Registered Office: 1 Jesmond Business Court, 217 Jesmond Road, Newcastle upon Tyne, NE2 1LA
Activities: Other business support service activities n.e.c.
Officers: Elizabeth Averill Leng [1980] Director

Nusafe Europe Limited
Incorporated: 23 October 2014 *Employees:* 20
Net Worth: £142,058 *Total Assets:* £1,207,885
Registered Office: Unit 6 Dean & Chapter Industrial Estate, Ferryhill, Co Durham, DL17 8LH
Activities: Wholesale of clothing and footwear
Shareholders: John Thomas Carruth; Gerry Carruth; Pauline Joan Carruth
Officers: Gerry Carruth [1981] Director; John Thomas Carruth [1962] Director

Nvent Solutions (UK) Limited
Incorporated: 10 February 1999 *Employees:* 76
Net Worth: £10,002,000 *Total Assets:* £23,693,000
Registered Office: 3 Rutherford Road, Stephenson Industrial Estate, Washington, Tyne & Wear, NE37 3HX
Activities: Manufacture of other electronic and electric wires and cables
Parent: Nvent UK Holdings Limited
Officers: Willem Gheysens [1974] Director/Financial Controller [Belgian]; Sylvain Henri Corneel Lemmens [1957] Director [Belgian]; David Martin [1970] Sales Director

NVM Private Equity LLP
Incorporated: 27 March 2014 *Employees:* 16
Net Worth: £1,910,565 *Total Assets:* £4,590,893
Registered Office: Time Central, 32 Gallowgate, Newcastle upon Tyne, NE1 4SN
Officers: James Vaughan Arrowsmith [1968] Member; Mauro Andrea Biagioni [1978] Member; Martin Ian Green [1964] Member; Peter Struan Hodson [1972] LLP Member; Andrew William Leach [1957] LLP Member; Timothy Roland Levett [1949] LLP Member; David Mathew Rolfe [1975] LLP Member; Charles Stephen Winward [1969] LLP Member

NWG Bioenergy Limited
Incorporated: 16 April 2015
Net Worth: £636,000 *Total Assets:* £13,106,000
Registered Office: Northumbria House, Abbey Road, Durham, DH1 5FJ
Activities: Manufacture of gas
Parent: Northumbrian Water Projects Limited
Officers: James Henry John King [1966] Director/Manager; Jonathan Quain [1971] Director/Accountant; Graham Brinsley Southall [1965] Director

NWG Commercial Solutions Limited
Incorporated: 26 February 2016 *Employees:* 11
Net Worth: £1,154,000 *Total Assets:* £22,626,000
Registered Office: Northumbria House, Abbey Road, Pity Me, Durham, DH1 5FJ
Activities: Management consultancy activities other than financial management
Parent: Northumbrian Water Group Limited
Officers: Martin Parker, Secretary; Christopher Ian Johns [1970] Director/Accountant; Heidi Mottram [1965] Director/Chief Executive Officer; Martin Parker [1959] Director/Solicitor

Nxpower (UK) Limited
Incorporated: 5 October 2005 *Employees:* 31
Net Worth: £596,338 *Total Assets:* £3,382,519
Registered Office: Unit B11 Kingsway Interchange, Eleventh Avenue, Team Valley Trading Estate, Gateshead, Tyne & Wear, NE11 0JY
Activities: Manufacture of computers and peripheral equipment
Major Shareholder: Wei-Lun Tai
Officers: Ping Hsu Lin [1966] Director [Taiwanese]

NY Construction Ltd
Incorporated: 6 January 2005 *Employees:* 4
Net Worth: £875,934 *Total Assets:* £1,304,088
Registered Office: Unit 14 Ellerbeck Way, Stokesley Industrial Park, Stokesley, Cleveland, TS9 7AE
Activities: Construction of other civil engineering projects n.e.c.
Major Shareholder: Robin Cope
Officers: Robin Cope, Secretary/Director; Robin Cope [1958] Director

NYT (Holdings) Limited
Incorporated: 31 March 2004 *Employees:* 199
Net Worth: £2,712,481 *Total Assets:* £12,042,025
Registered Office: c/o North Yorkshire Timber Co Ltd, Standard House, Thurston Road, Northallerton Business Park, Northallerton, N Yorks, DL6 2NA
Activities: Activities of other holding companies n.e.c.
Parent: Thornbridge Sawmills Limited
Officers: John Alexander George Douglas [1964] Finance Director; Nicholas Peter Kershaw [1972] Director; Neil Andrew McGill [1977] Investment Director; Stuart Whiteford [1990] Director

NZR Limited
Incorporated: 22 October 2009 *Employees:* 254
Net Worth Deficit: £11,741,000 *Total Assets:* £11,515,000
Registered Office: 1a Dukesway Court, Team Valley Trading Estate, Gateshead, Tyne & Wear, NE11 0PJ
Activities: Licenced restaurants
Parent: Steakhouse Holdings Limited
Officers: Phillip Nigel Blain, Secretary; David James Horrocks [1959] Financial Director; Ian Imrie [1955] Director; Kurt Stan Wolfgang Zdesar [1972] Director/Restaurateur [Australian]

O Communications Ltd
Incorporated: 11 March 2008 *Employees:* 13
Net Worth: £811,470 *Total Assets:* £1,086,412
Registered Office: Richmond House, Old Brewery Court, Sandyford Road, Newcastle upon Tyne, NE2 1XG
Activities: Public relations and communications activities
Shareholders: Kari Helen Owers; Robin Keith Owers
Officers: Robin Keith Owers, Secretary/Designer; Kari Helen Owers [1973] Director/PR & Marketing; Robin Keith Owers [1974] Director/Designer

Michael O'Connor (Carpets) Limited
Incorporated: 27 March 1981
Net Worth: £839,100 *Total Assets:* £1,677,028
Registered Office: 8-10 Holmeside, Sunderland, Tyne & Wear, SR1 3JE
Activities: Retail sale of electrical household appliances in specialised stores
Shareholders: Christopher O'Connor; Robert Stevens
Officers: Robert Stevens, Secretary; Christopher O'Connor [1975] Director; Robert Stevens [1967] Director

O'Neill Richmonds Law Firm Limited
Incorporated: 19 March 2013
Net Worth: £242,865 *Total Assets:* £1,035,488
Registered Office: 1-2 Lansdowne Terrace East, Newcastle upon Tyne, NE3 1HL
Activities: Solicitors
Major Shareholder: John Murdo O'Neill
Officers: Peter William Amos [1953] Director/Solicitor; Saleem Mohammed Asfar [1971] Director/Solicitor; Michael Geoffrey Barton Baker [1946] Director; Rodney Patrick William Etherington [1973] Director/Solicitor; Christine Jennifer Lowes [1952] Director; John Murdo O'Neill [1957] Director; Robert Richard Hamilton Twyford [1978] Director/Solicitor

Oak Learning Trust
Incorporated: 6 March 2017 *Employees:* 96
Net Worth: £9,793,251 *Total Assets:* £11,397,351
Registered Office: George Washington Primary School, Well Bank Road, Washington, Tyne & Wear, NE37 1NL
Activities: Primary education
Officers: Penelope Best [1959] Director; Francis Cain [1949] Director/Retired; Frank Carroll [1944] Director/Retired; Thomas David Frederick Lillie [1983] Director/Lawyer; Councillor Graeme Ferguson Miller [1962] Director; Ian Neil Oswald [1967] Company Owner Director; Dr Ailsa Munro Taylor [1969] Director/Headteacher; Ralph Wood Thoburn [1962] Director/Chartered Accountant; Reverend Julie Wing [1962] Director/Vicar

Oak Park Healthcare Limited
Incorporated: 7 April 2009 *Employees:* 38
Net Worth Deficit: £479,442 *Total Assets:* £3,972,666
Registered Office: RSM UK Tax and Accounting Limited, 1 St James' Gate, Newcastle upon Tyne, NE1 4AD
Activities: Residential care activities for the elderly and disabled
Parent: Darrington Healthcare (Yorkshire) Limited
Officers: Eric George Dixon [1954] Director; Stephen Dixon [1957] Director; Shaun Ian Lucas [1945] Director; Iain Alston Murphy [1953] Director

Oak Road and Whitby Motor Factors Limited
Incorporated: 1 June 2010
Net Worth: £580,244 *Total Assets:* £980,886
Registered Office: First Floor Suite, 6 High Street, Sedgefield, Stockton on Tees, Cleveland, TS21 3AR
Activities: Retail trade of motor vehicle parts and accessories
Major Shareholder: John David Martin
Officers: Alan Paul Brown, Secretary; John David Martin [1945] Director/Motor Parts Retailer; Sarah Powlowski [1979] Director

Oakdale (Contracts) Limited
Incorporated: 12 August 1996 *Employees:* 30
Net Worth: £1,901,990 *Total Assets:* £3,075,824
Registered Office: Teal House, 10 Teal Farm Way, Teal Farm Park, Washington, Tyne & Wear, NE38 8BG
Activities: Manufacture of concrete products for construction purposes
Officers: Gavin David Cordwell-Smith, Secretary; Gavin David Cordwell-Smith [1976] Director; Michael Philip Jonas [1959] Director

Oakenclough Buildings Limited
Incorporated: 15 July 2004 *Employees:* 14
Net Worth: £378,462 *Total Assets:* £1,213,611
Registered Office: J F Potts, Wallsend Road, North Shields, Tyne & Wear, NE29 7FN
Activities: Other specialised construction activities n.e.c.
Shareholder: Glen Michael John Brady
Officers: Joanne Mary Brady, Secretary; Glen Michael John Brady [1967] Director

Oakland Homes (North East) Limited
Incorporated: 10 July 2009
Registered Office: Dove Crag, Hillside West, Rothbury, Northumberland, NE65 7YN
Activities: Construction of domestic buildings
Shareholders: Keith Storey; Michael Courty
Officers: Keith Reginald Storey, Secretary; Michael George Courty [1965] Director/Property Developer; Keith Reginald Storey [1960] Director/Property Developer

Oaks Properties Limited
Incorporated: 17 February 1994 *Employees:* 4
Net Worth: £3,171,921 *Total Assets:* £6,890,337
Registered Office: The Basement, 25 Osborne Road, Jesmond, Newcastle upon Tyne, NE2 2AH
Activities: Real estate agencies
Shareholders: Om Krishan Puri; Arun Krishan Puri
Officers: Om Krishan Puri [1934] Director/Property Developer

Oaktree Homes (Durham) Limited
Incorporated: 30 May 2007 *Employees:* 1
Net Worth Deficit: £399,484 *Total Assets:* £4,501,619
Registered Office: The Sycamores, Mount House Drive, Gateshead, Tyne & Wear, NE9 7UF
Activities: Development of building projects
Shareholder: Alexander Colin Keith
Officers: Alexander Colin Keith [1960] Director

Oaktree Leasing Ltd
Incorporated: 27 January 2016 *Employees:* 3
Net Worth Deficit: £15,548 *Total Assets:* £824,126
Registered Office: Seaham Harbour Dock Co, Cargo Durham Distribution Centre, Seaham, Co Durham, SR7 7NZ
Activities: Sale of new cars and light motor vehicles
Major Shareholder: Thomas Edmund Carr Stuart
Officers: Thomas Edmund Carr Stuart [1941] Director

Oakview Properties Limited
Incorporated: 6 July 1988
Net Worth: £1,003,775 *Total Assets:* £1,735,456
Registered Office: 32 Cambridge Terrace, Gateshead, Tyne & Wear, NE8 1RP
Activities: Buying and selling of own real estate
Officers: Berta Kaufman, Secretary; Berta Kaufman [1932] Director; Chaim Yehuda Alexander Kaufman [1956] Director

Oakwell Gate Property Company Limited (The)
Incorporated: 10 June 1932 *Employees:* 6
Net Worth: £1,453,450 *Total Assets:* £1,607,317
Registered Office: Spring Cottage, Broomhaugh, Riding Mill, Northumberland, NE44 6EG
Activities: Other service activities n.e.c.
Officers: Charles William Roland Heslop, Secretary; Benjamin Michael Heslop [1976] Director/Yacht Consultant; Charles William Roland Heslop [1955] Director/Company Secretary; Geoffrey Edward Roland Heslop [1927] Director; Jonathan Heslop [1962] Director/Solicitor; Michael Hugh Heslop [1948] Director; Richard James Heslop [1960] Director/Chartered Surveyor

Oakwood House Property and Developments (UK) Limited
Incorporated: 21 March 2006
Net Worth Deficit: £38,838 *Total Assets:* £1,140,819
Registered Office: 33 Kellaw Road, Darlington, Co Durham, DL1 4YA
Activities: Other letting and operating of own or leased real estate
Officers: Christopher Andrew Sanders, Secretary; Mark Brooks [1977] Director/Landscaper; Jonathan Coates [1973] Director Glazing & Conservator; Julie-Ann Foxton [1974] Director; Daniel Charles Key [1977] Director/Consultant; Christopher Andrew Sanders [1966] Director/Solicitor

Oar Properties Limited
Incorporated: 14 February 2002
Net Worth Deficit: £345,620 *Total Assets:* £1,640,736
Registered Office: 18 Grosvenor Road, Jesmond, Newcastle upon Tyne, NE2 2RR
Activities: Other letting and operating of own or leased real estate
Officers: Sarah Suhail Din [1988] Director; Zaida Niaz Din [1963] Director

Oasis Aquila Housing Ltd
Incorporated: 30 November 2004 *Employees:* 78
Net Worth: £2,342,286 *Total Assets:* £3,353,358
Registered Office: 11 Walker Terrace, Gateshead, Tyne & Wear, NE8 1EB
Activities: Other accommodation
Officers: David William Smith, Secretary; Chris Aldridge [1984] Director/Acquisitions Surveyor; Bishop Mark Watts Bryant [1949] Director/Bishop; Ian Elliott [1962] Director/Facilities Manager, Richmondshire District Council; Kate Louise Ginks [1978] Managing Director; Nicholas William Salisbury [1956] Director/Consultant; Dr Anna Caroline Wroe [1974] Director/Consultant Nephrologist

Oberlin Filter Limited
Incorporated: 4 January 1999
Registered Office: 2 Hurworth Road, Aycliffe Business Park, Newton Aycliffe, Co Durham, DL5 6UD
Activities: Manufacture of other special-purpose machinery n.e.c.
Parent: Production Services Company Inc.
Officers: Gillian Shevels, Secretary; Micheal Ignatowski [1954] Director [American]; Andrew Thomas Oberlin [1977] Managing Director [American]; Thomas Oberlin [1943] Director [American]

Ocean Marine.Co.Uk Limited
Incorporated: 2 November 2007
Registered Office: The Old School House, Workshop Stores, East Chevington, Red Row, Northumberland, NE61 5AU
Activities: Sea and coastal passenger water transport
Major Shareholder: Alan Anderson
Officers: Alan James Anderson [1963] Director

Oceana Business Park Limited
Incorporated: 28 June 2013
Registered Office: 1st Floor, Northumbria House, Oceana Business Park, Davy Bank, Wallsend, Tyne & Wear, NE28 6UZ
Activities: Other accommodation
Major Shareholder: Martin Oliver
Officers: Martin Oliver [1961] Director/Property Management

Oceana Group (Holdings) Limited
Incorporated: 11 September 2003
Registered Office: 1st Floor, Northumbria House, Oceana Business Park, Davy Bank, Wallsend, Tyne & Wear, NE28 6UZ
Activities: Buying and selling of own real estate
Shareholder: Tony Mann
Officers: Tony Mann [1942] Director/Property Developer

Oceantec Marine Limited
Incorporated: 22 October 2004
Registered Office: Oceantec Marine Limited, Grindon Way, Heighington Lane Business Park, Newton Aycliffe, Co Durham, DL5 6SH
Activities: Machining
Officers: Rachel Mansfield, Secretary; Andrew David McKenna [1977] Director/Manufacturing Manager; David McKenna [1953] Director

Octagon Green Solutions Limited
Incorporated: 11 December 2012 *Employees:* 2
Net Worth: £1,954,868 *Total Assets:* £3,781,673
Registered Office: Blaydon Quarry Landfill Site, Lead Road, Greenside, Blaydon, Gateshead, Tyne & Wear, NE21 4SX
Activities: Remediation activities and other waste management services
Major Shareholder: Kevin John Wanless
Officers: Kevin John Wanless [1972] Director

Odin Shipping Limited
Incorporated: 28 October 1977
Net Worth: £731,638 *Total Assets:* £953,655
Registered Office: East Quay House, South Dock, Sunderland, Tyne & Wear, SR1 2EE
Activities: Other transportation support activities
Major Shareholder: Svend-Erik Hansson
Officers: Peter Dickson, Secretary; Peter Dickson [1960] Director/Manager; Svend Erik Hansson [1941] Director/Shipbroker [Danish]

Odyssey Systems Limited
Incorporated: 2 July 1990
Net Worth: £3,784,241 *Total Assets:* £4,530,604
Registered Office: Lockheed Court, Preston Farm, Stockton on Tees, Cleveland, TS18 3SH
Activities: Wired telecommunications activities
Major Shareholder: Michael Odysseas
Officers: Christine Louise Gilbert, Secretary; Christine Louise Gilbert [1957] Sales Director; Andrew Middlemiss [1971] Director/Management Accountant; Michael Odysseas [1968] Director/Sales Consultant

Off Shore Fuels Limited
Incorporated: 15 November 1974 *Employees:* 4
Net Worth: £739,461 *Total Assets:* £844,971
Registered Office: 3 Worset Lane, Hartlepool, Cleveland, TS26 0LJ
Activities: Wholesale of other fuels and related products
Shareholder: Michael Jeffrey Smith
Officers: Michael Jeffrey Smith, Secretary; Paul Andrew Lancaster [1965] Director; Geoffrey Smith [1943] Director; Michael Jeffrey Smith [1974] Director

Offerfair Limited
Incorporated: 10 September 1999 *Employees:* 3
Net Worth: £3,227,119 *Total Assets:* £6,810,426
Registered Office: 9-10 Parsons Road, Parsons Industrial Estate, Washington, Tyne & Wear, NE37 1HB
Activities: Buying and selling of own real estate
Major Shareholder: Roger Peter Willems
Officers: Philip John Stratford [1962] Director/Chief Executive Officer; Roger Peter Willems [1947] Managing Director

Offshore Renewable Energy Catapult
Incorporated: 7 February 2003 *Employees:* 133
Net Worth: £6,139,000 *Total Assets:* £82,424,000
Registered Office: Offshore House, Albert Street, Blyth, Northumberland, NE24 1LZ
Activities: Other professional, scientific and technical activities n.e.c.
Officers: Shareen Bibi Gault, Secretary; Lesley Anne Glover [1956] Director/Vice Principal for External Affairs; Frederick Stanislaus Hallsworth [1953] Independent Non-Executive Director; Dr Colin William Hood [1955] Director; Andrew John Jamieson [1967] Director/Chief Executive; Julia Elizabeth King [1954] Director/Vice Chancellor; Professor Sir James Rufus McDonald [1957] Director/University Principal & Vice Chancellor; Hugh Peter McNeal [1970] Director/Chief Executive; Andrew Mill [1951] Director; Alan Geoffrey Moore [1949] Director; Andrew Peter Lindsay Walls [1968] Finance Director

Offshore Support Vessels IV Limited
Incorporated: 21 June 1966
Net Worth: £1,083,000 *Total Assets:* £1,132,000
Registered Office: c/o Endeavour Partnership LLP, Tobias House, St Mark's Court, Teesdale Business Park, Stockton on Tees, Cleveland, TS17 6QW
Activities: Support activities for petroleum and natural gas mining
Parent: Vroon Offshore UK Limited
Officers: Graeme Paul Sheach, Secretary; Craig Harvie [1967] Director/Manager; Graeme Paul Sheach [1966] Director/Chartered Accountant

Offshore Support Vessels V Limited
Incorporated: 26 June 2001
Net Worth: £11,839,000 *Total Assets:* £42,964,000
Registered Office: c/o Endeavour Partnership LLP, Tobias House, St Mark's Court, Teesdale Business Park, Stockton on Tees, Cleveland, TS17 6QW
Activities: Support activities for petroleum and natural gas mining
Parent: Vroon Offshore UK Limited
Officers: Graeme Paul Sheach, Secretary; Craig Harvie [1967] Director/Manager; Graeme Paul Sheach [1966] Director/Chartered Accountant

OFL4 LLP
Incorporated: 30 April 2013
Net Worth: £468,223 *Total Assets:* £1,236,394
Registered Office: 32 Portland Terrace, Newcastle upon Tyne, NE2 1QP
Officers: Thomas Francis Eyre Speir [1941] Member; Sandra Judith Anne Lourenco [1944] LLP Member; Stacy John Owens [1976] LLP Member

OGI Groundwater Specialists Limited
Incorporated: 4 December 1989 *Employees:* 12
Net Worth: £689,406 *Total Assets:* £1,495,273
Registered Office: One St John's Court, St Johns Road, Meadowfield Industrial Estate, Meadowfield, Co Durham, DH7 8TP
Activities: Architectural activities
Major Shareholder: Dr Stephen David Thomas
Officers: Dr Stephen David Thomas [1957] Director/Civil Engineer

Oil Consultants Holdco Limited
Incorporated: 18 November 2010 *Employees:* 36
Net Worth: £868,837 *Total Assets:* £10,009,722
Registered Office: Parsons House, Parsons Industrial Estate, Washington, Tyne & Wear, NE37 1EZ
Activities: Other activities of employment placement agencies
Officers: Mark James Clayton, Secretary; Mark James Clayton [1989] Finance Director; Deborah Marie Cooper [1963] Director; Claire Fielding [1967] Director; Richard Fielding [1967] Director; Geoffrey Lennox [1956] Director; Jane Elizabeth Lennox [1956] Director; Helen Mary Smith [1962] Director

Oil Consultants Limited
Incorporated: 9 June 2003 *Employees:* 29
Net Worth: £6,755,360 *Total Assets:* £8,172,950
Registered Office: Parsons House, Parsons Industrial Estate, Washington, Tyne & Wear, NE37 1EZ
Activities: Support activities for petroleum and natural gas mining
Parent: Oil Consultants Holdco Limited
Officers: Mark James Clayton, Secretary; Mark James Clayton [1989] Finance Director; Richard Fielding [1967] Director; Geoffrey Lennox [1956] Director; Helen Mary Smith [1962] Director

Oil NRG Ltd
Incorporated: 30 May 2007 *Employees:* 47
Net Worth: £1,535,560 *Total Assets:* £13,550,093
Registered Office: Baltic Works, Baltic Street, Hartlepool, Cleveland, TS25 1PW
Activities: Wholesale of other fuels and related products
Officers: Gary Martin Nicholl [1968] Director [Irish]; Charles Frederick Peart [1966] Managing Director; Roger David Hunter Peart [1972] Managing Director; Timothy Charles Maxwell Shepherd [1967] Sales Director

W A Old & Son Limited
Incorporated: 9 May 2003 *Employees:* 8
Net Worth: £582,876 *Total Assets:* £1,083,382
Registered Office: Anndale, Stannerford Road, Crawcrook, Ryton, Tyne & Wear, NE40 3SN
Activities: Freight transport by road
Officers: Anthony Steven Old, Secretary; Steven William Old [1957] Director/Haulage Contractor

Old Exchange Darlington Limited
Incorporated: 18 October 2012 *Employees:* 3
Net Worth: £427,170 *Total Assets:* £1,995,323
Registered Office: 2nd Floor, Tirrem House, 16 High Street, Yarm, Cleveland, TS15 9AE
Activities: Other letting and operating of own or leased real estate
Officers: Andrew Loughran Preston [1966] Director/Property Investor; Graham Michael Senior [1970] Director/Chartered Surveyor; Graham Kevin Sizer [1969] Director/Chartered Accountant

Oldgate Finance Limited
Incorporated: 26 April 2001 *Employees:* 4
Net Worth: £44,013 *Total Assets:* £1,069,805
Registered Office: 12 Stanley Street, Blyth, Northumberland, NE24 2BU
Activities: Other credit granting n.e.c.
Shareholders: Duncan Michael Weir; Karen Weir
Officers: Karen Weir, Secretary; Duncan Michael Weir [1971] Director/Insurance Broker; Karen Weir [1971] Director/Insurance Broker

Oldgreen Limited
Incorporated: 21 November 2013
Net Worth: £220,949 *Total Assets:* £1,033,139
Registered Office: 7 Segedunum Business Centre, Station Road, Wallsend, Tyne & Wear, NE28 6HQ
Activities: Wholesale of sugar and chocolate and sugar confectionery
Major Shareholder: Chase Manders
Officers: Chase James Bailey Earl Manders [1981] Director

Oldham & Openshaw DP Limited
Incorporated: 24 April 2012
Net Worth: £1,211,861 *Total Assets:* £1,512,623
Registered Office: 178 York Road, Hartlepool, Cleveland, TS26 9EA
Activities: Other retail sale of food in specialised stores
Major Shareholder: Mike Racz
Officers: Mike Racz, Secretary; Mike Racz [1982] Director/Franchisee

On A Roll Sandwich Company Limited
Incorporated: 10 November 2006 *Employees:* 172
Net Worth: £1,864,657 *Total Assets:* £6,978,527
Registered Office: The Pantry, Barton Road, Middlesbrough, Cleveland, TS2 1RY
Activities: Manufacture of other food products n.e.c.
Shareholders: James McLay Stoddart; Helen Beverley Stoddart
Officers: Helen Beverley Stoddart, Secretary; James McLay Stoddart [1964] Director/Caterer

On Medical Limited
Incorporated: 7 April 2006 *Employees:* 58
Net Worth: £15,316,407 *Total Assets:* £16,798,716
Registered Office: Saxon House, 50-52 Heaton Road, Byker, Newcastle upon Tyne, NE6 1SL
Activities: General medical practice activities
Parent: Winn Holding Limited
Officers: Jeffery John Winn, Secretary; Iain Stuart Richardson [1973] Director/Chartered Accountant; Jeffery John Winn [1965] Director/Solicitor

On Track Retail Limited
Incorporated: 23 September 2014 *Employees:* 26
Net Worth: £140,000 *Total Assets:* £3,365,000
Registered Office: 3rd Floor, 41-51 Grey Street, Newcastle upon Tyne, NE1 6EE
Activities: Other business support service activities n.e.c.
Parent: Go-Ahead Holding Limited
Officers: Carolyn Ferguson, Secretary; Simon Patrick Butcher [1967] Finance Director; Enrique Fernandez-Pino [1966] Director [Spanish]; Alistair Byron Lees [1970] Director; Barry Royston Shaw [1945] Director; Katherine Taylor [1977] Director

On-Hire Limited
Incorporated: 31 January 2000 *Employees:* 15
Net Worth: £30,333,892 *Total Assets:* £40,438,044
Registered Office: Saxon House, Heaton Road, Newcastle upon Tyne, NE6 1SE
Activities: Renting and leasing of cars and light motor vehicles
Parent: Winn Holding Limited
Officers: Jeffery John Winn, Secretary; Iain Stuart Richardson [1973] Director/Chartered Accountant; Jeffery John Winn [1965] Solicitor Managing Director

One Premium Fitness Limited
Incorporated: 17 November 2015 *Employees:* 2
Net Worth Deficit: £349,150 *Total Assets:* £935,802
Registered Office: Fleming Business Centre, Burdon Terrace, Newcastle upon Tyne, NE2 3AE
Activities: Fitness facilities
Shareholders: Andrew William Graham Wylie; Wylie Childrens Settlement Trust
Officers: Kerry Louise McDonnell, Secretary; Andrew Mark Simpson, Secretary; Jackie Boylan [1971] Director; Paul James Ferris [1965] Director; Alan Shearer [1970] Director; Andrew Mark Simpson [1975] Director; Andrew William Graham Wylie [1959] Director

One Real Estate Development Limited
Incorporated: 21 January 2016
Net Worth Deficit: £7,394 *Total Assets:* £1,296,164
Registered Office: Room 2, 17b Windsor Terrace, Jesmond, Newcastle upon Tyne, NE2 4HE
Activities: Other letting and operating of own or leased real estate
Major Shareholder: Mohsin Latif Rashid
Officers: Mohsin Latif Rashid [1992] Director/Graduate Surveyor

Onyx Scientific Limited
Incorporated: 14 March 2000
Net Worth: £3,583,398 *Total Assets:* £4,797,612
Registered Office: Units 97 & 98 Silverbriar, Sunderland Enterprise Park East, Sunderland, Tyne & Wear, SR5 2TQ
Activities: Manufacture of basic pharmaceutical products
Parent: Ipca Laboratories Ltd
Officers: Denise Bowser [1971] Commercial Director; Pranay Godha [1972] Executive Director [Indian]; Nathan Vincent Lane [1972] Finance Director; Derek John Londesbrough [1970] Director of Chemistry

Ops Catering Limited
Incorporated: 14 March 2013 *Employees:* 130
Net Worth: £328,245 *Total Assets:* £1,284,997
Registered Office: 511 Durham Road, Low Fell, Gateshead, Tyne & Wear, NE9 5EY
Activities: Take-away food shops and mobile food stands
Major Shareholder: Owen Bradford
Officers: Owen Bradford [1964] Director; Paul Taylor [1969] Director; Steven Taylor [1969] Director

Opsec Security Group Limited
Incorporated: 23 December 1982
Net Worth: £69,760,000 *Total Assets:* £81,322,000
Registered Office: 40 Phoenix Road, Washington, Tyne & Wear, NE38 0AD
Activities: Other manufacturing n.e.c.
Parent: Orca Bidco Limited
Officers: Michael William Angus, Secretary/Accountant; Michael William Angus [1964] Director/Accountant; Michael John Currie [1975] Director/Chartered Accountant

Opsec Security Limited
Incorporated: 10 March 1986 *Employees:* 163
Net Worth: £12,539,000 *Total Assets:* £19,296,000
Registered Office: 40 Phoenix Road, Washington, Tyne & Wear, NE38 0AD
Activities: Other manufacturing n.e.c.
Parent: Opsec Security Group Limited
Officers: Michael John Currie, Secretary; David Andrew Bowden [1972] Operations Director; Michael John Currie [1975] Director

Optimise Neurotherapy Centre Limited
Incorporated: 6 April 2010
Net Worth: £758,217 *Total Assets:* £869,765
Registered Office: 34 Frederick Street, Sunderland, Tyne & Wear, SR1 1LP
Activities: Other human health activities
Major Shareholder: Sue Raine
Officers: Sue Raine [1965] Director

Optimus Global Limited
Incorporated: 6 August 2001
Net Worth: £988,322 *Total Assets:* £1,329,846
Registered Office: 22 Southgate Mews, Morpeth, Northumberland, NE61 2BW
Activities: Wholesale of hardware, plumbing and heating equipment and supplies
Shareholder: Shahram Dalvand
Officers: Imei Dalvand, Secretary; Shahram Dalvand [1960] Managing Director

Opus Building Services Limited
Incorporated: 9 May 2006 *Employees:* 74
Net Worth: £472,041 *Total Assets:* £1,555,370
Registered Office: Unit 7 Boldon Court, Boldon Colliery, Co Durham, NE35 9LZ
Activities: Electrical installation
Shareholders: Gavin Austin Richardson; Ian King
Officers: Ian King, Secretary; Ian King [1965] Director/Builder; Gavin Austin Richardson [1975] Director/Electrician

R.H. Orange & Son Limited
Incorporated: 16 July 2001 *Employees:* 25
Net Worth: £996,192 *Total Assets:* £1,628,375
Registered Office: Unit 106 North East Fruit & Vegetable Market, Team Valley Trading Estate, Gateshead, Tyne & Wear, NE11 0QY
Activities: Wholesale of sugar and chocolate and sugar confectionery
Shareholders: Michael Robert Orange; Lisa Beattie; Patricia Orange
Officers: Lisa Beattie, Secretary; Michael Robert Orange [1965] Director/Manager

Orange Box Self Storage Ltd
Incorporated: 12 December 2000
Registered Office: 25 Pallion West Industrial Estate, Sunderland, Tyne & Wear, SR4 6SJ
Activities: Operation of warehousing and storage facilities for land transport activities
Shareholders: Keith Wilson; Denise Wilson
Officers: Denise Wilson, Secretary/Civil Servant; Carl Allen Hedley [1980] Director/Container Trader; Keith Wilson [1963] Director/Container Trader

Orange Plant Limited
Incorporated: 14 March 2001 *Employees:* 30
Net Worth: £1,135,240 *Total Assets:* £4,075,382
Registered Office: Express Works, Brunswick Industrial Estate, Newcastle upon Tyne, NE13 7BA
Activities: Support services to forestry
Major Shareholder: Patricia Lilian Chapman
Officers: Philip Nathan Blackburn, Secretary; Joanna Chapman [1975] Director/Manager; Patricia Lilian Chapman [1950] Director

Orca Bidco Limited
Incorporated: 12 October 2015 *Employees:* 452
Net Worth: £52,047,712 *Total Assets:* £87,025,776
Registered Office: 40 Phoenix Road, Washington, Tyne & Wear, NE38 0AD
Activities: Other manufacturing n.e.c.
Parent: Orca Holdings Limited
Officers: Michael William Angus [1964] Director; Hazem Ben-Gacem [1970] Director/Finance; Richard Stewart Cremona [1957] Director/Chief Executive [American]; Richard Fuller [1962] Director; Gilbert Benjamin Kamieniecky [1981] Director [German]; Federico Minoli [1949] Director [Italian]; Roberta Vezzoli [1986] Director [Italian]

Orchard Garden Properties Limited
Incorporated: 6 September 2013
Registered Office: 5 Orchard Gardens, Whitburn, Sunderland, Tyne & Wear, SR6 9JW
Activities: Development of building projects
Major Shareholder: Robert Burns
Officers: Doreen Burns [1952] Director; Robert Burns [1951] Director

Orchard Homecare Services Limited
Incorporated: 1 August 2000 *Employees:* 163
Net Worth: £660,751 *Total Assets:* £848,346
Registered Office: 2 Ashfield Terrace, Chester-le-Street, Co Durham, DH3 3PD
Activities: Other business support service activities n.e.c.
Shareholders: Peter Thomas Alderson; Barbara Alderson
Officers: Barbara Alderson, Secretary/Director; Barbara Alderson [1959] Director; Peter Thomas Alderson [1958] Director/Proprietor

Orchard Information Systems Limited
Incorporated: 27 March 1985 *Employees:* 175
Net Worth: £949,730 *Total Assets:* £12,947,307
Registered Office: 3rd Floor, Central Square, Forth Street, Newcastle upon Tyne, NE1 3PJ
Activities: Business and domestic software development
Major Shareholder: Peter Anthony Hunt
Officers: Ian David Shard, Secretary; Lucy Victoria Winwood Armstrong [1968] Director; Patrick Alan Clarke [1965] Director/Chief Executive [Irish]; John Andrew Hunt [1977] Director; Daniel John Tobin [1974] Commercial Director

Orchidsoft Limited
Incorporated: 17 March 1999 *Employees:* 39
Net Worth: £1,337,846 *Total Assets:* £3,106,067
Registered Office: 4 Bankside, The Watermark, Gateshead, Tyne & Wear, NE11 9SY
Activities: Business and domestic software development
Major Shareholder: Ajay Sood
Officers: Honey Sood, Secretary; Neville Bearpark [1959] Director/Chartered Accountant; Alex Buchan [1961] Investor Director; Alex Marsh [1984] Investor Director; Mark John Rooks [1978] Director/Senior Software Engineer; Sukhvinder Singh Ryatt [1969] Director; Ajay Sood [1967] Managing Director; David Ronald Tiplady Thompson [1945] Director/Chairman; Alan Langley Willis [1972] Director/Software Consultant

Orderelite Limited
Incorporated: 6 December 1996
Registered Office: 7 Bankside, The Watermark, Gateshead, Tyne & Wear, NE11 9SY
Activities: Management of real estate on a fee or contract basis
Shareholders: Priyanka Singh; Rishi Singh; Prativa Singh
Officers: Prativa Singh [1953] Director; Priyanka Singh [1974] Director; Rishi Singh [1977] Director

Ore Catapult Development Services Limited
Incorporated: 25 November 2005
Net Worth: £2,810,000 *Total Assets:* £3,907,000
Registered Office: Offshore House, Albert Street, Blyth, Northumberland, NE24 1LZ
Activities: Other professional, scientific and technical activities n.e.c.
Officers: Andrew Peter Lindsay Walls, Secretary; Christopher Joseph Hill [1968] Innovation Engineering and Programmes Director; Andrew John Jamieson [1967] Director/Chief Executive; Anthony Lawrence Quinn [1962] Director/Engineer; Andrew Peter Lindsay Walls [1968] Finance Director

Oregon Estates Limited
Incorporated: 21 November 2013 *Employees:* 2
Net Worth: £955,094 *Total Assets:* £6,186,191
Registered Office: 3rd Floor, One Trinity Gardens, Broad Chare, Newcastle upon Tyne, NE1 2HF
Activities: Other letting and operating of own or leased real estate
Major Shareholder: Alison Morgan
Officers: Alison Morgan [1962] Director; Oliver Allan Morgan [1989] Director

The Original Produce Company (Middlesbrough) Limited
Incorporated: 28 February 2002 *Employees:* 24
Net Worth: £516,825 *Total Assets:* £991,122
Registered Office: Fresh Produce & Flower Centre, Unit 1 Easter Park, Barton Road, Middlesbrough, Cleveland, TS2 1RY
Activities: Wholesale of fruit and vegetables
Shareholders: Jill Scott; John Charles Bell
Officers: Jill Scott, Secretary/Director; John Charles Bell [1960] Director; Jill Scott [1961] Director

Ors Contracting Limited
Incorporated: 26 August 1994 *Employees:* 36
Net Worth: £626,927 *Total Assets:* £1,046,915
Registered Office: Unit 11 Hunter House Industrial Estate, Tofts Road East, Hartlepool, Cleveland, TS25 2BE
Activities: Construction of commercial buildings
Shareholders: John O'Connor; Roy James O'Connor
Officers: Mary Daphne O'Connor, Secretary; John O'Connor [1950] Director; Mary Daphne O'Connor [1953] Director; Roy James O'Connor [1978] Director

Orwin Limited
Incorporated: 3 January 2003
Net Worth: £663,293 *Total Assets:* £6,543,921
Registered Office: 3 Brockwell Road, Crowther, Washington, Tyne & Wear, NE38 0AF
Activities: Manufacture of other general-purpose machinery n.e.c.
Parent: Whiteley Murphy Ltd
Officers: Christopher Whiteley, Secretary/Managing Director; Brian Gerard Murphy [1969] Director/Management Consultant; Christopher Whiteley [1961] Managing Director

Osbit Limited
Incorporated: 11 October 2000 *Employees:* 47
Net Worth: £3,198,580 *Total Assets:* £6,447,530
Registered Office: Broomhaugh House, Broomhaugh, Riding Mill, Northumberland, NE44 6AW
Activities: Manufacture of other fabricated metal products n.e.c.
Major Shareholder: Antony David Trapp
Officers: Dr Antony David Trapp, Secretary; Dr Stephen Agar [1959] Director/Engineer; Stephen William Bedford [1963] Director/Engineer; Robbie Paul Blakeman [1976] Director/Mechanical Engineer; Rosamund Evelyn Blomfield-Smith [1949] Director; Terence Joseph Courtney [1954] Director; Mark Arnold Bowes Hatton [1962] Director/Financial Consultant; Brendon Matthew Hayward [1980] Director/Engineer; Antony David Trapp [1945] Director

Osborne Engineering Limited
Incorporated: 17 March 1983 *Employees:* 51
Net Worth: £2,891,456 *Total Assets:* £4,106,243
Registered Office: Unit 19 Atley Way, North Nelson Industrial Estate, Cramlington, Northumberland, NE23 1WA
Activities: Machining
Parent: AM Holdings Ltd (Bvi)
Officers: Rahul Hazra, Secretary; Kerry Ann Hardwick [1973] Director; Rahul Hazra [1970] Director [Indian]; Stewart Hicks [1970] Director [Australian]; Ziad Abou Nasr [1969] Director [Lebanese]

Osborne Motor Transport Limited
Incorporated: 2 April 1998 *Employees:* 44
Net Worth: £858,972 *Total Assets:* £1,330,593
Registered Office: Commercial Road, South Shields, Tyne & Wear, NE33 1RQ
Activities: Freight transport by road
Major Shareholder: Stanley James Kidney
Officers: Stanley James Kidney, Secretary; Stanley James Kidney [1944] Director/Haulier

Osborne Orthodontics Ltd
Incorporated: 14 March 2007
Net Worth: £775,793 *Total Assets:* £1,373,775
Registered Office: 3 Nile Street, North Shields, Tyne & Wear, NE29 0BE
Activities: Dental practice activities
Officers: Dr Christine Tsangaraki-Osborne, Secretary; Erik Hereward Osborne [1969] Director/Orthodontist; Dr Christine Tsangaraki-Osborne [1970] Director/Dentist

Osborne Professional Services Limited
Incorporated: 17 March 2004 *Employees:* 65
Net Worth: £970,768 *Total Assets:* £2,037,442
Registered Office: 5 Osborne Terrace, Jesmond, Newcastle upon Tyne, NE2 1SQ
Activities: Other service activities n.e.c.
Shareholder: Paul Hughes
Officers: Paul Hughes, Secretary/Solicitor; Howard Barry Gold [1943] Director/Solicitor; Paul Hughes [1965] Director/Solicitor; John Phillip Nicholson [1973] Director/Solicitor

Oskap (Commercial) Limited
Incorporated: 9 August 2004
Net Worth: £86,519 *Total Assets:* £1,270,517
Registered Office: 7 Acorn Road, Newcastle upon Tyne, NE2 2DJ
Activities: Buying and selling of own real estate
Parent: Oskap Limited
Officers: Kamni Margaret Puri, Secretary/Chartered Accountant; Arun Krishan Puri [1966] Director; Kamni Margaret Puri [1966] Director/Chartered Accountant

Oskap Limited
Incorporated: 14 December 1998
Net Worth: £2,468,040 *Total Assets:* £6,179,532
Registered Office: 46 Mitchell Avenue, Jesmond, Newcastle upon Tyne, NE2 3LA
Activities: Other letting and operating of own or leased real estate
Shareholders: Arun Krishan Puri; Kamni Margaret Puri
Officers: Kamni Margaret Puri, Secretary/Chartered Accountant; Arun Krishan Puri [1966] Director/Project Manager; Kamni Margaret Puri [1966] Director/Chartered Accountant

OSO Hotwater (U.K.) Limited
Incorporated: 3 December 1993 *Employees:* 16
Net Worth: £1,157,028 *Total Assets:* £2,181,630
Registered Office: Endeavour House, Colmet Court, Queensway South, Team Valley Trading Estate, Gateshead, Tyne & Wear, NE11 0EF
Activities: Other service activities n.e.c.
Major Shareholder: Sigurd Braathen
Officers: Philip Edward Grange, Secretary; Jonas Aartun [1980] Director/Solicitor [Norwegian]; Andrew Elms [1965] Director/Sales Manager; Michael Stuart Elsy [1968] Managing Director; Lars Odegard [1964] Sales Director [Norwegian]; David Sidney Wilkes [1964] Director/Sales Manager

Ostrada Limited
Incorporated: 14 May 2014
Registered Office: Unit 2 Team Valley Business Centre, Earlsway, Team Valley Trading Estate, Gateshead, Tyne & Wear, NE11 0QH
Activities: Non-specialised wholesale trade
Major Shareholder: Adrian Roswell
Officers: Adrian Roswell [1975] Director

Otolift Stairlifts Limited
Incorporated: 1 December 2011
Net Worth: £172,139 *Total Assets:* £1,341,522
Registered Office: Unit 53 Consett Business Park, Consett, Co Durham, DH8 6BN
Activities: Wholesale of other machinery and equipment
Officers: LEA Dobby, Secretary; LEA Dobby [1970] Director; Andre Ooms [1978] Director [Dutch]

Otterburn Investments Limited
Incorporated: 23 September 2003
Net Worth: £472,082 *Total Assets:* £892,287
Registered Office: Otterburn Mill, Otterburn, Northumberland, NE19 1JT
Activities: Other letting and operating of own or leased real estate
Parent: Otterburn Holdings Ltd
Officers: Nigel Owen, Secretary; Nigel Owen [1966] Director/Retailer; Euan James Pringle [1952] Director/Retailer

Oubas LLP
Incorporated: 1 December 2011
Net Worth: £1,245,613 *Total Assets:* £1,738,154
Registered Office: Highfield House, Slaley Grange, Slaley, Northumberland, NE47 0AD
Officers: Joanna Chapman [1975] Member; Patricia Lilian Chapman [1950] Member

Our Children 1st
Incorporated: 21 February 2017
Net Worth: £5,573,000 *Total Assets:* £6,183,000
Registered Office: Pallister Park Primary School, Gribdale Road, Pallister Park, Middlesbrough, Cleveland, TS3 8PW
Activities: Other education n.e.c.
Officers: Helen Louise Bone [1977] Director/School Business Manager; Ray Brown [1948] Director/Retired; Len Clarke [1949] Director/Retired; Julie Marie Davies [1971] Director/Manager; Ros Jessop [1957] Director; Catherine Jones [1971] Director/Deputy Headteacher; Jane Thackstone [1969] Director/Assistant Head; Stuart Williams [1988] Director/Safeguarding Consultant

Our Lady of Light Catholic Academy Trust
Incorporated: 8 July 2015 *Employees:* 224
Net Worth Deficit: £1,050,341 *Total Assets:* £1,157,394
Registered Office: St Patrick's Catholic College, Baysdale Road, Thornaby, Stockton on Tees, Cleveland, TS17 9DE
Activities: Pre-primary education
Officers: Lucy Elizabeth Emmerson, Secretary; Kevin Duffy [1963] Director/Diocesan Schools Commissioner; James David Farquhar [1976] Director/Chartered Accountant; Dr James Nevison [1977] Director/Medical Doctor; Janet O'Neill [1959] Director/Educational Psychologist; Anne-Marie Frances Stephenson [1976] Director/Teacher; Josephine Wilson [1959] Director/Headteacher

Ouseburn Learning Trust
Incorporated: 4 September 2014
Net Worth: £47,165,828 *Total Assets:* £47,166,428
Registered Office: Cragside Primary School, Cragside, Newcastle upon Tyne, NE7 7EL
Activities: Other education n.e.c.
Officers: Lucy Rebecca Backhurst [1971] Director/Head of Recruitment & Admissions; Dr Wasim Baqir [1969] Director/Pharmacist - NHS England; Karen Blackburn [1969] Director/Headteacher; Professor Margaret Anne Defeyter [1962] Director/Academic Professor; Jane Edminson [1962] Director/Local Government Officer; Deirdre Fawcett [1960] Director of Human Resources; Sandra Furno [1962] Director/Headteacher; Suzanne Lisa Hendey [1969] Director/Central Support Manager; Rebecca Louise Kroese [1967] Director/Headteacher; Clive Peter Maddison [1964] Director/Headteacher; Allan Willi Marks [1956] Director/Parish Priest; Shirley Anne Mills [1954] Director; Ailsa Elizabeth Nokes [1969] Director/Senior Healthcare Manager; Deborah Mary Tyler [1967] Director/Local Government Manager (Education); Gary Wallis-Clarke [1970] Director/Headteacher; Miles Clifford Maynard Wallis-Clarke [1966] Director; Benjamin Wassall [1977] Director/Headteacher; Alice Alexandra Witherow [1969] Director

Ouseburn Trust
Incorporated: 18 January 1996 *Employees:* 7
Net Worth: £1,262,744 *Total Assets:* £1,344,627
Registered Office: 53-55 Lime Street, Newcastle upon Tyne, NE1 2PQ
Activities: Renting and operating of Housing Association real estate
Officers: Raymond Geoffrey Bland [1952] Director/Chartered Engineer; Jon Dale Bolland [1949] Director/Retired; Susan Bright [1956] Director/Accounts Manager; Noel Anthony Gates [1965] Director/Chief Executive [Irish]; Dr Myra Giesen [1962] Director/University Lecturer [American]; Brenda Grey [1949] Director/Retired Civil Servant; Catherine Sarah Hindle [1974] Director/Head of Operations and Tourism; Geoffrey Kell [1960] Director/Writer; Hugh Philip Massey [1952] Director/Architect; Paul Francis Murphy [1961] Director/Chartered Surveyor; Sheila Spencer [1954] Director/Housing Researcher

Ouston Farms Limited
Incorporated: 29 September 1977 *Employees:* 6
Net Worth: £5,272,288 *Total Assets:* £6,319,523
Registered Office: Trench Hall, Ravensworth, Gateshead, Tyne & Wear, NE11 0HQ
Activities: Mixed farming
Officers: Dora Oates, Secretary; Charlotte Hodgson [1970] Director/Manager; Dora Oates [1946] Director/Teacher; William Snowdon Oates [1943] Director/Farmer; Louise Riley [1972] Director/Teacher

Outer West Learning Trust
Incorporated: 17 March 2014
Net Worth: £17,918,300 *Total Assets:* £17,920,552
Registered Office: Throckley Primary School, Hexham Road, Throckley, Newcastle upon Tyne, NE15 9DY
Activities: Primary education
Officers: Joanne Mary Clifford Swan [1964] Director/Principal Lecturer; Susan Diane Hall [1958] Director/Headteacher; Joanne Lockey [1969] Director/Civil Servant; Justine Jayne Massingham [1973] Director/Grants Manager; Robert William Morgan [1951] Director/Retired; Mark Jeremy Outterside [1967] Director/Headteacher; Stuart David Pickup [1977] Director/Headteacher; Helen Linda Richarson [1950] Director/Educational Consultant; Helen Elizabeth Simpson [1963] Director/Headteacher; Clare Helen Smith [1965] Director/Museums Education Manager; Louise Thompson [1973] Director/Headteacher; Angela Pauline Tinning [1973] Director/Finance Officer; Deborah Mary Tyler [1967] Director/Local Government Officer

Outlet Properties Limited
Incorporated: 22 February 1999 *Employees:* 2
Net Worth: £342,633 *Total Assets:* £813,555
Registered Office: St Georges Vicarage, Eastgate Bank, Mickley, Stocksfield, Northumberland, NE43 7LS
Activities: Other letting and operating of own or leased real estate
Officers: Christine Cuthbert, Secretary; Peter Cuthbert [1956] Director

Overdrive (North East) Limited
Incorporated: 4 January 2007 *Employees:* 2
Net Worth: £740,004 *Total Assets:* £1,079,988
Registered Office: 33 Station Road, Stannington, Morpeth, Northumberland, NE61 6DX
Activities: Sale of used cars and light motor vehicles
Shareholders: Jason Miller; Nichola Miller
Officers: Jason Miller, Secretary; Nichola Miller [1980] Director

Overs and Rich Limited
Incorporated: 10 February 1975 *Employees:* 11
Net Worth: £1,026,537 *Total Assets:* £1,133,682
Registered Office: Expresso Amusements, 19 Market Place, Bedlington, Northumberland, NE22 5TN
Activities: Other amusement and recreation activities n.e.c.
Parent: Treatview Limited
Officers: Stephen Overs [1964] Director/Amusement Caterer

Ovington Boats Limited
Incorporated: 7 May 1997 *Employees:* 31
Net Worth: £1,472,806 *Total Assets:* £2,142,776
Registered Office: Tanners Bank, North Shields, Tyne & Wear, NE30 1JH
Activities: Other manufacturing n.e.c.
Parent: Ovington Holdings Limited
Officers: Nigel John Carruthers [1966] Operations Director; John Paul Coyles [1973] Director/Chartered Accountant; Christopher John Turner [1972] Director/Businessman

Ovington Holdings Limited
Incorporated: 1 December 2005
Net Worth: £1,074,718 *Total Assets:* £1,074,718
Registered Office: 31 Tanners Bank, North Shields, Tyne & Wear, NE30 1JH
Activities: Activities of other holding companies n.e.c.
Shareholders: Kathryn Rebekah Turner; Christopher John Turner
Officers: Christopher John Turner [1972] Director/Boat Builder

Owben Ltd
Incorporated: 21 May 2012
Net Worth: £852,639 *Total Assets:* £1,253,002
Registered Office: Unit 3 Stratford Road, Pattinson Industrial Estate, Washington, Tyne & Wear, NE38 8QP
Activities: Installation of industrial machinery and equipment
Shareholders: Lee Spencer Finney; John Paul Hope; Richard Alan Walsh
Officers: Lee Spencer Finney [1974] Director/Management; John Paul Hope [1970] Director; Richard Alan Walsh [1975] Director/Management

Clive Owen LLP
Incorporated: 16 March 2005 *Employees:* 77
Net Worth: £1,640,291 *Total Assets:* £2,179,186
Registered Office: 140 Coniscliffe Road, Darlington, Co Durham, DL3 7RT
Officers: Angus Ian Allan [1967] Member; Rosemary Annie Anderson [1966] Member; Neville William Baldry [1961] Member; Christopher Paul Beaumont [1968] Member; Nicola Jane Bellerby [1971] Member; William James Catterick [1982] Member; Terence Anthony Doyle [1953] Member; Gary John Ellis [1963] Member; Simon Paul Hook [1980] Member; Antony William Luckett [1961] Member; Alan David Moore [1962] Member; Kevin Shotton [1981] Member

Owens Business Developments Limited
Incorporated: 3 December 1999
Net Worth: £387,938 *Total Assets:* £1,304,534
Registered Office: 9 Bonnyrigg Close, Ingleby Barwick, Stockton on Tees, Cleveland, TS17 0PG
Activities: Other letting and operating of own or leased real estate
Shareholder: John Owens
Officers: John Owens, Secretary; Gillian Owens [1966] Director/Development Manager; John Owens [1953] Director/Accountant; Michele Owens [1956] Director/Administrator; Terry Owens [1947] Director/Business Consultant

Owens Nutrition Limited
Incorporated: 4 September 2000 *Employees:* 10
Net Worth: £1,369,838 *Total Assets:* £1,816,022
Registered Office: Owens Nutrition Ltd, Frigidale Mill, Great Smeaton, Northallerton, N Yorks, DL6 2NF
Activities: Manufacture of prepared feeds for farm animals
Shareholders: Andrew Owens; Jane Owens; Margaret Mary Owens
Officers: Andrew Owens, Secretary/Director; Andrew Owens [1965] Director; Jane Owens [1966] Director; Margaret Mary Owens [1938] Director

P & I Design Limited
Incorporated: 26 July 1978 *Employees:* 14
Net Worth: £451,309 *Total Assets:* £1,229,613
Registered Office: 2 Reed Street, Gladstone Industrial Estate, Thornaby, Cleveland, TS17 7AF
Activities: Business and domestic software development
Officers: Michael Robert Edwards, Secretary; John Ernest Edwards [1940] Director; Mary Elizabeth Peterson Edwards [1939] Director; Michael Robert Edwards [1964] Director/Computer Programmer; Martin Morgan [1968] Managing Director; Philip Jonathan Parkin [1959] Managing Director; David Raymond Ransome [1951] Director; Pauline Ransome [1952] Director

P & P Caravan Services Limited
Incorporated: 9 November 2006
Net Worth: £269,083 *Total Assets:* £2,697,231
Registered Office: RMT, Gosforth Park Avenue, Newcastle upon Tyne, NE12 8EG
Activities: Maintenance and repair of motor vehicles
Shareholders: Patrick Joseph Doherty; Patrick Alexious Carlin
Officers: Patrick Alexious Carlin, Secretary; Patrick Alexious Carlin [1948] Director; Patrick Joseph Doherty [1955] Director

P J M Properties Limited
Incorporated: 26 September 2002
Net Worth: £1,699 *Total Assets:* £1,366,187
Registered Office: 5 Victoria Avenue, Bishop Auckland, Co Durham, DL14 7JH
Activities: Other letting and operating of own or leased real estate
Major Shareholder: Kevin Davis
Officers: Kevin Davis, Secretary; Maria Davis [1982] Director; Jo Ann Elizabeth Flatt [1975] Director; Paul Steele [1971] Director

P North Group Limited
Incorporated: 20 November 2009
Net Worth: £77,899 *Total Assets:* £1,816,287
Registered Office: 264-266 Durham Road, Gateshead, Tyne & Wear, NE8 4JR
Activities: Buying and selling of own real estate
Shareholders: Simon Christopher Ragg; Karen Liddle; David James Steven
Officers: Karen Liddle [1967] Director/Chartered Accountant; John Charles Priestley [1956] Director; Simon Christopher Ragg [1965] Director; David James Steven [1966] Director

P&A Food Management Services Limited
Incorporated: 20 July 1998 *Employees:* 370
Net Worth: £780,689 *Total Assets:* £3,995,927
Registered Office: Suite 1 & 4 Kingsfield House, Carthorpe, Bedale, N Yorks, DL8 2LL
Activities: Other food services
Parent: Contract Catering Services (P&A) Holdings Limited
Officers: David John Hall, Secretary; David John Hall [1969] Finance Director; Edward Arthur Naylor [1956] Managing Director

P&R Construction Limited
Incorporated: 15 March 2013 *Employees:* 6
Net Worth: £274,858 *Total Assets:* £4,841,790
Registered Office: Roseville Court, Blair Avenue, Ingleby Barwick, Stockton on Tees, Cleveland, TS17 5BL
Activities: Development of building projects
Major Shareholder: Sukhraj Singh
Officers: Sukhraj Singh [1964] Director

P+HS Architects Limited
Incorporated: 20 January 2004 *Employees:* 55
Net Worth: £1,543,204 *Total Assets:* £2,780,296
Registered Office: The Old Station, Station Road, Stokesley, Middlesbrough, Cleveland, TS9 7AB
Activities: Architectural activities
Shareholders: Alan Christopher Dennis; Joe Andrew Robert Biggs
Officers: Natalie Jayne Stirland, Secretary; James Richard Almond [1980] Director/Project Manager; Philip Bentley [1972] Director/Architect; Joe Andrew Robert Biggs [1958] Director/Architect; Alan Christopher Dennis [1958] Director/Architect; Catherine Anne Lake [1974] Director/Architect; Derek Alexander Shepherd [1979] Director/Architect; Adrian Taylor [1962] Director/Architectural Technologist

P.D.Q. Engineering Limited
Incorporated: 2 December 1986 *Employees:* 40
Net Worth: £1,818,299 *Total Assets:* £2,487,286
Registered Office: Industrial Road, Hertburn Industrial Estate, Washington, Tyne & Wear, NE37 2SA
Activities: Machining
Officers: Gayle Jackson, Secretary; Paul Antony Jackson, Secretary/Managing Director; Paul Antony Jackson [1965] Managing Director; Richard John Mellett [1973] Commercial Director

P.J.Engineering Products Limited
Incorporated: 15 February 1985 *Employees:* 36
Net Worth: £614,746 *Total Assets:* £2,672,136
Registered Office: Renown Engineering Ltd, Northumberland Business Park West, Cramlington, Northumberland, NE23 7RH
Activities: Manufacture of other fabricated metal products n.e.c.
Parent: Renown Group Limited
Officers: Katherine Carmichael Hamilton, Secretary; John Desmond Hamilton [1958] Director

PAC Holdings Limited
Incorporated: 18 January 1988
Net Worth: £1,074,885 *Total Assets:* £1,074,887
Registered Office: 15 Blackwell Scar, Darlington, Co Durham, DL3 8DL
Activities: Buying and selling of own real estate
Major Shareholder: Paul Anthony Chrisp
Officers: Constance Marilyn Chrisp, Secretary; Paul Anthony Chrisp [1951] Director

Pacifica Appliance Services Limited
Incorporated: 16 November 2004 *Employees:* 254
Net Worth: £709,061 *Total Assets:* £7,143,405
Registered Office: Pacifica House, Rainton Business Park, Houghton-le-Spring, Co Durham, DH4 5RA
Activities: Repair of household appliances and home and garden equipment
Parent: Pacifca Group Ltd
Officers: Scott Pallister, Secretary/Director; Kevin Brown [1968] Director/Repair of Domestic Appointment; Paul Richard Feek [1971] Director; Scott Pallister [1980] Director

Pacifica Group Limited
Incorporated: 19 August 2005 *Employees:* 346
Net Worth: £1,424,513 *Total Assets:* £12,750,594
Registered Office: Pacifica House, Rainton Business Park, Houghton-le-Spring, Co Durham, DH4 5RA
Activities: Combined office administrative service activities
Shareholders: Scott Pallister; Paul Richard Feek; Kevin Brown
Officers: Scott Pallister, Secretary; Kevin Brown [1968] Director/Repair of Domestic Appointment; Paul Richard Feek [1971] Director; Alan Johnson [1961] Non-Executive Director Chairman; Scott Pallister [1980] Director; Paul Thomas Ralphs [1968] IT Director

Pacifica Home Services Limited
Incorporated: 17 November 2003 *Employees:* 47
Net Worth: £1,082,451 *Total Assets:* £4,677,203
Registered Office: Pacifica Group, Rainton Business Park, Houghton-le-Spring, Co Durham, DH4 5RA
Activities: Other business support service activities n.e.c.
Parent: Pacifca Group
Officers: Scott Pallister, Secretary; Kevin Brown [1968] Director/Repair of Domestic Appointment; Philip Pallister [1981] Director; Scott Pallister [1980] Director

Paignton Limited
Incorporated: 17 May 2011 *Employees:* 49
Net Worth: £1,654,551 *Total Assets:* £3,151,746
Registered Office: 140 Coniscliffe Road, Darlington, Co Durham, DL3 7RT
Activities: Other service activities n.e.c.
Shareholder: Simon Andrew Wright
Officers: Debra Wright [1964] Director; Simon Andrew Wright [1964] Director

Pakway Limited
Incorporated: 8 March 2016 *Employees:* 13
Net Worth: £115,853 *Total Assets:* £2,001,117
Registered Office: Unit 16 Cherry Way, Dubmire Industrial Estate, Houghton-le-Spring, Co Durham, DH4 5RJ
Activities: Manufacture of plastic packing goods
Major Shareholder: Monji Mami
Officers: Jeffrey Brunskill [1960] Director; Farah Mami [1987] Strategy Director [French]

Palace Housing Company Ltd
Incorporated: 7 September 2012
Registered Office: 43 Coniscliffe Road, Darlington, Co Durham, DL3 7EH
Activities: Buying and selling of own real estate
Major Shareholder: Steven Green
Officers: Steven Green [1978] Director/Artist

Palintest Limited
Incorporated: 18 March 1975 *Employees:* 106
Net Worth: £3,603,160 *Total Assets:* £10,320,231
Registered Office: Palintest House, Kingsway, Team Valley Trading Estate, Gateshead, Tyne & Wear, NE11 0NS
Activities: Other manufacturing n.e.c.
Parent: Halma PLC
Officers: Lynn Spence, Secretary; Kenneth Simon Bowman [1963] Technical Director; Kevin Richard Davis [1970] Operations Director; Lesley Henderson [1967] Sales Director; Kim Thye Lee [1975] Managing Director [Malaysian]; Lynn Spence [1963] Finance Director

Pallett Hill Sand & Gravel Co. Limited
Incorporated: 27 April 1960
Registered Office: 9 St Paulinus Crescent, Catterick Village, Richmond, N Yorks, DL10 7UB
Activities: Mixed farming
Major Shareholder: Geoffrey Simpson
Officers: Peter Edward Nesbitt, Secretary; Geoffrey Maxwell Simpson [1952] Director/Farmer

Pallion Engineering Limited
Incorporated: 5 February 1991 *Employees:* 6
Net Worth Deficit: £207,364 *Total Assets:* £2,287,074
Registered Office: Pallion Yard, Pallion, Sunderland, Tyne & Wear, SR4 6LL
Activities: Manufacture of other fabricated metal products n.e.c.
Shareholders: Pantelis Kollakis; Diane Kollakis; Dimitrios Manios
Officers: Peter Callaghan, Secretary; Jeremy Flax [1960] Director; Alexander William Kollakis [1980] Director/Property Developer

Palmer (U.K.) Limited
Incorporated: 2 June 1981 *Employees:* 6
Net Worth: £1,310,969 *Total Assets:* £1,747,626
Registered Office: Unit BT 6019, Tofts Farm Industrial Estate, Brenda Road, Hartlepool, Cleveland, TS25 2BS
Activities: Wholesale of chemical products
Parent: Palmer International Inc
Officers: Roberta Palmer Body [1939] Director [American]; Kevin Palmer [1969] Director [American]

Palringo Limited
Incorporated: 29 April 2006 *Employees:* 53
Net Worth Deficit: £4,275,484 *Total Assets:* £6,190,087
Registered Office: 4 Arcot Court, South Nelson Industrial Estate, Cramlington, Northumberland, NE23 1BB
Activities: Other software publishing
Officers: Professor Jarek Rosinski, Secretary/Engineer; Izzat Aziz Ahmad Abou-Amarah [1979] Director/CEO - Impulse Telecom; AVP - Investment NTEC [Kuwaiti]; Stephen Francis Dunford [1957] Director/Chairman; Hermant Khatwani [1982] Director [Indian]; Gary Andrew Knight [1972] Director; Professor Jarek Rosinski [1958] Director; Martin Rosinski [1984] Director/Chief Technology Officer; Monish Suri [1966] Director/General Partner

Panda Motor Vehicles Ltd
Incorporated: 17 January 2012
Net Worth: £788,662 *Total Assets:* £1,745,860
Registered Office: Wearside Autoparc, The Parade, Sunderland, Tyne & Wear, SR2 8NT
Activities: Sale of used cars and light motor vehicles
Major Shareholder: Peter Ingram
Officers: Peter Ingram [1968] Director/Motor Dealer

Pantheon Macroeconomics Ltd.
Incorporated: 14 November 2009 *Employees:* 8
Net Worth: £196,144 *Total Assets:* £1,233,704
Registered Office: Quayside House, 110 Quayside, Newcastle upon Tyne, NE1 3DX
Activities: Other publishing activities
Shareholders: Ian Charles Shepherdson; Christine Anne Shepherdson
Officers: Ian Charles Shepherdson, Secretary; Christine Anne Shepherdson [1967] Director/Accountant; Ian Charles Shepherdson [1965] Director/Economist

Paper Dove Company Limited
Incorporated: 27 January 1997 *Employees:* 11
Net Worth: £1,535,119 *Total Assets:* £1,826,913
Registered Office: 8 South Acomb Farm, Bywell, Stocksfield, Northumberland, NE43 7AQ
Activities: Other publishing activities
Officers: David Leonard, Secretary/Business Manager; Anne Maria Bygate [1963] Production Director; David Leonard [1961] Strategic Director; Louise Ann McAlindon [1977] Managing Director

Par Petroleum Limited
Incorporated: 11 March 1991 *Employees:* 9
Net Worth: £1,867,347 *Total Assets:* £4,039,622
Registered Office: Par House, Lumley Sixth Pit, Woodstone Village, Houghton-le-Spring, Co Durham, DH4 6DU
Activities: Agents involved in the sale of fuels, ores, metals and industrial chemicals
Shareholders: Peter Roy-Toole; Carol Roy-Toole
Officers: Leanne Roy Hardy, Secretary; Leanne Roy Hardy [1978] Finance Director; Stuart Hardy [1978] Director; Carol Roy-Toole [1942] Director; Peter Roy-Toole [1943] Managing Director; Simon Roy Toole [1972] Operations Director

Paragon Financial Investments Limited
Incorporated: 24 April 2014
Net Worth Deficit: £398,403 *Total Assets:* £5,473,824
Registered Office: Pallion Trading Estate, Sunderland, Tyne & Wear, SR4 6ST
Activities: Activities of head offices
Parent: Paragon Group Limited
Officers: Patrick James Crean [1963] Director/Chief Executive Officer [Irish]; Laurent Thierry Salmon [1963] Director [French]

Paragon Group UK Limited
Incorporated: 30 June 1955 *Employees:* 585
Net Worth: £7,766,000 *Total Assets:* £33,587,000
Registered Office: Paragon Group UK Ltd, Pallion Trading Estate, Sunderland, Tyne & Wear, SR4 6ST
Activities: Printing n.e.c.
Parent: Paragon Transaction (U.K.) Ltd
Officers: Richard Joseph Cahill, Secretary; Patrick James Crean [1963] Director/Businessman [Irish]; Laurent Thierry Salmon [1963] Finance Director [French]; Sean Aongus Shine [1963] Director/Consultant [Irish]

Paragon Rapid Technologies Ltd
Incorporated: 6 August 2003 *Employees:* 61
Net Worth: £1,513,705 *Total Assets:* £3,972,606
Registered Office: Aviation Way, Durham Tees Valley Airport, Darlington, Co Durham, DL2 1NA
Activities: Manufacture of other plastic products
Shareholders: Phillip Laurence Adamson; Peter Humphrey
Officers: Phillip Laurence Adamson, Secretary; Phillip Laurence Adamson [1974] Director/General Manager; Peter Humphrey [1973] Director/Workshop Manager

Paragon Transaction (U.K.) Limited
Incorporated: 13 October 2004
Net Worth: £29,482,696 *Total Assets:* £38,614,908
Registered Office: Pallion Trading Estate, Sunderland, Tyne & Wear, SR4 6ST
Activities: Activities of other holding companies n.e.c.
Parent: Grenadier Holdings PLC
Officers: Richard Joseph Cahill, Secretary; Patrick James Crean [1963] Director [Irish]; Laurent Thierry Salmon [1963] Finance Director [French]; Sean Aongus Shine [1963] Director [Irish]

Paramount Home Improvements (U.K.) Limited
Incorporated: 16 August 2007
Net Worth: £244,572 *Total Assets:* £4,052,277
Registered Office: Unit 1c North Tyne Industrial Estate, Whitley Road, Benton, Newcastle upon Tyne, NE12 9SZ
Activities: Activities of construction holding companies
Parent: Pennine Newcastle Limited
Officers: Michael Alexander Giscombe [1967] Director; Gregory Kane [1975] Director; Sarah Lyn Van Haazel [1975] Director

Park Electrical Distributors Limited
Incorporated: 7 April 1992 *Employees:* 72
Net Worth: £1,054,031 *Total Assets:* £8,702,353
Registered Office: Unit 3 Queens Park, Earlsway, Team Valley Trading Estate, Gateshead, Tyne & Wear, NE11 0QD
Activities: Wholesale of radio, television goods & electrical household appliances (other than records, tapes, CDs)
Major Shareholder: Barry Wilkinson
Officers: Hazel Wilkinson, Secretary/Nurse; Ian Michael Aitchison [1965] Commercial Director; Bridget Harold [1976] Director; Craig Hopwood [1971] Director; Simon Joseph John Mooney [1965] Director; Barry Wilkinson [1964] Director; Hazel Wilkinson [1962] Director

Park Lane Garages (Teeside) Limited
Incorporated: 28 July 2004 *Employees:* 7
Net Worth: £698,119 *Total Assets:* £1,241,595
Registered Office: 132 Park Lane, Middlesbrough, Cleveland, TS1 3LL
Activities: Retail sale of automotive fuel in specialised stores
Major Shareholder: Mohammed Anwar
Officers: Mobeen Anwar [1980] Director; Mohammed Anwar [1957] Director/Shopkeeper

Park Lane NE Ltd
Incorporated: 30 September 2010
Registered Office: 2b North Sands Business Centre, Liberty Way, Sunderland, Tyne & Wear, SR6 0QA
Activities: Public houses and bars
Major Shareholder: John Alfred Dickman
Officers: John Alfred Dickman [1952] Director/Publican; Karen Dickman [1962] Director/Publican

Park Lets Limited
Incorporated: 29 August 2002 *Employees:* 5
Net Worth: £3,431,690 *Total Assets:* £7,943,560
Registered Office: 73 St Georges Terrace, Newcastle upon Tyne, NE2 2DL
Activities: Other accommodation
Shareholder: Raman Kohli
Officers: Raman Kohli, Secretary; Pradeep Kumar Kohli [1960] Director/Property Management [Indian]; Raman Kohli [1962] Director/Company Secretary

Park Parade Homes LLP
Incorporated: 26 September 2007
Net Worth Deficit: £176,301 *Total Assets:* £809,885
Registered Office: 32 Portland Terrace, Newcastle upon Tyne, NE2 1QP
Officers: Louise Clare Vardy [1974] Member; Richard Angus Reginald Vardy [1973] Member

Park Resorts Limited
Incorporated: 29 December 2000 *Employees:* 2,214
Net Worth: £132,993,000 *Total Assets:* £698,424,000
Registered Office: 2nd Floor, One Gosforth Park Way, Gosforth Business Park, Newcastle upon Tyne, NE12 8ET
Activities: Recreational vehicle parks, trailer parks and camping grounds
Parent: PD Parks Limited
Officers: Judith Ann Archibold, Secretary; Ian Kellett [1963] Director; John Anthony Waterworth [1963] Director

Park Spring Wind Farm Limited
Incorporated: 7 January 2015
Net Worth: £4,498,000 *Total Assets:* £12,810,000
Registered Office: Alexander House, 1 Mandarin Road, Rainton Bridge Business Park, Houghton-le-Spring, Co Durham, DH4 5RA
Activities: Production of electricity
Parent: EDF Energy Renewables Holdings Limited
Officers: Susan Elizabeth Lind, Secretary; Matthieu Thomas Hue [1975] Director [French]; Hassaan Majid [1968] Director

Park View Academy
Incorporated: 18 July 2011 *Employees:* 7
Net Worth: £5,373,000 *Total Assets:* £7,771,000
Registered Office: Park View School, Church Chare, Chester-le-Street, Co Durham, DH3 3QA
Activities: General secondary education
Officers: Hilary Bolton, Secretary; Philip Andrew Adamson [1973] Director/Headteacher; Janet Shelagh Carr [1961] Director/Exams and Assessment Manager; Margaret Stewart Caygill [1943] Director/Retired; Gillian Crawford [1962] Director/Retired; Dr William Forster Dennison [1941] Director/Education; Meg Dodd [1958] Director/Retired; Michael Goulding [1952] Director/Retired; Melanie Howie [1965] Director/Parish Councillor; Jonathan Robert Jarvis [1983] Director/Teacher; Simon Lindsay [1963] Director/Academies Lead Officer; Mustafaa Malik [1975] Director/Headteacher; David Alan Roberts [1980] Director/Scientist; Victoria Stevenson [1981] Director/Solicitor; Kirsty Tate [1973] Director/Assistant Headteacher; Iain Robert Veitch [1963] Director/Headteacher

Parkdean Caravan Parks Limited
Incorporated: 14 September 2004 *Employees:* 365
Net Worth: £7,670,000 *Total Assets:* £48,256,000
Registered Office: Second Floor, 1 Gosforth Park Way, Gosforth Business Park, Newcastle upon Tyne, NE12 8ET
Activities: Recreational vehicle parks, trailer parks and camping grounds
Parent: PD Parks Limited
Officers: Judith Ann Archibold, Secretary; Ian Kellett [1963] Director; John Anthony Waterworth [1963] Director

Parkdean Holiday Parks Limited
Incorporated: 9 October 2000 *Employees:* 722
Net Worth: £61,889,000 *Total Assets:* £194,916,000
Registered Office: 2nd Floor, One Gosforth Park Way, Gosforth Business Park, Newcastle upon Tyne, NE12 8ET
Activities: Recreational vehicle parks, trailer parks and camping grounds
Parent: PD Parks Limited
Officers: Judith Ann Archibold, Secretary; Ian Kellett [1963] Director; John Anthony Waterworth [1963] Director

Parkdean Holidays Limited
Incorporated: 25 October 1999
Net Worth: £440,000 *Total Assets:* £3,262,000
Registered Office: 2nd Floor, One Gosforth Park Way, Gosforth Business Park, Newcastle upon Tyne, NE12 8ET
Activities: Activities of head offices
Parent: PD Parks Limited
Officers: Judith Ann Archibold, Secretary; Ian Kellett [1963] Director; John Anthony Waterworth [1963] Director/Chief Executive

Parkdean Resorts Limited
Incorporated: 22 July 2015 *Employees:* 3
Net Worth: £780,857,024 *Total Assets:* £1,119,100,032
Registered Office: 2nd Floor, One Gosforth Park Way, Gosforth Business Park, Newcastle upon Tyne, NE12 8ET
Activities: Activities of head offices
Parent: Richmond UK Bidco Limited
Officers: Juidth Archibold, Secretary; Ian Gill [1974] Director; Ian Kellett [1963] Director; John Anthony Waterworth [1963] Director

Parkdean Resorts UK Limited
Incorporated: 3 March 2006
Net Worth: £474,409,984 *Total Assets:* £872,081,984
Registered Office: 2nd Floor, One Gosforth Park Way, Gosforth Business Park, Newcastle upon Tyne, NE12 8ET
Activities: Activities of head offices
Parent: Parkdean Resorts Limited
Officers: Judith Ann Archibold, Secretary; Ian Gill [1974] Director; Mark Simon Harper [1966] Director; Ian Kellett [1963] Director; John Anthony Waterworth [1963] Director

R. Parker (Wall & Floor Tiling Contractors) Limited
Incorporated: 20 November 1975 *Employees:* 36
Net Worth: £916,697 *Total Assets:* £1,303,452
Registered Office: 6 Octavian Way, Team Valley Trading Estate, Gateshead, Tyne & Wear, NE11 0HZ
Activities: Floor and wall covering
Shareholders: Mark James Parker; Norma Scott Parker
Officers: Norma Scott Parker, Secretary; Mark James Parker [1973] Director/Tiling Contractor; Norma Scott Parker [1941] Director

Parker Prestige Limited
Incorporated: 19 October 2016
Net Worth: £100,100 *Total Assets:* £804,591
Registered Office: The Garage, Dundas Street, Richmond, N Yorks, DL10 7AB
Activities: Sale of used cars and light motor vehicles
Shareholder: Ian Ralph Parker
Officers: Ian Ralph Parker, Secretary; Carole Parker [1953] Director; Craig Ian Ralph Parker [1982] Director; Ian Ralph Parker [1959] Director; Scott Lewis Edward Parker [1985] Director

Parkside Care Limited
Incorporated: 6 February 2008 *Employees:* 96
Net Worth: £76,770 *Total Assets:* £2,123,837
Registered Office: 48 Linskill Terrace, North Shields, Tyne & Wear, NE30 2EW
Activities: Residential care activities for the elderly and disabled
Shareholders: Margaret Kerr; Robert Kerr
Officers: Alister Robert Kerr [1982] Director; Andrew Stewart Kerr [1979] Director/Chartered Accountant; Robert Kerr [1950] Director

Parlour Product Holding Limited
Incorporated: 1 April 2008
Net Worth: £7,753,000 *Total Assets:* £11,130,000
Registered Office: c/o A Share & Sons Limited, 45-49 Villiers Street, Sunderland, Tyne & Wear, SR1 1HA
Activities: Retail sale of carpets, rugs, wall and floor coverings in specialised stores
Parent: Parlour Product Topco Limited
Officers: Christopher James Russell Muir, Secretary; David Knight [1958] Director/Chief Executive; Christopher James Russell Muir [1975] Director/Chief Financial Officer

Parlour Product Topco Limited
Incorporated: 1 April 2008
Net Worth: £23,415,000 *Total Assets:* £23,423,000
Registered Office: c/o A Share & Sons Limited, 45-49 Villiers Street, Sunderland, Tyne & Wear, SR1 1HA
Activities: Retail sale of carpets, rugs, wall and floor coverings in specialised stores
Parent: SCS Group PLC
Officers: Christopher James Russell Muir, Secretary; David Knight [1958] Director/Chief Executive; Christopher James Russell Muir [1975] Director/Chief Financial Officer

Parmley Graham Limited
Incorporated: 28 January 1921 *Employees:* 102
Net Worth: £3,723,000 *Total Assets:* £16,546,000
Registered Office: Parmley Graham Ltd, South Shore Road, Gateshead, Tyne & Wear, NE8 3AE
Activities: Wholesale of electronic and telecommunications equipment and parts
Major Shareholder: Michael Wilson
Officers: Mark Berry, Secretary; Mark Berry [1971] Finance Director; George Mackey [1960] Sales Director; Kathleen Wilson [1940] Director; Michael Wilson [1939] Director; Nicholas John Wilson [1963] Managing Director

Parmley Technologies Limited
Incorporated: 8 August 2000
Net Worth: £1,574,844 *Total Assets:* £2,312,963
Registered Office: Unit 1 Neptune Court, Orion Business Park, North Shields, Tyne & Wear, NE29 7UW
Activities: Other manufacturing n.e.c.
Major Shareholder: Derek Christopher Parmley
Officers: Derek Christopher Parmley [1967] Director

Derek Parnaby Cyclones International Limited
Incorporated: 20 July 1973 *Employees:* 102
Net Worth: £11,935,614 *Total Assets:* £13,342,263
Registered Office: Chilton Industrial Estate, Chilton, Ferryhill, Co Durham, DL17 0SH
Activities: Manufacture of other special-purpose machinery n.e.c.
Major Shareholder: Adrian Parnaby
Officers: Pauline Isobel Lerigo, Secretary; Thomas Henry Iveson [1950] Director/Commissioning Engineer; Pauline Isobel Lerigo [1960] Director/Secretary; Adrian Parnaby [1958] Director

Parnell Products Ltd
Incorporated: 24 April 2006
Net Worth: £538,205 *Total Assets:* £814,649
Registered Office: The Shieling, Nedderton Village, Bedlington, Northumberland, NE22 6AX
Activities: Retail sale of medical and orthopaedic goods in specialised stores (not incl. hearing aids) n.e.c.
Major Shareholder: Philip Parnell
Officers: Janice Parnell, Secretary; Philip Parnell [1948] Director

Parsons Containers Limited
Incorporated: 22 November 2000
Net Worth: £1,457,811 *Total Assets:* £2,609,431
Registered Office: The Manor House, West End, Sedgefield, Stockton on Tees, Cleveland, TS21 2BW
Activities: Other letting and operating of own or leased real estate
Shareholders: Ean Eric Parsons; Ian Philipson
Officers: Jane Skilbeck, Secretary; Ean Eric Parsons [1959] Director; Ian Philipson [1952] Director

Parsons Group Limited
Incorporated: 26 September 2007 *Employees:* 6
Net Worth: £806,997 *Total Assets:* £10,812,148
Registered Office: Waterloo House, Thornton Street, Newcastle upon Tyne, NE1 4AP
Activities: Other specialised construction activities n.e.c.
Parent: Patrick Parsons Holdings Limited
Officers: Stuart Marshall, Secretary; Nicholas Mark Beckwith [1973] Director; Conor John Murphy [1965] Director/Structural Engineer [Irish]; Dr Grant Vincent Richardson [1967] Director; Peter Vincent Stienlet [1969] Director; Douglas Roy Tidswell [1961] Director

Patrick Parsons Limited
Incorporated: 1 February 1989 *Employees:* 152
Net Worth Deficit: £661,779 *Total Assets:* £5,586,990
Registered Office: Waterloo House, Thornton Street, Newcastle upon Tyne, NE1 4AP
Activities: Other specialised construction activities n.e.c.
Parent: Parsons Group Limited
Officers: Stuart Marshall, Secretary; Nicholas Mark Beckwith [1973] Director; Conor John Murphy [1965] Director/Structural Engineer [Irish]; Dr Grant Vincent Richardson [1967] Director; Peter Vincent Stienlet [1969] Director/Consulting Engineer; Doug Roy Tidswell [1961] Director; Mark Turner [1965] Director/Structural Engineer

Ewart Parsons,Limited
Incorporated: 23 October 1933
Net Worth: £1,347,096 *Total Assets:* £1,347,096
Registered Office: Parsons Business Centre, Brenda Road, Hartlepool, Cleveland, TS25 2BJ
Activities: Sale of other motor vehicles
Officers: David Lawn, Secretary; Timothy Dunningham [1953] Director; Richard Christopher Irvine [1952] Director/Fleet Engineer; David Lawn [1948] Director/Accountant

Partner Construction Limited
Incorporated: 18 October 2010 *Employees:* 45
Net Worth: £2,001,845 *Total Assets:* £11,987,113
Registered Office: Units 11 & 12, Parsons Road, Parsons Industrial Estate, Washington, Tyne & Wear, NE37 1HB
Activities: Construction of domestic buildings
Parent: Partner Group U.K. Limited
Officers: Richard Barrett, Secretary; Neil Patrick Armstrong [1969] Director/Group Chief Executive Officer [Irish]; Richard James Barrett [1971] Finance Director; Ryan John Brennan [1971] Commercial Director; Ian Craggs [1976] Director/Chief Financial Officer; Leigh David Cresswell [1979] Director; Shaun Hastings [1958] Group Director; Frank James Lincoln [1968] Operations Director

Partner Contracting Limited
Incorporated: 18 February 1998
Net Worth: £799,997 *Total Assets:* £7,717,707
Registered Office: Units 11 & 12, Parsons Road, Parsons Industrial Estate, Washington, Tyne & Wear, NE37 1HB
Activities: Construction of domestic buildings
Parent: Partner Construction Limited
Officers: Richard Barrett, Secretary; Neil Patrick Armstrong [1969] Director/Group Chief Executive Officer [Irish]; Richard James Barrett [1971] Finance Director; Ryan John Brennan [1971] Commercial Director; Ian Craggs [1976] Director/Chief Financial Officer; Leigh Creswell [1979] Director; Shaun Hastings [1958] Group Director; Frank James Lincoln [1968] Operations Director

Partner Group U.K. Limited
Incorporated: 11 February 2011 *Employees:* 45
Net Worth: £2,610,146 *Total Assets:* £12,557,286
Registered Office: Units 11 & 12, Parsons Road, Parsons Industrial Estate, Washington, Tyne & Wear, NE37 1HB
Activities: Buying and selling of own real estate
Parent: Fastflow Group Limited
Officers: Richard Barrett, Secretary; Neil Patrick Armstrong [1969] Director/Group Chief Executive Officer [Irish]; Richard James Barrett [1971] Finance Director; Ryan John Brennan [1971] Commercial Director; Ian Craggs [1976] Director/Chief Financial Officer; Leigh David Cresswell [1979] Director; Shaun Hastings [1958] Group Director

Partners in Hygiene Limited
Incorporated: 21 September 2006 *Employees:* 350
Net Worth: £636,524 *Total Assets:* £2,693,231
Registered Office: Goosepool House, Over Dinsdale, Darlington, Co Durham, DL2 1PW
Activities: Specialised cleaning services
Shareholders: David Sydney Twemlow; Malcolm John Twemlow; Peter Ernest Barker
Officers: Christina Barker, Secretary; Peter Ernest Barker [1960] Director; David Sydney Twemlow [1966] Director; Malcolm John Twemlow [1965] Director

Pass (Portable Appliance Safety Services) Ltd
Incorporated: 7 June 2002 *Employees:* 64
Net Worth: £2,674,613 *Total Assets:* £5,529,521
Registered Office: 1 Wilson Street, Thornaby, Stockton on Tees, Cleveland, TS17 7AR
Activities: Technical testing and analysis
Shareholders: Barry Atkins; Lyndsey Atkins
Officers: Barry Atkins [1972] Managing Director; Lyndsey Atkins [1979] Director

Pat Telford Limited
Incorporated: 15 December 1966
Registered Office: 3 Simonside, Seaton Sluice, Whitley Bay, Tyne & Wear, NE26 4BN
Activities: Other letting and operating of own or leased real estate
Shareholders: Daniel Lawrenson; Pauline Lawrenson
Officers: Pauline Lawrenson, Secretary; Daniel John Lawrenson [1947] Director; Pauline Lawrenson [1949] Director/Company Secretary

R & D Patterson Limited
Incorporated: 23 January 2002
Net Worth Deficit: £166,393 *Total Assets:* £1,206,790
Registered Office: 32 Saltwell View, Gateshead, Tyne & Wear, NE8 4NT
Activities: Wholesale of dairy products, eggs and edible oils and fats
Shareholders: Robert Patterson; Dianne Patterson
Officers: Dianne Patterson, Secretary; Robert Patterson [1952] Director/Dairyman

Patterson Ryan Limited
Incorporated: 29 March 2001 *Employees:* 8
Net Worth: £312,707 *Total Assets:* £1,082,190
Registered Office: 66 Potter Street, Wallsend, Tyne & Wear, NE28 6TZ
Activities: Forging, pressing, stamping and roll-forming of metal; powder metallurgy
Major Shareholder: John Strother Shallcross
Officers: Michelle Frances Shallcross, Secretary; Benjamin John Strother Shallcross [1978] Director/Engineer; John Strother Shallcross [1946] Director/Welding Engineer

Keith Pattinson Limited
Incorporated: 18 March 1987 *Employees:* 198
Net Worth: £3,358,250 *Total Assets:* £4,189,725
Registered Office: Mercantile House, Silverlink, Wallsend, Tyne & Wear, NE28 9NY
Activities: Real estate agencies
Major Shareholder: Keith Alan Pattinson
Officers: Raymond McIntosh [1956] Director/Chartered Surveyor; Susan Marie Moore [1978] Finance Director; Caroline Jane Pattinson [1981] Director; Keith Alan Pattinson [1949] Director/Chartered Surveyor; Valerie Jane Pattinson [1953] Director/Clerk

M. Pattison & Co. Limited
Incorporated: 14 December 1920
Net Worth: £1,516,816 *Total Assets:* £1,913,961
Registered Office: 71 Willowtree Avenue, Gilesgate Moor, Durham, DH1 1DZ
Activities: Other letting and operating of own or leased real estate
Shareholders: John Brian Holloway; Amy Victoria Holloway
Officers: Vera Yvonne Holloway, Secretary; Amy Victoria Holloway [1942] Director; John Brian Holloway [1939] Director/Furniture Retailer

James Paul Services To Industry Limited
Incorporated: 8 April 1994 *Employees:* 28
Net Worth: £591,250 *Total Assets:* £2,309,667
Registered Office: 34 Metcalfe Road, Skippers Lane Industrial Estate, Middlesbrough, Cleveland, TS6 6PT
Activities: Other specialised construction activities n.e.c.
Officers: Donna White, Secretary; Kevin McMullen [1967] Contracts Director; Timothy John Snaith [1966] Director; Gary White [1971] Director

Pauls Property Investment Limited
Incorporated: 6 October 2000
Net Worth: £422,677 *Total Assets:* £1,464,198
Registered Office: 21 Clayton Street, Newcastle upon Tyne, NE1 5PN
Activities: Renting and operating of Housing Association real estate
Shareholder: Arjun Vedhara
Officers: Kamal Vedhara, Secretary; Arjun Vedhara [1979] Director

Pax Christi Catholic Partnership
Incorporated: 7 January 2015 *Employees:* 157
Net Worth Deficit: £1,329,152 *Total Assets:* £3,166,419
Registered Office: Pax Christi Catholic Partnership, Ridge Terrace, Bedlington, Northumberland, NE22 6ED
Activities: General secondary education
Officers: Lee Barrett [1979] Director/Priest; Ann Lesley Borthwick [1957] Director/Retired; Marc Robert Breeze [1989] Director/Accountant; Catherine Mary D'Arcy [1956] Director/Retired Headteacher [Irish]; Paul Mills [1978] Director/Civil Servant; Keith Owen Pugh [1947] Director/Retired Civil Engineer

J.G. Paxton and Sons Limited
Incorporated: 1 February 1983 *Employees:* 64
Net Worth: £4,780,891 *Total Assets:* £11,715,955
Registered Office: Abbey Road, Pity Me, Durham, DH1 5DQ
Activities: Repair of other equipment
Shareholder: William John Paxton
Officers: William John Paxton, Secretary; Christine Patricia Paxton [1962] Director/Administrator; William John Paxton [1956] Director/Agricultural Engineer; Peter Joseph Tallentire [1974] Managing Director

Payapps.Com (UK) Ltd
Incorporated: 22 December 2015 *Employees:* 3
Net Worth Deficit: £536,099 *Total Assets:* £1,690,394
Registered Office: 305-306 Cobalt Business Exchange, Cobalt Park Way, Wallsend, Tyne & Wear, NE28 9NZ
Activities: Business and domestic software development
Parent: Zuuse Limited
Officers: Natalie Sue Cappiello [1974] Director/Chief Financial Officer [Australian]; Jason Charles Lilienstein [1974] Director/Chief Executive Officer [Australian]

PBI Aqaba Industrial Estate LLP
Incorporated: 10 January 2003
Net Worth: £4,556,132 *Total Assets:* £5,409,671
Registered Office: Sintons LLP, The Cube, Barrack Road, Newcastle upon Tyne, NE4 6DB
Officers: Zeev Sheldon Fink [1943] Member; Adiviye Irem Yuceel [1999] Member

PBU (UK) Ltd
Incorporated: 8 September 2006 *Employees:* 43
Net Worth: £3,085,570 *Total Assets:* £7,655,277
Registered Office: 1 Hutton House, Sedgefield, Stockton on Tees, Cleveland, TS21 2EP
Activities: Site preparation
Shareholders: Paul Bradley; Lee Gardiner Porter
Officers: Paula Bradley, Secretary; Paul Bradley [1972] Director; Lee Gardiner Porter [1974] Director

PC Investments Limited
Incorporated: 31 May 1946 *Employees:* 5
Net Worth: £1,268,590 *Total Assets:* £1,531,921
Registered Office: 53 Briardene Crescent, Whitley Bay, Tyne & Wear, NE26 4AD
Activities: Other letting and operating of own or leased real estate
Shareholders: Ian Henry Smith; Gregg Hamilton Smith; Douglas Iain Smith
Officers: Ian Henry Smith, Secretary; Douglas Iain Smith [1973] Director/Manager; Gordon James Smith [1976] Director/Executive Officer (DWP); Gregg Hamilton Smith [1975] Director/Manager; Ian Henry Smith [1947] Director/Printer; Rachel Louise Smith [1975] Director/Housewife

PCCA (UK) Holdings Limited
Incorporated: 28 January 2014 *Employees:* 82
Net Worth: £1,177,013 *Total Assets:* £15,541,523
Registered Office: Unit 2 Regents Drive, Low Prudhoe Industrial Estate, Prudhoe, Northumberland, NE42 6PX
Activities: Manufacture of pharmaceutical preparations
Parent: PCCA
Officers: Sharon Clift [1976] Managing Director; Jimmy Ray Smith [1960] Director/Company President [American]; Lester David Sparks [1943] Director [American]

PCCA Limited
Incorporated: 14 May 1999 *Employees:* 82
Net Worth: £920,245 *Total Assets:* £4,594,779
Registered Office: Unit 2 Regents Drive, Low Prudhoe Industrial Estate, Low Prudhoe, Northumberland, NE42 6PX
Activities: Manufacture of pharmaceutical preparations
Parent: PCCA (UK) Holdings Limited
Officers: Sharon Clift [1976] Director; Jimmy Ray Smith [1960] Director/Company President [American]; Lester David Sparks [1943] Director [American]

PCL Investments (NE) LLP
Incorporated: 14 April 2012
Net Worth: £2,276,964 *Total Assets:* £3,436,463
Registered Office: 7 Bankside, The Watermark, Gateshead, Tyne & Wear, NE11 9SY
Officers: Daljit Singh Rehill [1964] Member; Gurbaskh Kaur Rehill [1936] Member; Narinder Singh Rehill [1965] Member

PCR Holdings Limited
Incorporated: 23 September 2005 *Employees:* 69
Net Worth: £7,020,969 *Total Assets:* £8,095,104
Registered Office: Courville House, 34 Ellerbeck Court, Stokesley Business Park, Stokesley, Cleveland, TS9 5PT
Activities: Activities of other holding companies n.e.c.
Major Shareholder: Peter Charles Richardson
Officers: Paul Geoffrey Flintoft, Secretary; Geoffrey Ablett [1965] Director; David John Richardson [1968] Director; John Foster Richardson [1931] Director Chairman; Peter Charles Richardson [1958] Managing Director; Teresa Beryl Richardson [1933] Director

PD Co Holdings (UK) Limited
Incorporated: 4 January 2013
Net Worth: £935,926 *Total Assets:* £14,151,332
Registered Office: 3rd Floor, Citygate, St James Boulevard, Newcastle upon Tyne, NE1 4JE
Activities: Activities of other holding companies n.e.c.
Parent: PDZ (UK) Limited
Officers: Dylan Browne, Secretary; Simon Mark Kersey [1973] Director/Business Executive; Benjamin Rade Stoikovich [1973] Director/Mining Engineer

PD Group Management Limited
Incorporated: 9 August 1988 *Employees:* 179
Net Worth: £9,071,000 *Total Assets:* £111,601,000
Registered Office: 17-27 Queen's Square, Middlesbrough, Cleveland, TS2 1AH
Activities: Activities of head offices
Parent: PD Portco Limited
Officers: Dermot Michael Russell, Secretary; Johannes Franciscus Calje [1972] Director [Dutch]; Jeremy Mark Hopkinson [1955] Director; Dermot Michael Russell [1965] Director/Accountant

PD Logistics Limited
Incorporated: 24 May 1979 *Total Assets:* £53,404,000
Net Worth: £4,000,000 *Total Assets:* £53,404,000
Registered Office: 17-27 Queen's Square, Middlesbrough, Cleveland, TS2 1AH
Activities: Non-trading company
Parent: PD Portco Limited
Officers: Dermot Michael Russell, Secretary; Johannes Franciscus Calje [1972] Director [Dutch]; Jeremy Mark Hopkinson [1955] Director; Dermot Michael Russell [1965] Director/Accountant

PD Parks Limited
Incorporated: 3 March 2006
Net Worth: £681,236,992 *Total Assets:* £681,401,984
Registered Office: 2nd Floor, One Gosforth Park Way, Gosforth Business Park, Newcastle upon Tyne, NE12 8ET
Activities: Activities of head offices
Parent: Parkdean Resorts UK Limited
Officers: Judith Ann Archibold, Secretary; Ian Kellett [1963] Director; John Anthony Waterworth [1963] Director

PD Port Services Limited
Incorporated: 18 November 1975 *Employees:* 405
Net Worth: £10,951,000 *Total Assets:* £87,778,000
Registered Office: 17-27 Queen's Square, Middlesbrough, Cleveland, TS2 1AH
Activities: Freight transport by road
Parent: PD Portco Limited
Officers: Dermot Michael Russell, Secretary; Johannes Franciscus Calje [1972] Director [Dutch]; Jeremy Mark Hopkinson [1955] Director; Dermot Michael Russell [1965] Director/Accountant

PD Portco Limited
Incorporated: 14 March 2001 *Employees:* 731
Net Worth: £205,228,992 *Total Assets:* £489,836,992
Registered Office: 17-27 Queen's Square, Middlesbrough, Cleveland, TS2 1AH
Activities: Activities of head offices
Parent: Ports Holdings Limited
Officers: Dermot Michael Russell, Secretary; Johannes Franciscus Calje [1972] Director [Dutch]; Jeremy Mark Hopkinson [1955] Director; David John Robinson [1964] Director; Dermot Michael Russell [1965] Director/Accountant

PD Ports Acquisitions (UK) Limited
Incorporated: 1 December 2005
Net Worth: £261,190,000 *Total Assets:* £465,761,984
Registered Office: 17-27 Queen's Square, Middlesbrough, Cleveland, TS2 1AH
Activities: Activities of head offices
Parent: Brookfield Ports (UK) Limited
Officers: Michael John Botha [1970] Director/Senior Vice President [Canadian]; Johannes Franciscus Calje [1972] Director [Dutch]; Jeremy Mark Hopkinson [1955] Director; Gabriele Montesi [1981] Director/Investment Professional [Italian]; Felipe Ortiz [1979] Director/Senior VP [Colombian]; David John Robinson [1964] Director; Paul Lucas Sim [1974] Director/Lawyer [Australian]

PD Ports Group Limited
Incorporated: 2 July 1986
Net Worth: £6,314,000 *Total Assets:* £354,299,008
Registered Office: 17-27 Queens Square, Middlesbrough, Cleveland, TS2 1AH
Activities: Activities of head offices
Parent: PD Ports Management Limited
Officers: Dermot Michael Russell, Secretary; Johannes Franciscus Calje [1972] Director [Dutch]; Jeremy Mark Hopkinson [1955] Director; David John Robinson [1964] Director; Dermot Michael Russell [1965] Director/Accountant

PD Ports Hull Limited
Incorporated: 16 November 1936
Net Worth: £5,437,000 *Total Assets:* £9,188,000
Registered Office: 17-27 Queens Square, Middlesbrough, Cleveland, TS2 1AH
Activities: Cargo handling for water transport activities
Parent: PD Ports Humber Limited
Officers: Dermot Michael Russell, Secretary; Johannes Franciscus Calje [1972] Director [Dutch]; Jeremy Mark Hopkinson [1955] Director; Dermot Michael Russell [1965] Director/Accountant

PD Ports Humber Limited
Incorporated: 12 June 2007
Net Worth: £852,000 *Total Assets:* £23,902,000
Registered Office: 17-27 Queen's Square, Middlesbrough, Cleveland, TS2 1AH
Activities: Activities of head offices
Parent: PD Ports Group Limited
Officers: Linda Moore, Secretary; Johannes Franciscus Calje [1972] Director [Dutch]; Jeremy Mark Hopkinson [1955] Director; Dermot Michael Russell [1965] Director/Accountant

PD Ports Limited
Incorporated: 9 June 2009 *Employees:* 1,232
Net Worth: £125,836,000 *Total Assets:* £647,417,984
Registered Office: 17-27 Queens Square, Middlesbrough, Cleveland, TS2 1AH
Activities: Activities of other holding companies n.e.c.
Officers: Michael John Botha [1970] Director/Senior Vice President [Canadian]; Johannes Franciscus Calje [1972] Director [Dutch]; Jeremy Mark Hopkinson [1955] Director; Gabriele Montesi [1981] Director/Investment Professional [Italian]; Felipe Ortiz [1979] Director/Senior Vice President [Colombian/British]; David John Robinson [1964] Director of Operations; Paul Lucas Sim [1974] Director/Lawyer [Australian]

PD Ports Management Limited
Incorporated: 24 March 2004 *Employees:* 6
Net Worth: £173,476,000 *Total Assets:* £295,124,992
Registered Office: 17-27 Queens Square, Middlesbrough, Cleveland, TS2 1AH
Activities: Activities of head offices
Parent: PD Ports Acquisitions (UK) Limited
Officers: Michael John Botha [1970] Director/Senior Vice President [Canadian]; Johannes Franciscus Calje [1972] Director [Dutch]; Jeremy Mark Hopkinson [1955] Director; Gabriele Montesi [1981] Director/Investment Professional [Italian]; Felipe Ortiz [1979] Director/Senior VP [Colombian]; David John Robinson [1964] Director; Paul Lucas Sim [1974] Director/Lawyer [Australian]

PD Ports Properties Limited
Incorporated: 31 October 1977 *Employees:* 2
Net Worth: £2,400,000 *Total Assets:* £3,208,000
Registered Office: 17-27 Queen's Square, Middlesbrough, Cleveland, TS2 1AH
Activities: Renting and operating of Housing Association real estate
Parent: PD Ports Humber Limited
Officers: Dermot Michael Russell, Secretary; Johannes Franciscus Calje [1972] Director [Dutch]; Dermot Michael Russell [1965] Director/Accountant

PD Shipping & Inspection Services Limited
Incorporated: 9 July 1956 *Employees:* 26
Net Worth: £3,419,000 *Total Assets:* £5,029,000
Registered Office: 17-27 Queen's Square, Middlesbrough, Cleveland, TS2 1AH
Activities: Service activities incidental to water transportation
Parent: PD Ports Humber Limited
Officers: Dermot Michael Russell, Secretary; Johannes Franciscus Calje [1972] Director [Dutch]; Jeremy Mark Hopkinson [1955] Director; Dermot Michael Russell [1965] Director/Accountant

PD Teesport Limited
Incorporated: 2 August 1991 *Employees:* 274
Net Worth: £198,198,000 *Total Assets:* £515,783,008
Registered Office: 17-27 Queen's Square, Middlesbrough, Cleveland, TS2 1AH
Activities: Freight transport by road
Parent: PD Portco Limited
Officers: Dermot Michael Russell, Secretary; Johannes Franciscus Calje [1972] Director [Dutch]; Jeremy Mark Hopkinson [1955] Director; Russell Warren McCallion [1956] Director; Dermot Michael Russell [1965] Director/Accountant

PDE (NE) Limited
Incorporated: 15 August 2014
Net Worth: £2,947 *Total Assets:* £1,032,117
Registered Office: Unit 14a Airport Industrial Estate, Kingston Park, Newcastle upon Tyne, NE3 2EF
Activities: Other letting and operating of own or leased real estate
Major Shareholder: Paul Dummett
Officers: Christine Dummett [1961] Director; Paul Dummett [1991] Director/Professional Football Player; Robert Ian Dummett [1961] Director

PDL Solutions (Europe) Limited
Incorporated: 10 May 2001 *Employees:* 34
Net Worth: £1,220,891 *Total Assets:* £1,538,811
Registered Office: 1 Tanners Yard, Hexham, Northumberland, NE46 3NY
Activities: Engineering related scientific and technical consulting activities
Shareholders: Paul William Robert Charlton; Sally Linsley Charlton
Officers: Paul William Robert Charlton, Secretary; Monica Elizabeth Binks [1970] Director; Paul William Robert Charlton [1965] Director; Sally Linsley Charlton [1963] Director; Alexander Roff [1984] Director/Mechanical Engineer; Michael Williams [1971] Director/Engineer; John Robert Wilson [1956] IT Director

PDZ (UK) Limited
Incorporated: 2 January 2013
Net Worth Deficit: £861,502 *Total Assets:* £12,165,678
Registered Office: 3rd Floor, Citygate, St James Boulevard, Newcastle upon Tyne, NE1 4JE
Activities: Activities of other holding companies n.e.c.
Parent: PDZ Holdings Pty Limited
Officers: Dylan Browne, Secretary; Simon Mark Kersey [1973] Director/Business Executive; Benjamin Rade Stoikovich [1973] Director/Mining Engineer

Pea Soup Limited
Incorporated: 30 September 2003
Registered Office: 7 Eggleston Court, Riverside Park, Middlesbrough, Cleveland, TS2 1RU
Activities: Retail sale via mail order houses or via Internet
Major Shareholder: Benedict Baxter
Officers: Diana Baxter, Secretary/Retail and Services; Benedict Baxter [1980] Director/Retail and Services

The Peacock Group Limited
Incorporated: 18 February 2016 *Employees:* 183
Net Worth: £1,939,955 *Total Assets:* £4,680,894
Registered Office: Unit C1, Benfield Business Park, Benfield Road, Newcastle upon Tyne, NE6 4NQ
Activities: Activities of other holding companies n.e.c.
Shareholders: Christopher David Peacock; John Colin Peacock
Officers: Terence Edmund Gumbley [1949] Director; Christopher David Peacock [1973] Director; John Colin Peacock [1944] Director

Peacocks (Surgical and Medical Equipment) Limited
Incorporated: 4 February 1956 *Employees:* 14
Net Worth: £986,856 *Total Assets:* £2,590,737
Registered Office: Unit C1, Benfield Industrial Estate, Benfield Road, Newcastle upon Tyne, NE6 4NQ
Activities: Wholesale of other machinery and equipment
Shareholders: Christopher David Peacock; John Colin Peacock
Officers: Gary Edward Cooper [1971] Director/Engineer; Christopher David Peacock [1973] Director/Sales; John Colin Peacock [1944] Director; David William Stevens [1976] Finance Director

Peacocks Medical Group Limited
Incorporated: 4 February 1956 *Employees:* 172
Net Worth: £1,044,700 *Total Assets:* £5,199,656
Registered Office: Unit C1, Benfield Business Park, Benfield Road, Newcastle upon Tyne, NE6 4NQ
Activities: Manufacture of medical and dental instruments and supplies
Shareholders: Christopher David Peacock; John Colin Peacock
Officers: Terence Edmund Gumbley [1949] Director; Christopher David Peacock [1973] Director; John Colin Peacock [1944] Director; David William Stevens [1976] Managing Director; Mark Steven Turner [1978] Commercial Director

Pear Tree Honey Farm Limited
Incorporated: 19 December 2006
Net Worth: £1,117,225 *Total Assets:* £1,138,093
Registered Office: Moor House, Middleton Tyas, Richmond, N Yorks, DL10 6RT
Activities: Manufacture of other food products n.e.c.
Shareholders: John Irvin Whent; John Irvin Whent
Officers: John Irvin Whent, Secretary/Bee Keeper; John Irvin Whent [1947] Director/Bee Keeper; Paul Irvin Whent [1980] Director/Bee Keeper

Pear Tree Projects Limited
Incorporated: 30 October 1992 *Employees:* 74
Net Worth: £3,979,118 *Total Assets:* £5,868,649
Registered Office: Pear Tree House, Bolam, Darlington, Co Durham, DL2 2UP
Activities: Other service activities n.e.c.
Shareholders: David Anthony John Bartlett; Andrea Sarah Bartlett
Officers: Andrea Sarah Bartlett, Secretary/Property Developer; Andrea Sarah Bartlett [1970] Director/Company Secretary; David Anthony John Bartlett [1966] Director/Property-Care Services Manager

Pearie Law Windfarm Limited
Incorporated: 27 October 2015
Net Worth: £9,770,000 *Total Assets:* £30,388,000
Registered Office: Alexander House, 1 Mandarin Road, Rainton Bridge Business Park, Houghton-le-Spring, Co Durham, DH4 5RA
Activities: Construction of utility projects for electricity and telecommunications
Parent: EDF Energy Renewables Holdings Limited
Officers: Susan Elizabeth Lind, Secretary; Matthieu Thomas Hue [1975] Director [French]; Hassaan Majid [1968] Director

E.Pearson and Sons (Teesside) Limited
Incorporated: 15 May 2015 *Employees:* 82
Net Worth: £1,045,077 *Total Assets:* £4,315,542
Registered Office: 1 Mickleton Road, Riverside Park Industrial Estate, Middlesbrough, Cleveland, TS2 1RH
Activities: Removal services
Officers: Stephen Vaughn Hayward [1955] Director

Pearson Caulfield Limited
Incorporated: 28 October 2011 *Employees:* 19
Net Worth: £323,133 *Total Assets:* £1,732,464
Registered Office: Newgate Chambers, 1 Newgate Street, Newcastle upon Tyne, NE1 5RE
Activities: Barristers at law
Shareholders: Paul Anthony Caulfield; Lewis Francis Pearson
Officers: Paul Anthony Caulfield [1957] Director; John James Langers [1979] Director/Solicitor; John Paul Oxnard [1961] Director/Solicitor; Lewis Francis Pearson [1949] Director

Pearson Engineering Limited
Incorporated: 10 January 1985 *Employees:* 63
Net Worth: £56,282,000 *Total Assets:* £60,357,000
Registered Office: Armstrong Works, Scotswood Road, Newcastle upon Tyne, NE15 6UX
Activities: Manufacture of other special-purpose machinery n.e.c.
Parent: Reece Group Limited
Officers: Richard James Beatson [1964] Business Development Director; Simon Paul Gilroy [1975] Director/Engineer; Craig Priday [1966] Managing Director; John Peter Reece [1961] Director; Jason Anthony Riby [1968] Engineering Director; Mark Robert Tom Welstead [1965] Director

Peart Property (Bowburn) Limited
Incorporated: 14 August 2015
Net Worth: £187,745 *Total Assets:* £2,498,865
Registered Office: Baltic Works, Baltic Street, Hartlepool, Cleveland, TS25 1PW
Activities: Other letting and operating of own or leased real estate
Shareholders: Charles Frederick Peart; Roger David Hunter Peart
Officers: Charles Frederick Peart [1966] Director; Roger David Hunter Peart [1972] Director

Peart Property Limited
Incorporated: 23 February 2010
Net Worth: £2,215,454 *Total Assets:* £5,754,233
Registered Office: Baltic Works, Baltic Street, Hartlepool, Cleveland, TS25 1PW
Activities: Renting and leasing of other machinery, equipment and tangible goods n.e.c.
Shareholders: Charles Frederick Peart; Roger David Hunter Peart
Officers: Charles Frederick Peart [1966] Managing Director; Roger David Hunter Peart [1972] Managing Director

William Peat (Barnard Castle) Limited
Incorporated: 10 December 1956 *Employees:* 4
Net Worth: £837,000 *Total Assets:* £847,168
Registered Office: Oaklands, Darlington Road, Barnard Castle, Co Durham, DL12 8TA
Activities: Mixed farming
Shareholders: Roger Allan Peat; John Richard Peat
Officers: Roger Allan Peat, Secretary; John Richard Peat [1950] Director/Farmer; Martin Peat [1983] Director/Veterinary Surgeon; Roger Allan Peat [1956] Director/Farmer; Susan Peat [1949] Director

Pebbletree Ltd
Incorporated: 10 October 2005 *Employees:* 27
Net Worth: £2,014,640 *Total Assets:* £2,427,365
Registered Office: Suite 1e, North Sands Business Centre, Liberty Way, Sunderland, Tyne & Wear, SR6 0QA
Activities: Other telecommunications activities
Shareholders: Robert Thornton; Janni Jensen
Officers: Robert Thornton, Secretary; Janni Jensen [1980] Managing Director [Danish]; Robert Thornton [1975] Technical Director

Pecks House Developments Ltd
Incorporated: 18 September 2003
Registered Office: 7a Studley Terrace, Fenham, Newcastle upon Tyne, NE4 5PA
Activities: Buying and selling of own real estate
Major Shareholder: Shaban Suleman
Officers: Shaban Suleman [1967] Director

Pecks House Leisure Limited
Incorporated: 20 April 1989
Registered Office: 511 Durham Road, Low Fell, Gateshead, Tyne & Wear, NE9 5EY
Activities: Other letting and operating of own or leased real estate
Shareholders: Michael O'Neill; Marisa O'Neill
Officers: Angela Maria Franchesca O'Neill, Secretary; Michael John O'Neill [1959] Property Director

Pee Gee Limited
Incorporated: 16 October 2002
Net Worth: £1,027,513 *Total Assets:* £1,443,286
Registered Office: 8d Bowes Road, Middlesbrough, Cleveland, TS2 1LU
Activities: Repair of other equipment
Major Shareholder: Nigel Peter Gough
Officers: Karen Louise Coston, Secretary; Nigel Peter Gough [1977] Director

Peel Jones Copper Products Limited
Incorporated: 21 March 1968
Net Worth: £1,407,921 *Total Assets:* £2,614,527
Registered Office: Maynard Foundry, Carlin How, Saltburn-by-the-Sea, N Yorks, TS13 4EY
Activities: Casting of other non-ferrous metals
Parent: Archibald Young Limited
Officers: Ian Robert Young, Secretary; Peter David Garner [1945] Foundry Director; Andrew Sutherland Young [1977] Director/Manager; Ian Robert Young [1945] Director

Peel Street Developments Limited
Incorporated: 7 August 2007 *Employees:* 1
Net Worth: £2,444,698 *Total Assets:* £3,976,302
Registered Office: Trinity House, Thurston Road, Northallerton, N Yorks, DL6 2NA
Activities: Activities of head offices
Shareholders: Jeremy Robin Stephenson; Abigail Louisa Stephenson
Officers: Abigail Louisa Stephenson, Secretary; Jeremy Robin Stephenson [1962] Director

Peel Street Properties Limited
Incorporated: 31 July 1961
Registered Office: Trinity House, Thurston Road, Northallerton, N Yorks, DL6 2NA
Activities: Other letting and operating of own or leased real estate
Major Shareholder: Jeremy Stephenson
Officers: Abigail Louisa Stephenson, Secretary; Jeremy Robin Stephenson [1962] Director

Pegasus Material Handling Ltd
Incorporated: 6 May 2003
Net Worth: £667,166 *Total Assets:* £967,619
Registered Office: 25 Brindley Road, Hertburn Industrial Estate, Washington, Tyne & Wear, NE37 2SB
Activities: Wholesale of other machinery and equipment
Shareholders: Vera Wilson; Robert Wilson
Officers: Vera Wilson, Secretary; Robert Wilson [1955] Director/Field Service Engineer; Vera Wilson [1952] Director/Administrator

Peikko UK Limited
Incorporated: 12 May 2006 *Employees:* 9
Net Worth: £446,534 *Total Assets:* £1,427,339
Registered Office: Peikko UK Ltd, Beaumont Way, Aycliffe Business Park, Newton Aycliffe, Co Durham, DL5 6SN
Activities: Manufacture of metal structures and parts of structures
Parent: Peikko Group Oy
Officers: John Graeme Metcalfe [1964] Director; Topi Anselmi Paananen [1971] Director [Finnish]; Jukka-Pekka Tapio Turva [1974] Director [Finnish]

The Pen Shop Limited
Incorporated: 17 June 1943
Net Worth: £1,682,952 *Total Assets:* £4,523,310
Registered Office: 24 Newgate Street, Morpeth, Northumberland, NE61 1BA
Activities: Other retail sale of new goods in specialised stores (not commercial art galleries and opticians)
Parent: T&G Allan Holdings Limited
Officers: Colin Peter McClymont [1956] Director; Sally McClymont [1961] Director

P. S. Pendergood Limited
Incorporated: 4 July 2008 *Employees:* 8
Net Worth: £610,100 *Total Assets:* £847,154
Registered Office: 76-78 Oxford Road, Hartlepool, Cleveland, TS25 5SA
Activities: Dispensing chemist in specialised stores
Major Shareholder: Paul Steve Pendergood
Officers: Glynis Pendergood, Secretary; Paul Steve Pendergood [1981] Director/Pharmacy

Penhill Investments Limited
Incorporated: 1 February 2010
Net Worth: £317,149 *Total Assets:* £805,232
Registered Office: Oak House, Market Place, Bedale, N Yorks, DL8 1AU
Activities: Other business support service activities n.e.c.
Major Shareholder: James Richard Jarratt Harrison-Topham
Officers: James Richard Jarratt Harrison-Topham [1965] Director/Property Manager; Joanna Patricia Harrison-Topham [1965] Director

Pennine Contracts Ltd
Incorporated: 5 October 2006
Net Worth: £639,612 *Total Assets:* £985,719
Registered Office: Unit B5 The Avenue, Eleventh Avenue North, Team Valley Trading Estate, Gateshead, Tyne & Wear, NE11 0NJ
Activities: Other construction installation
Major Shareholder: Marc James Lucas
Officers: Marc James Lucas, Secretary; Marc James Lucas [1981] Director

Pennine Enterprises Ltd
Incorporated: 10 July 2013
Net Worth Deficit: £42,771 *Total Assets:* £828,298
Registered Office: Barningham Coach House, Barningham, Richmond, N Yorks, DL11 7DW
Activities: Plumbing, heat and air-conditioning installation
Shareholders: Andrew Phillip Howard; Edward Mark Somerset Milbank
Officers: Andrew Phillip Howard [1972] Director; Edward Mark Somerset Millbank [1973] Director

Pennine Newcastle Limited
Incorporated: 28 February 2014
Net Worth: £2,121,776 *Total Assets:* £3,714,498
Registered Office: Unit 1c Chollerton Drive, North Tyne Industrial Estate, Whitley Road, Longbenton, Newcastle upon Tyne, NE12 9SZ
Activities: Activities of other holding companies n.e.c.
Parent: Conservatory Outlet Group Limited
Officers: Michael Alexander Giscombe [1967] Director; Gregory Kane [1975] Director; Sarah Lyn Van Haazel [1975] Director

Pensave Limited
Incorporated: 27 May 2005 *Employees:* 75
Net Worth: £3,383,871 *Total Assets:* £7,442,869
Registered Office: Detchant, Belford, Northumberland, NE70 7PF
Activities: Activities of head offices
Major Shareholder: Timothy Wyndam Basil Smalley
Officers: Timothy Wyndam Basil Smalley, Secretary/Manufacturer; John Haddon Lovett [1951] Director; Rosanna Smalley [1966] Director [Irish]; Timothy Wyndam Basil Smalley [1960] Director/Manufacturer

Penshaw Estates Limited
Incorporated: 25 February 2000 *Employees:* 14
Net Worth Deficit: £442,683 *Total Assets:* £1,735,498
Registered Office: Rainton Business Park, Mercantile Road, Houghton-le-Spring, Co Durham, DH4 5PH
Activities: Agents involved in the sale of food, beverages and tobacco
Major Shareholder: Matthew Roseberry
Officers: Joanne Roseberry, Secretary/Riding School Proprietress; Jean Roseberry [1944] Director/Hotelier; Joanne Roseberry [1969] Director/Riding School Proprietress; Matthew Roseberry [1944] Director/Builder; Michael Anthony Roseberry [1966] Director/Professional Cricketer

Penton House Limited
Incorporated: 11 April 2012 *Employees:* 2
Net Worth: £1,420,547 *Total Assets:* £1,431,367
Registered Office: Greenbank House, Sotherby Road, Middlesbrough, Cleveland, TS3 8BT
Activities: Remediation activities and other waste management services
Shareholders: Robin Evershed; Gillian Ruth Evershed
Officers: Gillian Ruth Evershed, Secretary; Robin Evershed [1978] Director

People First Care Ltd
Incorporated: 5 February 2007 *Employees:* 79
Net Worth: £187,823 *Total Assets:* £1,180,586
Registered Office: The Granary, Town Farm, Great Whittington, Northumberland, NE19 2HA
Activities: Medical nursing home activities
Shareholders: Simon Michael Fitton; Sarah Elizabeth Fitton
Officers: Simon Michael Fitton, Secretary; Sarah Elizabeth Fitton [1963] Director/HR Consultant; Simon Michael Fitton [1965] Director/Chartered Surveyor

The People's Kitchen Limited
Incorporated: 14 April 1993
Net Worth: £1,035,829 *Total Assets:* £1,042,756
Registered Office: 56 Bath Lane, Newcastle upon Tyne, NE4 5SQ
Activities: Other social work activities without accommodation n.e.c.
Officers: Michael Ian Spriggs, Secretary; Jackie Boardman [1970] Director; Jenny Harrison [1987] Director/Charity Worker; Michael Ian Spriggs [1956] Director; David William Yellowley [1965] Director/Civil Servant

Peratech Holdco Ltd
Incorporated: 24 February 2014 *Employees:* 26
Net Worth: £5,879,800 *Total Assets:* £6,331,262
Registered Office: Old Repeater Station, 851 Gatherley Road, Brompton on Swale, Richmond, N Yorks, DL10 7JH
Activities: Activities of production holding companies
Shareholder: Tranquil Capital Limited
Officers: Douglas Stuart Balderston [1968] Director; Dr William Max Beckenbaugh [1946] Director/Technical Consulting [American]; Dr Sven Harmsen [1967] Investment Director [German]; Michael Dean Levin [1965] Director [American]; Jonathan Sharif Marx Stark [1969] Director [American]; Ewan Peter Stradling [1971] Director; Simon Tobelem [1969] Director/Businessman [French]

The Percy Hedley Foundation
Incorporated: 12 October 1984 *Employees:* 1,012
Net Worth: £10,323,000 *Total Assets:* £24,727,000
Registered Office: Hampeth Lodge, Station Road, Forest Hall, Newcastle upon Tyne, NE12 8YY
Activities: Primary education
Officers: Sarah Jane Turner, Secretary; David Robson Arthur [1954] Director/Managing Partner Accountants; Ajeet Chadda [1982] Director; Lisa Charles-Jones [1970] HR Director; Angela Curran [1961] Director/Solicitor; Sarah Fitzpatrick [1974] Director/Lawyer; Dr Mary Gibson [1943] Director/Retired; Raymond Johnstone [1963] Director of Rail and Infrastructure; Susan Jopling [1968] Director/IT Service General Manager; Jonathan David Jowett [1962] Director/Company Secretary; Damon Kent [1972] Director of Campus Northumbria University; Angela May Russell [1967] Finance Director; Dr Nicholas Spencer [1978] Director/Senior Lecturer; Anne Woods [1958] Director/Head of Finance

Perfect Care Limited
Incorporated: 15 December 2010
Net Worth: £741,233 *Total Assets:* £984,830
Registered Office: 10-12 High Street, Spennymoor, Co Durham, DL16 6DB
Activities: Other social work activities without accommodation n.e.c.
Shareholders: John Patrick Moran; Barbara Anne Moran
Officers: Barbara Anne Moran, Secretary; Barbara Anne Moran [1962] Director/Executive; John Patrick Moran [1968] Director/Business Executive

Perfect Image Limited
Incorporated: 30 September 1991 *Employees:* 91
Net Worth: £2,582,893 *Total Assets:* £4,839,737
Registered Office: Equinox House, Silver Fox Way, Cobalt Business Park, Wallsend, Tyne & Wear, NE27 0QJ
Activities: Information technology consultancy activities
Shareholders: Ruth Robson; Andrew John Robson
Officers: Ruth Robson, Secretary/Accountant; Gael Comrie Morris [1966] Director; William Henry Morris [1965] Director; Andrew John Robson [1970] Director/Computer Consultant; Ruth Robson [1968] Director/Accountant

Performance Horizon Group Limited
Incorporated: 12 March 2010 *Employees:* 175
Net Worth: £4,331,000 *Total Assets:* £29,063,000
Registered Office: 8th Floor, West One, Forth Banks, Newcastle upon Tyne, NE1 3PA
Activities: Other information technology service activities
Shareholder: DN Capital-Global Venture Capital II LP
Officers: Louise Hall, Secretary; Malcolm Steven Cowley [1978] Director; Paul William Fellows [1972] Director; Anuja Royan [1983] Director/Venture Capitalist [Canadian]; Steve Schlenker [1968] Director/Venture Capital Investor [American]; Ian David Sigalow [1979] Director/Venture Capitalist [American]; Steven Walske [1952] Director/Venture Capital [American]

Permatt Fork Lift Trucks Limited
Incorporated: 26 May 1999 *Employees:* 23
Net Worth: £804,641 *Total Assets:* £2,558,397
Registered Office: T O'Sullivan & Co, Verdemar House, 230 Park View, Whitley Bay, Tyne & Wear, NE26 3QR
Activities: Renting and leasing of trucks and other heavy vehicles
Major Shareholder: Mark Andrew Percy
Officers: Michelle Frances Percy, Secretary; Joanne McIntyre [1972] Director; Mark Andrew Percy [1967] Managing Director

Permoid Industries Limited
Incorporated: 2 January 1991 *Employees:* 176
Net Worth: £1,961,217 *Total Assets:* £5,170,345
Registered Office: Horndale Avenue, Aycliffe Industrial Estate, Newton Aycliffe, Co Durham, DL5 6DW
Activities: Other manufacturing n.e.c.
Officers: Brian William Beckett, Secretary; Walid El Hage [1968] Managing Director

Pern Consumer Products Limited
Incorporated: 21 February 2007 *Employees:* 6
Net Worth: £790,957 *Total Assets:* £1,133,240
Registered Office: Quantum House, Hobson Industrial Estate, Burnopfield, Co Durham, NE16 6EA
Activities: Wholesale of perfume and cosmetics
Officers: Amanda Miller, Secretary; Andrew Paul Matthews [1976] Operations Director; David Alan Sanson [1959] Quality Director; Michael James Tagg [1982] Finance Director

Peron Limited
Incorporated: 5 August 2011
Net Worth: £418,835 *Total Assets:* £828,837
Registered Office: Thornton House, Brighouse Road, Riverside Park, Middlesbrough, Cleveland, TS2 1RT
Activities: Other engineering activities
Shareholders: James Gareth Orpen; Charles Jeremy Orpen
Officers: Charles Jeremy Orpen [1983] Director; James Gareth Orpen [1948] Director/Engineer

Ron Perry & Son Limited
Incorporated: 4 December 1978 *Employees:* 30
Net Worth: £2,336,023 *Total Assets:* £5,503,728
Registered Office: A19 Test and Tune, Elwick, Hartlepool, Cleveland, TS27 3HH
Activities: Retail sale of automotive fuel in specialised stores
Shareholders: Ronald Charles Perry; Lesley Alexis Perry
Officers: Lesley Alexis Perry, Secretary; Anne Marie Rose Cowan [1987] Director; Lesley Alexis Perry [1959] Director/Riding School Proprietor; Ronald Daniel Perry [1984] Director; Ronald Charles Perry [1956] Director

Ron Perry (A19 Test & Tune) Limited
Incorporated: 15 February 1989 *Employees:* 12
Net Worth: £447,215 *Total Assets:* £1,105,985
Registered Office: A19 Test and Tune, Elwick, Hartlepool, Cleveland, TS27 3HH
Activities: Maintenance and repair of motor vehicles
Parent: Ron Perry & Son Limited
Officers: Anne Marie Rose Cowan, Secretary; Anne Marie Rose Cowan [1987] Director; Lesley Alexis Perry [1959] Director/Riding School Proprietor; Ronald Daniel Perry [1984] Director; Ronald Charles Perry [1956] Director/Garage Proprietor

Perry Process Equipment Limited
Incorporated: 16 January 1990 *Employees:* 18
Net Worth: £2,005,977 *Total Assets:* £2,988,816
Registered Office: Station Road, Aycliffe Industrial Estate, Newton Aycliffe, Co Durham, DL5 6EQ
Activities: Agents involved in the sale of machinery, industrial equipment, ships and aircraft
Shareholder: Jerome Paul Epstein
Officers: Darren Bentham [1961] Managing Director; Gregg Paul Epstein [1959] Director/Business Executive [American]; Jerome Paul Epstein [1935] Director/Business Executive [American]; David Goodman [1948] Director/Business Executive [American]; Kenneth Miller [1951] Director/Business Executive [American]

Petards Joyce-Loebl Limited
Incorporated: 29 September 1987 *Employees:* 92
Net Worth: £4,520,000 *Total Assets:* £9,343,000
Registered Office: 390 Princesway, Team Valley Trading Estate, Gateshead, Tyne & Wear, NE11 0TU
Activities: Manufacture of communication equipment other than telegraph, and telephone apparatus and equipment
Shareholders: Petards Group PLC; Petards Group PLC
Officers: James Patrick Murray, Secretary; Osman Abdullah [1945] Director; Osman Abdullah [1945] Director; Raschid Michael Abdullah [1944] Director

H.S. Petch & Sons Limited
Incorporated: 5 September 1962 *Employees:* 13
Net Worth: £3,797,949 *Total Assets:* £4,316,355
Registered Office: Whitegate Farm, Newton under Roseberry, Great Ayton, Middlesbrough, Cleveland, TS9 6QP
Activities: Mixed farming
Shareholders: David Martin Petch; Herbert David Petch
Officers: David Martin Petch, Secretary; Christine Ruth Knight [1963] Director; David Martin Petch [1956] Director/Farmer; Heather Mary Petch [1959] Charity Director; Herbert David Petch [1928] Director/Farmer; Rodger Petch [1957] Director

S.G. Petch Limited
Incorporated: 9 March 1990 *Employees:* 328
Net Worth: £7,391,631 *Total Assets:* £42,452,692
Registered Office: McMullen Road, Darlington, Co Durham, DL1 1XZ
Activities: Sale of new cars and light motor vehicles
Major Shareholder: Stephen Guy Petch
Officers: Simon David Rees, Secretary; Shaun Burke [1960] Director/General Manager; Andrew Hodgson [1968] Director/Manager; Samantha Marie Petch [1977] Director/Manager; Stephen Guy Petch [1947] Director/Garage Proprietor; Simon David Rees [1956] Director/Accountant

Peterlee Fire Company Limited
Incorporated: 11 April 2001 *Employees:* 44
Net Worth: £165,572 *Total Assets:* £771,838
Registered Office: Unit 6 Seaview Industrial Estate, Horden, Peterlee, Co Durham, SR8 4TQ
Activities: Other professional, scientific and technical activities n.e.c.
Officers: Arthur Alan Chapman, Secretary; Arthur Alan Chapman [1953] Director/Manager; Alan Gage [1959] Director/Engineer

Peterlee Glass Company Limited
Incorporated: 19 October 1977 *Employees:* 34
Net Worth: £1,633,182 *Total Assets:* £3,610,077
Registered Office: Glass House, Mill Hill, North West Industrial Estate, Peterlee, Co Durham, SR8 2HR
Activities: Glazing
Parent: United Glass Group Ltd
Officers: Mark Edward Harrison [1977] Director; Graeme Hawes [1975] Director

Peterleefour Limited
Incorporated: 4 August 2016
Net Worth: £3,888 *Total Assets:* £1,607,688
Registered Office: 7 Holyrood Avenue, Darlington, Co Durham, DL3 8AZ
Activities: Other service activities n.e.c.
Shareholders: George Andrew Fotheringham; George Andrew Fotheringham
Officers: George Andrew Fotheringham [1957] Director/Chartered Accountant

Petersen Stainless Rigging Limited
Incorporated: 12 June 1978 *Employees:* 54
Net Worth: £1,572,970 *Total Assets:* £2,102,222
Registered Office: Cowen Road, Blaydon on Tyne, Tyne & Wear, NE21 5TW
Activities: Manufacture of metal structures and parts of structures
Officers: Harold Bell [1981] Director/Trainee Quantity Surveyor; Kevin Bell [1979] Director/Sales Manager; Norman Bell [1946] Director/Chartered Accountant; Aries Kornelis Dijkhuizen [1973] Director/Development Manager [Dutch]; Shelley Jane Wales [1968] Director/Operations Manager

PFC Marine Ltd
Incorporated: 11 February 2004 *Employees:* 15
Net Worth: £264,159 *Total Assets:* £998,203
Registered Office: Unit 8 Seaview Industrial Estate, Peterlee, Co Durham, SR8 4TQ
Activities: Other professional, scientific and technical activities n.e.c.
Parent: Peterlee Fire Company Ltd
Officers: Arthur Alan Chapman, Secretary; Arthur Alan Chapman [1953] Director; Peter Cox [1952] Director/Fire Protection; Alan Gage [1959] Director/Fire Protection; Craig Reilly [1975] Operations Director

PFS (Newcastle) Limited
Incorporated: 9 July 2015
Net Worth Deficit: £58,702 *Total Assets:* £1,684,096
Registered Office: 7-9 Groat Market, Newcastle upon Tyne, NE1 1UQ
Activities: Other letting and operating of own or leased real estate
Major Shareholder: Rajiv Vadhera
Officers: Rajiv Vadhera [1975] Director

PGM Investments Ltd
Incorporated: 11 April 2014
Net Worth: £471,241 *Total Assets:* £1,609,889
Registered Office: c/o Cygnet Family Law Ltd, Ground Floor, Portland House, West Dyke Road, Redcar, Cleveland, TS10 1DH
Activities: Other letting and operating of own or leased real estate
Major Shareholder: Peter George Medd
Officers: Lisa Smith, Secretary; Peter George Medd [1953] Director/Lawyer

PGS Law LLP
Incorporated: 29 February 2012 *Employees:* 30
Net Worth: £751,387 *Total Assets:* £904,566
Registered Office: Law Court Chambers, Waterloo Square, South Shields, Tyne & Wear, NE33 1AW
Officers: William Joseph Dryden [1964] Member; Ian William Farrer [1979] Member; Carolyne Deborah Hargreaves [1973] Member; Chris Ellwood Potts [1956] Member; Keith Swan [1966] Member; William Anthony Ward [1962] Member

PHA Limited
Incorporated: 27 October 2008
Net Worth: £15,076,283 *Total Assets:* £31,210,886
Registered Office: Citygate, St James Boulevard, Newcastle upon Tyne, NE1 4JE
Activities: Other letting and operating of own or leased real estate
Parent: BPT Limited
Officers: Adam McGhin, Secretary; Helen Christine Gordon [1959] Director; Adam McGhin [1978] Director/Solicitor; Mark Jeremy Robson [1959] Director/Chartered Surveyor; Vanessa Kate Simms [1975] Director

Pharma Nord (UK) Limited
Incorporated: 19 July 1988 *Employees:* 35
Net Worth: £2,435,962 *Total Assets:* £3,867,796
Registered Office: Telford Court, Morpeth, Northumberland, NE61 2DB
Activities: Non-specialised wholesale trade
Officers: Peter Irwin Aitchison, Secretary; Bent Henriksen [1938] Managing Director [Danish]; Sven Moesgaard [1954] Director [Danish]; Eli Wallin [1954] Director [Danish]

PHCC Developments (Commonfield) Limited
Incorporated: 20 September 2006
Net Worth: £352,031 *Total Assets:* £1,231,930
Registered Office: 25 Lamonby Way, Cramlington, Northumberland, NE23 7XW
Activities: Development of building projects
Parent: Primary Health Care Centres (Developments) Ltd
Officers: Deborah Ann Chisholm, Secretary; Christine Neve [1976] Director

PHCC Developments (West Kensington) Limited
Incorporated: 20 April 2009
Net Worth: £55,247 *Total Assets:* £1,407,034
Registered Office: 25 Lamonby Way, Cramlington, Northumberland, NE23 7XW
Activities: Development of building projects
Parent: Primary Health Care Centres (Developments) Ltd
Officers: Deborah Chisholm, Secretary; Christine Neve [1976] Director

Philadelphia Structures Ltd
Incorporated: 25 September 1997 *Employees:* 38
Net Worth: £1,342,011 *Total Assets:* £2,209,857
Registered Office: 4 Palmer Road, South West Industrial Estate, Peterlee, Co Durham, SR8 2HU
Activities: Manufacture of metal structures and parts of structures
Shareholders: Steven Defty; Richard William Little
Officers: Steven Defty, Secretary/Director; Steven Defty [1965] Director; Richard William Little [1959] Director

Phillips Chemists Limited
Incorporated: 13 January 2010 *Employees:* 15
Net Worth: £503,232 *Total Assets:* £1,429,141
Registered Office: 9 Alhambra Terrace, Fishburn, Stockton on Tees, Cleveland, TS21 4BU
Activities: Dispensing chemist in specialised stores
Shareholder: Alan Phillips
Officers: Jane Wright, Secretary; Alan Phillips [1943] Director/Pharmacist; Colin Vallance [1962] Director/Pharmacist; Jane Wright [1957] Director/Pharmacist

Phoenix Civil Engineering Limited
Incorporated: 11 July 1994
Net Worth: £1,157,204 *Total Assets:* £1,421,125
Registered Office: 7 Oaktree Close, Middleton St George, Darlington, Co Durham, DL2 1HJ
Activities: Construction of roads and motorways
Major Shareholder: Peter Allan Smith
Officers: Valerie Joan Stott, Secretary; Peter Allan Smith [1947] Director/Engineer

Phoenix Coaches (NE) Limited
Incorporated: 3 June 2013
Net Worth Deficit: £41,602 *Total Assets:* £1,056,308
Registered Office: Northumberland Taxi & Coach Centre, Albion Way, Blyth, Northumberland, NE24 5BW
Activities: Other urban, suburban or metropolitan passenger land transport (not underground, metro or similar)
Parent: Readypay Ltd
Officers: Kenneth Turner [1974] Operations Director

Phoenix Eye Ltd
Incorporated: 4 September 2007 *Employees:* 1,084
Net Worth: £880,814 *Total Assets:* £7,324,753
Registered Office: Patrick House, Gosforth Park Avenue, Gosforth Business Park, Newcastle upon Tyne, NE12 8EG
Activities: Security systems service activities
Shareholder: Neill Aidan Winch
Officers: Neill Aidan Winch, Secretary/Director; Colin George Austin [1968] Director; Stephen William Howe [1967] Director; Neill Aidan Winch [1964] Director

Phoenix House (Sunderland) Limited
Incorporated: 17 October 2014
Registered Office: 1 Kingswood Drive, Darras Hall, Ponteland, Newcastle upon Tyne, NE20 9PL
Activities: Development of building projects
Parent: SSG Property Limited
Officers: Dr Akash Ghai [1979] Director; Promila Sehgal [1948] Director; Dr Deepinder Singh Somal [1961] Director

Phoenix Passive Fire Protection Limited
Incorporated: 3 April 2014 *Employees:* 7
Net Worth: £681,307 *Total Assets:* £1,112,670
Registered Office: Watsons Yard, Barrington Road, Bedlington, Northumberland, NE22 7AH
Activities: Other construction installation
Shareholders: Paul Murther; Ronald Leyland; Michael Darbyshire
Officers: Michael Darbyshire [1959] Director; Ronald Leyland [1965] Director; Paul Murther [1972] Director

Phoenix Security Holdings Limited
Incorporated: 11 May 2016 *Employees:* 1,084
Net Worth: £880,914 *Total Assets:* £7,324,853
Registered Office: Patrick House, Gosforth Park Avenue, Gosforth Business Park, Newcastle upon Tyne, NE12 8EG
Activities: Private security activities
Shareholder: Neill Aidan Winch
Officers: Stephen William Howe [1967] Director; Donna Winch [1976] Director; Neill Aidan Winch [1964] Director

Phoenix Steel Holdings Limited
Incorporated: 23 July 2013 *Employees:* 67
Net Worth: £4,199,814 *Total Assets:* £7,625,791
Registered Office: Phoenix Steel Holdings, Amos Ayre Place, Simonside Industrial Estate, South Shields, Tyne & Wear, NE34 9PB
Activities: Activities of production holding companies
Major Shareholder: James Mullen
Officers: Vincent Conroy [1968] Director; Ian Fuesdale [1963] Director; James Mullen [1963] Director

Phoenix Steel Limited
Incorporated: 24 April 1998 *Employees:* 67
Net Worth: £4,035,831 *Total Assets:* £7,332,680
Registered Office: Phoenix Steel Limited, Amos Ayre Place, Simonside Industrial Estate, South Shields, Tyne & Wear, NE34 9PB
Activities: Wholesale of metals and metal ores
Major Shareholder: James Mullen
Officers: Ian Fuesdale, Secretary/Manager; Vincent Conroy [1968] Director/Steel Sales; Ian Fuesdale [1963] Director/Manager; James Mullen [1963] Director/Manager; Peter Shiels [1963] Director

Phoenix Theatre (Blyth)
Incorporated: 20 June 2012
Net Worth: £1,565,910 *Total Assets:* £1,639,837
Registered Office: 37a Beaconsfield Street, Blyth, Northumberland, NE24 2DS
Activities: Performing arts
Shareholders: David George Garrett; Paul Brian Worth
Officers: Susan Davey [1953] Director/Retired RGN; David George Garrett [1948] Director; Donald Cooper Macmillan Montgomery [1972] Director/Minister of Religion; Alison Thoburn [1957] Director; Paul Brian Worth [1961] Director

PHP Architects Limited
Incorporated: 23 December 2005 *Employees:* 8
Net Worth: £994,348 *Total Assets:* £1,181,934
Registered Office: 10 Lumley Court, Chester-le-Street, Co Durham, DH2 1AN
Activities: Architectural activities
Shareholders: Graeme Charles Hodgson; Fausto Antonio Almeida Matos Pereira
Officers: Fausto Antonio Almeida Matos Pereira, Secretary; Graeme Charles Hodgson [1973] Director/Architect; Fausto Antonio Almeida Matos Pereira [1967] Director/Architect [Portuguese]

Phusion IM Limited
Incorporated: 5 March 1992 *Employees:* 22
Net Worth: £797,856 *Total Assets:* £1,335,784
Registered Office: 16 Earls Nook, Belasis Business Park, Billingham, Cleveland, TS23 4EF
Activities: Data processing, hosting and related activities
Major Shareholder: Stephen John Pearson
Officers: Alexandra Jane Hayward, Secretary; Alexandra Jane Hayward [1967] Managing Director; Stephen John Pearson [1957] Director/Executive Chairman

Pickerings Europe Limited
Incorporated: 27 June 1996 *Employees:* 329
Net Worth: £24,169,000 *Total Assets:* £39,284,000
Registered Office: P O Box 19, Globe Elevator Works, Stockton on Tees, Cleveland, TS20 2AD
Activities: Repair of other equipment
Major Shareholder: John Donald Read Fothergill
Officers: Stephen Angus, Secretary; Ian Andrew Bowers [1963] Service Director; Paul Brooks [1972] Director; John Donald Read Fothergill [1961] Director; Gary Daniel Rains [1966] Sales Director

Richard Pickles Limited
Incorporated: 14 September 1988 *Employees:* 2
Net Worth: £1,340,012 *Total Assets:* £1,425,053
Registered Office: 246 Park View, Whitley Bay, Tyne & Wear, NE26 3QX
Activities: Other letting and operating of own or leased real estate
Major Shareholder: Richard Pickles
Officers: Amy Pickles, Secretary; Amy Pickles [1985] Operations Director; Richard Pickles [1949] Director

PII Group Limited
Incorporated: 22 August 1997 *Employees:* 442
Net Worth: £41,315,000 *Total Assets:* £94,730,000
Registered Office: Atley Way, North Nelson Industrial Estate, Cramlington, Northumberland, NE23 1WW
Activities: Other service activities n.e.c.
Officers: Michael Bellamy [1962] Director/General Manager; Sanjeet Chadda [1978] Director/Chartered Accountant; Kristopher Ryan McBride [1974] Director/CFO - GE Measurement & Control [American]

PII Limited
Incorporated: 26 August 1997 *Employees:* 221
Net Worth: £45,176,000 *Total Assets:* £89,165,000
Registered Office: Atley Way, North Nelson Industrial Estate, Cramlington, Northumberland, NE23 1WW
Activities: Other service activities n.e.c.
Parent: PII Group Limited
Officers: Michael Bellamy [1962] Director/General Manager; Sanjeet Chadda [1978] Director/Chartered Accountant; Kevin Johnson [1963] Director/Engineer

PIMCO 2852 Limited
Incorporated: 19 February 2010
Net Worth: £1,582,896 *Total Assets:* £12,554,880
Registered Office: Wilton Group Head Office, Port Clarence Offshore Base, Port Clarence Road, Middlesbrough, Cleveland, TS2 1RZ
Activities: Activities of head offices
Parent: Wilton Universal Group Limited
Officers: Christine Stobbs, Secretary; Steven Brian Pearson [1972] Director; William Scott [1961] Director/Engineer; Christine Stobbs [1973] Finance Director

Pink Boutique Limited
Incorporated: 8 February 2012
Net Worth: £1,219,124 *Total Assets:* £2,706,878
Registered Office: Unit 2 Newburn Industrial Estate, Shelley Road, Newcastle upon Tyne, NE15 9RT
Activities: Retail sale via mail order houses or via Internet
Shareholders: Alice Rowen Hall; Julie Blackie
Officers: Julie Blackie, Secretary; Julie Blackie [1954] Director/Manager; Alice Rowen Hall [1988] Director/Manager

Pinkney Building Contractors Limited
Incorporated: 12 December 2006 *Employees:* 60
Net Worth: £454,988 *Total Assets:* £1,332,279
Registered Office: West Park Farm, Tow Law, Bishop Auckland, Co Durham, DL13 4NR
Activities: Other building completion and finishing
Shareholders: Jordan Mae Pinkney; Cameron Joseph Pinkney; Richard Pinkney
Officers: Richard Pinkney [1969] Director/Builder

Pinnacle Re-Tec Limited
Incorporated: 27 September 2006 *Employees:* 29
Net Worth: £180,294 *Total Assets:* £1,681,896
Registered Office: Hownsgill Drive, Delves Lane Industrial Estate, Consett, Co Durham, DH8 9HU
Activities: Manufacture of metal structures and parts of structures
Major Shareholder: Tobias Francois Heintz
Officers: Gordon Walter Adam, Secretary; Gordon Walter Adam [1950] Director; Tobias Francois Heintz [1968] Director [German]

Pinpin Ltd
Incorporated: 26 April 2013 *Employees:* 63
Net Worth: £824,764 *Total Assets:* £1,535,526
Registered Office: 70 Victoria Road, Darlington, Co Durham, DL1 5JG
Activities: Other amusement and recreation activities n.e.c.
Parent: Lane7 Ltd
Officers: Timothy James Wilks [1978] Director

Pioneering Care Partnership
Incorporated: 7 January 1998 *Employees:* 83
Net Worth: £1,639,178 *Total Assets:* £1,878,878
Registered Office: Pioneering Care Centre, Carers Way, Newton Aycliffe, Co Durham, DL5 4SF
Activities: Other service activities n.e.c.
Officers: Carol Gaskarth, Secretary; Heather Brewster [1957] Director/Retired; Carol Briggs [1944] Director/Service User; David Cockburn [1967] Director; Brenda Davidson [1963] Director/Solicitor; Irena Marta Evans [1939] Director/Retired; Barry Knevitt [1958] Director/Retired; Marilyn Isobelle Mohan [1953] Director; Brian Crawford Wilson [1948] Director/Service User

Pipe Equipment Specialists Limited
Incorporated: 3 March 1995 *Employees:* 10
Net Worth: £1,081,010 *Total Assets:* £1,266,146
Registered Office: 66a Dukesway, Teesside Industrial Estate, Thornaby, Stockton on Tees, Cleveland, TS17 9LT
Activities: Manufacture of other special-purpose machinery n.e.c.
Parent: Indutrade UK
Officers: Andrew Johannes Cousins [1968] Director; David John Lyes [1970] Director; Peter Ian Rowlands [1968] Director; Peter Scott [1958] Sales Director

Pipeline Engineering & Supply Co. Limited
Incorporated: 27 March 1997 *Employees:* 68
Net Worth: £646,000 *Total Assets:* £8,317,000
Registered Office: Gatherley Road Industrial Estate, Catterick Bridge, Richmond, N Yorks, DL10 7JG
Activities: Manufacture of other plastic products
Parent: Circor International
Officers: Nicholas Bowerman, Secretary; Rajeev Bhalla [1963] Director [American]; Nicholas Bowerman [1975] Finance Director; Jonathan Gallagher [1969] Director/Operations

Pipeline Precision Engineering Ltd
Incorporated: 28 August 2009
Registered Office: 30 Yoden Way, Peterlee, Co Durham, SR8 1AL
Activities: Machining
Shareholders: Stewart Walker; Simon Hannar
Officers: Simon Lee Hannar [1974] Director

Pipetawse Limited
Incorporated: 25 September 1981 *Employees:* 57
Net Worth: £1,040,010 *Total Assets:* £2,164,056
Registered Office: Fabrication Division, New Hartley Drive, Double Row, Seaton Delaval, Whitley Bay, Tyne & Wear, NE25 0PP
Activities: Manufacture of tubes, pipes, hollow profiles and related fittings, of steel
Shareholder: Patricia Ann Armstrong
Officers: Laurie Wilson, Secretary; Patricia Ann Armstrong [1942] Director; Thomas William Armstrong [1962] Managing Director

Piramal Healthcare UK Limited
Incorporated: 21 February 2005 *Employees:* 519
Net Worth: £39,544,904 *Total Assets:* £79,694,360
Registered Office: Whalton Road, Morpeth, Northumberland, NE61 3YA
Activities: Other business support service activities n.e.c.
Officers: Christopher Michael Leahy, Secretary; Kay Hussain [1971] Managing Director - Pharmaceuticals; Christopher Michael Leahy [1972] Director/Accountant; Vivek Valsaraj [1973] Director [Indian]; Mark John Wright [1977] Director/Site Lead

Pitman Press Limited
Incorporated: 8 March 1984 *Employees:* 3
Net Worth Deficit: £1,013,797 *Total Assets:* £14,693,670
Registered Office: 8 Springfield Close, Ovington, Northumberland, NE42 6EL
Activities: Non-trading company
Major Shareholder: Jacques Francis Veyrat
Officers: Matthew William Robson, Secretary; Matthew William Robson [1954] Director/Barrister

PJA Distribution Limited
Incorporated: 26 May 2010 *Employees:* 48
Net Worth: £955,398 *Total Assets:* £1,998,815
Registered Office: 1 Sadler Forster Way, Teesside Industrial Estate, Stockton on Tees, Cleveland, TS17 9JY
Activities: Other retail sale of new goods in specialised stores (not commercial art galleries and opticians)
Shareholders: Andrew John Simpson; Andrea Simpson
Officers: Andrea Shiela Simpson, Secretary; Andrew John Simpson [1979] Director

PJS Brickwork Limited
Incorporated: 15 October 1998
Registered Office: PJS House, 9-11 Harris Street, Middlesbrough, Cleveland, TS1 5EF
Activities: Construction of commercial buildings
Shareholders: Michael Neale; Paul Stephenson
Officers: Paul Stephenson, Secretary; Michael Neale [1965] Director/Builder; Paul Stephenson [1967] Director/Builder

PJS Properties Limited
Incorporated: 4 March 2003
Registered Office: PJS House, 9-11 Harris Street, Middlesbrough, Cleveland, TS1 5EF
Activities: Other letting and operating of own or leased real estate
Shareholders: Michael Neale; Paul Stephenson
Officers: Michael Neale, Secretary; Michael Neale [1965] Director/Builder; Paul Stephenson [1967] Director/Builder

Planit Project Services Limited
Incorporated: 11 December 1998
Net Worth: £153,810 *Total Assets:* £1,038,627
Registered Office: Cherrygarth, Larners Hill, Great Ayton, Middlesbrough, Cleveland, TS9 6HH
Activities: Other letting and operating of own or leased real estate
Major Shareholder: Nicholas Stuart Turner
Officers: Nicholas Stuart Turner [1955] Director/Project Management and Support

Plant Services (Gateshead) Limited
Incorporated: 24 February 1967 *Employees:* 30
Net Worth: £686,822 *Total Assets:* £1,532,171
Registered Office: Tyne Slipway West Works, River Drive, South Shields, Tyne & Wear, NE33 1LH
Activities: Manufacture of other furniture
Parent: P.S.T.(U.K.) Limited
Officers: Gareth Treharne [1985] Director; Stephen Joseph Treharne [1956] Director

Plasterpiece Limited
Incorporated: 1 May 1997 *Employees:* 7
Net Worth: £764,151 *Total Assets:* £875,379
Registered Office: Plasterpiece, Shaftesbury Avenue, South Shields, Tyne & Wear, NE34 9PH
Activities: Other retail sale in non-specialised stores
Officers: Skye Alexander Ferry, Secretary; Christopher Ferry [1959] Managing Director; Skye-Alexander Ferry [1988] Director

Plastic Mouldings Northern Limited
Incorporated: 5 September 2005 *Employees:* 22
Net Worth: £1,025,433 *Total Assets:* £1,532,096
Registered Office: 72 Kingsway, Bishop Auckland, Co Durham, DL14 7JF
Activities: Manufacture of other plastic products
Shareholders: Mark Rigg; Freddie Bourdais
Officers: Freddy Gregory Bourdais, Secretary; Freddy Gregory Bourdais [1970] Sales Director [French]; Mark Anthony Rigg [1973] Director/Production

Platinum Properties (GB) Limited
Incorporated: 12 February 2004
Net Worth: £83,779 *Total Assets:* £819,120
Registered Office: 98 Langley Avenue, Thornaby, Stockton on Tees, Cleveland, TS17 7HF
Activities: Other letting and operating of own or leased real estate
Shareholder: Imran Rahman
Officers: Imran Rahman, Secretary; Imran Rahman [1978] Director/Sales Manager; Masood Rahman [1976] Director/Production Operator

Plaxica Limited
Incorporated: 30 July 2008
Net Worth: £242,722 *Total Assets:* £892,654
Registered Office: The Wilton Centre, Wilton, Redcar, Cleveland, TS10 4RF
Activities: Other research and experimental development on natural sciences and engineering
Shareholders: Invesco Ltd; Imperial Innovations Businesses LLP
Officers: George Dunstan Cooke, Secretary; Robert Harold Bahns [1964] Director/Investment Banker; Dunstan Cooke [1976] Business Director and Company Secretary; Philip James Goodier [1966] Director; Paul Mulhollem [1949] Director [American]

Players Bars Investments Limited
Incorporated: 7 April 2014 *Employees:* 86
Net Worth: £18,781 *Total Assets:* £1,225,796
Registered Office: 2nd Floor, Alderman Fenwick House, 98-100 Pilgrim Street, Newcastle upon Tyne, NE1 6SQ
Activities: Public houses and bars
Shareholders: Denise Codona; Gordon James Codona; Jonathan Dean Codona
Officers: Gordon James Codona [1979] Director; Jonathan Dean Codona [1982] Director

Plazawise Limited
Incorporated: 24 May 1978
Registered Office: 22 The Willow Chase, Long Newton, Stockton on Tees, Cleveland, TS21 1PD
Activities: Other letting and operating of own or leased real estate
Shareholders: Gregory Richard Stewart Brownlee; Alistair David Brownlee
Officers: Gillian Margaret Brownlee, Secretary; Barry Brownlee [1940] Director; Gillian Margaret Brownlee [1945] Director/Secretary

Pleasant Residential Ltd
Incorporated: 23 March 2015
Net Worth: £129,414 *Total Assets:* £1,802,323
Registered Office: 1 St Pauls Drive, Houghton-le-Spring, Co Durham, DH4 7SH
Activities: Other letting and operating of own or leased real estate
Shareholders: Sara Shakila Hasan; Serena Alice Hasan
Officers: Sara Shakila Hasan, Secretary; Sara Shakila Hasan [1996] Director; Serena Alice Hasan [1997] Director

Pleasure Leisure Limited
Incorporated: 8 August 2013 *Employees:* 2
Net Worth: £133,858 *Total Assets:* £1,565,504
Registered Office: 14 Scotswood Road, Newcastle upon Tyne, NE4 7JB
Activities: Other business support service activities n.e.c.
Shareholders: John Michael Little; David Fisher
Officers: David Fisher [1980] Director/Entrepreneur; John Michael Little [1965] Sales Director

Plenary Project Solutions Limited
Incorporated: 22 May 2007 *Employees:* 2
Net Worth: £733,179 *Total Assets:* £1,245,039
Registered Office: Plenary BV House, Queens Square, Middlesbrough, Cleveland, TS2 1PA
Activities: Other engineering activities
Shareholders: Daniel John McGlade; Christine McGlade
Officers: Christine McGlade, Secretary; Daniel John McGlade [1951] Director

Plessey Checks Farming Limited
Incorporated: 28 January 2014
Net Worth: £8,252,405 *Total Assets:* £8,774,087
Registered Office: Blagdon Estate Office, Seaton Burn, Newcastle upon Tyne, NE13 6DE
Activities: Mixed farming
Shareholders: Viscount Matthew White Ridley; William Mark Wood; Earl George Dominic Percy
Officers: Christopher Brian Stonehouse, Secretary; The Hon Matthew White Ridley [1993] Director; Viscount Matthew White Ridley [1958] Director/Writer/Landowner; William Mark Wood [1947] Director/Chartered Surveyor

Plimsoll Publishing Limited
Incorporated: 20 February 1987 *Employees:* 21
Net Worth: £961,356 *Total Assets:* £1,602,160
Registered Office: Scotswood House, Thornaby Place, Thornaby, Stockton on Tees, Cleveland, TS17 6SB
Activities: Other publishing activities
Officers: Elizabeth Anne McMorris, Secretary/Director; Elizabeth Anne McMorris [1966] Director; Daniel James Turkington [1976] Managing Director; Donald James Turkington [1938] Director/Chairman

P. Plunkett (Tiling Contractors) Limited
Incorporated: 24 February 1978 *Employees:* 53
Net Worth: £1,480,417 *Total Assets:* £2,382,160
Registered Office: Dukes Way, Low Prudhoe Industrial Estate, Prudhoe, Northumberland, NE42 6PQ
Activities: Floor and wall covering
Officers: Claire Muncer, Secretary; Steven Allsopp [1972] Contracts Director; David Baker [1970] Director/Contracts Manager; Mark Forster [1965] Estimating Director; Mark Henderson [1969] Director; John Peter Plunkett [1978] Director; Linda Plunkett [1949] Director; Patrick Plunkett [1946] Director/Chairman; Paul David Plunkett [1973] Director; Geoffrey Ian Williams [1959] Managing Director

Plymouth Citybus Limited
Incorporated: 27 March 1986 *Employees:* 545
Net Worth: £4,413,000 *Total Assets:* £18,366,000
Registered Office: 3rd Floor, 41-51 Grey Street, Newcastle upon Tyne, NE1 6EE
Activities: Other urban, suburban or metropolitan passenger land transport (not underground, metro or similar)
Parent: Go-Ahead Holding Limited
Officers: Carolyn Ferguson, Secretary; David Allen Brown [1960] Director; Simon Patrick Butcher [1967] Finance Director; Mark Brian Horide [1964] Engineering Director; Richard Charles Barrington Stevens [1968] Director

PMK Hague Investments Limited
Incorporated: 13 May 2014
Net Worth: £1,130,035 *Total Assets:* £1,131,406
Registered Office: 13a Bedale Hall, Bedale, N Yorks, DL8 1AA
Activities: Management consultancy activities other than financial management
Major Shareholder: Paul Martin King
Officers: Maria King, Secretary; Paul Martin King [1967] Director

PMK Limited
Incorporated: 1 June 1999 *Employees:* 4
Net Worth: £1,243,921 *Total Assets:* £1,332,504
Registered Office: 13a Bedale Hall, Bedale, N Yorks, DL8 1AA
Activities: Management consultancy activities other than financial management
Major Shareholder: Paul Martin King
Officers: Amy Roseland King, Secretary; Paul Martin King [1967] Director; Deborah Ward [1963] Director

PMP (Partnership) Ltd
Incorporated: 3 November 2010
Registered Office: 15 West House, Avenue, Durham, DH1 4FH
Activities: Other letting and operating of own or leased real estate
Shareholders: Nicola Fitches; Philip McGowan
Officers: Nicola Jayne Fitches [1972] Director/Nurse Practitioner; Philip Luke McGowan [1960] Director

The PNE Foundation
Incorporated: 23 September 2010
Net Worth: £752,189 *Total Assets:* £763,331
Registered Office: Ground Floor, Unit 3, 7-15 Pink Lane, Newcastle upon Tyne, NE1 5DW
Activities: Non-trading company
Officers: Tracey Joanne Moore, Secretary; Irene Lawrie Allcroft [1962] Director; Nathaniel Richard Mathwin Clark [1957] Director; Andrew Ceri Jones [1965] Director; David Thomas Mitchell [1964] Director/Client Partner and VP; Tracey Joanne Moore [1969] Director/Development Manager; John Howard Oswald [1952] Director/Chartered Accountant; Caroline Pilling [1965] Director/Communications Manager; Timothy Ralph Smith [1959] Director/Solicitor

Pneumatic Power Source Limited
Incorporated: 19 July 1994 *Employees:* 16
Net Worth: £1,135,618 *Total Assets:* £1,406,808
Registered Office: Ellison Road, Dunston, Gateshead, Tyne & Wear, NE8 2QU
Activities: Other service activities n.e.c.
Shareholders: Lesley Smith; Andrew Smith; David Leslie Sterling
Officers: Lesley Smith, Secretary; Andrew Smith [1955] Director/Compressor Engineering; David Leslie Sterling [1957] Director/Service Engineer

Pokrok 111 Limited
Incorporated: 28 July 2006
Net Worth: £38,168 *Total Assets:* £803,726
Registered Office: 58 Durham Road, Birtley, Chester-le-Street, Co Durham, DH3 2QJ
Activities: Buying and selling of own real estate
Shareholders: George Clark; Susan Jackson
Officers: Susan Jackson, Secretary; George Clark [1959] Leisure Club Director; Susan Jackson [1951] Leisure Club Director

Pola Minerals Limited
Incorporated: 5 November 1992 *Employees:* 16
Net Worth: £1,816,371 *Total Assets:* £3,273,054
Registered Office: Ninth Avenue East, Team Valley Trading Estate, Gateshead, Tyne & Wear, NE11 0EJ
Activities: Non-specialised wholesale trade
Major Shareholder: David James Winters
Officers: John Joseph Liddle, Secretary; David James Winters [1956] Director/Mineral Processor

Polar (N.E.) Limited
Incorporated: 19 July 1983 *Employees:* 91
Net Worth: £215,901 *Total Assets:* £2,271,390
Registered Office: Unit 9 Stephenson Court, Skippers Lane Industrial Estate, Middlesbrough, Cleveland, TS6 6UT
Activities: Glazing
Shareholders: Alexander Wolfgang Baxter; Raymond Hill
Officers: Richard Patton Dunn, Secretary; Alexander Wolfgang Baxter [1956] Director; Richard Patton Dunn [1970] Managing Director; James Hill [1988] Operations Director; Raymond Hill [1956] Director

Pollock Properties UK Limited
Incorporated: 23 November 2006
Registered Office: Former TA Centre, Longlands Road, Brambles Farm, Middlesbrough, Cleveland, TS3 8DR
Activities: Other letting and operating of own or leased real estate
Major Shareholder: Jamie Pollock
Officers: Jamie Pollock [1974] Director

Polyfoam XPS Limited
Incorporated: 5 August 2016 *Employees:* 36
Net Worth: £5,890,526 *Total Assets:* £15,545,257
Registered Office: Hunter House Industrial Estate, Hartlepool, Cleveland, TS25 2BE
Activities: Manufacture of plastic plates, sheets, tubes and profiles
Shareholders: Theodoros Roussis; Gunhilde Van Gorp
Officers: Stuart Bell [1964] Director; Patrick Cabuy [1961] Director [Belgian]; Filip Van Camfort [1969] Director [Belgian]

Polymer Compounders Limited
Incorporated: 18 March 1993 *Employees:* 29
Net Worth: £678,515 *Total Assets:* £2,489,295
Registered Office: 10 Yarm Road, Stockton on Tees, Cleveland, TS18 3NA
Activities: Manufacture of other plastic products
Major Shareholder: John Gibson
Officers: John Gibson [1935] Director; Joy Christine Gibson [1936] Director; Grahame Phillip Houlder [1960] Director

Polyphotonix Limited
Incorporated: 26 March 2008 *Employees:* 17
Net Worth Deficit: £126,966 *Total Assets:* £872,850
Registered Office: National Centre for Printable Electronics, Netpark, Sedgefield, Co Durham, TS21 3FG
Activities: Management consultancy activities other than financial management
Shareholder: CPI Innovation Services Ltd
Officers: Martin Neil Holland [1962] Operations Director; David Ian Johnston [1965] Director/Chief Operating Officer; Richard Anthony Kirk [1966] Director; Deborah Rachael Sharpe [1988] Director/Solicitor

Pondbank Ltd
Incorporated: 24 August 2005
Registered Office: 7 Oxford Terrace, Gateshead, Tyne & Wear, NE8 1RQ
Activities: Development of building projects
Shareholder: Henry Phillip Hirsch
Officers: Regina Hirsh, Secretary; Henry Phillip Hirsch [1947] Director/Surveyor; Regina Hirsch [1950] Director/Social Worker

Ponton Road LLP
Incorporated: 14 August 2014
Net Worth Deficit: £57,728 *Total Assets:* £67,095,916
Registered Office: Seaton Burn House, Dudley Lane, Seaton Burn, Newcastle upon Tyne, NE13 6BE

Popcorn Limited
Incorporated: 20 January 1998
Net Worth: £2,054,023 *Total Assets:* £2,417,057
Registered Office: 31 High Street, Stokesley, Cleveland, TS9 5AD
Activities: Event catering activities
Officers: Wendy Deans, Secretary; Andrew Deans [1963] Director; Wendy Deans [1961] Director

Poppypride Limited
Incorporated: 4 June 2013
Net Worth: £151,124 *Total Assets:* £988,643
Registered Office: Wynyard Park House, Wynyard Avenue, Wynyard, Cleveland, TS22 5TB
Activities: Other activities of employment placement agencies
Officers: Michael Morris, Secretary; Dr Art Sanchez [1971] Director [American]

Popular Care Ltd
Incorporated: 16 January 2006 *Employees:* 167
Net Worth: £2,079,613 *Total Assets:* £7,858,765
Registered Office: 31-40 West Parade, Newcastle upon Tyne, NE4 7LB
Activities: Other human health activities
Shareholders: Aran Handa; Arvan Handa
Officers: Varghese Thomas, Secretary/Businessman; Aran Handa [1955] Director; Arvan Handa [1952] Director; Varghese Thomas [1970] Director/Businessman; Merly Varghese [1972] Director/Business Lady

Pornic Limited
Incorporated: 15 October 2002
Net Worth: £2,499,087 *Total Assets:* £2,504,038
Registered Office: B3 Kingfisher House, Team Valley Trading Estate, Gateshead, Tyne & Wear, NE11 0JQ
Activities: Non-trading company
Parent: Metcalfe Holdings Limited
Officers: Jonathan Mills, Secretary; Daniel Walker Metcalfe [1963] Director; Jonathan Robert Mills [1968] Director

Port Clarence Land Limited
Incorporated: 13 January 2012 *Employees:* 3
Net Worth: £566,752 *Total Assets:* £1,977,763
Registered Office: 2nd Floor, 16 High Street, Yarm, Cleveland, TS15 9AE
Activities: Other letting and operating of own or leased real estate
Shareholders: Graham Kevin Sizer; Andrew Loughran Preston; Graham Michael Senior
Officers: Andrew Loughran Preston [1966] Director/Property Investor; Graham Michael Senior [1970] Director/Chartered Surveyor; Graham Kevin Sizer [1969] Director/Chartered Accountant

Port Clarence Logistics Limited
Incorporated: 7 March 2006 *Employees:* 4
Net Worth: £7,601,783 *Total Assets:* £10,583,534
Registered Office: Port Clarence Offshore Base, Port Clarence Road, Port Clarence, Middlesbrough, Cleveland, TS2 1RZ
Activities: Other letting and operating of own or leased real estate
Shareholders: William Scott; Stephen Glenn
Officers: Christine Stobbs, Secretary; Stephen Glenn [1959] Director; Paul Joseph Johnson [1955] Director; Steven Brian Pearson [1972] Director; William Scott [1961] Director

Port of Tyne Distribution Limited
Incorporated: 17 February 1999 *Employees:* 71
Net Worth: £2,375,000 *Total Assets:* £3,084,000
Registered Office: Maritime House, Tyne Dock, South Shields, Tyne & Wear, NE34 9PT
Activities: Freight transport by road
Officers: Steven Robert Harrison [1967] Port Operations Director; Andrew Noel Moffat [1956] Finance & Commercial Director; Mark Anthony Stoner [1969] Director/Chief Financial Officer

Port Ventures Ltd
Incorporated: 7 March 2011
Net Worth: £529 *Total Assets:* £1,013,615
Registered Office: 4 Endeavour Close, Hartlepool, Cleveland, TS25 1EY
Activities: Other service activities n.e.c.
Major Shareholder: Alastair Port
Officers: Christopher Port [1984] Director; Daniel Port [1992] Director

Portalclad Limited
Incorporated: 18 May 1998
Net Worth: £465,257 *Total Assets:* £793,043
Registered Office: Unit 1 Proctor Court, Boeing Way, Preston Farm Industrial Estate, Stockton on Tees, Cleveland, TS18 3TE
Activities: Development of building projects
Shareholder: Phillip Hall
Officers: Philip Davison Hall, Secretary/Consultant; Amanda Hall [1970] Director/Secretary; Philip Davison Hall [1967] Director/Consultant

Charles Porter Holdings Limited
Incorporated: 16 October 2007
Net Worth: £1,533,089 *Total Assets:* £1,591,671
Registered Office: 2 The Riding School, Aske, Richmond, N Yorks, DL10 5HJ
Activities: Other service activities n.e.c.
Shareholders: Charles David Porter; Alison Porter
Officers: Charles David Porter, Secretary; Gerard Holmes [1962] Director; Alison Porter [1965] Director; Charles David Porter [1964] Director/Management Consultant

Portland House Holdings Limited
Incorporated: 8 September 1989
Net Worth: £9,663,157 *Total Assets:* £9,667,795
Registered Office: Citygate, St James Boulevard, Newcastle upon Tyne, NE1 4JE
Activities: Development of building projects
Parent: Northumberland & Durham Property Trust Limited
Officers: Adam McGhin, Secretary; Helen Christine Gordon [1959] Director; Adam McGhin [1978] Director/Solicitor; Mark Jeremy Robson [1959] Director/Chartered Surveyor; Vanessa Kate Simms [1975] Director

Portland Investments (AM) Limited
Incorporated: 3 November 2010
Net Worth: £3,500,227 *Total Assets:* £3,680,284
Registered Office: Portland House, South Street, Durham, DH1 4QP
Activities: Fund management activities
Major Shareholder: Alison Morgan
Officers: Alison Morgan [1962] Director

Portland Residential Limited
Incorporated: 22 October 1998
Net Worth: £270,314 *Total Assets:* £6,868,598
Registered Office: 17 Windsor Terrace, Jesmond, Newcastle upon Tyne, NE2 4HE
Activities: Other letting and operating of own or leased real estate
Officers: Nasir Rashid, Secretary/Property Owner; Sayeed Ahmed [1956] Director/Property Owner; Nasir Rashid [1964] Director/Property Owner

Portrack Handling Limited
Incorporated: 29 May 1991 *Employees:* 90
Net Worth: £900,661 *Total Assets:* £1,396,686
Registered Office: 9 Belasis Court, Billingham, Cleveland, TS23 4AZ
Activities: Other professional, scientific and technical activities n.e.c.
Shareholder: Norman Davison
Officers: Ian William Davison, Secretary; Norman Davison [1937] Managing Director; Peter Frederick Davison [1967] Director/Operations Manager

Ports Holdings Limited
Incorporated: 14 March 2001 *Employees:* 1,060
Net Worth: £257,084,992 *Total Assets:* £602,779,008
Registered Office: 17-27 Queen's Square, Middlesbrough, Cleveland, TS2 1AH
Activities: Activities of head offices
Parent: PD Ports Group Limited
Officers: Michael John Botha [1970] Director/Senior Vice President [Canadian]; Johannes Franciscus Calje [1972] Director [Dutch]; Jeremy Mark Hopkinson [1955] Director; Gabriele Montesi [1981] Director/Investment Professional [Italian]; Felipe Ortiz [1979] Director/Senior VP [Colombian]; David John Robinson [1964] Director; Paul Lucas Sim [1974] Director/Lawyer [Australian]

Posi-Thread (U.K.) Ltd.
Incorporated: 21 June 1985 *Employees:* 26
Net Worth: £115,834 *Total Assets:* £1,486,358
Registered Office: 4 Bridgewater Road, Hertburn Industrial Estate, District 11, Washington, Tyne & Wear, NE37 2SG
Activities: Manufacture of other special-purpose machinery n.e.c.
Officers: Harry Joseph Ehrenberg [1948] Director [Stateless]

Positive Solutions (Financial Services) Ltd.
Incorporated: 12 November 1996
Net Worth: £28,333,000 *Total Assets:* £37,638,000
Registered Office: Riverside House, The Waterfront, Newcastle upon Tyne, NE15 8NY
Activities: Financial intermediation not elsewhere classified
Parent: Intrinsic Financial Services Limited
Officers: Darren William John Sharkey [1970] Director/Chartered Accountant [Irish]; Andrew Bernard Thompson [1968] Director

Nicholas Postgate Catholic Academy Trust
Incorporated: 4 September 2014 *Employees:* 240
Net Worth: £1,852,000 *Total Assets:* £4,204,000
Registered Office: Trinity Catholic College, Saltersgill Avenue, Middlesbrough, Cleveland, TS4 3JW
Activities: Primary education
Officers: James William Brown [1974] Director/Solicitor; Kevin Duffy [1963] Director of Schools - Diocese of Middlesbrough; Hugh Martin Hegarty [1969] Director; Joseph Hughes [1951] Director/Retired; Nicholas Mack [1961] Director/Retired Solicitor; Maureen McCullagh [1950] Director/Retired Teacher; Rev Derek Lynn Turnham [1952] Director/Catholic Priest; John Anthony Walton [1948] Director/Chartered Accountant; Josephine Wilson [1959] Director/Former Headteacher

Oswald Potter Farms (Kirklington) Limited
Incorporated: 25 March 1977
Registered Office: The Old Rectory, Kirklington, Bedale, N Yorks, DL8 2NB
Activities: Growing of cereals (except rice), leguminous crops and oil seeds
Major Shareholder: Michael Potter
Officers: Benjamin Richard Potter [1975] Director/Farmer; Michael Potter [1946] Director/Farmer

Thomas Potter Limited
Incorporated: 17 October 2006 *Employees:* 15
Net Worth: £1,239,274 *Total Assets:* £1,780,779
Registered Office: Factory D, Western Approach Industrial Estate, South Shields, Tyne & Wear, NE33 5NN
Activities: Wholesale of hardware, plumbing and heating equipment and supplies
Shareholders: David Harland; Pamela Harland
Officers: Pamela Harland, Secretary; David Harland [1948] Managing Director; Pamela Harland [1945] Director/Secretary

Potts Print (UK) Limited
Incorporated: 29 July 1954 *Employees:* 159
Net Worth: £4,029,473 *Total Assets:* £11,157,977
Registered Office: Atlas House, Nelson Park, Cramlington, Northumberland, NE23 1WG
Activities: Printing n.e.c.
Shareholders: Michael Sanford-Couch; Clare Sandford-Couch
Officers: Stephanie Tobin, Secretary; Carla Victoria Armstrong [1983] Director; Ian James Bensley [1961] Director; John Conway [1970] Marketing Director; Mark Washington Devine [1963] Commercial Director; Robert Shaun Johnson [1964] Managing Director; Keith Thomas McHugh [1969] Director; Michael John Sandford-Couch [1965] Director/Chief Executive; Daniel Vincent Tobin [1973] Sales Director; Stephanie Tobin [1980] Director; Brian Watson [1969] Director; Ian Robert White [1978] Director

Pout and Foster (N E) Limited
Incorporated: 21 April 2011
Net Worth: £5,419,596 *Total Assets:* £5,576,726
Registered Office: 90-91 Mainsforth Terrace, Hartlepool, Cleveland, TS25 1NR
Activities: Activities of other holding companies n.e.c.
Major Shareholder: Simon David Foster
Officers: Diane Foster [1971] Director/Company Secretary; Simon David Foster [1963] Director

Pout and Foster Limited
Incorporated: 20 March 1975 *Employees:* 16
Net Worth Deficit: £862,387 *Total Assets:* £2,545,189
Registered Office: 90-91 Mainsforth Terrace, Hartlepool, Cleveland, TS25 1NR
Activities: Wholesale of waste and scrap
Parent: Pout & Foster (NE) Limited
Officers: Diane Foster [1971] Director/Company Secretary; Simon David Foster [1963] Director

Power Efficiency Holdings Limited
Incorporated: 4 December 2007
Net Worth: £3,836,000 *Total Assets:* £3,838,000
Registered Office: Shared Services Centre, Q3 Office, Quorum Business Park, Benton Lane, Newcastle upon Tyne, NE12 8EX
Activities: Management consultancy activities other than financial management
Parent: Engie Services Limited
Officers: Sarah Gregory, Secretary; Gary Proctor [1966] Director

Power Topco Limited
Incorporated: 2 March 2016 *Employees:* 226
Net Worth: £1,483,000 *Total Assets:* £47,107,000
Registered Office: Roundhouse Road, Faverdale Industrial Estate, Darlington, Co Durham, DL3 0UR
Activities: Wholesale of other machinery and equipment
Parent: Project Polka Bidco Limited
Officers: Matthew Barker [1979] Director; James Scott Browning [1966] Director; Ian James Calvesbert [1966] Director; Paul Gibson [1980] Director; Richard Damon Smith [1974] Director

Power Wholesale Limited
Incorporated: 8 May 1964 *Employees:* 39
Net Worth: £2,044,442 *Total Assets:* £4,222,480
Registered Office: 100-104 High West Street, Gateshead, Tyne & Wear, NE8 1NA
Activities: Wholesale of electronic and telecommunications equipment and parts
Officers: Neil William Cornish, Secretary/Managing Director; Keith Victor Cornish [1963] Director/Support Services; Neil William Cornish [1969] Director/Manager; Stephen Cornish [1957] Director/Systems Engineer

PPG (NE) Limited
Incorporated: 24 April 2007
Net Worth: £216,519 *Total Assets:* £1,639,744
Registered Office: Carlton House, Carlton in Cleveland, Middlesbrough, Cleveland, TS9 7DJ
Activities: Other letting and operating of own or leased real estate
Major Shareholder: Neil Patterson
Officers: Joanne Ellen Patterson, Secretary; Joanne Ellen Patterson [1965] Director; Neil Patterson [1954] Director

Praesto Consulting UK Ltd
Incorporated: 11 September 2007
Net Worth: £1,011,118 *Total Assets:* £3,391,542
Registered Office: 9 Ropner Gardens, Middleton St George, Darlington, Co Durham, DL2 1FB
Activities: Information technology consultancy activities
Shareholders: Jeremy Michael Ranson; Kerrie Ranson
Officers: Jeremy Michael Ranson [1977] Director/IT Consultancy Manager

Pragmatic Printing Limited
Incorporated: 29 October 2010 *Employees:* 45
Net Worth: £14,806,951 *Total Assets:* £17,026,104
Registered Office: National Centre for Printable Electronics, Thomas Wright Way, Netpark, Sedgefield, Co Durham, TS21 3FG
Activities: Manufacture of electronic components
Shareholder: Cambridge Innovation Capital PLC
Officers: Gordon Michael Campbell, Secretary; Adam Neil Christian Bastin [1978] Director/Mergers & Acquisitions; Gordon Michael Campbell [1967] Director; Victor Christou [1966] Director/Venture Capitalist; David Nicholas Edwards [1959] Director/Consultant [British/American]; Philip Hudson [1953] Director/Investor; Dr Richard David Price [1975] Director/Chief Operating Officer; Scott Darren White [1973] Director/Chief Executive Officer

PRD Property Management Limited
Incorporated: 6 July 2015
Net Worth: £24,919 *Total Assets:* £848,281
Registered Office: 6 Queen's Court, Third Avenue, Team Valley Trading Estate, Gateshead, Tyne & Wear, NE11 0BU
Activities: Other letting and operating of own or leased real estate
Shareholders: Paul Victor Lodge; Dianne Lodge; Richard Paul Lodge
Officers: Dianne Lodge [1957] Director/Administration Manager; Paul Victor Lodge [1957] Director/Transport Manager; Richard Paul Lodge [1977] Director/Transport Manager; Robert Steven Lodge [1987] Director/Transport Driver

Precision 2000 Limited
Incorporated: 12 January 1998 *Employees:* 21
Net Worth: £1,822,600 *Total Assets:* £2,420,488
Registered Office: Princesway North, Team Valley Trading Estate, Gateshead, Tyne & Wear, NE11 0TU
Activities: Machining
Officers: Gary Burgess [1971] Director; Andrew Robert Pearson [1972] Director; Richard Pearson [1944] Director

Precision Geomatics Limited
Incorporated: 17 September 2003
Net Worth: £606,412 *Total Assets:* £2,301,759
Registered Office: Precision House, Colima Avenue, Sunderland, Tyne & Wear, SR5 3XE
Activities: Renting and leasing of construction and civil engineering machinery and equipment
Major Shareholder: Gwyneth Bell
Officers: Carole Anne Bookless, Secretary; Gwyneth Bell [1948] Director; Carole Anne Bookless [1965] Company Secretary/Director

Precision Hydraulic Cylinders (UK) Limited
Incorporated: 15 October 2001 *Employees:* 88
Net Worth: £10,213,567 *Total Assets:* £14,731,863
Registered Office: Bassington Industrial Estate, Cramlington, Northumberland, NE23 8AE
Activities: Manufacture of fluid power equipment
Officers: Christopher Scott Barclay [1958] Director/Chief Executive Officer [American]

Precision Labelling Systems Limited
Incorporated: 15 July 2004 *Employees:* 17
Net Worth: £1,358,503 *Total Assets:* £1,725,124
Registered Office: Plews Way, Leeming Bar Industrial Estate, Leeming Bar, Northallerton, N Yorks, DL7 9UL
Activities: Manufacture of other general-purpose machinery n.e.c.
Shareholders: Michael David Kent; David Geoffrey Keighley
Officers: David Geoffrey Keighley, Secretary; David Geoffrey Keighley [1964] Director; Michael David Kent [1970] Director

Precision Toolroom Services & Machining Limited
Incorporated: 16 October 1998 *Employees:* 20
Net Worth: £150,060 *Total Assets:* £825,446
Registered Office: 9 Hurworth Road, Aycliffe Industrial Park, Newton Aycliffe, Co Durham, DL5 6UD
Activities: Manufacture of other special-purpose machinery n.e.c.
Major Shareholder: Stephen Metcalfe
Officers: Stephen Metcalfe, Secretary; Stephen Metcalfe [1962] Executive Director

Prefere Resins UK Limited
Incorporated: 31 July 2013 *Employees:* 41
Net Worth: £8,886,000 *Total Assets:* £17,950,000
Registered Office: Aycliffe Industrial Park, Heighington Lane, Newton Aycliffe, Co Durham, DL5 6UE
Activities: Manufacture of other chemical products n.e.c.
Officers: David Green, Secretary; David Green [1963] Director/Vice President of Finance and Controlling; Arno Knebelkamp [1963] Director/Chief Executive Officer [German]; Anja Monika Plugge [1969] Director/Vice President Operations [German]

Preferred Management Solutions (PMS) Ltd
Incorporated: 10 September 2010 *Employees:* 47
Net Worth: £140,185 *Total Assets:* £963,556
Registered Office: 5 Blue Sky Way, Monkton Business Park South, Hebburn, Tyne & Wear, NE31 2EQ
Activities: Development of building projects
Shareholders: Dean George Rae; Anthony James Morrison Taylor
Officers: Dean George Rae [1976] Director; Anthony James Morrison Taylor [1981] Director

Premier Care Homes Limited
Incorporated: 19 December 1986 *Employees:* 132
Net Worth: £4,837,295 *Total Assets:* £10,241,008
Registered Office: Picktree Court Care Home, Picktree Lane, Chester-le-Street, Co Durham, DH3 3SP
Activities: Residential nursing care facilities
Shareholders: John Colin Oates; Eileen Oates
Officers: John Collin Oates, Secretary; Eileen Oates [1946] Director; John Collin Oates [1947] Director; Jon Paul Oates [1978] Director; Michelle Oates [1975] Director

Premier Commercial Properties (UK) LLP
Incorporated: 3 April 2008
Net Worth: £2,227,508 *Total Assets:* £2,228,058
Registered Office: 53 The Broadway, North Shields, Tyne & Wear, NE30 2LL
Officers: Philip Henderson [1950] Member; Mark David Henderson [1977] LLP Member

Premier Dawn Properties Limited
Incorporated: 25 October 1999
Net Worth: £78,214,000 *Total Assets:* £144,588,000
Registered Office: 2nd Floor, One Gosforth Park Way, Gosforth Business Park, Newcastle upon Tyne, NE12 8ET
Activities: Non-trading company
Parent: Upperbay Limited
Officers: Judith Ann Archibold, Secretary; Ian Kellett [1963] Director; John Anthony Waterworth [1963] Managing Director

Premier Estate Properties Ltd
Incorporated: 7 February 2013
Net Worth Deficit: £29,274 *Total Assets:* £1,054,761
Registered Office: Euro House, Earlsway, Team Valley Trading Estate, Gateshead, Tyne & Wear, NE11 0RQ
Activities: Other letting and operating of own or leased real estate
Officers: Surinder Singh Galsinh, Secretary; Surinder Singh Galsinh [1954] Director/Business Owner; Taranvir Singh Galsinh [1980] Director/Manager; Satbachan Singh Pannu [1946] Director; Nisha Postletwaite [1975] Director/Manager

Premier Fluid Solutions Limited
Incorporated: 4 March 2005 *Employees:* 9
Net Worth: £513,162 *Total Assets:* £782,626
Registered Office: 37-38 Market Street, Ferryhill, Co Durham, DL17 8JH
Activities: Other specialised construction activities n.e.c.
Major Shareholder: Nicholas Maxwell Cook
Officers: Nicholas Maxwell Cook [1969] Director/Sales Manager

Premier Leisure Limited
Incorporated: 1 August 2007
Net Worth: £892,877 *Total Assets:* £1,711,168
Registered Office: 35 Dean Road, South Shields, Tyne & Wear, NE33 4EA
Activities: Licenced restaurants
Major Shareholder: Satnam Singh
Officers: Gurminder Kaur, Secretary; Gurminder Kaur [1961] Director; Satnam Singh [1963] Director/Businessman

Premier Meats Limited
Incorporated: 26 September 1997 *Employees:* 41
Net Worth: £1,225,017 *Total Assets:* £1,630,165
Registered Office: Unit 1A/B Airport Industrial Estate, Kingston Park, Newcastle upon Tyne, NE3 2EF
Activities: Wholesale of meat and meat products
Parent: Premier Tenencias Limited
Officers: Celina Whittaker, Secretary; Celina Whittaker [1976] Director; Mark Lawrence Whittaker [1966] Managing Director

Premier Properties (UK) Limited
Incorporated: 25 February 2002
Net Worth: £1,219,894 *Total Assets:* £1,699,914
Registered Office: 53 The Broadway, Tynemouth, Tyne & Wear, NE30 2LL
Activities: Other letting and operating of own or leased real estate
Shareholder: Philip Henderson
Officers: Philip Henderson, Secretary; Mark David Henderson [1977] Director/Network Rail; Philip Henderson [1950] Director/Retired

Premier Scaffolding Services Limited
Incorporated: 11 December 1996 *Employees:* 64
Net Worth: £547,320 *Total Assets:* £1,108,986
Registered Office: Unit 10 Wagonway Road, Wagonway Industrial Estate, Hebburn, Tyne & Wear, NE31 1SP
Activities: Scaffold erection
Major Shareholder: Neil Robert Tatum
Officers: Carol Tatum, Secretary; Neil Robert Tatum [1965] Director/Scaffolder

Premier Tech Aqua Limited
Incorporated: 15 September 2008 *Employees:* 71
Net Worth Deficit: £803,200 *Total Assets:* £2,995,098
Registered Office: 2 Whitehouse Way, South West Industrial Estate, Peterlee, Co Durham, SR8 2RA
Activities: Manufacture of other plastic products
Officers: Martin Noel, Secretary; Jean Belanger [1965] Director/Engineer [Canadian]; Stephen Joyce [1960] Managing Director; Martin Noel [1968] Director/Accountant [Canadian]; Henri Ouellet [1964] Director/Engineer [Canadian]

Premier Traffic Management Limited
Incorporated: 27 November 2000 *Employees:* 129
Net Worth: £1,295,274 *Total Assets:* £3,682,012
Registered Office: Unit 13 Tudhoe Industrial Estate, Spennymoor, Co Durham, DL16 6TL
Activities: Other service activities incidental to land transportation, n.e.c.
Parent: PTM Holdings Limited
Officers: Jon Beamson [1964] Director; Richard George Elliott [1971] Director; Greig Neil Heywood [1972] Director/Traffic Management; David Thomas Moist [1972] Director; Michael John Rogan [1980] Health and Safety Director

Premier Truck Hire Limited
Incorporated: 1 December 2004 *Employees:* 22
Net Worth: £1,617,974 *Total Assets:* £2,428,702
Registered Office: St Matthews House, Haugh Lane, Hexham, Northumberland, NE46 3PU
Activities: Renting and leasing of trucks and other heavy vehicles
Shareholders: Tonia Denise Tailford; Maurice Eric Tailford
Officers: Tonia Denise Tailford, Secretary/Waste Disposal Plant Hire; Martyn John Tailford [1987] Director/Operations Manager; Maurice Eric Tailford [1956] Director/Waste Disposal Plant Hire; Tonia Denise Tailford [1961] Director/Waste Disposal Plant Hire

Premiertec Consulting Limited
Incorporated: 23 November 2004
Net Worth: £1,780,474 *Total Assets:* £4,496,572
Registered Office: Rotterdam House, 116 Quayside, Newcastle upon Tyne, NE1 3DY
Activities: Information technology consultancy activities
Parent: Claremont IT Services Limited
Officers: Steven James Anderson [1960] Director; Richard Owen Mac Innes Manby [1956] Director/Consultant; Roland James Miles [1970] Director/IT Consultant; Ian Monaghan [1968] Director/IT Consultant; Jonathan Douglas Stuart [1971] Director/Consultant; Mark Claude James Vivian [1966] Director/Consultant

Premo Fabrications Limited
Incorporated: 30 October 2009
Net Worth: £603,211 *Total Assets:* £3,302,520
Registered Office: Durham Way South, Aycliffe Business Park, Newton Aycliffe, Co Durham, DL5 6XN
Activities: Manufacture of basic iron and steel and of ferro-alloys
Major Shareholder: David Andrew Knowles
Officers: Beau Damean Stevens, Secretary; David Andrew Knowles [1970] Director; Beau Damean Stevens [1971] Director

Presmac Limited
Incorporated: 11 March 1999
Net Worth: £531,045 *Total Assets:* £814,935
Registered Office: Suite 3, Walker Davison House, High Street, Newburn, Newcastle upon Tyne, NE15 8LN
Activities: Other construction installation
Shareholders: Philip John Preston; John Michael MacLennan
Officers: Philip John Preston, Secretary/Plumber; John Michael MacLennan [1965] Director/Plumber; Philip John Preston [1970] Director/Plumber

Pressed Steel Products Limited
Incorporated: 23 June 1998
Net Worth: £1,432,778 *Total Assets:* £1,878,246
Registered Office: Unit 11 All Saints Industrial Estate, Shildon, Co Durham, DL4 2RD
Activities: Other letting and operating of own or leased real estate
Parent: Pressed Steel Products (Holdings) Ltd
Officers: Kamal Ashraf Abdul Razaq [1946] Director [Omani]; Heath Hindmarch [1967] Managing Director

Prestige Care (Redcar Sm) Limited
Incorporated: 28 August 2013 *Employees:* 57
Net Worth: £1,356,721 *Total Assets:* £5,728,066
Registered Office: c/o Prestige Group Head Office, Roseville Court, Ingleby Barwick, Stockton on Tees, Cleveland, TS17 5BL
Activities: Residential care activities for the elderly and disabled
Major Shareholder: Balbirk Kaur
Officers: Balbir Kaur [1939] Director [Indian]; Sukhraj Singh [1964] Director/Property Developer

Prestige Care Limited
Incorporated: 22 February 1995 *Employees:* 76
Net Worth: £1,566,430 *Total Assets:* £7,781,386
Registered Office: Roseville Court, Blair Avenue, Ingleby Barwick, Stockton on Tees, Cleveland, TS17 5BL
Activities: Residential nursing care facilities
Parent: Prestige Care Group Holdings Ltd
Officers: Sukhraj Singh [1964] Director/Property Owner

Prestige Properties (North East) Limited
Incorporated: 11 December 2006
Net Worth Deficit: £118,585 *Total Assets:* £2,931,410
Registered Office: Roseville Court, Blair Avenue, Ingleby Barwick, Stockton on Tees, Cleveland, TS17 5BL
Activities: Other letting and operating of own or leased real estate
Major Shareholder: Sukhraj Singh
Officers: Sukhraj Singh [1964] Director

Richard Preston & Son Limited
Incorporated: 28 November 1969 *Employees:* 208
Net Worth: £4,439,202 *Total Assets:* £10,394,385
Registered Office: Potto, Northallerton, N Yorks, DL6 3HX
Activities: Freight transport by road
Major Shareholder: Anne Preston MBE
Officers: Anne Preston [1937] Director; David Richard Preston [1962] Director/Distribution Manager

Prestons Transport Limited
Incorporated: 13 July 1962 *Employees:* 11
Net Worth: £3,740,596 *Total Assets:* £4,066,173
Registered Office: Levencroft, Leven Road, Yarm, Cleveland, TS15 9JJ
Activities: Freight transport by road
Major Shareholder: Aidan Preston
Officers: Susan Ann Boddy, Secretary; Aidan Preston [1942] Director/Haulage Contractor; Nigel Graham Preston [1964] Director/H & U Mechanic

Prestwick Care Limited
Incorporated: 22 December 2009 *Employees:* 200
Net Worth: £2,384,465 *Total Assets:* £3,127,275
Registered Office: Malhotra House, 7-9 Groat Market, Newcastle upon Tyne, NE1 1UQ
Activities: Residential nursing care facilities
Officers: Atul Malhotra [1981] Director; Devinder Mohan Malhotra [1967] Director; Varun Malhotra [1982] Director

Price Right Properties Limited
Incorporated: 29 March 2000 *Employees:* 3
Net Worth: £731,946 *Total Assets:* £2,683,543
Registered Office: 12 Lambeth Road, Linthorpe, Middlesbrough, Cleveland, TS5 6EB
Activities: Development of building projects
Shareholders: Shanaz Bi; Ali Akhtar Sadiq
Officers: Shanaz Bi Sadiq, Secretary; Ali Akhtar Sadiq [1968] Managing Director

Prima Cheese Limited
Incorporated: 17 September 2003 *Employees:* 97
Net Worth: £4,532,619 *Total Assets:* £13,346,014
Registered Office: 13 Partnership Court, Seaham Grange Industrial Estate, Seaham, Co Durham, SR7 0PX
Activities: Wholesale of dairy products, eggs and edible oils and fats
Shareholders: Behroz Noudoost Beni; Essmat Ansari Beni
Officers: Behroz Beni, Secretary/Executive; Behroz Beni [1948] Director/Executive; Essmat Ansari Beni [1948] Director/Executive [Iranian]; Nagma Ebanks-Beni [1972] Director/Cheese Making [Iranian]; Nima Noudoost-Beni [1983] Director/Executive

Primary Care Recruitment Ltd
Incorporated: 15 February 2007 *Employees:* 139
Net Worth: £185,296 *Total Assets:* £1,073,442
Registered Office: 10 Lansdowne Terrace, Gosforth, Newcastle upon Tyne, NE3 1HN
Activities: Temporary employment agency activities
Shareholders: Joanne Elisabeth Wood; Bradley John Wood
Officers: Joanne Elisabeth Wood, Secretary; Bradley John Wood [1970] Director/Engineer; Joanne Elisabeth Wood [1966] Director

Prime Horizontal Limited
Incorporated: 7 November 1997 *Employees:* 11
Net Worth: £1,793,050 *Total Assets:* £3,468,981
Registered Office: Maritime House, Harbour Walk, The Marina, Hartlepool, Cleveland, TS24 0UX
Activities: Other specialised construction activities n.e.c.
Officers: James Robin Baxter [1944] Director; Simon Andrew Kench [1969] Director; John Duane Teer [1949] Director [American]

Primex Plastics Limited
Incorporated: 10 June 1997 *Employees:* 54
Net Worth: £3,622,329 *Total Assets:* £5,290,423
Registered Office: Beaumont Way, Aycliffe Industrial Park, Newton Aycliffe, Co Durham, DL5 6SN
Activities: Manufacture of plastic plates, sheets, tubes and profiles
Shareholders: Dr John Farber; Maya Farber
Officers: Gia Incardone, Secretary; Michael John Cramer [1955] Director/President [American]; Timothy Robert Schultz [1956] Director/Vice President of Sales and Marketing [American]

Primrose House Ltd
Incorporated: 24 April 2015
Net Worth: £681,597 *Total Assets:* £2,285,680
Registered Office: Houghton House, New Road, Team Valley Trading Estate, Gateshead, Tyne & Wear, NE11 0JU
Activities: Residential nursing care facilities
Parent: Exclusive Care Group Ltd
Officers: Jennifer Pamela Houghton [1946] Director; Jill Yvette Houghton [1965] Director

Primula Limited
Incorporated: 5 June 1936 *Employees:* 82
Net Worth: £5,865,567 *Total Assets:* £11,497,000
Registered Office: Kingsway, Team Valley Trading Estate, Gateshead, Tyne & Wear, NE11 0ST
Activities: Butter and cheese production
Parent: Kavli UK Limited
Officers: Lynn Hayes, Secretary; Paul Robert Lewney [1967] Director; Erik Volden [1961] Director [Norwegian]

Prince Bishops Homes Limited
Incorporated: 1 October 2008
Net Worth: £2,762,994 *Total Assets:* £30,425,916
Registered Office: Number Five, Gosforth Park Avenue, Gosforth Business Park, Newcastle upon Tyne, NE12 8EG
Activities: Other letting and operating of own or leased real estate
Parent: Karbon Homes Limited
Officers: Richard Dean Fryer, Secretary; Robert Armstrong [1962] Sales Director; Charlotte Elise Carpenter [1971] Director; Paul Fiddaman [1965] Director/Group Chief Executive; Anne Mulroy [1953] Director/Retired; Michael Alexander Pattison [1962] Director/Chartered Surveyor; Clive Rook [1953] Director/Estate Agent; Adrian Mark Stanley [1960] Director/Lawyer

Pringle Building Services Limited
Incorporated: 19 February 1992 *Employees:* 30
Net Worth: £778,878 *Total Assets:* £2,417,951
Registered Office: Stephenson Way, Barrington Industrial Estate, Bedlington, Northumberland, NE22 7DL
Activities: Construction of commercial buildings
Major Shareholder: David Sean Pringle
Officers: David Sean Pringle, Secretary; David Sean Pringle [1968] Managing Director; John David Pringle [1939] Director

Print Demon Holdings Limited
Incorporated: 4 October 2013
Net Worth: £1 *Total Assets:* £1,001,950
Registered Office: Unit 2 Mercury Road, Richmond, N Yorks, DL10 4TQ
Activities: Public relations and communications activities
Major Shareholder: Peter John Broderick
Officers: Peter John Broderick [1989] Director/Service Manager

Print Demon Systems Limited
Incorporated: 16 February 2000
Net Worth: £901,975 *Total Assets:* £967,706
Registered Office: Unit 2 Mercury Road, Richmond, N Yorks, DL10 4TQ
Activities: Other information technology service activities
Officers: Rachel Clare Lambert, Secretary; John Howard Broderick [1960] Director/Computer Consultant; Peter John Broderick [1989] Technical Director

Print Ventures Limited
Incorporated: 2 June 2014
Net Worth Deficit: £193,505 *Total Assets:* £1,025,231
Registered Office: c/o Square One Law LLP, Anson House, The Fleming Business Centre, Jesmond, Newcastle upon Tyne, NE2 3AE
Activities: Other construction installation
Shareholders: Graham Stuart Lindsay Forrest; Kay Alberta Forrest
Officers: Graham Stuart Lindsay Forrest [1962] Director; Kay Alberta Forrest [1965] Director

Printbylaser Limited
Incorporated: 28 July 1997
Net Worth: £217,464 *Total Assets:* £4,586,529
Registered Office: Phoenix House, Angel Park, Drum Industrial Estate, Chester-le-Street, Co Durham, DH2 1AQ
Activities: Pre-press and pre-media services
Shareholders: Christine Stevenson; Eric Stevenson
Officers: Christine Stevenson, Secretary; Christopher Murley [1970] Director/Salesman; Eric Stevenson [1956] Director/Retailer

Prizepay Limited
Incorporated: 18 May 1989
Net Worth: £75,582 *Total Assets:* £1,224,372
Registered Office: 298 Wingrove Road North, Newcastle upon Tyne, NE4 9EE
Activities: Manufacture of other textiles n.e.c.
Officers: Aftab Ahmed Nemat, Secretary; Aftab Ahmed Nemat [1970] Director; Bushra Tufail [1966] Director

Pro - Fix Installations (North East) Limited
Incorporated: 13 December 2001 *Employees:* 22
Net Worth: £132,809 *Total Assets:* £1,579,899
Registered Office: The Crofters, 7 High Spen Court, High Spen, Rowlands Gill, Tyne & Wear, NE39 2EB
Activities: Joinery installation
Shareholders: Susan Jean Hawley; Richard Norman Hawley
Officers: Susan Jean Hawley, Secretary/Director; Richard Norman Hawley [1963] Director; Susan Jean Hawley [1964] Director; Emma Susan Lattimer [1988] Director

Pro-Flex Packaging Europe Ltd
Incorporated: 29 October 2007 *Employees:* 14
Net Worth: £762,837 *Total Assets:* £964,311
Registered Office: 49c Sadler Foster Way, Teesside Industrial Estate, Stockton on Tees, Cleveland, TS17 9JY
Activities: Manufacture of plastic packing goods
Shareholders: Allan Stephen John Leddra; Braid Logistics (UK) Limited
Officers: Andrew David Watson, Secretary; Colin Gee [1951] Director/Financial Advisor; Andrew David Watson [1968] Director

Process Control Equipment Limited
Incorporated: 15 April 1980 *Employees:* 52
Net Worth: £2,232,546 *Total Assets:* £9,295,544
Registered Office: Orchard House, Easterly Grange, Foxton, Sedgefield, Co Durham, TS21 2HX
Activities: Non-specialised wholesale trade
Shareholder: Barry James Jackson
Officers: Patricia Jackson, Secretary; Barry James Jackson [1947] Director; Patricia Jackson [1948] Director and Secretary; Richard Jackson [1974] Sales Director; Ben Williamson [1984] Finance Director

Procomm Site Services (Holdings) Limited
Incorporated: 4 January 2010 *Employees:* 6
Net Worth: £186,330 *Total Assets:* £5,896,447
Registered Office: P O Box 1949, Coverdale Court, Wilton International, Redcar, Cleveland, TS10 4YG
Activities: Activities of head offices
Parent: Porchester Equity Limited
Officers: Peter McCarthy, Secretary; Bernard John Cranny [1965] Director; David Christopher Harbord [1961] Director; Peter McCarthy [1961] Finance Director; Stephen John Smith [1957] Director; Mark Edward Thistlethwayte [1964] Director; Nicholas Leslie Wood [1962] Director

Procomm Site Services Limited
Incorporated: 28 January 2002 *Employees:* 91
Net Worth: £11,001,545 *Total Assets:* £21,830,076
Registered Office: P O Box 1949, Coverdale Court, Wilton International, Redcar, Cleveland, TS10 4YG
Activities: Renting and leasing of other machinery, equipment and tangible goods n.e.c.
Parent: Procomm Site Services (Holdings) Limited
Officers: Peter McCarthy, Secretary; Bernard John Cranny [1965] Sales Director; David Christopher Harbord [1961] Director; Peter McCarthy [1961] Finance Director; Stephen John Smith [1957] Director; Mark Edward Thistlethwayte [1964] Director; Nicholas Leslie Wood [1962] Director

Procters Coaches (North Yorkshire) Limited
Incorporated: 17 April 2000 *Employees:* 71
Net Worth: £3,130,629 *Total Assets:* £5,611,037
Registered Office: Tutin Road, Leeming Bar Industrial Estate, Northallerton, N Yorks, DL7 9UJ
Activities: Other passenger land transport
Parent: Procters Coaches (North Yorkshire No3) Limited
Officers: Claire Elizabeth Alenius, Secretary; Kevin John Procter [1964] Director/Coach Proprietor

Thos. Proctor & Son Limited
Incorporated: 22 December 1919
Registered Office: Proctor House, Dukesway, Team Valley Trading Estate, Gateshead, Tyne & Wear, NE11 0NW
Activities: Non-specialised wholesale trade
Shareholders: Robin Hancock; Timothy Hancock
Officers: Kevin Berry, Secretary; John Michael Gilroy [1953] Managing Director; Timothy John Pennington Hancock [1955] Director/Corporate Finance Executive; Richard Cecil Pelly [1951] Director/Royal Navy Captain; Andrew Philip Searle [1977] Director/Consultant

Prodrive (Joinery & Shop Fitting) Limited
Incorporated: 19 December 2002 *Employees:* 18
Net Worth: £310,587 *Total Assets:* £784,744
Registered Office: Station Yard, Station Road, Stokesley, Middlesbrough, Cleveland, TS9 7AB
Activities: Joinery installation
Shareholders: Ann Downes; Gary Downes
Officers: Ann Downes, Secretary; Gary Downes [1963] Director

Prodrive Property Maintenance Limited
Incorporated: 20 November 2001 *Employees:* 10
Net Worth: £632,156 *Total Assets:* £1,166,678
Registered Office: Field Buildings, Telford Road, Middlesbrough, Cleveland, TS3 8BL
Activities: Other building completion and finishing
Shareholders: Ian Donald Boyes; David Mark Hynes
Officers: Claire Elizabeth Angus, Secretary; Ian Donald Boyes [1963] Director/Construction; David Mark Hynes [1961] Director/Builder

Proflex Packaging Co Ltd
Incorporated: 20 October 2009 *Employees:* 12
Net Worth: £1,293,408 *Total Assets:* £1,562,220
Registered Office: 49A/B Sadler Forster Way, Teesside Industrial Estate, Stockton on Tees, Cleveland, TS17 9JY
Activities: Manufacture of plastic packing goods
Major Shareholder: Allan Stephen John Leddra
Officers: Andrew David Watson, Secretary; Colin Gee [1951] Director/Banker; Allan Stephen John Leddra [1962] Director; Andrew David Watson [1968] Director

Profound Services Limited
Incorporated: 17 October 2006 *Employees:* 30
Net Worth: £1,273,682 *Total Assets:* £2,314,846
Registered Office: 30 Yoden Way, Peterlee, Co Durham, SR8 1AL
Activities: Management consultancy activities other than financial management
Major Shareholder: Steven Ward
Officers: Brian Ward, Secretary; Brian Ward [1980] Director; David Ward [1957] Director; Gary Ward [1979] Director; Steven Ward [1958] Managing Director

Project Advisors International (U.K.) Ltd.
Incorporated: 25 March 2003 *Employees:* 5
Net Worth: £2,049,467 *Total Assets:* £2,344,667
Registered Office: 14 Manchester Street, Morpeth, Northumberland, NE61 1BH
Activities: Other business support service activities n.e.c.
Shareholders: Andrew Parry; Carol Parry
Officers: Carol Parry, Secretary; Andrew Parry [1970] Director/Quantity Surveyor

Project Bond Bidco Limited
Incorporated: 30 September 2013
Net Worth Deficit: £14,101,000 *Total Assets:* £51,936,000
Registered Office: Seal Sands, Middlesbrough, Cleveland, TS2 1UB
Activities: Activities of head offices
Parent: Lianhe Chemical Technology Co. Ltd
Officers: Lee Paul Kingsbury [1972] Director; Dr Nigel Christopher Parkinson [1968] Director; Minghui Xu [1971] Finance Director [Chinese]

Project Bond Holdco Limited
Incorporated: 4 October 2013 *Employees:* 304
Net Worth Deficit: £2,811,000 *Total Assets:* £77,811,000
Registered Office: Seal Sands, Middlesbrough, Cleveland, TS2 1UB
Activities: Activities of head offices
Parent: Lianhetech Europe Limited
Officers: Lee Paul Kingsbury [1972] Director; Dr Nigel Christopher Parkinson [1968] Director; Minghui Xu [1971] Finance Director [Chinese]

Project Bridal Designer Outlet Limited
Incorporated: 22 September 2015 *Employees:* 8
Net Worth: £27,944 *Total Assets:* £978,314
Registered Office: 43 Coniscliffe Road, Darlington, Co Durham, DL3 7EH
Activities: Retail sale of clothing in specialised stores
Shareholders: Phillip William Johnson; Julie Johnson
Officers: Julie Johnson [1961] Director/Sales Adviser; Phillip William Johnson [1961] Sales Director

Project Genesis Limited
Incorporated: 5 March 1993
Net Worth: £96,096 *Total Assets:* £8,022,312
Registered Office: Ravensworth House, 1 Ravensworth Street, Bedlington, Northumberland, NE22 7JP
Activities: Development of building projects
Shareholders: Dysart Developments Limited; Project Genesis Nominees Ltd
Officers: Lyn Joan Binks, Company Secretary; Lyn Joan Binks [1960] Director/Company Secretary; William Coxall [1950] Director/Civil Engineer [British Virgin Islander]; Morris Robert Muter [1954] Director; Christian Swinburne [1968] Director/Solicitor

Project North East
Incorporated: 18 April 1983 *Employees:* 24
Net Worth: £2,460,695 *Total Assets:* £4,653,776
Registered Office: Unit 3, Ground Floor, 7-15 Pink Lane, Newcastle upon Tyne, NE1 5DW
Activities: Other professional, scientific and technical activities n.e.c.
Officers: Tracey Joanne Moore, Secretary; Irene Lawrie Allcroft [1962] Director; Andrew Ceri Jones [1965] Director; David Thomas Mitchell [1964] Director/Manager; Tracey Joanne Moore [1969] Director/Development Manager; John Howard Oswald [1952] Director/Chartered Accountant; Caroline Pilling [1965] Director/Manager; Timothy Ralph Smith [1959] Director/Solicitor

Project Tulip Topco Limited
Incorporated: 4 May 2016 *Employees:* 196
Net Worth Deficit: £13,024,971 *Total Assets:* £30,666,716
Registered Office: Olliver, Aske, Richmond, N Yorks, DL10 5HX
Activities: Activities of financial services holding companies
Parent: Propharma Group MIS Holdings Limited
Officers: Dawn Gail Sherman, Secretary; Robert Hugh Chestnut [1961] Director [American]; Derek Everett Feagans [1972] Director [American]; Arjen Huijs [1976] Finance Director [Dutch]; Dawn Gail Sherman [1967] Director [American]; Andreas Gerardus Cornelis Johannes Van de Sande [1960] Director/Chief Executive Officer [Dutch]

Proofgolden Limited
Incorporated: 4 April 1991 *Employees:* 14
Net Worth: £1,209,369 *Total Assets:* £2,688,920
Registered Office: Glen C Rodger Limited, Cragside House, Heaton Road, Newcastle upon Tyne, NE6 1SE
Activities: Travel agency activities
Major Shareholder: David Eddleston
Officers: David Eddleston [1953] Director/Travel Agent; Janet Raine Eddleston [1956] Director/Tour Operator

Propertees Ltd
Incorporated: 19 October 2016
Net Worth: £474,744 *Total Assets:* £1,084,784
Registered Office: Brunel House, Brunel Road, Middlesbrough, Cleveland, TS6 6JA
Activities: Letting and operating of conference and exhibition centres
Major Shareholder: Simon Colin Scotchbrook
Officers: Simon Colin Scotchbrook [1973] Director

Property Rental Services Limited
Incorporated: 6 March 2008
Net Worth: £373,920 *Total Assets:* £2,042,197
Registered Office: 10 Langholm Road, East Boldon, Co Durham, NE36 0ED
Activities: Other letting and operating of own or leased real estate
Shareholder: David Murray
Officers: Elaine Forrest, Secretary; Clarence Forrest [1952] Director; Elaine Forrest [1958] Director; Jason Allan Lilley [1970] Director; David Murray [1961] Director; Norman Russell [1957] Director

Propharma Group MIS Holdings Limited
Incorporated: 6 November 2013 *Employees:* 323
Net Worth: £8,579,610 *Total Assets:* £10,462,714
Registered Office: Olliver, Aske, Richmond, N Yorks, DL10 5HX
Activities: Other information service activities n.e.c.
Parent: Propharma MIS Holdings LLC
Officers: Dawn Gail Sherman, Secretary; Robert Hugh Chestnut [1961] Director/Chief Financial Officer [American]; Derek Everett Feagans [1972] Director [American]; Dawn Gail Sherman [1967] Director [American]

Propharma Group MIS Limited
Incorporated: 20 November 1998 *Employees:* 291
Net Worth: £10,583,328 *Total Assets:* £12,203,950
Registered Office: Olliver, Aske, Richmond, N Yorks, DL10 5HX
Activities: Other information service activities n.e.c.
Parent: Propharma Group MIS Holdings Limited
Officers: Robert Hugh Chestnut [1961] Director/Chief Financial Officer [American]; Derek Everett Feagans [1972] Director [American]; Dawn Gail Sherman [1967] Director [American]

Propipe Ltd
Incorporated: 22 December 1997 *Employees:* 40
Net Worth: £1,368,034 *Total Assets:* £3,082,441
Registered Office: Unit 2 Queens Meadow Business Park, Hartlepool, Cleveland, TS25 5TE
Activities: Other manufacturing n.e.c.
Officers: Warren Findlay, Secretary; Michael Black [1964] Director; Warren Findlay [1974] Finance Director; David John Forster [1967] Director; Robert McKnight [1971] Director; John Spraggon [1962] Project Director

Prospero Growth Limited
Incorporated: 1 July 2014
Net Worth: £3,144,193 *Total Assets:* £3,153,971
Registered Office: 140 Coniscliffe Road, Darlington, Co Durham, DL3 7RT
Activities: Security dealing on own account
Shareholders: Isabella Moyes; James Moyes; Amy Moyes-Reader
Officers: Matthew Christopher Bennett [1964] Director/Solicitor; Elizabeth Kate Gardner [1983] Director; Antony William Luckett [1961] Director/Accountant; Janice Rosalind Moyes [1953] Director

Protec The Cap Company Limited
Incorporated: 9 July 1993 *Employees:* 15
Net Worth: £2,064,146 *Total Assets:* £2,266,038
Registered Office: RMT, Gosforth Park Avenue, Gosforth, Newcastle upon Tyne, NE12 8EG
Activities: Non-specialised wholesale trade
Major Shareholder: Dieter Brenning
Officers: Thomas Franz Willi Ohl, Secretary; Dieter Brenning [1951] Managing Director [German]; Thomas Franz Willi Ohl [1963] Director [German]

Protection Installation Services Ltd
Incorporated: 17 April 2007 *Employees:* 14
Net Worth: £446,481 *Total Assets:* £896,009
Registered Office: 9 Stirling Court, Team Valley Trading Estate, Gateshead, Tyne & Wear, NE11 0JF
Activities: Manufacture of electricity distribution and control apparatus
Major Shareholder: Ian Robert McLean
Officers: Linda Ann Whing, Secretary; David Dalton [1965] Director/Electrical Fitter; Ian Robert McLean [1960] Director; Gary Steven Whing [1972] Director/Electrical Fitter; Kevin William Whing [1966] Managing Director

The Protector Group Limited
Incorporated: 13 October 1997 *Employees:* 352
Net Worth: £1,347,814 *Total Assets:* £6,000,549
Registered Office: Protector House, Station Approach, Team Valley Trading Estate, Gateshead, Tyne & Wear, NE11 0ZF
Activities: Security systems service activities
Shareholders: Mercer Street Security Systems Limited; Mercer Street Marketing and Consulting Limited
Officers: Alan Crawford Fletcher, Secretary; Donna Louise Harvey, Secretary; Alan Crawford Fletcher [1969] Director/Solicitor; Donna Saunders MacDonald [1965] Finance Director; Kenneth Slater [1956] Director; Lord John Stevens [1942] Director

Protex (UK) Systems Limited
Incorporated: 5 December 2011 *Employees:* 4
Net Worth: £946,755 *Total Assets:* £1,097,422
Registered Office: Gloster House, Falcon Court, Preston Farm Business Park, Stockton on Tees, Cleveland, TS18 3TX
Activities: Other professional, scientific and technical activities n.e.c.
Major Shareholder: David Glenn Orr
Officers: David Glenn Orr [1972] Director; Kirsty Ailsa Orr [1973] Director

Protherm (UK) Limited
Incorporated: 4 March 1993 *Employees:* 55
Net Worth: £443,107 *Total Assets:* £2,060,264
Registered Office: Infinity House, Sotherby Road, Middlesbrough, Cleveland, TS3 8BT
Activities: Manufacture of other fabricated metal products n.e.c.
Officers: Vanessa Kilvington, Secretary; Paul Ward Healey [1966] Director/Ventilation; Timothy Kilvington [1964] Director

Proto (GB) Ltd
Incorporated: 7 August 2009 *Employees:* 5
Net Worth: £765,302 *Total Assets:* £807,198
Registered Office: 300 Westgate Road, Newcastle upon Tyne, NE4 5QT
Activities: Retail sale of leather goods in specialised stores
Shareholders: Krishan Vedhara; Shashi Bala; Anil Kumar
Officers: Krishan Vedhara [1983] Director

Protomed Limited
Incorporated: 30 July 2007 *Employees:* 16
Net Worth Deficit: £3,039,088 *Total Assets:* £1,974,495
Registered Office: Quantum House, Hobson Industrial Estate, Burnopfield, Co Durham, NE16 6EA
Activities: Other human health activities
Parent: Quantum Pharmaceutical Limited
Officers: Amanda Miller, Secretary; Baldev Raj Bange [1973] Operations Director; David Alan Sanson [1959] Quality Director; Michael James Tagg [1982] Finance Director

Proton Power Systems PLC
Incorporated: 7 February 2006 *Employees:* 74
Net Worth Deficit: £64,662,000 *Total Assets:* £3,260,000
Registered Office: St Ann's Wharf, 112 Quayside, Newcastle upon Tyne, NE99 1SB
Activities: Activities of head offices
Major Shareholder: Dr Faiz Francois Nahab
Officers: Roman Blaise Kotlarzewski, Secretary; Helmut Gierse [1950] Director/Engineer [German]; Sebastian Goldner [1980] Director/Electrical Engineer [German]; Roman Blaise Kotlarzewski [1958] Director/Chartered Accountant; Manfred Limbrunner [1969] Director/Mechanical Engineer [German]; Dr Faiz Francois Nahab [1942] Director

Provenance Developments Limited
Incorporated: 28 June 2016 *Employees:* 2
Net Worth Deficit: £927 *Total Assets:* £1,052,023
Registered Office: c/o Union Property Services Limited, Cobalt 3.1, Silver Fox Way, Cobalt Business Park, Wallsend, Tyne & Wear, NE27 0QJ
Activities: Development of building projects
Parent: Provenance Group Limited
Officers: Varsha Sehgal, Secretary; Melanie Kathryn Brown [1967] Director; Varsha Sehgal [1977] Director

Providence Fishing Company Limited
Incorporated: 8 March 1999
Net Worth: £1,013,776 *Total Assets:* £1,107,597
Registered Office: 15 Hatfield Drive, Seghill, Northumberland, NE23 7TU
Activities: Marine fishing
Major Shareholder: Kevin Caffrey
Officers: Eileen Caffrey, Secretary; Kevin Edward Caffrey [1956] Director/Fisherman

Prudhoe Community Partnership
Incorporated: 27 March 2006 *Employees:* 3
Net Worth: £327,247 *Total Assets:* £1,377,310
Registered Office: Spetchells Centre, Front Street, Prudhoe, Northumberland, NE42 5AA
Activities: Other information service activities n.e.c.
Officers: George Charles Hepburn, Secretary; Margaret Boonstra [1955] Director/Pastor; Pauline Edwards [1961] Director/Retail Trader; Doreen Elwell [1944] Director/Retired; George Charles Hepburn [1949] Director/Retired; Vesta Moore [1949] Director/Retired; Margaret Ann Phillips [1950] Director/Retired; Joan Russell [1946] Director/Retired; Richard William Shrimpton [1964] Director/Horticulturist; Kate Stanforth [1994] Director/Volunteer Charity Champion; Caroline Lucy Warburton [1953] Director/Retired; Iain Watt [1968] Director/Shop Manager

Prudhoe Estates LLP
Incorporated: 1 December 2014
Net Worth: £1,801,247 *Total Assets:* £1,985,800
Registered Office: Quayside House, 110 Quayside, Newcastle upon Tyne, NE1 3DX

Pryme Group Limited
Incorporated: 4 February 1976 *Employees:* 69
Net Worth: £2,234,205 *Total Assets:* £2,950,566
Registered Office: L5, 19 High Flatworth, Tyne Tunnel Trading Estate, North Shields, Tyne & Wear, NE29 7UT
Activities: Machining
Officers: Kerrie Rae Doreen Murray, Secretary; Angus John Gray [1966] Director/Engineer; Murray McKay Kerr [1981] Director; Kerrie Rae Doreen Murray [1983] Director

Psi Global Ltd
Incorporated: 30 March 1976 *Employees:* 84
Net Worth: £1,550,349 *Total Assets:* £5,543,335
Registered Office: Glenarm Road, Wynyard Business Park, Wynyard, Billingham, Cleveland, TS22 5FE
Activities: Other manufacturing n.e.c.
Shareholders: The G S Hunter 1991 Settlement; Susanne Phyllis Hunter
Officers: Daniel Stuart Hunter, Secretary/Director; Ian Davis [1964] Director; Daniel Stuart Hunter [1971] Commercial Director; Jon Sherwood Hunter [1965] Director; Susanne Phyllis Hunter [1945] Director; Hans Gunther Alexander Waltl [1958] Director [Austrian]

PSP Architectural Ltd
Incorporated: 29 November 2007
Net Worth: £813,050 *Total Assets:* £3,332,932
Registered Office: Unit 11 All Saints Industrial Estate, Shildon, Co Durham, DL4 2RD
Activities: Architectural activities
Parent: Pressed Steel Products (Holdings) Ltd
Officers: Kamal Ashraf Abdul Razaq [1946] Director [Omani]; Heath Hindmarch [1967] Managing Director; Tamer Ayoub Qaqish [1977] Director

Psyche Holdings Limited
Incorporated: 24 September 1997
Net Worth: £1,498,340 *Total Assets:* £1,508,520
Registered Office: The Psyche Building, 175-187 Linthorpe Road, Middlesbrough, Cleveland, TS1 4AG
Activities: Non-trading company
Major Shareholder: Stephen Cochrane
Officers: Susan Thomas, Secretary; Stephen Cochrane [1959] Director/Fashion Retailer

Psyche Limited
Incorporated: 10 August 1993 *Employees:* 69
Net Worth: £1,507,338 *Total Assets:* £3,585,501
Registered Office: The Psyche Building, 175-187 Linthorpe Road, Middlesbrough, Cleveland, TS1 4AG
Activities: Retail sale of clothing in specialised stores
Parent: Psyche Holdings Ltd
Officers: Susan Thomas, Secretary; Stephen Cochrane [1959] Director/Fashion Retailer

PT Wood Finishes LLP
Incorporated: 15 April 2009
Net Worth: £304,566 *Total Assets:* £874,371
Registered Office: Unit 6 Churchill Industrial Estate, Blaydon Industrial Park, Chainbridge Road, Blaydon on Tyne, Tyne & Wear, NE21 5AB

PTM Holdings Limited
Incorporated: 18 January 2008
Net Worth: £3,148,951 *Total Assets:* £4,316,526
Registered Office: 13 Tudhoe Industrial Estate, Spennymoor, Co Durham, DL16 6TL
Activities: Non-trading company
Parent: Berm Holdings Limited
Officers: Jon Beamson [1964] Director; Richard George Elliott [1971] Director; David Thomas Moist [1972] Director; Michael John Rogan [1980] Director

Pullan Barnes Limited
Incorporated: 16 September 2008 *Employees:* 19
Net Worth: £982,549 *Total Assets:* £1,119,065
Registered Office: Stephenson House, Richard Street, Hetton-le-Hole, Co Durham, DH5 9HW
Activities: Accounting and auditing activities
Shareholders: Michael Barnes; Keith Pullan; Yasmin Bari
Officers: Yasmin Bari, Secretary; Yasmin Bari [1969] Director/Accountant; Michael Barnes [1965] Director/Accountant; Keith Pullan [1955] Director/Accountant

Mike Pulman Holdings Limited
Incorporated: 16 August 2010 *Employees:* 182
Net Worth: £2,660,000 *Total Assets:* £17,279,000
Registered Office: Pulman, Abbey Road, Framwellgate Moor, Durham, DH1 5HA
Activities: Activities of other holding companies n.e.c.
Major Shareholder: Mike Pulman
Officers: Ian David Buckle, Secretary; Ian David Buckle [1966] Director/Chartered Accountant; Emma Pulman [1987] Director; Jane Pulman [1985] Director; Michael Pulman [1963] Director/Motor Retailer

Mike Pulman Limited
Incorporated: 13 July 1998 *Employees:* 117
Net Worth: £2,355,000 *Total Assets:* £10,735,000
Registered Office: Abbey Road, Framwellgate Moor, Durham, DH1 5HA
Activities: Sale of new cars and light motor vehicles
Major Shareholder: Michael Pulman
Officers: Ian David Buckle, Secretary; Ian David Buckle [1966] Director/Chartered Accountant; Michael Pulman [1963] Director/Motor Retailer

Pulman Seat Limited
Incorporated: 26 May 2010 *Employees:* 31
Net Worth: £305,000 *Total Assets:* £2,212,000
Registered Office: Pulman, Abbey Road, Framwellgate Moor, Durham, DH1 5HA
Activities: Sale of new cars and light motor vehicles
Major Shareholder: Michael Pulman
Officers: Ian David Buckle, Secretary; Ian David Buckle [1966] Director/Chartered Accountant; Michael Pulman [1963] Director/Motor Retailer

Punch Bowl Investments Limited
Incorporated: 29 April 2014
Net Worth: £3,049 *Total Assets:* £4,106,048
Registered Office: c/o Vale of Mowbray Holdings Ltd, 20 Leases Road, Leeming Bar, Northallerton, N Yorks, DL7 9AW
Activities: Other letting and operating of own or leased real estate
Major Shareholder: John Gatenby
Officers: Mark Gatenby, Secretary; John Gatenby [1946] Director

Punch Property Solutions Limited
Incorporated: 24 April 2014
Registered Office: Kensington House, 3 Kensington, Bishop Auckland, Co Durham, DL14 6HX
Activities: Other letting and operating of own or leased real estate
Shareholders: Joshua Cullerton; Paul Cook; Darryl Cullerton; John Cullerton
Officers: Paul Stewart Cook [1976] Director; Darryl John Cullerton [1986] Director; John Cullerton [1967] Director; Joshua Phillip Cullerton [1991] Director

The Punjab Kitchen Ltd
Incorporated: 5 July 1993 *Employees:* 96
Net Worth: £7,373,946 *Total Assets:* £8,469,262
Registered Office: Eldon House, Eldon Street, Rekendyke Industrial Estate, South Shields, Tyne & Wear, NE33 5BU
Activities: Manufacture of prepared meals and dishes
Officers: Mohammed Ishaq, Secretary; Naseem Ahmed [1982] Director; Amina Gani [1983] Director; Mohammed Ishaq [1953] Director/Businessman; Yaqoob Ishaq [1979] Director; Yasmine Ishaq [1956] Director/Businesswoman

Purdy Lodge Limited
Incorporated: 16 December 1992
Registered Office: Adderstone Garage, Belford, Northumberland, NE70 7JU
Activities: Hotels and similar accommodation
Major Shareholder: Valerie Davidson
Officers: Valerie Jacqueline Davidson, Secretary; James William Davidson [1947] Director/Garage Proprietor; Valerie Jacqueline Davidson [1949] Director/Company Secretary

Pure Fishing (UK) Ltd.
Incorporated: 21 September 1988 *Employees:* 131
Net Worth Deficit: £3,891,000 *Total Assets:* £34,838,000
Registered Office: Willowburn Trading Estate, Alnwick, Northumberland, NE66 2PF
Activities: Non-specialised wholesale trade
Parent: Shakespeare International Limited
Officers: Brian James Decker [1976] Director/Attorney [American]; Ben Hartley [1976] Director/Attorney

Purification Solutions UK Limited
Incorporated: 3 December 2015
Net Worth Deficit: £1,553 *Total Assets:* £860,887
Registered Office: Nano Purification Solutions Ltd, Dukesway, Team Valley Trading Estate, Gateshead, Tyne & Wear, NE11 0PZ
Activities: Manufacture of wire products, chain and springs
Parent: Purification Solutions LLC
Officers: Michael Leslie Eccles [1974] Director/Engineer; David Anthony Gilligan [1968] Director/Operations Manager; David Arthur Peters [1962] Managing Director [American]

Purity Global Limited
Incorporated: 21 September 2004
Net Worth: £237,056 *Total Assets:* £1,884,729
Registered Office: Westwaters Oakmere, Belmont Business Park, Durham, DH1 1TW
Activities: Wholesale of household goods (other than musical instruments) n.e.c
Shareholders: Brian Robin Matson; Derek Calvert Haggerstone
Officers: Derek Calvert Haggerstone [1950] Director; Brian Matson [1969] Director

K W Purvis Limited
Incorporated: 1 December 2011
Net Worth: £1,384,731 *Total Assets:* £4,526,374
Registered Office: 2 The Peth Stables, Walkergate, Alnwick, Northumberland, NE66 1NB
Activities: Construction of roads and motorways
Major Shareholder: David Purvis
Officers: David Purvis [1954] Director

PWS Distributors Limited
Incorporated: 27 January 1988 *Employees:* 290
Net Worth: £26,112,392 *Total Assets:* £61,485,940
Registered Office: P O Box 20, Station Road, Aycliffe Business Park, Newton Aycliffe, Co Durham, DL5 6XJ
Activities: Wholesale of household goods (other than musical instruments) n.e.c
Officers: Jonathan Barclay Whisker, Secretary; Kevin Francis Gay [1967] IT & Operations Director; Aidan Jackson [1965] Marketing Director; Wesley McKenna [1971] Sales Director; Mark William Winspear Stephenson [1962] Director; Jonathan Barclay Whisker [1964] Financial Director

PX (TGPP) Limited
Incorporated: 15 April 2002 *Employees:* 3
Net Worth: £783,048 *Total Assets:* £4,426,914
Registered Office: PX House, Westpoint Road, Stockton on Tees, Cleveland, TS17 6BF
Activities: Distribution of gaseous fuels through mains
Parent: PX Holdings Limited
Officers: Mark William Kenrick [1958] Director; Lee Nadine Smail [1971] Director/Accountant; Daniel Philip David Weatherill [1974] Director/Solicitor

PX Engineering Consultants Limited
Incorporated: 31 January 2006 *Employees:* 18
Net Worth: £1,481,807 *Total Assets:* £3,628,231
Registered Office: P X House, Westpoint Road, Stockton on Tees, Cleveland, TS17 6BF
Activities: Engineering design activities for industrial process and production
Parent: PX Holdings Limited
Officers: Mark William Kenrick [1958] Director; Lee Nadine Smail [1971] Director/Accountant; Daniel Philip David Weatherill [1974] Director/Solicitor

PX Holdings Limited
Incorporated: 15 April 2002 *Employees:* 3
Net Worth: £1,448,442 *Total Assets:* £5,451,627
Registered Office: PX House, Westpoint Road, Stockton on Tees, Cleveland, TS17 6BF
Activities: Activities of head offices
Parent: PX Group Limited
Officers: Mark William Kenrick [1958] Director; Lee Nadine Smail [1971] Director/Accountant; Daniel Philip David Weatherill [1974] Director/Solicitor

PX Limited
Incorporated: 14 February 2002 *Employees:* 319
Net Worth: £4,039,986 *Total Assets:* £18,151,180
Registered Office: PX House, Westpoint Road, Stockton on Tees, Cleveland, TS17 6BF
Activities: Production of electricity
Parent: PX Holdings Limited
Officers: Mark William Kenrick [1958] Director; Lee Nadine Smail [1971] Director/Accountant; Daniel Philip David Weatherill [1974] Director/Solicitor

PX UK Holdco1 Limited
Incorporated: 22 March 2016 *Employees:* 341
Net Worth Deficit: £612,707 *Total Assets:* £51,714,892
Registered Office: PX House, Westpoint Road, Thornaby, Stockton on Tees, Cleveland, TS17 6BF
Activities: Activities of other holding companies n.e.c.
Officers: Luis Pais Correia [1963] Director; Tushar Kantilal Doshi [1964] Director; Mark William Kenrick [1958] Director; Christopher James Picotte [1970] Director/Investor [American]; James Granville Potter [1980] Director [American]; Graeme David Sword [1968] Director

PX UK Holdco2 Limited
Incorporated: 22 March 2016 *Employees:* 5
Net Worth Deficit: £92,754 *Total Assets:* £37,192,212
Registered Office: PX House, Westpoint Road, Thornaby, Stockton on Tees, Cleveland, TS17 6BF
Activities: Activities of other holding companies n.e.c.
Parent: PX UK Holdco1 Limited
Officers: Luis Pais Correia [1963] Director; Mark William Kenrick [1958] Director; Christopher James Picotte [1970] Director/Investor [American]; James Granville Potter [1980] Director [American]; Graeme David Sword [1968] Director/Partner

PX UK Holdco3 Limited
Incorporated: 22 March 2016 *Employees:* 5
Net Worth Deficit: £2,232,286 *Total Assets:* £35,556,864
Registered Office: PX House, Westpoint Road, Thornaby, Stockton on Tees, Cleveland, TS17 6BF
Activities: Activities of other holding companies n.e.c.
Parent: PX UK Holdco2 Limited
Officers: Luis Pais Correia [1963] Director; Mark William Kenrick [1958] Director; Christopher James Picotte [1970] Director/Investor [American]; James Granville Potter [1980] Director [American]; Graeme David Sword [1968] Director/Partner

Q Laser Ltd
Incorporated: 23 January 2012
Net Worth: £336,915 *Total Assets:* £996,259
Registered Office: Unit 22a Cherry Way, Dubmire Industrial Estate, Houghton-le-Spring, Co Durham, DH4 5RJ
Activities: Machining
Major Shareholder: Colin Graham Hewitt
Officers: Colin Graham Hewitt [1963] Sales Director

Q.A. (Weld Tech) Limited
Incorporated: 13 February 1980 *Employees:* 80
Net Worth: £2,593,043 *Total Assets:* £3,608,837
Registered Office: Q A (Weld Tech) Limited, Bowes Road, Riverside Park Industrial Estate, Middlesbrough, Cleveland, TS2 1LU
Activities: Manufacture of other fabricated metal products n.e.c.
Major Shareholder: Charles Peter Tighe
Officers: Charles Peter Tighe, Secretary; Richard Lawton Knowles [1968] Director/Engineer; David Pickles [1968] Operations Director; Charles Peter Tighe [1946] Director

Q.A. International Certification Limited
Incorporated: 22 July 1992
Net Worth: £663,825 *Total Assets:* £766,484
Registered Office: Dudley Court, Dudley Road, Darlington, Co Durham, DL1 4GG
Activities: Other service activities n.e.c.
Shareholders: Elizabeth Ann Duffield; Alan Carter
Officers: Alan Carter [1963] Director/Certification Scheme Manager; Elizabeth Ann Duffield [1961] Director/Manager

Q9 Cladding Solutions Ltd
Incorporated: 16 December 2011 *Employees:* 13
Net Worth: £288,210 *Total Assets:* £1,415,970
Registered Office: The Stables, Arlaw Banks, Winston, Darlington, Co Durham, DL2 3PX
Activities: Construction of commercial buildings
Officers: Kathryn Joy Race, Secretary; Simon Kellett [1964] Director; Glen Race [1957] Director

QC Investments Limited
Incorporated: 10 May 2013
Registered Office: c/o Joseph Miller & Co, Floor A, Milburn House, Dean Street, Newcastle upon Tyne, NE1 1LE
Activities: Other letting and operating of own or leased real estate
Shareholders: Stefan Cross; Dr Alison Steele
Officers: Stefan Tylney Cross [1960] Director; Dr Alison Mary Steele [1961] Director

QE Facilities Limited
Incorporated: 30 April 2014 *Employees:* 531
Net Worth: £22,965,000 *Total Assets:* £65,142,000
Registered Office: Estates Department, Queen Elizabeth Hospital, Queen Elizabeth Avenue, Sheriff Hill, Gateshead, Tyne & Wear, NE9 6SX
Activities: Combined facilities support activities
Parent: Gateshead Health NHS Foundation Trust
Officers: Robert Anderson, Secretary; Shaun Bowron [1956] Director/Semi-Retired Business Consultant and NED; Peter Harding [1961] NHS Director; Anthony Joseph Robson [1964] Director/Accountant

Quality Food Service Limited
Incorporated: 14 July 2002 *Employees:* 39
Net Worth: £683,364 *Total Assets:* £1,514,828
Registered Office: Fresh Produce & Flower Centre, Unit 1 Easter Park, Barton Road, Riverside Park, Middlesbrough, Cleveland, TS2 1RY
Activities: Other food services
Shareholders: John Charles Bell; Jill Scott
Officers: Jill Scott, Secretary/Director; John Charles Bell [1960] Director; Jill Scott [1961] Director

Quality Tooling (North East) Limited
Incorporated: 7 September 1998 *Employees:* 16
Net Worth: £592,436 *Total Assets:* £866,171
Registered Office: 5 Back Norfolk Street, Sunderland, Tyne & Wear, SR1 1EA
Activities: Wholesale of machine tools
Major Shareholder: Sydney Walton
Officers: Sydney Walton [1940] Managing Director

Quantum Controls Ltd
Incorporated: 1 December 2000 *Employees:* 39
Net Worth: £2,360,757 *Total Assets:* £4,323,356
Registered Office: 6a Dukes Way, Low Prudhoe Industrial Estate, Prudhoe, Northumberland, NE42 6PQ
Activities: Manufacture of other electrical equipment
Shareholder: Kevin Brown
Officers: Craig Anthony Bell [1971] Director/Chartered Accountant; Kevin Brown [1971] Director

Quantum Pharma 2014 Limited
Incorporated: 17 October 2014
Net Worth: £21,200,000 *Total Assets:* £50,064,000
Registered Office: Quantum House, Hobson Industrial Estate, Burnopfield, Co Durham, NE16 6EA
Activities: Manufacture of pharmaceutical preparations
Parent: Quantum Pharma Holdings Limited
Officers: Amanda Miller, Secretary; David John Bryant [1967] Director/Chief Business Officer; Richard John Paling [1970] Director/Group Financial Controller

Quantum Pharma Group Limited
Incorporated: 17 December 2008 *Employees:* 8
Net Worth Deficit: £5,815,000 *Total Assets:* £70,794,000
Registered Office: Quantum House, Hobson Industrial Estate, Burnopfield, Hobson, Co Durham, NE16 6EA
Activities: Activities of head offices
Officers: Amanda Miller, Secretary; David John Bryant [1967] Director/Chief Business Officer; Richard John Paling [1970] Director/Group Financial Controller

Quantum Pharma Holdings Limited
Incorporated: 17 October 2014 *Employees:* 454
Net Worth: £46,614,000 *Total Assets:* £90,823,000
Registered Office: Quantum House, Hobson Industrial Estate, Burnopfield, Co Durham, NE16 6EA
Activities: Manufacture of pharmaceutical preparations
Parent: Clinigen Group PLC
Officers: Amanda Miller, Secretary; David John Bryant [1967] Director/Chief Business Officer; Richard John Paling [1970] Director/Group Financial Controller

Quantum Pharmaceutical Limited
Incorporated: 24 September 2004 *Employees:* 263
Net Worth: £15,500,000 *Total Assets:* £66,999,000
Registered Office: Quantum House, Hobson Industrial Estate, Burnopfield, Co Durham, NE16 6EA
Activities: Manufacture of pharmaceutical preparations
Parent: Quantum Pharma Group Limited
Officers: Amanda Miller, Secretary; Andrew Paul Matthews [1976] Operations Director; David Alan Sanson [1959] Technical Director; Michael James Tagg [1982] Finance Director

QuantuMDx Group Limited
Incorporated: 4 March 2008 *Employees:* 66
Net Worth: £9,080,277 *Total Assets:* £12,824,881
Registered Office: Lugano Building, 57 Melbourne Street, Newcastle upon Tyne, NE1 2JQ
Activities: Other human health activities
Officers: Norman Kribs, Secretary; Riccardo Braglia [1960] Director/Entrepreneur and CEO [Swiss/Italian]; Professor Sir John Burn [1952] Director/University Professor; Timothy Chia [1950] Director [Singaporean]; Jonathan James O'Halloran [1975] Director; Elaine Harrington Warburton OBE [1963] Director; Nigel Grenville Williams [1964] Director

Quarrington Renewable Gas Ltd
Incorporated: 23 December 2014
Net Worth Deficit: £915,414 *Total Assets:* £4,543,180
Registered Office: Quarrington Farm, Old Quarrington, Co Durham, DH6 5NN
Activities: Production of electricity
Shareholders: Quarrington Farms Ltd; Foresight Group LLP
Officers: Philip David Johnson [1960] Director; Timothy Rodney Spring [1958] Director/Financier; Ariel Max Vegoda [1977] Director/Solicitor

Quartz Electrical & Mechanical Services Limited
Incorporated: 24 July 1996 *Employees:* 47
Net Worth: £508,057 *Total Assets:* £2,113,522
Registered Office: Thornton House, Brighouse Business Village, Riverside Park, Middlesbrough, Cleveland, TS2 1RT
Activities: Electrical installation
Major Shareholder: James Gareth Orpen
Officers: Gavin Kendall [1972] Director/Electrical Engineer; Andrew Learmonth [1973] Director/Accountant; Liam McDermott [1973] Director/Mechanical Engineer; James Gareth Orpen [1948] Director

Quartztec Europe Limited
Incorporated: 10 September 1962 *Employees:* 36
Net Worth: £1,306,991 *Total Assets:* £2,526,120
Registered Office: Acomb House, The Green, Acomb, Hexham, Northumberland, NE46 4PH
Activities: Manufacture and processing of other glass, including technical glassware
Shareholder: Ron Jackman
Officers: Marc Spence, Secretary; Ronald Robert Jackman [1957] Managing Director; Marc Spence [1979] Finance Director; Christopher Scott Thompson [1956] Director/Chief Executive; Generald Thurgood [1946] Director

Quay North LLP
Incorporated: 7 August 2003
Net Worth: £408,013 *Total Assets:* £1,048,388
Registered Office: Clayton House, Walbottle Road, Newcastle upon Tyne, NE15 9RU
Officers: Mark Richard Greenwell [1968] Member; Tracey Greenwell [1970] Member

Quay Timber Ltd
Incorporated: 23 June 2011 *Employees:* 9
Net Worth: £423,554 *Total Assets:* £783,205
Registered Office: Quay Timber, Hume Street, Newcastle upon Tyne, NE6 1LN
Activities: Wholesale of wood, construction materials and sanitary equipment
Major Shareholder: Mark Fawcett
Officers: Mark Fawcett [1967] Director/Timber Merchant

Quays Hotels Limited
Incorporated: 19 April 2010
Net Worth Deficit: £485,601 *Total Assets:* £14,142,053
Registered Office: c/o Tindle's LLP, Scotswood House, Teesdale South, Thornaby Place, Stockton on Tees, Cleveland, TS17 6SB
Activities: Hotels and similar accommodation
Parent: CPS Haulage (Tyneside) Limited
Officers: Robert Ralph Tindle [1957] Director/Chartered Accountant; Michael Whinham [1939] Director

Quayside Frozen Foods (Newcastle) Limited
Incorporated: 23 May 1983 *Employees:* 32
Net Worth: £1,738,828 *Total Assets:* £3,199,082
Registered Office: Dukesway, Team Valley Trading Estate, Gateshead, Tyne & Wear, NE11 0PZ
Activities: Non-specialised wholesale trade
Shareholders: William Lane; Brenda Lane
Officers: Brenda Lane, Secretary; Brenda Lane [1948] Director; William Lane [1946] Director

Quayside Pharmacy Limited
Incorporated: 29 April 1992 *Employees:* 34
Net Worth: £985,222 *Total Assets:* £1,409,379
Registered Office: Crawhall Road, Newcastle upon Tyne, NE1 2BL
Activities: Other human health activities
Shareholders: Arun Kumar Jassal; Sunita Jassal
Officers: Sunita Jassal, Secretary; Arun Kumar Jassal [1957] Director/Pharmacist; Sunita Jassal [1960] Director/Store Manageress [Indian]

Qubic Tax Advisory Limited
Incorporated: 24 June 2016
Net Worth: £720,973 *Total Assets:* £988,942
Registered Office: St Ann's Quay, 118 Quayside, Newcastle upon Tyne, NE1 3BD
Activities: Tax consultancy
Parent: ILS Estates (UK) Limited
Officers: Neil Daran Devapal [1979] Director/Solicitor; David Michael Graham [1978] Director/Accountant; Andrew Neil Stevenson [1978] Director/Solicitor

Qubic Tax Ltd
Incorporated: 15 January 2008 *Employees:* 1
Net Worth: £1,837,078 *Total Assets:* £6,501,488
Registered Office: 118 Quayside, St Anns Quay, Newcastle upon Tyne, NE1 3BD
Activities: Tax consultancy
Parent: Qubic Associate Group Limited
Officers: David Michael Graham [1978] Director/Accountant

Queensberry Design Limited
Incorporated: 21 October 2002 *Employees:* 29
Net Worth: £1,563,862 *Total Assets:* £2,079,846
Registered Office: Suite 2a, Metro House, Metro Centre, Gateshead, Tyne & Wear, NE11 9NH
Activities: Architectural activities
Shareholder: Sarah Jane Paylor
Officers: Sarah Jane Paylor, Secretary; Mark Darren Paylor [1971] Director; Sarah Jane Paylor [1981] Director/Secretary

Queensway Dental Laboratory Limited
Incorporated: 29 August 2014 *Employees:* 13
Net Worth: £31,711 *Total Assets:* £1,239,839
Registered Office: 170 Queensway, Billingham, Stockton on Tees, Cleveland, TS23 2NT
Activities: Dental practice activities
Shareholder: Richard James Elliott
Officers: Dr Paul Anthony Averley [1967] Director/Dentist; Dr William Carter [1981] Director/Dentist; Richard James Elliott [1977] Director/Dental Technician; Dr Ian Anthony Lane [1974] Director/Dentist; Dr Uzma Olbrich [1973] Director/Dentist

Queribus Ltd
Incorporated: 15 June 2011
Net Worth: £1,149,930 *Total Assets:* £1,603,085
Registered Office: 43 Coniscliffe Road, Darlington, Co Durham, DL3 7EH
Activities: Activities of other holding companies n.e.c.
Shareholders: Michael John Sutter; Lesley Sheila Sutter
Officers: Lesley Sheila Sutter [1957] Director/Company Secretary; Michael John Sutter [1958] Director/Chartered Accountant

Quick Developments Limited
Incorporated: 2 March 2006
Net Worth: £51,936 *Total Assets:* £772,009
Registered Office: Lily Estate, Ponteland Road, Throckley, Newcastle upon Tyne, NE15 9EP
Activities: Buying and selling of own real estate
Officers: Brenda Collard, Secretary; Brenda Collard [1958] Director; David Collard [1956] Director

Quickly Finance Limited
Incorporated: 6 July 2007 *Employees:* 323
Net Worth: £530,001 *Total Assets:* £5,845,371
Registered Office: Fasttrack House, Pearson Way, Thornaby, Stockton on Tees, Cleveland, TS17 6PT
Activities: Other service activities n.e.c.
Parent: Quickly Group Holdings Limited
Officers: Colin Hartness, Secretary; Colin Robert Hartness [1962] Director

Quickly Group Holdings Limited
Incorporated: 27 February 2012 *Employees:* 323
Net Worth: £588,706 *Total Assets:* £5,904,059
Registered Office: Fasttrack House, Pearson Way, Thornaby, Stockton on Tees, Cleveland, TS17 6PT
Activities: Activities of head offices
Shareholders: Colin Robert Hartness; Duncan Adrian John Crocker
Officers: Colin Hartness, Secretary; Duncan Adrian Crocker [1961] Director; Colin Robert Hartness [1962] Director

Chris Quigley Education Limited
Incorporated: 7 September 2007 *Employees:* 7
Net Worth: £1,648,859 *Total Assets:* £1,911,112
Registered Office: Sandy View Buildings, Front Street, Burnopfield, Co Durham, NE16 6PU
Activities: Primary education
Shareholders: Christopher Quigley; Nicola Louise Quigley
Officers: Nicola Louise Quigley, Secretary; Christopher Quigley [1968] Director; Nicola Louise Quigley [1969] Director

WJM Quigley Limited
Incorporated: 2 June 1995
Registered Office: 1 Brandon Road, Esh Winning, Co Durham, DH7 9PH
Activities: Construction of other civil engineering projects n.e.c.
Major Shareholder: William Quigley
Officers: Angela Mary Ann White, Secretary; William Quigley [1946] Director/Builder; Angela Mary Ann White [1956] Director/Company Secretary

R and R Hands Road Transport Limited
Incorporated: 1 December 2005 *Employees:* 28
Net Worth: £1,470,277 *Total Assets:* £2,657,962
Registered Office: 6B Dukes Way, Low Prudhoe Industrial Estate, Prudhoe, Northumberland, NE42 6PQ
Activities: Freight transport by road
Shareholder: Richard Rex Hands
Officers: Richard Rex Hands, Secretary/Haulier; Martin Rex Hands [1985] Director/Fleet Manager; Philip Richard Hands [1987] Director/Haulier; Richard Rex Hands [1957] Director/Haulier

R D Consulting and Education Limited
Incorporated: 26 April 2011
Net Worth: £471,384 *Total Assets:* £921,655
Registered Office: 123 Kenton Road, Newcastle upon Tyne, NE3 4NN
Activities: Other retail sale not in stores, stalls or markets
Shareholder: Rahul Dharmadhikari
Officers: Dr Deepali Dharmadhikari [1973] Director; Rahul Dharmadhikari [1972] Director

R J Construction & Development Limited
Incorporated: 2 February 2006
Net Worth: £239,662 *Total Assets:* £1,263,255
Registered Office: 4 Lynford Gardens, Sunderland, Tyne & Wear, SR2 9AY
Activities: Other letting and operating of own or leased real estate
Officers: Rhonda Jane Bradford, Secretary/Director; David Richard Thomas Bradford [1970] Director/Property Development; Rhonda Jane Bradford [1979] Director

R J Utility Services Ltd
Incorporated: 20 October 1997 *Employees:* 86
Net Worth: £2,072,036 *Total Assets:* £3,341,732
Registered Office: Patterson Street, Blaydon on Tyne, Tyne & Wear, NE21 5TZ
Activities: Construction of other civil engineering projects n.e.c.
Shareholder: Eamon O'Hara
Officers: Eamon Ohara, Secretary; Robert Thomas Henderson [1961] Director/Project Manager; Eamon Ohara [1968] Director

R&M Diagnostics Limited
Incorporated: 20 January 2011 *Employees:* 4
Net Worth: £856,911 *Total Assets:* £915,363
Registered Office: 14 Saxilby Drive, Whitebridge Park, Gosforth, Newcastle upon Tyne, NE3 5LS
Activities: General medical practice activities
Shareholders: Rajendranath Sinha; Mital Sharma Sinha
Officers: Dr. Mitul Sharma Sinha [1970] Director/Doctor; Dr. Rajendranath Sinha [1967] Director/Doctor

R&R Ice Cream UK Limited
Incorporated: 21 March 1967 *Employees:* 907
Net Worth: £203,268,000 *Total Assets:* £285,327,008
Registered Office: Richmond House, Leeming Bar, Northallerton, N Yorks, DL7 9UL
Activities: Manufacture of ice cream
Parent: Richmond Foods Limited
Officers: Marcello Mattia, Secretary; Michael John Fraine [1966] Director; Phil Karl Griffin [1972] Marketing Director; Marcello Mattia [1965] Director [Italian]; Ibrahim Mahmood Ibrahim Najafi [1958] Director; Samuel David Wrist [1976] Director

R&R Packaging Limited
Incorporated: 7 June 2011 *Employees:* 13
Net Worth: £122,150 *Total Assets:* £976,035
Registered Office: Unit 1d Admiral Business Park, Nelson Way, Cramlington, Northumberland, NE23 1WG
Activities: Non-specialised wholesale trade
Shareholders: Robert White Jnr; Robert Harrison White Snr
Officers: Robert Harrison White Jnr [1972] Director; Robert Harrison White Snr [1949] Director

R&R PIK Limited
Incorporated: 23 April 2013
Net Worth Deficit: £56,074,520 *Total Assets:* £224,768,656
Registered Office: Richmond House, Leeming Bar, Northallerton, N Yorks, DL7 9UL
Activities: Activities of production holding companies
Parent: Riviera Acquisitions Limited
Officers: Marcello Mattia, Secretary; Phil Karl Griffin [1972] Director; Marcello Mattia [1965] Director [Italian]; Ibrahim Mahmood Ibrahim Najafi [1958] Director

The R.D.A. Centre in Cleveland Limited
Incorporated: 26 March 1997 *Employees:* 23
Net Worth: £989,985 *Total Assets:* £994,965
Registered Office: The Unicorn Centre, Stainton Way, Hemlington, Middlesbrough, Cleveland, TS8 9LX
Activities: Sports and recreation education
Officers: Ian Nigel Scrutton, Secretary; Julie Marion Elphee [1953] Director/Personal Assistant; Susan Gaffney [1963] Managing Director; Joan Northernd [1949] Director/Mental Health Support; Carole Judith Preston [1953] Director/Teacher; Jacqueline Rubin [1953] Director/Retired; Ian Nigel Scrutton [1944] Director/Retired; Garry Michael Toulouse [1962] Director/Retired; Patricia White [1952] Director/Retired Educationalist

R.F.I. Limited
Incorporated: 12 February 1985
Net Worth: £751,130 *Total Assets:* £757,875
Registered Office: Joseph Miller & Co, Floor A, Milburn House, Dean Street, Newcastle upon Tyne, NE1 1LE
Activities: Non-trading company
Shareholder: Brian Dixon
Officers: Maureen Dixon, Secretary; Bryan Dixon [1948] Director; Gary Bryan Dixon [1973] Director; Maureen Dixon [1949] Director

R.M. & K. Fashions Limited
Incorporated: 26 May 1976 *Employees:* 3
Net Worth: £1,050,358 *Total Assets:* £1,681,795
Registered Office: 36 Willow Way, Darras Hall, Ponteland, Northumberland, NE20 9RF
Activities: Other letting and operating of own or leased real estate
Major Shareholder: Kiran Chopra
Officers: Kiran Chopra [1953] Director/Property Investor; Reena Chopra [1985] Director; Sunny Chopra [1985] Director

RACZ Group Ltd
Incorporated: 28 September 2015 *Employees:* 1
Net Worth: £38,108 *Total Assets:* £2,488,873
Registered Office: 178 York Road, Hartlepool, Cleveland, TS26 9EA
Activities: Activities of open-ended investment companies
Major Shareholder: Mike Racz
Officers: Mike Racz [1982] Director

Radecal Limited
Incorporated: 30 July 2008
Registered Office: Unit 19 Whitworth Road, Armstrong, Washington, Tyne & Wear, NE37 1PP
Activities: Other retail sale not in stores, stalls or markets
Major Shareholder: Chris Economides
Officers: Chris Dionysios Economides [1974] Director

Rail Management Services Limited
Incorporated: 4 March 1992
Net Worth Deficit: £3,468,207 *Total Assets:* £1,415,294
Registered Office: Stanhope Station, Station Road, Stanhope, Bishop Auckland, Co Durham, DL13 2YS
Activities: Repair and maintenance of other transport equipment n.e.c.
Parent: British American Railway Services Limited
Officers: Edwin Ellis [1954] Director [American]; Hugh Michael McConville [1961] Director [American]

Rainton Construction Limited
Incorporated: 23 March 1992 *Employees:* 247
Net Worth: £5,296,965 *Total Assets:* £15,375,269
Registered Office: Davison House, Rennys Lane, Dragonville Industrial Estate, Durham, DH1 2RS
Activities: Construction of roads and motorways
Parent: MGL Group Limited
Officers: Gary Anthony Smith, Secretary; David Anthony Elliott [1969] Contracts Director; Kenneth John Forbes [1954] Estimating Director; Gary Anthony Smith [1967] Director/Accountant

Rainton Meadows Arena Limited
Incorporated: 3 August 1984 *Employees:* 15
Net Worth: £150,670 *Total Assets:* £1,448,391
Registered Office: Rainton Business Park, Mercantile Road, Houghton-le-Spring, Co Durham, DH4 5PH
Activities: Public houses and bars
Major Shareholder: Matthew Roseberry
Officers: Michael Anthony Roseberry, Secretary; Matthew Roseberry [1944] Director/Builder; Michael Anthony Roseberry [1966] Director/Hotelier

Raisco Limited
Incorporated: 19 April 2007 *Employees:* 22
Net Worth: £684,729 *Total Assets:* £2,844,001
Registered Office: 43 Coniscliffe Road, Darlington, Co Durham, DL3 7EH
Activities: Manufacture of metal structures and parts of structures
Parent: Gracloem Holdings Ltd
Officers: Julie Raistrick, Company Secretary; Paul Edward Dickinson [1959] Operations Director; Gary Raistrick [1974] Managing Director; Julie Raistrick [1975] Director/Company Secretary

G Ramage & Sons Windows Limited
Incorporated: 19 December 1984 *Employees:* 14
Net Worth: £684,211 *Total Assets:* £929,274
Registered Office: Ramage House, Samson Close, George Stephenson Industrial Estate, Killingworth, Newcastle upon Tyne, NE12 6DX
Activities: Painting
Shareholders: Ian George Ramage; Andrew Ramage
Officers: George Ramage, Secretary/Director; Andrew Ramage [1966] Director; Ian George Ramage [1971] Director/Glazier

Ramage Transport Limited
Incorporated: 5 July 1984 *Employees:* 123
Net Worth: £2,439,859 *Total Assets:* £5,282,436
Registered Office: New York Way, Shiremoor, Tyne & Wear, NE27 0QE
Activities: Freight transport by road
Major Shareholder: Raymond Robin Ramage
Officers: Denise Carole Hodgson, Secretary; Denise Carole Hodgson [1966] Director/Transport and Office Manager; Denise Ann Ramage [1956] Director; Raymond Robin Ramage [1957] Managing Director

Ramsay Services Investments Limited
Incorporated: 13 March 2003
Registered Office: Fourth Floor, Central Exchange Buildings, 93a Grey Street, Newcastle upon Tyne, NE1 6EG
Activities: Other letting and operating of own or leased real estate
Major Shareholder: Ian Lawson
Officers: Ian Ramsay Lawson [1954] Director

Ramscove Limited
Incorporated: 23 April 1990 *Employees:* 3
Net Worth: £11,157,963 *Total Assets:* £13,530,085
Registered Office: Sadberge Hall, Sadberge, Darlington, Co Durham, DL2 1RL
Activities: Management consultancy activities other than financial management
Shareholders: David John Soley; Susan Jane Soley
Officers: Susan Jane Soley, Secretary; David John Soley [1949] Director/Management Consultant; Susan Jane Soley [1956] Director/Secretary

Ramsdens Financial Limited
Incorporated: 12 April 1995 *Employees:* 570
Net Worth: £27,520,000 *Total Assets:* £40,709,000
Registered Office: Unit 16 Parkway Centre, Coulby Newham, Middlesbrough, Cleveland, TS8 0TJ
Activities: Financial intermediation not elsewhere classified
Parent: Ramsdens Holdings PLC
Officers: Kevin Nigel Brown, Secretary; Jason John Carr [1972] I.T.Director; Martin Clyburn [1981] Finance Director; Michael Johnson [1973] Operations Director; Peter Edward Kenyon [1965] Operations Director; Andrew David Meehan [1955] Director

Ramsdens Holdings PLC
Incorporated: 12 December 2013 *Employees:* 552
Net Worth: £23,395,000 *Total Assets:* £31,303,000
Registered Office: Unit 16 Parkway Centre, Coulby Newham, Middlesbrough, Cleveland, TS8 0TJ
Activities: Activities of financial services holding companies
Officers: Kevin Nigel Brown, Secretary; Martin Clyburn [1981] Finance Director; Simon Edward Herrick [1963] Director/Chartered Accountant; Peter Edward Kenyon [1965] Director; Andrew David Meehan [1955] Director; Stephen John Smith [1957] Director/Chartered Accountant

Ramside Estates Limited
Incorporated: 2 August 1963 *Employees:* 529
Net Worth: £22,762,376 *Total Assets:* £35,920,072
Registered Office: Ramside Hall Hotel, Carrville, Durham, DH1 1TD
Activities: Hotels and similar accommodation
Officers: Karen Wilson, Secretary; John Richard Adamson [1965] Director/Hotel Manager; Marian Ethel Adamson [1940] Director; Helen Roseberry [1967] Director; Karen Wison [1973] Director/Certified Chartered Accountant

Ramside Holdings Limited
Incorporated: 13 July 2007 *Employees:* 569
Net Worth: £19,844,290 *Total Assets:* £33,555,128
Registered Office: Ramside Hall Hotel, Carrville, Durham, DH1 1TD
Activities: Hotels and similar accommodation
Officers: Karen Wilson, Secretary; John Richard Adamson [1965] Director; Marian Ethel Adamson [1940] Director

Rand Rocket Limited
Incorporated: 31 December 1986 *Employees:* 13
Net Worth: £42,418 *Total Assets:* £987,805
Registered Office: AB Care House, Hownsgill Industrial Park, Consett, Co Durham, DH8 7NU
Activities: Wholesale of pharmaceutical goods
Shareholder: Randolph Vickers
Officers: Karen Lesley Vickers, Secretary; David Vickers [1962] Managing Director; Karen Lesley Vickers [1959] Director/Freelance Arts & Crafts Teacher

Randall Orchard Construction Limited
Incorporated: 14 October 1992 *Employees:* 56
Net Worth: £2,304,169 *Total Assets:* £3,192,954
Registered Office: 7 Mercury Road, Gallowfields Trading Estate, Richmond, N Yorks, DL10 4TQ
Activities: Development of building projects
Parent: Randall Orchard Holdings Ltd
Officers: Joanne Katherine Newton, Secretary; Graeme Richard Newton [1968] Director; Joanne Katherine Newton [1965] Director/Company Secretary

Randstad Limited
Incorporated: 20 May 1976 *Employees:* 31
Net Worth: £3,747,187 *Total Assets:* £4,280,862
Registered Office: 37 Crow Hall Road, Nelson Park, Cramlington, Northumberland, NE23 1WH
Activities: Retail trade of motor vehicle parts and accessories
Shareholders: June Elizabeth Dowd; Anthony John Dowd
Officers: June Elizabeth Dowd, Secretary; Anthony John Dowd [1950] Director; June Elizabeth Dowd [1952] Director; Martin Christopher Dowd [1964] Director/Accountant; Phillip Dowd [1979] Director/Buyer

Alan Ransome Sporting Goods Group Limited
Incorporated: 27 August 1974 *Employees:* 37
Net Worth: £4,150,489 *Total Assets:* £5,075,240
Registered Office: Queensway, Middlesbrough, Cleveland, TS3 8TF
Activities: Wholesale of clothing and footwear
Major Shareholder: Alan Edward Ransome
Officers: Peter Spellman, Secretary; Alan Edward Ransome [1946] Director

Rapid (UK) Engineering Services Limited
Incorporated: 8 July 2010 *Employees:* 11
Net Worth: £94,535 *Total Assets:* £798,026
Registered Office: Unit 3 Fergusons Business Park West, Sleekburn, Bedlington, Northumberland, NE22 7DH
Activities: Manufacture of tubes, pipes, hollow profiles and related fittings, of steel
Shareholder: Neil Elwell
Officers: Neil Elwell [1976] Director/Engineer; Michael James Lawson [1977] Director/Engineer; Tammie Irene Lawson [1979] Director; Heidi Lazenby [1977] Director; Kevin Lazenby [1979] Director/Engineer

Rapid Response Transport (UK) Limited
Incorporated: 10 February 2003 *Employees:* 40
Net Worth: £983,773 *Total Assets:* £1,258,910
Registered Office: Blue House, Point Road, Portrack Industrial Estate, Portrack Grange Road, Stockton on Tees, Cleveland, TS18 2PW
Activities: Freight transport by road
Shareholders: Graeme Keith Heward; Michelle Dawn Heward
Officers: Graeme Keith Heward, Secretary/Director; Graeme Keith Heward [1965] Director; Michelle Dawn Heward [1972] Director

Rasmi Electronics Limited
Incorporated: 30 July 1974 *Employees:* 45
Net Worth: £964,743 *Total Assets:* £2,314,197
Registered Office: Unit 14a, Tanfield Lea Industrial Estate, Stanley, Co Durham, DH9 9UU
Activities: Manufacture of electric lighting equipment
Shareholders: Dr Parwathappa Surendra; Boguimila Anna Surendra
Officers: Bogumila Anna Surendra, Secretary; Anjali Paula Hampton [1974] Director/Administrator; Dr Parwathappa Surendra [1939] Director/Electrical Engineer

Rasmi Lighting Limited
Incorporated: 9 July 2008 *Employees:* 3
Net Worth Deficit: £149,576 *Total Assets:* £861,560
Registered Office: Rasmi House, Morrison Road, Annfield Plain, Co Durham, DH9 7RX
Activities: Manufacture of electric lighting equipment
Shareholders: Dr Parwathappa Surendra; Bogumila Anna Surendra
Officers: Anjali Hampton [1974] Director; Bogmuila Anna Surendra [1943] Director; Dr Parwathappa Surendra [1939] Managing Director

Rathbone Training
Incorporated: 1 November 2011 *Employees:* 225
Net Worth Deficit: £11,552,000 *Total Assets:* £2,448,000
Registered Office: Newcastle College, Rye Hill Campus, Scotswood Road, Newcastle upon Tyne, NE4 7SA
Activities: General secondary education
Parent: NCG Corporation
Officers: Graeme Roland Dodd [1968] Finance Director; Peter Rene Lauener [1954] Director/Retired - Civil Servant; Christopher Payne [1964] Group Director; Ian Webber [1971] Director

Ravendale Foods Limited
Incorporated: 6 December 1982 *Employees:* 100
Net Worth: £5,192,324 *Total Assets:* £9,240,603
Registered Office: Unit 2 Lope Hill Road, Leadgate Industrial Estate, Consett, Co Durham, DH8 7RN
Activities: Production of meat and poultry meat products
Shareholders: Brenda Gray; Raymond Alan Gray
Officers: Brenda Gray, Secretary; Brenda Gray [1953] Director/Company Secretary; Raymond Alan Gray [1952] Director

Ravenside Ltd
Incorporated: 26 March 2014
Net Worth: £366,842 *Total Assets:* £1,335,266
Registered Office: 10 Rydal Street, Gateshead, Tyne & Wear, NE8 1HG
Activities: Buying and selling of own real estate
Officers: Eliezer Halberstadt [1986] Director; David Schleider [1959] Director/Property Developer; Lionel Spitzer [1969] Director/Company Manager

Ravensworth Golf Club,Limited (The)
Incorporated: 19 April 1912
Net Worth: £611,628 *Total Assets:* £1,347,309
Registered Office: Angel View, Longbank, Wrekenton, Gateshead, Tyne & Wear, NE9 7NE
Activities: Operation of sports facilities
Officers: Lynn Stearman, Secretary; Phillip Cyril Byrne [1971] Director/Civil Servant; Alan Day [1947] Director/Retired; Aidan Peter Heslop [1957] Director/General Manager; Susan McArdle [1950] Director/Retired; John Parker [1971] Director; Andrew Purdy [1966] Director/Electrician; Peter Whybrow [1964] Director/Repairs and Maintenance Manager

Ravensworth Homes LLP
Incorporated: 5 December 2002
Net Worth: £1,024,544 *Total Assets:* £4,491,820
Registered Office: Davison House, Rennys Lane, Dragonville Industrial Estate, Durham, DH1 2RS
Officers: Alan Davison [1940] Member; David Anthony Elliott [1969] Member; Gary Anthony Smith [1967] Member

Ravensworth Properties Limited
Incorporated: 4 August 1983 *Employees:* 2
Net Worth: £2,076,086 *Total Assets:* £4,831,743
Registered Office: Ravensworth House, Fifth Avenue Business Park, Team Valley Trading Estate, Gateshead, Tyne & Wear, NE11 0HF
Activities: Other letting and operating of own or leased real estate
Parent: Tolent Construction Limited
Officers: Andrew David Clark, Secretary; Andrew David Clark [1965] Director; John Gibbon Wood [1944] Director

Ravensworth Property Developments LLP
Incorporated: 4 May 2005
Net Worth: £2,211,629 *Total Assets:* £10,204,771
Registered Office: Davison House, Dragonville Industrial Estate, Rennys Lane, Durham, DH1 2RS
Officers: Geoff Clark [1970] Member; David Anthony Elliott [1969] Member; Gary Anthony Smith [1967] Member

Ray & Company (Hairdressers Sundries Men) Limited
Incorporated: 15 November 1946 *Employees:* 34
Net Worth: £1,151,979 *Total Assets:* £1,864,499
Registered Office: Trade Hair Supplies, Lingfield Way, Yarm Road Business Park, Darlington, Co Durham, DL1 4PZ
Activities: Wholesale of perfume and cosmetics
Officers: Virginia Ann Sliufko, Secretary; Christopher Harry Sliufko [1987] Director; Olivia Mary Sliufko [1982] Director; Paul Anthony Garth Sliufko [1954] Director; Thomas Guy Sliufko [1985] Director/Manager

Ray & Sons Limited
Incorporated: 18 February 1999
Registered Office: Hadrian House, Front Street, Chester-le-Street, Co Durham, DH3 3DB
Activities: Other letting and operating of own or leased real estate
Major Shareholder: Usman Ali
Officers: Shahnaz Ali, Secretary; Usman Ali [1984] Director

Les Rayner Foxhunters Motor Company Ltd.
Incorporated: 26 August 1993
Net Worth: £468,854 *Total Assets:* £1,366,990
Registered Office: Foxhunters Industrial Estate, Foxhunters Road, Whitley Bay, Tyne & Wear, NE25 8UG
Activities: Sale of used cars and light motor vehicles
Major Shareholder: Guy Edward Rayner
Officers: Guy Edward Rayner [1982] Director/Businessman

Raytec Limited
Incorporated: 10 August 2005 *Employees:* 66
Net Worth: £8,280,913 *Total Assets:* £10,115,878
Registered Office: Unit 15 Wansbeck Business Park, Rotary Parkway, Ashington, Northumberland, NE63 8QW
Activities: Manufacture of other electrical equipment
Officers: Toru Kamimura [1960] Director [Japanese]; David Lambert [1978] Director; Kenshi Miyamoto [1959] Director [Japanese]; Masakazu Nagano [1960] Business Development Director [Japanese]; Barry Thompson [1969] Divisional Director; Masashi Ueda [1982] Director [Japanese]; Anthony Gerard John Whiting [1964] Director

Razorblue Ltd
Incorporated: 22 May 2006 *Employees:* 21
Net Worth: £461,784 *Total Assets:* £1,319,151
Registered Office: Razorblue House, 12 Bailey Court, Colburn Business Park, Catterick Garrison, N Yorks, DL9 4QL
Activities: Information technology consultancy activities
Parent: Razorblue Group Limited
Officers: Rachel Jayne Atkinson, Secretary; Jonathan Anderson [1986] Director; Rachel Jayne Atkinson [1982] Finance Director; Daniel James Kitchen [1989] Director/Chief Executive; Rachel Victoria Kitchen [1990] Director/Chartered Accountant; David Raper [1966] Operations Director; Alan Timothy [1956] Director; Mark Wilkinson [1983] Sales Director

RBV Energy Limited
Incorporated: 13 January 2000
Net Worth: £2,294,490 *Total Assets:* £4,671,656
Registered Office: Unit 3 Centurion House, New York Way, New York Industrial Park, Newcastle upon Tyne, NE27 0QF
Activities: Manufacture of other fabricated metal products n.e.c.
Shareholders: Richard John Betteridge; Ronald Richard Brown; Ian Michael Storey
Officers: Ronald Richard Brown, Secretary/Engineering Sales; Anne Lucille Betteridge [1966] Director; Richard John Betteridge [1963] Director/Engineering Sales; Ronald Richard Brown [1962] Director/Engineering Sales; Sonia Brown [1962] Director; Ian Michael Storey [1959] Director/General Manager; Lynn Storey [1961] Director

RDS Driving Services Limited
Incorporated: 10 September 2010 *Employees:* 90
Net Worth Deficit: £615,642 *Total Assets:* £1,814,840
Registered Office: Pavilion 6, Coxwold Way, Belasis Hall Technology Park, Billingham, Cleveland, TS23 4EA
Activities: Driving school activities
Parent: Driving Success Limited
Officers: Simon Liddiard Clarke, Secretary; Ian McIntosh [1956] Director; Philip Richard Weston [1966] Director/Private Equity

Re:Production Limited
Incorporated: 13 December 2010 *Employees:* 12
Net Worth: £660,990 *Total Assets:* £1,509,696
Registered Office: The Studios, Swordfish House, Amethyst Road, Newcastle Business Park, Newcastle upon Tyne, NE4 7YL
Activities: Video production activities
Shareholders: Philip Greenwood; Stephen James Hunneysett
Officers: Leann Greenwood [1977] Director/Administrator; Philip Greenwood [1978] Director; Ruth Hunneysett [1974] Director/Administrator; Stephen James Hunneysett [1963] Director

Read Holdings Limited
Incorporated: 21 August 2000
Net Worth: £6,459,000 *Total Assets:* £33,553,000
Registered Office: Cleveland House, Norton Road, Stockton on Tees, Cleveland, TS20 2AQ
Activities: Activities of head offices
Major Shareholder: John Donald Read Fothergill
Officers: John Philip Pickering, Secretary; John Donald Read Fothergill [1961] Director; John Philip Pickering [1954] Director/Chartered Accountant

Read Limited
Incorporated: 15 November 1887 *Employees:* 4
Net Worth Deficit: £547,000 *Total Assets:* £24,317,000
Registered Office: Cleveland House, Norton Road, Stockton on Tees, Cleveland, TS20 2AQ
Activities: Manufacture of lifting and handling equipment
Major Shareholder: John Donald Read Fothergill
Officers: Stephen Angus, Secretary; John Donald Read Fothergill [1961] Director; John Philip Pickering [1954] Director

K.W. Reader & Sons Limited
Incorporated: 24 April 1992 *Employees:* 65
Net Worth: £1,455,510 *Total Assets:* £5,484,639
Registered Office: The Dunes, Sea Road, South Shields, Tyne & Wear, NE33 2LD
Activities: Retail sale of beverages in specialised stores
Major Shareholder: Kenneth William Reader
Officers: Gillian Reader, Secretary; Gillian Reader [1965] Director; Kenneth William Reader [1964] Director/Amusement Caterer

Readman Steel Limited
Incorporated: 24 November 2005 *Employees:* 19
Net Worth: £2,455,437 *Total Assets:* £4,194,327
Registered Office: Cochranes Wharf, Dockside Road, Middlesbrough, Cleveland, TS3 6AW
Activities: Manufacture of tubes, pipes, hollow profiles and related fittings, of steel
Parent: W.G.R. (Steels) Limited
Officers: Wayne Ashton Britton, Secretary; Wayne Ashton Britton [1971] Director; Richard William Readman [1960] Director

Ready Mix Tees Valley Ltd
Incorporated: 21 February 2008 *Employees:* 11
Net Worth Deficit: £324,618 *Total Assets:* £972,053
Registered Office: 1-4 Puddlers Road, South Bank, Middlesbrough, Cleveland, TS6 6TX
Activities: Other manufacturing n.e.c.
Shareholder: James Edward Greenwood
Officers: James Edward Greenwood, Secretary; James Edward Greenwood [1971] Director/Manager

Readypay Limited
Incorporated: 4 July 1990 *Employees:* 21
Net Worth: £837,386 *Total Assets:* £3,827,988
Registered Office: Northumberland Taxi & Coach Centre, South Albion Retail Park, Albion Way, Blyth, Northumberland, NE24 5BW
Activities: Renting and leasing of cars and light motor vehicles
Shareholders: Hugh Magill Hurst; Alexander Hugh Magill Hurst
Officers: Alexander Hurst, Secretary; Alexander Hurst [1988] Director; Hugh Magill Hurst [1951] Director/Taxi Proprietor

Real Time Claims Limited
Incorporated: 19 February 2007
Net Worth: £144,238 *Total Assets:* £4,465,118
Registered Office: 3rd Floor, Generator Studios, Trafalgar Street, Newcastle upon Tyne, NE1 2LA
Activities: Financial intermediation not elsewhere classified
Major Shareholder: Stuart Phillipson Bell
Officers: Stuart Phillipson Bell [1947] Director

Real Time Money Ltd.
Incorporated: 25 February 2011
Net Worth Deficit: £1,032,207 *Total Assets:* £1,032,945
Registered Office: Generator Studios, Trafalgar Street, Newcastle upon Tyne, NE1 2LA
Activities: Financial intermediation not elsewhere classified
Major Shareholder: Stuart Phillipson Bell
Officers: Stuart Phillipson Bell [1947] Director

Reality Enterprise Ltd
Incorporated: 20 March 2007 *Employees:* 100
Net Worth: £814,589 *Total Assets:* £1,281,137
Registered Office: 14 Captain Cook Square, Middlesbrough, Cleveland, TS1 5UB
Activities: Retail sale of other second-hand goods in stores (not incl. antiques)
Major Shareholder: Rafakat Ali
Officers: Safeena Kauser Ali, Secretary/Audit Facilitator; Rafakat Ali [1972] Managing Director; Safeena Kauser Ali [1978] Director/Audit Facilitator

Adina Reay Limited
Incorporated: 22 August 2013 *Employees:* 1
Net Worth Deficit: £236,975 *Total Assets:* £978,064
Registered Office: 25 Broad Chare, Quayside, Newcastle upon Tyne, NE1 3DQ
Activities: Manufacture of women's underwear
Major Shareholder: Sharon Lake
Officers: Sharon Lake [1967] Director/Clothing Manufacturer

Reay Security Limited
Incorporated: 3 August 1994
Net Worth: £1,472,145 *Total Assets:* £2,009,995
Registered Office: Arms Evertyne House, Quay Road, Dun Cow Quay, Blyth, Northumberland, NE24 2AS
Activities: Other service activities n.e.c.
Parent: Reay Security Holdings Limited
Officers: Diane Gorman, Secretary; Dianne Gorman [1967] Director/Office Manager; Steven Robert Reay [1964] Director

REC Consultancy Services Limited
Incorporated: 26 November 2007
Net Worth: £1,211,935 *Total Assets:* £2,430,255
Registered Office: 43 Coniscliffe Road, Darlington, Co Durham, DL3 7EH
Activities: Management consultancy activities other than financial management
Shareholders: DM Services (Banchory) Ltd; Lanof (UK) Ltd
Officers: Richard Edwin Clarke [1959] Director; David Telford MacKay [1960] Director

Red & Racz Ltd
Incorporated: 3 October 2015 *Employees:* 100
Net Worth: £277,755 *Total Assets:* £5,463,522
Registered Office: 178 York Road, Hartlepool, Cleveland, TS26 9EA
Activities: Unlicenced restaurants and cafes
Shareholders: Red Miracle Management Limited; RACZ Investment Ltd
Officers: Mike Racz [1982] Director/Franchisee; Arvinder Singh Salariya [1964] Director/Franchisee

Red House Investments Limited
Incorporated: 5 June 2015 *Employees:* 1
Net Worth: £73,133 *Total Assets:* £2,199,902
Registered Office: 246 Park View, Whitley Bay, Tyne & Wear, NE26 3QX
Activities: Financial intermediation not elsewhere classified
Major Shareholder: Michael Anthony Potts
Officers: Michael Anthony Potts [1953] Director

Red House School Limited
Incorporated: 1 April 1936 *Employees:* 52
Net Worth: £2,799,456 *Total Assets:* £6,867,039
Registered Office: Red House, 36 The Green, Norton, Stockton on Tees, Cleveland, TS20 1DX
Activities: Pre-primary education
Officers: Amanda Louise Mallen-Beadle, Secretary; Simon Jonathan Ashforth [1974] Regional Commercial Director Balfour Beatty; John Paul Card [1981] Recruitment Director; Gavin David Cordwell-Smith [1976] Director; Sean Michael Costigan [1969] Director/Business Owner; Mark Stephen Craggs [1968] Director/Farmer; Victoria Louise Duncan [1973] Director/Solicitor; Jeremy Henning [1968] Director/Doctor; Kate Elizabeth Huddart [1975] Director/Pharmacist; Amanda Louise Mallen-Beadle [1973] Director/Chartered Accountant; Dr Amar Rangan [1966] Director/Surgeon; Neil Simpson [1971] Director/Commercial Banker; Guy Taylor [1969] Director; Amy Witham [1975] Director/Accountant; Sven David Wright [1968] Managing Director

Red I55 Ltd
Incorporated: 13 December 2011 *Employees:* 2
Net Worth: £1,349,426 *Total Assets:* £1,869,359
Registered Office: Bulman House, Regent Centre, Gosforth, Newcastle upon Tyne, NE3 3LS
Activities: Engineering related scientific and technical consulting activities
Shareholders: Michael John Rudd; Vicki Rudd
Officers: Paul Cheesmond, Secretary; Michael John Rudd [1957] Director

Red Marine (Holdings) Limited
Incorporated: 27 March 2012
Net Worth: £3,172,338 *Total Assets:* £3,353,634
Registered Office: Tynedale House, Hexham Business Park, Burn Lane, Hexham, Northumberland, NE46 3RU
Activities: Activities of other holding companies n.e.c.
Shareholders: Joseph Orrell; Richard Derek Kent
Officers: Toby James Bailey [1971] Director; Richard Derek Kent [1968] Director/Engineer; Joseph Orrell [1976] Director/Engineer

Red Marine Engineering Limited
Incorporated: 21 July 2008 *Employees:* 18
Net Worth: £764,650 *Total Assets:* £1,084,170
Registered Office: Tynedale House, Hexham Business Park, Burn Lane, Hexham, Northumberland, NE46 3RU
Activities: Construction of other civil engineering projects n.e.c.
Parent: Red Marine (Holdings) Limited
Officers: Toby James Bailey [1971] Director; Richard Derek Kent [1968] Director/Engineer; Joseph Orrell [1976] Director/Engineer

Red Oak Ltd
Incorporated: 17 August 1982 *Employees:* 19
Net Worth: £1,618,789 *Total Assets:* £2,306,542
Registered Office: Sandgate House, 102 Quayside, Newcastle upon Tyne, NE1 3DX
Activities: Other information technology service activities
Shareholders: James Peter Land; Dr Julie Elizabeth Land
Officers: Julie Elizabeth Land, Secretary; Philip Alexander Blyth [1979] Financial Director; James Peter Land [1957] Director/Manager; Dr Julie Elizabeth Land [1959] Director; Mark William Philip [1967] Worksafe Services Director; Warren Lee Thomson [1983] Operations Director

Red Poppy (UK) Limited
Incorporated: 19 March 2010 *Employees:* 1,151
Net Worth: £8,504,000 *Total Assets:* £93,162,000
Registered Office: 1a Dukesway Court, Team Valley Trading Estate, Gateshead, Tyne & Wear, NE11 0PJ
Activities: Activities of head offices
Parent: Red Poppy (Gibraltar) Limited
Officers: Phillip Nigel Blain, Secretary; David James Horrocks [1959] Financial Director; Ian Imrie [1955] Director

Red Ridge Developments Limited
Incorporated: 4 August 2000
Net Worth: £271,687 *Total Assets:* £1,248,857
Registered Office: 158 Heaton Park Road, Heaton, Newcastle upon Tyne, NE6 5NR
Activities: Other letting and operating of own or leased real estate
Shareholders: Bizerka Horne; Imogen Horne; Rowan Horne
Officers: Biserka Stringer Horne, Secretary; Imogen Horne [1993] Director/Property Consultant; Peter Horne [1957] Director/Property Developer; Rowan Horne [1996] Director/Property Manager; Biserka Stringer Horne [1991] Director/Property Consultant

Red Ridge Residential Limited
Incorporated: 9 June 2000
Net Worth: £1,168,555 *Total Assets:* £3,429,367
Registered Office: 158 Heaton Park Road, Heaton, Newcastle upon Tyne, NE6 5NR
Activities: Other letting and operating of own or leased real estate
Major Shareholder: Peter David Horne
Officers: Dr Helen Barbara Stringer, Secretary/Speech Therapist-Teacher; Peter Horne [1957] Director/Property Developer; Dr Helen Barbara Stringer [1958] Director/Doctor

Redbale Limited
Incorporated: 15 January 2002
Registered Office: 7 Brenkley Way, Blezard Business Park, Seaton Burn, Tyne & Wear, NE13 6DS
Activities: Management of real estate on a fee or contract basis
Major Shareholder: Christopher Humble
Officers: Stephen Leslie Doberman, Secretary; Christopher Owen Humble [1959] Director

Redbead Limited
Incorporated: 22 April 2004
Net Worth: £348,227 *Total Assets:* £884,130
Registered Office: 234a Chillingham Road, Newcastle upon Tyne, NE6 5LP
Activities: Other letting and operating of own or leased real estate
Shareholder: Vineh Jerath
Officers: Vineh Jerath, Secretary/Self Employed; Roopika Jerath [1981] Director/Self Employed; Vineh Jerath [1978] Director/Self Employed

Redcar Bulk Terminal Limited
Incorporated: 11 October 2010 *Employees:* 81
Net Worth: £11,596,000 *Total Assets:* £16,415,000
Registered Office: Lackenby Main Office, Lackenby Works, Middlesbrough, Cleveland, TS6 7RP
Activities: Cargo handling for water transport activities
Shareholders: British Steel Limited; Sahaviriya Steel Industries UK Limited
Officers: Steven Antony Mason [1975] Finance Director; Garry O'Malley [1954] Director

Redcar Racecourse Limited
Incorporated: 14 June 1875 *Employees:* 20
Net Worth: £2,880,127 *Total Assets:* £4,579,741
Registered Office: The Racecourse, Redcar, Cleveland, TS10 2BY
Activities: Operation of sports facilities
Officers: John Francis Sanderson, Secretary/Racecourse Executive; Alison Jill Baptiste [1965] Director/Chartered Civil Engineer; John Leslie Garrett [1963] Director/Financial Analyst; John Joseph Andrew Sanderson [1977] Director/Racecourse Executive; John Francis Sanderson [1941] Director; Mark Lawrence Dundas Zetland [1937] Director/Corporate Body

Redcar Scaffolding Specialists Ltd
Incorporated: 2 July 2012
Net Worth: £119 *Total Assets:* £911,966
Registered Office: Beaumont Accountancy Services, 1st Floor, Enterprise House, 202-206 Linthorpe Road, Middlesbrough, Cleveland, TS1 3QW
Activities: Scaffold erection
Shareholders: Ron Stocks; Bernard Knight
Officers: Bernard Knight [1966] Director; Ronald Mark Stocks [1966] Director/Scaffolder

The Redemption Food Company Limited
Incorporated: 11 February 2004 *Employees:* 35
Net Worth: £417,949 *Total Assets:* £2,032,958
Registered Office: Unit 5a Number One Industrial Estate, Consett, Co Durham, DH8 6SR
Activities: Manufacture of other food products n.e.c.
Major Shareholder: Robert James Clarke
Officers: Robert James Clarke [1961] Director; Mark William Crow [1968] Director

The Redemption Holding Company (UK) Limited
Incorporated: 24 June 2016
Net Worth: £225,842 *Total Assets:* £1,120,140
Registered Office: Unit 5a Number One Industrial Estate, Consett, Co Durham, DH8 6SR
Activities: Manufacture of prepared meals and dishes
Major Shareholder: Robert James Clarke
Officers: Robert James Clarke [1961] Director; Mark William Crow [1968] Director

Redesdale Properties LLP
Incorporated: 22 January 2008
Net Worth: £327,029 *Total Assets:* £3,870,597
Registered Office: Howden Close, Newcastle Road, Corbridge, Northumberland, NE45 5LS
Officers: Andrew Peter Barratt [1982] Member; Angela Margaret Barratt [1957] Member; Peter Arthur Barratt [1955] Member

Redfern Building Services Limited
Incorporated: 31 January 1990
Registered Office: 24 Longfield Road, South Church Enterprise Park, Bishop Auckland, Co Durham, DL14 6XB
Activities: Construction of commercial buildings
Shareholders: Paul Redfern; Jack Redfern
Officers: Paul Redfern, Secretary; Jack Watson Redfern [1947] Director/Builder; Paul Redfern [1977] Director/Surveyor

Redgate Lodge Limited
Incorporated: 30 October 2012
Net Worth: £461,091 *Total Assets:* £1,527,297
Registered Office: 246 Park View, Whitley Bay, Tyne & Wear, NE26 3QX
Activities: Sale of used cars and light motor vehicles
Shareholders: Scott William Sibley; Jane Sibley
Officers: Jane Sibley [1969] Director; Scott William Sibley [1972] Director

Redhead Roofing LLP
Incorporated: 29 March 2006
Net Worth: £762,008 *Total Assets:* £1,310,860
Registered Office: 27 Hartley Court, Brunswick Industrial Estate, Newcastle upon Tyne, NE13 7BA
Officers: Juliet Elizabeth Hall [1959] Member; Stuart Adam Hall [1960] Member; Stephen Speak [1960] Member

Redrose Manufacturing Limited
Incorporated: 31 January 1995
Net Worth: £799,093 *Total Assets:* £1,352,948
Registered Office: Unit 21A/B Cherry Way, Dubmire Industrial Estate, Houghton-le-Spring, Co Durham, DH4 5RJ
Activities: Manufacture of basic pharmaceutical products
Major Shareholder: Nadia Mahan
Officers: David Goodings [1966] Managing Director; Nadia Mahan [1977] Director; Thomas Mahan [1943] Director

Redwood Engineering Company Ltd
Incorporated: 8 November 2013
Registered Office: 15 Bankside, The Watermark, Gateshead, Tyne & Wear, NE11 9SY
Activities: Manufacture of other special-purpose machinery n.e.c.
Shareholders: Stephen Dean; Facelift (GB) Ltd
Officers: Stephen Dean [1956] Director

The Reece Foundation
Incorporated: 5 September 2007
Net Worth: £24,832,072 *Total Assets:* £25,277,724
Registered Office: Armstrong Works, Scotswood Road, Newcastle upon Tyne, NE15 6UX
Activities: Other business support service activities n.e.c.
Officers: Anne Dorothy Reece, Secretary; Simon Paul Gilroy [1965] Director/Engineer; Eric Morgan [1945] Director/Retired; Anne Dorothy Reece [1956] Director; John Peter Reece [1961] Director/Engineer

Reece Group Limited
Incorporated: 11 May 2011 *Employees:* 462
Net Worth: £137,707,008 *Total Assets:* £148,674,000
Registered Office: Armstrong Works, Scotswood Road, Newcastle upon Tyne, NE15 6UX
Activities: Activities of head offices
Shareholders: Anne Dorothy Reece; John Peter Reece
Officers: Graeme Cook [1975] Managing Director; Ryan Dennis Lamb [1987] Finance Director; Craig Priday [1966] Managing Director; Anne Dorothy Reece [1956] Director; John Peter Reece [1961] Director

Reece Property Limited
Incorporated: 8 February 2013
Net Worth Deficit: £5,283,434 *Total Assets:* £20,194,204
Registered Office: Armstrong Works, Scotswood Road, Newcastle upon Tyne, NE15 6UX
Activities: Buying and selling of own real estate
Parent: Reece Group Limited
Officers: Ryan Dennis Lamb, Secretary; John Peter Reece [1961] Director

Reece Treasury Management Limited
Incorporated: 19 February 2015
Net Worth: £3,041,000 *Total Assets:* £62,946,000
Registered Office: Armstrong Works, Scotswood Road, Newcastle upon Tyne, NE15 6UX
Activities: Activities of head offices
Parent: Reece Group Limited
Officers: Ryan Dennis Lamb, Secretary; John Peter Reece [1961] Director

The Reed Group Ltd
Incorporated: 2 March 2016 *Employees:* 55
Net Worth: £1,332,941 *Total Assets:* £5,113,227
Registered Office: 43 Coniscliffe Road, Darlington, Co Durham, DL3 7EH
Activities: Activities of other holding companies n.e.c.
Major Shareholder: Christopher Stephen Reed
Officers: Christopher Stephen Reed [1984] Director

Gavin Reed Limited
Incorporated: 13 January 1965
Net Worth: £247,026 *Total Assets:* £871,586
Registered Office: Sunniside Garage, Sunniside, Whickham, Tyne & Wear, NE16 5EE
Activities: Development of building projects
Major Shareholder: Dougal Gavin Wynn Reed
Officers: Dougal Gavin Wynn Reed, Secretary; Dougal Gavin Wynn Reed [1961] Director/Manager; Joan Evelyn Reed [1931] Director/Housewife

Richard Reed Ltd
Incorporated: 8 February 2006
Net Worth: £153,730 *Total Assets:* £960,681
Registered Office: 3-6 Frederick Street, Sunderland, Tyne & Wear, SR1 1NA
Activities: Solicitors
Shareholder: Richard Reed (Holding) Limited
Officers: Alexander Phillip Moir [1980] Director/Solicitor; Laura Mary Peel [1980] Director/Solicitor; David John Place [1974] Director; Sarah Jane Reid [1977] Director/Solicitor; Barry Cosmo Wood [1960] Director/Solicitor

Reed Thermoformed Packaging Ltd.
Incorporated: 13 April 2016 *Employees:* 12
Net Worth: £490,558 *Total Assets:* £2,291,880
Registered Office: Unit 2 Albany Road, Gateshead, Tyne & Wear, NE8 3AT
Activities: Manufacture of plastic packing goods
Shareholders: Harry Reed; Jonathan Oliver Catto
Officers: Jonathan Oliver Catto [1984] Director; Kevin Mark Jones [1975] Director; Harry Reed [1954] Director; Kevin John Witheford [1958] Director

Reeds (Bray) Cranes Limited
Incorporated: 23 February 2004
Net Worth: £743,694 *Total Assets:* £2,839,424
Registered Office: Unit A, Penshaw Way, Portobella Industrial Estate, Birtley, Co Durham, DH3 2SA
Activities: Other specialised construction activities n.e.c.
Shareholders: Peter Bray; Karen Bray
Officers: Peter Bray, Secretary/Managing Director; Karen Bray [1961] Director; Peter Bray [1958] Managing Director

Rees Turnbull Limited
Incorporated: 12 February 2002
Net Worth: £186,377 *Total Assets:* £963,486
Registered Office: Jopling & Turnbull Ltd, Factory Road, Blaydon, Tyne & Wear, NE21 5RU
Activities: Renting and operating of Housing Association real estate
Shareholders: Thomas Alexander Turnbull; David Llewellyn Rees
Officers: Thomas Alexander Turnbull, Secretary/Director; David Llewellyn Rees [1974] Director/Sportsman; Thomas Alexander Turnbull [1974] Director

Reethorn Investments Limited
Incorporated: 16 February 1962 *Employees:* 1
Net Worth: £965,271 *Total Assets:* £1,023,405
Registered Office: 3 Kingfisher Court, Bowesfield Park, Stockton on Tees, Cleveland, TS18 3EX
Activities: Development of building projects
Shareholders: Nigel Robert Goodman; Anne Isabel Goodman Deceased
Officers: Nigel Robert Goodman, Secretary; Nigel Robert Goodman [1966] Director

Regal Amusements (North East) Limited
Incorporated: 4 January 1993 *Employees:* 9
Net Worth: £989,057 *Total Assets:* £1,046,506
Registered Office: Regal Amusements, Unit 5 Newport Road, Middlesbrough Bus Station, Middlesbrough, Cleveland, TS1 5EA
Activities: Gambling and betting activities
Major Shareholder: Ian Winch Henry
Officers: Ian Winch Henry, Secretary/Director; Ian Winch Henry [1964] Director

Regal Motors (Ashington) Limited
Incorporated: 24 April 1978
Net Worth: £1,653,679 *Total Assets:* £1,713,929
Registered Office: Camborne House, South View, Ashington, Northumberland, NE63 0SF
Activities: Travel agency activities
Shareholders: Pauline Trevithick; Melvyn Trevithick
Officers: Christina Trevithick, Secretary; Christina Trevithick [1971] Director/Office Manager; Melvyn Trevithick [1940] Director; Pauline Trevithick [1940] Director

Regeneration (North East) LLP
Incorporated: 1 October 2007
Net Worth: £1,341,933 *Total Assets:* £1,556,698
Registered Office: Express Group, 398A Princesway North, Team Valley Trading Estate, Gateshead, Tyne & Wear, NE11 0TY

Regent Leisure Limited
Incorporated: 10 October 2006
Net Worth: £733,860 *Total Assets:* £2,550,505
Registered Office: Beaumont Accountancy, First Floor, Enterprise House, 202-206 Linthorpe Road, Middlesbrough, Cleveland, TS1 3QW
Activities: Hotels and similar accommodation
Shareholder: Craig Beadnall
Officers: Harry Beadnall, Secretary; Aimee Beadnall [1993] Director/Accounts Manager; Anne Beadnall [1940] Director; Craig Beadnall [1971] Director; Faye Beadnall [1992] Director/Restaurant Manageress; Harry Beadnall [1940] Director; Lynn Beardnall [1968] Director

Reger Holding Limited
Incorporated: 30 May 2007 *Employees:* 3
Net Worth: £2,721,517 *Total Assets:* £15,201,488
Registered Office: First Floor, Finchale House, Belmont Business Park, Durham, DH1 1TW
Activities: Other letting and operating of own or leased real estate
Officers: Helen Austin, Secretary; John Corbitt Barnsley [1948] Director/Accountant; Spencer Trerise Glanville [1972] Director; Robert William Jefferson [1950] Director/Chartered Accountant

Reger Property Limited
Incorporated: 11 July 2007 *Employees:* 3
Net Worth: £2,204,197 *Total Assets:* £8,005,180
Registered Office: First Floor, Finchale House, Belmont Business Park, Durham, DH1 1TW
Activities: Other letting and operating of own or leased real estate
Officers: Helen Austin, Secretary; John Corbitt Barnsley [1948] Director/Accountant; Spencer Trerise Glanville [1972] Director; Robert William Jefferson [1950] Director/Chartered Accountant

Reial Property Investments Limited
Incorporated: 16 May 1947
Net Worth: £1,358,887 *Total Assets:* £2,029,950
Registered Office: 3rd Floor, Citygate, St James' Boulevard, Newcastle upon Tyne, NE1 4JE
Activities: Other letting and operating of own or leased real estate
Major Shareholder: Nicholas Baxter Ellis
Officers: Nicholas Baxter Ellis [1954] Director

Reid Street Primary School
Incorporated: 6 June 2011 *Employees:* 59
Net Worth: £1,660,000 *Total Assets:* £2,486,000
Registered Office: Reid Street Primary School, Reid Street, Darlington, Co Durham, DL3 6EX
Activities: Primary education
Officers: Angela Robinson, Secretary; Trevor Norman Alley [1953] Operations Director; Paula Anne Ayto [1966] Director/Principal of Reid Street Primary School; Catherine Bond [1987] Director; Tracey Charlton [1962] Director/Higher Level Teaching Assistant; Karina Faye Dare [1969] Director/Property Strategy Manager; Councillor Stephen James Harker [1963] Director/Software Designer; Jane Elizabeth Knowlson [1967] Director/Assistant Headteacher; Adrian Peter Marsh [1978] Director/Local Government Officer; Morvyn Anne Sanderson [1978] Director/Youth Worker; Carol Linda Saunders [1958] Director/Administration; Laura Margaret Swanston [1983] Director/Early Years Practitioner

Reiver Finance Limited
Incorporated: 20 August 2003
Net Worth Deficit: £66,144,000 *Total Assets:* £214,320,992
Registered Office: Northumbria House, Abbey Road, Pity Me, Durham, DH1 5FJ
Activities: Other business support service activities n.e.c.
Parent: Reiver Holdings Limited
Officers: Martin Parker, Secretary; Christopher Ian Johns [1970] Director/Accountant

Remondis JBT Limited
Incorporated: 13 March 2003 *Employees:* 148
Net Worth: £6,998,608 *Total Assets:* £12,655,831
Registered Office: Stephenson Way, Barrington Industrial Estate, Bedlington, Northumberland, NE22 7DL
Activities: Treatment and disposal of non-hazardous waste
Parent: Remondis Waste Solutions Ltd
Officers: Graham Andrew Palmer, Secretary; Graham Andrew Palmer [1971] Director; Steve Patterson [1968] Director; Christian Tauchmann [1985] Director [German]

Remondis Waste Solutions Limited
Incorporated: 13 January 1992 *Employees:* 1
Net Worth: £2,886,091 *Total Assets:* £11,428,393
Registered Office: Admin Office, Stephenson Way, Barrington Industrial Estate, Bedlington, Northumberland, NE22 7DL
Activities: Other business support service activities n.e.c.
Parent: Remondis International GmbH
Officers: Stephen Patterson [1968] Director; Christian Tauchmann [1985] Director [German]

Renaissance (Padiham) Limited
Incorporated: 17 January 2003 *Employees:* 4
Net Worth Deficit: £3,424,000 *Total Assets:* £1,944,000
Registered Office: West Terrace, Esh Winning, Co Durham, DH7 9PT
Activities: Development of building projects
Parent: Renaissance Land Regeneration Limited
Officers: Gregory Mark Liggins [1984] Director; Guy Warwick Pugh [1956] Director/Civil Engineer

Renaissance Land (D20) Limited
Incorporated: 10 October 2005 *Employees:* 5
Net Worth Deficit: £4,712,000 *Total Assets:* £1,697,000
Registered Office: West Terrace, Esh Winning, Co Durham, DH7 9PT
Activities: Development of building projects
Parent: Renaissance Land Regeneration Ltd
Officers: Gregory Mark Liggins [1984] Director; Guy Warwick Pugh [1956] Director/Civil Engineer

Renaissance Land Regeneration Limited
Incorporated: 19 January 2004 *Employees:* 148
Net Worth Deficit: £7,651,000 *Total Assets:* £2,744,000
Registered Office: West Terrace, Esh Winning, Co Durham, DH7 9PT
Activities: Development of building projects
Parent: C A Blackwell (Contracts) Ltd
Officers: Gregory Mark Liggins [1984] Director; Guy Warwick Pugh [1956] Director/Civil Engineer

Rend-Tech North East Ltd
Incorporated: 29 May 2009 *Employees:* 25
Net Worth: £667,131 *Total Assets:* £917,902
Registered Office: Bracken House, Salters Lane, Sedgefield, Stockton on Tees, Cleveland, TS21 3EE
Activities: Other building completion and finishing
Shareholders: Simon Nicholas Fletcher; Susan Fletcher
Officers: Simon Nicholas Fletcher [1972] Director; Susan Fletcher [1974] Director

Render Alarms Limited
Incorporated: 3 October 1989 *Employees:* 17
Net Worth: £461,303 *Total Assets:* £969,603
Registered Office: 6 Longlands Road, Longlands, Middlesbrough, Cleveland, TS4 2JL
Activities: Security systems service activities
Major Shareholder: Anthony Render
Officers: Wendy Hilary Render, Secretary; David Jon Almond [1963] Director/Engineer; Anthony Render [1953] Director/Alarm Engineer; Wendy Hilary Render [1953] Director/Administration; Geoffrey Michael Williams [1956] Director/Engineer

Rennyco Limited
Incorporated: 8 January 1986 *Employees:* 15
Net Worth: £602,997 *Total Assets:* £783,525
Registered Office: Westree Buildings, Whessoe Road, Darlington, Co Durham, DL3 0XE
Activities: Other construction installation
Major Shareholder: Mark Stephen Rennison
Officers: Mark Stephen Rennison [1962] Director/Farmer

Renolit (U.K.) Limited
Incorporated: 26 June 1978 *Employees:* 2
Net Worth: £27,839,000 *Total Assets:* £27,839,000
Registered Office: c/o Renolit Cramlington Limited, Station Road, Cramlington, Northumberland, NE23 8AQ
Activities: Activities of production holding companies
Officers: Simon Mark Wilson, Secretary; David Sean Hall [1963] Director/General Manager; Michael Thomas Kundel [1964] Director [German]

Renolit Cramlington Limited
Incorporated: 6 July 1925 *Employees:* 297
Net Worth: £23,408,000 *Total Assets:* £33,775,000
Registered Office: Station Road, Cramlington, Northumberland, NE23 8AQ
Activities: Manufacture of other plastic products
Parent: Renolit (U.K.) Limited
Officers: Simon Mark Wilson, Secretary; David Sean Hall [1963] Director/General Manager; Michael Thomas Kundel [1964] Director/Manager [German]; Simon Mark Wilson [1970] Director/Manager; Pierre Paul Marius Winant [1957] Director/Manager [Luxembourger]

Renown Engineering Limited
Incorporated: 17 February 1969 *Employees:* 89
Net Worth: £3,202,321 *Total Assets:* £5,632,902
Registered Office: Dudley Lane, Dudley, Cramlington, Northumberland, NE23 7RH
Activities: Manufacture of other fabricated metal products n.e.c.
Parent: Renown Group Limited
Officers: Katherine Carmichael Hamilton, Secretary; John Desmond Hamilton [1958] Director/Engineer; Katherine Carmichael Hamilton [1958] Director

Renown Group Limited
Incorporated: 20 July 2006 *Employees:* 153
Net Worth: £361,406 *Total Assets:* £4,900,273
Registered Office: Renown Engineering Ltd, Northumberland Business Park West, Cramlington, Northumberland, NE23 7RH
Activities: Dormant company
Major Shareholder: John Desmond Hamilton
Officers: Katherine Carmichael Hamilton, Secretary; James Henry Currer Briggs [1965] Director; John Desmond Hamilton [1958] Director/Engineer; Katherine Carmichael Hamilton [1958] Director

Replay Associates Limited
Incorporated: 14 July 2004
Net Worth: £7,284,349 *Total Assets:* £18,367,224
Registered Office: Old Vicarage, Spennithorne, Leyburn, N Yorks, DL8 5PR
Activities: Other letting and operating of own or leased real estate
Officers: Pamela Leathley, Secretary; Gordon Ian Leathley [1964] Director; Ian Leathley [1943] Director; John Winston Leathley [1969] Director; Kenneth Andrew Leathley [1967] Director; Pamela Leathley [1943] Director

Reproflex 3 Limited
Incorporated: 8 October 1996 *Employees:* 35
Net Worth: £217,305 *Total Assets:* £2,277,978
Registered Office: 27 Moorland Way, Nelson Park, Nelson Industrial Estate, Cramlington, Northumberland, NE23 1WE
Activities: Packaging activities
Shareholders: Andrew Graham Hewitson; Trevor Martin Lowes
Officers: Andrew Graham Hewitson, Secretary; Andrew Graham Hewitson [1974] Director; Trevor Martin Lowes [1966] Director

Resource Management Solutions (North East) Ltd
Incorporated: 9 November 2000 *Employees:* 35
Net Worth: £528,319 *Total Assets:* £3,517,428
Registered Office: 3 Victoria Road, Darlington, Co Durham, DL1 5SJ
Activities: Other activities of employment placement agencies
Officers: Leon Thomas Butt, Secretary; Carole Martin [1962] Director/Recruitment

Responsive Engineering Limited
Incorporated: 13 December 2002 *Employees:* 334
Net Worth: £6,513,360 *Total Assets:* £17,154,378
Registered Office: Armstrong Works, Scotswood Road, Newcastle upon Tyne, NE15 6UX
Activities: Manufacture of metal structures and parts of structures
Parent: Responsive Engineering (Holdings) Limited
Officers: Graeme Cook [1975] Managing Director; John Peter Reece [1961] Director

Restaurant Design Associates Ltd
Incorporated: 2 February 2007 *Employees:* 20
Net Worth: £545,819 *Total Assets:* £2,166,830
Registered Office: 5 Apollo Court, Monkton Business Park South, Hebburn, Tyne & Wear, NE31 2ES
Activities: Other professional, scientific and technical activities n.e.c.
Shareholders: Roy David Addyman; Judith Addyman
Officers: Neil Richard Addyman [1984] Director/Project Manager; Roy David Addyman [1956] Director; Alexander David Bradley [1986] Director/Commercial Manager; Nicholas Andrew George Bradley [1983] Director/Designer

Retirement Bridge Group Holdings Limited
Incorporated: 15 October 2015 *Employees:* 24
Net Worth: £102,513,000 *Total Assets:* £337,985,984
Registered Office: Cross House, Westgate Road, Newcastle upon Tyne, NE1 4XX
Activities: Buying and selling of own real estate
Parent: Retirement Bridge Investments Limited
Officers: Paul Trevor Barber [1967] Director; Stephen James Groves [1975] Director; Ashish Kashyap [1979] Director; Antony Lewis Pierce [1976] Finance Director

Retirement Bridge Housing Limited
Incorporated: 26 July 2006
Net Worth: £55,925,616 *Total Assets:* £90,830,944
Registered Office: Cross House, Westgate Road, Newcastle upon Tyne, NE1 4XX
Activities: Buying and selling of own real estate
Parent: Retirement Bridge Group Holdings Limited
Officers: Paul Trevor Barber [1967] Director; Antony Lewis Pierce [1976] Finance Director

Retirement Bridge Limited
Incorporated: 9 February 2005
Net Worth: £59,488,732 *Total Assets:* £59,488,732
Registered Office: Cross House, Westgate Road, Newcastle upon Tyne, NE1 4XX
Activities: Buying and selling of own real estate
Parent: Retirement Bridge Group Holdings Limited
Officers: Paul Trevor Barber [1967] Director; Ashish Kashyap [1979] Director; Antony Lewis Pierce [1976] Finance Director

Retirement Bridge Management Limited
Incorporated: 1 February 2005
Net Worth: £8,989,957 *Total Assets:* £9,031,718
Registered Office: Cross House, Westgate Road, Newcastle upon Tyne, NE1 4XX
Activities: Buying and selling of own real estate
Parent: Retirement Bridge Limited
Officers: Paul Trevor Barber [1967] Director; Ashish Kashyap [1979] Director; Antony Lewis Pierce [1976] Finance Director

Retirement Housing No. 1 (2007) Limited
Incorporated: 24 August 2007
Net Worth Deficit: £22,566,376 *Total Assets:* £28,889,856
Registered Office: Cross House, Westgate Road, Newcastle upon Tyne, NE1 4XX
Activities: Buying and selling of own real estate
Parent: Retirement Bridge Housing Limited
Officers: Paul Trevor Barber [1967] Director; Antony Lewis Pierce [1976] Finance Director

Rettig (UK) Limited
Incorporated: 23 March 1960 *Employees:* 315
Net Worth: £8,298,000 *Total Assets:* £36,897,000
Registered Office: Eastern Avenue, Team Valley Trading Estate, Gateshead, Tyne & Wear, NE11 0PG
Activities: Manufacture of central heating radiators and boilers
Parent: Rettig ICC BV
Officers: Tracy Hails, Secretary; Antonius Johannes Aarts [1969] Finance Director [Dutch]; Stig Bjorkqvist [1960] Director/Chief Finance Officer [Finnish]; Mike Conlon [1966] Group Managing Director; Linda Currie [1973] Director/Chief Personnel Officer; Barry Lynch [1975] Managing Director

Returnable Packaging Services Limited
Incorporated: 19 September 2002
Net Worth: £437,997 *Total Assets:* £1,194,564
Registered Office: Low Lane, Maltby, Middlesbrough, Cleveland, TS8 0BW
Activities: Packaging activities
Major Shareholder: Gary Hudson
Officers: Gary Hudson, Secretary/Management Consultant; Owen Heathcliffe Hines [1968] Business Development Director; Gary Hudson [1955] Director; Thomas Gary Hudson [1984] Marketing Director

Reversionary Assets 2 Limited
Incorporated: 12 October 2001
Net Worth: £156,343 *Total Assets:* £1,733,215
Registered Office: High Farm, Battersby, Middlesbrough, Cleveland, TS9 6LU
Activities: Buying and selling of own real estate
Shareholder: Paul Collins McInnes
Officers: Stefanie-Jayne McInnes, Secretary; Carl Hattersley [1963] Director/Surveyor; Paul Collins McInnes [1968] Director/Farmer; Richard Jonathan Rose [1958] Director

Reversions Financing (No.1) 2011 Limited
Incorporated: 22 September 2011
Net Worth: £19,663,612 *Total Assets:* £176,675,328
Registered Office: Cross House, Westgate Road, Newcastle upon Tyne, NE1 4XX
Activities: Other business support service activities n.e.c.
Parent: Reversions Financing Limited
Officers: Paul Trevor Barber [1967] Director; Antony Lewis Pierce [1976] Finance Director

Reversions Financing Limited
Incorporated: 22 September 2011
Net Worth: £48,233,416 *Total Assets:* £48,233,416
Registered Office: Cross House, Westgate Road, Newcastle upon Tyne, NE1 4XX
Activities: Other business support service activities n.e.c.
Parent: Retirement Bridge Group Holdings Limited
Officers: Paul Trevor Barber [1967] Director; Ashish Kashyap [1979] Director; Antony Lewis Pierce [1976] Finance Director

Reviloo Ltd
Incorporated: 4 March 2016
Net Worth: £4,199,207 *Total Assets:* £4,397,407
Registered Office: 27 Stargate Industrial Estate, Ryton, Tyne & Wear, NE40 3DG
Activities: Other building completion and finishing
Major Shareholder: Jamie Douglas
Officers: Jamie Douglas [1976] Director

Reynolds & Law (Stainless) Limited
Incorporated: 6 December 1984 *Employees:* 7
Net Worth: £918,115 *Total Assets:* £1,095,688
Registered Office: 59-69 Heaton Park Road, Newcastle upon Tyne, NE6 1SQ
Activities: Wholesale of metals and metal ores
Officers: Jill Mutch, Secretary; David George Mutch [1960] Director; Kevin Grant Mutch [1963] Director

RH Marine UK Ltd
Incorporated: 19 April 1996 *Employees:* 34
Net Worth: £1,154,000 *Total Assets:* £1,959,000
Registered Office: 409 Venture Court, Queens Meadow Business Park, Hartlepool, Cleveland, TS25 5TG
Activities: Repair and maintenance of ships and boats
Parent: RH Marine B.V
Officers: Stefan Jacobus Marinus Braat [1975] Finance Director [Dutch]; Hugo Alexander Loudon [1967] Managing Director [Dutch]

RHJ Maintenance Ltd
Incorporated: 9 November 2005
Net Worth: £479,310 *Total Assets:* £1,314,676
Registered Office: 246 Park View, Whitley Bay, Tyne & Wear, NE26 3QX
Activities: Non-trading company
Shareholders: Catherine Anne Jobson; Robert Henry Jobson
Officers: Catherine Anne Jobson, Secretary; Catherine Anne Jobson [1957] Director/Secretary; Robert Henry Jobson [1954] Director/Engineer

RI & Mr Ridley Limited
Incorporated: 16 February 2017 *Employees:* 4
Net Worth: £20,769 *Total Assets:* £754,675
Registered Office: Stokoe Rodger, St Matthews House, Haugh Lane, Hexham, Northumberland, NE46 3PU
Activities: Mixed farming
Parent: RIR (Farming & Vehicles) Limited
Officers: Donna Ridley, Secretary; Andrew John Ridley [1983] Director; Mary Rose Ridley [1948] Director; Robert Anthony Ridley [1978] Director; Robert Ridley [1948] Director/Farmer

Riba Enterprises Ltd
Incorporated: 28 April 1970 *Employees:* 257
Net Worth: £1,223,692 *Total Assets:* £14,732,381
Registered Office: The Old Post Office, St Nicholas Street, Newcastle upon Tyne, NE1 1RH
Activities: Retail sale via mail order houses or via Internet
Parent: Williams Topco Limited
Officers: Irena Dawn Peel, Secretary; Irena Dawn Peel [1969] Director/Chartered Accountant; Richard Paul Waterhouse [1966] Director/Chief Executive; Helen Lisa Whitfield [1968] Director/Accountant

Ribbon Academy Trust
Incorporated: 5 July 2012 *Employees:* 95
Net Worth: £2,823,000 *Total Assets:* £4,876,000
Registered Office: The Ribbon, Barnes Road, Seaham, Co Durham, SR7 9QR
Activities: Primary education
Officers: Stephen George Ball [1970] Director/Senior Lecturer; William Grant Burnett [1944] Director/Retired; Patricia Lynne Coulson [1970] Director/Learning and Development Manager; Amy Janet Duke [1992] Director/Teacher; Louise Victoria Hall [1968] Director/Police Officer; Michael Morton [1963] Director/Pharmacist; Vicky Patchett [1980] Director/Teacher; Victoria Ann Raby [1977] Director; Ashleigh Sheridan [1973] Director/Headteacher; Ian Stephenson [1970] Director/Local Government Officer

Ribchester Smith & Law Limited
Incorporated: 20 August 2013 *Employees:* 9
Net Worth: £613,558 *Total Assets:* £1,158,722
Registered Office: Sutherland House, 5-7 The Friars, Newcastle upon Tyne, NE1 5XE
Activities: Accounting and auditing activities
Shareholders: Wing Tak Jack Law; Josephine Lai Yung Law
Officers: David Maurice Armstrong [1960] Director/Chartered Accountant; John David Holloway [1970] Director/Chartered Accountant; Josephine Lai Yung Law [1956] Director/Accountant; Wing Tak Jack Law [1954] Director/Chartered Accountant; Robert William Ribchester [1981] Director/Chartered Accountant

Ribchesters Group Limited
Incorporated: 29 August 2013 *Employees:* 17
Net Worth: £622,591 *Total Assets:* £1,467,319
Registered Office: Finchale House, Belmont Business Park, Durham, DH1 1TW
Activities: Accounting and auditing activities
Shareholders: David Maurice Armstrong; John David Holloway
Officers: David Maurice Armstrong [1960] Director/Chartered Accountant; John David Holloway [1970] Director/Chartered Accountant; Robert William Ribchester [1981] Director/Chartered Accountant

P.C.Richardson & Co.(Middlesbrough),Limited
Incorporated: 11 March 1924 *Employees:* 48
Net Worth: £4,850,347 *Total Assets:* £5,803,552
Registered Office: Courville House, 34 Ellerbeck Court, Stokesley Business Park, Stokesley, Cleveland, TS9 5PT
Activities: Other specialised construction activities n.e.c.
Parent: PCR Holdings Limited
Officers: Paul Geoffrey Flintoft, Secretary; Geoffrey Ablett [1965] Director; David John Richardson [1968] Director; John Foster Richardson [1931] Director/Chairman; Peter Charles Richardson [1958] Managing Director; Teresa Beryl Richardson [1933] Director

Kevin Richardson Plantmasteruk Ltd
Incorporated: 24 October 2014 *Employees:* 2
Net Worth: £414,022 *Total Assets:* £1,181,571
Registered Office: Tower Farm, Ludworth, Co Durham, DH6 1NQ
Activities: Wholesale of mining, construction and civil engineering machinery
Major Shareholder: Kevin Alan Richardson
Officers: Kevin Alan Richardson [1963] Director/Dealer

Richmond Contracts Projects Limited
Incorporated: 2 April 2009 *Employees:* 16
Net Worth: £774,248 *Total Assets:* £1,082,886
Registered Office: 2 Thornfield Business Park, Standard Way, Northallerton, N Yorks, DL6 2XQ
Activities: Other building completion and finishing
Parent: RCP Holdings Limited
Officers: Peter Jagger [1950] Director; Christopher James Souter [1987] Director; Nicola Louise Walker [1976] Director

Richmond Fire Engineers Ltd
Incorporated: 16 March 1992 *Employees:* 17
Net Worth: £1,385,451 *Total Assets:* £2,024,853
Registered Office: 30 Firby Road, Gallowfields Trading Estate, Richmond, N Yorks, DL10 4ST
Activities: Other specialised construction activities n.e.c.
Parent: Richmond Fire Holdings Limited
Officers: Christopher Bryce Ryde [1977] Director; Lee John Smith [1972] Director

Richmond Foods Limited
Incorporated: 11 January 1991
Net Worth: £8,630,000 *Total Assets:* £66,526,000
Registered Office: Richmond House, Leeming Bar, Northallerton, N Yorks, DL7 9UL
Activities: Non-trading company
Parent: Ruby Acquisitions Limited
Officers: Marcello Mattia, Secretary; Phil Karl Griffin [1972] Director; Marcello Mattia [1965] Director [Italian]; Ibrahim Mahmood Ibrahim Najafi [1958] Director/Chief Operating Officer

Richmond UK Holdco Limited
Incorporated: 22 December 2016
Net Worth: £431,500,000 *Total Assets:* £1,699,299,968
Registered Office: 2nd Floor, One Gosforth Park Way, Gosforth Business Park, Newcastle upon Tyne, NE12 8ET
Activities: Activities of other holding companies n.e.c.
Parent: Richmond UK Top Holdco Limited
Officers: Judith Ann Archibold, Secretary; Chrisanth Werner Gradischnig [1984] Investment Director [Austrian]; Ian Kellett [1963] Director; Anthony David Morgan [1972] Managing Director; Simon Thomas Perry [1954] Director; Martin Anthony Robinson [1962] Director; John Anthony Waterworth [1961] Director/Chief Executive

Richmond UK Top Holdco Limited
Incorporated: 21 December 2016 *Employees:* 5,349
Net Worth: £431,500,000 *Total Assets:* £1,699,299,968
Registered Office: 2nd Floor, One Gosforth Park Way, Gosforth Business Park, Newcastle upon Tyne, NE12 8ET
Activities: Activities of other holding companies n.e.c.
Officers: Judith Ann Archibold, Secretary; Chrisanth Werner Gradischnig [1984] Investment Director [Austrian]; Ian Kellett [1963] Director; Anthony David Morgan [1972] Managing Director; Simon Thomas Perry [1954] Director; Martin Anthony Robinson [1962] Director; John Anthony Waterworth [1963] Director/Chief Executive

Richmondshire Building Preservation Trust Ltd
Incorporated: 15 January 2003 *Employees:* 9
Net Worth: £2,459,811 *Total Assets:* £2,523,840
Registered Office: The Station, Station Yard, Richmond, N Yorks, DL10 4LD
Activities: Other letting and operating of own or leased real estate
Officers: John Crossley Culpan, Secretary; Roger George Frier [1947] Director; James William Gravenor [1950] Director; John Philip Roger Harris [1942] Director/Retired Teacher; Ian Dennis Hepworth [1947] Director/Retired; June Margaret Mather [1959] Director/Chartered Surveyor; Catriona Marcia McLuckie [1951] Director/Business Proprietor; Dennis McLuckie [1953] Director and Project Manager; Margaret Joyce Steele [1960] Director/Chartered Surveyor; Philip Leonard James Upton [1956] Director; John Joseph Yates [1947] Director/Self Employed

Riddochhill Developments Limited
Incorporated: 31 March 2006
Net Worth: £2,503,389 *Total Assets:* £9,336,702
Registered Office: Stotforth Hill House, Windlestone, Rushyford, Co Durham, DL17 0NF
Activities: Development of building projects
Parent: Hall Construction Services Limited
Officers: Neville John Hall [1956] Director; Stephen Hall [1954] Director; Garry Hutchinson [1955] Director

Ringrose Properties Limited
Incorporated: 7 August 1995
Net Worth: £483,549 *Total Assets:* £989,888
Registered Office: Ottiwell Lodge, Snaizeholme, Hawes, N Yorks, DL8 3NB
Activities: Other letting and operating of own or leased real estate
Shareholders: Peter Borrie; Mark Borrie
Officers: Peter Borrie, Secretary; Mark Borrie [1965] Director; Peter Borrie [1962] Director/Farmer

Ringtons Holdings Limited
Incorporated: 17 November 1987 *Employees:* 622
Net Worth: £74,695,968 *Total Assets:* £97,098,616
Registered Office: Algernon Road, Newcastle upon Tyne, NE6 2YN
Activities: Tea processing
Officers: Peter Nigel Hastings Smith, Secretary; Colin John Smith [1961] Director; John David Smith [1951] Director; Peter Nigel Hastings Smith [1954] Director; Simon Montgomery Smith [1956] Director; Julia Clare Thompson [1979] Director

Ringtons Limited
Incorporated: 26 September 1956 *Employees:* 521
Net Worth: £24,096,112 *Total Assets:* £36,915,668
Registered Office: 10-22 Algernon Road, Heaton, Newcastle upon Tyne, NE6 2YN
Activities: Other retail sale not in stores, stalls or markets
Parent: Ringtons Holdings Limited
Officers: Peter Nigel Hastings Smith, Secretary; David Nicholas Brown [1964] Finance Director; Jonathan Richard Malton [1964] Director; Colin John Smith [1961] Production Director; John David Smith [1951] Director; Peter Nigel Hastings Smith [1954] Director; Simon Montgomery Smith [1956] Director; Julia Clare Thompson [1979] Director

Ritchie-Bland Estates Ltd
Incorporated: 28 March 2013 *Employees:* 5
Net Worth Deficit: £976,289 *Total Assets:* £2,582,549
Registered Office: Innovation House, Centurion Way, Darlington, Co Durham, DL3 0UP
Activities: Raising of horses and other equines
Major Shareholder: Gary Ritchie-Bland
Officers: Hazel Ritchie-Bland, Secretary; Gary Ritchie-Bland [1965] Director; Laura Ritchie-Bland [1992] Director

River Tees Multi-Academy Trust
Incorporated: 6 November 2015 *Employees:* 49
Net Worth: £3,906,447 *Total Assets:* £4,930,187
Registered Office: Complementary Education, Sulby Avenue, Middlesbrough, Cleveland, TS3 8RD
Activities: Other education n.e.c.
Officers: Mark Harrison Bruce [1959] Director/Retired; Leanne Victoria Chilton [1981] Director/Local Government Officer; Christina Jones [1967] Director; David Jones [1979] Director/Recruitment Consultant; Gary James MacDonald [1978] Finance Director; Jacqueline Lesley Robinson [1971] Finance Director; David Sanders [1956] Director/Retired

Riverdale Paper PLC
Incorporated: 30 March 1993 *Employees:* 50
Net Worth: £6,854,111 *Total Assets:* £9,387,097
Registered Office: Earlsway, Team Valley Trading Estate, Gateshead, Tyne & Wear, NE11 0RQ
Activities: Other service activities n.e.c.
Officers: Dorothy Riccalton, Secretary; Dorothy Riccalton [1948] Director/Company Secretary; Graeme Riccalton [1975] Production Director; Iain Riccalton [1978] Operations Director; Louise Marie Riccalton [1980] Director/Marketing Analyst; Stuart Riccalton [1948] Director/Paper Merchant; Victoria Claire Riccalton [1978] Director/Marketing Manager

Rivergreen Developments PLC
Incorporated: 14 July 1992 *Employees:* 18
Net Worth: £3,194,446 *Total Assets:* £5,577,173
Registered Office: The Rivergreen Centre, Aykley Heads, Durham, DH1 5TS
Activities: Development of building projects
Parent: Rivergreen Limited
Officers: Jeana Cobangbang Candler, Secretary; Peter Haswell Candler [1953] Director; Philip Anthony Ganley [1956] Director/Property Developer; Clive Leonard Oliphant [1956] Director/Chartered Engineer

Rivergreen Limited
Incorporated: 12 July 1995 *Employees:* 18
Net Worth: £4,849,124 *Total Assets:* £12,059,361
Registered Office: The Rivergreen Centre, Aykley Heads, Durham, DH1 5TS
Activities: Other letting and operating of own or leased real estate
Shareholders: Peter Haswell Candler; Philip Anthony Ganley
Officers: Jeana Cobangbang Candler, Secretary; Peter Haswell Candler [1953] Director; Philip Anthony Ganley [1956] Director

Rivermeade Signs Limited
Incorporated: 1 April 1997
Net Worth: £334,908 *Total Assets:* £2,127,367
Registered Office: Lancaster Road, Dunston, Gateshead, Tyne & Wear, NE11 9JG
Activities: Other manufacturing n.e.c.
Major Shareholder: Mark Graeme Harrison
Officers: Nigel Robert Ball, Secretary; Nigel Robert Ball [1966] Director; Mark Graeme Harrison [1964] Director; Peter Erling Wessel [1957] Director; Lindsay Charles John Wilcox [1947] Director

Riverside Acquisitions Limited
Incorporated: 19 July 2007
Net Worth Deficit: £4,985,123 *Total Assets:* £21,602,210
Registered Office: 4th Floor, Central Square, Forth Street, Newcastle upon Tyne, NE1 3PJ
Activities: Financial management
Parent: VCS (Holdings UK) Limited
Officers: Manolis Kotzabasakis [1959] Director [Greek]; Kelly E Lang [1961] Director/Chief Financial Officer/Accountant [American]

The Riverside Events LLP
Incorporated: 19 November 2009 *Employees:* 30
Net Worth: £220,374 *Total Assets:* £805,996
Registered Office: Emirates Durham International Cricket Ground, Riverside, Chester-le-Street, Co Durham, DH3 3QR

The Riverside Learning Trust
Incorporated: 23 October 2014
Net Worth: £18,188,272 *Total Assets:* £18,190,746
Registered Office: Walker Technology College, Waverdale Avenue, Walker, Newcastle upon Tyne, NE6 4AW
Activities: Other education n.e.c.
Officers: Michael Collier, Secretary; Michael Collier [1968] Director/Headteacher; Sheila Kingsland [1959] Director/Senior Advisor for SEN and Special Schools; Councillor David Leslie Wood [1948] Director/City Councillor

Riverside Leisure Promotions Limited
Incorporated: 3 April 1997
Net Worth: £338,213 *Total Assets:* £1,059,434
Registered Office: Unit 9A Cannon Park Way, Cannon Park Industrial Estate, Middlesbrough, Cleveland, TS1 5JU
Activities: Operation of arts facilities
Shareholder: John Edward Sidney Davey
Officers: Alma Davey, Secretary; John Derek Cooper [1963] Director/Manager; John Edward Sidney Davey [1949] Managing Director

Riverside Primary Academy
Incorporated: 13 June 2012 *Employees:* 46
Net Worth: £2,884,371 *Total Assets:* £3,586,922
Registered Office: Riverside Primary Academy, Colliery Road, Dunston, Gateshead, Tyne & Wear, NE11 9DX
Activities: Primary education
Officers: Gabrielle Teresa Rutherford, Secretary; Fiona Brown [1976] Director/Teaching Assistant; Joanne Earl [1974] Director/Trainee Teacher; Elizabeth Fearon [1970] Director/Civil Servant; Julie Marie Goodfellow [1965] Director/Headteacher; Paul Stephen Marshall [1976] Director/Facilities Manager; John McGowan [1949] Director/Retired; Robin William Purser [1983] Director/Head of Business Support; Linda Robinson [1957] Director/Retired; Gabrielle Teresa Rutherford [1962] Director/Business Manager; Lieanne Smith [1979] Director/Teacher; Paul Arthur Tomlinson [1956] Director

Riviera Acquisitions Limited
Incorporated: 22 March 2013 *Employees:* 2
Net Worth Deficit: £37,994,392 *Total Assets:* £272,101,152
Registered Office: Richmond House, Leeming Bar, Northallerton, N Yorks, DL7 9UL
Activities: Activities of production holding companies
Parent: Riviera Topco Limited
Officers: Marcello Mattia, Secretary; Phil Griffin [1972] Director; Marcello Mattia [1965] Director [Italian]; Ibrahim Mahmood Ibrahim Najafi [1958] Director

Riviera Topco Limited
Incorporated: 22 March 2013
Net Worth: £10,496 *Total Assets:* £254,074,176
Registered Office: Richmond House, Leeming Bar, Northallerton, N Yorks, DL7 9UL
Activities: Activities of production holding companies
Officers: Marcello Mattia, Secretary; Philip Karl Griffin [1972] Director; Marcello Mattia [1965] Director [Italian]; Ibrahim Mahmood Ibrahim Najafi [1958] Director

RJY Investments (North East) Ltd
Incorporated: 14 July 2014
Net Worth: £204,210 *Total Assets:* £772,115
Registered Office: c/o Teescraft Engineering Ltd, 1-3 Longfield Road, South Church Enterprise Park, Bishop Auckland, Co Durham, DL14 6XB
Activities: Activities of other holding companies n.e.c.
Major Shareholder: Robert John Yorke
Officers: John Clifford Laverick, Secretary; Robert John Yorke [1971] Director

RLDOM Ltd
Incorporated: 2 June 2006
Net Worth: £53,388 *Total Assets:* £789,102
Registered Office: AKV Buildings, Hackworth Industrial Park, Shildon, Co Durham, DL4 1HF
Activities: Other letting and operating of own or leased real estate
Officers: Robert Leslie Dominick [1963] Director/Publican; Kevin Michael Everitt [1958] Director

RMB Automotive Ltd
Incorporated: 23 April 2003 *Employees:* 183
Net Worth: £3,619,065 *Total Assets:* £19,749,696
Registered Office: RMB Automotive Limited, Cygnet Drive, Bowesfield Farm, Stockton-on-Tees, Cleveland, TS18 3DZ
Activities: Sale of new cars and light motor vehicles
Shareholders: Robert Douglas Bennett; Morag Bennett
Officers: Sarah Waddington, Secretary/Accountant; Morag Bennett [1966] Director/Marketing Manager; Robert Bennett [1957] Director/Self Employed; Sarah Waddington [1971] Finance Director

RMH Lamps, Lighting & Electrical Limited
Incorporated: 16 November 2006 *Employees:* 15
Net Worth: £769,082 *Total Assets:* £959,946
Registered Office: Unit 8c Spectrum Business Park, Seaham, Co Durham, SR7 7PS
Activities: Electrical installation
Major Shareholder: Michael Harries
Officers: Michael Harries [1979] Director/Lamps, Lighting and Electrical

RMT Accountants & Business Advisors Ltd
Incorporated: 22 December 2006 *Employees:* 66
Net Worth: £1,010,932 *Total Assets:* £2,823,902
Registered Office: RMT, Gosforth Park Avenue, Newcastle upon Tyne, NE12 8EG
Activities: Accounting and auditing activities
Shareholders: Michael Andrew Pott; Stephen Derek Slater; Julie Maxine Pott
Officers: Julie Maxine Pott, Secretary; Anthony Andreasen [1978] Tax Director; Paul Robert Gainford [1977] Director/Accountant; Richard Willoughby Humphreys [1970] Director/Tax Advisor; Julie Maxine Pott [1958] Director/Chartered Accountant; Michael Andrew Pott [1962] Director/Accountant; Stephen Derek Slater [1968] Director/Chartered Accountant

Ro-Bal Steel Fabrications Limited
Incorporated: 26 February 2009 *Employees:* 15
Net Worth: £755,457 *Total Assets:* £1,700,752
Registered Office: 20-22 Brindley Road, Hertburn Estate, Hertburn, Washington, Tyne & Wear, NE37 2SF
Activities: Other construction installation
Major Shareholder: Roberto Balzi
Officers: Roberto Balzi, Secretary; Roberto Balzi [1973] Director/Steel Fabricator

Road Link (A69) Limited
Incorporated: 14 November 1995 *Employees:* 11
Net Worth: £1,710,621 *Total Assets:* £6,928,667
Registered Office: Stocksfield Hall, Stocksfield, Northumberland, NE43 7TN
Activities: Other urban, suburban or metropolitan passenger land transport (not underground, metro or similar)
Parent: Roadlink (A69) Holdings Ltd
Officers: Clive Robert Franklin, Secretary; Simon Alexander Carr [1958] Director; John Kenneth Fowler [1963] Director/Chartered Accountant; Gianluigi Geddo [1958] Director/Manager [Italian]; John Trevor Sutcliffe [1959] Director

Roade Windfarm Limited
Incorporated: 7 June 2013
Net Worth: £4,560,000 *Total Assets:* £12,776,000
Registered Office: Alexander House, 1 Mandarin Road, Rainton Bridge Business Park, Houghton-le-Spring, Co Durham, DH4 5RA
Activities: Production of electricity
Parent: EDF Energy Renewables Holdings Limited
Officers: Susan Elizabeth Lind, Secretary; Matthieu Thomas Hue [1975] Director [French]; Hassaan Majid [1968] Director

Roadsafe Corporate Group Limited
Incorporated: 6 July 2012 *Employees:* 91
Net Worth: £321,938 *Total Assets:* £1,676,600
Registered Office: Railsafe House, Whiteley Road, Blaydon, Tyne & Wear, NE21 5NJ
Activities: Other specialised construction activities n.e.c.
Major Shareholder: Peter Scott
Officers: Peter Scott [1961] Director

Roballo Engineering Company Limited
Incorporated: 24 November 1975 *Employees:* 62
Net Worth: £2,325,000 *Total Assets:* £7,541,000
Registered Office: Mill Hill, North West Industrial Estate, Peterlee, Co Durham, SR8 2HR
Activities: Manufacture of bearings, gears, gearing and driving elements
Parent: Thyssenkrupp UK PLC
Officers: Julie Elizabeth Cripps, Secretary; Edward Francis Flood [1960] Managing Director; Winfried Schulte [1964] Director/Executive Board [German]; Arno Karl Schuppert [1957] Director/Executive Board [German]; Wilfried Otto Spintig [1963] Director Production [German]

Robert and Roberts Limited
Incorporated: 14 February 2006 *Employees:* 23
Net Worth: £2,992 *Total Assets:* £2,504,729
Registered Office: Neville Pharmacy, 6 Neville Parade, Newton Aycliffe, Co Durham, DL5 5DH
Activities: Dispensing chemist in specialised stores
Major Shareholder: Robert Michael Pitt
Officers: Gemma Katherine Pitt, Secretary; Robert Michael Pitt [1976] Director/Pharmacist

David Robert Limited
Incorporated: 1 September 2006 *Employees:* 4
Net Worth: £115,482 *Total Assets:* £1,128,629
Registered Office: St Matthews House, Haugh Lane, Hexham, Northumberland, NE46 3PU
Activities: Buying and selling of own real estate
Shareholders: Alistair Robert Knowles; Jonathan David Knowles
Officers: Susan Knowles, Secretary; Alistair Robert Knowles [1978] Director/Builder; Jonathan David Knowles [1982] Director/Builder

Robertson Simpson Limited
Incorporated: 6 March 2002
Net Worth: £1,027,418 *Total Assets:* £2,232,824
Registered Office: Unit 4 Staithes, The Watermark, Gateshead, Tyne & Wear, NE11 9SN
Activities: Architectural activities
Parent: Robertson Simpson Group Limited
Officers: Alison Robertson, Secretary; Alison Robertson [1971] Director/Accountant; Richard Mark Robertson [1972] Director/Building Surveyor; Paul James Tully [1980] Director

Robinson Construction Limited
Incorporated: 6 February 2004
Net Worth: £289,780 *Total Assets:* £1,077,898
Registered Office: 54 Racecourse Road, Gallowfields Trading Estate, Richmond, N Yorks, DL10 4TG
Activities: Other specialised construction activities n.e.c.
Shareholders: Amanda Robinson; Graham Adam Robinson
Officers: Amanda Robinson, Secretary; Amanda Robinson [1964] Director; Graham Adam Robinson [1966] Director

Robinson Dane Limited
Incorporated: 9 April 2001 *Employees:* 1
Net Worth: £1,482,847 *Total Assets:* £1,627,046
Registered Office: Bulman House, Regent Centre, Gosforth, Newcastle upon Tyne, NE3 3LS
Activities: Other business support service activities n.e.c.
Major Shareholder: Christine Mary Robinson
Officers: Christine Mary Robinson [1946] Director

Gus Robinson Developments Limited
Incorporated: 15 January 1982 *Employees:* 43
Net Worth: £815,856 *Total Assets:* £4,718,497
Registered Office: Stranton House, West View Road, Hartlepool, Cleveland, TS24 0BW
Activities: Development of building projects
Major Shareholder: Daniel Augustine Robinson
Officers: Judith Robinson, Secretary; Jeanette Henderson [1965] Finance Director; Judith Robinson [1951] Director

C G Robinson Limited
Incorporated: 18 March 2003
Net Worth: £2,575,935 *Total Assets:* £6,638,184
Registered Office: Robinson Plant Hire, Sandy Leas Lane, Elton, Stockton-on-Tees, Cleveland, TS21 1BT
Activities: Other specialised construction activities n.e.c.
Major Shareholder: Craig Gareth Robinson
Officers: Dulcie Robinson, Secretary; Craig Gareth Robinson [1972] Director/Plant Dealer

F. Peter Robinson Limited
Incorporated: 16 July 1957 *Employees:* 8
Net Worth: £2,989,958 *Total Assets:* £6,250,694
Registered Office: Northumberland Street, Darlington, Co Durham, DL3 7HJ
Activities: Other letting and operating of own or leased real estate
Shareholders: Frederick Peter Robinson; Stephanie Jane Robinson
Officers: Heather Viveca Choules, Secretary; David Philip Elstob [1984] Director/Chartered Surveyor; Frederick Peter Robinson [1954] Director/Auctioneer; Stephanie Jane Robinson [1966] Director/Broadcast Journalist

Geoffrey Robinson Limited
Incorporated: 16 February 1972 *Employees:* 115
Net Worth: £2,038,720 *Total Assets:* £6,047,398
Registered Office: Macklin Avenue, Cowpen Industrial Estate, Billingham, Cleveland, TS23 4ET
Activities: Electrical installation
Major Shareholder: Geoffrey Robinson
Officers: Susan Patricia Bentley, Secretary; Geoffrey Robinson [1946] Director/Chairman; Neal Geoffrey Robinson [1969] Managing Director; James Smithson [1961] Director; John Twigger [1956] Director; Paul Ronald Walker [1966] Operations Director

Walton Robinson Ltd
Incorporated: 16 February 2000
Net Worth: £1,185,018 *Total Assets:* £1,317,728
Registered Office: 101 Percy Street, Newcastle upon Tyne, NE1 7RY
Activities: Management of real estate on a fee or contract basis
Parent: Westlands Acquisitions Limited
Officers: Richard Paul Ponton, Secretary; Jaimie Lawton [1977] Director; Richard Paul Ponton [1977] Director; Mark Smith [1988] Director/General Manager; Mark Adam Walton [1974] Director/Property Management

Brian Robinson Machinery Limited
Incorporated: 21 October 2004 *Employees:* 23
Net Worth: £176,813 *Total Assets:* £1,877,564
Registered Office: Bungalow Farm, Birkby Lane, East Cowton, Northallerton, N Yorks, DL7 0DX
Activities: Wholesale of agricultural machinery, equipment and supplies
Shareholders: Brian Derrick Robinson; Christine Michelle Robinson
Officers: Brian Derrick Robinson [1960] Director

Robinsons Darlington LLP
Incorporated: 20 March 2012
Registered Office: 19a Old Elvet, Durham, DH1 3HL
Officers: George Robinson [1957] Member; Simon Anthony Wright [1961] Member

Robinsons Durham Limited
Incorporated: 21 February 2012 *Employees:* 69
Net Worth: £1,379,509 *Total Assets:* £1,629,044
Registered Office: 19a Old Elvet, Durham, DH1 3HL
Activities: Real estate agencies
Officers: Sharon Ann Turnbull, Secretary; George Robinson [1957] Director/Estate Agent; Pamela Fay Robinson [1956] Director/Estate Agent

Robinsons Tees Valley Ltd
Incorporated: 19 October 2000
Net Worth: £1,597,649 *Total Assets:* £1,857,291
Registered Office: 19a Old Elvet, Durham, DH1 3HL
Activities: Real estate agencies
Shareholders: George Robinson; Simon Anthony Wright
Officers: Simon Wright, Secretary; George Robinson [1957] Director; Simon Anthony Wright [1961] Director

W. Robson (Farm) Limited
Incorporated: 24 December 1985 *Employees:* 4
Net Worth: £1,776,777 *Total Assets:* £2,195,996
Registered Office: High Westhouse Farm, Tow Law, Bishop Auckland, Co Durham, DL13 4DE
Activities: Raising of dairy cattle
Shareholders: William Robson; Daphnie Robson
Officers: Daphne Robson, Secretary; Daphne Robson [1951] Director/Secretary; William Robson [1948] Director/Builder

M R Robson Electricity Services Ltd
Incorporated: 14 March 2006 *Employees:* 9
Net Worth: £3,222,388 *Total Assets:* £3,446,554
Registered Office: High Swinhope Shield, Sparty Lea, Hexham, Northumberland, NE47 9UU
Activities: Development of building projects
Shareholders: Michael Renwick Robson; Alison Robson
Officers: Alison Robson, Secretary; Alison Robson [1963] Director/Secretary; Michael Renwick Robson [1958] Director/Contractor

Robson Laidler Accountants Limited
Incorporated: 25 June 2015 *Employees:* 63
Net Worth: £1,008 *Total Assets:* £2,336,326
Registered Office: Fernwood House, Fernwood Road, Jesmond, Newcastle upon Tyne, NE2 1TJ
Activities: Accounting and auditing activities
Officers: Peter Charles [1966] Director/Chartered Accountant; Edwin Constable [1959] Director/Certified Chartered Accountant; Michael Thomas Moran [1971] Director/Chartered Accountant; Amy Park [1985] Director/Chartered Accountant; Graham Martin Purvis [1966] Director/Tax Advisor; Michael Smith [1983] Director/Accountant; Martin Wardle [1976] Director/Chartered Tax Adviser

Robsons General Wares Limited
Incorporated: 17 March 1955 *Employees:* 2
Net Worth: £597,780 *Total Assets:* £762,632
Registered Office: Stephenson House, Richard Street, Hetton-le-Hole, Co Durham, DH5 9HW
Activities: Other letting and operating of own or leased real estate
Major Shareholder: Lynda Hedley
Officers: Lisa Deborah Graham, Secretary; Lynda Hedley [1948] Director/Manageress

Rock Farms Limited
Incorporated: 8 January 1957 *Employees:* 11
Net Worth: £1,100,062 *Total Assets:* £1,709,714
Registered Office: Rock, Alnwick, Northumberland, NE66 3SE
Activities: Growing of cereals (except rice), leguminous crops and oil seeds
Shareholders: Charles Jay Bosanquet; Frederick Charles Bosanquet; Lalage Ann Bosanquet; Frederick Charles Bosanquet
Officers: Charles Jay Bosanquet, Secretary; Charles Jay Bosanquet [1949] Director/Landowner & Farmer; Frederick Charles Bosanquet [1981] Director/Teacher; Lalage Ann Bosanquet [1949] Director/Teacher; Theodore William Bosanquet [1983] Director/Journalist; Octavia Lucy Gilmour [1984] Director/Student

Rock Haulage Limited
Incorporated: 8 August 2005 *Employees:* 15
Net Worth: £453,780 *Total Assets:* £766,308
Registered Office: Rock NAB, Rock, Alnwick, Northumberland, NE66 2TL
Activities: Freight transport by road
Major Shareholder: William David Purvis
Officers: William David Purvis, Secretary; William David Purvis [1950] Director/Haulier

Rockbit UK Limited
Incorporated: 15 April 2003
Net Worth: £455,864 *Total Assets:* £1,249,516
Registered Office: Units 2b & 2c Buddle Industrial Estate, Benton Way, Wallsend, Tyne & Wear, NE28 6DL
Activities: Manufacture of other fabricated metal products n.e.c.
Officers: David Geoffrey Morley, Secretary; John Paul Cravagan [1984] Operations Director; David Geoffrey Morley [1969] Managing Director

Rockliffe Court Healthcare Limited
Incorporated: 22 July 1997
Net Worth: £773,744 *Total Assets:* £854,689
Registered Office: 29 The Green, Hurworth on Tees, Co Durham, DL2 2AA
Activities: Dispensing chemist in specialised stores
Shareholders: Dr Ian Michael Murray Bagshaw; Dr Victoria Bagshaw; Dr Gillian Barbara Glyn Williams
Officers: Dr Gillian Barbara Glyn Williams, Secretary/Medical Practitioner; Dr Ian Michael Murray Bagshaw [1941] Director/Medical Practitioner; Victoria Bagshaw [1943] Director/Practice Manager; Dr Gillian Barbara Glyn Williams [1956] Director/Medical Practitioner

Rockliffe Hall Limited
Incorporated: 19 October 2006 *Employees:* 321
Net Worth: £27,397,000 *Total Assets:* £71,100,000
Registered Office: Rockliffe Hall, Hurworth on Tees, Darlington, Co Durham, DL2 2DU
Activities: Hotels and similar accommodation
Parent: The Gibson O'Neill Company Limited
Officers: Jeremy Robin Bloom, Secretary; Jeremy Robin Bloom [1957] Director; Anthony Warwick Brindle [1950] Director; Stephen Gibson [1958] Director

Roflow Limited
Incorporated: 2 July 1990 *Employees:* 40
Net Worth: £410,497 *Total Assets:* £1,358,738
Registered Office: 6 Hanlon Court, Royal Industrial Estate, Jarrow, Tyne & Wear, NE32 3HR
Activities: Manufacture of metal structures and parts of structures
Major Shareholder: Thomas Pringle Robson
Officers: Gillian Robson, Secretary; Thomas Pringle Robson [1962] Engineer Director

Mike Rogerson Estate Agents Limited
Incorporated: 10 January 2001
Net Worth: £264,260 *Total Assets:* £1,266,758
Registered Office: 16 Laburnum Terrace, Ashington, Northumberland, NE63 0XX
Activities: Real estate agencies
Major Shareholder: Michael George Rogerson
Officers: Jean Rogerson, Secretary; Michael George Rogerson [1968] Director/Surveyor

Rohni's International Limited
Incorporated: 12 April 2002
Net Worth: £1,938,725 *Total Assets:* £3,253,066
Registered Office: 75-76 Baker Road, Nelson Park West, Cramlington, Northumberland, NE23 1WL
Activities: Wholesale of clothing and footwear
Shareholder: Rajesh Kumar Thamman
Officers: Rita Rani Thamman, Secretary; Prem Lata Thamman [1967] Director; Rajesh Kumar Thamman [1962] Director/Wholesaler; Rita Rani Thamman [1953] Director

Rokshaw Limited
Incorporated: 24 July 2012 *Employees:* 39
Net Worth: £57,000 *Total Assets:* £1,355,438
Registered Office: Unit 5a East Way, Rivergreen Industrial Estate, Sunderland, Tyne & Wear, SR4 6AD
Activities: Other professional, scientific and technical activities n.e.c.
Shareholders: Richard James Hodgson; Jonathan Simon Hodgson; Jonathan Simon Hodgson; Richard James Hodgson
Officers: Jonathan Simon Hodgson [1976] Director; Richard James Hodgson [1979] Sales Director

Romag PPM Limited
Incorporated: 30 January 2010 *Employees:* 5
Net Worth: £3,285,850 *Total Assets:* £3,491,702
Registered Office: Leadgate Industrial Estate, Lope Hill Road, Consett, Co Durham, DH8 7RS
Activities: Other manufacturing n.e.c.
Parent: Romag Holdings Limited
Officers: Paul Cruddace [1968] Sales Director

Romaldrose Limited
Incorporated: 31 August 2012 *Employees:* 25
Net Worth Deficit: £233,143 *Total Assets:* £939,763
Registered Office: Headlam Hall Hotel, Headlam, Gainford, Darlington, Co Durham, DL2 3HA
Activities: Hotels and similar accommodation
Parent: Headlam Leisure Limited
Officers: Suzanne Clare Metcalfe, Secretary; Cheryl Dawn Robinson [1976] Director; John Hugh Robinson [1937] Director/Farmer & Hotelier; Thomas Giles John Robinson [1971] Managing Director

Roman Limited
Incorporated: 27 October 1987 *Employees:* 206
Net Worth: £4,478,950 *Total Assets:* £11,222,885
Registered Office: Whitworth Avenue, Aycliffe Industrial Park, Newton Aycliffe, Co Durham, DL5 6YN
Activities: Other manufacturing n.e.c.
Officers: Deborah Louise Green, Company Secretary; Jonathan Malcolm Franks [1961] Finance Director; David Charles Osborne [1970] Sales Director; Generald Charles Osborne [1940] Chairman/Director; Kathryn Isabelle Osborne [1967] Director; Pamela Osborne [1932] Director; Julian Pearson [1968] Commercial Director; Simon Marc Teasdale [1963] Sales Director; John Wright [1956] Operations Director

Romanby Golf Course Limited
Incorporated: 23 September 1991 *Employees:* 16
Net Worth: £1,582,522 *Total Assets:* £2,496,812
Registered Office: Yafforth Road, Romanby, Northallerton, N Yorks, DL7 0PE
Activities: Other sports activities
Shareholder: Brian William Craven
Officers: Brian William Craven, Secretary; Wouter Boomsma [1947] Executive Director [Dutch]; Brian William Craven [1954] Director

Romano's Limited
Incorporated: 21 January 1999
Net Worth: £703,686 *Total Assets:* £872,902
Registered Office: 63 Front Street, Cleadon, Sunderland, Tyne & Wear, SR6 7PG
Activities: Licenced restaurants
Shareholders: Paolo Minchella; Romano Antonio Minchella
Officers: Paolo Minchella, Secretary/Restaurant; Paolo Minchella [1957] Director/Restaurateur; Romano Antonio Minchella [1949] Director/Restaurateur

Romero Catholic Education Trust
Incorporated: 4 November 2011 *Employees:* 172
Net Worth: £445,811 *Total Assets:* £3,602,377
Registered Office: St John's Catholic School and Sixth Form College, Woodhouse Lane, Bishop Auckland, Co Durham, DL14 6JT
Activities: General secondary education
Officers: Victoria Anne Howard, Secretary; Anthony Patrick Byrne [1955] Director/NHS Manager; Lisa Marie Byron-Ledwith [1969] Director/Headteacher; Joanna Foster [1975] Director/Civil Servant; Alan Gregory [1944] Director/Retired; Bob Hall [1944] Director/Retired; David Hart [1967] Director/Procurement Management; Geoffrey David O'Hehir [1947] Director/Certified Chartered Accountant; Lawrence Albert Petterson [1955] Director/Solicitor; Generald Summerbell [1947] Director/Retired; Dennis Tindall [1946] Director/Catholic Priest; Ann Mary Wake [1953] Director/Retired; Mary Wood [1945] Director/Retired

George Ronald Limited
Incorporated: 3 March 2008 *Employees:* 52
Net Worth: £559,424 *Total Assets:* £2,819,798
Registered Office: 22 Foyle Street, Sunderland, Tyne & Wear, SR1 1LE
Activities: Other residential care activities n.e.c.
Shareholder: Paul Martyn Stafford
Officers: Janet Stafford, Secretary; Paul Martyn Stafford [1955] Director/Chartered Accountant

Ronan Engineering Limited
Incorporated: 1 June 1977 *Employees:* 5
Net Worth: £1,362,344 *Total Assets:* £1,487,958
Registered Office: 1 Tilley Road, Crowther Industrial Estate, Washington, Tyne & Wear, NE38 0AE
Activities: Manufacture of electronic industrial process control equipment
Major Shareholder: John Adrian Hewitson
Officers: John Adrian Hewitson [1925] Director/Engineer [American]

Ronbar Factors Limited
Incorporated: 15 February 1977 *Employees:* 33
Net Worth: £4,952,857 *Total Assets:* £7,040,629
Registered Office: 2 Crowther Road, Crowther Industrial Estate, Washington, Tyne & Wear, NE38 0AQ
Activities: Manufacture of other electrical equipment
Major Shareholder: Margaret Gibbon Buckingham
Officers: Tracey Dembry, Secretary; Darren Buckingham [1971] Managing Director; Margaret Gibbon Buckingham [1934] Director/Secretary; Tracey Dembry [1965] Director/Financial Controller; Margaret Lynne Ebdale [1956] Director/Logistics Manager

Ronco Engineering Limited
Incorporated: 17 February 1992 *Employees:* 30
Net Worth: £538,678 *Total Assets:* £1,285,043
Registered Office: Unit 1 Bowburn North Industrial Estate, Bowburn, Co Durham, DH6 5PF
Activities: Manufacture of basic iron and steel and of ferro-alloys
Parent: Altec Engineering Limited
Officers: Martin Reid, Secretary; Simon Alexander McIntosh [1965] Director/Certified Chartered Accountant; Alastair Waite [1960] Director

Ronsbrook Services Limited
Incorporated: 6 June 1995 *Employees:* 1
Net Worth: £4,080,095 *Total Assets:* £5,423,197
Registered Office: 37 Belsay Gardens, Fawdon, Newcastle upon Tyne, NE3 2AU
Activities: Renting and operating of Housing Association real estate
Shareholders: Zahir Ahmad; Saghir Ahmad
Officers: Zahir Ahmad, Secretary; Saghir Ahmad [1951] Director; Zahir Ahmad [1946] Director

The Roof Truss Company (Northern) Ltd
Incorporated: 16 May 1991 *Employees:* 27
Net Worth: £1,046,106 *Total Assets:* £1,844,657
Registered Office: 2 Rainhill Close, Stephenson Industrial Estate, Washington, Tyne & Wear, NE37 3HU
Activities: Other manufacturing n.e.c.
Major Shareholder: Kevin Gray
Officers: Kevin Gray [1957] Director; Lisa Marie Short [1975] Director/Finance Manager

Rooster Enterprises Limited
Incorporated: 23 September 2005
Net Worth: £127,996 *Total Assets:* £1,191,496
Registered Office: Unit 7 Hatfield Way, South Church Enterprise Park, Bishop Auckland, Co Durham, DL14 6XF
Activities: Activities of other holding companies n.e.c.
Parent: Gilbertson & Page Limited
Officers: Kim Kong Wong, Secretary; Alexander Joseph Dale [1957] Director; Christopher Arthur Cory Ware [1972] Director; Richard Ivor Wakefield Ware [1939] Director; Kim Kong Wong [1959] Director [Malaysian]

Rootwise Limited
Incorporated: 9 March 2004 *Employees:* 3
Net Worth: £626,538 *Total Assets:* £941,722
Registered Office: Cote Hill Farm, Caldwell, Richmond, N Yorks, DL11 7UA
Activities: Retail sale of flowers, plants, seeds, fertilizers, pet animals and pet food in specialised stores
Shareholder: Gordon William Coggrave
Officers: Deborah Anne Coggrave, Secretary; Deborah Anne Coggrave [1955] Director; Gordon William Coggrave [1955] Director/Farmer

Ropers Caravan World (Catterick) Limited
Incorporated: 26 March 2009
Net Worth: £1,659,629 *Total Assets:* £1,860,959
Registered Office: Gatherley Road, Catterick Bridge, Richmond, N Yorks, DL10 7SL
Activities: Other retail sale of new goods in specialised stores (not commercial art galleries and opticians)
Parent: Ropers Leisure Limited
Officers: Roger Michael Roper, Secretary; Richard Simon Roper [1964] Director; Roger Michael Roper [1962] Director

Ropers Leisure Limited
Incorporated: 26 March 2009 *Employees:* 30
Net Worth: £450,315 *Total Assets:* £1,579,523
Registered Office: Gatherley Road, Catterick Bridge, Richmond, N Yorks, DL10 7SL
Activities: Other retail sale of new goods in specialised stores (not commercial art galleries and opticians)
Shareholders: Roger Michael Roper; Richard Simon Roper
Officers: Roger Michael Roper, Secretary; Margaret Roper [1937] Director; Richard Simon Roper [1964] Director; Roger Michael Roper [1962] Director

Rose Wood Academy
Incorporated: 5 December 2013 *Employees:* 57
Net Worth: £3,010,000 *Total Assets:* £3,544,000
Registered Office: Rose Wood Academy, The Garth, Coulby Farm Way, Coulby Newham, Middlesbrough, Cleveland, TS8 0UG
Activities: Primary education
Officers: Catherine Barnett [1975] Director/Housewife; Lisa Anne Carney [1972] Director/Deputy Headteacher; Paul Cowley [1972] Director/Headmaster; Robert William Lacy [1968] Director/Business Executive; Helen Claire Malbon [1972] Director/Headteacher; Jill Patterson [1960] Director/Teacher; Linda Seaman [1962] Director/HLTA; Sarah Louise Slater [1977] Director

Roseberry Care Centres GB Limited
Incorporated: 15 June 2007 *Employees:* 1,155
Net Worth Deficit: £266,704 *Total Assets:* £3,233,534
Registered Office: Roseberry Care Centres GB Ltd, 1st Floor, Valley View Care Centres, Back Lane, Penshaw, Houghton-le-Spring, Co Durham, DH4 7ER
Activities: Residential care activities for the elderly and disabled
Major Shareholder: Ronald Michael McNamara
Officers: Marie Summerson, Secretary; Elaine McNamara [1965] Director; Ronald Michael McNamara [1959] Director/Chief Executive [Irish]

Roseberry Specialist Care Centres Limited
Incorporated: 7 August 2009 *Employees:* 23
Net Worth Deficit: £262,935 *Total Assets:* £1,070,253
Registered Office: Roseberry Specialist Care Centres, 1st Floor, Valley View Care Centres, Back Lane, Penshaw, Houghton-le-Spring, Co Durham, DH4 7ER
Activities: Other residential care activities n.e.c.
Major Shareholder: Ronald Michael McNamara
Officers: Marie Summerson, Secretary; Elaine McNamara [1965] Director/Chairman; Leanne McNamara [1983] Director/Head of HR; Ronald Michael McNamara [1959] Director/Chief Executive [Irish]

Rosedene Nurseries Limited
Incorporated: 12 March 2002 *Employees:* 161
Net Worth: £392,243 *Total Assets:* £917,461
Registered Office: Hemlington Initiative Centre, Cass House Road, Hemlington, Middlesbrough, Cleveland, TS8 9QW
Activities: Pre-primary education
Shareholders: John Michael McCullagh; Clare Alexis McCullagh
Officers: Alice Sarah McCullagh [1991] Director; Clare Alexis McCullagh [1964] Director/Nursery Owner; John Michael McCullagh [1963] Director/Engineer; Sam Alexander McCullagh [1995] Director; Tom Oliver McCullagh [1997] Director

Roseframe Limited
Incorporated: 24 July 1996
Net Worth: £381,419 *Total Assets:* £774,105
Registered Office: 511 Durham Road, Gateshead, Tyne & Wear, NE9 5EY
Activities: Other letting and operating of own or leased real estate
Shareholders: Amit Bahanda; Corrina Leigh Mulholland
Officers: Amit Bahanda [1981] Director/IT Manager; Corrina Leigh Mulholland [1976] Director

Rosen (UK) Limited
Incorporated: 8 February 1996 *Employees:* 104
Net Worth: £1,291,856 *Total Assets:* £3,457,131
Registered Office: Floor 2, Q5 Quorum Business Park, Benton Lane, Newcastle upon Tyne, NE12 8BS
Activities: Other professional, scientific and technical activities n.e.c.
Major Shareholder: Marlene Elisabeth Rosen-Helming
Officers: Carolyn Ann Riley, Secretary; Martin Nesbitt [1966] Director/Operations Manager; Roland Palmer-Jones [1970] Director/Engineering Consultant; Carolyn Ann Riley [1982] Director/Accountant

Roseville (Hambleton Grove) Limited
Incorporated: 24 February 2012
Registered Office: Hadrian Offices, 3 Keel Row, The Watermark, Gateshead, Tyne & Wear, NE11 9SZ
Activities: Development of building projects
Parent: Hadrian Healthcare Holdings Limited
Officers: Jasvinder Singh Gill, Secretary; Ian Watson [1962] Director/Business Owner/Chairman

Roseville (Hillgate) Limited
Incorporated: 23 June 2014
Net Worth Deficit: £23,749 *Total Assets:* £979,488
Registered Office: 76 Eastern Way, Darras Hall, Ponteland, Northumberland, NE20 9RE
Activities: Buying and selling of own real estate
Parent: Roseville Asset Management Limited
Officers: Stephen Foster [1954] Director; David William Nicholson [1950] Director

Roseville Asset Management Limited
Incorporated: 16 February 2009
Net Worth: £2,217,577 *Total Assets:* £2,225,148
Registered Office: 76 Eastern Way, Darras Hall, Ponteland, Northumberland, NE20 9RE
Activities: Development of building projects
Shareholders: Stephen Foster; David William Nicholson
Officers: Stephen Foster, Secretary; Stephen Foster [1954] Director/Chartered Surveyor; David William Nicholson [1950] Director

Rosewood Care LLP
Incorporated: 27 November 2008
Net Worth: £620,978 *Total Assets:* £3,801,188
Registered Office: 7 Kyle Road, TEAMS, Gateshead, Tyne & Wear, NE8 2YE
Officers: Mohammad Amjad Ahmad [1968] Member; Mohammad Afzal Ahmad [1967] Member; Ali Asghar [1960] Member; Varghese Thomas [1970] LLP Member

Rosewood HR Services Ltd
Incorporated: 24 July 2013
Net Worth: £130,299 *Total Assets:* £2,048,991
Registered Office: 7 Kyle Road, Bensham, Gateshead, Tyne & Wear, NE8 2YE
Activities: Human resources provision and management of human resources functions
Shareholders: Mohammad Afzal Ahmad; Mohammad Amjad Ahmad; Ali Asghar; Rosewood Care LLP
Officers: Mohammad Amjad Ahmad [1968] Director; Mohammad Afzal Ahmad [1967] Director; Ali Asghar [1960] Director; Varghese Thomas [1970] Director

Rosh Engineering Limited
Incorporated: 28 May 1981
Net Worth: £1,225,410 *Total Assets:* £2,163,596
Registered Office: Unit 4 Riverside Court, Factory Road, Blaydon on Tyne, Tyne & Wear, NE21 5SA
Activities: Repair of other equipment
Major Shareholder: Ian Gareth Dormer
Officers: Dr. Julia Lindsey Newton, Secretary; Ian Gareth Dormer [1964] Director; Dr. Julia Lindsey Newton [1967] Director/Doctor; Paul Scott [1980] Director/Engineer

Rotary Power Ltd.
Incorporated: 24 April 1968 *Employees:* 125
Net Worth: £601,000 *Total Assets:* £10,455,000
Registered Office: 11 Glasshouse Street, St Peters, Newcastle upon Tyne, NE6 1BS
Activities: Manufacture of pumps
Parent: British Engines (UK) Limited
Officers: Joanne Alicea Wilkes, Secretary; Richard Dodd [1974] Group Product & Engineering Director; Laura Joicey [1976] Director/Group Chief Financial Officer; Alexander Harold Lamb [1971] Director; Jonathan Charles Lamb [1977] Group Manufacturing Director

Roth Properties LLP
Incorporated: 22 March 2010
Net Worth: £725,437 *Total Assets:* £1,462,877
Registered Office: 5 Maling Court, Union Street, Newcastle upon Tyne, NE2 1BP
Officers: Ian Robert Baggett [1972] Member; Nicola Baggett [1976] Member; Drew Swinburne [1970] Member; Fiona Swinburne [1977] Member

Rothbury Estates UK Limited
Incorporated: 26 July 2007
Net Worth Deficit: £73,632 *Total Assets:* £1,273,708
Registered Office: Unit 12 Ennerdale Road, Kitty Brewster Industrial Estate, Blyth, Northumberland, NE24 4RT
Activities: Other letting and operating of own or leased real estate
Officers: Martin Anthony Buckley, Secretary; Catherine Buckley [1960] Director [Irish]; Martin Anthony Buckley [1956] Director/Chartered Accountant [Irish]

Rothbury Motors Limited
Incorporated: 14 May 1973
Registered Office: Rothbury Motors Ltd, Lionheart Enterprise Park, Alnwick, Northumberland, NE66 2HT
Activities: Other passenger land transport
Officers: Maryam Manzoor, Secretary; Maryam Manzoor [1978] Director

Rothco Properties Ltd
Incorporated: 16 May 2003
Net Worth: £307 *Total Assets:* £759,906
Registered Office: 6 Craigton House, Queen Street, Redcar, Cleveland, TS10 1DL
Activities: Buying and selling of own real estate
Officers: Joanne Berry, Secretary; Martin Robert Shutt [1970] Managing Director

Roundel Manufacturing Limited
Incorporated: 21 September 1981 *Employees:* 228
Net Worth: £9,092,869 *Total Assets:* £13,407,986
Registered Office: 5-8 Sedling Road, Wear Industrial Estate, Washington, Tyne & Wear, NE38 9BZ
Activities: Manufacture of kitchen furniture
Shareholder: Lindsey Oman
Officers: Elizabeth Ann Oman, Secretary; James Thomas Bebbington [1962] Sales & Commercial Director; Lee Blythe [1978] Purchasing Director; Elizabeth Ann Oman [1950] Director/Credit Controller; Geoffrey Kershaw Oman [1944] Director; Lindsey Oman [1949] Managing Director; Margaret Elizabeth Oman [1944] Director/Administrator; Tristram Lindsey Oman [1981] Managing Director - Nixons; Graham Parkin [1941] Director

Routes Healthcare (North East) Limited
Incorporated: 27 April 2000 *Employees:* 96
Net Worth: £1,262,610 *Total Assets:* £1,460,804
Registered Office: First Floor, The Grainger Suite, Dobson House, Newcastle upon Tyne, NE3 3PF
Activities: Other social work activities without accommodation n.e.c.
Parent: Routes Healthcare (North) Limited
Officers: Andrew Healing [1969] Commercial Director; Elaine Young [1965] Managing Director

Rowan Specialist Interiors Limited
Incorporated: 6 August 1999 *Employees:* 17
Net Worth: £3,137,636 *Total Assets:* £4,134,503
Registered Office: 12 Saltmeadows Road, Gateshead, Tyne & Wear, NE8 3AH
Activities: Other construction installation
Major Shareholder: George Rowan
Officers: Lynn Rowan, Secretary; George Rowan [1958] Director

Roxburgh Group Limited
Incorporated: 21 July 2010 *Employees:* 5
Net Worth: £461,170 *Total Assets:* £1,952,611
Registered Office: 7 Shawwell Business Centre, Stagshaw Road, Corbridge, Northumberland, NE45 5PE
Activities: Other professional, scientific and technical activities n.e.c.
Parent: Roxburgh Holdings Limited
Officers: Lee Stenhouse [1971] Director/Consultant; David Robert Wilkinson [1967] Director/Engineer

Roxburgh Holdings Limited
Incorporated: 18 January 2016
Net Worth: £2,000,400 *Total Assets:* £2,000,780
Registered Office: 7 Shawwell Business Centre, Stagshaw Road, Corbridge, Northumberland, NE45 5PE
Activities: Activities of other holding companies n.e.c.
Shareholders: Lee Stenhouse; David Robert Wilkinson
Officers: Lee Stenhouse [1971] Director; David Robert Wilkinson [1967] Director

Royal IHC Limited
Incorporated: 3 April 1997 *Employees:* 192
Net Worth: £25,928,000 *Total Assets:* £48,541,000
Registered Office: Unit 11 Stocksfield Hall, Stocksfield, Northumberland, NE43 7TN
Activities: Manufacture of metal structures and parts of structures
Parent: IHC Merwede UK Limited
Officers: Andrew Briggs, Secretary; Paul Craig Hardisty [1961] Managing Director; Dave Alexander Andre Joseph Antoon Georges Vander Heyde [1967] Director/Chief Financial Officer [Belgian]

Royston Limited
Incorporated: 16 August 1978 *Employees:* 68
Net Worth: £2,964,237 *Total Assets:* £5,888,640
Registered Office: Unit 3 Walker Riverside, Wincomblee Road, Newcastle upon Tyne, NE6 3PF
Activities: Repair of machinery
Parent: Royston Power Generation Limited
Officers: Graham Ross Denholm, Secretary; Lawrence Joseph Brown [1955] Director/Chartered Accountant; Graham Ross Denholm [1964] Director/Accountant; Neil Stratford Graham [1958] Technical Director; Sarah Wade [1975] Director

Royston Power Generation Limited
Incorporated: 28 August 2007 *Employees:* 77
Net Worth: £1,692,050 *Total Assets:* £5,347,646
Registered Office: Unit 3 Walker Riverside, Wincomblee Road, Newcastle upon Tyne, NE6 3PF
Activities: Activities of head offices
Shareholder: Lawrence Brown
Officers: Graham Ross Denholm, Secretary; Lawrence Joseph Brown [1955] Director; Graham Ross Denholm [1964] Director/Accountant; Neil Stratford Graham [1958] Technical Director; Sarah Wade [1975] Director

RPMR Limited
Incorporated: 8 September 2005 *Employees:* 1
Net Worth: £3,002,521 *Total Assets:* £3,012,856
Registered Office: 43 Coniscliffe Road, Darlington, Co Durham, DL3 7EH
Activities: Other letting and operating of own or leased real estate
Shareholders: Michael Donald Gordon; Patricia Mary Gordon
Officers: Michael Donald Gordon [1956] Director/Chartered Accountant

RPS Switchgear Ltd
Incorporated: 18 February 2013 *Employees:* 6
Net Worth: £399,221 *Total Assets:* £1,682,983
Registered Office: 3 West Quay Court, Sunderland, Tyne & Wear, SR5 2TE
Activities: Manufacture of electricity distribution and control apparatus
Shareholder: Paul Anthony Dowell
Officers: Paul Anthony Dowell [1964] Director/Electrical Engineer

RPU Group PLC
Incorporated: 16 August 1960 *Employees:* 7
Net Worth: £7,525,083 *Total Assets:* £19,782,664
Registered Office: 22 Akenside Terrace, Newcastle upon Tyne, NE2 1TN
Activities: Development of building projects
Officers: Madeline Frances Upton, Secretary; Simon Harland [1978] Director/Chartered Surveyor; Shona Marion Jellett [1984] Director/Barrister; Ian Alexander MacKay [1952] Director/Accountant; James Alexander Metcalf [1974] Director/Chartered Surveyor; Nigel Matthew Upton [1963] Director/Property Manager; Philip Peter Ferguson Upton [1958] Director/Chartered Accountant

RS Industrial Services (Tyne & Wear) Limited
Incorporated: 5 April 2012 *Employees:* 13
Net Worth Deficit: £173,936 *Total Assets:* £2,069,270
Registered Office: 190 Kingsway South, Team Valley Trading Estate, Gateshead, Tyne & Wear, NE11 0SH
Activities: Engineering design activities for industrial process and production
Parent: RS Industrial Group Limited
Officers: Jane-Louise Riley, Secretary; Michael John Riley [1968] Director; Neil Sanderson [1969] Director

RS Industrial Services Limited
Incorporated: 27 September 2001 *Employees:* 49
Net Worth: £1,442,386 *Total Assets:* £3,907,520
Registered Office: RS Business Centre, 2 Cassel Court, Haverton Hill Road, Billingham, Cleveland, TS23 1RB
Activities: Engineering design activities for industrial process and production
Parent: R S Industrial Group Limited
Officers: Lisa Sanderson, Secretary; Michael John Riley [1968] Director/Technical Sales Engineer; Neil Sanderson [1969] Director/Crane Projects Engineer

RSD Marine Ltd
Incorporated: 12 July 2010 *Employees:* 1
Net Worth: £1,174,284 *Total Assets:* £1,243,422
Registered Office: 43 Coniscliffe Road, Darlington, Co Durham, DL3 7EH
Activities: Activities of other holding companies n.e.c.
Parent: The Reed Group Ltd
Officers: Christopher Reed [1984] Director/Project Engineer

RSL One Limited
Incorporated: 28 April 2005 *Employees:* 4
Net Worth: £683,203 *Total Assets:* £889,702
Registered Office: 7 Bankside, The Watermark, Gateshead, Tyne & Wear, NE11 9SY
Activities: Other engineering activities
Shareholders: Dennis White; Frederick Roberts
Officers: Fred Roberts, Secretary; Fred Roberts [1947] Director; Dennis White [1948] Director

RTC North Limited
Incorporated: 19 April 1989 *Employees:* 60
Net Worth: £2,036,576 *Total Assets:* £2,705,008
Registered Office: Loftus House, Colima House, Sunderland Enterprise Park, Sunderland, Tyne & Wear, SR5 3XB
Activities: Other professional, scientific and technical activities n.e.c.
Officers: Martin Carl Porton, Secretary; Andrew Lewis Esson [1963] Director/Chartered Engineer; Dr Timothy Hammond [1961] Director Commercialisation & Economic Development; John Joseph Harrison [1960] Commercial Director; Sarah Hart [1972] Director/Business Development Manager; Dr Stanley Derek Higgins [1953] Director/Chief Executive; Dr Anthony Ikwue [1961] Director; Christopher Alun Jones [1966] Director/Research and Development Manager; Dr Martin McGurk [1971] Innovation Director; James Ollivere [1974] Director; Dr David George Parker [1950] Director/Manager; Martin Carl Porton [1966] Director; Michael Alan Smith [1958] Director/Chartered Accountant; Dr Nicola Claire Wesley [1979] Innovation Director; Laura Mary Woods [1955] Director (HE)

Rubb Buildings Limited
Incorporated: 21 April 1977 *Employees:* 52
Net Worth: £1,641,548 *Total Assets:* £2,446,018
Registered Office: Dukes Way, Team Valley Trading Estate, Gateshead, Tyne & Wear, NE11 0QE
Activities: Manufacture of other fabricated metal products n.e.c.
Shareholders: Jan Erik Torgersen; Truls Torgersen
Officers: Finn Atle Haldorsen, Secretary; Finn Atle Haldorsen [1966] Director/Marketing [Norwegian]; Ian Hindmoor [1981] Managing Director; Truls Torgersen [1957] Director [Norwegian]; William Flett Wood [1946] Director/Engineer

Rubicon Pastimes Limited
Incorporated: 23 February 1996 *Employees:* 89
Net Worth: £2,409,319 *Total Assets:* £5,607,015
Registered Office: 12-14 The Front, Seaton Carew, Hartlepool, Cleveland, TS25 1BS
Activities: Other amusement and recreation activities n.e.c.
Shareholder: Stanley Lloyd Nichols
Officers: Helen Nichols, Secretary; Helen Nichols [1968] Director/Office Manager; Stanley Lloyd Nichols [1969] Director

Ruby Acquisitions Limited
Incorporated: 10 April 2006
Net Worth: £88,831,000 *Total Assets:* £187,855,008
Registered Office: Richmond House, Leeming Bar, Northallerton, N Yorks, DL7 9UL
Activities: Activities of production holding companies
Parent: Froneri International PLC
Officers: Marcello Mattia, Secretary; Phil Karl Griffin [1972] Director; Marcello Mattia [1965] Director [Italian]; Ibrahim Mahmood Ibrahim Najafi [1958] Director

Ruby Homes Limited
Incorporated: 6 April 2006
Registered Office: 32-34 Wear Street, Low Southwick, Sunderland, Tyne & Wear, SR5 2BU
Officers: Thomas Eastick Foster, Secretary; Thomas Eastick Foster [1935] Director/Taxi Proprietor

Bob Rudd Leisure Limited
Incorporated: 5 January 1995 *Employees:* 99
Net Worth: £1,401,233 *Total Assets:* £5,140,581
Registered Office: Hawthorn House, Brunswick Industrial Estate, Brunswick Village, Newcastle upon Tyne, NE13 7BA
Activities: Renting and leasing of media entertainment equipment
Parent: Bob Rudd Limited
Officers: Robert Rudd, Secretary/Manager; Charlotte Rudd [1988] HR Director; Nicholas David Rudd [1987] Operations and Marketing Director; Robert Rudd [1947] Director/Manager; Sharon Jean Rudd [1956] Director/Administrator

Bob Rudd Limited
Incorporated: 27 October 2014
Net Worth: £601 *Total Assets:* £1,080,989
Registered Office: Hawthorn House, Brunswick Industrial Estate, Brunswick Village, Newcastle upon Tyne, NE13 7BA
Activities: Renting and leasing of media entertainment equipment
Major Shareholder: Nicholas David Rudd
Officers: Charlotte Rudd [1988] Director; Mr Nicholas David Rudd [1987] Director; Robert Rudd [1947] Director; Sharon Jean Rudd [1956] Director

Ruff 'n' Tumble Adventure World Limited
Incorporated: 6 November 2003
Net Worth: £250,694 *Total Assets:* £929,109
Registered Office: Unit 3 Park 2000, Millennium Way, Newton Aycliffe, Co Durham, DL5 6AR
Activities: Other amusement and recreation activities n.e.c.
Officers: Darren Ashley Peckitt, Secretary; Andrea Louise Peckitt [1973] Operations Director; Darren Ashley Peckitt [1970] Managing Director

Rushyford Transport Services Limited
Incorporated: 26 November 1987 *Employees:* 19
Net Worth: £727,872 *Total Assets:* £1,004,562
Registered Office: Stotforth Hill Farm, Windlestone, Rushyford, Co Durham, DL17 0NF
Activities: Freight transport by road
Parent: Epplton Quarry Products Limited
Officers: Neville John Hall [1956] Director/Civil Engineer; Stephen Hall [1954] Director/Civil Engineering Contractor

Howard Russell Construction Limited
Incorporated: 23 June 1997
Net Worth: £1,461,526 *Total Assets:* £3,304,101
Registered Office: 7-8 Apex Business Village, Annitsford, Cramlington, Northumberland, NE23 7BF
Activities: Construction of commercial buildings
Major Shareholder: David Varty
Officers: Andrea Styles, Secretary; Ian Thomas Goss [1957] Director; Craig Richard Muldoon [1983] Director; Andrea Styles [1969] Director; David Varty [1955] Director; Barry Wilkinson [1972] Director

C.W. Russell Ltd
Incorporated: 7 April 2006
Net Worth: £501,855 *Total Assets:* £1,543,050
Registered Office: 14-15 Hareland Courtyard Offices, Moor Road, Melsonby, Richmond, N Yorks, DL10 5NY
Activities: Other business support service activities n.e.c.
Major Shareholder: Charles William Russell
Officers: Elizabeth Anne Russell, Secretary; Charles William Russell [1967] Director

Russell Network Solutions Limited
Incorporated: 18 May 2011 *Employees:* 2
Net Worth: £543,348 *Total Assets:* £1,224,527
Registered Office: Communications House, Keel Row, The Watermark, Gateshead, Tyne & Wear, NE11 9SZ
Activities: Other telecommunications activities
Shareholders: Kelvyn Gracie; Lawrence Ralph McCaughey
Officers: Kelvyn Gracie, Secretary; Kelvyn Gracie [1951] Director; Lawrence Ralph McCaughey [1957] Director

Russell Telecom Limited
Incorporated: 1 November 1990 *Employees:* 35
Net Worth: £249,204 *Total Assets:* £929,016
Registered Office: Communications House, Unit 11, Keel Row, The Watermark, Gateshead, Tyne & Wear, NE11 9SZ
Activities: Other telecommunications activities
Parent: Russell Systems Telecom Limited
Officers: Lawrence Ralph McCaughey, Secretary; Kelvyn Gracie [1951] Director; Lawrence Ralph McCaughey [1957] Director

Rust Resources Limited
Incorporated: 7 April 1992 *Employees:* 7
Net Worth: £700,403 *Total Assets:* £1,240,446
Registered Office: Parsons House, Parsons Road, Washington, Tyne & Wear, NE37 1EZ
Activities: Other activities of employment placement agencies
Parent: Rust Resources Holdco Limited
Officers: Richard Fielding [1967] Director; Louise Michelle Guiliano [1980] Director; Geoffrey Lennox [1956] Director; Helen Mary Smith [1962] Director; David Ernest Spencer [1962] Director

G. Rutherford & Co. Limited
Incorporated: 16 October 1936 *Employees:* 50
Net Worth: £1,198,479 *Total Assets:* £1,823,284
Registered Office: 10-16 Bridge Street, Morpeth, Northumberland, NE61 1NJ
Activities: Other retail sale in non-specialised stores
Officers: Catherine Bates [1958] Director; Seymour Jobling [1948] Director/Company Secretary; Anne Elizabeth Petrie [1948] Director; Audrey Rutherford [1924] Director; George Richard Rutherford [1952] Managing Director

Rutherford Association Football Club
Incorporated: 18 February 2008 *Employees:* 2
Net Worth: £774,079 *Total Assets:* £777,175
Registered Office: Rutherford AFC, Coach Road, Lobley Hill, Gateshead, Tyne & Wear, NE11 0HH
Activities: Activities of sport clubs
Officers: Sara Jaqueline Coxon [1987] Director/Club House Manager; Robert John Dixon [1957] Director; Ian Innes [1968] Director/HMRC; James Tate [1976] Director/Manager

S V Rutter Ltd
Incorporated: 16 October 1979 *Employees:* 28
Net Worth: £1,797,226 *Total Assets:* £3,273,899
Registered Office: Suite 7, S V Rutter Business Centre, 126 Great Lime Road, Newcastle upon Tyne, NE12 6RU
Activities: Construction of commercial buildings
Major Shareholder: Stanley Victor Rutter
Officers: Anne Michele Rutter, Secretary; Anne Michele Rutter [1953] Secretary & Director; Stanley Victor Rutter [1953] Builder & Director; Tony Andrew Rutter [1977] Director/Manager

Ryan Offshore Limited
Incorporated: 24 November 2009 *Employees:* 3
Net Worth: £94,211 *Total Assets:* £1,022,091
Registered Office: 4 The Square, Shields Road, Sunderland, Tyne & Wear, SR6 8JJ
Activities: Sea and coastal freight water transport
Shareholders: Hilary Tewari; Executors of Ram Kishore Tewari, Deceased
Officers: Robin Tewari [1983] Director

Ryder Architecture Limited
Incorporated: 5 October 1984 *Employees:* 138
Net Worth: £2,185,862 *Total Assets:* £5,717,542
Registered Office: Cooper's Studios, 14-18 Westgate Road, Newcastle upon Tyne, NE1 3NN
Activities: Architectural activities
Officers: Graeme Richard Hurworth, Secretary; Peter Buchan [1953] Director/Architect; Mark Richard Thompson [1965] Director/Project Manager

George Rye & Sons Limited
Incorporated: 7 August 1975 *Employees:* 31
Net Worth: £2,224,402 *Total Assets:* £4,542,290
Registered Office: Lunar House, Unit 1 Easter Park, Baker Road, Nelson Park West, Cramlington, Northumberland, NE23 1WQ
Activities: Wholesale of clothing and footwear
Shareholders: Michael Edward Rye; Edward Martin Rye
Officers: Michael Edward Rye, Secretary; Thomas Alexander Richardson [1949] Sales Director; Cindy Mary Rye [1945] Director; Edward Martin Rye [1972] Director; Michael Edward Rye [1948] Director

Ryhope Infant School Academy
Incorporated: 5 August 2014 *Employees:* 39
Net Worth: £1,812,070 *Total Assets:* £2,437,578
Registered Office: Ryhope Infant School Academy, Shaftesbury Avenue, Ryhope, Sunderland, Tyne & Wear, SR2 0RT
Activities: Primary education
Officers: Suzanne Brown [1945] Director; Craig Davidge [1983] Director/Business Manager; Alison Guthrie [1970] Director/Civil Servant; Holly Anne Hays [1979] Director/Microbiologist; Rachel Elizabeth Leonard [1972] Director/Trustee; Susan Reed [1969] Director/Headteacher; Janet Mary Wardle [1957] Director/Nursery Nurse

Ryka Developments Limited
Incorporated: 29 September 2016
Net Worth Deficit: £151,198 *Total Assets:* £2,302,612
Registered Office: Keel House, Garth Heads, Newcastle upon Tyne, NE1 2JE
Activities: Other letting and operating of own or leased real estate
Shareholder: Stewart Adam Watson
Officers: Stewart Adam Watson [1992] Director

S A Day Care Ltd
Incorporated: 26 November 2014
Net Worth: £193 *Total Assets:* £1,230,746
Registered Office: 12 Sinderby Lane, Nunthorpe, Middlesbrough, Cleveland, TS7 0RP
Activities: Pre-primary education
Major Shareholder: Shafq Naiman Anwar
Officers: Shafq Naiman Anwar [1971] Director

S and B EPS Limited
Incorporated: 24 June 1982 *Employees:* 41
Net Worth: £1,493,499 *Total Assets:* £4,404,447
Registered Office: Grieves Row, Dudley, Cramlington, Tyne & Wear, NE23 7PY
Activities: Other manufacturing n.e.c.
Shareholder: Jean Smith
Officers: Henry Christopher Smith, Secretary; Paul Banks [1965] Technical Director; Darryl Davison [1971] Operations Director; Diane Louise Davison [1981] Financial Director; Darren Christopher Smith [1968] Managing Director; Henry Christopher Smith [1945] Director; Jean Smith [1946] Director

S F Wind Ltd
Incorporated: 22 November 2010 *Employees:* 2
Net Worth Deficit: £69,887 *Total Assets:* £1,221,195
Registered Office: West 2, Asama Court, Newcastle Business Park, Newcastle upon Tyne, NE4 7YD
Activities: Production of electricity
Shareholders: Christopher James Fewster; Michael Fewster
Officers: Christopher James Fewster [1968] Managing Director; Michael Fabian Fewster [1967] Director

S J I Holdings Limited
Incorporated: 8 August 2005
Net Worth: £3,000 *Total Assets:* £908,179
Registered Office: Centre for Advanced Industry, Coble Dene, Royal Quays, North Shields, Tyne & Wear, NE29 6DE
Activities: Activities of head offices
Officers: Stephen Charles Thompson, Secretary; Andrew Paul Hartley [1965] Director/Engineer; Camille Elias Karam [1958] Director/Financial Advisor [American]; Peter Rossiter [1945] Director/Engineer; Dieter Rottsieper [1959] Director [German]; Stephen Charles Thompson [1975] Director/Chartered Accountant

S T R Enterprises Limited
Incorporated: 30 September 1996 *Employees:* 201
Net Worth: £5,315,653 *Total Assets:* £14,802,300
Registered Office: Waverley House, 30 The Oval, Forest Hall, Newcastle upon Tyne, NE12 9PP
Activities: Hotels and similar accommodation
Shareholders: Elizabeth Anne Sanderson; John Taylor Sanderson
Officers: Elizabeth Anne Sanderson, Secretary/Business Consultant; Christopher Spencer Sanderson [1974] Director/Business Consultant; Elizabeth Anne Sanderson [1945] Director/Business Consultant; John Taylor Sanderson [1944] Managing Director; Richard Alexander Sanderson [1979] Director

S&A Builders Merchants (Holdings) Limited
Incorporated: 30 November 2015
Net Worth: £2,073,002 *Total Assets:* £2,073,002
Registered Office: Harmire Enterprise Park, Barnard Castle, Co Durham, DL12 8EH
Activities: Activities of other holding companies n.e.c.
Parent: S&A BM Limited
Officers: Glynis Catterson [1965] Finance Director; Joe Catterson [1994] Director; John Leslie Catterson [1961] Director; Sarah Eve Catterson [1997] Director

S&A Builders Merchants Limited
Incorporated: 27 November 2015 *Employees:* 27
Net Worth: £2,100,445 *Total Assets:* £3,499,354
Registered Office: Harmire Enterprise Park, Barnard Castle, Co Durham, DL12 8EH
Activities: Agents involved in the sale of timber and building materials
Shareholder: Glynis Catterson
Officers: Glynis Catterson [1965] Finance Director; Joe Catterson [1994] Director; John Leslie Catterson [1961] Director; Sarah Eve Catterson [1997] Director

S&A Fabrications (Holdings) Limited
Incorporated: 30 November 2015
Net Worth: £1,271,002 *Total Assets:* £1,271,002
Registered Office: Harmire Enterprise Park, Barnard Castle, Co Durham, DL12 8EH
Activities: Activities of construction holding companies
Shareholders: John Joseph Allinson; Gepffrey Simpson
Officers: John Joseph Allinson [1951] Director; Geoffrey Simpson [1951] Managing Director

S&A Fabrications Limited
Incorporated: 27 November 2015 *Employees:* 30
Net Worth: £1,012,945 *Total Assets:* £1,693,699
Registered Office: Harmire Enterprise Park, Barnard Castle, Co Durham, DL12 8EH
Activities: Manufacture of metal structures and parts of structures
Shareholders: John Joseph Allinson; Geoffrey Simpson
Officers: John Joseph Allinson [1951] Director; Simon Charles Pelly [1973] Sales & Marketing Director; Geoffrey Simpson [1951] Managing Director

S&I Developments Ltd
Incorporated: 23 April 2003 *Employees:* 2
Net Worth: £275,958 *Total Assets:* £2,428,653
Registered Office: 25 Roseberry Road, Billingham, Cleveland, TS23 2SD
Activities: Development of building projects
Major Shareholder: Steven Wastell
Officers: Stephen Jones, Secretary; Barnaby James Wastell [1988] Director/Property Developer; Steven Wastell [1957] Director

S. & S. Precision Engineering (Washington) Limited
Incorporated: 13 March 1985 *Employees:* 14
Net Worth: £1,378,908 *Total Assets:* £1,691,875
Registered Office: 23 Rainhill Close, Stephenson Industrial Estate, District 12, Washington, Tyne & Wear, NE37 3HN
Activities: Manufacture of other fabricated metal products n.e.c.
Officers: Lesley Bunker, Secretary; David Staines [1968] Director/Precision Engineer; Ian Staines [1969] Director/Precision Engineer

S.A.L. Leisure Limited
Incorporated: 5 November 1982
Net Worth: £3,288,905 *Total Assets:* £3,632,868
Registered Office: 362c Dukesway, Team Valley Trading Estate, Gateshead, Tyne & Wear, NE11 0PZ
Activities: Gambling and betting activities
Parent: S.A.L Leisure Holdings Ltd
Officers: Neil Paramore, Secretary; Tom Allison [1963] Director; Paul David Hyman [1969] Director; Zane Cedomir Mersich [1972] Managing Director; Neil Paramore [1962] Financial Director

S.C.H. Site Services Ltd
Incorporated: 19 January 2005 *Employees:* 37
Net Worth: £1,451,364 *Total Assets:* £2,846,164
Registered Office: Whinbank Road, Aycliffe Industrial Estate, Newton Aycliffe, Co Durham, DL5 6AY
Activities: Manufacture of metal structures and parts of structures
Parent: Finley Holdings Limited
Officers: Julie Raistrick, Secretary; Andrew Braid [1974] Director; Gary John Finley [1980] Managing Director; John Finley [1952] Sales Director; Valerie Finley [1952] Director/Secretary; Julie Raistrick [1975] Director

S.D.S.K Limited
Incorporated: 3 March 1989
Net Worth: £1,234,014 *Total Assets:* £1,396,870
Registered Office: Sheenwynds, Wellfield Road, Murton, Seaham, Co Durham, SR7 9HN
Activities: Other letting and operating of own or leased real estate
Shareholders: Dr Daljit Singh Rangar; Dr Rani Rangar
Officers: Dr Daljit Singh Rangar, Secretary; Dr Daljit Singh Rangar [1951] Director/Medical Doctor; Dr Rani Rangar [1949] Director/Medical Doctor

S.E.L.F. (North East) Limited
Incorporated: 9 January 1995 *Employees:* 34
Net Worth: £2,227,095 *Total Assets:* £2,657,674
Registered Office: West Lodge, Warden Law Lane, Silksworth, Sunderland, Tyne & Wear, SR3 2PD
Activities: Residential care activities for learning difficulties, mental health and substance abuse
Shareholders: Malcolm Moore Snr; Jacqueline Yvonne Moore
Officers: Jacqueline Yvonne Moore, Secretary; Calvin Moore [1973] Director; Jacqueline Yvonne Moore [1947] Director; Malcolm Moore [1948] Director; Malcolm Moore Jnr [1984] Director

S.I.E. Industrial Limited
Incorporated: 6 April 1982 *Employees:* 15
Net Worth: £634,553 *Total Assets:* £1,468,511
Registered Office: Faraday House, Station Road, Pattinson South Industrial Estate, Washington, Tyne & Wear, NE38 8LW
Activities: Manufacture of other special-purpose machinery n.e.c.
Shareholders: Gareth Paul Bowen; Paul Bowen
Officers: Gareth Paul Bowen [1984] Director/Sales Manager; Paul Bowen [1955] Director

S.J.B. Recycling Limited
Incorporated: 30 March 2004 *Employees:* 21
Net Worth: £1,737,732 *Total Assets:* £2,400,919
Registered Office: Mount View, Standard Way Business Park, Northallerton, N Yorks, DL6 2YD
Activities: Recovery of sorted materials
Parent: North Yorkshire County Council
Officers: Alexander Boyle, Secretary; David Raymond Bowe [1962] Director/Local Government Officer; Alexander Boyle [1970] Finance Director; Martin Howard Buckley [1945] Director; Geoffrey Douglas Derham [1962] Director; Neil James Ferris [1969] Director/Local Government Officer; John Phillips [1954] Director; Cllr Andrew Michael Waller [1969] Director/Local Authority Member; John Keith Weighell [1942] Director/Farmer

S.M.P. (Services) Limited
Incorporated: 18 February 1986
Net Worth: £1,842,532 *Total Assets:* £1,842,532
Registered Office: Offshore Technology Park, 1 Rendle Road, Walker, Newcastle upon Tyne, NE6 3NH
Activities: Temporary employment agency activities
Major Shareholder: Bruce Stewart Shepherd
Officers: Shaun David Ward, Secretary; Violet Dryden [1934] Director/Company Secretary; Bruce Stewart Shepherd [1946] Director/Transport Manager

S.R. Transport Services Limited
Incorporated: 21 November 2001 *Employees:* 27
Net Worth: £532,673 *Total Assets:* £1,341,411
Registered Office: 42 Swan Road, Swan Industrial Estate, Washington, Tyne & Wear, NE38 8JJ
Activities: Freight transport by road
Shareholder: Savva Roberts
Officers: Jillian Connolly, Secretary; Savva Roberts [1970] Director/Haulier MD

S.W. Durham Training Limited
Incorporated: 13 October 1967 *Employees:* 30
Net Worth: £3,669,778 *Total Assets:* £4,474,378
Registered Office: Durham Way South, Aycliffe Business Park, Newton Aycliffe, Co Durham, DL5 6AT
Activities: Technical and vocational secondary education
Officers: Judith Eva Layfield, Secretary; Paul Aither [1982] Director/Site Electrical Engineer; Graham Currie [1970] Finance Director; Natalie Davison [1969] Director/College Principal; Andrew Arthur Dunn [1964] Director; Pamela Petty [1968] Managing Director; Stephen John Rose [1957] Director/Plant Manager; Andrew Scott [1963] Director/Engineering Manager

Sabic Global Limited
Incorporated: 8 July 1987 *Employees:* 2
Net Worth: £39,442,796 *Total Assets:* £39,448,048
Registered Office: Wilton Centre, Redcar, Cleveland, TS10 4RF
Activities: Other business support service activities n.e.c.
Officers: John Middleton, Secretary; Ronald Napier Grant [1957] Finance Director; John Christopher Middleton [1973] Director/Legal Counsel

Sabic Innovative Plastics ABS UK Limited
Incorporated: 25 March 1970 *Employees:* 22
Net Worth: £3,718,000 *Total Assets:* £4,064,000
Registered Office: The Wilton Centre, Redcar, Cleveland, TS10 4RF
Activities: Manufacture of plastics in primary forms
Officers: John Christopher Middleton, Secretary; Stephen John Jones [1959] Director/Site Manager

Sabic Innovative Plastics Limited
Incorporated: 4 December 1969 *Employees:* 6
Net Worth: £5,515,000 *Total Assets:* £5,929,000
Registered Office: The Wilton Centre, Redcar, Cleveland, TS10 4RF
Activities: Wholesale of petroleum and petroleum products
Officers: John Christopher Middleton, Secretary; Mark Bachelor [1977] Director/Senior Accountant; John Christopher Middleton [1973] Director/Legal Counsel

Sabic Tees Holdings Limited
Incorporated: 24 November 2006
Net Worth: £168,824,640 *Total Assets:* £457,437,696
Registered Office: The Wilton Centre, Wilton, Redcar, Cleveland, TS10 4RF
Activities: Manufacture of other organic basic chemicals
Officers: John Middleton, Secretary; Ronald Napier Grant [1957] Finance Director; John Christopher Middleton [1973] Director/Legal Counsel

Sabic UK Limited
Incorporated: 2 August 2001 *Employees:* 8
Net Worth: £7,062,000 *Total Assets:* £75,519,000
Registered Office: Wilton Centre, Redcar, Cleveland, TS10 4RF
Activities: Manufacture of other organic basic chemicals
Officers: John Middleton, Secretary; Mark Bachelor [1977] Director/Senior Accountant; John Christopher Middleton [1973] Director/Legal Counsel

Sabic UK Petrochemicals Limited
Incorporated: 5 May 1999 *Employees:* 605
Net Worth: £451,900,000 *Total Assets:* £839,699,968
Registered Office: The Wilton Centre, Wilton, Redcar, Cleveland, TS10 4RF
Activities: Manufacture of other organic basic chemicals
Parent: Sabic Tees Holdings Limited
Officers: John Middleton, Secretary; Ronald Napier Grant [1957] Finance & IT Director; John Christopher Middleton [1973] Director/Legal Counsel; Daren Smith [1966] Site Director

Sabre Rail Services Limited
Incorporated: 18 June 1987 *Employees:* 89
Net Worth: £2,945,825 *Total Assets:* £4,809,061
Registered Office: Grindon Way, Heighington Lane Business Park, Newton Aycliffe, Co Durham, DL5 6SH
Activities: Manufacture of railway locomotives and rolling stock
Major Shareholder: Glenys Thompson
Officers: Glenys Thompson, Secretary; Stephen Mark Thompson [1979] Managing Director

Sacred Heart Partnership of Schools
Incorporated: 9 November 2011 *Employees:* 188
Net Worth: £16,663,000 *Total Assets:* £18,213,000
Registered Office: Sacred Heart Catholic High School, Fenham Hall Drive, Newcastle upon Tyne, NE4 9YH
Activities: General secondary education
Officers: Anita Bath [1965] Director/Headteacher; Veronica Goatman [1950] Director/Retired; Gill Hardy [1968] Director/Product Researcher; David John Harrison [1964] Director; Denise Mary Kendall [1951] Director/Headteacher; Professor Kathleen McCourt [1952] Director/Retired; Juliet Patricia Scullion [1978] Director/Patent Counsel; Hilary Christine Thompson [1959] Director/Network

Sacriston Community and Sports Trust
Incorporated: 4 August 2003
Net Worth: £991,306 *Total Assets:* £992,344
Registered Office: The Fulforth Centre, Front Street, Sacriston, Co Durham, DH7 6JT
Activities: Other amusement and recreation activities n.e.c.
Officers: Linda Elizabeth Surtees, Secretary; Margaret Ayton [1952] Director/Retired; Diane Bloomfield [1943] Director/Clerk; Hugh Dixon [1950] Director/Retired; Robert Graeme Ludlow [1970] Funeral Director; John Metcalf [1940] Director/Project Worker; Frank Morrell [1942] Director/Retired; Derek Leslie Robson [1946] Director/Retired; Linda Elizabeth Surtees [1957] Director/Human Resources Manager

Saddle Skedaddle Limited
Incorporated: 25 February 1999 *Employees:* 21
Net Worth: £185,634 *Total Assets:* £933,064
Registered Office: The Cycle Hub, Quayside, Newcastle upon Tyne, NE6 1BU
Activities: Tour operator activities
Shareholders: Andrew John Straw; David Paul Snedker
Officers: David Paul Snedker, Secretary/Director; Alan John Holmes [1950] Director; David Paul Snedker [1964] Director/General Manager; Andrew John Straw [1965] Commercial Director; Michael Edward D'Arcy Walton [1943] Director

Saddlers Land and Property Limited
Incorporated: 13 May 2013 *Employees:* 1
Net Worth: £274,468 *Total Assets:* £4,876,385
Registered Office: 22 South Street, Durham, DH1 4QP
Activities: Buying and selling of own real estate
Major Shareholder: Simon John Williams
Officers: Simon John Williams [1972] Director/Architect

Saddlestone West Limited
Incorporated: 12 September 2013
Registered Office: Baldwins, Wynyard Park House, Wynyard Avenue, Wynyard, Cleveland, TS22 5TB
Activities: Other service activities n.e.c.
Officers: Joseph Christopher Musgrave [1965] Director

Shaun Sadler Holdings Limited
Incorporated: 16 February 2012 *Employees:* 100
Net Worth: £2,743,988 *Total Assets:* £5,441,663
Registered Office: Connor House, Pilgrims Way, Bede Industrial Estate, Jarrow, Tyne & Wear, NE32 3EW
Activities: Manufacture of other fabricated metal products n.e.c.
Major Shareholder: Shaun William Sadler
Officers: Shaun William Sadler [1970] Managing Director

Safe & Sure Fire Protection Limited
Incorporated: 6 October 1994 *Employees:* 16
Net Worth: £1,213,609 *Total Assets:* £1,373,801
Registered Office: Unit 2 Mill Lane, Langley Moor Industrial Estate, Langley Moor, Co Durham, DH7 8HE
Activities: Repair of electrical equipment
Major Shareholder: Colin Hunt
Officers: Elaine Hunt, Secretary; Colin Hunt [1959] Director; Margaret Hunt [1960] Director

Safe-Line Marine After Sales Ltd
Incorporated: 30 June 2003 *Employees:* 10
Net Worth: £1,415,617 *Total Assets:* £1,600,772
Registered Office: 28 Royal Industrial Estate, Jarrow, Tyne & Wear, NE32 3HR
Activities: Repair and maintenance of ships and boats
Shareholders: John William Convery; Michael Christopher Grant
Officers: Michael Grant, Secretary; John Convery [1962] Technical Director; Michael Grant [1960] Managing Director

Safechem Limited
Incorporated: 2 April 1986 *Employees:* 24
Net Worth: £2,253,679 *Total Assets:* £3,142,755
Registered Office: Drum House, Drum Industrial Estate, Chester-le-Street, Co Durham, DH2 1SR
Activities: Wholesale of chemical products
Shareholders: Nigel Laurence Bruce; Christine Bruce
Officers: Christine Bruce [1958] Director/Secretary; Jonathon Bruce [1981] Director/Stores Manager; Nigel Laurence Bruce [1951] Managing Director; Emma Lumley [1978] Director/Office Manageress

Saferad Limited
Incorporated: 22 July 1996
Net Worth: £1,915,732 *Total Assets:* £3,300,521
Registered Office: 6 Stockley Grove, Brancepeth, Co Durham, DH7 8DU
Activities: Manufacture of irradiation, electromedical and electrotherapeutic equipment
Major Shareholder: Teresa Ann Wass
Officers: Teresa Ann Wass, Company Secretary; Malcolm Laing Wass [1949] Director/Engineer; Teresa Ann Wass [1952] Director

Safety Systems Distribution Limited
Incorporated: 19 June 1998 *Employees:* 9
Net Worth: £953,505 *Total Assets:* £1,323,941
Registered Office: Unit 11b, Hobson Industrial Estate, Burnopfield, Co Durham, NE16 6EA
Activities: Electrical installation
Shareholders: Neil Robson; James Trueman
Officers: Neil Robson, Secretary/Director; Neil Robson [1955] Director; James Trueman [1954] Director

Safinah Limited
Incorporated: 9 October 1998 *Employees:* 14
Net Worth: £1,104,500 *Total Assets:* £1,609,622
Registered Office: 5 The Watermark, Gateshead, Tyne & Wear, NE11 9SZ
Activities: Other professional, scientific and technical activities n.e.c.
Parent: TPO Holding Danmark ApS
Officers: Rachel Coundon, Company Secretary; Dr Mohamed Raouf Abdul Karim Al-Kattan [1956] Director/Naval Architect; Steen Hartvig [1972] Director [Danish]; Tommy Meier Paulsen [1969] Director [Danish]; Doctor Tor Egil Svensen [1955] Director/Professor [Norwegian]; Peter Wilhelmsen [1971] Director [Danish]

Saft Limited
Incorporated: 16 June 1937 *Employees:* 95
Net Worth: £9,772,000 *Total Assets:* £12,098,000
Registered Office: River Drive, South Shields, Tyne & Wear, NE33 2TR
Activities: Manufacture of batteries and accumulators
Parent: Saft Finance SARL
Officers: Stephen John Harrison, Secretary; Igal Carmi [1954] Director [Israeli]; Tessa Collinson [1973] Director/General Manager; John Nicholas Taylor [1958] Director/Sales Manager

Sage (UK) Ltd
Incorporated: 14 March 1972 *Employees:* 2,222
Net Worth: £301,008,992 *Total Assets:* £522,297,984
Registered Office: North Park, Newcastle upon Tyne, NE13 9AA
Activities: Other software publishing
Parent: Sage Holding Company Limited
Officers: Miranda Craig, Secretary; Victoria Louise Bradin [1978] Director/General Counsel and Company Secretary; Adam Mark Richard Parker [1971] Finance Director; Sarah Jane Rolls [1974] Director/Accountant

Sage Brazilian Investment One Limited
Incorporated: 4 April 2012
Net Worth: £39,159,000 *Total Assets:* £84,939,000
Registered Office: The Sage Group PLC, North Park, Newcastle upon Tyne, NE13 9AA
Activities: Financial intermediation not elsewhere classified
Parent: Sage Holding Company Limited
Officers: Miranda Craig, Secretary; Victoria Louise Bradin [1978] Director/General Counsel and Company Secretary; John-Henry Fredrik Liepe [1974] Financial Director [Swedish]; Sarah Jane Rolls [1974] Director/Accountant

Sage Brazilian Investment Two Limited
Incorporated: 4 April 2012
Net Worth: £10,820,000 *Total Assets:* £10,820,000
Registered Office: The Sage Group PLC, North Park, Newcastle upon Tyne, NE13 9AA
Activities: Financial intermediation not elsewhere classified
Parent: Sage Holding Company Limited
Officers: Miranda Craig, Secretary; Victoria Louise Bradin [1978] Director/General Counsel and Company Secretary; John-Henry Fredrik Liepe [1974] Finance Director [Swedish]; Sarah Jane Rolls [1974] Director/Accountant

Sage Euro Hedgeco 1
Incorporated: 6 September 2013
Net Worth: £89,184,320 *Total Assets:* £89,184,320
Registered Office: North Park, Newcastle upon Tyne, NE13 9AA
Activities: Activities of other holding companies n.e.c.
Parent: Sage Treasury Company Limited
Officers: Miranda Craig, Secretary; Victoria Louise Bradin [1978] Director/General Counsel and Company Secretary; John-Henry Fredrik Liepe [1974] Financial Director [Swedish]; Sarah Jane Rolls [1974] Director/Accountant

Sage Far East Investments Limited
Incorporated: 12 May 2004
Net Worth: £10,721,000 *Total Assets:* £10,721,000
Registered Office: North Park, Newcastle upon Tyne, NE13 9AA
Activities: Financial intermediation not elsewhere classified
Parent: Sage Holding Company Limited
Officers: Miranda Craig, Secretary; Victoria Louise Bradin [1978] Director/General Counsel and Company Secretary; John-Henry Fredrik Liepe [1974] Financial Director [Swedish]; Sarah Jane Rolls [1974] Director/Accountant

Sage Global Services Limited
Incorporated: 24 March 2015
Net Worth Deficit: £165,999,008 *Total Assets:* £61,004,000
Registered Office: North Park, Newcastle upon Tyne, NE13 9AA
Activities: Other business support service activities n.e.c.
Parent: Sage Holding Company Limited
Officers: Miranda Craig, Secretary; Victoria Louise Bradin [1978] Director/General Counsel and Company Secretary; John-Henry Fredrik Liepe [1974] Director [Swedish]; Sarah Jane Rolls [1974] Director/Accountant

The Sage Group PLC.
Incorporated: 16 March 1988 *Employees:* 8
Net Worth: £1,168,000,000 *Total Assets:* £3,223,000,064
Registered Office: North Park, Newcastle upon Tyne, NE13 9AA
Activities: Activities of head offices
Officers: Victoria Louise Bradin, Secretary; Neil Anthony Berkett [1955] Director [British/New Zealander]; Donald Hood Brydon [1945] Director; Daniel Blair Crump [1961] Director/President [American]; John William Drummond Hall [1949] Director; Stephen Hare [1961] Director; Jonathan Anton George Howell [1962] Director; Soni Jiandani [1966] Director/Technology Executive [American]; Catherine Jane Keers [1965] Director

Sage Holding Company Limited
Incorporated: 5 December 2012
Net Worth: £3,455,436,032 *Total Assets:* £3,605,821,952
Registered Office: North Park, Newcastle upon Tyne, NE13 9AA
Activities: Activities of production holding companies
Parent: The Sage Group PLC
Officers: Miranda Craig, Secretary; Victoria Louise Bradin [1978] Director/General Counsel and Company Secretary; John-Henry Fredrik Liepe [1974] Finance Director [Swedish]; Sarah Jane Rolls [1974] Director/Accountant

Sage Holdings Limited
Incorporated: 5 August 1998
Net Worth: £609,070,016 *Total Assets:* £611,094,016
Registered Office: North Park, Newcastle upon Tyne, NE13 9AA
Activities: Activities of head offices
Parent: Sage Whitley Limited
Officers: Miranda Craig, Secretary; John-Henry Fredrik Liepe [1974] Financial Director [Swedish]; Adam Mark Richard Parker [1971] Finance Director; Claire Marcia Vaughan [1961] Director/Solicitor

Sage Multi Academy Trust
Incorporated: 9 March 2012 *Employees:* 45
Net Worth: £1,337,000 *Total Assets:* £1,913,000
Registered Office: Neasham Road, Middleton St George, Darlington, Co Durham, DL2 1LD
Activities: Primary education
Officers: Lilian Shutt, Secretary; Adrian Timothy Clarke [1974] Director/Analytical Chemist; Jean Fletcher [1954] Director; Janine Gleeson [1965] Director/Headteacher; Shirley Anne Gray [1975] Director/Volunteer Officer; Richard John Huysers [1973] Director/Health & Safety Executive; Joanna Jane Morrison [1971] Director/Territory Development Manager; Janis Maureen Robson [1947] Director; Rodger Victor Desmond Sansom [1945] Director; Reverend Adrian Thorp [1955] Director/Interim Priest in Charge; Dominic Jon Vizzard [1979] Director/Website Designer; Pauline Roberta Weighell [1947] Director/Retired; Ann Williams [1946] Director/Retired HR Manager

Sage Online Holdings Limited
Incorporated: 21 March 2011
Net Worth: £94,311,000 *Total Assets:* £94,311,000
Registered Office: North Park, Newcastle upon Tyne, NE13 9AA
Activities: Other software publishing
Parent: Sage Holding Company Limited
Officers: Miranda Craig, Secretary; Victoria Louise Bradin [1978] Director/General Counsel and Company Secretary; John-Henry Fredrik Liepe [1974] Director [Swedish]; Sarah Jane Rolls [1974] Director/Accountant

Sage Overseas Limited.
Incorporated: 22 June 1990 *Employees:* 11
Net Worth: £75,901,000 *Total Assets:* £435,548,992
Registered Office: North Park, Newcastle upon Tyne, NE13 9AA
Activities: Activities of head offices
Parent: Sage Holding Company Limited
Officers: Miranda Craig, Secretary; David John Bailey [1971] Finance Director; Victoria Louise Bradin [1978] Director/General Counsel and Company Secretary; John-Henry Fredrik Liepe [1974] Financial Director [Swedish]; Sarah Jane Rolls [1974] Director/Accountant

Sage Pay (GB) Limited
Incorporated: 13 September 1999 *Employees:* 2
Net Worth: £5,208,579 *Total Assets:* £6,930,706
Registered Office: North Park, Newcastle upon Tyne, NE13 9AA
Activities: Information technology consultancy activities
Parent: Sage Pay Europe Limited
Officers: Miranda Craig, Secretary; Victoria Louise Bradin [1978] Director/General Counsel and Company Secretary; Adam Mark Richard Parker [1971] Finance Director; Sarah Jane Rolls [1974] Director/Accountant

Sage Pay Europe Limited
Incorporated: 13 January 2011 *Employees:* 79
Net Worth: £127,162,000 *Total Assets:* £164,810,000
Registered Office: North Park, Newcastle upon Tyne, NE13 9AA
Activities: Information technology consultancy activities
Parent: Sage Online Holdings Limited
Officers: Miranda Craig, Secretary; Victoria Louise Bradin [1978] Director/General Counsel and Company Secretary; Adam Mark Richard Parker [1971] Finance Director; Sarah Jane Rolls [1974] Director/Accountant

Sage Payments (UK) Ltd.
Incorporated: 26 June 2013 *Employees:* 15
Net Worth: £2,476,000 *Total Assets:* £12,272,000
Registered Office: North Park, Newcastle upon Tyne, NE13 9AA
Activities: Financial intermediation not elsewhere classified
Parent: Sage (UK) Ltd
Officers: David Antony Coleman [1962] Director; Seamus Smith [1968] Director

Sage People Limited
Incorporated: 20 April 2007 *Employees:* 87
Net Worth: £7,509,113 *Total Assets:* £14,958,091
Registered Office: North Park, Newcastle upon Tyne, NE13 9AA
Activities: Other information technology service activities
Parent: Sage Holding Company Limited
Officers: Miranda Craig, Secretary; Victoria Louise Bradin [1978] Director/General Counsel & Company Secretary; John-Henry Fredrik Liepe [1974] Director, Financial Accounting & Control [Swedish]; Sarah Jane Rolls [1974] Director/Accountant

Sage Treasury Company Limited
Incorporated: 5 December 2012
Net Worth: £48,522,000 *Total Assets:* £4,396,947,968
Registered Office: North Park, Newcastle upon Tyne, NE13 9AA
Activities: Activities of financial services holding companies
Parent: The Sage Group PLC
Officers: Miranda Craig, Secretary; Victoria Louise Bradin [1978] Director/General Counsel and Company Secretary; Lesley Ann Flowerdew [1967] Director/VP Group Tax & Treasury/Chartered Accountant; Sarah Jane Rolls [1974] Director/Accountant

Sage USD Hedgeco 1
Incorporated: 6 September 2013
Net Worth: £22,646,416 *Total Assets:* £22,646,416
Registered Office: North Park, Newcastle upon Tyne, NE13 9AA
Activities: Activities of other holding companies n.e.c.
Parent: Sage Treasury Company Limited
Officers: Miranda Craig, Secretary; Victoria Louise Bradin [1978] Director/General Counsel and Company Secretary; John-Henry Fredrik Liepe [1974] Financial Director [Swedish]; Sarah Jane Rolls [1974] Director/Accountant

Sage Wealth Management Limited
Incorporated: 8 November 2010 *Employees:* 4
Net Worth: £129,843 *Total Assets:* £974,810
Registered Office: 5 West Walk, Bowes Offices, Lambton Park, Chester-le-Street, Co Durham, DH3 4AN
Activities: Fund management activities
Shareholders: Michael Sage; Lisa Sage
Officers: Lisa Michelle Sage [1986] Director; Michael John Sage [1982] Director

Sagesoft
Incorporated: 16 February 1990
Net Worth: £1,487,890,816 *Total Assets:* £1,490,019,584
Registered Office: North Park, Newcastle upon Tyne, NE13 9AA
Activities: Information technology consultancy activities
Parent: Sage Holding Company Limited
Officers: Miranda Craig, Secretary; Victoria Louise Bradin [1978] Director/General Counsel and Company Secretary; John-Henry Fredrik Liepe [1974] Finance Director [Swedish]; Sarah Jane Rolls [1974] Director/Accountant

SAI Automotive Washington Limited
Incorporated: 13 October 1989 *Employees:* 236
Net Worth: £6,278,000 *Total Assets:* £35,942,000
Registered Office: Staithes Road, Pattinson Industrial Estate, Washington, Tyne & Wear, NE38 8NW
Activities: Manufacture of other parts and accessories for motor vehicles
Parent: SAI Automotive Fradley Ltd
Officers: Jose Manuel Membrillera [1969] Director [Spanish]

Saint & Clark Limited
Incorporated: 22 November 1963
Registered Office: 86b Heaton Road, Newcastle upon Tyne, NE6 5HL
Activities: Other letting and operating of own or leased real estate
Major Shareholder: Gary Clark
Officers: Gary Clark [1962] Director/Electrician

Saint John of God Hospitaller Services
Incorporated: 5 January 2005 *Employees:* 706
Net Worth Deficit: £25,000 *Total Assets:* £2,544,000
Registered Office: St Bede's House, Morton Park, Darlington, Co Durham, DL1 4XZ
Activities: Residential nursing care facilities
Officers: Brian Jeffrey Boggon [1957] Director/Retired; Niall Brannigan [1947] Director/Brother - Hospitaller Order of Saint John of God [Irish]; William Martin Forkan [1942] Director/Brother in Religious Order [Irish]; Edward Francis [1941] Director; Generald Edward Kidd [1967] Director/Solicitor; Anthony David Moore [1951] Director; Robert Moore [1944] Director

Saks (Education) Limited
Incorporated: 23 October 1998 *Employees:* 33
Net Worth: £906,755 *Total Assets:* £1,492,844
Registered Office: 55-59 Duke Street, Darlington, Co Durham, DL3 7SD
Activities: Other education n.e.c.
Major Shareholder: Stephen Kee
Officers: Stephen Kee [1957] Director

Saks Hair (Holdings) Limited
Incorporated: 10 November 1988 *Employees:* 1
Net Worth: £302,669 *Total Assets:* £996,086
Registered Office: 2 Peel Court, St Cuthberts Way, Darlington, Co Durham, DL1 1GB
Activities: Hairdressing and other beauty treatment
Shareholders: Dennis Cheesebrough; Swan Kee Limited
Officers: Dennis Cheesebrough, Secretary; Dennis Cheesebrough [1945] Director; Stephen Kee [1957] Director

Sale PFI Limited
Incorporated: 26 February 2002 *Employees:* 3
Net Worth: £1,814,000 *Total Assets:* £12,142,000
Registered Office: Shared Services Centre, Q3 Office, Quorum Business Park, Benton Lane, Newcastle upon Tyne, NE12 8EX
Activities: Combined facilities support activities
Parent: Engie FM Limited
Officers: Sarah Gregory, Secretary; Samuel Hockman [1982] Director; Bilal Hashim Lala [1963] Finance Director

Salecycle Limited
Incorporated: 5 February 2010 *Employees:* 159
Net Worth: £4,173,776 *Total Assets:* £5,032,800
Registered Office: Ground Floor, Alexander House, 1 Mandarin Road, Rainton Bridge Industrial Park, Houghton-le-Spring, Co Durham, DH4 5RA
Activities: Business and domestic software development
Officers: Trevor Michael Peter Nicholson, Secretary; Bernard Callaghan [1959] Director; Gerard Dominic Callaghan [1967] Director; Paul Michael Callaghan [1952] Director; Dominic Richard Edmunds [1978] Director; John Peter Eggleston [1975] Director; Steven Nelson [1965] Director; Trevor Michael Peter Nicholson [1973] Finance Director; Christopher James Wilds [1975] Director

Salem Tube International Limited
Incorporated: 20 January 1993 *Employees:* 33
Net Worth: £3,496,152 *Total Assets:* £10,989,730
Registered Office: 114-116 High Street, Gosforth, Newcastle upon Tyne, NE3 1HB
Activities: Other manufacturing n.e.c.
Major Shareholder: Howard Ions
Officers: Paul Callighan [1967] Sales Director; Howard Ions [1956] Director/Sales Manager

Saltwell Park Agencies Limited
Incorporated: 24 February 2006 *Employees:* 2
Net Worth: £1,149,560 *Total Assets:* £2,287,349
Registered Office: Belle Vue House, Belle Vue Bank, Low Fell, Gateshead, Tyne & Wear, NE9 6BT
Activities: Sale of new cars and light motor vehicles
Shareholders: Bernard Gerard Carney; April Carney
Officers: Bernard Gerard Carney, Secretary; April Carney [1963] Director; Bernard Gerard Carney [1964] Director/Motor Dealer

Saltwell Park Developments Ltd
Incorporated: 18 September 2012
Net Worth: £2,021,483 *Total Assets:* £2,310,259
Registered Office: Belle Vue House, Belle Vue Bank, Low Fell, Gateshead, Tyne & Wear, NE9 6BT
Activities: Development of building projects
Officers: April Carney [1963] Director; Bernard Gerard Carney [1964] Director

Saluci Limited
Incorporated: 29 November 2013
Registered Office: Barrington House, 41-45 Yarm Lane, Stockton on Tees, Cleveland, TS18 3EA
Activities: Other letting and operating of own or leased real estate
Major Shareholder: Paul Messham
Officers: Paul Anthony Messham [1965] Director

Sameach
Incorporated: 16 April 2002
Net Worth: £1,115,730 *Total Assets:* £1,358,902
Registered Office: Y Halberstadt, 81 Bewick Road, Gateshead, Tyne & Wear, NE8 1RR
Activities: Activities of other membership organisations n.e.c.
Officers: Judith Halberstadt, Secretary; Yechezkel Michael Halberstadt [1972] Director/Consultant; Menachem Yaakov Salzer [1982] Director/Accountant

L. Sampson & Son Limited
Incorporated: 29 May 1956 *Employees:* 6
Net Worth: £826,284 *Total Assets:* £1,115,530
Registered Office: Acclom House, Well, Bedale, N Yorks, DL8 2QF
Activities: Mixed farming
Shareholders: Leonard Mark Sampson; Heather Louise Sampson
Officers: Heather Louise Sampson, Secretary; Heather Louise Sampson [1956] Director/Administrator; Leonard Thomas Henry Sampson [1988] Director/Farmer; Leonard Mark Sampson [1953] Director/Farmer

Samson Aviation Services Limited
Incorporated: 27 March 1991 *Employees:* 7
Net Worth: £1,840,960 *Total Assets:* £1,916,159
Registered Office: General Aviation Terminal, Southside, Newcastle International Airport, Woolsington, Newcastle upon Tyne, NE13 8BT
Activities: Agents involved in the sale of fuels, ores, metals and industrial chemicals
Parent: Newcastle International Airport Limited
Officers: Kirstin Hofbeck, Secretary; Mark Allan Hunt [1977] Director/Chief Financial Officer; Nicholas Vaughan Jones [1973] Director/Chief Executive; Richard Andrew Knight [1967] Operations Director

Samsung C&T ECUK Limited
Incorporated: 3 July 2012 *Employees:* 37
Net Worth Deficit: £38,012,064 *Total Assets:* £36,701,696
Registered Office: Whessoe Technology Centre, Alderman Best Way, Morton Palms, Darlington, Co Durham, DL1 4WB
Activities: Engineering design activities for industrial process and production
Officers: Yi Heon Hyun [1971] Director/CFO of Whessoe Engineering Ltd. [South Korean]

Sandco 1053 Limited
Incorporated: 23 October 2007
Registered Office: Houghton House, New Road, Team Valley Trading Estate, Gateshead, Tyne & Wear, NE11 0JU
Activities: Buying and selling of own real estate
Major Shareholder: George Houghton
Officers: George Houghton [1940] Director

Sandco 1184 Limited
Incorporated: 19 September 1978 *Employees:* 5
Net Worth: £125,000 *Total Assets:* £927,741
Registered Office: Ford Depositories, Walker Road, Newcastle upon Tyne, NE6 2HL
Activities: Activities of head offices
Parent: Sandco 1184 Limited
Officers: Peta Ann Hoult, Secretary; Anabel Kate Hoult [1969] Director; Charles Wilson Hoult [1967] Director; Frederick Wilson Hoult [1938] Director; Peta Ann Hoult [1938] Director/Journalist; Dr Sarah Louise Hoult [1965] Director/General Practitioner

Sandco 830 Limited
Incorporated: 9 March 2004
Net Worth: £475,064 *Total Assets:* £1,014,016
Registered Office: Henson House, Planet Place, Stephenson Industrial Estate, Newcastle upon Tyne, NE12 6RZ
Activities: Other letting and operating of own or leased real estate
Officers: Abigail Clare Miller, Secretary/Property Consultant; John Muckian [1971] Director; David Nathan Wilson [1973] Managing Director

Sandco F.P.S. Limited
Incorporated: 22 November 1999 *Employees:* 149
Net Worth: £7,357,539 *Total Assets:* £18,368,812
Registered Office: South Tyne Mill, Hexham, Northumberland, NE46 3SD
Activities: Other business support service activities n.e.c.
Shareholders: Peter Gerard Duxbury; Pauline Duxbury
Officers: Peter Gerard Duxbury, Secretary/Manager; Pauline Duxbury [1962] Director/Purchasing Manager; Peter Gerard Duxbury [1960] Director/Manager

Sanders Plant & Waste Management Limited
Incorporated: 16 March 2007 *Employees:* 42
Net Worth: £557,213 *Total Assets:* £4,662,552
Registered Office: 40 Butterwell Drive, Pegswood, Morpeth, Northumberland, NE61 6YE
Activities: Renting and leasing of construction and civil engineering machinery and equipment
Shareholders: Carl Joseph Sanders; Lynne Sanders
Officers: Lynne Sanders, Secretary; Carl Joseph Sanders [1959] Director; Lynne Sanders [1960] Director

Barry Sanderson (Property) Limited
Incorporated: 24 May 2005
Net Worth: £1,590,207 *Total Assets:* £1,691,629
Registered Office: Unit 5 Frontier Court, Leechmere Industrial Estate, Sunderland, Tyne & Wear, SR2 9TX
Activities: Activities of head offices
Shareholders: Barry Richard Sanderson; Owen Sanderson
Officers: Barry Richard Sanderson [1948] Director

Sanderson Young Ltd
Incorporated: 2 November 1998 *Employees:* 36
Net Worth: £384,455 *Total Assets:* £1,222,113
Registered Office: The Old Bank, 30 High Street, Gosforth, Newcastle upon Tyne, NE3 1LL
Activities: Real estate agencies
Parent: Sanderson Young Group Limited
Officers: Duncan Graham Young [1964] Director/Estate Agent

Sandgate Park Limited
Incorporated: 12 May 2015 *Employees:* 1
Net Worth: £61,503 *Total Assets:* £1,956,974
Registered Office: 3 Vinovia Place, Stockton on Tees, Cleveland, TS17 5LU
Activities: Other letting and operating of own or leased real estate
Officers: Stephen Cornfield [1969] Director; John Brian Harrison [1966] Director

Sandman Hotel Group (UK) Limited
Incorporated: 11 February 2009 *Employees:* 43
Net Worth: £1,914,317 *Total Assets:* £8,733,909
Registered Office: Sandman Signature Hotel, Gallowgate, Newcastle upon Tyne, NE1 4SD
Activities: Hotels and similar accommodation
Officers: Mitchell Rockford Gaglardi [1980] Director/Hotel and Restaurant Consultant [Canadian]

Sandwath Contracting Limited
Incorporated: 13 December 2011
Net Worth: £112,966 *Total Assets:* £796,803
Registered Office: Sandwath House, Forcett, Richmond, N Yorks, DL11 7SE
Activities: Mixed farming
Shareholders: Nicholas Anthony Johnson; Anne Victoria Johnson
Officers: Anne Victoria Johnson [1967] Director; Nicholas Anthony Johnson [1961] Director/Farmer

Sangenic International Ltd.
Incorporated: 15 April 1977 *Employees:* 110
Net Worth: £54,910,000 *Total Assets:* £82,497,000
Registered Office: Mayborn House, Balliol Business Park, Newcastle upon Tyne, NE12 8EW
Activities: Manufacture of other plastic products
Parent: Mayborn Group Limited
Officers: Neal Austin [1966] Global Operations Director; Edward Chapman [1964] Director; Stephen William Parkin [1969] Director/Marketing; James William Matthew Taylor [1974] Director/Chief Financial Officer

Sansec Development (Stevenage) Limited
Incorporated: 14 February 2000 *Employees:* 6
Net Worth: £3,575,810 *Total Assets:* £5,413,315
Registered Office: 53 Millview Drive, Tynemouth, North Shields, Tyne & Wear, NE30 2QD
Activities: Other letting and operating of own or leased real estate
Major Shareholder: Prudence Bailey Harvey
Officers: Rebecca Bailey Chapman, Secretary; Rebecca Bailey Chapman [1979] Director/Secretary; Benjamin Playfair Harvey [1982] Director; John Playfair Harvey [1942] Director; Mary Jane Harvey [1970] Director; Prudence Bailey Harvey [1955] Director; Emma Jill Wade [1972] Director

Sapphire Technologies Limited
Incorporated: 10 April 1996 *Employees:* 47
Net Worth: £1,088,000 *Total Assets:* £5,007,000
Registered Office: North Point, Faverdale North, Darlington, Co Durham, DL3 0PH
Activities: Information technology consultancy activities
Parent: Kiplun Ltd
Officers: Joseph Andrew Deane, Secretary; Annabel Berry [1976] Director; Richard James Guy Davies [1953] Director; Joseph Andrew Deane [1968] Director/Chartered Accountant; David Generald Lannin [1972] Director; Alan Moffat [1961] Director; Mayan Kantilal Shah [1966] Director

Sarens (UK) Ltd
Incorporated: 29 November 1988 *Employees:* 129
Net Worth: £13,035,000 *Total Assets:* £33,673,000
Registered Office: Booth House, Riverside Park Road, Middlesbrough, Cleveland, TS2 1UT
Activities: Other specialised construction activities n.e.c.
Officers: Allison Jane Hedley, Secretary; Grant Roy Mitchell [1952] Managing Director; Ludo Sarens [1952] Director [Belgian]; Marc Victor Felicitas Maria Sarens [1956] Director [Belgian]

Sashless Window Co. Limited
Incorporated: 5 April 1972 *Employees:* 39
Net Worth: £717,926 *Total Assets:* £1,124,198
Registered Office: 32 Standard Way, Standard Way Industrial Estate, Northallerton, N Yorks, DL6 2XA
Activities: Manufacture of other products of wood; manufacture of articles of cork, straw and plaiting materials
Major Shareholder: Redvers Chown
Officers: Ann Valerie Chown, Secretary; Alastair Paul Chown [1960] Managing Director; Ann Valerie Chown [1943] Director; John Francis Chown [1929] Director; Jonathan David Chown [1964] Director; Redvers Chown [1935] Director; James Kevin Clark [1958] Sales Director

Satcom Global Aura Limited
Incorporated: 18 March 2016
Net Worth: £25,335 *Total Assets:* £841,117
Registered Office: Satcom Global, Tanners Bank, North Shields, Tyne & Wear, NE30 1JH
Activities: Satellite telecommunications activities
Officers: Robert Alan Howes, Secretary; Robert Alan Howes [1955] Director/Accountant; Ian Andrew Robinson [1961] Director

N I Sattar Holdings Limited
Incorporated: 19 June 2014
Net Worth: £60,967 *Total Assets:* £827,687
Registered Office: 53 Reid Park Road, Jesmond, Newcastle upon Tyne, NE2 2ER
Activities: Activities of head offices
Shareholders: Dr Naweed Sattar; Irrm Nazir Sattar
Officers: Irrm Nazir Sattar [1969] Director/Pharmacist; Naweed Sattar [1968] Director/Doctor

Savisto Limited
Incorporated: 28 October 2014 *Employees:* 1
Net Worth: £450,165 *Total Assets:* £1,175,020
Registered Office: 1 Sadler Forster Way, Teesside Industrial Estate, Stockton on Tees, Cleveland, TS17 9JY
Activities: Retail sale via mail order houses or via Internet
Shareholders: Andrew John Simpson; Andrea Simpson
Officers: Andrea Sheila Simpson, Secretary; Andrea Sheila Simpson [1976] Director; Andrew John Simpson [1979] Director

Savona Imports Limited
Incorporated: 5 September 2013 *Employees:* 2
Net Worth: £1,039,703 *Total Assets:* £1,480,489
Registered Office: Beaumont Accountancy, First Floor, Enterprise House, 202-206 Linthorpe Road, Middlesbrough, Cleveland, TS1 3QW
Activities: Other retail sale in non-specialised stores
Major Shareholder: Wayne Kevin Spriggs
Officers: Wayne Kevin Spriggs [1974] Director/Import Export & Manufacture; Jason Lee Wood [1970] Director/Import Export & Manufacture

Sayers Property Limited
Incorporated: 6 March 2014 *Employees:* 1
Net Worth Deficit: £8,306 *Total Assets:* £813,882
Registered Office: Tutin Road, Leeming Bar Industrial Estate, Northallerton, N Yorks, DL7 9UJ
Activities: Construction of domestic buildings
Major Shareholder: Clifford Sayer
Officers: Clifford Sayer [1965] Director

Sayers Road Tanker Rentals Limited
Incorporated: 1 November 2001
Net Worth: £3,106,516 *Total Assets:* £5,988,156
Registered Office: Tutin Road, Leeming Bar Industrial Estate, Northallerton, N Yorks, DL7 9UJ
Activities: Maintenance and repair of motor vehicles
Major Shareholder: Clifford Sayer
Officers: Louise Chambers, Secretary; Clifford Sayer [1965] Director/Tanker Manufacture

Sayers Road Tankers Engineering Limited
Incorporated: 3 January 2008 *Employees:* 46
Net Worth: £1,038,531 *Total Assets:* £2,509,524
Registered Office: Tutin Road, Leeming Bar Industrial Estate, Northallerton, N Yorks, DL7 9UJ
Activities: Other service activities n.e.c.
Major Shareholder: Clifford Sayer
Officers: Louise Chambers, Secretary; Clifford Sayer [1965] Director

M.J. Scaife Limited
Incorporated: 3 April 1995
Net Worth: £1,077,397 *Total Assets:* £1,081,871
Registered Office: Yearby Farm, Yearby, Redcar, Cleveland, TS11 8HF
Activities: Non-trading company
Shareholders: Michael John Scaife; Patricia Scaife; M J Scaife 1990 Discretionary Settlement
Officers: Patricia Scaife, Secretary/Director; Michael John Scaife [1946] Director; Patricia Scaife [1945] Director

Scanman UK Limited
Incorporated: 21 June 2010 *Employees:* 10
Net Worth: £126,614 *Total Assets:* £1,364,395
Registered Office: Unit 1 Whorlton Road, Riverside Park Industrial Estate, Middlesbrough, Cleveland, TS2 1QJ
Activities: Manufacture of printed labels
Major Shareholder: Peter Neil Scanlon
Officers: Peter Scanlon, Secretary; Peter Scanlon [1969] Director/General Manager

Scarlet Band Bus and Coach Limited
Incorporated: 26 March 2008 *Employees:* 54
Net Worth: £797,449 *Total Assets:* £1,345,624
Registered Office: Welfare Garages, High Street, West Cornforth, Ferryhill, Co Durham, DL17 9LA
Activities: Other passenger land transport
Major Shareholder: Graeme Hopkins Torrance
Officers: Andrew Paul Dolan, Secretary; Graeme Hopkins Torrance [1956] Director

Schiedel Chimney Systems Limited
Incorporated: 25 February 2004 *Employees:* 110
Net Worth Deficit: £14,152,000 *Total Assets:* £9,905,000
Registered Office: Crowther Industrial Estate, Washington, Tyne & Wear, NE38 0AQ
Activities: Activities of head offices
Parent: Schiedel GmbH & Co KG
Officers: Shaun Goodings, Secretary; Michael Christopher Ball [1971] Managing Director; Alessandro Cappellini [1970] Director

Schofield Dyers & Finishers Limited
Incorporated: 9 November 2007
Registered Office: Time Central, 32 Gallowgate, Newcastle upon Tyne, NE1 4BF
Activities: Finishing of textiles
Major Shareholder: Aidan Queen
Officers: Aidan Wilson Queen, Secretary; Aidan Wilson Queen [1952] Finance Director

Schofield, Maddison & Carling Limited
Incorporated: 23 December 2011
Registered Office: Stoneridge, The Green, Brafferton, Darlington, Co Durham, DL1 3LA
Activities: Management consultancy activities other than financial management
Shareholder: Peter Schofield
Officers: Peter William Schofield, Secretary; John Carling [1965] Director/Financial Adviser; Susan Carling [1963] Director; Lucy Emma Crow [1979] Director/Housewife; Michael Maddison [1950] Director/Accountant; Claire Schofield [1962] Director/Secretary; Peter William Schofield [1954] Director/Financial Adviser

Scholle IPN UK Ltd.
Incorporated: 18 November 1997 *Employees:* 73
Net Worth: £5,113,883 *Total Assets:* £7,074,504
Registered Office: Unit 12a Follingsby Close, Follingsby Park, Wardley, Gateshead, Tyne & Wear, NE10 8YG
Activities: Manufacture of plastic packing goods
Parent: Scholle IPN Corporation
Officers: Thomas John Bickford [1953] Director/President and Chief Executive Officer [American]; Jasper Moonen [1985] Director/Corporate Lawyer [Dutch]; Jerry Trousdale [1966] Director/C.F.O./Executive [American]

Scigrip Adhesives Limited
Incorporated: 19 August 2010 *Employees:* 31
Net Worth: £567,346 *Total Assets:* £2,803,708
Registered Office: Unit 22 Bentall Business Park, Glover Road, Washington, Tyne & Wear, NE37 3JD
Activities: Other business support service activities n.e.c.
Officers: William Barton [1954] Director/Chief Financial Officer [American]; David Glenn Marschall [1956] Director/Financial Advisor [American]; George Carroll Moore [1955] Director [American]

Scollen & Wright Funeral Service Limited
Incorporated: 15 May 2009 *Employees:* 16
Net Worth: £578,467 *Total Assets:* £932,210
Registered Office: 37 Blind Lane, Silksworth, Sunderland, Tyne & Wear, SR3 1AS
Activities: Funeral and related activities
Major Shareholder: Alan Scollen
Officers: Nigel Edward Marston, Secretary; Alan Scollen [1963] Funeral Director

Scott Bros. Enterprises Limited
Incorporated: 15 May 2003
Net Worth: £1,188,067 *Total Assets:* £1,533,658
Registered Office: Scott Business Park, Haverton Hill Road, Billingham, Cleveland, TS23 1PY
Activities: Collection of non-hazardous waste
Parent: Scott Bros. Holdings Limited
Officers: Ian William Fraser [1948] Director; David John Scott [1971] Director

Scott Bros. Environmental Services Limited
Incorporated: 20 September 1995 *Employees:* 1
Net Worth: £8,093,382 *Total Assets:* £10,587,841
Registered Office: Scott Business Park, Haverton Hill Road, Billingham, Stockton on Tees, Cleveland, TS23 1PY
Activities: Other service activities incidental to land transportation, n.e.c.
Parent: Scott Bros. Holdings Limited
Officers: Ian William Fraser [1948] Director; David John Scott [1971] Director

Scott Bros. Holdings Limited
Incorporated: 15 May 2003 *Employees:* 120
Net Worth: £23,364,876 *Total Assets:* £28,390,208
Registered Office: Scott Business Park, Haverton Hill Road, Billingham, Cleveland, TS23 1PY
Activities: Activities of head offices
Major Shareholder: David Scott
Officers: Ian William Fraser [1948] Director; David John Scott [1971] Director; Peter George Scott [1976] Director

Scott Bros. Limited
Incorporated: 1 August 2007 *Employees:* 120
Net Worth: £2,137,154 *Total Assets:* £6,329,881
Registered Office: Scott Business Park, Haverton Hill Road, Billingham, Cleveland, TS23 1PY
Activities: Collection of non-hazardous waste
Parent: Scott Bros. Holdings Limited
Officers: Robert John Borthwick [1963] Director; Ian William Fraser [1948] Director; Peter George Scott [1976] Director

Scott Bros. Recycling Limited
Incorporated: 23 April 2003 *Employees:* 32
Net Worth Deficit: £79,161 *Total Assets:* £1,846,648
Registered Office: Scott Business Park, Haverton Hill Road, Billingham, Cleveland, TS23 1PY
Activities: Recovery of sorted materials
Parent: Scott Bros. Holdings Limited
Officers: Robert John Borthwick [1963] Director; David John Scott [1971] Director

Alex Scott Cars Limited
Incorporated: 11 February 2003 *Employees:* 24
Net Worth: £615,014 *Total Assets:* £2,475,201
Registered Office: Morpeth Road Garage, Guidepost, Choppington, Northumberland, NE62 5AR
Activities: Sale of used cars and light motor vehicles
Shareholders: Alexander Scott; Allison Margaret Scott
Officers: Allison Margaret Scott, Secretary/Bank Manager; Alexander Scott [1943] Director/Car Dealer; Allison Margaret Scott [1960] Director/Bank Official; James Talbot Scott [1979] Director/Car Dealer; Jonathan Mark Scott [1974] Director/Car Dealer

A.& J.Scott Limited
Incorporated: 20 December 1972 *Employees:* 152
Net Worth: £10,492,296 *Total Assets:* £16,735,571
Registered Office: Station Sawmills, Wooperton, Alnwick, Northumberland, NE66 4XW
Activities: Sawmilling and planing of wood
Major Shareholder: Andrew Scott
Officers: Judith Scott, Secretary; Ian Barfoot [1956] Sales Director; Rosemary Margaret Bertram [1958] Finance Director; Neil Waugh Somervell Campbell [1955] Forestry Director; Andrew Scott [1957] Director/Chairman; Robert Scott [1989] Managing Director

R & H Scott Limited
Incorporated: 26 February 2003 *Employees:* 9
Net Worth: £1,341,998 *Total Assets:* £1,690,475
Registered Office: The Haven, Church Lane, Wark, Hexham, Northumberland, NE48 3LX
Activities: Freight transport by road
Major Shareholder: Ann Helen Scott
Officers: Ann Helen Scott, Secretary; Robert William Scott [1965] Director/Haulier

Kirsten Scott Limited
Incorporated: 20 May 2009
Net Worth: £839,157 *Total Assets:* £841,563
Registered Office: 7 Collingwood Street, Newcastle upon Tyne, NE1 1JE
Activities: Solicitors
Major Shareholder: Kirsten Amanda Scott
Officers: Mark Laverick, Secretary; Kirsten Amanda Scott [1960] Director/Solicitor

Scott Logic Limited
Incorporated: 28 February 2005 *Employees:* 222
Net Worth: £10,915,651 *Total Assets:* £15,701,010
Registered Office: 1 St James' Gate, Newcastle upon Tyne, NE1 4AD
Activities: Other business support service activities n.e.c.
Major Shareholder: Gary Scott
Officers: Dr Helen Estyn-Jones, Secretary; Michael Edward Brown [1950] Director; Colin Nigel Eberhardt [1975] Director; Gary Scott [1970] Director; Nigel Charles Wilson [1971] Director

G. Scott of York Limited
Incorporated: 17 November 2005
Net Worth Deficit: £316,233 *Total Assets:* £1,134,875
Registered Office: East Farm, Great Whittington, Northumberland, NE19 2HP
Activities: Other letting and operating of own or leased real estate
Shareholders: Timothy Oliver; Sarah Oliver
Officers: Sarah Oliver, Secretary; Sarah Oliver [1964] Director/Secretary; Timothy John Oliver [1967] Director/Farmer

Scott-Chem Limited
Incorporated: 21 January 1981 *Employees:* 24
Net Worth: £727,781 *Total Assets:* £1,122,564
Registered Office: Unit 3 Roseberry Shopping Centre, Roseberry Road, Redcar, Cleveland, TS10 4NY
Activities: Dispensing chemist in specialised stores
Parent: N & R Gupta Limited
Officers: Nitin Gupta, Secretary; Nitin Gupta [1970] Director/Pharmacist; Rachna Gupta [1974] Director/Tutor

Scotts of Whittington Limited
Incorporated: 8 April 2010 *Employees:* 6
Net Worth: £503,967 *Total Assets:* £942,317
Registered Office: Great Whittington, Northumberland, NE19 2HP
Activities: Construction of other civil engineering projects n.e.c.
Shareholders: Alfred Wood; Margaret Henderson Wood
Officers: Alfred Wood [1945] Director; Christopher Wood [1969] Director; Kevin Wood [1976] Director; Margaret Henderson Wood [1948] Director

SCR UKI Ltd
Incorporated: 12 February 2014
Registered Office: 1 Greencroft Industrial Park, Stanley, Co Durham, DH9 7YA
Activities: Other business support service activities n.e.c.
Officers: Stuart Grant Junor [1980] Director

Screen Services (NE) Limited
Incorporated: 31 August 1999 *Employees:* 31
Net Worth: £1,079,872 *Total Assets:* £1,400,666
Registered Office: Cartmel Business Centre, Shields Road, Pelaw, Gateshead, Tyne & Wear, NE10 0QD
Activities: Printing n.e.c.
Major Shareholder: Jason Charlton
Officers: Nicholasina Charlton, Secretary; Jason Charlton [1969] Director/Screen Printer

SCS Structures Ltd
Incorporated: 13 September 2000
Registered Office: Unit 1 Proctor Court, Boeing Way, Preston Farm Industrial Estate, Stockton on Tees, Cleveland, TS18 3TE
Activities: Development of building projects
Major Shareholder: Philip Davison Hall
Officers: Philip Davison Hall, Secretary; Amanda Hall [1970] Director/Accounts Manager

SDY Limited
Incorporated: 7 August 2003 *Employees:* 17
Net Worth: £180,719 *Total Assets:* £1,208,481
Registered Office: 440 Dukesway, Team Valley Trading Estate, Gateshead, Tyne & Wear, NE11 0PZ
Activities: Retail sale of electrical household appliances in specialised stores
Shareholders: Gary Bunt; Paul Skinner; Katie Jane Skinner
Officers: Paul Skinner, Secretary; Gary Bunt [1968] Director; Paul Skinner [1969] Director

Sea Island Developments (Ponteland) Limited
Incorporated: 1 November 2016
Net Worth Deficit: £9,615 *Total Assets:* £968,199
Registered Office: West 2, Asama Court, Newcastle Business Park, Newcastle upon Tyne, NE4 7YD
Activities: Development of building projects
Parent: Sea Island Developments Limited
Officers: Victoria Jane Ponton [1978] Director; Edward James Walton [1987] Director; Mark Adam Walton [1974] Director; Philip George Walton [1949] Director

Sea Island Developments Limited
Incorporated: 14 October 2016
Net Worth: £799,989 *Total Assets:* £899,989
Registered Office: West 2, Asama Court, Newcastle Business Park, Newcastle upon Tyne, NE4 7YD
Activities: Development of building projects
Major Shareholder: Philip George Walton
Officers: Victoria Jane Ponton [1978] Director; Edward James Walton [1987] Director; Mark Adam Walton [1974] Director; Philip George Walton [1949] Director

Seaham Harbour Dock Company
Employees: 53
Net Worth: £1,050,000 *Total Assets:* £3,227,000
Registered Office: Cargo Durham Distribution Centre, Seaham, Co Durham, SR7 7NZ
Activities: Cargo handling for water transport activities
Major Shareholder: Mark Alexander Vernon Gatehouse
Officers: David Sydney Martin, Secretary; Christine Ann Gatehouse [1955] Director; Mark Alexander Vernon Gatehouse [1949] Director; Alan Burgoyne Luscombe [1958] Director; David Sydney Martin [1955] Director

Seatechs Limited
Incorporated: 10 November 2006 *Employees:* 6
Net Worth: £1,105,219 *Total Assets:* £1,942,713
Registered Office: Enterprise Centre, Brougham Terrace, Hartlepool, Cleveland, TS24 8EY
Activities: Other activities of employment placement agencies
Shareholders: Paul Anthony Cave; Beverley Cave
Officers: Beverley Cave, Secretary; Paul Anthony Cave [1954] Director

Seateks Engineering Limited
Incorporated: 12 June 2007 *Employees:* 2
Net Worth: £938,778 *Total Assets:* £1,021,345
Registered Office: 7a Ashville Avenue, Eaglescliffe, Stockton on Tees, Cleveland, TS16 9AU
Activities: Other engineering activities
Major Shareholder: Paul Robert Cairns
Officers: Diane Elizabeth Cairns, Secretary; Andrew Robert Amor [1978] Director; Diane Elizabeth Cairns [1962] Director; Paul Robert Cairns [1967] Director/Engineer

Seatgeek Sport Limited
Incorporated: 20 September 2011 *Employees:* 10
Net Worth: £333,738 *Total Assets:* £817,263
Registered Office: Rowlands House, Portobello Road, Birtley, Chester-le-Street, Co Durham, DH3 2RY
Activities: Other sports activities
Officers: Jon David Groetzinger [1984] Director/Manager [American]; John Bradford Tacy [1980] Director/Manager [American]

Seaton Developments Limited
Incorporated: 21 February 2002
Net Worth Deficit: £149,892 *Total Assets:* £978,326
Registered Office: The Barn, Rennington, Alnwick, Northumberland, NE66 3RR
Activities: Buying and selling of own real estate
Parent: Seaton Rest Homes Limited
Officers: Janice Carty [1950] Secretary Director; David Andrew Whitehead [1977] Director

Seaton Healthcare Limited
Incorporated: 23 September 2008 *Employees:* 25
Net Worth: £574,744 *Total Assets:* £2,138,347
Registered Office: 30 Bowes Street, Blyth, Northumberland, NE24 1BD
Activities: Dispensing chemist in specialised stores
Shareholders: Narinder Dave Singh Sangha; Harpreet Singh Kullar
Officers: Narinder Dave Singh Sangha, Secretary; Harpreet Singh Kullar [1979] Director/Pharmacist; Narinder Dave Singh Sangha [1975] Director/Pharmacist

Seaton Trust Limited
Incorporated: 20 June 1938 *Employees:* 4
Net Worth: £8,240,360 *Total Assets:* £8,415,040
Registered Office: 49 Park View, Whitley Bay, Tyne & Wear, NE26 2TP
Activities: Management of real estate on a fee or contract basis
Officers: Ian Dawson Jefferson, Secretary; Ian Geoffrey Firth [1949] Director/Solicitor; Ian Richard Harris [1950] Director/Chartered Surveyor; Ian Dawson Jefferson [1956] Director/Chartered Surveyor; James George Summers [1956] Director/Chartered Accountant

Seaward Electronic Limited
Incorporated: 28 October 1982 *Employees:* 154
Net Worth: £3,753,126 *Total Assets:* £5,899,074
Registered Office: 18 Bracken Hill, South West Industrial Estate, Peterlee, Co Durham, SR8 2SW
Activities: Manufacture of electronic measuring, testing etc. equipment, not for industrial process control
Parent: GMC Instruments UK Limited
Officers: Mark Marsh [1971] Finance Director; Dr Hans-Peter Manfred Opitz [1957] Managing Director [German]; Thomas Talbot [1957] Director; Andrew Richard Upton [1969] Director/Sales; Matthias Wist [1964] Managing Director [German]; Dr Manyin Thomas Ying [1970] Engineering Director

Sebastian Enterprises Ltd
Incorporated: 31 January 2006
Net Worth Deficit: £84,282 *Total Assets:* £2,079,969
Registered Office: 11 Finkle Street, Richmond, N Yorks, DL10 4QA
Activities: Management consultancy activities other than financial management
Major Shareholder: Christine Louise Fernandes
Officers: Steven Douglas Smith, Secretary; Christine Louise Fernandes [1971] Director/Manager; Steven Douglas Smith [1957] Director/Manager

Secon Solar Limited
Incorporated: 9 July 2003 *Employees:* 14
Net Worth: £1,143,885 *Total Assets:* £2,194,310
Registered Office: Unit 87 Business & Innovation Centre, Wearfield, Sunderland Enterprise Park, Sunderland, Tyne & Wear, SR5 2TH
Activities: Wholesale of electronic and telecommunications equipment and parts
Parent: Secon Holdings Limited
Officers: Pauline Skinner, Secretary; Chris Jackson Caldwell [1987] Director; Kevin James Carling [1955] Director; Paul Hind [1965] Director

Security Centres Securus Limited
Incorporated: 9 February 1989
Net Worth Deficit: £570,183 *Total Assets:* £1,151,656
Registered Office: 9-18 Ruby Court, Wesley Drive, Benton Square Industrial Estate, Newcastle upon Tyne, NE12 9UP
Activities: Other professional, scientific and technical activities n.e.c.
Parent: Securus Group Limited
Officers: Anthony Denis Kane [1959] Director; John Stewart [1968] Director

Security Print Solutions Limited
Incorporated: 10 June 1982 *Employees:* 72
Net Worth: £4,599,082 *Total Assets:* £7,576,065
Registered Office: Northumbria House, No 1 Industrial Estate, Consett, Co Durham, DH8 6TW
Activities: Manufacture of paper stationery
Shareholders: James Crowther; Michael Crowther
Officers: James Crowther, Secretary; David Anthony Clough [1972] Director; Paul Andrew Craig [1968] Director; James Crowther [1947] Managing Director; Michael Crowther [1950] Director; Claire Elizabeth Duggins [1967] Director; Graham Christopher McGuire [1946] Director; Stephen Wilson [1961] Director

Security Systems and Alarms Inspection Board
Incorporated: 5 June 1990 *Employees:* 37
Net Worth: £1,019,438 *Total Assets:* £1,487,450
Registered Office: 7-11 Earsdon Road, West Monkseaton, Whitley Bay, Tyne & Wear, NE25 9SX
Activities: Security systems service activities
Officers: Alan Fidler, Secretary; Alexander Paul Carmichael [1957] Director/Chief Executive; Mark Robert Peretti [1968] Director; Geoffrey Tate [1944] Director/Chief Executive

Sedbury Property Limited
Incorporated: 30 April 2001 *Employees:* 2
Net Worth: £888,372 *Total Assets:* £913,777
Registered Office: The Cottage, Sedbury East Farm, Gilling West, Richmond, N Yorks, DL10 5ER
Activities: Other letting and operating of own or leased real estate
Shareholders: Norman Hughes; Janet Hughes
Officers: Janet Hughes, Secretary/Director; Janet Hughes [1965] Director; Norman Hughes [1960] Director/Electrician

Michael Sehgal & Sons Limited
Incorporated: 5 June 1990 *Employees:* 5
Net Worth: £2,411,375 *Total Assets:* £2,519,920
Registered Office: 28-40 Scotswood Road, Newcastle upon Tyne, NE4 7JB
Activities: Wholesale of clothing and footwear
Officers: Robin Sehgal, Secretary; Jai Deip Sehgal [1967] Director/Draper; Kiran Sehgal [1970] Director/Manager; Purnima Sehgal [1974] Director/Chartered Accountant; Robin Sehgal [1969] Director/Draper; Veena Sehgal [1944] Director

Sehgal Commercial Properties Limited
Incorporated: 1 October 1974
Net Worth: £621,790 *Total Assets:* £1,707,846
Registered Office: 234a Chillingham Road, Heaton, Newcastle upon Tyne, NE6 5LP
Activities: Other letting and operating of own or leased real estate
Shareholder: Micky Sehgal
Officers: Micky Sehgal, Secretary/Director; Micky Sehgal [1959] Director; Sushill Kumar Steven Sehgal [1959] Director

Michael Sehgal Property Company Limited
Incorporated: 16 July 1998 *Employees:* 5
Net Worth: £4,054,526 *Total Assets:* £12,913,216
Registered Office: 28-40 Scotswood Road, Newcastle upon Tyne, NE4 7JB
Activities: Buying and selling of own real estate
Officers: Robin Sehgal, Secretary; Jai Deip Sehgal [1967] Director/Wholesaler; Kiran Sehgal [1970] Director; Purnima Sehgal [1974] Director; Robin Sehgal [1969] Director/Wholesaler

Sekura (Holdings) Limited
Incorporated: 16 April 2015 *Employees:* 92
Net Worth: £1,459,723 *Total Assets:* £3,157,678
Registered Office: 12 Walton Road, Pattinson North, Washington, Tyne & Wear, NE38 8QA
Activities: Activities of other holding companies n.e.c.
Major Shareholder: Charles Hill
Officers: Michelle Ayre [1963] Director; Charles Hill [1948] Director

Sekura Trade Frames Limited
Incorporated: 15 March 1996 *Employees:* 92
Net Worth: £2,470,855 *Total Assets:* £4,159,511
Registered Office: 12 Walton Road, Pattinson North, Washington, Tyne & Wear, NE38 8QA
Activities: Other manufacturing n.e.c.
Major Shareholder: Charles Hill
Officers: Michelle Ayre, Secretary/Accounts Manager; Michelle Ayre [1963] Director/Accounts Manager; Charles Hill [1948] Sales Director

Select Control Systems Limited
Incorporated: 14 August 1998 *Employees:* 20
Net Worth: £571,646 *Total Assets:* £843,634
Registered Office: 19i White Rose Way, Follingsby Park, Gateshead, Tyne & Wear, NE10 8YX
Activities: Manufacture of other electrical equipment
Shareholder: Kathleen Dodds
Officers: Stephen Paul Dodds [1957] Director/Accountant; Keith Ratcliffe [1954] Director/Foreman Electrician

Select Prime Sites UK Ltd
Incorporated: 19 December 2003
Net Worth: £1,405,455 *Total Assets:* £3,869,001
Registered Office: 359 Prince Edward Road, South Shields, Tyne & Wear, NE34 7LZ
Activities: Take-away food shops and mobile food stands
Officers: Herydal Singh Gill, Secretary; Herydal Singh Gill [1963] Director; Jasvir Singh Gill [1986] Director; Kulwant Kaur Gill [1962] Director; Sukhpreet Gill [1988] Director

Select Property Developments Limited
Incorporated: 2 March 2001
Net Worth: £3,848,434 *Total Assets:* £11,672,337
Registered Office: Henson Group, Henson House, Planet Place, Stephenson Industrial Estate, Newcastle upon Tyne, NE12 6RZ
Activities: Buying and selling of own real estate
Shareholders: David Nathan Wilson; Richard Nigel Wilson
Officers: Richard Nigel Wilson, Secretary/Trainee Manager; David Nathan Wilson [1973] Director; Richard Nigel Wilson [1971] Director/Trainee Manager

Sembcorp Holdings Limited
Incorporated: 25 September 2008
Net Worth: £69,392,000 *Total Assets:* £134,500,992
Registered Office: Sembcorp UK Headquarters, Wilton International, Middlesbrough, Cleveland, TS90 8WS
Activities: Activities of head offices
Officers: Stephen Christopher Hands, Secretary; Dan Chen [1975] Director/Senior Vice President, Finance [Singaporean]; Stephen Christopher Hands [1968] Director/Solicitor

Sembcorp Investments (China) Limited
Incorporated: 5 May 2009
Net Worth Deficit: £5,424,000 *Total Assets:* £28,790,000
Registered Office: Sembcorp UK Headquarters, Wilton International, Middlesbrough, Cleveland, TS90 8WS
Activities: Activities of head offices
Parent: Sembcorp Holdings Limited
Officers: Stephen Christopher Hands, Secretary; Dan Chen [1975] Director/Senior Vice President, Finance [Singaporean]; Stephen Christopher Hands [1968] Director/Solicitor

Sembcorp Investments Limited
Incorporated: 29 January 1988 *Employees:* 2
Net Worth: £15,829,000 *Total Assets:* £16,218,000
Registered Office: Sembcorp UK Headquarters, Wilton International, Middlesbrough, Cleveland, TS90 8WS
Activities: Other business support service activities n.e.c.
Parent: Sembcorp Holdings Limited
Officers: Christopher Stephen Hands, Secretary; Dan Chen [1975] Director/Senior Vice President, Finance [Singaporean]; Stephen Christopher Hands [1968] Director/Solicitor

Sembcorp Utilities (UK) Limited
Incorporated: 14 January 2003 *Employees:* 171
Net Worth: £78,169,000 *Total Assets:* £158,344,992
Registered Office: Sembcorp UK Headquarters, Wilton International, Middlesbrough, Cleveland, TS90 8WS
Activities: Other manufacturing n.e.c.
Officers: Stephen Christopher Hands, Secretary; Nauman Ahmad [1970] Director/Business Executive [Pakistani]; Graham John Cockroft [1963] Director/Group Chief Financial Officer [New Zealander]; Stephen Christopher Hands [1968] Director/Senior Vice President; Neil Garry McGregor [1955] Director/Group President & CEO [New Zealander]; Sriram Narayanan [1970] Director/Business Executive [Indian]

Sembcorp Utilities Services Limited
Incorporated: 19 April 1999
Net Worth: £47,050,000 *Total Assets:* £56,752,000
Registered Office: Sembcorp UK Headquarters, Wilton International, Middlesbrough, Cleveland, TS90 8WS
Activities: Management consultancy activities other than financial management
Parent: Sembcorp Holdings Limited
Officers: Stephen Christopher Hands, Secretary; Dan Chen [1975] Director/Senior Vice President, Finance [Singaporean]; Stephen Christopher Hands [1968] Director/Solicitor

Sendrig Construction Limited
Incorporated: 27 March 1981 *Employees:* 18
Net Worth: £4,195,725 *Total Assets:* £4,970,630
Registered Office: Andrew House, 4 Benton Terrace, Jesmond, Newcastle upon Tyne, NE2 1QU
Activities: Construction of commercial buildings
Major Shareholder: Rita Lee
Officers: Michael Kevin Lee [1980] Director; Rita Lee [1954] Director

Seneca Global Energy Limited
Incorporated: 4 January 2012 *Employees:* 11
Net Worth: £2,626,426 *Total Assets:* £7,616,546
Registered Office: Maritime House, Harbour Walk, Hartlepool, Cleveland, TS24 0UX
Activities: Production of electricity
Shareholder: Seneca Investments and Developments Limited
Officers: Mark Edward Betts [1966] Director/Finance Manager; Paul Anthony Hornshaw [1972] Director; Christopher Tute [1952] Director

Seneca Investments and Developments Limited
Incorporated: 12 February 2004 *Employees:* 2
Net Worth: £11,614,822 *Total Assets:* £12,809,947
Registered Office: Maritime House, Harbour Walk, The Marina, Hartlepool, Cleveland, TS24 0UX
Activities: Renting and leasing of construction and civil engineering machinery and equipment
Major Shareholder: Neil Elliott
Officers: Mark Edward Betts [1966] Director/Finance Manager; Neil Elliott [1975] Director

Sentinel Homes Limited
Incorporated: 17 September 1992
Net Worth: £1,692,408 *Total Assets:* £2,002,688
Registered Office: Sentinel House, Morton Road, Darlington, Co Durham, DL1 4PT
Activities: Dormant company
Officers: Christopher Hunter [1977] Director/Chief Risk Officer; Christopher Ben White [1978] Finance Director

Servbet Limited
Incorporated: 15 June 1999
Registered Office: 37 Chapel House Road, Chapel House, Newcastle upon Tyne, NE5 5AJ
Activities: Other letting and operating of own or leased real estate
Major Shareholder: Sunil Satyapal Khanna
Officers: Sunil Satyapal Khanna [1957] Director/Businessman

Service Engineering Marine Limited
Incorporated: 19 April 1999 *Employees:* 4
Net Worth: £1,368,118 *Total Assets:* £1,416,877
Registered Office: 31 Bridge Street, Seaton Burn, Newcastle upon Tyne, NE13 6EN
Activities: Other engineering activities
Shareholders: Richard Ferguson; Christine Ferguson
Officers: Christine Ferguson, Secretary; Richard Ferguson [1962] Director/Engineer

Service Engines (Newcastle) Limited
Incorporated: 8 March 1946 *Employees:* 18
Net Worth: £1,653,637 *Total Assets:* £3,436,754
Registered Office: Great Lime Road, West Moor, Newcastle upon Tyne, NE12 6RU
Activities: Repair of machinery
Major Shareholder: Alan Robert Frame
Officers: Alan Robert Frame, Secretary; Alan Robert Frame [1950] Director/Engineer

SES Securus Limited
Incorporated: 28 February 2012
Net Worth: £334 *Total Assets:* £2,140,334
Registered Office: 9-18 Ruby Court, Wesley Drive, Benton Square Industrial Estate, Newcastle upon Tyne, NE12 9UP
Activities: Activities of head offices
Parent: Securus Group Limited
Officers: Anthony Denis Kane [1959] Director; John Stewart [1968] Director

Seven Stories, The National Centre for Children's Books Limited
Incorporated: 7 June 1996 *Employees:* 58
Net Worth: £5,688,884 *Total Assets:* £5,906,941
Registered Office: 30 Lime Street, Ouseburn Valley, Newcastle upon Tyne, NE1 2PQ
Activities: Cultural education
Officers: Kathryn Chaplin, Secretary/Chief Executive; Douglas Dodds [1956] Director/Curator; Matthew Grenby [1970] Director/Professor; Nick Kemp [1969] Managing Director; Deirdre McDermott [1966] Director/Editor [Irish]; Matthew Thomas McWhinnie [1970] Director/Head of Marketing; Linda Moore [1952] Director/Retired; Julia Dawn Morrison [1959] Director/Leadership Coach; Catriona Nicholson [1942] Director/Lecturer in English; Sarah Catherine Pelham [1967] Director/Lawyer; Antony Lewis Pierce [1976] Finance Director; Andrew Mark Robinson [1964] Director/Consultant; Manohari Saravanamuttu [1972] Director/Marketing Consultant

Alan Sewell Limited
Incorporated: 13 July 2001
Registered Office: Sadler Lane Garage, Sadler Lane, Evenwood, Bishop Auckland, Co Durham, DL14 9SH
Activities: Maintenance and repair of motor vehicles
Officers: Olwyn Anderson, Secretary; David Scott Metcalfe [1961] Director/Motor Engineer; Alan William Sewell [1943] Director/Motor Engineer

G.W. Seymour Transport Limited
Incorporated: 2 July 1974
Net Worth: £918,384 *Total Assets:* £923,599
Registered Office: Stockton House, Grangefield Road, Stockton on Tees, Cleveland, TS18 4AB
Activities: Freight transport by road
Parent: T.J.Thomson & Son Ltd
Officers: Richard John Turner, Secretary/Director; David Brian Turner [1959] Director; Richard John Turner [1970] Director

SGG Property Developments Limited
Incorporated: 17 October 2002 *Employees:* 1
Net Worth: £375,343 *Total Assets:* £760,174
Registered Office: The Skiff Inn, Clasper Way, Swalwell, Gateshead, Tyne & Wear, NE16 3BE
Activities: Licenced restaurants
Shareholders: Giuseppe Iannitello; Laura Eve Farini
Officers: Guiseppe Ianitello [1945] Director [Italian]

SGS Timber Haulage Limited
Incorporated: 18 May 1998 *Employees:* 6
Net Worth: £209,538 *Total Assets:* £1,158,130
Registered Office: Stonehaugh Garage, Stonehaugh Wark, Hexham, Northumberland, NE48 3DY
Activities: Freight transport by road
Shareholder: Robert William Scott
Officers: Robert William Scott, Secretary/Haulier; Peter Gilbertson [1959] Director/Haulier; Robert William Scott [1965] Director/Haulier; John David Swan [1969] Director/Haulier

Shaheen Medical Services Limited
Incorporated: 16 March 2001
Net Worth: £944,885 *Total Assets:* £1,165,350
Registered Office: Exchange Building, 66 Church Street, Hartlepool, Cleveland, TS24 7DN
Activities: General medical practice activities
Officers: Maas Abdel Kader Shaheen, Secretary/Surgeon Consultant; Summer Fearnley [1979] Director/Architect; Lynne Shaheen [1951] Director/Company Secretary; Maas Abdel Kader Shaheen [1947] Director/Surgeon Consultant; Salaam Shaheen [1982] Director/Certified Accountant; Tamara Stewart [1979] Director/Teacher

Shapwells Developments Limited
Incorporated: 16 September 1952 *Employees:* 2
Net Worth: £2,610,826 *Total Assets:* £2,632,933
Registered Office: Victoria House, Bondgate Within, Alnwick, Northumberland, NE66 1TA
Activities: Development of building projects
Major Shareholder: Geoffrey Metcalfe
Officers: David Nicholas Metcalfe [1961] Managing Director; Geoffrey Metcalfe [1934] Director/Chairman; Ursula Gail Simpson [1959] Director

A. Share & Sons Limited
Incorporated: 1 February 1937 *Employees:* 1,970
Net Worth: £40,181,000 *Total Assets:* £104,130,000
Registered Office: 45-49 Villiers Street, Sunderland, Tyne & Wear, SR1 1HA
Activities: Retail sale of carpets, rugs, wall and floor coverings in specialised stores
Parent: Parlour Product Holding Limited
Officers: Christopher James Russell Muir, Secretary; Paul Joseph Burke [1964] Sales Director; Gary George Kemp [1961] Logistics Director; David Knight [1958] Director/Chief Executive; Marie Liston [1973] Human Resources Director; Christopher James Russell Muir [1975] Director/Chief Financial Officer; Simon Arthur Nicholson [1963] Furniture Buying Director; John McDaid Pattison [1969] Commercial Director; Elaine Ray [1973] Business Development Director; Mark Richard Sherburn [1963] HR Director

Shared Vision Learning Trust
Incorporated: 6 June 2011 *Employees:* 78
Net Worth: £4,135,000 *Total Assets:* £5,171,000
Registered Office: West Park Academy, Alderman Leach Drive, Darlington, Co Durham, DL2 2GF
Activities: Primary education
Officers: Sarah Roberts, Secretary; John Barrie Armstrong [1940] Director/Retired Councillor; John Robert Barrigan [1970] Director/Project Lead with DFE; Dorothy Dodds [1949] Director/Retired; John William Earley [1985] Director/Operations Manager; Jenna-Marie Ford [1985] Director/Deputy Principal; David John Fraser [1984] Director/Teacher; Lewis Charles Goodwin [1978] Director/Solicitor; Heather Anne Hebden [1969] Director/Nurse; Samantha Ruth Hirst-Caraher [1968] Director/Deputy Headteacher; John McKellar [1951] Director/Retired; Abigail Sarah Rowcroft [1976] Director/Housewife

Sharewave Limited
Incorporated: 17 August 2001
Net Worth Deficit: £214,000 *Total Assets:* £1,010,000
Registered Office: Metnor House, Mylord Crescent, Killingworth, Newcastle upon Tyne, NE12 5YD
Activities: Development of building projects
Parent: Metnor Group Limited
Officers: Dr Adam Boyd Langman, Secretary; Keith Andrew Atkinson [1961] Director; Adam Boyd Langman [1962] Director; Stephen Rankin [1964] Director

Shark Club (UK) Limited
Incorporated: 8 December 2010 *Employees:* 111
Net Worth Deficit: £420,586 *Total Assets:* £864,162
Registered Office: The Sandman Signature, Gallowgate, Newcastle upon Tyne, NE1 4SD
Activities: Licenced restaurants
Officers: Mitchell Rockford Gaglardi [1980] Director/Hotel and Restaurant Consultant [Canadian]

Sharperton Developments Limited
Incorporated: 20 February 2003 *Employees:* 4
Net Worth: £492,935 *Total Assets:* £1,806,717
Registered Office: 105 Moorside North, Fenham, Newcastle upon Tyne, NE4 9DY
Activities: Other letting and operating of own or leased real estate
Shareholders: Patricia Ann Holmes; Charlotte Frances Holmes
Officers: John Colin Fitzpatrick, Secretary; Christian David Holmes [1974] Director/Furniture Retailer; Daniel Christian Holmes [1969] Director/Software Analyst; Jonathan Hill Holmes [1967] Director/Chartered Surveyor; Ralph Mark Holmes [1965] Director/Chartered Surveyor

Sharpness Point Limited
Incorporated: 21 May 2014 *Employees:* 85
Net Worth: £2,832,740 *Total Assets:* £5,517,755
Registered Office: 34-36 South Parade, Whitley Bay, Tyne & Wear, NE26 2RQ
Activities: Hotels and similar accommodation
Shareholders: Edward James Hastie; Martina Hastie
Officers: Edward James Hastie [1945] Director/Hotelier; Martina Hastie [1940] Director/Hotelier; Nigel Anton Hastie [1973] Director/Hotelier; Trevor Edward Hastie [1971] Director/Hotelier

Sharpsmart Limited
Incorporated: 30 July 2001
Net Worth: £1,619,372 *Total Assets:* £6,837,379
Registered Office: Unit 44 Enterprise City, Meadowfield Avenue, Spennymoor, Co Durham, DL16 6JF
Activities: Collection of non-hazardous waste
Major Shareholder: Danny Daniels
Officers: Dean Justin McPhee, Secretary; Danny Boulas Daniels [1964] Director [Australian]

Shaw & Company Solicitors Limited
Incorporated: 31 March 2008
Net Worth: £47,387 *Total Assets:* £977,242
Registered Office: Three Indian Kings House, 31 Quayside, Newcastle upon Tyne, NE1 3DE
Activities: Solicitors
Major Shareholder: Christopher Mark Shaw
Officers: Mary Ann Reay [1961] Director/Solicitor; Christopher Mark Shaw [1962] Director/Solicitor

Sheers Limited
Incorporated: 13 January 1978 *Employees:* 30
Net Worth: £241,178 *Total Assets:* £1,353,050
Registered Office: Unit G7, Morton Park Way, Darlington, Co Durham, DL1 4PQ
Activities: Construction of water projects
Shareholders: Judith Marion Warren; Roy Warren
Officers: Judith Marion Warren, Secretary; Paul Rogers [1968] Director/Administrator; Roy Warren [1950] Director/Water Supply Engineer

Shelcorp 2008 Ltd
Incorporated: 16 June 2008 *Employees:* 39
Net Worth: £1,073,000 *Total Assets:* £2,037,000
Registered Office: Unit 2 Park Road Industrial Estate, Consett, Co Durham, DH8 5PY
Activities: Non-trading company
Parent: Suez Advanced Solutions UK Limited
Officers: Joan Knight, Secretary; Simon Timothy Dyke Turner [1965] Director

Shelford Sales LLP
Incorporated: 10 February 2012
Total Assets: £1,275,443
Registered Office: 9 King Charles Tower, Shield Field, Newcastle upon Tyne, NE2 1XX

Shellbraes Property Ltd
Incorporated: 19 May 2014
Net Worth: £31,859 *Total Assets:* £835,124
Registered Office: Shellbraes Farm, Great Whittington, Northumberland, NE19 2HQ
Activities: Buying and selling of own real estate
Major Shareholder: Katharine Jennifer Abraham
Officers: Katharine Jennifer Abraham [1976] Director

Edgar F Shepherd Ltd
Incorporated: 7 May 2010 *Employees:* 31
Net Worth: £4,405,382 *Total Assets:* £5,681,888
Registered Office: Twinsburn Farm, Heighington, Darlington, Co Durham, DL2 2TU
Activities: Treatment and disposal of non-hazardous waste
Major Shareholder: Edgar Foster Shepherd
Officers: Barbara Shepherd [1937] Director/Traditional Grocer; Edgar Foster Shepherd [1934] Director/Farmer and Wood Shavings Sawdust; Nigel Edgar Charles Herbert Shepherd [1978] Director/Sawdust & Shavings Processor; Simon Edgar Charles Herbert Shepherd [1970] Financial Director

Shepherd Offshore Group Limited
Incorporated: 11 December 2007 *Employees:* 97
Net Worth: £72,031,784 *Total Assets:* £86,605,840
Registered Office: Offshore Technology Park, 1 Rendle Road, Walker, Newcastle upon Tyne, NE6 3NH
Activities: Other letting and operating of own or leased real estate
Officers: Shaun David Ward, Secretary; Bruce Stewart Shepherd [1946] Director; Charles Henry Shepherd [1976] Managing Director; Philippa Jean Shepherd [1973] Director; Shaun David Ward [1964] Director/Accountant

Shepherd Offshore Limited
Incorporated: 8 May 1946 *Employees:* 32
Net Worth: £27,818,578 *Total Assets:* £55,920,536
Registered Office: Offshore Technology Park, 1 Rendle Road, Walker, Newcastle upon Tyne, NE6 3NH
Activities: Buying and selling of own real estate
Parent: Shepherd Offshore Group Limited
Officers: Shaun David Ward, Secretary; Bruce Stewart Shepherd [1946] Director/Transport Manager; Charles Henry Shepherd [1976] Managing Director; Philippa Jean Shepherd [1973] Director; Shaun David Ward [1964] Director/Accountant

Shepherd Offshore Services Limited
Incorporated: 8 September 1970 *Employees:* 55
Net Worth: £14,862,374 *Total Assets:* £16,608,872
Registered Office: Offshore Technology Park, 1 Rendle Road, Walker, Newcastle upon Tyne, NE6 3NH
Activities: Management of real estate on a fee or contract basis
Parent: Shepherd Offshore Group Limited
Officers: Shaun David Ward, Secretary; Bruce Stewart Shepherd [1946] Director/Transport Manager; Charles Henry Shepherd [1976] Managing Director; Philippa Jean Shepherd [1973] Director; Shaun David Ward [1964] Director/Accountant

Shepherds Dene
Incorporated: 23 June 2010 *Employees:* 9
Net Worth: £2,652,889 *Total Assets:* £2,686,208
Registered Office: Time Central, 32 Gallowgate, Newcastle upon Tyne, NE1 4BF
Activities: Activities of extraterritorial organisations and bodies
Officers: Robert Charles Philips Dower, Director/Retired Architect; Judith Margaret Grieve [1952] Director/Clerk in Holy Orders; John Edwin Hirst [1954] Director/University Lecturer; Robert Keith Hopper [1945] Director/Retired Vicar; The Venerable Ian Jagger [1955] Director/Clerk in Holy Orders; John Roland McManners [1946] Director/Clergyman; Geoffrey Vincent Miller [1956] Director/Clerk in Holy Orders; Derek Edward Thomas Nicholson [1940] Director/Retired University Registrar; Elisabeth Flora Rowark [1965] IT Director

Sherwoods (Darlington) Limited
Incorporated: 29 November 1993 *Employees:* 175
Net Worth: £2,423,660 *Total Assets:* £13,703,086
Registered Office: Chesnut Street, Darlington, Co Durham, DL1 1RJ
Activities: Sale of new cars and light motor vehicles
Major Shareholder: Alasdair MacConachie
Officers: Kevin John Smith, Secretary; Christopher David Elvidge [1962] Director; Alasdair MacConachie [1946] Director/Chairman; Simon Robert Allan MacConachie [1978] Managing Director; Kevin John Smith [1975] Finance Director

SHG Holdings Limited
Incorporated: 10 December 2007
Net Worth: £560,000 *Total Assets:* £9,719,000
Registered Office: Vertu House, Fifth Avenue Business Park, Team Valley Trading Estate, Gateshead, Tyne & Wear, NE11 0XA
Activities: Sale of new cars and light motor vehicles
Parent: Vertu Motors PLC
Officers: Karen Anderson, Secretary; Karen Anderson [1971] Finance Director; David Paul Crane [1967] Commercial Director; Robert Thomas Forrester [1969] Director; Michael Sherwin [1959] Finance Director

Billy Shiel Farne Islands Boats Limited
Incorporated: 25 March 2014 *Employees:* 6
Net Worth: £968,453 *Total Assets:* £1,844,722
Registered Office: Third Floor, Citygate, St James Boulevard, Newcastle upon Tyne, NE1 4JE
Activities: Sea and coastal passenger water transport
Major Shareholder: William Shiel
Officers: William Shiel [1972] Director

Shield Engineering Cramlington LLP
Incorporated: 9 July 2010
Net Worth: £913,912 *Total Assets:* £913,912
Registered Office: Bassington Drive, Bassington Industrial Estate, Cramlington, Northumberland, NE23 8AD
Officers: Thomas Jones [1955] Member; John Peace [1949] Member

Shield Therapeutics PLC
Incorporated: 3 September 2015 *Employees:* 29
Net Worth: £48,396,000 *Total Assets:* £52,384,000
Registered Office: Studio 6, 3rd Floor, Northern Design Centre, Baltic Business Quarter, Gateshead Quays, Gateshead, Tyne & Wear, NE8 3DF
Activities: Other human health activities
Shareholder: Nestle SA
Officers: Lucy Kate Bailey, Secretary; Hans Peter Hasler [1956] Director [Swiss]; Rolf Karl Heinz Hoffmann [1959] Director [German]; James Karis [1948] Director [American]; Peter Llewellyn-Davies [1958] Director; Carl Andrew Sterritt [1968] Director

Shiellow Wood Limited
Incorporated: 26 April 2006
Net Worth: £22,231 *Total Assets:* £997,093
Registered Office: Whitton Grange, Whitton, Rothbury, Northumberland, NE65 7RL
Activities: Logging
Shareholders: John Michael Monaghan; Ruth Margaret Monaghan
Officers: Ruth Robson, Secretary; Hannah Campbell [1970] Director/Consultant Pathologist; John Michael Monaghan [1942] Director/Surgeon; Ruth Margaret Monaghan [1942] Director/Retired; Ruth Robson [1968] Director/Accountant

Shilbottle Community Hall Limited
Incorporated: 12 February 2009
Net Worth: £1,050,602 *Total Assets:* £1,057,348
Registered Office: Shilbottle Community Hall, Grange Road, Shilbottle, Alnwick, Northumberland, NE66 2XH
Activities: Fitness facilities
Officers: Gillian Bray, Secretary; Gillian Bray [1964] Director/Teacher; Rev David Edward Cant [1949] Director/Retired; Gethyn Edmunds [1946] Director/IT; Mary Hamilton [1946] Director/Retired; Margaret Brida Knox [1971] Director/Housewife; Alistair MacKay [1952] Director/Retired; Denise MacKay [1954] Director/Retired; Joan Verity [1948] Director/Retired

Shildon Estates LLP
Incorporated: 26 April 2007
Net Worth Deficit: £402,877 *Total Assets:* £6,034,539
Registered Office: Bankside 14, The Watermark, Gateshead, Tyne & Wear, NE11 9SY
Officers: Catherine Jane Canon [1964] Member; Elliott Allan Ward [1966] Member

Shining Thought Limited
Incorporated: 13 February 2009
Net Worth: £22,683 *Total Assets:* £886,250
Registered Office: c/o Hillman & Co, Technology Court, Bradbury Road, Newton Aycliffe, Co Durham, DL5 6DA
Activities: Financial management
Officers: James Peter Forde [1992] Director

Shire Aggregates Bulk Limited
Incorporated: 17 February 2003
Net Worth: £106,304 *Total Assets:* £2,121,369
Registered Office: Gatherley Road Industrial Estate, Brompton on Swale, Richmond, N Yorks, DL10 7JQ
Activities: Quarrying of ornamental and building stone, limestone, gypsum, chalk and slate
Shareholders: Jonathan Mark Simpson; Tina Amanda Simpson
Officers: Jonathan Mark Simpson, Secretary/Director; Jonathan Mark Simpson [1975] Director; Tina Amanda Simpson [1967] Director

The Shiremoor Press Limited
Incorporated: 18 October 2005 *Employees:* 28
Net Worth: £299,725 *Total Assets:* £753,519
Registered Office: Shiremoor Press House, Mylord Crescent, Camperdown Industrial Estate, Newcastle upon Tyne, NE12 5UJ
Activities: Printing n.e.c.
Major Shareholder: Keith Whisson
Officers: Lisa Whisson, Secretary; Joseph Peter Burke [1962] Director; Lynne Hoult [1964] Director; Keith Whisson [1964] Director/Printer

Shout Digital Limited
Incorporated: 6 June 2009 *Employees:* 22
Net Worth: £904,227 *Total Assets:* £1,051,496
Registered Office: Keel House, Garth Heads, Newcastle upon Tyne, NE1 2JE
Activities: Other information technology service activities
Major Shareholder: Gary Geoffrey Boon
Officers: Sharon Theresa Boon, Secretary; Gary Geoffrey Boon [1971] Director

Showermania Limited
Incorporated: 22 October 2008 *Employees:* 5
Net Worth: £728,046 *Total Assets:* £1,148,318
Registered Office: Unit 5d Humshaugh Close, North Tyne Industrial Estate, Whitley Road, Benton, Newcastle upon Tyne, NE12 9SZ
Activities: Retail sale via mail order houses or via Internet
Shareholder: William Bell
Officers: Terry Burrows, Secretary; William Bell [1954] Director; Laura Burrows [1962] Director; Stanley Courtney [1976] Director; Neil Opie [1975] Director; Natalie Ross [1981] Director

SIG Combibloc Limited
Incorporated: 16 November 1973 *Employees:* 13
Net Worth: £3,843,000 *Total Assets:* £4,389,000
Registered Office: Alexander House, 1 Mandarin Road, Rainton Bridge Business Park, Houghton-le-Spring, Co Durham, DH4 5RA
Activities: Combined office administrative service activities
Officers: Malcolm Allum [1961] Director/Manager

Siglion Developments LLP
Incorporated: 7 August 2014
Net Worth: £1,948,958 *Total Assets:* £2,793,923
Registered Office: Echo 24 Building, West Wear Street, Sunderland, Tyne & Wear, SR1 1XD

Siglion Investments LLP
Incorporated: 7 August 2014
Net Worth: £10,168,909 *Total Assets:* £29,514,688
Registered Office: Echo 24 Building, West Wear Street, Sunderland, Tyne & Wear, SR1 1XD

Siglion LLP
Incorporated: 6 August 2014
Net Worth: £10,141,250 *Total Assets:* £11,242,989
Registered Office: Echo 24 Building, West Wear Street, Sunderland, Tyne & Wear, SR1 1XD

Sigma Holdings Limited
Incorporated: 17 May 1983 *Employees:* 5
Net Worth: £9,954,000 *Total Assets:* £22,984,000
Registered Office: Vertu House, Fifth Avenue Business Park, Team Valley Trading Estate, Gateshead, Tyne & Wear, NE11 0XA
Activities: Activities of head offices
Parent: Vertu Motors PLC
Officers: Karen Anderson, Secretary; Karen Anderson [1971] Finance Director; David Paul Crane [1967] Commercial Director; Robert Thomas Forrester [1969] Director; Michael Sherwin [1959] Finance Director

Sigma Plantfinder Limited
Incorporated: 27 June 2014
Net Worth: £125,579 *Total Assets:* £1,748,276
Registered Office: John Boyle Road, Middlesbrough, Cleveland, TS6 6TY
Activities: Agents involved in the sale of machinery, industrial equipment, ships and aircraft
Officers: Adrian Dennis James [1948] Director; Barrie Kurt James [1986] Director; Reuben Mark James [1988] Director

Signature Fencing and Flooring Systems Europe Limited
Incorporated: 18 August 2010 *Employees:* 4
Net Worth: £2,279,670 *Total Assets:* £2,363,774
Registered Office: Kensington House, 3 Kensington, Bishop Auckland, Co Durham, DL14 6HX
Activities: Floor and wall covering
Officers: Anthony Paul Booth [1975] Director; David Lee Egbert [1952] Director/Chief Financial Officer [American]; Pradeep Saha [1967] Director [American]

Silbury Motors Limited
Incorporated: 12 October 2006
Net Worth: £507,496 *Total Assets:* £2,318,920
Registered Office: 246 Park View, Whitley Bay, Tyne & Wear, NE26 3QX
Activities: Sale of new cars and light motor vehicles
Major Shareholder: Terence McLeod
Officers: Terence McLeod [1960] Director/Motor Retailer

Silk Family Law Limited
Incorporated: 10 March 2010
Net Worth: £731,132 *Total Assets:* £1,498,477
Registered Office: One Trinity, Broad Chare, Newcastle upon Tyne, NE1 2HF
Activities: Solicitors
Shareholders: Ian Leslie Kennerley; Margaret Ann Simpson; Kim Theresa Fellowes
Officers: Kim Theresa Fellowes [1968] Director/Solicitor; Ian Leslie Kennerley [1961] Director/Barrister; Wayne Lynn [1970] Director/Solicitor; Margaret Ann Simpson [1959] Director/Solicitor

Silver Street (Durham) Properties Limited
Incorporated: 24 March 1999
Net Worth: £1,376,138 *Total Assets:* £1,611,647
Registered Office: 1 Streetgate Park, Sunniside, Co Durham, NE16 5LD
Activities: Renting and operating of Housing Association real estate
Shareholders: Alexander John Turnbull and Donna Anne Rutherford Discretionary Settlement 2017; Alexander John Turnbull; Donna Ann Rutherford
Officers: Alexander John Turnbull, Secretary; Donna Ann Rutherford [1960] Director/Self-Employed Retailer; Alexander John Turnbull [1956] Director/Sales Manager

Silverlink Software Limited
Incorporated: 9 January 2008 *Employees:* 31
Net Worth: £2,881,024 *Total Assets:* £6,943,765
Registered Office: Cobalt Business Exchange, Cobalt Park Way, Wallsend, Tyne & Wear, NE28 9NZ
Activities: Business and domestic software development
Major Shareholder: John Connelly
Officers: William Tombs, Secretary; Stephen Frederick Hopkins [1950] Director/Certified Chartered Accountant; Kingsley Guy Manning [1952] Director; Tim Quainton [1959] Director; Iain Sinclair Smith [1965] Director

Silvia Properties Limited
Incorporated: 25 May 1988
Net Worth: £1,660,944 *Total Assets:* £2,121,618
Registered Office: 120b Borough Road, Middlesbrough, Cleveland, TS1 2ES
Activities: Other letting and operating of own or leased real estate
Shareholders: Michael John Addison; Jacqueline Ann Addison
Officers: Jacqueline Ann Addison, Secretary; Jacqueline Ann Addison [1960] Director/Teacher; Michael John Addison [1956] Director/Solicitor; Nicole Louise Addison [1993] Director/Student; Richard John Addison [1994] Director/Student

Simco (Engineers) Limited
Incorporated: 5 December 1973 *Employees:* 22
Net Worth: £3,534,516 *Total Assets:* £3,747,018
Registered Office: Monksway, Bede Trading Estate, Jarrow, Tyne & Wear, NE32 3HJ
Activities: Manufacture of other fabricated metal products n.e.c.
Major Shareholder: Hugh Donald Imrie
Officers: Hugh Donald Imrie, Secretary; Kevin Heyhurst [1959] Director/Accountant; Gordon Ian Imrie [1961] Director/Engineer; Hugh Donald Imrie [1934] Director/Engineer; Peter Andrew Thomson [1948] Director/Engineer

Simply Sugar Ltd
Incorporated: 17 November 2014
Net Worth: £54,419 *Total Assets:* £837,608
Registered Office: 7 Segedunum Business Centre, Station Road, Wallsend, Tyne & Wear, NE28 6HQ
Activities: Retail sale of bread, cakes, flour confectionery and sugar confectionery in specialised stores
Major Shareholder: Chase James Bailey Earl Manders
Officers: Chase Manders [1981] Director

Simpson Coulson Limited
Incorporated: 29 November 2012
Net Worth: £241,251 *Total Assets:* £841,879
Registered Office: The Pavilion, 1 Belasis Court, Belasis Hall Technology Park, Billingham, Cleveland, TS23 4AZ
Activities: Construction of other civil engineering projects n.e.c.
Major Shareholder: John Lees
Officers: John Lees [1957] Director/Civil Structural Engineer

Simpson Fuels Limited
Incorporated: 4 March 2004 *Employees:* 7
Net Worth: £624,861 *Total Assets:* £1,077,125
Registered Office: Ferngrove Farm, Copley Bent, Butterknowle, Bishop Auckland, Co Durham, DL13 5QS
Activities: Other retail sale not in stores, stalls or markets
Shareholders: Richard Simpson; Lisa Joanne Simpson
Officers: Lisa Joanne Simpson, Secretary; Lisa Joanne Simpson [1967] Director; Richard Simpson [1963] Director

Simpson Print Limited
Incorporated: 13 July 1972 *Employees:* 126
Net Worth: £2,036,971 *Total Assets:* £8,211,440
Registered Office: Influence Park, Rutherford Road, Stephenson, Washington, Tyne & Wear, NE37 3HX
Activities: Manufacture of other articles of paper and paperboard n.e.c.
Parent: Simpson Group Limited
Officers: David Lee Dowson [1981] Director; Mark Jerrard [1963] Director; Sarah Tishler [1969] Director; Dean Andre Williams [1970] Director

Stephen A. Sims (Cars) Limited
Incorporated: 7 September 1990 *Employees:* 29
Net Worth: £914,845 *Total Assets:* £4,159,949
Registered Office: Stephen A Sims (Cars) Limited, McMullen Road, Darlington, Co Durham, DL1 1XT
Activities: Sale of new cars and light motor vehicles
Major Shareholder: Stephen Andrew Sims
Officers: Stuart Bromley, Secretary; Stephen Andrew Sims [1955] Director/Motor Dealer

Sincera Ltd
Incorporated: 19 October 2011
Net Worth: £128,119 *Total Assets:* £938,050
Registered Office: Lynefield Park, Ashington, Northumberland, NE63 9YH
Activities: Combined facilities support activities
Major Shareholder: Martyn Lee
Officers: Martyn Lee, Secretary; Martyn Lee [1979] Director/Engineer

Alexander Sinclair (N.E.) Limited
Incorporated: 17 August 1989 *Employees:* 45
Net Worth: £653,210 *Total Assets:* £1,171,973
Registered Office: Unit C3, Bentley Avenue, Cowpen Lane Industrial Estate, Billingham, Cleveland, TS23 4BU
Activities: Roofing activities
Shareholders: Lee Joseph Faso; John Paul Faso
Officers: Lee Joseph Faso, Secretary/Director; Iole Faso [1954] Director; John Paul Faso [1980] Director; Lee Joseph Faso [1977] Company Secretary/Director; Luigi Faso [1947] Director

Singer Machines Limited
Incorporated: 9 September 2003 *Employees:* 9
Net Worth: £1,390,251 *Total Assets:* £1,565,939
Registered Office: 217-219 Whitley Road, Whitley Bay, Tyne & Wear, NE26 2SY
Activities: Repair of household appliances and home and garden equipment
Shareholders: Andrea Elizabeth Mills; Colin Steven Mills
Officers: Andrea Elizabeth Mills, Secretary; Andrea Elizabeth Mills [1963] Director; Colin Steven Mills [1962] Director

Singh Family Partnership LLP
Incorporated: 19 September 2016
Net Worth: £1,312,983 *Total Assets:* £2,314,808
Registered Office: Yoden House, 30 Yoden Way, Peterlee, Co Durham, SR8 1AL
Officers: Clare Amanda Rizzo-Singh [1963] Member; Sevak Singh [1954] Member

Singisetti Srinivas Limited
Incorporated: 3 June 2014
Net Worth: £376,879 *Total Assets:* £986,308
Registered Office: Kinsey Jones, 4 Lansdowne Court, Newcastle upon Tyne, NE3 1HN
Activities: Specialists medical practice activities
Major Shareholder: Dr Singisetti Srinivas
Officers: Dr Singisetti Srinivas [1974] Director [Indian]

Sintons Limited Liability Partnership
Incorporated: 13 October 2003 *Employees:* 190
Net Worth: £3,526,065 *Total Assets:* £8,889,084
Registered Office: The Cube, Barrack Road, Newcastle upon Tyne, NE4 6DB
Officers: Angus Stanley John Fraser Ashman [1966] Member; Matthew Robin Collen [1968] Member; Mark Sinclair Dobbin [1973] Member; Steven James Freeman [1968] Member; Frank Matthewson [1959] Member; James Christopher McCabe [1965] Member; Mark Quigley [1965] Member; Karen Tracy Simms [1971] Member; Timothy Andrew Smith [1964] Member; Christopher Jonathan Welch [1965] Member; Donna Louise Anderson [1985] LLP Member; Victoria Armstrong [1978] LLP Member; Anna Louise Barton [1979] LLP Member; Suzanne Claire Davidson [1975] LLP Member; Philip Davison [1964] LLP Member; Adrian Dye [1980] LLP Member; Katherine Marianne Jenkins [1980] LLP Member; Keith John Land [1973] LLP Member; Paul Anthony Liddle [1956] LLP Member; Alok Loomba [1980] LLP Member; Amanda Louise Maskery [1979] LLP Member; Jane Ann Meikle [1977] LLP Member; Paul Nickalls [1972] LLP Member; Christopher Neil Patton [1979] LLP Member; Laura Victoria Peace [1979] LLP Member; Alexander Thomas Rayner [1985] LLP Member; Kathryn Louise Riddell [1967] LLP Member; Graeme Ritzema [1959] LLP Member; Sarah Jane Smith [1969] LLP Member; Joanne Cresswell Willits [1970] LLP Member; Tom Henry Wills [1981] LLP Member; John Paul Woodford [1978] LLP Member

Sirap UK Limited
Incorporated: 16 October 1990 *Employees:* 118
Net Worth: £10,435,000 *Total Assets:* £15,903,000
Registered Office: Salters Lane, Sedgefield, Co Durham, TS21 3EE
Activities: Manufacture of plastic packing goods
Major Shareholder: Graeme Richard Hart
Officers: Susan Foster [1967] Director

Sirius Civil Engineering Limited
Incorporated: 21 June 2004 *Employees:* 9
Net Worth: £381,756 *Total Assets:* £1,213,008
Registered Office: Russel House, Mill Road, Langley Moor, Co Durham, DH7 8HJ
Activities: Construction of other civil engineering projects n.e.c.
Officers: Douglas Mill, Secretary/Accountant; Patrick Edward Kane [1970] Director; Douglas Mill [1962] Director; Matthew James Powell [1968] Director; Paul John Taylor [1967] Director

Sirius Demolition Ltd
Incorporated: 18 August 2008 *Employees:* 18
Net Worth: £889,690 *Total Assets:* £1,159,980
Registered Office: Russel House, Mill Road, Langley Moor, Co Durham, DH7 8HJ
Activities: Treatment and disposal of hazardous waste
Parent: Sirius Engineering Group Ltd
Officers: Douglas Mill, Secretary/Director; Phillip Stephen Collings [1972] Director; Patrick Edward Kane [1970] Director; Douglas Mill [1962] Director; Matthew James Powell [1968] Director; Paul John Taylor [1967] Director

Sirius Engineering Group Ltd
Incorporated: 10 February 2003 *Employees:* 178
Net Worth: £4,824,563 *Total Assets:* £8,440,170
Registered Office: Russel House, Mill Road, Langley Moor, Co Durham, DH7 8HJ
Activities: Activities of head offices
Officers: Douglas Mill, Secretary/Director; Patrick Edward Kane [1970] Director; Douglas Mill [1962] Director; Matthew James Powell [1968] Director; Paul John Taylor [1967] Director

Sirius Geotechnical Ltd
Incorporated: 24 February 2003 *Employees:* 32
Net Worth: £182,963 *Total Assets:* £758,500
Registered Office: Russel House, Mill Road, Langley Moor, Co Durham, DH7 8HJ
Activities: Test drilling and boring
Parent: Sirius Engineering Group Ltd
Officers: Douglas Mill, Secretary/Accountant; Patrick Edward Kane [1970] Director; Douglas Mill [1962] Director; Matthew James Powell [1968] Director; Paul John Taylor [1967] Director

Sirius Remediation Limited
Incorporated: 7 August 2003 *Employees:* 87
Net Worth: £2,202,154 *Total Assets:* £4,567,870
Registered Office: Russel House, Mill Road, Langley Moor, Co Durham, DH7 8HJ
Activities: Remediation activities and other waste management services
Parent: Sirius Engineering Group Ltd
Officers: Douglas Mill, Secretary; Patrick Edward Kane [1970] Director; Douglas Mill [1962] Director; Matthew James Powell [1968] Director; Paul John Taylor [1967] Director

Sirius Renewable Energy Limited
Incorporated: 7 October 2013
Net Worth: £7,870,522 *Total Assets:* £8,347,450
Registered Office: Russel House, Mill Road, Langley Moor, Co Durham, DH7 8HJ
Activities: Other specialised construction activities n.e.c.
Officers: Douglas Mill, Secretary; Nicholas John Davies [1967] Director; Patrick Edward Kane [1970] Director; Douglas Mill [1962] Director; Matthew James Powell [1968] Director; Paul John Taylor [1967] Director

Sirrah Properties Limited
Incorporated: 7 April 2011
Net Worth: £197,782 *Total Assets:* £1,266,103
Registered Office: 165 West Road, Newcastle upon Tyne, NE15 6PQ
Activities: Buying and selling of own real estate
Officers: Adil Mahmood Khan [1979] Director/Sales; Kashif Khan [1978] Director/Solicitor

Sistine Properties (Leeds) Limited
Incorporated: 19 September 2007
Registered Office: Faceby Manor, Carlton in Cleveland, Middlesbrough, Cleveland, TS9 7DP
Activities: Other letting and operating of own or leased real estate
Parent: Sistine Properties (Thetford) Limited
Officers: Paula Scott, Secretary; Paula Marie Scott [1969] Director [New Zealander]; Philip Henry Scott [1964] Director

Sistine Properties (Thetford) Limited
Incorporated: 15 September 2008 *Employees:* 2
Net Worth: £12,189,643 *Total Assets:* £13,941,376
Registered Office: Faceby Manor, Carlton in Cleveland, Middlesbrough, Cleveland, TS9 7DP
Activities: Other letting and operating of own or leased real estate
Officers: Paula Marie Scott, Secretary; Paula Marie Scott [1969] Director [New Zealander]; Philip Henry Scott [1964] Director

Site and Field Services Limited
Incorporated: 23 August 2004 *Employees:* 40
Net Worth: £1,046,127 *Total Assets:* £2,319,339
Registered Office: 1 Freeman Way, North Seaton Industrial Estate, Ashington, Northumberland, NE63 0YB
Activities: Manufacture of metal structures and parts of structures
Major Shareholder: Peter Tighe
Officers: Raymond Murray [1952] Operations Director; Brian Peter Shaw [1971] Finance Director; Peter Tighe [1941] Director

Sitelink Communications Limited
Incorporated: 22 July 1971
Net Worth: £2,450,229 *Total Assets:* £2,958,172
Registered Office: 18 Bridgewater Road, Hertburn Industrial Estate, Washington, Tyne & Wear, NE37 2SG
Activities: Retail sale of telecommunications equipment other than mobile telephones
Major Shareholder: Michael Gordon Hunter
Officers: Lorna Margaret Hunter, Secretary; Lorna Margaret Hunter [1946] Director/Company Secretary

Skelton Farming Limited
Incorporated: 10 March 2005 *Employees:* 9
Net Worth: £7,408,732 *Total Assets:* £17,667,380
Registered Office: Estate Office, North Terrace, Skelton, Saltburn-by-the-Sea, N Yorks, TS12 2ES
Activities: Mixed farming
Major Shareholder: Anthony Charles Philip Wharton
Officers: Neil Colver, Secretary; Anthony Charles Philip Wharton [1946] Director/Land Owner

Skelton Primary School
Incorporated: 17 September 2013 *Employees:* 82
Net Worth: £2,585,163 *Total Assets:* £3,631,308
Registered Office: Skelton Primary School, Station Lane, Skelton, Saltburn-by-the-Sea, N Yorks, TS12 2LR
Activities: Primary education
Officers: Laura Allan [1983] Director/Teacher; Geoffrey Edward Bland [1952] Director/Retired; Julia Brallisford [1973] Director/Assistant Head; Matthew Brayshaw [1967] Director/Post Manager; Christopher John Farrel [1971] Director; Jason Garratt [1969] Director/Project Manager; Tracy Jane Hill [1971] Director/Unqualified Teacher; Emma Anne McLeod [1983] Director/Student; Jennifer Shields [1991] Director/Teacher; Sarah Elizabeth Walker [1966] Director/Headteacher

Skills Training Academy Limited
Incorporated: 26 June 2014
Net Worth: £280,000 *Total Assets:* £1,134,186
Registered Office: Endeavour House, Colmet Court, Queensway South, Team Valley Trading Estate, Gateshead, Tyne & Wear, NE11 0EF
Activities: Other education n.e.c.
Parent: TRN (Train) Holdings Limited
Officers: Neil James Ackroyd [1974] Director; Mark Hewitt [1972] Director; David James Taylor [1975] Director/Consultant

SKR Holdings Limited
Incorporated: 3 November 2015
Net Worth: £47,833,000 *Total Assets:* £63,311,000
Registered Office: Metnor House, Mylord Crescent, Newcastle upon Tyne, NE12 5YD
Activities: Activities of head offices
Major Shareholder: Stephen Rankin
Officers: Kim Rankin [1959] Director; Stephen Rankin [1964] Director

Sky Scaffolding (Whitby) Limited
Incorporated: 23 May 2002
Net Worth: £1,261,951 *Total Assets:* £1,854,180
Registered Office: 7 Eggleston Court, Middlesbrough, Cleveland, TS2 1RU
Activities: Renting and leasing of construction and civil engineering machinery and equipment
Shareholders: Tony Coates; Amanda Michelle Coates; Tony Coates; Amanda Michelle Coates
Officers: Tony Coates, Secretary; Amanda Michelle Coates [1962] Director/Hairdresser; Tony Coates [1966] Director/Scaffolding

Skyline Retail Limited
Incorporated: 1 July 2010 *Employees:* 28
Net Worth: £507,934 *Total Assets:* £1,160,566
Registered Office: 24 Elvet Bridge, Durham, DH1 3AA
Activities: Retail sale of watches and jewellery in specialised stores
Officers: William John Bramwell, Secretary; Jill Bramwell [1956] Director; Peter Bramwell [1947] Director; William John Bramwell [1954] Director

Slaters Electricals Limited
Incorporated: 2 December 1946 *Employees:* 50
Net Worth: £2,857,925 *Total Assets:* £4,673,704
Registered Office: Scotswood Bridge Works, Blaydon on Tyne, Tyne & Wear, NE21 5TE
Activities: Manufacture of electric motors, generators and transformers
Parent: Slaters Electricals Holdings Limited
Officers: Michael Matson, Secretary; Gary John Atkinson [1961] Sales Director; Martin William McGuirk [1969] Projects and Sourcing Director; Simon Francis Riddell [1961] Director; James Leo Slater [1983] Director/Treasurer; Peter John Slater [1948] Director; Geoffrey Willis [1964] Director

Sleekburn Estates Limited
Incorporated: 5 August 1983
Net Worth: £1,293,052 *Total Assets:* £2,047,554
Registered Office: Ravensworth House, 1 Ravensworth Street, Bedlington, Northumberland, NE22 7JP
Activities: Development of building projects
Parent: May Investments Limited
Officers: Joan Muter, Secretary; Lyn Joan Binks [1960] Director; Joan Muter [1935] Director; Morris Robert Muter [1954] Director

Slim & Save Ltd
Incorporated: 13 October 2011
Registered Office: The Black Path, Portrack Lane, Stockton on Tees, Cleveland, TS18 2HE
Activities: Other service activities n.e.c.
Shareholders: Karen Barclay; Robert Anthony Barclay
Officers: Karen Barclay [1976] Director; Robert Anthony Barclay [1969] Director

SLJH Limited
Incorporated: 1 August 2016
Net Worth: £2,300,200 *Total Assets:* £2,300,200
Registered Office: Wansbeck Workspace, Rotary Parkway, Ashington, Northumberland, NE63 8QZ
Activities: Development of building projects
Shareholders: Arch (Development Projects) Limited; Hodgson Newcastle Limited
Officers: Duncan Neil Bowman [1972] Director/Chartered Surveyor; Paul Stanton Czerepok [1973] Director/Accountant; Joel James Hodgson [1992] Director; Lindsay Ann Hodgson [1957] Director; Stephen Hodgson [1958] Director

SLP Developments Limited
Incorporated: 30 May 2007
Net Worth: £271,342 *Total Assets:* £880,826
Registered Office: Lion House, 400 Durham Road, Birtley, Chester-le-Street, Co Durham, DH3 1LS
Activities: Development of building projects
Parent: Triplechance Holdings Limited
Officers: Stevie-Lee Pattinson, Secretary; Robert Pattinson [1934] Director; Stevie-Lee Pattinson [1969] Director

SLW (Holdings) Limited
Incorporated: 13 June 2014 *Employees:* 197
Net Worth: £9,363,941 *Total Assets:* £15,383,942
Registered Office: Sycamorecare Centre, Nookside, Grindon, Sunderland, Tyne & Wear, SR4 8PQ
Activities: Hotels and similar accommodation
Shareholder: Linda Ann Wrout
Officers: Linda Ann Wrout [1956] Director; Shelia Wrout [1933] Director

SLW (Thornbury) Limited
Incorporated: 10 November 2016
Net Worth Deficit: £1,400 *Total Assets:* £1,014,273
Registered Office: Sycamore Lodge, Nookside, Grindon, Sunderland, Tyne & Wear, SR4 8PQ
Activities: Residential nursing care facilities
Shareholder: Linda Ann Wrout
Officers: Linda Ann Wrout [1956] Director/Care Home Operator; Shelia Wrout [1933] Director/Care Home Operator

SLW Limited
Incorporated: 19 April 1995 *Employees:* 135
Net Worth: £4,405,636 *Total Assets:* £9,772,270
Registered Office: Sycamore Lodge, Nookside, Grindon, Sunderland, Tyne & Wear, SR4 8PQ
Activities: Residential care activities for the elderly and disabled
Officers: Florence Wright, Secretary; Linda Ann Wrout [1956] Director; Shelia Wrout [1933] Director

SM Comedy Limited
Incorporated: 1 July 2010 *Employees:* 3
Net Worth: £1,208,905 *Total Assets:* £1,299,592
Registered Office: Applause Accountancy Services Limited, 60 Beamish View, Birtley, Co Durham, DH3 1RS
Activities: Performing arts
Major Shareholder: Sarah Jane Millican
Officers: Valerie McNamara King [1945] Director; Sarah Jane Millican [1975] Director/Comedian

SM Farms Limited
Incorporated: 10 March 1998
Net Worth: £1,860,145 *Total Assets:* £2,007,757
Registered Office: West Bitchfield Tower, Belsay, Northumberland, NE20 0JP
Activities: Mixed farming
Shareholders: Stewart Malcolm Manners; Lesley Susan Helen Manners
Officers: Stewart Malcolm Manners, Secretary; Lesley Susan Helen Manners [1962] Director/Farmer; Stewart Malcolm Manners [1952] Director/Farmer

Smallburn Properties Ltd
Incorporated: 10 September 2014
Net Worth: £199,762 *Total Assets:* £1,165,403
Registered Office: PJ's Hotel, Station Road, Percy Main, North Shields, Tyne & Wear, NE29 6HN
Activities: Buying and selling of own real estate
Shareholder: Andrew Tom Beale
Officers: Andrew Tom Beale [1973] Director/Businessman; Amar Jaber [1977] Director/Businessman

Smart Multi Academy Trust
Incorporated: 29 June 2016 *Employees:* 401
Net Worth: £5,680,610 *Total Assets:* £11,315,265
Registered Office: Wyndham Primary School, Montagu Avenue, Newcastle upon Tyne, NE3 4SB
Activities: Primary education
Officers: Gillian Helen Caleary [1975] Director; James Charles Clark [1956] Director/Academic Head of Education; Anthony Hodge [1969] Assistant Director; Marie Danielle Leddy [1984] Director/Higher Executive Officer; Dr Helen Vivienne Roberts [1950] Director/Retired; Simon John Taylor [1970] Director

Smart Real Estate Limited
Incorporated: 18 May 1995 *Employees:* 1
Net Worth: £562,233 *Total Assets:* £1,123,927
Registered Office: Floor 11, Cale Cross House, 156 Pilgrim Street, Newcastle upon Tyne, NE1 6SU
Activities: Activities of real estate investment trusts
Major Shareholder: Leslie Norman Smart
Officers: Leslie Norman Smart [1960] Director/Property Investor and Landlord

SMC Motors Limited
Incorporated: 1 March 2006 *Employees:* 12
Net Worth: £471,028 *Total Assets:* £760,874
Registered Office: Chester Road, Stanley, Co Durham, DH9 0TJ
Activities: Sale of new cars and light motor vehicles
Shareholders: Julia Maria Taylor; Keith Taylor
Officers: Keith Taylor, Secretary/Motor Trader; Julia Maria Taylor [1965] Director/Motor Dealer; Keith Taylor [1965] Director/Motor Trader

SMD Offshore Support Limited
Incorporated: 6 October 1987 *Employees:* 15
Net Worth: £1,716,321 *Total Assets:* £1,847,902
Registered Office: Turbinia Works, Davy Bank, Wallsend, Tyne & Wear, NE28 6UZ
Activities: Temporary employment agency activities
Parent: Specialist Machine Developments (SMD) Limited
Officers: Richard Hedley Howarth, Secretary/Director; Jian Chen [1972] Director [Chinese]; Richard Hedley Howarth [1963] Director; Hua Zhang [1976] Director [Chinese]; Dongkui Zhu [1972] Director [Chinese]

SMH Equipment Limited
Incorporated: 7 October 2013 *Employees:* 38
Net Worth Deficit: £445,548 *Total Assets:* £1,922,592
Registered Office: 29-33 Maxwell Street, South Shields, Tyne & Wear, NE33 4PU
Activities: Manufacture of other plastic products
Parent: Global Decontamination Solutions Limited
Officers: Damian Meehan [1955] Director/Chairman and CEO of SMH Group; Dean Thomas Rowe [1979] Commercial Director

SMH Products Limited
Incorporated: 15 September 1994 *Employees:* 86
Net Worth: £4,583,635 *Total Assets:* £11,174,139
Registered Office: SMH House, Maxwell Street, South Shields, Tyne & Wear, NE33 4PU
Activities: Manufacture of other plastic products
Parent: Global Decontamination Solutions Limited
Officers: Guy Russell Barker [1964] Sales Director; Paul Cameron [1980] Finance Director; Dean Joseph Clark [1966] Sales Director; James Craig Leese [1968] Operations Director; Damian Meehan [1955] Director; Dean Thomas Rowe [1979] Director

W. Smith (Durham) Limited
Incorporated: 29 May 1974
Net Worth: £1,358,098 *Total Assets:* £2,624,257
Registered Office: 1 New House Road, Esh Winning, Co Durham, DH7 9JU
Activities: Dispensing chemist in specialised stores
Shareholders: Indira Sarania; Indira Sarania; Jayprakash Sarania
Officers: Indira Sarania, Secretary; Jayprakash Sarania [1957] Director; Valabhdas Padma Viramgama [1932] Director

Reuben Smith (Plant Hire) Limited
Incorporated: 19 June 1979
Registered Office: Kensington House, 3 Kensington, Bishop Auckland, Co Durham, DL14 6HX
Activities: Other specialised construction activities n.e.c.
Officers: Susan Smith, Secretary; Reuben Smith [1944] Director; Steven Smith [1980] Director; Susan Smith [1947] Director

William Smith Group 1832 Limited
Incorporated: 5 April 1965 *Employees:* 96
Net Worth: £5,308,086 *Total Assets:* £7,326,137
Registered Office: Grove Works, Queen Street, Barnard Castle, Co Durham, DL12 8JQ
Activities: Manufacture of other fabricated metal products n.e.c.
Major Shareholder: Mark Adrian Smith
Officers: Lesley Smith, Secretary; Lesley Ann Hennedy [1955] Director; Lesley Smith [1959] Director; Mark Adrian Smith [1958] Director/Technician; Nicola Smith [1985] Director; Norma Lilian Smith [1934] Director/Company Secretary; Robert James Smith [1987] Director

G A Smith Limited
Incorporated: 12 October 2007 *Employees:* 129
Net Worth: £11,317,374 *Total Assets:* £15,669,003
Registered Office: Rashercap, Felton, Morpeth, Northumberland, NE65 9NZ
Activities: Site preparation
Major Shareholder: George Albert Fairbairn Smith
Officers: Jacqueline Rochester Pringle, Secretary; George Albert Fairbairn Smith [1954] Director

John B.Smith Limited
Incorporated: 3 July 1946 *Employees:* 23
Net Worth: £1,243,099 *Total Assets:* £1,623,623
Registered Office: Dugdale Street, Stockton on Tees, Cleveland, TS18 2NE
Activities: Sawmilling and planing of wood
Shareholder: Michael John Scaife
Officers: Alyson Taylor, Secretary; Michael John Scaife [1954] Director; Andrew Taylor [1967] Director

D.J.R. Smith Limited
Incorporated: 26 July 1993 *Employees:* 38
Net Worth: £867,648 *Total Assets:* £1,803,239
Registered Office: c/o Tindle's Chartered Accountants, Scotswood House, Teesdale South, Thornaby Place, Stockton on Tees, Cleveland, TS17 6SB
Activities: Electrical installation
Parent: DJR Holdings Limited
Officers: Philip John O'Brien, Secretary; David Andrew Askin [1978] Director; Philip John O'Brien [1959] Director; Jonathan Obrien [1984] Director

Smithers-Oasis Europe Limited
Incorporated: 14 June 2004 *Employees:* 364
Net Worth Deficit: £2,918,000 *Total Assets:* £28,637,000
Registered Office: Crowther Road, Crowther Industrial Estate, Washington, Tyne & Wear, NE38 0AQ
Activities: Manufacture of other plastic products
Parent: Smithers-Oasis Company
Officers: Paul Frederick Southwick, Secretary; Robin McLaughlin Kilbride [1959] Director/President & Chief Operating [American]; Eduard Kremer [1963] Director [German]; Stephen Kenneth Short [1960] Managing Director; James Stull [1970] Director [American]

Smithers-Oasis U.K. Limited
Incorporated: 29 January 1981 *Employees:* 116
Net Worth: £3,397,000 *Total Assets:* £9,004,000
Registered Office: Crowther Road, Crowther Industrial Estate, Washington, Tyne & Wear, NE38 0AQ
Activities: Manufacture of other plastic products
Parent: Smithers-Oasis Company
Officers: Paul Frederick Southwick, Secretary; Robin McLaughlin Kilbride [1959] Director [American]; Stephen Kenneth Short [1960] Managing Director; James Stull [1970] Director [American]

Smithfield Timber Limited
Incorporated: 8 June 1990 *Employees:* 19
Net Worth: £405,113 *Total Assets:* £995,437
Registered Office: Westerby Road, East Middlesbrough Industrial Estate, Middlesbrough, Cleveland, TS3 8TD
Activities: Agents involved in the sale of timber and building materials
Shareholders: John Bousfield; Kathleen Bousfield
Officers: Kathleen Bousfield, Secretary; John Bousfield [1976] Director/Manager; Kathleen Bousfield [1945] Director/Secretary; William Bousfield [1984] Director

Smokies Entertainments Limited
Incorporated: 23 October 1975 *Employees:* 161
Net Worth: £4,236,657 *Total Assets:* £12,244,264
Registered Office: 24 Woolsington Park South, Woolsington, Newcastle upon Tyne, NE13 8BJ
Activities: Hotels and similar accommodation
Officers: Saroj Rani Chawla, Secretary; Mukesh Raj Chawla [1954] Director; Neel Chawla [1986] Director; Saroj Rani Chawla [1955] Director

SMT Electrical Contractors Limited
Incorporated: 8 September 1997
Registered Office: Great Lime Road, Killingworth, Newcastle upon Tyne, NE12 6RU
Activities: Electrical installation
Officers: Simon Thomas Weatherley, Secretary/Director; Christopher Dawson [1983] Director; John Trevor Dawson [1957] Director; Ronald Alan Fullerton [1967] Director/Electrical Engineer; Simon Thomas Weatherley [1962] Director

Smurf Property Portfolios Limited
Incorporated: 16 January 2001
Registered Office: 30 Yoden Way, Peterlee, Co Durham, SR8 1AL
Activities: Other letting and operating of own or leased real estate
Officers: Scott Norman Murphy, Secretary; Shaun Christopher Murphy [1959] Financial Director

Howard Snaith Limited
Incorporated: 17 January 2003
Net Worth: £1,153,548 *Total Assets:* £1,190,482
Registered Office: Milburn House, Hexham Business Park, Burn Lane, Hexham, Northumberland, NE46 3RU
Activities: Other passenger land transport
Shareholders: Howard James Snaith; Alison Marina Snaith
Officers: Howard Robert Snaith [1993] Director; Howard James Snaith [1928] Director/Coach Travel

Snippersgate '88 Limited
Incorporated: 2 August 1982
Net Worth: £1,339,332 *Total Assets:* £1,705,946
Registered Office: South Hetton Road, Easington Lane, Houghton-le-Spring, Co Durham, DH5 0LG
Activities: Sale of used cars and light motor vehicles
Major Shareholder: David Alan Walpert
Officers: Edith Walpert, Secretary; Edward Guy Lawson [1955] Company Sales Director; David Alan Walpert [1949] Managing Director

Snop UK Limited
Incorporated: 19 May 2009 *Employees:* 187
Net Worth: £317,975 *Total Assets:* £9,868,865
Registered Office: Rainhill Road, Washington, Tyne & Wear, NE37 3HP
Activities: Manufacture of other parts and accessories for motor vehicles
Shareholder: Anais Pinaire
Officers: Michel Henri Pinaire [1963] Director [French]

Snorkel Europe Limited
Incorporated: 28 October 2008 *Employees:* 226
Net Worth Deficit: £7,793,000 *Total Assets:* £21,211,000
Registered Office: Vigo Centre, Birtley Road, Washington, Tyne & Wear, NE38 9DA
Activities: Manufacture of lifting and handling equipment
Shareholders: Tanfield Group PLC; Snorkel International Holdings LLC; Xtreme Manufacturing LLC
Officers: Charles David Brooks, Secretary; Don Francis Ahern [1953] Director/Business Owner [American]; Charles David Brooks [1962] Director; Brendan Joseph Campbell [1965] Director

Kevin Snowdon Groundworks Limited
Incorporated: 1 September 2004 *Employees:* 31
Net Worth: £570,442 *Total Assets:* £1,266,217
Registered Office: Wellfield House, Front Street, Craghead, Stanley, Co Durham, DH9 6DU
Activities: Construction of commercial buildings
Major Shareholder: Kevin Snowdon
Officers: Kevin Snowdon [1965] Director/Groundworks

SNS Management & Solutions Limited
Incorporated: 6 November 2009
Net Worth: £17,443 *Total Assets:* £868,718
Registered Office: 81 Freebrough Road, Moorsholm, Saltburn-by-the-Sea, N Yorks, TS12 3JB
Activities: Freight rail transport
Major Shareholder: David Michael Eltherington
Officers: David Michael Eltherington [1967] Director/Management Consultant

Soccarena Limited
Incorporated: 22 November 2000
Registered Office: New Ferens Park, Belmont Industrial Estate, Durham, DH1 1GG
Activities: Operation of sports facilities
Major Shareholder: Austin Alfred Carney
Officers: Austin Alfred Carney [1963] Director/Consultant

Soccer Sensations Hull Limited
Incorporated: 25 January 2005 *Employees:* 12
Net Worth: £103,596 *Total Assets:* £1,799,771
Registered Office: 7 Bankside, The Watermark, Gateshead, Tyne & Wear, NE11 9SY
Activities: Activities of sport clubs
Major Shareholder: Donald Ian Sinclair
Officers: Ian Sinclair [1964] Director

Socialrel8 Ltd
Incorporated: 17 November 2011 *Employees:* 14
Net Worth: £1,331,064 *Total Assets:* £1,690,451
Registered Office: Digital City, Bridge Street West, The Boho Zone, Middlesbrough, Cleveland, TS2 1AE
Activities: Business and domestic software development
Shareholder: Jaime Alexander Scott
Officers: Clare Louise Scott, Secretary; Michelle Dinsmore [1970] Director; Jaime Alexander Scott [1970] Director

Society for Education Limited
Incorporated: 14 November 2003
Net Worth: £453,120 *Total Assets:* £1,336,148
Registered Office: 36-38 Gladstone Terrace, Gateshead, Tyne & Wear, NE8 4EF
Activities: Other education n.e.c.
Officers: Benjamin Samuel Halle, Secretary; Shulamith Bamberger [1945] Director/Secretary; Ruth Green [1988] Director/Housewife

Sohech Ltd
Incorporated: 12 September 2016
Net Worth: £3,231,000 *Total Assets:* £3,231,000
Registered Office: 38 Heathfield Place, East Park Road, Low Fell, Gateshead, Tyne & Wear, NE9 5AS
Activities: Buying and selling of own real estate
Major Shareholder: James Anthony Johnson
Officers: James Anthony Johnson [1949] Director; Richard Frederick Johnson [1974] Director

Soil Machine Dynamics Limited
Incorporated: 25 October 1971 *Employees:* 223
Net Worth: £7,550,953 *Total Assets:* £34,808,352
Registered Office: Turbinia Works, Davy Bank, Wallsend, Tyne & Wear, NE28 6UZ
Activities: Manufacture of other special-purpose machinery n.e.c.
Parent: Specialist Machine Developments (SMD) Limited
Officers: Richard Hedley Howarth, Secretary; Paul Robert Atkinson [1964] Engineering Director; Jian Chen [1972] Director [Chinese]; Richard Hedley Howarth [1963] Director/Engineer; Michael Thomas Jones [1968] Director/Chartered Engineer; Hua Zhang [1976] Director [Chinese]; Dongkui Zhu [1972] Director [Chinese]

Solar Solve Limited
Incorporated: 27 May 1988 *Employees:* 13
Net Worth: £1,117,217 *Total Assets:* £1,303,181
Registered Office: 7 Waldridge Way, South Shields, Tyne & Wear, NE34 9PZ
Activities: Other manufacturing n.e.c.
Major Shareholder: John Heron Lightfoot
Officers: Lilian Lightfoot, Secretary; John Heron Lightfoot [1943] Director/Chairman; Julie Lightfoot [1969] Managing Director; Lilian Lightfoot [1943] Director/Secretary

Solehawk Limited
Incorporated: 20 March 1989 *Employees:* 163
Net Worth: £8,155,966 *Total Assets:* £13,789,525
Registered Office: 31-40 West Parade, Newcastle upon Tyne, NE4 7LB
Activities: Medical nursing home activities
Shareholders: Aran Handa; Arvan Handa
Officers: Arvan Handa, Secretary; Aran Handa [1955] Director/Hotel Proprietor; Arvan Handa [1952] Director/Hotel Manager

Solmek Limited
Incorporated: 11 October 2000 *Employees:* 22
Net Worth: £1,467,729 *Total Assets:* £2,192,558
Registered Office: 12 Yarm Road, Stockton on Tees, Cleveland, TS18 3NA
Activities: Other engineering activities
Major Shareholder: Gary Raymond Dresser
Officers: Gary Raymond Dresser [1965] Director/Engineer; Deryck Simpson [1959] Director/Engineer; Richard Woods [1981] Director

Sone Products Holdings Ltd
Incorporated: 16 October 2013
Net Worth: £2,543,765 *Total Assets:* £2,926,445
Registered Office: Station Field Road, Tanfield Lea Industrial Estate South, Tanfield Lea, Stanley, Co Durham, DH9 9QX
Activities: Manufacture of other plastic products
Shareholders: Raymond Oliver; Hans Rainer Stork; Walter Schmidt
Officers: Raymond Oliver [1964] Director; Walter Schmidt [1955] Director [German]; Hans Rainer Stork [1958] Director [German]

Sone Products Ltd
Incorporated: 10 June 2010
Net Worth: £1,265,710 *Total Assets:* £2,428,257
Registered Office: Station Field Road, Tanfield Lea Industrial Estate South, Tanfield Lea, Stanley, Co Durham, DH9 9QX
Activities: Manufacture of other plastic products
Parent: Sone Products Holdings Ltd
Officers: Raymond Oliver [1964] Director; Herr Walter Schmidt [1955] Director [German]; Hans Rainer Stork [1958] Director [German]

Sonicedge Limited
Incorporated: 14 August 1995 *Employees:* 3
Net Worth: £74,744 *Total Assets:* £5,266,178
Registered Office: Sherburn Hill, Co Durham, DH6 1PS
Activities: Other manufacturing n.e.c.
Parent: GT Timber Ltd
Officers: Suzanne Claire Penrose, Secretary; Suzanne Claire Penrose [1987] Finance Director; Douglas John Wentworth [1953] Director; Jillian Anne Wentworth [1990] Director

Soretrac (U.K.) Limited
Incorporated: 18 June 1981 *Employees:* 12
Net Worth: £234,401 *Total Assets:* £1,353,401
Registered Office: Hurworth Road, Aycliffe Industrial Estate, Newton Aycliffe, Co Durham, DL5 6UD
Activities: Packaging activities
Major Shareholder: Olivier Claude Kahn
Officers: Daniel Whiteley, Secretary; Olivier Claude Kahn [1973] Director/President [French]; Daniel Whiteley [1968] Director

Sotech Limited
Incorporated: 14 July 1982 *Employees:* 49
Net Worth: £1,878,993 *Total Assets:* £4,446,908
Registered Office: Unit 2 Traynor Way, Whitehouse Business Park, Peterlee, Co Durham, SR8 2RU
Activities: Manufacture of metal structures and parts of structures
Major Shareholder: John Alan Egginton
Officers: Christine Egginton, Secretary; John Alan Egginton [1948] Managing Director

Sound Training for Reading Ltd
Incorporated: 30 July 2009
Net Worth: £512,145 *Total Assets:* £1,021,170
Registered Office: Boho 4, Gibson House, Cleveland Street, Middlesbrough, Cleveland, TS2 1AY
Activities: General secondary education
Major Shareholder: Catherine Parkinson
Officers: Catherine Mary Parkinson [1957] Director/Teacher; Andrew Loughran Preston [1966] Director; Claire Preston [1968] Director; Alastair Waite [1960] Director

Soundbitelearning UK Limited
Incorporated: 1 September 2006 *Employees:* 24
Net Worth Deficit: £2,234,154 *Total Assets:* £757,332
Registered Office: Newcastle Enterprise Centres, 6 Charlotte Square, Newcastle upon Tyne, NE1 4XF
Activities: General secondary education
Shareholder: Christopher John Courage
Officers: Ian Thompson, Secretary; Christopher John Courage [1962] Director; Anthony St John Coxon [1968] Director; Ian Thompson [1954] Director/Chartered Accountant

South Causey Limited
Incorporated: 24 November 2004
Net Worth: £1,640,169 *Total Assets:* £3,811,572
Registered Office: 1 Jesmond Business Court, Jesmond Road, Newcastle upon Tyne, NE2 1LA
Activities: Hotels and similar accommodation
Major Shareholder: Susan Jane Moiser
Officers: Susan Jane Moiser, Secretary/Director; Jean Gibson [1939] Director; Philip James Moiser [1962] Director; Susan Jane Moiser [1963] Director

South Durham Health C.I.C.
Incorporated: 12 October 2011 *Employees:* 7
Net Worth Deficit: £16,738 *Total Assets:* £2,034,796
Registered Office: RMT Accountants & Business Advisors Limited, Gosforth Park Avenue, Newcastle upon Tyne, NE12 8EG
Activities: General medical practice activities
Officers: Jill Moulton, Secretary; Dr Mirza Hassan [1983] Director/Medical Doctor; Dr Rajiv Israel Mansingh [1976] Director/Doctor; Dr Sanna Moss [1980] Director/Medical Practitioner; Dr Diane Elizabeth Robinson [1972] Director/General Practitioner; Nitish Nitish Sahoo [1979] Director/Medical Doctor (General Practitioner); Dr Kamalpreet Singh Sidhu [1980] Director/Medical Doctor; Dr James Edward Staines [1951] Director/Medical Doctor

South Durham Structures Limited
Incorporated: 11 May 1981 *Employees:* 29
Net Worth: £1,051,004 *Total Assets:* £1,948,263
Registered Office: Dovecot Hill, South Church Enterprise Park, Bishop Auckland, Co Durham, DL14 6XR
Activities: Other specialised construction activities n.e.c.
Shareholders: Brian Peter Hope; Margaret Ann Hope
Officers: Brian Peter Hope, Secretary; Keith Corner [1963] Director; Brian Peter Hope [1950] Director/Chartered Accountant; Margaret Ann Hope [1951] Director/Secretary

South Hereford Garages Limited
Incorporated: 3 May 1973 *Employees:* 214
Net Worth: £12,399,000 *Total Assets:* £23,616,000
Registered Office: Vertu House, Fifth Avenue Business Park, Team Valley Trading Estate, Gateshead, Tyne & Wear, NE11 0XA
Activities: Sale of new cars and light motor vehicles
Parent: SHG Holdings Limited
Officers: Karen Anderson, Secretary; Karen Anderson [1971] Finance Director; David Paul Crane [1967] Commercial Director; Robert Thomas Forrester [1969] Director; Mike Rich [1961] Group Operations Director; Michael Sherwin [1959] Finance Director

South Lakeland Group Limited
Incorporated: 8 June 2006
Net Worth: £48,113,000 *Total Assets:* £48,113,000
Registered Office: 2nd Floor, One Gosforth Park Way, Gosforth Business Park, Newcastle upon Tyne, NE12 8ET
Activities: Activities of head offices
Parent: PD Parks Limited
Officers: Judith Ann Archibold, Secretary; Ian Kellett [1963] Director; John Anthony Waterworth [1963] Director

South Lakeland Parks Limited
Incorporated: 10 March 1994 *Employees:* 232
Net Worth: £9,389,000 *Total Assets:* £56,336,000
Registered Office: 2nd Floor, One Gosforth Park Way, Gosforth Business Park, Newcastle upon Tyne, NE12 8ET
Activities: Recreational vehicle parks, trailer parks and camping grounds
Parent: South Lakeland Group Limited
Officers: Judith Ann Archibold, Secretary; Ian Kellett [1963] Director; John Anthony Waterworth [1963] Director

South Northumberland Cricket Club Limited
Incorporated: 22 October 1927 *Employees:* 4
Net Worth: £3,185,673 *Total Assets:* £3,370,810
Registered Office: Roseworth Terrace, Newcastle upon Tyne, NE3 1LU
Activities: Activities of sport clubs
Officers: Gordon Donald Halliday, Secretary; Alan Crawford Fletcher [1969] Director; Gordon Donald Halliday [1950] Director/Town Planner; Geoffrey William Robson [1958] Director/Chartered Accountant; John Martin Ruddick [1961] Director/Sales Manager; Thomas Robin Seymour [1978] Director; Michael John Smalley [1976] Director/Teacher; Simon David West [1978] Director/Recruitment Consultant

South Shore Developments (Monkton) Limited
Incorporated: 1 June 2005
Net Worth Deficit: £739,000 *Total Assets:* £784,000
Registered Office: 14 Bankside, The Watermark, Gateshead, Tyne & Wear, NE11 9SY
Activities: Buying and selling of own real estate
Officers: Ian Clark, Secretary; Catherine Jane Canon [1964] Director; Ian Clark [1959] Director/Accountant; William George Robertson [1945] Director; Elliott Allan Ward [1966] Director

South Shore Developments Limited
Incorporated: 21 April 2004 *Employees:* 2
Net Worth: £9,766,807 *Total Assets:* £19,825,640
Registered Office: 1 St James' Gate, Newcastle upon Tyne, NE99 1YQ
Activities: Other letting and operating of own or leased real estate
Major Shareholder: William George Robertson
Officers: Ian Clark, Secretary; Ian Clark [1959] Director; Sonya Billie Edgar [1972] Director; Dr Elliot Cardno Robertson [1973] Director; Hilda Mary Robertson [1948] Director; William George Robertson [1945] Managing Director

South Shore One Limited
Incorporated: 19 July 2004
Net Worth: £2,833,947 *Total Assets:* £5,069,292
Registered Office: Unit 2 Jubilee House, York Road, Hartlepool, Cleveland, TS26 9EN
Activities: Buying and selling of own real estate
Parent: Mowden Park Estate Company Limited
Officers: Julie Margaret Rigali, Secretary; David Nigel Williams [1943] Director; Edward Richard Thomas Yuill [1978] Managing Director; Phillip Guy Yuill [1954] Director; Victoria Mary Yuill [1951] Director

South Tyne Building Supplies Limited
Incorporated: 16 March 2001
Net Worth: £2,623,304 *Total Assets:* £3,031,695
Registered Office: Corstorphine House, Portberry Street, South Shields, Tyne & Wear, NE33 1QX
Activities: Wholesale of wood, construction materials and sanitary equipment
Shareholders: Kevin Gerard Parker; Carole Ann Parker
Officers: Carole Ann Parker, Secretary; Adam Parker [1978] Director/Builders Merchant; Carole Ann Parker [1953] Director/Builders Merchant; Kevin Gerard Parker [1946] Director/Builders Merchant

South Tyneside Homes Limited
Incorporated: 3 March 2005 *Employees:* 662
Net Worth Deficit: £32,005,000 *Total Assets:* £10,281,000
Registered Office: Town Hall and Civic Offices, Westoe Road, South Shields, Tyne & Wear, NE33 2RL
Activities: Management of real estate on a fee or contract basis
Officers: Brian Scott, Secretary; Gary Craig [1958] Director/Architect; Laverne Elrick [1948] Director/Retired; Ian Farrar [1975] Commercial Director; Cllr James Foreman [1947] Director; Sarah Kate French [1979] Director; Michael Laidler [1950] Director; Cllr Edward Malcolm [1955] Director/Welfare Home Officer; Margaret Mary Peacock [1956] Director/Councillor; James Sewell [1947] Director/Councillor; Gwen Smith [1983] Director/Local Government Officer; Joyce Smith [1937] Director/Retired

South Tyneside Housing Ventures Trust Limited
Incorporated: 26 July 2013
Net Worth Deficit: £351,252 *Total Assets:* £30,637,816
Registered Office: Unit 4 Heddon Way, Middlefields Industrial Estate, South Shields, Tyne & Wear, NE34 0NT
Activities: Renting and operating of Housing Association real estate
Officers: Brian Scott, Secretary; Julie Anne Allison [1970] Director/Accountant; Angela Anderson [1973] Director/Business Owner - Recruitment and Training; Victoria Stewart Beattie [1962] Director; Arthur Modral Chadwick [1942] Director/Retired; Peter Davidson [1945] Director/Chairman NHS Foundation Trust; Paul William Fellows [1972] Director; Kenneth Fudge [1955] Director/Tutor; Richard Edmund Porthouse [1951] Director/Retired; Sheila Mary Stephenson [1942] Director/Councillor

Southampton Geothermal Heating Company Limited (The)
Incorporated: 8 September 1986 *Employees:* 2
Net Worth: £4,288,000 *Total Assets:* £11,436,000
Registered Office: Shared Services Centre, Q3 Office, Quorum Business Park, Benton Lane, Newcastle upon Tyne, NE12 8EX
Activities: Distribution of electricity
Parent: Engie Urban Energy Group Limited
Officers: Sarah Gregory, Secretary; Andrew David Hart [1969] Managing Director; Lee Kitchen [1979] Director/Accountant

Southampton Orthodontic Centre Limited
Incorporated: 2 April 2009 *Employees:* 8
Net Worth: £118,207 *Total Assets:* £815,456
Registered Office: Third Floor, Citygate, St James Boulevard, Newcastle upon Tyne, NE1 4JE
Activities: Dental practice activities
Parent: Braces for You Limited
Officers: Dr Rupinder Kaur Sidhu [1974] Director

Southbay Civil Engineering Limited
Incorporated: 25 July 2007 *Employees:* 46
Net Worth: £573,718 *Total Assets:* £2,603,724
Registered Office: The Bailey, Cumberland Road, North Shields, Tyne & Wear, NE29 8RD
Activities: Construction of water projects
Major Shareholder: Gordon Iain Green
Officers: Paul Stephenson [1969] Director/Civil Engineer

Southhill Farm Services Ltd
Incorporated: 1 March 2010
Net Worth: £774,344 *Total Assets:* £804,735
Registered Office: The Estate Office, Harbour House, Plawsworth, Chester-le-Street, Co Durham, DH3 4EJ
Activities: Other business support service activities n.e.c.
Shareholders: Frank Nicholson; Sir Paul Douglas Nicholson; Mark Thomas Nicholson
Officers: Mark Thomas Nicholson, Secretary; Frank Nicholson [1954] Director/Business Consultant; Mark Thomas Nicholson [1950] Director/Farmer; Sir Paul Douglas Nicholson [1938] Director

Southlands Management Limited
Incorporated: 7 December 1981
Net Worth: £4,780,896 *Total Assets:* £6,128,891
Registered Office: Southlands, The Avenue, Eaglescliffe, Stockton on Tees, Cleveland, TS16 9AS
Activities: Buying and selling of own real estate
Shareholders: Ian Jacob Waller; Martin Trevor Corney
Officers: Ian Jacob Waller, Secretary; Martin Trevor Corney [1965] Director/Builder; Ian Jacob Waller [1952] Director

Southlands Motor Company Ltd
Incorporated: 4 April 2012
Net Worth: £297,306 *Total Assets:* £1,427,102
Registered Office: Unit 2 Foxhunters Road, Whitley Bay, Tyne & Wear, NE25 8UG
Activities: Sale of used cars and light motor vehicles
Major Shareholder: Darren Leigh Thomson
Officers: Darren Thomson, Secretary; Darren Thomson [1971] Director; Marie Thomson [1974] Director

Southmoor Golf Club
Incorporated: 10 December 2014
Net Worth: £234,089 *Total Assets:* £756,146
Registered Office: The Middles, Craghead, Stanley, Co Durham, DH9 6AG
Activities: Activities of sport clubs
Officers: Douglas Mill, Secretary; Guy Anthony Carr [1964] Director/IT Consultant; Peter Johnson [1945] Director; Douglas Mill [1962] Director

Southmoor Multi Academy Trust
Incorporated: 5 April 2012 *Employees:* 204
Net Worth: £16,720,000 *Total Assets:* £21,241,000
Registered Office: Southmoor Academy, Ryhope Road, Sunderland, Tyne & Wear, SR2 7TF
Activities: Other education n.e.c.
Officers: Dr John William Brown [1952] Director/Financial Advisor; Helen Catcherside [1966] Director/Registered General Nurse; Robert Alderson Edmonds [1958] Director/Process Plant Operator; Stephen Francis Garrett [1972] Director/Principal Southmoor Academy; Dr Philip Ingram [1960] Director/Headteacher; Alison Mary Lawson [1959] Regional Director NDCS; Emma Young [1975] Director/Sales Assistant

Southview Leisure Park Limited
Incorporated: 15 September 2006 *Employees:* 181
Net Worth: £35,091,000 *Total Assets:* £73,441,000
Registered Office: 2nd Floor, One Gosforth Park Way, Gosforth Business Park, Newcastle upon Tyne, NE12 8ET
Activities: Holiday centres and villages
Parent: PD Parks Limited
Officers: Judith Ann Archibold, Secretary; Ian Kellett [1963] Director; John Anthony Waterworth [1963] Director

Souvenir Scenic Studios Ltd.
Incorporated: 14 February 1994
Registered Office: Oakmere, Belmont Business Park, Durham, DH1 1TW
Activities: Artistic creation
Shareholders: Jeanette Kenny; Simon Kenny
Officers: Jeanette Alison Kenny, Company Secretary; Jeanette Alison Kenny [1959] Director; Simon David Kenny [1962] Director/Scenic Artist

Sovereign Adavo (Wallsend) LLP
Incorporated: 18 June 2013
Net Worth: £1,781,191 *Total Assets:* £3,015,024
Registered Office: The Town Hall, High Street East, Wallsend, Tyne & Wear, NE28 7RR
Officers: Kerry Anne Alexander [1981] Member; Mark Henry Black [1981] Member

Sovereign Care (North East) Ltd
Incorporated: 17 February 2003
Net Worth: £87,789 *Total Assets:* £1,521,351
Registered Office: Game Keepers Cottage, Limestone Lane, Ponteland, Northumberland, NE20 0DD
Activities: Residential care activities for the elderly and disabled
Shareholders: Linda Janet Hunter; Stephen Hunter
Officers: Linda Janet Hunter, Secretary; Linda Janet Hunter [1960] Director/Care Home; Stephen Hunter [1960] Director/Care Home

Sovereign Reversions Holdings Limited
Incorporated: 3 May 2011
Net Worth: £5,902,000 *Total Assets:* £5,978,000
Registered Office: Cross House, Westgate Road, Newcastle upon Tyne, NE1 4XX
Activities: Buying and selling of own real estate
Parent: New Sovereign Reversions Limited
Officers: Paul Trevor Barber [1967] Director/Chief Executive; Antony Lewis Pierce [1976] Finance Director

Sovereign Reversions Limited
Incorporated: 9 March 1992
Net Worth: £18,785,000 *Total Assets:* £34,381,000
Registered Office: Cross House, Westgate Road, Newcastle upon Tyne, NE1 4XX
Activities: Buying and selling of own real estate
Parent: New Sovereign Reversions Limited
Officers: Paul Trevor Barber [1967] Director/Chief Executive; Antony Lewis Pierce [1976] Finance Director

Space Architecture (Europe) Limited
Incorporated: 21 February 2003 *Employees:* 78
Net Worth: £2,233,179 *Total Assets:* £6,001,696
Registered Office: Spaceworks, Benton Park Road, Benton, Newcastle upon Tyne, NE7 7LX
Activities: Architectural activities
Parent: Space Group (Europe) Ltd
Officers: Neil McGlew, Secretary; Robert James Charlton [1969] Director

Spark Ecommerce Group Limited
Incorporated: 13 April 2012 *Employees:* 195
Net Worth Deficit: £1,059,871 *Total Assets:* £3,730,901
Registered Office: Follingsby Avenue, Follingsby Park, Gateshead, Tyne & Wear, NE10 8HQ
Activities: Activities of head offices
Officers: Peter Bruce Slee, Secretary; Noel Christopher Lambert [1958] Director [Irish]; Peter Bruce Slee [1961] Director; Barry Abraham Stiefel [1949] Director [German]

Spark Etail Limited
Incorporated: 3 March 2011 *Employees:* 12
Net Worth: £552,355 *Total Assets:* £990,026
Registered Office: 1 Follingsby Avenue, Follingsby Park, Gateshead, Tyne & Wear, NE10 8HQ
Activities: Retail sale via mail order houses or via Internet
Parent: Spark Ecommerce Group Limited
Officers: Noel Christopher Lambert [1958] Director [Irish]; Peter Bruce Slee [1961] Director

Spark of Genius North East LLP
Incorporated: 30 April 2013 *Employees:* 75
Net Worth: £2,000 *Total Assets:* £2,230,988
Registered Office: King Edwin School, Mill Lane, Norton, Stockton on Tees, Cleveland, TS20 1LG

Spark Response Limited
Incorporated: 11 March 1999 *Employees:* 183
Net Worth: £598,855 *Total Assets:* £3,502,056
Registered Office: Follingsby Avenue, Follingsby Park, Gateshead, Tyne & Wear, NE10 8HQ
Activities: Management consultancy activities other than financial management
Parent: Spark E-Commerce Group Limited
Officers: Peter Bruce Slee, Secretary; Noel Christopher Lambert [1958] Director [Irish]; Peter Bruce Slee [1961] Director; Barry Abraham Stiefel [1949] Director [German]

Spartan UK Limited
Incorporated: 12 January 2001 *Employees:* 116
Net Worth: £28,781,692 *Total Assets:* £73,321,768
Registered Office: Ropery Road, TEAMS, Gateshead, Tyne & Wear, NE8 2RD
Activities: Forging, pressing, stamping and roll-forming of metal; powder metallurgy
Major Shareholder: Rinat Akhmetov
Officers: Iuliia Dankova [1978] Director of The Controlling Department [Ukrainian]; Viktor Dembytskyy [1966] Director [Ukrainian]; Aleksandr Pogozhev [1966] Director/Chief Executive Officer [Russian]

Specialist Alarm Services Limited
Incorporated: 12 March 1981 *Employees:* 23
Net Worth: £3,485,566 *Total Assets:* £4,540,394
Registered Office: Hinde House, Elswick East Terrace, George Street Industrial Estate, Newcastle upon Tyne, NE4 7LJ
Activities: Manufacture of consumer electronics
Parent: Caring Technology Limited
Officers: Daniel Philip Adam Eastwood [1970] Technical Director; Bryan Christopher Smith [1965] Sales Director

Specialist Castings Ltd
Incorporated: 23 September 2013 *Employees:* 8
Net Worth: £91,932 *Total Assets:* £971,729
Registered Office: 1 Tatham Street, Sunderland, Tyne & Wear, SR1 2AG
Activities: Manufacture of basic iron and steel and of ferro-alloys
Major Shareholder: Christopher David Jennings
Officers: Catherine Camilla Jennings, Secretary; Catherine Camilla Jennings [1965] Director/Operations Manager; Christopher David Jennings [1965] Director

Specialist IT Services Group Limited
Incorporated: 27 March 2008 *Employees:* 22
Net Worth: £783,458 *Total Assets:* £2,615,641
Registered Office: 1 Berrymoor Court, Northumberland Business Park, Cramlington, Northumberland, NE23 7RZ
Activities: Information technology consultancy activities
Officers: Paul William Watson, Secretary; Phil Cambers [1976] Director/Senior IT Account Manager; Russell Henderson [1978] Director/Technical Architect; Geoff Hodgson [1961] Director; Michael Hugh Humphrey [1978] Director; Paul Rutherford [1968] Director/Technical Architect; Paul William Watson [1970] Director/Technical Architect

Specialist Machine Developments (Smd) Limited
Incorporated: 13 March 2008 *Employees:* 245
Net Worth Deficit: £2,778,395 *Total Assets:* £80,676,344
Registered Office: Turbinia Works, Davy Bank, Wallsend, Tyne & Wear, NE28 6UZ
Activities: Manufacture of other special-purpose machinery n.e.c.
Parent: State-Owned Assets Supervisions and Administration Commission of The State Council
Officers: Richard Hedley Howarth, Secretary; Jian Chen [1972] Director [Chinese]; Richard Hedley Howarth [1963] Director; Michael Thomas Jones [1968] Director/Chartered Engineer; Xiong Li [1964] Director [Chinese]; Hua Zhang [1976] Director [Chinese]; Dongkui Zhu [1972] Director [Chinese]

Specialist Panels UK Limited
Incorporated: 31 March 2009
Net Worth: £638,305 *Total Assets:* £947,040
Registered Office: 9 Drysdale Court, Brunswick Village, Newcastle upon Tyne, NE13 7EX
Activities: Other manufacturing n.e.c.
Shareholder: Robert Parkin
Officers: Peter Anthony Moody, Secretary/Director; Brian Camp [1958] Director; Peter Anthony Moody [1965] Director; Robert Parkin [1966] Director

Specma Samwon Ltd
Incorporated: 28 April 2003 *Employees:* 28
Net Worth: £3,021,440 *Total Assets:* £3,591,127
Registered Office: 3 Northfield Way, Newton Aycliffe, Co Durham, DL5 6EJ
Activities: Manufacture of other fabricated metal products n.e.c.
Officers: Patricia Anne Bake, Secretary; Charl Erasmus [1974] Commercial Director; Morten Kjaer Graakjear [1978] Director/Sales Executive [Danish]; Mats Lundgren [1953] Director [Swedish]; Garry Charles Quickfall [1956] Director

Spectrum Industrial Limited
Incorporated: 11 June 1976 *Employees:* 11
Net Worth: £1,082,197 *Total Assets:* £1,240,598
Registered Office: 19-24 Bedesway, Bede Industrial Estate, Jarrow, Tyne & Wear, NE32 3EG
Activities: Manufacture of soap and detergents
Shareholder: Wayne Evan Carr
Officers: Margaret Rose Carr, Secretary; Dean Alexander Carr [1961] Director/Print Manager; Harry James Carr [1936] Director; Margaret Rose Carr [1939] Director; Wayne Evan Carr [1968] Director/Works Manager

Speedbrand Limited
Incorporated: 21 April 1986 *Employees:* 2
Net Worth: £669,127 *Total Assets:* £788,810
Registered Office: 101 Galgate, Barnard Castle, Co Durham, DL12 8ES
Activities: Other letting and operating of own or leased real estate
Shareholders: Kathleen Veronica Elliott; Mark Elliott
Officers: Kathleen Veronica Elliott, Secretary; Kathleen Veronica Elliott [1958] Director/Secretary; Mark Elliott [1957] Director/Manager

Speedclad Limited
Incorporated: 4 February 2008 *Employees:* 56
Net Worth: £1,590,528 *Total Assets:* £3,897,494
Registered Office: Thurston House, Thornfield Business Park, Standard Way, Northallerton, N Yorks, DL6 2XQ
Activities: Construction of commercial buildings
Shareholder: Anthony Blake
Officers: Neil Allen Mercer, Secretary; Anthony Blake [1965] Commercial Director; Fraser Scott Brown [1971] Director; Paul Dingle [1962] Director; Rebecca Elizabeth Forward [1975] Business Services Director; Peter Hurst [1968] Director

M Spence Surfacing Limited
Incorporated: 18 June 2015 *Employees:* 14
Net Worth: £426,559 *Total Assets:* £990,944
Registered Office: Low West Thickley Farm, Brusselton Lane, Shildon, Co Durham, DL4 1QD
Activities: Construction of roads and motorways
Major Shareholder: Michael Spence
Officers: Caroline Spence [1983] Director; Michael James Spence [1984] Director/Paving & Surfacing

Spinks The Chemists Limited
Incorporated: 28 May 1952 *Employees:* 25
Net Worth: £1,130,616 *Total Assets:* £2,743,868
Registered Office: 379 Princesway South, Team Valley Trading Estate, Gateshead, Tyne & Wear, NE11 0TU
Activities: Dispensing chemist in specialised stores
Parent: Northcare Limited
Officers: Ruth Alexandria Downie [1983] Director/Pharmacist; David James Gulliford [1988] Director; Eric James Gulliford [1947] Director; Dr Peter Gulliford [1949] Director; Ross Edward Hepplewhite [1982] Director/Pharmacist

Spirit Regeneration & Development Co LLP
Incorporated: 31 March 2006
Net Worth: £31,841 *Total Assets:* £2,683,261
Registered Office: Three Rivers House, Abbeywoods Business Park, Pity Me, Durham, DH1 5TG

Spiro-Gills Thermal Products Ltd
Incorporated: 27 August 2016 *Employees:* 24
Net Worth: £15,279 *Total Assets:* £1,048,226
Registered Office: West Chirton Industrial Estate, Gloucester Road, North Shields, Tyne & Wear, NE29 8RQ
Activities: Manufacture of other special-purpose machinery n.e.c.
Parent: Diesel Marine International Limited
Officers: Alan Leslie Gray, Secretary; Peter Lindsey Jackson [1941] Director; Richard Kevin Woodmansey [1954] Director/Engineer

Spreckley Limited
Incorporated: 15 March 2001 *Employees:* 20
Net Worth: £1,124,017 *Total Assets:* £2,510,222
Registered Office: Unit B, Merlin Way, New York Industrial Park, Newcastle upon Tyne, NE27 0QG
Activities: Printing n.e.c.
Parent: Elanders Ltd
Officers: Paul Richard Jacques, Secretary; Christopher Michael Hewitt [1965] Managing Director; Paul Richard Jacques [1965] Finance Director

Springboard Sunderland Trust
Incorporated: 9 April 1987 *Employees:* 93
Net Worth: £1,784,037 *Total Assets:* £3,402,795
Registered Office: The Alec Dickson Centre, Rivergreen Industry Centre, Pallion, Sunderland, Tyne & Wear, SR4 6AD
Activities: Other education n.e.c.
Officers: David Edward Barker, Secretary; Jonathan Bryan Nicholson [1957] Director/Senior Assistant Principal; Denise Wilson [1954] Director/Retired Company Secretary; John Colin Wilson [1954] Director/Retired

Springfield Cars Limited
Incorporated: 26 April 1988 *Employees:* 99
Net Worth: £7,832,701 *Total Assets:* £12,238,890
Registered Office: 3 Crowther Road, Crowther, Washington, Tyne & Wear, NE38 0AQ
Activities: Sale of new cars and light motor vehicles
Major Shareholder: Ronald Price
Officers: Linda Irene Price, Secretary; Graeme Price [1969] Director/Customer Services; Linda Irene Price [1948] Director; Martyn Jon Price [1972] Director; Ronald Price [1947] Director/Dealer Principal

Springfield Properties (Ncle) Limited
Incorporated: 4 August 1997
Net Worth: £1,110,199 *Total Assets:* £1,495,172
Registered Office: Bermuda House, 1a Dinsdale Place, Newcastle upon Tyne, NE2 1BD
Activities: Management of real estate on a fee or contract basis
Major Shareholder: Mark James Duggan
Officers: Jean Duggan, Secretary; Mark James Duggan [1969] Director

Springs Roofing Limited
Incorporated: 5 March 1985 *Employees:* 80
Net Worth: £4,099,503 *Total Assets:* £7,088,116
Registered Office: Kimblesworth Industrial Estate, Kimblesworth, Chester-le-Street, Co Durham, DH2 3QT
Activities: Roofing activities
Parent: Northern Bear PLC
Officers: Wendy Ann Edgell, Secretary; Richard David Gordon [1983] Commercial Director; Graham Roy Jennings [1956] Director; Keith Alfred Muldoon [1962] Director; Steven Mark Roberts [1966] Director; Matthew Rowley [1976] Contracts Director; Keith Soulsby [1956] Director; Paul Soulsby [1982] Contracts Director

SPS Electrical Wholesalers Limited
Incorporated: 29 May 2014 *Employees:* 5
Net Worth: £6,449 *Total Assets:* £851,369
Registered Office: 16 Saltmeadows Road, Gateshead, Tyne & Wear, NE8 3AH
Activities: Wholesale of electronic and telecommunications equipment and parts
Shareholders: Anthony John McNally; Alan Smith
Officers: Anthony John McNally [1955] Director/Accountant; Alan Smith [1951] Director

Square One Law LLP
Incorporated: 22 February 2011
Net Worth: £1,595,478 *Total Assets:* £2,477,092
Registered Office: Anson House, Fleming Business Centre, Burdon Terrace, Jesmond, Newcastle upon Tyne, NE2 3AE
Officers: Ian Michael Gilthorpe [1953] Member; Gillian Hall [1972] Member; Mark Lazenby [1976] Member; Jean Pierre Van Zyl [1971] Member; Neil Kenneth Warwick [1968] Member; Marie-Louise Bozonet [1979] LLP Member; Helen Grace Brain [1975] LLP Member; Peter David Clegg [1978] LLP Member; Charles Ellis Fielding [1980] LLP Member; Barnabas Webster Frith [1956] LLP Member; John Canfield Hammill [1975] LLP Member; Adrian Edward Hill [1958] LLP Member; Simon John Loy [1965] LLP Member; Roisin Mary Patton [1982] LLP Member; Michael David Shuker [1977] LLP Member; Gillian Marie Tatt [1968] LLP Member

Square Peg Properties Limited
Incorporated: 11 December 2015
Net Worth: £2,303,067 *Total Assets:* £4,569,603
Registered Office: Tutin Road, Leeming Bar Industrial Estate, Northallerton, N Yorks, DL7 9UJ
Activities: Other letting and operating of own or leased real estate
Major Shareholder: Kevin John Procter
Officers: Claire Elizabeth Alenius, Secretary; Kevin John Procter [1964] Director/Coach Proprietor

Squirrels UK Limited
Incorporated: 30 March 2007 *Employees:* 25
Net Worth: £3,655,020 *Total Assets:* £7,036,508
Registered Office: Unit S, 3 Narvik Way, Tyne Tunnel Trading Estate, North Shields, Tyne & Wear, NE29 7XJ
Activities: Other business support service activities n.e.c.
Officers: Patricia Ada Rice, Secretary; David Leonard Brind [1972] Director; John Frederick Hope [1969] Group Operations Director; Patricia Ada Rice [1957] Director; David Terrence Yolland [1965] Sales Director; Paul Victor Young [1957] Director

SRJ Energy Ltd
Incorporated: 7 July 2014
Net Worth: £66,526 *Total Assets:* £820,993
Registered Office: 2 Matamba Terrace, Sunderland, Tyne & Wear, SR4 7AZ
Activities: Retail sale in non-specialised stores with food, beverages or tobacco predominating
Major Shareholder: Kavitha Thirumalai
Officers: Kavitha Thirumalai [1980] Director/Manager

SRSS Ltd
Incorporated: 1 August 2006
Net Worth: £9,915 *Total Assets:* £813,179
Registered Office: 4 Exelby Close, Whitebridge Park, Newcastle upon Tyne, NE3 5LG
Activities: Activities of mortgage finance companies
Major Shareholder: Sunil Satyapal Khanna
Officers: Sunil Satyapal Khanna [1957] Director/Businessman

SS Healthfoods Limited
Incorporated: 1 August 2007
Registered Office: 172 Whitley Road, Whitley Bay, Tyne & Wear, NE26 2TA
Activities: Other retail sale of new goods in specialised stores (not commercial art galleries and opticians)
Shareholders: Veneta Callan; Diana Mancheva
Officers: John Callan, Secretary; Veneta Dobrinova Callan [1976] Director; Diana Borisova Mancheva [1958] Director [Bulgarian]

SSDOS Limited
Incorporated: 7 May 2009
Net Worth: £813,704 *Total Assets:* £842,861
Registered Office: Unit 2 Standing Stone, Matfen, Northumberland, NE20 0RG
Activities: Activities of other holding companies n.e.c.
Shareholder: Gary George Ritson
Officers: Gary George Ritson, Secretary; Simon John Buckton [1971] Sales Director; Andrew John Neal [1976] Director/Service Manager; Gary George Ritson [1964] Director

SSL Healthcare Ltd
Incorporated: 28 September 2010 *Employees:* 102
Net Worth: £1,031,397 *Total Assets:* £3,261,520
Registered Office: Kensington House, 3 Kensington, Bishop Auckland, Co Durham, DL14 6HX
Activities: Other service activities n.e.c.
Shareholders: Stephen Metcalf; Susan Metcalf; Louise Harvey
Officers: Louise Harvey [1973] Director; Stephen Metcalf [1952] Director; Susan Metcalf [1954] Director

St (Edrom) Limited
Incorporated: 27 May 2004 *Employees:* 1
Net Worth: £752,677 *Total Assets:* £889,472
Registered Office: 19 Fenkle Street, Alnwick, Northumberland, NE66 1HW
Activities: Other business support service activities n.e.c.
Shareholders: Stella Tennant; David Maximilien Lasnet
Officers: Stella Tennant [1970] Director

St Aidan's Church of England Academy Limited
Incorporated: 15 March 2007 *Employees:* 53
Net Worth: £9,496,000 *Total Assets:* £11,448,000
Registered Office: St Aidan's, Hundens Lane, Darlington, Co Durham, DL1 1LL
Activities: General secondary education
Officers: Anita Susan Blackburn [1952] Director/Vice Principal; Marc Edward Crossland [1967] Director/Self Employed; Mike Davison [1951] Director/Retired/Educational Consultant; John Frank de Martino [1944] Director/Accountant; Nicole Gibbon [1970] Director/Principal; Anita Inglis [1970] Director/Group Head of Business Improvement; Christine Anne Large [1961] Director/Teacher; Ruth Lowbridge [1953] Director/Academy Ambassador; Steven Simpson [1967] Director/Estates Officer; David Barrie Spenceley [1966] Director/Teacher

St Aidan's Education Trust
Incorporated: 13 March 2013 *Employees:* 109
Net Worth: £5,378,396 *Total Assets:* £6,977,272
Registered Office: St Aidan's Catholic Academy, Willowbank Road, Ashbrooke, Sunderland, Tyne & Wear, SR2 7HJ
Activities: General secondary education
Shareholders: Bishop Seamus Cunningham; Catherine Mary Emmerson
Officers: Madeleine Louise Hope, Secretary; Doctor Catherine Mary Emmerson [1961] Director/Hospital Doctor; Charles Stewart Ferguson [1959] Director/Mortgage Broker; Michael McCoy [1963] Director/Catholic Priest; Kevin James Shepherd [1971] Director/Headteacher; Peter Robin Wood [1943] Director/Retired

St Bede's Catholic Academy (Lanchester)
Incorporated: 9 May 2012 *Employees:* 172
Net Worth Deficit: £1,586,381 *Total Assets:* £1,755,505
Registered Office: St Bede's Catholic School & Sixth Form College, Consett Road, Lanchester, Co Durham, DH7 0RD
Activities: General secondary education
Officers: Simon Chapman-Ward [1984] Director/Finance Officer; John David Dixon [1952] Director/Retired; Margaret Mary Gray [1949] Director/Retired; Neville Harrison [1962] Director/Headteacher; Anthony Stuart Isles [1963] Director/NHS-Health Visitor; Julia Patricia Leech [1966] Director/Bank Official; Kathleen Mary Noon [1979] Director/Teacher; Katherine Marie Nugent [1967] Director/Human Resources Manager; Gillian Pace [1959] Director/Road Safety Officer; Joseph Park [1937] Director/Catholic Priest; Andrea Diane Parker [1970] Director/Teacher; Lesley Ann Pinkerton [1966] Director/School Business Manager; Gail Roberts [1960] Director/Specialist Podiatrist in NHS; Martin Walker [1972] Programme Director

St Bede's RC Primary School
Incorporated: 28 May 2012 *Employees:* 38
Net Worth: £428,000 *Total Assets:* £986,000
Registered Office: St Bede's RC Primary School, Kingsway, Darlington, Co Durham, DL1 3ES
Activities: Primary education
Officers: Deborah Bowman [1969] Director/Church Secretary; Alba Amalia Brown [1977] Director/Senior Finance Assistant; Deborah Fox [1965] Director of Education; Doreen Elizabeth King [1956] Director/Headteacher; Gerard MacKowski [1958] Director/Civil Servant; Emily Ann Millward [1980] Director/Teacher; Karen Helen Mulholland [1971] Director/General Adviser; Neil Francis Oxley [1963] Director/Civil Servant; Rose-Marie Rochester [1979] Director/Teacher [Irish]; David Russell [1962] Director/Roman Catholic Priest; Paul Bryan Storey [1967] Director/Software Engineer; Marianne Theresa Taylor [1954] Director/Educational Psychologist

St Benedict's Hospice, Sunderland
Incorporated: 26 March 1993 *Employees:* 3
Net Worth: £1,616,696 *Total Assets:* £1,684,081
Registered Office: St Benedict's Hospice, St Benedicts Way, Ryhope, Sunderland, Tyne & Wear, SR2 0NY
Activities: Hospital activities
Officers: Kenneth Alan Stenger, Secretary; Janice Margaret Bray [1952] Director/Retired; Claire McLaughlin [1970] Director/Civil Servant; Derek Moss [1958] Director/Property Developer; John Trevor Thorne [1948] Director/Chartered Accountant; Chimanlal Himatlal Trivedy [1945] Managing Director; William Paul Usher [1956] Director/Property Developer; Dr Martin Joseph Walker [1953] Director/Retired

St Chad's Community Project
Incorporated: 5 January 2001 *Employees:* 22
Net Worth: £803,725 *Total Assets:* £908,352
Registered Office: 21 Liddell Terrace, Bensham, Gateshead, Tyne & Wear, NE8 1YN
Activities: Other social work activities without accommodation n.e.c.
Officers: The Venerable John Venerable John Stuart Bain [1955] Director/Clerk in Holy Orders; Valerie Barron [1965] Director/Charity Worker; Abigail Joanne Bick [1972] Director/Fund Raising Manager; Lesya Bourn [1970] Director/Sales Assistant [Ukrainian]; Elisabeth Bryant [1951] Director/Practice Nurse; Margaret Mary Gilley [1954] Director/Minister of Religion; Margaret O'Hara [1946] Director/Retired; Clare Talbot Jones [1981] Company Secretary/Director

St Cuthbert's Care
Incorporated: 23 June 1982 *Employees:* 322
Net Worth: £6,407,119 *Total Assets:* £7,653,254
Registered Office: St Cuthbert's House, West Road, Newcastle upon Tyne, NE15 7PY
Activities: Residential nursing care facilities
Officers: Nicholas Alexander Gilbert, Secretary; Moira Helen Ashman [1966] Director/Chief Executive; John Richard Devine [1976] Director/Solicitor; Michael George Dickson [1951] Managing Director; Dermott James Donnelly [1967] Director/Catholic Priest; Nicholas Alexander Gilbert [1971] Finance Director; Dr Jeremiah Joseph Kelliher [1956] Director/General Practitioner [Irish]; Paul Burnett Moran [1962] Director/Chartered Accountant; Kathleen Urwin [1958] Director/Manager Charity Sector

St Cuthbert's Catholic High School
Incorporated: 20 January 2012 *Employees:* 113
Net Worth: £2,664,000 *Total Assets:* £4,054,000
Registered Office: St Cuthbert's Catholic High School, Gretna Road, Newcastle upon Tyne, NE15 7PX
Activities: General secondary education
Officers: Mark Clasper [1982] Director/Architect; Carol Davison [1959] Director/Teacher; Dominic Joseph Dimambro [1968] Director/Property Developer; David Johnson [1949] Director/Retired; Reverend Simon Lerche [1971] Director/Roman Catholic Priest; Louise Anne Lockey [1968] Director/Requirements Manager; Ann Logan [1948] Director/Retired; John FitzGenerald Noone [1964] Managing Director - Insurance Broking Firm; Bridget Rutherford [1962] Director/Teacher; Ashley Elizabeth Simpson [1973] Director/Solicitor; Veronica Mary Stonor [1967] Director

St Helen's Farm Limited
Incorporated: 8 May 2007 *Employees:* 40
Net Worth: £2,588,835 *Total Assets:* £4,856,329
Registered Office: Kingsway, Team Valley Trading Estate, Gateshead, Tyne & Wear, NE11 0ST
Activities: Liquid milk and cream production
Parent: Kavli UK Limited
Officers: Lynn Hayes, Secretary; Paul Robert Lewney [1967] Director; Erik Volden [1961] Director [Norwegian]

St James' Central 4 & 5 Limited
Incorporated: 4 June 2015
Net Worth: £123 *Total Assets:* £1,867,420
Registered Office: Picton Manor, Ellison Place, Newcastle upon Tyne, NE1 8XG
Activities: Construction of domestic buildings
Officers: Victoria Jane Kalbraier, Secretary; Paul Clement [1965] Director; Robert William Kalbraier [1985] Director; Paul David Pestell [1969] Director/Chartered Accountant

St James' Central Investments Limited
Incorporated: 15 April 2015
Net Worth: £51,309 *Total Assets:* £2,641,320
Registered Office: Picton Manor, Ellison Place, Newcastle upon Tyne, NE1 8XG
Activities: Activities of venture and development capital companies
Officers: Victoria Jane Kalbraier, Secretary; Paul Clement [1965] Director; Robert William Kalbraier [1985] Director; Paul David Pestell [1969] Director/Chartered Accountant

St John's Church of England Academy
Incorporated: 11 April 2012 *Employees:* 32
Net Worth: £860,000 *Total Assets:* £1,371,000
Registered Office: St John's Church of England Academy, Fenby Avenue, Darlington, Co Durham, DL1 4UB
Activities: Primary education
Officers: Peter Cooke, Secretary; Michelle Brown [1966] Director/Deputy Headteacher; Valerie Cadd [1942] Director/Retired Teacher; Mark William Doswell [1978] Director/Business Operations Manager; William John Harrison [1948] Director/Retired; Jennie Marie Hazlewood [1971] Director; Christine Anne Large [1961] Director/Headteacher; Andrew Linsley [1978] Director/Postman; Christine Marsh [1959] Director/Chartered Management Accountant; Janet Pattinson [1959] Director/Pensions Administrator; Susan Plummer [1944] Director; Susan Railton [1962] Director; Edward George Robinson [1951] Director

St Thomas More Partnership of Schools
Incorporated: 6 January 2012 *Employees:* 260
Net Worth: £5,325,085 *Total Assets:* £7,589,018
Registered Office: St Thomas More Catholic School, Croftdale Road, Blaydon, Tyne & Wear, NE21 4BQ
Activities: General secondary education
Officers: James Thomson, Secretary; John Scott Hayes [1967] Director/Local Government Officer; Barbara Ann Lowery [1956] Director/Retired GP [Irish]; Richard Edward Paisley [1977] Director; Ewan Jonathan Parkinson [1962] Director/Headteacher; Kevin Gerard Joseph Robertson [1972] Director/Solicitor; Michael Whalen [1948] Director/RC Priest

St Thomas More Roman Catholic Academy
Incorporated: 11 November 2011 *Employees:* 177
Net Worth: £8,712,393 *Total Assets:* £10,641,063
Registered Office: St Thomas More Roman Catholic Academy, Lynn Road, North Shields, Tyne & Wear, NE29 8LF
Activities: General secondary education
Shareholder: Deborah Fox
Officers: Anthony Gollings, Secretary; Rosemary Anderson [1968] Director/HR Manager; Helen MacKenzie Bell [1962] Director/Teacher; Salome Mary Bolton [1973] Director/Lecturer [Irish]; David Campbell [1967] Director/Pharmacist; Julie Anne Connolly [1976] Director/Family Partner Supporting Families; Catherine Mary Edwards [1967] Director/Librarian; Andrew James Faley [1954] Director/Parish Priest; Colin Finlay [1952] Director/Retired Assistant Headteacher; Lisa Hagan [1968] Director/Teacher; Christopher John Hughes [1960] Director/Parish Priest; Catherine Rose Jeffrey [1963] Director/Accountant; Clare Louise Langley [1972] Director/Police Officer; Richard John Dent Lowery [1966] Finance Director; Dr Angela Jane MacOscar [1971] Director/Product Research Manager; Conrad Masiiwa [1967] Director/Business IT Analyst/Project Manager; Michael Ronan [1948] Director/Retired; Fiona Mary Stevenson [1960] Director/Assistant Headteacher; Bernadette Swallow [1959] Director/Retired; David Paul Watson [1971] Director/Headteacher; Christine Wright [1959] Director/Retired

St Trinity Limited
Incorporated: 1 December 2009
Net Worth: £614,000 *Total Assets:* £2,600,000
Registered Office: Newcastle House, Albany Court, Newcastle Business Park, Newcastle upon Tyne, NE4 7YB
Activities: Management of real estate on a fee or contract basis
Parent: LSL Property Services PLC
Officers: Sapna Bedi FitzGenerald, Secretary; Helen Elizabeth Buck [1960] Director; Adam Robert Castleton [1964] Director; Paul Hardy [1976] Director; James Charles McAuley [1954] Director

St. Anthony of Padua Community Association
Incorporated: 6 June 1986 *Employees:* 124
Net Worth: £2,860,720 *Total Assets:* £3,376,724
Registered Office: Community Centre, Welbeck Road, Walker, Newcastle upon Tyne, NE6 3BT
Activities: Social work activities without accommodation for the elderly and disabled
Officers: Catherine Mary Attwell [1972] HR Director; Julie Campbell [1966] Director/Nurse Practitioner; Michael Donnelly [1958] Director/Headteacher; James Joseph McLaughlin [1936] Director/Retired; Benjamin David Nixon [1982] Director/Solicitor; Timothy Patrick O'Grady [1947] Director Education Project; Daryn Robinson [1977] Director; Robert Edward Stanley [1951] Director

St. Anthony's Girls' Catholic Academy
Incorporated: 28 February 2012 *Employees:* 167
Net Worth: £490,851 *Total Assets:* £1,367,126
Registered Office: St Anthony's Girls' Catholic Academy, Thornhill Terrace, Sunderland, Tyne & Wear, SR2 7JN
Activities: General secondary education
Officers: Julie Liddell, Secretary; Julia May Adamson [1966] Director/Teacher; Emma Jayne Ashton [1975] Director; Angela Maria Bashton [1957] Director; Jane Catherine Carlin [1945] Director/Retired Teacher; Michael Louis Flores [1948] Director; Maureen Ann Galbraith [1950] Director; Anne Gleeson [1938] Director/Retired Teacher [Irish]; Marc James Lyden-Smith [1982] Director/Priest; Katherine Lucy Richardson-Dunn [1969] Director/Pupil Support Manager; Andrea Maria Shanks [1961] Director/Associate Dean in Law; Monica Anne Shepherd [1957] Director/Headteacher; Samantha Kerry Ward [1973] Director/Teacher

St. Astier Limited
Incorporated: 30 January 2003
Net Worth: £732,271 *Total Assets:* £1,569,942
Registered Office: 11 Enterprise Court, Seaham Grange Industrial Estate, Seaham, Co Durham, SR7 0PS
Activities: Other specialised construction activities n.e.c.
Shareholders: Ranson Og; Carol Ann Og
Officers: Carol Ann Og, Secretary; Carol Ann Og [1964] Director/Building Contractor; Ranson Og [1962] Director/Specialist Building Contractor

St. Camillus Care Group Ltd
Incorporated: 27 May 2015 *Employees:* 13
Net Worth Deficit: £160,267 *Total Assets:* £1,666,333
Registered Office: 37 Side, Newcastle upon Tyne, NE1 3JE
Activities: Licenced restaurants
Shareholders: John Heron; Stephen Talbot
Officers: John Heron [1973] Director/Property Developer; Stephen Talbot [1971] Director

St. Chad's College
Incorporated: 4 May 1910 *Employees:* 48
Net Worth: £10,297,300 *Total Assets:* £10,821,604
Registered Office: 18 North Bailey, Durham, DH1 3RH
Activities: First-degree level higher education
Officers: Alistair John Jenkins, Secretary; Julia Atherley [1997] Director/Student; Professor Sarah Jane Banks [1955] Director/Academic; Alan Arthur Buckle [1959] Director/Adviser & Trustee; Paul Geoffrey Chandler [1961] Director; Professor Howell Martyn Evans [1956] Director/Principal; Jenny Haworth [1966] Director/Strategic Planner; Dr Margaret Jane Masson [1961] Director/College Principal; Joseph Nelson [1993] Director/Student; Sean Bernard Power [1978] Director/Development; Richard David Pratt [1955] Director/Clerk in Holy Orders; Elisabeth Rowark [1965] Director; Susan Shaw [1949] Director/Freelance Research; Richard Taylor [1962] Director/Archivist; Professor Claire Louise Harrison Warwick [1967] Director/Pro-Vice-Chancellor (Research); Hilaire Wong [1996] Director/Student [Chinese]; The Rev Barry Mark Woodruff [1959] Catholic Priest (Westminster); Charity Director

St. Cuthbert Newcastle Estates Limited
Incorporated: 25 April 1928 *Employees:* 6
Net Worth: £8,001,211 *Total Assets:* £9,251,544
Registered Office: The Cube, Barrack Road, Newcastle upon Tyne, NE4 6DB
Activities: Other letting and operating of own or leased real estate
Officers: James Whaley Heppell, Secretary; Judith Ann Bishop [1962] Director/Surveyor; James Whaley Heppell [1947] Director/Surveyor; Sarah Jane Nash [1980] Director/Accountant; Peter Charles Anthony Smith [1949] Director/Chartered Surveyor

St. Cuthbert's Hospice Durham
Incorporated: 28 December 1987 *Employees:* 92
Net Worth: £6,372,796 *Total Assets:* £6,511,757
Registered Office: St Cuthbert's Hospice, Park House Road, Durham, DH1 3QF
Activities: Medical nursing home activities
Officers: Richard Hugh Langdon, Secretary/Solicitor; Janet Ann Brown [1951] Director/Retired; Sheila Mary Chapman [1960] Director/PR and Marketing Consultant; John Davison [1957] Director/Solicitor; Ian Roberts Dewhirst [1948] Director/Retired; Dr Patricia Anne Flanagan [1957] Director/Doctor; Dr Angela Galloway [1954] Director/Retired; John Graydon [1956] Director/Head of Estates and Facilities; Simon Paul Jefferson [1974] Director/Commercial Account Manager; Angela Lorraine Lamb [1958] Director; Gillian Louise MacArthur [1959] Retired Director of Nursing & Midwifery; Dr James Lees McMichael [1958] Director/General Practitioner; Naomi Morrow [1993] Director/Head of Innovation; Dr Catherine Lorraine O'Donnell [1968] Director of Transformation and Partnerships; Sandra Ann Ruskin [1947] Director/Retired; Kevin Whitfield [1960] Managing Director

St. Joseph's Catholic Education Trust
Incorporated: 6 June 2013 *Employees:* 160
Net Worth Deficit: £1,610,347 *Total Assets:* £1,544,486
Registered Office: St Josephs Catholic Academy, Mill Lane, Hebburn, Tyne & Wear, NE31 2ET
Activities: General secondary education
Officers: Christine Henderson, Secretary; Martin Clephane [1970] Director/Headteacher; Rev Adrian Dixon [1956] Director/Clergy; Tracey Fairweather [1975] Director/Housewife; Angela Harrison [1972] Director/Teacher; Joseph Hughes [1951] Director/Retired; Stephen Jobling [1974] Director/Data Manager; Generaldine Kilgour [1971] Director/Civil Servant; Michael McDonagh [1968] Director/Teacher; Debra Phippen [1969] Director/School Staff; Thomas Brendan Tapping [1963] Director; Lynne Thompson [1966] Director/School Staff; Virginia Mary Wiblin [1948] Director/Retired

St. Martin's Care Limited
Incorporated: 14 September 1993 *Employees:* 528
Net Worth: £2,612,974 *Total Assets:* £9,629,964
Registered Office: Anson House, Fleming Business Centre, Burdon Terrace, Jesmond, Newcastle upon Tyne, NE2 3AE
Activities: Other human health activities
Officers: Kevin Pattison [1962] Director

St. Mary's Catholic School Trust
Incorporated: 5 July 2013 *Employees:* 122
Net Worth: £13,323,080 *Total Assets:* £14,535,355
Registered Office: St Mary's Catholic School, Benton Park Road, Newcastle upon Tyne, NE7 7PE
Activities: General secondary education
Officers: Michael Donnelly [1958] Director/Headteacher; Nicholas Dominic Edgar [1976] Director/Investment Manager; John Martin Foster [1963] Director/Headteacher; Malcolm Geoffrey Gregor [1932] Director/Retired Solicitor; John Martin McConnell [1964] HR Director; David Andrew McDyer [1967] Director/Police Superintendent; Michael McGhee [1962] Operations Director; Angela Ness [1962] Director/Headmistress; Stormont James Eltringham Smith [1961] Director/Pilot; Nicola Taylor [1967] Director/Teacher; Anthony Edward Woods-Waters [1960] Director

St. Mary's Chare Developments Limited
Incorporated: 17 March 1972
Net Worth: £2,119,224 *Total Assets:* £2,663,542
Registered Office: Unit 1 Hexham Auction Mart, Tyne Green, Hexham, Northumberland, NE46 3SG
Activities: Buying and selling of own real estate
Officers: Geoffrey Raymond Hubbuck, Secretary; Derek William Hubbuck [1951] Director/Agricultural Merchant; Geoffrey Raymond Hubbuck [1957] Director/Agricultural Merchant

St. Oswald's Catholic Academy Trust
Incorporated: 5 March 2014 *Employees:* 170
Net Worth: £1,730,000 *Total Assets:* £4,090,000
Registered Office: St Peter's Catholic Voluntary Academy, Normanby Road, South Bank, Middlesbrough, Cleveland, TS6 6SP
Activities: Primary education
Officers: Jane Marie Edmends [1968] Director/Clerical Officer; Zahida Sarah Hammond [1973] Director/Headmistress; Nicola Lynne Jamalizadeh [1980] Director/Headteacher; Jill Margaret Miller [1969] Director/Company Secretary; Lindsay Anne Phelps [1983] Director/Headmistress; Christine Anne Ruddy [1953] Director/Headteacher; Robert Iain Sim [1957] Director/Chief Executive; Lesley Anne Wilson M.B.E. [1961] Director/Civil Servant

St. Oswald's Hospice Limited
Incorporated: 9 April 1974 *Employees:* 277
Net Worth: £14,071,144 *Total Assets:* £14,686,304
Registered Office: Regent Avenue, Gosforth, Newcastle upon Tyne, NE3 1EE
Activities: Other human health activities
Officers: Helen Alice Eadington, Secretary/Corporate and Support Services; Dr Stephen Michael Blades [1960] Director/Doctor; Janet Clarke [1947] Director/Retired Pharmaceutical Manager; Dorothy Clasper [1943] Director/Retired Civil Servant; Christine English [1960] Principal Lecturer/Director of Outreach; Kersi Fanibunda [1936] Director/Retired Dental Consultant; Julie Harrison [1958] Director/Solicitor; Brian Kyle Hedley [1951] Director/Retired Accountant; Kim Gail Jobson [1961] Director/Head of Human Resources & Organisational Development; Marie Liston [1973] Director of Human Resources; Dr Helen Hunter Lucraft [1950] Director/Retired Consultant Clinical Oncologist; Mike Paul Robson [1955] Director/Accountant

St.John's College,Durham
Incorporated: 2 January 1911 *Employees:* 112
Net Worth: £19,726,654 *Total Assets:* £21,687,532
Registered Office: 3 South Bailey, Durham, DH1 3RJ
Activities: First-degree level higher education
Officers: Caragh Beth Aylett [1995] Director/Student President; Dr Rebecca Bouveng [1980] Director/Academic [Swedish]; Susanne Mai Bradley [1965] Director/HR Consultant; The Venerable Sarah Ruth Bullock [1964] Director/Minister of Religion; Bridget Marye Cass [1952] Director/Charity Executive; Angela Cook [1961] Director/Accountant; Dr Michael John Gilmore [1958] Director/Higher Education; Ian Richard Harris [1950] Director/Chartered Surveyor; James Herbert Harrison [1953] Director/GP; Professor Michel Anthony Higton [1971] Director/University Lecturer; Claire Rachel Jones [1990] Director/Student; Elizabeth Jane Holden Lane [1966] Director/Bishop; Richard Derrick Mayland [1953] Director; Professor Geoffrey Alastair Moore [1955] Director/Lecturer; James William Scobie Newcome [1953] Director/Minister of Religion; Kelly Pattinson [1971] Director/Finance Assistant; Revd Dr Philip James John Plyming [1974] Director/College Warden; Nigel Rhyl Robson [1951] Retired Solicitor, Currently Part Time Director; Margaret Mugabi Sentamu [1951] Director/Consultant; Kevin Shotton [1981] Director/Chartered Accountant; David Adam Wilkinson [1963] Director/Lecturer

St.Julian's Estate Limited (The)
Incorporated: 3 March 1905 *Employees:* 4
Net Worth: £7,967,915 *Total Assets:* £12,882,843
Registered Office: St Ann's Wharf, 112 Quayside, Newcastle upon Tyne, NE1 3DX
Activities: Other letting and operating of own or leased real estate
Parent: Lambton Share Property Company Limited
Officers: Robert Alexander Dickinson [1964] Director/Solicitor; Lady Agnes Harriet Frances Mary Joicey [1956] Director; Lord James Michael Joicey [1953] Director

Stablewood Developments Limited
Incorporated: 14 May 2008
Net Worth: £490,362 *Total Assets:* £1,237,603
Registered Office: Stablewood House, Lucker Road, Lucker, Belford, Northumberland, NE70 7JQ
Activities: Non-trading company
Shareholders: Tina Anne Johnson; Kevin Johnson
Officers: Tina Anne Johnson, Secretary/Clerical Assistant; Daniel James Johnson [1987] Director; Jonathon Matthew Johnson [1990] Director; Kevin Johnson [1962] Director; Martyn Leigh Johnson [1986] Director; Tina Anne Johnson [1962] Director

Stackpole Investments Limited
Incorporated: 12 September 2006
Net Worth: £8,823,094 *Total Assets:* £8,823,094
Registered Office: Office G5, Ground Floor, Metropolitan House, Longrigg Road, Swalwell, Gateshead, Tyne & Wear, NE16 3AS
Activities: Activities of head offices
Parent: Johnson Electric International (UK) Limited
Officers: Christopher John Hasson [1963] Director; Jeffrey L. Obermayer [1955] Director [American]

Stadium Consumer Products Limited
Incorporated: 1 November 2001 *Employees:* 16
Net Worth: £326,824 *Total Assets:* £942,194
Registered Office: Stadium North, Tofts Farm Industrial Estate, Brenda Road, Hartlepool, Cleveland, TS25 2DH
Activities: Agents involved in the sale of furniture, household goods, hardware and ironmongery
Major Shareholder: Julie Anne Morrisey
Officers: Julie Anne Morrisey, Secretary/Managing Director; Julie Anne Morrisey [1964] Managing Director; Stephen Bernard Morrisey [1963] Director

Stadium Export Services Limited
Incorporated: 9 June 1995 *Employees:* 20
Net Worth: £764,004 *Total Assets:* £1,182,165
Registered Office: 11 Glasshouse Street, St Peters, Newcastle upon Tyne, NE6 1BS
Activities: Manufacture of wooden containers
Parent: British Engines (UK) Limited
Officers: Joanne Alicea Wilkes, Secretary; Laura Joicey [1976] Director/Group Chief Financial Officer; Alexander Harold Lamb [1971] Director; Jonathan Charles Lamb [1977] Group Manufacturing Director; Brian Andrew Smith [1964] Director/Chief Executive Officer (CEO)

B.M. Stafford & Sons Ltd
Incorporated: 1 February 2007 *Employees:* 41
Net Worth: £536,985 *Total Assets:* £2,360,249
Registered Office: Milburn House, Hetton Lyons Industrial Estate, Houghton-le-Spring, Co Durham, DH5 0RH
Activities: Freight transport by road
Shareholder: Mark Milburn Stafford
Officers: Mark Milburn Stafford, Secretary/Haulage Contractor; Mark Milburn Stafford [1977] Director/Haulage Contractor

Staindrop Academy
Incorporated: 6 July 2011
Registered Office: Staindrop School, Cleatlam Lane, Staindrop, Darlington, Co Durham, DL2 3JU
Activities: General secondary education
Officers: Helen Overfield, Secretary; Julian Christopher Brown [1966] Director; Paul Hunton [1967] Director; Stephen James Leech [1974] Director/Lecturer

Stairrods (UK) Limited
Incorporated: 19 September 1985 *Employees:* 25
Net Worth: £814,636 *Total Assets:* £1,427,999
Registered Office: Unit 6 Park Road, North Industrial Estate, Blackhill, Consett, Co Durham, DH8 5UN
Activities: Copper production
Officers: John Ronald Raine, Secretary; Stuart Brown [1954] Director; John Ronald Raine [1959] Director

Staithes Lane Properties Limited
Incorporated: 8 February 2016 *Employees:* 4
Net Worth: £135,489 *Total Assets:* £2,453,375
Registered Office: Braefoot, Longhorsley, Morpeth, Northumberland, NE65 8UU
Activities: Other letting and operating of own or leased real estate
Shareholder: Sally Ann Booth
Officers: Jane Michelle Barwick-Nesbit [1961] Director/Veterinary Surgeon; Sally Ann Booth [1963] Director/Veterinary Surgeon; John Richard Robert Prescott [1972] Director/Veterinary Surgeon

Stamford Farms Ltd
Incorporated: 15 June 2012
Registered Office: Stamford, Alnwick, Northumberland, NE66 3RY
Activities: Mixed farming
Shareholders: Kathryn Elizabeth Robertson; Iain George Robertson
Officers: Kathryn Elizabeth Robertson, Secretary; Iain George Robertson [1961] Director/Farmer; Kathryn Elizabeth Robertson [1965] Director/Property and General Manager

Stampflat Limited
Incorporated: 9 December 2004 *Employees:* 3
Net Worth: £18,646,720 *Total Assets:* £20,951,254
Registered Office: First Floor, Finchale House, Belmont Business Park, Durham, DH1 1TW
Activities: Other letting and operating of own or leased real estate
Officers: Helen Austin, Secretary; John Corbitt Barnsley [1948] Director; Spencer Glanville [1972] Director; Robert William Jefferson [1950] Director/Chartered Accountant

Standard Aviation Limited
Incorporated: 3 June 1982
Net Worth: £577,000 *Total Assets:* £1,692,000
Registered Office: 1a Dukesway Court, Team Valley Trading Estate, Gateshead, Tyne & Wear, NE11 0PJ
Activities: Non-scheduled passenger air transport
Parent: Falcombe Holdings Limited
Officers: Phillip Nigel Blain, Secretary; David James Horrocks [1959] Director/Chartered Accountant; Ian Imrie [1955] Director

Standard Security Services Limited
Incorporated: 19 March 2003 *Employees:* 7
Net Worth: £1,254,158 *Total Assets:* £2,228,848
Registered Office: 1 Jesmond Business Court, Jesmond Road, Newcastle upon Tyne, NE2 1LA
Activities: Private security activities
Shareholder: Suzette Scott
Officers: Suzette Scott, Secretary; Samantha Jayne Scott [1985] Director; Suzette Scott [1962] Director

Standing Stone Drawing Office Supplies Limited
Incorporated: 14 May 2004 *Employees:* 15
Net Worth: £312,960 *Total Assets:* £879,083
Registered Office: Unit 2 Standing Stone, Matfen, Northumberland, NE20 0RQ
Activities: Other retail sale in non-specialised stores
Parent: SSDOS Limited
Officers: Gary George Ritson, Secretary; Simon John Buckton [1971] Director; Andrew John Neal [1976] Director/Technical Service Manager; Gary George Ritson [1964] Director

Stanfam Properties Limited
Incorporated: 30 July 2001
Net Worth Deficit: £30,518 *Total Assets:* £1,345,837
Registered Office: Spaceworks, Benton Park Road, Newcastle upon Tyne, NE7 7LX
Activities: Other accommodation
Officers: Loretta Mary Stanley, Secretary; Mark Anthony Stanley [1974] Director; Martin Luke Stanley [1986] Director; Roy Robert Edward Stanley [1951] Director; Maria Kathryn Thrall [1980] Director

Stanley Learning Partnership
Incorporated: 16 September 2016 *Employees:* 80
Net Worth: £5,875,000 *Total Assets:* £7,838,000
Registered Office: Unit G3, Tanfield Lea Business Centre, Tanfield Lea Industrial Estate North, Tanfield Lea, Stanley, Co Durham, DH9 9DB
Activities: Pre-primary education
Officers: Henry Peter Broome [1982] Director/IT Consultancy; Tracy Davinson [1967] Director/Teacher; Eric Dodd [1957] Director/Retired; Stephen Down [1969] Director/Best Interest Assessor; Thomas Harpe [1946] Director/Retired; Heather Kemp [1954] Director/Headteacher; Liam Kenneth McMahon [1986] Director/Financial Adviser; Malcolm Webb [1946] Director/Retired; Christine Weightman [1969] Director/Support Worker; Emily Hannah White [1981] Director/Lawyer and Legal Tutor; Professor David Ainsley Wooff [1957] Director/Retired

Stanners Equipment Limited
Incorporated: 9 July 1980 *Employees:* 25
Net Worth: £2,211,465 *Total Assets:* £2,808,585
Registered Office: Coopies Lane, Morpeth, Northumberland, NE61 6JN
Activities: Wholesale of other machinery and equipment
Shareholders: James William Michael Stanners; John Duncan Stanners
Officers: John Duncan Stanners, Secretary; James William Michael Stanners [1968] Director; John Duncan Stanners [1954] Director; John Stanners Jnr [1986] Director

Stannington Estates Limited
Incorporated: 23 May 2003
Net Worth Deficit: £59,622 *Total Assets:* £839,297
Registered Office: 51 Station Road, Stannington, Morpeth, Northumberland, NE61 6NH
Activities: Buying and selling of own real estate
Major Shareholder: Mark Lindsay Buckland
Officers: Mark Lindsay Buckland, Secretary; Claire Louise Buckland [1966] Director/HR & Training Manager; Mark Lindsay Buckland [1962] Director/Self Employed

Star Meats Limited
Incorporated: 11 December 2012 *Employees:* 71
Net Worth: £573,371 *Total Assets:* £1,288,540
Registered Office: 3a Gresley Road, South West Industrial Estate, Peterlee, Co Durham, SR8 2LU
Activities: Wholesale of meat and meat products
Parent: GFC Group Limited
Officers: Nathan Hepurker [1984] Director

Stargate Developments (2015) Limited
Incorporated: 24 April 2015
Net Worth: £1,229,905 *Total Assets:* £1,249,806
Registered Office: Manor House, Cresswell, Morpeth, Northumberland, NE61 5LE
Activities: Other letting and operating of own or leased real estate
Officers: Louise Wright, Secretary; Michael Keith Wright [1952] Director

Stargate Precision Engineering Limited
Incorporated: 3 August 1995 *Employees:* 13
Net Worth: £634,995 *Total Assets:* £844,997
Registered Office: L5, 19 High Flatworth, Tyne Tunnel Trading Estate, North Shields, Tyne & Wear, NE29 7UT
Activities: Other business support service activities n.e.c.
Parent: Pryme Group Ltd
Officers: Kerrie Rae Doreen Murray, Secretary; Angus John Gray [1966] Director/Engineer; Murray McKay Kerr [1981] Director; Kerrie Rae Doreen Murray [1983] Director

Starkold Building Services Limited
Incorporated: 18 April 2000 *Employees:* 15
Net Worth: £566,186 *Total Assets:* £1,333,748
Registered Office: Old Engineering Works, Rennys Lane, Durham, DH1 2RS
Activities: Construction of other civil engineering projects n.e.c.
Major Shareholder: Darren James Grooms
Officers: Joanne Grooms, Secretary; Darren James Grooms [1969] Director

Starrs Contract Services Limited
Incorporated: 19 September 1986 *Employees:* 11
Net Worth: £2,388,656 *Total Assets:* £2,843,521
Registered Office: 1 Meadow Close, Ormesby, Middlesbrough, Cleveland, TS7 9AY
Activities: Other specialised construction activities n.e.c.
Major Shareholder: Ronanld Bedingfield
Officers: Ronald Bedingfield [1950] Director/Erector

Starstruck Limited
Incorporated: 8 November 2001
Net Worth: £396,224 *Total Assets:* £2,863,854
Registered Office: 55 Carr House Drive, Framwellgate Moor, Durham, DH1 5LT
Activities: Other letting and operating of own or leased real estate
Shareholder: Jayprakash Sarania
Officers: Jayprakash Sarania, Secretary; Jayprakash Sarania [1957] Director; Mukesh Viramgama [1964] Director

Statebourne (Cryogenic) Limited
Incorporated: 17 April 1969 *Employees:* 79
Net Worth: £2,515,732 *Total Assets:* £6,472,029
Registered Office: 18 Parsons Road, Washington, Tyne & Wear, NE37 1EZ
Activities: Manufacture of other fabricated metal products n.e.c.
Shareholders: David Haley; James Carr Haley
Officers: David Haley [1953] Director; James Carr Haley [1966] International Marketing Director; Brian Makepeace [1961] Production Director

Stateplus Limited
Incorporated: 23 September 2005 *Employees:* 1
Net Worth: £242,021 *Total Assets:* £1,733,944
Registered Office: Third Floor, Citygate, St James Boulevard, Newcastle upon Tyne, NE1 4JE
Activities: Other letting and operating of own or leased real estate
Shareholders: Tracey Laureles; Lyn Dayson
Officers: Lyn Dayson, Secretary; Lyn Dayson [1972] Director; Robert Nicholson [1945] Director

Statex Press (Northern) Limited
Incorporated: 14 January 1994 *Employees:* 80
Net Worth: £712,174 *Total Assets:* £2,588,156
Registered Office: 6 Airport Industrial Estate, Newcastle upon Tyne, NE3 2EF
Activities: Printing n.e.c.
Officers: Susan Maitland, Secretary/Finance & HR Director; James Edward Dark [1956] Director; Neil Richard MacRay [1977] Regional Sales Director; Susan Maitland [1957] Finance & HR Director; Steven Alan Miller [1957] Production Director; Graham Minett [1965] Director; Kerry Minett [1964] Executive Director; Christopher Noel Nellist [1971] Sales Director

Station Developments Limited
Incorporated: 4 March 1991 *Employees:* 3
Net Worth: £2,368,688 *Total Assets:* £3,124,965
Registered Office: Ravensworth House, 1 Ravensworth Street, Bedlington, Northumberland, NE22 7JP
Activities: Development of building projects
Parent: Millhouse Group Holdings Limited
Officers: Sandra Orr, Secretary; Viscount Terence Devonport [1944] Director/Landowner; Cllr Raymond Glindon [1946] Director; Morris Robert Muter [1954] Director

The Station Hotel (Newcastle) Limited
Incorporated: 13 November 1985 *Employees:* 1,531
Net Worth: £96,513,000 *Total Assets:* £254,664,000
Registered Office: 31-40 West Parade, Newcastle upon Tyne, NE4 7LB
Activities: Hotels and similar accommodation
Shareholders: Aran Handa; Arvan Handa; Roshan Lal Handa
Officers: Handa Aran, Secretary; Aran Handa [1955] Director/Hotel Proprietor; Arvan Handa [1952] Director/Hotel Manager; Roshan Lal Handa [1928] Director/Chairman [Indian]

Station Taxis (Sunderland) Limited
Incorporated: 13 November 1985
Net Worth: £1,007,341 *Total Assets:* £1,231,338
Registered Office: Taxi Kiosk, Central Station, Sunderland, Tyne & Wear, SR1 3HR
Activities: Taxi operation
Officers: George Dixon Daley [1963] Director; Trevor Evans Hines [1947] Director/Hackney Carriage Licenced Operator; Michael McCardle [1955] Director/Taxi Driver; Duncan Small [1963] Director; James Henry Usher [1960] Director/Taxi Driver; James Wilson [1965] Director

Steadfast Secure Storage Ltd
Incorporated: 10 January 2007 *Employees:* 20
Net Worth: £384,831 *Total Assets:* £1,142,028
Registered Office: 1 Hackworth Road, North West Industrial Estate, Peterlee, Co Durham, SR8 2JQ
Activities: Other service activities n.e.c.
Shareholder: Michael Robert Harbord
Officers: David Watson, Secretary; Michael Robert Harbord [1958] Director; David Watson [1961] Sales Director

Steadfast Security Solutions Limited
Incorporated: 2 August 2010
Net Worth: £286,258 *Total Assets:* £835,978
Registered Office: 1 Hackworth Road, North West Industrial Estate, Peterlee, Co Durham, SR8 2JQ
Activities: Private security activities
Major Shareholder: David Watson
Officers: David Watson, Secretary; David Watson [1961] Director

Steakhouse Holdings Limited
Incorporated: 22 October 2009
Total Assets: £2,800,000
Registered Office: 1a Dukesway Court, Team Valley Trading Estate, Gateshead, Tyne & Wear, NE11 0PJ
Activities: Activities of other holding companies n.e.c.
Parent: Falcombe Holdings Limited
Officers: Phillip Nigel Blain, Secretary; David James Horrocks [1959] Financial Director; Ian Imrie [1955] Director

Steel River Limited
Incorporated: 15 February 1996
Net Worth: £2,905,391 *Total Assets:* £3,004,838
Registered Office: Rowlands House, Portobello Road, Birtley, Chester-le-Street, Co Durham, DH3 2RY
Activities: Buying and selling of own real estate
Officers: David Patrick Brown [1955] Director

Stella Property Investments Limited
Incorporated: 18 December 2013 *Employees:* 4
Net Worth Deficit: £452,434 *Total Assets:* £3,435,163
Registered Office: Mariners Park, Shaftesbury Avenue, South Shields, Tyne & Wear, NE32 3UP
Activities: Buying and selling of own real estate
Major Shareholder: Geoffrey Thompson
Officers: Keith Finnigan [1963] Managing Director; Geoffrey Thompson [1962] Director

Stelling LLP
Incorporated: 14 September 2006
Net Worth: £1,043,109 *Total Assets:* £1,054,937
Registered Office: The Annexe, The Garden House, Stelling Hall, Newton, Stocksfield, Northumberland, NE43 7UR
Officers: Elizabeth Claire Wright [1968] Member; Alexandra Louise Farrington [1972] LLP Member; Pamela Wright [1942] LLP Member

Stelrad Limited
Incorporated: 31 May 1988 *Employees:* 301
Net Worth: £3,655,000 *Total Assets:* £42,612,000
Registered Office: 69-75 Side, Newcastle upon Tyne, NE1 3JE
Activities: Manufacture of central heating radiators and boilers
Parent: Stelrad Radiator Holdings Limited
Officers: Leigh Antony Wilcox, Secretary; Trevor Terence Harvey [1956] Director/Chief Executive Officer; George John Letham [1957] Director

Stelrad Management Limited
Incorporated: 8 August 2000 *Employees:* 12
Net Worth Deficit: £1,793,000 *Total Assets:* £1,031,000
Registered Office: 69-75 The Side, Newcastle upon Tyne, NE1 3JE
Activities: Activities of head offices
Parent: Stelrad Radiator Holdings Limited
Officers: Leigh Antony Wilcox, Secretary; Trevor Terence Harvey [1956] Director/Chief Executive Officer; George John Letham [1957] Director

Stelrad Radiator Group Limited
Incorporated: 5 September 2014 *Employees:* 1,312
Net Worth: £22,904,000 *Total Assets:* £140,640,992
Registered Office: 69-75 Side, Newcastle upon Tyne, NE1 3JE
Activities: Activities of head offices
Officers: Leigh Wilcox, Secretary; Nicholas Dawborn Tyrrell Armstrong [1986] Director/Investment Manager [Australian]; Robert Keith Ellis [1951] Director; Trevor Terence Harvey [1956] Director; Edmund Alfred Lazarus [1968] Director; George John Letham [1957] Director

Stelrad Radiator Holdings Limited
Incorporated: 28 April 2000
Net Worth: £17,375,000 *Total Assets:* £53,023,000
Registered Office: 69-75 Side, Newcastle upon Tyne, NE1 3JE
Activities: Activities of head offices
Parent: Stelrad Radiator Group Limited
Officers: Leigh Antony Wilcox, Secretary; Trevor Terence Harvey [1956] Director; George John Letham [1957] Director

Stenness Estates Limited
Incorporated: 10 January 1995
Registered Office: Springhill, Aydon Road, Corbridge, Northumberland, NE45 5DL
Activities: Other letting and operating of own or leased real estate
Major Shareholder: William Clouston
Officers: Kim Ann Clouston, Secretary; Kim Ann Clouston [1964] Director; William Stuart James Clouston [1965] Director/Chartered Town Planner

Stephenson Coates Limited
Incorporated: 6 July 2010 *Employees:* 15
Net Worth: £694,096 *Total Assets:* £1,067,370
Registered Office: West 2, Asama Court, Newcastle Business Park, Newcastle upon Tyne, NE4 7YD
Activities: Accounting and auditing activities
Officers: Paul William Docherty [1960] Director/Chartered Tax Advisor; John Howard Oswald [1952] Director/Chartered Accountant

Stephenson Gobin Limited
Incorporated: 13 July 1972 *Employees:* 49
Net Worth: £1,984,777 *Total Assets:* £2,512,654
Registered Office: 11 Glasshouse Street, St Peters, Newcastle upon Tyne, NE6 1BS
Activities: Other manufacturing n.e.c.
Parent: British Engines (UK) Limited
Officers: Joanne Alicea Wilkes, Secretary; Andrew Joseph Collinson [1974] Director/Chief Executive Officer; Richard Dodd [1974] Group Product & Engineering Director; Laura Joicey [1976] Director/Group Chief Financial Officer; Alexander Harold Lamb [1971] Group Chairman and Director; Jonathan Charles Lamb [1977] Group Manufacturing Director

Stephenson Hotel Limited
Incorporated: 14 August 2012 *Employees:* 187
Net Worth Deficit: £11,811,424 *Total Assets:* £42,788,024
Registered Office: Boiler Shop, 20 South Street, Newcastle upon Tyne, NE1 3PE
Activities: Development of building projects
Major Shareholder: William David Clouston
Officers: Martyn Bowes [1964] Director/Financial Consultant; Pamela Fry Clouston [1950] Director; Richard Donald Carr Clouston [1977] Director; William David Clouston [1946] Company Secretary/Director

Stephenson Quarter Developments Limited
Incorporated: 17 March 2004
Net Worth Deficit: £10,074,253 *Total Assets:* £4,412,963
Registered Office: Stockbridge House, Trinity Gardens, Newcastle upon Tyne, NE1 2HJ
Activities: Development of building projects
Major Shareholder: William David Clouston
Officers: Martyn Bowes [1964] Director/Financial Consultant; Martyn Bowes [1964] Director/Financial Consultant; William David Clouston [1946] Company Secretary/Director

Stephenson Rocket Limited
Incorporated: 10 August 2012
Net Worth: £363,603 *Total Assets:* £1,110,285
Registered Office: Boiler Shop, 20 South Street, Newcastle upon Tyne, NE1 3PE
Activities: Development of building projects
Major Shareholder: William David Clouston
Officers: Martyn Bowes [1964] Director; Richard Donald Carr Clouston [1977] Director; William David Clouston [1946] Company Secretary/Director

Sterling GP Limited
Incorporated: 25 June 2013 *Employees:* 40
Net Worth: £353,399 *Total Assets:* £2,210,580
Registered Office: Unit 7 Burdon Way, Stokesley Business Park, Stokesley, Cleveland, TS9 5PY
Activities: Manufacture of trailers and semi-trailers
Major Shareholder: Antony Adrian James
Officers: Antony Adrian James [1970] Director/General Manager

Sterling Pharma Solutions Limited
Incorporated: 16 February 2006 *Employees:* 366
Net Worth: £17,489,000 *Total Assets:* £49,927,000
Registered Office: Dudley, Cramlington, Northumberland, NE23 7QG
Activities: Manufacture of basic pharmaceutical products
Major Shareholder: Arun Kumar Pillai
Officers: Dr Rashmi Barbhaiya [1952] Director/Independent Advisor [American]; Kevin Peter Cook [1964] Director/President; Bharat Dhirajlal Shah [1947] Director [Indian]; Ian Dermot Shott [1957] Director/Business Executive; Deepak Calian Vaidya [1945] Director [Indian]; John Wiper [1962] Operations Director

Sterling Property Portfolio Limited
Incorporated: 31 December 1998
Net Worth: £1,098,402 *Total Assets:* £5,218,721
Registered Office: Clayton House, Walbottle Road, Newcastle upon Tyne, NE15 9RU
Activities: Other letting and operating of own or leased real estate
Major Shareholder: Mark Richard Greenwell
Officers: Mark Richard Greenwell [1968] Director/Property Developer

Sterling Trust Professional (North East) Limited
Incorporated: 18 May 2010 *Employees:* 12
Net Worth: £682,703 *Total Assets:* £1,314,440
Registered Office: 12 Parsons Court, Welbury Way, Aycliffe Industrial Park, Newton Aycliffe, Co Durham, DL5 6ZE
Activities: Life insurance
Major Shareholder: Jeffrey Grantham
Officers: Jeffrey Grantham [1963] Director

Stessa 3006 Ltd
Incorporated: 20 May 2014 *Employees:* 2
Net Worth: £769,970 *Total Assets:* £4,711,940
Registered Office: Newfield House, 9 Field House, Close, Hepscott, Northumberland, NE61 6LU
Activities: Other letting and operating of own or leased real estate
Shareholders: Anna Judith Thompson; Geoffrey Adam Thompson
Officers: Anna Judith Thompson, Secretary; Anna Judith Thompson [1984] Director; Geoffrey Adam Thompson [1987] Director

Stevenson of Oxbridge Limited
Incorporated: 10 October 1984 *Employees:* 35
Net Worth: £1,169,018 *Total Assets:* £3,172,278
Registered Office: 87-91 Oxbridge Lane, Stockton on Tees, Cleveland, TS18 4AR
Activities: Retail sale in non-specialised stores with food, beverages or tobacco predominating
Shareholders: Ian Andrew Stevenson; John Richard Stevenson
Officers: Ian Hurren, Secretary; John Francis Alexander Heagney [1952] Director; Ian Andrew Stevenson [1951] Managing Director; John Richard Stevenson [1978] Director/Manager

Stevenson Properties Limited
Incorporated: 10 October 2002
Net Worth: £1,185,903 *Total Assets:* £1,441,798
Registered Office: 87-91 Oxbridge Lane, Stockton on Tees, Cleveland, TS18 4AR
Activities: Other letting and operating of own or leased real estate
Major Shareholder: Ian Andrew Stevenson
Officers: Ian Hurren, Secretary; Ian Andrew Stevenson [1951] Managing Director; John Richard Stevenson [1978] Director

Stewart & Harris Limited
Incorporated: 6 January 2004
Net Worth: £655,027 *Total Assets:* £1,833,184
Registered Office: Waterloo House, Thornton Street, Newcastle upon Tyne, NE1 4AP
Activities: Engineering related scientific and technical consulting activities
Officers: Stuart Marshall, Secretary; Nicholas Mark Beckwith [1973] Director; Conor John Murphy [1965] Director/Structural Engineer [Irish]; Dr Grant Vincent Richardson [1967] Director; Peter Vincent Stienlet [1969] Director; Doug Roy Tidswell [1961] Director; Mark Turner [1965] Director

Stiller Warehousing & Distribution Limited
Incorporated: 27 March 1996 *Employees:* 139
Net Worth: £2,921,815 *Total Assets:* £5,835,950
Registered Office: Stiller Warehousing, Ridgeway, Aycliffe Business Park, Newton Aycliffe, Co Durham, DL5 6SP
Activities: Operation of warehousing and storage facilities for land transport activities
Major Shareholder: Paul William Stiller
Officers: Andrea Howes, Secretary; Brian Simpson [1968] Operations Director; Gillian Stiller [1959] Director/Accountant; Matthew Paul Stiller [1985] Managing Director; Paul William Stiller [1958] Managing Director

Stockdale & Reid Limited
Incorporated: 31 October 2001
Registered Office: 51-52 Howard Street, North Shields, Tyne & Wear, NE30 1AP
Activities: Solicitors
Shareholders: Peter William Amos; John Denoon Reid
Officers: Peter William Amos, Secretary/Solicitor; Peter William Amos [1953] Director/Solicitor; John Denoon Reid [1946] Director/Solicitor

Stockton Arts Centre
Incorporated: 15 November 2002 *Employees:* 58
Net Worth: £1,410,839 *Total Assets:* £1,680,926
Registered Office: Arc, Dovecot Street, Stockton on Tees, Cleveland, TS18 1LL
Activities: Operation of arts facilities
Officers: Simi Kumar, Secretary; Aaron Joseph David Bowman [1990] Director; Kate Concinnity Craddock [1979] Director/Senior Lecturer; Ishtiaq Din [1969] Director/Writer; Patrick James Masheder [1968] Managing Director; John McCann [1967] Director of Finance & Operations; Jane Elizabeth Robinson [1978] Director/Freelance Charity Fundraising Consultant; Lynne Snowball [1955] Director/Retired

Stockton Casting Company Limited (The)
Incorporated: 8 October 1947 *Employees:* 31
Net Worth: £1,847,053 *Total Assets:* £2,683,823
Registered Office: Unit 2 South Church Enterprise Park, Bishop Auckland, Co Durham, DL14 6XB
Activities: Casting of iron
Officers: John Clifford Laverick, Secretary; John Clifford Laverick [1942] Director; Alexander Jones Ramsay [1956] Technical Director; Robert John Yorke [1971] Director

Stockton Machine Company Limited
Incorporated: 14 October 2004
Net Worth: £112,862 *Total Assets:* £843,130
Registered Office: 4 Royce Avenue, Cowpen Industrial Estate, Billingham, Cleveland, TS23 4BX
Activities: Machining
Shareholder: Denise Smith
Officers: Mark Allan Smith [1970] Director/Engineer

Stokesley Golf Range Limited
Incorporated: 20 July 2011
Registered Office: Tresanton, Ayton Road, Stokesley, Middlesbrough, Cleveland, TS9 5JW
Activities: Operation of sports facilities
Officers: Andrew Marsay [1974] Director/Farmer; John George Marsay [1944] Director/Farmer; Kevin Marsay [1980] Director/Farmer; Susan Marie Marsay [1951] Director/Farmer

Stokesley Hardware Co. Limited
Incorporated: 19 May 1978 *Employees:* 2
Net Worth: £8,326,902 *Total Assets:* £13,089,360
Registered Office: Unit 6 Roseberry Court, Ellerbeck Way, Stokesley, Cleveland, TS9 5QT
Activities: Other letting and operating of own or leased real estate
Shareholders: Paula Mary Warburton; Martin Donnelly
Officers: Brenda Rosemary Dicken, Secretary; Mark Terence Dicken [1969] Director; Susan Elizabeth Dicken [1970] Director

Stokesley Tractors Ltd
Incorporated: 12 October 2012 *Employees:* 8
Net Worth: £277,753 *Total Assets:* £1,044,282
Registered Office: Hill House Farm, Redmarshall Road, Redmarshall, Stockton on Tees, Cleveland, TS21 1EW
Activities: Sale of other motor vehicles
Shareholders: Christiana Ann Farrow; Martina Farrow; Ambrose Farrow
Officers: Ambrose Farrow [1971] Director/Machinery Dealer; Christiana Ann Farrow [1969] Director

Stone Hill Park Limited
Incorporated: 17 September 2014
Net Worth: £2,423,215 *Total Assets:* £9,051,471
Registered Office: Baldwins, Wynyard Park House, Wynyard Avenue, Wynyard, Cleveland, TS22 5TB
Activities: Buying and selling of own real estate
Parent: Invicta Asset Management Limited
Officers: Pauline Anne Bradley [1961] Director; Trevor Cartner [1960] Director; Joseph Christopher Musgrave [1965] Director/Developer

E. J. Stone Limited
Incorporated: 4 January 2001
Net Worth: £1,325,233 *Total Assets:* £2,660,806
Registered Office: c/o Nicholson & Morgan Solicitors, 14 Bell Villas, Ponteland, Northumberland, NE20 9BE
Activities: Manufacture of other articles of concrete, plaster and cement
Shareholders: Michael Charles Clippingdale; Northumberland Property Investments Ltd
Officers: Andrew William Morgan, Secretary; Michael Charles Clippingdale [1957] Director

Stone Technical Services Group Limited
Incorporated: 24 January 2000
Net Worth: £371,296 *Total Assets:* £1,181,322
Registered Office: Stone Technical Services Group Limited, Kellaw Road, Darlington, Co Durham, DL1 4YA
Activities: Other specialised construction activities n.e.c.
Major Shareholder: David Stone
Officers: Grahame Stone, Secretary; David Stone [1962] Managing Director; Grahame Stone [1965] Director

Stonegrave Aggregates Limited
Incorporated: 27 November 1970 *Employees:* 62
Net Worth: £7,039,231 *Total Assets:* £12,302,900
Registered Office: Aycliffe Quarry, Aycliffe Village, Co Durham, DL5 6NB
Activities: Treatment and disposal of non-hazardous waste
Major Shareholder: John Wade
Officers: John Wade, Secretary; Paul William Monkhouse [1957] Director/Contracts Manager; John Wade [1943] Director; Bruce David Whitley [1959] Director/Operations Manager

Tim Stonock Limited
Incorporated: 4 July 2017
Net Worth: £100 *Total Assets:* £1,516,780
Registered Office: 5 West Terrace, Durham, DH1 4RN
Activities: Activities of head offices
Major Shareholder: Timothy Stonock
Officers: Timothy Stonock [1985] Director

Chris Stonock Limited
Incorporated: 15 May 2007 *Employees:* 65
Net Worth: £1,093,253 *Total Assets:* £1,521,108
Registered Office: 53 Front Street, Chester-le-Street, Co Durham, DH3 3BH
Activities: Real estate agencies
Parent: Tim Stonock Limited
Officers: Timothy Stonock [1985] Director

Storage and Handling Equipment Limited
Incorporated: 26 October 1999 *Employees:* 10
Net Worth: £4,550,662 *Total Assets:* £11,704,218
Registered Office: SHE House, Macklin Avenue, Cowpen Lane Industrial Estate, Billingham, Cleveland, TS23 4BY
Activities: Manufacture of lifting and handling equipment
Major Shareholder: John Robert Beamson
Officers: Dawn Stebbings, Secretary; John Robert Beamson [1944] Director

The Storage Company UK Limited
Incorporated: 25 March 1999
Registered Office: Metropolitan House, Longrigg, Swalwell, Newcastle upon Tyne, NE16 3AS
Activities: Other letting and operating of own or leased real estate
Major Shareholder: Lynn Gate
Officers: Hazel Stephenson, Secretary; Lynn Gate [1961] Director

Storage Equipment Safety Service Limited
Incorporated: 29 January 1997 *Employees:* 59
Net Worth: £1,351,797 *Total Assets:* £1,968,569
Registered Office: The National Warehouse Safety, South Nelson Road, South Nelson Industrial Estate, Cramlington, Northumberland, NE23 1EG
Activities: Other professional, scientific and technical activities n.e.c.
Shareholders: Philip Pinel; Linda Pinel
Officers: Deborah Wheatley, Secretary/Accounts Manager; Doreen Doris Atchinson [1964] Business Operations Director; Michelle Douglas [1975] Marketing Director; Michael Thomas Pace [1947] Technical Director; Linda Pinel [1950] Director; Philip Pinel [1949] Director; Marion Swan [1952] HR & Quality Director; Deborah Wheatley [1963] Financial Director

Storey & Edmondson (Builders) Limited
Incorporated: 27 July 2000
Net Worth: £1,036,322 *Total Assets:* £1,234,540
Registered Office: Dove Crag, Hillside West, Rothbury, Morpeth, Northumberland, NE65 7YN
Activities: Development of building projects
Shareholders: Keith Reginald Storey; Kirstine Angela Storey
Officers: Keith Reginald Storey, Secretary; Keith Reginald Storey [1960] Director/Builder; Kirstine Angela Storey [1968] Director/Classroom Assistant

Stott Holdings Limited
Incorporated: 22 July 1998
Net Worth: £711,518 *Total Assets:* £1,000,002
Registered Office: View Logistics, Park View Road East, Hartlepool, Cleveland, TS25 1HT
Activities: Activities of head offices
Parent: Whitestone Carpets Holdings Ltd
Officers: Stephen Maurice Martin Byrne [1960] Director; Geoffrey Brendon Wilding [1963] Director [New Zealander]

Peter Stott Properties Ltd
Incorporated: 3 July 2001 *Employees:* 1
Net Worth: £310,831 *Total Assets:* £1,906,521
Registered Office: Low Burn Hall Farm, Darlington Road, Durham, DH1 3ST
Activities: Construction of domestic buildings
Officers: Victoria Stott, Secretary; Victoria Louise Jenkins [1973] Director/Scientist; Peter Robert Stott [1968] Director/Property Developer

STP Construction Limited
Incorporated: 9 July 2002 *Employees:* 32
Net Worth: £664,597 *Total Assets:* £3,791,621
Registered Office: Woodside House, Woodside Walk, Whinfield Industrial Estate, Rowlands Gill, Tyne & Wear, NE39 1EH
Activities: Construction of other civil engineering projects n.e.c.
Officers: Ian Cowling, Secretary; Ian Cowling [1963] Director/Contracts Manager; John Smailes [1956] Director/Chartered Surveyor

Straight Line Holdings North East Limited
Incorporated: 3 July 2014
Net Worth: £2,468,933 *Total Assets:* £3,770,509
Registered Office: Unit 2 Ruby Park, Brunswick Industrial Estate, Brunswick Village, Newcastle upon Tyne, NE13 7BA
Activities: Activities of other holding companies n.e.c.
Major Shareholder: Richard Paul Gilbert
Officers: Richard Paul Gilbert [1979] Director; Simon Christopher Reay [1979] Director

Straightline (NE) Limited
Incorporated: 29 February 1980 *Employees:* 29
Net Worth: £286,733 *Total Assets:* £1,058,620
Registered Office: Unit 1-3 Ruby Park, Brunswick Industrial Estate, Brunswick Village, Newcastle upon Tyne, NE13 7BA
Activities: Other building completion and finishing
Major Shareholder: Richard Paul Gilbert
Officers: Kevin Peter Bucas [1980] Director; Richard Paul Gilbert [1979] Director; Keith Newbegin [1949] Director/Consultant; Simon Christopher Reay [1979] Director/Construction

The Charlotte Straker Project
Incorporated: 16 October 1992 *Employees:* 61
Net Worth: £1,135,888 *Total Assets:* £1,175,949
Registered Office: Charlotte Straker House, Cookson Close, Corbridge, Northumberland, NE45 5HB
Activities: Other residential care activities n.e.c.
Officers: Neil Elliott Braithwaite, Secretary; Gavin MacFarlane Black [1949] Director/Chartered Surveyor; Lady Anna Margaret Blackett [1959] Director; Neil Elliott Braithwaite [1954] Director/Solicitor; Dr William F Cunningham [1951] Director/General Practitioner; Richard Alan Dixon [1942] Director/Retired Chartered Electrical Engineer; Berenice Groves [1967] Director of Operations; Mary Elizabeth Angela Jones [1950] Director; Michael Francis Pottage [1951] Director/Project Manager; Margaret Ann Wagstaff [1943] Director/Retired; Peter Wood [1943] Director/Retired Banker; Lesley Woodcock [1964] Director

Stranton Academy Trust
Incorporated: 7 June 2013 *Employees:* 156
Net Worth: £9,599,322 *Total Assets:* £11,222,664
Registered Office: Stranton Academy, Southburn Terrace, Hartlepool, Cleveland, TS25 1SQ
Activities: Primary education
Officers: Gillian Danby [1956] Director/Senior Executive [British/Canadian]; Peter Grenville Gowland [1950] Director/Retired Project Development Officer; Peter Hart [1982] Director; Peter Ingham [1968] Director/Retired; Victoria Kelly [1979] Director/Development Lead - Teach First; Neil Nottingham [1978] Director/Headteacher; Dr Shirley-Anne Paul [1981] Director/Researcher; Sandra Elaine Saint [1970] Director/Education Advisor; Michael Andrew Sumpter [1961] Director

Strathearn Leisure Parks Limited
Incorporated: 1 July 1959
Net Worth: £1,538,169 *Total Assets:* £4,944,760
Registered Office: Seafield Park, Seahouses, Northumberland, NE68 7SP
Activities: Other reservation service activities n.e.c.
Officers: Allison Britton, Secretary; John Kenneth Britton [1947] Director; Andrew William Howard [1971] Director/Chartered Surveyor; Simon Ian Manners [1971] Director/Caravan Operator; John Douglas Stuart [1966] Director

Strathmore Bondgate Limited
Incorporated: 12 September 2006
Net Worth: £100 *Total Assets:* £1,594,090
Registered Office: East Farm, East Farm Mews, Medomsley, Co Durham, DH8 6TU
Activities: Development of building projects
Shareholder: Alistdair Barclay Brown
Officers: Alistdair Barclay Brown, Secretary; Alistdair Barclay Brown [1959] Director/Lawyer; Dr Stuart Robertson Brown [1967] Director/Physicist; James Alexander Johnston [1968] Director/Construction Engineer

Strathmore Holdings Limited
Incorporated: 17 June 2002
Net Worth: £829,138 *Total Assets:* £1,751,625
Registered Office: East Farm, East Farm Mews, Medomsley, Co Durham, DH8 6TU
Activities: Development of building projects
Officers: Alistdair Barclay Brown, Secretary; Alistdair Barclay Brown [1959] Director/Lawyer; Dr Stuart Robertson Brown [1967] Director/Physicist; James Alexander Johnston [1968] Director/Construction Engineer

Strathmore Renewables Ltd
Incorporated: 4 June 2013
Net Worth Deficit: £51,393 *Total Assets:* £1,296,693
Registered Office: Strathmore House, Cleatlam, Darlington, Co Durham, DL2 3QS
Activities: Production of electricity
Shareholders: John Arthur Botes; Marion Boyes; Michael James Boyes
Officers: John Arthur Boyes [1956] Director; Marion Boyes [1957] Director; Michael James Boyes [1993] Director

J. O. Straughan & Co. Limited
Incorporated: 15 December 1986 *Employees:* 13
Net Worth: £2,059,244 *Total Assets:* £3,875,907
Registered Office: Netherton Park Steads, Stannington, Morpeth, Northumberland, NE61 6EF
Activities: Growing of cereals (except rice), leguminous crops and oil seeds
Shareholders: Sandra Dickinson; Aileen Callaghan
Officers: Aileen Callaghan, Secretary/Finance & Admin Officer; Aileen Callaghan [1958] Director/Finance & Admin Officer; Roger Walton Dickinson [1955] Director/Agricultural Contractor; Sheena Straughan [1956] Director/Teaching Assistant

W. L. Straughan & Son Limited
Incorporated: 4 December 2002 *Employees:* 46
Net Worth: £932,608 *Total Assets:* £2,516,848
Registered Office: Lane Farm, Bedlington, Northumberland, NE22 6AA
Activities: Landscape service activities
Parent: WLS (2016) Limited
Officers: Denise Straughan, Secretary; Denise Straughan [1959] Director/Administrator; Philip Nigel Straughan [1954] Director/Environmental Contractor

Streonshalh Limited
Incorporated: 18 September 1998
Net Worth: £2,183,507 *Total Assets:* £2,187,201
Registered Office: 55 Cleveland Avenue, Darlington, Co Durham, DL3 7HF
Activities: Activities of other holding companies n.e.c.
Major Shareholder: Stephen Paul Ness
Officers: John Jeffrey Everrett Ness, Secretary; Stephen Paul Ness [1963] Director

Strickland Tucker LLP
Incorporated: 24 July 2003
Total Assets: £786,187
Registered Office: Clarendon House, Market Place, Middleham, N Yorks, DL8 4NP
Officers: Benjamin Michael John Strickland [1968] Member; Ian Lawrence Tucker [1964] Member

The John Strutt Conservation Foundation
Incorporated: 18 November 2010 *Employees:* 1
Net Worth: £4,822,391 *Total Assets:* £4,859,546
Registered Office: John G Hills FRICS, Estate Office, Leyburn, N Yorks, DL8 5EW
Activities: Non-trading company
Officers: Christine Mary Berry [1959] Director; Sarah Caroline Bradley [1943] Director/Retired; Robert William Dunning [1948] Director; James Simon Radford Elliott [1945] Director/Retired Chartered Surveyor; Edward Anthony Hewetson [1976] Director; Sir Martin Wyatt Holdgate [1931] Director/Retired Civil Servant; Christopher Metcalfe-Gibson [1942] Director; Doctor Stephen David Ward [1943] Director; Peter Welsh [1952] Director/Ecologist

Student Accommodation (UK) Limited
Incorporated: 8 June 2011
Net Worth: £45,782 *Total Assets:* £1,394,011
Registered Office: Patrick House, Gosforth Park Avenue, Gosforth Business Park, Newcastle upon Tyne, NE12 8EG
Activities: Other accommodation
Shareholder: Neill Aidan Winch
Officers: Neill Aidan Winch, Secretary; Stephen William Howe [1967] Director; Donna Winch [1976] Director; Neill Aidan Winch [1964] Director

Student Accommodation Services Limited
Incorporated: 11 June 2004
Net Worth: £609,633 *Total Assets:* £2,756,893
Registered Office: 21 North Bridge Street, Sunderland, Tyne & Wear, SR5 1AB
Activities: Renting and operating of Housing Association real estate
Major Shareholder: Richard Wooler
Officers: Victoria Anne Bianchi, Secretary; Victoria Anne Bianchi [1986] Director/Property Lettings Manager; Richard Wooler [1950] Director

Student Loans Company Limited
Incorporated: 5 July 1989 *Employees:* 181
Net Worth Deficit: £28,240,000 *Total Assets:* £144,728,992
Registered Office: Memphis Building, Lingfield Point, McMullen Road, Darlington, Co Durham, DL1 1RW
Activities: Other credit granting n.e.c.
Parent: Secretary of State for Education
Officers: Gary Stuart Womersley, Secretary; Christian Norman Brodie [1957] Director/Banker; Antonia Mary Cox [1963] Director/Councillor; Mary Elizabeth Curnock Cook [1958] Director; Simon Peter Devonshire [1967] Director; Natalie Cecilia Elphicke [1970] Director/Chief Executive; David Peter Anthony Gravells [1949] Director; Paula Elizabeth Sussex [1964] Director/Chief Executive; Professor Andrew Brian Wathey [1958] Director/Chief Executive

Sturton Grange Developments Limited
Incorporated: 7 February 2001
Net Worth: £899,598 *Total Assets:* £1,696,828
Registered Office: Fernwood House, Fernwood Road, Jesmond, Newcastle upon Tyne, NE2 1TJ
Activities: Development of building projects
Shareholders: Thomas Batey; Richard John Betteridge
Officers: Thomas Batey, Secretary; Thomas Batey [1949] Director; Richard John Betteridge [1963] Director

Sty.Com Limited
Incorporated: 23 October 2000 *Employees:* 48
Net Worth: £1,106,317 *Total Assets:* £3,039,501
Registered Office: Richmond Court, Morton Road, Darlington, Co Durham, DL1 4PT
Activities: Retail sale via mail order houses or via Internet
Shareholders: Sabena Al Badr; Haya Al Badr
Officers: Kevin Iceton, Secretary; Colin William Eglington [1951] Director/Manager; Margaret Eglington [1953] Purchasing and Operations Director; Kevin Iceton [1973] Director/Accountant; Simon Martin [1966] Director; Michael John Wood [1950] Director/Solicitor; Matthew Young [1978] Director

Subsea Energy Solutions Ltd
Incorporated: 10 October 2011 *Employees:* 13
Net Worth: £534,272 *Total Assets:* £942,667
Registered Office: Unit 4 Chartermark Way, Colburn Business Park, Catterick Road, Catterick Garrison, N Yorks, DL9 4QJ
Activities: Other manufacturing n.e.c.
Parent: Subsea Energy Solutions Holdings Ltd
Officers: Paul Kenneth Boddy [1969] Director/Manufacturer; Philip Ashley Ross Stanyon [1974] Sales Director

Subsea Innovation Limited
Incorporated: 5 October 1995 *Employees:* 32
Net Worth: £601,155 *Total Assets:* £7,312,912
Registered Office: Innovation House, Centurion Way, Darlington, Co Durham, DL3 0UP
Activities: Manufacture of other special-purpose machinery n.e.c.
Parent: Tekmar Group PLC
Officers: Susan Ann Hurst [1966] Finance Director; Alasdair MacDonald [1965] Director; James Thomas Ritchie-Bland [1990] Director; David Andrew Thompson [1970] Technical Director

Success Bidco 2 Limited
Incorporated: 7 April 2016 *Employees:* 1,324
Net Worth: £162,060,000 *Total Assets:* £358,792,992
Registered Office: Mayborn House, Balliol Business Park, Newcastle upon Tyne, NE12 8EW
Activities: Activities of other holding companies n.e.c.
Officers: Stephen William Parkin [1969] Director/Chief Executive Officer; James William Matthew Taylor [1974] Director

Sudfeld Limited
Incorporated: 12 July 2000
Net Worth: £1,067,103 *Total Assets:* £1,758,233
Registered Office: 34-36 South Parade, Whitley Bay, Tyne & Wear, NE26 2RQ
Activities: Non-trading company
Officers: Edward James Hastie, Secretary; Edward James Hastie [1945] Director; Martina Hastie [1940] Director; Nigel Anton Hastie [1973] Director/Developer; Trevor Edward Hastie [1971] Director

Suffolk Electrical Services Limited
Incorporated: 2 November 1977
Net Worth: £978,043 *Total Assets:* £1,811,803
Registered Office: 9-18 Ruby Court, Wesley Drive, Benton Square Industrial Estate, Newcastle upon Tyne, NE12 9UP
Activities: Electrical installation
Parent: SES Securus Limited
Officers: Anthony Denis Kane [1959] Director; John Stewart [1968] Director

Sugarfayre Ltd.
Incorporated: 23 October 1991 *Employees:* 108
Net Worth: £6,581,421 *Total Assets:* £7,469,580
Registered Office: Culpitt Ltd, Jubilee Industrial Estate, Ashington, Northumberland, NE63 8UQ
Activities: Manufacture of other food products n.e.c.
Parent: Culpitt Ltd
Officers: Donna George, Secretary; John Anderson [1959] Director [American]; Helen Jane Johnson [1965] Marketing Director; Simon Mark Keogh [1971] Finance Director; Gary Peter Quinn [1982] Supply Chain Director; Thomas Wylie [1967] Managing Director

Suiker Limited
Incorporated: 11 September 2014
Registered Office: 24 St Cuthberts Way, Darlington, Co Durham, DL1 1GB
Activities: Buying and selling of own real estate
Major Shareholder: Joshua Malcolm Hanson
Officers: Joshua Malcolm Hanson [1977] Director/Property Developer; Mathew James Hanson [1979] Director

David Summerfield Limited
Incorporated: 28 July 1947 *Employees:* 30
Net Worth: £7,022,051 *Total Assets:* £7,378,678
Registered Office: 70 Parklands, Ponteland, Northumberland, NE20 9LN
Activities: Retail sale of watches and jewellery in specialised stores
Shareholders: Raymond Smith; Linda Smith
Officers: Raymond Smith [1951] Director/Jeweller

Summerhouse Development Limited
Incorporated: 6 September 2011 *Employees:* 2
Net Worth: £24,729 *Total Assets:* £2,703,586
Registered Office: 81 Bondgate, Darlington, Co Durham, DL3 7JT
Activities: Development of building projects
Major Shareholder: Andrew John Schoorlemmer
Officers: John Gladney Harrison, Secretary; Carole Budge [1958] Director; John Gladney Harrison [1965] Director/Chartered Building Surveyor

Summers-Inman Construction and Property Consultants LLP
Incorporated: 17 October 2002 *Employees:* 88
Net Worth Deficit: £203,585 *Total Assets:* £3,470,259
Registered Office: Bevan House, Sir Bobby Robson Way, Newcastle upon Tyne, NE13 9BA
Officers: David Paul Blakey [1968] Member; Aynsley Robinson Frizzell Cheatley [1974] Member; David Carel Cronje [1974] Member; Mark Andrew Dutton [1968] Member; Ian Ross Griffiths [1966] Member; Lee Anthony Orchard [1982] Member; Steve Turner [1962] Member

Sun Valley Holdings
Incorporated: 10 June 1974
Net Worth: £3,152,000 *Total Assets:* £3,739,000
Registered Office: 1a Duksway Court, Team Valley Trading Estate, Gateshead, Tyne & Wear, NE11 0PJ
Activities: Other letting and operating of own or leased real estate
Parent: Falcombe
Officers: Phillip Nigel Blain, Secretary; David James Horrocks [1959] Director/Chartered Accountant; Ian Imrie [1955] Managing Director

Sunderland Accommodation Services Limited
Incorporated: 11 June 2004
Net Worth: £631,970 *Total Assets:* £1,847,574
Registered Office: 21 North Bridge Street, Sunderland, Tyne & Wear, SR5 1AB
Activities: Renting and operating of Housing Association real estate
Major Shareholder: Richard Wooler
Officers: Victoria Anne Branchi, Secretary; Victoria Anne Bianchi [1986] Director/Property Lettings Manager; Richard Wooler [1950] Director

Sunderland Association Football Club,Limited (The)
Incorporated: 12 August 1896 *Employees:* 589
Net Worth Deficit: £116,743,000 *Total Assets:* £144,671,008
Registered Office: The Sunderland Stadium of Light, Sunderland, Tyne & Wear, SR5 1SU
Activities: Operation of sports facilities
Parent: Sunderland Limited
Officers: Angela Lowes, Secretary; Anthony Joseph Davison [1974] Managing Director; Stewart James Donald [1974] Director; Neil James Fox [1969] Director; Angela Lowes [1973] Director/Financial Accountant; Charles Harry Finlayson Methven [1976] Director

Sunderland Care and Support (Holding Company) Limited
Incorporated: 9 September 2013 *Employees:* 5
Net Worth: £37,143 *Total Assets:* £2,909,471
Registered Office: Civic Centre, Burdon Road, Sunderland, Tyne & Wear, SR2 7DN
Activities: Other social work activities without accommodation n.e.c.
Parent: Sunderland City Council
Officers: Patrick Melia, Secretary; Councillor Jill Elaine Fletcher [1960] Director/Councillor; Philip Foster [1963] Director/Chief Operating Officer; Councillor Anne Lawson [1954] Director/Councillor; Darren Anthony Lough [1969] Director/Chief Finance Officer; Councillor Amy Wilson [1961] Director/Councillor

Sunderland Care and Support Limited
Incorporated: 9 September 2013 *Employees:* 967
Net Worth Deficit: £15,134,661 *Total Assets:* £7,641,272
Registered Office: Civic Centre, Burdon Road, Sunderland, Tyne & Wear, SR2 7DN
Activities: Other social work activities without accommodation n.e.c.
Parent: Sunderland Care and Support (Holding Company) Limited
Officers: Patrick Melia, Secretary; Councillor Jill Elaine Fletcher [1960] Director/Councillor; Philip Foster [1963] Director/Chief Operating Officer; Councillor Anne Lawson [1954] Director/Councillor; Darren Anthony Lough [1969] Director/Chief Finance Officer; Councillor Amy Wilson [1961] Director/Councillor

Sunderland Counselling Service
Incorporated: 7 February 1997 *Employees:* 87
Net Worth: £1,007,430 *Total Assets:* £1,072,817
Registered Office: 51 John Street, Sunderland, Tyne & Wear, SR1 1QN
Activities: Other human health activities
Officers: Bernard Greener, Secretary/Support Worker; Laura Helen Bruton [1981] Director/NHS Manager; Bernard Greener [1950] Director/Support Worker; Anne Loadman [1959] Director/Specialist Teacher in Mental Health; Linda Morris [1961] Director/Accountancy Assistant; Carl Sketchley [1968] Director/Manager; Eileen Mary Watt [1953] Director/Occupational Health Nurse Advisor

Sunderland Engineering Training Association Limited
Incorporated: 12 June 1978 *Employees:* 17
Net Worth: £923,513 *Total Assets:* £1,000,227
Registered Office: 17 Sedling Road, Wear Industrial Estate, Washington, Tyne & Wear, NE38 9BZ
Activities: Post-secondary non-tertiary education
Officers: Robin Jeremy Lockwood, Secretary; David Bartell [1978] Director; Ian Scurfield [1967] Director/Operations; Gill Usher [1972] Director/HR Manager

Sunderland FC Hotels Limited
Incorporated: 22 November 2013 *Employees:* 70
Net Worth Deficit: £1,788,000 *Total Assets:* £12,788,000
Registered Office: Hilton Garden Inn Sunderland, Vaux Brewery Way, Sunderland, Tyne & Wear, SR5 1SU
Activities: Hotels and similar accommodation
Parent: Sunderland FC Development LLP
Officers: Janet Lee Feggett, Secretary; Per-Magnus Andersson [1965] Director [Swedish]; Janet Lee Feggett [1962] Director/Certified Public Accountant [American]

Sunderland Home Care Associates (20-20) Limited
Incorporated: 15 May 1998 *Employees:* 417
Net Worth: £3,041,385 *Total Assets:* £3,395,038
Registered Office: Elliott House, Mainsforth Terrace West, Sunderland, Tyne & Wear, SR2 8JX
Activities: Other social work activities without accommodation n.e.c.
Parent: Sunderland Home Care Associates Trustees 20 20 Employee Benefit Trust
Officers: Rachael Louise Blyth, Secretary; Joan Margaret Hutchinson [1960] Director/Manager; Shaun Andrew Jackson [1966] Director/Co-ordinator

Sunderland Hotels Limited
Incorporated: 5 March 2009 *Employees:* 75
Net Worth: £4,551,311 *Total Assets:* £8,310,255
Registered Office: 24 Woolsington Park South, Woolsington, Newcastle upon Tyne, NE13 8BJ
Activities: Hotels and similar accommodation
Officers: Saroj Rani Chawla, Secretary; Mukesh Raj Chawla [1954] Director; Neel Chawla [1986] Director; Saroj Rani Chawla [1955] Director; Tina Chawla [1986] Director

Sunderland Lifestyle Partnership Limited
Incorporated: 28 May 2015
Net Worth: £965,928 *Total Assets:* £3,822,857
Registered Office: Sunderland Aquatic and Wellness Centre, Stadium Park, Sunderland, Tyne & Wear, SR5 1SU
Activities: Operation of sports facilities
Officers: David John Bibby [1961] Director/Accountant; Fiona Carole Brown [1966] Director; Paul Dowling [1974] Director; John Kelly [1962] Director; Martin Miles [1970] Director

Sunderland Limited
Incorporated: 23 April 1996 *Employees:* 1,009
Net Worth Deficit: £33,878,000 *Total Assets:* £234,874,000
Registered Office: The Sunderland Stadium of Light, Sunderland, Tyne & Wear, SR5 1SU
Activities: Operation of sports facilities
Parent: Madrox Partners Limited
Officers: Angela Lowes, Secretary; Anthony Joseph Davison [1974] Managing Director; Stewart James Donald [1974] Director; Neil James Fox [1969] Director; Angela Lowes [1973] Director/Financial Accountant; Charles Harry Finlayson Methven [1976] Director; Juan Sartori [1981] Director/Businessman [Uruguayan]

Sunderland Marina Ltd
Incorporated: 29 October 1996 *Employees:* 13
Net Worth: £2,130,795 *Total Assets:* £2,894,154
Registered Office: Marine Activities Centre, North Dock, Roker, Sunderland, Tyne & Wear, SR6 0PN
Activities: Operation of sports facilities
Parent: Marine Activities Centre, Sunderland
Officers: Tom Wills, Secretary; Michael Hendy [1966] Director/Accountant; Patrick Thomas Murray [1963] Managing Director

Sunderland Marine Insurance Company Limited
Incorporated: 17 February 1882 *Employees:* 55
Net Worth: £59,454,544 *Total Assets:* £191,877,520
Registered Office: The Quayside, Newcastle upon Tyne, NE1 3DU
Activities: Non-life insurance
Officers: Alan Stuart Rowland, Secretary; Jacobus Martinus de Groot [1960] Director/Lawyer [Dutch]; Trevor Frank Hart [1944] Director/Retired; Paul Andrew Jennings [1962] Director; Peter Medwell Johnson [1948] Director/Chartered Accountant; Frederick Joseph Mattera [1951] Director/Commercial Fisherman [American]; Pratap Baburao Shirke [1948] Director; Sir Peter Ivan Talijancich [1945] Joint Managing Director [New Zealander]; Alan Andrew Wilson [1955] Director

Sundram International Limited
Incorporated: 26 January 2016
Net Worth: £26,119,250 *Total Assets:* £32,280,974
Registered Office: Central Square South, Orchard Street, Newcastle upon Tyne, NE1 3XX
Activities: Activities of production holding companies
Officers: Narayansamy Balakrishnan [1951] Director/President - Fasteners and Hot Forgings [Indian]; David Bartle [1966] Director/General Manager; Ramachandran Dilipkumar [1966] Director [Indian]; Stephen Rose [1957] Director

Sunley Farms (Richmond) Limited
Incorporated: 12 July 1966
Net Worth: £1,339,587 *Total Assets:* £1,890,576
Registered Office: Lownethwaite Farm, Reeth Road, Richmond, N Yorks, DL10 4SE
Activities: Other letting and operating of own or leased real estate
Shareholders: Michael Charles John Sunley; Catherine Jean Sunley
Officers: Catherine Jean Sunley, Secretary/Chartered Accountant; Catherine Jean Sunley [1964] Director/Company Secretary; Michael Charles John Sunley [1960] Director

Sunnyside Academy
Incorporated: 5 December 2013 *Employees:* 112
Net Worth: £3,884,334 *Total Assets:* £5,147,996
Registered Office: Sunnyside Academy, Manor Farm Way, Coulby Newham, Middlesbrough, Cleveland, TS8 0RJ
Activities: Pre-primary education
Officers: Daniel Burns [1992] Director/Teaching Assistant; Nicola Susan Fox [1973] Director/Housewife; Colin Spence Geddes [1969] Director/Civil Servant; Clare Anne Hall [1969] Director/Deputy Headteacher; Margaret Madden [1951] Director/Retired; Rebecca Rathmell [1983] Director/Assistant Headteacher; Helen Louise Robinson [1979] Director/Office Manager; Julie Patricia Sutton [1969] Director/Headteacher; Deborah Susan Whitehead [1965] Director/Store Manager

Sunter Limited
Incorporated: 23 April 1998 *Employees:* 67
Net Worth: £1,605,997 *Total Assets:* £2,577,708
Registered Office: Unit 14 Hetton Lyons Industrial Estate, Hetton-le-Hole, Co Durham, DH5 0RH
Activities: Other construction installation
Shareholder: Terence Sunter
Officers: Kevin Stubbs [1968] Director; Lee Terence Sunter [1975] Director; Maureen Sunter [1945] Director; Terence Sunter [1947] Director

Superkrush Films Limited
Incorporated: 4 May 2006 *Employees:* 9
Net Worth: £565,894 *Total Assets:* £978,809
Registered Office: 5 Mulgrave Terrace, Gateshead, Tyne & Wear, NE8 1PQ
Activities: Motion picture production activities
Shareholders: Christopher Jon Taylor; Nicholas Todd
Officers: Caroline Metcalfe [1959] Director; Christopher Jon Taylor [1976] Director/Film Producer; Nicholas Todd [1983] Director/Video Producer

Superlec Electrical Distributors Limited
Incorporated: 14 October 1981 *Employees:* 17
Net Worth: £4,759,564 *Total Assets:* £5,245,432
Registered Office: Riverside Park Road, Middlesbrough, Cleveland, TS2 1QW
Activities: Wholesale of hardware, plumbing and heating equipment and supplies
Shareholders: Alastair Powell; Michael Powell
Officers: Janice Robson, Secretary; Alastair Powell [1952] Director; Michael Powell [1957] Director

Supportive SRC Ltd
Incorporated: 3 April 2000 *Employees:* 117
Net Worth: £573,774 *Total Assets:* £843,136
Registered Office: Chapter House, Unit 7a Dean & Chapter Industrial Estate, Ferryhill, Co Durham, DL17 8LH
Activities: Other social work activities without accommodation n.e.c.
Officers: John Davison, Secretary; Ian Brown [1963] Director/Business Consultant; Kathleen Conroy [1943] Director/Retired; John Davison [1960] Director; Robert George Evans [1947] Director/Solicitor; Joanne Tracy Hall [1980] Director/Sales, Lettings and Consultancy; Wayne Martin Hall [1973] Director/Property Manager; Jill Lax [1962] Director/Compliance Lead; Councillor Brian Meek [1938] Director/Retired Miner; Andrew Munro [1965] Director/Software Engineer; David Ian Rayner [1959] Director/Loss Assessor - Property Damage; Alison Schreiber [1970] Director/Human Resources Consultancy; Michael Frank Smith [1947] Director/Retired; Linda Tyman [1955] Director/Retired

Supreme Health Care Limited
Incorporated: 16 September 1992 *Employees:* 21
Net Worth: £803,663 *Total Assets:* £1,050,090
Registered Office: Holmside Residential Home, Station Road, Bedlington, Northumberland, NE22 5PP
Activities: Residential care activities for the elderly and disabled
Shareholders: Mukesh Raj Chawla; Neel Chawla
Officers: Mukesh Raj Chawla, Secretary; Mukesh Raj Chawla [1954] Director/Consultant; Neel Chawla [1986] Director

Supreme Knitwear Manufacturing Company Limited
Incorporated: 27 November 1975 *Employees:* 13
Net Worth: £305,953 *Total Assets:* £3,554,601
Registered Office: Durham Tees Valley Business Centre, Primrose Hill Business Park, Orde Wingate Way, Durham Road, Stockton on Tees, Cleveland, TS19 0GA
Activities: Development of building projects
Shareholder: Khawer Din
Officers: Khawer Din, Secretary; Babar Din [1957] Director; Khawer Din [1958] Director; Nasser Din [1960] Director; Zarina Din [1932] Director

Supreme Property Developments Limited
Incorporated: 8 August 1990 *Employees:* 2
Net Worth: £666,313 *Total Assets:* £2,270,127
Registered Office: Durham Tees Valley Business Centre, Primrose Hill Business Park, Orde Wingate Way, Durham Road, Stockton on Tees, Cleveland, TS19 0GA
Activities: Buying and selling of own real estate
Shareholder: Khawer Din
Officers: Khawer Din, Secretary; Babar Din [1957] Director; Khawer Din [1958] Director; Nasser Din [1960] Director

Sure Wind Marine Limited
Incorporated: 28 April 2009
Net Worth Deficit: £1,572,061 *Total Assets:* £1,674,181
Registered Office: Suites 24 & 25, Dobson House, Regent Centre, Gosforth, Newcastle upon Tyne, NE3 3PF
Activities: Sea and coastal passenger water transport
Parent: Sure Wind Holdings Ltd
Officers: Michael Christopher Comninos [1986] Director

Surgo Construction Limited
Incorporated: 12 December 1928 *Employees:* 78
Net Worth: £3,388,981 *Total Assets:* £14,326,285
Registered Office: Albany Court, Monarch Road, Newcastle upon Tyne, NE4 7YB
Activities: Construction of commercial buildings
Parent: Hawkpost Limited
Officers: Steven Christopher Coombes, Secretary; Jeffrey Robson Alexander [1960] Marketing Director; Martin Lawrence Blight [1970] Estimating Director; David Blyth [1973] Commercial Director; Jeffrey Charlton [1956] Director/Contract Manager; Ian Walker [1949] Surveying Director; James Grant Walker [1978] Director/Surveyor

Surtec (North East) Limited
Incorporated: 25 July 2002 *Employees:* 12
Net Worth: £249,968 *Total Assets:* £1,019,929
Registered Office: The Former Tarmac Site, Littleburn Road, Langley Moor, Co Durham, DH7 8HJ
Activities: Other engineering activities
Major Shareholder: Barry Grimes
Officers: Barry Grimes [1953] Director/Engineer

Sutton Services International Limited
Incorporated: 19 July 1991 *Employees:* 43
Net Worth: £367,114 *Total Assets:* £818,557
Registered Office: Unit 8 Mercury Orion Way, Orion Business Park, North Shields, Tyne & Wear, NE29 7SN
Activities: Other specialised construction activities n.e.c.
Parent: RKM Capital Limited
Officers: Christopher Stewart Johnston [1982] Director; Peter Kilgour [1952] Director/HVAC Engineer; Andrew John Lawlor [1979] Director; Colin McCluskey [1955] Director/Engineer; William Joseph McCluskey [1954] Director/HVAC Engineer; Paul Martin Rowledge [1951] Director/HVAC Engineer; Matthew Smith [1982] Director

Svitzer Eastlands Limited
Incorporated: 25 February 1987 *Employees:* 213
Net Worth: £58,518,000 *Total Assets:* £76,875,000
Registered Office: Tees Wharf, Dockside Road, Middlesbrough, Cleveland, TS3 6AB
Activities: Non-trading company
Parent: Svitzer Holding UK Limited
Officers: David Anthony Noakes, Secretary; Anthony Howard Brown [1955] Director/Accountant; Kasper Friis Nilaus [1975] Director [Danish]; David Anthony Noakes [1965] Director/Company Secretary

Svitzer Holding UK Limited
Incorporated: 21 December 1999
Net Worth: £34,771,000 *Total Assets:* £98,749,000
Registered Office: Tees Wharf, Dockside Road, Middlesbrough, Cleveland, TS3 6AB
Activities: Activities of other holding companies n.e.c.
Parent: A P Moller Maersk A/S
Officers: David Anthony Noakes, Secretary; Kasper Friis Nilaus [1975] Director [Danish]; Matthijs Schot [1975] Finance Director [Dutch]; Knud Lind Winkler [1971] Director/Chief Financial Officer [Danish]

Svitzer Marine Limited
Incorporated: 1 March 1901 *Employees:* 434
Net Worth: £90,238,000 *Total Assets:* £137,007,008
Registered Office: Tees Wharf, Dockside Road, Middlesbrough, Cleveland, TS3 6AB
Activities: Sea and coastal freight water transport
Parent: Svitzer Holding UK Limited
Officers: David Anthony Noakes, Secretary; Anthony Howard Brown [1955] Director/Accountant; Kasper Friis Nilaus [1975] Director [Danish]; Matthijs Schot [1975] Finance Director [Dutch]

SVP Health Care Limited
Incorporated: 28 March 1988 *Employees:* 31
Net Worth: £584,062 *Total Assets:* £2,354,368
Registered Office: The Haining, Melbury Road, Jesmond Park East, Newcastle upon Tyne, NE7 7DE
Activities: Residential care activities for the elderly and disabled
Shareholders: Dr Sandeep Dewan; Dr Vini Dewan
Officers: Dr Vini Dewan, Secretary; Pooja Dewan [1987] Director/Care Worker; Dr Sandeep Dewan [1948] Director/Doctor; Sonia Dewan [1989] Director/Adviser; Dr Vini Dewan [1955] Director/Doctor

SW Mawdesley Limited
Incorporated: 3 July 2015
Net Worth: £48,544 *Total Assets:* £2,734,315
Registered Office: 25 Roseberry Road, Billingham, Cleveland, TS23 2SD
Activities: Development of building projects
Major Shareholder: Steven Wastell
Officers: Barnaby James Wastell [1988] Director/Property Developer; Steven Wastell [1957] Director/Builder

Harry Swaddle Limited
Incorporated: 29 June 1971 *Employees:* 4
Net Worth: £1,765,221 *Total Assets:* £2,016,363
Registered Office: 32 Portland Terrace, Newcastle upon Tyne, NE2 1QP
Activities: Other letting and operating of own or leased real estate
Shareholders: Angela Louise Evans; Anthony Nicholas Swaddle; Jennifer Susan Swaddle; Timothy Patrick Swaddle
Officers: Jennifer Susan Swaddle, Secretary; Angela Louise Evans [1951] Director/Secretary; Anthony Nicholas Swaddle [1955] Director/Manager; Jennifer Susan Swaddle [1949] Director/Manageress; Timothy Patrick Swaddle [1953] Director/Manager

S.T. Swaddle Ltd
Incorporated: 5 April 1971 *Employees:* 3
Net Worth: £1,665,898 *Total Assets:* £1,729,954
Registered Office: 32 Portland Terrace, Newcastle upon Tyne, NE2 1QP
Activities: Other letting and operating of own or leased real estate
Officers: Patricia Dorothy Swaddle, Secretary; Helen Elizabeth Swaddle [1953] Director; Patricia Susan Swaddle [1949] Director; Patricia Dorothy Swaddle [1923] Director/Secretary

Swale Scaffolding Limited
Incorporated: 20 June 1986
Registered Office: Gatherley Road Industrial Estate, Brompton on Swale, Richmond, N Yorks, DL10 7JQ
Activities: Other specialised construction activities n.e.c.
Major Shareholder: Gillian Pepe
Officers: Gillian Margaret Pepe [1960] Director; Sarah Louise Richardson [1969] Director/Finance; Paul Stephen Ward [1974] Director/Quantity Surveyor

Swale Valley Construction Limited
Incorporated: 19 February 2010
Net Worth: £20,518 *Total Assets:* £870,899
Registered Office: 26 Crofts Avenue, Richmond, N Yorks, DL10 4AZ
Activities: Construction of domestic buildings
Major Shareholder: Simon Robert Smith
Officers: Simon Robert Smith, Secretary; Abigail Louise Pardoe Smith [1990] Director; Charles Robert Pardoe Smith [1987] Director; Simon Robert Smith [1957] Director

Swale View Caravan Sales Limited
Incorporated: 23 April 2004 *Employees:* 2
Net Worth: £358,834 *Total Assets:* £1,009,328
Registered Office: Buena Vista, Swale View Caravan Park, Richmond, N Yorks, DL10 4SF
Activities: Other holiday and other collective accommodation
Shareholders: Andrew Philip Carter; Eileen Lamont Carter
Officers: Eileen Lamont Carter, Secretary/Caravan Site Operator; Andrew Philip Carter [1954] Director/Caravan Site Operator; Eileen Lamont Carter [1959] Director/Caravan Site Operator

Swaledale Homes Limited
Incorporated: 24 November 2014 *Employees:* 4
Net Worth Deficit: £102,929 *Total Assets:* £1,566,199
Registered Office: Brewery House, Richmond Road, Brompton on Swale, Richmond, N Yorks, DL10 7HE
Activities: Other accommodation
Officers: Deborah Ann Chaplin [1967] Director

Thomas Swan & Co.Limited
Incorporated: 31 December 1925 *Employees:* 167
Net Worth: £18,314,100 *Total Assets:* £27,576,710
Registered Office: Administration Offices, Rotary Way, Consett, Co Durham, DH8 7ND
Activities: Manufacture of other inorganic basic chemicals
Parent: Thomas Swan Holdings Ltd
Officers: Ian George Bonas [1942] Director; David Paul Gresham [1948] Director; Ernest Arthur Richardson [1950] Director/Accountant Venture Capitalist; Harry MacKlyn Swan [1976] Managing Director; Thomas MacKlyn Swan [1942] Director

Joseph Swan Academy
Incorporated: 15 February 2012 *Employees:* 118
Net Worth: £12,575,219 *Total Assets:* £14,902,200
Registered Office: Joseph Swan Academy, Saltwell Road South, Gateshead, Tyne & Wear, NE9 6LE
Activities: General secondary education
Officers: Claire Johnson, Secretary; Andrea Atkinson [1970] Director; Christopher Bland [1982] Director/Teacher; Peter De-Vere [1956] Director; Helen Michaela Harold [1966] Director/Process Improvement Manager; Alison Kinsey [1970] Director; Julie Morrow [1968] Director/Occupational Therapist; William Joseph Roberts [1978] Director/Education Recruitment Manager; Jacqueline Robson [1976] Director/Teacher; Jayne Marie Robson [1960] Director/Senior Administrator; Heather Elizabeth Scott [1970] Director/Headteacher; Victoria Jane Whalen [1976] Director/Teacher

Thomas Swan Holdings Limited
Incorporated: 15 September 2015 *Employees:* 167
Net Worth: £5,299,000 *Total Assets:* £27,399,000
Registered Office: Administration Offices, Rotary Way, Consett, Co Durham, DH8 7ND
Activities: Activities of production holding companies
Officers: Ian George Bonas [1942] Director; David Paul Gresham [1948] Director/Retired; Ernest Arthur Richardson [1950] Director/Accountant; Harry MacKlyn Swan [1976] Director/Manager

Swan Hunter (NE) Limited
Incorporated: 30 November 2006 *Employees:* 2
Net Worth Deficit: £965,064 *Total Assets:* £3,094,107
Registered Office: Station Road, Wallsend, Tyne & Wear, NE28 6EQ
Activities: Other engineering activities
Parent: Swan Hunter (Lars) Limited
Officers: Gerard Nico Kroese [1970] Director/Engineer [Dutch]

Swan Kee Limited
Incorporated: 4 May 2012
Net Worth: £928,206 *Total Assets:* £2,111,776
Registered Office: 24 St Cuthberts Way, Darlington, Co Durham, DL1 1GB
Activities: Activities of other holding companies n.e.c.
Major Shareholder: Stephen Kee
Officers: Stephen Kee [1957] Director

Swandene Furniture Limited
Incorporated: 21 May 1970
Net Worth: £333,193 *Total Assets:* £1,031,925
Registered Office: 22 Sedling Road, Wear Industrial Estate, Washington, Tyne & Wear, NE38 9BZ
Activities: Manufacture of other furniture
Shareholders: Paul Gerard Buckley; Timothy James Buckley
Officers: Timothy James Buckley, Secretary; Gerard David Buckley [1976] Director; Paul Gerard Buckley [1952] Director/Financial Manager; Timothy James Buckley [1979] Director; Alan Morritt [1959] Director; Alan Pattison [1956] Director/Joiner

Swarco Traffic Limited
Incorporated: 25 May 1989 *Employees:* 64
Net Worth: £1,842,526 *Total Assets:* £5,921,731
Registered Office: 7 Mercury Road, Gallowfields Trading Estate, Richmond, N Yorks, DL10 4TQ
Activities: Other manufacturing n.e.c.
Parent: Swarco Traffic Systems GmbH
Officers: Berony Anne Abraham, Secretary; Berony Anne Abraham [1955] Operations Director; Jeremy Peter Cowling [1967] Director; Carl James Dyer [1968] Director/Head of Systems Integration

Swarland Brick Company Limited (The)
Incorporated: 6 February 1937 *Employees:* 7
Net Worth: £2,187,610 *Total Assets:* £2,233,480
Registered Office: Thrunton, Whittingham, Alnwick, Northumberland, NE66 4SD
Activities: Freshwater fishing
Officers: Jillian Blythe, Secretary; Jillian Blythe [1963] Finance Director; Joseph Christopher Blythe [1955] Director/Brick Manufacturer

Sweetdreams Limited
Incorporated: 28 April 1998 *Employees:* 10
Net Worth: £274,407 *Total Assets:* £785,111
Registered Office: 32 Brenkley Way, Blezard Business Park, Seaton Burn, Newcastle upon Tyne, NE13 6DS
Activities: Manufacture of cocoa and chocolate confectionery
Major Shareholder: Matthew John Stephenson
Officers: Catherine Anne Stephenson, Secretary/Marketing Manager; Catherine Anne Stephenson [1972] Director; Matthew John Stephenson [1973] Director/Salesperson

Swift Brake & Clutch Limited
Incorporated: 14 July 1999
Net Worth: £785,949 *Total Assets:* £1,031,578
Registered Office: Railway Street, Newcastle upon Tyne, NE4 7AD
Activities: Retail trade of motor vehicle parts and accessories
Shareholder: Edward Paisley
Officers: Richard Edward Paisley, Secretary; Edward Paisley [1953] Director/Businessman; Richard Edward Paisley [1977] Director/Businessman

Swiftpage International Limited
Incorporated: 11 February 2013 *Employees:* 57
Net Worth Deficit: £3,698,716 *Total Assets:* £2,175,611
Registered Office: Ground Floor, Q15 Quorum Business Park, Benton Lane, Newcastle upon Tyne, NE12 8BU
Activities: Other information technology service activities
Officers: Henry John Oechsle III [1962] Director [American]

W.Swinbank & Sons Limited
Incorporated: 21 March 1961 *Employees:* 9
Net Worth: £1,753,535 *Total Assets:* £3,881,166
Registered Office: Greystones, Caldwell, Richmond, N Yorks, DL11 7UB
Activities: Growing of cereals (except rice), leguminous crops and oil seeds
Officers: Brian Victor Swinbank, Secretary; Brian Victor Swinbank [1945] Director/Farmer; David Andrew Swinbank [1975] Director/Farmer; Ralph Watson Swinbank [1972] Director/Farmer

Swinburne Horticultural Services Limited
Incorporated: 27 February 2002 *Employees:* 29
Net Worth: £1,328,955 *Total Assets:* £1,615,219
Registered Office: 50a Durham Road, Blackhill, Consett, Co Durham, DH8 8NP
Activities: Other service activities n.e.c.
Officers: David Lowes Swinburne, Secretary; David Lowes Swinburne [1961] Director; Jeremy Swinburne [1965] Director; Michael Swinburne [1962] Director

Swinburne Maddison LLP
Incorporated: 29 June 2010 *Employees:* 56
Net Worth: £905,975 *Total Assets:* £1,138,927
Registered Office: Venture House, Aykley Heads Business Centre, Durham, DH1 5TS
Officers: Andrew John Davison [1957] Member; Jonathan Michael Moreland [1968] Member; Simon Andrew Robinson [1960] Member; Kate Elizabeth Stephenson [1980] Member; Martyn William Tennant [1982] Member; Victoria Elizabeth Walton [1977] Member; Carolyn Beal [1978] LLP Member; David Joseph Low [1984] LLP Member; Alex Arthur Wilby [1981] LLP Member

Swiss Land Limited
Incorporated: 5 January 2006 *Employees:* 3
Net Worth: £2,673,138 *Total Assets:* £12,380,942
Registered Office: 2nd Floor, Building 7, Queens Park, Queensway, Team Valley Trading Estate, Gateshead, Tyne & Wear, NE11 0QD
Activities: Dormant company
Parent: UK Land Estates Limited
Officers: Emilia Keleditis [1977] Director [Greek]; Alan Keith Taylor [1963] Director; Christopher John Whitfield [1964] Director

Sycamore Homes Limited
Incorporated: 7 August 1987
Net Worth: £488,740 *Total Assets:* £756,267
Registered Office: 138 Westoe Road, South Shields, Tyne & Wear, NE33 3PF
Activities: Construction of other civil engineering projects n.e.c.
Major Shareholder: Alan Dixon
Officers: David Dixon, Secretary; Alan Dixon [1964] Director/Builder

Sycamore Property Developments Limited
Incorporated: 1 August 2001
Net Worth: £1,896,198 *Total Assets:* £6,007,301
Registered Office: Oak House, Durham Road, Birtley, Chester-le-Street, Co Durham, DH3 2TB
Activities: Construction of domestic buildings
Shareholder: Gordon Obrien
Officers: Gordon John O'Brien, Secretary/Demolition Controller; Gordon John O'Brien [1962] Director/Demolition Controller; Michael Obrien [1967] Director/Demolition Controller

Symetri Limited
Incorporated: 20 August 1996 *Employees:* 20
Net Worth Deficit: £1,747,588 *Total Assets:* £3,138,528
Registered Office: Dobson House, The Grainger Suite, Regent Centre, Gosforth, Newcastle upon Tyne, NE3 3PF
Activities: Retail sale of computers, peripheral units and software in specialised stores
Parent: Addnode Group AB
Officers: Johan Fredrik Andersson [1974] Director/Chief Financial Officer [Swedish]; John Bartle [1957] Managing Director; Rolf Kjaernsli [1958] Director [Norwegian]; Boel Ingela Elisabet Norlander [1962] Director [Swedish]

Synergy Compliance Limited
Incorporated: 17 July 2003
Net Worth: £731,727 *Total Assets:* £1,256,170
Registered Office: The Mill House, Market Place, Houghton-le-Spring, Co Durham, DH5 8AH
Activities: Activities of other membership organisations n.e.c.
Major Shareholder: Vicki Elizabeth Peck
Officers: Peter John Thompson, Secretary; Vicki Elizabeth Peck [1964] Compliance Director; Peter John Thompson [1957] Compliance Director

Syntex Engineering Services Limited
Incorporated: 8 April 1983
Net Worth: £426,026 *Total Assets:* £980,236
Registered Office: 32-33 Brewsdale Road, Lawson Industrial Estate, Middlesbrough, Cleveland, TS3 6LJ
Activities: Other specialised construction activities n.e.c.
Officers: Patrick Anthony Finn, Secretary; Patrick Anthony Finn [1943] Director [Irish]; Sally Anne Finn [1976] Director/H and S Consultant [Irish]

Synthetiq Limited
Incorporated: 12 May 2014
Registered Office: 5 Drake Court, Middlesbrough, Cleveland, TS2 1RS
Activities: Other business support service activities n.e.c.
Major Shareholder: James Pearl
Officers: James Pearl [1972] Managing Director

T C & C Ltd
Incorporated: 9 June 2014
Net Worth: £361,778 *Total Assets:* £802,716
Registered Office: Unit 4 Princess Court, Low Prudhoe Industrial Estate, Prudhoe, Northumberland, NE42 6PL
Activities: Sale of used cars and light motor vehicles
Major Shareholder: Daniel Noel Colpitts
Officers: Daniel Colpitts [1985] Director/Motor Trader

T C Developments North East Ltd
Incorporated: 11 September 2001 *Employees:* 2
Net Worth: £1,285,266 *Total Assets:* £1,589,203
Registered Office: 23 Yarm Road, Stockton on Tees, Cleveland, TS18 3NJ
Activities: Other professional, scientific and technical activities n.e.c.
Officers: Anthony Norman Cuthbert [1963] Director/Property Developer

T J D Properties Limited
Incorporated: 14 August 1998
Net Worth: £1,033,538 *Total Assets:* £9,079,386
Registered Office: Moor Chambers, 26 Front Street, Framwellgate Moor, Durham, DH1 5EJ
Activities: Buying and selling of own real estate
Officers: Andrew John Davison, Secretary; Andrew John Davison [1957] Director; David McLaughlin [1947] Director/Chartered Accountant; Anthony Moorley [1948] Director; Kenneth Alexander Robertson Prain [1938] Director

T M A Property Consultants Limited
Incorporated: 6 June 2008
Net Worth: £155,039 *Total Assets:* £3,052,739
Registered Office: Suites 1 and 2, Cheviot House, Beaminster Way East, Kingston Park, Newcastle upon Tyne, NE3 2ER
Activities: Quantity surveying activities
Major Shareholder: Timothy Robert Weightman
Officers: Julia Ann Weightman [1963] Director/Administration; Timothy Robert Weightman [1962] Director

T R M Marketing Limited
Incorporated: 10 December 1998 *Employees:* 5
Net Worth: £2,698,089 *Total Assets:* £5,077,515
Registered Office: The Archways, Headlam Hall, Headlam, Darlington, Co Durham, DL2 3HA
Activities: Other business support service activities n.e.c.
Major Shareholder: Timothy Robert Metcalfe
Officers: Timothy Robert Metcalfe, Secretary/Furniture Component Agent; Suzanne Clare Metcalfe [1963] Director; Timothy Robert Metcalfe [1958] Director/Furniture Component Agent

T&G Automotive Ltd
Incorporated: 15 December 1981 *Employees:* 45
Net Worth: £2,725,521 *Total Assets:* £4,905,535
Registered Office: Unit 12 All Saints Industrial Estate, Darlington Road, Shildon, Co Durham, DL4 2RD
Activities: Manufacture of other tanks, reservoirs and containers of metal
Officers: Konrad Gehle [1940] Director [German]

T-Mac Technologies Limited
Incorporated: 8 October 2004
Net Worth: £67,069 *Total Assets:* £1,394,701
Registered Office: Utilitywise House, 3 & 4 Cobalt Park Way, Cobalt Business Park, New York, Tyne & Wear, NE28 9EJ
Activities: Technical testing and analysis
Parent: Utilitywise PLC
Officers: Richard Stephen Laker [1976] Director; Richard Brinsley Sheridan [1964] Director

T.A. Plastic Supplies Limited
Incorporated: 22 August 1977 *Employees:* 8
Net Worth: £590,610 *Total Assets:* £1,098,954
Registered Office: Tudhoe Industrial Estate, Spennymoor, Co Durham, DL16 6TL
Activities: Non-specialised wholesale trade
Parent: Tap Ltd
Officers: Agnes Humphreys, Secretary; Stephen Averre [1959] Director; Susan Brown [1962] Director; John Pattenden Humphreys [1966] Director; Trevor Joseph Humphreys [1944] Director

T.A.P. Limited
Incorporated: 18 January 1988
Net Worth: £902,836 *Total Assets:* £956,657
Registered Office: Tudhoe Industrial Estate, Spennymoor, Co Durham, DL16 6TL
Activities: Activities of head offices
Major Shareholder: Trevor Joseph Humphreys
Officers: Trevor Joseph Humphreys, Secretary; Agnes Humphreys [1948] Director; John Pattenden Humphreys [1966] Director/Works Manager; Trevor Joseph Humphreys [1944] Director

T.M.G. Joinery (UK) Limited
Incorporated: 3 August 2000
Registered Office: Skippers Lane Industrial Estate, Middlesbrough, Cleveland, TS6 6HA
Activities: Joinery installation
Parent: T.M.G. Joinery (Holdings) Limited
Officers: Graham Leo McDonald [1963] Director

T.P. Enterprises Limited
Incorporated: 13 March 1986 *Employees:* 2
Net Worth: £295,808 *Total Assets:* £1,406,561
Registered Office: Meadowfield Avenue, Green Lane Industrial Estate, Spennymoor, Co Durham, DL16 6YJ
Activities: Activities of head offices
Major Shareholder: Stephan Taylor
Officers: Barbara Winn, Secretary; Adam Taylor [1973] Director Salesman; Lesley Taylor [1948] Director/Consultant; Stephan Cyril Taylor [1947] Director/Manager

T.W.R. Trade Frames Limited
Incorporated: 29 March 2004 *Employees:* 21
Net Worth: £901,883 *Total Assets:* £2,014,906
Registered Office: Lauhen House, 3-4 Whitehouse Way, South West Industrial Estate, Peterlee, Co Durham, SR8 2RA
Activities: Other manufacturing n.e.c.
Major Shareholder: Terence William Richardson
Officers: Laura Elizabeth Richardson [1990] Director; Terence William Richardson [1957] Director

Taemar Limited
Incorporated: 24 February 2005 *Employees:* 22
Net Worth: £107,983 *Total Assets:* £2,314,072
Registered Office: Unit 5 Maling Court, Union Street, Newcastle upon Tyne, NE2 1BP
Activities: Development of building projects
Major Shareholder: Ian Robert Baggett
Officers: Ian Robert Baggett [1972] Director; Allison Jane Harrison [1964] Director

Martin Tait Redheads Ltd.
Incorporated: 20 April 1977
Net Worth: £1,343,199 *Total Assets:* £2,873,447
Registered Office: Buxton House, 1 Buxton Street, Newcastle upon Tyne, NE1 6NJ
Activities: Advertising agencies
Major Shareholder: Howard William Tait
Officers: Colette Thompson, Secretary; Howard William Tait [1949] Director; Kathleen Veronica Tait [1949] Director

Tait Walker Financial Services Limited
Incorporated: 12 January 2006 *Employees:* 24
Net Worth: £753,192 *Total Assets:* £1,143,125
Registered Office: Bulman House, Regent Centre, Gosforth, Newcastle upon Tyne, NE3 3LS
Activities: Activities of insurance agents and brokers
Parent: Tait Walker LLP
Officers: Andrew John Moorby [1965] Director/Accountant; Mark Andrew Parkinson [1974] Director; Alastair Rowan Wilson [1974] Director/Tax Advisor

Tait Walker LLP
Incorporated: 16 September 2008 *Employees:* 152
Net Worth: £2,268,826 *Total Assets:* £4,692,359
Registered Office: Bulman House, Regent Centre, Gosforth, Newcastle upon Tyne, NE3 3LS
Officers: Simon Brown [1975] Member; Mark Richard Cail Brunton [1963] Member; Brian Anthony Laidlaw [1971] Member; Andrew John Moorby [1965] Member; Mark Andrew Parkinson [1974] Member; Stephen Charles Plaskitt [1969] Member; Christopher Ian Potter [1978] Member; Michael Alan Smith [1958] Member; Alastair Rowan Wilson [1974] Member

Talbot House Trust North East
Incorporated: 16 June 1995 *Employees:* 45
Net Worth: £429,936 *Total Assets:* £1,955,457
Registered Office: Hexham Road, Walbottle, Newcastle upon Tyne, NE15 8HW
Activities: Primary education
Officers: Deirdre Pearson, Secretary; Louise Cannell-Mirza [1983] Director/Solicitor; Rev Allison Joan Harding [1965] Director/Reverend; Benjamin Ross Henderson [1984] Director/Teacher; Christopher Denys Matthews [1943] Director/Retired Consultant; Linda Tarbit [1960] Director/Housewife

The Talent Group UK Limited
Incorporated: 30 January 2001
Net Worth: £893,494 *Total Assets:* £1,144,258
Registered Office: Tanfield Lea Business Centre, Tanfield Lea Industrial Estate North, Tanfield Lea, Stanley, Co Durham, DH9 9DB
Activities: Management consultancy activities other than financial management
Major Shareholder: George Heydon
Officers: George Heydon [1961] Director/Consultant

Tallantyre Wallcoverings Limited
Incorporated: 13 March 1978 *Employees:* 20
Net Worth: £542,489 *Total Assets:* £812,001
Registered Office: 43-45 Newgate Street, Morpeth, Northumberland, NE61 1AT
Activities: Retail sale of textiles in specialised stores
Major Shareholder: Robin Tallantyre
Officers: Michelle Leah Edge, Secretary; Gillian Martin [1976] Director/Interior Designer; Martin Edward Robert Tallantyre [1974] Director/Manager; Robert Tallantyre [1942] Retailer/Director

Tan International Limited
Incorporated: 18 November 1982 *Employees:* 40
Net Worth: £4,528,570 *Total Assets:* £6,570,720
Registered Office: Bulman House, Regent Centre, Gosforth, Newcastle upon Tyne, NE3 3LS
Activities: Wholesale of chemical products
Major Shareholder: Christopher Thomas Irvine
Officers: Christopher Thomas Irvine, Secretary; Christopher Thomas Irvine [1968] Director; Alan Graham Martin [1954] Director

Tancred Gravel Limited
Incorporated: 27 April 1953 *Employees:* 4
Net Worth: £1,595,897 *Total Assets:* £2,157,308
Registered Office: Scorton, Richmond, N Yorks, DL10 6AA
Activities: Operation of gravel and sand pits; mining of clays and kaolin
Shareholder: Stephen Robert Collins as Executor for David Willi Barker
Officers: Andrew Barker [1976] Director; Rachel Margaret Lawson [1966] Director; Mark Andrew William Westgarth [1970] Director/Farmer

Tandem Properties Limited
Incorporated: 2 February 2007
Net Worth Deficit: £317,512 *Total Assets:* £1,107,744
Registered Office: Holywood House, Wolsingham, Bishop Auckland, Co Durham, DL13 3HE
Activities: Other business support service activities n.e.c.
Shareholder: Robert Angus Hill
Officers: Anne Hill, Secretary; Andrea Cassidy [1975] Director/Teacher; Emma Hill [1979] Director/Marketing; Robert Angus Hill [1950] Director

Tanfield Engineering Systems Limited
Incorporated: 14 March 2012 *Employees:* 100
Net Worth: £115,544 *Total Assets:* £4,543,413
Registered Office: Tanfield Engineering Systems, Tanfield Lea Industrial Estate, Stanley, Co Durham, DH9 9NX
Activities: Manufacture of other fabricated metal products n.e.c.
Major Shareholder: Kevin David Harris
Officers: Kevin David Harris [1963] Director

Tanfield Group PLC
Incorporated: 30 August 2000 *Employees:* 3
Net Worth: £36,522,000 *Total Assets:* £36,613,000
Registered Office: Sandgate House, 102 Quayside, Newcastle upon Tyne, NE1 3DX
Activities: Manufacture of other general-purpose machinery n.e.c.
Officers: Daryn Robinson, Secretary; Martin Hugh Charles Groak [1950] Director/Business Consultant; Daryn Ashley Robinson [1977] Director and Company Secretary

Tanfield Metal Spinners Ltd
Incorporated: 8 May 1998
Registered Office: 6 Parsons Road, Parsons Industrial Estate, Washington, Tyne & Wear, NE37 1HB
Activities: Manufacture of metal structures and parts of structures
Shareholder: David Haley
Officers: Paul Rushton, Secretary; David Haley [1953] Financial Director; James Carr Haley [1966] Director; Derek Lonsdale [1956] Managing Director; Paul Rushton [1964] Commercial Director

Tangent Construction Limited
Incorporated: 13 June 2000
Net Worth: £416,787 *Total Assets:* £818,259
Registered Office: 6 Queens Court North, Third Avenue, Team Valley Trading Estate, Gateshead, Tyne & Wear, NE11 0BU
Activities: Construction of commercial buildings
Shareholders: Lynn Sutheran; Stephen Edward Sutheran
Officers: Liam Sutheran [1989] Director; Lynn Sutheran [1958] Director; Stephen Edward Sutheran [1955] Director/Civil Engineer

Taniya Properties Ltd
Incorporated: 4 April 2011
Net Worth Deficit: £356,946 *Total Assets:* £2,916,646
Registered Office: c/o Hillman & Co, Technology Court, Bradbury Road, Newton Aycliffe, Co Durham, DL5 6DA
Activities: Buying and selling of own real estate
Officers: Seema Jagota, Secretary; Aminur Choudhury [1971] Director; Taniya Choudhury [1982] Director; Seema Jagota [1973] Director; Javaid Nazir [1969] Director

Tantallon Homes Limited
Incorporated: 12 November 2014 *Employees:* 2
Net Worth Deficit: £4,249 *Total Assets:* £1,008,523
Registered Office: 53 Moor Crescent, Gosforth, Newcastle upon Tyne, NE3 4AQ
Activities: Construction of domestic buildings
Major Shareholder: Charlotte Simmonds
Officers: Charlotte Jayne Simmonds [1993] Director; Peter John Stoker [1956] Director

Tao Sustainable Power Solutions (UK) Ltd
Incorporated: 11 December 2009 *Employees:* 2
Net Worth: £1,836,000 *Total Assets:* £2,137,000
Registered Office: 1 Queens Park, Team Valley Trading Estate, Gateshead, Tyne & Wear, NE11 0QD
Activities: Manufacture of tools
Parent: TWC3N Limited
Officers: Carlos Augusto Martins Das Neves [1966] Director [Portuguese]; Charles Ian Rendell [1966] Director/Chartered Accountant

Taopix Group Limited
Incorporated: 29 November 2016
Net Worth: £786,477 *Total Assets:* £1,566,497
Registered Office: The Greenhouse, Meadowfield Industrial Estate, Ponteland, Northumberland, NE20 9SD
Activities: Activities of head offices
Major Shareholder: James Paterson Gray
Officers: Hayley Samantha Gray, Secretary; James Paterson Gray [1978] Director

Taopix Limited
Incorporated: 17 May 2007 *Employees:* 25
Net Worth: £400,896 *Total Assets:* £1,036,429
Registered Office: The Greenhouse, Meadowfield Industrial Estate, Ponteland, Northumberland, NE20 9SD
Activities: Other software publishing
Shareholders: Hayley Samantha Gray; James Paterson Gray
Officers: James Paterson Gray [1978] Director

Tom Tappin,Limited
Incorporated: 20 March 1939 *Employees:* 83
Net Worth: £4,001,661 *Total Assets:* £4,182,842
Registered Office: 3rd Floor, 41-51 Grey Street, Newcastle upon Tyne, NE1 6EE
Activities: Tour operator activities
Parent: The City of Oxford Motor Services Limited
Officers: Carolyn Ferguson, Secretary; David Allen Brown [1960] Director; Simon Patrick Butcher [1967] Finance Director; Luke Carl Marion [1980] Director/Chartered Accountant; Philip Richard Southall [1976] Director; Raymond Woodhouse [1953] Director/Engineering

Taprich Limited
Incorporated: 6 October 1989 *Employees:* 13
Net Worth: £931,451 *Total Assets:* £1,715,660
Registered Office: 17 Queens Street, Queens Arcade, Darlington, Co Durham, DL3 6SH
Activities: Other retail sale of new goods in specialised stores (not commercial art galleries and opticians)
Parent: Taprich (Holdings) Limited
Officers: Maxine Dobbing, Secretary; Alex Dobbing [1955] Director/Jeweller; Maxine Dobbing [1976] Director

Taradina Number Two Limited
Incorporated: 9 October 2014
Net Worth: £996,643 *Total Assets:* £1,249,626
Registered Office: Wynyard Park House, Wynyard Avenue, Wynyard, Cleveland, TS22 5TB
Activities: Development of building projects
Officers: Joseph Christopher Musgrave [1965] Director

Tarcon Limited
Incorporated: 20 February 2013
Registered Office: Hughes House, Cargo Fleet Road, Middlesbrough, Cleveland, TS3 6AG
Activities: Construction of roads and motorways
Shareholders: Philip Hughes; Donal Hughes
Officers: Christopher Roystone Brown [1981] Commercial Director; Anthony Constantine [1961] Operations Director; Donal James Hughes [1975] Director; Philip Gerard Hughes [1982] Director

T.B. Tarn Limited
Incorporated: 1 February 2010 *Employees:* 14
Net Worth: £231,538 *Total Assets:* £1,397,679
Registered Office: Thorndale Farm, Melsonby, Richmond, N Yorks, DL10 5NJ
Activities: Combined facilities support activities
Shareholders: Kurtis Barrie Tarn; Thomas Barrie Tarn; Wesley Thomas Tarn
Officers: Thomas Barrie Tarn, Secretary; Kurtis Barrie Tarn [1972] Director/Engineer; Thomas Barrie Tarn [1944] Director/Executive; Wesley Thomas Tarn [1979] Director/Executive

Tascomp Holdings Limited
Incorporated: 2 March 2016
Net Worth: £892,479 *Total Assets:* £2,541,968
Registered Office: Newburgh Court, Belasis Hall Technology Park, Billingham, Stockton on Tees, Cleveland, TS23 4EE
Activities: Activities of other holding companies n.e.c.
Shareholders: Ashley Tizard; Alan Edward Williamson; Ann Lesley Forster
Officers: Ashley Tizard [1968] Director/Project Manager; Alan Edward Williamson [1964] Director/Project Manager

Tascomp Limited
Incorporated: 10 March 1978
Registered Office: Newburgh Court, Belasis Hall Technology Park, Billingham, Cleveland, TS23 4EE
Activities: Business and domestic software development
Parent: Tascomp Holdings Limited
Officers: Ashley Tizard [1968] Director; Alan Edward Williamson [1964] Director/Software Development Manager

Tau Properties Limited
Incorporated: 25 November 2002
Net Worth: £27,165 *Total Assets:* £1,134,570
Registered Office: 22 Ladypark, Gateshead, Tyne & Wear, NE11 0HD
Activities: Other holiday and other collective accommodation
Shareholders: John Russell Scott; Philip Howard Scott
Officers: Philip Howard Scott, Secretary/Director; John Russell Scott [1963] Director; Philip Howard Scott [1967] Director

Tavistock Hospitality Limited
Incorporated: 6 February 2014 *Employees:* 89
Net Worth: £3,043,629 *Total Assets:* £6,744,159
Registered Office: Cottage rear of Roker Hotel, Roker Terrace, Sunderland, Tyne & Wear, SR6 9ND
Activities: Hotels and similar accommodation
Shareholders: Mark Hird; Nicola Foster-Hird
Officers: Steven Andrew Akers [1981] Finance Director; Nicola Jane Foster Hird [1972] Director; Jonathan Graham [1974] Director; Mark Hird [1973] Director

Tavistock House Day Nursery Limited
Incorporated: 22 October 2002
Net Worth: £1,395,093 *Total Assets:* £1,533,525
Registered Office: Tavistock House, Borough Road, Sunderland, Tyne & Wear, SR1 1PG
Activities: Pre-primary education
Officers: Gillian Hopkins, Secretary; David Downey [1957] Director; Gillian Hopkins [1959] Director; Norman Vincent [1959] Director/Accountant; Norman Vincent Senior [1927] Director/Retired

Tax Incentivised Savings Association
Incorporated: 17 April 1998 *Employees:* 30
Net Worth: £583,354 *Total Assets:* £1,776,192
Registered Office: Dakota House, 25 Falcon Court, Preston Farm Business Park, Stockton on Tees, Cleveland, TS18 3TX
Activities: Other education n.e.c.
Officers: Carol Lesley Knight, Secretary; Larry Banda [1961] Director; Elissa Bayer [1953] Director; John David Brasington [1946] Director/Consultant; David Martin Dalton-Brown [1959] Executive Director; Richard David Freeman [1954] Director; Jane Sarah Goodland [1972] Responsible Business Director; Carol Lesley Knight [1953] Director; Julian Witold Korek [1952] Director/Accountant; Gregg McClymont [1976] Director; Katrina Therese Sartorius [1974] Director; Patrick Joseph Shea [1963] Director [American]; Clive John Shelton [1955] Director; Tony Stenning [1970] Director/MD, UK Retail; David Jason White [1970] Director; David Ian White [1959] Director/Chief Executive

J & S Taylor (Site Services) Ltd
Incorporated: 10 February 2003
Net Worth: £1,042,710 *Total Assets:* £1,381,592
Registered Office: Thistle Road, Littleburn Industrial Estate, Langley Moor, Co Durham, DH7 8HJ
Activities: Other business support service activities n.e.c.
Officers: Barbara Taylor, Secretary; Barbara Taylor [1957] Director/Secretary

A.V.Taylor Limited
Incorporated: 5 June 1972 *Employees:* 20
Net Worth: £323,502 *Total Assets:* £1,046,761
Registered Office: 82-84 Shields Road, Newcastle upon Tyne, NE6 1DS
Activities: Wholesale trade of motor vehicle parts and accessories
Shareholders: Colin Lee; Eileen Lee
Officers: Jane Lee, Secretary; Colin Lee [1961] Director; Eileen Lee [1967] Director; Jane Lee [1936] Director/Secretary

MJ & A Taylor Limited
Incorporated: 12 January 2004
Net Worth: £865,763 *Total Assets:* £1,022,858
Registered Office: 226 Park Road, South Moor, Stanley, Co Durham, DH9 7AN
Activities: Dispensing chemist in specialised stores
Parent: Blue House Retail Limited
Officers: Babar Arshad [1987] Director/Pharmacist

Neal Taylor Management Limited
Incorporated: 23 August 2012
Net Worth: £2,766,434 *Total Assets:* £3,214,549
Registered Office: 1st Floor, 5 Cattle Market, Hexham, Northumberland, NE46 1NJ
Activities: Management consultancy activities other than financial management
Shareholders: Clive William Lantsbery; Patricia Baker; Michael James Baker
Officers: Michael James Baker [1973] Director; Patricia Baker [1945] Director; Clive William Lantsbery [1940] Director

Taylor Packaging (Bishop Auckland) Limited
Incorporated: 11 July 2002 *Employees:* 18
Net Worth: £1,214,912 *Total Assets:* £2,024,314
Registered Office: Meadowfield Avenue, Green Lane Industrial Estate, Spennymoor, Co Durham, DL16 6YJ
Activities: Non-specialised wholesale trade
Parent: T.P. Enterprises Limited
Officers: Barbara O'Hare, Secretary; Barbara O'Hare [1965] Director; Adam Taylor [1973] Director; Stephan Cyril Taylor [1947] Managing Director; Lesley Taylor Mbe [1948] Director

Taylored Estates Limited
Incorporated: 3 September 2015
Net Worth: £295,369 *Total Assets:* £4,087,542
Registered Office: 2 St Peters Road, Wallsend, Tyne & Wear, NE28 7LG
Activities: Construction of domestic buildings
Shareholder: Timothy Peter Shearing
Officers: Stephen David Leightley [1963] Director; Tim Peter Shearing [1979] Director; Andrew Edward David Taylor [1985] Director

Taylored Properties (NE) Ltd
Incorporated: 11 March 2008
Registered Office: 2 St Peters Road, Wallsend, Tyne & Wear, NE28 7LG
Activities: Buying and selling of own real estate
Major Shareholder: Andrew Taylor
Officers: Andrew Taylor, Secretary; Andrew Edward David Taylor [1985] Director/Property Developer; John Bentley Taylor [1947] Director/Retired; Susan Elizabeth Taylor [1947] Director/Retired

Taylored Property Group Limited
Incorporated: 9 April 2008
Net Worth: £1,400,039 *Total Assets:* £6,292,661
Registered Office: 2 St Peters Road, Wallsend, Tyne & Wear, NE28 7LG
Activities: Development of building projects
Shareholder: Tinothy Peter Shearing
Officers: Tim Peter Shearing, Secretary; Stephen David Leightley [1963] Director; Tim Peter Shearing [1979] Director; Andrew Edward David Taylor [1985] Director/Property Developer

Taylormade Timber Products Ltd
Incorporated: 15 May 1957 *Employees:* 171
Net Worth: £13,956,043 *Total Assets:* £21,421,552
Registered Office: Sherburn Hill, Co Durham, DH6 1PS
Activities: Other manufacturing n.e.c.
Parent: Sonicedge Limited
Officers: Suzanne Claire Penrose, Secretary; Suzanne Claire Penrose [1987] Finance Director; Douglas John Wentworth [1953] Director; Jillian Anne Wentworth [1990] Managing Director

Taylors Football Souvenirs Limited
Incorporated: 20 June 2003
Registered Office: Wynbury Stables, Main Street, West Witton, Leyburn, N Yorks, DL8 4LR
Activities: Retail sale via mail order houses or via Internet
Shareholders: Wolf Karadzic; Jill Karadzic
Officers: Jill Carol Karadzic, Secretary; Nicole Clare Jones [1983] Director; Jill Carol Karadzic [1963] Director/Administrator; Stefan Peter Karadzic [1984] Director; Wolf Stefan Marko Karadzic [1963] Director/Operations Manager

TBT Catering Limited
Incorporated: 17 March 2014
Net Worth: £344,593 *Total Assets:* £2,142,722
Registered Office: 511 Durham Road, Low Fell, Gateshead, Tyne & Wear, NE9 5EY
Activities: Take-away food shops and mobile food stands
Shareholders: Owen Bradford; Paul Taylor; Steven Taylor
Officers: Owen Bradford [1964] Director; Paul Taylor [1969] Director; Steven Taylor [1969] Director

TC Industries of Europe Limited
Incorporated: 5 June 1984 *Employees:* 69
Net Worth: £6,487,894 *Total Assets:* £7,532,934
Registered Office: Skinningrove Works, Carlin How, Saltburn-by-the-Sea, N Yorks, TS13 4EE
Activities: Manufacture of other fabricated metal products n.e.c.
Parent: TCR Corp.
Officers: Robert Fremont Berry, Secretary; George Albert Berry IV [1952] Director [American]; Thomas Zander Hayward Jr [1940] Director [American]; Jeff Quarrie [1961] Director/Business Executive [Canadian]

TCC Holdings Ltd
Incorporated: 21 September 2006
Net Worth: £1,788,942 *Total Assets:* £3,111,997
Registered Office: c/o Town Centre Citroen, Ferryboat Lane, Sunderland, Tyne & Wear, SR5 3JN
Activities: Other letting and operating of own or leased real estate
Parent: BTCO No 1 Ltd
Officers: Stephen Smith [1950] Director

TCUK Homes Limited
Incorporated: 1 February 2013
Net Worth: £25,588 *Total Assets:* £6,338,210
Registered Office: Unit D13 Marquis Court, Team Valley Trading Estate, Gateshead, Tyne & Wear, NE11 0RU
Activities: Renting and operating of Housing Association real estate
Officers: Valerie Bell, Secretary; Stephen Bell [1968] Director/Chief Executive; Arthur Modral Chadwick [1942] Director/Retired; Lynn Hall [1967] Director/Housing Solutions Manager; Zoey Hawthorne [1964] Director/Property Management & Development; Alexander Thomas Michael Shiel [1959] Director/Solicitor; James Nicholas Hampton Walder [1976] Director/Financial Controller

TDG Brand Communications Limited
Incorporated: 13 May 1953 *Employees:* 39
Net Worth: £346,944 *Total Assets:* £1,535,778
Registered Office: Mill House, Haddricks Mill Road, Newcastle upon Tyne, NE3 1QL
Activities: Advertising agencies
Parent: TDG Holdings Limited
Officers: Joanne Clare Chater, Secretary; Jeremy Hall [1964] Director/Accountant; Grant Marshall [1960] Director/Graphic Designer; Rosemary Patricia Parker Blair [1959] Director/Design Consultant; Alistair Quinn [1962] Director/Design Consultant

TDX (Europe) Limited
Incorporated: 6 September 2013 *Employees:* 104
Net Worth: £3,226,019 *Total Assets:* £14,647,826
Registered Office: 3 Princes Park, Princesway North, Gateshead, Tyne & Wear, NE11 0NF
Activities: Activities of head offices
Major Shareholder: Mark Steven Prinn
Officers: Trevor James Marr [1955] Director; Mark Steven Prinn [1975] Director

Team Build Construction Limited
Incorporated: 17 January 2003 *Employees:* 24
Net Worth: £324,234 *Total Assets:* £1,148,218
Registered Office: 39b Colbourne Crescent, Nelson Park, Cramlington, Northumberland, NE23 1WB
Activities: Construction of commercial buildings
Officers: Janine Davis, Secretary; Gary Davis [1966] Director/Contract Manager; Christopher Dixon [1966] Director/Commercial Manager

Team Fostering
Incorporated: 16 January 2001 *Employees:* 65
Net Worth: £3,686,957 *Total Assets:* £4,069,691
Registered Office: Unit 6 Hedley Court, Orion Business Park, North Shields, Tyne & Wear, NE29 7ST
Activities: Other social work activities without accommodation n.e.c.
Officers: Hayley Lavinia Eleanor Payne, Secretary; Mark Alden [1964] Director/Bank Manager; Jane Clare Butler [1961] Director; Rosemarie Holden [1955] Director; Walter Samuel Egerton Young [1965] Director/Consultant

Team Stokes Limited
Incorporated: 22 July 2010
Net Worth: £1,269,003 *Total Assets:* £1,269,003
Registered Office: 17a Doctors Lane, Hutton Rudby, Yarm, Cleveland, TS15 0EQ
Activities: Production of electricity
Major Shareholder: Philip Anthony Stokes
Officers: Philip Anthony Stokes [1956] Director/Consultant

Teatime Tasties Limited
Incorporated: 28 September 2000 *Employees:* 63
Net Worth: £2,314,087 *Total Assets:* £4,486,292
Registered Office: Unit S3, Narvik Way, Tyne Tunnel Trading Estate, North Shields, Tyne & Wear, NE29 7XJ
Activities: Wholesale of sugar and chocolate and sugar confectionery
Officers: Patricia Ada Rice, Secretary; David Leonard Brind [1972] Director; John Frederick Hope [1969] Group Operations Director; Patricia Ada Rice [1951] Finance Director; Paul Victor Young [1957] Director

Techflow Marine Ltd
Incorporated: 11 July 2005 *Employees:* 38
Net Worth: £4,534,082 *Total Assets:* £11,726,640
Registered Office: Unit 4 Silverton Court, Northumberland Business Park, Cramlington, Northumberland, NE23 7RY
Activities: Other manufacturing n.e.c.
Shareholder: Kenneth Brian Beattie
Officers: Bryan Percy Beattie [1932] Director; Kenneth Brian Beattie [1953] Director; Graham Osmond Clark [1956] Director/Accountant; John Colin Fitzpatrick [1955] Director/Chartered Accountant; James Straker [1962] Director/Engineer

Technical Engineering Resource (Aerospace) Limited
Incorporated: 2 October 2014 *Employees:* 9
Net Worth: £274,912 *Total Assets:* £864,756
Registered Office: 1 Trimdon Grange Industrial Estate, Trimdon Grange, Trimdon Station, Cleveland, TS29 6PA
Activities: Manufacture of other transport equipment n.e.c.
Parent: DLI Engineering Limited
Officers: Barry Michael Wells [1946] Director

Technical Housing Solutions Limited
Incorporated: 28 August 2008
Net Worth: £1,507,036 *Total Assets:* £1,756,901
Registered Office: 10 Summerhouse Grove, Darlington, Co Durham, DL3 8UE
Activities: Other engineering activities
Shareholders: Daniel Charles Key; Ellen Key
Officers: Ellen Key, Secretary; Daniel Charles Key [1977] Director

Technical Investment Solutions Ltd
Incorporated: 19 December 2001
Net Worth: £954,543 *Total Assets:* £985,032
Registered Office: Juniper House, Station Road, Piercebridge, Darlington, Co Durham, DL2 3TS
Activities: Other activities auxiliary to insurance and pension funding
Shareholders: Steven Harry Sayer; Jillian Sayer
Officers: Jillian Sayer, Secretary; Steven Harry Sayer [1960] Director/Financial Advisor Trust and ES

Technical Options (Europe) Ltd
Incorporated: 24 October 1996 *Employees:* 2
Net Worth: £630,718 *Total Assets:* £980,940
Registered Office: Verdemar House, 230 Park View, Whitley Bay, Tyne & Wear, NE26 3QR
Activities: Other professional, scientific and technical activities n.e.c.
Major Shareholder: Michael Brian Farnham
Officers: Therese Cunningham, Secretary; Michael Brian Farnham [1949] Director/Engineer

Technimark Limited
Incorporated: 10 September 2009 *Employees:* 65
Net Worth: £7,145,523 *Total Assets:* £8,146,804
Registered Office: Kirkcarrion Estate, Gas Lane, Middleton in Teesdale, Barnard Castle, Co Durham, DL12 0TN
Activities: Manufacture of other plastic products
Officers: Brad Wellington [1968] Director/President [American]

Technocopy Ltd.
Incorporated: 2 September 1992 *Employees:* 16
Net Worth: £1,344,390 *Total Assets:* £1,799,186
Registered Office: 106-108 North Road, Darlington, Co Durham, DL1 2EQ
Activities: Renting and leasing of office machinery and equipment (including computers)
Shareholders: Bradley Fraser Woods; Bradley Fraser Woods; Bradley Fraser Woods
Officers: Bradley Fraser Woods, Secretary; Bradley Fraser Woods [1964] Managing Director; Linda Joyce Woods [1964] Director

Technology Services Group Limited
Incorporated: 1 July 2003 *Employees:* 358
Net Worth: £2,118,000 *Total Assets:* £14,227,000
Registered Office: Q11 Quorum Business Park, Benton Lane, Newcastle upon Tyne, NE12 8BU
Activities: Information technology consultancy activities
Shareholder: Andrew William Graham Wylie
Officers: Joanne Walker, Secretary; Steven James Lynn [1979] Finance Director; David Coulson Stonehouse [1955] Director/Accountant; Andrew William Graham Wylie [1959] Director

Technowash Limited
Incorporated: 12 July 2000 *Employees:* 56
Net Worth: £163,581 *Total Assets:* £2,433,729
Registered Office: 8-10 Standard Way, Standard Way Business Park, Northallerton, N Yorks, DL6 2XE
Activities: Manufacture of other special-purpose machinery n.e.c.
Parent: Safety-Kleen UK Limited
Officers: Anthony Thomas Grayson, Secretary; Andrew Gregory Firth [1964] Director; Anthony Thomas Grayson [1963] Director/Engineer; Andrew Patrick Griffith [1968] Director; Philippe Robert Francis Mauguy [1960] Director [French]; Steven Edward Price [1964] Director

Techwax Limited
Incorporated: 24 May 1991 *Employees:* 48
Net Worth: £1,989,107 *Total Assets:* £3,251,541
Registered Office: Unit 4b Whinbank Park, Whinbank Road, Aycliffe Industrial Park, Newton Aycliffe, Co Durham, DL5 6AY
Activities: Manufacture of other chemical products n.e.c.
Parent: ISP Holdings (U.K.) Ltd
Officers: Julie Charlton, Secretary; Arnoldus Hendrikus Hermanus Bosgoed [1972] Director Finance & Control EMEA [Dutch]; Kevin Higgins [1985] Director/Treasury Manager [American]; Christophe Nicolas Roland Le Louarn [1962] Director/Senior Controller [French]

Teekay Marine Solutions Ltd
Incorporated: 14 May 1984
Net Worth: £2,132,202 *Total Assets:* £2,571,379
Registered Office: 1 The Cloisters, Sunderland, Tyne & Wear, SR2 7BD
Activities: Service activities incidental to water transportation
Parent: Teekay Marine Holdings Ltd
Officers: Christopher McGreevy, Secretary; Anne Elizabeth Liversedge [1968] Director/Solicitor

Tees & Hartlepool Yacht Club Limited
Incorporated: 9 July 1997
Net Worth: £180,994 *Total Assets:* £779,599
Registered Office: West Harbour, Hartlepool, Cleveland, TS24 0SP
Activities: Activities of sport clubs
Officers: Ian Lynch, Secretary; Stuart Armstrong [1958] Director/Retired Teacher; Graeme Richard Boagey [1963] Director/Chartered Accountant; Malcolm Iveson Boagey [1948] Director/Teacher; Russell James Garner [1963] Director/Retired; Clare Hope [1978] Director/Teaching Assistant; Phillip Hope [1977] Director/Quantity Surveyor; Christine Hughes [1946] Director/Retired Bank Clerk; Dr Anthony Gould Jones [1960] Director/Scientist; Stuart John Lawson [1972] Director; Ian Lynch [1970] Director/Clerk; Neil MacKechnie [1951] Director; Elizabeth McCormack [1956] Director/Manager; Stephen William Passmore [1955] Director/Quality Manager; Robert Michael Walker [1958] Director/Surveyor

Tees and Hartlepool Pilotage Company Limited
Incorporated: 23 April 1920 *Employees:* 18
Net Worth: £16,172,000 *Total Assets:* £64,583,000
Registered Office: 17-27 Queen's Square, Middlesbrough, Cleveland, TS2 1AH
Activities: Sea and coastal freight water transport
Parent: PD Portco Limited
Officers: Dermot Michael Russell, Secretary; Johannes Franciscus Calje [1972] Director [Dutch]; Jeremy Mark Hopkinson [1955] Director; Dermot Michael Russell [1965] Director/Accountant

Tees Components Limited
Incorporated: 1 October 1963 *Employees:* 64
Net Worth: £4,416,726 *Total Assets:* £5,613,356
Registered Office: North Skelton, Saltburn-by-the-Sea, N Yorks, TS12 2AP
Activities: Manufacture of metal structures and parts of structures
Parent: Tees Components (Holdings) Limited
Officers: Jean Wood, Secretary; Sharon Lesley Lane [1978] Director/General Manager; Clive Leslie Wood [1949] Managing Director; Jean Wood [1949] Director/CS

Tees Components Property Company Limited
Incorporated: 3 April 1998
Net Worth: £1,527,187 *Total Assets:* £2,732,788
Registered Office: North Skelton, Saltburn-by-the-Sea, N Yorks, TS12 2AP
Activities: Other letting and operating of own or leased real estate
Parent: Jeave 4 Limited
Officers: Jean Wood, Secretary; Clive Leslie Wood [1949] Managing Director; Jean Wood [1949] Director/CS

Tees Insulation (International) Limited
Incorporated: 17 October 1996 *Employees:* 41
Net Worth: £197,460 *Total Assets:* £1,085,522
Registered Office: 138 Lynn Street, Hartlepool, Cleveland, TS24 7LX
Activities: Other construction installation
Shareholders: Tees Group Limited; Tees Group
Officers: Anthony Thomas McCarte, Secretary/Director; Anthony Thomas McCarte [1955] Director; Brian Paul McCarte [1957] Director; Paul McCarte [1967] Director/Engineer; John Paul Moore [1969] Director

Tees Licensed Foyboatmens' Association Limited
Incorporated: 30 May 1963 *Employees:* 53
Net Worth: £545,431 *Total Assets:* £990,218
Registered Office: Graving Dock, Dockside Road, Middlesbrough, Cleveland, TS3 8AT
Activities: Other transportation support activities
Officers: Neil Todd, Secretary; Gavin Allen [1971] Director/Boatman; John Appleton [1966] Director/Foyboatmen; Ryan Ludrecius [1979] Director/Boatman; Lee Richard Scott [1971] Director/Foyboatman; Carl Swinnerton [1964] Director/Foyboatman; David Todd [1986] Director/Boatman

Tees Valley Chinese Community Centre Ltd
Incorporated: 9 September 2003
Net Worth: £796,126 *Total Assets:* £797,279
Registered Office: Swan House, Westpoint Road, Thornaby, Stockton on Tees, Cleveland, TS17 6BP
Activities: Other amusement and recreation activities n.e.c.
Officers: Jimmy Chow, Secretary; Shirley Chan [1937] Director; Danny Chau [1940] Director/Retired Businessman; Jackie Tin Cheung [1953] Director/Trustee; Esperanza Chow [1956] Director/Self Caterer; Jimmy Chow [1944] Director/Retired; Tom Ha [1948] Director; Lai Tong Ho [1950] Director/Shop Owner; Stephen Ho [1943] Director/Self Employed Caterer; Lai Choi Leung [1947] Director; Kew Lim [1946] Director/Health Visitor [Chinese/British]; Choon Dee Neoh [1951] Director/Teacher [Malaysian/Chinese]; Edward Wong [1948] Director/Chef; Paul Kwok Ying Wong [1944] Director/Self Employed Caterer; Peter Wong [1947] Director/Retired

Tees Valley Community Church
Incorporated: 8 March 2006 *Employees:* 10
Net Worth: £1,642,532 *Total Assets:* £1,668,643
Registered Office: Tees Valley Community Church, Oakwood Centre, Cleasby Way, Durham Lane Industrial Estate, Eaglescliffe, Stockton on Tees, Cleveland, TS16 0RD
Activities: Activities of religious organisations
Officers: Christopher Vale, Secretary; Graham Bond [1947] Director/Retired; Martin Andrew Dunkley [1961] Director/Church Leader Doctor; Andrew Malbon [1965] Director/Shop Assistant; Julie Marley [1964] Director/Solicitor; Christopher John Vale [1978] Director/Pastor; Janet Clare Bourdillon West [1953] Director/Retired

Tees Valley Community Foundation
Incorporated: 10 June 2005 *Employees:* 5
Net Worth: £14,581,421 *Total Assets:* £14,638,532
Registered Office: Wallace House, Falcon Court, Preston Farm Industrial Estate, Stockton on Tees, Cleveland, TS18 3TX
Activities: Other professional, scientific and technical activities n.e.c.
Officers: Peter William Rowley, Secretary; Wendy Lorraine John [1983] Director/Solicitor; Neil Kenley [1960] Director; Professor Eileen Martin [1949] Director/Deputy Vice Chancellor; Heather Ann O'Driscoll [1961] Director/Chartered Accountant; Keith Smith [1957] Director/Retired Accountant; Jeffrey Taylor [1953] Director/Stockbroker

Tees Valley Components Limited
Incorporated: 15 November 2005 *Employees:* 27
Net Worth: £242,131 *Total Assets:* £948,169
Registered Office: Unit 1 Portrack Grange Close, Stockton on Tees, Cleveland, TS18 2PH
Activities: Other business support service activities n.e.c.
Parent: MJM Developments (Portrack Grange) Limited
Officers: James Robert McCulloch, Secretary; Mark James [1974] Director/Salesman; James Robert McCulloch [1977] Director/Salesman

Tees Valley Trailers Limited
Incorporated: 13 December 2004 *Employees:* 3
Net Worth: £2,400,606 *Total Assets:* £4,276,476
Registered Office: Dinsdale House, Riverside Park Road, Middlesbrough, Cleveland, TS2 1UT
Activities: Other service activities incidental to land transportation, n.e.c.
Major Shareholder: Gary Stuart Dawson
Officers: Craig Lloyd, Secretary; Gary Stuart Dawson [1970] Director; John Ellis Young [1970] Financial Director

Teescraft Engineering Limited
Incorporated: 6 April 1981 *Employees:* 63
Net Worth: £4,121,670 *Total Assets:* £6,089,568
Registered Office: Unit 2 South Church Enterprise Park, Bishop Auckland, Co Durham, DL14 6XB
Activities: Machining
Major Shareholder: Robert John Yorke
Officers: John Clifford Laverick, Secretary/Director; John Clifford Laverick [1942] Director; Robert John Yorke [1971] Director; Stephen Yorke [1963] Director/Logistics Manager

Teesdale South Limited
Incorporated: 22 December 2000
Net Worth Deficit: £316,888 *Total Assets:* £4,263,726
Registered Office: Mandale House, 5 Neville Road, North Tees Industrial Estate, Stockton on Tees, Cleveland, TS18 2RD
Activities: Development of building projects
Parent: Arkgrove Limited
Officers: Joseph Darragh, Secretary; Paula Davidson, Secretary; Joseph Darragh [1966] Director; David Ian Harriman [1956] Director

Teesnap Limited
Incorporated: 7 March 1997
Net Worth: £161,855 *Total Assets:* £4,426,130
Registered Office: Teesside University, Middlesbrough, Cleveland, TS1 3BA
Activities: Technical and vocational secondary education
Officers: Helen Cutting, Secretary; Professor Paul Croney [1963] Director/Vice Chancellor & Chief Executive; Malcolm Douglas Page [1967] Director/Chief Operating Officer

Teesside Estates Limited
Incorporated: 15 September 2006
Net Worth: £495,873 *Total Assets:* £1,517,636
Registered Office: 53 Market Place, Richmond, N Yorks, DL10 4JJ
Activities: Renting and operating of Housing Association real estate
Officers: Zarar Gulbahar, Secretary; Balqis Akhtar Gulbahar [1952] Director/Housewife Property Owner; Mohammed Gulbahar [1944] Director

Teesside High School Limited
Incorporated: 1 October 1956 *Employees:* 90
Net Worth: £2,058,616 *Total Assets:* £4,427,001
Registered Office: Teesside High School, The Avenue, Eaglescliffe, Stockton on Tees, Cleveland, TS16 9AT
Activities: Other education n.e.c.
Officers: Charles Geoffrey Watson, Secretary; Charles Anthony Stewart Atha [1962] Director/Solicitor; Trevor Cook [1955] Director/Governor; Alison Greenwood [1965] Director/Marketing Consultant; Anna Guest [1971] Director/Solicitor; Dennis Henry Lister [1938] Director/Retired; Dr Angela Marie Steele [1968] Director/GP; Robert James Stone [1948] Director; Robert Ralph Tindle [1957] Director/Accountant; Andrew Warrior [1968] Director/Senior Building Surveyor; Charles Geoffrey Watson [1943] Director/Retired; Trevor George Watson [1946] Director/Governor

Teesside Hospice Care Foundation
Incorporated: 9 June 1982 *Employees:* 94
Net Worth: £6,515,268 *Total Assets:* £7,210,038
Registered Office: 1 Northgate Road, Middlesbrough, Cleveland, TS5 5NW
Activities: Specialists medical practice activities
Officers: Erica Marie Turner, Secretary; Elaine Claire Criddle [1958] Director; Prof Brian Footitt [1944] Director of Nursing; John Leslie Fysh [1945] Director/Retired; Robert Morgan Jewell [1949] Director/Retired Accountant; Ann O'Hanlon [1956] Director; William Richard Pickersgill [1947] Director; David Addison Swallow [1951] Director/Chartered Accountant; Erica Marie Turner [1985] Director/Solicitor; Thomas Anthony Waites [1943] Director & Manager; Paul Everett Whitaker [1940] Director/Accountant

Teesside Industrial Controls Limited
Incorporated: 10 August 2005 *Employees:* 23
Net Worth: £496,762 *Total Assets:* £2,348,789
Registered Office: Portrack Grange Road, Stockton on Tees, Cleveland, TS18 2PF
Activities: Wholesale of electronic and telecommunications equipment and parts
Shareholders: Peter Thomas Atkinson; Paul Richard Stevenson
Officers: Peter Thomas Atkinson [1968] Director/Sales Manager; Jamie Dickinson [1977] Director; Paul Richard Stevenson [1968] Director/Sales Manager

Teesside Industrial Solutions Ltd
Incorporated: 2 November 2011 *Employees:* 3
Net Worth: £983,158 *Total Assets:* £1,234,362
Registered Office: Acklam Hall, Hall Drive, Middlesbrough, Cleveland, TS5 7DY
Activities: Other specialised construction activities n.e.c.
Shareholder: Gary King
Officers: Darrin Minto [1969] Director/Welding Inspector

Teesside Insurance Consultants Limited
Incorporated: 6 August 1986 *Employees:* 32
Net Worth: £637,569 *Total Assets:* £1,447,194
Registered Office: 2 Kingfisher Court, Kingfisher Way, Bowesfield Park, Stockton on Tees, Cleveland, TS18 3EX
Activities: Activities of insurance agents and brokers
Parent: Erimus Holdings Teesside Limited
Officers: Christine Nolan, Secretary; Paul James Davison [1973] Director; Shaun David Edward Hughes [1962] Director; Ian David Miller [1981] Director/Insurance Broker; Scott Stephen Pinnell [1976] Director

Teesside Learning Trust
Incorporated: 10 March 2010 *Employees:* 266
Net Worth: £35,188,000 *Total Assets:* £39,141,000
Registered Office: Freebrough Academy, Linden Road, Brotton, Saltburn-by-the-Sea, N Yorks, TS12 2SJ
Activities: General secondary education
Officers: Jonathan Madoc Anthony [1956] Director/Chief Education Officer; John Baker [1946] Director; Kelly Britton-Hawes [1985] Director/Careers Education Lead Officer; Reverend Adam Gaunt [1979] Director/Reverend; Linda Halbert [1959] Director/Chief Executive; Andrew David Haslam [1971] Director/Insolvency Practitioner; Rachel Clare Price [1971] Director/Property, Facilities Solution & Compliance Manager; Martin Walker [1983] Director/Finance Manager; Patricia White [1952] Director

Teesside Pain Management Limited
Incorporated: 8 April 2010 *Employees:* 1
Net Worth: £549,001 *Total Assets:* £966,443
Registered Office: c/o Joseph Miller & Co, Floor A, Milburn House, Dean Street, Newcastle upon Tyne, NE1 1LE
Activities: Other human health activities
Shareholders: Sujata Gulve; Dr Ashish Pralhad Gulve
Officers: Dr Ashish Pralhad Gulve [1968] Director; Sujata Gulve [1973] Director

Teesside Precision Engineering Ltd
Incorporated: 30 December 2009
Net Worth: £1,123,876 *Total Assets:* £1,302,007
Registered Office: Teesside Precision Engineering Ltd, Skippers Lane Industrial Estate, Middlesbrough, Cleveland, TS6 6HA
Activities: Machining
Major Shareholder: David James Dean
Officers: David Dean, Secretary; David James Dean [1972] Managing Director; Sacha Dean [1971] Director

Teesside Properties (2) Limited
Incorporated: 20 December 1993
Net Worth: £963,224 *Total Assets:* £1,391,158
Registered Office: 9 Stephenson Street, Thornaby, Cleveland, TS17 6AL
Activities: Other letting and operating of own or leased real estate
Shareholders: Philip Arthur Thompson; Dr Stephen Anthony Thompson
Officers: Susan Evelyn Thompson, Secretary; Philip Arthur Thompson [1945] Director

Teesside Properties Limited
Incorporated: 22 September 1993
Net Worth: £618,628 *Total Assets:* £1,245,885
Registered Office: 9 Stephenson Street, Thornaby, Cleveland, TS17 6AL
Activities: Other letting and operating of own or leased real estate
Shareholders: Matthew Philip Thompson; Katie Jane Thompson
Officers: Susan Evelyn Thompson, Secretary; Philip Arthur Thompson [1945] Director

Teesside Transport Commercial Services Limited
Incorporated: 4 November 1971
Net Worth: £2,569,406 *Total Assets:* £4,700,234
Registered Office: 1a Bolckow Road, Grangetown, Middlesbrough, Cleveland, TS6 7BN
Activities: Freight transport by road
Shareholder: Richard Adrian Fox
Officers: David Ballantyne Fox [1977] Director; Richard Adrian Fox [1964] Director/Haulage Contractor

Teesside Windfarm Limited
Incorporated: 26 September 2008
Net Worth: £109,697,000 *Total Assets:* £289,017,984
Registered Office: Alexander House, 1 Mandarin Road, Rainton Bridge Business Park, Houghton-le-Spring, Co Durham, DH4 5RA
Activities: Production of electricity
Parent: EDF Energy Renewables Holdings Limited
Officers: Susan Elizabeth Lind, Secretary; Matthieu Thomas Hue [1975] Director [French]; Hassaan Majid [1968] Director

Tekmar Energy Limited
Incorporated: 27 June 2007 *Employees:* 102
Net Worth: £13,823,000 *Total Assets:* £19,866,000
Registered Office: Unit 1 Park 2000, Millennium Way, Aycliffe Business Park, Newton Aycliffe, Co Durham, DL5 6AR
Activities: Other manufacturing n.e.c.
Parent: Tekmar Holdings Limited
Officers: Russell Edmondson [1978] Operations Director; Sue Hurst [1966] Finance Director; Alasdair MacDonald [1965] Director/Chairman; James Thomas Ritchie-Bland [1990] Director; Terence Henry Sheldrake [1963] Director

Tekmar Holdings Limited
Incorporated: 1 August 2011 *Employees:* 6
Net Worth Deficit: £20,163,000 *Total Assets:* £28,179,000
Registered Office: Unit 1 Park 2000, Millennium Way, Aycliffe Business Park, Newton Aycliffe, Co Durham, DL5 6AR
Activities: Activities of head offices
Parent: Tekmar Limited
Officers: Sue Hurst [1966] Finance Director; Alasdair MacDonald [1965] Director/Chairman; James Thomas Ritchie-Bland [1990] Director/Operation Manager

Tekmar Limited
Incorporated: 19 August 2011 *Employees:* 113
Net Worth Deficit: £13,205,000 *Total Assets:* £31,411,000
Registered Office: Unit 1 Park 2000, Millennium Way, Aycliffe Business Park, Newton Aycliffe, Co Durham, DL5 6AR
Activities: Activities of head offices
Parent: Tekmar Group PLC
Officers: Sue Hurst [1966] Finance Director; Alasdair MacDonald [1965] Director/Chairman; James Thomas Ritchie-Bland [1990] Director/Operations Manager

Temp-Team Limited
Incorporated: 15 January 1987 *Employees:* 29
Net Worth: £637,467 *Total Assets:* £1,671,958
Registered Office: Yours Business Network, Delta Bank Road, Metro Riverside Park, Gateshead, Tyne & Wear, NE11 9DJ
Activities: Temporary employment agency activities
Parent: Juhler Holding AS
Officers: Sandra May Kennedy, Secretary; Christopher William Bone [1979] Managing Director; Rachel Louise Young [1977] Operations Director

Malcolm Tempest Limited
Incorporated: 15 January 1970 *Employees:* 21
Net Worth Deficit: £6,091 *Total Assets:* £848,437
Registered Office: High Parks, Newton-le-Willows, Bedale, N Yorks, DL8 1TP
Activities: Unlicenced restaurants and cafes
Major Shareholder: Malcolm Tempest
Officers: Ann Margaret Wheatley, Secretary; Malcolm Tempest [1947] Director/Architect; Ann Margaret Wheatley [1941] Director/Secretary

Templeman Retailing and Vending Limited
Incorporated: 3 July 2008 *Employees:* 106
Net Worth: £3,697,491 *Total Assets:* £8,193,989
Registered Office: c/o Templeman Retailing and Vending Limited, Earlsway, Team Valley Trading Estate, Gateshead, Tyne & Wear, NE11 0RQ
Activities: Other service activities n.e.c.
Major Shareholder: Wendy Margaret Templeman
Officers: Kevin Templeman [1989] Director; Wendy Margaret Templeman [1965] Director

Templeman Trading Limited
Incorporated: 2 April 2008 *Employees:* 106
Net Worth: £5,959,365 *Total Assets:* £10,809,070
Registered Office: c/o Templeman Retailing and Vending Limited, Earlsway, Team Valley Trading Estate, Gateshead, Tyne & Wear, NE11 0RQ
Activities: Activities of other holding companies n.e.c.
Major Shareholder: Wendy Margaret Templeman
Officers: Wendy Margaret Templeman, Secretary; Kevin Templeman [1989] Director; Wendy Margaret Templeman [1965] Director; William Neil Templeman [1962] Managing Director

Templeton LPA Limited
Incorporated: 18 February 2008 *Employees:* 24
Net Worth: £555,849 *Total Assets:* £1,005,591
Registered Office: Newcastle House, Albany Court, Newcastle Business Park, Newcastle upon Tyne, NE4 7YB
Activities: Management of real estate on a fee or contract basis
Parent: First Complete Ltd
Officers: Sapna Bedi FitzGenerald, Secretary; Helen Elizabeth Buck [1960] Director; David James Burgess [1953] Director; Adam Robert Castleton [1964] Director; Paul Hardy [1976] Director; James Charles McAuley [1954] Director

Tendercrave Limited
Incorporated: 12 November 1997 *Employees:* 2
Net Worth: £1,002,386 *Total Assets:* £1,266,530
Registered Office: Sterling House, Brunswick Industrial Estate, Wideopen, Newcastle upon Tyne, NE13 7BA
Activities: Sale of new cars and light motor vehicles
Major Shareholder: Brian Stanners
Officers: Brian Stanners [1946] Director/Motor Engineer

Tenmanor Limited
Incorporated: 20 February 1985
Net Worth: £819,890 *Total Assets:* £821,638
Registered Office: c/o Ward Hadaway Solicitors, Sandgate House, 102 Quayside, Newcastle upon Tyne, NE1 3DX
Activities: Other business support service activities n.e.c.
Shareholders: Nicholas James Scullion; Dorothy Neilan Scullion
Officers: Dorothy Neilan Scullion, Secretary; Dorothy Neilan Scullion [1947] Director; Nicholas James Scullion [1947] Director/Solicitor

Tennant Street Medical Practice LLP
Incorporated: 27 March 2013
Net Worth: £258,226 *Total Assets:* £3,609,114
Registered Office: c/o Tennant Street Medical Centre, Tennant Street, Stockton on Tees, Cleveland, TS18 2AT
Officers: Dr Jonathan Berry [1965] Member; Dr Iain Charles Bonavia [1964] Member; Dr Claire Victoria Green [1978] Member; Dr Rupert Noel Smith [1974] Member

Tennants of Yorkshire Antique and Fine Art Auctioneers Limited
Incorporated: 4 May 1988 *Employees:* 97
Net Worth: £5,269,461 *Total Assets:* £11,683,181
Registered Office: Harmby Road, Leyburn, N Yorks, DL8 5SG
Activities: Other business support service activities n.e.c.
Shareholders: Rodney Michael Tennant; Lesley Jane Tennant
Officers: Lesley Jean Tennant, Secretary; Audrey Ann Fall [1954] Director/Accounts Manager; Jeremy Michael Pattison [1974] Director/Auctioneer; Alison Clare Tennant [1983] Director/Personal Assistant; Jane Michelle Tennant [1987] Director/Personal Assistant; Lesley Jean Tennant [1954] Director/Company Secretary; Rodney Michael Tennant [1947] Director/Auctioneer and Valuer; Caroline Louise Thomas [1981] Director/Accountant

Tesmonard Europe Limited
Incorporated: 19 March 1999 *Employees:* 14
Net Worth: £2,368,687 *Total Assets:* £2,430,258
Registered Office: 136 Fowler Street, South Shields, Tyne & Wear, NE33 1PZ
Activities: Other activities of employment placement agencies
Shareholders: Terence James Kane; Thomas Leonard Sullivan
Officers: Terence James Kane, Secretary; Terence James Kane [1959] Director; Thomas Leonard Sullivan [1955] Director; Raymond Turnbull [1954] Director

Testerworld Limited
Incorporated: 10 April 1986 *Employees:* 513
Net Worth: £15,521,000 *Total Assets:* £60,638,000
Registered Office: 7 Regents Drive, Prudhoe, Northumberland, NE42 6PX
Activities: Wholesale of pharmaceutical goods
Parent: Calmband Limited
Officers: Mark Gulliford [1969] Director; David Horry [1964] Director/Chairman; Leslie King [1958] Director/Sales Manager; Haydn Peter Smith [1966] Group IT Director; Derek Andrew Wilson [1964] Director/Chartered Accountant

Tew Engineering Limited
Incorporated: 18 September 1973 *Employees:* 63
Net Worth: £10,146,347 *Total Assets:* £11,885,437
Registered Office: 5 Osborne Terrace, Jesmond, Newcastle upon Tyne, NE2 1SQ
Activities: Manufacture of other special-purpose machinery n.e.c.
Parent: Tew Holdings 2008 Limited
Officers: Peter David Vaughan Jones [1966] Director; John Francis Kasel [1965] Director [American]; Suzanne Roberts [1974] Director; Neil Sheffield [1972] Director

Tew Holdings (2012) Limited
Incorporated: 15 October 2012 *Employees:* 4
Net Worth: £3,422,947 *Total Assets:* £4,308,390
Registered Office: 5 Osborne Terrace, Jesmond, Newcastle upon Tyne, NE2 1SQ
Activities: Manufacture of other electrical equipment
Parent: L.B. Foster Rail Technologies (UK) Limited
Officers: Peter David Vaughan Jones [1966] Director; John Francis Kasel [1965] Director [American]; Suzanne Roberts [1974] Director

Teward Bros Ltd
Incorporated: 3 February 2000 *Employees:* 49
Net Worth: £2,566,697 *Total Assets:* £6,135,980
Registered Office: New View, Staindrop, Barnard Castle, Co Durham, DL2 3JT
Activities: Demolition
Major Shareholder: Jeffrey Gilbert Teward
Officers: Ruth Teward, Secretary/Farmer; Jeffrey Gilbert Teward [1969] Director/Contractor

Texon (Newco 2) Ltd
Incorporated: 11 January 2005
Net Worth Deficit: £34,965,000 *Total Assets:* £4,635,000
Registered Office: Skelton Industrial Estate, Skelton, Saltburn-by-the-Sea, N Yorks, TS12 2LH
Activities: Activities of head offices
Parent: Texon International Group Limited
Officers: Gary Ian Hollins [1966] Director/Operations Manager; Emma Richardson [1970] Director; Andrew Richard Stansbie [1966] Director/Accountant

Texon International Group Limited
Incorporated: 11 January 2005
Net Worth: £3,403,000 *Total Assets:* £24,638,000
Registered Office: Skelton Industrial Estate, Skelton, Saltburn-by-the-Sea, N Yorks, TS12 2LH
Activities: Activities of head offices
Parent: Torque Group International Wealth Limited
Officers: Hon Yin Wilson Lai [1987] Director/Investment Manager [Chinese]; Wing Yee Agnes Lee [1971] Director [Chinese]; Bruno Paul Yves Ghislain Seghin [1957] Director [Belgian]; Raphael Jules L. Timsonet [1970] Director [Belgian]; Jelle Adrianus Gerardus Tolsma [1969] Director [Dutch]

Texon Non Woven Ltd
Incorporated: 15 November 2004 *Employees:* 88
Net Worth: £31,712,000 *Total Assets:* £34,174,000
Registered Office: Skelton Industrial Estate, Skelton, Saltburn-by-the-Sea, N Yorks, TS12 2LH
Activities: Manufacture of non-wovens and articles made from non-wovens, except apparel
Parent: Texon International Group Limited
Officers: Gary Ian Hollins [1966] Director/Operations Manager; Emma Richardson [1970] Director; Andrew Richard Stansbie [1966] Director/Accountant

Texon Overseas
Incorporated: 9 December 1986
Net Worth Deficit: £14,489,000 *Total Assets:* £21,592,000
Registered Office: Skelton Industrial Estate, Skelton, Saltburn-by-the-Sea, N Yorks, TS12 2LH
Activities: Activities of head offices
Parent: Texon (Newco 2) Ltd
Officers: Gary Ian Hollins [1966] Director/Operations Manager; Emma Richardson [1970] Director; Andrew Richard Stansbie [1966] Director/Accountant

TFLX Limited
Incorporated: 10 February 2006 *Employees:* 59
Net Worth: £8,222,171 *Total Assets:* £15,110,840
Registered Office: 2nd Floor, Grainger Chambers, Hood Street, Newcastle upon Tyne, NE1 6JQ
Activities: Manufacture of other rubber products
Parent: Techflow Flexibles (Holdings) Limited
Officers: Bryan Percy Beattie [1932] Director; Kenneth Brian Dargue Beattie [1953] Director; Graham Osmond Clark [1956] Director/Accountant; John Colin Fitzpatrick [1955] Director/Chartered Accountant

TGA Consulting Engineers LLP
Incorporated: 13 June 2007 *Employees:* 40
Net Worth: £815,278 *Total Assets:* £1,025,030
Registered Office: Salvus House, Aykley Heads, Durham, DH1 5TS
Officers: Graeme John Carr [1965] Member; Scott Thomas Graham [1974] Member; Jason Stephen Jobes [1979] Member; Stephen James Olley [1969] Member; David Nicholas Reynolds [1959] Member; Michael Edwin Waugh [1955] Member

TGMgroup Limited
Incorporated: 13 June 2000
Net Worth: £1,434,000 *Total Assets:* £7,141,000
Registered Office: Admiral Way, Doxford International Business Park, Sunderland, Tyne & Wear, SR3 3XP
Activities: Other passenger land transport
Officers: Lorna Edwards, Secretary; Jason Bush [1967] Director; Simon Oliver Loh [1983] Director; Laura Kiri Wakefield [1982] Director

TGT Holidays Limited
Incorporated: 6 September 2002 *Employees:* 13
Net Worth: £475,957 *Total Assets:* £2,231,083
Registered Office: Townfoot Garage, Haltwhistle, Northumberland, NE49 0EJ
Activities: Travel agency activities
Shareholders: Catherine Margaret Sinclair; Andrew John Sinclair
Officers: Catherine Margaret Sinclair, Secretary; Andrew John Sinclair [1968] Director/Tour Operator

Thames Travel (Wallingford) Limited
Incorporated: 21 March 2001 *Employees:* 117
Net Worth: £606,000 *Total Assets:* £4,256,000
Registered Office: 3rd Floor, 41-51 Grey Street, Newcastle upon Tyne, NE1 6EE
Activities: Other urban, suburban or metropolitan passenger land transport (not underground, metro or similar)
Parent: Go-Ahead Holding Limited
Officers: Carolyn Ferguson, Secretary; David Allen Brown [1960] Director; Simon Patrick Butcher [1967] Finance Director; Luke Carl Marion [1980] Director/Chartered Accountant; Philip Richard Southall [1976] Director; Raymond Woodhouse [1953] Director/Engineering

Tharsus Group Limited
Incorporated: 29 March 2012 *Employees:* 202
Net Worth: £4,528,346 *Total Assets:* £13,100,259
Registered Office: Birmayne House, Cowley Road, Blyth Riverside Business Park, Blyth, Northumberland, NE24 5TF
Activities: Other manufacturing n.e.c.
Major Shareholder: Brian Andrew Palmer
Officers: Brian Palmer, Secretary; Brian Andrew Palmer [1966] Director; Peter Allen Sayer [1966] Director; John Sutherland [1955] Director; David Peter Swan [1972] Technical Director; David John Williams [1953] Director/Chairman

Tharsus Limited
Incorporated: 30 October 2007 *Employees:* 128
Net Worth: £3,983,118 *Total Assets:* £11,375,646
Registered Office: Birmayne House, Cowley Road, Blyth Riverside Business Park, Blyth, Northumberland, NE24 5TF
Activities: Other manufacturing n.e.c.
Parent: Tharsus Group Limited
Officers: Brian Palmer, Secretary; John William Lucas [1958] Director/Engineer; Brian Andrew Palmer [1966] Director; David Peter Swan [1972] Director

That LB Properties Limited
Incorporated: 20 June 2003
Registered Office: Verdemar House, 230 Park View, Whitley Bay, Tyne & Wear, NE26 3QR
Activities: Development of building projects
Shareholders: Iain Bailey; Minnie Little
Officers: Minnie Little, Secretary/Director; Iain Robert Bailey [1972] Director/Property Developer; Minnie Little [1962] Director

THDA Ltd
Incorporated: 29 January 2003 *Employees:* 14
Net Worth: £427,262 *Total Assets:* £906,609
Registered Office: Waterloo House, Thornton Street, Newcastle upon Tyne, NE1 4AP
Activities: Engineering related scientific and technical consulting activities
Parent: Parsons Group Limited
Officers: Stuart Marshall, Secretary; Nicholas Mark Beckwith [1973] Director; Stuart Hodgkiss [1968] Director; Conor John Murphy [1965] Director/Structural Engineer [Irish]; Dr Grant Vincent Richardson [1967] Director; Peter Vincent Stienlet [1969] Director; Doug Roy Tidswell [1961] Director; Paul Adrian Tinley [1960] Director; Mark Turner [1965] Director/Structural Engineer

Theakston Estate Company Limited
Incorporated: 6 July 2011
Net Worth Deficit: £5,830 *Total Assets:* £1,290,502
Registered Office: Southlands, The Avenue, Eaglescliffe, Stockton on Tees, Cleveland, TS16 9AS
Activities: Buying and selling of own real estate
Parent: Theakston Estates Limited
Officers: Martin Trevor Corney [1965] Director

Theakston Estates (Mickle Hill) Limited
Incorporated: 16 May 2011
Net Worth Deficit: £20,759 *Total Assets:* £3,323,000
Registered Office: Southlands, The Avenue, Eaglescliffe, Stockton on Tees, Cleveland, TS16 9AS
Activities: Other letting and operating of own or leased real estate
Officers: Jarrod Colin Best [1977] Director; Martin Trevor Corney [1965] Director; David James Shann [1973] Director/Company Secretary; Ian Jacob Waller [1952] Director

Theakston Estates (North East) Limited
Incorporated: 16 February 2011
Net Worth: £1,820,603 *Total Assets:* £2,007,419
Registered Office: Southlands, The Avenue, Eaglescliffe, Stockton on Tees, Cleveland, TS16 9AS
Activities: Buying and selling of own real estate
Parent: Theakston Estates Limited
Officers: Martin Trevor Corney [1965] Director/Property Developer; Ian Jacob Waller [1952] Director/Property Developer

Theakston Estates Limited
Incorporated: 27 April 1981 *Employees:* 6
Net Worth: £15,613,515 *Total Assets:* £34,028,764
Registered Office: Southlands, The Avenue, Eaglescliffe, Cleveland, TS16 9AS
Activities: Buying and selling of own real estate
Shareholders: Ian Jacob Waller; Martin Trevor Corney
Officers: Ian Jacob Waller, Secretary; Martin Trevor Corney [1965] Director; Ian Jacob Waller [1952] Director

Theakston Waller Limited
Incorporated: 16 April 1974 *Employees:* 1
Net Worth: £2,360,144 *Total Assets:* £2,410,004
Registered Office: Southlands, The Avenue, Eaglescliffe, Cleveland, TS16 9AS
Activities: Buying and selling of own real estate
Major Shareholder: Ian Jacob Waller
Officers: Ian Jacob Waller, Secretary; Martin Trevor Corney [1965] Director/Builder; Ian Jacob Waller [1952] Director

Theakston-Laing Limited
Incorporated: 13 December 1978 *Employees:* 4
Net Worth: £987,735 *Total Assets:* £1,271,556
Registered Office: Southlands, The Avenue, Eaglescliffe, Cleveland, TS16 9AS
Activities: Buying and selling of own real estate
Shareholders: Ian Jacob Waller; Martin Trevor Corney
Officers: Ian Jacob Waller, Secretary; Martin Trevor Corney [1965] Director; Ian Jacob Waller [1952] Director

Theatre Leisure Limited
Incorporated: 18 February 2013
Net Worth: £304,169 *Total Assets:* £830,347
Registered Office: 34 Frederick Street, Sunderland, Tyne & Wear, SR1 1LP
Activities: Public houses and bars
Shareholders: David Guy; Lee Robson
Officers: David Guy [1967] Director/Publican; Lee Robson [1973] Director/Property Developer

Theme Bins (International) Ltd
Incorporated: 11 September 1991
Net Worth: £707,218 *Total Assets:* £1,162,917
Registered Office: Nest Road, Felling Industrial Estate, Gateshead, Tyne & Wear, NE10 0ES
Activities: Manufacture of other plastic products
Shareholders: Paul Andrew Hewitt; Terence William Wilson
Officers: Terence William Wilson, Secretary; Paul Andrew Hewitt [1958] Director/Design Consultant; Terence William Wilson [1959] Director/Leisure Consultant

Thermal Insulation Contractors Association
Incorporated: 13 February 1985 *Employees:* 19
Net Worth: £1,815,958 *Total Assets:* £2,227,485
Registered Office: Tica House, 34 Allington Way, Yarm Road Business Park, Darlington, Co Durham, DL1 4QB
Activities: Other education n.e.c.
Officers: Jennifer Rush, Secretary; Karl Bramwell [1977] Director/General Manager; Matthew Edward Broughton [1968] Director; Richard Lewis Cardiss [1980] Director/Executive Operations Manager; Peter Coles [1962] Contracts Director; Roger Alan Doble [1965] Managing Director; Alan Gosling [1956] Director; Simon Roger Jones [1976] Managing Director; Marion Helen Marsland [1968] Director/Chief Executive; Pauline Palmer [1969] Health & Safety Director; James Graham Soady [1954] Contracts Director; Thomas Stark [1961] Director/Engineer; Ian John Tattersall [1964] Managing Director

Thermal Transfer Technology Limited
Incorporated: 9 October 1992 *Employees:* 95
Net Worth: £3,901,555 *Total Assets:* £5,312,342
Registered Office: Hall Dene Way, Seaham Grange Industrial Estate, Seaham, Co Durham, SR7 0PU
Activities: Manufacture of other fabricated metal products n.e.c.
Officers: Iain Pearson, Secretary/Accountant; Stuart John Barnes [1966] Production Director; Derek Hill [1970] Sales Director; Iain Pearson [1957] Director/Accountant; Anders Gudme Thomsen [1960] Director [Danish]; Kevin Tumilty [1985] Director

Thermalmate UK Limited
Incorporated: 6 August 2008
Net Worth: £746,827 *Total Assets:* £1,333,643
Registered Office: Call Hill Farm, Eaglescliffe, Stockton on Tees, Cleveland, TS16 0QU
Activities: Manufacture of other plastic products
Shareholder: Paul David Lawrence
Officers: Amber Lawrence, Secretary; Jamie David Lawrence, Secretary; Amber Lawrence [1993] Director/Printer; Jamie David Lawrence [1989] Director/Printing and Distribution; Joel Lawrence [1987] Director/Printing and Distribution; Paul Lawrence [1956] Director/Promotional Goods; Victoria Lawrence [1960] Director/Promotional Goods

Thermodynamix (Holdings) Limited
Incorporated: 22 June 2004
Net Worth: £731,291 *Total Assets:* £950,605
Registered Office: 3 Princes Park, Princesway North, Team Valley Trading Estate, Gateshead, Tyne & Wear, NE11 0NF
Activities: Activities of head offices
Parent: TDX (Europe) Limited
Officers: Neil Atkinson [1964] Director; Trevor James Marr [1955] Director/Accountant; Mark Steven Prinn [1975] Sales Director

Thermodynamix Thermoforming Specialist Services Limited
Incorporated: 7 July 1999 *Employees:* 104
Net Worth: £4,961,858 *Total Assets:* £16,247,866
Registered Office: 3 Princes Park, Princesway North, Team Valley Trading Estate, Gateshead, Tyne & Wear, NE11 0NF
Activities: Manufacture of other plastic products
Parent: Thermodynamix (Holdings) Limited
Officers: Neil Atkinson [1964] Director; Trevor James Marr [1955] Director/Accountant; Mark Steven Prinn [1975] Sales Director

Thermon (U.K.) Limited
Incorporated: 4 October 1979 *Employees:* 18
Net Worth: £2,432,062 *Total Assets:* £3,733,115
Registered Office: Seventh Avenue, Team Valley Trading Estate, Gateshead, Tyne & Wear, NE11 0JW
Activities: Manufacture of other electronic and electric wires and cables
Parent: Thermon Europe BV
Officers: Jay Carl Peterson, Secretary; John Allison [1963] Director; Jay Carl Peterson [1957] Director/Executive [American]

Thimbleby Farms Limited
Incorporated: 16 February 1996
Net Worth Deficit: £359,988 *Total Assets:* £5,750,857
Registered Office: York House, Thornfield Business Park, Standard Way Business Park, Northallerton, N Yorks, DL6 2XQ
Activities: Mixed farming
Shareholders: Andrea Shelley; Andrew Shelley
Officers: Andrea Shelley, Secretary; Andrea Shelley [1961] Director; Andrew Edgar Shelley [1960] Director

Think Limited
Incorporated: 25 October 2002 *Employees:* 58
Net Worth: £2,077,698 *Total Assets:* £4,778,969
Registered Office: 55 Degrees North, Pilgrim Street, Newcastle upon Tyne, NE1 6BF
Activities: Ready-made interactive leisure and entertainment software development
Shareholders: Tarek Antoine Nseir; Proven VCT
Officers: Anita RajDevelopment, Secretary; Richard James Curtis [1969] Director/Strategy Partner; Natalie Sarah Gross [1971] Managing Director; Malcolm Kennedy Hunt Moss [1959] Director/Venture Capitalist; Tarek Antoine Nseir [1981] Director; Anita RajDevelopment [1974] Director

Think Synergy Limited
Incorporated: 27 April 2004
Net Worth: £253,000 *Total Assets:* £1,639,000
Registered Office: Riverside House, The Waterfront, Newcastle upon Tyne, NE15 8NY
Activities: Financial intermediation not elsewhere classified
Parent: Positive Solutions (Financial Services) Limited
Officers: Darren William John Sharkey [1970] Director/Chartered Accountant [Irish]; Andrew Bernard Thompson [1968] Director

Third Eye Technologies Limited
Incorporated: 20 August 1996
Registered Office: Unit 33F, Number One Industrial Estate, Consett, Co Durham, DH8 6SZ
Activities: Other service activities n.e.c.
Officers: Paul Anthony Smith [1966] Director

J. Thirlwell & Sons Limited
Incorporated: 7 June 1960
Registered Office: Millers Bridge, Swalwell, Gateshead, Tyne & Wear, NE16 3BP
Activities: Other passenger land transport
Shareholders: Ian Arnott Thirlwell; Susan Marion Searl; John Swaddle Thirlwell
Officers: Susan Marion Searl, Secretary; Susan Marion Searl [1954] Director/Secretary; Ian Arnott Thirlwell [1959] Director/Motor Engineer; John Swaddle Thirlwell [1957] Director/Clerk

Thirston Property & Investments Limited
Incorporated: 1 February 2012
Net Worth: £7,448 *Total Assets:* £1,004,985
Registered Office: Bulman House, Regent Centre, Gosforth, Newcastle upon Tyne, NE3 3LS
Activities: Dormant company
Major Shareholder: Stephen Cowell
Officers: Stephen Cowell [1951] Director/Chief Executive; Cheryl Patricia Foreman [1958] Director

Thirteen Properties Limited
Incorporated: 12 July 2006
Net Worth: £12,303 *Total Assets:* £954,705
Registered Office: 17 Wellington Road, Dunston, Gateshead, Tyne & Wear, NE11 9HB
Activities: Other letting and operating of own or leased real estate
Shareholder: Paul Anthony Barrass
Officers: Paul Barrass, Secretary; Paul Barrass [1974] Director/Engineering Assessor; Linda Mather [1965] Director

Thistle Property Developments Ltd.
Incorporated: 12 April 2011
Net Worth: £984,285 *Total Assets:* £1,801,660
Registered Office: Yours Business Networks, Suite B, 7-8 Delta Bank Road, Gateshead, Tyne & Wear, NE11 9DJ
Activities: Other letting and operating of own or leased real estate
Major Shareholder: Derek William Stephen
Officers: Derek William Stephen [1950] Director

Ken Thomas Site Clearance Limited
Incorporated: 29 January 2007
Net Worth: £178,144 *Total Assets:* £1,261,194
Registered Office: The Old Brickworks, Tanfield, Stanley, Co Durham, DH9 9UY
Activities: Other specialised construction activities n.e.c.
Parent: Colton Group Limited
Officers: Marian Teresa Thompson, Secretary; Hugh Finton Colton [1939] Director; Jessie Agnes Colton [1934] Director; Paul Fintan Colton [1964] Director; Marian Teresa Thompson [1963] Director

Walter Thompson (Contractors) Limited
Incorporated: 3 January 1946 *Employees:* 86
Net Worth: £2,518,496 *Total Assets:* £6,975,379
Registered Office: Construction House, Northallerton, N Yorks, DL7 8ED
Activities: Construction of commercial buildings
Shareholder: Susan Bridget Greenwell
Officers: Derek John Greenwell, Secretary; Paul Blades [1963] Director; Derek John Greenwell [1948] Director Company Secretary; Paul John Hammerton [1969] Managing Director; Keith Brian Noddings [1972] Finance Director; Richard Andrew Salt [1970] Commercial Director; Graham Michael Shepherd [1974] Director

Edward Thompson (Printers) Limited
Incorporated: 21 December 1962 *Employees:* 72
Net Worth: £3,218,332 *Total Assets:* £13,625,583
Registered Office: Sheepfolds Industrial Estate, Richmond Street, Sunderland, Tyne & Wear, SR5 1BQ
Activities: Printing n.e.c.
Shareholders: Patrick Gerard Cronin; Philip John Cronin
Officers: Morven Sheridan Cronin, Secretary; David Christopher Bate [1965] Director; Patrick Gerard Cronin [1965] Director; Philip John Cronin [1964] Director

W. & M. Thompson (Quarries) Limited
Incorporated: 11 November 1975 *Employees:* 42
Net Worth: £4,492,573 *Total Assets:* £10,729,145
Registered Office: Princess Way, Low Prudhoe, Northumberland, NE42 6PL
Activities: Operation of gravel and sand pits; mining of clays and kaolin
Major Shareholder: John Thompson
Officers: John Thompson, Secretary; John Hedley Burdon [1958] Director; Frank William Hurst [1955] Director/Company Accountant; John Thompson [1966] Director/Contracts Manager; John Thompson [1942] Director/Haulage Contractor

Thompson (Wholesale Meat) Limited
Incorporated: 29 January 1993 *Employees:* 41
Net Worth: £1,496,428 *Total Assets:* £2,041,420
Registered Office: Marshall Green Abattoir, Witton-le-Wear, Bishop Auckland, Co Durham, DL14 0AQ
Activities: Processing and preserving of meat
Shareholders: Mark Thompson; John Thompson
Officers: John Thompson, Secretary; John Thompson [1947] Director/Farmer; Mark Thompson [1974] Director/Manager

Thompson Bros (South Shields) Limited
Incorporated: 18 August 1936
Net Worth: £1,272,220 *Total Assets:* £1,291,039
Registered Office: 106 Fowler Street, South Shields, Tyne & Wear, NE33 1PZ
Activities: Retail sale of electrical household appliances in specialised stores
Major Shareholder: Charles Timothy Allinson
Officers: Charles Timothy Allinson, Secretary; Charles Timothy Allinson [1961] Managing Director

Thompson Contracts Limited
Incorporated: 15 December 1989 *Employees:* 35
Net Worth: £533,450 *Total Assets:* £1,439,177
Registered Office: Unit A, Site 1, Cold Hesledon Industrial Estate, Seaham, Co Durham, SR7 8ST
Activities: Other manufacturing n.e.c.
Major Shareholder: Alan Robson
Officers: Lesley Robson, Secretary; Alan Robson [1959] Director/Contract Furnisher; Lesley Robson [1960] Director

S.M.Thompson Limited
Incorporated: 11 October 1950 *Employees:* 27
Net Worth: £2,338,811 *Total Assets:* £3,079,537
Registered Office: Marathon Works, Dormor Way, South Bank, Middlesbrough, Cleveland, TS6 6XH
Activities: Non-specialised wholesale trade
Major Shareholder: Howard Leslie Thompson
Officers: Harvey James Thompson [1977] Director; Holly Joanne Thompson [1979] Director; Howard Leslie Thompson [1947] Director/Steel Merchant

Thompson Power Tool Services UK Ltd
Incorporated: 30 March 2007 *Employees:* 64
Net Worth: £312,075 *Total Assets:* £1,561,350
Registered Office: 5 Wincomblee Road, Walker Riverside, Newcastle upon Tyne, NE6 3PF
Activities: Repair of other equipment
Shareholders: Adam John Thompson; John Thompson; Linda Thompson
Officers: Mr Tim Luckhurst-Matthews, Secretary; Kristian Lee Simpson [1974] Group Operations Director; Adam John Thompson [1983] Director; John Thompson [1953] Sales Director; Linda Thompson [1954] Director/Accounts Clerk

Thompson Ventures Limited
Incorporated: 20 March 2014
Net Worth: £3,342 *Total Assets:* £1,545,034
Registered Office: Maritime House, Harbour Walk, The Marina, Hartlepool, Cleveland, TS24 0UX
Activities: Other service activities n.e.c.
Major Shareholder: Andrew Paul Thompson
Officers: Andrew Paul Thompson [1962] Director

Garth Thompson Wealth Management Limited
Incorporated: 12 January 2010
Net Worth: £259,854 *Total Assets:* £958,969
Registered Office: Brockencote, Slaley Road, Riding Mill, Northumberland, NE44 6HX
Activities: Financial intermediation not elsewhere classified
Shareholders: Garth McCaul Thompson; Sunniva Hjelmervik Thompson
Officers: Garth McCaul Thompson [1968] Director/Financial Advisor; Sunniva Hjelmervik Thompson [1978] Director [Norwegian]

Thompsons of Prudhoe Holding Ltd.
Incorporated: 6 March 1957 *Employees:* 289
Net Worth: £14,603,167 *Total Assets:* £27,896,028
Registered Office: Princess Way, Low Prudhoe, Northumberland, NE42 6PL
Activities: Other business support service activities n.e.c.
Major Shareholder: John Thompson
Officers: John Thompson Snr, Secretary; Helen Margaret Hillary [1968] Director/Financial Assistant; John Thompson [1966] Director/Contracts Manager; John Thompson Snr [1942] Director/Haulage Contractor

Thompsons of Prudhoe Limited
Incorporated: 19 August 1974 *Employees:* 235
Net Worth: £8,000,938 *Total Assets:* £18,491,542
Registered Office: Princess Way, Prudhoe, Northumberland, NE42 6PL
Activities: Demolition
Officers: John Thompson, Secretary; John Hedley Burdon [1958] Director/Contracts Manager; Frank William Hurst [1955] Director/Company Accountant; Kevin Paul Robson [1962] Director/Quantity Surveyor; Nicholas Derek Shilling [1976] Director/Contracts Manager; John Thompson [1966] Director/Contracts Manager; John Thompson [1942] Director/Haulage Contractor

T.J.Thomson & Son Limited
Incorporated: 30 September 1959 *Employees:* 17
Net Worth: £3,892,733 *Total Assets:* £6,585,073
Registered Office: Stockton House, Grangefield Road, Stockton on Tees, Cleveland, TS18 4AB
Activities: Wholesale of waste and scrap
Shareholders: David Brian Turner; Richard John Turner
Officers: Margaret Turner, Secretary; David Brian Turner [1959] Director; Margaret Turner [1931] Director; Richard John Turner [1970] Director

Thomson Bros (Newcastle) Limited
Incorporated: 11 April 1933 *Employees:* 6
Net Worth: £823,508 *Total Assets:* £1,042,366
Registered Office: Mylord Crescent, Camperdown Industrial Estate, Newcastle upon Tyne, NE12 5UJ
Activities: Other service activities n.e.c.
Major Shareholder: Douglas Sinclair Neill
Officers: Dr Karen Jane Neill, Secretary; Douglas Sinclair Neill [1948] Managing Director

Thomson West Limited
Incorporated: 16 May 1974
Net Worth: £1,087,593 *Total Assets:* £1,239,645
Registered Office: Ground Floor, Finchale House, Belmont Business Park, Durham, DH1 1TW
Activities: Other letting and operating of own or leased real estate
Shareholder: Peter William West
Officers: Philippa Anne West, Secretary; Peter William West [1944] Director; Philippa Anne West [1990] Director/Accountant

Thor Car Parts and Accessories Limited
Incorporated: 28 April 2015 *Employees:* 23
Net Worth: £205,502 *Total Assets:* £1,442,246
Registered Office: Unit 6 & 7 Teal Farm Way, Washington, Tyne & Wear, NE38 8BG
Activities: Wholesale trade of motor vehicle parts and accessories
Parent: Thor Motor Factors Ltd
Officers: David Anthony Harbison [1959] Director; Raj Morjaria [1965] Director; Rajshi Odedra [1952] Director

Thornex Limited
Incorporated: 19 May 2014
Net Worth: £270,396 *Total Assets:* £1,015,925
Registered Office: Wynyard Park House, Wynyard Avenue, Wynyard, Billingham, Cleveland, TS22 5TB
Activities: Development of building projects
Shareholders: Trevor Cartner; Joseph Christopher Musgrave
Officers: Trevor Cartner [1960] Director; Joseph Christopher Musgrave [1965] Director

Thorngate Place Properties Limited
Incorporated: 1 April 2005
Net Worth: £1,735 *Total Assets:* £1,175,799
Registered Office: 118 Coniscliffe Road, Darlington, Co Durham, DL3 7RW
Activities: Other letting and operating of own or leased real estate
Major Shareholder: David Liddle
Officers: David Liddle [1962] Director/Property Developer

Thornley Properties Limited
Incorporated: 31 January 1986
Net Worth: £243,058 *Total Assets:* £1,254,382
Registered Office: Albert House, Albert Drive, Gateshead, Tyne & Wear, NE9 6EH
Activities: Buying and selling of own real estate
Officers: Andrew Francis Craig, Secretary; Andrew Francis Craig [1955] Director/Estate Agent; Ian David Craig [1950] Director/Mechanical Engineer

R. Thornton & Co. Ltd.
Incorporated: 7 September 1992 *Employees:* 35
Net Worth: £761,660 *Total Assets:* £2,219,205
Registered Office: Linton Colliery, Linton, Morpeth, Northumberland, NE61 5SD
Activities: Site preparation
Parent: M.J. Hickey Plant Hire & Contracts Limited
Officers: Jacqueline Hickey, Secretary; Scott Beresford [1953] Director; Thomas Anthony Hickey [1964] Director

Thornton Brothers Limited
Incorporated: 2 August 1996
Net Worth: £1,075,245 *Total Assets:* £3,653,752
Registered Office: North Seaton Industrial Estate, Ashington, Northumberland, NE63 0YB
Activities: Maintenance and repair of motor vehicles
Shareholders: George Thornton; Sharon Thornton; Keith Thornton; Susan Thornton
Officers: Susan Thornton, Secretary; George Thornton [1952] Director/Garage Proprietor; Keith Thornton [1958] Director/Garage Proprietor; Sharon Thornton [1962] Director/Admin/Accounts; Susan Thornton [1958] Director/Admin/Accounts

Thornton Investments Ltd
Incorporated: 3 December 2009
Net Worth Deficit: £807,406 *Total Assets:* £1,041,585
Registered Office: Exchange Building, 66 Church Street, Hartlepool, Cleveland, TS24 7DN
Activities: Activities of head offices
Shareholders: Christopher Scott Agar; Susan Ann Agar
Officers: Christopher Scott Agar [1966] Director; Susan Ann Agar [1961] Director

Thornton Print Limited
Incorporated: 15 February 1993 *Employees:* 28
Net Worth: £1,524,558 *Total Assets:* £2,418,853
Registered Office: North Tyne Industrial Estate, Whitley Road, Benton, Newcastle upon Tyne, NE12 9SZ
Activities: Printing n.e.c.
Parent: DNR Limited
Officers: Doreen Mallen [1947] Director; Scott Mallen [1975] Director; Paul David Thompson [1969] Director/Finance

The Thoroughbred Agency Ltd
Incorporated: 11 February 2003
Net Worth: £55,551 *Total Assets:* £1,218,878
Registered Office: Trenholme House Farm, Osmotherley, Northallerton, N Yorks, DL6 3QA
Activities: Other letting and operating of own or leased real estate
Major Shareholder: Nigel David Tutty
Officers: Karen Joy Tutty, Secretary; Nigel David Tutty [1960] Managing Director; Phillipa Louise Tutty [1990] Director/Secretary

Thoroughbred Homes Limited
Incorporated: 8 November 1996
Net Worth: £467,283 *Total Assets:* £1,665,867
Registered Office: Trenholme House Farm, Osmotherley, Northallerton, N Yorks, DL6 3QA
Activities: Construction of domestic buildings
Major Shareholder: Nigel David Tutty
Officers: Karen Joy Tutty [1964] Director; Nigel David Tutty [1960] Director

The Three Rivers Learning Trust
Incorporated: 7 November 2011 *Employees:* 404
Net Worth: £22,045,420 *Total Assets:* £29,293,344
Registered Office: Time Central, 32 Gallowgate, Newcastle upon Tyne, NE1 4BF
Activities: Primary education
Officers: Paula Jane Reeves, Secretary; Dr Peter Gerard Allan [1961] Director/Chartered Engineer; Karen Margaret Barwick [1964] Director; Paul Stephen Carvin [1957] Director/Property Developer; Amy Chaudhuri [1986] Director/Head of HR; Andrew Forsyth Lister [1965] Director/Local Government Officer; Colin Pearson [1947] Director/Retired; Hilary June Rimmer [1951] Director/Retired; Simon Taylor [1962] Director/Headteacher; Sylvie Walker-Barras [1969] Director/Management Accountant; Reverend Simon James Hithersay White [1965] Director/Rector

Three Tuns Developments Limited
Incorporated: 4 July 2016
Net Worth Deficit: £207,858 *Total Assets:* £6,776,183
Registered Office: Workwear Express, 8-11 Cathedral Park, Belmont Industrial Estate, Durham, DH1 1TF
Activities: Other letting and operating of own or leased real estate
Officers: Andrew John Ward [1972] Director/Developer; Simon John Williams [1972] Director/Developer

Thrift Energy Limited
Incorporated: 5 March 2012 *Employees:* 19
Net Worth: £185,574 *Total Assets:* £1,004,108
Registered Office: Unit 10 Kingsway House, Kingsway, Team Valley Trading Estate, Gateshead, Tyne & Wear, NE11 0HW
Activities: Other specialised construction activities n.e.c.
Shareholders: Derek Brian Campbell; Kenneth Gilbert Wombwell
Officers: Robert Peter Browne [1983] Director/Manager; Derek Brian Campbell [1949] Director/Construction Manager; Joshua Dominic Raffo [1991] Director

Thrower Stone Investments Limited
Incorporated: 27 June 2005
Registered Office: 163 Alexandra Road, Gateshead, Tyne & Wear, NE8 1RB
Activities: Buying and selling of own real estate
Major Shareholder: Joseph Zvi Schleider
Officers: Joseph Zvi Schleider [1985] Director

Thursby Homes Limited
Incorporated: 14 June 2016
Net Worth Deficit: £315,767 *Total Assets:* £2,924,962
Registered Office: Keel House, Garth Heads, Newcastle upon Tyne, NE1 2JE
Activities: Buying and selling of own real estate
Shareholders: Adamson Holding Company Ltd; Tier One Capital Ltd
Officers: Jonathan Mark Prime [1960] Director; Tony Patrick Whelan [1963] Director

Thyssenkrupp Access Limited
Incorporated: 10 April 1974 *Employees:* 139
Net Worth: £20,971,000 *Total Assets:* £26,765,000
Registered Office: Unit E3 Eagle Court, De Havilland Avenue, Preston Farm Business Park, Stockton on Tees, Cleveland, TS18 3TB
Activities: Agents specialised in the sale of other particular products
Parent: Thyssenkrupp UK PLC
Officers: Malcolm Whetton, Secretary; Mauro Augusto Carneiro [1968] Director; Sarah Kane [1978] Finance Director; Andrew Warbrick [1975] Managing Director

TI Geosciences Ltd
Incorporated: 25 March 2008 *Employees:* 4
Net Worth: £416,000 *Total Assets:* £2,841,000
Registered Office: Beaumont House, Beaumont Street, Darlington, Co Durham, DL1 5RW
Activities: Other professional, scientific and technical activities n.e.c.
Officers: Rodney Vincent Norman [1956] Director [South African]; Martijn Schouten [1975] Director [Dutch]; David Alexander Andre Joseph Vander Heyde [1967] Director [Belgian]

Tier One Capital Investments Limited
Incorporated: 25 August 2015
Net Worth Deficit: £64,389 *Total Assets:* £988,662
Registered Office: Keel House, Garth Heads, Newcastle upon Tyne, NE1 2JE
Activities: Management consultancy activities other than financial management
Officers: Stephen William Black [1981] Managing Director; Ian Michael McElroy [1980] Managing Director

Tiger Lifting UK Limited
Incorporated: 18 August 2011
Net Worth: £1,815,307 *Total Assets:* £3,241,138
Registered Office: Bulman House, Regent Centre, Gosforth, Newcastle upon Tyne, NE3 3LS
Activities: Manufacture of lifting and handling equipment
Shareholders: Alice Mary Inglis; David Inglis; Chang-Feng Tsao; Chang-Ping Tsao; Cheony-Sun Tsao
Officers: Alice Mary Inglis [1967] Director; David Inglis [1970] Managing Director; Chang-Feng Tsao [1960] Director [Chinese]; Chang-Ping Tsao [1952] Director [Chinese]; Cheony-Sun Tsao [1957] Director [Chinese]

Tiger T Investments LLP
Incorporated: 7 April 2014
Net Worth: £3,559,810 *Total Assets:* £4,145,114
Registered Office: 4 Osborne Villas, Jesmond, Newcastle upon Tyne, NE2 1JU
Officers: Anthony Ronald Tailford [1967] Member; Melissa Polly Tailford [1969] Member

Tiles Porcelain Limited
Incorporated: 14 February 2007 *Employees:* 19
Net Worth: £1,994,658 *Total Assets:* £2,282,525
Registered Office: Buytiles.Com, Unit 1, off Littleburn Road, Littleburn Industrial Estate, Langley Moor, Co Durham, DH7 8JF
Activities: Retail sale of hardware, paints and glass in specialised stores
Officers: Jason Colling, Secretary; Tracey Bryden [1970] Director; David Colling [1937] Director; Jason Colling [1972] Director; Joyce Colling [1939] Director; Claire Louise Glendenning [1979] Director; Douglas Glendenning [1951] Director; Lynda Glendenning [1953] Director; Paul Glendenning [1976] Director/Manager; Jeanne Rutter [1949] Director; Keith Rutter [1947] Director; Darren Wragg [1974] Director/Manager; Kate Wragg [1982] Director; Mary Olwen Wragg [1939] Director

The Tiling Company (Northern) Limited
Incorporated: 21 May 2008 *Employees:* 7
Net Worth: £657,853 *Total Assets:* £1,128,690
Registered Office: 1st Floor, West House, Redburn Road, Westerhope, Newcastle upon Tyne, NE5 1NB
Activities: Floor and wall covering
Shareholders: Nicholas Simon Burr; Russell Tristan Burr
Officers: Nicholas Simon Burr [1968] Director; Russell Tristan Burr [1970] Director; Christopher Hutton [1955] Director

Tilly Bailey & Irvine LLP
Incorporated: 2 September 2005 *Employees:* 153
Net Worth: £1,409,091 *Total Assets:* £3,040,562
Registered Office: York Chambers, York Road, Hartlepool, Cleveland, TS26 9DP
Officers: John Robert Ellwood [1955] Member; Carolyn Jane Tilly [1966] Member; Martin Leigh Brown [1953] LLP Member; Nicola Jayne Dalzell [1972] LLP Member; Helen Clare Dexter [1971] LLP Member; Mark Harry Ellis [1964] LLP Member; John Bernard Hall [1952] LLP Member; Alison Leith [1971] LLP Member; Craig James Malarkey [1981] LLP Member; Kirstey Maloney [1972] LLP Member; Robert Neil Taylor [1967] LLP Member; John Walters [1955] LLP Member

Timber Plant & Haulage Ltd.
Incorporated: 14 July 1999 *Employees:* 3
Net Worth: £1,600,625 *Total Assets:* £2,358,133
Registered Office: Blackaburn, Wark, Hexham, Northumberland, NE48 3DU
Activities: Logging
Shareholder: Robert Graham Dover
Officers: Graham Dover, Secretary; Robert Baty [1959] Director/Machine Operator; Graham Dover [1960] Director/Machine Operator

Timberway Limited
Incorporated: 10 November 2015
Net Worth: £16,132 *Total Assets:* £1,217,485
Registered Office: Unit 7 Bentall Business Park, Washington, Tyne & Wear, NE37 3JD
Activities: Wholesale of wood, construction materials and sanitary equipment
Shareholders: Christopher Burke; Anthony Ferris
Officers: Christopher Burke [1962] Director; Anthony Ferris [1962] Director

Time Properties Limited
Incorporated: 30 June 2010
Net Worth: £3,580,890 *Total Assets:* £5,635,126
Registered Office: Unit 1 Imperial Food Park, Imperial Avenue, South Bank, Middlesbrough, Cleveland, TS6 6BA
Activities: Other letting and operating of own or leased real estate
Officers: Dr Dissanayake Hitihamu [1944] Director; Naushad Mahomed Ismail Abdoola [1960] Director; Shaukat Alli Moosa [1946] Director [South African]

Timec 1289 Limited
Incorporated: 19 August 2010 *Employees:* 70
Net Worth Deficit: £845,080 *Total Assets:* £4,424,822
Registered Office: 2 Cook Way, North West Industrial Estate, Peterlee, Co Durham, SR8 2HY
Activities: Activities of other holding companies n.e.c.
Parent: Grantham Enterprises Limited
Officers: Kevin Robert Wills, Secretary; Jeffrey Grantham [1963] Director; Michelle Woodward [1971] Director/Chartered Accountant

Timec 1306 Limited
Incorporated: 3 February 2011
Net Worth: £502,829 *Total Assets:* £1,886,018
Registered Office: Lady Stephenson Library, Welbeck Road, Newcastle upon Tyne, NE6 2PA
Activities: Book publishing
Shareholder: Graeme Robert Campbell Nicol
Officers: Laura Vaughan, Secretary; Michael Denis Barker [1976] Commercial Director; Kourosh Manoucheri [1955] Director; Graeme Robert Campbell Nicol [1968] Director/Chief Executive; Malcolm Andrew Vaughan [1961] Director

Timec 1484 Limited
Incorporated: 19 December 2014 *Employees:* 84
Net Worth: £9,953,743 *Total Assets:* £17,098,760
Registered Office: Cleadon House, Cleadon Lane, East Boldon, Co Durham, NE36 0AJ
Activities: Demolition
Shareholder: Gordon O'Brien
Officers: Gordon John O'Brien [1962] Director/Demolition Controller; Michael O'Brien [1967] Director/Demolition Controller

Timec 1526 Limited
Incorporated: 6 November 2015
Net Worth: £20,862 *Total Assets:* £1,032,816
Registered Office: Hadrian Offices, 3 Keel Row, The Watermark, Gateshead, Tyne & Wear, NE11 9SZ
Activities: Other human health activities
Officers: Jasvinder Singh Gill, Secretary; David William Nicholson [1950] Director; Ian Watson [1962] Director

Tiplady Tanker Services Ltd
Incorporated: 28 January 2009 *Employees:* 2
Net Worth: £278,817 *Total Assets:* £754,788
Registered Office: West Roods, Boldron, Barnard Castle, Co Durham, DL12 9RQ
Activities: Collection of non-hazardous waste
Shareholders: Derek Mark Tiplady; Penelope Forster Wilson
Officers: Penelope Forster Wilson, Secretary; Derek Mark Tiplady [1976] Director/Contractor

Tirsul Limited
Incorporated: 24 April 1989 *Employees:* 41
Net Worth: £1,392,581 *Total Assets:* £2,549,500
Registered Office: 91-95 Blandford Street, Newcastle upon Tyne, NE1 3PZ
Activities: Other human health activities
Shareholders: Rajan Malhotra; Rajesh Malhotra
Officers: Darshan Kumar Malhotra [1948] Director; Kusam Malhotra [1951] Director/Administrator; Rajan Malhotra [1986] Director/Hotel Manager; Rajesh Malhotra [1974] Director/Hotel Manager; Tripta Devi Malhotra [1948] Director/Company Secretary

Titan Property (Newcastle) Limited
Incorporated: 6 February 2004
Net Worth: £507,472 *Total Assets:* £1,237,808
Registered Office: 14 Regent Terrace, Gateshead, Tyne & Wear, NE8 1LU
Activities: Other service activities n.e.c.
Shareholders: Mohammed Shahid; Yasmin Shahid; Medina Shahid
Officers: Shahid Mohammed [1969] Director

Titan Trailers Industries Limited
Incorporated: 19 May 2011 *Employees:* 24
Net Worth: £1,008,726 *Total Assets:* £3,125,585
Registered Office: Holden Close, Kingsway Sidings, Middlesbrough, Cleveland, TS6 7AL
Activities: Manufacture of other transport equipment n.e.c.
Major Shareholder: Michael Patrick Kloepfer
Officers: Michael Patrick Kloepfer [1955] Director [Canadian]; Michelle Caralee Kloepfer [1986] Director/International Sales and Special Projects Manager [Canadian]; Sandra Kloepfer [1957] Director [Canadian]

Tivoli Properties Limited
Incorporated: 15 May 2013
Net Worth Deficit: £26,689 *Total Assets:* £783,273
Registered Office: Normanhurst, Westoe Village, South Shields, Tyne & Wear, NE33 3EB
Activities: Development of building projects
Shareholders: Christopher Daniel Bond; Janette Bond
Officers: Christopher Daniel Bond [1962] Director; Janette Bond [1961] Director/Bio Medical Scientist

TLC (Car Care) Limited
Incorporated: 14 August 2003 *Employees:* 511
Net Worth: £302,599 *Total Assets:* £2,823,419
Registered Office: 49 Front Street, Framwellgate Moor, Durham, DH1 5BL
Activities: Maintenance and repair of motor vehicles
Shareholders: Graham Stuart Lucas; Ileen Sives
Officers: Graham Stuart Lucas, Secretary/Car Valeting; Graham Stuart Lucas [1968] Director/Car Valeting; Ileen Sives [1947] Director/Vehicle Valeting

TLW LLP
Incorporated: 13 July 2005 *Employees:* 30
Net Worth: £1,726,923 *Total Assets:* £2,335,641
Registered Office: 9 Hedley Court, Orion Business Park, North Shields, Tyne & Wear, NE29 7ST

TMH Associates Ltd
Incorporated: 12 March 2014
Net Worth: £6,850 *Total Assets:* £807,947
Registered Office: Third Floor, Citygate, St James Boulevard, Newcastle upon Tyne, NE1 4JE
Activities: Activities of other holding companies n.e.c.
Shareholders: Helen Elizabeth Ryder; Teresa Robinson; Mark Corbett Garner
Officers: Mark Corbett Garner [1972] Director/Dentist; Teresa Robinson [1970] Director/Dental Surgeon; Helen Elizabeth Ryder [1967] Director/Dentist

W. Todd (Builders) Limited
Incorporated: 1 October 1998
Net Worth: £1,749,094 *Total Assets:* £1,770,906
Registered Office: B3 Kingfisher House, Kingsway, Team Valley Trading Estate, Gateshead, Tyne & Wear, NE11 0JQ
Activities: Development of building projects
Shareholders: Andrea Smiles; Barbara Stewart
Officers: Vivian Todd, Secretary; Andrea Smiles [1979] Director/Administrator; Barbara Stewart [1984] Director/Administrator

Todd and Cue (RMS) Limited
Incorporated: 10 July 2001 *Employees:* 2
Net Worth: £1,349,994 *Total Assets:* £1,350,000
Registered Office: Kingfisher House, Kingsway, Team Valley Trading Estate, Gateshead, Tyne & Wear, NE11 0JS
Activities: Other business support service activities n.e.c.
Shareholders: Mark Armstrong; Julie Rea; Glenn Stephen Cue
Officers: Mark Armstrong [1972] Director/Insurance Broker; Glenn Stephen Cue [1983] Director/Insurance Broker; Julie Rea [1967] Director/Insurance Broker

Todd and Cue Limited
Incorporated: 22 February 1979 *Employees:* 29
Net Worth: £2,223,512 *Total Assets:* £3,728,841
Registered Office: A2 Kingfisher House, Kingsway, Team Valley Trading Estate, Gateshead, Tyne & Wear, NE11 0JQ
Activities: Non-life insurance
Parent: Todd & Cue (RMS) Ltd
Officers: Mark Armstrong [1972] Director/Insurance Broker; Glenn Stephen Cue [1983] Director/Insurance Broker; Julie Rea [1967] Director/Insurance Broker

Todd Waste Management Group Limited
Incorporated: 25 September 2008 *Employees:* 57
Net Worth: £2,998,323 *Total Assets:* £5,963,408
Registered Office: c/o Yorwaste Limited, Mount View, Standard Way Business Park, Northallerton, N Yorks, DL6 2YD
Activities: Collection of non-hazardous waste
Parent: Yorwaste Limited
Officers: Richard Robert Bate [1964] Director; Alexander Boyle [1970] Finance Director

Todds Highway Maintenance Limited
Incorporated: 8 November 1996 *Employees:* 29
Net Worth: £2,985,513 *Total Assets:* £4,008,790
Registered Office: Henson Road, Yarm Road Business Park, Darlington, Co Durham, DL1 4QD
Activities: Construction of roads and motorways
Shareholders: Graeme Malcolm Todd; Darren James Todd
Officers: Malcolm Todd, Secretary/Director; Claire Louise Todd [1976] Director; Darren James Todd [1967] Director; Graeme Malcolm Todd [1971] Director; Malcolm Todd [1947] Director

Tofco CPP Limited
Incorporated: 1 August 2006 *Employees:* 21
Net Worth: £691,856 *Total Assets:* £1,523,615
Registered Office: Meadowfield Industrial Estate, Ponteland, Northumberland, NE20 9SJ
Activities: Manufacture of electric lighting equipment
Officers: Kevin James Doherty [1971] Commercial Director; David John Hodgkins [1959] Director; Susan Hodgkins [1960] Director; Alison Paice [1965] Director; Noel Raymond Toft [1955] Director

Tokyo and York Limited
Incorporated: 16 February 2009
Net Worth: £750,001 *Total Assets:* £750,001
Registered Office: The Lodge, Gatherley Moor Farm, Gilling West, Richmond, N Yorks, DL10 5LJ
Activities: Activities of head offices
Officers: Joe Mulhall [1966] Director/Clerk

Tolent Construction Limited
Incorporated: 8 December 1989 *Employees:* 415
Net Worth: £14,219,974 *Total Assets:* £68,640,504
Registered Office: Ravensworth House, Fifth Avenue Business Park, Team Valley Trading Estate, Gateshead, Tyne & Wear, NE11 0HF
Activities: Construction of commercial buildings
Parent: Tolent PLC
Officers: Andrew David Clark, Secretary; Andrew David Clark [1965] Director/Chartered Accountant; Andrew Ian McLeod [1964] Director; Paul William Webster [1962] Director/Engineer; John Gibbon Wood [1944] Director

Tolent Homes Limited
Incorporated: 24 March 1993 *Employees:* 2
Net Worth Deficit: £4,575,737 *Total Assets:* £3,863,199
Registered Office: Ravensworth House, Fifth Avenue Business Park, Team Valley Trading Estate, Gateshead, Tyne & Wear, NE11 0HF
Activities: Other letting and operating of own or leased real estate
Parent: Tolent PLC
Officers: Andrew David Clark, Secretary; Andrew David Clark [1965] Director; John Gibbon Wood [1944] Director

Tolent Living Limited
Incorporated: 23 March 2015 *Employees:* 12
Net Worth: £261,806 *Total Assets:* £4,182,909
Registered Office: Ravensworth House, Fifth Avenue Business Park, Team Valley Trading Estate, Gateshead, Tyne & Wear, NE11 0HF
Activities: Construction of domestic buildings
Parent: Tolent Construction Limited
Officers: Andrew David Clark, Secretary; Andrew David Clark [1965] Director/Chartered Accountant; Andrew Ian McLeod [1964] Managing Director; Paul William Webster [1962] Director/Engineer; John Gibbon Wood [1944] Director

Tolent PLC
Incorporated: 30 July 1999 *Employees:* 440
Net Worth: £6,660,000 *Total Assets:* £65,936,000
Registered Office: Ravensworth House, Fifth Avenue Business Park, Team Valley Trading Estate, Gateshead, Tyne & Wear, NE11 0HF
Activities: Activities of head offices
Officers: Andrew David Clark, Secretary; Olivier Alexander Johannes Aebi [1968] Director/Engineer [Swiss]; Craig Anderson [1959] Director/Chartered Accountant; Andrew David Clark [1965] Director; Ian Michael Lawson [1957] Director; Andrew Ian McLeod [1964] Director; Dr Alexander Wolfgang Ospelt [1967] Director/Solicitor [Liechtensteiner]; Paul William Webster [1962] Director/Engineer; John Gibbon Wood [1944] Director

Tolent Solutions Limited
Incorporated: 15 March 2007 *Employees:* 73
Net Worth: £2,775,723 *Total Assets:* £13,085,623
Registered Office: Ravensworth House, Fifth Avenue, Team Valley Trading Estate, Gateshead, Tyne & Wear, NE11 0HF
Activities: Development of building projects
Parent: Tolent Construction Limited
Officers: Andrew David Clark, Secretary; Andrew David Clark [1965] Director/Chartered Accountant; Andrew Ian McLeod [1964] Managing Director; Paul William Webster [1962] Director/Engineer; John Gibbon Wood [1944] Director/Engineer

Tombola Limited
Incorporated: 7 December 1999 *Employees:* 372
Net Worth: £28,293,640 *Total Assets:* £37,188,032
Registered Office: Rose Line Building, Wylam Wharf, Low Street, Sunderland, Tyne & Wear, SR1 2JR
Activities: Other information technology service activities
Major Shareholder: Philip John Cronin
Officers: Alison Jane Cronin, Secretary; Alison Jane Cronin [1964] Director; James Edward Cronin [1989] Director; Michael Andrew Cronin [1989] Director; Philip John Cronin [1964] Director; Robert Adam Cronin [1992] Director

Tomlinson,Hall & Company Limited
Incorporated: 27 March 1954
Net Worth: £1,826,866 *Total Assets:* £2,425,983
Registered Office: Lagonda Road, Cowpen Lane Industrial Estate, Billingham, Cleveland, TS23 4JA
Activities: Manufacture of pumps
Shareholders: John Anthony Keville; Adrian Hall
Officers: Paul Anthony Dixon, Secretary; Allan Marc Dale [1972] Director/Sales Manager; John Anthony Keville [1950] Managing Director and Engineer; Colin Simpson [1961] Director/Sales Manager

Tompkins Investments Limited
Incorporated: 14 December 2010
Net Worth Deficit: £8,333,000 *Total Assets:* £5,769,000
Registered Office: Beaumont House, Beaumont Street, Darlington, Co Durham, DL1 5RW
Activities: Other professional, scientific and technical activities n.e.c.
Major Shareholder: Arthur Charles Tompkins
Officers: Peter Nicholas Holley [1950] Director/Financial Consultant; Angela Rosemary Tompkins [1949] Director; Arthur Charles Tompkins [1947] Director; Sophie Jane Tompkins [1988] Director/Legal Counsel

Tompkins UK Limited
Incorporated: 9 January 2007 *Employees:* 58
Net Worth: £6,335,000 *Total Assets:* £19,790,000
Registered Office: Beaumont House, Beaumont Street, Darlington, Co Durham, DL1 5RW
Activities: Other professional, scientific and technical activities n.e.c.
Officers: Mark Ewart Aldridge [1950] Director/Active Chairman; Angela Rosemary Tompkins [1949] Director; Arthur Charles Tompkins [1947] Director; Jason Edward Tompkins [1974] Managing Director; Nicholas Stewart Charles Tompkins [1972] Director; Sophie Jane Tompkins [1988] Director/Solicitor

H. Tones & Sons Limited
Incorporated: 16 July 1976 *Employees:* 18
Net Worth: £1,216,415 *Total Assets:* £1,788,704
Registered Office: Brenda Road, Hartlepool, Cleveland, TS25 1PE
Activities: Sale of used cars and light motor vehicles
Shareholder: James Tones
Officers: James Tones, Secretary/Managing Director; James Tones [1955] Managing Director; Luke Tones [1990] Director/Manager; Matthew Tones [1986] Director/Motor Dealer

Tong Ltd
Incorporated: 11 May 2012
Net Worth: £59,004 *Total Assets:* £1,050,394
Registered Office: West 2, Asama Court, Newcastle Business Park, Newcastle upon Tyne, NE4 7YD
Activities: Hotels and similar accommodation
Major Shareholder: Tong Zheng
Officers: Tong Zheng, Secretary; Dr Tong Zheng [1980] Director/Investment [Chinese]

Tonks 2000 Limited
Incorporated: 11 May 2000
Net Worth: £962,768 *Total Assets:* £1,394,827
Registered Office: 11 Hunter Road, South West Industrial Estate, Peterlee, Co Durham, SR8 2LX
Activities: Collection of non-hazardous waste
Major Shareholder: Geoffrey Edward Tonks
Officers: Michael Stuart Armstrong, Secretary; Geoffrey Edward Tonks [1956] Director/Workshop Manager

Top Drawer Properties Limited
Incorporated: 30 July 2004
Net Worth: £576,469 *Total Assets:* £937,979
Registered Office: Yoden House, 30 Yoden Way, Peterlee, Co Durham, SR8 1AL
Activities: Residential care activities for learning difficulties, mental health and substance abuse
Major Shareholder: Gerald Phillips
Officers: Christina Lias, Secretary; Generald Phillips [1955] Director/General Builder

Top Line Promotions Limited
Incorporated: 15 April 2004
Net Worth: £133,284 *Total Assets:* £1,573,125
Registered Office: 111 Runnymede Road, Darras Hall, Ponteland, Northumberland, NE20 9HL
Activities: Other sports activities
Shareholders: Steven Taylor; Sheila Taylor; Alfred Taylor
Officers: Sheila Margaret Taylor, Secretary; Alfred Taylor [1949] Director/Security Officer; Sheila Taylor [1951] Director/Secretary; Steven Vincent Taylor [1986] Director/Footballer

Topside Group Limited
Incorporated: 1 July 1992
Net Worth: £847,337 *Total Assets:* £2,030,825
Registered Office: Topside House, Daimler Drive, Cowpen Lane Industrial Estate, Billingham, Cleveland, TS23 4JD
Activities: Other construction installation
Officers: Elaine Caroline Prior, Secretary; Craig Grierson Curry [1975] Director/Operations Manager; Stephen Allen Prior [1970] Director/Draughtsman

Torque Group International Fortune Limited
Incorporated: 22 March 2016 *Employees:* 357
Net Worth Deficit: £1,976,145 *Total Assets:* £117,116,584
Registered Office: Skelton Industrial Estate, Skelton, Saltburn-by-the-Sea, N Yorks, TS12 2LH
Activities: Activities of head offices
Officers: Hon Yin Wilson Lai [1987] Director/Investment Manager [Chinese]; Wing Yee Agnes Lee [1971] Director [Chinese]; Bruno Paul Yves Ghislain Seghin [1957] Director [Belgian]; Raphael Jules L. Timsonet [1970] Director [Belgian]; Jelle Adrianus Gerardus Tolsma [1969] Director [Dutch]

Torque Group International Wealth Limited
Incorporated: 22 March 2016
Net Worth Deficit: £11,038,142 *Total Assets:* £87,985,232
Registered Office: Skelton Industrial Estate, Skelton, Saltburn-by-the-Sea, N Yorks, TS12 2LH
Activities: Activities of head offices
Parent: Torque Group International Fortune Limited
Officers: Hon Yin Wilson Lai [1987] Director/Investment Manager [Chinese]; Wing Yee Agnes Lee [1971] Director [Chinese]; Bruno Paul Yves Ghislain Seghin [1957] Director [Belgian]; Raphael Jules L. Timsonet [1970] Director [Belgian]; Jelle Adrianus Gerardus Tolsma [1969] Director [Dutch]

Total Bolt Solutions Limited
Incorporated: 30 May 2012 *Employees:* 15
Net Worth: £781,812 *Total Assets:* £1,948,540
Registered Office: Total Bolt Solutions Ltd (TBS), John Boyle Road, Southbank, Middlesbrough, Cleveland, TS6 6TY
Activities: Wholesale of hardware, plumbing and heating equipment and supplies
Major Shareholder: Roy Cowie
Officers: Ian Pringle Cowie [1953] Director; Roy Cowie [1975] Managing Director; Clive South [1969] Director

Total Business Computers Ltd
Incorporated: 31 January 1995
Net Worth: £1,228,580 *Total Assets:* £2,087,609
Registered Office: Albany House, East Gateshead Industrial Estate, Albany Road, Gateshead, Tyne & Wear, NE8 3DG
Activities: Retail sale of computers, peripheral units and software in specialised stores
Major Shareholder: Robert Stephen Winter
Officers: Susan Patricia Jones, Secretary; Shaun Christopher Carter [1968] Director/Copier Engineer; Susan Patricia Jones [1963] Director/Company Secretary; Stephen John Thompson [1965] Sales Director; Robert Stephen Winter [1959] Director/Salesman [New Zealander]

Total Communications and Security Limited
Incorporated: 11 January 1993 *Employees:* 18
Net Worth: £167,423 *Total Assets:* £1,075,534
Registered Office: 10 Bailey Court, Colburn Business Park, Catterick Garrison, N Yorks, DL9 4QL
Activities: Retail sale of mobile telephones
Major Shareholder: Christopher James Nichols
Officers: Margaret Elaine Parkington, Secretary; Emma Louise Johnson [1978] Director; Christopher James Nichols [1954] Director/Telephone Salesman; Daniel Robert Andrew Parkington [1982] Director; Margaret Elaine Parkington [1952] Director; Michael James Kenneth Parkington [1979] Director

Total Courier Solutions Limited
Incorporated: 18 December 2003
Net Worth: £939,789 *Total Assets:* £1,068,951
Registered Office: 194 Western Way, Darras Hall, Ponteland, Northumberland, NE20 9NB
Activities: Renting and leasing of cars and light motor vehicles
Officers: Tracey Jane Beswick, Secretary; Tracey Beswick, Secretary; Tracey Jane Beswick [1968] Director; Tracy Marie Harris [1967] Director

Total Electrical Solutions UK Limited
Incorporated: 24 September 2004
Net Worth: £831,921 *Total Assets:* £1,118,225
Registered Office: Meadowlea, Finghall, Leyburn, N Yorks, DL8 5ND
Activities: Wholesale of electronic and telecommunications equipment and parts
Shareholders: Michael David Russell; Sharron Louise Russell
Officers: Sharron Louise Russell, Secretary; Michael David Russell [1972] Director; Sharron Louise Russell [1969] Director

Total Gutter Maintenance Limited
Incorporated: 24 July 1997 *Employees:* 36
Net Worth: £623,923 *Total Assets:* £1,105,383
Registered Office: Suite 4, Mile House, Business Park, Darlington Road, Northallerton, N Yorks, DL6 2NW
Activities: Specialised cleaning services
Shareholders: Susan Margaret Ellis; Keith Ellis
Officers: Susan Margaret Ellis, Secretary/Accountant; Jon Brett Ellis [1977] Managing Director; Keith Ellis [1953] Director/Chairman; Susan Margaret Ellis [1956] Director/Accountant; Samantha Jo Williams [1978] Quality & Business Systems Director

Total Maintenance & Engineering Limited
Incorporated: 13 July 1995 *Employees:* 23
Net Worth: £351,824 *Total Assets:* £786,384
Registered Office: L5, 19 High Flatworth, Tyne Tunnel Trading Estate, North Shields, Tyne & Wear, NE29 7UT
Activities: Other service activities n.e.c.
Parent: Pryme Goup Ltd
Officers: Kerrie Rae Doreen Murray, Secretary; Angus John Gray [1966] Director/Engineer; Murray McKay Kerr [1981] Director; Kerrie Rae Doreen Murray [1983] Director/Chartered Accountant

Total Oynx Limited
Incorporated: 25 August 2011 *Employees:* 6
Net Worth: £3,167,459 *Total Assets:* £6,421,439
Registered Office: Riverview Park, Abbey Lane, Barnard Castle, Co Durham, DL12 9TJ
Activities: Holiday centres and villages
Major Shareholder: Frank Maguire Snr
Officers: Andrew Maguire [1994] Director; Frank Maguire Snr [1969] Director

Total Reclaim Limited
Incorporated: 13 November 2009 *Employees:* 19
Net Worth Deficit: £460,018 *Total Assets:* £842,453
Registered Office: Merchant House, 30 Cloth Market, Newcastle upon Tyne, NE1 1EE
Activities: Other service activities n.e.c.
Major Shareholder: Mark Stephen Salkeld
Officers: Drew Cessford [1992] Director

Total Recycling Services Limited
Incorporated: 12 August 2009 *Employees:* 92
Net Worth: £2,115,000 *Total Assets:* £10,322,000
Registered Office: Lingfield Way, Yarm Road Business Park, Darlington, Co Durham, DL1 4PZ
Activities: Collection of non-hazardous waste
Major Shareholder: Robert Jones
Officers: Andrew Mark Dobson [1974] Operations Director; Alex Foreman [1978] Director; Carol Gee [1970] Finance Director; Barry Jackson [1981] Director/Chartered Accountant; Robert Jones [1975] Director; Ross Smith [1966] Director/Chairman; Susan Woodward [1974] Commercial Director

Total Resources (UK) Limited
Incorporated: 24 July 2014
Net Worth: £911,902 *Total Assets:* £2,559,930
Registered Office: 8 Didcot Way, Boldon Business Park, Boldon Colliery, Co Durham, NE35 9PD
Activities: Other service activities n.e.c.
Shareholder: Leslie Thompson
Officers: John William Smart [1940] Director; Leslie Thompson [1960] Director/Highway Manager

Tourmaster Travel Limited
Incorporated: 21 January 1999
Net Worth: £467,379 *Total Assets:* £1,809,341
Registered Office: Kitty Brewster Bridge, Staithes Quay, Bedlington, Northumberland, NE22 7BS
Activities: Other passenger land transport
Shareholders: John Cooper; Jane Cooper
Officers: Jane Cooper, Secretary/Administration; Jane Cooper [1962] Director; John Cooper [1958] Director/Coach Operator

Towertop Limited
Incorporated: 19 October 1998
Registered Office: St Matthews House, Haugh Lane, Hexham, Northumberland, NE46 3PU
Activities: Other letting and operating of own or leased real estate
Major Shareholder: David Knowles
Officers: Susan Knowles, Secretary; David Robert Knowles [1947] Director/Builder

Town Centre Automobiles Ltd.
Incorporated: 31 March 2015
Net Worth: £750,472 *Total Assets:* £1,517,472
Registered Office: Town Centre Citroen, Ferryboat Lane, Sunderland, Tyne & Wear, SR5 3JN
Activities: Other retail sale not in stores, stalls or markets
Major Shareholder: Stephen Smith
Officers: Stephen Smith [1950] Director/Motor Mechanic

Town Centre Garage (Sunderland) Limited
Incorporated: 26 January 1978 *Employees:* 33
Net Worth: £1,534,525 *Total Assets:* £3,394,799
Registered Office: Ferryboat Lane, Sunderland, Tyne & Wear, SR5 3JN
Activities: Sale of new cars and light motor vehicles
Parent: TCC Holdings Ltd
Officers: Geoffrey Brackenborough [1955] Director/After Sales Manager; Christopher Michael Marshall [1983] Director/Sales Manager; Stephen Smith [1950] Director

Town Farm (Wall) Limited
Incorporated: 11 February 1997
Net Worth: £730,615 *Total Assets:* £792,260
Registered Office: Town Farm, Wall, Hexham, Northumberland, NE46 4DU
Activities: Mixed farming
Major Shareholder: John Dixon Lamb
Officers: Susan Elizabeth Lamb, Secretary; John Dixon Lamb [1949] Director/Farmer; Susan Elizabeth Lamb [1963] Director/Company Secretary

Townglow Ltd
Incorporated: 2 March 2011
Net Worth: £566,647 *Total Assets:* £2,738,889
Registered Office: 5a Station Terrace, East Boldon, Co Durham, NE36 0LJ
Activities: Other letting and operating of own or leased real estate
Major Shareholder: Saleem Hakim
Officers: Saleem Hakim [1969] Director/Manager

Trading North East Limited
Incorporated: 27 November 2012
Net Worth Deficit: £41,906 *Total Assets:* £890,231
Registered Office: Merrifield Hall, Low Coniscliffe, Darlington, Co Durham, DL2 2NG
Activities: Wholesale of waste and scrap
Shareholders: Henry Hartley Ward; Robert Ward
Officers: Henry Hartley Ward [1994] Director; Robert Ward [1993] Director

The Traidcraft Exchange
Incorporated: 10 March 1995 *Employees:* 43
Net Worth: £1,072,000 *Total Assets:* £1,397,000
Registered Office: Kingsway North, Gateshead, Tyne & Wear, NE11 0NE
Activities: Other service activities n.e.c.
Officers: Andrew James Biggs, Secretary; Jennifer Edith Borden [1949] Director/Consultant; Mathew Edmundson [1973] Director; Balram Gidoomal [1950] Director/Consultant; Sarah Elizabeth Hughes [1953] Director/Consultant; Christopher John Moorhouse [1952] Director/Consultant; David Huw Neale [1962] Director; Robin Dean Roth [1966] Director

Traidcraft Public Limited Company
Incorporated: 11 October 1977 *Employees:* 86
Net Worth: £3,136,000 *Total Assets:* £4,518,000
Registered Office: Kingsway, Team Valley Trading Estate, Gateshead, Tyne & Wear, NE11 0NE
Activities: Non-specialised wholesale trade
Officers: Jennifer Edith Borden [1949] Director/Consultant; Mathew Edmundson [1973] Director; Balram Gidoomal [1950] Director/Consultant; Sarah Elizabeth Hughes [1953] Director/Consultant; Christopher John Moorhouse [1952] Director/Consultant; David Huw Neale [1962] Director; Robin Dean Roth [1966] Director

Training and Development Resource Limited
Incorporated: 23 February 1996 *Employees:* 74
Net Worth: £1,445,869 *Total Assets:* £2,607,530
Registered Office: Q1 Quorum Business Park, Benton Lane, Newcastle upon Tyne, NE12 8EX
Activities: Other education n.e.c.
Officers: Xue Li, Secretary; Tracey Ann Bowman [1963] Director/Human Resources Manager; Lawrence Joseph Brown [1955] Director; Ronald Dodd [1937] Director/Group Consultant (Engineering); Barrie Stuart Hensby [1952] Director; David Trotter [1944] Director/Consultant; Ian Young [1957] Managing Director

Training Support for Industry Limited
Incorporated: 23 January 2006 *Employees:* 7
Net Worth: £319,219 *Total Assets:* £947,050
Registered Office: Easington Lea Farm, Easington Colliery, Peterlee, Co Durham, SR8 3UP
Activities: Other business support service activities n.e.c.
Shareholders: David Robinson; Lisa Jane Robinson; Stephen John Robinson; Elizabeth Rosemary Robinson
Officers: Elizabeth Rosemary Robinson, Secretary; David Robinson [1955] Director; Elizabeth Rosemary Robinson [1959] Company Secretary/Director; Lisa Jane Robinson [1982] Director/Training Support

Transcare Solutions Limited
Incorporated: 12 September 2000 *Employees:* 60
Net Worth: £473,000 *Total Assets:* £2,329,000
Registered Office: Arriva PLC, 1 Admiral Way, Doxford International Business Park, Sunderland, Tyne & Wear, SR3 3XP
Activities: Non-life insurance
Parent: Arriva UK Bus Holdings Limited
Officers: Lorna Edwards, Secretary; Lorna Edwards [1984] Director; Peter Simon Youel [1967] Director

Transcend Bloodstock Limited Liability Partnership
Incorporated: 24 June 2004
Net Worth: £2,925,142 *Total Assets:* £2,926,951
Registered Office: Nelson House, The Fleming Business Centre, Jesmond, Newcastle upon Tyne, NE2 3AE
Officers: Andrea Wylie [1972] Member; Andrew William Graham Wylie [1959] Member

Transend Solutions Limited
Incorporated: 1 March 2002 *Employees:* 29
Net Worth: £1,211,792 *Total Assets:* £3,602,209
Registered Office: 9 Chapell Lane South, Wynyard Park Business Village, Wynyard, Cleveland, TS22 5FG
Activities: Business and domestic software development
Shareholders: Elaine Cook; David Anthony Cook
Officers: Paul Nicholas Janes, Secretary; Stephen Brailsford [1965] Software Development Director; David Anthony Cook [1962] Director; Elaine Cook [1963] Director; Paul Nicholas Janes [1962] Director; Victoria Anne Janes [1963] Director; Anthony Rafe Munro-Martin [1962] Director/Computer Software

Transped Limited
Incorporated: 18 July 1997 *Employees:* 20
Net Worth: £744,323 *Total Assets:* £2,698,037
Registered Office: South Harbour, Blyth, Northumberland, NE24 3PB
Activities: Service activities incidental to water transportation
Parent: Blyth Harbour Commission
Officers: Karen Maria Johnson, Secretary; Christopher Hill [1960] Sales Director; Martin Lawlor [1964] Director/Chief Executive; Oran Kenneth Hindhaugh Robson [1969] Director/Chartered Accountant; Alan Stewart Todd [1970] Director/Engineer

Travelsure Coaches Limited
Incorporated: 23 July 2013 *Employees:* 40
Net Worth: £208,607 *Total Assets:* £2,068,770
Registered Office: T/A Travelsure, Station Road, Belford, Northumberland, NE70 7DT
Activities: Operation of bus and coach passenger facilities at bus and coach stations
Officers: Amy Miller [1982] Director; Barrie Patterson [1954] Director; Karen Patterson [1955] Director; Mark Patterson [1976] Director

Treatview Limited
Incorporated: 23 September 1983 *Employees:* 32
Net Worth: £1,211,219 *Total Assets:* £3,151,611
Registered Office: 19 Market Place, Bedlington, Northumberland, NE22 5TN
Activities: Gambling and betting activities
Major Shareholder: Stephen Overs
Officers: Stephen Overs [1964] Director/Amusement Caterer

Treeview Properties Limited
Incorporated: 22 November 2000
Net Worth: £369,528 *Total Assets:* £840,456
Registered Office: 53 The Broadway, North Shields, Tyne & Wear, NE30 2LL
Activities: Buying and selling of own real estate
Major Shareholder: Philip Henderson
Officers: Philip Henderson, Secretary; Mark David Henderson [1977] Director/Network Rail; Philip Henderson [1950] Director of Property Companies

Trend International Group Limited
Incorporated: 15 August 1979 *Employees:* 55
Net Worth: £1,346,335 *Total Assets:* £3,309,890
Registered Office: Trend House, Mylord Crescent, Camperdown Industrial Estate, Killingworth, Newcastle upon Tyne, NE12 5RF
Activities: Other manufacturing n.e.c.
Major Shareholder: John-Paul Cowan
Officers: Sarah Jane Kay Cowan, Secretary; John-Paul Cowan [1975] Managing Director

Trend International Holdings Limited
Incorporated: 6 February 2008 *Employees:* 4
Net Worth: £424,403 *Total Assets:* £765,599
Registered Office: Trend House, Mylord Crescent, Camperdown Industrial Estate, Killingworth, Newcastle upon Tyne, NE12 5RF
Activities: Activities of head offices
Major Shareholder: John-Paul Cowan
Officers: Sarah Jane Kay Cowan, Secretary; John-Paul Paul Cowan [1975] Managing Director; Robert Graham Wilson [1953] Director

Trewicks Accident Repair Centre Limited
Incorporated: 11 September 1968
Net Worth: £301,919 *Total Assets:* £863,780
Registered Office: 94/4 Carrmere Road, Leechmere Industrial Estate, Sunderland, Tyne & Wear, SR2 9TE
Activities: Maintenance and repair of motor vehicles
Officers: Roger Andrew Collings, Secretary; Roger Andrew Collings [1961] Director; Robert George Taylor [1957] Director

TRI Construction Limited
Incorporated: 19 November 2015 *Employees:* 8
Net Worth: £681,251 *Total Assets:* £1,759,323
Registered Office: Suite 2e, Building 7, Queens Park, Team Valley Trading Estate, Gateshead, Tyne & Wear, NE11 0QD
Activities: Development of building projects
Parent: TRI Construction Holdings Limited
Officers: Jack Robert Bruce [1987] Director; Graham Urwin [1977] Director; Keith John Wigham [1966] Director/Construction Manager

Tribo - Synthetics Limited
Incorporated: 19 October 2004
Net Worth: £463,568 *Total Assets:* £1,083,468
Registered Office: 1 Belasis Court, Belasis Technology Park, Billingham, Cleveland, TS23 4AZ
Activities: Agents involved in the sale of fuels, ores, metals and industrial chemicals
Shareholders: Sandra Maddalena Teresa Johnstone; Sandra Maddalena Teresa Johnstone
Officers: Sandra Johnstone, Secretary; Jason Johnstone [1974] Commercial Director; Sandra Maddalena Teresa Johnstone [1949] Director/Accounts Manager

Tricogen Laboratories Limited
Incorporated: 22 April 1949 *Employees:* 48
Net Worth: £1,983,073 *Total Assets:* £3,653,428
Registered Office: Whitworth Avenue, Aycliffe Business Park, Newton Aycliffe, Co Durham, DL5 6YN
Activities: Other manufacturing n.e.c.
Major Shareholder: Paul Anthony Garth Sliufko
Officers: Virginia Ann Sliufko, Secretary; Christopher Harry Sliufko [1987] Director; Olivia Mary Sliufko [1982] Director; Paul Anthony Garth Sliufko [1954] Director; Thomas Guy Sliufko [1985] Director/Manager

Tricomm Housing (Holdings) Limited
Incorporated: 30 August 2001
Net Worth: £199,998 *Total Assets:* £9,843,361
Registered Office: Citygate, St James Boulevard, Newcastle upon Tyne, NE1 4JE
Activities: Development of building projects
Shareholders: H I Tricomm Holdings Limited; Infrastructure Investors Defence Housing (Bristol) Limited
Officers: Adam McGhin, Secretary; Helen Christine Gordon [1959] Director; Adam McGhin [1978] Director/Solicitor; Vanessa Kate Simms [1975] Director

Tricomm Housing Limited
Incorporated: 30 August 2001
Net Worth: £39,589,000 *Total Assets:* £136,250,000
Registered Office: Citygate, St James Boulevard, Newcastle upon Tyne, NE1 4JE
Activities: Development of building projects
Parent: Tricomm Housing (Holdings) Limited
Officers: Adam McGhin, Secretary; Helen Christine Gordon [1959] Director; Adam McGhin [1978] Director/Solicitor; Andrew Philip Saunderson [1975] Director; Vanessa Kate Simms [1975] Director

Trims Gym Limited
Incorporated: 23 February 1996 *Employees:* 35
Net Worth: £498,420 *Total Assets:* £1,004,806
Registered Office: c/o Parklands Care Home, New Road, Crook, Co Durham, DL15 8LN
Activities: Other business support service activities n.e.c.
Officers: Tarsem Lal Chopra, Secretary/Director; Tarsem Lal Chopra [1952] Director

The Trinity Catholic Multi Academy Trust
Incorporated: 22 December 2011 *Employees:* 129
Net Worth: £3,090,805 *Total Assets:* £5,031,131
Registered Office: Cardinal Hume Catholic School, Old Durham Road, Gateshead, Tyne & Wear, NE9 6RZ
Activities: General secondary education
Officers: Anne Louise Levy, Secretary; Grainne Magella Bolton [1960] Director/IT Specialist; Peter Cantwell [1983] Director/Solicitor; Christopher Allan Coxon [1955] Director/IT Specialist; Maria Elliott [1968] Director/Headteacher; Martin Gannon [1958] Director/Gateshead Council Leader; Thomas Graham [1943] Director/Retired Civil Servant; Nicholas Simon Hurn [1961] Director/Headteacher; Judith Anne Lawson [1954] Director/Travel Agent; Jennifer Anne Margaret McKeague [1952] Director/Retired Teacher; James Sinclair [1950] Director/Retired Teacher; Michael Leslie Stuart [1939] Director/Retired Deputy Headteacher; Edward Thompson [1953] Director/Teacher

Tripak Ltd
Incorporated: 9 July 1979 *Employees:* 22
Net Worth: £1,260,861 *Total Assets:* £2,388,486
Registered Office: Europa House, Stoneygate Lane, Felling, Gateshead, Tyne & Wear, NE10 0LX
Activities: Manufacture of corrugated paper and paperboard, sacks and bags
Major Shareholder: Avigdor Wolf Gluck
Officers: Deborah Gluck, Secretary; Avigdor Wolf Gluck [1951] Managing Director; David Gluck [1993] Managing Director (Joint); Samuel Simon Gluck [1978] Financial Director

Triple Air-Technology Ltd
Incorporated: 18 November 2009 *Employees:* 8
Net Worth: £224,327 *Total Assets:* £820,425
Registered Office: 41 Colbourne Crescent, Nelson Park, Cramlington, Northumberland, NE23 1WB
Activities: Wholesale of other machinery and equipment
Shareholders: David Alexander Stewart; Eileen Andrews
Officers: Eileen Andrews [1956] Director/Business Development Manager; David Alexander Stewart [1959] Director/Engineer

Triple T Engineering Limited
Incorporated: 6 December 1985 *Employees:* 22
Net Worth: £3,818,707 *Total Assets:* £4,061,168
Registered Office: Hackworth Industrial Park, Shildon, Co Durham, DL4 1HF
Activities: Machining
Major Shareholder: Timothy Paul Tarn
Officers: Marilyn Tarn, Secretary; Marilyn Tarn [1953] Director; Timothy Paul Tarn [1951] Director/Mechanical Engineer

Tripnovel Limited
Incorporated: 15 November 1990 *Employees:* 34
Net Worth: £4,705,679 *Total Assets:* £5,418,524
Registered Office: 4 Sycamore Close, Jesmond, Newcastle upon Tyne, NE2 2TG
Activities: Public houses and bars
Shareholder: Frederick John Plater
Officers: Deirdra Mary Plater, Secretary; Deirdra Mary Plater [1952] Director; Frederick John Plater [1954] Director

Tripsdale Technology Ltd
Incorporated: 18 May 2010
Net Worth: £830,928 *Total Assets:* £832,553
Registered Office: 2 The Acres, Stokesley, Cleveland, TS9 5QA
Activities: Non-trading company
Shareholders: Paul Donald Bartlett; Julie Ann Bartlett
Officers: Julie Ann Bartlett [1960] Director/Retired; Paul Donald Bartlett [1960] Director/Chartered Engineer

TRN (Train) Ltd.
Incorporated: 1 March 2001 *Employees:* 31
Net Worth: £1,488,448 *Total Assets:* £1,676,402
Registered Office: Endeavour House, Colmet Court, Queensway South, Team Valley Trading Estate, Gateshead, Tyne & Wear, NE11 0EF
Activities: Other education n.e.c.
Parent: Skills Training Academy Ltd
Officers: Neil James Ackroyd [1974] Director; Mark Hewitt [1972] Director; David James Taylor [1975] Director/Consultant

Trojan Scaffolding (NE) Ltd
Incorporated: 3 March 2011
Net Worth: £252,236 *Total Assets:* £828,128
Registered Office: Shibdon View, Shibdon Road, Blaydon on Tyne, Tyne & Wear, NE21 5NW
Activities: Scaffold erection
Major Shareholder: Steven James Parker
Officers: Steven Parker [1980] Director

Tropic Properties Limited
Incorporated: 30 September 1997 *Employees:* 1
Net Worth: £3,746,259 *Total Assets:* £7,332,910
Registered Office: 2 Richmond Terrace, Gateshead, Tyne & Wear, NE8 1RN
Activities: Other letting and operating of own or leased real estate
Officers: Judith Fried, Secretary [Swiss]; Jerry Fried [1950] Director [American]; Rachel Iwanier [1981] Director/Property Manager

Trotec Laser Limited
Incorporated: 20 December 2006 *Employees:* 36
Net Worth: £1,965,441 *Total Assets:* £2,873,393
Registered Office: 9 Didcot Way, Boldon Business Park, Boldon Colliery, Co Durham, NE35 9PD
Activities: Wholesale of other machinery and equipment
Parent: Trodat Trotec Holding GmbH
Officers: Martin Dawson Horne [1970] Managing Director; Andreas Penz [1964] Managing Director [Austrian]

Trout Hotels (Cumbria) Limited
Incorporated: 13 October 1988 *Employees:* 56
Net Worth: £3,756,522 *Total Assets:* £5,644,545
Registered Office: 1st Floor Offices, Grandstand Garage, Kenton Road, Gosforth, Newcastle upon Tyne, NE3 4NB
Activities: Hotels and similar accommodation
Shareholder: Nigel John Mills
Officers: Philip Peter Ferguson Upton, Secretary; Shona Marion Jellett [1984] Director/Barrister; Geoffrey Lurie [1934] Director/Solicitor; Nigel John Mills [1958] Director/Chartered Accountant; Alasdair Douglas Upton [1989] Director/I.T.Consultant; Lorna Elspeth Upton [1997] Director/Student; Philip Peter Ferguson Upton [1958] Director/Chartered Accountant

Truck Technics Limited
Incorporated: 1 June 2007 *Employees:* 30
Net Worth: £400,483 *Total Assets:* £1,226,208
Registered Office: Washfold Farm, Moor Road, Leyburn, N Yorks, DL8 5LZ
Activities: Maintenance and repair of motor vehicles
Officers: David James Metcalfe, Secretary; Andrew Philip Metcalfe [1970] Director; Brian John Metcalfe [1966] Director; David James Metcalfe [1964] Director; Kenneth Tyrala [1978] Director/Mechanic

True Potential Adviser Services LLP
Incorporated: 8 March 2007 *Employees:* 37
Net Worth: £17,328,116 *Total Assets:* £17,852,904
Registered Office: Newburn House, Newburn Riverside, Newcastle upon Tyne, NE15 8NX
Officers: Daniel George Harrison [1981] Member; David George Harrison [1950] Member; Mark Henderson [1961] Member; Neil Andrew Johnson [1964] Member

True Potential Group Limited
Incorporated: 15 December 2015 *Employees:* 299
Net Worth: £142,034,000 *Total Assets:* £155,412,000
Registered Office: Newburn House, Gateway West, Newburn Riverside, Newcastle upon Tyne, NE15 8NX
Activities: Financial management
Shareholder: David George Harrison
Officers: Bradford Eric Bernstein [1967] Director [American]; Peter John Coward [1956] Non-Executive Director; Earl William Glasgow [1967] Director; Kyle Adams Griswold [1982] Director [American]; Daniel George Harrison [1981] Director/Business Partner; David George Harrison [1950] Director; Mark Henderson [1961] Director/Senior Partner; Neil Andrew Johnson [1964] Director; George Adam Peebles [1954] Non-Executive Director

True Potential Investments LLP
Incorporated: 29 June 2010 *Employees:* 95
Net Worth: £50,481,788 *Total Assets:* £55,138,200
Registered Office: Newburn House, Newburn Riverside, Newcastle upon Tyne, NE15 8NX
Officers: Daniel George Harrison [1981] Member; Mark Henderson [1961] Member; Peter John Coward [1956] LLP Member; George Adam Peebles [1954] LLP Member

True Potential LLP
Incorporated: 5 December 2012 *Employees:* 212
Net Worth: £10,803,000 *Total Assets:* £18,232,000
Registered Office: Newburn House, Gateway West, Newburn Riverside, Newcastle upon Tyne, NE15 8NX

True Potential Wealth Management LLP
Incorporated: 21 July 2010 *Employees:* 11
Net Worth: £4,437,941 *Total Assets:* £9,965,249
Registered Office: Newburn House, Newburn Riverside, Newcastle upon Tyne, NE15 8NX
Officers: Earl William Glasgow [1967] Member; Neil Andrew Johnson [1964] Member; Hilary Ellen Austin [1966] LLP Member; Peter John Coward [1956] LLP Member; Stephen John Hutton [1962] LLP Member; George Adam Peebles [1954] LLP Member; Neil Rayner [1973] LLP Member; Jamie Allan Sexton [1986] LLP Member

True Solicitors LLP
Incorporated: 22 February 2012 *Employees:* 202
Net Worth: £3,938,536 *Total Assets:* £11,045,120
Registered Office: Percy House, Percy Street, Newcastle upon Tyne, NE1 4PW
Officers: Kieran Magee [1966] Member; Stephen McCourt [1967] Member; Andrew Stephen Milnes [1978] Member

Trumark Properties Limited
Incorporated: 9 September 2008 *Employees:* 95
Net Worth: £2,743,431 *Total Assets:* £5,902,612
Registered Office: Roker Terrace, Sunderland, Tyne & Wear, SR6 9ND
Activities: Manufacture of beer
Shareholders: Mark Hird; Nicola Foster Hird
Officers: Steven Andrew Akers [1981] Finance Director; Nicola Jane Foster-Hird [1972] Director; Jonathan Graham [1974] Operations Director; Mark Hird [1973] Director

Trumeau Limited
Incorporated: 25 January 2007
Net Worth: £1,000 *Total Assets:* £1,925,332
Registered Office: 2nd Floor, Building 7, Queens Park, Queensway, Team Valley Trading Estate, Gateshead, Tyne & Wear, NE11 0QD
Activities: Buying and selling of own real estate
Shareholders: Ronan Keating; UK Land Estates Limited
Officers: Ronan Keating [1977] Director [Irish]; Emilia Keladitis [1977] Director; Alan McEvoy [1966] Director [Irish]; Alan Keith Taylor [1963] Director; Christopher John Whitfield [1964] Director

TS Developments Ltd
Incorporated: 16 September 2005
Net Worth: £879,949 *Total Assets:* £2,085,513
Registered Office: The Imperial Centre, Grange Road, Darlington, Co Durham, DL1 5NQ
Activities: Other activities of employment placement agencies
Major Shareholder: Claire Emma Watson
Officers: Claire Emma Watson [1973] Director

TS Plant Sales (NE) Ltd.
Incorporated: 20 May 2015 *Employees:* 6
Net Worth: £181,898 *Total Assets:* £2,553,615
Registered Office: Millennium House, 49a High Street, Yarm, Cleveland, TS15 9BH
Activities: Wholesale of agricultural machinery, equipment and supplies
Shareholders: Timothy Wilson; James Taylor
Officers: James Taylor [1976] Director; Timothy Wilson [1972] Director

Tsing Hing Limited
Incorporated: 26 April 1991
Net Worth: £1,440,688 *Total Assets:* £2,448,848
Registered Office: 231 Scotswood Road, Newcastle upon Tyne, NE4 7AW
Activities: Non-specialised wholesale trade
Shareholder: Nigel Hin for Tsang
Officers: Nigel Hin for Tsang, Secretary; Janis Shuk Fan Tsang [1959] Director; Nigel Hin for Tsang [1966] Director

TT2 (Holdings) Limited
Incorporated: 20 August 2007 *Employees:* 53
Net Worth Deficit: £66,983,912 *Total Assets:* £267,644,000
Registered Office: Tyne Tunnels, Wallsend, Tyne & Wear, NE28 0PD
Activities: Activities of head offices
Shareholders: Aberdeen Infrastructure (No. 3) Limited; Infrared Infrastructure Yield Holdings Limited
Officers: Guillaume Raoul Fernand Albaric [1975] Director [French]; Michael Andrew Donn [1972] Director/Banker; Charles Andre Paradis [1958] Director/Chief Operating Officer [French]; Andrew Leslie Tennant [1958] Director/Banker; Rachel Louise Turnbull [1978] Director/Asset Manager; Mark Christopher Wayment [1958] Director/Asset Manager

TT2 Limited
Incorporated: 20 August 2007 *Employees:* 53
Net Worth Deficit: £66,983,928 *Total Assets:* £267,643,984
Registered Office: Tyne Tunnels, Wallsend, Tyne & Wear, NE28 0PD
Activities: Other service activities incidental to land transportation, n.e.c.
Parent: TT2 (Holdings) Limited
Officers: Guillaume Raoul Fernand Albaric [1975] Director [French]; Michael Andrew Donn [1972] Director/Banker; Charles Andre Paradis [1958] Director/Chief Operating Officer [French]; Andrew Leslie Tennant [1958] Director/Banker; Rachel Louise Turnbull [1978] Director/Asset Manager; Mark Christopher Wayment [1958] Director/Asset Manager

TTE Apprenticeships Limited
Incorporated: 3 April 2009 *Employees:* 6
Net Worth: £10 *Total Assets:* £1,328,172
Registered Office: Edison House, Middlesbrough Road East, South Bank, Middlesbrough, Cleveland, TS6 6TZ
Activities: Technical and vocational secondary education
Officers: Andrea Preston, Secretary; Ainsley Cheetham [1951] Director/Educational Consultant; Steven John Grant [1960] Group Managing Director; Keith Leslie [1951] Director; Sara Louise Marshall [1972] Group Operations Director; Andrea Preston [1969] Finance Director

TTE International Limited
Incorporated: 25 April 2001 *Employees:* 5
Net Worth: £2,031,988 *Total Assets:* £3,371,466
Registered Office: Edison House, Middlesbrough Road East, South Bank, Middlesbrough, Cleveland, TS6 6TZ
Activities: Other education n.e.c.
Parent: The TTE Technical Training Group
Officers: Andrea Preston, Secretary; John Philip Arbuckle [1954] Director/Engineering Consultant; Steven John Grant [1960] Managing Director; Keith Leslie [1951] Director; Sara Louise Marshall [1972] Group Operations Director; Andrea Preston [1969] Finance Director

The TTE Technical Training Group
Incorporated: 13 March 1989 *Employees:* 121
Net Worth: £677,162 *Total Assets:* £6,963,288
Registered Office: The TTE Technical Training Group, Edison House, Middlesbrough Road East, South Bank, Middlesbrough, Cleveland, TS6 6TZ
Activities: Other education n.e.c.
Officers: Andrea Preston, Secretary; John Philip Arbuckle [1954] Director/Engineering Consultant; Ainsley Cheetham [1951] Director/Consultant; Keith Leslie [1951] Director/Retired; Keith Mutimer [1950] Director/Operations Manager; Lynn Perry [1973] Director/Head of People Transformation

TTR Barnes Limited
Incorporated: 24 September 2001 *Employees:* 3
Net Worth: £1,591,368 *Total Assets:* £1,955,889
Registered Office: 3-5 Grange Terrace, Sunderland, Tyne & Wear, SR2 7DG
Activities: Accounting and auditing activities
Parent: TTRB Limited
Officers: Allan Russell, Secretary; David James Cook [1968] Director/Accountant; Allan Russell [1956] Director/Accountant; John Trevor Thorne [1948] Director

Tudhoe Learning Trust
Incorporated: 26 October 2012 *Employees:* 253
Net Worth: £9,172,738 *Total Assets:* £14,423,274
Registered Office: Tudhoe Colliery Primary School, Front Street, Tudhoe, Spennymoor, Co Durham, DL16 6TJ
Activities: Primary education
Officers: Gillian Dixon Pigott, Secretary; Allison Boustead [1983] Director/Deputy Headteacher; David Bowes [1945] Director/Retired; David Collins [1972] Relationship Director Banking; Vivienne Ingleton [1952] Director/Retired; Mike Simpson [1947] Director/Retired; James Hastings Smith [1964] Director/Executive Headteacher; Derek Turner [1942] Director/Retired; Ivan Whitfield [1963] University Employee (Director of Service Function)

Stephen Tuer Farms Ltd
Incorporated: 10 November 2004
Net Worth: £343,250 *Total Assets:* £3,370,990
Registered Office: Hutton Grange, Hutton Bonville, Northallerton, N Yorks, DL6 2PT
Activities: Growing of cereals (except rice), leguminous crops and oil seeds
Major Shareholder: Stephen Andrew Tuer
Officers: Mary Alleen Tuer, Secretary; Stephen Andrew Tuer [1971] Director/Farmer

Tunstall Developments Limited
Incorporated: 15 July 2008
Net Worth Deficit: £608,314 *Total Assets:* £2,485,630
Registered Office: Bridgend Works, Ryhope, Sunderland, Tyne & Wear, SR2 0NJ
Activities: Development of building projects
Officers: Joanne Elaine Laidler, Company Secretary; Denise Laidler [1962] Director; Joanne Elaine Laidler [1964] Director/Company Secretary; Angela Laidler Hall [1968] Director/Housewife

Tup Tup Palace Limited
Incorporated: 25 July 2008 *Employees:* 131
Net Worth: £2,168,890 *Total Assets:* £2,758,692
Registered Office: 7 St Nicholas Street, Newcastle upon Tyne, NE1 1RE
Activities: Licenced clubs
Shareholder: Aaron Matthew Mellor
Officers: Nigel Holliday [1979] Director; Aaron Matthew Mellor [1970] Director; Chris Penfold [1985] Director/Financial Controller; Matthew Joseph Smyth [1980] Director; Nicholas Mark Woodhead [1974] Director

Turbo Power Systems Limited
Incorporated: 18 December 1992 *Employees:* 112
Net Worth: £2,303,000 *Total Assets:* £7,104,000
Registered Office: 1 Queens Park, Queensway North, Team Valley Trading Estate, Gateshead, Tyne & Wear, NE11 0QD
Activities: Manufacture of electric motors, generators and transformers
Parent: TWC3N Limited
Officers: Charles Rendell, Secretary; Ian Robert Baggett [1972] Director; Dr Nigel Jakeman [1974] Director/Engineer; Carlos Augusto Martins Das Neves [1966] Director [Portuguese]; Charles Ian Rendell [1966] Director/Chartered Accountant

Turboactive Limited
Incorporated: 16 April 1997 *Employees:* 20
Net Worth: £1,688,061 *Total Assets:* £1,888,193
Registered Office: Evolution, Wynyard Avenue, Wynyard Business Park, Billingham, Cleveland, TS22 5TB
Activities: Retail trade of motor vehicle parts and accessories
Major Shareholder: Mark Watson
Officers: Stephen Bush, Secretary; Stephen Bush [1954] Managing Director; Mark Watson [1968] Managing Director

Turbocharger Solutions Limited
Incorporated: 18 July 2012
Net Worth: £862,013 *Total Assets:* £1,731,511
Registered Office: c/o Turbo Solutions, Red Barnes Way, Darlington, Co Durham, DL1 2RR
Activities: Wholesale trade of motor vehicle parts and accessories
Shareholders: Timothy Robert Waterson; Tim Waterson Property Developments Limited
Officers: Louise Waterson, Secretary; Louise Waterson [1976] Director; Timothy Robert Waterson [1975] Director

Turkey Mill Investments Limited
Incorporated: 28 May 1997 *Employees:* 8
Net Worth: £9,026,133 *Total Assets:* £21,518,080
Registered Office: Murky Hill Offices, Cow Lane, Middleton Tyas, Richmond, N Yorks, DL10 6RW
Activities: Other letting and operating of own or leased real estate
Shareholders: Adrian John Speir; Ralph Congreve
Officers: Adrian John Speir, Secretary; Ralph Congreve [1953] Director/Chartered Surveyor; Douglas James Lawson [1958] Director/Chartered Surveyor; Katharine Judith Lawson [1962] Director; Thomas Clifford Sheldon [1952] Director/Chartered Surveyor; Adrian John Speir [1949] Director

E. Turnbull & Son Limited
Incorporated: 7 April 1924 *Employees:* 12
Net Worth: £814,543 *Total Assets:* £1,606,134
Registered Office: Albion Road, North Shields, Tyne & Wear, NE29 0HE
Activities: Funeral and related activities
Shareholders: James Henry Turnbull; Jonathan Turnbull
Officers: Barbara Anne Turnbull, Secretary; Amanda Jane Broadhead [1960] Director; James Henry Turnbull [1934] Funeral Director; Jonathan James Turnbull [1960] Director/Chartered Accountant

Turnbull Family Investments Limited
Incorporated: 20 May 2016 *Employees:* 2
Net Worth: £627,256 *Total Assets:* £38,361,704
Registered Office: Elwick Hall, Elwick, Hartlepool, Cleveland, TS27 3EJ
Activities: Activities of investment trusts
Officers: Peter Francis Riley [1947] Director/Financial Consultant; Geoffrey Turnbull [1946] Director; Sandra Elizabeth Turnbull [1947] Director

VB Turnbull Limited
Incorporated: 6 July 2011 *Employees:* 3
Net Worth: £7,390,675 *Total Assets:* £18,170,320
Registered Office: The Farmhouse, Hedley Hill Farm, Cornsay Colliery, Co Durham, DH7 9EX
Activities: Development of building projects
Parent: Vestbrown Limited
Officers: Donna Ann Rutherford Turnbull, Secretary; Michael Francis Hogan [1944] Director; Alexander John Turnbull [1956] Director

Turner & Wrights Limited
Incorporated: 19 June 1996 *Employees:* 68
Net Worth: £7,225,062 *Total Assets:* £19,230,256
Registered Office: Unit S3, Narvik Way, Tyne Tunnel Trading Estate, North Shields, Tyne & Wear, NE29 7XJ
Activities: Wholesale of sugar and chocolate and sugar confectionery
Officers: Patricia Ada Rice, Secretary; David Leonard Brind [1972] Financial Director; John Frederick Hope [1969] Director; Paul Victor Young [1957] Director/Accountant

Sam Turner and Sons Limited
Incorporated: 18 December 1945 *Employees:* 177
Net Worth: £8,078,578 *Total Assets:* £10,559,353
Registered Office: Darlington Road, Northallerton, N Yorks, DL6 2XB
Activities: Wholesale of agricultural machinery, equipment and supplies
Shareholder: Charles Edward Turner
Officers: John Samuel Turner, Secretary; Benjamin Matthew Turner [1980] Director; Charles Edward Turner [1974] Director/Agricultural Merchant; Charles Michael Turner [1948] Director/Agricultural Merchant; John Samuel Turner [1946] Director/Agricultural Merchant; Mark Samuel Turner [1970] Director/Agricultural Merchant

Turners Fabrications Limited
Incorporated: 19 July 2005
Net Worth: £572,000 *Total Assets:* £1,131,376
Registered Office: Walkerville Industrial Estate, Colburn, Richmond, N Yorks, DL9 4RR
Activities: Manufacture of other tanks, reservoirs and containers of metal
Shareholders: Julie Turner; Peter Anthony Turner
Officers: Peter Anthony Turner, Secretary/Engineer; Julie Turner [1964] Director; Peter Anthony Turner [1962] Director/Engineer

Turnkey Air Conditioning Limited
Incorporated: 24 December 1998
Net Worth: £108,334 *Total Assets:* £2,332,365
Registered Office: Ground Floor, 2 Apollo Court, Koppers Way, Monkton Business Park South, Hebburn, Tyne & Wear, NE31 2ES
Activities: Plumbing, heat and air-conditioning installation
Parent: TKAC Holdings Limited
Officers: Kirstie Swirles, Secretary; Jonathan Reginald Batty [1965] Director; Christopher Stopforth [1954] Director; Mitchell Ashley Swirles [1968] Director

J B Tustain Motors Holdings Limited
Incorporated: 2 February 2010 *Employees:* 129
Net Worth: £1,765,414 *Total Assets:* £11,550,440
Registered Office: 13 Freeman Way, North Seaton Industrial Estate, Ashington, Northumberland, NE63 0YB
Activities: Activities of head offices
Officers: David Storey, Secretary; Brian William Baxter [1968] Director; David Storey [1966] Director; Elizabeth Beatrice Tustain [1947] Director; John Bernard Tustain [1945] Director/Retired

Tustain Motors Limited
Incorporated: 30 July 2009 *Employees:* 106
Net Worth: £1,631,517 *Total Assets:* £6,058,699
Registered Office: 13 Freeman Way, North Seaton Industrial Estate, Ashington, Northumberland, NE63 0YB
Activities: Sale of new cars and light motor vehicles
Parent: J B Tustain Motors Holdings Limited
Officers: David Storey, Secretary; Brian William Baxter [1968] Director; David Storey [1966] Director; John Bernard Tustain [1945] Director/Retired

Tustain Motors Northumberland Limited
Incorporated: 8 December 2015 *Employees:* 13
Net Worth: £22,809 *Total Assets:* £1,875,979
Registered Office: 13 Freeman Way, North Seaton Industrial Estate, Ashington, Northumberland, NE63 0YB
Activities: Sale of new cars and light motor vehicles
Parent: J B Tustain Motors Holdings Limited
Officers: Brian William Baxter [1968] Director; David Storey [1966] Director; John Bernard Tustain [1945] Director

TVG Systems Limited
Incorporated: 29 December 1998 *Employees:* 22
Net Worth: £914,186 *Total Assets:* £1,539,638
Registered Office: 1 Target, Chartermark Way, Colburn Business Park, Colburn, N Yorks, DL9 4QJ
Activities: Repair and maintenance of other transport equipment n.e.c.
Major Shareholder: Graeme Michael Frankland
Officers: Graeme Michael Frankland, Secretary; Graeme Michael Frankland [1958] Director; Claire Freeman Palmer [1964] Financial Director

TVG Telematics Ltd
Incorporated: 7 March 2007 *Employees:* 24
Net Worth: £613,067 *Total Assets:* £1,653,940
Registered Office: 1 Target, Chartermark Way, Colburn Business Park, Colburn, N Yorks, DL9 4QJ
Activities: Wholesale of electronic and telecommunications equipment and parts
Major Shareholder: Graeme Michael Frankland
Officers: Claire Freeman Palmer, Secretary; Graeme Michael Frankland [1958] Director/Automotive Electronics; Claire Freeman Palmer [1964] Financial Director

TVG Vision Ltd
Incorporated: 14 April 2009 *Employees:* 2
Net Worth: £237,268 *Total Assets:* £1,937,494
Registered Office: Unit 1 Target, Chartermark Way, Colburn Business Park, Catterick Garrison, N Yorks, DL9 4QJ
Activities: Non-specialised wholesale trade
Major Shareholder: Graeme Michael Frankland
Officers: Claire Palmer, Secretary; Graeme Michael Frankland [1958] Director; Claire Freeman Palmer [1964] Director

Tweedmouth House Care Limited
Incorporated: 18 November 2002
Net Worth: £874,576 *Total Assets:* £1,069,360
Registered Office: Douglas Home and Company Ltd, 19 Fenkle Street, Alnwick, Northumberland, NE66 1HW
Activities: Other human health activities
Shareholders: Christopher Thomlinson; Patricia Thomlinson
Officers: Patricia Thomlinson, Secretary/Registered General Nurse; Christopher Thomlinson [1946] Director/Nursing Home Owner; Patricia Thomlinson [1947] Director/Registered General Nurse

Twice Brewed LLP
Incorporated: 13 March 2015 *Employees:* 52
Net Worth: £589,564 *Total Assets:* £1,223,721
Registered Office: A6 Kingfisher House, Kingsway, Team Valley Trading Estate, Gateshead, Tyne & Wear, NE11 0JQ
Officers: Edward Marcus Reuben Straker [1991] Member; Reuben Thomas Coppin Straker [1956] Member; The Hon Sophie Henrietta Straker [1960] Member

Twin Services Limited
Incorporated: 8 February 1982 *Employees:* 35
Net Worth: £664,106 *Total Assets:* £2,125,426
Registered Office: 9 Bowesfield Crescent, Stockton-on-Tees, Cleveland, TS18 3BL
Activities: Construction of commercial buildings
Parent: Jamas Building Services Limited
Officers: Peter Ian Kemp [1969] Director/Senior Designer/Estimator; Ruth Kemp [1970] Director/Accounts Manager; Thomas Stanley Levell [1976] Director/Designer/Estimator

Twizell Poultry (Ponteland) Limited
Incorporated: 14 April 1983
Net Worth: £136,936 *Total Assets:* £780,198
Registered Office: Twizell Cottage, Ponteland, Northumberland, NE20 0AL
Activities: Raising of poultry
Shareholder: Thomas Jonathan Goodwill
Officers: Elizabeth Sarah Goodwill, Secretary; Elizabeth Sarah Goodwill [1932] Director; Henry Rutter Routledge Goodwill [1925] Director; Thomas Jonathan Goodwill [1960] Director

Two Trees Woolley Limited
Incorporated: 16 September 2013
Net Worth: £182,734 *Total Assets:* £2,422,438
Registered Office: 1 University Boulevard, Middlesbrough, Cleveland, TS1 3BB
Activities: Other letting and operating of own or leased real estate
Major Shareholder: Faraz Ahmed Khaliq
Officers: Faraz Ahmed Khaliq [1984] Director/Chartered Accountant; Mohammed Arif Mushtaq [1962] Director

Twoplustwo Commercial Services Limited
Incorporated: 20 July 2007
Net Worth: £251,052 *Total Assets:* £945,404
Registered Office: Glen Cottage, Slaley, Hexham, Northumberland, NE47 0BN
Activities: Other business support service activities n.e.c.
Parent: WMB (Holdings) Limited
Officers: Julie Coulson Murrell, Secretary; Robert Hugh Blair [1981] Director; Samantha Jane Langlands [1971] Director/Management Accountant; Julie Coulson Murrell [1970] Director/Quantity Surveyor; Stewart Arthur Murrell [1973] Director/Quantity Surveyor; Paul Walker [1968] Director/Commercial Manager; Anna Woods [1978] Director; Joe Woods [1973] Director/Quantity Surveyor

TYK Limited
Incorporated: 8 October 1988 *Employees:* 26
Net Worth: £697,827 *Total Assets:* £4,113,456
Registered Office: Chilton Way, Chilton Industrial Estate, Chilton, Ferryhill, Co Durham, DL17 0SD
Activities: Manufacture of refractory products
Officers: Jean-Pierre Lefebvre, Secretary; Jean-Pierre Lefebvre [1973] Plant Director [French]; Nobutaka Ushigome [1964] Director [Japanese]

Tyne & Wear Holdings Limited
Incorporated: 27 June 2006 *Employees:* 222
Net Worth: £11,562,032 *Total Assets:* £23,364,860
Registered Office: Wessyngton House, Industrial Road, Hertburn Industrial Estate, Washington, Tyne & Wear, NE37 2SA
Activities: Activities of head offices
Parent: Greendale Holdings Limited
Officers: Michael John Williamson, Secretary; David Norris Cooper [1975] Production Director; John Russell Croisdale [1960] Managing Director; Michael John Williamson [1965] Financial Director

Tyne and Wear Building Preservation Trust Limited
Incorporated: 15 August 1979 *Employees:* 2
Net Worth: £1,954,979 *Total Assets:* £2,112,139
Registered Office: Bulman House, Regent Centre, Gosforth, Newcastle upon Tyne, NE3 3LS
Activities: Operation of historical sites and buildings and similar visitor attractions
Officers: Martin David Hulse, Secretary; Shona Alexander [1959] Director; Margaret Bozic [1950] Director; Ian Maurice Burns [1945] Director; Ronald Denton Clark [1938] Director/Retired; Dr. John Michael Daniels [1945] Director/Deputy Headteacher; Dr Neveen Ahmed Hamza [1967] Director/Senior Lecturer; John McElroy [1951] Director/Public Relations; Michael Murphy [1958] Director/Business Consultant; Katie Sussams [1970] Director of Operations; John Thompson [1941] Director/Heritage Consultant; Michael Roger Thompson [1961] Director

Tyne Coast Academy Trust
Incorporated: 29 November 2012 *Employees:* 44
Net Worth: £2,310,000 *Total Assets:* £2,777,000
Registered Office: Tyne Coast College, St Georges Avenue, South Shields, Tyne & Wear, NE34 6ET
Activities: Other education n.e.c.
Officers: Neil Longstaff, Secretary; Dr Ana Lopes [1975] Director/Lecturer in HRM [Portuguese]; Bashir Ahmed Malik [1939] Director; Christine Susan Smith [1950] Director; Raymond Staward [1950] Director; Maxine Tennet [1974] Director of Operations; Les Watson [1951] Director/Retired; Andrew Richard Watts [1970] Director-Charitable Trust; Robert James Whitelaw [1944] Director/Chartered Accountant; Dr Lindsey Janet Whiterod [1970] Director/College Chief Executive

Tyne Electro Diesel Limited
Incorporated: 4 July 1990 *Employees:* 14
Net Worth: £1,298,380 *Total Assets:* £1,495,845
Registered Office: 5-7 Noble Street, Newcastle upon Tyne, NE4 7PD
Activities: Repair and maintenance of other transport equipment n.e.c.
Shareholders: Kenneth Bramley; Jonathan Chaytor
Officers: Margaret Lesley Bramley, Secretary; Kenneth Bramley [1946] Director/Engineer; Peter Robinson [1958] Director

Tyne Gangway (Structures) Limited
Incorporated: 13 October 2009
Net Worth: £679,825 *Total Assets:* £1,743,046
Registered Office: Unit 2 Stephenson Street, Howdon Quays, Wallsend, Tyne & Wear, NE28 6UE
Activities: Manufacture of other fabricated metal products n.e.c.
Parent: Lift-Rite Holdings Limited
Officers: Alasdair MacDonald [1965] Director; Kenneth McDonald [1964] Director; John Peter Reece [1961] Director

Tyne Insulation Supplies Limited
Incorporated: 15 January 1987 *Employees:* 23
Net Worth: £2,949,798 *Total Assets:* £5,458,228
Registered Office: Unit 21 Orion Way, Orion Business Park, North Shields, Tyne & Wear, NE29 7SN
Activities: Wholesale of wood, construction materials and sanitary equipment
Shareholder: Kathleen McKenna
Officers: Kathleen McKenna, Secretary/Director; David McKenna [1955] Director; Kathleen McKenna [1956] Director and Company Secretary; Neil Robert Topping [1964] Sales Director

Tyne Logistics Company Limited
Incorporated: 7 December 1990 *Employees:* 56
Net Worth: £6,834,000 *Total Assets:* £7,873,000
Registered Office: Maritime House, Tyne Dock, South Shields, Tyne & Wear, NE34 9PT
Activities: Freight transport by road
Officers: Steven Robert Harrison [1967] Port Operations Director; Andrew Noel Moffat [1956] Director/Chief Executive Officer; Mark Anthony Stoner [1969] Director/Chief Financial Officer

Tyne Mills Motor Company Limited
Incorporated: 2 July 1986 *Employees:* 1
Net Worth: £1,358,781 *Total Assets:* £2,214,540
Registered Office: Tyne Mills Industrial Estate, Hexham, Northumberland, NE46 1XL
Activities: Sale of new cars and light motor vehicles
Major Shareholder: John Robert Woods
Officers: John Woods, Secretary; John Robert Woods [1953] Director

Tyne Moulds & Machinery Company Limited
Incorporated: 22 November 1976
Net Worth: £3,043,889 *Total Assets:* £3,963,672
Registered Office: 8 Segedunum Business Centre, Station Road, Wallsend, Tyne & Wear, NE28 6HQ
Activities: Manufacture of other plastic products
Officers: Ramy Zack, Secretary; Ramy Zack [1959] Managing Director

Tyne North Training Limited
Incorporated: 27 October 1970 *Employees:* 20
Net Worth: £1,688,616 *Total Assets:* £1,950,041
Registered Office: Embleton Avenue, Wallsend, Tyne & Wear, NE28 9NJ
Activities: Technical and vocational secondary education
Officers: Michael Needham, Secretary; Stanley Armstrong [1954] Director/Technical Training & Development Manager; Colin Pratt [1963] Director/Operations Manager; Thomas Ian Selkirk [1943] Director

Tyne Properties Limited
Incorporated: 1 March 1999 *Employees:* 1
Net Worth: £3,205,734 *Total Assets:* £7,774,993
Registered Office: The Old Post Office, 63 Saville Street, North Shields, Tyne & Wear, NE30 1AY
Activities: Other letting and operating of own or leased real estate
Shareholders: Mutahir Hassan Rizvi; Raza Mujitiba Rizvi; Sidra Rubina Naz Bruce
Officers: Sidra Rubina Naz Bruce [1966] Director; Hassan Rizvi [1972] Director/Property Owner; Raza Mujtiba Rizvi [1964] Director

Tyne Property Limited
Incorporated: 9 December 2009
Net Worth: £959,264 *Total Assets:* £992,430
Registered Office: 3 Hedley Court, Orion Business Park, Orion Way, North Shields, Tyne & Wear, NE29 7ST
Activities: Other letting and operating of own or leased real estate
Shareholder: Johann Bernhard Schulte
Officers: Graham Colin Bates [1980] Director/Accountant; Charis Charilaou [1972] Director/Accountant [Cypriot]

Tyne Region North Limited
Incorporated: 16 September 1993 *Employees:* 14
Net Worth: £14,787,049 *Total Assets:* £26,020,742
Registered Office: Sandgate House, 102 Quayside, Newcastle upon Tyne, NE1 3DX
Activities: Buying and selling of own real estate
Major Shareholder: Geoffrey Simon Walton
Officers: Peter Michael Tanner, Secretary; Peter Michael Tanner [1963] Director/Estate Agent; Annabel Jayne Walton [1987] Director

Tyne Region North Properties Limited
Incorporated: 26 July 2011
Net Worth Deficit: £1,878,447 *Total Assets:* £10,376,637
Registered Office: Sandgate House, 102 Quayside, Newcastle upon Tyne, NE1 3DX
Activities: Other letting and operating of own or leased real estate
Major Shareholder: Geoffrey Simon Walton
Officers: Peter Michael Tanner [1963] Director/Estate Agent; Annabel Jayne Walton [1987] Director

Tyne Region North Stepney Limited
Incorporated: 27 July 2011
Net Worth Deficit: £1,374,519 *Total Assets:* £15,247,644
Registered Office: Sandgate House, 102 Quayside, Newcastle upon Tyne, NE1 3DX
Activities: Other letting and operating of own or leased real estate
Major Shareholder: Geoffrey Simon Walton
Officers: Peter Michael Tanner [1963] Director/Estate Agent; Annabel Jayne Walton [1987] Director

Tyne Subsea Limited
Incorporated: 7 August 2014 *Employees:* 3
Net Worth: £306,197 *Total Assets:* £7,389,055
Registered Office: 11 Glasshouse Street, St Peters, Newcastle upon Tyne, NE6 1BS
Activities: Technical testing and analysis
Parent: Bel Valves Limited
Officers: Joanne Alicea Wilkes, Secretary; Richard Dodd [1974] Director; Bruce Michael Amos Heppenstall [1970] Director; Nicholas George Wright [1965] Director/Academic Engineer

Tyne Tees Ceramics Limited
Incorporated: 7 April 1983
Net Worth: £707,944 *Total Assets:* £1,030,721
Registered Office: Unit 20 The Avenue North, Team Valley Trading Estate, Gateshead, Tyne & Wear, NE11 0NJ
Activities: Other retail sale in non-specialised stores
Shareholders: Anthony Craven; John Paul Craven
Officers: Clare Craven, Secretary; Anthony Craven [1941] Sales Director; Clare Craven [1983] Director; John Paul Craven [1976] Director/Sales Manager

Tyne Tees Entertainments Limited
Incorporated: 5 November 1984 *Employees:* 48
Net Worth: £6,207,659 *Total Assets:* £6,745,649
Registered Office: 10 The Esplanade, Redcar, Cleveland, TS10 3AA
Activities: Other amusement and recreation activities n.e.c.
Officers: Elsie Gail Caris, Secretary; Elsie Gail Caris [1962] Director; George Caris [1990] Director; George Caris [1958] Director

Tyne Tees Thermal Limited
Incorporated: 10 August 2006 *Employees:* 34
Net Worth: £453,722 *Total Assets:* £1,063,509
Registered Office: Unit 8 Ruby Park, Brunswick Industrial Estate, Brunswick Village, Newcastle upon Tyne, NE13 7BA
Activities: Plumbing, heat and air-conditioning installation
Shareholders: Debra Louise Moody; Christopher Edward Morton
Officers: Evelyn Morton, Secretary; Nicholas Hunter [1973] Director; Debra Louise Moody [1947] Director; Christopher Edward Morton [1967] Director; Evelyn Morton [1947] Director

Tyne Tees Vehicle Repair Group Limited
Incorporated: 30 July 2008 *Employees:* 32
Net Worth: £3,383,437 *Total Assets:* £4,637,840
Registered Office: Swan Road, Swan Industrial Estate, Washington, Tyne & Wear, NE38 8JJ
Activities: Maintenance and repair of motor vehicles
Major Shareholder: Darren Norton
Officers: Darren Norton, Secretary; Darren Norton [1970] Director

Tyne Valves Limited
Incorporated: 2 March 2004 *Employees:* 6
Net Worth: £884,023 *Total Assets:* £1,323,578
Registered Office: Unit 23 Blaydon Business Centre, Cowen Road, Blaydon on Tyne, Tyne & Wear, NE21 5TW
Activities: Wholesale of hardware, plumbing and heating equipment and supplies
Shareholders: David Hill; Brian Hill
Officers: Brian Hill [1960] Director/Sales Engineer

Tynedale Agricultural Society Ltd
Incorporated: 5 October 2006 *Employees:* 2
Net Worth: £976,241 *Total Assets:* £989,313
Registered Office: Hexham Auction Mart, Tyne Green, Hexham, Northumberland, NE46 3SG
Activities: Activities of other membership organisations n.e.c.
Officers: Judith Kathryn Willis, Secretary; John William Bell [1938] Director/Farmer; David Carr [1974] Director/Farmer; Chris Chomse [1958] Director/Sales Manager; Michael Roger Douglas [1948] Director/Architect; Thomas Arnold Harrison [1976] Director/Waterboard - Farmer; Gawin Ian Holmes [1948] Director/Chartered Surveyor; Robert Henry Mole [1939] Director/Retired; Robert John Raine [1964] Director/Farmer; John Alfred Rowland [1961] Director/Farmer; Mark Scandle [1970] Director/Territory Manager; James Wardle [1974] Director/Farmer; John Woodman [1953] Director/Farmer

Tynedale Family Funeral Directors Limited
Incorporated: 11 November 2011 *Employees:* 13
Net Worth: £196,919 *Total Assets:* £839,854
Registered Office: Tynedale House, Stanhope Road, South Shields, Tyne & Wear, NE33 4TB
Activities: Funeral and related activities
Shareholders: Mark Anthony Cook; Diane Cook
Officers: Diane Cook [1970] Director/Receptionist; Mark Anthony Cook [1968] Director/Undertaker

Tynedale Roadstone Limited
Incorporated: 9 March 1999 *Employees:* 21
Net Worth: £2,682,510 *Total Assets:* £8,421,204
Registered Office: Davison House, Rennys Lane, Dragonville Industrial Estate, Durham, DH1 2RS
Activities: Other manufacturing n.e.c.
Parent: MGL Group Limited
Officers: Deborah Jane Milnthorp, Secretary; David Anthony Elliott [1969] Director; Gary Anthony Smith [1967] Director/Accountant

Tynegrain Agriculture Limited
Incorporated: 24 September 1982 *Employees:* 1
Net Worth: £418,084 *Total Assets:* £847,540
Registered Office: Tynegrain, Tyne Dock, South Shields, Tyne & Wear, NE34 9PL
Activities: Post-harvest crop activities
Officers: William Mark Wood, Secretary; Geoffrey Orpeth Alderslade [1959] Director/Farmer; Richard Allinson [1957] Director/Agronomist; Gary John Bright [1969] Director; Robert John Davison [1954] Director/Farmer; David John Gibson [1966] Director/Farmer; Andrew Robert Graham [1969] Director/Farmer; David William Hall [1956] Director/Farm Manager; Peter Alan Jackson [1958] Director/Farmer; Christopher James Stephenson [1973] Director/Farmer; William Taylor [1958] Director/Lecturer Farm Manager

Tynehead (Property) Limited
Incorporated: 25 October 1907
Net Worth: £1,382,139 *Total Assets:* £3,233,845
Registered Office: 3rd Floor, 86 Pilgrim Street, Newcastle upon Tyne, NE1 6SG
Activities: Other letting and operating of own or leased real estate
Officers: Cristina Virginia de Giorgi, Secretary; Aldo Pasquale de Giorgi [1969] Director/Restaurateur; Anne de Giorgi [1938] Director/Retired; Cristina Virginia de Giorgi [1966] Director/Business Manager; Joseph Mario de Giorgi [1965] Director/Restaurateur; Maria Rosanna de Giorgi [1963] Director/Teacher; Mario Pasquale de Gorgi [1933] Director/Restaurateur [Italian]

Tynemanagement NE Limited
Incorporated: 18 May 2015
Net Worth Deficit: £7,755 *Total Assets:* £2,868,704
Registered Office: 9 Consett Park Terrace, Consett, Co Durham, DH8 8ET
Activities: Other letting and operating of own or leased real estate
Major Shareholder: Desmond Young
Officers: Desmond Young [1963] Director/Landlord

Tyneside Autoparc Limited
Incorporated: 15 October 2002
Net Worth: £677,907 *Total Assets:* £4,470,473
Registered Office: 140 Coniscliffe Road, Darlington, Co Durham, DL3 7RT
Activities: Other letting and operating of own or leased real estate
Parent: St Margaret's Trustee's Ltd
Officers: Geoffrey William Dawson [1949] Director

Tyneside Badminton Centre CIC
Incorporated: 15 December 2011
Net Worth: £23,233 *Total Assets:* £766,020
Registered Office: Bowness Road, Slatyford, Newcastle upon Tyne, NE5 2TA
Activities: Operation of sports facilities
Officers: Stephen John Abbott [1953] Director; Peter James McLane [1956] Director; Stephen Porter [1970] Director; Michael Andrew Woodward [1963] Director

Tyneside Cinema
Incorporated: 10 May 1973 *Employees:* 76
Net Worth: £4,194,030 *Total Assets:* £5,941,966
Registered Office: Newe House, 10 Pilgrim Street, Newcastle upon Tyne, NE1 6QG
Activities: Motion picture projection activities
Officers: Lucy Joanne Smyth, Secretary; Lucy Victoria Winwood Armstrong [1968] Director/Chief Executive; Clare Binns [1979] Deputy Managing Director; Timothy James Neil Davies-Pugh [1966] Investment Director; Steven Hugh Montague Kyffin [1959] Director/Designer & University Executive Dean; Heather Markham [1979] Director/Solicitor; Keith Michael Proudfoot [1952] Regional Director at ICAEW; Nicholas Robert Shottel [1963] Brand Director

Tyneside Estate Office Limited
Incorporated: 23 November 1961 *Employees:* 2
Net Worth: £1,552,187 *Total Assets:* £2,458,323
Registered Office: Saville Chambers, 5 North Street, Newcastle upon Tyne, NE1 8DF
Activities: Management of real estate on a fee or contract basis
Shareholders: David Scott Cowper; Pauline Jill Nisbet
Officers: Caroline Anna Cowper, Secretary; Pauline Jill Nisbet, Secretary; Caroline Anna Cowper [1946] Director; David Scott Cowper [1942] Director/Chartered Surveyor; Pauline Jill Nisbet [1945] Director

Tyneside Express Transport Limited
Incorporated: 27 April 2000 *Employees:* 42
Net Worth: £290,307 *Total Assets:* £1,197,405
Registered Office: Unit 2 BRS Complex, Earlsway, Team Valley Trading Estate, Gateshead, Tyne & Wear, NE11 0UU
Activities: Freight transport by road
Shareholders: Darren Robert Casey; Margaret Casey; Shaun Casey
Officers: Darren Robert Casey [1965] Director/Transport Manager; Margaret Casey [1968] Director

Tyneside Foodservice Limited
Incorporated: 21 September 1979
Net Worth: £1,942,865 *Total Assets:* £3,293,740
Registered Office: Patterson Street, Blaydon Haughs Industrial Estate, Blaydon, Tyne & Wear, NE21 5SD
Activities: Non-specialised wholesale of food, beverages and tobacco
Officers: Stephen Walton, Secretary; Peter Henderson [1965] Sales Director; John Alan Hervin [1975] Purchasing Director; Christopher John Walton [1965] Director/Depot Manager; Stephen Walton [1967] Director/Office Manager

Tyneside Group Limited
Incorporated: 24 October 2012 *Employees:* 9
Net Worth: £178,566 *Total Assets:* £1,156,293
Registered Office: Picton Manor, Ellison Place, Newcastle upon Tyne, NE1 8XG
Activities: Activities of head offices
Shareholders: Norma Joy Kalbraier; Robert William Kalbraier
Officers: Victoria Jane Kalbraier, Secretary; Paul Clement [1965] Director; Robert William Kalbraier [1985] Director; Paul David Pestell [1969] Director/Chartered Accountant

Tyneside Investments Limited
Incorporated: 11 January 2012 *Employees:* 2
Net Worth: £787,830 *Total Assets:* £875,031
Registered Office: Bridge House, 96 High West Street, Gateshead, Tyne & Wear, NE8 1NA
Activities: Buying and selling of own real estate
Officers: Eliezer Halberstadt, Secretary; Bernard Dunner [1981] Director; Eliezer Halberstadt [1986] Director/Manager

Tyneside Leisure World Limited
Incorporated: 18 January 2012
Net Worth: £233,221 *Total Assets:* £1,905,472
Registered Office: c/o Catterick Caravan & Camping Centre Limited, Gatherley Road, Brompton on Swale, Richmond, N Yorks, DL10 7JB
Activities: Sale of other motor vehicles
Parent: Leisure World Group Limited
Officers: Christopher Michael Kinsell, Secretary; Christopher Michael Kinsell [1973] Director; Matthew Alexander Kinsell [1979] Director

Tyneside Surgical Services Limited
Incorporated: 23 April 2007
Net Worth: £2,562,119 *Total Assets:* £3,454,748
Registered Office: RMT Accountants & Business Advisors, Gosforth Park Avenue, Newcastle upon Tyne, NE12 8EG
Activities: Hospital activities
Major Shareholder: Hamdy Yousef Hafez Ashour
Officers: Mark Mercer-Jones, Secretary; Hamdy Yousef Hafez Ashour [1957] Director; Mark Andrew Mercer-Jones [1964] Director/Surgeon

Tyneview Diagnostics Limited
Incorporated: 8 November 2012
Net Worth: £768,087 *Total Assets:* £898,383
Registered Office: 15 Stonecroft Gardens, Newcastle upon Tyne, NE7 7GD
Activities: Specialists medical practice activities
Major Shareholder: Vimbai Chasi
Officers: Dr Ishmael Chasi [1972] Director/Radiologist; Vimbai Chasi [1973] Director

Tyneview Properties Limited
Incorporated: 16 December 2015
Net Worth: £29,268 *Total Assets:* £885,023
Registered Office: 15 Stonecroft Gardens, Newcastle upon Tyne, NE7 7GD
Activities: Other letting and operating of own or leased real estate
Major Shareholder: Vimbai Chasi
Officers: Dr Ishmael Chasi [1972] Director/Radiologist; Vimbai Chasi [1973] Director

Tynexe Limited
Incorporated: 21 October 1986
Net Worth: £6,258,256 *Total Assets:* £6,512,122
Registered Office: Democratic Services Division, Newcastle City Council, Civic Centre, Newcastle upon Tyne, NE99 2BN
Activities: Other letting and operating of own or leased real estate
Shareholders: The Armstrong Centre Company Limited; Dysart Developments North East Limited
Officers: Linda Scott, Secretary; Councillor Robin Arthur John Ashby [1947] Director; Councillor Generald William Bell [1961] Director/Retired; Lyn Joan Binks [1960] Director; Councillor Anita Anne Lower [1957] Director/Councillor; Joyce McCarty [1953] Director/Retired; Morris Robert Muter [1954] Director; Roland Mark Short [1966] Managing Director (Development & Construction)

Tynexe Residential Limited
Incorporated: 16 July 2014
Net Worth Deficit: £490 *Total Assets:* £802,475
Registered Office: Democratic Services Division, Newcastle City Council, Civic Centre, Newcastle upon Tyne, NE99 2BN
Activities: Development of building projects
Parent: Tynexe Limited
Officers: Councillor Robin Arthur John Ashby [1947] Director; Councillor Generald William Bell [1961] Director/Councillor; Lyn Joan Binks [1960] Director; Councillor Anita Anne Lower [1957] Director/Councillor; Joyce McCarty [1953] Director/Councillor; Morris Robert Muter [1954] Director; Roland Mark Short [1966] Managing Director (Development & Construction)

Tyre Spot Limited
Incorporated: 16 September 1993 *Employees:* 108
Net Worth: £3,697,620 *Total Assets:* £8,121,714
Registered Office: Drum Road, Birtley, Chester-le-Street, Co Durham, DH3 2AF
Activities: Wholesale trade of motor vehicle parts and accessories
Shareholders: John Thomas Shaw; Pauline Shaw; Johnathon William Shaw
Officers: Pauline Shaw, Company Secretary; John Thomas Shaw [1945] Director/Tyre Dealer; Johnathon William Shaw [1978] Director/Manager; Pauline Shaw [1949] Director/Company Secretary

Tysoft Software Ltd
Incorporated: 4 March 2013
Net Worth: £622,042 *Total Assets:* £783,176
Registered Office: 11 Cloverfield Avenue, Fawdon, Newcastle upon Tyne, NE3 3NJ
Activities: Business and domestic software development
Major Shareholder: Brian Leslie Harper
Officers: Brian Leslie Harper [1981] Director/Software Designer

U L Medicines Limited
Incorporated: 21 February 2007 *Employees:* 23
Net Worth: £7,824,905 *Total Assets:* £9,696,005
Registered Office: Quantum House, Hobson Industrial Estate, Burnopfield, Co Durham, NE16 6EA
Activities: Wholesale of pharmaceutical goods
Officers: Amanda Miller, Secretary; Graeme Petrie [1973] Managing Director Interim; David Alan Sanson [1959] Quality Director; Michael James Tagg [1982] Finance Director

U.C.O.S. Holdings Limited
Incorporated: 29 June 2002 *Employees:* 113
Net Worth: £5,149,106 *Total Assets:* £7,748,239
Registered Office: Meadow Court, Dukesway, Team Valley Trading Estate, Gateshead, Tyne & Wear, NE11 0PZ
Activities: Activities of head offices
Officers: Paul William Dawson, Secretary/Accountant; Mark Andrew Bryce [1968] Sales Director; Warren Michael Colby [1971] Sales Director; John Ellis [1966] Sales Director; Michael David Nelson [1968] Sales Director; John Watson [1960] Managing Director

Uber Limited
Incorporated: 3 June 2004 *Employees:* 2
Net Worth Deficit: £8,073 *Total Assets:* £1,468,234
Registered Office: 34-36 South Parade, Whitley Bay, Tyne & Wear, NE26 2RQ
Activities: Other letting and operating of own or leased real estate
Officers: Trevor Edward Hastie, Secretary; Edward James Hastie [1945] Director; Trevor Edward Hastie [1971] Director

Ubisoft CRC Ltd
Incorporated: 23 June 2014 *Employees:* 142
Net Worth: £502,000 *Total Assets:* £1,973,000
Registered Office: The Hub, Haymarket, Newcastle upon Tyne, NE1 7PF
Activities: Activities of call centres
Officers: Yves Guillemot [1960] Director [French]

Ubisoft Reflections Limited
Incorporated: 19 April 2006 *Employees:* 232
Net Worth: £57,357,960 *Total Assets:* £66,415,180
Registered Office: 5th Floor, Partnership House, Regent Farm Road, Newcastle upon Tyne, NE3 3AF
Activities: Ready-made interactive leisure and entertainment software development
Parent: Ubisoft Limited
Officers: Claude Michel Marcel Guillemot, Secretary/Chief Executive Officer [French]; Yves Marie Remy Guillemot [1960] Director/Chief Executive Officer [French]

UK & Ireland SAP User Group Limited
Incorporated: 18 January 2000 *Employees:* 10
Net Worth: £621,084 *Total Assets:* £1,168,575
Registered Office: Unit 3b Lockheed Court, Preston Farm Industrial Estate, Stockton on Tees, Cleveland, TS18 3SH
Activities: Activities of business and employers membership organisations
Officers: Gillian Bowness, Secretary/Solicitor; Philip Samuel Adams [1973] Director/Manager; Alan Thomas Bowling [1958] Director/Manager; Paul Anthony Cooper [1967] Director/IT Manager; Michael Paul Dean [1951] Director/Consultant; Brian Kenneth Froom [1962] Director/Information Security Manager; Ralph Martin Lewis [1955] Director; Costantino Petrosellini [1968] Director/IT Manager [British/Italian]; Michael John Thomas Reaney [1955] Director/Project Manager; Fiona Warburg [1976] Director/IT Manager

UK Asbestos Specialists Ltd
Incorporated: 26 February 2003
Net Worth: £595,229 *Total Assets:* £818,115
Registered Office: Suite 7, The Eco Centre, Windmill Way, Hebburn, Tyne & Wear, NE31 1SR
Activities: Other education n.e.c.
Shareholders: Marion Agnes Cooper; Leslie Cooper
Officers: Leslie Cooper, Secretary/Consultant; Leslie Cooper [1960] Director/Consultant; Marion Agnes Cooper [1961] Director

UK Bathrooms Limited
Incorporated: 15 January 2002 *Employees:* 3
Net Worth: £280,434 *Total Assets:* £1,044,845
Registered Office: Kinnair & Company, Aston House, Redburn Road, Newcastle upon Tyne, NE5 1NB
Activities: Wholesale of wood, construction materials and sanitary equipment
Officers: Paul Brian Kidwell, Secretary; Anthony Paul Colin Kidwell [1987] Director; Ruou Liang [1976] Director [Chinese]

UK Docks Marine Services North Limited
Incorporated: 9 February 1977 *Employees:* 30
Net Worth: £1,060,801 *Total Assets:* £1,636,475
Registered Office: River Drive, South Shields, Tyne & Wear, NE33 1LH
Activities: Building of ships and floating structures
Parent: Wilson Group Holdings Limited
Officers: Gary Wilson, Secretary; Christopher Wilson [1970] Director/Marine Engineer; Gary Wilson [1974] Director/Marine Engineer; Harold Wilson [1942] Director/Ship Repair Consultant; Jonathan Wilson [1976] Director/Marine Engineer

UK Docks Marine Services South Limited
Incorporated: 31 July 2000 *Employees:* 16
Net Worth: £44,022 *Total Assets:* £910,181
Registered Office: River Drive, South Shields, Tyne & Wear, NE33 1LH
Activities: Building of ships and floating structures
Major Shareholder: Harold Wilson
Officers: Gary Wilson, Secretary; David Paul Barley [1962] Operations Director; Christopher Wilson [1970] Director; Gary Wilson [1974] Director; Harold Wilson [1942] Director; Jonathan Wilson [1976] Director

UK Docks Marine Services Teesside Limited
Incorporated: 31 March 2011 *Employees:* 42
Net Worth: £214,824 *Total Assets:* £1,925,650
Registered Office: River Drive, South Shields, Tyne & Wear, NE33 1LH
Activities: Building of ships and floating structures
Major Shareholder: Harold Wilson
Officers: Christopher Wilson [1970] Director; Gary Wilson [1974] Director; Harold Wilson [1942] Director; Jonathan Wilson [1976] Director

UK Independent Medical Services Limited
Incorporated: 10 September 2002 *Employees:* 192
Net Worth: £5,740,053 *Total Assets:* £22,083,832
Registered Office: Brenner House, Rainton Bridge Business Park, Houghton-le-Spring, Co Durham, DH4 5RA
Activities: Other professional, scientific and technical activities n.e.c.
Parent: Examworks UK Limited
Officers: Paul Gray, Secretary; Paul Robert Gray [1967] Director/Accountant; Paul Charles Healey [1956] Director; Christopher Nairns [1975] Director

UK Industrial Tapes Limited
Incorporated: 17 February 1997 *Employees:* 46
Net Worth: £721,491 *Total Assets:* £3,742,492
Registered Office: Brumwell House, Westway Industrial Park, Throckley, Newcastle upon Tyne, NE15 9EW
Activities: Wholesale of other intermediate products
Shareholders: Brian Matthew Welch; Ruth Welch
Officers: Brian Matthew Welch [1963] Managing Director; Matthew David Welch [1991] Director; Michael Brian Welch [1994] Director; Ruth Welch [1964] Sales Director

UK Land Estates (Partnership) Limited
Incorporated: 12 March 2002
Net Worth Deficit: £44,881,000 *Total Assets:* £139,632,000
Registered Office: 2nd Floor, Building 7, Queens Park, Queensway, Team Valley Trading Estate, Gateshead, Tyne & Wear, NE11 0QD
Activities: Development of building projects
Parent: UK Land Estates Partnership (Holdings) Limited
Officers: Jerome Christian Kathleen Anselme [1974] Director [French]; Michael O'Shaughnessy [1972] Director [American]; Joseph Martin Pedlow [1962] Director [British/American]; Richard Alexander Pellatt [1976] Director; Stephen Smith [1953] Director; Alan Keith Taylor [1963] Treasury Director; Christopher John Whitfield [1963] Director

UK Land Estates Limited
Incorporated: 22 October 2003 *Employees:* 1
Net Worth: £3,912,358 *Total Assets:* £24,747,104
Registered Office: 2nd Floor, Building 7, Queens Park, Queensway, Team Valley Trading Estate, Gateshead, Tyne & Wear, NE11 0QD
Activities: Development of building projects
Parent: Estate Capital Limited
Officers: Emilia Keleditis [1977] Director [Greek]; Alan Keith Taylor [1963] Director; Christopher John Whitfield [1964] Director

UK Land Estates Partnership (Holdings) Limited
Incorporated: 8 July 2011
Net Worth: £125,052,000 *Total Assets:* £258,044,992
Registered Office: 2nd Floor, Building 7, Queens Park, Queensway, Team Valley Trading Estate, Gateshead, Tyne & Wear, NE11 0QD
Activities: Activities of head offices
Major Shareholder: Christopher John Whitfield
Officers: Jerome Christian Kathleen Anselme [1974] Director [French]; Michael O'Shaughnessy [1972] Director [American]; Joseph Martin Pedlow [1962] Director [British/American]; Richard Alexander Pellatt [1976] Director; Stephen Smith [1953] Director; Alan Keith Taylor [1963] Director; Christopher John Whitfield [1963] Director

UK Land Investments Limited
Incorporated: 1 October 2014
Net Worth: £4,806,337 *Total Assets:* £11,685,315
Registered Office: 2nd Floor, Building 7, Queens Park, Queensway, Team Valley Trading Estate, Gateshead, Tyne & Wear, NE11 0QD
Activities: Other letting and operating of own or leased real estate
Shareholder: Christopher John Whitfield
Officers: Lord James William Eustace Percy [1965] Director; Alan Keith Taylor [1963] Director; Christopher John Whitfield [1963] Director; Roderick Charles St John Wilson [1961] Director

UK National Limited
Incorporated: 20 June 2005 *Employees:* 35
Net Worth: £1,452,081 *Total Assets:* £2,438,288
Registered Office: 4 Wass Way, Durham Lane Industrial Estate, Eaglescliffe, Stockton on Tees, Cleveland, TS16 0RG
Activities: Other business support service activities n.e.c.
Shareholders: Julia Parker; Alan Parker
Officers: Julia Parker, Secretary; Alan Parker [1960] Director/Manager; Dean Parker [1987] Director/Gas Engineer; Julia Parker [1963] Director/Business Proprietor; Sonny Parker [1983] Commercial Director

UK Warranty Limited
Incorporated: 3 August 2011 *Employees:* 15
Net Worth: £59,767 *Total Assets:* £2,093,891
Registered Office: Pacifica House, Rainton Business Park, Houghton-le-Spring, Co Durham, DH4 5RA
Activities: Activities of insurance agents and brokers
Officers: Scott Pallister, Secretary; Kevin Brown [1968] Director/Executive Chairman; Paul Richard Feek [1971] Director; Neil Martin [1966] Director; Jonathan Negri [1968] Sales Director; Scott Pallister [1980] Director; Keith William Wardell [1957] Director

UKLEP (2003) Limited
Incorporated: 18 September 2003
Net Worth: £731,982 *Total Assets:* £32,933,600
Registered Office: 2nd Floor, Building 7, Queens Park, Queensway, Team Valley Trading Estate, Gateshead, Tyne & Wear, NE11 0QD
Activities: Other business support service activities n.e.c.
Parent: UK Land Estates (Partnership) Limited
Officers: Jerome Christian Kathleen Anselme [1974] Director [French]; Michael O'Shaughnessy [1972] Director [American]; Joseph Martin Pedlow [1962] Director [British/American]; Richard Alexander Pellatt [1976] Director; Stephen Smith [1953] Director; Alan Keith Taylor [1963] Treasury Director; Christopher John Whitfield [1963] Director

ULookUBook Travel Limited
Incorporated: 10 September 2013
Net Worth: £1,258,352 *Total Assets:* £1,258,684
Registered Office: 3rd Floor, Tyne House, Side, Newcastle upon Tyne, NE1 3JA
Activities: Activities of other holding companies n.e.c.
Major Shareholder: Stephen Campion
Officers: David Kenneth Young, Secretary; Stephen Campion [1967] Director; Susan Winter [1963] Director

Ultralight Outdoor Gear Limited
Incorporated: 17 July 2007 *Employees:* 14
Net Worth: £705,175 *Total Assets:* £1,088,023
Registered Office: Unit 9 Pioneer Court, Morton Palms Business Park, Darlington, Co Durham, DL1 4WD
Activities: Retail sale of sports goods, fishing gear, camping goods, boats and bicycles
Shareholders: Mark Derek Richardson; Mark Richardson
Officers: Mark Derek Richardson, Secretary; Elizabeth Richardson [1951] Director/School Secretary; Mark Derek Richardson [1961] Director/Manager

Ultramap Limited
Incorporated: 7 January 2013 *Employees:* 2
Net Worth: £384,064 *Total Assets:* £825,254
Registered Office: Grainger Suite, Regent Centre, Gosforth, Newcastle upon Tyne, NE3 3PF
Activities: Business and domestic software development
Shareholders: Martin Connelly; Andrew James Desforges
Officers: Martin Connelly, Secretary; Martin Connelly [1961] Commercial Director; Andrew James Desforges [1964] Director of Operations

Unasys Limited
Incorporated: 22 August 2000
Net Worth: £962,882 *Total Assets:* £1,337,698
Registered Office: Boho One, Bridge Street West, Middlesbrough, Cleveland, TS2 1AE
Activities: Other engineering activities
Shareholder: Michael Vincent Flynn
Officers: Adrian Mark Johnston, Secretary; Michael Vincent John Flynn [1960] Director/Mechanical Engineer

Underpressure Pipeline Solutions Limited
Incorporated: 7 February 2005 *Employees:* 13
Net Worth: £831,351 *Total Assets:* £1,129,409
Registered Office: Connor House, 30 Pilgrims Way, Bede Industrial Estate, Jarrow, Tyne & Wear, NE32 3EW
Activities: Repair of other equipment
Shareholders: Shaun William Sadler; John Swan; UTS Group Limited
Officers: Paul Douthwaite [1973] Director; Shaun William Sadler [1970] Director

Underwater Cutting Solutions Ltd
Incorporated: 2 February 2004
Net Worth: £5,605,608 *Total Assets:* £5,863,254
Registered Office: Hawthorn Cottage, Brunton Quarry, North Gosforth, Newcastle upon Tyne, NE13 6PH
Activities: Manufacture of other special-purpose machinery n.e.c.
Major Shareholder: Ronald Wraith
Officers: Ronald Wraith, Secretary/Rigger Foreman; Ronald Wraith [1961] Director/Rigger Foreman

Underwood Hall Limited
Incorporated: 9 April 1996 *Employees:* 63
Net Worth: £357,467 *Total Assets:* £2,242,686
Registered Office: Wentworth Grange, Riding Mill, Northumberland, NE44 6DZ
Activities: Residential care activities for the elderly and disabled
Major Shareholder: Phyllis Rose Lee
Officers: Julian Leslie Lee, Secretary; Jeffrey Isaac Lee [1964] Director; Julian Leslie Lee [1969] Director; Phyllis Rose Lee [1942] Director/Proprietor

Unika Group Limited
Incorporated: 17 December 2007 *Employees:* 5
Net Worth: £9,269,653 *Total Assets:* £9,287,312
Registered Office: Unika House, New York Way, New York Industrial Park, Newcastle upon Tyne, NE27 0QF
Activities: Activities of head offices
Shareholders: Paul Robert Rogers; Martin Francis Wrightson
Officers: Lee Etherington, Secretary; Lee Etherington [1970] Director; Annika Rogers [1976] Director [Estonian]; Paul Robert Rogers [1961] Marketing Director; Martin Francis Wrightson [1962] Director; Suzanne Wrightson [1962] Director

Union Electric Steel UK Limited
Incorporated: 17 January 1920 *Employees:* 237
Net Worth: £26,903,000 *Total Assets:* £44,689,000
Registered Office: P O Box 21, Union Electric Steel UK Limited, Coulthards Lane, Gateshead, Tyne & Wear, NE8 3DX
Activities: Manufacture of basic iron and steel and of ferro-alloys
Parent: Ampco UES Sub, Inc
Officers: David Attle, Secretary; Rose Hoover, Secretary/Corporate Executive [American]; William John Garrett [1972] Managing Director; Rose Hoover [1955] Director/Corporate Executive [American]; Brett McBrayer [1966] Director/CEO Ampco-Pittsburgh Corporation [American]; Rodney Lee Scagline [1967] Director/Executive Vice President [American]

Union Property Development Limited
Incorporated: 12 June 2015 *Employees:* 4
Net Worth: £2,401,367 *Total Assets:* £17,223,722
Registered Office: c/o Union Property Services Limited, Cobalt 3.1, Silver Fox Way, Cobalt Business Park, Wallsend, Tyne & Wear, NE27 0QJ
Activities: Development of building projects
Major Shareholder: Raj Kumar Sehgal
Officers: Naresh Abrol [1973] Director; Mukesh Kumar Sehgal [1949] Director; Promila Sehgal [1948] Director; Raj Kumar Sehgal [1975] Director

Union Property Services Limited
Incorporated: 3 March 2014 *Employees:* 14
Net Worth: £147,431 *Total Assets:* £1,141,204
Registered Office: Cobalt 3.1, Silver Fox Way, Cobalt Business Park, Newcastle upon Tyne, NE27 0QJ
Activities: Management of real estate on a fee or contract basis
Major Shareholder: Raj Kumar Sehgal
Officers: Naresh Abrol [1973] Director; Mukesh Kumar Sehgal [1949] Director; Promila Sehgal [1948] Director; Raj Kumar Sehgal [1975] Director; Varsha Sehgal [1977] Director

Union Retail Properties Limited
Incorporated: 5 May 1993 *Employees:* 3
Net Worth: £17,027,240 *Total Assets:* £43,598,580
Registered Office: c/o Union Property Services Ltd, Cobalt 3.1, Silver Fox Way, Cobalt Business Park, Wallsend, Tyne & Wear, NE27 0QJ
Activities: Buying and selling of own real estate
Parent: Norham House 3 Limited
Officers: Mukesh Kumar Sehgal [1949] Director; Promila Sehgal [1948] Director; Raj Kumar Sehgal [1975] Director

Unipres (UK) Limited
Incorporated: 14 September 1987 *Employees:* 1,396
Net Worth: £75,051,000 *Total Assets:* £168,375,008
Registered Office: Cherry Blossom Way, Sunderland, Tyne & Wear, SR5 3NT
Activities: Forging, pressing, stamping and roll-forming of metal; powder metallurgy
Parent: Unipres Corporation
Officers: Andrew Fawell, Secretary; John Cruddace [1959] Director; Gary Graham [1963] Director; Hideo Kanazawa [1959] Director [Japanese]; Yukihiko Morita [1959] Director [Japanese]; Masanobu Yoshizawa [1953] Director [Japanese]

United British Caravans Limited
Incorporated: 30 November 2006 *Employees:* 27
Net Worth: £3,203,000 *Total Assets:* £5,560,000
Registered Office: UBC, Sandy Lane, Wideopen, Newcastle upon Tyne, NE3 5HE
Activities: Other retail sale of new goods in specialised stores (not commercial art galleries and opticians)
Parent: Xander Developments Ltd
Officers: Alexander Lloyd Levington, Secretary; Thomas Frederick Lambert [1948] Director; Alexander Lloyd Levington [1973] Director/General Manager

United Carlton Digital Solutions Limited
Incorporated: 6 March 2006 *Employees:* 31
Net Worth: £1,995,788 *Total Assets:* £2,820,451
Registered Office: Meadow Court, Dukesway, Team Valley Trading Estate, Gateshead, Tyne & Wear, NE11 0PZ
Activities: Other information technology service activities
Parent: Ucos Holdings Ltd
Officers: Paul William Dawson, Secretary/Accountant; Mark Andrew Bryce [1968] Sales Director; Warren Michael Colby [1971] Sales Director; John Ellis [1966] Sales Director; Adam Mark Fawcett [1974] Sales Director; Michael David Nelson [1968] Sales Director; Nicholas Jeremy Speight [1973] Director/Sales Executive; John Watson [1960] Sales Director

United Carlton Office Systems Limited
Incorporated: 1 April 1987 *Employees:* 76
Net Worth: £4,027,808 *Total Assets:* £8,668,211
Registered Office: Meadow Court, Dukesway, Team Valley Trading Estate, Gateshead, Tyne & Wear, NE11 0PZ
Activities: Wholesale of other office machinery and equipment
Parent: Ucos Holdings Ltd
Officers: Paul William Dawson, Secretary/Accountant; Mark Andrew Bryce [1968] Director/Sales Executive; Warren Michael Colby [1971] Director/Sales Manager; Paul William Dawson [1959] Director/Accountant; John Ellis [1966] Director/Sales Executive; Michael David Nelson [1968] Director/Salesman; John Watson [1960] Director/Sales Manager

United Healthcare Developments Limited
Incorporated: 26 June 2000 *Employees:* 7
Net Worth: £19,615,584 *Total Assets:* £45,081,880
Registered Office: Hanover House, 13 Victoria Road, Darlington, Co Durham, DL1 5SF
Activities: Other letting and operating of own or leased real estate
Parent: United Healthcare Holdings Limited
Officers: Katherine Susan Brown, Secretary; David Colin Currer Brown [1965] Director/Surveyor; Katherine Susan Brown [1965] Director

The United Reformed Church (Northern Province) Trust Limited
Incorporated: 13 March 1914 *Employees:* 7
Net Worth: £10,575,927 *Total Assets:* £10,795,570
Registered Office: 4 College Lane, Newcastle upon Tyne, NE1 8JJ
Activities: Activities of other holding companies n.e.c.
Officers: Dr Andrew Hamnett, Secretary; William Ian Buchanan [1948] Director/Part-Time Lecturer; Dr Heather Jean Finlayson [1952] Director/University Lecturer; John Christopher Gilmour Forrest [1940] Director/Retired; Revd David Grosch-Miller [1948] Director/Minister of Religion; Dr Andrew Hamnett [1947] Director; Revd Dr Anthony Paul Haws [1946] Director/Retired; Carol Hogg [1948] Director/Retired; Joseph Cecil Kennedy [1942] Director/Retired; Michael John Louis [1944] Director/Retired; Peter Brooke Matthew [1942] Director; Janet Ruth Tomlin [1937] Director/Chartered Accountant (Retired)

Unity City Academy Trust
Incorporated: 21 January 2002 *Employees:* 145
Net Worth: £18,486,000 *Total Assets:* £21,389,000
Registered Office: Unity City Academy, Ormesby Road, Middlesbrough, Cleveland, TS3 8RE
Activities: General secondary education
Officers: Helen Dao Carter, Secretary; David Thomas Hatchett [1978] Executive Director; Howard Gowland Leighton [1957] Director/Sports Coach; Kevin Luke Parish [1971] Director of HR; Gemma Clare Simon [1979] Director; Michael Thompson [1955] Director; Stella Trantor [1973] Director/Learning Support Assistant; Robert David Turner [1962] Director/Education Professional; Beverley Whitfield [1978] Director/Teacher

Unity Tech Group Ltd
Incorporated: 30 November 2016
Net Worth: £601,257 *Total Assets:* £1,605,924
Registered Office: Brunel House, Brunel Road, Middlesbrough, Cleveland, TS6 6JA
Activities: Activities of head offices
Officers: Simon Colin Scotchbrook [1973] Director; David Ronald Tiplady Thompson [1945] Director

Universal Coatings & Services Limited
Incorporated: 27 October 1999 *Employees:* 78
Net Worth: £1,625,252 *Total Assets:* £3,245,909
Registered Office: Port Clarence Offshore Base, Port Clarence Road, Middlesbrough, Cleveland, TS2 1RZ
Activities: Other manufacturing n.e.c.
Parent: Wilton Engineering Services Limited
Officers: Christine Stobbs, Secretary; Stephen Glenn [1959] Director; Paul Joseph Johnson [1955] Director; William Scott [1961] Director; Christine Stobbs [1973] Finance Director

Universal Systems Solutions (Security) Limited
Incorporated: 26 February 2004 *Employees:* 20
Net Worth: £198,791 *Total Assets:* £1,070,174
Registered Office: Unit 4 Boldon Court, Burford Way, Boldon Colliery, Co Durham, NE35 9PY
Activities: Other specialised construction activities n.e.c.
Shareholders: Kevin Bruce; Brian Joseph Fascoine
Officers: Michelle Reay, Secretary; Kevin Bruce [1957] Director; Brian Fascione [1962] Director; John Frederick Ramsay [1960] Director/Contracts Manager

Universal Wolf Limited
Incorporated: 21 August 1997 *Employees:* 95
Net Worth: £1,226,265 *Total Assets:* £4,604,593
Registered Office: Universal Wolf Ltd, Birmayne House, Cowley Road, Blyth Riverside Business Park, Blyth, Northumberland, NE24 5TF
Activities: Manufacture of metal structures and parts of structures
Parent: Tharsus Group Limited
Officers: Brian Palmer, Secretary; Brian Andrew Palmer [1966] Director; Robert Wight Palmer [1939] Director

University of Northumbria at Newcastle Developments Limited
Incorporated: 29 April 1997 *Employees:* 2
Net Worth: £1,664 *Total Assets:* £1,623,038
Registered Office: Sutherland Building, College Street, Newcastle upon Tyne, NE1 8ST
Activities: First-degree level higher education
Parent: University of Northumbria at Newcastle
Officers: Professor Andrew Brian Wathey [1958] Director/Vice-Chancellor and CEO

University of Sunderland Enterprises Limited
Incorporated: 29 January 1990
Net Worth: £485,000 *Total Assets:* £1,101,000
Registered Office: 4th Floor, Edinburgh Building, City Campus, Chester Road, Sunderland, Tyne & Wear, SR1 3SD
Activities: Other business support service activities n.e.c.
Officers: Doreen Reveley, Secretary; Ben Dale [1970] Director of Finance; Dr Anthony Ikwue [1961] University Director of Enterprise and Innovation; Stephen Colin Knight [1960] Director/University Chief Operating Officer

Unsworth Unsworth & Co. Limited
Incorporated: 30 April 2007
Net Worth: £172,844 *Total Assets:* £852,801
Registered Office: Hadrian House, Crowther Road, Crowther Industrial Estate, Washington, Tyne & Wear, NE38 0AQ
Activities: Non-trading company
Shareholders: Alan John Unsworth; Elizabeth Rutherford Unsworth
Officers: Alan John Unsworth, Secretary; Alan John Unsworth [1970] Director

UNW LLP
Incorporated: 25 March 2002 *Employees:* 90
Net Worth: £2,681,934 *Total Assets:* £3,502,334
Registered Office: Citygate, St James Boulevard, Newcastle upon Tyne, NE1 4JE
Officers: Neville Bearpark [1959] Member; Stephen Lant [1963] Member; Andrew James Granville Wilson [1960] Member; Anne Victoria Hallowell [1968] LLP Member; John Healey [1982] LLP Member; Mark Raymond Hetherington [1967] LLP Member; Paul Kaiser [1956] LLP Member; Charles Edward Dorning Linaker [1956] LLP Member; Michael James Morris [1974] LLP Member; Lee Muter [1969] LLP Member; David Redhead [1970] LLP Member; Hazel Marie Smith [1979] LLP Member; Alan Moore Suggett [1953] LLP Member; David Ward [1972] LLP Member

Unwind Me Limited
Incorporated: 14 February 2008 *Employees:* 5
Net Worth: £1,052,222 *Total Assets:* £1,458,470
Registered Office: 5 Jupiter Court, Orion Business Park, North Shields, Tyne & Wear, NE29 7SE
Activities: Retail sale via mail order houses or via Internet
Major Shareholder: Sanjay Nayyar
Officers: Anju Nayyar, Director/Secretary; Anju Nayyar [1975] Director Secretary; Sanjay Nayyar [1972] Director

UPA (UK) Limited
Incorporated: 15 January 2013 *Employees:* 11
Net Worth Deficit: £151,583 *Total Assets:* £2,707,948
Registered Office: Evenwood Industrial Estate, Copeland Road, Evenwood, Co Durham, DL14 9SF
Activities: Renting and leasing of construction and civil engineering machinery and equipment
Parent: C.A. Group (Holdings) Limited
Officers: Des Webster, Secretary; Neil James Alderson [1976] Commercial Director; Martin Lowther [1967] Director; Peter William Rowe [1961] Director; Desmond Joseph Webster [1963] Managing Director

Upnorth Engineering Services Limited
Incorporated: 4 February 2002 *Employees:* 99
Net Worth: £6,076,510 *Total Assets:* £13,303,114
Registered Office: Merlin House, Princesway, Team Valley Trading Estate, Gateshead, Tyne & Wear, NE11 0NF
Activities: Other engineering activities
Major Shareholder: Stewart Alan Grierson
Officers: Vickie Grierson, Secretary; Stewart Alan Grierson [1978] Director/Engineer; Vickie Grierson [1977] Financial Director; John Alexander Soulsby [1983] Operations Director

Upperbay Limited
Incorporated: 30 July 1999 *Employees:* 304
Net Worth: £50,624,000 *Total Assets:* £82,787,000
Registered Office: 2nd Floor, One Gosforth Park Way, Gosforth Business Park, Newcastle upon Tyne, NE12 8ET
Activities: Recreational vehicle parks, trailer parks and camping grounds
Parent: PD Parks Limited
Officers: Judith Ann Archibold, Secretary; Ian Kellett [1963] Director; John Anthony Waterworth [1963] Director/Chief Executive

Urban Lifestyle Limited
Incorporated: 7 May 2013
Net Worth: £303,155 *Total Assets:* £2,454,740
Registered Office: 190 Linthorpe Road, Middlesbrough, Cleveland, TS1 3RF
Activities: Other accommodation
Officers: Julian Charles Oliver Pilling [1971] Director

Utex Industries UK Limited
Incorporated: 20 March 2002 *Employees:* 50
Net Worth: £1,708,376 *Total Assets:* £4,492,028
Registered Office: Jubilee Industrial Estate, Ashington, Northumberland, NE63 8UA
Activities: Manufacture of other rubber products
Officers: Scott Mason, Secretary; Michael Balas [1964] Director/President/CEO [American]; George Albert Malcolm Duhrin [1951] Operations Director; Jairo Parra Suarez [1961] Director/Treasurer and International Controller [Colombian]; Pete Sanchez [1956] Director/Finance [American]

Utilergy Gas Limited
Incorporated: 12 April 2012
Net Worth: £156,563 *Total Assets:* £1,608,138
Registered Office: Site 8, Unit 1 Cold Hesledon Industrial Estate, Cold Hesledon, Seaham, Co Durham, SR7 8ST
Activities: Management consultancy activities other than financial management
Officers: David Bailey [1970] Director; Jeannie Elizabeth Bailey [1974] Director; Andrea Gardner [1971] Director; Simon Matthew Gardner [1971] Director

Utilergy Limited
Incorporated: 23 November 2006
Net Worth: £369,201 *Total Assets:* £1,061,144
Registered Office: Site 8, Unit 1 Cold Hesledon Industrial Estate, Cold Hesledon, Seaham, Co Durham, SR7 8ST
Activities: Management consultancy activities other than financial management
Officers: Simon Matthew Gardner, Secretary; David Bailey [1970] Director; Jeannie Elizabeth Bailey [1974] Director; Andrea Gardner [1971] Director; Simon Matthew Gardner [1971] Director

Utility Alliance Ltd
Incorporated: 10 February 2015 *Employees:* 49
Net Worth: £554,917 *Total Assets:* £1,129,537
Registered Office: Tranquility House, Harbour Walk, Hartlepool, Cleveland, TS24 0UX
Activities: Trade of electricity
Shareholders: Darren Sutherland; Robert James Moore; Phillip John Moore
Officers: Phillip John Moore [1980] Director; Robert James Moore [1978] Director; Darren Sutherland [1963] Director

Utility ROV Services Limited
Incorporated: 6 December 2013 *Employees:* 19
Net Worth Deficit: £2,396,014 *Total Assets:* £5,438,560
Registered Office: Great North House, Sandyford Road, Newcastle upon Tyne, NE1 8ND
Activities: Other manufacturing n.e.c.
Major Shareholder: Peter Lee
Officers: Patrick John Crawford [1983] Director/Engineer; Peter Lee [1966] Director [Canadian]

Utility Services (N.E.) Limited
Incorporated: 29 December 2005 *Employees:* 45
Net Worth: £1,640,830 *Total Assets:* £3,636,493
Registered Office: 14 Citywest Business Park, St Johns Road, Meadowfield, Co Durham, DH7 8ER
Activities: Construction of other civil engineering projects n.e.c.
Officers: Louise O'Connor, Secretary; Louise O'Connor [1974] Director; Patrick George O'Connor [1975] Director/Executive; Christopher Michael Stephenson [1983] Director

Utility Support Solutions Limited
Incorporated: 8 June 2011
Net Worth: £372,892 *Total Assets:* £2,275,205
Registered Office: Penshaw Way, Portobello Industrial Estate, Chester-le-Street, Co Durham, DH3 2SA
Activities: Construction of roads and motorways
Officers: Gavin Paul Johnston [1964] Director

Utilitywise PLC
Incorporated: 19 June 2006 *Employees:* 1,629
Net Worth: £59,388,952 *Total Assets:* £102,674,568
Registered Office: Utilitywise House, 3 & 4 Cobalt Park Way, Cobalt Business Park, New York, Tyne & Wear, NE28 9EJ
Activities: Distribution of electricity
Officers: Natalie Claire Gerrard, Secretary; Kathleen Child-Villiers [1965] Director [American]; Debra Davies [1963] Director; Brendan Peter Flattery [1964] Director; Richard Stephen Laker [1976] Director; Richard Brinsley Sheridan [1964] Director/Chief Operating Officer; Simon Waugh [1958] Director

UTS Engineering Limited
Incorporated: 2 April 2001 *Employees:* 87
Net Worth: £2,490,372 *Total Assets:* £4,668,712
Registered Office: Connor House, Pilgrims Way, Bede Industrial Estate, Jarrow, Tyne & Wear, NE32 3EW
Activities: Treatment and coating of metals
Parent: UTS Group Limited
Officers: Giles Gavin Johnston [1977] Director; Shaun William Sadler [1970] Director; Thomas Wilkinson [1958] Director/Engineering Manager; Daniel Wilson [1983] Director

UTS Group Limited
Incorporated: 2 April 2001
Net Worth: £510,203 *Total Assets:* £1,082,523
Registered Office: Connor House, 30 Pilgrims Way, Bede Industrial Estate, Jarrow, Tyne & Wear, NE32 3EW
Activities: Other business support service activities n.e.c.
Major Shareholder: Shaun Sadler
Officers: Shaun William Sadler [1970] Director

V.H. Bio Limited
Incorporated: 13 February 1991 *Employees:* 12
Net Worth: £1,383,523 *Total Assets:* £2,790,264
Registered Office: Unit 11b Station Approach, Team Valley Trading Estate, Gateshead, Tyne & Wear, NE11 0ZF
Activities: Wholesale of chemical products
Major Shareholder: Alison Joan Wortley
Officers: Alison Joan Wortley [1972] Technical Director

VA Property Developments Limited
Incorporated: 30 April 2015
Net Worth: £39,679 *Total Assets:* £1,056,366
Registered Office: Aston House, Redburn Road, Newcastle upon Tyne, NE5 1NB
Activities: Development of building projects
Major Shareholder: Gavin Renganaden Venchard
Officers: Gavin Renganaden Venchard [1959] Director/Dentist

Vale of Mowbray Holdings Limited
Incorporated: 11 June 2004 *Employees:* 247
Net Worth: £7,331,876 *Total Assets:* £19,328,004
Registered Office: 20 Leases Road, Leeming Bar, Northallerton, N Yorks, DL7 9AW
Activities: Production of meat and poultry meat products
Major Shareholder: John Gatenby
Officers: Mark Jonathon Gatenby [1972] Director/Operations Manager; Giles Francis John Penn [1967] Director/Financial Controller

Vale of Mowbray Limited
Incorporated: 25 July 1995 *Employees:* 247
Net Worth: £9,559,656 *Total Assets:* £21,458,016
Registered Office: 20 Leases Road, Leeming Bar, N Yorks, DL7 9AW
Activities: Production of meat and poultry meat products
Parent: Vale of Mowbray Holdings Limited
Officers: Mark Jonathon Gatenby [1972] Director/Operations Manager; Giles Francis John Penn [1967] Director/Financial Controller

Vale Ventures Limited
Incorporated: 8 September 2015
Net Worth Deficit: £120,250 *Total Assets:* £931,266
Registered Office: 54-56 Keswick Street, Gateshead, Tyne & Wear, NE8 1TQ
Activities: Buying and selling of own real estate
Officers: Martin Zvi Oppenheimer [1989] Director

LV Valenbeck Limited
Incorporated: 21 March 2006 *Employees:* 48
Net Worth: £394,350 *Total Assets:* £1,399,388
Registered Office: Bailey Industrial Estate, Ellison Street, Jarrow, Tyne & Wear, NE32 3JU
Activities: Manufacture of wooden containers
Officers: Lee Woolams, Secretary; Colin Ainsley [1957] Managing Director; Lee Woolams [1978] Finance Director

Valens Contracts Limited
Incorporated: 18 May 1992
Net Worth: £999,553 *Total Assets:* £3,301,740
Registered Office: c/o RMT Accountants, Gosforth Park Avenue, Newcastle upon Tyne, NE12 8EG
Activities: Other service activities n.e.c.
Officers: Dr Christopher Marr, Secretary; Dr Alistair Blair [1969] Director/Doctor; Dr Rakesh Chopra [1961] Director/GP; Dr Zoe Claire Crichton [1975] Director/General Practitioner; Dr Lindsay John Gilfillan [1961] Director/GP; Stephen Andrew Hinchliffe [1967] Director/Doctor; Dr Adrian Allan Jefferies [1976] Director/GP; Dr Sarah Emma Jones [1971] Director/GP; Dr Margaret Jacinta Marie Manship [1967] Director/General Practitioner; Dr Christopher Marr [1959] Director/Medical Practitioner; Dr Catherine Frances McKinney [1973] Director/GP; Dr. Aamir Munir [1972] Director/GP; Dr Caroline Elizabeth Phipps [1982] Director/General Practitioner; Dr Christopher John Prank [1963] Director/GP; Dr Suzanne Louise Renner [1974] Director/General Practitioner; Dr Barnaby Colin Rookwood [1970] Director/GP; Dr. Donna Marie Wall [1977] Director/GP; Dr John Richard Warrington [1973] Director/GP; Dr Rebecca Joanne Wright [1973] Director/GP

Valiant Sheep Limited
Incorporated: 4 January 1991
Net Worth: £2,016,137 *Total Assets:* £2,151,137
Registered Office: Gloucester Road, West Chirton Industrial Estate, North Shields, Tyne & Wear, NE29 8RQ
Activities: Activities of head offices
Parent: Diesel Marine International Limited
Officers: Alan Leslie Gray, Secretary/Accountant; Peter Lindsey Jackson [1941] Director; Richard Kevin Woodmansey [1954] Director

Validus Investments Limited
Incorporated: 16 October 2015 *Employees:* 2
Net Worth Deficit: £17,821 *Total Assets:* £872,050
Registered Office: c/o RMT Accountants & Business Advisors Ltd, Gosforth Park Avenue, Newcastle upon Tyne, NE12 8EG
Activities: Other letting and operating of own or leased real estate
Shareholders: Magnus Ainsworth McGillivray; Steven Vincent Taylor
Officers: Magnus Ainsworth McGillivray [1979] Director; Steven Vincent Taylor [1986] Director

Vallum Properties Limited
Incorporated: 2 June 1994
Net Worth: £1,659,672 *Total Assets:* £2,284,587
Registered Office: Fernwood House, Fernwood Road, Jesmond, Newcastle upon Tyne, NE2 1TJ
Activities: Other letting and operating of own or leased real estate
Major Shareholder: Michael St. John Way
Officers: Roderick David Adams, Secretary/Solicitor; Michael St. John Way [1942] Director

Valmont Stainton Limited
Incorporated: 23 August 1999 *Employees:* 114
Net Worth: £10,759,000 *Total Assets:* £16,793,000
Registered Office: Unit 5 Dukesway, Teesside Industrial Estate, Stockton on Tees, Cleveland, TS17 9LT
Activities: Manufacture of metal structures and parts of structures
Officers: Roger Andrew Massey, Secretary; Mark Charles Jaksich [1957] Director/Accountant [American]; Roger Andrew Massey [1969] Director [American]; Neil Richard Stainthorpe [1963] Director; Jamie Austin Taylor [1971] Director; David William Tweed [1972] Director

Valued Properties Limited
Incorporated: 6 February 1962 *Employees:* 1
Net Worth: £2,818,085 *Total Assets:* £2,924,335
Registered Office: 63 High Street, Marske-by-the-Sea, Redcar, Cleveland, TS11 6JW
Activities: Other letting and operating of own or leased real estate
Officers: Andrea Kay, Secretary; Derek Stanley Bainbridge [1951] Director/Motor Engineer; Andrea Kay [1962] Director/Office Manageress

The Van Centre (Richmond) Limited
Incorporated: 21 February 2000 *Employees:* 4
Net Worth: £2,553,943 *Total Assets:* £2,968,007
Registered Office: Scorton Road, Brompton on Swale, N Yorks, DL10 7EQ
Activities: Sale of new cars and light motor vehicles
Shareholder: Michelle Robertson
Officers: Michelle Robertson, Secretary/Director; Michelle Robertson [1965] Director; William Fraser Robertson [1963] Director

Van Hessen UK Casings Ltd
Incorporated: 1 June 1979 *Employees:* 12
Net Worth: £1,417,376 *Total Assets:* £3,908,318
Registered Office: 12 The Parade, Sunderland, Tyne & Wear, SR2 8NT
Activities: Production of meat and poultry meat products
Parent: Van Hessen UK Holding Ltd
Officers: Marie Remmer, Secretary; Robert Martijn Schouten [1977] Director [Dutch]

Van Hessen UK Holding Ltd
Incorporated: 10 November 1986
Net Worth: £1,770,455 *Total Assets:* £1,770,455
Registered Office: Charlton & Co, Chartered Accountants, Saville Chambers, 4 Saville Street, South Shields, Tyne & Wear, NE33 2PR
Activities: Activities of head offices
Officers: Marcel Van Der Toorn, Secretary; Elliot Joseph Simon [1974] Managing Director [Dutch]; Jan Willem Vreeburg [1964] Director [Dutch]

Van Mildert Landlord and Tenant Protection Limited
Incorporated: 3 November 2009 *Employees:* 59
Net Worth: £1,561,961 *Total Assets:* £2,125,280
Registered Office: DCS House, Camperdown Industrial Estate, Newcastle upon Tyne, NE12 5UJ
Activities: Non-life insurance
Parent: Millex Investments Limited
Officers: Christian Alexis Balshen [1979] Director; Nicholas Mark Ryman Richards [1966] Director; Mark Vincent Rijkse [1968] Director [New Zealander]; Steven Gary Simons [1972] Director; Mark Anthony Stewart [1956] Director

Vandewiele UK Limited
Incorporated: 16 June 2006 *Employees:* 28
Net Worth: £745,053 *Total Assets:* £827,026
Registered Office: Textile House, Dukesway, Team Valley Trading Estate, Gateshead, Tyne & Wear, NE11 0LF
Activities: Engineering design activities for industrial process and production
Officers: Debra Ann Almond, Secretary/Accountant; John Robert Harding [1960] Director; Jason James Kent [1969] Director/General Manager; Bram Hugo Willem Vanderjeugt [1966] Director/Engineer [Belgian]

Vantec Europe Limited
Incorporated: 12 January 1990 *Employees:* 930
Net Worth: £18,969,870 *Total Assets:* £35,641,512
Registered Office: 3 Infiniti Drive, Hillthorn Business Park, Washington, Tyne & Wear, NE37 3HG
Activities: Other service activities incidental to land transportation, n.e.c.
Parent: Hitachi Transport System Limited
Officers: Abigail Curry, Secretary/Accountant; Riichiro Hirano [1964] Director/Chief Executive [Japanese]; Martin Kendall [1967] Managing Director; Hirotaka Takada [1962] Director/Executive Officer [Japanese]

Vapourlites Limited
Incorporated: 12 September 2011 *Employees:* 19
Net Worth: £858,162 *Total Assets:* £1,648,020
Registered Office: 4 Whitworth Road, South West Industrial Estate, Peterlee, Co Durham, SR8 2LY
Activities: Retail sale via mail order houses or via Internet
Shareholders: John Benjamin Quinney; Charles David Bloom
Officers: Charles David Bloom [1966] Director; John Benjamin Quinney [1968] Director/Computer Sales

Vardy 1985 Investments Limited
Incorporated: 24 October 2013 *Employees:* 2
Net Worth: £172,115 *Total Assets:* £1,813,330
Registered Office: 32 Portland Terrace, Newcastle upon Tyne, NE2 1QP
Activities: Financial management
Parent: Peter Vardy 1985 A&M Settlement
Officers: Sir Peter Vardy [1947] Director; Richard Angus Reginald Vardy [1973] Director

George Vardy Limited
Incorporated: 10 December 1980 *Employees:* 32
Net Worth: £1,117,721 *Total Assets:* £1,911,721
Registered Office: Richard Street, Hetton-le-Hole, Co Durham, DH5 9HN
Activities: Other specialised construction activities n.e.c.
Major Shareholder: George Vardy
Officers: Doreen Vardy, Secretary; Sara Middleton [1988] Director/Accountant; Louise Reay [1975] Director; Doreen Vardy [1932] Director/Secretary; George James Vardy [1995] Director; George Vardy [1953] Director/Plant Hire Contractor

Vardy Property (Teesside) Limited
Incorporated: 10 August 2006
Net Worth: £1,896,101 *Total Assets:* £3,698,655
Registered Office: 32 Portland Terrace, Newcastle upon Tyne, NE2 1QP
Activities: Buying and selling of own real estate
Parent: Vardy Property Group Limited
Officers: Sir Peter Vardy [1947] Director/Chairman; Richard Angus Reginald Vardy [1973] Managing Director

Vardy Property Aberdeen Ltd
Incorporated: 26 October 2005
Net Worth: £960,981 *Total Assets:* £5,981,606
Registered Office: 32 Portland Terrace, Newcastle upon Tyne, NE2 1QP
Activities: Buying and selling of own real estate
Major Shareholder: Sir Peter Vardy
Officers: Sir Peter Vardy [1947] Director/Chairman; Richard Angus Reginald Vardy [1973] Director

Vardy Property Group Limited
Incorporated: 8 July 2002 *Employees:* 3
Net Worth: £221,662 *Total Assets:* £9,807,455
Registered Office: 32 Portland Terrace, Newcastle upon Tyne, NE2 1QP
Activities: Buying and selling of own real estate
Shareholders: Richard Angus Reginald Vardy; Louise Clare Vardy
Officers: Louise Clare Vardy [1974] Director; Sir Peter Vardy [1947] Director/Chairman; Richard Angus Reginald Vardy [1973] Managing Director

Vardy Property LLP
Incorporated: 23 April 2008
Net Worth: £2,952,218 *Total Assets:* £2,956,173
Registered Office: 32 Portland Terrace, Newcastle upon Tyne, NE2 1QP
Officers: Louise Clare Vardy [1974] Member; Richard Angus Reginald Vardy [1973] Member

Vaulkhard Group Limited
Incorporated: 1 April 1999 *Employees:* 279
Net Worth: £13,280,441 *Total Assets:* £23,506,896
Registered Office: Bealim House, 17-25 Gallowgate, Newcastle upon Tyne, NE1 4SG
Activities: Other letting and operating of own or leased real estate
Shareholders: Oliver Tom Vaulkhard; Harry Vaulkhard
Officers: Sarah Barbara Cook [1972] Director; Harry Vaulkhard [1985] Director; Oliver Tom Vaulkhard [1971] Director

Vaulkhard Investment Properties Limited
Incorporated: 12 January 1994
Net Worth: £1,768,653 *Total Assets:* £2,168,876
Registered Office: Bealim House, 17-25 Gallowgate, Newcastle upon Tyne, NE1 4SG
Activities: Other letting and operating of own or leased real estate
Shareholders: Oliver Tom Vaulkhard; Harry Vaulkhard
Officers: Sarah Barbara Cook [1972] Director; Harry Vaulkhard [1985] Director; Oliver Tom Vaulkhard [1971] Director

Vaulkhard Leisure Limited
Incorporated: 26 November 2004 *Employees:* 243
Net Worth: £2,719,974 *Total Assets:* £13,141,100
Registered Office: Bealim House, 17-25 Gallowgate, Newcastle upon Tyne, NE1 4SG
Activities: Public houses and bars
Shareholders: Oliver Tom Vaulkhard; Harry Vaulkhard
Officers: Oliver Tom Vaulkhard, Secretary/Director; Sarah Barbara Cook [1972] Operations Director; Harry Vaulkhard [1985] Director; Oliver Tom Vaulkhard [1971] Director

Vauxhall Holiday Park Limited
Incorporated: 4 March 1960 *Employees:* 167
Net Worth: £5,198,000 *Total Assets:* £9,637,000
Registered Office: 2nd Floor, One Gosforth Park Way, Gosforth Business Park, Newcastle upon Tyne, NE12 8ET
Activities: Recreational vehicle parks, trailer parks and camping grounds
Parent: Parkdean Resorts Limited
Officers: Judith Archibold, Secretary; Ian Gill [1974] Director; Ian Kellett [1963] Director; John Anthony Waterworth [1963] Director

VCS (Holdings UK) Limited
Incorporated: 25 January 2013 *Employees:* 104
Net Worth Deficit: £20,634,404 *Total Assets:* £37,471,528
Registered Office: 4th Floor, Central Square, Forth Street, Newcastle upon Tyne, NE1 3PJ
Activities: Other business support service activities n.e.c.
Parent: Viewpoint, Inc.
Officers: Manolis Kotzabasakis [1959] Director [Greek]; Kelly E Lang [1961] Director/Chief Financial Officer/Accountant [American]

Vectis Auctions Limited
Incorporated: 3 January 1997 *Employees:* 29
Net Worth: £510,502 *Total Assets:* £1,113,424
Registered Office: Fleck Way, Teesside Industrial Estate, Thornaby, Stockton on Tees, Cleveland, TS17 9JZ
Activities: Other business support service activities n.e.c.
Parent: The Hambleton Group Limited
Officers: Georgina Goodall, Secretary; Bryan Walter Goodall [1948] Director; Georgina Goodall [1947] Director; Jonathan James Goodall [1973] Director; Kathryn Holly Robson [1975] Director; Victoria Weall [1966] Director

Vector Power Solutions Limited
Incorporated: 19 September 2002 *Employees:* 8
Net Worth: £1,164,585 *Total Assets:* £1,413,391
Registered Office: The Axis Building, Maingate, Kingsway North, Team Valley Trading Estate, Gateshead, Tyne & Wear, NE11 0NQ
Activities: Agents specialised in the sale of other particular products
Officers: Kenneth George Chapman, Secretary; Keith Allan [1967] Director; June Chapman [1949] Director; Kenneth George Chapman [1950] Director/Engineer; Maria Rita Hindle [1955] Director; Paul Joseph Hindle [1956] Director/Electrical Engineer

Vega Environmental Consultants Limited
Incorporated: 18 November 1988 *Employees:* 34
Net Worth: £559,516 *Total Assets:* £887,457
Registered Office: Church Building, Station Road, Seaton Delaval, Whitley Bay, Tyne & Wear, NE25 0PT
Activities: Environmental consulting activities
Major Shareholder: Edward Brown
Officers: Alison Brown, Secretary; Alison Brown [1959] Director/Company Secretary; Edward Brown [1962] Director; Ronald Brown [1964] Director

The Vehicle Group Limited
Incorporated: 27 November 2008 *Employees:* 90
Net Worth: £746,366 *Total Assets:* £2,247,689
Registered Office: 1 Target, Chartermark Way, Colburn Business Park, Colburn, N Yorks, DL9 4QJ
Activities: Agents specialised in the sale of other particular products
Major Shareholder: Graeme Michael Frankland
Officers: Graeme Michael Frankland [1958] Director; Claire Freeman Palmer [1964] Financial Director

Vehicle Lease and Service Limited
Incorporated: 10 August 1998 *Employees:* 76
Net Worth: £5,796,716 *Total Assets:* £32,877,600
Registered Office: Centre for Advanced Industry, 3rd Floor, Coble Dene, Royal Quays, North Shields, Tyne & Wear, NE29 6DE
Activities: Renting and leasing of cars and light motor vehicles
Shareholders: NWG Commercial Solutions Limited; Northern Electric PLC
Officers: Joanne Wheatley, Secretary; Louise Bennett [1986] Director/Treasurer and Investor Reporting Manager; Stewart Hazon [1971] Director/Group Financial Controller; Daniel George Frederick Keating [1968] Managing Director; Stephen John Lockwood [1965] Director/Accountant; John Edward McGovern [1958] Director/Chartered Civil Engineer; Richard Ian Murray [1967] Director/Engineer; Gareth David Pearson [1967] Director/Head of Operational Services; Neil Rutherford [1969] Director/Accountant

Vehicle Movements (North East) Limited
Incorporated: 2 July 1986
Net Worth: £2,318,069 *Total Assets:* £3,136,884
Registered Office: Sandy Lane, North Gosforth, Newcastle upon Tyne, NE3 5HE
Activities: Freight transport by road
Officers: Moira Ann Hogg, Secretary; Colin James Hogg [1966] Director; David Hogg [1971] Director; James Murray Hogg [1960] Director; Dr Jennifer Murray Hogg [1963] Director/Doctor; John Murray Hogg [1934] Director/Haulage Contractor; Paul Hogg [1973] Director; Deborah Anne Scott [1962] Director; Alyson Mary Summerhill [1959] Director/Secretary; Joanne Topping [1969] Director

Velocity UK Limited
Incorporated: 8 July 1997 *Employees:* 42
Net Worth: £637,579 *Total Assets:* £3,419,695
Registered Office: Armstrong Works, Scotswood Road, Newcastle upon Tyne, NE15 6UX
Activities: Manufacture of equipment for concrete crushing and screening and roadworks
Parent: Velocity Works Limited
Officers: Dominic Gardner [1980] Director; John Peter Reece [1961] Director

Venator Materials PLC
Incorporated: 28 April 2017
Net Worth: £883,742,592 *Total Assets:* £1,488,084,992
Registered Office: Titanium House, Hanzard Drive, Wynyard Park, Stockton on Tees, Cleveland, TS22 5FD
Activities: Activities of other holding companies n.e.c.
Parent: Huntsman Corporation
Officers: Russell Robert Stolle, Secretary; Douglas D Delano Anderson [1949] Director/Dean and Professor at Utah State University [American]; Daniele Ferrari [1961] Director/CEO of Eni SpA [Italian]; Peter Riley Huntsman [1963] Director/Business Executive [American]; Sir Robert Margetts [1946] Director/Deputy Chairman of OJSC Uralkali; Kathy Dawn Patrick [1960] Director/Attorney [American]; Simon Turner [1963] Director/President

Venator Materials UK Limited
Incorporated: 24 December 1964 *Employees:* 603
Net Worth: £152,603,008 *Total Assets:* £269,433,984
Registered Office: Titanium House, Hanzard Drive, Wynyard Park, Stockton on Tees, Cleveland, TS22 5FD
Activities: Manufacture of dyes and pigments
Parent: Venator P&A Holdings UK Limited
Officers: Richard Justin James Phillipson, Secretary; Kurt David Ogden [1968] Director/Finance [American]; John Jeffrey Pehrson [1975] Director [American]; Richard Justin James Phillipson [1968] Director/Solicitor; Russell Robert Stolle [1962] Director/Attorney [American]

Venator P&A Holdings UK Limited
Incorporated: 5 May 1999
Net Worth: £234,416,992 *Total Assets:* £268,370,000
Registered Office: Titanium House, Hanzard Drive, Wynyard Park, Stockton on Tees, Cleveland, TS22 5FD
Activities: Manufacture of other chemical products n.e.c.
Parent: Venator Materials International UK Limited
Officers: Richard Justin James Phillipson, Secretary; Kurt David Ogden [1968] Director/Finance [American]; John Jeffrey Pehrson [1975] Director [American]; Richard Justin James Phillipson [1968] Director/Solicitor; Russell Robert Stolle [1962] Director/Attorney [American]

Venator Pigments UK Limited
Incorporated: 14 June 1989 *Employees:* 130
Net Worth: £23,637,000 *Total Assets:* £34,611,000
Registered Office: Titanium House, Hanzard Drive, Wynyard Park, Stockton on Tees, Cleveland, TS22 5FD
Activities: Manufacture of dyes and pigments
Parent: Creambay Limited
Officers: Richard Justin James Phillipson, Secretary; Kurt David Ogden [1968] Director/Finance [American]; John Jeffrey Pehrson [1975] Director [American]; Richard Justin James Phillipson [1968] Director/Solicitor; Russell Robert Stolle [1962] Director/Attorney [American]; Simon Turner [1963] Director/President

M S Vernon Limited
Incorporated: 29 January 2014 *Employees:* 4
Net Worth: £275,878 *Total Assets:* £813,520
Registered Office: Coatsey Moor Farm, Heighington, Darlington, Co Durham, DL2 2XW
Activities: Growing of cereals (except rice), leguminous crops and oil seeds
Major Shareholder: Stewart Vernon
Officers: Gail Vernon [1961] Director/Farmer; Helen Browning Vernon [1938] Director/Farmer; Stewart Vernon [1959] Director/Farmer

Vertellus Specialties Holdings UK Limited
Incorporated: 29 October 2003 *Employees:* 224
Net Worth Deficit: £9,681,000 *Total Assets:* £38,265,000
Registered Office: St Anns Wharf, 112 Quayside, Newcastle upon Tyne, NE1 3DX
Activities: Activities of other holding companies n.e.c.
Officers: William David Dunn [1966] Director and Chief Financial Officer [American]; Anne Marie Frye [1966] Director/Attorney [American]

Vertellus Specialties UK Limited
Incorporated: 20 October 1993 *Employees:* 224
Net Worth: £2,745,000 *Total Assets:* £35,513,000
Registered Office: St Ann's Wharf, 112 Quayside, Newcastle upon Tyne, NE1 3DX
Activities: Manufacture of other inorganic basic chemicals
Parent: Vertellus Specialties Holdings UK Limited
Officers: William David Dunn [1966] Director and Chief Financial Officer [American]; Anne Marie Frye [1966] Director/Attorney [American]

Vertu Motors (Amc) Limited
Incorporated: 7 February 2007
Net Worth: £2,000,001 *Total Assets:* £3,696,815
Registered Office: Vertu House, Fifth Avenue Business Park, Team Valley Trading Estate, Gateshead, Tyne & Wear, NE11 0XA
Activities: Activities of other holding companies n.e.c.
Parent: Vertu Motors PLC
Officers: Karen Anderson, Secretary; Karen Anderson [1971] Finance Director; Robert Thomas Forrester [1969] Director; Michael Sherwin [1959] Finance Director

Vertu Motors (Chingford) Limited
Incorporated: 7 February 2007 *Employees:* 49
Net Worth: £1,944,000 *Total Assets:* £4,403,000
Registered Office: Vertu House, Fifth Avenue Business Park, Team Valley Trading Estate, Gateshead, Tyne & Wear, NE11 0XA
Activities: Sale of new cars and light motor vehicles
Parent: Vertu Motors PLC
Officers: Karen Anderson, Secretary; Karen Anderson [1971] Finance Director; David Paul Crane [1967] Director; Robert Thomas Forrester [1969] Director; Colin Kent [1957] Director; Michael Sherwin [1959] Finance Director

Vertu Motors (Knaresborough) Limited
Incorporated: 7 April 2015
Net Worth: £218,000 *Total Assets:* £2,980,000
Registered Office: Vertu House, Fifth Avenue Business Park, Team Valley Trading Estate, Gateshead, Tyne & Wear, NE11 0XA
Activities: Buying and selling of own real estate
Parent: Vertu Motors PLC
Officers: Karen Anderson, Secretary; Karen Anderson [1971] Finance Director; David Paul Crane [1967] Commercial Director; Robert Thomas Forrester [1969] Director; Michael Sherwin [1959] Finance Director

Vertu Motors (Property) Limited
Incorporated: 11 January 2007
Net Worth: £2,540,000 *Total Assets:* £204,256,992
Registered Office: Vertu House, Fifth Avenue Business Park, Team Valley Trading Estate, Gateshead, Tyne & Wear, NE11 0XA
Activities: Buying and selling of own real estate
Parent: Vertu Motors PLC
Officers: Karen Anderson, Secretary; Karen Anderson [1971] Finance Director; David Paul Crane [1967] Commercial Director; Robert Thomas Forrester [1969] Finance Director; Michael Sherwin [1959] Finance Director

Vertu Motors (Vmc) Limited
Incorporated: 5 June 1961 *Employees:* 611
Net Worth: £25,867,000 *Total Assets:* £61,004,000
Registered Office: Vertu House, Fifth Avenue Business Park, Team Valley Trading Estate, Gateshead, Tyne & Wear, NE11 0XA
Activities: Sale of new cars and light motor vehicles
Parent: Vertu Motors PLC
Officers: Karen Anderson, Secretary; Karen Anderson [1971] Finance Director; David Paul Crane [1967] Commercial Director; Robert Thomas Forrester [1969] Director; Colin Kent [1957] Director; Michael Sherwin [1959] Finance Director

Vertu Motors PLC
Incorporated: 1 November 2006 *Employees:* 5,271
Net Worth: £264,418,000 *Total Assets:* £969,068,032
Registered Office: Vertu House, Fifth Avenue Business Park, Team Valley Trading Estate, Gateshead, Tyne & Wear, NE11 0XA
Activities: Sale of new cars and light motor vehicles
Officers: Karen Anderson, Secretary; Pauline Ann Best [1963] People Director; David Paul Crane [1967] Commercial Director; Robert Thomas Forrester [1969] Director; Andrew Paul Goss [1958] Director/Consultant; Peter Jones [1956] Director; Kenneth Lever [1953] Director; Michael Sherwin [1959] Finance Director; Nigel Cleator Stead [1949] Director

Vestbrown (Esh) Limited
Incorporated: 25 October 2011
Net Worth: £7,163,661 *Total Assets:* £8,068,915
Registered Office: The Fam House, Hedley Hill Farm, Cornsay Colliery, Co Durham, DH7 9EX
Activities: Activities of construction holding companies
Officers: Marie Elizabeth McQuaid, Secretary; Michael Francis Hogan [1944] Director; Marie Elizabeth McQuaid [1978] Director

Vestbrown Limited
Incorporated: 20 September 1982
Net Worth: £11,420,801 *Total Assets:* £16,479,364
Registered Office: The Farm House, Hedley Hill Farm, Cornsay Colliery, Co Durham, DH7 9EX
Activities: Buying and selling of own real estate
Parent: Vestbrown (Newco) Limited
Officers: Michael Francis Hogan [1944] Director/Fencing Contractor

VHV Investments UK Limited
Incorporated: 13 May 2013
Net Worth: £2,124,080 *Total Assets:* £9,241,125
Registered Office: 32 Portland Terrace, Newcastle upon Tyne, NE2 1QP
Activities: Activities of investment trusts
Major Shareholder: Sir Peter Vardy
Officers: Lady Margaret Barr Vardy [1950] Director; Sir Peter Vardy [1947] Director

Vianet Group PLC
Incorporated: 28 January 2005 *Employees:* 174
Net Worth: £25,014,000 *Total Assets:* £34,717,000
Registered Office: 1 Surtees Way, Surtees Business Park, Stockton on Tees, Cleveland, TS18 3HR
Activities: Other service activities n.e.c.
Officers: Mark Hardwick Foster, Secretary/Chartered Accountant; David Charles Coplin [1970] Director; Stewart William Darling [1964] Commercial Director; James William Dickson [1959] Director; Mark Hardwick Foster [1962] Director/Chartered Accountant; Christopher Williams [1948] Director

Vicari Properties Services Limited
Incorporated: 29 March 1999
Net Worth: £103,171 *Total Assets:* £816,802
Registered Office: Kingfisher House, Kingfisher Way, Stockton on Tees, Cleveland, TS18 3EX
Activities: Other letting and operating of own or leased real estate
Shareholders: Maria Vicari; Gaetano Vicari
Officers: Domenica Vicari [1975] Director; Francesca Vicari [1972] Director; Gaetano Vicari [1939] Director/Sole Trader [Italian]; Maria Vicari [1943] Director/Sole Trader [Italian]

Stanley Vickers Limited
Incorporated: 15 March 1956 *Employees:* 21
Net Worth: £2,265,553 *Total Assets:* £3,929,818
Registered Office: Snowdon Road, Middlesbrough, Cleveland, TS2 1LG
Activities: Manufacture of plastic plates, sheets, tubes and profiles
Major Shareholder: Hassan Hafdani Zarei
Officers: Sara Melissa Phillips [1986] Director; Hassan Hafdani Zarei [1953] Director/Engineer

Vickers Scott Investment Company Limited
Incorporated: 3 January 1935 *Employees:* 5
Net Worth: £612,503 *Total Assets:* £939,485
Registered Office: Back Ellison Road, Dunston, Gateshead, Tyne & Wear, NE11 9TS
Activities: Development of building projects
Officers: John Vickers Scott, Secretary; Susan Mary Burfoot [1958] Director/Caterer; Betty Mary Scott [1923] Director/Retired; David Vickers Scott [1961] Director/Leisure Centre Manager; John Vickers Scott [1954] Director

Victor Products Holdings Ltd
Incorporated: 26 July 1929
Net Worth: £2,900,717 *Total Assets:* £3,088,113
Registered Office: c/o Victor Products Ltd, Unit 3a Tyne Dock East Side, Port of Tyne, South Shields, Tyne & Wear, NE33 5SQ
Activities: Activities of head offices
Parent: Federal Signal UK Holdings Limited
Officers: Daniel Anthony Dupre [1956] Director/Attorney [American]; Ian Hudson [1976] Director/VP, Interim CFO, Federal Signal Corporation; Jennifer Lynn Sherman [1964] Director/Chief Administrative Officer and General Counsel [American]; Svetlana Vinokur [1979] Director/VP Treasurer [American]

Victor Products Ltd
Incorporated: 11 March 2008 *Employees:* 14
Net Worth: £4,016,511 *Total Assets:* £5,001,309
Registered Office: Unit 3a Tyne Dock East Side, Port of Tyne, South Shields, Tyne & Wear, NE33 5SQ
Activities: Manufacture of electric lighting equipment
Parent: Victor Products Holdings Ltd
Officers: Daniel Anthony Dupre [1956] Director/Attorney [American]; Michael Ejupi [1965] Director/VP Taxes [American]; Ian Hudson [1976] Director/VP Interim CFO; Svetlana Vinokur [1979] Director/VP Treasurer [American]

Victoria Chemist Ltd
Incorporated: 6 October 2005
Net Worth: £1,503,981 *Total Assets:* £1,695,941
Registered Office: 15 Westwood Avenue, Linthorpe, Middlesbrough, Cleveland, TS5 5PX
Activities: Other human health activities
Shareholders: Zulfiqar Rafiq; Rehana Akhtar
Officers: Rehana Akhtar, Secretary; Zulfiqar Ali Rafiq [1979] Director

View Developments Limited
Incorporated: 13 May 2004
Net Worth: £102,212 *Total Assets:* £916,328
Registered Office: 7 Hartford Road, Darlington, Co Durham, DL3 8EY
Activities: Buying and selling of own real estate
Shareholder: Joanne Elizabeth Glendenning
Officers: David Antony Glendenning, Secretary; Emma Jayne Carrigan [1978] Director; Sean Kidson Carrigan [1971] Director/Engineer; David Antony Glendenning [1971] Director/Firefighter; Joanne Elizabeth Glendenning [1973] Director

View Logistics Limited
Incorporated: 2 October 2007 *Employees:* 119
Net Worth: £442,678 *Total Assets:* £2,463,413
Registered Office: View Logistics, Park View Road East, Hartlepool, Cleveland, TS25 1HT
Activities: Wholesale of textiles
Parent: Whitestone Carpets Holdings Ltd
Officers: Tanya Kelly, Secretary; Clive Nicholas Beckett [1969] Sales Director; Stephen Maurice Martin Byrne [1960] Director/Chairman; Stephen Donlan [1966] Managing Director; Nicholas Michael Finlay [1969] Sales Director; Vincent Holden [1956] Managing Director; Geoffrey Brendon Wilding [1963] Director [New Zealander]; Philip Yates [1975] Director/Operations Manager

Viewley Hill Academy
Incorporated: 5 December 2013 *Employees:* 44
Net Worth: £2,427,000 *Total Assets:* £2,849,000
Registered Office: Viewley Hill Academy, Andover Way, Hemlington, Middlesbrough, Cleveland, TS8 9HL
Activities: Primary education
Officers: Wendy Atkinson [1969] Director/Teaching Assistant; Paula Louise Bowler [1979] Director/School Business Manager; Paul Cowley [1980] Director/Headteacher; Gillan Dorman-Smith [1954] Director/School Adviser; Helen Claire Malbon [1972] Director/Headteacher; Joanne Measor [1970] Director/School Business Manager; Rachel Louise Moffat [1979] Director/Volunteer; Leah Shadforth [1992] Director/Teacher; Lesley Elizabeth Sinclair [1952] Director/Headteacher; Kenneth Edwin Stone [1956] Director/Pastor; Jane Caroline Thirkell [1981] Director/Finance Controller

Viewpoint Construction Software Ltd
Incorporated: 15 March 2000 *Employees:* 104
Net Worth: £4,858,493 *Total Assets:* £12,444,966
Registered Office: 4th Floor, Central Square, Forth Street, Newcastle upon Tyne, NE1 3PJ
Activities: Business and domestic software development
Parent: Riverside Acquistions Limited
Officers: Manolis Kotzabasakis [1959] Director [Greek]; Kelly E Lang [1961] Director/Chief Financial Officer/Accountant [American]

Vigilant Homes (UK) Limited
Incorporated: 24 September 2004
Net Worth: £35,597 *Total Assets:* £1,090,552
Registered Office: 212 Tedco Business Works, Henry Robson Way, South Shields, Tyne & Wear, NE33 1RF
Activities: Construction of domestic buildings
Major Shareholder: Kenneth Collins
Officers: Kenneth Collins, Secretary; Kenneth Collins [1960] Director/Bricklayer

Villafirst Investment Properties Limited
Incorporated: 4 February 1987
Net Worth: £350,121 *Total Assets:* £803,905
Registered Office: Hallgarth, Lincoln Hill, Humshaugh, Northumberland, NE46 4BE
Activities: Other letting and operating of own or leased real estate
Major Shareholder: Eileen Willey
Officers: Eileen Willey, Secretary/Director; Eileen Willey [1955] Director; Peter Gilhespy Willey [1951] Director/Chartered Accountant

The Vindolanda Trust
Incorporated: 19 August 2014 *Employees:* 36
Net Worth: £8,014,591 *Total Assets:* £8,496,422
Registered Office: Chesterholm Museum, Bardon Mill, Hexham, Northumberland, NE47 7JN
Activities: Operation of historical sites and buildings and similar visitor attractions
Officers: Dr Hans Christian Ib Anderson [1951] Director/Retired [Danish]; Gary Calland [1969] Director/General Manager; Terence Francis Carroll [1948] Director/Consultant; Professor Ian Haynes [1967] Director/Professor of Archaeology; Veryan Steele Johnston [1956] Director/Consultant; Professor David Mattingly [1958] Director/University Professor; Lawrence John Thompson [1938] Director/Retired; Dr Peter Richard Wilson [1957] Director/Consultant; Helen Louise Woodford [1975] Director/Solicitor

The Virgin Money Foundation
Incorporated: 25 February 2015
Net Worth: £1,984,200 *Total Assets:* £3,912,500
Registered Office: Jubilee House, Gosforth, Newcastle upon Tyne, NE3 4PL
Activities: Other business support service activities n.e.c.
Officers: Katie Marshall, Secretary; Tim Arthur [1970] Creative Director; Joanne Jane Curry [1972] Director/Chief Executive of Voluntary Sector Organisation; Timothy James Neil Davies-Pugh [1966] Director; Ruth Ibegbuna [1976] Director; Emma Margaret Morris [1974] Director/Psychotherapy Services; William Stephen Pearson [1961] Director/Senior Advisor; Edward Cecil Wakefield [1973] Director

Virgin Money Holdings (UK) PLC
Incorporated: 4 August 1995 *Employees:* 3,140
Net Worth: £1,670,499,968 *Total Assets:* £35,055,599,616
Registered Office: Jubilee House, Gosforth, Newcastle upon Tyne, NE3 4PL
Activities: Activities of head offices
Officers: Katie Jane Marshall, Secretary; Peter Douglas Bole [1969] Director/Chartered Accountant; Eva Kristina Eisenschimmel [1962] Director/Customer Experience; Jayne-Anne Gadhia [1961] Director/Accountant; Geeta Gopalan [1964] Director; Colin Denis Keogh [1953] Director; Patrick Charles Kingdon McCall [1964] Corporate Operations Director; Norman Cardie McLuskie [1944] Director; Darren Scott Pope [1965] Director; Amy Stirling [1969] Director/Accountant

Virgin Money Management Services Limited
Incorporated: 27 June 1995
Net Worth: £3,468,000 *Total Assets:* £3,548,000
Registered Office: Jubilee House, Gosforth, Newcastle upon Tyne, NE3 4PL
Activities: Other business support service activities n.e.c.
Parent: Virgin Money Holdings (UK) PLC
Officers: Katie Jane Marshall, Secretary; Marian MacDonald Martin [1967] Risk Director; Chad William Ryan [1969] Director/Accountant

Virgin Money Personal Financial Service Limited
Incorporated: 27 June 1995
Net Worth: £4,887,000 *Total Assets:* £6,022,000
Registered Office: Jubilee House, Gosforth, Newcastle upon Tyne, NE3 4PL
Activities: Financial intermediation not elsewhere classified
Parent: Virgin Money Holdings (UK) PLC
Officers: Katie Jane Marshall, Secretary; Peter Douglas Bole [1969] Director/Chartered Accountant; Jayne-Anne Gadhia [1961] Director/Chief Executive Officer; Marian MacDonald Martin [1967] Risk Director

Virgin Money PLC
Incorporated: 3 July 2009 *Employees:* 3,140
Net Worth: £1,691,200,000 *Total Assets:* £34,915,201,024
Registered Office: Jubilee House, Gosforth, Newcastle upon Tyne, NE3 4PL
Activities: Banks
Parent: Virgin Money Holdings (UK) PLC
Officers: Katie Jane Marshall, Secretary; Peter Douglas Bole [1969] Director/Chartered Accountant; Eva Kristina Eisenschimmel [1962] Director/Customer Experience; Jayne-Anne Gadhia [1961] Director/Accountant; Geeta Gopalan [1964] Director; Colin Denis Keogh [1953] Director; Marian MacDonald Martin [1967] Risk Director; Norman Cardie McLuskie [1944] Director; Darren Scott Pope [1965] Director

Virgin Money Unit Trust Managers Limited
Incorporated: 12 December 1994
Net Worth: £12,543,000 *Total Assets:* £15,731,000
Registered Office: Jubilee House, Gosforth, Newcastle upon Tyne, NE3 4PL
Activities: Activities of unit trusts
Parent: Virgin Money Holdings (UK) PLC
Officers: Katie Jane Marshall, Secretary; Peter Douglas Bole [1969] Director; Jayne-Anne Gadhia [1961] Director/Chief Executive Officer; Colin Denis Keogh [1953] Director; Marian MacDonald Martin [1967] Risk Director

The Viridis Group Ltd
Incorporated: 15 June 2015
Registered Office: The Old Brickworks, Eldon, Co Durham, DL14 8EA
Activities: Remediation activities and other waste management services
Shareholders: John Anthony Wood; John Jones
Officers: David Langhorne [1963] Director

Viscatain Ltd
Incorporated: 4 May 2016
Net Worth: £1,389,567 *Total Assets:* £1,742,504
Registered Office: 1 Coburg Street, Gateshead, Tyne & Wear, NE8 1NS
Activities: Management consultancy activities other than financial management
Parent: Viscatain LLC
Officers: Robert John Groves [1979] Director; William Borden James [1965] Director [American]

Vishay Ltd.
Incorporated: 1 September 1966 *Employees:* 11
Net Worth: £5,473,000 *Total Assets:* £12,387,000
Registered Office: Suite 7a, Tower House, St Catherines Court, Sunderland Enterprise Park, Sunderland, Tyne & Wear, SR5 3XJ
Activities: Activities of head offices
Parent: E-Sil Components
Officers: Laura Mary Bell, Secretary; Laura Mary Bell [1955] Director; Generald Walter Paul [1949] Director [German]

Vision Academy Learning Trust
Incorporated: 24 June 2016 *Employees:* 272
Net Worth: £21,769,864 *Total Assets:* £23,558,908
Registered Office: Egglescliffe School, Urlay Nook Road, Stockton on Tees, Cleveland, TS16 0LA
Activities: Primary education
Officers: David Michael Blake [1965] Director; Kathryn Van Der Graaf [1978] Strategic Accounts Director; Josephine Louise Graham [1981] Director/Financial Controller/Qualified Accountant; Charlotte Irving [1973] Director/Agency Manager; Richard George Long [1956] Director/Retired; Jill Amanda McGuire [1967] Director/Registered Childcare Provider; Karen Norton [1966] Director/Headteacher; Janet Richards [1953] Director/Retired School Teacher; Simon Gerard White [1965] Director/Headteacher

Vision Building Services Limited
Incorporated: 8 April 2008 *Employees:* 61
Net Worth: £1,553,500 *Total Assets:* £2,875,983
Registered Office: 6 Crofton Court, Crofton Road, Stockton on Tees, Cleveland, TS18 2QR
Activities: Other building completion and finishing
Shareholders: Martin Henry Bruton; Tina Bruton
Officers: Tina Bruton, Secretary; Martin Henry Bruton [1963] Director/Builder

Vision Learning Trust Limited
Incorporated: 25 July 2016 *Employees:* 121
Net Worth: £7,134,000 *Total Assets:* £8,616,000
Registered Office: Hill View Infant School, Helvellyn Road, Sunderland, Tyne & Wear, SR2 9JJ
Activities: Primary education
Officers: Linda Jobson, Secretary; Patricia Joan Bevan [1965] Director/Headteacher; Michael William Foster [1957] Director/Retired; Steven Andrew Little [1975] Director/Head of HR; Jonathan Bryan Nicholson [1957] Director/Retired; Peter Nicol [1964] Director/Local Government Officer; Gary Patrick Reid [1977] Site Director; Paul Rushworth [1975] Director/Solicitor; Claire Louise Smith [1976] Director/Headteacher; Malcolm Snaith [1951] Director/Chartered Accountant

Visitech International Limited
Incorporated: 16 December 1998 *Employees:* 8
Net Worth: £612,216 *Total Assets:* £1,760,372
Registered Office: Unit 92 Silverbriar, Sunderland Enterprise Park East, Sunderland, Tyne & Wear, SR5 2TQ
Activities: Manufacture of electronic measuring, testing etc. equipment, not for industrial process control
Major Shareholder: Dr Jafer Sadeq Shablee
Officers: Doctor Jafer Sadeq Sheblee [1960] Director

Vistech Services Ltd
Incorporated: 25 August 2010 *Employees:* 87
Net Worth: £126,607 *Total Assets:* £770,600
Registered Office: Boho Six Offices, 5 Linthorpe Road, Middlesbrough, Cleveland, TS1 1RE
Activities: Private security activities
Major Shareholder: Christopher John Mallory Taylor
Officers: Christopher John Mallory Taylor [1986] Director/Business Consultant

Visual Concept Ltd
Incorporated: 1 February 2005 *Employees:* 17
Net Worth: £1,260,378 *Total Assets:* £1,545,710
Registered Office: 38a Bellingham Drive, North Tyne Industrial Estate, Newcastle upon Tyne, NE12 9SZ
Activities: Glazing
Shareholders: Paul Anthony Davidson; Paul Martin Price
Officers: Paul Martin Price, Secretary; Paul Anthony Davidson [1971] Director/Contracts Manager; Paul Martin Price [1965] Director/Estimator

Visualsoft Holdings Limited
Incorporated: 5 June 2014 *Employees:* 234
Net Worth: £4,800,110 *Total Assets:* £9,469,780
Registered Office: Visualsoft House, Princes Wharf, Thornaby, Stockton on Tees, Cleveland, TS17 6QY
Activities: Information technology consultancy activities
Major Shareholder: Dean Richard Benson
Officers: Dean Richard Benson [1975] Director; David Duke [1978] Marketing Director; Timothy Johnson [1977] Director; Mark John Leader [1972] Director/Chief Commercial Officer

Visualsoft Limited
Incorporated: 23 October 1998 *Employees:* 234
Net Worth: £4,144,860 *Total Assets:* £7,214,059
Registered Office: Visualsoft House, Princes Wharf, Thornaby, Stockton on Tees, Cleveland, TS17 6QY
Activities: Business and domestic software development
Parent: Visualsoft Holdings Limited
Officers: Dean Richard Benson, Secretary; Dean Richard Benson [1975] Director/Chief Executive Officer; David Duke [1978] Director/Chief Marketing Officer; Neil Innes [1981] Director; Timothy Johnson [1977] Director/Chief Business Development Officer; Mark John Leader [1972] Director/Chief Commercial Officer; Marc Keith McDermott [1976] Director/Accountant

Viswanath & Co Limited
Incorporated: 20 February 2003
Net Worth: £476,761 *Total Assets:* £1,013,493
Registered Office: 1 The Wynd, Wynyard, Billingham, Cleveland, TS22 5QE
Activities: General medical practice activities
Shareholders: Yirupaiahgari Krishnaiah Setty Viswanath; Gowrilatha Viswanath
Officers: Gowrilatha Viswanath, Secretary/Assistant [Indian]; Gowrilatha Viswanath [1972] Director/Assistant [Indian]; Yirupaiahgari Krishnaiah Setty Viswanath [1965] Director/Consultant Surgeon

Vixen Properties Limited
Incorporated: 27 November 2009
Net Worth: £1,253,597 *Total Assets:* £1,839,596
Registered Office: Unit 73 Jay Avenue, Teesside Industrial Estate, Thornaby, Stockton on Tees, Cleveland, TS17 9LZ
Activities: Other letting and operating of own or leased real estate
Officers: Aidan John Mallon [1957] Managing Director

Vixen Surface Treatments Limited
Incorporated: 19 November 2009 *Employees:* 72
Net Worth: £1,178,660 *Total Assets:* £2,550,006
Registered Office: 73 Jay Avenue, Thornaby, Cleveland, TS17 9LZ
Activities: Manufacture of other general-purpose machinery n.e.c.
Major Shareholder: Aidan John Mallon
Officers: Aidan John Mallon [1957] Managing Director

Vizsec Holdings Limited
Incorporated: 10 March 2016
Net Worth Deficit: £28,887 *Total Assets:* £1,326,187
Registered Office: Vizsec House, Robson Avenue, Teesside Industrial Estate, Stockton on Tees, Cleveland, TS17 9LS
Activities: Electrical installation
Shareholders: Richard Alan Waldren; Marc Stephen Dee; Steven Bland; Alison Elizabeth Dawson
Officers: Steven Bland [1970] Director/Project Manager; Alison Elizabeth Dawson [1969] Director/Bookkeeper; Marc Stephen Dee [1984] Director/Senior Security Engineer; Richard Alan Waldron [1977] Director/General Manager

VMS Live 2011 Ltd
Incorporated: 4 May 2011 *Employees:* 5
Net Worth: £347,313 *Total Assets:* £1,144,260
Registered Office: 17 Woodbine Avenue, Newcastle upon Tyne, NE3 4EU
Activities: Operation of arts facilities
Major Shareholder: Stephen Forster
Officers: Michael Ian Cleghorn, Secretary; Carl Bathgate [1974] Operations Director; Stephen Forster [1964] Director; Richard Antony Maides [1968] Director/General Manager

The Vocational Learning Trust
Incorporated: 19 July 2005
Net Worth: £1,490,798 *Total Assets:* £1,537,759
Registered Office: The Work Place, Heighington Lane, Aycliffe Business Park, Newton Aycliffe, Co Durham, DL5 6AH
Activities: Other education n.e.c.
Officers: Andrew Gilmore, Secretary/Accountant; Andrew Gilmore [1969] Director/Accountant; Ian Stewart Kershaw [1945] Director/Education Consultant; Michael Bernard McGarry [1972] Director/Solicitor; Keith Mitchell [1950] Director/Retired; Robin David Morton [1972] Construction Director; Craig Alistair Peterson [1969] Director; Jane Other Ritchie [1949] Director/Retired

Voicentric Limited
Incorporated: 22 October 2002
Net Worth: £683,218 *Total Assets:* £1,241,192
Registered Office: 3rd Floor, Bridge House, North Road, Durham, DH1 4PW
Activities: Other professional, scientific and technical activities n.e.c.
Shareholders: Mary Madeleine Jordan; Wyndam Paul Williams
Officers: Mary Madeleine Jordan [1957] Director; Wyndham Paul Williams [1957] Director/Call Centre Manager

Voltigeur Estates Ltd.
Incorporated: 18 June 2001
Net Worth: £203,851 *Total Assets:* £772,644
Registered Office: 69a York Road, Hartlepool, Cleveland, TS26 8AH
Activities: Other letting and operating of own or leased real estate
Major Shareholder: Alan Colin Ridden
Officers: David Ridden, Secretary; Alan Colin Ridden [1960] Director/Engineer

Volume Trading (Europe) Limited
Incorporated: 8 January 2010
Net Worth: £491,810 *Total Assets:* £1,160,088
Registered Office: 36 Ash Grove, Kirklevington, Cleveland, TS15 9NQ
Activities: Agents involved in the sale of timber and building materials
Shareholder: Barry Dunn
Officers: Barbara Ann Dunn [1963] Director; Barry Dunn [1943] Managing Director; Mark Richardson [1975] Director

Vroon Shipping U.K. Ltd.
Incorporated: 6 January 2004
Net Worth: £6,531,067 *Total Assets:* £16,754,845
Registered Office: Tobias House, St Mark's Court, Teesdale Business Park, Stockton on Tees, Cleveland, TS17 6QW
Activities: Sea and coastal freight water transport
Officers: Herman Frans Mathilde Marks [1960] Director [Dutch]; Graeme Paul Sheach [1966] Director/Chartered Accountant

W & M Holding Company Limited
Incorporated: 4 December 2012 *Employees:* 76
Net Worth: £10,381,877 *Total Assets:* £17,273,912
Registered Office: Unit 3c Admiral Business Park, Nelson Way, Nelson Park West, Cramlington, Northumberland, NE23 1WG
Activities: Dormant company
Shareholders: Anthony Wallett; Gary Middlemiss
Officers: Anthony Wallett [1965] Director

W & M Wholesale Limited
Incorporated: 2 May 1991 *Employees:* 72
Net Worth: £10,329,973 *Total Assets:* £17,860,528
Registered Office: Unit 3c Admiral Business Park, Nelson Way, Nelson Park West, Cramlington, Northumberland, NE23 1WG
Activities: Wholesale of clothing and footwear
Parent: W & M Holding Company Ltd
Officers: Gary Middlemiss, Secretary; Gary Middlemiss [1961] Director; Anthony Wallett [1965] Director

W & W Peeled Potatoes Limited
Incorporated: 7 September 1994 *Employees:* 16
Net Worth: £501,570 *Total Assets:* £839,214
Registered Office: Carlbury Road, Newton Aycliffe, Co Durham, DL5 6BH
Activities: Other processing and preserving of fruit and vegetables
Shareholders: Wendy Waller; David Waller
Officers: Geoffrey Waller, Secretary; David Waller [1955] Director; Geoffrey Waller [1962] Director; John Waller [1958] Director

W Dot Homes Limited
Incorporated: 30 May 2000 *Employees:* 1
Net Worth Deficit: £141,669 *Total Assets:* £757,263
Registered Office: 42 Greystoke Park, Newcastle upon Tyne, NE3 2DZ
Activities: Construction of domestic buildings
Major Shareholder: William Ian Waites
Officers: William Ian Waites, Secretary; William Ian Waites [1950] Director/Solicitor

W M T Entertainments (No 2) Limited
Incorporated: 30 January 1961
Net Worth: £3,038,229 *Total Assets:* £3,107,302
Registered Office: Churchill House, 12 Mosley Street, Newcastle upon Tyne, NE1 1DE
Activities: Other letting and operating of own or leased real estate
Officers: Graham Testo [1970] Director/Amusement Caterer; Waine Maxwell Testo [1968] Director/Amusement Caterer

W.G.R. (Steels) Limited
Incorporated: 13 July 1988
Net Worth: £1,723,403 *Total Assets:* £2,751,327
Registered Office: Cochranes Wharf, Dockside Road, Middlesbrough, Cleveland, TS3 6AW
Activities: Wholesale of metals and metal ores
Major Shareholder: Richard William Readman
Officers: Wayne Ashton Britton, Secretary; Wayne Ashton Britton [1971] Director; Richard William Readman [1960] Director

W.I.P (Work in Progress) Limited
Incorporated: 28 March 2003 *Employees:* 3
Net Worth: £7,202,435 *Total Assets:* £12,520,137
Registered Office: 32 Portland Terrace, Newcastle upon Tyne, NE2 1QP
Activities: Manufacture of footwear
Shareholders: Christopher Patrick Maughan; Dragonfly Venture Group Limited
Officers: Christopher Patrick Maughan, Secretary; Christopher Patrick Maughan [1963] Director

W.I.P. (Workwear) Limited
Incorporated: 16 April 2007 *Employees:* 1
Net Worth: £737,848 *Total Assets:* £1,565,264
Registered Office: 32 Portland Terrace, Newcastle upon Tyne, NE2 1QP
Activities: Manufacture of workwear
Shareholders: Christopher Patrick Maughan; Dragonfly Venture Group Limited
Officers: Steven John Bowen, Secretary; Christopher Patrick Maughan [1963] Director

W.J.(Bill) Tillston Limited
Incorporated: 25 September 1956 *Employees:* 9
Net Worth: £540,394 *Total Assets:* £1,434,443
Registered Office: 52 Yarm Lane, Stockton on Tees, Cleveland, TS18 1ER
Activities: Sale, maintenance and repair of motorcycles and related parts and accessories
Major Shareholder: Robert William Tillston
Officers: Robert William Tillston, Secretary; Peter Robinson [1946] Director/Manager; Robert William Tillston [1947] Director

W.O.W! (Welcome To Our World) Limited
Incorporated: 2 April 2004 *Employees:* 61
Net Worth: £1,045,685 *Total Assets:* £1,255,136
Registered Office: 7 The Grove, Forest Hall, Newcastle upon Tyne, NE12 9PE
Activities: Pre-primary education
Shareholders: Paul Caven; Leigh Caven
Officers: Paul Caven, Secretary/Director/Owner; Leigh Caven [1970] Director/Owner; Paul Caven [1962] Director/Owner

Wack Wholesale (Building Supplies) Ltd
Incorporated: 12 February 2010 *Employees:* 19
Net Worth: £280,656 *Total Assets:* £1,006,930
Registered Office: Unit 8 Arcot Court, Nelson Industrial Estate West, Cramlington, Northumberland, NE23 1BB
Activities: Wholesale of wood, construction materials and sanitary equipment
Major Shareholder: Keith White
Officers: Keith White, Secretary; Wayne Grassie [1983] Director/Salesman; Keith White [1972] Director/Chairman

John Wade (Haulage) Limited
Incorporated: 19 February 1980 *Employees:* 54
Net Worth: £3,680,487 *Total Assets:* £5,006,957
Registered Office: Aycliffe Quarry, Aycliffe Village, Darlington, Co Durham, DL5 6NB
Activities: Freight transport by road
Major Shareholder: John Wade
Officers: John Wade, Secretary; Paul William Monkhouse [1957] Director/Contracts Manager; John Wade [1943] Director; Bruce David Whitley [1959] Director/Operations Manager

John Wade (Holdings) Limited
Incorporated: 16 April 1997 *Employees:* 118
Net Worth: £15,411,203 *Total Assets:* £21,502,488
Registered Office: Aycliffe Quarry, Aycliffe Village, Co Durham, DL5 6NB
Activities: Activities of other holding companies n.e.c.
Major Shareholder: John Wade
Officers: John Wade, Secretary; Paul William Monkhouse [1957] Director; John Wade [1943] Director; Bruce David Whitley [1959] Director

Alan Wadkins Limited
Incorporated: 3 February 1966 *Employees:* 15
Net Worth: £1,364,607 *Total Assets:* £1,587,585
Registered Office: Chesnut Street, Darlington, Co Durham, DL1 1QL
Activities: Retail sale of hardware, paints and glass in specialised stores
Major Shareholder: Michael Alan Wadkins
Officers: Amanda Jane Wadkins, Secretary; Michael Wadkins [1961] Director

Waggies Limited
Incorporated: 30 October 2013
Net Worth: £28,609 *Total Assets:* £793,497
Registered Office: Unit 3e Enterprise House, Valley Street North, Darlington, Co Durham, DL1 1GY
Activities: Activities of other holding companies n.e.c.
Shareholders: Peter Robert Loft; Christopher James Wallace
Officers: Christopher James Wallace [1962] Director

Wainstones Energy Limited
Incorporated: 30 September 2008
Net Worth Deficit: £14,188,277 *Total Assets:* £25,883,276
Registered Office: 4 Ellerbeck Way, Stokesley Business Park, Stokesley, Middlesbrough, Cleveland, TS9 5JZ
Activities: Production of electricity
Parent: Carlton Power Limited
Officers: Jayne Margaret Hodgson, Secretary; Michael Fred Shaw Benson [1964] Director/Engineer; Keith Clarke [1960] Director; Jayne Margaret Hodgson [1963] Finance Director; David John Philpot [1961] Director/Legal Counsel; Matthew Ian Shields [1944] Director/Engineer; Alan White [1961] Finance Director

Wainstones Estates Limited
Incorporated: 18 May 2016 *Employees:* 2
Net Worth Deficit: £141,781 *Total Assets:* £1,180,704
Registered Office: 4 Ellerbeck Way, Stokesley Business Park, Stokesley, Middlesbrough, Cleveland, TS9 5JZ
Activities: Other holiday and other collective accommodation
Parent: Carlton Investments (Holdings) Limited
Officers: Jayne Margaret Hodgson, Secretary; Keith Clarke [1960] Director; Jayne Margaret Hodgson [1963] Director/Company Secretary; David John Philpot [1961] General Counsel and Director

Wainstones Investments Limited
Incorporated: 14 August 1995 *Employees:* 12
Net Worth: £75,914,376 *Total Assets:* £76,700,360
Registered Office: 4 Ellerbeck Way, Stokesley Business Park, Stokesley, Middlesbrough, Cleveland, TS9 5JZ
Activities: Activities of venture and development capital companies
Parent: Carlton Investment (Holdings) Ltd
Officers: Jayne Margaret Hodgson, Secretary/Development; Michael Fred Shaw Benson [1964] Director/Engineer; Keith Clarke [1960] Director/Engineer; Jayne Margaret Hodgson [1963] Finance Director; David John Philpot [1961] Director/Legal Counsel; Matthew Ian Shields [1944] Director/Engineer; Alan White [1961] Finance Director

Fred Walker (Estates) Limited
Incorporated: 17 July 1979 *Employees:* 3
Net Worth: £2,595,357 *Total Assets:* £4,172,242
Registered Office: 624 Yarm Road, Eaglescliffe, Stockton on Tees, Cleveland, TS16 0DQ
Activities: Other letting and operating of own or leased real estate
Major Shareholder: Pamela Margaret Walker
Officers: Geoffrey Alan Walker, Secretary; Geoffrey Alan Walker [1948] Director/Accountant; Martin Kenneth Walker [1974] Director/Landscape Gardener; Pamela Margaret Walker [1949] Director/Housewife

T.T.Walker (Newcastle) Limited
Incorporated: 6 June 1952 *Employees:* 3
Net Worth: £1,163,318 *Total Assets:* £3,486,557
Registered Office: Bulman House, Regent Centre, Gosforth, Newcastle upon Tyne, NE3 3LS
Activities: Mixed farming
Shareholders: Alastair Temperley Sym; Malcolm Douglas Sym
Officers: Malcolm Douglas Sym, Secretary; Alastair Temperley Sym [1960] Director/Information Technology Technician; Malcolm Douglas Sym [1957] Director/Farmer

Tom Walker and Sons Limited
Incorporated: 1 December 1982
Net Worth: £1,099,659 *Total Assets:* £2,057,425
Registered Office: Thorpe Leazes Farm, Thorpe Thewles, Stockton on Tees, Cleveland, TS21 3HZ
Activities: Butter and cheese production
Shareholders: Peter Thomas Walker; Pauline Mary Chapman; Michael Eugene Walker
Officers: Pauline Mary Chapman, Company Secretary & Director; Pauline Mary Chapman [1965] Company Secretary & Director; Michael Eugene Walker [1958] Director; Peter Thomas Walker [1955] Director

Walker Filtration Limited
Incorporated: 24 May 1983 *Employees:* 225
Net Worth: £19,670,134 *Total Assets:* £25,183,352
Registered Office: Birtley Road, Washington, Tyne & Wear, NE38 9DA
Activities: Manufacture of electronic measuring, testing etc. equipment, not for industrial process control
Parent: Atlas Copco Airpower N.V.
Officers: Alex Bongaerts [1960] Director [Belgian]; Sean Fairest [1964] Director; Lianne Walker Powell [1970] Director; Ben Paul Karl Van Hove [1971] Director [Belgian]

Walkway Windfarm Limited
Incorporated: 26 September 2008
Net Worth: £7,281,000 *Total Assets:* £14,966,000
Registered Office: Alexander House, 1 Mandarin Road, Rainton Bridge Business Park, Houghton-le-Spring, Co Durham, DH4 5RA
Activities: Production of electricity
Parent: EDF Energy Renewables Holdings Limited
Officers: Susan Elizabeth Lind, Secretary; Matthieu Thomas Hue [1975] Director [French]; Hassaan Majid [1968] Director

Wallsend Boys Club
Incorporated: 18 August 2005 *Employees:* 2
Net Worth: £1,725,148 *Total Assets:* £1,728,218
Registered Office: Bigges Main, Rheydt Avenue, Wallsend, Tyne & Wear, NE28 8SX
Activities: Other sports activities
Officers: Allan John Henderson, Secretary; John Bell [1953] Director/Chartered Accountant; Robin Cairns [1966] Director; Stephen Terence Dale [1961] Director/Independent Financial Advisor; Allan John Henderson [1961] Director/Solicitor; Alan Jarvis [1959] Director; Charles Peter Kirkley [1942] Director/Football Academy Recruitment Officer; Sidney Sharp [1948] Director/Safety Manager; Neil Watson [1961] Director

Wallsend Memorial Hall & People's Centre
Incorporated: 19 January 2011
Net Worth: £748,007 *Total Assets:* £2,012,468
Registered Office: 10 Frank Street, Wallsend, Tyne & Wear, NE28 6RN
Activities: Cultural education
Officers: Neil Anthony Barker [1949] Director/Architect; Thomas James Docherty [1955] Director/Domiciliary Care Worker; Michael Hemsley Hardy [1954] Director/Solicitor; John Hunter [1944] Director/Retired; Michael Lisle [1967] Director; Maureen Louise Madden [1950] Director; Dr John David Matthews [1960] Director/General Medical Practitioner; Michael Riley [1956] Director; Alan Robson [1952] Director/Retired; Lesley Anne Spillard [1954] Director/Councillor; Brian Nicholas Topping [1949] Director/Retired

Walton Logging Limited
Incorporated: 9 March 1999 *Employees:* 9
Net Worth: £1,378,819 *Total Assets:* £3,244,535
Registered Office: West Orchard House, Allendale Road, Hexham, Northumberland, NE46 2DE
Activities: Support services to forestry
Shareholders: Colin Robert Robertson; Kerry Robertson
Officers: Colin Robert Robertson [1968] Director/Forestry Manager; Kerry Robertson [1969] Director/Secretary

Waltons Clark Whitehill Limited
Incorporated: 10 March 2014
Net Worth: £370 *Total Assets:* £1,594,900
Registered Office: Maritime House, Harbour Walk, The Marina, Hartlepool, Cleveland, TS24 0UX
Activities: Accounting and auditing activities
Officers: Paul Christopher Andrew Harrison, Secretary; George Michael Hardey [1972] Director/Chartered Tax Advisor; Paul Christopher Andrew Harrison [1974] Director/Chartered Accountant; Heather Ann O'Driscoll [1961] Director/Chartered Accountant; Graeme Leslie Surtees [1962] Director/Chartered Tax Advisor

Wansbeck (Morpeth) Limited
Incorporated: 6 May 2004
Net Worth: £231,942 *Total Assets:* £784,655
Registered Office: The Walled Garden, Longhirst, Morpeth, Northumberland, NE61 3LJ
Activities: Other letting and operating of own or leased real estate
Officers: Lawrence Daniel Carey, Secretary; Daniel Paul Carey [1981] Director/Solicitor; Lawrence Daniel Carey [1951] Director/Chartered Accountant; Gary Paul Virgo [1964] Director/Engineer

T. M. Ward (Darlington) Limited
Incorporated: 14 August 1992
Net Worth: £476,316 *Total Assets:* £2,309,633
Registered Office: Victoria Building, 14 Elwin Lane, Darlington, Co Durham, DL1 5RX
Activities: Construction of other civil engineering projects n.e.c.
Parent: Faverdale Recycling Centre Limited
Officers: Martyn Andrew Jackson [1966] Director; John Anthony Ward [1957] Director/Manager

Ward A Limited
Incorporated: 27 April 2006
Net Worth: £513,079 *Total Assets:* £839,541
Registered Office: 189 Elwick Road, Hartlepool, Cleveland, TS26 9NP
Activities: Other service activities n.e.c.
Major Shareholder: Anthony Ward
Officers: Helen Ward, Secretary; Anthony Ward [1967] Director/Salesman

D. Ward Automotive Limited
Incorporated: 16 January 2004
Registered Office: 10 Peel Street, Bishop Auckland, Co Durham, DL14 7LF
Activities: Retail trade of motor vehicle parts and accessories
Shareholders: Derek Ward; Lynn Ward
Officers: Lynn Ward, Secretary/Director; Derek Ward [1953] Director; Genette Ward [1979] Director; Lynn Ward [1955] Director; Stewart Neil Ward [1977] Director

Ward Bros (Malton) Limited
Incorporated: 11 September 2000 *Employees:* 135
Net Worth: £339,890 *Total Assets:* £4,184,456
Registered Office: Ward Bros (Malton) Ltd, Dormor Way, South Bank, Middlesbrough, Cleveland, TS6 6XH
Activities: Freight transport by road
Shareholders: Steven John Ward; David William Ward; Brenda Jean Ward
Officers: Brenda Jean Ward, Secretary; David William Ward [1956] Director/Mechanical Engineer; Steven John Ward [1963] Director/Mechanical Engineer

Ward Bros. (Plant Hire) Limited
Incorporated: 26 March 1971 *Employees:* 38
Net Worth: £2,251,936 *Total Assets:* £4,205,428
Registered Office: Thistle Road, Littleburn Industrial Estate, Langley Moor, Co Durham, DH7 8HZ
Activities: Recovery of sorted materials
Shareholders: Angus Moffat Ward; John Stewart Ward
Officers: Anthony William Plumb [1956] Director/Office Manager; Angus Moffat Ward [1940] Director; John Stewart Ward [1949] Director

Ward Bros. (Steel) Limited
Incorporated: 27 July 1976 *Employees:* 76
Net Worth: £1,107,472 *Total Assets:* £10,867,774
Registered Office: Cleveland House, Cleveland Street, Darlington, Co Durham, DL1 2PE
Activities: Recovery of sorted materials
Officers: Billy Ward [1978] Director; Nathan Ward [1982] Director

J. & J. Ward Limited
Incorporated: 2 April 2001 *Employees:* 72
Net Worth: £1,724,160 *Total Assets:* £18,530,308
Registered Office: The Garage, Patrick Brompton, Bedale, N Yorks, DL8 1JP
Activities: Freight transport by road
Parent: Bulk Logistics Group Limited
Officers: David Andrew Castle [1952] Director; David Keith Edghill [1979] Director; Paul William Tolmie [1961] Director; Michael James Ward [1968] Director

J & J Ward Properties Limited
Incorporated: 1 April 2016
Net Worth: £6,491,949 *Total Assets:* £6,681,400
Registered Office: The Garage, Patrick Brompton, Bedale, N Yorks, DL8 1JP
Activities: Buying and selling of own real estate
Officers: June Rose Ward, Secretary; Michael James Ward [1968] Director/Haulage Contractor

James H Ward Properties Limited
Incorporated: 22 August 2007
Net Worth: £1,059,319 *Total Assets:* £1,364,569
Registered Office: Cleveland House, Cleveland Street, Darlington, Co Durham, DL1 2PE
Activities: Other letting and operating of own or leased real estate
Major Shareholder: James Henry Ward
Officers: Esther Ward, Secretary; James Henry Ward [1973] Director

Angela Ward Properties LLP
Incorporated: 24 October 2016
Net Worth: £1,373,131 *Total Assets:* £1,434,922
Registered Office: Franklin House, Stockton Road, Sedgefield, Stockton on Tees, Cleveland, TS21 2AG
Officers: Angela Marie Ward [1975] Member

Ward Property Investments Limited
Incorporated: 10 July 2007
Net Worth Deficit: £990 *Total Assets:* £1,435,871
Registered Office: Cleveland House, Cleveland Street, Darlington, Co Durham, DL1 2PE
Activities: Other letting and operating of own or leased real estate
Officers: Robert Ward Junior, Secretary; Billy Ward [1978] Director; James Henry Ward [1973] Director; Nathan Ward [1982] Director; Robert Ward [1945] Director; Robert Ward Jnr [1970] Director

Ward Recycling Limited
Incorporated: 13 February 2002 *Employees:* 126
Net Worth: £3,377,812 *Total Assets:* £7,082,529
Registered Office: The Bungalow, Warlaby Lane, Ainderby Steeple, Northallerton, N Yorks, DL7 9JX
Activities: Collection of non-hazardous waste
Officers: Mark Stephen Ward, Secretary; Michael James Ward [1968] Sales Director

Ward Timber Limited
Incorporated: 5 September 2002
Net Worth: £1,373,509 *Total Assets:* £2,049,294
Registered Office: Rogerley Sawmills, Frosterley, Bishop Auckland, Co Durham, DL13 2QE
Activities: Sawmilling and planing of wood
Major Shareholder: Frank Alistair Ward
Officers: Gillian Mary Ward, Secretary; Audrey Ward [1930] Director; Frank Alistair Ward [1963] Director/Timber Merchant; Gillian Mary Ward [1966] Director/Secretary

William A.Wardman Limited
Incorporated: 11 March 1964 *Employees:* 11
Net Worth Deficit: £3,770,109 *Total Assets:* £4,076,765
Registered Office: Thrushwood Farm, Yearby, Redcar, Cleveland, TS11 8HD
Activities: Growing of cereals (except rice), leguminous crops and oil seeds
Shareholders: William Norman Wardman; Linda Marie Wardman
Officers: William Norman Wardman, Secretary; Linda Marie Wardman [1964] Director; William Norman Wardman [1965] Director/Farmer

Warm Protection Products Limited
Incorporated: 30 September 1987 *Employees:* 13
Net Worth: £408,550 *Total Assets:* £888,604
Registered Office: Unit 5 Throckley Way, Middlefields Industrial Estate, South Shields, Tyne & Wear, NE34 0NU
Activities: Other manufacturing n.e.c.
Officers: James Chapman, Secretary; James Chapman [1952] Director; Susan Elizabeth Chapman [1953] Director; Dennis Ivan Wadey [1953] Director; Wendy Alison Wadey [1966] Director

Warm Zones C.I.C
Incorporated: 8 December 2000 *Employees:* 39
Net Worth: £661,260 *Total Assets:* £9,470,701
Registered Office: 2nd Floor, 9 Portland Terrace, Jesmond, Newcastle upon Tyne, NE2 1QQ
Activities: Other service activities n.e.c.
Officers: Rebecca Jane Parker, Secretary; Layla Barke-Jones [1983] Director/Solicitor; Andrew Mavor Brown [1956] Director/Retired; David Howard Connor [1968] Director; Claire Julia Harrold [1968] Managing Director; Philip Hudson [1960] Director/Retired; Charles Owen Lewis [1976] Director; Matthew Luke Osborn [1976] Director; Rebecca Jane Parker [1969] Finance Director; Jayne Carole Pitkeathley [1961] Director

Ken Warne Limited
Incorporated: 31 October 1975 *Employees:* 24
Net Worth: £546,730 *Total Assets:* £1,259,319
Registered Office: 17-19 Cleveland Terrace, Darlington, Co Durham, DL3 7HD
Activities: Other retail sale in non-specialised stores
Shareholders: Kevin Anthony Warne; Peter David Warne
Officers: Kevin Anthony Warne, Secretary/Supermarket Director; Kevin Anthony Warne [1955] Director/Executive; Peter David Warne [1952] Director/Executive

Warner of Wingate Limited
Incorporated: 22 February 1967 *Employees:* 2
Net Worth: £1,056,023 *Total Assets:* £1,216,369
Registered Office: Colliery Yard, Wingate, Cleveland, TS28 5LJ
Activities: Sale of other motor vehicles
Shareholders: Philip Winetroube; Mary Theresa Winetroube
Officers: Mary Theresa Winetroube, Secretary; Philip Winetroube [1968] Director/Motor Trader

Warren Court Limited
Incorporated: 2 October 1995
Net Worth: £11,941,776 *Total Assets:* £12,068,604
Registered Office: Citygate, St James Boulevard, Newcastle upon Tyne, NE1 4JE
Activities: Development of building projects
Parent: Northumberland & Durham Property Trust Limited
Officers: Adam McGhin, Secretary; Helen Christine Gordon [1959] Director; Adam McGhin [1978] Director/Solicitor; Mark Jeremy Robson [1959] Director/Chartered Surveyor; Vanessa Kate Simms [1975] Director

Warrens Group Limited
Incorporated: 1 August 1986 *Employees:* 60
Net Worth: £5,435,391 *Total Assets:* £17,211,688
Registered Office: Eden Hall, Hamsterley, Bishop Auckland, Co Durham, DL13 3QG
Activities: Treatment and disposal of non-hazardous waste
Shareholders: Antony Michael Warren; John Adam Ralph Warren
Officers: Elizabeth Elsie Warren, Secretary; Antony Michael Warren [1978] Director/Manager; Elizabeth Elsie Warren [1954] Director/Secretary; John Adam Ralph Warren [1972] Director/Manager; John Neville Ralph Warren [1950] Director/Animal By Products Collector

Warrior Assault Systems Limited
Incorporated: 17 April 2009
Net Worth: £661,921 *Total Assets:* £1,328,839
Registered Office: 53 Greens Grove, Hartburn, Stockton on Tees, Cleveland, TS18 5AW
Activities: Manufacture of other wearing apparel and accessories n.e.c.
Shareholders: Melanie Louise Baxtrem; Mark David Dexter
Officers: Mark David Dexter, Secretary; Melanie Louise Baxtrem [1972] Director; Mark David Dexter [1965] Director

Wartsila Puregas Solutions Limited
Incorporated: 12 March 2012 *Employees:* 7
Net Worth: £1,713,732 *Total Assets:* £3,277,834
Registered Office: Business & Innovation Centre, Enterprise Park, Sunderland, Tyne & Wear, SR5 2TA
Activities: Engineering related scientific and technical consulting activities
Parent: Purac Puregas AB
Officers: Jan Molin, Secretary; Andrew David Dickinson [1967] Director; Kjetil Hovland [1966] Director [Norwegian]; Timo Ensio Koponen [1969] Director/Vice President [Finnish]

Washington Components Limited
Incorporated: 30 April 1999 *Employees:* 34
Net Worth: £1,142,524 *Total Assets:* £1,538,284
Registered Office: Prestex House, Hertburn Industrial Estate, Washington, Tyne & Wear, NE37 2SF
Activities: Other engineering activities
Shareholders: Anthony Sutherland; Joan Teresa Sutherland
Officers: Anthony Sutherland, Secretary/Engineering; Anthony Sutherland [1951] Director/Engineering; Joan Teresa Sutherland [1953] Director/Engineering

Washington Direct Mail Limited
Incorporated: 9 December 1983 *Employees:* 24
Net Worth: £145,203 *Total Assets:* £1,547,208
Registered Office: Unit M79 Kingsway South, Team Valley Trading Estate, Gateshead, Tyne & Wear, NE11 0SH
Activities: Printing n.e.c.
Major Shareholder: Lynn Beasley
Officers: John Edward Robinson, Secretary; David Beasley [1988] Customer Service Director; Jon Beasley [1985] IT Director; Lynn Beasley [1954] Director

Washington Investments Limited
Incorporated: 12 May 2006
Registered Office: 9 Armstrong Road, Armstrong Industrial Estate, Washington, Tyne & Wear, NE37 1PR
Activities: Manufacture of basic iron and steel and of ferro-alloys
Shareholders: Peter Gatens; Philip Gatens
Officers: Peter Anthony Gatens, Secretary; Peter Anthony Gatens [1958] Director/Engineer; Philip Henry Gatens [1960] Director/Engineer

Washington Metalworks Limited
Incorporated: 11 February 1985 *Employees:* 205
Net Worth: £1,355,565 *Total Assets:* £8,050,604
Registered Office: Washington Metalworks, Bath Road, Gateshead, Tyne & Wear, NE10 0LH
Activities: Manufacture of other fabricated metal products n.e.c.
Shareholders: WMW Group Limited; Steven John Tate
Officers: Judith Anne Tate, Secretary; Paul Atkinson [1967] Finance Director; Paul Francis McGowan [1963] Commercial Director; William Snaith [1955] Non-Executive Director Analysis and Strategy; Thomas Swinburn [1959] Manufacturing Director; Stephen John Tate [1959] Director

Washington Waterjet Limited
Incorporated: 15 February 2008 *Employees:* 16
Net Worth: £825,824 *Total Assets:* £1,374,045
Registered Office: 14 Sedling Road, Wear Industrial Estate, Washington, Tyne & Wear, NE38 9BZ
Activities: Machining
Shareholders: Peter Robinson; Terry Stewart
Officers: Terence Stewart, Secretary; Peter Robinson [1955] Director/Sales; Terence Stewart [1965] Director/Management

Wassenburg Limited
Incorporated: 8 September 1997 *Employees:* 58
Net Worth: £1,908,929 *Total Assets:* £5,098,045
Registered Office: Sandgate House, 102 Quayside, Newcastle upon Tyne, NE1 3DX
Activities: Manufacture of other special-purpose machinery n.e.c.
Parent: Hoya Corporation
Officers: Robert Salter [1954] Director; Arno Wassenburg [1973] Director [Dutch]; Ronald Wassenburg [1970] Director [Dutch]

Waterloo Estates Limited
Incorporated: 21 May 2015
Net Worth: £36,003 *Total Assets:* £3,715,149
Registered Office: 45 Grasmere Street, Gateshead, Tyne & Wear, NE8 1TS
Activities: Other letting and operating of own or leased real estate
Officers: Fanny Bodner, Secretary; Michael Martin Bodner [1951] Director; Steven Anthony Bodner [1961] Director

Waterloo House Rest Home Limited
Incorporated: 3 February 2010
Net Worth: £2,438,800 *Total Assets:* £3,515,866
Registered Office: The Park Hotel, Grand Parade, Tynemouth, Tyne & Wear, NE30 4JQ
Activities: Dormant company
Officers: Jaswant Singh Gill [1968] Director; Sewa Singh Gill [1945] Director

Waters Waste Services Ltd
Incorporated: 9 February 2011
Net Worth: £2,908,316 *Total Assets:* £3,848,644
Registered Office: Waters Waste Services Ltd, 9 Ellerbeck Way, Stokesley, Middlesbrough, Cleveland, TS9 5JZ
Activities: Sewerage
Shareholders: Universal Tanker Group Limited; Simon Gunn
Officers: Simon Gunn [1955] Director; Toby Gunn [1981] Director

Waterseal (Waterbar & Sealants) Limited
Incorporated: 20 May 1980 *Employees:* 50
Net Worth: £813,093 *Total Assets:* £1,847,679
Registered Office: Unit 27 Dragonville Industrial Park, Durham, DH1 2XH
Activities: Other specialised construction activities n.e.c.
Parent: Waterseal Holdings Limited
Officers: Grant James Weston [1972] Director/Engineer; Guy Lapique Weston [1968] Director/Contracts Manager

The Waterside Palace Restaurant Co Ltd
Incorporated: 23 April 1996
Net Worth: £1,156,577 *Total Assets:* £1,349,794
Registered Office: 29 Forth Banks, Newcastle upon Tyne, NE1 3SG
Activities: Licenced restaurants
Shareholders: Tak Keung Lau; Pat Kiu Lau
Officers: Tak Keung Lau, Secretary/Restaurateur; Pat Kiu Lau [1953] General Director; Tak Keung Lau [1951] Director

Waterstons Limited
Incorporated: 3 August 1999 *Employees:* 106
Net Worth: £2,195,955 *Total Assets:* £3,428,285
Registered Office: Liddon House, Belmont Business Park, Durham, DH1 1TW
Activities: Business and domestic software development
Shareholders: Robert Michael Waterston; Sally Ann Waterston
Officers: Michael Stirrup, Secretary; Susan Jane Bell [1971] Director/Chief Executive Officer; Leanne Cullen [1979] Operations Director; Alistair William McLeod [1972] Business Development Director; Robert Morrow [1942] Director; Ajaib Singh [1966] Projects Director; Michael Paul Stirrup [1978] Finance & Human Resources Director; Robert Michael Waterston [1947] Director/Chairman; Sally Ann Waterston [1948] Director/Chairman

Watkins Hire Limited
Incorporated: 16 July 1998 *Employees:* 83
Net Worth: £13,180,000 *Total Assets:* £16,303,000
Registered Office: Unit B, Colima Avenue, Sunderland Enterprise Park, Sunderland, Tyne & Wear, SR5 3XE
Activities: Renting and leasing of other machinery, equipment and tangible goods n.e.c.
Parent: Carrier Rental Systems (UK) Limited
Officers: Simon Boniface, Secretary; Laura Jayne Wilcock, Secretary; Steven Blaby [1979] Director/Accountant; Archibald Ziwanemoyo Hungwe [1973] Director/General Manager; Simon Ross Harden McMullen [1969] Financial Director

T E Watson & Co. Limited
Incorporated: 8 December 1982
Net Worth: £3,242,606 *Total Assets:* £3,616,527
Registered Office: Old Acres Hall Farm, Sedgefield, Stockton on Tees, Cleveland, TS21 3HS
Activities: Growing of cereals (except rice), leguminous crops and oil seeds
Shareholders: Robin Derek Watson; Anthony Edwin Watson
Officers: Enid Watson, Secretary; Anthony Edwin Watson [1962] Director/Farmer; Enid Watson [1930] Director/Farmer; Robin Derek Watson [1955] Director/Farmer; Thomas Edwin Watson [1926] Director/Farmer

AG Watson & Sons Limited
Incorporated: 16 August 2011 *Employees:* 4
Net Worth: £1,696,003 *Total Assets:* £3,053,303
Registered Office: Nunstainton Grange, Rushyford, Ferryhill, Co Durham, DL17 0LH
Activities: Mixed farming
Shareholders: Clifford Gordon Watson; John Terence Watson
Officers: John Terence Watson [1958] Director

A Watson Associates Limited
Incorporated: 29 April 2010
Registered Office: A6 Kingfisher House, Team Valley Trading Estate, Gateshead, Tyne & Wear, NE11 0JQ
Activities: Accounting and auditing activities
Shareholders: Alan Watson; Beverley Watson
Officers: Alan Watson [1958] Director/Accountant

Watson Burton LLP
Incorporated: 24 November 2003 *Employees:* 107
Net Worth: £750,000 *Total Assets:* £3,392,481
Registered Office: 1 St James Gate, Newcastle upon Tyne, NE99 1YQ
Officers: Christopher Graham [1966] Member; Richard John Palmer [1967] LLP Member; Duncan Bryson Reid [1971] LLP Member

J Watson Haulage Limited
Incorporated: 26 January 2009 *Employees:* 31
Net Worth: £829,631 *Total Assets:* £1,113,533
Registered Office: Limerick Road, Dormanstown, Redcar, Cleveland, TS10 5JU
Activities: Freight transport by road
Parent: Gruden Acquisition Inc
Officers: Colin Garnett [1963] Director; Joseph Troy [1963] Director [American]; John Wilson [1974] Director [American]

Watson Investments Limited
Incorporated: 19 March 2003
Net Worth Deficit: £45,699 *Total Assets:* £879,489
Registered Office: 2 Murray Court, Chester-le-Street, Co Durham, DH2 2UD
Activities: Other letting and operating of own or leased real estate
Officers: Barry Rundle, Secretary; Barry Rundle [1952] Director/Accountant

John Watson Joinery Ltd
Incorporated: 21 December 1982 *Employees:* 57
Net Worth: £631,754 *Total Assets:* £2,314,380
Registered Office: Usworth Road Industrial Estate, Belle Vue Way, Hartlepool, Cleveland, TS25 1JZ
Activities: Other manufacturing n.e.c.
Shareholders: John Watson; Betty Dunlop Watson
Officers: Betty Dunlop Watson, Secretary; John Watson, Secretary/Director; Stephen John Kirtley [1955] Sales Director; June Mary Maley [1946] Sales Director; Edward Watson [1978] Director/Sales Manager; John Watson [1946] Director/Builder

Watson Woodhouse Solicitors LLP
Incorporated: 13 June 2013 *Employees:* 72
Net Worth: £195,766 *Total Assets:* £1,011,332
Registered Office: 102-108 Borough Road, Middlesbrough, Cleveland, TS1 2HJ
Officers: Neil Andrew Douglas [1963] Member; Sean Peter Grainger [1954] Member; James Watson [1957] Member; Nicolas John Martin Woodhouse [1955] Member

Watsons Haulage Limited
Incorporated: 4 December 2013 *Employees:* 13
Net Worth: £430,817 *Total Assets:* £1,785,822
Registered Office: Barrington Road, Bedlington, Northumberland, NE22 7AJ
Activities: Freight transport by road
Shareholders: Kevin Watson; Paul Watson
Officers: Kevin Watson [1966] Director; Paul Watson [1969] Director

Wave Aluminium Profiles Limited
Incorporated: 27 February 2013 *Employees:* 5
Net Worth: £742,002 *Total Assets:* £846,293
Registered Office: Unit 401 Princesway Central, Team Valley Trading Estate, Gateshead, Tyne & Wear, NE11 0TU
Activities: Manufacture of metal structures and parts of structures
Parent: Worthington Armstrong U.K. Limited
Officers: Willem Antonius Middel [1967] Vice President and Managing Director of EMEA [Dutch]; Doug Wisel [1970] Director/Vice President/CFO [American]

WBE Limited
Incorporated: 22 April 2013 *Employees:* 4
Net Worth: £1,617,157 *Total Assets:* £1,884,858
Registered Office: Newbrough Cottage, Newbrough, Hexham, Northumberland, NE47 5AS
Activities: Management consultancy activities other than financial management
Major Shareholder: Shelley Wilkinson
Officers: Wilkinson Jenkins [1980] Director; Jonathan Peter Wilkinson [1979] Director/Professional Rugby Player; Phillip Mark Wilkinson [1952] Director

Wear Referrals Limited
Incorporated: 8 February 2010 *Employees:* 89
Net Worth: £4,096,874 *Total Assets:* £5,254,638
Registered Office: Veterinary Hospital, Bradbury, Stockton on Tees, Cleveland, TS21 2ES
Activities: Other business support service activities n.e.c.
Parent: Linnaeus Group Bidco Limited
Officers: Paul Daryl Coxon [1965] Director; Lynne Victoria Hill [1954] Director [Irish]

Wear Valley Renewables C.I.C.
Incorporated: 4 December 2013
Net Worth: £58,648 *Total Assets:* £1,453,928
Registered Office: Crook Golf Club, Low Jobs Hill, Crook, Co Durham, DL15 9AA
Activities: Trade of electricity
Officers: John Malcolm Elliott [1943] Director; David Hanlon [1957] Director; Kevin McCormick [1954] Director/Retired; Thomas Alan Race [1950] Director/Retired

Weardale Motor Services Limited
Incorporated: 23 November 1961 *Employees:* 50
Net Worth: £3,934,933 *Total Assets:* £5,861,025
Registered Office: The Garage, Stanhope, Bishop Auckland, Co Durham, DL13 2YQ
Activities: Other passenger land transport
Shareholder: Ian Gibson
Officers: Allyson Margaret Gibson-Hewison, Secretary; Anthony Maurice Gibson [1966] Director/Mechanic; Ian Gibson [1973] Director/PSV Driver; Roland Stanley Gibson [1939] Director/P S V Operator; Sylvia Gibson [1932] Director/P S V Operator; Allyson Margaret Gibson Hewison [1963] Director/Administrator

Weardale Railways CIC
Incorporated: 2 June 1993 *Employees:* 3
Net Worth Deficit: £2,409,350 *Total Assets:* £3,204,679
Registered Office: Stanhope Station, Station Road, Stanhope, Bishop Auckland, Co Durham, DL13 2YS
Activities: Freight rail transport
Officers: Edwin Ellis [1954] Director [American]; Hugh Michael McConville [1961] Director [American]; Stephen Raine [1946] Director/Retired; Anthony Slack [1952] Director

Wearmouth Construction and Plant Limited
Incorporated: 2 May 1984 *Employees:* 308
Net Worth: £5,633,333 *Total Assets:* £13,728,367
Registered Office: Wearmouth House, Innovation Court, Yarm Road, Stockton on Tees, Cleveland, TS18 3DA
Activities: Construction of commercial buildings
Shareholders: Robert Alan Wearmouth Jnr; Susan Linda Wearmouth
Officers: Susan Linda Wearmouth, Secretary; Gary Keith Humphreys [1970] Commercial Director; Robert Alan Wearmouth [1961] Director/Builder; Susan Linda Wearmouth [1963] Director/Secretary

Wearmouth Learning Trust
Incorporated: 8 November 2013 *Employees:* 130
Net Worth: £9,559,496 *Total Assets:* £11,324,077
Registered Office: Monkwearmouth Academy, Torver Crescent, Seaburn Dene, Sunderland, Tyne & Wear, SR6 8LG
Activities: General secondary education
Officers: Melissa Dobrianski, Secretary; Maynard Alison [1968] Director/College Principal; Christopher John Burns [1972] Finance Director; John Cogdon [1949] Director; Philip Curtis [1958] Director/Retired; Paul Francis Gowans [1956] Director/Business Development Manager; Julie Rimmer [1963] Director/School Improvement Partner; Stephen William Wilkinson [1957] Director/Headteacher

Wearside Accommodation Services Limited
Incorporated: 2 November 2010
Net Worth: £514,535 *Total Assets:* £6,792,571
Registered Office: 21 North Bridge Street, Sunderland, Tyne & Wear, SR5 1AB
Activities: Other accommodation
Shareholders: Victoria Anne Bianchi; Richard James Wooler
Officers: Victoria Anne Bianchi, Secretary; Richard Wooler [1950] Director

Wearside Golf Club Limited (The)
Incorporated: 30 December 1899
Registered Office: Wearside Golf Club Limited, Coxgreen, Sunderland, Tyne & Wear, SR4 9JT
Activities: Operation of sports facilities
Officers: Robert Harrison Stanbridge Willis, Secretary; Christopher David Barnfather [1983] Director; Peter Tunnah Dewar [1949] Director/Dental Surgeon; James William Dutton [1949] Director; Marjorie Allen Fletcher [1944] Director/Retired; Keith Dane Hodson [1954] Director/Bookmaker; Graham Percival Hope [1948] Director/Retired; Gavin Raitt [1969] Director; David Smith [1959] Director; Ian Smith [1965] Director; Robert Harrison Stanbridge Willis [1953] Director/Retired

Wearside Plumbing Supplies Limited
Incorporated: 10 June 1994 *Employees:* 22
Net Worth: £517,275 *Total Assets:* £1,208,771
Registered Office: 14 Wilson Street North, Sheepfolds Industrial Estate, Monkwearmouth, Sunderland, Tyne & Wear, SR5 1BB
Activities: Wholesale of hardware, plumbing and heating equipment and supplies
Major Shareholder: Barry Richard Sanderson
Officers: Michelle Gayle Stewart, Secretary; Barry Richard Sanderson [1948] Director/Plumber; Mark John Smith [1971] Director/Manager

Websters (Farmers) Limited
Incorporated: 17 May 1966 *Employees:* 7
Net Worth: £1,050,022 *Total Assets:* £4,231,946
Registered Office: Mowbray Hill, Well, Bedale, N Yorks, DL8 2QL
Activities: Growing of cereals (except rice), leguminous crops and oil seeds
Officers: Rachel Carolyn Webster, Secretary; David Anthony Webster [1948] Director/Farmer; Samuel David Webster [1978] Director/Farmer

Webworks Internet (UK) Limited
Incorporated: 2 December 2009 *Employees:* 30
Net Worth: £1,158,826 *Total Assets:* £1,286,744
Registered Office: Business Central Darlington, 2 Union Square, Central Park, Darlington, Co Durham, DL1 1GL
Activities: Specialised design activities
Major Shareholder: Gerard Brogan
Officers: Gerard Brogan [1969] Director

B. Weightman Ltd.
Incorporated: 29 January 2003
Net Worth: £774,162 *Total Assets:* £1,425,804
Registered Office: Estuary House, Steppey Lane, Lesbury, Alnwick, Northumberland, NE66 3PU
Activities: Development of building projects
Shareholders: Brian Weightman; Diana Elizabeth Weightman
Officers: Diana Elizabeth Weightman, Secretary; Brian Weightman [1962] Director/Businessman; Diana Elizabeth Weightman [1963] Director/Secretary

Welbeck C P
Incorporated: 20 December 1928
Net Worth: £2,793,000 *Total Assets:* £35,893,000
Registered Office: 1a Dukesway Court, Team Valley Trading Estate, Gateshead, Tyne & Wear, NE11 0PJ
Activities: Other letting and operating of own or leased real estate
Parent: Welbeck CP Holding Limited
Officers: Phillip Nigel Blain, Secretary; David James Horrocks [1959] Director/Chartered Accountant; Ian Imrie [1955] Director

Welbilt (Halesowen) Limited
Incorporated: 3 August 1976 *Employees:* 119
Net Worth: £6,556,000 *Total Assets:* £40,612,000
Registered Office: St Ann's Wharf, 112 Quayside, Newcastle upon Tyne, NE1 3DX
Activities: Manufacture of machinery for food, beverage and tobacco processing
Parent: Merrychef Limited
Officers: Adrian David Gray [1962] Director/Accountant; John Albert James Rourke [1967] Director; Mark Anthony Smith [1968] Director/Vice President Beverage EMEA/APAC

Welbilt UK Limited
Incorporated: 23 October 1991 *Employees:* 284
Net Worth: £26,907,000 *Total Assets:* £40,570,000
Registered Office: St Ann's Wharf, 112 Quayside, Newcastle upon Tyne, NE1 3DX
Activities: Manufacture of machinery for food, beverage and tobacco processing
Parent: Welbilt (Halesowen) Limited
Officers: Adrian David Gray [1962] Director/Accountant; John Albert James Rourke [1967] Director

Peter Weldon & Co Limited
Incorporated: 24 November 2004
Net Worth: £696,679 *Total Assets:* £1,221,727
Registered Office: 87 Station Road, Ashington, Northumberland, NE63 8RS
Activities: Accounting and auditing activities
Shareholders: Peter Weldon; Violet Lesley Weldon
Officers: Peter Weldon [1957] Director

The Welfare Dwellings Trust Limited
Incorporated: 25 January 1989
Net Worth: £11,040,000 *Total Assets:* £26,501,000
Registered Office: Cross House, Westgate Road, Newcastle upon Tyne, NE1 4XX
Activities: Development of building projects
Parent: Sovereign Reversions Limited
Officers: Paul Trevor Barber [1967] Director/Chief Executive; Ashish Kashyap [1979] Investment Director; Antony Lewis Pierce [1976] Finance Director

Welkin Investments Ltd
Incorporated: 15 January 2010
Net Worth Deficit: £2,715 *Total Assets:* £889,667
Registered Office: Exchange Building, 66 Church Street, Hartlepool, Cleveland, TS24 7DN
Activities: Buying and selling of own real estate
Parent: Thornton Investments Ltd
Officers: Christopher Scott Agar [1966] Director

Wellbark Property Limited
Incorporated: 25 May 2006
Net Worth Deficit: £1,176,174 *Total Assets:* £21,624,724
Registered Office: First Floor, Finchale House, Belmont Business Park, Durham, DH1 1TW
Activities: Other letting and operating of own or leased real estate
Officers: Helen Austin, Secretary; John Corbitt Barnsley [1948] Director; Spencer Trerise Glanville [1972] Director; Robert William Jefferson [1950] Director/Chartered Accountant

Wellburn Care Homes Limited
Incorporated: 27 November 1985 *Employees:* 548
Net Worth: £23,748,424 *Total Assets:* £51,841,600
Registered Office: Tyne View House, 9 Grange Road, Newburn, Newcastle upon Tyne, NE15 8ND
Activities: Residential care activities for the elderly and disabled
Shareholders: Rachel Buckland; Simon William Beckett
Officers: Richard David Guppy, Secretary; Simon William Beckett [1944] Director/Chartered Surveyor; Rachel Buckland [1973] Director/Interior Designer; Stephen William Buckland [1971] Director; Christopher John Davey [1952] Director/Chartered Accountant; Richard David Guppy [1966] Director; Susan Margaret McKinney [1964] Director

Wellsprings Properties Ltd
Incorporated: 9 March 2000 *Employees:* 4
Net Worth: £1,394,221 *Total Assets:* £4,047,622
Registered Office: Whitfield House, Whitfield Court, St Johns Road, Meadowfield Industrial Estate, Meadowfield, Co Durham, DH7 8XL
Activities: Buying and selling of own real estate
Major Shareholder: Kevin Whitfield
Officers: Anne Whitfield, Secretary; Amy Victoria Whitfield [1990] Director/Property; Kevin Whitfield [1960] Director

Wellstream Finance Limited
Incorporated: 26 November 2002
Net Worth: £15,841,000 *Total Assets:* £16,168,000
Registered Office: Wellstream House, Wincomblee Road, Walker Riverside, Newcastle upon Tyne, NE6 3PF
Activities: Other business support service activities n.e.c.
Officers: David Russell Justiss [1976] Director [American]; Federico Romani [1975] Director [Italian]

Wellway Pharmacy Limited
Incorporated: 9 February 1995 *Employees:* 18
Net Worth: £110,622 *Total Assets:* £785,214
Registered Office: The Surgery, Wellway, Morpeth, Northumberland, NE61 1BJ
Activities: Dispensing chemist in specialised stores
Officers: Dr Alistair Stewart Blair [1969] Director/Medical Practitioner; Dr Zoe Claire Crichton [1975] Director/General Practitioner; Stephen Andrew Hinchliffe [1967] Director/Medical Practitioner; Sukhpreet Singh Kullar [1980] Director/Pharmacist; Dr Margaret Jacinta Marie Manship [1967] Director/General Practitioner; Dr Christopher Marr [1959] Director/Medical Practitioner; Dr Caroline Elizabeth Phipps [1982] Director/Doctor; Dr Suzanne Louise Renner [1974] Director/General Practitioner; Sharon Louise Williams [1972] Director/Pharmacist

E.B. & C.A. Welsh Limited
Incorporated: 30 June 2006 *Employees:* 9
Net Worth: £1,040,205 *Total Assets:* £1,558,510
Registered Office: 37-38 Market Street, Ferryhill, Co Durham, DL17 8JH
Activities: Recreational vehicle parks, trailer parks and camping grounds
Officers: Ann Godrica Watson, Secretary/Park Home Proprietor; Julie Anderson [1977] Director; Charlotte Brown [1990] Director; Emma Brown [1980] Director/Farmer Accountant; Suzanne Coverdale [1982] Director; Zoe MacDonald [1978] Director; Ann Godrica Watson [1951] Director/Park Home Proprietor; Eric John Welsh [1945] Director/Park Home Proprietor; Graham Welsh [1979] Director; Michael Welsh [1977] Director; Peter Welsh [1972] Director

Welwyn Components Limited
Incorporated: 6 January 1920 *Employees:* 291
Net Worth: £18,403,000 *Total Assets:* £31,248,000
Registered Office: Welwyn Electronics Park, Bedlington, Northumberland, NE22 7AA
Activities: Manufacture of electronic components
Parent: TT Electronics Group Holdings Limited
Officers: Lynton David Boardman, Secretary; Guy Paul Millard [1971] Director; Barry Peters [1958] Director; Timothy Hal Roberts [1970] Director

Wemyss Bay Caravan Park Limited
Incorporated: 9 April 1969
Net Worth: £11,819,000 *Total Assets:* £18,918,000
Registered Office: Second Floor, One Gosforth Park Way, Gosforth Business Park, Newcastle upon Tyne, NE12 8ET
Activities: Recreational vehicle parks, trailer parks and camping grounds
Parent: PD Parks Limited
Officers: Judith Ann Archibold, Secretary; Ian Kellett [1963] Director; John Anthony Waterworth [1963] Director

Wensley Roofing Limited
Incorporated: 13 November 1996 *Employees:* 54
Net Worth: £3,002,044 *Total Assets:* £4,848,404
Registered Office: Station House, Station Road, Chester-le-Street, Co Durham, DH3 3DU
Activities: Roofing activities
Parent: Northern Bear PLC
Officers: Wendy Ann Edgell, Secretary; Alan Chapman [1956] Director/Contracts Manager; Robert Dodds [1968] Director/Accounts; Graham Roy Jennings [1956] Director; Steven Raymond Luke [1980] Director; Steven Mark Roberts [1966] Director; Keith Soulsby [1956] Director/Roofing Contractor

Wensleydale Bacon Limited
Incorporated: 7 July 1983 *Employees:* 23
Net Worth: £1,660,343 *Total Assets:* £2,550,963
Registered Office: Tennant Close, Standard Way Business Park, Northallerton, N Yorks, DL6 2XL
Activities: Wholesale of meat and meat products
Shareholders: Thomas Ralph Stockdale; Carolyn Elizabeth Stockdale
Officers: Carolyn Stockdale, Secretary; Thomas Ralph Stockdale [1953] Director/Bacon Wholesaler; Malcolm Stuart Stokoe [1944] Director/Office Manager

Wensleydale Dairy Products Limited
Incorporated: 29 July 1992 *Employees:* 239
Net Worth: £5,153,983 *Total Assets:* £17,249,696
Registered Office: The Creamery, Gayle Lane, Hawes, N Yorks, DL8 3RN
Activities: Butter and cheese production
Officers: Sally Rachel Bowen, Secretary; Sally Rachel Bowen [1973] Finance Director; Lee Coates [1966] Operations Director; Sarah Elizabeth Emmett-Lee [1967] Commercial Director; David Alwyne James Hartley [1962] Director/Production Manager; Philip Keith Jones [1960] Director; David John Salkeld [1956] Director/Chairman

The Wensleydale Property Company Limited
Incorporated: 10 March 1998 *Employees:* 10
Net Worth: £2,061,665 *Total Assets:* £2,273,447
Registered Office: Hilltop East, Newton-le-Willows, Bedale, N Yorks, DL8 1TP
Activities: Other letting and operating of own or leased real estate
Shareholder: Kenneth Woolley
Officers: John Bernard Liddle, Secretary; John Joicey Dickinson [1953] Director/Chartered Surveyor/Land Agent; Tobyn Benedict Dickinson [1981] Director; John Bernard Liddle [1946] Farm Manager and Director; Charles Guy Corban Ropner [1959] Director/Sales Executive; Dominic Adam Ropner [1968] Director/Supplier of Memorial Stones; Edith Avril Ropner [1930] Director/Housewife; Jonathan Mark Ropner [1954] Director/Construction Superintendent; Paul Benedict Peat Ropner [1965] Director/Self Employed Businessman; Kenneth Woolley [1946] Director [American]

Wensleydale Railway PLC
Incorporated: 20 October 2000 *Employees:* 13
Net Worth: £691,989 *Total Assets:* £1,508,542
Registered Office: Leeming Bar Station, Leases Road, Leeming Bar, Northallerton, N Yorks, DL7 9AR
Activities: Passenger rail transport, interurban
Officers: Malcolm John Lynch, Secretary; Stephen Davies [1959] Managing Director; Alex Michael Dudiak [1965] Director/Chief Engineering Officer; Graham Harris [1954] Director; Richard James Holt [1972] Director/Management Consultant; Carl Anthony Les [1949] Director; Russell Frederick Lord [1954] Director; David Walker [1949] Director

Wentworth Northern Properties Limited
Incorporated: 5 March 1992
Net Worth: £378,194 *Total Assets:* £772,381
Registered Office: Morningside, Newbrough, Hexham, Northumberland, NE47 5AR
Activities: Other letting and operating of own or leased real estate
Major Shareholder: Ian Kingsley Donkin
Officers: Ian Kingsley Donkin [1959] Director; Michael Peter Donkin [1989] Director/Business Manager

Wescott Industrial Services Ltd
Incorporated: 8 March 2010
Net Worth: £570,906 *Total Assets:* £1,734,529
Registered Office: Unit 9 B/C Plus, 10 Tyne Point Industrial Estate, Shaftesbury Avenue, Jarrow, Tyne & Wear, NE32 3UP
Activities: Technical testing and analysis
Shareholders: Thomas Whittleton; Kevin Carruthers
Officers: Kevin Carruthers [1979] Director; Matthew Thomas Doyle [1990] Director; Mark Duffy [1970] Director; Tom Whittleton [1965] Managing Director

Wescott Medical Limited
Incorporated: 7 October 1991
Net Worth: £672,555 *Total Assets:* £860,424
Registered Office: Unit 3b Drum Industrial Estate, Chester-le-Street, Co Durham, DH2 1AG
Activities: Manufacture of medical and dental instruments and supplies
Shareholders: Neville Stebbings; Susan Stebbings
Officers: Neville Stebbings [1957] Director/Medical Equipment Marketing; Susan Stebbings [1957] Director/Medical Equipment Marketing

Wessington Cryogenics Limited
Incorporated: 10 February 1984 *Employees:* 93
Net Worth: £1,676,847 *Total Assets:* £4,343,826
Registered Office: 2 Gadwall Road, Rainton Bridge South, Houghton-le-Spring, Co Durham, DH4 5NL
Activities: Manufacture of other tanks, reservoirs and containers of metal
Officers: Debbie Bell, Secretary; Edwin Marshall Rowe [1936] Director/Engineer; Paul Rowe [1966] Director/Engineer; Gillian Southern [1962] Director/Engineering

West Denton Indoor Bowls Club Limited
Incorporated: 28 January 2014
Net Worth: £133,668 *Total Assets:* £2,231,219
Registered Office: West Denton Indoor Bowls Hall, Hillhead Road, West Denton, Newcastle upon Tyne, NE5 1DN
Activities: Operation of sports facilities
Officers: David Lee [1947] Director/Retired; Elizabeth Ann Lennie [1947] Director/Retired; William Lennie [1944] Director/Retired; Generald McCue [1947] Director/Retired; Raymond Duff Rodgers [1942] Director/Retired; James Scott Russell [1930] Director/Retired; Karen Weites [1952] Director/Retired

West End Schools Trust
Incorporated: 23 January 2015
Net Worth: £15,878,188 *Total Assets:* £15,878,788
Registered Office: Bridgewater, Delaval Road, Newcastle upon Tyne, NE15 6NL
Activities: Primary education
Officers: Helen Victoria Thomson, Secretary; John Richard Anderson [1965] Director/School Governor; Tracey Anne Caffrey [1973] Director/Headteacher; Revd George Robert Curry [1951] Director/Clerk; David Michael Drewe [1957] Director; Professor Christopher Kenneth Drinkwater [1944] Director/Retired; Jane Dube [1967] Director/Headteacher; Margaret Fisher [1945] Director/Retired; Kathryn Herron [1972] Director/Headteacher; David Gilroy Jones [1964] Director/Manager; David McLeod [1970] Director/Headteacher; Jane Mullarkey [1967] Director/Headteacher; Diva Kumar Nair [1992] Director/Financial Controller; Alison Margaret Priestley [1961] Director/Service Manager; Samantha Jane Robson [1969] Director/Headteacher; Lynn Stephenson [1948] Director/Board Member Your Homes Newcastle; Judith Sword [1955] Director; Peter John Stuart Thomson [1952] Director/Retired; Liz Todd [1958] Director/University Professor

West Hartlepool Rugby Football Club Limited
Incorporated: 20 September 1999 *Employees:* 12
Net Worth Deficit: £16,941 *Total Assets:* £1,183,969
Registered Office: Brinkburn, Catcote Road, Hartlepool, Cleveland, TS25 4HA
Activities: Other sports activities
Officers: Godfrey Hainsworth, Secretary; Graham Frankland [1958] Director/Local Government Officer; Peter Norman Olsen [1948] Director/Chartered Accountant; Leslie William Burton Smith [1946] Director/Teacher; Kathryn Elaine Waites [1975] Director/Clerk

West Waterlooville Developments Limited
Incorporated: 19 April 1995
Net Worth: £6,767,938 *Total Assets:* £61,569,144
Registered Office: Citygate, St James Boulevard, Newcastle upon Tyne, NE1 4JE
Activities: Development of building projects
Parent: Grainger Housing & Developments Limited
Officers: Adam McGhin, Secretary; Helen Christine Gordon [1959] Director; Michael Paul Keaveney [1967] Director; Adam McGhin [1978] Director/Solicitor; Vanessa Kate Simms [1975] Director

Westbrook Cycles Limited
Incorporated: 10 March 2009 *Employees:* 11
Net Worth: £1,082,086 *Total Assets:* £1,174,054
Registered Office: 2 Market Place, Stokesley, Cleveland, TS9 5DG
Activities: Retail sale of sports goods, fishing gear, camping goods, boats and bicycles
Shareholders: Paul Rex Craig Richardson; Samantha Jane Richardson
Officers: Paul Rex Craig Richardson [1969] Director/Manager; Samantha Jane Richardson [1973] Director/Manager

Westerhope Limited
Incorporated: 7 August 2014 *Employees:* 19
Net Worth: £605,666 *Total Assets:* £1,954,603
Registered Office: Fernwood House, Fernwood Road, Jesmond, Newcastle upon Tyne, NE2 1TJ
Activities: Dental practice activities
Major Shareholder: Dr Shabinuddin Chohan
Officers: Jacqueline Callear [1988] Director; Dr Shabinuddin Chohan [1971] Director/Dentist

Westgarth Haulage Limited
Incorporated: 13 March 2008 *Employees:* 10
Net Worth: £2,040,096 *Total Assets:* £2,319,600
Registered Office: Pond Dale, Gilling West, Richmond, N Yorks, DL10 5LB
Activities: Freight transport by road
Shareholders: Paul Anthony Hall Westgarth; Timothy Peter Westgarth
Officers: Peter Leslie Westgarth, Secretary/Farmer; Paul Anthony Hall Westgarth [1967] Director/Farmer; Timothy Peter Westgarth [1973] Director/Farmer

G. & M. Westgarth Limited
Incorporated: 3 April 1996 *Employees:* 28
Net Worth: £4,234,886 *Total Assets:* £11,462,633
Registered Office: Newsham Hall, Newsham, Richmond, N Yorks, DL11 7RA
Activities: Raising of swine and pigs
Major Shareholder: Mark Andrew William Westgarth
Officers: Mark Andrew William Westgarth, Secretary; George William Westgarth [1938] Director/Farmer; Mark Andrew William Westgarth [1970] Director/Farmer

Westland Way 3 LLP
Incorporated: 18 January 2010
Net Worth: £1,029,844 *Total Assets:* £2,871,232
Registered Office: 3 George Stephenson Court, Preston Farm, Stockton on Tees, Cleveland, TS18 3FB

Westline Distributors Limited
Incorporated: 6 March 1987 *Employees:* 15
Net Worth: £573,052 *Total Assets:* £1,330,671
Registered Office: Bede House, Westline Industrial Estate, Birtley, Chester-le-Street, Co Durham, DH2 1AU
Activities: Manufacture of metal structures and parts of structures
Parent: Bede Group Ltd
Officers: Joy Christine Crawley, Secretary; George Henry Gibbon [1961] Director; Kenneth Kirsop [1954] Director; Linda Deborah Lewins [1964] Director

Westminster Day Nurseries Limited
Incorporated: 22 May 1998 *Employees:* 50
Net Worth: £1,827,531 *Total Assets:* £2,229,762
Registered Office: The Willows, 6 Kingswood, Langley Park, Co Durham, DH7 9WA
Activities: Pre-primary education
Shareholders: Trevor Graham; Susan Graham
Officers: Susan Graham, Secretary; Susan Graham [1956] Director/Nursery Nurse; Trevor Graham [1954] Director/Childrens Nursery

Westone Wholesale Limited
Incorporated: 26 April 1983 *Employees:* 5
Net Worth: £5,507,186 *Total Assets:* £9,282,724
Registered Office: Unit S3, Narvik Way, Tyne Tunnel Trading Estate, North Shields, Tyne & Wear, NE29 7XJ
Activities: Wholesale of sugar and chocolate and sugar confectionery
Officers: Patricia Ada Rice, Secretary; David Leonard Brind [1972] Director; John Frederick Hope [1969] Group Operations Director; Paul Victor Young [1957] Director

Westray Recruitment Consultants Limited
Incorporated: 29 January 1990 *Employees:* 271
Net Worth: £69,234 *Total Assets:* £1,213,742
Registered Office: Valley House, Kingsway South, Team Valley Trading Estate, Gateshead, Tyne & Wear, NE11 0JW
Activities: Temporary employment agency activities
Parent: Westray Holdings Limited
Officers: Steven Hodgson, Secretary; Steven Hodgson [1976] Director; Maureen Wright [1961] Managing Director

Westside Properties & Developments Limited
Incorporated: 4 October 2012 *Employees:* 1
Net Worth: £144,851 *Total Assets:* £1,347,678
Registered Office: 37-38 Market Street, Ferryhill, Co Durham, DL17 8JH
Activities: Buying and selling of own real estate
Major Shareholder: Kevin Crabtree
Officers: Lynsey Anne Ibbetson [1972] Director

Weststar Holidays Limited
Incorporated: 2 January 1987 *Employees:* 400
Net Worth: £7,929,000 *Total Assets:* £20,344,000
Registered Office: 2nd Floor, One Gosforth Park Way, Gosforth Business Park, Newcastle upon Tyne, NE12 8ET
Activities: Recreational vehicle parks, trailer parks and camping grounds
Parent: PD Parks Limited
Officers: Judith Ann Archibold, Secretary; Ian Kellett [1963] Director; John Anthony Waterworth [1963] Director

Westway Developments (North East) Limited
Incorporated: 20 March 2007
Net Worth Deficit: £150,403 *Total Assets:* £976,438
Registered Office: 32 Saltwell View, Gateshead, Tyne & Wear, NE8 4NT
Activities: Buying and selling of own real estate
Shareholders: Stephen Hamilton; John Robert Watkins
Officers: Stephen Hamilton, Secretary; Stephen Hamilton [1964] Director/Local Government Officer; Jonathan Robert Watkins [1959] Director/Structural Engineer

Whale Hill Limited
Incorporated: 29 September 2015
Net Worth: £25,239 *Total Assets:* £1,090,884
Registered Office: Lakeside House, Kingfisher Way, Stockton on Tees, Cleveland, TS18 3NB
Activities: Other human health activities
Major Shareholder: David Graham Jarvis
Officers: David Graham Jarvis, Secretary; Sukhy Chahal [1988] Director/Pharmacist; David Graham Jarvis [1966] Director/Pharmacist

Wharton Construction Limited
Incorporated: 2 September 1985 *Employees:* 46
Net Worth: £933,896 *Total Assets:* £2,123,053
Registered Office: Kellaw Road, Yarm Road Business Park, Darlington, Co Durham, DL1 4YA
Activities: Construction of other civil engineering projects n.e.c.
Major Shareholder: Peter Wharton
Officers: Sandra Wharton, Secretary; Christopher Paul Lee [1970] Director/Senior Quantity Surveyor; Matthew Ross Wharton [1983] Director/Quantity Surveyor; Peter Wharton [1949] Director/Engineer; Sandra Wharton [1949] Director/Secretary

Wheatley Hill Community Association
Incorporated: 9 March 2004 *Employees:* 7
Net Worth: £901,253 *Total Assets:* £914,287
Registered Office: Wheatley Hill Community Association, Stephens Terrace, Wheatley Hill, Co Durham, DH6 3JS
Activities: Other business support service activities n.e.c.
Officers: Robert Potts, Secretary/Retired; Freda Elizabeth Coxon [1937] Director/Retired; Diane Metcalfe [1941] Director/Retired; Jake Miller [1994] Director/Support Worker; Robert Potts [1944] Director/Retired; John Walter Probert [1957] Director/Business Advisor; Barry Robinson [1946] Director/Retired; Evelyn Robson [1940] Director/Retired

Wheatley Hill Property Company Limited
Incorporated: 5 September 2012
Net Worth Deficit: £260,771 *Total Assets:* £2,190,667
Registered Office: 8 Sutherland Grange, New Herrington, Houghton-le-Spring, Co Durham, DH4 4UT
Activities: General medical practice activities
Shareholder: Joseph Chandy
Officers: Raymond Priestman, Secretary; Joseph Chandy [1970] Director/Practice Developer; Dr Sanjay Kailashnath Gupta [1976] Director/Doctor [Indian]; Dr Nand Kishore Mahto [1948] Director/Doctor; Dr Harbhajan Singh Mangat [1951] Director/Doctor; Dr Ko Ko Naing [1963] Director/Doctor

Whessoe Engineering Limited
Incorporated: 14 December 2007
Registered Office: Whessoe Technology Centre, Alderman Best Way, Morton Palms, Darlington, Co Durham, DL1 4WB
Activities: Other engineering activities
Officers: Yi Heon Hyun [1971] Director [South Korean]; Steve Un Kim [1956] Director [Canadian]; Leonard Taylor [1958] Director/Chief Executive

Whickham Golf Club Limited (The)
Incorporated: 24 June 1938 *Employees:* 15
Net Worth: £593,036 *Total Assets:* £854,526
Registered Office: Hollinside Park, Fellside Road, Whickham, Gateshead, Tyne & Wear, NE16 5BA
Activities: Operation of sports facilities
Officers: Irene Patricia Hutton, Secretary; Leslie John Britton [1944] Director; Peter John Brown [1961] Director/Retired; Philip Coldron [1948] Director/Retired; Hayley Gobin [1985] Director/Civil Servant (Overseas Pension Officer); Kenneth Greatbatch [1948] Director; Ian Harvey [1990] Director/Regional Development Officer; David Hutchinson [1961] Director

Whickham Salerooms Limited
Incorporated: 10 March 2010 *Employees:* 10
Net Worth: £806,657 *Total Assets:* £1,627,456
Registered Office: Back Row, Whickham, Gateshead, Tyne & Wear, NE16 4AB
Activities: Retail of furniture, lighting, and similar (not musical instruments or scores) in specialised store
Shareholders: Alan David Dumighan; Paul Richard Dumighan; Jason Mark Dumighan
Officers: Alan David Dumighan [1947] Director/Businessman; Jason Mark Dumighan [1969] Director/Businessman; Paul Richard Dumighan [1973] Director/Businessman

Whickham School and Sports College
Incorporated: 4 August 2011 *Employees:* 146
Net Worth: £4,205,000 *Total Assets:* £6,123,000
Registered Office: Whickham School and Sports College, Burnthouse Lane, Whickham, Gateshead, Tyne & Wear, NE16 5AR
Activities: General secondary education
Officers: Hazel Davison, Secretary; Simon Alexander [1982] Director/Teacher; Sasha Lyn Ban [1969] Director/Senior Lecturer; Councillor David Berry Bradford [1953] Director/Retired; Cllr Malcolm Alfred Brain [1958] Director/Probation Officer; Catherine Joy Enlund [1979] Director/Teacher; Steven James Haigh [1960] Director/Headteacher; Ross Hogarth-Willis [1978] Director; Rhonda Elizabeth Jones [1979] Director/Child Workforce Adopter [American]; Moira Ledger [1950] Director/Retired; Geoffrey Little [1964] Director/Chartered Accountant; Graham Ian Maitland [1970] Director/Engineer; Vicki McLeod [1968] Director/Education; Adrian William Oakes [1972] Director/Policeman; Melanie Louise Pears [1965] Director/Solicitor; Michael Ronald Phillips [1975] Director/Manager; Geessien Alida Potse [1961] Director [Dutch]; Emma Ridley [1973] Director/Social Worker; Anthony Wilson [1959] Director

Whitburn Church of England Academy
Incorporated: 9 December 2010 *Employees:* 140
Net Worth: £14,179,000 *Total Assets:* £15,933,000
Registered Office: Whitburn Church of England Academy, Rackly Way, Whitburn, Sunderland, Tyne & Wear, SR6 7EF
Activities: General secondary education
Officers: Gillian Elizabeth Hodgson, Secretary; Hilary Margaret Al Ajdiri [1952] Director/Retired Assistant Headteacher; Christine Alder [1948] Director/Retired; Susan Alison Beech [1965] Director/IT Analyst/Programmer; Nicholas Clougher [1970] Director/Teacher; Ian Dale Fawdon [1964] Director of Learning and Development; Alan Hardie [1966] Director/Principal of Academy; Paul Anthony MacKings [1961] Director; Barry Morris [1960] Director/Human Resources Advisor (Schools); Timothy Mulford [1974] Director/Teacher; Jean Mulley [1940] Director/Retired Headteacher; Milda Small [1959] Director/Retired Clerk; Roderick Matthew Stuart [1971] Director/Head of Communications; Andrea Louise Tobin [1966] Director/Accountant

Whitchester Farm Limited
Incorporated: 13 June 1975 *Employees:* 1
Net Worth: £4,122,405 *Total Assets:* £5,744,604
Registered Office: Frankham Farm, Fourstones, Hexham, Northumberland, NE47 5DL
Activities: Growing of cereals (except rice), leguminous crops and oil seeds
Shareholders: John Spence; Emma Spence
Officers: Emma Spence, Secretary; John Spence, Secretary; Emma Spence [1967] Company Secretary/Director; John Spence [1955] Director/Farmer

White Bros. (N'cle-on-Tyne) Limited
Incorporated: 1 December 1987 *Employees:* 46
Net Worth: £1,154,508 *Total Assets:* £1,794,726
Registered Office: Unit 4-5 Gosforth Industrial Estate, Newcastle upon Tyne, NE3 1XD
Activities: Manufacture of other fabricated metal products n.e.c.
Major Shareholder: Peter James Harding
Officers: Peter James Harding [1952] Director/Chartered Accountant; Stephen Paul Roberts [1969] Director/Chartered Accountant; Gavin Wragby [1971] Director

The White Hart Hawes Limited
Incorporated: 11 August 2011
Registered Office: O'Reilly Chartered Accountants, Kiln Hill, Market Place, Hawes, N Yorks, DL8 3RA
Activities: Unlicenced restaurants and cafes
Shareholders: Matthew Kirkbride; Pat Kirkbride; Professor Max Robinson
Officers: Pat Kirkbride, Secretary; Mathew Robert Kirkbride [1988] Director; Pat Kirkbride [1959] Director; Professor Max Robinson [1945] Director

T.A. and N. White Limited
Incorporated: 12 October 1982 *Employees:* 2
Net Worth: £933,185 *Total Assets:* £977,545
Registered Office: Unit E4, Park Road South Industrial Estate, Blackhill, Consett, Co Durham, DH8 5PY
Activities: Other letting and operating of own or leased real estate
Shareholders: Norma White; Thomas Anthony White
Officers: Norma White, Secretary; Norma White [1943] Director/Administrator; Thomas Anthony White [1945] Director/Vehicle Trader

George F. White LLP
Incorporated: 16 May 2003 *Employees:* 91
Net Worth: £797,575 *Total Assets:* £1,501,399
Registered Office: 6 Market Street, Alnwick, Northumberland, NE66 1TL
Officers: Simon Checkley Britton [1974] Member; Andrew John Entwistle [1972] Member; Richard Kenneth Garland [1979] Member; Sally Alexandra Hart [1985] Member; David Robyn Peat [1963] Member; George Francis White [1952] Member; Michael Alasdair Young [1970] Member

Whitehall Executive Developments Limited
Incorporated: 28 September 2000
Net Worth: £1,649,535 *Total Assets:* £3,372,365
Registered Office: Stonehaven Manor, Iveston Lane, Consett, Co Durham, DH8 7TB
Activities: Construction of domestic buildings
Shareholders: Paul Stobbs; Jane Louise Stobbs
Officers: Paul Stobbs, Secretary; Jane Louise Stobbs [1968] Director/Property Developer; Mark Anthony Stobbs [1965] Director; Paul Stobbs [1966] Director/Property Developer

Whitehead Alloys Limited
Incorporated: 23 September 1980 *Employees:* 18
Net Worth: £3,848,919 *Total Assets:* £5,224,893
Registered Office: Buck Street, Middlesbrough, Cleveland, TS2 1LW
Activities: Aluminium production
Shareholder: William Albert Edward Whitehead
Officers: Andrew Spalding, Secretary; Andrew Spalding [1957] Director; Gloria Whitehead [1942] Director/Secretary; William Whitehead [1962] Director; William Albert Edward Whitehead [1937] Director

Whitehouse Funeral Service Limited
Incorporated: 7 August 2009 *Employees:* 24
Net Worth: £343,463 *Total Assets:* £927,492
Registered Office: Cockerton House, 11 West Auckland Road, Darlington, Co Durham, DL3 9EJ
Activities: Funeral and related activities
Shareholders: Charles Melvin Whitehouse; Charles John Whitehouse
Officers: Charles Melvin Whitehouse, Secretary; Charles John Whitehouse [1971] Director; Charles Melvin Whitehouse [1948] Director

Whiterock Bid Support Limited
Incorporated: 29 July 2013
Net Worth: £1,419,779 *Total Assets:* £1,977,594
Registered Office: York House, Thornfield Business Park, Standard Way Business Park, Northallerton, N Yorks, DL6 2XQ
Activities: Management consultancy activities other than financial management
Shareholders: Colin Howell; Kelly Howell
Officers: Colin Howell [1963] Director; Kelly Howell [1979] Director

Whiteside Residential Limited
Incorporated: 21 October 2013
Net Worth: £169,049 *Total Assets:* £1,951,507
Registered Office: Bankside 14, The Watermark, Gateshead, Tyne & Wear, NE11 9SY
Activities: Other letting and operating of own or leased real estate
Officers: Elliott Allan Ward [1966] Director; Lorna Grace Ward [1969] Director

Whitestone Weavers Limited
Incorporated: 3 June 1991 *Employees:* 1
Net Worth: £3,521,761 *Total Assets:* £9,238,898
Registered Office: View Logistics, Park View Road East, Hartlepool, Cleveland, TS25 1HT
Activities: Wholesale of textiles
Parent: Whitestone Carpets Holdings Ltd
Officers: Tanya Kelly, Secretary; Stephen Maurice Martin Byrne [1960] Director/Salesman; Vincent Holden [1956] Sales Director; Geoffrey Brendon Wilding [1963] Director [New Zealander]

Whitewell Hotels Limited
Incorporated: 23 February 1998 *Employees:* 7
Net Worth Deficit: £1,138,338 *Total Assets:* £4,752,759
Registered Office: 18 Grosvenor Road, Jesmond, Newcastle upon Tyne, NE2 2RP
Activities: Other letting and operating of own or leased real estate
Shareholder: Zaida Niaz Din
Officers: Hasan Din [1994] Director; Sarah Suhail Din [1988] Director; Zaida Niaz Din [1963] Director/Hotelier

Whitewell Properties Limited
Incorporated: 19 March 1998
Net Worth: £3,330,203 *Total Assets:* £5,325,267
Registered Office: 18 Grosvenor Road, Jesmond, Newcastle upon Tyne, NE2 2RP
Activities: Other letting and operating of own or leased real estate
Officers: Hasan Din [1994] Director; Sarah Suhail Din [1988] Director; Zaida Niaz Din [1963] Director/Hotelier

M.Whitfield Limited
Incorporated: 20 February 1935 *Employees:* 75
Net Worth: £1,708,690 *Total Assets:* £2,465,678
Registered Office: St Aidans Terrace, Trimdon Station, Cleveland, TS29 6BT
Activities: Dispensing chemist in specialised stores
Parent: PRWG Holdings Limited
Officers: Peter Robert Whitfield Grundy, Secretary; Stuart John Bowman [1967] Director/Pharmacist; John Whitfield Grundy [1947] Director/Optician; Peter Robert Whitfield Grundy [1951] Director/Qualified Chemist

G. Whitfield Limited
Incorporated: 28 February 1957
Net Worth: £1,305,587 *Total Assets:* £2,312,882
Registered Office: 1a Church Street, Houghton-le-Spring, Co Durham, DH4 4DN
Activities: Dispensing chemist in specialised stores
Shareholders: Karen Valerie Gaines; Fiona Claire Kerry
Officers: Valerie Karen Gaines, Secretary; Clifford Rowland Gaines [1962] Director/Pharmacist; Valerie Karen Gaines [1965] Director/Pharmacist; Fiona Claire Kerry [1965] Director/Pharmacist; Valerie Catmore Whitfield [1936] Director/Pharmacist; George Whitfield Jnr [1936] Director/Pharmacist

Whitley Bay Golf Club Ltd (The)
Incorporated: 20 May 1912 *Employees:* 16
Net Worth: £500,734 *Total Assets:* £931,637
Registered Office: Claremont Road, Whitley Bay, Tyne & Wear, NE26 3UF
Activities: Activities of sport clubs
Officers: Dawn Lesley Ridley, Secretary; James Douglas [1953] Director/Retired; John Wilfrid Hewison [1944] Director/Retired; Graham Holland [1958] Director/Optician; Dr Anthony Hood [1949] Director/Retired; Duncan Keady [1961] Director/Building Inspector; Andrew Potter [1980] Director/Accountant; Margaret Waterson [1949] Director/Retired; John Wymer [1951] Director/Retired

J. & J. Whittaker (Chemist) Limited
Incorporated: 12 May 1989 *Employees:* 10
Net Worth: £1,890,470 *Total Assets:* £2,006,192
Registered Office: 32 Wansbeck Road South, Gosforth, Newcastle upon Tyne, NE3 3HQ
Activities: Other retail sale in non-specialised stores
Parent: Horsley Properties Limited
Officers: Sunil Maini, Secretary; Sunil Maini [1967] Director/Pharmacist; Bhavna Patel [1970] Director/Pharmacist

Whitworth Hall Developments Limited
Incorporated: 4 December 2013 *Employees:* 47
Net Worth Deficit: £1,246,643 *Total Assets:* £2,216,095
Registered Office: Avenue One, Chilton Industrial Estate, Chilton, Ferryhill, Co Durham, DL17 0SH
Activities: Hotels and similar accommodation
Major Shareholder: Adrian Parnaby
Officers: Pauline Isobel Lerigo [1960] Director; Adrian Parnaby [1958] Director; Ben Parnaby [1987] Director; Ian Parnaby [1984] Director

WHL 2013 Holdings Limited
Incorporated: 1 November 2013 *Employees:* 83
Net Worth: £17,093,000 *Total Assets:* £20,291,000
Registered Office: Unit B, Colima Avenue, Sunderland Enterprise Park, Sunderland, Tyne & Wear, SR5 3XE
Activities: Renting and leasing of other machinery, equipment and tangible goods n.e.c.
Shareholders: Carrier Rental Systems (UK) Limited; Baird Capital Partners Europe II LP
Officers: Simon Boniface, Secretary; Laura Jayne Wilcock, Secretary; Steven Blaby [1979] Director/Accountant; Archibald Ziwanemoyo Hungwe [1973] Director/General Manager; Simon Ross Harden McMullen [1969] Financial Director

WHL 2013 Limited
Incorporated: 6 November 2013 *Employees:* 2
Net Worth: £15,506,000 *Total Assets:* £15,673,000
Registered Office: Unit B, Colima Avenue, Sunderland Enterprise Park, Sunderland, Tyne & Wear, SR5 3XE
Activities: Renting and leasing of other machinery, equipment and tangible goods n.e.c.
Parent: WHL 2013 Holdings Limited
Officers: Simon Boniface, Secretary; Laura Jayne Wilcock, Secretary; Steven Blaby [1979] Director/Accountant; Archibald Ziwanemoyo Hungwe [1973] Director/General Manager; Simon Ross Harden McMullen [1969] Financial Director

WHP Facilities Ltd
Incorporated: 5 March 2009 *Employees:* 58
Net Worth: £491,640 *Total Assets:* £854,880
Registered Office: Riverside House, Delta Bank Road, Metro Riverside Park, Gateshead, Tyne & Wear, NE11 9DJ
Activities: Other business support service activities n.e.c.
Officers: Caroline Farquhar [1972] Finance Director; Nigel John Hall [1959] Director/Engineer; Michael James Ketley [1975] Operations Director; Ian Lichfield [1967] Director/Chief Executive Officer; Trevor James Murch [1949] Director/Chairman; David Miller Weir [1956] Director/Chemical & Process Engineer

WHP Investments UK Ltd
Incorporated: 27 June 2016 *Employees:* 58
Net Worth Deficit: £8,245,614 *Total Assets:* £3,571,885
Registered Office: Riverside House, Delta Bank Road, Metro Riverside Park, Gateshead, Tyne & Wear, NE11 9DJ
Activities: Activities of head offices
Shareholders: Endless IV (GP) LP; Endless LLP
Officers: Caroline Farquhar [1972] Finance Director; Nigel John Hall [1959] Managing Director; Michael James Ketley [1975] Operations Director; Ian Lichfield [1967] Director/Chief Executive Officer; Trevor James Murch [1949] Director/Chairman; David Miller Weir [1956] Technical Director

Whymar Limited
Incorporated: 21 March 2002
Net Worth: £5,979,115 *Total Assets:* £7,057,458
Registered Office: Brake House, 72 Middleton Lane, Middleton St George, Darlington, Co Durham, DL2 1AD
Activities: Development of building projects
Major Shareholder: John McCardle
Officers: Gillian Frances McArdle, Secretary/Accounts Clerk; John McArdle [1953] Director/Solicitor

Wight Developments Limited
Incorporated: 6 May 2003
Registered Office: 15 Staindrop Road, West Auckland, Bishop Auckland, Co Durham, DL14 9JU
Activities: Development of building projects
Major Shareholder: Robert Gillard
Officers: David Scott, Secretary; Robert Gillard [1948] Director

Wilkinson Landscapes Limited
Incorporated: 28 February 1995
Net Worth: £888,156 *Total Assets:* £1,384,271
Registered Office: East Brocks Farm, Eaglescliffe, Stockton on Tees, Cleveland, TS16 0QH
Activities: Landscape service activities
Shareholders: Jonathan Peter Wilkinson; Thomas Michael Wilkinson
Officers: Thomas Michael Wilkinson, Secretary/Landscape Director; Jonathon Peter Wilkinson [1963] Landscape Director; Thomas Michael Wilkinson [1961] Landscape Director

Stephen Willcox Builder Limited
Incorporated: 2 April 2003 *Employees:* 3
Net Worth: £1,807,161 *Total Assets:* £1,931,439
Registered Office: Drakeside, Hawthorn Terrace, Shilbottle, Northumberland, NE66 2XX
Activities: Construction of domestic buildings
Shareholders: Stephen George Willcox; Emma Marie Willcox
Officers: Emma Marie Willcox, Secretary; Emma Marie Willcox [1975] Director/Manager; Stephen George Willcox [1968] Director/Manager

Williams & Spenceley Limited
Incorporated: 21 February 1986
Net Worth: £834,343 *Total Assets:* £1,133,951
Registered Office: Howlish Hall, Coundon, Bishop Auckland, Co Durham, DL14 8ED
Activities: Residential nursing care facilities
Parent: New Albion Limited
Officers: Yoel Eliahu Etel [1966] Director [French]

Henry Williams Group Limited
Incorporated: 2 March 1989 *Employees:* 11
Net Worth: £1,440,934 *Total Assets:* £2,436,577
Registered Office: Dodsworth Street, Darlington, Co Durham, DL1 2NJ
Activities: Activities of production holding companies
Parent: Con Mech Group Ltd
Officers: Derek Neil, Secretary; Christine Ames [1962] Director; David Brookes [1977] Director; Steven Adrian Cotton [1964] Director; Robert James Dilley [1972] Director; Robert Howard Stapleton Dilley [1946] Director/Chairman; Derek Neil [1964] Financial Director

Henry Williams Limited
Incorporated: 8 December 1988 *Employees:* 116
Net Worth: £4,058,556 *Total Assets:* £6,784,996
Registered Office: Henry Williams Group Ltd, Dodsworth Street, Darlington, Co Durham, DL1 2NJ
Activities: Forging, pressing, stamping and roll-forming of metal; powder metallurgy
Officers: Derek Neil, Secretary; Christine Ames [1962] Director; David Brookes [1977] Director; Steven Adrian Cotton [1964] Sales & Marketing Director; Robert James Dilley [1972] Director; Robert Howard Stapleton Dilley [1946] Director/Chairman; Alan Herron [1964] Director; Andrew John Lazenby [1965] Director; Derek Neil [1964] Financial Director; Micheal Wilson [1962] Director

Williamson Construction Equipment Limited
Incorporated: 11 January 1985 *Employees:* 14
Net Worth: £1,507,820 *Total Assets:* £1,621,615
Registered Office: Wesley Drive, Benton Square Industrial Estate, Newcastle upon Tyne, NE12 9UP
Activities: Renting and leasing of construction and civil engineering machinery and equipment
Shareholders: William George Williamson; David Williamson
Officers: William George Williamson, Secretary; David Williamson [1948] Director; William George Williamson [1934] Director/Certified Accountant

A. Williamson Limited
Incorporated: 4 February 1987 *Employees:* 13
Net Worth: £932,161 *Total Assets:* £1,053,467
Registered Office: 6 Finlay Court, South Shields, Tyne & Wear, NE34 9QA
Activities: Other service activities n.e.c.
Shareholders: Anthony Williamson; Heather Williamson
Officers: Heather Williamson, Secretary; Anthony Williamson [1956] Director; Heather Williamson [1956] Director/Secretary

Williamson Network Limited
Incorporated: 22 April 2015
Net Worth: £1,022,462 *Total Assets:* £1,423,648
Registered Office: Unit G6, Narvik Way, Tyne Tunnel Trading Estate, North Shields, Tyne & Wear, NE29 7XJ
Activities: Agents involved in the sale of a variety of goods
Officers: David Keele [1983] Director

Willington Healthcare Limited
Incorporated: 9 March 2016
Net Worth: £15,302 *Total Assets:* £2,334,420
Registered Office: Lakeside House, Kingfisher Way, Stockton on Tees, Cleveland, TS18 3NB
Activities: Other business support service activities n.e.c.
Major Shareholder: David Graham Jarvis
Officers: David Graham Jarvis, Secretary; David Graham Jarvis [1966] Director/Pharmacist; Kevin Alan Simpson [1958] Director/Pharmacist

D.H. Willis & Sons Limited
Incorporated: 21 October 2002
Registered Office: Carrbeck House, Gilling West, Richmond, N Yorks, DL10 5LN
Activities: Raising of other cattle and buffaloes
Shareholders: Timothy David Willis; Mark William Willis
Officers: Mark William Willis [1966] Director/Farmer Engineer; Timothy David Willis [1964] Director

J.A.Willis (Northallerton) Limited
Incorporated: 22 April 1960 *Employees:* 9
Net Worth: £645,900 *Total Assets:* £1,949,128
Registered Office: Sowber Gate, Newby Wiske, Northallerton, N Yorks, DL7 9ER
Activities: Growing of cereals (except rice), leguminous crops and oil seeds
Shareholder: Doreen Willis
Officers: Robert Thomas Willis, Secretary; Doreen Willis [1930] Director; Matthew John Willis [1965] Director/Poultry Farmer

Tom Willoughby Limited
Incorporated: 25 September 1961 *Employees:* 95
Net Worth: £1,521,928 *Total Assets:* £5,137,864
Registered Office: Construction House, Northallerton, N Yorks, DL7 8ED
Activities: Development of building projects
Shareholder: Susan Bridget Greenwell
Officers: Derek John Greenwell, Secretary; Paul Blades [1963] Director; Derek John Greenwell [1948] Director Company Secretary; William Darren Johnson [1969] Director; Keith Brian Noddings [1972] Finance Director

Willow Bridge Properties Limited
Incorporated: 15 December 1972
Net Worth: £760,400 *Total Assets:* £771,543
Registered Office: Waterfall Lodge, Carlton Village, Carlton, Stockton on Tees, Cleveland, TS21 1EA
Activities: Other letting and operating of own or leased real estate
Shareholder: Eric Arthur Clayton
Officers: Eric Arthur Clayton [1936] Director

Willow Group Ltd
Incorporated: 25 April 2005
Net Worth: £67,148 *Total Assets:* £1,231,979
Registered Office: 264-266 Durham Road, Gateshead, Tyne & Wear, NE8 4JR
Activities: Other letting and operating of own or leased real estate
Officers: Sharon Louise Oliver, Secretary; Gary Charlton [1983] Director/Developer; Ian Andrew Charlton [1960] Director/Developer; Sharon Louise Charlton [1962] Director/Sales

Willow Park Healthcare Limited
Incorporated: 7 April 2009 *Employees:* 72
Net Worth: £1,570,458 *Total Assets:* £4,517,188
Registered Office: RSM UK Tax and Accounting Limited, 1 St James' Gate, Newcastle upon Tyne, NE1 4AD
Activities: Activities of head offices
Parent: Darrington Healthcare Ltd
Officers: Eric George Dixon [1954] Director; Stephen Dixon [1957] Director; Shaun Ian Lucas [1945] Director; Iain Alston Murphy [1953] Director

Willow View Care Limited
Incorporated: 12 October 2012
Net Worth: £294,934 *Total Assets:* £3,772,021
Registered Office: 1 Norton Court, Norton Road, Stockton on Tees, Cleveland, TS20 2BL
Activities: Other business support service activities n.e.c.
Shareholders: Apinder Singh Ghura; Khushninder Singh Ghura
Officers: Apinder Singh Ghura [1963] Director; Khushninder Singh Ghura [1967] Commercial Director

Willowbank Holiday Park Limited
Incorporated: 26 June 1998 *Employees:* 11
Net Worth: £2,549,427 *Total Assets:* £3,723,613
Registered Office: Ash House, Catterick, Richmond, N Yorks, DL10 7PH
Activities: Recreational vehicle parks, trailer parks and camping grounds
Shareholders: Richard Henry Darling; Judith Anne Darling
Officers: Judith Anne Darling, Secretary/Farmer; Judith Anne Darling [1946] Director/Farmer; Richard Henry Darling [1943] Director/Caravan Park Operator; Richard Simon Darling [1971] Director/IT Manager

Willowcrete Manufacturing Company Limited
Incorporated: 30 March 1950
Net Worth: £887,433 *Total Assets:* £1,175,763
Registered Office: Deptford Works, Deptford Terrace, Deptford, Sunderland, Tyne & Wear, SR4 6DD
Activities: Other service activities n.e.c.
Major Shareholder: Jeffrey Alan Broomfield
Officers: Jeffrey Alan Broomfield [1960] Director/Fencing Contractor; Terrence Lowes [1972] Director

Willson Developments Limited
Incorporated: 23 February 2011
Net Worth: £1,122,207 *Total Assets:* £1,125,975
Registered Office: Unit 2 Jubilee House, York Road, Hartlepool, Cleveland, TS26 9EN
Activities: Buying and selling of own real estate
Shareholder: Phillip Guy Yuill
Officers: Julie Margaret Rigali, Secretary; John Howard Short [1944] Director/Chartered Surveyor; Nicholas John Charles Short [1971] Director/Interior Architect; Edward Richard Thomas Yuill [1978] Director; Phillip Guy Yuill [1954] Director

Matthew H. Wilson & Son, Limited
Incorporated: 29 December 1928 *Employees:* 3
Net Worth: £1,830,969 *Total Assets:* £2,660,040
Registered Office: 39 Mitchell Avenue, Jesmond, Newcastle upon Tyne, NE2 3JY
Activities: Other letting and operating of own or leased real estate
Shareholder: Ronald Albert Wilaon
Officers: June Hilary Wilson, Secretary; June Hilary Wilson [1959] Director; Ronald Albert Wilson [1924] Director

Harry Wilson Associates Limited
Incorporated: 29 July 1988 *Employees:* 1
Net Worth: £845,184 *Total Assets:* £1,308,473
Registered Office: River Drive, South Shields, Tyne & Wear, NE33 1LH
Activities: Non-specialised wholesale trade
Major Shareholder: Harold Wilson
Officers: Gary Wilson, Secretary; Harold Wilson [1942] Director/Management Consultant

Keith Wilson Transport Limited
Incorporated: 20 March 2001
Registered Office: Oakmere, Belmont Business Park, Durham, DH1 1TW
Activities: Freight transport by road
Major Shareholder: Keith Wilson
Officers: Jennifer Wilson [1970] Director/Secretary; Keith Wilson [1962] Director/Haulier

Wilton Energy Limited
Incorporated: 9 October 2002
Net Worth: £35,000 *Total Assets:* £763,000
Registered Office: Sembcorp UK Headquarters, Wilton International, Middlesbrough, Cleveland, TS90 8WS
Activities: Trade of electricity
Parent: Sembcorp Utilities (UK) Limited
Officers: Stephen Christopher Hands, Secretary; Stephen Christopher Hands [1968] Director/Senior Vice President; Craig Hardaker [1971] Director/Senior Vice President; Meng Poh NG [1956] Director/Executive Vice President [Singaporean]

Wilton Engineering Services Limited
Incorporated: 4 July 1994 *Employees:* 18
Net Worth: £9,415,669 *Total Assets:* £16,391,216
Registered Office: Wilton Group Head Office, Port Clarence Offshore Base, Port Clarence Road, Middlesbrough, Cleveland, TS2 1RZ
Activities: Manufacture of metal structures and parts of structures
Parent: PIMCO 2852 Limited
Officers: Christine Stobbs, Secretary; Stephen Glenn [1959] Director/Engineer; Paul Joseph Johnson [1955] Director; Steven Brian Pearson [1972] Director; William Scott [1961] Director/Engineer; Christine Stobbs [1973] Finance Director

Wilton Universal Group Limited
Incorporated: 15 February 2013 *Employees:* 95
Net Worth Deficit: £1,656,077 *Total Assets:* £6,527,104
Registered Office: Wilton Group Head Office, Port Clarence Offshore Base, Port Clarence Road, Middlesbrough, Cleveland, TS2 1RZ
Activities: Activities of head offices
Shareholders: William Scott; Stephen Glenn
Officers: Christine Stobbs, Secretary; Stephen Glenn [1959] Director/Engineer; Paul Joseph Johnson [1955] Director; Steven Brian Pearson [1972] Director; William Scott [1961] Director; Christine Stobbs [1973] Finance Director

Windcrew Workboats Limited
Incorporated: 14 May 2010
Net Worth: £894,368 *Total Assets:* £1,445,308
Registered Office: 46 The Barns, Stanley, Co Durham, DH9 8BN
Activities: Sea and coastal freight water transport
Major Shareholder: Christopher Robert Church
Officers: Christopher Robert Church [1965] Director

Winder House Developments Limited
Incorporated: 28 October 2005
Net Worth Deficit: £24,822 *Total Assets:* £1,130,470
Registered Office: Lakeside House, Kingfisher Way, Stockton on Tees, Cleveland, TS18 3NB
Activities: Development of building projects
Shareholders: David Anthony Collier; John Patrick Joyce; Roy Alan Stephenson
Officers: David Anthony Collier [1958] Director/Solicitor; John Patrick Joyce [1954] Director; Roy Alan Stephenson [1955] Director

Windgrove Limited
Incorporated: 21 December 1961 *Employees:* 17
Net Worth: £147,067 *Total Assets:* £798,782
Registered Office: 69 High Street, Gosforth, Newcastle upon Tyne, NE3 4AT
Activities: Travel agency activities
Parent: Windgrove (Holdings) Limited
Officers: Jeanne Lally, Secretary; Anne Bromley [1964] Director/Travel Agent; Jeanne Lally [1956] Director/Travel Agent

Windmill (Heaton) Orthodontics Limited
Incorporated: 22 December 2015 *Employees:* 16
Net Worth: £171,567 *Total Assets:* £938,451
Registered Office: Third Floor, Citygate, St James Boulevard, Newcastle upon Tyne, NE1 4JE
Activities: Dental practice activities
Shareholders: Dr Ross Sherwood Hobson; Dr Shiv Bhagwanji Pabary
Officers: Ross Sherwood Hobson [1958] Director/Orthodontist; Shiv Pabary [1960] Director/Dentist

Window Fitters Warehouse Limited
Incorporated: 22 April 2009
Net Worth: £193,877 *Total Assets:* £1,224,777
Registered Office: 2-6 Franklin Street, South Shields, Tyne & Wear, NE33 1PR
Activities: Glazing
Officers: Anthony William Mordew [1969] Director

Windsor Nursing Home LLP
Incorporated: 23 January 2014 *Employees:* 80
Net Worth: £3,125,726 *Total Assets:* £4,813,100
Registered Office: 18 Sandgrove, Cleadon Village, Sunderland, Tyne & Wear, SR6 7RL
Officers: Purnima Sehgal [1974] Member; Doctor Inder Paul Vinayak [1941] Member; Doctor Veena Vinayak [1950] Member; Kiran Sehgal [1970] LLP Member; Amitabh Vinayak [1976] LLP Member; Chetan Vinayak [1977] LLP Member

The Wine Fusion Limited
Incorporated: 14 January 2008 *Employees:* 4
Net Worth Deficit: £47,359 *Total Assets:* £1,335,002
Registered Office: Unit 2 Greencroft Estates, Tower Road, Annfield Plain, Stanley, Co Durham, DH9 7XP
Activities: Manufacture of wine from grape
Parent: Lanchester Wine Cellars Limited
Officers: Adam Richard Black [1968] Director; Anthony Austin Cleary [1952] Director; Veronica Anne Cleary [1954] Director; Andrew George Porton [1974] Director/Wine Merchant; Mark Anthony Satchwell [1964] Director

Wine World Producers Limited
Incorporated: 30 August 2006
Net Worth: £2,185,323 *Total Assets:* £2,738,828
Registered Office: Yours Business Networks, Suite A, 7-8 Delta Bank Road, Gateshead, Tyne & Wear, NE11 9DJ
Activities: Wholesale of wine, beer, spirits and other alcoholic beverages
Officers: Davide Zondini, Secretary; Alfeo Martini [1968] Director [Italian]

Wing Hong & Company Limited
Incorporated: 5 July 2003 *Employees:* 46
Net Worth Deficit: £252,788 *Total Assets:* £1,584,012
Registered Office: 55 George Street, Newcastle upon Tyne, NE4 7JN
Activities: Wholesale of fruit and vegetables
Shareholders: Koon Kiu Cheng; Po Fat Cheng
Officers: Ken Ying Cheng, Secretary/Director; David Cheng [1967] Director; Ken Ying Cheng [1969] Director

Wingrove Motor Company Limited
Incorporated: 10 August 1925 *Employees:* 93
Net Worth: £2,777,723 *Total Assets:* £9,339,945
Registered Office: Silverlink Business Park, Wallsend, Tyne & Wear, NE28 9ND
Activities: Sale of new cars and light motor vehicles
Shareholders: Peter Dalkin; Lindsay Dalkin
Officers: Peter Dalkin, Secretary; Peter Dalkin [1940] Director/Garage Proprietor; Louise Parker [1963] Director

Winkfield Properties Limited
Incorporated: 13 August 1990
Net Worth: £848,286 *Total Assets:* £895,793
Registered Office: 80 Hartington Road, Stockton on Tees, Cleveland, TS18 1HE
Activities: Other letting and operating of own or leased real estate
Officers: Dominic George Collinge Ferard, Secretary; Dominic George Collinge Ferard [1963] Director/Property Manager; Jo Tracy Ferard [1969] Director; Rupert Charles Hawkesworth Ferard [1966] Director/Property Manager; Sally Clare Ferard [1962] Director

Winn Solicitors Limited
Incorporated: 25 March 2004 *Employees:* 281
Net Worth: £8,017,113 *Total Assets:* £20,676,104
Registered Office: Winn Solicitors, Brinkburn Street, Byker, Newcastle upon Tyne, NE6 1PL
Activities: Solicitors
Parent: Winn Holding Limited
Officers: Jeffery John Winn, Secretary; Christopher Birkett [1971] Sales Director; Iain Stuart Richardson [1973] Director/Chartered Accountant; Jeffery John Winn [1965] Director/Solicitor

Winning Homes Limited
Incorporated: 26 March 2001
Net Worth: £539,952 *Total Assets:* £878,808
Registered Office: Office 64, Derwent Business Centre, Consett, Co Durham, DH8 6BN
Activities: Construction of domestic buildings
Officers: Joan Slater, Secretary; Joan Slater [1945] Director; John Robert Slater [1943] Director

Winning Lines Limited
Incorporated: 9 May 1994
Net Worth: £803,562 *Total Assets:* £847,620
Registered Office: Prospect Road, Crook, Co Durham, DL15 8JL
Activities: Wholesale of perfume and cosmetics
Major Shareholder: Harry Forrester Williams
Officers: Rita Williams, Secretary; Harry Forrester Williams [1940] Director/Company Buyer

Simon Winstanley Ltd
Incorporated: 10 May 2002
Registered Office: Unit 1 Beckside Court, Leyburn Business Park, Leyburn, N Yorks, DL8 5QA
Activities: Renting and leasing of other machinery, equipment and tangible goods n.e.c.
Shareholders: John Winstanley; Julie McGregor
Officers: Simon John Winstanley, Secretary/Director; Julie Margaret McGregor [1968] Director; John Edward Winstanley [1937] Director; Simon John Winstanley [1961] Director

Wirecard Card Solutions Limited
Incorporated: 8 December 2011
Net Worth: £33,683,000 *Total Assets:* £414,241,984
Registered Office: Third Floor, Grainger Chambers, 3-5 Hood Street, Newcastle upon Tyne, NE1 6JQ
Activities: Central banking
Officers: Oliver Bellenhaus [1973] Director/Executive Vice President [German]; Thomas Michael Richard Jennings [1981] Director; Thomas Kaeppner [1964] Managing Director [German]; Alexander Von Knoop [1972] Director [German]

Wise Academies
Incorporated: 8 February 2011 *Employees:* 184
Net Worth: £10,305,000 *Total Assets:* £13,133,000
Registered Office: Wise Academies Head Office, Borodin Avenue, Town End Farm, Sunderland, Tyne & Wear, SR5 4NX
Activities: Primary education
Officers: John Gary Robinson, Secretary; Zoe Carr [1973] Director/Chief Executive Officer; Christine Collins [1956] Director; Natalie Fountain [1980] Director; David Pearson [1956] Director/Chartered Surveyor; Paul James Smith [1976] Director/Group Health and Safety Manager; Margaret Elise Wright Stephenson [1953] Director; Robert Symonds [1973] Director; Nicola Sara Vokes [1966] Director/Chief Executive; John Gibbon Wood [1944] Director

Wise Financial Consulting Limited
Incorporated: 31 May 2007 *Employees:* 3
Net Worth: £682,170 *Total Assets:* £757,727
Registered Office: Maritime House, Harbour Walk, The Marina, Hartlepool, Cleveland, TS24 0UX
Activities: Other business support service activities n.e.c.
Major Shareholder: Gavin Michael Wise
Officers: Helen Donkin, Secretary; Gavin Michael Wise [1970] Director/Independent Financial Adviser

Wise Financial Property Limited
Incorporated: 16 December 2015
Net Worth: £3,542 *Total Assets:* £1,628,478
Registered Office: Maritime House, Harbour Walk, The Marina, Hartlepool, Cleveland, TS24 0UX
Activities: Other letting and operating of own or leased real estate
Major Shareholder: Gavin Michael Wise
Officers: Helen Donkin, Secretary; Gavin Michael Wise [1970] Director

Thomas Witter Carpets Limited
Incorporated: 27 February 2013 *Employees:* 2
Net Worth: £129,193 *Total Assets:* £2,240,003
Registered Office: Park View, Road East, Hartlepool, Cleveland, TS25 1HT
Activities: Wholesale of furniture, carpets and lighting equipment
Parent: Whitestone Carpets Holdings Ltd
Officers: Tanya Kelly, Secretary; Stephen Maurice Martin Byrne [1960] Director; Geoffrey Brendon Wilding [1963] Director [New Zealander]

Witton Care Limited
Incorporated: 14 February 2013
Net Worth: £696,418 *Total Assets:* £6,302,130
Registered Office: Unit 1 City West Business Park, St Johns Road, Meadowfield Industrial Estate, Meadowfield, Co Durham, DH7 8ER
Activities: Residential care activities for the elderly and disabled
Officers: Karon Ann Morgan [1963] Director; William Morgan [1951] Director

WM Utility Services Limited
Incorporated: 28 October 2008
Net Worth: £544,960 *Total Assets:* £897,174
Registered Office: 18 Linden Mews, Langley Park, Co Durham, DH7 9DZ
Activities: Construction of utility projects for electricity and telecommunications
Major Shareholder: Christopher Mark Welch
Officers: Christopher Mark Welch [1979] Director/Civil Engineer

Wolds Produce Ltd
Incorporated: 19 July 2006 *Employees:* 18
Net Worth: £288,390 *Total Assets:* £2,435,196
Registered Office: York House, Thornfield Business Park, Standard Way Business Park, Northallerton, N Yorks, DL6 2XQ
Activities: Support activities for crop production
Shareholders: Simon Bernard Tootell; Simon Charles Foster
Officers: Graham Douglas Bennett [1969] Sales Director; Timothy Malcolm Foggin [1969] Finance Director; Simon Charles Foster [1967] Director/Farmer; Simon Bernard Tootell [1965] Marketing Director

Wolviston Group Limited
Incorporated: 27 August 2004 *Employees:* 331
Net Worth: £2,398,908 *Total Assets:* £6,351,113
Registered Office: Wolviston House, 5 Falcon Court, Preston Farm, Stockton on Tees, Cleveland, TS18 3TS
Activities: Activities of head offices
Major Shareholder: Samantha Jane Anderson
Officers: Samantha Jane Anderson [1974] Director

Wolviston Management Services Limited
Incorporated: 19 July 1979 *Employees:* 367
Net Worth: £384,617 *Total Assets:* £5,271,879
Registered Office: Wolviston House, 5 Falcon Court, Preston Farm, Stockton on Tees, Cleveland, TS18 3TS
Activities: Temporary employment agency activities
Parent: Wolviston Group Limited
Officers: Samantha Jane Anderson [1974] Director

Women's Health in South Tyneside
Incorporated: 21 March 2007 *Employees:* 8
Net Worth: £1,195,331 *Total Assets:* £1,209,507
Registered Office: Salus House, 33 & 35 Mile End Road, South Shields, Tyne & Wear, NE33 1TA
Activities: Other human health activities
Officers: Eva Allen [1959] Director/Retired Nurse; Ruth Rachel Berkley [1955] Director/Equality & Diversity Officer; Catherine Anne Bull [1980] Director/Supervisor Family Support; Andonia di Stefano [1953] Director; Amy Lamb [1991] Director/Trainee Solicitor; Jeanette Telfer [1950] Director/Retired; Chris Westbury [1944] Director/Retired Social Worker

H Wood & Sons (Leyburn) Limited
Incorporated: 21 November 1957
Net Worth: £916,827 *Total Assets:* £925,505
Registered Office: Norfolk House, Market Place, Leyburn, N Yorks, DL8 5AQ
Activities: Other letting and operating of own or leased real estate
Major Shareholder: Adrian Walton
Officers: Adrian Walton, Secretary; Adrian Walton [1952] Director/Petrol Retailer; Nigel Walton [1960] Director/Petrol Retailer

Matthew Wood Developments Limited
Incorporated: 27 February 1995
Net Worth: £951,986 *Total Assets:* £2,322,958
Registered Office: 93 Great Lime Road, West Moor, Newcastle upon Tyne, NE12 7NJ
Activities: Other letting and operating of own or leased real estate
Shareholders: Sydney Matthew Wood Appleby; Maria Gertrude Appleby
Officers: Maria Gertrude Appleby, Secretary; Maria Gertrude Appleby [1951] Director/Secretary; Sydney Matthew Wood Appleby [1950] Director/Property Developer

J.W. Wood Limited
Incorporated: 29 July 1992
Net Worth: £1,406,076 *Total Assets:* £2,216,929
Registered Office: 7 Old Elvet, Durham, DH1 3HL
Activities: Other business support service activities n.e.c.
Major Shareholder: Keith Johnson
Officers: Ian Anthony Huntley, Secretary; John Burton [1964] Property Director; Keith Johnson [1947] Director/Chartered Surveyor; Patricia Johnson [1949] Director; Richard Johnson [1981] Director

Woodham Academy
Incorporated: 3 August 2012 *Employees:* 117
Net Worth: £5,118,000 *Total Assets:* £6,962,000
Registered Office: Woodham Academy, Washington Crescent, Newton Aycliffe, Co Durham, DL5 4AX
Activities: General secondary education
Officers: David Coates, Secretary; Sean Barnett [1964] Managing Director; Robert Cherrie [1976] Director/Fire and Rescue Service; John Strachan Denham [1946] Director/Retired Primary Headteacher; Richard Charles Eirew [1965] Director/Senior IT Service Manager; Christine Forsyth [1961] Director/Headteacher; Jonathan Jeffery French [1961] Director/Financial Advisor; Robert Michael Gales [1991] Director/Teacher; Richard Paul Heaven [1965] Director/HLTA; Ian Johnson [1981] Director/Telecommunications Worker; David Graham Knight [1957] Director/Financial Adviser; Arthur Marshall [1951] Retired Director; Steven Mark Mendelsohn [1961] Director/Self Employed Consultant; Diane Newton [1964] Director/Administrator; Brian Winwood [1966] Director/Self Employed

Woodham Christian Centre Ltd.
Incorporated: 28 April 1993
Net Worth: £1,051,659 *Total Assets:* £1,278,857
Registered Office: Bethany House, Village Close, Woodham Village, Newton Aycliffe, Co Durham, DL5 4UD
Activities: Residential nursing care facilities
Officers: Robert Foster, Secretary; Karen Horn [1974] Director/Housewife; Ruth Anne Horn [1959] Director/Landlord; William Horn [1948] Director/Private Landlord; Dr Winny Jose [1974] Director/Doctor GP [Indian]; Maureen Margaret Kersley [1945] Director/NHS Support Worker; Sheila Martin [1935] Director/Retired; Christine Mills [1947] Director/Occupational Therapist; Caraline Rowland [1972] Director/Care Home Manager; Ian Mark Rowland [1967] Director/Pastor; Geoffrey Walvin [1953] Director/Minister of Religion

Woodhorn Charitable Trust
Incorporated: 1 May 2009 *Employees:* 111
Net Worth: £1,244,009 *Total Assets:* £1,598,241
Registered Office: Woodhorn Museum, QEII Country Park, Ashington, Northumberland, NE63 9YF
Activities: Museums activities
Officers: Philip Ashley Browell [1956] Director/Solicitor; John Browne-Swinburne [1937] Director/Retired; John McMorrough Carr-Ellison [1952] Director and Farmer; Ian Lavery [1963] Director/Member of Parliament; Mai Lai Chun Mak [1959] Director/Chartered Accountant; Peter John Alan Robinson [1961] Director/Clerk in Holy Orders; Jeffrey George Watson [1947] Director/Councillor; Penelope Jane Wilkinson [1961] Director/Cultural Manager

Woodhouse Triangle Limited
Incorporated: 5 September 1995
Net Worth: £926,337 *Total Assets:* £2,418,591
Registered Office: Gisborough Hall, Whitby Road, Guisborough, Cleveland, TS14 6PT
Activities: Other letting and operating of own or leased real estate
Major Shareholder: The Honourable Thomas Peregrine Long Chaloner
Officers: The Honourable Thomas Peregrine Long Chaloner [1961] Director/Fruit Farmer; Peter Anthony Salvatore [1941] Director/Retired

Woodside North East Property Limited
Incorporated: 10 May 2010
Net Worth: £228,866 *Total Assets:* £5,410,712
Registered Office: Exchange Building, 66 Church Street, Hartlepool, Cleveland, TS24 7DN
Activities: Management of real estate on a fee or contract basis
Officers: Lamaan Mahmoud, Secretary; Raad Mahmoud [1958] Director

Woodside Park Estates Limited
Incorporated: 21 August 1975 *Employees:* 4
Net Worth: £1,369,399 *Total Assets:* £2,294,988
Registered Office: Woodside, Park Avenue, Hartlepool, Cleveland, TS26 0EA
Activities: Other holiday and other collective accommodation
Officers: Richard Michael Atkinson, Secretary/Director; Martin Graham Atkinson [1965] Director/Property Rentals; Mary Collingwood Atkinson [1931] Director; Richard Michael Atkinson [1963] Director; Susan Mary Gilbertson [1959] Director

Woodtech (Joinery) Limited
Incorporated: 23 April 1998
Net Worth: £750,344 *Total Assets:* £1,603,297
Registered Office: Unit 8 Newcomen Road, Skippers Lane Industrial Estate, Middlesbrough, Cleveland, TS6 6PS
Activities: Other manufacturing n.e.c.
Major Shareholder: Andrew John Simpson
Officers: Andrew John Simpson, Secretary; Andrew John Simpson [1966] Director; Stefanie Simpson [1980] Director

Woodview Estates Limited
Incorporated: 5 September 2011
Net Worth: £1,072,875 *Total Assets:* £4,263,553
Registered Office: c/o Templeman Retailing & Vending Limited, Earlsway, Team Valley Trading Estate, Gateshead, Tyne & Wear, NE11 0RQ
Activities: Other letting and operating of own or leased real estate
Major Shareholder: William Neil Templeman
Officers: William Neil Templeman [1962] Director

Woodydog Limited
Incorporated: 13 January 2015
Net Worth Deficit: £47,337 *Total Assets:* £1,064,065
Registered Office: The Archways, Headlam Hall, Headlam, Darlington, Co Durham, DL2 3HA
Activities: Other accommodation
Parent: TRM Marketing Limited
Officers: Suzanne Clare Metcalfe [1963] Director; Timothy Robert Metcalfe [1958] Director

H E Woolley Limited
Incorporated: 31 July 2000 *Employees:* 34
Net Worth: £875,598 *Total Assets:* £1,552,225
Registered Office: 1a Startforth Road, Middlesbrough, Cleveland, TS2 1PT
Activities: Other service activities n.e.c.
Major Shareholder: Sir Henry Robert Wilmot
Officers: Susan Clare Wilmot, Secretary; Sir Henry Robert Wilmot [1967] Director

Woolsington Bridge Nurseries Limited
Incorporated: 22 November 1963
Registered Office: The Old Vicarage, 63 Williams Park, Newcastle upon Tyne, NE12 8BL
Activities: Other service activities n.e.c.
Shareholders: Gabrielle Bernstone; Doreen Chipchase
Officers: Gabrielle Bernstone, Secretary; Gabrielle Bernstone [1946] Director; Allan Rankin [1960] Director

Les Woolston Haulage Limited
Incorporated: 12 March 2001 *Employees:* 21
Net Worth: £64,571 *Total Assets:* £796,361
Registered Office: 1-4 Puddlers Road, Southbank, Middlesbrough, Cleveland, TS6 6TX
Activities: Freight transport by road
Major Shareholder: Martin Sean Woolston
Officers: Martin Sean Woolston, Secretary; Leslie John Woolston [1945] Director/Haulier; Martin Sean Woolston [1969] Director/Haulage Contractor

Working Links (Employment) Limited
Incorporated: 6 March 2000 *Employees:* 1,241
Net Worth: £2,048,000 *Total Assets:* £52,123,000
Registered Office: Sun Alliance House, 16-26 Albert Road, Middlesbrough, Cleveland, TS1 1PR
Activities: Other activities of employment placement agencies
Parent: Aurelius Sigma Limited
Officers: Stephen Geoffrey Jones [1956] Director/Chief Operating Officer; Rajesh Patel [1970] Finance Director

Workspace & Storage Limited
Incorporated: 5 October 2011
Registered Office: Unit 5c Strand House, Locomotion Way, Camperdown Industrial Estate, Newcastle upon Tyne, NE12 5US
Activities: Management of real estate on a fee or contract basis
Major Shareholder: Paul Wallace
Officers: Jamie McGregor [1991] Director/Property Letting

Workwear Express Limited
Incorporated: 30 March 1999 *Employees:* 119
Net Worth: £1,317,913 *Total Assets:* £4,884,811
Registered Office: Units 8-12 Cathedral Park, Belmont Industrial Estate, Durham, DH1 1TF
Activities: Retail sale of clothing in specialised stores
Shareholders: Andrew John Ward; Angel Homes (Durham) Limited
Officers: Andrew John Ward, Secretary; Andrew John Ward [1972] Managing Director

Worldweary Limited
Incorporated: 5 June 2002
Registered Office: Wellington Chambers, 61 Saville Street, North Shields, Tyne & Wear, NE30 1AY
Activities: Other letting and operating of own or leased real estate
Officers: Claire Wheatley, Secretary; Catherine Maddison [1959] Director; John Alan Maddison [1959] Director/Property Consultant

Worthington Armstrong U.K. Limited
Incorporated: 11 February 1997 *Employees:* 34
Net Worth: £17,860,520 *Total Assets:* £19,821,532
Registered Office: Central Square South, Orchard Street, Newcastle upon Tyne, NE1 3XX
Activities: Manufacture of metal structures and parts of structures
Shareholders: Armstrong World Industries, Inc.; Worthington Industries, Inc.
Officers: Willem Antonius Middel [1967] VP and Managing Director EMEA [Dutch]; Bruce Andrew Rose [1970] Director/Vice President, Finance/CFO [American]; Doug Wisel [1970] Director/Vice President and CFO of Wave [American]

Wox Agri Services Ltd
Incorporated: 17 July 2008 *Employees:* 8
Net Worth: £264,163 *Total Assets:* £1,237,618
Registered Office: 71 Station Road, Stannington, Morpeth, Northumberland, NE61 6NQ
Activities: Wholesale of agricultural machinery, equipment and supplies
Shareholders: Geoffrey David Wox; Helen Wox
Officers: Geoffrey David Wox [1965] Director/Contractor; Helen Wox [1966] Director/Contractor

WPR Farms Ltd
Incorporated: 14 September 2016 *Employees:* 5
Net Worth: £940 *Total Assets:* £4,222,379
Registered Office: Burnt House Farm, Nedderton Village, Bedlington, Northumberland, NE22 6AZ
Activities: Growing of cereals (except rice), leguminous crops and oil seeds
Shareholders: Anthony Rutherford; Claire Anne Rutherford
Officers: Anthony Rutherford [1958] Director/Farmer; Claire Anne Rutherford [1956] Director/Farmer

Wraggs Seafoods Limited
Incorporated: 30 March 2001 *Employees:* 14
Net Worth: £939,908 *Total Assets:* £1,607,530
Registered Office: Unit 2 Park 2000, Millennium Way, Aycliffe Industrial Park, Newton Aycliffe, Co Durham, DL5 6AR
Activities: Wholesale of other food, including fish, crustaceans and molluscs
Major Shareholder: Richard Collins
Officers: Claire Elizabeth Carter, Secretary; Gustaf Baldvinsson [1957] Director [Icelander]; Thorsteinn Mar Baldvinsson [1952] Director [Icelander]; Claire Elizabeth Carter [1979] Director; Richard Collins [1954] Director; Kenneth Gary Lethem [1959] Director

Wright Construction (Durham) Limited
Incorporated: 3 February 1969 *Employees:* 8
Net Worth: £933,091 *Total Assets:* £1,160,253
Registered Office: 46 North End, Sedgefield, Stockton on Tees, Cleveland, TS21 3BT
Activities: Development of building projects
Major Shareholder: Sven David Wright
Officers: Jayne Wright, Secretary; Jayne Wright [1969] Director; Sven David Wright [1968] Director

Nigel Wright Consultancy Limited
Incorporated: 5 March 1999 *Employees:* 69
Net Worth: £4,000,000 *Total Assets:* £10,580,000
Registered Office: Lloyds Court, 78 Grey Street, Newcastle upon Tyne, NE1 6AF
Activities: Other activities of employment placement agencies
Parent: Nigel Wright Group Ltd
Officers: Mark Douglas Ingleson [1979] Finance Director; Mark Nicholas Simpson [1973] Director; Paul Jonathan Wilson [1960] Director/Chief Executive

Nigel Wright Employment Services Limited
Incorporated: 19 February 2007 *Employees:* 8
Net Worth: £4,099,000 *Total Assets:* £4,669,000
Registered Office: Lloyds Court, 78 Grey Street, Newcastle upon Tyne, NE1 6AF
Activities: Temporary employment agency activities
Parent: Nigel Wright Group Ltd
Officers: Mark Douglas Ingleson [1979] Finance Director; Mark Nicholas Simpson [1973] Director; Paul Jonathan Wilson [1960] Director/Chief Executive

Stuart Wright Funeral Service Limited
Incorporated: 26 February 2003 *Employees:* 15
Net Worth: £1,597,980 *Total Assets:* £2,043,014
Registered Office: 43 Front Street, Langley Park, Co Durham, DH7 9SA
Activities: Funeral and related activities
Shareholders: Edwin Stuart Bowes Wright; Lesley Frances Wright
Officers: Edwin Stuart Bowes Wright, Secretary; Edwin Stuart Bowes Wright [1968] Funeral Director

Nigel Wright Group Holdings Limited
Incorporated: 19 August 2009 *Employees:* 128
Net Worth Deficit: £7,741,000 *Total Assets:* £12,421,000
Registered Office: Lloyds Court 78 Grey Street, Newcastle upon Tyne, NE1 6AF
Activities: Activities of head offices
Shareholders: GPCP VII (GP) LLP; GPCP VII GP Limited
Officers: Dennis John Hall [1964] Director; Lars Sigve Herrem [1979] Director [Norwegian]; Mark Douglas Ingleson [1979] Finance Director; Mark Nicholas Simpson [1973] Director; Timothy Hugh Southcombe Trotter [1959] Director; Paul Jonathan Wilson [1960] Director/Chief Executive

Nigel Wright Group Limited
Incorporated: 5 May 2009
Net Worth: £691,000 *Total Assets:* £958,000
Registered Office: Lloyds Court, 78 Grey Street, Newcastle upon Tyne, NE1 6AF
Activities: Activities of head offices
Parent: Nigel Wright Group Holdings Ltd
Officers: Mark Douglas Ingleson [1979] Finance Director; Mark Nicholas Simpson [1973] Director; Paul Jonathan Wilson [1960] Director/Chief Executive

WV Associates Limited
Incorporated: 12 March 1984 *Employees:* 40
Net Worth: £1,422,234 *Total Assets:* £4,963,336
Registered Office: Unit 7 Hatfield Way, South Church Enterprise Park, Bishop Auckland, Co Durham, DL14 6XF
Activities: Other manufacturing n.e.c.
Parent: Rooster Enterprises Limited
Officers: Kim Kong Wong, Secretary; Alexander Joseph Dale [1957] Director; Eric William Deveney [1956] Sales Director; Patrick Anthony Dominick McGonigal [1980] Director; Christopher Arthur Cory Ware [1972] Director; Richard Ivor Wakefield Ware [1939] Director; Kim Kong Wong [1959] Director [Malaysian]

WW Medical Facilities Limited
Incorporated: 26 June 2015
Net Worth: £656,551 *Total Assets:* £2,383,515
Registered Office: 14-15 Harelands Courtyard Offices, Moor Road, Melsonby, Richmond, N Yorks, DL10 5NY
Activities: Development of building projects
Shareholders: Neil Whittingham; Beverley Quigley
Officers: Neil Joseph Whittingham [1966] Director; Martin David Scriven Williams [1977] Director

WW Residential Ltd
Incorporated: 19 December 2012
Net Worth Deficit: £50,150 *Total Assets:* £2,713,442
Registered Office: Harelands Courtyard Offices, Moor Road, Melsonby, Richmond, N Yorks, DL10 5NY
Activities: Development of building projects
Shareholder: Neil Joseph Whittingham
Officers: Neil Joseph Whittingham [1966] Director

Wylam Brewery Limited
Incorporated: 11 September 2000
Registered Office: South Houghton, Heddon on the Wall, Newcastle upon Tyne, NE15 0EZ
Activities: Manufacture of beer
Officers: Matthew Dunstan Boyle [1973] Director/Business Development Manager; Robert Cameron [1968] Director; Carina Elena McKenzie Curry [1979] Director/Office Administrator; David Jonathan Stone [1963] Director

Wylam Garage Limited
Incorporated: 21 April 1977 *Employees:* 22
Net Worth: £676,533 *Total Assets:* £2,644,161
Registered Office: 1 Burn Lane, Hexham, Northumberland, NE46 3HN
Activities: Sale of used cars and light motor vehicles
Shareholders: Dorothy Conley; Alan Ashburn Conley
Officers: Dorothy Conley, Secretary; Alan Ashburn Conley [1942] Director/Garage Proprietor; Dorothy Conley [1942] Director/Garage Proprietor; Sean Conley [1969] Director/Garage Proprietor

Wyn Construction Limited
Incorporated: 20 July 1992 *Employees:* 127
Net Worth: £1,817,063 *Total Assets:* £4,328,729
Registered Office: Hilltop Garage, Cornsay Village, Co Durham, DH7 9EL
Activities: Construction of other civil engineering projects n.e.c.
Shareholders: Roy Bainbridge; David Cowie
Officers: Roy Bainbridge, Secretary; Roy Bainbridge [1960] Director/Foreman; David Cowie [1961] Director/Foreman; Mark Horner [1972] Director/Commercial Manager; John Lee Osborne [1972] Operations Director

Wyn Limited
Incorporated: 5 June 2007
Net Worth: £1,187,383 *Total Assets:* £1,728,254
Registered Office: Hilltop Garage, Cornsay Village, Co Durham, DH7 9EL
Activities: Construction of other civil engineering projects n.e.c.
Officers: Roy Bainbridge, Secretary; Roy Bainbridge [1960] Director; David Cowie [1961] Director

Wyndham Court Limited
Incorporated: 27 June 2007 *Employees:* 100
Net Worth: £95,234 *Total Assets:* £3,951,863
Registered Office: Lion House, 400 Durham Road, Birtley, Co Durham, DH3 1LS
Activities: Residential care activities for the elderly and disabled
Parent: Lion Care Home Group
Officers: Robert Pattinson [1934] Director/Care Home Owner; Stevie-Lee Pattinson [1969] Director/Restaurateur

Wynyard Golf Club Ltd.
Incorporated: 27 September 2001 *Employees:* 39
Net Worth: £13,867,765 *Total Assets:* £19,748,544
Registered Office: Top Floor, Oriel House, Calverts Lane, Bishop Street, Stockton on Tees, Cleveland, TS18 1SW
Activities: Activities of sport clubs
Parent: Jomast Limited
Officers: Stuart John Monk [1949] Director

Wynyard Hall Limited
Incorporated: 30 November 2004 *Employees:* 188
Net Worth: £1,608,911 *Total Assets:* £3,071,509
Registered Office: Wynyard Hall, Wynyard, Billingham, Cleveland, TS22 5NF
Activities: Other business support service activities n.e.c.
Parent: Cameron Hall Developments Limited
Officers: Allison Antonopoulos [1960] Director; Mark James Antonopoulos [1988] Director; Sarah-Mae Antonopoulos [1990] Director/Administration Manager; Paul Anthony MacKings [1961] Director

Wynyard Homes Limited
Incorporated: 31 August 2011 *Employees:* 8
Net Worth: £378,364 *Total Assets:* £8,773,969
Registered Office: Maritime House, Harbour Walk, The Marina, Hartlepool, Cleveland, TS24 0UX
Activities: Construction of domestic buildings
Parent: Seneca Investments and Developments Limited
Officers: Colin Leslie Barnes [1960] Director/Town and Country Planner; Barry Miller [1954] Director; Roderick Charles St John Wilson [1961] Director/Land Agent

Wynyard Life Ltd
Incorporated: 10 September 2015 *Employees:* 2
Net Worth: £1,719,346 *Total Assets:* £2,284,441
Registered Office: 15 The Wickets, Seaton Carew, Hartlepool, Cleveland, TS25 2BD
Activities: Buying and selling of own real estate
Shareholder: Trevor Cartner
Officers: Jonathan Tones [1956] Director

Wynyard Motor Company Limited
Incorporated: 29 May 2012 *Employees:* 10
Net Worth: £736,258 *Total Assets:* £1,382,078
Registered Office: The Grange, Portrack Lane, Stockton on Tees, Cleveland, TS18 2PA
Activities: Sale of used cars and light motor vehicles
Shareholders: Anthony Edmond Spensley; Lee Edmund Spensley
Officers: Gregory Alan Ramsey [1984] Director/Car Sales Manager; Anthony Edmund Spensley [1949] Director; Lee Edmund Spensley [1970] Director

Wynyard Park Limited
Incorporated: 14 March 2005 *Employees:* 10
Net Worth Deficit: £2,579,047 *Total Assets:* £23,614,882
Registered Office: Wynyard Park House, Wynyard Avenue, Wynyard, Billingham, Cleveland, TS22 5TB
Activities: Development of building projects
Parent: Wynyard Park Holdings Ltd
Officers: Trevor Cartner [1960] Director/Chartered Surveyor; Joseph Christopher Musgrave [1965] Managing Director

Xander Developments Limited
Incorporated: 16 October 2013
Net Worth: £890,001 *Total Assets:* £2,153,497
Registered Office: United British Caravans, Sandy Lane, North Gosforth, Newcastle upon Tyne, NE3 5HE
Activities: Other retail sale not in stores, stalls or markets
Major Shareholder: Alexander Lloyd Levington
Officers: Thomas Frederick Lambert [1948] Director; Alexander Lloyd Levington [1973] Director

XC Trains Limited
Incorporated: 22 March 2002 *Employees:* 1,811
Net Worth: £34,596,000 *Total Assets:* £132,159,000
Registered Office: c/o Arriva PLC, 1 Admiral Way, Doxford International Business Park, Sunderland, Tyne & Wear, SR3 3XP
Activities: Passenger rail transport, interurban
Officers: Lorna Edwards, Secretary; Christopher Derek Dyne Burchell [1973] Director; Andre Cnossen [1965] Director [Dutch]; Andrew John Cooper [1958] Director; Amanda Furlong [1975] Director; Mary Elisabeth Courtney Hewitt [1979] Director; Desmond Peter Lowe [1963] Director; Joanne MacPhail [1977] Director; Lee Garreth Paxton [1983] Director; Jonathan Luke Roberts [1978] Director

XCEL County Durham
Incorporated: 24 September 2013 *Employees:* 36
Net Worth: £677,689 *Total Assets:* £2,143,820
Registered Office: Xcel Centre, Long Tens Way, Aycliffe Business Park, Newton Aycliffe, Co Durham, DL5 6AP
Activities: Other education n.e.c.
Officers: Kerina Lucy Clark, Secretary; Paul Benger [1964] Director; Jean Carter [1957] Director/NHS Consultancy; Kerina Lucy Clark [1973] Director/Centre Manager; John James Greenow [1968] Director/Minister of Religion; Rosemary Ann Laxton [1950] Director

XL Precision Technologies Limited
Incorporated: 22 December 1998 *Employees:* 61
Net Worth: £4,646,338 *Total Assets:* £5,858,740
Registered Office: Unit 79 Sadler Forster Way, Teesside Industrial Estate, Stockton on Tees, Cleveland, TS17 9JY
Activities: Manufacture of medical and dental instruments and supplies
Shareholders: Andrew Olaf Fischer; Ian Fisher; Alan Thomas Fletcher
Officers: Jonathan Charles Richardson, Secretary and Director; Andrew Olaf Fischer [1964] Director [German]; Ian Fisher [1950] Director; Alan Thomas Fletcher [1934] Director; Alan Thomas Graham [1961] Director; Jonathan Charles Richardson [1960] Secretary and Director; Colin Thompson [1949] Director/Engineer

Xtralite (Rooflights) Limited
Incorporated: 15 March 2001 *Employees:* 86
Net Worth: £3,812,789 *Total Assets:* £5,456,681
Registered Office: 7-9 Spencer Road, Blyth, Northumberland, NE24 5TG
Activities: Other manufacturing n.e.c.
Parent: Jet Group BV
Officers: Deborah Margaret Smith, Secretary; Ralf Stefan Paul Dahmer [1967] Director/Chief Executive [German]

Xtravagant Limited
Incorporated: 17 April 2001
Registered Office: c/o Union Property Services Ltd, Cobalt 3.1, Silver Fox Way, Cobalt Business Park, Newcastle upon Tyne, NE27 0QJ
Activities: Renting and operating of Housing Association real estate
Shareholders: Anita Mehan; Sanjeev Mehan
Officers: Promila Sehgal, Secretary; Anita Mehan [1971] Director; Sanjeev Mehan [1969] Director; Promila Sehgal [1948] Director

XYZ Limited
Incorporated: 21 August 1990
Registered Office: Victoria House, Bondgate Within, Alnwick, Northumberland, NE66 1TA
Activities: Development of building projects
Officers: Kathleen Bowley, Secretary; Kathleen Bowley [1947] Director; David John Houghton [1944] Director

Y&I Properties Limited
Incorporated: 30 December 2015
Net Worth: £55,174 *Total Assets:* £1,515,606
Registered Office: Gainford House, Chester-le-Street, Co Durham, DH3 3SR
Activities: Other letting and operating of own or leased real estate
Shareholder: Imran Khaliq
Officers: Yasser Khaliq, Secretary; Imran Khaliq [1987] Director

Yarm School
Incorporated: 30 May 2002 *Employees:* 220
Net Worth: £31,336,000 *Total Assets:* £40,910,000
Registered Office: Yarm School, The Friarage, Yarm, Stockton on Tees, Cleveland, TS15 9EJ
Activities: Pre-primary education
Officers: Kelly May Heward, Secretary; Olufemi Omoyoola Ajekigbe [1968] Director/Deputy Headteacher; Sarah Helen Anderson [1968] Director/Chartered Accountant; Paul Joseph Barron [1963] Director; Dr Paul Michael Chapman [1957] Director/Retired; Stephen Robert Davidson [1950] Director/Retired Headmaster; Christopher David de Jong [1958] Director/Management Consultant; Liam Dickinson Gamble [1987] Director/Veterinary Surgeon; Penelope Sarah Ann Jones [1957] Director/Retired; Ruth Margaret Langford [1959] Director/Dental Surgeon; Elizabeth Lynn Longstaff [1954] Director/Headmistress; Ian Frances Lovat [1955] Director/Retired; Kevin Shotton [1981] Director/Accountant; Dr Angela Jennifer Slater [1957] Director/Retired; Mark Thompson [1963] Director/Chief Executive Officer; Alexander Martin Turner [1975] Director/Senior Registrar of Paediatric Surgery

Yarm View Limited
Incorporated: 24 December 2014
Registered Office: 7 Bankside, The Watermark, Gateshead, Tyne & Wear, NE11 9SY
Activities: Hotels and similar accommodation
Shareholders: Victoria Clare Holden; Stephen John Holden
Officers: Stephen John Holden [1969] Director; Victoria Clare Holden [1973] Director/Hotelier

Yayla Enterprises Limited
Incorporated: 19 April 1993 *Employees:* 7
Net Worth: £204,883 *Total Assets:* £783,188
Registered Office: 16 Ashtree Close, Rowlands Gill, Tyne & Wear, NE39 1RA
Activities: Agents involved in the sale of food, beverages and tobacco
Officers: Vivien Sian Dogan, Secretary; Egemen Dogan [1959] Director/Manager

YMCA North Tyneside
Incorporated: 2 April 1992 *Employees:* 47
Net Worth: £6,507,010 *Total Assets:* £7,390,774
Registered Office: Church Way, North Shields, Tyne & Wear, NE29 0AB
Activities: Other service activities n.e.c.
Officers: Dean Titterton, Secretary; Carol Ann Groombridge [1952] Director/Self Employed; Russell John Hall [1972] Director/Solicitor; John William Hawksworth [1966] Director/Youth Worker; David Hodgson [1949] Director/Chartered Accountant; Samantha Kleis Meredith [1973] Marketing Director; Barbara Morris [1961] Director/Civil Servant; Louise Elizabeth Snelders [1974] Director/Senior Manager at Big Lottery; Louise Jane Stewart [1978] Director/Quantity Surveyor

YOLO (Newcastle) Limited
Incorporated: 9 June 2016 *Employees:* 5
Net Worth Deficit: £6,139 *Total Assets:* £946,878
Registered Office: Patrick House, Gosforth Park Avenue, Gosforth Business Park, Newcastle upon Tyne, NE12 8EG
Activities: Public houses and bars
Shareholder: Neill Aidan Winch
Officers: Stephen William Howe [1967] Director; Donna Winch [1976] Director; Neill Aidan Winch [1964] Director

Yorhold Limited
Incorporated: 4 December 1991
Net Worth: £3,750,007 *Total Assets:* £3,750,007
Registered Office: The Lodge, Gatherley Moor Farm, Gilling West, Richmond, N Yorks, DL10 5LJ
Activities: Activities of head offices
Major Shareholder: Joe Mulhall
Officers: Joe Mulhall [1966] Director/Product Research

Yorkshire Construction Contractors Limited
Incorporated: 19 March 2004
Net Worth: £1,294,846 *Total Assets:* £1,296,584
Registered Office: 80 Hartington Road, Stockton on Tees, Cleveland, TS18 1HE
Activities: Construction of domestic buildings
Officers: Dominic George Collinge Ferard, Secretary; Dominic George Collinge Ferard [1963] Director; Rupert Charles Hawkesworth Ferard [1966] Director

Yorkshire Dales Meat Company Ltd
Incorporated: 5 November 2004 *Employees:* 44
Net Worth: £143,824 *Total Assets:* £1,058,575
Registered Office: Mill Close, Patrick Brompton, Bedale, N Yorks, DL8 1JY
Activities: Processing and preserving of meat
Shareholders: Thomas Stephen Knox; Patricia Anne Knox
Officers: Thomas Stephen Knox, Secretary; Patricia Anne Knox [1957] Director; Thomas James Knox [1985] Director; Thomas Stephen Knox [1954] Director

Yorkshire Electricity Group PLC
Incorporated: 1 April 1989
Net Worth: £526,502,016 *Total Assets:* £577,644,032
Registered Office: Lloyds Court, 78 Grey Street, Newcastle upon Tyne, NE1 6AF
Activities: Activities of other holding companies n.e.c.
Parent: Yorkshire Power Group Limited
Officers: Jennifer Catherine Riley, Secretary; Thomas Edward Fielden [1970] Director/Chartered Accountant; Thomas Hugh France [1985] Director/Lawyer; Dr Philip Antony Jones [1968] Director/President and Chief Executive Officer

Yorkshire Independent Building Supplies Limited
Incorporated: 29 May 2002 *Employees:* 20
Net Worth Deficit: £120,305 *Total Assets:* £1,054,649
Registered Office: Thornton House, Harmby Road, Leyburn, N Yorks, DL8 5QA
Activities: Agents involved in the sale of timber and building materials
Parent: A R Calvert (Leyburn) Limited
Officers: Olive Ann Calvert, Secretary; Albert Richard Calvert [1928] Director/Builder; Andrew Daniel Calvert [1971] Director/Architectural Stone Supplier; Olive Ann Calvert [1944] Director; Paul Robert Sadler [1963] Director/Building Contractor (Management)

Yorkshire Power Group Limited
Incorporated: 19 July 1996
Net Worth: £463,795,008 *Total Assets:* £891,595,008
Registered Office: Lloyds Court, 78 Grey Street, Newcastle upon Tyne, NE1 6AF
Activities: Activities of other holding companies n.e.c.
Parent: Northern Powergrid UK Holdings
Officers: Jennifer Catherine Riley, Secretary; Thomas Edward Fielden [1970] Director/Chartered Accountant; Thomas Hugh France [1985] Director/Lawyer; Dr Philip Antony Jones [1968] Director/President and Chief Executive Officer

Yorkshire Tiger Limited
Incorporated: 22 February 2001 *Employees:* 272
Net Worth: £3,175,000 *Total Assets:* £7,518,000
Registered Office: 1 Admiral Way, Doxford International Business Park, Sunderland, Tyne & Wear, SR3 3XP
Activities: Other passenger land transport
Parent: Centrebus Holdings Limited
Officers: Lorna Edwards, Secretary; Matthew Thomas Ashton [1985] Director; David Cocker [1957] Director; Nigel Paul Featham [1964] Director; Thomas Robert Large [1985] Director

Yorwaste Limited
Incorporated: 25 November 1991 *Employees:* 193
Net Worth: £9,728,733 *Total Assets:* £32,063,124
Registered Office: Mount View, Standard Way, Northallerton, N Yorks, DL6 2YD
Activities: Collection of non-hazardous waste
Parent: North Yorkshire County Council
Officers: David Raymond Bowe [1962] Director/Local Government Officer; Alexander Boyle [1970] Finance Director; Martin Howard Buckley [1945] Director; Geoffrey Douglas Derham [1962] Director; Neil James Ferris [1969] Director/Local Government Officer; John Phillips [1954] Director; Cllr Andrew Michael Waller [1969] Director/Local Authority Member; John Keith Weighell [1942] Director/Farmer

Youll Construction Ltd
Incorporated: 28 March 2007 *Employees:* 22
Net Worth: £980,676 *Total Assets:* £1,853,593
Registered Office: Byers Garth Cottage, Byers Garth, Sherburn House, Durham, DH1 2SN
Activities: Construction of roads and motorways
Shareholders: Michael Youll; Judith Youll
Officers: Judith Youll, Secretary; Michael Youll [1965] Director

Vic Young (South Shields) Limited
Incorporated: 24 June 1988 *Employees:* 82
Net Worth: £7,854,959 *Total Assets:* £11,299,438
Registered Office: Newcastle Road, South Shields, Tyne & Wear, NE34 9QE
Activities: Sale of new cars and light motor vehicles
Shareholders: Alicia Rose Young; Victor Wyatt Young
Officers: Alicia Rose Young, Secretary; Alicia Rose Young [1945] Director; Victor Wyatt Young [1945] Director

R G Young Pharmacy Ltd
Incorporated: 6 May 2005
Registered Office: 33 Sheriffs Highway, Old Durham Road, Gateshead, Tyne & Wear, NE9 5PJ
Activities: Dispensing chemist in specialised stores
Major Shareholder: Robert Young
Officers: Jacqueline Ann Young, Secretary; Robert George Young [1960] Director/Pharmacist

Youngs RPS Limited
Incorporated: 4 April 2014 *Employees:* 26
Net Worth: £257,290 *Total Assets:* £987,870
Registered Office: Myenza Building, Priestpopple, Hexham, Northumberland, NE46 1PS
Activities: Real estate agencies
Officers: Michael Anthony Blake [1959] Director/Chartered Surveyor; Edward Roberts Boon [1979] Director/Chartered Surveyor; Graeme Cameron Stuart Bruce [1964] Director/Chartered Surveyor; Robert William Heath Hutchinson [1959] Director/Chartered Surveyor; Neil Mortimer [1952] Director/Estate Agent; Thomas Richard Oates [1974] Director/Chartered Surveyor; Charles Robert Raine [1969] Director/Chartered Surveyor; John Francis Turnbull [1953] Director/Chartered Surveyor

Your Care First Limited
Incorporated: 7 June 2005 *Employees:* 91
Net Worth: £708,564 *Total Assets:* £896,733
Registered Office: 200 Newburn Road, Throckley, Newcastle upon Tyne, NE15 9AH
Activities: Other human health activities
Major Shareholder: Sunny Okukpolor Humphreys
Officers: Sunny Okukpolor Humphreys, Secretary; Sunny Okukpolor Humphreys [1958] Director/Health Care

Your Homes Newcastle Limited
Incorporated: 17 March 2004 *Employees:* 726
Net Worth Deficit: £19,100,000 *Total Assets:* £19,304,000
Registered Office: Civic Centre, Barras Bridge, Newcastle upon Tyne, NE1 8PR
Activities: Renting and operating of Housing Association real estate
Parent: Newcastle City Council
Officers: Jill Louise Davison, Secretary; Alistair Stuart Chisholm [1966] Director/Head of Advice, Sector, Policy and Partnerships; Richard Anthony Clark [1948] Director/Retired; Lisa Michelle Doherty [1974] Director/Civil Servant; Anne Veronica Dunn [1949] Director/Retired; Doreen Huddart [1943] Director/Nurse; Kevin Joseph Lowry [1961] Director/Consultant; Joyce McCarty [1953] Director/Education Advisor; Malcolm Douglas Page [1967] Director/Accountant; Paul William Scope [1975] Director/Solicitor; Helen Mary Simpson [1959] Director/Consultant; Elaine Snaith [1958] Director/Retired; Josephine Catherine Totton [1956] Director/Chief Executive

Your-Move.co.uk Limited
Incorporated: 19 November 1984 *Employees:* 1,963
Net Worth: £27,304,000 *Total Assets:* £78,148,000
Registered Office: Newcastle House, Albany Court, Newcastle Business Park, Newcastle upon Tyne, NE4 7YB
Activities: Real estate agencies
Parent: Lending Solutions Holdings Ltd
Officers: Sapna Bedi FitzGenerald, Secretary/Solicitor; Oliver Thomas Blake [1971] Director; Helen Elizabeth Buck [1960] Director; Adam Robert Castleton [1964] Director; Simon Cox [1967] Director; Paul Hardy [1976] Finance Director; James Charles McAuley [1954] Sales Director

Cecil M. Yuill Limited
Incorporated: 18 January 2006
Net Worth: £1,447,782 *Total Assets:* £2,112,617
Registered Office: Unit 2 Jubilee House, York Road, Hartlepool, Cleveland, TS26 9EN
Activities: Buying and selling of own real estate
Shareholders: Phillip Guy Yuill; Patricia Margaret Wilson
Officers: Julie Margaret Rigali, Secretary; Emma Jane Holmes [1982] Director; David Nigel Williams [1943] Director; Edward Richard Thomas Yuill [1978] Managing Director; Phillip Guy Yuill [1954] Director; Victoria Mary Yuill [1951] Director

The YW Investment Company Limited
Incorporated: 22 December 2011
Net Worth: £110,899 *Total Assets:* £4,443,055
Registered Office: Unit 2 Jubilee House, York Road, Hartlepool, Cleveland, TS26 9EN
Activities: Other letting and operating of own or leased real estate
Shareholders: Trident Trust Company (Guernsey) Limited as Trustees of The CM Yuill 1972 Settlement-Phillip's Children's Fund; Trident Trust Company (Guernsey) Limited as Trustees of The CM Yuill 1972 Settlement-Patricia's Children's Fund
Officers: Julie Margaret Rigali, Secretary; Emma Jane Holmes [1982] Director; David Nigel Williams [1943] Director; Edward Richard Thomas Yuill [1978] Managing Director; Phillip Guy Yuill [1954] Director; Victoria Mary Yuill [1951] Director

Zapego Limited
Incorporated: 4 August 1987 *Employees:* 4
Net Worth: £1,714,477 *Total Assets:* £2,203,613
Registered Office: Wellington Chambers, 61 Saville Street, North Shields, Tyne & Wear, NE30 1AY
Activities: Other letting and operating of own or leased real estate
Officers: Claire Wheatley, Secretary; Catherine Maddison [1959] Director; John Alan Maddison [1959] Director/Property Consultant

Zenith Growth Limited
Incorporated: 13 May 2016
Net Worth: £989,818 *Total Assets:* £1,008,966
Registered Office: 140 Coniscliffe Road, Darlington, Co Durham, DL3 7RT
Activities: Security dealing on own account
Shareholders: Matilda Louise Gardner; Janice Rosalind Moyes; Janice Rosalind Moyes
Officers: Matthew Christopher Bennett [1964] Director/Solicitor; Elizabeth Kate Gardner [1983] Director; Janice Rosalind Moyes [1953] Director; Clive Faulkner Owen [1948] Director

Zenith Jewellery and Accessories UK Limited
Incorporated: 30 December 2009 *Employees:* 16
Net Worth: £1,072,753 *Total Assets:* £1,208,330
Registered Office: Swan House, Westpoint Road, Teesdale Business Park, Stockton on Tees, Cleveland, TS17 6BP
Activities: Other retail sale in non-specialised stores
Major Shareholder: Nassim Hussain
Officers: Khalid Hussain [1955] Director; Nassim Hussain [1961] Director

Zenith People Limited
Incorporated: 28 October 2008 *Employees:* 304
Net Worth: £58,548 *Total Assets:* £1,827,577
Registered Office: 10 Merchant Court, Monkton Business Park South, Hebburn, Tyne & Wear, NE31 2EX
Activities: Temporary employment agency activities
Parent: Messenger Holdings Limited
Officers: Angela Anderson [1973] Director

Zerolight Limited
Incorporated: 13 May 2014 *Employees:* 73
Net Worth Deficit: £114,998 *Total Assets:* £6,263,820
Registered Office: Live Works, 55-57 Quayside, Newcastle upon Tyne, NE1 3DE
Activities: Other information technology service activities
Parent: Prime Ventures
Officers: Brian Henry Jobling [1968] Director; Darren Jobling [1966] Director; Giles Henry Sharp [1970] Director/Chartered Accountant; Monish Suri [1966] Director/Venture Capital

Zerust (UK) Limited
Incorporated: 11 September 1996 *Employees:* 4
Net Worth: £509,508 *Total Assets:* £1,224,988
Registered Office: Meadowfield Avenue, Green Lane Industrial Estate, Spennymoor, Co Durham, DL16 6YJ
Activities: Agents specialised in the sale of other particular products
Shareholders: TP Enterprises Ltd; Northern Technologies International Corporation
Officers: Stephan Cyril Taylor, Secretary/Director; Vineet Dalal [1969] Director/Marketing [American]; Gregory Patrick Lynch [1967] Director/Company President [American]; Adam Taylor [1973] Director; Stephan Cyril Taylor [1947] Director

Zest Investment (Omagh) Limited
Incorporated: 25 September 2008 *Employees:* 2
Net Worth: £951,228 *Total Assets:* £4,550,000
Registered Office: 2nd Floor, 16 High Street, Yarm, Cleveland, TS15 9AE
Activities: Other human health activities
Parent: Zest Investment Group Limited
Officers: Philip Henry Scott [1964] Director; Graham Kevin Sizer [1969] Director

Zest Investment (Portadown) Limited
Incorporated: 25 September 2008 *Employees:* 2
Net Worth: £620,884 *Total Assets:* £4,250,000
Registered Office: 2nd Floor, 16 High Street, Yarm, Cleveland, TS15 9AE
Activities: Other human health activities
Parent: Zest Investment Group Limited
Officers: Philip Henry Scott [1964] Director; Graham Kevin Sizer [1969] Director

Zest Investment Group Limited
Incorporated: 29 August 2008 *Employees:* 379
Net Worth: £5,945,625 *Total Assets:* £16,178,444
Registered Office: 2nd Floor, 16 High Street, Yarm, Cleveland, TS15 9AE
Activities: Activities of head offices
Shareholder: Graham Kevin Sizer
Officers: Philip Henry Scott [1964] Director; Graham Kevin Sizer [1969] Director

Zetland Estates Limited
Incorporated: 25 March 1999 *Employees:* 2
Net Worth Deficit: £15,862 *Total Assets:* £11,515,562
Registered Office: The Estate Office, Aske Hall, Richmond, N Yorks, DL10 5HJ
Activities: Other letting and operating of own or leased real estate
Major Shareholder: Hon. Robin Lawrence Dundas
Officers: Amanda Jane Blenkiron, Secretary; Amanda Jane Blenkiron [1965] Director/Estate Secretary; Hon. Robin Lawrence Dundas [1965] Director/Estate Owner; Kathryn Ann Metcalfe [1981] Director/Accounts Manager

Zig Zag Cars Limited
Incorporated: 26 October 2004 *Employees:* 21
Net Worth: £58,219 *Total Assets:* £1,694,825
Registered Office: Tees Valley Mitsubishi, McMullen Road, Darlington, Co Durham, DL1 1XP
Activities: Sale of new cars and light motor vehicles
Major Shareholder: William Robson
Officers: Neal Anthony Gibson, Secretary; George Ellis [1977] Director/Motor Trader; Neal Anthony Gibson [1965] Managing Director; William Robson [1955] Director

Zigi Enterprises Limited
Incorporated: 12 February 1982 *Employees:* 12
Net Worth: £1,254,251 *Total Assets:* £1,464,247
Registered Office: 211-221 York Road, Hartlepool, Cleveland, TS26 9EE
Activities: Retail of furniture, lighting, and similar (not musical instruments or scores) in specialised store
Shareholders: Janice Holroyd; Peter Charles Shotton
Officers: Janice Holroyd, Secretary/Joint Managing Director; Janice Holroyd [1964] Joint Managing Director; Peter Charles Shotton [1966] Joint Managing Director

Zimb Johnson Bespoke Financial Planning Limited
Incorporated: 28 April 2005 *Employees:* 3
Net Worth: £1,034,304 *Total Assets:* £1,130,341
Registered Office: 1 The Bulrushes, Woodstock Way, Boldon Business Park, Boldon Colliery, Co Durham, NE35 9PF
Activities: Administration of financial markets
Parent: Fairstone Holdings Limited
Officers: Scott Hopkinson, Secretary; Lee Graham Hartley [1976] Director; Scott Hopkinson [1974] Director/Accountant

ZIV Automation UK Ltd
Incorporated: 8 July 2002 *Employees:* 10
Net Worth Deficit: £1,925,962 *Total Assets:* £7,017,907
Registered Office: 5 Bamburgh Court, Team Valley Trading Estate, Gateshead, Tyne & Wear, NE11 0TX
Activities: Construction of utility projects for electricity and telecommunications
Officers: Adrian Kearney [1960] Director/Engineer [Irish]; Nekane Vijandi Urrechaga [1969] Director [Spanish]

Zonat Limited
Incorporated: 21 January 2014 *Employees:* 2
Net Worth: £3,305,748 *Total Assets:* £14,452,635
Registered Office: Ravensworth House, Fifth Avenue, Team Valley Trading Estate, Gateshead, Tyne & Wear, NE11 0HF
Activities: Other letting and operating of own or leased real estate
Officers: Andrew David Clark, Secretary; Andrew David Clark [1965] Director/Chartered Accountant; Benjamin John Dunning [1977] Director

Zonic Investments Limited
Incorporated: 31 May 2016
Net Worth: £100 *Total Assets:* £1,078,290
Registered Office: Newton Red House, Mitford, Morpeth, Northumberland, NE61 3QW
Activities: Other letting and operating of own or leased real estate
Major Shareholder: David William Nicholson
Officers: David William Nicholson [1950] Director/Developer

Zubedo Limited
Incorporated: 16 October 2003
Net Worth: £1,336,000 *Total Assets:* £1,341,293
Registered Office: 3 Kingfisher Court, Bowesfield Park, Stockton on Tees, Cleveland, TS18 3EX
Activities: Business and domestic software development
Shareholders: Jonathan Paul Belch; Michael Andrew Belch; Michael Kason
Officers: Peter Belch, Secretary; Peter Belch [1947] Director/Company Secretary; Michael Kason [1954] Director/Chief Operating Officer

The Zurbaran Trust
Incorporated: 14 November 2011
Net Worth: £17,613,152 *Total Assets:* £17,618,554
Registered Office: Auckland Castle, Market Place, Bishop Auckland, Co Durham, DL14 7NR
Activities: Operation of arts facilities
Officers: Nicholas John Eldred, Secretary; Dr Jose Luis Colomer [1962] Director/Publisher [Spanish]; Anthony Stewart Worsley Mould [1955] Director/Art Consultant; Jane Mary Ruffer [1956] Director/Medical Practitioner; Jonathan Garnier Ruffer [1951] Director/Investment Manager; Dr Lindsay Raymonde Clifford Stainton [1947] Director/Curator and Author; Sir Stephen John Leadbetter Wright [1946] Director/Retired

Zynk Software Limited
Incorporated: 8 May 2002 *Employees:* 9
Net Worth: £596,315 *Total Assets:* £819,707
Registered Office: 6-8 Charlotte Square, Business Development Centre I6, Newcastle upon Tyne, NE1 4XF
Activities: Other information technology service activities
Parent: The Internetware Group Limited
Officers: Adam Patrick McCrory [1970] Managing Director

Zyro Limited
Incorporated: 23 May 1995 *Employees:* 212
Net Worth: £13,562,000 *Total Assets:* £33,901,000
Registered Office: Zyro Limited, Roundhouse Road, Faverdale Industrial Estate, Darlington, Co Durham, DL3 0UR
Activities: Non-specialised wholesale trade
Parent: Aghoco 1136 Limited
Officers: Matthew Barker [1979] Director/Chief Executive; James Scott Browning [1966] Director; Ian James Calvesbert [1966] Director; Paul Gibson [1980] Director; Richard Damon Smith [1974] Director

Zytronic Displays Limited
Incorporated: 7 April 1943 *Employees:* 185
Net Worth: £12,412,000 *Total Assets:* £14,808,000
Registered Office: Whiteley Road, Blaydon on Tyne, Tyne & Wear, NE21 5NJ
Activities: Manufacture of electronic components
Officers: Claire Louise Smith, Secretary; Mark Cambridge [1964] Director; Ian Crosby [1967] Director; Adrian John Leyland [1965] Director; Andrew Morrison [1976] Technical Director; Claire Louise Smith [1977] Director/Chartered Accountant

Zytronic PLC
Incorporated: 22 November 1999 *Employees:* 191
Net Worth: £26,801,000 *Total Assets:* £29,318,000
Registered Office: Whiteley Road, Blaydon on Tyne, Tyne & Wear, NE21 5NJ
Activities: Activities of head offices
Officers: Claire Smith, Secretary; David John Buffham [1959] Director; Mark Cambridge [1964] Director; Tudor Griffith Davies [1951] Director; Claire Louise Smith [1977] Director/Certified Chartered Accountant

Standard Industrial Classification

01110 Growing of cereals (except rice), leguminous crops and oil seeds

F. Brunton & Sons Limited
Dalesend Farms Limited
R. A. & S. Darling Farms (Hartlepool) Limited
Dawson Farms Limited
Dewhirst Holywell Enterprises Limited
Dunstanburgh Farm Limited
Emerald Biogas Ltd
Eshott South Farm Limited
C. W. J. Fall & Sons Limited
John T. Fall Limited
Gloag & Sons Limited
Hirst (Farmers) Limited
Holywell Farms Ltd
Lingy Moor Farming Ltd
The Manydown Company Limited
Oswald Potter Farms (Kirklington) Limited
Rock Farms Limited
J. O. Straughan & Co. Limited
W.Swinbank & Sons Limited
Stephen Tuer Farms Ltd
M S Vernon Limited
WPR Farms Ltd
William A.Wardman Limited
T E Watson & Co. Limited
Websters (Farmers) Limited
Whitchester Farm Limited
J.A.Willis (Northallerton) Limited

01130 Growing of vegetables and melons, roots and tubers

Blyth Star Enterprises Limited
M Dungait & Sons Limited

01270 Growing of beverage crops

The Endowment Fund for Tacri

01300 Plant propagation

Azure Charitable Enterprises

01410 Raising of dairy cattle

Haswell Moor Farms Ltd
High Hedley Hope Farm Limited
Leggott Farming Limited
Miresdale Dairy Limited
Modaim Limited
W. Robson (Farm) Limited

01420 Raising of other cattle and buffaloes

J A & M Boyes Limited
Cleveland & Highland Holdings Ltd
High Hedley Hope Farm Limited
Leggott Farming Limited
Lingy Moor Farming Ltd
J & D Longlands Ltd
Websters (Farmers) Limited
D.H. Willis & Sons Limited

01430 Raising of horses and other equines

Killashee House Limited
Ritchie-Bland Estates Ltd

01450 Raising of sheep and goats

John T. Fall Limited
Linhope Farming Company Limited
J & D Longlands Ltd
R C McInnes Limited
W. Robson (Farm) Limited

01460 Raising of swine and pigs

F. Brunton & Sons Limited
Donald Pig & Poultry Ltd
John T. Fall Limited
H.M. Pigs Limited
Hallikeld Limited
Middle Caves Ltd
Stephen Tuer Farms Ltd
G. & M. Westgarth Limited

01470 Raising of poultry

Blue Barns Poultry Farms Limited
Dinsdale Farming Limited
Donald Pig & Poultry Ltd
Grange Farm Eggs Ltd
Mill Poultry Limited
Modaim Limited
Musterfield Poultry Growers Ltd
Twizell Poultry (Ponteland) Limited
J.A.Willis (Northallerton) Limited

01490 Raising of other animals

Dromonby Bridge Farm Limited

01500 Mixed farming

Wm.Allison & Sons Limited
William Anderson Farmers Limited
Barker Bros. Limited
George W. Barker Limited
Barnaby Side Farms Limited
Blagdon Farming Limited
Burncastle Farming Company Ltd
Caledonian Trust PLC.
The Callaly Estates Company Limited
Chipchase Farms Limited
Crow Hall Farms Limited
Croxdale Farms Limited
J A Dent & Sons Limited
G H Farms Limited
Hartley Main Farms Limited
Hepburn Farm Limited
High Crane Limited
High Warden Farm Limited
Holmedale Valley Limited
Alan Jackson (Westcotes) Limited
Edgar Lawson Limited
A S & J K Leggott Limited
Lintz Green Farms Limited
Manners Farms Limited
Middleheads Limited
C.K.& D.Muir Limited
Murton Farm Estate Limited
Ouston Farms Limited
Pallett Hill Sand & Gravel Co. Limited
William Peat (Barnard Castle) Limited
H.S. Petch & Sons Limited
Plessey Checks Farming Limited
Rl & Mr Ridley Limited
W. Robson (Farm) Limited
SM Farms Limited
L. Sampson & Son Limited
Sandwath Contracting Limited
Skelton Farming Limited
Stamford Farms Ltd
Thimbleby Farms Limited
Town Farm (Wall) Limited
T.T.Walker (Newcastle) Limited
AG Watson & Sons Limited

01610 Support activities for crop production

S.Bainbridge Limited
M & D Bell Ltd
Dawson Farms Limited
Mrs J & J G Gill & Son Limited
J. O. Straughan & Co. Limited
M S Vernon Limited
D.H. Willis & Sons Limited
Wolds Produce Ltd

01621 Farm animal boarding and care

Appleton Grange Equestrian Centre Limited
Breckonborough Equestrian Limited

01629 Support activities for animal production (other than farm animal boarding)

Alnwick Farmers Livestock Auction Company Limited
The Darlington Farmers Auction Mart Company Limited
C. W. J. Fall & Sons Limited
Fox Formulated Feeds Limited
Hexham Auction Mart Company,Limited

01630 Post-harvest crop activities

J. O. Straughan & Co. Limited
Tynegrain Agriculture Limited

02100 Silviculture and other forestry activities

Cowie Forestry Limited

02200 Logging

Edmondson Logging Ltd
M.W. Herdman Forestry Solutions Limited
Shiellow Wood Limited
Timber Plant & Haulage Ltd.

02400 Support services to forestry

Forest Carbon Limited
M.W. Herdman Forestry Solutions Limited
Orange Plant Limited
Walton Logging Limited

03110 Marine fishing

Handyside Fishing Ltd
Providence Fishing Company Limited

03120 Freshwater fishing

Swarland Brick Company Limited (The)

05102 Open cast coal working

Coal Contractors Limited
Hall Construction Services Limited
Hargreaves Land Limited

06100 Extraction of crude petroleum

Clearmid Limited

08110 Quarrying of ornamental and building stone, limestone, gypsum, chalk and slate

A.D. Calvert Architectural Stone Supplies Limited
Dunhouse Quarry Co.Limited
Eppleton Quarry Products (Scunthorpe) Limited
Kearton Crushing and Screening Limited
Northumberland Stone Limited
Pallett Hill Sand & Gravel Co. Limited
Shire Aggregates Bulk Limited

08120 Operation of gravel and sand pits; mining of clays and kaolin

Eppleton Quarry Products (Middlesbrough) Ltd
Eppleton Quarry Products Limited
Tancred Gravel Limited
W. & M. Thompson (Quarries) Limited

08910 Mining of chemical and fertilizer minerals

Cleveland Potash Limited

08990 Other mining and quarrying n.e.c.

Harden Redstone Company Limited
W. & M. Thompson (Quarries) Limited

09100 Support activities for petroleum and natural gas mining

DM Services (Banchory) Ltd
Metalis Energy Limited
Offshore Support Vessels IV Limited
Offshore Support Vessels V Limited
Oil Consultants Limited

09900 Support activities for other mining and quarrying

Forward Sound Limited
Hargreaves Services (Blindwells) Limited
Hargreaves Technical Resources Limited

10110 Processing and preserving of meat

Holmesterne Farm Co. Limited
Istanbul Meats Limited
Linden Foods Burradon Limited
Thompson (Wholesale Meat) Limited
Yorkshire Dales Meat Company Ltd

10120 Processing and preserving of poultry meat

Kookaburra Limited
Meat Zone UK Limited

10130 Production of meat and poultry meat products

M.I. Dickson Limited
Euro Foods (GB) Limited
Newby Foods Limited
Ravendale Foods Limited
Vale of Mowbray Holdings Limited
Vale of Mowbray Limited
Van Hessen UK Casings Ltd

10200 Processing and preserving of fish, crustaceans and molluscs

Angelbond Limited
Coquet Island Shellfish Limited
Libra Seafood Processing Limited

10390 Other processing and preserving of fruit and vegetables

W & W Peeled Potatoes Limited

10410 Manufacture of oils and fats

The Kerfoot Group Limited

10511 Liquid milk and cream production

Embleton Hall Dairies Limited
Lanchester Dairies Limited
North Lakes Foods Limited
St Helen's Farm Limited

10512 Butter and cheese production

Primula Limited
St Helen's Farm Limited
Tom Walker and Sons Limited
Wensleydale Dairy Products Limited

10519 Manufacture of other milk products

St Helen's Farm Limited

10520 Manufacture of ice cream

Beckleberrys Limited
R&R Ice Cream UK Limited

10710 Manufacture of bread; manufacture of fresh pastry goods and cakes

Greggs PLC
It's All Good Limited

10720 Manufacture of rusks and biscuits; manufacture of preserved pastry goods and cakes

Baketime Limited
Greco Brothers Limited
Northumbrian Fine Foods Limited

10821 Manufacture of cocoa and chocolate confectionery

Sweetdreams Limited

10831 Tea processing

Ringtons Holdings Limited

10832 Production of coffee and coffee substitutes

Beanies The Flavour Co. Ltd.

10840 Manufacture of condiments and seasonings

Maysan Foods Limited
Moguntia Food Ingredients UK Limited

10850 Manufacture of prepared meals and dishes

Monde Nissin (UK) Limited
The Punjab Kitchen Ltd
The Redemption Holding Company (UK) Limited

10890 Manufacture of other food products n.e.c.

Culpitt Limited
F K Solutions (UK) Limited
JLM Global Foods Limited
Lowrie Foods Limited
Marlow Foods Limited
On A Roll Sandwich Company Limited
Pear Tree Honey Farm Limited
Primula Limited
The Redemption Food Company Limited
Sugarfayre Ltd.

10910 Manufacture of prepared feeds for farm animals

Equine Products U.K. Limited
Natural Stockcare Limited
Owens Nutrition Limited

11010 Distilling, rectifying and blending of spirits

The Lakes Distillery Company Limited

11020 Manufacture of wine from grape

The Wine Fusion Limited

11050 Manufacture of beer

Brewing and Distilling Company Limited
Camerons Brewery Limited
H.B.Clark & Co.(Successors) Limited
Trumark Properties Limited
Wylam Brewery Limited

11070 Manufacture of soft drinks; production of mineral waters and other bottled waters

Cawingredients Limited
Clearly Drinks Limited
Fentimans Ltd.
Northumbrian Ice Cream Company Limited

13300 Finishing of textiles

Elite Embroidery Limited
Schofield Dyers & Finishers Limited

13921 Manufacture of soft furnishings

BGRP Limited
Baileys Blinds Limited

13931 Manufacture of woven or tufted carpets and rugs

Gaskell MacKay Carpets Limited
Griffith Textile Machines Limited

13939 Manufacture of other carpets and rugs

All Floors (Services) Limited

13950 Manufacture of non-wovens and articles made from non-wovens, except apparel

Texon Non Woven Ltd

13990 Manufacture of other textiles n.e.c.

Prizepay Limited

14120 Manufacture of workwear

W.I.P. (Workwear) Limited

14131 Manufacture of other men's outerwear

J Barbour and Sons (Manufacturing) Limited
Montane Ltd

14132 Manufacture of other women's outerwear

J Barbour and Sons (Manufacturing) Limited
Montane Ltd

14142 Manufacture of women's underwear

Adina Reay Limited

14190 Manufacture of other wearing apparel and accessories n.e.c.

J.Barbour & Sons,Limited
Montane Ltd
Warrior Assault Systems Limited

15110 Tanning and dressing of leather; dressing and dyeing of fur

Furniture Clinic Limited

15200 Manufacture of footwear

Alt Berg Limited
Dragonfly Venture (Trading) Limited
Dragonfly Venture (UK) Limited
Dragonfly Venture Group Ltd
W.I.P (Work in Progress) Limited

16100 Sawmilling and planing of wood

Bedmax Limited
Percy A.Hudson Limited
M.H.Southern & Company Limited
MH Southern (Holdings) Limited
T.O. Mounter & Sons Limited
A.& J.Scott Limited
John B.Smith Limited
Ward Timber Limited

16210 Manufacture of veneer sheets and wood-based panels

Invertec Holdings Ltd.
Invertec Interiors Limited

16230 Manufacture of other builders' carpentry and joinery

Bridgman IBC Limited
Conduit Construction Network Limited
Grove Reed Joinery Limited
H. Jarvis Ltd
Kennek Construction Limited

16240 Manufacture of wooden containers

Evergreen Pallet Solutions (UK) Limited
A.& J.Scott Limited
Stadium Export Services Limited
LV Valenbeck Limited

16290 Manufacture of other products of wood; manufacture of articles of cork, straw and plaiting materials

Appletree Joinery Products Limited
Blyth Star Enterprises Limited
D.A.F. Timber Limited
J A Sales and Service Limited
Sashless Window Co. Limited

17120 Manufacture of paper and paperboard

Fourstones Paper Mill Company Limited

17211 Manufacture of corrugated paper and paperboard, sacks and bags

Encore Packaging Solutions Limited
Tripak Ltd

17219 Manufacture of other paper and paperboard containers

Durham Box Company Limited
Encore Packaging Solutions Limited
John Harrison (Stockton) Limited
LV Valenbeck Limited

17220 Manufacture of household and sanitary goods and of toilet requisites

Atlas Washroom Systems Limited

17230 Manufacture of paper stationery

Encore Envelopes Limited
Security Print Solutions Limited

17240 Manufacture of wallpaper

Belgravia Decor Limited

17290 Manufacture of other articles of paper and paperboard n.e.c.

Corespec Ltd
Encore Packaging Solutions Limited
Simpson Print Limited

18110 Printing of newspapers

Howarth Limited

18121 Manufacture of printed labels

Scanman UK Limited

18129 Printing n.e.c.

Agne Limited
Aztec Print North East Limited
Azure Charitable Enterprises
B.Print & Display Limited
BLP (Northern) Limited
Bath Press Limited
CPI Antony Rowe Ltd
CPI Books Ltd
CPI Colour Ltd
CPI William Clowes Ltd
Class Fundraising Limited
Datasupplies (Stationery) Limited
Elanders Ltd
First Choice Labels Limited
First2print Ltd
W.H. Forster (Printers) Limited
Gate 7 Limited
Harlow Printing Limited
MV Print Limited
Mallen Print Limited
Metro Repro Limited
New Century Services Limited
Paragon Group UK Limited
Potts Print (UK) Limited
Screen Services (NE) Limited
The Shiremoor Press Limited
Spreckley Limited
Statex Press (Northern) Limited
Edward Thompson (Printers) Limited
Thornton Print Limited
Washington Direct Mail Limited

18130 Pre-press and pre-media services

Elanders Ltd
Printbylaser Limited

18140 Binding and related services

Elanders Ltd

19100 Manufacture of coke oven products

Monckton Coke & Chemical Company Limited (The)

20120 Manufacture of dyes and pigments

Billions Europe Ltd
Huntsman (Holdings) UK
Venator Materials UK Limited
Venator Pigments UK Limited

20130 Manufacture of other inorganic basic chemicals

Applied Graphene Materials PLC
Applied Graphene Materials UK Limited
Chemson Limited
INEOS Compounds Aycliffe Limited
INEOS Compounds Holdings Limited
R. Mason Chemicals Limited
Thomas Swan & Co.Limited
Venator Pigments UK Limited
Vertellus Specialties UK Limited

20140 Manufacture of other organic basic chemicals

Cornerstone Chemical Company Limited
Fine Organics Limited
Huntsman (Holdings) UK
Sabic Tees Holdings Limited
Sabic UK Limited
Sabic UK Petrochemicals Limited

20160 Manufacture of plastics in primary forms

Lucite International Speciality Polymers and Resins Limited
Lucite International UK Limited
Millfield Enterprises (Manufacturing) Limited
Novares Peterlee Limited
Sabic Innovative Plastics ABS UK Limited

20200 Manufacture of pesticides and other agrochemical products

Chemian Technology Limited
Chiltern Farm Chemicals Limited
Exwold Technology Limited
Fine Organics Limited

20301 Manufacture of paints, varnishes and similar coatings, mastics and sealants

John Davey Limited
Esschem Europe Limited

20411 Manufacture of soap and detergents

Spectrum Industrial Limited

20520 Manufacture of glues

Huntsman Advanced Materials (UK) Limited

20530 Manufacture of essential oils

Chemian Technology Limited

20590 Manufacture of other chemical products n.e.c.

Agma Limited
Chemian Technology Limited
Chemoxy International Limited
Ensus UK Limited
Exwold Technology Limited
Fine & Performance Chemicals Limited
Fluid Technology Generation Limited
Fulbeck Limited
High Force Research Limited
Huntsman (Holdings) UK
Huntsman Polyurethanes (UK) Limited
Hutton Chemicals Limited
INEOS Nitriles (UK) Limited
ISP Holdings (U.K.) Ltd.
International Processplants (Europe) Limited
Kilfrost Group Limited
Kilfrost Limited
Liquiform Limited
Lotte Chemical UK Limited
Microchem Limited
Prefere Resins UK Limited
Techwax Limited
Venator P&A Holdings UK Limited
Venator Pigments UK Limited

20600 Manufacture of man-made fibres

Aptec Products Limited
Century Composites Limited

21100 Manufacture of basic pharmaceutical products

Fine Organics Limited
Getinge UK Limited
MacLeods Pharma UK Limited
Onyx Scientific Limited
Redrose Manufacturing Limited
Sterling Pharma Solutions Limited

21200 Manufacture of pharmaceutical preparations

Fujifilm Diosynth Biotechnologies UK Limited
Hyperdrug Pharmaceuticals Ltd
Ipca Laboratories UK Limited
PCCA (UK) Holdings Limited
PCCA Limited
Quantum Pharma 2014 Limited
Quantum Pharma Holdings Limited
Quantum Pharmaceutical Limited

22110 Manufacture of rubber tyres and tubes; retreading and rebuilding of rubber tyres

G.B. Bandag Ltd

22190 Manufacture of other rubber products

Aldona Seals Ltd
Deerness Rubber Company Limited
Henry Gallacher Limited
Millennium Conveyor Services Limited
TFLX Limited
Utex Industries UK Limited

22210 Manufacture of plastic plates, sheets, tubes and profiles

Bay Plastics Limited
Dupont Teijin Films U.K. Limited
Polyfoam XPS Limited
Primex Plastics Limited
Stanley Vickers Limited

22220 Manufacture of plastic packing goods

A & K Ecofilm Limited
Faerch Plast Manufacturing Limited
Moulded Packaging Solutions Ltd
Pakway Limited
Pro-Flex Packaging Europe Ltd
Proflex Packaging Co Ltd
Reed Thermoformed Packaging Ltd.
Scholle IPN UK Ltd.
Sirap UK Limited

22230 Manufacture of builders ware of plastic

Bay Plastics Limited
Millfield Enterprises Limited
Millfield GRP Products Limited
Polyfoam XPS Limited

22290 Manufacture of other plastic products

Aanco (UK) Limited
Aldona Seals Ltd
Allflex UK Group Limited
Armour Plastics Limited
Bay Plastics Limited
City Signs and Display Limited
E.S.P. Plastics Ltd
Entek International Limited
FM Coatings Limited
Flat Free Tyres Limited
Formula Plastics Limited
Grayson Spa Limited
International Pipeline Products Limited
JKL Mouldings Limited
Kasai UK Ltd
Labone Castleside Limited
M & S Plastics Limited
Marmax Products Limited
Mayborn (UK) Limited
Millfield Composites Limited
Millfield Enterprises Limited
Millfield GRP Products Limited
Mold Systems Limited
Naturalight Systems Limited
Nifco UK Limited
North East Panels Limited
Northumbria Blow Mouldings Limited
Paragon Rapid Technologies Ltd
Pipeline Engineering & Supply Co. Limited
Plastic Mouldings Northern Limited
Polyfoam XPS Limited
Polymer Compounders Limited
Premier Tech Aqua Limited
Renolit Cramlington Limited
SMH Equipment Limited
SMH Products Limited
Sangenic International Ltd.
Smithers-Oasis Europe Limited
Smithers-Oasis U.K. Limited
Sone Products Holdings Ltd
Sone Products Ltd
Technimark Limited
Theme Bins (International) Ltd
Thermalmate UK Limited
Thermodynamix Thermoforming Specialist Services Limited
Tyne Moulds & Machinery Company Limited

23120 Shaping and processing of flat glass

Clayton Glass Limited

23140 Manufacture of glass fibres

Bastion Glassfibre Rod & Sections Limited
East Coast Fibreglass Supplies Limited

23190 Manufacture and processing of other glass, including technical glassware

Heraeus Quartz UK Limited
Multi-Lab Limited
Newcastle Optical Engineering Limited
Quartztec Europe Limited

23200 Manufacture of refractory products

TYK Limited

23320 Manufacture of bricks, tiles and construction products, in baked clay

W. McGovern & Co. Limited

23440 Manufacture of other technical ceramic products

Blundell Production Equipment Limited
International Syalons (Newcastle) Limited

23490 Manufacture of other ceramic products n.e.c.

Magneco Metrel U.K. Limited

23610 Manufacture of concrete products for construction purposes

Lynx Precast Limited
Oakdale (Contracts) Limited

23630 Manufacture of ready-mixed concrete

Gilbert Birdsall Limited
North East Concrete Limited

23690 Manufacture of other articles of concrete, plaster and cement

E. J. Stone Limited

23700 Cutting, shaping and finishing of stone

Dunhouse Quarry Co.Limited
F Jones (Cleveland) Limited
North East Granite Company Limited

23990 Manufacture of other non-metallic mineral products n.e.c.

A.D. Calvert Architectural Stone Supplies Limited

24100 Manufacture of basic iron and steel and of ferro-alloys

Almet Sheet Metal Fabrication Limited
Katmex Seaham Limited
Allan Liddle (Steel) Limited
Premo Fabrications Limited
Ronco Engineering Limited
Specialist Castings Ltd
Union Electric Steel UK Limited
Washington Investments Limited

24200 Manufacture of tubes, pipes, hollow profiles and related fittings, of steel

Pipetawse Limited
Rapid (UK) Engineering Services Limited
Readman Steel Limited

24420 Aluminium production

Corrpro Companies Europe Limited
Hadrian Architectural Glazing Systems Limited
Whitehead Alloys Limited

24440 Copper production

Stairrods (UK) Limited

24450 Other non-ferrous metal production

Corrpro Companies Europe Limited
Doby Cleats Limited

24510 Casting of iron

Stockton Casting Company Limited (The)

24520 Casting of steel

Bonds Foundry Company Limited
Darwins Holdings Limited
A.M. Graham Fabrications Limited

24540 Casting of other non-ferrous metals

Peel Jones Copper Products Limited
Specialist Castings Ltd

25110 Manufacture of metal structures and parts of structures

AAP Metal Fabrication Services Ltd
ADM Pressings Limited
AW Fabrication Limited
Allerton Steel Limited
Apollo Facility Management Ltd
Arlington Automotive NE Limited
John Aynsley (Architectural Metalwork) Limited
BTS Fabrications Limited
Barrier (Offshore) Engineering Limited
Bede Group Limited
Billingham Machine Company Limited
Bonds Foundry Company Limited
DJ Camp Ltd
Castle Fabrication & Installation Limited
Cleveland Sitesafe Limited
Cramlington Precision Forge Limited
Creative Cutting Services Limited
D.C. Handrails and Ironwork Parts Limited
Donyal Engineering Limited
Dormor Machine and Engineering Company Limited
Durham Sheet Metal Works Limited
EEW Offshore Structures (Britain) Limited
EOS Facades Limited
Eldrett Finch Limited
Finley Structures Ltd
Ford Component Manufacturing Limited
Glendale Engineering (Milfield) Limited
Hydram Engineering Limited
JW Installations UK Limited
KC Engineering Bearings Ltd
Landon Engineering (Castle Works) Limited
Liebherr Sunderland Works Limited
Marine Fabricators Limited
Mech-Tool Engineering Limited
Naturalight Systems Limited
Newbridge Engineering Limited
G.Nicholson (Engineers) Limited
Peikko UK Limited
Petersen Stainless Rigging Limited
Philadelphia Structures Ltd
Pinnacle Re-Tec Limited
Raisco Limited
Responsive Engineering Limited
Roflow Limited
Royal IHC Limited
S&A Fabrications Limited
S.C.H. Site Services Ltd
Site and Field Services Limited
Sotech Limited
Tanfield Metal Spinners Ltd
Tees Components Limited
Universal Wolf Limited
Valmont Stainton Limited
Wave Aluminium Profiles Limited
Westline Distributors Limited
Wilton Engineering Services Limited
Worthington Armstrong U.K. Limited

25120 Manufacture of doors and windows of metal

Autoroll UK Limited
Crown Doors and Shutters Limited
Essential Aluminium Limited
Hadrian Architectural Glazing Systems Limited
NEOS Protect Limited

25210 Manufacture of central heating radiators and boilers

Rettig (UK) Limited
Stelrad Limited

25290 Manufacture of other tanks, reservoirs and containers of metal

G T Project Engineering Limited
T&G Automotive Ltd
Turners Fabrications Limited
Wessington Cryogenics Limited

25300 Manufacture of steam generators, except central heating hot water boilers

Gecomac Limited

25500 Forging, pressing, stamping and roll-forming of metal; powder metallurgy

ADM Pressings Limited
Automotive Chassis Products UK Limited
Elring Klinger (Great Britain) Limited
The Expanded Metal Company Limited
Gestamp Tallent Limited
Patterson Ryan Limited
Spartan UK Limited
Unipres (UK) Limited
Wave Aluminium Profiles Limited
Henry Williams Limited
Worthington Armstrong U.K. Limited

25610 Treatment and coating of metals

Ionbond UK Limited
Monitor Coatings Limited
UTS Engineering Limited

25620 Machining

Aavid Thermacore Europe Limited
Arlington Automotive NE Limited
Bel Engineering (UK) Limited
Billingham Machine Company Limited
Blue Diamond Engineering Limited
Cavendish (Northern) Limited
Clifton Engineering (North East) Limited
Design and Security Services Limited
Diamond Chain (UK) Limited
Dormor Machine and Engineering Company Limited
Durham Precision Engineering Limited
Express Engineering (Gateshead) Limited
Express Engineering (Industrial Products) Limited
G T Project Engineering Limited
G.V. Engineering Limited
Hargreaves Engineering & Contracts Limited
Impress North East Limited
Industrial and Marine Hydraulics Limited
Millennium Conveyor Services Limited
Newcastle Tool & Gauge Limited
Northdale Rotary Engineering Limited
Oceantec Marine Limited
Osborne Engineering Limited
P.D.Q. Engineering Limited
Pipeline Precision Engineering Ltd
Precision 2000 Limited
Pryme Group Limited
Q Laser Ltd
Responsive Engineering Limited
Stockton Machine Company Limited
Tees Components Limited
Teescraft Engineering Limited
Teesside Precision Engineering Ltd
Triple T Engineering Limited
Utex Industries UK Limited
Washington Waterjet Limited
Wave Aluminium Profiles Limited
Worthington Armstrong U.K. Limited

25720 Manufacture of locks and hinges

A.L.M. Products Limited

25730 Manufacture of tools

A H Engineering (North East) Limited
Durham Precision Engineering Limited
Manchester Alloys and Metals Limited
Mold Systems Limited
Tao Sustainable Power Solutions (UK) Ltd

25910 Manufacture of steel drums and similar containers

Metal Drum Company Limited (The)

25930 Manufacture of wire products, chain and springs

Patterson Ryan Limited
Petersen Stainless Rigging Limited
Purification Solutions UK Limited

25940 Manufacture of fasteners and screw machine products

Berger Closures Limited
Ford Component Manufacturing Limited
Hawk Fasteners Limited
Petersen Stainless Rigging Limited

26110 Manufacture of electronic components

Axenic Limited
C.R.D. Devices Ltd.
CTG Limited
Canford Audio PLC
Cleveland Circuits Limited
Cleveland Technologies Limited
Faraday Printed Circuits Limited
Feller (UK) Limited
Hindley Circuits Limited
Isocom Components 2004 Limited
Isocom Limited
Lintron Electronics Limited
Pragmatic Printing Limited
Welwyn Components Limited
Zytronic Displays Limited

26120 Manufacture of loaded electronic boards

Benchmark Electronics Limited
Connor Solutions Limited
Martel Instruments Limited

26200 Manufacture of computers and peripheral equipment

Amtech Automated Micro Technology Limited
Nxpower (UK) Limited

26301 Manufacture of telegraph and telephone apparatus and equipment

Lintron Electronics Limited

26309 Manufacture of communication equipment other than telegraph, and telephone apparatus and equipment

Petards Joyce-Loebl Limited

26400 Manufacture of consumer electronics

Specialist Alarm Services Limited

26511 Manufacture of electronic measuring, testing etc. equipment, not for industrial process control

Analox Military Systems Limited
Analox Sensor Technology Limited
Arquer Diagnostics Limited
Bruker JV UK Ltd
Eco Monitoring Utility Systems Limited
Kromek Limited
Seaward Electronic Limited
Visitech International Limited
Walker Filtration Limited

26512 Manufacture of electronic industrial process control equipment

Amtech Automated Micro Technology Limited
Identec Limited
Integrated Display Systems Limited
Lintron Electronics Limited
Mowden Controls Limited
Ronan Engineering Limited

26514 Manufacture of non-electronic industrial process control equipment

Bureau of Analysed Samples Limited

26600 Manufacture of irradiation, electromedical and electrotherapeutic equipment

Saferad Limited

26702 Manufacture of photographic and cinematographic equipment

Petards Joyce-Loebl Limited

27110 Manufacture of electric motors, generators and transformers

Carroll & Meynell Transformers Limited
Houghton International Electrical Services Limited
Slaters Electricals Limited
Turbo Power Systems Limited

27120 Manufacture of electricity distribution and control apparatus

Armah Switchgear Limited
The British Electrical & Manufacturing Company Limited
Northern Switchgear & Controls Limited
Protection Installation Services Ltd
RPS Switchgear Ltd

27200 Manufacture of batteries and accumulators

Alexander Technologies Europe Limited
Cell Pack Solutions Limited
Hyperdrive Innovation Ltd
Saft Limited

27320 Manufacture of other electronic and electric wires and cables

Controle Mesure Regulation (UK) Limited
Mineral Insulated Cable Company Limited
Nvent Solutions (UK) Limited
Thermon (U.K.) Limited

27400 Manufacture of electric lighting equipment

Carbon8 Ltd
Hacel Lighting Limited
Invertec Holdings Ltd.
Invertec Interiors Limited
Rasmi Electronics Limited
Rasmi Lighting Limited
Tofco CPP Limited
Victor Products Ltd

27510 Manufacture of electric domestic appliances

Ebac Industrial Products Limited

27900 Manufacture of other electrical equipment

Advanced Electronics Limited
Apex Cables Limited
Barkell Limited
Borgwarner Gateshead Limited
Canford Audio PLC
Clover Controls Limited
D-Line (Europe) Limited
Erico Europa (G.B.) Limited
H.V.R. International Limited
HVR Limited
Hawkridge Management Limited
Johnson Electric International (UK) Limited
NEL Technologies Limited
Petards Joyce-Loebl Limited
Quantum Controls Ltd
Raytec Limited
Ronbar Factors Limited
Select Control Systems Limited
Tew Holdings (2012) Limited
Victor Products Ltd
Henry Williams Limited

28120 Manufacture of fluid power equipment

IHC FHP Limited
Industrial and Marine Hydraulics Limited
Precision Hydraulic Cylinders (UK) Limited

28131 Manufacture of pumps

Haskel Europe Ltd
Hydraulic & Offshore Supplies Limited
Metnor (Great Yarmouth) Limited
Pinnacle Re-Tec Limited
Rotary Power Ltd.
Tomlinson,Hall & Company Limited

28132 Manufacture of compressors

Haskel Europe Ltd
Hydraulic & Offshore Supplies Limited
Kail and Co. Limited

28140 Manufacture of taps and valves

Alpha Process Controls (International) Limited
Bel Valves Limited
DLI Engineering Limited
Evolution Valves Limited

28150 Manufacture of bearings, gears, gearing and driving elements

Algernon Precision Engineering Limited
Delta Precision Engineering North East Limited
G.B. Belting Ltd
KC Engineering Bearings Ltd
Michell Bearings Limited
Roballo Engineering Company Limited

28220 Manufacture of lifting and handling equipment

A-Tech Fabrications Limited
B.& B. Attachments Limited
Durham Lifting Limited
Read Limited
Snorkel Europe Limited
Storage and Handling Equipment Limited
Tiger Lifting UK Limited

28250 Manufacture of non-domestic cooling and ventilation equipment

BMM Heaters Limited
Roflow Limited

28290 Manufacture of other general-purpose machinery n.e.c.

ABS Precision Limited
Advance Automated Systems Limited
Armour Plastics Limited
Express Engineering (Aerospace) Limited
Express Engineering (Gateshead) Limited
Fillworth (UK) Limited
Hart Door Systems Limited
IK-UK Limited
C. C. Jensen Limited
Logic Manufacturing Limited
Newarc (Newcastle) Limited
Orwin Limited
Precision Labelling Systems Limited
SMH Equipment Limited
SMH Products Limited
Tanfield Group PLC
Vixen Surface Treatments Limited

28302 Manufacture of agricultural and forestry machinery other than tractors

Husqvarna UK Limited
Logic Manufacturing Limited
JJ Metcalfe & Son Ltd

28410 Manufacture of metal forming machinery

Advanced Cutting Tools Limited
M R B Schumag Ltd

28490 Manufacture of other machine tools

Armour Plastics Limited
Izumi Products UK Limited
Mill Masters International Limited

28921 Manufacture of machinery for mining

L.H. (Quarry Plant) Limited

28922 Manufacture of earthmoving equipment

Komatsu UK Limited

28923 Manufacture of equipment for concrete crushing and screening and roadworks

Velocity UK Limited

28930 Manufacture of machinery for food, beverage and tobacco processing

Manitowoc Group (UK) Limited
Welbilt (Halesowen) Limited
Welbilt UK Limited

28960 Manufacture of plastics and rubber machinery

SMH Products Limited

28990 Manufacture of other special-purpose machinery n.e.c.

Air Filters Limited
Aqualution Systems Ltd
Cavotec UK Limited
Cleveland Cascades Limited
Crabco Limited
Crabtree of Gateshead (Holdings) Limited
Crabtree of Gateshead Limited
Daikin Applied (UK) Limited
Draeger Safety UK Ltd
L.B. Foster Rail Technologies (UK) Limited
G T Project Engineering Limited
HTL Worldwide Ltd
Heinzmann UK Limited
Industrial Monitoring Systems Limited
Matthew James Services Limited
Labman Automation Limited
John Lilley & Gillie Limited
M M C (Europe) Limited
Messer Griesheim Limited
Nano-Purification Solutions Ltd
Oberlin Filter Limited
Osbit Limited
Derek Parnaby Cyclones International Limited
Pearson Engineering Limited
Pipe Equipment Specialists Limited
Posi-Thread (U.K.) Ltd.
Precision Toolroom Services & Machining Limited
Redwood Engineering Company Ltd
S.I.E. Industrial Limited
Soil Machine Dynamics Limited
Specialist Machine Developments (Smd) Limited
Spiro-Gills Thermal Products Ltd
Subsea Innovation Limited
Technowash Limited
Tew Engineering Limited
Underwater Cutting Solutions Ltd
Vixen Surface Treatments Limited
Wassenburg Limited

29100 Manufacture of motor vehicles

Devon Conversions Limited
Nissan Motor Manufacturing (UK) Limited

29201 Manufacture of bodies (coachwork) for motor vehicles (except caravans)

Faltec Europe Limited
Erwin Hymer Group Holdings UK Limited
Erwin Hymer Group UK Ltd
Lam-Plas (Durham) Limited

29202 Manufacture of trailers and semi-trailers

Sterling GP Limited

29203 Manufacture of caravans

Erwin Hymer Group UK Ltd

29310 Manufacture of electrical and electronic equipment for motor vehicles and their engines

Hyperdrive Innovation Ltd

29320 Manufacture of other parts and accessories for motor vehicles

Bremsen Technik Reman Limited
Gestamp Washington UK Limited
MSSL (GB) Limited
SAI Automotive Washington Limited
Snop UK Limited

30110 Building of ships and floating structures

Amble Boat Company Limited
B. Marshall Marine Limited
UK Docks Marine Services North Limited
UK Docks Marine Services South Limited
UK Docks Marine Services Teesside Limited

30120 Building of pleasure and sporting boats

Abel Yachts Limited
UK Docks Marine Services South Limited

30200 Manufacture of railway locomotives and rolling stock

The A1 Steam Locomotive Trust
Class G5 Locomotive Company Ltd
Sabre Rail Services Limited

30300 Manufacture of air and spacecraft and related machinery

CAV Advanced Technologies Limited
CAV Ice Protection Limited

30400 Manufacture of military fighting vehicles

Pearson Engineering Limited

30920 Manufacture of bicycles and invalid carriages

Automotive Group (Newcastle upon Tyne) Limited

30990 Manufacture of other transport equipment n.e.c.

Avid Technology Limited
CPD Bodies Limited
Dependable Bodies (Newcastle) Limited
FG Trailers Limited
Immi Ltd
Technical Engineering Resource (Aerospace) Limited
Titan Trailers Industries Limited

31010 Manufacture of office and shop furniture

H. & J. Forbes Limited
Grove Reed Joinery Limited
Newman Scott Limited

31020 Manufacture of kitchen furniture

Browns Bedrooms & Kitchens Ltd
Custom Design B.A. Limited
Mowlem and Company (Newcastle) Limited
Northeast Sheets & Panels Limited
Roundel Manufacturing Limited

31030 Manufacture of mattresses

Bishop's Beds Ltd

31090 Manufacture of other furniture

Ambic Limited
BHK (UK) Limited
Be Modern Limited
Bentincks Ltd
Bishop's Beds Ltd
Blue Aardvark Joinery Limited
Court Homemakers Limited
Delcor Ltd.
GKC Interiors (NE) Limited
Grove Reed Joinery Limited
Katell Limited
Plant Services (Gateshead) Limited
Swandene Furniture Limited

32120 Manufacture of jewellery and related articles

Alchemy Design & Works Limited

32500 Manufacture of medical and dental instruments and supplies

Altomed Limited
Arquer Diagnostics Limited
Easibathe Limited
Hart Biologicals Limited
Implants International Limited
Kromek Limited
Peacocks Medical Group Limited
Wescott Medical Limited
XL Precision Technologies Limited

32910 Manufacture of brooms and brushes

Brush Technology Limited
Cottam Brush Ltd

33110 Repair of fabricated metal products

MCE Group PLC

33120 Repair of machinery

Aconpex (UK) Limited
Banner Contracts (Halnaby) Limited
Bignall Group Ltd
The Cylinder Service Centre Limited
Londonderry Garage (S.E.) Limited
Royston Limited
Service Engines (Newcastle) Limited

33130 Repair of electronic and optical equipment

Lord Technical Limited

33140 Repair of electrical equipment

ADC Electrical Limited
Cenelec Standards Inspections Limited
DFP Services Limited
Digital Office Solutions Limited
Mastercopy Limited
Safe & Sure Fire Protection Limited

33150 Repair and maintenance of ships and boats

A & P Falmouth Limited
A & P Tees Limited
A M I Exchangers Limited
A&P GH 2006 Limited
A&P Group Limited
A&P Tyne Limited
Amble Boat Company Limited
Industrial and Marine Hydraulics Limited
RH Marine UK Ltd
Safe-Line Marine After Sales Ltd

33170 Repair and maintenance of other transport equipment n.e.c.

Dennis Dixon Limited
Forman Vehicle Services Limited
Hogarth Coachworks Limited
Houghton International Electrical Services Limited
Jarrow Coachworks Limited
Lockwell Limited
Midland Steel Traders Limited,
Rail Management Services Limited
Swarco Traffic Limited
TVG Systems Limited
Tyne Electro Diesel Limited

33190 Repair of other equipment

Bartram Walker Limited
Britannia Office Systems Limited
EVT Contractors Limited
Londonderry Garage (S.E.) Limited
J.G. Paxton and Sons Limited
Pee Gee Limited
Pickerings Europe Limited
Rosh Engineering Limited
Thompson Power Tool Services UK Ltd
Underpressure Pipeline Solutions Limited

33200 Installation of industrial machinery and equipment

Coolcheck Refrigeration Limited
EJM Engineered Systems Limited
Engie Urban Energy Limited
Gecomac Limited
Heat Tech Tooling Ltd
Independent Air Treatment Technology Limited
Industrial Energy Services Limited
Lacegold Electrical and Mechanical Services Limited
Londonderry Garage (S.E.) Limited
Oberlin Filter Limited
Owben Ltd
Specialist Alarm Services Limited
Underpressure Pipeline Solutions Limited

35110 Production of electricity

Banks Renewables (Marr Wind Farm) Limited
Barmoor Wind Power Limited
Blyth Offshore Demonstrator Limited
Boundary Lane Windfarm Limited
Braemore Wood Windfarm Limited
Burnfoot Windfarm Limited
Burnhead Moss Wind Farm Limited
Castleson Ltd
Cemmaes Windfarm Limited
Corriemoillie Windfarm Limited
Coventry District Energy Company Limited
WJ Drennan Limited
Duranta Teesside Limited
EDF Energy Renewables Limited
East London Energy Limited
Excel District Energy Company Limited
Fairfield Windfarm Limited
Great Orton Windfarm II Limited
High Hedley Hope Wind Limited
Higher Trevartha Solar Park Limited
Industrial & Community Wind Generation No. 2 Limited
Industrial Energy Services Limited
Infinite Sirius (Lounge) Limited
LCH Renewables Limited
Lanchester Properties Limited
Langage Solar Park Limited
Layfield Renewable Ltd
Leicester District Energy Company Limited
Llangwyryfon Windfarm Limited
Longpark Windfarm Limited
Lynemouth Power Limited
PX Limited
Park Spring Wind Farm Limited
Quarrington Renewable Gas Ltd
Roade Windfarm Limited
S F Wind Ltd
Sembcorp Utilities (UK) Limited
Seneca Global Energy Limited
Strathmore Renewables Ltd
Team Stokes Limited
Teesside Windfarm Limited
Wainstones Energy Limited
Walkway Windfarm Limited

35120 Transmission of electricity

Sembcorp Utilities (UK) Limited

35130 Distribution of electricity

Birmingham District Energy Company Limited
Northern Powergrid (Northeast) Limited
Northern Powergrid (Yorkshire) PLC
Southampton Geothermal Heating Company Limited (The)
Utilitywise PLC

35140 Trade of electricity

Birmingham District Energy Company Limited
East London Energy Limited
Energy24 Limited
Excel District Energy Company Limited
Southampton Geothermal Heating Company Limited (The)
Utility Alliance Ltd
Wear Valley Renewables C.I.C.
Wilton Energy Limited

35210 Manufacture of gas

Emerald Biogas Ltd
NWG Bioenergy Limited
PX Limited

35220 Distribution of gaseous fuels through mains

C & R Utilities Ltd
Engie FM Limited
L & G Utilities Ltd
PX (TGPP) Limited

35230 Trade of gas through mains

Ceres Energy Limited
PX (TGPP) Limited

35300 Steam and air conditioning supply

Birmingham District Energy Company Limited
Bloomsbury Heat & Power Limited
Coventry District Energy Company Limited
East London Energy Limited
Engie FM Limited
Excel District Energy Company Limited
Hadrian Air Conditioning and Refrigeration Company Limited
Southampton Geothermal Heating Company Limited (The)

36000 Water collection, treatment and supply

Anglian Water Business (National) Limited
Northumbrian Water Limited

37000 Sewerage

Aquajet Drain Cleaning Limited
Caledonian Environmental Levenmouth Treatment Services Limited
Craig Enterprises Limited
R.A. Dalton Limited
Dial-a-Loo Limited
Northumbrian Water Limited
Northumbrian Water Projects Limited
Waters Waste Services Ltd

38110 Collection of non-hazardous waste

Crossco (1371) Limited
R & J Farrow Limited
Fewsters Services Limited
A. McCall & Sons (Houghton-le-Spring) Limited
Scott Bros. Enterprises Limited
Scott Bros. Limited
Sharpsmart Limited
Tiplady Tanker Services Ltd
Todd Waste Management Group Limited
Tonks 2000 Limited
Total Recycling Services Limited
Ward Recycling Limited
Yorwaste Limited

38120 Collection of hazardous waste

Sharpsmart Limited
Total Recycling Services Limited

38210 Treatment and disposal of non-hazardous waste

1st Choice Skip Hire North East Ltd
Alab Environmental Services Limited
B2B Contracting Services Ltd.
Eco Tyre Disposals Ltd
R & J Farrow Limited
P A Moody Recycling Limited
Niramax Group Limited
North Tees Waste Management Limited
Remondis JBT Limited
Sharpsmart Limited
Edgar F Shepherd Ltd
Stonegrave Aggregates Limited
Total Recycling Services Limited
Warrens Group Limited
Yorwaste Limited

38220 Treatment and disposal of hazardous waste

Alab Environmental Services Limited
Fine Environmental Services Limited
North Tees Waste Management Limited
Sharpsmart Limited
Sirius Demolition Ltd
Todd Waste Management Group Limited
Total Recycling Services Limited

38310 Dismantling of wrecks

JSB (Metals) Limited

38320 Recovery of sorted materials

Accredited Processed Metals Limited
CRS (North-East) Limited
Crossco (1370) Limited
Emerald Biogas Ltd
Enviroclothes Limited
GES Recycling Ltd.
Graphite Resources (DEP) Limited
IK-ECO Limited
J & B Recycling Limited
S.J.B. Recycling Limited
Scott Bros. Recycling Limited
Todd Waste Management Group Limited
Ward Bros. (Plant Hire) Limited
Ward Bros. (Steel) Limited
Yorwaste Limited

39000 Remediation activities and other waste management services

AVG Imperial Ltd
AVG Power Limited
Able UK Limited
Borders Recycling Limited
IC & MJ Evershed Limited
Gunnergate Limited
Headway Point Limited
Octagon Green Solutions Limited
Penton House Limited
Sirius Demolition Ltd
Sirius Remediation Limited
The Viridis Group Ltd

42110 Construction of roads and motorways

AA Construction Utilities Ltd
DCS Maintenance Solutions NE Ltd
Debmat Surfacing Limited
T W Eason Limited
Hall Construction Services Limited
Holystone Civil Engineering Limited
Lee Construction (Ldg) Limited
Fred Mence (Construction) Limited
Northumbrian Roads Limited
Phoenix Civil Engineering Limited
K W Purvis Limited
Rainton Construction Limited
M Spence Surfacing Limited
Tarcon Limited
Todds Highway Maintenance Limited
Utility Support Solutions Limited
Youll Construction Ltd

42130 Construction of bridges and tunnels

Crestfix Limited
Herrenknecht International Limited

42210 Construction of utility projects for fluids

Compac Services (NE) Limited

42220 Construction of utility projects for electricity and telecommunications

Beck Burn Windfarm Limited
Doocey North East Limited
Dorenell Windfarm Limited
Global Substation Solutions Limited
Hall Construction Services Limited
Leicester District Energy Company Limited
Pearie Law Windfarm Limited
WM Utility Services Limited
ZIV Automation UK Ltd

42910 Construction of water projects

Crestfix Limited
Esh-MWH Limited
Sheers Limited
Southbay Civil Engineering Limited

42990 Construction of other civil engineering projects n.e.c.

2020 Property Developments Limited
Able UK Limited
Absolute Civil Engineering Limited
Acomb Construction Limited
Applebridge Construction Limited
Arrowbuild & Civil Engineering Limited
Ashbrook Construction Services Limited
H.J. Banks (Construction) Limited
R.Bau Limited
Bloomsbury Heat & Power Limited
Brambledown Landscape Services Limited
C.A.T. Builders Limited
Cameron's Builders (Newcastle) Limited
David Carr (Durham) Limited
David A Clark Limited
Coal Contractors Limited
Complete Cladding Systems Limited
Crestfix Limited
Crownfold Limited
Engie Urban Energy Limited
Geofirma Soils Engineering Limited
Grainger (Commercial Developments) Limited
Groundwork Services (Durham) Ltd
H.S. Carlsteel Engineering Limited
HAB Northern Ltd
John Hellens (Contracts) Limited
Hewitson Group Ltd
Highway Construction Services Limited
Hodgson Sayers Limited
Holystone Civil Engineering Limited
Hughes Bros Construction Limited
J.K. Construction and Joinery Limited
D Jones Construction & Haulage Limited
K & L Groundworks Limited
R.D. Kearton & Sons Limited
L & A Reinforcements Ltd.
M A Utilities Ltd
MW Crane Hire Ltd
Fred Mence (Construction) Limited
NY Construction Ltd
North East Homes Limited
Northern Construction Solutions Limited
WJM Quigley Limited
R J Utility Services Ltd
Rainton Construction Limited
Red Marine Engineering Limited
Gus Robinson Developments Limited
STP Construction Limited
Scotts of Whittington Limited
Simpson Coulson Limited
Sirius Civil Engineering Limited
Southbay Civil Engineering Limited
Starkold Building Services Limited
Sycamore Homes Limited
Utility Services (N.E.) Limited
T. M. Ward (Darlington) Limited
Wharton Construction Limited
Wyn Construction Limited
Wyn Limited

43110 Demolition

A1 Environmental Services Ltd.
Able UK Limited
A.Buckler Haulage Limited
E C Groundworks Ltd
EVT Contractors Limited
Gnat UK Limited
John Hellens (Contracts) Limited
M.G.L. Demolition Limited
Sirius Demolition Ltd
Stonegrave Aggregates Limited
Teward Bros Ltd
Thompsons of Prudhoe Limited
Timec 1484 Limited
T. M. Ward (Darlington) Limited

43120 Site preparation

Arrowbuild & Civil Engineering Limited
Arrowcruit Limited
RB Blackburn Ltd
Colton Excavations Limited
E C Groundworks Ltd
EVT Contractors Limited
Grab & Deliver Limited
John Hellens (Contracts) Limited
M.J. Hickey Plant Hire & Contracts Limited
Fred Mence (Construction) Limited
PBU (UK) Ltd
G A Smith Limited
Thompson Power Tool Services UK Ltd
Thompsons of Prudhoe Limited
R. Thornton & Co. Ltd.
T. M. Ward (Darlington) Limited

43130 Test drilling and boring

Allied Exploration & Geotechnics Limited
Dunelm Geotechnical & Environmental Limited
Geo - Drill Limited
Geocore Site Investigations Limited
Herrenknecht International Limited
Sirius Geotechnical Ltd

43210 Electrical installation

Aardvarc Electrical Engineers Limited
Abca Systems Limited
F.A. Atkinson Limited
Bartram Walker Limited
Baydale Control Systems Limited
C.B.L. Cable Contractors Limited
CEL Securus Ltd
Cable Jointing Services Limited
The Castle Building Services Organisation Limited
Colledge Trundle & Hall Limited
Compac Services (NE) Limited
John Cullerton & Sons Limited
D & A Systems Limited
Dougal & Railton Limited
Dualbound Limited
John N Dunn Group Limited
E-Wire Northern Limited
EJM Engineered Systems Limited
Eco Drill (England) Limited
Engie Energy Services UK Limited
Excelsior Services (Student Accommodation) Limited
FG Trailers Limited
The Faraday Centre Limited
Global Substation Solutions Limited
Goldshield Securus Limited
H.T.B. Electrical Contractors Limited
Hepple Engineering Services Limited
ICS Integrated Cable Services Limited
ITC Plumbing and Heating Services Limited
Integrated Utility Services Limited
Intelect (UK) Limited
Intruder Detection & Surveillance Ltd.
Richard Irvin & Sons Limited
J.E.B. Contractors (UK) Limited
J.E.B. Contractors Limited
A. & J. Keith Limited
Kennedy Services Limited
Kennek Construction Limited
Nigel Lightfoot Electrical Contracting Limited
Lytestream Electrical Engineers & Contractors Limited
MRM Electrical Solutions Limited
Map Group (UK) Limited
Matrix Power Limited
Maval Electrical and Mechanical Engineering Company Limited
McNally and Thompson (UK Contracts) Limited
McVickers Limited
Nala Engineers Limited
Norstead Limited
Northumbrian Property Services Group Limited
Opus Building Services Limited
Quartz Electrical & Mechanical Services Limited
RMH Lamps, Lighting & Electrical Limited
Geoffrey Robinson Limited
M R Robson Electricity Services Ltd
SMT Electrical Contractors Limited
Safety Systems Distribution Limited
Sheers Limited
D.J.R. Smith Limited
Suffolk Electrical Services Limited
Vizsec Holdings Limited

43220 Plumbing, heat and air-conditioning installation

21 Degrees Limited
Aircon-Refrigeration Limited
F.A. Atkinson Limited
R.Bland Limited
P.F.Burridge & Sons Limited
The Castle Building Services Organisation Limited
Matthew Charlton,Limited
H Clarke & Sons Limited
Compac Services (NE) Limited
Cromex Limited
John N Dunn Group Limited
EHLUK Building Maintenance & Facility Services Ltd
EJM Engineered Systems Limited
Elite Maintenance & Installation Services Limited
Engie Energy Services UK Limited
Engie FM Limited
Engie Urban Energy Limited
Excelsior Services (Student Accommodation) Limited
Green Team Partnership Ltd
K Hewitt Holdings Limited
K. Hewitt and Co. Limited
ITC Plumbing and Heating Services Limited
Richard Irvin & Sons Limited
Kennedy Services Limited
Robert Kirkland (Blyth) Limited
Leybourne Urwin Limited
MNP Services Ltd.
H.Malone and Sons Limited
Mathewson Limited
Maval Electrical and Mechanical Engineering Company Limited
The Minel Group Ltd.
Norstead Limited
Northumbrian Property Services Group Limited
Pennine Enterprises Ltd
Geoffrey Robinson Limited
Turnkey Air Conditioning Limited
Tyne Tees Thermal Limited

43290 Other construction installation

01906302 Limited
G. Abbott & Co. Limited
Aquind Limited
Brynco Ltd
Burnell Fencing Limited
Commercial Insulation Services Ltd
Crownfold Limited
Datim Building Contractors Limited
Electronic Security Solutions Limited
G T Project Engineering Limited
Hadrian Technology Limited
Hambleton Steel Limited
Hertel (UK) Limited
I D Construction Services Ltd
Intumescent Protective Coatings Limited
JD Joinery & Building Services Limited
G D Lee Building Services Limited
M.G.N. Fire Protection Limited
MSD Construction (UK) Ltd
MW Crane Hire Ltd
Map Construction Services Ltd
The Minel Group Ltd.
N&T Civils Ltd
NIS Group Services Limited
North East Building Services Limited
Pennine Contracts Ltd
Phoenix Passive Fire Protection Limited
Presmac Limited
Print Ventures Limited
Rennyco Limited
Ro-Bal Steel Fabrications Limited
Rowan Specialist Interiors Limited
S.C.H. Site Services Ltd
Sheers Limited
Sunter Limited
Tees Insulation (International) Limited
Topside Group Limited

43310 Plastering

Kenmor Ceilings & Partitions Limited
Lawson & Cowell Ltd

43320 Joinery installation

Contract Joinery (North East) Limited
Damian Cronin Limited
Hesbro Limited
Howell Cummings Joinery Ltd
J.K. Construction and Joinery Limited
Karlin Timber Frame (NE) Limited
Newman Scott Limited
North East Homes Limited
Pro - Fix Installations (North East) Limited
Prodrive (Joinery & Shop Fitting) Limited
T.M.G. Joinery (UK) Limited

43330 Floor and wall covering

Johnson Wright (Flooring) Limited
Kenmor Ceilings & Partitions Limited
Level Flooring North East Limited
Newcastle Flooring Company Limited
Northern Floorcraft (Gateshead) Limited
R. Parker (Wall & Floor Tiling Contractors) Limited
P. Plunkett (Tiling Contractors) Limited
Signature Fencing and Flooring Systems Europe Limited
The Tiling Company (Northern) Limited

43341 Painting

Alldec (Northern) Limited
Architectural Powder Coatings Limited
Crownfold Limited
DW Contractors (Oxford) Ltd
Dunningham Decorators Limited
Glenwood Paint Supplies Limited
Hayton & Lamb Limited
Cyril John Limited
Colin Marshall Painting Contractors Ltd
G Ramage & Sons Windows Limited

43342 Glazing

Ace Aluminium & Architectural Services Ltd
Crownfold Limited
North Eastern Glass Limited
Peterlee Glass Company Limited
Polar (N.E.) Limited
Visual Concept Ltd
Window Fitters Warehouse Limited

43390 Other building completion and finishing

A.C.T Construction Services Limited
Able Construction (Northern) Limited
Advanced Industrial Solutions Limited
BSD (UK) Ltd
Gary Bluff Projects Limited
Brickwork Services Limited
P.F.Burridge & Sons Limited
Carmel Structures Limited
Castle Construction (North East) Limited
Commercial & Industrial Interiors Ltd
DOH Construction Limited
DSE (N.E.) Limited
Decke (Newcastle) Limited
Empire Property Concepts Limited
GTD Developments Limited
Horsley Properties Limited
Interceil Limited
CD Johnson Limited
Kelt Properties Limited
Kenmor Ceilings & Partitions Limited
LTS Refurbishment Limited
The Minel Group Ltd.
Monument (Survey:Design:Build) Ltd
Pinkney Building Contractors Limited
Prodrive Property Maintenance Limited
Rend-Tech North East Ltd
Reviloo Ltd
Richmond Contracts Projects Limited
Straightline (NE) Limited
Vision Building Services Limited

43910 Roofing activities

Alderclad Ltd
Barclay Roofing Limited
C.A. Group (Holdings) Limited
C.A. Group Limited
Chemplas Limited
Chemplas Roofing Services Ltd
Dufell Roofing Company Limited
G A Evans Roofing Contractors Limited
Findley Roofing & Building Limited
John Flowers Limited
Group Tegula Limited
Hathaway Roofing Limited
W.H.Hillerby & Sons Limited
Hodgson Sayers Limited
IPS Roofing Limited
Integrated Polymer Systems Limited
Midas Cladding Services Limited
Mitrepoint Limited
Ors Contracting Limited
Portalclad Limited
S&A Fabrications Limited
Alexander Sinclair (N.E.) Limited
Springs Roofing Limited
Wensley Roofing Limited

43991 Scaffold erection

J Gunn Scaffolding Limited
Hertel (UK) Limited
James Ingleford Scaffolding Limited
Interlink Scaffolding Ltd
Premier Scaffolding Services Limited
Redcar Scaffolding Specialists Ltd
Trojan Scaffolding (NE) Ltd

45111 Sale of new cars and light motor vehicles

Bob Alexander Limited
Arriva Bus & Coach Limited
Aston Workshop Limited
Atlas Garages (Morpeth) Limited
Autosense Limited
Simon Bailes Limited
Bescol Motors Limited
Blackshaw's Garage (Alnwick) Limited
Bridge End Motors Limited
Bristol Street First Investments Limited
Bristol Street Fourth Investments Limited
Cookswell Garage Limited
Cramlington Garages Limited
Croxdale Service Station Limited
Dapra York Limited
Albert Farnell Limited
Greenoaks (Maidenhead) Limited
Richard Hardie Limited
Hodgson Newcastle Limited
Ideal Caravan Sales Limited
Gordon Lamb Limited
Lingscars.Com Limited
Meadowfield Motors Limited
Milburn Motors Garages Limited
Motorcare (Alnwick) Limited
Nissan Trading Europe Limited
North East Truck & Van Limited
Northumbria Vehicle Co Ltd.
Oaktree Leasing Ltd
S.G. Petch Limited
Mike Pulman Limited
Pulman Seat Limited
RMB Automotive Ltd
Gavin Reed Limited
SHG Holdings Limited
SMC Motors Limited
Saltwell Park Agencies Limited
Sherwoods (Darlington) Limited
Silbury Motors Limited
Stephen A. Sims (Cars) Limited
South Hereford Garages Limited
Springfield Cars Limited
Tendercrave Limited
Town Centre Garage (Sunderland) Limited
Tustain Motors Limited
Tustain Motors Northumberland Limited
Tyne Mills Motor Company Limited
The Van Centre (Richmond) Limited
Vertu Motors (Chingford) Limited
Vertu Motors (Vmc) Limited
Vertu Motors PLC
Wingrove Motor Company Limited
Vic Young (South Shields) Limited
Zig Zag Cars Limited

45112 Sale of used cars and light motor vehicles

A690 Specialist Cars Limited
Acklam Car Centre Limited
Atlas Garages (Morpeth) Limited
Autosense Limited
Simon Bailes Limited
Bescol Motors Limited
Biscuit Vehicle Leasing Limited
Blackshaw's Garage (Alnwick) Limited
Bristol Street Fourth Investments Limited
Buy from Us Autopark Limited
Catterick Service Station Ltd.
Cleveland Motorhomes Limited
Commercial Vehicle Exports (Northern) Limited
Cookswell Garage Limited
Crowther Lodge Motor Company Limited
D. C. C. (Cars) Limited
Derek Slack Motors Limited
Driven Car Sales Limited
European Horseboxes Limited
Jack Ford Limited
Frecker Limited
Greenoaks (Maidenhead) Limited
Richard Hardie Limited
Icicle Vehicle Solutions Limited
Ideal Caravan Sales Limited
Gordon Lamb Limited
Lawson Cars Limited
Edgar Lawson Limited
Leo Car Company Limited
McDougal & Breen Ltd
Motorcare (Alnwick) Limited
Nova Finance Limited
Overdrive (North East) Limited
Panda Motor Vehicles Ltd
Parker Prestige Limited
S.G. Petch Limited
Mike Pulman Limited
Pulman Seat Limited
Les Rayner Foxhunters Motor Company Ltd.
Redgate Lodge Limited
C G Robinson Limited
Saltwell Park Agencies Limited
Alex Scott Cars Limited
Silbury Motors Limited
Snippersgate '88 Limited
Southlands Motor Company Ltd
T C & C Ltd
Tendercrave Limited
H. Tones & Sons Limited
Wingrove Motor Company Limited
Wylam Garage Limited
Wynyard Motor Company Limited

45190 Sale of other motor vehicles

Beadnell Bay Caravan Park Ltd
Ian Bell (Motor Cycles) Limited
Bell Truck Sales Limited
Bell Trucks (Holdings) Limited
Catterick Caravan & Camping Centre Limited
City Leasing (Sunderland) Limited
Ebor Leisure World Limited
European Horseboxes Limited
Harris (U.K.) Limited
Albert Hill Commercials Limited
Ideal Caravan Sales Limited
C.J. Leonard & Sons Limited
North East Truck & Van Limited
Ewart Parsons,Limited
J.G. Paxton and Sons Limited
Stokesley Tractors Ltd
Tyneside Leisure World Limited
The Van Centre (Richmond) Limited
Warner of Wingate Limited

45200 Maintenance and repair of motor vehicles

C F Abraham Limited
Aston Workshop Limited
Atlas Garages (Morpeth) Limited
B.E.L. Lift Trucks Limited
Simon Bailes Limited
Berryvale Ltd
Bescol Motors Limited
Blackshaw's Garage (Alnwick) Limited
Bristol Street First Investments Limited
Bristol Street Fourth Investments Limited
C.F.Motoring Services Ltd
Catterick Service Station Ltd.
Clarks Coachbuilders Limited
Cookswell Garage Limited
James Cooper & Son (Tyneside) Ltd
Croxdale Fast-Fit Limited
D. C. C. (Cars) Limited
Darlington Tyre & Auto Centre Limited
E L Denney & Son Limited
Greenoaks (Maidenhead) Limited
Hammer Services Ltd
Richard Hardie Limited
J & R A Hawkes & Sons Limited
Fred Henderson Limited
Ideal Caravan Sales Limited
Gordon Lamb Limited
Lawson Cars Limited
Edgar Lawson Limited
Mids Auto Services Limited
Motorcare (Alnwick) Limited
North East Truck & Van Limited
Northumbria Youth Action Limited
Nova Finance Limited
P & P Caravan Services Limited
J.G. Paxton and Sons Limited
Ron Perry (A19 Test & Tune) Limited
S.G. Petch Limited
Mike Pulman Limited
Pulman Seat Limited
Gavin Reed Limited
Sayers Road Tanker Rentals Limited
Alan Sewell Limited
TLC (Car Care) Limited
Tendercrave Limited
Thornton Brothers Limited
Trewicks Accident Repair Centre Limited
Truck Technics Limited
Tyne Tees Vehicle Repair Group Limited
Vertu Motors (Chingford) Limited
Vertu Motors (Vmc) Limited
Wingrove Motor Company Limited

45310 Wholesale trade of motor vehicle parts and accessories

4X4 Accessories & Tyres Limited
Baydale Estates Limited
Bremsen Technik (UK) Limited
CPS Drivelink Limited
Commercial Propshaft Services Limited
Denka Limited
Elring Parts Limited
Ford Parts (UK) Limited
Grantham Motor Company Limited
Harris (U.K.) Limited
Gordon Lamb Limited
N.P. Alliance Limited
Nissan Trading Europe Limited
A.V.Taylor Limited
Thor Car Parts and Accessories Limited
Turbocharger Solutions Limited
Tyre Spot Limited

45320 Retail trade of motor vehicle parts and accessories

Atlas Garages (Morpeth) Limited
Simon Bailes Limited
Bikesport (North East) Limited
Blackshaw's Garage (Alnwick) Limited
Cookswell Garage Limited
Eurojag Limited
Fleet Factors Limited
Greenoaks (Maidenhead) Limited
Richard Hardie Limited
N.E. Truck Spares Limited
North East Motor Salvage Limited
North East Truck & Van Limited
Oak Road and Whitby Motor Factors Limited
S.G. Petch Limited
Mike Pulman Limited
Pulman Seat Limited
Randstad Limited
Swift Brake & Clutch Limited
Turboactive Limited
Tyre Spot Limited
D. Ward Automotive Limited
Wingrove Motor Company Limited

45400 Sale, maintenance and repair of motorcycles and related parts and accessories

Michael Brandon Limited
Eagle Road Services Limited
M. & S. Motorcycles Limited
Newcastle Motorcycles Ltd
North East Accident Repair Centres Limited
W.J.(Bill) Tillston Limited

46110 Agents selling agricultural raw materials, livestock, textile raw materials and semi-finished goods

Charnley Marketing Limited
The Hawes Farmers' Auction Mart Company, Limited
J.S. Hubbuck Limited
The Leyburn Livestock Auction Mart Company Limited

46120 Agents involved in the sale of fuels, ores, metals and industrial chemicals

Dixons of Westerhope Limited
Epivalence Ltd
Exelby Services Limited
M. & G. Fuels Limited
Par Petroleum Limited
Samson Aviation Services Limited
Tribo - Synthetics Limited

46130 Agents involved in the sale of timber and building materials

J T Atkinson & Sons Limited
Brick Services Limited
James Burrell Limited
Crossling Limited
J.T.Dove,Limited
Durham Roofing Centre Limited
Gill & Robinson Limited
Green & Son Building Services Limited
Mastclimber Solutions UK Ltd.
F.E.Maughan Limited
McGovern Holdings Limited
Middleton Forge Limited
S&A Builders Merchants Limited
Smithfield Timber Limited
Volume Trading (Europe) Limited
Yorkshire Independent Building Supplies Limited

46140 Agents involved in the sale of machinery, industrial equipment, ships and aircraft

A1 Industrial Trucks Limited
Advanced Handling & Storage Limited
B.& B. Attachments Limited
Carbis Filtration Limited
Fairfield Industries Limited
GT Cleaning Machines Limited
Greenlay (Grass Machinery) Limited
Manissa Ltd
John Morfield Limited
Perry Process Equipment Limited
Sigma Plantfinder Limited

46150 Agents involved in the sale of furniture, household goods, hardware and ironmongery

Danesmoor Limited
Stadium Consumer Products Limited

46160 Agents involved in the sale of textiles, clothing, fur, footwear and leather goods

The Mountain Boot Company Limited
Nike (UK) Limited

46170 Agents involved in the sale of food, beverages and tobacco

Chamberlin Agencies Limited
Penshaw Estates Limited
Yayla Enterprises Limited

46180 Agents specialised in the sale of other particular products

Ken Brown Agencies Limited
C.R.T. Packaging (U.K.) Limited
John Clark Valves Limited
Eyeworks Industries Limited
GNS 2015 Limited
GNS Acquisitions Limited
Global Navigation Solutions Limited
Home and Leisure International Limited
In-House Inspired Room Design Ltd
Inkland Limited
Jotron UK Ltd
Quantum Controls Ltd
Thyssenkrupp Access Limited
Tynedale Roadstone Limited
Vector Power Solutions Limited
The Vehicle Group Limited
Zerust (UK) Limited

46190 Agents involved in the sale of a variety of goods

CPMC Limited
Evergreen Pallet Solutions (UK) Limited
N.OOR Jewellery Limited
Williamson Network Limited
Yayla Enterprises Limited

46210 Wholesale of grain, unmanufactured tobacco, seeds and animal feeds

Armstrong Richardson & Co.Limited
The Feed Warehouse Ltd
Grainco Limited

46310 Wholesale of fruit and vegetables

Thomas Baty (Newcastle upon Tyne) Limited
Hutchinsons Fruit & Veg Limited
JH Laidler & Son Limited
North East Wholesale Fruit & Vegetable Market Limited
The Original Produce Company (Middlesbrough) Limited
Wing Hong & Company Limited

46320 Wholesale of meat and meat products

George Bolam (Foods) Ltd
Warren Butterworth Catering Butchers Limited
Collins (Seafoods) Limited
Country Valley Wholesale Foods Limited
J. Freeman & Sons Limited
Great Park Food Company Ltd.
Holmesterne Farm Co. Limited
J.A. Jewitt (Farms) Limited
J.A. Jewitt (Meat) Limited
J.A.Jewitt
Lowrie Foods Limited
R.Manners & Sons Limited
Premier Meats Limited
Star Meats Limited
Wensleydale Bacon Limited
Wing Hong & Company Limited

46330 Wholesale of dairy products, eggs and edible oils and fats

Hall Farm Foods Limited
Hanover Dairies Limited
Lintz Hall Farm Limited
R & D Patterson Limited
Prima Cheese Limited
Wensleydale Dairy Products Limited

46342 Wholesale of wine, beer, spirits and other alcoholic beverages

Bon Coeur Fine Wines Limited
CKW Trading Limited
H.B.Clark & Co.(Successors) Limited
Elliston Fine Wines Limited
Greencroft Bottling Company Limited
Hameed Investments Limited
Kitwave Limited
Lanchester Wine Cellars Limited
Lanchester Wine Sales Limited
M.& M.Value Limited
Wine World Producers Limited

46350 Wholesale of tobacco products

Kitwave Limited
M.& M.Value Limited

46360 Wholesale of sugar and chocolate and sugar confectionery

Automatic Retailing (Northern) Limited
Kitwave Limited
Kitwave One Limited
M.& M.Value Limited
Oldgreen Limited
R.H. Orange & Son Limited
Teatime Tasties Limited
Turner & Wrights Limited
Westone Wholesale Limited

46380 Wholesale of other food, including fish, crustaceans and molluscs

Caterpak Limited
W. Hodgson (Hartlepool) Limited
Hodgson Fish Holdings Limited
Inshore Fisheries Limited
Italica UK Limited
Ky247 Limited
Libra Seafoods Limited
Wraggs Seafoods Limited

46390 Non-specialised wholesale of food, beverages and tobacco

2M Food Suppliers Limited
Henry Colbeck Limited
Country Valley Foods Ltd
David Miller Frozen Foods Limited
Tyneside Foodservice Limited

46410 Wholesale of textiles

Carpet Line Direct Limited
Firgate Limited
Gro-Group Holdings Limited
Gro-Group International Limited
View Logistics Limited
Whitestone Weavers Limited

46420 Wholesale of clothing and footwear

Barbour (Europe) Limited
Bebe Clothing (UK) Limited
Bebe Group Limited
Roland Burgess Limited
Nigel Cabourn Marketing Limited
Chan Commercial Ltd
The Clinkard Group Limited
Durham Footwear Distributors Limited
Inoveight Limited
Louietex Ltd
MBC Summit Holdings Limited
Nusafe Europe Limited
Alan Ransome Sporting Goods Group Limited
Rohni's International Limited
George Rye & Sons Limited
Michael Sehgal & Sons Limited
W & M Wholesale Limited

46439 Wholesale of radio, television goods & electrical household appliances (other than records, tapes, CDs)

The British Electrical & Manufacturing Company Limited
R. Dinning Limited
Jerry Fried & Co Limited
Harbro Electrical Wholesale Limited
Park Electrical Distributors Limited

46440 Wholesale of china and glassware and cleaning materials

Goodfellow & Goodfellow Ltd.
Innerglass Limited

46450 Wholesale of perfume and cosmetics

Additional Lengths Ltd
Create Images Ion Limited
Graham Hair and Beauty Limited
Millennium Nails Limited
Pern Consumer Products Limited
Ray & Company (Hairdressers Sundries Men) Limited
Winning Lines Limited

46460 Wholesale of pharmaceutical goods

Derma UK Limited
Doncaster Pharmaceuticals Group Limited
Doncaster Pharmaceuticals Limited
Durham Pharmaceuticals Limited
Fagron UK Ltd
Farah Chemists Limited
Fast Track Sourcing Limited
Islestone Limited
Rand Rocket Limited
Testerworld Limited
U L Medicines Limited

46470 Wholesale of furniture, carpets and lighting equipment

Baker Furniture Limited
Connection Flooring Limited
Createcity Limited
Dallas Carpets Limited
Kaydian Design Limited
Thomas Witter Carpets Limited

46491 Wholesale of musical instruments

Geneva Brasswind Limited

46499 Wholesale of household goods (other than musical instruments) n.e.c

A. & A. Carpets Limited
Fisher Outdoor Leisure Holdings Limited
Gro-Group Holdings Limited
Gro-Group International Limited
The Hill Cross Organisation Limited
Hill Giftware Limited
Homeware Essentials Limited
Kindred Living Limited
Mayborn (UK) Limited
PWS Distributors Limited
Park Electrical Distributors Limited
Purity Global Limited

46510 Wholesale of computers, computer peripheral equipment and software

Canford Audio PLC

46520 Wholesale of electronic and telecommunications equipment and parts

Canford Audio PLC
Parmley Graham Limited
Power Wholesale Limited
SPS Electrical Wholesalers Limited
Secon Solar Limited
TVG Telematics Ltd
Teesside Industrial Controls Limited
Total Electrical Solutions UK Limited

46610 Wholesale of agricultural machinery, equipment and supplies

Ben Burgess & Co Limited
Con Mech Group Limited
Newquip Limited
Orange Plant Limited
J.G. Paxton and Sons Limited
C G Robinson Limited
Brian Robinson Machinery Limited
TS Plant Sales (NE) Ltd.
Sam Turner and Sons Limited
Wox Agri Services Ltd

46620 Wholesale of machine tools

Blue Diamond Machine Tools Limited
EWM Hightec Welding UK Limited
Fairfield Industries Limited
Izumi Products UK Limited
Quality Tooling (North East) Limited

46630 Wholesale of mining, construction and civil engineering machinery

Fairfield Industries Limited
Herrenknecht International Limited
Kevin Richardson Plantmasteruk Ltd

46650 Wholesale of office furniture

Albany Office Equipment (Wholesale) Limited
Carson Office Environments Limited

46660 Wholesale of other office machinery and equipment

MIW Office Solutions Limited
United Carlton Office Systems Limited

46690 Wholesale of other machinery and equipment

Air Filters Limited
CCG Cable Terminations Limited
Container Sales (UK) Limited
Daikin Applied (UK) Limited
Draeger Safety UK Ltd
Eagle Welding & Engineering Supplies Limited
Edmi Europe Limited
GSLF Engineering Limited
Gecomac Limited
H T Process Control Ltd
Husqvarna UK Limited
L.D.H. Plant Limited
Newarc (Aberdeen) Limited
Novatech (UK) Limited
Otolift Stairlifts Limited
Peacocks (Surgical and Medical Equipment) Limited
Pegasus Material Handling Ltd
Perry Process Equipment Limited
Power Topco Limited
Stanners Equipment Limited
Triple Air-Technology Ltd
Trotec Laser Limited

46711 Wholesale of petroleum and petroleum products

Eagle Road Services Limited
Sabic Innovative Plastics Limited

46719 Wholesale of other fuels and related products

Off Shore Fuels Limited
Oil NRG Ltd

46720 Wholesale of metals and metal ores

Aluminium (Bar & Sheet) Limited
Carter Steel Limited
Chainbridge Steel (North East) Ltd
Chainbridge Steel Group Limited
Clarkes of Stillington Plate & Profiles Limited
Corbitts Limited
Hargreaves (UK) Services Limited
Holme Dodsworth (Est.1879) Limited
Holme Dodsworth (Non-Ferrous) Limited
Holme Dodsworth Metals Limited
J.T.P. (Non-Ferrous Stockholders) Limited
Manchester Alloys and Metals Limited
N.T. Steel Services Ltd
Phoenix Steel Limited
Reynolds & Law (Stainless) Limited
W.G.R. (Steels) Limited

46730 Wholesale of wood, construction materials and sanitary equipment

Ashley Timber Limited
James Burrell Limited
CMC North East Ltd
Crossling Limited
Decor Panel Limited
F.M. Steelstock Limited
Norseal Limited
North Yorkshire Timber Company Limited
Northern Lights Energy Limited
Polyfoam XPS Limited
Quay Timber Ltd
South Tyne Building Supplies Limited
Timberway Limited
Tyne Insulation Supplies Limited
UK Bathrooms Limited
Wack Wholesale (Building Supplies) Ltd

46740 Wholesale of hardware, plumbing and heating equipment and supplies

ATF Supplies Limited
Ability Supplies UK Limited
Crossling Limited
Decor Cladding Centre Ltd
J.T.Dove,Limited
Flame Heating Spares Limited
Go Geothermal Ltd
Heating Trade Supplies Group Limited
Heating World of Spares Limited
M B Distribution (Cleveland) Limited
Metalpoint Limited
Optimus Global Limited
Thomas Potter Limited
Superlec Electrical Distributors Limited
Total Bolt Solutions Limited
Tyne Valves Limited
Wack Wholesale (Building Supplies) Ltd
Wearside Plumbing Supplies Limited

46750 Wholesale of chemical products

Biochemica Water Limited
Devine Chemicals Limited
Fast Track Sourcing Limited
Liquiform Limited
Mineral & Chemical Services Ltd
Molekula Limited
NST Welding (UK) Limited
Palmer (U.K.) Limited
Safechem Limited
Tan International Limited
V.H. Bio Limited

46760 Wholesale of other intermediate products

Adaptive Trading Limited
Amitex LED Lighting Company Limited
Bede Group Limited
Cast Tec Limited
Central Plant (Northern) Limited
Cleveland Cable Company Limited
D.P. Fasteners Limited
Samuel Grant (North East) Limited
International Plastic Systems Limited
Lezora Limited
Chas. Long & Son (Aggregates) Limited
Mineral & Chemical Services Ltd
Superlec Electrical Distributors Limited
UK Industrial Tapes Limited
Westline Distributors Limited

46770 Wholesale of waste and scrap

J Denham Metals Ltd
Jebb Metals (Newcastle) Ltd
Pout and Foster Limited
T.J.Thomson & Son Limited
Trading North East Limited

47110 Retail sale in non-specialised stores with food, beverages or tobacco predominating

Sir John Fitzgerald,Limited
Lewis & Cooper Limited
Mazhar Ltd
SRJ Energy Ltd
Stevenson of Oxbridge Limited

47190 Other retail sale in non-specialised stores

Barkers (Northallerton) Limited
Blaydon UK Limited
R Campbell & Sons Limited
Con Mech Group Limited
Durham Markets Company Limited
The Feel Good Group Limited
Fenwick,Limited
Gillen's Limited
Gray & Son Robe Makers (Durham) Ltd
Ikonica Furniture Ltd
Junsterik Ltd
Plasterpiece Limited
G. Rutherford & Co. Limited
Savona Imports Limited
Standing Stone Drawing Office Supplies Limited
Tyne Tees Ceramics Limited
Ken Warne Limited
J. & J. Whittaker (Chemist) Limited
Zenith Jewellery and Accessories UK Limited

47210 Retail sale of fruit and vegetables in specialised stores

Hutchinsons Fruit & Veg Limited
Hutchinsons Fruit&Veg (Gateshead) Limited
JH Laidler & Son Limited
Modaim Limited

47220 Retail sale of meat and meat products in specialised stores

George Bolam (Foods) Ltd
M.I. Dickson Limited
Haswells Homer Hill Farm Shop Limited
Heck! Food Limited
B & T Kitson Limited

47240 Retail sale of bread, cakes, flour confectionery and sugar confectionery in specialised stores

Greggs PLC
Simply Sugar Ltd

47250 Retail sale of beverages in specialised stores

K.W. Reader & Sons Limited

47260 Retail sale of tobacco products in specialised stores

Eciggy UK Limited

47290 Other retail sale of food in specialised stores

Chester Le Street DP Limited
Consett DP Limited
Cross Lanes Organic Farm Limited
Dhillons Investment Properties Limited
Gills Fry Fry Limited
Greencroft Milk Supplies Limited
Middlesbrough DP Ltd
Modaim Limited
Oldham & Openshaw DP Limited
Wing Hong & Company Limited

47300 Retail sale of automotive fuel in specialised stores

Avor Garages (North East) Limited
Bewicke Service Station Limited
Catterick Service Station Ltd.
Cliff House Service Station Ltd
E L Denney & Son Limited
Exelby Services Limited
Houston Commercial Ltd
Kenworth Limited
Lion Garage (Bedlington) Limited
G.Nicholson (Engineers) Limited
Park Lane Garages (Teeside) Limited
Ron Perry & Son Limited
SRJ Energy Ltd
Stevenson of Oxbridge Limited

47410 Retail sale of computers, peripheral units and software in specialised stores

Invate Limited
Symetri Limited
Total Business Computers Ltd

47421 Retail sale of mobile telephones

Chrome PSG Limited
Cygnet Total Communications Limited
Total Communications and Security Limited

47429 Retail sale of telecommunications equipment other than mobile telephones

Sitelink Communications Limited

47510 Retail sale of textiles in specialised stores

Baileys Blinds Limited
Cotterhill Limited
Tallantyre Wallcoverings Limited

47520 Retail sale of hardware, paints and glass in specialised stores

Aycliffe Decorative Supplies Limited
Ebsonlodge Limited
HSA DIY Limited
Hardware Supply Company (Middlesbrough) Limited
JTM Plumbing Limited
F.E.Maughan Limited
Maxwells (Sunderland) Limited
Quay Timber Ltd
Tallantyre Wallcoverings Limited
Tiles Porcelain Limited
Alan Wadkins Limited

47530 Retail sale of carpets, rugs, wall and floor coverings in specialised stores

Balmoral Interiors Limited
Dickinson Brothers Limited
FM Trading (GB) Limited
Parlour Product Holding Limited
Parlour Product Topco Limited
A. Share & Sons Limited

47540 Retail sale of electrical household appliances in specialised stores

Adept Ecommerce Ltd
Dutchwest Distribution Limited
Andrew James UK Ltd
Michael O'Connor (Carpets) Limited
SDY Limited
Thompson Bros (South Shields) Limited

47591 Retail sale of musical instruments and scores

Geneva Brasswind Limited
J.G. Windows Limited

47599 Retail of furniture, lighting, and similar (not musical instruments or scores) in specialised store

Abri Trading Limited
At Home Furnishings Outlet Limited
Barker & Stonehouse Limited
Bench Marque (GBR) Limited
Bishop's Beds Ltd
Court Homemakers Limited
Delcor Ltd.
Exclusive Bedrooms North East Limited
Harbro Electrical Wholesale Limited
Hardware Supply Company (Middlesbrough) Limited
Homes Direct 365 Limited
Kebrico Limited
Leader Online Limited
Monomarket Limited
Mowlem and Company (London) Limited
Parlour Product Holding Limited
Parlour Product Topco Limited
A. Share & Sons Limited
Whickham Salerooms Limited
Zigi Enterprises Limited

47610 Retail sale of books in specialised stores

Barter Books Limited

47640 Retail sale of sports goods, fishing gear, camping goods, boats and bicycles

Ebor Leisure World Limited
Gilsan Sports Limited
Tyneside Leisure World Limited
Ultralight Outdoor Gear Limited
W & M Wholesale Limited
Westbrook Cycles Limited

47650 Retail sale of games and toys in specialised stores

Grainger Games (Holdings) Limited

47710 Retail sale of clothing in specialised stores

A & K Fashions Limited
Airport Retail UK Limited
Aphrodite Clothing Limited
Ashworth and Parker Limited
Barbour (Europe) Limited
Ebor Leisure World Limited
Gilsan Sports Limited
Jules B Limited
Project Bridal Designer Outlet Limited
Psyche Limited
Tyneside Leisure World Limited
Workwear Express Limited

47721 Retail sale of footwear in specialised stores

Barbour (Europe) Limited
The Clinkard Group Limited
Durham Footwear Distributors Limited
John Eliot (Footwear) Limited
Jules B Limited

47722 Retail sale of leather goods in specialised stores

Barbour (Europe) Limited
Proto (GB) Ltd

47730 Dispensing chemist in specialised stores

Alrahi & Singh Limited
Avenue Pharmacy (Sunderland) Limited
Beacon View Pharmacy Limited
Britton & Robson Limited
M.D. & A.G. Burdon Ltd
Chemcare Limited
Clemitsons Limited
Clevechem Limited
Coopers Chemist Gt.Ayton Limited
Coopers Chemist Marske Limited
Coopers Chemist Redcar Limited
ME Cronin Ltd
J.M.& W.Darling Limited
J. Dinning (Woodlands) Limited
T.S.C. Dobbin Limited
Empharm (North East) Limited
Fairman Chemists Limited
Flagg Court Pharmacy Limited
Fursewood Limited
Gaelpharm Ltd
Gill & Schofield Pharmaceutical Chemists Limited
N & R Gupta Limited
Hancock & Ainsley Limited
Hyperdrug Pharmaceuticals Ltd
Intrahealth Pharmacy Limited
J S Locum Services Limited
John Low Limited
Lydon Pharmacy Group Ltd.
G Mayes Ltd
Medicentre (Newcastle) Limited
Medichem Limited
Peter Milburn Chemist Limited
Mills Pharmacies Limited
P. S. Pendergood Limited
Phillips Chemists Limited
Robert and Roberts Limited
Rockliffe Court Healthcare Limited
Scott-Chem Limited
Seaton Healthcare Limited
W. Smith (Durham) Limited
Spinks The Chemists Limited
MJ & A Taylor Limited
Wellway Pharmacy Limited
G. Whitfield Limited
M.Whitfield Limited
J. & J. Whittaker (Chemist) Limited
R G Young Pharmacy Ltd

47749 Retail sale of medical and orthopaedic goods in specialised stores (not incl. hearing aids) n.e.c.

Parnell Products Ltd
Peacocks Medical Group Limited

47760 Retail sale of flowers, plants, seeds, fertilizers, pet animals and pet food in specialised stores

Armstrong Richardson & Co.Limited
Bon-Bloemen Ltd
Brambledown Contracts Group Limited
Cherry Hill Garden & Landscape Centre Ltd
Cleveland Country Store Limited
Con Mech Group Limited
Cowell's Garden Centre Limited
Epro (Wholesale) Limited
Lanchester Garden Centre Limited
Rootwise Limited

47770 Retail sale of watches and jewellery in specialised stores

Alchemy Design & Works Limited
Argentaurum Limited
Arodnap Limited
Bramwells Retail Limited
Galleria Retail Limited
Goldmart Limited
Skyline Retail Limited
David Summerfield Limited

47781 Retail sale in commercial art galleries

Norman Cornish Limited

47789 Other retail sale of new goods in specialised stores (not commercial art galleries and opticians)

T & G Allan Holdings Limited
Care-Ability Healthcare Limited
Clay's Garden Centre Ltd.
E L Denney & Son Limited
Durham Cathedral Trading Limited
Homecare Heating Supplies Teesside Limited
Homefair Blinds (U.K.) Limited
L. D. Mountain Centre Limited
G.W.Leader Limited
M. & S. Distributors Limited
Mlgo Limited
Newcastle Arts Centre Limited
Newcastle Jewellers Ltd.
PJA Distribution Limited
The Pen Shop Limited
Ropers Caravan World (Catterick) Limited
Ropers Leisure Limited
SS Healthfoods Limited
Taprich Limited
United British Caravans Limited

47799 Retail sale of other second-hand goods in stores (not incl. antiques)

Corbitts Limited
Reality Enterprise Ltd
Ropers Caravan World (Catterick) Limited
Ropers Leisure Limited

47810 Retail sale via stalls and markets of food, beverages and tobacco products

J.& H.B.Ibbitson (Sunderland) Limited

47890 Retail sale via stalls and markets of other goods

J.J. Blair & Sons Limited
R.H. Orange & Son Limited

47910 Retail sale via mail order houses or via Internet

4 Cool Technology Limited
Adept Professional Services Ltd
All Car Parts Limited
Armstrong Direct Limited
Ashworth and Parker Limited
Bold Bloc Design Limited
Crafter's Companion Limited
Direct Sports Limited
Ex-Pro Products Limited
Foxy Hair Extensions (NE) Ltd
I&K International Company Limited
Jewel First Limited
Jules B Limited
Modern Rugs Limited
Pea Soup Limited
Pink Boutique Limited
Riba Enterprises Ltd
SS Healthfoods Limited
Savisto Limited
Showermania Limited
Spark Etail Limited
Sty.Com Limited
Taylors Football Souvenirs Limited
Traidcraft Public Limited Company
Unwind Me Limited
Vapourlites Limited
W & M Wholesale Limited

47990 Other retail sale not in stores, stalls or markets

Advanced Productivity Group Limited
Ben Burgess & Co Limited
Colena Ltd.
Crafty Apps Limited
Decorating Direct Limited
Ecco Finishing Supplies Limited
Euro Super Abrasives Limited
Everris Limited
Franklin Steel Stockholders Ltd
Gro-Group Holdings Limited
Gro-Group International Limited
Hanover Dairies Limited
Heating Trade Supplies Group Limited
Integrated Polymer Systems (U.K.) Limited
JCM Retail Equipment Limited
Darren McCormick Jewellery Limited
National Numbers Limited
R D Consulting and Education Limited
Radecal Limited
Ringtons Limited
Simpson Fuels Limited
Town Centre Automobiles Ltd.
Xander Developments Limited

49100 Passenger rail transport, interurban

Arriva PLC
Arriva Rail North Limited
Arriva Trains Holdings Limited
Arriva UK Trains Limited
The Chiltern Railway Company Limited
Govia Thameslink Railway Limited
Grand Central Railway Company Limited
London & Birmingham Railway Limited
London & South Eastern Railway Limited
London and North Western Railway Company Limited
M40 Trains Limited
Wensleydale Railway PLC
XC Trains Limited

49200 Freight rail transport

Rail Management Services Limited
SNS Management & Solutions Limited
Weardale Railways CIC

49319 Other urban, suburban or metropolitan passenger land transport (not underground, metro or similar)

Anglian Bus Limited
Arriva Cymru Limited
Arriva Durham County Limited
Arriva Kent & Surrey Limited
Arriva Kent Thameside Limited
Arriva London North Limited
Arriva London South Limited
Arriva Merseyside Limited
Arriva Midlands Limited
Arriva Midlands North Limited
Arriva North West Limited
Arriva Northumbria Limited
Arriva PLC
Arriva The Shires Limited
Arriva Yorkshire Limited
Carousel Buses Limited
Centrebus Holdings Limited
H.C.Chambers & Son Limited
The City of Oxford Motor Services Limited
East Yorkshire Motor Services Limited
Eyms Group Limited
Go North East Limited
Go-Ahead London Rail Replacement Services Limited
Hedingham & District Omnibuses Ltd.
Konectbus Limited
London General Transport Services Limited
Phoenix Coaches (NE) Limited
Plymouth Citybus Limited
Road Link (A69) Limited
Thames Travel (Wallingford) Limited

49320 Taxi operation

Central Taxis Gateshead Ltd
Chevron Taxis Limited
Dean Taxis Limited
Hudsons 23 Limited
Juma Corporation Ltd
L A Taxis Ltd
Middlesbrough Borough Cars Limited
Noda Taxis Limited
North East Executive Limited
Station Taxis (Sunderland) Limited

49390 Other passenger land transport

Ambuline Limited
Arriva Transport Solutions Limited
Brighton & Hove Bus and Coach Company Limited
C & C Horse Transport Limited
DC Assets Limited
Durham City Coaches Limited
Garnetts Limited
Glen Valley Tours Ltd.
The Go-Ahead Group PLC
Green Mountain Travel Ltd
Jim Hughes Coaches Limited
Konectbus Limited
Lee's Coaches Limited
Longstaffs Travel Ltd
M & D Travel Limited
Network Ticketing Limited
Procters Coaches (North Yorkshire) Limited
Rothbury Motors Limited
Scarlet Band Bus and Coach Limited
Howard Snaith Limited
TGMgroup Limited
J. Thirlwell & Sons Limited
Tourmaster Travel Limited
Weardale Motor Services Limited
Yorkshire Tiger Limited

49420 Removal services

L & L Braines Limited
D. Collard Limited
E.Pearson and Sons (Teesside) Limited

50100 Sea and coastal passenger water transport

Absolute Pleasure Limited
Ocean Marine.Co.Uk Limited
Billy Shiel Farne Islands Boats Limited
Sure Wind Marine Limited

50200 Sea and coastal freight water transport

D & D Armstrong Limited
Casper Shipping Limited
FB Tankship III Limited
FB Tankship IV Limited
FC Tankship I Ltd
FC Tankship II Ltd
Felixarc Marine Limited
G.T.Gillie & Blair Limited
Logical Link Solutions Limited
PD Teesport Limited
Ryan Offshore Limited
Stadium Export Services Limited
Svitzer Marine Limited
Tees and Hartlepool Pilotage Company Limited
Vroon Shipping U.K. Ltd.
Windcrew Workboats Limited

50300 Inland passenger water transport

Just Sport (Pro Club) Ltd

51101 Scheduled passenger air transport

NIAL Services Limited
Newcastle International Airport Limited

51102 Non-scheduled passenger air transport

The Great North Air Ambulance Service
NAL Asset Management Limited
Standard Aviation Limited
Stephen Tuer Farms Ltd

51210 Freight air transport

Stadium Export Services Limited

52103 Operation of warehousing and storage facilities for land transport activities

Barrington Distribution Ltd
Containerships (UK) Ltd
Cool Retail Services Ltd
Datastor (North East) Limited
A.V.Dawson Limited
GCA Domestic Limited
Groveport Logistics Limited
Inbond Limited
International Cookware Limited
Lanchester Wine Cellars Limited
Logical Link Solutions Limited
Norsea Group (UK) Limited
Orange Box Self Storage Ltd
PD Port Services Limited
PD Teesport Limited
Plymouth Citybus Limited
Rapid Response Transport (UK) Limited
G A Smith Limited
Stiller Warehousing & Distribution Limited
Tyne Logistics Company Limited
View Logistics Limited

52213 Operation of bus and coach passenger facilities at bus and coach stations

Travelsure Coaches Limited

52219 Other service activities incidental to land transportation, n.e.c.

J.E.M Road Construction Ltd
Newcastle Park & Fly Limited
Premier Traffic Management Limited
Scott Bros. Environmental Services Limited
TT2 Limited
Tees Valley Trailers Limited
Vantec Europe Limited

52220 Service activities incidental to water transportation

GAC Netherlands Limited
G.T.Gillie & Blair Limited
PD Shipping & Inspection Services Limited
PD Teesport Limited
Svitzer Marine Limited
Teekay Marine Solutions Ltd
Transped Limited

52230 Service activities incidental to air transportation

NIAL Finance Limited
NIAL Group Limited
Samson Aviation Services Limited

52241 Cargo handling for water transport activities

Groveport Logistics Limited
Logical Link Solutions Limited
PD Port Services Limited
PD Ports Hull Limited
Redcar Bulk Terminal Limited
Seaham Harbour Dock Company

52242 Cargo handling for air transport activities

PD Shipping & Inspection Services Limited

52243 Cargo handling for land transport activities

Groveport Logistics Limited
Hutchinson Transport Limited
G A Smith Limited

52290 Other transportation support activities

Alpha Recovery Limited
Cleveland Containers Limited
Dancorr Limited
Den Hartogh Logistics Limited
G.T.Gillie & Blair Limited
Interbulk (Tankcontainers) Holdings Limited
Mann Haulage Limited
Odin Shipping Limited
Tees Licensed Foyboatmens' Association Limited
Transped Limited

53201 Licensed carriers

GFC Group Limited

53202 Unlicensed carriers

Excello Limited

55100 Hotels and similar accommodation

Ailantus Hotels Limited
Angel of Corbridge Limited
Bannatyne Hotels Limited
Beamish Hall Limited
Big Hearted Hospitality Company Limited
Boxpipe Limited
CB Inn Limited
Close House Hospitality Limited
Closegate Hotel Development (Durham) Limited
The Coach Inn Company Limited
Derwent Manor Ltd
Downs Holdings Limited
Durham Vale Developments Limited
Edgeman Limited
First Sight Estates Limited
GB Holiday Parks Limited
Gainford Hotels Limited
George Washington Golf and Country Club Limited
The Gibside Hotel Limited
Gosforth Park Hotels Limited
Greensfield Moor Development Limited
Grey Street Newcastle Ltd.
Grovekey Limited
Guisborough Hotels Limited
Headlam Leisure Limited
Helme Park Hall Limited
Hotel Operations Limited
Inn Collection Acquisitionco Limited
Kwik Corporate Lettings Limited
Lartington Hall Limited
Lindisfarne Inns (Bamburgh Castle) Limited
Lindisfarne Inns Limited
Little Haven Beach Limited
Marina Hotels Limited
Metro Inns Limited
Middleton Lodge Events Limited
Minhoco 24 Limited
Minhoco 27 Limited
Minhoco 30 Limited
Minhoco 35 Limited
Moorlands Holdings (N.E.) Limited
Movesun Limited
Mulberry Leisure Limited
Newton Hall (Northumberland) Limited
Norfolk Hotel Limited
North of England Estates Limited
Purdy Lodge Limited
Quays Hotels Limited
Ramside Estates Limited
Ramside Holdings Limited
Regent Leisure Limited
Rockliffe Hall Limited
Romaldrose Limited
S T R Enterprises Limited
SLW (Holdings) Limited
Sandman Hotel Group (UK) Limited
Sharpness Point Limited
Smokies Entertainments Limited
South Causey Limited
The Station Hotel (Newcastle) Limited
Sunderland FC Hotels Limited
Sunderland Hotels Limited
Tavistock Hospitality Limited
Tong Ltd
Trout Hotels (Cumbria) Limited
Trumark Properties Limited
Whitworth Hall Developments Limited
Yarm View Limited

55201 Holiday centres and villages

Cotterhill Limited
Dunham Leisure Limited
Hawthorn Parks Limited
Manor Park Holiday Park Limited
Southview Leisure Park Limited
Total Oynx Limited

55202 Youth hostels

Delta - North Consett Limited

55209 Other holiday and other collective accommodation

Fairfield House Limited
Ford Castle Adventure Ltd
GB Holiday Parks Limited
Holiday at Home Limited
Leisure Works (Yorkshire) Limited
MAV Investments Limited
Newton Hall (Northumberland) Limited
Northumberland Luxury Log Cabins Limited
Swale View Caravan Sales Limited
Tau Properties Limited
Wainstones Estates Limited
Woodside Park Estates Limited

55300 Recreational vehicle parks, trailer parks and camping grounds

Akebar Park Leisure Limited
Beadnell Links Limited
Bellingham Camping Limited
Bradley Mill Caravan Site Limited
Britton Leisure Limited
Bronte Caravan Park Limited
Callaly Leisure Limited
Felmoor Park Limited
GB Holiday Parks Limited
Haswells Homer Hill Farm Shop Limited
Legacy Resorts Limited
Mountgate Caravans Limited
Newhall Caravan Park Limited
Northumbrian Leisure Limited
Park Resorts Limited
Parkdean Caravan Parks Limited
Parkdean Holiday Parks Limited
South Lakeland Parks Limited
Upperbay Limited
Vauxhall Holiday Park Limited
E.B. & C.A. Welsh Limited
Wemyss Bay Caravan Park Limited
Weststar Holidays Limited
Willowbank Holiday Park Limited

55900 Other accommodation

Alexage Limited
Ascot Place Properties Limited
Jack Brodie (Wholesale) Limited
Burradon Farm Houses and Cottages Limited
Coatham House
The Cyrenians Ltd
DFI Properties Limited
Dartford Student Living Limited
R & R Edwards and Sons Limited
HGC Properties Limited
Haven (Tyneside) Ltd.
Key Homes (GB) Limited
Lake District Leisure Pursuits Limited
Leazes Homes Limited
Leven Estates Ltd
Maceachern HCH Ltd
Malhotra Property Limited
North Eastern Y.W.C.A.Trustees Limited
Oasis Aquila Housing Ltd
Oceana Business Park Limited
Park Lets Limited
Stanfam Properties Limited
Student Accommodation (UK) Limited
Swaledale Homes Limited
Urban Lifestyle Limited
Wearside Accommodation Services Limited
Woodydog Limited

56101 Licenced restaurants

40/46 The Side Newcastle Limited
ATFC Limited
Angel of Corbridge Limited
Arcwhiz 2000 Limited
BBL NE Limited
Bon Bon Leisure Limited
CLX Ltd
Cafe Twentyone Newcastle Limited
Colmans Caterers Limited
Cook & Barker Inn Limited
Endeavour Northern Limited
FLC Durham Limited
Guisborough Hotels Limited
Hop Vietnamese Limited
J3S Ltd
Jesmond Holdings Limited
Jesmond Leisure Limited
Jetsun Ltd
Kymel Trading Limited
Lanchester Garden Centre Limited
M J M Leisure Limited
Marshall Inns Limited
Mio Angelo Limited
NZR Limited
The New Pavilion Limited
Northumberland Castle and Country Lodgings Ltd
Premier Leisure Limited
Romano's Limited
S T R Enterprises Limited
SGG Property Developments Limited
Shark Club (UK) Limited
St. Camillus Care Group Ltd
Tavistock Hospitality Limited
Trumark Properties Limited
The Waterside Palace Restaurant Co Ltd

56102 Unlicenced restaurants and cafes

W. Liddy & Company Limited
Nucleus (GB) Limited
Nudo Sushi Box Ltd
Red & Racz Ltd
Malcolm Tempest Limited
The White Hart Hawes Limited

56103 Take-away food shops and mobile food stands

Coastline Fish and Chip Restaurant Limited
Dulai Enterprises Limited
Eat Fresh Investments Limited
Ops Catering Limited
Select Prime Sites UK Ltd
TBT Catering Limited

56210 Event catering activities

The Assembly Rooms (Newcastle) Limited
Creative Management Services Limited
International Centre for Life (Property) Limited
Popcorn Limited

56290 Other food services

Card Trix [Greetings] Limited
Country Harvest Frozen Foods Limited
EJM Engineered Systems Limited
Eden Farm Limited
Fullwell Mill Limited
J.R. Holland (Food Services) Limited
Lowrie Foods Limited
P&A Food Management Services Limited
Quality Food Service Limited

56301 Licenced clubs

Alta Vista Global Limited
Armstrong Hall Social Club Ltd
G & G Leisure Limited
Maymask (202) Limited
Tup Tup Palace Limited

56302 Public houses and bars

Angel of Corbridge Limited
Apartment 1 Limited
Asset Manager Solutions Limited
Beyond Leisure Limited
Chameleon Bar & Dining Limited
Cook & Barker Inn Limited
Drinx Leisure Limited
Durham Vale Developments Limited
Easteye Limited
Ebony Leisure Limited
Endeavour Northern Limited
The Head of Steam Limited
Hyena (Northern) Limited
Jesmond Court Limited
O Kay Automatics Limited
Keeping Inn Limited
Lindisfarne Inns (Bamburgh Castle) Limited
M J M Leisure Limited
Manners (Newcastle) Limited
Minhoco 12 Limited
Mistell Limited
Moores Leisure (Teesside) Limited
Newcastle upon Tyne World Headquarters Limited
Northumberland Castle and Country Lodgings Ltd
Park Lane NE Ltd
Players Bars Investments Limited
Rainton Meadows Arena Limited
S T R Enterprises Limited
Tavistock Hospitality Limited
Theatre Leisure Limited
Tripnovel Limited
Vaulkhard Leisure Limited
YOLO (Newcastle) Limited

58110 Book publishing

Cambridge Scholars Publishing Ltd
Timec 1306 Limited

58142 Publishing of consumer and business journals and periodicals

Alfol Limited
I2media Limited

58190 Other publishing activities

Alfol Limited
Pantheon Macroeconomics Ltd.
Paper Dove Company Limited
Plimsoll Publishing Limited

58210 Publishing of computer games

Filematch Limited
I6media Ltd

58290 Other software publishing

Aceviral.Com Ltd
Engica Technology Systems International Limited
For Skills Limited
Foster Findlay Associates Limited
Palringo Limited
Riba Enterprises Ltd
Sage (UK) Ltd
Sage Online Holdings Limited
Taopix Limited

59111 Motion picture production activities

Superkrush Films Limited

59112 Video production activities

Re:Production Limited

59113 Television programme production activities

Barking Dog (UK) Limited
Gary Beadle Promotions Limited
Headline Pictures (Peter Pan) Limited
Nova Marketing Consultancy Limited

59140 Motion picture projection activities

Alnwick District Playhouse Trust
Tyneside Cinema

59200 Sound recording and music publishing activities

Pea Soup Limited

60200 Television programming and broadcasting activities

JDE Management Limited

61100 Wired telecommunications activities

Advantex Network Solutions Limited
KBR I.T. and Networking Solutions Limited
Odyssey Systems Limited

61200 Wireless telecommunications activities

Activ Technology Limited
Apex Radio Systems Limited
Cellular Solutions (North East) Ltd.
Cellular Solutions Holdings Limited
E.E.M.I.T.S. Communications Limited
Impulsepay Ltd
KBR I.T. and Networking Solutions Limited
Universal Systems Solutions (Security) Limited

61300 Satellite telecommunications activities

And Group Limited
Broadband Satellite Services Limited
KBR I.T. and Networking Solutions Limited
MRM Electrical Solutions Limited
Satcom Global Aura Limited

61900 Other telecommunications activities

Communicate Technology PLC
Main-Tel (NE) Limited
Map Group (UK) Limited
N.T.E. Holdings Limited
N.T.E. Limited
Nice Network Ltd
Pebbletree Ltd
Russell Network Solutions Limited
Russell Telecom Limited

62011 Ready-made interactive leisure and entertainment software development

Double Eleven Limited
The Indie Stone Ltd
Think Limited
Ubisoft Reflections Limited

62012 Business and domestic software development

Actdesign (UK) Ltd
Adlink Technology Limited
Arjuna Technologies Limited
Casmaco Limited
Clarity Informatics Limited
Clover Controls Limited
Enigma Interactive Limited
For Skills Limited
Grid Smarter Cities Ltd
Hedgehog Lab Limited
Indigo Software Group Limited
Indigo Software Limited
Mandata (Holdings) Limited
Nicander Limited
Orchard Information Systems Limited
Orchidsoft Limited
P & I Design Limited
Payapps.Com (UK) Ltd
Salecycle Limited
Silverlink Software Limited
Socialrel8 Ltd
Tascomp Limited
Transend Solutions Limited
Tysoft Software Ltd
Ultramap Limited
Viewpoint Construction Software Ltd
Visualsoft Limited
Waterstons Limited
Zubedo Limited

62020 Information technology consultancy activities

Amtech Automated Micro Technology Limited
Askaris Information Technology Limited
Aspire Technology Solutions Ltd
Beaumont Colson Ltd.
Cartridge Tech Limited
Casmaco Limited
Cleardata UK Limited
Cleveland Systems Engineering Limited
Exis Technologies Limited
Hedgehog Lab Limited
ITC Service Limited
Increase Computers Limited
Industrial Technology Systems Limited
MC Ware IT Solutions Limited
Nonlinear Technologies Limited
Perfect Image Limited
Praesto Consulting UK Ltd
Premiertec Consulting Limited
Razorblue Ltd
Sage (UK) Ltd
Sage Online Holdings Limited
Sage Pay (GB) Limited
Sage Pay Europe Limited
Sagesoft
Sapphire Technologies Limited
Specialist IT Services Group Limited
Symetri Limited
Technology Services Group Limited
Think Limited
Visualsoft Holdings Limited
Visualsoft Limited
Waterstons Limited

62030 Computer facilities management activities

Atlas Cloud Limited
Waterstons Limited

62090 Other information technology service activities

Aceda Limited
Advantex Network Solutions Limited
Beyond360 Limited
Biostore Limited
Broadmedia Holdings Limited
Casmaco Limited
Edynamix Global Ltd
Edynamix UK Ltd
Grove Information Systems Limited
I.T. Professional Services Limited
ITC Service Limited
Sir Joseph Isherwood Limited
KBR I.T. and Networking Solutions Limited
Leighton Corporation Limited
Lexiauk Limited
Lindy Electronics Limited
Mandata (Management and Data Services) Ltd
Moltin Ltd
My Firms App Limited
Newcastle Systems Management Limited
Niche Technology UK Limited
Orchidsoft Limited
Pea Soup Limited
Performance Horizon Group Limited
Print Demon Systems Limited
Red Oak Ltd
Sage People Limited
Shout Digital Limited
Swiftpage International Limited
Tombola Limited
United Carlton Digital Solutions Limited
Visualsoft Limited
Waterstons Limited
Zerolight Limited
Zynk Software Limited

63110 Data processing, hosting and related activities

Colewood Internet Ltd
Datatrial Limited
Elanders Ltd
Phusion IM Limited
Ultramap Limited

63120 Web portals

Casmaco Limited
Lenton Marketing Limited
Ultramap Limited

63990 Other information service activities n.e.c.

Airowsafe Limited
Business Data Partners Limited
Citizens Advice Sunderland
Durham County Carers Support
The Five Lamps Organisation
Mediaworks UK Limited
Middlesbrough Voluntary Development Agency
My Sister's Place
Propharma Group MIS Holdings Limited
Propharma Group MIS Limited
Prudhoe Community Partnership
Riba Enterprises Ltd
Ultramap Limited

64110 Central banking

Wirecard Card Solutions Limited

64191 Banks

00741078 Limited
Atom Bank PLC
Virgin Money PLC

64201 Activities of agricultural holding companies

David Coates Agronomy Limited

64202 Activities of production holding companies

AKV Group Ltd
AVG Holdings (Cleveland) Limited
Clifton Holdings (North East) Limited
Connor Group Limited
Froneri Limited
Froneri South Africa Holdings Limited
GSH 2018 Limited
Genesis Brands Limited
Global Decontamination Solutions Limited
Impress North East (Holdings) Limited
New R & R Ice Cream Limited
Peratech Holdco Ltd
Phoenix Steel Holdings Limited
R&R PIK Limited
Renolit (U.K.) Limited
Riviera Acquisitions Limited
Riviera Topco Limited
Ruby Acquisitions Limited
Sage Holding Company Limited
Sundram International Limited
Thomas Swan Holdings Limited
Henry Williams Group Limited

64203 Activities of construction holding companies

Advent Development Holdings Ltd
Blue Aardvark Holdings Limited
John N Dunn Holdings Limited
F & I Holdings Ltd
Hawkpost Limited
Millhouse Group Holdings Limited
Newroc Ltd
Paramount Home Improvements (U.K.) Limited
S&A Fabrications (Holdings) Limited
Vestbrown (Esh) Limited

64204 Activities of distribution holding companies

Converse Pharma Limited
GNS Midco 1 Limited
GNS Midco 2 Limited
GNS Treasury Limited
Global Navigation Solutions Holdings Limited
M Rugs Limited

64205 Activities of financial services holding companies

ACS Invest UK Limited
Internet Insurance (Holdings) Limited
Project Tulip Topco Limited
Ramsdens Holdings PLC
Sage Treasury Company Limited

64301 Activities of investment trusts

Dissington Investments Limited
The North East Regional Investment Fund Partner Limited
Turnbull Family Investments Limited
VHV Investments UK Limited

64302 Activities of unit trusts

Virgin Money Unit Trust Managers Limited

64303 Activities of venture and development capital companies

St James' Central Investments Limited
Wainstones Investments Limited

64304 Activities of open-ended investment companies

Bede Investments Limited
Claire Errington Limited
MCQ Investments Limited
McCallum Currie Limited
Milbank Investments Ltd
RACZ Group Ltd

64306 Activities of real estate investment trusts

DFI Properties Limited
Smart Real Estate Limited

64910 Financial leasing

Advanced Vehicle Leasing (Stockton) Limited
FB Shipping Limited
FC Shipping Limited

64922 Activities of mortgage finance companies

Armstrong Nationwide Ltd.
Inveniam Home Loans Limited
Loanchoice Limited
SRSS Ltd

64929 Other credit granting n.e.c.

Carraway Finance Ltd
Dane Finance Limited
Gentoo Genie Limited
High Street Commercial Finance Limited
J.E. Laidler (North East) Limited
Lucite International Finco Limited
Oldgate Finance Limited
SRSS Ltd
Student Loans Company Limited

64991 Security dealing on own account

Cornucopia Investments Limited
Prospero Growth Limited
R D Consulting and Education Limited
Zenith Growth Limited

64992 Factoring

McCaffery Financial Limited

64999 Financial intermediation not elsewhere classified

ACS Invest UK Limited
Absolute Medicals Limited
Allay Redress Ltd.
Anglo Scottish Asset Finance Limited
Argent Wealth Limited
Avendus Capital (UK) Private Limited
Bowes Wealth Management Limited
Bridging Funding Limited
DHD Wealth Management Ltd
Emerchantpay Limited
Fairstone Financial Management Limited
Fairstone Group Limited
First Complete Limited
Grainger Finance (Tricomm) Limited
Grainger Finance Company Limited
Hase Osborne Asset Management Limited
The High Street GRP Contact Centre Limited
William Leech (Investments) Limited
William Leech Foundation Limited (The)
Bob Little & Co Limited
Lowes Financial Management Limited
The Minel Group Ltd.
Newcastle Financial Advisers Limited
Nielsen,Andersen & Company Limited
North Lodge Farming Limited
Northeastern Finance Limited
Northern 2 VCT PLC
Northern 3 VCT PLC
Northern Electric Finance PLC
Northern Transport Finance Limited
Northern Venture Trust PLC
Northstar Ventures Limited
Positive Solutions (Financial Services) Ltd.
Ramsdens Financial Limited
Real Time Claims Limited
Real Time Money Ltd.
Red House Investments Limited
Sage Brazilian Investment One Limited
Sage Brazilian Investment Two Limited
Sage Far East Investments Limited
Sage Payments (UK) Ltd.
Think Synergy Limited
Garth Thompson Wealth Management Limited
Virgin Money Personal Financial Service Limited
Virgin Money Unit Trust Managers Limited
Warren Court Limited

65110 Life insurance

Lycetts Financial Services Limited
Sterling Trust Professional (North East) Limited
Virgin Money Personal Financial Service Limited

65120 Non-life insurance

B.T.I.C. Limited
Biss Underwriting Limited
Collingwood Insurance Services (U.K.) Limited
Elliott Westland Insurance Brokers Limited
Gralenno Limited
Internet Insurance Services UK Ltd
Mechanical Breakdown and General Insurance Services Limited
North of England Protecting and Indemnity Association Limited (The)
Sterling Trust Professional (North East) Limited
Sunderland Marine Insurance Company Limited
Todd and Cue Limited
Transcare Solutions Limited
Van Mildert Landlord and Tenant Protection Limited
Virgin Money Personal Financial Service Limited

65201 Life reinsurance

Lycetts Financial Services Limited

65202 Non-life reinsurance

Internet Insurance Services UK Ltd

65300 Pension funding

Sterling Trust Professional (North East) Limited

66110 Administration of financial markets

Zimb Johnson Bespoke Financial Planning Limited

66120 Security and commodity contracts dealing activities

Exponential Derivatives Limited

66190 Activities auxiliary to financial intermediation n.e.c.

Arc Finance Group Limited
Bors Advisory Limited
Gale and Phillipson Investment Services Ltd

66210 Risk and damage evaluation

Cleveland Fire Brigade Risk Management Services C.I.C.

66220 Activities of insurance agents and brokers

Castle Insurance Services (North East) Ltd
Collingwood Insurance Services (U.K.) Limited
Henry F. Dodds Limited
Erimus Holdings Teesside Limited
Farmers & Mercantile Insurance Brokers Limited
Justships Ltd
Lycett, Browne-Swinburne & Douglass Limited
Tait Walker Financial Services Limited
Teesside Insurance Consultants Limited
UK Warranty Limited

66290 Other activities auxiliary to insurance and pension funding

Allay (UK) Ltd.
Collingwood Business Solutions Limited
Darras Consulting Limited
Horatio Holdings Limited
Justships Ltd
Lycetts Financial Services Limited
North East Actuarial Services Limited
Technical Investment Solutions Ltd

66300 Fund management activities

ACS Invest UK Limited
Growth Capital Ventures Limited
North East Finance (Holdco) Limited
North East Finance (Subco) Limited
Portland Investments (AM) Limited
Sage Wealth Management Limited

68201 Renting and operating of Housing Association real estate

21st Century Style Limited
Argyle Square Properties Limited
Budget Workspace Limited
C.C. Property Management Limited
CML Property Solutions Limited
Calibre Properties Limited
Clavering Management Limited
Cleveland Housing Trust Limited
J.T. Clough & Son Limited
Community Estates UK Limited
Emirates Ltd
Fox House Ltd
Greenbale Ltd
Keelman Homes Limited
Leader Property Limited
M.M. Knitwear (1982) Limited
Melford Contracts Limited
The Middlesbrough Empire Limited
Ouseburn Trust
PD Ports Properties Limited
Pauls Property Investment Limited
Pondbank Ltd
Rees Turnbull Limited
Ronsbrook Services Limited
Silver Street (Durham) Properties Limited
South Tyneside Housing Ventures Trust Limited
Student Accommodation Services Limited
Sunderland Accommodation Services Limited
TCUK Homes Limited
Teesside Estates Limited
Winder House Developments Limited
Xtravagant Limited
Your Homes Newcastle Limited

68202 Letting and operating of conference and exhibition centres

Crossco (281) Limited
Propertees Ltd

68310 Real estate agencies

The Agents Property Auction Limited
Arcada Trading Limited
Bolel Ltd
Andrew Craig Limited
DH Dowen Limited
IAM-Sold Ltd
Jesres (Property Lets) Co. Limited
Robin Jessop Holdings Limited
Juma Corporation Ltd
Lofthouse and Partners Limited
Sarah Mains Residential Limited
Migdal Developments (UK) Ltd
Next2buy Limited
Northumbria Coast and Country Cottages Limited
Oaks Properties Limited
Keith Pattinson Limited
Robinsons Durham Limited
Robinsons Tees Valley Ltd
Mike Rogerson Estate Agents Limited
Sanderson Young Ltd
Chris Stonock Limited
Youngs RPS Limited
Your-Move.co.uk Limited

68320 Management of real estate on a fee or contract basis

AAA Property (North East) Limited
AEDT Operations Limited
Adavo Ltd
Align Property Partners Limited
Alpha Developments (Bradford2) Ltd
Athenaeum Developments Limited
Barrasford Park Limited
Bridgewater (Home Reversions Number 1) Limited
Burnell Properties Limited
Campbell Properties Limited
Geo.A.Carter Limited
Cavendish (Northern) Property Developments Limited
Clifton Property Investments Limited
Coast & Country Connections Ltd.
James Cook Discovery Ltd
Cordrow Limited
Covion Limited
Cranbourne Estates Limited
DSONS Limited
Forte Freehold Management Limited
Forum Centrespace Limited
G.I. Fox Limited
The Gateshead Housing Company
Grainger Asset Management Limited
Grainger Ramp Limited
Grosvenor Gate Property Management Limited
Hameed Investments Limited
Hare Homes Limited
In Service Limited
Ivybank Limited
LO (Roscommon) Properties Limited
LSL Corporate Client Services Limited
Lambton Share Property Company Limited
Land Factor Limited
Legacy No.1 Limited
Looprevil (North East) Limited
MJM Developments (Portrack Grange) Limited
Michael Drapers Limited
Monte Cristo Residential Ltd
Thomas Morris Limited
Mynicehouse Limited
Naturalight Properties Ltd.
Natzone Limited
Newcastle Great Park (Estates) Limited
Newcastle Portland House Limited
Northern Electric Properties Limited
Orderelite Limited
Keith Pattinson Limited
Propertees Ltd
RPU Group PLC
Redbale Limited
Gavin Reed Limited
Walton Robinson Ltd
Seaton Trust Limited
Select Property Developments Limited
Shepherd Offshore Services Limited
South Tyneside Homes Limited
Springfield Properties (Ncle) Limited
St Trinity Limited
T J D Properties Limited
Templeton LPA Limited
Tyneside Estate Office Limited
Union Property Services Limited
Winkfield Properties Limited
Woodside North East Property Limited
Workspace & Storage Limited

69101 Barristers at law

Pearson Caulfield Limited

69102 Solicitors

Amakhala Limited
Askews Solicitors Limited
Kenneth M Barrow & Co Limited
Beecham Peacock North East Limited
Carr & Co Solicitors (NE) Limited
Coles Solicitors Limited
Cygnet Family Law Limited
D J M S Solicitors Ltd
John Donkin Solicitors Ltd
EMG Solicitors Limited
Geoffrey Forrester & Co Limited
Gibson & Co. Solicitors Ltd
Kidd & Spoor Solicitors Limited
Longden Walker and Renney (Solicitors) Limited
O'Neill Richmonds Law Firm Limited
Pearson Caulfield Limited
Richard Reed Ltd
Kirsten Scott Limited
Shaw & Company Solicitors Limited
Silk Family Law Limited
Stockdale & Reid Limited
Winn Solicitors Limited

69109 Activities of patent and copyright agents; other legal activities n.e.c.

Harbron Legal Ltd

69201 Accounting and auditing activities

Addison & Co (Teesdale) Limited
Cavu Corporate Finance Limited
Chuhan & Singh Partnership Limited
Dalts Ltd
Davies Tracey Limited
Hawik Limited
King Hope Ltd
Montpelier Professional Limited
Murray and Lamb Accountants Limited
Pullan Barnes Limited
RMT Accountants & Business Advisors Ltd
Ribchester Smith & Law Limited
Ribchesters Group Limited
Robson Laidler Accountants Limited
Stephenson Coates Limited
TTR Barnes Limited
Waltons Clark Whitehill Limited
A Watson Associates Limited
Peter Weldon & Co Limited

69202 Bookkeeping activities

King Hope Ltd
Northgate (CB) Limited
Ribchester Smith & Law Limited
Ribchesters Group Limited

69203 Tax consultancy

Christopher Bailey Tax Consultants Limited
Davies Tracey Limited
King Hope Ltd
Pullan Barnes Limited
Qubic Tax Advisory Limited
Qubic Tax Ltd
Ribchester Smith & Law Limited
Ribchesters Group Limited
Stephenson Coates Limited
Technical Investment Solutions Ltd

70210 Public relations and communications activities

O Communications Ltd
Print Demon Holdings Limited

70221 Financial management

ACS Invest UK Limited
Adderstone 1993 Limited
Dinnington Cottages Limited
Freeman Finance (North East) Limited
Leadgates Investments Limited
The Morpeth Practice Ltd
Pensave Limited
Riverside Acquisitions Limited
Shining Thought Limited
True Potential Group Limited
Vardy 1985 Investments Limited

71111 Architectural activities

Align Property Partners Limited
Building Design (Northern) Limited
Devereux Architecture Limited
Glasshus Ltd
Howarth Litchfield Partnership Limited
Identity Consult Limited
Iris Engineering & Technology Limited
OGI Groundwater Specialists Limited
P+HS Architects Limited
PHP Architects Limited
PSP Architectural Ltd
Queensberry Design Limited
Riba Enterprises Ltd
Robertson Simpson Limited
Ryder Architecture Limited
Space Architecture (Europe) Limited
Malcolm Tempest Limited

71121 Engineering design activities for industrial process and production

Autotech Engineering R&D UK Limited
B.C. & T. Consultants Limited
John Boyd Associates Limited
Cleveland Fire Brigade Risk Management Services C.I.C.
Contract Design (Northern) Limited
Global Substation Solutions Limited
Idec Power Services Limited
Idec Technical Services Limited
Iris Engineering & Technology Limited
Materials Processing Institute
Metrology Software Products Limited
PX Engineering Consultants Limited
RS Industrial Services (Tyne & Wear) Limited
RS Industrial Services Limited
Samsung C&T ECUK Limited
Vandewiele UK Limited

71122 Engineering related scientific and technical consulting activities

Ayton Consulting Limited
Engineering Support Partnership Ltd.
Global Substation Solutions Limited
Invenio Systems Limited
Iris Engineering & Technology Limited
Iris Project Solutions Ltd
Mactech Inspection Limited
Materials Processing Institute
PDL Solutions (Europe) Limited
PX Engineering Consultants Limited
PX Limited
Red I55 Ltd
Robertson Simpson Limited
Stewart & Harris Limited
THDA Ltd
Wartsila Puregas Solutions Limited

71129 Other engineering activities

4B Precision Engineering Ltd
Body Engineering Limited
Cad 21 Limited
Calibrate Inc Ltd
Cathie Associates Limited
William Coulthard and Company Limited
EDM Zone Limited
Express Lasers Limited
Falcon Engineering & Development Limited
GMS (Holdings) Limited
Global Manufacturing Supplies Limited
IKM Testing UK Limited
Industrial and Marine Hydraulics Limited
Iris Engineering & Technology Limited
Iris Project Solutions Ltd
JCP Consulting Engineers Limited
K Home International Limited
MJR Controls Limited
MacGregor (GBR) Limited
Marske Site Services Ltd.
Metcalfe Components (Sunderland) Limited
NRG Global Power Limited
Novares Peterlee Limited
PX Engineering Consultants Limited
Peron Limited
Perry Process Equipment Limited
Plenary Project Solutions Limited
RSL One Limited
Reece Group Limited
Reece Treasury Management Limited
Rivergreen Developments PLC
Seateks Engineering Limited
Service Engineering Marine Limited
Solmek Limited
Surtec (North East) Limited
Swan Hunter (NE) Limited
Technical Housing Solutions Limited
Tees Components Limited
Unasys Limited
Upnorth Engineering Services Limited
Washington Components Limited
Whessoe Engineering Limited

71200 Technical testing and analysis

Arc Environmental Limited
Argos Inspection Company Limited
Axiom Engineering Associates Limited
Derwentside Environmental Testing Services Limited
Dunelm Geotechnical & Environmental Limited
Geneius Laboratories Limited
Gilligan Engineering Services Limited
Kratos Communications Limited
NDT Electronic Services Ltd
Pass (Portable Appliance Safety Services) Ltd
T-Mac Technologies Limited
Tyne Subsea Limited
Valmont Stainton Limited
Wescott Industrial Services Ltd

72110 Research and experimental development on biotechnology

Arc Trinova Limited
CPI Innovation Services Limited
Centre for Process Innovation Limited
Complement Genomics Limited
Fujifilm Diosynth Biotechnologies UK Limited
Lamda (UK) Limited
Lamda Pharma Limited

72190 Other research and experimental development on natural sciences and engineering

Applied Graphene Materials PLC
Applied Graphene Materials UK Limited
Axenic Limited
Axiom Engineering Associates Limited
CPI Innovation Services Limited
Cambridge Photonics Limited
Centre for Process Innovation Limited
The Endowment Fund for Tacri
Griffith Textile Machines Limited
Honeyman Group Limited
IT-IS International Limited
JR Dynamics Limited
Kromek Limited
NDT Global Services Limited
Newchem Technologies Limited
Plaxica Limited
Polyphotonix Limited
Royal IHC Limited
Saferad Limited

73110 Advertising agencies

Coffee Design Limited
Different Advertising Design and Marketing Limited
Drummond Central Limited
FPP Design Limited
HDC Travel Limited
Inspired Agency Ltd
The Media Network Global Limited
Mercer Street Marketing and Consulting Limited
Mesh Marketing Limited
N21 Limited
TDG Brand Communications Limited
Martin Tait Redheads Ltd.

73120 Media representation services

CLC Enterprise Limited

73200 Market research and public opinion polling

Dipsticks Research Limited
Explain Market Research Limited

74100 Specialised design activities

Benchmark Electronics Limited
David Brown Automotive Limited
Alex Clark Art Ltd
Cleveland Fire Brigade Risk Management Services C.I.C.
Hyperdrive Innovation Ltd
Kratos Communications Limited
PX Engineering Consultants Limited
Webworks Internet (UK) Limited

74201 Portrait photographic activities

Joegraphic Ltd

74901 Environmental consulting activities

Applied Ecological Services Limited
Ayton Consulting Limited
Chemtech Environmental Limited
E3 Ecology Ltd
FWS Consultants Limited
Lucion Environmental Limited
Lucion Services Limited
Northern Archaeological Associates Limited
Sirius Renewable Energy Limited
Utilitywise PLC
Vega Environmental Consultants Limited

74902 Quantity surveying activities

Blake Newport Associates Limited
Hall & Partners (Special Projects) Limited
T M A Property Consultants Limited

74909 Other professional, scientific and technical activities n.e.c.

Aedis Regulatory Services Limited
Ayton Consulting Limited
BCTQ Maritime Corporate Limited
Barrier Architectural Services Limited
Bradley Hall Limited
Bulman Support Ltd
Carson Office Environments Limited
Cenelec Standards Inspections Limited
Ceres Energy Limited
Cleveland Fire Brigade Risk Management Services C.I.C.
Clic Time Holdings Limited
Consumer Refund Service Ltd
Contract Laboratory Services Limited
DNR Limited
Draeger Safety UK Ltd
Emerchantpay UK Services Ltd
The Endowment Fund for Tacri
Gilmour & Associates Limited
International Centre for Life Trust
Jiahua Europe Limited
Just Drama Based Training Ltd
MRM Electrical Solutions Limited
Manxguard Limited
Nitelites Limited
North of England Civic Trust
Offshore Renewable Energy Catapult
Ore Catapult Development Services Limited
PFC Marine Ltd
Peterlee Fire Company Limited
Portrack Handling Limited
Project North East
Protex (UK) Systems Limited
RTC North Limited
Restaurant Design Associates Ltd
Rokshaw Limited
Rosen (UK) Limited
Roxburgh Group Limited
Safinah Limited
Security Centres Securus Limited
Storage Equipment Safety Service Limited
T C Developments North East Ltd
TI Geosciences Ltd
Technical Options (Europe) Ltd
Tees Valley Community Foundation
Malcolm Tempest Limited
Tompkins Investments Limited
Tompkins UK Limited
UK Independent Medical Services Limited
Utilergy Limited
Voicentric Limited

74990 Non-trading company

A & P Ship Repairers Limited
Arriva International Limited
Arriva Motor Holdings Limited
Balkan Properties Limited
Banks Renewables (Armistead Wind Farm) Limited
Banks Renewables (Harting Rig Wind Farm) Limited
Banks Renewables (Hazlehead Wind Farm) Limited
Banks Renewables (Heysham South Wind Farm) Limited
Banks Renewables (Hook Moor Wind Farm) Limited
Banks Renewables (Kype Muir Wind Farm) Limited
Banks Renewables (Middle Muir Wind Farm) Limited
Banks Renewables (Moor House Wind Farm) Limited
Banks Renewables (Penny Hill Wind Farm) Limited
Bellway Housing Trust Limited
Blue Assistance Limited
Brunton Holdings Limited
Casper Shipping Holdings Limited
Chrysalis Grant Making Trust
Covion Holdings Limited
Crown Care Holdings Limited
Davison Tyne Metal Limited
J. Dinning (Investments) Limited
Doby Verrolec Limited
The Endowment Fund for Tacri
Engie Services Holding UK Limited
Essex and Suffolk Water Limited
Formica Finance Limited
Formica Holdco (UK) Limited
GLT Limited
John Gill Limited
Golftee LP 4 Limited
The Goshen Trust
Grainger Newbury Limited
Grainger PRS Limited
Grainger Trust Limited
Graza Limited
Greit Limited
Homefair (Holdings) Limited
JL Mechanical and Electrical Services Limited
Jomast Limited
Kuyt Limited
Kymel Limited
LGA Foundation
Leisure Centre Holdings
Lycetts Holdings Limited
MD5 Forensics Ltd
McIntyres Properties Limited
Medichem (Sunderland) Limited
Nicholson's Aircraft Seals Limited
PD Logistics Limited
The PNE Foundation
PTM Holdings Limited
Pitman Press Limited
Pornic Limited
Premier Dawn Properties Limited
Psyche Holdings Limited
R.F.I. Limited
RHJ Maintenance Ltd
Richmond Foods Limited
M.J. Scaife Limited
Shelcorp 2008 Ltd
Stablewood Developments Limited
The John Strutt Conservation Foundation
Sudfeld Limited
Svitzer Eastlands Limited
Tripsdale Technology Ltd
The United Reformed Church (Northern Province) Trust Limited
Unsworth Unsworth & Co. Limited

75000 Veterinary activities

Blythman & Partners Limited
Copeland Veterinary Practice Limited
Hadrian Limited
Hyperdrug Pharmaceuticals Ltd

77110 Renting and leasing of cars and light motor vehicles

Co-Wheels Car Club Community Interest Company
DHM Vehicle Rental Limited
DVS Autos Limited
Eagle Road Services Limited
Euro Contract Leasing Limited
Goode Durrant Administration Limited
Icicle Vehicle Solutions Limited
Metro Rental Limited
Motorcare (Alnwick) Limited
Northgate Vehicle Hire Limited
On-Hire Limited
Readypay Limited
Total Courier Solutions Limited
Vehicle Lease and Service Limited

77120 Renting and leasing of trucks and other heavy vehicles

Eagle Road Services Limited
Euro Contract Leasing Limited
W A Old & Son Limited
Permatt Fork Lift Trucks Limited
Premier Truck Hire Limited

77291 Renting and leasing of media entertainment equipment

Bob Rudd Leisure Limited
Bob Rudd Limited

77310 Renting and leasing of agricultural machinery and equipment

Cleveland Land Services (Guisborough) Limited
Hubbway Limited
Orange Plant Limited

77320 Renting and leasing of construction and civil engineering machinery and equipment

A.T. & P Rentals Ltd.
Abbey Plant Ltd
Arrowcruit Limited
Cleveland Land Services (Guisborough) Limited
D&K Hire Services Limited
EVT Contractors Limited
Flextime Limited
GAP Group Leasing Limited
GAP Group Limited
Herrenknecht International Limited
Hewitson Plant Hire Limited
M.J. Hickey Plant Hire & Contracts Limited
Hubbway Limited
Hughes Plant Hire Limited
Geoff Huntley Plant Limited
Kearton Farms Limited
J Kelly Plant Hire Limited
Kramar Limited
R.Lord & Co.(Newcastle) Limited
Lord Technical Limited
Mechplant (North East) Limited
John Nixon Limited
North East Plant Hire Limited
Precision Geomatics Limited
Sanders Plant & Waste Management Limited
Seneca Investments and Developments Limited
Service Engines (Newcastle) Limited
Sky Scaffolding (Whitby) Limited
R. Thornton & Co. Ltd.
UPA (UK) Limited
Williamson Construction Equipment Limited

77330 Renting and leasing of office machinery and equipment (including computers)

Document Solutions (UK) Limited
Technocopy Ltd.

77390 Renting and leasing of other machinery, equipment and tangible goods n.e.c.

A1 Industrial Trucks Limited
B & S (Rentals) Limited
Cool Assets Ltd
DP Plant Hire Limited
HMC Finance Limited
William Hackett Holdings Limited
Hatton Traffic Management Limited
Humbles Real Estate Limited
IHC FHP Limited
Inlec UK Limited
J A Sales and Service Limited
O Kay Automatics Limited
R.Lord & Co.(Newcastle) Limited
Metano Limited
Metnor (Great Yarmouth) Limited
Mobile Mini UK Limited
Modus Seabed Intervention Limited
Morfitt Waste Management Ltd
Northern Powergrid Metering Limited
Pea Soup Limited
Peart Property Limited
Procomm Site Services Limited
Quantum Controls Ltd
Rail Management Services Limited
SMH Products Limited
Sayers Road Tanker Rentals Limited
Thompson Power Tool Services UK Ltd
WHL 2013 Holdings Limited
WHL 2013 Limited
Watkins Hire Limited
Simon Winstanley Ltd

77400 Leasing of intellectual property and similar products, except copyright works

Team Stokes Limited

78109 Other activities of employment placement agencies

Arrowcruit Limited
B2B Staff Solutions Ltd
Baltic Recruitment Services Limited
CDM Recruitment Limited
Contact Centre Professional Limited
Firthmoor and District Community Association
Nigel Frank International Limited
Frank Recruitment Group Services Limited
Interocean Personnel Services (UK) Limited
JB Skills Training Ltd
Marske Site Services Ltd.
Mason Frank International Limited
NAS Group Durham Limited
Northern Recruitment Group Limited
Oil Consultants Holdco Limited
Poppypride Limited
Resource Management Solutions (North East) Ltd
Rust Resources Limited
Seatechs Limited
TS Developments Ltd
Tesmonard Europe Limited
Working Links (Employment) Limited
Nigel Wright Consultancy Limited

78200 Temporary employment agency activities

3KB Recruitment Group Ltd
B2B Staff Solutions Ltd
CDM Recruitment Limited
CY Partners Recruitment Ltd
Central Employment Agency (North East) Limited
Contract Design (Northern) Limited
Corepeople Recruitment Limited
Direkt Engineering Services Limited
Engineering Recruitment Services Ltd
First Class Supply & Training Limited
Fission Recruitment Services Limited
Gem Partnership Limited
Hargreaves Industrial Services Limited
Key Stage Recruitment Limited
MTREC Limited
Manning Limited
Marske Site Services Ltd.
Mason Frank International Limited
Northern Recruitment Group Limited
Nova Payroll Management Services Limited
Oil Consultants Holdco Limited
Poppypride Limited
Primary Care Recruitment Ltd
Resource Management Solutions (North East) Ltd
S.M.P. (Services) Limited
SMD Offshore Support Limited
Temp-Team Limited
Westray Recruitment Consultants Limited
Wolviston Management Services Limited
Nigel Wright Employment Services Limited
Zenith People Limited

78300 Human resources provision and management of human resources functions

B2B Staff Solutions Ltd
Centralus 003 Ltd
Centralus 004 Ltd
Cundall Limited
Gosforth 22 Limited
Mash Staffing Payroll Limited
NIAL Services Limited
Northern Recruitment Group Limited
Poppypride Limited
Resource Management Solutions (North East) Ltd
Rosewood HR Services Ltd

79110 Travel agency activities

Check in USA Limited
Dawson & Sanderson Limited
HDC Travel Limited
Hays Beds Limited
Hays Foreign Exchange Limited
Hays Transport Limited
Hays Travel Limited
Holiday Travel & Booking Agency Limited
Horncastle Executive Travel Limited
Christine Nugent Business Travel Limited
Proofgolden Limited
Regal Motors (Ashington) Limited
TGT Holidays Limited
Windgrove Limited

79120 Tour operator activities

Hays Tour Operating Limited
Lee's Coaches Limited
Saddle Skedaddle Limited
Tom Tappin,Limited
Travelsure Coaches Limited

79909 Other reservation service activities n.e.c.

Hospitality Guaranteed Limited
Strathearn Leisure Parks Limited

80100 Private security activities

Phoenix Security Holdings Limited
Standard Security Services Limited
Steadfast Security Solutions Limited
Vistech Services Ltd

80200 Security systems service activities

20/20 Vision Systems Limited
A E L Systems Ltd
Act Response Ltd
Barrier Surveillance Systems Limited
Cormeton Electronics Limited
Dynamic CCTV Limited
Dynamic CCTV Management Ltd
ITC Service Limited
Lyndon Systems Ltd
Phoenix Eye Ltd
The Protector Group Limited
Render Alarms Limited
Security Systems and Alarms Inspection Board
Universal Systems Solutions (Security) Limited

80300 Investigation activities

Acumen Investigation Services Ltd.
Armstrong Nationwide Ltd.

81100 Combined facilities support activities

Cenergist Limited
JW Colpitts & Co Limited
Engie FM Limited
Engie International FM Limited
Engie Services Limited
Engynious Clean Power (UK) Ltd
Engynious Schools PLC
Maxim Facilities Management Ltd
NE Property Management Limited
QE Facilities Limited
Sale PFI Limited
Sincera Ltd
T.B. Tarn Limited

81210 General cleaning of buildings

Arix Europe Limited
Blenheim Court Properties Limited
Clean It UK/Gumbusters Limited

81222 Specialised cleaning services

Aqueous 1st Kwikflow Limited
Partners in Hygiene Limited
Total Gutter Maintenance Limited

81223 Furnace and chimney cleaning services

Stone Technical Services Group Limited

81229 Other building and industrial cleaning activities

The Durham Company Limited
Stone Technical Services Group Limited

81299 Other cleaning services

Isotank Depot Services Limited

81300 Landscape service activities

J W Bainbridge Contractors Ltd
Cleveland Land Services (Guisborough) Limited
DKB Crop Protection Limited
Deerness Fencing & Landscaping Limited
Dixon Landscapes Limited
Graform Limited
Groundwork South Tyneside and Newcastle upon Tyne
Landscape Matters Limited
W. Marley Agricultural Contractors Limited
Stamford Farms Ltd
W. L. Straughan & Son Limited
Wilkinson Landscapes Limited

82110 Combined office administrative service activities

Calmor Limited
Cavotec International Limited
Direct Connections Limited
Fletcher Challenge Forest Industries Limited
NSA (Ventures) Limited
NSG Limited
Northern Ladies Annuity Society
Pacifica Group Limited
Prudhoe Community Partnership
SIG Combibloc Limited

82200 Activities of call centres

2 Touch BPO Services Ltd
Allay Claims Ltd
Convergys CMG UK Limited
Kura Financial Services Limited
MBL Solutions Limited
Ubisoft CRC Ltd

82301 Activities of exhibition and fair organisers

Harris (U.K.) Limited

82302 Activities of conference organisers

Cynergy UK Limited

82920 Packaging activities

Arix Europe Limited
Greencroft Bottling Company Limited
Reproflex 3 Limited
Returnable Packaging Services Limited
Soretrac (U.K.) Limited

84130 Regulation of and contribution to more efficient operation of businesses

Bloom Procurement Services Ltd

84220 Defence activities

Pearson Engineering Limited

84230 Justice and judicial activities

Achieving Real Change in Communities CIC
The Durham Tees Valley Community Rehabilitation Company Limited

84250 Fire service activities

MacDonald Martin Limited

85100 Pre-primary education

AAM & Sons Limited
Dame Allan's Schools
Argyle House Holdings Limited
The Ascent Academies' Trust
Aysgarth School Trust Limited
Brunton Nursery Limited
Castleview Group Training Limited
Choice Childcare Limited
Clever Clogs Day Nurseries Limited
Durham High School for Girls
ELG Developments Limited
Firthmoor and District Community Association
Hawks Road Community Nursery Limited
Little Learners Sunderland Limited
Monkton Infants School
Newcastle School for Boys
Northumberland Church of England Academy Trust
The Northumbrian Educational Trust Ltd
Northumbrian Trust Day Nurseries Limited
Our Lady of Light Catholic Academy Trust
Red House School Limited
Rosedene Nurseries Limited
S A Day Care Ltd
Stanley Learning Partnership
Sunnyside Academy
Tavistock House Day Nursery Limited
W.O.W! (Welcome To Our World) Limited
Westminster Day Nurseries Limited
Yarm School

85320 Technical and vocational secondary education

Academy 360
B L Training (Holdings) Limited
B L Training Limited
Baltic Training Services Limited
Cablecom Training Limited
Centre for Process Innovation Limited
Discovery Learning Limited
Gateshead College Foundation
Groundwork South Tyneside and Newcastle upon Tyne
ITEC North East Limited
Maersk Training Newcastle Limited
North East Autism Society
Northumberland Church of England Academy Trust
Rathbone Training
S.W. Durham Training Limited
TTE Apprenticeships Limited
Teesnap Limited
Tyne North Training Limited
Unity City Academy Trust

85410 Post-secondary non-tertiary education

The Ascent Academies' Trust
Delta - North Consett Limited
Genius Bidco Limited
Genius Holdco Limited
Learning Concepts Limited
S.W. Durham Training Limited
Sunderland Engineering Training Association Limited
Yarm School

85421 First-degree level higher education

Newcastle University Students' Union
The Reece Foundation
St. Chad's College
St.John's College,Durham
Teesnap Limited
University of Northumbria at Newcastle Developments Limited
University of Sunderland Enterprises Limited

85422 Post-graduate level higher education

Northumbria London Campus Limited
St. Chad's College
St.John's College,Durham
University of Northumbria at Newcastle Developments Limited
University of Sunderland Enterprises Limited

85510 Sports and recreation education

Newcastle United Foundation
The R.D.A. Centre in Cleveland Limited

85520 Cultural education

CISV International Limited
Seven Stories, The National Centre for Children's Books Limited
Wallsend Memorial Hall & People's Centre

85530 Driving school activities

Plymouth Citybus Limited
RDS Driving Services Limited

85590 Other education n.e.c.

Adventure Sunderland
Bahr Academy
Barnard Castle School
CACDP
Catcote Futures
The Cedars Academy Trust
Challenging Learning Ltd
Changing Futures North East
Communicators Training Associates Limited
Contact Centre Professional Limited
The Education Village Academy Trust
Education and Services for People with Autism Limited
The Faraday Centre Limited
Finchale Training College
Foundation of Light
GJPS Trust Fund
Hartlepool Aspire Trust
Horizons Specialist Academy Trust
International Centre for Life Trust
The Intraining Group Limited
J and K Training Ltd
Kilton Thorpe Specialist Academy
Learning Concepts Limited
Learning at Work Limited
Marrick Priory Trust
Middlesbrough Environment City Trust Limited
N A College Limited
NAC Training Limited
Newcastle East Mixed Multi Academy Trust
Newcastle Special Schools Trust
North Tyneside Learning Trust
Our Children 1st
Ouseburn Learning Trust
Outer West Learning Trust
Rathbone Training
Red Oak Ltd
River Tees Multi-Academy Trust
The Riverside Learning Trust
S.W. Durham Training Limited
Saks (Education) Limited
Skills Training Academy Limited
Society for Education Limited
Southmoor Multi Academy Trust
Springboard Sunderland Trust
TRN (Train) Ltd.
TTE International Limited
The TTE Technical Training Group
Tax Incentivised Savings Association
Teesside High School Limited
Thermal Insulation Contractors Association
Training and Development Resource Limited
Tyne Coast Academy Trust
UK Asbestos Specialists Ltd
University of Northumbria at Newcastle Developments Limited
The Vocational Learning Trust
XCEL County Durham

85600 Educational support services

Changing Health Limited
Creativity, Culture and Education
The Education Village Academy Trust
For Skills Limited
Invate Limited
Keyfort Group Limited
NCFE
Neat Active Limited
Newcastle Special Schools Trust
Northern Grid for Learning
St. Camillus Care Group Ltd
Stanley Learning Partnership

86101 Hospital activities

Centre for Sports Injury Surgery Limited
City Hospitals Independent Commercial Enterprises Limited
Darlington & District Hospice Movement
Hartlepool Hospice Limited (The)
St Benedict's Hospice, Sunderland
Tyneside Surgical Services Limited

86102 Medical nursing home activities

Carewell (Health Care) Limited
Grace House North East
Middleton Hall Limited
People First Care Ltd
Solehawk Limited
St. Cuthbert's Hospice Durham

86210 General medical practice activities

Bans Healthcare Ltd
Bentley Medical Practice Limited
Community Based Care Health Limited
Crispin (Pharmacy) Limited
Euro GPS Limited
Freeman Clinics Limited
Dr W Hassan Ltd
G.W. Herdman (Chemists) Limited
Immunodiagnostic Systems Holdings Public Limited Company
Inderjeet Medicals Limited
Intrahealth Limited
North East Eye Care Limited
On Medical Limited
R&M Diagnostics Limited
Shaheen Medical Services Limited
South Durham Health C.I.C.
Viswanath & Co Limited
Wheatley Hill Property Company Limited

86220 Specialists medical practice activities

Derwentside Hospice Care Foundation
The Great North Air Ambulance Service
Kotur Limited
Lool Shulan Ltd
R D Consulting and Education Limited
Singisetti Srinivas Limited
South Durham Health C.I.C.
St. Cuthbert's Hospice Durham
Teesside Hospice Care Foundation
Tyneview Diagnostics Limited

86230 Dental practice activities

Anglesea Terrace Orthodontic Practice Ltd
Ashford Orthodontics Limited
The Cosmetic Dental Clinic Limited
Epsom Dental Centre Ltd
Infinity Dental Services (IDS) Ltd
LJWC Limited
Northumbria Dental Care Limited
Osborne Orthodontics Ltd
Queensway Dental Laboratory Limited
Southampton Orthodontic Centre Limited
Westerhope Limited
Windmill (Heaton) Orthodontics Limited

87100 Residential nursing care facilities

Ascot Care North East Limited
Aspire Healthcare Limited
Burlam House Limited
Clovely Care Limited
Crown Care IV Limited
Crown Care V Limited
Crown Care VI Limited
Crown Care VII Limited
Darrington Healthcare Ltd
Eastbourne House Ltd
Enhanced Elderly Care Limited
Exclusive Care Group Ltd
HC-ONE Beamish Limited
HC-ONE Limited
The Hamilton Portfolio (Care Homes) Limited
Herrington Mews Ltd
Ideal Care (North) Limited
Kay Care Services Ltd
Malhotra Care Homes Limited
Middleton Hall Limited
Moorlands Care Homes (N.E.) Limited
Premier Care Homes Limited
Prestige Care Limited
Prestwick Care Limited
Primrose House Ltd
SLW (Holdings) Limited
SLW (Thornbury) Limited
Saint John of God Hospitaller Services
St Cuthbert's Care
St. Cuthbert's Hospice Durham
Williams & Spenceley Limited
Woodham Christian Centre Ltd.

87200 Residential care activities for learning difficulties, mental health and substance abuse

Ashdown Care Homes Ltd
Aspire Healthcare Limited
Azure Charitable Enterprises
Blyth Star Enterprises Limited
Careline Lifestyles (UK) Ltd
Cherry Orchards Care Ltd
Cleveland Alzheimer's Residential Centre Limited
Coquet Trust
Flexible Support Options Limited
Gainford Care Homes Limited
The Hawthorns Lodge Limited
Mental Health Concern
North East Autism Society
S.E.L.F. (North East) Limited
Saint John of God Hospitaller Services
St Cuthbert's Care
Top Drawer Properties Limited

87300 Residential care activities for the elderly and disabled

Abbeyfield (Darlington) Society Limited (The)
Abbeyfield Newcastle upon Tyne Society Limited (The)
Atlas Care Homes Limited
Burlam House Limited
Philip Cussins House
Danick Limited
Darnley Bidco Limited
Dipton Care Home Limited
East Cleveland M.S. Home
Eastbourne House Ltd
Eothen Homes Limited
Exclusive Care Group Ltd
GMA Healthcare Ltd
Genhawk Limited
Gracelands Care Home Limited
Greta Cottage Limited
HC-ONE Beamish Limited
HC-ONE Limited
Hadrian Healthcare (Knaresborough) Limited
Hadrian Healthcare (Oulton) Limited
Herrington Mews Ltd
Hornby Healthcare Limited
The Hospital of God at Greatham
Lambton House Ltd
Lion Care Home Group Limited
Malhotra Care Homes (Sunderland) Limited
Malhotra Care Homes Limited
Meridian Healthcare Limited
Moorlands Holdings (N.E.) Limited
Motherdale Limited
North East Care Homes Limited
Northumbria Care Limited
Oak Park Healthcare Limited
Parkside Care Limited
The Percy Hedley Foundation
Premier Care Homes Limited
Prestige Care (Redcar Sm) Limited
Roseberry Care Centres GB Limited
SLW Limited
SVP Health Care Limited
Saint John of God Hospitaller Services
Sovereign Care (North East) Ltd
Supreme Health Care Limited
Underwood Hall Limited
Wellburn Care Homes Limited
Willow View Care Limited
Witton Care Limited
Wyndham Court Limited
Your Care First Limited

87900 Other residential care activities n.e.c.

3.13
Artemis Support Limited
Belmont View Limited
Darlington & District Hospice Movement
Education and Services for People with Autism Limited
Elpha Lodge Residential Care Home Limited
Harbour Support Services
Holme Farm Residential Village Limited
Howard House Care Limited
Humankind Charity
Intobeige Limited
Little Acorns London Beach Farm Limited
Northridge Healthcare Limited
Oasis Aquila Housing Ltd
George Ronald Limited
Roseberry Specialist Care Centres Limited
St Cuthbert's Care
The Charlotte Straker Project
Talbot House Trust North East

88100 Social work activities without accommodation for the elderly and disabled

Age Concern Tyneside South
Age UK North Tyneside
Age UK Northumberland
Age UK Sunderland
Azure Charitable Enterprises
Bell View (Belford)
Care and Share Associates One (2014) Limited
Coquet Trust
Dale Care Limited
Disability North
Keyfort Group Limited
New Beginnings (North East) Limited
The Percy Hedley Foundation
Saint John of God Hospitaller Services
St. Anthony of Padua Community Association

88910 Child day-care activities

Ladybird's Childrens Nursery Limited
Rosedene Nurseries Limited

88990 Other social work activities without accommodation n.e.c.

Arc Adoption North East Limited
Aspire Healthcare Limited
Blyth Star Enterprises Limited
Blyth Valley Disabled Forum Ltd
Cares Group Holdings Limited
Community Foundation Serving Tyne & Wear and Northumberland
Daisy Chain Project Teesside
Darlington & District Hospice Movement
Darlington Mind Limited
East Durham Partnership Limited
Education and Services for People with Autism Limited
Friends of Biala Limited
HH Community Care Limited
Hartlepool People Limited
Hospitaller Order of Saint John of God
Humankind Charity
Interactive Development Support Limited
Journey Enterprises Ltd
Mental Health Concern
Middlesbrough and Stockton Mind Limited
The Multiple Sclerosis Research and Relief Fund
NECA
National Energy Action
The Northstar Foundation
Oasis Aquila Housing Ltd
The People's Kitchen Limited
Perfect Care Limited
Routes Healthcare (North East) Limited
St Chad's Community Project
St Cuthbert's Care
St. Camillus Care Group Ltd
Sunderland Care and Support (Holding Company) Limited
Sunderland Care and Support Limited
Sunderland Home Care Associates (20-20) Limited
Supportive SRC Ltd
Team Fostering

90010 Performing arts

Eleven Arches
North Music Trust
Northern Stage (Theatrical Productions) Limited
Phoenix Theatre (Blyth)
SM Comedy Limited

90020 Support activities to performing arts

Alnwick District Playhouse Trust
The Customs House Trust Limited
Newcastle Theatre Royal Trust Limited
North Music Trust

90030 Artistic creation

Allendale Creative Artists Community Interest Company
The Customs House Trust Limited
Terry Deary Limited
Limekent Limited
North East Theatre Trust Limited
North Music Trust
Souvenir Scenic Studios Ltd.

90040 Operation of arts facilities

Allendale Creative Artists Community Interest Company
Alnwick District Playhouse Trust
Baltic Flour Mills Visual Arts Trust
The Customs House Trust Limited
Dance North
Liveworks (Newcastle upon Tyne) Ltd
Newcastle Theatre Royal Trust Limited
North East Theatre Trust Limited
North Music Trust
Northern Stage (Theatrical Productions) Limited
Riverside Leisure Promotions Limited
Stockton Arts Centre
VMS Live 2011 Ltd
The Zurbaran Trust

91011 Library activities

Active Northumberland
The Literary & Philosophical Society of Newcastle upon Tyne

91012 Archives activities

Seven Stories, The National Centre for Children's Books Limited

91020 Museums activities

The Bowes Museum
Durham Cathedral Open Treasure Limited
Seven Stories, The National Centre for Children's Books Limited
Woodhorn Charitable Trust

91030 Operation of historical sites and buildings and similar visitor attractions

Active Northumberland
The Auckland Castle Trust
Georgian Theatre (Richmond) Trust Limited (The)
Howick Trustees Limited
International Centre for Life Trust
North of England Civic Trust
Richmondshire Building Preservation Trust Ltd
Tyne and Wear Building Preservation Trust Limited
The Vindolanda Trust
Woodhorn Charitable Trust

91040 Botanical and zoological gardens and nature reserves activities

Durham Wildlife Trust
The John Strutt Conservation Foundation

92000 Gambling and betting activities

Chisholm Bookmakers Limited
Edenpace Limited
K.Johnson Limited
Leaguenotion
Luxury Leisure
Megabet UK Ltd.
J. Noble & Sons Limited
Wm. Noble (Automatics) Limited
K.W. Reader & Sons Limited
Regal Amusements (North East) Limited
S.A.L. Leisure Limited
Treatview Limited

93110 Operation of sports facilities

Active Northumberland
The Bedlingtonshire Golf Club Limited
Blackwell Grange Golf Club Limited
Delta - North Consett Limited
Durham Cricket C.I.C.
Eaglescliffe and District Golf Company Limited
Firthmoor and District Community Association
Russell Foster Tyne and Wear Sports Foundation
Guy Sports Limited
Hartlepool Golf Club Limited
Jesmond Community Leisure
Match Day Centres Ltd
Neat Active Limited
Newburn Riverside Recreation Association Limited
Newcastle Rugby KP Limited
Newcastle United Football Company Limited
Newcastle United Limited
North of England Estates Limited
Northumberland CTC (Properties) Limited
Ravensworth Golf Club,Limited (The)
Redcar Racecourse Limited
Soccarena Limited
Stokesley Golf Range Limited
Sunderland Association Football Club,Limited (The)
Sunderland Lifestyle Partnership Limited
Sunderland Limited
Sunderland Marina Ltd
Tyneside Badminton Centre CIC
Wearside Golf Club Limited (The)
West Denton Indoor Bowls Club Limited
Whickham Golf Club Limited (The)

93120 Activities of sport clubs

Arcot Hall Golf Club Limited
Ashbrooke Sports Club Limited
Belle Vue Community, Sports & Youth Centre Limited
Blue Flames Sporting Club Limited
Close House Golf Club Limited
Darlington Cricket and Athletic Club C.I.C.
Darlington Mowden Park Rugby Football Club Limited
Darlington Rugby Football Club Limited
Durham City Golf Club Limited
Houghton-le-Spring Golf Club,Limited (The)
Matfen Golf Limited
Middlesbrough Football & Athletic Company (1986) Limited
The Morpeth Golf Club Limited
Newcastle Rugby Limited
Rutherford Association Football Club
Soccer Sensations Hull Limited
South Northumberland Cricket Club Limited
Southmoor Golf Club
Tees & Hartlepool Yacht Club Limited
Whitley Bay Golf Club Ltd (The)
Wynyard Golf Club Ltd.

93130 Fitness facilities

Bannatyne Fitness (2) Limited
Bannatyne Fitness Limited
Bannatyne's Health Club (Fairfield) Limited
Competition Line (U.K.) Limited
One Premium Fitness Limited
Shilbottle Community Hall Limited

93199 Other sports activities

Ashington Leisure Partnership
Ceefox Sports Consultancy Limited
Darlington Arena Limited
Durham County Football Association Limited
Newcastle Climbing Centre Limited
Newcastle United Foundation
Northumberland Golf Club Limited (The)
Northumberland Rugby Football Union Limited
Northumbria Calvert Trust
Nova International Limited
Nova Marketing Consultancy Limited
Nova Marketing Limited
Romanby Golf Course Limited
Seatgeek Sport Limited
Soccarena Limited
Top Line Promotions Limited
Wainstones Estates Limited
Wallsend Boys Club
West Hartlepool Rugby Football Club Limited

93210 Activities of amusement parks and theme parks

Allsafety Limited
K.W. Reader & Sons Limited

93290 Other amusement and recreation activities n.e.c.

Alfol Limited
Argrennan Manor House Limited
C. and R. Limited
Denemouth Caravan Park Limited
Endeavour Northern Limited
Farmtastic Valley Limited
GB Holiday Parks Limited
Hartlepool Marina Limited
Lane7 Aberdeen Ltd
Last Night Limited
Middlesbrough & District Motor Club Limited
Northumbria Leisure Limited
Overs and Rich Limited
Pinpin Ltd
K.W. Reader & Sons Limited
Rubicon Pastimes Limited
Ruff 'n' Tumble Adventure World Limited
S T R Enterprises Limited
Sacriston Community and Sports Trust
Tees Valley Chinese Community Centre Ltd
Tyne Tees Entertainments Limited
Wheatley Hill Community Association

94110 Activities of business and employers membership organisations

Citizens Advice County Durham
Groundwork North East
Markbourn Limited
Newcastle Gateshead Initiative Limited
North East England Chamber of Commerce
Northern Housing Consortium Limited
Tax Incentivised Savings Association
Thermal Insulation Contractors Association
UK & Ireland SAP User Group Limited
Whymar Limited

94120 Activities of professional membership organisations

Association of International Accountants (The)
The British Sociological Association
Peter Fergusson Properties Limited

94910 Activities of religious organisations

Christchurch Claypath Durham
The Christian Institute
City Church Newcastle
Destiny Church Tees Valley
Dhammakaya North United Kingdom
Durham Diocesan Board of Finance
Emmanuel Church Durham
Harnham Buddhist Monastery Trust
Hartridge Buddhist Monastery Trust
Joel Memorial Limited
Kings Church Darlington
Newcastle Christian Life Centre
Newcastle Diocesan Board of Finance Limited (The)
Newcastle Diocesan Education Board Limited
Newcastle Diocesan Society
Tees Valley Community Church
The United Reformed Church (Northern Province) Trust Limited

94990 Activities of other membership organisations n.e.c.

CISV International Limited
Catalyst Stockton-on-Tees Limited
Durham Wildlife Trust
East Durham Community Development Trust Limited
Fawside
Grainger (Octavia Hill) Limited
Hexham and Tynedale Community Trust
Longhoughton Community and Sports Centre Trust
Middlesbrough Voluntary Development Agency
Newbiggin-By-The Sea Heritage Partnership Ltd
Newcastle Council for Voluntary Service
Newcastle NE1 Limited
Newcastle upon Tyne Y.M.C.A.
Northumberland Wildlife Trust Limited
Sameach
Synergy Compliance Limited
Tees Valley Chinese Community Centre Ltd
Tynedale Agricultural Society Ltd

95110 Repair of computers and peripheral equipment

Centrex Computing Services Limited

95120 Repair of communication equipment

Sitelink Communications Limited

95220 Repair of household appliances and home and garden equipment

Pacifica Appliance Services Limited
Singer Machines Limited

95250 Repair of watches, clocks and jewellery

Newcastle Jewellers Ltd.
David Summerfield Limited

96010 Washing and (dry-)cleaning of textile and fur products

The Ashbank Group Limited

96020 Hairdressing and other beauty treatment

Contemporary Franchising Ltd
Saks (Education) Limited
Saks Hair (Holdings) Limited

96030 Funeral and related activities

J.C. Atkinson and Son Limited
J Barthram & Son Limited
Borthwick Marble & Granite Ltd
H Duckworth Limited
Fawcett & Hetherington Funeral Service Limited
Scollen & Wright Funeral Service Limited
E. Turnbull & Son Limited
Tynedale Family Funeral Directors Limited
Whitehouse Funeral Service Limited
Stuart Wright Funeral Service Limited

96040 Physical well-being activities

Age Concern Durham County
Journey Enterprises Ltd

97000 Activities of households as employers of domestic personnel

Leavendale Properties Ltd

98000 Residents property management

Atlantic Metropolitan (U.K.) Limited
GKP Solutions Ltd
Hebburn Properties (NE) Limited
KJT Properties Ltd
Kingston Property Services Limited
Matwest Ltd

99000 Activities of extraterritorial organisations and bodies

Ever 1209 Limited
Shepherds Dene

99999 Dormant company

Arch Building Supplies Limited
Chatswell Properties Ltd
The Chrome Group Limited
Cofathec Energy Services Limited
Engie DE Holding Company Limited
Finders Midco Limited
Global Enterprise (EU) Limited
Hargreaves Maltby Limited
Hivehome Ltd
Jeave 2 Limited
Jeave 4 Limited
KWR Holdings Limited
Kelt Properties Limited
London & Regional Capital Ltd
Merrychef Limited
Mineral & Chemical Services (North East) Limited
Renown Group Limited
Sentinel Homes Limited
Swiss Land Limited
Thirston Property & Investments Limited
W & M Holding Company Limited
Waterloo House Rest Home Limited

Printed in 8pt Nimbus Sans L

Designed by URW++ Design and Development GmbH

Dellam Publishing Limited

2 Heath Drive, Sutton, Surrey, SM2 5RP

Fax: 020 8770 7478 email: enquiries@dellam.com

SAN: 0177881 EAN/GLN: 5030670177882

www.ingramcontent.com/pod-product-compliance
Lightning Source LLC
LaVergne TN
LVHW082012200926
848481LV00010B/2842

* 9 7 8 1 9 1 2 7 3 6 0 8 9 *